CRIMINAL PROCEDURE AND RACIAL INJUSTICE

EDITORIAL ADVISORS

Rachel E. Barkow
Vice Dean and Charles Seligson Professor of Law
Faculty Director, Zimroth Center on the Administration of Criminal Law
New York University School of Law

Erwin Chemerinsky
Dean and Jesse H. Choper Distinguished Professor of Law
University of California, Berkeley School of Law

Richard A. Epstein
Laurence A. Tisch Professor of Law
New York University School of Law
Peter and Kirsten Bedford Senior Fellow
The Hoover Institution
Senior Lecturer in Law
The University of Chicago

Ronald J. Gilson
Charles J. Meyers Professor of Law and Business
Stanford University
Marc and Eva Stern Professor of Law and Business
Columbia Law School

James E. Krier
Earl Warren DeLano Professor of Law Emeritus
The University of Michigan Law School

Tracey L. Meares
Walton Hale Hamilton Professor of Law
Director, The Justice Collaboratory
Yale Law School

Richard K. Neumann, Jr.
Alexander Bickel Professor of Law
Maurice A. Deane School of Law at Hofstra University

Robert H. Sitkoff
Austin Wakeman Scott Professor of Law
John L. Gray Professor of Law
Harvard Law School

David Alan Sklansky
Stanley Morrison Professor of Law
Faculty Co-Director, Stanford Criminal Justice Center
Stanford Law School

ASPEN CASEBOOK SERIES

CRIMINAL PROCEDURE AND RACIAL INJUSTICE

JAMES C. REHNQUIST

TRACEY MACLIN
*Raymond & Miriam Ehrlich Chair in
U.S. Constitutional Law
University of Florida Levin College of Law*

Copyright © 2025 Aspen Publishing. All Rights Reserved.

Thank you for complying with copyright laws by not reproducing or distributing any part of this book in any form without permission. Aspen Publishing supports copyright because it encourages creativity and the sharing of knowledge and fosters a climate of fairness, progress, and innovation.

No part of this publication may be reproduced or transmitted in any form or by any means, electronic or mechanical, including photocopy, recording, or utilized by any information storage or retrieval system, without written permission from the publisher. Under no circumstances may any part of this publication be used in content generation software, systems, or tools such as those that utilize artificial intelligence processes or algorithms. For information about permissions or to request permissions online, visit us at www.AspenPublishing.com.

To contact Customer Service, e-mail customer.service@aspenpublishing.com, call 1-800-950-5259, or mail correspondence to:

> Aspen Publishing
> Attn: Order Department
> 1 Wall Street
> Burlington, MA 01803

Printed in the United States of America.

1 2 3 4 5 6 7 8 9 0

ISBN 979-8-8890-6114-4

Library of Congress Cataloging-in-Publication Data

Names: Rehnquist, James C., author. | Maclin, Tracey, author.
Title: Criminal procedure and racial injustice / James C. Rehnquist, Tracey Maclin, Raymond &
    Miriam Ehrlich Chair in U.S. Constitutional Law, University of Florida, Levin College of Law.
Description: First edition. | Burlington: Aspen Publishing, [2025] | Series: Aspen casebook series |
    Includes bibliographical references and index. | Summary: "Criminal Procedure casebook
    with an emphasis on race"—Provided by publisher.
Identifiers: LCCN 2024026348 (print) | LCCN 2024026349 (ebook) | ISBN 9798889061144
    (hardback) | ISBN 9798889061151 (ebook)
Subjects: LCSH: Race discrimination—Law and legislation—United States. | Civil rights—
    United States—Criminal provisions. | Criminal procedure—United States. | Right to counsel—
    United States. | Exclusionary rule (Evidence)—United States. | Tort liability of
    police—United States. | Police misconduct—Law and legislation—United States. |
    LCGFT: Casebooks (Law)
Classification: LCC KF4755.R45 2025 (print) | LCC KF4755 (ebook) |
    DDC 345.73/05—dc23/eng/20240614
LC record available at https://lccn.loc.gov/2024026348
LC ebook record available at https://lccn.loc.gov/2024026349

About Aspen Publishing

Aspen Publishing is a leading provider of educational content and digital learning solutions to law schools in the U.S. and around the world. Aspen provides best-in-class solutions for legal education through authoritative textbooks, written by renowned authors, and breakthrough products such as Connected eBooks, Connected Quizzing, and PracticePerfect.

The Aspen Casebook Series (famously known among law faculty and students as the "red and black" casebooks) encompasses hundreds of highly regarded textbooks in more than eighty disciplines, from large enrollment courses, such as Torts and Contracts to emerging electives such as Sustainability and the Law of Policing. Study aids such as the *Examples & Explanations* and the *Emanuel Law Outlines* series, both highly popular collections, help law students master complex subject matter.

Major products, programs, and initiatives include:

- **Connected eBooks** are enhanced digital textbooks and study aids that come with a suite of online content and learning tools designed to maximize student success. Designed in collaboration with hundreds of faculty and students, the Connected eBook is a significant leap forward in the legal education learning tools available to students.
- **Connected Quizzing** is an easy-to-use formative assessment tool that tests law students' understanding and provides timely feedback to improve learning outcomes. Delivered through CasebookConnect.com, the learning platform already used by students to access their Aspen casebooks, Connected Quizzing is simple to implement and integrates seamlessly with law school course curricula.
- **PracticePerfect** is a visually engaging, interactive study aid to explain commonly encountered legal doctrines through easy-to-understand animated videos, illustrative examples, and numerous practice questions. Developed by a team of experts, PracticePerfect is the ideal study companion for today's law students.
- The **Aspen Learning Library** enables law schools to provide their students with access to the most popular study aids on the market across all of their courses. Available through an annual subscription, the online library consists of study aids in e-book, audio, and video formats with full text search, note-taking, and highlighting capabilities.
- Aspen's **Digital Bookshelf** is an institutional-level online education bookshelf, consolidating everything students and professors need to ensure success. This program ensures that every student has access to affordable course materials from day one.
- **Leading Edge** is a community centered on thinking differently about legal education and putting those thoughts into actionable strategies. At the core of the program is the Leading Edge Conference, an annual gathering of legal education thought leaders looking to pool ideas and identify promising directions of exploration.

SUMMARY OF CONTENTS

Contents	ix
Preface	xix
Acknowledgments	xxi

CHAPTER I
Introductory Principles 1

CHAPTER II
**The Roots of Modern Constitutional Criminal Procedure:
The Supreme Court, Race, and the Post-Bellum South** 11

CHAPTER III
Police Interrogation and the Fifth Amendment 77

CHAPTER IV
The Fourth Amendment 211

CHAPTER V
The Exclusionary Rule, Its Exceptions, and Suppression Hearings 473

CHAPTER VI
Addressing Police Misconduct 551

CHAPTER VII
Grand Jury 627

CHAPTER VIII
Right to Counsel and the Defense Function 721

CHAPTER IX
The Prosecution Function 811

CHAPTER X
The Department of Justice and the Prosecution of Civil Rights Crimes 905

CHAPTER XI
Pleas and Plea Bargaining 975

CHAPTER XII
Discriminatory Enforcement 1059

CHAPTER XIII
The Jury I: Scope of the Right and Other Issues 1119

CHAPTER XIV
Eyewitness Identification 1185

CHAPTER XV
The Jury II: Race and Juries 1231

CHAPTER XVI
Incarceration: Bail, Pretrial Detention, and Sentencing 1321

Table of Cases 1429
Index 1437

CONTENTS

Preface	xix
Acknowledgments	xxi

CHAPTER I
Introductory Principles — 1

A. Stages of the Criminal Process	1
B. Players in the Criminal Justice System	3
C. Criminal Procedure versus Civil Procedure	5
D. Incorporation	6
E. State Constitutional Criminal Procedure	7

CHAPTER II
The Roots of Modern Constitutional Criminal Procedure: The Supreme Court, Race, and the Post-Bellum South — 11

A. Invalidation of Convictions Where Black People Were Excluded from Juries	12
Strauder v. West Virginia	*12*
B. Peonage Convictions	17
Bailey v. Alabama	*19*
Pollock v. Williams	*30*
Papachristou v. Jacksonville	*35*
C. Mob Convictions	40
Moore v. Dempsey	*40*
Powell v. Alabama	*45*
Norris v. Alabama	*54*
D. Coerced Confessions	60
Brown v. Mississippi	*60*
Lyons v. Oklahoma	*66*
Akins v. Texas	*72*

CHAPTER III
Police Interrogation and the Fifth Amendment — 77

A. Scope of the Right Against Self-Incrimination	78
Schmerber v. California	*78*
Kastigar v. United States	*81*
Oliver's Army	89
United States v. Hubbell	*92*
Griffin v. California	*101*

B. Police Interrogation: Voluntariness and the Road to *Miranda*		104
	Ashcraft v. Tennessee	*104*
	Spano v. New York	*109*
	Massiah v. United States	*114*
C. *Miranda*		118
	Miranda v. Arizona	*118*
D. *Miranda* in Practice I: Exceptions, Interrogation, and Custody		134
	1. *Miranda* Exceptions	134
	New York v. Quarles	*134*
	2. Interrogation	138
	Rhode Island v. Innis	*138*
	3. Custody	143
	Berkemer v. McCarty	*143*
	Stansbury v. California	*148*
	J.D.B. v. North Carolina	*151*
E. *Miranda* in Practice II: Waiver and Invocation of *Miranda* Rights		157
	Michigan v. Mosley	*157*
	Edwards v. Arizona	*161*
	Berghuis v. Thompkins	*166*
	Salinas v. Texas	*171*
	Doyle v. Ohio	*177*
F. Consequences of *Miranda* Violations		183
	Oregon v. Elstad	*184*
	Missouri v. Seibert	*191*
G. The Durability of *Miranda*		196
	Dickerson v. United States	*197*
	Vega v. Tekoh	*202*

CHAPTER IV

The Fourth Amendment 211

A. What Is a Search for Fourth Amendment Purposes?		211
	Katz v. United States	*213*
	Florida v. Riley	*218*
	Kyllo v. United States	*225*
	United States v. Jones	*230*
	Florida v. Jardines	*239*
	Carpenter v. United States	*243*
B. What Is a Seizure for Fourth Amendment Purposes? Race, Seizure, and Force		259
	1. Police Encounters and Seizures	260
	United States v. Mendenhall	*260*
	California v. Hodari D.	*266*
	United States v. Drayton	*269*
	2. Should Race Matter?	276
	State v. Sum	*277*
	3. Seizures and Police Use of Force	284
	Tennessee v. Garner	*285*
	Graham v. Connor	*291*
C. The Warrant Requirement and Its Exceptions		295
	1. Warrant Requirements: Search Warrants	296

a. Particularity		296
b. Probable Cause		297
Illinois v. Gates		*297*
c. Warrant Execution Issues		305
2. Plain View Exception		306
Horton v. California		*306*
3. Warrantless Arrests		311
Payton v. New York		*311*
Atwater v. City of Lago Vista		*319*
4. Search Incident to Arrest		329
Chimel v. California		*329*
United States v. Robinson		*333*
5. Consent Searches		341
Schneckloth v. Bustamonte		*341*
Illinois v. Rodriguez		*350*
6. Exigent Circumstances		356
Brigham City v. Stuart		*356*
7. Administrative or "Special Needs" Searches		359
a. Vehicle Checkpoints		360
City of Indianapolis v. Edmond		*361*
b. High School Students		367
Vernonia School District 47J v. Acton		*367*
8. The Automobile Exception		375
Carroll v. United States		*375*
Brinegar v. United States		*384*
California v. Carney		*387*
D. Exception to the Probable Cause Requirement: The *Terry* Doctrine		391
Terry v. Ohio		*392*
Minnesota v. Dickerson		*407*
Hiibel v. Sixth Judicial District Court of Nevada		*411*
Arizona v. Johnson		*416*
E. Race and Suspicion		421
1. *Terry* and Race		421
Illinois v. Wardlow		*424*
2. Border Searches and Racial Profiling		430
United States v. Brignoni-Ponce		*430*
3. Traffic Stops: Pretext, Policing, and Race		437
United States v. Laymon		*438*
Whren v. United States		*448*
State v. Soto		*454*
United States v. Johnson		*463*

CHAPTER V
The Exclusionary Rule, Its Exceptions, and Suppression Hearings

473

A. The Exclusionary Rule		473
Mapp v. Ohio		*474*
B. The Good Faith Exception		481
United States v. Leon		*481*
Herring v. United States		*491*

C. Attenuation	497
Hudson v. Michigan	497
Utah v. Strieff	503
D. Standing	512
Jones v. United States	512
Minnesota v. Carter	517
Byrd v. United States	521
E. Impeachment	528
Walder v. United States	528
Harris v. New York	530
United States v. Havens	532
James v. Illinois	536
F. Suppression Hearings	540
United States v. Matos	541
People v. McMurty	543
United States v. Restrepo	546

CHAPTER VI
Addressing Police Misconduct
551

A. Awakening of § 1983	552
Monroe v. Pape	552
B. Section 1983 Actions Against Municipalities	558
Monell v. Department of Social Services of the City of New York	558
Canton v. Harris	561
Connick v. Thompson	566
City of Los Angeles v. Lyons	573
Floyd v. City of New York	580
C. Qualified Immunity	588
Pierson v. Ray	588
Harlow v. Fitzgerald	594
Malley v. Briggs	599
Anderson v. Creighton	603
Saucier v. Katz	608
Mullenix v. Luna	615
Ziglar v. Abbasi	618
D. The Department of Justice and Structural Reform Litigation	620
United States v. City of Columbus	620

CHAPTER VII
Grand Jury
627

A. Introduction: Grand Jury Mythos	628
B. Race and Grand Jury Composition	629
Castaneda v. Partida	629
Vasquez v. Hillery	634
C. Grand Jury Independence and Informality	638
United States v. Costello	638
United States v. Williams	641
United States v. Cox	653

Contents **xiii**

D.	Grand Jury Subpoena Power	662
	United States v. Dionisio	*662*
	United States v. R. Enterprises, Inc.	*668*
E.	Grand Jury Secrecy	673
	United States v. Sells Engineering, Inc.	*674*
	United States v. Bryant	*680*
F.	Witnesses in the Grand Jury	682
	United States v. Mandujano	*683*
	United States v. Washington	*690*
G.	Prosecutorial Abuse of the Grand Jury's Powers	699
	United States v. Doe	*699*
	People v. Tyler	*703*
H.	The Indictment	709
	Kaley v. United States	*710*
I.	The Grand Jury and Investigation of Police Misconduct	718

CHAPTER VIII
Right to Counsel and the Defense Function

721

A.	Scope of the Right to Counsel	721
	Betts v. Brady	*722*
	Griffin v. Illinois	*727*
	Gideon v. Wainwright	*730*
	Gideon's Two Trials	736
	Douglas v. California	*738*
	Argersinger v. Hamlin	*740*
	Alabama v. Shelton	*745*
B.	Consequences of Representation by Counsel	749
	Brewer v. Williams	*750*
C.	Effective Assistance of Counsel: Standard of Performance	756
	Strickland v. Washington	*757*
	People v. Garrison	*767*
	Rompilla v. Beard	*770*
D.	Effective Assistance of Counsel: Indigent Defense Problems	776
	State v. A.N.J.	*776*
	State v. Wigley	*783*
	Missouri v. Pratte	*787*
E.	Zealous Advocacy	791
	Nix v. Whiteside	*792*
	Taylor v. Illinois	*799*
	McCoy v. Louisiana	*804*

CHAPTER IX
The Prosecution Function

811

A.	Discretion	812
	1. The Concern About Discretion	812
	Morrison v. Olson	*814*
	2. Prosecutorial Discretion in Charging Decisions and the Influence of Race	820
	a. Race and Charging Discretion	820
	b. The Prosecutor's Plenary Charging Power and Discretion	821
	United States v. Fokker Services B.V.	*822*

xiv   Contents

3. The Prosecutor's Discretion to Use Unsavory and Unreliable Witnesses and Tactics		832
Sherman v. United States		*832*
Jacobson v. United States		*836*
Hoffa v. United States		*842*
B. Prosecutor's Disclosure Obligations		848
1. Exculpatory Information		848
Brady v. Maryland		*848*
Giglio v. United States		*851*
United States v. Ruiz		*854*
Milke v. Ryan		*860*
2. Discovery Obligations		868
Williams v. Florida		*869*
Williams v. United States		*875*
3. Witness Statements		879
United States v. Jencks		*879*
C. Ethics and Accountability		886
1. General Ethical Obligations of Prosecutors		886
Berger v. United States		*887*
Rogue Cop?		890
2. Prosecutors' Lack of Accountability		891
3. Prosecutorial Misconduct Examples		892
United States v. Hardy		*893*
United States v. Coast of Maine Lobster Co.		*898*

CHAPTER X
The Department of Justice and the Prosecution of Civil Rights Crimes

905

A. Reconstruction Era Congressional Criminal Legislation	906
B. Federal Criminal Enforcement During Reconstruction	907
C. The Supreme Court and Reconstruction Legislation	909
D. The Department of Justice Civil Rights Section and the Disappointment of *Screws v. United States*	911
United States v. Classic	*912*
Screws v. United States	*918*
United States v. Crews	*931*
Williams v. United States	*935*
United States v. Price	*938*
E. Double Jeopardy, Successive Prosecutions, and Federal Civil Rights Enforcement	948
Abbate v. United States	*948*
Petite v. United States	*954*
Gamble v. United States	*961*

CHAPTER XI
Pleas and Plea Bargaining

975

A. Introduction: The Plea-Bargaining Controversy	976
1. Race and Plea Bargaining	976
2. Plea Bargaining History	977

B. The Plea Hearing: Waiver and Consequences		979
	Boykin v. Alabama	*979*
C. Guilty Pleas and Voluntariness		984
	Brady v. United States	*985*
	North Carolina v. Alford	*992*
D. Plea Bargaining, the Constitution, and Coercion		997
	Bordenkircher v. Hayes	*997*
	United States v. Goodwin	*1006*
E. The Supreme Court Discovers Plea Agreements Again		1011
	Padilla v. Kentucky	*1012*
	Missouri v. Frye	*1019*
F. The Enforceability of Plea Agreements: Breach and Collateral Waivers		1028
	Santobello v. New York	*1028*
	United States v. Raynor	*1032*
	United States v. Guillen	*1038*
	Watson v. United States	*1042*
	Hurlow v. United States	*1046*
	Class v. United States	*1052*

CHAPTER XII
Discriminatory Enforcement

1059

A. Discriminatory Prosecution: The Perfection of *Yick Wo v. Hopkins*		1060
	Yick Wo v. Hopkins	*1060*
	Oyler v. Boles	*1066*
B. Lower Courts and Selective Prosecution Claims		1068
	United States v. Robinson	*1068*
	United States v. Falk	*1072*
	United States v. Berrios	*1080*
C. The Supreme Court Steps Back In		1084
	Wayte v. United States	*1084*
	United States v. Armstrong	*1089*
D. Selective Investigation		1102
	People v. Harris	*1102*
	Butler v. Cooper	*1105*
	United States v. Conley	*1110*

CHAPTER XIII
The Jury I: Scope of the Right and Other Issues

1119

A. Scope of the Right to Trial by Jury		1119
	Duncan v. Louisiana	*1119*
	United States v. Gaudin	*1127*
	Ramos v. Louisiana	*1133*
B. Jury Nullification		1140
	United States v. Dougherty	*1140*
	United States v. Sepulveda	*1151*
C. Jury Knowledge of Potential Punishment		1153
	Rogers v. United States	*1154*
	Shannon v. United States	*1157*
	United States v. Trent	*1163*

Contents

D. Jury Instruction Issues: Reasonable Doubt, the *Allen* Charge, and Implicit Bias — 1170
1. Reasonable Doubt — 1170
   Sandoval v. California — *1170*
2. The *Allen* Charge — 1177
   United States v. Paniagua-Ramos — *1178*
3. Implicit Bias Instruction — 1184

CHAPTER XIV
Eyewitness Identification — 1185

A. Eyewitness Identification and the Right to Counsel — 1185
   United States v. Wade — *1185*
   Gilbert v. California — *1196*
   Kirby v. Illinois — *1198*
   United States v. Ash — *1201*
B. Eyewitness Identification and Due Process — 1206
   Stovall v. Denno — *1206*
   Manson v. Brathwaite — *1208*
   Perry v. New Hampshire — *1215*
   Commonwealth v. Gomes — *1221*
   United States v. Thoreen — *1226*

CHAPTER XV
The Jury II: Race and Juries — 1231

A. Race and the Sixth Amendment's Fair Cross-Section Requirement — 1231
   Taylor v. Louisiana — *1231*
   Duren v. Missouri — *1237*
B. Bias Challenges to Potential Jurors — 1242
   Ham v. South Carolina — *1242*
   Ristaino v. Ross — *1246*
   Turner v. Murray — *1250*
C. Race and Peremptory Challenges — 1257
   Batson v. Kentucky — *1259*
   Georgia v. McCollum — *1270*
   Hernandez v. New York — *1277*
   Flowers v. Mississippi — *1287*
D. Cross-Racial Identifications at Trial — 1303
   United States v. Hines — *1303*
   Commonwealth v. Bastaldo — *1308*
   People v. Boone — *1314*

CHAPTER XVI
Incarceration: Bail, Pretrial Detention, and Sentencing — 1321

A. Mass Incarceration — 1321
B. Bail and Pretrial Detention — 1322
   Stack v. Boyle — *1322*
   United States v. Salerno — *1326*
   United States v. Boustani — *1334*
   Odonnell v. Harris County, Texas — *1337*

C. The Sentencing Guidelines		1341
	Mistretta v. United States	*1343*
	United States v. Leviner	*1351*
	Booker v. United States	*1357*
D. Race and Sentencing		1368
	Maxwell v. Bishop	*1368*
	McCleskey v. Kemp	*1378*
	United States v. Clary	*1401*
	Belcher v. Connecticut	*1421*
Table of Cases		1429
Index		1437

PREFACE

This casebook brings a sustained emphasis on race to the traditional content of criminal procedure. To be clear, the book is not intended as a wholesale revision of the standard criminal procedure fare: It amply covers all the familiar subject matter areas, as the Table of Contents should make clear. But it integrates into these and other materials, wherever possible, the roles that racial prejudice and racial disparities have played and continue to play in our criminal justice system. For example, in a chapter on jury trials the book has a focus on *Batson v. Kentucky* and its progeny that is more extensive than counterpart books. For another example, in connection with *Terry v. Ohio*, the book looks deeply into the role that race—mostly implicitly—played not only in the Court's written decision but also in the trial court and appellate advocacy that produced that decision, including the direct and cross-examinations of Detective McFadden in the suppression hearing. The book also includes four race-orientated chapters not found in other criminal procedure casebooks: The Roots of Modern Constitutional Criminal Procedure (Chapter II), Race and Juries (Chapter XV), The Department of Justice and the Prosecution of Civil Rights Crimes (Chapter X), and Discriminatory Enforcement (Chapter XII).

An argument could be made that the DOJ prosecution chapter and another atypical chapter, Addressing Police Misconduct (Chapter VI), focusing on § 1983 and other civil remedies, aren't really "criminal procedure" topics. Fair enough. They are included for other reasons: the DOJ chapter because it permits an important historical and contemporary look into race and federal criminal enforcement, and the police misconduct chapter because, among other reasons, of the subject's increasing invocation by the Court as an alternative to the exclusionary rule.

These five unconventional chapters are not a package deal. They do not depend on each other or on any other chapters. A professor could fruitfully use some or all of these chapters, in whole or in part. Because the book aspires to something novel it does so modestly, aiming to permit maximum flexibility.

A secondary overarching goal of the book is to emphasize the role and power of prosecutors in the contemporary criminal justice system. As many scholars and judges have recognized, in our contemporary landscape of minimum mandatory sentences and unfettered plea bargaining, prosecutors not only exercise their historical function of making charging decisions but also, in the exercise of that power, significantly impact and even effectively determine the length of sentences. Chapter IX, The Prosecution Function, focuses on the powers, responsibilities, and obligations of prosecutors in this system. In keeping with this emphasis, and recognizing the reality that due to the prevalence of the notorious "trial penalty" in the modern plea-bargaining and sentencing regimes most criminal justice happens outside of a trial setting, the book also devotes more attention than most books to the grand jury (Chapter VII), pleas and plea bargaining (Chapter XI), and incarceration (Chapter XVI).

The book also focuses, more generally, on lawyering. Should the prosecutor have presented that piece of exculpatory information to the grand jury even if she wasn't required to under *Williams v. United States*? How could the cross-examination of the bank teller–cooperator in *Giglio v. United States* be improved? This emphasis comes from a conviction that encouraging

xix

students to think about what the lawyers did or did not do in the cases only enhances their understanding of the cases' doctrinal significance. Advocacy is not the enemy of the doctrine. Ideally, such a focus may even encourage a few students to pursue a career that includes time spent as a responsible and ethical prosecutor and/or a creative and aggressive defense attorney.

The book's pedagogical approach is conventional. It consists primarily of cases followed by a numbered Notes and Questions section. There are many Notes and Questions for each case, in keeping with the book's themes to encourage thinking and discussion not only about the case's doctrinal situation but also about racial implications where applicable, the decisions made or forgone by the lawyers in the case, and also (again where applicable) the historical context of the case. The expectation is that professors will assign to students only the Notes and Questions that they anticipate to be most fruitful based on their own interests and emphases.

The book also contains approximately 80 photographs, mostly of defendants, lawyers, or images establishing relevant historical, cultural, or geographical context.

The cases have been edited for space and relevance. Almost all case citations within cases have been removed except where the citation was of contextual relevance. Unlike these omissions, the removal of more substantial matter — e.g., sections, paragraphs, or sentences in cases — are noted by ellipses (. . .).

There are three versions of this casebook: a hardcover volume (which includes everything) and two paperback volumes, one for use in courses focusing on the investigative phase of criminal procedure and the other for use in courses focusing on the adjudicative phase. Both of the paperback volumes include the entirety of Chapter I, Introductory Principles, and Chapter II, Roots of Modern Constitutional Criminal Procedure. The chapter numbering and pagination of both paperback volumes remains identical to the pagination in the hardcover volume. In other words, the investigative volume includes Chapters I through VII of the hardcover volume, while the adjudicative volume begins with Chapters I and II of the main volume and then picks up with Chapter VIII of the main volume.

Mr. Rehnquist thanks his coauthor Tracey Maclin for believing in and joining this venture, and for the insight, expertise, and credibility he has brought to bear on it; Aspen Publishing, especially Joe Terry, who gave a non-academic lawyer the opportunity to take a shot at this book, as well as editors Anton Yakovlev and Kathy Langone for their excellent assistance throughout and Corinne Pulicay for her photograph procurement; the many reviewers who gave helpful comments and suggestions on early drafts, especially David Sklansky, William Ortman, Dan Medwed, and Barry Friedman; and to his former law firm Goodwin Procter LLP, and his good friends there, who provided both institutional and personal support for this effort, especially his former Goodwin assistant Shannen Flanagan. Lastly, and above all, he thanks to his family — his wife Anna; children Andy, Dana, Peter Grace, and Thomas; and daughters-in-law Leah, MK, Molly, and Erica — for their continuous and loyal support.

ACKNOWLEDGMENTS

The authors gratefully acknowledge permission to reprint excerpts from the following:

A chain gang, ca. 1898. Photograph. Library of Congress, https://www.loc.gov/resource/det.4a10700/.

A choke hold. Photograph. Expert Infantry via Flickr. Licensed under CC BY 2.0 DEED, https://creativecommons.org/licenses/by/2.0/.

A segregated bus terminal in Memphis, Tennessee. Photograph. Library of Congress, https://www.loc.gov/item/2017862145/.

Abe Fortas and President Johnson. Photograph. LBJ Library, http://www.lbjlibrary.net/collections/photo-archive/photolab-detail.html?id=940.

Alexander Butterfield. Photograph. Richard M. Nixon Presidential Library via Wikimedia Commons.

Amos T. Ackerman. Photograph. Library of Congress via Wikimedia Commons.

Andrew Volstead. Photograph. Library of Congress, https://www.loc.gov/pictures/item/2016857711/.

Anthony "Fat Tony" Salerno. Photograph. Wikimedia Commons.

Anthony Amsterdam. Photograph. Copyright © John Earle for NYU Law Magazine. Reprinted with permission from Anthony Amsterdam and NYU Law Magazine.

Attorney General Edwin Meese. Photograph. Wikimedia Commons.

Attorney General Robert Jackson. Photograph. Library of Congress, https://www.loc.gov/item/2016877860/.

Bar-Gill, Oren, et al. "Taking Warrants Seriously." *Northwestern University Law Review*, vol. 106, no. 4, 2012. Northwestern University Pritzker School of Law. Reprinted with permission from the authors.

Bay County Courthouse in Panama City, Florida. Photograph. Ebyabe via Wikimedia Commons. Licensed under CC BY-SA 3.0 DEED, https://creativecommons.org/licenses/by-sa/3.0/deed.en.

Benjamin Bristow. Photograph. Library of Congress via Wikimedia Commons.

Bibas, Stephanos. "Regulating the Plea-Bargaining Market: From Caveat Emptor to Consumer Protection Consumer Protection." *California Law Review*, vol. 99, 2011. University of California, Berkeley, School of Law.

Bobby Kennedy. Photograph. Wikimedia Commons.

Bobby Seale. Photograph. Wikimedia Commons.

Brown v. Mississippi Defendants on the cover of the NAACP's The Crisis. Photograph, April 1935. Vieilles Annonces via Flickr, www.flickr.com/photos/vieilles_annonces/5045426107.

Butler, Paul. "Mississippi Goddamn: Flowers v. Mississippi's Cheap Racial Justice." *The Supreme Court Review*, vol. 2019, May 2020. University of Chicago Press. Reprinted with permission from the author.

Butler, Paul. "Racially Based Jury Nullification: Black Power in the Criminal Justice System." *The Yale Law Journal*, vol. 105, no. 3, Dec. 1995. The Yale Law Journal Company, Inc. Reprinted with permission from the author.

Classic phone booth. Photograph. N9LXI via Wikimedia Commons. Licensed under CC BY-SA 3.0 DEED, https://creativecommons.org/licenses/by-sa/3.0/deed.en.

Cleveland Sellers. Video screenshot. Library of Congress, https://www.loc.gov/item/2015669180/.

Cole, David. "Gideon v. Wainright and Strickland v. Washington: Broken Promises." *Criminal Procedure Stories*, edited by Carol E. Steiker, Foundation Press, 2006.

Constance Baker Motley. Photograph. Wikimedia Commons.

EJI Memorial in Montgomery, Alabama. Photograph. Copyright © Roy Johnson/ Alamy Stock Photo.

Elise and Roy Olmstead, Seattle, 1925. Photograph. Museum of History & Industry Collection, https://digitalcollections.lib.washington.edu/digital/collection/imlsmohai/id/892.

Emory Bruckner. Photograph. Library of Congress, https://www.loc.gov/item/2014687743/.

Eric Foner. Photograph. Wikimedia Commons.

Epps, Daniel, and William Ortman. "The Informed Jury." *Vanderbilt Law Review*, vol. 75, no. 3, Apr. 2022. Vanderbilt University Law School. Reprinted with permission.

Evangelisto Ramos. Photograph. Copyright © Sophia Germer/NOLA.com/The Times-Picayune/The New Orleans Advocate.

Fountains of Wayne Lawn Ornament Store in Wayne, New Jersey. Photograph. Courtesy of the Manhattan Chowder Blog, 3.bp.blogspot.com/_XkZRvEeVzGA/Rl9TreEcTMI/AAAAAAAAASY/nMMhyjrDTiA/s1600-h/IMG_3569.JPG.

Frank Costello. Photograph. Library of Congress, http://loc.gov/pictures/resource/cph.3c20716/.

Fred T. Korematsu. Photograph. Courtesy of the family of Fred T. Korematsu via Wikimedia Commons. Licensed under CC BY 2.0, https://creativecommons.org/licenses/by/2.0.

Garrett, Brandon L. "Eyewitnesses and Exclusion." *Vanderbilt Law Review*, vol. 65, no. 2, Jan. 2012, p. Vanderbilt University Law School. Reprinted with permission from the author.

Gideon versus Wainright sign. Photograph. Ebyabe via Wikimedia Commons. Licensed under CC BY-SA 3.0 DEED, https://creativecommons.org/licenses/by-sa/3.0/deed.en.

Goldberg, Steven H. "Harmless Error: Constitutional Sneak Thief." *The Journal of Criminal Law and Criminology*, vol. 71, no. 4, 1980. Northwestern University School of Law.

Handheld Thermal Imaging Device. Photograph. Copyright © Ivan Smuk/Shutterstock.

Harold Cox. Photograph. Courtesy of Open Jurist, https://openjurist.org/judge/william-harold-cox.

Harvey Matusow. Screenshot from a March 15, 1955 news clip, https://digital.library.unt.edu/ark:/67531/metadc1940889/ (accessed March 26, 2024). University of North Texas Libraries, UNT Digital Library, UNT Libraries Special Collections.

Henry Hill and Ray Liotta. Photograph. Copyright © s_bukley/Deposit Photos.

Home of Ossian Sweet. Photograph. Andrew Jameson via Wikimedia Commons. Licensed under CC BY-SA 3.0 DEED, https://creativecommons.org/licenses/by-sa/3.0/deed.en.

In the Dark Podcast team. Photograph. Reprinted with permission from Dr. Alan Bean.

Irvin Younger. Photograph. Library of Congress, https://www.loc.gov/item/2020734212/.

J. Edgar Hoover in 1961. Photograph. Library of Congress, http://loc.gov/pictures/resource/ppmsc.03262/.

Jackson, Robert H. *The Federal Prosecutor*. www.justice.gov/sites/default/files/ag/legacy/2011/09/16/04-01-1940.pdf. Delivered at the Second Annual Conference of United States Attorneys, Washington, D. C.

James Batson and his mother. Photograph. Reprinted with permission from Sean Rameswaram.

Jimmy Hoffa. Photograph. New York World-Telegram and Sun collection, Library of Congress.

John Adams. Painting. National Gallery of Art, https://www.nga.gov/collection/art-object-page.42933.html.

Joy, Peter A. "Rationing Justice by Rationing Lawyers." *Washington University Journal of Law & Policy*, vol. 37, no. 1, 2011. Washington University in St. Louis School of Law .

Klarman, Michael. "The Racial Origins of Modern Criminal Procedure." *Michigan Law Review*, vol. 99, no. 1, Oct. 2000. University of Michigan Law School. Reprinted with permission of the author.

Kenneth Starr. Photograph. Gage Skidmore via Wikimedia Commons. Licensed under CC BY-SA 2.0 DEED, https://creativecommons.org/licenses/by-sa/2.0/deed.en.

Larry Dudley Hiibel. Photograph. Copyright © ZUMA Press, Inc. / Alamy Stock Photo.

Larry English, Robert McCoy's lawyer. Photograph. Reprinted with permission from Dash Media PR.

Len Bias. Photograph. Copyright © 1986 Associated Press.

Louis Stokes. Photograph. Via Wikimedia Commons.

Members of the Wickersham Commission. Photograph. Library of Congress, https://www.loc.gov/pictures/item/2016889308/.

Moorefielf Storey. Photograph. Wikimedia Commons.

NAACP Headquarters Flag. Photograph. Library of Congress, https://www.loc.gov/resource/ppmsca.09705/.

New Jersey Turnpike, Exit 3. Photograph. Famartin via Wikimedia Commons. Licensed under CC BY-SA 4.0 DEED, https://creativecommons.org/licenses/by-sa/4.0/deed.en.

Nick Katzenbach. Photograph. John F. Kennedy Presidential Library and Museum via Wikimedia Commons.

Officer Elton Hymon. Photograph. The National Newspaper Publishers Association (NNPA), nnpa.org/nnpa_newswire/wp-content/uploads/2019/03/Rev.-Elton-Hymon-corrected-731x1024.jpg.

Ossian Sweet. Photograph. Detroit Public Library, https://digitalcollections.detroitpubliclibrary.org/islandora/object/islandora:143138.

Post-mortem photograph of Robert Hall's bludgeoned body. Photograph. Library of Congress, https://www.loc.gov/pictures/item/2001701644/.

Robert McCoy and his counsel Larry English. Photograph. Courtesy of the Bossier Parish Sheriff's Office.

Rodney King. Photograph. Justin Hoch via Wikimedia Commons. Licensed under CC BY 3.0 DEED, https://creativecommons.org/licenses/by/3.0/deed.en.

Roy Wilkins, Walter White, and Thurgood Marshall. Photograph. Library of Congress, www.loc.gov/item/95518993/.

Schmidt, Benno C. Jr. "Juries, Jurisdiction, and Race Discrimination: The Lost Promise of Strauder v. West Virginia." *Texas Law Review*, vol. 61, no. 8, May 1982. University of Texas School of Law. Reprinted with permission.

Schmidt, Benno C. Jr. "Principle and Prejudice: The Supreme Court and Race in the Progressive Era. Part 2: The Peonage Cases." *Columbia Law Review*, vol. 82, 1982. Columbia Law School.

Scottsboro Defendants with Their Lawyer, Samuel Leibowitz. Photograph, 1932. Courtesy of the Morgan County (AL) Archives.

Stephen Trott. Photograph. Wikimedia Commons.

The Edward R. Roybal Federal Courthouse, Los Angeles, California. Photograph. DocFreeman24 via Wikimedia Commons. Licensed under CC BY-SA 4.0 DEED, https://creativecommons.org/licenses/by-sa/4.0/deed.en.

USDJ Fred James Cassibry. Photograph. Wikimedia Commons.

Veronia High School. Photograph. Tedder via Wikimedia Commons. Licensed under CC BY 3.0 DEED, https://creativecommons.org/licenses/by/3.0/deed.en.

Vorenberg, James. "Decent Restraint of Prosecutorial Power." *Harvard Law Review*, vol. 94, no. 7, May 1981. Copyright © Harvard Law School.

W.D. Lyons, NAACP defendant, handcuffed and standing next to six arresting officers and attorneys. Photograph. Library of Congress, www.loc.gov/item/95518936/.

Walter White. Photograph. Library of Congress, https://www.loc.gov/item/2017765010/.

Warren McClesky. Photograph. Copyright © Atlanta Journal-Constitution / Associated Press.

Wesley McKinley. Video screenshot. Boulder Public Library.

William A. Dunning. Photograph. *A History of Political Theories, Recent Times: Essays on Contemporary Developments in Political Theory*. The Macmillan Company, 1924.

Yick Wo Elementary School. Photograph. JACKDD via Flickr. Licensed under CC BY-SA 2.0 DEED, https://creativecommons.org/licenses/by-sa/2.0/.

CRIMINAL PROCEDURE AND RACIAL INJUSTICE

CHAPTER I

INTRODUCTORY PRINCIPLES

The history of American freedom is, in no small measure, the history of procedure.

Malinski v. New York, 324 U.S. 401 (1945) (Frankfurter, J.)

A. STAGES OF THE CRIMINAL PROCESS

Investigation. Almost all criminal prosecutions are preceded by some degree of government investigation. At one end of the spectrum are complex investigations featuring the use of the grand jury and/or electronic surveillance to develop evidence in complex fraud or racketeering cases. These investigations can take months or even years before any charges are brought. At the other end are more "reactive" cases, where police or other law enforcement agents respond in real time to facts they observe or information they receive from witnesses and proceed quickly to an arrest after perhaps only a handful of interviews. Generally speaking, during the investigative phase of a case—before any charges are brought—the police have more powers and criminal suspects have fewer rights than they do once charges are brought.

Arrest. An arrest is an indefinite curtailment by police of the liberty of a criminal suspect. An arrest usually but not always results in a criminal charge against the arrestee. An arrest has constitutional significance in two important respects. First, when a suspect is under arrest the suspect can only be interrogated by police after receiving *Miranda* warnings and waiving his rights to remain silent and to be represented by counsel in connection with the interrogation. Second, a person under arrest must either be released, or brought to court within 48 hours of the arrest where his detention must be justified by a showing of probable cause that he has committed a crime.

The Criminal Charge. The forms in which a criminal charge is brought vary by state and even within the federal system. The federal system requires a grand jury indictment for serious crimes, but approximately half the states have no such requirement. In the states without a grand jury indictment requirement, charges can be brought by "complaints" or "informations" that sometimes will require a subsequent preliminary hearing where a judge will make a determination whether the charge is supported by probable cause. The filing of criminal charges leads to the formal engagement of the judiciary in a criminal case for the first time.

Arraignment/Initial Appearance. Most states require some sort of an initial appearance in a criminal case, often called an arraignment, where several things usually happen: (1) the judge will ensure the defendant is aware of the charges against him, sometimes reading the defendant the written charges; (2) the defendant will enter an initial plea to the charges, almost always a plea of not guilty unless the defendant has already agreed to cooperate with the government's continuing investigation; (3) a hearing will be held as to the terms of the defendant's pretrial release, if any; and (4) arrangements will be made for the retention or appointment of counsel for the defendant, if they haven't already been made. (If defendant does have not have counsel at this initial appearance, steps (1) through (3) may be deferred until defendant is represented.)

Scheduling Conferences. At some point early in the case the court will set scheduling deadlines, often with input from the parties. The critical deadlines, in addition to a trial date, will be a deadline for motions to suppress and for the parties to discharge their disclosure obligations under the applicable federal or state rules. The court also may set deadlines for other motions, such as motions to dismiss the indictment or to obtain a bill of particulars (adding detail to the charges), or more specific trial-related deadlines regarding evidence, such as for the filing of motions in limine or for turning over witness and exhibit lists.

Plea Bargaining. Plea bargaining is not a "stage" of a criminal case, exactly, but it needs to be included here because over 95 percent of all criminal cases are resolved by a guilty plea by defendant. Plea bargaining can take place at any time, including during the investigative phase, at one extreme, and during or even after trial, at the other. Timing can be crucial to the plea bargaining process. Defendants will often be reluctant to plead guilty unless and until they know enough about the strength of the government's case, usually through reviewing discovery provided by the government (including exculpatory information), in order to negotiate effectively with the prosecutor and to make an intelligent decision as to their best interests. Prosecutors, on the other hand, are often most amenable to negotiating a plea early in the case, before they have invested significant effort in the case beyond what was necessary to bring charges.

If the parties reach an agreement the defendant will enter a plea of guilty before a judge, who will normally accept the plea, without considering its substantive fairness or merit, as long as she is convinced the defendant is making a voluntary, knowing, and intelligent waiver of his constitutional right to a jury trial and the attendant rights that go along with that right. A guilty plea is a criminal "conviction," the equivalent for almost all legal purposes of being found guilty by a jury at trial.

Trial. Trial will usually be before a jury, which must find defendant guilty beyond a reasonable doubt. The jury's decision must be unanimous. Federal law and most state law require a twelve-person jury but the constitutional minimum is only six. A federal defendant can waive his right to a jury trial and have the case tried before the judge (a "bench trial"), but only if the prosecutor and judge both agree. State practice on jury waivers varies. Many constitutional rights come into play at trial. For example, the Sixth Amendment requires that defendants be permitted to cross-examine the government's witnesses and to demand the attendance of their own witnesses, and the Fifth Amendment requires that if the defendant declines to testify the government cannot comment on that lack of evidence.

Sentencing. If defendant is convicted he will thereafter be sentenced, with the timing and content of that procedure largely a matter of state law and practice in state courts. In federal court sentencings usually occur two to three months after verdict. During the interim period the probation department prepares an often lengthy presentence report, which includes a personal history of the defendant, including any aggravating or mitigating information; a complete explanation of the defendant's criminal history; and an analysis of how the United States Sentencing Guidelines apply to the defendant's conduct. A sentencing hearing will be held where the parties will have an opportunity to dispute any aspect of the presentence report, including the opportunity to make arguments as to how the Guidelines should be applied in the case and what sentence is appropriate. The judge will resolve the disputes and impose the sentence.

Appeals. Defendants have a right to appeal from their conviction. They may challenge the jury's verdict on any of several grounds, including the following: the evidence was insufficient to support the jury's verdict; the trial judge made errors in her evidentiary rulings or instructions to the jury or erroneously admitted evidence that was illegally obtained by the government; the theory of the case was legally flawed, that is, the facts proven did not violate the statute that was charged; and so on. The defendant can also appeal his sentence as being too harsh although many prosecuting authorities, including the Department of Justice, will usually require a defendant who pleads guilty to agree to waive any sentencing appeal he may have. It is extremely difficult to prevail on appeal on any issue that was not contested at trial. Indeed, the record on appeal is confined to the record of what took place during the trial. It is also difficult to have the sentence stayed (delayed) while an appeal is pending.

Post-Conviction Relief. A defendant who loses on his "direct appeal," as most do, can subsequently bring a claim for post-conviction relief in either state or federal court, wherever his trial was. Post-conviction motions are commonly although not exclusively based on information that was not presented at trial, such as ineffective assistance of trial or appellate counsel or newly discovered physical evidence or witnesses. At the federal level and in some state systems the potential grounds for post-conviction relief have been substantially narrowed in the last few decades by statute as well as by judicial decisions.

B. PLAYERS IN THE CRIMINAL JUSTICE SYSTEM

Police and Other Law Enforcement Agents. Primary responsibility for investigating criminal activity and apprehending criminal suspects lies with local and other state and federal law enforcement agents. There are an estimated 18,000 separate police and law enforcement agencies in the United States, including local municipal police departments, county sheriff's offices, state troopers, and federal law enforcement agencies. The police department is the nation's largest, with approximately 36,000 officers; many small towns have their own independent police officers with fewer than ten officers. In most local police departments the senior police officer is called the chief of police; in larger cities the title is usually police commissioner. Both commissioners and chiefs are usually appointed by the mayor or an equivalent local municipal authority. Approximately 80 percent of police officers nationwide are members of a union.

Prosecutors. There are approximately 2,300 separate state prosecutor's offices in the United States, typically corresponding to a county or other local subdivision of a state. In Rhode Island the attorney general is responsible for all prosecutions in the entire state. In all but three states (Connecticut, Hawaii, and New Jersey) prosecutors are elected. The United States is the only country in the world where prosecutors are elected. The elected prosecutor in charge of the office is usually called the district attorney (or state's attorney or commonwealth's attorney) and the "line" prosecutors underneath her are usually called assistant district attorneys (ADAs).

At the federal level the President appoints the senior prosecutors, called United States attorneys, for each of the country's 94 judicial districts. While United States attorneys largely operate independently they are part of, and are ultimately responsible to, the Department of Justice. New United States attorneys are usually appointed each time there is a change in the political party of the President. The "line" attorneys under the U.S. attorney are called assistant United States attorneys (AUSAs).

Judges and Magistrates. All federal judges—including the trial judges of the 94 United States District Courts, the judges of the 12 United States Circuit Courts of Appeals, and the Supreme Court—are appointed by the President and must be confirmed by the Senate. State judges are selected by a variety of methods, including election, appointment, and combined methods that can include appointment from candidates recommended by a panel. At the federal level United States magistrate judges, appointed by the district court, are empowered to handle minor criminal cases and pretrial matters, including arraignments and conferences. They also authorize search warrants. Many states also have magistrate judges or their equivalent, who have authority over minor criminal and pretrial matters.

Defendants. Persons who have been charged with crimes are called defendants. Unless and until charges are brought by a prosecutor, persons on law enforcement radar may be called "suspects" or "targets" (in DOJ parlance) but it is the formal act of filing charges that makes someone a defendant. It is this formality that establishes a right to counsel, although the Supreme Court's *Miranda* decision also provides that persons subjected to custodial interrogation by police also have a right to counsel even if they have not been charged.

Defense Counsel. Defendants charged with felonies or lesser offenses that could result in substantial jail time have a constitutional right to counsel, including a right to court-appointed counsel if they cannot afford to pay for a lawyer. In federal court approximately 66 percent of felony defendants are represented by appointed counsel; in state courts 88 percent of felony defendants have appointed counsel. There are two main types of court-appointed counsel: employees of state-funded public defender organizations or members of the bar who are appointed to represent defendants in specific cases and are reimbursed on a schedule for the type of case and/or the amount of time spent on the case.

Jurors. Jurors are drawn at random from public sources such as residence lists, voter rolls, or automobile registries. For each criminal trial, a large pool of potential jurors (often called a "panel" or "venire") is summoned to court and the judge and parties engage in a "jury selection" process to cull from the pool the jurors who will actually hear the case. Potential jurors may be excused because of personal hardship, actual or apparent bias, or without any expressed reason based on a limited number of "peremptory" challenges by either party.

It is sometimes said that the jury is "the judge of the facts." Jurors "deliberate"—discuss the case—in secret after all the evidence has been heard and the judge has given the jury instructions on the law that governs the case. Juries are not supposed to discuss the case even among themselves until they have heard all of the evidence; the judge will also instruct them that they are not to seek to acquire any information about the case from sources (e.g., the internet or television) other than the evidence at trial. Jurors take an oath to follow the judge's instructions, including that they will not decide the case based on sympathy for or prejudice against any party.

Probation Officers. As noted above, probation officers in the federal system and in some state systems prepare pre-sentence reports, which are used at sentencing. Probation officers also "supervise" criminal defendants who are serving a term of probation as part of a criminal sentence. Probation officers are generally considered to be part of the judicial branch. Probation officers' supervision of the persons reporting to them includes regular in-person meetings or telephone communication and ensuring that probationers comply with any conditions of their probation or release, such as drug testing or making restitution payments to crime victims.

C. CRIMINAL PROCEDURE VERSUS CIVIL PROCEDURE

Unlike civil procedure, the law of criminal procedure is almost entirely constitutional. In the investigative phase of criminal cases, almost all of what police and prosecutors do — conduct searches for evidence, talk to suspects, employ technology in surveillance or search efforts, call witnesses to the grand jury — is regulated to some degree by the Constitution, usually the Fourth and Fifth Amendments. When investigations result in charges, the process by which the persons charged are brought to court, beginning with the arrest, and the standards for initially evaluating those charges are constitutional. If, as is the case over 95 percent of the time, the defendant pleads guilty rather than going to trial, his guilty plea must be accepted by a judge who is charged with ensuring that the defendant is making a knowing and voluntary waiver of his Sixth and Fifth Amendment rights.

When a defendant chooses to go to trial, the manner in which that trial must be conducted is driven by the Fourth, Fifth, and Sixth Amendments. The jury, for example, must be drawn from a fair cross-section of the community, in a nondiscriminatory manner, and peremptory challenges to jurors based on race and other impermissible reasons are prohibited. Evidence that was obtained by the government by illegal means is normally inadmissible under the Fourth Amendment. The defendant has a Sixth Amendment right to both cross-examine the government's witnesses and to require the testimony of defense witnesses. By virtue of the Fifth Amendment, the defendant is not required to testify in his own defense, and the jury must be instructed not to draw an adverse inference against the defendant who chooses not to testify. *See generally* William J. Stuntz, *Substance, Process and the Civil-Criminal Line*, 7 J. Contemp. L. Issues 1, 3-4 (1996).

Consider, by contrast, the law of civil procedure. While some constitutional requirements form the deep backdrop for issues regarding notice, personal and subject matter jurisdiction, and jury trial rights, these issues form a minor part of even a law school civil procedure curriculum, and are much less significant in practice. The bulk of the raw material of civil procedure — service of process, venue, removal, pleadings, joinder, class actions, challenges to pleadings and other motion practice, discovery, trial practice, etc. — are regulated primarily or only by statutes and federal and state rules of civil procedure. *Id.* at 4.

Another manifestation of this phenomenon is the degree to which judicial management can affect how a case proceeds. In civil cases judges have wide discretion to manage the scope and length of the discovery process, and are able to put limits on the sort of information to which the parties are entitled and the length of time the parties will have for discovery. In a criminal case, on the other hand, the scope and content of discovery is largely driven by constitutional (the government's obligation to turn over exculpatory information) or statutory (witness statements) requirements, and courts have less discretion. Similarly, a judge in a civil trial has broad discretion to make evidentiary rulings and to control the presentation of evidence, whereas the judge in a criminal case must always be mindful of the defendant's Sixth Amendment rights. William J. Stuntz, *The Uneasy Relationship Between Criminal Procedure and Criminal Justice*, 107 Yale L.J. 1, 13-14 (1997).

How is it that criminal procedure became the special concern of constitutional regulation? And is that a good thing?

As to the first question, no theory is perfect, but Professor Stuntz has observed that the universe of criminal suspects and defendants as a group — politically unpopular and disproportionately poor and minority — is the classic sort of group that has been and should be the subject of constitutional protection on account of their comparative political powerlessness. As to whether this is a good thing, Professor Stuntz says no: He contends that the cause of criminal justice would be (would have been?) better served by less constitutional criminal procedure and more constitutional substantive criminal law in areas—such as requiring specified levels of funding for indigent defense, regulating crime definition and sentencing, and bolstering the mens rea requirement—where the Supreme Court has largely stayed away. *Id.* at 76.

Professor Barry Friedman shares the view that constitutional law is a less than ideal means for regulating criminal procedure, and not just because the scope of that regulation may have deterred forays into criminal substance. Professor Friedman and Maria Ponomarenko argue that policing is too important and too pervasive to be subject only to the sort of ad hoc regulation afforded by judicial review, and should instead be regulated by substantive rules promulgated by the municipal and other accountable political bodies that operate police forces, under a model similar to that governing federal administrative agencies. Barry Friedman & Maria Ponomarenko, *Democratic Policing*, 90 N.Y.U. L. Rev. 1827 (2015).

D. INCORPORATION

Much of modern constitutional criminal procedure has resulted from the Supreme Court's "incorporation" of particular rights found in the Bill of Rights into the Due Process Clause of the Fourteenth Amendment, thereby making those rights applicable to the states. That history will be outlined here and will be largely omitted from the discussion of the cases in the following chapters.

The Bill of Rights originally was held to apply only to the federal government. *Barron ex rel. Tiernan v. Mayor of Baltimore*, 7 Pet. 243 (1833). The constitutional Amendments adopted in the aftermath of the Civil War fundamentally altered the country's federal system, however. Section 1 of the Fourteenth Amendment provides, among other things, that a State may not abridge "the privileges or immunities of citizens of the United States" or deprive "any person of life, liberty, or property, without due process of law." Although the Supreme Court originally restricted the application of these clauses, *see Slaughter-House Cases*, 16 Wall. 36, 79 (1873) (the privileges and immunities protected by the Fourteenth Amendment were only the rights that were uniquely of national citizenship); *United States v. Cruikshank*, 92 U.S. 542 (1876) (First Amendment right of peaceful assembly only protects against infringement by Congress), beginning in the late nineteenth century the Court began to consider whether other rights in the Bill of Rights applied to the states. *See Hurtado v. California*, 110 U.S. 516 (1884) (due process does not require grand jury indictment); *Twining v. New Jersey*, 211 U.S. 78 (1908) (Fifth Amendment right against compelled incrimination does not apply to the states); *Powell v. Alabama*, 287 U.S. 45 (1932) (right to counsel apples to states in certain capital cases).

In the 1960s, the Warren Court accelerated the process of incorporation, holding that the Due Process Clause fully incorporates most of the particular rights contained in the Bill of Rights. *See, e.g., Mapp v. Ohio*, 367 U.S. 643 (1961) (Fourth Amendment exclusionary rule); *Gideon v. Wainwright*, 372 U.S. 335 (1963) (Sixth Amendment right to counsel in *Malloy v. Hogan*, 378 U.S. 1 (1964) (Fifth Amendment right against compelled incrimination); *Pointer v. Texas*, 380 U.S. 400 (1965) (Sixth Amendment right to confrontation); *Washington v. Texas*, 388 U.S. 14 (1967) (Sixth Amendment right to compulsory process); *Duncan v. Louisiana*, 391 U.S. 145 (1968) (Sixth Amendment right to jury trial). By the end of that decade, only a handful of rights in the Bill of Rights had not been incorporated into the Due Process Clause.

Another, shorter series of incorporation cases began in 2010. In *McDonald v. City of Chicago*, 561 U.S. 742 (2010), the Court considered whether the Due Process Clause incorporated

Gary Duncan, the defendant in *Duncan v. Louisisana*

the Second Amendment right to keep and bear arms for self-defense purposes, a right that the Court had recently recognized as a matter of federal law in *District of Columbia v. Heller*, 554 U.S. 570 (2008). The Court held the Second Amendment right was incorporated because the right was "fundamental to our scheme of ordered liberty" and was "deeply rooted in this Nation's history and tradition." *McDonald*, 561 U.S. at 767. The Court has since applied this test to two of the last remaining unincorporated rights in the criminal procedure area. In *Timbs v. Indiana*, 586 U.S. 146 (2019), the Court held that the Eighth Amendment's Excessive Fines Clause was incorporated under the *McDonald* test. The Court noted, among other things, that even though almost all state constitutions had prohibited excessive fines by the time of the ratification of the Fourteenth Amendment, draconian fines in the Black Codes enacted following the Civil War had been instrumental in the schemes of peonage and involuntary servitude used to re-enslave southern Black people in that era and beyond. *Id.* at 153. *See* Chapter II *infra*. And in *Ramos v. Louisiana*, 140 S. Ct. 1390 (2020), the Court held that the Sixth Amendment's right to jury unanimity in criminal cases applied to the states, invalidating procedures in Louisiana and Oregon, whose origin the Court traced to efforts by those states to dilute the influence of Black people on juries. *Id.* at 87-88.

Today the only significant criminal procedure right that has not been incorporated is the Fifth Amendment's right to grand jury indictment. *See* Chapter VII *infra*. *See* Roger A. Fairfax Jr., *Interrogating the Nonincorporation of the Grand Jury Clause*, 43 Cardozo L. Rev. 855 (2022) (analyzing the case for incorporation of the grand jury right).

E. STATE CONSTITUTIONAL CRIMINAL PROCEDURE

This book focuses largely but not exclusively on federal law, specifically, federal courts' interpretations of the federal constitution as the source of the rules of criminal procedure. But it must always be remembered that the states have their own constitutions, often with identical or similar provisions as the federal constitution, and that state judges are not bound by federal courts' interpretations of the federal constitution in interpreting identical or analogous terms of state constitutions.

The focus on state constitutional law has increased in the last 50 years. By the early 1970s the Warren Court's wholesale expansion of individual rights was plainly over. President Nixon had by then substantially succeeded in remaking the Court in the form that he had promised in his law-and-order presidential campaigns of 1968 and 1972. This trend was acknowledged

Chapter I Introductory Principles

by Justice Brennan in an important 1977 law review article, William Brennan Jr., *State Constitutions and the Protection of Individual Rights*, 90 Harv. L. Rev. 489 (1977), in which he noted the Supreme Court's recent proclivities and encouraged state judges to view their own constitutions as robust sources of individual rights:

> But the point I want to stress here is that state courts cannot rest when they have afforded their citizens the full protections of the federal Constitution. State constitutions, too, are a font of individual liberties, their protections often extending beyond those required by the Supreme Court's interpretation of federal law. The legal revolution which has brought federal law to the fore must not be allowed to inhibit the independent protective force of state law—for without it, the full realization of our liberties cannot be guaranteed.

Id. at 491.

Even by 1977, Justice Brennan was able to point to multiple examples where state courts had interpreted their own state constitutions to be more protective of individual rights than the federal constitution as interpreted by Nixon's Burger Court. For example, in 1971 the Supreme Court held in *Harris v. New York*, 401 U.S. 222 (1971), that statements taken by police officers from a defendant without first giving *Miranda* warnings were nonetheless admissible to impeach a testifying defendant. *See* Chapter III *infra*. Justice Brennan noted that the California Supreme Court had explicitly renounced the United States Supreme Court's decision in *Harris*. In that case, after explaining its own view of the privilege against self-incrimination in the California Constitution, the court concluded: "We pause finally to reaffirm the independent nature of the California Constitution and our responsibility to sep-arately define and protect the rights of California citizens despite conflicting decisions of the United States Supreme Court interpreting the federal Constitution." *People v. Disbrow*, 545 P.2d 272, 280 (Cal. 1976).

Another example was the nature of the consent required to authorize a police officer to conduct a motor vehicle search. In *Schneckloth v. Bustamonte*, 412 U.S. 218 (1973), the Supreme Court rejected any requirement that such a consent must be intelligent and know-ing, and that the individual must be aware of his right to refuse to consent. In New Jersey, however, the state's highest court construed language in the New Jersey Constitution that was identical to the federal Fourth Amendment to require informed consent. "Under Art. I, par. 7 of our State Constitution the validity of a consent to search, even in a non-custodial situation, must be measured in terms of waiver, i.e., where the state seeks to justify a search on the basis of consent it has the burden of showing that the consent was voluntary, an essential element of which is knowledge of the right to refuse consent." *State v. Johnson*, 346 A.2d 66, 68 (N.J. 1975).

This trend continued long after in part because of Justice Brennan's influential article. For example, in 1984 the Supreme Court announced a major exception to its prior ruling in *Mapp v. Ohio*, 367 U.S. 643 (1961), which had held that illegally obtained evidence was inadmissible in state as well as federal court. In *United States v. Leon*, 469 U.S. 897 (1984), the Court held that *Mapp*'s exclusionary rule did not apply where the police officers acted in "good faith." A decade later, courts in eight states had rejected the *Leon* good faith exception. *See* Leigh A. Morrissey, *State Courts Reject Leon on State Constitutional Grounds: A Defense of Reactive Rulings*, 47 Vand. L. Rev. 917, 919 (1994). According to a 2023 survey in the Missis-sippi Law Journal, more states (17) have refused to follow *Leon* than any other Supreme Court criminal procedure decision. Christopher R. Green, et. al., *State-Court Departures from the Supreme Court: A Comprehensive Survey*, 92 Miss. L.J. 329, 330 (2023).

The availability of state constitutional law as a source of expanded individual rights should not be exaggerated, however. The vast majority of state courts follow federal Supreme Court precedent interpreting constitutional terms and principles that are common to both

John Adams

federal and state constitutions, either as a matter of deference or as a matter of independent agreement. For example, in *Whren v. United States*, 517 U.S. 806 (1996), the Supreme Court flatly and controversially rejected the argument that a police stop of a vehicle for a traffic violation could be challenged on the basis that the stop was "pretextual" — that is, that the stop was motivated by a reason other than enforcing traffic laws. *Id.* at 816-19. It declined to adopt a test that the validity of the stop depended on whether a reasonable officer "would have" made the stop regardless of the ulterior motive. *Id.* In the decades following *Whren*, 47 out of 50 states have followed the Supreme Court in also rejecting the "would have" test. *Commonwealth v. Long*, 485 Mass. 711, 727 & n.13 (2020). By contrast, only two states adopted some version of a "would have" test after *Whren*. See *State v. Gonzales*, 150 N.M. 74, 257 P.3d 894, 898 (2011) (question is whether, based on totality of circumstances, "the officer who made the stop would have done so even without the unrelated motive"); *State v. Ladson*, 138 Wash. 2d 343, 358-59, 979 P.2d 833 (1999) ("When determining whether a given stop is pretextual, the court should consider the totality of the circumstances, including both the subjective intent of the officer as well as the objective reasonableness of the officer's behavior.").

One of the most defendant-protective state constitutions is that of Massachusetts, which was the model on which the federal Constitution was based. Its author, more widely known as the second U.S. President, was John Adams, who also warrants a place in the criminal procedure pantheon on account of his successful trial defense of the British soldiers charged with murder arising out of the 1770 Boston Massacre.

CHAPTER II

THE ROOTS OF MODERN CONSTITUTIONAL CRIMINAL PROCEDURE: THE SUPREME COURT, RACE, AND THE POST-BELLUM SOUTH

The Supreme Court under the tenure of Chief Justice Earl Warren (1953-1969) has been widely credited with effecting a revolution in the American law of criminal procedure. Much of this was accomplished by the "incorporation" of constitutional rights into the Due Process Clause of the Fourteenth Amendment, thereby making them applicable to the states. *See* Chapter I *supra*. Not all of the criminal defendants in the seminal cases of the Warren Court revolution were Black, and the race of the defendant was only mentioned in one of them, *Duncan v. Louisiana*, 391 U.S. 145 (1968). *See* Chapter XIII *infra*.

Nonetheless it is generally accepted that the Warren Court revolution was actually, albeit implicitly, driven by race, specifically by the Court's concerns about racial injustice. *See* Burt Newborne, *The Gravitational Pull of Race on the Warren Court*, 2010 Sup. Ct. Rev. 59, 60 (2010) ("concern over racial injustice and state institutional failure was so intense during . . . [the] "Warren years" that it played a significant role in shaping many of the most important constitutional decisions of the Supreme Court"); Gabriel J. Chin, *Race and the Disappointing Right to Counsel*, 122 Yale L.J. 2236, 2239 (2013) (although Clarence Gideon was white, "*Gideon* was a race case, in that *Gideon* and the Court's other criminal procedure cases of the era were concerned with institutional racism"); Dan M. Kahan & Tracey L. Meares, *Foreword: The Coming Crisis of Criminal Procedure*, 86 Geo. L.J. 1153, 1153 (1998) ("Law enforcement was a key instrument of racial repression, in both the North and the South, before the 1960s civil rights revolution. Modern criminal procedure reflects the Supreme Court's admirable contribution to eradicating this incidence of American apartheid."); David Alan Sklansky, *Police and Democracy*, 103 Mich. L. Rev. 1699, 1805 (2005) ("[C]riminal procedure in the Warren Court era was famously preoccupied with issues of illegitimate inequality, particularly those associated with race."); William J. Stuntz, *The Uneasy Relationship Between Criminal Procedure and Criminal Justice*, 107 Yale L.J. 1, 5 (1997) ("The post-1960 constitutionalization of criminal procedure arose, in large part, out of the sense that the system was treating black suspects and defendants much worse than white ones. Warren-era constitutional criminal procedure began as a kind of antidiscrimination law.").

This chapter looks at a handful of seeds that were sown in race cases in the decades preceding the advent of the Warren Court. These cases sometimes provided precedent for important Warren Court decisions. This is not to suggest that these cases necessarily represent

Chapter II The Roots of Modern Constitutional Criminal Procedure

an awakening on the part of the Supreme Court at any particular point in time. The development of the Supreme Court's case law on matters of criminal procedure and race has always been and continues to be belated, halting, regressive, and inconsistent.

Section A looks at cases where the Court considers state exclusion of Black people from juries. Section B considers the Court's invalidation of certain state mechanisms for enforcing a regime of peonage in the South long after the Thirteenth Amendment was passed, a regime of involuntary servitude largely enabled by criminal law and procedure. Section C looks at cases where the Supreme Court invalidated state court "trials" that were dominated by the shadow of the mobs outside the courthouse. Section D examines the Court's initial consideration of coerced confessions.

The focus of this chapter borrows heavily from the concept developed in Professor Michael J. Klarman's article *The Racial Origins of Modern Criminal Procedure*, 99 Mich. L. Rev. 48 (2000). Professor Klarman writes:

> The constitutional law of state criminal procedure was born between the First and Second World Wars. Prior to 1920, the Supreme Court had upset the results of the state criminal justice system in just a handful of cases, all involving race discrimination in jury selection. By 1940, however, the Court had interpreted the Due Process Clause of the Fourteenth Amendment to invalidate state criminal convictions in a wide variety of settings: mob-dominated trials, violation of the right to counsel, coerced confessions, financially-biased judges, and knowingly perjured testimony by prosecution witnesses.
>
> . . .
>
> Altogether, the Supreme Court decided six landmark state criminal procedure cases during the interwar period. Four of these cases involved black defendants from southern states. This Article contends that the linkage between the birth of modern criminal procedure and southern black defendants is no fortuity. For the Court to assume the function of superintending the state criminal process required a departure from a century and a half of tradition and legal precedent, both grounded in federalism concerns. The Justices were not prepared to embark on such a novel enterprise in cases of marginal unfairness — where the police had interrogated a suspect a bit too vigorously or permitted defense counsel a little less time than optimal for preparing a case. On the contrary, the Court was willing to take this leap only when confronted with cases in which defendants were brutally tortured into confessing or the appointment of defense counsel in a capital case was a complete sham. Such flagrant injustices were not frequent occurrences in the United States during the 1920s and 1930s — except in the South, in cases involving black defendants charged with serious interracial crimes, usually rape or murder.

Id. at 48-49.

The four cases Professor Klarman refers to above — *Moore v. Dempsey*, 261 U.S. 86 (1923); *Powell v. Alabama*, 287 U.S. 45 (1932); *Norris v. Alabama*, 294 U.S. 587 (1935); and *Brown v. Mississippi*, 297 U.S. 278 (1936) — are considered below, among others.

A. INVALIDATION OF CONVICTIONS WHERE BLACK PEOPLE WERE EXCLUDED FROM JURIES

Strauder v. West Virginia
100 U.S. 303 (1879)

Mr. Justice STRONG delivered the opinion of the court.

The plaintiff in error, a colored man, was indicted for murder in the Circuit Court of Ohio County, in West Virginia, on the 20th of October, 1874, and upon trial was convicted and sentenced. The record was then removed to the Supreme Court of the State, and there the judgment of the Circuit Court was affirmed. The present case is a writ of error to that court, and it is now, in substance, averred that at the trial in the State court the defendant (now plaintiff in error) was denied rights to which he was entitled under the Constitution and laws of the United States.

• • •

The law of the State to which reference was made in the petition for removal and in the several motions was enacted on the 12th of March, 1873, and it is as follows: "All white male persons who are twenty-one years of age and who are citizens of this State shall be liable to serve as jurors, except as herein provided." The persons excepted are State officials.

In this court, several errors have been assigned, and the controlling questions underlying them all are, first, whether, by the Constitution and laws of the United States, every citizen of the United States has a right to a trial of an indictment against him by a jury selected and impanelled without discrimination against his race or color, because of race or color; and, second, if he has such a right, and is denied its enjoyment by the State in which he is indicted, may he cause the case to be removed into the Circuit Court of the United States?

It is to be observed that the first of these questions is not whether a colored man, when an indictment has been preferred against him, has a right to a grand or a petit jury composed in whole or in part of persons of his own race or color, but it is whether, in the composition or selection of jurors by whom he is to be indicted or tried, all persons of his race or color may be excluded by law, solely because of their race or color, so that by no possibility can any colored man sit upon the jury.

The questions are important, for they demand a construction of the recent amendments of the Constitution. If the defendant has a right to have a jury selected for the trial of his case without discrimination against all persons of his race or color, because of their race or color, the right, if not created, is protected by those amendments, and the legislation of Congress under them. The Fourteenth Amendment ordains that "all persons born or naturalized in the United States and subject to the jurisdiction thereof are citizens of the United States and of the State wherein they reside. No State shall make or enforce any laws which shall abridge the privileges or immunities of citizens of the United States, nor shall any State deprive any person of life, liberty, or property, without due process of law, nor deny to any person within its jurisdiction the equal protection of the laws."

This is one of a series of constitutional provisions having a common purpose; namely, securing to a race recently emancipated, a race that through many generations had been held in slavery, all the civil rights that the superior race enjoy. The true spirit and meaning of the amendments, as we said in the *Slaughter-House Cases*, cannot be understood without keeping in view the history of the times when they were adopted, and the general objects they plainly sought to accomplish. At the time when they were incorporated into the Constitution, it required little knowledge of human nature to anticipate that those who had long been regarded as an inferior and subject race would, when suddenly raised to the rank of citizenship, be looked upon with jealousy and positive dislike, and that State laws might be enacted or enforced to perpetuate the distinctions that had before existed. Discriminations against them had been habitual. It was well known that in some States laws making such discriminations then existed, and others might well be expected. The colored race, as a race, was abject and ignorant, and in that condition was unfitted to command the respect of those who had superior intelligence. Their training had left them mere children, and as such they needed the protection which a wise government extends to those who are unable to protect themselves. They especially needed protection against unfriendly action in the States where they were resident. It was in view of these considerations the Fourteenth Amendment was framed and adopted. It was designed to assure to the colored race the enjoyment of all the civil rights that under the law are enjoyed by white persons, and to give to that race the protection of the general government, in that enjoyment, whenever it should be denied by the States. It not only gave citizenship and the privileges of citizenship to persons of color, but it denied to any State the power to withhold from them the equal protection of the laws, and authorized Congress to enforce its provisions by appropriate legislation. To quote the language used by us in the *Slaughter-House Cases*, "No one can fail to be impressed with the one pervading purpose found in all the amendments, lying at the foundation of each, and without which none of them would have been suggested, — we mean the freedom of the slave race, the security and firm establishment of that freedom, and the protection of the newly made freeman and citizen from the oppressions of those who had formerly exercised unlimited dominion over them." So again: "The existence of laws in the States where the newly emancipated negroes resided, which discriminated with gross injustice and hardship against them as a class, was the evil to be remedied, and by it [the Fourteenth Amendment] such laws were forbidden. If, however, the States did not conform their laws to its requirements, then, by the fifth section of the article of amendment, Congress was authorized to enforce it by suitable legislation." And it was added, "We doubt very much whether any action of a State, not directed by way of discrimination against the negroes, as a class, will ever be held to come within the purview of this provision."

If this is the spirit and meaning of the amendment, whether it means more or not, it is to be construed liberally, to carry out the purposes of its framers. It ordains that no State shall make or enforce any laws which shall abridge the privileges or immunities of citizens of the United States (evidently referring to the newly made citizens, who, being citizens of the United States, are declared to be also citizens of the State in which they reside). It ordains that no State shall deprive any person of life, liberty, or property, without due process of law, or deny to any person within its jurisdiction the equal protection of the laws. What is this but declaring that the law in the States shall be the same for the black as for the white; that all persons, whether colored or white, shall stand equal before the laws of the States, and, in regard to the colored race, for whose protection the amendment was primarily designed, that no discrimination shall be made against them by law because of their color? The words of the amendment, it is true, are prohibitory, but they contain a necessary implication of a positive immunity, or right, most valuable to the colored race, — the right to exemption from unfriendly legislation against them distinctively as colored, — exemption from legal discriminations, implying inferiority in civil society, lessening the security of their enjoyment of the rights which others enjoy, and discriminations which are steps towards reducing them to the condition of a subject race.

That the West Virginia statute respecting juries — the statute that controlled the selection of the grand and petit jury in the case of the plaintiff in error — is such a discrimination ought not to be doubted. Nor would it be if the persons excluded by it were white men. If in those States where the colored people constitute a majority of the entire population a law should be enacted excluding all white men from jury service, thus denying to them the privilege of participating equally with the blacks in the administration of justice, we apprehend no one would be heard to claim that it would not be a denial to white men of the equal protection of the laws. Nor if a law should be passed excluding all naturalized Celtic Irishmen, would there be any doubt of its inconsistency with the spirit of the amendment. The very fact that colored people are singled out and expressly denied by a statute all right to participate in the administration of the law, as jurors, because of their color, though they are citizens, and may be in other respects fully qualified, is practically a brand upon them, affixed by the law, an assertion of their inferiority, and a stimulant to that race prejudice which is an impediment to securing to individuals of the race that equal justice which the law aims to secure to all others.

The right to a trial by jury is guaranteed to every citizen of West Virginia by the Constitution of that State, and the constitution of juries is a very essential part of the protection such a mode of trial is intended to secure. The very idea of a jury is a body of men composed of the peers or equals of the person whose rights it is selected or summoned to determine; that is, of his neighbors, fellows, associates, persons having the same legal status in society as that which he holds. Blackstone, in his Commentaries, says, "The right of trial by jury, or the country, is a trial by the peers of every Englishman, and is the grand bulwark of his liberties, and is secured to him by the Great Charter." It is also guarded by statutory enactments intended to make impossible what Mr. Bentham called "packing juries." It is well known that prejudices often exist against particular classes in the community, which sway the judgment of jurors, and which, therefore, operate in some cases to deny to persons of those classes the full enjoyment of that protection which others enjoy. Prejudice in a local community is held to be a reason for a change of venue. The framers of the constitutional amendment must have known full well the existence of such prejudice and its likelihood to continue against the manumitted slaves and their race, and that knowledge was doubtless a motive that led to the amendment. By their manumission and citizenship the colored race became entitled to the equal protection of the laws of the States in which they resided; and the apprehension that through prejudice they might be denied that equal protection, that is, that there might be discrimination against them, was the inducement to bestow upon the national government the power to enforce the provision that no State shall deny to them the equal protection of the laws. Without the apprehended existence of prejudice that portion of the amendment would have been unnecessary, and it might have been left to the States to extend equality of protection.

In view of these considerations, it is hard to see why the statute of West Virginia should not be regarded as discriminating against a colored man when he is put upon trial for an alleged criminal offence against the State. It is not easy to comprehend how it can be said that while every white man is entitled to a trial by a jury selected from persons of his own race or color, or, rather, selected without discrimination against his color, and a negro is not, the latter is equally protected by the law with the former. Is not protection of life and liberty against race or color prejudice, a right, a legal right, under the constitutional amendment? And how can it be maintained that compelling a colored man to submit to a trial for his life by a jury drawn from a panel from which the State has expressly excluded every man of his race, because of color alone, however well qualified in other respects, is not a denial to him of equal legal protection?

We do not say that within the limits from which it is not excluded by the amendment a State may not prescribe the qualifications of its jurors, and in so doing make discriminations. It may confine the selection to males, to freeholders, to citizens, to persons within certain ages, or to persons having educational qualifications. We do not believe the Fourteenth Amendment was ever intended to prohibit this. Looking at its history, it is clear it had no such purpose. Its aim was against discrimination because of race or color.

• • •

The Fourteenth Amendment makes no attempt to enumerate the rights it designed to protect. It speaks in general terms, and those are as comprehensive as possible. Its language is prohibitory; but every prohibition implies the existence of rights and immunities, prominent among which is an immunity from inequality of legal protection, either for life, liberty, or property. Any State action that denies this immunity to a colored man is in conflict with the Constitution.

[Justices Field and Clifford dissented.]

NOTES AND QUESTIONS

1. *Strauder* marks the first time the Supreme Court invalidated a state court criminal conviction. In one sense it is an easy case, as the West Virginia statute at issue explicitly excluded Black people from serving on juries. The opinion nonetheless reflects an expansive view of the Fourteenth Amendment — "[i]t speaks in general terms, and those areas are as comprehensive as possible" — and notably recognizes the "stigmatizing" effect of racial discrimination (the statute is "practically a brand upon [Black people], affixed by law").

2. What do you make of the caveats the Court includes? For example, the Court is careful to note that the issue "is not whether a colored man, when an indictment has been preferred against him, has a right to a grand or petit jury composed in whole or part of persons of his own race or color." The Court also notes that under the Fourteenth Amendment a state is free to "prescribe the qualifications of its jurors, and in doing so may make discriminations. It may confine the selection to males, to freeholders, to citizens, to persons within certain ages, or to persons having educational qualifications." Do these caveats dilute the significance of *Strauder*?

3. The Court just a year later considered a claim of racial discrimination in juror panels in a much different context in *Neal v. Delaware*, 130 U.S. 370 (1880), inasmuch as no facially discriminatory statute was at issue. In *Neal*, the state conceded that no Black people had *ever* served on grand or petit juries in the state courts of Delaware. That concession was accompanied, moreover, by the following statement from the Delaware chief justice: "[T] hat none but white men were selected is in nowise remarkable in view of the fact — too notorious to be ignored — that the great body of black men residing in this State are utterly unqualified by want of intelligence, experience, or moral integrity to sit on juries." *Id.* at 393-94. The state made no effort to rebut the defendant's allegation that, although Black people were approximately 20 percent of the population of Delaware, not a single Black person had ever served on a grand or petit jury; the state just contended that this evidence did not amount to discrimination. The state court agreed, concluding that defendant had failed to prove that Black people had been excluded from jury panels "because of their color." *Id.* at 395.

The Supreme Court held otherwise, invoking the reasoning of *Strauder*. The Court noted that the defendant's allegations coupled with the state's concession established a prima facie case of a Fourteenth Amendment violation, which the state had failed to rebut. *Id.* at 397. As to the state court's conclusion that defendant had not shown that Black people had been excluded because of their race, the Court observed:

> It was, we think, under all the circumstances, a violent presumption which the State court indulged, that such uniform exclusion of that race from juries, during a period of many years, was solely because, in the judgment of those officers, fairly exercised, the black race in Delaware were utterly disqualified, by want of intelligence, experience, or moral integrity, to sit on juries. The action of those officers in the premises is to be deemed the act of the State; and the refusal of the State court to redress the wrong by them committed was a denial of a right secured to the prisoner by the Constitution and laws of the United States.

Id. Why do you think the State might have made such an extraordinary concession in *Neal*?

4. The burden-shifting framework employed by the Court in *Neal* — where the government must rebut a prima facie case of discrimination to prove its absence — is a methodology that lay dormant for 50 years before being employed implicitly in *Norris v. Alabama*, 294 U.S. 587 (1935). And it has been used intermittently by courts in discrimination cases for the past several decades. What do you see as its pros and cons from a methodological standpoint? Are there certain factual scenarios where it makes more or less sense?

5. A less enduring aspect of *Neal*, declining over the years but never totally eliminated, is the evidence of overt racial animus by the Delaware chief justice. For another example of a law enforcement official saying the quiet part out loud, *see infra Brown v. Mississippi*, 297 U.S. 278 (1936) (conviction obtained by police admission of brutally coerced confessions violated due process).

6. In two other cases from the same approximate time period the Supreme Court overturned the convictions of Black defendants indicted by grand juries from which Black people had been systematically excluded, in circumstances where state courts had thrown transparently bogus procedural roadblocks in front of their discrimination claims. In *Carter v. Texas*, 177 U.S. 442 (1900), the trial court denied defendant's motion for leave to introduce witnesses in support of his well-founded motion to quash the indictment, noting that the defendant should have presented his claim to the grand jury at the time of its empanelment (i.e., before he was indicted and when he was presumably unaware of the existence of the empanelment of the grand jury). In *Rogers v. Alabama*, 192 U.S. 226 (1904), the trial court struck defendant's motion because the motion—at two pages—was "unnecessarily prolix."

Generally, however, challenges to discriminatory administration of juror selection practices were unsuccessful. The sad truth is that *Strauder* and *Neal* and their progeny had virtually no direct effect on the racial composition of juries in the South. Their teachings were ignored by state courts and, in the rare instances where Black people were empaneled, they could be eliminated through the exercise of peremptory challenges. *See* Benno C. Schmidt Jr., *Juries, Jurisdiction, and Race Discrimination: The Lost Promise of* Strauder v. West Virginia, 61 Tex. L. Rev. 1401, 1406-08 (1983) (footnotes omitted):

> "In the whole of Georgia & Alabama, and other Southern states not a negro juror is allowed to sit in the jury box in state courts," lamented Booker T. Washington toward the end of the nineteenth century. After his travels through the South the young Harvard historian Albert B. Hart wrote in 1912 that "Negroes, although still eligible to jury service, are rarely impaneled, even for the trial of a Negro." As late as World War II, Gunnar Myrdal could treat as a reality too obvious and accepted to require documentation that "if, as in the South, Negroes are kept out of jury service, the democratic safeguard of the jury system is easily turned into a means of minority subjugation."
>
> The exclusion of blacks was virtually total. Gilbert T. Stephenson, author of the informative 1910 study, Race Distinctions in American Law, attempted to determine how many blacks served on Southern juries by sending questionnaires to the court clerks in every Southern county in which blacks comprised more than half the population. The replies from Alabama, Florida, and Georgia indicated uniform exclusion. The court clerks from Virginia, South Carolina, Louisiana, Mississippi, and Missouri reported occasional black jurors in some counties, although uniform exclusion was said to be the rule. Kentucky and Oklahoma indicated occasional black participation on juries. Stephenson's survey was impressionistic, but it supports other reports by observers of the South in the period from roughly 1890 to 1930 that black jurors were rare indeed. Certainly the federal and state court reports are filled with cases in which black defendants protested to no avail against the unfairness of all-white grand and petit juries.

B. PEONAGE CONVICTIONS

In the 1910s the Supreme Court decided two cases involving Alabama criminal statutes that were part and parcel of the regimes of "peonage" through which most southern states had substantially re-enslaved Black people after the Civil War. State criminal justice systems were the engines of these regimes, as it was through convictions on trumped-up charges under vaguely worded and cynically targeted statutes (e.g., vagrancy) that Black people typically entered the peonage system. It is a mistake, however, to think of these cases as criminal convictions in any conventional sense: The defendants were almost always unrepresented, there were seldom jury trials, and the adjudicators were often small-town mayors or justices of the peace with connections to local business interests. *See* Benno C. Schmidt Jr., *Principle and Prejudice in the Progressive Era. Part 2: The Peonage Cases*, 82 Colum. L. Rev. 646, 650-53 (1983) (footnotes omitted):

> A more or less unbroken momentum of law and history carried peonage into the twentieth century. Despite the thirteenth amendment's command that "[n]either slavery nor involuntary servitude, except as a punishment for crime . . . shall exist within the United States," forcing blacks to work was the paramount concern of the Black Codes passed in the relaxed years of presidential reconstruction following the Civil War. Under the Codes, black males who did not enter employment contracts could be charged as criminal vagrants. Those who quit jobs for which they had contracted could be arrested and returned to their employers. Enticement laws prohibited other employers from hiring laborers already under contract. Black children could be "apprenticed" to their former masters by order of the probate courts. Indigents fined for petty offenses such as vagrancy avoided harsh punishment by contracting to work for private employers who paid their fines, and the force of the state's criminal law fell behind the employment obligation.
>
> . . .
>
> The pinnacle of the system of servitude during Reconstruction and after was convict labor. The convicts were leased to private interests by the state, toiled on state or county chain gangs,

Chain gang circa 1898

or were forced into criminal surety contracts under which a period of servitude for a private employer was exchanged for the wherewithal to pay a fine levied as a result of a criminal conviction often based on petty or trumped-up charges. The practice of leasing convicts began during Reconstruction when large numbers of blacks became convicts for the first time. Leased convict labor was the shame of the South.

. . .

The exhausting cruelty of the penal system made almost any private servitude preferable. To avoid the chain gang, black convicts signed up with private employers who would pay their fines in return for much longer periods of forced labor. But the chain gang buttressed the system of involuntary servitude even with regard to those blacks never caught in the toils of Southern justice. Contract breaches, switching jobs, failure to pay debts and simple idleness were surrounded with the threat of false accusations and criminal sanctions — a potent weapon in the hands of white employers who sought to bend blacks to their bidding.

Bailey v. Alabama
219 U.S. 219 (1911)

Mr. Justice HUGHES delivered the opinion of the court:

This is a writ of error to review a judgment of the supreme court of the state of Alabama, affirming a judgment of conviction in the Montgomery city court. The statute upon which the conviction was based is assailed as in violation of the 14th Amendment of the Constitution of the United States upon the ground that it deprived the plaintiff in error of his liberty without due process of law and denied him the equal protection of the laws, and also of the 13th Amendment, and of the act of Congress providing for the enforcement of that Amendment, in that the effect of the statute is to enforce involuntary servitude by compelling personal service in liquidation of a debt.

The statute in question is § 4730 of the Code of Alabama of 1896, as amended in 1903 and 1907. The section of the Code as it stood before the amendments provided that any person who, with intent to injure or defraud his employer, entered into a written contract for service, and thereby obtained from his employer money or other personal property, and with like intent and without just cause, and without refunding the money or paying for the property, refused to perform the service, should be punished as if he had stolen it. In 1903 the section was amended so as to make the refusal or failure to perform the service, or to refund the money, or pay for the property, without just cause, prima facie evidence of the intent to injure or defraud. This amendment was enlarged by that of 1907. The section, thus amended, reads as follows:

> Any person who, with intent to injure or defraud his employer, enters into a contract in writing for the performance of any act of service, and thereby obtains money or other personal property from such employer, and with like intent, and without just cause, and without refunding such money, or paying for such property, refuses or fails to perform such act or service, must on conviction be punished by a fine in double the damage suffered by the injured party, but not more than $300, one half of said fine to go to the county and one half to the party injured; and any person who, with intent to injure or defraud his landlord, enters into any contract in writing for the rent of land, and thereby obtains any money or other personal property from such landlord, and with like intent, without just cause, and without refunding such money, or paying for such property, refuses or fails to cultivate such land, or to comply with his contract relative thereto, must on conviction be punished by fine in double the damage suffered by the injured party, but not more than $300, one half of said fine to go to the county and one half to the party injured. And the refusal or failure of any person, who enters into such contract, to perform such act or service, or to cultivate such land, or refund such money, or pay for such property, without just

cause, shall be prima facie evidence of the intent to injure his employer or landlord or defraud him. That all laws and parts of laws in conflict with the provisions hereof be and the same are hereby repealed.

There is also a rule of evidence enforced by the courts of Alabama which must be regarded as having the same effect as if read into the statute itself, that the accused, for the purpose of rebutting the statutory presumption, shall not be allowed to testify "as to his uncommunicated motives, purpose, or intention."

Bailey, the plaintiff in error, was committed for detention on the charge of obtaining $15 under a contract in writing with intent to injure or defraud his employer. He sued out a writ of habeas corpus, challenging the validity of the statute. His discharge was refused, and the supreme court of the state affirmed the order, holding the statute to be constitutional. On writ of error from this court it was held that the case was brought here prematurely, and the questions now presented were expressly reserved.

Having failed to obtain his release on habeas corpus, Bailey was indicted on the following charge:

> The grand jury of said county charge that before the finding of this indictment Alonzo Bailey, with intent to injure or defraud his employer, the Riverside Company, a corporation, entered into a written contract to perform labor or services for the Riverside Company, a corporation, and obtained thereby the sum of $15 from the said the Riverside Company, and afterwards with like intent, and without just cause, failed or refused to perform such labor or services, or to refund such money, against the peace and dignity of the state of Alabama.

Motion to quash and a demurrer to the indictment were overruled. Upon the trial the following facts appeared: On December 26, 1907, Bailey entered into a written contract with the Riverside Company, which provided:

> That I, Lonzo Bailey, for and in consideration of the sum of $15 in money, this day in hand paid to me by said the Riverside Company, the receipt whereof I do hereby acknowledge, I, the said Lonzo Bailey, do hereby consent, contract, and agree to work and labor for the said Riverside Company as a farm hand on their Scott's Bend place in Montgomery county, Alabama, from the 30 day of December, 1907, to the 30 day of December, 1908, at and for the sum of $12 per month.
>
> And the said Lonzo Bailey agrees to render respectful and faithful service to the said the Riverside Company, and to perform diligently and actively all work pertaining to such employment, in accordance with the instructions of the said the Riverside Company or agent.
>
> And the said the Riverside Company, in consideration of the agreement above mentioned of the said Lonzo Bailey, hereby employs the said Lonzo Bailey as such farm hand for the time above set out, and agrees to pay the said Lonzo Bailey the sum of $10.75 per month.

The manager of the employing company testified that at the time of entering into this contract there were present only the witness and Bailey, and that the latter then obtained from the company the sum of $15; that Bailey worked under the contract throughout the month of January and for three or four days in February, 1908, and then, "without just cause, and without refunding the money, ceased to work for said Riverside Company, and has not since that time performed any service for said company in accordance with or under said contract, and has refused and failed to perform any further service thereunder, and has, without just cause, refused and failed to refund said $15." He also testified, in response to a question from the attorney for the defendant, and against the objection of the state, that Bailey was a negro. No other evidence was introduced.

The court, after defining the crime in the language of the statute, charged the jury, in accordance with its terms, as follows:

> And the refusal of any person who enters into such contract to perform such act or service, or refund such money, or pay for such property, without just cause, shall be prima facie evidence of the intent to injure his employer, or to defraud him.

Bailey excepted to these instructions, and requested the court to instruct the jury that the statute and the provision creating the presumption were invalid, and further that "the refusal or failure of the defendant to perform the service alleged in the indictment, or to refund the money obtained from the Riverside Company under the contract between it and the defendant, without cause, does not of itself make out a prima facie case of the defendant's intent to injure or defraud said Riverside Company."

The court refused these instructions and Bailey took exception.

The jury found the accused guilty, fixed the damages sustained by the injured party at $15, and assessed a fine of $30. Thereupon Bailey was sentenced by the court to pay the fine of $30 and the costs, and in default thereof to hard labor "for twenty days in lieu of said fine, and one hundred and sixteen days on account of said costs."

On appeal to the supreme court of the state, the constitutionality of the statute was again upheld and the judgment affirmed.

We at once dismiss from consideration the fact that the plaintiff in error is a black man. While the action of a state, through its officers charged with the administration of a law fair in appearance, may be of such a character as to constitute a denial of the equal protection of the laws (*Yick Wo v. Hopkins*), such a conclusion is here neither required nor justified. The statute, on its face, makes no racial discrimination, and the record fails to show its existence in fact. No question of a sectional character is presented, and we may view the legislation in the same manner as if it had been enacted in New York or in Idaho. Opportunities for coercion and oppression, in varying circumstances, exist in all parts of the Union, and the citizens of all the states are interested in the maintenance of the constitutional guaranties, the consideration of which is here involved.

Prior to the amendment of the year 1903, enlarged in 1907, the statute did not make the mere breach of the contract, under which the employee had obtained from his employer money which was not refunded or property which was not paid for, a crime. The essential ingredient of the offense was the intent of the accused to injure or defraud. To justify conviction, it was necessary that this intent should be established by competent evidence, aided only by such inferences as might logically be derived from the facts proved, and should not be the subject of mere surmise or arbitrary assumption.

This was the construction which the supreme court of Alabama placed upon the statute, as it then stood. . . .

We pass, then, to the consideration of the amendment, through the operation of which under the charge of the trial court this conviction was obtained. No longer was it necessary for the prosecution to comply with the rule of the Riley Case (supra) in order to establish the intent to injure or defraud which, as the court said, constituted the gist of the offense. It was "the difficulty in proving the intent, made patent by that decision," which "suggested the amendment of 1903." By this amendment it was provided, in substance, that the refusal or failure to perform the service contracted for, or to refund the money obtained, without just cause, should be prima facie evidence of the intent to injure or defraud.

But the refusal or failure to perform the service, without just cause, constitutes the breach of the contract. The justice of the grounds of refusal or failure must, of course, be determined by the contractual obligation assumed. Whatever the reason for leaving the service, if, judged by the terms of the contract, it is insufficient in law, it is not "just cause." The money received and repayable, nothing more being shown, constitutes a mere debt. The asserted difficulty of proving the intent to injure or defraud is thus made the occasion for dispensing with such proof, so far as the prima facie case is concerned. And the mere breach of a contract for personal service, coupled with the mere failure to pay a debt which was to be liquidated in the course of such service, is made sufficient to warrant a conviction.

It is no answer to say that the jury must find, and here found, that a fraudulent intent existed. The jury by their verdict cannot add to the facts before them. If nothing be shown but a mere breach of a contract of service and a mere failure to pay a debt, the jury have nothing else to go upon, and the evidence becomes nothing more because of their finding. Had it not been for this statutory presumption, supplied by the amendment, no one would be heard to say that Bailey could have been convicted.

Prima facie evidence is sufficient evidence to outweigh the presumption of innocence, and if not met by opposing evidence, to support a verdict of guilty. "It is such as, in judgment of law, is sufficient to establish the fact; and, if not rebutted, remains sufficient for the purpose."

We are not impressed with the argument that the supreme court of Alabama has construed the amendment to mean that the jury is not controlled by the presumption, if unrebutted, and still may find the accused not guilty. That court, in its opinion, said: "Again, it must be borne in mind that the rule of evidence fixed by the statute does not make it the duty of the jury to convict on the evidence referred to in the enactment, if unrebutted, whether satisfied thereby of the guilt of the accused beyond a reasonable doubt or not. On the contrary, with such evidence before them, the jury are still left free to find the accused guilty or not guilty, according as they may be satisfied of his guilt or not, by the whole evidence."

But the controlling construction of the statute is the affirmance of this judgment of conviction. It is not sufficient to declare that the statute does not make it the duty of the jury to convict, where there is no other evidence but the breach of the contract and the failure to pay the debt. The point is that, in such a case, the statute authorizes the jury to convict. It is not enough to say that the jury may not accept that evidence as alone sufficient; for the jury may accept it, and they have the express warrant of the statute to accept it as a basis for their verdict. And it is in this light that the validity of the statute must be determined.

It is urged that the time and circumstances of the departure from service may be such as to raise not only an inference, but a strong inference, of fraudulent intent. There was no need to create a statutory presumption, and it was not created for such a case. Where circumstances are shown permitting a fair inference of fraudulent purpose, the case falls within the rule of *Ex parte Riley* (supra), which governed prosecutions under the statute before the amendment was made. The "difficulty," which admittedly the amendment was intended to surmount, did not exist where natural inferences sufficed. Plainly, the object of the statute was to hit cases which were destitute of such inferences, and to provide that the mere breach of the contract and the mere failure to pay the debt might do duty in their absence.

While, in considering the natural operation and effect of the statute, as amended, we are not limited to the particular facts of the case at the bar, they present an illuminating illustration. We may briefly restate them. Bailey made a contract to work for a year at $12 a month. He received $15, and he was to work this out, being entitled monthly only to $10.75 of his wages. No one was present when he made the contract but himself and the manager of the employing company. There is not a particle of evidence of any circumstance indicating that he made the contract or received the money with any intent to injure or defraud his employer. On the contrary, he actually worked for upwards of a month. His motive in leaving does not appear, the only showing being that it was without legal excuse and that he did not repay the money received. For this he is sentenced to a fine of $30 and to imprisonment at hard labor, in default of the payment of the fine and costs, for 136 days. Was not the case the same in effect as if the statute had made it a criminal act to leave the service without just cause and without liquidating the debt? To say that he has been found guilty of an intent to injure or defraud his employer, and not merely for breaking his contract and not paying his debt, is a distinction without a difference to Bailey.

Consider the situation of the accused under this statutory presumption. If, at the outset, nothing took place but the making of the contract and the receipt of the money, he could show nothing else. If there was no legal justification for his leaving his employment, he could show none. If he had not paid the debt, there was nothing to be said as to that. The law of the state did not permit him to testify that he did not intend to injure or defraud. Unless he were fortunate enough to be able to command evidence of circumstances affirmatively showing good faith, he was helpless. He stood, stripped by the statute of the presumption of innocence, and exposed to conviction for fraud upon evidence only of breach of contract and failure to pay.

It is said that we may assume that a fair jury would convict only where the circumstances sufficiently indicated a fraudulent intent. Why should this be assumed in the face of the statute and upon this record? In the present case the jury did convict, although there is an absence of evidence sufficient to establish fraud under the familiar rule that fraud will not be presumed, and the obvious explanation of the verdict is that the trial court, in accordance with the statute, charged the jury that refusal to perform the service, or to repay the money, without just cause, constituted prima facie evidence of the commission of the offense which the statute defined. That is, the jury were told in effect that the evidence, under the statutory rule, was sufficient, and hence they treated it as such. There is no basis for an assumption that the jury would have acted differently if Bailey had worked for three months, or six months, or nine months, if in fact his debt had not been paid. The normal assumption is that the jury will follow the statute, and, acting in accordance with the authority it confers, will accept as sufficient what the statute expressly so describes.

It may further be observed that under the statute, there is no punishment for the alleged fraud if the service is performed or the money refunded. If the service is rendered in liquidation of the debt, there is no punishment; and if it is not rendered, and the money is not refunded, that fact alone is sufficient for conviction. By a statute passed by the legislature of Alabama in 1901, it was made a misdemeanor for any person who had made a written contract to labor for or serve another for any given time, to leave the service before the expiration of the contract, and without the consent of the employer, and to make a second contract of similar nature with another person without giving the second employer notice of the existence of the first contract. This was held unconstitutional upon the ground that it interfered with freedom of contract. But, judging it by its necessary operation and obvious effect, the fundamental purpose plainly was to compel, under the sanction of the criminal law, the enforcement of the contract for personal service, and the same purpose, tested by like criteria, breathes despite its different phraseology through the amendments of 1903 and 1907 of the statute here in question.

We cannot escape the conclusion that, although the statute in terms is to punish fraud, still its natural and inevitable effect is to expose to conviction for crime those who simply fail or refuse to perform contracts for personal service in liquidation of a debt; and judging its purpose by its effect, that it seeks in this way to provide the means of compulsion through which performance of such service may be secured. The question is whether such a statute is constitutional.

This court has frequently recognized the general power of every legislature to prescribe the evidence which shall be received, and the effect of that evidence, in the courts of its own government. In the exercise of this power numerous statutes have been enacted providing that proof of one fact shall be prima facie evidence of the main fact in issue; and where the inference is not purely arbitrary, and there is a rational relation between the two facts, and the accused is not deprived of a proper opportunity to submit all the facts bearing upon the issue, it has been held that such statutes do not violate the requirements of due process of law.

The latest expression upon this point is found in the case last cited, where the court, by Mr. Justice Lurton, said: "That a legislative presumption of one fact from evidence of another may not constitute a denial of due process of law, or a denial of the equal protection of the law, it is only essential that there shall be some rational connection between the fact proved and the ultimate fact presumed, and that the inference of one fact from proof of another shall not be so unreasonable as to be a purely arbitrary mandate. So, also, it must not, under guise of regulating the presentation of evidence, operate to preclude the party from the right to present his defense to the main fact thus presumed. If a legislative provision not unreasonable in itself, prescribing a rule of evidence, in either criminal or civil cases, does not shut out from the party affected a reasonable opportunity to submit to the jury in his defense all of the facts bearing upon the issue, there is no ground for holding that due process of law has been denied him."

In this class of cases where the entire subject-matter of the legislation is otherwise within state control, the question has been whether the prescribed rule of evidence interferes with the guaranteed equality before the law, or violates those fundamental rights and immutable principles of justice which are embraced within the conception of due process of law. But where the conduct or fact, the existence of which is made the basis of the statutory presumption, itself falls within the scope of a provision of the Federal Constitution, a further question arises. It is apparent that a constitutional prohibition cannot be transgressed indirectly by the creation of a statutory presumption any more than it can be violated by direct enactment. The power to create presumptions is not a means of escape from constitutional restrictions. And the state may not in this way interfere with matters withdrawn from its authority by the Federal Constitution, or subject an accused to conviction for conduct which it is powerless to proscribe.

In the present case it is urged that the statute as amended, through the operation of the presumption for which it provides, violates the 13th Amendment of the Constitution of the United States and the act of Congress passed for its enforcement.

The 13th Amendment provides:

Section 1. Neither slavery nor involuntary servitude, except as a punishment for crime whereof the party shall have been duly convicted, shall exist within the United States, or any place subject to their jurisdiction.

Section 2. Congress shall have power to enforce this article by appropriate legislation.

Pursuant to the authority thus conferred, Congress passed the [Antipeonage Act], as follows:

Sec. 1990. The holding of any person to service or labor under the system known as peonage is abolished and forever prohibited in the territory of New Mexico, or in any other territory or state of the United States; and all acts, laws, resolutions, orders, regulations, or usages of the territory of New Mexico, or of any other territory or state, which have heretofore established, maintained, or enforced, or by virtue of which any attempt shall hereafter be made to establish, maintain, or enforce, directly or indirectly, the voluntary or involuntary service or labor of any persons as peons, in liquidation of any debt or obligation, or otherwise, are declared null and void.

Sec. 5526. Every person who holds, arrests, returns, or causes to be held, arrested, or returned, or in any manner aids in the arrest or return, of any person to a condition of peonage, shall be punished by a fine of not less than one thousand nor more than five thousand dollars, or by imprisonment not less than one year nor more than five years, or by both.

The language of the 13th Amendment was not new. It reproduced the historic words of the ordinance of 1787 for the government of the Northwest territory, and gave them unrestricted application within the United States and all places subject to their jurisdiction. While the immediate concern was with African slavery, the Amendment was not limited to that. It was a charter of universal civil freedom for all persons, of whatever race, color, or estate, under the flag.

The words involuntary servitude have a "larger meaning than slavery."

"It was very well understood that, in the form of apprenticeship for long terms, as it had been practiced in the West India Islands, on the abolition of slavery by the English government, or by reducing the slaves to the condition of serfs attached to the plantation, the purpose of the article might have been evaded, if only the word 'slavery' had been used." The plain intention was to abolish slavery of whatever name and form and all its badges and incidents; to render impossible any state of bondage; to make labor free, by prohibiting that control by which the personal service of one man is disposed of or coerced for another's benefit, which is the essence of involuntary servitude.

While the Amendment was self-executing, so far as its terms were applicable to any existing condition, Congress was authorized to secure its complete enforcement by appropriate legislation. As was said in the Civil Rights Cases: "By its own unaided force and effect it abolished slavery, and established universal freedom. Still, legislation may be necessary and proper to meet all the various cases and circumstances to be affected by it, and to prescribe proper modes of redress for its violation in letter or spirit. And such legislation may be primary and direct in its character; for the Amendment is not a mere prohibition of state laws establishing or upholding slavery, but an absolute declaration that slavery or involuntary servitude shall not exist in any part of the United States."

The [Antipeonage Act] was a valid exercise of this express authority. It declared that all laws of any state, by virtue of which any attempt should be made "to establish, maintain, or enforce, directly or indirectly, the voluntary or involuntary service or labor of any person as peons, in liquidation of any debt or obligation, or otherwise," should be null and void.

Peonage is a term descriptive of a condition which has existed in Spanish America, and especially in Mexico. The essence of the thing is compulsory service in payment of a debt. A peon is one who is compelled to work for his creditor until his debt is paid. And in this explicit and comprehensive enactment, Congress was not concerned with mere names or manner of description, or with a particular place or section of the country. It was concerned with a fact, wherever it might exist; with a condition, however named and wherever it might be established, maintained, or enforced.

The fact that the debtor contracted to perform the labor which is sought to be compelled does not withdraw the attempted enforcement from the condemnation of the statute. The full intent of the constitutional provision could be defeated with obvious facility if, through the guise of contracts under which advances had been made, debtors could be held to compulsory service. It is the compulsion of the service that the statute inhibits, for when that occurs, the condition of servitude is created, which would be not less involuntary because of the original agreement to work out the indebtedness. The contract exposes the debtor to liability for the loss due to the breach, but not to enforced labor.

* * *

The act of Congress, nullifying all state laws by which it should be attempted to enforce the "service or labor of any persons as peons, in liquidation of any debt or obligation, or otherwise," necessarily embraces all legislation which seeks to compel the service or labor by making it a crime to refuse or fail to perform it. Such laws would furnish the readiest means of compulsion. The 13th Amendment prohibits involuntary servitude except as punishment for crime. But the exception, allowing full latitude for the enforcement of penal laws, does not destroy the prohibition. It does not permit slavery or involuntary servitude to be established or maintained through the operation of the criminal law by making it a crime to refuse to submit to the one or to render the service which would constitute the other. The state may impose involuntary servitude as a punishment for crime, but it may not compel one man to labor for another in payment of a debt, by punishing him as a criminal if he does not perform the service or pay the debt.

If the statute in this case had authorized the employing company to seize the debtor, and hold him to the service until he paid the $15, or had furnished the equivalent in labor, its invalidity would not be questioned. It would be equally clear that the state could not authorize its constabulary to prevent the servant from escaping, and to force him to work out his debt. But the state could not avail itself of the sanction of the criminal law to supply the compulsion any more than it could use or authorize the use of physical force. "In contemplation of the law, the compulsion to such service by the fear of punishment under a criminal statute is more powerful than any guard which the employer could station."

What the state may not do directly it may not do indirectly. If it cannot punish the servant as a criminal for the mere failure or refusal to serve without paying his debt, it is not permitted to accomplish the same result by creating a statutory presumption which, upon proof of no other fact, exposes him to conviction and punishment. Without imputing any actual motive to oppress, we must consider the natural operation of the statute here in question, and it is apparent that it furnishes a convenient instrument for the coercion which the Constitution and the act of Congress forbid; an instrument of compulsion peculiarly effective as against the poor and the ignorant, its most likely victims. There is no more important concern than to safeguard the freedom of labor upon which alone can enduring prosperity be based. The provision designed to secure it would soon become a barren form if it were possible to establish a statutory presumption of this sort, and to hold over the heads of laborers the threat of punishment for crime, under the name of fraud, but merely upon evidence of failure to work out their debts. The act of Congress deprives of effect all legislative measures of any state through which, directly or indirectly, the prohibited thing, to wit, compulsory service to secure the payment of a debt, may be established or maintained; and we conclude that § 4730, as amended, of the Code of Alabama, in so far as it makes the refusal or failure to perform the act or service, without refunding the money or paying for the property prima facie evidence of the commission received of the crime which the section defines, is in conflict with the 13th Amendment, and the legislation authorized by that Amendment, and is therefore invalid.

• • •

Mr. Justice HOLMES, dissenting:

We all agree that this case is to be considered and decided in the same way as if it arose in Idaho or New York. Neither public document nor evidence discloses a law which, by its administration, is made something different from what it appears on its face, and therefore the fact that in Alabama it mainly concerns the blacks does not matter. *Yick Wo v. Hopkins* does not apply. I shall begin, then, by assuming for the moment what I think is not true, and shall try to show not to be true, that this statute punishes the mere refusal to labor according to contract as a crime, and shall inquire whether there would be anything contrary to the 13th Amendment or the statute if it did, supposing it to have been enacted in the state of New York. I cannot believe it. The 13th Amendment does not outlaw contracts for labor. That would be at least as great a misfortune for the laborer as for the man that employed him. For it certainly would affect the terms of the bargain unfavorably for the laboring man if it were understood that the employer could do nothing in case the laborer saw fit to break his word. But any legal liability for breach of a contract is a disagreeable consequence which tends to make the contractor do as he said he would. Liability to an action for damages has that tendency as well a fine. If the mere imposition of such consequences as tend to make a man keep to his promise is the creation of peonage when the contract happens to be for labor, I do not see why the allowance of a civil action is not, as well as an indictment ending in fine. Peonage is service to a private master at which a man is kept by bodily compulsion against his will. But the creation of the ordinary legal motives for right conduct does not produce it. Breach of a legal contract without excuse is wrong conduct, even if the contract is for labor; and if a state adds to civil liability a criminal liability to fine, it simply intensifies the legal motive for doing right; it does not make the laborer a slave.

But if a fine may be imposed, imprisonment may be imposed in case of a failure to pay it. Nor does it matter if labor is added to the imprisonment. Imprisonment with hard labor is not stricken from the statute books. On the contrary, involuntary servitude as a punishment for crime is excepted from the prohibition of the 13th Amendment in so many words. Also the power of the states to make breach of contract a crime is not done away with by the abolition of slavery. But if breach of contract may be made a crime at all, it may be made a crime with all the consequences usually attached to crime. There is produced a sort of illusion if a contract to labor ends in compulsory labor in a prison. But compulsory work for no private master in a jail is not peonage. If work in a jail is not condemned in itself, without regard to what the conduct is it punishes, it may be made a consequence of any conduct that the state has power to punish at all. I do not blink the fact that the liability to imprisonment may work as a motive when a fine without it would not, and that it may induce the laborer to keep on when he would like to leave. But it does not strike me as an objection to a law that it is effective. If the contract is one that ought not to be made, prohibit it. But if it is a perfectly fair and proper contract, I can see no reason why the state should not throw its weight on the side of performance. There is no relation between its doing so in the manner supposed, and allowing a private master to use private force upon a laborer who wishes to leave.

But all that I have said so far goes beyond the needs of the case as I understand it. I think it a mistake to say that this statute attaches its punishment to the mere breach of a contract to labor. It does not purport to do so; what it purports to punish is fraudulently obtaining money by a false pretense of an intent to keep the written contract in consideration of which the money is advanced. (It is not necessary to cite cases to show that such an intent may be the subject of a material false representation.) But the import of the statute is supposed to be changed by the provision, that a refusal to perform, coupled with a failure to return the money advanced, shall be prima facie evidence of fraudulent intent. I agree that if the statute created a conclusive presumption, it might be held to make a disguised change in the substantive law. But it only makes the conduct prima facie evidence — a very different matter. Is it not evidence that a man had a fraudulent intent if he receives an advance upon a contract over night and leaves in the morning? I should have thought that it very plainly was. Of course, the statute is in general terms, and applies to a departure at any time without excuse or repayment, but that does no harm except on a tacit assumption that this law is not administered as it would be in New York, and that juries will act with prejudice against the laboring man. For prima facie evidence is only evidence, and as such may be held by the jury insufficient to make out guilt. This was decided by the supreme court of Alabama in this case, and we should be bound by their construction of the statute, even if we thought it wrong. But I venture to add that I think it entirely right. This being so, I take it that a fair jury would acquit, if the only evidence were a departure after eleven months' work, and if it received no color from some special well-known course of events. But the matter well may be left to a jury, because their experience as men of the world may teach them that in certain conditions it is so common for laborers to remain during a part of the season, receiving advances, and then to depart at the period of need, in the hope of greater wages at a neighboring plantation, that when a laborer follows that course there is a fair inference of fact that he intended it from the beginning.

The Alabama statute, as construed by the state court and as we must take it, merely says, as a court might say, that the prosecution may go to the jury. This means, and means only, that the court cannot say, from its knowledge of the ordinary course of events, that the jury could not be justified by its knowledge in drawing the inference from the facts proved. In my opinion, the statute embodies little if anything more than what I should have told the jury was the law without it. The right of the state to regulate laws of evidence is admitted, and the statute does not go much beyond the common law.

I do not see how the result that I have reached thus far is affected by the rule laid down by the court, but not contained in the statute, that the prisoner cannot testify to his uncommunicated intentions, and therefore, it is assumed, would not be permitted to offer a naked denial of an intent to defraud. If there is an excuse for breaking the contract, it will be found in external circumstances, and can be proved. So the sum of the wrong supposed to be inflicted is that the intent to go off without repaying may be put further back than it would be otherwise. But if there is a wrong it lies in leaving the evidence to the jury — a wrong that is not affected by the letting in or keeping out an item of evidence on the other side. I have stated why I think it was not a wrong.

To sum up, I think that obtaining money by fraud may be made a crime as well as murder or theft; that a false representation, expressed or implied, at the time of making a contract of labor, that one intends to perform it, and thereby obtaining an advance, may be declared a case of fraudulently obtaining money as well as any other; that if made a crime it may be punished like any other crime; and that an unjustified departure from the promised service without repayment may be declared a sufficient case to go to the jury for their judgment; all without in any way infringing the 13th Amendment or the statutes of the United States.

Mr. Justice LURTON concurs in this dissent.

NOTES AND QUESTIONS

1. The Court is at pains to ignore the elephant in the room: that *Bailey* is a race case. Indeed, *Bailey* is not just a case about race but a case where the conviction at the heart of the case is emblematic of the means by which Black people were re-enslaved after the Civil War. It would be odd enough if the Court simply ignored the racial dimension of the case but it goes further, affirmatively denying that race is a factor. *See id.* at 231 ("We at once dismiss from consideration the fact that the plaintiff in error is a black man. . . . The statute, on its face, makes no racial discrimination, and the record fails to show its existence in fact. No question of a sectional character is presented and we may view the legislation in the same manner as if it had been enacted in New York or in Idaho."). Idaho had been admitted to the Union in 1890, 25 years after the end of the Civil War, as the forty-third state. The dissent also accepts this premise: "that in Alabama [the statute] mainly concerns the blacks does not matter." *Id.* at 245 (Holmes, J., dissenting).

2. Why did the Court pretend this was not a race case? The southern peonage system at issue had by the time *Bailey* was decided in 1911 been the subject of wide reporting. The racial aspect of this particular case was no secret, moreover. The press covered it as a race case. And both the defendant and the United States as amicus in their briefs emphasized the racial impact of the Alabama statute. As the Court points out, at trial Bailey's attorney asked just one question of the government's sole witness, the manager of the company that had employed Bailey: whether Bailey was a Negro. And the United States' brief argued that all reported convictions under the statute were of farm laborers, the majority of whom were Black, and that the law thus violated the rule of *Yick Wo v. Hopkins*, 118 U.S. 356 (1886), imposing coercive legal burdens on a particular class "with an evil eye and an unequal hand."

3. Before reaching the federal statutory and constitutional issues, the Court addressed the statute's rebuttable presumption—that intent to defraud can be inferred from the mere fact of the breach of a labor contract—a presumption that the Alabama legislature had added to the statute after a prior version that criminalized a contractual breach itself was struck down by the Alabama Supreme Court. *Ex parte Riley*, 94 Ala. 82, 83 (1891). The Court concludes that inasmuch as the statute *authorizes* conviction without evidence of fraud that "its natural purpose and effect is to expose to conviction for crime those who simply fail or refuse to perform contracts for personal service . . . [and thereby] provide[s] the means of compulsion through which performance of such service is secured." 219 U.S. at 238. In his dissent Justice Holmes takes issue with this characterization, and points out factual scenarios where "a fair jury would acquit" notwithstanding the presumption. Does the dissent have a valid point? Is it possible for defendants to rebut the presumption? How so? Are these hypotheticals relevant given that in Bailey's case the only evidence of fraud was his breach of the contract? Note that Justice Holmes also chastises the majority, despite its disclaimers, for proceeding on "the tacit assumption that this law is not administered as it would be in New York, and that juries will act with prejudice against the laboring men." Fair point?

4. Once the Court had declared the "natural and inevitable effect" of the statute it had little trouble finding that it violated both the Antipeonage Act and the Thirteenth Amendment. In consecutive sentences the Court was able to both hint at the known but unstated premises of the statute and also dress its decision in the garb of laissez-faire economics:

> What the state may not do directly it may not do indirectly. If it cannot punish the servant as a criminal for the mere failure or refusal to serve without paying his debt, it is not permitted to accomplish the same result by creating a statutory presumption which, upon proof of no other fact, exposes him to conviction and punishment. Without imputing any actual motive to oppress, we must consider the natural operation of the statute here in question . . ., and it is apparent that it furnishes a convenient instrument for coercion which the Constitution and the act of Congress forbid; an instrument of compulsion peculiarly effective as against the poor and the ignorant, its most likely victims. There is no more important concern than to safeguard the freedom of labor upon which alone can enduring prosperity be based.

Id. at 244-45. Why the paean to "freedom of labor," a theme that had scarcely been implied in the opinion prior to this punch line?

5. Justice Holmes rejected the premise that the state could not criminalize the breach of a labor contract. *Id.* at 246-47. In rigidly moralistic fashion he reasoned, "[b]reach of a legal contract without excuse is wrong conduct, even if the contract is for labor; and if a state adds to civil liability a criminal liability to fine, it simply intensifies the legal motive for doing right; it does not make the laborer a slave." *Id.* at 246. Does this strike you as correct? Are there constitutional limits on the type of conduct a state can criminalize?

———————

Just three years after *Bailey*, in *United States v. Reynolds*, 235 U.S. 133 (1914), the Court considered a different aspect of Alabama's neoslavery regime, namely, its criminal-surety system. Under this system a criminal defendant would "confess judgment" to a charge and an employer would step in to pay the defendant's fines and court costs in exchange for entering into a labor contract with the employer to pay off the debt. Breach of such a labor contract was itself a crime, enforceable by the employer. The defendant's motivation in agreeing to the surety arrangement was usually to avoid the alternative of the dreaded chain gang.

In *Reynolds*, the defendant employer was indicted for violating the federal Antipeonage Act. He had entered into a surety relationship on behalf of Rivers, who had been convicted of petit larceny and fined $15 with $43.75 of costs. Reynolds paid these amounts to the court and Rivers contracted with Reynolds to work for him as a farmhand for 9 months and 24 days at the rate of $6 a month. After about a month, Rivers stopped working and was arrested upon a warrant initiated by Reynolds, charging him with violating the labor contract. He was convicted on the charge, and fined one cent with $87.05 in costs. He again confessed judgment and entered into contract with a second defendant employer to work for 14 months and 15 days at the same rate. *Id.* at 139-40.

While acknowledging that the Thirteenth Amendment explicitly authorized involuntary servitude as punishment for crime, the Court found the surety arrangement in violation of both the Amendment and the statute, as by criminalizing a breach of a labor contract the state requires the worker "under pain of recurring prosecutions [to] be kept at labor, to satisfy the demands of the employer." *Id.* at 150. The majority opinion did not say a word about race.

The decision was unanimous, although Holmes added a one-paragraph concurrence, apparently to explain his deviation from his position in *Bailey*:

> There seems to me nothing in the 13th Amendment or the Revised Statutes that prevents a state from making a breach of contract, as well a reasonable contract for labor as for other matters, a crime and punishing it as such. But impulsive people with little intelligence or foresight may be expected to lay hold of anything that affords a relief from present pain, even though it will cause greater trouble by and by. The successive contracts, each for a longer term than the last, are the inevitable, and must be taken to have been the contemplated, outcome of the Alabama laws. On this ground I am inclined to agree that the statutes in question disclosed the attempt to maintain service that the Revised Statutes forbid.

Justice Holmes's petulant little paragraph is remarkable. Having been unwilling to acknowledge and explicitly disavowing the racial backdrop of the criminal regime at issue in *Bailey*, he relies overtly on a repugnant racial stereotype to justify his agreement with the majority in *Reynolds*. Rather than condemn the white Alabamans who established the criminal-surety system—a system that he seems to acknowledge was intended to doom Black people to successive periods of servitude—he castigates Black people for needing special dispensation from otherwise sound economic principles.

The Court's decisions in *Bailey* and *Reynolds* did not, to say the least, put an end to peonage in the South. While the Great Migration of Black people from the South to the North and a lessened demand for manual labor in the following decades decreased the extent of the practice, vestiges of the practice continued into the 1960s. *See* Tamar R. Birckhead, *The New Peonage*, 72 Wash. & Lee L. Rev. 1595, 1625-26 (2015).

As the next case shows, not only did peonage systems continue into the middle of the twentieth century, some southern courts and legislatures aided and abetted their survival by ignoring or disingenuously interpreting Supreme Court precedent.

Pollock v. Williams
322 U.S. 4 (1942)

Mr. Justice JACKSON delivered the opinion of the Court.

Appellant Pollock questions the validity of a statute of the State of Florida making it a misdemeanor to induce advances with intent to defraud by a promise to perform labor and further making failure to perform labor for which money has been obtained prima facie evidence of intent to defraud. It conflicts, he says, with the Thirteenth Amendment to the Federal Constitution and with the antipeonage statute enacted by Congress thereunder. Claims also are made under the due process and equal protection clauses of the Fourteenth Amendment which we find it unnecessary to consider.

B. Peonage Convictions 31

Pollock was arrested January 5, 1943, on a warrant issued three days before which charged that on the 17th of October, 1942, he did "with intent to injure and defraud under and by reason of a contract and promise to perform labor and service, procure and obtain money, to-wit: the sum of $5.00, as advances from one J. V. O'Albora, a corporation, contrary to the statute in such cases made and provided, and against the peace and dignity of the State of Florida." He was taken before the county judge on the same day, entered a plea of guilty, and was sentenced to pay a fine of $100 and in default to serve sixty days in the county jail. He was immediately committed.

On January 11, 1943, a writ of habeas corpus was issued by the judge of the circuit court, directed to the jail keeper, who is appellee here. Petition for the writ challenged the constitutionality of the statutes under which Pollock was confined and set forth that "at the trial aforesaid, he was not told that he was entitled to counsel, and that counsel would be provided for him if he wished, and he did not know that he had such right. Petitioner was without funds and unable to employ counsel. He further avers that he did not understand the nature of the charge against him, but understood that if he owed any money to his prior employer and had quit his employment without paying the same, he was guilty, which facts he admitted." The Sheriff's return makes no denial of these allegations, but merely sets forth that he holds the prisoner by virtue of the commitment "based upon the judgment and conviction as set forth in the petition." The Supreme Court of Florida has said that "undenied allegations of the petition are taken as true."

The Circuit Court held the statutes under which the case was prosecuted to be unconstitutional and discharged the prisoner. The Supreme Court of Florida reversed. It read our decisions in *Bailey v. Alabama* and *Taylor v. Georgia* to hold that similar laws are not in conflict with the Constitution in so far as they denounce the crime, but only in declaring the prima facie evidence rule. It stated that its first impression was that the entire Florida act would fall, as did that of Georgia, but on reflection it concluded that our decisions were called forth by operation of the presumption, and did not condemn the substantive part of the statute where the presumption was not brought into play. As the prisoner had pleaded guilty, the Florida court thought the presumption had played no part in this case, and therefore remanded the prisoner to custody. An appeal to this Court was taken and probable jurisdiction noted.

Florida advances no argument that the presumption section of this statute is constitutional, nor could it plausibly do so in view of our decisions. It contends, however, (1) that we can give no consideration to the presumption section because it was not in fact brought into play in the case, by reason of the plea of guilty; (2) that so severed the section denouncing the crime is constitutional.

These issues emerge from an historical background against which the Florida legislation in question must be appraised.

The Thirteenth Amendment to the Federal Constitution, made in 1865, declares that involuntary servitude shall not exist within the United States and gives Congress power to enforce the article by appropriate legislation. Congress on March 2, 1867, enacted that all laws or usages of any state "by virtue of which any attempt shall hereafter be made to establish, maintain, or enforce, directly or indirectly, the voluntary or involuntary service or labor of any persons as peons, in liquidation of any debt or obligation, or otherwise," are null and void, and denounced it as a crime to hold, arrest, or return a person to the condition of peonage. Congress thus raised both a shield and a sword against forced labor because of debt.

Clyatt v. United States was a case from Florida in which the Federal Act was used as a sword and an employer convicted under it. This Court sustained it as constitutional and said of peonage: "It may be defined as a status or condition of compulsory service, based upon the indebtedness of the peon to the master. The basal fact is indebtedness. Peonage is sometimes classified as voluntary or involuntary; but this implies simply a difference in the mode of origin, but none in the character of the servitude. The one exists where the debtor voluntarily contracts to enter the service of his creditor. The other is forced upon the debtor by some provision of law. . . . A clear distinction exists between peonage and the voluntary performance of labor or rendering of services in payment of a debt. In the latter case the debtor, though contracting to pay his indebtedness by labor or service, and subject, like any other contractor, to an action for damages for breach of that contract, can elect at any time to break it, and no law or force compels performance or a continuance of the service."

Then came the twice-considered case of *Bailey v. Alabama*, in which the Act and the Constitution were raised as a shield against conviction of a laborer under an Alabama act substantially the same as the one before us now. Bailey, a Negro, had obtained $15 from a corporation on a written agreement to work for a year at $12 per month, $10.75 to be paid him and $1.25 per month to apply on his debt. In about a month he quit. He was convicted, fined $30, or in default sentenced to hard labor for 20 days in lieu of the fine and 116 days on account of costs. The Court considered that the portion of the state law defining the crime would require proof of intent to defraud, and so did not strike down that part; nor was it expressly sustained, nor was it necessarily reached, for the prima facie evidence provision had been used to obtain a conviction. This Court held the presumption, in such a context, to be unconstitutional.

Later came *United States v. Reynolds* and *United States v. Broughton* in which the Act of 1867 was sword again. Reynolds and Broughton were indicted under it. The Alabama Code authorized one under some circumstances to become surety for a convict, pay his fine, and be reimbursed by labor. Reynolds and Broughton each got himself a convict to work out fines and costs as a farm hand at $6.00 per month. After a time each convict refused to labor further and, under the statute, each was convicted for the refusal. This Court said, "Thus, under pain of recurring prosecutions, the convict may be kept at labor, to satisfy the demands of his employer." It held the Alabama statute unconstitutional and employers under it subject to prosecution.

In *Taylor v. Georgia* the Federal Act was again applied as a shield, against conviction by resort to the presumption, of a Negro laborer, under a Georgia statute in effect like the one before us now. We made no effort to separate valid from invalid elements in the statute, although the substantive and procedural provisions were, as here, in separate, and separately numbered, sections. We said, "We think that the sections of the Georgia Code upon which this conviction rests are repugnant to the Thirteenth Amendment and to the Act of 1867, and that the conviction must therefore be reversed." Only recently in a case from Northern Florida a creditor-employer was indicted under the Federal Act for arresting a debtor to peonage, and we sustained the indictment. *United States v. Gaskin.*

These cases decided by this Court under the Act of 1867 came either from Florida or one of the adjoining states. And these were but a part of the stir caused by the Federal Antipeonage Act and its enforcement in this same region. This is not to intimate that this section, more than others, was sympathetic with peonage, for this evil has never had general approval anywhere, and its sporadic appearances have been neither sectional nor racial. It is mentioned, however, to indicate that the Legislature of Florida acted with almost certain knowledge in designing its successive "labor fraud" acts in relation to our series of peonage decisions. The present Act is the latest of a lineage, in which its antecedents were obviously associated with the practice of peonage. This history throws some light on whether the present state act is one "by virtue of which any attempt shall hereafter be made" to "enforce involuntary servitude," in which event the Federal Act declares it void.

In 1891, the Legislature created an offense of two elements: obtaining money or property upon a false promise to perform service, and abandonment of service without just cause and without restitution of what had been obtained. In 1905, this Court decided *Clyatt*, indicating that any person, including public officers, even if acting under state law, might be guilty of violating the Federal Act. In 1907, the Florida Legislature enacted a new statute, nearly identical in terms with that of Alabama. In 1911, in *Bailey v. Alabama*, this Court held such an act unconstitutional. In 1913, the Florida Legislature repealed the 1907 act, but reenacted in substance the section denouncing the crime, omitting the presumption of intent from the failure to perform the service or make restitution. In 1919, the Florida Supreme Court held this act, standing alone, void under the authority of *Bailey v. Alabama*. Whereupon, at the session of 1919, the present statute was enacted, including the prima facie evidence provisions, notwithstanding these decisions by the Supreme Court of Florida and by this Court. The Supreme Court of Florida later upheld a conviction under this statute on a plea of guilty, but declined to pass on the presumption section, because, as in the present case, the plea of guilty was thought to make its consideration unnecessary. The statute was re-enacted without substantial change in 1941. Again in 1943 it was re-enacted despite the fact that the year before we held a very similar Georgia statute unconstitutional in its entirety.

II

The State contends that we must exclude the prima facie evidence provision from consideration because in fact it played no part in producing this conviction. Such was the holding of the State Supreme Court. We are not concluded by that holding, however, but under the circumstances are authorized to make an independent determination.

What the prisoner actually did that constituted the crime cannot be gleaned from the record. The charge is cast in the words of the statute and is largely a conclusion. It affords no information except that Pollock obtained $5 from a corporation in connection with a promise to work which he failed to perform, and that his doing so was fraudulent. If the conclusion that the prisoner acted with intent to defraud rests on facts and not on the prima facie evidence provisions of the statute, none are stated in the warrant or appear in the record. None were so set forth that he could deny them. He obtained the money on the 14th of October, 1942, and the warrant was not sought until January 2, 1943. Whether the original advancement was more or less than $5, what he represented or promised in obtaining it, whether he worked a time and quit, or whether he never began work at all are undisclosed. About all that appears is that he obtained an advancement of $5 from a corporation and failed to keep his agreement to work it out. He admitted those facts and the law purported to supply the element of intent. He admitted the conclusion of guilt which the statute made prima facie thereon. He was fined $20 for each dollar of his debt, and in default of payment was required to atone for it by serving time at the rate of less than 9¢ per day.

Especially in view of the undenied assertions in Pollock's petition we cannot doubt that the presumption provision had a coercive effect in producing the plea of guilty. The statute laid its undivided weight upon him. The legislature had not even included a separability clause. Of course the function of the prima facie evidence section is to make it possible to convict where proof of guilt is lacking. No one questions that we clearly have held that such a presumption is prohibited by the Constitution and the federal statute. The Florida Legislature has enacted and twice re-enacted it since we so held. We cannot assume it was doing an idle thing. Since the presumption was known to be unconstitutional and of no use in a contested case, the only explanation we can find for its persistent appearance in the statute is its extra-legal coercive effect in suppressing defenses. It confronted this defendant. There was every probability that a law so recently and repeatedly enacted by the legislature would be followed by the trial court, whose judge was not required to be a lawyer. The possibility of obtaining relief by appeal was not bright, as the event proved, for Pollock had to come all the way to this Court and was required, and quite regularly, to post a supersedeas bond of $500, a hundred times the amount of his debt. He was an illiterate Negro laborer in the toils of the law for the want of $5. Such considerations bear importantly on the decision of a prisoner even if aided by counsel, as Pollock was not, whether to plead guilty and hope for leniency or to fight. It is plain that, had his plight after conviction not aroused outside help, Pollock himself would have been unheard in any appellate court.

In the light of its history, there is no reason to believe that the law was generally used or especially useful merely to punish deceit. Florida has a general and comprehensive statute making it a crime to obtain money or property by false pretenses or commit "gross fraud or cheat at common law." These appear to authorize prosecution for even the petty amount involved here. We can conceive reasons, even if unconstitutional ones, which might lead well-intentioned persons to apply this Act as a means to make otherwise shiftless men work, but if in addition to this general fraud protection employers as a class are so susceptible to imposition that they need extra legislation, or workmen so crafty and subtle as to constitute a special menace, we do not know it, nor are we advised of such facts.

We think that a state which maintains such a law in face of the court decisions we have recited may not be heard to say that a plea of guilty under the circumstances is not due to pressure of its statutory threat to convict him on the presumption.

As we have seen, Florida, persisted in putting upon its statute books a provision creating a presumption of fraud from the mere nonperformance of a contract for labor service three times after the courts ruled that such a provision violates the prohibition against peonage. To attach no meaning to such action, to say that legally speaking there was no such legislation, is to be blind to fact. Since the Florida Legislature deemed these repeated enactments to be important, we take the Legislature at its own word. Such a provision is on the statute books for those who are arrested for the crime, and it is on the statute books for us in considering the practical meaning of what Florida has done.

III

We are induced by the evident misunderstanding of our decisions by the Florida Supreme Court, in what we are convinced was a conscientious and pains-taking study of them, to make more explicit the basis of constitutional invalidity of this type of statute.

• • •

We impute to the Legislature no intention to oppress, but we are compelled to hold that the Florida Act of 1919 [is] by virtue of the Thirteenth Amendment and the Antipeonage Act of the United States, null and void. The judgment of the court below is reversed and the cause is remanded for further proceedings not inconsistent with this opinion.

[Chief Justice Stone and Justice Reed dissented.]

NOTES AND QUESTIONS

1. Justice Jackson memorably describes the federal Antipeonage Act as "both a shield and a sword" against forced labor because of debt. As to the sword, he references *Clyatt v. United States*, 197 U.S. 207 (1905), where the Court upheld the statute as constitutional although it reversed the conviction on evidentiary grounds. Although the Court in *Clyatt* defined the concept of peonage, *Clyatt*, and its definition of peonage, are barely mentioned in either *Bailey* or *Reynolds*.

2. The Florida Supreme Court found Pollock's conviction lawful because, inasmuch as he pleaded guilty, the statutory presumption that was found fatal in *Bailey* never went into operation. Does this reasoning have any superficial plausibility? What if the record in the case showed that Pollock had admitted to obtaining identical advances from multiple employers at the same time and then left town? Would the result be different?

3. The Court concludes that the presumption provision of the Florida statute "had a coercive effect in producing the plea of guilty." How can this be true given that Pollock appears to claim on appeal—which is almost certainly true, given his lack of counsel—that he "did not understand the nature of the charge against him"? Pollock does say that he understood that "if he owed any money to his prior employer and had quit his employment without paying the same" he would be guilty. Is this understanding tantamount to an understanding of the charge against him?

4. Justice Jackson's opinion is restrained in some respects, yet he is plainly "frustrated"—to put it mildly—with the Florida Supreme Court and the Florida legislature. He walks though the relevant Supreme Court case law—*Bailey, Reynolds*, and the 1942 case of *Taylor v. Georgia*, in which the Court struck down a virtually identical Georgia statute—as if providing a remedial tutorial for the Florida court. As to the Florida legislature his displeasure is more overt. He observes that "the Legislature acted with almost certain knowledge in designing its successive 'labor fraud' acts in relation to our series of peonage decisions," and suggests that the legislature's purpose was the presumption's "extra-legal coercive effect in suppressing defenses." He even has a sentence suggesting that Florida's conduct "estops" it from defending the statute:

> We think that a state which maintains such a law in face of the court decisions we have recited may not be heard to say that a plea of guilty under the circumstances is not due to pressure of its statutory threat to convict him on the presumption.

This is unusually forceful language for the Supreme Court to use in any context. Do you see any evidence that Justice Jackson's "frustration" extends to the actual operation of the state's criminal justice system?

5. Note also Justice Jackson's expressed sympathy to Pollock as compared to the Court's opinions in *Bailey* and *Reynolds*. Not only does he mention Pollock's race multiple times but he notes that without "outside help" Pollock would have been unheard in any appellate court, and the Florida statute would have affected him the same way it affected countless other uncounseled defendants.

The vagrancy statutes that fueled the peonage system in the South, and provided other avenues for assertions of white supremacy, were not outlawed by the Supreme Court until the 1970s in the following case, *Papachristou v. Jacksonville*, although the Court does so without critically examining their pedigree. But vagrancy prosecutorial regimes were not limited to the South. By the 1960s all 50 states and the District of Columbia had vagrancy statutes, which were often enforced against disfavored groups—civil rights activists, gays and lesbians, political dissidents, and, of course, hippies. Risa Goluboff, Vagrant Nation: Police Power, Constitutional Change and the Making of the 1960s 2-3 (2016). And by the time *Papachristou* was decided in 1972, the Supreme Court had already held in *Terry v. Ohio*, 392 U.S. 1 (1968), that police could stop and frisk persons based on "reasonable suspicion," which substantially compensated the police for any loss of authority due to the invalidation of vagrancy laws. *Id.* at 11. *See* Chapter IV *infra*.

Papachristou v. Jacksonville
405 U.S. 156 (1972)

Mr. Justice DOUGLAS delivered the opinion of the Court.

This case involves eight defendants who were convicted in a Florida municipal court of violating a Jacksonville, Florida, vagrancy ordinance. Their convictions, entailing fines and jail

Chapter II The Roots of Modern Constitutional Criminal Procedure

sentences (some of which were suspended), were affirmed by the Florida Circuit The case is here on a petition for certiorari, which we granted. For reasons which will appear, we reverse.

At issue are five consolidated cases. Margaret Papachristou, Betty Calloway, Eugene Eddie Melton, and Leonard Johnson were all arrested early on a Sunday morning, and charged with vagrancy—"prowling by auto."

Jimmy Lee Smith and Milton Henry were charged with vagrancy—"vagabonds."

Henry Edward Heath and a codefendant were arrested for vagrancy—"loitering" and "common thief."

Thomas Owen Campbell was charged with vagrancy—"common thief."

Hugh Brown was charged with vagrancy—"disorderly loitering on street" and "disorderly conduct—resisting arrest with violence."

The facts are stipulated. Papachristou and Calloway are white females. Melton and Johnson are black males. Papachristou was enrolled in a job-training program sponsored by the State Employment Service at Florida Junior College in Jacksonville. Calloway was a typing and shorthand teacher at a state mental institution located near Jacksonville. She was the owner of the automobile in which the four defendants were arrested. Melton was a Vietnam war veteran who had been released from the Navy after nine months in a veterans' hospital. On the date of his arrest he was a part-time computer helper while attending college as a full-time student in Jacksonville. Johnson was a tow-motor operator in a grocery chain warehouse and was a lifelong resident of Jacksonville.

At the time of their arrest the four of them were riding in Calloway's car on the main thoroughfare in Jacksonville. They had left a restaurant owned by Johnson's uncle where they had eaten and were on their way to a nightclub. The arresting officers denied that the racial mixture in the car played any part in the decision to make the arrest. The arrest, they said, was made because the defendants had stopped near a used-car lot which had been broken into several times. There was, however, no evidence of any breaking and entering on the night in question.

Of these four charged with "prowling by auto" none had been previously arrested except Papachristou who had once been convicted of a municipal offense.

Jimmy Lee Smith and Milton Henry (who is not a petitioner) were arrested between 9 and 10 a.m. on a weekday in downtown Jacksonville, while waiting for a friend who was to lend them a car so they could apply for a job at a produce company. Smith was a part-time produce worker and part-time organizer for a Negro political group. He had a common-law wife and three children supported by him and his wife. He had been arrested several times but convicted only once. Smith's companion, Henry, was an 18-year-old high school student with no previous record of arrest.

This morning it was cold, and Smith had no jacket, so they went briefly into a dry cleaning shop to wait, but left when requested to do so. They thereafter walked back and forth two or three times over a two-block stretch looking for their friend. The store owners, who apparently were wary of Smith and his companion, summoned two police officers who searched the men and found neither had a weapon. But they were arrested because the officers said they had no identification and because the officers did not believe their story.

Heath and a codefendant were arrested for "loitering" and for "common thief." Both were residents of Jacksonville, Heath having lived there all his life and being employed at an automobile body shop. Heath had previously been arrested but his codefendant had no arrest record. Heath and his companion were arrested when they drove up to a residence shared by Heath's girl friend and some other girls. Some police officers were already there in the process of arresting another man. When Heath and his companion started backing out of the driveway, the officers signaled to them to stop and asked them to get out of the car, which they did. Thereupon they and the automobile were searched. Although no contraband or incriminating evidence was found, they were both arrested, Heath being charged with being a "common thief" because he was reputed to be a thief. The codefendant was charged with "loitering" because he was standing in the driveway, an act which the officers admitted was done only at their command.

Campbell was arrested as he reached his home very early one morning and was charged with "common thief." He was stopped by officers because he was traveling at a high rate of speed, yet no speeding charge was placed against him.

Brown was arrested when he was observed leaving a downtown Jacksonville hotel by a police officer seated in a cruiser. The police testified he was reputed to be a thief, narcotics pusher, and generally opprobrious character. The officer called Brown over to the car, intending at that time to arrest him unless he had a good explanation for being on the street. Brown walked over to the police cruiser, as commanded, and the officer began to search him, apparently preparatory to placing him in the car. In the process of the search he came on two small packets which were later found to contain heroin. When the officer touched the pocket where the packets were, Brown began to resist. He was charged with "disorderly loitering on street" and "disorderly conduct — resisting arrest with violence." While he was also charged with a narcotics violation, that charge was nolled.

Jacksonville's ordinance and Florida's statute were derived from early English law. . . .

This ordinance is void for vagueness, both in the sense that it "fails to give a person of ordinary intelligence fair notice that his contemplated conduct is forbidden by the statute," and because it encourages arbitrary and erratic arrests and convictions.

Living under a rule of law entails various suppositions, one of which is that "(all persons) are entitled to be informed as to what the State commands or forbids."

Lanzetta is one of a well-recognized group of cases insisting that the law give fair notice of the offending conduct. In the field of regulatory statutes governing business activities, where the acts limited are in a narrow category, greater leeway is allowed.

The poor among us, the minorities, the average householder are not in business and not alerted to the regulatory schemes of vagrancy laws; and we assume they would have no understanding of their meaning and impact if they read them. Nor are they protected from being caught in the vagrancy net by the necessity of having a specific intent to commit an unlawful act.

The Jacksonville ordinance makes criminal activities which by modern standards are normally innocent. "Nightwalking" is one. Florida construes the ordinance not to make criminal one night's wandering, only the "habitual" wanderer or, as the ordinance describes it, "common night walkers." We know, however, from experience that sleepless people often walk at night, perhaps hopeful that sleep-inducing relaxation will result.

Luis Munoz-Marin, former Governor of Puerto Rico, commented once that "loafing" was a national virtue in his Commonwealth and that it should be encouraged. It is, however, a crime in Jacksonville.

"(P)ersons able to work but habitually living upon the earnings of their wives or minor children" — like habitually living "without visible means of support" — might implicate unemployed pillars of the community who have married rich wives.

"(P)ersons able to work but habitually living upon the earnings of their wives or minor children" may also embrace unemployed people out of the labor market, by reason of a recession or disemployed by reason of technological or so-called structural displacements.

Persons "wandering or strolling" from place to place have been extolled by Walt Whitman and Vachel Lindsay. The qualification "without any lawful purpose or object" may be a trap for innocent acts. Persons "neglecting all lawful business and habitually spending their time by frequenting . . . places where alcoholic beverages are sold or served" would literally embrace many members of golf clubs and city clubs.

Walkers and strollers and wanderers may be going to or coming from a burglary. Loafers or loiterers may be "casing" a place for a holdup. Letting one's wife support him is an intra-family matter, and normally of no concern to the police. Yet it may, of course, be the setting for numerous crimes.

The difficulty is that these activities are historically part of the amenities of life as we have known them. They are not mentioned in the Constitution or in the Bill of Rights. These unwritten amenities have been in part responsible for giving our people the feeling of independence and self-confidence, the feeling of creativity. These amenities have dignified the right of dissent and have honored the right to be nonconformists and the right to defy submissiveness. They have encouraged lives of high spirits rather than hushed, suffocating silence.

They are embedded in Walt Whitman's writings, especially in his "Song of the Open Road." They are reflected too, in the spirit of Vachel Lindsay's "I Want to Go Wandering," and by Henry D. Thoreau.

This aspect of the vagrancy ordinance before us is suggested by what this Court said in 1876 about a broad criminal statute enacted by Congress: "It would certainly be dangerous if the legislature could set a net large enough to catch all possible offenders, and leave it to the courts to step inside and say who could be rightfully detained, and who should be set at large."

• • •

Where the list of crimes is so all-inclusive and generalized as the one in this ordinance, those convicted may be punished for no more than vindicating affronts to police authority:

> The common ground which brings such a motley assortment of human troubles before the magistrates in vagrancy-type proceedings is the procedural laxity which permits "conviction" for almost any kind of conduct and the existence of the House of Correction as an easy and convenient dumping-ground for problems that appear to have no other immediate solution.

Foote, *Vagrancy-Type Law and Its Administration*, 104 U. Pa. L. Rev. 603, 631.

Another aspect of the ordinance's vagueness appears when we focus, not on the lack of notice given a potential offender, but on the effect of the unfettered discretion it places in the hands of the Jacksonville police. Caleb Foote, an early student of this subject, has called the vagrancy-type law as offering "punishment by analogy." Such crimes, though long common in Russia, are not compatible with our constitutional system. We allow our police to make arrests only on "probable cause," a Fourth and Fourteenth Amendment standard applicable to the States as well as to the Federal Government. Arresting a person on suspicion, like arresting a person for investigation, is foreign to our system, even when the arrest is for past criminality. Future criminality, however, is the common justification for the presence of vagrancy statutes. Florida has, indeed, construed her vagrancy statute "as necessary regulations," inter alia, "to deter vagabondage and prevent crimes."

A direction by a legislature to the police to arrest all "suspicious" persons would not pass constitutional muster. A vagrancy prosecution may be merely the cloak for a conviction which could not be obtained on the real but undisclosed grounds for the arrest.

Those generally implicated by the imprecise terms of the ordinance — poor people, nonconformists, dissenters, idlers — may be required to comport themselves according to the life style deemed appropriate by the Jacksonville police and the courts. Where, as here, there are no standards governing the exercise of the discretion granted by the ordinance, the scheme permits and encourages an arbitrary and discriminatory enforcement of the law. It furnishes a convenient tool for "harsh and discriminatory enforcement by local prosecuting officials, against particular groups deemed to merit their displeasure." It results in a regime in which the poor and the unpopular are permitted to "stand on a public sidewalk . . . only at the whim of any police officer." Under this ordinance, "(I)f some carefree type of fellow is satisfied to work just so much, and no more, as will pay for one square meal, some wine, and a flophouse daily, but a court thinks this kind of living subhuman, the fellow can be forced to raise his sights or go to jail as a vagrant."

A presumption that people who might walk or loaf or loiter or stroll or frequent houses where liquor is sold, or who are supported by their wives or who look suspicious to the police are to become future criminals is too precarious for a rule of law. The implicit presumption in these generalized vagrancy standards — that crime is being nipped in the bud — is too extravagant to deserve extended treatment. Of course, vagrancy statutes are useful to the police. Of course, they are nets making easy the roundup of so-called undesirables. But the rule of law implies equality and justice in its application. Vagrancy laws of the Jacksonville type teach that the scales of justice are so tipped that even-handed administration of the law is not possible. The rule of law, evenly applied to minorities as well as majorities, to the poor as well as the rich, is the great mucilage that holds society together.

The Jacksonville ordinance cannot be squared with our constitutional standards and is plainly unconstitutional.

NOTES AND QUESTIONS

1. Although vagrancy statutes were a central driver of the peonage system in the South, the Court fails to acknowledge as much, rooting their pedigree only in "early English law." This may be true insofar as it goes, although recent research demonstrates that vagrancy laws were passed and reinvigorated in southern states as an explicit response to Reconstruction. *See* D. Blackmon, Slavery by Another Name: The Re-enslavement of Black America from the Civil War to World War II (2009), at 53 ("Every Southern state except Arkansas and Tennessee had passed laws by the end of 1865 outlawing vagrancy and so vaguely defining it that virtually any freed slave not under the protection of a white man could be arrested for the crime."). Assuming the Court was aware of this traditional use of vagrancy laws, why not mention that fact in the opinion? The Court is not otherwise reticent about race in the opinion.

2. The Court notes two evils of unduly vague criminal statutes: (a) they fail to provide fair notice of the conduct that is forbidden by the statute, and (b) they encourage arbitrary enforcement. Which are the lesser and greater of these two evils? As to the former, the Court observes that "the poor among us, the minorities, the average householder are not in business and not alerted to the regulatory schemes of vagrancy laws; and we assume they would have no understanding of their meaning and impact if they read them." What is the point here? Would whites or "above average householders" understand these laws and their potential impact? The Court also points out that the Jacksonville ordinance criminalizes "normally innocent" conduct, and in a riff on "the amenities of life" extols the virtues of loafing, wandering, strolling, etc. Is this a function of the ordinance's vagueness or is it a different problem?

3. The facts of *Papachristou* could hardly better demonstrate the dangers of arbitrary enforcement. Not only are the charges ludicrous but the defendants include a pair of mixed-race couples (white females and black males) and "an organizer for a Negro political group." The Court notes that one of the black males was a Vietnam war veteran and the other was a lifelong Jacksonville resident, and that the "organizer" had been arrested several times but convicted only once.

Just a few years after *Papachristou*, in *Kolender v. Lawson*, 461 U.S. 352 (1983), the Court considered a void-for-vagueness challenge to a California statute that made it a crime for a person who is loitering or wandering on the streets, if approached by a police officer, to fail

40 Chapter II The Roots of Modern Constitutional Criminal Procedure

to present "credible and reliable" identification and to "account for their presence." Appellee Lawson (the case was a civil rights action; Lawson filed a lawsuit challenging the constitutionality of the statute) had been arrested or detained under this statute on 15 occasions, but prosecuted only twice and convicted once. *Id.* at 354-55. As interpreted by California courts, the statute vested the inquiring police officer with full discretion to determine whether a suspect had sufficiently identified himself and accounted for his presence. The Supreme Court found the statute unconstitutional "because it encourages arbitrary enforcement by failing to describe with sufficient particularity what a suspect must do in order to satisfy the statute." *Id.* at 361.

Despite grounding its decision on the evil of arbitrary enforcement the Court avoided mentioning that Lawson was a Black man. Why not, in 1983?

The Court explicitly roots its holding in the evil of "arbitrary enforcement" rather than "fair notice." How does the statute fare as to "fair notice"? Would "an average householder" reading the statute know what conduct is prohibited?

C. MOB CONVICTIONS

The next set of cases involve Black defendants who were prosecuted for crimes against white victims. The "trials" were held within days of the crimes, in courthouses that were surrounded by white mobs that surely would have lynched the defendants but for the presence of armed militia. The all-white juries deliberated for just minutes before imposing the death penalty. In each case there was a substantial question as to the defendants' innocence.

The first case, *Moore v. Dempsey*, 261 U.S. 86 (1923), arose out of a large-scale racial altercation in Phillips County, Arkansas in the fall of 1919. Phillips County was a typical Deep South cotton county with a Black majority of approximately three to one. When local Black sharecroppers after World War I held meetings to consider unionization and to seek legal redress for their landlords' peonage practices, the white community became enraged and spread rumors of a Black conspiracy to murder white planters throughout the county. Whites fired shots into a Black union meeting at a church; Black people returned the gunfire, killing a white man; widespread mayhem ensued. Marauding bands of whites, some of whom came to the county from adjoining counties, went on a rampage against Black people, killing as many as 250 of them. Seventy-nine Black people (and no whites) were prosecuted as a result of the riot, including Frank Moore. *See generally* Klarman, *The Racial Origins of Modern Criminal Procedure, supra* at 50-51.

Moore v. Dempsey
261 U.S. 86 (1923)

Mr. Justice HOLMES delivered the opinion of the Court.

This is an appeal from an order of the District Court for the Eastern District of Arkansas dismissing a writ of habeas corpus upon demurrer, the presiding judge certifying that there was probable cause for allowing the appeal. There were two cases originally, but by agreement they were consolidated into one. The appellants are five negroes who were convicted of murder in the first degree and sentenced to death by the Court of the State of Arkansas. The ground of the petition for the writ is that the proceedings in the State Court, although a trial in form, were only a form, and that the appellants were hurried to conviction under the pressure of a mob without any regard for their rights and without according to them due process of law.

The case stated by the petition is as follows, and it will be understood that while we put it in narrative form, we are not affirming the facts to be as stated but only what we must take them to be, as they are admitted by the demurrer: On the night of September 30, 1919, a number of colored people assembled in their church were attacked and fired upon by a body of white men. and in the disturbance that followed a white man was killed. The report of the killing caused great excitement and was followed by the hunting down and shooting of many negroes and also by the killing on October 1 of one Clinton Lee, a white man, for whose murder the petitioners were indicted. They seem to have been arrested with many others on the same day. The petitioners say that Lee must have been killed by other whites, but that we leave on one side as what we have to deal with is not the petitioners' innocence or guilt but solely the question whether their constitutional rights have been preserved. They say that their meeting was to employ counsel for protection against extortions practiced upon them by the landowners and that the landowners tried to prevent their effort, but that again we pass by as not directly bearing upon the trial. It should be mentioned, however, that O. S. Bratton, a son of the counsel who is said to have been contemplated and who took part in the argument here, arriving for consultation on October 1, is said to have barely escaped being mobbed; that he was arrested and confined during the month on a charge of murder and on October 31 was indicted for barratry, but later in the day was told that he would be discharged but that he must leave secretly by a closed automobile to take the train at West Helena, four miles away, to avoid being mobbed. It is alleged that the judge of the Court in which the petitioners were tried facilitated the departure and went with Bratton to see him safely off.

A Committee of Seven was appointed by the Governor in regard to what the committee called the "insurrection" in the county. The newspapers daily published inflammatory articles. On the 7th a statement by one of the committee was made public to the effect that the present trouble was "a deliberately planned insurrection of the negroes against the whites, directed by an organization known as the 'Progressive Farmers' and 'Household Union of America' established for the purpose of banding negroes together for the killing of white people." According to the statement the organization was started by a swindler to get money from the blacks.

Shortly after the arrest of the petitioners a mob marched to the jail for the purpose of lynching them but were prevented by the presence of United States troops and the promise of some of the Committee of Seven and other leading officials that if the mob would refrain, as the petition puts it, they would execute those found guilty in the form of law. The Committee's own statement was that the reason that the people refrained from mob violence was "that this Committee gave our citizens their solemn promise that the law would be carried out." According to affidavits of two white men and the colored witnesses on whose testimony the petitioners were convicted, produced by the petitioners since the last decision of the Supreme Court hereafter mentioned, the Committee made good their promise by calling colored witnesses and having them whipped and tortured until they would say what was wanted, among them being the two relied on to prove the petitioners' guilt. However this may be, a grand jury of white men was organized on October 27 with one of the Committee of Seven and, it is alleged, with many of a posse organized to fight the blacks, upon it, and on the morning of the 29th the indictment was returned. On November 3 the petitioners were brought into Court, informed that a certain lawyer was appointed their counsel and were placed on trial before a white jury—blacks being systematically excluded from both grand and petit juries. The Court and neighborhood were thronged with an adverse crowd that threatened the most dangerous consequences to anyone interfering with the desired result. The counsel did not venture to demand delay or a change of venue, to challenge a juryman or to ask for separate trials. He had had no preliminary consultation with the accused, called no witnesses for the defence although they could have been produced, and did not put the defendants on the stand. The trial lasted about three-quarters of an hour and in less than five minutes the jury brought in a verdict of guilty of murder in the first degree. According to the allegations and affidavits there never was a chance for the petitioners to be acquitted; no juryman could have voted for an acquittal and continued to live Phillips County and if any prisoner by any chance had been acquitted by a jury he could not have escaped the mob.

The averments as to the prejudice by which the trial was environed have some corroboration in appeals to the Governor, about a year later, earnestly urging him not to interfere with the execution of the petitioners. One came from five members of the Committee of Seven, and stated in addition to what has been quoted heretofore that "all our citizens are of the opinion that the law should take its course." Another from a part of the American Legion protests against a contemplated commutation of the sentence of four of the petitioners and repeats that a "solemn promise was given by the leading citizens of the community that it the guilty parties were not lynched, and let the law take its course, that justice would be done and the majesty of the law upheld." A meeting of the Helena Rotary Club attended by members representing, as it said, seventy-five of the leading industrial and commercial enterprises of Helena, passed a resolution approving and supporting the action of the American Legion post. The Lions Club of Helena at a meeting attended by members said to represent sixty of the leading industrial and commercial enterprises of the city passed a resolution to the same effect. In May of the same year, a trial of six other negroes was coming on and it was represented to the Governor by the white citizens and officials of Phillips County that in all probability those negroes would be lynched. It is alleged that in order to appease the mob spirit and in a measure secure the safety of the six the Governor fixed the date for the execution of the petitioners at June 10, 1921, but that the execution was stayed by proceedings in Court; we presume the proceedings before the Chancellor to which we shall advert.

In *Frank v. Mangum*, it was recognized of course that if in fact a trial is dominated by a mob so that there is an actual interference with the course of justice, there is a departure from due process of law; and that "if the State, supplying no corrective process, carries into execution a judgment of death or imprisonment based upon a verdict thus produced by mob domination, the State deprives the accused of his life or liberty without due process of law." We assume in accordance with that case that the corrective process supplied by the State may be so adequate that interference by habeas corpus ought not to be allowed. It certainly is true that mere mistakes of law in the course of a trial are not to be corrected in that way. But if the case is that the whole proceeding is a mask — that counsel, jury and judge were swept to the fatal end by an irresistible wave of public passion, and that the State Courts failed to correct the wrong, neither perfection in the machinery for correction nor the possibility that the trial court and counsel saw no other way of avoiding an immediate outbreak of the mob can prevent this Court from securing to the petitioners their constitutional rights.

In this case a motion for a new trial on the ground alleged in this petition was overruled and upon exceptions and appeal to the Supreme Court the judgment was affirmed. The Supreme Court said that the complaint of discrimination against petitioners by the exclusion of colored men from the jury came too late and by way of answer to the objection that no fair trial could be had in the circumstances, stated that it could not say "that this must necessarily have been the case"; that eminent counsel was appointed to defend the petitioners, that the trial was had according to law, the jury correctly charged, and the testimony legally sufficient. On June 8, 1921, two days before the date fixed for their execution, a petition for habeas corpus was presented to the Chancellor and he issued the writ and an injunction against the execution of the petitioners; but the Supreme Court of the State held that the Chancellor had no jurisdiction under the state law whatever might be the law of the United States. The present petition perhaps was suggested by the language of the Court: "What the result would be of an application to a Federal Court we need not inquire." It was presented to the District

Court on September 21. We shall not say more concerning the corrective process afforded to the petitioners than that it does not seem to us sufficient to allow a Judge of the United States to escape the duty of examining the facts for himself when if true as alleged they make the trial absolutely void. We have confined the statement to facts admitted by the demurrer. We will not say that they cannot be met, but it appears to us unavoidable that the District Judge should find whether the facts alleged are true and whether they can be explained so far as to leave the state proceedings undisturbed.

Order reversed. The case to stand for hearing before the District Court.

[Justices Sutherland and McReynolds dissented.]

NOTES AND QUESTIONS

1. Both the majority and dissenting opinions mention *Frank v. Magnum*, 237 U.S. 309 (1915), in which just eight years earlier on somewhat comparable facts the Supreme Court had affirmed the denial of a writ of habeas corpus. Leo Frank, a Jewish businessman in Atlanta, was charged with the murder of a girl who worked at the factory he managed. His trial was also dominated by the threat of mob violence. After Frank failed in the Supreme Court, Georgia's governor commuted his sentence to life imprisonment, whereafter a mob seized him from the state prison farm where he was held and lynched him.

The two cases are difficult to reconcile. Professor Klarman attributes the transformation to a heightened national sensitivity to the evils of lynching to which the Court—even though its membership was more conservative in 1923 than 1915—was not immune. Klarman, *The Racial Origins of Modern Criminal Procedure*, supra at 60. After a resurgence in lynchings after World War I the NAACP waged a large-scale publicity campaign in support of a proposed federal anti-lynching act, the Dyer Bill. Although the bill passed in the House it was killed by filibuster in the Senate, as over two hundred such proposals were to do in the first half of

The Equal Justice Initiative's National Memorial for Peace and Justice, Montgomery, Alabama. Each of the Memorial's 800 metal plates represents a county where one of the known 4,400 terror lynchings in the United States between 1877 and 1950 occurred, along with the victims' names.

the twentieth century. But the bill had received wide recognition and had been endorsed by President Coolidge and other prominent politicians.

The Equal Justice Initiative has documented at least 4,742 lynchings in the United States between 1882 and 1968. Seven presidents petitioned Congress for anti-lynching legislation and the House passed three bills but the Senate blocked all efforts. Congress finally based the largely symbolic Emmit Till Act in 2022, codified at 18 U.S.C. § 249(a), adding lynching to the actions prohibited by the federal Hate Crimes Act.

2. The NAACP played an active role in *Moore v. Dempsey*. The facts on the ground were developed by Walter White, the organization's investigator par excellence, who was able to get local witnesses to open up to him in part because he was so light-skinned and fair that he was not perceived as Black. The NAACP also gave financial support to the appellate litigation, and Boston lawyer Moorefield Storey, the NAACP's first president and its leading advocate for the Dyer Bill, argued *Moore* before the Supreme Court. This was one of the NAACP's earliest and most successful litigation efforts, and helped shape its strategy for the coming decades. The NAACP continued to be cautious, however, about the cases that it took on.

Moorfield Storey

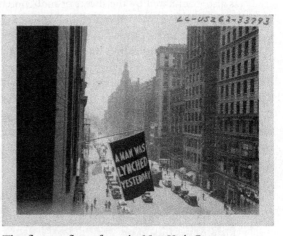

This flag was flown from the New York City headquarters of the NAACP from 1936-1938.

3. Note that the Court in *Moore*, in attempting to distinguish *Frank*, condemns the entire state judicial system of Arkansas, including its appellate courts, requiring federal judicial intervention where "the whole proceeding is a mask—that counsel, jury and judge were swept to the fatal end by an irresistible wave of public passion, and that the State courts failed to correct the wrong." Magdalen Zier argues that whatever limited effect *Moore* may have as a criminal procedure precedent, this aspect of *Moore*'s reasoning served as an important development in state action doctrine, helping pave the way for such landmark cases as *Shelley v. Kraemer*, 334 U.S. 1, 15-16, 20 (1948) (citing *Moore* in finding state action in judicial enforcement of racially restrictive housing covenants) and *Monroe v. Pape*, 365 U.S. 167, 171-87 (1961) (finding state action where even low-level state actors, such as police officers, could violate 42 U.S.C. § 1983). *See* Comment, *Crimes of Omission: State Action Doctrine and Anti-Lynching Legislation in the Jim Crow Era*, 73 Stan. L. Rev. 777, 815-17 (2021).

C. Mob Convictions

Walter White, NAACP investigator

The Supreme Court's next major venture into criminal procedure came in appeals from the convictions of nine young Black men in Scottsboro, Alabama.

Powell v. Alabama
287 U.S. 45 (1932)

Mr. Justice SUTHERLAND delivered the opinion of the Court.

The petitioners, hereinafter referred to as defendants, are negroes charged with the crime of rape, committed upon the persons of two white girls. The crime is said to have been committed on March 25, 1931. The indictment was returned in a state court of first instance on March 31, and the record recites that on the same day the defendants were arraigned and entered pleas of not guilty. There is a further recital to the effect that upon the arraignment they were represented by counsel. But no counsel had been employed, and aside from a statement made by the trial judge several days later during a colloquy immediately preceding the trial, the record does not disclose when, or under what circumstances, an appointment of counsel was made, or who was appointed. During the colloquy referred to, the trial judge, in response to a question, said that he had appointed all the members of the bar for the purpose of arraigning the defendants and then of course anticipated that the members of the bar would continue to help the defendants if no counsel appeared. Upon the argument here both sides accepted that as a correct statement of the facts concerning the matter.

There was a severance upon the request of the state, and the defendants were tried in three several groups, as indicated above. As each of the three cases was called for trial, each defendant was arraigned, and, having the indictment read to him, entered a plea of not guilty. Whether the original arraignment and pleas were regarded as ineffective is not shown. Each of the three trials was completed within a single day. Under the Alabama statute the punishment for rape is to be fixed by the jury, and in its discretion may be from ten years imprisonment to death. The juries found defendants guilty and imposed the death penalty upon all. The trial court overruled motions for new trials and sentenced the defendants in accordance with the verdicts. The judgments were affirmed by the state supreme court. Chief Justice Anderson thought the defendants had not been accorded a fair trial and strongly dissented.

In this court the judgments are assailed upon the grounds that the defendants, and each of them, were denied due process of law and the equal protection of the laws, in contravention of the Fourteenth Amendment, specifically as follows: (1) They were not given a fair, impartial, and deliberate trial; (2) they were denied the right of counsel, with the accustomed incidents of consultation and opportunity of preparation for trial; and (3) they were tried before juries from which qualified members of their own race were systematically excluded. These questions were properly raised and saved in the courts below.

The only one of the assignments which we shall consider is the second, in respect of the denial of counsel; and it becomes unnecessary to discuss the facts of the case or the circumstances surrounding the prosecution except in so far as they reflect light upon that question.

The record shows that on the day when the offense is said to have been committed, these defendants, together with a number of other negroes, were upon a freight train on its way through Alabama. On the same train were seven white boys and the two white girls. A fight took place between the negroes and the white boys, in the course of which the white boys, with the exception of one named Gilley, were thrown off the train. A message was sent ahead, reporting the fight and asking that every negro be gotten off the train. The participants in the fight, and the two girls, were in an open gondola car. The two girls testified that each of them was assaulted by six different negroes in turn, and they identified the seven defendants as having been among the number. None of the white boys was called to testify, with the exception of Gilley, who was called in rebuttal.

Before the train reached Scottsboro, Ala., a sheriff's posse seized the defendants and two other negroes. Both girls and the negroes then were taken to Scottsboro, the county seat. Word of their coming and of the alleged assault had preceded them, and they were met at Scottsboro by a large crowd. It does not sufficiently appear that the defendants were seriously threatened with, or that they were actually in danger of, mob violence; but it does appear that the attitude of the community was one of great hostility. The sheriff thought it necessary to call for the militia to assist in safeguarding the prisoners. Chief Justice Anderson pointed out in his opinion that every step taken from the arrest and arraignment to the sentence was accompanied by the military. Soldiers took the defendants to Gadsden for safe-keeping, brought them back to Scottsboro for arraignment, returned them to Gadsden for safe-keeping while awaiting trial, escorted them to Scottsboro for trial a few days later, and guarded the courthouse and grounds at every stage of the proceedings. It is perfectly apparent that the proceedings, from beginning to end, took place in an atmosphere of tense, hostile, and excited public sentiment. During the entire time, the defendants were closely confined or were under military guard. The record does not disclose their ages, except that one of them was nineteen; but the record clearly indicates that most, if not all, of them were youthful, and they are constantly referred to as "the boys." They were ignorant and illiterate. All of them were residents of other states, where alone members of their families or friends resided.

However guilty defendants, upon due inquiry, might prove to have been, they were, until convicted, presumed to be innocent. It was the duty of the court having their cases in charge to see that they were denied no necessary incident of a fair trial. With any error of the state court involving alleged contravention of the state statutes or Constitution we, of course, have nothing to do. The sole inquiry which we are permitted to make is whether the federal Constitution was contravened, and as to that, we confine ourselves, as already suggested, to the inquiry whether the defendants were in substance denied the right of counsel, and if so, whether such denial infringes the due process clause of the Fourteenth Amendment.

C. Mob Convictions

47

First. The record shows that immediately upon the return of the indictment defendants were arraigned and pleaded not guilty. Apparently they were not asked whether they had, or were able to employ, counsel, or wished to have counsel appointed; or whether they had friends or relatives who might assist in that regard if communicated with. That it would not have been an idle ceremony to have given the defendants reasonable opportunity to communicate with their families and endeavor to obtain counsel is demonstrated by the fact that very soon after conviction, able counsel appeared in their behalf. This was pointed out by Chief Justice Anderson in the course of his dissenting opinion. "They were nonresidents," he said, "and had little time or opportunity to get in touch with their families and friends who were scattered throughout two other states, and time has demonstrated that they could or would have been represented by able counsel had a better opportunity been given by a reasonable delay in the trial of the cases judging from the number and activity of counsel that appeared immediately or shortly after their conviction."

It is hardly necessary to say that the right to counsel being conceded, a defendant should be afforded a fair opportunity to secure counsel of his own choice. Not only was that not done here, but such designation of counsel as was attempted was either so indefinite or so close upon the trial as to amount to a denial of effective and substantial aid in that regard. This will be amply demonstrated by a brief review of the record.

April 6, six days after indictment, the trials began. When the first case was called, the court inquired whether the parties were ready for trial. The state's attorney replied that he was ready to proceed. No one answered for the defendants or appeared to represent or defend them. Mr. Roddy, a Tennessee lawyer not a member of the local bar, addressed the court, saying that he had not been employed, but that people who were interested had spoken to him about the case. He was asked by the court whether he intended to appear for the defendants, and answered that he would like to appear along with counsel that the court might appoint. The record then proceeds:

The Court:	If you appear for these defendants, then I will not appoint counsel; if local counsel are willing to appear and assist you under the circumstances all right, but I will not appoint them.
Mr. Roddy:	Your Honor has appointed counsel, is that correct?
The Court:	I appointed all the members of the bar for the purpose of arraigning the defendants and then of course I anticipated them to continue to help them if no counsel appears.
Mr. Roddy:	Then I don't appear then as counsel but I do want to stay in and not be ruled out in this case.
The Court:	Of course I would not do that—
Mr. Roddy:	I just appear here through the courtesy of Your Honor.
The Court:	Of course I give you that right. . . .

And then, apparently addressing all the lawyers present, the court inquired:

	. . . Well are you all willing to assist?
Mr. Moody:	Your Honor appointed us all and we have been proceeding along every line we know about it under Your Honor's appointment.
The Court:	The only thing I am trying to do is, if counsel appears for these defendants I don't want to impose on you all, but if you feel like counsel from Chattanooga—
Mr. Moody:	I see his situation of course and I have not run out of anything yet. Of course, if Your Honor purposes to appoint us, Mr. Parks, I am willing to go on with it. Most of the bar have been down and conferred with these defendants in this case; they did not know what else to do.

The Court:	The thing, I did not want to impose on the members of the bar if counsel unqualifiedly appears; if you all feel like Mr. Roddy is only interested in a limited way to assist, then I don't care to appoint—
Mr. Parks:	Your Honor, I don't feel like you ought to impose on any member of the local bar if the defendants are represented by counsel.
The Court:	That is what I was trying to ascertain, Mr. Parks.
Mr. Parks:	Of course if they have counsel, I don't see the necessity of the Court appointing anybody; if they haven't counsel, of course I think it is up to the Court to appoint counsel to represent them.
The Court:	I think you are right about it Mr. Parks and that is the reason I was trying to get an expression from Mr. Roddy.
Mr. Roddy:	I think Mr. Parks is entirely right about it, if I was paid down here and employed, it would be a different thing, but I have not prepared this case for trial and have only been called into it by people who are interested in these boys from Chattanooga. Now, they have not given me an opportunity to prepare the case and I am not familiar with the procedure in Alabama, but I merely came down here as a friend of the people who are interested and not as paid counsel, and certainly I haven't any money to pay them and nobody I am interested in had me to come down here has put up any fund of money to come down here and pay counsel. If they should do it I would be glad to turn it over — a counsel but I am merely here at the solicitation of people who have become interested in this case without any payment of fee and without any preparation for trial and I think the boys would be better off if I step entirely out of the case according to my way of looking at it and according to my lack of preparation for it and not being familiar with the procedure in Alabama. . . .

Mr. Roddy later observed:

	If there is anything I can do to be of help to them, I will be glad to do it; I am interested to that extent.
The Court:	Well gentlemen, if Mr. Roddy only appears as assistant that way, I think it is proper that I appoint members of this bar to represent them, I expect that is right. If Mr. Roddy will appear, I wouldn't of course, I would not appoint anybody. I don't see, Mr. Roddy, how I can make a qualified appointment or a limited appointment. Of course, I don't mean to cut off your assistance in any way — Well gentlemen, I think you understand it.
Mr. Moody:	I am willing to go ahead and help Mr. Roddy in anything I can do about it, under the circumstances.
The Court:	All right, all the lawyers that will; of course I would not require a lawyer to appear if—
Mr. Moody:	I am willing to go ahead and help Mr. Roddy in anything I can do about it, under the circumstances.
The Court:	All right, all the lawyers that will, of course, I would not require a lawyer to appear if—
Mr. Moody:	I am willing to do that for him as a member of the bar; I will go ahead and help do anything I can do.
The Court:	All right.

And in this casual fashion the matter of counsel in a capital case was disposed of.

It thus will be seen that until the very morning of the trial no lawyer had been named or definitely designated to represent the defendants. Prior to that time, the trial judge had "appointed all the members of the bar" for the limited "purpose of arraigning the defendants." Whether they would represent the defendants thereafter, if no counsel appeared in their behalf, was a matter of speculation only, or, as the judge indicated, of mere anticipation on the part of the court. Such a designation, even if made for all purposes, would, in our opinion, have fallen far short of meeting, in any proper sense, a requirement for the appointment of counsel. How many lawyers were members of the bar does not appear; but, in the very nature of things, whether many or few, they would not, thus collectively named, have been given that clear appreciation of responsibility or impressed with that individual sense of duty which should and naturally would accompany the appointment of a selected member of the bar, specifically named and assigned.

That this action of the trial judge in respect of appointment of counsel was little more than an expansive gesture, imposing no substantial or definite obligation upon any one, is borne out by the fact that prior to the calling of the case for trial on April 6, a leading member of the local bar accepted employment on the side of the prosecution and actively participated in the trial. It is true that he said that before doing so he had understood Mr. Roddy would be employed as counsel for the defendants. This the lawyer is question, of his own accord, frankly stated to the court; and no doubt he acted with the utmost good faith. Probably other members of the bar had a like understanding. In any event, the circumstance lends emphasis to the conclusion that during perhaps the most critical period of the proceedings against these defendants, that is to say, from the time of their arraignment until the beginning of their trial, when consultation, thorough-going investigation and preparation were vitally important, the defendants did not have the aid of counsel in any real sense, although they were as much entitled to such aid during that period as at the trial itself.

Nor do we think the situation was helped by what occurred on the morning of the trial. At that time, as appears from the colloquy printed above, Mr. Roddy stated to the court that he did not appear as counsel, but that he would like to appear along with counsel that the court might appoint; that he had not been given an opportunity to prepare the case; that he was not familiar with the procedure in Alabama, but merely came down as a friend of the people who were interested; that he thought the boys would be better off if he should step entirely out of the case. Mr. Moody, a member of the local bar, expressed a willingness to help Mr. Roddy in anything he could do under the circumstances. To this the court responded: "All right, all the lawyers that will; of course I would not require a lawyer to appear if—." And Mr. Moody continued: "I am willing to do that for him as a member of the bar; I will go ahead and help do anything I can do." With this dubious understanding, the trials immediately proceeded. The defendants, young, ignorant, illiterate, surrounded by hostile sentiment, haled back and forth under guard of soldiers, charged with an atrocious crime regarded with especial horror in the community where they were to be tried, were thus put in peril of their lives within a few moments after counsel for the first time charged with any degree of responsibility began to represent them.

It is not enough to assume that counsel thus precipitated into the case thought there was no defense, and exercised their best judgment in proceeding to trial without preparation. Neither they nor the court could say what a prompt and thorough-going investigation might disclose as to the facts. No attempt was made to investigate. No opportunity to do so was given. Defendants were immediately hurried to trial. Chief Justice Anderson, after disclaiming any intention to criticize harshly counsel who attempted to represent defendants at the trials, said: ". . . The record indicates that the appearance was rather pro forma than zealous and active. . . ." Under the circumstances disclosed, we hold that defendants were not accorded the right of counsel in any substantial sense. To decide otherwise, would simply be to ignore actualities. This conclusion finds ample support in the reasoning of an overwhelming array of state decisions. . . .

It is true that great and inexcusable delay in the enforcement of our criminal law is one of the grave evils of our time. Continuances are frequently granted for unnecessarily long periods of time, and delays incident to the disposition of motions for new trial and hearings upon appeal have come in many cases to be a distinct reproach to the administration of justice. The prompt disposition of criminal cases is to be commended and encouraged. But in reaching that result a defendant, charged with a serious crime, must not be stripped of his right to have sufficient time to advise with counsel and prepare his defense. To do that is not to proceed promptly in the calm spirit of regulated justice but to go forward with the haste of the mob.

• • •

Second. The Constitution of Alabama (Const. 1901, s 6) provides that in all criminal prosecutions the accused shall enjoy the right to have the assistance of counsel; and a state statute (Code 1923, s 5567) requires the court in a capital case, where the defendant is unable to employ counsel, to appoint counsel for him. The state Supreme Court held that these provisions had not been infringed, and with that holding we are powerless to interfere. The question, however, which it is our duty, and within our power, to decide, is whether the denial of the assistance of counsel contravenes the due process clause of the Fourteenth Amendment to the Federal Constitution.

If recognition of the right of a defendant charged with a felony to have the aid of counsel depended upon the existence of a similar right at common law as it existed in England when our Constitution was adopted, there would be great difficulty in maintaining it as necessary to due process. Originally, in England, a person charged with treason or felony was denied the aid of counsel, except in respect of legal questions which the accused himself might suggest. At the same time parties in civil cases and persons accused of misdemeanors were entitled to the full assistance of counsel. After the revolution of 1688, the rule was abolished as to treason, but was otherwise steadily adhered to until 1836, when by act of Parliament the full right was granted in respect of felonies generally.

An affirmation of the right to the aid of counsel in petty offenses, and its denial in the case of crimes of the gravest character, where such aid is most needed, is so outrageous and so obviously a perversion of all sense of proportion that the rule was constantly, vigorously and sometimes passionately assailed by English statesmen and lawyers. As early as 1758, Blackstone, although recognizing that the rule was settled at common law, denounced it as not in keeping with the rest of the humane treatment of prisoners by the English law. "For upon what face of reason," he says "can that assistance be denied to save the life of a man, which yet is allowed him in prosecutions for every petty trespass?" One of the grounds upon which Lord Coke defended the rule was that in felonies the court itself was counsel for the prisoner. But how can a judge, whose functions are purely judicial, effectively discharge the obligations of counsel for the accused? He can and should see to it that in the proceedings before the court the accused shall be dealt with justly and fairly. He cannot investigate the facts, advise and direct the defense, or participate in those necessary conferences between counsel and accused which sometimes partake of the inviolable character of the confessional.

The [English] rule was rejected by the colonies. . . .

• • •

It never has been doubted by this court, or any other so far as we know, that notice and hearing are preliminary steps essential to the passing of an enforceable judgment, and that they, together with a legally competent tribunal having jurisdiction of the case, constitute basic elements of the constitutional requirement of due process of law. The words of Webster, so often quoted, that by "the law of the land" is intended "a law which hears before it condemns," have been repeated in varying forms of expression in a multitude of decisions. . . .

What, then, does a hearing include? Historically and in practice, in our own country at least, it has always included the right to the aid of counsel when desired and provided by the party asserting the right. The right to be heard would be, in many cases, of little avail if it did not comprehend the right to be heard by counsel. Even the intelligent and educated layman has small and sometimes no skill in the science of law. If charged with crime, he is incapable, generally, of determining for himself whether the indictment is good or bad. He is unfamiliar with the rules of evidence. Left without the aid of counsel he may be put on trial without a proper charge, and convicted upon incompetent evidence, or evidence irrelevant to the issue or otherwise inadmissible. He lacks both the skill and knowledge adequately to prepare his defense, even though he have a perfect one. He requires the guiding hand of counsel at every step in the proceedings against him. Without it, though he be not guilty, he faces the danger of conviction because he does not know how to establish his innocence. If that be true of men of intelligence, how much more true is it of the ignorant and illiterate, or those of feeble intellect. If in any case, civil or criminal, a state or federal court were arbitrarily to refuse to hear a party by counsel, employed by and appearing for him, it reasonably may not be doubted that such a refusal would be a denial of a hearing, and, therefore, of due process in the constitutional sense.

• • •

In the light of the facts outlined in the forepart of this opinion — the ignorance and illiteracy of the defendants, their youth, the circumstances of public hostility, the imprisonment and the close surveillance of the defendants by the military forces, the fact that their friends and families were all in other states and communication with them necessarily difficult, and above all that they stood in deadly peril of their lives — we think the failure of the trial court to give them reasonable time and opportunity to secure counsel was a clear denial of due process.

But passing that, and assuming their inability, even if opportunity had been given, to employ counsel, as the trial court evidently did assume, we are of opinion that, under the circumstances just stated, the necessity of counsel was so vital and imperative that the failure of the trial court to make an effective appointment of counsel was likewise a denial of due process within the meaning of the Fourteenth Amendment. Whether this would be so in other criminal prosecutions, or under other circumstances, we need not determine. All that it is necessary now to decide, as we do decide, is that in a capital case, where the defendant is unable to employ counsel, and is incapable adequately of making his own defense because of ignorance, feeble-mindedness, illiteracy, or the like, it is the duty of the court, whether requested or not, to assign counsel for him as a necessary requisite of due process of law; and that duty is not discharged by an assignment at such a time or under such circumstances as to preclude the giving of effective aid in the preparation and trial of the case. To hold otherwise would be to ignore the fundamental postulate, already adverted to, "that there are certain immutable principles of justice which inhere in the very idea of free government which no member of the Union may disregard." In a case such as this, whatever may be the rule in other cases, the right to have counsel appointed, when necessary, is a logical corollary from the constitutional right to be heard by counsel. . . .

• • •

Let us suppose the extreme case of a prisoner charged with a capital offense, who is deaf and dumb, illiterate, and feeble-minded, unable to employ counsel, with the whole power of the state arrayed against him, prosecuted by counsel for the state without assignment of counsel for his defense, tried, convicted, and sentenced to death. Such a result, which, if carried into execution, would be little short of judicial murder, it cannot be doubted would be a gross violation of the guarantee of due process of law; and we venture to think that no appellate court, state or federal, would hesitate so to decide. The duty of the trial court to appoint counsel under such circumstances is clear, as it is clear under circumstances such as are disclosed by the record here; and its power to do so, even in the absence of a statute, can not be questioned. Attorneys are officers of the court, and are bound to render service when required by such an appointment.

The United States by statute and every state in the Union by express provision of law, or by the determination of its courts, make it the duty of the trial judge, where the accused is unable to employ counsel, to appoint counsel for him. In most states the rule applies broadly to all criminal prosecutions, in others it is limited to the more serious crimes, and in a very limited number, to capital cases. A rule adopted with such unanimous accord reflects, if it does not establish the inherent right to have counsel appointed at least in cases like the present, and lends convincing support to the conclusion we have reached as to the fundamental nature of that right.

The judgments must be reversed and the causes remanded for further proceedings not inconsistent with this opinion.

[Justices Butler and McReynolds dissented.]

NOTES AND QUESTIONS

1. Of the three grounds for appeal presented to it — mob-dominated trial, insufficient right to counsel, discrimination in jury selection — the Supreme Court chose right to counsel. Why that choice? There was recent precedent in *Moore v. Dempsey* on the first ground, although the trials in *Powell* were not quite as egregious as in *Moore*: the trials lasted hours not 45 minutes; the prosecution severed the defendants into three groups; defense counsel cross-examined prosecution witnesses. There was also some constitutional precedent in the juror discrimination arena, although far from consistent, in *Strauder* and *Neal*. *See supra*. Assuming the Court wanted to take the most cautious path to reversal, which is likely, which ground for decision would be the least threatening to white supremacist criminal justice regimes?

2. It is unclear from the Court's opinion what lawyer or lawyers actually conducted the meager defense at the trials. But the Court has little trouble finding that the defendants were "in substance denied the right to counsel." It notes the "casual fashion" in which the trial court dealt with the issue — appointing all members of the local bar at the arraignment as counsel and apparently again on the morning of trial — and that, inasmuch as none of the "appointees" joined the prosecution team the appointment was nothing but an "expansive gesture." Why do you think the trial court might have handled the appointment in this manner?

3. The trials were held just 6 days after the indictment and arraignment and just 12 days after young men were arrested. The Court says nothing critical about this accelerated schedule, which was presumably due to the mob atmosphere, although it does state that defendants "should have been afforded a fair opportunity to secure counsel of their own choosing," and implies that defendants would have been entitled to a reasonable delay in order to do so. How important is this observation to the Court's decision? What if defendants had not been able to secure their own counsel and the trial court had unambiguously appointed counsel for defendants at their arraignment? Different result? If these had been the facts might the Court have decided the case on a different ground? Putting aside the obvious conflicts of interest with a lawyer or multiple lawyers representing nine defendants charged in a single criminal episode, is six days enough time to prepare a defense, which the Court acknowledges requires "consultation, thoroughgoing investigation and preparation"? The Court doesn't shed

C. Mob Convictions   53

any light on this question—it didn't need to—but it does generally acknowledge "that great and inexcusable delays in the enforcement of our criminal law is one of the grave evils of our time." *Id.* at 59.

4. The Court recognizes that the Alabama Constitution enshrines the right to counsel in a criminal case and that a state statute requires the appointment of counsel for an indigent defendant in a capital case. *Id.* at 59-60. Because the Alabama Supreme Court had found these provisions satisfied in *Powell*, however, the Court could only reverse the conviction on the right-to-counsel issue by finding a violation of a new federal right to counsel that would bind states under the Fourteenth Amendment. The two dissenters take no issue with the majority's conclusion that the Sixth Amendment right should be "incorporated" into the Fourteenth Amendment. Was the Court's conclusion in this regard compelling? Why or why not? What about the Court's related conclusion—which it called a "logical corollary" of the first conclusion—that under certain circumstances courts were required to appoint counsel for indigent defendants? What bases were available to the Court in reaching these two conclusions?

5. The Court finds the right to counsel to be fundamental in part because it is derivative of, and essential to, the undoubtedly fundamental "right to be heard." *Id.* at 68. The Court continues:

> What, then, does a hearing include? Historically and in practice, in our own country at least, it has always included the right to the aid of counsel when desired and provided by the party asserting the right. The right to be heard would be, in many cases, of little avail if it did not comprehend the right to be heard by counsel. Even the intelligent and educated layman has small and sometimes no skill in the science of law. If charged with crime, he is incapable, generally, of determining for himself whether the indictment is good or bad. He is unfamiliar with the rules of evidence. Left without the aid of counsel he may be put on trial without a proper charge, and convicted upon incompetent evidence, or evidence irrelevant to the issue or otherwise inadmissible. He lacks both the skill and knowledge adequately to prepare his defense, even though he have a perfect one. He requires the guiding hand of counsel at every step in the proceedings against him. Without it, though he be not guilty, he faces the danger of conviction because he does not know how to establish his innocence. If that be true of men of intelligence, how much more true is it of the ignorant and illiterate, or those of feeble intellect. If in any case, civil or criminal, a state or federal court were arbitrarily to refuse to hear a party by counsel, employed by and appearing for him, it reasonably may not be doubted that such a refusal would be a denial of a hearing, and, therefore, of due process in the constitutional sense.

Id. at 68-69. While perhaps a statement of the obvious, this is powerful and compelling language, a ringing endorsement of the right to and necessity of counsel. Yet the Court in *Powell* narrowly limits its holding to the exceptional circumstances of the case: "the ignorance and illiteracy of the defendants, their youth, the circumstances of public hostility, the imprisonment and the close surveillance of the defendants by the military forces, the fact that their friends and families were all in other states and communication with them necessarily difficult, and above all that they stood in peril of their lives." *Id.* at 70. These are serious limitations. Presumably the Court was hesitant to impose on courts the burden, and perhaps cost, of an obligation to appoint counsel for indigent defendants in all capital cases or some subset of non-capital cases. But did it need to make the limited nature of its holding so explicit? Wouldn't the "holding" of *Powell* be tied to the circumstances of the case in any event?

6. Given this caveat, what does the federal right recognized in *Powell* truly accomplish? Is it that the right to counsel must be of meaningful substance, and "not discharged by an assignment at such a time or circumstances as to preclude the giving of effective aid in the trial of the case"?

Norris v. Alabama
294 U.S. 587 (1935)

Mr. Chief Justice HUGHES delivered the opinion of the Court.

Petitioner, Clarence Norris, is one of nine negro boys who were indicted in March, 1931, in Jackson county, Ala., for the crime of rape. On being brought to trial in that county, eight were convicted. The Supreme Court of Alabama reversed the conviction of one of these and affirmed that of seven, including Norris. This Court reversed the judgments of conviction upon the ground that the defendants had been denied due process of law in that the trial court had failed in the light of the circumstances disclosed, and of the inability of the defendants at that time to obtain counsel, to make an effective appointment of counsel to aid them in preparing and presenting their defense. *Powell v. Alabama.*

After the remand, a motion for change of venue was granted and the cases were transferred to Morgan county. Norris was brought to trial in November, 1933. At the outset, a motion was made on his behalf to quash the indictment upon the ground of the exclusion of negroes from juries in Jackson county where the indictment was found. A motion was also made to quash the trial venire in Morgan county upon the ground of the exclusion of negroes from juries in that county. In relation to each county, the charge was of long-continued, systematic, and arbitrary exclusion of qualified negro citizens from service on juries, solely because of their race and color, in violation of the Constitution of the United States. The state joined issue on this charge and after hearing the evidence, which we shall presently review, the trial judge denied both motions, and exception was taken. The trial then proceeded and resulted in the conviction of Norris who was sentenced to death. On appeal, the Supreme Court of the state considered and decided the federal question which Norris had raised and affirmed the judgment. We granted a writ of certiorari.

First. There is no controversy as to the constitutional principle involved. That principle, long since declared, was not challenged, but was expressly recognized, by the Supreme Court of the state. Summing up precisely the effect of earlier decisions, this Court thus stated the principle in *Carter v. Texas*, in relation to exclusion from service on grand juries: "Whenever by any action of a state, whether through its Legislature, through its courts, or through its executive or administrative officers, all persons of the African race are excluded, solely because of their race or color, from serving as grand jurors in the criminal prosecution of a person of the African race, the equal protection of the laws is denied to him, contrary to the Fourteenth Amendment of the Constitution of the United States." *Strauder v. West Virginia; Neal v. Delaware.* This statement was repeated in the same terms in *Rogers v. Alabama*, 192 U.S. 226, 231, 24 S. Ct. 257, 48 L. Ed. 417, and again in *Martin v. Texas*, 200 U.S. 316, 319, 26 S. Ct. 338, 50 L. Ed. 497. The principle is equally applicable to a similar exclusion of negroes from service on petit juries. And although the state statute defining the qualifications of jurors may be fair on its face, the constitutional provision affords protection against action of the state through its administrative officers in effecting the prohibited discrimination.

The question is of the application of this established principle to the facts disclosed by the record. That the question is one of fact does not relieve us of the duty to determine whether in truth a federal right has been denied. When a federal right has been specially set up and claimed in a state court, it is our province to inquire not merely whether it was denied in express terms but also whether it was denied in substance and effect. If this requires an examination of evidence, that examination must be made. Otherwise, review by this Court would fail of its purpose in safeguarding constitutional rights. Thus, whenever a conclusion of law of a state court as to a federal right and findings of fact are so intermingled that the latter

C. Mob Convictions

control the former, it is incumbent upon us to analyze the facts in order that the appropriate enforcement of the federal right may be assured.

Second. The evidence on the motion to quash the indictment. In 1930, the total population of Jackson county, where the indictment was found, was 36,881, of whom 2,688 were negroes. The male population over twenty-one years of age numbered 8,801, and of these 666 were negroes.

The qualifications of jurors were thus prescribed by the state statute: "The jury commission shall place on the jury roll and in the jury box the names of all male citizens of the county who are generally reputed to be honest and intelligent men, and are esteemed in the community for their integrity, good character and sound judgment, but no person must be selected who is under twenty-one or over sixty-five years of age, or, who is an habitual drunkard, or who, being afflicted with a permanent disease or physical weakness is unfit to discharge the duties of a juror, or who cannot read English, or who has ever been convicted of any offense involving moral turpitude. If a person cannot read English and has all the other qualifications prescribed herein and is a freeholder or householder, his name may be placed on the jury roll and in the jury box."

Defendant adduced evidence to support the charge of unconstitutional discrimination in the actual administration of the statute in Jackson county. The testimony, as the state court said, tended to show that "in a long number of years no negro had been called for jury service in that county." It appeared that no negro had served on any grand or petit jury in that county within the memory of witnesses who had lived there all their lives. Testimony to that effect was given by men whose ages ran from fifty to seventy-six years. Their testimony was uncontradicted. It was supported by the testimony of officials. The clerk of the jury commission and the clerk of the circuit court had never known of a negro serving on a grand jury in Jackson county. The court reporter, who had not missed a session in that county in twenty-four years, and two jury commissioners testified to the same effect. One of the latter, who was a member of the commission which made up the jury roll for the grand jury which found the indictment, testified that he had "never known of a single instance where any negro sat on any grand or petit jury in the entire history of that county."

That testimony in itself made out a prima facie case of the denial of the equal protection which the Constitution guarantees. *See Neal v. Delaware, supra.* The case thus made was supplemented by direct testimony that specified negroes, thirty or more in number, were qualified for jury service. Among these were negroes who were members of school boards, or trustees, of colored schools, and property owners and householders. It also appeared that negroes from that county had been called for jury service in the federal court. Several of those who were thus described as qualified were witnesses. While there was testimony which cast doubt upon the qualifications of some of the negroes who had been named, and there was also general testimony by the editor of a local newspaper who gave his opinion as to the lack of "sound judgment" of the "good negroes" in Jackson county, we think that the definite testimony as to the actual qualifications of individual negroes, which was not met by any testimony equally direct, showed that there were negroes in Jackson county qualified for jury service.

The question arose whether names of negroes were in fact on the jury roll. The books containing the jury roll for Jackson county for the year 1930-31 were produced. They were produced from the custody of a member of the jury commission which, in 1931, had succeeded the commission which had made up the jury roll from which the grand jury in question had been drawn. On the pages of this roll appeared the names of six negroes. They were entered, respectively, at the end of the precinct lists which were alphabetically arranged. The genuineness of these entries was disputed. It appeared that after the jury roll in question had been made up, and after the new jury commission had taken office, one of the new commissioners directed the new clerk to draw lines after the names which had been placed on the roll by the preceding commission. These lines, on the pages under consideration, were red lines, and the clerk of the old commission testified that they were not put in by him. The entries made by the new clerk, for the new jury roll, were below these lines.

The names of the six negroes were in each instance written immediately above the red lines. An expert of long experience testified that these names were superimposed upon the red lines, that is, that they were written after the lines had been drawn. The expert was not cross-examined and no testimony was introduced to contradict him. In denying the motion to quash, the trial judge expressed the view that he would not "be authorized to presume that somebody had committed a crime" or to presume that the jury board "had been unfaithful to their duties and allowed the books to be tampered with." His conclusion was that names of negroes were on the jury roll.

We think that the evidence did not justify that conclusion. The Supreme Court of the state did not sustain it. That court observed that the charge that the names of negroes were fraudulently placed on the roll did not involve any member of the jury board, and that the charge "was, by implication at least, laid at the door of the clerk of the board." The court, reaching its decision irrespective of that question, treated that phase of the matter as "wholly immaterial" and hence passed it by "without any expression of opinion thereon."

The state court rested its decision upon the ground that even if it were assumed that there was no name of a negro on the jury roll, it was not established that race or color caused the omission. The court pointed out that the statute fixed a high standard of qualifications for and that the jury commission was vested with a wide discretion. The court adverted to the fact that more white citizens possessing age qualifications had been omitted from the jury roll than the entire negro population of the county, and regarded the testimony as being to the effect that "the matter of race, color, politics, religion or fraternal affiliations" had not been discussed by the commission and had not entered into their consideration, and that no one had been excluded because of race or color.

The testimony showed the practice of the jury commission. One of the commissioners who made up the jury roll in question, and the clerk of that commission, testified as to the manner of its preparation. The other two commissioners of that period did not testify. It was shown that the clerk, under the direction of the commissioners, made up a preliminary list which was based on the registration list of voters, the polling list and the tax list, and apparently also upon the telephone directory. The clerk testified that he made up a list of all male citizens between the ages of twenty-one and sixty-five years without regard to their status or qualifications. The commissioner testified that the designation "col." was placed after the names of those who were colored. In preparing the final jury roll, the preliminary list was checked off as to qualified jurors with the aid of men whom the commissioners called in for that purpose from the different precincts. And the commissioner testified that in the selections for the jury roll no one was "automatically or systematically" excluded, or excluded on account of race or color; that he "did not inquire as to color," that was not discussed.

But, in appraising the action of the commissioners, these statements cannot be divorced from other testimony. As we have seen, there was testimony, not overborne or discredited, that there were in fact negroes in the county qualified for jury service. That testimony was direct and specific. After eliminating those persons as to whom there was some evidence of lack of qualifications, a considerable number of others remained. The fact that the testimony as to these persons, fully identified, was not challenged by evidence appropriately direct, cannot be brushed aside. There is no ground for an assumption that the names of these negroes were not on the preliminary list. The inference to be drawn from the testimony is that they were on that preliminary list, and were designated on that list as the names of negroes, and that they were not placed on the jury roll. There was thus presented a test of the practice of the commissioners. Something more than mere general asseverations was required. Why were these names excluded from the jury roll? Was it because of the lack of statutory qualifications? Were the qualifications of negroes actually and properly considered?

The testimony of the commissioner on this crucial question puts the case in a strong light. That testimony leads to the conclusion that these or other negroes were not excluded on account of age, or lack of esteem in the community for integrity and judgment, or because of disease or want of any other qualification. The commissioner's answer to specific inquiry upon this point was that negroes were "never discussed."

We are of the opinion that the evidence required a different result from that reached in the state court. We think that the evidence that for a generation or longer no negro had been called for service on any jury in Jackson county, that there were negroes qualified for jury service, that according to the practice of the jury commission their names would normally appear on the preliminary list of male citizens of the requisite age but that no names of negroes were placed on the jury roll, and the testimony with respect to the lack of appropriate consideration of the qualifications of negroes, established the discrimination which the Constitution forbids. The motion to quash the indictment upon that ground should have been granted.

Third. The evidence on the motion to quash the trial venire. The population of Morgan county, where the trial was had, was larger than that of Jackson county, and the proportion of negroes was much greater. The total population of Morgan county in 1930 was 46,176, and of this number 8,311 were negroes.

Within the memory of witnesses, long resident there, no negro had ever served on a jury in that county or had been called for such service. Some of these witnesses were over fifty years of age and had always lived in Morgan county. Their testimony was not contradicted. A clerk of the circuit court, who had resided in the county for thirty years, and who had been in office for over four years, testified that during his official term approximately 2,500 persons had been called for jury service and that not one of them was a negro; that he did not recall "ever seeing any single person of the colored race serve on any jury in Morgan County."

There was abundant evidence that there were a large number of negroes in the county who were qualified for jury service. Men of intelligence, some of whom were college graduates, testified to long lists (said to contain nearly 200 names) of such qualified negroes, including many business men, owners of real property and householders. When defendant's counsel proposed to call many additional witnesses in order to adduce further proof of qualifications of negroes for jury service, the trial judge limited the testimony, holding that the evidence was cumulative.

We find no warrant for a conclusion that the names of any of the negroes as to whom this testimony was given, or of any other negroes, were placed on the jury rolls. No such names were identified. The evidence that for many years no negro had been called for jury service itself tended to show the absence of the names of negroes from the jury rolls, and the state made no effort to prove their presence. The trial judge limited the defendant's proof "to the present year, the present jury roll." The sheriff of the county, called as a witness for defendants, scanned the jury roll and after "looking over every single name on that jury roll, from A to Z," was unable to point out "any single negro on it."

For this long-continued, unvarying, and wholesale exclusion of negroes from jury service we find no justification consistent with the constitutional mandate. We have carefully examined the testimony of the jury commissioners upon which the state court based its decision. One of these commissioners testified in person and the other two submitted brief affidavits. By the state act in force at the time the jury roll in question was made up, the clerk of the jury board was required to obtain the names of all male citizens of the county over twenty-one and under sixty-five years of age, and their occupation, place of residence, and place of business. The qualifications of those who were to be placed on the jury roll were the same as those prescribed by the earlier statute which we have already quoted. The member of the jury board, who testified orally, said that a list was made up which included the names of all male citizens of suitable age; that black residents were not excluded from this general list; that in compiling the jury roll he did not consider race or color; that no one was excluded for that reason; and that he had placed on the jury roll the names of persons possessing the qualifications under the statute. The affidavits of the other members of the board contained general statements to the same effect.

We think that this evidence failed to rebut the strong prima facie case which defendant had made. That showing as to the long-continued exclusion of negroes from jury service, and as to the many negroes qualified for that service, could not be met by mere generalities. If, in the presence of such testimony as defendant adduced, the mere general assertions by officials of their performance of duty were to be accepted as in adequate justification for the complete exclusion of negroes from jury service, the constitutional provision—adopted with special reference to their protection—would be but a vain and illusory requirement. The general attitude of the jury commissioner is shown by the following extract from his testimony: "I do not know of any negro in Morgan County over twenty-one and under sixty-five who is generally reputed to be honest and intelligent and who is esteemed in the community for his integrity, good character and sound judgment, who is not an habitual drunkard, who isn't afflicted with a permanent disease or physical weakness which would render him unfit to discharge the duties of a juror, and who can read English, and who has never been convicted of a crime involving moral turpitude." In the light of the testimony given by defendant's witnesses, we find it impossible to accept such a sweeping characterization of the lack of qualifications of negroes in Morgan county. It is so sweeping, and so contrary to the evidence as to the many qualified negroes, that it destroys the intended effect of the commissioner's testimony.

In *Neal v. Delaware, supra,* decided over fifty years ago, this Court observed that it was a "violent presumption," in which the state court had there indulged, that the uniform exclusion of negroes from juries, during a period of many years, was solely because, in the judgment of the officers, charged with the selection of grand and petit jurors, fairly exercised, "the black race in Delaware were utterly disqualified by want of intelligence, experience, or moral integrity, to sit on juries." Such a presumption at the present time would be no less violent with respect to the exclusion of the negroes of Morgan county. And, upon the proof contained in the record now before us, a conclusion that their continuous and total exclusion from juries was because there were none possessing the requisite qualifications, cannot be sustained.

We are concerned only with the federal question which we have discussed, and in view of the denial of the federal right suitably asserted, the judgment must be reversed and the cause remanded for further proceedings not inconsistent with this opinion.

It is so ordered.

Mr. Justice McREYNOLDS did not hear the argument and took no part in the consideration and decision of this case.

NOTES AND QUESTIONS

1. The retrials of the Scottsboro defendants were led by New York lawyer Samuel Leibowitz, who had been retained by the Internal Labor Defense (ILD), the legal arm of the Communist Party. After the original convictions the cases of the "Scottsboro Boys" became a national and even international cause célèbre. In addition, a bitter feud arose between the Communist Party and the NAACP over which organization would lead the appeals and

Scottsboro defendants with their lawyer, Samuel Leibowitz

(if any) retrials. The Communist Party had immediately denounced the convictions while the NAACP had moved more cautiously, and the Communists ultimately gained the upper hand and litigation control, simultaneously launching protests and supporting rallies in the North. See Michael Klarman, Powell v. Alabama: The Supreme Court Confronts "Legal Lynchings," at 5-6, 16 in Criminal Procedure Stories (Carol S. Steiker ed., 2006).

   2. Leibowitz was able to launch vigorous challenges to the racial composition of both the grand jury in Jackson County, where defendants had been indicted, and the petit jury in Morgan County, where the new trials would be held. He was able to put on dozens of witnesses, including current and former jury commissioners, court clerks, a handwriting expert, and Black witnesses who were plainly qualified for jury service but had never been called for jury duty. Although it is true that the judges that oversaw this pretrial litigation ultimately denied the defendants' motions to quash, unwilling to reach the conclusions the factual records warranted, the defendants' ability to compile such a record was itself something of an achievement. It marked progress from the turn-of-the-century cases, see supra, where many such challenges were shut off without any factual inquiry whatsoever.

   3. The coup de grace of this pretrial litigation was the discovery that a jury commissioner had falsified the addition of names of Black persons to one of the juror rolls. At oral argument in the Supreme Court Leibowitz made inspired use of this evidence:

> He brought to the counsel table the actual books containing the jury roll for Jackson County, Alabama, which had been made part of the record below and had been filed with the Clerk's office. During his argument, Leibowitz piqued the Chief Justice's curiosity about the books. Leibowitz declared that the forgery in the jury rolls was fraud "not only against the defendants but against this very court itself." At this point, Hughes asked whether Leibowitz could prove

the forgery, and Leibowitz offered to exhibit the jury rolls. "Let's see them," demanded Hughes. According to Professor Don Carter, "One by one, the eight justices examined the names in question under a magnifying glass while Leibowitz explained the mechanics of the forgery." For the first time in the history of the United States a federal judge laid his hands directly on hard evidence of jury discrimination by state jury selection officials. At Hughes' right shoulder, the fastidious Willis Van Devanter, the senior Associate Justice, craned to look at the books. In the expectant hush of the courtroom, Van Devanter was heard to whisper to Hughes: "Why it's as plain as punch."

See Benno C. Schmidt Jr., *Juries, Jurisdiction, and Race Discrimination: The Lost Promise of* Strauder v. West Virginia, 61 Tex. L. Rev. 1401, 1478-79 (1983) (footnotes omitted).

4. As in *Neal, supra,* the Supreme Court found that defendants had made out a prima facie case of discrimination as to both the petit and grand juries, which the state failed to rebut. 294 U.S. at 591, 598. The means to that end was a thorough and independent review of the facts, which was far from standard practice. The Court stated at the outset of its opinion:

> That the question is one of fact does not relieve us of the duty to determine whether in truth a federal right has been denied. When a federal right has been specially set up and claimed in a state court, it is our province to inquire not merely whether it was denied in express terms but also whether it was denied in substance and effect. If this requires an examination of evidence, that examination must be made. Otherwise, review by this Court would fail of its purpose in safeguarding constitutional rights. Thus, whenever a conclusion of law of a state court as to a federal right and findings of fact are so intermingled that the latter control the former, it is incumbent upon us to analyze the facts in order that the appropriate enforcement of the federal right may be assured.

Id. at 589. Are there any reasonable limits that, in more normal circumstances, should be placed on appellate courts' review of lower courts' factfinding? In what ways in *Norris* are the legal right and the findings of fact "intermingled"? Did the Supreme Court essentially draw different inferences from the facts than the trial court did?

D. COERCED CONFESSIONS

Brown v. Mississippi
297 U.S. 278 (1936)

Mr. Chief Justice HUGHES delivered the opinion of the Court.

The question in this case is whether convictions, which rest solely upon confessions shown to have been extorted by officers of the state by brutality and violence, are consistent with the due process of law required by the Fourteenth Amendment of the Constitution of the United States.

Petitioners were indicted for the murder of one Raymond Stewart, whose death occurred on March 30, 1934. They were indicted on April 4, 1934, and were then arraigned and pleaded not guilty. Counsel were appointed by the court to defend them. Trial was begun the next morning and was concluded on the following day, when they were found guilty and sentenced to death.

Aside from the confessions, there was no evidence sufficient to warrant the submission of the case to the jury. After a preliminary inquiry, testimony as to the confessions was received over the objection of defendants' counsel. Defendants then testified that the confessions were false and had been procured by physical torture. The case went to the jury with instructions, upon the request of defendants' counsel, that if the jury had reasonable doubt as to the confessions having resulted from coercion, . . . they were not to be considered as evidence. On their [appeal] to the Supreme Court of the State, defendants assigned as error the inadmissibility of the confessions. The judgment was affirmed.

Defendants then moved in the Supreme Court of the State to arrest the judgment and for a new trial on the ground that all the evidence against them was obtained by coercion and brutality known to the court and to the district attorney, and that defendants had been denied the benefit of counsel or opportunity to confer with counsel in a reasonable manner. The motion was supported by affidavits. At about the same time, defendants filed in the Supreme Court a "suggestion of error" explicitly challenging the proceedings of the trial, in the use of the confessions and with respect to the alleged denial of representation by counsel, as violating the due process clause of the Fourteenth Amendment of the Constitution of the United States. The state court entertained the suggestion of error, considered the federal question, and decided it against defendants' contentions. Two judges dissented. We granted a writ of certiorari.

The grounds of the decision were (1) that immunity from self-incrimination is not essential to due process of law; and (2) that the failure of the trial court to exclude the confessions after the introduction of evidence showing their incompetency, in the absence of a request for such exclusion, did not deprive the defendants of life or liberty without due process of law; and that even if the trial court had erroneously overruled a motion to exclude the confessions, the ruling would have been mere error reversible on appeal, but not a violation of constitution right.

The opinion of the state court did not set forth the evidence as to the circumstances in which the confessions were procured. That the evidence established that they were procured by coercion was not questioned. The state court said: "After the state closed its case on the merits, the appellants, for the first time, introduced evidence from which it appears that the confessions were not made voluntarily but were coerced." There is no dispute as to the facts upon this point, and as they are clearly and adequately stated in the dissenting opinion of Judge Griffith (with whom Judge Anderson concurred), showing both the extreme brutality of the measures to extort the confessions and the participation of the state authorities, we quote this part of his opinion in full, as follows:

> The crime with which these defendants, all ignorant negroes, are charged, was discovered about 1 o'clock p.m. on Friday, March 30, 1934. On that night one Dial, a deputy sheriff, accompanied by others, came to the home of Ellington, one of the defendants, and requested him to accompany them to the house of the deceased, and there a number of white men were gathered, who began to accuse the defendant of the crime. Upon his denial they seized him, and with the participation of the deputy they hanged him by a rope to the limb of a tree, and, having let him down, they hung him again, and when he was let down the second time, and he still protested his innocence, he was tied to a tree and whipped, and, still declining to accede to the demands that he confess, he was finally released, and he returned with some difficulty to his home, suffering intense pain and agony. The record of the testimony shows that the signs of the rope on his neck were plainly visible during the so-called trial. A day or two thereafter the said deputy, accompanied by another, returned to the home of the said defendant and arrested him, and departed with the prisoner towards the jail in an adjoining county, but went by a route which led into the state of Alabama; and while on the way, in that state, the deputy stopped and again severely whipped the defendant, declaring that he would continue the whipping until he confessed, and the defendant then agreed to confess to such a statement as the deputy would dictate, and he did so, after which he was delivered to jail.
>
> The other two defendants, Ed Brown and Henry Shields, were also arrested and taken to the same jail. On Sunday night, April 1, 1934, the same deputy, accompanied by a number of white men, one of whom was also an officer, and by the jailer, came to the jail, and the two last

named defendants were made to strip and they were laid over chairs and their backs were cut to pieces with a leather strap with buckles on it, and they were likewise made by the said deputy definitely to understand that the whipping would be continued unless and until they confessed, and not only confessed, but confessed in every matter of detail as demanded by those present; and in this manner the defendants confessed the crime, and, as the whippings progressed and were repeated, they changed or adjusted their confession in all particulars of detail so as to conform to the demands of their torturers. When the confessions had been obtained in the exact form and contents as desired by the mob, they left with the parting admonition and warning that, if the defendants changed their story at any time in any respect from that last stated, the perpetrators of the outrage would administer the same or equally effective treatment.

Further details of the brutal treatment to which these helpless prisoners were subjected need not be pursued. It is sufficient to say that in pertinent respects the transcript reads more like pages torn from some medieval account than a record made within the confines of a modern civilization which aspires to an enlightened constitutional government.

All this having been accomplished, on the next day, that is, on Monday, April 2, when the defendants had been given time to recuperate somewhat from the tortures to which they had been subjected, the two sheriffs, one of the county where the crime was committed, and the other of the county of the jail in which the prisoners were confined, came to the jail, accompanied by eight other persons, some of them deputies, there to hear the free and voluntary confession of these miserable and abject defendants. The sheriff of the county of the crime admitted that he had heard of the whipping, but averred that he had no personal knowledge of it. He admitted that one of the defendants, when brought before him to confess, was limping and did not sit down, and that this particular defendant then and there stated that he had been strapped so severely that he could not sit down, and, as already stated, the signs of the rope on the neck of another of the defendants were plainly visible to all. Nevertheless the solemn farce of hearing the free and voluntary confessions was gone through with, and these two sheriffs and one other person then present were the three witnesses used in court to establish the so-called confessions, which were received by the court and admitted in evidence over the objections of the defendants duly entered of record as each of the said three witnesses delivered their alleged testimony. There was thus enough before the court when these confessions were first offered to make known to the court that they were not, beyond all reasonable doubt, free and voluntary; and the failure of the court then to exclude the confessions is sufficient to reverse the judgment, under every rule of procedure that has heretofore been prescribed, and hence it was not necessary subsequently to renew the objections by motion or otherwise.

The spurious confessions having been obtained — and the farce last mentioned having been gone through with on Monday, April 2d — the court, then in session, on the following day, Tuesday, April 3, 1934, ordered the grand jury to reassemble on the succeeding day, April 4, 1934, at 9 o'clock, and on the morning of the day last mentioned the grand jury returned an indictment against the defendants for murder. Late that afternoon the defendants were brought from the jail in the adjoining county and arraigned, when one or more of them offered to plead guilty, which the court declined to accept, and, upon inquiry whether they had or desired counsel, they stated that they had none, and did not suppose that counsel could be of any assistance to them. The court thereupon appointed counsel, and set the case for trial for the following morning at 9 o'clock, and the defendants were returned to the jail in the adjoining county about thirty miles away.

The defendants were brought to the courthouse of the county on the following morning, April 5th, and the so-called trial was opened, and was concluded on the next day, April 6, 1934, and resulted in a pretended conviction with death sentences. The evidence upon which the conviction was obtained was the so-called confessions. Without this evidence, a peremptory instruction to find for the defendants would have been inescapable. The defendants were put on the stand, and by their testimony the facts and the details thereof as to the manner by which the confessions were extorted from them were fully developed, and it is further disclosed by the record that the same deputy, Dial, under whose guiding hand and active participation the tortures to coerce the confessions were administered, was actively in the performance of the supposed duties of a court deputy in the courthouse and in the presence of the prisoners during what is denominated, in complimentary terms, the trial of these defendants. This deputy was put on the stand by the state in rebuttal, and admitted the whippings. It is interesting to note that in his testimony with reference to the whipping of the defendant Ellington, and in response to the inquiry as to how severely he was whipped, the deputy stated, "Not too much for a negro; not as much as I would have done if it were left to me." Two others who had participated in these whippings were introduced and admitted it — not a single witness was introduced who denied it. The facts are not only undisputed, they are admitted, and admitted to have been done by officers of the state, in conjunction with other participants, and all this was definitely well known to everybody connected with the trial, and during the trial, including the state's prosecuting attorney and the trial judge presiding.

The state stresses the statement in *Twining v. New Jersey* that "exemption from compulsory self-incrimination in the courts of the states is not secured by any part of the Federal Constitution," and the statement in *Snyder v. Massachusetts* that "the privilege against self-incrimination may be withdrawn and the accused put upon the stand as a witness for the state." But the question of the right of the state to withdraw the privilege against self-incrimination is not here involved. The compulsion to which the quoted statements refer is that of the processes of justice by which the accused may be called as a witness and required to testify. Compulsion by torture to extort a confession is a different matter.

The state is free to regulate the procedure of its courts in accordance with its own conceptions of policy, unless in so doing it "offends some principle of justice so rooted in the traditions and conscience of our people as to be ranked as fundamental." The state may abolish trial by jury. It may dispense with indictment by a grand jury and substitute complaint or information. But the freedom of the state in establishing its policy is the freedom of constitutional government and is limited by the requirement of due process of law. Because a state may dispense with a jury trial, it does not follow that it may substitute trial by ordeal. The rack and torture chamber may not be substituted for the witness stand. The state may not permit an accused to be hurried to conviction under mob domination — where the whole proceeding is but a mask — without supplying corrective process. *Moore v. Dempsey*. The state may not deny to the accused the aid of counsel. *Powell v. Alabama*. Nor may a state, through the action of its officers, contrive a conviction through the pretense of a trial which in truth is "but used as a means of depriving a defendant of liberty through a deliberate deception of court and jury by the presentation of testimony known to be perjured." *Mooney v. Holohan*. And the trial equally is a mere pretense where the state authorities have contrived a conviction resting solely upon confessions obtained by violence. The due process clause requires "that state action, whether through one agency or another, shall be consistent with the fundamental principles of liberty and justice which lie at the base of all our civil and political institutions." It would be difficult to conceive of methods more revolting to the sense of justice than those taken to procure the confessions of these petitioners, and the use of the confessions thus obtained as the basis for conviction and sentence was a clear denial of due process.

It is in this view that the further contention of the State must be considered. That contention rests upon the failure of counsel for the accused, who had objected to the admissibility of the confessions, to move for their exclusion after they had been introduced and the fact of coercion had been proved. It is a contention which proceeds upon a misconception of the nature of petitioners' complaint. That complaint is not of the commission of mere error, but of a wrong so fundamental that it made the whole proceeding a mere pretense of a trial and rendered the conviction and sentence wholly void. We are not concerned with a mere question of state practice, or whether counsel assigned to petitioners were competent or mistakenly assumed that their first objections were sufficient. In an earlier case the Supreme Court of the State had recognized the duty of the court to supply corrective process where due process of law had been denied. In *Fisher v. State*, 145 Miss. 116, the court said: "Coercing the supposed state's criminals into confessions and using such confessions so coerced from them against them in trials has been the curse of all countries. It was the chief iniquity, the crowning infamy of the Star Chamber, and the Inquisition, and other similar institutions. The Constitution recognized the evils that lay behind these practices and prohibited them in this country. . . . The duty of maintaining constitutional rights of a person on trial for his life rises above mere rules of procedure, and wherever the court is clearly satisfied that such violations exist, it will refuse to sanction such violations and will apply the corrective."

In the instant case, the trial court was fully advised by the undisputed evidence of the way in which the confessions had been procured. The trial court knew that there was no other evidence upon which conviction and sentence could be based. Yet it proceeded to permit conviction and to pronounce sentence. The conviction and sentence were void for want of the essential elements of due process, and the proceeding thus vitiated could be challenged in any appropriate manner. It was challenged before the Supreme Court of the State by the express invocation of the Fourteenth Amendment. That court entertained the challenge, considered the federal question thus presented, but declined to enforce petitioners' constitutional right. The court thus denied a federal right fully established and specially set up and claimed, and the judgment must be reversed.

It is so ordered.

NOTES AND QUESTIONS

1. One of the remarkable aspects of *Brown* is that the coerced confessions were the only evidence the prosecution offered against the three defendants. There are at least two possible explanations for this: (a) no other evidence against them could be found after investigation; or (b) the state simply didn't bother to look for evidence once it had the confessions. As to the latter explanation, consider that the Mississippi Supreme Court had previously reversed convictions based on confessions coerced by violence, *Brown v. State*, 36 So. 73 (Miss. 1904), a fact that the U.S. Supreme Court notes in its opinion. Of course, from the state's perspective, there was always a chance that the facts of the coercion would never come to light, or that the defendant would not appeal. Or that the defendant would be lynched before trial. In any event, the lack of any non-confession evidence against the defendants suggests the likelihood of their innocence, which — as in the cases above — made it more likely that there would be potential financial support for appellate litigation and that the U.S. Supreme Court would hear the case.

2. The Mississippi Supreme Court affirms on two grounds, one of which is a procedural default by defense counsel. What error did defense counsel make? What does the U.S. Supreme Court make of this reasoning?

3. For the facts of the case the Court relies almost entirely on the dissenting opinion of Mississippi Supreme Court Justice Griffith, which it quotes at length. Why might the Supreme Court have done this?

4. Another remarkable aspect of *Brown* is that the only real issue in the case — whether the confessions were coerced — was not the subject of a swearing contest. The facts of the coercion, testified to by the defendants, were admitted by the law enforcement and civilian assailants. In light of this factual record, what is the likely effect, if any, of *Brown* on law enforcement tactics? *See* Mark Tushnet, Making Civil Rights Law: Thurgood Marshall and the Supreme Court, 1936-1961 (1994), at 57 ("The police did not stop using those tactics;

instead, having been told that they could not use the third degree, the police began to deny that the confessions they obtained resulted from improper tactics.").

Four of the cases highlighted in this chapter—*Moore*, *Powell*, *Norris*, and *Brown*—are widely regarded as landmark cases in the Supreme Court's constitutionalization of criminal procedure. Yet their actual impact is uncertain. *Moore* did not end mob-dominated trials. *Powell*, narrow to begin with, could be complied with by appointing counsel for a defendant just a few days before trial. *Norris* did not do much at all to change the racial composition of juries in the South, and to the extent any Black persons made their way on to grand juries, they could be outvoted and they could be removed from petit juries though peremptory challenges. *Brown* did not end coerced confessions, although it may have taught the police not to admit to them. *See* Klarman, *The Racial Origins of Modern Criminal Procedure*, *supra* at 78-83. And it wasn't as if counsel was readily available to help impecunious Black criminal defendants take advantage of the legal precedent that began to emerge, even at trial not to mention appellate litigation:

> The criminal procedure cases that reached the Supreme Court were atypical in this regard. The NAACP financed the appellate litigation in *Moore*; the ILD in *Powell* and *Norris*; and the NAACP, the CIC, and the ASWPL in *Brown*. None of these cases could have gotten to the Supreme Court without outside financial assistance. The Phillips County race riot and

Brown v. Mississippi defendants Henry Shields, Arthur Ellington, and Ed Brown on the cover of the NAACP's April 1935 edition of *The Crisis*. The magazine's first editor was W.E.B. DuBois. It has been in continuous circulation since 1910.

the alleged rapes and ensuing trials at Scottsboro captured national attention. Because these criminal cases revealed southern Jim Crow at its worst, they provided outstanding fundraising opportunities. The NAACP and the ILD, respectively, became involved at the early stages of litigation and raised large sums of money to finance appeals. *Brown v. Mississippi* was more of a garden variety murder case. Only the extraordinary efforts of local appointed counsel, who covered some of the legal costs from his own pocket, kept the case alive long enough for outside organizations to become involved and finance an appeal to the Supreme Court.

In the run-of-the-mill criminal case, indigent black defendants were represented not by elite legal talent hired by the NAACP or the ILD, but rather by court-appointed lawyers. Generally these lawyers were white, and they could not always be counted upon to defend aggressively the rights of their black clients, since doing so could be injurious to their careers as well as potentially hazardous to their health. For example, a tacit agreement existed among prosecutors and defense counsel in many southern counties not to raise the issue of black exclusion from juries. When a white ILD lawyer challenged that tacit agreement in a Maryland murder case in 1931, he had to endure death threats and subsequent retaliatory disbarment proceedings. The ILD lawyer representing the Scottsboro Boys in their first round of retrials, Samuel Leibowitz, was besieged with death threats after he questioned in court the honesty of county jury commissioners and of the white women who had alleged rape. The court-appointed white defense attorney in *Brown v. Mississippi* ruined a promising political career by pursuing the case so aggressively. In the wake of Scottsboro, two white ILD lawyers lost their lives for defending three blacks charged with raping and killing a white woman in Tuscaloosa, Alabama.

Id. at 84-85.

Nor was it a sure thing that getting a case to the Supreme Court would result in a faithful application of the principles set forth in cases such as *Moore*, *Powell*, *Norris*, and *Brown*, as the next two cases will show.

Lyons v. Oklahoma
322 U.S. 596 (1944)

Mr. Justice REED delivered the opinion of the Court.

This writ brings to this Court for review a conviction obtained with the aid of a confession which furnished, if voluntary, material evidence to support the conviction. As the questioned confession followed a previous confession which was given on the same day and which was admittedly involuntary, the issue is the voluntary character of the second confession under the circumstances which existed at the time and place of its signature and, particularly, because of the alleged continued influence of the unlawful inducements which vitiated the prior confession.

The petitioner was convicted in the state district court of Choctaw County, Oklahoma, on an information charging him and another with the crime of murder. The jury fixed his punishment at life imprisonment. The conviction was affirmed by the Criminal Court of Appeals, and this Court granted certiorari upon the petitioner's representation that there had been admitted against him an involuntary confession procured under circumstances which made its use in evidence a violation of his rights under the due process clause of the Fourteenth Amendment.

Prior to Sunday, December 31, 1939, Elmer Rogers lived with his wife and three small sons in a tenant house situated a short distance northwest of Fort Towson, Choctaw County, Oklahoma. Late in the evening of that day Mr. and Mrs. Rogers and a four year old son Elvie were murdered at their home and the house was burned to conceal the crime.

Suspicion was directed toward the petitioner Lyons and a confederate, Van Bizzell. On January 11, 1940. Lyons was arrested by a special policeman and another officer whose exact official status is not disclosed by the record. The first formal charge that appears is at Lyons' hearing before a magistrate on January 27, 1940. Immediately after his arrest there was an interrogation of about two hours at the jail. After he had been in jail eleven days he was again questioned, this time in the county prosecutor's office. This interrogation began about six-thirty in the evening, and on the following morning between two and four produced a confession. This questioning is the basis of the objection to the introduction as evidence of a second confession which was obtained later in the day at the state penitentiary at McAlester by Warden Jess Dunn and introduced in evidence at the trial. There was also a third confession, oral, which was admitted on the trial without objection by petitioner. This was given to a guard at the penitentiary two days after the second. Only the petitioner, police, prosecuting and penitentiary officials were present at any of these interrogations, except that a private citizen who drove the car that brought Lyons to McAlester witnessed this second confession.

William Douglas Lyons, handcuffed and in the company of the six arresting police officers

Lyons is married and was twenty-one or two years of age at the time of the arrest. The extent of his education or his occupation does not appear. He signed the second confession. From the transcript of his evidence, there is no indication of a subnormal intelligence. He had served two terms in the penitentiary—one for chicken stealing and one for burglary. Apparently he lived with various relatives.

While petitioner was competently represented before and at the trial, counsel was not supplied him until after his preliminary examination, which was subsequent to the confessions. His wife and family visited him between his arrest and the first confession. There is testimony by Lyons of physical abuse by the police officers at the time of his arrest and first interrogation on January 11th. His sister visited him in jail shortly afterwards and testified as to marks of violence on his body and a blackened eye. Lyons says that this violence was accompanied by threats of further harm unless he confessed. This evidence was denied in toto by officers who were said to have participated.

Eleven days later the second interrogation occurred. Again the evidence of assault is conflicting. Eleven or twelve officials were in and out of the prosecutor's small office during the night. Lyons says that he again suffered assault. Denials of violence were made by all the participants accused by Lyons except the county attorney, his assistant, the jailer and a highway patrolman. Disinterested witnesses testified to statements by an investigator which tended to implicate that officer in the use of force, and the prosecutor in cross-examination used language which gave color to defendant's charge. It is not disputed that the inquiry continued until two-thirty in the morning before an oral confession was obtained and that a pan of the victims' bones was placed in Lyon's lap by his interrogators to bring about his confession. As the confession obtained at this time was not offered in evidence, the only bearing these events have here is their tendency to show that the later confession at McAlester was involuntary.

After the oral confession in the early morning hours of January 23, Lyons was taken to the scene of the crime and subjected to further questioning about the instruments which were used to commit the murders. He was returned to the jail about eight-thirty a.m. and left there until early afternoon. After that the prisoner was taken to a nearby town of Antlers, Oklahoma. Later in the day a deputy sheriff and a private citizen took the petitioner to the penitentiary. There, sometime between eight and eleven o'clock on that same evening, the petitioner signed the second confession.

When the confession which was given at the penitentiary was offered, objection was made on the ground that force was practiced to secure it and that even if no force was then practiced, the fear instilled by the prisoner's former treatment at Hugo on his first and second interrogations continued sufficiently coercive in its effect to require the rejection of the second confession.

The judge in accordance with Oklahoma practice and, after hearing evidence from the prosecution and the defense in the absence of the jury, first passed favorably upon its admissibility as a matter of law, and then, after witnesses testified before the jury as to the voluntary character of the confession, submitted the guilt or innocence of the defendant to the jury under a full instruction, approved by the Criminal Court of Appeals, to the effect that voluntary confessions are admissible against the person making them but are to be "carefully scrutinized and received with great caution" by the jury and rejected if obtained by punishment, intimidation or threats. It was added that the mere fact that a confession was made in answer to inquiries "while under arrest or in custody" does not prevent consideration of the evidence if made "freely and voluntarily." The instruction did not specifically cover the defendant's contention, embodied in a requested instruction, that the second confession sprang from the fear engendered by the treatment he had received at Hugo.

The mere questioning of a suspect while in the custody of police officers is not prohibited either as a matter of common law or due process. The question of how specific an instruction in a state court must be upon the involuntary character of a confession is, as a matter of procedure or practice, solely for the courts of the state. When the state-approved instruction fairly raises the question of whether or not the challenged confession was voluntary, as this instruction did, the requirements of due process, under the Fourteenth Amendment, are satisfied and this Court will not require a modification of local practice to meet views that it might have as to the advantages of concreteness. The instruction given satisfies the legal requirements of the State of Oklahoma as to the particularity with which issues must be presented to its juries, and in view of the scope of that instruction, it was sufficient to preclude any claim of violation of the Fourteenth Amendment.

The federal question presented is whether the second confession was given under such circumstances that its use as evidence at the trial constitutes a violation of the due process clause of the Fourteenth Amendment, which requires that state criminal proceedings "shall be consistent with the fundamental principles of liberty and justice."

No formula to determine this question by its application to the facts of a given case can be devised. Here improper methods were used to obtain a confession, but that confession was not used at the trial. Later, in another place and with different persons present, the accused again told the facts of the crime. Involuntary confessions, of course, may be given either simultaneously with or subsequently to unlawful pressures, force or threats. The question of whether those confessions subsequently given are themselves voluntary depends on the inferences as to the continuing effect of the coercive practices which may fairly be drawn from the surrounding circumstances. The voluntary or involuntary character of a confession is determined by a conclusion as to whether the accused, at the time he confesses, is in possession of "mental freedom" to confess to or deny a suspected participation in a crime.

When conceded facts exist which are irreconcilable with such mental freedom, regardless of the contrary conclusions of the triers of fact, whether judge or jury, this Court cannot avoid responsibility for such injustice by leaving the burden of adjudication solely in other hands. But where there is a dispute as to whether the acts which are charged to be coercive actually occurred, or where different inferences may fairly be drawn from admitted facts, the trial judge and the jury are not only in a better position to appraise the truth or falsity of the defendant's assertions from the demeanor of the witnesses but the legal duty is upon them to make the decision.

Review here deals with circumstances which require examination into the possibility as to whether the judge and jury in the trial court could reasonably conclude that the McAlester confession was voluntary. The fact that there is evidence which would justify a contrary conclusion is immaterial. To triers of fact is left the determination of the truth or error of the testimony of prisoner and official alike. It is beyond question that if the triers of fact accepted as true the evidence of the immediate events at McAlester, which were detailed by Warden Dunn and the other witnesses, the verdict would be that the confession was voluntary, so that the petitioner's case rests upon the theory that the McAlester confession was the unavoidable outgrowth of the events at Hugo.

The Fourteenth Amendment does not protect one who has admitted his guilt because of forbidden inducements against the use at trial of his subsequent confessions under all possible circumstances. The admissibility of the later confession depends upon the same test — is it voluntary. Of course the fact that the earlier statement was obtained from the prisoner by coercion is to be considered in appraising the character of the later confession. The effect of earlier abuse may be so clear as to forbid any other inference than that it dominated the mind of the accused to such an extent that the later confession is involuntary. If the relation between the earlier and later confession is not so close that one must say the facts of one control the character of the other, the inference is one for the triers of fact and their conclusion, in such an uncertain situation, that the confession should be admitted as voluntary, cannot be a denial of due process.

* * *

Petitioner suggests a presumption that earlier abuses render subsequent confessions involuntary unless there is clear and definite evidence to overcome the presumption. We need not analyze this contention further than to say that in this case there is evidence for the state which, if believed, would make it abundantly clear that the events at Hugo did not bring about the confession at McAlester.

In our view, the earlier events at Hugo do not lead unescapably to the conclusion that the later McAlester confession was brought about by the earlier mistreatments. The McAlester confession was separated from the early morning statement by a full twelve hours. It followed the prisoner's transfer from the control of the sheriff's force to that of the warden. One person who had been present during a part of the time while the Hugo interrogation was in progress was present at McAlester, it is true, but he was not among those charged with abusing Lyons during the questioning at Hugo. There was evidence from others present that Lyons readily confessed without any show of force or threats within a very short time of his surrender to Warden Dunn and after being warned by Dunn that anything he might say would be used against him and that he should not "make a statement unless he voluntarily wanted to." Lyons, as a former inmate of the institution, was acquainted with the warden. The petitioner testified to nothing in the past that would indicate any reason for him to fear mistreatment there. The fact that Lyons, a few days later, frankly admitted the killings to a sergeant of the prison guard, a former acquaintance from his own locality, under circumstances free of coercion suggests strongly that the petitioner had concluded that it was wise to make a clean breast of his guilt and that his confession to Dunn was voluntary. The answers to the warden's questions, as transcribed by a prison stenographer, contain statements correcting and supplementing the questioner's information and do not appear to be mere supine attempts to give the desired response to leading questions.

The Fourteenth Amendment is a protection against criminal trials in state courts conducted in such a manner as amounts to a disregard of "that fundamental fairness essential to the very concept of justice," and in a way that "necessarily prevent(s) a fair trial." A coerced confession is offensive to basic standards of justice, not because the victim has a legal grievance against the police, but because declarations procured by torture are not premises from which a civilized forum will infer guilt. The Fourteenth Amendment does not provide review of mere error in jury verdicts, even though the error concerns the voluntary character of a confession. We cannot say that an inference of guilt based in part upon Lyons' McAlester confession is so illogical and unreasonable as to deny the petitioner a fair trial.

Affirmed.

Mr. Justice DOUGLAS concurs in the result.

Mr. Justice RUTLEDGE dissents.

Mr. Justice MURPHY, dissenting.

This flagrant abuse by a state of the rights on an American citizen accused of murder ought not to be approved. The Fifth Amendment prohibits the federal government from convicting a defendant on evidence that he was compelled to give against himself. Decisions of this Court in effect have held that the Fourteenth Amendment makes this prohibition applicable to the states. It is our duty to apply that constitutional prohibition in this case.

Even though approximately twelve hours intervened between the two confessions and even assuming that there was no violence surrounding the second confession, it is inconceivable under these circumstances that the second confession was free from the coercive atmosphere that admittedly impregnated the first one. The whole confession technique used here constituted one single, continuing transaction. To conclude that the brutality inflicted at the time of the first confession suddenly lost all of its effect in the short space of twelve hours is to close one's eyes to the realities of human nature. An individual does not that easily forget the type of torture that accompanied petitioner's previous refusal to confess, nor does a person like petitioner so quickly recover from the gruesome effects of having had a pan of human bones placed on his knees in order to force incriminating testimony from him. Moreover, the trial judge refused petitioner's request that the jury be charged that the second confession was not free and voluntary if it was obtained while petitioner was still suffering from the inhuman treatment he had previously received. Thus it cannot be said that we are confronted with a finding by the trier of facts that the coercive effect of the prior brutality had completely worn off by the time the second confession was signed.

Presumably, therefore, this decision means that state officers are free to force a confession from an individual by ruthless methods, knowing full well that they dare not use such a confession at the trial, and then, as a part of the same continuing transaction and before the effects of the coercion can fairly be said to have completely worn off, procure another confession without any immediate violence being inflicted. The admission of such a tainted confession does not accord with the Fourteenth Amendment's command that a state shall not convict a defendant on evidence that he was compelled to give against himself.

Mr. Justice BLACK concurs in this opinion.

NOTES AND QUESTIONS

1. The Court concludes that deference must be given to the judge and jury's conclusion that the confession admitted into evidence at trial was voluntary. How does this square with the *Norris* Court's statements on the Supreme Court's obligations with respect to state-court factfinding?

Lyons's trial defense team, led by 32-year-old Thurgood Marshall (on the right)

2. The Court's discussion of the facts tells you right where this is headed. Perhaps most remarkable is the Court's statement that, with respect to the interrogation that produced the confession, "the evidence of assault is conflicting." Yet in the very next sentence we learn that

Chapter II The Roots of Modern Constitutional Criminal Procedure

"[denials] of violence were made by all of the [11 or 12] interrogation participants accused by Lyons *except the county attorney, his assistant, the jailer, and a highway patrolman.*" That is not disputed evidence. Four representatives of the state admitted that violence occurred; the other seven or eight lied.

3. Note that the ultimate question of voluntariness was an issue for the jury, not a preliminary matter for the court to decide. Does it make sense that the jury and not the court should decide this issue, which is at bottom an evidentiary issue — should the confession be admitted into evidence for the jury's consideration? The court also refused to give the jury the instruction requested by the defendant, that the second confession could not be considered voluntary if it was attributable to the defendant's inhumane treatment during the physically coerced confession made earlier. Do you think the relationship between the two confessions is a matter of common sense and that therefore a specific instruction was not necessary inasmuch as the jury was instructed that confessions must be "carefully scrutinized and received with great caution" and rejected if obtained by intimidation or threats? What effect, if any, might the instruction requested by the defendant have had?

4. The Court notes that the second confession was given to, among others, the warden of the penitentiary to which Lyons had been transferred, and that the warden had warned him that anything he said would be used against him. What effect might that have had on the voluntariness of Lyons's subsequent statements? What do you make of the Court's observation that Lyons "was acquainted with the warden"?

5. The dissent states that "it is inconceivable under these circumstances that the second confession was free from the coercive atmosphere that admittedly tainted the first one." Can you disagree with that point and still agree with the dissent?

Akins v. Texas
325 U.S. 398 (1945)

Mr. Justice REED delivered the opinion of the Court.

This certiorari brings here for review a judgment of the Criminal District Court of Dallas County, Texas, sentencing petitioner to execution on a jury verdict which found petitioner guilty of murder with malice and assessed the penalty at death.

Certiorari was sought to the Court of Criminal Appeals of the State of Texas, which had affirmed the judgment, on a petition which claimed discrimination on account of his race, against the petitioner, who is a Negro, under the equal protection and due process clauses of the Fourteenth Amendment of the Constitution of the United States. Certiorari was allowed because of the importance in the administration of criminal justice of the alleged racial discrimination which was relied upon to support the claim of violation of constitutional rights. This discrimination was said to consist of an arbitrary and purposeful limitation by the Grand Jury Commissioners of the number of Negroes to one who was to be placed upon the grand jury panel of sixteen for the term of court at which the indictment against petitioner was found. This is petitioner's only complaint as to racial discrimination. No other errors in the proceedings are pointed out.

The Fourteenth Amendment forbids any discrimination against a race in the selection of a grand jury. An allegation of discriminatory practices in selecting a grand jury panel challenges an essential element of proper judicial procedure — the requirement of fairness on the part of the judicial arm of government in dealing with persons charged with criminal offenses. It cannot lightly be concluded that officers of the courts disregard this accepted standard of justice.

The order overruling the motion to quash the indictment was made after evidence and without opinion. That motion set out the alleged purposeful limitation on racial representation which is pressed here. The Court of Criminal Appeals, however, without a written analysis of the testimony, said in an opinion that it failed "to find any evidence of discrimination. On the contrary, the evidence shows an effort on the part of the authorities to comply with the holding of this court and of the Supreme Court of the United States upon the question of discrimination." Although this opinion of the Court of Criminal Appeals does not refer to proportional racial representation on juries, recent decisions of that court had previously disapproved that procedure. We think, therefore, that the conclusions of the state courts show that in their judgment there was no proven racial discrimination by limitation in this case. Otherwise there would have been a reversal by the Court of Criminal Appeals.

As will presently appear, the transcript of the evidence presents certain inconsistencies and conflicts of testimony in regard to limiting the number of negroes on the grand jury. Therefore, the trier of fact who heard the witnesses in full and observed their demeanor on the stand has a better opportunity than a reviewing court to reach a correct conclusion as to the existence of that type of discrimination. While our duty, in reviewing a conviction upon a complaint that the procedure through which it was obtained violates due process and equal protection under the Fourteenth Amendment, calls for our examination of evidence to determine for ourselves whether a federal constitutional right has been denied, expressly or in substance and effect, *Norris v. State of Alabama*, we accord in that examination great respect to the conclusions of the state judiciary. That respect leads us to accept the conclusion of the trier on disputed issues "unless it is so lacking in support in the evidence that to give it effect would work that fundamental unfairness which is at war with due process."

The regular statutory practice for the selection of grand jurors was followed in this case. Under the Texas statutes jury commissioners appointed by the judge of the trial court select a list of sixteen grandjurymen from which list twelve are chosen as a grand jury. Qualifications for grandjurymen are set out in Article 339. The Commissioners are instructed by the court as to their duties. This method of selection leaves a wide range of choice to the commissioners. Its validity, however, has been accepted by this Court. Petitioner does not attack it now. Its alternative would be a list composed of all eligibles within the trial court's jurisdiction and selection of the panel by lot.

Petitioner's sole objection to the grand jury is that the "commissioners deliberately, intentionally and purposely limited the number of the Negro race that should be selected on said grand jury panel to one member." Fairness in selection has never been held to require proportional representation of races upon a jury. Purposeful discrimination is not sustained by a showing that on a single grand jury the number of members of one race is less than that race's proportion of the eligible individuals. The number of our races and nationalities stands in the way of evolution of such a conception of due process or equal protection. Defendants under our criminal statutes are not entitled to demand representatives of their racial inheritance upon juries before whom they are tried. But such defendants are entitled to require that those who are trusted with jury selection shall not pursue a course of conduct which results in discrimination "in the selection of jurors on racial grounds." Our directions that indictments be quashed when Negroes, although numerous in the community, were excluded from grand jury lists have been based on the theory that their continual exclusion indicated discrimination and not on the theory that racial groups must be recognized. The mere fact of inequality in the number selected does not in itself show discrimination. A purpose to discriminate must be present which may be proven by systematic exclusion of eligible jurymen of the proscribed race or by unequal application of the law to such an extent as to show intentional discrimination. Cf. *Snowden v. Hughes*, 321 U.S. 1, 8, 64 S. Ct. 397, 401. Any such discrimination which affects an accused will make his conviction unlawful.

The history and record of this case gives evidence that the courts of Texas which are charged with the trial of petitioner endeavored to comply with the federal constitutional requirements as to the selection of grand juries, according to the interpretation of this Court in *Hill v. Texas, supra*. Not only did the Court of Criminal Appeals reverse a former conviction of petitioner on its authority but the judge, now deceased, of the criminal district court of Dallas instructed the three jury commissioners, who selected this grand jury list, as testified to by each of them, that there should be no discrimination against anyone because of his color.

Hill v. Texas, supra, was decided June 1, 1942. The trial court has four terms a year — January, April, July and October. After the *Hill* decision, the jury commissioners who were appointed at the July 1942 term to select grand jurors for the October 1942 term, placed a Negro on the grand jury list although he did not serve. Under the instructions of the judge as just detailed, the commissioners for the January 1943 term, at which petitioner was indicted, placed a Negro on the list and he served as a grand juror. Prior to the decision in the *Hill* case, it does not appear that any colored person had ever served on a grand jury in Dallas County.

On the precise act of discrimination by the jury commissioners which is asserted by petitioner, that is the deliberate, intentional and purposeful limitation to one of the number of Negroes on the grand jury panel, the record shows as follows. About fifteen and one-half per cent of the population of Dallas County, Texas, is negro. A substantial percentage of them are qualified to serve as grand jurors. No exact comparison can be made between the white and negro citizens as to the percentage of each race which is eligible. On the strictly mathematical basis of population, a grand jury of twelve would have 1.8552 negro members on the average. Of course, the qualifications for grand jury service would affect the proportion of eligibles from the two races. As one member of the Negro race served upon the grand jury which indicted petitioner and one had appeared upon the other grand jury list which had been selected after the decision in *Hill v. Texas, supra*, we cannot say that the omission from each of the two lists of all but one of the members of a race which composed some fifteen per cent of the population alone proved racial discrimination.

In connection with that fact of omission, we must appraise the testimony offered to show the intentional limitation. Besides the language quoted in note 4, supra, which relates particularly to the court's instructions, other relevant evidence of such intention is found only in the testimony of the commissioners. They made these statements as to their intentions:

Commissioner Wells: "There was nothing said about the number and nothing was said about the number on the panel. . . . We had no intention of placing more than one negro on the panel. When we did that we had finished with the negro. That was the suggestion of the others and what Judge Adams thought about the selection of the grand jury. . . . Judge Adams did not tell us to put one negro or five negroes on the grand jury. Yes, we just understood to see that negroes had representation on the grand jury, and we went out to see this particular one because we did not know him. . . . Among the white people whose names might go on the grand jury, unless I knew them personally and knew their qualifications, we went out and talked to them. No, we did not discriminate against a white man or a negro. I attempted not to."

Commissioner Tennant: "We three did not go to see any other negroes, that is the only one. I did not have any intention of putting more than one on the list; I could not think of anybody; I would have if I could have thought of another one, and putting one on."

D. Coerced Confessions   75

Commissioner Douglas: "Yes, sir, there were other negroes' names mentioned besides the one we selected; we did not go talk to them; we liked this one, and our intentions were to get just one negro on the grand jury; that is right. No, I did not have any intention of placing more than one negro on the grand jury. . . . We never agreed to select any certain number, but when we found one with all the qualifications of a grand juror we felt like that was satisfactory representation. . . . No, sir, we did not have in mind to put any set number of representatives of the various races. . . . We did not agree to put eleven negroes and one white man on, no. That is right, all that we were endeavoring to get a fair and impartial grand jury without any discrimination against any race on earth. We did not have in mind, or the other commissioners, to put any set number on of any race, white, yellow or what-not."

A careful examination of these statements in connection with all the other evidence leaves us unconvinced that the commissioners deliberately and intentionally limited the number of Negroes on the grand jury list. The judge who heard the witnesses on the motion to quash did not find that type of discrimination. The law of their state, the instructions of the judge, their oath of office required them to choose prospective jurors on their statutory qualifications and without regard to their color or the number of representatives of various races who might appear upon the list. We cannot say the commissioners violated these obligations.

This conclusion makes it unnecessary to decide whether a purposeful limitation of jurors by race to the approximate proportion that the eligible jurymen of the race so limited bears to the total eligibles is invalid under the Fourteenth Amendment.

The judgment is affirmed.

Affirmed.

Mr. Justice RUTLEDGE concurs in the result.

THE CHIEF JUSTICE and Mr. Justice BLACK dissent.

Mr. Justice MURPHY, dissenting.

The equal protection clause of the Fourteenth Amendment entitles every person, whose life, liberty or property is in issue, to the benefits of grand and petit juries chosen without regard to race, color or creed. This constitutional principle is a fundamental tenet of the American faith in the jury system. The absence of such a principle would give free rein to those who wittingly or otherwise act to undermine the very foundations of this system and would make juries ready weapons for officials to oppress those accused individuals who by chance are numbered among unpopular or inarticulate minorities.

The State of Texas in this instance appears to have made a sincere effort to obey this constitutional mandate in selecting the grand jury which indicted the Negro petitioner. Until this Court's decision in 1942 in *Hill v. State of Texas*, no Negro ever served on a grand jury in Dallas County, Texas, where this case arose. In an attempt to comply with that decision the three jury commissioners were careful here to appoint one Negro to the sixteen-member grand jury panel; he qualified and served on the twelve-man jury. Thus it cannot be said that Texas has systematically and completely excluded Negroes from the grand jury. But that fact alone does not guarantee compliance with the Fourteenth Amendment, however commendable may be the attempt. Racial limitation no less than racial exclusion in the formation of juries is an evil condemned by the equal protection clause. "The Amendment nullifies sophisticated as well as simple-minded modes of discrimination." This case must therefore be reviewed with that in mind.

Petitioner, as a Negro, "cannot claim, as matter of right, that his race shall have a representation on the jury," inasmuch as "a mixed jury in a particular case is not essential to the equal protection of the laws." But petitioner, as a human being endowed with all the rights specified in the Constitution, can claim that no racial or religious exclusion, limitation or other form of discrimination shall enter into the selection of any jury which indicts or tries him.

It follows that the State of Texas, in insisting upon one Negro representative on the grand jury panel, has respected no right belonging to petitioner. On the contrary, to the extent that this insistence amounts to a definite limitation of Negro grand jurors, a clear constitutional right has been directly invaded. The equal protection clause guarantees petitioner not only the right to have Negroes considered as prospective veniremen but also the right to have them considered without numerical or proportional limitation. If a jury is to be fairly chosen from a cross section of the community it must be done without limiting the number of persons of a particular color, racial background or faith — all of which are irrelevant factors in setting qualifications for jury service. This may in a particular instance result in the selection of one, six, twelve or even no Negroes on a jury panel. The important point, however, is that the selections must in no way be limited or restricted by such irrelevant factors.

In this case the State of Texas has candidly admitted before us "that none of the three (jury commissioners) intended to place more than one Negro upon the grand jury drawn by them." Commissioner Wells testified that "We had no intention of placing more than one Negro on the panel. When we did that we had finished with the Negro." In the words of Commissioner Tennant, "We three did not go to see any other Negroes, that is the only one. I did not have any intention of putting more than one on the list." Finally, as Commissioner Douglas stated, "Yes, sir, there were other Negroes' names mentioned besides the one we selected; we did not go talk to them; we liked this one, and our intentions were to get just one Negro on the grand jury; that is right. No, I did not have any intention of placing more than one Negro on the grand jury."

Clearer proof of intentional and deliberate limitation on the basis of color would be difficult to produce. The commissioners' declarations that they did not intend to discriminate and their other inconsistent statements cited by the Court fade into insignificance beside the admitted and obvious fact that they intended to and did limit the number of Negroes on the jury panel. By limiting the number to one they thereby excluded the possibility that two or more Negroes might be among the persons qualified to serve. All those except the one Negro were required to be of white color. At the same time, by insisting upon one Negro, they foreclosed the possibility of choosing sixteen white men on the panel. They refused, in brief, to disregard the factor of color in selecting the jury personnel. To that extent they have disregarded petitioner's right to the equal protection of the laws. To that extent they have ignored the ideals of the jury system. Our affirmance of this judgment thus tarnishes the fact that we of this nation are one people undivided in ability or freedom by differences in race, color or creed.

NOTES AND QUESTIONS

1. After describing the Fourteenth Amendment principle and legal precedents at issue, the Court states that it "cannot lightly be concluded that officers of the courts disregard this accepted standard of justice." Why not? Is there some kind of a presumption of regularity when state officials are accused of unconstitutional conduct? Would such a presumption affect the result here?

2. The Court also notes that because the evidence contains "certain inconsistencies and conflicts of testimony" it must show deference to "the trier of fact who heard the witnesses in full and observed their demeanor." This point is largely uncontroversial as a general matter. But is the predicate — testimonial inconsistencies and conflicts — accurate here?

CHAPTER III

POLICE INTERROGATION AND THE FIFTH AMENDMENT

This chapter focuses on the Fifth Amendment, particularly as it is implicated in the context of police interrogations of suspects and arrestees.

Section A examines the overall scope of the Fifth Amendment right—or as some would say, privilege—against self-incrimination. This section looks at the Supreme Court's requirement that the Amendment's protection applies only to conduct that is "testimonial or communicative" in nature; the extent to which the right can be abrogated by a government grant of immunity to a witness, compelling the witness to testify; and the rule preventing a prosecutor from impairing the exercise of the right by commenting on a defendant's decision not to testify in a criminal trial.

Section B considers the backdrop to the Supreme Court's seminal decision in *Miranda v. Arizona*, 384 U.S. 436 (1966), which imposed certain requirements on police interrogation in order to protect the Fifth Amendment rights of suspects and arrestees in police custody. The backdrop includes a look at a series of cases leading up to *Miranda* in which the Court considered due process challenges to confessions on the grounds that they were "involuntary," a mode of analysis mostly—but not totally—displaced by *Miranda*.

Section C looks at the *Miranda* decision.

Sections D and E examine how the *Miranda* decision was implemented in practice, largely in a manner that can charitably be described as "grudging." Section D looks at how the Court recognized exceptions to the *Miranda* requirements, and diluted the threshold prerequisites of the doctrine by narrowly defining the terms "interrogation" and "custody." Section E looks at the how the Court further weakened *Miranda*—or confined it, if you will—by making it easy to "waive" *Miranda* rights while at the same time making it hard to "invoke" *Miranda* rights.

Section F looks at the consequences of *Miranda* violations, including cases where police employed a "successive interrogation" technique designed to circumvent the obligation to provide *Miranda* warnings until they were essentially useless. This section also looks at cases where the Court held there could be no violation of *Miranda* unless a suspect's unwarned statement was introduced into evidence against the suspect in a trial.

Section G considers the durability of *Miranda*. Despite the stingy implementation of the doctrine in the decades after it squeaked into existence, and efforts by Congress to legislate it away, the core of *Miranda* was affirmed—almost enthusiastically—by a 7-2 vote of the Court in 2000, in a decision noting that *Miranda* warnings have become "part of our national culture." A 2022 decision by a much different Court, finding in a civil rights action that the constitutional requirement of *Miranda* warnings is not "law" under 42 U.S.C. § 1983, raises the prospect that the apparent entrenchment of *Miranda* in 2000 may have been fleeting.

A. SCOPE OF THE RIGHT AGAINST SELF-INCRIMINATION

This first case considers the requirement that the Fifth Amendment only applies to conduct that is "testimonial or communicative."

Schmerber v. California
384 U.S. 757 (1966)

Mr. Justice BRENNAN delivered the opinion of the Court.

Petitioner was convicted in Los Angeles Municipal Court of the criminal offense of driving an automobile while under the influence of intoxicating liquor. He had been arrested at a hospital while receiving treatment for injuries suffered in an accident involving the automobile that he had apparently been driving. At the direction of a police officer, a blood sample was then withdrawn from petitioner's body by a physician at the hospital. The chemical analysis of this sample revealed a percent by weight of alcohol in his blood at the time of the offense which indicated intoxication, and the report of this analysis was admitted in evidence at the trial. Petitioner objected to receipt of this evidence of the analysis on the ground that the blood had been withdrawn despite his refusal, on the advice of his counsel, to consent to the test. He contended that in that circumstance the withdrawal of the blood and the admission of the analysis in evidence denied him due process of law under the Fourteenth Amendment, as well as specific guarantees of the Bill of Rights secured against the States by that Amendment: his privilege against self-incrimination under the Fifth Amendment; his right to counsel under the Sixth Amendment; and his right not to be subjected to unreasonable searches and seizures in violation of the Fourth Amendment. The Appellate Department of the California Superior Court rejected these contentions and affirmed the conviction. We affirm.

THE PRIVILEGE AGAINST SELF-INCRIMINATION CLAIM

We therefore must now decide whether the withdrawal of the blood and admission in evidence of the analysis involved in this case violated petitioner's privilege. We hold that the privilege protects an accused only from being compelled to testify against himself, or otherwise provide the State with evidence of a testimonial or communicative nature, and that the withdrawal of blood and use of the analysis in question in this case did not involve compulsion to these ends.

It could not be denied that in requiring petitioner to submit to the withdrawal and chemical analysis of his blood the State compelled him to submit to an attempt to discover evidence that might be used to prosecute him for a criminal offense. He submitted only after the police officer rejected his objection and directed the physician to proceed. The officer's direction to the physician to administer the test over petitioner's objection constituted compulsion for the purposes of the privilege. The critical question, then, is whether petitioner was thus compelled "to be a witness against himself."

If the scope of the privilege coincided with the complex of values it helps to protect, we might be obliged to conclude that the privilege was violated. In *Miranda v. Arizona*, the Court said of the interests protected by the privilege: "All these policies point to one overriding thought: the constitutional foundation underlying the privilege is the respect a government — state or federal — must accord to the dignity and integrity of its citizens. To maintain a 'fair state-individual balance,' to require the government 'to shoulder the entire load,' . . . to respect the inviolability of the human personality, our accusatory system of criminal justice demands that the government seeking to punish an individual produce the evidence against him by its own independent labors, rather than by the cruel, simple expedient of compelling it from his own mouth." The withdrawal of blood necessarily involves puncturing the skin for extraction, and the percent by weight of alcohol in that blood, as established by chemical analysis, is evidence of criminal guilt. Compelled submission fails on one view to respect the "inviolability of the human personality." Moreover, since it enables the State to rely on evidence forced from the accused, the compulsion violates at least one meaning of the requirement that the State procure the evidence against an accused "by its own independent labors."

As the passage in *Miranda* implicitly recognizes, however, the privilege has never been given the full scope which the values it helps to protect suggest. History and a long line of authorities in lower courts have consistently limited its protection to situations in which the State seeks to submerge those values by obtaining the evidence against an accused through "the cruel, simple expedient of compelling it from his own mouth. . . . In sum, the privilege is fulfilled only when the person is guaranteed the right 'to remain silent unless he chooses to speak in the unfettered exercise of his own will.'" The leading case in this Court is *Holt v. United States*. There the question was whether evidence was admissible that the accused, prior to trial and over his protest, put on a blouse that fitted him. It was contended that compelling the accused to submit to the demand that he model the blouse violated the privilege. Mr. Justice Holmes, speaking for the Court, rejected the argument as "based upon an extravagant extension of the 5th Amendment," and went on to say: "(T)he prohibition of compelling a man in a criminal court to be witness against himself is a prohibition of the use of physical or moral compulsion to extort communications from him, not an exclusion of his body as evidence when it may be material. The objection in principle would forbid a jury to look at a prisoner and compare his features with a photograph in proof."

It is clear that the protection of the privilege reaches an accused's communications, whatever form they might take, and the compulsion of responses which are also communications, for example, compliance with a subpoena to produce one's papers. On the other hand, both federal and state courts have usually held that it offers no protection against compulsion to submit to fingerprinting, photographing, or measurements, to write or speak for identification, to appear in court, to stand, to assume a stance, to walk, or to make a particular gesture. The distinction which has emerged, often expressed in different ways, is that the privilege is a bar against compelling "communications" or "testimony," but that compulsion which makes a suspect or accused the source of "real or physical evidence" does not violate it.

Although we agree that this distinction is a helpful framework for analysis, we are not to be understood to agree with past applications in all instances. There will be many cases in which such a distinction is not readily drawn. Some tests seemingly directed to obtain "physical evidence," for example, lie detector tests measuring changes in body function during interrogation, may actually be directed to eliciting responses which are essentially testimonial. To compel a person to submit to testing in which an effort will be made to determine his guilt or innocence on the basis of physiological responses, whether willed or not, is to evoke the spirit and history of the Fifth Amendment. Such situations call to mind the principle that the protection of the privilege "is as broad as the mischief against which it seeks to guard."

In the present case, however, no such problem of application is presented. Not even a shadow of testimonial compulsion upon or enforced communication by the accused was involved either in the extraction or in the chemical analysis. Petitioner's testimonial capacities were in no way implicated; indeed, his participation, except as a donor, was irrelevant to the results of the test, which depend on chemical analysis and on that alone. Since the blood test evidence, although an incriminating product of compulsion, was neither petitioner's testimony nor evidence relating to some communicative act or writing by the petitioner, it was not inadmissible on privilege grounds.

• • •

Chapter III Police Interrogation and The Fifth Amendment

We thus conclude that the present record shows no violation of petitioner's right under the Fourth and Fourteenth Amendments to be free of unreasonable searches and seizures. It bears repeating, however, that we reach this judgment only on the facts of the present record. The integrity of an individual's person is a cherished value of our society. That we today hold that the Constitution does not forbid the States minor intrusions into an individual's body under stringently limited conditions in no way indicates that it permits more substantial intrusions, or intrusions under other conditions.

Affirmed.

NOTES AND QUESTIONS

1. The Court uses a lengthy quote from *Miranda*, decided one week earlier, to describe the values protected by the Fifth Amendment:

> All these policies point to one overriding thought: the constitutional foundation underlying the privilege is the respect a government — state or federal — must accord to the dignity and integrity of its citizens. To maintain a "fair state-individual balance," to require the government "to shoulder the entire load, . . . to respect the inviolability of the human personality, our accusatory system of criminal justice demands that the government seeking to punish an individual produce the evidence against him by its own independent labors, rather than by the cruel, simple expedient of compelling it from his own mouth."

Miranda, 384 U.S. at 460. The Court acknowledges, however, that the Fifth Amendment's language is narrower than its values, and only forbids compelling a person "to be a witness against himself." Here, the government was plainly not content to prosecute Schmerber by "its own independent labors."

After *Schmerber* was argued, Justice Brennan was purportedly unsure how he would vote. He ultimately voted to affirm and, according to Bernard Schwartz, Super Chief: Earl Warren and His Supreme Court — A Judicial Biography 594 (1983), he said that "a comprehensive opinion should be written limiting the scope of the Fifth Amendment. That, he felt, would soften the impact of the *Miranda* decision."

2. How persuasive as a matter of language and logic, if not precedent, is the Court's view that being "a witness" requires action that is testimonial or communicative in nature? What would the result be here if the scope of the privilege were "as broad as the mischief against which it seeks to guard," as the Court had described it in 1892 in *Counselman v. Hitchcock*, 142 U.S. 547, 562 (1892)?

3. Is there nonetheless an argument based even on the precedents the Court cites that the blood sample evidence at issue is testimonial? What do you make of Justice Black's argument in dissent that the entire purpose of the extraction of the blood sample was so that its characteristics could be used in the testimony of a witness against Schmerber?

4. Is the result here surprising given the civil libertarian reputation of the Warren Court and the physically coercive nature of the "compulsion" — described by Justice Fortas in dissent as "a tort" — in this context? To reach a contrary result here would the Court's decision in *Holt* have to be overturned? How about the cases requiring submission to fingerprinting, photographing, etc.?

5. Justice Douglas dissents on his view that both the Fourth and Fifth Amendment are animated by a "a right of privacy":

> We are dealing with the right of privacy which we have held to be within the penumbra of some specific guarantees of the Bill of Rights. *Griswold v. State of Connecticut*. Thus, the Fifth Amendment marks "a zone of privacy" which the Government may not force a person to surrender. Likewise the Fourth Amendment recognizes that right when it guarantees the right of

A. Scope of the Right Against Self-Incrimination **81**

the people to be secure "in their persons." No clearer invasion of this right of privacy can be imagined than forcible bloodletting of the kind involved here.

Why don't the nature of the intrusion and the right of privacy provide a basis for persuasively distinguishing *Holt*? Would a different result in *Schmerber* have fortified the notion of a constitutional right to a "zone of privacy" thereby bolstering the constitutionality of *Roe v. Wade*, 410 U.S. 113 (1973), decided just seven years later?

In *California v. Byers*, 402 U.S. 424 (1971), the Court upheld against a Fifth Amendment challenge a "hit and run" statute that required a motorist involved in a car accident to stop at the scene and give his name and address. The Court reasoned that the statute's purpose was primarily regulatory, and that an "organized society" necessarily imposes demands on its citizens — filing tax returns, making SEC disclosures, etc. — that create some risk of prosecution. It noted that in *United States v. Sullivan*, 274 U.S. 424 (1927), one among many anti-defendant Supreme Court cases from the Prohibition era, the Court had rejected the Fifth Amendment claim of a "bootlegger" who argued that listing his source of income on his tax return would incriminate him for violating the Volstead Act.

The California Supreme Court had upheld the statute by imposing a judicially created "use" restriction in any criminal prosecution where the state sought to offer evidence of statutory disclosures. Why isn't that an adequate result? For analysis of a different variety of a self-identification statute under the Fifth Amendment *see* Chapter IV, *infra* (discussing *Hiibel v. Sixth Judicial District of Nevada*, 542 U.S. 177 (2004)).

In *Pennsylvania v. Muniz*, 496 U.S. 582 (1990), the Court considered *Schmerber's* "testimonial" requirement in the context of the police's administration of sobriety tests to a DUI suspect who was under arrest but had not been read his *Miranda* warnings. The Court found that admission of the suspect's "slurred" responses to administrative questions (e.g., name, age, address) was nontestimonial as the statements were not being offered for their content but rather as something akin to physical evidence. *Id.* at 592. But the Court ruled otherwise regarding the suspect's inability to answer the question, "Do you know the date of your sixth birthday?" A response to this question, the Court held, was testimonial inasmuch as the answer by its content — and not simply by the manner of its delivery — incriminated the suspect. *Id.* at 594-98.

In the next case the Court considers the government's ability to circumvent the Fifth Amendment's requirements by granting immunity to a witness and thereby compelling the witness's testimony, a procedure that in theory should eliminate the possibility of the witness's prosecution based on the immunized testimony.

Kastigar v. United States
406 U.S. 441 (1972)

Mr. Justice POWELL delivered the opinion of the Court.

This case presents the question whether the United States Government may compel testimony from an unwilling witness, who invokes the Fifth Amendment privilege against compulsory self-incrimination, by conferring on the witness immunity from use of the compelled testimony in subsequent criminal proceedings, as well as immunity from use of evidence derived from the testimony.

Petitioners were subpoenaed to appear before a United States grand jury in the Central District of California on February 4, 1971. The Government believed that petitioners were likely to assert their Fifth Amendment privilege. Prior to the scheduled appearances, the Government applied to the District Court for an order directing petitioners to answer questions and produce evidence before the grand jury under a grant of immunity conferred pursuant to 18 U.S.C. ss 6002, 6003. Petitioners opposed issuance of the order, contending primarily that the scope of the immunity provided by the statute was not coextensive with the scope of the privilege against self-incrimination, and therefore was not sufficient to supplant the privilege and compel their testimony. The District Court rejected this contention, and ordered petitioners to appear before the grand jury and answer its questions under the grant of immunity.

Petitioners appeared but refused to answer questions, asserting their privilege against compulsory self-incrimination. They were brought before the District Court, and each persisted in his refusal to answer the grand jury's questions, notwithstanding the grant of immunity. The court found both in contempt, and committed them to the custody of the Attorney General until either they answered the grand jury's questions or the term of the grand jury expired. The Court of Appeals for the Ninth Circuit affirmed. This Court granted certiorari to resolve the important question whether testimony may be compelled by granting immunity from the use of compelled testimony and evidence derived therefrom ("use and derivative use" immunity), or whether it is necessary to grant immunity from prosecution for offenses to which compelled testimony relates ("transactional" immunity).

I

The power of government to compel persons to testify in court or before grand juries and other governmental agencies is firmly established in Anglo-American jurisprudence. The power with respect to courts was established by statute in England as early as 1562, and Lord Bacon observed in 1612 that all subjects owed the King their "knowledge and discovery." While it is not clear when grand juries first resorted to compulsory process to secure the attendance and testimony of witnesses, the general common-law principle that "the public has a right to every man's evidence" was considered an "indubitable certainty" that "cannot be denied" by 1742. The power to compel testimony, and the corresponding duty to testify, are recognized in the Sixth Amendment requirements that an accused be confronted with the witnesses against him, and have compulsory process for obtaining witnesses in his favor. The first Congress recognized the testimonial duty in the Judiciary Act of 1789, which provided for compulsory attendance of witnesses in the federal courts. Mr. Justice White noted the importance of this essential power of government in his concurring opinion in *Murphy v. Waterfront Comm'n* (1964):

> Among the necessary and most important of the powers of the States as well as the Federal Government to assure the effective functioning of government in an ordered society is the broad power to compel residents to testify in court or before grand juries or agencies. Such testimony constitutes one of the Government's primary sources of information.

But the power to compel testimony is not absolute. There are a number of exemptions from the testimonial duty, the most important of which is the Fifth Amendment privilege against compulsory self-incrimination. The privilege reflects a complex of our fundamental values and aspirations, and marks an important advance in the development of our liberty. It can be asserted in any proceeding, civil or criminal, administrative or judicial, investigatory or adjudicatory; and it protects against any disclosures which the witness reasonably believes could be used in a criminal prosecution or could lead to other evidence that might be so used. This Court has been zealous to safeguard the values which underlie the privilege.

Immunity statutes, which have historical roots deep in Anglo-American jurisprudence, are not incompatible with these values. Rather, they seek a rational accommodation between the imperatives of the privilege and the legitimate demands of government to compel citizens to testify. The existence of these statutes reflects the importance of testimony, and the fact that many offenses are of such a character that the only persons capable of giving useful testimony are those implicated in the crime. Indeed, their origins were in the context of such offenses, and their primary use has been to investigate such offenses. Congress included immunity statutes in many of the regulatory measures adopted in the first half of this century. Indeed, prior to the enactment of the statute under consideration in this case, there were in force over 50 federal immunity statutes. In addition, every State in the Union, as well as the District of Columbia and Puerto Rico, has one or more such statutes. The commentators, and this Court on several occasions, have characterized immunity statutes as essential to the effective enforcement of various criminal statutes. As Mr. Justice Frankfurter observed, such statutes have "become part of our constitutional fabric."

II

Petitioners contend, first, that the Fifth Amendment's privilege against compulsory self-incrimination, which is that "(n)o person . . . shall be compelled in any criminal case to be a witness against himself," deprives Congress of power to enact laws that compel self-incrimination, even if complete immunity from prosecution is granted prior to the compulsion of the incriminatory testimony. In other words, petitioners assert that no immunity statute, however drawn, can afford a lawful basis for compelling incriminatory testimony. They ask us to reconsider and overrule *Brown v. Walker* (1896), and *Ullmann v. United States, supra,* decisions that uphold the constitutionality of immunity statutes.

We find no merit to this contention and reaffirm the decisions in *Brown* and *Ullmann.*

III

Petitioners' second contention is that the scope of immunity provided by the federal witness immunity statute, 18 U.S.C. s 6002, is not coextensive with the scope of the Fifth Amendment privilege against compulsory self-incrimination, and therefore is not sufficient to supplant the privilege and compel testimony over a claim of the privilege. The statute provides that when a witness is compelled by district court order to testify over a claim of the privilege:

> the witness may not refuse to comply with the order on the basis of his privilege against self-incrimination; but no testimony or other information compelled under the order (or any information directly or indirectly derived from such testimony or other information) may be used against the witness in any criminal case, except a prosecution for perjury, giving a false statement, or otherwise failing to comply with the order.

The constitutional inquiry, rooted in logic and history, as well as in the decisions of this Court, is whether the immunity granted under this statute is coextensive with the scope of the privilege. If so, petitioners' refusals to answer based on the privilege were unjustified, and the judgments of contempt were proper, for the grant of immunity has removed the dangers against which the privilege protects. If, on the other hand, the immunity granted is not as comprehensive as the protection afforded by the privilege, petitioners were justified in refusing to answer, and the judgments of contempt must be vacated.

Petitioners draw a distinction between statutes that provide transactional immunity and those that provide, as does the statute before us, immunity from use and derivative use. They contend that a statute must at a minimum grant full transactional immunity in order to be coextensive with the scope of the privilege. In support of this contention, they rely on

Counselman v. Hitchcock (1892), the first case in which this Court considered a constitutional challenge to an immunity statute. The statute, a reenactment of the Immunity Act of 1868, provided that no "evidence obtained from a party or witness by means of a judicial proceeding . . . shall be given in evidence, or in any manner used against him . . . in any court of the United States. . . ." Notwithstanding a grant of immunity and order to testify under the revised 1868 Act, the witness, asserting his privilege against compulsory self-incrimination, refused to testify before a federal grand jury. He was consequently adjudged in contempt of court. On appeal, this Court construed the statute as affording a witness protection only against the use of the specific testimony compelled from him under the grant of immunity. This construction meant that the statute "could not, and would not, prevent the use of his testimony to search out other testimony to be used in evidence against him." Since the revised 1868 Act, as construed by the Court, would permit the use against the immunized witness of evidence derived from his compelled testimony, it did not protect the witness to the same extent that a claim of the privilege would protect him. Accordingly, under the principle that a grant of immunity cannot supplant the privilege, and is not sufficient to compel testimony over a claim of the privilege, unless the scope of the grant of immunity is coextensive with the scope of the privilege, the witness' refusal to testify was held proper. In the course of its opinion, the Court made the following statement, on which petitioners heavily rely:

> We are clearly of opinion that no statute which leaves the party or witness subject to prosecution after he answers the criminating question put to him, can have the effect of supplanting the privilege conferred by the Constitution of the United States. (The immunity statute under consideration) does not supply a complete protection from all the perils against which the constitutional prohibition was designed to guard, and is not a full substitute for that prohibition. In view of the constitutional provision, a statutory enactment, to be valid, must afford absolute immunity against future prosecution for the offence to which the question relates.

Sixteen days after the *Counselman* decision, a new immunity bill was introduced by Senator Cullom, who urged that enforcement of the Interstate Commerce Act would be impossible in the absence of an effective immunity statute. The bill, which became the Compulsory Testimony Act of 1893, was drafted specifically to meet the broad language in *Counselman* set forth above. The new Act removed the privilege against self-incrimination in hearings before the Interstate Commerce Commission and provided that:

> no person shall be prosecuted or subjected to any penalty or forfeiture for or on account of any transaction, matter or thing, concerning which he may testify, or produce evidence, documentary or otherwise . . . .

This transactional immunity statute became the basic form for the numerous federal immunity statutes until 1970, when, after re-examining applicable constitutional principles and the adequacy of existing law, Congress enacted the statute here under consideration. The new statute, which does not "afford (the) absolute immunity against future prosecution" referred to in *Counselman*, was drafted to meet what Congress judged to be the conceptual basis of *Counselman*, as elaborated in subsequent decisions of the Court, namely, that immunity from the use of compelled testimony and evidence derived therefrom is coextensive with the scope of the privilege.

The statute's explicit proscription of the use in any criminal case of "testimony or other information compelled under the order (or any information directly or indirectly derived from such testimony or other information)" is consonant with Fifth Amendment standards. We hold that such immunity from use and derivative use is coextensive with the scope of the privilege against self-incrimination, and therefore is sufficient to compel testimony over a claim of the privilege. While a grant of immunity must afford protection commensurate with that afforded by the privilege, it need not be broader. Transactional immunity, which accords full immunity from prosecution for the offense to which the compelled testimony relates, affords the witness considerably broader protection than does the Fifth Amendment privilege. The privilege has never been construed to mean that one who invokes it cannot subsequently be prosecuted. Its sole concern is to afford protection against being "forced to give testimony leading to the infliction of 'penalties affixed to . . . criminal acts.'" Immunity from the use of compelled testimony, as well as evidence derived directly and indirectly therefrom, affords this protection. It prohibits the prosecutorial authorities from using the compelled testimony in any respect, and it therefore insures that the testimony cannot lead to the infliction of criminal penalties on the witness.

Our holding is consistent with the conceptual basis of *Counselman*. The *Counselman* statute, as construed by the Court, was plainly deficient in its failure to prohibit the use against the immunized witness of evidence derived from his compelled testimony. The Court repeatedly emphasized this deficiency, noting that the statute:

> could not, and would not, prevent the use of his testimony to search out other testimony to be used in evidence against him or his property, in a criminal proceeding . . . ;

that it:

> could not prevent the obtaining and the use of witnesses and evidence which should be attributable directly to the testimony he might give under compulsion and on which he might be convicted, when otherwise, and if he had refused to answer, he could not possibly have been convicted, ibid.;

and that it:

> affords no protection against that use of compelled testimony which consists in gaining therefrom a knowledge of the details of a crime, and of sources of information which may supply other means of convicting the witness or party.

The basis of the Court's decision was recognized in *Ullmann v. United States* (1956), in which the Court reiterated that the *Counselman* statute was insufficient:

> because the immunity granted was incomplete, in that it merely forbade the use of the testimony given and failed to protect a witness from future prosecution based on knowledge and sources of information obtained from the compelled testimony.

IV

Although an analysis of prior decisions and the purpose of the Fifth Amendment privilege indicates that use and derivative-use immunity is coextensive with the privilege, we must consider additional arguments advanced by petitioners against the sufficiency of such immunity. We start from the premise, repeatedly affirmed by this Court, that an appropriately broad immunity grant is compatible with the Constitution.

Petitioners argue that use and derivative-use immunity will not adequately protect a witness from various possible incriminating uses of the compelled testimony: for example, the prosecutor or other law enforcement officials may obtain leads, names of witnesses, or other information not otherwise available that might result in a prosecution. It will be difficult and perhaps impossible, the argument goes, to identify, by testimony or cross-examination, the subtle ways in which the compelled testimony may disadvantage a witness, especially in the jurisdiction granting the immunity.

This argument presupposes that the statute's prohibition will prove impossible to enforce. The statute provides a sweeping proscription of any use, direct or indirect, of the compelled testimony and any information derived therefrom:

> (N)o testimony or other information compelled under the order (or any information directly or indirectly derived from such testimony or other information) may be used against the witness in any criminal case. . . .

This total prohibition on use provides a comprehensive safeguard, barring the use of compelled testimony as an "investigatory lead," and also barring the use of any evidence obtained by focusing investigation on a witness as a result of his compelled disclosures.

A person accorded this immunity under 18 U.S.C. s 6002, and subsequently prosecuted, is not dependent for the preservation of his rights upon the integrity and good faith of the prosecuting authorities.

This burden of proof, which we reaffirm as appropriate, is not limited to a negation of taint; rather, it imposes on the prosecution the affirmative duty to prove that the evidence it proposes to use is derived from a legitimate source wholly independent of the compelled testimony.

This is very substantial protection, commensurate with that resulting from invoking the privilege itself. The privilege assures that a citizen is not compelled to incriminate himself by his own testimony. It usually operates to allow a citizen to remain silent when asked a question requiring an incriminatory answer. This statute, which operates after a witness has given incriminatory testimony, affords the same protection by assuring that the compelled testimony can in no way lead to the infliction of criminal penalties. The statute, like the Fifth Amendment, grants neither pardon nor amnesty. Both the statute and the Fifth Amendment allow the government to prosecute using evidence from legitimate independent sources.

The statutory proscription is analogous to the Fifth Amendment requirement in cases of coerced confessions. A coerced confession, as revealing of leads as testimony given in exchange for immunity, is inadmissible in a criminal trial, but it does not bar prosecution. Moreover, a defendant against whom incriminating evidence has been obtained through a grant of immunity may be in a stronger position at trial than a defendant who asserts a Fifth Amendment coerced-confession claim. One raising a claim under this statute need only show that he testified under a grant of immunity in order to shift to the government the heavy burden of proving that all of the evidence it proposes to use was derived from legitimate independent sources. On the other hand, a defendant raising a coerced-confession claim under the Fifth Amendment must first prevail in a voluntariness hearing before his confession and evidence derived from it become inadmissible.

There can be no justification in reason or policy for holding that the Constitution requires an amnesty grant where, acting pursuant to statute and accompanying safeguards, testimony is compelled in exchange for immunity from use and derivative use when no such amnesty is required where the government, acting without colorable right, coerces a defendant into incriminating himself.

We conclude that the immunity provided by 18 U.S.C. s 6002 leaves the witness and the prosecutorial authorities in substantially the same position as if the witness had claimed the Fifth Amendment privilege. The immunity therefore is coextensive with the privilege and suffices to supplant it. The judgment of the Court of Appeals for the Ninth Circuit accordingly is

Affirmed.

[Justice Douglas dissented.]

Mr. Justice MARSHALL, dissenting.

Today the Court holds that the United States may compel a witness to give incriminating testimony, and subsequently prosecute him for crimes to which that testimony relates. I cannot believe the Fifth Amendment permits that result.

The Fifth Amendment gives a witness an absolute right to resist interrogation, if the testimony sought would tend to incriminate him. A grant of immunity may strip the witness of the right to refuse to testify, but only if it is broad enough to eliminate all possibility that the testimony will in fact operate to incriminate him. It must put him in precisely the same position, vis-a-vis the government that has compelled his testimony, as he would have been in had he remained silent in reliance on the privilege.

The Court recognizes that an immunity statute must be tested by that standard, that the relevant inquiry is whether it "leaves the witness and the prosecutorial authorities in substantially the same position as if the witness had claimed the Fifth Amendment privilege." I assume, moreover, that in theory that test would be met by a complete ban on the use of the compelled testimony, including all derivative, use, however remote and indirect. But I cannot agree that a ban on use will in practice be total, if it remains open for the government to convict the witness on the basis of evidence derived from a legitimate independent source. The Court asserts that the witness is adequately protected by a rule imposing on the government a heavy burden of proof if it would establish the independent character of evidence to be used against the witness. But in light of the inevitable uncertainties of the fact-finding process, a greater margin of protection is required in order to provide a reliable guarantee that the witness is in exactly the same position as if he had not testified. That margin can be provided only by immunity from prosecution for the offenses to which the testimony relates, i.e., transactional immunity.

I do not see how it can suffice merely to put the burden of proof on the government. First, contrary to the Court's assertion, the Court's rule does leave the witness "dependent for the preservation of his rights upon the integrity and good faith of the prosecuting authorities." For the information relevant to the question of taint is uniquely within the knowledge of the prosecuting authorities. They alone are in a position to trace the chains of information and investigation that lead to the evidence to be used in a criminal prosecution. A witness who suspects that his compelled testimony was used to develop a lead will be hard pressed indeed to ferret out the evidence necessary to prove it. And of course it is no answer to say he need not prove it, for though the Court puts the burden of proof on the government, the government will have no difficulty in meeting its burden by mere assertion if the witness produces no contrary evidence. The good faith of the prosecuting authorities is thus the sole safeguard of the witness' rights. Second, even their good faith is not a sufficient safeguard. For the paths of information through the investigative bureaucracy may well be long and winding, and even a prosecutor acting in the best of faith cannot be certain that somewhere in the depths of his investigative apparatus, often including hundreds of employees, there was not some prohibited use of the compelled testimony. The Court today sets out a loose net to trap tainted evidence and prevent its use against the witness, but it accepts an intolerably great risk that tainted evidence will in fact slip through that net.

In my view the Court turns reason on its head when it compares a statutory grant of immunity to the "immunity" that is inadvertently conferred by an unconstitutional interrogation. The exclusionary rule of evidence that applies in that situation has nothing whatever to do with this case. Evidence obtained through a coercive interrogation, like evidence obtained through an illegal search, is excluded at trial because the Constitution prohibits such methods of gathering evidence. The exclusionary rules provide a partial and inadequate remedy to some victims of illegal police conduct, and a similarly partial and inadequate deterrent to police officers. An immunity statute, on the other hand, is much more ambitious than any exclusionary rule. It does not merely attempt to provide a remedy for past police misconduct, which never should have occurred. An immunity statute operates in advance of the event, and it authorizes — even encourages — interrogation that would otherwise be prohibited by the Fifth Amendment. An immunity statute thus differs from an exclusionary rule of evidence in at least two critical respects.

First, because an immunity statute gives constitutional approval to the resulting interrogation, the government is under an obligation here to remove the danger of incrimination completely and absolutely, whereas in the case of the exclusionary rules it may be sufficient to shield the witness from the fruits of the illegal search or interrogation in a partial and reasonably adequate manner. For when illegal police conduct has occurred, the exclusion of evidence does not purport to purge the conduct of its unconstitutional character. The constitutional violation remains, and may provide the basis for other relief, such as a civil action for or a criminal prosecution of the responsible officers (see 18 U.S.C. ss 241, 242). The Constitution does not authorize police officers to coerce confessions or to invade privacy without cause, so long as no use is made of the evidence they obtain. But this Court has held that the Constitution does authorize the government to compel a witness to give potentially incriminating testimony, so long as no incriminating use is made of the resulting evidence. Before the government puts its seal of approval on such an interrogation, it must provide an absolutely reliable guarantee that it will not use the testimony in any way at all in aid of prosecution of the witness. The only way to provide that guarantee is to give the witness immunity from prosecution for crimes to which his testimony relates.

Second, because an immunity statute operates in advance of the interrogation, there is room to require a broad grant of transactional immunity without imperiling large numbers of otherwise valid convictions. An exclusionary rule comes into play after the interrogation or search has occurred; and the decision to question or to search is often made in haste, under pressure, by an officer who is not a lawyer. If an unconstitutional interrogation or search were held to create transactional immunity, that might well be regarded as an excessively high price to pay for the "constable's blunder." An immunity statute, on the other hand, creates a framework in which the prosecuting attorney can make a calm and reasoned decision whether to compel testimony and suffer the resulting ban on prosecution, or to forgo the testimony.

For both these reasons it is clear to me that an immunity statute must be tested by a standard far more demanding than that appropriate for an exclusionary rule fashioned to deal with past constitutional violations. Measured by that standard, the statute approved today by the Court fails miserably. I respectfully dissent.

NOTES AND QUESTIONS

1. The Court describes the rule that "the public has a right to every man's evidence" as a "common law principle." What does this mean? Does the rule exist independently of statutory authority for a public body — a court, an agency, a legislative committee — to subpoena witnesses to testify? Is the rule of constitutional dimension?

2. The Court notes the longstanding history of immunity statutes and the rule established in *Counselman v. Hitchcock* that the Fifth Amendment requires an immunity statute to "afford absolute immunity against future prosecution for the offence to which the question relates." 142 U.S. at 585-86. Thus so-called transactional immunity became the normal price the government had to pay for compelling testimony from 1892 to 1970.

Is the *Counselman* formulation of a "transactional immunity" rule self-executing? Does it depend on the proceeding in which the testimony is given? Will it always be obvious, for example, in the sometimes freewheeling and sprawling arena of a grand jury investigation, *see* Chapter VII *infra*, what "offence" a question relates to?

Note also that one of the government's concerns about transactional immunity was that savvy and gutsy witnesses could, upon receiving immunity, attempt to take an "immunity bath" by testifying to crimes not directly related to the prosecutor's inquiry.

3. The Court concludes that the new 1970 federal immunity statute, 18 U.S.C. §§ 6002-6003, satisfies the Fifth Amendment even though it only prohibits the use and derivative use of immunized testimony. It describes transactional immunity as providing a witness with "considerably broader protection" than the Fifth Amendment. Do you agree? Wouldn't a textual interpretation of the Fifth Amendment prohibit immunity altogether in criminal cases, in that even where a witness is immunized he is still "providing evidence against himself"?

On the other hand, can you think of circumstances where a prohibition on the use and derivative use of immunized testimony might provide greater protection than transactional immunity? Consider an immunized gang member's testimony in a grand jury investigation of a gang murder where the gang member testifies about the structure and operations of the gang. Would transactional immunity necessarily prohibit the use of such testimony in a subsequent prosecution of the witness on drug charges arising out of his gang activities?

4. The Court doesn't mention the one-sided nature of the immunity statute, an asymmetry of which defense attorneys are keenly aware. Under 18 U.S.C. § 6003 only the Department of Justice is authorized to obtain an order immunizing a witness and compelling his testimony. This gives the government a powerful investigative tool to obtain testimony from witnesses who will help the government's case. The defense, on the other hand, can only in the rarest of circumstances prevail on a court to authorize immunity for a defense witness. *See* Leonard N. Sosnov, *Separation of Powers Shell Game: The Federal Witness Immunity Act*, 73 Temp. L. Rev. 171, 213-14 (2000) (discussing the extremely narrow circumstances where a defendant can obtain judicially ordered use immunity for a defense witness).

Consider a health care fraud investigation where sales representatives have engaged in illegal sales activity but disagree about whether the illegal practices were known to senior management. The government can immunize the witnesses who admit the practices were known to management and stealthily imply that the witnesses who dispute this view might be committing perjury — whether or not it truly believes they are lying — so that they will be afraid to testify. Accordingly, if senior executives are prosecuted, they will likely be unable to adduce favorable testimony from the nervous representatives, who will assert the Fifth Amendment to protect themselves.

5. In *New Jersey v. Portash*, 440 U.S. 450 (1979), the Court held that the Fifth Amendment prohibited the government from using immunized testimony to impeach a defendant. The government had relied on the Court's decision in *Harris v. New York*, 401 U.S. 222 (1971), *see infra*, that a defendant could be impeached by statements he had made in a confession that had been ruled inadmissible because he had not been given proper *Miranda* warnings. The Court in *Portash*, however, said that the "crucial distinction" between the two situations was the issue of coercion: "Testimony given in response to a grant of immunity is the essence of coerced testimony."

OLIVER'S ARMY

In *United States v. North*, 910 F.2d 843 (D.C. Cir. 1990), the D.C. Circuit grappled with the "heavy burden" the government would have to discharge under *Kastigar* in proving the absence of "taint" if it elects to prosecute someone who had given immunized testimony. This case illustrates the concerns expressed by Justice Marshall in his *Kastigar* dissent about the "good faith" of prosecutors and "the inevitable uncertainties of the fact-finding process."

In November of 1986, a Lebanese newspaper reported that the United States had secretly and illegally sold weapons to Iran. Congress immediately established two committees charged with investigating the sales of arms to Iran, the diversion of proceeds therefrom to rebels (or "Contras") fighting in Nicaragua, and the attempted cover-up of these activities.

The saga, which was in the news almost daily for almost two years, became popularly if unpoetically known as "the Iran/Contra affair."

At the center of things was Lieutenant Colonel Oliver L. North, a former member of the National Security Council (NSC) staff. *Id.* at 851. When North was subpoenaed to testify before the Iran/Contra congressional committees he asserted his Fifth Amendment rights, but the government compelled his testimony by a grant of use immunity pursuant to 18 U.S.C. § 6002. Thus immunized, North testified for six days. His testimony was carried live on national television and radio, replayed on news shows, and analyzed in the public media. *Id.*

Contemporaneously with the congressional investigation, and pursuant to the Independent Counsel statute, 28 U.S.C. §§ 591-599, the Special Division of the D.C. Circuit appointed Lawrence E. Walsh as Independent Counsel (IC) and charged him with the investigation and prosecution of any criminal wrongdoing by government officials in the Iran/Contra events. As a result of the efforts of the IC, North was indicted and tried on 12 counts arising from his role in the Iran/Contra affair. After extensive pretrial proceedings and a 12-week trial, North was convicted in May of 1989 on 3 counts: aiding and abetting an endeavor to obstruct Congress in violation of 18 U.S.C. §§ 1505 and 2 ("Count 6"); destroying, altering, or removing official NSC documents in violation of 18 U.S.C. § 2071 ("Count 9"); and accepting an illegal gratuity, consisting of a security system for his home, in violation of 18 U.S.C. § 201(c)(1)(B) ("Count 10").

North appealed his convictions on multiple grounds, including that his prosecution was tainted by the government's indirect use of his congressional testimony in violation of 18 U.S.C. § 6002 and *Kastigar.* The D.C. Circuit reversed the convictions. It found that the trial court insufficiently discharged its responsibilities under *Kastigar* to hold the government to its "heavy burden" of proving the absence of taint. Further, while the D.C. Circuit acknowledged that the prosecution team scrupulously avoided any exposure to the North testimony, it found that multiple government witnesses had their memories refreshed by North's testimony, which in itself was a fatal "indirect use" of the testimony. The Court also noted that the IC had warned Congress in advance not to immunize witnesses as any such grants of immunity "would create serious — and perhaps insurmountable — barriers to the prosecution of immunized witnesses." *Id.* at 863.

Do you think North was prosecuted, at least in part, due to the dynamic that the prosecutor was an appointed Independent Counsel who was specifically charged with "the investigation and prosecution of any criminal wrongdoing by government officials in the Iran/Contra Affair"?

Put differently, do you think the United States Attorney for the District of Columbia would have prosecuted North?

What level of deference, if any, should a prosecutor have afforded the congressional decision to immunize North?

Chapter IX, *infra*, includes a section on the "Independent Prosecutor Problem."

On its terms the Fifth Amendment speaks not to "testimony" but to the act of being a "witness": "No person . . . shall be compelled to be a witness against himself." But does the Fifth Amendment apply to a court order or other compulsory process requiring the production of documents or other tangible items? For a long time the answer was yes. In *Boyd v. United States*, 116 U.S. 616 (1886), the Supreme Court held that a court order requiring a partnership to produce an incriminating invoice in connection with a civil forfeiture proceeding was a violation of the Fifth Amendment inasmuch as it compelled the owner of the papers to be a witness against himself. *Id.* at 634-35. (*Boyd* also held that the order worked a violation of the Fourth Amendment as the invoice was a private paper. *Id.*)

Boyd was eventually drained of all meaning, gradually then suddenly, beginning with a pair of Fourth Amendment cases. *Warden v. Hayden*, 387 U.S. 294 (1967), overruled *Gouled v. United States*, 255 U.S. 298 (1921), and allowed for searches for mere evidence of crime and not just fruits or instrumentalities. *Andresen v. Maryland*, 427 U.S. 463 (1976), subsequently held that a search warrant for potentially incriminating private papers did not independently offend the Fifth Amendment. On the Fifth Amendment front, two cases from the 1960s clarified that the Fifth Amendment protects against only compelled communications or testimony, but not obtaining incriminating evidence from the suspect. *See United States v. Wade*, 388 U.S. 218, 221-23 (1967) (holding that compelled participation in lineup did not violate Fifth Amendment); *Schmerber, supra*, 384 U.S. 757, 767 (1966) (holding withdrawal of defendant's blood sample is not violative of Fifth Amendment). On another Fifth Amendment front, the Court held that neither collective entities nor their individual representatives are shielded from the compelled production of records of the entity on Fifth Amendment grounds. *See Bellis v. United States*, 417 U.S. 85, 88 (1974) (ruling that artificial entities, such as corporations, do not have Fifth Amendment privilege); *Braswell v. United States*, 487 U.S. 99, 103-04 (1988) (reaffirming that the longstanding "collective entities doctrine" remained valid and unaffected by new analyses of document production in *Fisher* and *Doe I*).

The "suddenly" aspect of *Boyd*'s demise came in *Fisher v. United States*, 425 U.S. 391 (1976), where the Court explicitly renounced *Boyd* in considering the application of the Fifth Amendment to IRS summonses served on two attorneys directing them to produce accountants' workpapers relating to the attorneys' clients. *Id.* at 394-95. The Court found that the summonses did not violate the Fifth Amendment for multiple reasons: (1) no testimonial communications or authentication of the papers were required of the clients; (2) the documents were the accountants' papers, not the clients, and had been prepared by the accountants; (3) the papers were prepared voluntarily; and (4) the existence of the papers was known to the government. *Id.* at 409-14.

But the Court went beyond this holding and attempted to articulate a framework for what has become known as the "act of production" doctrine, based on the recognition that producing evidence does have certain "communicative aspects of its own." *Id.* at 410. These include the tacit admissions that the requested material exists, is in the possession or control of the order recipient, and is responsive to what the order requests. *Id.* The determination of whether, in light of these issues, the act of production is both "testimonial" and "incriminating," the Court stated, will depend on the facts and circumstances of individual cases. On the facts in *Fisher*, however, the Court found that production required no testimonial communication because (1) the existence of the documents was a foregone conclusion, (2) responding to the summons would not require the client to authenticate the documents, and (3) there was nothing incriminating in the client seeking accounting or legal assistance in connection with his tax returns. *Id.* at 411-13.

Fisher explicitly declined to rule whether the Fifth Amendment would protect a taxpayer from having to produce his own tax records. *Id.* at 414. That question was answered eight years later in *United States v. Doe*, 465 U.S. 605 (1984) (*Doe I*). *Doe I* held that the contents of voluntarily prepared business records had no Fifth Amendment protection from production in response to grand jury subpoenas. *Id.* at 610-11. Because the documents' creation was not compelled, there was no Fifth Amendment violation. *Id.* As to the "act of production" raised in *Fisher*, however, the Court deferred—without analysis or explanation—to the district court's finding, with which the court of appeals agreed, that producing the documents would have communicated the records' existence and authenticity, and that they were in the possession of the recipient. *Id.* at 614. The government had conceded, moreover, that the documents were potentially incriminating. *Id.* at 608. Accordingly, the Court held that production of the

Chapter III Police Interrogation and The Fifth Amendment

documents would be required only by a grant of act of production immunity under 18 U.S.C. §§ 6002 and 6003.

In sum, the contours of the "act of production" doctrine were substantially uncertain when Independent Counsel Kenneth Starr sought to press the matter in the D.C. Circuit and then the Supreme Court in response to an assertion of the Fifth Amendment by an Arkansas lawyer named Webster Hubbell.

United States v. Hubbell
530 U.S. 27 (2000)

Justice STEVENS delivered the opinion of the Court.

The two questions presented concern the scope of a witness' protection against compelled self-incrimination: (1) whether the Fifth Amendment privilege protects a witness from being compelled to disclose the existence of incriminating documents that the Government is unable to describe with reasonable particularity; and (2) if the witness produces such documents pursuant to a grant of immunity, whether 18 U.S.C. § 6002 prevents the Government from using them to prepare criminal charges against him.

I

This proceeding arises out of the second prosecution of respondent, Webster Hubbell, commenced by the Independent Counsel appointed in August 1994 to investigate possible violations of federal law relating to the Whitewater Development Corporation. The first prosecution was terminated pursuant to a plea bargain. In December 1994, respondent pleaded guilty to charges of mail fraud and tax evasion arising out of his billing practices as a member of an Arkansas law firm from 1989 to 1992, and was sentenced to 21 months in prison. In the plea agreement, respondent promised to provide the Independent Counsel with "full, complete, accurate, and truthful information" about matters relating to the Whitewater investigation.

The second prosecution resulted from the Independent Counsel's attempt to determine whether respondent had violated that promise. In October 1996, while respondent was incarcerated, the Independent Counsel served him with a subpoena duces tecum calling for the production of 11 categories of documents before a grand jury sitting in Little Rock, Arkansas. On November 19, he appeared before the grand jury and invoked his Fifth Amendment privilege against self-incrimination. In response to questioning by the prosecutor, respondent initially refused "to state whether there are documents within my possession, custody, or control responsive to the Subpoena." App. 62. Thereafter, the prosecutor produced an order, which had previously been obtained from the District Court pursuant to 18 U.S.C. § 6003(a), directing him to respond to the subpoena and granting him immunity "to the extent allowed by law." Respondent then produced 13,120 pages of documents and records and responded to a series of questions that established that those were all of the documents in his custody or control that were responsive to the commands in the subpoena, with the exception of a few documents he claimed were shielded by the attorney-client and attorney work-product privileges.

The contents of the documents produced by respondent provided the Independent Counsel with the information that led to this second prosecution. On April 30, 1998, a grand jury in the District of Columbia returned a 10-count indictment charging respondent with various tax-related crimes and mail and wire fraud. The District Court dismissed the indictment relying, in part, on the ground that the Independent Counsel's use of the subpoenaed documents

A. Scope of the Right Against Self-Incrimination

violated § 6002 because all of the evidence he would offer against respondent at trial derived either directly or indirectly from the testimonial aspects of respondent's immunized act of producing those documents. Noting that the Independent Counsel had admitted that he was not investigating tax-related issues when he issued the subpoena, and that he had "'learned about the unreported income and other crimes from studying the records' contents,'" the District Court characterized the subpoena as "the quintessential fishing expedition."

The Court of Appeals vacated the judgment and remanded for further proceedings. The majority concluded that the District Court had incorrectly relied on the fact that the Independent Counsel did not have prior knowledge of the contents of the subpoenaed documents. The question the District Court should have addressed was the extent of the Government's independent knowledge of the documents' existence and authenticity, and of respondent's possession or control of them. It explained:

> On remand, the district court should hold a hearing in which it seeks to establish the extent and detail of the [G]overnment's knowledge of Hubbell's financial affairs (or of the paperwork documenting it) on the day the subpoena issued. It is only then that the court will be in a position to assess the testimonial value of Hubbell's response to the subpoena. Should the Independent Counsel prove capable of demonstrating with reasonable particularity a prior awareness that the exhaustive litany of documents sought in the subpoena existed and were in Hubbell's possession, then the wide distance evidently traveled from the subpoena to the substantive allegations contained in the indictment would be based upon legitimate intermediate steps. To the extent that the information conveyed through Hubbell's compelled act of production provides the necessary linkage, however, the indictment deriving therefrom is tainted.

In the opinion of the dissenting judge, the majority failed to give full effect to the distinction between the contents of the documents and the limited testimonial significance of the act of producing them. In his view, as long as the prosecutor could make use of information contained in the documents or derived therefrom without any reference to the fact that respondent had produced them in response to a subpoena, there would be no improper use of the testimonial aspect of the immunized act of production. In other words, the constitutional privilege and the statute conferring use immunity would only shield the witness from the use of any information resulting from his subpoena response "beyond what the prosecutor would receive if the documents appeared in the grand jury room or in his office unsolicited and unmarked, like manna from heaven."

On remand, the Independent Counsel acknowledged that he could not satisfy the "reasonable particularity" standard prescribed by the Court of Appeals and entered into a conditional plea agreement with respondent. In essence, the agreement provides for the dismissal of the charges unless this Court's disposition of the case makes it reasonably likely that respondent's "act [of] production immunity" would not pose a significant bar to his prosecution. The case is not moot, however, because the agreement also provides for the entry of a guilty plea and a sentence that will not include incarceration if we should reverse and issue an opinion that is sufficiently favorable to the Government to satisfy that condition. Despite that agreement, we granted the Independent Counsel's petition for a writ of certiorari in order to determine the precise scope of a grant of immunity with respect to the production of documents in response to a subpoena. We now affirm.

II

It is useful to preface our analysis of the constitutional issue with a restatement of certain propositions that are not in dispute. The term "privilege against self-incrimination" is not an entirely accurate description of a person's constitutional protection against being "compelled in any criminal case to be a witness against himself."

The word "witness" in the constitutional text limits the relevant category of compelled incriminating communications to those that are "testimonial" in character. As Justice Holmes observed, there is a significant difference between the use of compulsion to extort communications from a defendant and compelling a person to engage in conduct that may be incriminating. Thus, even though the act may provide incriminating evidence, a criminal suspect may be compelled to put on a shirt, to provide a blood sample or handwriting exemplar, or to make a recording of his voice. The act of exhibiting such physical characteristics is not the same as a sworn communication by a witness that relates either express or implied assertions of fact or belief. Similarly, the fact that incriminating evidence may be the byproduct of obedience to a regulatory requirement, such as filing an income tax return, maintaining required records, or reporting an accident, does not clothe such required conduct with the testimonial privilege.

More relevant to this case is the settled proposition that a person may be required to produce specific documents even though they contain incriminating assertions of fact or belief because the creation of those documents was not "compelled" within the meaning of the privilege. Our decision in *Fisher v. United States* (1976), dealt with summonses issued by the Internal Revenue Service (IRS) seeking working papers used in the preparation of tax returns. Because the papers had been voluntarily prepared prior to the issuance of the summonses, they could not be "said to contain compelled testimonial evidence, either of the taxpayers or of anyone else." Accordingly, the taxpayer could not "avoid compliance with the subpoena merely by asserting that the item of evidence which he is required to produce contains incriminating writing, whether his own or that of someone else." It is clear, therefore, that respondent Hubbell could not avoid compliance with the subpoena served on him merely because the demanded documents contained incriminating evidence, whether written by others or voluntarily prepared by himself.

On the other hand, we have also made it clear that the act of producing documents in response to a subpoena may have a compelled testimonial aspect. We have held that "the act of production" itself may implicitly communicate "statements of fact." By "producing documents in compliance with a subpoena, the witness would admit that the papers existed, were in his possession or control, and were authentic." Moreover, as was true in this case, when the custodian of documents responds to a subpoena, he may be compelled to take the witness stand and answer questions designed to determine whether he has produced everything demanded by the subpoena. The answers to those questions, as well as the act of production itself, may certainly communicate information about the existence, custody, and authenticity of the documents. Whether the constitutional privilege protects the answers to such questions, or protects the act of production itself, is a question that is distinct from the question whether the unprotected contents of the documents themselves are incriminating.

Finally, the phrase "in any criminal case" in the text of the Fifth Amendment might have been read to limit its coverage to compelled testimony that is used against the defendant in the trial itself. It has, however, long been settled that its protection encompasses compelled statements that lead to the discovery of incriminating evidence even though the statements themselves are not incriminating and are not introduced into evidence. Thus, a half century ago we held that a trial judge had erroneously rejected a defendant's claim of privilege on the ground that his answer to the pending question would not itself constitute evidence of the charged offense. As we explained:

> The privilege afforded not only extends to answers that would in themselves support a conviction under a federal criminal statute but likewise embraces those which would furnish a link in the chain of evidence needed to prosecute the claimant for a federal crime.

Compelled testimony that communicates information that may "lead to incriminating evidence" is privileged even if the information itself is not inculpatory. It is the Fifth

Amendment's protection against the prosecutor's use of incriminating information derived directly or indirectly from the compelled testimony of the respondent that is of primary relevance in this case.

III

Acting pursuant to 18 U.S.C. § 6002, the District Court entered an order compelling respondent to produce "any and all documents" described in the grand jury subpoena and granting him "immunity to the extent allowed by law." In *Kastigar v. United States* (1972), we upheld the constitutionality of § 6002 because the scope of the "use and derivative-use" immunity that it provides is coextensive with the scope of the constitutional privilege against self-incrimination.

The protection against the derivative use of compelled testimony distinguishes § 6002 from the 1868 statute that had been held invalid in *Counselman v. Hitchcock* (1892), because it merely provided "use" immunity, as well as from the more recent federal statutes that broadly provide "transactional" immunity. In *Kastigar* the petitioners argued that, under our reasoning in *Counselman*, nothing less than full transactional immunity from prosecution for any offense to which compelled testimony relates could suffice to supplant the privilege. In rejecting that argument, we stressed the importance of § 6002's "explicit proscription" of the use in any criminal case of "'testimony or other information compelled under the order (or any information directly or indirectly derived from such testimony or other information).'" We particularly emphasized the critical importance of protection against a future prosecution "'based on knowledge and sources of information obtained from the compelled testimony.'"

We also rejected the petitioners' argument that derivative-use immunity under § 6002 would not obviate the risk that the prosecutor or other law enforcement officials may use compelled testimony to obtain leads, names of witnesses, or other information not otherwise available to support a prosecution. That argument was predicated on the incorrect assumption that the derivative-use prohibition would prove impossible to enforce. But given that the statute contains a "comprehensive safeguard" in the form of a "sweeping proscription of any use, direct or indirect, of the compelled testimony and any information derived therefrom," we concluded that a person who is prosecuted for matters related to testimony he gave under a grant of immunity does not have the burden of proving that his testimony was improperly used. Instead, we held that the statute imposes an affirmative duty on the prosecution, not merely to show that its evidence is not tainted by the prior testimony, but "to prove that the evidence it proposes to use is derived from a legitimate source wholly independent of the compelled testimony." Requiring the prosecution to shoulder this burden ensures that the grant of immunity has "le[ft] the witness and the Federal Government in substantially the same position as if the witness had claimed his privilege in the absence of a grant of immunity."

The "compelled testimony" that is relevant in this case is not to be found in the contents of the documents produced in response to the subpoena. It is, rather, the testimony inherent in the act of producing those documents. The disagreement between the parties focuses entirely on the significance of that testimonial aspect.

IV

The Government correctly emphasizes that the testimonial aspect of a response to a subpoena duces tecum does nothing more than establish the existence, authenticity, and custody of items that are produced. We assume that the Government is also entirely correct in its submission that it would not have to advert to respondent's act of production in order to prove the existence, authenticity, or custody of any documents that it might offer in evidence at a criminal trial; indeed, the Government disclaims any need to introduce any of the documents produced by respondent into evidence in order to prove the charges against him. It follows, according to the Government, that it has no intention of making improper "use" of respondent's compelled testimony.

The question, however, is not whether the response to the subpoena may be introduced into evidence at his criminal trial. That would surely be a prohibited "use" of the immunized act of production. But the fact that the Government intends no such use of the act of production leaves open the separate question whether it has already made "derivative use" of the testimonial aspect of that act in obtaining the indictment against respondent and in preparing its case for trial. It clearly has.

It is apparent from the text of the subpoena itself that the prosecutor needed respondent's assistance both to identify potential sources of information and to produce those sources. See Appendix, infra. Given the breadth of the description of the 11 categories of documents called for by the subpoena, the collection and production of the materials demanded was tantamount to answering a series of interrogatories asking a witness to disclose the existence and location of particular documents fitting certain broad descriptions. The assembly of literally hundreds of pages of material in response to a request for "any and all documents reflecting, referring, or relating to any direct or indirect sources of money or other things of value received by or provided to" an individual or members of his family during a 3-year period, Appendix, infra, at 2048-2050, is the functional equivalent of the preparation of an answer to either a detailed written interrogatory or a series of oral questions at a discovery deposition. Entirely apart from the contents of the 13,120 pages of materials that respondent produced in this case, it is undeniable that providing a catalog of existing documents fitting within any of the 11 broadly worded subpoena categories could provide a prosecutor with a "lead to incriminating evidence," or "a link in the chain of evidence needed to prosecute."

Indeed, the record makes it clear that that is what happened in this case. The documents were produced before a grand jury sitting in the Eastern District of Arkansas in aid of the Independent Counsel's attempt to determine whether respondent had violated a commitment in his first plea agreement. The use of those sources of information eventually led to the return of an indictment by a grand jury sitting in the District of Columbia for offenses that apparently are unrelated to that plea agreement. What the District Court characterized as a "fishing expedition" did produce a fish, but not the one that the Independent Counsel expected to hook. It is abundantly clear that the testimonial aspect of respondent's act of producing subpoenaed documents was the first step in a chain of evidence that led to this prosecution. The documents did not magically appear in the prosecutor's office like "manna from heaven." They arrived there only after respondent asserted his constitutional privilege, received a grant of immunity, and — under the compulsion of the District Court's order — took the mental and physical steps necessary to provide the prosecutor with an accurate inventory of the many sources of potentially incriminating evidence sought by the subpoena. It was only through respondent's truthful reply to the subpoena that the Government received the incriminating documents of which it made "substantial use . . . in the investigation that led to the indictment."

For these reasons, we cannot accept the Government's submission that respondent's immunity did not preclude its derivative use of the produced documents because its "possession of the documents [was] the fruit only of a simple physical act — the act of producing the documents." It was unquestionably necessary for respondent to make extensive use of "the contents of his own mind" in identifying the hundreds of documents responsive to the requests in the subpoena. The assembly of those documents was like telling an inquisitor the combination to a wall safe, not like being forced to surrender the key to a strongbox. The Government's anemic view of respondent's act of production as a mere physical act that is principally nontestimonial in character and can be entirely divorced from its "implicit" testimonial aspect so as to constitute a "legitimate, wholly independent source" (as required by *Kastigar*) for the documents produced simply fails to account for these realities.

In sum, we have no doubt that the constitutional privilege against self-incrimination protects the target of a grand jury investigation from being compelled to answer questions designed to elicit information about the existence of sources of potentially incriminating evidence. That constitutional privilege has the same application to the testimonial aspect of a response to a subpoena seeking discovery of those sources. Before the District Court, the Government arguably conceded that respondent's act of production in this case had a testimonial aspect that entitled him to respond to the subpoena by asserting his privilege against self-incrimination. On appeal and again before this Court, however, the Government has argued that the communicative aspect of respondent's act of producing ordinary business records is insufficiently "testimonial" to support a claim of privilege because the existence and possession of such records by any businessman is a "foregone conclusion" under our decision in *Fisher*. This argument both misreads *Fisher* and ignores our subsequent decision in *United States v. Doe* (1984).

As noted in Part II, supra, *Fisher* involved summonses seeking production of working papers prepared by the taxpayers' accountants that the IRS knew were in the possession of the taxpayers' attorneys. In rejecting the taxpayers' claim that these documents were protected by the Fifth Amendment privilege, we stated:

> It is doubtful that implicitly admitting the existence and possession of the papers rises to the level of testimony within the protection of the Fifth Amendment. The papers belong to the accountant, were prepared by him, and are the kind usually prepared by an accountant working on the tax returns of his client. Surely the Government is in no way relying on the "truthtelling" of the taxpayer to prove the existence of or his access to the documents. . . . The existence and location of the papers are a foregone conclusion and the taxpayer adds little or nothing to the sum total of the Government's information by conceding that he in fact has the papers.

Whatever the scope of this "foregone conclusion" rationale, the facts of this case plainly fall outside of it. While in *Fisher* the Government already knew that the documents were in the attorneys' possession and could independently confirm their existence and authenticity through the accountants who created them, here the Government has not shown that it had any prior knowledge of either the existence or the whereabouts of the 13,120 pages of documents ultimately produced by respondent. The Government cannot cure this deficiency through the overbroad argument that a businessman such as respondent will always possess general business and tax records that fall within the broad categories described in this subpoena. The *Doe* subpoenas also sought several broad categories of general business records, yet we upheld the District Court's finding that the act of producing those records would involve testimonial self-incrimination.

Given our conclusion that respondent's act of production had a testimonial aspect, at least with respect to the existence and location of the documents sought by the Government's subpoena, respondent could not be compelled to produce those documents without first receiving a grant of immunity under § 6003. As we construed § 6002 in *Kastigar*, such immunity is coextensive with the constitutional privilege. *Kastigar* requires that respondent's motion to dismiss the indictment on immunity grounds be granted unless the Government proves that the evidence it used in obtaining the indictment and proposed to use at trial was derived from legitimate sources "wholly independent" of the testimonial aspect of respondent's immunized conduct in assembling and producing the documents described in the subpoena. The Government, however, does not claim that it could make such a showing. Rather, it contends that its prosecution of respondent must be considered proper unless someone — presumably respondent — shows that "there is some substantial relation between the compelled testimonial communications implicit in the act of production (as opposed to the act of production standing alone) and some aspect of the information used in the investigation or the evidence presented at trial." We could not accept this submission without repudiating the basis for our conclusion in *Kastigar* that the statutory guarantee of use and derivative-use immunity is as broad as the constitutional privilege itself. This we are not prepared to do.

Accordingly, the indictment against respondent must be dismissed. The judgment of the Court of Appeals is affirmed.

It is so ordered.

APPENDIX TO OPINION OF THE COURT

On October 31, 1996, upon application by the Independent Counsel, a subpoena was issued commanding respondent to appear and testify before the grand jury of the United States District Court for the Eastern District of Arkansas on November 19, 1996, and to bring with him various documents described in a "Subpoena Rider" as follows:

A. Any and all documents reflecting, referring, or relating to any direct or indirect sources of money or other things of value received by or provided to Webster Hubbell, his wife, or children from January 1, 1993 to the present, including but not limited to the identity of employers or clients of legal or any other type of work.

B. Any and all documents reflecting, referring, or relating to any direct or indirect sources of money of other things of value received by or provided to Webster Hubbell, his wife, or children from January 1, 1993 to the present, including but not limited to billing memoranda, draft statements, bills, final statements, and/or bills for work performed or time billed from January 1, 1993 to the present.

C. Copies of all bank records of Webster Hubbell, his wife, or children for all accounts from January 1, 1993 to the present, including but not limited to all statements, registers and ledgers, cancelled checks, deposit items, and wire transfers.

D. Any and all documents reflecting, referring, or relating to time worked or billed by Webster Hubbell from January 1, 1993 to the present, including but not limited to original time sheets, books, notes, papers, and/or computer records.

E. Any and all documents reflecting, referring, or relating to expenses incurred by and/or disbursements of money by Webster Hubbell during the course of any work performed or to be performed by Mr. Hubbell from January 1, 1993 to the present.

F. Any and all documents reflecting, referring, or relating to Webster Hubbell's schedule of activities, including but not limited to any and all calendars, day-timers, time books, appointment books, diaries, records of reverse telephone toll calls, credit card calls, telephone message slips, logs, other telephone records, minutes, databases, electronic mail messages, travel records, itineraries, tickets for transportation of any kind, payments, bills, expense backup documentation, schedules, and/or any other document or database that would disclose Webster Hubbell's activities from January 1, 1993 to the present.

G. Any and all documents reflecting, referring, or relating to any retainer agreements or contracts for employment of Webster Hubbell, his wife, or his children from January 1, 1993 to the present.

H. Any and all tax returns and tax return information, including but not limited to all W-2s, form 1099s, schedules, draft returns, work papers, and backup documents filed, created or held by or on behalf of Webster Hubbell, his wife, his children, and/or any business in which he, his wife, or his children holds or has held an interest, for the tax years 1993 to the present.

I. Any and all documents reflecting, referring, or relating to work performed or to be performed or on behalf of the City of Los Angeles, California, the Los Angeles Department of Airports or any other Los Angeles municipal Governmental entity, Mary Leslie, and/or Alan S. Arkatov, including but not limited to correspondence, retainer agreements, contracts, time sheets, appointment calendars, activity calendars, diaries, billing statements, billing memoranda, telephone records, telephone message slips, telephone credit card statements, itineraries, tickets for transportation, payment records, expense receipts, ledgers, check registers, notes, memoranda, electronic mail, bank deposit items, cashier's checks, traveler's checks, wire transfer records and/or other records of financial transactions.

J. Any and all documents reflecting, referring, or relating to work performed or to be performed by Webster Hubbell, his wife, or his children on the recommendation, counsel or other influence of Mary Leslie and/or Alan S. Arkatov, including but not limited to correspondence, retainer agreements, contracts, time sheets, appointment calendars, activity calendars, diaries, billing statements, billing memoranda, telephone records, telephone message slips, telephone credit card statements, itineraries, tickets for transportation, payment records, expense receipts, ledgers, check registers, notes, memoranda, electronic mail, bank deposit items, cashier's checks, traveler's checks, wire transfer records and/or other records of financial transactions.

K. Any and all documents related to work performed or to be performed for or on behalf of Lippo Ltd. (formerly Public Finance (H.K.) Ltd.), the Lippo Group, the Lippo Bank, Mochtar Riady, James Riady, Stephen Riady, John Luen Wai Lee, John Huang, Mark W. Grobmyer, C. Joseph Giroir, Jr., or any affiliate, subsidiary, or corporation owned or controlled by or related to the aforementioned entities or individuals, including but not limited to correspondence, retainer agreements, contracts, time sheets, appointment calendars, activity calendars, diaries, billing statements, billing memoranda, telephone records, telephone message slips, telephone credit card statements, itineraries, tickets for transportation, payment records, expense receipts, ledgers, check registers, notes, memoranda, electronic mail, bank deposit items, cashier's checks, traveler's checks, wire transfer records and/or other records of financial transactions.

NOTES AND QUESTIONS

Kenneth Starr, Independent Counsel in the Whitewater/Clinton investigations

1. Pursuant to the Ethics in Government Act of 1978, on August 5, 1994, upon the application of Attorney General Janet Reno, Kenneth Starr was appointed as Independent Counsel by a special three-judge division of the D.C. Circuit.

The appointing order gave him authority to investigate:

> whether any individuals or entities have committed a violation of any federal criminal law . . . relating in any way to James B. McDougal's, President William Jefferson Clinton's, or Mrs. Hillary Rodham Clinton's relationships with Madison Guaranty Savings & Loan Association, Whitewater Development Corporation, or Capital Management Services, Inc.

United States v. Hubbell, 11 F. Supp. 2d 25, 27 (D.D.C. 1998), *rev'd, vacated by* 167 F.3d 552 (1999), *aff'd*, 530 U.S. 27 (2000). That original grant of authority, expanded multiple times by the Special Division under the "related to" provision in the statute, lead to prosecutions of Webster Hubbell, a Clinton family friend and professional colleague of Hillary Rodham Clinton at the Rose law firm in Little Rock, Arkansas. *Id.* at 28. In December 1994 Hubbell pleaded guilty to tax and mail fraud charges arising out of overbilling of clients. *Id.*

2. It is unclear whether the Court is sensitive to the ironies of Hubbell's multiple prosecutions by the Independent Counsel. In the first paragraph of Part I of its decision it refers to the substance of the Independent Counsel's original grant of authority ("Whitewater

Development Corporation") and then, without comment on any relationship, describes the subject of Hubbell's previous conviction ("billing practices" at an Arkansas law firm). And while it describes the instant prosecution as based on an alleged failure to "cooperate" with the Whitewater investigation, the Court refers, again without comment, to the subpoena at issue—described by the district court as "the quintessential fishing expedition"—that sought from Hubbell nothing but personal financial information, that is, materials apparently unrelated to his "cooperation" with the investigation. The Court does note in a footnote that the district court dismissed the indictment of Hubbell not only on the immunity issue before it, but also on the ground that the Independent Counsel had exceeded his jurisdiction in bringing the case against Hubbell, although that decision was reversed by the D.C. Circuit.

3. Take a close look at the subpoena categories, located in the Appendix. While it is true that an individual subpoena is just one piece of an investigation, and the perspective of a defendant is inherently imperfect, there are exceptions. What do these subpoena topics have to do with Hubbell's "cooperation" with the Independent Counsel? Is it more likely that the Independent Counsel is simply trying—for the second time—to pressure Hubbell into serving up incriminating information on the Clintons?

4. As the Court notes, even the most damning of documents in a defendant's possession are not covered by the Fifth Amendment privilege because their creation was not compelled by the government. But because producing such documents in response to a subpoena or other compulsory process has a testimonial component, a witness can nonetheless assert the Fifth Amendment privilege, as Hubbell did here, in response to the subpoena. But once he received "act-of-production immunity" under 18 U.S.C. § 6002 that privilege is eliminated, and he can be compelled to answer questions about the production, but not the contents, of the documents.

5. The Independent Counsel claims it can prove its tax evasion case against Hubbell without using either the documents produced by Hubbell or his testimony about their production. How could this be accomplished? Why does this matter?

6. In what precise ways were Hubbell's act of producing the documents testimonial?

7. The government essentially conceded that it had used the documents produced by Hubbell in preparing the indictment, and that it could not satisfy the showing the Court of Appeals required it to make on remand. Is that concession fatal? Is this an application of *Kastigar*?

8. Professor Mosteller notes that while *Hubbell* says nothing about overruling *Fisher* on the "act of production" doctrine, it is clear that the significance of *Fisher* has been narrowed to the proposition that requiring the production of incriminating documents from a target does not violate the Fifth Amendment if the government can establish advance knowledge of the existence and location of the requested documents and if the production requires no selection by the target. Robert P. Mosteller, *Cowboy Prosecutors and Subpoenas for Incriminating Evidence: The Consequences and Correction of Excess*, 58 Wash. & Lee L. Rev. 487, 520 (2001). He also makes the point that the Department of Justice would have been much better off, institutionally, had the Independent Counsel not pursued this matter. *See id.* at 488 ("The [Independent Counsel's] recklessness severely impaired the value of use immunity applied to subpoenas for documents from the perspective of prosecutors.").

The core of the Fifth Amendment's protection is that a criminal defendant cannot be forced to testify in his own defense in a criminal trial. But is the prosecution permitted to comment on the defendant's decision not to testify in his defense? A federal statute had since 1878 prohibited such comment in federal prosecutions. Shortly after holding that the Fifth Amendment applied to the states in *Malloy v. Hogan*, 378 U.S. 1 (1965), the Court considered whether the Amendment prohibited such comment in state prosecutions.

A. Scope of the Right Against Self-Incrimination

101

Griffin v. California
380 U.S. 609 (1965)

Mr. Justice DOUGLAS delivered the opinion of the Court.

Petitioner was convicted of murder in the first degree after a jury trial in a California court. He did not testify at the trial on the issue of guilt, though he did testify at the separate trial on the issue of penalty. The trial court instructed the jury on the issue of guilt, stating that a defendant has a constitutional right not to testify. But it told the jury:

> As to any evidence or facts against him which the defendant can reasonably be expected to deny or explain because of facts within his knowledge, if he does not testify or if, though he does testify, he fails to deny or explain such evidence, the jury may take that failure into consideration as tending to indicate the truth of such evidence and as indicating that among the inferences that may be reasonably drawn therefrom those unfavorable to the defendant are the more probable.

It added, however, that no such inference could be drawn as to evidence respecting which he had no knowledge. It stated that failure of a defendant to deny or explain the evidence of which he had knowledge does not create a presumption of guilt nor by itself warrant an inference of guilt nor relieve the prosecution of any of its burden of proof.

Petitioner had been seen with the deceased the evening of her death, the evidence placing him with her in the alley where her body was found. The prosecutor made much of the failure of petitioner to testify:

> The defendant certainly knows whether Essie Mae had this beat up appearance at the time he left her apartment and went down the alley with her.
>
> What kind of a man is it that would want to have sex with a woman that beat up if she was beat up at the time he left?
>
> He would know that. He would know how she got down the alley. He would know how the blood got on the bottom of the concrete steps. He would know how long he was with her in that box. He would know how her wig got off. He would know whether he beat her or mistreated her. He would know whether he walked away from that place cool as a cucumber when he saw Mr. Villasenor because he was conscious of his own guilt and wanted to get away from that damaged or injured woman.
>
> These things he has not seen fit to take the stand and deny or explain.
>
> And in the whole world, if anybody would know, this defendant would know.
>
> Essie Mae is dead, she can't tell you her side of the story. The defendant won't.

The death penalty was imposed and the California Supreme Court affirmed. The case is here on a writ of certiorari which we granted to consider whether comment on the failure to testify violated the Self-Incrimination Clause of the Fifth Amendment which we made applicable to the States by the Fourteenth in *Malloy v. Hogan*, decided after the Supreme Court of California had affirmed the present conviction.

If this were a federal trial, reversible error would have been committed. It is said, however, that the *Wilson* decision rested not on the Fifth Amendment, but on an Act of Congress. That indeed is the fact, as the opinion of the Court in the *Wilson* case states. But that is the beginning, not the end, of our inquiry. The question remains whether, statute or not, the comment rule, approved by California, violates the Fifth Amendment.

We think it does. It is in substance a rule of evidence that allows the State the privilege of tendering to the jury for its consideration the failure of the accused to testify. No formal offer of proof is made as in other situations; but the prosecutor's comment and the court's acquiescence are the equivalent of an offer of evidence and its acceptance. The Court in the *Wilson* case stated:

> . . . the act was framed with a due regard also to those who might prefer to rely upon the presumption of innocence which the law gives to every one, and not wish to be witnesses. It is not

Chapter III Police Interrogation and The Fifth Amendment

every one who can safely venture on the witness stand, though entirely innocent of the charge against him. Excessive timidity, nervousness when facing others and attempting to explain transactions of a suspicious character, and offenses charged against him, will often confuse and embarrass him to such a degree as to increase rather than remove prejudices against him. It is not every one, however honest, who would therefore willingly be placed on the witness stand. The statute, in tenderness to the weakness of those who from the causes mentioned might refuse to ask to be witnesses, particularly when they may have been in some degree compromised by their association with others, declares that the failure of a defendant in a criminal action to request to be a witness shall not create any presumption against him.

If the words "fifth Amendment" are substituted for "act" and for "statute" the spirit of the Self-Incrimination Clause is reflected. For comment on the refusal to testify is a remnant of the "inquisitorial system of criminal justice," which the Fifth Amendment outlaws. It is a penalty imposed by courts for exercising a constitutional privilege. It cuts down on the privilege by making its assertion costly. It is said, however, that the inference of guilt for failure to testify as to facts peculiarly within the accused's knowledge is in any event natural and irresistible, and that comment on the failure does not magnify that inference into a penalty for asserting a constitutional privilege. What the jury may infer, given no help from the court, is one thing. What it may infer when the court solemnizes the silence of the accused into evidence against him is quite another. That the inference of guilt is not always so natural or irresistible is brought out in the *Modesto* opinion itself:

> Defendant contends that the reason a defendant refuses to testify is that his prior convictions will be introduced in evidence to impeach him ((Cal.) Code Civ. Proc. s 2051) and not that he is unable to deny the accusations. It is true that the defendant might fear that his prior convictions will prejudice the jury, and therefore another possible inference can be drawn from his refusal to take the stand.

We said in *Malloy v. Hogan* that "the same standards must determine whether an accused's silence in either a federal or state proceeding is justified." We take that in its literal sense and hold that the Fifth Amendment, in its direct application to the Federal Government and in its bearing on the States by reason of the Fourteenth Amendment, forbids either comment by the prosecution on the accused's silence or instructions by the court that such silence is evidence of guilt.

Reversed.

[Justice Harlan concurred. Justices White and Stewart dissented.]

NOTES AND QUESTIONS

1. Consider closely the instruction the trial court gave the jury after informing it of the defendant's right not to testify:

> As to any evidence or facts against him which the defendant can reasonably be expected to deny or explain because of facts within his knowledge, if he does not testify or if, though he does testify, he fails to deny or explain such evidence, the jury may take that failure into consideration as tending to indicate the truth of such evidence and as indicating that among the inferences that may be reasonably drawn therefrom those unfavorable to the defendant are the more probable.

Putting aside whether this instruction impermissibly comments on the defendant's failure to testify, and also putting aside whether the instruction is comprehensible, is this instruction even consistent with the government's burden to prove its case beyond a reasonable doubt?

2. Note the Court's sensitive recognition in the 1893 *Wilson* case of the reasons for the federal statute prohibiting comment on a defendant's failure to testify in a federal criminal case, which the Court adopts as "the spirit" of the Fifth Amendment.

Would you say the "no comment" rule as applied to the states is a constitutional rule, driven by the Fifth Amendment itself, or rather a rule that simply reinforces a constitutional guarantee? Could you describe it as a "prophylactic rule," aimed to prevent Fifth Amendment violations?

3. The Court acknowledges that the jury may nonetheless draw its own inference of guilt from the defendant's refusal to testify, whether encouraged by the court or not. Do you agree that juries are likely draw such an inference?

4. The "no comment" rule is a continual source of prosecutorial misconduct cases, as there are innumerable ways in which prosecutors can intentionally, carelessly, or inadvertently comment on the witness's failure to testify, including in some circumstances by referring to the government's evidence as "undisputed" or "unopposed." *See* Chapter IX *infra*.

5. *Griffin* has been widely criticized since it was decided, and Justice Thomas has explicitly called for the case to be "reexamined." *Mitchell v. United States*, 526 U.S. 314, 342 (1999) (Thomas, J., dissenting). For references to criticism of *Griffin*, *see* Tracey Maclin, *Is Silence Golden?*, 65 Ariz. L. Rev. 43, 47-48 & nn.12-19 (2023). Professor Maclin defends *Griffin* because allowing the state to argue for an inference of guilt from a defendant's silence undermines the defendant's absolute right not to testify against himself. *Id.* at 49.

The Court in *Kastigar* made it clear that a witness can assert the Fifth Amendment privilege in any proceeding, including civil proceedings. The Fifth Amendment "not only protects the individual against being involuntarily called as a witness against himself in a criminal prosecution but also privileges him not to answer official questions put to him in any other proceeding, civil or criminal, formal or informal, where the answers might incriminate him in future criminal proceedings." *Lefkowitz v. Turley*, 414 U.S. 70, 77 (1973). Accordingly, although corporations and other "collective entities" do not have Fifth Amendment rights (e.g., *United States v. Braswell*, 487 U.S. 99 (1988)), individuals in all manner of civil litigation can assert the privilege in depositions, responses to interrogatories, or any other form of questioning or examination.

But there are important differences between the assertion of the Fifth Amendment in a civil as opposed to a criminal proceeding. Among other things, unlike in criminal cases after *Griffin*, in a civil case an adverse inference may be drawn from the assertion of the Fifth Amendment. *Baxter v. Palmigiano*, 425 U.S. 308 (1976). Typically, if a party takes the Fifth Amendment in a civil trial, the judge will instruct the jury that an adverse inference may — not shall — be drawn from the witness's assertion. The nature of the inference that will be permitted depends on the facts and circumstances of the case, and there is considerable variation among the states and even the federal circuits about the circumstances in which an adverse inference will be permitted.

Further, while the popular conception of the Fifth Amendment may be that it affords a right to remain silent (*but see Salinas v. Texas*, 570 U.S. 178 (2013); *infra* at Section E), in a civil proceeding the right must be asserted on a question-by-question basis. Part of this is so that a court will be able to determine what adverse inferences, if any, are permissible. But there also may be judicial scrutiny of Fifth Amendment assertions in civil proceedings to ensure that they are justified. The scope of the right extends not only to "answers that would in themselves support a conviction under a federal criminal statute," but also to answers "which would furnish a link in the chain of evidence needed to prosecute the claimant for a federal crime." *Hoffman v. United States*, 341 U.S. 479, 486 (1951). Courts typically will uphold

Chapter III Police Interrogation and The Fifth Amendment

assertions of the privilege unless the possibility of criminal exposure is extremely remote. *In re Folding Carton Antitrust Litigation*, 609 F.2d 867 (7th Cir. 1979).

B. POLICE INTERROGATION: VOLUNTARINESS AND THE ROAD TO *MIRANDA*

In an ideal world of criminal justice the government would prosecute based entirely on "its own independent labors," *Miranda*, 384 U.S. at 360, without resorting to interrogation at all. But the law has forever countenanced some forms of interrogation even as it recognized the danger of coerced and false confessions. That danger could no longer be considered speculative in the twenty-first century, as the evidence mounted that in a significant percentage of cases where defendants were exonerated by DNA evidence they had been convicted based at least in part on confessions.

In *Brown v. Mississippi*, *see* Chapter II *supra*, the Court found that the extortion of a confession by physical coercion was a violation of due process. After *Brown* the Court increasingly was confronted with confessions induced by more subtle means of coercion, and decided no fewer than 30 such cases between *Brown* and *Miranda*. *Dickerson v. United States*, 530 U.S. 428, 433 (2000). Referring to this period unsentimentally in 2004, the Court described "the old way of doing things" by "litigating the voluntariness of any statement in nearly every instance." *Missouri v. Seibert*, 542 U.S. 600, 609 (2004).

Two of those instances follow.

Ashcraft v. Tennessee
322 U.S. 143 (1944)

Mr. Justice BLACK delivered the opinion of the Court.

About three o'clock on the morning of Thursday, June 5, 1941, Mrs. Zelma Ida Ashcraft got in her automobile at her home in Memphis, Tennessee, and set out on a trip to visit her mother's home in Kentucky. Late in the afternoon of the same day her car was observed a few miles out of Memphis, standing on the wrong side of a road which she would likely have taken on her journey. Just off the road, in a slough, her lifeless body was found. On her head were cut places inflicted by blows sufficient to have caused her death. Petitioner Ware, age 20, a Negro, was indicted in a state court and found guilty of her murder. Petitioner Ashcraft, age 45, a white man, husband of the deceased, charged with having hired Ware to commit the murder, was tried jointly with Ware and convicted as an accessory before the fact. Both were sentenced to ninety-nine years in the state penitentiary. The Supreme Court of Tennessee affirmed the convictions.

In applying to us for certiorari, Ware and Ashcraft urged that alleged confessions were used at their trial which had been extorted from them by state law enforcement officers in violation of the Fourteenth Amendment, and that "solely and alone" on the basis of these confessions they had been convicted. Their contentions raised a federal question which the record showed to be substantial and we brought both cases here for review. Upon oral argument before this Court Tennessee's legal representatives conceded that the convictions could not be sustained without the confessions but defended their use upon the ground that they were not compelled but were "freely and voluntarily made."

The record discloses that neither the trial court nor the Tennessee Supreme Court actually held as a matter of fact that petitioners' confessions were "freely and voluntarily made." The trial court heard evidence on the issue out of the jury's hearing, but did not itself determine from that evidence that the confessions were voluntary. Instead it over-ruled Ashcraft's objection to the use of his alleged confession with the statement that, "This Court is not able to hold, as a matter of law, that reasonable minds might not differ on the question of whether or not that alleged confession was voluntarily obtained." And it likewise over-ruled Ware's objection to use of his alleged confession, stating that "the reasonable minds of twelve men might . . . differ as to . . . whether Ware's confession was voluntary, and . . . therefore, that is a question of fact for the jury to pass on." Nor did the State Supreme Court review the evidence pertaining to the confessions and affirmatively hold them voluntary. In sustaining the petitioners' convictions, one Justice dissenting, it went no further than to point out that, "The trial judge . . . held . . . he could not say that the confessions were not voluntarily made and, therefore, permitted them to go to the jury," and to declare that it, likewise, was "unable to say that the confessions were not freely and voluntarily made."

If, therefore, the question of the voluntariness of the two confessions was actually decided at all it was by the jury. And the jury was charged generally on the subject of the two confessions as follows:

> I further charge you that if verbal or written statements made by the defendants freely and voluntarily and without fear of punishment or hope of reward, have been proven to you in this case, you may take them into consideration with all of the other facts and circumstances in the case. . . . In statements made at the time of the arrest, you may take into consideration the condition of the minds of the prisoners owing to their arrest and whether they were influenced by motives of hope or fear, to make the statements. Such a statement is competent evidence against the defendant who makes it and is not competent evidence against the other defendant. . . . You cannot consider it for any purpose against the other defendant.

Concerning Ashcraft's alleged confession this general charge constituted the sole instruction to the jury. But with regard to Ware's alleged confession the jury further was instructed:

> It is his (Ware's) further theory that he was induced by the fear of violence at the hands of a mob and by fear of the officers of the law to confess his guilt of the crime charged against him, but that such confession was false and that he had nothing whatsoever to do with, and no knowledge of the alleged crime. If you believe the theory of the defendant, Ware, . . . it is your duty to acquit him.

Having submitted the two alleged confessions to the jury in this manner, the trial court instructed the jury that:

> what the proof may show you, if anything, that the defendants have said against themselves, the law presumes to be true, but anything the defendants have said in their own behalf, you are not obliged to believe. . . .

This treatment of the confessions by the two State courts, the manner of the confessions' submission to the jury, and the emphasis upon the great weight to be given confessions make all the more important the kind of "independent examination" of petitioners' claims which, in any event, we are bound to make. Our duty to make that examination could not have been "foreclosed by the finding of a court, or the verdict of a jury, or both." We proceed therefore to consider the evidence relating to the circumstances out of which the alleged confessions came.

First, as to Ashcraft. Ashcraft was born on an Arkansas farm. At the age of eleven he left the farm and became a farm hand working for others. Years later he gravitated into construction work, finally becoming a skilled dragline and steam shovel operator. Uncontradicted evidence in the record was that he had acquired for himself "an excellent reputation." In 1929 he married the deceased Zelma Ida Ashcraft. Childless, they accumulated, apparently through Ashcraft's earnings, a very modest amount of jointly held property including bank accounts and an equity in the home in which they lived. The Supreme Court of Tennessee found "nothing to show but what the home life of Ashcraft and the deceased was pleasant and happy." Several of Mrs. Ashcraft's friends who were guests at the Ashcraft home on the night before her tragic death testified that both husband and wife appeared to be in a happy frame of mind.

The officers first talked to Ashcraft about 6 p.m. on the day of his wife's murder as he was returning home from work. Informed by them of the tragedy, he was taken to an undertaking establishment to identify her body which previously had been identified only by a driver's license. From there he was taken to the county jail where he conferred with the officers until about 2 a.m. No clues of ultimate value came from this conference, though it did result in the officers' holding and interrogating the Ashcrafts' maid and several of her friends. During the following week the officers made extensive investigations in Ashcraft's neighborhood and elsewhere and further conferred with Ashcraft himself on several occasions, but none of these activities produced tangible evidence pointing to the identity of the murderer.

Then, early in the evening of Saturday, June 14, the officers came to Ashcraft's home and "took him into custody." In the words of the Tennessee Supreme Court,

> They took him to an office or room on the northwest corner of the fifth Floor of the Shelby County jail. This office is equipped with all sorts of crime and detective devices such as a fingerprint outfit, cameras, high-powered lights, and such other devices as might be found in a homicide investigating office. . . . It appears that the officers placed Ashcraft at a table in this room on the fifth floor of the county jail with a light over his head and began to quiz him. They questioned him in relays until the following Monday morning, June 16, 1941, around nine-thirty or ten o'clock. It appears that Ashcraft from Saturday evening at seven o'clock until Monday morning at approximately nine-thirty never left this homicide room of the fifth floor.

Testimony of the officers shows that the reason they questioned Ashcraft "in relays" was that they became so tired they were compelled to rest. But from 7:00 Saturday evening until 9:30 Monday morning Ashcraft had no rest. One officer did say that he gave the suspect a single five minutes respite, but except for this five minutes the procedure consisted of one continuous stream of questions.

As to what happened in the fifth-floor jail room during this thirty-six hour secret examination the testimony follows the usual pattern and is in hopeless conflict. Ashcraft swears that the first thing said to him when he was taken into custody was, "Why in hell did you kill your wife?"; that during the course of the examination he was threatened and abused in various ways; and that as the hours passed his eyes became blinded by a powerful electric light, his body became weary, and the strain on his nerves became unbearable. The officers, on the other hand, swear that throughout the questioning they were kind and considerate. They say that they did not accuse Ashcraft of the murder until four hours after he was brought to the jail building, though they freely admit that from that time on their barrage of questions was constantly directed at him on the assumption that he was the murderer. Together with other persons whom they brought in on Monday morning to witness the culmination of the thirty-six hour ordeal the officers declare that at that time Ashcraft was "cool," "calm," "collected," "normal"; that his vision was unimpaired and his eyes not bloodshot; and that he showed no outward signs of being tired or sleepy.

As to whether Ashcraft actually confessed there is a similar conflict of testimony. Ashcraft maintains that although the officers incessantly attempted by various tactics of intimidation to entrap him into a confession, not once did he admit knowledge concerning or participation in the crime. And he specifically denies the officers' statements that he accused Ware of the crime, insisting that in response to their questions he merely gave them the name of Ware as one of several men who occasionally had ridden with him to work. The officers' version of what happened, however, is that about 11 p.m. on Sunday night, after twenty-eight hours' constant questioning, Ashcraft made a statement that Ware had overpowered him at his

B. Police Interrogation: Voluntariness and the Road to *Miranda*

home and abducted the deceased, and was probably the killer. About midnight the officers found Ware and took him into custody, and, according to their testimony, Ware made a self-incriminating statement as of early Monday morning, and at 5:40 a.m. signed by mark a written confession in which appeared the statement that Ashcraft had hired him to commit the murder. This alleged confession of Ware was read to Ashcraft about six o'clock Monday morning, whereupon Ashcraft is said substantially to have admitted its truth in a detailed statement taken down by a reporter. About 9:30 Monday morning a transcript of Ashcraft's purported statement was read to him. The State's position is that he affirmed its truth but refused to sign the transcript, saying that he first wanted to consult his lawyer. As to this latter 9:30 episode the officers' testimony is reinforced by testimony of the several persons whom they brought in to witness the end of the examination.

In reaching our conclusion as to the validity of Ashcraft's confession we do not resolve any of the disputed questions of fact relating to the details of what transpired within the confession chamber of the jail or whether Ashcraft actually did confess. Such disputes, we may say, are an inescapable consequence of secret inquisitorial practices. And always evidence concerning the inner details of secret inquisitions is weighted against an accused, particularly where, as here, he is charged with a brutal crime, or where, as in many other cases, his supposed offense bears relation to an unpopular economic, political, or religious cause.

Our conclusion is that if Ashcraft made a confession it was not voluntary but compelled. We reach this conclusion from facts which are not in dispute at all. Ashcraft, a citizen of excellent reputation, was taken into custody by police officers. Ten days' examination of the Ashcrafts' maid, and of several others, in jail where they were held, had revealed nothing whatever against Ashcraft. Inquiries among his neighbors and business associates likewise had failed to unearth one single tangible clue pointing to his guilt. For thirty-six hours after Ashcraft's seizure during which period he was held incommunicado, without sleep or rest, relays of officers, experienced investigators, and highly trained lawyers questioned him without respite. From the beginning of the questioning at 7 o'clock on Saturday evening until 6 o'clock on Monday morning Ashcraft denied that he had anything to do with the murder of his wife. And at a hearing before a magistrate about 8:30 Monday morning Ashcraft pleaded not guilty to the charge of murder which the officers had sought to make him confess during the previous thirty-six hours.

We think a situation such as that here shown by uncontradicted evidence is so inherently coercive that its very existence is irreconcilable with the possession of mental freedom by a lone suspect against whom its full coercive force is brought to bear. It is inconceivable that any court of justice in the land, conducted as our courts are, open to the public, would permit prosecutors serving in relays to keep a defendant witness under continuous cross examination for thirty-six hours without rest or sleep in an effort to extract a "voluntary" confession. Nor can we, consistently with Constitutional due process of law, hold voluntary a confession where prosecutors do the same thing away from the restraining influences of a public trial in an open court room.

The Constitution of the United States stands as a bar against the conviction of any individual in an American court by means of a coerced confession. There have been, and are now, certain foreign nations with governments dedicated to an opposite policy: governments which convict individuals with testimony obtained by police organizations possessed of an unrestrained power to seize persons suspected of crimes against the state, hold them in secret custody, and wring from them confessions by physical or mental torture. So long as the Constitution remains the basic law of our Republic, America will not have that kind of government.

Second, as to Ware. Ashcraft and Ware were jointly tried, and were convicted on the theory that Ashcraft hired Ware to perform the murder. Ware's conviction was sustained by the

Tennessee Supreme Court on the assumption that Ashcraft's confession was properly admitted and his conviction valid. Whether it would have been sustained had the court reached the conclusion we have reached as to Ashcraft we cannot know. Doubt as to what the State court would have done under the changed circumstances brought about by our reversal of its decision as to Ashcraft is emphasized by the position of the State's representatives in this Court. They have asked that if we reverse Ashcraft's conviction we also reverse Ware's.

In disposing of cases before us it is our responsibility to make such disposition as justice may require. "And in determining what justice does require, the Court is bound to consider any change, either in fact or in law, which has supervened since the judgment was entered." Application of this guiding principle to the case at hand requires that we send Ware's case back to the Tennessee Supreme Court. Should that Court in passing on Ware's conviction in the light of our ruling as to Ashcraft adopt the State Attorney General's view and reverse the conviction there then would be no occasion for our passing on the federal question here raised by Ware. Under these circumstances we vacate the judgment of the Tennessee Supreme Court affirming Ware's conviction, and remand his case to that court for further proceedings.

The judgment affirming Ashcraft's conviction is reversed and the cause is remanded to the Supreme Court of Tennessee for proceedings not inconsistent with this opinion. It is so ordered.

NOTES AND QUESTIONS

1. Note that the trial judge made no assessment of the confessions besides finding that reasonable jurors could disagree as to whether the confessions were "freely and voluntarily made." The Supreme Court makes no ruling as to this procedural practice, as it determines that it must do an "independent examination" of the confessions regardless.

Is there anything about the power of confessions as evidence that makes their voluntariness particularly ill-suited to consideration by a jury in the first instance? Consider that confession evidence will almost always come in through the testimony of a police officer who participated in the interrogation, and the circumstances of the questioning can usually only be rebutted if the defendant testifies.

2. The trial judge instructed the jury that the statements by the defendant were "competent evidence" against the defendant and, further, that statements by the defendants "against themselves, the law presumes to be true." While the Federal Rules of Evidence make admissions against interest an exception to the hearsay rule, Fed. R. Evid. 804(b)(3), and therefore admissible in evidence, such statements are not "presumed to be true."

3. Do the personal characteristics of Mr. E. E. Ashcraft matter to the result here? The Court describes his circumstances in detail and in its conclusion it calls him a "citizen of excellent reputation." Does the Court do this because it senses that Ashcraft did not really confess? Or because even the best citizens can have their will overborne by interrogation that is "inherently coercive"?

4. The Court wrings its hands at the "hopeless conflict" in the testimony surrounding what actually transpired in the interrogation itself. The conflict extends not only to the circumstances of the interrogation but also as to what Ashcraft actually said. It concludes that the undisputed evidence reveals an interrogation that was "inherently coercive."

Note that *Ashcraft* was decided on May 1, 1944, just five weeks before the D-Day invasion of Normandy, at a time when the ultimate fate of Western Europe was by no means assured. This may explain the Court's acknowledgment of "certain foreign nations" with an "opposite policy" to a prohibition of coerced confessions.

5. In footnotes the Court refers to findings of the "Wickersham Report," the memorialized findings of a national commission charged in 1929 by President Hoover to study the

The members of the Wickersham Commission

widespread failure of state and local police to enforce Prohibition. Its conclusion was that Prohibition laws were not rigorously enforced. The commission's most notable findings, ironically, were in the area of abusive and coercive police interrogation tactics. The Court cites some of the commission's findings relevant here: that the "third degree" interrogation tactics often take place in a "back room" selected for its privacy and that "persistent questioning continuing hour after hour, sometimes by relays of officers" causing a "deprivation of sleep is the most effective torture and certain to produce any confession desired."

Some but by no means all of the Court's coerced confessions came out of the South.

Spano v. New York
360 U.S. 215 (1959)

Mr. Chief Justice WARREN delivered the opinion of the Court.
    This is another in the long line of cases presenting the question whether a confession was properly admitted into evidence under the Fourteenth Amendment. As in all such cases, we are forced to resolve a conflict between two fundamental interests of society; its interest in prompt and efficient law enforcement, and its interest in preventing the rights of its individual members from being abridged by unconstitutional methods of law enforcement. Because of the delicate nature of the constitutional determination which we must make, we cannot escape the responsibility of making our own examination of the record. *Norris v. State of Alabama.*
    The State's evidence reveals the following: Petitioner Vincent Joseph Spano is a derivative citizen of this country, having been born in Messina, Italy. He was 25 years old at the time of the shooting in question and had graduated from junior high school. He had a record of regular employment. The shooting took place on January 22, 1957.

On that day, petitioner was drinking in a bar. The decedent, a former professional boxer weighing almost 200 pounds who had fought in Madison Square Garden, took some of petitioner's money from the bar. Petitioner followed him out of the bar to recover it. A fight ensued, with the decedent knocking petitioner down and then kicking him in the head three or four times. Shock from the force of these blow caused petitioner to vomit. After the bartender applied some ice to his head, petitioner left the bar, walked to his apartment, secured a gun, and walked eight or nine blocks to a candy store where the decedent was frequently to be found. He entered the store in which decedent, three friends of decedent, at least two of whom were ex-convicts, and a boy who was supervising the store were present. He fired five shots, two of which entered the decedent's body, causing his death. The boy was the only eyewitness; the three friends of decedent did not see the person who fired the shot. Petitioner then disappeared for the next week or so.

On February 1, 1957, the Bronx County Grand Jury returned an indictment for first-degree murder against petitioner. Accordingly, a bench warrant was issued for his arrest, commanding that he be forthwith brought before the court to answer the indictment, or, if the court had adjourned for the term, that he be delivered into the custody of the Sheriff of Bronx County.

On February 3, 1957, petitioner called one Gaspar Bruno, a close friend of 8 or 10 years' standing who had attended school with him. Bruno was a fledgling police officer, having at that time not yet finished attending police academy. According to Bruno's testimony, petitioner told him "that he took a terrific beating, that the deceased hurt him real bad and he dropped him a couple of times and he was dazed; he didn't know what he was doing and that he went and shot at him." Petitioner told Bruno that he intended to get a lawyer and give himself up. Bruno relayed this information to his superiors.

The following day, February 4, at 7:10 p.m., petitioner, accompanied by counsel, surrendered himself to the authorities in front of the Bronx County Building, where both the office of the Assistant District Attorney who ultimately prosecuted his case and the court-room in which he was ultimately tried were located. His attorney had cautioned him to answer no questions, and left him in the custody of the officers. He was promptly taken to the office of the Assistant District Attorney and at 7:15 p.m. the questioning began, being conducted by Assistant District Attorney Goldsmith, Lt. Gannon, Detectives Farrell, Lehrer and Motta, and Sgt. Clarke. The record reveals that the questioning was both persistent and continuous. Petitioner, in accordance with his attorney's instructions, steadfastly refused to answer. Detective Motta testified: "He refused to talk to me." "He just looked up to the ceiling and refused to talk to me." Detective Farrell testified:

Q. And you started to interrogate him? A. That is right.
Q. What did he say? A. He said "you would have to see my attorney. I tell you nothing but my name."
Q. Did you continue to examine him? A. Verbally, yes, sir.

He asked one officer, Detective Ciccone, if he could speak to his attorney, but that request was denied. Detective Ciccone testified that he could not find the attorney's name in the telephone book. He was given two sandwiches, coffee and cake at 11 p.m.

At 12:15 a.m. on the morning of February 5, after five hours of questioning in which it became evident that petitioner was following his attorney's instructions, on the Assistant District Attorney's orders petitioner was transferred to the 46th Squad, Ryer Avenue Police Station. The Assistant District Attorney also went to the police station and to some extent continued to participate in the interrogation. Petitioner arrived at 12:30 and questioning was

B. Police Interrogation: Voluntariness and the Road to *Miranda*

resumed at 12:40. The character of the questioning is revealed by the testimony of Detective Farrell:

> **Q.** Who did you leave him in the room with? A. With Detective Lehrer and Sergeant Clarke came in and Mr. Goldsmith came in or Inspector Halk came in. It was back and forth. People just came in, spoke a few words to the defendant or they listened a few minutes and they left.

But petitioner persisted in his refusal to answer, and again requested permission to see his attorney, this time from Detective Lehrer. His request was again denied.

It was then that those in charge of the investigation decided that petitioner's close friend, Bruno, could be of use. He had been called out on the case around 10 or 11 p.m., although he was not connected with the 46th Squad or Precinct in any way. Although, in fact, his job was in no way threatened, Bruno was told to tell petitioner that petitioner's telephone call had gotten him "in a lot of trouble," and that he should seek to extract sympathy from petitioner for Bruno's pregnant wife and three children. Bruno developed this theme with petitioner without success, and petitioner, also without success, again sought to see his attorney, a request which Bruno relayed unavailingly to his superiors. After this first session with petitioner, Bruno was again directed by Lt. Gannon to play on petitioner's sympathies, but again no confession was forthcoming. But the Lieutenant a third time ordered Bruno falsely to importune his friend to confess but again petitioner clung to his attorney's advice. Inevitably, in the fourth such session directed by the Lieutenant, lasting a full hour, petitioner succumbed to his friend's prevarications and agreed to make a statement. Accordingly, at 3:25 a.m. the Assistant District Attorney, a stenographer, and several other law enforcement officials entered the room where petitioner was being questioned, and took his statement in question and answer form with the Assistant District Attorney asking the questions. The statement was completed at 4:05 a.m.

But this was not the end. At 4:30 a.m. three detectives took petitioner to Police Headquarters in Manhattan. On the way they attempted to find the bridge from which petitioner said he had thrown the murder weapon. They crossed the Triborough Bridge into Manhattan, arriving at Police Headquarters at 5 a.m., and left Manhattan for the Bronx at 5:40 a.m. via the Willis Avenue Bridge. When petitioner recognized neither bridge as the one from which he had thrown the weapon, they re-entered Manhattan via the Third Avenue Bridge, which petitioner stated was the right one, and then returned to the Bronx well after 6 a.m. During that trip the officers also elicited a statement from petitioner that the deceased was always "on (his) back," "always pushing" him and that he was "not sorry" he had shot the deceased. All three detectives testified to that statement at the trial.

Court opened at 10 a.m. that morning, and petitioner was arraigned at 10:15.

At the trial, the confession was introduced in evidence over appropriate objections. The jury was instructed that it could rely on it only if it was found to be voluntary. The jury returned a guilty verdict and petitioner was sentenced to death. The New York Court of Appeals affirmed the conviction over three dissents, and we granted certiorari to resolve the serious problem presented under the Fourteenth Amendment.

Petitioner's first contention is that his absolute right to counsel in a capital case, became operative on the return of an indictment against him, for at that time he was in every sense a defendant in a criminal case, the grand jury having found sufficient cause to believe that he had committed the crime. He argues accordingly that following indictment no confession obtained in the absence of counsel can be used without violating the Fourteenth Amendment. We find it unnecessary to reach that contention, for we find use of the confession obtained here inconsistent with the Fourteenth Amendment under traditional principles.

Chapter III Police Interrogation and The Fifth Amendment

The abhorrence of society to the use of involuntary confessions does not turn alone on their inherent untrustworthiness. It also turns on the deep-rooted feeling that the police must obey the law while enforcing the law; that in the end life and liberty can be as much endangered from illegal methods used to convict those thought to be criminals as from the actual criminals themselves. Accordingly, the actions of police in obtaining confessions have come under scrutiny in a long series of cases. Those cases suggest that in recent years law enforcement officials have become increasingly aware of the burden which they share, along with our courts, in protecting fundamental rights of our citizenry, including that portion of our citizenry suspected of crime. The facts of no case recently in this Court have quite approached the brutal beatings in *Brown v. State of Mississippi*, or the 36 consecutive hours of questioning present in *Ashcraft v. State of Tennessee*. But as law enforcement officers become more responsible, and the methods used to extract confessions more sophisticated, our duty to enforce federal constitutional protections does not cease. It only becomes more difficult because of the more delicate judgments to be made. Our judgment here is that, on all the facts, this conviction cannot stand.

Petitioner was a foreign-born young man of 25 with no past history of law violation or of subjection to official interrogation, at least insofar as the record shows. He had progressed only one-half year into high school and the record indicates that he had a history of emotional instability. He did not make a narrative statement, but was subject to the leading questions of a skillful prosecutor in a question and answer confession. He was subjected to questioning not by a few men, but by many. They included Assistant District Attorney Goldsmith, one Hyland of the District Attorney's Office, Deputy Inspector Halks, Lieutenant Gannon, Detective Ciccone, Detective Motta, Detective Lehrer, Detective Marshal, Detective Farrell, Detective Leira, Detective Murphy, Detective Murtha, Sergeant Clarke, Patrolman Bruno and Stenographer Baldwin. All played some part, and the effect of such massive official interrogation must have been felt. Petitioner was questioned for virtually eight straight hours before he confessed, with his only respite being a transfer to an arena presumably considered more appropriate by the police for the task at hand. Nor was the questioning conducted during normal business hours, but began in early evening, continued into the night, and did not bear fruition until the not-too-early morning. The drama was not played out, with the final admissions obtained, until almost sunrise. In such circumstances slowly mounting fatigue does, and is calculated to, play its part. The questioners persisted in the face of his repeated refusals to answer on the advice of his attorney, and they ignored his reasonable requests to contact the local attorney whom he had already retained and who had personally delivered him into the custody of these officers in obedience to the bench warrant.

The use of Bruno, characterized in this Court by counsel for the State as a "childhood friend" of petitioner's, is another factor which deserves mention in the totality of the situation. Bruno's was the one face visible to petitioner in which he could put some trust. There was a bond of friendship between them going back a decade into adolescence. It was with this material that the officers felt that they could overcome petitioner's will. They instructed Bruno falsely to state that petitioner's telephone call had gotten him into trouble, that his job was in jeopardy, and that loss of his job would be disastrous to his three children, his wife and his unborn child. And Bruno played this part of a worried father, harried by his superiors, in not one, but four different acts, the final one lasting an hour. Petitioner was apparently unaware of John Gay's famous couplet:

An open foe may prove a curse, But a pretended friend is worse,

and he yielded to his false friend's entreaties.

We conclude that petitioner's will was overborne by official pressure, fatigue and sympathy falsely aroused after considering all the facts in their post-indictment setting. Here a

B. Police Interrogation: Voluntariness and the Road to *Miranda*   **113**

grand jury had already found sufficient cause to require petitioner to face trial on a charge of first-degree murder, and the police had an eyewitness to the shooting. The police were not therefore merely trying to solve a crime, or even to absolve a suspect. They were rather concerned primarily with securing a statement from defendant on which they could convict him. The undeviating intent of the officers to extract a confession from petitioner is therefore patent. When such an intent is shown, this Court has held that the confession obtained must be examined with the most careful scrutiny, and has reversed a conviction on facts less compelling than these. Accordingly, we hold that petitioner's conviction cannot stand under the Fourteenth Amendment.

Reversed.

NOTES AND QUESTIONS

1. Chief Justice Warren describes the defendant, Joseph Spano, as a "derivative citizen," whatever that may mean. How if at all might Spano's personal characteristics—his age, his education, his employment status, his "citizenship"—be relevant?

2. How significant to the result here is it that, at the time of his confession, Spano was already under indictment? That he had already retained counsel? That the government had a witness to the alleged murder?

Four Justices concurred, noting that Spano had counsel and/or had been indicted, facts that were sufficient grounds themselves for reversal.

3. The Court distinguishes between police action aimed to "extract a confession" as opposed to action "merely to solve a crime." Should the circumstances and status of the investigation matter in a constitutional sense? Should the police get more leeway when a crime is unsolved or unwitnessed?

4. What is the significance to the result that the assistant district attorney who ultimately prosecuted the case, a "skillful" cross-examiner, participated in the interrogation, including relocating to the police station to continue the interrogation after five hours at the D.A.'s office? Would it have been ethical for the ADA to participate in the deception of the defendant by his friend Bruno?

5. Are there any limits on the deception a police officer can use in questioning a suspect? Note that the Court does not explicitly say that the deception of Spano was unconstitutionally coercive. Was the length of the questioning of Spano unconstitutionally coercive?

The Court's reference to a suspect's need for counsel in the Fifth Amendment interrogation context can sometimes be difficult to take seriously. In some instances, the Court seems to harbor the illusion that a criminal suspect is actually in need of advice about whether to submit to questioning by the police. But the Court knows better, and has known better since at least as long as Justice Robert Jackson had been on the Court, as this excerpt from his concurring opinion in *Watts v. Indiana*, 338 U.S. 49 (1949), makes clear:

> Amid much that is irrelevant or trivial one serious situation seems to me to stand out in these cases. The suspect neither had nor was advised of his right to get counsel. This presents a real dilemma in a free society. To subject one without counsel to questioning which may and is intended to convict him, is a real peril to individual freedom. To bring in a lawyer means a real peril to solution of the crime because, under our adversary system, he deems that his sole duty is to protect his client—guilty or innocent—and that in such a capacity he owes no duty whatever to help society solve its crime problem. Under this conception of criminal procedure, any

Chapter III Police Interrogation and The Fifth Amendment

lawyer worth his salt will tell the suspect in no uncertain terms to make no statement to police under any circumstances.

If the State may arrest on suspicion and interrogate without counsel, there is no denying the fact that it largely negates the benefits of the constitutional guaranty of the right to assistance of counsel. Any lawyer who has ever been called into a case after his client has "told all" and turned any evidence he has over to the Government, knows how helpless he is to protect his client against the facts thus disclosed.

Id. at 59.

The Court further reflected on the meaning of the right to counsel in the interrogation context in the next case, where the defendant, like the defendant in *Spano*, was already under indictment and represented by counsel when the interrogation occurred.

Massiah v. United States
377 U.S. 201 (1964)

Mr. Justice STEWART delivered the opinion of the Court.

The petitioner was indicted for violating the federal narcotics laws. He retained a lawyer, pleaded not guilty, and was released on bail. While he was free on bail a federal agent succeeded by surreptitious means in listening to incriminating statements made by him. Evidence of these statements was introduced against the petitioner at his trial over his objection. He was convicted, and the Court of Appeals affirmed. We granted certiorari to consider whether, under the circumstances here presented, the prosecution's use at the trial of evidence of the petitioner's own incriminating statements deprived him of any right secured to him under the Federal Constitution.

The petitioner, a merchant seaman, was in 1958 a member of the crew of the S. S. Santa Maria. In April of that year federal customs officials in New York received information that he was going to transport a quantity of narcotics aboard that ship from South America to the United States. As a result of this and other information, the agents searched the Santa Maria upon its arrival in New York and found in the afterpeak of the vessel five packages containing about three and a half pounds of cocaine. They also learned of circumstances, not here relevant, tending to connect the petitioner with the cocaine. He was arrested, promptly arraigned, and subsequently indicted for possession of narcotics aboard a United States vessel. In July a superseding indictment was returned, charging the petitioner and a man named Colson with the same substantive offense, and in separate counts charging the petitioner, Colson, and others with having conspired to possess narcotics aboard a United States vessel, and to import, conceal, and facilitate the sale of narcotics. The petitioner, who had retained a lawyer, pleaded not guilty and was released on bail, along with Colson.

A few days later, and quite without the petitioner's knowledge, Colson decided to cooperate with the government agents in their continuing investigation of the narcotics activities in which the petitioner, Colson, and others had allegedly been engaged. Colson permitted an agent named Murphy to install a Schmidt radio transmitter under the front seat of Colson's automobile, by means of which Murphy, equipped with an appropriate receiving device, could overhear from some distance away conversations carried on in Colson's car.

On the evening of November 19, 1959, Colson and the petitioner held a lengthy conversation while sitting in Colson's automobile, parked on a New York street. By prearrangement with Colson, and totally unbeknown to the petitioner, the agent Murphy sat in a car parked out of sight down the street and listened over the radio to the entire conversation. The petitioner made several incriminating statements during the course of this conversation.

At the petitioner's trial these incriminating statements were brought before the jury through Murphy's testimony, despite the insistent objection of defense counsel. The jury convicted the petitioner of several related narcotics offenses, and the convictions were affirmed by the Court of Appeals.

The petitioner argues that it was an error of constitutional dimensions to permit the agent Murphy at the trial to testify to the petitioner's incriminating statements which Murphy had overheard under the circumstances disclosed by this record. This argument is based upon two distinct and independent grounds. First, we are told that Murphy's use of the radio equipment violated the petitioner's rights under the Fourth Amendment, and, consequently, that all evidence which Murphy thereby obtained was, under the rule of *Weeks v. United States*, inadmissible against the petitioner at the trial. Secondly, it is said that the petitioner's Fifth and Sixth Amendment rights were violated by the use in evidence against him of incriminating statements which government agents had deliberately elicited from him after he had been indicted and in the absence of his retained counsel. Because of the way we dispose of the case, we do not reach the Fourth Amendment issue.

In *Spano v. New York*, this Court reversed a state criminal conviction because a confession had been wrongly admitted into evidence against the defendant at his trial. In that case the defendant had already been indicted for first-degree murder at the time he confessed. The Court held that the defendant's conviction could not stand under the Fourteenth Amendment. While the Court's opinion relied upon the totality of the circumstances under which the confession had been obtained, four concurring Justices pointed out that the Constitution required reversal of the conviction upon the sole and specific ground that the confession had been deliberately elicited by the police after the defendant had been indicted, and therefore at a time when he was clearly entitled to a lawyer's help. It was pointed out that under our system of justice the most elemental concepts of due process of law contemplate that an indictment be followed by a trial, "in an orderly courtroom, presided over by a judge, open to the public, and protected by all the procedural safeguards of the law. It was said that a Constitution which guarantees a defendant the aid of counsel at such a trial could surely vouchsafe no less to an indicted defendant under interrogation by the police in a completely extrajudicial proceeding. Anything less, it was said, might deny a defendant 'effective representation by counsel at the only stage when legal aid and advice would help him.'"

Ever since this Court's decision in the *Spano* case, the New York courts have unequivocally followed this constitutional rule. "Any secret interrogation of the defendant, from and after the finding of the indictment, without the protection afforded by the presence of counsel, contravenes the basic dictates of fairness in the conduct of criminal causes and the fundamental rights of persons charged with crime."

This view no more than reflects a constitutional principle established as long ago as *Powell v. Alabama*, where the Court noted that ". . . during perhaps the most critical period of the proceedings . . . that is to say, from the time of their arraignment until the beginning of their trial, when consultation, thorough-going investigation and preparation (are) vitally important, the defendants . . . (are) as much entitled to such aid (of counsel) during that period as at the trial itself." And since the *Spano* decision the same basic constitutional principle has been broadly reaffirmed by this Court.

Here we deal not with a state court conviction, but with a federal case, where the specific guarantee of the Sixth Amendment directly applies. We hold that the petitioner was denied the basic protections of that guarantee when there was used against him at his trial evidence of his own incriminating words, which federal agents had deliberately elicited from him after he had been indicted and in the absence of his counsel. It is true that in the *Spano* case the defendant was interrogated in a police station, while here the damaging testimony was elicited from the defendant without his knowledge while he was free on bail. But, as Judge Hays pointed out in his dissent in the Court of Appeals, "if such a rule is to have any efficacy it must apply to indirect and surreptitious interrogations as well as those conducted in the jailhouse. In this case, Massiah was more seriously imposed upon . . . because he did not even know that he was under interrogation by a government agent."

The Solicitor General, in his brief and oral argument, has strenuously contended that the federal law enforcement agents had the right, if not indeed the duty, to continue their investigation of the petitioner and his alleged criminal associates even though the petitioner had been indicted. He points out that the Government was continuing its investigation in order to uncover not only the source of narcotics found on the S. S. Santa Maria, but also their intended buyer. He says that the quantity of narcotics involved was such as to suggest that the petitioner was part of a large and well-organized ring, and indeed that the continuing investigation confirmed this suspicion, since it resulted in criminal charges against many defendants. Under these circumstances the Solicitor General concludes that the Government agents were completely "justified in making use of Colson's cooperation by having Colson continue his normal associations and by surveilling them."

We may accept and, at least for present purposes, completely approve all that this argument implies, Fourth Amendment problems to one side. We do not question that in this case, as in many cases, it was entirely proper to continue an investigation of the suspected criminal activities of the defendant and his alleged confederates, even though the defendant had already been indicted. All that we hold is that the defendant's own incriminating statements, obtained by federal agents under the circumstances here disclosed, could not constitutionally be used by the prosecution as evidence against him at his trial.

Reversed.

[Justices White, Clark, and Harlan dissented.]

NOTES AND QUESTIONS

1. The Court states that "under our system of justice the most elemental concepts of due process contemplate that an indictment be followed by a trial, 'in an orderly courtroom, presided over by a judge, open to the public, and protected by all the procedural safeguards of the law'" (citing and quoting from) *Spano v. New York*, 360 U.S. 315, 327 (1959). What is the point of this observation? Is there tension between this observation and the Court's later statement that it may in some cases "be entirely proper to continue an investigation of the suspected activities of the defendant and his alleged confederates, even though the defendant had already been indicted"? In what category of cases is this sort of post-indictment investigation appropriate?

The Court quotes with apparent approval the line from the dissenting judge in the Second Circuit, who noted that Massiah was "more seriously imposed upon" than the defendant in *Spano*, who was openly, and not surreptitiously, interrogated. Do you agree with this sentiment? Is the Court nostalgic for some bygone norms of criminal justice, where the police observed recognized boundaries? Is it clear that the government's use of Colson to secretly record his conversations with Massiah would have been permissible prior to indictment? What if Massiah had hired an attorney prior to indictment because he had got wind of the government's investigation, and the government was aware of this representation?

2. Is it fair to read *Massiah* as recognizing what might be thought of as a "defensive" component of the right to counsel? If this understanding of *Massiah* is correct, what is the

B. Police Interrogation: Voluntariness and the Road to *Miranda* 117

relevance of the Court's citation to and reliance on such right-to-counsel cases as *Powell, Gideon,* and *Johnson v. Zerbst?*

What might the contours of such a defensive right to counsel be? Is this view compatible with the language of the Sixth Amendment, which speaks in terms of the "assistance of counsel"? The dissent points out that this "new rule" rests on the likelihood that, if counsel were to participate in any attempt to interrogate a defendant post-indictment, counsel would advise defendant not to say anything. Is the dissent correct? Does such advice amount to "assistance of counsel"?

3. Unfortunately, the opinion does not include the recorded conversation between Colson (the cooperator) and Massiah. Does it seem likely that Colson's conversation with Massiah had the benefit of substantive input from Murphy, the agent? Suppose Colson had not been given the recording device but had been directed by Murphy on how to handle the conversation and had immediately reported the substance of the conversation to Murphy after it ended. What result? Consider further the situation where Colson is cooperating with Murphy but receives neither recording equipment nor instruction from Murphy on how to handle the conversation and, instead, has the conversation entirely of his own volition but then reports admissions by Massiah to Murphy?

The dissent makes several interesting points in addition to its general lament that the new rule will make it harder to convict criminals. First, it points out that Massiah's statements to Colson are suppressed without any showing of coercion, which at this point (pre-*Miranda*) was the standard used in confession cases. Second, the dissent argues that the rule exceeds the Fifth Amendment bar on self-incrimination, which does not bar voluntary pretrial admissions. Third, there is no suggestion that the government in any way interfered with Massiah's relationship with his counsel. What is the best response to these points, individually or collectively?

Miranda v. Arizona, 384 U.S. 436 (1966), decided seven years after *Spano* and two years after *Massiah,* was to fundamentally and forever change the landscape of police interrogation. But the concept of voluntariness—though eclipsed by the "warnings" required by *Miranda*—did not cease to be relevant. In *Colorado v. Connelly,* 479 U.S. 157 (1986), 20 years after *Miranda,* the Court held that an unprompted confession by a person with a history of mental illness was voluntary for due process purposes even though there was undisputed medical evidence that, at the moment of confession, the defendant was experiencing "command hallucinations" and thus lacked "the ability to make free and rational choices." *Id.* at 161. The Court held that coercive police activity was "a necessary predicate" to establishing a constitutional violation. Dissenting, Justice Brennan argued that due to the enormous power of a confession as a type of evidence, an involuntary confession should be admissible only where bulwarked by "substantial indicia of reliability" extrinsic to the confession itself, evidence that was totally lacking in *Connelly. Id.* at 184.

In *Arizona v. Fulminante,* 499 U.S. 279 (1991), defendant was incarcerated in federal prison on a felon-in-possession firearms charge. He had previously been a suspect in the murder of his stepdaughter but had not been charged. A fellow federal prisoner, who was also an FBI informant, heard rumors about the defendant's having been a suspect in a child murder. He offered to arrange for the defendant's protection in prison, but agreed to do so only if the defendant came clean about his involvement in the murder. The defendant's subsequent confession to the informant was found to be involuntary and hence inadmissible inasmuch as it was induced by "a credible threat of physical violence." *Id.* at 288.

C. *MIRANDA*

We turn now to the centerpiece of the Warren Court revolution, the best-known case name ever, the Supreme Court's 1966 decision in *Miranda v. Arizona*, 384 U.S. 436 (1966). The term "revolution" is not hyperbole. Consider that in a state court criminal prosecution in 1960 the Fourth, Fifth, and Sixth Amendments played no role. Just eight years later in such a prosecution, illegally obtained evidence could be suppressed, *Mapp v. Ohio*, 367 U.S. 643 (1961); indigent felony defendants had to be afforded counsel, *Gideon v. Wainwright*, 372 U.S. 335 (1963); a person could not be subpoenaed to give testimony that might incriminate him, *Malloy v. Hogan*, 378 U.S. 1 (1964); warnings were required for custodial interrogations, *Miranda*; and states were required to provide jury trials in serious criminal cases, *Duncan v. Louisiana*, 391 U.S. 145 (1968). *See* Stephen Schulhofer, Miranda v. Arizona: *A Modest But Important Legacy* 157, in Criminal Procedure Stories (Carol Steiker ed., 2006). The authors of these five opinions had not come to the Court ordained with civil libertarian credentials, moreover. Four of the five of them—Justices Clark (*Mapp*), White (*Duncan*), Black (*Gideon*) and Warren (*Miranda*)—had been state or federal prosecutors.

The immediate predicate to *Miranda* was what the Court calls in *Miranda* the "spirited debate" engendered by its decision just two years earlier in *Escobedo v. Illinois*, 378 U.S. 478 (1964). In *Escobedo*, the police interrogated a suspect in custody at the police station, all the while denying his requests for counsel and preventing his retained attorney, who had come to the police station, from consulting with him. The suspect eventually made incriminating statements that were admitted against him at trial. The Court overturned the conviction, holding the statements "constitutionally inadmissible."

<hr>

Miranda v. Arizona
384 U.S. 436 (1966)

Mr. Chief Justice WARREN delivered the opinion of the Court.

The cases before us raise questions which go to the roots of our concepts of American criminal jurisprudence: the restraints society must observe consistent with the Federal Constitution in prosecuting individuals for crime. More specifically, we deal with the admissibility of statements obtained from an individual who is subjected to custodial police interrogation and the necessity for procedures which assure that the individual is accorded his privilege under the Fifth Amendment to the Constitution not to be compelled to incriminate himself.

We dealt with certain phases of this problem recently in *Escobedo*. There, as in the four cases before us, law enforcement officials took the defendant into custody and interrogated him in a police station for the purpose of obtaining a confession. The police did not effectively advise him of his right to remain silent or of his right to consult with his attorney. Rather, they confronted him with an alleged accomplice who accused him of having perpetrated a murder. When the defendant denied the accusation and said "I didn't shoot Manuel, you did it," they handcuffed him and took him to an interrogation room. There, while handcuffed and standing, he was questioned for four hours until he confessed. During this interrogation, the police denied his request to speak to his attorney, and they prevented his retained attorney, who had come to the police station, from consulting with him. At his trial, the State, over his objection, introduced the confession against him. We held that the statements thus made were constitutionally inadmissible.

This case has been the subject of judicial interpretation and spirited legal debate since it was decided two years ago. Both state and federal courts, in assessing its implications, have arrived at varying conclusions. A wealth of scholarly material has been written tracing its ramifications and underpinnings. Police and prosecutor have speculated on its range and desirability. We granted certiorari in these cases in order further to explore some facets of the problems, thus exposed, of applying the privilege against self-incrimination to in-custody interrogation, and to give concrete constitutional guidelines for law enforcement agencies and courts to follow.

We start here, as we did in *Escobedo*, with the premise that our holding is not an innovation in our jurisprudence, but is an application of principles long recognized and applied in other settings. We have undertaken a thorough re-examination of the *Escobedo* decision and the principles it announced, and we reaffirm it. That case was but an explication of basic rights that are enshrined in our Constitution — that "No person . . . shall be compelled in any criminal case to be a witness against himself," and that "the accused shall . . . have the Assistance of Counsel" — rights which were put in jeopardy in that case through official overbearing. These precious rights were fixed in our Constitution only after centuries of persecution and struggle. And in the words of Chief Justice Marshall, they were secured "for ages to come, and . . . designed to approach immortality as nearly as human institutions can approach it."

Over 70 years ago, our predecessors on this Court eloquently stated:

> The maxim "Nemo tenetur seipsum accusare," had its origin in a protest against the inquisitorial and manifestly unjust methods of interrogating accused persons, which (have) long obtained in the continental system, and, until the expulsion of the Stuarts from the British throne in 1688, and the erection of additional barriers for the protection of the people against the exercise of arbitrary power, (were) not uncommon even in England. While the admissions or confessions of the prisoner, when voluntarily and freely made, have always ranked high in the scale of incriminating evidence, if an accused person be asked to explain his apparent connection with a crime under investigation, the ease with which the questions put to him may assume an inquisitorial character, the temptation to press the witness unduly, to browbeat him if he be timid or reluctant, to push him into a corner, and to entrap him into fatal contradictions, which is so painfully evident in many of the earlier state trials, notably in those of Sir Nicholas Throckmorton, and Udal, the Puritan minister, made the system so odious as to give rise to a demand for its total abolition. The change in the English criminal procedure in that particular seems to be founded upon no statute and no judicial opinion, but upon a general and silent acquiescence of the courts in a popular demand. But, however adopted, it has become firmly embedded in English, as well as in American jurisprudence. So deeply did the iniquities of the ancient system impress themselves upon the minds of the American colonists that the States, with one accord, made a denial of the right to question an accused person a part of their fundamental law, so that a maxim, which in England was a mere rule of evidence, became clothed in this country with the impregnability of a constitutional enactment.

In stating the obligation of the judiciary to apply these constitutional rights, this Court declared in *Weems v. United States* (1910):

> . . . our contemplation cannot be only of what has been, but of what may be. Under any other rule a constitution would indeed be as easy of application as it would be deficient in efficacy and power. Its general principles would have little value, and be converted by precedent into impotent and lifeless formulas. Rights declared in words might be lost in reality. And this has been recognized. The meaning and vitality of the Constitution have developed against narrow and restrictive construction.

This was the spirit in which we delineated, in meaningful language, the manner in which the constitutional rights of the individual could be enforced against overzealous police practices. It was necessary in *Escobedo*, as here, to insure that what was proclaimed in the Constitution had not become but a "form of words," in the hands of government officials. And it is in this spirit, consistent with our role as judges, that we adhere to the principles of *Escobedo* today.

Our holding will be spelled out with some specificity in the pages which follow but briefly stated it is this: the prosecution may not use statements, whether exculpatory or inculpatory, stemming from custodial interrogation of the defendant unless it demonstrates the use of procedural safeguards effective to secure the privilege against self-incrimination. By custodial interrogation, we mean questioning initiated by law enforcement officers after a person has been taken into custody or otherwise deprived of his freedom of action in any significant way. As for the procedural safeguards to be employed, unless other fully effective means are devised to inform accused persons of their right of silence and to assure a continuous opportunity to exercise it, the following measures are required. Prior to any questioning, the person must be warned that he has a right to remain silent, that any statement he does make may be used as evidence against him, and that he has a right to the presence of an attorney, either retained or appointed. The defendant may waive effectuation of these rights, provided the waiver is made voluntarily, knowingly and intelligently. If, however, he indicates in any manner and at any stage of the process that he wishes to consult with an attorney before speaking there can be no questioning. Likewise, if the individual is alone and indicates in any manner that he does not wish to be interrogated, the police may not question him. The mere fact that he may have answered some questions or volunteered some statements on his own does not deprive him of the right to refrain from answering any further inquiries until he has consulted with an attorney and thereafter consents to be questioned.

1

The constitutional issue we decide in each of these cases is the admissibility of statements obtained from a defendant questioned while in custody or otherwise deprived of his freedom of action in any significant way. In each, the defendant was questioned by police officers, detectives, or a prosecuting attorney in a room in which he was cut off from the outside world. In none of these cases was the defendant given a full and effective warning of his rights at the outset of the interrogation process. In all the cases, the questioning elicited oral admissions, and in three of them, signed statements as well which were admitted at their trials. They all thus share salient features—incommunicado interrogation of individuals in a police-dominated atmosphere, resulting in self-incriminating statements without full warnings of constitutional rights.

An understanding of the nature and setting of this in-custody interrogation is essential to our decisions today. The difficulty in depicting what transpires at such interrogations stems from the fact that in this country they have largely taken place incommunicado. From extensive factual studies undertaken in the early 1930's, including the famous Wickersham Report to Congress by a Presidential Commission, it is clear that police violence and the "third degree" flourished at that time. In a series of cases decided by this Court long after these studies, the police resorted to physical brutality—beatings, hanging, whipping—and to sustained and protracted questioning incommunicado in order to extort confessions. The Commission on Civil Rights in 1961 found much evidence to indicate that "some policemen still resort to physical force to obtain confessions." The use of physical brutality and violence is not, unfortunately, relegated to the past or to any part of the country. Only recently in Kings County, New York, the police brutally beat, kicked and placed lighted cigarette butts on the back of a potential witness under interrogation for the purpose of securing a statement incriminating a third party.

The examples given above are undoubtedly the exception now, but they are sufficiently widespread to be the object of concern. Unless a proper limitation upon custodial interrogation is achieved—such as these decisions will advance—there can be no assurance that practices of this nature will be eradicated in the foreseeable future. The conclusion of the Wickersham Commission Report, made over 30 years ago, is still pertinent:

> To the contention that the third degree is necessary to get the facts, the reporters aptly reply in the language of the present Lord Chancellor of England (Lord Sankey): "It is not admissible to do a great right by doing a little wrong. . . . It is not sufficient to do justice by obtaining a proper result by irregular or improper means." Not only does the use of the third degree involve a flagrant violation of law by the officers of the law, but it involves also the dangers of false confessions, and it tends to make police and prosecutors less zealous in the search for objective evidence. As the New York prosecutor quoted in the report said, "It is a short cut and makes the police lazy and unenterprising." Or, as another official quoted remarked: "If you use your fists, you are not so likely to use your wits." We agree with the conclusion expressed in the report, that "The third degree brutalizes the police, hardens the prisoner against society, and lowers the esteem in which the administration of justice is held by the public."

Again we stress that the modern practice of in-custody interrogation is psychologically rather than physically oriented. As we have stated before, "this Court has recognized that coercion can be mental as well as physical, and that the blood of the accused is not the only hallmark of an unconstitutional inquisition." Interrogation still takes place in privacy. Privacy results in secrecy and this in turn results in a gap in our knowledge as to what in fact goes on in the interrogation rooms. A valuable source of information about present police practices, however, may be found in various police manuals and texts which document procedures employed with success in the past, and which recommend various other effective tactics. These texts are used by law enforcement agencies themselves as guides. It should be noted that these texts professedly present the most enlightened and effective means presently used to obtain statements through custodial interrogation. By considering these texts and other data, it is possible to describe procedures observed and noted around the country.

* * *

II

We sometimes forget how long it has taken to establish the privilege against self-incrimination, the sources from which it came and the fervor with which it was defended. Its roots go back into ancient times. Perhaps the critical historical event shedding light on its origins and evolution was the trial of one John Lilburn, a vocal anti-Stuart Leveller, who was made to take the Star Chamber Oath in 1637. The oath would have bound him to answer to all questions posed to him on any subject. The Trial of John Lilburn and John Wharton. He resisted the oath and declaimed the proceedings, stating:

> Another fundamental right I then contended for, was, that no man's conscience ought to be racked by oaths imposed, to answer to questions concerning himself in matters criminal, or pretended to be so.

On account of the Lilburn Trial, Parliament abolished the inquisitorial Court of Star Chamber and went further in giving him generous reparation. The lofty principles to which Lilburn had appealed during his trial gained popular acceptance in England. These sentiments worked their way over to the Colonies and were implanted after great struggle into the Bill of Rights. Those who framed our Constitution and the Bill of Rights were ever aware of subtle encroachments on individual liberty. They knew that "illegitimate and unconstitutional practices get their first footing . . . by silent approaches and slight deviations from legal modes of procedure." The privilege was elevated to constitutional status and has always been "as broad as the mischief against which it seeks to guard." *Counselman*. We cannot depart from this noble heritage.

Thus we may view the historical development of the privilege as one which groped for the proper scope of governmental power over the citizen. As a "noble principle often transcends its origins," the privilege has come rightfully to be recognized in part as an individual's substantive right, a "right to a private enclave where he may lead a private life. That right is the hallmark of our democracy." We have recently noted that the privilege against self-incrimination — the essential mainstay of our adversary system — is founded on a complex of values. All these policies point to one overriding thought: the constitutional foundation underlying the privilege is the respect a government — state or federal — must accord to the dignity and integrity of its citizens. To maintain a "fair state-individual balance," to require the government "to shoulder the entire load," to respect the inviolability of the human personality, our accusatory system of criminal justice demands that the government seeking to punish an individual produce the evidence against him by its own independent labors, rather than by the cruel, simple expedient of compelling it from his own mouth. In sum, the privilege is fulfilled only when the person is guaranteed the right "to remain silent unless he chooses to speak in the unfettered exercise of his own will."

The question in these cases is whether the privilege is fully applicable during a period of custodial interrogation. We are satisfied that all the principles embodied in the privilege apply to informal compulsion exerted by law-enforcement officers during in-custody questioning. An individual swept from familiar surroundings into police custody, surrounded by antagonistic forces, and subjected to the techniques of persuasion described above cannot be otherwise than under compulsion to speak. As a practical matter, the compulsion to speak in the isolated setting of the police station may well be greater than in courts or other official investigations, where there are often impartial observers to guard against intimidation or trickery.

This question, in fact, could have been taken as settled in federal courts almost 70 years ago, when, in *Bram v. United States*, this Court held:

> In criminal trials, in the courts of the United States, wherever a question arises whether a confession is incompetent because not voluntary, the issue is controlled by that portion of the fifth amendment . . . commanding that no person "shall be compelled in any criminal case to be a witness against himself."

In *Bram*, the Court reviewed the British and American history and case law and set down the Fifth Amendment standard for compulsion which we implement today:

> Much of the confusion which has resulted from the effort to deduce from the adjudged cases what would be a sufficient quantum of proof to show that a confession was or was not voluntary has arisen from a misconception of the subject to which the proof must address itself. The rule is not that, in order to render a statement admissible, the proof must be adequate to establish that the particular communications contained in a statement were voluntarily made, but it must be sufficient to establish that the making of the statement was voluntary; that is to say, that, from the causes which the law treats as legally sufficient to engender in the mind of the accused hope or fear in respect to the crime charged, the accused was not involuntarily impelled to make a statement when but for the improper influences he would have remained silent.

The Court has adhered to this reasoning. In 1924, Mr. Justice Brandeis wrote for a unanimous Court in reversing a conviction resting on a compelled confession. He stated:

> In the federal courts, the requisite of voluntariness is not satisfied by establishing merely that the confession was not induced by a promise or a threat. A confession is voluntary in law if, and only if, it was, in fact, voluntarily made. A confession may have been given voluntarily, although

it was made to police officers, while in custody, and in answer to an examination conducted by them. But a confession obtained by compulsion must be excluded whatever may have been the character of the compulsion, and whether the compulsion was applied in a judicial proceeding or otherwise.

In addition to the expansive historical development of the privilege and the sound policies which have nurtured its evolution, judicial precedent thus clearly establishes its application to incommunicado interrogation. In fact, the Government concedes this point as well established.

Because of the adoption by Congress of Rule 5(a) of the Federal Rules of Criminal Procedure, and the Court's effectuation of that Rule in *McNabb v. United States*, we have had little occasion in the past quarter century to reach the constitutional issues in dealing with federal interrogations.

Our decision in *Malloy v. Hogan* (1964) necessitates an examination of the scope of the privilege in state cases as well. In *Malloy*, we squarely held the privilege applicable to the States, and held that the substantive standards underlying the privilege applied with full force to state court proceedings. Aside from the holding itself, the reasoning in *Malloy* made clear what had already become apparent—that the substantive and procedural safeguards surrounding admissibility of confessions in state cases had become exceedingly exacting, reflecting all the policies embedded in the privilege. The voluntariness doctrine in the state cases, as *Malloy* indicates, encompasses all interrogation practices which are likely to exert such pressure upon an individual as to disable him from making a free and rational choice. The implications of this proposition were elaborated in our decision in *Escobedo*, decided one week after *Malloy* applied the privilege to the States.

Our holding there stressed the fact that the police had not advised the defendant of his constitutional privilege to remain silent at the outset of the interrogation, and we drew attention to that fact at several points in the decision. This was no isolated factor, but an essential ingredient in our decision. The entire thrust of police interrogation there, as in all the cases today, was to put the defendant in such an emotional state as to impair his capacity for rational judgment. The abdication of the constitutional privilege—the choice on his part to speak to the police—was not made knowingly or competently because of the failure to apprise him of his rights; the compelling atmosphere of the in-custody interrogation, and not an independent decision on his part, caused the defendant to speak.

A different phase of the *Escobedo* decision was significant in its attention to the absence of counsel during the questioning. There, as in the cases today, we sought a protective device to dispel the compelling atmosphere of the interrogation. In *Escobedo*, however, the police did not relieve the defendant of the anxieties which they had created in the interrogation rooms. Rather, they denied his request for the assistance of counsel. This heightened his dilemma, and made his later statements the product of this compulsion. The denial of the defendant's request for his attorney thus undermined his ability to exercise the privilege—to remain silent if he chose or to speak without any intimidation, blatant or subtle. The presence of counsel, in all the cases before us today, would be the adequate protective device necessary to make the process of police interrogation conform to the dictates of the privilege. His presence would insure that statements made in the government-established atmosphere are not the product of compulsion.

It was in this manner that *Escobedo* explicated another facet of the pre-trial privilege, noted in many of the Court's prior decisions: the protection of rights at trial. That counsel is present when statements are taken from an individual during interrogation obviously enhances the integrity of the fact-finding processes in court. The presence of an attorney, and the warnings delivered to the individual, enable the defendant under otherwise compelling circumstances to tell his story without fear, effectively, and in a way that eliminates the evils in the interrogation process. Without the protections flowing from adequate warning and the rights of counsel, "all the careful safeguards erected around the giving of testimony, whether by an accused or any other witness, would become empty formalities in a procedure where the most compelling possible evidence of guilt, a confession, would have already been obtained at the unsupervised pleasure of the police."

III

Today, then, there can be no doubt that the Fifth Amendment privilege is available outside of criminal court proceedings and serves to protect persons in all settings in which their freedom of action is curtailed in any significant way from being compelled to incriminate themselves. We have concluded that without proper safeguards the process of in-custody interrogation of persons suspected or accused of crime contains inherently compelling pressures which work to undermine the individual's will to resist and to compel him to speak where he would not otherwise do so freely. In order to combat these pressures and to permit a full opportunity to exercise the privilege against self-incrimination, the accused must be adequately and effectively apprised of his rights and the exercise of those rights must be fully honored.

It is impossible for us to foresee the potential alternatives for protecting the privilege which might be devised by Congress or the States in the exercise of their creative rule-making capacities. Therefore we cannot say that the Constitution necessarily requires adherence to any particular solution for the inherent compulsions of the interrogation process as it is presently conducted. Our decision in no way creates a constitutional straitjacket which will handicap sound efforts at reform, nor is it intended to have this effect. We encourage Congress and the States to continue their laudable search for increasingly effective ways of protecting the rights of the individual while promoting efficient enforcement of our criminal laws. However, unless we are shown other procedures which are at least as effective in apprising accused persons of their right of silence and in assuring a continuous opportunity to exercise it, the following safeguards must be observed.

At the outset, if a person in custody is to be subjected to interrogation, he must first be informed in clear and unequivocal terms that he has the right to remain silent. For those unaware of the privilege, the warning is needed simply to make them aware of it — the threshold requirement for an intelligent decision as to its exercise. More important, such a warning is an absolute prerequisite in overcoming the inherent pressures of the interrogation atmosphere. It is not just the subnormal or woefully ignorant who succumb to an interrogator's imprecations, whether implied or expressly stated, that the interrogation will continue until a confession is obtained or that silence in the face of accusation is itself damning and will bode ill when presented to a jury. Further, the warning will show the individual that his interrogators are prepared to recognize his privilege should he choose to exercise it.

The Fifth Amendment privilege is so fundamental to our system of constitutional rule and the expedient of giving an adequate warning as to the availability of the privilege so simple, we will not pause to inquire in individual cases whether the defendant was aware of his rights without a warning being given. Assessments of the knowledge the defendant possessed, based on information as to his age, education, intelligence, or prior contact with authorities, can never be more than speculation; a warning is a clearcut fact. More important, whatever the background of the person interrogated, a warning at the time of the interrogation is indispensable to overcome its pressures and to insure that the individual knows he is free to exercise the privilege at that point in time.

The warning of the right to remain silent must be accompanied by the explanation that anything said can and will be used against the individual in court. This warning is needed in order to make him aware not only of the privilege, but also of the consequences of forgoing it. It is only through an awareness of these consequences that there can be any assurance of real understanding and intelligent exercise of the privilege. Moreover, this warning may serve to make the individual more acutely aware that he is faced with a phase of the adversary system—that he is not in the presence of persons acting solely in his interest.

The circumstances surrounding in-custody interrogation can operate very quickly to overbear the will of one merely made aware of his privilege by his interrogators. Therefore, the right to have counsel present at the interrogation is indispensable to the protection of the Fifth Amendment privilege under the system we delineate today. Our aim is to assure that the individual's right to choose between silence and speech remains unfettered throughout the interrogation process. A once-stated warning, delivered by those who will conduct the interrogation, cannot itself suffice to that end among those who most require knowledge of their rights. A mere warning given by the interrogators is not alone sufficient to accomplish that end. Prosecutors themselves claim that the admonishment of the right to remain silent without more "will benefit only the recidivist and the professional." Even preliminary advice given to the accused by his own attorney can be swiftly overcome by the secret interrogation process. Thus, the need for counsel to protect the Fifth Amendment privilege comprehends not merely a right to consult with counsel prior to questioning, but also to have counsel present during any questioning if the defendant so desires.

The presence of counsel at the interrogation may serve several significant subsidiary functions as well. If the accused decides to talk to his interrogators, the assistance of counsel can mitigate the dangers of untrustworthiness. With a lawyer present the likelihood that the police will practice coercion is reduced, and if coercion is nevertheless exercised the lawyer can testify to it in court. The presence of a lawyer can also help to guarantee that the accused gives a fully accurate statement to the police and that the statement is rightly reported by the prosecution at trial.

An individual need not make a pre-interrogation request for a lawyer. While such request affirmatively secures his right to have one, his failure to ask for a lawyer does not constitute a waiver. No effective waiver of the right to counsel during interrogation can be recognized unless specifically made after the warnings we here delineate have been given. The accused who does not know his rights and therefore does not make a request may be the person who most needs counsel. As the California Supreme Court has aptly put it:

> Finally, we must recognize that the imposition of the requirement for the request would discriminate against the defendant who does not know his rights. The defendant who does not ask for counsel is the very defendant who most needs counsel. We cannot penalize a defendant who, not understanding his constitutional rights, does not make the formal request and by such failure demonstrates his helplessness. To require the request would be to favor the defendant whose sophistication or status had fortuitously prompted him to make it.

Accordingly we hold that an individual held for interrogation must be clearly informed that he has the right to consult with a lawyer and to have the lawyer with him during interrogation under the system for protecting the privilege we delineate today. As with the warnings of the right to remain silent and that anything stated can be used in evidence against him, this warning is an absolute prerequisite to interrogation. No amount of circumstantial evidence that the person may have been aware of this right will suffice to stand in its stead. Only through such a warning is there ascertainable assurance that the accused was aware of this right.

If an individual indicates that he wishes the assistance of counsel before any interrogation occurs, the authorities cannot rationally ignore or deny his request on the basis that the individual does not have or cannot afford a retained attorney. The financial ability of the individual has no relationship to the scope of the rights involved here. The privilege against self-incrimination secured by the Constitution applies to all individuals. The need for counsel in order to protect the privilege exists for the indigent as well as the affluent. In fact, were we to limit these constitutional rights to those who can retain an attorney, our decisions today would be of little significance. The cases before us as well as the vast majority of confession cases with which we have dealt in the past involve those unable to retain counsel. While authorities are not required to relieve the accused of his poverty, they have the obligation not to take advantage of indigence in the administration of justice. Denial of counsel to the indigent at the time of interrogation while allowing an attorney to those who can afford one would be no more supportable by reason or logic than the similar situation at trial and on appeal struck down in *Gideon*.

In order fully to apprise a person interrogated of the extent of his rights under this system then, it is necessary to warn him not only that he has the right to consult with an attorney, but also that if he is indigent a lawyer will be appointed to represent him. Without this additional warning, the admonition of the right to consult with counsel would often be understood as meaning only that he can consult with a lawyer if he has one or has the funds to obtain one. The warning of a right to counsel would be hollow if not couched in terms that would convey to the indigent—the person most often subjected to interrogation—the knowledge that he too has a right to have counsel present. As with the warnings of the right to remain silent and of the general right to counsel, only by effective and express explanation to the indigent of this right can there be assurance that he was truly in a position to exercise it.

Once warnings have been given, the subsequent procedure is clear. If the individual indicates in any manner, at any time prior to or during questioning, that he wishes to remain silent, the interrogation must cease. At this point he has shown that he intends to exercise his Fifth Amendment privilege; any statement taken after the person invokes his privilege cannot be other than the product of compulsion, subtle or otherwise. Without the right to cut off questioning, the setting of in-custody interrogation operates on the individual to overcome free choice in producing a statement after the privilege has been once invoked. If the individual states that he wants an attorney, the interrogation must cease until an attorney is present. At that time, the individual must have an opportunity to confer with the attorney and to have him present during any subsequent questioning. If the individual cannot obtain an attorney and he indicates that he wants one before speaking to police, they must respect his decision to remain silent.

This does not mean, as some have suggested, that each police station must have a "station house lawyer" present at all times to advise prisoners. It does mean, however, that if police propose to interrogate a person they must make known to him that he is entitled to a lawyer and that if he cannot afford one, a lawyer will be provided for him prior to any interrogation. If authorities conclude that they will not provide counsel during a reasonable period of time in which investigation in the field is carried out, they may refrain from doing so without violating the person's Fifth Amendment privilege so long as they do not question him during that time.

If the interrogation continues without the presence of an attorney and a statement is taken, a heavy burden rests on the government to demonstrate that the defendant knowingly and intelligently waived his privilege against self-incrimination and his right to retained or appointed counsel. This Court has always set high standards of proof for the waiver of constitutional rights, and we reassert these standards as applied to in custody interrogation. Since the State is responsible for establishing the isolated circumstances under which the interrogation takes place and has the only means of making available corroborated evidence of warnings given during incommunicado interrogation, the burden is rightly on its shoulders.

An express statement that the individual is willing to make a statement and does not want an attorney followed closely by a statement could constitute a waiver. But a valid waiver will not be presumed simply from the silence of the accused after warnings are given or simply from the fact that a confession was in fact eventually obtained.

Whatever the testimony of the authorities as to waiver of rights by an accused, the fact of lengthy interrogation or incommunicado incarceration before a statement is made is strong evidence that the accused did not validly waive his rights. In these circumstances the fact that the individual eventually made a statement is consistent with the conclusion that the compelling influence of the interrogation finally forced him to do so. It is inconsistent with any notion of a voluntary relinquishment of the privilege. Moreover, any evidence that the accused was threatened, tricked, or cajoled into a waiver will, of course, show that the defendant did not voluntarily waive his privilege. The requirement of warnings and waiver of rights is a fundamental with respect to the Fifth Amendment privilege and not simply a preliminary ritual to existing methods of interrogation.

The warnings required and the waiver necessary in accordance with our opinion today are, in the absence of a fully effective equivalent, prerequisites to the admissibility of any statement made by a defendant. No distinction can be drawn between statements which are direct confessions and statements which amount to "admissions" of part or all of an offense. The privilege against self-incrimination protects the individual from being compelled to incriminate himself in any manner; it does not distinguish degrees of incrimination. Similarly, or precisely the same reason, no distinction may be drawn between inculpatory statements and statements alleged to be merely "exculpatory." If a statement made were in fact truly exculpatory it would, of course, never be used by the prosecution. In fact, statements merely intended to be exculpatory by the defendant are often used to impeach his testimony at trial or to demonstrate untruths in the statement given under interrogation and thus to prove guilt by implication. These statements are incriminating in any meaningful sense of the word and may not be used without the full warnings and effective waiver required for any other statement. In *Escobedo* itself, the defendant fully intended his accusation of another as the slayer to be exculpatory as to himself.

The principles announced today deal with the protection which must be given to the privilege against self-incrimination when the individual is first subjected to police interrogation while in custody at the station or otherwise deprived of his freedom of action in any significant way. It is at this point that our adversary system of criminal proceedings commences, distinguishing itself at the outset from the inquisitorial system recognized in some countries. Under the system of warnings we delineate today or under any other system which may be devised and found effective, the safeguards to be erected about the privilege must come into play at this point.

Our decision is not intended to hamper the traditional function of police officers in investigating crime. When an individual is in custody on probable cause, the police may, of course, seek out evidence in the field to be used at trial against him. Such investigation may include inquiry of persons not under restraint. General on-the-scene questioning as to facts surrounding a crime or other general questioning of citizens in the fact-finding process is not affected by our holding. It is an act of responsible citizenship for individuals to give whatever information they may have to aid in law enforcement. In such situations the compelling atmosphere inherent in the process of in-custody interrogation is not necessarily present.

In dealing with statements obtained through interrogation, we do not purport to find all confessions inadmissible. Confessions remain a proper element in law enforcement. Any statement given freely and voluntarily without any compelling influences is, of course, admissible in evidence. The fundamental import of the privilege while an individual is in custody is not whether he is allowed to talk to the police without the benefit of warnings and counsel, but whether he can be interrogated. There is no requirement that police stop a person who enters a police station and states that he wishes to confess to a crime, or a person who calls the police to offer a confession or any other statement he desires to make. Volunteered statements of any kind are not barred by the Fifth Amendment and their admissibility is not affected by our holding today.

To summarize, we hold that when an individual is taken into custody or otherwise deprived of his freedom by the authorities in any significant way and is subjected to questioning, the privilege against self-incrimination is jeopardized. Procedural safeguards must be employed to protect the privilege and unless other fully effective means are adopted to notify the person of his right of silence and to assure that the exercise of the right will be scrupulously honored, the following measures are required. He must be warned prior to any questioning that he has the right to remain silent, that anything he says can be used against him in a court of law, that he has the right to the presence of an attorney, and that if he cannot afford an attorney one will be appointed for him prior to any questioning if he so desires. Opportunity to exercise these rights must be afforded to him throughout the interrogation. After such warnings have been given, and such opportunity afforded him, the individual may knowingly and intelligently waive these rights and agree to answer questions or make a statement. But unless and until such warnings and waiver are demonstrated by the prosecution at trial, no evidence obtained as a result of interrogation can be used against him.

IV

A recurrent argument made in these cases is that society's need for interrogation outweighs the privilege. This argument is not unfamiliar to this Court. The whole thrust of our foregoing discussion demonstrates that the Constitution has prescribed the rights of the individual when confronted with the power of government when it provided in the Fifth Amendment that an individual cannot be compelled to be a witness against himself. That right cannot be abridged. As Mr. Justice Brandeis once observed:

> Decency, security, and liberty alike demand that government officials shall be subjected to the same rules of conduct that are commands to the citizen. In a government of laws, existence of the government will be imperiled if it fails to observe the law scrupulously. Our government is the potent, the omnipresent teacher. For good or for ill, it teaches the whole people by its example. Crime is contagious. If the government becomes a lawbreaker, it breeds contempt for law; it invites every man to become a law unto himself; it invites anarchy. To declare that in the administration of the criminal law the end justifies the means . . . would bring terrible retribution. Against that pernicious doctrine this court should resolutely set its face. *Olmstead.*

In this connection, one of our country's distinguished jurists has pointed out: "The quality of a nation's civilization can be largely measured by the methods it uses in the enforcement of its criminal law."

If the individual desires to exercise his privilege, he has the right to do so. This is not for the authorities to decide. An attorney may advise his client not to talk to police until he has had an opportunity to investigate the case, or he may wish to be present with his client during any police questioning. In doing so an attorney is merely exercising the good professional judgment he has been taught. This is not cause for considering the attorney a menace to law enforcement. He is merely carrying out what he is sworn to do under his oath — to protect to the extent of his ability the rights of his client. In fulfilling this responsibility the attorney plays a vital role in the administration of criminal justice under our Constitution.

In announcing these principles, we are not unmindful of the burdens which law enforcement officials must bear, often under trying circumstances. We also fully recognize the obligation of all citizens to aid in enforcing the criminal laws. This Court, while protecting individual rights, has always given ample latitude to law enforcement agencies in the legitimate exercise of their duties. The limits we have placed on the interrogation process should not constitute an undue interference with a proper system of law enforcement. As we have noted, our decision does not in any way preclude police from carrying out their traditional investigatory functions. Although confessions may play an important role in some convictions, the cases before us present graphic examples of the overstatement of the "need" for confessions. In each case authorities conducted interrogations ranging up to five days in duration despite the presence, through standard investigating practices, of considerable evidence against each defendant.

It is also urged that an unfettered right to detention for interrogation should be allowed because it will often redound to the benefit of the person questioned. When police inquiry determines that there is no reason to believe that the person has committed any crime, it is said, he will be released without need for further formal procedures. The person who has committed no offense, however, will be better able to clear himself after warnings with counsel present than without. It can be assumed that in such circumstances a lawyer would advise his client to talk freely to police in order to clear himself.

Custodial interrogation, by contrast, does not necessarily afford the innocent an opportunity to clear themselves. A serious consequence of the present practice of the interrogation alleged to be beneficial for the innocent is that many arrests "for investigation" subject large numbers of innocent persons to detention and interrogation. In one of the cases before us, police held four persons, who were in the defendant's house at the time of the arrest, in jail for five days until defendant confessed. At that time they were finally released. Police stated that there was "no evidence to connect them with any crime." Available statistics on the extent of this practice where it is condoned indicate that these four are far from alone in being subjected to arrest, prolonged detention, and interrogation without the requisite probable cause.

Over the years the Federal Bureau of Investigation has compiled an exemplary record of effective law enforcement while advising any suspect or arrested person, at the outset of an interview, that he is not required to make a statement, that any statement may be used against him in court, that the individual may obtain the services of an attorney of his own choice and, more recently, that he has a right to free counsel if he is unable to pay. A letter received from the Solicitor General in response to a question from the Bench makes it clear that the present pattern of warnings and respect for the rights of the individual followed as a practice by the FBI is consistent with the procedure which we delineate today. It states:

> At the oral argument of the above cause, Mr. Justice Fortas asked whether I could provide certain information as to the practices followed by the Federal Bureau of Investigation. I have directed these questions to the attention of the Director of the Federal Bureau of Investigation and am submitting herewith a statement of the questions and of the answers which we have received.
>
> "(1) When an individual is interviewed by agents of the Bureau, what warning is given to him?
>
> "The standard warning long given by Special Agents of the FBI to both suspects and persons under arrest is that the person has a right to say nothing and a right to counsel, and that any statement he does make may be used against him in court.
>
> "After passage of the Criminal Justice Act of 1964, which provides free counsel for Federal defendants unable to pay, we added to our instructions to Special Agents the requirement that any person who is under arrest for an offense under FBI jurisdiction, or whose arrest is contemplated following the interview, must also be advised of his right to free counsel if he is unable to pay, and the fact that such counsel will be assigned by the Judge. At the same time, we broadened the right to counsel warning to read counsel of his own choice, or anyone else with whom he might wish to speak.
>
> "(2) When is the warning given?
>
> "The FBI warning is given to a suspect at the very outset of the interview. The warning may be given to a person arrested as soon as practicable after the arrest, but in any event it must precede the interview with the person for a confession or admission of his own guilt.

"(3) What is the Bureau's practice in the event that (a) the individual requests counsel and (b) counsel appears?

"When the person who has been warned of his right to counsel decides that he wishes to consult with counsel before making a statement, the interview is terminated at that point. It may be continued, however, as to all matters other than the person's own guilt or innocence. If he is indecisive in his request for counsel, there may be some question on whether he did or did not waive counsel. Situations of this kind must necessarily be left to the judgment of the interviewing Agent.

"A person being interviewed and desiring to consult counsel by telephone must be permitted to do so. When counsel appears in person, he is permitted to confer with his client in private.

"(4) What is the Bureau's practice if the individual requests counsel, but cannot afford to retain an attorney?

"If any person being interviewed after warning of counsel decides that he wishes to consult with counsel before proceeding further the interview is terminated, as shown above. FBI Agents do not pass judgment on the ability of the person to pay for counsel. They do, however, advise those who have been arrested for an offense under FBI jurisdiction, or whose arrest is contemplated following the interview, of a right to free counsel if they are unable to pay, and the availability of such counsel from the Judge."

The practice of the FBI can readily be emulated by state and local enforcement agencies. The argument that the FBI deals with different crimes than are dealt with by state authorities does not mitigate the significance of the FBI experience.

The experience in some other countries also suggests that the danger to law enforcement in curbs on interrogation is overplayed. The English procedure since 1912 under the Judges' Rules is significant. As recently strengthened, the Rules require that a cautionary warning be given an accused by a police officer as soon as he has evidence that affords reasonable grounds for suspicion; they also require that any statement made be given by the accused without questioning by police. The right of the individual to consult with an attorney during this period is expressly recognized.

The safeguards present under Scottish law may be even greater than in England. Scottish judicial decisions bar use in evidence of most confessions obtained through police interrogation. In India, confessions made to police not in the presence of a magistrate have been excluded by rule of evidence since 1872, at a time when it operated under British law. Identical provisions appear in the Evidence Ordinance of Ceylon, enacted in 1895. Similarly, in our country the Uniform Code of Military Justice has long provided that no suspect may be interrogated without first being warned of his right not to make a statement and that any statement he makes may be used against him. Denial of the right to consult counsel during interrogation has also been proscribed by military tribunals. There appears to have been no marked detrimental effect on criminal law enforcement in these jurisdictions as a result of these rules. Conditions of law enforcement in our country are sufficiently similar to permit reference to this experience as assurance that lawlessness will not result from warning an individual of his rights or allowing him to exercise them. Moreover, it is consistent with our legal system that we give at least as much protection to these rights as is given in the jurisdictions described. We deal in our country with rights grounded in a specific requirement of the Fifth Amendment of the Constitution, whereas other jurisdictions arrived at their conclusions on the basis of principles of justice not so specifically defined.

It is also urged upon us that we withhold decision on this issue until state legislative bodies and advisory groups have had an opportunity to deal with these problems by rule making. We have already pointed out that the Constitution does not require any specific code of procedures for protecting the privilege against self-incrimination during custodial interrogation. Congress and the States are free to develop their own safeguards for the privilege, so long as they are fully as effective as those described above in informing accused persons of their right of silence and in affording a continuous opportunity to exercise it. In any event, however, the issues presented are of constitutional dimensions and must be determined by the courts. The admissibility of a statement in the face of a claim that it was obtained in violation of the defendant's constitutional rights is an issue the resolution of which has long since been undertaken by this Court. Judicial solutions to problems of constitutional dimension have evolved decade by decade. As courts have been presented with the need to enforce constitutional rights, they have found means of doing so. That was our responsibility when *Escobedo* was before us and it is our responsibility today. Where rights secured by the Constitution are involved, there can be no rule making or legislation which would abrogate them.

V

Because of the nature of the problem and because of its recurrent significance in numerous cases, we have to this point discussed the relationship of the Fifth Amendment privilege to police interrogation without specific concentration on the facts of the cases before us. We turn now to these facts to consider the application to these cases of the constitutional principles discussed above. In each instance, we have concluded that statements were obtained from the defendant under circumstances that did not meet constitutional standards for protection of the privilege.

. . .

[Justices Harlan, Stewart, and White dissented.]

NOTES AND QUESTIONS

Ernesto Miranda

1. Is the premise of the Court's decision that custodial interrogation is inherently coercive? The Court defines "custodial" as when a person is "taken into custody or otherwise deprived of his freedom in any meaningful way." Is there a reason the Court does not equate "custody" with "under arrest"?

2. The Court devotes most of Part II of its opinion to examples of interrogation techniques from "police manuals," largely omitted here, most of which are at least manipulative if not rooted in outright deception. Why not regulate interrogation techniques rather than require warnings? Is the concern that the techniques themselves are essential to law enforcement?

The Court is mindful that, particularly in the wake of *Escobedo*, its audience is a large one. Accordingly it takes pains to note that "our decision does not in any way preclude police from carrying out their traditional investigatory functions." Doesn't this statement at least implicitly condone the interrogation techniques itemized in the opinion? *See* Christopher Slobogin, *Manipulation of Suspects and Unrecorded Questioning: After Fifty Years of* Miranda *Jurisprudence, Still Two (Or Maybe Three) Remaining Issues*, 97 B.U. L. Rev. 1157, 1158 (2017) (noting that the Court has rarely addressed the subject of manipulative interrogation techniques).

3. In describing *Escobedo* the Court notes that the interrogators' denial of the suspect's right to talk to his lawyer "undermined his ability to exercise the privilege to remain silent if he chose or to speak without any intimidation, blatant or subtle." In the same vein the Court notes how the presence of counsel at an interrogation can mitigate the dangers of untrustworthiness by deterring coercive tactics and by keeping an accurate record of events.

Does the Court really believe that a lawyer "worth his salt" would have permitted Escobedo to speak to his interrogators under those circumstances? Is the Court trying, albeit disingenuously, to avoid the inference that the presence of counsel means the end of interrogation?

4. The Court caveats its holding as follows:

[T]he Constitution does not require any specific code of procedures for protecting the privilege against self-incrimination during custodial interrogation. Congress and the States are free to develop their own safeguards for the privilege, so long as they are fully as effective as those described above in informing accused persons of their right of silence and in affording a continuous opportunity to exercise it. In any event, however, the issues presented are of constitutional dimensions and must be determined by the courts.

What does it mean that the issues in *Miranda* are of a constitutional dimension? The idea for allowing the states a modicum of flexibility in service of the Fifth Amendment privilege was made to Chief Justice Warren by Justice Brennan as a measure to appease critics of the Court and make the opinion more acceptable to the general public. Letter from Justice William J. Brennan to Chief Justice Earl Warren 2-4 (May 11, 1966) (on file with the Library of Congress).

The extent to which *Miranda* is "constitutional" is an issue that will recur for decades. Read on.

5. In rejecting the view that unfettered interrogation is a law enforcement necessity, the Court lavishes praise on the standard warnings the FBI voluntarily chooses to give Gideon to suspects and arrestees, which closely resemble the warnings the Court requires in its holding. The Court states that the FBI's practices "can readily be emulated by state and local enforcement agencies."

The Court is dismissive of the argument that the FBI experience is not analogous to the situations of thousands of state and local agencies, as "the FBI deals with different crimes than are dealt with by state authorities." The Court's only real response is in a footnote, which states:

Among the crimes within the enforcement jurisdiction of the FBI are kidnapping, 18 U.S.C. s 1201 (1964 ed.), white slavery, 18 U.S.C. ss 2421-2423 (1964 ed.), bank robbery, 18 U.S.C. s 2113 (1964 ed.), interstate transportation and sale of stolen property, 18 U.S.C. ss 2311-2317 (1964 ed.), all manner of conspiracies, 18 U.S.C. s 371 (1964 ed.), and violations of civil rights, 18 U.S.C. ss 241-242 (1964 ed.). *See also* 18 U.S.C. s 1114 (1964 ed.) (murder of officer or employee of the United States).

384 U.S. at 486 n.56. Is this an adequate response to the argument that the FBI experience is not analogous?

6. The Court's required four-part warning — actually three warnings and a "cutoff right" — was criticized as something that a legislature, and not a court, should impose. Do you agree? Does it matter that the Court did not mandate specific language to be used or insist that these were the only warnings that could make a custodial interrogation constitutional?

7. The first and most famous of the warnings is the right to remain silent. The Court refers to this right as if it were a preexisting bedrock constitutional principle, so well established as to need no elaboration or explanation. But was it? Is it? Did the right exist before *Miranda*? *See* Tracey Maclin, *The Right to Silence v. the Fifth Amendment*, 2016 U. Chi. Legal F. 255, 258 & n.15 (agreeing with Professor Kamisar that there was no general right to remain silent prior to *Miranda*, although whether a suspect was advised of such a right was a factor in determining the voluntariness of a confession). *See* Yale Kamisar, *A Rejoinder to Professor Schauer's Commentary*, 88 Wash. L. Rev. 171, 172-73 (2013).

8. *Miranda* says nothing at all about race, but one academic attributes it to concerns about racial injustice in the South:

> In retrospect, *Miranda* seems most understandable as an exaggerated response to the times rather than as an enunciation of a natural right mined at last from the Constitution. *Miranda* was a child of the racially troubled 1960's and our tragic legacy of slavery. It was decided when blood was actually being spilled in the streets. There were civil rights protests in the South and civil disorders in urban areas elsewhere. On national television, black protesters [and their supporters] were bullied and beaten, black rioters beaten and shot. *Miranda* itself was decided not only in the shadow of the police practices exposed in *Brown v. Mississippi* and *Chambers v. Florida* but also in the more recent past of the third degree applied particularly to southern blacks.

Gerald M. Caplan, *Questioning* Miranda, 38 Vand. L. Rev. 1417, 1470 (1985). *See* Chapter II *supra*.

9. After the Supreme Court's decision Miranda was retried without his confession being offered in evidence and was again convicted. In the wake of the *Miranda* decision, many police departments distributed to their officers printed *Miranda* warnings on cards. While out on parole in the mid-1970s, Miranda sold autographed "*Miranda* warnings" cards for $1.50 outside the courthouse in downtown Phoenix. Miranda was fatally stabbed in a bar fight in Phoenix in 1976. One of the murder suspects refused to talk to police, invoking his *Miranda* rights.

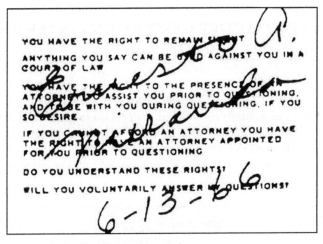

Autographed *Miranda* warnings card

Miranda drew heat from the outset. Law enforcement authorities complained loudly that the police had been "handcuffed" by the decision, echoing the concerns of the Court's dissenters. Congress piled on too, as the emergence of crime as a national issue was well underway by 1966. As part of the Omnibus Crime Control and Safe Streets Act of 1968, Congress claimed to "overrule" *Miranda* and declare that voluntariness was the only criterion for the admissibility of a confession in federal court. 18 U.S.C. § 3501. In furtherance of a national public focus on crime, Richard Nixon campaigned successfully for President in 1968 on the same message of law and order that Barry Goldwater had used (unsuccessfully) four years earlier, and ultimately was able to remake the Supreme Court as he had promised on the campaign trail. Stephen Schulhofer, Miranda v. Arizona: *A Modest But Important Legacy* 164, in Criminal Procedure Stories (Carol Steiker ed., 2006).

134   Chapter III Police Interrogation and The Fifth Amendment

The resulting Burger Court demonized *Miranda*. It denigrated the *Miranda* decision in a snarky tone that was then unusual for Supreme Court opinions, found exceptions to the doctrine's applicability, degraded some of its core principles, and criticized its semi-constitutional foundation. Yet somehow *Miranda* survived. When Edwin Meese, attorney general under President Reagan in the 1980s, wanted to do *Miranda* in by invoking § 3501 in federal prosecutions he was talked out of it by his own solicitor general, Republican Charles Fried. *Id*. at 165. It had already turned out by the 1980s that police officials did not view *Miranda* as the law enforcement bogeyman they had feared it would be. *Id*. As Professor Schulhofer put it, *Miranda* had instead become for the police "a legitimating symbol of their own professionalism, a highly public affirmation of their respect for the rights of suspects and for the rule of law." In *Dickerson v. United States*, 530 U.S. 428 (2000), the Court refused to overrule *Miranda*, rejecting the claim that it could be displaced by § 3501, and observing that *Miranda* warnings "have become part of our national culture." *See infra.*

This is not to say that the *Miranda* doctrine was not materially weakened in the following decades. Exceptions were found. Central doctrinal terms like "interrogation" and "custody" were narrowly interpreted. Much of the weakening of the original conception of *Miranda* took place in connection with law enforcement conduct occurring before, during, and after indisputably appropriate warnings were given to suspects. The Court had stated in *Miranda* that "[o]nce warnings have been given the subsequent procedure is clear." It was not to be so simple.

D. *MIRANDA* IN PRACTICE I: EXCEPTIONS, INTERROGATION, AND CUSTODY

1. *Miranda* Exceptions

One of the earliest of the cases sometimes called *Miranda* "exceptions" held that a statement obtained in violation of *Miranda* could be used to cross-examine a testifying defendant. *Harris v. New York*, 401 U.S. 222 (1971). This case is fully considered in Chapter V *infra* in discussing the impeachment exception to the exclusionary rule.

The next case makes no bones about its status as an "exception" to *Miranda*.

New York v. Quarles
467 U.S. 649 (1984)

Justice REHNQUIST delivered the opinion of the Court.

Respondent Benjamin Quarles was charged in the New York trial court with criminal possession of a weapon. The trial court suppressed the gun in question, and a statement made by respondent, because the statement was obtained by police before they read respondent his "Miranda rights." That ruling was affirmed on appeal through the New York Court of Appeals. We granted certiorari and we now reverse. We conclude that under the circumstances involved in this case, overriding considerations of public safety justify the officer's failure to provide *Miranda* warnings before he asked questions devoted to locating the abandoned weapon.

On September 11, 1980, at approximately 12:30 a.m., Officer Frank Kraft and Officer Sal Scarring were on road patrol in Queens, N.Y., when a young woman approached their car. She told them that she had just been raped by a black male, approximately six feet tall, who was wearing a black jacket with the name "Big Ben" printed in yellow letters on the back. She told the officers that the man had just entered an A & P supermarket located nearby and that the man was carrying a gun.

The officers drove the woman to the supermarket, and Officer Kraft entered the store while Officer Scarring radioed for assistance. Officer Kraft quickly spotted respondent, who matched the description given by the woman, approaching a checkout counter. Apparently upon seeing the officer, respondent turned and ran toward the rear of the store, and Officer Kraft pursued him with a drawn gun. When respondent turned the corner at the end of an aisle, Officer Kraft lost sight of him for several seconds, and upon regaining sight of respondent, ordered him to stop and put his hands over his head.

Although more than three other officers had arrived on the scene by that time, Officer Kraft was the first to reach respondent. He frisked him and discovered that he was wearing a shoulder holster which was then empty. After handcuffing him, Officer Kraft asked him where the gun was. Respondent nodded in the direction of some empty cartons and responded, "the gun is over there." Officer Kraft thereafter retrieved a loaded .38-caliber revolver from one of the cartons, formally placed respondent under arrest, and read him his *Miranda* rights from a printed card. Respondent indicated that he would be willing to answer questions without an attorney present. Officer Kraft then asked respondent if he owned the gun and where he had purchased it. Respondent answered that he did own it and that he had purchased it in Miami, Fla.

In the subsequent prosecution of respondent for criminal possession of a weapon, the judge excluded the statement, "the gun is over there," and the gun because the officer had not given respondent the warnings required by our decision in *Miranda* before asking him where the gun was located. The judge excluded the other statements about respondent's ownership of the gun and the place of purchase, as evidence tainted by the prior *Miranda* violation.

The Court of Appeals granted leave to appeal and affirmed by a 4-3 vote. It concluded that respondent was in "custody" within the meaning of *Miranda* during all questioning and rejected the State's argument that the exigencies of the situation justified Officer Kraft's failure to read respondent his *Miranda* rights until after he had located the gun. The court declined to recognize an exigency exception to the usual requirements of *Miranda* because it found no indication from Officer Kraft's testimony at the suppression hearing that his subjective motivation in asking the question was to protect his own safety or the safety of the public. For the reasons which follow, we believe that this case presents a situation where concern for public safety must be paramount to adherence to the literal language of the prophylactic rules enunciated in *Miranda*.

The Fifth Amendment guarantees that "[n]o person . . . shall be compelled in any criminal case to be a witness against himself." In *Miranda* this Court for the first time extended the Fifth Amendment privilege against compulsory self-incrimination to individuals subjected to custodial interrogation by the police. The Fifth Amendment itself does not prohibit all incriminating admissions; "[a]bsent some officially coerced self-accusation, the Fifth Amendment privilege is not violated by even the most damning admissions." The *Miranda* Court, however, presumed that interrogation in certain custodial circumstances is inherently coercive and held that statements made under those circumstances are inadmissible unless the suspect is specifically informed of his *Miranda* rights and freely decides to forgo those rights. The prophylactic *Miranda* warnings therefore are "not themselves rights protected by the Constitution but [are] instead measures to insure that the right against compulsory self-incrimination [is] protected." Requiring *Miranda* warnings before custodial interrogation provides "practical reinforcement" for the Fifth Amendment right.

In this case we have before us no claim that respondent's statements were actually compelled by police conduct which overcame his will to resist. Thus the only issue before us is whether Officer Kraft was justified in failing to make available to respondent the procedural safeguards associated with the privilege against compulsory self-incrimination since *Miranda*.

The New York Court of Appeals was undoubtedly correct in deciding that the facts of this case come within the ambit of the *Miranda* decision as we have subsequently interpreted it. We agree that respondent was in police custody because we have noted that "the ultimate inquiry is simply whether there is a 'formal arrest or restraint on freedom of movement' of the degree associated with a formal arrest." Here Quarles was surrounded by at least four police officers and was handcuffed when the questioning at issue took place. As the New York Court of Appeals observed, there was nothing to suggest that any of the officers were any longer concerned for their own physical safety. The New York Court of Appeals' majority declined to express an opinion as to whether there might be an exception to the *Miranda* rule if the police had been acting to protect the public, because the lower courts in New York had made no factual determination that the police had acted with that motive.

We hold that on these facts there is a "public safety" exception to the requirement that *Miranda* warnings be given before a suspect's answers may be admitted into evidence, and that the availability of that exception does not depend upon the motivation of the individual officers involved. In a kaleidoscopic situation such as the one confronting these officers, where spontaneity rather than adherence to a police manual is necessarily the order of the day, the application of the exception which we recognize today should not be made to depend on post hoc findings at a suppression hearing concerning the subjective motivation of the arresting officer. Undoubtedly most police officers, if placed in Officer Kraft's position, would act out of a host of different, instinctive, and largely unverifiable motives—their own safety, the safety of others, and perhaps as well the desire to obtain incriminating evidence from the suspect.

Whatever the motivation of individual officers in such a situation, we do not believe that the doctrinal underpinnings of *Miranda* require that it be applied in all its rigor to a situation in which police officers ask questions reasonably prompted by a concern for the public safety. The *Miranda* decision was based in large part on this Court's view that the warnings which it required police to give to suspects in custody would reduce the likelihood that the suspects would fall victim to constitutionally impermissible practices of police interrogation in the presumptively coercive environment of the station house. The dissenters warned that the requirement of *Miranda* warnings would have the effect of decreasing the number of suspects who respond to police questioning. The *Miranda* majority, however, apparently felt that whatever the cost to society in terms of fewer convictions of guilty suspects, that cost would simply have to be borne in the interest of enlarged protection for the Fifth Amendment privilege.

The police in this case, in the very act of apprehending a suspect, were confronted with the immediate necessity of ascertaining the whereabouts of a gun which they had every reason to believe the suspect had just removed from his empty holster and discarded in the supermarket. So long as the gun was concealed somewhere in the supermarket, with its actual whereabouts unknown, it obviously posed more than one danger to the public safety: an accomplice might make use of it, a customer or employee might later come upon it.

In such a situation, if the police are required to recite the familiar *Miranda* warnings before asking the whereabouts of the gun, suspects in Quarles' position might well be deterred from responding. Procedural safeguards which deter a suspect from responding were deemed acceptable in *Miranda* in order to protect the Fifth Amendment privilege; when the primary social cost of those added protections is the possibility of fewer convictions, the *Miranda* majority was willing to bear that cost. Here, had *Miranda* warnings deterred Quarles from responding to Officer Kraft's question about the whereabouts of the gun, the cost would have been something more than merely the failure to obtain evidence useful in convicting Quarles. Officer Kraft needed an answer to his question not simply to make his case against Quarles but to insure that further danger to the public did not result from the concealment of the gun in a public area.

We conclude that the need for answers to questions in a situation posing a threat to the public safety outweighs the need for the prophylactic rule protecting the Fifth Amendment's privilege against self-incrimination. We decline to place officers such as Officer Kraft in the untenable position of having to consider, often in a matter of seconds, whether it best serves society for them to ask the necessary questions without the *Miranda* warnings and render whatever probative evidence they uncover inadmissible, or for them to give the warnings in order to preserve the admissibility of evidence they might uncover but possibly damage or destroy their ability to obtain that evidence and neutralize the volatile situation confronting them.

In recognizing a narrow exception to the *Miranda* rule in this case, we acknowledge that to some degree we lessen the desirable clarity of that rule. At least in part in order to preserve its clarity, we have over the years refused to sanction attempts to expand our *Miranda* holding. As we have in other contexts, we recognize here the importance of a workable rule "to guide police officers, who have only limited time and expertise to reflect on and balance the social and individual interests involved in the specific circumstances they confront." But as we have pointed out, we believe that the exception which we recognize today lessens the necessity of that on-the-scene balancing process. The exception will not be difficult for police officers to apply because in each case it will be circumscribed by the exigency which justifies it. We think police officers can and will distinguish almost instinctively between questions necessary to secure their own safety or the safety of the public and questions designed solely to elicit testimonial evidence from a suspect.

The facts of this case clearly demonstrate that distinction and an officer's ability to recognize it. Officer Kraft asked only the question necessary to locate the missing gun before advising respondent of his rights. It was only after securing the loaded revolver and giving the warnings that he continued with investigatory questions about the ownership and place of purchase of the gun. The exception which we recognize today, far from complicating the thought processes and the on-the-scene judgments of police officers, will simply free them to follow their legitimate instincts when confronting situations presenting a danger to the public safety.

We hold that the Court of Appeals in this case erred in excluding the statement, "the gun is over there," and the gun because of the officer's failure to read respondent his *Miranda* rights before attempting to locate the weapon. Accordingly we hold that it also erred in excluding the subsequent statements as illegal fruits of a *Miranda* violation. We therefore reverse and remand for further proceedings not inconsistent with this opinion.

[Justice O'Connor wrote a concurring opinion. Justices Marshall, Brennan, and Stevens dissented.]

NOTES AND QUESTIONS

1. In *Quarles* the Court stated in no uncertain terms that it was finding a "public safety exception" to *Miranda*. A difficulty the Court elided was that the New York Court of Appeals, perhaps astutely reading the room in which its decision would ultimately be evaluated, had explicitly held that, in view of the arresting officer's testimony that the situation was "under control" at the time of the unwarned questioning of the defendant about the location of the gun, there was no record evidence of exigent circumstances posing a risk to public safety. *People v. Quarles*, 444 N.E.2d 984, 985 (N.Y. 1982).

Was the "objective evidence" of a risk to public safety sufficient to warrant an exception to *Miranda*?

2. In reaching this conclusion the Court described the *Miranda* warnings as "prophylactic" and cited its decision in *Michigan v. Tucker*, 417 U.S. 182 (1974), where it had stated that *Miranda* warnings were "not themselves rights protected by the Constitution." This drumbeat would continue through *Dickerson* and beyond.

3. The police officer who questioned Quarles as to the location of the gun had been living under *Miranda* for his whole career or at least the last 18 years of it. Yet he apparently recognized that under the circumstances a single unwarned question of the suspect was necessary. When that question was answered the officer administered *Miranda* warnings and further questioning followed after the suspect waived his rights.

If the lesson of *Quarles* is that this is how we want police officers to behave, is a "public safety" exception even necessary?

Is another part of the lesson that the state should not be penalized by the suppression of evidence when police act as we want them to? Was Quarles's unwarned statement necessary to his conviction? If you were the prosecutor at trial, operating in a world where *Miranda* had been the law for 18 years, how would you have made the decision whether to offer the unwarned statement in evidence?

4. The Court describes *Quarles* as a "narrow exception," and it has not addressed the exception's dimensions in any subsequent case. The exception's history in lower courts is another story. *See* Jim Weller, *The Legacy of* Quarles: *A Summary of the Public Safety Exception to* Miranda *in the Federal Courts*, 49 Baylor L. Rev. 1107, 1113 (1997) (summarizing expansions of the public safety exception by the federal circuit courts).

5. The *Quarles* exception has been heavily relied on by law enforcement in the twenty-first century in connection with the investigation of terrorist activities. The interrogation of the suspected perpetrator of the Boston Marathon bombing, Dzhokhar Tsarnaev, since convicted, is itself the focus of two law review articles. *See* Joanna Wright, *Applying* Miranda's *Public Safety Exception to Dzhokhar Tsarnaev: Restricting Criminal Procedure Rights by Expanding Judicial Exceptions*, 113 Colum. L. Rev. Sidebar 136 (2013); Brian Gallini, *The Unlikely Meeting Between Dzhokhar Tsarnaev and Benjamin Quarles*, 66 Case W. Rsrv. L. Rev. 393 (2015).

2. Interrogation

To precisely what kind of police communication does *Miranda* apply? Is all questioning "interrogation"? Do declarative statements that are not explicitly framed as questions count? The Court addressed these issues for the first time in the next case.

Rhode Island v. Innis
446 U.S. 291 (1980)

Mr. Justice STEWART delivered the opinion of the Court.

In *Miranda* the Court held that, once a defendant in custody asks to speak with a lawyer, all interrogation must cease until a lawyer is present. The issue in this case is whether the respondent was "interrogated" in violation of the standards promulgated in the *Miranda* opinion.

I

On the night of January 12, 1975, John Mulvaney, a Providence, R.I., taxicab driver, disappeared after being dispatched to pick up a customer. His body was discovered four days later buried in a shallow grave in Coventry, R.I. He had died from a shotgun blast aimed at the back of his head.

On January 17, 1975, shortly after midnight, the Providence police received a telephone call from Gerald Aubin, also a taxicab driver, who reported that he had just been robbed by a man wielding a sawed-off shotgun. Aubin further reported that he had dropped off his assailant near Rhode Island College in a section of Providence known as Mount Pleasant. While at the Providence police station waiting to give a statement, Aubin noticed a picture of his assailant on a bulletin board. Aubin so informed one of the police officers present. The officer prepared a photo array, and again Aubin identified a picture of the same person. That person was the respondent. Shortly thereafter, the Providence police began a search of the Mount Pleasant area.

At approximately 4:30 a.m. on the same date, Patrolman Lovell, while cruising the streets of Mount Pleasant in a patrol car, spotted the respondent standing in the street facing him. When Patrolman Lovell stopped his car, the respondent walked towards it. Patrolman Lovell then arrested the respondent, who was unarmed, and advised him of his so-called *Miranda* rights. While the two men waited in the patrol car for other police officers to arrive, Patrolman Lovell did not converse with the respondent other than to respond to the latter's request for a cigarette.

Within minutes, Sergeant Sears arrived at the scene of the arrest, and he also gave the respondent the *Miranda* warnings. Immediately thereafter, Captain Leyden and other police officers arrived. Captain Leyden advised the respondent of his *Miranda* rights. The respondent stated that he understood those rights and wanted to speak with a lawyer. Captain Leyden then directed that the respondent be placed in a "caged wagon," a four-door police car with a wire screen mesh between the front and rear seats, and be driven to the central police station. Three officers, Patrolmen Gleckman, Williams, and McKenna, were assigned to accompany the respondent to the central station. They placed the respondent in the vehicle and shut the doors. Captain Leyden then instructed the officers not to question the respondent or intimidate or coerce him in any way. The three officers then entered the vehicle, and it departed.

While en route to the central station, Patrolman Gleckman initiated a conversation with Patrolman McKenna concerning the missing shotgun. As Patrolman Gleckman later testified:

A. At this point, I was talking back and forth with Patrolman McKenna stating that I frequent this area while on patrol and [that because a school for handicapped children is located nearby,] there's a lot of handicapped children running around in this area, and God forbid one of them might find a weapon with shells and they might hurt themselves.

Patrolman McKenna apparently shared his fellow officer's concern:

A. I more or less concurred with him [Gleckman] that it was a safety factor and that we should, you know, continue to search for the weapon and try to find it.

Id., at 53.

While Patrolman Williams said nothing, he overheard the conversation between the two officers:

A. He [Gleckman] said it would be too bad if the little—I believe he said a girl—would pick up the gun, maybe kill herself.

The respondent then interrupted the conversation, stating that the officers should turn the car around so he could show them where the gun was located. At this point, Patrolman McKenna radioed back to Captain Leyden that they were returning to the scene of the arrest and that the respondent would inform them of the location of the gun. At the time the respondent indicated that the officers should turn back, they had traveled no more than a mile, a trip encompassing only a few minutes.

The police vehicle then returned to the scene of the arrest where a search for the shotgun was in progress. There, Captain Leyden again advised the respondent of his *Miranda* rights.

The respondent replied that he understood those rights but that he "wanted to get the gun out of the way because of the kids in the area in the school." The respondent then led the police to a nearby field, where he pointed out the shotgun under some rocks by the side of the road.

On March 20, 1975, a grand jury returned an indictment charging the respondent with the kidnaping, robbery, and murder of John Mulvaney. Before trial, the respondent moved to suppress the shotgun and the statements he had made to the police regarding it. After an evidentiary hearing at which the respondent elected not to testify, the trial judge found that the respondent had been "repeatedly and completely advised of his *Miranda* rights." He further found that it was "entirely understandable that [the officers in the police vehicle] would voice their concern [for the safety of the handicapped children] to each other." The judge then concluded that the respondent's decision to inform the police of the location of the shotgun was "a waiver, clearly, and on the basis of the evidence that I have heard, and [sic] intelligent waiver, of his [*Miranda*] right to remain silent." Thus, without passing on whether the police officers had in fact "interrogated" the respondent, the trial court sustained the admissibility of the shotgun and testimony related to its discovery. That evidence was later introduced at the respondent's trial, and the jury returned a verdict of guilty on all counts.

On appeal, the Rhode Island Supreme Court, in a 3-2 decision, set aside the respondent's conviction. Relying at least in part on this Court's decision in *Brewer v. Williams*, the court concluded that the respondent had invoked his Miranda right to counsel and that, contrary to *Miranda*'s mandate that, in the absence of counsel, all custodial interrogation then cease, the police officers in the vehicle had "interrogated" the respondent without a valid waiver of his right to counsel. It was the view of the state appellate court that, even though the police officers may have been genuinely concerned about the public safety and even though the respondent had not been addressed personally by the police officers, the respondent nonetheless had been subjected to "subtle coercion" that was the equivalent of "interrogation" within the meaning of the *Miranda* opinion. Moreover, contrary to the holding of the trial court, the appellate court concluded that the evidence was insufficient to support a finding of waiver. Having concluded that both the shotgun and testimony relating to its discovery were obtained in violation of the *Miranda* standards and therefore should not have been admitted into evidence, the Rhode Island Supreme Court held that the respondent was entitled to a new trial.

We granted certiorari to address for the first time the meaning of "interrogation" under *Miranda*.

II

In its *Miranda* opinion, the Court concluded that in the context of "custodial interrogation" certain procedural safeguards are necessary to protect a defendant's Fifth and Fourteenth Amendment privilege against compulsory self-incrimination. More specifically, the Court held that "the prosecution may not use statements, whether exculpatory or inculpatory, stemming from custodial interrogation of the defendant unless it demonstrates the use of procedural safeguards effective to secure the privilege against self-incrimination." Those safeguards included the now familiar *Miranda* warnings—namely, that the defendant be informed "that he has the right to remain silent, that anything he says can be used against him in a court of law, that he has the right to the presence of an attorney, and that if he cannot afford an attorney one will be appointed for him prior to any questioning if he so desires"—or their equivalent.

The Court in the *Miranda* opinion also outlined in some detail the consequences that would result if a defendant sought to invoke those procedural safeguards. With regard to the right to the presence of counsel, the Court noted:

> Once warnings have been given, the subsequent procedure is clear. . . . If the individual states that he wants an attorney, the interrogation must cease until an attorney is present. At that time, the individual must have an opportunity to confer with the attorney and to have him present during

any subsequent questioning. If the individual cannot obtain an attorney and he indicates that he wants one before speaking to police, they must respect his decision to remain silent.

In the present case, the parties are in agreement that the respondent was fully informed of his *Miranda* rights and that he invoked his *Miranda* right to counsel when he told Captain Leyden that he wished to consult with a lawyer. It is also uncontested that the respondent was "in custody" while being transported to the police station.

The issue, therefore, is whether the respondent was "interrogated" by the police officers in violation of the respondent's undisputed right under *Miranda* to remain silent until he had consulted with a lawyer. In resolving this issue, we first define the term "interrogation" under *Miranda* before turning to a consideration of the facts of this case.

A

The starting point for defining "interrogation" in this context is, of course, the Court's *Miranda* opinion. There the Court observed that "[b]y custodial interrogation, we mean questioning initiated by law enforcement officers after a person has been taken into custody or otherwise deprived of his freedom of action in any significant way." This passage and other references throughout the opinion to "questioning" might suggest that the *Miranda* rules were to apply only to those police interrogation practices that involve express questioning of a defendant while in custody.

We do not, however, construe the *Miranda* opinion so narrowly. The concern of the Court in *Miranda* was that the "interrogation environment" created by the interplay of interrogation and custody would "subjugate the individual to the will of his examiner" and thereby undermine the privilege against compulsory self-incrimination. The police practices that evoked this concern included several that did not involve express questioning. For example, one of the practices discussed in *Miranda* was the use of line-ups in which a coached witness would pick the defendant as the perpetrator. This was designed to establish that the defendant was in fact guilty as a predicate for further interrogation. A variation on this theme discussed in *Miranda* was the so-called "reverse line-up" in which a defendant would be identified by coached witnesses as the perpetrator of a fictitious crime, with the object of inducing him to confess to the actual crime of which he was suspected in order to escape the false prosecution. The Court in *Miranda* also included in its survey of interrogation practices the use of psychological ploys, such as to "posi[t]" "the guilt of the subject," to "minimize the moral seriousness of the offense," and "to cast blame on the victim or on society." It is clear that these techniques of persuasion, no less than express questioning, were thought, in a custodial setting, to amount to interrogation.

This is not to say, however, that all statements obtained by the police after a person has been taken into custody are to be considered the product of interrogation. As the Court in *Miranda* noted:

> Confessions remain a proper element in law enforcement. Any statement given freely and voluntarily without any compelling influences is, of course, admissible in evidence. The fundamental import of the privilege while an individual is in custody is not whether he is allowed to talk to the police without the benefit of warnings and counsel, but whether he can be interrogated. . . . Volunteered statements of any kind are not barred by the Fifth Amendment and their admissibility is not affected by our holding today.

It is clear therefore that the special procedural safeguards outlined in *Miranda* are required not where a suspect is simply taken into custody, but rather where a suspect in custody is subjected to interrogation. "Interrogation," as conceptualized in the *Miranda* opinion, must reflect a measure of compulsion above and beyond that inherent in custody itself.

We conclude that the *Miranda* safeguards come into play whenever a person in custody is subjected to either express questioning or its functional equivalent. That is to say, the term "interrogation" under *Miranda* refers not only to express questioning, but also to any words or actions on the part of the police (other than those normally attendant to arrest and custody) that the police should know are reasonably likely to elicit an incriminating response from the suspect. The latter portion of this definition focuses primarily upon the perceptions of the suspect, rather than the intent of the police. This focus reflects the fact that the *Miranda* safeguards were designed to vest a suspect in custody with an added measure of protection against coercive police practices, without regard to objective proof of the underlying intent of the police. A practice that the police should know is reasonably likely to evoke an incriminating response from a suspect thus amounts to interrogation. But, since the police surely cannot be held accountable for the unforeseeable results of their words or actions, the definition of interrogation can extend only to words or actions on the part of police officers that they should have known were reasonably likely to elicit an incriminating response.

B

Turning to the facts of the present case, we conclude that the respondent was not "interrogated" within the meaning of *Miranda*. It is undisputed that the first prong of the definition of "interrogation" was not satisfied, for the conversation between Patrolmen Gleckman and McKenna included no express questioning of the respondent. Rather, that conversation was, at least in form, nothing more than a dialogue between the two officers to which no response from the respondent was invited.

Moreover, it cannot be fairly concluded that the respondent was subjected to the "functional equivalent" of questioning. It cannot be said, in short, that Patrolmen Gleckman and McKenna should have known that their conversation was reasonably likely to elicit an incriminating response from the respondent. There is nothing in the record to suggest that the officers were aware that the respondent was peculiarly susceptible to an appeal to his conscience concerning the safety of handicapped children. Nor is there anything in the record to suggest that the police knew that the respondent was unusually disoriented or upset at the time of his arrest.

The case thus boils down to whether, in the context of a brief conversation, the officers should have known that the respondent would suddenly be moved to make a self-incriminating response. Given the fact that the entire conversation appears to have consisted of no more than a few off hand remarks, we cannot say that the officers should have known that it was reasonably likely that Innis would so respond. This is not a case where the police carried on a lengthy harangue in the presence of the suspect. Nor does the record support the respondent's contention that, under the circumstances, the officers' comments were particularly "evocative." It is our view, therefore, that the respondent was not subjected by the police to words or actions that the police should have known were reasonably likely to elicit an incriminating response from him.

The Rhode Island Supreme Court erred, in short, in equating "subtle compulsion" with interrogation. That the officers' comments struck a responsive chord is readily apparent. Thus, it may be said, as the Rhode Island Supreme Court did say, that the respondent was subjected to "subtle compulsion." But that is not the end of the inquiry. It must also be established that a suspect's incriminating response was the product of words or actions on the part of the police that they should have known were reasonably likely to elicit an incriminating response. This was not established in the present case.

For the reasons stated, the judgment of the Supreme Court of Rhode Island is vacated, and the case is remanded to that court for further proceedings not inconsistent with this opinion.

It is so ordered.

[Justices Stevens, Marshall, and Brennan dissented.]

D. *Miranda* in Practice I: Exceptions, Interrogation, and Custody   **143**

NOTES AND QUESTIONS

1. Suppose the prosecution had decided to defend the police conduct not on the ground that it wasn't interrogation but rather on a "public safety" exception as the prosecution was to do a few years later in *Quarles*. Is this a stronger or weaker case for such an exception than *Quarles*?

2. In a footnote the Court states that "[t]he record in no way suggests that the officers' remarks were designed to elicit a response." Do you agree?

As support for this assertion the Court states that the trial judge, after hearing the officers' testimony, concluded that it was "entirely understandable that [the officers] would voice their concern [for the safety of the handicapped children] to each other." Is the trial judge's conclusion inconsistent with an intent to elicit a response from the defendant?

3. Should it matter—as the dissent points out, citing the leading authority on police interrogation tactics—that appealing to the defendant's sense of "decency" is a "classic interrogation technique"? Should that fact be relevant to whether the officers should have known their statements "were reasonably likely to elicit an incriminating response"?

Did the Court correctly apply the "reasonable likelihood" test here?

4. Why wasn't this case remanded so the trial court could apply the test the Court prescribes? If it had been remanded, and you had represented Innis, how would you try to prove the officers intended to elicit an incriminating response and reasonably believed they could get one? What information would you subpoena to use at the suppression hearing?

Consider whether each of the following statements made to a suspect in custody who had received *Miranda* warnings and invoked his rights amount to interrogation under *Innis*:

- You could really help yourself here, you know.
- Any cooperation will be brought to the attention of the assistant U.S. attorney.
- There could be immigration consequences here.
- We've got a warrant for your apartment too.

3. Custody

Prior to the next case, *Berkemer v. McCarty*, 468 U.S. 420 (1984), the Court had seldom dealt with any difficulty regarding the definition of "custody" for *Miranda* purposes. In two fairly straightforward cases where the defendants had voluntarily appeared for questioning, the Court had essentially just restated what it had held in *Miranda*, that custody is when "a person is taken into custody or otherwise deprived of his freedom in any significant way." 384 U.S. at 444. *See Oregon v. Mathiason*, 429 U.S. 492 (1977) (per curiam); *California v. Beheler*, 463 U.S. 112 (1983).

In *Berkemer* the Court considers whether the amount of detention associated with a "routine" traffic stop amounts to custody for *Miranda* purposes.

Berkemer v. McCarty
468 U.S. 420 (1984)

Justice MARSHALL delivered the opinion of the Court.

This case presents two related questions: First, does our decision in *Miranda* govern the admissibility of statements made during custodial interrogation by a suspect accused of a misdemeanor traffic offense? Second, does the roadside questioning of a motorist detained pursuant to a traffic stop constitute custodial interrogation for the purposes of the doctrine enunciated in *Miranda*?

I

A

The parties have stipulated to the essential facts. On the evening of March 31, 1980, Trooper Williams of the Ohio State Highway Patrol observed respondent's car weaving in and out of a lane on Interstate Highway 270. After following the car for two miles, Williams forced respondent to stop and asked him to get out of the vehicle. When respondent complied, Williams noticed that he was having difficulty standing. At that point, "Williams concluded that [respondent] would be charged with a traffic offense and, therefore, his freedom to leave the scene was terminated." However, respondent was not told that he would be taken into custody. Williams then asked respondent to perform a field sobriety test, commonly known as a "balancing test." Respondent could not do so without falling.

While still at the scene of the traffic stop, Williams asked respondent whether he had been using intoxicants. Respondent replied that "he had consumed two beers and had smoked several joints of marijuana a short time before." Respondent's speech was slurred, and Williams had difficulty understanding him. Williams thereupon formally placed respondent under arrest and transported him in the patrol car to the Franklin County Jail.

At the jail, respondent was given an intoxilyzer test to determine the concentration of alcohol in his blood. The test did not detect any alcohol whatsoever in respondent's system. Williams then resumed questioning respondent in order to obtain information for inclusion in the State Highway Patrol Alcohol Influence Report. Respondent answered affirmatively a question whether he had been drinking. When then asked if he was under the influence of alcohol, he said, "I guess, barely." Williams next asked respondent to indicate on the form whether the marihuana he had smoked had been treated with any chemicals. In the section of the report headed "Remarks," respondent wrote, "No ang[el] dust or PCP in the pot. Rick McCarty."

At no point in this sequence of events did Williams or anyone else tell respondent that he had a right to remain silent, to consult with an attorney, and to have an attorney appointed for him if he could not afford one.

B

Respondent was charged with operating a motor vehicle while under the influence of alcohol and/or drugs. Under Ohio law, that offense is a first-degree misdemeanor and is punishable by fine or imprisonment for up to six months. Incarceration for a minimum of three days is mandatory.

Respondent moved to exclude the various incriminating statements he had made to Trooper Williams on the ground that introduction into evidence of those statements would violate the Fifth Amendment insofar as he had not been informed of his constitutional rights prior to his interrogation. When the trial court denied the motion, respondent pleaded "no contest" and was found guilty. He was sentenced to 90 days in jail, 80 of which were suspended, and was fined $300, $100 of which were suspended.

On appeal to the Franklin County Court of Appeals, respondent renewed his constitutional claim. Relying on a prior decision by the Ohio Supreme Court, which held that the rule announced in *Miranda* "is not applicable to misdemeanors," the Court of Appeals rejected respondent's argument and affirmed his conviction. The Ohio Supreme Court dismissed respondent's appeal on the ground that it failed to present a "substantial constitutional question."

Respondent then filed an action for a writ of habeas corpus in the District Court for the Southern District of Ohio. The District Court dismissed the petition, holding that "*Miranda* warnings do not have to be given prior to in custody interrogation of a suspect arrested for a traffic offense."

D. *Miranda* in Practice I: Exceptions, Interrogation, and Custody

A divided panel of the Court of Appeals for the Sixth Circuit reversed, holding that "*Miranda* warnings must be given to all individuals prior to custodial interrogation, whether the offense investigated be a felony or a misdemeanor traffic offense." In applying this principle to the facts of the case, the Court of Appeals distinguished between the statements made by respondent before and after his formal arrest. The postarrest statements, the court ruled, were plainly inadmissible; because respondent was not warned of his constitutional rights prior to or "[a]t the point that Trooper Williams took [him] to the police station," his ensuing admissions could not be used against him. The court's treatment of respondent's prearrest statements was less clear. It eschewed a holding that "the mere stopping of a motor vehicle triggers *Miranda*," but did not expressly rule that the statements made by respondent at the scene of the traffic stop could be used against him. In the penultimate paragraph of its opinion, the court asserted that "[t]he failure to advise [respondent] of his constitutional rights rendered at least some of his statements inadmissible," suggesting that the court was uncertain as to the status of the prearrest confessions. "Because [respondent] was convicted on inadmissible evidence," the court deemed it necessary to vacate his conviction and order the District Court to issue a writ of habeas corpus. Ibid. However, the Court of Appeals did not specify which statements, if any, could be used against respondent in a retrial.

We granted certiorari to resolve confusion in the federal and state courts regarding the applicability of our ruling in *Miranda* to interrogations involving minor offenses and to questioning of motorists detained pursuant to traffic stops.

II

. . .

III

To assess the admissibility of the self-incriminating statements made by respondent prior to his formal arrest, we are obliged to address a second issue concerning the scope of our decision in *Miranda*: whether the roadside questioning of a motorist detained pursuant to a routine traffic stop should be considered "custodial interrogation." Respondent urges that it should, on the ground that *Miranda* by its terms applies whenever "a person has been taken into custody or otherwise deprived of his freedom of action in any significant way." Petitioner contends that a holding that every detained motorist must be advised of his rights before being questioned would constitute an unwarranted extension of the *Miranda* doctrine.

It must be acknowledged at the outset that a traffic stop significantly curtails the "freedom of action" of the driver and the passengers, if any, of the detained vehicle. Under the law of most States, it is a crime either to ignore a policeman's signal to stop one's car or, once having stopped, to drive away without permission. Certainly few motorists would feel free either to disobey a directive to pull over or to leave the scene of a traffic stop without being told they might do so. Partly for these reasons, we have long acknowledged that "stopping an automobile and detaining its occupants constitute a 'seizure' within the meaning of [the Fourth] Amendmen[t], even though the purpose of the stop is limited and the resulting detention quite brief."

However, we decline to accord talismanic power to the phrase in the *Miranda* opinion emphasized by respondent. Fidelity to the doctrine announced in *Miranda* requires that it be enforced strictly, but only in those types of situations in which the concerns that powered the decision are implicated. Thus, we must decide whether a traffic stop exerts upon a detained person pressures that sufficiently impair his free exercise of his privilege against self-incrimination to require that he be warned of his constitutional rights.

Two features of an ordinary traffic stop mitigate the danger that a person questioned will be induced "to speak where he would not otherwise do so freely." First, detention of a motorist pursuant to a traffic stop is presumptively temporary and brief. The vast majority of roadside detentions last only a few minutes. A motorist's expectations, when he sees a policeman's light flashing behind him, are that he will be obliged to spend a short period of time answering questions and waiting while the officer checks his license and registration, that he may then be given a citation, but that in the end he most likely will be allowed to continue on his way. In this respect, questioning incident to an ordinary traffic stop is quite different from stationhouse interrogation, which frequently is prolonged, and in which the detainee often is aware that questioning will continue until he provides his interrogators the answers they seek.

Second, circumstances associated with the typical traffic stop are not such that the motorist feels completely at the mercy of the police. To be sure, the aura of authority surrounding an armed, uniformed officer and the knowledge that the officer has some discretion in deciding whether to issue a citation, in combination, exert some pressure on the detainee to respond to questions. But other aspects of the situation substantially offset these forces. Perhaps most importantly, the typical traffic stop is public, at least to some degree. Passersby, on foot or in other cars, witness the interaction of officer and motorist. This exposure to public view both reduces the ability of an unscrupulous policeman to use illegitimate means to elicit self-incriminating statements and diminishes the motorist's fear that, if he does not cooperate, he will be subjected to abuse. The fact that the detained motorist typically is confronted by only one or at most two policemen further mutes his sense of vulnerability. In short, the atmosphere surrounding an ordinary traffic stop is substantially less "police dominated" than that surrounding the kinds of interrogation at issue in *Miranda* itself, and in the subsequent cases in which we have applied *Miranda*.

In both of these respects, the usual traffic stop is more analogous to a so-called "Terry stop," see *Terry v. Ohio* (1968), than to a formal arrest. Under the Fourth Amendment, we have held, a policeman who lacks probable cause but whose "observations lead him reasonably to suspect" that a particular person has committed, is committing, or is about to commit a crime, may detain that person briefly in order to "investigate the circumstances that provoke suspicion." "[T]he stop and inquiry must be 'reasonably related in scope to the justification for their initiation.'" Typically, this means that the officer may ask the detainee a moderate number of questions to determine his identity and to try to obtain information confirming or dispelling the officer's suspicions. But the detainee is not obliged to respond. And, unless the detainee's answers provide the officer with probable cause to arrest him, he must then be released. The comparatively nonthreatening character of detentions of this sort explains the absence of any suggestion in our opinions that *Terry* stops are subject to the dictates of *Miranda*. The similarly noncoercive aspect of ordinary traffic stops prompts us to hold that persons temporarily detained pursuant to such stops are not "in custody" for the purposes of *Miranda*.

Respondent contends that to "exempt" traffic stops from the coverage of *Miranda* will open the way to widespread abuse. Policemen will simply delay formally arresting detained motorists, and will subject them to sustained and intimidating interrogation at the scene of their initial detention. The net result, respondent contends, will be a serious threat to the rights that the *Miranda* doctrine is designed to protect.

We are confident that the state of affairs projected by respondent will not come to pass. It is settled that the safeguards prescribed by *Miranda* become applicable as soon as a suspect's freedom of action is curtailed to a "degree associated with formal arrest." If a motorist who has been detained pursuant to a traffic stop thereafter is subjected to treatment that renders him "in custody" for practical purposes, he will be entitled to the full panoply of protections prescribed by *Miranda*.

Admittedly, our adherence to the doctrine just recounted will mean that the police and lower courts will continue occasionally to have difficulty deciding exactly when a suspect has been taken into custody. Either a rule that *Miranda* applies to all traffic stops or a rule that a suspect need not be advised of his rights until he is formally placed under arrest would provide a clearer, more easily administered line. However, each of these two alternatives has drawbacks that make it unacceptable. The first would substantially impede the enforcement of the Nation's traffic laws — by compelling the police either to take the time to warn all detained motorists of their constitutional rights or to forgo use of self-incriminating statements made by those motorists — while doing little to protect citizens' Fifth Amendment rights. The second would enable the police to circumvent the constraints on custodial interrogations established by *Miranda*.

Turning to the case before us, we find nothing in the record that indicates that respondent should have been given *Miranda* warnings at any point prior to the time Trooper Williams placed him under arrest. For the reasons indicated above, we reject the contention that the initial stop of respondent's car, by itself, rendered him "in custody." And respondent has failed to demonstrate that, at any time between the initial stop and the arrest, he was subjected to restraints comparable to those associated with a formal arrest. Only a short period of time elapsed between the stop and the arrest. At no point during that interval was respondent informed that his detention would not be temporary. Although Trooper Williams apparently decided as soon as respondent stepped out of his car that respondent would be taken into custody and charged with a traffic offense, Williams never communicated his intention to respondent. A policeman's unarticulated plan has no bearing on the question whether a suspect was "in custody" at a particular time; the only relevant inquiry is how a reasonable man in the suspect's position would have understood his situation. Nor do other aspects of the interaction of Williams and respondent support the contention that respondent was exposed to "custodial interrogation" at the scene of the stop. From aught that appears in the stipulation of facts, a single police officer asked respondent a modest number of questions and requested him to perform a simple balancing test at a location visible to passing motorists. Treatment of this sort cannot fairly be characterized as the functional equivalent of formal arrest.

We conclude, in short, that respondent was not taken into custody for the purposes of *Miranda* until Williams arrested him. Consequently, the statements respondent made prior to that point were admissible against him. . . .

NOTES AND QUESTIONS

1. While acknowledging that traffic stops undeniably involve a degree of "deprivation of freedom," the Court distinguishes questioning during traffic stops from custodial interrogation on several grounds: They are presumptively temporary and brief, take place in public view, usually involve fewer police, and are "comparatively nonthreatening." Which of these reasons do you find the most persuasive? Least persuasive?

In the almost 40 years since *Berkemer* was decided there has been an enormous increase in the criminal penalties for driving-under-the-influence violations. *See Birchfield v. North Dakota*, 579 U.S. 438, 448-49 (2016) (noting the toughening of drunk-driving laws). Are traffic stops, accordingly, still comparatively nonthreatening compared to custodial interrogation?

2. The Court analogizes the curtailment of freedom in traffic stops to *Terry* stops, *see* Chapter IV *infra*, both being presumptively brief detentions based on reasonable suspicion. Is that an apt analogy? In what ways are the two police interdictions different?

148 Chapter III Police Interrogation and The Fifth Amendment

3. As the Court points out, in a *Terry* stop the detainee is not obliged to respond to the officer's inquiries and the detainee's silence cannot be used against him. Is the same true in a traffic stop?

4. Can an ordinary traffic stop escalate into a situation that would be more analogous to custodial detention such that *Miranda* warnings would be required before interrogation?

Stansbury v. California
511 U.S. 318 (1994)

PER CURIAM.

This case concerns the rules for determining whether a person being questioned by law enforcement officers is held in custody, and thus entitled to the warnings required by *Miranda*. We hold, not for the first time, that an officer's subjective and undisclosed view concerning whether the person being interrogated is a suspect is irrelevant to the assessment whether the person is in custody.

I

Ten-year-old Robyn Jackson disappeared from a playground in Baldwin Park, California, at around 6:30 p.m. on September 28, 1982. Early the next morning, about 10 miles away in Pasadena, Andrew Zimmerman observed a large man emerge from a turquoise American sedan and throw something into a nearby flood control channel. Zimmerman called the police, who arrived at the scene and discovered the girl's body in the channel. There was evidence that she had been raped, and the cause of death was determined to be asphyxia complicated by blunt force trauma to the head.

Lieutenant Thomas Johnston, a detective with the Los Angeles County Sheriff's Department, investigated the homicide. From witnesses interviewed on the day the body was discovered, he learned that Robyn had talked to two ice cream truck drivers, one being petitioner Robert Edward Stansbury, in the hours before her disappearance. Given these contacts, Johnston thought Stansbury and the other driver might have some connection with the homicide or knowledge thereof, but for reasons unimportant here Johnston considered only the other driver to be a leading suspect. After the suspect driver was brought in for interrogation, Johnston asked Officer Lee of the Baldwin Park Police Department to contact Stansbury to see if he would come in for questioning as a potential witness.

Lee and three other plainclothes officers arrived at Stansbury's trailer home at about 11:00 that evening. The officers surrounded the door and Lee knocked. When Stansbury answered, Lee told him the officers were investigating a homicide to which Stansbury was a possible witness and asked if he would accompany them to the police station to answer some questions. Stansbury agreed to the interview and accepted a ride to the station in the front seat of Lee's police car.

At the station, Lieutenant Johnston, in the presence of another officer, questioned Stansbury about his whereabouts and activities during the afternoon and evening of September 28. Neither Johnston nor the other officer issued *Miranda* warnings. Stansbury told the officers (among other things) that on the evening of the 28th he spoke with the victim at about 6:00, returned to his trailer home after work at 9:00, and left the trailer at about midnight in his housemate's turquoise, American-made car. This last detail aroused Johnston's suspicions, as the turquoise car matched the description of the one Andrew Zimmerman had observed in Pasadena. When Stansbury, in response to a further question, admitted to prior convictions for rape, kidnaping, and child molestation, Johnston terminated the interview and another officer advised Stansbury of his *Miranda* rights. Stansbury declined to make further statements, requested an attorney, and was arrested. Respondent State of California charged Stansbury with first-degree murder and other crimes.

Stansbury filed a pretrial motion to suppress all statements made at the station, and the evidence discovered as a result of those statements. The trial court denied the motion in relevant part, ruling that Stansbury was not "in custody"—and thus not entitled to *Miranda* warnings—until he mentioned that he had taken his housemate's turquoise car for a midnight drive. Before that stage of the interview, the trial court reasoned, "the focus in [Lieutenant Johnston's] mind certainly was on the other ice cream [truck] driver"; only "after Mr. Stansbury made the comment . . . describing the . . . turquoise-colored automobile" did Johnston's suspicions "shif[t] to Mr. Stansbury." Based upon its conclusion that Stansbury was not in custody until Johnston's suspicions had focused on him, the trial court permitted the prosecution to introduce in its case in chief the statements Stansbury made before that time. At trial, the jury convicted Stansbury of first-degree murder, rape, kidnaping, and lewd act on a child under the age of 14, and fixed the penalty for the first-degree murder at death.

The California Supreme Court affirmed. Before determining whether Stansbury was in custody during the interview at the station, the court set out what it viewed as the applicable legal standard:

> In deciding the custody issue, the totality of the circumstances is relevant, and no one factor is dispositive. However, the most important considerations include (1) the site of the interrogation, (2) whether the investigation has focused on the subject, (3) whether the objective indicia of arrest are present, and (4) the length and form of questioning.

The court proceeded to analyze the second factor in detail, in the end accepting the trial court's factual determination "that suspicion focused on [Stansbury] only when he mentioned that he had driven a turquoise car on the night of the crime." The court "conclude[d] that [Stansbury] was not subject to custodial interrogation before he mentioned the turquoise car," and thus approved the trial court's ruling that *Miranda* did not bar the admission of statements Stansbury made before that point.

We granted certiorari.

II

We held in *Miranda* that a person questioned by law enforcement officers after being "taken into custody or otherwise deprived of his freedom of action in any significant way" must first "be warned that he has a right to remain silent, that any statement he does make may be used as evidence against him, and that he has a right to the presence of an attorney, either retained or appointed." . . .

Our decisions make clear that the initial determination of custody depends on the objective circumstances of the interrogation, not on the subjective views harbored by either the interrogating officers or the person being questioned.

Berkemer reaffirmed the conclusions reached in *Beckwith*. *Berkemer* concerned the roadside questioning of a motorist detained in a traffic stop. We decided that the motorist was not in custody for purposes of *Miranda* even though the traffic officer "apparently decided as soon as [the motorist] stepped out of his car that [the motorist] would be taken into custody and charged with a traffic offense." The reason, we explained, was that the officer "never communicated his intention to" the motorist during the relevant questioning. The lack of communication was crucial, for under *Miranda* "[a] policeman's unarticulated plan has no bearing on the question whether a suspect was 'in custody' at a particular time"; rather, "the only relevant inquiry is how a reasonable man in the suspect's position would have understood his situation." Other cases of ours have been consistent in adhering to this understanding of the custody element of *Miranda*.

It is well settled, then, that a police officer's subjective view that the individual under questioning is a suspect, if undisclosed, does not bear upon the question whether the individual is in custody for purposes of *Miranda*. The same principle obtains if an officer's undisclosed assessment is that the person being questioned is not a suspect. In either instance, one cannot expect the person under interrogation to probe the officer's innermost thoughts. Save as they are communicated or otherwise manifested to the person being questioned, an officer's evolving but unarticulated suspicions do not affect the objective circumstances of an interrogation or interview, and thus cannot affect the *Miranda* custody inquiry. "The threat to a citizen's Fifth Amendment rights that *Miranda* was designed to neutralize has little to do with the strength of an interrogating officer's suspicions."

An officer's knowledge or beliefs may bear upon the custody issue if they are conveyed, by word or deed, to the individual being questioned. Those beliefs are relevant only to the extent they would affect how a reasonable person in the position of the individual being questioned would gauge the breadth of his or her "'freedom of action.'" Even a clear statement from an officer that the person under interrogation is a prime suspect is not, in itself, dispositive of the custody issue, for some suspects are free to come and go until the police decide to make an arrest. The weight and pertinence of any communications regarding the officer's degree of suspicion will depend upon the facts and circumstances of the particular case. In sum, an officer's views concerning the nature of an interrogation, or beliefs concerning the potential culpability of the individual being questioned, may be one among many factors that bear upon the assessment whether that individual was in custody, but only if the officer's views or beliefs were somehow manifested to the individual under interrogation and would have affected how a reasonable person in that position would perceive his or her freedom to leave. (Of course, instances may arise in which the officer's undisclosed views are relevant in testing the credibility of his or her account of what happened during an interrogation; but it is the objective surroundings, and not any undisclosed views, that control the *Miranda* custody inquiry.)

We decide on this state of the record that the California Supreme Court's analysis of whether Stansbury was in custody is not consistent in all respects with the foregoing principles. Numerous statements in the court's opinion are open to the interpretation that the court regarded the officers' subjective beliefs regarding Stansbury's status as a suspect (or nonsuspect) as significant in and of themselves, rather than as relevant only to the extent they influenced the objective conditions surrounding his interrogation. So understood, the court's analysis conflicts with our precedents. The court's apparent conclusion that Stansbury's *Miranda* rights were triggered by virtue of the fact that he had become the focus of the officers' suspicions, is incorrect as well. Our cases make clear, in no uncertain terms, that any inquiry into whether the interrogating officers have focused their suspicions upon the individual being questioned (assuming those suspicions remain undisclosed) is not relevant for purposes of *Miranda*.

The State acknowledges that Lieutenant Johnston's and the other officers' subjective and undisclosed suspicions (or lack thereof) do not bear upon the question whether Stansbury was in custody, for purposes of *Miranda*, during the station house interview. It maintains, however, that the objective facts in the record support a finding that Stansbury was not in custody until his arrest. Stansbury, by contrast, asserts that the objective circumstances show that he was in custody during the entire interrogation. We think it appropriate for the California Supreme Court to consider this question in the first instance. We therefore reverse its judgment and remand the case for further proceedings not inconsistent with this opinion.

NOTES AND QUESTIONS

1. Note that Stansbury was interrupted in his "trailer home" at 11:00 p.m. by four police officers, who "asked" if he would come to the police station with them and answer some questions. From a reasonable person in Stansbury's position, does this feel like an invitation you can refuse? How does it cut that he "accepted a ride" to the station in the police car? That there were four officers who came to visit to extend this invitation?

2. What was the question that elicited Stansbury's response that he had prior convictions for rape, kidnapping, and child molestation? How could this question not "convey" the interrogator's belief that Stansbury was a suspect?

3. Does it matter that Stansbury was in all likelihood lured by deceptive means to go to the police station?

4. Why do the police officer's intentions not matter unless they are communicated to the individual who is questioned? Is it really because they are not relevant to the inquiry whether a reasonable person would feel he is free to leave? Or is it because the Court wants to avoid litigation over the police officer's state of mind in every *Miranda* case where custody is an issue?

This next case considers whether the interrogation of a minor presents special circumstances relevant to the application of *Miranda* requirements.

J.D.B v. North Carolina
564 U.S. 261 (2011)

Justice SOTOMAYOR delivered the opinion of the Court.

This case presents the question whether the age of a child subjected to police questioning is relevant to the custody analysis of *Miranda*. It is beyond dispute that children will often feel bound to submit to police questioning when an adult in the same circumstances would feel free to leave. Seeing no reason for police officers or courts to blind themselves to that commonsense reality, we hold that a child's age properly informs the *Miranda* custody analysis.

I

A

Petitioner J.D.B. was a 13-year-old, seventh-grade student attending class at Smith Middle School in Chapel Hill, North Carolina when he was removed from his classroom by a uniformed police officer, escorted to a closed-door conference room, and questioned by police for at least half an hour.

This was the second time that police questioned J.D.B. in the span of a week. Five days earlier, two home break-ins occurred, and various items were stolen. Police stopped and questioned J.D.B. after he was seen behind a residence in the neighborhood where the crimes occurred. That same day, police also spoke to J.D.B.'s grandmother—his legal guardian—as well as his aunt.

Police later learned that a digital camera matching the description of one of the stolen items had been found at J.D.B.'s middle school and seen in J.D.B.'s possession. Investigator DiCostanzo, the juvenile investigator with the local police force who had been assigned to the case, went to the school to question J.D.B. Upon arrival, DiCostanzo informed the uniformed police officer on detail to the school (a so-called school resource officer), the assistant principal, and an administrative intern that he was there to question J.D.B. about the break-ins.

Although DiCostanzo asked the school administrators to verify J.D.B.'s date of birth, address, and parent contact information from school records, neither the police officers nor the school administrators contacted J.D.B.'s grandmother.

The uniformed officer interrupted J.D.B.'s afternoon social studies class, removed J.D.B. from the classroom, and escorted him to a school conference room. There, J.D.B. was met by DiCostanzo, the assistant principal, and the administrative intern. The door to the conference room was closed. With the two police officers and the two administrators present, J.D.B. was questioned for the next 30 to 45 minutes. Prior to the commencement of questioning, J.D.B. was given neither *Miranda* warnings nor the opportunity to speak to his grandmother. Nor was he informed that he was free to leave the room.

Questioning began with small talk — discussion of sports and J.D.B.'s family life. DiCostanzo asked, and J.D.B. agreed, to discuss the events of the prior weekend. Denying any wrongdoing, J.D.B. explained that he had been in the neighborhood where the crimes occurred because he was seeking work mowing lawns. DiCostanzo pressed J.D.B. for additional detail about his efforts to obtain work; asked J.D.B. to explain a prior incident, when one of the victims returned home to find J.D.B. behind her house; and confronted J.D.B. with the stolen camera. The assistant principal urged J.D.B. to "do the right thing," warning J.D.B. that "the truth always comes out in the end."

Eventually, J.D.B. asked whether he would "still be in trouble" if he returned the "stuff." In response, DiCostanzo explained that return of the stolen items would be helpful, but "this thing is going to court" regardless. DiCostanzo then warned that he may need to seek a secure custody order if he believed that J.D.B. would continue to break into other homes. When J.D.B. asked what a secure custody order was, DiCostanzo explained that "it's where you get sent to juvenile detention before court."

After learning of the prospect of juvenile detention, J.D.B. confessed that he and a friend were responsible for the break-ins. DiCostanzo only then informed J.D.B. that he could refuse to answer the investigator's questions and that he was free to leave. Asked whether he understood, J.D.B. nodded and provided further detail, including information about the location of the stolen items. Eventually J.D.B. wrote a statement, at DiCostanzo's request. When the bell rang indicating the end of the schoolday, J.D.B. was allowed to leave to catch the bus home.

B

Two juvenile petitions were filed against J.D.B., each alleging one count of breaking and entering and one count of larceny. J.D.B.'s public defender moved to suppress his statements and the evidence derived therefrom, arguing that suppression was necessary because J.D.B. had been "interrogated by police in a custodial setting without being afforded *Miranda* warning[s]," and because his statements were involuntary under the totality of the circumstances test. After a suppression hearing at which DiCostanzo and J.D.B. testified, the trial court denied the motion, deciding that J.D.B. was not in custody at the time of the schoolhouse interrogation and that his statements were voluntary. As a result, J.D.B. entered a transcript of admission to all four counts, renewing his objection to the denial of his motion to suppress, and the court adjudicated J.D.B. delinquent.

We granted certiorari to determine whether the *Miranda* custody analysis includes consideration of a juvenile suspect's age.

II

A

Any police interview of an individual suspected of a crime has "coercive aspects to it." Only those interrogations that occur while a suspect is in police custody, however, "heighte[n] the risk" that statements obtained are not the product of the suspect's free choice.

By its very nature, custodial police interrogation entails "inherently compelling pressures." Even for an adult, the physical and psychological isolation of custodial interrogation can "undermine the individual's will to resist and . . . compel him to speak where he would not otherwise do so freely." Indeed, the pressure of custodial interrogation is so immense that it "can induce a frighteningly high percentage of people to confess to crimes they never committed." *Corley v. United States* (2009) (citing Drizin & Leo, The Problem of False Confessions in the Post-DNA World, 82 N.C. L. Rev. 891, 906-907 (2004)); see also *Miranda*, 384 U.S., at 455, n. 23. That risk is all the more troubling—and recent studies suggest, all the more acute—when the subject of custodial interrogation is a juvenile. See Brief for Center on Wrongful Convictions of Youth et al. as Amici Curiae 21-22 (collecting empirical studies that "illustrate the heightened risk of false confessions from youth").

Recognizing that the inherently coercive nature of custodial interrogation "blurs the line between voluntary and involuntary statements," this Court in *Miranda* adopted a set of prophylactic measures designed to safeguard the constitutional guarantee against self-incrimination. Prior to questioning, a suspect "must be warned that he has a right to remain silent, that any statement he does make may be used as evidence against him, and that he has a right to the presence of an attorney, either retained or appointed."

Because these measures protect the individual against the coercive nature of custodial interrogation, they are required "'only where there has been such a restriction on a person's freedom as to render him "in custody." ' " As we have repeatedly emphasized, whether a suspect is "in custody" is an objective inquiry.

"Two discrete inquiries are essential to the determination: first, what were the circumstances surrounding the interrogation; and second, given those circumstances, would a reasonable person have felt he or she was at liberty to terminate the interrogation and leave. Once the scene is set and the players' lines and actions are reconstructed, the court must apply an objective test to resolve the ultimate inquiry: was there a formal arrest or restraint on freedom of movement of the degree associated with formal arrest."

Rather than demarcate a limited set of relevant circumstances, we have required police officers and courts to "examine all of the circumstances surrounding the interrogation," including any circumstance that "would have affected how a reasonable person" in the suspect's position "would perceive his or her freedom to leave." On the other hand, the "subjective views harbored by either the interrogating officers or the person being questioned" are irrelevant. The test, in other words, involves no consideration of the "actual mindset" of the particular suspect subjected to police questioning.

The benefit of the objective custody analysis is that it is "designed to give clear guidance to the police." Police must make in-the-moment judgments as to when to administer *Miranda* warnings. By limiting analysis to the objective circumstances of the interrogation, and asking how a reasonable person in the suspect's position would understand his freedom to terminate questioning and leave, the objective test avoids burdening police with the task of anticipating the idiosyncrasies of every individual suspect and divining how those particular traits affect each person's subjective state of mind.

B

The State and its amici contend that a child's age has no place in the custody analysis, no matter how young the child subjected to police questioning. We cannot agree. In some circumstances, a child's age "would have affected how a reasonable person" in the suspect's position "would perceive his or her freedom to leave." That is, a reasonable child subjected to police questioning will sometimes feel pressured to submit when a reasonable adult would feel free to go. We think it clear that courts can account for that reality without doing any damage to the objective nature of the custody analysis.

A child's age is far "more than a chronological fact." Such conclusions apply broadly to children as a class. And, they are self-evident to anyone who was a child once himself, including any police officer or judge.

Time and again, this Court has drawn these commonsense conclusions for itself. We have observed that children "generally are less mature and responsible than adults"; that they "often lack the experience, perspective, and judgment to recognize and avoid choices that could be detrimental to them"; that they "are more vulnerable or susceptible to . . . outside pressures" than adults, and so on. Addressing the specific context of police interrogation, we have observed that events that "would leave a man cold and unimpressed can overawe and overwhelm a lad in his early teens." Describing no one child in particular, these observations restate what "any parent knows"—indeed, what any person knows—about children generally.

Our various statements to this effect are far from unique. The law has historically reflected the same assumption that children characteristically lack the capacity to exercise mature judgment and possess only an incomplete ability to understand the world around them. Like this Court's own generalizations, the legal disqualifications placed on children as a class—e.g., limitations on their ability to alienate property, enter a binding contract enforceable against them, and marry without parental consent—exhibit the settled understanding that the differentiating characteristics of youth are universal.

Indeed, even where a "reasonable person" standard otherwise applies, the common law has reflected the reality that children are not adults. In negligence suits, for instance, where liability turns on what an objectively reasonable person would do in the circumstances, "[a]ll American jurisdictions accept the idea that a person's childhood is a relevant circumstance" to be considered.

As this discussion establishes, "[o]ur history is replete with laws and judicial recognition" that children cannot be viewed simply as miniature adults. *Eddings*, 455 U.S., at 115-116, 102 S. Ct. 869. We see no justification for taking a different course here. So long as the child's age was known to the officer at the time of the interview, or would have been objectively apparent to any reasonable officer, including age as part of the custody analysis requires officers neither to consider circumstances "unknowable" to them, nor to "anticipat[e] the frailties or idiosyncrasies" of the particular suspect whom they question. The same "wide basis of community experience" that makes it possible, as an objective matter, "to determine what is to be expected" of children in other contexts, and likewise makes it possible to know what to expect of children subjected to police questioning.

In other words, a child's age differs from other personal characteristics that, even when known to police, have no objectively discernible relationship to a reasonable person's understanding of his freedom of action. *Alvarado*, holds, for instance, that a suspect's prior interrogation history with law enforcement has no role to play in the custody analysis because such experience could just as easily lead a reasonable person to feel free to walk away as to feel compelled to stay in place. Because the effect in any given case would be "contingent [on the] psycholog[y]" of the individual suspect, the Court explained, such experience cannot be considered without compromising the objective nature of the custody analysis. A child's age, however, is different. Precisely because childhood yields objective conclusions like those we have drawn ourselves—among others, that children are "most susceptible to influence" and "outside pressures"—considering age in the custody analysis in no way involves a determination of how youth "subjectively affect[s] the mindset" of any particular child."

In fact, in many cases involving juvenile suspects, the custody analysis would be nonsensical absent some consideration of the suspect's age. This case is a prime example. Were the court precluded from taking J.D.B.'s youth into account, it would be forced to evaluate the circumstances present here through the eyes of a reasonable person of average years. In other words, how would a reasonable adult understand his situation, after being removed from a seventh-grade social studies class by a uniformed school resource officer; being encouraged by his assistant principal to "do the right thing"; and being warned by a police investigator of the prospect of juvenile detention and separation from his guardian and primary caretaker? To describe such an inquiry is to demonstrate its absurdity. Neither officers nor courts can reasonably evaluate the effect of objective circumstances that, by their nature, are specific to children without accounting for the age of the child subjected to those circumstances.

Indeed, although the dissent suggests that concerns "regarding the application of the *Miranda* custody rule to minors can be accommodated by considering the unique circumstances present when minors are questioned in school," the effect of the schoolhouse setting cannot be disentangled from the identity of the person questioned. A student—whose presence at school is compulsory and whose disobedience at school is cause for disciplinary action—is in a far different position than, say, a parent volunteer on school grounds to chaperone an event, or an adult from the community on school grounds to attend a basketball game. Without asking whether the person "questioned in school" is a "minor" the coercive effect of the schoolhouse setting is unknowable.

· · ·

Reviewing the question de novo today, we hold that so long as the child's age was known to the officer at the time of police questioning, or would have been objectively apparent to a reasonable officer, its inclusion in the custody analysis is consistent with the objective nature of that test. This is not to say that a child's age will be a determinative, or even a significant, factor in every case. It is, however, a reality that courts cannot simply ignore.

III

The State and its amici offer numerous reasons that courts must blind themselves to a juvenile defendant's age. None is persuasive.

To start, the State contends that a child's age must be excluded from the custody inquiry because age is a personal characteristic specific to the suspect himself rather than an "external" circumstance of the interrogation. Despite the supposed significance of this distinction, however, at oral argument counsel for the State suggested without hesitation that at least some undeniably personal characteristics—for instance, whether the individual being questioned is blind—are circumstances relevant to the custody analysis. Thus, the State's quarrel cannot be that age is a personal characteristic, without more.

The State further argues that age is irrelevant to the custody analysis because it "go[es] to how a suspect may internalize and perceive the circumstances of an interrogation." But the same can be said of every objective circumstance that the State agrees is relevant to the custody analysis: Each circumstance goes to how a reasonable person would "internalize and perceive" every other. Indeed, this is the very reason that we ask whether the objective circumstances "add up to custody" instead of evaluating the circumstances one by one.

In the same vein, the State and its amici protest that the "effect of . . . age on [the] perception of custody is internal." But the whole point of the custody analysis is to determine whether, given the circumstances, "a reasonable person [would] have felt he or she was . . . at liberty to terminate the interrogation and leave." Because the *Miranda* custody inquiry turns on the mindset of a reasonable person in the suspect's position, it cannot be the case that a circumstance is subjective simply because it has an "internal" or "psychological" impact on perception. Were that so, there would be no objective circumstances to consider at all.

Relying on our statements that the objective custody test is "designed to give clear guidance to the police," the State next argues that a child's age must be excluded from the analysis in order to preserve clarity. Similarly, the dissent insists that the clarity of the custody analysis will be destroyed unless a "one-size-fits-all reasonable-person test" applies. In reality, however, ignoring a juvenile defendant's age will often make the inquiry more artificial, and thus only add confusion. And in any event, a child's age, when known or apparent, is hardly an obscure factor to assess. Though the State and the dissent worry about gradations among children of different ages, that concern cannot justify ignoring a child's age altogether. Just as police officers are competent to account for other objective circumstances that are a matter of degree such as the length of questioning or the number of officers present, so too are they competent to evaluate the effect of relative age. Indeed, they are competent to do so even though an interrogation room lacks the "reflective atmosphere of a [jury] deliberation room." The same is true of judges, including those whose childhoods have long since passed. In short, officers and judges need no imaginative powers, knowledge of developmental psychology, training in cognitive science, or expertise in social and cultural anthropology to account for a child's age. They simply need the common sense to know that a 7-year-old is not a 13-year-old and neither is an adult.

There is, however, an even more fundamental flaw with the State's plea for clarity and the dissent's singular focus on simplifying the analysis: Not once have we excluded from the custody analysis a circumstance that we determined was relevant and objective, simply to make the fault line between custodial and noncustodial "brighter." Indeed, were the guiding concern clarity and nothing else, the custody test would presumably ask only whether the suspect had been placed under formal arrest. But we have rejected that "more easily administered line," recognizing that it would simply "enable the police to circumvent the constraints on custodial interrogations established by *Miranda*."

Finally, the State and the dissent suggest that excluding age from the custody analysis comes at no cost to juveniles' constitutional rights because the due process voluntariness test independently accounts for a child's youth. To be sure, that test permits consideration of a child's age, and it erects its own barrier to admission of a defendant's inculpatory statements at trial. But *Miranda*'s procedural safeguards exist precisely because the voluntariness test is an inadequate barrier when custodial interrogation is at stake. To hold, as the State requests, that a child's age is never relevant to whether a suspect has been taken into custody—and thus to ignore the very real differences between children and adults—would be to deny children the full scope of the procedural safeguards that *Miranda* guarantees to adults.

• • •

The question remains whether J.D.B. was in custody when police interrogated him. We remand for the state courts to address that question, this time taking account of all of the relevant circumstances of the interrogation, including J.D.B.'s age at the time. The judgment of the North Carolina Supreme Court is reversed, and the case is remanded for proceedings not inconsistent with this opinion.

NOTES AND QUESTIONS

1. This is one of the Supreme Court's first opinions in which it openly acknowledges not just the theoretical possibility of false confessions but data demonstrating the fact of false confessions. If anything, the Court understates the problem of false confessions by juveniles. By the time of this decision most of America was aware of the wrongful conviction of the "Central Park Five," in which five juveniles were convicted of assault and rape based on their confessions, only to have the real perpetrator surface years later and confess, leading to the convictions of the Central Park Five being vacated. *See generally* N. Jeremi Duru, *The Central Park Five, the Scottsboro Boys, and the Myth of the Bestial Black Man*, 25 Cardozo L. Rev. 1315, 1320 (2004). *See also The Central Park Five* (Sundance Selects 2012); *When They See Us* (Netflix 2019).

2. Did the presence of the school administrators likely add to or lessen the custodial nature of the interrogation?

3. On remand, how should the trial court go about taking into account the fact of J.D.B.'s youth in making the custody determination? Will this be purely the subject of expert testimony? Will the trial court have discretion not to take expert testimony on the issue? Will J.D.B. be allowed to testify as to whether he believed he was free to refuse the interview? What is the significance of the fact that J.D.B. was required to be in school?

4. What do you think of the dissent's slippery slope argument — that age is no different than intelligence, education, occupation, etc. — and that all such factors will inevitably become part of a fact-intensive custody standard?

E. *MIRANDA* IN PRACTICE II: WAIVER AND INVOCATION OF *MIRANDA* RIGHTS

Michigan v. Mosley
423 U.S. 96 (1975)

Mr. Justice STEWART delivered the opinion of the Court.

The respondent, Richard Bert Mosley, was arrested in Detroit, Mich., in the early afternoon of April 8, 1971, in connection with robberies that had recently occurred at the Blue Goose Bar and the White Tower Restaurant on that city's lower east side. The arresting officer, Detective James Cowie of the Armed Robbery Section of the Detroit Police Department, was acting on a tip implicating Mosley and three other men in the robberies. After effecting the arrest, Detective Cowie brought Mosley to the Robbery, Breaking and Entering Bureau of the Police Department, located on the fourth floor of the departmental headquarters building. The officer advised Mosley of his rights under this Court's decision in *Miranda* and had him read and sign the department's constitutional rights notification certificate. After filling out the necessary arrest papers, Cowie began questioning Mosley about the robbery of the White Tower Restaurant. When Mosley said he did not want to answer any questions about the robberies, Cowie promptly ceased the interrogation. The completion of the arrest papers and the questioning of Mosley together took approximately 20 minutes. At no time during the questioning did Mosley indicate a desire to consult with a lawyer, and there is no claim that the procedures followed to this point did not fully comply with the strictures of the *Miranda* opinion. Mosley was then taken to a ninth-floor cell block.

Shortly after 6 p.m., Detective Hill of the Detroit Police Department Homicide Bureau brought Mosley from the cell block to the fifth-floor office of the Homicide Bureau for questioning about the fatal shooting of a man named Leroy Williams. Williams had been killed on January 9, 1971, during a holdup attempt outside the 101 Ranch Bar in Detroit. Mosley had not been arrested on this charge or interrogated about it by Detective Cowie. Before questioning Mosley about this homicide, Detective Hill carefully advised him of his "*Miranda* rights." Mosley read the notification form both silently and aloud, and Detective Hill then read and explained the warnings to him and had him sign the form. Mosley at first denied any involvement in the Williams murder, but after the officer told him that Anthony Smith had confessed to participating in the slaying and had named him as the "shooter," Mosley made a statement implicating himself in the homicide. The interrogation by Detective Hill lasted approximately 15 minutes, and at no time during its course did Mosley ask to consult with a lawyer or indicate that he did not want to discuss the homicide. In short, there is no claim that the procedures followed during Detective Hill's interrogation of Mosley, standing alone, did not fully comply with the strictures of the *Miranda* opinion.

Mosley was subsequently charged in a one-count information with first-degree murder. Before the trial he moved to suppress his incriminating statement on a number of grounds, among them the claim that under the doctrine of the *Miranda* case it was constitutionally impermissible for Detective Hill to question him about the Williams murder after he had told Detective Cowie that he did not want to answer any questions about the robberies. The trial court denied the motion to suppress after an evidentiary hearing, and the incriminating statement was subsequently introduced in evidence against Mosley at his trial. The jury convicted Mosley of first-degree murder, and the court imposed a mandatory sentence of life imprisonment.

On appeal to the Michigan Court of Appeals, Mosley renewed his previous objections to the use of his incriminating statement in evidence. The appellate court reversed the judgment of conviction, holding that Detective Hill's interrogation of Mosley had been a per se violation of the *Miranda* doctrine. Accordingly, without reaching Mosley's other contentions, the Court remanded the case for a new trial with instructions that Mosley's statement be suppressed as evidence. After further appeal was denied by the Michigan Supreme Court, the State filed a petition for certiorari here. We granted the writ because of the important constitutional question presented.

In the *Miranda* case this Court promulgated a set of safeguards to protect the there-delineated constitutional rights of persons subjected to custodial police interrogation. In sum, the Court held in that case that unless law enforcement officers give certain specified warnings before questioning a person in custody, and follow certain specified procedures during the course of any subsequent interrogation, any statement made by the person in custody cannot over his objection be admitted in evidence against him as a defendant at trial, even though the statement may in fact be wholly voluntary.

Neither party in the present case challenges the continuing validity of the *Miranda* decision, or of any of the so-called guidelines it established to protect what the Court there said was a person's constitutional privilege against compulsory self-incrimination. The issue in this case, rather, is whether the conduct of the Detroit police that led to Mosley's incriminating statement did in fact violate the *Miranda* "guidelines," so as to render the statement inadmissible in evidence against Mosley at his trial. Resolution of the question turns almost entirely on the interpretation of a single passage in the *Miranda* opinion, upon which the Michigan appellate court relied in finding a per se violation of *Miranda*:

> Once warnings have been given, the subsequent procedure is clear. If the individual indicates in any manner, at any time prior to or during questioning, that he wishes to remain silent, the interrogation must cease. At this point he has shown that he intends to exercise his Fifth Amendment privilege; any statement taken after the person invokes his privilege cannot be other than the product of compulsion, subtle or otherwise. Without the right to cut off questioning, the setting of in-custody interrogation operates on the individual to overcome free choice in producing a statement after the privilege has been once invoked.

This passage states that "the interrogation must cease" when the person in custody indicates that "he wishes to remain silent." It does not state under what circumstances, if any, a resumption of questioning is permissible. The passage could be literally read to mean that a person who has invoked his "right to silence" can never again be subjected to custodial interrogation by any police officer at any time or place on any subject. Another possible construction of the passage would characterize "any statement taken after the person invokes his privilege" as "the product of compulsion" and would therefore mandate its exclusion from evidence, even if it were volunteered by the person in custody without any further interrogation whatever. Or the passage could be interpreted to require only the immediate cessation of questioning, and to permit a resumption of interrogation after a momentary respite.

It is evident that any of these possible literal interpretations would lead to absurd and unintended results. To permit the continuation of custodial interrogation after a momentary cessation would clearly frustrate the purposes of *Miranda* by allowing repeated rounds of questioning to undermine the will of the person being questioned. At the other extreme, a blanket prohibition against the taking of voluntary statements or a permanent immunity from further interrogation, regardless of the circumstances, would transform the *Miranda* safeguards into wholly irrational obstacles to legitimate police investigative activity, and deprive suspects of an opportunity to make informed and intelligent assessments of their interests. Clearly, therefore, neither this passage nor any other passage in the *Miranda* opinion can sensibly be read to create a per se proscription of indefinite duration upon any further questioning by any police officer on any subject, once the person in custody has indicated a desire to remain silent.

A reasonable and faithful interpretation of the *Miranda* opinion must rest on the intention of the Court in that case to adopt "fully effective means . . . to notify the person of his right of silence and to assure that the exercise of the right will be scrupulously honored. . . ." The critical safeguard identified in the passage at issue is a person's "right to cut off questioning." Through the exercise of his option to terminate questioning he can control the time at which questioning occurs, the subjects discussed, and the duration of the interrogation. The requirement that law enforcement authorities must respect a person's exercise of that option counteracts the coercive pressures of the custodial setting. We therefore conclude that the admissibility of statements obtained after the person in custody has decided to remain silent depends under *Miranda* on whether his "right to cut off questioning" was "scrupulously honored."

A review of the circumstances leading to Mosley's confession reveals that his "right to cut off questioning" was fully respected in this case. Before his initial interrogation, Mosley was carefully advised that he was under no obligation to answer any questions and could remain silent if he wished. He orally acknowledged that he understood the *Miranda* warnings and then signed a printed notification-of-rights form. When Mosley stated that he did not want to discuss the robberies, Detective Cowie immediately ceased the interrogation and did not try either to resume the questioning or in any way to persuade Mosley to reconsider his position. After an interval of more than two hours, Mosley was questioned by another police officer at another location about an unrelated holdup murder. He was given full and complete *Miranda* warnings at the outset of the second interrogation. He was thus reminded again that he could remain silent and could consult with a lawyer, and was carefully given a full and fair opportunity to exercise these options. The subsequent questioning did not undercut Mosley's previous decision not to answer Detective Cowie's inquiries. Detective Hill did not resume the interrogation about the White Tower Restaurant robbery or inquire about the Blue Goose Bar robbery, but instead focused exclusively on the Leroy Williams homicide, a crime different in nature and in time and place of occurrence from the robberies for which Mosley had been arrested and interrogated by Detective Cowie. Although it is not clear from the record how much Detective Hill knew about the earlier interrogation, his questioning of Mosley about an unrelated homicide was quite consistent with a reasonable interpretation of Mosley's earlier refusal to answer any questions about the robberies.

This is not a case, therefore, where the police failed to honor a decision of a person in custody to cut off questioning, either by refusing to discontinue the interrogation upon request or by persisting in repeated efforts to wear down his resistance and make him change his mind. In contrast to such practices, the police here immediately ceased the interrogation, resumed questioning only after the passage of a significant period of time and the provision of

160 Chapter III Police Interrogation and The Fifth Amendment

a fresh set of warnings, and restricted the second interrogation to a crime that had not been a subject of the earlier interrogation.

For these reasons, we conclude that the admission in evidence of Mosley's incriminating statement did not violate the principles of *Miranda*. Accordingly, the judgment of the Michigan Court of Appeals is vacated, and the case is remanded to that court for further proceedings not inconsistent with this opinion.

[Justices Marshall and Brennan dissented.]

NOTES AND QUESTIONS

1. The Court's references to *Miranda* could hardly be more grudging. Note the following examples of what can only be described as petulance: "In the *Miranda* case this Court," instead of "In *Miranda* we . . ."; the gratuitous reference to the inadmissibility of a statement "even though the statement may in fact be wholly voluntary"; the characterization of the decision's required warnings as "so-called guidelines"; and the apparent disappointment that "[n]either party in the present case challenges the continuing validity of the *Miranda* decision."

2. The Court states that Mosley was "arrested . . . in connection with" recent robberies based on a tip. What does "in connection with" mean in this context? Was there an arrest warrant issued? Was there probable cause for his arrest for the recent robberies?

Information relegated to a footnote supplies the answer to these questions: "The officer testified that information supplied by an anonymous caller was the sole basis for his arrest of Mosley."

In short, there was not probable cause for Mosley's arrest. What does this fact suggest to you about the lack of clarity in the record about "how much defendant Hill knew about the earlier interrogation"? Shouldn't this have been a focus of the defense attorney's cross-examination of the officers at the suppression hearing? How did Detective Hill learn that Mosley, a suspect in Hill's homicide investigation, was being held in the same building?

The dissent points out that, contrary to the Court's description of the subject of Detective Hill's questioning as an "unrelated holdup murder," the tip received by Detective Cowie included information about that murder.

3. Do you agree that it would be an "absurd and unintended result" for *Miranda* to be interpreted as "a permanent immunity from further interrogation"? The Court states that such a "blanket prohibition" has two evils: imposing "irrational obstacles to legitimate police investigative activity" and "depriv[ing] suspects of an opportunity to make informed and intelligent assessments of their interests." Are the police here engaged in "legitimate police activity"? Won't Mosley be able to make an informed decision if (and when) he is lawfully arrested and has the advice of counsel?

4. The Court notes that Mosley never indicated a desire to consult with a lawyer. Would this have made a difference? If Mosley had uttered those words, would he have been entitled to a "permanent immunity" as to further questioning?

If Mosley were resolute in his desire not to talk to the police — to exercise his right to remain silent — why would he have thought a lawyer necessary?

5. The Court seems to view it as material that the second interrogation was two hours later and in another location (in the same building) by a different police officer (from the same department) about a different (more serious) crime. Why do any of these factors matter?

6. Note that the Supreme Court had held just a few months earlier in *Gerstein v. Pugh*, 420 U.S. 103 (1975), that a person arrested without a warrant must "promptly" be brought before a magistrate to establish probable cause for continued detention. Many more years

E. *Miranda* in Practice II: Waiver and Invocation of *Miranda* Rights   **161**

would pass before the Court, in *County of Riverside v. McLaughlin*, 500 U.S. 44 (1991), specified 48 hours as the time within which the police must comply with *Gerstein*.

Edwards v. Arizona
451 U.S. 477 (1981)

Justice WHITE delivered the opinion of the Court.

We granted certiorari in this case limited to Q 1 presented in the petition, which in relevant part was "whether the Fifth, Sixth, and Fourteenth Amendments require suppression of a post-arrest confession, which was obtained after Edwards had invoked his right to consult counsel before further interrogation. . . ."

I

On January 19, 1976, a sworn complaint was filed against Edwards in Arizona state court charging him with robbery, burglary, and first-degree murder. An arrest warrant was issued pursuant to the complaint, and Edwards was arrested at his home later that same day. At the police station, he was informed of his rights as required by *Miranda*. Petitioner stated that he understood his rights, and was willing to submit to questioning. After being told that another suspect already in custody had implicated him in the crime, Edwards denied involvement and gave a taped statement presenting an alibi defense. He then sought to "make a deal." The interrogating officer told him that he wanted a statement, but that he did not have the authority to negotiate a deal. The officer provided Edwards with the telephone number of a county attorney. Petitioner made the call, but hung up after a few moments. Edwards then said: "I want an attorney before making a deal." At that point, questioning ceased and Edwards was taken to county jail.

At 9:15 the next morning, two detectives, colleagues of the officer who had interrogated Edwards the previous night, came to the jail and asked to see Edwards. When the detention officer informed Edwards that the detectives wished to speak with him, he replied that he did not want to talk to anyone. The guard told him that "he had" to talk and then took him to meet with the detectives. The officers identified themselves, stated they wanted to talk to him, and informed him of his *Miranda* rights. Edwards was willing to talk, but he first wanted to hear the taped statement of the alleged accomplice who had implicated him. After listening to the tape for several minutes, petitioner said that he would make a statement so long as it was not tape-recorded. The detectives informed him that the recording was irrelevant since they could testify in court concerning whatever he said. Edwards replied: "I'll tell you anything you want to know, but I don't want it on tape." He thereupon implicated himself in the crime.

Prior to trial, Edwards moved to suppress his confession on the ground that his *Miranda* rights had been violated when the officers returned to question him after he had invoked his right to counsel. The trial court initially granted the motion to suppress, but reversed its ruling when presented with a supposedly controlling decision of a higher Arizona court. The court stated without explanation that it found Edwards' statement to be voluntary. Edwards was tried twice and convicted. Evidence concerning his confession was admitted at both trials.

On appeal, the Arizona Supreme Court held that Edwards had invoked both his right to remain silent and his right to counsel during the interrogation conducted on the night of January 19. The court then went on to determine, however, that Edwards had waived both rights during the January 20 meeting when he voluntarily gave his statement to the detectives after again being informed that he need not answer questions and that he need not answer without the advice of counsel: "The trial court's finding that the waiver and confession were voluntarily and knowingly made is upheld."

Because the use of Edwards' confession against him at his trial violated his rights under the Fifth and Fourteenth Amendments as construed in *Miranda* we reverse the judgment of the Arizona Supreme Court.

II

In *Miranda* the Court determined that the Fifth and Fourteenth Amendments' prohibition against compelled self-incrimination required that custodial interrogation be preceded by advice to the putative defendant that he has the right to remain silent and also the right to the presence of an attorney. The Court also indicated the procedures to be followed subsequent to the warnings. If the accused indicates that he wishes to remain silent, "the interrogation must cease." If he requests counsel, "the interrogation must cease until an attorney is present."

Miranda thus declared that an accused has a Fifth and Fourteenth Amendment right to have counsel present during custodial interrogation. Here, the critical facts as found by the Arizona Supreme Court are that Edwards asserted his right to counsel and his right to remain silent on January 19, but that the police, without furnishing him counsel, returned the next morning to confront him and as a result of the meeting secured incriminating oral admissions. Contrary to the holdings of the state courts, Edwards insists that having exercised his right on the 19th to have counsel present during interrogation, he did not validly waive that right on the 20th. For the following reasons, we agree.

First, the Arizona Supreme Court applied an erroneous standard for determining waiver where the accused has specifically invoked his right to counsel. It is reasonably clear under our cases that waivers of counsel must not only be voluntary, but must also constitute a knowing and intelligent relinquishment or abandonment of a known right or privilege, a matter which depends in each case "upon the particular facts and circumstances surrounding that case, including the background, experience, and conduct of the accused."

Considering the proceedings in the state courts in the light of this standard, we note that in denying petitioner's motion to suppress, the trial court found the admission to have been "voluntary," without separately focusing on whether Edwards had knowingly and intelligently relinquished his right to counsel. The Arizona Supreme Court, in a section of its opinion entitled "Voluntariness of Waiver," stated that in Arizona, confessions are prima facie involuntary and that the State had the burden of showing by a preponderance of the evidence that the confession was freely and voluntarily made. The court stated that the issue of voluntariness should be determined based on the totality of the circumstances as it related to whether an accused's action was "knowing and intelligent and whether his will [was] overborne." Once the trial court determines that "the confession is voluntary, the finding will not be upset on appeal absent clear and manifest error." The court then upheld the trial court's finding that the "waiver and confession were voluntarily and knowingly made."

In referring to the necessity to find Edwards' confession knowing and intelligent the State Supreme Court cited *Schneckloth*. Yet, it is clear that *Schneckloth* does not control the issue presented in this case. The issue in *Schneckloth* was under what conditions an individual could be found to have consented to a search and thereby waived his Fourth Amendment rights. The Court declined to impose the "intentional relinquishment or abandonment of a known right or privilege" standard and required only that the consent be voluntary under the totality of the circumstances. The Court specifically noted that the right to counsel was a prime example of those rights requiring the special protection of the knowing and intelligent waiver standard, but held that "[t]he considerations that informed the Court's holding in *Miranda* are simply inapplicable in the present case." *Schneckloth* itself thus emphasized that the voluntariness of a consent or an admission on the one hand, and a knowing and intelligent waiver on the other, are discrete inquiries. Here, however sound the conclusion of the state courts as to the voluntariness of Edwards' admission may be, neither the trial court nor the Arizona Supreme Court undertook to focus on whether Edwards understood his right to counsel and intelligently and knowingly relinquished it. It is thus apparent that the decision below misunderstood the requirement for finding a valid waiver of the right to counsel, once invoked.

Second, although we have held that after initially being advised of his *Miranda* rights, the accused may himself validly waive his rights and respond to interrogation, the Court has strongly indicated that additional safeguards are necessary when the accused asks for counsel; and we now hold that when an accused has invoked his right to have counsel present during custodial interrogation, a valid waiver of that right cannot be established by showing only that he responded to further police-initiated custodial interrogation even if he has been advised of his rights. We further hold that an accused, such as Edwards, having expressed his desire to deal with the police only through counsel, is not subject to further interrogation by the authorities until counsel has been made available to him, unless the accused himself initiates further communication, exchanges, or conversations with the police.

Miranda itself indicated that the assertion of the right to counsel was a significant event and that once exercised by the accused, "the interrogation must cease until an attorney is present." Our later cases have not abandoned that view. In *Mosley*, the Court noted that *Miranda* had distinguished between the procedural safeguards triggered by a request to remain silent and a request for an attorney and had required that interrogation cease until an attorney was present only if the individual stated that he wanted counsel. In *Fare v. Michael C.*, the Court referred to *Miranda*'s "rigid rule that an accused's request for an attorney is per se an invocation of his Fifth Amendment rights, requiring that all interrogation cease." And just last Term, in a case where a suspect in custody had invoked his *Miranda* right to counsel, the Court again referred to the "undisputed right" under *Miranda* to remain silent and to be free of interrogation "until he had consulted with a lawyer." *Rhode Island v. Innis*. We reconfirm these views and, to lend them substance, emphasize that it is inconsistent with *Miranda* and its progeny for the authorities, at their instance, to reinterrogate an accused in custody if he has clearly asserted his right to counsel.

In concluding that the fruits of the interrogation initiated by the police on January 20 could not be used against Edwards, we do not hold or imply that Edwards was powerless to countermand his election or that the authorities could in no event use any incriminating statements made by Edwards prior to his having access to counsel. Had Edwards initiated the meeting on January 20, nothing in the Fifth and Fourteenth Amendments would prohibit the police from merely listening to his voluntary, volunteered statements and using them against him at the trial. The Fifth Amendment right identified in *Miranda* is the right to have counsel present at any custodial interrogation. Absent such interrogation, there would have been no infringement of the right that Edwards invoked and there would be no occasion to determine whether there had been a valid waiver.

But this is not what the facts of this case show. Here, the officers conducting the interrogation on the evening of January 19 ceased interrogation when Edwards requested counsel as he had been advised he had the right to do. The Arizona Supreme Court was of the opinion that this was a sufficient invocation of his *Miranda* rights, and we are in accord. It is also clear that without making counsel available to Edwards, the police returned to him the next day. This was not at his suggestion or request. Indeed, Edwards informed the detention officer that he did not want to talk to anyone. At the meeting, the detectives told Edwards that they wanted to talk to him and again advised him of his *Miranda* rights. Edwards stated that he would talk, but what prompted this action does not appear. He listened at his own request to part of the taped statement made by one of his alleged accomplices and then made an incriminating

164 Chapter III Police Interrogation and The Fifth Amendment

statement, which was used against him at his trial. We think it is clear that Edwards was subjected to custodial interrogation on January 20 within the meaning of *Rhode Island v. Innis*, and that this occurred at the instance of the authorities. His statement made without having had access to counsel, did not amount to a valid waiver and hence was inadmissible.

Accordingly, the holding of the Arizona Supreme Court that Edwards had waived his right to counsel was infirm, and the judgment of that court is reversed.

NOTES AND QUESTIONS

1. Unlike Mosley, Edwards was lawfully under arrest. So an arrest warrant had issued, based on a determination by a magistrate or judge that there was probable cause to believe that Edwards had committed the charged offenses. If this is the case, why the urgency on the part of the detectives? Did they fear a lawyer would be on the scene soon?

2. In his first interrogation, after being given *Miranda* warnings, Edwards was told that another suspect had implicated him in the crime. After hearing this, Edwards provided the detectives with an alibi defense and then stated that he "wanted to make a deal" after first consulting an attorney.

Why would Edwards want to "make a deal" if he had an alibi? Did the detectives really need to get an explicit confession after this exchange? Isn't it likely that a competent defense attorney, knowing about the first interrogation, would have advised Edwards to make a deal?

3. Judging by Edwards's behavior the next day it would seem that the detectives had been telling the truth when they told Edwards they had a taped statement of an accomplice that implicated Edwards. But they could have lied about that fact in the interrogation with virtual impunity. *See Frazier v. Cupp*, 394 U.S. 731 (1969) (false representation by interrogator that defendant's companion had confessed to the murder and implicated defendant does not render subsequent confession involuntary).

4. Why is the right to counsel, at issue here, treated so differently than the right to remain silent at issue in *Mosley*? The Court suggests that if Edwards had initiated the second meeting, there would have been no *Miranda* violation. Why shouldn't the same rule apply in a *Mosley* scenario where a suspect has asserted not his right to counsel but his right to remain silent?

5. In *Oregon v. Bradshaw*, 462 U.S. 1039 (1983), and *Davis v. United States*, 512 U.S. 452 (1994), the Court made it difficult for defendants to suppress statements they claimed resulted from violations of *Edwards*. In *Bradshaw*, the defendant was given *Miranda* warnings in connection with a murder investigation, denied any involvement, then asserted his right to counsel. *Id.* at 1041-42. Shortly thereafter, as he was about to be transported from the police station to a local jail, Bradshaw asked a police officer, "What is going to happen to me now?" *Id.* at 1042. This inquiry led to some colloquy and then to an unsuccessful polygraph, after which Bradshaw incriminated himself. *Id.* The Supreme Court ultimately found that Bradshaw had "initiated" a discussion under *Edwards*, and had thus withdrawn his previous assertion of the right to counsel, even though it acknowledged that his language was ambiguous. *Id.* at 1045-46. Per Justice Marshall, the four dissenters interpreted the defendant's question as more likely a question about where he was going than it was indicative of a desire to resume the interrogation. *Id.* at 1055 (Marshall, J., dissenting).

In *Davis*, after 90 minutes of interrogation the defendant said, "Maybe I should talk to a lawyer?" The interrogators asked him follow-up questions designed to enable him to clarify his request, which he did not, and then they re-Mirandized him and resumed questioning, eliciting incriminating information that was used to convict him. 512 U.S. at 455. The Supreme Court held that only an unambiguous request could trigger the protection of *Edwards*. Both *Bradshaw* and *Davis* have been sharply criticized by commentators. *See, e.g.,* Marcy Strauss, *Understanding* Davis v. United States, 40 Loy. L.A. L. Rev. 1011, 1012 (2006) (concluding that *Davis* will eviscerate the *Miranda* guarantees, particularly for women and minorities who may be less likely to speak in clear, declarative terms).

6. The Supreme Court eventually clarified that *Edwards* did not impose an "eternal" prohibition on a resumption of questioning once a suspect had invoked his right to counsel. In *Maryland v. Shatzer*, 559 U.S. 98 (2010), the Court held that a two-week "break in custody" is sufficient to dispel the coercive effects of custody, and defended the legislative feel of its announced ruling—the second interrogation in *Shatzer* of the defendant was more than two years after the first—on the ground that "law officers need to know" what is lawful. The Court could have cited *Miranda*, of course, as a justification for its giving such detailed guidance to the police. It did not, instead noting its decision in *County of Riverside v. McLaughlin*, 500 U.S. 44 (1991), which specified 48 hours as the time within which the police must comply with *Gerstein v. Pugh*.

The Court considered the significance of counsel to an arrestee again in *Moran v. Burbine*, 475 U.S. 412 (1986). Brian Burbine was arrested—as was Mosley—"in connection with" a burglary in Cranston, Rhode Island, after a confidential informant had implicated him in a notorious unsolved murder in neighboring Providence. In short, as with Mosley, there was no probable cause for his arrest. Burbine was given *Miranda* warnings but refused to answer questions by a Cranston police detective.

A few hours later he was questioned again, by Providence police, and after being given *Miranda* warnings, and explicitly stating that he did not want an attorney, confessed to the murder. So far, does *Mosley* control? But here's the wrinkle: Between the two interrogations Burbine's sister, having learned of her brother's arrest, arranged for him to have a lawyer. That lawyer called the Cranston police station, identified herself as Burbine's lawyer, and was told that Burbine would not be questioned. The factual record was unclear as to exactly what transpired in the police station with respect to the lawyer's phone call, but the Court held that "the state of mind of the police is irrelevant to the question of the intelligence and voluntariness of respondent's election to abandon his rights." *Id.* at 423. Three Justices dissented, noting a recurring pattern in state court cases of the police affirmatively deceiving attorneys who are seeking to consult with clients under arrest.

The Court had more directly dealt with the issue of a "waiver" of *Miranda* rights before *Edwards* and *Moran* in *North Carolina v. Butler*, 441 U.S. 369 (1979). In that case the defendant was provided with the FBI's standard "Advice of Rights" form, which he read and thereafter stated that he understood. *Id.* at 370-71. He agreed to talk but refused to sign the portion of the form indicating "waiver" and said, "I will talk to you but I am not signing any form." And then he began answering questions and inculpated himself. The Court found that although the burden of proving waiver was on the government, Butler's decision to speak to agents after refusing to sign the form was sufficient evidence of waiver and that nothing more "explicit" was required. In dissent, Justice Brennan argued that fidelity to *Miranda* required an express waiver requirement, and that "ambiguity be interpreted against the interrogator."

Revisiting the issue of *Miranda* waiver 30 years after *Butler*, the Court held that while a waiver need not be explicit an assertion of the right to remain silent must be unambiguous.

Berghuis v. Thompkins
560 U.S. 370 (2010)

Justice KENNEDY delivered the opinion of the Court.

The United States Court of Appeals for the Sixth Circuit, in a habeas corpus proceeding challenging a Michigan conviction for first-degree murder and certain other offenses, ruled that there had been two separate constitutional errors in the trial that led to the jury's guilty verdict. First, the Court of Appeals determined that a statement by the accused, relied on at trial by the prosecution, had been elicited in violation of *Miranda*. . . .

On January 10, 2000, a shooting occurred outside a mall in Southfield, Michigan. Among the victims was Samuel Morris, who died from multiple gunshot wounds. The other victim, Frederick France, recovered from his injuries and later testified. Thompkins, who was a suspect, fled. About one year later he was found in Ohio and arrested there.

Two Southfield police officers traveled to Ohio to interrogate Thompkins, then awaiting transfer to Michigan. The interrogation began around 1:30 p.m. and lasted about three hours. The interrogation was conducted in a room that was 8 by 10 feet, and Thompkins sat in a chair that resembled a school desk (it had an arm on it that swings around to provide a surface to write on). At the beginning of the interrogation, one of the officers, Detective Helgert, presented Thompkins with a form derived from the *Miranda* rule. It stated:

> "NOTIFICATION OF CONSTITUTIONAL RIGHTS AND STATEMENT
> "1. You have the right to remain silent.
> "2. Anything you say can and will be used against you in a court of law.
> "3. You have a right to talk to a lawyer before answering any questions and you have the right to have a lawyer present with you while you are answering any questions.
> "4. If you cannot afford to hire a lawyer, one will be appointed to represent you before any questioning, if you wish one.
> "5. You have the right to decide at any time before or during questioning to use your right to remain silent and your right to talk with a lawyer while you are being questioned."

Brief for Petitioner 60 (some capitalization omitted).

Helgert asked Thompkins to read the fifth warning out loud. Thompkins complied. Helgert later said this was to ensure that Thompkins could read, and Helgert concluded that Thompkins understood English. Helgert then read the other four *Miranda* warnings out loud and asked Thompkins to sign the form to demonstrate that he understood his rights. Thompkins declined to sign the form. The record contains conflicting evidence about whether Thompkins then verbally confirmed that he understood the rights listed on the form.

Officers began an interrogation. At no point during the interrogation did Thompkins say that he wanted to remain silent, that he did not want to talk with the police, or that he wanted an attorney. Thompkins was "[l]argely" silent during the interrogation, which lasted about three hours. He did give a few limited verbal responses, however, such as "yeah," "no," or "I don't know." And on occasion he communicated by nodding his head. Thompkins also said that he "didn't want a peppermint" that was offered to him by the police and that the chair he was "sitting in was hard."

About 2 hours and 45 minutes into the interrogation, Helgert asked Thompkins, "Do you believe in God?" Thompkins made eye contact with Helgert and said "Yes," as his eyes "well[ed] up with tears." Helgert asked, "Do you pray to God?" Thompkins said "Yes." Helgert asked, "Do you pray to God to forgive you for shooting that boy down?" Thompkins answered "Yes" and looked away. Thompkins refused to make a written confession, and the interrogation ended about 15 minutes later.

Thompkins was charged with first-degree murder, assault with intent to commit murder, and certain firearms-related offenses. He moved to suppress the statements made during the interrogation. He argued that he had invoked his Fifth Amendment right to remain silent, requiring police to end the interrogation at once, that he had not waived his right to remain silent, and that his inculpatory statements were involuntary. The trial court denied the motion.

. . .

The jury found Thompkins guilty on all counts. He was sentenced to life in prison without parole.

III

The *Miranda* Court formulated a warning that must be given to suspects before they can be subjected to custodial interrogation. The substance of the warning still must be given to suspects today. A suspect in custody must be advised as follows:

"He must be warned prior to any questioning that he has the right to remain silent, that anything he says can be used against him in a court of law, that he has the right to the presence of an attorney, and that if he cannot afford an attorney one will be appointed for him prior to any questioning if he so desires."

All concede that the warning given in this case was in full compliance with these requirements. The dispute centers on the response — or nonresponse — from the suspect.

A

Thompkins makes various arguments that his answers to questions from the detectives were inadmissible. He first contends that he "invoke[d] his privilege" to remain silent by not saying anything for a sufficient period of time, so the interrogation should have "cease[d]" before he made his inculpatory statements.

This argument is unpersuasive. In the context of invoking the *Miranda* right to counsel, the Court in *Davis* held that a suspect must do so "unambiguously." If an accused makes a statement concerning the right to counsel "that is ambiguous or equivocal" or makes no statement, the police are not required to end the interrogation, or ask questions to clarify whether the accused wants to invoke his or her *Miranda* rights.

The Court has not yet stated whether an invocation of the right to remain silent can be ambiguous or equivocal, but there is no principled reason to adopt different standards for determining when an accused has invoked the *Miranda* right to remain silent and the *Miranda* right to counsel.

There is good reason to require an accused who wants to invoke his or her right to remain silent to do so unambiguously. A requirement of an unambiguous invocation of *Miranda* rights results in an objective inquiry that "avoid[s] difficulties of proof and . . . provide[s] guidance to officers" on how to proceed in the face of ambiguity. If an ambiguous act, omission, or statement could require police to end the interrogation, police would be required to make difficult decisions about an accused's unclear intent and face the consequence of suppression "if they guess wrong." Suppression of a voluntary confession in these circumstances would place a significant burden on society's interest in prosecuting criminal activity. Treating an ambiguous or equivocal act, omission, or statement as an invocation of *Miranda* rights "might add marginally to *Miranda*'s goal of dispelling the compulsion inherent in custodial interrogation." But "as *Miranda* holds, full comprehension of the rights to remain silent and request an attorney are sufficient to dispel whatever coercion is inherent in the interrogation process."

Thompkins did not say that he wanted to remain silent or that he did not want to talk with the police. Had he made either of these simple, unambiguous statements, he would have invoked his "'right to cut off questioning.'" Here he did neither, so he did not invoke his right to remain silent.

B

We next consider whether Thompkins waived his right to remain silent. Even absent the accused's invocation of the right to remain silent, the accused's statement during a custodial interrogation is inadmissible at trial unless the prosecution can establish that the accused "in fact knowingly and voluntarily waived [*Miranda*] rights" when making the statement. The waiver inquiry "has two distinct dimensions": waiver must be "voluntary in the sense that it was the product of a free and deliberate choice rather than intimidation, coercion, or deception," and "made with a full awareness of both the nature of the right being abandoned and the consequences of the decision to abandon it."

Some language in *Miranda* could be read to indicate that waivers are difficult to establish absent an explicit written waiver or a formal, express oral statement. *Miranda* said "a valid waiver will not be presumed simply from the silence of the accused after warnings are given or simply from the fact that a confession was in fact eventually obtained." In addition, the *Miranda* Court stated that "a heavy burden rests on the government to demonstrate that the defendant knowingly and intelligently waived his privilege against self-incrimination and his right to retained or appointed counsel."

The course of decisions since *Miranda*, informed by the application of *Miranda* warnings in the whole course of law enforcement, demonstrates that waivers can be established even absent formal or express statements of waiver that would be expected in, say, a judicial hearing to determine if a guilty plea has been properly entered. Cf. Fed. Rule Crim. Proc. 11. The main purpose of *Miranda* is to ensure that an accused is advised of and understands the right to remain silent and the right to counsel. Thus, "[i]f anything, our subsequent cases have reduced the impact of the *Miranda* rule on legitimate law enforcement while reaffirming the decision's core ruling that unwarned statements may not be used as evidence in the prosecution's case in chief."

One of the first cases to decide the meaning and import of *Miranda* with respect to the question of waiver was *North Carolina v. Butler*. The *Butler* Court, after discussing some of the problems created by the language in *Miranda*, established certain important propositions. *Butler* interpreted the *Miranda* language concerning the "heavy burden" to show waiver, in accord with usual principles of determining waiver, which can include waiver implied from all the circumstances. And in a later case, the Court stated that this "heavy burden" is not more than the burden to establish waiver by a preponderance of the evidence.

The prosecution therefore does not need to show that a waiver of *Miranda* rights was express. An "implicit waiver" of the "right to remain silent" is sufficient to admit a suspect's statement into evidence. *Butler* made clear that a waiver of *Miranda* rights may be implied through "the defendant's silence, coupled with an understanding of his rights and a course of conduct indicating waiver." The Court in *Butler* therefore "retreated" from the "language and tenor of the *Miranda* opinion," which "suggested that the Court would require that a waiver . . . be 'specifically made.'"

If the State establishes that a *Miranda* warning was given and the accused made an uncoerced statement, this showing, standing alone, is insufficient to demonstrate "a valid waiver" of *Miranda* rights. Where the prosecution shows that a *Miranda* warning was given and that it was understood by the accused, an accused's uncoerced statement establishes an implied waiver of the right to remain silent.

E. *Miranda* in Practice II: Waiver and Invocation of *Miranda* Rights   **169**

Although *Miranda* imposes on the police a rule that is both formalistic and practical when it prevents them from interrogating suspects without first providing them with a *Miranda* warning, it does not impose a formalistic waiver procedure that a suspect must follow to relinquish those rights. As a general proposition, the law can presume that an individual who, with a full understanding of his or her rights, acts in a manner inconsistent with their exercise has made a deliberate choice to relinquish the protection those rights afford. As *Butler* recognized, *Miranda* rights can therefore be waived through means less formal than a typical waiver on the record in a courtroom, cf. Fed. Rule Crim. Proc. 11, given the practical constraints and necessities of interrogation and the fact that *Miranda*'s main protection lies in advising defendants of their rights.

The record in this case shows that Thompkins waived his right to remain silent. There is no basis in this case to conclude that he did not understand his rights; and on these facts it follows that he chose not to invoke or rely on those rights when he did speak. First, there is no contention that Thompkins did not understand his rights; and from this it follows that he knew what he gave up when he spoke. There was more than enough evidence in the record to conclude that Thompkins understood his *Miranda* rights. Thompkins received a written copy of the *Miranda* warnings; Detective Helgert determined that Thompkins could read and understand English; and Thompkins was given time to read the warnings. Thompkins, furthermore, read aloud the fifth warning, which stated that "you have the right to decide at any time before or during questioning to use your right to remain silent and your right to talk with a lawyer while you are being questioned." He was thus aware that his right to remain silent would not dissipate after a certain amount of time and that police would have to honor his right to be silent and his right to counsel during the whole course of interrogation. Those rights, the warning made clear, could be asserted at any time. Helgert, moreover, read the warnings aloud.

Second, Thompkins' answer to Detective Helgert's question about whether Thompkins prayed to God for forgiveness for shooting the victim is a "course of conduct indicating waiver" of the right to remain silent. If Thompkins wanted to remain silent, he could have said nothing in response to Helgert's questions, or he could have unambiguously invoked his *Miranda* rights and ended the interrogation. The fact that Thompkins made a statement about three hours after receiving a *Miranda* warning does not overcome the fact that he engaged in a course of conduct indicating waiver. Police are not required to rewarn suspects from time to time. Thompkins' answer to Helgert's question about praying to God for forgiveness for shooting the victim was sufficient to show a course of conduct indicating waiver. This is confirmed by the fact that before then Thompkins had given sporadic answers to questions throughout the interrogation.

Third, there is no evidence that Thompkins' statement was coerced. Thompkins does not claim that police threatened or injured him during the interrogation or that he was in any way fearful. The interrogation was conducted in a standard-sized room in the middle of the afternoon. It is true that apparently he was in a straight-backed chair for three hours, but there is no authority for the proposition that an interrogation of this length is inherently coercive. Indeed, even where interrogations of greater duration were held to be improper, they were accompanied, as this one was not, by other facts indicating coercion, such as an incapacitated and sedated suspect, sleep and food deprivation, and threats. The fact that Helgert's question referred to Thompkins' religious beliefs also did not render Thompkins' statement involuntary. "[T]he Fifth Amendment privilege is not concerned 'with moral and psychological pressures to confess emanating from sources other than official coercion.'" In these circumstances, Thompkins knowingly and voluntarily made a statement to police, so he waived his right to remain silent.

Thompkins next argues that, even if his answer to Detective Helgert could constitute a waiver of his right to remain silent, the police were not allowed to question him until they obtained a waiver first. *Butler* forecloses this argument. The *Butler* Court held that courts can infer a waiver of *Miranda* rights "from the actions and words of the person interrogated." This principle would be inconsistent with a rule that requires a waiver at the outset. The *Butler* Court thus rejected the rule proposed by the *Butler* dissent, which would have "requir[ed] the police to obtain an express waiver of [*Miranda* rights] before proceeding with interrogation." This holding also makes sense given that "the primary protection afforded suspects subject[ed] to custodial interrogation is the *Miranda* warnings themselves." The *Miranda* rule and its requirements are met if a suspect receives adequate *Miranda* warnings, understands them, and has an opportunity to invoke the rights before giving any answers or admissions. Any waiver, express or implied, may be contradicted by an invocation at any time. If the right to counsel or the right to remain silent is invoked at any point during questioning, further interrogation must cease.

Interrogation provides the suspect with additional information that can put his or her decision to waive, or not to invoke, into perspective. As questioning commences and then continues, the suspect has the opportunity to consider the choices he or she faces and to make a more informed decision, either to insist on silence or to cooperate. When the suspect knows that *Miranda* rights can be invoked at any time, he or she has the opportunity to reassess his or her immediate and long-term interests. Cooperation with the police may result in more favorable treatment for the suspect; the apprehension of accomplices; the prevention of continuing injury and fear; beginning steps toward relief or solace for the victims; and the beginning of the suspect's own return to the law and the social order it seeks to protect.

In order for an accused's statement to be admissible at trial, police must have given the accused a *Miranda* warning. If that condition is established, the court can proceed to consider whether there has been an express or implied waiver of *Miranda* rights. In making its ruling on the admissibility of a statement made during custodial questioning, the trial court, of course, considers whether there is evidence to support the conclusion that, from the whole course of questioning, an express or implied waiver has been established. Thus, after giving a *Miranda* warning, police may interrogate a suspect who has neither invoked nor waived his or her *Miranda* rights. On these premises, it follows the police were not required to obtain a waiver of Thompkins' *Miranda* rights before commencing the interrogation.

In sum, a suspect who has received and understood the *Miranda* warnings, and has not invoked his *Miranda* rights, waives the right to remain silent by making an uncoerced statement to the police. Thompkins did not invoke his right to remain silent and stop the questioning. Understanding his rights in full, he waived his right to remain silent by making a voluntary statement to the police. The police, moreover, were not required to obtain a waiver of Thompkins' right to remain silent before interrogating him.

[Justices Sotomayor, Stevens, Breyer, and Ginsburg dissented.]

NOTES AND QUESTIONS

1. Why would the police officers travel from Southfield, Michigan to Ohio to question the defendant given that he was awaiting transfer to Michigan? Why would they continue the interrogation after Thompkins refused to sign the form?

2. Consider carefully the description of the right to counsel in item 3 on the form:

You have a right to talk to a lawyer before answering any questions and you have the right to have a lawyer present with you while you are answering any questions.

Is this warning accurate? Is it misleading? Does this description make clear that the right to have counsel does not mean that you lose the right to remain silent? In other words, does the language suggest that you only have the right to counsel if you agree to answer questions? What are the likely consequences of such a misunderstanding of the right to counsel?

The Court has been lax about the actual content of *Miranda* warnings. "[N]o talismanic incantation [is] required to satisfy [*Miranda's*] strictures." *California v. Prysock*, 453 U.S. 355, 359 (1981) (per curiam). The inquiry is simply whether the warnings reasonably communicated to a suspect his rights. *Duckworth v. Eagan*, 492 U.S. 195 (1989).

3. The police officer appears to have admitted that Thompkins was "largely silent" during the three-hour interrogation, and that Thompkins only gave a handful of verbal responses. But why isn't the factual record better? What else happened in the interrogation room in the other 2 hours and 40 minutes of interrogation? Did either officer have notes reflecting Thompkins's verbal acknowledgment that he understood his rights?

4. The Court holds that since an invocation of the right to counsel must be done "unambiguously," so must an invocation of the right to remain silent. Is the analogy apt? Can you invoke the right to counsel without speaking?

5. Note the three reasons the Court gives for its finding that Thompkins waived his right to silence. Does the Court hold the prosecution to its burden of proving waiver? Is the fact of silence—itself—irrelevant to the waiver finding?

6. Would the case have come out differently if Thompkins had said literally nothing after he refused to sign the form? What would Thompkins have needed to say to "invoke" his right to remain silent? Would "I'm not talking" be sufficient? How about simply "silence" or "shut up"? Would those words have acted as the proverbial "cutoff" and precluded any further questioning?

Would simply saying "lawyer" or "lawyer!" be enough to invoke the right to counsel?

Salinas v. Texas
570 U.S. 178 (2013)

Justice ALITO announced the judgment of the Court and delivered an opinion in which THE CHIEF JUSTICE and Justice KENNEDY join.

Without being placed in custody or receiving *Miranda* warnings, petitioner voluntarily answered the questions of a police officer who was investigating a murder. But petitioner balked when the officer asked whether a ballistics test would show that the shell casings found at the crime scene would match petitioner's shotgun. Petitioner was subsequently charged with murder, and at trial prosecutors argued that his reaction to the officer's question suggested that he was guilty. Petitioner claims that this argument violated the Fifth Amendment, which guarantees that "[n]o person . . . shall be compelled in any criminal case to be a witness against himself."

Petitioner's Fifth Amendment claim fails because he did not expressly invoke the privilege against self-incrimination in response to the officer's question. It has long been settled that the privilege "generally is not self-executing" and that a witness who desires its protection "'must claim it.'" Although "no ritualistic formula is necessary in order to invoke the privilege," a witness does not do so by simply standing mute. Because petitioner was required to assert the privilege in order to benefit from it, the judgment of the Texas Court of Criminal Appeals rejecting petitioner's Fifth Amendment claim is affirmed.

I

On the morning of December 18, 1992, two brothers were shot and killed in their Houston home. There were no witnesses to the murders, but a neighbor who heard gunshots saw someone run out of the house and speed away in a dark-colored car. Police recovered six shotgun shell casings at the scene. The investigation led police to petitioner, who had been a guest at a party the victims hosted the night before they were killed. Police visited petitioner at his home, where they saw a dark blue car in the driveway. He agreed to hand over his shotgun for ballistics testing and to accompany police to the station for questioning.

Petitioner's interview with the police lasted approximately one hour. All agree that the interview was noncustodial, and the parties litigated this case on the assumption that he was not read *Miranda* warnings. For most of the interview, petitioner answered the officer's questions. But when asked whether his shotgun "would match the shells recovered at the scene of the murder," petitioner declined to answer. Instead, petitioner "[l]ooked down at the floor, shuffled his feet, bit his bottom lip, cl[e]nched his hands in his lap, [and] began to tighten up." After a few moments of silence, the officer asked additional questions, which petitioner answered.

Following the interview, police arrested petitioner on outstanding traffic warrants. Prosecutors soon concluded that there was insufficient evidence to charge him with the murders, and he was released. A few days later, police obtained a statement from a man who said he had heard petitioner confess to the killings. On the strength of that additional evidence, prosecutors decided to charge petitioner, but by this time he had absconded. In 2007, police discovered petitioner living in the Houston area under an assumed name.

Petitioner did not testify at trial. Over his objection, prosecutors used his reaction to the officer's question during the 1993 interview as evidence of his guilt. The jury found petitioner guilty, and he received a 20-year sentence. On direct appeal to the Court of Appeals of Texas, petitioner argued that prosecutors' use of his silence as part of their case in chief violated the Fifth Amendment. The Court of Appeals rejected that argument, reasoning that petitioner's prearrest, pre-Miranda silence was not "compelled" within the meaning of the Fifth Amendment. The Texas Court of Criminal Appeals took up this case and affirmed on the same ground.

We granted certiorari, to resolve a division of authority in the lower courts over whether the prosecution may use a defendant's assertion of the privilege against self-incrimination during a noncustodial police interview as part of its case in chief. But because petitioner did not invoke the privilege during his interview, we find it unnecessary to reach that question.

II

A

The privilege against self-incrimination "is an exception to the general principle that the Government has the right to everyone's testimony." To prevent the privilege from shielding information not properly within its scope, we have long held that a witness who "'desires the protection of the privilege . . . must claim it'" at the time he relies on it.

That requirement ensures that the Government is put on notice when a witness intends to rely on the privilege so that it may either argue that the testimony sought could not be self-incriminating, or cure any potential self-incrimination through a grant of immunity. The express invocation requirement also gives courts tasked with evaluating a Fifth Amendment claim a contemporaneous record establishing the witness' reasons for refusing to answer. In these ways, insisting that witnesses expressly invoke the privilege "assures that the Government obtains all the information to which it is entitled."

We have previously recognized two exceptions to the requirement that witnesses invoke the privilege, but neither applies here. First, we held in *Griffin v. California* that a criminal defendant need not take the stand and assert the privilege at his own trial. That exception reflects the fact that a criminal defendant has an "absolute right not to testify." Since a defendant's reasons for remaining silent at trial are irrelevant to his constitutional right to do so, requiring that he expressly invoke the privilege would serve no purpose; neither a showing that his testimony would not be self-incriminating nor a grant of immunity could force him to speak. Because petitioner had no comparable unqualified right during his interview with police, his silence falls outside the *Griffin* exception.

Second, we have held that a witness' failure to invoke the privilege must be excused where governmental coercion makes his forfeiture of the privilege involuntary. Thus, in *Miranda*, we said that a suspect who is subjected to the "inherently compelling pressures" of an unwarned custodial interrogation need not invoke the privilege. Due to the uniquely coercive nature of custodial interrogation, a suspect in custody cannot be said to have voluntarily forgone the privilege "unless [he] fails to claim [it] after being suitably warned."

For similar reasons, we have held that threats to withdraw a governmental benefit such as public employment sometimes make exercise of the privilege so costly that it need not be affirmatively asserted. And where assertion of the privilege would itself tend to incriminate, we have allowed witnesses to exercise the privilege through silence. The principle that unites all of those cases is that a witness need not expressly invoke the privilege where some form of official compulsion denies him "a 'free choice to admit, to deny, or to refuse to answer.'"

Petitioner cannot benefit from that principle because it is undisputed that his interview with police was voluntary. As petitioner himself acknowledges, he agreed to accompany the officers to the station and "was free to leave at any time during the interview." That places petitioner's situation outside the scope of *Miranda* and other cases in which we have held that various forms of governmental coercion prevented defendants from voluntarily invoking the privilege. The dissent elides this point when it cites our precedents in this area for the proposition that "[c]ircumstances, rather than explicit invocation, trigger the protection of the Fifth Amendment." The critical question is whether, under the "circumstances" of this case, petitioner was deprived of the ability to voluntarily invoke the Fifth Amendment. He was not. We have before us no allegation that petitioner's failure to assert the privilege was involuntary, and it would have been a simple matter for him to say that he was not answering the officer's question on Fifth Amendment grounds. Because he failed to do so, the prosecution's use of his noncustodial silence did not violate the Fifth Amendment.

B

Petitioner urges us to adopt a third exception to the invocation requirement for cases in which a witness stands mute and thereby declines to give an answer that officials suspect would be incriminating. Our cases all but foreclose such an exception, which would needlessly burden the Government's interests in obtaining testimony and prosecuting criminal activity. We therefore decline petitioner's invitation to craft a new exception to the "general rule" that a witness must assert the privilege to subsequently benefit from it.

Our cases establish that a defendant normally does not invoke the privilege by remaining silent. In *Roberts* for example, we rejected the Fifth Amendment claim of a defendant who remained silent throughout a police investigation and received a harsher sentence for his failure to cooperate. In so ruling, we explained that "if [the defendant] believed that his failure to cooperate was privileged, he should have said so at a time when the sentencing court could have determined whether his claim was legitimate." A witness does not expressly invoke the privilege by standing mute.

We have also repeatedly held that the express invocation requirement applies even when an official has reason to suspect that the answer to his question would incriminate the witness. Thus, in *Murphy* we held that the defendant's self-incriminating answers to his probation officer were properly admitted at trial because he failed to invoke the privilege. In reaching that conclusion, we rejected the notion "that a witness must 'put the Government on notice by formally availing himself of the privilege' only when he alone 'is reasonably aware of the incriminating tendency of the questions.'"

Petitioner does not dispute the vitality of either of those lines of precedent but instead argues that we should adopt an exception for cases at their intersection. Thus, petitioner would have us hold that although neither a witness' silence nor official suspicions are enough to excuse the express invocation requirement, the invocation requirement does not apply where a witness is silent in the face of official suspicions. For the same reasons that neither of those factors is sufficient by itself to relieve a witness of the obligation to expressly invoke the privilege, we conclude that they do not do so together. A contrary result would do little to protect those genuinely relying on the Fifth Amendment privilege while placing a needless new burden on society's interest in the admission of evidence that is probative of a criminal defendant's guilt.

Petitioner's proposed exception would also be very difficult to reconcile with *Berghuis v. Thompkins.* There, we held in the closely related context of post-*Miranda* silence that a defendant failed to invoke the privilege when he refused to respond to police questioning for 2 hours and 45 minutes. If the extended custodial silence in that case did not invoke the privilege, then surely the momentary silence in this case did not do so either.

Petitioner and the dissent attempt to distinguish *Berghuis* by observing that it did not concern the admissibility of the defendant's silence but instead involved the admissibility of his subsequent statements. But regardless of whether prosecutors seek to use silence or a confession that follows, the logic of *Berghuis* applies with equal force: A suspect who stands mute has not done enough to put police on notice that he is relying on his Fifth Amendment privilege.

In support of their proposed exception to the invocation requirement, petitioner and the dissent argue that reliance on the Fifth Amendment privilege is the most likely explanation for silence in a case such as this one. But whatever the most probable explanation, such silence is "insolubly ambiguous." To be sure, someone might decline to answer a police officer's question in reliance on his constitutional privilege. But he also might do so because he is trying to think of a good lie, because he is embarrassed, or because he is protecting someone else. Not every such possible explanation for silence is probative of guilt, but neither is every possible explanation protected by the Fifth Amendment. Petitioner alone knew why he did not answer the officer's question, and it was therefore his "burden . . . to make a timely assertion of the privilege."

At oral argument, counsel for petitioner suggested that it would be unfair to require a suspect unschooled in the particulars of legal doctrine to do anything more than remain silent in order to invoke his "right to remain silent." But popular misconceptions notwithstanding, the Fifth Amendment guarantees that no one may be "compelled in any criminal case to be a witness against himself"; it does not establish an unqualified "right to remain silent." A witness' constitutional right to refuse to answer questions depends on his reasons for doing so, and courts need to know those reasons to evaluate the merits of a Fifth Amendment claim.

In any event, it is settled that forfeiture of the privilege against self-incrimination need not be knowing. Statements against interest are regularly admitted into evidence at criminal trials, see Fed. Rule of Evid. 804(b)(3), and there is no good reason to approach a defendant's silence any differently.

C

Finally, we are not persuaded by petitioner's arguments that applying the usual express invocation requirement where a witness is silent during a noncustodial police interview will prove unworkable in practice. Petitioner and the dissent suggest that our approach will "unleash complicated and persistent litigation" over what a suspect must say to invoke the privilege, but our cases have long required that a witness assert the privilege to subsequently benefit from it.

That rule has not proved difficult to apply. Nor did the potential for close cases dissuade us from adopting similar invocation requirements for suspects who wish to assert their rights and cut off police questioning during custodial interviews.

Notably, petitioner's approach would produce its own line-drawing problems, as this case vividly illustrates. When the interviewing officer asked petitioner if his shotgun would match the shell casings found at the crime scene, petitioner did not merely remain silent; he made movements that suggested surprise and anxiety. At precisely what point such reactions transform "silence" into expressive conduct would be a difficult and recurring question that our decision allows us to avoid.

We also reject petitioner's argument that an express invocation requirement will encourage police officers to "'unfairly "tric[k]"'" suspects into cooperating. Petitioner worries that officers could unduly pressure suspects into talking by telling them that their silence could be used in a future prosecution. But as petitioner himself concedes, police officers "have done nothing wrong" when they "accurately stat[e] the law." We found no constitutional infirmity in government officials telling the defendant in *Murphy* that he was required to speak truthfully to his parole officer, and we see no greater danger in the interview tactics petitioner identifies. So long as police do not deprive a witness of the ability to voluntarily invoke the privilege, there is no Fifth Amendment violation.

• • •

Before petitioner could rely on the privilege against self-incrimination, he was required to invoke it. Because he failed to do so, the judgment of the Texas Court of Criminal Appeals is affirmed.

[Justices Breyer, Ginsburg, Sotomayor, and Kagan dissented.]

NOTES AND QUESTIONS

1. What do you think would have happened here if Salinas had refused to turn over the shotgun and accompany the officer to the station? Would the officer have arrested him and taken him in for a custodial interrogation where he would have had to give *Miranda* warnings? Do you think the officer was instead hoping to do a noncustodial interrogation so he could avoid his *Miranda* obligations? How would a police officer weigh the pros and cons of which approach to use? Why does the Court not say how many officers came to Salinas's house? Would that be relevant as to the intent of the officer(s)?

2. The plurality opinion conveniently omits any reference to the police officer's lie that seems to have induced Salinas to go to the police station (just to "clear him as a suspect"). Of course the fact of a police lie normally has no legal consequence. But why doesn't either the plurality or the dissent explain more about the substance of the hour of questioning other than the single exchange about the shotgun? The dissent suggests the shotgun question was a change of subject, implying that Salinas was lulled into a false sense of security before having the "money" question sprung on him. What about the questioning that occurred after the silence?

3. The plurality casually notes that "[f]ollowing the interview, police arrested petitioner on outstanding traffic warrants." Was the plan all along to arrest him on these warrants, either with or without his initial voluntary cooperation? Was this approach of Salinas originally on a track to be more like *Mosley* or *Burbine*, where a suspect is arrested on a semi-pretextual lesser crime, sometimes without probable cause, but then—once in custody and as the pressure mounts—to be questioned on a more serious crime? Note that it was explicitly settled by *Colorado v. Spring*, 479 U.S. 564, 574 (1987), that a suspect's waiver of his *Miranda* rights was not involuntary because the suspect was unaware of which crimes he might be questioned about.

4. Did defense counsel give up too easily on the custody issue? Is it dispositive that Salinas appears to have voluntarily gone to the police station? Does it matter that the officers had received the shotgun from Salinas's father in connection with the execution of a search warrant at Salinas's house that day (facts from the state appellate opinion)? Why did Salinas's counsel appear to allow him to testify at the suppression hearing that he felt he "was free to leave" during the interrogation? Did he still feel free to leave after being asked the question about the shotgun? Did the shotgun question "convey" to Salinas that he was a suspect and thereby make the interrogation from that point forward custodial? *See Stansbury v. California*, 511 U.S. 318, 325 (1994) (officer's views as to whether witness is a suspect not relevant unless "conveyed" to individual being questioned). What if at some point in the interrogation the officer had said "I think you're lying to me" or "I just might have to arrest you"? Would a reasonable person still feel "free to leave"?

Even if litigating custody for *Miranda* applicability purposes was a long shot, note that one of the "exceptions" the Court finds to the rule that the Fifth Amendment has to be asserted is where a witness has been subjected to "some form of official compulsion." It might have been worth trying to establish that even if the interrogation was not "custodial" for *Miranda* purposes it was "custodial-ish" and thus within that line of cases.

5. Once Salinas made the horrible decision to agree to be interviewed, what were his options when the shotgun question came up? What words did he need to say to invoke the Fifth Amendment, which everyone seems to assume—at least for the sake of argument—applies here? Would he have had to include the term "Fifth Amendment" as the Court suggests? What if he had simply said, "I'm not going to answer that"? Or, uneducated and/or confused, "I'm taking the Sixth" on that? Assuming those answers successfully invoked the right, could the interrogator have kept going with more questioning after the invocation? Would the prosecutor have been allowed to use the defendant's invocation of his right to silence against him at trial just as he was allowed to use his actual silence against him?

What if Salinas had responded to the shotgun question by wordlessly getting up and leaving, which he had every right to do? Could the officer testify about his exit at trial?

6. The Court says a witness must assert the privilege in order to provide "notice" to the government. Do any of the justifications the Court provides for the "notice" rationale even remotely apply in the context of an interrogation? In his dissenting opinion Justice Breyer establishes that all the cases the plurality relies on for the "invocation requirement" are readily distinguishable, as they were all situations where there were specific reasons the questioner needed to know whether the witness was taking the Fifth.

7. Is the fact that the *Miranda* warnings have become "part of our national culture," as the Court said in *Dickerson*, relevant here? In other words, is the widespread cultural understanding that Americans have a "right to remain silent" relevant to how a reasonable person in Salinas's position would have understood his options in dealing with the shotgun question? Note that the actual words "Fifth Amendment" are not normally part of the *Miranda* warnings that are heard in the movies or on television.

8. The Court brushes off the policy concern that after *Salinas* the police could pressure suspects into agreeing to be questioned by telling them, in effect, that their silence can be used against them in court. The Court says that there is nothing wrong with police officers accurately stating the law, and dismisses those concerns. What it could have added, as this case makes clear, is that there is also nothing wrong with police officers lying to a witness in order to get him to agree to being questioned.

E. *Miranda* in Practice II: Waiver and Invocation of *Miranda* Rights   **177**

But is it true that a witness's silence can be used against them in court? Doesn't it depend on whether the interrogation is voluntary (it can be used) or custodial (it can't)? And might it also depend on whether the witness sufficiently invoked the Fifth Amendment or not? Recall that the circuit split on which the Court granted cert—still undecided after *Salinas*—was over whether comments on assertions of the Fifth Amendment in a noncustodial interview were permissible.

9. Justice Thomas and Justice Scalia concur only in the judgment in *Salinas*. Justice Thomas renews his call for overturning *Griffin v. California* on the ground that the Fifth Amendment is only a "trial right," precluding a person from being compelled to testify against himself in court, and that Salinas had no Fifth Amendment rights during his interview.

Does Justice Thomas's textualist view of the Fifth Amendment also require overturning *Kastigar* and invalidating all immunity statutes?

10. One of the priceless things about *Salinas* is the plurality's description of the Fifth Amendment as "an exception to the general principle that the Government has the right to everyone's testimony." The ten amendments found in the Bill of Rights are not often described as "exceptions."

A separate and older line of cases deals with a defendant's "right to silence" in the context of a defendant's post-arrest silence.

Doyle v. Ohio
426 U.S. 610 (1976)

Mr. Justice POWELL delivered the opinion of the Court.

The question in these consolidated cases is whether a state prosecutor may seek to impeach a defendant's exculpatory story, told for the first time at trial, by cross-examining the defendant about his failure to have told the story after receiving *Miranda* warnings at the time of his arrest. We conclude that use of the defendant's post-arrest silence in this manner violates due process, and therefore reverse the convictions of both petitioners.

I

Petitioners Doyle and Wood were arrested together and charged with selling 10 pounds of marihuana to a local narcotics bureau informant. They were convicted in the Common Pleas Court of Tuscarawas County, Ohio, in separate trials held about one week apart. The evidence at their trials was identical in all material respects.

The State's witnesses sketched a picture of a routine marihuana transaction. William Bonnell, a well-known "street person" with a long criminal record, offered to assist the local narcotics investigation unit in setting up drug "pushers" in return for support in his efforts to receive lenient treatment in his latest legal problems. The narcotics agents agreed. A short time later, Bonnell advised the unit that he and Doyle had arranged a "buy" of 10 pounds of marihuana and needed $1,750 to pay for it. Since the banks were closed and time was short, the agents were able to collect only $1,320. Bonnell took this money and left for the rendezvous, under surveillance by four narcotics agents in two cars. As planned, he met petitioners in a bar in Dover, Ohio. From there, he and petitioner Wood drove in Bonnell's pickup truck to the nearby town of New Philadelphia, Ohio, while petitioner Doyle drove off to obtain the marihuana and then meet them at a prearranged location in New Philadelphia. The narcotics agents followed the Bonnell truck. When Doyle arrived at Bonnell's waiting

Chapter III Police Interrogation and The Fifth Amendment

truck in New Philadelphia, the two vehicles proceeded to a parking lot where the transaction took place. Bonnell left in his truck, and Doyle and Wood departed in Doyle's car. They quickly discovered that they had been paid $430 less than the agreed-upon price, and began circling the neighborhood looking for Bonnell. They were stopped within minutes by New Philadelphia police acting on radioed instructions from the narcotics agents. One of those agents, Kenneth Beamer, arrived on the scene promptly, arrested petitioners, and gave them *Miranda* warnings. A search of the car, authorized by warrant, uncovered the $1,320.

At both trials, defense counsel's cross-examination of the participating narcotics agents was aimed primarily at establishing that due to a limited view of the parking lot, none of them had seen the actual transaction but had seen only Bonnell standing next to Doyle's car with a package under his arm, presumably after the transaction. Each petitioner took the stand at his trial and admitted practically everything about the State's case except the most crucial point: who was selling marihuana to whom. According to petitioners, Bonnell had framed them. The arrangement had been for Bonnell to sell Doyle 10 pounds of marihuana. Doyle had left the Dover bar for the purpose of borrowing the necessary money, but while driving by himself had decided that he only wanted one or two pounds instead of the agreed-upon 10 pounds. When Bonnell reached Doyle's car in the New Philadelphia parking lot, with the marihuana under his arm, Doyle tried to explain his change of mind. Bonnell grew angry, threw the $1,320 into Doyle's car, and took all 10 pounds of the marihuana back to his truck. The ensuing chase was the effort of Wood and Doyle to catch Bonnell to find out what the $1,320 was all about.

Petitioners' explanation of the events presented some difficulty for the prosecution, as it was not entirely implausible and there was little if any direct evidence to contradict it. As part of a wide-ranging cross-examination for impeachment purposes, and in an effort to undercut the explanation, the prosecutor asked each petitioner at his respective trial why he had not told the frameup story to Agent Beamer when he arrested petitioners. In the first trial, that of petitioner Wood, the following colloquy occurred:

Q. (By the prosecutor.) Mr. Beamer did arrive on the scene?
A. (by Wood.) Yes, he did.
Q. And I assume you told him all about what happened to you?
A. No.
Q. You didn't tell Mr. Beamer?
A. No.
Q. You didn't tell Mr. Beamer this guy put $1,300 in your car?
A. No, sir.
Q. And we can't understand any reason why anyone would put money in your car and you were chasing him around town and trying to give it back?
A. I didn't understand that.
Q. You mean you didn't tell him that?
A. Tell him what?
Q. Mr. Wood, if that is all you had to do with this and you are innocent, when Mr. Beamer arrived on the scene why didn't you tell him?
Q. But in any event you didn't bother to tell Mr. Beamer anything about this?
A. No, sir.

Defense counsel's timely objections to the above questions of the prosecutor were overruled. The cross-examination of petitioner Doyle at his trial contained a similar exchange, and again defense counsel's timely objections were overruled.

Each petitioner appealed to the Court of Appeals, Fifth District, Tuscarawas County, alleging, Inter alia, that the trial court erred in allowing the prosecutor to cross-examine the petitioner at his trial about his post-arrest silence. The Court of Appeals affirmed the convictions, stating as to the contentions about the post-arrest silence:

> This was not evidence offered by the state in its case in chief as confession by silence or as substantive evidence of guilt but rather cross examination of a witness as to why he had not told the same story earlier at his first opportunity.
> We find no error in this. It goes to credibility of the witness.

The Supreme Court of Ohio denied further review. We granted certiorari to decide whether impeachment use of a defendant's post-arrest silence violates any provision of the Constitution, a question left open last Term in *United States v. Hale* (1975), and on which the Federal Courts of Appeals are in conflict.

II

The State pleads necessity as justification for the prosecutor's action in these cases. It argues that the discrepancy between an exculpatory story at trial and silence at time of arrest gives rise to an inference that the story was fabricated somewhere along the way, perhaps to fit within the seams of the State's case as it was developed at pretrial hearings. Noting that the prosecution usually has little else with which to counter such an exculpatory story, the State seeks only the right to cross-examine a defendant as to post-arrest silence for the limited purpose of impeachment. In support of its position the State emphasizes the importance of cross-examination in general, and relies upon those cases in which this Court has permitted use for impeachment purposes of post-arrest statements that were inadmissible as evidence of guilt because of an officer's failure to follow *Miranda*'s dictates. Thus, although the State does not suggest petitioners' silence could be used as evidence of guilt, it contends that the need to present to the jury all information relevant to the truth of petitioners' exculpatory story fully justifies the cross-examination that is at issue.

Despite the importance of cross-examination, we have concluded that the *Miranda* decision compels rejection of the State's position. The warnings mandated by that case, as a prophylactic means of safeguarding Fifth Amendment rights, require that a person taken into custody be advised immediately that he has the right to remain silent, that anything he says may be used against him, and that he has a right to retained or appointed counsel before submitting to interrogation. Silence in the wake of these warnings may be nothing more than the arrestee's exercise of these *Miranda* rights. Thus, every post-arrest silence is insolubly ambiguous because of what the State is required to advise the person arrested. Moreover, while it is true that the *Miranda* warnings contain no express assurance that silence will carry no penalty, such assurance is implicit to any person who receives the warnings. In such circumstances, it would be fundamentally unfair and a deprivation of due process to allow the arrested person's silence to be used to impeach an explanation subsequently offered at trial. Mr. Justice White, concurring in the judgment in *United States v. Hale*, put it very well:

> (W)hen a person under arrest is informed, as *Miranda* requires, that he may remain silent, that anything he says may be used against him, and that he may have an attorney if he wishes, it seems to me that it does not comport with due process to permit the prosecution during the trial to call attention to his silence at the time of arrest and to insist that because he did not speak about the facts of the case at that time, as he was told he need not do, an unfavorable inference might be drawn as to the truth of his trial testimony. . . . Surely Hale was not informed here that his silence, as well as his words, could be used against him at trial. Indeed, anyone would reasonably conclude from *Miranda* warnings that this would not be the case.

We hold that the use for impeachment purposes of petitioners' silence, at the time of arrest and after receiving *Miranda* warnings, violated the Due Process Clause of the Fourteenth

Amendment. The State has not claimed that such use in the circumstances of this case might have been harmless error. Accordingly, petitioners' convictions are reversed and their causes remanded to the state courts for further proceedings not inconsistent with this opinion.

So ordered.

Mr. Justice STEVENS, with whom Mr. Justice BLACKMUN and Mr. Justice REHNQUIST join, dissenting.

Petitioners assert that the prosecutor's cross-examination about their failure to mention the purported "frame" until they testified at trial violated their constitutional right to due process and also their constitutional privilege against self-incrimination. I am not persuaded by the first argument; though there is merit in a portion of the second, I do not believe it warrants reversal of these state convictions.

I

The Court's due process rationale has some of the characteristics of an estoppel theory. If (a) the defendant is advised that he may remain silent, and (b) he does remain silent, then we (c) presume that his decision was made in reliance on the advice, and (d) conclude that it is unfair in certain cases, though not others, to use his silence to impeach his trial testimony. The key to the Court's analysis is apparently a concern that the *Miranda* warning, which is intended to increase the probability that a person's response to police questioning will be intelligent and voluntary, will actually be deceptive unless we require the State to honor an unstated promise not to use the accused's silence against him.

In my judgment there is nothing deceptive or prejudicial to the defendant in the *Miranda* warning. Nor do I believe that the fact that such advice was given to the defendant lessens the probative value of his silence, or makes the prosecutor's cross-examination about his silence any more unfair than if he had received no such warning.

This is a case in which the defendants' silence at the time of their arrest was graphically inconsistent with their trial testimony that they were the unwitting victims of a "frameup" in which the police did not participate. If defendants had been framed, their failure to mention that fact at the time of their arrest is almost inexplicable; for that reason, under accepted rules of evidence, their silence is tantamount to a prior inconsistent statement and admissible for purposes of impeachment.

Indeed, there is irony in the fact that the *Miranda* warning provides the only plausible explanation for their silence. If it were the true explanation, I should think that they would have responded to the questions on cross-examination about why they had remained silent by stating that they relied on their understanding of the advice given by the arresting officers. Instead, however, they gave quite a different jumble of responses. Those response negate the Court's presumption that their silence was induced by reliance on deceptive advice.

Since the record requires us to put to one side the Court's presumption that the defendants' silence was the product of reliance on the *Miranda* warning, the Court's entire due process rationale collapses. For without reliance on the waiver, the case is no different than if no warning had been given, and nothing in the Court's opinion suggests that there would be any unfairness in using petitioners' prior inconsistent silence for impeachment purposes in such a case.

Indeed, as a general proposition, if we assume the defendant's silence would be admissible for impeachment purposes if no *Miranda* warning had been given, I should think that the warning would have a tendency to salvage the defendant's credibility as a witness. If the defendant is a truthful witness, and if his silence is the consequence of his understanding of the *Miranda* warning, he may explain that fact when he is on the stand. Even if he is untruthful,

E. *Miranda* in Practice II: Waiver and Invocation of *Miranda* Rights **181**

the availability of that explanation puts him in a better position than if he had received no warning. In my judgment, the risk that a truthful defendant will be deceived by the *Miranda* warning and also will be unable to explain his honest misunderstanding is so much less than the risk that exclusion of the evidence will merely provide a shield for perjury that I cannot accept the Court's due process rationale.

Accordingly, if we assume that the use of a defendant's silence for impeachment purposes would be otherwise unobjectionable, I find no merit in the notion that he is denied due process of law because he received a *Miranda* warning.

II

Petitioners argue that the State violated their Fifth Amendment privilege against self-incrimination by asking the jury to draw an inference of guilt from their constitutionally protected silence. They challenge both the prosecutor's cross-examination and his closing argument.

A

Petitioners claim that the cross-examination was improper because it referred to their silence at the time of their arrest, to their failure to testify at the preliminary hearing, and to their failure to reveal the "frame" prior to trial. Their claim applies to the testimony of each defendant at his own trial, and also to the testimony each gave as a witness at the trial of the other. Since I think it quite clear that a defendant may not object to the violation of another person's privilege, I shall only discuss the argument that a defendant may not be cross-examined about his own prior inconsistent silence.

In support of their objections to the cross-examination about their silence at the time of arrest, petitioners primarily rely on the statement in *Miranda* that the prosecution may not use at trial the fact that the defendant stood mute or claimed the privilege in the face of accusations during custodial interrogation. There are two reasons why that statement does not adequately support petitioners' argument.

First, it is not accurate to say that the petitioners "stood mute or claimed the privilege in the face of accusations." Neither petitioner claimed the privilege and petitioner Doyle did not even remain silent. The case is not one in which a description of the actual conversation between the defendants and the police would give rise to any inference of guilt if it were not so flagrantly inconsistent with their trial testimony. Rather than a claim of privilege, we simply have a failure to advise the police of a "frame" at a time when it most surely would have been mentioned if petitioners' trial testimony were true. That failure gave rise to an inference of guilt only because it belied their trial testimony.

Second, the dictum in the footnote in *Miranda* relies primarily upon *Griffin v. California*, which held that the Fifth Amendment, as incorporated in the Fourteenth, prohibited the prosecution's use of the defendant's silence in its case in chief. But as long ago as *Raffel v. United States*, this Court recognized the distinction between the prosecution's affirmative use of the defendant's prior silence and the use of prior silence for impeachment purposes. *Raffel* expressly held that the defendant's silence at a prior trial was admissible for purposes of impeachment despite the application in federal prosecutions of the prohibition that Griffin found in the Fifth Amendment. *Raffel.*

Moreover, Mr. Chief Justice Warren, the author of the Court's opinion in *Miranda*, joined the opinion in *Walder v. United States*, which squarely held that a valid constitutional objection to the admissibility of evidence as part of the Government's case in chief did not bar the use of that evidence to impeach the defendant's trial testimony. The availability of an objection to the affirmative use of improper evidence does not provide the defendant "with a shield against contradiction of his untruths." The need to ensure the integrity of the

182   Chapter III Police Interrogation and The Fifth Amendment

truth-determining function of the adversary trial process has provided the predicate for an unbroken line of decisions so holding.

Although I have no doubt concerning the propriety of the cross-examination about petitioners' failure to mention the purported "frame" at the time of their arrest, a more difficult question is presented by their objection to the questioning about their failure to testify at the preliminary hearing and their failure generally to mention the "frame" before trial. Unlike the failure to make the kind of spontaneous comment that discovery of a "frame" would be expected to prompt, there is no significant inconsistency between petitioners' trial testimony and their adherence to counsel's advice not to take the stand at the preliminary hearing; moreover, the decision not to divulge their defense prior to trial is probably attributable to counsel rather than to petitioners. Nevertheless, unless and until this Court overrules *Raffel v. United States*, I think a state court is free to regard the defendant's decision to take the stand as a waiver of his objection to the use of his failure to testify at an earlier proceeding or his failure to offer his version of the events prior to trial.

B

In my judgment portions of the prosecutor's argument to the jury overstepped permissible bounds. In each trial, he commented upon the defendant's silence not only as inconsistent with his testimony that he had been "framed," but also as inconsistent with the defendant's innocence. Comment on the lack of credibility of the defendant is plainly proper; it is not proper, however, for the prosecutor to ask the jury to draw a direct inference of guilt from silence — to argue, in effect, that silence is inconsistent with innocence. But since the two inferences perjury and guilt are inextricably intertwined because they have a common source, it would be unrealistic to permit comment on the former but to find reversible error in the slightest reference to the latter. In the context of the entire argument and the entire trial, I am not persuaded that the rather sophisticated distinction between permissible comment on credibility and impermissible comment on an inference of guilt justifies a reversal of these state convictions.

Accordingly, although I have some doubt concerning the propriety of the cross-examination about the preliminary hearing and consider a portion of the closing argument improper, I would affirm these convictions.

NOTES AND QUESTIONS

1. The Court says that a defendant's silence in response to *Miranda* warnings is "insolubly ambiguous." The dissent rejects this view, claiming that the defendants' silence here is "almost inexplicable" and "tantamount to a prior inconsistent statement" and thus fair ground for impeachment. Which view do you find more persuasive?

Why do you think the defendants might not have shared with the arresting officers their "frame up" defense?

2. The dissent suggests that the presumption that the defendants' silence was the product of *Miranda* warnings is unwarranted because if that were in fact the reason, the defendants could have testified to that effect. Do you agree? Would it be unfair to require a defendant to so testify?

3. Do you agree that it is implicit in the *Miranda* warnings that a defendant's silence cannot be used against him? Put somewhat differently, how would it affect the character of *Miranda* warnings if they included a statement to the effect that "if you choose to remain silent that silence can be used against you"?

4. Why do you think the Court bases its holding on the Due Process Clause of the Fourteenth Amendment instead of the Fifth Amendment?

Four years later, in *Jenkins v. Anderson*, 447 U.S. 231 (1980), the Court revisited the issue of the government's use at trial of a defendant's silence, this time prior to his arrest. Defendant Dennis Seay Jenkins was charged with murder. The defense was self-defense. The defendant turned himself in two weeks after the killing. *Id.* at 232. The defendant testified, explained how he acted in self-defense, but admitted on cross-examination that he had waited two weeks before turning himself in, a fact the prosecutor emphasized in closing argument in arguing that the defense was fabricated. *Id.* at 233-34. The Court held the impeachment was permissible. It found *Doyle* distinguishable because there, unlike in *Jenkins*, government action (giving *Miranda* warnings) had induced the defendant's silence. *Id.* at 241.

In *Fletcher v. Weir*, 455 U.S. 603 (1982), the defendant was also accused of murder and also testified that he had acted in self-defense. He was impeached at trial on his silence during the time period (of unclear length) between his arrest and when he was given *Miranda* warnings. *Id.* at 603-04. The court of appeals found that *Doyle* was applicable inasmuch as the government's arrest of the defendant effectively induced his silence. *Id.* at 605-06. The Court reversed, finding the lack of "the sort of affirmative assurances embodied in the *Miranda* warnings" to be dispositive. *Id.* at 607.

In both of these post-*Doyle* cases the Court emphasized that the states were free to apply their own rules of evidence to govern the use of pre-arrest and post-arrest silence. What is the best evidentiary argument that the admission of pre-arrest and/or post-arrest silence for impeachment purposes is more prejudicial than probative? Does *Miranda*'s role in popular culture figure into either scenario?

Since the *Doyle/Jenkins/Weir* trilogy, several circuits have considered whether a defendant's pre-arrest or pre-*Miranda* silence can be used not just for impeachment but substantively, as part of the government's case-in-chief. The Fifth, Ninth, and Eleventh Circuits have all held that the government may use pre-arrest silence in its case-in-chief. *United States v. Oplinger*, 150 F.3d 1061, 1067 (9th Cir. 1998) (holding government may use pre-arrest silence in its case-in-chief); *United States v. Zanabria*, 74 F.3d 590 (5th Cir. 1996) (same); *United States v. Rivera*, 944 F.2d 1563, 1568 (11th Cir. 1991) (same). Four circuits have found such use prohibited by the Constitution. *See Coppola v. Powell*, 878 F.2d 1562, 1568 (1st Cir. 1989) (holding pre-arrest silence cannot be used in the government's case-in-chief); *United States ex rel. Savory v. Lane*, 832 F.2d 1011, 1018 (7th Cir. 1987) (holding government cannot use pre-arrest silence in its case-in-chief); *United States v. Caro*, 637 F.2d 869, 876 (2d Cir. 1981) (suggesting government cannot comment on a defendant's silence in its case-in-chief). *See* David S. Romantz, *"You Have the Right to Remain Silent": A Case for the Use of Silence as Substantive Proof of the Criminal Defendant's Guilt*, 38 Ind. L. Rev. 1, 28-29 (2005).

F. CONSEQUENCES OF *MIRANDA* VIOLATIONS

The next two cases feature a "successive interrogation" technique in which the police conduct an interrogation without *Miranda* warnings followed by a second interrogation after warnings are given.

Chapter III Police Interrogation and The Fifth Amendment

Oregon v. Elstad
470 U.S. 298 (1985)

Justice O'CONNOR delivered the opinion of the Court.

This case requires us to decide whether an initial failure of law enforcement officers to administer the warnings required by *Miranda*, without more, "taints" subsequent admissions made after a suspect has been fully advised of and has waived his *Miranda* rights. Respondent, Michael James Elstad, was convicted of burglary by an Oregon trial court. The Oregon Court of Appeals reversed, holding that respondent's signed confession, although voluntary, was rendered inadmissible by a prior remark made in response to questioning without benefit of *Miranda* warnings. We granted certiorari and we now reverse.

I

In December 1981, the home of Mr. and Mrs. Gilbert Gross, in the town of Salem, Polk County, Ore., was burglarized. Missing were art objects and furnishings valued at $150,000. A witness to the burglary contacted the Polk County Sheriff's office, implicating respondent Michael Elstad, an 18-year-old neighbor and friend of the Grosses' teenage son. Thereupon, Officers Burke and McAllister went to the home of respondent Elstad, with a warrant for his arrest. Elstad's mother answered the door. She led the officers to her son's room where he lay on his bed, clad in shorts and listening to his stereo. The officers asked him to get dressed and to accompany them into the living room. Officer McAllister asked respondent's mother to step into the kitchen, where he explained that they had a warrant for her son's arrest for the burglary of a neighbor's residence. Officer Burke remained with Elstad in the living room. He later testified:

> I sat down with Mr. Elstad and I asked him if he was aware of why Detective McAllister and myself were there to talk with him. He stated no, he had no idea why we were there. I then asked him if he knew a person by the name of Gross, and he said yes, he did, and also added that he heard that there was a robbery at the Gross house. And at that point I told Mr. Elstad that I felt he was involved in that, and he looked at me and stated, "Yes, I was there."

The officers then escorted Elstad to the back of the patrol car. As they were about to leave for the Polk County Sheriff's office, Elstad's father arrived home and came to the rear of the patrol car. The officers advised him that his son was a suspect in the burglary. Officer Burke testified that Mr. Elstad became quite agitated, opened the rear door of the car and admonished his son: "I told you that you were going to get into trouble. You wouldn't listen to me. You never learn."

Elstad was transported to the Sheriff's headquarters and approximately one hour later, Officers Burke and McAllister joined him in McAllister's office. McAllister then advised respondent for the first time of his *Miranda* rights, reading from a standard card. Respondent indicated he understood his rights, and, having these rights in mind, wished to speak with the officers. Elstad gave a full statement, explaining that he had known that the Gross family was out of town and had been paid to lead several acquaintances to the Gross residence and show them how to gain entry through a defective sliding glass door. The statement was typed, reviewed by respondent, read back to him for correction, initialed and signed by Elstad and both officers. As an afterthought, Elstad added and initialed the sentence, "After leaving the house Robby & I went back to [the] van & Robby handed me a small bag of grass." Respondent concedes that the officers made no threats or promises either at his residence or at the Sheriff's office.

F. Consequences of *Miranda* Violations

Respondent was charged with first-degree burglary. He was represented at trial by retained counsel. Elstad waived his right to a jury, and his case was tried by a Circuit Court Judge. Respondent moved at once to suppress his oral statement and signed confession. He contended that the statement he made in response to questioning at his house "let the cat out of the bag," citing *United States v. Bayer* (1947), and tainted the subsequent confession as "fruit of the poisonous tree," citing *Wong Sun v. United States* (1963). The judge ruled that the statement, "I was there," had to be excluded because the defendant had not been advised of his *Miranda* rights. The written confession taken after Elstad's arrival at the Sheriff's office, however, was admitted in evidence. The court found:

"[H]is written statement was given freely, voluntarily and knowingly by the defendant after he had waived his right to remain silent and have counsel present which waiver was evidenced by the card which the defendant had signed. [It] was not tainted in any way by the previous brief statement between the defendant and the Sheriff's Deputies that had arrested him."

Elstad was found guilty of burglary in the first degree. He received a 5-year sentence and was ordered to pay $18,000 in restitution.

Following his conviction, respondent appealed to the Oregon Court of Appeals, relying on *Wong Sun* and *Bayer*. The State conceded that Elstad had been in custody when he made his statement, "I was there," and accordingly agreed that this statement was inadmissible as having been given without the prescribed Miranda warnings. But the State maintained that any conceivable "taint" had been dissipated prior to the respondent's written confession by McAllister's careful administration of the requisite warnings. The Court of Appeals reversed respondent's conviction, identifying the crucial constitutional inquiry as "whether there was a sufficient break in the stream of events between [the] inadmissible statement and the written confession to insulate the latter statement from the effect of what went before." The Oregon court concluded:

Regardless of the absence of actual compulsion, the coercive impact of the unconstitutionally obtained statement remains, because in a defendant's mind it has sealed his fate. It is this impact that must be dissipated in order to make a subsequent confession admissible. In determining whether it has been dissipated, lapse of time, and change of place from the original surroundings are the most important considerations.

Because of the brief period separating the two incidents, the "cat was sufficiently out of the bag to exert a coercive impact on [respondent's] later admissions."

The State of Oregon petitioned the Oregon Supreme Court for review, and review was declined. This Court granted certiorari to consider the question whether the Self-Incrimination Clause of the Fifth Amendment requires the suppression of a confession, made after proper *Miranda* warnings and a valid waiver of rights, solely because the police had obtained an earlier voluntary but unwarned admission from the defendant.

II

The arguments advanced in favor of suppression of respondent's written confession rely heavily on metaphor. One metaphor, familiar from the Fourth Amendment context, would require that respondent's confession, regardless of its integrity, voluntariness, and probative value, be suppressed as the "tainted fruit of the poisonous tree" of the *Miranda* violation. A second metaphor questions whether a confession can be truly voluntary once the "cat is out of the bag." Taken out of context, each of these metaphors can be misleading. They should not be used to obscure fundamental differences between the role of the Fourth Amendment exclusionary rule and the function of *Miranda* in guarding against the prosecutorial use of compelled statements as prohibited by the Fifth Amendment. The Oregon court assumed and respondent here contends that a failure to administer *Miranda* warnings necessarily breeds the same consequences as police infringement of a constitutional right, so that evidence uncovered following an unwarned statement must be suppressed as "fruit of the poisonous tree." We believe this view misconstrues the nature of the protections afforded by *Miranda* warnings and therefore misreads the consequences of police failure to supply them.

A

. . .

Respondent's contention that his confession was tainted by the earlier failure of the police to provide *Miranda* warnings and must be excluded as "fruit of the poisonous tree" assumes the existence of a constitutional violation. This figure of speech is drawn from *Wong Sun*, in which the Court held that evidence and witnesses discovered as a result of a search in violation of the Fourth Amendment must be excluded from evidence. The *Wong Sun* doctrine applies as well when the fruit of the Fourth Amendment violation is a confession. It is settled law that "a confession obtained through custodial interrogation after an illegal arrest should be excluded unless intervening events break the causal connection between the illegal arrest and the confession so that the confession is 'sufficiently an act of free will to purge the primary taint.'"

But as we explained in *Quarles* and *Tucker*, a procedural *Miranda* violation differs in significant respects from violations of the Fourth Amendment, which have traditionally mandated a broad application of the "fruits" doctrine. The purpose of the Fourth Amendment exclusionary rule is to deter unreasonable searches, no matter how probative their fruits. Where a Fourth Amendment violation "taints" the confession, a finding of voluntariness for the purposes of the Fifth Amendment is merely a threshold requirement in determining whether the confession may be admitted in evidence. Beyond this, the prosecution must show a sufficient break in events to undermine the inference that the confession was caused by the Fourth Amendment violation.

The *Miranda* exclusionary rule, however, serves the Fifth Amendment and sweeps more broadly than the Fifth Amendment itself. It may be triggered even in the absence of a Fifth Amendment violation. The Fifth Amendment prohibits use by the prosecution in its case in chief only of compelled testimony. Failure to administer *Miranda* warnings creates a presumption of compulsion. Consequently, unwarned statements that are otherwise voluntary within the meaning of the Fifth Amendment must nevertheless be excluded from evidence under *Miranda*. Thus, in the individual case, *Miranda*'s preventive medicine provides a remedy even to the defendant who has suffered no identifiable constitutional harm.

But the *Miranda* presumption, though irrebuttable for purposes of the prosecution's case in chief, does not require that the statements and their fruits be discarded as inherently tainted. Despite the fact that patently voluntary statements taken in violation of *Miranda* must be excluded from the prosecution's case, the presumption of coercion does not bar their use for impeachment purposes on cross-examination. *Harris v. New York* (1971). The Court in *Harris* rejected as an "extravagant extension of the Constitution," the theory that a defendant who had confessed under circumstances that made the confession inadmissible, could thereby enjoy the freedom to "deny every fact disclosed or discovered as a 'fruit' of his confession, free from confrontation with his prior statements" and that the voluntariness of his confession would be totally irrelevant. Where an unwarned statement is preserved for use in situations that fall outside the sweep of the *Miranda* presumption, "the primary criterion of admissibility [remains] the 'old' due process voluntariness test."

In *Michigan v. Tucker, supra*, the Court was asked to extend the *Wong Sun* fruits doctrine to suppress the testimony of a witness for the prosecution whose identity was discovered as the result of a statement taken from the accused without benefit of full *Miranda* warnings. As in respondent's case, the breach of the *Miranda* procedures in *Tucker* involved no actual compulsion. The Court concluded that the unwarned questioning "did not abridge respondent's constitutional privilege . . . but departed only from the prophylactic standards later laid down by this Court in *Miranda* to safeguard that privilege." Since there was no actual infringement of the suspect's constitutional rights, the case was not controlled by the doctrine expressed in that fruits of a constitutional violation must be suppressed. In deciding "how sweeping the judicially imposed consequences" of a failure to administer *Miranda* warnings should be, the *Tucker* Court noted that neither the general goal of deterring improper police conduct nor the Fifth Amendment goal of assuring trustworthy evidence would be served by suppression of the witness' testimony. The unwarned confession must, of course, be suppressed, but the Court ruled that introduction of the third-party witness' testimony did not violate Tucker's Fifth Amendment rights.

We believe that this reasoning applies with equal force when the alleged "fruit" of a non-coercive *Miranda* violation is neither a witness nor an article of evidence but the accused's own voluntary testimony. As in *Tucker*, the absence of any coercion or improper tactics undercuts the twin rationales—trustworthiness and deterrence—for a broader rule. Once warned, the suspect is free to exercise his own volition in deciding whether or not to make a statement to the authorities. The Court has often noted: "'[A] living witness is not to be mechanically equated with the proffer of inanimate evidentiary objects illegally seized. . . . [T]he living witness is an individual human personality whose attributes of will, perception, memory and volition interact to determine what testimony he will give.'"

Because *Miranda* warnings may inhibit persons from giving information, this Court has determined that they need be administered only after the person is taken into "custody" or his freedom has otherwise been significantly restrained. Unfortunately, the task of defining "custody" is a slippery one, and "policemen investigating serious crimes [cannot realistically be expected to] make no errors whatsoever." If errors are made by law enforcement officers in administering the prophylactic *Miranda* procedures, they should not breed the same irremediable consequences as police infringement of the Fifth Amendment itself. It is an unwarranted extension of *Miranda* to hold that a simple failure to administer the warnings, unaccompanied by any actual coercion or other circumstances calculated to undermine the suspect's ability to exercise his free will, so taints the investigatory process that a subsequent voluntary and informed waiver is ineffective for some indeterminate period. Though *Miranda* requires that the unwarned admission must be suppressed, the admissibility of any subsequent statement should turn in these circumstances solely on whether it is knowingly and voluntarily made.

B

The Oregon court, however, believed that the unwarned remark compromised the voluntariness of respondent's later confession. It was the court's view that the prior answer and not the unwarned questioning impaired respondent's ability to give a valid waiver and that only lapse of time and change of place could dissipate what it termed the "coercive impact" of the inadmissible statement. When a prior statement is actually coerced, the time that passes between confessions, the change in place of interrogations, and the change in identity of the interrogators all bear on whether that coercion has carried over into the second confession. The failure of police to administer *Miranda* warnings does not mean that the statements received have actually been coerced, but only that courts will presume the privilege against compulsory self-incrimination has not been intelligently exercised. Of the courts that have considered whether a properly warned confession must be suppressed because it was preceded by an unwarned but clearly voluntary admission, the majority have explicitly or implicitly recognized that *Westover*'s requirement of a break in the stream of events is inapposite. In these circumstances, a careful and thorough administration of *Miranda* warnings serves to cure the condition that rendered the unwarned statement inadmissible. The warning conveys the relevant information and thereafter the suspect's choice whether to exercise his privilege to remain silent should ordinarily be viewed as an "act of free will."

The Oregon court nevertheless identified a subtle form of lingering compulsion, the psychological impact of the suspect's conviction that he has let the cat out of the bag and, in so doing, has sealed his own fate. But endowing the psychological effects of voluntary unwarned admissions with constitutional implications would, practically speaking, disable the police from obtaining the suspect's informed cooperation even when the official coercion proscribed by the Fifth Amendment played no part in either his warned or unwarned confessions. As the Court remarked in *Bayer*:

> [A]fter an accused has once let the cat out of the bag by confessing, no matter what the inducement, he is never thereafter free of the psychological and practical disadvantages of having confessed. He can never get the cat back in the bag. The secret is out for good. In such a sense, a later confession may always be looked upon as fruit of the first. But this Court has never gone so far as to hold that making a confession under circumstances which preclude its use, perpetually disables the confessor from making a usable one after those conditions have been removed.

Even in such extreme cases as *Lyons v. Oklahoma* (1944), in which police forced a full confession from the accused through unconscionable methods of interrogation, the Court has assumed that the coercive effect of the confession could, with time, be dissipated.

This Court has never held that the psychological impact of voluntary disclosure of a guilty secret qualifies as state compulsion or compromises the voluntariness of a subsequent informed waiver. The Oregon court, by adopting this expansive view of Fifth Amendment compulsion, effectively immunizes a suspect who responds to pre-*Miranda* warning questions from the consequences of his subsequent informed waiver of the privilege of remaining silent. This immunity comes at a high cost to legitimate law enforcement activity, while adding little desirable protection to the individual's interest in not being compelled to testify against himself. When neither the initial nor the subsequent admission is coerced, little justification exists for permitting the highly probative evidence of a voluntary confession to be irretrievably lost to the factfinder.

There is a vast difference between the direct consequences flowing from coercion of a confession by physical violence or other deliberate means calculated to break the suspect's will and the uncertain consequences of disclosure of a "guilty secret" freely given in response to an unwarned but noncoercive question, as in this case. Justice Brennan's contention that it is impossible to perceive any causal distinction between this case and one involving a confession that is coerced by torture is wholly unpersuasive. Certainly, in respondent's case, the causal connection between any psychological disadvantage created by his admission and his ultimate decision to cooperate is speculative and attenuated best. It is difficult to tell with certainty what motivates a suspect to speak. A suspect's confession may be traced to factors as disparate as "a prearrest event such as a visit with a minister" or an intervening event such as the exchange of words respondent had with his father. We must conclude that, absent deliberately coercive or improper tactics in obtaining the initial statement, the mere fact that a suspect has made an unwarned admission does not warrant a presumption of compulsion. A subsequent administration of *Miranda* warnings to a suspect who has given a voluntary but unwarned statement ordinarily should suffice to remove the conditions that precluded admission of the earlier statement. In such circumstances, the finder of fact may reasonably conclude that the suspect made a rational and intelligent choice whether to waive or invoke his rights.

III

Though belated, the reading of respondent's rights was undeniably complete. McAllister testified that he read the *Miranda* warnings aloud from a printed card and recorded Elstad's responses. There is no question that respondent knowingly and voluntarily waived his right to remain silent before he described his participation in the burglary. It is also beyond dispute that respondent's earlier remark was voluntary, within the meaning of the Fifth Amendment. Neither the environment nor the manner of either "interrogation" was coercive. The initial conversation took place at midday, in the living room area of respondent's own home, with his mother in the kitchen area, a few steps away. Although in retrospect the officers testified that respondent was then in custody, at the time he made his statement he had not been informed that he was under arrest. The arresting officers' testimony indicates that the brief stop in the living room before proceeding to the station house was not to interrogate the suspect but to notify his mother of the reason for his arrest.

The State has conceded the issue of custody and thus we must assume that Burke breached *Miranda* procedures in failing to administer *Miranda* warnings before initiating the discussion in the living room. This breach may have been the result of confusion as to whether the brief exchange qualified as "custodial interrogation" or it may simply have reflected Burke's reluctance to initiate an alarming police procedure before McAllister had spoken with respondent's mother. Whatever the reason for Burke's oversight, the incident had none of the earmarks of coercion. Nor did the officers exploit the unwarned admission to pressure respondent into waiving his right to remain silent.

Respondent, however, has argued that he was unable to give a fully informed waiver of his rights because he was unaware that his prior statement could not be used against him. Respondent suggests that Officer McAllister, to cure this deficiency, should have added an additional warning to those given him at the Sheriff's office. Such a requirement is neither practicable nor constitutionally necessary. In many cases, a breach of *Miranda* procedures may not be identified as such until long after full *Miranda* warnings are administered and a valid confession obtained. The standard *Miranda* warnings explicitly inform the suspect of his right to consult a lawyer before speaking. Police officers are ill-equipped to pinch-hit for counsel, construing the murky and difficult questions of when "custody" begins or whether a given unwarned statement will ultimately be held admissible.

This Court has never embraced the theory that a defendant's ignorance of the full consequences of his decisions vitiates their voluntariness. If the prosecution has actually violated the defendant's Fifth Amendment rights by introducing an inadmissible confession at trial, compelling the defendant to testify in rebuttal, the rule announced in *Harrison* precludes use of that testimony on retrial. "Having 'released the spring' by using the petitioner's unlawfully obtained confessions against him, the Government must show that its illegal action did not induce his testimony." But the Court has refused to find that a defendant who confesses, after being falsely told that his codefendant has turned State's evidence, does so involuntarily. The Court has also rejected the argument that a defendant's ignorance that a prior coerced confession could not be admitted in evidence compromised the voluntariness of his guilty plea. Likewise, in *California v. Beheler, supra*, the Court declined to accept defendant's contention that, because he was unaware of the potential adverse consequences of statements he made to the police, his participation in the interview was involuntary. Thus we have not held that the sine qua non for a knowing and voluntary waiver of the right to remain silent is a full and complete appreciation of all of the consequences flowing from the nature and the quality of the evidence in the case.

IV

When police ask questions of a suspect in custody without administering the required warnings, *Miranda* dictates that the answers received be presumed compelled and that they be excluded from evidence at trial in the State's case in chief. The Court has carefully adhered to this principle, permitting a narrow exception only where pressing public safety concerns demanded. The Court today in no way retreats from the bright-line rule of *Miranda*. We do not imply that good faith excuses a failure to administer *Miranda* warnings; nor do we condone inherently coercive police tactics or methods offensive to due process that render the initial admission involuntary and undermine the suspect's will to invoke his rights once they are read to him. A handful of courts have, however, applied our precedents relating to confessions obtained under coercive circumstances to situations involving wholly voluntary admissions, requiring a passage of time or break in events before a second, fully warned statement can be deemed voluntary. Far from establishing a rigid rule, we direct courts to avoid one; there is no warrant for presuming coercive effect where the suspect's initial inculpatory statement, though technically in violation of *Miranda*, was voluntary. The relevant inquiry is whether, in fact, the second statement was also voluntarily made. As in any such inquiry, the finder of fact must examine the surrounding circumstances and the entire course of police conduct with respect to the suspect in evaluating the voluntariness of his statements. The fact that a suspect chooses to speak after being informed of his rights is, of course, highly probative. We find that the dictates of *Miranda* and the goals of the Fifth Amendment proscription against use of compelled testimony are fully satisfied in the circumstances of this case by barring use of the unwarned statement in the case in chief. No further purpose is served by imputing "taint" to subsequent statements obtained pursuant to a voluntary and knowing waiver. We hold today that a suspect who has once responded to unwarned yet uncoercive questioning is not thereby disabled from waiving his rights and confessing after he has been given the requisite *Miranda* warnings.

The judgment of the Court of Appeals of Oregon is reversed, and the case is remanded for further proceedings not inconsistent with this opinion.

[Justices Brennan, Marshall, and Stevens dissented.]

NOTES AND QUESTIONS

1. The selection of every fact for inclusion in an opinion is purposeful. And the Court here mentions some very random details about 18-year old defendant Michael Elstad that must be meant to affect our view of him. He was found by the police in his room "clad in shorts and listening to his stereo." Was he a slacker? He added a gratuitous note to his written statement that he acquired a "bag of grass" in connection with the burglary. A pothead? His dad yelled at the defendant as he was being escorted away, "I told you that you were going to get into trouble. You wouldn't listen to me. You never learn." A bad kid? Or maybe a rough home situation? He was represented at trial by "retained counsel." A rich kid?

Or was the detail about the "bag of grass" added to show the cathartic purification of the soul that attends confessions?

Would it be too much to expect the 18-year old son of a man who yells at his kid in front of police officers to invoke his right of silence when given *Miranda* warnings?

2. The State conceded that the questioning at the Elstads' home was custodial. Should it have? Did the officer's statement that "I feel you were involved" render it custodial? But the Court finds nonetheless that the initial interrogation was not "coercive." However the interrogation is described colloquially, isn't one of the points of *Miranda* that custodial interrogation is "inherently coercive"?

3. The Court uncritically accepts the officers' explanation for the purpose of their visit to the Elstads' home: that they had not stopped by to interrogate the defendant at all but rather to notify his mother of the reason for the arrest. Is this believable? And how could "retained counsel" have allowed that testimony to stand unquestioned? (Of course, it's possible the officers were superbly cross-examined and simply lied at the suppression hearing.)

If the officers were telling the truth, why did both officers approach Michael in his room *before* notifying his mother of the reason for their visit? (And why on earth would the mother let them in and show them to her son's room?) And why did the officers immediately separate the defendant from his mother once he came down the stairs? Note that all the police manuals encourage so-called incommunicado interrogation whereby the suspect is isolated and cannot receive support or advice from family members or counsel.

4. Is the brevity of the questioning of Michael in the house relevant, as the Court seems to find? Was it brief only because it was immediately successful, and Michael "let the cat out of the bag" without much resistance? Did the interrogation need to go much further once the defendant admitted—or as the Court has it, made a "remark"—that he "was there" and a longer, warned interrogation was in the offing?

5. Will police after *Elstad* be incentivized to use the successive-interrogation ploy in future cases? The dissent offers a litany of case law and police interrogation manuals demonstrating the widespread nature of the successive-interrogation ploy and multiple variations on the theme.

6. Do you agree with the Court that any "psychological impact" of defendant's admission at his home ("I was there") had on his subsequent waiver of his rights at the police station was "speculative and attenuated"? Would a reasonable person in Michael's position have believed he had "let the cat out of the bag" by saying "I was there"? Would you?

In 1998 Professor Charles Weisselberg wrote an article based on police training materials received through discovery in civil litigation against California police departments alleging systemic *Miranda* violations. Charles D. Weisselberg, *Saving* Miranda, 84 Cornell L. Rev. 109 (1998). The materials showed that officers were encouraged to ignore a person's *Miranda* rights when necessary to serve law enforcement goals such as developing impeachment material (should the person testify), obtaining physical evidence, locating a crime scene, and identifying other accomplices and witnesses. *Id.* at 134. One training bulletin advised that officers had "little to lose and perhaps something to gain" by questioning "outside *Miranda*." *Id.* at 133.

It turns out that police agencies and the lawyers that advise them pay attention to Supreme Court opinions on police tactics. The successive-interrogation technique validated by the Court in *Elstad* was not ignored in police training manuals, as the next case makes clear.

Missouri v. Seibert
542 U.S. 600 (2004)

Justice SOUTER announced the judgment of the Court and delivered an opinion in which Justice STEVENS, Justice GINSBURG, and Justice BREYER join.

This case tests a police protocol for custodial interrogation that calls for giving no warnings of the rights to silence and counsel until interrogation has produced a confession. Although such a statement is generally inadmissible, since taken in violation of *Miranda*, the interrogating officer follows it with *Miranda* warnings and then leads the suspect to cover the same ground a second time. The question here is the admissibility of the repeated statement. Because this midstream recitation of warnings after interrogation and unwarned confession could not effectively comply with *Miranda*'s constitutional requirement, we hold that a statement repeated after a warning in such circumstances is inadmissible.

I

Respondent Patrice Seibert's 12-year-old son Jonathan had cerebral palsy, and when he died in his sleep she feared charges of neglect because of bedsores on his body. In her presence, two of her teenage sons and two of their friends devised a plan to conceal the facts surrounding Jonathan's death by incinerating his body in the course of burning the family's mobile home, in which they planned to leave Donald Rector, a mentally ill teenager living with the family, to avoid any appearance that Jonathan had been unattended. Seibert's son Darian and a friend set the fire, and Donald died.

Five days later, the police awakened Seibert at 3 a.m. at a hospital where Darian was being treated for burns. In arresting her, Officer Kevin Clinton followed instructions from Rolla, Missouri, Officer Richard Hanrahan that he refrain from giving *Miranda* warnings. After Seibert had been taken to the police station and left alone in an interview room for 15 to 20 minutes, Officer Hanrahan questioned her without *Miranda* warnings for 30 to 40 minutes, squeezing her arm and repeating "Donald was also to die in his sleep." After Seibert finally admitted she knew Donald was meant to die in the fire, she was given a 20-minute coffee and cigarette break. Officer Hanrahan then turned on a tape recorder, gave Seibert the *Miranda* warnings, and obtained a signed waiver of rights from her. He resumed the questioning with "Ok, 'Trice, we've been talking for a little while about what happened on Wednesday the twelfth, haven't we?" and confronted her with her prewarning statements:

Hanrahan:	"Now, in discussion you told us, you told us that there was a[n] understanding about Donald."
Seibert:	"Yes."
Hanrahan:	"Did that take place earlier that morning?"
Seibert:	"Yes."
Hanrahan:	"And what was the understanding about Donald?"
Seibert:	"If they could get him out of the trailer, to take him out of the trailer."
Hanrahan:	"And if they couldn't?"
Seibert:	"I, I never even thought about it. I just figured they would."
Hanrahan:	"'Trice, didn't you tell me that he was supposed to die in his sleep?"
Seibert:	"If that would happen, 'cause he was on that new medicine, you know. . . ."
Hanrahan:	"The Prozac? And it makes him sleepy. So he was supposed to die in his sleep?"
Seibert:	"Yes."

After being charged with first-degree murder for her role in Donald's death, Seibert sought to exclude both her prewarning and postwarning statements. At the suppression hearing, Officer Hanrahan testified that he made a "conscious decision" to withhold *Miranda* warnings, thus resorting to an interrogation technique he had been taught: question first, then give the warnings, and then repeat the question "until I get the answer that she's already provided once. He acknowledged that Seibert's ultimate statement was "largely a repeat of information . . . obtained" prior to the warning.

The trial court suppressed the prewarning statement but admitted the responses given after the *Miranda* recitation. A jury convicted Seibert of second-degree murder. On appeal, the Missouri Court of Appeals affirmed, treating this case as indistinguishable from *Oregon v. Elstad.*

The Supreme Court of Missouri reversed, holding that "[i]n the circumstances here, where the interrogation was nearly continuous, . . . the second statement, clearly the product of the invalid first statement, should have been suppressed." The court distinguished *Elstad* on the ground that warnings had not intentionally been withheld there, and reasoned that "Officer Hanrahan's intentional omission of a *Miranda* warning was intended to deprive Seibert of the opportunity knowingly and intelligently to waive her *Miranda* rights." Since there were "no circumstances that would seem to dispel the effect of the *Miranda* violation," the court held that the postwarning confession was involuntary and therefore inadmissible. To allow the police to achieve an "end run" around *Miranda*, the court explained, would encourage *Miranda* violations and diminish *Miranda*'s role in protecting the privilege against self-incrimination. Three judges dissented, taking the view that Elstad applied even though the police intentionally withheld *Miranda* warnings before the initial statement, and believing that "Seibert's unwarned responses to Officer Hanrahan's questioning did not prevent her from waiving her rights and confessing."

We granted certiorari to resolve a split in the Courts of Appeals. We now affirm.

II

. . .

III

There are those, of course, who preferred the old way of doing things, giving no warnings and litigating the voluntariness of any statement in nearly every instance. In the aftermath of *Miranda*, Congress even passed a statute seeking to restore that old regime, 18 U.S.C. § 3501, although the Act lay dormant for years until finally invoked and challenged in *Dickerson*. *Dickerson* reaffirmed *Miranda* and held that its constitutional character prevailed against the statute.

The technique of interrogating in successive, unwarned and warned phases raises a new challenge to *Miranda*. Although we have no statistics on the frequency of this practice, it is not confined to Rolla, Missouri. An officer of that police department testified that the strategy of withholding *Miranda* warnings until after interrogating and drawing out a confession was promoted not only by his own department, but by a national police training organization and other departments in which he had worked. Consistently with the officer's testimony, the Police Law Institute, for example, instructs that "officers may conduct a two-stage interrogation. . . . At any point during the pre-*Miranda* interrogation, usually after arrestees have confessed, officers may then read the *Miranda* warnings and ask for a waiver. If the arrestees waive their *Miranda* rights, officers will be able to repeat any subsequent incriminating statements later in court." The upshot of all this advice is a question-first practice of some popularity, as one can see from the reported cases describing its use, sometimes in obedience to departmental policy.

IV

When a confession so obtained is offered and challenged, attention must be paid to the conflicting objects of *Miranda* and question-first. *Miranda* addressed "interrogation practices . . . likely . . . to disable [an individual] from making a free and rational choice" about speaking, and held that a suspect must be "adequately and effectively" advised of the choice the Constitution guarantees." The object of question-first is to render *Miranda* warnings ineffective by waiting for a particularly opportune time to give them, after the suspect has already confessed.

Just as "no talismanic incantation [is] required to satisfy [*Miranda*'s] strictures," it would be absurd to think that mere recitation of the litany suffices to satisfy *Miranda* in every conceivable circumstance. "The inquiry is simply whether the warnings reasonably 'conve[y] to [a suspect] his rights as required by *Miranda*.'" The threshold issue when interrogators question first and warn later is thus whether it would be reasonable to find that in these circumstances the warnings could function "effectively" as *Miranda* requires. Could the warnings effectively advise the suspect that he had a real choice about giving an admissible statement at that juncture? Could they reasonably convey that he could choose to stop talking even if he had talked earlier? For unless the warnings could place a suspect who has just been interrogated in a position to make such an informed choice, there is no practical justification for accepting the formal warnings as compliance with *Miranda*, or for treating the second stage of interrogation as distinct from the first, unwarned and inadmissible segment.

There is no doubt about the answer that proponents of question-first give to this question about the effectiveness of warnings given only after successful interrogation, and we think their answer is correct. By any objective measure, applied to circumstances exemplified here, it is likely that if the interrogators employ the technique of withholding warnings until after interrogation succeeds in eliciting a confession, the warnings will be ineffective in preparing the suspect for successive interrogation, close in time and similar in content. After all, the reason that question-first is catching on is as obvious as its manifest purpose, which is to get a confession the suspect would not make if he understood his rights at the outset; the sensible underlying assumption is that with one confession in hand before the warnings, the interrogator can count on getting its duplicate, with trifling additional trouble. Upon hearing warnings only in the aftermath of interrogation and just after making a confession, a suspect would hardly think he had a genuine right to remain silent, let alone persist in so believing once the police began to lead him over the same ground again. A more likely reaction on a suspect's part would be perplexity about the reason for discussing rights at that point, bewilderment being an unpromising frame of mind for knowledgeable decision. What is worse, telling a suspect that "anything you say can and will be used against you," without expressly excepting the statement just given, could lead to an entirely reasonable inference that what he has just said will be used, with subsequent silence being of no avail. Thus, when *Miranda* warnings are inserted in the midst of coordinated and continuing interrogation, they are likely to mislead and "depriv[e] a defendant of knowledge essential to his ability to understand the nature of his rights and the consequences of abandoning them." By the same token, it would ordinarily be unrealistic to treat two spates of integrated and proximately conducted questioning as independent interrogations subject to independent evaluation simply because *Miranda* warnings formally punctuate them in the middle.

V

Missouri argues that a confession repeated at the end of an interrogation sequence envisioned in a question-first strategy is admissible on the authority of *Oregon v. Elstad*, but the argument disfigures that case. In *Elstad*, the police went to the young suspect's house to take him into custody on a charge of burglary. Before the arrest, one officer spoke with the suspect's mother, while the other one joined the suspect in a "brief stop in the living room," where the officer said he "felt" the young man was involved in a burglary. The suspect acknowledged he had been at the scene. This Court noted that the pause in the living room "was not to interrogate the suspect but to notify his mother of the reason for his arrest," and described the incident as having "none of the earmarks of coercion." The Court, indeed, took care to mention that the officer's initial failure to warn was an "oversight" that "may have been the result of confusion as to whether the brief exchange qualified as 'custodial interrogation' or . . . may simply have reflected . . . reluctance to initiate an alarming police procedure before [an officer] had spoken with respondent's mother." At the outset of a later and systematic station house interrogation going well beyond the scope of the laconic prior admission, the suspect was given *Miranda* warnings and made a full confession. In holding the second statement admissible and voluntary, *Elstad* rejected the "cat out of the bag" theory that any short, earlier admission, obtained in arguably innocent neglect of *Miranda*, determined the character of the later, warned confession, *Elstad*; on the facts of that case, the Court thought any causal connection between the first and second responses to the police was "speculative and attenuated." Although the *Elstad* Court expressed no explicit conclusion about either officer's state of mind, it is fair to read *Elstad* as treating the living room conversation as a good-faith *Miranda* mistake, not only open to correction by careful warnings before systematic questioning in that particular case, but posing no threat to warn-first practice generally.

The contrast between *Elstad* and this case reveals a series of relevant facts that bear on whether *Miranda* warnings delivered midstream could be effective enough to accomplish their object: the completeness and detail of the questions and answers in the first round of interrogation, the overlapping content of the two statements, the timing and setting of the first and the second, the continuity of police personnel, and the degree to which the interrogator's questions treated the second round as continuous with the first. In *Elstad*, it was not unreasonable to see the occasion for questioning at the station house as presenting a markedly different experience from the short conversation at home; since a reasonable person in the suspect's shoes could have seen the station house questioning as a new and distinct experience, the *Miranda* warnings could have made sense as presenting a genuine choice whether to follow up on the earlier admission.

At the opposite extreme are the facts here, which by any objective measure reveal a police strategy adapted to undermine the *Miranda* warnings. The unwarned interrogation was conducted in the station house, and the questioning was systematic, exhaustive, and managed with psychological skill. When the police were finished there was little, if anything, of incriminating potential left unsaid. The warned phase of questioning proceeded after a pause of only 15 to 20 minutes, in the same place as the unwarned segment. When the same officer who had conducted the first phase recited the *Miranda* warnings, he said nothing to counter the probable misimpression that the advice that anything Seibert said could be used against her also applied to the details of the inculpatory statement previously elicited. In particular, the police did not advise that her prior statement could not be used. Nothing was said or done to dispel the oddity of warning about legal rights to silence and counsel right after the police had led her through a systematic interrogation, and any uncertainty on her part about a right to stop talking about matters previously discussed would only have been aggravated by the way Officer Hanrahan set the scene by saying "we've been talking for a little while about what happened on Wednesday the twelfth, haven't we?" The impression that the further questioning was a mere continuation of the earlier questions and responses was fostered by references back to the confession already given. It would have been reasonable to regard the two sessions as parts of a continuum, in which it would have been unnatural to refuse to repeat at the second stage what had been said before. These circumstances must be seen as challenging the comprehensibility and efficacy of the *Miranda* warnings to the point that a reasonable person in the suspect's shoes would not have understood them to convey a message that she retained a choice about continuing to talk.

VI

Strategists dedicated to draining the substance out of *Miranda* cannot accomplish by training instructions what *Dickerson* held Congress could not do by statute. Because the question-first tactic effectively threatens to thwart *Miranda*'s purpose of reducing the risk that a coerced confession would be admitted, and because the facts here do not reasonably support a conclusion that the warnings given could have served their purpose, Seibert's postwarning statements are inadmissible. The judgment of the Supreme Court of Missouri is affirmed.

NOTES AND QUESTIONS

1. Officer Hanrahan is to be commended for his truthful testimony at the suppression hearing. He not only admitted to being trained to use the successive-interrogation technique but acknowledged that its purpose was to get a suspect to essentially ratify a previously unwarned confession. Would the case have come out differently if he had not been so forthcoming?

2. The Court finds that the successive-interrogation technique at issue here is "by any objective measure . . . a police strategy adapted to undermine the *Miranda* warnings," and in fact it rendered the *Miranda* warnings given before the second interrogation ineffective. But the Court ties its holding to the specific facts of Hanrahan's interrogations and not to his admission of its purpose.

Do you see any room for creative successive-interrogation proponents to get around *Seibert*? What if the suspect was questioned the second time after a much longer interval? By a different officer? In a different place? What if the second interrogation covered new subjects?

3. Justice Breyer in a concurring opinion grounds his vote in the fruits-of-the-poisonous-tree doctrine, which was rejected by the Court in a footnote in reliance on the precedent of *Elstad*, rather than the sufficiency of the *Miranda* warnings. Which approach is preferable?

4. The Court otherwise distinguishes *Elstad*, as "it is fair to read *Elstad* as treating the living room 'conversation' as a good faith *Miranda* mistake." That certainly is a fair reading of *Elstad*. But the Court then identifies a laundry list of factual differences between *Elstad* and *Seibert*. Do you see any of these differences as being material to whether the *Miranda* warnings before the second interrogation would have "made sense," as the Court puts it?

5. What if before the second interrogation the suspect was advised, in addition to receiving the *Miranda* warnings, that nothing she had said up until now could be "used against her"? Would this suffice to make the *Miranda* warnings effective?

6. The vigorous dissent by Justice O'Connor, who wrote for the Court in *Elstad*, criticizes Justice Kennedy's concurring opinion for injecting the interrogating officer's "state of mind" into the analysis, as it adds a third step of analysis into every "two stage interrogation case." Are the four dissenters suggesting that "two stage interrogation cases" are here to stay notwithstanding *Seibert*?

G. THE DURABILITY OF *MIRANDA*

As noted above, there was speculation about *Miranda*'s staying power from its inception. Just two years after the decision Congress passed a statute, 18 U.S.C. § 3501, purporting to overrule *Miranda* in federal cases and replace it with a "voluntariness" test. That test included among a list of factors to be considered whether the suspect had received the equivalent of the warnings that *Miranda* had required. Although the Supreme Court once referred to § 3501 as "the statute governing the admissibility of confessions in federal prosecutions," *United States v. Alvarez-Sanchez*, 511 U.S. 350, 351 (1994), the Court for over 30 years never considered whether the statute overruled *Miranda*. *Davis v. United States*, 512 U.S. 452, 457 n.* (1994). Several lower courts have found that § 3501, rather than *Miranda*, governs the admissibility of confessions in federal courts. *See United States v. Crocker*, 510 F.2d 1129, 1137 (10th Cir. 1975); *United States v. Rivas-Lopez*, 988 F. Supp. 1424, 1430-36 (D. Utah 1997).

Remarkably the Department of Justice—including under the "tough on crime" Republican administrations of Nixon, Reagan, and Bush and the "tough on crime" Democratic administration of Clinton—never pressed the point in court. Justice Scalia publicly complained about the department's refusal to invoke § 3501 in 1994. *See Davis*, 512 U.S. at 453-54 (Scalia, J., concurring) (noting that "the provision has been studiously avoided by every Administration . . . since its enactment more than 25 years ago"). He also stated that the department's passivity had "caused the federal judiciary to confront a host of '*Miranda*' issues that might be entirely irrelevant under federal law," and "may have produced—during an era of intense national concern about the problem of run-away crime—the acquittal and the nonprosecution of many dangerous felons." *Id.* at 457. In fact, after initially declining to take a position on the applicability of § 3501, the Clinton Administration eventually asserted that it believed the statute to be unconstitutional. Letter from Janet Reno, Attorney General, to Congress (Sept. 10, 1997).

Charles Thomas Dickerson was arrested in 1997 and charged with bank robbery. Dickerson had incriminated himself to the FBI, but there was a factual dispute over whether he had been given proper *Miranda* warnings. At an evidentiary hearing the trial judge found that the testifying FBI agent lacked credibility and suppressed the confession. *Dickerson v. United States*, 971 F. Supp. 1023 (E.D. Va. 1997). The government appealed to the Fourth Circuit, which sua sponte held that 18 U.S.C. § 3501 was applicable because *Miranda* was not a constitutional holding and, since the confession was voluntary, reversed the district court's suppression ruling. *Dickerson v. United States*, 166 F.3d 667 (4th Cir. 1999).

The Supreme Court granted certiorari.

Dickerson v. United States
530 U.S. 428 (2000)

Chief Justice REHNQUIST delivered the opinion of the Court.

In *Miranda* we held that certain warnings must be given before a suspect's statement made during custodial interrogation could be admitted in evidence. In the wake of that decision, Congress enacted 18 U.S.C. § 3501, which in essence laid down a rule that the admissibility of such statements should turn only on whether or not they were voluntarily made. We hold that *Miranda*, being a constitutional decision of this Court, may not be in effect overruled by an Act of Congress, and we decline to overrule *Miranda* ourselves. We therefore hold that *Miranda* and its progeny in this Court govern the admissibility of statements made during custodial interrogation in both state and federal courts.

Petitioner Dickerson was indicted for bank robbery, conspiracy to commit bank robbery, and using a firearm in the course of committing a crime of violence, all in violation of the applicable provisions of Title 18 of the United States Code. Before trial, Dickerson moved to suppress a statement he had made at a Federal Bureau of Investigation field office, on the grounds that he had not received "*Miranda* warnings" before being interrogated. The District Court granted his motion to suppress, and the Government took an interlocutory appeal to the United States Court of Appeals for the Fourth Circuit. That court, by a divided vote, reversed the District Court's suppression order. It agreed with the District Court's conclusion that petitioner had not received *Miranda* warnings before making his statement. But it went on to hold that § 3501, which in effect makes the admissibility of statements such as Dickerson's turn solely on whether they were made voluntarily, was satisfied in this case. It then concluded that our decision in *Miranda* was not a constitutional holding, and that, therefore, Congress could by statute have the final say on the question of admissibility.

Because of the importance of the questions raised by the Court of Appeals' decision, we granted certiorari and now reverse.

We begin with a brief historical account of the law governing the admission of confessions. Prior to *Miranda*, we evaluated the admissibility of a suspect's confession under a voluntariness test. The roots of this test developed in the common law, as the courts of England and then the United States recognized that coerced confessions are inherently untrustworthy. Over time, our cases recognized two constitutional bases for the requirement that a confession be voluntary to be admitted into evidence: the Fifth Amendment right against self-incrimination and the Due Process Clause of the Fourteenth Amendment.

While *Bram* was decided before *Brown* and its progeny, for the middle third of the 20th century our cases based the rule against admitting coerced confessions primarily, if not exclusively, on notions of due process. We applied the due process voluntariness test in "some 30 different cases decided during the era that intervened between *Brown* and *Escobedo*." Those cases refined the test into an inquiry that examines "whether a defendant's will was overborne" by the circumstances surrounding the giving of a confession. The due process test takes into consideration "the totality of all the surrounding circumstances—both the characteristics of the accused and the details of the interrogation." The determination "depend[s] upon a weighing of the circumstances of pressure against the power of resistance of the person confessing."

We have never abandoned this due process jurisprudence, and thus continue to exclude confessions that were obtained involuntarily. But our decisions in *Malloy v. Hogan* (1964) and *Miranda* changed the focus of much of the inquiry in determining the admissibility of suspects' incriminating statements.

In *Miranda*, we noted that the advent of modern custodial police interrogation brought with it an increased concern about confessions obtained by coercion. Because custodial police interrogation, by its very nature, isolates and pressures the individual, we stated that "[e]ven without employing brutality, the 'third degree' or [other] specific stratagems, . . . custodial interrogation exacts a heavy toll on individual liberty and trades on the weakness of individuals." We concluded that the coercion inherent in custodial interrogation blurs the line between voluntary and involuntary statements, and thus heightens the risk that an individual will not be "accorded his privilege under the Fifth Amendment . . . not to be compelled to incriminate himself." Accordingly, we laid down "concrete constitutional guidelines for law enforcement agencies and courts to follow." Those guidelines established that the admissibility in evidence of any statement given during custodial interrogation of a suspect would depend on whether the police provided the suspect with four warnings. These warnings (which have come to be known colloquially as "*Miranda* rights") are: a suspect "has the right to remain silent, that anything he says can be used against him in a court of law, that he has the right to the presence of an attorney, and that if he cannot afford an attorney one will be appointed for him prior to any questioning if he so desires."

Two years after *Miranda* was decided, Congress enacted § 3501. That section provides, in relevant part:

> (a) In any criminal prosecution brought by the United States or by the District of Columbia, a confession . . . shall be admissible in evidence if it is voluntarily given. Before such confession is received in evidence, the trial judge shall, out of the presence of the jury, determine any issue as to voluntariness. If the trial judge determines that the confession was voluntarily made it shall be admitted in evidence and the trial judge shall permit the jury to hear relevant evidence on the issue of voluntariness and shall instruct the jury to give such weight to the confession as the jury feels it deserves under all the circumstances.
>
> (b) The trial judge in determining the issue of voluntariness shall take into consideration all the circumstances surrounding the giving of the confession, including (1) the time elapsing between arrest and arraignment of the defendant making the confession, if it was made after arrest and before arraignment, (2) whether such defendant knew the nature of the offense with which he was charged or of which he was suspected at the time of making the confession, (3) whether or not such defendant was advised or knew that he was not required to make any statement and that any such statement could be used against him, (4) whether or not such defendant had been advised prior to questioning of his right to the assistance of counsel; and

G. The Durability of *Miranda*   **199**

(5) whether or not such defendant was without the assistance of counsel when questioned and when giving such confession.

The presence or absence of any of the above-mentioned factors to be taken into consideration by the judge need not be conclusive on the issue of voluntariness of the confession.

Given § 3501's express designation of voluntariness as the touchstone of admissibility, its omission of any warning requirement, and the instruction for trial courts to consider a nonexclusive list of factors relevant to the circumstances of a confession, we agree with the Court of Appeals that Congress intended by its enactment to overrule *Miranda*. Because of the obvious conflict between our decision in *Miranda* and § 3501, we must address whether Congress has constitutional authority to thus supersede *Miranda*. If Congress has such authority, § 3501's totality-of-the-circumstances approach must prevail over *Miranda*'s requirement of warnings; if not, that section must yield to *Miranda*'s more specific requirements.

The law in this area is clear. This Court has supervisory authority over the federal courts, and we may use that authority to prescribe rules of evidence and procedure that are binding in those tribunals. Congress retains the ultimate authority to modify or set aside any judicially created rules of evidence and procedure that are not required by the Constitution.

But Congress may not legislatively supersede our decisions interpreting and applying the Constitution. This case therefore turns on whether the *Miranda* Court announced a constitutional rule or merely exercised its supervisory authority to regulate evidence in the absence of congressional direction. Recognizing this point, the Court of Appeals surveyed *Miranda* and its progeny to determine the constitutional status of the *Miranda* decision. Relying on the fact that we have created several exceptions to *Miranda*'s warnings requirement and that we have repeatedly referred to the *Miranda* warnings as "prophylactic," *New York v. Quarles*, and "not themselves rights protected by the Constitution," *Michigan v. Tucker*, the Court of Appeals concluded that the protections announced in *Miranda* are not constitutionally required.

We disagree with the Court of Appeals' conclusion, although we concede that there is language in some of our opinions that supports the view taken by that court. But first and foremost of the factors on the other side — that *Miranda* is a constitutional decision — is that both *Miranda* and two of its companion cases applied the rule to proceedings in state courts. Since that time, we have consistently applied *Miranda*'s rule to prosecutions arising in state courts. It is beyond dispute that we do not hold a supervisory power over the courts of the several States. With respect to proceedings in state courts, our "authority is limited to enforcing the commands of the United States Constitution."

The *Miranda* opinion itself begins by stating that the Court granted certiorari "to explore some facets of the problems . . . of applying the privilege against self-incrimination to in-custody interrogation, and to give concrete constitutional guidelines for law enforcement agencies and courts to follow." In fact, the majority opinion is replete with statements indicating that the majority thought it was announcing a constitutional rule. Indeed, the Court's ultimate conclusion was that the unwarned confessions obtained in the four cases before the Court in *Miranda* "were obtained from the defendant under circumstances that did not meet constitutional standards for protection of the privilege."

Additional support for our conclusion that *Miranda* is constitutionally based is found in the *Miranda* Court's invitation for legislative action to protect the constitutional right against coerced self-incrimination. After discussing the "compelling pressures" inherent in custodial police interrogation, the *Miranda* Court concluded that, "[i]n order to combat these pressures and to permit a full opportunity to exercise the privilege against self-incrimination, the accused must be adequately and effectively apprised of his rights and the exercise of those rights must be fully honored." However, the Court emphasized that it could not foresee "the potential alternatives for protecting the privilege which might be devised by Congress or the

States," and it accordingly opined that the Constitution would not preclude legislative solutions that differed from the prescribed *Miranda* warnings but which were "at least as effective in apprising accused persons of their right of silence and in assuring a continuous opportunity to exercise it."

The Court of Appeals also relied on the fact that we have, after our *Miranda* decision, made exceptions from its rule in cases such as *New York v. Quarles* and *Harris v. New York*. But we have also broadened the application of the *Miranda* doctrine in cases such as *Doyle v. Ohio* (1976), and *Arizona v. Roberson* (1988). These decisions illustrate the principle — not that *Miranda* is not a constitutional rule — but that no constitutional rule is immutable. No court laying down a general rule can possibly foresee the various circumstances in which counsel will seek to apply it, and the sort of modifications represented by these cases are as much a normal part of constitutional law as the original decision.

The Court of Appeals also noted that in *Oregon v. Elstad* we stated that "'[t]he *Miranda* exclusionary rule . . . serves the Fifth Amendment and sweeps more broadly than the Fifth Amendment itself.'" Our decision in that case — refusing to apply the traditional "fruits" doctrine developed in Fourth Amendment cases — does not prove that *Miranda* is a nonconstitutional decision, but simply recognizes the fact that unreasonable searches under the Fourth Amendment are different from unwarned interrogation under the Fifth Amendment.

As an alternative argument for sustaining the Court of Appeals' decision, the court-invited amicus curiae contends that the section complies with the requirement that a legislative alternative to *Miranda* be equally as effective in preventing coerced confessions. We agree with the amicus' contention that there are more remedies available for abusive police conduct than there were at the time *Miranda* was decided to hold that a suspect may bring a federal cause of action under the Due Process Clause for police misconduct during custodial interrogation. But we do not agree that these additional measures supplement § 3501's protections sufficiently to meet the constitutional minimum. *Miranda* requires procedures that will warn a suspect in custody of his right to remain silent and which will assure the suspect that the exercise of that right will be honored. As discussed above, § 3501 explicitly eschews a requirement of preinterrogation warnings in favor of an approach that looks to the administration of such warnings as only one factor in determining the voluntariness of a suspect's confession. The additional remedies cited by amicus do not, in our view, render them, together with § 3501, an adequate substitute for the warnings required by *Miranda*.

The dissent argues that it is judicial overreaching for this Court to hold § 3501 unconstitutional unless we hold that the *Miranda* warnings are required by the Constitution, in the sense that nothing else will suffice to satisfy constitutional requirements. But we need not go further than *Miranda* to decide this case. In *Miranda*, the Court noted that reliance on the traditional totality-of-the-circumstances test raised a risk of overlooking an involuntary custodial confession, a risk that the Court found unacceptably great when the confession is offered in the case in chief to prove guilt. The Court therefore concluded that something more than the totality test was necessary. As discussed above, § 3501 reinstates the totality test as sufficient. Section 3501 therefore cannot be sustained if *Miranda* is to remain the law.

Whether or not we would agree with *Miranda*'s reasoning and its resulting rule, were we addressing the issue in the first instance, the principles of stare decisis weigh heavily against overruling it now.

We do not think there is such justification for overruling *Miranda*. *Miranda* has become embedded in routine police practice to the point where the warnings have become part of our national culture. While we have overruled our precedents when subsequent cases have undermined their doctrinal underpinnings, we do not believe that this has happened to the *Miranda* decision. If anything, our subsequent cases have reduced the impact of the *Miranda* rule on legitimate law enforcement while reaffirming the decision's core ruling that unwarned statements may not be used as evidence in the prosecution's case in chief.

The disadvantage of the *Miranda* rule is that statements which may be by no means involuntary, made by a defendant who is aware of his "rights," may nonetheless be excluded and a guilty defendant go free as a result. But experience suggests that the totality-of-the-circumstances test which § 3501 seeks to revive is more difficult than *Miranda* for law enforcement officers to conform to, and for courts to apply in a consistent manner. The requirement that *Miranda* warnings be given does not, of course, dispense with the voluntariness inquiry. But as we said in *Berkemer*, "[c]ases in which a defendant can make a colorable argument that a self-incriminating statement was 'compelled' despite the fact that the law enforcement authorities adhered to the dictates of *Miranda* are rare."

In sum, we conclude that *Miranda* announced a constitutional rule that Congress may not supersede legislatively. Following the rule of stare decisis, we decline to overrule *Miranda* ourselves. The judgment of the Court of Appeals is therefore

Reversed.

NOTES AND QUESTIONS

1. The Court does not retreat from any of its previous decisions finding "exceptions" to *Miranda* or failing to treat the decision as if it were a full-blown constitutional right as opposed to a "prophylactic rule"—or even from its acknowledgment in *Elstad* that *Miranda* "sweeps more broadly than the Fifth Amendment itself." Do you understand how the Fourth Circuit could have concluded from these decisions that *Miranda* was not a "constitutional rule"?

The Supreme Court concludes that, notwithstanding these limits on the doctrine, *Miranda* is nonetheless a "constitutional decision." Is the Court's reasoning on this point persuasive?

2. Is the fact that *Miranda* has been held to apply in state court proceedings—that is, that the Court itself has treated *Miranda* as a constitutional rule—dispositive on this issue?

3. If § 3501 had displaced *Miranda*, how much would this have altered the behavior of federal law enforcement agents in the field, given that whether warnings were given is a factor in the statutory voluntariness test?

4. Do you think the outcome in *Dickerson* was attributable in part to the fact-intensive nature of the voluntariness test under § 3501? To the Court's previous experience with the voluntariness test prior to *Miranda*? To the comparative administrative ease of *Miranda* warnings?

5. Should the DOJ's nonenforcement of § 3501 have had any impact on the Court's decision in *Dickerson*? Was the DOJ a reliable proxy for law enforcement generally?

6. What do you make of the Court's comment that *Miranda* warnings "have become part of the national culture"? Does this mean that *Miranda* might have been more vulnerable to being overturned earlier, before it had been incorporated into the zeitgeist?

Indeed, confining *Miranda*'s impact to the "national" culture may be an understatement. Professor Frederick Schauer has observed that on Russian television shows Russian police officers administer *Miranda* warnings to arrestees even though Russian law has no such requirement. Frederick Schauer, *The* Miranda *Warning*, 88 Wash. L. Rev. 155, 155 (2013).

Dickerson seemed to have settled for good *Miranda*'s stability as a Supreme Court precedent. Or maybe not.

Just three years after *Dickerson*, in a civil action under 42 U.S.C. § 1983, a plurality of the Court in an opinion by Justice Thomas embraced a conception of the Fifth Amendment as purely a "trial right." (This view was in rough alignment with Justice Thomas's concurrence ten years later in *Salinas*, where he called for overturning *Griffin v. California*.) In *Chavez v. Martinez*, 538 U.S. 760 (2003), a badly injured man was questioned by police in the hospital without receiving *Miranda* warnings. He was never charged with a crime. The plurality held that he had no claim for a "deprivation of rights" under § 1983 because he was not charged and therefore his statements were not used against him at trial. The decision has been heavily criticized. *See* Tracey Maclin, *The Prophylactic Fifth Amendment*, 97 B.U. L. Rev. 1047, 1059-77 (2017) (arguing, inter alia, that *Chavez* ignores substantial precedent recognizing Fifth Amendment violations where statements were not used against a defendant at trial).

Chavez did not directly involve the constitutionality of *Miranda* but it did reflect a willingness by some members of the Court to think "creatively" about the Fifth Amendment.

A year later, in *United States v. Patane*, 542 U.S. 630 (2004), the implications of *Dickerson* were very much on the table. A DEA agent and a local police officer went to the home of Samuel Patane to investigate tips that he was harassing his ex-girlfriend, despite being under a no-contact restraining order, and that he illegally possessed a .40 Glock pistol. Patane invoked his *Miranda* rights, but the agent continued to question him about the gun and eventually Patane relented and directed the officer to it. Patane was charged with being a felon in possession under 18 U.S.C. § 922(g)(1); the district court granted a motion to suppress the gun; and the Tenth Circuit affirmed, reasoning that the gun was the fruit of the poisonous tree and that *Dickerson*'s holding that *Miranda* was a constitutional rule had essentially overruled *Elstad*'s earlier holding that the "fruits" doctrine was inapplicable to *Miranda* violations.

The Supreme Court, in another plurality opinion, reversed. It found that *Dickerson* did not warrant an extension of *Miranda* to the "fruits" context, and that *Miranda* only requires that a defendant's unwarned statements be inadmissible at trial, not derivative physical evidence. The opinion again invoked the conception of the Fifth Amendment as being only a "trial right," as it had done in *Chavez*.

Justice Souter, joined by Justices Stevens and Ginsburg, worried about the incentives *Patane* would provide to law enforcement. And the incentives that the Court's decisions provide were very much in mind — or at least should have been — given that *Patane* was decided the same day as *Missouri v. Seibert*. Justice Souter wrote: "There is no way to read this case except as an unjustifiable invitation to law enforcement officers to flout *Miranda* when there may be physical evidence to be gained. The incentive is an odd one, coming from the Court on the same day it decides *Missouri v. Seibert, ante*, 542 U.S. 600, 124 S. Ct. 2601. I respectfully dissent."

Although it may have seemed self-explanatory, the next case considers what *Dickerson* meant in holding that *Miranda* was a "constitutional rule." Not that much, it turns out, to a majority of the Court.

Vega v. Tekoh
597 U.S. 134 (2022)

Justice ALITO delivered the opinion of the Court.

This case presents the question whether a plaintiff may sue a police officer under Rev. Stat. § 1979, 42 U.S.C. § 1983, based on the allegedly improper admission of an "un-Mirandized" statement in a criminal prosecution. The case arose out of the interrogation of respondent, Terence Tekoh, by petitioner, Los Angeles County Sheriff's Deputy Carlos Vega. Deputy Vega

G. The Durability of *Miranda*   **203**

questioned Tekoh at his place of employment and did not give him a *Miranda* warning. Tekoh was prosecuted, and his confession was admitted into evidence, but the jury returned a verdict of not guilty. Tekoh then sued Vega under § 1983, and the United States Court of Appeals for the Ninth Circuit held that the use of Tekoh's un-Mirandized statement provided a valid basis for a § 1983 claim against Vega. We now reject this extension of our *Miranda* case law.

I

In March 2014, Tekoh was working as a certified nursing assistant at a Los Angeles medical center. When a female patient accused him of sexually assaulting her, the hospital staff reported the accusation to the Los Angeles County Sheriff's Department, and Deputy Vega responded. Vega questioned Tekoh at length in the hospital, and Tekoh eventually provided a written statement apologizing for inappropriately touching the patient's genitals. The parties dispute whether Vega used coercive investigatory techniques to extract the statement, but it is undisputed that he never informed Tekoh of his rights under *Miranda* which held that during a custodial interrogation police officers must inform a suspect that "he has the right to remain silent, that anything he says can be used against him in a court of law, that he has the right to the presence of an attorney, and that if he cannot afford an attorney one will be appointed for him prior to any questioning."

Tekoh was arrested and charged in California state court with unlawful sexual penetration. At Tekoh's first trial, the judge held that *Miranda* had not been violated because Tekoh was not in custody when he provided the statement, but the trial resulted in a mistrial. When Tekoh was retried, a second judge again denied his request to exclude the confession. This trial resulted in acquittal, and Tekoh then brought this action under 42 U.S.C. § 1983 against Vega and several other defendants seeking damages for alleged violations of his constitutional rights, including his Fifth Amendment right against compelled self-incrimination.

When this § 1983 case was first tried, the jury returned a verdict in favor of Vega, but the judge concluded that he had given an improper jury instruction and thus granted a new trial. Before the second trial, Tekoh asked the court to instruct the jury that it was required to find that Vega violated the Fifth Amendment right against compelled self-incrimination if it determined that he took a statement from Tekoh in violation of *Miranda* and that the statement was then improperly used against Tekoh at his criminal trial. The District Court declined, reasoning that *Miranda* established a prophylactic rule and that such a rule could not alone provide a ground for § 1983 liability. Instead, the jury was asked to decide whether Tekoh's Fifth Amendment right had been violated. The court instructed the jury to determine, based on "the totality of all the surrounding circumstances," whether Tekoh's statement had been "improperly coerced or compelled," and the court explained that "[a] confession is improperly coerced or compelled . . . if a police officer uses physical or psychological force or threats not permitted by law to undermine a person's ability to exercise his or her free will." The jury found in Vega's favor, and Tekoh appealed.

A Ninth Circuit panel reversed, holding that the "use of an un-Mirandized statement against a defendant in a criminal proceeding violates the Fifth Amendment and may support a § 1983 claim" against the officer who obtained the statement. The panel acknowledged that this Court has repeatedly said that *Miranda* adopted prophylactic rules designed to protect against constitutional violations and that the decision did not hold that the contravention of those rules necessarily constitutes a constitutional violation. But the panel thought that our decision in *Dickerson* "made clear that the right of a criminal defendant against having an un-Mirandized statement introduced in the prosecution's case in chief is indeed a right secured by the Constitution." Therefore the panel concluded that Tekoh could establish a violation of his Fifth Amendment right against compelled self-incrimination simply by showing that *Miranda* had been violated. The panel thus remanded the case for a new trial.

II

Section 1983 provides a cause of action against any person acting under color of state law who "subjects" a person or "causes [a person] to be subjected . . . to the deprivation of any rights, privileges, or immunities secured by the Constitution and laws." The question we must decide is whether a violation of the *Miranda* rules provides a basis for a claim under § 1983. We hold that it does not.

A

If a *Miranda* violation were tantamount to a violation of the Fifth Amendment, our answer would of course be different. The Fifth Amendment, made applicable to the States by the Fourteenth Amendment, *Malloy v. Hogan* (1964), provides that "[n]o person . . . shall be compelled in any criminal case to be a witness against himself." This Clause "permits a person to refuse to testify against himself at a criminal trial in which he is a defendant" and "also 'privileges him not to answer official questions put to him in any other proceeding, civil or criminal, formal or informal, where the answers might incriminate him in future criminal proceedings.'" In addition, the right bars the introduction against a criminal defendant of out-of-court statements obtained by compulsion.

In *Miranda*, the Court concluded that additional procedural protections were necessary to prevent the violation of this important right when suspects who are in custody are interrogated by the police. To afford this protection, the Court required that custodial interrogation be preceded by the now-familiar warnings mentioned above, and it directed that statements obtained in violation of these new rules may not be used by the prosecution in its case-in-chief.

In this case, the Ninth Circuit held—and Tekoh now argues—that a violation of *Miranda* constitutes a violation of the Fifth Amendment right against compelled self-incrimination, but that is wrong. *Miranda* itself and our subsequent cases make clear that *Miranda* imposed a set of prophylactic rules. Those rules, to be sure, are "constitutionally based," *Dickerson*, but they are prophylactic rules nonetheless.

B

Miranda itself was clear on this point. *Miranda* did not hold that a violation of the rules it established necessarily constitute a Fifth Amendment violation, and it is difficult to see how it could have held otherwise. For one thing, it is easy to imagine many situations in which an un-Mirandized suspect in custody may make self-incriminating statements without any hint of compulsion. In addition, the warnings that the Court required included components, such as notification of the right to have retained or appointed counsel present during questioning, that do not concern self-incrimination per se but are instead plainly designed to safeguard that right. And the same is true of *Miranda*'s detailed rules about the waiver of the right to remain silent and the right to an attorney.

At no point in the opinion did the Court state that a violation of its new rules constituted a violation of the Fifth Amendment right against compelled self-incrimination. Instead, it claimed only that those rules were needed to safeguard that right during custodial interrogation.

In accordance with this understanding of the nature of the rules it imposed, the *Miranda* Court stated quite clearly that the Constitution did not itself require "adherence to any particular solution for the inherent compulsions of the interrogation process" and that its decision "in no way create[d] a constitutional straitjacket." The opinion added that its new rules might not be needed if Congress or the States adopted "other procedures which are at least as effective," and the opinion suggested that there might not have been any actual Fifth Amendment violations in the four cases that were before the Court. The Court could not have said any of these things if a violation of the *Miranda* rules necessarily constituted a violation of the Fifth Amendment.

Since *Miranda*, the Court has repeatedly described the rules it adopted as "prophylactic."

C

After *Miranda* was handed down, the Court engaged in the process of charting the dimensions of these new prophylactic rules. As we would later spell out, this process entailed a weighing of the benefits and costs of any clarification of the rules' scope.

Some post-*Miranda* decisions found that the balance of interests justified restrictions that would not have been possible if *Miranda* represented an explanation of the meaning of the Fifth Amendment right as opposed to a set of rules designed to protect that right. For example, in *Harris v. New York*, the Court held that a statement obtained in violation of *Miranda* could be used to impeach the testimony of a defendant, even though an involuntary statement obtained in violation of the Fifth Amendment could not have been employed in this way. Engaging in the process we described in *Shatzer*, the *Harris* Court considered the benefits of forbidding impeachment but dismissed "the speculative possibility" that this would discourage "impermissible police conduct," and on the other side of the scale, it feared that barring impeachment would turn *Miranda* into "a license to use perjury by way of a defense."

A similar analysis was used in *Michigan v. Tucker*, where the Court held that the "fruits" of an un-Mirandized statement can be admitted. The Court noted that "the 'fruits' of police conduct which actually infringe[s]" a defendant's constitutional rights must be suppressed. Because there had been only a *Miranda* violation in that case, the *Wong Sun* rule of automatic exclusion was found to be inapplicable. Instead, the Court asked whether the *Miranda* rules' prophylactic purposes justified the exclusion of the fruits of the violation, and after "balancing the interests involved," it held that exclusion was not required.

In *New York v. Quarles*, the Court held that statements obtained in violation of *Miranda* need not be suppressed when the questioning is conducted to address an ongoing "public safety" concern.

Finally, in *Elstad*, the Court again distinguished between a constitutional violation and a violation of *Miranda*. In that case, a suspect in custody was initially questioned without receiving a *Miranda* warning, and the statements made at that time were suppressed. But the suspect was later given *Miranda* warnings, chose to waive his *Miranda* rights, and signed a written confession. Asked to decide whether this confession was admissible, the Court followed the reasoning in *Tucker* and again held that the fruit-of-the-poisonous-tree rule that applies to constitutional violations does not apply to violations of *Miranda*. The Court refused to exclude the signed confession and emphasized that an officer's error "in administering the prophylactic *Miranda* procedures . . . should not breed the same irremediable consequences as police infringement of the Fifth Amendment itself."

It is hard to see how these decisions could stand if a violation of *Miranda* constituted a violation of the Fifth Amendment.

D

While these decisions imposed limits on *Miranda*'s prophylactic rules, other decisions found that the balance of interests called for expansion. . . .

• • •

Thus, all the post-*Miranda* cases we have discussed acknowledged the prophylactic nature of the *Miranda* rules and engaged in cost-benefit analysis to define the scope of these prophylactic rules.

E

Contrary to the decision below and Tekoh's argument here, our decision in *Dickerson* did not upset the firmly established prior understanding of *Miranda* as a prophylactic decision. *Dickerson* involved a federal statute, 18 U.S.C. § 3501, that effectively overruled *Miranda* by making the admissibility of a statement given during custodial interrogation turn solely on whether it was made voluntarily. The Court held that Congress could not abrogate *Miranda* by statute because *Miranda* was a "constitutional decision" that adopted a "constitutional rule," and the Court noted that these rules could not have been made applicable to the States if it did not have that status.

At the same time, however, the Court made it clear that it was not equating a violation of the *Miranda* rules with an outright Fifth Amendment violation. For one thing, it reiterated *Miranda*'s observation that "the Constitution would not preclude legislative solutions that differed from the prescribed *Miranda* warnings but which were 'at least as effective in apprising accused persons'" of their rights.

Even more to the point, the Court rejected the dissent's argument that § 3501 could not be held unconstitutional unless "*Miranda* warnings are required by the Constitution, in the sense that nothing else will suffice to satisfy constitutional requirements." The Court's answer, in substance, was that the *Miranda* rules, though not an explication of the meaning of the Fifth Amendment right, are rules that are necessary to protect that right (at least until a better alternative is found and adopted). Thus, in the words of the *Dickerson* Court, the *Miranda* rules are "constitutionally based" and have "constitutional underpinnings." But the obvious point of these formulations was to avoid saying that a *Miranda* violation is the same as a violation of the Fifth Amendment right.

What all this boils down to is basically as follows. The *Miranda* rules are prophylactic rules that the Court found to be necessary to protect the Fifth Amendment right against compelled self-incrimination. In that sense, *Miranda* was a "constitutional decision" and it adopted a "constitutional rule" because the decision was based on the Court's judgment about what is required to safeguard that constitutional right. And when the Court adopts a constitutional prophylactic rule of this nature, *Dickerson* concluded, the rule has the status of a "La[w] of the United States" that is binding on the States under the Supremacy Clause (as *Miranda* implicitly held, since three of the four decisions it reversed came from state court), and the rule cannot be altered by ordinary legislation.

This was a bold and controversial claim of authority, but we do not think that *Dickerson* can be understood any other way without (1) taking the insupportable position that a *Miranda* violation is tantamount to a violation of the Fifth Amendment, (2) calling into question the prior decisions that were predicated on the proposition that a *Miranda* violation is not the same as a constitutional violation, and (3) excising from the United States Reports a mountain of statements describing the *Miranda* rules as prophylactic.

Subsequent cases confirm that *Dickerson* did not upend the Court's understanding of the *Miranda* rules as prophylactic.

In sum, a violation of *Miranda* does not necessarily constitute a violation of the Constitution, and therefore such a violation does not constitute "the deprivation of [a] right . . . secured by the Constitution." 42 U.S.C. § 1983.

III

This conclusion does not necessarily dictate reversal because a § 1983 claim may also be based on "the deprivation of any rights, privileges, or immunities secured by the . . . *laws*." (Emphasis added.) It may thus be argued that the *Miranda* rules constitute federal "law" and that an abridgment of those rules can therefore provide the ground for a § 1983 claim. But whatever

G. The Durability of *Miranda*   **207**

else may be said about this argument, it cannot succeed unless Tekoh can persuade us that this "law" should be expanded to include the right to sue for damages under § 1983.

As we have noted, "[a] judicially crafted" prophylactic rule should apply "only where its benefits outweigh its costs," and here, while the benefits of permitting the assertion of *Miranda* claims under § 1983 would be slight, the costs would be substantial.

Miranda rests on a pragmatic judgment about what is needed to stop the violation at trial of the Fifth Amendment right against compelled self-incrimination. That prophylactic purpose is served by the suppression at trial of statements obtained in violation of *Miranda* and by the application of that decision in other recognized contexts. Allowing the victim of a *Miranda* violation to sue a police officer for damages under § 1983 would have little additional deterrent value, and permitting such claims would cause many problems.

Allowing a claim like Tekoh's would disserve "judicial economy," by requiring a federal judge or jury to adjudicate a factual question (whether Tekoh was in custody when questioned) that had already been decided by a state court. This re-adjudication would not only be wasteful; it would undercut the "'strong judicial policy against the creation of two conflicting resolutions'" based on the same set of facts. And it could produce "unnecessary friction" between the federal and state court systems by requiring the federal court entertaining the § 1983 claim to pass judgment on legal and factual issues already settled in state court.

Allowing § 1983 suits based on *Miranda* claims could also present many procedural issues, such as whether a federal court considering a § 1983 claim would owe any deference to a trial court's factual findings; whether forfeiture and plain error rules carry over from the criminal trial; whether harmless-error rules apply; and whether civil damages are available in instances where the unwarned statement had no impact on the outcome of the criminal case.

We therefore refuse to extend *Miranda* in the way Tekoh requests. *Miranda, Dickerson,* and the other cases in that line provide sufficient protection for the Fifth Amendment right against compelled self-incrimination. "The identification of a *Miranda* violation and its consequences . . . ought to be determined at trial." *Chavez v. Martinez* (2003). And except in unusual circumstances, the "exclusion of unwarned statements" should be "a complete and sufficient remedy."

• • •

Because a violation of *Miranda* is not itself a violation of the Fifth Amendment, and because we see no justification for expanding *Miranda* to confer a right to sue under § 1983, the judgment of the Court of Appeals is reversed, and the case is remanded for further proceedings consistent with this opinion.

It is so ordered.

Justice KAGAN, with whom Justice BREYER and Justice SOTOMAYOR join, dissenting.

The Court's decision in *Miranda* affords well-known protections to suspects who are interrogated by police while in custody. Those protections derive from the Constitution: *Dickerson* tells us in no uncertain terms that *Miranda* is a "constitutional rule." And that rule grants a corresponding right: If police fail to provide the *Miranda* warnings to a suspect before interrogating him, then he is generally entitled to have any resulting confession excluded from his trial. From those facts, only one conclusion can follow—that *Miranda*'s protections are a "right[ ]" "secured by the Constitution" under the federal civil rights statute. 42 U.S.C. § 1983. Yet the Court today says otherwise. It holds that *Miranda* is not a constitutional right enforceable through a § 1983 suit. And so it prevents individuals from obtaining any redress when police violate their rights under *Miranda*. I respectfully dissent.

Miranda responded to problems stemming from the interrogation of suspects "incommunicado" and "in a police-dominated atmosphere." In such an environment, *Miranda* said, there are "pressures" which may "compel [a suspect] to speak where he would not otherwise do so freely." And so *Miranda* found a "necessity for procedures which assure that the individual is accorded his" Fifth Amendment privilege "not to be compelled to incriminate himself." *Miranda* set out protocols (including the now-familiar warnings) that would safeguard the constitutional privilege against self-incrimination. And *Miranda* held that if police failed to follow those requirements (without substituting equally effective ones), the prosecution could not use at trial a statement obtained from the interrogation.

The question in this case is whether *Miranda*'s protections are a "right[ ]" that is "secured by the Constitution" within the meaning of § 1983. If the answer is yes, then a person may sue a state actor who deprives him of the right. In past cases, the Court has given a broad construction to § 1983's broad language. Under § 1983 (as elsewhere), a "right[ ]" is anything that creates specific "obligations binding on [a] governmental unit" that an individual may ask the judiciary to enforce. And the phrase "secured by the Constitution" also has a capacious meaning. It refers to any right that is "protect[ed] or ma[de] certain" by the country's foundational charter.

Begin with whether *Miranda* is "secured by the Constitution." We know that it is, because the Court's decision in *Dickerson* says so. *Dickerson* tells us again and again that *Miranda* is a "constitutional rule." It is a "constitutional decision" that sets forth "'concrete constitutional guidelines.'" *Miranda* "is constitutionally based"; or again, it has a "constitutional basis." It is "of constitutional origin"; it has "constitutional underpinnings." And—one more—*Miranda* sets a "constitutional minimum." Over and over, *Dickerson* labels *Miranda* a rule stemming from the Constitution.

Dickerson also makes plain that *Miranda* has all the substance of a constitutional rule—including that it cannot be "abrogate[d]" by any "legislation. In *Dickerson*, the Court considered a federal statute whose obvious purpose was to override *Miranda*. *Dickerson* held that *Miranda* is a "constitutional decision" that cannot be "overruled by" any "Act of Congress." To be sure, Congress may devise "legislative solutions that differ[ ] from the prescribed *Miranda* warnings," but only if those solutions are "'at least as effective.'" *Dickerson* therefore instructs (as noted above) that *Miranda* sets a "constitutional minimum." No statute may provide lesser protection than that baseline.

And *Dickerson* makes clear that the constitutional substance of *Miranda* does not end there. Rules arising from "the United States Constitution" are applicable in state-court proceedings, but non-constitutional rules are not. Too, constitutional rules are enforceable in federal-court habeas proceedings, where a prisoner is entitled to claim he "is in custody in violation of the Constitution." 28 U.S.C. § 2254(a). *Miranda* checks both boxes. The Court has "consistently applied *Miranda*'s rule to prosecutions arising in state courts." And prisoners may claim *Miranda* violations in federal-court habeas proceedings. So *Dickerson* is unequivocal: *Miranda* is set in constitutional stone.

Miranda's constitutional rule gives suspects a correlative "right[ ]." § 1983. Under *Miranda*, a suspect typically has a right to be tried without the prosecutor using his un-Mirandized statement. And we know how that right operates in the real world. Suppose a defendant standing trial was able to show the court that he gave an un-Mirandized confession during a custodial interrogation. The court would have no choice but to exclude it from the prosecutor's case. As one judge below put it: "*Miranda* indisputably creates individual legal rights that are judicially enforceable."

The majority basically agrees with everything I've just explained. It concurs that, per *Dickerson*, *Miranda* "adopted a 'constitutional rule.'" How could it not? That *Miranda* is a constitutional rule is what *Dickerson* said (and said and said). The majority also agrees that *Miranda* "directed that statements obtained in violation of [its] rules may not be used by the prosecution in its case-in-chief"—which is simply another way of saying that *Miranda* grants suspects a right to the exclusion of those statements from the prosecutor's case.

So how does the majority hold that a violation of *Miranda* is not a "deprivation of [a] right[ ]" "secured by the Constitution"? § 1983. How does it agree with my premises, but not my conclusion? The majority's argument is that "a violation of *Miranda* does not necessarily constitute a violation of the Constitution," because *Miranda*'s rules are "prophylactic." The idea is that the Fifth Amendment prohibits the use only of statements obtained by compulsion, whereas *Miranda* excludes non-compelled statements too. That is why, the majority says, the Court has been able to recognize exceptions permitting certain uses of un-Mirandized statements at trial (when it could not do so for compelled statements).

But none of that helps the majority's case. Let's assume, as the majority says, that *Miranda* extends beyond — in order to safeguard — the Fifth Amendment's core guarantee. Still, *Miranda* is enforceable through § 1983. It remains a constitutional rule, as *Dickerson* held (and the majority agrees). And it grants the defendant a legally enforceable entitlement — in a word, a right — to have his confession excluded. So, to refer back to the language of § 1983, *Miranda* grants a "right[ ]" "secured by the Constitution." Whether that right to have evidence excluded safeguards a yet deeper constitutional commitment makes no difference to § 1983. The majority has no response to that point — except to repeat what our argument assumes already.

Compare the majority's holding today to a prior decision, in which the Court "rejected [an] attempt[ ] to limit the types of constitutional rights that are encompassed within" § 1983. There, the Court held that a plaintiff could sue under § 1983 for a violation of the so-called dormant Commerce Clause, which safeguards interstate commerce. To the Court, it did not matter that the Commerce Clause might be viewed as "merely allocat[ing] power between the Federal and State Governments" over interstate commerce, rather than as "confer[ring] 'rights.'" Nor did it matter that the dormant Commerce Clause's protection is only "implied" by the constitutional text. The dormant Commerce Clause, the Court said, still provides a "right" — in the "ordinary" sense of being "'[a] legally enforceable claim of one person against another.'" That describes *Miranda* to a tee. And if a right implied from Congress's constitutional authority over interstate commerce is enforceable under § 1983, how could it be that *Miranda* — which the Court has found necessary to safeguard the personal protections of the Fifth Amendment — is not also enforceable? The majority again has no answer.

* * *

Today, the Court strips individuals of the ability to seek a remedy for violations of the right recognized in *Miranda*. The majority observes that defendants may still seek "the suppression at trial of statements obtained" in violation of *Miranda*'s procedures. But sometimes, such a statement will not be suppressed. And sometimes, as a result, a defendant will be wrongly convicted and spend years in prison. He may succeed, on appeal or in habeas, in getting the conviction reversed. But then, what remedy does he have for all the harm he has suffered? The point of § 1983 is to provide such redress — because a remedy "is a vital component of any scheme for vindicating cherished constitutional guarantees." The majority here, as elsewhere, injures the right by denying the remedy. *See, e.g., Egbert v. Boule* (2022). I respectfully dissent.

NOTES AND QUESTIONS

1. For a closer look at 42 U.S.C. § 1983, and in particular its use in remedying police misconduct such as that alleged to have been committed by Officer Vega, *see* Chapter VI *infra*.

2. The Court labels as "a bold and controversial claim" the holding of a case that was 23 years old and decided by a vote of 7-2. As support for this point the Court cites in a footnote the dissenting opinion in *Dickerson* and the titles of three law review articles (from the 1970s and 1980s) that appear to represent a "debate" about the "authority" of the Supreme Court to make prophylactic rules. Didn't *Dickerson* settle this "debate"? Didn't *Miranda* itself settle this debate?

3. The language of § 1983 is simple. The pertinent part provides:

> Every person who, under color of any statute, ordinance, regulation, custom, or usage, of any State or Territory or the District of Columbia, subjects, or causes to be subjected, any citizen of the United States or other person within the jurisdiction thereof to the deprivation of any rights, privileges, or immunities secured by the *Constitution and laws*, shall be liable . . .

Note how the Court carves up its presentation of § 1983's language in order to advance its position that alleging a deprivation of a right secured by "law" as opposed to "the Constitution" is some sort of an exotic vehicle for recovery under § 1983.

Is there any doubt that *Miranda* is "law"? Why isn't that the end of the inquiry?

4. Even if *Miranda* was "merely a prophylactic rule," wasn't the cost-benefit analysis the Court proceeds to do in determining whether a violation would be redressable under § 1983 already done by Congress in including the word "law" without qualification in the statute?

5. A federal criminal statute, 18 U.S.C. § 242, enacted by the same Reconstruction-era Congress that passed the original version of § 1983, contains similar language:

> Whoever, under color of any law, statute, ordinance, regulation, or custom, willfully subjects any person in any State, Territory, Commonwealth, Possession, or District to the deprivation of any rights, privileges, or immunities secured or protected by the Constitution or laws of the United States . . . shall be [punished].

Might the current Court similarly interpret the term "law" in this criminal statute to not include *Miranda* violations based on its own cost-benefit analysis? Is the same cost-benefit analysis that was done in *Tekoh* equally applicable to § 242? *See* Chapter X *infra*.

6. The Court says that "allowing a claim like Tekoh's would disserve "judicial economy . . . by requiring a federal judge or jury to adjudicate a factual question (whether Tekoh was in custody when questioned) that had already been decided by a state court." Isn't this true of many (or all) § 1983 actions? For example, in an action based on an allegedly illegal search, wouldn't the federal court have to independently determine whether the search was unconstitutional?

Recall that in *Chavez* the plurality held there was no § 1983 claim precisely because the plaintiff's statements had *not* been offered previously in court.

CHAPTER IV

THE FOURTH AMENDMENT

Section A of this chapter examines how the Supreme Court has determined what constitutes a search for Fourth Amendment purposes, a journey that is as much about technology—wiretaps, beepers, pen registers, thermal imaging, GPS devices, cellphones—as legal doctrine. Section B looks at the law regarding search's sister, seizure, with a particular focus on how race has been considered in this context. Section C examines the warrant "requirement" and its many exceptions: plain view, warrantless arrests, searches incident to arrest, consent searches, exigent circumstances, administrative or "special need" searches, and the automobile exception. Section D looks at another exception—the *Terry* doctrine and its elimination of a probable cause requirement for a search or seizure. Section E focuses on race and suspicion, with particular emphasis on the racial origin and impact of *Terry*, racial profiling, and traffic stops.

A. WHAT IS A SEARCH FOR FOURTH AMENDMENT PURPOSES?

Much of the Court's analysis of whether a particular government intrusion amounts to a "search" for Fourth Amendment purposes is, even today, governed at least in part by the "reasonable expectation of privacy" test that is attributable to *Katz v. United States*, 389 U.S. 347 (1967). But *Katz* must be understood against the backdrop of the decision it overruled, *Olmstead v. United* States, 277 U.S. 438, 455-56 (1928), and the government's investigative excesses of the Prohibition era.

Roy Olmstead was a Seattle policeman who dabbled in smuggling liquor into the country from Canada during Prohibition. After he was caught and fired from the police force, he became a full-time and hugely successful rum-runner. His bootlegging empire included fleets of cars, ships, motorboats, and dozens of employees and associates, not counting his former police force colleagues whom he bribed generously. Federal Prohibition agents in Seattle were atypically, let's say, aggressive. They not only cared about detecting and prosecuting violations of Prohibition laws, unlike many of their fellow agents, but were willing to be creative. Although the Treasury Department, the agents' employer, prohibited wiretapping, as did Washington state law and the FBI under Attorney General (later Justice) Harlan Fiske Stone, the agents nonetheless tapped into several phone lines used by Olmstead and his associates. They listened for months. Based on the evidence obtained from these wiretaps Olmstead and his codefendants were convicted in federal court of violations of the Volstead Act. *See* Daniel Okrent, Last Call: The Rise and Fall of Prohibition 284-86 (2010).

The Supreme Court rejected Olmstead's Fourth Amendment challenge for the simple reason that there was no violation of Olmstead's property rights and therefore no "search": "There was no entry of the houses or offices of the defendants." *Olmstead*, 277 U.S. at 464. Justice Brandeis famously dissented. He found the lack of a property right "immaterial." *Id.* at 479. The Founders, he claimed, conferred, as against the government, the right to be let alone—the most comprehensive of rights and the right most valued by civilized men. To protect, that right, every unjustifiable intrusion by the government upon the privacy of the individual, whatever the means employed, must be deemed a violation of the Fourth Amendment.

Id. at 478. Justice Brandeis also warned that "[t]he progress of science in furnishing the government with means of espionage is not likely to stop with wire tapping. Ways may some day be developed by which the government, without removing papers from secret drawers, can reproduce them in court. . . ." *Id.* at 473-74.

A less well-known aspect of the dissent was Justice Brandeis's denunciation of the Justice Department, which he asserted had assumed "moral responsibility" for the Prohibition agents' illegal wiretapping by using its fruits in a federal prosecution.

Elise and Roy Olmstead, Seattle, 1925

That is more or less where things stood doctrinally until the 1960s. On the one hand, the Court after *Olmstead* expressed criticism of the ethics of wiretapping in considering the government's use of intercepted communications in the prosecutions of another bootlegger, Frank Nardone, and reversed his convictions by interpreting a statute prohibiting "divulging" such communications as a bar to admissibility. *United States v. Nardone*, 302 U.S. 379, 382 (1937) (reversing conviction and finding intercepted statements inadmissible); *United States v. Nardone*, 308 U.S. 338, 340-43 (1939) (reversing retrial conviction for use of evidence derived from intercepted communications). On the other hand, the Court refused to find a Fourth Amendment violation where agents used a "detectaphone," a device that amplified sound waves, which agents used to eavesdrop from an adjacent room on statements made by the target on the telephone, relying on the "trespass" principle of *Olmstead*. *Goldman v. United States*, 316 U.S. 129 (1942).

Two cases in the 1960s set the stage for *Katz*. In *Silverman v. United States*, 365 U.S. 505 (1961), the Court found a Fourth Amendment search where agents inserted a "spike mike" into a shared wall in the defendants' rowhouse in order to eavesdrop on conversations. *Id.* at 506-07. The Court found this "encroachment" to be a Fourth Amendment search even though there had been no "technical trespass under . . . local property law." *Id.* at 511. And shortly before *Katz* was decided, the Court issued its decision in *Berger v. New York*, 388 U.S. 41 (1967), striking down on Fourth Amendment grounds a New York statute that authorized judges to issue warrants to law enforcement agents for bugging or wiretapping. The opinion for the Court held that the warrants lacked probable cause to be issued, were insufficiently particular, had no time limit, and did not have a means for providing notice to the targets. *Id.* at 55-63. The many opinions in *Berger* left it unclear how many Justices believed that electronic eavesdropping could ever satisfy the Fourth Amendment warrant requirement.

In the next handful of cases the Court considers whether law enforcement use of some sort of technology, in the broadest sense of the term, constitutes a "search" under the Fourth Amendment. In none of these cases did the government have a search warrant, which it could have obtained if it had been able to persuade a magistrate or judge that it had probable cause to believe criminal activity was afoot and it could have drawn up a sufficiently particularized warrant describing what and where it wanted to search. Ask yourself as you read these cases, why did the police or agents not get a warrant? There are usually three possible explanations: They could not satisfy the warrant requirements. They didn't want to bother with a warrant. They had already tried to get a warrant and failed.

Consider also in these cases, as the Court roots the Fourth Amendment in the protection of "privacy," what privacy can mean in these varied contexts. Does privacy mean secrecy? Does privacy mean, if not absolute secrecy, at least control over who has access to personal information? Do people "assume the risk"—and reasonably so—of compromising their privacy by sharing information with some third parties?

Katz v. United States
389 U.S. 347 (1967)

Mr. Justice STEWART delivered the opinion of the Court.

The petitioner was convicted in the District Court for the Southern District of California under an eight-count indictment charging him with transmitting wagering information by telephone from Los Angeles to Miami and Boston in violation of a federal statute. At trial the Government was permitted, over the petitioner's objection, to introduce evidence of the petitioner's end of telephone conversation, overheard by FBI agents who had attached an electronic listening and recording device to the outside of the public telephone booth from which he had placed his calls. In affirming his conviction, the Court of Appeals rejected the contention that the recordings had been obtained in violation of the Fourth Amendment, because "(t)here was no physical entrance into the area occupied by (the petitioner)." We granted certiorari in order to consider the constitutional questions thus presented.

The petitioner had phrased those questions as follows:

A. Whether a public telephone booth is a constitutionally protected area so that evidence obtained by attaching an electronic listening recording device to the top of such a booth is obtained in violation of the right to privacy of the user of the booth.

B. Whether physical penetration of a constitutionally protected area is necessary before a search and seizure can be said to be violative of the Fourth Amendment to the United States Constitution.

We decline to adopt this formulation of the issues. In the first place the correct solution of Fourth Amendment problems is not necessarily promoted by incantation of the phrase "constitutionally protected area." Secondly, the Fourth Amendment cannot be translated into a general constitutional "right to privacy." That Amendment protects individual privacy against certain kinds of governmental intrusion, but its protections go further, and often have nothing to do with privacy at all. Other provisions of the Constitution protect personal privacy from other forms of governmental invasion. But the protection of a person's general right to privacy—his right to be let alone by other people—is, like the protection of his property and of his very life, left largely to the law of the individual States.

Because of the misleading way the issues have been formulated, the parties have attached great significance to the characterization of the telephone booth from which the petitioner placed his calls. The petitioner has strenuously argued that the booth was a "constitutionally protected area." The Government has maintained with equal vigor that it was not. But this effort to decide whether or not a given "area," viewed in the abstract, is "constitutionally protected" deflects attention from the problem presented by this case. For the Fourth Amendment protects people, not places. What a person knowingly exposes to the public, even in his own home or office, is not a subject of Fourth Amendment protection. But what he seeks to preserve as private, even in an area accessible to the public, may be constitutionally protected.

The Government stresses the fact that the telephone booth from which the petitioner made his calls was constructed partly of glass, so that he was as visible after he entered it as he would have been if he had remained outside. But what he sought to exclude when he entered the booth was not the intruding eye—it was the uninvited ear. He did not shed his right to do so simply because he made his calls from a place where he might be seen. No less than an individual in a business office, in a friend's apartment, or in a taxicab, a person in a telephone booth may rely upon the protection of the Fourth Amendment. One who occupies it, shuts the door behind him, and pays the toll that permits him to place a call is surely entitled to assume that the words he utters into the mouthpiece will not be broadcast to the world. To read the Constitution more narrowly is to ignore the vital role that the public telephone has come to play in private communication.

The Government contends, however, that the activities of its agents in this case should not be tested by Fourth Amendment requirements, for the surveillance technique they employed involved no physical penetration of the telephone booth from which the petitioner placed his calls. It is true that the absence of such penetration was at one time thought to foreclose further Fourth Amendment inquiry, for that Amendment was thought to limit only searches and seizures of tangible property. But "(t)he premise that property interests control the right of the Government to search and seize has been discredited." Thus, although a closely divided Court supposed in *Olmstead* that surveillance without any trespass and without the seizure of any material object fell outside the ambit of the Constitution, we have since departed from the narrow view on which that decision rested. Indeed, we have expressly held that the Fourth Amendment governs not only the seizure of tangible items, but extends as well to the recording of oral statements overheard without any "technical trespass under . . . local property law." Once this much is acknowledged, and once it is recognized that the Fourth Amendment protects people—and not simply "areas"—against unreasonable searches and seizures it becomes clear that the reach of that Amendment cannot turn upon the presence or absence of a physical intrusion into any given enclosure.

We conclude that the underpinnings of *Olmstead* and *Goldman* have been so eroded by our subsequent decisions that the "trespass" doctrine there enunciated can no longer be regarded as controlling. The Government's activities in electronically listening to and recording the petitioner's words violated the privacy upon which he justifiably relied while using the telephone booth and thus constituted a "search and seizure" within the meaning of the Fourth Amendment. The fact that the electronic device employed to achieve that end did not happen to penetrate the wall of the booth can have no constitutional significance.

The question remaining for decision, then, is whether the search and seizure conducted in this case complied with constitutional standards. In that regard, the Government's position is that its agents acted in an entirely defensible manner: They did not begin their electronic surveillance until investigation of the petitioner's activities had established a strong probability that he was using the telephone in question to transmit gambling information to persons in other States, in violation of federal law. Moreover, the surveillance was limited, both in scope and in duration, to the specific purpose of establishing the contents of the petitioner's unlawful telephonic communications. The agents confined their surveillance to the brief periods during which he used the telephone booth, and they took great care to overhear only the conversations of the petitioner himself.

Accepting this account of the Government's actions as accurate, it is clear that this surveillance was so narrowly circumscribed that a duly authorized magistrate, properly notified of the need for such investigation, specifically informed of the basis on which it was to proceed, and clearly apprised of the precise intrusion it would entail, could constitutionally have authorized, with appropriate safeguards, the very limited search and seizure that the Government asserts in fact took place. Only last Term we sustained the validity of such an authorization, holding that, under sufficiently "precise and discriminate circumstances," a federal court may empower government agents to employ a concealed electronic device "for the narrow and particularized purpose of ascertaining the truth of the . . . allegations" of a "detailed factual affidavit alleging the commission of a specific criminal offense." Discussing that holding, the Court in *Berger v. State of New York*, said that "the order authorizing the use of the electronic device" in *Osborn* "afforded similar protections to those . . . of conventional warrants authorizing the seizure of tangible evidence." Through those protections, "no greater invasion of privacy was permitted than was necessary under the circumstances." Here, too, a similar judicial order could have accommodated "the legitimate needs of law enforcement" by authorizing the carefully limited use of electronic surveillance.

The Government urges that, because its agents relied upon the decisions in *Olmstead* and *Goldman*, and because they did no more here than they might properly have done with prior judicial sanction, we should retroactively validate their conduct. That we cannot do. It is apparent that the agents in this case acted with restraint. Yet the inescapable fact is that this restraint was imposed by the agents themselves, not by a judicial officer. They were not required, before commencing the search, to present their estimate of probable cause for detached scrutiny by a neutral magistrate. They were not compelled, during the conduct of the search itself, to observe precise limits established in advance by a specific court order. Nor were they directed, after the search had been completed, to notify the authorizing magistrate in detail of all that had been seized. In the absence of such safeguards, this Court has never sustained a search upon the sole ground that officers reasonably expected to find evidence of a particular crime and voluntarily confined their activities to the least intrusive means consistent with that end. Searches conducted without warrants have been held unlawful "notwithstanding facts unquestionably showing probable cause," for the Constitution requires "that the deliberate, impartial judgment of a judicial officer . . . be interposed between the citizen and the police. . . ." "Over and over again this Court has emphasized that the mandate of the (Fourth) Amendment requires adherence to judicial processes," and that searches conducted outside the judicial process, without prior approval by judge or magistrate, are per se unreasonable under the Fourth Amendment — subject only to a few specifically established and well-delineated exceptions.

It is difficult to imagine how any of those exceptions could ever apply to the sort of search and seizure involved in this case. Even electronic surveillance substantially contemporaneous with an individual's arrest could hardly be deemed an "incident" of that arrest. Nor could the use of electronic surveillance without prior authorization be justified on grounds of "hot pursuit." And, of course, the very nature of electronic surveillance precludes its use pursuant to the suspect's consent.

The Government does not question these basic principles. Rather, it urges the creation of a new exception to cover this case. It argues that surveillance of a telephone booth should be exempted from the usual requirement of advance authorization by a magistrate upon a showing of probable cause. We cannot agree. Omission of such authorization

> bypasses the safeguards provided by an objective predetermination of probable cause, and substitutes instead the far less reliable procedure of an after-the-event justification for the . . . search, too likely to be subtly influenced by the familiar shortcomings of hindsight judgment.

And bypassing a neutral predetermination of the scope of a search leaves individuals secure from Fourth Amendment violations "only in the discretion of the police."

These considerations do not vanish when the search in question is transferred from the setting of a home, an office, or a hotel room to that of a telephone booth. Wherever a man may be, he is entitled to know that he will remain free from unreasonable searches and seizures. The government agents here ignored "the procedure of antecedent justification . . . that is central to the Fourth Amendment," a procedure that we hold to be a constitutional precondition of the kind of electronic surveillance involved in this case. Because the surveillance here failed to meet that condition, and because it led to the petitioner's conviction, the judgment must be reversed.

NOTES AND QUESTIONS

1. The Court firmly denounces the framing of the Fourth Amendment issue in terms of property interests. No more "trespass." No more "constitutionally protected area." Because, we are told, the Fourth Amendment "protects people not places." But doesn't where the people are, and what they are doing, bear on what protection the Fourth Amendment provides?

Even in *Katz* itself, weren't the physical characteristics of a phone booth relevant to the outcome?

2. In *Berger* it had been unclear how many of the Justices thought electronic eavesdropping could satisfy the Fourth Amendment warrant requirement. *Katz* answers this question unambiguously. But strangely the Court in *Katz* also says that in this case the government could have gotten a warrant given that its eavesdropping was "narrowly circumscribed." Even that is debatable — they appear to have intercepted 100 percent of Katz's calls from the phone booth for a week.

But what about probable cause? What facts in the opinion indicate the agents had probable cause to believe Katz was engaged in criminal activity? The record before the Court included information that Katz attracted the agents' attention after a tip from an informant. *See generally* David A. Sklansky, Katz v. United States: *The Limits of Aphorism*, in Criminal Procedure Stories 224 (Carol Steiker ed., 2007). But that doesn't establish probable cause without independent corroboration.

The agents observed Katz regularly walking to the phone booth to make telephone calls. Isn't that a purely innocuous activity? To paraphrase the Court, to infer illicit activity from using a pay phone "is to ignore the vital role that the public telephone has come to play in private communication."

3. Justice Harlan's concurring opinion puts a helpful gloss on the Court's pithy but useless "people not places" slogan:

> My understanding of the rule that has emerged from prior decisions is that there is a twofold requirement, first that a person have exhibited an actual (subjective) expectation of privacy and, second, that the expectation be one that society is prepared to recognize as "reasonable."

389 U.S. at 516. Although sometimes criticized for the circularity of the objective component of the standard, *see, e.g., Minnesota v. Carter*, 525 U.S. 83, 97 (1998) (Scalia, J., concurring), this was a standard that courts could and did apply in subsequent Fourth Amendment cases.

Why should a person's subjective view of what is private affect what protection the Fourth Amendment affords?

4. Though often praised for its vindication of privacy interests, *Katz* made explicit that the Fourth Amendment did not embody a generalized constitutional right to privacy. 389 U.S. at 510. Justice Brandeis's *Olmstead* dissent was not acknowledged in the opinion, although the Court in a footnote does make reference to his famous law review article on the protection of privacy rights through private tort actions. *See* Samuel D. Warren & Louis Brandeis, *The Right to Privacy*, 4 Harv. L. Rev. 193 (1890).

5. The most profound immediate response to *Katz* was not judicial but legislative. In 1968, Congress enacted comprehensive federal wiretapping legislation as part of the Omnibus Crime Control and Safe Streets Act. Title III of the act permitted wiretapping but imposed procedural requirements (probable cause, time limits, notice, minimization, etc.) flowing directly from *Berger* and *Katz*. To this day, the primary regulation of wiretapping is legislative not judicial. *See* Orin Kerr, *The Fourth Amendment and New Technologies: Constitutional Myths and the Case for Caution*, 102 Mich. L. Rev. 801, 805 (2004) (arguing that legislative rules are preferable to judicial interpretations of the Fourth Amendment in regulating new technologies).

Classic phone booth

Katz belongs in a museum. Its co-starring character, a public telephone booth, once such a common feature of public life, has largely disappeared. The activity for which Charlie Katz was charged, betting on sporting events, is now ubiquitous and wholly legal in many states. Crime rates were sufficiently low when Katz was under investigation that the FBI could devote several agents to the pursuit of one gambler, who was not even (as far as we are told) a bookie.

Katz is also a reminder that the doctrinal stakes involved in cases that reach the Supreme Court often exceed the stakes to the litigants. Katz's jury-waived trial lasted two days. The evidence included the telephone recordings, records seized from his hotel rooms, and a police officer who offered "expert testimony" about the gambling jargon on the recordings. Katz was found guilty and fined $300, the equivalent of about $2,700 today. *See generally* David A. Sklansky, Katz v. United States: *The Limits of Aphorism*, in Criminal Procedure Stories 223-33 (Carol Steiker ed., 2007).

The Court applied *Katz*'s "reasonable expectations of privacy" test to all manner of law enforcement techniques, some involving technology (aerial surveillance, beepers, pen

Chapter IV The Fourth Amendment

registers) and some more old school (using informants, looking through trash), in the ensuing decades. In *United States v. White*, 401 U.S. 745 (1971), the Court found no search where an informant recorded his conversations with a defendant because a person has no reasonable expectation of privacy in what he says to another person. Similarly, in *Smith v. Maryland*, 442 U.S. 735 (1979), the government's use of a "pen register," a device that records the numbers dialed on a telephone, was not a search because the defendant shared such numbers with the phone company, a third party. That physical location still mattered to the "reasonable expectations of privacy" test, however, was seen in a pair of cases involving government use of beepers as an investigative tool. *United States v. Knotts*, 460 U.S. 276 (1983); *United States v. Karo*, 468 U.S. 705 (1984). The "home" as a physical structure as opposed to a metaphor also retained significance. In *Oliver v. United States*, 466 U.S. 170 (1984), a warrantless search of "open fields" on a defendant's property, but distant from his home, was not forbidden by the Fourth Amendment; neither was a warrantless search of garbage bags defendants left for curbside collection. *California v. Greenwood*, 486 U.S. 35 (1988).

Florida v. Riley
488 U.S. 445 (1989)

Justice WHITE announced the judgment of the Court and delivered an opinion in which THE CHIEF JUSTICE, Justice SCALIA, and Justice KENNEDY join.

On certification to it by a lower state court, the Florida Supreme Court addressed the following question: "Whether surveillance of the interior of a partially covered greenhouse in a residential backyard from the vantage point of a helicopter located 400 feet above the greenhouse constitutes a 'search' for which a warrant is required under the Fourth Amendment and Article I, § 12 of the Florida Constitution." The court answered the question in the affirmative, and we granted the State's petition for certiorari challenging that conclusion.

Respondent Riley lived in a mobile home located on five acres of rural property. A greenhouse was located 10 to 20 feet behind the mobile home. Two sides of the greenhouse were enclosed. The other two sides were not enclosed but the contents of the greenhouse were obscured from view from surrounding property by trees, shrubs, and the mobile home. The greenhouse was covered by corrugated roofing panels, some translucent and some opaque. At the time relevant to this case, two of the panels, amounting to approximately 10% of the roof area, were missing. A wire fence surrounded the mobile home and the greenhouse, and the property was posted with a "DO NOT ENTER" sign.

This case originated with an anonymous tip to the Pasco County Sheriff's office that marijuana was being grown on respondent's property. When an investigating officer discovered that he could not see the contents of the greenhouse from the road, he circled twice over respondent's property in a helicopter at the height of 400 feet. With his naked eye, he was able to see through the openings in the roof and one or more of the open sides of the greenhouse and to identify what he thought was marijuana growing in the structure. A warrant was obtained based on these observations, and the ensuing search revealed marijuana growing in the greenhouse. Respondent was charged with possession of marijuana under Florida law. The trial court granted his motion to suppress; the Florida Court of Appeals reversed but certified the case to the Florida Supreme Court, which quashed the decision of the Court of Appeals and reinstated the trial court's suppression order.

We agree with the State's submission that our decision in *California v. Ciraolo* (1986), controls this case. There, acting on a tip, the police inspected the back-yard of a particular house while flying in a fixed-wing aircraft at 1,000 feet. With the naked eye the officers saw what they concluded was marijuana growing in the yard. A search warrant was obtained on the strength of this airborne inspection, and marijuana plants were found. The trial court refused to suppress this evidence, but a state appellate court held that the inspection violated the Fourth and Fourteenth Amendments to the United States Constitution, and that the warrant was therefore invalid. We in turn reversed, holding that the inspection was not a search subject to the Fourth Amendment. We recognized that the yard was within the curtilage of the house, that a fence shielded the yard from observation from the street, and that the occupant had a subjective expectation of privacy. We held, however, that such an expectation was not reasonable and not one "that society is prepared to honor." Our reasoning was that the home and its curtilage are not necessarily protected from inspection that involves no physical invasion. "'What a person knowingly exposes to the public, even in his own home or office, is not a subject of Fourth Amendment protection.'" As a general proposition, the police may see what may be seen "from a public vantage point where [they have] a right to be," Thus the police, like the public, would have been free to inspect the backyard garden from the street if their view had been unobstructed. They were likewise free to inspect the yard from the vantage point of an aircraft flying in the navigable airspace as this plane was. "In an age where private and commercial flight in the public airways is routine, it is unreasonable for respondent to expect that his marijuana plants were constitutionally protected from being observed with the naked eye from an altitude of 1,000 feet. The Fourth Amendment simply does not require the police traveling in the public airways at this altitude to obtain a warrant in order to observe what is visible to the naked eye."

We arrive at the same conclusion in the present case. In this case, as in *Ciraolo*, the property surveyed was within the curtilage of respondent's home. Riley no doubt intended and expected that his greenhouse would not be open to public inspection, and the precautions he took protected against ground-level observation. Because the sides and roof of his greenhouse were left partially open, however, what was growing in the greenhouse was subject to viewing from the air. Under the holding in Ciraolo, Riley could not reasonably have expected the contents of his greenhouse to be immune from examination by an officer seated in a fixed-wing aircraft flying in navigable airspace at an altitude of 1,000 feet or, as the Florida Supreme Court seemed to recognize, at an altitude of 500 feet, the lower limit of the navigable airspace for such an aircraft. Here, the inspection was made from a helicopter, but as is the case with fixed-wing planes, "private and commercial flight [by helicopter] in the public airways is routine" in this country, *Ciraolo*, and there is no indication that such flights are unheard of in Pasco County, Florida. Riley could not reasonably have expected that his greenhouse was protected from public or official observation from a helicopter had it been flying within the navigable airspace for fixed-wing aircraft.

Nor on the facts before us, does it make a difference for Fourth Amendment purposes that the helicopter was flying at 400 feet when the officer saw what was growing in the greenhouse through the partially open roof and sides of the structure. We would have a different case if flying at that altitude had been contrary to law or regulation. But helicopters are not bound by the lower limits of the navigable airspace allowed to other aircraft. Any member of the public could legally have been flying over Riley's property in a helicopter at the altitude of 400 feet and could have observed Riley's greenhouse. The police officer did no more. This is not to say that an inspection of the curtilage of a house from an aircraft will always pass muster under the Fourth Amendment simply because the plane is within the navigable airspace specified by law. But it is of obvious importance that the helicopter in this case was not violating the law, and there is nothing in the record or before us to suggest that helicopters flying at 400 feet are sufficiently rare in this country to lend substance to respondent's claim that he reasonably anticipated that his greenhouse would not be subject to observation from that altitude. Neither is there any intimation here that the helicopter interfered with respondent's normal use of the greenhouse or of other parts of the curtilage. As far as this record reveals, no intimate details connected with the use of the home or curtilage were observed, and there was no undue noise, and no wind, dust, or threat of injury. In these circumstances, there was no violation of the Fourth Amendment.

The judgment of the Florida Supreme Court is accordingly reversed.

[Justice O'Connor wrote an opinion concurring in the judgment. Justice Blackmun wrote a separate disappointing opinion.]

Justice BRENNAN, with whom Justice MARSHALL and Justice STEVENS join, dissenting.

The Court holds today that police officers need not obtain a warrant based on probable cause before circling in a helicopter 400 feet above a home in order to investigate what is taking place behind the walls of the curtilage. I cannot agree that the Fourth Amendment to the Constitution, which safeguards "[t]he right of the people to be secure in their persons, houses, papers, and effects, against unreasonable searches and seizures," tolerates such an intrusion on privacy and personal security.

<h1 style="text-align:center">I</h1>

The opinion for a plurality of the Court reads almost as if *Katz* had never been decided. Notwithstanding the disclaimers of its final paragraph, the opinion relies almost exclusively on the fact that the police officer conducted his surveillance from a vantage point where, under applicable Federal Aviation Administration regulations, he had a legal right to be. *Katz* teaches, however, that the relevant inquiry is whether the police surveillance "violated the privacy upon which [the defendant] justifiably relied" — or, as Justice Harlan put it, whether the police violated an "expectation of privacy . . . that society is prepared to recognize as 'reasonable.'" The result of that inquiry in any given case depends ultimately on the judgment "whether, if the particular form of surveillance practiced by the police is permitted to go unregulated by constitutional restraints, the amount of privacy and freedom remaining to citizens would be diminished to a compass inconsistent with the aims of a free and open society."

The plurality undertakes no inquiry into whether low-level helicopter surveillance by the police of activities in an enclosed backyard is consistent with the "aims of a free and open society." Instead, it summarily concludes that Riley's expectation of privacy was unreasonable because "[a]ny member of the public could legally have been flying over Riley's property in a helicopter at the altitude of 400 feet and could have observed Riley's greenhouse." This observation is, in turn, based solely on the fact that the police helicopter was within the airspace within which such craft are allowed by federal safety regulations to fly.

I agree, of course, that "[w]hat a person knowingly exposes to the public . . . is not a subject of Fourth Amendment protection." But I cannot agree that one "knowingly exposes [an area] to the public" solely because a helicopter may legally fly above it. Under the plurality's exceedingly grudging Fourth Amendment theory, the expectation of privacy is defeated if a single member of the public could conceivably position herself to see into the area in question without doing anything illegal. It is defeated whatever the difficulty a person would have in so positioning herself, and however infrequently anyone would in fact do so. In taking this view the plurality ignores the very essence of *Katz*. The reason why there is no reasonable expectation of privacy in an area that is exposed to the public is that little diminution in "the amount of privacy and freedom remaining to citizens" will result from police surveillance of something that any passerby readily sees. To pretend, as the plurality opinion does, that the same is true when the police use a helicopter to peer over high fences is, at best, disingenuous.

Notwithstanding the plurality's statistics about the number of helicopters registered in this country, can it seriously be questioned that Riley enjoyed virtually complete privacy in his backyard greenhouse, and that that privacy was invaded solely by police helicopter surveillance? Is the theoretical possibility that any member of the public (with sufficient means) could also have hired a helicopter and looked over Riley's fence of any relevance at all in determining whether Riley suffered a serious loss of privacy and personal security through the police action?

In *Ciraolo*, we held that whatever might be observed from the window of an airplane flying at 1,000 feet could be deemed unprotected by any reasonable expectation of privacy. That decision was based on the belief that airplane traffic at that altitude was sufficiently common that no expectation of privacy could inure in anything on the ground observable with the naked eye from so high. Indeed, we compared those airways to "public thoroughfares," and made the obvious point that police officers passing by a home on such thoroughfares were not required by the Fourth Amendment to "shield their eyes." Seizing on a reference in *Ciraolo* to the fact that the police officer was in a position "where he ha[d] a right to be," today's plurality professes to find this case indistinguishable because FAA regulations do not impose a minimum altitude requirement on helicopter traffic; thus, the officer in this case too made his observations from a vantage point where he had a right to be.

It is a curious notion that the reach of the Fourth Amendment can be so largely defined by administrative regulations issued for purposes of flight safety. It is more curious still that the plurality relies to such an extent on the legality of the officer's act, when we have consistently refused to equate police violation of the law with infringement of the Fourth Amendment. But the plurality's willingness to end its inquiry when it finds that the officer was in a position he had a right to be in is misguided for an even more fundamental reason. Finding determinative the fact that the officer was where he had a right to be is, at bottom, an attempt to analogize surveillance from a helicopter to surveillance by a police officer standing on a public road and viewing evidence of crime through an open window or a gap in a fence. In such a situation, the occupant of the home may be said to lack any reasonable expectation of privacy in what can be seen from that road—even if, in fact, people rarely pass that way.

The police officer positioned 400 feet above Riley's backyard was not, however, standing on a public road. The vantage point he enjoyed was not one any citizen could readily share. His ability to see over Riley's fence depended on his use of a very expensive and sophisticated piece of machinery to which few ordinary citizens have access. In such circumstances it makes no more sense to rely on the legality of the officer's position in the skies than it would to judge the constitutionality of the wiretap in Katz by the legality of the officer's position outside the telephone booth. The simple inquiry whether the police officer had the legal right to be in the position from which he made his observations cannot suffice, for we cannot assume that Riley's curtilage was so open to the observations of passersby in the skies that he retained little privacy or personal security to be lost to police surveillance. The question before us must be not whether the police were where they had a right to be, but whether public observation of Riley's curtilage was so commonplace that Riley's expectation of privacy in his backyard could not be considered reasonable. To say that an invasion of Riley's privacy from the skies was not impossible is most emphatically not the same as saying that his expectation of privacy within his enclosed curtilage was not "one that society is prepared to recognize as 'reasonable.'" While, as we held in *Ciraolo*, air traffic at elevations of 1,000 feet or more may be so common that whatever could be seen with the naked eye from that elevation is unprotected by the Fourth Amendment, it is a large step from there to say that the Amendment offers no protection against low-level helicopter surveillance of enclosed curtilage areas. To take this step is error enough. That the plurality does so with little analysis beyond its determination that the police complied with FAA regulations is particularly unfortunate.

II

Equally disconcerting is the lack of any meaningful limit to the plurality's holding. It is worth reiterating that the FAA regulations the plurality relies on as establishing that the officer was where he had a right to be set no minimum flight altitude for helicopters. It is difficult, therefore, to see what, if any, helicopter surveillance would run afoul of the plurality's rule that there exists no reasonable expectation of privacy as long as the helicopter is where it has a right to be.

Only in its final paragraph does the plurality opinion suggest that there might be some limits to police helicopter surveillance beyond those imposed by FAA regulations:

> Neither is there any intimation here that the helicopter interfered with respondent's normal use of the greenhouse or of other parts of the curtilage. As far as this record reveals, no intimate details connected with the use of the home or curtilage were observed, and there was no undue noise, and no wind, dust, or threat of injury. In these circumstances, there was no violation of the Fourth Amendment.

I will deal with the "intimate details" below. For the rest, one wonders what the plurality believes the purpose of the Fourth Amendment to be. If through noise, wind, dust, and threat of injury from helicopters the State "interfered with respondent's normal use of the greenhouse or of other parts of the curtilage," Riley might have a cause of action in inverse condemnation, but that is not what the Fourth Amendment is all about. Nowhere is this better stated than in Justice White's opinion for the Court in *Camara*: "The basic purpose of this Amendment, as recognized in countless decisions of this Court, is to safeguard the privacy and security of individuals against arbitrary invasions by governmental officials."

If indeed the purpose of the restraints imposed by the Fourth Amendment is to "safeguard the privacy and security of individuals," then it is puzzling why it should be the helicopter's noise, wind, and dust that provides the measure of whether this constitutional safeguard has been infringed. Imagine a helicopter capable of hovering just above an enclosed courtyard or patio without generating any noise, wind, or dust at all—and, for good measure, without posing any threat of injury. Suppose the police employed this miraculous tool to discover not only what crops people were growing in their greenhouses, but also what books they were reading and who their dinner guests were. Suppose, finally, that the FAA regulations remained unchanged, so that the police were undeniably "where they had a right to be." Would today's plurality continue to assert that "[t]he right of the people to be secure in their persons, houses, papers, and effects, against unreasonable searches and seizures" was not infringed by such surveillance? Yet that is the logical consequence of the plurality's rule that, so long as the police are where they have a right to be under air traffic regulations, the Fourth Amendment is offended only if the aerial surveillance interferes with the use of the backyard as a garden spot. Nor is there anything in the plurality's opinion to suggest that any different rule would apply were the police looking from their helicopter, not into the open curtilage, but through an open window into a room viewable only from the air.

III

Perhaps the most remarkable passage in the plurality opinion is its suggestion that the case might be a different one had any "intimate details connected with the use of the home or curtilage [been] observed." What, one wonders, is meant by "intimate details"? If the police had observed Riley embracing his wife in the backyard greenhouse, would we then say that his reasonable expectation of privacy had been infringed? Where in the Fourth Amendment or in our cases is there any warrant for imposing a requirement that the activity observed must be "intimate" in order to be protected by the Constitution?

It is difficult to avoid the conclusion that the plurality has allowed its analysis of Riley's expectation of privacy to be colored by its distaste for the activity in which he was engaged. It is indeed easy to forget, especially in view of current concern over drug trafficking, that the scope of the Fourth Amendment's protection does not turn on whether the activity disclosed by a search is illegal or innocuous. But we dismiss this as a "drug case" only at the peril of our own liberties. Justice Frankfurter once noted that "[i]t is a fair summary of history to say that the safeguards of liberty have frequently been forged in controversies involving not very nice people," and nowhere is this observation more apt than in the area of the Fourth Amendment, whose words have necessarily been given meaning largely through decisions suppressing evidence of criminal activity. The principle enunciated in this case determines what limits the Fourth Amendment imposes on aerial surveillance of any person, for any reason. If the Constitution does not protect Riley's marijuana garden against such surveillance, it is hard to see how it will prohibit the government from aerial spying on the activities of a law-abiding citizen on her fully enclosed outdoor patio. As Professor Amsterdam has eloquently written: "The question is not whether you or I must draw the blinds before we commit a crime. It is whether you and I must discipline ourselves to draw the blinds every time we enter a room, under pain of surveillance if we do not."

IV

I find little to disagree with Justice O'Connor's concurrence, apart from its closing paragraphs. A majority of the Court thus agrees that the fundamental inquiry is not whether the police were where they had a right to be under FAA regulations, but rather whether Riley's expectation of privacy was rendered illusory by the extent of public observation of his backyard from aerial traffic at 400 feet.

What separates me from Justice O'Connor is essentially an empirical matter concerning the extent of public use of the airspace at that altitude, together with the question of how to resolve that issue. I do not think the constitutional claim should fail simply because "there is reason to believe" that there is "considerable" public flying this close to earth or because Riley "introduced no evidence to the contrary before the Florida courts." I should think that this might be an apt occasion for the application of Professor Davis' distinction between "adjudicative" and "legislative" facts. If so, I think we could take judicial notice that, while there may be an occasional privately owned helicopter that flies over populated areas at an altitude of 400 feet, such flights are a rarity and are almost entirely limited to approaching or leaving airports or to reporting traffic congestion near major roadways. And, as the concurrence agrees, at 699, the extent of police surveillance traffic cannot serve as a bootstrap to demonstrate public use of the airspace.

If, however, we are to resolve the issue by considering whether the appropriate party carried its burden of proof, I again think that Riley must prevail. Because the State has greater access to information concerning customary flight patterns and because the coercive power of the State ought not be brought to bear in cases in which it is unclear whether the prosecution is a product of an unconstitutional, warrantless search, the burden of proof properly rests with the State and not with the individual defendant. The State quite clearly has not carried this burden.

V

The issue in this case is, ultimately, "how tightly the Fourth Amendment permits people to be driven back into the recesses of their lives by the risk of surveillance." The Court today approves warrantless helicopter surveillance from an altitude of 400 feet. While Justice O'Connor's opinion gives reason to hope that this altitude may constitute a lower limit, I find considerable cause for concern in the fact that a plurality of four Justices would remove virtually all constitutional barriers to police surveillance from the vantage point of helicopters. The Fourth Amendment demands that we temper our efforts to apprehend criminals with a concern for the impact on our fundamental liberties of the methods we use. I hope it will be a matter of concern to my colleagues that the police surveillance methods they would sanction were among those described 40 years ago in George Orwell's dread vision of life in the 1980s:

> The black-mustachio'd face gazed down from every commanding corner. There was one on the house front immediately opposite. BIG BROTHER IS WATCHING YOU, the caption said. . . . In the far distance a helicopter skimmed down between the roofs, hovered for an instant like a bluebottle, and darted away again with a curving flight. It was the Police Patrol, snooping into people's windows.

Nineteen Eighty-Four 4 (1949).

Who can read this passage without a shudder, and without the instinctive reaction that it depicts life in some country other than ours? I respectfully dissent.

NOTES AND QUESTIONS

1. All of the opinions here seem to ignore the elephant in the room: the credibility of the police officer's testimony at the suppression hearing that he was able to identify with his naked eye from a distance of 400' — 1.3 times the length of a football field — what he "thought" were marijuana plants in a greenhouse defendant's backyard. Bad defense lawyering? A credulous judge? Or maybe just a bad record due to the fact that the suppression motion was granted on the ground that the surveillance constituted a warrantless search? *See* Adam M. Gershowitz & Caroline E. Lewis, *Laundering Police Lies*, 2023 Wis. L. Rev. 1187, 1229-30 (2023) (describing *Florida v. Riley* as a leading example of the Supreme Court countenancing farfetched police testimony). *See generally* Bennett Capers, *Crime, Legitimacy and Testilying*, 83 Ind. L.J. 835 (2008).

2. Note that Michael Riley came to the attention of police only by the way of an anonymous tip. And the police went airborne only after they were unable to see the contents of the greenhouse from the road, a detail that makes mighty curious the plurality opinion's reference to the line from *Ciraolo* that officers need not "shield their eyes" when on public streets. In short, the only basis for finding probable cause for the ultimate search of the property was the officer's "naked eye" observation.

What does *Riley* teach about the role of the "subject expectation of privacy" aspect of the *Katz* test? That it doesn't matter? That it's a one-way factor, only relevant if a person does *not* manifest such an expectation?

3. Riley's expectation of privacy was unreasonable, we are told, because "there is reason to believe that there is considerable public use of airspace at altitudes of 400' and above."

What is the basis for this conclusion, other than the FAA regulations that are discussed? And don't the regulations only mean the location of the helicopter was legal, not that it was common? And why does the legality of the helicopter's location matter one way or the other? Recall that in *Olmstead* the fact that the agents' wiretapping was illegal was irrelevant.

4. Is the extent of the use of the airspace a purely factual issue? In her concurring opinion Justice O'Connor suggests that it is, and says the burden of proof is defendant's, which was not met here. How would a defendant meet such a burden? Would a defendant's testimony that she had never before seen a helicopter anywhere near her home be relevant? Would data — countywide, statewide, national — on the incidence and elevation of helicopter travel be required?

What do you make of the dissent's point that a court should be able to take "judicial notice" of the fact that helicopter flights over homes at an elevation of 400' are a rarity?

5. Is the result in *Riley* required by the Court's previous decision in *Ciraolo*? If so, is it because the facts of the case are sufficiently close that *Ciraolo* is controlling precedent? Or is it because after *Ciraolo* it was no longer reasonable to have an expectation of privacy in curtilage that was visible from airspace? Does the "objective reasonableness" of an expectation of privacy turn to any degree on what the Supreme Court has held in previous cases?

6. What is the constitutional significance of "curtilage" after *Riley*?

7. Should the cultural association of helicopters with intrusive police investigative activity—note Justice Brennan's quote from *1984*, or the terrifying helicopter scene from *Goodfellas* (1990)—have any bearing on reasonable expectations of privacy? Should the nature of the technology used by the police be part of the mix?

Classic paperback edition of George Orwell's *1984*

Ray Liotta as Henry Hill near the end of *Goodfellas* as police helicopters appear to be closing in on him.

Law enforcement's use of modern technology was very much the issue in the next few cases.

Kyllo v. United States
533 U.S. 27 (2000)

Justice SCALIA delivered the opinion of the Court.

This case presents the question whether the use of a thermal-imaging device aimed at a private home from a public street to detect relative amounts of heat within the home constitutes a "search" within the meaning of the Fourth Amendment.

I

In 1991 Agent William Elliott of the United States Department of the Interior came to suspect that marijuana was being grown in the home belonging to petitioner Danny Kyllo, part of a triplex on Rhododendron Drive in Florence, Oregon. Indoor marijuana growth typically requires high-intensity lamps. In order to determine whether an amount of heat was emanating from petitioner's home consistent with the use of such lamps, at 3:20 a.m. on January 16, 1992, Agent Elliott and Dan Haas used an Agema Thermovision 210 thermal imager to scan the triplex. Thermal imagers detect infrared radiation, which virtually all objects emit but which is not visible to the naked eye. The imager converts radiation into images based on relative warmth—black is cool, white is hot, shades of gray connote relative differences; in that respect, it operates somewhat like a video camera showing heat images. The scan of Kyllo's home took only a few minutes and was performed from the passenger seat of Agent Elliott's vehicle across the street from the front of the house and also from the street in back of the house. The scan showed that the roof over the garage and a side wall of petitioner's home were relatively hot compared to the rest of the home and substantially warmer than neighboring homes in the triplex. Agent Elliott concluded that petitioner was using halide lights to grow marijuana in his house, which indeed he was. Based on tips from informants, utility bills, and the thermal imaging, a Federal Magistrate Judge issued a warrant authorizing a search of petitioner's home, and the agents found an indoor growing operation involving more than 100 plants. Petitioner was indicted on one count of manufacturing marijuana, in violation of 21 U.S.C. § 841(a)(1). He unsuccessfully moved to suppress the evidence seized from his home and then entered a conditional guilty plea.

The Court of Appeals for the Ninth Circuit remanded the case for an evidentiary hearing regarding the intrusiveness of thermal imaging. On remand the District Court found that the Agema 210 "is a non-intrusive device which emits no rays or beams and shows a crude visual image of the heat being radiated from the outside of the house"; it "did not show any people or activity within the walls of the structure"; "[t]he device used cannot penetrate walls or windows to reveal conversations or human activities"; and "[n]o intimate details of the home were observed." Based on these findings, the District Court upheld the validity of the warrant that relied in part upon the thermal imaging, and reaffirmed its denial of the motion to suppress. The [Ninth Circuit] held that petitioner had shown no subjective expectation of privacy because he had made no attempt to conceal the heat escaping from his home, and even if he had, there was no objectively reasonable expectation of privacy because the imagery "did not expose any intimate details of Kyllo's life," only "amorphous 'hot spots' on the roof and exterior wall." We granted certiorari.

II

The Fourth Amendment provides that "[t]he right of the people to be secure in their persons, houses, papers, and effects, against unreasonable searches and seizures, shall not be violated." "At the very core" of the Fourth Amendment "stands the right of a man to retreat into his own home and there be free from unreasonable governmental intrusion." With few exceptions, the question whether a warrantless search of a home is reasonable and hence constitutional must be answered no.

On the other hand, the antecedent question whether or not a Fourth Amendment "search" has occurred is not so simple under our precedent. The permissibility of ordinary visual surveillance of a home used to be clear because, well into the 20th century, our Fourth Amendment jurisprudence was tied to common-law trespass. Visual surveillance was unquestionably lawful because "'the eye cannot by the laws of England be guilty of a trespass.'" We have since decoupled violation of a person's Fourth Amendment rights from trespassory violation of his property, but the lawfulness of warrantless visual surveillance of a home has still been preserved. As we observed in *Ciraolo*, "[t]he Fourth Amendment protection of the home has never been extended to require law enforcement officers to shield their eyes when passing by a home on public thoroughfares."

One might think that the new validating rationale would be that examining the portion of a house that is in plain public view, while it is a "search" despite the absence of trespass, is not an "unreasonable" one under the Fourth Amendment. But in fact we have held that visual observation is no "search" at all—perhaps in order to preserve somewhat more intact our doctrine that warrantless searches are presumptively unconstitutional. In assessing when a search is not a search, we have applied somewhat in reverse the principle first enunciated in *Katz*. *Katz* involved eavesdropping by means of an electronic listening device placed on the outside of a telephone booth—a location not within the catalog ("persons, houses, papers, and effects") that the Fourth Amendment protects against unreasonable searches. We held that the Fourth Amendment nonetheless protected Katz from the warrantless eavesdropping because he "justifiably relied" upon the privacy of the telephone booth. As Justice Harlan's oft-quoted concurrence described it, a Fourth Amendment search occurs when the government violates a subjective expectation of privacy that society recognizes as reasonable. We have subsequently applied this principle to hold that a Fourth Amendment search does not occur—even when the explicitly protected location of a house is concerned—unless "the individual manifested a subjective expectation of privacy in the object of the challenged search," and "society [is] willing to recognize that expectation as reasonable." We have applied this test in holding that it is not a search for the police to use a pen register at the phone company to determine what numbers were dialed in a private home, and we have applied the test on two different occasions in holding that aerial surveillance of private homes and surrounding areas does not constitute a search.

The present case involves officers on a public street engaged in more than naked-eye surveillance of a home. We have previously reserved judgment as to how much technological enhancement of ordinary perception from such a vantage point, if any, is too much. While we upheld enhanced aerial photography of an industrial complex in *Dow Chemical*, we noted that we found "it important that this is not an area immediately adjacent to a private home, where privacy expectations are most heightened."

III

It would be foolish to contend that the degree of privacy secured to citizens by the Fourth Amendment has been entirely unaffected by the advance of technology. For example, as the cases discussed above make clear, the technology enabling human flight has exposed to public view (and hence, we have said, to official observation) uncovered portions of the house and its curtilage that once were private. The question we confront today is what limits there are upon this power of technology to shrink the realm of guaranteed privacy.

The *Katz* test—whether the individual has an expectation of privacy that society is prepared to recognize as reasonable—has often been criticized as circular, and hence subjective and unpredictable. While it may be difficult to refine *Katz* when the search of areas such as telephone booths, automobiles, or even the curtilage and uncovered portions of residences is at issue, in the case of the search of the interior of homes—the prototypical and hence most commonly litigated area of protected privacy—there is a ready criterion, with roots deep in the common law, of the minimal expectation of privacy that exists, and that is acknowledged to be reasonable. To withdraw protection of this minimum expectation would be to permit police technology to erode the privacy guaranteed by the Fourth Amendment. We think that obtaining by sense-enhancing technology any information regarding the interior of the home that could not otherwise have been obtained without physical "intrusion into a constitutionally protected area," constitutes a search—at least where (as here) the technology in question is not in general public use. This assures preservation of that degree of privacy against government that existed when the Fourth Amendment was adopted. On the basis of this criterion, the information obtained by the thermal imager in this case was the product of a search.

The Government maintains, however, that the thermal imaging must be upheld because it detected "only heat radiating from the external surface of the house." The dissent makes this its leading point, contending that there is a fundamental difference between what it calls "off-the-wall" observations and "through-the-wall" surveillance." But just as a thermal imager captures only heat emanating from a house, so also a powerful directional microphone picks up only sound emanating from a house-and a satellite capable of scanning from many miles away would pick up only visible light emanating from a house. We rejected such a mechanical interpretation of the Fourth Amendment in *Katz*, where the eavesdropping device picked up only sound waves that reached the exterior of the phone booth. Reversing that approach would leave the homeowner at the mercy of advancing technology — including imaging technology that could discern all human activity in the home. While the technology used in the present case was relatively crude, the rule we adopt must take account of more sophisticated systems that are already in use or in development. The dissent's reliance on the distinction between "off-the-wall" and "through-the-wall" observation is entirely incompatible with the dissent's belief, which we discuss below, that thermal-imaging observations of the intimate details of a home are impermissible. The most sophisticated thermal-imaging devices continue to measure heat "off-the-wall" rather than "through-the-wall"; the dissent's disapproval of those more sophisticated thermal-imaging devices, is an acknowledgement that there is no substance to this distinction. As for the dissent's extraordinary assertion that anything learned through "an inference" cannot be a search, that would validate even the "through-the-wall" technologies that the dissent purports to disapprove. Surely the dissent does not believe that the through-the-wall radar or ultrasound technology produces an 8-by-10 Kodak glossy that needs no analysis (i.e., the making of inferences). And, of course, the novel proposition that inference insulates a search is blatantly contrary to *Karo*, where the police "inferred" from the activation of a beeper that a certain can of ether was in the home. The police activity was held to be a search, and the search was held unlawful.

The Government also contends that the thermal imaging was constitutional because it did not "detect private activities occurring in private areas." It points out that in *Dow Chemical* we observed that the enhanced aerial photography did not reveal any "intimate details." *Dow Chemical*, however, involved enhanced aerial photography of an industrial complex, which does not share the Fourth Amendment sanctity of the home. The Fourth Amendment's protection of the home has never been tied to measurement of the quality or quantity of information obtained. In *Silverman*, for example, we made clear that any physical invasion of the structure of the home, "by even a fraction of an inch," was too much, and there is certainly no exception to the warrant requirement for the officer who barely cracks open the front door and sees nothing but the nonintimate rug on the vestibule floor. In the home, our cases show, all details are intimate details, because the entire area is held safe from prying government eyes. Thus, in *Karo, supra*, the only thing detected was a can of ether in the home; and in *Arizona v. Hicks* (1987), the only thing detected by a physical search that went beyond what officers lawfully present could observe in "plain view" was the registration number of a phonograph turntable. These were intimate details because they were details of the home, just as was the detail of how warm — or even how relatively warm — Kyllo was heating his residence.

Limiting the prohibition of thermal imaging to "intimate details" would not only be wrong in principle; it would be impractical in application, failing to provide "a workable accommodation between the needs of law enforcement and the interests protected by the Fourth Amendment." To begin with, there is no necessary connection between the sophistication of the surveillance equipment and the "intimacy" of the details that it observes — which means that one cannot say (and the police cannot be assured) that use of the relatively crude equipment at issue here will always be lawful. The Agema Thermovision 210 might disclose, for example, at what hour each night the lady of the house takes her daily sauna and bath — a detail that many would consider "intimate"; and a much more sophisticated system might detect nothing more intimate than the fact that someone left a closet light on. We could not, in other words, develop a rule approving only that through-the-wall surveillance which identifies objects no smaller than 36 by 36 inches, but would have to develop a jurisprudence specifying which home activities are "intimate" and which are not. And even when (if ever) that jurisprudence were fully developed, no police officer would be able to know in advance whether his through-the-wall surveillance picks up "intimate" details — and thus would be unable to know in advance whether it is constitutional.

The dissent's proposed standard — whether the technology offers the "functional equivalent of actual presence in the area being searched" — would seem quite similar to our own at first blush. The dissent concludes that *Katz* was such a case, but then inexplicably asserts that if the same listening device only revealed the volume of the conversation, the surveillance would be permissible. Yet if, without technology, the police could not discern volume without being actually present in the phone booth, Justice Stevens should conclude a search has occurred. The same should hold for the interior heat of the home if only a person present in the home could discern the heat. Thus the driving force of the dissent, despite its recitation of the above standard, appears to be a distinction among different types of information — whether the "homeowner would even care if anybody noticed." The dissent offers no practical guidance for the application of this standard, and for reasons already discussed, we believe there can be none. The people in their houses, as well as the police, deserve more precision.

We have said that the Fourth Amendment draws "a firm line at the entrance to the house." That line, we think, must be not only firm but also bright — which requires clear specification of those methods of surveillance that require a warrant. While it is certainly possible to conclude from the videotape of the thermal imaging that occurred in this case that no "significant" compromise of the homeowner's privacy has occurred, we must take the long view, from the original meaning of the Fourth Amendment forward.

The Fourth Amendment is to be construed in the light of what was deemed an unreasonable search and seizure when it was adopted, and in a manner which will conserve public interests as well as the interests and rights of individual citizens." *Carroll v. United States* (1925).

Where, as here, the Government uses a device that is not in general public use, to explore details of the home that would previously have been unknowable without physical intrusion, the surveillance is a "search" and is presumptively unreasonable without a warrant.

Since we hold the Thermovision imaging to have been an unlawful search, it will remain for the District Court to determine whether, without the evidence it provided, the search warrant issued in this case was supported by probable cause — and if not, whether there is any other basis for supporting admission of the evidence that the search pursuant to the warrant produced.

The judgment of the Court of Appeals is reversed; the case is remanded for further proceedings consistent with this opinion.

NOTES AND QUESTIONS

1. Does the result here reveal itself in the first paragraph of the Court's analysis, with the Court's reminder that the home is at the "very core" of the Fourth Amendment's protection? Does the Court's recitation of the Fourth Amendment's language — "persons, houses, papers, and effects" — portend revitalized interest in a textualist approach to the Amendment?

2. The Court finds it material that thermal imaging is "sense enhancing" technology. The point seems to be that the technology permits police officers who are situated in perfectly legitimate investigative locations—across the street from Kyllo's home—to improve on what they could discern with their own eyes and ears and thereby defeat reasonable expectations of privacy. Don't devices such as binoculars confer a similar sensory "enhancement"?

3. Why does the Court limit its holding to "sense enhancing" technology that is "not in general public use"? What if at some point every police department in the country gets an Agema Thermovision 210 or its equivalent and uses it routinely but only after getting a search warrant? General public use? Does "public use" mean that the use has to spread to include uses for purposes other than law enforcement? In 2024, just 24 years after *Kyllo*, dozens of different types of thermal imaging devices could be purchased on Amazon for under $500.

Handheld thermal imaging device

4. "With few exceptions, the question whether a warrantless search of a home is reasonable and hence constitutional must be answered no," says the Court in *Kyllo*. Is the use of thermal imagery only found to be a search here because it was directed at a home? What if it was directed at Kyllo's garage? Or a greenhouse in his backyard?

5. The Court says that it has "decoupled" Fourth Amendment violations from notions of trespass. Is that how you read *Katz*, as a decoupling?

United States v. Jones
565 U.S. 400 (2012)

Justice SCALIA delivered the opinion of the Court.

We decide whether the attachment of a Global-Positioning-System (GPS) tracking device to an individual's vehicle, and subsequent use of that device to monitor the vehicle's movements on public streets, constitutes a search or seizure within the meaning of the Fourth Amendment.

I

In 2004 respondent Antoine Jones, owner and operator of a nightclub in the District of Columbia, came under suspicion of trafficking in narcotics and was made the target of an investigation by a joint Federal Bureau of Investigation and Metropolitan Police Department task force. Officers employed various investigative techniques, including visual surveillance of the nightclub, installation of a camera focused on the front door of the club, and a pen register and wiretap covering Jones's cellular phone.

Based in part on information gathered from these sources, in 2005 the Government applied to the United States District Court for the District of Columbia for a warrant authorizing the use of an electronic tracking device on the Jeep Grand Cherokee registered to Jones's wife. A warrant issued, authorizing installation of the device in the District of Columbia and within 10 days.

On the 11th day, and not in the District of Columbia but in Maryland, agents installed a GPS tracking device on the undercarriage of the Jeep while it was parked in a public parking lot. Over the next 28 days, the Government used the device to track the vehicle's movements, and once had to replace the device's battery when the vehicle was parked in a different public lot in Maryland. By means of signals from multiple satellites, the device established the vehicle's location within 50 to 100 feet, and communicated that location by cellular phone to a Government computer. It relayed more than 2,000 pages of data over the 4-week period.

The Government ultimately obtained a multiple-count indictment charging Jones and several alleged co-conspirators with, as relevant here, conspiracy to distribute and possess with intent to distribute five kilograms or more of cocaine and 50 grams or more of cocaine base, in violation of 21 U.S.C. §§ 841 and 846. Before trial, Jones filed a motion to suppress evidence obtained through the GPS device. The District Court granted the motion only in part, suppressing the data obtained while the vehicle was parked in the garage adjoining Jones's residence. It held the remaining data admissible, because "'[a] person traveling in an automobile on public thoroughfares has no reasonable expectation of privacy in his movements from one place to another.'" Jones's trial in October 2006 produced a hung jury on the conspiracy count.

In March 2007, a grand jury returned another indictment, charging Jones and others with the same conspiracy. The Government introduced at trial the same GPS-derived locational data admitted in the first trial, which connected Jones to the alleged conspirators' stash house that contained $850,000 in cash, 97 kilograms of cocaine, and 1 kilogram of cocaine base. The jury returned a guilty verdict, and the District Court sentenced Jones to life imprisonment.

The United States Court of Appeals for the District of Columbia Circuit reversed the conviction because of admission of the evidence obtained by warrantless use of the GPS device which, it said, violated the Fourth Amendment. The D.C. Circuit denied the Government's petition for rehearing en banc, with four judges dissenting. We granted certiorari.

II

A

The Fourth Amendment provides in relevant part that "[t]he right of the people to be secure in their persons, houses, papers, and effects, against unreasonable searches and seizures, shall not be violated." It is beyond dispute that a vehicle is an "effect" as that term is used in the Amendment. We hold that the Government's installation of a GPS device on a target's vehicle, and its use of that device to monitor the vehicle's movements, constitutes a "search."

It is important to be clear about what occurred in this case: The Government physically occupied private property for the purpose of obtaining information. We have no doubt that such a physical intrusion would have been considered a "search" within the meaning of the Fourth Amendment when it was adopted.

The text of the Fourth Amendment reflects its close connection to property, since otherwise it would have referred simply to "the right of the people to be secure against unreasonable searches and seizures"; the phrase "in their persons, houses, papers, and effects" would have been superfluous.

Consistent with this understanding, our Fourth Amendment jurisprudence was tied to common-law trespass, at least until the latter half of the 20th century.

Our later cases, of course, have deviated from that exclusively property-based approach. In *Katz* we said that "the Fourth Amendment protects people, not places," and found a violation in attachment of an eavesdropping device to a public telephone booth. Our later cases have applied the analysis of Justice Harlan's concurrence in that case, which said that a violation occurs when government officers violate a person's "reasonable expectation of privacy."

The Government contends that the Harlan standard shows that no search occurred here, since Jones had no "reasonable expectation of privacy" in the area of the Jeep accessed by Government agents (its underbody) and in the locations of the Jeep on the public roads, which were visible to all. But we need not address the Government's contentions, because Jones's Fourth Amendment rights do not rise or fall with the *Katz* formulation. At bottom, we must "assur[e] preservation of that degree of privacy against government that existed when the Fourth Amendment was adopted." As explained, for most of our history the Fourth Amendment was understood to embody a particular concern for government trespass upon the areas ("persons, houses, papers, and effects") it enumerates. *Katz* did not repudiate that understanding. Less than two years later the Court upheld defendants' contention that the Government could not introduce against them conversations between other people obtained by warrantless placement of electronic surveillance devices in their homes. The opinion rejected the dissent's contention that there was no Fourth Amendment violation "unless the conversational privacy of the homeowner himself is invaded."

More recently, the Court unanimously rejected the argument that although a "seizure" had occurred "in a 'technical' sense" when a trailer home was forcibly removed, no Fourth Amendment violation occurred because law enforcement had not "invade[d] the [individuals'] privacy." *Katz*, the Court explained, established that "property rights are not the sole measure of Fourth Amendment violations," but did not "snuf[f] out the previously recognized protection for property." As Justice Brennan explained in his concurrence in *Knotts*, *Katz* did not erode the principle "that, when the Government does engage in physical intrusion of a constitutionally protected area in order to obtain information, that intrusion may constitute a violation of the Fourth Amendment." We have embodied that preservation of past rights in our very definition of "reasonable expectation of privacy" which we have said to be an expectation "that has a source outside of the Fourth Amendment, either by reference to concepts of real or personal property law or to understandings that are recognized and permitted by society."

The Government contends that several of our post-*Katz* cases foreclose the conclusion that what occurred here constituted a search. It relies principally on two cases in which we rejected Fourth Amendment challenges to "beepers," electronic tracking devices that represent another form of electronic monitoring. The first case, *Knotts*, upheld against Fourth Amendment challenge the use of a "beeper" that had been placed in a container of chloroform, allowing law enforcement to monitor the location of the container. We said that there had been no infringement of Knotts' reasonable expectation of privacy since the information obtained—the location of the automobile carrying the container on public roads, and the location of the off-loaded container in open fields near Knotts' cabin—had been voluntarily conveyed to the public. But as we have discussed, the *Katz* reasonable-expectation-of-privacy test has been added to, not substituted for, the common-law trespassory test. The holding in *Knotts* addressed only the former, since the latter was not at issue. The beeper had been placed in the container before it came into Knotts' possession, with the consent of the then-owner. Knotts did not challenge that installation, and we specifically declined to consider its effect on the Fourth Amendment analysis. *Knotts* would be relevant, perhaps, if the Government were making the argument that what would otherwise be an unconstitutional search is not such where it produces only public information. The Government does not make that argument, and we know of no case that would support it.

The second "beeper" case, *United States v. Karo* (1984), does not suggest a different conclusion. There we addressed the question left open by *Knotts*, whether the installation of a beeper in a container amounted to a search or seizure. As in *Knotts*, at the time the beeper was installed the container belonged to a third party, and it did not come into possession of the defendant until later. Thus, the specific question we considered was whether the installation "with the consent of the original owner constitute[d] a search or seizure . . . when the container is delivered to a buyer having no knowledge of the presence of the beeper." We held not. The Government, we said, came into physical contact with the container only before it belonged to the defendant Karo; and the transfer of the container with the unmonitored beeper inside did not convey any information and thus did not invade Karo's privacy. That conclusion is perfectly consistent with the one we reach here. Karo accepted the container as it came to him, beeper and all, and was therefore not entitled to object to the beeper's presence, even though it was used to monitor the container's location. Jones, who possessed the Jeep at the time the Government trespassorily inserted the information-gathering device, is on much different footing.

The Government also points to our exposition in *New York v. Class* (1986), that "[t]he exterior of a car . . . is thrust into the public eye, and thus to examine it does not constitute a 'search.'" That statement is of marginal relevance here since, as the Government acknowledges, "the officers in this case did more than conduct a visual inspection of respondent's vehicle." By attaching the device to the Jeep, officers encroached on a protected area. In *Class* itself we suggested that this would make a difference, for we concluded that an officer's momentary reaching into the interior of a vehicle did constitute a search.

Finally, the Government's position gains little support from our conclusion in *Oliver v. United States* (1984), that officers' information-gathering intrusion on an "open field" did not constitute a Fourth Amendment search even though it was a trespass at common law. Quite simply, an open field, unlike the curtilage of a home, is not one of those protected areas enumerated in the Fourth Amendment. The Government's physical intrusion on such an area — unlike its intrusion on the "effect" at issue here — is of no Fourth Amendment significance.

B

The concurrence begins by accusing us of applying "18th-century tort law." That is a distortion. What we apply is an 18th-century guarantee against unreasonable searches, which we believe must provide at a minimum the degree of protection it afforded when it was adopted. The concurrence does not share that belief. It would apply exclusively *Katz*'s reasonable-expectation-of-privacy test, even when that eliminates rights that previously existed.

The concurrence faults our approach for "present[ing] particularly vexing problems" in cases that do not involve physical contact, such as those that involve the transmission of electronic signals. We entirely fail to understand that point. For unlike the concurrence, which would make *Katz* the exclusive test, we do not make trespass the exclusive test. Situations involving merely the transmission of electronic signals without trespass would remain subject to *Katz* analysis.

In fact, it is the concurrence's insistence on the exclusivity of the *Katz* test that needlessly leads us into "particularly vexing problems" in the present case. This Court has to date not deviated from the understanding that mere visual observation does not constitute a search. We accordingly held in *Knotts* that "[a] person traveling in an automobile on public thoroughfares has no reasonable expectation of privacy in his movements from one place to another." Thus, even assuming that the concurrence is correct to say that "[t]raditional surveillance" of Jones for a 4-week period "would have required a large team of agents, multiple vehicles, and perhaps aerial assistance," our cases suggest that such visual observation is constitutionally permissible. It may be that achieving the same result through electronic means, without an accompanying trespass, is an unconstitutional invasion of privacy, but the present case does not require us to answer that question.

And answering it affirmatively leads us needlessly into additional thorny problems. The concurrence posits that "relatively short-term monitoring of a person's movements on public streets" is okay, but that "the use of longer term GPS monitoring in investigations of *most offenses*" is no good (emphasis added). That introduces yet another novelty into our jurisprudence. There is no precedent for the proposition that whether a search has occurred depends on the nature of the crime being investigated. And even accepting that novelty, it remains unexplained why a 4-week investigation is "surely" too long and why a drug-trafficking conspiracy involving substantial amounts of cash and narcotics is not an "extraordinary offens[e]" which may permit longer observation. What of a 2-day monitoring of a suspected purveyor of stolen electronics? Or of a 6-month monitoring of a suspected terrorist? We may have to grapple with these "vexing problems" in some future case where a classic trespassory search is not involved and resort must be had to *Katz* analysis; but there is no reason for rushing forward to resolve them here.

• • •

Justice ALITO, with whom Justice GINSBURG, Justice BREYER, and Justice KAGAN join, concurring in the judgment.

This case requires us to apply the Fourth Amendment's prohibition of unreasonable searches and seizures to a 21st-century surveillance technique, the use of a Global Positioning System (GPS) device to monitor a vehicle's movements for an extended period of time. Ironically, the Court has chosen to decide this case based on 18th-century tort law. By attaching a small GPS device to the underside of the vehicle that respondent drove, the law enforcement officers in this case engaged in conduct that might have provided grounds in 1791 for a suit for trespass to chattels. And for this reason, the Court concludes, the installation and use of the GPS device constituted a search.

This holding, in my judgment, is unwise. It strains the language of the Fourth Amendment; it has little if any support in current Fourth Amendment case law; and it is highly artificial.

I would analyze the question presented in this case by asking whether respondent's reasonable expectations of privacy were violated by the long-term monitoring of the movements of the vehicle he drove.

I

A

The Fourth Amendment prohibits "unreasonable searches and seizures," and the Court makes very little effort to explain how the attachment or use of the GPS device fits within these terms. The Court does not contend that there was a seizure. A seizure of property occurs when there is "some meaningful interference with an individual's possessory interests in that property," *United States v. Jacobsen* (1984), and here there was none. Indeed, the success of the surveillance technique that the officers employed was dependent on the fact that the GPS did not interfere in any way with the operation of the vehicle, for if any such interference had been detected, the device might have been discovered.

The Court does claim that the installation and use of the GPS constituted a search, but this conclusion is dependent on the questionable proposition that these two procedures cannot be separated for purposes of Fourth Amendment analysis. If these two procedures are analyzed separately, it is not at all clear from the Court's opinion why either should be regarded as a search. It is clear that the attachment of the GPS device was not itself a search; if the device had not functioned or if the officers had not used it, no information would have been obtained. And the Court does not contend that the use of the device constituted a search either. On the contrary, the Court accepts the holding in *Knotts* that the use of a surreptitiously planted electronic device to monitor a vehicle's movements on public roads did not amount to a search.

The Court argues—and I agree—that "we must 'assur[e] preservation of that degree of privacy against government that existed when the Fourth Amendment was adopted.'" But it is almost impossible to think of late-18th-century situations that are analogous to what took place in this case. (Is it possible to imagine a case in which a constable secreted himself somewhere in a coach and remained there for a period of time in order to monitor the movements of the coach's owner?) The Court's theory seems to be that the concept of a search, as originally understood, comprehended any technical trespass that led to the gathering of evidence, but we know that this is incorrect. At common law, any unauthorized intrusion on private property was actionable, but a trespass on open fields, as opposed to the "curtilage" of a home, does not fall within the scope of the Fourth Amendment because private property outside the curtilage is not part of a "hous[e]" within the meaning of the Fourth Amendment.

B

'The Court's reasoning in this case is very similar to that in the Court's early decisions involving wiretapping and electronic eavesdropping, namely, that a technical trespass followed by the gathering of evidence constitutes a search. In the early electronic surveillance cases, the Court concluded that a Fourth Amendment search occurred when private conversations were monitored as a result of an "unauthorized physical penetration into the premises occupied" by the defendant. *Silverman v. United States.* In *Silverman*, police officers listened to conversations in an attached home by inserting a "spike mike" through the wall that this house shared with the vacant house next door. This procedure was held to be a search because the mike made contact with a heating duct on the other side of the wall and thus "usurp[ed] . . . an integral part of the premises."

By contrast, in cases in which there was no trespass, it was held that there was no search. Thus, in *Olmstead*, the Court found that the Fourth Amendment did not apply because "[t]he taps from house lines were made in the streets near the houses." Similarly, the Court concluded that no search occurred in *Goldman*, where a "detectaphone" was placed on the outer wall of defendant's office for the purpose of overhearing conversations held within the room.

This trespass-based rule was repeatedly criticized. In *Olmstead*, Justice Brandeis wrote that it was "immaterial where the physical connection with the telephone wires . . . was made. Although a private conversation transmitted by wire did not fall within the literal words of the Fourth Amendment, he argued, the Amendment should be understood as prohibiting "every unjustifiable intrusion by the Government upon the privacy of the individual."

Katz finally did away with the old approach, holding that a trespass was not required for a Fourth Amendment violation. *Katz* involved the use of a listening device that was attached to the outside of a public telephone booth and that allowed police officers to eavesdrop on one end of the target's phone conversation. This procedure did not physically intrude on the area occupied by the target, but the *Katz* Court "repudiate[ed]" the old doctrine, and held that "[t]he fact that the electronic device employed . . . did not happen to penetrate the wall of the booth can have no constitutional significance." What mattered, the Court now held, was whether the conduct at issue "violated the privacy upon which [the defendant] justifiably relied while using the telephone booth." *Katz*.

Under this approach, as the Court later put it when addressing the relevance of a technical trespass, "an actual trespass is neither necessary nor sufficient to establish a constitutional violation." In *Oliver*, the Court wrote:

> The existence of a property right is but one element in determining whether expectations of privacy are legitimate. "The premise that property interests control the right of the Government to search and seize has been discredited." *Katz*.

II

The majority suggests that two post-*Katz* decisions — *Soldal v. Cook County* (1992), and *Alderman v. United States* (1969) — show that a technical trespass is sufficient to establish the existence of a search, but they provide little support.

In *Soldal*, the Court held that towing away a trailer home without the owner's consent constituted a seizure even if this did not invade the occupants' personal privacy. But in the present case, the Court does not find that there was a seizure, and it is clear that none occurred.

In *Alderman*, the Court held that the Fourth Amendment rights of homeowners were implicated by the use of a surreptitiously planted listening device to monitor third-party conversations that occurred within their home. *Alderman* is best understood to mean that the homeowners had a legitimate expectation of privacy in all conversations that took place under their roof.

In sum, the majority is hard pressed to find support in post-*Katz* cases for its trespass-based theory.

III

Disharmony with a substantial body of existing case law is only one of the problems with the Court's approach in this case.

I will briefly note four others. First, the Court's reasoning largely disregards what is really important (the use of a GPS for the purpose of long-term tracking) and instead attaches great significance to something that most would view as relatively minor (attaching to the bottom of a car a small, light object that does not interfere in any way with the car's operation). Attaching such an object is generally regarded as so trivial that it does not provide a basis for recovery under modern tort law. *See* Prosser & Keeton § 14, at 87 (harmless or trivial contact with personal property not actionable); D. Dobbs, Law of Torts 124 (2000) (same). But under the Court's reasoning, this conduct may violate the Fourth Amendment. By contrast, if long-term monitoring can be accomplished without committing a technical trespass — suppose, for example, that the Federal Government required or persuaded auto manufacturers to include a GPS tracking device in every car — the Court's theory would provide no protection.

Second, the Court's approach leads to incongruous results. If the police attach a GPS device to a car and use the device to follow the car for even a brief time, under the Court's theory, the Fourth Amendment applies. But if the police follow the same car for a much longer period using unmarked cars and aerial assistance, this tracking is not subject to any Fourth Amendment constraints.

A. What Is a Search for Fourth Amendment Purposes? **237**

In the present case, the Fourth Amendment applies, the Court concludes, because the officers installed the GPS device after respondent's wife, to whom the car was registered, turned it over to respondent for his exclusive use. But if the GPS had been attached prior to that time, the Court's theory would lead to a different result. The Court proceeds on the assumption that respondent "had at least the property rights of a bailee," but a bailee may sue for a trespass to chattel only if the injury occurs during the term of the bailment. So if the GPS device had been installed before respondent's wife gave him the keys, respondent would have no claim for trespass—and, presumably, no Fourth Amendment claim either.

Third, under the Court's theory, the coverage of the Fourth Amendment may vary from State to State. If the events at issue here had occurred in a community-property State or a State that has adopted the Uniform Marital Property Act, respondent would likely be an owner of the vehicle, and it would not matter whether the GPS was installed before or after his wife turned over the keys. In non-community-property States, on the other hand, the registration of the vehicle in the name of respondent's wife would generally be regarded as presumptive evidence that she was the sole owner.

Fourth, the Court's reliance on the law of trespass will present particularly vexing problems in cases involving surveillance that is carried out by making electronic, as opposed to physical, contact with the item to be tracked. For example, suppose that the officers in the present case had followed respondent by surreptitiously activating a stolen vehicle detection system that came with the car when it was purchased. Would the sending of a radio signal to activate this system constitute a trespass to chattels? Trespass to chattels has traditionally required a physical touching of the property. In recent years, courts have wrestled with the application of this old tort in cases involving unwanted electronic contact with computer systems, and some have held that even the transmission of electrons that occurs when a communication is sent from one computer to another is enough. But may such decisions be followed in applying the Court's trespass theory? Assuming that what matters under the Court's theory is the law of trespass as it existed at the time of the adoption of the Fourth Amendment, do these recent decisions represent a change in the law or simply the application of the old tort to new situations?

IV

A

The *Katz* expectation-of-privacy test avoids the problems and complications noted above, but it is not without its own difficulties. It involves a degree of circularity, and judges are apt to confuse their own expectations of privacy with those of the hypothetical reasonable person to which the *Katz* test looks. In addition, the *Katz* test rests on the assumption that this hypothetical reasonable person has a well-developed and stable set of privacy expectations. But technology can change those expectations. Dramatic technological change may lead to periods in which popular expectations are in flux and may ultimately produce significant changes in popular attitudes. New technology may provide increased convenience or security at the expense of privacy, and many people may find the tradeoff worthwhile. And even if the public does not welcome the diminution of privacy that new technology entails, they may eventually reconcile themselves to this development as inevitable.

On the other hand, concern about new intrusions on privacy may spur the enactment of legislation to protect against these intrusions. This is what ultimately happened with respect to wiretapping. After *Katz*, Congress did not leave it to the courts to develop a body of Fourth Amendment case law governing that complex subject. Instead, Congress promptly enacted a comprehensive statute, and since that time, the regulation of wiretapping has been governed primarily by statute and not by case law. In an ironic sense, although *Katz* overruled *Olmstead*,

Chief Justice Taft's suggestion in the latter case that the regulation of wiretapping was a matter better left for Congress, has been borne out.

B

Recent years have seen the emergence of many new devices that permit the monitoring of a person's movements. In some locales, closed-circuit television video monitoring is becoming ubiquitous. On toll roads, automatic toll collection systems create a precise record of the movements of motorists who choose to make use of that convenience. Many motorists purchase cars that are equipped with devices that permit a central station to ascertain the car's location at any time so that roadside assistance may be provided if needed and the car may be found if it is stolen.

Perhaps most significant, cell phones and other wireless devices now permit wireless carriers to track and record the location of users—and as of June 2011, it has been reported, there were more than 322 million wireless devices in use in the United States. For older phones, the accuracy of the location information depends on the density of the tower network, but new "smart phones," which are equipped with a GPS device, permit more precise tracking. For example, when a user activates the GPS on such a phone, a provider is able to monitor the phone's location and speed of movement and can then report back real-time traffic conditions after combining ("crowdsourcing") the speed of all such phones on any particular road. Similarly, phone-location-tracking services are offered as "social" tools, allowing consumers to find (or to avoid) others who enroll in these services. The availability and use of these and other new devices will continue to shape the average person's expectations about the privacy of his or her daily movements.

V

In the precomputer age, the greatest protections of privacy were neither constitutional nor statutory, but practical. Traditional surveillance for any extended period of time was difficult and costly and therefore rarely undertaken. The surveillance at issue in this case—constant monitoring of the location of a vehicle for four weeks—would have required a large team of agents, multiple vehicles, and perhaps aerial assistance. Only an investigation of unusual importance could have justified such an expenditure of law enforcement resources. Devices like the one used in the present case, however, make long-term monitoring relatively easy and cheap. In circumstances involving dramatic technological change, the best solution to privacy concerns may be legislative. A legislative body is well situated to gauge changing public attitudes, to draw detailed lines, and to balance privacy and public safety in a comprehensive way.

To date, however, Congress and most States have not enacted statutes regulating the use of GPS tracking technology for law enforcement purposes. The best that we can do in this case is to apply existing Fourth Amendment doctrine and to ask whether the use of GPS tracking in a particular case involved a degree of intrusion that a reasonable person would not have anticipated.

Under this approach, relatively short-term monitoring of a person's movements on public streets accords with expectations of privacy that our society has recognized as reasonable. But the use of longer term GPS monitoring in investigations of most offenses impinges on expectations of privacy. For such offenses, society's expectation has been that law enforcement agents and others would not—and indeed, in the main, simply could not—secretly monitor and catalogue every single movement of an individual's car for a very long period. In this case, for four weeks, law enforcement agents tracked every movement that respondent made in the vehicle he was driving. We need not identify with precision the point at which the tracking of this vehicle became a search, for the line was surely crossed before the 4-week mark. Other cases may present more difficult questions. But where uncertainty exists with respect to whether a certain period of GPS surveillance is long enough to constitute a Fourth Amendment search, the police may always seek a warrant. We also need not consider whether prolonged GPS monitoring in the context of investigations involving extraordinary offenses would similarly intrude on a constitutionally protected sphere of privacy. In such cases, long-term tracking might have been mounted using previously available techniques.

For these reasons, I conclude that the lengthy monitoring that occurred in this case constituted a search under the Fourth Amendment. I therefore agree with the majority that the decision of the Court of Appeals must be affirmed. . . .

NOTES AND QUESTIONS

1. What is the relationship between the "trespass" test and the "reasonable expectation of privacy" test after *Jones*? Is a trespass a sufficient condition for a Fourth Amendment violation even if not a necessary condition? Is the Court correct that the latter test has "added to not substituted for" the former test?

2. The government contends, in what appears to be something of an eleventh-hour Hail Mary pass, that even if the use of the GPS monitoring device was a search, it was supported by "reasonable suspicion" and thus constitutional. What is your reaction to this argument? How does the government's use of GPS monitoring here compare to a permissible *Terry* stop?

3. In her concurring opinion Justice Sotomayor questions the continuing validity of the Court's third-party cases, pointing out Justice Marshall's observation in dissent in *Smith v. Maryland*, 442 U.S. 735, 749 (1979) (Marshall, J., dissenting): "Privacy is not a discrete commodity, possessed absolutely or not at all. Those who disclose certain facts to a bank or phone company for a limited business purpose need not assume that this information will be released to other persons for other purposes."

Should the issue be reframed as a reasonable expectation of privacy with respect to the government?

4. Justice Alito's concurrence suggests that some shorter period of surveillance than the 28 days here might not constitute a search. What is the relevance of the duration of the monitoring?

5. What are the pros and cons of legislative solutions to government use of technology for investigative purposes?

With respect to living "technology," the Court rejected the notion that police use of drug-sniffing dogs was a search given the limited nature of both the intrusion and the information derived. *United States v. Place*, 462 U.S. 696 (1983). *See also Illinois v. Caballes*, 543 U.S. 205 (2005) (subjecting vehicle pulled over for traffic stop to canine sniff does not violate Fourth Amendment where duration of stop not unreasonably extended; no legitimate expectation of privacy inasmuch as dog only able to detect illegal substances).

But traditional notions of property and home can still be trump cards.

Florida v. Jardines
569 U.S. 1 (2013)

Justice SCALIA delivered the opinion of the Court.

We consider whether using a drug-sniffing dog on a homeowner's porch to investigate the contents of the home is a "search" within the meaning of the Fourth Amendment.

I

In 2006, Detective William Pedraja of the Miami-Dade Police Department received an unverified tip that marijuana was being grown in the home of respondent Joelis Jardines. One month later, the Department and the Drug Enforcement Administration sent a joint surveillance team to Jardines' home. Detective Pedraja was part of that team. He watched the home for fifteen minutes and saw no vehicles in the driveway or activity around the home, and could not see inside because the blinds were drawn. Detective Pedraja then approached Jardines' home accompanied by Detective Douglas Bartelt, a trained canine handler who had just arrived at the scene with his drug-sniffing dog. The dog was trained to detect the scent of marijuana, cocaine, heroin, and several other drugs, indicating the presence of any of these substances through particular behavioral changes recognizable by his handler.

Detective Bartelt had the dog on a six-foot leash, owing in part to the dog's "wild" nature, and tendency to dart around erratically while searching. As the dog approached Jardines' front porch, he apparently sensed one of the odors he had been trained to detect, and began energetically exploring the area for the strongest point source of that odor. As Detective Bartelt explained, the dog "began tracking that airborne odor by . . . tracking back and forth," engaging in what is called "bracketing," "back and forth, back and forth." Detective Bartelt gave the dog "the full six feet of the leash plus whatever safe distance [he could] give him" to do this—he testified that he needed to give the dog "as much distance as I can." And Detective Pedraja stood back while this was occurring, so that he would not "get knocked over" when the dog was "spinning around trying to find" the source.

After sniffing the base of the front door, the dog sat, which is the trained behavior upon discovering the odor's strongest point. Detective Bartelt then pulled the dog away from the door and returned to his vehicle. He left the scene after informing Detective Pedraja that there had been a positive alert for narcotics.

On the basis of what he had learned at the home, Detective Pedraja applied for and received a warrant to search the residence. When the warrant was executed later that day, Jardines attempted to flee and was arrested; the search revealed marijuana plants, and he was charged with trafficking in cannabis.

At trial, Jardines moved to suppress the marijuana plants on the ground that the canine investigation was an unreasonable search. The trial court granted the motion, and the Florida Third District Court of Appeal reversed. On a petition for discretionary review, the Florida Supreme Court quashed the decision of the Third District Court of Appeal and approved the trial court's decision to suppress, holding (as relevant here) that the use of the trained narcotics dog to investigate Jardines' home was a Fourth Amendment search unsupported by probable cause, rendering invalid the warrant based upon information gathered in that search.

We granted certiorari, limited to the question of whether the officers' behavior was a search within the meaning of the Fourth Amendment.

II

The Fourth Amendment provides in relevant part that the "right of the people to be secure in their persons, houses, papers, and effects, against unreasonable searches and seizures, shall not be violated." The Amendment establishes a simple baseline, one that for much of our history formed the exclusive basis for its protections: When "the Government obtains information by physically intruding" on persons, houses, papers, or effects, "a 'search' within the original meaning of the Fourth Amendment" has "undoubtedly occurred."

That principle renders this case a straightforward one. The officers were gathering information in an area belonging to Jardines and immediately surrounding his house—in the curtilage of the house, which we have held enjoys protection as part of the home itself. And they gathered that information by physically entering and occupying the area to engage in conduct not explicitly or implicitly permitted by the homeowner.

A

The Fourth Amendment "indicates with some precision the places and things encompassed by its protections": persons, houses, papers, and effects. The Fourth Amendment does not, therefore, prevent all investigations conducted on private property; for example, an officer may (subject to *Katz*) gather information in what we have called "open fields" — even if those fields are privately owned — because such fields are not enumerated in the Amendment's text.

But when it comes to the Fourth Amendment, the home is first among equals. At the Amendment's "very core" stands "the right of a man to retreat into his own home and there be free from unreasonable governmental intrusion." This right would be of little practical value if the State's agents could stand in a home's porch or side garden and trawl for evidence with impunity; the right to retreat would be significantly diminished if the police could enter a man's property to observe his repose from just outside the front window.

We therefore regard the area "immediately surrounding and associated with the home" — what our cases call the curtilage — as "part of the home itself for Fourth Amendment purposes." That principle has ancient and durable roots. Just as the distinction between the home and the open fields is "as old as the common law," so too is the identity of home and what Blackstone called the "curtilage or homestall," for the "house protects and privileges all its branches and appurtenants." This area around the home is "intimately linked to the home, both physically and psychologically," and is where "privacy expectations are most heightened."

While the boundaries of the curtilage are generally "clearly marked," the "conception defining the curtilage" is at any rate familiar enough that it is "easily understood from our daily experience." Here there is no doubt that the officers entered it: The front porch is the classic exemplar of an area adjacent to the home and "to which the activity of home life extends."

B

Since the officers' investigation took place in a constitutionally protected area, we turn to the question of whether it was accomplished through an unlicensed physical intrusion. While law enforcement officers need not "shield their eyes" when passing by the home "on public thoroughfares," an officer's leave to gather information is sharply circumscribed when he steps off those thoroughfares and enters the Fourth Amendment's protected areas. In permitting, for example, visual observation of the home from "public navigable airspace," we were careful to note that it was done "in a physically nonintrusive manner." "[O]ur law holds the property of every man so sacred, that no man can set his foot upon his neighbour's close without his leave." As it is undisputed that the detectives had all four of their feet and all four of their companion's firmly planted on the constitutionally protected extension of Jardines' home, the only question is whether he had given his leave (even implicitly) for them to do so. He had not.

"A license may be implied from the habits of the country," notwithstanding the "strict rule of the English common law as to entry upon a close." We have accordingly recognized that "the knocker on the front door is treated as an invitation or license to attempt an entry, justifying ingress to the home by solicitors, hawkers and peddlers of all kinds." This implicit license typically permits the visitor to approach the home by the front path, knock promptly, wait briefly to be received, and then (absent invitation to linger longer) leave. Complying with the terms of that traditional invitation does not require fine-grained legal knowledge; it is generally managed without incident by the Nation's Girl Scouts and trick-or-treaters. Thus, a police officer not armed with a warrant may approach a home and knock, precisely because that is "no more than any private citizen might do."

But introducing a trained police dog to explore the area around the home in hopes of discovering incriminating evidence is something else. There is no customary invitation to do that. An invitation to engage in canine forensic investigation assuredly does not inhere in the very act of hanging a knocker. To find a visitor knocking on the door is routine (even if sometimes unwelcome); to spot that same visitor exploring the front path with a metal detector, or marching his bloodhound into the garden before saying hello and asking permission, would inspire most of us to—well, call the police. The scope of a license—express or implied—is limited not only to a particular area but also to a specific purpose. Consent at a traffic stop to an officer's checking out an anonymous tip that there is a body in the trunk does not permit the officer to rummage through the trunk for narcotics. Here, the background social norms that invite a visitor to the front door do not invite him there to conduct a search.

The State points to our decisions holding that the subjective intent of the officer is irrelevant. See *Ashcroft v. al-Kidd* (2011); *Whren v. United States* (1996). But those cases merely hold that a stop or search that is objectively reasonable is not vitiated by the fact that the officer's real reason for making the stop or search has nothing to do with the validating reason. Thus, the defendant will not be heard to complain that although he was speeding the officer's real reason for the stop was racial harassment. Here, however, the question before the court is precisely whether the officer's conduct was an objectively reasonable search. As we have described, that depends upon whether the officers had an implied license to enter the porch, which in turn depends upon the purpose for which they entered. Here, their behavior objectively reveals a purpose to conduct a search, which is not what anyone would think he had license to do.

III

The State argues that investigation by a forensic narcotics dog by definition cannot implicate any legitimate privacy interest. The State cites for authority our decisions in *United States v. Place*, (1983), *United States v. Jacobsen* (1984), and *Illinois v. Caballes* (2005), which held, respectively, that canine inspection of luggage in an airport, chemical testing of a substance that had fallen from a parcel in transit, and canine inspection of an automobile during a lawful traffic stop, do not violate the "reasonable expectation of privacy" described in *Katz*.

Just last Term, we considered an argument much like this. *Jones* held that tracking an automobile's whereabouts using a physically-mounted GPS receiver is a Fourth Amendment search. The Government argued that the *Katz* standard "show[ed] that no search occurred," as the defendant had "no 'reasonable expectation of privacy'" in his whereabouts on the public roads—a proposition with at least as much support in our case law as the one the State marshals here. But because the GPS receiver had been physically mounted on the defendant's automobile (thus intruding on his "effects"), we held that tracking the vehicle's movements was a search: a person's "Fourth Amendment rights do not rise or fall with the *Katz* formulation." The *Katz* reasonable-expectations test "has been added to, not substituted for," the traditional property-based understanding of the Fourth Amendment, and so is unnecessary to consider when the government gains evidence by physically intruding on constitutionally protected areas.

Thus, we need not decide whether the officers' investigation of Jardines' home violated his expectation of privacy under *Katz*. One virtue of the Fourth Amendment's property-rights baseline is that it keeps easy cases easy. That the officers learned what they learned only by physically intruding on Jardines' property to gather evidence is enough to establish that a search occurred.

For a related reason we find irrelevant the State's argument (echoed by the dissent) that forensic dogs have been commonly used by police for centuries. This argument is apparently directed to our holding in *Kyllo* that surveillance of the home is a search where "the Government uses a device that is not in general public use" to "explore details of the home that would previously have been unknowable without physical intrusion." But the implication of that statement (inclusio unius est exclusio alterius) is that when the government uses a physical intrusion to explore details of the home (including its curtilage), the antiquity of the tools that they bring along is irrelevant.

• • •

The government's use of trained police dogs to investigate the home and its immediate surroundings is a "search" within the meaning of the Fourth Amendment. The judgment of the Supreme Court of Florida is therefore affirmed.

[Justices Alito, Kennedy, and Breyer and Chief Justice Roberts dissented.]

NOTES AND QUESTIONS

1. Do you agree that this is a "straightforward" case? Because of *Kyllo*? Because of *Jones*?

2. Consider the first use of drug-sniffing dogs. Is such "technology" similar to the thermal imaging in *Kyllo* in that it is "sense enhancing"? Does the use of drug-sniffing dogs ever come into "general public use" within the meaning of *Kyllo*?

3. Did the defendant have a reasonable expectation of privacy in his porch area, even though it was accessible to trick-or-treaters and the like? Should the answer depend on common law notions of "license"?

4. In her concurring opinion Justice Kagan analogizes *Jardines* to a stranger (or a policeman) standing on a porch with "super high-powered binoculars" with which he can see into every nook and cranny of the home. Based on this analogy she concludes that *Jardines* involves a search under both a property theory and a *Katz* theory. Do you agree?

5. "But when it comes to the Fourth Amendment, the home is first among equals," the Court says, and *Kyllo* and *Jardines* certainly seem to be examples of this. For a contrary view, see Ric Simmons, Lange, Caniglia, *and the Myth of Home Exceptionalism*, 54 Ariz. St. L.J. 145 (2022).

Carpenter v. United States
585 U.S. 296 (2018)

Chief Justice ROBERTS delivered the opinion of the Court.

This case presents the question whether the Government conducts a search under the Fourth Amendment when it accesses historical cell phone records that provide a comprehensive chronicle of the user's past movements.

I

A

There are 396 million cell phone service accounts in the United States — for a Nation of 326 million people. Cell phones perform their wide and growing variety of functions by connecting to a set of radio antennas called "cell sites." Although cell sites are usually mounted on a tower, they can also be found on light posts, flagpoles, church steeples, or the sides of buildings. Cell sites typically have several directional antennas that divide the covered area into sectors.

Cell phones continuously scan their environment looking for the best signal, which generally comes from the closest cell site. Most modern devices, such as smartphones, tap into the wireless network several times a minute whenever their signal is on, even if the owner is not using one of the phone's features. Each time the phone connects to a cell site, it generates a time-stamped record known as cell-site location information (CSLI). The precision of this information depends on the size of the geographic area covered by the cell site. The greater the concentration of cell sites, the smaller the coverage area. As data usage from cell phones has increased, wireless carriers have installed more cell sites to handle the traffic. That has led to increasingly compact coverage areas, especially in urban areas.

Wireless carriers collect and store CSLI for their own business purposes, including finding weak spots in their network and applying "roaming" charges when another carrier routes data through their cell sites. In addition, wireless carriers often sell aggregated location records to data brokers, without individual identifying information of the sort at issue here. While carriers have long retained CSLI for the start and end of incoming calls, in recent years phone companies have also collected location information from the transmission of text messages and routine data connections. Accordingly, modern cell phones generate increasingly vast amounts of increasingly precise CSLI.

B

In 2011, police officers arrested four men suspected of robbing a series of Radio Shack and (ironically enough) T-Mobile stores in Detroit. One of the men confessed that, over the previous four months, the group (along with a rotating cast of getaway drivers and lookouts) had robbed nine different stores in Michigan and Ohio. The suspect identified 15 accomplices who had participated in the heists and gave the FBI some of their cell phone numbers; the FBI then reviewed his call records to identify additional numbers that he had called around the time of the robberies.

Based on that information, the prosecutors applied for court orders under the Stored Communications Act to obtain cell phone records for petitioner Timothy Carpenter and several other suspects. That statute, as amended in 1994, permits the Government to compel the disclosure of certain telecommunications records when it "offers specific and articulable facts showing that there are reasonable grounds to believe" that the records sought "are relevant and material to an ongoing criminal investigation." 18 U.S.C. § 2703(d). Federal Magistrate Judges issued two orders directing Carpenter's wireless carriers—MetroPCS and Sprint—to disclose "cell/site sector [information] for [Carpenter's] telephone[ ] at call origination and at call termination for incoming and outgoing calls" during the four-month period when the string of robberies occurred. The first order sought 152 days of cell-site records from MetroPCS, which produced records spanning 127 days. The second order requested seven days of CSLI from Sprint, which produced two days of records covering the period when Carpenter's phone was "roaming" in northeastern Ohio. Altogether the Government obtained 12,898 location points cataloging Carpenter's movements—an average of 101 data points per day.

Carpenter was charged with six counts of robbery and an additional six counts of carrying a firearm during a federal crime of violence. See 18 U.S.C. §§ 924(c), 1951(a). Prior to trial, Carpenter moved to suppress the cell-site data provided by the wireless carriers. He argued that the Government's seizure of the records violated the Fourth Amendment because they had been obtained without a warrant supported by probable cause. The District Court denied the motion.

A. What Is a Search for Fourth Amendment Purposes?

At trial, seven of Carpenter's confederates pegged him as the leader of the operation. In addition, FBI agent Christopher Hess offered expert testimony about the cell-site data. Hess explained that each time a cell phone taps into the wireless network, the carrier logs a time-stamped record of the cell site and particular sector that were used. With this information, Hess produced maps that placed Carpenter's phone near four of the charged robberies. In the Government's view, the location records clinched the case: They confirmed that Carpenter was "right where the . . . robbery was at the exact time of the robbery." App. 131 (closing argument). Carpenter was convicted on all but one of the firearm counts and sentenced to more than 100 years in prison.

The Court of Appeals for the Sixth Circuit affirmed. The court held that Carpenter lacked a reasonable expectation of privacy in the location information collected by the FBI because he had shared that information with his wireless carriers. Given that cell phone users voluntarily convey cell-site data to their carriers as "a means of establishing communication," the court concluded that the resulting business records are not entitled to Fourth Amendment protection.

We granted certiorari.

II

A

. . .

B

The case before us involves the Government's acquisition of wireless carrier cell-site records revealing the location of Carpenter's cell phone whenever it made or received calls. This sort of digital data — personal location information maintained by a third party — does not fit neatly under existing precedents. Instead, requests for cell-site records lie at the intersection of two lines of cases, both of which inform our understanding of the privacy interests at stake.

The first set of cases addresses a person's expectation of privacy in his physical location and movements. In *Knotts* we considered the Government's use of a "beeper" to aid in tracking a vehicle through traffic. Police officers in that case planted a beeper in a container of chloro-form before it was purchased by one of Knotts's co-conspirators. The officers (with intermit-tent aerial assistance) then followed the automobile carrying the container from Minneapolis to Knotts's cabin in Wisconsin, relying on the beeper's signal to help keep the vehicle in view. The Court concluded that the "augment[ed]" visual surveillance did not constitute a search because "[a] person traveling in an automobile on public thoroughfares has no reasonable expectation of privacy in his movements from one place to another." Since the movements of the vehicle and its final destination had been "voluntarily conveyed to anyone who wanted to look."

This Court in *Knotts*, however, was careful to distinguish between the rudimentary track-ing facilitated by the beeper and more sweeping modes of surveillance. The Court empha-sized the "limited use which the government made of the signals from this particular beeper" during a discrete "automotive journey." Significantly, the Court reserved the question whether "different constitutional principles may be applicable" if "twenty-four hour surveillance of any citizen of this country [were] possible."

Three decades later, the Court considered more sophisticated surveillance of the sort envi-sioned in Knotts and found that different principles did indeed apply. In *Jones*, FBI agents installed a GPS tracking device on Jones's vehicle and remotely monitored the vehicle's move-ments for 28 days. The Court decided the case based on the Government's physical trespass of the vehicle. At the same time, five Justices agreed that related privacy concerns would be raised by, for example, "surreptitiously activating a stolen vehicle detection system" in Jones's car to track Jones himself, or conducting GPS tracking of his cell phone. Since GPS monitoring of a vehicle tracks "every movement" a person makes in that vehicle, the concurring Justices concluded that "longer term GPS monitoring in investigations of most offenses impinges on expectations of privacy"—regardless whether those movements were disclosed to the public at large.

In a second set of decisions, the Court has drawn a line between what a person keeps to himself and what he shares with others. We have previously held that "a person has no legitimate expectation of privacy in information he voluntarily turns over to third parties." That remains true "even if the information is revealed on the assumption that it will be used only for a limited purpose." As a result, the Government is typically free to obtain such information from the recipient without triggering Fourth Amendment protections.

This third-party doctrine largely traces its roots to *Miller*. While investigating Miller for tax evasion, the Government subpoenaed his banks, seeking several months of canceled checks, deposit slips, and monthly statements. The Court rejected a Fourth Amendment challenge to the records collection. For one, Miller could "assert neither ownership nor possession" of the documents; they were "business records of the banks." For another, the nature of those records confirmed Miller's limited expectation of privacy, because the checks were "not confidential communications but negotiable instruments to be used in commercial transactions," and the bank statements contained information "exposed to [bank] employees in the ordinary course of business." The Court thus concluded that Miller had "take[n] the risk, in revealing his affairs to another, that the information [would] be conveyed by that person to the Government."

Three years later, *Smith* applied the same principles in the context of information conveyed to a telephone company. The Court ruled that the Government's use of a pen register—a device that recorded the outgoing phone numbers dialed on a landline telephone—was not a search. Noting the pen register's "limited capabilities," the Court "doubt[ed] that people in general entertain any actual expectation of privacy in the numbers they dial." Telephone subscribers know, after all, that the numbers are used by the telephone company "for a variety of legitimate business purposes," including routing calls. And at any rate, the Court explained, such an expectation "is not one that society is prepared to recognize as reasonable." When Smith placed a call, he "voluntarily conveyed" the dialed numbers to the phone company by "expos[ing] that information to its equipment in the ordinary course of business." Once again, we held that the defendant "assumed the risk" that the company's records "would be divulged to police."

III

The question we confront today is how to apply the Fourth Amendment to a new phenomenon: the ability to chronicle a person's past movements through the record of his cell phone signals. Such tracking partakes of many of the qualities of the GPS monitoring we considered in *Jones*. Much like GPS tracking of a vehicle, cell phone location information is detailed, encyclopedic, and effortlessly compiled.

At the same time, the fact that the individual continuously reveals his location to his wireless carrier implicates the third-party principle of *Smith* and *Miller*. But while the third-party doctrine applies to telephone numbers and bank records, it is not clear whether its logic extends to the qualitatively different category of cell-site records. After all, when *Smith* was decided in 1979, few could have imagined a society in which a phone goes wherever its owner goes, conveying to the wireless carrier not just dialed digits, but a detailed and comprehensive record of the person's movements.

We decline to extend *Smith* and *Miller* to cover these novel circumstances. Given the unique nature of cell phone location records, the fact that the information is held by a third party does not by itself overcome the user's claim to Fourth Amendment protection. Whether the Government employs its own surveillance technology as in Jones or leverages the technology of a wireless carrier, we hold that an individual maintains a legitimate expectation of privacy in the record of his physical movements as captured through CSLI. The location information obtained from Carpenter's wireless carriers was the product of a search.

A

A person does not surrender all Fourth Amendment protection by venturing into the public sphere. To the contrary, "what [one] seeks to preserve as private, even in an area accessible to the public, may be constitutionally protected." A majority of this Court has already recognized that individuals have a reasonable expectation of privacy in the whole of their physical movements. Prior to the digital age, law enforcement might have pursued a suspect for a brief stretch, but doing so "for any extended period of time was difficult and costly and therefore rarely undertaken." For that reason, "society's expectation has been that law enforcement agents and others would not—and indeed, in the main, simply could not—secretly monitor and catalogue every single movement of an individual's car for a very long period."

Allowing government access to cell-site records contravenes that expectation. Although such records are generated for commercial purposes, that distinction does not negate Carpenter's anticipation of privacy in his physical location. Mapping a cell phone's location over the course of 127 days provides an all-encompassing record of the holder's whereabouts. As with GPS information, the time-stamped data provides an intimate window into a person's life, revealing not only his particular movements, but through them his "familial, political, professional, religious, and sexual associations." These location records "hold for many Americans the 'privacies of life.'" And like GPS monitoring, cell phone tracking is remarkably easy, cheap, and efficient compared to traditional investigative tools. With just the click of a button, the Government can access each carrier's deep repository of historical location information at practically no expense.

In fact, historical cell-site records present even greater privacy concerns than the GPS monitoring of a vehicle we considered in *Jones*. Unlike the bugged container in *Knotts* or the car in *Jones*, a cell phone—almost a "feature of human anatomy," tracks nearly exactly the movements of its owner. While individuals regularly leave their vehicles, they compulsively carry cell phones with them all the time. A cell phone faithfully follows its owner beyond public thoroughfares and into private residences, doctor's offices, political headquarters, and other potentially revealing locales.

Moreover, the retrospective quality of the data here gives police access to a category of information otherwise unknowable. In the past, attempts to reconstruct a person's movements were limited by a dearth of records and the frailties of recollection. With access to CSLI, the Government can now travel back in time to retrace a person's whereabouts, subject only to the retention polices of the wireless carriers, which currently maintain records for up to five years. Critically, because location information is continually logged for all of the 400 million devices in the United States—not just those belonging to persons who might happen to come under investigation—this newfound tracking capacity runs against everyone. Unlike with the GPS device in *Jones*, police need not even know in advance whether they want to follow a particular individual, or when.

Whoever the suspect turns out to be, he has effectively been tailed every moment of every day for five years, and the police may—in the Government's view—call upon the results of that surveillance without regard to the constraints of the Fourth Amendment. Only the few without cell phones could escape this tireless and absolute surveillance.

The Government and Justice Kennedy contend, however, that the collection of CSLI should be permitted because the data is less precise than GPS information. Not to worry, they maintain, because the location records did "not on their own suffice to place [Carpenter] at the crime scene"; they placed him within a wedge-shaped sector ranging from one-eighth to four square miles. Yet the Court has already rejected the proposition that "inference insulates a search." From the 127 days of location data it received, the Government could, in combination with other information, deduce a detailed log of Carpenter's movements, including when he was at the site of the robberies. And the Government thought the CSLI accurate enough to highlight it during the closing argument of his trial.

At any rate, the rule the Court adopts "must take account of more sophisticated systems that are already in use or in development." While the records in this case reflect the state of technology at the start of the decade, the accuracy of CSLI is rapidly approaching GPS-level precision. As the number of cell sites has proliferated, the geographic area covered by each cell sector has shrunk, particularly in urban areas. In addition, with new technology measuring the time and angle of signals hitting their towers, wireless carriers already have the capability to pinpoint a phone's location within 50 meters.

Accordingly, when the Government accessed CSLI from the wireless carriers, it invaded Carpenter's reasonable expectation of privacy in the whole of his physical movements.

B

The Government's primary contention to the contrary is that the third-party doctrine governs this case. In its view, cell-site records are fair game because they are "business records" created and maintained by the wireless carriers. The Government (along with Justice Kennedy) recognizes that this case features new technology, but asserts that the legal question nonetheless turns on a garden-variety request for information from a third-party witness.

The Government's position fails to contend with the seismic shifts in digital technology that made possible the tracking of not only Carpenter's location but also everyone else's, not for a short period but for years and years. Sprint Corporation and its competitors are not your typical witnesses. Unlike the nosy neighbor who keeps an eye on comings and goings, they are ever alert, and their memory is nearly infallible. There is a world of difference between the limited types of personal information addressed in *Smith* and *Miller* and the exhaustive chronicle of location information casually collected by wireless carriers today. The Government thus is not asking for a straightforward application of the third-party doctrine, but instead a significant extension of it to a distinct category of information.

The third-party doctrine partly stems from the notion that an individual has a reduced expectation of privacy in information knowingly shared with another. But the fact of "diminished privacy interests does not mean that the Fourth Amendment falls out of the picture entirely." *Smith* and *Miller*, after all, did not rely solely on the act of sharing. Instead, they considered "the nature of the particular documents sought" to determine whether "there is a legitimate 'expectation of privacy' concerning their contents." *Smith* pointed out the limited capabilities of a pen register; as explained in *Riley*, telephone call logs reveal little in the way of "identifying information." *Miller* likewise noted that checks were "not confidential communications but negotiable instruments to be used in commercial transactions." In mechanically applying the third-party doctrine to this case, the Government fails to appreciate that there are no comparable limitations on the revealing nature of CSLI.

The Court has in fact already shown special solicitude for location information in the third-party context. In *Knotts*, the Court relied on *Smith* to hold that an individual has no reasonable expectation of privacy in public movements that he "voluntarily conveyed to anyone who wanted to look." But when confronted with more pervasive tracking, five Justices agreed that longer term GPS monitoring of even a vehicle traveling on public streets constitutes a search. Justice Gorsuch wonders why "someone's location when using a phone" is sensitive, and Justice Kennedy assumes that a person's discrete movements "are not particularly private." Yet this case is not about "using a phone" or a person's movement at a particular time. It is about a detailed chronicle of a person's physical presence compiled every day, every moment, over several years. Such a chronicle implicates privacy concerns far beyond those considered in *Smith* and *Miller*.

Neither does the second rationale underlying the third-party doctrine—voluntary exposure—hold up when it comes to CSLI. Cell phone location information is not truly "shared" as one normally understands the term. In the first place, cell phones and the services they provide are "such a pervasive and insistent part of daily life" that carrying one is indispensable to participation in modern society. Second, a cell phone logs a cell-site record by dint of its operation, without any affirmative act on the part of the user beyond powering up. Virtually any activity on the phone generates CSLI, including incoming calls, texts, or e-mails and countless other data connections that a phone automatically makes when checking for news, weather, or social media updates. Apart from disconnecting the phone from the network, there is no way to avoid leaving behind a trail of location data. As a result, in no meaningful sense does the user voluntarily "assume[ ] the risk" of turning over a comprehensive dossier of his physical movements.

We therefore decline to extend *Smith* and *Miller* to the collection of CSLI. Given the unique nature of cell phone location information, the fact that the Government obtained the information from a third party does not overcome Carpenter's claim to Fourth Amendment protection. The Government's acquisition of the cell-site records was a search within the meaning of the Fourth Amendment.

· · ·

Our decision today is a narrow one. We do not express a view on matters not before us: real-time CSLI or "tower dumps" (a download of information on all the devices that connected to a particular cell site during a particular interval). We do not disturb the application of *Smith* and *Miller* or call into question conventional surveillance techniques and tools, such as security cameras. Nor do we address other business records that might incidentally reveal location information. Further, our opinion does not consider other collection techniques involving foreign affairs or national security. As Justice Frankfurter noted when considering new innovations in airplanes and radios, the Court must tread carefully in such cases, to ensure that we do not "embarrass the future."

IV

Having found that the acquisition of Carpenter's CSLI was a search, we also conclude that the Government must generally obtain a warrant supported by probable cause before acquiring such records. Although the "ultimate measure of the constitutionality of a governmental search is 'reasonableness,'" our cases establish that warrantless searches are typically unreasonable where "a search is undertaken by law enforcement officials to discover evidence of criminal wrongdoing." Thus, "[i]n the absence of a warrant, a search is reasonable only if it falls within a specific exception to the warrant requirement."

The Government acquired the cell-site records pursuant to a court order issued under the Stored Communications Act, which required the Government to show "reasonable grounds" for believing that the records were "relevant and material to an ongoing investigation." 18 U.S.C. § 2703(d). That showing falls well short of the probable cause required for a warrant. The Court usually requires "some quantum of individualized suspicion" before a search or seizure may take place. Under the standard in the Stored Communications Act, however, law enforcement need only show that the cell-site evidence might be pertinent to an ongoing investigation — a "gigantic" departure from the probable cause rule, as the Government explained below. Consequently, an order issued under Section 2703(d) of the Act is not a permissible mechanism for accessing historical cell-site records. Before compelling a wireless carrier to turn over a subscriber's CSLI, the Government's obligation is a familiar one — get a warrant.

Justice Alito contends that the warrant requirement simply does not apply when the Government acquires records using compulsory process. Unlike an actual search, he says, subpoenas for documents do not involve the direct taking of evidence; they are at most a "constructive search" conducted by the target of the subpoena. Given this lesser intrusion on personal privacy, Justice Alito argues that the compulsory production of records is not held to the same probable cause standard. In his view, this Court's precedents set forth a categorical rule — separate and distinct from the third-party doctrine — subjecting subpoenas to lenient scrutiny without regard to the suspect's expectation of privacy in the records.

But this Court has never held that the Government may subpoena third parties for records in which the suspect has a reasonable expectation of privacy. Almost all of the examples Justice Alito cites, contemplated requests for evidence implicating diminished privacy interests or for a corporation's own books. The lone exception, of course, is *Miller*, where the Court's analysis of the third-party subpoena merged with the application of the third-party doctrine.

Justice Alito overlooks the critical issue. At some point, the dissent should recognize that CSLI is an entirely different species of business record — something that implicates basic Fourth Amendment concerns about arbitrary government power much more directly than corporate tax or payroll ledgers. When confronting new concerns wrought by digital technology, this Court has been careful not to uncritically extend existing precedents.

If the choice to proceed by subpoena provided a categorical limitation on Fourth Amendment protection, no type of record would ever be protected by the warrant requirement. Under Justice Alito's view, private letters, digital contents of a cell phone — any personal information reduced to document form, in fact — may be collected by subpoena for no reason other than "official curiosity." Justice Kennedy declines to adopt the radical implications of this theory, leaving open the question whether the warrant requirement applies "when the Government obtains the modern-day equivalents of an individual's own 'papers' or 'effects,' even when those papers or effects are held by a third party." That would be a sensible exception, because it would prevent the subpoena doctrine from overcoming any reasonable expectation of privacy. If the third-party doctrine does not apply to the "modern-day equivalents of an individual's own 'papers' or 'effects,'" then the clear implication is that the documents should receive full Fourth Amendment protection. We simply think that such protection should extend as well to a detailed log of a person's movements over several years.

This is certainly not to say that all orders compelling the production of documents will require a showing of probable cause. The Government will be able to use subpoenas to acquire records in the overwhelming majority of investigations. We hold only that a warrant is required in the rare case where the suspect has a legitimate privacy interest in records held by a third party.

Further, even though the Government will generally need a warrant to access CSLI, case-specific exceptions may support a warrantless search of an individual's cell-site records under certain circumstances. "One well-recognized exception applies when ' "the exigencies of the situation" make the needs of law enforcement so compelling that [a] warrantless search is objectively reasonable under the Fourth Amendment.'" Such exigencies include the need to pursue a fleeing suspect, protect individuals who are threatened with imminent harm, or prevent the imminent destruction of evidence.

As a result, if law enforcement is confronted with an urgent situation, such fact-specific threats will likely justify the warrantless collection of CSLI. Lower courts, for instance, have approved warrantless searches related to bomb threats, active shootings, and child abductions. Our decision today does not call into doubt warrantless access to CSLI in such circumstances. While police must get a warrant when collecting CSLI to assist in the mine-run criminal investigation, the rule we set forth does not limit their ability to respond to an ongoing emergency.

• • •

As Justice Brandeis explained in his famous dissent, the Court is obligated—as "[s]ubtler and more far-reaching means of invading privacy have become available to the Government"—to ensure that the "progress of science" does not erode Fourth Amendment protections. Here the progress of science has afforded law enforcement a powerful new tool to carry out its important responsibilities. At the same time, this tool risks Government encroachment of the sort the Framers, "after consulting the lessons of history," drafted the Fourth Amendment to prevent.

We decline to grant the state unrestricted access to a wireless carrier's database of physical location information. In light of the deeply revealing nature of CSLI, its depth, breadth, and comprehensive reach, and the inescapable and automatic nature of its collection, the fact that such information is gathered by a third party does not make it any less deserving of Fourth Amendment protection. The Government's acquisition of the cell-site records here was a search under that Amendment.

The judgment of the Court of Appeals is reversed, and the case is remanded for further proceedings consistent with this opinion.

[Justices Kennedy, Thomas, Gorsuch, and Alito dissented.]

Justice GORSUCH, dissenting.

In the late 1960s this Court suggested for the first time that a search triggering the Fourth Amendment occurs when the government violates an "expectation of privacy" that "society is prepared to recognize as 'reasonable.'" *Katz*. Then, in a pair of decisions in the 1970s applying the *Katz* test, the Court held that a "reasonable expectation of privacy" doesn't attach to information shared with "third parties." *Smith v. Maryland*; *United States v. Miller*. By these steps, the Court came to conclude, the Constitution does nothing to limit investigators from searching records you've entrusted to your bank, accountant, and maybe even your doctor.

What's left of the Fourth Amendment? Today we use the Internet to do most everything. Smartphones make it easy to keep a calendar, correspond with friends, make calls, conduct banking, and even watch the game. Countless Internet companies maintain records about us and, increasingly, for us. Even our most private documents—those that, in other eras, we would have locked safely in a desk drawer or destroyed—now reside on third party servers. *Smith* and *Miller* teach that the police can review all of this material, on the theory that no one reasonably expects any of it will be kept private. But no one believes that, if they ever did.

What to do? It seems to me we could respond in at least three ways. The first is to ignore the problem, maintain *Smith* and *Miller*, and live with the consequences. If the confluence of these decisions and modern technology means our Fourth Amendment rights are reduced to nearly nothing, so be it. The second choice is to set *Smith* and *Miller* aside and try again using the *Katz* "reasonable expectation of privacy" jurisprudence that produced them. The third is to look for answers elsewhere.

• • •

Start with the first option. *Smith* held that the government's use of a pen register to record the numbers people dial on their phones doesn't infringe a reasonable expectation of privacy because that information is freely disclosed to the third party phone company. *Miller* held that a bank account holder enjoys no reasonable expectation of privacy in the bank's records of his account activity. That's true, the Court reasoned, "even if the information is revealed on the assumption that it will be used only for a limited purpose and the confidence placed in the third party will not be betrayed." Today the Court suggests that *Smith* and *Miller* distinguish between kinds of information disclosed to third parties and require courts to decide whether to "extend" those decisions to particular classes of information, depending on their sensitivity. But as the Sixth Circuit recognized and Justice Kennedy explains, no balancing test of this kind can be found in *Smith* and *Miller*. Those cases announced a categorical rule: Once you disclose information to third parties, you forfeit any reasonable expectation of privacy you might have had in it. And even if *Smith* and *Miller* did permit courts to conduct a balancing contest of the kind the Court now suggests, it's still hard to see how that would help the petitioner in this case. Why is someone's location when using a phone so much more sensitive than who he was talking to (*Smith*) or what financial transactions he engaged in (*Miller*)? I do not know and the Court does not say.

The problem isn't with the Sixth Circuit's application of *Smith* and *Miller* but with the cases themselves. Can the government demand a copy of all your e-mails from Google or Microsoft without implicating your Fourth Amendment rights? Can it secure your DNA from 23 and Me without a warrant or probable cause? *Smith* and *Miller* say yes it can — at least without running afoul of *Katz*. But that result strikes most lawyers and judges today — me included — as pretty unlikely. In the years since its adoption, countless scholars, too, have come to conclude that the "third-party doctrine is not only wrong, but horribly wrong." Kerr, The Case for the Third-Party Doctrine, 107 Mich. L. Rev. 561, 563, n. 5, 564 (2009) (collecting criticisms but defending the doctrine (footnotes omitted)). The reasons are obvious. "As an empirical statement about subjective expectations of privacy," the doctrine is "quite dubious." Baude & Stern, The Positive Law Model of the Fourth Amendment, 129 Harv. L. Rev. 1821, 1872 (2016). People often do reasonably expect that information they entrust to third parties, especially information subject to confidentiality agreements, will be kept private. Meanwhile, if the third party doctrine is supposed to represent a normative assessment of when a person should expect privacy, the notion that the answer might be "never" seems a pretty unattractive societal prescription.

What, then, is the explanation for our third party doctrine? The truth is, the Court has never offered a persuasive justification. The Court has said that by conveying information to a third party you "'assum[e] the risk'" it will be revealed to the police and therefore lack a reasonable expectation of privacy in it. But assumption of risk doctrine developed in tort law. It generally applies when "by contract or otherwise [one] expressly agrees to accept a risk of harm" or impliedly does so by "manifest[ing] his willingness to accept" that risk and thereby "take[s] his chances as to harm which may result from it. That rationale has little play in this context. Suppose I entrust a friend with a letter and he promises to keep it secret until he delivers it to an intended recipient. In what sense have I agreed to bear the risk that he will turn around, break his promise, and spill its contents to someone else? More confusing still, what have I done to "manifest my willingness to accept" the risk that the government will pry the document from my friend and read it without his consent?

One possible answer concerns knowledge. I know that my friend might break his promise, or that the government might have some reason to search the papers in his possession. But knowing about a risk doesn't mean you assume responsibility for it. Whenever you walk down the sidewalk you know a car may negligently or recklessly veer off and hit you, but that hardly means you accept the consequences and absolve the driver of any damage he may do to you.

Some have suggested the third party doctrine is better understood to rest on consent than assumption of risk. "So long as a person knows that they are disclosing information to a third party," the argument goes, "their choice to do so is voluntary and the consent valid." I confess I still don't see it. Consenting to give a third party access to private papers that remain my property is not the same thing as consenting to a search of those papers by the government. Perhaps there are exceptions, like when the third party is an undercover government agent. But otherwise this conception of consent appears to be just assumption of risk relabeled—you've "consented" to whatever risks are foreseeable.

Another justification sometimes offered for third party doctrine is clarity. You (and the police) know exactly how much protection you have in information confided to others: none. As rules go, "the king always wins" is admirably clear. But the opposite rule would be clear too: Third party disclosures never diminish Fourth Amendment protection (call it "the king always loses"). So clarity alone cannot justify the third party doctrine.

In the end, what do *Smith* and *Miller* add up to? A doubtful application of *Katz* that lets the government search almost whatever it wants whenever it wants. The Sixth Circuit had to follow that rule and faithfully did just that, but it's not clear why we should.

• • •

There's a second option. What if we dropped *Smith* and *Miller*'s third party doctrine and retreated to the root *Katz* question whether there is a "reasonable expectation of privacy" in data held by third parties? Rather than solve the problem with the third party doctrine, I worry this option only risks returning us to its source: After all, it was *Katz* that produced *Smith* and *Miller* in the first place.

Katz's problems start with the text and original understanding of the Fourth Amendment, as Justice Thomas thoughtfully explains today. The Amendment's protections do not depend on the breach of some abstract "expectation of privacy" whose contours are left to the judicial imagination. Much more concretely, it protects your "person," and your "houses, papers, and effects." Nor does your right to bring a Fourth Amendment claim depend on whether a judge happens to agree that your subjective expectation to privacy is a "reasonable" one. Under its plain terms, the Amendment grants you the right to invoke its guarantees whenever one of your protected things (your person, your house, your papers, or your effects) is unreasonably searched or seized. Period.

History too holds problems for *Katz*. Little like it can be found in the law that led to the adoption of the Fourth Amendment or in this Court's jurisprudence until the late 1960s. The Fourth Amendment came about in response to a trio of 18th century cases "well known to the men who wrote and ratified the Bill of Rights, [and] famous throughout the colonial population." Stuntz, The Substantive Origins of Criminal Procedure, 105 Yale L.J. 393, 397 (1995). The first two were English cases invalidating the Crown's use of general warrants to enter homes and search papers. *Entick v. Carrington; Wilkes v. Wood; Boyd v. United States*. The third was American: the Boston Writs of Assistance Case, which sparked colonial outrage at the use of writs permitting government agents to enter houses and business, breaking open doors and chests along the way, to conduct searches and seizures—and to force third parties to help them. No doubt the colonial outrage engendered by these cases rested in part on the government's intrusion upon privacy. But the framers chose not to protect privacy in some ethereal way dependent on judicial intuitions. They chose instead to protect privacy in particular places and things—"persons, houses, papers, and effects"—and against particular threats—"unreasonable" governmental "searches and seizures."

Even taken on its own terms, *Katz* has never been sufficiently justified. In fact, we still don't even know what its "reasonable expectation of privacy" test is. Is it supposed to pose an empirical question (what privacy expectations do people actually have) or a normative one (what expectations should they have)? Either way brings problems. If the test is supposed to be an empirical one, it's unclear why judges rather than legislators should conduct it. Legislators are responsive to their constituents and have institutional resources designed to help them discern and enact majoritarian preferences. Politically insulated judges come armed with only the attorneys' briefs, a few law clerks, and their own idiosyncratic experiences. They are hardly the representative group you'd expect (or want) to be making empirical judgments for hundreds of millions of people. Unsurprisingly, too, judicial judgments often fail to reflect public views. Consider just one example. Our cases insist that the seriousness of the offense being investigated does not reduce Fourth Amendment protection. Yet scholars suggest that most people are more tolerant of police intrusions when they investigate more serious crimes. And I very much doubt that this Court would be willing to adjust its *Katz* cases to reflect these findings even if it believed them.

Maybe, then, the *Katz* test should be conceived as a normative question. But if that's the case, why (again) do judges, rather than legislators, get to determine whether society should be prepared to recognize an expectation of privacy as legitimate? Deciding what privacy interests should be recognized often calls for a pure policy choice, many times between incommensurable goods—between the value of privacy in a particular setting and society's interest in combating crime. Answering questions like that calls for the exercise of raw political will belonging to legislatures, not the legal judgment proper to courts. When judges abandon legal judgment for political will we not only risk decisions where "reasonable expectations of privacy" come to bear "an uncanny resemblance to those expectations of privacy" shared by Members of this Court. We also risk undermining public confidence in the courts themselves.

My concerns about *Katz* come with a caveat. Sometimes, I accept, judges may be able to discern and describe existing societal norms. That is particularly true when the judge looks to positive law rather than intuition for guidance on social norms. So there may be some occasions where *Katz* is capable of principled application—though it may simply wind up approximating the more traditional option I will discuss in a moment. Sometimes it may also be possible to apply *Katz* by analogizing from precedent when the line between an existing case and a new fact pattern is short and direct. But so far this Court has declined to tie itself to any significant restraints like these.

As a result, *Katz* has yielded an often unpredictable—and sometimes unbelievable—jurisprudence. *Smith* and *Miller* are only two examples; there are many others. Take *Florida v. Riley*, which says that a police helicopter hovering 400 feet above a person's property invades no reasonable expectation of privacy. Try that one out on your neighbors. Or *California v. Greenwood*, which holds that a person has no reasonable expectation of privacy in the garbage he puts out for collection. In that case, the Court said that the homeowners forfeited their privacy interests because "[i]t is common knowledge that plastic garbage bags left on or at the side of a public street are readily accessible to animals, children, scavengers, snoops, and other members of the public." But the habits of raccoons don't prove much about the habits of the country. I doubt, too, that most people spotting a neighbor rummaging through their garbage would think they lacked reasonable grounds to confront the rummager. Making the decision all the stranger, California state law expressly protected a homeowner's property rights in discarded trash. Yet rather than defer to that as evidence of the people's habits and reasonable expectations of privacy, the Court substituted its own curious judgment.

Resorting to *Katz* in data privacy cases threatens more of the same. Just consider. The Court today says that judges should use *Katz*'s reasonable expectation of privacy test to decide what Fourth Amendment rights people have in cell-site location information, explaining that "no single rubric definitively resolves which expectations of privacy are entitled to protection." But then it offers a twist. Lower courts should be sure to add two special principles to their *Katz* calculus: the need to avoid "arbitrary power" and the importance of "plac[ing] obstacles in the way of a too permeating police surveillance." While surely laudable, these principles don't offer lower courts much guidance. The Court does not tell us, for example, how far to carry either principle or how to weigh them against the legitimate needs of law enforcement. At what point does access to electronic data amount to "arbitrary" authority? When does police surveillance become "too permeating"? And what sort of "obstacles" should judges "place" in law enforcement's path when it does? We simply do not know.

The Court's application of these principles supplies little more direction. The Court declines to say whether there is any sufficiently limited period of time "for which the Government may obtain an individual's historical [location information] free from Fourth Amendment scrutiny." But then it tells us that access to seven days' worth of information does trigger Fourth Amendment scrutiny — even though here the carrier "produced only two days of records." Why is the relevant fact the seven days of information the government asked for instead of the two days of information the government actually saw? Why seven days instead of ten or three or one? And in what possible sense did the government "search" five days' worth of location information it was never even sent? We do not know.

Later still, the Court adds that it can't say whether the Fourth Amendment is triggered when the government collects "real-time CSLI or 'tower dumps' (a download of information on all the devices that connected to a particular cell site during a particular interval)." But what distinguishes historical data from real-time data, or seven days of a single person's data from a download of everyone's data over some indefinite period of time? Why isn't a tower dump the paradigmatic example of "too permeating police surveillance" and a dangerous tool of "arbitrary" authority — the touchstones of the majority's modified *Katz* analysis? On what possible basis could such mass data collection survive the Court's test while collecting a single person's data does not? Here again we are left to guess. At the same time, though, the Court offers some firm assurances. It tells us its decision does not "call into question conventional surveillance techniques and tools, such as security cameras." That, however, just raises more questions for lower courts to sort out about what techniques qualify as "conventional" and why those techniques would be okay even if they lead to "permeating police surveillance" or "arbitrary police power."

Nor is this the end of it. After finding a reasonable expectation of privacy, the Court says there's still more work to do. Courts must determine whether to "extend" *Smith* and *Miller* to the circumstances before them. So apparently *Smith* and *Miller* aren't quite left for dead; they just no longer have the clear reach they once did. How do we measure their new reach? The Court says courts now must conduct a second *Katz*-like balancing inquiry, asking whether the fact of disclosure to a third party outweighs privacy interests in the "category of information" so disclosed. But how are lower courts supposed to weigh these radically different interests? Or assign values to different categories of information? All we know is that historical cell-site location information (for seven days, anyway) escapes *Smith* and *Miller*'s shorn grasp, while a lifetime of bank or phone records does not. As to any other kind of information, lower courts will have to stay tuned.

In the end, our lower court colleagues are left with two amorphous balancing tests, a series of weighty and incommensurable principles to consider in them, and a few illustrative examples that seem little more than the product of judicial intuition. In the Court's defense, though, we have arrived at this strange place not because the Court has misunderstood *Katz*. Far from it. We have arrived here because this is where *Katz* inevitably leads.

• • •

There is another way. From the founding until the 1960s, the right to assert a Fourth Amendment claim didn't depend on your ability to appeal to a judge's personal sensibilities about the "reasonableness" of your expectations or privacy. It was tied to the law. The Fourth

Amendment protects "the right of the people to be secure in their persons, houses, papers and effects, against unreasonable searches and seizures." True to those words and their original understanding, the traditional approach asked if a house, paper or effect was yours under law. No more was needed to trigger the Fourth Amendment. Though now often lost in *Katz*'s shadow, this traditional understanding persists. *Katz* only "supplements, rather than displaces the traditional property-based understanding of the Fourth Amendment."

Beyond its provenance in the text and original understanding of the Amendment, this traditional approach comes with other advantages. Judges are supposed to decide cases based on "democratically legitimate sources of law"—like positive law or analogies to items protected by the enacted Constitution—rather than "their own biases or personal policy preferences." A Fourth Amendment model based on positive legal rights "carves out significant room for legislative participation in the Fourth Amendment context," too, by asking judges to consult what the people's representatives have to say about their rights. Nor is this approach hobbled by *Smith* and *Miller*, for those cases are just limitations on *Katz*, addressing only the question whether individuals have a reasonable expectation of privacy in materials they share with third parties. Under this more traditional approach, Fourth Amendment protections for your papers and effects do not automatically disappear just because you share them with third parties.

Given the prominence *Katz* has claimed in our doctrine, American courts are pretty rusty at applying the traditional approach to the Fourth Amendment. We know that if a house, paper, or effect is yours, you have a Fourth Amendment interest in its protection. But what kind of legal interest is sufficient to make something yours? And what source of law determines that? Current positive law? The common law at 1791, extended by analogy to modern times? Both? Much work is needed to revitalize this area and answer these questions. I do not begin to claim all the answers today, but (unlike with *Katz*) at least I have a pretty good idea what the questions are. And it seems to me a few things can be said.

First, the fact that a third party has access to or possession of your papers and effects does not necessarily eliminate your interest in them. Ever hand a private document to a friend to be returned? Toss your keys to a valet at a restaurant? Ask your neighbor to look after your dog while you travel? You would not expect the friend to share the document with others; the valet to lend your car to his buddy; or the neighbor to put Fido up for adoption. Entrusting your stuff to others is a bailment. A bailment is the "delivery of personal property by one person (the bailor) to another (the bailee) who holds the property for a certain purpose." A bailee normally owes a legal duty to keep the item safe, according to the terms of the parties' contract if they have one, and according to the "implication[s] from their conduct" if they don't. A bailee who uses the item in a different way than he's supposed to, or against the bailor's instructions, is liable for conversion. This approach is quite different from *Smith* and *Miller*'s (counter)-intuitive approach to reasonable expectations of privacy; where those cases extinguish Fourth Amendment interests once records are given to a third party, property law may preserve them.

Our Fourth Amendment jurisprudence already reflects this truth. In *Ex parte Jackson* (1878), this Court held that sealed letters placed in the mail are "as fully guarded from examination and inspection, except as to their outward form and weight, as if they were retained by the parties forwarding them in their own domiciles." The reason, drawn from the Fourth Amendment's text, was that "[t]he constitutional guaranty of the right of the people to be secure in their papers against unreasonable searches and seizures extends to *their* papers, thus closed against inspection, wherever they may be." Ibid. (emphasis added). It did not matter that letters were bailed to a third party (the government, no less). The sender enjoyed the same Fourth Amendment protection as he does "when papers are subjected to search in one's own household." Ibid.

These ancient principles may help us address modern data cases too. Just because you entrust your data—in some cases, your modern-day papers and effects—to a third party may not mean you lose any Fourth Amendment interest in its contents. Whatever may be left of *Smith* and *Miller*, few doubt that e-mail should be treated much like the traditional mail it has largely supplanted—as a bailment in which the owner retains a vital and protected legal interest.

Second, I doubt that complete ownership or exclusive control of property is always a necessary condition to the assertion of a Fourth Amendment right. Where houses are concerned, for example, individuals can enjoy Fourth Amendment protection without fee simple title. Both the text of the Amendment and the common law rule support that conclusion. "People call a house 'their' home when legal title is in the bank, when they rent it, and even when they merely occupy it rent free." That rule derives from the common law. That is why tenants and resident family members—though they have no legal title—have standing to complain about searches of the houses in which they live.

Another point seems equally true: just because you have to entrust a third party with your data doesn't necessarily mean you should lose all Fourth Amendment protections in it. Not infrequently one person comes into possession of someone else's property without the owner's consent. Think of the finder of lost goods or the policeman who impounds a car. The law recognizes that the goods and the car still belong to their true owners, for "where a person comes into lawful possession of the personal property of another, even though there is no formal agreement between the property's owner and its possessor, the possessor will become a constructive bailee when justice so requires." At least some of this Court's decisions have already suggested that use of technology is functionally compelled by the demands of modern life, and in that way the fact that we store data with third parties may amount to a sort of involuntary bailment too.

Third, positive law may help provide detailed guidance on evolving technologies without resort to judicial intuition. State (or sometimes federal) law often creates rights in both tangible and intangible things. In the context of the Takings Clause we often ask whether those state-created rights are sufficient to make something someone's property for constitutional purposes. A similar inquiry may be appropriate for the Fourth Amendment. Both the States and federal government are actively legislating in the area of third party data storage and the rights users enjoy. State courts are busy expounding common law property principles in this area as well. If state legislators or state courts say that a digital record has the attributes that normally make something property, that may supply a sounder basis for judicial decisionmaking than judicial guesswork about societal expectations.

Fourth, while positive law may help establish a person's Fourth Amendment interest there may be some circumstances where positive law cannot be used to defeat it. *Ex parte Jackson* reflects that understanding. There this Court said that "[n]o law of Congress" could authorize letter carriers "to invade the secrecy of letters." 96 U.S., at 733. So the post office couldn't impose a regulation dictating that those mailing letters surrender all legal interests in them once they're deposited in a mailbox. If that is right, *Jackson* suggests the existence of a constitutional floor below which Fourth Amendment rights may not descend. Legislatures cannot pass laws declaring your house or papers to be your property except to the extent the police wish to search them without cause. As the Court has previously explained, "we must 'assur[e] preservation of that degree of privacy against government that existed when the Fourth Amendment was adopted.'" Nor does this mean protecting only the specific rights known at the founding; it means protecting their modern analogues too. So, for example, while thermal imaging was unknown in 1791, this Court has recognized that using that technology to look inside a home constitutes a Fourth Amendment "search" of that "home" no less than a physical inspection might.

Fifth, this constitutional floor may, in some instances, bar efforts to circumvent the Fourth Amendment's protection through the use of subpoenas. No one thinks the government can evade *Jackson*'s prohibition on opening sealed letters without a warrant simply by issuing a subpoena to a postmaster for "all letters sent by John Smith" or, worse, "all letters sent by John Smith concerning a particular transaction." So the question courts will confront will be this: What other kinds of records are sufficiently similar to letters in the mail that the same rule should apply?

It may be that, as an original matter, a subpoena requiring the recipient to produce records wasn't thought of as a "search or seizure" by the government implicating the Fourth Amendment, but instead as an act of compelled self-incrimination implicating the Fifth Amendment. But the common law of searches and seizures does not appear to have confronted a case where private documents equivalent to a mailed letter were entrusted to a bailee and then subpoenaed. As a result, "[t]he common-law rule regarding subpoenas for documents held by third parties entrusted with information from the target is . . . unknown and perhaps unknowable." Given that (perhaps insoluble) uncertainty, I am content to adhere to *Jackson* and its implications for now.

To be sure, we must be wary of returning to the doctrine of *Boyd v. United States*. *Boyd* invoked the Fourth Amendment to restrict the use of subpoenas even for ordinary business records and, as Justice Alito notes, eventually proved unworkable. But if we were to overthrow *Jackson* too and deny Fourth Amendment protection to any subpoenaed materials, we would do well to reconsider the scope of the Fifth Amendment while we're at it. Our precedents treat the right against self-incrimination as applicable only to testimony, not the production of incriminating evidence. But there is substantial evidence that the privilege against self-incrimination was also originally understood to protect a person from being forced to turn over potentially incriminating evidence.

What does all this mean for the case before us? To start, I cannot fault the Sixth Circuit for holding that *Smith* and *Miller* extinguish any *Katz*-based Fourth Amendment interest in third party cell-site data. That is the plain effect of their categorical holdings. Nor can I fault the Court today for its implicit but unmistakable conclusion that the rationale of *Smith* and *Miller* is wrong; indeed, I agree with that. The Sixth Circuit was powerless to say so, but this Court can and should. At the same time, I do not agree with the Court's decision today to keep *Smith* and *Miller* on life support and supplement them with a new and multilayered inquiry that seems to be only *Katz*-squared. Returning there, I worry, promises more trouble than help. Instead, I would look to a more traditional Fourth Amendment approach. Even if *Katz* may still supply one way to prove a Fourth Amendment interest, it has never been the only way. Neglecting more traditional approaches may mean failing to vindicate the full protections of the Fourth Amendment.

Our case offers a cautionary example. It seems to me entirely possible a person's cell-site data could qualify as his papers or effects under existing law. Yes, the telephone carrier holds the information. But 47 U.S.C. § 222 designates a customer's cell-site location information as "customer proprietary network information," and gives customers certain rights to control use of and access to CPNI about themselves. The statute generally forbids a carrier to "use, disclose, or permit access to individually identifiable" CPNI without the customer's consent, except as needed to provide the customer's telecommunications services. It also requires the carrier to disclose CPNI "upon affirmative written request by the customer, to any person designated by the customer." § 222(c)(2). Congress even afforded customers a private cause of action for damages against carriers who violate the Act's terms. § 207. Plainly, customers have substantial legal interests in this information, including at least some right to include, exclude, and control its use. Those interests might even rise to the level of a property right.

The problem is that we do not know anything more. Before the district court and court of appeals, Mr. Carpenter pursued only a *Katz* "reasonable expectations" argument. He did not invoke the law of property or any analogies to the common law, either there or in his petition for certiorari. Even in his merits brief before this Court, Mr. Carpenter's discussion of his positive law rights in cell-site data was cursory. He offered no analysis, for example, of what rights state law might provide him in addition to those supplied by § 222. In these circumstances, I cannot help but conclude — reluctantly — that Mr. Carpenter forfeited perhaps his most promising line of argument.

Unfortunately, too, this case marks the second time this Term that individuals have forfeited Fourth Amendment arguments based on positive law by failing to preserve them. Litigants have had fair notice since at least *United States v. Jones* (2012) and *Florida v. Jardines* (2013) that arguments like these may vindicate Fourth Amendment interests even where *Katz* arguments do not. Yet the arguments have gone unmade, leaving courts to the usual *Katz* handwaving. These omissions do not serve the development of a sound or fully protective Fourth Amendment jurisprudence.

NOTES AND QUESTIONS

1. The FBI and the prosecutors probably thought that the fact that they received a court order under a federal statute protected their acquisition of the CSLI. But why didn't they get a search warrant just to be sure? Do you see any reason why they could not have gotten a search warrant?

2. Why does it matter that the use of CSLI is easy and cheap? Is the point simply that the use of such technology is likely to be frequent and commonplace?

3. Does the comparative lack of precision of CSLI provide a basis for distinguishing *Jones*? Given the lack of precision, does the use of CSLI really permit the government to retrospectively "tail" someone?

4. Justice Alito in dissent claims that two aspects of the Court's decision are "revolutionary" (a) treating a judicial production order as a "search" under the Fourth Amendment and (b) allowing a defendant to object to the "search" of a third party's property. Are both of these criticisms a function of the reality that the CSLI is in the possession of a third party?

5. Justice Alito also expresses a preference for legislative solutions over Fourth Amendment case law in dealing with problems of "rapidly changing technology." Here, there was just such a legislative resolution, the Stored Communications Act, which permitted a court order to issue based on the government's mere showing that information was "relevant and material" to an "ongoing investigation." Is this a meaningful layer of judicial scrutiny?

B. WHAT IS A SEIZURE FOR FOURTH AMENDMENT PURPOSES? RACE, SEIZURE, AND FORCE

There are three essential categories of seizure for Fourth Amendment purposes. The most extreme form of seizure is an arrest, a clear manifestation or exertion of force by a police officer that constitutionally requires probable cause to believe the restrained individual has committed a crime. The least extreme is a temporary detention of an individual for questioning and sometimes frisking that constitutionally only requires "reasonable suspicion." *See infra*. In this category the person approached normally may have the right to ignore the questioner and walk away. In between is a mushier category where a reasonable person would not feel free to leave but has not been arrested.

The next case considers the circumstances of a woman being approached in the Detroit airport by DEA agents using a "drug courier profile." Do not lose focus on the consequences

Chapter IV The Fourth Amendment

of the determination whether a law enforcement encounter rises to the level of a seizure. If it does, the encounter would have to have been justified by "reasonable suspicion" on the officers' part, a concept that will be explored in more depth *infra*.

1. Police Encounters and Seizures

United States v. Mendenhall

446 U.S. 544 (1980)

Mr. Justice STEWART announced the judgment of the Court and delivered an opinion in which Mr. Justice REHNQUIST joined.

The respondent was brought to trial in the United States District Court for the Eastern District of Michigan on a charge of possessing heroin with intent to distribute it. She moved to suppress the introduction at trial of the heroin as evidence against her on the ground that it had been acquired from her through an unconstitutional search and seizure by agents of the Drug Enforcement Administration (DEA). The District Court denied the respondent's motion, and she was convicted after a trial upon stipulated facts. The Court of Appeals reversed, finding the search of the respondent's person to have been unlawful. We granted certiorari to consider whether any right of the respondent guaranteed by the Fourth Amendment was violated in the circumstances presented by this case.

I

At the hearing in the trial court on the respondent's motion to suppress, it was established how the heroin she was charged with possessing had been obtained from her. The respondent arrived at the Detroit Metropolitan Airport on a commercial airline flight from Los Angeles early in the morning on February 10, 1976. As she disembarked from the airplane, she was observed by two agents of the DEA, who were present at the airport for the purpose of detecting unlawful traffic in narcotics. After observing the respondent's conduct, which appeared to the agents to be characteristic of persons unlawfully carrying narcotics, the agents approached her as she was walking through the concourse, identified themselves as federal agents, and asked to see her identification and airline ticket. The respondent produced her driver's license, which was in the name of Sylvia Mendenhall, and, in answer to a question of one of the agents, stated that she resided at the address appearing on the license. The airline ticket was issued in the name of "Annette Ford." When asked why the ticket bore a name different from her own, the respondent stated that she "just felt like using that name." In response to a further question, the respondent indicated that she had been in California only two days. Agent Anderson then specifically identified himself as a federal narcotics agent and, according to his testimony, the respondent "became quite shaken, extremely nervous. She had a hard time speaking."

After returning the airline ticket and driver's license to her, Agent Anderson asked the respondent if she would accompany him to the airport DEA office for further questions. She did so, although the record does not indicate a verbal response to the request. The office, which was located up one flight of stairs about 50 feet from where the respondent had first been approached, consisted of a reception area adjoined by three other rooms. At the office the agent asked the respondent if she would allow a search of her person and handbag and told her that she had the right to decline the search if she desired. She responded: "Go ahead." She then handed Agent Anderson her purse, which contained a receipt for an airline ticket that had been issued to "F. Bush" three days earlier for a flight from Pittsburgh through Chicago to Los Angeles. The agent asked whether this was the ticket that she had used for her flight to California, and the respondent stated that it was.

A female police officer then arrived to conduct the search of the respondent's person. She asked the agents if the respondent had consented to be searched. The agents said that she had, and the respondent followed the policewoman into a private room. There the policewoman again asked the respondent if she consented to the search, and the respondent replied that she did. The policewoman explained that the search would require that the respondent remove her clothing. The respondent stated that she had a plane to catch and was assured by the policewoman that if she were carrying no narcotics, there would be no problem. The respondent then began to disrobe without further comment. As the respondent removed her clothing, she took from her undergarments two small packages, one of which appeared to contain heroin, and handed both to the policewoman. The agents then arrested the respondent for possessing heroin.

It was on the basis of this evidence that the District Court denied the respondent's motion to suppress. The court concluded that the agents' conduct in initially approaching the respondent and asking to see her ticket and identification was a permissible investigative stop under the standards of *Terry v. Ohio*, finding that this conduct was based on specific and articulable facts that justified a suspicion of criminal activity. The court also found that the respondent had not been placed under arrest or otherwise detained when she was asked to accompany the agents to the DEA office, but had accompanied the agents "'voluntarily in a spirit of apparent cooperation.'" It was the court's view that no arrest occurred until after the heroin had been found. Finally, the trial court found that the respondent "gave her consent to the search [in the DEA office] and . . . such consent was freely and voluntarily given."

The Court of Appeals reversed the respondent's subsequent conviction.

II

The Fourth Amendment provides that "the right of the people to be secure in their persons, houses, papers, and effects, against unreasonable searches and seizures, shall not be violated. . . ." There is no question in this case that the respondent possessed this constitutional right of personal security as she walked through the Detroit Airport, for "the Fourth Amendment protects people, not places." Here the Government concedes that its agents had neither a warrant nor probable cause to believe that the respondent was carrying narcotics when the agents conducted a search of the respondent's person. It is the Government's position, however, that the search was conducted pursuant to the respondent's consent, and thus was excepted from the requirements of both a warrant and probable cause. Evidently, the Court of Appeals concluded that the respondent's apparent consent to the search was in fact not voluntarily given and was in any event the product of earlier official conduct violative of the Fourth Amendment. We must first consider, therefore, whether such conduct occurred, either on the concourse or in the DEA office at the airport.

A

The Fourth Amendment's requirement that searches and seizures be founded upon an objective justification, governs all seizures of the person, "including seizures that involve only a brief detention short of traditional arrest. Accordingly, if the respondent was "seized" when the DEA agents approached her on the concourse and asked questions of her, the agents' conduct in doing so was constitutional only if they reasonably suspected the respondent of wrongdoing. But "[o]bviously, not all personal intercourse between policemen and citizens involves 'seizures' of persons. Only when the officer, by means of physical force or show of authority, has in some way restrained the liberty of a citizen may we conclude that a 'seizure' has occurred."

The distinction between an intrusion amounting to a "seizure" of the person and an encounter that intrudes upon no constitutionally protected interest is illustrated by the facts of *Terry v. Ohio*, which the Court recounted as follows: "Officer McFadden approached the three men, identified himself as a police officer and asked for their names. . . . When the men 'mumbled something' in response to his inquiries, Officer McFadden grabbed petitioner Terry, spun him around so that they were facing the other two, with Terry between McFadden and the others, and patted down the outside of his clothing." Obviously the officer "seized" Terry and subjected him to a "search" when he took hold of him, spun him around, and patted down the outer surfaces of his clothing. What was not determined in that case, however, was that a seizure had taken place before the officer physically restrained Terry for purposes of searching his person for weapons. The court "assume[d] that up to that point no intrusion upon constitutionally protected rights had occurred." The Court's assumption appears entirely correct in view of the fact, noted in the concurring opinion of Mr. Justice White, that "[t]here is nothing in the Constitution which prevents a policeman from addressing questions to anyone on the streets." Police officers enjoy "the liberty (again, possessed by every citizen) to address questions to other persons," although "ordinarily the person addressed has an equal right to ignore his interrogator and walk away."

We adhere to the view that a person is "seized" only when, by means of physical force or a show of authority, his freedom of movement is restrained. Only when such restraint is imposed is there any foundation whatever for invoking constitutional safeguards. The purpose of the Fourth Amendment is not to eliminate all contact between the police and the citizenry, but "to prevent arbitrary and oppressive interference by enforcement officials with the privacy and personal security of individuals." As long as the person to whom questions are put remains free to disregard the questions and walk away, there has been no intrusion upon that person's liberty or privacy as would under the Constitution require some particularized and objective justification.

Moreover, characterizing every street encounter between a citizen and the police as a "seizure," while not enhancing any interest secured by the Fourth Amendment, would impose wholly unrealistic restrictions upon a wide variety of legitimate law enforcement practices. The Court has on other occasions referred to the acknowledged need for police questioning as a tool in the effective enforcement of the criminal laws. "Without such investigation, those who were innocent might be falsely accused, those who were guilty might wholly escape prosecution, and many crimes would go unsolved. In short, the security of all would be diminished.

We conclude that a person has been "seized" within the meaning of the Fourth Amendment only if, in view of all of the circumstances surrounding the incident, a reasonable person would have believed that he was not free to leave. Examples of circumstances that might indicate a seizure, even where the person did not attempt to leave, would be the threatening presence of several officers, the display of a weapon by an officer, some physical touching of the person of the citizen, or the use of language or tone of voice indicating that compliance with the officer's request might be compelled. In the absence of some such evidence, otherwise inoffensive contact between a member of the public and the police cannot, as a matter of law, amount to a seizure of that person.

On the facts of this case, no "seizure" of the respondent occurred. The events took place in the public concourse. The agents wore no uniforms and displayed no weapons. They did not summon the respondent to their presence, but instead approached her and identified themselves as federal agents. They requested, but did not demand to see the respondent's identification and ticket. Such conduct without more, did not amount to an intrusion upon any constitutionally protected interest. The respondent was not seized simply by reason of the fact that the agents approached her, asked her if she would show them her ticket and identification, and posed to her a few questions. Nor was it enough to establish a seizure that the person asking the questions was a law enforcement official. In short, nothing in the record suggests that the respondent had any objective reason to believe that she was not free to end the conversation in the concourse and proceed on her way, and for that reason we conclude that the agents' initial approach to her was not a seizure.

Our conclusion that no seizure occurred is not affected by the fact that the respondent was not expressly told by the agents that she was free to decline to cooperate with their inquiry, for the voluntariness of her responses does not depend upon her having been so informed. We also reject the argument that the only inference to be drawn from the fact that the respondent acted in a manner so contrary to her self-interest is that she was compelled to answer the agents' questions. It may happen that a person makes statements to law enforcement officials that he later regrets, but the issue in such cases is not whether the statement was self-protective, but rather whether it was made voluntarily.

. . .

B

Although we have concluded that the initial encounter between the DEA agents and the respondent on the concourse at the Detroit Airport did not constitute an unlawful seizure, it is still arguable that the respondent's Fourth Amendment protections were violated when she went from the concourse to the DEA office. Such a violation might in turn infect the subsequent search of the respondent's person.

The District Court specifically found that the respondent accompanied the agents to the office "'voluntarily in a spirit of apparent cooperation.'" Notwithstanding this determination by the trial court, the Court of Appeals evidently concluded that the agents' request that the respondent accompany them converted the situation into an arrest requiring probable cause in order to be found lawful. But because the trial court's finding was sustained by the record, the Court of Appeals was mistaken in substituting for that finding its view of the evidence.

The question whether the respondent's consent to accompany the agents was in fact voluntary or was the product of duress or coercion, express or implied, is to be determined by the totality of all the circumstances, and is a matter which the Government has the burden of proving. The respondent herself did not testify at the hearing. The Government's evidence showed that the respondent was not told that she had to go to the office, but was simply asked if she would accompany the officers. There were neither threats nor any show of force. The respondent had been questioned only briefly, and her ticket and identification were returned to her before she was asked to accompany the officers.

On the other hand, it is argued that the incident would reasonably have appeared coercive to the respondent, who was 22 years old and had not been graduated from high school. It is additionally suggested that the respondent, a female and a Negro, may have felt unusually threatened by the officers, who were white males. While these factors were not irrelevant, neither were they decisive, and the totality of the evidence in this case was plainly adequate to support the District Court's finding that the respondent voluntarily consented to accompany the officers to the DEA office.

C

Because the search of the respondent's person was not preceded by an impermissible seizure of her person, it cannot be contended that her apparent consent to the subsequent search was infected by an unlawful detention. There remains to be considered whether the respondent's consent to the search was for any other reason invalid. The District Court explicitly credited the officers' testimony and found that the "consent was freely and voluntarily given." There was more than enough evidence in this case to sustain that view. First, we note that the respondent, who was 22 years old and had an 11th-grade education, was plainly capable of a knowing consent. Second, it is especially significant that the respondent was twice expressly told that she was free to decline to consent to the search, and only thereafter explicitly consented to it. Although the Constitution does not require "proof of knowledge of a right to refuse as the sine qua non of an effective consent to a search," such knowledge was highly relevant to the determination that there had been consent. And, perhaps more important for present purposes, the fact that the officers themselves informed the respondent that she was free to withhold her consent substantially lessened the probability that their conduct could reasonably have appeared to her to be coercive.

Counsel for the respondent has argued that she did in fact resist the search, relying principally on the testimony that when she was told that the search would require the removal of her clothing, she stated to the female police officer that "she had a plane to catch." But the trial court was entitled to view the statement as simply an expression of concern that the search be conducted quickly. The respondent had twice unequivocally indicated her consent to the search, and when assured by the police officer that there would be no problem if nothing were turned up by the search, she began to undress without further comment.

Counsel for the respondent has also argued that because she was within the DEA office when she consented to the search, her consent may have resulted from the inherently coercive nature of those surroundings. But in view of the District Court's finding that the respondent's presence in the office was voluntary, the fact that she was there is little or no evidence that she was in any way coerced. And in response to the argument that the respondent would not voluntarily have consented to a search that was likely to disclose the narcotics that she carried, we repeat that the question is not whether the respondent acted in her ultimate self-interest, but whether she acted voluntarily.

III

We conclude that the District Court's determination that the respondent consented to the search of her person "freely and voluntarily" was sustained by the evidence and that the Court of Appeals was, therefore, in error in setting it aside. Accordingly, the judgment of the Court of Appeals is reversed, and the case is remanded to that court for further proceedings.

[Justices White, Marshall, Brennan, and Stevens dissented.]

NOTES AND QUESTIONS

1. This is a case about the meaning of "seizure" under the Fourth Amendment. But in working toward a definition of that term the Court also underscores the legitimate authority of police officers to engage in what might be called "consensual encounters," as recognized in *Terry v. Ohio*, 328 U.S. 1, 8, 10-11 (1968). *See* Aliza Hochman Bloom, *Long Overdue: Confronting Race in the Fourth Amendment's Free-to-Leave Analysis*, 65 Howard L.J. 1, 8-18 (2021) (discussing the significance of the consensual encounter category of police interaction).

2. The Court defines a "seizure" under the Fourth Amendment as a law enforcement interaction where, under the totality of the circumstances, "a reasonable person would have believed that he was not free to leave." Does "free to leave" mean a belief that one could leave combined with the belief that the officer would abandon any further investigative effort, including asking questions of, or following, a person?

3. The Court provides examples of law enforcement "force or a show of authority" that likely would constitute a seizure: display of a weapon, physical contact, the use of an aggressive tone. How might the nature of the questioning by the officer affect the seizure analysis?

The Court also acknowledges that the person's individual characteristics, including race (Sylvia Mendenhall was a Black woman) age, and gender, may be relevant to the totality of the circumstances insofar as they bear on whether the individual felt free to leave. Would it even be relevant whether the individual subjectively believed she was not free to leave?

If the agent had not returned her identification before continuing to question Mendenhall, would that have turned the interaction into a seizure? What if the officer had asked her to accompany him to the office before returning the identification?

4. Three Justices, concurring, would have found reasonable suspicion justifying a seizure based to some unspecified degree on the DEA's drug courier profile, and cited statistics from an unrelated district court case on the efficacy of that profile. To the extent those statistics were relevant to a reasonable suspicion, shouldn't they have been subject to cross-examination at the suppression hearing?

5. Why do you think Sylvia Mendenhall did not testify at her suppression hearing? Note that the factual record established at the hearing was entirely the result of law enforcement testimony. Isn't it likely she would have been able to provide additional details about her interaction with the agents that would have been relevant as to the officers' manifestations of authority, or to her own assessment of the situation?

If she had testified at the hearing, could she have been questioned about whether she had been in possession of heroin? The Supreme Court in 1968 held that a defendant's testimony at a suppression hearing—sometimes necessary to establish standing to contest an illegal search—cannot be used against the defendant on the question of guilt or innocence although it can be used to impeach the credibility of a testifying defendant at trial. *Simmons v. United States*, 390 U.S. 27 (1968). *See* Chapter V *infra*.

If the DEA had opposed the motion solely on the basis of the drug courier profile, would her testimony have been necessary?

The Court applied the *Mendenhall* standard in several cases over the next decade, each time concluding that a reasonable person in the defendant's position would have felt "free to leave." The defendants in these cases were Black people or other minorities, although the defendant's race was never mentioned, raising the possibility that the observations about race in *Mendenhall* were only a cruel head fake. In *Florida v. Royer*, 460 U.S. 491 (1983), plainclothes DEA agents singled out and approached Royer pursuant to their drug courier profile inasmuch as he was nervous, young, had paid cash for his ticket, and had checked heavy luggage. The Court held that the DEA's approach and questioning of Royer about his identification and travel intentions did not rise to the level of a seizure until the moment when they identified themselves as agents and asked him to accompany them to another room, while retaining his ticket, as before that particular point a reasonable person would have felt free to leave. *Id.* at 502. *See infra* Section E.

In *INS v. Delgado*, 466 U.S. 210 (1984), the Court held that raids of two factories by INS agents, and systematic questioning of the entire work forces at both factories regarding potential immigration offenses, was not a seizure under *Mendenhall*. The Court noted that the mere questioning about their identification issues (despite the subject's sensitivity in this particular context) did not amount to a seizure, as it had previously held to similar effect in *Royer*, and that reasonable persons in the workers' position would have felt free to leave. It reached this conclusion even though some of the INS agents—all of whom were badged, armed, and

266 Chapter IV The Fourth Amendment

carried handcuffs—had been strategically situated at the factories' exits, as if to inhibit that very feeling. *Id.* at 218.

The Court noted that the workers' freedom of movement had already been curtailed by their conditions of employment, suggesting that similar investigative activity in a different environment—say, a law firm?—might have different consequences. None of the opinions do justice to the facts "on the ground" in *Delgado*, which included that several workers who attempted to exit the factory during the raid were arrested by the agents. Brief for Respondents at 30, *INS v. Delgado*, 466 U.S. 210 (1984) (No. 82-1271). In a dissenting opinion, Justice Brennan stated that the Court's opinion had a "studied air of unreality." *Id.* at 226 (Brennan, J., dissenting).

Finally, in *Michigan v. Chesternut*, 486 U.S. 567 (1988), a police car pursued Chesternut as he began running away after observing the police car. After following him around a corner and catching up with him, the police drive alongside him for a "short distance." Although one of the officers described the action as "a chase," and the Court agreed the police actions may have been "somewhat intimidating," the Court held that a reasonable person would have felt free to leave. The Court did not acknowledge that "leaving" is exactly what Chesternut was trying to do all along.

Not satisfied with so much police success on the seizure front, the Court in the next case changed the *Mendenhall* test to make seizures even more difficult to establish.

California v. Hodari D.
499 U.S. 621 (1991)

Justice SCALIA delivered the opinion of the Court.

Late one evening in April 1988, Officers Brian McColgin and Jerry Pertoso were on patrol in a high-crime area of Oakland, California. They were dressed in street clothes but wearing jackets with "Police" embossed on both front and back. Their unmarked car proceeded west on Foothill Boulevard, and turned south onto 63rd Avenue. As they rounded the corner, they saw four or five youths huddled around a small red car parked at the curb. When the youths saw the officers' car approaching they apparently panicked, and took flight. The respondent here, Hodari D., and one companion ran west through an alley; the others fled south. The red car also headed south, at a high rate of speed.

The officers were suspicious and gave chase. McColgin remained in the car and continued south on 63rd Avenue; Pertoso left the car, ran back north along 63rd, then west on Foothill Boulevard, and turned south on 62nd Avenue. Hodari, meanwhile, emerged from the alley onto 62nd and ran north. Looking behind as he ran, he did not turn and see Pertoso until the officer was almost upon him, whereupon he tossed away what appeared to be a small rock. A moment later, Pertoso tackled Hodari, handcuffed him, and radioed for assistance. Hodari was found to be carrying $130 in cash and a pager; and the rock he had discarded was found to be crack cocaine.

In the juvenile proceeding brought against him, Hodari moved to suppress the evidence relating to the cocaine. The court denied the motion without opinion. The California Court of Appeal reversed, holding that Hodari had been "seized" when he saw Officer Pertoso running towards him, that this seizure was unreasonable under the Fourth Amendment, and that the evidence of cocaine had to be suppressed as the fruit of that illegal seizure. The California Supreme Court denied the State's application for review. We granted certiorari.

As this case comes to us, the only issue presented is whether, at the time he dropped the drugs, Hodari had been "seized" within the meaning of the Fourth Amendment. If so, respondent argues, the drugs were the fruit of that seizure and the evidence concerning them was properly excluded. If not, the drugs were abandoned by Hodari and lawfully recovered by the police, and the evidence should have been admitted. (In addition, of course, Pertoso's seeing the rock of cocaine, at least if he recognized it as such, would provide reasonable suspicion for the unquestioned seizure that occurred when he tackled Hodari.)

We have long understood that the Fourth Amendment's protection against "unreasonable . . . seizures" includes seizure of the person. From the time of the founding to the present, the word "seizure" has meant a "taking possession." For most purposes at common law, the word connoted not merely grasping, or applying physical force to, the animate or inanimate object in question, but actually bringing it within physical control.

"There can be constructive detention, which will constitute an arrest, although the party is never actually brought within the physical control of the party making an arrest. This is accomplished by merely touching, however slightly, the body of the accused, by the party making the arrest and for that purpose, although he does not succeed in stopping or holding him even for an instant; as where the bailiff had tried to arrest one who fought him off by a fork, the court said, 'If the bailiff had touched him, that had been an arrest. . . .'"

To say that an arrest is effected by the slightest application of physical force, despite the arrestee's escape, is not to say that for Fourth Amendment purposes there is a continuing arrest during the period of fugitivity. If, for example, Pertoso had laid his hands upon Hodari to arrest him, but Hodari had broken away and had then cast away the cocaine, it would hardly be realistic to say that that disclosure had been made during the course of an arrest. The present case, however, is even one step further removed. It does not involve the application of any physical force; Hodari was untouched by Officer Pertoso at the time he discarded the cocaine. His defense relies instead upon the proposition that a seizure occurs "when the officer, by means of physical force or show of authority, has in some way restrained the liberty of a citizen." Hodari contends (and we accept as true for purposes of this decision) that Pertoso's pursuit qualified as a "show of authority" calling upon Hodari to halt. The narrow question before us is whether, with respect to a show of authority as with respect to application of physical force, a seizure occurs even though the subject does not yield. We hold that it does not.

The language of the Fourth Amendment, of course, cannot sustain respondent's contention. The word "seizure" readily bears the meaning of a laying on of hands or application of physical force to restrain movement, even when it is ultimately unsuccessful. ("She seized the purse-snatcher, but he broke out of her grasp.") It does not remotely apply, however, to the prospect of a policeman yelling "Stop, in the name of the law!" at a fleeing form that continues to flee. That is no seizure. Nor can the result respondent wishes to achieve be produced — indirectly, as it were — by suggesting that Pertoso's uncomplied-with show of authority was a common-law arrest, and then appealing to the principle that all common-law arrests are seizures. An arrest requires either physical force (as described above) or, where that is absent, submission to the assertion of authority.

"Mere words will not constitute an arrest, while, on the other hand, no actual, physical touching is essential. The apparent inconsistency in the two parts of this statement is explained by the fact that an assertion of authority and purpose to arrest followed by submission of the arrestee constitutes an arrest. There can be no arrest without either touching or submission."

We do not think it desirable, even as a policy matter, to stretch the Fourth Amendment beyond its words and beyond the meaning of arrest, as respondent urges. Street pursuits always place the public at some risk, and compliance with police orders to stop should therefore be encouraged. Only a few of those orders, we must presume, will be without adequate basis, and since the addressee has no ready means of identifying the deficient ones it almost invariably is the responsible course to comply. Unlawful orders will not be deterred, moreover, by sanctioning through the exclusionary rule those of them that are not obeyed. Since policemen do not command "Stop!" expecting to be ignored, or give chase hoping to be outrun, it fully suffices to apply the deterrent to their genuine, successful seizures.

Respondent contends that his position is sustained by the so-called *Mendenhall* test. In seeking to rely upon that test here, respondent fails to read it carefully. It says that a person has been seized "only if," not that he has been seized "whenever"; it states a necessary, but not a sufficient, condition for seizure — or, more precisely, for seizure effected through a "show of authority." *Mendenhall* establishes that the test for existence of a "show of authority" is an objective one: not whether the citizen perceived that he was being ordered to restrict his movement, but whether the officer's words and actions would have conveyed that to a reasonable person. Application of this objective test was the basis for our decision in the other case principally relied upon by respondent, *Chesternut, supra*, where we concluded that the police cruiser's slow following of the defendant did not convey the message that he was not free to disregard the police and go about his business. We did not address in *Chesternut*, however, the question whether, if the *Mendenhall* test was met — if the message that the defendant was not free to leave had been conveyed — a Fourth Amendment seizure would have occurred.

Quite relevant to the present case, however, was our decision in *Brower v. Inyo County* (1989). In that case, police cars with flashing lights had chased the decedent for 20 miles — surely an adequate "show of authority" — but he did not stop until his fatal crash into a police-erected blockade. The issue was whether his death could be held to be the consequence of an unreasonable seizure in violation of the Fourth Amendment. We did not even consider the possibility that a seizure could have occurred during the course of the chase because, as we explained, that "show of authority" did not produce his stop. And we discussed an opinion of Justice Holmes, involving a situation not much different from the present case, where revenue agents had picked up containers dropped by moonshiners whom they were pursuing without adequate warrant. The containers were not excluded as the product of an unlawful seizure because "[t]he defendant's own acts, and those of his associates, disclosed the jug, the jar and the bottle — and there was no seizure in the sense of the law when the officers examined the contents of each after they had been abandoned." The same is true here.

In sum, assuming that Pertoso's pursuit in the present case constituted a "show of authority" enjoining Hodari to halt, since Hodari did not comply with that injunction he was not seized until he was tackled. The cocaine abandoned while he was running was in this case not the fruit of a seizure, and his motion to exclude evidence of it was properly denied. We reverse the decision of the California Court of Appeal, and remand for further proceedings not inconsistent with this opinion.

[Justices Stevens and Marshall dissented.]

NOTES AND QUESTIONS

1. Is *Hodari D.* based on a fair reading of *Mendenhall*? Put differently, is it reasonable to interpret *Mendenhall* as establishing only a necessary condition of a seizure and not also a sufficient condition of a seizure?

2. Does the Court in *Hodari D.* equate seizure with arrest?

3. If Hodari had yielded to the police officer's pursuit (and hung on to the cocaine) he may have thereby been under "arrest." Was there probable cause for his arrest? Was there

B. What Is a Seizure for Fourth Amendment Purposes? Race, Seizure, and Force

"reasonable suspicion" to temporarily detain him? The Court makes this observation in footnote 1:

> California conceded below that Officer Pertoso did not have the "reasonable suspicion" required to justify stopping Hodari, *see Terry v. Ohio*, 392 U.S. 1 (1968). That it would be unreasonable to stop, for brief inquiry, young men who scatter in panic upon the mere sighting of the police is not self-evident, and arguably contradicts proverbial common sense. *See* Proverbs 28:1 ("The wicked flee when no man pursueth"). We do not decide that point here, but rely entirely upon the State's concession.

Do you agree with Justice Scalia's point about a connection between flight and suspicion? Does Proverbs 28:1 consider the possibility that to some persons, especially Black people and other minorities, the pursuers themselves may reasonably be regarded as wicked? *See infra* Section E.

4. The Court doubled down on the common law of arrests in *Torres v. Madrid*, 592 U.S. 306 (2021), where a police officer shot and hit a car driven by a woman trying to escape the officers, whom she had mistakenly believed were car jackers, and had accordingly rebuffed their approach to her vehicle. In a 5-4 decision featuring a dispute over competing originalist interpretations of "arrest," the majority found an "arrest" and therefore a "seizure" even though the woman was not successfully apprehended.

5. According to the 2023 survey in the *Mississippi Law Journal* referenced in Chapter I, 16 states have refused to follow *Hodari D*, the second most states (after *Leon*) than any other Supreme Court criminal procedure decision. Christopher R. Green et. al., *State-Court Departures from the Supreme Court: A Comprehensive Survey*, 92 Miss. L.J. 329, 330 (2023).

United States v. Drayton
536 U.S. 194 (2002)

Justice KENNEDY delivered the opinion of the Court.

The Fourth Amendment permits police officers to approach bus passengers at random to ask questions and to request their consent to searches, provided a reasonable person would understand that he or she is free to refuse. *Florida v. Bostick*. his case requires us to determine whether officers must advise bus passengers during these encounters of their right not to cooperate.

I

On February 4, 1999, respondents Christopher Drayton and Clifton Brown, Jr., were traveling on a Greyhound bus en route from Ft. Lauderdale, Florida, to Detroit, Michigan. The bus made a scheduled stop in Tallahassee, Florida. The passengers were required to disembark so the bus could be refueled and cleaned. As the passengers reboarded, the driver checked their tickets and then left to complete paperwork inside the terminal. As he left, the driver allowed three members of the Tallahassee Police Department to board the bus as part of a routine drug and weapons interdiction effort. The officers were dressed in plain clothes and carried concealed weapons and visible badges.

Once onboard Officer Hoover knelt on the driver's seat and faced the rear of the bus. He could observe the passengers and ensure the safety of the two other officers without blocking the aisle or otherwise obstructing the bus exit. Officers Lang and Blackburn went to the rear of the bus. Blackburn remained stationed there, facing forward. Lang worked his way toward the front of the bus, speaking with individual passengers as he went. He asked the passengers about their travel plans and sought to match passengers with luggage in the overhead racks. To avoid blocking the aisle, Lang stood next to or just behind each passenger with whom he spoke.

According to Lang's testimony, passengers who declined to cooperate with him or who chose to exit the bus at any time would have been allowed to do so without argument. In Lang's experience, however, most people are willing to cooperate. Some passengers go so far as to commend the police for their efforts to ensure the safety of their travel. Lang could recall five to six instances in the previous year in which passengers had declined to have their luggage searched. It also was common for passengers to leave the bus for a cigarette or a snack while the officers were on board. Lang sometimes informed passengers of their right to refuse to cooperate. On the day in question, however, he did not.

Respondents were seated next to each other on the bus. Drayton was in the aisle seat, Brown in the seat next to the window. Lang approached respondents from the rear and leaned over Drayton's shoulder. He held up his badge long enough for respondents to identify him as a police officer. With his face 12-to-18 inches away from Drayton's, Lang spoke in a voice just loud enough for respondents to hear:

> I'm Investigator Lang with the Tallahassee Police Department. We're conducting bus interdiction [sic], attempting to deter drugs and illegal weapons being transported on the bus. Do you have any bags on the bus?

Both respondents pointed to a single green bag in the overhead luggage rack. Lang asked, "Do you mind if I check it?," and Brown responded, "Go ahead." Lang handed the bag to Officer Blackburn to check. The bag contained no contraband.

Officer Lang noticed that both respondents were wearing heavy jackets and baggy pants despite the warm weather. In Lang's experience drug traffickers often use baggy clothing to conceal weapons or narcotics. The officer thus asked Brown if he had any weapons or drugs in his possession. And he asked Brown: "Do you mind if I check your person?" Brown answered, "Sure," and cooperated by leaning up in his seat, pulling a cell phone out of his pocket, and opening up his jacket. Lang reached across Drayton and patted down Brown's jacket and pockets, including his waist area, sides, and upper thighs. In both thigh areas, Lang detected hard objects similar to drug packages detected on other occasions. Lang arrested and handcuffed Brown. Officer Hoover escorted Brown from the bus.

Lang then asked Drayton, "Mind if I check you?" Drayton responded by lifting his hands about eight inches from his legs. Lang conducted a patdown of Drayton's thighs and detected hard objects similar to those found on Brown. He arrested Drayton and escorted him from the bus. A further search revealed that respondents had duct-taped plastic bundles of powder cocaine between several pairs of their boxer shorts. Brown possessed three bundles containing 483 grams of cocaine. Drayton possessed two bundles containing 295 grams of cocaine.

Respondents were charged with conspiring to distribute cocaine, in violation of 21 U.S.C. §§ 841(a)(1) and 846, and with possessing cocaine with intent to distribute it, in violation of § 841(a)(1). They moved to suppress the cocaine, arguing that the consent to the patdown search was invalid. Following a hearing at which only Officer Lang testified, the United States District Court for the Northern District of Florida denied their motions to suppress. The District Court determined that the police conduct was not coercive and respondents' consent to the search was voluntary. The District Court pointed to the fact that the officers were dressed in plain clothes, did not brandish their badges in an authoritative manner, did not make a general announcement to the entire bus, and did not address anyone in a menacing tone of voice. It noted that the officers did not block the aisle or the exit, and stated that it was "obvious that [respondents] can get up and leave, as can the people ahead of them." The District Court concluded: "[E]verything that took place between Officer Lang and Mr. Drayton and

Mr. Brown suggests that it was cooperative. There was nothing coercive, there was nothing confrontational about it."

The Court of Appeals for the Eleventh Circuit reversed and remanded with instructions to grant respondents' motions to suppress.

We granted certiorari. The respondents, we conclude, were not seized and their consent to the search was voluntary; and we reverse.

II

Law enforcement officers do not violate the Fourth Amendment's prohibition of unreasonable seizures merely by approaching individuals on the street or in other public places and putting questions to them if they are willing to listen. Even when law enforcement officers have no basis for suspecting a particular individual, they may pose questions, ask for identification, and request consent to search luggage—provided they do not induce cooperation by coercive means. If a reasonable person would feel free to terminate the encounter, then he or she has not been seized.

The Court has addressed on a previous occasion the specific question of drug interdiction efforts on buses. In *Bostick*, two police officers requested a bus passenger's consent to a search of his luggage. The passenger agreed, and the resulting search revealed cocaine in his suitcase. The Florida Supreme Court suppressed the cocaine. In doing so it adopted a per se rule that due to the cramped confines onboard a bus the act of questioning would deprive a person of his or her freedom of movement and so constitute a seizure under the Fourth Amendment.

This Court reversed. *Bostick* first made it clear that for the most part per se rules are inappropriate in the Fourth Amendment context. The proper inquiry necessitates a consideration of "all the circumstances surrounding the encounter." The Court noted next that the traditional rule, which states that a seizure does not occur so long as a reasonable person would feel free "to disregard the police and go about his business," is not an accurate measure of the coercive effect of a bus encounter. A passenger may not want to get off a bus if there is a risk it will depart before the opportunity to reboard. A bus rider's movements are confined in this sense, but this is the natural result of choosing to take the bus; it says nothing about whether the police conduct is coercive. The proper inquiry "is whether a reasonable person would feel free to decline the officers' requests or otherwise terminate the encounter." Finally, the Court rejected Bostick's argument that he must have been seized because no reasonable person would consent to a search of luggage containing drugs. The reasonable person test, the Court explained, is objective and "presupposes an innocent person."

In light of the limited record, *Bostick* refrained from deciding whether a seizure occurred. The Court, however, identified two factors "particularly worth noting" on remand. First, although it was obvious that an officer was armed, he did not remove the gun from its pouch or use it in a threatening way. Second, the officer advised the passenger that he could refuse consent to the search.

* * *

Applying the *Bostick* framework to the facts of this particular case, we conclude that the police did not seize respondents when they boarded the bus and began questioning passengers. The officers gave the passengers no reason to believe that they were required to answer the officers' questions. When Officer Lang approached respondents, he did not brandish a weapon or make any intimidating movements. He left the aisle free so that respondents could exit. He spoke to passengers one by one and in a polite, quiet voice. Nothing he said would suggest to a reasonable person that he or she was barred from leaving the bus or otherwise terminating the encounter.

There were ample grounds for the District Court to conclude that "everything that took place between Officer Lang and [respondents] suggests that it was cooperative" and that there "was nothing coercive [or] confrontational" about the encounter. There was no application of force, no intimidating movement, no overwhelming show of force, no brandishing of weapons, no blocking of exits, no threat, no command, not even an authoritative tone of voice. It is beyond question that had this encounter occurred on the street, it would be constitutional. The fact that an encounter takes place on a bus does not on its own transform standard police questioning of citizens into an illegal seizure. Indeed, because many fellow passengers are present to witness officers' conduct, a reasonable person may feel even more secure in his or her decision not to cooperate with police on a bus than in other circumstances.

Respondents make much of the fact that Officer Lang displayed his badge. And while neither Lang nor his colleagues were in uniform or visibly armed, those factors should have little weight in the analysis. Officers are often required to wear uniforms and in many circumstances this is cause for assurance, not discomfort. Much the same can be said for wearing sidearms. That most law enforcement officers are armed is a fact well known to the public. The presence of a holstered firearm thus is unlikely to contribute to the coerciveness of the encounter absent active brandishing of the weapon.

Officer Hoover's position at the front of the bus also does not tip the scale in respondents' favor. Hoover did nothing to intimidate passengers, and he said nothing to suggest that people could not exit and indeed he left the aisle clear. In *Delgado*, the Court determined there was no seizure even though several uniformed INS officers were stationed near the exits of the factory. The Court noted: "The presence of agents by the exits posed no reasonable threat of detention to these workers, . . . the mere possibility that they would be questioned if they sought to leave the buildings should not have resulted in any reasonable apprehension by any of them that they would be seized or detained in any meaningful way."

Finally, the fact that in Officer Lang's experience only a few passengers have refused to cooperate does not suggest that a reasonable person would not feel free to terminate the bus encounter. In Lang's experience it was common for passengers to leave the bus for a cigarette or a snack while the officers were questioning passengers. And of more importance, bus passengers answer officers' questions and otherwise cooperate not because of coercion but because the passengers know that their participation enhances their own safety and the safety of those around them. "While most citizens will respond to a police request, the fact that people do so, and do so without being told they are free not to respond, hardly eliminates the consensual nature of the response."

Drayton contends that even if Brown's cooperation with the officers was consensual, Drayton was seized because no reasonable person would feel free to terminate the encounter with the officers after Brown had been arrested. The Court of Appeals did not address this claim; and in any event the argument fails. The arrest of one person does not mean that everyone around him has been seized by police. If anything, Brown's arrest should have put Drayton on notice of the consequences of continuing the encounter by answering the officers' questions. Even after arresting Brown, Lang addressed Drayton in a polite manner and provided him with no indication that he was required to answer Lang's questions.

We turn now from the question whether respondents were seized to whether they were subjected to an unreasonable search, i.e., whether their consent to the suspicionless search was involuntary. In circumstances such as these, where the question of voluntariness pervades both the search and seizure inquiries, the respective analyses turn on very similar facts. And, as the facts above suggest, respondents' consent to the search of their luggage and their persons was voluntary. Nothing Officer Lang said indicated a command to consent to the search. Rather, when respondents informed Lang that they had a bag on the bus, he asked for their permission to check it. And when Lang requested to search Brown and Drayton's persons, he asked first if they objected, thus indicating to a reasonable person that he or she was free to refuse. Even after arresting Brown, Lang provided Drayton with no indication that he was required to consent to a search. To the contrary, Lang asked for Drayton's permission to search him ("Mind if I check you?"), and Drayton agreed.

The Court has rejected in specific terms the suggestion that police officers must always inform citizens of their right to refuse when seeking permission to conduct a warrantless consent search. "While knowledge of the right to refuse consent is one factor to be taken into account, the government need not establish such knowledge as the sine qua non of an effective consent." Nor do this Court's decisions suggest that even though there are no per se rules, a presumption of invalidity attaches if a citizen consented without explicit notification that he or she was free to refuse to cooperate. Instead, the Court has repeated that the totality of the circumstances must control, without giving extra weight to the absence of this type of warning. Although Officer Lang did not inform respondents of their right to refuse the search, he did request permission to search, and the totality of the circumstances indicates that their consent was voluntary, so the searches were reasonable.

In a society based on law, the concept of agreement and consent should be given a weight and dignity of its own. Police officers act in full accord with the law when they ask citizens for consent. It reinforces the rule of law for the citizen to advise the police of his or her wishes and for the police to act in reliance on that understanding. When this exchange takes place, it dispels inferences of coercion.

• • •

The judgment of the Court of Appeals is reversed, and the case is remanded for further proceedings consistent with this opinion.

Justice SOUTER, with whom Justice STEVENS and Justice GINSBURG join, dissenting.

Anyone who travels by air today submits to searches of the person and luggage as a condition of boarding the aircraft. It is universally accepted that such intrusions are necessary to hedge against risks that, nowadays, even small children understand. The commonplace precautions of air travel have not, thus far, been justified for ground transportation, however, and no such conditions have been placed on passengers getting on trains or buses. There is therefore an air of unreality about the Court's explanation that bus passengers consent to searches of their luggage to "enhanc[e] their own safety and the safety of those around them." Nor are the other factual assessments underlying the Court's conclusion in favor of the Government more convincing.

The issue we took to review is whether the police's examination of the bus passengers, including respondents, amounted to a suspicionless seizure under the Fourth Amendment. If it did, any consent to search was plainly invalid as a product of the illegal seizure.

Florida v. Bostick (1991), established the framework for determining whether the bus passengers were seized in the constitutional sense. In that case, we rejected the position that police questioning of bus passengers was a per se seizure, and held instead that the issue of seizure was to be resolved under an objective test considering all circumstances: whether a reasonable passenger would have felt "free to decline the officers' requests or otherwise terminate the encounter." We thus applied to a bus passenger the more general criterion, whether the person questioned was free "to ignore the police presence and go about his business."

Before applying the standard in this case, it may be worth getting some perspective from different sets of facts. A perfect example of police conduct that supports no colorable claim of seizure is the act of an officer who simply goes up to a pedestrian on the street and asks him a question. A pair of officers questioning a pedestrian, without more, would presumably support the same conclusion. Now consider three officers, one of whom stands behind the pedestrian, another at his side toward the open sidewalk, with the third addressing questions to the pedestrian a foot or two from his face. Finally, consider the same scene in a narrow alley. On such barebones facts, one may not be able to say a seizure occurred, even in the last case, but one can say without qualification that the atmosphere of the encounters differed significantly from the first to the last examples. In the final instance there is every reason to believe that the pedestrian would have understood, to his considerable discomfort, what Justice Stewart described as the "threatening presence of several officers." The police not only carry legitimate authority but also exercise power free from immediate check, and when the attention of several officers is brought to bear on one civilian the imbalance of immediate power is unmistakable. We all understand this, as well as we understand that a display of power rising to Justice Stewart's "threatening" level may overbear a normal person's ability to act freely, even in the absence of explicit commands or the formalities of detention. As common as this understanding is, however, there is little sign of it in the Court's opinion. My own understanding of the relevant facts and their significance follows.

When the bus in question made its scheduled stop in Tallahassee, the passengers were required to disembark while the vehicle was cleaned and refueled. When the passengers returned, they gave their tickets to the driver, who kept them and then left himself, after giving three police officers permission to board the bus in his absence. Although they were not in uniform, the officers displayed badges and identified themselves as police. One stationed himself in the driver's seat by the door at the front, facing back to observe the passengers. The two others went to the rear, from which they worked their way forward, with one of them speaking to passengers, the other backing him up. They necessarily addressed the passengers at very close range; the aisle was only 15 inches wide, and each seat only 18. The quarters were cramped further by the overhead rack, 19 inches above the top of the passenger seats. The passenger by the window could not have stood up straight, and the face of the nearest officer was only a foot or 18 inches from the face of the nearest passenger being addressed. During the exchanges, the officers looked down, and the passengers had to look up if they were to face the police. The officer asking the questions spoke quietly. He prefaced his requests for permission to search luggage and do a body patdown by identifying himself by name as a police investigator "conducting bus interdiction" and saying, "'We would like for your cooperation. Do you have any luggage on the bus?'"

Thus, for reasons unexplained, the driver with the tickets entitling the passengers to travel had yielded his custody of the bus and its seated travelers to three police officers, whose authority apparently superseded the driver's own. The officers took control of the entire passenger compartment, one stationed at the door keeping surveillance of all the occupants, the others working forward from the back. With one officer right behind him and the other one forward, a third officer accosted each passenger at quarters extremely close and so cramped that as many as half the passengers could not even have stood to face the speaker. None was asked whether he was willing to converse with the police or to take part in the enquiry. Instead the officer said the police were "conducting bus interdiction," in the course of which they "would like . . . cooperation." The reasonable inference was that the "interdiction" was not a consensual exercise, but one the police would carry out whatever the circumstances; that they would prefer "cooperation" but would not let the lack of it stand in their way. There was no contrary indication that day, since no passenger had refused the cooperation requested, and there was no reason for any passenger to believe that the driver would return and the trip resume until the police were satisfied. The scene was set and an atmosphere of obligatory participation was established by this introduction. Later requests to search prefaced with "Do you mind . . ." would naturally have been understood in the terms with which the encounter began.

It is very hard to imagine that either Brown or Drayton would have believed that he stood to lose nothing if he refused to cooperate with the police, or that he had any free choice

B. What Is a Seizure for Fourth Amendment Purposes? Race, Seizure, and Force — **275**

to ignore the police altogether. No reasonable passenger could have believed that, only an uncomprehending one. It is neither here nor there that the interdiction was conducted by three officers, not one, as a safety precaution. The fact was that there were three, and when Brown and Drayton were called upon to respond, each one was presumably conscious of an officer in front watching, one at his side questioning him, and one behind for cover, in case he became unruly, perhaps, or "cooperation" was not forthcoming. The situation is much like the one in the alley, with civilians in close quarters, unable to move effectively, being told their cooperation is expected. While I am not prepared to say that no bus interrogation and search can pass the *Bostick* test without a warning that passengers are free to say no, the facts here surely required more from the officers than a quiet tone of voice. A police officer who is certain to get his way has no need to shout.

It is true of course that the police testified that a bus passenger sometimes says no, but that evidence does nothing to cast the facts here in a different light. We have no way of knowing the circumstances in which a passenger elsewhere refused a request; maybe that has happened only when the police have told passengers they had a right to refuse (as the officers sometimes advised them). Nor is it fairly possible to see the facts of this case differently by recalling *Delgado* as precedent. In that case, a majority of this Court found no seizure when a factory force was questioned by immigration officers, with an officer posted at every door leading from the workplace. Whether that opinion was well reasoned or not, the facts as the Court viewed them differed from the case here. *Delgado* considered an order granting summary judgment in favor of respondents, with the consequence that the Court was required to construe the record and all issues of fact favorably to the Immigration and Naturalization Service. The Court therefore emphasized that even after "th[e] surveys were initiated, the employees were about their ordinary business, operating machinery and performing other job assignments." In this case, however, Brown and Drayton were seemingly pinned-in by the officers and the customary course of events was stopped flat. The bus was going nowhere, and with one officer in the driver's seat, it was reasonable to suppose no passenger would tend to his own business until the officers were ready to let him.

In any event, I am less concerned to parse this case against *Delgado* than to apply *Bostick*'s totality of circumstances test, and to ask whether a passenger would reasonably have felt free to end his encounter with the three officers by saying no and ignoring them thereafter. In my view the answer is clear. The Court's contrary conclusion tells me that the majority cannot see what Justice Stewart saw, and I respectfully dissent.

NOTES AND QUESTIONS

1. The Court revisits the seizure question it had deferred in *Florida v. Bostick*, 501 U.S. 429 (1991), due to a limited record on the issue in that case. In *Bostick*, notably, the officers had informed the passenger that he could refuse consent to the search.

2. Drayton argues that the dynamic of his interaction with the police changed once his traveling companion and virtual seatmate was handcuffed and arrested before his eyes. The Court responds to this argument by stating that the arrest "should have put Drayton on notice of the consequences of continuing the encounter by answering the officers' questions."

But what is the relevance of this "notice" to the "coerciveness" of the altercation, which the Court seems to think is a proxy for whether cooperation could be refused?

3. In connection with acknowledging the officer's testimony that it was common for passengers to step off the bus for a cigarette or a snack — presumably after being questioned, although the Court doesn't clarify and maybe the record didn't either — the Court offers this observation:

276 Chapter IV The Fourth Amendment

> And of more importance, bus passengers answer officers' questions and otherwise cooperate not because of coercion but because the passengers know that their participation enhances their own safety and the safety of those around them.

This sentiment does not appear to be either directly or even indirectly based on any evidence from the suppression hearing. The sentiment reflects yet another example of "a studied air of unreality." It is also rank supposition that no police officer would be permitted to testify to in court.

Professor Bennett Capers collects and discusses these little civics tutorials that the Court so often imparts — mostly in cases with minority defendants — in Bennett Capers, Essay, *Criminal Procedure and the Good Citizen*, 118 Colum. L. Rev. 653, 670 (2018).

4. The dissent points to three factual circumstances that in its view the Court fails to acknowledge: the location of the officers at the bus's exits, which it reinforces by the "narrow alley" analogy; the cramped, almost claustrophobic quarters of the bus, including not just its narrowness but the physical location of the interrogating officers; and the bus driver's apparent abandonment of authority to the police officers, for at least the indefinite future. Which of these factors is most supportive of the dissent's conclusion that an "atmosphere of obligatory participation was established"?

What do you make of the Court's point that the lack of freedom of movement was largely a function of the "choice" to travel by bus as opposed to any action by law enforcement? *See ACLU Amicus Brief, Florida v. Bostick*, 501 U.S. 429 (1991) at 8 n.19 (noting that drug raids on buses disproportionally affect minorities). Are Fourth Amendment seizure rules different for people who work in factories (as in *Delgado*) and take buses?

5. There appears to be substantial case law on drug interdiction bus searches. Any wonder why police officers continue to use this tactic?

All of the Court's seizure case law has an "air of unreality" about it. Most reasonable people would not "feel free to leave" almost any encounter with police. Some courts have acknowledged that this is the actual "reality" of such interactions. "[A]s a practical matter, citizens almost never feel free to end an encounter initiated by the police." *State v. Jones*, 172 N.H. 774, 777 (2020) (quoting *State v. Rodriguez*, 172 N.J. 117, 796 A.2d 857, 863 (2002)); *United States v. Tanguay*, 918 F.3d 1, 5-6 (1st Cir. 2019) ("few people . . . would ever feel free to walk away from any police questioning"); *United States v. Thompson*, 546 F.3d 1223, 1226 n.1 (10th Cir. 2008) (describing the notion that a reasonable person would feel free to disregard the police as potentially "unrealistic"). Academics unanimously agree. *See* Tracey Maclin, *The Decline of the Right of Locomotion: The Fourth Amendment on the Streets*, 75 Cornell L. Rev. 1258, 1301 n.205 (1990) (listing sources).

2. Should Race Matter?

Professor Maclin suggested over 30 years ago that the Court should discard the notion of using a hypothesized reasonable person to judge the constitutionality of police encounters. Instead, taking *Mendenhall* seriously, in assessing the coercive nature of an interaction the Court should take the citizen's race into account, and how race might have influenced the person's perception of the encounter. *See* Tracey Maclin, *Black and Blue Encounters — Some Preliminary Thoughts About Fourth Amendment Seizures: Should Race Matter?*, 26 Val. L. Rev. 243, 250 (1991). Because of widespread fear of police violence in the Black community, Black people have "internalized racial obedience toward, and fear of, the police." Devon W. Carbado, *(E)racing the Fourth Amendment*, 100 Mich. L. Rev. 946, 966 (2002).

A handful of state and federal courts have discussed whether race should matter in the seizure context. The most unequivocal affirmative answer to Professor Maclin's question — Should race matter? — has come from the Supreme Court of Washington, which held in *State v. Sum*, 199 Wash. 2d 627, 656 (2022) (en banc) that courts "must" consider the race and ethnicity of the allegedly seized person in assessing an encounter.

State v. Sum
199 Wash. 2d 627 (2022) (en banc)

Yu, J.

This case concerns the analysis that courts must apply to determine whether a person has been seized by law enforcement for purposes of article I, section 7 of the Washington Constitution. It is well established that an encounter with law enforcement rises to the level of a seizure if "considering all the circumstances, an individual's freedom of movement is restrained and the individual would not believe [they are] free to leave or decline a request due to an officer's use of force or display of authority." Today, we are asked whether "all the circumstances" of the encounter includes the race and ethnicity of the allegedly seized person.

As the parties correctly agree, the answer is yes. Our precedent has always required that the seizure inquiry be made in light of the totality of the circumstances, and we have never stated that race and ethnicity cannot be relevant circumstances. However, we have not explicitly held that in interactions with law enforcement, race and ethnicity matter. We do so today. Furthermore, to ensure that all the circumstances of a law enforcement encounter are properly considered, including race and ethnicity, we take this opportunity to clarify the seizure inquiry as a matter of independent state law, taking guidance from GR 37.

As set forth in this court's precedent, the seizure inquiry is an objective test in which the allegedly seized person has the burden to show that a seizure occurred. To aid courts in the application of this test, we now clarify that a person is seized for purposes of article I, section 7 if, based on the totality of the circumstances, an objective observer could conclude that the person was not free to leave, to refuse a request, or to otherwise terminate the encounter due to law enforcement's display of authority or use of physical force. For purposes of this analysis, an objective observer is aware that implicit, institutional, and unconscious biases, in addition to purposeful discrimination, have resulted in disproportionate police contacts, investigative seizures, and uses of force against Black, Indigenous, and other People of Color (BIPOC) in Washington. Finally, in accordance with our precedent, if the person shows there was a seizure, then the burden shifts to the State to prove that the seizure was lawfully justified by a warrant or an applicable exception to the warrant requirement.

Based on the totality of the circumstances presented in this case, we hold that petitioner Palla Sum was seized when a sheriff's deputy requested Sum's identification while implying that Sum was under investigation for car theft. As the State properly concedes, at that time, the deputy did not have a warrant, reasonable suspicion, or any other lawful authority to seize Sum. As a result, Sum was unlawfully seized, and the false name and birth date he gave to the deputy must be suppressed. We therefore reverse the Court of Appeals and remand to the trial court for further proceedings.

FACTUAL BACKGROUND AND PROCEDURAL HISTORY

On April 9, 2019, Pierce County Sheriff's Deputy Mark Rickerson was on patrol, driving an unmarked police vehicle through an area where there were "some problem houses" that Deputy Rickerson liked to "keep an eye on." At 9:15 a.m., the deputy noticed a Honda Civic parked near the entry gate to a church parking lot.

The Honda was not blocking the entry gate, and there is no indication that it was parked illegally. Nevertheless, the car attracted the deputy's attention because "it was parked there."

278 Chapter IV The Fourth Amendment

The location was significant to Deputy Rickerson because "four or five months before . . . another deputy in [his] unit arrested another subject there in a stolen vehicle." Within that same four- to five-month time frame, an unnamed person approached Deputy Rickerson in a nearby grocery store parking lot to tell the deputy that they were "concerned about all the vehicles that were parking there that didn't belong in the area."

As Deputy Rickerson observed the Honda, he saw Sum, who "was slumped over and appeared to be unconscious in the driver's seat." At that point, the deputy decided to conduct "a social contact" and parked nearby, "making sure to leave enough room so as not to block the Honda Civic or prevent it from leaving." Before getting out of his police vehicle, Deputy Rickerson conducted a records check of the Honda's license plate and discovered a report of sale, although it was not clear when the sale had occurred. The records check also showed that the car had not been reported stolen, but the records did not state the name of the current owner. Deputy Rickerson noted the last four digits of the vehicle identification number (VIN) associated with the Honda's license plate, then approached the driver's side of the car on foot, wearing his full uniform.

As he approached, Deputy Rickerson noticed another man in the car, who was in the front passenger seat. Both Sum and the passenger "appeared to be unconscious and did not notice Rickerson approach." Before attempting to wake them, Deputy Rickerson checked the Honda's public VIN to confirm that it matched the license plates. The deputy then knocked on the driver's side window. After "seven to eight seconds," Sum "slowly woke up" and "rolled the window down slightly."

Deputy Rickerson asked Sum what he and his passenger were doing there, and Sum responded that they "were waiting for a friend." The deputy then asked Sum who owned the Honda. Sum said the Honda was not his, and he identified the owner "with the given name, but not the surname, of an individual." At the suppression hearing, Deputy Rickerson could not recall the name Sum provided.

Deputy Rickerson next asked Sum and his passenger for identification, and Sum "asked him why he wanted it." The deputy responded "that the two men were sitting in an area known for stolen vehicles and that [Sum] did not appear to know to whom the vehicle he was sitting in belonged." Sum provided a false name and date of birth. The passenger gave his true name and birth date.

Deputy Rickerson walked back to his patrol vehicle to check the names Sum and his passenger provided. While the deputy was in his vehicle, Sum started the Honda's engine, "backed up quickly, and then took off," driving partially on the sidewalk and over some grass. Deputy Rickerson activated his emergency lights and started pursuing the Honda, soon joined by another deputy in a separate vehicle. Sum drove at a high rate of speed through a stop sign and multiple red lights before ultimately crashing in someone's front yard. Deputy Rickerson handcuffed Sum and read him the *Miranda* warnings.

A search of Sum's person incident to arrest turned up the Honda's title and registration, which showed that the car did, in fact, belong to Palla Sum. He had purchased it two weeks earlier. The search of Sum's person also uncovered a small holster in his pants, and when the Honda was later searched pursuant to a warrant, police discovered a pistol.

Sum was charged by amended information with unlawful possession of a firearm in the first degree, attempting to elude a pursuing police vehicle, and making a false or misleading statement to a public servant. The original and amended charging documents both specify that Sum's race is "ASIAN/PACIFIC ISLAND[ER]."

Sum filed a pretrial motion to suppress pursuant to CrR 3.6, contending that he was unlawfully seized without reasonable suspicion when Deputy Rickerson requested Sum's identification while implying that Sum was under investigation for car theft. The court denied Sum's motion to suppress, ruling that "[b]ecause Rickerson did not retain [Sum]'s physical identification to conduct his records check, [Sum] was not seized when Rickerson asked him to identify himself." Sum was convicted of all three charges by a jury. Like the charging documents, Sum's felony judgment and sentence states that his race is "Asian/Pacific Islander." His ethnicity is listed as "Non-Hispanic."

Sum appealed, and the Court of Appeals affirmed in an unpublished opinion, holding that Sum was not seized by the deputy's request for identification because "merely asking for identification is properly characterized as a social contact." Sum petitioned for review, reiterating his previous arguments and further contending for the first time that "there is no justification—aside from unacceptably ignoring the issue of race altogether—for courts considering the totality of the circumstances to disregard the effect of race as one of the circumstances affecting evaluation of police contact."

We granted Sum's petition for review and accepted for filing a joint amici brief by the King County Department of Public Defense, the American Civil Liberties Union of Washington, the Fred T. Korematsu Center for Law and Equality, and the Washington Defender Association. We now reverse.

$$\bullet \quad \bullet \quad \bullet$$

As discussed above, the parties correctly agree that race and ethnicity can be relevant to the seizure inquiry, and we further hold that Sum's race is relevant to the seizure inquiry in this case. Although this decision flows directly from our precedent, Washington case law provides no guidance as to how a court is to consider the allegedly seized person's race or ethnicity because we have never done so before. Moreover, some of the analysis offered in this case indicates there is a need to reiterate that the seizure inquiry depends on the totality of the circumstances, rather than a list of factors. We therefore clarify the seizure inquiry, taking guidance from GR 37. In doing so, we do not disavow our precedent, and we do not suggest that any particular case would have had a different outcome pursuant to the clarification we announce today.

1. The seizure analysis must properly account for all the circumstances of Sum's encounter with Deputy Rickerson

On the ultimate question of when Sum was seized, the State contends that "Sum was not seized until he drove off at a high rate of speed, over grass and the sidewalk, and Deputy Rickerson activated his lights in pursuit." To reach this conclusion, the State focuses on the circumstances that were not present in Sum's encounter with Deputy Rickerson. For instance, as the State correctly notes, there were not multiple officers, Deputy Rickerson did not physically block Sum's car from leaving, the deputy did not "activate[ ] his lights or siren," and he did not "display[ ] his weapon, physically touch[ ] Sum, or use[ ] language or tone indicating mandatory compliance." The Court of Appeals took a similar approach in its seizure analysis. Likewise, the trial court appears to have placed dispositive weight on the fact that Deputy "Rickerson did not retain [Sum]'s physical identification to conduct his records check"; that was the only reason the court identified in its written ruling concluding that Sum was not seized.

Without question, each of those circumstances, if present, would weigh in favor of holding that Sum was seized. However, the lack of those particular circumstances fails to show that Sum was not seized. To the contrary, because the seizure inquiry depends on "all the circumstances," there will always be factual distinctions between cases. As a result, our precedent requires courts to carefully assess "all surrounding circumstances" that are presented in each encounter, rather than focusing on the circumstances that are not presented, or considering each encounter against a predetermined set of factors. Nevertheless, we recognize that this requirement can be difficult to apply with consistency and objectivity. We therefore take this opportunity to clarify the article I, section 7 seizure analysis as a matter of independent state law.

2. GR 37 appropriately guides our clarification of the seizure inquiry

In order to provide courts and parties with a clearer framework for conducting an article I, section 7 seizure analysis, we take guidance from GR 37. GR 37 was adopted to bring increased clarity, consistency, and justice to jury selection, an area of law where all three qualities have long proved elusive. Many of the same concerns arise in the context of warrantless seizures.

This court adopted GR 37 in an effort "to eliminate the unfair exclusion of potential jurors based on race or ethnicity." GR 37 replaces the *Batson* test, which "has done very little to make juries more diverse or to prevent prosecutors from exercising race-based challenges." The differences between GR 37 and *Batson* are informative in contexts beyond jury selection, including the seizure analysis required by article I, section 7.

For instance, in order to bring a successful *Batson* challenge, a defendant must show that a peremptory challenge was motivated by "purposeful discrimination." GR 37, by contrast, provides that a "court need not find purposeful discrimination" and, instead, must deny the peremptory challenge if "an objective observer could view race or ethnicity as a factor." GR 37(e). This shift away from purposeful discrimination "take[s] the focus off of the credibility and integrity of the attorneys and ease[s] the accusatory strain of sustaining a *Batson* challenge," which "simplif[ies] the task of reducing racial bias in our criminal justice system, both conscious and unconscious."

Similar concerns are presented in the warrantless seizure context, where it is well known that BIPOC are wrongfully subject to excessive police scrutiny. Nevertheless, purposeful, explicit discrimination may be absent or impossible to prove in individual cases because "identifying the influence of racial bias generally, and implicit racial bias specifically, presents unique challenges." Beyond the problem of proof, GR 37's rejection of the need to show purposeful discrimination also better aligns with the objective seizure inquiry required by our precedent, which holds that the "subjective intent of police is irrelevant to the question [of] whether a seizure occurred unless it is conveyed to the defendant."

Another relevant difference between *Batson* and GR 37 is that *Batson* permits a party to exercise their peremptory challenges on an apparently discriminatory basis, so long as the party can "articulate a neutral explanation" to justify their actions. The list of potential "neutral explanations" is limitless, and "[p]roffered reasons sometimes involve subtle observations about a prospective juror's appearance or demeanor, which are easily alleged but often extremely difficult to scrutinize." GR 37 addresses this concern by specifying that "allegations that the prospective juror was sleeping, inattentive, or staring or failing to make eye contact; exhibited a problematic attitude, body language, or demeanor; or provided unintelligent or confused answers" cannot be a valid basis for a peremptory challenge without "corroboration by the judge or opposing counsel verifying the behavior" because such allegations "have historically been associated with improper discrimination in jury selection in Washington State." GR 37(i). Moreover, as noted above, GR 37 also provides a list of presumptively invalid reasons for exercising peremptory challenges, such as prior contacts with, and distrust of, law enforcement, which "have been associated with improper discrimination in jury selection in Washington State."

These presumptively invalid reasons for exercising peremptory challenges reflect that unless carefully drawn, facially neutral standards can have a disproportionate impact in jury selection. The same is true in the seizure context. As discussed above, BIPOC are subject to excessive police contacts, investigative seizures, and uses of force by law enforcement. Moreover, the BIPOC community, as a whole, is generally well aware of such patterns of excessive police scrutiny. As a result, "generations of children have had to grow up with 'the Talk,'" in which parents must educate their children "about how to interact with law enforcement so no officer will have any reason to misperceive them as a threat and take harmful or fatal action against them." "Against that awareness," an encounter with law enforcement would certainly feel "more pointed and coercive." Thus, "[t]he fear of harm and resulting protective conditioning to submit to avoid harm at the hands of police is relevant to whether there was a seizure because feeling 'free' to leave or terminate an encounter with police officers is rooted in an assessment of the consequences of doing so."

A final relevant point of comparison between *Batson* and GR 37 is the perspective from which the ultimate determination is made. A successful *Batson* challenge requires the trial judge to "decide[ ] that the facts establish, prima facie, purposeful discrimination," and that the State failed to "come forward with a neutral explanation for [its] action." However, *Batson* does not specify from whose perspective "purposeful discrimination" and "neutral explanations" are to be evaluated. As a result, "[g]iven the inevitably clumsy fit between any objectively measurable standard and the subjective decisionmaking at issue, [we should not be] surprised to find studies and anecdotal reports suggesting that, despite *Batson*, the discriminatory use of peremptory challenges remains a problem."

GR 37 seeks to address this problem by explicitly providing that (1) the analysis must be made from the perspective of "an objective observer," (2) the necessary showing is made if the objective observer "could view race or ethnicity as a factor in the use of the peremptory challenge," and (3) an objective observer "is aware that implicit, institutional, and unconscious biases, in addition to purposeful discrimination, have resulted in the unfair exclusion of potential jurors in Washington State." Thus, "GR 37 was written in terms of possibilities, not actualities," and the rule "teaches that peremptory strikes exercised against prospective jurors who appear to be members of racial or ethnic minority groups must be treated with skepticism and considerable caution."

The seizure context presents similar issues. Washington's seizure test is intended to be "'a purely objective one'" based on what a hypothetical "reasonable person" in the defendant's position would have believed under the same circumstances. However, without more specific guidance, the perspective of a "reasonable person" is measured from the perspective of the judicial decision-maker. Judicial officers are especially well situated to know their legal rights and may also be unusually likely to expect that their rights, if asserted, will be respected by law enforcement. This commonsense observation is not to suggest that judicial perspectives are unreasonable; we merely acknowledge that it is unrealistic to equate the perspective of a judicial officer with the perspective of a "reasonable person" in this context. Therefore, following GR 37's example and reframing the seizure inquiry to focus on what an objective observer could believe about a person's encounter with law enforcement provides a valuable safeguard.

Thus, there are relevant parallels between the contexts of jury selection and warrantless seizures, showing that GR 37 should guide our clarification of the seizure inquiry.

3. We now clarify the analysis that courts must apply when determining whether a person has been seized by law enforcement

As provided by our precedent, the article I, section 7 seizure inquiry is an objective test in which the allegedly seized person has the burden of showing that a seizure occurred. To properly apply this test, we now clarify that a person has been seized as a matter of independent state law if, based on the totality of the circumstances, an objective observer could conclude that the person was not free to leave, to refuse a request, or to otherwise terminate a police encounter due to law enforcement's display of authority or use of physical force. For purposes of this analysis, an objective observer is aware that implicit, institutional, and unconscious biases, in addition to purposeful discrimination, have resulted in disproportionate police contacts, investigative seizures, and uses of force against BIPOC in Washington.

Moreover, in determining whether there has been a seizure in light of all the circumstances of the encounter, courts may take guidance from some of the circumstances specified in GR 37, in addition to case law and the contentions of the parties. For instance, "the number and types of questions posed" or requests made of the allegedly seized person, and the extent to which similar law enforcement encounters are "disproportionately associated with a race or ethnicity" may be relevant considerations, among others.

Finally, in accordance with our precedent, if the person shows that there was a seizure, then the burden shifts to the State to prove that the seizure was supported by a warrant or "was justified by an exception to the warrant requirement." Our opinion today is not intended to modify or clarify the warrant requirement or any of its exceptions.

D. Given the totality of the circumstances, we hold that Deputy Rickerson seized Sum before Sum identified himself with a false name and birth date

As discussed above, although Sum's race is relevant to the seizure inquiry, it is certainly not dispositive. We must instead consider all of the circumstances to determine whether an objective observer could conclude that Sum was not free to refuse Deputy Rickerson's request for identification based on the deputy's display of authority. The answer is yes.

The circumstances, as found by the trial court, were as follows. Sum, a person of color, was asleep in his car, which was parked on a public street in a "high-crime area." At 9:15 in the morning, Sum was awoken by a sheriff's deputy in full uniform knocking on the car window next to where Sum was sleeping. Deputy Rickerson did not ask about Sum's health or safety, and he did not ask if Sum and his passenger required assistance. Instead, the deputy asked what Sum and his passenger were doing, clearly implying that they did not belong there.

Sum answered that "they were visiting a friend across the street." This answer proved insufficient to satisfy the deputy's interest in Sum and his passenger because Deputy Rickerson next asked "to whom the Honda Civic belonged." Sum provided a name, but this also failed to satisfy the deputy because he then requested Sum's identification. When Sum "asked him why he wanted" identification, the deputy "explained that the two men were sitting in an area known for stolen vehicles and that [Sum] did not appear to know to whom the vehicle he was sitting in belonged."

Assuming, without deciding, that Sum was not already seized, then Deputy Rickerson's explanation was certainly "the tipping point at which the weight of the circumstances transformed a simple encounter into a seizure." At that point, it would have been clear to any reasonable person that Deputy Rickerson wanted Sum's identification because he suspected Sum of car theft. Indeed, the deputy stated as much, and we have recognized that law enforcement's subjective intent is relevant if "it is conveyed to the defendant." "[T]he number and types" of Deputy Rickerson's questions and requests further indicated his investigative purpose, despite the lack of reasonable suspicion. It is also "no secret" that "suspicionless stop[s]" are "disproportionately associated" with people of color.

Thus, this case is not like others in which we have held that a seizure does not occur "merely because a police officer engages [a person] in conversation in a public place and asks for identification." There were far more circumstances at play here.

Based on the totality of the circumstances, an objective observer could easily conclude that if Sum had refused to identify himself and requested to be left alone, Deputy Rickerson would have failed to honor Sum's request because the deputy was investigating Sum for car theft. In other words, an objective observer could conclude that Sum was not free to refuse Deputy Rickerson's request due to the deputy's display of authority. At that point, Sum was seized. As the State correctly concedes, this seizure was not supported by a warrant, reasonable suspicion, or any other authority of law.

Thus, the false name and birth date that Sum gave to Deputy Rickerson was the product of an unlawful seizure. Sum's false statement must be suppressed because "[o]ur state exclusionary rule requires the suppression of evidence obtained in violation of article I, section 7."

CONCLUSION

Today, we formally recognize what has always been true: in interactions with law enforcement, race and ethnicity matter. Therefore, courts must consider the race and ethnicity of the allegedly seized person as part of the totality of the circumstances when deciding whether there was a seizure for purposes of article I, section 7. Here, in light of all the circumstances of Sum's encounter with Deputy Rickerson, we hold that Sum was unlawfully seized before he provided a false name and birth date to the deputy, so his false statement must be suppressed. We reverse the Court of Appeals and remand to the trial court for further proceedings consistent with this opinion.

NOTES AND QUESTIONS

Fred Korematsu

1. The court insists that the question of whether a seizure occurred is "a purely objective one" under Washington law. How is it possible to account for race or ethnicity in applying an objective test?

2. The court also relies on the fact that under Washington law the seizure inquiry requires consideration of the totality of the circumstances. Is there tension between this requirement and the "objective" nature of the test?

3. Washington's GR 37 rejected the federal framework derived from *Batson v. Kentucky*, 476 U.S. 79 (1986), for determining whether a party has improperly discriminated in exercising peremptory challenges. *See* Chapter XV *infra*. In short, the rule supplants *Batson*'s requirement of proof of "purposeful discrimination" with an "objective observer" test. How does the court import this aspect of GR 37 into its seizure analysis? Does this aspect of the decision seem forced?

4. How does the court use Sum's ethnicity in determining that a seizure occurred here prior to Sum's false statements? Was the fact of his ethnicity necessary to the court's conclusion?

5. For a discussion of *Sum*, *see* Aliza Hochman Bloom, *"What Has Always Been True": The Washington Supreme Court Decides That Seizure Law Must Account for Racial Disparity in Policing*, 107 Minn. L. Rev. Headnotes 1 (2022).

6. An amicus brief in *Sum* was filed by the Fred T. Korematsu Center for Law and Equality, a public interest organization named for pioneering civil rights hero Fred Korematsu that has the mission to use legal research, litigation advocacy, and clinical education to achieve durable social change related to racial equality and social justice.

Sum was not the first case to acknowledge the use of race as a factor in seizure analysis but it is the most emphatic. In *United States v. Washington*, 490 F.3d 765, 773-74 (9th Cir. 2007), the Ninth Circuit found that one factor tipping the balance in favor of finding a seizure in a white police officer's encounter with a Black man was the recently publicized shootings of Black men by white Portland police officers. Similar reasoning prevailed in *Dozier v. United States*, 220 A.3d 933 (D.C. 2019). In evaluating whether a consensual encounter had escalated into a seizure, the D.C. Circuit found that race surely bore on whether a reasonable person in the defendant's position would have believed he was free to leave. "As is known from well-publicized and documented examples, an African-American man facing armed policemen would reasonably be especially apprehensive" in defendant's situation, having been "perceived by hyper vigilant police officers expecting to find criminal activity in a particular area." *Id.* at 944. In *United States v. Smith*, 794 F.3d 681 (7th Cir. 2015), citing the observation about the potential relevance of race in *Mendenhall*, the Seventh Circuit found that it did not need to consider race in finding a seizure in the case at hand, but observed: "We do not deny the relevance of race in everyday police encounters with citizens in Milwaukee and around the country. Nor do we ignore empirical data demonstrating the existence of racial profiling, police brutality, and other racial disparities in the criminal justice system." *Id.* at 688. *See also State v. Jones*, 172 N.H. 774, 780-81 (2020) ("race is an appropriate circumstance to consider in conducting the totality of the circumstances seizure analysis").

Two federal circuits have explicitly rejected the use of race in evaluating police encounters. In *United States v. Easley*, 911 F.3d 1074 (10th Cir. 2018), the Tenth Circuit stated: "There is no uniform life experience for persons of color, and there are surely divergent attitudes toward law enforcement officers among members of the population. Thus, there is no uniform way to apply a reasonable person test that adequately accounts for racial differences consistent with an objective standard for Fourth Amendment seizures." *Id.* at 1082.

The Eleventh Circuit echoed *Easley*'s concerns in *United States v. Knights*, 989 F.3d 1281 (11th Cir. 2021), and also noted that consideration of race as a factor might run afoul of the Equal Protection Clause. *Id.* at 1287-89. In a concurring opinion in *Knights*, Judge Rosenbaum acknowledged the equal protection issue and advocated for the adoption of a rule requiring police officers to inform persons being questioned of their right to end the encounter. Professor Carbado argues that *not* taking race into account in seizure analysis is tantamount to imposing a racial preference for whites. Devon W. Carbado, Unreasonable: Black Lives, Police Power, and the Fourth Amendment 62 (2022).

In the debate over whether seizure analysis should account for race, both sides have enlisted *J.D.B v. North Carolina*, 564 U.S. 261 (2011), *see* Chapter III *supra*, where the Supreme Court held that a child's age must be considered in determining whether a valid waiver of *Miranda* rights occurred. Professor Carbado, for example, suggests that "reasonable children" and "reasonable black persons"—for very different reasons, obviously—might view their "freedom to leave" differently than white adults. *See also Sum*, 199 Wash. 2d at 642 (discussing *J.D.B.*). On the other hand, in *Knights* the Eleventh Circuit cited *J.D.B.* as a basis for distinguishing between age, a chronological fact that has an "objectively discernible relationship to a reasonable person's understanding of his freedom of action," and other personal characteristics such as race that do not.

3. Seizures and Police Use of Force

Prior to 1985, the Supreme Court had not clarified the constitutional source, if any, of claims that police used excessive force in connection with arrests or other citizen encounters. In the two cases that follow it held that such claims flow from the Fourth Amendment's requirement that "seizures" must be "reasonable." Because a successful allegation of an unreasonable seizure is not a defense to an otherwise valid criminal charge, and does not require the exclusion of evidence, these claims—as in the next two cases—are typically brought as civil damages actions under 42 U.S.C. § 1983. *See* Chapter VI *infra*.

B. What Is a Seizure for Fourth Amendment Purposes? Race, Seizure, and Force

Tennessee v. Garner
471 U.S. 1 (1985)

Justice WHITE delivered the opinion of the Court.

This case requires us to determine the constitutionality of the use of deadly force to prevent the escape of an apparently unarmed suspected felon. We conclude that such force may not be used unless it is necessary to prevent the escape and the officer has probable cause to believe that the suspect poses a significant threat of death or serious physical injury to the officer or others.

I

At about 10:45 p.m. on October 3, 1974, Memphis Police Officers Elton Hymon and Leslie Wright were dispatched to answer a "prowler inside call." Upon arriving at the scene they saw a woman standing on her porch and gesturing toward the adjacent house. She told them she had heard glass breaking and that "they" or "someone" was breaking in next door. While Wright radioed the dispatcher to say that they were on the scene, Hymon went behind the house. He heard a door slam and saw someone run across the backyard. The fleeing suspect, who was appellee-respondent's decedent, Edward Garner, stopped at a 6-feet-high chain link fence at the edge of the yard. With the aid of a flashlight, Hymon was able to see Garner's face and hands. He saw no sign of a weapon, and, though not certain, was "reasonably sure" and "figured" that Garner was unarmed. He thought Garner was 17 or 18 years old and about 5'5" or 5'7" tall. While Garner was crouched at the base of the fence, Hymon called out "police, halt" and took a few steps toward him. Garner then began to climb over the fence. Convinced that if Garner made it over the fence he would elude capture, Hymon shot him. The bullet hit Garner in the back of the head. Garner was taken by ambulance to a hospital, where he died on the operating table. Ten dollars and a purse taken from the house were found on his body.

In using deadly force to prevent the escape, Hymon was acting under the authority of a Tennessee statute and pursuant to Police Department policy. The statute provides that "[i]f, after notice of the intention to arrest the defendant, he either flee or forcibly resist, the officer may use all the necessary means to effect the arrest." The Department policy was slightly more restrictive than the statute, but still allowed the use of deadly force in cases of burglar. The incident was reviewed by the Memphis Police Firearm's Review Board and presented to a grand jury. Neither took any action.

Garner's father then brought this action in the Federal District Court for the Western District of Tennessee, seeking damages under 42 U.S.C. § 1983 for asserted violations of Garner's constitutional rights. The complaint alleged that the shooting violated the Fourth, Fifth, Sixth, Eighth, and Fourteenth Amendments of the United States Constitution. It named as defendants Officer Hymon, the Police Department, its Director, and the Mayor and city of Memphis. After a 3-day bench trial, the District Court entered judgment for all defendants. It dismissed the claims against the Mayor and the Director for lack of evidence. It then concluded that Hymon's actions were authorized by the Tennessee statute, which in turn was constitutional. Hymon had employed the only reasonable and practicable means of preventing Garner's escape. Garner had "recklessly and heedlessly attempted to vault over the fence to escape, thereby assuming the risk of being fired upon."

• • •

II

Whenever an officer restrains the freedom of a person to walk away, he has seized that person. While it is not always clear just when minimal police interference becomes a seizure, there can be no question that apprehension by the use of deadly force is a seizure subject to the reasonableness requirement of the Fourth Amendment.

A

A police officer may arrest a person if he has probable cause to believe that person committed a crime. Petitioners and appellant argue that if this requirement is satisfied the Fourth Amendment has nothing to say about how that seizure is made. This submission ignores the many cases in which this Court, by balancing the extent of the intrusion against the need for it, has examined the reasonableness of the manner in which a search or seizure is conducted. To determine the constitutionality of a seizure "[w]e must balance the nature and quality of the intrusion on the individual's Fourth Amendment interests against the importance of the governmental interests alleged to justify the intrusion." We have described "the balancing of competing interests" as "the key principle of the Fourth Amendment." Because one of the factors is the extent of the intrusion, it is plain that reasonableness depends on not only when a seizure is made, but also how it is carried out.

• • •

In each of these cases, the question was whether the totality of the circumstances justified a particular sort of search or seizure.

B

The same balancing process applied in the cases cited above demonstrates that, notwithstanding probable cause to seize a suspect, an officer may not always do so by killing him. The intrusiveness of a seizure by means of deadly force is unmatched. The suspect's fundamental interest in his own life need not be elaborated upon. The use of deadly force also frustrates the interest of the individual, and of society, in judicial determination of guilt and punishment. Against these interests are ranged governmental interests in effective law enforcement. It is argued that overall violence will be reduced by encouraging the peaceful submission of suspects who know that they may be shot if they flee. Effectiveness in making arrests requires the resort to deadly force, or at least the meaningful threat thereof. "Being able to arrest such individuals is a condition precedent to the state's entire system of law enforcement."

Without in any way disparaging the importance of these goals, we are not convinced that the use of deadly force is a sufficiently productive means of accomplishing them to justify the killing of nonviolent suspects. The use of deadly force is a self-defeating way of apprehending a suspect and so setting the criminal justice mechanism in motion. If successful, it guarantees that that mechanism will not be set in motion. And while the meaningful threat of deadly force might be thought to lead to the arrest of more live suspects by discouraging escape attempts, the presently available evidence does not support this thesis. The fact is that a majority of police departments in this country have forbidden the use of deadly force against nonviolent suspects. If those charged with the enforcement of the criminal law have abjured the use of deadly force in arresting nondangerous felons, there is a substantial basis for doubting that the use of such force is an essential attribute of the arrest power in all felony cases. Petitioners and appellant have not persuaded us that shooting nondangerous fleeing suspects is so vital as to outweigh the suspect's interest in his own life.

The use of deadly force to prevent the escape of all felony suspects, whatever the circumstances, is constitutionally unreasonable. It is not better that all felony suspects die than that they escape. Where the suspect poses no immediate threat to the officer and no threat to others, the harm resulting from failing to apprehend him does not justify the use of deadly force to do so. It is no doubt unfortunate when a suspect who is in sight escapes, but the fact that the police arrive a little late or are a little slower afoot does not always justify killing the suspect. A police officer may not seize an unarmed, nondangerous suspect by shooting him dead. The Tennessee statute is unconstitutional insofar as it authorizes the use of deadly force against such fleeing suspects.

It is not, however, unconstitutional on its face. Where the officer has probable cause to believe that the suspect poses a threat of serious physical harm, either to the officer or to others, it is not constitutionally unreasonable to prevent escape by using deadly force. Thus, if the suspect threatens the officer with a weapon or there is probable cause to believe that he has committed a crime involving the infliction or threatened infliction of serious physical harm, deadly force may be used if necessary to prevent escape, and if, where feasible, some warning has been given. As applied in such circumstances, the Tennessee statute would pass constitutional muster.

III

A

It is insisted that the Fourth Amendment must be construed in light of the common-law rule, which allowed the use of whatever force was necessary to effect the arrest of a fleeing felon, though not a misdemeanant.

The State and city argue that because this was the prevailing rule at the time of the adoption of the Fourth Amendment and for some time thereafter, and is still in force in some States, use of deadly force against a fleeing felon must be "reasonable." It is true that this Court has often looked to the common law in evaluating the reasonableness, for Fourth Amendment purposes, of police activity. On the other hand, it "has not simply frozen into constitutional law those law enforcement practices that existed at the time of the Fourth Amendment's passage." Because of sweeping change in the legal and technological context, reliance on the common-law rule in this case would be a mistaken literalism that ignores the purposes of a historical inquiry.

B

It has been pointed out many times that the common-law rule is best understood in light of the fact that it arose at a time when virtually all felonies were punishable by death. "Though effected without the protections and formalities of an orderly trial and conviction, the killing of a resisting or fleeing felon resulted in no greater consequences than those authorized for punishment of the felony of which the individual was charged or suspected." Courts have also justified the common-law rule by emphasizing the relative dangerousness of felons.

Neither of these justifications makes sense today. Almost all crimes formerly punishable by death no longer are or can be. And while in earlier times "the gulf between the felonies and the minor offences was broad and deep," today the distinction is minor and often arbitrary. Many crimes classified as misdemeanors, or nonexistent, at common law are now felonies. These changes have undermined the concept, which was questionable to begin with, that use of deadly force against a fleeing felon is merely a speedier execution of someone who has already forfeited his life. They have also made the assumption that a "felon" is more dangerous than a misdemeanant untenable. Indeed, numerous misdemeanors involve conduct more dangerous than many felonies.

There is an additional reason why the common-law rule cannot be directly translated to the present day. The common-law rule developed at a time when weapons were rudimentary.

288 Chapter IV The Fourth Amendment

Deadly force could be inflicted almost solely in a hand-to-hand struggle during which, necessarily, the safety of the arresting officer was at risk. Handguns were not carried by police officers until the latter half of the last century. Only then did it become possible to use deadly force from a distance as a means of apprehension. As a practical matter, the use of deadly force under the standard articulation of the common-law rule has an altogether different meaning—and harsher consequences—now than in past centuries.

One other aspect of the common-law rule bears emphasis. It forbids the use of deadly force to apprehend a misdemeanant, condemning such action as disproportionately severe.

In short, though the common-law pedigree of Tennessee's rule is pure on its face, changes in the legal and technological context mean the rule is distorted almost beyond recognition when literally applied.

C

In evaluating the reasonableness of police procedures under the Fourth Amendment, we have also looked to prevailing rules in individual jurisdictions. Some 19 States have codified the common-law rule, though in two of these the courts have significantly limited the statute. Four States, though without a relevant statute, apparently retain the common-law rule. Two States have adopted the Model Penal Code's provision verbatim. Eighteen others allow, in slightly varying language, the use of deadly force only if the suspect has committed a felony involving the use or threat of physical or deadly force, or is escaping with a deadly weapon, or is likely to endanger life or inflict serious physical injury if not arrested. Louisiana and Vermont, though without statutes or case law on point, do forbid the use of deadly force to prevent any but violent felonies. The remaining States either have no relevant statute or case law, or have positions that are unclear.

It cannot be said that there is a constant or overwhelming trend away from the common-law rule. In recent years, some States have reviewed their laws and expressly rejected abandonment of the common-law rule. Nonetheless, the long-term movement has been away from the rule that deadly force may be used against any fleeing felon, and that remains the rule in less than half the States.

This trend is more evident and impressive when viewed in light of the policies adopted by the police departments themselves. Overwhelmingly, these are more restrictive than the common-law rule. The Federal Bureau of Investigation and the New York City Police Department, for example, both forbid the use of firearms except when necessary to prevent death or grievous bodily harm. For accreditation by the Commission on Accreditation for Law Enforcement Agencies, a department must restrict the use of deadly force to situations where "the officer reasonably believes that the action is in defense of human life . . . or in defense of any person in immediate danger of serious physical injury." A 1974 study reported that the police department regulations in a majority of the large cities of the United States allowed the firing of a weapon only when a felon presented a threat of death or serious bodily harm. Overall, only 7.5% of departmental and municipal policies explicitly permit the use of deadly force against any felon; 86.8% explicitly do not. In light of the rules adopted by those who must actually administer them, the older and fading common-law view is a dubious indicium of the constitutionality of the Tennessee statute now before us.

D

Actual departmental policies are important for an additional reason. We would hesitate to declare a police practice of long standing "unreasonable" if doing so would severely hamper effective law enforcement. But the indications are to the contrary. There has been no suggestion that crime has worsened in any way in jurisdictions that have adopted, by legislation or departmental policy, rules similar to that announced today. Amici noted that "[a]fter extensive research and consideration, [they] have concluded that laws permitting police officers to use deadly force to apprehend unarmed, non-violent fleeing felony suspects actually do not protect citizens or law enforcement officers, do not deter crime or alleviate problems caused by crime, and do not improve the crime-fighting ability of law enforcement agencies." The submission is that the obvious state interests in apprehension are not sufficiently served to warrant the use of lethal weapons against all fleeing felons.

Nor do we agree with petitioners and appellant that the rule we have adopted requires the police to make impossible, split-second evaluations of unknowable facts. We do not deny the practical difficulties of attempting to assess the suspect's dangerousness. However, similarly difficult judgments must be made by the police in equally uncertain circumstances. Nor is there any indication that in States that allow the use of deadly force only against dangerous suspects, the standard has been difficult to apply or has led to a rash of litigation involving inappropriate second-guessing of police officers' split-second decisions. Moreover, the highly technical felony/misdemeanor distinction is equally, if not more, difficult to apply in the field. An officer is in no position to know, for example, the precise value of property stolen, or whether the crime was a first or second offense. Finally, as noted above, this claim must be viewed with suspicion in light of the similar self-imposed limitations of so many police departments.

IV

The District Court concluded that Hymon was justified in shooting Garner because state law allows, and the Federal Constitution does not forbid, the use of deadly force to prevent the escape of a fleeing felony suspect if no alternative means of apprehension is available. This conclusion made a determination of Garner's apparent dangerousness unnecessary. The court did find, however, that Garner appeared to be unarmed, though Hymon could not be certain that was the case. Restated in Fourth Amendment terms, this means Hymon had no articulable basis to think Garner was armed.

In reversing, the Court of Appeals accepted the District Court's factual conclusions and held that "the facts, as found, did not justify the use of deadly force." We agree. Officer Hymon could not reasonably have believed that Garner — young, slight, and unarmed — posed any threat. Indeed, Hymon never attempted to justify his actions on any basis other than the need to prevent an escape. The District Court stated in passing that "[t]he facts of this case did not indicate to Officer Hymon that Garner was 'non-dangerous.'" This conclusion is not explained, and seems to be based solely on the fact that Garner had broken into a house at night. However, the fact that Garner was a suspected burglar could not, without regard to the other circumstances, automatically justify the use of deadly force. Hymon did not have probable cause to believe that Garner, whom he correctly believed to be unarmed, posed any physical danger to himself or others.

The dissent argues that the shooting was justified by the fact that Officer Hymon had probable cause to believe that Garner had committed a nighttime burglary. While we agree that burglary is a serious crime, we cannot agree that it is so dangerous as automatically to justify the use of deadly force. The FBI classifies burglary as a "property" rather than a "violent" crime. Although the armed burglar would present a different situation, the fact that an unarmed suspect has broken into a dwelling at night does not automatically mean he is physically dangerous. This case demonstrates as much. In fact, the available statistics demonstrate that burglaries only rarely involve physical violence. During the 10-year period from 1973-1982, only 3.8% of all burglaries involved violent crime.

• • •

The judgment of the Court of Appeals is affirmed, and the case is remanded for further proceedings consistent with this opinion.

[Justices O'CONNOR and REHNQUIST and Chief Justice BURGER dissented.]

Memphis police officer Elton Hymon

NOTES AND QUESTIONS

1. Note that the predicate for the Tennessee statute and the common law "fleeing felon" rule is that the officer has probable cause to arrest. Is it obvious that Officer Hymon had probable cause to arrest Edward Garner when he observed him going over the fence?

Does the Court do a convincing job explaining why the common law rule should not carry over to the present day, given the differences in criminal penalties and police and firearms practices?

If *Garner* were to be reconsidered today from a purely originalist perspective, would the result be different?

2. In balancing the relevant interests in determining the appropriate situations justifying the use of deadly force, the Court considers not only the state of state law on the subject but also actual police practices in weighing the law enforcement interests at stake. Is this a sensible approach? Do you see any downsides to using this factor?

3. Would this case have come out differently if Officer Hymon observed a gun in Garner's hand as he was making his way over the fence? What if Garner had a gun in his hand and, upon seeing Hymon, turned and ran back into the house?

4. The Court does not mention race. Both Officer Hymon and Edward Garner were Black. The Garner family's lawyer, famed Memphis civil rights activist and defense attorney Walter Bailey, argued in his brief to the Supreme Court that the discretion afforded police in using deadly force against nondangerous fleeing property crime suspects violated the Equal Protection Clause. He pointed to statistics showing that, as compared to similarly situated white suspects, Black suspects were twice as likely to be shot at, four times as likely to be wounded, and 40 percent more likely to be killed. (Interestingly Bailey's statistics revealed no racial disparity in police shooting of fleeing violent crime suspects.) *Tennessee v. Garner*, Brief for Appellee-Respondent, 1984 WL 566020, at *99-100.

5. Consider how easy it would have been for Officer Hymon to testify that "he thought" Garner had a gun. And there was a more insidious alternative to that "embellishment." Interviewed in 2019 by a reporter for the *New Tri-State Defender*, retired Officer Elton Hymon gave context for the case that became *Tennessee v. Garner*. Hymon had only been on the force for five months and was still getting acclimated to police culture. "The N word was used often without hesitation and several white officers proudly notched their revolvers for every African-American they had killed," he said. Hymon also disclosed the widespread practice of officers carrying with them a "drop gun," which could be placed on or near a shot or killed suspect in order to manufacture a justifiable use of force.

6. In the same article, Attorney Bailey credited Officer Hymon's truthful testimony (and failure to use a drop gun) with the Garners' litigation success. Officer Hymon probably deserves even more credit than that, as the number of persons shot and killed by police decreased dramatically after *Garner*, as many police departments abandoned the common law rule to comply with the decision. Cynthia Lee, *Reforming the Law on Police Use of Deadly Force: De-Escalation, Preseizure Conduct, and Imperfect Self-Defense*, 2018 U. Ill. L. Rev. 629, 641 (citing Abraham N. Tennenbaum, *The Influence of the* Garner *Decision on Police Use of Deadly Force*, 85 J. Crim. L. & Criminology 241, 255-56 (1994) (finding that overall police shootings declined by 16 percent following the *Garner* decision)).

Bailey, a longtime Memphis civil rights lawyer, had earlier represented Dr. Martin Luther King Jr. in connection with the 1968 sanitation workers' strike. His portrait was unveiled at the National Civil Rights Museum in Memphis in December 2022.

The Court applied *Garner* over two decades later in a case involving a different sort of deadly force. In *Scott v. Harris*, 550 U.S. 372 (2007), the Court reversed a denial of summary judgment for a defendant police officer alleged to have unreasonably used deadly force by ramming his police car into the plaintiff's car in a high-speed chase. Finding that a video-tape of the encounter so clearly showed that the officer's use of force was not excessive, the Court — substituting itself for a "reasonable jury" — entered judgment for the police officer. Justice Stevens, who dissented, the district judge, and three members of the court of appeals panel all reached a different conclusion.

Three academics used the videotape of the high-speed chase in *Harris* to do a study to test the Court's conclusion as to what a "reasonable jury" could have found. They found that 75 percent of the 1,350 participants in the study found that the use of deadly force was justified, although the results varied significantly depending on the demographics, politics, and values of the participants. Dan M. Kahan et al., *Whose Eyes Are You Going to Believe?* Scott v. Harris *and the Perils of Cognitive Illiberalism*, 122 Harv. L. Rev. 837, 838 (2009).

In the next case the Court considered how to evaluate allegations of improper uses of force by police that are not deadly but only "excessive."

Graham v. Connor
490 U.S. 386 (1989)

Chief Justice REHNQUIST delivered the opinion of the Court.

This case requires us to decide what constitutional standard governs a free citizen's claim that law enforcement officials used excessive force in the course of making an arrest, investigatory stop, or other "seizure" of his person. We hold that such claims are properly analyzed under the Fourth Amendment's "objective reasonableness" standard, rather than under a substantive due process standard.

In this action under 42 U.S.C. § 1983, petitioner Dethorne Graham seeks to recover damages for injuries allegedly sustained when law enforcement officers used physical force against him during the course of an investigatory stop. Because the case comes to us from a decision of the Court of Appeals affirming the entry of a directed verdict for respondents, we

292 Chapter IV The Fourth Amendment

take the evidence hereafter noted in the light most favorable to petitioner. On November 12, 1984, Graham, a diabetic, felt the onset of an insulin reaction. He asked a friend, William Berry, to drive him to a nearby convenience store so he could purchase some orange juice to counteract the reaction. Berry agreed, but when Graham entered the store, he saw a number of people ahead of him in the check outline. Concerned about the delay, he hurried out of the store and asked Berry to drive him to a friend's house instead.

Respondent Connor, an officer of the Charlotte, North Carolina, Police Department, saw Graham hastily enter and leave the store. The officer became suspicious that something was amiss and followed Berry's car. About one-half mile from the store, he made an investigative stop. Although Berry told Connor that Graham was simply suffering from a "sugar reaction," the officer ordered Berry and Graham to wait while he found out what, if anything, had happened at the convenience store. When Officer Connor returned to his patrol car to call for backup assistance, Graham got out of the car, ran around it twice, and finally sat down on the curb, where he passed out briefly.

In the ensuing confusion, a number of other Charlotte police officers arrived on the scene in response to Officer Connor's request for backup. One of the officers rolled Graham over on the sidewalk and cuffed his hands tightly behind his back, ignoring Berry's pleas to get him some sugar. Another officer said: "I've seen a lot of people with sugar diabetes that never acted like this. Ain't nothing wrong with the M.F. but drunk. Lock the S.B. up." Several officers then lifted Graham up from behind, carried him over to Berry's car, and placed him face down on its hood. Regaining consciousness, Graham asked the officers to check in his wallet for a diabetic decal that he carried. In response, one of the officers told him to "shut up" and shoved his face down against the hood of the car. Four officers grabbed Graham and threw him headfirst into the police car. A friend of Graham's brought some orange juice to the car, but the officers refused to let him have it. Finally, Officer Connor received a report that Graham had done nothing wrong at the convenience store, and the officers drove him home and released him.

At some point during his encounter with the police, Graham sustained a broken foot, cuts on his wrists, a bruised forehead, and an injured shoulder; he also claims to have developed a loud ringing in his right ear that continues to this day. He commenced this action under 42 U.S.C. § 1983 against the individual officers involved in the incident, all of whom are respondents here, alleging that they had used excessive force in making the investigatory stop, in violation of "rights secured to him under the Fourteenth Amendment to the United States Constitution and 42 U.S.C. § 1983." The case was tried before a jury. At the close of petitioner's evidence, respondents moved for a directed verdict. In ruling on that motion, the District Court considered the following four factors, which it identified as "[t]he factors to be considered in determining when the excessive use of force gives rise to a cause of action under § 1983": (1) the need for the application of force; (2) the relationship between that need and the amount of force that was used; (3) the extent of the injury inflicted; and (4) "[w]hether the force was applied in a good faith effort to maintain and restore discipline or maliciously and sadistically for the very purpose of causing harm." Finding that the amount of force used by the officers was "appropriate under the circumstances," that "[t]here was no discernable injury inflicted," and that the force used "was not applied maliciously or sadistically for the very purpose of causing harm," but in "a good faith effort to maintain or restore order in the face of a potentially explosive situation," the District Court granted respondents' motion for a directed verdict.

A divided panel of the Court of Appeals for the Fourth Circuit affirmed. . . . We granted certiorari and now reverse.

• • •

We reject this notion that all excessive force claims brought under § 1983 are governed by a single generic standard. As we have said many times, § 1983 "is not itself a source of substantive rights," but merely provides "a method for vindicating federal rights elsewhere conferred." In addressing an excessive force claim brought under § 1983, analysis begins by identifying the specific constitutional right allegedly infringed by the challenged application of force. In most instances, that will be either the Fourth Amendment's prohibition against unreasonable seizures of the person, or the Eighth Amendment's ban on cruel and unusual punishments, which are the two primary sources of constitutional protection against physically abusive governmental conduct. The validity of the claim must then be judged by reference to the specific constitutional standard which governs that right, rather than to some generalized "excessive force" standard.

Where, as here, the excessive force claim arises in the context of an arrest or investigatory stop of a free citizen, it is most properly characterized as one invoking the protections of the Fourth Amendment, which guarantees citizens the right "to be secure in their persons . . . against unreasonable . . . seizures" of the person. This much is clear from our decision in *Garner*. In *Garner*, we addressed a claim that the use of deadly force to apprehend a fleeing suspect who did not appear to be armed or otherwise dangerous violated the suspect's constitutional rights, notwithstanding the existence of probable cause to arrest. Though the complaint alleged violations of both the Fourth Amendment and the Due Process Clause, we analyzed the constitutionality of the challenged application of force solely by reference to the Fourth Amendment's prohibition against unreasonable seizures of the person, holding that the "reasonableness" of a particular seizure depends not only on when it is made, but also on how it is carried out. Today we make explicit what was implicit in *Garner*'s analysis, and hold that all claims that law enforcement officers have used excessive force—deadly or not—in the course of an arrest, investigatory stop, or other "seizure" of a free citizen should be analyzed under the Fourth Amendment and its "reasonableness" standard, rather than under a "substantive due process" approach. Because the Fourth Amendment provides an explicit textual source of constitutional protection against this sort of physically intrusive governmental conduct, that Amendment, not the more generalized notion of "substantive due process," must be the guide for analyzing these claims.

Determining whether the force used to effect a particular seizure is "reasonable" under the Fourth Amendment requires a careful balancing of "'the nature and quality of the intrusion on the individual's Fourth Amendment interests'" against the countervailing governmental interests at stake. Our Fourth Amendment jurisprudence has long recognized that the right to make an arrest or investigatory stop necessarily carries with it the right to use some degree of physical coercion or threat thereof to effect it. Because "[t]he test of reasonableness under the Fourth Amendment is not capable of precise definition or mechanical application," however, its proper application requires careful attention to the facts and circumstances of each particular case, including the severity of the crime at issue, whether the suspect poses an immediate threat to the safety of the officers or others, and whether he is actively resisting arrest or attempting to evade arrest by flight.

The "reasonableness" of a particular use of force must be judged from the perspective of a reasonable officer on the scene, rather than with the 20/20 vision of hindsight. The Fourth Amendment is not violated by an arrest based on probable cause, even though the wrong person is arrested, nor by the mistaken execution of a valid search warrant on the wrong premises. With respect to a claim of excessive force, the same standard of reasonableness at the moment applies: "Not every push or shove, even if it may later seem unnecessary in the peace of a judge's chambers," violates the Fourth Amendment. The calculus of reasonableness must embody allowance for the fact that police officers are often forced to make split-second judgments—in circumstances that are tense, uncertain, and rapidly evolving—about the amount of force that is necessary in a particular situation.

As in other Fourth Amendment contexts, however, the "reasonableness" inquiry in an excessive force case is an objective one: the question is whether the officers' actions are "objectively reasonable" in light of the facts and circumstances confronting them, without regard to their underlying intent or motivation. An officer's evil intentions will not make a Fourth Amendment violation out of an objectively reasonable use of force; nor will an officer's good intentions make an objectively unreasonable use of force constitutional.

Because petitioner's excessive force claim is one arising under the Fourth Amendment, the Court of Appeals erred in analyzing it under the four-part *Johnson v. Glick* test. That test, which requires consideration of whether the individual officers acted in "good faith" or "maliciously and sadistically for the very purpose of causing harm," is incompatible with a proper Fourth Amendment analysis. We do not agree with the Court of Appeals' suggestion that the "malicious and sadistic" inquiry is merely another way of describing conduct that is objectively unreasonable under the circumstances. Whatever the empirical correlations between "malicious and sadistic" behavior and objective unreasonableness may be, the fact remains that the "malicious and sadistic" factor puts in issue the subjective motivations of the individual officers, which our prior cases make clear has no bearing on whether a particular seizure is "unreasonable" under the Fourth Amendment. Nor do we agree with the Court of Appeals' conclusion, that because the subjective motivations of the individual officers are of central importance in deciding whether force used against a convicted prisoner violates the Eighth Amendment, it cannot be reversible error to inquire into them in deciding whether force used against a suspect or arrestee violates the Fourth Amendment. Differing standards under the Fourth and Eighth Amendments are hardly surprising: the terms "cruel" and "punishments" clearly suggest some inquiry into subjective state of mind, whereas the term "unreasonable" does not. Moreover, the less protective Eighth Amendment standard applies "only after the State has complied with the constitutional guarantees traditionally associated with criminal prosecutions." The Fourth Amendment inquiry is one of "objective reasonableness" under the circumstances, and subjective concepts like "malice" and "sadism" have no proper place in that inquiry.

Because the Court of Appeals reviewed the District Court's ruling on the motion for directed verdict under an erroneous view of the governing substantive law, its judgment must be vacated and the case remanded to that court for reconsideration of that issue under the proper Fourth Amendment standard.

NOTES AND QUESTIONS

1. Compare the four-factor test that some courts had been applying in excessive force claims to the test announced by the Court in *Graham*. What are the most important differences between the two tests?

2. Does the Court's conclusion that excessive force claims should be analyzed as unreasonable seizures under the Fourth Amendment follow inevitably from the decision in *Garner*?

3. The test announced in *Graham* has been widely criticized as being, among other things, overly deferential to police. Do you agree? The Court cautions that the test must account for the "tense, uncertain, and rapidly evolving" circumstances in which police must make "split-second judgments." Is this layer of deference baked into every evaluation of police use of force or only where such circumstances are present?

4. A leading scholar on police misconduct, Professor Rachel Harmon, has offered this critique of the *Graham v. Connor* test:

Graham permits courts to consider any circumstance in determining whether force is reasonable without providing a standard for measuring relevance, it gives little instruction on how to weigh relevant factors, and it apparently requires courts to consider the severity of the underlying crime in all cases, a circumstance that is sometimes irrelevant and misleading in determining whether force is reasonable. Thus, *Graham* has largely left judges and juries to their intuitions, and what direction it does give sometimes steers them off course.

Rachel A. Harmon, *When Is Police Violence Justified?*, 102 Nw. U. L. Rev. 1119, 1130-31 (2008). Fair criticism? Do you agree that the severity of the crime should not always be relevant? Does the open-ended nature of the test leave the jury with too much discretion to decide the issue? Does that discretion cut for or against police officer defendants in civil damages actions?

5. Does the irrelevance of the police officer's subjective intentions to the reasonableness of the seizure mean that statements made by the officer in connection with the application of force will be relevant only as they may bear on the objective considerations? Consider, for example, the statements made by the officer questioning the legitimacy of Graham's sugar reaction. Are they relevant? Consider the following hypothetical statements made by an officer in subduing a suspect who is resisting arrest:

> "Stay cool, I'm not going to hurt you."
> "Let's do this the easy way, not the hard way."
> "I'm going to have to mess you up."

Relevant to the objective test? Admissible regardless?

6. As in *Garner*, the Court in *Graham* does not mention race. Officer Connor was Black; the race of his codefendant officers does not appear to be publicly available. Graham was Black. Cynthia Lee, *Reforming the Law on Police Use of Deadly Force: De-Escalation, Pre-Seizure Conduct, and Imperfect Self-Defense*, 2018 U. Ill. L. Rev. 629, 643 (citation omitted).

7. Seven years prior to *Graham*, in *Harlow v. Fitzgerald*, 457 U.S. 800 (1982), the Court had held that police officers enjoyed qualified immunity from suits for damages unless they violated "clearly established law," and that officers' subjective intentions were not relevant to the inquiry. *See* Chapter VI *infra*. Does the open-ended, totality-of-the-circumstances nature of the *Graham* test make it unlikely that an excessive force plaintiff will be able to prove that the conduct at issue violated precedent that was "clearly established" at any meaningful level of detail? *Id.*

8. Litigation of Fourth Amendment excessive force claims often involves "use of force" expert witnesses. Indeed, one of the important advantages in the federal (compared to the state) prosecution of the Los Angeles Police Department officers in the Rodney King trials was the prosecution's presentation of such a "use of force" expert. *See* Chapter X *infra*. Such litigation also often focuses on internal police department "use of force" policies. For an argument that courts too often rely on such internal policies to shape what constitutes excessive force as a constitutional matter, *see generally* Osagie K. Obasogie & Zachary Newman, *The Endogenous Fourth Amendment: An Empirical Assessment of How Police Understandings of Excessive Force Become Constitutional Law*, 104 Cornell L. Rev. 1281 (2019).

C. THE WARRANT REQUIREMENT AND ITS EXCEPTIONS

The next few subsections focus on special issues that arise in connection with search warrants. Arrest warrants are less often the subject of litigation, although the proliferation of so-called bench warrants, which can authorize the arrest of a person for comparatively trivial reasons (e.g., failure to appear in court or to pay a traffic ticket), raise enormous problems. *See* Chapter V *infra*.

1. Warrant Requirements: Search Warrants

The Fourth Amendment provides: "no Warrants shall issue, but upon probable cause, supported by Oath or affirmation, and particularly describing the place to be searched, and the persons or things to be seized." U.S. Const. amend. IV. "The chief evil that prompted the framing and adoption of the Fourth Amendment was the 'indiscriminate searches and seizures' conducted by the British 'under the authority of general warrants.'" *Payton v. New York*, 445 U.S. 573, 583 (1980). Thus the particularity and probable cause requirements aim to prevent a "general, exploratory rummaging in a person's belongings." *Coolidge v. New Hampshire*, 403 U.S. 443, 467 (1971). The two requirements are related: Together they limit the officer's authority to a search only of "the specific areas and things for which there is probable cause to search." *Maryland v. Garrison*, 480 U.S. 79, 84 (1987).

The warrant requirement is a microcosm of the separation of powers, a check of the judiciary upon the executive. As the Supreme Court has put it:

> The point of the Fourth Amendment, which often is not grasped by zealous officers, is not that it denies law enforcement the support of the usual inferences that reasonable men draw from evidence. Its protection consists in requiring that those inferences be drawn by a neutral and detached magistrate instead of being judged by the officer engaged in the often competitive enterprise of ferreting out crime.

Johnson v. United States, 333 U.S. 10, 13-14 (1948).

The Supreme Court was once fond of saying that searches without warrants are "per se unreasonable." *Katz v. United States*, 389 U.S. 347, 357 (1967). But in the intervening decades the number and breadth of the exceptions to the warrant "requirement," *see infra*, have expanded. For a strong argument that the warrant requirement should be, well, taken more seriously, *see generally* Oren Bar-Gill & Barry Friedman, *Taking Warrants Seriously*, 106 Nw. U. L. Rev. 1609 (2012) (arguing that a serious ex ante warrant requirement will be much clearer and more effective than a deterrence model focused on the exclusionary rule).

It must not be lost in the doctrinal shuffle that a search warrant is not an abstraction but a document. The theory is that the searching officer is guided by the language of the warrant—by its words—when executing a search.

a. Particularity

As to particularity, the idea is that the scope of discretion of the searching officer must be as small as possible. *Marron v. United States*, 275 U.S. 192 (1927) ("As to what is to be taken, nothing is left to the discretion of the officer executing the warrant"). Some courts break the requirement into three necessary criteria. *United States v. Galpin*, 720 F.3d 436, 445 (2d Cir. 2013). First, the warrant must identify the specific offense for which the police or agents have established probable cause. *Id*. Second, the warrant must, as the plain language of the Amendment commands, "describe the place to be searched." *Id*. at 445-46. And third, it must "specify the items to be seized by their relation to designated crimes." *Id*. at 446. In most contexts, a warrant must also require the specification of a time frame that would limit the scope of a search. Overbreadth is a fatal warrant flaw at the intersection of particularity and probable cause. A warrant is overbroad where its "description of the objects to be seized . . . is broader than can be justified by the probable cause upon which the warrant is based." *Galpin*, 720 F.3d at 446.

The particularity must be supplied by the text of the warrant itself, along with any documents attached to and incorporated in the warrant. *Groh v. Ramirez*, 540 U.S. 551, 557, (2004). That some other document, such as the application for the warrant, provides further specificity will not save an insufficiently particularized warrant. The purpose of this

C. The Warrant Requirement and Its Exceptions

requirement, loftier than the technicality it appears to be, is twofold: first, any document adding particularity must actually in theory serve to guide the searching officer during the search, and therefore must be present at the search location with, and part of, the warrant; second, the owner of the property being searched has the right to inspect any document that functions as part of the warrant. *See* Fed. R. Crim. P. 41(f)(B) (requiring officer to provide a copy of the warrant to the person whose property was searched).

Special caution is necessary when warrants target electronically stored information, as many do now. As the Second Circuit has recognized, where the property to be searched is a computer hard drive, "the particularity requirement assumes even greater importance." *Galpin*, 720 F.3d at 446. That is because the seizure of a computer hard drive, and its subsequent retention by the government, can give the government possession of a vast trove of personal information about the person to whom the drive belongs, much of which may be entirely irrelevant to the criminal investigation that led to the seizure. *United States v. Ganias*, 824 F.3d 199, 217 (2d Cir. 2016) (en banc). *See supra Carpenter v. United States*, 585 U.S. 296 (2018). "The potential for privacy violations in such a context is compounded by the nature of digital storage." *Galpin*, 720 F.3d at 447. Indeed, the government, once it has obtained authorization to search a hard drive, may in theory claim that the contents of every file it chose to open were in plain view and thereby available to it regardless of the scope of the warrant, rendering the Fourth Amendment irrelevant. *United States v. Comprehensive Drug Testing, Inc., (BALCO)*, 621 F.3d 1162, 1176 (9th Cir. 2010) (en banc) (per curiam). Accordingly, a "heightened sensitivity to the particularity requirement in the context of digital searches" is necessary. *Galpin*, 720 F.3d at 447.

b. Probable Cause

Illinois v. Gates
462 U.S. 213 (1983)

Justice REHNQUIST delivered the opinion of the Court.

Respondents Lance and Susan Gates were indicted for violation of state drug laws after police officers, executing a search warrant, discovered marijuana and other contraband in their automobile and home. Prior to trial the Gates moved to suppress evidence seized during this search. The Illinois Supreme Court affirmed the decisions of lower state courts granting the motion. It held that the affidavit submitted in support of the State's application for a warrant to search the Gates' property was inadequate under this Court's decisions in *Aguilar v. Texas* (1964) and *Spinelli v. United States* (1969).

We granted certiorari to consider the application of the Fourth Amendment to a magistrate's issuance of a search warrant on the basis of a partially corroborated anonymous informant's tip. After receiving briefs and hearing oral argument on this question, however, we requested the parties to address an additional question:

> Whether the rule requiring the exclusion at a criminal trial of evidence obtained in violation of the Fourth Amendment, *Mapp v. Ohio* (1961); *Weeks v. United States* (1914), should to any extent be modified, so as, for example, not to require the exclusion of evidence obtained in the reasonable belief that the search and seizure at issue was consistent with the Fourth Amendment.

We decide today, with apologies to all, that the issue we framed for the parties was not presented to the Illinois courts and, accordingly, do not address it. Rather, we consider the question originally presented in the petition for certiorari, and conclude that the Illinois Supreme Court read the requirements of our Fourth Amendment decisions too restrictively. Initially,

298 Chapter IV The Fourth Amendment

however, we set forth our reasons for not addressing the question regarding modification of the exclusionary rule framed in our order.

• • •

II

We now turn to the question presented in the State's original petition for certiorari, which requires us to decide whether respondents' rights under the Fourth and Fourteenth Amendments were violated by the search of their car and house. A chronological statement of events usefully introduces the issues at stake. Bloomingdale, Ill., is a suburb of Chicago located in DuPage County. On May 3, 1978, the Bloomingdale Police Department received by mail an anonymous handwritten letter which read as follows:

> This letter is to inform you that you have a couple in your town who strictly make their living on selling drugs. They are Sue and Lance Gates, they live on Greenway, off Bloomingdale Rd. in the condominiums. Most of their buys are done in Florida. Sue his wife drives their car to Florida, where she leaves it to be loaded up with drugs, then Lance flys down and drives it back. Sue flys back after she drops the car off in Florida. May 3 she is driving down there again and Lance will be flying down in a few days to drive it back. At the time Lance drives the car back he has the trunk loaded with over $100,000.00 in drugs. Presently they have over $100,000.00 worth of drugs in their basement.
>
> They brag about the fact they never have to work, and make their entire living on pushers.
>
> I guarantee if you watch them carefully you will make a big catch. They are friends with some big drugs dealers, who visit their house often.
>
> Lance & Susan Gates
>
> Greenway
>
> in Condominiums

The letter was referred by the Chief of Police of the Bloomingdale Police Department to Detective Mader, who decided to pursue the tip. Mader learned, from the office of the Illinois Secretary of State, that an Illinois driver's license had been issued to one Lance Gates, residing at a stated address in Bloomingdale. He contacted a confidential informant, whose examination of certain financial records revealed a more recent address for the Gates, and he also learned from a police officer assigned to O'Hare Airport that "L. Gates" had made a reservation on Eastern Airlines flight 245 to West Palm Beach, Fla., scheduled to depart from Chicago on May 5 at 4:15 p.m.

Mader then made arrangements with an agent of the Drug Enforcement Administration for surveillance of the May 5 Eastern Airlines flight. The agent later reported to Mader that Gates had boarded the flight, and that federal agents in Florida had observed him arrive in West Palm Beach and take a taxi to the nearby Holiday Inn. They also reported that Gates went to a room registered to one Susan Gates and that, at 7:00 a.m. the next morning, Gates and an unidentified woman left the motel in a Mercury bearing Illinois license plates and drove northbound on an interstate frequently used by travelers to the Chicago area. In addition, the DEA agent informed Mader that the license plate number on the Mercury registered to a Hornet station wagon owned by Gates. The agent also advised Mader that the driving time between West Palm Beach and Bloomingdale was approximately 22 to 24 hours.

C. The Warrant Requirement and Its Exceptions

Mader signed an affidavit setting forth the foregoing facts, and submitted it to a judge of the Circuit Court of DuPage County, together with a copy of the anonymous letter. The judge of that court thereupon issued a search warrant for the Gates' residence and for their automobile. The judge, in deciding to issue the warrant, could have determined that the modus operandi of the Gates had been substantially corroborated. As the anonymous letter predicted, Lance Gates had flown from Chicago to West Palm Beach late in the afternoon of May 5th, had checked into a hotel room registered in the name of his wife, and, at 7:00 a.m. the following morning, had headed north, accompanied by an unidentified woman, out of West Palm Beach on an interstate highway used by travelers from South Florida to Chicago in an automobile bearing a license plate issued to him.

At 5:15 a.m. on March 7th, only 36 hours after he had flown out of Chicago, Lance Gates, and his wife, returned to their home in Bloomingdale, driving the car in which they had left West Palm Beach some 22 hours earlier. The Bloomingdale police were awaiting them, searched the trunk of the Mercury, and uncovered approximately 350 pounds of marijuana. A search of the Gates' home revealed marijuana, weapons, and other contraband. The Illinois Circuit Court ordered suppression of all these items, on the ground that the affidavit submitted to the Circuit Judge failed to support the necessary determination of probable cause to believe that the Gates' automobile and home contained the contraband in question. This decision was affirmed in turn by the Illinois Appellate Court and by a divided vote of the Supreme Court of Illinois.

The Illinois Supreme Court concluded—and we are inclined to agree—that, standing alone, the anonymous letter sent to the Bloomingdale Police Department would not provide the basis for a magistrate's determination that there was probable cause to believe contraband would be found in the Gates' car and home. The letter provides virtually nothing from which one might conclude that its author is either honest or his information reliable; likewise, the letter gives absolutely no indication of the basis for the writer's predictions regarding the Gates' criminal activities. Something more was required, then, before a magistrate could conclude that there was probable cause to believe that contraband would be found in the Gates' home and car.

The Illinois Supreme Court also properly recognized that Detective Mader's affidavit might be capable of supplementing the anonymous letter with information sufficient to permit a determination of probable cause. In holding that the affidavit in fact did not contain sufficient additional information to sustain a determination of probable cause, the Illinois court applied a "two-pronged test," derived from our decision in *Spinelli*. The Illinois Supreme Court, like some others, apparently understood *Spinelli* as requiring that the anonymous letter satisfy each of two independent requirements before it could be relied on. According to this view, the letter, as supplemented by Mader's affidavit, first had to adequately reveal the "basis of knowledge" of the letter writer—the particular means by which he came by the information given in his report. Second, it had to provide facts sufficiently establishing either the "veracity" of the affiant's informant, or, alternatively, the "reliability" of the informant's report in this particular case.

The Illinois court, alluding to an elaborate set of legal rules that have developed among various lower courts to enforce the "two-pronged test," found that the test had not been satisfied. First, the "veracity" prong was not satisfied because, "there was simply no basis [for] . . . conclud[ing] that the anonymous person [who wrote the letter to the Bloomingdale Police Department] was credible." The court indicated that corroboration by police of details contained in the letter might never satisfy the "veracity" prong, and in any event, could not do so if, as in the present case, only "innocent" details are corroborated. In addition, the letter gave no indication of the basis of its writer's knowledge of the Gates' activities. The Illinois court understood *Spinelli* as permitting the detail contained in a tip to be used to infer that the informant had a reliable basis for his statements, but it thought that the anonymous letter failed to provide sufficient detail to permit such an inference. Thus, it concluded that no showing of probable cause had been made.

We agree with the Illinois Supreme Court that an informant's "veracity," "reliability" and "basis of knowledge" are all highly relevant in determining the value of his report. We do not agree, however, that these elements should be understood as entirely separate and independent requirements to be rigidly exacted in every case, which the opinion of the Supreme Court of Illinois would imply. Rather, as detailed below, they should be understood simply as closely intertwined issues that may usefully illuminate the commonsense, practical question whether there is "probable cause" to believe that contraband or evidence is located in a particular place.

III

This totality-of-the-circumstances approach is far more consistent with our prior treatment of probable cause than is any rigid demand that specific "tests" be satisfied by every informant's tip. Perhaps the central teaching of our decisions bearing on the probable cause standard is that it is a "practical, nontechnical conception." *Brinegar* (1949). "In dealing with probable cause, . . . as the very name implies, we deal with probabilities. These are not technical; they are the factual and practical considerations of everyday life on which reasonable and prudent men, not legal technicians, act." Our observation in *United States v. Cortez* (1981), regarding "particularized suspicion," is also applicable to the probable cause standard:

> The process does not deal with hard certainties, but with probabilities. Long before the law of probabilities was articulated as such, practical people formulated certain common-sense conclusions about human behavior; jurors as factfinders are permitted to do the same — and so are law enforcement officers. Finally, the evidence thus collected must be seen and weighed not in terms of library analysis by scholars, but as understood by those versed in the field of law enforcement.

As these comments illustrate, probable cause is a fluid concept — turning on the assessment of probabilities in particular factual contexts — not readily, or even usefully, reduced to a neat set of legal rules. Informants' tips doubtless come in many shapes and sizes from many different types of persons. As we said in *Adams v. Williams*, "Informants' tips, like all other clues and evidence coming to a policeman on the scene may vary greatly in their value and reliability." Rigid legal rules are ill-suited to an area of such diversity. "One simple rule will not cover every situation."

Moreover, the "two-pronged test" directs analysis into two largely independent channels — the informant's "veracity" or "reliability" and his "basis of knowledge." There are persuasive arguments against according these two elements such independent status. Instead, they are better understood as relevant considerations in the totality-of-the-circumstances analysis that traditionally has guided probable cause determinations: a deficiency in one may be compensated for, in determining the overall reliability of a tip, by a strong showing as to the other, or by some other indicia of reliability.

If, for example, a particular informant is known for the unusual reliability of his predictions of certain types of criminal activities in a locality, his failure, in a particular case, to thoroughly set forth the basis of his knowledge surely should not serve as an absolute bar to a finding of probable cause based on his tip. Likewise, if an unquestionably honest citizen comes forward with a report of criminal activity — which if fabricated would subject him to criminal liability — we have found rigorous scrutiny of the basis of his knowledge unnecessary. *Adams v. Williams, supra.* Conversely, even if we entertain some doubt as to an informant's motives, his explicit and detailed description of alleged wrongdoing, along with a statement that the event was observed first-hand, entitles his tip to greater weight than might otherwise be the case. Unlike a totality-of-the-circumstances analysis, which permits a balanced assessment of the relative weights of all the various indicia of reliability (and unreliability) attending an informant's tip, the "two-pronged test" has encouraged an excessively technical dissection of informants' tips, with undue attention being focused on isolated issues that cannot sensibly be divorced from the other facts presented to the magistrate.

As early as *Locke v. United States* (1813), Chief Justice Marshall observed, in a closely related context, that "the term 'probable cause,' according to its usual acceptation, means less than evidence which would justify condemnation. . . . It imports a seizure made under circumstances which warrant suspicion." More recently, we said that "the quanta . . . of proof" appropriate in ordinary judicial proceedings are inapplicable to the decision to issue a warrant. Finely-tuned standards such as proof beyond a reasonable doubt or by a preponderance of the evidence, useful in formal trials, have no place in the magistrate's decision. While an effort to fix some general, numerically precise degree of certainty corresponding to "probable cause" may not be helpful, it is clear that "only the probability, and not a prima facie showing, of criminal activity is the standard of probable cause."

We also have recognized that affidavits "are normally drafted by nonlawyers in the midst and haste of a criminal investigation. Technical requirements of elaborate specificity once exacted under common law pleading have no proper place in this area." Likewise, search and arrest warrants long have been issued by persons who are neither lawyers nor judges, and who certainly do not remain abreast of each judicial refinement of the nature of "probable cause." The rigorous inquiry into the *Spinelli* prongs and the complex superstructure of evidentiary and analytical rules that some have seen implicit in our *Spinelli* decision, cannot be reconciled with the fact that many warrants are—quite properly, ibid.—issued on the basis of nontechnical, common-sense judgments of laymen applying a standard less demanding than those used in more formal legal proceedings. Likewise, given the informal, often hurried context in which it must be applied, the "built-in subtleties," of the "two-pronged test" are particularly unlikely to assist magistrates in determining probable cause.

Similarly, we have repeatedly said that after-the-fact scrutiny by courts of the sufficiency of an affidavit should not take the form of de novo review. A magistrate's "determination of probable cause should be paid great deference by reviewing courts." "A grudging or negative attitude by reviewing courts toward warrants," is inconsistent with the Fourth Amendment's strong preference for searches conducted pursuant to a warrant "courts should not invalidate . . . warrant[s] by interpreting affidavit[s] in a hypertechnical, rather than a commonsense, manner." [sic]

If the affidavits submitted by police officers are subjected to the type of scrutiny some courts have deemed appropriate, police might well resort to warrantless searches, with the hope of relying on consent or some other exception to the warrant clause that might develop at the time of the search. In addition, the possession of a warrant by officers conducting an arrest or search greatly reduces the perception of unlawful or intrusive police conduct, by assuring "the individual whose property is searched or seized of the lawful authority of the executing officer, his need to search, and the limits of his power to search." Reflecting this preference for the warrant process, the traditional standard for review of an issuing magistrate's probable cause determination has been that so long as the magistrate had a "substantial basis for . . . conclud[ing]" that a search would uncover evidence of wrongdoing, the Fourth Amendment requires no more. We think reaffirmation of this standard better serves the purpose of encouraging recourse to the warrant procedure and is more consistent with our traditional deference to the probable cause determinations of magistrates than is the "two-pronged test."

Finally, the direction taken by decisions following *Spinelli* poorly serves "the most basic function of any government": "to provide for the security of the individual and of his property." The strictures that inevitably accompany the "two-pronged test" cannot avoid seriously impeding the task of law enforcement. If, as the Illinois Supreme Court apparently thought, that test must be rigorously applied in every case, anonymous tips seldom would be of greatly diminished value in police work. Ordinary citizens, like ordinary witnesses, see Federal Rules of Evidence 701, Advisory Committee Note (1976), generally do not provide extensive recitations of the basis of their everyday observations. Likewise, as the Illinois Supreme Court observed in this case, the veracity of persons supplying anonymous tips is by hypothesis largely unknown, and unknowable. As a result, anonymous tips seldom could survive a rigorous application of either of the *Spinelli* prongs. Yet, such tips, particularly when supplemented by independent police investigation, frequently contribute to the solution of otherwise "perfect crimes." While a conscientious assessment of the basis for crediting such tips is required by the Fourth Amendment, a standard that leaves virtually no place for anonymous citizen informants is not.

For all these reasons, we conclude that it is wiser to abandon the "two-pronged test" established by our decisions in *Aguilar* and *Spinelli*. In its place we reaffirm the totality-of-the-circumstances analysis that traditionally has informed probable cause determinations. The task of the issuing magistrate is simply to make a practical, common-sense decision whether, given all the circumstances set forth in the affidavit before him, including the "veracity" and "basis of knowledge" of persons supplying hearsay information, there is a fair probability that contraband or evidence of a crime will be found in a particular place. And the duty of a reviewing court is simply to ensure that the magistrate had a "substantial basis for . . . conclud[ing]" that probable cause existed. We are convinced that this flexible, easily applied standard will better achieve the accommodation of public and private interests that the Fourth Amendment requires than does the approach that has developed from *Aguilar* and *Spinelli*.

Our earlier cases illustrate the limits beyond which a magistrate may not venture in issuing a warrant. A sworn statement of an affiant that "he has cause to suspect and does believe that" liquor illegally brought into the United States is located on certain premises will not do. An affidavit must provide the magistrate with a substantial basis for determining the existence of probable cause, and the wholly conclusory statement at issue in *Nathanson* failed to meet this requirement. An officer's statement that "affiants have received reliable information from a credible person and believe" that heroin is stored in a home, is likewise inadequate. As in *Nathanson*, this is a mere conclusory statement that gives the magistrate virtually no basis at all for making a judgment regarding probable cause. Sufficient information must be presented to the magistrate to allow that official to determine probable cause; his action cannot be a mere ratification of the bare conclusions of others. In order to ensure that such an abdication of the magistrate's duty does not occur, courts must continue to conscientiously review the sufficiency of affidavits on which warrants are issued. But when we move beyond the "bare bones" affidavits present in cases such as *Nathanson* and *Aguilar*, this area simply does not lend itself to a prescribed set of rules, like that which had developed from *Spinelli*. Instead, the flexible, common-sense standard articulated in *Jones*, *Ventresca*, and *Brinegar* better serves the purposes of the Fourth Amendment's probable cause requirement.

Justice Brennan's dissent suggests in several places that the approach we take today somehow downgrades the role of the neutral magistrate, because *Aguilar* and *Spinelli* "preserve the role of magistrates as independent arbiters of probable cause. . . ." Quite the contrary, we believe, is the case. The essential protection of the warrant requirement of the Fourth Amendment is in "requiring that [the usual inferences which reasonable men draw from evidence] be drawn by a neutral and detached magistrate instead of being judged by the officer engaged in the often competitive enterprise of ferreting out crime." *Johnson*. Nothing in our opinion in any way lessens the authority of the magistrate to draw such reasonable inferences as he will from the material supplied to him by applicants for a warrant; indeed, he is freer than under the regime of *Aguilar* and *Spinelli* to draw such inferences, or to refuse to draw them if he is so minded.

The real gist of Justice Brennan's criticism seems to be a second argument, somewhat at odds with the first, that magistrates should be restricted in their authority to make probable cause determinations by the standards laid down in *Aguilar* and *Spinelli*, and that such findings "should not be authorized unless there is some assurance that the information on which they are based has been obtained in a reliable way by an honest or credible person." However, under our opinion magistrates remain perfectly free to exact such assurances as they deem necessary, as well as those required by this opinion, in making probable cause determinations. Justice Brennan would apparently prefer that magistrates be restricted in their findings of probable cause by the development of an elaborate body of case law dealing with the "veracity" prong of the *Spinelli* test, which in turn is broken down into two "spurs"—the informant's "credibility" and the "reliability" of his information, together with the "basis of knowledge" prong of the *Spinelli* test. That such a labyrinthine body of judicial refinement bears any relationship to familiar definitions of probable cause is hard to imagine. Probable cause deals "with probabilities. These are not technical; they are the factual and practical considerations of everyday life on which reasonable and prudent men, not legal technicians, act." *Brinegar*.

Justice Brennan's dissent also suggests that "words such as 'practical,' 'nontechnical,' and 'common sense,' as used in the Court's opinion, are but code words for an overly-permissive attitude towards police practices in derogation of the rights secured by the Fourth Amendment." An easy, but not a complete, answer to this rather florid statement would be that nothing we know about Justice Rutledge suggests that he would have used the words he chose in *Brinegar* in such a manner. More fundamentally, no one doubts that "under our Constitution only measures consistent with the Fourth Amendment may be employed by government to cure [the horrors of drug trafficking]"; but this agreement does not advance the inquiry as to which measures are, and which measures are not, consistent with the Fourth Amendment. "Fidelity" to the commands of the Constitution suggests balanced judgment rather than exhortation. The highest "fidelity" is achieved neither by the judge who instinctively goes furthest in upholding even the most bizarre claim of individual constitutional rights, any more than it is achieved by a judge who instinctively goes furthest in accepting the most restrictive claims of governmental authorities. The task of this Court, as of other courts, is to "hold the balance true," and we think we have done that in this case.

IV

Our decisions applying the totality-of-the-circumstances analysis outlined above have consistently recognized the value of corroboration of details of an informant's tip by independent police work. In *Jones v. United States*, we held that an affidavit relying on hearsay "is not to be deemed insufficient on that score, so long as a substantial basis for crediting the hearsay is presented." We went on to say that even in making a warrantless arrest an officer "may rely upon information received through an informant, rather than upon his direct observations, so long as the informant's statement is reasonably corroborated by other matters within the officer's knowledge." Likewise, we recognized the probative value of corroborative efforts of police officials in *Aguilar*—the source of the "two-pronged test"—by observing that if the police had made some effort to corroborate the informant's report at issue, "an entirely different case" would have been presented.

Our decision in *Draper v. United States* (1959), however, is the classic case on the value of corroborative efforts of police officials. There, an informant named Hereford reported that Draper would arrive in Denver on a train from Chicago on one of two days, and that he would be carrying a quantity of heroin. The informant also supplied a fairly detailed physical description of Draper, and predicted that he would be wearing a light colored raincoat, brown slacks and black shoes, and would be walking "real fast." Hereford gave no indication of the basis for his information.

On one of the stated dates police officers observed a man matching this description exit a train arriving from Chicago; his attire and luggage matched Hereford's report and he was walking rapidly. We explained in *Draper* that, by this point in his investigation, the arresting officer "had personally verified every facet of the information given him by Hereford except whether petitioner had accomplished his mission and had the three ounces of heroin on his person or in his bag. And surely, with every other bit of Hereford's information being thus personally verified, [the officer] had 'reasonable grounds' to believe that the remaining unverified bit of Hereford's information—that Draper would have the heroin with him—was likewise true."

The showing of probable cause in the present case was fully as compelling as that in *Draper*. Even standing alone, the facts obtained through the independent investigation of Mader and the DEA at least suggested that the Gates were involved in drug trafficking. In addition to being a popular vacation site, Florida is well-known as a source of narcotics and other illegal drugs. Lance Gates' flight to Palm Beach, his brief, overnight stay in a motel, and apparent immediate return north to Chicago in the family car, conveniently awaiting him in West Palm Beach, is as suggestive of a pre-arranged drug run, as it is of an ordinary vacation trip.

In addition, the magistrate could rely on the anonymous letter, which had been corroborated in major part by Mader's efforts—just as had occurred in *Draper*. The Supreme Court of Illinois reasoned that *Draper* involved an informant who had given reliable information on previous occasions, while the honesty and reliability of the anonymous informant in this case were unknown to the Bloomingdale police. While this distinction might be an apt one at the time the police department received the anonymous letter, it became far less significant after Mader's independent investigative work occurred. The corroboration of the letter's predictions that the Gates' car would be in Florida, that Lance Gates would fly to Florida in the next day or so, and that he would drive the car north toward Bloomingdale all indicated, albeit not with certainty, that the informant's other assertions also were true. "Because an informant is right about some things, he is more probably right about other facts"—including the claim regarding the Gates' illegal activity. This may well not be the type of "reliability" or "veracity" necessary to satisfy some views of the "veracity prong" of *Spinelli*, but we think it suffices for the practical, common-sense judgment called for in making a probable cause determination. It is enough, for purposes of assessing probable cause, that "corroboration through other sources of information reduced the chances of a reckless or prevaricating tale," thus providing "a substantial basis for crediting the hearsay."

Finally, the anonymous letter contained a range of details relating not just to easily obtained facts and conditions existing at the time of the tip, but to future actions of third parties ordinarily not easily predicted. The letter writer's accurate information as to the travel plans of each of the Gates was of a character likely obtained only from the Gates themselves, or from someone familiar with their not entirely ordinary travel plans. If the informant had access to accurate information of this type a magistrate could properly conclude that it was not unlikely that he also had access to reliable information of the Gates' alleged illegal activities. Of course, the Gates' travel plans might have been learned from a talkative neighbor or travel agent; under the "two-pronged test" developed from *Spinelli*, the character of the details in the anonymous letter might well not permit a sufficiently clear inference regarding the letter writer's "basis of knowledge." But, as discussed previously, probable cause does not demand the certainty we associate with formal trials. It is enough that there was a fair probability that the writer of the anonymous letter had obtained his entire story either from the

Gates or someone they trusted. And corroboration of major portions of the letter's predictions provides just this probability. It is apparent, therefore, that the judge issuing the warrant had a "substantial basis for . . . conclud[ing]" that probable cause to search the Gates' home and car existed. The judgment of the Supreme Court of Illinois therefore must be

Reversed.

[Justices Brennan, Marshall, and Stevens dissented.]

NOTES AND QUESTIONS

1. The Court repeatedly refers to the *Aguilar-Spinelli* test as if it were some indecipherable object of interpretation by Talmudic scholars. It is "an elaborate set of legal rules." The inquiry it demands turns on a "complex superstructure" of evidentiary and analytical rules. This is overstated. *Aguilar* required that for an informant's tip to establish probable cause there must be some basis provided for both the informant's source of knowledge and the reliability of the information provided. *Aguilar v. Texas*, 378 U.S. 108, 114-15 (1964). *Spinelli v. United States*, 393 U.S. 410, 413 (1969), added that corroboration of the details of the tip could satisfy the "reliability" prong.

2. How did the tip at issue in *Gates* fail under the traditional *Aguilar-Spinelli* test? Justice Stevens dissents, joined by Justice Brennan, and argues that the affidavit failed to establish probable cause under even the new "totality of the circumstances" test, inasmuch as the tipster was mistaken about Susan Gates's return travel to Chicago and that the fact of the Gateses' 22-hour nonstop car trip from West Palm Beach to Chicago was unknown to the magistrate when he issued the warrant. Do you agree?

3. Note that after accepting certiorari in *Gates* the government asked the parties for additional briefing on whether the Court should consider a "good faith" exception to the exclusionary rule under which exclusion would not be required where the government had a reasonable belief that the search and seizure at issue was constitutional. The Court did not reach the issue in *Gates*, but adopted such a rule the following year in *United States v. Leon*, 468 U.S. 897 (1984). *See* Chapter V *infra*. Would the existence of such an exception have precluded the exclusion of evidence in *Gates*?

The Supreme Court really doesn't like being pinned down on the meaning of probable cause. It says things like "probable cause is a fluid concept — turning on the assessment of probabilities in particular factual contexts — not readily, or even usefully, reduced to a neat set of legal rules." *Gates*, 462 U.S. at 232. And this: "In evaluating probable cause in any given case, a judge must make a practical common-sense decision whether, given all the circumstances set forth in the affidavit before him, there is a fair probability that contraband or evidence of a crime will be found in a particular place." *Id.* at 238. Although the magistrate judge issuing a warrant is normally entitled to some degree of deference, a reviewing court "may properly conclude that . . . a warrant was invalid because the [magistrate judge's] probable-cause determination reflected an improper analysis of the totality of circumstances." *Leon*, 468 U.S. at 915.

c. Warrant Execution Issues

Police officers' lawful presence at a location where a search has been judicially authorized confers on the officers some ancillary authority consistent with the authority to conduct the search. Accordingly, officers may take reasonable steps to prevent the flight of property occupants, minimize the risk of harm to the officers, and facilitate the orderly completion of the search. *See Muehler v. Mena*, 544 U.S. 93 (2005) (detention of house occupants in handcuffs

306   Chapter IV The Fourth Amendment

during two- to three-hour search of home does not violate Fourth Amendment). On the other hand, a warrant to search a bar and a bartender did not authorize pat-downs of bar patrons. *Ybarra v. Illinois*, 444 U.S. 85, 91 (1979).

The Supreme Court has held that the common law included a general "knock and announce" requirement on officers executing a search warrant, subject to exception for competing law enforcement interests. *Wilson v. Arkansas*, 514 U.S. 927 (1995) (common law knock-and-announce requirement rule applies absent circumstances suggesting a risk of violence to officers or reason to believe evidence will be destroyed). In *Richards v. Wisconsin*, 520 U.S. 385 (1997), the Court considered the constitutionality of a Wisconsin rule that categorically approved no-knock warrants in all felony drug investigations. The Court held that while drug investigations do tend to involve the type of risks identified in *Wilson*, the rule was overly broad in that not all executions of search warrants in drug investigations run such risks, and that other broad categories of investigations could be similarly characterized.

2. Plain View Exception

The plain view doctrine is about leverage. The rationale for the exception is that where police are lawfully in a private location by virtue of a warrant or an exception to the warrant requirement they may leverage that lawful position to take notice of patently incriminating evidence they observe that may not be related to the basis for their lawful presence. Officers need not avert their eyes to incriminating material, in other words.

In *Coolidge v. New Hampshire*, 403 U.S. 443 (1971), a plurality of the Court suppressed the government's evidentiary use of two automobiles that it had seized from defendant's driveway — in "plain view" — in connection with the defendant's arrest, as the incriminating character of the cars only became apparent after their interiors were searched. The Court held that the incriminating character of the evidence in plain view must be "immediately apparent" and a search cannot be artificially prolonged in the hopes of stumbling upon incriminating evidence. Among the questions that remained open after *Coolidge* were (1) what level of suspicion or cause did an officer need to justify a seizure of the incriminating item, and (2) did the discovery of the incriminating evidence have to be, as the *Coolidge* plurality stated, "inadvertent."

In *Arizona v. Hicks*, 480 U.S. 321 (1987), a police officer entered the defendant's apartment under exigent circumstances to investigate a gunshot fired from defendant's apartment into the apartment below it. Upon seeing high-end stereo equipment in the otherwise "squalid" apartment, and suspecting the equipment might be stolen, the officer took a closer look and turned the turntable over to obtain its serial number. It ultimately turned out that the turntable was stolen, a determination made possible by knowledge of the serial number. The Court found the plain view doctrine inapplicable because the officer had lacked probable cause for the search that his moving of the turntable entailed.

In the next case the Court considers whether the plain view doctrine only applies where the discovery of the incriminating evidence was "inadvertent."

Horton v. California
496 U.S. 128 (1990)

Justice STEVENS delivered the opinion of the Court.

In this case we revisit an issue that was considered, but not conclusively resolved, in *Coolidge v. New Hampshire* (1971): Whether the warrantless seizure of evidence of crime in plain view is prohibited by the Fourth Amendment if the discovery of the evidence was not

C. The Warrant Requirement and Its Exceptions

inadvertent. We conclude that even though inadvertence is a characteristic of most legitimate "plain-view" seizures, it is not a necessary condition.

I

Petitioner was convicted of the armed robbery of Erwin Wallaker, the treasurer of the San Jose Coin Club. When Wallaker returned to his home after the Club's annual show, he entered his garage and was accosted by two masked men, one armed with a machine gun and the other with an electrical shocking device, sometimes referred to as a "stun gun." The two men shocked Wallaker, bound and handcuffed him, and robbed him of jewelry and cash. During the encounter sufficient conversation took place to enable Wallaker subsequently to identify petitioner's distinctive voice. His identification was partially corroborated by a witness who saw the robbers leaving the scene and by evidence that petitioner had attended the coin show.

Sergeant LaRault, an experienced police officer, investigated the crime and determined that there was probable cause to search petitioner's home for the proceeds of the robbery and for the weapons used by the robbers. His affidavit for a search warrant referred to police reports that described the weapons as well as the proceeds, but the warrant issued by the Magistrate only authorized a search for the proceeds, including three specifically described rings.

Pursuant to the warrant, LaRault searched petitioner's residence, but he did not find the stolen property. During the course of the search, however, he discovered the weapons in plain view and seized them. Specifically, he seized an Uzi machine gun, a .38-caliber revolver, two stun guns, a handcuff key, a San Jose Coin Club advertising brochure, and a few items of clothing identified by the victim. LaRault testified that while he was searching for the rings, he also was interested in finding other evidence connecting petitioner to the robbery. Thus, the seized evidence was not discovered "inadvertently."

The trial court refused to suppress the evidence found in petitioner's home and, after a jury trial, petitioner was found guilty and sentenced to prison. The California Court of Appeal affirmed. It rejected petitioner's argument that our decision in *Coolidge* required suppression of the seized evidence that had not been listed in the warrant because its discovery was not inadvertent. The court relied on the California Supreme Court's decision in *North v. Superior Court*. In that case the court noted that the discussion of the inadvertence limitation on the "plain-view" doctrine in Justice Stewart's opinion in *Coolidge* had been joined by only three other Members of this Court and therefore was not binding on it. The California Supreme Court denied petitioner's request for review.

Because the California courts' interpretation of the "plain-view" doctrine conflicts with the view of other courts and because the unresolved issue is important, we granted certiorari.

II

• • •

The criteria that generally guide "plain-view" seizures were set forth in *Coolidge v. New Hampshire* (1971). The Court held that the police, in seizing two automobiles parked in plain view on the defendant's driveway in the course of arresting the defendant, violated the Fourth Amendment. Accordingly, particles of gunpowder that had been subsequently found in vacuum sweepings from one of the cars could not be introduced in evidence against the defendant. The State endeavored to justify the seizure of the automobiles, and their subsequent search at the police station, on four different grounds, including the "plain-view" doctrine. The scope of that doctrine as it had developed in earlier cases was fairly summarized in these three paragraphs from Justice Stewart's opinion:

> It is well established that under certain circumstances the police may seize evidence in plain view without a warrant. But it is important to keep in mind that, in the vast majority of cases, any

308 Chapter IV The Fourth Amendment

evidence seized by the police will be in plain view, at least at the moment of seizure. The problem with the "plain view" doctrine has been to identify the circumstances in which plain view has legal significance rather than being simply the normal concomitant of any search, legal or illegal.

An example of the applicability of the "plain view" doctrine is the situation in which the police have a warrant to search a given area for specified objects, and in the course of the search come across some other article of incriminating character. Where the initial intrusion that brings the police within plain view of such an article is supported, not by a warrant, but by one of the recognized exceptions to the warrant requirement, the seizure is also legitimate. Thus the police may inadvertently come across evidence while in "hot pursuit" of a fleeing suspect. And an object that comes into view during a search incident to arrest that is appropriately limited in scope under existing law may be seized without a warrant. Finally, the "plain view" doctrine has been applied where a police officer is not searching for evidence against the accused, but nonetheless inadvertently comes across an incriminating object.

What the "plain view" cases have in common is that the police officer in each of them had a prior justification for an intrusion in the course of which he came inadvertently across a piece of evidence incriminating the accused. The doctrine serves to supplement the prior justification—whether it be a warrant for another object, hot pursuit, search incident to lawful arrest, or some other legitimate reason for being present unconnected with a search directed against the accused—and permits the warrantless seizure. Of course, the extension of the original justification is legitimate only where it is immediately apparent to the police that they have evidence before them; the "plain view" doctrine may not be used to extend a general exploratory search from one object to another until something incriminating at last emerges.

Justice Stewart then described the two limitations on the doctrine that he found implicit in its rationale: First, that "plain view alone is never enough to justify the warrantless seizure of evidence," and second, that "the discovery of evidence in plain view must be inadvertent." Id., at 469.

Justice Stewart's analysis of the "plain-view" doctrine did not command a majority, and a plurality of the Court has since made clear that the discussion is "not a binding precedent." Justice Harlan, who concurred in the Court's judgment and in its response to the dissenting opinions, did not join the plurality's discussion of the "plain-view" doctrine. The decision nonetheless is a binding precedent. Before discussing the second limitation, which is implicated in this case, it is therefore necessary to explain why the first adequately supports the Court's judgment.

It is, of course, an essential predicate to any valid warrantless seizure of incriminating evidence that the officer did not violate the Fourth Amendment in arriving at the place from which the evidence could be plainly viewed. There are, moreover, two additional conditions that must be satisfied to justify the warrantless seizure. First, not only must the item be in plain view; its incriminating character must also be "immediately apparent." Thus, in *Coolidge*, the cars were obviously in plain view, but their probative value remained uncertain until after the interiors were swept and examined microscopically. Second, not only must the officer be lawfully located in a place from which the object can be plainly seen, but he or she must also have a lawful right of access to the object itself. As the United States has suggested, Justice Harlan's vote in *Coolidge* may have rested on the fact that the seizure of the cars was accomplished by means of a warrantless trespass on the defendant's property. In all events, we are satisfied that the absence of inadvertence was not essential to the Court's rejection of the State's "plain-view" argument in *Coolidge*.

III

Justice Stewart concluded that the inadvertence requirement was necessary to avoid a violation of the express constitutional requirement that a valid warrant must particularly describe the things to be seized. He explained:

The rationale of the exception to the warrant requirement, as just stated, is that a plain-view seizure will not turn an initially valid (and therefore limited) search into a "general" one, while the inconvenience of procuring a warrant to cover an inadvertent discovery is great. But where the discovery is anticipated, where the police know in advance the location of the evidence and intend to seize it, the situation is altogether different. The requirement of a warrant to seize imposes no inconvenience whatever, or at least none which is constitutionally cognizable in a legal system that regards warrantless searches as "per se unreasonable" in the absence of "exigent circumstances."

   If the initial intrusion is bottomed upon a warrant that fails to mention a particular object, though the police know its location and intend to seize it, then there is a violation of the express constitutional requirement of "Warrants . . . particularly describing . . . [the] things to be seized.

We find two flaws in this reasoning. First, evenhanded law enforcement is best achieved by the application of objective standards of conduct, rather than standards that depend upon the subjective state of mind of the officer. The fact that an officer is interested in an item of evidence and fully expects to find it in the course of a search should not invalidate its seizure if the search is confined in area and duration by the terms of a warrant or a valid exception to the warrant requirement. If the officer has knowledge approaching certainty that the item will be found, we see no reason why he or she would deliberately omit a particular description of the item to be seized from the application for a search warrant. Specification of the additional item could only permit the officer to expand the scope of the search. On the other hand, if he or she has a valid warrant to search for one item and merely a suspicion concerning the second, whether or not it amounts to probable cause, we fail to see why that suspicion should immunize the second item from seizure if it is found during a lawful search for the first. The hypothetical case put by Justice White in his concurring and dissenting opinion in *Coolidge* is instructive:

> Let us suppose officers secure a warrant to search a house for a rifle. While staying well within the range of a rifle search, they discover two photographs of the murder victim, both in plain sight in the bedroom. Assume also that the discovery of the one photograph was inadvertent but finding the other was anticipated. The Court would permit the seizure of only one of the photographs. But in terms of the "minor" peril to Fourth Amendment values there is surely no difference between these two photographs: the interference with possession is the same in each case and the officers' appraisal of the photograph they expected to see is no less reliable than their judgment about the other. And in both situations the actual inconvenience and danger to evidence remain identical if the officers must depart and secure a warrant.

Second, the suggestion that the inadvertence requirement is necessary to prevent the police from conducting general searches, or from converting specific warrants into general warrants, is not persuasive because that interest is already served by the requirements that no warrant issue unless it "particularly describ[es] the place to be searched and the persons or things to be seized." Scrupulous adherence to these requirements serves the interests in limiting the area and duration of the search that the inadvertence requirement inadequately protects. Once those commands have been satisfied and the officer has a lawful right of access, however, no additional Fourth Amendment interest is furthered by requiring that the discovery of evidence be inadvertent. If the scope of the search exceeds that permitted by the terms of a validly issued warrant or the character of the relevant exception from the warrant requirement, the subsequent seizure is unconstitutional without more. Thus, in the case of a search incident to a lawful arrest, "[i]f the police stray outside the scope of an authorized *Chimel* search they are already in violation of the Fourth Amendment, and evidence so seized will be excluded; adding a second reason for excluding evidence hardly seems worth the candle." Similarly, the object of a warrantless search of an automobile also defines its scope:

> The scope of a warrantless search of an automobile thus is not defined by the nature of the container in which the contraband is secreted. Rather, it is defined by the object of the search and the places in which there is probable cause to believe that it may be found. Just as probable

cause to believe that a stolen lawnmower may be found in a garage will not support a warrant to search an upstairs bedroom, probable cause to believe that undocumented aliens are being transported in a van will not justify a warrantless search of a suitcase. Probable cause to believe that a container placed in the trunk of a taxi contains contraband or evidence does not justify a search of the entire cab.

In this case, the scope of the search was not enlarged in the slightest by the omission of any reference to the weapons in the warrant. Indeed, if the three rings and other items named in the warrant had been found at the outset — or if petitioner had them in his possession and had responded to the warrant by producing them immediately — no search for weapons could have taken place. Again, Justice White's concurring and dissenting opinion in *Coolidge* is instructive:

> Police with a warrant for a rifle may search only places where rifles might be and must terminate the search once the rifle is found; the inadvertence rule will in no way reduce the number of places into which they may lawfully look.

As we have already suggested, by hypothesis the seizure of an object in plain view does not involve an intrusion on privacy. If the interest in privacy has been invaded, the violation must have occurred before the object came into plain view and there is no need for an inadvertence limitation on seizures to condemn it. The prohibition against general searches and general warrants serves primarily as a protection against unjustified intrusions on privacy. But reliance on privacy concerns that support that prohibition is misplaced when the inquiry concerns the scope of an exception that merely authorizes an officer with a lawful right of access to an item to seize it without a warrant.

In this case the items seized from petitioner's home were discovered during a lawful search authorized by a valid warrant. When they were discovered, it was immediately apparent to the officer that they constituted incriminating evidence. He had probable cause, not only to obtain a warrant to search for the stolen property, but also to believe that the weapons and handguns had been used in the crime he was investigating. The search was authorized by the warrant; the seizure was authorized by the "plain-view" doctrine. The judgment is affirmed.

NOTES AND QUESTIONS

1. Are you curious as to why Sergeant LaRault was able to obtain a search warrant only for the "proceeds" of the robbery and not for the weapons used in the robbery, not even the comparatively rare (and thus specific) "stun gun"? Do you think the robbery victim was probably better able to particularly describe the items he was dispossessed of than the weapons used in the robbery?

2. The officer honestly testified at the suppression hearing that in executing the search warrant he was looking not just for what the warrant authorized but also for other evidence pertaining to the robbery. Suppose you were the assistant district attorney in charge of this prosecution and that you had been involved not only in the suppression hearing but also the obtaining of the warrant. How would you have advised Sergeant LaRault about his execution of the warrant (if he had asked) bearing in mind (a) the "half a loaf" nature of the warrant and (b) the uncertainty of *Coolidge*'s "inadvertence" requirement? How would you have prepared him for the suppression hearing on this issue?

3. What is the relevance of the fact that Officer LaRault did not seize other guns that were also in plain view?

4. Do you believe the incriminating character of the handcuff key was immediately apparent? Do you think it was immediately apparent that it was a handcuff key?

C. The Warrant Requirement and Its Exceptions

5. What if Officer LaRault had observed a clear baggie containing a white powdery substance on the kitchen table? In the bathroom on the sink?

6. What do you think of the dissent's argument that eliminating the "inadvertence" requirement gives the police an incentive to hold back information in applying for a warrant?

3. Warrantless Arrests

An arrest is the quintessential seizure under the Fourth Amendment. An arrest is not only a substantial curtailment of freedom in itself—an arrestee does not have to be brought before a judicial officer for consideration of bail for 48 hours, *County of Riverside v. McLaughlin*, 500 U.S. 44 (1991)—but it is the first step in a prosecution that may result in a further and substantially more extreme deprivation of liberty. Even more consequential to the arrestee in many cases are the further invasions of freedom that are occasioned and legitimated by an arrest: searches of the arrestee's person and immediate surroundings, sometimes including the arrestee's vehicle, as "incident" to the arrest.

Yet warrantless arrests are not really an "exception" to the warrant requirement inasmuch as there has never been any such uniform requirement. *Carroll v. United States*, 267 U.S. 132 (1925), described the common law: "The usual rule is that a police officer may arrest without warrant one believed by the officer upon reasonable cause to have been guilty of a felony. . . ." This was confirmed to still be good law 50 years later in *United States v. Watson*, 423 U.S. 41 (1976), where the Court held that where probable cause exists a warrantless arrest of a suspect in a public place on a felony charge was constitutional, despite the lack of exigency, at least where—as in *Watson*—such an arrest was authorized by a federal statute. The probable cause requirement for an arrest was absolute, however. A person could not be detained for questioning—even if given *Miranda* warnings—under circumstances similar to an arrest without probable cause. *Dunaway v. New York*, 442 U.S. 200, 208 (1979).

Statutory authority for an arrest is not a silver bullet, though. In the next case, *Payton v. New York*, 445 U.S. 573 (1980), the Court held that probable cause to arrest did not justify the warrantless entry of the suspect's home absent exigent circumstances, notwithstanding a New York statute authorizing such an arrest. Another case of "home exceptionalism"?

Payton v. New York
445 U.S. 573 (1980)

Mr. Justice STEVENS delivered the opinion of the Court.

These appeals challenge the constitutionality of New York statutes that authorize police officers to enter a private residence without a warrant and with force, if necessary, to make a routine felony arrest.

The important constitutional question presented by this challenge has been expressly left open in a number of our prior opinions. In *United States v. Watson*, we upheld a warrantless "midday public arrest," expressly noting that the case did not pose "the still unsettled question . . . 'whether and under what circumstances an officer may enter a suspect's home to make a warrantless arrest.'" The question has been answered in different ways by other appellate courts. The Supreme Court of Florida rejected the constitutional attack, as did the New York Court of Appeals in this case. The courts of last resort in 10 other States, however, have held that unless special circumstances are present, warrantless arrests in the home are unconstitutional. Of the seven United States Courts of Appeals that have considered the question, five have expressed the opinion that such arrests are unconstitutional.

Chapter IV The Fourth Amendment

Last Term we noted probable jurisdiction of these appeals in order to address that question. After hearing oral argument, we set the case for reargument this Term. We now reverse the New York Court of Appeals and hold that the Fourth Amendment to the United States Constitution, made applicable to the States by the Fourteenth Amendment, prohibits the police from making a warrantless and nonconsensual entry into a suspect's home in order to make a routine felony arrest.

We first state the facts of both cases in some detail and put to one side certain related questions that are not presented by these records. We then explain why the New York statutes are not consistent with the Fourth Amendment and why the reasons for upholding warrantless arrests in a public place do not apply to warrantless invasions of the privacy of the home.

I

On January 14, 1970, after two days of intensive investigation, New York detectives had assembled evidence sufficient to establish probable cause to believe that Theodore Payton had murdered the manager of a gas station two days earlier. At about 7:30 a. m. on January 15, six officers went to Payton's apartment in the Bronx, intending to arrest him. They had not obtained a warrant. Although light and music emanated from the apartment, there was no response to their knock on the metal door. They summoned emergency assistance and, about 30 minutes later, used crowbars to break open the door and enter the apartment. No one was there. In plain view, however, was a .30-caliber shell casing that was seized and later admitted into evidence at Payton's murder trial.

In due course Payton surrendered to the police, was indicted for murder, and moved to suppress the evidence taken from his apartment. The trial judge held that the warrantless and forcible entry was authorized by the New York Code of Criminal Procedure, and that the evidence in plain view was properly seized. He found that exigent circumstances justified the officers' failure to announce their purpose before entering the apartment as required by the statute. He had no occasion, however, to decide whether those circumstances also would have justified the failure to obtain a warrant, because he concluded that the warrantless entry was adequately supported by the statute without regard to the circumstances. The Appellate Division, First Department, summarily affirmed.

On March 14, 1974, Obie Riddick was arrested for the commission of two armed robberies that had occurred in 1971. He had been identified by the victims in June 1973, and in January 1974 the police had learned his address. They did not obtain a warrant for his arrest. At about noon on March 14, a detective, accompanied by three other officers, knocked on the door of the Queens house where Riddick was living. When his young son opened the door, they could see Riddick sitting in bed covered by a sheet. They entered the house and placed him under arrest. Before permitting him to dress, they opened a chest of drawers two feet from the bed in search of weapons and found narcotics and related paraphernalia. Riddick was subsequently indicted on narcotics charges. At a suppression hearing, the trial judge held that the warrantless entry into his home was authorized by the revised New York statute, and that the search of the immediate area was reasonable under *Chimel v. California*. The Appellate Division, Second Department, affirmed the denial of the suppression motion.

The New York Court of Appeals, in a single opinion, affirmed the convictions of both Payton and Riddick. The court recognized that the question whether and under what circumstances an officer may enter a suspect's home to make a warrantless arrest had not been settled either by that court or by this Court. In answering that question, the majority of four judges relied primarily on its perception that there is a

> . . . substantial difference between the intrusion which attends an entry for the purpose of searching the premises and that which results from an entry for the purpose of making an

C. The Warrant Requirement and Its Exceptions

arrest, and [a] significant difference in the governmental interest in achieving the objective of the intrusion in the two instances.

The majority supported its holding by noting the "apparent historical acceptance" of warrantless entries to make felony arrests, both in the English common law and in the practice of many American States.

Three members of the New York Court of Appeals dissented on this issue because they believed that the Constitution requires the police to obtain a "warrant to enter a home in order to arrest or seize a person, unless there are exigent circumstances." Starting from the premise that, except in carefully circumscribed instances, "the Fourth Amendment forbids police entry into a private home to search for and seize an object without a warrant," the dissenters reasoned that an arrest of the person involves an even greater invasion of privacy and should therefore be attended with at least as great a measure of constitutional protection. The dissenters noted "the existence of statutes and the American Law Institute imprimatur codifying the common-law rule authorizing warrantless arrests in private homes" and acknowledged that "the statutory authority of a police officer to make a warrantless arrest in this State has been in effect for almost 100 years," but concluded that "neither antiquity nor legislative unanimity can be determinative of the grave constitutional question presented" and "can never be a substitute for reasoned analysis."

Before addressing the narrow question presented by these appeals, we put to one side other related problems that are not presented today. Although it is arguable that the warrantless entry to effect Payton's arrest might have been justified by exigent circumstances, none of the New York courts relied on any such justification. The Court of Appeals majority treated both Payton's and Riddick's cases as involving routine arrests in which there was ample time to obtain a warrant, and we will do the same. Accordingly, we have no occasion to consider the sort of emergency or dangerous situation, described in our cases as "exigent circumstances," that would justify a warrantless entry into a home for the purpose of either arrest or search.

Nor do these cases raise any question concerning the authority of the police, without either a search or arrest warrant, to enter a third party's home to arrest a suspect. The police broke into Payton's apartment intending to arrest Payton, and they arrested Riddick in his own dwelling. We also note that in neither case is it argued that the police lacked probable cause to believe that the suspect was at home when they entered. Finally, in both cases we are dealing with entries into homes made without the consent of any occupant. In *Payton*, the police used crowbars to break down the door and in *Riddick*, although his 3-year-old son answered the door, the police entered before Riddick had an opportunity either to object or to consent.

II

It is familiar history that indiscriminate searches and seizures conducted under the authority of "general warrants" were the immediate evils that motivated the framing and adoption of the Fourth Amendment. Indeed, as originally proposed in the House of Representatives, the draft contained only one clause, which directly imposed limitations on the issuance of warrants, but imposed no express restrictions on warrantless searches or seizures. As it was ultimately adopted, however, the Amendment contained two separate clauses, the first protecting the basic right to be free from unreasonable searches and seizures and the second requiring that warrants be particular and supported by probable cause. The Amendment provides:

> The right of the people to be secure in their persons, houses, papers, and effects, against unreasonable searches and seizures, shall not be violated, and no Warrants shall issue, but upon probable cause, supported by Oath or affirmation, and particularly describing the place to be searched, and the persons or things to be seized.

It is thus perfectly clear that the evil the Amendment was designed to prevent was broader than the abuse of a general warrant. Unreasonable searches or seizures conducted without any warrant at all are condemned by the plain language of the first clause of the Amendment. Almost a century ago the Court stated in resounding terms that the principles reflected in the Amendment "reached farther than the concrete form" of the specific cases that gave it birth, and "apply to all invasions on the part of the government and its employees of the sanctity of a man's home and the privacies of life." Without pausing to consider whether that broad language may require some qualification, it is sufficient to note that the warrantless arrest of a person is a species of seizure required by the Amendment to be reasonable. Indeed, as Mr. Justice Powell noted in his concurrence in *United States v. Watson*, the arrest of a person is "quintessentially a seizure."

The simple language of the Amendment applies equally to seizures of persons and to seizures of property. Our analysis in this case may therefore properly commence with rules that have been well established in Fourth Amendment litigation involving tangible items. As the Court reiterated just a few years ago, the "physical entry of the home is the chief evil against which the wording of the Fourth Amendment is directed. And we have long adhered to the view that the warrant procedure minimizes the danger of needless intrusions of that sort.

It is a "basic principle of Fourth Amendment law" that searches and seizures inside a home without a warrant are presumptively unreasonable. Yet it is also well settled that objects such as weapons or contraband found in a public place may be seized by the police without a warrant. The seizure of property in plain view involves no invasion of privacy and is presumptively reasonable, assuming that there is probable cause to associate the property with criminal activity. The distinction between a warrantless seizure in an open area and such a seizure on private premises was plainly stated in *G. M. Leasing Corp. v. United States*:

> It is one thing to seize without a warrant property resting in an open area or seizable by levy without an intrusion into privacy, and it is quite another thing to effect a warrantless seizure of property, even that owned by a corporation, situated on private premises to which access is not otherwise available for the seizing officer.

As the late Judge Leventhal recognized, this distinction has equal force when the seizure of a person is involved. Writing on the constitutional issue now before us for the United States Court of Appeals for the District of Columbia Circuit sitting en banc, Judge Leventhal first noted the settled rule that warrantless arrests in public places are valid. He immediately recognized, however, that

> [a] greater burden is placed . . . on officials who enter a home or dwelling without consent. Freedom from intrusion into the home or dwelling is the archetype of the privacy protection secured by the Fourth Amendment.

His analysis of this question then focused on the long-settled premise that, absent exigent circumstances, a warrantless entry to search for weapons or contraband is unconstitutional even when a felony has been committed and there is probable cause to believe that incriminating evidence will be found within. He reasoned that the constitutional protection afforded to the individual's interest in the privacy of his own home is equally applicable to a warrantless entry for the purpose of arresting a resident of the house; for it is inherent in such an entry that a search for the suspect may be required before he can be apprehended. Judge Leventhal concluded that an entry to arrest and an entry to search for and to seize property implicate the same interest in preserving the privacy and the sanctity of the home, and justify the same level of constitutional protection.

C. The Warrant Requirement and Its Exceptions

This reasoning has been followed in other Circuits. Thus, the Second Circuit recently summarized its position:

> To be arrested in the home involves not only the invasion attendant to all arrests but also an invasion of the sanctity of the home. This is simply too substantial an invasion to allow without a warrant, at least in the absence of exigent circumstances, even when it is accomplished under statutory authority and when probable cause is clearly present.

We find this reasoning to be persuasive and in accord with this Court's Fourth Amendment decisions.

The majority of the New York Court of Appeals, however, suggested that there is a substantial difference in the relative intrusiveness of an entry to search for property and an entry to search for a person. It is true that the area that may legally be searched is broader when executing a search warrant than when executing an arrest warrant in the home. This difference may be more theoretical than real, however, because the police may need to check the entire premises for safety reasons, and sometimes they ignore the restrictions on searches incident to arrest.

But the critical point is that any differences in the intrusiveness of entries to search and entries to arrest are merely ones of degree rather than kind. The two intrusions share this fundamental characteristic: the breach of the entrance to an individual's home. The Fourth Amendment protects the individual's privacy in a variety of settings. In none is the zone of privacy more clearly defined than when bounded by the unambiguous physical dimensions of an individual's home—a zone that finds its roots in clear and specific constitutional terms: "The right of the people to be secure in their . . . houses . . . shall not be violated." That language unequivocally establishes the proposition that "[a]t the very core [of the Fourth Amendment] stands the right of a man to retreat into his own home and there be free from unreasonable governmental intrusion." In terms that apply equally to seizures of property and to seizures of persons, the Fourth Amendment has drawn a firm line at the entrance to the house. Absent exigent circumstances, that threshold may not reasonably be crossed without a warrant.

III

Without contending that *United States v. Watson* decided the question presented by these appeals, New York argues that the reasons that support the *Watson* holding require a similar result here. In *Watson* the Court relied on (a) the well-settled common-law rule that a warrantless arrest in a public place is valid if the arresting officer had probable cause to believe the suspect is a felon; (b) the clear consensus among the States adhering to that well-settled common-law rule; and (c) the expression of the judgment of Congress that such an arrest is "reasonable." We consider each of these reasons as it applies to a warrantless entry into a home for the purpose of making a routine felony arrest.

A

An examination of the common-law understanding of an officer's authority to arrest sheds light on the obviously relevant, if not entirely dispositive, consideration of what the Framers of the Amendment might have thought to be reasonable. Initially, it should be noted that the common-law rules of arrest developed in legal contexts that substantially differ from the cases now before us. In these cases, which involve application of the exclusionary rule, the issue is whether certain evidence is admissible at trial. At common law, the question whether an arrest was authorized typically arose in civil damages actions for trespass or false arrest, in which a constable's authority to make the arrest was a defense. Additionally, if an officer was killed while attempting to effect an arrest, the question whether the person resisting the arrest was guilty of murder or manslaughter turned on whether the officer was acting within the bounds of his authority.

A study of the common law on the question whether a constable had the authority to make warrantless arrests in the home on mere suspicion of a felony—as distinguished from an officer's right to arrest for a crime committed in his presence—reveals a surprising lack of judicial decisions and a deep divergence among scholars.

The most cited evidence of the common-law rule consists of an equivocal dictum in a case actually involving the sheriff's authority to enter a home to effect service of civil process. In *Semayne's Case*, the Court stated:

> In all cases when the King is party, the Sheriff (if the doors be not open) may break the party's house, either to arrest him, or to do other execution of the K.'s process, if otherwise he cannot enter. But before he breaks it, he ought to signify the cause of his coming, and to make request to open doors; and that appears well by the stat. of Westm. 1. c. 17. (which it but an affirmance of the common law) as hereafter appears, for the law without a default in the owner abhors the destruction or breaking of any house (which is for the habitation and safety of man) by which great damage and inconvenience might ensue to the party, when no default is in him; for perhaps he did not know of the process, of which, if he had notice, it is to be presumed that he would obey it, and that appears by the book in 18 E. 2. Execut. 252. where it is said, that the K.'s officer who comes to do execution, &c. may open the doors which are shut, and break them, if he cannot have the keys; which proves, that he ought first to demand them, 7 E. 3.16. (Footnotes omitted.)

This passage has been read by some as describing an entry without a warrant. The context strongly implies, however, that the court was describing the extent of authority in executing the King's writ. This reading is confirmed by the phrase "either to arrest him, or to do other execution of the K.'s process" and by the further point that notice was necessary because the owner may "not know of the process." In any event, the passage surely cannot be said unambiguously to endorse warrantless entries.

The common-law commentators disagreed sharply on the subject. Three distinct views were expressed. Lord Coke, widely recognized by the American colonists "as the greatest authority of his time on the laws of England," clearly viewed a warrantless entry for the purpose of arrest to be illegal. Burn, Foster, and Hawkins agreed, as did East and Russell, though the latter two qualified their opinions by stating that if an entry to arrest was made without a warrant, the officer was perhaps immune from liability for the trespass if the suspect was actually guilty. Blackstone, Chitty, and Stephen took the opposite view, that entry to arrest without a warrant was legal, though Stephen relied on Blackstone who, along with Chitty, in turn relied exclusively on Hale. But Hale's view was not quite so unequivocally expressed. Further, Hale appears to rely solely on a statement in an early Yearbook, quoted in *Burdett v. Abbot*:

> that for felony, or suspicion of felony, a man may break open the house to take the felon; for it is for the commonweal to take them.

Considering the diversity of views just described, however, it is clear that the statement was never deemed authoritative. Indeed, in *Burdett*, the statement was described as an "extrajudicial opinion."

It is obvious that the common-law rule on warrantless home arrests was not as clear as the rule on arrests in public places. Indeed, particularly considering the prominence of Lord Coke, the weight of authority as it appeared to the Framers was to the effect that a warrant was required, or at the minimum that there were substantial risks in proceeding without one. The common-law sources display a sensitivity to privacy interests that could not have been lost on the Framers. The zealous and frequent repetition of the adage that a "man's house is his castle," made it abundantly clear that both in England and in the Colonies "the freedom of one's house" was one of the most vital elements of English liberty.

C. The Warrant Requirement and Its Exceptions

Thus, our study of the relevant common law does not provide the same guidance that was present in *Watson*. Whereas the rule concerning the validity of an arrest in a public place was supported by cases directly in point and by the unanimous views of the commentators, we have found no direct authority supporting forcible entries into a home to make a routine arrest and the weight of the scholarly opinion is somewhat to the contrary. Indeed, the absence of any 17th- or 18th-century English cases directly in point, together with the unequivocal endorsement of the tenet that "a man's house is his castle," strongly suggests that the prevailing practice was not to make such arrests except in hot pursuit or when authorized by a warrant. In all events, the issue is not one that can be said to have been definitively settled by the common law at the time the Fourth Amendment was adopted.

B

A majority of the States that have taken a position on the question permit warrantless entry into the home to arrest even in the absence of exigent circumstances. At this time, 24 States permit such warrantless entries; 15 States clearly prohibit them, though 3 States do so on federal constitutional grounds alone; and 11 States have apparently taken no position on the question.

But these current figures reflect a significant decline during the last decade in the number of States permitting warrantless entries for arrest. Recent dicta in this Court raising questions about the practice, and Federal Courts of Appeals' decisions on point, have led state courts to focus on the issue. Virtually all of the state courts that have had to confront the constitutional issue directly have held warrantless entries into the home to arrest to be invalid in the absence of exigent circumstances. Three state courts have relied on Fourth Amendment grounds alone, while seven have squarely placed their decisions on both federal and state constitutional grounds. A number of other state courts, though not having had to confront the issue directly, have recognized the serious nature of the constitutional question. Apparently, only the Supreme Court of Florida and the New York Court of Appeals in this case have expressly upheld warrantless entries to arrest in the face of a constitutional challenge.

A longstanding, widespread practice is not immune from constitutional scrutiny. But neither is it to be lightly brushed aside. This is particularly so when the constitutional standard is as amorphous as the word "reasonable," and when custom and contemporary norms necessarily play such a large role in the constitutional analysis. In this case, although the weight of state-law authority is clear, there is by no means the kind of virtual unanimity on this question that was present in *United States v. Watson*, with regard to warrantless arrests in public places. Only 24 of the 50 States currently sanction warrantless entries into the home to arrest, and there is an obvious declining trend. Further, the strength of the trend is greater than the numbers alone indicate. Seven state courts have recently held that warrantless home arrests violate their respective State Constitutions. That is significant because by invoking a state constitutional provision, a state court immunizes its decision from review by this Court. This heightened degree of immutability underscores the depth of the principle underlying the result.

C

No congressional determination that warrantless entries into the home are "reasonable" has been called to our attention. None of the federal statutes cited in the Watson opinion reflects any such legislative judgment. Thus, that support for the *Watson* holding finds no counterpart in this case.

Mr. Justice Powell, concurring in *United States v. Watson*, stated:

> But logic sometimes must defer to history and experience. The Court's opinion emphasizes the historical sanction accorded warrantless felony arrests [in public places].

In this case, however, neither history nor this Nation's experience requires us to disregard the overriding respect for the sanctity of the home that has been embedded in our traditions since the origins of the Republic.

IV

The parties have argued at some length about the practical consequences of a warrant requirement as a precondition to a felony arrest in the home. In the absence of any evidence that effective law enforcement has suffered in those States that already have such a requirement, we are inclined to view such arguments with skepticism. More fundamentally, however, such arguments of policy must give way to a constitutional command that we consider to be unequivocal.

Finally, we note the State's suggestion that only a search warrant based on probable cause to believe the suspect is at home at a given time can adequately protect the privacy interests at stake, and since such a warrant requirement is manifestly impractical, there need be no warrant of any kind. We find this ingenious argument unpersuasive. It is true that an arrest warrant requirement may afford less protection than a search warrant requirement, but it will suffice to interpose the magistrate's determination of probable cause between the zealous officer and the citizen. If there is sufficient evidence of a citizen's participation in a felony to persuade a judicial officer that his arrest is justified, it is constitutionally reasonable to require him to open his doors to the officers of the law. Thus, for Fourth Amendment purposes, an arrest warrant founded on probable cause implicitly carries with it the limited authority to enter a dwelling in which the suspect lives when there is reason to believe the suspect is within.

Because no arrest warrant was obtained in either of these cases, the judgments must be reversed and the cases remanded to the New York Court of Appeals for further proceedings not inconsistent with this opinion.

It is so ordered.

NOTES AND QUESTIONS

1. The police officers who arrested Payton and Reddick did not bother to get arrest warrants, presumably because they were relying on the New York statute that authorized officers to enter a private residence, without a warrant, to effectuate an arrest. Were there any obstacles to them getting a warrant on these facts? Could they demonstrate probable cause?

2. The Court notes that no congressional legislation appears to authorize a warrantless entry into a home to effectuate an arrest. What difference would such legislation make? Is the result in *Payton* not required by the Constitution? Could Congress statutorily override *Payton*?

3. The New York Court of Appeals found a substantial difference between the intrusiveness of the entry of a home to search for property and an entry to make an arrest. Is the Court's response to this point — that the difference is more theoretical than real because police may ignore the constitutional limits on searches incident to arrest — satisfactory?

4. It is clear from *Payton* that an arrest warrant authorizes police to enter, by force if necessary, the home of the subject of the warrant to effectuate an arrest. What about the home of a third party, where police have probable cause to believe the subject is in that home? The Supreme Court confronted this question the year after *Payton* in *Steagald v. United States*, 451 U.S. 204 (1981), where DEA agents, armed with an arrest warrant for one Lyons, believed him to be in Steagald's home. Without obtaining a search warrant or consent, and in the absence of exigent circumstances, the agents entered the home and discovered cocaine belonging to Steagald but not Lyons. *Id.* at 206. The Court reversed the conviction because the arrest warrant for a third party was insufficient to protect Steagald's Fourth Amendment privacy interests. *Id.* at 212.

The next case — on extreme facts — considers whether the Fourth Amendment prohibits a warrantless arrest on a misdemeanor charge.

Atwater v. City of Lago Vista
532 U.S. 318 (2001)

Justice SOUTER delivered the opinion of the Court.

The question is whether the Fourth Amendment forbids a warrantless arrest for a minor criminal offense, such as a misdemeanor seatbelt violation punishable only by a fine. We hold that it does not.

I

A

In Texas, if a car is equipped with safety belts, a front-seat passenger must wear one, and the driver must secure any small child riding in front. Violation of either provision is "a misdemeanor punishable by a fine not less than $25 or more than $50." Texas law expressly authorizes "[a]ny peace officer [to] arrest without warrant a person found committing a violation" of these seatbelt laws, although it permits police to issue citations in lieu of arrest.

In March 1997, petitioner Gail Atwater was driving her pickup truck in Lago Vista, Texas, with her 3-year-old son and 5-year-old daughter in the front seat. None of them was wearing a seatbelt. Respondent Bart Turek, a Lago Vista police officer at the time, observed the seatbelt violations and pulled Atwater over. According to Atwater's complaint (the allegations of which we assume to be true for present purposes), Turek approached the truck and "yell[ed]" something to the effect of "[w]e've met before" and "[y]ou're going to jail." He then called for backup and asked to see Atwater's driver's license and insurance documentation, which state law required her to carry. When Atwater told Turek that she did not have the papers because her purse had been stolen the day before, Turek said that he had "heard that story two-hundred times."

Atwater asked to take her "frightened, upset, and crying" children to a friend's house nearby, but Turek told her, "[y]ou're not going anywhere." As it turned out, Atwater's friend learned what was going on and soon arrived to take charge of the children. Turek then handcuffed Atwater, placed her in his squad car, and drove her to the local police station, where booking officers had her remove her shoes, jewelry, and eyeglasses, and empty her pockets. Officers took Atwater's "mug shot" and placed her, alone, in a jail cell for about one hour, after which she was taken before a magistrate and released on $310 bond.

Atwater was charged with driving without her seatbelt fastened, failing to secure her children in seatbelts, driving without a license, and failing to provide proof of insurance. She ultimately pleaded no contest to the misdemeanor seatbelt offenses and paid a $50 fine; the other charges were dismissed.

B

Atwater and her husband, petitioner Michael Haas, filed suit in a Texas state court under 42 U.S.C. § 1983 against Turek and respondents City of Lago Vista and Chief of Police Frank Miller. So far as concerns us, petitioners (whom we will simply call Atwater) alleged that respondents (for simplicity, the City) had violated Atwater's Fourth Amendment "right to be free from unreasonable seizure," and sought compensatory and punitive damages.

• • •

We granted certiorari to consider whether the Fourth Amendment, either by incorporating common-law restrictions on misdemeanor arrests or otherwise, limits police officers' authority to arrest without warrant for minor criminal offenses. We now affirm.

• • •

III

While it is true here that history, if not unequivocal, has expressed a decided, majority view that the police need not obtain an arrest warrant merely because a misdemeanor stopped short of violence or a threat of it, Atwater does not wager all on history. Instead, she asks us to mint a new rule of constitutional law on the understanding that when historical practice fails to speak conclusively to a claim grounded on the Fourth Amendment, courts are left to strike a current balance between individual and societal interests by subjecting particular contemporary circumstances to traditional standards of reasonableness. Atwater accordingly argues for a modern arrest rule, one not necessarily requiring violent breach of the peace, but nonetheless forbidding custodial arrest, even upon probable cause, when conviction could not ultimately carry any jail time and when the government shows no compelling need for immediate detention.

If we were to derive a rule exclusively to address the uncontested facts of this case, Atwater might well prevail. She was a known and established resident of Lago Vista with no place to hide and no incentive to flee, and common sense says she would almost certainly have buckled up as a condition of driving off with a citation. In her case, the physical incidents of arrest were merely gratuitous humiliations imposed by a police officer who was (at best) exercising extremely poor judgment. Atwater's claim to live free of pointless indignity and confinement clearly outweighs anything the City can raise against it specific to her case.

But we have traditionally recognized that a responsible Fourth Amendment balance is not well served by standards requiring sensitive, case-by-case determinations of government need, lest every discretionary judgment in the field be converted into an occasion for constitutional review. Often enough, the Fourth Amendment has to be applied on the spur (and in the heat) of the moment, and the object in implementing its command of reasonableness is to draw standards sufficiently clear and simple to be applied with a fair prospect of surviving judicial second-guessing months and years after an arrest or search is made. Courts attempting to strike a reasonable Fourth Amendment balance thus credit the government's side with an essential interest in readily administrable rules.

At first glance, Atwater's argument may seem to respect the values of clarity and simplicity, so far as she claims that the Fourth Amendment generally forbids warrantless arrests for minor crimes not accompanied by violence or some demonstrable threat of it (whether "minor crime" be defined as a fine-only traffic offense, a fine-only offense more generally, or a misdemeanor.) But the claim is not ultimately so simple, nor could it be, for complications arise the moment we begin to think about the possible applications of the several criteria Atwater proposes for drawing a line between minor crimes with limited arrest authority and others not so restricted.

One line, she suggests, might be between "jailable" and "fine-only" offenses, between those for which conviction could result in commitment and those for which it could not. The trouble with this distinction, of course, is that an officer on the street might not be able to tell. It is not merely that we cannot expect every police officer to know the details of frequently complex penalty schemes, but that penalties for ostensibly identical conduct can vary on account of facts difficult (if not impossible) to know at the scene of an arrest. Is this the first offense or is the suspect a repeat offender? Is the weight of the marijuana a gram above or a gram below the fine-only line? Where conduct could implicate more than one criminal prohibition, which one will the district attorney ultimately decide to charge? And so on.

But Atwater's refinements would not end there. She represents that if the line were drawn at nonjailable traffic offenses, her proposed limitation should be qualified by a proviso authorizing warrantless arrests where "necessary for enforcement of the traffic laws or when [an] offense would otherwise continue and pose a danger to others on the road." The proviso only compounds the difficulties. Would, for instance, either exception apply to speeding? At oral argument, Atwater's counsel said that "it would not be reasonable to arrest a driver for speeding unless the speeding rose to the level of reckless driving." But is it not fair to expect that the chronic speeder will speed again despite a citation in his pocket, and should that not qualify as showing that the "offense would . . . continue" under Atwater's rule? And why, as a constitutional matter, should we assume that only reckless driving will "pose a danger to others on the road" while speeding will not?

There is no need for more examples to show that Atwater's general rule and limiting proviso promise very little in the way of administrability. It is no answer that the police routinely make judgments on grounds like risk of immediate repetition; they surely do and should. But there is a world of difference between making that judgment in choosing between the discretionary leniency of a summons in place of a clearly lawful arrest, and making the same judgment when the question is the lawfulness of the warrantless arrest itself. It is the difference between no basis for legal action challenging the discretionary judgment, on the one hand, and the prospect of evidentiary exclusion or (as here) personal § 1983 liability for the misapplication of a constitutional standard, on the other. Atwater's rule therefore would not only place police in an almost impossible spot but would guarantee increased litigation over many of the arrests that would occur. For all these reasons, Atwater's various distinctions between permissible and impermissible arrests for minor crimes strike us as "very unsatisfactory line[s]" to require police officers to draw on a moment's notice.

One may ask, of course, why these difficulties may not be answered by a simple tie breaker for the police to follow in the field: if in doubt, do not arrest. The first answer is that in practice the tie breaker would boil down to something akin to a least-restrictive-alternative limitation, which is itself one of those "ifs, ands, and buts" rules, generally thought inappropriate in working out Fourth Amendment protection. Beyond that, whatever help the tie breaker might give would come at the price of a systematic disincentive to arrest in situations where even Atwater concedes that arresting would serve an important societal interest. An officer not quite sure that the drugs weighed enough to warrant jail time or not quite certain about a suspect's risk of flight would not arrest, even though it could perfectly well turn out that, in fact, the offense called for incarceration and the defendant was long gone on the day of trial. Multiplied many times over, the costs to society of such underenforcement could easily outweigh the costs to defendants of being needlessly arrested and booked, as Atwater herself acknowledges.

Just how easily the costs could outweigh the benefits may be shown by asking, as one Member of this Court did at oral argument, "how bad the problem is out there." The very fact that the law has never jelled the way Atwater would have it leads one to wonder whether warrantless misdemeanor arrests need constitutional attention, and there is cause to think the answer is no. So far as such arrests might be thought to pose a threat to the probable-cause requirement, anyone arrested for a crime without formal process, whether for felony or misdemeanor, is entitled to a magistrate's review of probable cause within 48 hours, and there is no reason to think the procedure in this case atypical in giving the suspect a prompt opportunity to request release. Many jurisdictions, moreover, have chosen to impose more restrictive safeguards through statutes limiting warrantless arrests for minor offenses. It is of course easier to devise a minor-offense limitation by statute than to derive one through the Constitution, simply because the statute can let the arrest power turn on any sort of practical consideration without having to subsume it under a broader principle. It is, in fact, only natural that States should resort to this sort of legislative regulation, for, as Atwater's own amici emphasize, it is in the interest of the police to limit petty-offense arrests, which carry costs that are simply too great to incur without good reason. Finally, and significantly, under current doctrine the preference for categorical treatment of Fourth Amendment claims gives way to individualized review when a defendant makes a colorable argument that an arrest, with or without a warrant, was "conducted in an extraordinary manner, unusually harmful to [his] privacy or even physical interests."

The upshot of all these influences, combined with the good sense (and, failing that, the political accountability) of most local lawmakers and law-enforcement officials, is a dearth of horribles demanding redress. Indeed, when Atwater's counsel was asked at oral argument for any indications of comparably foolish, warrantless misdemeanor arrests, he could offer only one. We are sure that there are others, but just as surely the country is not confronting anything like an epidemic of unnecessary minor-offense arrests. That fact caps the reasons for rejecting Atwater's request for the development of a new and distinct body of constitutional law.

Accordingly, we confirm today what our prior cases have intimated: the standard of probable cause "applie[s] to all arrests, without the need to 'balance' the interests and circumstances involved in particular situations." If an officer has probable cause to believe that an individual has committed even a very minor criminal offense in his presence, he may, without violating the Fourth Amendment, arrest the offender.

IV

Atwater's arrest satisfied constitutional requirements. There is no dispute that Officer Turek had probable cause to believe that Atwater had committed a crime in his presence. She admits that neither she nor her children were wearing seatbelts, as required by Tex. Transp. Code Ann. § 545.413 (1999). Turek was accordingly authorized (not required, but authorized) to make a custodial arrest without balancing costs and benefits or determining whether or not Atwater's arrest was in some sense necessary.

Nor was the arrest made in an "extraordinary manner, unusually harmful to [her] privacy or . . . physical interests." Atwater's arrest was surely "humiliating," as she says in her brief, but it was no more "harmful to . . . privacy or . . . physical interests" than the normal custodial arrest. She was handcuffed, placed in a squad car, and taken to the local police station, where officers asked her to remove her shoes, jewelry, and glasses, and to empty her pockets. They then took her photograph and placed her in a cell, alone, for about an hour, after which she was taken before a magistrate, and released on $310 bond. The arrest and booking were inconvenient and embarrassing to Atwater, but not so extraordinary as to violate the Fourth Amendment.

• • •

Justice O'CONNOR, with whom Justice STEVENS, Justice GINSBURG, and Justice BREYER join, dissenting.

The Fourth Amendment guarantees the right to be free from "unreasonable searches and seizures." The Court recognizes that the arrest of Gail Atwater was a "pointless indignity" that

C. The Warrant Requirement and Its Exceptions

served no discernible state interest, ante, and yet holds that her arrest was constitutionally permissible. Because the Court's position is inconsistent with the explicit guarantee of the Fourth Amendment, I dissent.

I

A full custodial arrest, such as the one to which Ms. Atwater was subjected, is the quintessential seizure. When a full custodial arrest is effected without a warrant, the plain language of the Fourth Amendment requires that the arrest be reasonable. It is beyond cavil that "[t]he touchstone of our analysis under the Fourth Amendment is always 'the reasonableness in all the circumstances of the particular governmental invasion of a citizen's personal security.'"

We have "often looked to the common law in evaluating the reasonableness, for Fourth Amendment purposes, of police activity." But history is just one of the tools we use in conducting the reasonableness inquiry. And when history is inconclusive, as the majority amply demonstrates it is in this case, see ante, we will "evaluate the search or seizure under traditional standards of reasonableness by assessing, on the one hand, the degree to which it intrudes upon an individual's privacy and, on the other, the degree to which it is needed for the promotion of legitimate governmental interests."

The majority gives a brief nod to this bedrock principle of our Fourth Amendment jurisprudence, and even acknowledges that "Atwater's claim to live free of pointless indignity and confinement clearly outweighs anything the City can raise against it specific to her case." But instead of remedying this imbalance, the majority allows itself to be swayed by the worry that "every discretionary judgment in the field [will] be converted into an occasion for constitutional review." It therefore mints a new rule that "[i]f an officer has probable cause to believe that an individual has committed even a very minor criminal offense in his presence, he may, without violating the Fourth Amendment, arrest the offender." This rule is not only unsupported by our precedent, but runs contrary to the principles that lie at the core of the Fourth Amendment.

As the majority tacitly acknowledges, we have never considered the precise question presented here, namely, the constitutionality of a warrantless arrest for an offense punishable only by fine. Indeed, on the rare occasions that Members of this Court have contemplated such an arrest, they have indicated disapproval.

To be sure, we have held that the existence of probable cause is a necessary condition for an arrest. And in the case of felonies punishable by a term of imprisonment, we have held that the existence of probable cause is also a sufficient condition for an arrest. In *Watson*, however, there was a clear and consistently applied common law rule permitting warrantless felony arrests. Accordingly, our inquiry ended there and we had no need to assess the reasonableness of such arrests by weighing individual liberty interests against state interests.

Here, however, we have no such luxury. The Court's thorough exegesis makes it abundantly clear that warrantless misdemeanor arrests were not the subject of a clear and consistently applied rule at common law. We therefore must engage in the balancing test required by the Fourth Amendment. While probable cause is surely a necessary condition for warrantless arrests for fine-only offenses, any realistic assessment of the interests implicated by such arrests demonstrates that probable cause alone is not a sufficient condition.

Our decision in *Whren v. United States* (1996), is not to the contrary. The specific question presented there was whether, in evaluating the Fourth Amendment reasonableness of a traffic stop, the subjective intent of the police officer is a relevant consideration. We held that it is not, and stated that "[t]he making of a traffic stop . . . is governed by the usual rule that probable cause to believe the law has been broken 'outbalances' private interest in avoiding police contact."

We of course did not have occasion in *Whren* to consider the constitutional preconditions for warrantless arrests for fine-only offenses. Nor should our words be taken beyond their context. There are significant qualitative differences between a traffic stop and a full custodial arrest. While both are seizures that fall within the ambit of the Fourth Amendment, the latter entails a much greater intrusion on an individual's liberty and privacy interests. As we have said, "[a] motorist's expectations, when he sees a policeman's light flashing behind him, are that he will be obliged to spend a short period of time answering questions and waiting while the officer checks his license and registration, that he may be given a citation, but that in the end he most likely will be allowed to continue on his way." Thus, when there is probable cause to believe that a person has violated a minor traffic law, there can be little question that the state interest in law enforcement will justify the relatively limited intrusion of a traffic stop. It is by no means certain, however, that where the offense is punishable only by fine, "probable cause to believe the law has been broken [will] 'outbalanc[e]' private interest in avoiding" a full custodial arrest. Justifying a full arrest by the same quantum of evidence that justifies a traffic stop — even though the offender cannot ultimately be imprisoned for her conduct — defies any sense of proportionality and is in serious tension with the Fourth Amendment's proscription of unreasonable seizures.

A custodial arrest exacts an obvious toll on an individual's liberty and privacy, even when the period of custody is relatively brief. The arrestee is subject to a full search of her person and confiscation of her possessions. If the arrestee is the occupant of a car, the entire passenger compartment of the car, including packages therein, is subject to search as well. The arrestee may be detained for up to 48 hours without having a magistrate determine whether there in fact was probable cause for the arrest. Because people arrested for all types of violent and nonviolent offenses may be housed together awaiting such review, this detention period is potentially dangerous. And once the period of custody is over, the fact of the arrest is a permanent part of the public record.

We have said that "the penalty that may attach to any particular offense seems to provide the clearest and most consistent indication of the State's interest in arresting individuals suspected of committing that offense." If the State has decided that a fine, and not imprisonment, is the appropriate punishment for an offense, the State's interest in taking a person suspected of committing that offense into custody is surely limited, at best. This is not to say that the State will never have such an interest. A full custodial arrest may on occasion vindicate legitimate state interests, even if the crime is punishable only by fine. Arrest is the surest way to abate criminal conduct. It may also allow the police to verify the offender's identity and, if the offender poses a flight risk, to ensure her appearance at trial. But when such considerations are not present, a citation or summons may serve the State's remaining law enforcement interests every bit as effectively as an arrest.

Because a full custodial arrest is such a severe intrusion on an individual's liberty, its reasonableness hinges on "the degree to which it is needed for the promotion of legitimate governmental interests." In light of the availability of citations to promote a State's interests when a fine-only offense has been committed, I cannot concur in a rule which deems a full custodial arrest to be reasonable in every circumstance. Giving police officers constitutional carte blanche to effect an arrest whenever there is probable cause to believe a fine-only misdemeanor has been committed is irreconcilable with the Fourth Amendment's command that seizures be reasonable. Instead, I would require that when there is probable cause to believe that a fine-only offense has been committed, the police officer should issue a citation unless the officer is "able to point to specific and articulable facts which, taken together with rational inferences from those facts, reasonably warrant [the additional] intrusion" of a full custodial arrest.

The majority insists that a bright-line rule focused on probable cause is necessary to vindicate the State's interest in easily administrable law enforcement rules. Probable cause itself, however, is not a model of precision. "The quantum of information which constitutes probable cause—evidence which would 'warrant a man of reasonable caution in the belief' that a [crime] has been committed—must be measured by the facts of the particular case." The rule I propose—which merely requires a legitimate reason for the decision to escalate the seizure into a full custodial arrest—thus does not undermine an otherwise "clear and simple" rule.

While clarity is certainly a value worthy of consideration in our Fourth Amendment jurisprudence, it by no means trumps the values of liberty and privacy at the heart of the Amendment's protections. What the *Terry* rule lacks in precision it makes up for in fidelity to the Fourth Amendment's command of reasonableness and sensitivity to the competing values protected by that Amendment. Over the past 30 years, it appears that the *Terry* rule has been workable and easily applied by officers on the street.

At bottom, the majority offers two related reasons why a bright-line rule is necessary: the fear that officers who arrest for fine-only offenses will be subject to "personal [42 U.S.C.] § 1983 liability for the misapplication of a constitutional standard," and the resulting "systematic disincentive to arrest . . . where . . . arresting would serve an important societal interest." These concerns are certainly valid, but they are more than adequately resolved by the doctrine of qualified immunity.

Qualified immunity was created to shield government officials from civil liability for the performance of discretionary functions so long as their conduct does not violate clearly established statutory or constitutional rights of which a reasonable person would have known. This doctrine is "the best attainable accommodation of competing values," namely, the obligation to enforce constitutional guarantees and the need to protect officials who are required to exercise their discretion.

In *Anderson v. Creighton* (1987), we made clear that the standard of reasonableness for a search or seizure under the Fourth Amendment is distinct from the standard of reasonableness for qualified immunity purposes. If a law enforcement officer "reasonably but mistakenly conclude[s]" that the constitutional predicate for a search or seizure is present, he "should not be held personally liable."

This doctrine thus allays any concerns about liability or disincentives to arrest. If, for example, an officer reasonably thinks that a suspect poses a flight risk or might be a danger to the community if released, he may arrest without fear of the legal consequences. Similarly, if an officer reasonably concludes that a suspect may possess more than four ounces of marijuana and thus might be guilty of a felony, the officer will be insulated from liability for arresting the suspect even if the initial assessment turns out to be factually incorrect. As we have said, "officials will not be liable for mere mistakes in judgment." Of course, even the specter of liability can entail substantial social costs, such as inhibiting public officials in the discharge of their duties. We may not ignore the central command of the Fourth Amendment, however, to avoid these costs.

II

The record in this case makes it abundantly clear that Ms. Atwater's arrest was constitutionally unreasonable. Atwater readily admits—as she did when Officer Turek pulled her over—that she violated Texas' seatbelt law. While Turek was justified in stopping Atwater, neither law nor reason supports his decision to arrest her instead of simply giving her a citation. The officer's actions cannot sensibly be viewed as a permissible means of balancing Atwater's Fourth Amendment interests with the State's own legitimate interests.

There is no question that Officer Turek's actions severely infringed Atwater's liberty and privacy. Turek was loud and accusatory from the moment he approached Atwater's car. Atwater's young children were terrified and hysterical. Yet when Atwater asked Turek to lower his voice because he was scaring the children, he responded by jabbing his finger in Atwater's face and saying, "You're going to jail." Having made the decision to arrest, Turek did not inform Atwater of her right to remain silent. He instead asked for her license and insurance information.

Atwater asked if she could at least take her children to a friend's house down the street before going to the police station. But Turek—who had just castigated Atwater for not caring for her children—refused and said he would take the children into custody as well. Only the intervention of neighborhood children who had witnessed the scene and summoned one of Atwater's friends saved the children from being hauled to jail with their mother.

With the children gone, Officer Turek handcuffed Ms. Atwater with her hands behind her back, placed her in the police car, and drove her to the police station. Ironically, Turek did not secure Atwater in a seatbelt for the drive. At the station, Atwater was forced to remove her shoes, relinquish her possessions, and wait in a holding cell for about an hour. A judge finally informed Atwater of her rights and the charges against her, and released her when she posted bond. Atwater returned to the scene of the arrest, only to find that her car had been towed.

Ms. Atwater ultimately pleaded no contest to violating the seatbelt law and was fined $50. Even though that fine was the maximum penalty for her crime, and even though Officer Turek has never articulated any justification for his actions, the city contends that arresting Atwater was constitutionally reasonable because it advanced two legitimate interests: "the enforcement of child safety laws and encouraging [Atwater] to appear for trial."

It is difficult to see how arresting Atwater served either of these goals any more effectively than the issuance of a citation. With respect to the goal of law enforcement generally, Atwater did not pose a great danger to the community. She had been driving very slowly—approximately 15 miles per hour—in broad daylight on a residential street that had no other traffic. Record 380. Nor was she a repeat offender; until that day, she had received one traffic citation in her life—a ticket, more than 10 years earlier, for failure to signal a lane change. Although Officer Turek had stopped Atwater approximately three months earlier because he thought that Atwater's son was not wearing a seatbelt, Turek had been mistaken. Moreover, Atwater immediately accepted responsibility and apologized for her conduct. Thus, there was every indication that Atwater would have buckled herself and her children in had she been cited and allowed to leave.

With respect to the related goal of child welfare, the decision to arrest Atwater was nothing short of counterproductive. Atwater's children witnessed Officer Turek yell at their mother and threaten to take them all into custody. Ultimately, they were forced to leave her behind with Turek, knowing that she was being taken to jail. Understandably, the 3-year-old boy was "very, very, very traumatized." After the incident, he had to see a child psychologist regularly, who reported that the boy "felt very guilty that he couldn't stop this horrible thing . . . he was powerless to help his mother or sister." Both of Atwater's children are now terrified at the sight of any police car. According to Atwater, the arrest "just never leaves us. It's a conversation we have every other day, once a week, and it's—it raises its head constantly in our lives."

Citing Atwater surely would have served the children's interests well. It would have taught Atwater to ensure that her children were buckled up in the future. It also would have taught the children an important lesson in accepting responsibility and obeying the law. Arresting Atwater, though, taught the children an entirely different lesson: that "the bad person could just as easily be the policeman as it could be the most horrible person they could imagine."

Respondents also contend that the arrest was necessary to ensure Atwater's appearance in court. Atwater, however, was far from a flight risk. A 16-year resident of Lago Vista, population 2,486, Atwater was not likely to abscond. Although she was unable to produce her driver's license because it had been stolen, she gave Officer Turek her license number and address. In addition, Officer Turek knew from their previous encounter that Atwater was a local resident.

The city's justifications fall far short of rationalizing the extraordinary intrusion on Gail Atwater and her children. Measuring "the degree to which [Atwater's custodial arrest was] needed for the promotion of legitimate governmental interests," against "the degree to which it intrud[ed] upon [her] privacy," it can hardly be doubted that Turek's actions were disproportionate to Atwater's crime. The majority's assessment that "Atwater's claim to live free of pointless indignity and confinement clearly outweighs anything the City can raise against it specific to her case," is quite correct. In my view, the Fourth Amendment inquiry ends there.

III

The Court's error, however, does not merely affect the disposition of this case. The per se rule that the Court creates has potentially serious consequences for the everyday lives of Americans. A broad range of conduct falls into the category of fine-only misdemeanors. In Texas alone, for example, disobeying any sort of traffic warning sign is a misdemeanor punishable only by fine, as is failing to pay a highway toll, and driving with expired license plates. Nor are fine-only crimes limited to the traffic context. In several States, for example, littering is a criminal offense punishable only by fine.

To be sure, such laws are valid and wise exercises of the States' power to protect the public health and welfare. My concern lies not with the decision to enact or enforce these laws, but rather with the manner in which they may be enforced. Under today's holding, when a police officer has probable cause to believe that a fine-only misdemeanor offense has occurred, that officer may stop the suspect, issue a citation, and let the person continue on her way. Or, if a traffic violation, the officer may stop the car, arrest the driver, see ante, at 1557, search the driver, search the entire passenger compartment of the car including any purse or package inside, and impound the car and inventory all of its contents. Although the Fourth Amendment expressly requires that the latter course be a reasonable and proportional response to the circumstances of the offense, the majority gives officers unfettered discretion to choose that course without articulating a single reason why such action is appropriate.

Such unbounded discretion carries with it grave potential for abuse. The majority takes comfort in the lack of evidence of "an epidemic of unnecessary minor-offense arrests." But the relatively small number of published cases dealing with such arrests proves little and should provide little solace. Indeed, as the recent debate over racial profiling demonstrates all too clearly, a relatively minor traffic infraction may often serve as an excuse for stopping and harassing an individual. After today, the arsenal available to any officer extends to a full arrest and the searches permissible concomitant to that arrest. An officer's subjective motivations for making a traffic stop are not relevant considerations in determining the reasonableness of the stop. But it is precisely because these motivations are beyond our purview that we must vigilantly ensure that officers' poststop actions—which are properly within our reach—comport with the Fourth Amendment's guarantee of reasonableness.

The Court neglects the Fourth Amendment's express command in the name of administrative ease. In so doing, it cloaks the pointless indignity that Gail Atwater suffered with the mantle of reasonableness. I respectfully dissent.

NOTES AND QUESTIONS

1. The upshot of the exhaustive Part II of the Court's opinion (not included here) is that unlike the common law rule with respect to felonies, there is no historical consensus on whether warrants were required for arrests for minor criminal offenses. Accordingly, as the

Gail Atwater

dissent notes, this typically leads to a balancing test: a weighing of the severity of the intrusion against the needs of law enforcement.

The Court does not conduct the usual balancing test it would do in such cases. As a matter of the devil's advocacy, what is the best argument to be made for the government under a balancing test?

2. Instead of engaging in balancing analysis, the Court criticizes possible versions of any "rule" that would result from a decision in Atwater's favor, noting the complexity of traffic codes and the difficulties of "administrability" of any rule. None of this, of course, is Atwater's fault. At some level, shouldn't the state of Texas—and its law enforcement agents—have to pay some price for a motor vehicle code that criminalizes a first-offense failure to wear a seatbelt?

Further, how can police officers, who feast on traffic code violations for pretextual vehicle stops, *see infra*, and thus as gateways to more serious criminal matters, be heard to complain about the complexity of the state's regulation of motor vehicles? Shouldn't they be required to take the bitter with the sweet?

3. The dissent unflinchingly catalogues the seriousness of the intrusion on personal liberty that an arrest entails. It also notes the potential for racial bias to affect the exercise of the enormous discretion *Atwater* affords to police officers. It would have been nice if the metes and bounds of a search incident to an arrest had first arisen in a case like Gail Atwater's, and not drug cases in the 1970s and 1980s. *See infra*.

4. The dissent notes that "the rule" of *Atwater* has pernicious effects on a larger societal scale given the lack of any constitutional limits on the ability of state and federal government to criminalize conduct. Does *Whren* necessarily mean, as the dissent suggests, that the subjective motivation of a police officer's decision to arrest someone on a misdemeanor charge is irrelevant? *See* Part V *infra*.

5. Two years before *Atwater*, in *Knowles v. Iowa*, 525 U.S. 113 (1998), the Court had rejected the concept of a "search-incident-to-citation," holding that only custodial arrests justified incidental searches. Does Atwater incentivize police officers to do pretextual traffic-violation custodial arrests of persons they suspect of more serious wrongdoing in order to conduct searches of their person and inventory searches of their vehicle? Note that they may be able to execute such a plan regardless of whether state law permits a warrantless arrest for the violation chosen by the officer. *See Virginia v. Moore*, 553 U.S. 164 (2008) (search incident to arrest that was supported by probable cause, though unlawful under Virginia law, does not violate Fourth Amendment).

It should not surprise that *Atwater* has been harshly criticized. *See* Richard S. Fraser, *What Were They Thinking: Fourth Amendment Unreasonableness in* Atwater v. City of Lago Vista, 71 Fordham L. Rev. 329, 331 n.4 (2002) (citing criticism); *id*. at 407-15 (proposing a reasonable and workable arrest limitation rule that could easily have been adopted by the Court in *Atwater*: "arrest for a fine-only traffic violation should only be permitted if the officer has a reasonable, articulable basis to believe that custodial arrest is needed to verify identity, ensure payment of the fine, prevent imminent bodily harm, or prevent immediate repetition of the violation"); Thomas Y. Davies, *The Fictional Character of Law-and-Order Originalism: A Case Study of the Distortions and Evasions of Framing-Era Arrest Doctrine in* Atwater v. Lago Vista, 37 Wake Forest L. Rev. 239, 246 (2002) (contrary to the Court's conclusion, "[t]he historical

C. The Warrant Requirement and Its Exceptions 329

authorities regarding arrest authority actually show that warrantless misdemeanor arrests for minor offenses were usually unlawful, except in some categories of minor offenses that gave rise to an unusual need for a prompt arrest—the position advocated by Gail Atwater's counsel and endorsed by the four dissenting justices in *Atwater*").

Stepping back from it all, Professor Rachel Harmon asks "Why Arrest"? Rachel Harmon, *Why Arrest?*, 115 Mich. L. Rev. 307 (2016). Professor Harmon points out that the Fourth Amendment does not generally regulate arrests other than by the warrant (sometimes) and probable cause requirements, which overlooks the substantial costs of arrests to society (potentially violent confrontations with police; collateral consequences to arrestees, e.g., loss of income/job). *Id.*at 313-15. For many misdemeanors and other nonviolent offenses, she argues, arrests are unnecessary and the costs of proceeding by way of summonses to appear (a marginally increased incidence of failures to appear) are significantly lower than the costs of arrests. *Id.* at 334-36.

4. Search Incident to Arrest

The search-incident-to-arrest exception to the warrant requirement was first recognized by the Court in dictum in *Weeks v. United States*, 232 U.S. 383, 392 (1914), a case better known for mandating the exclusionary rule in federal prosecutions. The modern scope of the search-incident-to-arrest exception came into shape in *Chimel v. California*, 395 U.S. 752 (1969).

Chimel v. California
395 U.S. 752 (1969)

Mr. Justice STEWART delivered the opinion of the Court.

This case raises basic questions concerning the permissible scope under the Fourth Amendment of a search incident to a lawful arrest.

The relevant facts are essentially undisputed. Late in the afternoon of September 13, 1965, three police officers arrived at the Santa Ana, California, home of the petitioner with a warrant authorizing his arrest for the burglary of a coin shop. The officers knocked on the door, identified themselves to the petitioner's wife, and asked if they might come inside. She ushered them into the house, where they waited 10 or 15 minutes until the petitioner returned home from work. When the petitioner entered the house, one of the officers handed him the arrest warrant and asked for permission to "look around." The petitioner objected, but was advised that "on the basis of the lawful arrest," the officers would nonetheless conduct a search. No search warrant had been issued.

Accompanied by the petitioner's wife, the officers then looked through the entire three-bedroom house, including the attic, the garage, and a small workshop. In some rooms the search was relatively cursory. In the master bedroom and sewing room, however, the officers directed the petitioner's wife to open drawers and "to physically move contents of the drawers from side to side so that (they) might view any items that would have come from (the) burglary." After completing the search, they seized numerous items—primarily coins, but also several medals, tokens, and a few other objects. The entire search took between 45 minutes and an hour.

At the petitioner's subsequent state trial on two charges of burglary, the items taken from his house were admitted into evidence against him, over his objection that they had been unconstitutionally seized. He was convicted, and the judgments of conviction were affirmed by both the California Court of Appeal, and the California Supreme Court. Both courts accepted the petitioner's contention that the arrest warrant was invalid because the supporting affidavit was set out in conclusory terms, but held that since the arresting officers had procured the warrant "in good faith," and since in any event they had had sufficient information to constitute probable cause for the petitioner's arrest, that arrest had been lawful. From this conclusion the appellate courts went on to hold that the search of the petitioner's home had been justified, despite the absence of a search warrant, on the ground that it had been incident to a valid arrest. We granted certiorari in order to consider the petitioner's substantial constitutional claims.

Without deciding the question, we proceed on the hypothesis that the California courts were correct in holding that the arrest of the petitioner was valid under the Constitution. This brings us directly to the question whether the warrantless search of the petitioner's entire house can be constitutionally justified as incident to that arrest. The decisions of this Court bearing upon that question have been far from consistent, as even the most cursory review makes evident.

Approval of a warrantless search incident to a lawful arrest seems first to have been articulated by the Court in 1914 as dictum in *Weeks v. United States*, in which the Court stated:

> What then is the present case? Before answering that inquiry specifically, it may be well by a process of exclusion to state what it is not. It is not an assertion of the right on the part of the Government, always recognized under English and American law, to search the person of the accused when legally arrested to discover and seize the fruits or evidences of crime.

That statement made no reference to any right to search the place where an arrest occurs, but was limited to a right to search the "person." Eleven years later the case of *Carroll v. United States*, brought the following embellishment of the Weeks statement:

> When a man is legally arrested for an offense, whatever is found upon his person or in his control which it is unlawful for him to have and which may be used to prove the offense may be seized and held as evidence in the prosecution.

* * *

Only last Term in *Terry v. Ohio*, we emphasized that "the police must, whenever practicable, obtain advance judicial approval of searches and seizures through the warrant procedure," and that "(t)he scope of (a) search must be 'strictly tied to and justified by' the circumstances which rendered its initiation permissible." The search undertaken by the officer in that "stop and frisk" case was sustained under that test, because it was no more than a "protective . . . search for weapons." But in a companion case, *Sibron v. New York*, we applied the same standard to another set of facts and reached a contrary result, holding that a policeman's action in thrusting his hand into a suspect's pocket had been neither motivated by nor limited to the objective of protection. Rather, the search had been made in order to find narcotics, which were in fact found.

A similar analysis underlies the "search incident to arrest" principle, and marks its proper extent. When an arrest is made, it is reasonable for the arresting officer to search the person arrested in order to remove any weapons that the latter might seek to use in order to resist arrest or effect his escape. Otherwise, the officer's safety might well be endangered, and the arrest itself frustrated. In addition, it is entirely reasonable for the arresting officer to search for and seize any evidence on the arrestee's person in order to prevent its concealment or destruction. And the area into which an arrestee might reach in order to grab a weapon or evidentiary items must, of course, be governed by a like rule. A gun on a table or in a drawer in front of one who is arrested can be as dangerous to the arresting officer as one concealed in the clothing of the person arrested. There is ample justification, therefore, for a search of the arrestee's person and the area "within his immediate control" — construing that phrase to mean the area from within which he might gain possession of a weapon or destructible evidence.

C. The Warrant Requirement and Its Exceptions 331

There is no comparable justification, however, for routinely searching any room other than that in which an arrest occurs—or, for that matter, for searching through all the desk drawers or other closed or concealed areas in that room itself. Such searches, in the absence of well-recognized exceptions, may be made only under the authority of a search warrant. The "adherence to judicial processes" mandated by the Fourth Amendment requires no less.

This is the principle that underlay our decision in *Preston v. United States*. In that case three men had been arrested in a parked car, which had later been towed to a garage and searched by police. We held that search to have been unlawful under the Fourth Amendment, despite the contention that it had been incidental to a valid arrest. Our reasoning was straightforward:

> The rule allowing contemporaneous searches is justified, for example, by the need to seize weapons and other things which might be used to assault an officer or effect an escape, as well as by the need to prevent the destruction of evidence of the crime—things which might easily happen where the weapon or evidence is on the accused's person or under his immediate control. But these justifications are absent where a search is remote in time or place from the arrest.

The same basic principle was reflected in our opinion last Term in *Sibron*. That opinion dealt with *Peters v. New York*, as well as with Sibron's case, and *Peters* involved a search that we upheld as incident to a proper arrest. We sustained the search, however, only because its scope had been "reasonably limited" by the "need to seize weapons" and "to prevent the destruction of evidence," to which *Preston* had referred. We emphasized that the arresting officer "did not engage in an unrestrained and thorough going examination of Peters and his personal effects. He seized him to cut short his flight, and he searched him primarily for weapons."

It is argued in the present case that it is "reasonable" to search a man's house when he is arrested in it. But that argument is founded on little more than a subjective view regarding the acceptability of certain sorts of police conduct, and not on consideration relevant to Fourth Amendment interests. Under such an unconfined analysis, Fourth Amendment protection in this area would approach the evaporation point. It is not easy to explain why, for instance, it is less subjectively "reasonable" to search a man's house when he is arrested on his front lawn—or just down the street—than it is when he happens to be in the house at the time of arrest. As Mr. Justice Frankfurter put it:

> To say that the search must be reasonable is to require some criterion of reason. It is no guide at all either for a jury or for district judges or the police to say that an "unreasonable search" is forbidden—that the search must be reasonable. What is the test of reason which makes a search reasonable? The test is the reason underlying and expressed by the Fourth Amendment: the history and experience which it embodies and the safeguards afforded by it against the evils to which it was a response.

Thus, although "(t)he recurring questions of the reasonableness of searches" depend upon "the facts and circumstances—the total atmosphere of the case," those facts and circumstances must be viewed in the light of established Fourth Amendment principles.

It would be possible, of course, to draw a line between *Rabinowitz* and *Harris* on the one hand, and this case on the other. For *Rabinowitz* involved a single room, and *Harris* a four-room apartment, while in the case before us an entire house was searched. But such a distinction would be highly artificial. The rationale that allowed the searches and seizures in *Rabinowitz* and *Harris* would allow the searches and seizures in this case. No consideration relevant to the Fourth Amendment suggests any point of rational limitation, once the search is allowed to go beyond the area from which the person arrested might obtain weapons or evidentiary items. The only reasoned distinction is one between a search of the person arrested and the area within his reach on the one hand, and more extensive searches on the other.

The petitioner correctly points out that one result of decisions such as *Rabinowitz* and *Harris* is to give law enforcement officials the opportunity to engage in searches not justified by probable cause, by the simple expedient of arranging to arrest suspects at home rather than elsewhere. We do not suggest that the petitioner is necessarily correct in his assertion that such a strategy was utilized here, but the fact remains that had he been arrested earlier in the day, at his place of employment rather than at home, no search of his house could have been made without a search warrant. In any event, even apart from the possibility of such police tactics, the general point so forcefully made by Judge Learned Hand in *United States v. Kirschenblatt*, remains:

> After arresting a man in his house, to rummage at will among his papers in search of whatever will convict him, appears to us to be indistinguishable from what might be done under a general warrant; indeed, the warrant would give more protection, for presumably it must be issued by a magistrate. True, by hypothesis the power would not exist, if the supposed offender were not found on the premises; but it is small consolation to know that one's papers are safe only so long as one is not at home.

Rabinowitz and *Harris* have been the subject of critical commentary for many years, and have been relied upon less and less in our own decisions. It is time, for the reasons we have stated, to hold that on their own facts, and insofar as the principles they stand for are inconsistent with those that we have endorsed today, they are no longer to be followed.

Application of sound Fourth Amendment principles to the facts of this case produces a clear result. The search here went far beyond the petitioner's person and the area from within which he might have obtained either a weapon or something that could have been used as evidence against him. There was no constitutional justification, in the absence of a search warrant, for extending the search beyond that area. The scope of the search was, therefore, "unreasonable" under the Fourth and Fourteenth Amendments and the petitioner's conviction cannot stand.

Reversed.

NOTES AND QUESTIONS

1. The Court accepts *Weeks*'s negative definition of the valid purpose of a search incident to arrest, namely, that it is not "to discover and seize the fruits or evidences of crime." Why this strange locution? And why should a search for "fruits or evidence" be an impermissible purpose of a search incident to arrest?

2. The Court ultimately holds—after a lengthy discussion of 50 years of inconsistent precedents on this subject that is omitted here—that the scope of a search incident to an arrest must be limited to a search of the person of the arrestee and the area subject to his immediate control, for the narrow purposes of removing weapons that could be used to effect an escape or evidence that might be concealed or destroyed. To what extent is the permissible scope issue a function of the presumption in favor of warrants? Is the scope issue also driven by the fear that agents could game the timing and place of arrests to get around the warrant requirement?

3. Did Chimel's wife impliedly consent to the search by showing the officers around the house and guiding them in their search? Did she have authority to consent even after Chimel refused to give them their permission? Does it matter in what form the Chimels owned or occupied the property?

4. How important was it to the result here that the search the Court found to exceed the proper scope was of Chimel's home? Suppose that instead he had been arrested at his place of business, in—let's say—a large private office in an office building, and that the officers had searched the entire office?

C. The Warrant Requirement and Its Exceptions

Just four years later the Court dramatically expanded the permissible scope of a search incident to arrest.

United States v. Robinson
414 U.S. 218 (1973)

Mr. Justice REHNQUIST delivered the opinion of the Court.

Respondent Robinson was convicted in United States District Court for the District of Columbia of the possession and facilitation of concealment of heroin in violation of 26 U.S.C. s 4704(a) (1964 ed.), and 21 U.S.C. s 174 (1964 ed.). He was sentenced to concurrent terms of imprisonment for these offenses. On his appeal to the Court of Appeals for the District of Columbia Circuit, that court first remanded the case to the District Court for an evidentiary hearing concerning the scope of the search of respondent's person which had occurred at the time of his arrest. The District Court made findings of fact and conclusions of law adverse to respondent, and he again appealed. This time the Court of Appeals en banc reversed the judgment of conviction, holding that the heroin introduced in evidence against respondent had been obtained as a result of a search which violated the Fourth Amendment to the United States Constitution. We granted certiorari.

On April 23, 1968, at approximately 11 p.m., Officer Richard Jenks, a 15-year veteran of the District of Columbia Metropolitan Police Department, observed the respondent driving a 1965 Cadillac near the intersection of 8th and C Streets, N.E., in the District of Columbia. Jenks, as a result of previous investigation following a check of respondent's operator's permit four days earlier, determined there was reason to believe that respondent was operating a motor vehicle after the revocation of his operator's permit. This is an offense defined by statute in the District of Columbia which carries a mandatory minimum jail term, a mandatory minimum fine, or both. D.C. Code Ann. s 40-302(d) (1967).

Jenks signaled respondent to stop the automobile, which respondent did, and all three of the occupants emerged from the car. At that point Jenks informed respondent that he was under arrest for "operating after revocation and obtaining a permit by misrepresentation." It was assumed by the Court of Appeals, and is conceded by the respondent here, that Jenks had probable cause to arrest respondent, and that he effected a full custody arrest.

In accordance with procedures prescribed in police department instructions, Jenks then began to search respondent. He explained at a subsequent hearing that he was "face-to-face" with the respondent, and "placed (his) hands on (the respondent), my right-hand to his left breast like this (demonstrating) and proceeded to pat him down thus (with the right hand)." During this patdown, Jenks felt an object in the left breast pocket of the heavy coat respondent was wearing, but testified that he "couldn't tell what it was" and also that he "couldn't actually tell the size of it." Jenks then reached into the pocket and pulled out the object, which turned out to be a "crumpled up cigarette package." Jenks testified that at this point he still did not know what was in the package:

> As I felt the package I could feel objects in the package but I couldn't tell what they were. . . . I knew they weren't cigarettes.

The officer then opened the cigarette pack and found 14 gelatin capsules of white powder which he thought to be, and which later analysis proved to be, heroin. Jenks then continued his search of respondent to completion, feeling around his waist and trouser legs, and examining the remaining pockets. The heroin seized from the respondent was admitted into evidence at the trial which resulted in his conviction in the District Court.

The opinion for the plurality judges of the Court of Appeals, written by Judge Wright, the concurring opinion of Chief Judge Bazelon, and the dissenting opinion of Judge Wilkey, concurred in by three judges, gave careful and comprehensive treatment to the authority of a police officer to search the person of one who has been validly arrested and taken into custody. We conclude that the search conducted by Jenks in this case did not offend the limits imposed by the Fourth Amendment, and we therefore reverse the judgment of the Court of Appeals.

I

It is well settled that a search incident to a lawful arrest is a traditional exception to the warrant requirement of the Fourth Amendment. This general exception has historically been formulated into two distinct propositions. The first is that a search may be made of the person of the arrestee by virtue of the lawful arrest. The second is that a search may be made of the area within the control of the arrestee.

Examination of this Court's decisions shows that these two propositions have been treated quite differently. The validity of the search of a person incident to a lawful arrest has been regarded as settled from its first enunciation, and has remained virtually unchallenged until the present case. The validity of the second proposition, while likewise conceded in principle, has been subject to differing interpretations as to the extent of the area which may be searched.

Because the rule requiring exclusion of evidence obtained in violation of the Fourth Amendment was first enunciated in *Weeks v. United States* (1914), it is understandable that virtually all of this Court's search-and-seizure law has been developed since that time. In *Weeks*, the Court made clear its recognition of the validity of a search incident to a lawful arrest:

> What then is the present case? Before answering that inquiry specifically, it may be well by a process of exclusion to state what it is not. It is not an assertion of the right on the part of the Government, always recognized under English and American law, to search the person of the accused when legally arrested to discover and seize the fruits or evidences of crime. This right has been uniformly maintained in many cases.

Agnello v. United States (1925), decided 11 years after *Weeks*, repeats the categorical recognition of the validity of a search incident to lawful arrest:

> The right without a search warrant contemporaneously to search persons lawfully arrested while committing crime and to search the place where the arrest is made in order to find and seize things connected with the crime as its fruits or as the means by which it was committed, as well as weapons and other things to effect an escape from custody, is not to be doubted.

Throughout the series of cases in which the Court has addressed the second proposition relating to a search incident to a lawful arrest — the permissible area beyond the person of the arrestee which such a search may cover — no doubt has been expressed as to the unqualified authority of the arresting authority to search the person of the arrestee. In *Chimel*, where the Court overruled *Rabinowitz* and *Harris* as to the area of permissible search incident to a lawful arrest, full recognition was again given to the authority to search the person of the arrestee:

> When an arrest is made, it is reasonable for the arresting officer to search the person arrested in order to remove any weapons that the latter might seek to use in order to resist arrest or effect his escape. Otherwise, the officer's safety might well be endangered, and the arrest itself frustrated. In addition, it is entirely reasonable for the arresting officer to search for and seize any evidence on the arrestee's person in order to prevent its concealment or destruction.

C. The Warrant Requirement and Its Exceptions

Three years after the decision in *Chimel, supra,* we upheld the validity of a search in which heroin had been taken from the person of the defendant after his arrest on a weapons charge, in *Adams v. Williams* (1972), saying:

> Under the circumstances surrounding Williams' possession of the gun seized by Sgt. Connolly, the arrest on the weapons charge was supported by probable cause, and the search of his person and of the car incident to that arrest was lawful.

Last Term, we again reaffirmed the traditional statement of the authority to search incident to a valid arrest.

Thus the broadly stated rule, and the reasons for it, have been repeatedly affirmed in the decisions of this Court since *Weeks v. United States,* supra, nearly 60 years ago. Since the statements in the cases speak not simply in terms of an exception to the warrant requirement, but in terms of an affirmative authority to search, they clearly imply that such searches also meet the Fourth Amendment's requirement of reasonableness.

II

In its decision of this case, the Court of Appeals decided that even after a police officer lawfully places a suspect under arrest for the purpose of taking him into custody, he may not ordinarily proceed to fully search the prisoner. He must, instead, conduct a limited frisk of the outer clothing and remove such weapons that he may, as a result of that limited frisk, reasonably believe and ascertain that the suspect has in his possession. While recognizing that *Terry v. Ohio* (1968), dealt with a permissible "frisk" incident to an investigative stop based on less than probable cause to arrest, the Court of Appeals felt that the principles of that case should be carried over to this probable-cause arrest for driving while one's license is revoked. Since there would be no further evidence of such a crime to be obtained in a search of the arrestee, the court held that only a search for weapons could be justified.

Terry v. Ohio, supra, did not involve an arrest for probable cause, and it made quite clear that the "protective frisk" for weapons which it approved might be conducted without probable cause. Id., at 21-22, 24-25, 88 S. Ct. at 1879-1880, 1881-1882. This Court's opinion explicitly recognized that there is a "distinction in purpose, character, and extent between a search incident to an arrest and a limited search for weapons."

> The former, although justified in part by the acknowledged necessity to protect the arresting officer from assault with a concealed weapon, *Preston v. United State* (1964), is also justified on other grounds, ibid., and can therefore involve a relatively extensive exploration of the person. A search for weapons in the absence of probable cause to arrest, however, must, like any other search, be strictly circumscribed by the exigencies which justify its initiation. *Warden v. Hayden* (1967) (Mr. Justice Fortas, concurring). Thus it must be limited to that which is necessary for the discovery of weapons which might be used to harm the officer or others nearby, and may realistically be characterized as something less than a "full" search, even though it remains a serious intrusion.
>
> . . . An arrest is a wholly different kind of intrusion upon individual freedom from a limited search for weapons, and the interests each is designed to serve are likewise quite different. An arrest is the initial stage of a criminal prosecution. It is intended to vindicate society's interest in having its laws obeyed, and it is inevitably accompanied by future interference with the individual's freedom of movement, whether or not trial or conviction ultimately follows. The protective search for weapons, on the other hand, constitutes brief, though far from inconsiderable, intrusion upon the sanctity of the person.

Terry, therefore, affords no basis to carry over to a probable-cause arrest the limitations this Court placed on a stop-and-frisk search permissible without probable cause.

The Court of Appeals also relied on language in *Peters v. New York* (1968), a companion case to *Terry*. There the Court held that the police officer had authority to search Peters because he had probable cause to arrest him, and went on to say:

> (T)he incident search was obviously justified "by the need to seize weapons and other things which might be used to assault an officer or effect an escape, as well as by the need to prevent the destruction of evidence of the crime." *Preston v. United States* (1964). Moreover, it was reasonably limited in scope by these purposes. Officer Lasky did not engage in an unrestrained and thorough-going examination of Peters and his personal effects.

It is, of course, possible to read the second sentence from this quotation as imposing a novel limitation on the established doctrine set forth in the first sentence. It is also possible to read it as did Mr. Justice Harlan in his opinion concurring in the result:

> The second possible source of confusion is the Court's statement that "Officer Lasky did not engage in an unrestrained and thorough-going examination of Peters and his personal effects." Since the Court found probable cause to arrest Peters, and since an officer arresting on probable cause is entitled to make a very full incident search, I assume that this is merely a factual observation. As a factual matter, I agree with it.

We do not believe that the Court in *Peters* intended in one unexplained and unelaborated sentence to impose a novel and far-reaching limitation on the authority to search the person of an arrestee incident to his lawful arrest. While the language from *Peters* was quoted with approval in *Chimel*, it is preceded by a full exposition of the traditional and unqualified authority of the arresting officer to search the arrestee's person. We do not believe that either *Terry* or *Peters*, when considered in the light of the previously discussed statements of this Court, justified the sort of limitation upon that authority which the Court of Appeals fashioned in this case.

III

Virtually all of the statements of this Court affirming the existence of an unqualified authority to search incident to a lawful arrest are dicta. We would not, therefore, be foreclosed by principles of stare decisis from further examination into history and practice in order to see whether the sort of qualifications imposed by the Court of Appeals in this case were in fact intended by the Framers of the Fourth Amendment or recognized in cases decided prior to *Weeks*. Unfortunately such authorities as exist are sparse. Such common-law treatises as Blackstone's Commentaries and Holmes' Common Law are simply silent on the subject. Pollock and Maitland, in their History of English Law, describe the law of arrest as "rough and rude" before the time of Edward I, but do not address the authority to search incident to arrest.

The issue was apparently litigated in the English courts in *Dillon v. O'Brien*, 16 Cox C.C. 245 (Exch. Ireland, 1887), cited in *Weeks v. United States*, supra, There Baron Palles said:

> But the interest of the State in the person charged being brought to trial in due course necessarily extends, as well to the preservation of material evidence of his guilt or innocence, as to his custody for the purpose of trial. His custody is of no value if the law is powerless to prevent the abstraction or destruction of this evidence, without which a trial would be no more than an empty form. But if there be a right to production or preservation of this evidence, I cannot see how it can be enforced otherwise than by capture.

Spalding v. Preston (1848), represents an early holding in this country that evidence may be seized from one who is lawfully arrested. in *Closson v. Morrison* (1867), the Court made the following statement:

> (W)e think that an officer would also be justified in taking from a person whom he had arrested for crime, any deadly weapon he might find upon him, such as a revolver, a dirk, a knife, a sword cane, a slung shot, or a club, though it had not been used or intended to be used in the

C. The Warrant Requirement and Its Exceptions

commission of the offence for which the prisoner had been arrested, and even though no threats of violence towards the officer had been made. A due regard for his own safety on the part of the officer, and also for the public safety, would justify a sufficient search to ascertain if such weapons were carried about the person of the prisoner, or were in his possession, and if found, to seize and hold them until the prisoner should be discharged, or until they could be otherwise properly disposed of.

So we think it might be with money or other articles of value, found upon the prisoner, by means of which, if left in his possession, he might procure his escape, or obtain tools, or implements, or weapons with which to effect his escape. We think the officer arresting a man for crime, not only may, but frequently should, make such searches and seizures; that in many cases they might be reasonable and proper, and courts would hold him harmless for so doing, when he acts in good faith, and from a regard to his own or the public safety, or the security of his prisoner.

Similarly, in *Holker v. Hennessey* (1897), the Supreme Court of Missouri said:

Generally speaking, in the absence of a statute, an officer has no right to take any property from the person of the prisoner except such as may afford evidence of the crime charged, or means of identifying the criminal, or may be helpful in making an escape.

Then Associate Judge Cardozo of the New York Court of Appeals summarized his understanding of the historical basis for the authority to search incident to arrest in these words:

The basic principle is this: Search of the person is unlawful when the seizure of the body is a trespass, and the purpose of the search is to discover grounds as yet unknown for arrest or accusation (citation omitted). Search of the person becomes lawful when grounds for arrest and accusation have been discovered, and the law is in the act of subjecting the body of the accused to its physical dominion.

The distinction may seem subtle, but in truth it is founded in shrewd appreciation of the necessities of government. We are not to strain an immunity to the point at which human nature rebels against honoring it in conduct. The peace officer empowered to arrest must be empowered to disarm. If he many disarm, he may search, lest a weapon be concealed. The search being lawful, he retains what he finds if connected with the crime.

People v. Chiagles (1923).

While these earlier authorities are sketchy, they tend to support the broad statement of the authority to search incident to arrest found in the successive decisions of this Court, rather than the restrictive one which was applied by the Court of Appeals in this case. The scarcity of case law before *Weeks* is doubtless due in part to the fact that the exclusionary rule there enunciated had been first adopted only 11 years earlier in Iowa; but it would seem to be also due in part to the fact that the issue was regarded as well settled.

The Court of Appeals in effect determined that the only reason supporting the authority for a full search incident to lawful arrest was the possibility of discovery of evidence or fruits. Concluding that there could be no evidence or fruits in the case of an offense such as that with which respondent was charged, it held that any protective search would have to be limited by the conditions laid down in *Terry* for a search upon less than probable cause to arrest. Quite apart from the fact that *Terry* clearly recognized the distinction between the two types of searches, and that a different rule governed one than governed the other, we find additional reason to disagree with the Court of Appeals.

The justification or reason for the authority to search incident to a lawful arrest rests quite as much on the need to disarm the suspect in order to take him into custody as it does on the need to preserve evidence on his person for later use at trial. The standards traditionally governing a search incident to lawful arrest are not, therefore, commuted to the stricter *Terry* standards by the absence of probable fruits or further evidence of the particular crime for which the arrest is made.

Nor are we inclined, on the basis of what seems to us to be a rather speculative judgment, to qualify the breadth of the general authority to search incident to a lawful custodial arrest on an assumption that persons arrested for the offense of driving while their licenses have been revoked are less likely to possess dangerous weapons than are those arrested for other crimes. It is scarcely open to doubt that the danger to an officer is far greater in the case of the extended exposure which follows the taking of a suspect into custody and transporting him to the police station than in the case of the relatively fleeting contact resulting from the typical *Terry*-type stop. This is an adequate basis for treating all custodial arrests alike for purposes of search justification.

But quite apart from these distinctions, our more fundamental disagreement with the Court of Appeals arises from its suggestion that there must be litigated in each case the issue of whether or not there was present one of the reasons supporting the authority for a search of the person incident to a lawful arrest. We do not think the long line of authorities of this Court dating back to *Weeks*, or what we can glean from the history of practice in this country and in England, requires such a case-by-case adjudication. A police officer's determination as to how and where to search the person of a suspect whom he has arrested is necessarily a quick ad hoc judgment which the Fourth Amendment does not require to be broken down in each instance into an analysis of each step in the search. The authority to search the person incident to a lawful custodial arrest, while based upon the need to disarm and to discover evidence, does not depend on what a court may later decide was the probability in a particular arrest situation that weapons or evidence would in fact be found upon the person of the suspect. A custodial arrest of a suspect based on probable cause is a reasonable intrusion under the Fourth Amendment; that intrusion being lawful, a search incident to the arrest requires no additional justification. It is the fact of the lawful arrest which establishes the authority to search, and we hold that in the case of a lawful custodial arrest a full search of the person is not only an exception to the warrant requirement of the Fourth Amendment, but is also a "reasonable" search under that Amendment.

IV

The search of respondent's person conducted by Officer Jenks in this case and the seizure from him of the heroin, were permissible under established Fourth Amendment law. While thorough, the search partook of none of the extreme or patently abusive characteristics which were held to violate the Due Process Clause of the Fourteenth Amendment in *Rochin v. California* (1952). Since it is the fact of custodial arrest which gives rise to the authority to search, it is of no moment that Jenks did not indicate any subjective fear of the respondent or that he did not himself suspect that respondent was armed. Having in the course of a lawful search come upon the crumpled package of cigarettes, he was entitled to inspect it; and when his inspection revealed the heroin capsules, he was entitled to seize them as "fruits, instrumentalities, or contraband" probative of criminal conduct. The judgment of the Court of Appeals holding otherwise is reversed.

Reversed.

NOTES AND QUESTIONS

1. Is this a pretextual arrest? Was Robinson really arrested simply because he was driving with a revoked driver's license? Officer Jenks plainly had his eye on Robinson—he had been monitoring his driving records—and it couldn't have been only for driving with a revoked driver's license.

C. The Warrant Requirement and Its Exceptions

2. The court of appeals analogizes the scope of a search incident to arrest to a *Terry* stop and frisk, as both involve a search for weapons. What is wrong with that analogy? Why does the Supreme Court reject it? If the analogy were controlling, what should the officer have done when he felt the "crumpled up cigarette pack"?

3. The crime at issue here, driving with a revoked license, is unusual in that it is almost impossible to contend that the defendant would be in possession of evidence or fruits of the commission of the crime. So the permissible purpose and scope of the search should be limited to a search for weapons. The Court rejects the argument that the need for a weapons search should be determined on a case-by-case basis, and holds that such a search is always justified. Does this make sense? Is the potential for violent confrontation inherent in any arrest, regardless of the underlying charge? If so, what does this say about whether arrests for nonviolent, minor offenses such as this one should be the norm? Did the scope of the permissible scope of the search extend to Washington's car?

4. Does the Court's conclusion that Officer Jenks was entitled to "inspect" the cigarette pack once he felt it seem like a non sequitur in view of the opinion's emphasis on officer safety up to that point? Are there any limits to the scope of the search of the person incident to arrest after *Robinson*?

Robinson is an early example of the ominous power that the police wield by virtue of their traffic law enforcement responsibilities. Here, a routine traffic violation ultimately justified an arrest, which justified an all-encompassing search of the person, which in turn eventually leads to a drug conviction. For discussion of how law enforcement weaponized its traffic regulatory powers in investigating drug crimes, *see infra* Section E. The Court used a similar bright-line approach to searches incident to arrest in *New York v. Belton*, 453 U.S. 454 (1981), holding — under a broad reading — that the arrest of the recent occupant of a vehicle justified a search incident to that arrest of the entire passenger compartment of the vehicle and any containers therein.

Recall at this juncture Justice O'Connor's warning in her *Atwater* dissent about the risk of racial profiling where police are given broad discretionary power. In that dissent she also notes the holding in *Whren v. United States*, 517 U.S. 806 (1996), which will be addressed fully *infra*. In short, *Whren* held that the Fourth Amendment doesn't prohibit pretextual vehicle stops where there is probable cause for the traffic violation supporting the stop. So the upshot of the combination of *Robinson*, *Belton*, *Whren*, and *Atwater* is that a motorist can be stopped for a traffic violation, even if the stop is pretextual (*Whren*), can be arrested for that violation (*Atwater*), and can have his person (*Robinson*) and car (*Belton*) searched incident to that arrest. In short, in the discretionary regime in which even a conservative member of the Supreme Court admits is fraught with potential for racial profiling, the police can with impunity effectively select a motorist virtually at random and have their person and car searched. *See* Donald A. Dripps, *The Fourth Amendment and the Fallacy of Composition: Determinacy versus Legitimacy in a Regime of Bright-Line Rules*, 74 Miss. L.J. 341, 392-92 (2004) (describing the "Iron Triangle" of *Belton*, *Whren*, and *Atwater*, which "means in practice that police have general search power over anyone traveling by automobile"). *See* Frank Rudy Cooper, *Post-Racialism and Searches Incident to Arrest*, 44 Ariz. St. L.J. 113, 147 (2012) ("Police officers racially profile all the time. The point of racial profiling is to catch them 'dirty.' The search incident to arrest is the primary means of potentially catching the prey.").

In *Arizona v. Gant*, 556 U.S. 332 (2009), the Court clarified — or overruled — *Belton*, at least in part, holding that the passenger area of a vehicle cannot be searched incident to an arrest after the arrestee has been secured and cannot access the interior of the vehicle. The Court may have realized *Belton* was ripe for reconsideration when it learned that at the suppression hearing in *Gant* the arresting officer, when asked why he searched the passenger area of the car, could only respond: "Because the law says we can." The Court did find that the passenger area could nonetheless be searched if it was reasonable to believe that evidence relevant to the crime of arrest might be found, but no such reasonable belief was available here as Gant was charged only with driving with a suspended license. Four Justices dissented on stare decisis grounds.

Gant does not, however, mean that the police cannot search a car after the car's driver has been arrested. The vehicle of an arrestee under some circumstances can be impounded by the police and searched under the administrative exception for "inventory searches." *Florida v. Wells*, 495 U.S. 1 (1990). Such searches serve to protect an owner's property while it is in the custody of the police, to insure against claims of lost, stolen, or vandalized property, and to guard the police from danger. *Id.* at 4. They are permissible where performed pursuant to standardized criteria or established routine — for the purpose of producing an inventory — and must not be a ruse for a general rummaging in order to discover incriminating evidence. *Id.*

Being afoot, rather than in a vehicle, hardly insulates one from the powers wielded by police "search-incident-to-arrest" powers. Individuals in public areas can be approached by police for no reason at all and questioned. If their freedom to leave the interaction has not been curtailed, they have not been "seized," *see supra*, and no level of suspicion for the encounter is required. A wholesale practice of precisely such interactions was infamously described as "pedestrian checks" by the police department in Ferguson, Missouri. *See* U.S. Dept. of Justice, Civil Rights Division, Investigation of the Ferguson Police Department (2015) (hereinafter DOJ Ferguson Report) at 16-20. *See* Devon W. Carbado, Unreasonable: Black Lives, Police Power, and the Fourth Amendment 41-44 (2022) (discussing Ferguson Police Department's "ped checks"). In these interactions the police are almost always able to acquire the names of the persons they approach, which enables the police to remotely determine if the individuals have any outstanding warrants. The existence of such warrants — including bench warrants for comparably minor civil violations such as traffic violations or failures to appear in court — justifies an arrest that in turn justifies a search incident to that arrest. Justice O'Connor's concerns about the potential for racial profiling, of course, are at least as applicable in this context as in the traffic stop context.

Indeed, this was precisely the fact pattern in *Utah v. Strieff*, 579 U.S. 232, 235-36 (2016): An individual was stopped and questioned by police, showed identification, was subsequently arrested when the police were able to learn remotely of an outstanding warrant for an unpaid traffic ticket, and was convicted of drug possession when the search incident to his arrest turned up methamphetamine in a pocket. (*Strieff* is discussed more thoroughly in the chapter on the exclusionary rule, *see* Chapter V, *infra*.) Bench warrants of this type are commonplace, as is their use as a method of policing. The DOJ Ferguson Report found that of the 21,000 persons living in Ferguson, 16,000 people had outstanding warrants against them. DOJ Ferguson Report, at 6, 55. Ferguson may be an extreme example but there is no reason to think it is an outlier, as other DOJ investigations have shown. For example, in a single year in New Orleans, officers "made nearly 60,000 arrests, of which about 20,000 were of people with outstanding traffic or misdemeanor warrants from neighboring parishes for such infractions as unpaid tickets." Dept. of Justice, Civil Rights Div., Investigation of the New Orleans Police Department 29 (2011).

The Court turned down an opportunity to further expand search-incident-to-arrest powers in 2014. In *Riley v. California*, 573 U.S. 373 (2014), the Court considered whether the police may without a warrant search digital information on a cell phone seized from an arrestee as an incident to that arrest. The Court rejected a categorical application of *Robinson* in this context, as a search of the type of information a person has on his cell phone "bears

C. The Warrant Requirement and Its Exceptions

little resemblance" to the type of physical search at issue in *Robinson*. Ultimately the Court found that neither of the twin *Chimel* rationales justified the search while, on the other hand, the intrusion on an individual's privacy was extreme, employing reasoning similar to that in *Carpenter v. United Carpenter States*, 585 U.S. 296 (2018), *supra*.

In *Birchfield v. North Dakota*, 579 U.S. 438 (2016), the Court considered statutory schemes under which motorists arrested on drunk-driving charges are required, under an "implied consent" theory, to undergo warrantless blood alcohol tests. Refusal of the tests was itself a crime. Analyzing these schemes under the "search incident to arrest" framework, the Court found that breath tests were permissible but the more invasive blood tests—involving a physical piercing of the skin, and generating information beyond blood alcohol content—were not. The Court dismissed almost out of hand the suggestion that such tests should require a warrant:

> In order to persuade a magistrate that there is probable cause for a search warrant, the officer would typically recite the same facts that led the officer to find that there was probable cause for arrest, namely, that there is probable cause to believe that a BAC breath test will reveal that the motorist's blood alcohol level is over the limit. . . . [T]he facts that establish probable cause are largely the same from one drunk-driving stop to the next and consist largely of the officer's own characterization of his or her observations—for example, that there was a strong odor of alcohol, that the motorist wobbled when attempting to stand, that the motorist paused when reciting the alphabet or counting backwards, and so on. A magistrate would be in a poor position to challenge such characterizations.

Is the Court trying to say that police officers simply recite boilerplate language to justify probable cause for drunk-driving arrests?

Wouldn't the possibility of judicial scrutiny cause police to take more care in preparing their police reports knowing they needed a factual basis for their arrest that would be put into an affidavit? Might the possibility of judicial scrutiny also cause them to be more thorough and disciplined in reaching the probable cause conclusion in the first place?

5. Consent Searches

Schneckloth v. Bustamonte
412 U.S. 218 (1973)

Mr. Justice STEWART delivered the opinion of the Court.

It is well settled under the Fourth and Fourteenth Amendments that a search conducted without a warrant issued upon probable cause is "per se unreasonable . . . subject only to a few specifically established and well-delineated exceptions." It is equally well settled that one of the specifically established exceptions to the requirements of both a warrant and probable cause is a search that is conducted pursuant to consent. The constitutional question in the present case concerns the definition of "consent" in this Fourth and Fourteenth Amendment context.

I

The respondent was brought to trial in a California court upon a charge of possessing a check with intent to defraud. He moved to suppress the introduction of certain material as evidence against him on the ground that the material had been acquired through an unconstitutional search and seizure. In response to the motion, the trial judge conducted an evidentiary hearing where it was established that the material in question had been acquired by the State under the following circumstances:

While on routine patrol in Sunnyvale, California, at approximately 2:40 in the morning, Police Officer James Rand stopped an automobile when he observed that one headlight and its license plate light were burned out. Six men were in the vehicle. Joe Alcala and the respondent, Robert Bustamonte, were in the front seat with Joe Gonzales, the driver. Three older men were seated in the rear. When, in response to the policeman's question, Gonzales could not produce a driver's license, Officer Rand asked if any of the other five had any evidence of identification. Only Alcala produced a license, and he explained that the car was his brother's. After the six occupants had stepped out of the car at the officer's request and after two additional policemen had arrived, Officer Rand asked Alcala if he could search the car. Alcala replied, "Sure, go ahead." Prior to the search no one was threatened with arrest and, according to Officer Rand's uncontradicted testimony, it "was all very congenial at this time." Gonzales testified that Alcala actually helped in the search of the car, by opening the trunk and glove compartment. In Gonzales' words: "(T)he police officer asked Joe (Alcala), he goes, 'Does the trunk open?' And Joe said, 'Yes.' He went to the car and got the keys and opened up the trunk." Wadded up under the left rear seat, the police officers found three checks that had previously been stolen from a car wash.

The trial judge denied the motion to suppress, and the checks in question were admitted in evidence at Bustamonte's trial. On the basis of this and other evidence he was convicted, and the California Court of Appeal for the First Appellate District affirmed the conviction.

• • •

II

It is important to make it clear at the outset what is not involved in this case. The respondent concedes that a search conducted pursuant to a valid consent is constitutionally permissible.

The precise question in this case, then, is what must the prosecution prove to demonstrate that a consent was "voluntarily" given. And upon that question there is a square conflict of views between the state and federal courts that have reviewed the search involved in the case before us. The Court of Appeals for the Ninth Circuit concluded that it is an essential part of the State's initial burden to prove that a person knows he has a right to refuse consent. The California courts have followed the rule that voluntariness is a question of fact to be determined from the totality of all the circumstances, and that the state of a defendant's knowledge is only one factor to be taken into account in assessing the voluntariness of a consent.

A

The most extensive judicial exposition of the meaning of "voluntariness" has been developed in those cases in which the Court has had to determine the "voluntariness" of a defendant's confession for purposes of the Fourteenth Amendment.

• • •

Similar considerations lead us to agree with the courts of California that the question whether a consent to a search was in fact "voluntary" or was the product of duress or coercion, express or implied, is a question of fact to be determined from the totality of all the circumstances. While knowledge of the right to refuse consent is one factor to be taken into account, the government need not establish such knowledge as the sine qua non of an effective consent. As with police questioning, two competing concerns must be accommodated in determining the meaning of a "voluntary" consent — the legitimate need for such searches and the equally important requirement of assuring the absence of coercion.

C. The Warrant Requirement and Its Exceptions

In situations where the police have some evidence of illicit activity, but lack probable cause to arrest or search, a search authorized by a valid consent may be the only means of obtaining important and reliable evidence. In the present case for example, while the police had reason to stop the car for traffic violations, the State does not contend that there was probable cause to search the vehicle or that the search was incident to a valid arrest of any of the occupants. Yet, the search yielded tangible evidence that served as a basis for a prosecution, and provided some assurance that others, wholly innocent of the crime, were not mistakenly brought to trial. And in those cases where there is probable cause to arrest or search, but where the police lack a warrant, a consent search may still be valuable. If the search is conducted and proves fruitless, that in itself may convince the police that an arrest with its possible stigma and embarrassment is unnecessary, or that a far more extensive search pursuant to a warrant is not justified. In short, a search pursuant to consent may result in considerably less inconvenience for the subject of the search, and, properly conducted, is a constitutionally permissible and wholly legitimate aspect of effective police activity.

But the Fourth and Fourteenth Amendments require that a consent not be coerced, by explicit or implicit means, by implied threat or covert force. For, no matter how subtly the coercion was applied, the resulting "consent" would be no more than a pretext for the unjustified police intrusion against which the Fourth Amendment is directed. In the words of the classic admonition in *Boyd v. United States*:

> It may be that it is the obnoxious thing in its mildest and least repulsive form; but illegitimate and unconstitutional practices get their first footing in that way, namely, by silent approaches and slight deviations from legal modes of procedure. This can only be obviated by adhering to the rule that constitutional provisions for the security of person and property should be liberally construed. A close and literal construction deprives them of half their efficacy, and leads to gradual depreciation of the right, as if it consisted more in sound than in substance. It is the duty of courts to be watchful for the constitutional rights of the citizen, and against any stealthy encroachments thereon.

The problem of reconciling the recognized legitimacy of consent searches with the requirement that they be free from any aspect of official coercion cannot be resolved by any infallible touchstone. To approve such searches without the most careful scrutiny would sanction the possibility of official coercion; to place artificial restrictions upon such searches would jeopardize their basic validity. Just as was true with confessions, the requirement of a "voluntary" consent reflects a fair accommodation of the constitutional requirements involved. In examining all the surrounding circumstances to determine if in fact the consent to search was coerced, account must be taken of subtly coercive police questions, as well as the possibly vulnerable subjective state of the person who consents. Those searches that are the product of police coercion can thus be filtered out without undermining the continuing validity of consent searches. In sum, there is no reason for us to depart in the area of consent searches, from the traditional definition of "voluntariness."

The approach of the Court of Appeals for the Ninth Circuit finds no support in any of our decisions that have attempted to define the meaning of "voluntariness." Its ruling, that the State must affirmatively prove that the subject of the search knew that he had a right to refuse consent, would, in practice, create serious doubt whether consent searches could continue to be conducted. There might be rare cases where it could be proved from the record that a person in fact affirmatively knew of his right to refuse—such as a case where he announced to the police that if he didn't sign the consent form, "you (police) are going to get a search warrant"; or a case where by prior experience and training a person had clearly and convincingly demonstrated such knowledge. But more commonly where there was no evidence of any coercion, explicit or implicit, the prosecution would nevertheless be unable to demonstrate that the subject of the search in fact had known of his right to refuse consent.

The very object of the inquiry—the nature of a person's subjective understanding—underlines the difficulty of the prosecution's burden under the rule applied by the Court of Appeals in this case. Any defendant who was the subject of a search authorized solely by his consent could effectively frustrate the introduction into evidence of the fruits of that search by simply failing to testify that he in fact knew he could refuse to consent. And the near impossibility of meeting this prosecutorial burden suggests why this Court has never accepted any such litmus-paper test of voluntariness. It is instructive to recall the fears of then Justice Traynor of the California Supreme Court:

> (I)t is not unreasonable for officers to seek interviews with suspects or witnesses or to call upon them at their homes for such purposes. Such inquiries, although courteously made and not accompanied with any assertion of a right to enter or search or secure answers, would permit the criminal to defeat his prosecution by voluntarily revealing all of the evidence against him and then contending that he acted only in response to an implied assertion of unlawful authority.

One alternative that would go far toward proving that the subject of a search did know he had a right to refuse consent would be to advise him of that right before eliciting his consent. That, however, is a suggestion that has been almost universally repudiated by both federal and state courts, and, we think, rightly so. For it would be thoroughly impractical to impose on the normal consent search the detailed requirements of an effective warning. Consent searches are part of the standard investigatory techniques of law enforcement agencies. They normally occur on the highway, or in a person's home or office, and under informal and unstructured conditions. The circumstances that prompt the initial request to search may develop quickly or be a logical extension of investigative police questioning. The police may seek to investigate further suspicious circumstances or to follow up leads developed in questioning persons at the scene of a crime. These situations are a far cry from the structured atmosphere of a trial where, assisted by counsel if he chooses, a defendant is informed of his trial rights. And, while surely a closer question, these situations are still immeasurably, far removed from "custodial interrogation" where, in *Miranda* we found that the Constitution required certain now familiar warnings as a prerequisite to police interrogation. Indeed, in language applicable to the typical consent search, we refused to extend the need for warnings:

> Our decision is not intended to hamper the traditional function of police officers in investigating crime. . . . When an individual is in custody on probable cause, the police may, of course, seek out evidence in the field to be used at trial against him. Such investigation may include inquiry of persons not under restraint. General on-the-scene questioning as to facts surrounding a crime or other general questioning of citizens in the fact-finding process is not affected by our holding. It is an act of responsible citizenship for individuals to give whatever information they may have to aid in law enforcement.

Consequently, we cannot accept the position of the Court of Appeals in this case that proof of knowledge of the right to refuse consent is a necessary prerequisite to demonstrating a "voluntary" consent. Rather it is only by analyzing all the circumstances of an individual consent that it can be ascertained whether in fact it was voluntary or coerced. It is this careful sifting of the unique facts and circumstances of each case that is evidenced in our prior decisions involving consent searches.

* * *

In short, neither this Court's prior cases, nor the traditional definition of "voluntariness" requires proof of knowledge of a right to refuse as the sine qua non of an effective consent to a search.

It is said, however, that a "consent" is a "waiver" of a person's rights under the Fourth and Fourteenth Amendments. The argument is that by allowing the police to conduct a search, a person "waives" whatever right he had to prevent the police from searching. It is argued that under the doctrine of *Johnson v. Zerbst*, to establish such a "waiver" the State must demonstrate "an intentional relinquishment or abandonment of a known right or privilege."

But these standards were enunciated in *Johnson* in the context of the safeguards of a fair criminal trial. Our cases do not reflect an uncritical demand for a knowing and intelligent waiver in every situation where a person has failed to invoke a constitutional protection. As Mr. Justice Black once observed for the Court: "Waiver is a vague term used for a great variety of purposes, good and bad, in the law." With respect to procedural due process, for example, the Court has acknowledged that waiver is possible, while explicitly leaving open the question whether a "knowing and intelligent" waiver need be shown.

The requirement of a "knowing" and "intelligent" waiver was articulated in a case involving the validity of a defendant's decision to forego a right constitutionally guaranteed to protect a fair trial and the reliability of the truth-determining process. *Johnson v. Zerbst* dealt with the denial of counsel in a federal criminal trial. There the Court held that under the Sixth Amendment a criminal defendant is entitled to the assistance of counsel, and that if he lacks sufficient funds to retain counsel, it is the Government's obligation to furnish him with a lawyer. As Mr. Justice Black wrote for the Court: "The Sixth Amendment stands as a constant admonition that if the constitutional safeguards it provides be lost, justice will not 'still be done.' It embodies a realistic recognition of the obvious truth that the average defendant does not have the professional legal skill to protect himself when brought before a tribunal with power to take his life or liberty, wherein the prosecution is presented by experienced and learned counsel. That which is simple, orderly, and necessary to the lawyer—to the untrained layman may appear intricate, complex and mysterious." To preserve the fairness of the trial process the Court established an appropriately heavy burden on the Government before waiver could be found—"an intentional relinquishment or abandonment of a known right or privilege."

Almost without exception, the requirement of a knowing and intelligent waiver has been applied only to those rights which the Constitution guarantees to a criminal defendant in order to preserve a fair trial. Hence, and hardly surprisingly in view of the facts of *Johnson* itself, the standard of a knowing and intelligent waiver has most often been applied to test the validity of a waiver of counsel, either at trial, or upon a guilty plea. And the Court has also applied the *Johnson* criteria to assess the effectiveness of a waiver of other trial rights such as the right to confrontation, to a jury trial, and to a speedy trial, and the right to be free from twice being placed in jeopardy. Guilty pleas have been carefully scrutinized to determine whether the accused knew and understood all the rights to which he would be entitled at trial, and that he had intentionally chosen to forgo them. And the Court has evaluated the knowing and intelligent nature of the waiver of trial rights in trial-type situations, such as the waiver of the privilege against compulsory self-incrimination before an administrative agency or a congressional committee, or the waiver of counsel in a juvenile proceeding.

The guarantees afforded a criminal defendant at trial also protect him at certain stages before the actual trial, and any alleged waiver must meet the strict standard of an intentional relinquishment of a "known" right. But the "trial" guarantees that have been applied to the "pretrial" stage of the criminal process are similarly designed to protect the fairness of the trial itself.

$$\bullet \quad \bullet \quad \bullet$$

Hence, in *Wade* and *Gilbert* the Court held "that a post-indictment pretrial lineup at which the accused is exhibited to identifying witnesses is a critical stage of the criminal prosecution; that police conduct of such a lineup without notice to and in the absence of his counsel denies the accused his Sixth (and Fourteenth) Amendment right to counsel. . . ." Accordingly, the

Court indicated that the standard of a knowing and intelligent waiver must be applied to test the waiver of counsel at such a lineup. The Court stressed the necessary interrelationship between the presence of counsel at a post-indictment lineup before trial and the protection of the trial process itself:

> Insofar as the accused's conviction may rest on a courtroom identification in fact the fruit of a suspect pretrial identification which the accused is helpless the subject to effective scrutiny at trial, the accused is deprived of that right of cross-examination which is an essential safeguard to his right to confront the witnesses against him. And even though cross-examination is a precious safeguard to a fair trial, it cannot be viewed as an absolute assurance of accuracy and reliability. Thus in the present context, where so many variables and pitfalls exist, the first line of defense must be the prevention of unfairness and the lessening of the hazards of eyewitness identification at the lineup itself. The trial which might determine the accused's fate may well not be that in the courtroom but that at the pretrial confrontation, with the State aligned against the accused, the witness the sole jury, and the accused unprotected against the overreaching, intentional or unintentional, and with little or no effective appeal from the judgment there rendered by the witness — "that's the man."

And in *Miranda* the Court found that custodial interrogation by the police was inherently coercive, and consequently held that detailed warnings were required to protect the privilege against compulsory self-incrimination. The Court made it clear that the basis for decision was the need to protect the fairness of the trial itself:

> That counsel is present when statements are taken from an individual during interrogation obviously enhances the integrity of the fact-finding processes in court. The presence of an attorney, and the warnings delivered to the individual, enable the defendant under otherwise compelling circumstances to tell his story without fear, effectively, and in a way that eliminates the evils in the interrogation process. Without the protections flowing from adequate warnings and the rights of counsel, "all the careful safeguards erected around the giving of testimony, whether by an accused or any other witness, would become empty formalities in a procedure where the most compelling possible evidence of guilt, a confession, would have already been obtained at the unsupervised pleasure of the police."

The standards of *Johnson* were, therefore, found to be a necessary prerequisite to a finding of a valid waiver.

There is a vast difference between those rights that protect a fair criminal trial and the rights guaranteed under the Fourth Amendment. Nothing, either in the purposes behind requiring a "knowing" and "intelligent" waiver of trial rights, or in the practical application of such a requirement suggests that it ought to be extended to the constitutional guarantee against unreasonable searches and seizures.

A strict standard of waiver has been applied to those rights guaranteed to a criminal defendant to insure that he will be accorded the greatest possible opportunity to utilize every facet of the constitutional model of a fair criminal trial. Any trial conducted in derogation of that model leaves open the possibility that the trial reached an unfair result precisely because all the protections specified in the Constitution were not provided. A prime example is the right to counsel. For without that right, a wholly innocent accused faces the real and substantial danger that simply because of his lack of legal expertise he may be convicted. As Mr. Justice Harlan once wrote: "The sound reason why (the right to counsel) is so freely extended for a criminal trial is the severe injustice risked by confronting an untrained defendant with a range of technical points of law, evidence, and tactics familiar to the prosecutor but not to himself." The Constitution requires that every effort be made to see to it that a defendant in a criminal case has not unknowingly relinquished the basic protections that the Framers thought indispensable to a fair trial.

The protections of the Fourth Amendment are of a wholly different order, and have nothing whatever to do with promoting the fair ascertainment of truth at a criminal trial. Rather, as Mr. Justice Frankfurter's opinion for the Court put it in *Wolf v. Colorado*, the Fourth Amendment protects the "security of one's privacy against arbitrary intrusion by the police. . . ." In declining to apply the exclusionary rule of *Mapp v. Ohio* to convictions that had become final before rendition of that decision, the Court emphasized that "there is no likelihood of unreliability or coercion present in a search-and-seizure case." The Fourth Amendment "is not an adjunct to the ascertainment of truth." The guarantees of the Fourth Amendment stand "as a protection of quite different constitutional values—values reflecting the concern of our society for the right of each individual to be let alone. To recognize this is no more than to accord those values undiluted respect."

Nor can it even be said that a search, as opposed to an eventual trial, is somehow "unfair" if a person consents to a search. While the Fourth and Fourteenth Amendments limit the circumstances under which the police can conduct a search, there is nothing constitutionally suspect in a person's voluntarily allowing a search. The actual conduct of the search may be precisely the same as if the police had obtained a warrant. And, unlike those constitutional guarantees that protect a defendant at trial, it cannot be said every reasonable presumption ought to be indulged against voluntary relinquishment. We have only recently stated: "(I) t is no part of the policy underlying the Fourth and Fourteenth Amendments to discourage citizens from aiding to the utmost of their ability in the apprehension of criminals." Rather, the community has a real interest in encouraging consent, for the resulting search may yield necessary evidence for the solution and prosecution of crime, evidence that may insure that a wholly innocent person is not wrongly charged with a criminal offense.

Those cases that have dealt with the application of the *Johnson v. Zerbst* rule make clear that it would be next to impossible to apply to a consent search the standard of "an intentional relinquishment or abandonment of a known right or privilege." To be true to *Johnson* and its progeny, there must be examination into the knowing and understanding nature of the waiver, an examination that was designed for a trial judge in the structured atmosphere of a courtroom. As the Court expressed it in *Johnson*:

> The constitutional right of an accused to be represented by counsel invokes, of itself, the protection of a trial court, in which the accused—whose life or liberty is at stake—is without counsel. This protecting duty imposes the serious and weighty responsibility upon the trial judge of determining whether there is an intelligent and competent waiver by the accused. While an accused may waive the right to counsel, whether there is a proper waiver should be clearly determined by the trial court, and it would be fitting and appropriate for that determination to appear upon the record.

It would be unrealistic to expect that in the informal, unstructured context of a consent search, a policeman, upon pain of tainting the evidence obtained, could make the detailed type of examination demanded by *Johnson*. And, if for this reason a diluted form of "waiver" were found acceptable, that would itself be ample recognition of the fact that there is no universal standard that must be applied in every situation where a person foregoes a constitutional right.

Similarly, a "waiver" approach to consent searches would be thoroughly inconsistent with our decisions that have approved "third party consents." . . .

In short, there is nothing in the purposes or application of the waiver requirements of *Johnson v. Zerbst* that justifies, much less compels, the easy equation of a knowing waiver with a consent search. To make such an equation is to generalize from the broad rhetoric of some of our decisions, and to ignore the substance of the differing constitutional guarantees. We decline to follow what one judicial scholar has termed "the domino method of constitutional adjudication . . . wherein every explanatory statement in a previous opinion is made the basis for extension to a wholly different situation."

D

Much of what has already been said disposes of the argument that the Court's decision in the *Miranda* case requires the conclusion that knowledge of a right to refuse is an indispensable element of a valid consent. The considerations that informed the Court's holding in *Miranda* are simply inapplicable in the present case. In *Miranda* the Court found that the techniques of police questioning and the nature of custodial surroundings produce an inherently coercive situation. The Court concluded that "(u)nless adequate protective devices are employed to dispel the compulsion inherent in custodial surroundings, no statement obtained from the defendant can truly be the product of his free choice." And at another point the Court noted that "without proper safeguards the process of in-custody interrogation of persons suspected or accused of crime contains inherently compelling pressures which work to undermine the individual's will to resist and to compel him to speak where he would not otherwise do so freely."

In this case, there is no evidence of any inherently coercive tactics—either from the nature of the police questioning or the environment in which it took place. Indeed, since consent searches will normally occur on a person's own familiar territory, the specter of incommunicado police interrogation in some remote station house is simply inapposite. There is no reason to believe, under circumstances such as are present here, that the response to a policeman's question is presumptively coerced; and there is, therefore, no reason to reject the traditional test for determining the voluntariness of a person's response. *Miranda*, of course, did not reach investigative questioning of a person not in custody, which is most directly analogous to the situation of a consent search, and it assuredly did not indicate that such questioning ought to be deemed inherently coercive.

It is also argued that the failure to require the Government to establish knowledge as a prerequisite to a valid consent, will relegate the Fourth Amendment to the special province of "the sophisticated, v. knowledgeable and the privileged." We cannot agree. The traditional definition of voluntariness we accept today has always taken into account evidence of minimal schooling, low intelligence, and the lack of any effective warnings to a person of his rights; and the voluntariness of any statement taken under those conditions has been carefully scrutinized to determine whether it was in fact voluntarily given.

E

Our decision today is a narrow one. We hold only that when the subject of a search is not in custody and the State attempts to justify a search on the basis of his consent, the Fourth and Fourteenth Amendments require that it demonstrate that the consent was in fact voluntarily given, and not the result of duress or coercion, express or implied. Voluntariness is a question of fact to be determined from all the circumstances, and while the subject's knowledge of a right to refuse is a factor to be taken into account, the prosecution is not required to demonstrate such knowledge as a prerequisite to establishing a voluntary consent. Because the California court followed these principles in affirming the respondent's conviction, and because the Court of Appeals for the Ninth Circuit in remanding for an evidentiary hearing required more, its judgment must be reversed.

[Justices Douglas, Brennan, and Marshall dissented.]

NOTES AND QUESTIONS

1. The case could not begin with a more quintessential traffic stop: a burned-out headlight and license plate light. The Court notes that the testimony of Officer Rand that the mood of the stop was "all very congenial" was uncontradicted. Maybe it really was congenial.

But what risks do you think Bustamonte would have run by taking the stand and offering a different account of the mood?

2. Do you think most people understand that they have a right to refuse to consent to a vehicle search? Do you think that, even if they do understand that they have such a right in the abstract, they think that they can exercise it without penalty (e.g., further questioning, a ticket instead of a citation, arrest, etc.)? Do you think people understand that their consent to a vehicle search includes consent to a search the scope of which, as here, extends to areas underneath the seats? To removal of door panels in some cases? To a search that can last over an hour?

3. As you saw in Chapter III *supra*, the Court seven years earlier in *Miranda* had rejected the due process "voluntariness" test (the Court's discussion of which is omitted here) for analyzing allegedly coercive confessions, in part due to its lack of administrative ease. Why employ it here?

4. In doing "balancing" here the Court offers about as unapologetic, ends-justifying-means appraisal of the law enforcement interests as can be imagined:

> In situations where the police have some evidence of illicit activity, but lack probable cause to arrest or search, a search authorized by a valid consent may be the only means of obtaining important and reliable evidence. In the present case for example, while the police had reason to stop the car for traffic violations, the State does not contend that there was probable cause to search the vehicle or that the search was incident to a valid arrest of any of the occupants. Yet, the search yielded tangible evidence that served as a basis for a prosecution, and provided some assurance that others, wholly innocent of the crime, were not mistakenly brought to trial. And in those cases where there is probable cause to arrest or search, but where the police lack a warrant, a consent search may still be valuable. If the search is conducted and proves fruitless, that in itself may convince the police that an arrest with its possible stigma and embarrassment is unnecessary, or that a far more extensive search pursuant to a warrant is not justified. In short, a search pursuant to consent may result in considerably less inconvenience for the subject of the search, and, properly conducted, is a constitutionally permissible and wholly legitimate aspect of effective police activity.

Id. at 227-28. Of course, depending on California law, after *Atwater* it may be constitutionally permissible to arrest at least the driver for the traffic code violations.

This spirit is also reflected in the Court's civics lesson on the virtue of consent: "the community has a real interest in encouraging consent, for the resulting search may yield necessary evidence for the solution and prosecution of crime, evidence that may insure that a wholly innocent person is not wrongly charged with a criminal offense." As a rule of thumb, you can always tell that the defendant is losing when the Court justifies a police practice by invoking the exoneration of innocent people.

5. The Court seems to genuinely resist conceptualizing a consent to a car search as a "waiver" of Fourth Amendment rights. It even cites gratuitously from a case saying that waiver can be for both "good and bad" purposes, and also cites two civil cases — civil cases! — for the proposition that waiver need not always be "knowing and intelligent." What possible explanation is there for such resistance to the well-established concept of waiver?

6. Is there any basis for the Court's distinction in this context between Fourth Amendment rights and rights that ensure a fair trial? How does the guilty plea — a waiver of the right to a jury trial, among other things — figure into this construct?

7. The Court contends it would be "next to impossible" to import into a traffic stop the full-blown colloquy required for determining whether a waiver was knowing and intelligent in other contexts. Is such a colloquy required? How about something like *Miranda* but shorter?

8. Very few people refuse to consent to a search of their car. *See* Kathryne M. Young & Christin L. Munsch, *Fact and Fiction in Constitutional Criminal Procedure*, 66 S.C. L. Rev. 445 (2014). Moreover, as Professors Young and Munsch find, rights assertion in police-citizen encounters differs based on social class and other background factors: lower socioeconomic status is associated with a greater reluctance to assert constitutional rights in interactions with the police. *Id.* at 476. Professor Carbado confirms that race may often be at play in the dynamic of the consent search inquiry:

> If Black Americans believe that police officers are likely to perceive Black people as criminally suspect, they may feel extra pressure to consent to say yes to consent to searches to disconfirm that stereotype. Black Americans might also feel pressured to say yes to consent searches on the view that saying no carries the risk of both prolonging the encounter and escalating the situation.

Devon W. Carbado, Unreasonable: Black Lives, Police Power, and the Fourth Amendment 51 (2022).

***

Schneckloth is still good law 50 years later, even as traffic stops have morphed into a critical and relentless law enforcement weapon that may not have been fully anticipated in 1973. If anything, the Court has extended its reach. In *Ohio v. Robinette*, 519 U.S. 33 (1996), the driver of the car, Robert Robinette, was stopped for speeding. The police officer wrote up a warning and handed it Robinette. The purpose of the stop had ended. Rather than return to his cruiser, however, the officer began to ask Robinette questions about whether there was any contraband in the car. Robinette responded in the negative. The officer then asked Robinette—"just one more thing"—if he could search the car. Robinette consented and drugs were found. The Court rejected the bright-line Ohio traffic-stop rule that once the purpose of the stop was over the driver had to be advised he was free to leave. Echoing the reasoning of *Schneckloth* the Court said such a requirement would be "unrealistic." Dissenting, Justice Stevens stated what would appear to most people to be obvious: "Repeated decisions by ordinary citizens to surrender [their self-interest] cannot satisfactorily be explained on any hypothesis other than an assumption that they believed they had had a legal duty to do so." *Id.* at 48.

Consent issues have reached the Supreme Court in other contexts, such as a third party's consent to the search of shared living space. In *United States v. Matlock*, 415 U.S. 164 (1974), the Court held that a warrantless entry and search is permissible if consent to the search were given by a third party with common authority over the premises. Quaintly, the Court noted in *Matlock* that a woman's statement authorizing consent to search the bedroom in the premises she shared with her boyfriend was admissible at the boyfriend's trial as an admission-against-interest because "cohabitation" was a crime under state law.

It's unclear when and whether law enforcement determined that *Matlock* gave it the ability to leverage domestic acrimony into an extra exception to the warrant requirement. Fourteen years after *Matlock*, in *Illinois v. Rodriguez*, 497 U.S. 177 (1990), police were able to leverage a woman's alleged physical abuse by her boyfriend into the latter's arrest on drug charges.

Illinois v. Rodriguez
497 U.S. 177 (1990)

Justice SCALIA delivered the opinion of the Court.

In *United States v. Matlock*, this Court reaffirmed that a warrantless entry and search by law enforcement officers does not violate the Fourth Amendment's proscription of "unreasonable searches Illinois and seizures" if the officers have obtained the consent of a third party who possesses common authority over the premises. The present case presents an issue we expressly reserved in *Matlock*: Whether a warrantless entry is valid when based upon the consent of a third party whom the police, at the time of the entry, reasonably believe to possess common authority over the premises, but who in fact does not do so.

I

Respondent Edward Rodriguez was arrested in his apartment by law enforcement officers and charged with possession of illegal drugs. The police gained entry to the apartment with the consent and assistance of Gail Fischer, who had lived there with respondent for several months. The relevant facts leading to the arrest are as follows.

On July 26, 1985, police were summoned to the residence of Dorothy Jackson on South Wolcott in Chicago. They were met by Ms. Jackson's daughter, Gail Fischer, who showed signs of a severe beating. She told the officers that she had been assaulted by respondent Edward Rodriguez earlier that day in an apartment on South California. Fischer stated that Rodriguez was then asleep in the apartment, and she consented to travel there with the police in order to unlock the door with her key so that the officers could enter and arrest him. During this conversation, Fischer several times referred to the apartment on South California as "our" apartment, and said that she had clothes and furniture there. It is unclear whether she indicated that she currently lived at the apartment, or only that she used to live there.

The police officers drove to the apartment on South California, accompanied by Fischer. They did not obtain an arrest warrant for Rodriguez, nor did they seek a search warrant for the apartment. At the apartment, Fischer unlocked the door with her key and gave the officers permission to enter. They moved through the door into the living room, where they observed in plain view drug paraphernalia and containers filled with white powder that they believed (correctly, as later analysis showed) to be cocaine. They proceeded to the bedroom, where they found Rodriguez asleep and discovered additional containers of white powder in two open attaché cases. The officers arrested Rodriguez and seized the drugs and related paraphernalia.

Rodriguez was charged with possession of a controlled substance with intent to deliver. He moved to suppress all evidence seized at the time of his arrest, claiming that Fischer had vacated the apartment several weeks earlier and had no authority to consent to the entry. The Cook County Circuit Court granted the motion, holding that at the time she consented to the entry Fischer did not have common authority over the apartment. The Court concluded that Fischer was not a "usual resident" but rather an "infrequent visitor" at the apartment on South California, based upon its findings that Fischer's name was not on the lease, that she did not contribute to the rent, that she was not allowed to invite others to the apartment on her own, that she did not have access to the apartment when respondent was away, and that she had moved some of her possessions from the apartment. The Circuit Court also rejected the State's contention that, even if Fischer did not possess common authority over the premises, there was no Fourth Amendment violation if the police reasonably believed at the time of their entry that Fischer possessed the authority to consent.

The Appellate Court of Illinois affirmed the Circuit Court in all respects. The Illinois Supreme Court denied the State's petition for leave to appeal, and we granted certiorari.

II

The Fourth Amendment generally prohibits the warrantless entry of a person's home, whether to make an arrest or to search for specific objects. *Payton v. New York* (1980); *Johnson v. United States* (1948). The prohibition does not apply, however, to situations in which voluntary consent has been obtained, either from the individual whose property is searched, see *Schneckloth v. Bustamonte* (1973), or from a third party who possesses common authority over the premises, see *United States v. Matlock*. The State of Illinois contends that that exception applies in the present case.

352 Chapter IV The Fourth Amendment

As we stated in *Matlock*, "[c]ommon authority" rests "on mutual use of the property by persons generally having joint access or control for most purposes. . . ." The burden of establishing that common authority rests upon the State. On the basis of this record, it is clear that burden was not sustained. The evidence showed that although Fischer, with her two small children, had lived with Rodriguez beginning in December 1984, she had moved out on July 1, 1985, almost a month before the search at issue here, and had gone to live with her mother. She took her and her children's clothing with her, though leaving behind some furniture and household effects. During the period after July 1 she sometimes spent the night at Rodriguez's apartment, but never invited her friends there, and never went there herself when he was not home. Her name was not on the lease nor did she contribute to the rent. She had a key to the apartment, which she said at trial she had taken without Rodriguez's knowledge (though she testified at the preliminary hearing that Rodriguez had given her the key). On these facts the State has not established that, with respect to the South California apartment, Fischer had "joint access or control for most purposes." To the contrary, the Appellate Court's determination of no common authority over the apartment was obviously correct.

III

A

The State contends that, even if Fischer did not in fact have authority to give consent, it suffices to validate the entry that the law enforcement officers reasonably believed she did. Before reaching the merits of that contention, we must consider a jurisdictional objection: that the decision below rests on an adequate and independent state ground. Respondent asserts that the Illinois Constitution provides greater protection than is afforded under the Fourth Amendment, and that the Appellate Court relied upon this when it determined that a reasonable belief by the police officers was insufficient.

When a state-court decision is clearly based on state law that is both adequate and independent, we will not review the decision. *Michigan v. Long* (1983). But when "a state court decision fairly appears to rest primarily on federal law, or to be interwoven with the federal law," we require that it contain a "'plain statement' that [it] rests upon adequate and independent state grounds"; otherwise, "we will accept as the most reasonable explanation that the state court decided the case the way it did because it believed that federal law required it to do so." Here, the Appellate Court's opinion contains no "plain statement" that its decision rests on state law. The opinion does not rely on (or even mention) any specific provision of the Illinois Constitution, nor even the Illinois Constitution generally. Even the Illinois cases cited by the opinion rely upon no constitutional provisions other than the Fourth and Fourteenth Amendments of the United States Constitution. We conclude that the Appellate Court of Illinois rested its decision on federal law.

B

On the merits of the issue, respondent asserts that permitting a reasonable belief of common authority to validate an entry would cause a defendant's Fourth Amendment rights to be "vicariously waived." We disagree.

We have been unyielding in our insistence that a defendant's waiver of his trial rights cannot be given effect unless it is "knowing" and "intelligent." We would assuredly not permit, therefore, evidence seized in violation of the Fourth Amendment to be introduced on the basis of a trial court's mere "reasonable belief" — derived from statements by unauthorized persons — that the defendant has waived his objection. But one must make a distinction between, on the one hand, trial rights that derive from the violation of constitutional

C. The Warrant Requirement and Its Exceptions   **353**

guarantees and, on the other hand, the nature of those constitutional guarantees themselves. As we said in *Schneckloth*:

> There is a vast difference between those rights that protect a fair criminal trial and the rights guaranteed under the Fourth Amendment. Nothing, either in the purposes behind requiring a "knowing" and "intelligent" waiver of trial rights, or in the practical application of such a requirement suggests that it ought to be extended to the constitutional guarantee against unreasonable searches and seizures.

What Rodriguez is assured by the trial right of the exclusionary rule, where it applies, is that no evidence seized in violation of the Fourth Amendment will be introduced at his trial unless he consents. What he is assured by the Fourth Amendment itself, however, is not that no government search of his house will occur unless he consents; but that no such search will occur that is "unreasonable." There are various elements, of course, that can make a search of a person's house "reasonable" — one of which is the consent of the person or his cotenant. The essence of respondent's argument is that we should impose upon this element a requirement that we have not imposed upon other elements that regularly compel government officers to exercise judgment regarding the facts: namely, the requirement that their judgment be not only responsible but correct.

The fundamental objective that alone validates all unconsented government searches is, of course, the seizure of persons who have committed or are about to commit crimes, or of evidence related to crimes. But "reasonableness," with respect to this necessary element, does not demand that the government be factually correct in its assessment that that is what a search will produce. Warrants need only be supported by "probable cause," which demands no more than a proper "assessment of probabilities in particular factual contexts. . . ." If a magistrate, based upon seemingly reliable but factually inaccurate information, issues a warrant for the search of a house in which the sought-after felon is not present, has never been present, and was never likely to have been present, the owner of that house suffers one of the inconveniences we all expose ourselves to as the cost of living in a safe society; he does not suffer a violation of the Fourth Amendment.

Another element often, though not invariably, required in order to render an unconsented search "reasonable" is, of course, that the officer be authorized by a valid warrant. Here also we have not held that "reasonableness" precludes error with respect to those factual judgments that law enforcement officials are expected to make. In *Maryland v. Garrison* (1987), a warrant supported by probable cause with respect to one apartment was erroneously issued for an entire floor that was divided (though not clearly) into two apartments. We upheld the search of the apartment not properly covered by the warrant. We said:

> [T]he validity of the search of respondent's apartment pursuant to a warrant authorizing the search of the entire third floor depends on whether the officers' failure to realize the overbreadth of the warrant was objectively understandable and reasonable. Here it unquestionably was. The objective facts available to the officers at the time suggested no distinction between [the suspect's] apartment and the third-floor premises.

The ordinary requirement of a warrant is sometimes supplanted by other elements that render the unconsented search "reasonable." Here also we have not held that the Fourth Amendment requires factual accuracy. A warrant is not needed, for example, where the search is incident to an arrest. In *Hill v. California* (1971), we upheld a search incident to an arrest, even though the arrest was made of the wrong person. We said:

> The upshot was that the officers in good faith believed Miller was Hill and arrested him. They were quite wrong as it turned out, and subjective good-faith belief would not in itself justify either the arrest or the subsequent search. But sufficient probability, not certainty, is the

touchstone of reasonableness under the Fourth Amendment and on the record before us the officers' mistake was understandable and the arrest a reasonable response to the situation facing them at the time.

It would be superfluous to multiply these examples. It is apparent that in order to satisfy the "reasonableness" requirement of the Fourth Amendment, what is generally demanded of the many factual determinations that must regularly be made by agents of the government—whether the magistrate issuing a warrant, the police officer executing a warrant, or the police officer conducting a search or seizure under one of the exceptions to the warrant requirement—is not that they always be correct, but that they always be reasonable. As we put it in *Brinegar v. United States* (1949):

> Because many situations which confront officers in the course of executing their duties are more or less ambiguous, room must be allowed for some mistakes on their part. But the mistakes must be those of reasonable men, acting on facts leading sensibly to their conclusions of probability.

We see no reason to depart from this general rule with respect to facts bearing upon the authority to consent to a search. Whether the basis for such authority exists is the sort of recurring factual question to which law enforcement officials must be expected to apply their judgment; and all the Fourth Amendment requires is that they answer it reasonably. The Constitution is no more violated when officers enter without a warrant because they reasonably (though erroneously) believe that the person who has consented to their entry is a resident of the premises, than it is violated when they enter without a warrant because they reasonably (though erroneously) believe they are in pursuit of a violent felon who is about to escape.

Stoner v. California (1964) is in our view not to the contrary. There, in holding that police had improperly entered the defendant's hotel room based on the consent of a hotel clerk, we stated that "the rights protected by the Fourth Amendment are not to be eroded . . . by unrealistic doctrines of 'apparent authority.'" It is ambiguous, of course, whether the word "unrealistic" is descriptive or limiting—that is, whether we were condemning as unrealistic all reliance upon apparent authority, or whether we were condemning only such reliance upon apparent authority as is unrealistic. Similarly ambiguous is the opinion's earlier statement that "there [is no] substance to the claim that the search was reasonable because the police, relying upon the night clerk's expressions of consent, had a reasonable basis for the belief that the clerk had authority to consent to the search." Was there no substance to it because it failed as a matter of law, or because the facts could not possibly support it? At one point the opinion does seem to speak clearly:

> It is important to bear in mind that it was the petitioner's constitutional right which was at stake here, and not the night clerk's nor the hotel's. It was a right, therefore, which only the petitioner could waive by word or deed, either directly or through an agent.

But as we have discussed, what is at issue when a claim of apparent consent is raised is not whether the right to be free of searches has been waived, but whether the right to be free of unreasonable searches has been violated. Even if one does not think the *Stoner* opinion had this subtlety in mind, the supposed clarity of its foregoing statement is immediately compromised, as follows:

> It is true that the night clerk clearly and unambiguously consented to the search. But there is nothing in the record to indicate that the *police had any basis whatsoever to believe that* the night clerk had been authorized by the petitioner to permit the police to search the petitioner's room.

The italicized language should have been deleted, of course, if the statement two sentences earlier meant that an appearance of authority could never validate a search. In the last analysis, one must admit that the rationale of *Stoner* was ambiguous—and perhaps deliberately so. It

C. The Warrant Requirement and Its Exceptions

is at least a reasonable reading of the case, and perhaps a preferable one, that the police could not rely upon the obtained consent because they knew it came from a hotel clerk, knew that the room was rented and exclusively occupied by the defendant, and could not reasonably have believed that the former had general access to or control over the latter. Similarly ambiguous in its implications (the Court's opinion does not even allude to, much less discuss the effects of, "reasonable belief") is *Chapman v. United States*. In sum, we were correct in *Matlock*, when we regarded the present issue as unresolved.

As *Stoner* demonstrates, what we hold today does not suggest that law enforcement officers may always accept a person's invitation to enter premises. Even when the invitation is accompanied by an explicit assertion that the person lives there, the surrounding circumstances could conceivably be such that a reasonable person would doubt its truth and not act upon it without further inquiry. As with other factual determinations bearing upon search and seizure, determination of consent to enter must "be judged against an objective standard: would the facts available to the officer at the moment . . . 'warrant a man of reasonable caution in the belief'" that the consenting party had authority over the premises? If not, then warrantless entry without further inquiry is unlawful unless authority actually exists. But if so, the search is valid.

• • •

In the present case, the Appellate Court found it unnecessary to determine whether the officers reasonably believed that Fischer had the authority to consent, because it ruled as a matter of law that a reasonable belief could not validate the entry. Since we find that ruling to be in error, we remand for consideration of that question. The judgment of the Illinois Appellate Court is reversed, and the case is remanded for further proceedings not inconsistent with this opinion.

So ordered.

NOTES AND QUESTIONS

1. Note the issue as to whether the Appellate Court of Illinois rested its decision that the search was legal on an adequate and independent state law ground. Why should the Court need to require such unmistakable clarity that a decision was grounded in state law? Why didn't the Appellate Court make its decision clear if that was its intention?

2. What do you think of the police officers' questioning of Fischer as to whether Rodriguez dealt in narcotics, a question to which she did not respond, a fact pointed out by the dissent but not the majority? Were the police really going to Rodriguez's house in order to arrest him for battery?

3. Why is this case not considered under the good faith exception to the exclusionary rule instead of as a third-party consent to search case?

4. The dissent accuses the majority of failing to analyze the consent issue in terms of the defendant's reasonable expectations of privacy, as it had done in *Matlock*, where it had held that a joint tenant assumes the risk that her cotenant might permit a common area to be searched. Did Rodriguez have a reasonable expectation of privacy here? Should a joint tenant really be seen as assuming the risk that his or her cotenant will consent to a search of the premises by law enforcement?

In *Georgia v. Randolph*, 547 U.S. 103 (2006), events led police to the exterior of a house where a bitterly feuding and separated husband and wife had lived together until a few weeks earlier. Janet Randolph told police that her husband was a drug user and that the house contained evidence of that usage. *Id.* Her husband, Scott Randolph, refused to give the police

Chapter IV The Fourth Amendment

permission to search the house; Janet Randolph enthusiastically gave it to them. *Id.* The police entered the house with Janet, who led them to drug paraphernalia and cocaine. *Id.* The Court held that the *Matlock* rule does not apply where a person who also has common authority over the premises is physically present and refuses to give consent. *Id.* at 108, 123.

In *Fernandez v. California*, 571 U.S. 292 (2014), the Court again considered the issue of the authority of a joint tenant to consent to a search in the face of an objecting cotenant. In the course of investigating a robbery, the police came to the home of a woman who appeared to have been injured in a fight. A man who turned out to be the woman's cotenant appeared at the door and refused to let the police enter the apartment. The man was arrested and ultimately taken to the police station, where he was identified as the perpetrator of the robbery. *Id.* at 295-96. The police later returned to the apartment and received the woman's consent to search the home, where they found evidence inculpating the defendant in the robbery. *Id.* at 296. The Court refused to "extend" *Randolph* to this situation given that the defendant was not present when his cotenant gave permission for the search. The Court refused to consider the intent of the officers in removing the objecting cotenant from the scene, even though it was not clear that they had probable cause to arrest him. *Id.* at 295-96.

6. Exigent Circumstances

The Supreme Court has long recognized that sometimes "exigent circumstances" justify a warrantless entry and search as an urgent investigative need that would go unmet if a warrant were required. As the term suggests, both the exigency and the circumstances are case-specific, but some general categories recur. *See Ker v. California*, 374 U.S. 23 (1963) (plurality opinion) (to prevent the imminent destruction of evidence); *United States v. Santana*, 427 U.S. 38 (1976) (to engage in hot pursuit of a fleeing suspect). In *Welsh v. Wisconsin*, 466 U.S. 740 (1984), the Court found that a warrantless entry of a home to arrest a drunk-driving suspect was not justified where the only exigency was the preservation of the suspect's blood alcohol level. The Court frequently states that "searches and seizures inside a home without a warrant are presumptively unreasonable." *Groh v. Ramirez*, 540 U.S. 551, 559 (2004).

Brigham City v. Stuart
547 U.S. 398 (2006)

Chief Justice ROBERTS delivered the opinion of the Court.

In this case we consider whether police may enter a home without a warrant when they have an objectively reasonable basis for believing that an occupant is seriously injured or imminently threatened with such injury. We conclude that they may.

I

This case arises out of a melee that occurred in a Brigham City, Utah, home in the early morning hours of July 23, 2000. At about 3 a.m., four police officers responded to a call regarding a loud party at a residence. Upon arriving at the house, they heard shouting from inside, and proceeded down the driveway to investigate. There, they observed two juveniles drinking beer in the backyard. They entered the backyard, and saw—through a screen door and windows—an altercation taking place in the kitchen of the home. According to the testimony of one of the officers, four adults were attempting, with some difficulty, to restrain a juvenile. The juvenile eventually "broke free, swung a fist and struck one of the adults in the face." The officer testified that he observed the victim of the blow spitting blood into a nearby

C. The Warrant Requirement and Its Exceptions   357

sink. The other adults continued to try to restrain the juvenile, pressing him up against a refrigerator with such force that the refrigerator began moving across the floor. At this point, an officer opened the screen door and announced the officers' presence. Amid the tumult, nobody noticed. The officer entered the kitchen and again cried out, and as the occupants slowly became aware that the police were on the scene, the altercation ceased.

The officers subsequently arrested respondents and charged them with contributing to the delinquency of a minor, disorderly conduct, and intoxication. In the trial court, respondents filed a motion to suppress all evidence obtained after the officers entered the home, arguing that the warrantless entry violated the Fourth Amendment. The court granted the motion, and the Utah Court of Appeals affirmed.

Before the Supreme Court of Utah, Brigham City argued that although the officers lacked a warrant, their entry was nevertheless reasonable on either of two grounds. The court rejected both contentions and, over two dissenters, affirmed. First, the court held that the injury caused by the juvenile's punch was insufficient to trigger the so-called "emergency aid doctrine" because it did not give rise to an "objectively reasonable belief that an unconscious, semi-conscious, or missing person feared injured or dead [was] in the home." Furthermore, the court suggested that the doctrine was inapplicable because the officers had not sought to assist the injured adult, but instead had acted "exclusively in their law enforcement capacity."

The court also held that the entry did not fall within the exigent circumstances exception to the warrant requirement. This exception applies, the court explained, where police have probable cause and where "a reasonable person [would] believe that the entry was necessary to prevent physical harm to the officers or other persons." Under this standard, the court stated, the potential harm need not be as serious as that required to invoke the emergency aid exception. Although it found the case "a close and difficult call," the court nevertheless concluded that the officers' entry was not justified by exigent circumstances.

We granted certiorari in light of differences among state courts and the Courts of Appeals concerning the appropriate Fourth Amendment standard governing warrantless entry by law enforcement in an emergency situation.

II

It is a "'basic principle of Fourth Amendment law that searches and seizures inside a home without a warrant are presumptively unreasonable.'"

One exigency obviating the requirement of a warrant is the need to assist persons who are seriously injured or threatened with such injury. "'The need to protect or preserve life or avoid serious injury is justification for what would be otherwise illegal absent an exigency or emergency.'" Accordingly, law enforcement officers may enter a home without a warrant to render emergency assistance to an injured occupant or to protect an occupant from imminent injury.

Respondents do not take issue with these principles, but instead advance two reasons why the officers' entry here was unreasonable. First, they argue that the officers were more interested in making arrests than quelling violence. They urge us to consider, in assessing the reasonableness of the entry, whether the officers were "indeed motivated primarily by a desire to save lives and property." The Utah Supreme Court also considered the officers' subjective motivations relevant.

Our cases have repeatedly rejected this approach. An action is "reasonable" under the Fourth Amendment, regardless of the individual officer's state of mind, "as long as the circumstances, viewed objectively, justify [the] action." The officer's subjective motivation is irrelevant. It therefore does not matter here—even if their subjective motives could be so neatly unraveled—whether the officers entered the kitchen to arrest respondents and gather evidence against them or to assist the injured and prevent further violence.

As respondents note, we have held in the context of programmatic searches conducted without individualized suspicion — such as checkpoints to combat drunk driving or drug trafficking — that "an inquiry into programmatic purpose" is sometimes appropriate. But this inquiry is directed at ensuring that the purpose behind the program is not "ultimately indistinguishable from the general interest in crime control." It has nothing to do with discerning what is in the mind of the individual officer conducting the search.

Respondents further contend that their conduct was not serious enough to justify the officers' intrusion into the home. They rely on *Welsh v. Wisconsin* (1984), in which we held that "an important factor to be considered when determining whether any exigency exists is the gravity of the underlying offense for which the arrest is being made." This contention, too, is misplaced. *Welsh* involved a warrantless entry by officers to arrest a suspect for driving while intoxicated. There, the "only potential emergency" confronting the officers was the need to preserve evidence (i.e., the suspect's blood-alcohol level) — an exigency that we held insufficient under the circumstances to justify entry into the suspect's home. Here, the officers were confronted with ongoing violence occurring within the home. Welsh did not address such a situation.

We think the officers' entry here was plainly reasonable under the circumstances. The officers were responding, at 3 o'clock in the morning, to complaints about a loud party. As they approached the house, they could hear from within "an altercation occurring, some kind of a fight." "It was loud and it was tumultuous." The officers heard "thumping and crashing" and people yelling "stop, stop" and "get off me." As the trial court found, "it was obvious that . . . knocking on the front door" would have been futile. The noise seemed to be coming from the back of the house; after looking in the front window and seeing nothing, the officers proceeded around back to investigate further. They found two juveniles drinking beer in the backyard. From there, they could see that a fracas was taking place inside the kitchen. A juvenile, fists clenched, was being held back by several adults. As the officers watch, he breaks free and strikes one of the adults in the face, sending the adult to the sink spitting blood.

In these circumstances, the officers had an objectively reasonable basis for believing both that the injured adult might need help and that the violence in the kitchen was just beginning. Nothing in the Fourth Amendment required them to wait until another blow rendered someone "unconscious" or "semi-conscious" or worse before entering. The role of a peace officer includes preventing violence and restoring order, not simply rendering first aid to casualties; an officer is not like a boxing (or hockey) referee, poised to stop a bout only if it becomes too one-sided.

The manner of the officers' entry was also reasonable. After witnessing the punch, one of the officers opened the screen door and "yelled in police." When nobody heard him, he stepped into the kitchen and announced himself again. Only then did the tumult subside. The officer's announcement of his presence was at least equivalent to a knock on the screen door. Indeed, it was probably the only option that had even a chance of rising above the din. Under these circumstances, there was no violation of the Fourth Amendment's knock-and-announce rule. Furthermore, once the announcement was made, the officers were free to enter; it would serve no purpose to require them to stand dumbly at the door awaiting a response while those within brawled on, oblivious to their presence.

Accordingly, we reverse the judgment of the Supreme Court of Utah, and remand the case for further proceedings not inconsistent with this opinion.

C. The Warrant Requirement and Its Exceptions

359

NOTES AND QUESTIONS

1. Does the nature of the "exigent circumstances" exception justify an exception to the Court's general Fourth Amendment rule that police officers' subjective motivation is irrelevant? Aren't inquiries under this exception always going to be fact-specific regardless?

2. Does the Court persuasively distinguish *Welsh*? What if all the persons scuffling had been—or appeared to be—juveniles? What if the officers had not observed any exchange of blows but had overheard threats of violence amid the tumult?

3. In *Kentucky v. King*, 563 U.S. 452 (2011), the Court considered an exception that many lower courts had carved out of the exigent circumstances doctrine where the exigency had been created by the conduct of the police. The rationale for the exception was that the police should not be able to exploit an exigency of their own making—such as by approaching a person or property that was under surveillance—to get around the warrant requirement. The Court essentially rejected the lower courts' exception, holding that as long as the police did not violate the Fourth Amendment by their conduct the fact that the conduct may have induced the exigency—such as the imminent destruction of evidence due to police in the vicinity—the exigent circumstances doctrine applied in full force.

4. The Court returned to the significance of the severity of the crime under investigation in *Lange v. California*, 141 S. Ct. 2011 (2021). A police officer on patrol in his vehicle followed defendant Arthur Lange after Lange attracted attention by playing loud music with his windows down and honking his horn. By the time the officer turned on his overhead lights to signal that Lange should pull over they were a hundred feet from Lange's home. Lange pulled into his driveway and entered the garage. The officer followed him into the garage and administered field sobriety tests that Lange failed. Lange was charged with misdemeanor drink driving.

The Court held that the result was not automatically determined by *Santana*, the Court's "hot pursuit" precedent, inasmuch as *Santana* was a felony drug case. Emphasizing the sanctity of the home, the Court rejected a categorical "hot pursuit" exigency for misdemeanants, and held that all circumstances must be considered:

> The flight of a suspected misdemeanant does not always justify a warrantless entry into a home. An officer must consider all the circumstances in a pursuit case to determine whether there is a law enforcement emergency. On many occasions, the officer will have good reason to enter—to prevent imminent harms of violence, destruction of evidence, or escape from the home. But when the officer has time to get a warrant, he must do so—even though the misdemeanant fled.

Id. at 2025. The case was remanded for application of this newly announced test. How do you think Lange will fare under it? Should the dissipation in the body of one's blood alcohol content be considered "destruction of evidence" for purposes of the exigent circumstances exception? Do fleeing suspects almost always—by virtue of the presence of police and their flight therefrom—create a risk of destruction of evidence?

7. Administrative or "Special Needs" Searches

An enormous and varied category of government searches lives largely outside the strictures of the Fourth Amendment. These searches often don't require warrants, probable cause, or even individualized suspicion. They fall into none of the above exceptions to the warrant requirement. As a category, they are sometimes called "administrative" or "suspicionless" or "special needs" searches. They are often justified by the fact that the regulatory authority under which they occur does not have criminal investigation and prosecution as its purpose, or at least not its primary purpose. Sometimes these searches are considered "special" just because they target high school kids.

An early example of such an administrative search was blessed in *Camara v. Municipal Court of City and County of San Francisco*, 387 U.S. 523 (1967), where the Court sanctioned city officials' inspection of buildings in a specified location for compliance with health-and-safety housing codes pursuant to an "area warrant" but without any individualized cause or suspicion as to particular buildings. The Court did not dismiss entirely the interests of the private citizens whose residences were searched but under the circumstances found them to be outweighed by the government's interests. *See also Michigan v. Tyler*, 436 U.S. 499 (1978) (allowing warrantless entry for purposes of fighting fire and for reasonable inspection of premises to determine cause of blaze).

In *New York v. Burger*, 482 U.S. 691 (1987), the Court upheld the constitutionality of a warrantless inspection of an automobile "junkyard" on the ground that the business was "closely regulated" and therefore any exalted expectation of privacy was unrealistic. This was a classic example of the circularity of the reasonable expectation of privacy doctrine: Because a state statute authorizes warrantless inspections of the business the proprietor's expectation of privacy was unreasonable. The Court was clearly thinking "chop shop," not junkyard, as was the New York legislature. The Court upheld the warrantless intrusion even though the regulatory framework was plainly law enforcement adjacent, at a minimum: The stated purpose of the regulatory scheme was to "deter motor vehicle theft," the inspections were done by police officers, and one of the records required to be maintained by the statute was called a "police book."

A warrantless search of a home was even upheld in *Griffin v. Wisconsin*, 483 U.S. 868 (1987). Joseph Griffin had been sentenced to probation after being convicted of disorderly conduct. The probation department got a tip that Griffin had a gun at his home, which—for a probationer—would have required approval by his probation officer, which had not been given. Under a statute authorizing a warrantless search of a probationer's home based on "reasonable grounds" to believe "contraband" would be found there, a probation officer (with three police officers) searched Griffin's home and found a gun. The Court found the warrantless search among the "exceptions when special needs, beyond the normal need for law enforcement, make the warrant and probable-cause requirement impracticable." *Id.* at 873. Observing, correctly, that probation is a form of punishment, the Court found that the regulatory regime for supervision of probationers justified the intrusion, in particular as it pertained to Griffin's "rehabilitation." (Ironically the federal Sentencing Reform Act of 1986—a year earlier than *Griffin* was decided—had explicitly renounced rehabilitation as a goal of federal sentencing.)

a. Vehicle Checkpoints

Sometimes the government isn't satisfied with its ability to stop and search cars without warrants, or to pull them over for trivial traffic code violations. Sometimes the government just passes a law that requires vehicles to pull themselves over for inspection at a checkpoint. Sometimes it works.

In *United States v. Martinez-Fuerte*, 428 U.S. 543 (1976), discussed further below in the section on racial profiling, the Court considered the constitutionality of immigration checkpoints designed to intercept illegal "aliens" that were located less than 100 miles from the Mexican border. Balancing the interests—the permitted intrusion was comparatively minor; stopping illegal immigration is hard—the Court found the checkpoints passed Fourth Amendment scrutiny. Just two years later, in *Delaware v. Prouse*, 440 U.S. 648, 663 (1979), in invalidating a suspicionless stop of a motorist, the Court—in a truly remarkable "write your congressperson" manner—suggested that a similar type of vehicle checkpoint for the regulatory purpose of verifying drivers' licenses and vehicle registrations might be permissible:

> This holding does not preclude the State of Delaware or other States from developing methods for spot checks that involve less intrusion or that do not involve the unconstrained exercise of discretion. Questioning of all oncoming traffic at roadblock-type stops is one possible alternative.

Id. at 663. Yikes. Could you imagine how such discretion would be exercised in practice?

The first case involving a vehicle checkpoint—Michigan cleverly called it a "sobriety checkpoint program," as if it were a therapeutic modality—reached the Court 11 years later. In *Michigan Dep't of State Police v. Sitz*, 496 U.S. 444 (1990), the Court upheld the checkpoint program due to its aim of combating the dangers of drunk driving notwithstanding the obvious overlap between safety and law enforcement interests in that context. *Id.* at 451.

In the next case the Court considered a less crafty attempt to use checkpoints.

City of Indianapolis v. Edmond
531 U.S. 32 (2000)

Justice O'CONNOR delivered the opinion of the Court.

In *Michigan Dept. of State Police v. Sitz* and *United States v. Martinez-Fuerte* we held that brief, suspicionless seizures at highway checkpoints for the purposes of combating drunk driving and intercepting illegal immigrants were constitutional. We now consider the constitutionality of a highway checkpoint program whose primary purpose is the discovery and interdiction of illegal narcotics.

I

In August 1998, the city of Indianapolis began to operate vehicle checkpoints on Indianapolis roads in an effort to interdict unlawful drugs. The city conducted six such roadblocks between August and November that year, stopping vehicles and arresting 104 motorists. Fifty-five arrests were for drug-related crimes, while 49 were for offenses unrelated to drugs. The overall "hit rate" of the program was thus approximately nine percent.

The parties stipulated to the facts concerning the operation of the checkpoints by the Indianapolis Police Department (IPD) for purposes of the preliminary injunction proceedings instituted below. At each checkpoint location, the police stop a predetermined number of vehicles. Approximately 30 officers are stationed at the checkpoint. Pursuant to written directives issued by the chief of police, at least one officer approaches the vehicle, advises the driver that he or she is being stopped briefly at a drug checkpoint, and asks the driver to produce a license and registration. The officer also looks for signs of impairment and conducts an open-view examination of the vehicle from the outside. A narcotics-detection dog walks around the outside of each stopped vehicle.

The directives instruct the officers that they may conduct a search only by consent or based on the appropriate quantum of particularized suspicion. The officers must conduct each stop in the same manner until particularized suspicion develops, and the officers have no discretion to stop any vehicle out of sequence. The city agreed in the stipulation to operate the checkpoints in such a way as to ensure that the total duration of each stop, absent reasonable suspicion or probable cause, would be five minutes or less.

The affidavit of Indianapolis Police Sergeant Marshall DePew, although it is technically outside the parties' stipulation, provides further insight concerning the operation of the checkpoints. According to Sergeant DePew, checkpoint locations are selected weeks in advance based on such considerations as area crime statistics and traffic flow. The checkpoints are generally operated during daylight hours and are identified with lighted signs reading, "'NARCOTICS CHECKPOINT—MILE AHEAD, NARCOTICS K-9 IN USE, BE PREPARED TO STOP.'" Once a group of cars has been stopped, other traffic proceeds without interruption until all the stopped cars have been processed or diverted for further processing. Sergeant DePew also stated that the average stop for a vehicle not subject to further processing lasts two to three minutes or less.

Respondents James Edmond and Joell Palmer were each stopped at a narcotics checkpoint in late September 1998. Respondents then filed a lawsuit on behalf of themselves and the class of all motorists who had been stopped or were subject to being stopped in the future at the Indianapolis drug checkpoints. Respondents claimed that the roadblocks violated the Fourth Amendment of the United States Constitution and the search and seizure provision of the Indiana Constitution. Respondents requested declaratory and injunctive relief for the class, as well as damages and attorney's fees for themselves.

Respondents then moved for a preliminary injunction. Although respondents alleged that the officers who stopped them did not follow the written directives, they agreed to the stipulation concerning the operation of the checkpoints for purposes of the preliminary injunction proceedings. The parties also stipulated to certification of the plaintiff class. The United States District Court for the Southern District of Indiana agreed to class certification and denied the motion for a preliminary injunction, holding that the checkpoint program did not violate the Fourth Amendment. A divided panel of the United States Court of Appeals for the Seventh Circuit reversed, holding that the checkpoints contravened the Fourth Amendment. The panel denied rehearing. We granted certiorari, and now affirm.

II

The Fourth Amendment requires that searches and seizures be reasonable. A search or seizure is ordinarily unreasonable in the absence of individualized suspicion of wrongdoing. While such suspicion is not an "irreducible" component of reasonableness, we have recognized only limited circumstances in which the usual rule does not apply. For example, we have upheld certain regimes of suspicionless searches where the program was designed to serve "special needs, beyond the normal need for law enforcement." We have also allowed searches for certain administrative purposes without particularized suspicion of misconduct, provided that those searches are appropriately limited.

We have also upheld brief, suspicionless seizures of motorists at a fixed Border Patrol checkpoint designed to intercept illegal aliens, and at a sobriety checkpoint aimed at removing drunk drivers from the road. In addition, in *Delaware v. Prouse*, we suggested that a similar type of roadblock with the purpose of verifying drivers' licenses and vehicle registrations would be permissible. In none of these cases, however, did we indicate approval of a checkpoint program whose primary purpose was to detect evidence of ordinary criminal wrongdoing.

In *Martinez-Fuerte*, we entertained Fourth Amendment challenges to stops at two permanent immigration checkpoints located on major United States highways less than 100 miles from the Mexican border. We noted at the outset the particular context in which the constitutional question arose, describing in some detail the "formidable law enforcement problems" posed by the northbound tide of illegal entrants into the United States. These problems had also been the focus of several earlier cases addressing the constitutionality of other Border Patrol traffic-checking operations. In *Martinez-Fuerte*, we found that the balance tipped in favor of the Government's interests in policing the Nation's borders. In so finding, we emphasized the difficulty of effectively containing illegal immigration at the border itself. We also stressed the impracticality of the particularized study of a given car to discern whether it was transporting illegal aliens, as well as the relatively modest degree of intrusion entailed by the stops.

Our subsequent cases have confirmed that considerations specifically related to the need to police the border were a significant factor in our *Martinez-Fuerte* decision.

In *Sitz*, we evaluated the constitutionality of a Michigan highway sobriety checkpoint program. The *Sitz* checkpoint involved brief, suspicionless stops of motorists so that police officers could detect signs of intoxication and remove impaired drivers from the road. Motorists who exhibited signs of intoxication were diverted for a license and registration check and, if warranted, further sobriety tests. This checkpoint program was clearly aimed at reducing the immediate hazard posed by the presence of drunk drivers on the highways, and there was an obvious connection between the imperative of highway safety and the law enforcement practice at issue. The gravity of the drunk driving problem and the magnitude of the State's interest in getting drunk drivers off the road weighed heavily in our determination that the program was constitutional.

In *Prouse*, we invalidated a discretionary, suspicionless stop for a spot check of a motorist's driver's license and vehicle registration. The officer's conduct in that case was unconstitutional primarily on account of his exercise of "standardless and unconstrained discretion." We nonetheless acknowledged the States' "vital interest in ensuring that only those qualified to do so are permitted to operate motor vehicles, that these vehicles are fit for safe operation, and hence that licensing, registration, and vehicle inspection requirements are being observed." Accordingly, we suggested that "[q]uestioning of all oncoming traffic at roadblock-type stops" would be a lawful means of serving this interest in highway safety.

We further indicated in *Prouse* that we considered the purposes of such a hypothetical roadblock to be distinct from a general purpose of investigating crime. The State proffered the additional interests of "the apprehension of stolen motor vehicles and of drivers under the influence of alcohol or narcotics" in its effort to justify the discretionary spot check. We attributed the entirety of the latter interest to the State's interest in roadway safety. Ibid. We also noted that the interest in apprehending stolen vehicles may be partly subsumed by the interest in roadway safety. Ibid. We observed, however, that "[t]he remaining governmental interest in controlling automobile thefts is not distinguishable from the general interest in crime control." Not only does the common thread of highway safety thus run through *Sitz* and *Prouse*, but *Prouse* itself reveals a difference in the Fourth Amendment significance of highway safety interests and the general interest in crime control.

III

It is well established that a vehicle stop at a highway checkpoint effectuates a seizure within the meaning of the Fourth Amendment. The fact that officers walk a narcotics-detection dog around the exterior of each car at the Indianapolis checkpoints does not transform the seizure into a search. Just as in *Place*, an exterior sniff of an automobile does not require entry into the car and is not designed to disclose any information other than the presence or absence of narcotics. Like the dog sniff in *Place*, a sniff by a dog that simply walks around a car is "much less intrusive than a typical search." Rather, what principally distinguishes these checkpoints from those we have previously approved is their primary purpose.

As petitioners concede, the Indianapolis checkpoint program unquestionably has the primary purpose of interdicting illegal narcotics. In their stipulation of facts, the parties repeatedly refer to the checkpoints as "drug checkpoints" and describe them as "being operated by the City of Indianapolis in an effort to interdict unlawful drugs in Indianapolis." In addition, the first document attached to the parties' stipulation is entitled "DRUG CHECKPOINT CONTACT OFFICER DIRECTIVES BY ORDER OF THE CHIEF OF POLICE." These directives instruct officers to "[a]dvise the citizen that they are being stopped briefly at a drug checkpoint." The second document attached to the stipulation is entitled "1998 Drug Road Blocks" and contains a statistical breakdown of information relating to the checkpoints conducted. Further, according to Sergeant DePew, the checkpoints are identified with lighted signs reading, "'NARCOTICS CHECKPOINT ___ MILE AHEAD, NARCOTICS K-9 IN USE, BE PREPARED TO STOP.'" Finally, both the District Court and the Court of Appeals recognized that the primary purpose of the roadblocks is the interdiction of narcotics.

We have never approved a checkpoint program whose primary purpose was to detect evidence of ordinary criminal wrongdoing. Rather, our checkpoint cases have recognized only limited exceptions to the general rule that a seizure must be accompanied by some measure of individualized suspicion. We suggested in *Prouse* that we would not credit the "general interest in crime control" as justification for a regime of suspicionless stops. Consistent with this suggestion, each of the checkpoint programs that we have approved was designed primarily to serve purposes closely related to the problems of policing the border or the necessity of ensuring roadway safety. Because the primary purpose of the Indianapolis narcotics checkpoint program is to uncover evidence of ordinary criminal wrongdoing, the program contravenes the Fourth Amendment.

Petitioners propose several ways in which the narcotics-detection purpose of the instant checkpoint program may instead resemble the primary purposes of the checkpoints in *Sitz* and *Martinez-Fuerte*. Petitioners state that the checkpoints in those cases had the same ultimate purpose of arresting those suspected of committing crimes. Brief for Petitioners. Securing the border and apprehending drunk drivers are, of course, law enforcement activities, and law enforcement officers employ arrests and criminal prosecutions in pursuit of these goals. If we were to rest the case at this high level of generality, there would be little check on the ability of the authorities to construct roadblocks for almost any conceivable law enforcement purpose. Without drawing the line at roadblocks designed primarily to serve the general interest in crime control, the Fourth Amendment would do little to prevent such intrusions from becoming a routine part of American life.

Petitioners also emphasize the severe and intractable nature of the drug problem as justification for the checkpoint program. There is no doubt that traffic in illegal narcotics creates social harms of the first magnitude. The law enforcement problems that the drug trade creates likewise remain daunting and complex, particularly in light of the myriad forms of spin-off crime that it spawns. The same can be said of various other illegal activities, if only to a lesser degree. But the gravity of the threat alone cannot be dispositive of questions concerning what means law enforcement officers may employ to pursue a given purpose. Rather, in determining whether individualized suspicion is required, we must consider the nature of the interests threatened and their connection to the particular law enforcement practices at issue. We are particularly reluctant to recognize exceptions to the general rule of individualized suspicion where governmental authorities primarily pursue their general crime control ends.

Nor can the narcotics-interdiction purpose of the checkpoints be rationalized in terms of a highway safety concern similar to that present in *Sitz*. The detection and punishment of almost any criminal offense serves broadly the safety of the community, and our streets would no doubt be safer but for the scourge of illegal drugs. Only with respect to a smaller class of offenses, however, is society confronted with the type of immediate, vehicle-bound threat to life and limb that the sobriety checkpoint in *Sitz* was designed to eliminate.

Petitioners also liken the anticontraband agenda of the Indianapolis checkpoints to the antismuggling purpose of the checkpoints in *Martinez-Fuerte*. Petitioners cite this Court's conclusion in *Martinez-Fuerte* that the flow of traffic was too heavy to permit "particularized study of a given car that would enable it to be identified as a possible carrier of illegal aliens," and claim that this logic has even more force here. The problem with this argument is that the same logic prevails any time a vehicle is employed to conceal contraband or other evidence of a crime. This type of connection to the roadway is very different from the close connection to roadway safety that was present in *Sitz* and *Prouse*. Further, the Indianapolis checkpoints are far removed from the border context that was crucial in *Martinez-Fuerte*. While the difficulty of examining each passing car was an important factor in validating the law enforcement technique employed in *Martinez-Fuerte*, this factor alone cannot justify a regime of suspicionless searches or seizures. Rather, we must look more closely at the nature of the public interests that such a regime is designed principally to serve.

The primary purpose of the Indianapolis narcotics checkpoints is in the end to advance "the general interest in crime control." We decline to suspend the usual requirement of individualized suspicion where the police seek to employ a checkpoint primarily for the ordinary enterprise of investigating crimes. We cannot sanction stops justified only by the generalized and ever-present possibility that interrogation and inspection may reveal that any given motorist has committed some crime.

Of course, there are circumstances that may justify a law enforcement checkpoint where the primary purpose would otherwise, but for some emergency, relate to ordinary crime control. For example, as the Court of Appeals noted, the Fourth Amendment would almost certainly permit an appropriately tailored roadblock set up to thwart an imminent terrorist attack or to catch a dangerous criminal who is likely to flee by way of a particular route. The exigencies created by these scenarios are far removed from the circumstances under which authorities might simply stop cars as a matter of course to see if there just happens to be a felon leaving the jurisdiction. While we do not limit the purposes that may justify a checkpoint program to any rigid set of categories, we decline to approve a program whose primary purpose is ultimately indistinguishable from the general interest in crime control.

Petitioners argue that our prior cases preclude an inquiry into the purposes of the checkpoint program. For example, they cite *Whren v. United States* (1996), and *Bond v. United States*, 529 (2000) to support the proposition that "where the government articulates and pursues a legitimate interest for a suspicionless stop, courts should not look behind that interest to determine whether the government's 'primary purpose' is valid." These cases, however, do not control the instant situation.

In *Whren*, we held that an individual officer's subjective intentions are irrelevant to the Fourth Amendment validity of a traffic stop that is justified objectively by probable cause to believe that a traffic violation has occurred. We observed that our prior cases "foreclose any argument that the constitutional reasonableness of traffic stops depends on the actual motivations of the individual officers involved." In so holding, we expressly distinguished cases where we had addressed the validity of searches conducted in the absence of probable cause.

Whren therefore reinforces the principle that, while "[s]ubjective intentions play no role in ordinary, probable-cause Fourth Amendment analysis," programmatic purposes may be relevant to the validity of Fourth Amendment intrusions undertaken pursuant to a general scheme without individualized suspicion. Accordingly, *Whren* does not preclude an inquiry into programmatic purpose in such contexts. It likewise does not preclude an inquiry into programmatic purpose here.

Last Term in *Bond*, we addressed the question whether a law enforcement officer violated a reasonable expectation of privacy in conducting a tactile examination of carry-on luggage in the overhead compartment of a bus. In doing so, we simply noted that the principle of *Whren* rendered the subjective intent of an officer irrelevant to this analysis. While, as petitioners correctly observe, the analytical rubric of *Bond* was not "ordinary, probable-cause Fourth Amendment analysis," nothing in *Bond* suggests that we would extend the principle of *Whren* to all situations where individualized suspicion was lacking. Rather, subjective intent was irrelevant in *Bond* because the inquiry that our precedents required focused on the objective effects of the actions of an individual officer. By contrast, our cases dealing with intrusions that occur pursuant to a general scheme absent individualized suspicion have often required an inquiry into purpose at the programmatic level.

Petitioners argue that the Indianapolis checkpoint program is justified by its lawful secondary purposes of keeping impaired motorists off the road and verifying licenses and registrations. If this were the case, however, law enforcement authorities would be able to establish checkpoints for virtually any purpose so long as they also included a license or sobriety check. For this reason, we examine the available evidence to determine the primary purpose of the

Chapter IV The Fourth Amendment

checkpoint program. While we recognize the challenges inherent in a purpose inquiry, courts routinely engage in this enterprise in many areas of constitutional jurisprudence as a means of sifting abusive governmental conduct from that which is lawful. As a result, a program driven by an impermissible purpose may be proscribed while a program impelled by licit purposes is permitted, even though the challenged conduct may be outwardly similar. While reasonableness under the Fourth Amendment is predominantly an objective inquiry, our special needs and administrative search cases demonstrate that purpose is often relevant when suspicionless intrusions pursuant to a general scheme are at issue.

It goes without saying that our holding today does nothing to alter the constitutional status of the sobriety and border checkpoints that we approved in *Sitz* and *Martinez-Fuerte*, or of the type of traffic checkpoint that we suggested would be lawful in *Prouse*. The constitutionality of such checkpoint programs still depends on a balancing of the competing interests at stake and the effectiveness of the program. When law enforcement authorities pursue primarily general crime control purposes at checkpoints such as here, however, stops can only be justified by some quantum of individualized suspicion.

Our holding also does not affect the validity of border searches or searches at places like airports and government buildings, where the need for such measures to ensure public safety can be particularly acute. Nor does our opinion speak to other intrusions aimed primarily at purposes beyond the general interest in crime control. Our holding also does not impair the ability of police officers to act appropriately upon information that they properly learn during a checkpoint stop justified by a lawful primary purpose, even where such action may result in the arrest of a motorist for an offense unrelated to that purpose. Finally, we caution that the purpose inquiry in this context is to be conducted only at the programmatic level and is not an invitation to probe the minds of individual officers acting at the scene. Because the primary purpose of the Indianapolis checkpoint program is ultimately indistinguishable from the general interest in crime control, the checkpoints violate the Fourth Amendment. The judgment of the Court of Appeals is, accordingly, affirmed.

NOTES AND QUESTIONS

1. The Court discusses the checkpoint program in a fair amount of detail but is cryptic about how the checkpoint locations are determined, saying only that they are "based on such considerations as area crime statistics and traffic flow." What else would you like to know about the selection of locations? Would there be any legal issues if all the locations were located in areas with predominantly minority populations? At a more general level, do you see any legal issues if police disproportionately patrol areas with predominantly minority populations?

2. The Court concludes that "the Indianapolis checkpoint program has the primary purpose of interdicting illegal narcotics." Should it matter that the trial court, which denied a motion to preliminarily enjoin the program, found that another purpose of the program was checking licenses and registrations?

3. Could better lawyering have saved the city's checkpoint program? Large urban cities and their police departments sometimes have excellent lawyers, fully capable of reading Supreme Court precedent—such as *Sitz*—and advising accordingly. Couldn't the city's lawyers have created a self-serving document outlining the program—there doesn't seem to have been one here—that explicitly announces the program's dual purposes? Why in the world did the city's lawyers enter into a stipulation that calls the very intrusions at issue—the checkpoints—"drug checkpoints"?

Admittedly, the use of a canine drug-sniff at each and every stop might have given the game away regardless.

4. Does the Court persuasively distinguish the forbidden inquiry into purpose required by *Whren* from the permitted inquiry into "programmatic" purpose here? If the program had been better dressed up in "dual purpose" clothing, would *Whren* have precluded consideration of whether the regulatory part of the clothing was pretextual?

5. Do these statistics—104 arrests (55 for drugs; 49 for other) out of 1,161 vehicles stopped—suggest to you the program was successful or unsuccessful? Would you need to know more about the other 49 arrests? More about whether charges were brought based on the arrests and, if so, to what end (prior to the Seventh Circuit decision reversing the denial of the injunction)? More about how many vehicles were stopped for "further processing"? Demographic information about the occupants of the vehicles subjected to "further processing"?

b. High School Students

As seen in the next case, the Supreme Court is fond of duly noting—right before it denies them their rights—that high school students do not "shed their constitutional rights . . . at the schoolhouse gate." *Tinker v. Des Moines Independent Community School Dist.*, 393 U.S. 503 (1969) (school district could not discipline students for protesting Vietnam War by wearing black armbands absent reasonable prospect of disruption of school activities). In *New Jersey v. T.L.O.*, 469 U.S. 325 (1985), the Court held that a search of a high school student's purse would be governed by a flexible "reasonableness" standard and did not require a showing of probable cause, given the different interests and responsibilities in the school environment.

In the next case, the Court considers a suspicionless drug-testing program directed at all students in a school district who participate in interscholastic athletics.

Vernonia School District 47J v. Acton
515 U.S. 646 (1995)

Justice SCALIA delivered the opinion of the Court.

The Student Athlete Drug Policy adopted by School District 47J in the town of Vernonia, Oregon, authorizes random urinalysis drug testing of students who participate in the District's school athletics programs. We granted certiorari to decide whether this violates the Fourth and Fourteenth Amendments to the United States Constitution.

I

A

Petitioner Vernonia School District 47J (District) operates one high school and three grade schools in the logging community of Vernonia, Oregon. As elsewhere in small-town America, school sports play a prominent role in the town's life, and student athletes are admired in their schools and in the community.

Drugs had not been a major problem in Vernonia schools. In the mid-to-late 1980's, however, teachers and administrators observed a sharp increase in drug use. Students began to speak out about their attraction to the drug culture, and to boast that there was nothing the school could do about it. Along with more drugs came more disciplinary problems. Between 1988 and 1989 the number of disciplinary referrals in Vernonia schools rose to more than twice the number reported in the early 1980's, and several students were suspended. Students became increasingly rude during class; outbursts of profane language became common.

368   Chapter IV The Fourth Amendment

Not only were student athletes included among the drug users but, as the District Court found, athletes were the leaders of the drug culture. This caused the District's administrators particular concern, since drug use increases the risk of sports-related injury. Expert testimony at the trial confirmed the deleterious effects of drugs on motivation, memory, judgment, reaction, coordination, and performance. The high school football and wrestling coach witnessed a severe sternum injury suffered by a wrestler, and various omissions of safety procedures and misexecutions by football players, all attributable in his belief to the effects of drug use.

Initially, the District responded to the drug problem by offering special classes, speakers, and presentations designed to deter drug use. It even brought in a specially trained dog to detect drugs, but the drug problem persisted. According to the District Court:

> [T]he administration was at its wits end and . . . a large segment of the student body, particularly those involved in interscholastic athletics, was in a state of rebellion. Disciplinary actions had reached "epidemic proportions." The coincidence of an almost three-fold increase in classroom disruptions and disciplinary reports along with the staff's direct observations of students using drugs or glamorizing drug and alcohol use led the administration to the inescapable conclusion that the rebellion was being fueled by alcohol and drug abuse as well as the student's misperceptions about the drug culture.

At that point, District officials began considering a drug-testing program. They held a parent "input night" to discuss the proposed Student Athlete Drug Policy (Policy), and the parents in attendance gave their unanimous approval. The school board approved the Policy for implementation in the fall of 1989. Its expressed purpose is to prevent student athletes from using drugs, to protect their health and safety, and to provide drug users with assistance programs.

B

The Policy applies to all students participating in interscholastic athletics. Students wishing to play sports must sign a form consenting to the testing and must obtain the written consent of their parents. Athletes are tested at the beginning of the season for their sport. In addition, once each week of the season the names of the athletes are placed in a "pool" from which a student, with the supervision of two adults, blindly draws the names of 10% of the athletes for random testing. Those selected are notified and tested that same day, if possible.

The student to be tested completes a specimen control form which bears an assigned number. Prescription medications that the student is taking must be identified by providing a copy of the prescription or a doctor's authorization. The student then enters an empty locker room accompanied by an adult monitor of the same sex. Each boy selected produces a sample at a urinal, remaining fully clothed with his back to the monitor, who stands approximately 12 to 15 feet behind the student. Monitors may (though do not always) watch the student while he produces the sample, and they listen for normal sounds of urination. Girls produce samples in an enclosed bathroom stall, so that they can be heard but not observed. After the sample is produced, it is given to the monitor, who checks it for temperature and tampering and then transfers it to a vial.

The samples are sent to an independent laboratory, which routinely tests them for amphetamines, cocaine, and marijuana. Other drugs, such as LSD, may be screened at the request of the District, but the identity of a particular student does not determine which drugs will be tested. The laboratory's procedures are 99.94% accurate. The District follows strict procedures regarding the chain of custody and access to test results. The laboratory does not know the identity of the students whose samples it tests. It is authorized to mail written test reports only to the superintendent and to provide test results to District personnel by telephone only after the requesting official recites a code confirming his authority. Only the superintendent, principals, vice-principals, and athletic directors have access to test results, and the results are not kept for more than one year.

If a sample tests positive, a second test is administered as soon as possible to confirm the result. If the second test is negative, no further action is taken. If the second test is positive, the athlete's parents are notified, and the school principal convenes a meeting with the student and his parents, at which the student is given the option of (1) participating for six weeks in an assistance program that includes weekly urinalysis, or (2) suffering suspension from athletics for the remainder of the current season and the next athletic season. The student is then retested prior to the start of the next athletic season for which he or she is eligible. The Policy states that a second offense results in automatic imposition of option (2); a third offense in suspension for the remainder of the current season and the next two athletic seasons.

C

In the fall of 1991, respondent James Acton, then a seventh grader, signed up to play football at one of the District's grade schools. He was denied participation, however, because he and his parents refused to sign the testing consent forms. The Actons filed suit, seeking declaratory and injunctive relief from enforcement of the Policy on the grounds that it violated the Fourth and Fourteenth Amendments to the United States Constitution and Article I, § 9, of the Oregon Constitution. After a bench trial, the District Court entered an order denying the claims on the merits and dismissing the action. The United States Court of Appeals for the Ninth Circuit reversed, holding that the Policy violated both the Fourth and Fourteenth Amendments and Article I, § 9, of the Oregon Constitution. We granted certiorari.

II

The Fourth Amendment to the United States Constitution provides that the Federal Government shall not violate "[t]he right of the people to be secure in their persons, houses, papers, and effects, against unreasonable searches and seizures. . . ." We have held that the Fourteenth Amendment extends this constitutional guarantee to searches and seizures by state officers, including public school officials. In *Skinner v. Railway Labor Executives' Assn.* (1989), we held that state-compelled collection and testing of urine, such as that required by the Policy, constitutes a "search" subject to the demands of the Fourth Amendment.

As the text of the Fourth Amendment indicates, the ultimate measure of the constitutionality of a governmental search is "reasonableness." At least in a case such as this, where there was no clear practice, either approving or disapproving the type of search at issue, at the time the constitutional provision was enacted, whether a particular search meets the reasonableness standard "'is judged by balancing its intrusion on the individual's Fourth Amendment interests against its promotion of legitimate governmental interests.'" Where a search is undertaken by law enforcement officials to discover evidence of criminal wrongdoing, this Court has said that reasonableness generally requires the obtaining of a judicial warrant. Warrants cannot be issued, of course, without the showing of probable cause required by the Warrant Clause. But a warrant is not required to establish the reasonableness of all government searches; and when a warrant is not required (and the Warrant Clause therefore not applicable), probable cause is not invariably required either. A search unsupported by probable cause can be constitutional, we have said, "when special needs, beyond the normal need for law enforcement, make the warrant and probable-cause requirement impracticable." *Griffin v. Wisconsin* (1987).

We have found such "special needs" to exist in the public school context. There, the warrant requirement "would unduly interfere with the maintenance of the swift and informal disciplinary procedures [that are] needed," and "strict adherence to the requirement that searches be based upon probable cause" would undercut "the substantial need of teachers and administrators for freedom to maintain order in the schools." The school search we approved in *T.L.O.*, while not based on probable cause, was based on individualized suspicion of wrongdoing. As we explicitly acknowledged, however, "'the Fourth Amendment imposes no irreducible requirement of such suspicion.'" We have upheld suspicionless searches and seizures to conduct drug testing of railroad personnel involved in train accidents; to conduct random drug testing of federal customs officers who carry arms or are involved in drug interdiction; and to maintain automobile checkpoints looking for illegal immigrants and contraband.

III

The first factor to be considered is the nature of the privacy interest upon which the search here at issue intrudes. The Fourth Amendment does not protect all subjective expectations of privacy, but only those that society recognizes as "legitimate." What expectations are legitimate varies, of course, with context, depending, for example, upon whether the individual asserting the privacy interest is at home, at work, in a car, or in a public park. In addition, the legitimacy of certain privacy expectations vis-à-vis the State may depend upon the individual's legal relationship with the State. For example, in *Griffin*, we held that, although a "probationer's home, like anyone else's, is protected by the Fourth Amendmen[t]," the supervisory relationship between probationer and State justifies "a degree of impingement upon [a probationer's] privacy that would not be constitutional if applied to the public at large." Central, in our view, to the present case is the fact that the subjects of the Policy are (1) children, who (2) have been committed to the temporary custody of the State as schoolmaster.

Traditionally at common law, and still today, unemancipated minors lack some of the most fundamental rights of self-determination—including even the right of liberty in its narrow sense, i.e., the right to come and go at will. They are subject, even as to their physical freedom, to the control of their parents or guardians. When parents place minor children in private schools for their education, the teachers and administrators of those schools stand in loco parentis over the children entrusted to them. In fact, the tutor or schoolmaster is the very prototype of that status. As Blackstone describes it, a parent "may . . . delegate part of his parental authority, during his life, to the tutor or schoolmaster of his child; who is then in loco parentis, and has such a portion of the power of the parent committed to his charge, viz. that of restraint and correction, as may be necessary to answer the purposes for which he is employed."

In *T.L.O.* we rejected the notion that public schools, like private schools, exercise only parental power over their students, which of course is not subject to constitutional constraints. Such a view of things, we said, "is not entirely 'consonant with compulsory education laws,' and is inconsistent with our prior decisions treating school officials as state actors for purposes of the Due Process and Free Speech Clauses." But while denying that the State's power over schoolchildren is formally no more than the delegated power of their parents, *T.L.O.* did not deny, but indeed emphasized, that the nature of that power is custodial and tutelary, permitting a degree of supervision and control that could not be exercised over free adults. "[A] proper educational environment requires close supervision of schoolchildren, as well as the enforcement of rules against conduct that would be perfectly permissible if undertaken by an adult." While we do not, of course, suggest that public schools as a general matter have such a degree of control over children as to give rise to a constitutional "duty to protect," we have acknowledged that for many purposes "school authorities ac[t] in loco parentis," with the power and indeed the duty to "inculcate the habits and manners of civility." Thus, while children assuredly do not "shed their constitutional rights . . . at the schoolhouse gate," the nature of those rights is what is appropriate for children in school.

Fourth Amendment rights, no less than First and Fourteenth Amendment rights, are different in public schools than elsewhere; the "reasonableness" inquiry cannot disregard the schools' custodial and tutelary responsibility for children. For their own good and that of their classmates, public school children are routinely required to submit to various physical examinations, and to be vaccinated against various diseases. According to the American Academy of Pediatrics, most public schools "provide vision and hearing screening and dental and dermatological checks. . . . Others also mandate scoliosis screening at appropriate grade levels." In the 1991-1992 school year, all 50 States required public school students to be vaccinated against diphtheria, measles, rubella, and polio. Particularly with regard to medical examinations and procedures, therefore, "students within the school environment have a lesser expectation of privacy than members of the population generally."

Legitimate privacy expectations are even less with regard to student athletes. School sports are not for the bashful. They require "suiting up" before each practice or event, and showering and changing afterwards. Public school locker rooms, the usual sites for these activities, are not notable for the privacy they afford. The locker rooms in Vernonia are typical: No individual dressing rooms are provided; shower heads are lined up along a wall, unseparated by any sort of partition or curtain; not even all the toilet stalls have doors. As the United States Court of Appeals for the Seventh Circuit has noted, there is "an element of 'communal undress' inherent in athletic participation."

There is an additional respect in which school athletes have a reduced expectation of privacy. By choosing to "go out for the team," they voluntarily subject themselves to a degree of regulation even higher than that imposed on students generally. In Vernonia's public schools, they must submit to a preseason physical exam (James testified that his included the giving of a urine sample), they must acquire adequate insurance coverage or sign an insurance waiver, maintain a minimum grade point average, and comply with any "rules of conduct, dress, training hours and related matters as may be established for each sport by the head coach and athletic director with the principal's approval." Somewhat like adults who choose to participate in a "closely regulated industry," students who voluntarily participate in school athletics have reason to expect intrusions upon normal rights and privileges, including privacy.

IV

Having considered the scope of the legitimate expectation of privacy at issue here, we turn next to the character of the intrusion that is complained of. We recognized in *Skinner* that collecting the samples for urinalysis intrudes upon "an excretory function traditionally shielded by great privacy." We noted, however, that the degree of intrusion depends upon the manner in which production of the urine sample is monitored. Under the District's Policy, male students produce samples at a urinal along a wall. They remain fully clothed and are only observed from behind, if at all. Female students produce samples in an enclosed stall, with a female monitor standing outside listening only for sounds of tampering. These conditions are nearly identical to those typically encountered in public restrooms, which men, women, and especially schoolchildren use daily. Under such conditions, the privacy interests compromised by the process of obtaining the urine sample are in our view negligible.

The other privacy-invasive aspect of urinalysis is, of course, the information it discloses concerning the state of the subject's body, and the materials he has ingested. In this regard it is significant that the tests at issue here look only for drugs, and not for whether the student is, for example, epileptic, pregnant, or diabetic. Moreover, the drugs for which the samples are screened are standard, and do not vary according to the identity of the student. And finally, the results of the tests are disclosed only to a limited class of school personnel who have a need to know; and they are not turned over to law enforcement authorities or used for any internal disciplinary function.

Respondents argue, however, that the District's Policy is in fact more intrusive than this suggests, because it requires the students, if they are to avoid sanctions for a falsely positive test, to identify in advance prescription medications they are taking. We agree that this raises some cause for concern. In *Von Raab*, we flagged as one of the salutary features of the Customs Service drug-testing program the fact that employees were not required to disclose medical information unless they tested positive, and, even then, the information was supplied to a licensed physician rather than to the Government employer. On the other hand, we have never indicated that requiring advance disclosure of medications is per se unreasonable. Indeed, in *Skinner* we held that it was not "a significant invasion of privacy." It can be argued that, in *Skinner*, the disclosure went only to the medical personnel taking the sample, and the Government personnel analyzing it; and that disclosure to teachers and coaches — to persons who personally know the student — is a greater invasion of privacy. Assuming for the sake of argument that both those propositions are true, we do not believe they establish a difference that respondents are entitled to rely on here.

The General Authorization Form that respondents refused to sign, which refusal was the basis for James's exclusion from the sports program, said only (in relevant part): "I . . . authorize the Vernonia School District to conduct a test on a urine specimen which I provide to test for drugs and/or alcohol use. I also authorize the release of information concerning the results of such a test to the Vernonia School District and to the parents and/or guardians of the student." While the practice of the District seems to have been to have a school official take medication information from the student at the time of the test, that practice is not set forth in, or required by, the Policy, which says simply: "Student athletes who . . . are or have been taking prescription medication must provide verification (either by a copy of the prescription or by doctor's authorization) prior to being tested." It may well be that, if and when James was selected for random testing at a time that he was taking medication, the School District would have permitted him to provide the requested information in a confidential manner — for example, in a sealed envelope delivered to the testing lab. Nothing in the Policy contradicts that, and when respondents choose, in effect, to challenge the Policy on its face, we will not assume the worst. Accordingly, we reach the same conclusion as in *Skinner*: that the invasion of privacy was not significant.

V

Finally, we turn to consider the nature and immediacy of the governmental concern at issue here, and the efficacy of this means for meeting it. In both *Skinner* and *Von Raab*, we characterized the government interest motivating the search as "compelling." Relying on these cases, the District Court held that because the District's program also called for drug testing in the absence of individualized suspicion, the District "must demonstrate a 'compelling need' for the program." The Court of Appeals appears to have agreed with this view. It is a mistake, however, to think that the phrase "compelling state interest," in the Fourth Amendment context, describes a fixed, minimum quantum of governmental concern, so that one can dispose of a case by answering in isolation the question: Is there a compelling state interest here? Rather, the phrase describes an interest that appears important enough to justify the particular search at hand, in light of other factors that show the search to be relatively intrusive upon a genuine expectation of privacy. Whether that relatively high degree of government concern is necessary in this case or not, we think it is met.

That the nature of the concern is important — indeed, perhaps compelling — can hardly be doubted. Deterring drug use by our Nation's schoolchildren is at least as important as enhancing efficient enforcement of the Nation's laws against the importation of drugs, which was the governmental concern in *Von Raab*, or deterring drug use by engineers and trainmen, which was the governmental concern in *Skinner*. School years are the time when the physical, psychological, and addictive effects of drugs are most severe. "Maturing nervous systems are more critically impaired by intoxicants than mature ones are; childhood losses in learning are lifelong and profound"; "children grow chemically dependent more quickly than adults, and their record of recovery is depressingly poor." And of course the effects of a drug-infested school are visited not just upon the users, but upon the entire student body and faculty, as the educational process is disrupted. In the present case, moreover, the necessity for the State to act is magnified by the fact that this evil is being visited not just upon individuals at large, but upon children for whom it has undertaken a special responsibility of care and direction. Finally, it must not be lost sight of that this program is directed more narrowly to drug use by school athletes, where the risk of immediate physical harm to the drug user or those with whom he is playing his sport is particularly high. Apart from psychological effects, which include impairment of judgment, slow reaction time, and a lessening of the perception of pain, the particular drugs screened by the District's Policy have been demonstrated to pose substantial physical risks to athletes. Amphetamines produce an "artificially induced heart rate increase, [p]eripheral vasoconstriction, [b]lood pressure increase, and [m]asking of the normal fatigue response," making them a "very dangerous drug when used during exercise of any type." Marijuana causes "[i]rregular blood pressure responses during changes in body position," "[r]eduction in the oxygen-carrying capacity of the blood," and "[i]nhibition of the normal sweating responses resulting in increased body temperature." Cocaine produces "[v]asoconstriction[,] [e]levated blood pressure," and "[p]ossible coronary artery spasms and myocardial infarction."

As for the immediacy of the District's concerns: We are not inclined to question — indeed, we could not possibly find clearly erroneous — the District Court's conclusion that "a large segment of the student body, particularly those involved in interscholastic athletics, was in a state of rebellion," that "[d]isciplinary actions had reached 'epidemic proportions,'" and that "the rebellion was being fueled by alcohol and drug abuse as well as by the student's misperceptions about the drug culture." That is an immediate crisis of greater proportions than existed in *Skinner*, where we upheld the Government's drug-testing program based on findings of drug use by railroad employees nationwide, without proof that a problem existed on the particular railroads whose employees were subject to the test. And of much greater proportions than existed in *Von Raab*, where there was no documented history of drug use by any customs officials.

As to the efficacy of this means for addressing the problem: It seems to us self-evident that a drug problem largely fueled by the "role model" effect of athletes' drug use, and of particular danger to athletes, is effectively addressed by making sure that athletes do not use drugs. Respondents argue that a "less intrusive means to the same end" was available, namely, "drug testing on suspicion of drug use." We have repeatedly refused to declare that only the "least intrusive" search practicable can be reasonable under the Fourth Amendment. Respondents' alternative entails substantial difficulties — if it is indeed practicable at all. It may be impracticable, for one thing, simply because the parents who are willing to accept random drug testing for athletes are not willing to accept accusatory drug testing for all students, which transforms the process into a badge of shame. Respondents' proposal brings the risk that teachers will impose testing arbitrarily upon troublesome but not drug-likely students. It generates the expense of defending lawsuits that charge such arbitrary imposition, or that simply demand greater process before accusatory drug testing is imposed. And not least of all, it adds to the ever-expanding diversionary duties of schoolteachers the new function of spotting and bringing to account drug abuse, a task for which they are ill prepared, and which is not readily compatible with their vocation. In many respects, we think, testing based on "suspicion" of drug use would not be better, but worse.

VI

Taking into account all the factors we have considered above—the decreased expectation of privacy, the relative unobtrusiveness of the search, and the severity of the need met by the search—we conclude Vernonia's Policy is reasonable and hence constitutional.

We caution against the assumption that suspicionless drug testing will readily pass constitutional muster in other contexts. The most significant element in this case is the first we discussed: that the Policy was undertaken in furtherance of the government's responsibilities, under a public school system, as guardian and tutor of children entrusted to its care. Just as when the government conducts a search in its capacity as employer (a warrantless search of an absent employee's desk to obtain an urgently needed file, for example), the relevant question is whether that intrusion upon privacy is one that a reasonable employer might engage in; so also when the government acts as guardian and tutor the relevant question is whether the search is one that a reasonable guardian and tutor might undertake. Given the findings of need made by the District Court, we conclude that in the present case it is.

We may note that the primary guardians of Vernonia's schoolchildren appear to agree. The record shows no objection to this districtwide program by any parents other than the couple before us here—even though, as we have described, a public meeting was held to obtain parents' views. We find insufficient basis to contradict the judgment of Vernonia's parents, its school board, and the District Court, as to what was reasonably in the interest of these children under the circumstances.

The Ninth Circuit held that Vernonia's Policy not only violated the Fourth Amendment, but also, by reason of that violation, contravened Article I, § 9, of the Oregon Constitution. Our conclusion that the former holding was in error means that the latter holding rested on a flawed premise. We therefore vacate the judgment, and remand the case to the Court of Appeals for further proceedings consistent with this opinion.

[Justices Souter, Stevens, and O'Connor dissented.]

NOTES AND QUESTIONS

1. What inferences can you draw from the opening line of the opinion:

> As elsewhere in small-town America, school sports play a prominent role in the town's life, and student athletes are admired in their schools and in the community.

Id. at 648. Any doubt that Justice Scalia was from a city? And did not play sports in high school?

2. Note the meticulous attention to detail in the four-paragraph description of the school district's drug-testing program. Is there any doubt at this point in the opinion who is going to win?

3. The Court relies, as it did in *T.L.O.*, on the notion that the state's power over schoolchildren is both "custodial and tutelary," which permits "a degree of supervision and control that could not be exercised over free adults." Do you accept this premise? If so, is the greater degree of control permitted more a function of the compulsory nature of public education or the educational mission of public education?

4. Do you agree with the Court that high school athletes have reduced legitimate expectations in their urine because they may shower in locker rooms and to some extent experience "communal undress"? Because they have to comply with other requirements (a physical, GPA, etc.) not imposed on the student body at large?

Are these two points necessary to the Court's conclusion, or could this drug-testing regime be applied to the entire student body?

Is the school's purported concern for sports-related injury to members of the Loggers (including the football and wrestling coach's testimony) plausible?

Vernonia High, home of the Loggers

5. Is there anything preventing the local district attorney from serving a grand jury subpoena for the high school's drug-testing records and prosecuting those students who tested positive?

6. Just five years later, in *Bd. of Educ. v. Earls*, 536 U.S. 822 (2002), the Court upheld on virtually identical reasoning a school district's drug-testing regime for all students participating in "competitive extracurricular activities." The Court did not find it necessary to revisit the sports-related implications of *Vernonia*. In dissent, however, Justice Ginsburg distinguished *Vernonia* in part on the basis of her view of the superiority of non-athletic extracurricular activities over the interscholastic sports at issue in *Vernonia*.

As noted in *Vernonia*, the Court has upheld drug-testing regimens in other contexts under the special needs/administrative exception. *See, e.g., Skinner v. Railway Labor Executives' Assn.*, 489 U.S. 602 (1989); *Treasury Employees v. Von Raab*, 489 U.S. 656 (1989). It has rejected as too broad, however, a Georgia law requiring every candidate for state office to take and pass a drug test. *Chandler v. Miller*, 520 U.S. 305 (1997).

8. The Automobile Exception

Carroll v. United States
267 U.S. 132 (1925)

Mr. Chief Justice TAFT, after stating the case as above, delivered the opinion of the Court.

The constitutional and statutory provisions involved in this case include the Fourth Amendment and the National Prohibition Act.

Chapter IV The Fourth Amendment

The Fourth Amendment is in part as follows:

> The right of the people to be secure in their persons, houses, papers and effects against unreasonable searches and seizures shall not be violated, and no warrants shall issue but upon probable cause, supported by oath or affirmation, and particularly describing the place to be searched, and the persons or things to be seized.

Section 25, title 2, of the National Prohibition Act, passed to enforce the Eighteenth Amendment, makes it unlawful to have or possess any liquor intended for use in violating the act, or which has been so used, and provides that no property rights shall exist in such liquor. A search warrant may issue and such liquor, with the containers thereof, may be seized under the warrant and be ultimately destroyed. The section further provides:

> No search warrant shall issue to search any private dwelling occupied as such unless it is being used for the unlawful sale of intoxicating liquor, or unless it is in part used for some business purpose such as a store, shop, saloon, restaurant, hotel, or boarding house. The term "private dwelling" shall be construed to include the room or rooms used and occupied not transiently but solely as a residence in an apartment house, hotel, or boarding house.

Section 26, title 2, under which the seizure herein was made, provides in part as follows:

> When the commissioner, his assistants, inspectors, or any officer of the law shall discover any person in the act of transporting in violation of the law, intoxicating liquors in any wagon, buggy, automobile, water or air craft, or other vehicle, it shall be his duty to seize any and all intoxicating liquors found therein being transported contrary to law. Whenever intoxicating liquors transported or possessed illegally shall be seized by an officer he shall take possession of the vehicle and team or automobile, boat, air or water craft, or any other conveyance, and shall arrest any person in charge thereof.

The section then provides that the court upon conviction of the person so arrested shall order the liquor destroyed, and except for good cause shown shall order a sale by public auction of the other property seized, and that the proceeds shall be paid into the Treasury of the United States.

By section 6 of an act supplemental to the National Prohibition it is provided that if any officer or agent or employee of the United States engaged in the enforcement of the Prohibition Act or this Amendment, "shall search any private dwelling," as defined in that act, "without a warrant directing such search," or "shall without a search warrant maliciously and without reasonable cause search any other building or property," he shall be guilty of a misdemeanor and subject to fine or imprisonment or both.

In the passage of the supplemental act through the Senate, amendment No. 32, known as the Stanley Amendment, was adopted, the relevant part of which was as follows:

> Sec. 6. That any officer, agent or employee of the United States engaged in the enforcement of this act or the National Prohibition Act, or any other law of the United States, who shall search or attempt to search the property or premises of any person without previously securing a search warrant, as provided by law, shall be guilty of a misdemeanor and upon conviction thereof shall be fined not to exceed $1,000, or imprisoned not to exceed one year, or both so fined and imprisoned in the discretion of the court.

This amendment was objected to in the House, and the judiciary committee, to whom it was referred, reported to the House of Representatives the following as a substitute:

> Sec. 6. That no officer, agent or employee of the United States, while engaged in the enforcement of this act, the National Prohibition Act, or any law in reference to the manufacture or taxation of, or traffic in, intoxicating liquor, shall search any private dwelling without a warrant directing such search, and no such warrant shall issue unless there is reason to believe

C. The Warrant Requirement and Its Exceptions

such dwelling is used as a place in which liquor is manufactured for sale or sold. The term "private dwelling" shall be construed to include the room or rooms occupied not transiently, but solely as a residence in an apartment house, hotel, or boarding house. Any violation of any provision of this paragraph shall be punished by a fine of not to exceed $1,000 or imprisonment not to exceed one year, or both such fine and imprisonment, in the discretion of the court.

In its report the committee spoke in part as follows:

> It appeared to the committee that the effect of the Senate amendment No. 32, if agreed to by the House, would greatly cripple the enforcement of the National Prohibition Act and would otherwise seriously interfere with the government in the enforcement of many other laws, as its scope is not limited to the prohibition law, but applies equally to all laws where prompt action is necessary. There are on the statute books of the United States a number of laws authorizing search without a search warrant. Under the common law and agreeable to the Constitution search may in many cases be legally made without a warrant. The Constitution does not forbid search, as some parties contend, but it does forbid unreasonable search. This provision in regard to search is as a rule contained in the various state Constitutions, but notwithstanding that fact search without a warrant is permitted in many cases, and especially is that true in the enforcement of liquor legislation.
>
> The Senate amendment prohibits all search or attempt to search any property or premises without a search warrant. The effect of that would necessarily be to prohibit all search, as no search can take place if it is not on some property or premises.
>
> Not only does this amendment prohibit search of any lands but it prohibits the search of all property. It will prevent the search of the common bootlegger and his stock in trade, though caught and arrested in the act of violating the law. But what is perhaps more serious, it will make it impossible to stop the rum-running automobiles engaged in like illegal traffic. It would take from the officers the power that they absolutely must have to be of any service, for if they cannot search for liquor without a warrant they might as well be discharged. It is impossible to get a warrant to stop an automobile. Before a warrant could be secured the automobile would be beyond the reach of the officer with its load of illegal liquor disposed of.

The conference report resulted, so far as the difference between the two houses was concerned, in providing for the punishment of any officer, agent, or employee of the government who searches a "private dwelling" without a warrant, and for the punishment of any such officer, etc., who searches any "other building or property" where, and only where, he makes the search without a warrant "maliciously and without probable cause." In other words, it left the way open for searching an automobile or vehicle of transportation without a warrant, if the search was not malicious or without probable cause.

The intent of Congress to make a distinction between the necessity for a search warrant in the searching of private dwellings and in that of automobiles and other road vehicles in the enforcement of the Prohibition Act is thus clearly established by the legislative history of the Stanley Amendment. Is such a distinction consistent with the Fourth Amendment? We think that it is. The Fourth Amendment does not denounce all searches or seizures, but only such as are unreasonable.

The leading case on the subject of search and seizure is *Boyd v. United States*, 116 U.S. 616. An Act of Congress authorized a court of the United States in revenue cases, on motion of the government attorney, to require the defendant to produce in court his private books, invoices, and papers on pain in case of refusal of having the allegations of the attorney in his motion taken as confessed. This was held to be unconstitutional and void as applied to suits for penalties or to establish a forfeiture of goods, on the ground that under the Fourth Amendment the compulsory production of invoices to furnish evidence for forfeiture of goods constituted an unreasonable search even where made upon a search warrant, and was also a violation of the

Fifth Amendment, in that it compelled the defendant in a criminal case to produce evidence against himself or be in the attitude of confessing his guilt.

In *Weeks v. United States*, it was held that a court in a criminal prosecution could not retain letters of the accused seized in his house, in his absence and without his authority, by a United States marshal holding no warrant for his arrest and none for the search of his premises, to be used as evidence against him, the accused having made timely application to the court for an order for the return of the letters.

In *Silverthorne Lumber Co. v. United States* a writ of error was brought to reverse a judgment of contempt of the District Court, fining the company and imprisoning one Silverthorne, its president, until he should purge himself of contempt in not producing books and documents of the company before the grand jury to prove violation of the statutes of the United States by the company and Silverthorne. Silverthorne had been arrested, and while under arrest the marshal had gone to the office of the company without a warrant and made a clean sweep of all books, papers, and documents found there and had taken copies and photographs of the papers. The District Court ordered the return of the originals, but impounded the photographs and copies. This was held to be an unreasonable search of the property and possessions of the corporation and a violation of the Fourth Amendment and the judgment for contempt was reversed.

In *Gouled v. United States*, the obtaining through stealth by a representative of the government from the office of one suspected of defrauding the government of a paper which had no pecuniary value in itself, but was only to be used as evidence against its owner, was held to be a violation of the Fourth Amendment. It was further held that when the paper was offered in evidence and duly objected to it must be ruled inadmissible because obtained through an unreasonable search and seizure and also in violation of the Fifth Amendment because working compulsory incrimination.

In *Amos v. United States*, it was held that where concealed liquor was found by government officers without a search warrant in the home of the defendant, in his absence, and after a demand made upon his wife, it was inadmissible as evidence against the defendant, because acquired by an unreasonable seizure.

In none of the cases cited is there any ruling as to the validity under the Fourth Amendment of a seizure without a warrant of contraband goods in the course of transportation and subject to forfeiture or destruction.

On reason and authority the true rule is that if the search and seizure without a warrant are made upon probable cause, that is, upon a belief, reasonably arising out of circumstances known to the seizing officer, that an automobile or other vehicle contains that which by law is subject to seizure and destruction, the search and seizure are valid. The Fourth Amendment is to be construed in the light of what was deemed an unreasonable search and seizure when it was adopted, and in a manner which will conserve public interests as well as the interests and rights of individual citizens.

In *Boyd v. United States* as already said, the decision did not turn on whether a reasonable search might be made without a warrant; but for the purpose of showing the principle on which the Fourth Amendment proceeds, and to avoid any misapprehension of what was decided, the court, speaking through Mr. Justice Bradley, used language which is of particular significance and applicability here. It was there said:

> The search for and seizure of stolen or forfeited goods, or goods liable to duties and concealed to avoid the payment thereof, are totally different things from a search for and seizure of a man's private books and papers for the purpose of obtaining information therein contained, or of using them as evidence against him. The two things differ *toto coelo*. In the one case, the government is entitled to the possession of the property; in the other it is not. The seizure of stolen goods is authorized by the common law; and the seizure of goods forfeited for a breach of the

revenue laws, or concealed to avoid the duties payable on them, has been authorized by English statutes for at least two centuries past; and the like seizures have been authorized by our own revenue acts from the commencement of the government.

. . .

We have made a somewhat extended reference to these statutes to show that the guaranty of freedom from unreasonable searches and seizures by the Fourth Amendment has been construed, practically since the beginning of the government, as recognizing a necessary difference between a search of a store, dwelling house, or other structure in respect of which a proper official warrant readily may be obtained and a search of a ship, motor boat, wagon, or automobile for contraband goods, where it is not practicable to secure a warrant, because the vehicle can be quickly moved out of the locality or jurisdiction in which the warrant must be sought.

Having thus established that contraband goods concealed and illegally transported in an automobile or other vehicle may be searched for without a warrant, we come now to consider under what circumstances such search may be made. It would be intolerable and unreasonable if a prohibition agent were authorized to stop every automobile on the chance of finding liquor, and thus subject all persons lawfully using the highways to the inconvenience and indignity of such a search. Travelers may be so stopped in crossing an international boundary because of national self-protection reasonably requiring one entering the country to identify himself as entitled to come in, and his belongings as effects which may be lawfully brought in. But those lawfully within the country, entitled to use the public highways, have a right to free passage without interruption or search unless there is known to a competent official, authorized to search, probable cause for believing that their vehicles are carrying contraband or illegal merchandise. Section 26, title 2, of the National Prohibition Act, like the second section of the act of 1789, for the searching of vessels, like the provisions of the act of 1815, and section 3601, Revised Statutes, for searching vehicles for smuggled goods, and like the act of 1822, and that of 1834 and section 2140, R. S., and the act of 1917 for the search of vehicles and automobiles for liquor smuggled into the Indian country, was enacted primarily to accomplish the seizure and destruction of contraband goods; secondly, the automobile was to be forfeited; and, thirdly, the driver was to be arrested. Under section 29, title 2, of the act the latter might be punished by not more than $500 fine for the first offense, not more than $1,000 fine and 90 days' imprisonment for the second offense, and by a fine of $500 or more and by not more than 2 years' imprisonment for the third offense. Thus he is to be arrested for a misdemeanor for his first and second offenses, and for a felony if he offends the third time.

The main purpose of the act obviously was to deal with the liquor and its transportation, and to destroy it. The mere manufacture of liquor can do little to defeat the policy of the Eighteenth Amendment and the Prohibition Act, unless the for bidden product can be distributed for illegal sale and use. Section 26 was intended to reach and destroy the forbidden liquor in transportation and the provisions for forfeiture of the vehicle and the arrest of the transporter were incidental. The rule for determining what may be required before a seizure may be made by a competent seizing official is not to be determined by the character of the penalty to which the transporter may be subjected. Under section 28, title 2, of the Prohibition Act, the Commissioner of Internal Revenue, his assistants, agents and inspectors are to have the power and protection in the enforcement of the act conferred by the existing laws relating to the manufacture or sale of intoxicating liquors. Officers who seize under section 26 of the Prohibition Act are therefore protected by section 970 of the Revised Statutes, providing that:

> When, in any prosecution commenced on account of the seizure of any vessel, goods, wares, or merchandise, made by any collector or other officer, under any act of Congress authorizing such seizure, judgment is rendered for the claimant, but it appears to the court that there was

reasonable cause of seizure, the court shall cause a proper certificate thereof to be entered, and the claimant shall not, in such case, be entitled to costs, nor shall the person who made the seizure, nor the prosecutor, be liable to suit or judgment on account of such suit or prosecution: Provided, that the vessel, goods, wares, or merchandise be, after judgment, forthwith returned to such claimant or his agent.

It follows from this that, if an officer seizes an automobile or the liquor in it without a warrant, and the facts as subsequently developed do not justify a judgment of condemnation and forfeiture, the officer may escape costs or a suit for damages by a showing that he had reasonable or probable cause for the seizure. The measure of legality of such a seizure is, therefore, that the seizing officer shall have reasonable or probable cause for believing that the automobile which he stops and seizes has contraband liquor therein which is being illegally transported.

We here find the line of distinction between legal and illegal seizures of liquor in transport in vehicles. It is certainly a reasonable distinction. It gives the owner of an automobile or other vehicle seized under section 26, in absence of probable cause, a right to have restored to him the automobile, it protects him under the *Weeks* and *Amos* cases from use of the liquor as evidence against him, and it subjects the officer making the seizures to damages. On the other hand, in a case showing probable cause, the government and its officials are given the opportunity which they should have, to make the investigation necessary to trace reasonably suspected contraband goods and to seize them.

Such a rule fulfills the guaranty of the Fourth Amendment. In cases where the securing of a warrant is reasonably practicable, it must be used and when properly supported by affidavit and issued after judicial approval protects the seizing officer against a suit for damages. In cases where seizure is impossible except without warrant, the seizing officer acts unlawfully and at his peril unless he can show the court probable cause.

But we are pressed with the argument that if the search of the automobile discloses the presence of liquor and leads under the statue to the arrest of the person in charge of the automobile, the right of seizure should be limited by the common-law rule as to the circumstances justifying an arrest without a warrant for a misdemeanor. The usual rule is that a police officer may arrest without warrant one believed by the officer upon reasonable cause to have been guilty of a felony, and that he may only arrest without a warrant one guilty of a misdemeanor if committed in his presence. The rule is sometimes expressed as follows:

> In cases of misdemeanor, a peace officer like a private person has at common law no power of arresting without a warrant except when a breach of the peace has been committed in his presence or there is reasonable ground for supposing that a breach of peace is about to be committed or renewed in his presence.

The reason for arrest for misdemeanors without warrant at common law was promptly to suppress breaches of the peace, while the reason for arrest without warrant on a reliable report of a felony was because the public safety and the due apprehension of criminals charged with heinous offenses required that such arrests should be made at once without warrant. The argument for defendants is that, as the misdemeanor to justify arrest without warrant must be committed in the presence of the police officer, the offense is not committed in his presence unless he can by his senses detect that the liquor is being transported, no matter how reliable his previous information by which he can identify the automobile as loaded with it.

So it is that under the rule contended for by defendants the liquor if carried by one who has been already twice convicted of the same offense may be seized on information other than the senses, while if he has been only once convicted it may not be seized unless the presence of the liquor is detected by the senses as the automobile concealing it rushes by. This is certainly a very unsatisfactory line of difference when the main object of the section is to forfeit and suppress the liquor, the arrest of the individual being only incidental as shown by the lightness of the penalty. In England at the common law the difference in punishment between felonies and misdemeanors was very great. Under our present federal statutes, it is much less important and Congress may exercise a relatively wide discretion in classing particular offenses as felonies or misdemeanors. As the main purpose of section 26 was seizure and forfeiture, it is not so much the owner as the property that offends. The language of the section provides for seizure when the officer of the law "discovers" any one in the act of transporting the liquor by automobile or other vehicle. Certainly it is a very narrow and technical construction of this word which would limit it to what the officer sees, hears or smells as the automobile rolls by and excludes therefrom when he identifies the car the convincing information that he may previously have received as to the use being made of it.

We do not think such a nice distinction is applicable in the present case. When a man is legally arrested for an offense, whatever is found upon his person or in his control which it is unlawful for him to have and which may be used to prove the offense may be seized and held as evidence in the prosecution. The argument of defendants is based on the theory that the seizure in this case can only be thus justified. If their theory were sound, their conclusion would be. The validity of the seizure then would turn wholly on the validity of the arrest without a seizure. But the theory is unsound. The right to search and the validity of the seizure are not dependent on the right to arrest. They are dependent on the reasonable cause the seizing officer has for belief that the contents of the automobile offend against the law. The seizure in such a proceeding comes before the arrest as section 26 indicates. It is true that section 26, title 2, provides for immediate proceedings against the person arrested and that upon conviction the liquor is to be destroyed and the automobile or other vehicle is to be sold, with the saving of the interest of a lienor who does not know of its unlawful use; but it is evident that if the person arrested is ignorant of the contents of the vehicle, or if he escapes, proceedings can be had against the liquor for destruction or other disposition under section 25 of the same title. The character of the offense for which, after the contraband liquor is found and seized, the driver can be prosecuted does not affect the validity of the seizure.

This conclusion is in keeping with the requirements of the Fourth Amendment and the principles of search and seizure of contraband forfeitable property; and it is a wise one because it leaves the rule one which is easily applied and understood and is uniform.

Finally, was there probable cause?

• • •

In *The Apollon*, the question was whether the seizure of a French vessel at a particular place was upon probable cause that she was there for the purpose of smuggling. In this discussion Mr. Justice Story, who delivered the judgment of the court, said:

> It has been very justly observed at the bar that the court is bound to take notice of public facts and geographical positions, and that this remote part of the country has been infested, at different periods, by smugglers, is matter of general notoriety, and may be gathered from the public documents of the government.

We know in this way that Grand Rapids is about 152 miles from Detroit, and that Detroit and its neighborhood along the Detroit river, which is the international boundary, is one of the most active centers for introducing illegally into this country spirituous liquors for distribution into the interior. It is obvious from the evidence that the prohibition agents were engaged in a regular patrol along the important highways from Detroit to Grand Rapids to stop and seize liquor carried in automobiles. They knew or had convincing evidence to make them believe that the Carroll boys, as they called them, were so-called "bootleggers" in Grand Rapids; i.e., that they were engaged in plying the unlawful trade of selling such liquor in that city. The officers had soon after noted their going from Grand Rapids half way to Detroit, and attempted to follow them to that city to see where they went, but they escaped observation. Two months later these officers suddenly met the same men on their way westward presumably from Detroit. The partners in the original combination to sell liquor in Grand Rapids were together in the same automobile they had been in the night when they tried to furnish the whisky to the officers, which was thus identified as part of the firm equipment. They were coming from the direction of the great source of supply for their stock to Grand Rapids, where they plied their trade. That the officers, when they saw the defendants, believed that they were carrying liquor, we can have no doubt, and we think it is equally clear that they had reasonable cause for thinking so. Emphasis is put by defendants' counsel on the statement made by one of the officers that they were not looking for defendants at the particular time when they appeared. We do not perceive that it has any weight. As soon as they did appear, the officers were entitled to use their reasoning faculties upon all the facts of which they had previous knowledge in respect to the defendants.

The necessity for probable cause in justifying seizures on land or sea, in making arrests without warrant for past felonies, and in malicious prosecution and false imprisonment cases has led to frequent definition of the phrase. In *Stacey v. Emery*, a suit for damages for seizure by a collector, this court defined probable cause as follows:

> If the facts and circumstances before the officer are such as to warrant a man of prudence and caution in believing that the offense has been committed, it is sufficient.

$$\bullet \quad \bullet \quad \bullet$$

In the light of these authorities, and what is shown by this record, it is clear the officers here had justification for the search and seizure. This is to say that the facts and circumstances within their knowledge and of which they had reasonably trustworthy information were sufficient in themselves to warrant a man of reasonable caution in the belief that intoxicating liquor was being transported in the automobile which they stopped and searched.

Counsel finally argue that the defendants should be permitted to escape the effect of the conviction because the court refused on motion to deliver them the liquor when, as they say, the evidence adduced on the motion was much less than that shown on the trial, and did not show probable cause. The record does not make it clear what evidence was produced in support of or against the motion. But, apart from this, we think the point is without substance here. If the evidence given on the trial was sufficient, as we think it was, to sustain the introduction of the liquor as evidence, it is immaterial that there was an inadequacy of evidence when application was made for its return. A conviction on adequate and admissible evidence should not be set aside on such a ground. The whole matter was gone into at the trial, so no right of the defendants was infringed.

Counsel for the government contend that Kiro, the defendant who did not own the automobile, could not complain of the violation of the Fourth Amendment in the use of the liquor as evidence against him, whatever the view taken as to Carroll's rights. Our conclusion as to the whole case makes it unnecessary for us to discuss this aspect of it.

NOTES AND QUESTIONS

1. In parts of the opinion mostly omitted here, the Court goes into some detail about congressional legislation regarding search and seizure, both in connection with Prohibition — a movement with not only its own constitutional amendment but multiple implementing statutes — and otherwise. The Court notes that the Volstead Act established a dichotomy between automobiles and dwellings, explicitly requiring warrants for searches for the latter but not the former. The Court also notes that other legislation over the previous century more generally permitted warrantless searches of ships and other vessels.

Why would the Court look to such congressional "precedent" in applying the Fourth Amendment? Part of the answer may be due to the fact that federal case law on the subject was scanty — prior to Prohibition federal law enforcement agents were few and far between and there was not much federal criminal law for them to enforce. Federal customs officials — the investigators in *Boyd v. United States* (*see* Chapter III *supra*) — were an exception.

2. *Carroll* nonetheless established new Fourth Amendment law by dispensing with the warrant requirement, and the corresponding judicial oversight of police action, for a "reasonable or probable cause" standard that would be applied by law enforcement agents in the field. Chief Justice Taft, though an avowed opponent of Prohibition as a matter of policy, was an equally forceful proponent of what he viewed as the rule of law. Daniel Okrent, Last Call: The Rise and Fall of Prohibition 282-83 (2010). Despite the matter-of-fact tone of the opinion, Taft was well aware that the Court was making brand new law, as he privately confided in letters to his son and fellow Justice Van Devanter. Sarah A. Seo, Policing the Open Road: How Cars Transformed American Freedom 138 (2019).

3. Another novel aspect of *Carroll* was its abrogation of the common law of arrests. Prior to *Carroll* a warrantless arrest on a misdemeanor charge — first and second violations of the Volstead Act were misdemeanors — required that the arresting officer personally witness the crime. The Court shrugged off this requirement as a concession to law enforcement necessity, noting that the difference between felonies and misdemeanors was more important under English common law than today. This is a classic example of the Court confronting new technology and concluding that the impact of that technology on law enforcement requires ignoring or modifying existing precedent. Not all such clashes are resolved in favor of the government, but most are.

4. Ironically Justice Brandeis, the passionate spokesperson for the interests of privacy in his *Olmstead* dissent just three years later, and in the *Harvard Law Review* 35 years earlier, joined the Court's opinion. The explanation, according to Professor Seo and others, may lie in the fact that Brandeis was something of a Luddite or what we would now call a technophobe, who never owned a car and viewed cars as an urban menace. Seo, Policing the Open Road, *supra* at 131-32. Brandeis may have in some way seen automobiles as of a piece with the new and evolving forms of privacy-reducing technology that animated his *Olmstead* dissent.

5. Does the *Carroll* exception apply only to automobiles that are actually in motion, or is it a categorical rule, owing to the inherent mobility of an automobile? Consider a car parked on a street or in a driveway, for two days, a week, a month. Is a warrant required for a search?

6. Do you agree with the Court that the officers had "probable cause" for the search and seizure of "the Carroll boys'" car? Note that the ultraconservative Justice McReynolds says the stop was made "on mere suspicion." To what extent does it appear that the Court defers to the officers' "expertise"?

7. Can *Carroll* be read as a compromise insofar as it imposes a "reasonableness" requirement even as it abandons the "warrant" requirement?

Carroll was controversial from its inception yet its reach was somewhat unclear. Arguably, perhaps hopefully, it could be read to authorize warrantless automobile searches only where Congress had authorized them by statute, as it had done in the Volstead Act. *See* Tracey Maclin, *Cops and Cars: How the Automobile Drove Fourth Amendment Law*, 99 B.U. L. Rev. 2317, 2342-43 (2019) (reviewing Seo, Policing the Open Road, *supra*). *See United States v. Di Re*, 332 U.S. 581, 585 (1948) (noting that the Court had never held that *Carroll* applied in the absence of federal legislation).

The answer came in 1949, in another illegal liquor case, even though federal Prohibition had long since been repealed. In *Brinegar v. United States*, 338 U.S. 160 (1949), on facts

384 Chapter IV The Fourth Amendment

remarkably similar to those in *Carroll*, the Court upheld a warrantless search of a car in the absence of legislation even as it acknowledged that the facts of both *Carroll* and *Brinegar* hovered somewhere "between mere suspicion and probable cause." *Id.* at 176. Even more explicitly than in *Carroll*, the Court articulated its deference to a police officer's "act of judgment," and noted that officers in the field must be given "leeway." *Id.*

Professor Seo reports that the Court in *Brinegar* was in genuine conflict about whether *Carroll* should be overturned, and that Justice Jackson's dissent—which follows—started off as the majority opinion. Seo, Policing the Open Road, *supra* at 164.

Brinegar v. United States
338 U.S. 160 (1949) (Jackson, J., dissenting)

Mr. Justice JACKSON, dissenting.

When this Court recently has promulgated a philosophy that some rights derived from the Constitution are entitled to "a preferred position," I have not agreed. We cannot give some constitutional rights a preferred position without relegating others to a deferred position; we can establish no firsts without thereby establishing seconds. Indications are not wanting that Fourth Amendment freedoms are tacitly marked as secondary rights, to be relegated to a deferred position.

The Fourth Amendment states:

> The right of the people to be secure in their persons, houses, papers, and effects, against unreasonable searches and seizures, shall not be violated, and no Warrants shall issue, but upon probable cause, supported by Oath or affirmation, and particularly describing the place to be searched, and the persons or things to be seized.

These, I protest, are not mere second-class rights but belong in the catalog of indispensable freedoms. Among deprivations of rights, none is so effective in cowing a population, crushing the spirit of the individual and putting terror in every heart. Uncontrolled search and seizure is one of the first and most effective weapons in the arsenal of every arbitrary government. And one need only briefly to have dwelt and worked among a people possessed of many admirable qualities but deprived of these rights to know that the human personality deteriorates and dignity and self-reliance disappear where homes, persons and possessions are subject at any hour to unheralded search and seizure by the police.

But the right to be secure against searches and seizures is one of the most difficult to protect. Since the officers are themselves the chief invaders, there is no enforcement outside of court.

Only occasional and more flagrant abuses come to the attention of the courts, and then only those where the search and seizure yields incriminating evidence and the defendant is at least sufficiently compromised to be indicted. If the officers raid a home, an office, or stop and search an automobile but find nothing incriminating, this invasion of the personal liberty of the innocent too often finds no practical redress. There may be, and I am convinced that there are, many unlawful searches of homes and automobiles of innocent people which turn up nothing incriminating, in which no arrest is made, about which courts do nothing, and about which we never hear.

Courts can protect the innocent against such invasions indirectly and through the medium of excluding evidence obtained against those who frequently are guilty. Federal courts have used this method of enforcement of the Amendment, in spite of its unfortunate consequences on law enforcement, although many state courts do not. This inconsistency does not disturb me, for local excesses or invasions of liberty are more amenable to political correction, the

Amendment was directed only against the new and centralized government, and any really dangerous threat to the general liberties of the people can come only from this source. We must therefore look upon the exclusion of evidence in federal prosecutions if obtained in violation of the Amendment as a means of extending protection against the central government's agencies. So a search against Brinegar's car must be regarded as a search of the car of Everyman.

We must remember that the extent of any privilege of search and seizure without warrant which we sustain, the officers interpret and apply themselves and will push to the limit. We must remember, too, that freedom from unreasonable search differs from some of the other rights of the Constitution in that there is no way the innocent citizen can invoke advance protection. For example, any effective interference with freedom of the press, or free speech, or religion, usually requires a course of suppressions against which the citizen can and often does go to the court and obtain an injunction. Other rights, such as that to an impartial jury or the aid of counsel, are within the supervisory power of the courts themselves. Such a right as just compensation for the taking of private property may be vindicated after the act in terms of money.

But an illegal search and seizure usually is a single incident, perpetrated by surprise, conducted in haste, kept purposely beyond the court's supervision and limited only by the judgment and moderation of officers whose own interests and records are often at stake in the search. There is no opportunity for injunction or appeal to disinterested intervention. The citizen's choice is quietly to submit to whatever the officers undertake or to resist at risk of arrest or immediate violence.

And we must remember that the authority which we concede to conduct searches and seizures without warrant may be exercised by the most unfit and ruthless officers as well as by the fit and responsible, and resorted to in case of petty misdemeanors as well as in the case of the gravest felonies.

• • •

I do not, of course, contend that officials may never stop a car on the highway without the halting being considered an arrest or a search. Regulations of traffic, identifications where proper, traffic census, quarantine regulations, and many other causes give occasion to stop cars in circumstances which do not imply arrest or charge of crime. And to trail or pursue a suspected car to its destination, to observe it and keep it under surveillance, is not in itself an arrest nor a search. But when a car is forced off the road, summoned to stop by a siren, and brought to a halt under such circumstances as are here disclosed, we think the officers are then in the position of one who has entered a home: the search at its commencement must be valid and cannot be saved by what it turns up.

The findings of the two courts below make it clear that this search began and proceeded through critical and coercive phases without the justification of probable cause. What it yielded cannot save it. I would reverse the judgment.

NOTES

1. All criminal procedure cases should be read from the perspective of Justice Jackson's Everyman.

2. Justice Jackson spoke with uncommon authority on the Court on the realities of law enforcement proclivities, having previous experience as a general practitioner for 15 years, a Department of Justice prosecutor for 5 years, and, ultimately, Attorney General of the United

States. Thus, his warning that the powers accorded to law enforcement "may be exercised by the most unfit and ruthless officers as well as by the fit and responsible" carry a special ring of truth. Recall also his reference in *Johnson v. United States, supra,* to the "competitive enterprise" of law enforcement. 333 U.S. 10, 13-14.

In the decades following *Brinegar,* the automobile exceptionalism of *Carroll* was layered into all cases where cars touched the Fourth Amendment. And cars touched the Fourth Amendment everywhere, especially as both the general population and police forces became increasingly mobile. The Court upheld warrantless searches of cars even in situations where it was indisputable that the rationale for the exception — "automobility," to use Professor Seo's term — was inapplicable. In *Chambers v. Mahoney,* 399 U.S. 42 (1970), a car's occupants were arrested for armed robbery and the vehicle was impounded by police and taken to the police station. It was searched at the station without a warrant — even though it was immobilized and the officers had all the time in the world — and incriminating evidence was found and used at the defendants' trial. The Court upheld the search because it was supported by probable cause.

The *Carroll* principle was further extended by the Court — ultimately — through a line of cases that began in 1977. *See* Maclin, *Cops and Cars, supra* at 2355-61; Seo, Policing the Open Road, *supra* at 247-53. In *United States v. Chadwick,* 433 U.S. 1 (1977), federal narcotics agents in Boston had probable cause to search for drugs in a footlocker that was on a train heading their way. When the train arrived at South Station and the footlocker was placed in the trunk of a waiting car by its transporters, the agents pounced: They arrested the individuals and seized the footlocker, which they later opened at their office, finding marijuana. The Court held that while the agents had been permitted to seize the footlocker from the trunk, they could not open it without a warrant, since a person has a heightened privacy expectation in luggage. In *Arkansas v. Sanders,* 442 U.S. 753 (1979), a similar result was reached with respect to a suitcase in the trunk of a moving taxi. Then in *United States v. Ross,* 456 U.S. 798 (1982), the Court held that probable cause to search an entire car — the police had information that the defendant was selling drugs "out of his car" and kept the drugs in the car's trunk — included authority to search containers in the trunk. So, to review the bidding: A warrant was required for the search of a container in a car under *Chadwick* and *Sanders* unless there was probable cause to search the entire car, as there was in *Ross.*

A majority of the Court was to find this state of affairs untenable, even though probable cause determinations were always circumstances-dependent. Nine years after *Ross,* in a case with a factual resemblance to *Sanders* — officers observed a man place a bag likely containing marijuana in a car trunk — the Court seized on and exaggerated the confusion engendered by the *Ross* dichotomy to overrule *Chadwick* and *Sanders.* In *California v. Acevedo,* 500 U.S. 565 (1991), the automobile exception of *Carroll* was extended to containers simply by virtue of their placement in an automobile. Maclin, *Cops and Cars, supra* at 2359 ("*Acevedo* is an extension of *Carroll*"). Confusion remained, however. As Justice Stevens observed in dissent, "it is anomalous to prohibit a search of a briefcase while the owner is carrying it exposed on a public street yet to permit a search once the owner has placed the briefcase in the locked trunk of his car." Justice Stevens also famously noted in his *Acevedo* dissent that "decisions like the one today will support the conclusion that this Court has become a loyal foot soldier in the Executive's fight against crime." While some see *Acevedo* as the apotheosis of automobile exceptionalism, others have recognized it as emblematic of a different Fourth Amendment trend. *See* Erik Luna, *Drug Exceptionalism,* 47 Vill. L. Rev. 753, 755-56 (2002) ("Legal commentators have likewise identified a 'drug exception' to the Bill of Rights created through judicial acquiescence to the activities of narcotics agents.").

C. The Warrant Requirement and Its Exceptions

A subsidiary yet equally important legacy of *Carroll* that traveled into the future along with the automobility exception was the notion of judicial deference to police officer expertise. Such deference was explicitly relied on by the Court in upholding the police officers' judgments in *Carroll* and *Brinegar*, and was part of the *Carroll* playbook that the Court relied on in embracing a "reasonable suspicion" Fourth Amendment standard in *Terry v. Ohio, see infra*, and continues to be relied on today. In 1996 this notion of law enforcement deference was enshrined in, of all places, the appellate review standard for probable cause and reasonable suspicion determinations, as the Court held that appellate courts should give due weight not only to trial judges' factual findings but also to the conclusions of "local law enforcement officers." *Ornelas v. United States*, 517 U.S. 690 (1996).

It was only a matter of time before the Court considered a case involving the ultimate Fourth Amendment hybrid — a mobile home.

California v. Carney
471 U.S. 386 (1985)

Chief Justice BURGER delivered the opinion of the Court.

We granted certiorari to decide whether law enforcement agents violated the Fourth Amendment when they conducted a warrantless search, based on probable cause, of a fully mobile "motor home" located in a public place.

I

On May 31, 1979, Drug Enforcement Agency Agent Robert Williams watched respondent, Charles Carney, approach a youth in downtown San Diego. The youth accompanied Carney to a Dodge Mini Motor Home parked in a nearby lot. Carney and the youth closed the window shades in the motor home, including one across the front window. Agent Williams had previously received uncorroborated information that the same motor home was used by another person who was exchanging marihuana for sex. Williams, with assistance from other agents, kept the motor home under surveillance for the entire one and one-quarter hours that Carney and the youth remained inside. When the youth left the motor home, the agents followed and stopped him. The youth told the agents that he had received marijuana in return for allowing Carney sexual contacts.

At the agents' request, the youth returned to the motor home and knocked on its door; Carney stepped out. The agents identified themselves as law enforcement officers. Without a warrant or consent, one agent entered the motor home and observed marihuana, plastic bags, and a scale of the kind used in weighing drugs on a table. Agent Williams took Carney into custody and took possession of the motor home. A subsequent search of the motor home at the police station revealed additional marihuana in the cupboards and refrigerator.

Respondent was charged with possession of marihuana for sale. At a preliminary hearing, he moved to suppress the evidence discovered in the motor home. The Magistrate denied the motion, upholding the initial search as a justifiable search for other persons, and the subsequent search as a routine inventory search.

Respondent renewed his suppression motion in the Superior Court. The Superior Court also rejected the claim, holding that there was probable cause to arrest respondent, that the search of the motor home was authorized under the automobile exception to the Fourth Amendment's warrant requirement, and that the motor home itself could be seized without a warrant as an instrumentality of the crime. Respondent then pleaded nolo contendere to the charges against him, and was placed on probation for three years.

Respondent appealed from the order placing him on probation. The California Court of Appeal affirmed, reasoning that the vehicle exception applied to respondent's motor home.

The California Supreme Court reversed the conviction. The Supreme Court did not disagree with the conclusion of the trial court that the agents had probable cause to arrest respondent and to believe that the vehicle contained evidence of a crime; however, the court held that the search was unreasonable because no warrant was obtained, rejecting the State's argument that the vehicle exception to the warrant requirement should apply. That court reached its decision by concluding that the mobility of a vehicle "is no longer the prime justification for the automobile exception; rather, 'the answer lies in the diminished expectation of privacy which surrounds the automobile.'" The California Supreme Court held that the expectations of privacy in a motor home are more like those in a dwelling than in an automobile because the primary function of motor homes is not to provide transportation but to "provide the occupant with living quarters."

We granted certiorari. We reverse.

II

The Fourth Amendment protects the "right of the people to be secure in their persons, houses, papers, and effects, against unreasonable searches and seizures." This fundamental right is preserved by a requirement that searches be conducted pursuant to a warrant issued by an independent judicial officer. There are, of course, exceptions to the general rule that a warrant must be secured before a search is undertaken; one is the so-called "automobile exception" at issue in this case. This exception to the warrant requirement was first set forth by the Court 60 years ago in *Carroll*. There, the Court recognized that the privacy interests in an automobile are constitutionally protected; however, it held that the ready mobility of the automobile justifies a lesser degree of protection of those interests. The Court rested this exception on a long-recognized distinction between stationary structures and vehicles:

> [T]he guaranty of freedom from unreasonable searches and seizures by the Fourth Amendment has been construed, practically since the beginning of Government, as recognizing a necessary difference between a search of a store, dwelling house or other structure in respect of which a proper official warrant readily may be obtained, and a search of a ship, motor boat, wagon or automobile, for contraband goods, where it is not practicable to secure a warrant because the vehicle can be quickly moved out of the locality or jurisdiction in which the warrant must be sought.

The capacity to be "quickly moved" was clearly the basis of the holding in *Carroll*, and our cases have consistently recognized ready mobility as one of the principal bases of the automobile exception. In *Chambers*, for example, commenting on the rationale for the vehicle exception, we noted that "the opportunity to search is fleeting since a car is readily movable." More recently, in *United States v. Ross* (1982), we once again emphasized that "an immediate intrusion is necessary" because of "the nature of an automobile in transit. . . ." The mobility of automobiles, we have observed, "creates circumstances of such exigency that, as a practical necessity, rigorous enforcement of the warrant requirement is impossible."

However, although ready mobility alone was perhaps the original justification for the vehicle exception, our later cases have made clear that ready mobility is not the only basis for the exception. The reasons for the vehicle exception, we have said, are twofold. "Besides the element of mobility, less rigorous warrant requirements govern because the expectation of privacy with respect to one's automobile is significantly less than that relating to one's home or office."

Even in cases where an automobile was not immediately mobile, the lesser expectation of privacy resulting from its use as a readily mobile vehicle justified application of the vehicular exception. In some cases, the configuration of the vehicle contributed to the lower expectations of privacy; for example, we held in *Cardwell v. Lewis* that, because the passenger compartment of a standard automobile is relatively open to plain view, there are lesser expectations of privacy. But even when enclosed "repository" areas have been involved, we have concluded that the lesser expectations of privacy warrant application of the exception. We have applied the exception in the context of a locked car trunk, a sealed package in a car trunk, a closed compartment under the dashboard, the interior of a vehicle's upholstery, or sealed packages inside a covered pickup truck.

These reduced expectations of privacy derive not from the fact that the area to be searched is in plain view, but from the pervasive regulation of vehicles capable of traveling on the public highways. As we explained in *South Dakota v. Opperman*, an inventory search case:

> Automobiles, unlike homes, are subjected to pervasive and continuing governmental regulation and controls, including periodic inspection and licensing requirements. As an everyday occurrence, police stop and examine vehicles when license plates or inspection stickers have expired, or if other violations, such as exhaust fumes or excessive noise, are noted, or if headlights or other safety equipment are not in proper working order.

The public is fully aware that it is accorded less privacy in its automobiles because of this compelling governmental need for regulation. Historically, "individuals always [have] been on notice that movable vessels may be stopped and searched on facts giving rise to probable cause that the vehicle contains contraband, without the protection afforded by a magistrate's prior evaluation of those facts." In short, the pervasive schemes of regulation, which necessarily lead to reduced expectations of privacy, and the exigencies attendant to ready mobility justify searches without prior recourse to the authority of a magistrate so long as the overriding standard of probable cause is met.

When a vehicle is being used on the highways, or if it is readily capable of such use and is found stationary in a place not regularly used for residential purposes—temporary or otherwise—the two justifications for the vehicle exception come into play. First, the vehicle is obviously readily mobile by the turn of an ignition key, if not actually moving. Second, there is a reduced expectation of privacy stemming from its use as a licensed motor vehicle subject to a range of police regulation inapplicable to a fixed dwelling. At least in these circumstances, the overriding societal interests in effective law enforcement justify an immediate search before the vehicle and its occupants become unavailable.

While it is true that respondent's vehicle possessed some, if not many of the attributes of a home, it is equally clear that the vehicle falls clearly within the scope of the exception laid down in *Carroll* and applied in succeeding cases. Like the automobile in *Carroll*, respondent's motor home was readily mobile. Absent the prompt search and seizure, it could readily have been moved beyond the reach of the police. Furthermore, the vehicle was licensed to "operate on public streets; [was] serviced in public places; . . . and [was] subject to extensive regulation and inspection." And the vehicle was so situated that an objective observer would conclude that it was being used not as a residence, but as a vehicle.

Respondent urges us to distinguish his vehicle from other vehicles within the exception because it was capable of functioning as a home. In our increasingly mobile society, many vehicles used for transportation can be and are being used not only for transportation but for shelter, i.e., as a "home" or "residence." To distinguish between respondent's motor home and an ordinary sedan for purposes of the vehicle exception would require that we apply the exception depending upon the size of the vehicle and the quality of its appointments. Moreover, to fail to apply the exception to vehicles such as a motor home ignores the fact that a motor home lends itself easily to use as an instrument of illicit drug traffic and other illegal activity. In *United States v. Ross*, we declined to distinguish between "worthy" and "unworthy" containers, noting that "the central purpose of the Fourth Amendment forecloses such a distinction." We decline today to distinguish between "worthy" and "unworthy" vehicles which are either on the public roads and highways, or situated such that it is reasonable to conclude that the vehicle is not being used as a residence.

Our application of the vehicle exception has never turned on the other uses to which a vehicle might be put. The exception has historically turned on the ready mobility of the vehicle, and on the presence of the vehicle in a setting that objectively indicates that the vehicle is being used for transportation. These two requirements for application of the exception ensure that law enforcement officials are not unnecessarily hamstrung in their efforts to detect and prosecute criminal activity, and that the legitimate privacy interests of the public are protected. Applying the vehicle exception in these circumstances allows the essential purposes served by the exception to be fulfilled, while assuring that the exception will acknowledge legitimate privacy interests.

III

The question remains whether, apart from the lack of a warrant, this search was unreasonable. Under the vehicle exception to the warrant requirement, "[o]nly the prior approval of the magistrate is waived; the search otherwise [must be such] as the magistrate could authorize."

This search was not unreasonable; it was plainly one that the magistrate could authorize if presented with these facts. The DEA agents had fresh, direct, uncontradicted evidence that the respondent was distributing a controlled substance from the vehicle, apart from evidence of other possible offenses. The agents thus had abundant probable cause to enter and search the vehicle for evidence of a crime notwithstanding its possible use as a dwelling place.

The judgment of the California Supreme Court is reversed, and the case is remanded for further proceedings not inconsistent with this opinion.

NOTES AND QUESTIONS

1. The Court acknowledges that the Dodge Mini Motor Home carries many indicia of domesticity: curtains, cupboards, a refrigerator, etc.

But why is the record so bad here? The lawyers on both sides must have known what was at stake in this suppression hearing, as the case presented the classic hybrid between an automobile and a home. Even its name—Motor Home—embraced this duality.

Why are we only told that the vehicle was located "in a nearby lot." What kind of lot? A parking lot? Was the lot public or private property?

Where was the vehicle when the agents observed it recently?

2. The dissent does not make the point that the DEA agents could have avoided any risk involved in getting a warrant simply by continuing to keep the vehicle under surveillance while one agent got a warrant. If the vehicle were to try to take off in the meantime, the surveilling agents could have stopped it and executed a warrantless arrest, as it would seem clear that if the vehicle were actually moving the automobile exception would come into play.

3. Perhaps defensive about relying too heavily on the automobile's mobility on the facts of this case, and after the shame of *Chambers*, the Court in the 1970s and 1980s and especially in *Carney* began to lean hard into the "closely regulated" trope that it would rely on two years later in upholding a warrantless search of a junkyard in *New York v. Burger*, 482 U.S. 691 (1987), and the correlative notion that people have a lessened expectation of privacy in their cars.

Is this persuasive? Consider the regulation of your car. You have to have a license to drive it. You have to have insurance. When driving it, you have to comply with numerous safety regulations: wearing seatbelts, signaling for turns, stopping at stop signs, observing speed limits. You have to take the car to a garage for an annual or biannual inspection. If you get stopped while impaired, depending on the state, you may have to take a blood alcohol test or risk significant collateral consequences, for example, suspension of license or a criminal offense. Do any of these regulatory tentacles reach into and compromise the private space within the four (or two or three) doors of the car? Recall that in *Burger* the regulatory regime at issue explicitly authorized warrantless searches of junkyards.

4. The reliance on a reduced expectation of privacy in automobiles did not fade away with time, or yield to a more nuanced and disciplined view of people's relationship with their cars. This reduced expectation of privacy was explicitly relied on, reflexively it would seem, in *Wyoming v. Houghton*, 526 U.S. 295 (1999), where the Court found that the scope of a car search justified by probable cause to believe the car contained contraband extended to a purse in the backseat.

Are people who are driven to work by chauffeurs driving government vehicles capable of adequately assessing people's reasonable expectations of privacy in their cars?

Do people's actual expectations of privacy in their cars sometimes, and under some circumstances, exceed those in their homes? *See* Elizabeth Merritt, Note, *VanLife: An Argument to Reconsider the Automobile Exception and Ensure Fourth Amendment Protections for All Citizens*, 56 Ind. L. Rev. 599, 599-600 (2023) (acknowledging the increasingly widespread of people living in their vans (vanlife) and arguing that the automobile exception should not apply in such cases). What are the Fourth Amendment consequences, if any, of the answer to that question?

5. Concepts of "home" may sometimes still trump the automobile exception, however. *See Collins v. Virginia*, 584 U.S. 586 (2018) (search of motorcycle parked in a covered portion of driveway abutting the house requires a warrant, notwithstanding the automobile exception, inasmuch as that area is "curtilage" under cases such as *Florida v. Jardines*, 569 U.S. 1, 6 (2013)).

We now turn from exceptions to the warrant requirement to what will prove to be a gaping exception to the probable cause requirement.

D. EXCEPTION TO THE PROBABLE CAUSE REQUIREMENT: THE *TERRY* DOCTRINE

By the time the constitutionality of police "stop and frisk" encounters reached the Supreme Court in 1968 both the term and the practice were familiar to the Court. Police had been stopping people on the streets and questioning and frisking them without probable cause for decades. *See* Sam B. Warner, *The Uniform Arrest Act*, 28 Va. L. Rev. 315, 320 (1942) ("Every day large numbers of persons are questioned by police officers. This questioning, without immediate arrest, is essential to proper policing."). Because these encounters, sometimes called "field interrogation" or "patrol," often did not result in prosecutions—in which resultant statements or physical evidence might be challenged—they usually stayed below the legal radar. People who were the "victims" of such arguably unconstitutional encounters, moreover, may quite reasonably have seen little upside in "pressing charges" against a police officer given their small damages, the uncertainty of any remedial vehicles (§ 1983 was not resuscitated until 1960), and a not unrealistic risk of retaliation.

This state of affairs began to change in the 1960s, as crime rates began to rise. New York enacted a statute that affirmatively authorized stop and frisk, N.Y. Code Crim. Proc. § 180-a (1964), and the incidence of field interrogation was otherwise increasing. Lawrence P. Tiffany,

Chapter IV The Fourth Amendment

Field Interrogation: Administrative, Judicial and Legislative Approaches, 43 Denv. L.J. 389, 389 (1966) ("A common police practice, probably in all localities, is to stop and question suspects on the street when there are insufficient grounds to arrest."). Police officers, however, were unsure of the legality of such stops. Loren G. Stern, *Stop and Frisk: An Historical Answer to a Modern Problem*, 58 J. Crim. L. Criminology & Police Sci. 532, 533 (1967). Lower courts were increasingly being confronted with constitutional challenges to the practice in the wake of *Mapp* and *Gideon*. And a commission created by President Johnson recommended that states define the authority for such police encounters. President's Commission on Law Enforcement and Administration of Justice, Task Force Report: The Police 183 (1967). *See generally* John Q. Barrett, Terry v. Ohio: *The Fourth Amendment Reasonableness of Police Stops and Frisks Based on Less Than Probable Cause*, in Criminal Procedure Stories 299-300 (Carol Steiker ed., 2005).

Terry v. Ohio
392 U.S. 1 (1968)

Mr. Chief Justice WARREN delivered the opinion of the Court.

This case presents serious questions concerning the role of the Fourth Amendment in the confrontation on the street between the citizen and the policeman investigating suspicious circumstances.

Petitioner Terry was convicted of carrying a concealed weapon and sentenced to the statutorily prescribed term of one to three years in the penitentiary. Following the denial of a pretrial motion to suppress, the prosecution introduced in evidence two revolvers and a number of bullets seized from Terry and a codefendant, Richard Chilton, by Cleveland Police Detective Martin McFadden. At the hearing on the motion to suppress this evidence, Officer McFadden testified that while he was patrolling in plain clothes in downtown Cleveland at approximately 2:30 in the afternoon of October 31, 1963, his attention was attracted by two men, Chilton and Terry, standing on the corner of Huron Road and Euclid Avenue. He had never seen the two men before, and he was unable to say precisely what first drew his eye to them. However, he testified that he had been a policeman for 39 years and a detective for 35 and that he had been assigned to patrol this vicinity of downtown Cleveland for shoplifters and pickpockets for 30 years. He explained that he had developed routine habits of observation over the years and that he would "stand and watch people or walk and watch people at many intervals of the day." He added: "Now, in this case when I looked over they didn't look right to me at the time."

His interest aroused, Officer McFadden took up a post of observation in the entrance to a store 300 to 400 feet away from the two men. "I get more purpose to watch them when I seen their movements," he testified. He saw one of the men leave the other one and walk southwest on Huron Road, past some stores. The man paused for a moment and looked in a store window, then walked on a short distance, turned around and walked back toward the corner, pausing once again to look in the same store window. He rejoined his companion at the corner, and the two conferred briefly. Then the second man went through the same series of motions, strolling down Huron Road, looking in the same window, walking on a short distance, turning back, peering in the store window again, and returning to confer with the first man at the corner. The two men repeated this ritual alternately between five and six times apiece—in all, roughly a dozen trips. At one point, while the two were standing together on the corner, a third man approached them and engaged them briefly in conversation. This man then left the two others and walked west on Euclid Avenue. Chilton and Terry resumed their

D. Exception to the Probable Cause Requirement: The *Terry* Doctrine

measured pacing, peering and conferring. After this had gone on for 10 to 12 minutes, the two men walked off together, heading west on Euclid Avenue, following the path taken earlier by the third man.

By this time Officer McFadden had become thoroughly suspicious. He testified that after observing their elaborately casual and oft-repeated reconnaissance of the store window on Huron Road, he suspected the two men of "casing a job, a stick-up," and that he considered it his duty as a police officer to investigate further. He added that he feared "they may have a gun." Thus, Officer McFadden followed Chilton and Terry and saw them stop in front of Zucker's store to talk to the same man who had conferred with them earlier on the street corner. Deciding that the situation was ripe for direct action, Officer McFadden approached the three men, identified himself as a police officer and asked for their names. At this point his knowledge was confined to what he had observed. He was not acquainted with any of the three men by name or by sight, and he had received no information concerning them from any other source. When the men "mumbled something" in response to his inquiries, Officer McFadden grabbed petitioner Terry, spun him around so that they were facing the other two, with Terry between McFadden and the others, and patted down the outside of his clothing. In the left breast pocket of Terry's overcoat Officer McFadden felt a pistol. He reached inside the overcoat pocket, but was unable to remove the gun. At this point, keeping Terry between himself and the others, the officer ordered all three men to enter Zucker's store. As they went in, he removed Terry's overcoat completely, removed a .38-caliber revolver from the pocket and ordered all three men to face the wall with their hands raised. Officer McFadden proceeded to pat down the outer clothing of Chilton and the third man, Katz. He discovered another revolver in the outer pocket of Chilton's overcoat, but no weapons were found on Katz. The officer testified that he only patted the men down to see whether they had weapons, and that he did not put his hands beneath the outer garments of either Terry or Chilton until he felt their guns. So far as appears from the record, he never placed his hands beneath Katz' outer garments. Officer McFadden seized Chilton's gun, asked the proprietor of the store to call a police wagon, and took all three men to the station, where Chilton and Terry were formally charged with carrying concealed weapons.

On the motion to suppress the guns the prosecution took the position that they had been seized following a search incident to a lawful arrest. The trial court rejected this theory, stating that it "would be stretching the facts beyond reasonable comprehension" to find that Officer McFadden had had probable cause to arrest the men before he patted them down for weapons. However, the court denied the defendants' motion on the ground that Officer McFadden, on the basis of his experience, "had reasonable cause to believe . . . that the defendants were conducting themselves suspiciously, and some interrogation should be made of their action." Purely for his own protection, the court held, the officer had the right to pat down the outer clothing of these men, who he had reasonable cause to believe might be armed. The court distinguished between an investigatory "stop" and an arrest, and between a "frisk" of the outer clothing for weapons and a full-blown search for evidence of crime. The frisk, it held, was essential to the proper performance of the officer's investigatory duties, for without it "the answer to the police officer may be a bullet, and a loaded pistol discovered during the frisk is admissible."

After the court denied their motion to suppress, Chilton and Terry waived jury trial and pleaded not guilty. The court adjudged them guilty, and the Court of Appeals for the Eighth Judicial District, Cuyahoga County, affirmed. The Supreme Court of Ohio dismissed their appeal on the ground that no "substantial constitutional question" was involved. We granted certiorari, to determine whether the admission of the revolvers in evidence violated petitioner's rights under the Fourth Amendment, made applicable to the States by the Fourteenth. We affirm the conviction.

I.

The Fourth Amendment provides that "the right of the people to be secure in their persons, houses, papers, and effects, against unreasonable searches and seizures, shall not be violated. . . ." This inestimable right of personal security belongs as much to the citizen on the streets of our cities as to the homeowner closeted in his study to dispose of his secret affairs. For, as this Court has always recognized:

> No right is held more sacred, or is more carefully guarded, by the common law, than the right of every individual to the possession and control of his own person, free from all restraint or interference of others, unless by clear and unquestionable authority of law.

We have recently held that "the Fourth Amendment protects people, not places," *Katz v. United States* (1967), and wherever an individual may harbor a reasonable "expectation of privacy," he is entitled to be free from unreasonable governmental intrusion. Of course, the specific content and incidents of this right must be shaped by the context in which it is asserted. For "what the Constitution forbids is not all searches and seizures, but unreasonable searches and seizures." The question is whether in all the circumstances of this on-the-street encounter, his right to personal security was violated by an unreasonable search and seizure.

We would be less than candid if we did not acknowledge that this question thrusts to the fore difficult and troublesome issues regarding a sensitive area of police activity — issues which have never before been squarely presented to this Court. Reflective of the tensions involved are the practical and constitutional arguments pressed with great vigor on both sides of the public debate over the power of the police to "stop and frisk" — as it is sometimes euphemistically termed — suspicious persons.

On the one hand, it is frequently argued that in dealing with the rapidly unfolding and often dangerous situations on city streets the police are in need of an escalating set of flexible responses, graduated in relation to the amount of information they possess. For this purpose it is urged that distinctions should be made between a "stop" and an "arrest" (or a "seizure" of a person), and between a "frisk" and a "search." Thus, it is argued, the police should be allowed to "stop" a person and detain him briefly for questioning upon suspicion that he may be connected with criminal activity. Upon suspicion that the person may be armed, the police should have the power to "frisk" him for weapons. If the "stop" and the "frisk" give rise to probable cause to believe that the suspect has committed a crime, then the police should be empowered to make a formal "arrest," and a full incident "search" of the person. This scheme is justified in part upon the notion that a "stop" and a "frisk" amount to a mere "minor inconvenience and petty indignity," which can properly be imposed upon the citizen in the interest of effective law enforcement on the basis of a police officer's suspicion.

On the other side the argument is made that the authority of the police must be strictly circumscribed by the law of arrest and search as it has developed to date in the traditional jurisprudence of the Fourth Amendment. It is contended with some force that there is not — and cannot be — a variety of police activity which does not depend solely upon the voluntary cooperation of the citizen and yet which stops short of an arrest based upon probable cause to make such an arrest. The heart of the Fourth Amendment, the argument runs, is a severe requirement of specific justification for any intrusion upon protected personal security, coupled with a highly developed system of judicial controls to enforce upon the agents of the State the commands of the Constitution. Acquiescence by the courts in the compulsion inherent in the field interrogation practices at issue here, it is urged, would constitute an abdication of judicial control over, and indeed an encouragement of, substantial interference with liberty and personal security by police officers whose judgment is necessarily colored by their primary involvement in "the often competitive enterprise of ferreting out crime." This, it is argued, can only serve to exacerbate police-community tensions in the crowded centers of our Nation's cities.

In this context we approach the issues in this case mindful of the limitations of the judicial function in controlling the myriad daily situations in which policemen and citizens confront each other on the street. The State has characterized the issue here as "the right of a police officer . . . to make an on-the-street stop, interrogate and pat down for weapons (known in street vernacular as 'stop and frisk')." But this is only partly accurate. For the issue is not the abstract propriety of the police conduct, but the admissibility against petitioner of the evidence uncovered by the search and seizure. Ever since its inception, the rule excluding evidence seized in violation of the Fourth Amendment has been recognized as a principal mode of discouraging lawless police conduct. Thus its major thrust is a deterrent one, and experience has taught that it is the only effective deterrent to police misconduct in the criminal context, and that without it the constitutional guarantee against unreasonable searches and seizures would be a mere "form of words." Courts which sit under our Constitution cannot and will not be made party to lawless invasions of the constitutional rights of citizens by permitting unhindered governmental use of the fruits of such invasions. Thus in our system evidentiary rulings provide the context in which the judicial process of inclusion and exclusion approves some conduct as comporting with constitutional guarantees and disapproves other actions by state agents. A ruling admitting evidence in a criminal trial, we recognize, has the necessary effect of legitimizing the conduct which produced the evidence, while an application of the exclusionary rule withholds the constitutional imprimatur.

The exclusionary rule has its limitations, however, as a tool of judicial control. It cannot properly be invoked to exclude the products of legitimate police investigative techniques on the ground that much conduct which is closely similar involves unwarranted intrusions upon constitutional protections. Moreover, in some contexts the rule is ineffective as a deterrent. Street encounters between citizens and police officers are incredibly rich in diversity. They range from wholly friendly exchanges of pleasantries or mutually useful information to hostile confrontations of armed men involving arrests, or injuries, or loss of life. Moreover, hostile confrontations are not all of a piece. Some of them begin in a friendly enough manner, only to take a different turn upon the injection of some unexpected element into the conversation. Encounters are initiated by the police for a wide variety of purposes, some of which are wholly unrelated to a desire to prosecute for crime. Doubtless some police "field interrogation" conduct violates the Fourth Amendment. But a stern refusal by this Court to condone such activity does not necessarily render it responsive to the exclusionary rule. Regardless of how effective the rule may be where obtaining convictions is an important objective of the police, it is powerless to deter invasions of constitutionally guaranteed rights where the police either have no interest in prosecuting or are willing to forgo successful prosecution in the interest of serving some other goal.

Proper adjudication of cases in which the exclusionary rule is invoked demands a constant awareness of these limitations. The wholesale harassment by certain elements of the police community, of which minority groups, particularly Negroes, frequently complain, will not be stopped by the exclusion of any evidence from any criminal trial. Yet a rigid and unthinking application of the exclusionary rule, in futile protest against practices which it can never be used effectively to control, may exact a high toll in human injury and frustration of efforts to prevent crime. No judicial opinion can comprehend the protean variety of the street encounter, and we can only judge the facts of the case before us. Nothing we say today is to be taken as indicating approval of police conduct outside the legitimate investigative sphere. Under our decision, courts still retain their traditional responsibility to guard against police conduct which is over-bearing or harassing, or which trenches upon personal security without the objective evidentiary justification which the Constitution requires. When such conduct is identified, it must be condemned by the judiciary and its fruits must be excluded from evidence in criminal trials. And, of course, our approval of legitimate and restrained investigative conduct undertaken on the basis of ample factual justification should in no way discourage the employment of other remedies than the exclusionary rule to curtail abuses for which that sanction may prove inappropriate.

Having thus roughly sketched the perimeters of the constitutional debate over the limits on police investigative conduct in general and the background against which this case presents itself, we turn our attention to the quite narrow question posed by the facts before us: whether it is always unreasonable for a policeman to seize a person and subject him to a limited search for weapons unless there is probable cause for an arrest. Given the narrowness of this question, we have no occasion to canvass in detail the constitutional limitations upon the scope of a policeman's power when he confronts a citizen without probable cause to arrest him.

II

Our first task is to establish at what point in this encounter the Fourth Amendment becomes relevant. That is, we must decide whether and when Officer McFadden "seized" Terry and whether and when he conducted a "search." There is some suggestion in the use of such terms as "stop" and "frisk" that such police conduct is outside the purview of the Fourth Amendment because neither action rises to the level of a "search" or "seizure" within the meaning of the Constitution. We emphatically reject this notion. It is quite plain that the Fourth Amendment governs "seizures" of the person which do not eventuate in a trip to the station house and prosecution for crime — "arrests" in traditional terminology. It must be recognized that whenever a police officer accosts an individual and restrains his freedom to walk away, he has "seized" that person. And it is nothing less than sheer torture of the English language to suggest that a careful exploration of the outer surfaces of a person's clothing all over his or her body in an attempt to find weapons is not a "search," Moreover, it is simply fantastic to urge that such a procedure performed in public by a policeman while the citizen stands helpless, perhaps facing a wall with his hands raised, is a "petty indignity." It is a serious intrusion upon the sanctity of the person, which may inflict great indignity and arouse strong resentment, and it is not to be undertaken lightly.

The danger in the logic which proceeds upon distinctions between a "stop" and an "arrest," or "seizure" of the person, and between a "frisk" and a "search" is twofold. It seeks to isolate from constitutional scrutiny the initial stages of the contact between the policeman and the citizen. And by suggesting a rigid all-or-nothing model of justification and regulation under the Amendment, it obscures the utility of limitations upon the scope, as well as the initiation, of police action as a means of constitutional regulation. This Court has held in the past that a search which is reasonable at its inception may violate the Fourth Amendment by virtue of its intolerable intensity and scope. The scope of the search must be "strictly tied to and justified by" the circumstances which rendered its initiation permissible.

The distinctions of classical "stop-and-frisk" theory thus serve to divert attention from the central inquiry under the Fourth Amendment — the reasonableness in all the circumstances of the particular governmental invasion of a citizen's personal security. "Search" and "seizure" are not talismans. We therefore reject the notions that the Fourth Amendment does not come into play at all as a limitation upon police conduct if the officers stop short of something called a "technical arrest" or a "full-blown search."

In this case there can be no question, then, that Officer McFadden "seized" petitioner and subjected him to a "search" when he took hold of him and patted down the outer surfaces of his clothing. We must decide whether at that point it was reasonable for Officer McFadden to have interfered with petitioner's personal security as he did. And in determining whether the seizure and search were "unreasonable" our inquiry is a dual one — whether the officer's action was justified at its inception, and whether it was reasonably related in scope to the circumstances which justified the interference in the first place.

III

If this case involved police conduct subject to the Warrant Clause of the Fourth Amendment, we would have to ascertain whether "probable cause" existed to justify the search and seizure which took place. However, that is not the case. We do not retreat from our holdings that the police must, whenever practicable, obtain advance judicial approval of searches and seizures through the warrant procedure, or that in most instances failure to comply with the warrant requirement can only be excused by exigent circumstances. But we deal here with an entire rubric of police conduct — necessarily swift action predicated upon the on-the-spot observations of the officer on the beat — which historically has not been, and as a practical matter could not be, subjected to the warrant procedure. Instead, the conduct involved in this case must be tested by the Fourth Amendment's general proscription against unreasonable searches and seizures.

Nonetheless, the notions which underlie both the warrant procedure and the requirement of probable cause remain fully relevant in this context. In order to assess the reasonableness of Officer McFadden's conduct as a general proposition, it is necessary "first to focus upon the governmental interest which allegedly justifies official intrusion upon the constitutionally protected interests of the private citizen," for there is "no ready test for determining reasonableness other than by balancing the need to search (or seize) against the invasion which the search (or seizure) entails." And in justifying the particular intrusion the police officer must be able to point to specific and articulable facts which, taken together with rational inferences from those facts, reasonably warrant that intrusion. The scheme of the Fourth Amendment becomes meaningful only when it is assured that at some point the conduct of those charged with enforcing the laws can be subjected to the more detached, neutral scrutiny of a judge who must evaluate the reasonableness of a particular search or seizure in light of the particular circumstances. And in making that assessment it is imperative that the facts be judged against an objective standard: would the facts available to the officer at the moment of the seizure or the search "warrant a man of reasonable caution in the belief" that the action taken was appropriate? Anything less would invite intrusions upon constitutionally guaranteed rights based on nothing more substantial than inarticulate hunches, a result this Court has consistently refused to sanction. And simple "good faith on the part of the arresting officer is not enough. . . . If subjective good faith alone were the test, the protections of the Fourth Amendment would evaporate, and the people would be 'secure in their persons, houses, papers and effects,' only in the discretion of the police."

Applying these principles to this case, we consider first the nature and extent of the governmental interests involved. One general interest is of course that of effective crime prevention and detection; it is this interest which underlies the recognition that a police officer may in appropriate circumstances and in an appropriate manner approach a person for purposes of investigating possibly criminal behavior even though there is no probable cause to make an arrest. It was this legitimate investigative function Officer McFadden was discharging when he decided to approach petitioner and his companions. He had observed Terry, Chilton, and Katz go through a series of acts, each of them perhaps innocent in itself, but which taken together warranted further investigation. There is nothing unusual in two men standing together on a street corner, perhaps waiting for someone. Nor is there anything suspicious about people in such circumstances strolling up and down the street, singly or in pairs. Store windows, moreover, are made to be looked in. But the story is quite different where, as here, two men hover about a street corner for an extended period of time, at the end of which it becomes apparent that they are not waiting for anyone or anything; where these men pace alternately along an identical route, pausing to stare in the same store window roughly 24 times; where each completion of this route is followed immediately by a conference between the two men on the corner; where they are joined in one of these conferences by a third man who leaves swiftly; and where the two men finally follow the third and rejoin him a couple of blocks away. It would have been poor police work indeed for an officer of 30 years' experience in the detection of thievery from stores in this same neighborhood to have failed to investigate this behavior further.

The crux of this case, however, is not the propriety of Officer McFadden's taking steps to investigate petitioner's suspicious behavior, but rather, whether there was justification for McFadden's invasion of Terry's personal security by searching him for weapons in the course of that investigation. We are now concerned with more than the governmental interest in investigating crime; in addition, there is the more immediate interest of the police officer in taking steps to assure himself that the person with whom he is dealing is not armed with a weapon that could unexpectedly and fatally be used against him. Certainly it would be unreasonable to require that police officers take unnecessary risks in the performance of their duties. American criminals have a long tradition of armed violence, and every year in this country many law enforcement officers are killed in the line of duty, and thousands more are wounded. Virtually all of these deaths and a substantial portion of the injuries are inflicted with guns and knives.

In view of these facts, we cannot blind ourselves to the need for law enforcement officers to protect themselves and other prospective victims of violence in situations where they may lack probable cause for an arrest. When an officer is justified in believing that the individual whose suspicious behavior he is investigating at close range is armed and presently dangerous to the officer or to others, it would appear to be clearly unreasonable to deny the officer the power to take necessary measures to determine whether the person is in fact carrying a weapon and to neutralize the threat of physical harm.

We must still consider, however, the nature and quality of the intrusion on individual rights which must be accepted if police officers are to be conceded the right to search for weapons in situations where probable cause to arrest for crime is lacking. Even a limited search of the outer clothing for weapons constitutes a severe, though brief, intrusion upon cherished personal security, and it must surely be an annoying, frightening, and perhaps humiliating experience. Petitioner contends that such an intrusion is permissible only incident to a lawful arrest, either for a crime involving the possession of weapons or for a crime the commission of which led the officer to investigate in the first place. However, this argument must be closely examined.

Petitioner does not argue that a police officer should refrain from making any investigation of suspicious circumstances until such time as he has probable cause to make an arrest; nor does he deny that police officers in properly discharging their investigative function may find themselves confronting persons who might well be armed and dangerous. Moreover, he does not say that an officer is always unjustified in searching a suspect to discover weapons. Rather, he says it is unreasonable for the policeman to take that step until such time as the situation evolves to a point where there is probable cause to make an arrest. When that point has been reached, petitioner would concede the officer's right to conduct a search of the suspect for weapons, fruits or instrumentalities of the crime, or "mere" evidence, incident to the arrest.

There are two weaknesses in this line of reasoning however. First, it fails to take account of traditional limitations upon the scope of searches, and thus recognizes no distinction in purpose, character, and extent between a search incident to an arrest and a limited search for weapons. The former, although justified in part by the acknowledged necessity to protect the arresting officer from assault with a concealed weapon, is also justified on other grounds, and can therefore involve a relatively extensive exploration of the person. A search for weapons in the absence of probable cause to arrest, however, must, like any other search, be strictly circumscribed by the exigencies which justify its initiation. Thus it must be limited to that which is necessary for the discovery of weapons which might be used to harm the officer or others nearby, and may realistically be characterized as something less than a "full" search, even though it remains a serious intrusion.

A second, and related, objection to petitioner's argument is that it assumes that the law of arrest has already worked out the balance between the particular interests involved here—the neutralization of danger to the policeman in the investigative circumstance and the sanctity of the individual. But this is not so. An arrest is a wholly different kind of intrusion upon individual freedom from a limited search for weapons, and the interests each is designed to serve are likewise quite different. An arrest is the initial stage of a criminal prosecution. It is intended to vindicate society's interest in having its laws obeyed, and it is inevitably accompanied by future interference with the individual's freedom of movement, whether or not trial or conviction ultimately follows. The protective search for weapons, on the other hand, constitutes a brief, though far from inconsiderable, intrusion upon the sanctity of the person. It does not follow that because an officer may lawfully arrest a person only when he is apprised of facts sufficient to warrant a belief that the person has committed or is committing a crime, the officer is equally unjustified, absent that kind of evidence, in making any intrusions short of an arrest. Moreover, a perfectly reasonable apprehension of danger may arise long before the officer is possessed of adequate information to justify taking a person into custody for the purpose of prosecuting him for a crime. Petitioner's reliance on cases which have worked out standards of reasonableness with regard to "seizures" constituting arrests and searches incident thereto is thus misplaced. It assumes that the interests sought to be vindicated and the invasions of personal security may be equated in the two cases, and thereby ignores a vital aspect of the analysis of the reasonableness of particular types of conduct under the Fourth Amendment.

Our evaluation of the proper balance that has to be struck in this type of case leads us to conclude that there must be a narrowly drawn authority to permit a reasonable search for weapons for the protection of the police officer, where he has reason to believe that he is dealing with an armed and dangerous individual, regardless of whether he has probable cause to arrest the individual for a crime. The officer need not be absolutely certain that the individual is armed; the issue is whether a reasonably prudent man in the circumstances would be warranted in the belief that his safety or that of others was in danger. And in determining whether the officer acted reasonably in such circumstances, due weight must be given, not to his inchoate and unparticularized suspicion or "hunch," but to the specific reasonable inferences which he is entitled to draw from the facts in light of his experience. *Cf. Brinegar v. United States.*

IV

We must now examine the conduct of Officer McFadden in this case to determine whether his search and seizure of petitioner were reasonable, both at their inception and as conducted. He had observed Terry, together with Chilton and another man, acting in a manner he took to be preface to a "stick-up." We think on the facts and circumstances Officer McFadden detailed before the trial judge a reasonably prudent man would have been warranted in believing petitioner was armed and thus presented a threat to the officer's safety while he was investigating his suspicious behavior. The actions of Terry and Chilton were consistent with McFadden's hypothesis that these men were contemplating a daylight robbery—which, it is reasonable to assume, would be likely to involve the use of weapons—and nothing in their conduct from the time he first noticed them until the time he confronted them and identified himself as a police officer gave him sufficient reason to negate that hypothesis. Although the trio had departed the original scene, there was nothing to indicate abandonment of an intent to commit a robbery at some point. Thus, when Officer McFadden approached the three men gathered before the display window at Zucker's store he had observed enough to make it quite reasonable to fear that they were armed; and nothing in their response to his hailing them, identifying himself as a police officer, and asking their names served to dispel that reasonable belief. We cannot say his decision at that point to seize Terry and pat his clothing for weapons was the product of a volatile or inventive imagination, or was undertaken simply as an act of harassment; the record evidences the tempered act of a policeman who in the course of an investigation had to make a quick decision as to how to protect himself and others from possible danger, and took limited steps to do so.

The manner in which the seizure and search were conducted is, of course, as vital a part of the inquiry as whether they were warranted at all. The Fourth Amendment proceeds as much by limitations upon the scope of governmental action as by imposing preconditions upon its initiation. The entire deterrent purpose of the rule excluding evidence seized in violation of the Fourth Amendment rests on the assumption that "limitations upon the fruit to be gathered tend to limit the quest itself." Thus, evidence may not be introduced if it was discovered by means of a seizure and search which were not reasonably related in scope to the justification for their initiation.

We need not develop at length in this case, however, the limitations which the Fourth Amendment places upon a protective seizure and search for weapons. These limitations will have to be developed in the concrete factual circumstances of individual cases. Suffice it to note that such a search, unlike a search without a warrant incident to a lawful arrest, is not justified by any need to prevent the disappearance or destruction of evidence of crime. The sole justification of the search in the present situation is the protection of the police officer and others nearby, and it must therefore be confined in scope to an intrusion reasonably designed to discover guns, knives, clubs, or other hidden instruments for the assault of the police officer.

The scope of the search in this case presents no serious problem in light of these standards. Officer McFadden patted down the outer clothing of petitioner and his two companions. He did not place his hands in their pockets or under the outer surface of their garments until he had felt weapons, and then he merely reached for and removed the guns. He never did invade Katz' person beyond the outer surfaces of his clothes, since he discovered nothing in his patdown which might have been a weapon. Officer McFadden confined his search strictly to what was minimally necessary to learn whether the men were armed and to disarm them once he discovered the weapons. He did not conduct a general exploratory search for whatever evidence of criminal activity he might find.

V

We conclude that the revolver seized from Terry was properly admitted in evidence against him. At the time he seized petitioner and searched him for weapons, Officer McFadden had reasonable grounds to believe that petitioner was armed and dangerous, and it was necessary for the protection of himself and others to take swift measures to discover the true facts and neutralize the threat of harm if it materialized. The policeman carefully restricted his search to what was appropriate to the discovery of the particular items which he sought. Each case of this sort will, of course, have to be decided on its own facts. We merely hold today that where a police officer observes unusual conduct which leads him reasonably to conclude in light of his experience that criminal activity may be afoot and that the persons with whom he is dealing may be armed and presently dangerous, where in the course of investigating this behavior he identifies himself as a policeman and makes reasonable inquiries, and where nothing in the initial stages of the encounter serves to dispel his reasonable fear for his own or others' safety, he is entitled for the protection of himself and others in the area to conduct a carefully

D. Exception to the Probable Cause Requirement: The *Terry* Doctrine

limited search of the outer clothing of such persons in an attempt to discover weapons which might be used to assault him. Such a search is a reasonable search under the Fourth Amendment, and any weapons seized may properly be introduced in evidence against the person from whom they were taken

Affirmed.

• • •

Mr. Justice WHITE, concurring.

I join the opinion of the Court, reserving judgment, however, on some of the Court's general remarks about the scope and purpose of the exclusionary rule which the Court has fashioned in the process of enforcing the Fourth Amendment.

Also, although the Court puts the matter aside in the context of this case, I think an additional word is in order concerning the matter of interrogation during an investigative stop. There is nothing in the Constitution which prevents a policeman from addressing questions to anyone on the streets. Absent special circumstances, the person approached may not be detained or frisked but may refuse to cooperate and go on his way. However, given the proper circumstances, such as those in this case, it seems to me the person may be briefly detained against his will while pertinent questions are directed to him. Of course, the person stopped is not obliged to answer, answers may not be compelled, and refusal to answer furnishes no basis for an arrest, although it may alert the officer to the need for continued observation. In my view, it is temporary detention, warranted by the circumstances, which chiefly justifies the protective frisk for weapons. Perhaps the frisk itself, where proper, will have beneficial results whether questions are asked or not. If weapons are found, an arrest will follow. If none are found, the frisk may nevertheless serve preventive ends because of its unmistakable message that suspicion has been aroused. But if the investigative stop is sustainable at all, constitutional rights are not necessarily violated if pertinent questions are asked and the person is restrained briefly in the process.

Mr. Justice DOUGLAS, dissenting.

I agree that petitioner was "seized" within the meaning of the Fourth Amendment. I also agree that frisking petitioner and his companions for guns was a "search." But it is a mystery how that "search" and that "seizure" can be constitutional by Fourth Amendment standards, unless there was "probable cause" to believe that (1) a crime had been committed or (2) a crime was in the process of being committed or (3) a crime was about to be committed.

The opinion of the Court disclaims the existence of "probable cause." If loitering were in issue and that was the offense charged, there would be "probable cause" shown. But the crime here is carrying concealed weapons; and there is no basis for concluding that the officer had "probable cause" for believing that that crime was being committed. Had a warrant been sought, a magistrate would, therefore, have been unauthorized to issue one, for he can act only if there is a showing of "probable cause." We hold today that the police have greater authority to make a "seizure" and conduct a "search" than a judge has to authorize such action. We have said precisely the opposite over and over again.

In other words, police officers up to today have been permitted to effect arrests or searches without warrants only when the facts within their personal knowledge would satisfy the constitutional standard of probable cause. At the time of their "seizure" without a warrant they must possess facts concerning the person arrested that would have satisfied a magistrate that "probable cause" was indeed present. The term "probable cause" rings a bell of certainty that is not sounded by phrases such as "reasonable suspicion." Moreover, the meaning of "probable cause" is deeply imbedded in our constitutional history. As we stated in *Henry v. United States*:

The requirement of probable cause has roots that are deep in our history. The general warrant, in which the name of the person to be arrested was left blank, and the writs of assistance, against which James Otis inveighed, both perpetuated the oppressive practice of allowing the police to arrest and search on suspicion. Police control took the place of judicial control, since no showing of "probable cause" before a magistrate was required.

That philosophy (rebelling against these practices) later was reflected in the Fourth Amendment. And as the early American decisions both before and immediately after its adoption show, common rumor or report, suspicion, or even "strong reason to suspect" was not adequate to support a warrant for arrest. And that principle has survived to this day. . . .

. . . It is important, we think, that this requirement (of probable cause) be strictly enforced, for the standard set by the Constitution protects both the officer and the citizen. If the officer acts with probable cause, he is protected even though it turns out that the citizen is innocent. . . . And while a search without a warrant is, within limits, permissible if incident to a lawful arrest, if an arrest without a warrant is to support an incidental search, it must be made with probable cause. . . . This immunity of officers cannot fairly be enlarged without jeopardizing the privacy or security of the citizen.

The infringement on personal liberty of any "seizure" of a person can only be "reasonable" under the Fourth Amendment if we require the police to possess "probable cause" before they seize him. Only that line draws a meaningful distinction between an officer's mere inkling and the presence of facts within the officer's personal knowledge which would convince a reasonable man that the person seized has committed, is committing, or is about to commit a particular crime. "In dealing with probable cause, . . . as the very name implies, we deal with probabilities. These are not technical; they are the factual and practical considerations of everyday life on which reasonable and prudent men, not legal technicians, act."

To give the police greater power than a magistrate is to take a long step down the totalitarian path. Perhaps such a step is desirable to cope with modern forms of lawlessness. But if it is taken, it should be the deliberate choice of the people through a constitutional amendment. Until the Fourth Amendment, which is closely allied with the Fifth, is rewritten, the person and the effects of the individual are beyond the reach of all government agencies until there are reasonable grounds to believe (probable cause) that a criminal venture has been launched or is about to be launched.

There have been powerful hydraulic pressures throughout our history that bear heavily on the Court to water down constitutional guarantees and give the police the upper hand. That hydraulic pressure has probably never been greater than it is today.

Yet if the individual is no longer to be sovereign, if the police can pick him up whenever they do not like the cut of his jib, if they can "seize" and "search" him in their discretion, we enter a new regime. The decision to enter it should be made only after a full debate by the people of this country.

NOTES AND QUESTIONS

1. *Terry* tries very hard not to be a case about race, even as it acknowledges the "harassment" about which "Negroes frequently complain" and in a footnote references the report of the President's Commission on Law Enforcement and Administration of Justice cited above, and its finding that "stop and frisk" practices are a "major source of friction between the police and minority groups." But *Terry* of course is all about race. The racial implications of *Terry* will be explored more fully in the next section.

2. The legal proposition for which *Terry* became known is that the limited type of search and seizure reflected in a "stop and frisk" — also known eventually as a *Terry* stop — satisfies the Fourth Amendment based on a showing not of probable cause but only of "reasonable suspicion." Yet the term "reasonable suspicion" is nowhere in the opinion. Did the Court not want to make explicit the standard it was substituting for probable cause in this context? Did it believe a vaguer concept of untethered reasonableness was more palatable?

3. In its conclusion the Court connects Detective McFadden's actions to his reasonable conclusion that "criminal activity may be afoot." But do the facts of the case suggest that a temporal limitation to ongoing or imminent criminal activity is warranted? What were the two men doing when they were apprehended?

4. Does the rule in *Terry* actually make police officers safer? Aren't police officers always going to do what they believe they need to do to protect themselves during an encounter with civilians? Is the only real-world consequence of *Terry* that the evidence officers come upon in frisks will not be subject to the exclusionary rule?

As to officer safety: Officer McFadden said nothing at all in the suppression hearing about safety, protection, or even why he frisked the three men. When asked if he knew the men had guns, he replied "[a]bsolutely not." Transcript of Suppression Hearing, reprinted in State of Ohio v. Richard D. Chilton *and* State of Ohio v. John W. Terry: *The Suppression Hearing and Trial Transcripts*, 72 St. John's L. Rev. 1387, Appendix B at 1419 (John Q. Barrett ed., 1998) (hereinafter Suppression Hearing Transcript).

5. *Terry* is sometimes described as a compromise because the Court found that a stop and frisk was a "search and seizure" within the meaning of the Fourth Amendment. Is that really a compromise? Is there any serious argument that the "stop" half is anything but a seizure, at least insofar as a reasonable person would not feel free to leave? Any serious argument that the "frisk" half is not a search?

6. The Court assumes that a classic "stop" has the requisite curtailment of freedom to amount to a seizure: "It must be recognized that whenever a police officer accosts an individual and restrains his freedom to walk away, he has 'seized' that person." But does the stopped person also have an obligation to respond to the officer's questioning? Justice White concurs for the sole purpose of answering this question in the negative:

> Of course, the person stopped is not obliged to answer, answers may not be compelled, and refusal to answer furnishes no basis for an arrest, although it may alert the officer to the need for continued observation.

Do you agree that this follows from the rest of *Terry*? On what basis? Fifth Amendment? Justice White's observation would not hold the day when the Court began to consider the constitutionality of so-called stop-and-identify statutes. *See infra.*

7. Professor Seo has observed that the Court used the same playbook in *Terry* as it had earlier used in *Carroll.* It dispensed with the Fourth Amendment's probable cause requirement in *Terry* just as it had dispensed with the Fourth Amendment's warrant requirement in *Carroll,* and in both instances the Court ushered in an era of police discretion, based only on "reasonableness," to be filtered through the policeman's expertise. Seo, Policing the Open Road, *supra* at 151-55. In both cases, moreover, the Court appeared to be reaching a "compromise," a view some academics have accepted. *Id. See, e.g.,* Stephen A. Saltzburg, Terry v. Ohio: *A Practically Perfect Doctrine*, 72 St. John's L. Rev. 911 (1998).

Others have not. Professor Carbado sees the decision as Solomonic in the more accurate historical sense: "Like Solomon, [Chief Justice] Warren only feigned compromise, but in reality he handed the entire baby to the government, wrapped in the blanket of *reasonable suspicion.*" Carbado, Unreasonable, *supra* at 126.

8. Officer safety is of course a laudable goal. But note that in *Terry* the frisk of Terry results not only in preserving the safety of the encounter but also in yielding all the evidence needed to convict Terry of a firearms offense, an all too common result. What if the *Terry* rule had a proviso that any evidence yielded as a result of a frisk was inadmissible? Sort of a reverse good faith exception? For one thing, this would reduce the collateral consequences of an arguably subconstitutional encounter. For another, it would ensure that *Terry* frisks were only done where there were legitimate officer safety concerns and not as pretextual searches for evidence.

The reverse good faith exception would be conceptually similar to the tradeoff in the federal immunity statute. *See* 18 U.S.C. § 6001 (conditioning the compulsion of immunized testimony on the requirement that the government may not make any direct or indirect use of the testimony).

9. Do you see any foreshadowing of Justice Douglas's opinion for the Court in *Papachristou (see* Chapter II, *supra*), striking down a Florida vagrancy statute, in his *Terry* dissent here, just four years earlier? Do you think the decision in *Papachristou*—by an already more conservative Court than in *Terry*—was easier for the Court to reach inasmuch as it had already enabled police by endorsing the "reasonable suspicion" standard for an investigative stop. In other words, after *Terry* did the police even need the power conferred by vagrancy statutes?

The Court did specify in *Terry* that the "justification" for the intrusion could not simply be an "inarticulate hunch." "[T]he police officer must be able to point to specific and articulable facts which, taken together with rational inferences from those facts, reasonably warrant that intrusion." The Court later in the opinion put a deadly gloss on the term "rational inferences," restating it as "the specific reasonable inferences which he is entitled to draw from the facts in light of his experience."

Refreshingly candid in this regard, the Court doesn't try to sugarcoat Detective McFadden's experience. He had been on the lookout in downtown Cleveland for "shoplifters and pickpockets for 30 years." Despite the narrowness of his beat, McFadden nonetheless deduces that an "armed robbery" is afoot. What do armed robberies have in common with pickpocketing and shoplifting, besides being illegal? Nothing in the opinion suggests that McFadden has any experience investigating armed robbery.

John W. Terry

Martin McFadden

And as to his specific interpretation of the men's odd behavior as "casing the place," as a predicate to an "armed robbery," consider this exchange in the suppression hearing when the judge—unforgivably—jumped into the examination and got an answer from McFadden that he probably wasn't expecting:

Q. Have you ever had any experience in observing the activities of individuals in casing a place?
A. To be truthful with you, no.
Q. You never observed anybody casing a place?
A. No.
Q. But you have had the experience of a detective in apprehending, and doing your police job as assigned?
A: Yes.

Suppression Hearing Transcript at 1420.

The Court nonetheless saw fit to bless Detective McFadden's expertise and experience, assuming it uncritically, as courts have often unthoughtfully done and will probably continue to do. *See generally* Anna Lvovsky, *The Judicial Presumption of Police Expertise*, 130 Harv. L. Rev. 1995 (2017).

Terry is sometimes seen as inconsistent with the legacy of the Warren Court. But as Professor Maclin and others have observed, by 1968, having taken a public beating over its 1966 *Miranda* decision, the Warren Court had lost some of its civil libertarian mojo. *See* Tracey Maclin, Terry v. Ohio's *Fourth Amendment Legacy: Black Men and Police Discretion*, 72 St. John's L. Rev. 1271, 1277-78 (1998). *See also* Yale Kamisar, *The Warren Court (Was It Really So Defense-Minded?), The Burger Court (Is it Really So Prosecution-Oriented?), and Police Investigatory Practices*, in The Burger Court: The Counter Revolution That Wasn't 67 (Vincent Blasi ed., 1983) ("In its final years, 'the Warren Court,' I think it may be argued, was not the same Court that had produced *Miranda* or *Mapp*.").

This plaque honoring Detective McFadden, sponsored by the Cleveland Police Historical Society and the Ohio Historical Society, was erected in 2003 on Euclid Avenue in downtown Cleveland.

There were also cultural and political realities that of course influenced the Court. In the 12 months between the grant of certiorari and the decision in *Terry*, there had been what were then inaptly called "race riots" in 13 cities, most notably in Newark and Detroit, during the "long hot summer" of 1967; the assassination by gun of Martin Luther King Jr. on April 4, 1968, precipitating "race riots" in 100 cities, and of presidential candidate Robert Kennedy, on June 5, five days before the decision in *Terry*. During this same period Richard Nixon was hard on the campaign trail for the 1968 presidential election with his anti-crime message, vowing to make over the Supreme Court with "strict constructionists." And crime rates were, in fact, soaring. Not only Congress but President Johnson was chomping at the bit for tough-on-crime legislation. Perhaps poetically, the Omnibus Crime Control and Safe Streets Act of 1968, the most significant general criminal legislation passed perhaps ever by Congress, became effective on June 10, 1968, the same day the decision in *Terry* was handed down. This, of course, was precisely what Justice Douglas was referring to in his dissent in *Terry*:

> There have been powerful hydraulic pressures throughout our history that bear heavily on the Court to water down constitutional guarantees and give the police the upper hand. That hydraulic pressure has probably never been greater than it is today.

398 U.S. at 38 (Douglas, J., dissenting).

Chief Justice Warren's law clerk at the time stated later that *Terry* was the product of perceived political necessity. The Court was unwilling to be seen as the body that had "tied the hands of the police" in an age of escalating street violence. Earl C. Dudley Jr., *Terry v. Ohio, the Warren Court and the Fourth Amendment: A Law Clerk's Perspective*, 72 St. John's L. Rev. 891, 893 (1998). *See also* Bennett Capers, *Crime, Legitimacy and Testilying*, 83 Ind. L.J. 835, 862-65 (2008).

President Johnson announced he would not run for reelection on March 31, 1968. Chief Justice Warren retired effective June 30, 1968. An era was over.

The street-level impact of *Terry* was enormous, especially after the 1982 publication in *The Atlantic* of the influential "Broken Windows" article by criminologists George Kelling and James Q. Wilson, which advocated for prompt police attention to low-grade criminality as a deterrent to more serious crime. Ben Grunwald & Jeffrey Fagan, *The End of Intuition-Based High-Crime Areas*, 107 Cal. L. Rev. 345, 357 (2019). Almost overnight, field interrogation was everywhere and no level of urban hijinks was too innocuous for police inquiry. *Id. See also* Debra Livingston, *Police Discretion and the Quality of Life in Public Places: Courts, Communities, and the New Policing*, 97 Colum. L. Rev. 551 (1997). As occasions for *Terry* stops spread with the popularization of broken windows policing, police officers quickly discovered that when and if they wanted to it was fairly simple to escalate—even unilaterally—a *Terry* stop into a situation where there was probable cause to arrest, especially for such "contempt of cop" misdemeanors as obstruction, disorderly conduct, and the like. *See* Alexandra Napatoff, *A Stop Is Just a Stop:* Terry's *Formalism*, 15 Ohio St. J. Crim. L. 113, 121 (2017).

Terry, while cast originally as a narrow exception to the probable cause requirement, was read generously by the reconstituted Burger Court in the 1970s and 1980s. In *Pennsylvania v. Mimms*, 434 U.S. 106 (1977), for example, the Court held that police may order persons out of a car during a routine traffic stop as a matter of routine, without any quantum of suspicion, purely as a means to protect the safety of the officers. *Id.* at 111. Further, if the police officers have reasonable suspicion that the passengers may be armed—an observed "bulge" under a passenger's sport coat satisfied that test in *Mimms*—the officers may frisk them for weapons. In *Michigan v. Long*, 463 U.S. 1032 (1983), the Court upheld the frisk of an apparently drunk driver and search of the front compartment area of the vehicle where officers saw a

D. Exception to the Probable Cause Requirement: The *Terry* Doctrine

hunting knife on front floor board. And in *Maryland v. Buie*, 494 U.S. 325 (1990), the Court found that *Terry* justified a "protective sweep" of the premises in connection with the execution of an arrest warrant in a home to protect the safety of the officers and others, where the officers reasonably believed other dangerous persons might be present.

In the next case the Court considers the extent to which the "frisk" warranted under *Terry* can serve as a gateway to investigation unrelated to securing the safety of the questioning officers. The frisker here, an unnamed Minneapolis officer, purports to have a superhero's sense of touch rivaled only by Tommy, the mythical "deaf, dumb, and blind kid" of The Who's eponymous rock opera.

Minnesota v. Dickerson
508 U.S. 366 (1993)

Justice WHITE delivered the opinion of the Court.

In this case, we consider whether the Fourth Amendment permits the seizure of contraband detected through a police officer's sense of touch during a protective patdown search.

I

On the evening of November 9, 1989, two Minneapolis police officers were patrolling an area on the city's north side in a marked squad car. At about 8:15 p.m., one of the officers observed respondent leaving a 12-unit apartment building on Morgan Avenue North. The officer, having previously responded to complaints of drug sales in the building's hallways and having executed several search warrants on the premises, considered the building to be a notorious "crack house." According to testimony credited by the trial court, respondent began walking toward the police but, upon spotting the squad car and making eye contact with one of the officers, abruptly halted and began walking in the opposite direction. His suspicion aroused, this officer watched as respondent turned and entered an alley on the other side of the apartment building. Based upon respondent's seemingly evasive actions and the fact that he had just left a building known for cocaine traffic, the officers decided to stop respondent and investigate further.

The officers pulled their squad car into the alley and ordered respondent to stop and submit to a patdown search. The search revealed no weapons, but the officer conducting the search did take an interest in a small lump in respondent's nylon jacket. The officer later testified:

> [A]s I pat-searched the front of his body, I felt a lump, a small lump, in the front pocket. I examined it with my fingers and it slid and it felt to be a lump of crack cocaine in cellophane.

The officer then reached into respondent's pocket and retrieved a small plastic bag containing one fifth of one gram of crack cocaine. Respondent was arrested and charged in Hennepin County District Court with possession of a controlled substance.

Before trial, respondent moved to suppress the cocaine. The trial court first concluded that the officers were justified under *Terry* in stopping respondent to investigate whether he might be engaged in criminal activity. The court further found that the officers were justified in frisking respondent to ensure that he was not carrying a weapon. Finally, analogizing to the "plain-view" doctrine, under which officers may make a warrantless seizure of contraband found in plain view during a lawful search for other items, the trial court ruled that the officers' seizure of the cocaine did not violate the Fourth Amendment:

> To this Court there is no distinction as to which sensory perception the officer uses to conclude that the material is contraband. An experienced officer may rely upon his sense of smell in DWI stops or in recognizing the smell of burning marijuana in an automobile. The sound of a shotgun being racked would clearly support certain reactions by an officer. The sense of touch, grounded in experience and training, is as reliable as perceptions drawn from other senses. "Plain feel," therefore, is no different than plain view and will equally support the seizure here.

His suppression motion having failed, respondent proceeded to trial and was found guilty.

On appeal, the Minnesota Court of Appeals reversed. The court agreed with the trial court that the investigative stop and protective patdown search of respondent were lawful under *Terry* because the officers had a reasonable belief based on specific and articulable facts that respondent was engaged in criminal behavior and that he might be armed and dangerous. The court concluded, however, that the officers had overstepped the bounds allowed by *Terry* in seizing the cocaine. In doing so, the Court of Appeals "decline [d] to adopt the plain feel exception" to the warrant requirement.

The Minnesota Supreme Court affirmed. Like the Court of Appeals, the State Supreme Court held that both the stop and the frisk of respondent were valid under *Terry*, but found the seizure of the cocaine to be unconstitutional. The court expressly refused "to extend the plain view doctrine to the sense of touch" on the grounds that "the sense of touch is inherently less immediate and less reliable than the sense of sight" and that "the sense of touch is far more intrusive into the personal privacy that is at the core of the [F]ourth [A]mendment." The court thus appeared to adopt a categorical rule barring the seizure of any contraband detected by an officer through the sense of touch during a patdown search for weapons. The court further noted that "[e]ven if we recognized a 'plain feel' exception, the search in this case would not qualify" because "[t]he pat search of the defendant went far beyond what is permissible under *Terry*." Id., As the State Supreme Court read the record, the officer conducting the search ascertained that the lump in respondent's jacket was contraband only after probing and investigating what he certainly knew was not a weapon.

We granted certiorari to resolve a conflict among the state and federal courts over whether contraband detected through the sense of touch during a patdown search may be admitted into evidence. We now affirm.

II

A

The Fourth Amendment, made applicable to the States by way of the Fourteenth Amendment, guarantees "[t]he right of the people to be secure in their persons, houses, papers, and effects, against unreasonable searches and seizures." Time and again, this Court has observed that searches and seizures "'conducted outside the judicial process, without prior approval by judge or magistrate, are per se unreasonable under the Fourth Amendment—subject only to a few specifically established and well delineated exceptions.'" One such exception was recognized in *Terry*, which held that "where a police officer observes unusual conduct which leads him reasonably to conclude in light of his experience that criminal activity may be afoot . . .," the officer may briefly stop the suspicious person and make "reasonable inquiries" aimed at confirming or dispelling his suspicions.

Terry further held that "[w]hen an officer is justified in believing that the individual whose suspicious behavior he is investigating at close range is armed and presently dangerous to the officer or to others," the officer may conduct a patdown search "to determine whether the person is in fact carrying a weapon." "The purpose of this limited search is not to discover evidence of crime, but to allow the officer to pursue his investigation without fear of violence. . . ." Rather, a protective search—permitted without a warrant and on the basis

D. Exception to the Probable Cause Requirement: The *Terry* Doctrine

of reasonable suspicion less than probable cause—must be strictly "limited to that which is necessary for the discovery of weapons which might be used to harm the officer or others nearby." If the protective search goes beyond what is necessary to determine if the suspect is armed, it is no longer valid under *Terry* and its fruits will be suppressed.

These principles were settled 25 years ago when, on the same day, the Court announced its decisions in *Terry* and *Sibron*. The question presented today is whether police officers may seize nonthreatening contraband detected during a protective patdown search of the sort permitted by *Terry*. We think the answer is clearly that they may, so long as the officers' search stays within the bounds marked by *Terry*.

B

We have already held that police officers, at least under certain circumstances, may seize contraband detected during the lawful execution of a *Terry* search. In *Michigan v. Long*, for example, police approached a man who had driven his car into a ditch and who appeared to be under the influence of some intoxicant. As the man moved to reenter the car from the roadside, police spotted a knife on the floorboard. The officers stopped the man, subjected him to a patdown search, and then inspected the interior of the vehicle for other weapons. During the search of the passenger compartment, the police discovered an open pouch containing marijuana and seized it. This Court upheld the validity of the search and seizure under *Terry*. The Court held first that, in the context of a roadside encounter, where police have reasonable suspicion based on specific and articulable facts to believe that a driver may be armed and dangerous, they may conduct a protective search for weapons not only of the driver's person but also of the passenger compartment of the automobile. Of course, the protective search of the vehicle, being justified solely by the danger that weapons stored there could be used against the officers or bystanders, must be "limited to those areas in which a weapon may be placed or hidden." The Court then held: "If, while conducting a legitimate *Terry* search of the interior of the automobile, the officer should, as here, discover contraband other than weapons, he clearly cannot be required to ignore the contraband, and the Fourth Amendment does not require its suppression in such circumstances."

The Court in *Long* justified this latter holding by reference to our cases under the "plain-view" doctrine. Under that doctrine, if police are lawfully in a position from which they view an object, if its incriminating character is immediately apparent, and if the officers have a lawful right of access to the object, they may seize it without a warrant. If, however, the police lack probable cause to believe that an object in plain view is contraband without conducting some further search of the object—i.e., if "its incriminating character [is not] 'immediately apparent,'"—the plain-view doctrine cannot justify its seizure.

We think that this doctrine has an obvious application by analogy to cases in which an officer discovers contraband through the sense of touch during an otherwise lawful search. The rationale of the plain-view doctrine is that if contraband is left in open view and is observed by a police officer from a lawful vantage point, there has been no invasion of a legitimate expectation of privacy and thus no "search" within the meaning of the Fourth Amendment—or at least no search independent of the initial intrusion that gave the officers their vantage point. The warrantless seizure of contraband that presents itself in this manner is deemed justified by the realization that resort to a neutral magistrate under such circumstances would often be impracticable and would do little to promote the objectives of the Fourth Amendment. The same can be said of tactile discoveries of contraband. If a police officer lawfully pats down a suspect's outer clothing and feels an object whose contour or mass makes its identity immediately apparent, there has been no invasion of the suspect's privacy beyond that already authorized by the officer's search for weapons; if the object is contraband, its warrantless seizure would be justified by the same practical considerations that inhere in the plain-view context.

The Minnesota Supreme Court rejected an analogy to the plain-view doctrine on two grounds: first, its belief that "the sense of touch is inherently less immediate and less reliable than the sense of sight," and second, that "the sense of touch is far more intrusive into the personal privacy that is at the core of the [F]ourth [A]mendment." We have a somewhat different view. First, *Terry* itself demonstrates that the sense of touch is capable of revealing the nature of an object with sufficient reliability to support a seizure. The very premise of *Terry*, after all, is that officers will be able to detect the presence of weapons through the sense of touch and *Terry* upheld precisely such a seizure. Even if it were true that the sense of touch is generally less reliable than the sense of sight, that only suggests that officers will less often be able to justify seizures of unseen contraband. Regardless of whether the officer detects the contraband by sight or by touch, however, the Fourth Amendment's requirement that the officer have probable cause to believe that the item is contraband before seizing it ensures against excessively speculative seizures. The court's second concern—that touch is more intrusive into privacy than is sight—is inapposite in light of the fact that the intrusion the court fears has already been authorized by the lawful search for weapons. The seizure of an item whose identity is already known occasions no further invasion of privacy. Accordingly, the suspect's privacy interests are not advanced by a categorical rule barring the seizure of contraband plainly detected through the sense of touch.

III

It remains to apply these principles to the facts of this case. Respondent has not challenged the finding made by the trial court and affirmed by both the Court of Appeals and the State Supreme Court that the police were justified under *Terry* in stopping him and frisking him for weapons. Thus, the dispositive question before this Court is whether the officer who conducted the search was acting within the lawful bounds marked by *Terry* at the time he gained probable cause to believe that the lump in respondent's jacket was contraband. The State District Court did not make precise findings on this point, instead finding simply that the officer, after feeling "a small, hard object wrapped in plastic" in respondent's pocket, "formed the opinion that the object . . . was crack . . . cocaine." The District Court also noted that the officer made "no claim that he suspected this object to be a weapon," a finding affirmed on appeal. The Minnesota Supreme Court, after "a close examination of the record," held that the officer's own testimony "belies any notion that he 'immediately'" recognized the lump as crack cocaine. Rather, the court concluded, the officer determined that the lump was contraband only after "squeezing, sliding and otherwise manipulating the contents of the defendant's pocket"—a pocket which the officer already knew contained no weapon.

Under the State Supreme Court's interpretation of the record before it, it is clear that the court was correct in holding that the police officer in this case overstepped the bounds of the "strictly circumscribed" search for weapons allowed under *Terry*. Where, as here, "an officer who is executing a valid search for one item seizes a different item," this Court rightly "has been sensitive to the danger . . . that officers will enlarge a specific authorization, furnished by a warrant or an exigency, into the equivalent of a general warrant to rummage and seize at will." Here, the officer's continued exploration of respondent's pocket after having concluded that it contained no weapon was unrelated to "[t]he sole justification of the search [under *Terry*:] . . . the protection of the police officer and others nearby." It therefore amounted to the sort of evidentiary search that *Terry* expressly refused to authorize and that we have condemned in subsequent cases.

Once again, the analogy to the plain-view doctrine is apt. In *Arizona v. Hicks*, this Court held invalid the seizure of stolen stereo equipment found by police while executing a valid search for other evidence. Although the police were lawfully on the premises, they obtained probable cause to believe that the stereo equipment was contraband only after moving the equipment

D. Exception to the Probable Cause Requirement: The *Terry* Doctrine   **411**

to permit officers to read its serial numbers. The subsequent seizure of the equipment could not be justified by the plain-view doctrine, this Court explained, because the incriminating character of the stereo equipment was not immediately apparent; rather, probable cause to believe that the equipment was stolen arose only as a result of a further search—the moving of the equipment—that was not authorized by a search warrant or by any exception to the warrant requirement. The facts of this case are very similar. Although the officer was lawfully in a position to feel the lump in respondent's pocket, because *Terry* entitled him to place his hands upon respondent's jacket, the court below determined that the incriminating character of the object was not immediately apparent to him. Rather, the officer determined that the item was contraband only after conducting a further search, one not authorized by *Terry* or by any other exception to the warrant requirement. Because this further search of respondent's pocket was constitutionally invalid, the seizure of the cocaine that followed is likewise unconstitutional.

IV

For these reasons, the judgment of the Minnesota Supreme Court is
   Affirmed.

NOTES AND QUESTIONS

1. Is the case for reasonable suspicion ironclad here? Is criminal activity "afoot"? What is the probative value of "walking away"? Do you see irony in the notion that "walking away" can contribute to the basis for reasonable suspicion for a *Terry* stop, while at the same time a reasonable belief in the ability to "walk away" signifies the absence of a seizure?

2. The Court notes the police officer's "interest" in a "lump" in a jacket pocket. The Court seemingly legitimates this interest even though the only constitutional basis for the officer's hands on the defendant is to search for weapons. Isn't the officer just supposed to ignore the "lump" because it isn't a weapon?

Is the officer's testimony that "by feel" he had determined that he had felt "a lump of cocaine wrapped in cellophane" even remotely credible? Wasn't he cross-examined on this conclusion? What's in the record? Why does the Court just seem to accept this?

3. The Court recognizes the theoretical possibility of a "plain feel" exception but finds it inapplicable here, apparently because the officer continued his search even after its original and legitimate purpose of looking for weapons was over. Can you imagine a scenario where the exception would be applicable?

In the next case the Court considers what happens when a *Terry* stop doesn't go as planned, as well as whether Justice White's concurring opinion in *Terry* on "the right to remain" silent still has legs.

Hiibel v. Sixth Judicial District Court of Nevada
542 U.S. 177 (2004)

Justice KENNEDY delivered the opinion of the Court.

The petitioner was arrested and convicted for refusing to identify himself during a stop allowed by *Terry*. He challenges his conviction under the Fourth and Fifth Amendments to the United States Constitution, applicable to the States through the Fourteenth Amendment.

I

The sheriff's department in Humboldt County, Nevada, received an afternoon telephone call reporting an assault. The caller reported seeing a man assault a woman in a red and silver GMC truck on Grass Valley Road. Deputy Sheriff Lee Dove was dispatched to investigate. When the officer arrived at the scene, he found the truck parked on the side of the road. A man was standing by the truck, and a young woman was sitting inside it. The officer observed skid marks in the gravel behind the vehicle, leading him to believe it had come to a sudden stop.

The officer approached the man and explained that he was investigating a report of a fight. The man appeared to be intoxicated. The officer asked him if he had "any identification on [him]," which we understand as a request to produce a driver's license or some other form of written identification. The man refused and asked why the officer wanted to see identification. The officer responded that he was conducting an investigation and needed to see some identification. The unidentified man became agitated and insisted he had done nothing wrong. The officer explained that he wanted to find out who the man was and what he was doing there. After continued refusals to comply with the officer's request for identification, the man began to taunt the officer by placing his hands behind his back and telling the officer to arrest him and take him to jail. This routine kept up for several minutes: The officer asked for identification 11 times and was refused each time. After warning the man that he would be arrested if he continued to refuse to comply, the officer placed him under arrest.

We now know that the man arrested on Grass Valley Road is Larry Dudley Hiibel. Hiibel was charged with "willfully resist[ing], delay[ing] or obstruct[ing] a public officer in discharging or attempting to discharge any legal duty of his office" in violation of Nev. Rev. Stat. (NRS) § 199.280 (2003). The government reasoned that Hiibel had obstructed the officer in carrying out his duties under § 171.123, a Nevada statute that defines the legal rights and duties of a police officer in the context of an investigative stop. Section 171.123 provides in relevant part:

> 1. Any peace officer may detain any person whom the officer encounters under circumstances which reasonably indicate that the person has committed, is committing or is about to commit a crime. . . .
>
>   3. The officer may detain the person pursuant to this section only to ascertain his identity and the suspicious circumstances surrounding his presence abroad. Any person so detained shall identify himself, but may not be compelled to answer any other inquiry of any peace officer.

Hiibel was tried in the Justice Court of Union Township. The court agreed that Hiibel's refusal to identify himself as required by § 171.123 "obstructed and delayed Dove as a public officer in attempting to discharge his duty" in violation of § 199.280. Hiibel was convicted and fined $250. The Sixth Judicial District Court affirmed, rejecting Hiibel's argument that the application of § 171.123 to his case violated the Fourth and Fifth Amendments. On review the Supreme Court of Nevada rejected the Fourth Amendment challenge in a divided opinion. Hiibel petitioned for rehearing, seeking explicit resolution of his Fifth Amendment challenge. The petition was denied without opinion. We granted certiorari.

II

NRS § 171.123(3) is an enactment sometimes referred to as a "stop and identify" statute. . . .

Stop and identify statutes often combine elements of traditional vagrancy laws with provisions intended to regulate police behavior in the course of investigatory stops. The statutes vary from State to State, but all permit an officer to ask or require a suspect to disclose his identity. A few States model their statutes on the Uniform Arrest Act, a model code that permits an officer to stop a person reasonably suspected of committing a crime and "demand of him his name, address, business abroad and whither he is going." Other statutes are based on the text proposed by the American Law Institute as part of the Institute's Model Penal Code. The provision, originally designated § 250.12, provides that a person who is loitering "under circumstances which justify suspicion that he may be engaged or about to engage in crime commits a violation if he refuses the request of a peace officer that he identify himself and give a reasonably credible account of the lawfulness of his conduct and purposes." In some States, a suspect's refusal to identify himself is a misdemeanor offense or civil violation; in others, it is a factor to be considered in whether the suspect has violated loitering laws. In other States, a suspect may decline to identify himself without penalty.

Stop and identify statutes have their roots in early English vagrancy laws that required suspected vagrants to face arrest unless they gave "a good Account of themselves," a power that itself reflected common-law rights of private persons to "arrest any suspicious night-walker, and detain him till he give a good account of himself . . . ." In recent decades, the Court has found constitutional infirmity in traditional vagrancy laws. In *Papachristou v. Jacksonville* (1972), the Court held that a traditional vagrancy law was void for vagueness. Its broad scope and imprecise terms denied proper notice to potential offenders and permitted police officers to exercise unfettered discretion in the enforcement of the law.

The Court has recognized similar constitutional limitations on the scope and operation of stop and identify statutes. In *Brown v. Texas* (1979), the Court invalidated a conviction for violating a Texas stop and identify statute on Fourth Amendment grounds. The Court ruled that the initial stop was not based on specific, objective facts establishing reasonable suspicion to believe the suspect was involved in criminal activity. Absent that factual basis for detaining the defendant, the Court held, the risk of "arbitrary and abusive police practices" was too great and the stop was impermissible. Four Terms later, the Court invalidated a modified stop and identify statute on vagueness grounds. The California law in *Kolender* required a suspect to give an officer "'credible and reliable'" identification when asked to identify himself. The Court held that the statute was void because it provided no standard for determining what a suspect must do to comply with it, resulting in "'virtually unrestrained power to arrest and charge persons with a violation.'"

The present case begins where our prior cases left off. Here there is no question that the initial stop was based on reasonable suspicion, satisfying the Fourth Amendment requirements noted in *Brown*. Further, the petitioner has not alleged that the statute is unconstitutionally vague, as in *Kolender*. Here the Nevada statute is narrower and more precise. The statute in *Kolender* had been interpreted to require a suspect to give the officer "credible and reliable" identification. In contrast, the Nevada Supreme Court has interpreted NRS § 171.123(3) to require only that a suspect disclose his name. As we understand it, the statute does not require a suspect to give the officer a driver's license or any other document. Provided that the suspect either states his name or communicates it to the officer by other means—a choice, we assume, that the suspect may make—the statute is satisfied and no violation occurs.

III

Hiibel argues that his conviction cannot stand because the officer's conduct violated his Fourth Amendment rights. We disagree.

Asking questions is an essential part of police investigations. In the ordinary course a police officer is free to ask a person for identification without implicating the Fourth Amendment. "[I]nterrogation relating to one's identity or a request for identification by the police does not, by itself, constitute a Fourth Amendment seizure." Beginning with *Terry*, the Court has recognized that a law enforcement officer's reasonable suspicion that a person may be involved in criminal activity permits the officer to stop the person for a brief time and take additional steps to investigate further. To ensure that the resulting seizure is constitutionally reasonable, a *Terry* stop must be limited. The officer's action must be "'justified at its inception, and . . . reasonably related in scope to the circumstances which justified the interference in the first place.'" For example, the seizure can not continue for an excessive period of time, or resemble a traditional arrest.

Our decisions make clear that questions concerning a suspect's identity are a routine and accepted part of many *Terry* stops.

Obtaining a suspect's name in the course of a *Terry* stop serves important government interests. Knowledge of identity may inform an officer that a suspect is wanted for another offense, or has a record of violence or mental disorder. On the other hand, knowing identity may help clear a suspect and allow the police to concentrate their efforts elsewhere. Identity may prove particularly important in cases such as this, where the police are investigating what appears to be a domestic assault. Officers called to investigate domestic disputes need to know whom they are dealing with in order to assess the situation, the threat to their own safety, and possible danger to the potential victim.

Although it is well established that an officer may ask a suspect to identify himself in the course of a *Terry* stop, it has been an open question whether the suspect can be arrested and prosecuted for refusal to answer. Petitioner draws our attention to statements in prior opinions that, according to him, answer the question in his favor. In *Terry*, Justice White stated in a concurring opinion that a person detained in an investigative stop can be questioned but is "not obliged to answer, answers may not be compelled, and refusal to answer furnishes no basis for an arrest." The Court cited this opinion in dicta in *Berkemer v. McCarty*, (1984), a decision holding that a routine traffic stop is not a custodial stop requiring the protections of *Miranda*. In the course of explaining why *Terry* stops have not been subject to *Miranda*, the Court suggested reasons why *Terry* stops have a "nonthreatening character," among them the fact that a suspect detained during a *Terry* stop "is not obliged to respond" to questions. According to petitioner, these statements establish a right to refuse to answer questions during a *Terry* stop.

We do not read these statements as controlling. The passages recognize that the Fourth Amendment does not impose obligations on the citizen but instead provides rights against the government. As a result, the Fourth Amendment itself cannot require a suspect to answer questions. This case concerns a different issue, however. Here, the source of the legal obligation arises from Nevada state law, not the Fourth Amendment. Further, the statutory obligation does not go beyond answering an officer's request to disclose a name. As a result, we cannot view the dicta in *Berkemer* or Justice White's concurrence in *Terry* as answering the question whether a State can compel a suspect to disclose his name during a *Terry* stop.

The principles of *Terry* permit a State to require a suspect to disclose his name in the course of a *Terry* stop. The reasonableness of a seizure under the Fourth Amendment is determined "by balancing its intrusion on the individual's Fourth Amendment interests against its promotion of legitimate government interests." The Nevada statute satisfies that standard. The request for identity has an immediate relation to the purpose, rationale, and practical demands of a *Terry* stop. The threat of criminal sanction helps ensure that the request for identity does not become a legal nullity. On the other hand, the Nevada statute does not alter the nature of the stop itself: it does not change its duration or its location. A state law requiring a suspect to disclose his name in the course of a valid *Terry* stop is consistent with Fourth Amendment prohibitions against unreasonable searches and seizures.

Petitioner argues that the Nevada statute circumvents the probable-cause requirement, in effect allowing an officer to arrest a person for being suspicious. According to petitioner, this creates a risk of arbitrary police conduct that the Fourth Amendment does not permit.

These are familiar concerns; they were central to the opinion in *Papachristou*, and also to the decisions limiting the operation of stop and identify statutes in *Kolender* and *Brown*. Petitioner's concerns are met by the requirement that a *Terry* stop must be justified at its inception and "reasonably related in scope to the circumstances which justified" the initial stop. Under these principles, an officer may not arrest a suspect for failure to identify himself if the request for identification is not reasonably related to the circumstances justifying the stop. The Court noted a similar limitation in *Hayes*, where it suggested that Terry may permit an officer to determine a suspect's identity by compelling the suspect to submit to fingerprinting only if there is "a reasonable basis for believing that fingerprinting will establish or negate the suspect's connection with that crime." It is clear in this case that the request for identification was "reasonably related in scope to the circumstances which justified" the stop. The officer's request was a commonsense inquiry, not an effort to obtain an arrest for failure to identify after a *Terry* stop yielded insufficient evidence. The stop, the request, and the State's requirement of a response did not contravene the guarantees of the Fourth Amendment.

• • •

The judgment of the Nevada Supreme Court is
Affirmed.

NOTES AND QUESTIONS

1. Every fact selected for inclusion in a case is purposeful. The skid marks in the gravel? Why? And why defendant's middle name?

2. Is the Court's description of Sheriff Dove's encounter with Larry Dudley Hiibel slanted? Sure, Larry Dudley is being a pain in the ass, but why does the Court not acknowledge Dove's harassment of him? Asking for identification once might have been "a commonsense inquiry" as the Court describes it. But 11 times? It wasn't like there were no other investigation avenues available to Dove. For one thing, the alleged victim, per the tip, is just sitting in the truck, apparently being ignored, while Dove goes *mano a mano* with Hiibel. Might she have relevant information? Are there other witnesses in the neighborhood? How about running the plate on the truck? Does Dove actually care about finding out what happened, or does he just want to win his showdown with Larry Dudley?

3. The Court states that "stop and identify" statutes like the Nevada statute at issue here contain provisions "intended to regulate police behavior." Do you agree? What provisions in the Nevada statute appear to have this purpose?

4. The Court also states that there is "no question" that Dove's "stop" of Hiibel was supported by reasonable suspicion. Do you agree? Under what circumstances should an anonymous tip be able to serve as the basis for reasonable suspicion? Isn't the original justification for *Terry* the purported expertise and experience that police officers bring to bear on situations they observe?

5. The Court sings a love song to the importance of questioning, as if the point were debatable. But it never acknowledges the peril that answering may bring. For example, if a person being questioned has an outstanding warrant, and gives his name to a police officer, the officer can easily learn of the warrant and the person will immediately become arrestable—and searchable incident to that arrest. These are essentially the facts of *Utah v. Strieff*, 579 U.S. 232 (2016), *see infra*, where questioning of the defendant—*without* reasonable suspicion—leads to the production of identification, discovery of a warrant for traffic violation, arrest, search incident to arrest, discovery of drugs, then prosecution, then conviction and jail.

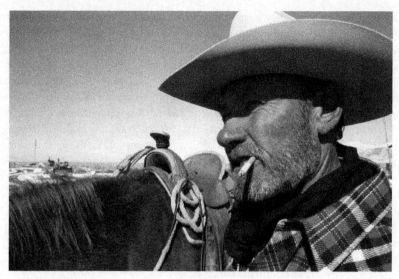
Larry Dudley Hiibel

6. None of this was presumably on Justice White's mind when he wrote his concurrence in *Terry* 36 years prior to *Hiibel*. But does anything in *Terry* itself compel the conclusion the Court reaches here?

7. Does the Court satisfactorily address its explicit reliance on Justice White's *Terry* concurrence in *Berkemer v. McCarty*, 468 U.S. 420 (1984). What is the relevance of the fact that a state statute purports to compel a person to speak? Isn't this tantamount to saying that a state law could abrogate *Terry* by, say, permitting a frisk for contraband as well as weapons?

8. The Court notes that an important interest served by learning a suspect's name is that it "may inform an officer that a suspect is wanted for another offense." Acquiring such knowledge, of course, requires the intermediate step of the officer remotely consulting a criminal records database, which the officer can easily do. But is that intermediate step consistent with *Terry*, which requires that the search and seizure be "reasonably related in scope to the circumstances which justified the interference in the first place"? 392 U.S. at 20.

The next case deals with a police officer's "reasonable suspicion" as to whether automobile passengers in a traffic stop might be "armed and dangerous" such that they can be frisked for the protection of the officers.

Arizona v. Johnson
555 U.S. 323 (2009)

Justice GINSBURG delivered the opinion of the Court.

This case concerns the authority of police officers to "stop and frisk" a passenger in a motor vehicle temporarily seized upon police detection of a traffic infraction. In a pathmarking decision, *Terry*, the Court considered whether an investigatory stop (temporary detention) and frisk (patdown for weapons) may be conducted without violating the Fourth Amendment's ban on unreasonable searches and seizures. The Court upheld "stop and frisk" as constitutionally permissible if two conditions are met. First, the investigatory stop must be lawful.

D. Exception to the Probable Cause Requirement: The *Terry* Doctrine

That requirement is met in an on-the-street encounter, *Terry* determined, when the police officer reasonably suspects that the person apprehended is committing or has committed a criminal offense. Second, to proceed from a stop to a frisk, the police officer must reasonably suspect that the person stopped is armed and dangerous.

For the duration of a traffic stop, we recently confirmed, a police officer effectively seizes "everyone in the vehicle," the driver and all passengers. *Brendlin v. California* (2007). Accordingly, we hold that, in a traffic-stop setting, the first *Terry* condition—a lawful investigatory stop—is met whenever it is lawful for police to detain an automobile and its occupants pending inquiry into a vehicular violation. The police need not have, in addition, cause to believe any occupant of the vehicle is involved in criminal activity. To justify a patdown of the driver or a passenger during a traffic stop, however, just as in the case of a pedestrian reasonably suspected of criminal activity, the police must harbor reasonable suspicion that the person subjected to the frisk is armed and dangerous.

I

On April 19, 2002, Officer Maria Trevizo and Detectives Machado and Gittings, all members of Arizona's gang task force, were on patrol in Tucson near a neighborhood associated with the Crips gang. At approximately 9 p.m., the officers pulled over an automobile after a license plate check revealed that the vehicle's registration had been suspended for an insurance-related violation. Under Arizona law, the violation for which the vehicle was stopped constituted a civil infraction warranting a citation. At the time of the stop, the vehicle had three occupants—the driver, a front-seat passenger, and a passenger in the back seat, Lemon Montrea Johnson, the respondent here. In making the stop the officers had no reason to suspect anyone in the vehicle of criminal activity.

The three officers left their patrol car and approached the stopped vehicle. Machado instructed all of the occupants to keep their hands visible. He asked whether there were any weapons in the vehicle; all responded no. Machado then directed the driver to get out of the car. Gittings dealt with the front-seat passenger, who stayed in the vehicle throughout the stop. While Machado was getting the driver's license and information about the vehicle's registration and insurance, Trevizo attended to Johnson.

Trevizo noticed that, as the police approached, Johnson looked back and kept his eyes on the officers. When she drew near, she observed that Johnson was wearing clothing, including a blue bandana, that she considered consistent with Crips membership. She also noticed a scanner in Johnson's jacket pocket, which "struck [her] as highly unusual and cause [for] concern," because "most people" would not carry around a scanner that way "unless they're going to be involved in some kind of criminal activity or [are] going to try to evade the police by listening to the scanner." In response to Trevizo's questions, Johnson provided his name and date of birth but said he had no identification with him. He volunteered that he was from Eloy, Arizona, a place Trevizo knew was home to a Crips gang. Johnson further told Trevizo that he had served time in prison for burglary and had been out for about a year.

Trevizo wanted to question Johnson away from the front-seat passenger to gain "intelligence about the gang [Johnson] might be in." For that reason, she asked him to get out of the car. Johnson complied. Based on Trevizo's observations and Johnson's answers to her questions while he was still seated in the car, Trevizo suspected that "he might have a weapon on him." When he exited the vehicle, she therefore "patted him down for officer safety." During the patdown, Trevizo felt the butt of a gun near Johnson's waist. At that point Johnson began to struggle, and Trevizo placed him in handcuffs.

Johnson was charged in state court with, inter alia, possession of a weapon by a prohibited possessor. He moved to suppress the evidence as the fruit of an unlawful search. The trial court denied the motion, concluding that the stop was lawful and that Trevizo had cause to suspect Johnson was armed and dangerous. A jury convicted Johnson of the gun-possession charge.

A divided panel of the Arizona Court of Appeals reversed Johnson's conviction. Recognizing that "Johnson was [lawfully] seized when the officers stopped the car," the court nevertheless concluded that prior to the frisk the detention had "evolved into a separate, consensual encounter stemming from an unrelated investigation by Trevizo of Johnson's possible gang affiliation." Absent "reason to believe Johnson was involved in criminal activity," the Arizona appeals court held, Trevizo "had no right to pat him down for weapons, even if she had reason to suspect he was armed and dangerous."

II

A

We begin our consideration of the constitutionality of Officer Trevizo's patdown of Johnson by looking back to the Court's leading decision in *Terry. Terry* involved a stop for interrogation of men whose conduct had attracted the attention of a patrolling police officer. The officer's observation led him reasonably to suspect that the men were casing a jewelry shop in preparation for a robbery. He conducted a patdown, which disclosed weapons concealed in the men's overcoat pockets. This Court upheld the lower courts' determinations that the interrogation was warranted and the patdown, permissible.

Terry established the legitimacy of an investigatory stop "in situations where [the police] may lack probable cause for an arrest." When the stop is justified by suspicion (reasonably grounded, but short of probable cause) that criminal activity is afoot, the Court explained, the police officer must be positioned to act instantly on reasonable suspicion that the persons temporarily detained are armed and dangerous. Recognizing that a limited search of outer clothing for weapons serves to protect both the officer and the public, the Court held the patdown reasonable under the Fourth Amendment.

"[M]ost traffic stops," this Court has observed, "resemble, in duration and atmosphere, the kind of brief detention authorized in *Terry*." Furthermore, the Court has recognized that traffic stops are "especially fraught with danger to police officers." "'The risk of harm to both the police and the occupants [of a stopped vehicle] is minimized,'" we have stressed, "'if the officers routinely exercise unquestioned command of the situation.'" Three decisions cumulatively portray *Terry*'s application in a traffic-stop setting: *Pennsylvania v. Mimms*; *Maryland v. Wilson*; and *Brendlin v. California*.

In *Mimms*, the Court held that "once a motor vehicle has been lawfully detained for a traffic violation, the police officers may order the driver to get out of the vehicle without violating the Fourth Amendment's proscription of unreasonable searches and seizures." The government's "legitimate and weighty" interest in officer safety, the Court said, outweighs the "de minimis" additional intrusion of requiring a driver, already lawfully stopped, to exit the vehicle. Citing *Terry* as controlling, the Court further held that a driver, once outside the stopped vehicle, may be patted down for weapons if the officer reasonably concludes that the driver "might be armed and presently dangerous."

Wilson held that the *Mimms* rule applied to passengers as well as to drivers. Specifically, the Court instructed that "an officer making a traffic stop may order passengers to get out of the car pending completion of the stop." "[T]he same weighty interest in officer safety," the Court observed, "is present regardless of whether the occupant of the stopped car is a driver or passenger."

It is true, the Court acknowledged, that in a lawful traffic stop, "[t]here is probable cause to believe that the driver has committed a minor vehicular offense," but "there is no such reason to stop or detain the passengers." On the other hand, the Court emphasized, the risk of a violent encounter in a traffic-stop setting "stems not from the ordinary reaction of a motorist

D. Exception to the Probable Cause Requirement: The *Terry* Doctrine

stopped for a speeding violation, but from the fact that evidence of a more serious crime might be uncovered during the stop." "[T]he motivation of a passenger to employ violence to prevent apprehension of such a crime," the Court stated, "is every bit as great as that of the driver." Moreover, the Court noted, "as a practical matter, the passengers are already stopped by virtue of the stop of the vehicle," so "the additional intrusion on the passenger is minimal."

Completing the picture, *Brendlin* held that a passenger is seized, just as the driver is, "from the moment [a car stopped by the police comes] to a halt on the side of the road." A passenger therefore has standing to challenge a stop's constitutionality.

After *Wilson*, but before *Brendlin*, the Court had stated, in dictum, that officers who conduct "routine traffic stop[s]" may "perform a 'patdown' of a driver and any passengers upon reasonable suspicion that they may be armed and dangerous." That forecast, we now confirm, accurately captures the combined thrust of the Court's decisions in *Mimms*, *Wilson*, and *Brendlin*.

B

The Arizona Court of Appeals recognized that, initially, Johnson was lawfully detained incident to the legitimate stop of the vehicle in which he was a passenger. But, that court concluded, once Officer Trevizo undertook to question Johnson on a matter unrelated to the traffic stop, i.e., Johnson's gang affiliation, patdown authority ceased to exist, absent reasonable suspicion that Johnson had engaged, or was about to engage, in criminal activity. In support of the Arizona court's portrayal of Trevizo's interrogation of Johnson as "consensual," Johnson emphasizes Trevizo's testimony at the suppression hearing. Responding to the prosecutor's questions, Trevizo affirmed her belief that Johnson could have "refused to get out of the car" and "to turn around for the pat down."

It is not clear why the prosecutor, in opposing the suppression motion, sought to portray the episode as consensual. In any event, Trevizo also testified that she never advised Johnson he did not have to answer her questions or otherwise cooperate with her. And during cross-examination, Trevizo did not disagree when defense counsel asked "in fact, you weren't seeking [Johnson's] permission . . . ?" As the dissenting judge observed, "consensual" is an "unrealistic" characterization of the Trevizo–Johnson interaction. "[T]he encounter . . . took place within minutes of the stop"; the patdown followed "within mere moments" of Johnson's exit from the vehicle; beyond genuine debate, the point at which Johnson could have felt free to leave had not yet occurred.

A lawful roadside stop begins when a vehicle is pulled over for investigation of a traffic violation. The temporary seizure of driver and passengers ordinarily continues, and remains reasonable, for the duration of the stop. Normally, the stop ends when the police have no further need to control the scene, and inform the driver and passengers they are free to leave. An officer's inquiries into matters unrelated to the justification for the traffic stop, this Court has made plain, do not convert the encounter into something other than a lawful seizure, so long as those inquiries do not measurably extend the duration of the stop.

In sum, as stated in *Brendlin*, a traffic stop of a car communicates to a reasonable passenger that he or she is not free to terminate the encounter with the police and move about at will. Nothing occurred in this case that would have conveyed to Johnson that, prior to the frisk, the traffic stop had ended or that he was otherwise free "to depart without police permission." Officer Trevizo surely was not constitutionally required to give Johnson an opportunity to depart the scene after he exited the vehicle without first ensuring that, in so doing, she was not permitting a dangerous person to get behind her.

. . .

For the reasons stated, the judgment of the Arizona Court of Appeals is reversed, and the case is remanded for further proceedings not inconsistent with this opinion.

NOTES AND QUESTIONS

1. Automobile insurance is important. Accidents happen, and when they do it is important that persons who are hurt or whose cars are damaged have recourse to recover. But note here how a civil infraction based on an insurance violation leads directly to a passenger's incarceration.

Should police be able to pull people over for civil infractions?

The Court doesn't say whether the driver was given a "citation," the penalty for the civil infraction. Do you think the officers, members of Arizona's "gang task force," even carried blank citation forms to issue?

2. How do you think the police officers discovered the existence of the vehicle's suspended registration while they were "on patrol" in a "neighborhood associated with the Crips gang"? Were they just driving around running plate checks on any car they thought was sketchy? Are the police required to have any quantum of suspicion before running a plate? Should they be?

3. The Court suggests that the result in *Johnson* is the inevitable culmination of its prior precedents: *Pennsylvania v. Mimms*, 434 U.S. 106 (1977) (police can order driver to get out of car in the interests of officer safety); *Maryland v. Wilson*, 519 U.S. 408 (1997) (same for passengers); *Brendlin v. California*, 551 U.S. 249 (2007) (passenger ordered out of car is "seized."

Why should the traffic stop be allowed to extend even 30 seconds longer than necessary to address the purpose of the stop?

4. But note that the police officers' power, without any basis for suspicion, to order the occupants out of the car does not necessarily also entitle them to frisk for weapons. Reasonable suspicion is needed for that step. Was that established here? The Arizona appellate court did not appear to reach that issue, relying instead on the interrogation's detour into another area.

What was the officer's basis for suspecting Johnson was armed and dangerous? We know this: he had no identification; he was wearing a blue bandana (consistent with Crips membership); he had a scanner; he was from Eloy, Arizona (a town of 15,000 50 miles from Tucson); and he had done time in prison. Is that enough?

5. In *Rodriguez v. United States*, 575 U.S. 348 (2015), the police officer extended a traffic stop by seven to eight minutes after issuing the driver a written warning in order to conduct a canine sniff. The Court found that extension of the stop transformed it into an unreasonable seizure, distinguishing de minimis temporal extensions such as the one in *Johnson*.

Between 1990 and 2014 the Court considered three cases about the relationship between an anonymous tip and reasonable suspicion for Fourth Amendment purposes. These cases bear on situations like the encounter between Officer Dove and Larry Dudley Hiibel, above, and less directly on the use of anonymous informants and tipsters in establishing the probable cause needed for search warrant.

In *Alabama v. White*, 496 U.S. 325 (1990), police received an anonymous tip that a woman was in possession of cocaine and might shortly be leaving a specified apartment building at a specified time in a car the tipster described, bound for a motel the tipster named. Police followed up on the tip and were able to confirm that the tipster had accurately described the woman's movements. At that point — upon confirmation of the details of the tip — the officers' suspicion became reasonable. The Court acknowledged that *White* was a close case inasmuch as the tipster's knowledge of the woman's anticipated movements did not necessarily include any knowledge about whether the woman would be bringing the cocaine with her on her journey.

Florida v. JL, 529 U.S. 266 (2000), involved an anonymous tip that a young Black male at a specified bus stop wearing a plaid shirt was in possession of a gun. Officers approached the bus stop and saw three black males hanging out at the bus stop, doing nothing to arouse suspicion. One, who turned out to be JL, was wearing a plaid shirt. The officers approached JL and one of them frisked him, finding a gun. The Court affirmed the suppression of the gun. It found that an anonymous tip, without more and with only weak corroboration, does not establish reasonable suspicion for a *Terry* stop.

Finally, in *Navarette v. California*, 572 U.S. 393 (2014), police received an anonymous tip in a 911 call from a motorist saying that a truck — for which the tipster provided the make and model and plate number — had just run the motorist off the road at a specified mile marker on U.S. 1 in Mendocino, California. Police were able to locate the truck within 13 minutes at a location consistent with the information the tipster had supplied earlier. The police pulled the truck over a few minutes later and during an investigatory stop discovered 30 pounds of marijuana. The Court found that although this was another "close case," there was sufficient indicia of reliability attending the tip to justify a traffic stop based on reasonable suspicion of reckless driving.

The Court's most recent case evaluating a police officer's claim of reasonable suspicion is *Kansas v. Glover*, 589 U.S. 376 (2020). In *Glover*, an officer initiated an investigative traffic stop of an automobile on the ground that the car's owner — not the driver — had a revoked driver's license, inferring that the driver and the owner were one and the same despite the revocation. The Kansas Supreme Court found that the stop was based not on "reasonable suspicion" but only on the sort of "hunch" condemned in *Terry*. The Court reversed, finding that the degree of suspicion here was a matter of common sense and well within the *Terry* standard, which was below a "preponderance" standard or even a "probable cause" standard. The Court quoted from its 2004 decision in *United States v. Arvizu*, 534 U.S. 266 (2004), to the effect that the reasonable suspicion standard does not require officers to "rule out the possibility of innocent conduct."

E. RACE AND SUSPICION

1. *Terry* and Race

As noted above, the Court in *Terry* acknowledges race to some extent. It notes the "wholesale harassment" of which the "Negroes complain," and references in this regard the findings of the President's Commission on Law Enforcement and Administration of Justice, Task Force Report: The Police 183 (1967). But in virtually the same breath the Court both minimizes the "harassment," attributing it to only "certain elements" of the police, and also throws its hands in the air, noting the "limitations of the judicial function in controlling the myriad daily situations in which policemen and citizens confront each other in the street." The Court is equally "equivocal," to use Professor Maclin's word, in footnote 14, noting that the "friction" between the police and Black people "is not susceptible of control by means of the exclusionary rule" while at the same time stating that "the degree of community resentment aroused by particular practices is clearly relevant to assessment of the quality of the intrusion upon reasonable expectations of personal security caused by those practices." Tracey Maclin, Terry v. Ohio's *Fourth Amendment Legacy: Black Men and Police Discretion*, 72 St. John's L. Rev. 1271, 1284 (1998).

The Court also fails to acknowledge the explicit prediction and warning in the amicus brief of the NAACP Legal Defense and Educational Fund, Inc. In that brief, the LDF cited statistics showing that Black people were more prone to being stopped and frisked than white people. Observing that "many thousands of our citizens who have been or may be stopped and interrogated yearly, only to be released when the police find them innocent of any crime," the LDF explicitly warned that the police would exploit a diluted probable cause standard to engage in exploratory searches under the guise of protecting themselves. *See* Brief for the NAACP Legal Defense and Educational Fund, Inc., as Amicus Curiae at 4-5, *Sibron v. New York*, 392 U.S. 40 (1967) (No. 63) and *Terry v. Ohio*, 392 U.S. 1 (1967) (No. 67), reprinted in 66 Landmark Briefs and Arguments of the Supreme Court of the United States 577, 580-81 (Philip B. Kurland & Gerhard Casper eds., 1975). The NAACP's amicus brief was no outlier, either. By 1968 "objective evidence of police bias against Blacks had been well documented by scholars and observers of the police." Maclin, *Black Men and Police Discretion*, *supra* at 1311 (citations omitted).

But *Terry*'s silence on race runs even deeper. The Court fails to acknowledge that two of the three men that were stopped and frisked by Detective McFadden were Black. The trial court record reveals that the first two men observed by Detective McFadden, John Terry and Richard Chilton, were Black, and the third man, Katz, was white. *See* State of Ohio v. Richard D. Chilton *and* State of Ohio v. John W. Terry: *The Suppression Hearing and Trial Transcripts*, 72 St. John's L. Rev. app. at 1408 (1998) (John Q. Barrett ed.) [transcript] (reprinting suppression hearing testimony of Detective McFadden). *See generally* Anthony C. Thompson, *Stopping the Usual Suspects: Race and the Fourth Amendment*, 74 N.Y.U. L. Rev. 956, 962-74 (1999) (discussing the "constructed reality" of the Supreme Court's Fourth Amendment decisions, including *Terry*, where race is ignored). Even Justice Douglas's impassioned and prescient dissent, in which he remarked that "'probable cause' rings a bell of certainty that 'reasonable suspicion' does not," and bemoaned the impending era where a policeman can stop someone just because he doesn't like "the cut of his jib"—precisely as the NAACP was predicting—says nothing about race. *Id*. at 965-66.

So what? The Supreme Court fails to acknowledge race all the time. In *Terry*, however, the omission of race seems to have been more deliberate than usual. For one thing, the race of the

Louis Stokes. Less than six months after the decision in *Terry*, Stokes became the first Black person from Ohio to be elected to Congress.

two Black men was openly discussed at the suppression hearing. In describing Chilton and Terry's interaction with the "third man," Detective McFadden says the "white man came over and talked to these two colored men." Suppression Hearing Transcript at 1408. And at oral argument before the Supreme Court the lawyers for both the defendants and the state, both of whom were themselves Black, referred to the race of Terry and Chilton. Defense counsel Louis Stokes described his clients as "two Negro males." Barrett, *Terry v. Ohio, supra* at 302.

But in *Terry*, moreover, race indisputably mattered. It mattered in the implications of the Court's new rule in Black communities, as predicted by the NAACP. But it also mattered on the ground in Cleveland, on the street, that day in October 1963 when Detective McFadden's suspicions first became "aroused." Race was "afoot" on the streets of Cleveland.

Chief Justice Warren acknowledges in the case's second paragraph that Officer McFadden was "unable to say precisely what drew his eye to" the two Black men standing on a street corner that afternoon. The Court then describes Officer McFadden's experience, and his people-watching habits, and then presents to the reader—voilà—with McFadden's expert conclusion: "they didn't look right to me." The testimony is presented as if the men's actions didn't "look right." The more likely interpretation is that they didn't "look right" because they were Black. The Court studiously constrains this implication by omitting what McFadden had said in response to the previous question, which asked at what point he considered the men's actions unusual: "Well, to be truthful with you, I didn't like them. I was just attracted to them. . . ." Trial Transcript at 1456.

Further, the Court incorrectly states the source of McFadden's testimony. The quoted testimony that "they didn't look right to me" is not from the suppression hearing but from McFadden's trial testimony. Does that matter? Well, yes, because the issue before the Court is whether the gun found in the frisk of Terry should have been suppressed. The suppression hearing testimony was very different. Detective McFadden appears to have become emboldened at trial by the trial court's earlier denial of the defendants' suppression motion. At the suppression hearing he was much more cautious and circumspect, to the point where the prosecutor, Reuben Payne, must have been worried whether the trial court would be able to find any level of suspicion or expertise whatsoever. For one thing, as noted above, McFadden conceded that his expertise ran only to pickpocketing and shoplifting, and he further conceded that he had never observed a suspect "casing" a place. He was just as blunt when the court examined him about the reason for his suspicion:

Q. What caused you specifically to be attracted to those two individuals at the location that you have mentioned, or let me put it to you this way:

Supposing those two defendants here that are now in court were standing across the street from here, and doing the same activities that you observed them on Huron and Euclid, would you have had any cause for suspicion?

A. I really don't know.

Suppression Hearing Transcript at 1421. That answer was the last thing McFadden said at the suppression hearing. This answer may have been the basis for the Court's acknowledgment that McFadden couldn't say what "drew his eye" to the two Black men, but it could just as easily have been the basis for a conclusion that McFadden lacked any reasonable suspicion whatsoever to stop and frisk them.

It is difficult to resist the conclusion that Detective McFadden had his eye on Terry and Chilton because they were Black. If the attorneys or the trial court were sensitive to this fact there is no suggestion of any such awareness in the transcripts. Indeed, at oral argument before the Supreme Court the prosecutor, Reuben Payne, who like Louis Stokes handled the case from indictment all the way to the Supreme Court, characterized McFadden's testimony as "he didn't like their looks." This remark prompted an exchange with Justice Marshall—who had been on the Court for just two months—in which Payne clarified that McFadden had not "meant by that any reference to pigmentation or anything else."

Even if the lawyers and trial judge had perceived a racial dynamic at work, it certainly wasn't clear in 1964—or even today—how race discrimination maps on to the Fourth Amendment. On the one hand, the Supreme Court had held just one year before Terry's arrest, in *Oyler v. Boles*, 368 U.S. 448, 546 (1962), that prosecutors could not bring criminal charges based on unconstitutional considerations such as race. But *Oyler* had also stated that "the conscious exercise of some selectivity in enforcement is not in itself a federal constitutional violation," which gave some courts pause, *see* Chapter XII *infra*, and it certainly wasn't clear that *Oyler* applied in a Fourth Amendment context.

Professor Thompson has observed that the *Terry* Court's silence on race was part of a pattern: The Court was silent on race when it ostensibly may have played a role or risked playing a role in reasonable suspicion or probable cause determinations, yet openly acknowledged race and approved of its usage as a factor when the Court deemed it necessary to a particular police practice. Thompson, *Stopping the Usual Suspects*, *supra* at 977-78. The next subsection will explore this further.

To Professor Carbado, one of the most profound legacies of *Terry* is what he calls "prophylactic racial profiling." On this view, the regime of wholesale and pervasive police encounters with urban residents that are legally *permissible* under *Terry*, not even to mention the ones that are contrived or manufactured, have dangerously increased the level of police-civilian interaction in Black communities and thereby expose Black people to a heightened risk of police violence. Devon W. Carbado, *From Stop and Frisk to Shoot and Kill:* Terry v. Ohio's *Pathway to Police Violence*, 64 UCLA L. Rev. 1508, 1513, 1537 (2017).

One specific manifestation of the racial implications of *Terry* is in the specific factors that became regularly invoked to establish reasonable suspicion. The next case addresses two of them: "flight" and "high crime area." Of course, equally baked into the "reasonable suspicion" standard is the implicit racial bias police officers have in evaluating whether observed behaviors are "suspicious." *See* L. Song Richardson, *Cognitive Bias, Police Character, and the Fourth Amendment*, 44 Ariz. St. L.J. 267 (2012); L. Song Richardson, *Police Efficiency and the Fourth Amendment*, 87 Ind. L.J. 1143, 1145 (2012) (arguing that "[i]mplicit social cognition research demonstrates that implicit biases can affect whether police interpret an individual's ambiguous behaviors as suspicious").

Illinois v. Wardlow
528 U.S. 119 (2000)

Chief Justice REHNQUIST delivered the opinion of the Court.

Respondent Wardlow fled upon seeing police officers patrolling an area known for heavy narcotics trafficking. Two of the officers caught up with him, stopped him and conducted a protective patdown search for weapons. Discovering a .38-caliber handgun, the officers arrested Wardlow. We hold that the officers' stop did not violate the Fourth Amendment to the United States Constitution.

On September 9, 1995, Officers Nolan and Harvey were working as uniformed officers in the special operations section of the Chicago Police Department. The officers were driving the last car of a four car caravan converging on an area known for heavy narcotics trafficking in order to investigate drug transactions. The officers were traveling together because they expected to find a crowd of people in the area, including lookouts and customers.

As the caravan passed 4035 West Van Buren, Officer Nolan observed respondent Wardlow standing next to the building holding an opaque bag. Respondent looked in the direction of the officers and fled. Nolan and Harvey turned their car southbound, watched him as he ran through the gangway and an alley, and eventually cornered him on the street. Nolan then exited his car and stopped respondent. He immediately conducted a protective pat-down search for weapons because in his experience it was common for there to be weapons in the near vicinity of narcotics transactions. During the frisk, Officer Nolan squeezed the bag respondent was carrying and felt a heavy, hard object similar to the shape of a gun. The officer then opened the bag and discovered a .38-caliber handgun with five live rounds of ammunition. The officers arrested Wardlow.

The Illinois trial court denied respondent's motion to suppress, finding the gun was recovered during a lawful stop and frisk. Following a stipulated bench trial, Wardlow was convicted of unlawful use of a weapon by a felon. The Illinois Appellate Court reversed Wardlow's conviction, concluding that the gun should have been suppressed because Officer Nolan did not have reasonable suspicion sufficient to justify an investigative stop pursuant to *Terry*.

The Illinois Supreme Court agreed. While rejecting the Appellate Court's conclusion that Wardlow was not in a high crime area, the Illinois Supreme Court determined that sudden flight in such an area does not create a reasonable suspicion justifying a *Terry* stop. Relying on *Florida v. Royer*, the court explained that although police have the right to approach individuals and ask questions, the individual has no obligation to respond.

The Illinois Supreme Court also rejected the argument that flight combined with the fact that it occurred in a high crime area supported a finding of reasonable suspicion because the "high crime area" factor was not sufficient standing alone to justify a *Terry* stop.

This case, involving a brief encounter between a citizen and a police officer on a public street, is governed by the analysis we first applied in *Terry*. In *Terry*, we held that an officer may, consistent with the Fourth Amendment, conduct a brief, investigatory stop when the officer has a reasonable, articulable suspicion that criminal activity is afoot. While "reasonable suspicion" is a less demanding standard than probable cause and requires a showing considerably less than preponderance of the evidence, the Fourth Amendment requires at least a minimal level of objective justification for making the stop. The officer must be able to articulate more than an "inchoate and unparticularized suspicion or 'hunch'" of criminal activity.

Nolan and Harvey were among eight officers in a four-car caravan that was converging on an area known for heavy narcotics trafficking, and the officers anticipated encountering a large number of people in the area, including drug customers and individuals serving as lookouts. It was in this context that Officer Nolan decided to investigate Wardlow after observing him flee. An individual's presence in an area of expected criminal activity, standing alone, is not enough to support a reasonable, particularized suspicion that the person is committing a crime. But officers are not required to ignore the relevant characteristics of a location in determining whether the circumstances are sufficiently suspicious to warrant further investigation. Accordingly, we have previously noted the fact that the stop occurred in a "high crime area" among the relevant contextual considerations in a *Terry* analysis.

In this case, moreover, it was not merely respondent's presence in an area of heavy narcotics trafficking that aroused the officers' suspicion, but his unprovoked flight upon noticing the police. Our cases have also recognized that nervous, evasive behavior is a pertinent factor in determining reasonable suspicion. Headlong flight—wherever it occurs—is the consummate act of evasion: It is not necessarily indicative of wrongdoing, but it is certainly suggestive of such. In reviewing the propriety of an officer's conduct, courts do not have available empirical studies dealing with inferences drawn from suspicious behavior, and we cannot reasonably demand scientific certainty from judges or law enforcement officers where none exists. Thus, the determination of reasonable suspicion must be based on commonsense judgments and inferences about human behavior. We conclude Officer Nolan was justified in suspecting that Wardlow was involved in criminal activity, and, therefore, in investigating further.

Such a holding is entirely consistent with our decision in *Florida v. Royer* (1983), where we held that when an officer, without reasonable suspicion or probable cause, approaches an individual, the individual has a right to ignore the police and go about his business. And any "refusal to cooperate, without more, does not furnish the minimal level of objective justification needed for a detention or seizure." But unprovoked flight is simply not a mere refusal to cooperate. Flight, by its very nature, is not "going about one's business"; in fact, it is just the opposite. Allowing officers confronted with such flight to stop the fugitive and investigate further is quite consistent with the individual's right to go about his business or to stay put and remain silent in the face of police questioning.

Respondent and amici also argue that there are innocent reasons for flight from police and that, therefore, flight is not necessarily indicative of ongoing criminal activity. This fact is undoubtedly true, but does not establish a violation of the Fourth Amendment. Even in *Terry*, the conduct justifying the stop was ambiguous and susceptible of an innocent explanation. The officer observed two individuals pacing back and forth in front of a store, peering into the window and periodically conferring. All of this conduct was by itself lawful, but it also suggested that the individuals were casing the store for a planned robbery. *Terry* recognized that the officers could detain the individuals to resolve the ambiguity.

In allowing such detentions, *Terry* accepts the risk that officers may stop innocent people. Indeed, the Fourth Amendment accepts that risk in connection with more drastic police action; persons arrested and detained on probable cause to believe they have committed a crime may turn out to be innocent. The *Terry* stop is a far more minimal intrusion, simply allowing the officer to briefly investigate further. If the officer does not learn facts rising to the level of probable cause, the individual must be allowed to go on his way. But in this case the officers found respondent in possession of a handgun, and arrested him for violation of an Illinois firearms statute. No question of the propriety of the arrest itself is before us.

The judgment of the Supreme Court of Illinois is reversed, and the cause is remanded for further proceedings not inconsistent with this opinion.

NOTES AND QUESTIONS

1. Whether a location is a "high crime area" is, or at least should be, an empirical fact—despite the term's imprecision—yet the Court appears to permit it to be established as a basis for reasonable suspicion by the say-so of police officers. Here, the Court says only that the area in which Wardlow was observed was "known for heavy narcotics trafficking." To be more precise, they observed Wardlow as they were "converging" on that area. The dissent notes that the record was silent on whether the police cars were marked, how fast they were going, and whether the police had arrived in their "high crime area" destination when they saw Wardlow. It also appears defense counsel failed to cross-examine on how this drug-investigation juggernaut of a caravan was utterly derailed by the sight of one guy with an "opaque bag" who was running away from it.

Despite its apparently empirical nature, in most jurisdictions courts have generally relied on an officer's testimony that an area is a "high crime area" without much analysis as to the basis of that conclusion. *See* Andrew Guthrie Ferguson & Damien Bernache, *The "High*

Crime Area" Question: Requiring Verifiable and Quantifiable Evidence for Fourth Amendment Reasonable Suspicion Analysis, 57 Am. U. L. Rev. 1587, 1607 (2008).

Shouldn't police departments—at least large urban ones, like Chicago's—have reliable data on the rates of criminality in various portions of their city? If not in 2000, at least now? Wouldn't such information be important for officer safety, if nothing else?

2. Lower federal and state courts and police departments after *Terry* had seized on "high crime area" as a reasonable suspicion factor. Even the 1972 case the Court cites in *Wardlow* as precedent on this point, *Adams v. Williams,* 407 U.S. 143 (1972), was actually a case where a "high crime area" was part of the justification for a seizure during a *Terry* stop. *Wardlow* seems to have been influential, however. Between 2000 and 2019 over 4,500 federal and state cases cited it. Ben Grunwald & Jeffrey Fagan, *The End of Intuition-Based High-Crime Areas,* 107 Cal. L. Rev. 345, 363 & n.83 (2019). Westlaw's "citing references" feature on May 20, 2023, puts the tally at an even 6,000.

The increase in "citing references" could mean one of at least two things. One, since *Wardlow,* courts are increasingly recognizing that a "high crime area" is a factor in analyzing reasonable suspicion. Two, since *Wardlow,* police officers are increasingly trying to justify reasonable suspicion conclusions by referring to "high crime areas."

3. It is likely that the people who live in and are present on the streets of "high crime areas" will disproportionately be ethnic and racial minorities. Accordingly, just by going about their normal daily lives such persons are already 0-1, with one reasonable suspicion strike against them. For this reason, the Ninth Circuit has cautioned that "the citing of an area as 'high-crime' requires careful examination by the court, because such a description, unless properly limited and factually based, can easily serve as a proxy for race or ethnicity." *United States v. Montero-Camargo,* 208 F.3d 1122, 1138 (9th Cir. 2000).

Is the "high crime area" factor's disproportionate effect on minorities reason enough to preclude its use in establishing reasonable suspicion? Would police work really be hampered if *Terry* factors had to be about the person police want to stop and question and not just the neighborhood?

This aspect of reasonable suspicion effects a double whammy on minorities, who generate suspicion where they live as well as when they venture into areas where they do not. *See, e.g.,* Sheri Lynn Johnson, *Race and the Decision to Detain a Suspect,* 93 Yale L.J. 214, 226 (1983) (reviewing Arizona Supreme Court decision from 1975 in which court approved racial profiling of Hispanic man and stated: "That a person is observed in a neighborhood not frequented by persons of his ethnic background is quite often a basis for an officer's initial suspicion. To attempt by judicial fiat to say he may not do this ignores the practical aspects of good law enforcement") (citation omitted); Lawrence P. Tiffany et al., Detection of Crime 20 (Frank J. Remington ed., 1967) (stating, one year before *Terry,* that "[a] person of one race observed in an area which is largely inhabited by a different racial group may be stopped and questioned").

4. In *Montero-Camargo* the Court upheld a finding of reasonable suspicion based in part on a finding that a particular spot just before an immigration checkpoint in El Centro, California, where the defendant had apparently made a U-turn to avoid the checkpoint, was a "high crime area." Concurring, Judge Kozinski was skeptical about the court's conclusion as well as officers' "high crime area" characterizations generally:

> The [court's] opinion recognizes the danger in allowing the police to characterize an area as "high-crime" to establish a basis for reasonable suspicion, but then proceeds to do just that, based on nothing more than the personal experiences of two arresting agents. As I discuss above, the agents didn't even claim this was a high crime area, but let's say they had. What in this record would support their conclusion? Both agents testified only that they had detected criminal violations after stopping people in the area. How often? One agent said he'd been involved in 15-20 stops over eight and a half years, and "[could]n't recall any . . . where we

didn't have a violation of some sort." The other agent testified to "about a dozen" stops in the same period, all but one of which led to an arrest.

Without hesitation, the majority treats this as a crime wave, but is it really? Does an arrest every four months or so make for a high crime area? Can we rely on the vague and undocumented recollections of the officers here? Do the two officers' figures of "15-20" and "about a dozen" reflect separate pools of incidents, or do they include some where, as here, both officers were involved? Are such estimates sufficiently precise to tell us anything useful about the area? I wouldn't have thought so, although I could be persuaded otherwise. But my colleagues don't even pause to ask the questions. To them, it's a high crime area, because the officers say it's a high crime area.

Just as a man with a hammer sees every problem as a nail, so a man with a badge may see every corner of his beat as a high crime area. Police are trained to detect criminal activity and they look at the world with suspicious eyes. This is a good thing, because we rely on this suspicion to keep us safe from those who would harm us. But to rely on every cop's repertoire of war stories to determine what is a "high crime area"—and on that basis to treat otherwise innocuous behavior as grounds for reasonable suspicion—strikes me as an invitation to trouble. If the testimony of two officers that they made, at most, 32 arrests during the course of a decade is sufficient to turn the road here into a high crime area, then what area under police surveillance wouldn't qualify as one? There are street corners in our inner cities that see as much crime within a month—even a week. I would be most reluctant to give police the power to turn any area into a high crime area based on their unadorned personal experiences. . . .

Id. at 1143.

5. Professors Grunwald and Fagan note that *Wardlow* rests on three tacit empirical assumptions: first, that police officers are using the correct geographic scope when they characterize areas as "high crime"; second, that the officers' assessments of high crime areas are accurate; and third, that an assessment of a "high crime area" is predictive—that is, that persons' presence in a "high crime area" is probative of whether they are engaged in crime. Grunwald & Fagan, *End of Intuition-Based High-Crime Areas, supra* at 348-49.

The professors then tested these assumptions on the dataset of over 200 million police stops conducted by the NYPD between 2007 and 2012, where all police stops were required to be coded for reasonable suspicion in connection with the settlement of a lawsuit against the department. *Daniels v. New York*, 138 F. Supp. 2d 562 (S.D.N.Y. 2001). Professor Fagan was an expert statistical witness for the plaintiffs in *Floyd et al. v. City of New York*, 959 F. Supp. 2d 540 (S.D.N.Y. 2013), a follow-on action to *Daniels. See* Chapter VII *infra*.

Professors Grunwald and Fagan found that none of *Wardlow*'s assumptions were satisfied in practice. Grunwald & Fagan, *End of Intuition-Based High-Crime Areas, supra* at 370-96. They concluded:

> Our empirical investigation raises serious questions about whether *Wardlow*'s empirical assumptions are satisfied in practice. Indeed, at least based on administrative data from the NYPD during an era of intensive use of stop and frisk policing, implementation of the high-crime area standard appears haphazard at best, and discriminatory at worst. Officers call nearly every block in the city high crime. Their assessments of high-crime areas are only weakly correlated with actual crime rates. The suspect's race predicts whether an officer deems an area high crime as well as the actual crime rate itself. The racial composition of the area and the identity of the officer are stronger predictors of whether an officer deems an area high crime than the crime rate. And officers may even be using high-crime area as cover to bolster the appearance of constitutional validity in their weakest stops.

Id. at 396.

6. *Wardlow* is as much about "flight" as about high crime areas. Why do the Justices and the parties insist on using the term "unprovoked flight"? Isn't the type of flight we are talking about here always "provoked"—by the arrival of the police?

7. The Court places flight on one end of a continuum of evasive behavior, with "nervousness" at one end and "headlong flight" at the other. As a defense attorney at a suppression hearing, how would you go about cross-examining a police officer who testified about the defendant's behavior at either end of the spectrum?

8. The Court's seizure analysis emphasizes whether a reasonable person would "feel free to leave." And *Florida v. Royer*, 460 U.S. 491 (1983), *supra*, establishes that a person approached by police has every right to ignore the police and go about his business. Isn't "headlong flight" among the purest manifestations of a feeling of the freedom to leave? Put differently, isn't flight also a manifestation of a "refusal to cooperate"? Why should the police be able to draw a legally cognizable inference of suspicion from the pace at which a person expresses his freedom to leave or his refusal to cooperate?

9. The dissent notes that minorities may flee from the police, innocent or not, because they reasonably or unreasonably believe contact with the police may be dangerous. How can defense attorneys establish such a belief as a fact in litigating a motion to suppress? Judicial notice? Testimony from the defendant? Would a local history of police violence be required? Would an expert witness be needed?

10. In *Commonwealth v. Warren*, 58 N.E.3d 333 (Mass. 2016), the Massachusetts Supreme Judicial Court concluded that flight could not in itself support reasonable suspicion, especially the flight of a Black male. In relevant part the Court stated:

> *d. Flight.* We recognize that the defendant's evasive conduct during his successive encounters with police is a factor properly considered in the reasonable suspicion analysis. But evasive conduct in the absence of any other information tending toward an individualized suspicion that the defendant was involved in the crime is insufficient to support reasonable suspicion. "Were the rule otherwise, the police could turn a hunch into a reasonable suspicion by inducing the [flight] justifying the suspicion." Although flight is relevant to the reasonable suspicion analysis in appropriate circumstances, we add two cautionary notes regarding the weight to be given this factor.
>
> First, we perceive a factual irony in the consideration of flight as a factor in the reasonable suspicion calculus. Unless reasonable suspicion for a threshold inquiry already exists, our law guards a person's freedom to speak or not to speak to a police officer. A person also may choose to walk away, avoiding altogether any contact with police. Yet, because flight is viewed as inculpatory, we have endorsed it as a factor in the reasonable suspicion analysis. Where a suspect is under no obligation to respond to a police officer's inquiry, we are of the view that flight to avoid that contact should be given little, if any, weight as a factor probative of reasonable suspicion. Otherwise, our long-standing jurisprudence establishing the boundary between consensual and obligatory police encounters will be seriously undermined. Thus, in the circumstances of this case, the flight from [police officer] Anjos during the initial encounter added nothing to the reasonable suspicion calculus.
>
> Second, as set out by one of the dissenting Justices in the Appeals court opinion, where the suspect is a black male stopped by the police on the streets of Boston, the analysis of flight as a factor in the reasonable suspicion calculus cannot be divorced from the findings in a recent Boston Police Department (department) report documenting a pattern of racial profiling of black males in the city of Boston. According to the study, based on FIO data collected by the department, black men in the city of Boston were more likely to be targeted for police-civilian encounters such as stops, frisks, searches, observations, and interrogations. Black men were also disproportionally targeted for repeat police encounters. We do not eliminate flight as a factor in the reasonable suspicion analysis whenever a black male is the subject of an investigatory stop. However, in such circumstances, flight is not necessarily probative of a suspect's state of mind or consciousness of guilt. Rather, the finding that black males in Boston are disproportionately and repeatedly targeted for FIO encounters suggests a reason for flight totally unrelated to consciousness of guilt. Such an individual, when approached by the police, might just as easily be motivated by the desire to avoid the recurring indignity of being racially profiled as by the desire to hide criminal activity. Given this reality for black males in the city of Boston, a judge should, in appropriate cases, consider the report's findings in weighing flight as a factor in the reasonable suspicion calculus.

2. Border Searches and Racial Profiling

United States v. Brignoni-Ponce
422 U.S. 873 (1975)

Mr. Justice POWELL delivered the opinion of the Court.

This case raises questions as to the United States Border Patrol's authority to stop automobiles in areas near the Mexican border. It differs from our decision in in that the Border Patrol does not claim authority to search cars, but only to question the occupants about their citizenship and immigration status.

I

As a part of its regular traffic-checking operations in southern California, the Border Patrol operates a fixed checkpoint on Interstate Highway 5 south of San Clemente. On the evening of March 11, 1973, the checkpoint was closed because of inclement weather, but two officers were observing northbound traffic from a patrol car parked at the side of the highway. The road was dark, and they were using the patrol car's headlights to illuminate passing cars. They pursued respondent's car and stopped it, saying later that their only reason for doing so was that its three occupants appeared to be of Mexican descent. The officers questioned respondent and his two passengers about their citizenship and learned that the passengers were aliens who had entered the country illegally. All three were then arrested, and respondent was charged with two counts of knowingly transporting illegal immigrants, a violation of s 274(a)(2) of the Immigration and Nationality Act, 66 Stat. 228, 8 U.S.C. s 1324(a)(2). At trial respondent moved to suppress the testimony of and about the two passengers, claiming that this evidence was the fruit of an illegal seizure. The trial court denied the motion, the aliens testified at trial, and respondent was convicted on both counts.

Respondent's appeal was pending in the Court of Appeals for the Ninth Circuit when we announced our decision in *Almeida-Sanchez*, holding that the Fourth Amendment prohibits the use of roving patrols to search vehicles, without a warrant or probable cause, at points removed from the border and its functional equivalents. The Court of Appeals, sitting en banc, held that the stop in this case more closely resembled a roving-patrol stop than a stop at a traffic checkpoint, and applied the principles of *Almeida-Sanchez*. The court held that the Fourth Amendment, as interpreted in *Almeida-Sanchez*, forbids stopping a vehicle, even for the limited purpose of questioning its occupants, unless the officers have a "founded suspicion" that the occupants are aliens illegally in the country. The court refused to find that Mexican ancestry alone supported such a "founded suspicion" and held that respondent's motion to suppress should have been granted. We granted certiorari.

The Government does not challenge the Court of Appeals' factual conclusion that the stop of respondent's car was a roving-patrol stop rather than a checkpoint stop. Nor does it challenge the retroactive application of *Almeida-Sanchez*, or contend that the San Clemente checkpoint is the functional equivalent of the border. The only issue presented for decision is whether a roving patrol may stop a vehicle in an area near the border and question its occupants when the only ground for suspicion is that the occupants appear to be of Mexican ancestry. For the reasons that follow, we affirm the decision of the Court of Appeals.

II

The Government claims two sources of statutory authority for stopping cars without warrants in the border areas. Section 287(a)(1) of the Immigration and Nationality Act, 8 U.S.C. s 1357(a)(1), authorizes any officer or employee of the Immigration and Naturalization Service (INS) without a warrant, "to interrogate any alien or person believed to be an alien as to his right to be or to remain in the United States." There is no geographical limitation on this authority. The Government contends that, at least in the areas adjacent to the Mexican border, a person's apparent Mexican ancestry alone justifies belief that he or she is an alien and satisfies the requirement of this statute. Section 287(a)(3) of the Act, 8 U.S.C. s 1357(a)(3), authorizes agents, without a warrant,

> within a reasonable distance from any external boundary of the United States, to board and search for aliens any vessel within the territorial waters of the United States and any railway car, aircraft, conveyance, or vehicle. . . .

Under current regulations, this authority may be exercised anywhere within 100 miles of the border. 8 CFR s 287.1(a) (1975). The Border Patrol interprets the statute as granting authority to stop moving vehicles and question the occupants about their citizenship, even when its officers have no reason to believe that the occupants are aliens or that other aliens may be concealed in the vehicle. But "no Act of Congress can authorize a violation of the Constitution," and we must decide whether the Fourth Amendment allows such random vehicle stops in the border areas.

III

The Fourth Amendment applies to all seizures of the person, including seizures that involve only a brief detention short of traditional arrest. As with other categories of police action subject to Fourth Amendment constraints, the reasonableness of such seizures depends on a balance between the public interest and the individual's right to personal security free from arbitrary interference by law officers.

The Government makes a convincing demonstration that the public interest demands effective measures to prevent the illegal entry of aliens at the Mexican border. Estimates of the number of illegal immigrants in the United States vary widely. A conservative estimate in 1972 produced a figure of about one million, but the INS now suggests there may be as many as 10 or 12 million aliens illegally in the country. Whatever the number, these aliens create significant economic and social problems, competing with citizens and legal resident aliens for jobs, and generating extra demand for social services. The aliens themselves are vulnerable to exploitation because they cannot complain of substandard working conditions without risking deportation.

The Government has estimated that 85% of the aliens illegally in the country are from Mexico. The Mexican border is almost 2,000 miles long, and even a vastly reinforced Border Patrol would find it impossible to prevent illegal border crossings. Many aliens cross the Mexican border on foot, miles away from patrolled areas, and then purchase transportation from the border area to inland cities, where they find jobs and elude the immigration authorities. Others gain entry on valid temporary border-crossing permits, but then violate the conditions of their entry. Most of these aliens leave the border area in private vehicles, often assisted by professional "alien smugglers." The Border Patrol's traffic-checking operations are designed to prevent this inland movement. They succeed in apprehending some illegal entrants and smugglers, and they deter the movement of others by threatening apprehension and increasing the cost of illegal transportation.

Against this valid public interest we must weigh the interference with individual liberty that results when an officer stops an automobile and questions its occupants. The intrusion is modest. The Government tells us that a stop by a roving patrol "usually consumes no more than a minute." There is no search of the vehicle or its occupants, and the visual inspection is limited to those parts of the vehicle that can be seen by anyone standing alongside. According to the Government, "(a)ll that is required of the vehicle's occupants is a response to a brief question or two and possibly the production of a document evidencing a right to be in the United States."

Because of the limited nature of the intrusion, stops of this sort may be justified on facts that do not amount to the probable cause required for an arrest. In *Terry*, the Court declined expressly to decide whether facts not amounting to probable cause could justify an "investigative 'seizure'" short of an arrest, but it approved a limited search—a pat-down for weapons—for the protection of an officer investigating suspicious behavior of persons he reasonably believed to be armed and dangerous. The Court approved such a search on facts that did not constitute probable cause to believe the suspects guilty of a crime, requiring only that "the police officer . . . be able to point to specific and articulable facts which, taken together with rational inferences from those facts, reasonably warrant" a belief that his safety or that of others is in danger.

We elaborated on Terry in *Adams v. Williams* (1972), holding that a policeman was justified in approaching the respondent to investigate a tip that he was carrying narcotics and a gun.

> The Fourth Amendment does not require a policeman who lacks the precise level of information necessary for probable cause to arrest to simply shrug his shoulders and allow a crime to occur or a criminal to escape. On the contrary, *Terry* recognizes that it may be the essence of good police work to adopt an intermediate response. . . . A brief stop of a suspicious individual, in order to determine his identity or to maintain the status quo momentarily while obtaining more information, may be most reasonable in light of the facts known to the officer at the time.

These cases together establish that in appropriate circumstances the Fourth Amendment allows a properly limited "search" or "seizure" on facts that do not constitute probable cause to arrest or to search for contraband or evidence of crime. In both *Terry* and *Adams v. Williams* the investigating officers had reasonable grounds to believe that the suspects were armed and that they might be dangerous. The limited searches and seizures in those cases were a valid method of protecting the public and preventing crime. In this case as well, because of the importance of the governmental interest at stake, the minimal intrusion of a brief stop, and the absence of practical alternatives for policing the border, we hold that when an officer's observations lead him reasonably to suspect that a particular vehicle may contain aliens who are illegally in the country, he may stop the car briefly and investigate the circumstances that provoke suspicion. As in *Terry*, the stop and inquiry must be "reasonably related in scope to the justification for their initiation." The officer may question the driver and passengers about their citizenship and immigration status, and he may ask them to explain suspicious circumstances, but any further detention or search must be based on consent or probable cause.

We are unwilling to let the Border Patrol dispense entirely with the requirement that officers must have a reasonable suspicion to justify roving-patrol stops. In the context of border area stops, the reasonableness requirement of the Fourth Amendment demands something more than the broad and unlimited discretion sought by the Government. Roads near the border carry not only aliens seeking to enter the country illegally, but a large volume of legitimate traffic as well. San Diego, with a metropolitan population of 1.4 million, is located on the border. Texas has two fairly large metropolitan areas directly on the border: El Paso, with a population of 360,000, and the Brownsville-McAllen area, with a combined population of 320,000. We are confident that substantially all of the traffic in these cities is lawful and that relatively few of their residents have any connection with the illegal entry and transportation

E. Race and Suspicion 433

of aliens. To approve roving-patrol stops of all vehicles in the border area, without any suspicion that a particular vehicle is carrying illegal immigrants, would subject the residents of these and other areas to potentially unlimited interference with their use of the highways, solely at the discretion of Border Patrol officers. The only formal limitation on that discretion appears to be the administrative regulation defining the term "reasonable distance" in s 287(a)(3) to mean within 100 air miles from the border. 8 CFR s 287.1(a) (1975). Thus, if we approved the Government's position in this case, Border Patrol officers could stop motorists at random for questioning, day or night, anywhere within 100 air miles of the 2,000-mile border, on a city street, a busy highway, or a desert road, without any reason to suspect that they have violated any law.

We are not convinced that the legitimate needs of law enforcement require this degree of interference with lawful traffic. As we discuss in Part IV, infra, the nature of illegal alien traffic and the characteristics of smuggling operations tend to generate articulable grounds for identifying violators. Consequently, a requirement of reasonable suspicion for stops allows the Government adequate means of guarding the public interest and also protects residents of the border areas from indiscriminate official interference. Under the circumstances, and even though the intrusion incident to a stop is modest, we conclude that it is not "reasonable" under the Fourth Amendment to make such stops on a random basis.

The Government also contends that the public interest in enforcing conditions on legal alien entry justifies stopping persons who may be aliens for questioning about their citizenship and immigration status. Although we may assume for purposes of this case that the broad congressional power over immigration, authorizes Congress to admit aliens on condition that they will submit to reasonable questioning about their right to be and remain in the country, this power cannot diminish the Fourth Amendment rights of citizens who may be mistaken for aliens. For the same reasons that the Fourth Amendment forbids stopping vehicles at random to inquire if they are carrying aliens who are illegally in the country, it also forbids stopping or detaining persons for questioning about their citizenship on less than a reasonable suspicion that they may be aliens.

IV

The effect of our decision is to limit exercise of the authority granted by both s 287(a)(1) and s 287(a)(3). Except at the border and its functional equivalents, officers on roving patrol may stop vehicles only if they are aware of specific articulable facts, together with rational inferences from those facts, that reasonably warrant suspicion that the vehicles contain aliens who may be illegally in the country.

Any number of factors may be taken into account in deciding whether there is reasonable suspicion to stop a car in the border area. Officers may consider the characteristics of the area in which they encounter a vehicle. Its proximity to the border, the usual patterns of traffic on the particular road, and previous experience with alien traffic are all relevant. They also may consider information about recent illegal border crossings in the area. The driver's behavior may be relevant, as erratic driving or obvious attempts to evade officers can support a reasonable suspicion. Aspects of the vehicle itself may justify suspicion. For instance, officers say that certain station wagons, with large compartments for fold-down seats or spare tires, are frequently used for transporting concealed aliens. The vehicle may appear to be heavily loaded, it may have an extraordinary number of passengers, or the officers may observe persons trying to hide. The Government also points out that trained officers can recognize the characteristic appearance of persons who live in Mexico, relying on such factors as the mode of dress and haircut. In all situations the officer is entitled to assess the facts in light of his experience in detecting illegal entry and smuggling.

434   Chapter IV The Fourth Amendment

In this case the officers relied on a single factor to justify stopping respondent's car: the apparent Mexican ancestry of the occupants. We cannot conclude that this furnished reasonable grounds to believe that the three occupants were aliens. At best the officers had only a fleeting glimpse of the persons in the moving car, illuminated by headlights. Even if they saw enough to think that the occupants were of Mexican descent, this factor alone would justify neither a reasonable belief that they were aliens, nor a reasonable belief that the car concealed other aliens who were illegally in the country. Large numbers of native-born and naturalized citizens have the physical characteristics identified with Mexican ancestry, and even in the border area a relatively small proportion of them are aliens. The likelihood that any given person of Mexican ancestry is an alien is high enough to make Mexican appearance a relevant factor, but standing alone it does not justify stopping all Mexican-Americans to ask if they are aliens.

The judgment of the Court of Appeals is affirmed.

NOTES AND QUESTIONS

1. The Court actually seems skeptical of the agent's testimony at the suppression hearing that the individuals he saw and stopped — based on a fleeting glance in only the light of the cruiser's headlights — "appeared to be of Mexican descent." It states: "Even if they saw enough to think that the occupants were of Mexican descent this factor alone would justify neither a reasonable belief that they were aliens nor a reasonable belief that the car concealed other aliens who were illegally in the country. Such skepticism is unusual. Typically the conservative members of the Court accept police officer testimony uncritically.

If it is truly concerned about the ease with which an "appearance of Mexican descent" factor can be contrived, why does the Court permit it to be used at all, even as one of many factors?

Under the reasonable suspicion standard the Court requires for such stops, what percentage level of confidence would an agent need to have to conclude the occupants of a car "appeared to be of Mexican descent"?" 10 percent? 30 percent? More?

2. The Court also recognizes that "[l]arge numbers of native-born and naturalized citizens have the physical characteristics identified with Mexican ancestry, and even in the border area a relatively small proportion of them are aliens." In fact, as the attorney for Brignoni-Ponce pointed out at oral argument before the Supreme Court, only two of the three occupants of the car were Mexican: The driver was a Spanish-speaking Puerto Rican-American citizen and the other passenger was from Guatemala. Transcript of Oral Argument at 47, *Brignoni-Ponce*, 422 U.S. 873 (1975) (No. 74-114).

3. The lawyer for Brignoni-Ponce argued throughout his briefing that the use of race or ethnicity in determining suspicion was unconstitutional, citing among other authorities *Yick Wo v. Hopkins*, 118 U.S. 356 (1886), *see* Chapter XII *infra*, but conceded at oral argument that, at a minimum, it could not be the only factor.

Professor Kevin Johnson is critical of the attorney on this point:

> [T]he conventional — and overly narrow, client-centered — representation by Brignoni-Ponce's counsel has resulted in deep damage, with many thousands, if not millions, of Latina/os adversely affected.
>
> This history demonstrates the challenges of truly rebellious lawyering by lawyers committed to social justice. Such creative lawyering requires a long-term view of litigation and the impacts of the law on communities of people, not just individual clients. A broad vision is what Thurgood Marshall and a team of civil rights attorneys pursued for a generation before realizing the milestone victory in *Brown v. Board of Education*. Such a vision requires careful

E. Race and Suspicion   **435**

evaluation of compromises, strategies, long-term goals, and the human impacts of legal rules. In the end, the attorneys' short-term strategy in *Brignoni-Ponce*, although successful for the individual defendant, set back the rights of Latina/os for decades.

Kevin R. Johnson, *How Racial Profiling in America Became the Law of the Land:* United States v. Brignoni-Ponce *and* Whren v. United States *and the Need for Truly Rebellious Lawyering*, 98 Geo. L.J. 1005, 1044-45 (2010). Fair criticism? What does Professor Johnson mean by "overly narrow, client-centered" representation?

4. Why does the Court feel obligated to enshrine in the U.S. Reports a laundry list of factors the Border Patrol can use as a basis for reasonable suspicion? Is the Court blessing these factors in advance so that the agents can rely on them with impunity, confident that their reasonable suspicion conclusions will be bullet-proof in suppression hearings? Note that the bookend anchors in the long paragraph supplying these factors are *Carroll* and *Terry*, the textbook opinions on deference to police "expertise."

5. Just a year later, in *United States v. Martinez-Fuerte*, 428 U.S. 543 (1976), the Court addressed the constitutionality of fixed immigration checkpoints located between 50 and 100 miles from the Mexican border. At one of the three checkpoints at issue, a point agent would visually screen all incoming northbound traffic, which would have come to almost a complete halt at the checkpoint, and based on that cursory inspection would direct a subset of motorists to a secondary inspection site where they would be questioned about citizenship and immigration status. The Court concluded that the intrusion was sufficiently minimal that even a reasonable suspicion standard was unnecessary, and reached this conclusion even under the assumption that the referrals by the point agent to the secondary inspection site would be based on nothing more than "apparent Mexican ancestry."

In a heated dissent, Justice Brennan, joined only by Justice Marshall, accused the Court of continuing its "evisceration" of the Fourth Amendment and undermining its one-year old decision in *Brignoni-Ponce*.

Brignoni-Ponce and *Martinez-Fuerte* had a significant and long-lasting effect on the Border Patrol's ability to use ethnicity in immigration enforcement. Johnson, *Racial Profiling in America, supra* at 1027-30. Lower courts sometimes referred to the "*Brignoni-Ponce* factors" in analyzing reasonable suspicion, as if they had actually been the facts of a case rather than an advisory bulletin from the Supreme Court. The Court further assisted this effort by holding, in *INS v. Lopez-Mendoza*, 468 U.S. 1032, 1050-51 (1984), that the exclusionary rule did not apply in deportation proceedings unless the Fourth Amendment violation was "egregious."

But on the other hand, the factors on which an agent could base reasonable suspicion near the border were so numerous and varied it is a fair question whether the Court's blessing of "apparent Mexican ancestry" as a factor was even necessary. One Fifth Circuit judge, lamenting a "border exception" to the Fourth Amendment, observed that courts accept as justiciable suspicion in border searches "virtually everything and anything":

> The vehicle was suspiciously dirty and muddy, or the vehicle was suspiciously squeaky-clean; the driver was suspiciously dirty, shabbily dressed and unkept, or the driver was too clean; the vehicle was suspiciously traveling fast, or was traveling suspiciously slow (or even was traveling suspiciously at precisely the legal speed limit); the [old car, new car, big car, station wagon, camper, oilfield service truck, SUV, van] is the kind of vehicle typically used for smuggling aliens or drugs; the driver would not make eye contact with the agent, or the driver made eye contact too readily; the driver appeared nervous (or the driver even appeared too cool, calm, and collected); the time of day [early morning, mid-morning, late afternoon, early evening, late evening, middle of the night] is when "they" tend to smuggle contraband or aliens; the

vehicle was riding suspiciously low (overloaded), or suspiciously high (equipped with heavy duty shocks and springs); the passengers were slumped suspiciously in their seats, presumably to avoid detection, or the passengers were sitting suspiciously ramrod-erect; the vehicle suspiciously slowed when being overtaken by the patrol car traveling at a high rate of speed with its high-beam lights on, or the vehicle suspiciously maintained its same speed and direction despite being overtaken by a patrol car traveling at a high speed with its high-beam lights on; and on and on ad nauseam.

United States v. Zapata-Ibarra, 223 F.3d 281 (5th Cir. 2000) (Weiner, J., dissenting) (citations to 16 cases identifying these factors omitted).

Brignoni-Ponce and *Martinez-Fuerte* also provided a green light for profiling in other contexts. Bernard Harcourt, United States v. Brignoni-Ponce *and* United States v. Martinez-Fuerte: *The Road to Racial Profiling*, 323-24, 337-40, in Criminal Procedure Stories (Carol Steiker ed., 2006). The DEA had begun building a drug courier profile in the early 1970s, and had implemented an experimental pilot program at the Detroit Airport in the 1970s, even before Sylvia Mendenhall was apprehended there. *United States v. Mendenhall*, 446 U.S. 544 (1980). *See also Florida v. Royer*, 460 U.S. 491, 507 (1981) (describing the DEA's profile). The profile was implemented nationwide after *Brignoni-Ponce* and *Martinez-Fuerte*, and between 1976 and 1980 over 140 reported decisions involved DEA stops at airports based on the drug courier profile. Harcourt, *The Road to Racial Profiling*, *supra* at 337.

For obvious reasons, the DEA has never publicized or published a definitive drug courier profile. Nor is there necessarily a single profile, as much as DEA agents like to dress up what are sometimes little more than hunches in the clothing of "agencywide expertise." Professor David Cole has catalogued over 50 factors that DEA agents have offered in court as contributing to the basis for reasonable suspicion, including many—like those on Judge Wiener's list—that are mutually exclusive. *See* David Cole, No Equal Justice: Race and Class in the American Criminal Justice System 48-49 (1999) (e.g., "arrived late at night; arrived early in the morning; arrived in the afternoon").

DEA agents only infrequently acknowledge that race or ethnicity is part of their profile. In *United States v. Weaver*, 966 F.2d 391 (8th Cir. 1992), the DEA agent testified that one of the factors he relied on in doing a *Terry* stop of the defendant at the Kansas City airport was that he "was a roughly dressed young black male who might be a member of a Los Angeles street gang who had been bringing narcotics into the Kansas City area." The Court found that while the factor of race alone could not justify the stop, it could be used as one factor among others where the agent was in possession of "intelligence" that Black persons from Los Angeles were "flooding the Kansas City area with cocaine." David Cole is able to identify only five federal cases where agents openly admitted in court that race or ethnicity were among the factors in their suspicion conclusion. Cole, No Equal Justice, *supra* at 49 & nn.104-08.

There was a point in the 1990s that something of a consensus had emerged that "racial profiling"—undefined and in the abstract—was fundamentally wrong. Harcourt, *The Road to Racial Profiling*, *supra* at 346-47. Public opinion polls found widespread opposition to the practice. It was condemned by tough-on-crime Presidents George W. Bush and Bill Clinton. But any consensus collapsed in the wake of the 2001 terrorist attacks on the World Trade Center. *Id.* And the Supreme Court has subsequently eliminated any lingering doubt of its position on the subject, at least in the context of the Fourth Amendment. In 2011, the Court stated that its 1995 decision in *Whren v. United States*, 517 U.S. 806 (1996), meant that the Court "would not look behind an objectively reasonable traffic stop to determine whether racial profiling . . . was the real motive." *Ashcroft v. al-Kidd*, 563 U.S. 731, 739 (2011).

3. Traffic Stops: Pretext, Policing, and Race

The Supreme Court has historically been ambivalent about the intrusiveness of traffic stops. In 1979, in *Delaware v. Prouse*, 440 U.S. 648 (1979), the Court acknowledged the "substantial anxiety" such stops cause, and conceded that they curtail "freedom of movement, are inconvenient, and consume time." Just five years later, as traffic stops began to be increasingly weaponized in the war on drugs, the Court's leading civil libertarian, Justice Marshall, described traffic stops as benign—a "presumptively temporary and brief" form of detention. *Berkemer v. McCarty*, 468 U.S. 420, 437-38 (1984). *See* Chapter III, *supra*.

The Court has never considered the increased "anxiety," not to mention other increased emotions, experienced disproportionately by Black people and other minorities during traffic stops. *See* C. Epp et al., Pulled Over: How Police Stops Define Race and Citizenship 47, 124-33 (2014). *See, e.g.*, Angela J. Davis, *Race, Cops, and Traffic Stops*, 51 U. Miami L. Rev. 425, 425, 438-40 (1997); David Harris, *Factors for Reasonable Suspicion: When Black and Poor Means Stopped and Frisked*, 69 Ind. L.J. 659, 679-81 (1994); Tracey Maclin, *"Black and Blue Encounters"—Some Preliminary Thoughts About Fourth Amendment Seizures: Should Race Matter?*, 26 Val. U. L. Rev. 243, 251-53 (1991).

Law enforcement did not just stumble upon the utility of the traffic stop as an instrument of crime detection writ large, specifically, drug interdiction. A pioneer of the movement was a journalist and academic named Charles Remsberg, whose police academy textbook, *Tactics for Criminal Patrol: Vehicle Stops, Drug Discovery, and Officer Survival*, was used to train police throughout the country. Seo, Policing the Open Road, *supra* at 255-57. Remsberg's essential message was that police officers should leverage the ubiquitous traffic violations motorists commit as a matter of course into vehicle stops. And then those stops, in turn, can be leveraged into full-blown vehicle searches based on probable cause or, more likely, consent. *Id.* Among Remsberg's lessons was that most drivers are not aware they can refuse to consent to a search and will therefore consent. *Id. See generally* Epp et al., Pulled Over, *supra* at 8 (describing increased police attention on citizen encounters to enable further investigation).

Remsberg's views were evident in the DEA's Operation Pipeline, created in 1984 and still operating today, which was also used to train state and local law enforcement officers to use traffic stops as pretexts for drug interdiction. Officers learned how to lengthen a routine traffic stop and leverage it into a search for drugs by obtaining (or extorting) consent or obtaining (or manufacturing) probable cause. As of 2000, the DEA had trained more than 25,000 officers in 48 states in Pipeline tactics.

Operation Pipeline specifically teaches that the officers should have drivers exit their cars and ask them a series of questions about their origin, travel plans, and destination while looking for signs of nervousness or inconsistencies. After that line of questioning is apparently completed, the script—apparently deployed effectively in *Ohio v. Robinette, supra*—calls for officers to use the Columbo trope (from the humble detective in the eponymous 1970s television show) to cap off the inquiry—"just one more thing, sir"—and then to ask whether there are any drugs or guns in the car. And after receiving a "no" the officer says, "You don't mind if I search your car then, do you?" *See* Ricardo J. Bascuas, *Fourth Amendment Lessons from the Highway and the Subway: A Principled Approach to Suspicionless Searches*, 38 Rutgers L.J. 719, 761-66 (2007) (discussing Operation Pipeline).

The next case has it all: great judge, great facts, heroic lawyering—and, in a telling detail, a total repudiation of *Schneckloth*'s argument that requiring motorists' consent to a car search was unrealistic. This could have been the law.

Chapter IV The Fourth Amendment

United States v. Laymon
730 F. Supp. 332 (D. Colo. 1990)

ORDER GRANTING MOTION TO SUPPRESS EVIDENCE

CARRIGAN, District Judge.

Defendant Louis Laymon, Jr. has filed a motion to suppress evidence obtained by the government during a March 8, 1989 search of his automobile after a traffic stop on Interstate 70 in Eagle County, Colorado. Laymon is charged with violating Title 21 U.S.C. § 841(a)(1) and (b) (possession with intent to distribute cocaine) and Title 21 U.S.C. § 846 and Title 18 U.S.C. § 2 (conspiracy to possess cocaine with intent to distribute.) He is a 21-year-old Black resident of California.

Defendant contends: (1) that the search of his automobile was made following a pretextual traffic stop and therefore violated his Fourth Amendment right to be free from unreasonable searches and seizures, and (2) that the consent to search, given by him on a printed form he signed during the traffic stop, was the product of trickery, coercion or both, and not freely and voluntarily given. Plaintiff, the government, contends that the search was carried out pursuant to a voluntary consent following a valid traffic stop.

During extensive hearings both parties introduced evidence, including exhibits and the testimony of numerous witnesses. Briefs have been filed and the issues are ripe for decision. Jurisdiction is not questioned. This memorandum constitutes my findings of fact pursuant to Rule 12(e), Fed. R. Crim. P.

I. FINDINGS OF FACT

A. Pretextual Stop

On March 8, 1989, at about 2:10 p.m., the defendant Louis Laymon, Jr. was riding as a passenger in a vehicle titled or registered in the name of his sister, Edjunia Laymon, but actually owned by him. The vehicle, bearing California license plates, was being driven East toward Denver by Alvin Riley. Both Laymon and Riley are Black. Sergeant James Perry ("Perry"), of the Eagle County Sheriff's Department, who is White, observed the Laymon vehicle traveling eastbound well within the 65 mile per hour speed limit on Interstate 70 ("I-70"). Perry, although employed by the Eagle County Sheriff's Department, was assigned to the High Country Drug Task Force. At the time of the traffic stop here involved he was driving a sheriff's department vehicle that was unmarked except for decals on its sides. It had no overhead lights or other characteristics to distinguish or identify it as a police car when viewed from the front.

Perry testified that while following the Laymon vehicle he observed it gradually moving or edging toward the right shoulder of the road until the right front tire ultimately contacted the white line separating the travelled portion of the highway from the shoulder. He described this motion as "weaving." Perry did not assert, however, that the "weaving" he allegedly observed included any gross movement such as swerving. Both Riley and Laymon denied that Riley ever allowed the vehicle to come into contact with or cross the white shoulder stripe. Testimony and a videotape indicated that the highway through the area in question curves through mountainous terrain.

Perry stated that he became concerned by the car's "weaving" and he briefly signaled with his siren for the vehicle to stop. He testified that the car's occupants appeared not to notice the siren because they failed to stop. Perry also testified that he attempted to flash the red light or lights installed in or behind his car's grill. Again this effort elicited no apparent response from the vehicle.

Riley and Laymon testified that Perry never activated either his siren or his lights to signal Riley to stop the vehicle. Eagle County Sheriff A.J. Johnson testified that he recalled Perry having informed him at a later date that an electrical problem had prevented the red lights on Perry's vehicle from functioning properly. As stated, the patrol car had no overhead lights. I find that Sheriff Johnson was a credible witness and thus find that the car driven by Sergeant Perry had non-functioning red lights under its front grill, and therefore even if Perry did attempt to activate those lights, as he testified, they did not come on.

Finally, Perry testified, he pulled alongside the California vehicle and motioned the driver to pull over. Riley immediately complied. Riley and Laymon testified that neither had any idea who Perry was or what he wanted until he pulled alongside and motioned for Riley to pull over. They testified that they did not realize until Perry pulled alongside that the car behind them was a police car.

Perry, Riley and the defendant Laymon all testified that after pulling the Laymon vehicle over, Perry took Riley's driver's license and the vehicle registration and returned to his patrol car for five to ten minutes. While waiting for Perry to return, Riley got out and stood by the rear of the car. When Perry returned, he issued a written warning to Riley for weaving.

At this point, Perry's, Riley's and Laymon's testimony diverges drastically. Perry testified that after he issued the warning to Riley he approached Laymon, who was still in the front passenger seat, and asked him to step out of the car. He stated that he informed Laymon that the Eagle County Sheriff's Department had been having problems with people carrying narcotics, large amounts of cash and firearms through the county. Perry stated that he then asked Laymon for consent to search the vehicle, and Laymon voluntarily agreed. Perry testified that he returned to his vehicle to obtain a consent to search form, and that Laymon signed that consent form after fully reviewing it.

Riley testified that after Perry issued him the warning for weaving, Perry informed him that the Eagle County Sheriff's Department had been having problems with people transporting drugs and weapons. According to Riley, Perry then said that Laymon would also have to sign a warning for weaving. Riley stated that Perry then approached Laymon, who was seated in the front passenger seat, and that he (Riley) could not hear the verbal exchange between Perry and Laymon.

Laymon testified that Perry approached the passenger side of the car and told him to step out of the car. Laymon stated that he complied and Perry then told him that he would have to sign a warning for weaving. He stated that Perry put a piece of paper on the hood of the car for Laymon to sign, and that he (Laymon) signed it without examining or reading it to see what the document actually stated. Next, Laymon stated that Perry mentioned the drug trafficking problems and asked Laymon if he could search the vehicle.

Riley and Laymon both testified that Laymon had refused to allow Perry to search the car but that Perry then had declared forcefully that Laymon had already signed a consent to search form. Laymon testified that he thought he had only signed a warning for weaving and not a consent to search form.

At this point Perry's, Riley's and Laymon's testimony again becomes consistent. At about the time Perry commenced searching the vehicle, a second white uniformed officer drove up to the scene and told Riley and Laymon to step away from the vehicle and face away while Perry searched the vehicle.

Upon opening the vehicle's hatchback, Perry observed what appeared to be a glove compartment type door on an inside wall panel. Perry testified that he either forced open the compartment or simply turned the knob. Riley and Laymon testified that they heard a loud "popping" sound that they believed to be Perry breaking the compartment door. Upon opening the door Perry observed a box of Kleenex in front of a cardboard inside wall that appeared to be dislodged or out of place. When he removed the cardboard wall separating the glove box from the car's metal shell, Perry discovered plastic bags filled with what appeared to be cocaine. Riley and Laymon were immediately arrested.

Perry's credibility was seriously undermined by cross examination. Perry admitted that he had a history of stopping vehicles based upon a "drug courier profile." He testified that he had received training from the Drug Enforcement Administration and the Eagle County Sheriff's office regarding drug courier profiles.

Further, Officer Lee Roybal, formerly of the Eagle County Sheriff's Department and the chief training officer of the Drug Task Force, testified that the primary assignment of the Drug Task Force is drug interdiction, not traffic enforcement. He stated that it is the Colorado Highway Patrol's responsibility to enforce traffic laws on I-70, whereas the Drug Task Force investigates and attempts to curtail the transportation of illicit drugs on that highway. Clearly, at the time Perry stopped Laymon's car his primary responsibilities concerned narcotics laws and not traffic control.

Perry testified that in performing his Drug Task Force duties, he evaluates many factors to determine whether a particular person fits a drug courier profile. For example, Perry claimed that he considered whether the vehicle contained fast food wrappers, a map with cities marked, a radar detector, luggage in the passenger compartment rather than the trunk, and numerous other seemingly innocuous factors. Perry admitted, however, that during the period when he was stopping cars and seeking consents to search based solely upon the "profile," he could not have discerned these factors during his first observation of a vehicle because it would have been impossible for him to really examine a car's contents without first stopping it. These factors obviously could not have played a part in Perry's decision to stop a vehicle.

Perry was therefore forced to admit that his initial observation of a vehicle would give him only very limited information, including its make and model, whether its plates indicated that it was a rental vehicle, and the state of its registration as indicated by the license plates.

In evaluating Perry's credibility and the weight to be accorded his testimony, I have considered among other factors, his testimony that physical limitations on his vision make it difficult or impossible for him to discern whether a person is Black, Hispanic or Anglo. He testified that he suffers from both astigmatism and color blindness. His astigmatism requires him to wear glasses. With regard to his asserted color blindness, Perry swore that it is nearly impossible for him to distinguish among Black, Hispanic and White people. There was no hint of any medical opinion or other evidence to support that assertion.

Perry testified that the louvers on the back of Laymon's vehicle, rendered it impossible for him to identify the race of its occupants. Indeed, he went so far as to testify that even when he pulled alongside the defendant's vehicle, a few feet from it in broad daylight, his color blindness prevented him from determining that the driver and passenger were Black. On cross examination, however, he testified that in looking around the courtroom, he was able to distinguish Blacks, Whites and Hispanics, but that he could not always do so while on duty as a law officer. Laymon's and Riley's complexions are very dark and they are obviously Black. I find to be incredible Perry's testimony that he could not distinguish Black from non-Black drivers in broad daylight.

Additional evidence to support that finding as to credibility is found in prior testimony from an unrelated Eagle County case, *People v. Jose Fernando Encines*. Perry's testimony there contradicts his claim of vision restricting his ability to tell Blacks from Whites limitations by sight. He testified in that case that he had been able to identify by sight an Hispanic male who fit a description on a "wanted" poster in his office. He only observed that man in a car travelling toward him at approximately 65 m.p.h. while he was walking on I-70. After giving a motorist a ticket, he was walking back to his car on Interstate 70, when he observed the car coming. Perry chased Encines in his patrol car and discovered that Encines, although an Hispanic male, was not the same Hispanic male described on the "wanted" poster. Because

Perry was able to make an identification based upon race under those circumstances and based upon my evaluation of Perry's credibility, I find that he was able to and did determine the sex, approximate age and race of the occupants of the defendant's vehicle before stopping it. This conclusion is also supported by Riley's and Laymon's testimony that they had no knowledge that Perry was a police officer who wanted them to stop until Perry drove alongside their vehicle and signaled them to pull over.

Perry's daily activity logs, admitted into evidence, provided additional damage to his credibility. The logs were recorded from August 10, 1988 to May 8, 1989. The logs reflect that during this period, Perry made approximately 200 highway stops. Of that 200, 188 were stops of out of state vehicles. These logs also confirm that Perry's duties were primarily narcotics enforcement because he did not issue any traffic tickets during any of the recorded stops, but at most issued only traffic warnings.

Despite these entries in his own activity log, Perry testified that his pattern and practice of stopping individuals has nothing to do with a vehicle's state of registration. He testified that he stops all vehicles that violate traffic laws in his presence regardless of their place of origin.

In an apparent attempt to salvage lost credibility, Perry testified that if statistics prove that he overwhelmingly stops out of state vehicles, it is because during the ski season, most of the vehicles on I-70 in Eagle County are from out of state. Even a cursory examination of Perry's activity logs, however, belies this testimony. Officer Roybal testified that the ski season begins on Thanksgiving and ends in early April. Perry's daily logs show no change in the pattern of stopping out of state vehicles, regardless of the season, from August to May. Nor is there any claim by Perry that a disproportionately higher number of out of state skiers are Black or Hispanic than White.

More troubling than the evidence demonstrating that out of state travelers are at far greater risk of being subjected to highway stops in Eagle County, with all the implications that situation has in light of the Fourteenth Amendment's equal protection and privileges and immunities clauses, is the irrefutable evidence that Blacks and Hispanics were far more likely to be stopped by Perry than White, non-Hispanic motorists. This was proven by several items of evidence.

Perry testified that of all the stops he made from August 10, 1988 to May 8, 1989, only ten to fifteen percent involved Hispanic drivers. When confronted with the fact that approximately fifty percent of all of his consent to search forms obtained during that time period had been signed by motorists with Spanish surnames, Perry could only conclude that this alarming statistical disparity was coincidental. Of the remaining half, those not Spanish surnamed, at least some were Blacks who testified in this court about their encounters with Perry.

Jhenita and Janice Whitfield, two young Black women testified that they were stopped, while driving a car with California plates, for the alleged offense of failing to signal a sufficient distance prior to changing lanes on I-70, a four-lane highway. Along with their four infant children they testified that they were forced to stand alongside the highway in cold mountain weather for more than forty-five minutes while Perry searched their car, unpacking their luggage and rummaging through all their personal clothing and belongings. No contraband was found, and the only product of this exercise was the anger of these citizens who felt that they had been pressured to submit to the search because of their race. Perhaps ironically, one of them had served for years in the military service of the United States and had elected that service as her career.

Byron Boudreaux, a young black male, testified that he was stopped by Perry while driving a car with Oklahoma plates through Eagle County on I-70. Perry and two other officers informed him that they had received an anonymous tip that a man fitting his description was carrying drugs. Boudreaux testified that he was detained for approximately forty-five minutes while Perry and the other officers searched his car.

Aguinaldo Ferreria, a young Black male, was stopped by Perry while driving a car with California plates through Eagle County on I-70. Perry told him that he fit a description of someone suspected of carrying drugs. Ferreria was detained for about forty-five minutes while Perry conducted his search.

These Black drivers indicated that Perry gave them the impression the searches would be of the vehicle and would delay them only a few minutes, but the actual searches involved going through all their luggage and personal effects and took far longer.

Michael Misukanis, a young white male with hair longer than shoulder length, testified that he had been stopped by Perry while driving an old car with a loud engine and blotched body paint through Eagle County on I-70. His car carried California license plates. Perry told him that he fit a drug dealer description. Unlike the other victims who testified, Misukanis declined to give Perry consent to search his car. Perry persistently tried to pressure Misukanis to consent by stating that his refusal to consent indicated that he was transporting drugs. After an exchange lasting fifteen to twenty minutes, Misukanis asked Perry if he was going to be arrested for failing to sign the consent to search form. Finally, Perry allowed him to leave. There was no indication that Perry customarily informed those stopped that they were free to leave if they did not consent to a vehicle search. While not dispositive, the absence of such notice is a factor to be considered in determining whether a consent is voluntary.

The fact that Blacks and Hispanics are frequently targeted by the Eagle County Drug Task Force was further highlighted during the hearings on this matter, when Perry, Officer Roybal and Sheriff A.J. Johnson all testified that being Black or Hispanic was and is a factor in their drug courier profile on which they decide who to stop and search. Perry and Sheriff Johnson reluctantly made this admission, while Officer Roybal candidly admitted that race is part of the profile. Officer Roybal's admission is noteworthy and entitled to substantial weight because he was in charge of training for the Drug Task Force. This evidence was not contradicted.

Further evidence of a pattern, practice and habit of racist law enforcement is Perry's admission that in December of 1988 he had stopped three young Blacks with California license plates because he thought they might be gang members carrying drugs or weapons. Upon obtaining a "consent" to search, he found twenty pounds of cocaine. No charges were ever filed, however, because the Eagle County District Attorney concluded that Perry had violated the suspects' Fourth Amendment rights.

Perry testified that the arrest of the young blacks from Los Angeles taught him that "profiling" based on race was unconstitutional as a sole justification for stopping a vehicle. As a result of the District Attorney's refusing to file charges in that case, he asserted that he began to use traffic stops, rather than profiles, as his means of stopping vehicles. He claimed that his entire practice as a Drug Task Force officer changed and that he would no longer simply stop people because they were Black or Hispanic with out-of-state plates. However, the irrefutable evidence shows, and I find, that his practice was to stop disproportionately larger numbers of Blacks and Hispanics with out-of-state license plates on the pretext that they were committing some trivial traffic violation for which he would not have stopped Anglo drivers with Colorado license plates.

After the District Attorney refused to file the case involving the twenty pound cocaine seizure, Perry's activity logs markedly changed. His logs for the period prior to the December 1988 arrest, are filled with the notation "CI" meaning "criminal investigation" as the reason for the stop. Perry testified that the "CI" stops had been based solely on profiles.

After the December 1988 arrest, Perry entered "TE" as his reason for the stops, explaining that this stood for "traffic enforcement."

If Perry's own records are to be construed literally, Perry went from being a Drug Task Force officer who went for days at a time without ever concerning himself with any traffic violations, to a drug enforcement officer obsessed with traffic enforcement. The logs, however, reflect that Perry's routine was unaffected by his sudden passion for traffic enforcement. He still stopped approximately the same number of vehicles as he had stopped when he was admittedly unlawfully "profiling," and his primary focus remained on out of state vehicles. His consent forms continued to be signed by a disproportionately high percentage of Spanish surnamed people. In fact, from February to May 1989, Perry made 106 stops and obtained consents to search from twenty-eight persons. Fourteen, or one-half, of these individuals had Hispanic surnames. I reject as incredible the proffered explanation that this is explainable on the ground that Eagle County has a large number of Hispanic residents. The government presented no census or other statistics to support that contention, and even if true, it would not justify the disproportionately high number of stops and consents to search signed by Hispanic named travellers whose vehicles had out-of-state license plates. Surely most of them were not Eagle county residents.

The sworn testimony of Riley and Laymon provides further evidence of Perry's habit, practice and modus operandi to engage in pretextual stops. Their testimony, even when discounted by obvious factors likely to affect their credibility, is still more credible than Perry's after the other witnesses described his practices. Both unequivocally testified that Riley was not weaving at any time prior to being pulled over by Perry.

Further, there is no evidence that a reasonable officer would have made a stop under the circumstances of this case. Colorado Highway Patrolman Rogozik, testifying on behalf of the government, attempted to address this issue by stating what he personally would have done under the circumstances faced by Perry on March 8, 1989. This officer's testimony regarding his own practices, is irrelevant because it assumes that the Laymon vehicle was in fact weaving, and I find as a fact that it was not. Moreover Patrolman Rogozik gave no opinion as to what a reasonable, prudent officer would have done in Perry's situation even if the Laymon car had been weaving. Rather he testified only as to what he personally would have done. That falls short of meeting the standard set for the Tenth Circuit in *United States v. Guzman* (10th Cir. 1988).

I have considered Riley's and Laymon's testimony, Perry's testimony and his lack of credibility, the Highway Patrolman Rogozik's testimony and all the other evidence. I find as stated that the defendant's car did not weave or swerve in a manner that would have caused a reasonable, prudent police officer to pull it over for a traffic stop.

The inescapable conclusion from all the evidence is that Sergeant Perry engaged in a pattern and practice of making traffic stops based primarily on the most readily observable aspects of the vehicle that drew his attention as a Drug Task Force officer, i.e. out-of-state license plates and the driver's race or ethnicity. His failure to issue any traffic violation citations is further evidence that the traffic stops were merely subterfuges. I find as a fact that the alleged traffic stop in the instant case was pretextual.

B. Consent to Search

The period of time between the actual traffic stop and the issuance of the written warning for weaving was very brief. Perry claims that he returned the vehicle registration and the driver's licenses of both occupants before he asked Laymon for a consent to search the car. Riley and Laymon on the other hand, testified that Perry never asked Laymon for a consent to search, but instead deceived him into signing a consent to search by telling him that it was a warning for weaving. Riley's testimony before me is somewhat inconsistent with his testimony before the grand jury. Riley, testifying before the grand jury on this issue, stated:

Q. Did the officer force him to sign the form?
A. No. He did not tell him he had to or anything like that.

Q. In other words, Mr. Laymon freely signed it?

A. Yes.

Q. Mr. Laymon ever tell you what was going through his mind as to why he freely signed the form?

A. No.

Q. Did he ever tell you that he felt that he wouldn't be able to find the cocaine in the back of the car?

A. It was more or less we were just trying to be cool. (Transcript of Federal Grand Jury 88-1 (Denver), on April 12, 1989, at 33 and 34).

Therefore, it is somewhat suspicious, and casts serious doubt on Riley's and Laymon's credibility, that Riley deviated from his grand jury testimony when he testified before me that Perry had asked Laymon to sign a warning for weaving. Additionally, neither Riley nor Laymon testified that Perry coerced Laymon to sign the consent to search through the use of force or the threat of force. Further, Laymon testified that he had completed high school and is fully capable of reading and writing. Therefore, from all the evidence and circumstances surrounding Perry's acquisition of Laymon's signature on the search consent form, I find that Sergeant Perry's testimony on this point is more credible than that of Laymon and Riley and therefore I find that Laymon probably knew that he was signing a consent to search form and did not sign under the misapprehension that he was signing a warning for weaving.

II. CONCLUSIONS OF LAW

A. The Pretextual Stop Issue

Defendant contends that Perry conducted an unconstitutional pretextual stop of the defendant's vehicle that justifies suppressing the cocaine thereafter discovered. The Tenth Circuit has adopted an objective test for determining whether an investigatory stop is pretextual and therefore unconstitutional. The Court of Appeals has stated that:

> a court should ask "not whether the officer could validly have made the stop, but whether under the same circumstances a reasonable officer would have made the stop in the absence of the invalid purpose." "That an officer theoretically could validly have stopped the car for a possible traffic infraction [i]s not determinative. Similarly immaterial [i]s the actual subjective intent of the deputy. [A] stop [i]s unreasonable not because the officer secretly hope[s] to find evidence of a greater offence, but because it [i]s clear that an officer would have been uninterested in pursuing the lesser offence absent that hope." *United States v. Guzman* (10th Cir. 1988).

From my interpretation of the evidence, specifically Perry's demeanor and credibility, I already have determined that the alleged weaving of the defendant's car was a pretext for the invalid purpose of stopping it based on its California license plates and the race of its occupants. I find as a fact that Perry did not decide to stop the defendant's car until he pulled alongside and determined that Riley and Laymon were Black. The government has not carried its burden of proof to provide sufficient credible evidence that a reasonable, prudent officer would have made the stop absent the invalid purpose. Further, Perry's past habit and pattern of stopping vehicles based on a "profile" provides persuasive circumstantial evidence supporting a finding that he was uninterested in the alleged weaving as a traffic offense.

Lastly, Perry's lack of real interest in traffic law enforcement is strongly evidenced by his overall and consistent practice of not issuing traffic citations or "tickets," but merely warnings, and by his specific failure to follow-up by checking Riley's sobriety or competency to drive, a normal procedure for a police officer who observes a driver weaving.

Perry appeared to act in concert with and on instructions from the Eagle County Sheriff's Department and the Drug Task Force. He carried out policies that systematically violated the constitutionally protected rights of Blacks and Hispanics to travel and be free from unreasonable seizures on an equal basis with other persons travelling the highways of this nation. For these reasons, I conclude as a matter of law that on March 8, 1989 when Perry stopped his vehicle, the defendant suffered an unconstitutional pretextual stop amounting to a seizure that violated the Fourth Amendment.

This opinion does not hold that all "profile" investigatory stops are improper or unconstitutional. Higher courts have established guidelines for determining the validity of profile stops in the broad context. This case holds only that profile stops may not be predicated on unconstitutional discrimination based on race, ethnicity or state of residence.

Here the stop was tainted by violations of Laymon's rights guaranteed by the United States Constitution Amendment IV (freedom from unlawful seizures); Amendment I (freedom to travel); and Amendment XIV (right to equal protection of the law and freedom from discriminatory law enforcement based on race; equal access of citizens of other states to privileges and immunities accorded to citizens of Colorado, including travel without harassment on Colorado highways). Amendment XIV applies the First and Fourth Amendments to restrict state action such as that here involved. *Mapp v. Ohio* (1961) and its progeny require this court to suppress evidence obtained in violation of a defendant's Fourth Amendments rights.

B. Consent to Search

The question remains whether Laymon's consent to the search of his car was valid despite the constitutional violation. The government argues that the defendant's consent was free and voluntary and therefore it legitimized Perry's search.

The Tenth Circuit has stated that:

> When attempting to establish that there was voluntary consent after an illegal stop, however, the Government has a heavier burden to carry than when the consent is given after a permissible stop. . . .
>
> Moreover, when consent is obtained after an illegal arrest, the Government must establish a break in the causal connection between the illegality and the evidence thereby obtained.

In determining the voluntariness of the consent, Guzman stated:

> In *Brown v. Illinois* (1975), the Supreme Court held that where a confession is preceded by a Fourth Amendment violation, in determining the voluntariness of the confession the examining court must decide whether it was "'sufficiently an act of free will to purge the primary taint' [of the illegal arrest]." . . . Although the Court acknowledged that a determination of this issue is necessarily a complex one in which "no single fact is dispositive," . . . it placed special emphasis on three factors: "[t]he temporal proximity of the arrest and the confession, the presence of intervening circumstances, and particularly, the purpose and flagrancy of the official misconduct are all relevant."

These three elements of voluntariness clearly apply in this Circuit when evaluating consents to search following a Fourth Amendment violation.

The issue of consent is a question of fact. *Schneckloth v. Bustamonte* (1973). *Guzman* stated that:

> This Circuit has held that when a consent to search is preceded by a Fourth Amendment violation, the consent is valid only if it is voluntary in fact.

Ballard, interpreting prior Fifth Circuit case law, stated:

> The most significant factor relied upon by the court was a warning informing defendant of his right to refuse to permit the search. . . . The court reasoned: "While warnings prior to a consensual search may not have the same indispensability as those required prior to a confession . . . they do help insure that the consent is free, voluntary, and untainted by the arrest's possible illegality.

> In the instant case the presence of these warnings leads us to conclude that any coercion flowing from the possible illegality of appellant's arrest was dissipated." . . . Similarly . . . this court held that advising a defendant of his right to refuse to permit a search was a sufficient intervening occurrence to remove the influence of a prior fourth amendment violation.

Here the defendant signed the consent to search form after Perry had violated his Fourth Amendment rights by committing a pretextual stop. I find as a fact that the government has not met its burden to establish that Laymon's consent was "sufficiently an act of free will to purge the primary taint" of the illegal stop, and therefore I find and conclude that the alleged consent was not free or voluntary. The government has presented no evidence that Perry informed Laymon that he could refuse consent. Although the government is not required to make such a showing and its lack, standing alone, is not dispositive, this factor may be considered when evaluating the totality of the circumstances.

I find that the evidence demonstrates that Perry, in the past, conducted, and at least in this case, continued to conduct, stops on I-70 in a manner creating a coercive and intimidating atmosphere that most people, especially young minority citizens, would find coercive and impossible to resist. The testimony of Jhenita and Janice Whitfield, Byron Boudreaux, Aguinaldo Ferreria and Michael Misukanis, although not dispositive as to the totality of the circumstances present here, persuades me that Perry probably followed his normal habit, routine or practice to create a coercive atmosphere when he stopped Laymon. All of these individuals, with the exception of Misukanis, testified that they gave Perry consent to search because they felt intimidated and that they had no real alternative. Misukanis refused consent and was allowed to leave only after enduring Perry's unfounded accusations and pressure to consent for fifteen to twenty minutes.

If this nation were to win its "War on Drugs" at the cost of sacrificing its citizens' constitutional rights, it would be a Pyrrhic victory indeed. It ill behooves a great nation to compromise or sacrifice the freedoms of its citizens as the price of more efficient law enforcement. Many countries have written constitutions similar to ours that define the rights of their people in words as forceful and inspiring as those of the United States constitution. But for most people living under those other constitutions the rights so emphatically guaranteed them are hollow, because there is no practical means to enforce them. The rights they define are illusory and disappear like vapor in the face of governmental pressure. Our tradition is different. It requires judges and police officers, who are equally sworn to uphold the same Constitution, to enforce constitutionally guaranteed rights, even when their enforcement is unpopular and even when those rights are asserted on behalf of persons whose activities are considered despicable. If the rule of law—rather than the rule of man—is to prevail, there cannot be one set of search and seizure rules applicable to some and a different set applicable to others. We deal here with rights, not privileges. There must be one guarantee of rights for all. As a practical matter if we are not all free, none of us is really free, for exceptions which deny constitutional rights to some erode them for all. While we deal today only with denial of Mr. Laymon's rights, who knows which of us may be next.

A society cannot remain free or strong if it undermines its own principles. Law enforcement officials are not licensed to disregard the law—especially not the law enshrined in the Constitution. It is utter hypocrisy to celebrate as a national holiday the birthday of Martin Luther King, Jr. while applying to Blacks a practice of selective law enforcement in disregard of their constitutionally guaranteed status as equal citizens.

The Florida Supreme Court recently declared:

> Without doubt the inherently transient nature of drug courier activity presents difficult law enforcement problems. Roving patrols, random sweeps, and arbitrary searches or seizures would go far to eliminate such crime in this state [and nation]. Nazi Germany, Soviet Russia, and

Communist Cuba have demonstrated all too tellingly the effectiveness of such methods. Yet we are not a state that subscribes to the notion that ends justify means. History demonstrates that the adoption of repressive measures, even to eliminate a clear evil, usually results only in repression more mindless and terrifying than the evil that prompted them. Means have a disturbing tendency to become the end result. And as Judge Glickstein noted in his dissent in (Fla. App. 1986):

> "Occasionally the price we must pay to make innocent persons secure from unreasonable search and seizure of their persons or property is to let an offender go. Those who suffered harassment from King George III's forces would say that is not a great price to pay. So would residents of the numerous totalitarian and authoritarian states of our day." *Bostick v. State of Florida*, 554 So. 2d 1153 (Fla. 1989).

Considering Florida's past history in race relations and that it is probably the state most heavily impacted by drug trafficking, it would be ironic indeed if rights guaranteed by the Federal Constitution should be accorded greater protection in drug cases by the elected Florida state courts than by federal courts.

Although I have found that Laymon knew that he was signing a consent to search form, I further find as a fact that, under the circumstances existing at the time of his stop, any reasonable traveller, and especially two out-of-state young Black men in the company of two uniformed and armed white law officers on a roadside in rural Colorado, would not have felt that he could do anything other than sign the consent to search. In other words, I find as a fact that Laymon was coerced or intimidated into signing the consent to search. For this reason, I conclude that the government has not sustained its burden to demonstrate that his consent was "sufficiently an act of free will to purge the primary taint" of the illegal stop. Therefore, I conclude that the defendant is entitled to prevail on his motion to suppress.

Accordingly It Is Ordered that the defendant Laymon's motion to suppress is granted.

NOTES AND QUESTIONS

1. The Eagle County Police Department does not appear to be in the vanguard of progressive policing. But note its use of a simple standardized "consent form" to memorialize consents to searches. Recall how in *Schneckloth* and *Robinette* the Court said it would be "impractical" and "unrealistic" to require police to inform motorists of their right to refuse to consent to a search. Such printed *Miranda* warning cards and forms were in use shortly after the *Miranda* decision to memorialize an arrestee's consent to be interviewed; here a police department has implemented a similar system without any legal requirement to do so. Kudos Eagle County!

2. What great lawyering here by defense counsel. But note what made it all possible: an order from the court requiring the county to turn over the logs of Sergeant Perry's stops for a nine-month period, which probably required a threshold showing of pretext. For this to become dispositive evidence several other things were required: attendance at the suppression hearing of other "victims" — uncharged — of Perry's tactics; the court's willingness to view the matter through the perspective of Justice Jackson's Everyman in his *Brinegar* dissent; and, ultimately, candid (if criminal) testimony from Perry that he switched from relying solely on race for traffic stops to a system where he instead relied on trivial traffic violations.

(Note that the searches many of these Everyman witnesses consented to took almost an hour, almost surely longer than what they thought they were agreeing to.)

3. Judge Carrigan finds that the stop was unconstitutionally pretextual under the Tenth Circuit's rule in *Guzman*, which required an inquiry into whether a reasonable officer would have made the stop in the absence of the pretextual purpose. What difficulties do you see in courts' application of that test in contexts such as these? How do those difficulties compare to other Fourth Amendment tests, such as, for example, whether a person has a reasonable expectation of privacy?

4. Judge Carrigan makes an impassioned plea that civil rights cannot be sacrificed on the altar of the war on drugs, and notes the example of the Florida Supreme Court—"the state most heavily impacted by drug trafficking"—in recognizing individual rights.

In two years the Florida Supreme Court decision Judge Carrigan noted would be overturned by the United States Supreme Court. *Florida v. Bostick*, 501 U.S. 429 (1991). In five years, the United States Supreme Court would reject the Tenth Circuit's rule in *Guzman* relied on by Judge Carrigan, blessing traffic stops supported by probable cause regardless of a pretextual purpose. *Whren v. United States*, 517 U.S. 806 (1996).

We now turn to *Whren*.

Whren v. United States
517 U.S. 806 (1996)

Justice SCALIA delivered the opinion of the Court.

In this case we decide whether the temporary detention of a motorist who the police have probable cause to believe has committed a civil traffic violation is inconsistent with the Fourth Amendment's prohibition against unreasonable seizures unless a reasonable officer would have been motivated to stop the car by a desire to enforce the traffic laws.

I

On the evening of June 10, 1993, plainclothes vice-squad officers of the District of Columbia Metropolitan Police Department were patrolling a "high drug area" of the city in an unmarked car. Their suspicions were aroused when they passed a dark Pathfinder truck with temporary license plates and youthful occupants waiting at a stop sign, the driver looking down into the lap of the passenger at his right. The truck remained stopped at the intersection for what seemed an unusually long time—more than 20 seconds. When the police car executed a U-turn in order to head back toward the truck, the Pathfinder turned suddenly to its right, without signaling, and sped off at an "unreasonable" speed. The policemen followed, and in a short while overtook the Pathfinder when it stopped behind other traffic at a red light. They pulled up alongside, and Officer Ephraim Soto stepped out and approached the driver's door, identifying himself as a police officer and directing the driver, petitioner Brown, to put the vehicle in park. When Soto drew up to the driver's window, he immediately observed two large plastic bags of what appeared to be crack cocaine in petitioner Whren's hands. Petitioners were arrested, and quantities of several types of illegal drugs were retrieved from the vehicle.

Petitioners were charged in a four-count indictment with violating various federal drug laws, including 21 U.S.C. §§ 844(a) and 860(a). At a pretrial suppression hearing, they challenged the legality of the stop and the resulting seizure of the drugs. They argued that the stop had not been justified by probable cause to believe, or even reasonable suspicion, that petitioners were engaged in illegal drug-dealing activity; and that Officer Soto's asserted ground for approaching the vehicle—to give the driver a warning concerning traffic violations—was pretextual. The District Court denied the suppression motion, concluding that "the facts of the stop were not controverted," and "[t]here was nothing to really demonstrate that the actions of the officers were contrary to a normal traffic stop."

E. Race and Suspicion 449

Petitioners were convicted of the counts at issue here. The Court of Appeals affirmed the convictions, holding with respect to the suppression issue that, "regardless of whether a police officer subjectively believes that the occupants of an automobile may be engaging in some other illegal behavior, a traffic stop is permissible as long as a reasonable officer in the same circumstances could have stopped the car for the suspected traffic violation." We granted certiorari.

II

The Fourth Amendment guarantees "[t]he right of the people to be secure in their persons, houses, papers, and effects, against unreasonable searches and seizures." Temporary detention of individuals during the stop of an automobile by the police, even if only for a brief period and for a limited purpose, constitutes a "seizure" of "persons" within the meaning of this provision. An automobile stop is thus subject to the constitutional imperative that it not be "unreasonable" under the circumstances. As a general matter, the decision to stop an automobile is reasonable where the police have probable cause to believe that a traffic violation has occurred.

Petitioners accept that Officer Soto had probable cause to believe that various provisions of the District of Columbia traffic code had been violated. See 18 D.C. Mun. Regs. §§ 2213.4 (1995) ("An operator shall . . . give full time and attention to the operation of the vehicle"); 2204.3 ("No person shall turn any vehicle . . . without giving an appropriate signal"); 2200.3 ("No person shall drive a vehicle . . . at a speed greater than is reasonable and prudent under the conditions"). They argue, however, that "in the unique context of civil traffic regulations" probable cause is not enough. Since, they contend, the use of automobiles is so heavily and minutely regulated that total compliance with traffic and safety rules is nearly impossible, a police officer will almost invariably be able to catch any given motorist in a technical violation. This creates the temptation to use traffic stops as a means of investigating other law violations, as to which no probable cause or even articulable suspicion exists. Petitioners, who are both black, further contend that police officers might decide which motorists to stop based on decidedly impermissible factors, such as the race of the car's occupants. To avoid this danger, they say, the Fourth Amendment test for traffic stops should be, not the normal one (applied by the Court of Appeals) of whether probable cause existed to justify the stop; but rather, whether a police officer, acting reasonably, would have made the stop for the reason given.

A

Petitioners contend that the standard they propose is consistent with our past cases' disapproval of police attempts to use valid bases of action against citizens as pretexts for pursuing other investigatory agendas. We are reminded that in *Florida v. Wells* (1990), we stated that "an inventory search" must not be a ruse for a general rummaging in order to discover incriminating evidence"; that in *Colorado v. Bertine* (1987), in approving an inventory search, we apparently thought it significant that there had been "no showing that the police, who were following standardized procedures, acted in bad faith or for the sole purpose of investigation"; and that in *New York v. Burger* (1987), we observed, in upholding the constitutionality of a warrantless administrative inspection, that the search did not appear to be "a 'pretext' for obtaining evidence of . . . violation of . . . penal laws." But only an undiscerning reader would regard these cases as endorsing the principle that ulterior motives can invalidate police conduct that is justifiable on the basis of probable cause to believe that a violation of law has occurred. In each case we were addressing the validity of a search conducted in the absence of probable cause. Our quoted statements simply explain that the exemption from the need for probable cause (and warrant), which is accorded to searches made for the purpose of inventory or administrative regulation, is not accorded to searches that are not made for those purposes.

Petitioners also rely upon *Colorado v. Bannister* (1980) (per curiam), a case which, like this one, involved a traffic stop as the prelude to a plain-view sighting and arrest on charges wholly unrelated to the basis for the stop. Petitioners point to our statement that "[t]here was no evidence whatsoever that the officer's presence to issue a traffic citation was a pretext to confirm any other previous suspicion about the occupants" of the car. That dictum at most demonstrates that the Court in *Bannister* found no need to inquire into the question now under discussion; not that it was certain of the answer. And it may demonstrate even less than that: If by "pretext" the Court meant that the officer really had not seen the car speeding, the statement would mean only that there was no reason to doubt probable cause for the traffic stop.

It would, moreover, be anomalous, to say the least, to treat a statement in a footnote in the per curiam *Bannister* opinion as indicating a reversal of our prior law. Petitioners' difficulty is not simply a lack of affirmative support for their position. Not only have we never held, outside the context of inventory search or administrative inspection (discussed above), that an officer's motive invalidates objectively justifiable behavior under the Fourth Amendment; but we have repeatedly held and asserted the contrary. In *United States v. Villamonte-Marquez* (1983), we held that an otherwise valid warrantless boarding of a vessel by customs officials was not rendered invalid "because the customs officers were accompanied by a Louisiana state policeman, and were following an informant's tip that a vessel in the ship channel was thought to be carrying marihuana." We flatly dismissed the idea that an ulterior motive might serve to strip the agents of their legal justification. In *United States v. Robinson* (1973), we held that a traffic-violation arrest (of the sort here) would not be rendered invalid by the fact that it was "a mere pretext for a narcotics search," and that a lawful postarrest search of the person would not be rendered invalid by the fact that it was not motivated by the officer-safety concern that justifies such searches. And in *Scott v. United States* (1978), in rejecting the contention that wiretap evidence was subject to exclusion because the agents conducting the tap had failed to make any effort to comply with the statutory requirement that unauthorized acquisitions be minimized, we said that "[s]ubjective intent alone . . . does not make otherwise lawful conduct illegal or unconstitutional." We described *Robinson* as having established that "the fact that the officer does not have the state of mind which is hypothecated by the reasons which provide the legal justification for the officer's action does not invalidate the action taken as long as the circumstances, viewed objectively, justify that action."

We think these cases foreclose any argument that the constitutional reasonableness of traffic stops depends on the actual motivations of the individual officers involved. We of course agree with petitioners that the Constitution prohibits selective enforcement of the law based on considerations such as race. But the constitutional basis for objecting to intentionally discriminatory application of laws is the Equal Protection Clause, not the Fourth Amendment. Subjective intentions play no role in ordinary, probable-cause Fourth Amendment analysis.

B

Recognizing that we have been unwilling to entertain Fourth Amendment challenges based on the actual motivations of individual officers, petitioners disavow any intention to make the individual officer's subjective good faith the touchstone of "reasonableness." They insist that the standard they have put forward—whether the officer's conduct deviated materially from usual police practices, so that a reasonable officer in the same circumstances would not have made the stop for the reasons given—is an "objective" one.

But although framed in empirical terms, this approach is plainly and indisputably driven by subjective considerations. Its whole purpose is to prevent the police from doing under the guise of enforcing the traffic code what they would like to do for different reasons. Petitioners' proposed standard may not use the word "pretext," but it is designed to combat nothing other than the perceived "danger" of the pretextual stop, albeit only indirectly and over the run of cases. Instead of asking whether the individual officer had the proper state of mind, the petitioners would have us ask, in effect, whether (based on general police practices) it is plausible to believe that the officer had the proper state of mind.

Why one would frame a test designed to combat pretext in such fashion that the court cannot take into account actual and admitted pretext is a curiosity that can only be explained by the fact that our cases have foreclosed the more sensible option. If those cases were based only upon the evidentiary difficulty of establishing subjective intent, petitioners' attempt to root out subjective vices through objective means might make sense. But they were not based only upon that, or indeed even principally upon that. Their principal basis—which applies equally to attempts to reach subjective intent through ostensibly objective means—is simply that the Fourth Amendment's concern with "reasonableness" allows certain actions to be taken in certain circumstances, whatever the subjective intent. But even if our concern had been only an evidentiary one, petitioners' proposal would by no means assuage it. Indeed, it seems to us somewhat easier to figure out the intent of an individual officer than to plumb the collective consciousness of law enforcement in order to determine whether a "reasonable officer" would have been moved to act upon the traffic violation. While police manuals and standard procedures may sometimes provide objective assistance, ordinarily one would be reduced to speculating about the hypothetical reaction of a hypothetical constable—an exercise that might be called virtual subjectivity.

Moreover, police enforcement practices, even if they could be practicably assessed by a judge, vary from place to place and from time to time. We cannot accept that the search and seizure protections of the Fourth Amendment are so variable and can be made to turn upon such trivialities. The difficulty is illustrated by petitioners' arguments in this case. Their claim that a reasonable officer would not have made this stop is based largely on District of Columbia police regulations which permit plainclothes officers in unmarked vehicles to enforce traffic laws "only in the case of a violation that is so grave as to pose an immediate threat to the safety of others." This basis of invalidation would not apply in jurisdictions that had a different practice. And it would not have applied even in the District of Columbia, if Officer Soto had been wearing a uniform or patrolling in a marked police cruiser.

Petitioners argue that our cases support insistence upon police adherence to standard practices as an objective means of rooting out pretext. They cite no holding to that effect, and dicta in only two cases. In *Abel v. United States* (1960), the petitioner had been arrested by the Immigration and Naturalization Service (INS), on the basis of an administrative warrant that, he claimed, had been issued on pretextual grounds in order to enable the Federal Bureau of Investigation (FBI) to search his room after his arrest. We regarded this as an allegation of "serious misconduct," but rejected Abel's claims on the ground that "[a] finding of bad faith is . . . not open to us on th[e] record" in light of the findings below, including the finding that "'the proceedings taken by the [INS] differed in no respect from what would have been done in the case of an individual concerning whom [there was no pending FBI investigation].'" But it is a long leap from the proposition that following regular procedures is some evidence of lack of pretext to the proposition that failure to follow regular procedures proves (or is an operational substitute for) pretext. *Abel*, moreover, did not involve the assertion that pretext could invalidate a search or seizure for which there was probable cause—and even what it said about pretext in other contexts is plainly inconsistent with the views we later stated in *Robinson, Gustafson, Scott*, and *Villamonte-Marquez*. In the other case claimed to contain supportive dicta, *United States v. Robinson* (1973), in approving a search incident to an arrest for driving without a license, we noted that the arrest was "not a departure from established police department practice." That was followed, however, by the statement that "[w]e leave for another day questions which would arise on facts different from these." This is not even a dictum that purports to provide an answer, but merely one that leaves the question open.

III

In what would appear to be an elaboration on the "reasonable officer" test, petitioners argue that the balancing inherent in any Fourth Amendment inquiry requires us to weigh the governmental and individual interests implicated in a traffic stop such as we have here. That balancing, petitioners claim, does not support investigation of minor traffic infractions by plainclothes police in unmarked vehicles; such investigation only minimally advances the government's interest in traffic safety, and may indeed retard it by producing motorist confusion and alarm — a view said to be supported by the Metropolitan Police Department's own regulations generally prohibiting this practice. And as for the Fourth Amendment interests of the individuals concerned, petitioners point out that our cases acknowledge that even ordinary traffic stops entail "a possibly unsettling show of authority"; that they at best "interfere with freedom of movement, are inconvenient, and consume time" and at worst "may create substantial anxiety." That anxiety is likely to be even more pronounced when the stop is conducted by plainclothes officers in unmarked cars.

It is of course true that in principle every Fourth Amendment case, since it turns upon a "reasonableness" determination, involves a balancing of all relevant factors. With rare exceptions not applicable here, however, the result of that balancing is not in doubt where the search or seizure is based upon probable cause. That is why petitioners must rely upon cases like *Prouse* to provide examples of actual "balancing" analysis. There, the police action in question was a random traffic stop for the purpose of checking a motorist's license and vehicle registration, a practice that — like the practices at issue in the inventory search and administrative inspection cases upon which petitioners rely in making their "pretext" claim — involves police intrusion without the probable cause that is its traditional justification. Our opinion in *Prouse* expressly distinguished the case from a stop based on precisely what is at issue here: "probable cause to believe that a driver is violating any one of the multitude of applicable traffic and equipment regulations." It noted approvingly that "[t]he foremost method of enforcing traffic and vehicle safety regulations . . . is acting upon observed violations," which afford the "'quantum of individualized suspicion'" necessary to ensure that police discretion is sufficiently constrained. What is true of *Prouse* is also true of other cases that engaged in detailed "balancing" to decide the constitutionality of automobile stops, such as *Martinez-Fuerte*, which upheld checkpoint stops, and *Brignoni-Ponce*, which disallowed so-called "roving patrol" stops. The detailed "balancing" analysis was necessary because they involved seizures without probable cause.

Where probable cause has existed, the only cases in which we have found it necessary actually to perform the "balancing" analysis involved searches or seizures conducted in an extraordinary manner, unusually harmful to an individual's privacy or even physical interests — such as, for example, seizure by means of deadly force, see *Tennessee v. Garner* (1985), unannounced entry into a home, *see Wilson v. Arkansas* (1995), entry into a home without a warrant, *see Welsh v. Wisconsin* (1984), or physical penetration of the body. The making of a traffic stop out of uniform does not remotely qualify as such an extreme practice, and so is governed by the usual rule that probable cause to believe the law has been broken "outbalances" private interest in avoiding police contact.

Petitioners urge as an extraordinary factor in this case that the "multitude of applicable traffic and equipment regulations" is so large and so difficult to obey perfectly that virtually everyone is guilty of violation, permitting the police to single out almost whomever they wish for a stop. But we are aware of no principle that would allow us to decide at what point a code of law becomes so expansive and so commonly violated that infraction itself can no longer be the ordinary measure of the lawfulness of enforcement. And even if we could identify such exorbitant codes, we do not know by what standard (or what right) we would decide, as

E. Race and Suspicion   **453**

petitioners would have us do, which particular provisions are sufficiently important to merit enforcement.

For the run-of-the-mine case, which this surely is, we think there is no realistic alternative to the traditional common-law rule that probable cause justifies a search and seizure.

• • •

Here the District Court found that the officers had probable cause to believe that petitioners had violated the traffic code. That rendered the stop reasonable under the Fourth Amendment, the evidence thereby discovered admissible, and the upholding of the convictions by the Court of Appeals for the District of Columbia Circuit correct. The judgment is affirmed.

NOTES AND QUESTIONS

1. Note carefully how the police first had their suspicions "aroused" here. It had nothing to do with traffic. It was what most would think was an entirely benign observation: "a dark Pathfinder truck with temporary license plates and youthful occupants waiting at a stop sign, the driver looking down into the lap of the passenger at his right." Why would this arouse suspicion? In the 1990s motorists often consulted roadmaps, or printed out Mapquest directions for navigational guidance. Maybe the "youthful occupants" of the car were lost.

What if at the suppression hearing the police officers had admitted that they began observing the defendants and then followed the Pathfinder because its occupants were Black. Does *Whren* tell us that this would not be a Fourth Amendment violation? Would it be an Equal Protection Clause violation?

Would such an admission by the police bring the facts within the rule of *Oyler v. Boles*, 368 U.S. 448, 546 (1962) (prosecutors cannot bring criminal charges based on unconstitutional considerations such as race), *see* Chapter XII *infra*? For an affirmative answer to this question, *see* Gabriel J. Chin & Charles J. Vernon, *Reasonable but Unconstitutional: Racial Profiling and the Radical Objectivity of* Whren v. United States, 83 Geo. Wash. L. Rev. 882, 932-34 (2015) (arguing that in such a scenario the resulting arrest would be a fruit of the poisonous tree).

2. We are often aghast at the notion that a police officer who observes a motorist commit a traffic violation will—depending on state law—often have the power to pull the motorist over, arrest him, perform a search incident to that arrest, and impound the vehicle (which will then be searched). And of course a police officer can embellish or flat out lie about a perceived violation. But can we take at least some comfort in the fact that traffic violations—speeding, wearing a seatbelt, using a turn signal, etc.—are usually marked by bright lines?

Certainly not in Washington, D.C. The Court notes that Officer Soto had probable cause—his actual beliefs and testimony at the suppression hearing are irrelevant, of course—to believe the following terms of the D.C. traffic code had been violated: D.C. Mun. Regs. §§ 2213.4 (1995) ("An operator shall . . . give full time and attention to the operation of the vehicle"); 2204.3 ("No person shall turn any vehicle . . . without giving an appropriate signal"); 2200.3 ("No person shall drive a vehicle . . . at a speed greater than is reasonable and prudent under the conditions").

Each of these requirements has a layer of discretion baked into it, just adding additional layers of discretion to the powers of the police.

3. Officer Soto did actually testify at the suppression hearing. And it's a shame that not one Justice on the Supreme Court or one judge on the D.C. Circuit panel dissented, or at least concurred, in order to discuss his testimony. Officer Soto testified that he did not intend to issue a ticket to the driver for stopping too long at the stop sign—he lacked authority to do so—but that he wished to stop the Pathfinder to inquire why it sped off without signaling in a school area. *United States v. Whren*, 53 F.3d 371, 373 (D.C. Cir. 1995). There is no suggestion there was cross-examination on whether school was in session that "evening."

4. Why does the Court go out of its way to decide the Fourth Amendment racial bias issue? Note that defendants had not argued they were stopped because they were Black. They argued, rather, that allowing the police to have the discretion to pull over anyone who has committed a civil traffic violation creates a risk that decisions will be made for impermissible reasons, such as race. Note that this type of argument has had some success in death penalty challenges. *See* Chapter XVI *infra*.

Relatedly, how is it possible that *Whren* is a 9-0 decision?

5. Is *Whren* unusual in that the issue of pretext can be resolved on a purely objective basis in that (a) the traffic offenses were only civil violations and (b) the officers lacked authority to enforce the traffic laws under municipal regulations?

6. In two states, courts have interpreted state law to prohibit in at least some circumstances the sort of pretextual stop blessed in *Whren*. *See State v. Ladson*, 979 P.2d 833, 842 (Wash. 1999) (holding that while "police may enforce the traffic code . . . [t]hey may not, however, use that authority as a pretext or justification to avoid the warrant requirement for an unrelated criminal investigation"); *State v. Arreola*, 290 P.3d 983, 991 (Wash. 2012) (retreating from *Ladson* in a case involving a "mixed-motive" traffic stop). *See State v. Ochoa*, 206 P.3d 143, 148 (N.M. Ct. App. 2008) (refusing to follow *Whren* and finding its "analysis unpersuasive and incompatible with our state's distinctively protective standards for searches and seizures of automobiles").

For a discussion of how these and other courts have grappled with *Whren*, *see* Margaret Lawton, *State Responses to the* Whren *Decision*, 66 Case W. Rsrv. L. Rev. 1039 (2016).

For a "rewriting" of *Whren* in the voice of the late Justice Thurgood Marshall, see Devon W. Carbado & Jonathan Feingold, *Rewriting* Whren v. United States, 68 UCLA L. Rev. 1678 (2022).

7. A dataset of over 8 million traffic stops generated in the state of Washington in the period after the ban on pretext stops was essentially lifted in the *Arreola* case, *supra*, has confirmed what many have long suspected: that pretext stops disproportionately target drivers of color. *See* Stephen Rushin & Griffin Edwards, *An Empirical Assessment of Pretextual Stops and Racial Profiling*, 73 Stan. L. Rev. 637, 697 (2021) ("The data from Washington suggest that legal rules giving police officers increased discretion to conduct pretextual or mixed-motive traffic stops may contribute to inequality by facilitating racial profiling.").

Contemporaneous with *Whren* was a New Jersey case featuring data on racial profiling in traffic stops on the New Jersey Turnpike.

State v. Soto
734 A.2d 350 (N.J. 1996)

Robert E. Francis, J.S.C.

These are consolidated motions to suppress under the equal protection and due process clauses of the Fourteenth Amendment. Seventeen defendants of African ancestry claim that their arrests on the New Jersey Turnpike south of exit 3 between 1988 and 1991 result from discriminatory enforcement of the traffic laws by the New Jersey State Police. After a lengthy hearing, I find defendants have established a prima facie case of selective enforcement which the State has failed to rebut requiring suppression of all contraband and evidence seized.

E. Race and Suspicion   **455**

Defendants base their claim of institutional racism primarily on statistics. During discovery, each side created a database of all stops and arrests by State Police members patrolling the Turnpike between exits 1 and 7A out of the Moorestown Station for thirty-five randomly selected days between April 1988 and May 1991 from arrest reports, patrol charts, radio logs and traffic tickets. The databases are essentially the same. Both sides counted 3060 stops which the State found to include 1212 race identified stops (39.6%), the defense 1146 (37.4%).

To establish a standard against which to compare the stop data, the defense conducted a traffic survey and a violator survey. Dr. John Lamberth, Chairman of the Psychology Department at Temple University who I found is qualified as an expert in statistics and social psychology, designed both surveys.

The traffic survey was conducted over twenty-one randomly selected two and one-half hour sessions between June 11 and June 24, 1993 and between 8:00 a.m. and 8:00 p.m. at four sites, two northbound and two southbound, between exits 1 and 3 of the Turnpike. Teams supervised by Fred Last, Esq., of the Office of the Public Defender observed and recorded the number of vehicles that passed them except for large trucks, tractor-trailers, buses and government vehicles, how many contained a "black" occupant and the state of origin of each vehicle. Of the 42,706 vehicles counted, 13.5% had a black occupant. Dr. Lamberth testified that this percentage is consistent with the 1990 Census figures for the eleven states from where almost 90% of the observed vehicles were registered. He said it is also consistent with a study done by the Triangle Group for the U.S. Department of Transportation with which he was familiar.

The violator survey was conducted over ten sessions in four days in July 1993 by Mr. Last traveling between exits 1 and 3 in his vehicle at sixty miles per hour on cruise control after the speedometer had been calibrated and observing and recording the number of vehicles that passed him, the number of vehicles he passed and how many had a black occupant. Mr. Last counted a total of 2096 vehicles other than large trucks, tractor-trailers, buses and government vehicles of which 2062 or 98.1% passed him going in excess of sixty miles per hour including 306 with a black occupant equaling about 15% of those vehicles clearly speeding. Multiple violators, that is those violating the speed limit and committing some other moving violation like tailgating, also equaled about 15% black. Dr. Lamberth testified that the difference between the percentage of black violators and the percentage of black travelers from the surveys is statistically insignificant and that there is no evidence traffic patterns changed between the period April 1988 to May 1991 in the databases and June-July 1993 when the surveys were done.

Using 13.5% as the standard or benchmark against which to compare the stop data, Dr. Lamberth found that 127 or 46.2% of the race identified stops between exits 1 and 3 were of blacks constituting an absolute disparity of 32.7%, a comparative disparity of 242% (32.7% divided by 13.5%) and 16.35 standard deviations. By convention, something is considered statistically significant if it would occur by chance fewer than five times in a hundred (over two standard deviations). In case I were to determine that the appropriate stop data for comparison with the standard is the stop data for the entire portion of the Turnpike patrolled by the Moorestown Station in recognition of the fact that the same troopers patrol between exits 3 and 7A as patrol between exits 1 and 3, Dr. Lamberth found that 408 or 35.6% of the race identified stops between exits 1 and 7A were of blacks constituting an absolute disparity of 22.1%, a comparative disparity of 164% and 22.1 standard deviations.3 He opined it is highly unlikely such statistics could have occurred randomly or by chance.

Defendants also presented the testimony of Dr. Joseph B. Kadane, an eminently qualified statistician. Among his many credentials, Dr. Kadane is a full professor of statistics and social sciences at Carnegie Mellon University, headed the Department of Statistics there between 1972 and 1981 and is a Fellow of the American Statistical Association, having served on its board of directors and a number of its committees and held various editorships on its

Journal. Dr. Kadane testified that in his opinion both the traffic and violator surveys were well designed, carefully performed and statistically reliable for analysis. From the surveys and the defense database, he calculated that a black was 4.85 times as likely as a white to be stopped between exits 1 and 3. This calculation led him to "suspect" a racially non-neutral stopping policy. While he noted that the surveys were done in 1993 and compared to data from 1988 to 1991, he was nevertheless satisfied that the comparisons were useable and accurate within a few percent. He was not concerned that the violator survey failed to count cars going less than sixty miles per hour and travelling behind Mr. Last when he started a session. He was concerned, however, with the fact that only 37.4% of the stops in the defense database were race identified. In order to determine if the comparisons were sensitive to the missing racial data, he did calculations performed on the log odds of being stopped. Whether he assumed the probability of having one's race recorded if black and stopped is the same as if white and stopped or two or three times as likely, the log odds were still greater than .99 that blacks were stopped at higher rates than whites on the Turnpike between exits 1 and 3 during the period April 1988 to May 1991. He therefore concluded that the comparisons were not sensitive to the missing racial data.

Supposing that the disproportionate stopping of blacks was related to police discretion, the defense studied the traffic tickets issued by State Police members between exits 1 and 7A on the thirty-five randomly selected days broken down by State Police unit. There are 533 racially identified tickets in the databases issued by either the now disbanded Radar Unit, the Tactical Patrol Unit or general road troopers ("Patrol Unit"). The testimony indicates that the Radar Unit focused mainly on speeders using a radar van and chase cars and exercised limited discretion regarding which vehicles to stop. The Tac-Pac concentrates on traffic problems at specific locations and exercises somewhat more discretion as regards which vehicles to stop. Responsible to provide general law enforcement, the Patrol Unit exercises by far the most discretion among the three units. From Mr. Last's count, Dr. Lamberth computed that 18% of the tickets issued by the Radar Unit were to blacks, 23.8% of the tickets issued by the Tac-Pac were to blacks while 34.2% of the tickets issued by the Patrol Unit were to blacks. South of exit 3, Dr. Lamberth computed that 19.4% of the tickets issued by the Radar Unit were to blacks, 0.0% of the tickets issued by the Tac-Pac were to blacks while 43.8% of the tickets issued by the Patrol Unit were to blacks. In his opinion, the Radar Unit percentages are statistically consistent with the standard established by the violator survey, but the differences between the Radar Unit and the Patrol Unit between both exits 1 and 3 and 1 and 7A are statistically significant or well in excess of two standard deviations.

The State presented the testimony of Dr. Leonard Cupingood to challenge or refute the statistical evidence offered by the defense. I found Dr. Cupingood is qualified to give expert testimony in the field of statistics based on his Ph.D in statistics from Temple and his work experience with the Center for Forensic Economic Studies, a for profit corporation headquartered in Philadelphia. Dr. Cupingood collaborated with Dr. Bernard Siskin, his superior at the Center for Forensic Economic Studies and a former chairman of the Department of Statistics at Temple.

Dr. Cupingood had no genuine criticism of the defense traffic survey. Rather, he centered his criticism of the defense statistical evidence on the violator survey. Throughout his testimony he maintained that the violator survey failed to capture the relevant data which he opined was the racial mix of those speeders most likely to be stopped or the "tail of the distribution." He even recommended the State authorize him to design a study to collect this data, but the State declined. He was unclear, though, how he would design a study to ascertain in a safe way the vehicle going the fastest above the speed limit at a given time at a given location and the race of its occupants without involving the credibility of State Police members. In any event, his supposition that maybe blacks drive faster than whites above the speed limit was repudiated by all State Police members called by the State who were questioned about it.

E. Race and Suspicion   **457**

Colonel Clinton Pagano, Trooper Donald Nemeth, Trooper Stephen Baumann and Detective Timothy Grant each testified that blacks drive indistinguishably from whites. Moreover, Dr. Cupingood acknowledged that he knew of no study indicating that blacks drive worse than whites. Nor could he reconcile the notion with the evidence that 37% of the unticketed stops between exits 1 and 7A in his database were black and 63% of those between exits 1 and 3. Dr. James Fyfe, a criminal justice professor at Temple who the defense called in its rebuttal case and who I found is qualified as an expert in police science and police procedures, also testified that there is nothing in the literature or in his personal experience to support the theory that blacks drive differently from whites.

Convinced in his belief that the defense 15% standard or benchmark was open to question, Dr. Cupingood attempted to find the appropriate benchmark to compare with the databases. He did three studies of presumedly race-blind stops: night stops versus day stops; radar stops versus non-radar stops and drinking driving arrests triggered by calls for service.

In his study of night stops versus day stops, he compared the percentage of stops of blacks at night between exits 1 and 7A in the databases with the percentage of stops of blacks during daytime and found that night stops were 37.3% black versus 30.2% for daytime stops. Since he presumed the State Police generally cannot tell race at night, he concluded the higher percentage for night stops of blacks supported a standard well above 15%. His premise that the State Police generally cannot recognize race at night, however, is belied by the evidence. On July 16, 1994 between 9:40 p.m. and 11:00 p.m. Ahmad S. Corbitt, now an assistant deputy public defender, together with Investigator Minor of the Office of the Public Defender drove on the Turnpike at 55 miles per hour for a while and parked perpendicular to the Turnpike at a rest stop for a while to see if they could make out the races of the occupants of the vehicles they observed. Mr. Corbitt testified that the two could identify blacks versus whites about 80% of the time in the moving mode and close to 100% in the stationary mode. Over and above this proof is the fact the databases establish that the State Police only stopped an average of eight black occupied vehicles per night between exits 1 and 7A. Dr. Cupingood conceded a trooper could probably identify one or two black motorists per night.

Next, in his study of radar stops versus non-radar stops, Dr. Cupingood focused on the race identified tickets where radar was used in the databases and found that 28.5% of them were issued to blacks. Since he assumed that radar is race neutral, he suggested 28.5% might be the correct standard. As Dr. Kadane said in rebuttal, this study is fundamentally flawed because it assumes what is in question or that the people stopped are the best measure of who is eligible to be stopped. If racial prejudice were afoot, the standard would be tainted. In addition, although a radar device is race-blind, the operator may not be. Of far more significance is the defense study comparing the traffic tickets issued by the Radar, Tac-Pac and Patrol Units which shows again that where radar is used by a unit concerned primarily with speeders and acting with little or no discretion like the Radar Unit, the percentage of tickets issued to blacks is consistent with their percentage on the highway.

And lastly in his effort to find the correct standard, Dr. Cupingood considered a DUI study done by Lieutenant Fred Madden, Administrative Officer of the Records and Identification Section of the State Police. Lt. Madden tabulated DUI arrests between July 1988 and June 1991 statewide, statewide excluding the State Police, for Troop D of the State Police which patrols the entire length of the Turnpike, for Moorestown Station of Troop D and for Moorestown Station south of exit 3 broken down by race and between patrol related versus calls for service (i.e. accidents, motorist aids and other—the arrested motorist coming to the attention of the State Police by a toll-taker or civilian). Since Dr. Cupingood believed DUI arrests from calls for service were race neutral, he adopted the percentage of DUI arrests of blacks for the Moorestown Station from calls for service of 23% as a possible standard. Like his radar versus non-radar stop study, his use of the DUI arrest study is fundamentally flawed because he assumed what is in question. Further, he erred in assuming that DUI arrests from calls for service involve no discretion. While the encounters involve no discretion, the arrests surely do. He admitted that race/discretion may explain the following widespread statistics in the DUI arrest study:

Statewide (all departments)	12% black
Statewide (excluding State Police)	10.4% black
State Police	16% black
Troop D	23% black
Moorestown Station	34% black
Moorestown Station patrol related	41% black
Moorestown Station patrol related south of exit 3	50% black

After hearing the testimony of Kenneth Ruff and Kenneth Wilson, two former troopers called by the defense who were not reappointed at the end of their terms and who said they were trained and coached to make race based "profile" stops to increase their criminal arrests, the State asked Dr. Cupingood to study the race identified stops in his database and see how many possessed the profile characteristics cited by Ruff and Wilson, particularly how many were young (30 or under), black and male. Dr. Cupingood found that only 11.6% of the race identified stops were of young black males and only 6.6% of all stops were of young black males.

The defense then conducted a profile study of its own. It concentrated on the race identified stops of just blacks issued tickets and found that an adult black male was present in 88% of the cases where the gender of all occupants could be determined and that where gender and age could be determined, a black male 30 or younger was present in 63% of the cases. The defense study is more probative because it does concentrate on just stops of blacks issued tickets eliminating misleading comparisons with totals including whites or whites and a 62.6% group of race unknowns. Neither side, of course, could consider whether the blacks stopped and not issued tickets possessed profile characteristics since the databases contain no information about them.

Dr. Cupingood's so-called Mantel-Haentzel analysis ended the statistical evidence. He put forward this calculation of "expected black tickets" in an attempt to disprove the defense study showing the Patrol Unit, the unit with the most discretion, ticketed blacks at a rate not only well above the Radar and Tac-Pac Units, but also well above the standard fixed by the violator survey. The calculation insinuates that the Patrol Unit issued merely 5 excess tickets to blacks beyond what would have been expected. The calculation is worthless. First and foremost, Dr. Cupingood deleted the non-radar tickets which presumably involved a greater exercise of discretion. The role police discretion played in the issuance of tickets to blacks was the object of the defense study. Under the guise of comparing only things similarly situated, he thereupon deleted any radar tickets not issued in one of the four time periods he divided each of the thirty-five randomly selected days into for which there was not at least one race identified radar ticket issued by the Patrol Unit and at least one by the combined Radar, Tac-Pac Unit. He provided no justification for either creating the 140 time periods or combining the tickets of the Radar and Tac-Pac Units. To compound his defective analysis, he pooled the data in each time period into a single number and employed the resultant weighted average of the two units to compute the expected and excess, if any, tickets issued to blacks. By using weighted averages, he once again assumed the answer to the question he purported to address. He assumed the Patrol Unit gave the same number of tickets to blacks as did the Radar, Tac-Pac Unit, rather than test to see if it did. Even after "winnowing" the data, the comparison between the Patrol Unit and the Radar, Tac-Pac Unit is marginally statistically significant. Without winnowing, Dr. Kadane found the comparison of the radar tickets issued by the Patrol Unit to blacks with the radar tickets issued by the Radar, Tac-Pac Unit to blacks constituted 3.78 standard deviations which is distinctly above the 5% standard of statistical significance.

E. Race and Suspicion 459

The defense did not rest on its statistical evidence alone. Along with the testimony of former troopers Kenneth Ruff and Kenneth Wilson about having been trained and coached to make race based profile stops but whose testimony is weakened by bias related to their not having been reappointed at the end of their terms, the defense elicited evidence through cross-examination of State witnesses and a rebuttal witness, Dr. James Fyfe, that the State Police hierarchy allowed, condoned, cultivated and tolerated discrimination between 1988 and 1991 in its crusade to rid New Jersey of the scourge of drugs.

Conjointly with the passage of the Comprehensive Drug Reform Act of 1987 and to advance the Attorney General's Statewide Action Plan for Narcotics Enforcement issued in January 1988 which "directed that the enforcement of our criminal drug laws shall be the highest priority law enforcement activity," Colonel Pagano formed the Drug Interdiction Training Unit (DITU) in late 1987 consisting of two supervisors and ten other members, two from each Troop selected for their successful seizure statistics, ". . . to actually patrol with junior road personnel and provide critical on-the-job training in recognizing potential violators." State Police Plan For Action dated July 7, 1987, at p. 14. According to Colonel Pagano, the DITU program was intended to be one step beyond the existing coach program to impart to newer troopers insight into drug enforcement and the "criminal program" (patrol related arrests) in general. DITU was disbanded in or around July 1992.

No training materials remain regarding the training DITU members themselves received, and few training materials remain regarding the training DITU members provided the newer troopers except for a batch of checklists. Just one impact study was ever prepared regarding the effectiveness of the DITU program rather than periodic impact evaluations and studies as required by S.O.P. F4 dated January 12, 1989, but this one undated report marked D-62 in evidence only provided statistics about the number of investigations conducted, the number of persons involved and the quantity and value of drugs seized without indicating the race of those involved or the number of fruitless investigations broken down by race. In the opinion of Dr. Fyfe, retention of training materials is important for review of the propriety of the training and to discern agency policy, and preparation of periodic impact evaluations and studies is important not only to determine the effectiveness of the program from a numbers standpoint, but more than that to enable administration to monitor and control the quality of the program and its impact on the public, especially a crackdown program like DITU which placed so much emphasis on stopping drug transportation by the use of "consents" to search following traffic stops in order to prevent constitutional excesses.

Despite the paucity of training materials and lack of periodic and complete impact evaluations and studies, a glimpse of the work of DITU emerges from the preserved checklists and the testimony of Sergeants Brian Caffrey and David Cobb. Sergeant Caffrey was the original assistant supervisor of DITU and became the supervisor in 1989. Sergeant Cobb was an original member of DITU and became the assistant supervisor in 1989. Sergeant Caffrey left DITU sometime in 1992, Sergeant Cobb sometime in 1991. Both testified that a major purpose of DITU was to teach trainees tip-offs and techniques about what to look for and do to talk or "dig" their way into a vehicle after, not before, a motor vehicle stop to effectuate patrol related arrests. Both denied teaching or using race as a tip-off either before or after a stop. Nevertheless, Sergeant Caffrey condoned a comment by a DITU trainer during the time he was the supervisor of DITU stating:

> Trooper Fash previously had DITU training, and it showed in the way he worked. He has become a little reluctant to stop cars in lieu [sic] of the Channel 9 News Report. He was told as long as he uses Title 39 he can stop any car he wants. He enjoys DITU and would like to ride again.

As the defense observes in its closing brief, "Why would a trooper who is acting in a racially neutral fashion become reluctant to stop cars as a result of a news story charging that racial

460 Chapter IV The Fourth Amendment

minorities were being targeted [by the New Jersey State Police]?" Even A.A.G. Ronald Susswein, Deputy Director of the Division of Criminal Justice, acknowledged that this comment is incomplete because it fails to add the caveat, "as long as he doesn't also use race or ethnicity." Further, Sergeant Caffrey testified that "ethnicity is something to keep in mind" albeit not a tip-off and that he taught attendees at both the annual State Police in-service training session in March 1987 and the special State Police in-service training sessions in July and August 1987 that Hispanics are mainly involved in drug trafficking and showed them the film Operation Pipeline wherein the ethnicity of those arrested, mostly Hispanics, is prominently depicted. Dr. Fyfe criticized Sergeant Caffrey's teaching Hispanics are mainly involved and his showing Operation Pipeline as well as the showing of the Jamaican Posse film wherein only blacks are depicted as drug traffickers at the 1989 annual State Police in-service training session saying trainers should not teach what they do not intend their trainees to act upon. At a minimum, teaching Hispanics are mainly involved in drug trafficking and showing films depicting mostly Hispanics and blacks trafficking in drugs at training sessions worked at cross-purposes with concomitant instruction pointing out that neither race nor ethnicity may be considered in making traffic stops.

Key corroboration for finding the State Police hierarchy allowed and tolerated discrimination came from Colonel Pagano. Colonel Pagano was Superintendent of the State Police from 1975 to February 1990. He testified there was a noisy demand in the 1980s to get drugs off the streets. In accord, Attorney General Cary Edwards and he made drug interdiction the number one priority of law enforcement. He helped formulate the Attorney General's Statewide Action Plan for Narcotics Enforcement and established DITU within the State Police. He kept an eye on DITU through conversations with staff officers and Sergeants Mastella and Caffrey and review of reports generated under the traditional reporting system and D-62 in evidence. He had no thought DITU would engage in constitutional violations. He knew all State Police members were taught that they were guardians of the Constitution and that targeting any race was unconstitutional and poor police practice to boot. He recognized it was his responsibility to see that race was not a factor in who was stopped, searched and arrested. When he became Superintendent, he formed the Internal Affairs Bureau to investigate citizen complaints against State Police members to maintain the integrity of the Division. Substantiated deviations from regulations resulted in sanctions, additional training or counseling.

More telling, however, is what Colonel Pagano said and did, or did not do, in response to the Channel 9 exposé entitled "Without Just Cause" which aired in 1989 and which troubled Trooper Fash and what he did not do in response to complaints of profiling from the NAACP and ACLU and these consolidated motions to suppress and similar motions in Warren and Middlesex Counties. He said to Joe Collum of Channel 9 that "[violating rights of motorists was] of serious concern [to him], but no where near the concern that I think we have got to look to in trying to correct some of the problems we find with the criminal element in this State" and "the bottom line is that those stops were not made on the basis of *race alone*" (emphasis added). Since perhaps these isolated comments were said inadvertently or edited out of context, a truer reflection of his attitude about claims of racism would appear to be his videotaped remarks shown all members of the State Police at roll call in conjunction with the WOR series. Thereon he clearly said that he did not want targeting or discriminatory enforcement and that "[w]hen you put on this uniform, you leave your biases and your prejudices behind." But he also said as regarded the charge of a Trenton school principal named Jones that he had been stopped on the Turnpike and threatened, intimidated and assaulted by a trooper, "We know that the teacher assaulted the trooper. He didn't have a driver's license or a registration *for his fancy new Mercedes*" (emphasis added). And he called Paul McLemore, the first African-American trooper in New Jersey and now a practicing attorney and who spoke of

E. Race and Suspicion

discrimination within the ranks of the State Police, "an ingrate." And he told the members to "keep the heat on" and then assured them:

> . . . [H]ere at Division Headquarters we'll make sure that when the wheels start to squeak, we'll do whatever we can to make sure that you're supported out in the field. . . . Anything that goes toward implementing the Drug Reform Act is important. And, we'll handle the squeaky wheels here.

He admitted the Internal Affairs Bureau was not designed to investigate general complaints, so he could not refer the general complaints of discrimination to it for scrutiny. Yet he never requested the Analytical Unit to investigate stop data from radio logs, patrol charts and tickets or search and seizure data from arrest reports, operations reports, investigation reports and consent to search forms, not even after the Analytical Unit informed him in a report on arrests by region, race and crime that he had requested from it for his use in the WOR series that ". . . arrests are not a valid reflection of stops (data relative to stops with respect to race is not compiled)." The databases compiled for these motions attest, of course, to the fact that race identified stop data could have been compiled. He testified he could not launch an investigation into every general complaint because of limited resources and that there was insufficient evidence of discrimination in the Channel 9 series, the NAACP and ACLU complaints and the various motions to suppress for him to spend his "precious" resources. In short, he left the issue of discrimination up to the courts and months of testimony in this and other counties at State expense.

The right to be free from discrimination is firmly supported by the Fourteenth Amendment to the United States Constitution and the protections of Article I, paragraphs 1 and 5 of the New Jersey Constitution of 1947. To be sure, "[t]he eradication of the 'cancer of discrimination' has long been one of our State's highest priorities." It is indisputable, therefore, that the police may not stop a motorist based on race or any other invidious classification.

Generally, however, the inquiry for determining the constitutionality of a stop or a search and seizure is limited to "whether the conduct of the law enforcement officer who undertook the [stop or] search was objectively reasonable, without regard to his or her underlying motives or intent." Thus, it has been said that the courts will not inquire into the motivation of a police officer whose stop of a vehicle was based upon a traffic violation committed in his presence. But where objective evidence establishes "that a police agency has embarked upon an officially sanctioned or de facto policy of targeting minorities for investigation and arrest," any evidence seized will be suppressed to deter future insolence in office by those charged with enforcement of the law and to maintain judicial integrity.

Statistics may be used to make out a case of targeting minorities for prosecution of traffic offenses provided the comparison is between the racial composition of the motorist population violating the traffic laws and the racial composition of those arrested for traffic infractions on the relevant roadway patrolled by the police agency. While defendants have the burden of proving "the existence of purposeful discrimination," discriminatory intent may be inferred from statistical proof presenting a stark pattern or an even less extreme pattern in certain limited contexts. *Kennedy, supra*, implies that discriminatory intent may be inferred from statistical proof in a traffic stop context probably because only uniform variables (Title 39 violations) are relevant to the challenged stops and the State has an opportunity to explain the statistical disparity. "[A] selection procedure that is susceptible of abuse . . . supports the presumption of discrimination raised by the statistical showing." *Castaneda v. Partida* (1977).

Once defendants expose a prima facie case of selective enforcement, the State generally cannot rebut it by merely calling attention to possible flaws or unmeasured variables in defendants' statistics. Rather, the State must introduce specific evidence showing that either there actually are defects which bias the results or the missing factors, when properly organized and accounted for, eliminate or explain the disparity. Nor will mere denials or reliance on the good faith of the officers suffice.

Here, defendants have proven at least a de facto policy on the part of the State Police out of the Moorestown Station of targeting blacks for investigation and arrest between April 1988 and May 1991 both south of exit 3 and between exits 1 and 7A of the Turnpike. Their surveys satisfy *Wards Cove* [*Packing Co. v. Atonio*, 490 U.S. 642, (1989)], *supra*. The statistical disparities and standard deviations revealed are indeed stark. The discretion devolved upon general road troopers to stop any car they want as long as Title 39 is used evinces a selection process that is susceptible of abuse. The utter failure of the State Police hierarchy to monitor and control a crackdown program like DITU or investigate the many claims of institutional discrimination manifests its indifference if not acceptance. Against all this, the State submits only denials and the conjecture and flawed studies of Dr. Cupingood.

The eradication of illegal drugs from our State is an obviously worthy goal, but not at the expense of individual rights. As Justice Brandeis so wisely said dissenting in *Olmstead v. United States* (1928):

> Experience should teach us to be most on our guard to protect liberty when the government's purposes are beneficent. Men born to freedom are naturally alert to repel invasion of their liberty by evil-minded rulers. The greatest dangers to liberty lurk in insidious encroachment by men of zeal, well-meaning but without understanding.

Motions granted.

NOTES AND QUESTIONS

1. The data here are shocking but perhaps not surprising. But note the other powerful aspects of the defense case even in the absence of the existence of complete State Police training materials.

2. Note the central importance in the Drug Interdiction Training Unit, established 1987, of teaching trainees to "dig their way into a vehicle" after a traffic stop. This is consistent with the teachings of Remsberg and Operation Pipeline, *supra*.

New Jersey Turnpike, Exit 3

E. Race and Suspicion 463

3. Note the court's use of federal equal protection case law to conclude that defendants established a prima facie case (at least) of purposeful discrimination that the state was able to rebut. The decision in *Soto* pre-dated *Whren* by just three months.

If a car is parked and not moving, can there be a pretextual "traffic" stop? Do the government's interests in enforcing traffic codes apply equally to parking regulations? Are there any violations of law that are beyond the reach of *Terry* and *Whren*?

United States v. Johnson
874 F.3d 571 (7th Cir. 2017)

EASTERBROOK, Circuit Judge.

Police in Milwaukee saw a car stopped within 15 feet of a crosswalk, which is unlawful unless the car is "actually engaged in loading or unloading or in receiving or discharging passengers." Wis. Stat. § 346.53. One police car drew up parallel to the stopped car, while another drew up behind. Shining lights through the car's windows (it was after 7 p.m. in January), police saw a passenger in the back seat try to hide a firearm. Randy Johnson, the passenger, was prosecuted for possessing a weapon that, as a felon, he was forbidden to have. 18 U.S.C. § 922(g)(1). After the district court denied his motion to suppress the gun, Johnson entered a conditional guilty plea and was sentenced to 46 months' imprisonment. A panel of this court affirmed the conviction, but that decision was vacated when the full court decided to hear the appeal en banc.

Johnson concedes that the car was stopped 7 or 8 feet from a crosswalk. The district court held that this gave the police probable cause to issue a ticket, a process that entails a brief seizure of the car and its occupants. As Officer Conway approached he saw Johnson make movements that led him to infer that Johnson was hiding something such as alcohol, drugs, or a gun. Concerned for his safety, Conway ordered Johnson to get out of the car. Once the car's door was open, Conway saw a gun on the floor. This led to Johnson's arrest.

Johnson says that the judge should have suppressed the gun, because the statutory exception for receiving or discharging cargo or passengers means that the police did not have adequate reason to issue a ticket or even to approach the car until they had observed long enough to know that the car was not within the scope of the exception. The district court rejected that contention, as do we.

First, the district court found that, when the police approached, all four doors of the car were shut and no one was standing nearby, so that the exception was inapplicable. That finding is not clearly erroneous. Indeed, Johnson does not contest it.

Second, although Johnson contends that Wisconsin's judiciary would treat a driver's stop to buy something from a nearby store as within the "loading or unloading or . . . receiving or discharging passengers" exception, we need not address that issue of state law. Officers who had probable cause—recall that it has been stipulated that the car was within 15 feet of the crosswalk—were entitled to approach the car before resolving statutory exceptions. Police possessed of probable cause can hand out tickets (or make arrests) and leave to the judicial process the question whether a defense, exception, proviso, or other limitation applies. Parking-enforcement patrols approach stopped cars countless times every day. Depending on what they find, sometimes they write tickets and sometimes they don't. If the car is occupied, the difference may turn on what the driver says. The Fourth Amendment requires searches and seizures to be reasonable; it does not demand that police and other public officials resolve all possible exceptions before approaching a stopped car and asking the first question.

When denying Johnson's motion to suppress, the district court relied on *Whren v. United States*, (1996), which holds that probable cause to believe that a car's driver is engaged in speeding or another motor-vehicle violation supports a stop and arrest—and that the possibility of an ulterior motive, such as a desire to investigate drugs, does not matter, because analysis under the Fourth Amendment is objective. Johnson, who believes that the police had an ulterior motive for approaching his car, contends that *Whren* does not apply to infractions by stopped cars, which he labels parking violations rather than moving violations.

Yet *Whren* did not create a special rule for moving offenses. The two doctrines that underlie *Whren's* holding—(1) that probable cause justifies stops and arrests, even for fine-only offenses, and (2) that analysis of search-and-seizure issues disregards the officers' thoughts—are of general application.

We assumed in *United States v. Shields* (7th Cir. 2015), that *Whren* applies to parked as well as moving vehicles, and to parking violations as well as moving violations. Every other circuit that has addressed the issue expressly has so held. If there were to be a difference, it would be easier to deem "reasonable" (the constitutional standard) an officer's approach to a car already stopped than the halting of a car in motion. "[I]f police may pull over a vehicle if there is probable cause that a civil traffic violation has been committed, then [the police] surely did not violate the Fourth Amendment by walking up to [a suspect], who was sitting in a car that rested in a spot where it was violating one of [a city's] parking regulations."

The stop of a moving vehicle is more intrusive than approaching a parked car. Because the police approached Johnson's car with probable cause to believe that the driver was violating a traffic law, and the car was not moving, it is unnecessary to consider today how *Terry* applies when cars are in motion. It is enough to conclude that *Whren* applies to both parking and moving offenses.

We grant that the police did more than just stroll up: two squad cars, which bathed the parked car in bright light, implied that the occupants were not free to drive away. The district judge treated this as a seizure; so do we. But issuing a ticket always entails a brief seizure. Johnson concedes that the driver of a car approached with probable cause to investigate a parking offense is not entitled to leave. What is more, when the officers approached this parked car, no one was in the driver's seat. (The driver was inside a liquor store making a purchase.) So both as a matter of the suspects' legal entitlements and as a matter of brute fact, it did not make any difference whether the police approached with two cars rather than one, or whether the cars' spotlights were on. Johnson's car was not going anywhere.

The district court concluded that the way in which the stop was conducted was not responsible for the gun's discovery. That finding is not clearly erroneous. We therefore do not consider whether the officers' show of force was excessive under the circumstances. The United States contends that the use of two cars and searchlights was reasonable to reduce the risk the officers faced in making a nighttime stop in a high-crime area, circumstances in which a city will not rely on foot patrols to enforce traffic laws. The district court did not address that subject; we do not either.

Finally, it is worth noting that Johnson has never contended that the police considered the race of the car's occupants when deciding to approach it, or when deciding to use two cruisers rather than one. Indeed, Johnson has not contended that the police even observed the race of the car's occupants until after they approached it; recall that Johnson's principal contention is that police had the car in view for only an instant before deciding to approach. We therefore do not consider whether, and if so when, using racial criteria to select among potential targets of investigation would require the suppression of evidence.

Affirmed.

HAMILTON, Circuit Judge, joined by ROVNER and WILLIAMS, Circuit Judges, dissenting.

Five officers in two police cars seized the passengers of a stopped car. The officers swooped in on the car, suddenly parking close beside and behind it with bright lights shining in from both directions, opening the doors, pulling all the passengers out and handcuffing them. The district court found, and the majority and I agree, that the passengers were seized as the officers swarmed them, before the officers had any sign that one passenger had a firearm. The sole basis for this intrusive and even terrifying "investigatory stop"? A suspected parking violation . . . for parking too close to an unmarked crosswalk.

The majority errs by extending *Terry v. Ohio* (1968), and *Whren v. United States* (1996), to allow this pretextual seizure based on the suspected parking violation. This extension is not supported by existing law. It also runs contrary to the core Fourth Amendment standard of reasonableness. No other appellate court has tolerated such police tactics to address a suspected parking violation. Nor should we, at least absent extraordinary circumstances not present here. We should find a Fourth Amendment violation in this seizure of the passengers in the car idling outside a store.

As applied to moving traffic violations, Fourth Amendment doctrine has evolved in recent decades to give police officers so much discretion, including the power to conduct pretextual traffic stops, that some scholars have described this power as the "the twentieth-century version of the general warrant." Sarah A. Seo, The New Public, 125 Yale L.J. 1616, 1669 (2016); see also Barbara C. Salken, The General Warrant of the Twentieth Century? A Fourth Amendment Solution to Unchecked Discretion to Arrest for Traffic Offenses, 62 Temp. L. Rev. 221 (1989) (written before the most dramatic expansions of this discretion). The doctrinal evolution has enabled stops for what is often called "driving while black." See generally, e.g., David A. Harris, "Driving While Black" and All Other Traffic Offenses: The Supreme Court and Pretextual Traffic Stops, 87 J. Crim. L. & Criminology 544 (1997). Unless the target of such a seizure can offer evidence of racial motivation in the particular case, which is rarely available, such seizures are difficult to limit.

By extending *Terry* and *Whren* to the suspected parking violation in this case, the majority errs by taking the further step of enabling seizures that can be used for "parking while black." The majority's extension of doctrine is arguably defensible. But defensible does not mean correct. The police tactics here would never be tolerated in more affluent neighborhoods. This extension will further erode the Fourth Amendment, trading away privacy rights of some for the hope of more security for others, and stripping those targeted in searches of both security and privacy. We should find that the tactics in this case violated the Fourth Amendment. I respectfully dissent.

I

The Fourth Amendment provides: "The right of the people to be secure in their persons, houses, papers, and effects, against unreasonable searches and seizures, shall not be violated. . . ." "This inestimable right of personal security belongs as much to the citizen on the streets of our cities as to the homeowner closeted in his study to dispose of his secret affairs." In *Terry*, the Supreme Court struck a practical and necessary balance between protecting privacy and allowing effective law enforcement. *Terry* did so by allowing a brief investigatory stop in response to signs of an imminent armed robbery.

In applying *Terry*, "which is grounded in the standard of reasonableness embodied in the Fourth Amendment," the court "balances the nature and quality of the intrusion on personal security against the importance of the governmental interests alleged to justify the intrusion." When the governmental interest is based on a car parked too close to a crosswalk, the balance looks very different from the balance in *Terry*. The alleged governmental interests pale in comparison to the intrusion on personal security in this seizure.

Before digging into the doctrinal issues, consider the circumstances of this seizure. It was just after 7:30 p.m. on January 8, 2014 in Milwaukee. It was dark and very cold, during the memorable "Polar Vortex" of that winter. The air temperature was eight degrees Fahrenheit, with a wind-chill of twenty degrees below zero and eight inches of snow on the ground. The streets were quiet.

In a tough neighborhood in Milwaukee, five police officers were patrolling together in two squad cars. They were part of the Milwaukee Police Department's Neighborhood Task Force Street Crimes Unit assigned to patrol so-called "hot spots." As one officer testified, "part of our initiative is to look for smaller infractions and hope that possibly they may lead to bigger and better things," posing the danger of police overreach that was realized here.

In this search for "bigger and better things," the officers saw a car parked on a side street in front of a liquor store. The motor was running. The officer in charge saw an opportunity. The car was within fifteen feet of a crosswalk. That meant it might have been parked illegally.

The officer in charge made a split-second decision. The police cars quickly turned onto the side street and closed in on the parked car—one police car pulled up next to and a little in front of the parked car, and the other pulled up right behind it. From both directions, the police lit up the parked car with headlights and spotlights. The five officers got out of their cars and immediately opened the doors of the parked car, shined a flashlight at the passengers, and ordered the passengers out of the car and handcuffed them. One, defendant Johnson, was unlawfully in possession of a firearm that he had placed on the floor of the car.

The district court found, and the majority agrees, that the car's passengers were seized the moment the police cars pulled up next to and behind the parked car. From that moment, the passengers could not have felt free to walk away.

II

This was not a reasonable seizure. It cannot be justified as the constitutional equivalent of an officer strolling up to a parked car to see if the driver or passengers are willing to chat. The passengers in the car were seized, and in a sudden, terrifying, and unjustified way. Absent the most extraordinary circumstances, these intrusions on privacy and restraints on liberty—by police officers looking for "bigger and better things"—simply are not justifiable to write a parking ticket. And the government has not argued for any other ground to justify this seizure.

There are two distinct grounds for reversal here. The first is that the doctrines allowing pretextual traffic stops under the combination of *Terry* and *Whren* should not be extended to mere parking violations. The second and narrower ground is that even if such an extension might be available in theory, the police did not have a reasonable basis for this particular seizure.

On the first ground for reversal, the Supreme Court itself has not gone so far as to allow seizure of a person to investigate a possible parking violation. The core Fourth Amendment standard of reasonableness is what drove the balance between privacy and law enforcement in *Terry*. Extending *Terry* and *Whren* to allow police to use a mere parking violation as a pretext for seizing a car's passengers, and then using the occasion to remove them and handcuff them, loses sight of reasonableness and proportion.

Terry authorizes investigatory stops without a warrant when a police officer has a reasonable suspicion that a person is engaged or is about to engage in crime. The logic of *Terry* has been understood to authorize traffic stops for moving violations. Since *Whren*, Fourth Amendment law allows the police to carry out intrusive traffic stops based on the pretext of investigating a moving traffic violation.

This combination of constitutional decisions already enables a host of aggressive and intrusive police tactics. Police officers are trained to exploit those powers, as the officers tried to do here in their search for "bigger and better things." Officers who have probable cause for a trivial traffic violation can stop the car under *Whren* and then order all occupants out of the car, often question them in an intimidating way, visually inspect the interior of the car, often search at least portions of the vehicle's interior, and hold the driver and passengers while a drug-detection dog inspects the vehicle.

In these encounters, the danger of further escalation is always present. With authority to stop comes the authority to require the subject to submit to the stop, and to use reasonable force in doing so. The Fourth Amendment also allows police to arrest suspects for minor traffic infractions even if a court could impose only a fine, and arrested persons can be strip-searched, fingerprinted, photographed, and perhaps even subjected to a DNA test. Moreover, a *Terry* stop can even be justified by an officer's mistake of either law or fact.

Adding these doctrines together gives the police broad discretion to impose severe intrusions on the privacy and freedom of civilians going about their business. This potential is not entirely new. In 1940, the future Justice Jackson said: "We know that no local police force can strictly enforce the traffic laws, or it would arrest half the driving population on any given morning." R. Jackson, The Federal Prosecutor, Address Delivered at the Second Annual Conference of United States Attorneys, April 1, 1940, quoted in *Morrison v. Olson* (1988) (Scalia, J., dissenting); *see also, e.g.,* David A. Sklansky, Traffic Stops, Minority Motorists, and the Future of the Fourth Amendment, 1997 Sup. Ct. Rev. 271, 273 ("Since virtually everyone violates traffic laws at least occasionally, the upshot of these decisions is that police officers, if they are patient, can eventually pull over almost anyone they choose, order the driver and all passengers out of the car, and then ask for permission to search the vehicle without first making clear the detention is over.").

Courts usually examine these aspects of Fourth Amendment doctrine piecemeal, focusing on the one or two aspects most salient for the particular case. But when we consider a significant extension of Fourth Amendment authority, such as extending *Terry* and *Whren* to suspected parking violations, we must consider the cumulative effects of the doctrine. Those effects mean that authority to conduct an investigatory stop can trigger sweeping intrusions and even dangers. See Devon W. Carbado, From Stopping Black People to Killing Black People: The Fourth Amendment Pathways to Police Violence, 105 Calif. L. Rev. 125 (2017) (reviewing cumulative effects); Gabriel J. Chin & Charles J. Vernon, Reasonable but Unconstitutional: Racial Profiling and the Radical Objectivity of *Whren v. United States*, 83 Geo. Wash. L. Rev. 882, 884 n.2 (2015) (collecting literature on consequences of *Whren*).

The government's theory here is that the suspected parking violation justified the seizure of the passengers. The government sees no difference between parking violations and suspected traffic violations, so that all the police tactics permitted in a pretextual traffic stop under *Whren* can be used when a car might be parked illegally.

Relevant case law is both sparse and divided, perhaps because the notion of using such aggressive police tactics in response to parking violations seems so audacious. As noted, the Supreme Court has not extended these powers to the parking context. It should not do so, particularly with an eye toward practical consequences, including whether the cumulative effects of Fourth Amendment doctrine are reasonable and whether such intrusions may become "a routine part of American life."

In *United States v. Thornton* (7th Cir. 1999), two officers in a "high crime" neighborhood walked toward a car parked in a no-parking zone. They saw the driver get out of the car with what looked like a police-radio scanner. The officers patted down the driver and spotted what looked like a package of cocaine on the floor of the back seat. We said that whether "an illegally parked car, a crime-ridden neighborhood, the driver's sudden exit, and the driver's possession of a device that was monitoring police radio traffic adds up to sufficient suspicion to justify a *Terry* stop is a close call." In this case, by contrast, the police had much less to go on than the police had with that "close call" in *Thornton*. And the police tactics here were much more intrusive than walking up to the car, as in *Thornton*.

In *United States v. Shields* (7th Cir. 2015), the panel treated a parking violation as enough to support an investigatory *Terry* stop, though the real action in *Shields* concerned the driver's decision to flee from the officers.

These extensions of *Terry* to suspected parking violations remain few in number and are mistaken when there is no additional basis for the seizure. And at least two state supreme courts have taken a different view of the Fourth Amendment. See *State v. Duncan* (2002) (*Terry* did not extend to seizure to investigate suspected civil infractions such as possession of open container of alcohol in public); *State v. Holmes* (Minn. 1997) (*Terry* did not authorize seizure to investigate suspected parking violation). An illegally parked car is a far cry from the would-be robbers casing their target in *Terry v. Ohio*.

Extending *Terry* stops and the further intrusions they entail to pretextual parking violations loses sight of the core test of reasonableness and the balance at the core of *Terry* and the Fourth Amendment itself. "The makers of our Constitution . . . conferred, as against the Government, the right to be let alone — the most comprehensive of rights and the right most valued by civilized men. To protect that right, every unjustifiable intrusion by the Government upon the privacy of the individual, whatever the means employed, must be deemed a violation of the Fourth Amendment." We should find a violation of the Fourth Amendment in the unreasonable and intrusive seizure of the passengers in this case for the supposed purpose of investigating this parking violation.

III

Extending *Terry* and *Whren* to real parking violations is bad enough. The seizure here had even less foundation because the police did not have a reasonable basis for suspecting a parking violation. That is the second and narrower ground for reversal here.

The police relied on a Wisconsin statute that provides:

> No person shall stop or leave any vehicle standing in any of the following places except temporarily for the purpose of and while actually engaged in loading or unloading or in receiving or discharging passengers and while the vehicle is attended by a licensed operator so that it may promptly be moved in case of an emergency or to avoid obstruction of traffic:
>
> (1) In a loading zone.
> (2) In an alley in a business district.
> (3) Within 10 feet of a fire hydrant, unless a greater distance is indicated by an official traffic sign.
> (4) Within 4 feet of the entrance to an alley or a private road or driveway.
> (5) Closer than 15 feet to the near limits of a cross-walk.
> (6) Upon any portion of a highway where and at the time when parking is prohibited, limited or restricted by official traffic signs.

Wis. Stat. § 346.53.

The seized car and passengers could stand lawfully where they were if the car was there "temporarily for the purpose of and while actually engaged in loading or unloading or in receiving or discharging passengers and while the vehicle is attended by a licensed operator." That was all the police saw here: the driver had gone into a store, and the motor was running.

A car stopped in front of a store with its motor running is not itself suspicious. Given the sensible statutory proviso for cars that are loading and unloading, the police here could not reasonably decide, in the few seconds it took them to swoop in to seize this car and its passengers, that this seizure was justified.

Yet the majority treats what the police saw as suspicious enough to justify the seizure. That rationale overlooks the statute itself, which of course does not require the driver to "occupy" the car while loading or unloading. It requires only that the car be "attended" so it can be moved if needed. At the risk of stating the obvious, a driver making deliveries and pick-ups will not always occupy the vehicle, but he or she may "attend" it for these purposes.

To avoid the logic of the provision for loading and unloading, the majority cites cases from quite different contexts where police officers who receive conflicting information can make arrests and "leave to the judicial process the question whether a defense applies."

The majority's treatment of the loading-and-unloading proviso bears no practical relationship to reality or to what happened here on the streets of Milwaukee. Imagine that the police tried these tactics in Milwaukee's affluent east side. Citizens would be up in arms, and rightly so. No police officer could expect to keep his job if he treated a car standing in front of a store as worthy of such an intrusive *Terry* stop. The government's theory—that the seizure of a stopped car by the police would be justified because the occupants could always explain in court that they had merely stopped the car to make a purchase—invites intolerable intrusions on people just going about their business.

We have rejected similar efforts to authorize stops on grounds that would apply to a high proportion of people engaged in lawful behavior.

What made the officers decide so fast to swoop in to seize this car? On this record, the only explanation is the neighborhood, and the correlation with race is obvious. It is true that Johnson has not made an issue of race, but we should not close our eyes to the fact that this seizure and these tactics would never be tolerated in other communities and neighborhoods. If we tolerate these heavy-handed tactics here, we enable tactics that breed anger and resentment, and perhaps worse, toward the police.

Defendant Johnson is not a sympathetic champion of the Fourth Amendment, of course. That is not unusual in Fourth Amendment litigation. But the practical dangers of the majority's extension of *Terry* and *Whren* to suspected parking violations will sweep broadly. Who among us can say we have never overstayed a parking meter or parked a little too close to a crosswalk? We enforce the Fourth Amendment not for the sake of criminals but for the sake of everyone else who might be swept up by such intrusive and unjustified police tactics. I respectfully dissent.

NOTES AND QUESTIONS

1. Is there any doubt that the police had already figured out who was in, or at least who owned, the car before they pulled up and blocked it?

2. Why does the Court address the race of the car's occupants?

3. Is there a meaningful distinction between *Johnson* and *Whren*? What is the best argument as to why this sort of parking violation should be treated differently for *Terry* purposes than the sort of D.C. traffic code violations at issue on *Whren*? What is the best counter-argument?

4. The Court says the district court's finding that "the way in which the stop was conducted was not responsible for the gun's discovery" was not clearly erroneous. Do you agree?

5. Recall the limitation in *Terry* itself that both the search and seizure must be "reasonably related in scope to the circumstances which justified the interference in the first place." 392 U.S. at 20. Was the seizure here reasonably related to the parking violation that "justified it in the first place?" Was the search?

Professor Seo points out that automobile travel is the ultimate paradox of American culture. On the one hand, the car and the road—the "open road"—are icons of American freedom and imagination. On the other hand, an American in a car on the road is subject to a level of police scrutiny associated with repressive states. Seo, Policing the Open Road, *supra* at 159. For Black people and other minorities the term "paradox" here is misleading, as they have never been allowed to be full participants in the "American dream" half of the equation. As Nancy Leong describes it:

> American culture is steeped in the mythology of the open road. In our collective imagination, the road represents freedom, escape, friendship, romance, and above all, the possibility for a better life. But our shared dream of the open road comes to a halt in the mundane reality of the traffic stop—a judicially authorized policing procedure in which an officer may pull over a vehicle if she has cause to believe the driver has committed even the most minor traffic violation. . . . The traffic stop, I conclude, interrupts the open road narrative closely associated with the American dream. Those stopped most frequently—in particular, racial minorities—are consequently denied full participation in an abiding national fantasy.

Nancy Leong, *The Open Road and the Traffic Stop: Narratives and Counter Narratives of the American Dream*, 64 Fla. L. Rev. 305, 305 (2012).

Traffic stop reform may finally be afoot. Perhaps due to publicized shootings and other casualties of Black persons in connection with traffic stops (Philando Castile, Sandra Bland, Tyre Nichols, and others) many states and other jurisdictions are questioning whether the nation's 20 million traffic stops a year are worth the candle. Two states (Virginia and Oregon), four cities (Seattle, Philadelphia, Los Angeles, and Berkeley), and one county (Mecklenburg County, North Carolina) have adopted policies limiting traffic stops for minor infractions. A systematic study of stops in Fayetteville, North Carolina, found what would undoubtedly be true across the board. Traffic stops do not advance their ulterior law enforcement agenda (or at most do so inefficiently): just 3 percent of stops lead to search, only 20 percent of searches lead to the discovery of contraband, and only 50 percent of contraband discoveries result in an arrest—in short, just .3 percent of stops lead to an arrest. The same study also showed that Black drivers were three times more likely than white drivers to be searched after a stop. *See* Low-Level Traffic Stops Are Ineffective—And Sometimes Deadly. Why Are They Still Happening?, Vera Institute (Mar. 29, 2023).

Alternatively, would policing collapse if a warrant were required for a vehicle search after a traffic stop? The technology exists in many jurisdictions whereby an officer could apply for a warrant electronically from his vehicle and receive an answer within minutes. Oren Bar-Gill & Barry Friedman, *Taking Warrants Seriously*, 106 Nw. U. L. Rev. 1609, 1658-59 (2012). The obvious benefits to such a requirement would be that officers would go to the trouble only when they believed it truly necessary, and not as a matter of course or as a fishing expedition; that factual disputes about probable cause would be decreased; and that motorists would not be bullied into consenting to searches because they thought they had to.

Would this work? And at what cost to law enforcement? Professors Friedman and Bar-Gill make the following observations, comparing traffic stop data between Los Angeles and Pittsburgh while the latter was operating under a Department of Justice consent decree (*see* Chapter VI *infra*) that imposed quasi-warrant requirements for traffic stops:

> Comparing two jurisdictions in which traffic-stop data exists, there is evidence that a stringent ex ante warrant model can have a strong self-screening effect. While the total search rate in L.A. was 0.053 per capita, in Pittsburgh it was only 0.006 per capita. Why does the LAPD search almost ten times as often? One possible answer is that the Pittsburgh consent decree imposed a near-warrant level requirement on searches and seizures. Pittsburgh police officers were required to record every search and seizure in elaborate detail, including the location, basis

of the search, type of search conducted (warrantless, consent, etc.), demographic information about the search subject, and a description of what was searched. Subjects could only consent to searches after signing an officer's written form explaining their right to refuse.

Pittsburgh's decree monitors understood the impact of the consent decree, writing, "[S]upervisors and officers told us that officers were hesitant to conduct searches and to use force since the consent decree was signed. Of course, care in conducting searches and in the use of force was one of the goals of the decree." Our comparative data affirm these assessments: Pittsburgh's policing reforms resulted in fewer searches, as compared to other jurisdictions. Pittsburgh was performing about half as many total (auto and pedestrian) searches per capita than other jurisdictions were conducting per capita in the traffic-stop setting alone. What Part [this] suggests in theory seems to be borne out in practice: requiring officers to make a written justification makes a massive empirical difference. When the justification needs to be submitted to a magistrate, the difference might be even greater.

Although there may be reason to doubt the sharp difference between Los Angeles and Pittsburgh, if this difference is at all correct, then excluding arrests, the number of additional warrants required would be one-tenth, or roughly one million warrants. The two cities may be extremes on a continuum. Los Angeles officials may search more often than in most places. Pittsburgh officers may not have recorded all of their searches. Still, the data suggest a sharp decrease from our original estimate in the number of warrants needed under the permission model.

It also is interesting to note that despite the decrease in searches, police performance in Pittsburgh did not substantially deteriorate during the consent decree. Police morale was unaffected and crime rates, including homicides, either stayed the same or continued to steadily decrease. Officer activity on traffic-related matters remained relatively unchanged, and while felony clearance rates initially decreased, the rates bounced back to pre-decree levels towards the end of the decree. There is insufficient evidence to assess whether the Pittsburgh consent decree resulted in an overall increase or decrease in social welfare. But clearly the criminal justice system did not collapse or even suffer in any notable way.

Id. at 1667-68.

CHAPTER V

THE EXCLUSIONARY RULE, ITS EXCEPTIONS, AND SUPPRESSION HEARINGS

This chapter considers the exclusionary rule, once the glory of the Warren Court criminal procedure revolution, and its gradual erosion over the ensuing decades. Section A briefly introduces the rule itself, and the subsequent sections take on the most important exceptions: the good faith exception (Section B), the attenuation doctrine (Section C), standing (Section D), and impeachment (Section E). Section F looks at suppression hearings, the judicial proceedings in which motions to suppress evidence are litigated — that is, the court hearings in which defense counsel seeks to exclude evidence. This section pays particular attention to the problem of police perjury, or "testilying," a phenomenon that some judges and commentators have attributed to the advent of *Mapp v. Ohio* and its requirement that state courts exclude illegally obtained evidence.

A. THE EXCLUSIONARY RULE

As originally conceived as a matter of federal constitutional law, the exclusionary rule was seen as an inherent part of the Fourth Amendment, without which the constitutional guarantee would be a nullity. *See Weeks v. United States*, 232 U.S. 383, 393 (1914) ("If [illegally acquired materials can be] used in evidence against a citizen accused of an offense, the protection of the Fourth Amendment declaring his right to be secure against such searches and seizures is of no value, and, so far as those thus placed are concerned, might as well be stricken from the Constitution."); *Silverthorne Lumber Co. v. United States*, 251 U.S. 385, 392 (1920) ("The essence of a provision forbidding the acquisition of evidence in a certain way is that not merely evidence so acquired shall not be used before the Court but that it shall not be used at all.").

That premise went unquestioned in federal criminal prosecutions for decades. When the Court first applied the Fourth Amendment to the states, however, it decoupled the right from the remedy. In *Wolf v. Colorado*, 338 U.S. 25 (1949), the Court held that while the Fourth Amendment's substance applied to the states — via its incorporation — the Court declined to also apply the exclusionary rule remedy. The Court overruled that aspect of *Wolf* 12 years later in *Mapp v. Ohio*, 367 U.S. 643 (1961). The Court noted, among other things, that alternative state law remedies for enforcing the Fourth Amendment had proven ineffective and that the "imperative of judicial integrity" required the result. Echoing *Weeks*, it held that without the exclusionary rule the Fourth Amendment would only be a "valueless" "form of words."

Mapp v. Ohio
367 U.S. 643 (1961)

Mr. Justice CLARK delivered the opinion of the Court.

Appellant stands convicted of knowingly having had in her possession and under her control certain lewd and lascivious books, pictures, and photographs in violation of § 2905.34 of Ohio's Revised Code. As officially stated in the syllabus to its opinion, the Supreme Court of Ohio found that her conviction was valid though "based primarily upon the introduction in evidence of lewd and lascivious books and pictures unlawfully seized during an unlawful search of defendant's home. . . ."

On May 23, 1957, three Cleveland police officers arrived at appellant's residence in that city pursuant to information that "a person (was) hiding out in the home, who was wanted for questioning in connection with a recent bombing, and that there was a large amount of policy paraphernalia being hidden in the home." Miss Mapp and her daughter by a former marriage lived on the top floor of the two-family dwelling. Upon their arrival at that house, the officers knocked on the door and demanded entrance but appellant, after telephoning her attorney, refused to admit them without a search warrant. They advised their headquarters of the situation and undertook a surveillance of the house.

The officers again sought entrance some three hours later when four or more additional officers arrived on the scene. When Miss Mapp did not come to the door immediately, at least one of the several doors to the house was forcibly opened and the policemen gained admittance. Meanwhile Miss Mapp's attorney arrived, but the officers, having secured their own entry, and continuing in their defiance of the law, would permit him neither to see Miss Mapp nor to enter the house. It appears that Miss Mapp was halfway down the stairs from the upper floor to the front door when the officers, in this highhanded manner, broke into the hall. She demanded to see the search warrant. A paper, claimed to be a warrant, was held up by one of the officers. She grabbed the "warrant" and placed it in her bosom. A struggle ensued in which the officers recovered the piece of paper and as a result of which they hand-cuffed appellant because she had been "belligerent" in resisting their official rescue of the "warrant" from her person. Running roughshod over appellant, a policeman "grabbed" her, "twisted (her) hand," and she "yelled (and) pleaded with him" because "it was hurting." Appellant, in handcuffs, was then forcibly taken upstairs to her bedroom where the officers searched a dresser, a chest of drawers, a closet and some suitcases. They also looked into a photo album and through personal papers belonging to the appellant. The search spread to the rest of the second floor including the child's bedroom, the living room, the kitchen and a dinette. The basement of the building and a trunk found therein were also searched. The obscene materials for possession of which she was ultimately convicted were discovered in the course of that widespread search.

At the trial no search warrant was produced by the prosecution, nor was the failure to produce one explained or accounted for. At best, "There is, in the record, considerable doubt as to whether there ever was any warrant for the search of defendant's home." The Ohio Supreme Court believed a "reasonable argument" could be made that the conviction should be reversed "because the methods employed to obtain the (evidence) were such as to 'offend "a sense of justice,"'" but the court found determinative the fact that the evidence had not been taken "from defendant's person by the use of brutal or offensive physical force against defendant."

The State says that even if the search were made without authority, or otherwise unreasonably, it is not prevented from using the unconstitutionally seized evidence at trial, citing *Wolf*, in which this Court did indeed hold "that in a prosecution in a State court for a State crime the Fourteenth Amendment does not forbid the admission of evidence obtained by an unreasonable search and seizure." On this appeal, of which we have noted probable jurisdiction, it is urged once again that we review that holding.

I

Seventy-five years ago, in *Boyd v. United States*, considering the Fourth and Fifth Amendments as running "almost into each other" on the facts before it, this Court held that the doctrines of those Amendments

> apply to all invasions on the part of the government and its employees of the sanctity of a man's home and the privacies of life. It is not the breaking of his doors, and the rummaging of his drawers, that constitutes the essence of the offence; but it is the invasion of his indefeasible right of personal security, personal liberty and private property. . . . Breaking into a house and opening boxes and drawers are circumstances of aggravation; but any forcible and compulsory extortion of a man's own testimony or of his private papers to be used as evidence to convict him of crime or to forfeit his goods, is within the condemnation . . . (of those Amendments).

The Court noted that

> constitutional provisions for the security of person and property should be liberally construed. . . . It is the duty of courts to be watchful for the constitutional rights of the citizen, and against any stealthy encroachments thereon.

In this jealous regard for maintaining the integrity of individual rights, the Court gave life to Madison's prediction that "independent tribunals of justice . . . will be naturally led to resist every encroachment upon rights expressly stipulated for in the Constitution by the declaration of rights." Concluding, the Court specifically referred to the use of the evidence there seized as "unconstitutional."

Less than 30 years after *Boyd*, this Court, in *Weeks v. United States*, stated that

> the 4th Amendment . . . put the courts of the United States and Federal officials, in the exercise of their power and authority, under limitations and restraints (and) . . . forever secure(d) the people, their persons, houses, papers, and effects, against all unreasonable searches and seizures under the guise of law . . . and the duty of giving to it force and effect is obligatory upon all entrusted under our Federal system with the enforcement of the laws.

Specifically dealing with the use of the evidence unconstitutionally seized, the Court concluded:

> If letters and private documents can thus be seized and held and used in evidence against a citizen accused of an offense, the protection of the Fourth Amendment declaring his right to be secure against such searches and seizures is of no value, and, so far as those thus placed are concerned, might as well be stricken from the Constitution. The efforts of the courts and their officials to bring the guilty to punishment, praiseworthy as they are, are not to be aided by the sacrifice of those great principles established by years of endeavor and suffering which have resulted in their embodiment in the fundamental law of the land.

Finally, the Court in that case clearly stated that use of the seized evidence involved "a denial of the constitutional rights of the accused." Thus, in the year 1914, in the *Weeks* case, this Court "for the first time" held that "in a federal prosecution the Fourth Amendment barred the use of evidence secured through an illegal search and seizure." This Court has ever since required of federal law officers a strict adherence to that command which this Court has held to be a clear, specific, and constitutionally required — even if judicially implied — deterrent safeguard without insistence upon which the Fourth Amendment would have been reduced to "a form of words." It meant, quite simply, that "conviction by means of unlawful seizures and enforced confessions . . . should find no sanction in the judgments of the courts . . .," *Weeks v. United States, supra*, and that such evidence "shall not be used at all."

There are in the cases of this Court some passing references to the *Weeks* rule as being one of evidence. But the plain and unequivocal language of *Weeks*—and its later paraphrase in *Wolf*—to the effect that the *Weeks* rule is of constitutional origin, remains entirely undisturbed. In *Byars v. United States*, a unanimous Court declared that "the doctrine (cannot) . . . be tolerated under our constitutional system, that evidences of crime discovered by a federal officer in making a search without lawful warrant may be used against the victim of the unlawful search where a timely challenge has been interposed." The Court, in *Olmstead v. United States*, in unmistakable language restated the *Weeks* rule:

> The striking outcome of the *Weeks* case and those which followed it was the sweeping declaration that the Fourth Amendment, although not referring to or limiting the use of evidence in court, really forbade its introduction if obtained by government officers through a violation of the amendment.

In *McNabb v. United States*, we note this statement:

> (A) conviction in the federal courts, the foundation of which is evidence obtained in disregard of liberties deemed fundamental by the Constitution, cannot stand. *Boyd v. United States . . . Weeks v. United States.* . . . And this Court has, on Constitutional grounds, set aside convictions, both in the federal and state courts, which were based upon confessions "secured by protracted and repeated questioning of ignorant and untutored persons, in whose minds the power of officers was greatly magnified" or "who have been unlawfully held incommunicado without advice of friends or counsel". . . .

Significantly, in *McNabb*, the Court did then pass on to formulate a rule of evidence, saying, "(i)n the view we take of the case, however, it becomes unnecessary to reach the Constitutional issue (for) . . . (t)he principles governing the admissibility of evidence in federal criminal trials have not been restricted . . . to those derived solely from the Constitution."

II

In 1949, 35 years after *Weeks* was announced, this Court, in *Wolf* again for the first time, discussed the effect of the Fourth Amendment upon the States through the operation of the Due Process Clause of the Fourteenth Amendment. It said:

> (W)e have no hesitation in saying that were a State affirmatively to sanction such police incursion into privacy it would run counter to the guaranty of the Fourteenth Amendment.

Nevertheless, after declaring that the "security of one's privacy against arbitrary intrusion by the police" is "implicit in 'the concept of ordered liberty' and as such enforceable against the States through the Due Process Clause," and announcing that it "stoutly adhere(d)" to the *Weeks* decision, the Court decided that the *Weeks* exclusionary rule would not then be imposed upon the States as "an essential ingredient of the right." The Court's reasons for not considering essential to the right to privacy, as a curb imposed upon the States by the Due Process Clause, that which decades before had been posited as part and parcel of the Fourth Amendment's limitations upon federal encroachment of individual privacy, were bottomed on factual considerations.

While they are not basically relevant to a decision that the exclusionary rule is an essential ingredient of the Fourth Amendment as the right it embodies is vouchsafed against the States by the Due Process Clause, we will consider the current validity of the factual grounds upon which *Wolf* was based.

The Court in *Wolf* first stated that "(t)he contrariety of views of the States" on the adoption of the exclusionary rule of *Weeks* was "particularly impressive" and, in this connection that it could not "brush aside the experience of States which deem the incidence of such conduct by the police too slight to call for a deterrent remedy . . . by overriding the (States') relevant rules of evidence." While in 1949, prior to the *Wolf* case, almost two-thirds of the States were opposed to the use of the exclusionary rule, now, despite the *Wolf* case, more than half of those since passing upon it, by their own legislative or judicial decision, have wholly or partly adopted or adhered to the *Weeks* rule. Significantly, among those now following the rule is California, which, according to its highest court, was "compelled to reach that conclusion because other remedies have completely failed to secure compliance with the constitutional provisions. . . ." In connection with this California case, we note that the second basis elaborated in *Wolf* in support of its failure to enforce the exclusionary doctrine against the States was that "other means of protection" have been afforded "the right to privacy." The experience of California that such other remedies have been worthless and futile is buttressed by the experience of other States. The obvious futility of relegating the Fourth Amendment of the protection of other remedies has, moreover, been recognized by this Court since *Wolf.*

Likewise, time has set its face against what *Wolf* called the "weighty testimony" of *People v. Defore.* There Justice (then Judge) Cardozo, rejecting adoption of the *Weeks* exclusionary rule in New York, had said that "(t)he Federal rule as it stands is either too strict or too lax." However, the force of that reasoning has been largely vitiated by later decisions of this Court. These include the recent discarding of the "silver platter" doctrine which allowed federal judicial use of evidence seized in violation of the Constitution by state agents, *Elkins v. United States, supra*; the relaxation of the formerly strict requirements as to standing to challenge the use of evidence thus seized, so that now the procedure of exclusion, "ultimately referable to constitutional safeguards," is available to anyone even "legitimately on (the) premises" unlawfully searched, *Jones v. United States*; and finally, the formulation of a method to prevent state use of evidence unconstitutionally seized by federal agents, *Rea v. United States.* Because there can be no fixed formula, we are admittedly met with "recurring questions of the reasonableness of searches," but less is not to be expected when dealing with a Constitution, and, at any rate, "(r)easonableness is in the first instance for the (trial court) to determine."

It, therefore, plainly appears that the factual considerations supporting the failure of the *Wolf* Court to include the *Weeks* exclusionary rule when it recognized the enforceability of the right to privacy against the States in 1949, while not basically relevant to the constitutional consideration, could not, in any analysis, now be deemed controlling.

III

Some five years after *Wolf*, in answer to a plea made here Term after Term that we overturn its doctrine on applicability of the *Weeks* exclusionary rule, this Court indicated that such should not be done until the States had "adequate opportunity to adopt or reject the (*Weeks*) rule." *Irvine v. People of State of California*, supra. There again it was said:

> Never until June of 1949 did this Court hold the basic search-and-seizure prohibition in any way applicable to the states under the Fourteenth Amendment.

And only last Term, after again carefully re-examining the *Wolf* doctrine in *Elkins* the Court pointed out that "the controlling principles" as to search and seizure and the problem of admissibility "seemed clear" until the announcement in *Wolf* "that the Due Process Clause of the Fourteenth Amendment does not itself require state courts to adopt the exclusionary rule" of the *Weeks* case. At the same time, the Court pointed out, "the underlying constitutional doctrine which *Wolf* established . . . that the Federal Constitution . . . prohibits unreasonable searches and seizures by state officers" had undermined the "foundation upon which the admissibility of state seized evidence in a federal trial originally rested. . . ." The Court concluded that it was therefore obliged to hold, although it chose the narrower ground on which to do so, that all evidence obtained by an unconstitutional search and seizure was inadmissible in a federal court regardless of its source. Today we once again examine *Wolf*'s constitutional documentation of the right to privacy free from unreasonable state intrusion, and, after its dozen years on our books, are led by it to close the only courtroom door remaining open to evidence secured by official lawlessness in flagrant abuse of that basic right, reserved to all persons as a specific guarantee against that very same unlawful conduct. We hold that all evidence obtained by searches and seizures in violation of the Constitution is, by that same authority, inadmissible in a state court.

IV

Since the Fourth Amendment's right of privacy has been declared enforceable against the States through the Due Process Clause of the Fourteenth, it is enforceable against them by the same sanction of exclusion as is used against the Federal Government. Were it otherwise, then just as without the Weeks rule the assurance against unreasonable federal searches and seizures would be "a form of words" valueless and undeserving of mention in a perpetual charter of inestimable human liberties, so too, without that rule the freedom from state invasions of privacy would be so ephemeral and so neatly severed from its conceptual nexus with the freedom from all brutish means of coercing evidence as not to merit this Court's high regard as a freedom "implicit in the concept of ordered liberty." At the time that the Court held in *Wolf* that the Amendment was applicable to the States through the Due Process Clause, the cases of this Court, as we have seen, had steadfastly held that as to federal officers the Fourth Amendment included the exclusion of the evidence seized in violation of its provisions. Even *Wolf* "stoutly adhered" to that proposition. The right to privacy, when conceded operatively enforceable against the States, was not susceptible of destruction by avulsion of the sanction upon which its protection and enjoyment had always been deemed dependent under the *Boyd*, *Weeks* and *Silverthorne* cases. Therefore, in extending the substantive protections of due process to all constitutionally unreasonable searches — state or federal — it was logically and constitutionally necessary that the exclusion doctrine — an essential part of the right to privacy — be also insisted upon as an essential ingredient of the right newly recognized by the *Wolf* case. In short, the admission of the new constitutional right by *Wolf* could not consistently tolerate denial of its most important constitutional privilege, namely, the exclusion of the evidence which an accused had been forced to give by reason of the unlawful seizure. To hold otherwise is to grant the right but in reality to withhold its privilege and enjoyment. Only last year the Court itself recognized that the purpose of the exclusionary rule "is to deter — to compel respect for the constitutional guaranty in the only effectively available way — by removing the incentive to disregard it."

Indeed, we are aware of no restraint, similar to that rejected today, conditioning the enforcement of any other basic constitutional right. The right to privacy, no less important than any other right carefully and particularly reserved to the people, would stand in marked contrast to all other rights declared as "basic to a free society." This Court has not hesitated to enforce as strictly against the States as it does against the Federal Government the rights of free speech and of a free press, the rights to notice and to a fair, public trial, including, as it does, the right not to be convicted by use of a coerced confession, however logically relevant it be, and without regard to its reliability. And nothing could be more certain that that when a coerced confession is involved, "the relevant rules of evidence" are overridden without regard to "the incidence of such conduct by the police," slight or frequent. Why should not the same rule apply to what is tantamount to coerced testimony by way of unconstitutional seizure of goods, papers, effect, documents, etc.? We find that, as to the Federal Government, the Fourth and Fifth Amendments and, as to the States, the freedom from unconscionable invasions of privacy and the freedom from convictions based upon coerced confessions do enjoy an "intimate relation" in their perpetuation of "principles of humanity and civil liberty (secured) . . . only after years of struggle." They express "supplementing phases of the same constitutional purpose—to maintain inviolate large areas of personal privacy." The philosophy of each Amendment and of each freedom is complementary to, although not dependent upon, that of the other in its sphere of influence—the very least that together they assure in either sphere is that no man is to be convicted on unconstitutional evidence.

V

Moreover, our holding that the exclusionary rule is an essential part of both the Fourth and Fourteenth Amendments is not only the logical dictate of prior cases, but it also makes very good sense. There is no war between the Constitution and common sense. Presently, a federal prosecutor may make no use of evidence illegally seized, but a State's attorney across the street may, although he supposedly is operating under the enforceable prohibitions of the same Amendment. Thus the State, by admitting evidence unlawfully seized, serves to encourage disobedience to the Federal Constitution which it is bound to uphold. Moreover, as was said in *Elkins*, "(t)he very essence of a healthy federalism depends upon the avoidance of needless conflict between state and federal courts." Such a conflict, hereafter needless, arose this very Term, in *Wilson v. Schnettler*, in which, and in spite of the promise made by *Rea*, we gave full recognition to our practice in this regard by refusing to restrain a federal officer from testifying in a state court as to evidence unconstitutionally seized by him in the performance of his duties. Yet the double standard recognized until today hardly put such a thesis into practice. In non-exclusionary States, federal officers, being human, were by it invited to and did, as our cases indicate, step across the street to the State's attorney with their unconstitutionally seized evidence. Prosecution on the basis of that evidence was then had in a state court in utter disregard of the enforceable Fourth Amendment. If the fruits of an unconstitutional search had been inadmissible in both state and federal courts, this inducement to evasion would have been sooner eliminated. There would be no need to reconcile such cases as *Rea* and *Schnettler*, each pointing up the hazardous uncertainties of our heretofore ambivalent approach.

Federal-state cooperation in the solution of crime under constitutional standards will be promoted, if only by recognition of their now mutual obligation to respect the same fundamental criteria in their approaches. "However much in a particular case insistence upon such rules may appear as a technicality that inures to the benefit of a guilty person, the history of the criminal law proves that tolerance of shortcut methods in law enforcement impairs its enduring effectiveness." Denying shortcuts to only one of two cooperating law enforcement agencies tends naturally to breed legitimate suspicion of "working arrangements" whose results are equally tainted.

There are those who say, as did Justice (then Judge) Cardozo, that under our constitutional exclusionary doctrine "(t)he criminal is to go free because the constable has blundered." In some cases this will undoubtedly be the result. But, as was said in *Elkins*, "there is another consideration—the imperative of judicial integrity." The criminal goes free, if he must, but it is the law that sets him free. Nothing can destroy a government more quickly than its failure to observe its own laws, or worse, its disregard of the charter of its own existence. As Mr. Justice Brandeis, dissenting, said in *Olmstead v. United States*: "Our government is the potent, the omnipresent teacher. For good or for ill, it teaches the whole people by its example. . . . If the government becomes a lawbreaker, it breeds contempt for law; it invites every man to become a law unto himself; it invites anarchy." Nor can it lightly be assumed that, as a practical matter, adoption of the exclusionary rule fetters law enforcement. Only last year this Court expressly considered that contention and found that "pragmatic evidence of a sort" to the contrary was not wanting. The Court noted that

> The federal courts themselves have operated under the exclusionary rule of *Weeks* for almost half a century; yet it has not been suggested either that the Federal Bureau of Investigation has thereby been rendered ineffective, or that the administration of criminal justice in the federal courts has thereby been disrupted. Moreover, the experience of the states is impressive.... The movement towards the rule of exclusion has been halting but seemingly inexorable.

The ignoble shortcut to conviction left open to the State tends to destroy the entire system of constitutional restraints on which the liberties of the people rest. Having once recognized that the right to privacy embodied in the Fourth Amendment is enforceable against the States, and that the right to be secure against rude invasions of privacy by state officers is, therefore, constitutional in origin, we can no longer permit that right to remain an empty promise. Because it is enforceable in the same manner and to like effect as other basic rights secured by the Due Process Clause, we can no longer permit it to be revocable at the whim of any police officer who, in the name of law enforcement itself, chooses to suspend its enjoyment. Our decision, founded on reason and truth, gives to the individual no more than that which the Constitution guarantees him, to the police officer no less than that to which honest law enforcement is entitled, and, to the courts, that judicial integrity so necessary in the true administration of justice.

The judgment of the Supreme Court of Ohio is reversed and the cause remanded for further proceedings not inconsistent with this opinion.

NOTES AND QUESTIONS

Dollree Mapp

1. The Fourth Amendment violation here was particularly egregious. Cleveland police officers essentially broke into Dollree Mapp's home, lied to her about whether they had a search warrant, and arrested her when she demanded to see the warrant. Yet the Ohio Supreme Court, relying on *Wolf,* affirmed the conviction. The facts, of course, always matter. But does anything in the Supreme Court's opinion suggest that the invocation of the exclusionary rule depends on the egregiousness of the facts?

2. The Court notes Justice Cardozo's famous quip in opposition to the exclusionary rule, the logic of which he characterized as "the criminal is to go free because the constable has blundered." *People v. Defore*, 242 N.Y. 13, 21 (1926) (rejecting the exclusionary rule as a requirement in New York courts). The Court responds to this sentiment, a mainstay of exclusionary rule opponents, by making two related points: (a) it is the law that lets the criminal "go free," not the court; and (b) exclusion is required for the sake of "judicial integrity." In making this second point the Court relies on Justice Brandeis's dissent in *Olmstead v. United States*, 277 U.S. 438, 485 (1928), where he had dissented on the ground that the government's evidence was the product of illegal wiretapping.

Which of these two points is the more effective response to Justice Cardozo's quip?

3. The Court is sensitive to the fact that the decision in *Wolf,* which it overruled, was only 12 years old. It notes that whereas before *Wolf* two-thirds of the states were opposed to the exclusionary rule, by 1961 more than half of the states had wholly or partially adopted the rule by case law or legislation. It also singles out the experience of California, which had found that other, nonexclusionary remedies for Fourth Amendment violations had proven "worthless and futile." The leading role of two important state courts in *Mapp* is interesting: California, as an example for others to follow, and New York (through Justice Cardozo), as a relic to be left behind.

4. *Mapp* famously says that without the exclusionary rule the Fourth Amendment would be "valueless," and only "a form of words." The truth of the Court's statements about the centrality of the exclusionary rule to the Fourth Amendment was quickly proven. State police officials throughout the nation complained about the sea change inaugurated by *Mapp*, as if it had announced a new rule against illegal seizures and not simply a remedy. The New York City police commissioner described *Mapp* as a "tidal wave" and worried how his department could "implement" the decision.

The truth was, of course, that prior to *Mapp* state law enforcement had largely disregarded the requirements of the Fourth Amendment. *See* Yale Kamisar, Mapp v. Ohio*: The First Shot Fired in the Warren Court's Criminal Procedure Revolution*, in Criminal Procedure Stories 76-78 (Carol Steiker ed., 2006). In New York City the number of warrant applications increased from a handful before *Mapp* to 5,000 two years later. The theme was consistent nationwide. Warrants in Massachusetts were almost unknown before *Mapp*. They had also fallen into disuse in Philadelphia. *See* Sarah A. Seo, Policing the Open Road: How Cars Transformed American Freedom 197-98 (2019).

B. THE GOOD FAITH EXCEPTION

Hostility to *Mapp* eventually lead to erosion of the exclusionary rule, beginning with the "good faith exception" first established in the next case, *United States v. Leon*.

United States v. Leon
468 U.S. 897 (1984)

Justice WHITE delivered the opinion of the Court.

This case presents the question whether the Fourth Amendment exclusionary rule should be modified so as not to bar the use in the prosecution's case in chief of evidence obtained by officers acting in reasonable reliance on a search warrant issued by a detached and neutral magistrate but ultimately found to be unsupported by probable cause. To resolve this question, we must consider once again the tension between the sometimes competing goals of, on the one hand, deterring official misconduct and removing inducements to unreasonable invasions of privacy and, on the other, establishing procedures under which criminal defendants are "acquitted or convicted on the basis of all the evidence which exposes the truth."

I

In August 1981, a confidential informant of unproven reliability informed an officer of the Burbank Police Department that two persons known to him as "Armando" and "Patsy" were selling large quantities of cocaine and methaqualone from their residence at 620 Price Drive in Burbank, Cal. The informant also indicated that he had witnessed a sale of methaqualone by "Patsy" at the residence approximately five months earlier and had observed at that time a shoebox containing a large amount of cash that belonged to "Patsy." He further declared that "Armando" and "Patsy" generally kept only small quantities of drugs at their residence and stored the remainder at another location in Burbank.

On the basis of this information, the Burbank police initiated an extensive investigation focusing first on the Price Drive residence and later on two other residences as well. Cars parked at the Price Drive residence were determined to belong to respondents Armando Sanchez, who had previously been arrested for possession of marihuana, and Patsy Stewart, who had no criminal record. During the course of the investigation, officers observed an automobile belonging to respondent Ricardo Del Castillo, who had previously been arrested for possession of 50 pounds of marihuana, arrive at the Price Drive residence. The driver of that car entered the house, exited shortly thereafter carrying a small paper sack, and drove away. A check of Del Castillo's probation records led the officers to respondent Alberto Leon, whose telephone number Del Castillo had listed as his employer's. Leon had been arrested in 1980 on drug charges, and a companion had informed the police at that time that Leon was heavily involved in the importation of drugs into this country. Before the current investigation began, the Burbank officers had learned that an informant had told a Glendale police officer that Leon stored a large quantity of methaqualone at his residence in Glendale. During the course of this investigation, the Burbank officers learned that Leon was living at 716 South Sunset Canyon in Burbank.

Subsequently, the officers observed several persons, at least one of whom had prior drug involvement, arriving at the Price Drive residence and leaving with small packages; observed a variety of other material activity at the two residences as well as at a condominium at 7902 Via Magdalena; and witnessed a variety of relevant activity involving respondents' automobiles. The officers also observed respondents Sanchez and Stewart board separate flights for Miami. The pair later returned to Los Angeles together, consented to a search of their luggage that revealed only a small amount of marihuana, and left the airport. Based on these and other observations summarized in the affidavit, Officer Cyril Rombach of the Burbank Police Department, an experienced and well-trained narcotics investigator, prepared an application for a warrant to search 620 Price Drive, 716 South Sunset Canyon, 7902 Via Magdalena, and automobiles registered to each of the respondents for an extensive list of items believed to be related to respondents' drug-trafficking activities. Officer Rombach's extensive application was reviewed by several Deputy District Attorneys.

A facially valid search warrant was issued in September 1981 by a State Superior Court Judge. The ensuing searches produced large quantities of drugs at the Via Magdalena and Sunset Canyon addresses and a small quantity at the Price Drive residence. Other evidence was discovered at each of the residences and in Stewart's and Del Castillo's automobiles. Respondents were indicted by a grand jury in the District Court for the Central District of California and charged with conspiracy to possess and distribute cocaine and a variety of substantive counts.

The respondents then filed motions to suppress the evidence seized pursuant to the warrant. The District Court held an evidentiary hearing and, while recognizing that the case was a close one, granted the motions to suppress in part. It concluded that the affidavit was insufficient to establish probable cause, but did not suppress all of the evidence as to all of the respondents because none of the respondents had standing to challenge all of the searches. In response to a request from the Government, the court made clear that Officer Rombach had acted in good faith, but it rejected the Government's suggestion that the Fourth Amendment exclusionary rule should not apply where evidence is seized in reasonable, good-faith reliance on a search warrant.

The District Court denied the Government's motion for reconsideration, and a divided panel of the Court of Appeals for the Ninth Circuit affirmed. The Court of Appeals first concluded that Officer Rombach's affidavit could not establish probable cause to search the Price Drive residence. To the extent that the affidavit set forth facts demonstrating the basis of the informant's knowledge of criminal activity, the information included was fatally stale. The affidavit, moreover, failed to establish the informant's credibility. Accordingly, the Court of Appeals concluded that the information provided by the informant was inadequate under both prongs of the two-part test established in *Aguilar v. Texas* (1964), and *Spinelli v. United States* (1969). The officers' independent investigation neither cured the staleness nor corroborated the details of the informant's declarations. The Court of Appeals then considered whether the affidavit formed a proper basis for the search of the Sunset Canyon residence. In its view, the affidavit included no facts indicating the basis for the informants' statements concerning respondent Leon's criminal activities and was devoid of information establishing the informants' reliability. Because these deficiencies had not been cured by the police investigation, the District Court properly suppressed the fruits of the search. The Court of Appeals refused the Government's invitation to recognize a good-faith exception to the Fourth Amendment exclusionary rule.

The Government's petition for certiorari expressly declined to seek review of the lower courts' determinations that the search warrant was unsupported by probable cause and presented only the question "[w]hether the Fourth Amendment exclusionary rule should be modified so as not to bar the admission of evidence seized in reasonable, good-faith reliance on a search warrant that is subsequently held to be defective." We granted certiorari to consider the propriety of such a modification. Although it undoubtedly is within our power to consider the question whether probable cause existed under the "totality of the circumstances" test announced last Term in *Illinois v. Gates* (1983), that question has not been briefed or argued; and it is also within our authority, which we choose to exercise, to take the case as it comes to us, accepting the Court of Appeals' conclusion that probable cause was lacking under the prevailing legal standards.

We have concluded that, in the Fourth Amendment context, the exclusionary rule can be modified somewhat without jeopardizing its ability to perform its intended functions. Accordingly, we reverse the judgment of the Court of Appeals.

II

Language in opinions of this Court and of individual Justices has sometimes implied that the exclusionary rule is a necessary corollary of the Fourth Amendment, or that the rule is required by the conjunction of the Fourth and Fifth Amendments. These implications need not detain us long. The Fifth Amendment theory has not withstood critical analysis or the test of time, and the Fourth Amendment "has never been interpreted to proscribe the introduction of illegally seized evidence in all proceedings or against all persons."

A

The Fourth Amendment contains no provision expressly precluding the use of evidence obtained in violation of its commands, and an examination of its origin and purposes makes clear that the use of fruits of a past unlawful search or seizure "work[s] no new Fourth Amendment wrong." The wrong condemned by the Amendment is "fully accomplished" by the unlawful search or seizure itself, and the exclusionary rule is neither intended nor able to "cure the invasion of the defendant's rights which he has already suffered." The rule thus operates as "a judicially created remedy designed to safeguard Fourth Amendment rights generally through its deterrent effect, rather than a personal constitutional right of the party aggrieved."

Whether the exclusionary sanction is appropriately imposed in a particular case, our decisions make clear, is "an issue separate from the question whether the Fourth Amendment rights of the party seeking to invoke the rule were violated by police conduct." Only the former question is currently before us, and it must be resolved by weighing the costs and benefits of preventing the use in the prosecution's case in chief of inherently trustworthy tangible evidence obtained in reliance on a search warrant issued by a detached and neutral magistrate that ultimately is found to be defective.

The substantial social costs exacted by the exclusionary rule for the vindication of Fourth Amendment rights have long been a source of concern. "Our cases have consistently recognized that unbending application of the exclusionary sanction to enforce ideals of governmental rectitude would impede unacceptably the truth-finding functions of judge and jury. An objectionable collateral consequence of this interference with the criminal justice system's truth-finding function is that some guilty defendants may go free or receive reduced sentences as a result of favorable plea bargains. Particularly when law enforcement officers have acted in objective good faith or their transgressions have been minor, the magnitude of the benefit conferred on such guilty defendants offends basic concepts of the criminal justice system. Indiscriminate application of the exclusionary rule, therefore, may well "generat[e] disrespect for the law and administration of justice." Accordingly, "[a]s with any remedial device, the application of the rule has been restricted to those areas where its remedial objectives are thought most efficaciously served."

B

Close attention to those remedial objectives has characterized our recent decisions concerning the scope of the Fourth Amendment exclusionary rule. The Court has, to be sure, not seriously questioned, "in the absence of a more efficacious sanction, the continued application of the rule to suppress evidence from the [prosecution's] case where a Fourth Amendment violation has been substantial and deliberate. . . ." Nevertheless, the balancing approach that has evolved in various contexts — including criminal trials — "forcefully suggest[s] that the exclusionary rule be more generally modified to permit the introduction of evidence obtained in the reasonable good-faith belief that a search or seizure was in accord with the Fourth Amendment."

In *Stone v. Powell, supra*, the Court emphasized the costs of the exclusionary rule, expressed its view that limiting the circumstances under which Fourth Amendment claims could be raised in federal habeas corpus proceedings would not reduce the rule's deterrent effect, and held that a state prisoner who has been afforded a full and fair opportunity to litigate a Fourth Amendment claim may not obtain federal habeas relief on the ground that unlawfully obtained evidence had been introduced at his trial. Proposed extensions of the exclusionary rule to proceedings other than the criminal trial itself have been evaluated and rejected under the same analytic approach. In *United States v. Calandra*, for example, we declined to allow grand jury witnesses to refuse to answer questions based on evidence obtained from an unlawful search or seizure since "[a]ny incremental deterrent effect which might be achieved by extending the rule to grand jury proceedings is uncertain at best." Similarly, in *United States v. Janis*, supra, we permitted the use in federal civil proceedings of evidence illegally seized by state officials since the likelihood of deterring police misconduct through such an extension of the exclusionary rule was insufficient to outweigh its substantial social costs. In so doing, we declared that, "[i]f . . . the exclusionary rule does not result in appreciable deterrence, then, clearly, its use in the instant situation is unwarranted."

As cases considering the use of unlawfully obtained evidence in criminal trials themselves make clear, it does not follow from the emphasis on the exclusionary rule's deterrent value that "anything which deters illegal searches is thereby commanded by the Fourth Amendment." In determining whether persons aggrieved solely by the introduction of damaging evidence unlawfully obtained from their co-conspirators or co-defendants could seek suppression, for example, we found that the additional benefits of such an extension of the exclusionary rule would not outweigh its costs. Standing to invoke the rule has thus been limited to cases in which the prosecution seeks to use the fruits of an illegal search or seizure against the victim of police misconduct.

Even defendants with standing to challenge the introduction in their criminal trials of unlawfully obtained evidence cannot prevent every conceivable use of such evidence. Evidence obtained in violation of the Fourth Amendment and inadmissible in the prosecution's case in chief may be used to impeach a defendant's direct testimony. A similar assessment of the "incremental furthering" of the ends of the exclusionary rule led us to conclude in *United States v. Havens* (1980), that evidence inadmissible in the prosecution's case in chief or otherwise as substantive evidence of guilt may be used to impeach statements made by a defendant in response to "proper cross-examination reasonably suggested by the defendant's direct examination."

When considering the use of evidence obtained in violation of the Fourth Amendment in the prosecution's case in chief, moreover, we have declined to adopt a per se or "but for" rule that would render inadmissible any evidence that came to light through a chain of causation that began with an illegal arrest. We also have held that a witness' testimony may be admitted even when his identity was discovered in an unconstitutional search. The perception underlying these decisions — that the connection between police misconduct and evidence of crime may be sufficiently attenuated to permit the use of that evidence at trial — is a product of considerations relating to the exclusionary rule and the constitutional principles it is designed to protect. In short, the "dissipation of the taint" concept that the Court has applied in deciding whether exclusion is appropriate in a particular case "attempts to mark the point at which the detrimental consequences of illegal police action become so attenuated that the deterrent effect of the exclusionary rule no longer justifies its cost." Not surprisingly in view of this purpose, an assessment of the flagrancy of the police misconduct constitutes an important step in the calculus.

The same attention to the purposes underlying the exclusionary rule also has characterized decisions not involving the scope of the rule itself. We have not required suppression of the fruits of a search incident to an arrest made in good-faith reliance on a substantive criminal statute that subsequently is declared unconstitutional. Similarly, although the Court has been unwilling to conclude that new Fourth Amendment principles are always to have only prospective effect, no Fourth Amendment decision marking a "clear break with the past" has been applied retroactively. The propriety of retroactive application of a newly announced Fourth Amendment principle, moreover, has been assessed largely in terms of the contribution retroactivity might make to the deterrence of police misconduct.

As yet, we have not recognized any form of good-faith exception to the Fourth Amendment exclusionary rule. But the balancing approach that has evolved during the years of experience with the rule provides strong support for the modification currently urged upon us. As we discuss below, our evaluation of the costs and benefits of suppressing reliable physical evidence seized by officers reasonably relying on a warrant issued by a detached and neutral magistrate leads to the conclusion that such evidence should be admissible in the prosecution's case in chief.

III

A

Because a search warrant "provides the detached scrutiny of a neutral magistrate, which is a more reliable safeguard against improper searches than the hurried judgment of a law enforcement officer 'engaged in the often competitive enterprise of ferreting out crime,'" we have expressed a strong preference for warrants and declared that "in a doubtful or marginal case a search under a warrant may be sustainable where without one it would fall." Reasonable minds frequently may differ on the question whether a particular affidavit establishes probable cause, and we have thus concluded that the preference for warrants is most appropriately effectuated by according "great deference" to a magistrate's determination.

Deference to the magistrate, however, is not boundless. It is clear, first, that the deference accorded to a magistrate's finding of probable cause does not preclude inquiry into the knowing or reckless falsity of the affidavit on which that determination was based. Second, the courts must also insist that the magistrate purport to "perform his 'neutral and detached' function and not serve merely as a rubber stamp for the police." A magistrate failing to "manifest that neutrality and detachment demanded of a judicial officer when presented with a warrant application" and who acts instead as "an adjunct law enforcement officer" cannot provide valid authorization for an otherwise unconstitutional search.

Third, reviewing courts will not defer to a warrant based on an affidavit that does not "provide the magistrate with a substantial basis for determining the existence of probable cause." "Sufficient information must be presented to the magistrate to allow that official to determine probable cause; his action cannot be a mere ratification of the bare conclusions of others." Even if the warrant application was supported by more than a "bare bones" affidavit, a reviewing court may properly conclude that, notwithstanding the deference that magistrates deserve, the warrant was invalid because the magistrate's probable-cause determination reflected an improper analysis of the totality of the circumstances, or because the form of the warrant was improper in some respect.

Only in the first of these three situations, however, has the Court set forth a rationale for suppressing evidence obtained pursuant to a search warrant; in the other areas, it has simply excluded such evidence without considering whether Fourth Amendment interests will be advanced. To the extent that proponents of exclusion rely on its behavioral effects on judges and magistrates in these areas, their reliance is misplaced. First, the exclusionary rule is designed to deter police misconduct rather than to punish the errors of judges and magistrates. Second, there exists no evidence suggesting that judges and magistrates are inclined to ignore or subvert the Fourth Amendment or that lawlessness among these actors requires application of the extreme sanction of exclusion.

Third, and most important, we discern no basis, and are offered none, for believing that exclusion of evidence seized pursuant to a warrant will have a significant deterrent effect on the issuing judge or magistrate. Many of the factors that indicate that the exclusionary rule cannot provide an effective "special" or "general" deterrent for individual offending law enforcement officers apply as well to judges or magistrates. And, to the extent that the rule is thought to operate as a "systemic" deterrent on a wider audience, it clearly can have no such effect on individuals empowered to issue search warrants. Judges and magistrates are not adjuncts to the law enforcement team; as neutral judicial officers, they have no stake in the outcome of particular criminal prosecutions. The threat of exclusion thus cannot be expected significantly to deter them. Imposition of the exclusionary sanction is not necessary meaningfully to inform judicial officers of their errors, and we cannot conclude that admitting evidence obtained pursuant to a warrant while at the same time declaring that the warrant was somehow defective will in any way reduce judicial officers' professional incentives to comply with the Fourth Amendment, encourage them to repeat their mistakes, or lead to the granting of all colorable warrant requests.

B

If exclusion of evidence obtained pursuant to a subsequently invalidated warrant is to have any deterrent effect, therefore, it must alter the behavior of individual law enforcement officers or the policies of their departments. One could argue that applying the exclusionary rule in cases where the police failed to demonstrate probable cause in the warrant application deters future inadequate presentations or "magistrate shopping" and thus promotes the ends of the Fourth Amendment. Suppressing evidence obtained pursuant to a technically defective warrant supported by probable cause also might encourage officers to scrutinize more closely the form of the warrant and to point out suspected judicial errors. We find such arguments speculative and conclude that suppression of evidence obtained pursuant to a warrant should be ordered only on a case-by-case basis and only in those unusual cases in which exclusion will further the purposes of the exclusionary rule.

We have frequently questioned whether the exclusionary rule can have any deterrent effect when the offending officers acted in the objectively reasonable belief that their conduct did not violate the Fourth Amendment. "No empirical researcher, proponent or opponent of the rule, has yet been able to establish with any assurance whether the rule has a deterrent effect. . . ." But even assuming that the rule effectively deters some police misconduct and provides incentives for the law enforcement profession as a whole to conduct itself in accord with the Fourth Amendment, it cannot be expected, and should not be applied, to deter objectively reasonable law enforcement activity.

As we observed in *Michigan v. Tucker*, and reiterated in *United States v. Peltier*:

> The deterrent purpose of the exclusionary rule necessarily assumes that the police have engaged in willful, or at the very least negligent, conduct which has deprived the defendant of some right. By refusing to admit evidence gained as a result of such conduct, the courts hope to instill in those particular investigating officers, or in their future counterparts, a greater degree of care toward the rights of an accused. Where the official action was pursued in complete good faith, however, the deterrence rationale loses much of its force.
>
> If the purpose of the exclusionary rule is to deter unlawful police conduct, then evidence obtained from a search should be suppressed only if it can be said that the law enforcement officer had knowledge, or may properly be charged with knowledge, that the search was unconstitutional under the Fourth Amendment.

In short, where the officer's conduct is objectively reasonable,

> excluding the evidence will not further the ends of the exclusionary rule in any appreciable way; for it is painfully apparent that . . . the officer is acting as a reasonable officer would and should act in similar circumstances. Excluding the evidence can in no way affect his future conduct unless it is to make him less willing to do his duty.

This is particularly true, we believe, when an officer acting with objective good faith has obtained a search warrant from a judge or magistrate and acted within its scope. In most such cases, there is no police illegality and thus nothing to deter. It is the magistrate's responsibility to determine whether the officer's allegations establish probable cause and, if so, to issue a warrant comporting in form with the requirements of the Fourth Amendment. In the ordinary case, an officer cannot be expected to question the magistrate's probable-cause determination or his judgment that the form of the warrant is technically sufficient. "[O]nce the warrant issues, there is literally nothing more the policeman can do in seeking to comply with the law." Penalizing the officer for the magistrate's error, rather than his own, cannot logically contribute to the deterrence of Fourth Amendment violations.

C

We conclude that the marginal or nonexistent benefits produced by suppressing evidence obtained in objectively reasonable reliance on a subsequently invalidated search warrant cannot justify the substantial costs of exclusion. We do not suggest, however, that exclusion is always inappropriate in cases where an officer has obtained a warrant and abided by its terms. "[S]earches pursuant to a warrant will rarely require any deep inquiry into reasonableness," for "a warrant issued by a magistrate normally suffices to establish" that a law enforcement officer has "acted in good faith in conducting the search." Nevertheless, the officer's reliance on the magistrate's probable-cause determination and on the technical sufficiency of the warrant he issues must be objectively reasonable, and it is clear that in some circumstances the officer will have no reasonable grounds for believing that the warrant was properly issued.

Chapter V The Exclusionary Rule, its Exceptions, and Suppression Hearings

Suppression therefore remains an appropriate remedy if the magistrate or judge in issuing a warrant was misled by information in an affidavit that the affiant knew was false or would have known was false except for his reckless disregard of the truth. The exception we recognize today will also not apply in cases where the issuing magistrate wholly abandoned his judicial role in the manner condemned in *Lo-Ji Sales, Inc. v. New York* (1979); in such circumstances, no reasonably well trained officer should rely on the warrant. Nor would an officer manifest objective good faith in relying on a warrant based on an affidavit "so lacking in indicia of probable cause as to render official belief in its existence entirely unreasonable." Finally, depending on the circumstances of the particular case, a warrant may be so facially deficient—i.e., in failing to particularize the place to be searched or the things to be seized—that the executing officers cannot reasonably presume it to be valid.

In so limiting the suppression remedy, we leave untouched the probable-cause standard and the various requirements for a valid warrant. Other objections to the modification of the Fourth Amendment exclusionary rule we consider to be insubstantial. The good-faith exception for searches conducted pursuant to warrants is not intended to signal our unwillingness strictly to enforce the requirements of the Fourth Amendment, and we do not believe that it will have this effect. As we have already suggested, the good-faith exception, turning as it does on objective reasonableness, should not be difficult to apply in practice. When officers have acted pursuant to a warrant, the prosecution should ordinarily be able to establish objective good faith without a substantial expenditure of judicial time.

Nor are we persuaded that application of a good-faith exception to searches conducted pursuant to warrants will preclude review of the constitutionality of the search or seizure, deny needed guidance from the courts, or freeze Fourth Amendment law in its present state. There is no need for courts to adopt the inflexible practice of always deciding whether the officers' conduct manifested objective good faith before turning to the question whether the Fourth Amendment has been violated. Defendants seeking suppression of the fruits of allegedly unconstitutional searches or seizures undoubtedly raise live controversies which Art. III empowers federal courts to adjudicate. As cases addressing questions of good-faith immunity under 42 U.S.C. § 1983, and cases involving the harmless-error doctrine, make clear, courts have considerable discretion in conforming their decisionmaking processes to the exigencies of particular cases.

If the resolution of a particular Fourth Amendment question is necessary to guide future action by law enforcement officers and magistrates, nothing will prevent reviewing courts from deciding that question before turning to the good-faith issue. Indeed, it frequently will be difficult to determine whether the officers acted reasonably without resolving the Fourth Amendment issue. Even if the Fourth Amendment question is not one of broad import, reviewing courts could decide in particular cases that magistrates under their supervision need to be informed of their errors and so evaluate the officers' good faith only after finding a violation. In other circumstances, those courts could reject suppression motions posing no important Fourth Amendment questions by turning immediately to a consideration of the officers' good faith. We have no reason to believe that our Fourth Amendment jurisprudence would suffer by allowing reviewing courts to exercise an informed discretion in making this choice.

IV

When the principles we have enunciated today are applied to the facts of this case, it is apparent that the judgment of the Court of Appeals cannot stand. The Court of Appeals applied the prevailing legal standards to Officer Rombach's warrant application and concluded that the application could not support the magistrate's probable-cause determination. In so doing, the court clearly informed the magistrate that he had erred in issuing the challenged warrant. This aspect of the court's judgment is not under attack in this proceeding.

Having determined that the warrant should not have issued, the Court of Appeals understandably declined to adopt a modification of the Fourth Amendment exclusionary rule that this Court had not previously sanctioned. Although the modification finds strong support in our previous cases, the Court of Appeals' commendable self-restraint is not to be criticized. We have now reexamined the purposes of the exclusionary rule and the propriety of its application in cases where officers have relied on a subsequently invalidated search warrant. Our conclusion is that the rule's purposes will only rarely be served by applying it in such circumstances.

In the absence of an allegation that the magistrate abandoned his detached and neutral role, suppression is appropriate only if the officers were dishonest or reckless in preparing their affidavit or could not have harbored an objectively reasonable belief in the existence of probable cause. Only respondent Leon has contended that no reasonably well trained police officer could have believed that there existed probable cause to search his house; significantly, the other respondents advance no comparable argument. Officer Rombach's application for a warrant clearly was supported by much more than a "bare bones" affidavit. The affidavit related the results of an extensive investigation and, as the opinions of the divided panel of the Court of Appeals make clear, provided evidence sufficient to create disagreement among thoughtful and competent judges as to the existence of probable cause. Under these circumstances, the officers' reliance on the magistrate's determination of probable cause was objectively reasonable, and application of the extreme sanction of exclusion is inappropriate.

Accordingly, the judgment of the Court of Appeals is

Reversed.

NOTES AND QUESTIONS

1. Is the good faith exception fashioned by the Court dependent on the existence of a search warrant that had been approved by a detached and neutral magistrate? There is certainly much discussion of the importance of a warrant, but are there hints that the majority views the exception as broader?

2. Note the way the Department of Justice strategically litigated the case. First, DOJ asked the district court, which had granted defendants' motions to suppress in part, to make a finding that the officers had acted in good faith, which the district court did even though the officers' good faith was totally irrelevant under existing law. Second, it appealed from the district court's partial denial of the motion to suppress, even though much of the evidence obtained from the search was admissible. Third, the government petitioned for certiorari only on the issue of whether there should be a good faith exception, and not on whether the warrants were supported by probable cause.

The DOJ was not, however, just trying a Hail Mary pass here. There had been hints in at least two previous cases that the Court might be willing to recognize a good faith exception to the exclusionary rule. First, in his dissenting opinion in *Stone v. Powell*, 428 U.S. 465, 536 (1976), Justice White had proposed establishing a good faith exception to the exclusionary rule. And more recently, in *Illinois v. Gates*, 462 U.S. 213 (1983), the Court had asked for briefing on whether it should adopt the good faith exception, although it ultimately declined to reach the issue. *Id.* at 216-24.

3. Note that the Court relies entirely on the district court's finding — wholly gratuitous — that the police officer had acted in good faith. It doesn't reproduce, summarize, or in any way describe the affidavit filed in support of the search warrant applications, and does not explain how the affidavit fell short of establishing probable cause. The court of appeals, on the other hand, found that the informant's information was "fatally stale" and that the

Chapter V The Exclusionary Rule, its Exceptions, and Suppression Hearings

affidavit "failed to establish the informant's reliability," and thus the application failed under both prongs of the *Aguilar-Spinelli* test.

How could a warrant application resting on information that was "fatally stale" and that failed under both aspects of the applicable legal test have been made "in good faith."?

Is it significant that the police officer testified that the affidavit had been reviewed by several deputy district attorneys?

4. In a companion case to *Leon, Massachusetts v. Sheppard*, 468 U.S. 981 (1984), the Court found that a police officer had reasonably relied on a warrant issued by a judge even though the judge failed to conform the ultimately issued warrant to reflect edits the officer had made to the warrant form he had submitted. Relying on *Leon*, the Court held that the exclusionary rule did not apply because the officer had an "objectively reasonable belief" that the warrant was valid.

5. As the next cases will show, the scope of *Leon's* good faith exception to the exclusionary rule has been repeatedly extended by the Court. At least 20 state courts, however, interpreting state constitutions, have rejected *Leon*. *See* Joseph Blocher, *Reverse Incorporation of State Constitutional Law*, 84 S. Cal. L. Rev. 323, 373 (2011) ("Perhaps the Court will revisit *Leon's* reasoning and rule if that number reaches the fifty percent figure that seemed so significant in *Mapp*.").

It appeared to some that the "good faith exception" was limited to situations where search warrants had been issued by a "detached and neutral magistrate." That notion was dispelled in *Illinois v. Krull*, 480 U.S. 340 (1987), where the Court applied the exception in a case involving a warrantless administrative inspection of an automobile wrecking yard. In a prosecution based on the fruits of that inspection, the evidence was suppressed by the trial court because the statute authorizing the inspection had been found to be unconstitutional in that it conferred unbridled discretion on the searching officers. *Id.* at 344. The Supreme Court found the search to be within the good faith exception. Because the statute had not been found unconstitutional at the time of the search, and was not patently illegal, the officers were entitled to rely on it and no deterrent purpose would be served by suppressing the evidence the search yielded. *Id.* at 349-50. The Court dismissed any concerns that state legislatures needed incentives to deter them from passing unconstitutional statutes, and noted that the exclusionary rule focused only on police misconduct. *Id.* at 350. The Court also ignored that the effect of its ruling left no incentive for challenges to such potentially unconstitutional statutes because even successful actions would be remediless. *Id.* at 354. Justice O'Connor, the only Justice on the Court with any legislative experience (she had been an Arizona state senator), wrote a dissenting opinion in which Justices Brennan, Marshall, and Stevens joined. She reasoned, among other things, that legislatures did in fact need disincentives against passing unconstitutional statutes. *Id.* at 361, 366 (O'Connor, J., dissenting).

The Court's next significant good faith case was *Arizona v. Evans*, 514 U.S. 1 (1995). A police officer stopped Isaac Evans for driving the wrong way on a one-way street—right in front of apolice station—and upon entering Evans's name into a computerized criminal record database terminal in his car learned that Evans had an outstanding misdemeanor warrant for his arrest, based on his failure to appear in court to respond to alleged traffic violations. *Id.* at 4-5. Evans was arrested and in the search incident to that arrest, and subsequent search of his car, marijuana was discovered. *Id.* at 4.

It turned out the misdemeanor arrest warrant had been quashed 17 days earlier and was thus no longer effective. *Id.* Due to an error in the clerk's office, however, the judicial action quashing the warrant had not been communicated to the sheriff's office. *Id.* The Court found that excluding the evidence would not have any deterrent effect on police conduct, as the officer had acted objectively reasonably in reliance upon the police computer records. *Id.*

at 15-16. It also noted that the exclusionary rule's purpose was not aimed at deterring the conduct of judicial branch employees—the officials who had made the error here—and also that the error here was rare. *Id.*

The Court revisited the subject of a computer database error leading to an illegal arrest 12 years later.

Herring v. United States
555 U.S. 135 (2009)

Chief Justice ROBERTS delivered the opinion of the Court.

The Fourth Amendment forbids "unreasonable searches and seizures," and this usually requires the police to have probable cause or a warrant before making an arrest. What if an officer reasonably believes there is an outstanding arrest warrant, but that belief turns out to be wrong because of a negligent bookkeeping error by another police employee? The parties here agree that the ensuing arrest is still a violation of the Fourth Amendment, but dispute whether contraband found during a search incident to that arrest must be excluded in a later prosecution.

Our cases establish that such suppression is not an automatic consequence of a Fourth Amendment violation. Instead, the question turns on the culpability of the police and the potential of exclusion to deter wrongful police conduct. Here the error was the result of isolated negligence attenuated from the arrest. We hold that in these circumstances the jury should not be barred from considering all the evidence.

I

On July 7, 2004, Investigator Mark Anderson learned that Bennie Dean Herring had driven to the Coffee County Sheriff's Department to retrieve something from his impounded truck. Herring was no stranger to law enforcement, and Anderson asked the county's warrant clerk, Sandy Pope, to check for any outstanding warrants for Herring's arrest. When she found none, Anderson asked Pope to check with Sharon Morgan, her counterpart in neighboring Dale County. After checking Dale County's computer database, Morgan replied that there was an active arrest warrant for Herring's failure to appear on a felony charge. Pope relayed the information to Anderson and asked Morgan to fax over a copy of the warrant as confirmation. Anderson and a deputy followed Herring as he left the impound lot, pulled him over, and arrested him. A search incident to the arrest revealed methamphetamine in Herring's pocket, and a pistol (which as a felon he could not possess) in his vehicle.

There had, however, been a mistake about the warrant. The Dale County sheriff's computer records are supposed to correspond to actual arrest warrants, which the office also maintains. But when Morgan went to the files to retrieve the actual warrant to fax to Pope, Morgan was unable to find it. She called a court clerk and learned that the warrant had been recalled five months earlier. Normally when a warrant is recalled the court clerk's office or a judge's chambers calls Morgan, who enters the information in the sheriff's computer database and disposes of the physical copy. For whatever reason, the information about the recall of the warrant for Herring did not appear in the database. Morgan immediately called Pope to alert her to the mixup, and Pope contacted Anderson over a secure radio. This all unfolded in 10 to 15 minutes, but Herring had already been arrested and found with the gun and drugs, just a few hundred yards from the sheriff's office.

Herring was indicted in the District Court for the Middle District of Alabama for illegally possessing the gun and drugs, violations of 18 U.S.C. § 922(g)(1) and 21 U.S.C. § 844(a). He moved to suppress the evidence on the ground that his initial arrest had been illegal because the warrant had been rescinded. The Magistrate Judge recommended denying the motion because the arresting officers had acted in a good-faith belief that the warrant was still outstanding. Thus, even if there were a Fourth Amendment violation, there was "no reason to believe that application of the exclusionary rule here would deter the occurrence of any future mistakes." The District Court adopted the Magistrate Judge's recommendation, and the Court of Appeals for the Eleventh Circuit affirmed.

The Eleventh Circuit found that the arresting officers in Coffee County "were entirely innocent of any wrongdoing or carelessness." The court assumed that whoever failed to update the Dale County sheriff's records was also a law enforcement official, but noted that "the conduct in question [wa]s a negligent failure to act, not a deliberate or tactical choice to act." Ibid. Because the error was merely negligent and attenuated from the arrest, the Eleventh Circuit concluded that the benefit of suppressing the evidence "would be marginal or nonexistent), and the evidence was therefore admissible under the good-faith rule of *United States v. Leon* (1984).

Other courts have required exclusion of evidence obtained through similar police errors, so we granted Herring's petition for certiorari to resolve the conflict. We now affirm the Eleventh Circuit's judgment.

II

When a probable-cause determination was based on reasonable but mistaken assumptions, the person subjected to a search or seizure has not necessarily been the victim of a constitutional violation. The very phrase "probable cause" confirms that the Fourth Amendment does not demand all possible precision. And whether the error can be traced to a mistake by a state actor or some other source may bear on the analysis. For purposes of deciding this case, however, we accept the parties' assumption that there was a Fourth Amendment violation. The issue is whether the exclusionary rule should be applied.

A

The Fourth Amendment protects "[t]he right of the people to be secure in their persons, houses, papers, and effects, against unreasonable searches and seizures," but "contains no provision expressly precluding the use of evidence obtained in violation of its commands." Nonetheless, our decisions establish an exclusionary rule that, when applicable, forbids the use of improperly obtained evidence at trial. We have stated that this judicially created rule is "designed to safeguard Fourth Amendment rights generally through its deterrent effect."

In analyzing the applicability of the rule, *Leon* admonished that we must consider the actions of all the police officers involved. The Coffee County officers did nothing improper. Indeed, the error was noticed so quickly because Coffee County requested a faxed confirmation of the warrant.

The Eleventh Circuit concluded, however, that somebody in Dale County should have updated the computer database to reflect the recall of the arrest warrant. The court also concluded that this error was negligent, but did not find it to be reckless or deliberate. That fact is crucial to our holding that this error is not enough by itself to require "the extreme sanction of exclusion."

B

The fact that a Fourth Amendment violation occurred—i.e., that a search or arrest was unreasonable—does not necessarily mean that the exclusionary rule applies. Indeed, exclusion "has always been our last resort, not our first impulse," and our precedents establish important principles that constrain application of the exclusionary rule.

First, the exclusionary rule is not an individual right and applies only where it "'result[s] in appreciable deterrence.'" We have repeatedly rejected the argument that exclusion is a necessary consequence of a Fourth Amendment violation. Instead we have focused on the efficacy of the rule in deterring Fourth Amendment violations in the future.

In addition, the benefits of deterrence must outweigh the costs. "We have never suggested that the exclusionary rule must apply in every circumstance in which it might provide marginal deterrence." "[T]o the extent that application of the exclusionary rule could provide some incremental deterrent, that possible benefit must be weighed against [its] substantial social costs." The principal cost of applying the rule is, of course, letting guilty and possibly dangerous defendants go free—something that "offends basic concepts of the criminal justice system." "[T]he rule's costly toll upon truth-seeking and law enforcement objectives presents a high obstacle for those urging [its] application."

These principles are reflected in the holding of *Leon*: When police act under a warrant that is invalid for lack of probable cause, the exclusionary rule does not apply if the police acted "in objectively reasonable reliance" on the subsequently invalidated search warrant. We (perhaps confusingly) called this objectively reasonable reliance "good faith." Ibid., n. 23, 104 S. Ct. 3405. In a companion case, *Massachusetts v. Sheppard* (1984), we held that the exclusionary rule did not apply when a warrant was invalid because a judge forgot to make "clerical corrections" to it.

Shortly thereafter we extended these holdings to warrantless administrative searches performed in good-faith reliance on a statute later declared unconstitutional. Finally, in *Evans*, we applied this good-faith rule to police who reasonably relied on mistaken information in a court's database that an arrest warrant was outstanding. We held that a mistake made by a judicial employee could not give rise to exclusion for three reasons: The exclusionary rule was crafted to curb police rather than judicial misconduct; court employees were unlikely to try to subvert the Fourth Amendment; and "most important, there [was] no basis for believing that application of the exclusionary rule in [those] circumstances" would have any significant effect in deterring the errors. *Evans* left unresolved "whether the evidence should be suppressed if police personnel were responsible for the error," an issue not argued by the State in that case, but one that we now confront.

The extent to which the exclusionary rule is justified by these deterrence principles varies with the culpability of the law enforcement conduct. As we said in *Leon*, "an assessment of the flagrancy of the police misconduct constitutes an important step in the calculus" of applying the exclusionary rule. Similarly, in *Krull* we elaborated that "evidence should be suppressed 'only if it can be said that the law enforcement officer had knowledge, or may properly be charged with knowledge, that the search was unconstitutional under the Fourth Amendment.'"

Anticipating the good-faith exception to the exclusionary rule, Judge Friendly wrote that "[t]he beneficent aim of the exclusionary rule to deter police misconduct can be sufficiently accomplished by a practice . . . outlawing evidence obtained by flagrant or deliberate violation of rights."

Indeed, the abuses that gave rise to the exclusionary rule featured intentional conduct that was patently unconstitutional. In *Weeks*, a foundational exclusionary rule case, the officers had broken into the defendant's home (using a key shown to them by a neighbor), confiscated incriminating papers, then returned again with a U.S. Marshal to confiscate even more. Not only did they have no search warrant, which the Court held was required, but they could not have gotten one had they tried. They were so lacking in sworn and particularized information that "not even an order of court would have justified such procedure." *Silverthorne Lumber Co. v. United States* (1920), on which petitioner repeatedly relies, was similar; federal officials "without a shadow of authority" went to the defendants' office and "made a clean sweep" of every paper they could find. Even the Government seemed to acknowledge that the "seizure was an outrage."

Equally flagrant conduct was at issue in *Mapp v. Ohio* (1961), which overruled *Wolf v. Colorado* (1949), and extended the exclusionary rule to the States. Officers forced open a door to Ms. Mapp's house, kept her lawyer from entering, brandished what the court concluded was a false warrant, then forced her into handcuffs and canvassed the house for obscenity. An error that arises from nonrecurring and attenuated negligence is thus far removed from the core concerns that led us to adopt the rule in the first place. And in fact since *Leon*, we have never applied the rule to exclude evidence obtained in violation of the Fourth Amendment, where the police conduct was no more intentional or culpable than this.

To trigger the exclusionary rule, police conduct must be sufficiently deliberate that exclusion can meaningfully deter it, and sufficiently culpable that such deterrence is worth the price paid by the justice system. As laid out in our cases, the exclusionary rule serves to deter deliberate, reckless, or grossly negligent conduct, or in some circumstances recurring or systemic negligence. The error in this case does not rise to that level.

Our decision in *Franks v. Delaware* (1978), provides an analogy. In *Franks*, we held that police negligence in obtaining a warrant did not even rise to the level of a Fourth Amendment violation, let alone meet the more stringent test for triggering the exclusionary rule. We held that the Constitution allowed defendants, in some circumstances, "to challenge the truthfulness of factual statements made in an affidavit supporting the warrant," even after the warrant had issued. If those false statements were necessary to the Magistrate Judge's probable-cause determination, the warrant would be "voided." But we did not find all false statements relevant: "There must be allegations of deliberate falsehood or of reckless disregard for the truth," and "[a]llegations of negligence or innocent mistake are insufficient."

Both this case and *Franks* concern false information provided by police. Under *Franks*, negligent police miscommunications in the course of acquiring a warrant do not provide a basis to rescind a warrant and render a search or arrest invalid. Here, the miscommunications occurred in a different context—after the warrant had been issued and recalled—but that fact should not require excluding the evidence obtained.

The pertinent analysis of deterrence and culpability is objective, not an "inquiry into the subjective awareness of arresting officers." We have already held that "our good-faith inquiry is confined to the objectively ascertainable question whether a reasonably well trained officer would have known that the search was illegal" in light of "all of the circumstances." These circumstances frequently include a particular officer's knowledge and experience, but that does not make the test any more subjective than the one for probable cause, which looks to an officer's knowledge and experience, but not his subjective intent, *Whren v. United States* (1996).

We do not suggest that all recordkeeping errors by the police are immune from the exclusionary rule. In this case, however, the conduct at issue was not so objectively culpable as to require exclusion. In *Leon*, we held that "the marginal or nonexistent benefits produced by suppressing evidence obtained in objectively reasonable reliance on a subsequently invalidated search warrant cannot justify the substantial costs of exclusion." The same is true when evidence is obtained in objectively reasonable reliance on a subsequently recalled warrant.

If the police have been shown to be reckless in maintaining a warrant system, or to have knowingly made false entries to lay the groundwork for future false arrests, exclusion would certainly be justified under our cases should such misconduct cause a Fourth Amendment violation. We said as much in *Leon*, explaining that an officer could not "obtain a warrant on the basis of a 'bare bones' affidavit and then rely on colleagues who are ignorant of the circumstances under which the warrant was obtained to conduct the search." Petitioner's fears that our decision will cause police departments to deliberately keep their officers ignorant, are thus unfounded.

B. The Good Faith Exception   **495**

Justice Ginsburg's dissent also adverts to the possible unreliability of a number of databases not relevant to this case. In a case where systemic errors were demonstrated, it might be reckless for officers to rely on an unreliable warrant system. But there is no evidence that errors in Dale County's system are routine or widespread. Officer Anderson testified that he had never had reason to question information about a Dale County warrant, and both Sandy Pope and Sharon Morgan testified that they could remember no similar miscommunication ever happening on their watch. That is even less error than in the database at issue in *Evans*, where we also found reliance on the database to be objectively reasonable. Because no such showings were made here, the Eleventh Circuit was correct to affirm the denial of the motion to suppress.

• • •

Petitioner's claim that police negligence automatically triggers suppression cannot be squared with the principles underlying the exclusionary rule, as they have been explained in our cases. In light of our repeated holdings that the deterrent effect of suppression must be substantial and outweigh any harm to the justice system, we conclude that when police mistakes are the result of negligence such as that described here, rather than systemic error or reckless disregard of constitutional requirements, any marginal deterrence does not "pay its way." In such a case, the criminal should not "go free because the constable has blundered."

The judgment of the Court of Appeals for the Eleventh Circuit is affirmed.

NOTES AND QUESTIONS

1. The Court makes several observations about the type of "culpability" that will be required for exclusion. It notes that the exclusionary rule only serves "to deter deliberate, reckless, or grossly negligent conduct, or in some circumstances recurring or systemic negligence." How often do you think police violations fall in to these categories? Is a rogue police officer who commits the sort of flagrant constitutional violations the Court posits a better or worse candidate for deterrence that an officer who makes a mistake?

2. What do you understand the Court to mean in describing the "error" as "isolated negligence attenuated from the arrest"? How can the database error be seen as "attenuated" from the arrest where the existence of the warrant was in itself both the necessary and sufficient condition for the arrest? Would negligence in determining, say, reasonable suspicion for a *Terry* stop that led to an arrest be similarly "attenuated"?

3. Justice Ginsburg, dissenting along with Justices Stevens and Breyer, points out the inconsistency between the Court's exclusionary jurisprudence and the basic principles of tort law, which impose liability for negligence as an incentive for defendants to act with greater care. Fair analogy? Is there anything special about the deterrence rationale as applied to law enforcement that warrants a different approach?

What are the costs of overdeterrence in tort law? What are the costs of overdeterrence in the law enforcement context? Is it fair to think of the latter costs in terms of crimes going undetected or unprosecuted because police officers will take fewer risks? Or, alternatively, should those costs be viewed more broadly in terms of fewer violations of constitutional rights, even in those situations where there is not a prosecution and the exclusionary rule does not come into play?

4. Justice Ginsburg also stresses the enormous expansion of law enforcement databases, and how they can be called on instantly—as they were here—to find out if a person has an outstanding warrant, a state of affairs that can result in an immediate arrest and a search incident to that arrest. Shouldn't this terrifying power be subjected to a heightened degree of scrutiny? Should a police officer be permitted to embark on a database fishing expedition without probable cause or even reasonable suspicion? *See* Wayne A. Logan, *Policing Police Access to Criminal Justice Data,* 104 Iowa L. Rev. 619. 673-76 (2019) (discussing legislative restrictions on police access to certain database information).

5. The Court doesn't deem it worthy of inclusion in its opinion that Bennie Dean Herring had a target on his back. As the dissenting opinion notes:

> Investigator Mark Anderson . . . knew Herring from prior interactions: Herring had told the District Attorney, among others, of his suspicion that Anderson had been involved in the killing of a local teenager, and Anderson had pursued Herring to get him to drop the accusations. Informed that Herring was in the impoundment lot, Anderson asked the Coffee County warrant clerk whether there was an outstanding warrant for Herring's arrest.

Bennie Dean Herring

The Court presumably would have attached no legal relevance to this because of its fetish with ignoring police officers' "subjective motivations." But doesn't it hurt the Court's credibility when it fails to even acknowledge such information?

6. Commentators have debated the significance of *Herring* in that, on the one hand, it arguably involved only a "negligent bookkeeping error," as the Court framed the issue in the first paragraph of the opinion. Others disagree and focus on its statement that the exclusionary rule aims only "to deter deliberate, reckless, or grossly negligent conduct," and its references to the sort of "flagrant misconduct" at issue in *Weeks* and *Mapp. See* Albert W. Alschuler, Herring v. United States: *A Minnow or a Shark?*, 7 Ohio St. J. Crim. L. 463, 488-89 (2009) ("No decision prior to *Herring*, however, had suggested or implied that the exclusionary rule should be limited in the way the Court proposed.").

In *Davis v. United States*, 554 U.S. 229 (2011), the Court applied the exclusionary rule where a police officer searched the vehicle of a driver arrested for giving a false name. At the time the search was conducted it was in compliance with existing law (*New York v. Belton*), but while the defendant's appeal was pending *Arizona v. Gant* overruled *Belton. See* Chapter IV *supra*. The Court found the good faith exception applicable even though there was no evidence that the officer had actually relied on the authority of *Belton*. Dissenting, Justice Breyer openly wondered about the future of the exclusionary rule:

> If the Court means what it says, what will happen to the exclusionary rule, a rule that the Court adopted nearly a century ago for federal courts, and made applicable to state courts a half century ago through the Fourteenth Amendment? The Court has thought of that rule not as punishment for the individual officer or as reparation for the individual defendant but more generally as an effective way to secure enforcement of the Fourth Amendment's commands. This Court has deviated from the "suppression" norm in the name of "good faith" only a handful of times and in limited, atypical circumstances: where a magistrate has erroneously issued a warrant; where a database has erroneously informed police that they have a warrant; and where an unconstitutional statute purported to authorize the search.

Id. at 252, 257 (Breyer, J., dissenting). Professors Maclin and Rader argue that *Davis* represents an extension of *Herring* in that it applies the good faith exception to ordinary

Fourth Amendment violations, and not just situations — as in *Evans* and *Herring* — where the connection between the error and the violation is "attenuated." *See* Tracey Maclin & Jennifer Rader, *No More Chipping Away: The Roberts Court Uses an Axe to Take Out the Fourth Amendment Exclusionary Rule*, 81 Miss. L.J. 1183, 1206-07 (2011).

C. ATTENUATION

Attenuation of a different sort than at issue in *Herring* is its own categorical exception to the exclusionary rule. The attenuation doctrine applies in situations where the connection between police misconduct and illegally obtained evidence — the "fruit of the poisonous tree" — is indirect or "attenuated." Under this exception, evidence may be admissible where the misconduct is so distant or remote from the acquisition of the evidence that the original violation is effectively nullified. Usually the doctrine applies where there are intervening circumstances between the misconduct and the acquisition of the evidence sought to be suppressed. Related causation-based exceptions to the exclusionary rule are the "independent source" doctrine, which allows trial courts to admit evidence obtained in an unlawful search if officers acquired it from a separate, independent source, *Murray v. United States*, 487 U.S. 533 (1988), and the "inevitable discovery" doctrine, which permits the admission of evidence that would have been discovered even without the unconstitutional misconduct, *Nix v. Williams*, 467 U.S. 431 (1984).

The Court adopted a three-factor balancing test for application of the attenuation doctrine in *Brown v. Illinois*, 422 U.S. 590 (1975). This test requires analyzing (1) the temporal proximity of the unlawful police action and the seizure of evidence, (2) the presence of intervening circumstances, and (3) the existence of any purposeful or flagrant misconduct by a police officer. In *Brown*, the Court found that where the defendant had been illegally arrested without either probable cause or a warrant, and subsequently made admissions after being given *Miranda* warnings, that the *Miranda* warnings did not necessarily remove the taint of the illegal conduct.

The Court has applied the attenuation doctrine in numerous contexts before and after *Brown*, largely adhering to its general principles.

The next two cases, from 2006 and 2016 respectively, suggest this may no longer be the case.

Hudson v. Michigan
547 U.S. 586 (2006)

Justice SCALIA delivered the opinion of the Court, except as to Part IV.

We decide whether violation of the "knock-and-announce" rule requires the suppression of all evidence found in the search.

I

Police obtained a warrant authorizing a search for drugs and firearms at the home of petitioner Booker Hudson. They discovered both. Large quantities of drugs were found, including cocaine rocks in Hudson's pocket. A loaded gun was lodged between the cushion and armrest of the chair in which he was sitting. Hudson was charged under Michigan law with unlawful drug and firearm possession.

This case is before us only because of the method of entry into the house. When the police arrived to execute the warrant, they announced their presence, but waited only a short time — perhaps "three to five seconds" — before turning the knob of the unlocked front door and entering Hudson's home. Hudson moved to suppress all the inculpatory evidence, arguing that the premature entry violated his Fourth Amendment rights.

II

The common-law principle that law enforcement officers must announce their presence and provide residents an opportunity to open the door is an ancient one. Since 1917, when Congress passed the Espionage Act, this traditional protection has been part of federal statutory law, and is currently codified at 18 U.S.C. § 3109. We applied that statute in *Miller v. United States* (1958), and again in *Sabbath v. United States* (1968). Finally, in *Wilson*, we were asked whether the rule was also a command of the Fourth Amendment. Tracing its origins in our English legal heritage, we concluded that it was.

We recognized that the new constitutional rule we had announced is not easily applied. *Wilson* and cases following it have noted the many situations in which it is not necessary to knock and announce. It is not necessary when "circumstances presen[t] a threat of physical violence," or if there is "reason to believe that evidence would likely be destroyed if advance notice were given," or if knocking and announcing would be "futile," *Richards v. Wisconsin* (1997). We require only that police "have a reasonable suspicion . . . under the particular circumstances" that one of these grounds for failing to knock and announce exists, and we have acknowledged that "[t]his showing is not high."

When the knock-and-announce rule does apply, it is not easy to determine precisely what officers must do. How many seconds' wait are too few? Our "reasonable wait time" standard, is necessarily vague. *Banks* (a drug case, like this one) held that the proper measure was not how long it would take the resident to reach the door, but how long it would take to dispose of the suspected drugs—but that such a time (15 to 20 seconds in that case) would necessarily be extended when, for instance, the suspected contraband was not easily concealed. If our ex post evaluation is subject to such calculations, it is unsurprising that, ex ante, police officers about to encounter someone who may try to harm them will be uncertain how long to wait.

Happily, these issues do not confront us here. From the trial level onward, Michigan has conceded that the entry was a knock-and-announce violation. The issue here is remedy. *Wilson* specifically declined to decide whether the exclusionary rule is appropriate for violation of the knock-and-announce requirement. That question is squarely before us now.

III

A

In *Weeks v. United States* we adopted the federal exclusionary rule for evidence that was unlawfully seized from a home without a warrant in violation of the Fourth Amendment. We began applying the same rule to the States, through the Fourteenth Amendment, in *Mapp v. Ohio* (1961).

Suppression of evidence, however, has always been our last resort, not our first impulse. The exclusionary rule generates "substantial social costs," which sometimes include setting the guilty free and the dangerous at large. We have therefore been "cautio[us] against expanding" it, and "have repeatedly emphasized that the rule's 'costly toll' upon truth-seeking and law enforcement objectives presents a high obstacle for those urging [its] application." We have rejected "[i]ndiscriminate application" of the rule, and have held it to be applicable only "where its remedial objectives are thought most efficaciously served"—that is, "where its deterrence benefits outweigh its 'substantial social costs.'"

We did not always speak so guardedly. Expansive dicta in *Mapp*, for example, suggested wide scope for the exclusionary rule. But we have long since rejected that approach. As explained in *Arizona v. Evans* (1995): "In *Whiteley*, the Court treated identification of a Fourth Amendment violation as synonymous with application of the exclusionary rule to evidence secured incident to that violation. Subsequent case law has rejected this reflexive application of the exclusionary rule." We had said as much in *Leon*, a decade earlier, when we explained that "[w]hether the exclusionary sanction is appropriately imposed in a particular case . . . is 'an issue separate from the question whether the Fourth Amendment rights of the party seeking to invoke the rule were violated by police conduct.'"

In other words, exclusion may not be premised on the mere fact that a constitutional violation was a "but-for" cause of obtaining evidence. Our cases show that but-for causality is only a necessary, not a sufficient, condition for suppression. In this case, of course, the constitutional violation of an illegal manner of entry was not a but-for cause of obtaining the evidence. Whether that preliminary misstep had occurred or not, the police would have executed the warrant they had obtained, and would have discovered the gun and drugs inside the house. But even if the illegal entry here could be characterized as a but-for cause of discovering what was inside, we have "never held that evidence is 'fruit of the poisonous tree' simply because 'it would not have come to light but for the illegal actions of the police.'" Rather, but-for cause, or "causation in the logical sense alone," can be too attenuated to justify exclusion. Even in the early days of the exclusionary rule, we declined to

> hold that all evidence is "fruit of the poisonous tree" simply because it would not have come to light but for the illegal actions of the police. Rather, the more apt question in such a case is "whether, granting establishment of the primary illegality, the evidence to which instant objection is made has been come at by exploitation of that illegality or instead by means sufficiently distinguishable to be purged of the primary taint."

Attenuation can occur, of course, when the causal connection is remote. Attenuation also occurs when, even given a direct causal connection, the interest protected by the constitutional guarantee that has been violated would not be served by suppression of the evidence obtained. "The penalties visited upon the Government, and in turn upon the public, because its officers have violated the law must bear some relation to the purposes which the law is to serve." Thus, in *New York v. Harris* (1990), where an illegal warrantless arrest was made in Harris's house, we held:

> [S]uppressing [Harris's] statement taken outside the house would not serve the purpose of the rule that made Harris' in-house arrest illegal. The warrant requirement for an arrest in the home is imposed to protect the home, and anything incriminating the police gathered from arresting Harris in his home, rather than elsewhere, has been excluded, as it should have been; the purpose of the rule has thereby been vindicated.

For this reason, cases excluding the fruits of unlawful warrantless searches, say nothing about the appropriateness of exclusion to vindicate the interests protected by the knock-and-announce requirement. Until a valid warrant has issued, citizens are entitled to shield "their persons, houses, papers, and effects," from the government's scrutiny. Exclusion of the evidence obtained by a warrantless search vindicates that entitlement. The interests protected by the knock-and-announce requirement are quite different — and do not include the shielding of potential evidence from the government's eyes.

One of those interests is the protection of human life and limb, because an unannounced entry may provoke violence in supposed self-defense by the surprised resident. Another interest is the protection of property. Breaking a house (as the old cases typically put it) absent an announcement would penalize someone who "'did not know of the process, of which, if he had notice, it is to be presumed that he would obey it. . . .'" The knock-and-announce rule gives individuals "the opportunity to comply with the law and to avoid the destruction of property occasioned by a forcible entry." And thirdly, the knock-and-announce rule protects those elements of privacy and dignity that can be destroyed by a sudden entrance. It gives residents the "opportunity to prepare themselves for" the entry of the police. "The brief interlude between announcement and entry with a warrant may be the opportunity that an individual has to pull on clothes or get out of bed." In other words, it assures the opportunity to collect oneself before answering the door.

What the knock-and-announce rule has never protected, however, is one's interest in preventing the government from seeing or taking evidence described in a warrant. Since the interests that were violated in this case have nothing to do with the seizure of the evidence, the exclusionary rule is inapplicable.

B

Quite apart from the requirement of unattenuated causation, the exclusionary rule has never been applied except "where its deterrence benefits outweigh its 'substantial social costs.'" The costs here are considerable. In addition to the grave adverse consequence that exclusion of relevant incriminating evidence always entails (viz., the risk of releasing dangerous criminals into society), imposing that massive remedy for a knock-and-announce violation would generate a constant flood of alleged failures to observe the rule, and claims that any asserted *Richards* justification for a no-knock entry, had inadequate support. The cost of entering this lottery would be small, but the jackpot enormous: suppression of all evidence, amounting in many cases to a get-out-of-jail-free card. Courts would experience as never before the reality that "[t]he exclusionary rule frequently requires extensive litigation to determine whether particular evidence must be excluded." Unlike the warrant or *Miranda* requirements, compliance with which is readily determined (either there was or was not a warrant; either the *Miranda* warning was given, or it was not), what constituted a "reasonable wait time" in a particular case, or whether there was "reasonable suspicion" of the sort that would invoke the *Richards* exceptions, is difficult for the trial court to determine and even more difficult for an appellate court to review.

Another consequence of the incongruent remedy Hudson proposes would be police officers' refraining from timely entry after knocking and announcing. As we have observed, the amount of time they must wait is necessarily uncertain. If the consequences of running afoul of the rule were so massive, officers would be inclined to wait longer than the law requires—producing preventable violence against officers in some cases, and the destruction of evidence in many others. We deemed these consequences severe enough to produce our unanimous agreement that a mere "reasonable suspicion" that knocking and announcing "under the particular circumstances, would be dangerous or futile, or that it would inhibit the effective investigation of the crime," will cause the requirement to yield.

Next to these "substantial social costs" we must consider the deterrence benefits, existence of which is a necessary condition for exclusion. (It is not, of course, a sufficient condition: "[I]t does not follow that the Fourth Amendment requires adoption of every proposal that might deter police misconduct.") To begin with, the value of deterrence depends upon the strength of the incentive to commit the forbidden act. Viewed from this perspective, deterrence of knock-and-announce violations is not worth a lot. Violation of the warrant requirement sometimes produces incriminating evidence that could not otherwise be obtained. But ignoring knock-and-announce can realistically be expected to achieve absolutely nothing except the prevention of destruction of evidence and the avoidance of life-threatening resistance by occupants of the premises—dangers which, if there is even "reasonable suspicion" of their existence, suspend the knock-and-announce requirement anyway. Massive deterrence is hardly required.

It seems to us not even true, as Hudson contends, that without suppression there will be no deterrence of knock-and-announce violations at all. Of course even if this assertion were accurate, it would not necessarily justify suppression. Assuming (as the assertion must) that civil suit is not an effective deterrent, one can think of many forms of police misconduct that are similarly "undeterred." When, for example, a confessed suspect in the killing of a police officer, arrested (along with incriminating evidence) in a lawful warranted search, is subjected to physical abuse at the station house, would it seriously be suggested that the evidence must be excluded, since that is the only "effective deterrent"? And what, other than civil suit, is the "effective deterrent" of police violation of an already-confessed suspect's Sixth Amendment rights by denying him prompt access to counsel? Many would regard these violated rights as more significant than the right not to be intruded upon in one's nightclothes—and yet nothing but "ineffective" civil suit is available as a deterrent. And the police incentive for those violations is arguably greater than the incentive for disregarding the knock-and-announce rule.

We cannot assume that exclusion in this context is necessary deterrence simply because we found that it was necessary deterrence in different contexts and long ago. That would be forcing the public today to pay for the sins and inadequacies of a legal regime that existed almost half a century ago. Dollree Mapp could not turn to 42 U.S.C. § 1983, for meaningful relief; *Monroe v. Pape* (1961), which began the slow but steady expansion of that remedy, was decided the same Term as *Mapp*. It would be another 17 years before the § 1983 remedy was extended to reach the deep pocket of municipalities, *Monell v. New York City Dept. of Social Servs.* (1978). Citizens whose Fourth Amendment rights were violated by federal officers could not bring suit until 10 years after *Mapp*, with this Court's decision in *Bivens v. Six Unknown Fed. Narcotics Agents* (1971).

Hudson complains that "it would be very hard to find a lawyer to take a case such as this," but 42 U.S.C. § 1988(b) answers this objection. Since some civil-rights violations would yield damages too small to justify the expense of litigation, Congress has authorized attorney's fees for civil-rights plaintiffs. This remedy was unavailable in the heydays of our exclusionary-rule jurisprudence, because it is tied to the availability of a cause of action. For years after *Mapp*, "very few lawyers would even consider representation of persons who had civil rights claims against the police," but now "much has changed. Citizens and lawyers are much more willing to seek relief in the courts for police misconduct." The number of public-interest law firms and lawyers who specialize in civil-rights grievances has greatly expanded.

Hudson points out that few published decisions to date announce huge awards for knock-and-announce violations. But this is an unhelpful statistic. Even if we thought that only large damages would deter police misconduct (and that police somehow are deterred by "damages" but indifferent to the prospect of large § 1988 attorney's fees), we do not know how many claims have been settled, or indeed how many violations have occurred that produced anything more than nominal injury. It is clear, at least, that the lower courts are allowing colorable knock-and-announce suits to go forward, unimpeded by assertions of qualified immunity. As far as we know, civil liability is an effective deterrent here, as we have assumed it is in other contexts.

Another development over the past half-century that deters civil-rights violations is the increasing professionalism of police forces, including a new emphasis on internal police discipline. Even as long ago as 1980 we felt it proper to "assume" that unlawful police behavior would "be dealt with appropriately" by the authorities, but we now have increasing evidence that police forces across the United States take the constitutional rights of citizens seriously. There have been "wide-ranging reforms in the education, training, and supervision of police officers." Numerous sources are now available to teach officers and their supervisors what is required of them under this Court's cases, how to respect constitutional guarantees in various situations, and how to craft an effective regime for internal discipline. Failure to teach and enforce constitutional requirements exposes municipalities to financial liability. Moreover, modern police forces are staffed with professionals; it is not credible to assert that internal discipline, which can limit successful careers, will not have a deterrent effect. There is also evidence that the increasing use of various forms of citizen review can enhance police accountability.

Chapter V The Exclusionary Rule, its Exceptions, and Suppression Hearings

In sum, the social costs of applying the exclusionary rule to knock-and-announce violations are considerable; the incentive to such violations is minimal to begin with, and the extant deterrences against them are substantial—incomparably greater than the factors deterring warrantless entries when *Mapp* was decided. Resort to the massive remedy of suppressing evidence of guilt is unjustified.

IV

A trio of cases—confirms our conclusion that suppression is unwarranted in this case.

Like today's case, *Segura* involved a concededly illegal entry. Police conducting a drug crime investigation waited for Segura outside an apartment building; when he arrived, he denied living there. The police arrested him and brought him to the apartment where they suspected illegal activity. An officer knocked. When someone inside opened the door, the police entered, taking Segura with them. They had neither a warrant nor consent to enter, and they did not announce themselves as police—an entry as illegal as can be. Officers then stayed in the apartment for 19 hours awaiting a search warrant. Once alerted that the search warrant had been obtained, the police—still inside, having secured the premises so that no evidence could be removed—conducted a search. We refused to exclude the resulting evidence. We recognized that only the evidence gained from the particular violation could be excluded, and therefore distinguished the effects of the illegal entry from the effects of the legal search: "None of the information on which the warrant was secured was derived from or related in any way to the initial entry into petitioners' apartment. . . ." It was therefore "beyond dispute that the information possessed by the agents before they entered the apartment constituted an independent source for the discovery and seizure of the evidence now challenged." Ibid.

If the search in *Segura* could be "wholly unrelated to the prior entry," when the only entry was warrantless, it would be bizarre to treat more harshly the actions in this case, where the only entry was with a warrant. If the probable cause backing a warrant that was issued later in time could be an "independent source" for a search that proceeded after the officers illegally entered and waited, a search warrant obtained before going in must have at least this much effect.

In the second case, *Harris*, the police violated the defendant's Fourth Amendment rights by arresting him at home without a warrant, contrary to *Payton v. New York* (1980). Once taken to the station house, he gave an incriminating statement. We refused to exclude it. Like the illegal entry which led to discovery of the evidence in today's case, the illegal arrest in *Harris* began a process that culminated in acquisition of the evidence sought to be excluded. While Harris's statement was "the product of an arrest and being in custody," it "was not the fruit of the fact that the arrest was made in the house rather than someplace else." Likewise here: While acquisition of the gun and drugs was the product of a search pursuant to warrant, it was not the fruit of the fact that the entry was not preceded by knock-and-announce.

United States v. Ramirez, supra, involved a claim that police entry violated the Fourth Amendment because it was effected by breaking a window. We ultimately concluded that the property destruction was, under all the circumstances, reasonable, but in the course of our discussion we unanimously said the following: "[D]estruction of property in the course of a search may violate the Fourth Amendment, even though the entry itself is lawful and the fruits of the search are not subject to suppression." Had the breaking of the window been unreasonable, the Court said, it would have been necessary to determine whether there had been a "sufficient causal relationship between the breaking of the window and the discovery of the guns to warrant suppression of the evidence." What clearer expression could there be of the proposition that an impermissible manner of entry does not necessarily trigger the exclusionary rule?

• • •

C. Attenuation   **503**

For the foregoing reasons we affirm the judgment of the Michigan Court of Appeals.

[Justice Kennedy filed an opinion concurring in part and concurring in the judgment. Justice Breyer filed an opinion dissenting, in which Justices Stevens, Souter, and Ginsburg joined.]

NOTES AND QUESTIONS

1. Does *Hudson* mean that suppression can never be a remedy for violation of a knock-and-announce requirement?

2. The Court suggests that because 42 U.S.C § 1983 provides a civil remedy for persons aggrieved by Fourth Amendment violations the deterrence afforded by the exclusionary rule is less necessary than it once was. The Court makes this point without irony, failing to acknowledge how it over the previous years has largely gutted that civil remedy by conferring an expansive, judicially created, qualified immunity on defendant police officers in § 1983 actions. *See* Chapter VIII *infra.*

3. Note that the Court deviates from the general principles of *Brown*, to say nothing of its three-factor test, in finding that the interests that were violated in *Hudson* "have nothing to do with the seizure of the evidence," and—therefore, the Court implies—the exclusionary rule is inapplicable. Professors Maclin and Rader and others point out that this novel approach to attenuation makes vulnerable many cases finding Fourth Amendment violations based on the manner in which a search was executed. *See* Maclin & Rader, *No More Chipping Away, supra* at 1183, 1219-26.

The next case uses a more traditional application of the *Brown v. Illinois* test to justify a harsh result. Once again, computerized police criminal record databases figure prominently.

Utah v. Strieff
579 U.S. 232 (2016)

Justice THOMAS delivered the opinion of the Court.

To enforce the Fourth Amendment's prohibition against "unreasonable searches and seizures," this Court has at times required courts to exclude evidence obtained by unconstitutional police conduct. But the Court has also held that, even when there is a Fourth Amendment violation, this exclusionary rule does not apply when the costs of exclusion outweigh its deterrent benefits. In some cases, for example, the link between the unconstitutional conduct and the discovery of the evidence is too attenuated to justify suppression. The question in this case is whether this attenuation doctrine applies when an officer makes an unconstitutional investigatory stop; learns during that stop that the suspect is subject to a valid arrest warrant; and proceeds to arrest the suspect and seize incriminating evidence during a search incident to that arrest. We hold that the evidence the officer seized as part of the search incident to arrest is admissible because the officer's discovery of the arrest warrant attenuated the connection between the unlawful stop and the evidence seized incident to arrest.

I

This case began with an anonymous tip. In December 2006, someone called the South Salt Lake City police's drug-tip line to report "narcotics activity" at a particular residence.

Narcotics detective Douglas Fackrell investigated the tip. Over the course of about a week, Officer Fackrell conducted intermittent surveillance of the home. He observed visitors who left a few minutes after arriving at the house. These visits were sufficiently frequent to raise his suspicion that the occupants were dealing drugs.

One of those visitors was respondent Edward Strieff. Officer Fackrell observed Strieff exit the house and walk toward a nearby convenience store. In the store's parking lot, Officer Fackrell detained Strieff, identified himself, and asked Strieff what he was doing at the residence.

As part of the stop, Officer Fackrell requested Strieff's identification, and Strieff produced his Utah identification card. Officer Fackrell relayed Strieff's information to a police dispatcher, who reported that Strieff had an outstanding arrest warrant for a traffic violation. Officer Fackrell then arrested Strieff pursuant to that warrant. When Officer Fackrell searched Strieff incident to the arrest, he discovered a baggie of methamphetamine and drug paraphernalia.

The State charged Strieff with unlawful possession of methamphetamine and drug paraphernalia. Strieff moved to suppress the evidence, arguing that the evidence was inadmissible because it was derived from an unlawful investigatory stop. At the suppression hearing, the prosecutor conceded that Officer Fackrell lacked reasonable suspicion for the stop but argued that the evidence should not be suppressed because the existence of a valid arrest warrant attenuated the connection between the unlawful stop and the discovery of the contraband.

* * *

II

A

The Fourth Amendment protects "[t]he right of the people to be secure in their persons, houses, papers, and effects, against unreasonable searches and seizures." Because officers who violated the Fourth Amendment were traditionally considered trespassers, individuals subject to unconstitutional searches or seizures historically enforced their rights through tort suits or self-help. Thomas Y. Davies, *Recovering the Original Fourth Amendment*, 98 Mich. L. Rev. 547, 625 (1999). In the 20th century, however, the exclusionary rule—the rule that often requires trial courts to exclude unlawfully seized evidence in a criminal trial—became the principal judicial remedy to deter Fourth Amendment violations.

Under the Court's precedents, the exclusionary rule encompasses both the "primary evidence obtained as a direct result of an illegal search or seizure" and, relevant here, "evidence later discovered and found to be derivative of an illegality," the so-called "'fruit of the poisonous tree.'" But the significant costs of this rule have led us to deem it "applicable only . . . where its deterrence benefits outweigh its substantial social costs." "Suppression of evidence . . . has always been our last resort, not our first impulse."

We have accordingly recognized several exceptions to the rule. Three of these exceptions involve the causal relationship between the unconstitutional act and the discovery of evidence. First, the independent source doctrine allows trial courts to admit evidence obtained in an unlawful search if officers independently acquired it from a separate, independent source. *See Murray v. United States* (1988). Second, the inevitable discovery doctrine allows for the admission of evidence that would have been discovered even without the unconstitutional source. *See Nix v. Williams* (1984). Third, and at issue here, is the attenuation doctrine: Evidence is admissible when the connection between unconstitutional police conduct and the evidence is remote or has been interrupted by some intervening circumstance, so that "the interest protected by the constitutional guarantee that has been violated would not be served by suppression of the evidence obtained."

B

Turning to the application of the attenuation doctrine to this case, we first address a threshold question: whether this doctrine applies at all to a case like this, where the intervening circumstance that the State relies on is the discovery of a valid, pre-existing, and untainted arrest warrant. The Utah Supreme Court declined to apply the attenuation doctrine because it read our precedents as applying the doctrine only "to circumstances involving an independent act of a defendant's 'free will' in confessing to a crime or consenting to a search." In this Court, Strieff has not defended this argument, and we disagree with it, as well. The attenuation doctrine evaluates the causal link between the government's unlawful act and the discovery of evidence, which often has nothing to do with a defendant's actions. And the logic of our prior attenuation cases is not limited to independent acts by the defendant.

It remains for us to address whether the discovery of a valid arrest warrant was a sufficient intervening event to break the causal chain between the unlawful stop and the discovery of drug-related evidence on Strieff's person. The three factors articulated in *Brown v. Illinois* (1975) guide our analysis. First, we look to the "temporal proximity" between the unconstitutional conduct and the discovery of evidence to determine how closely the discovery of evidence followed the unconstitutional search. Second, we consider "the presence of intervening circumstances." Third, and "particularly" significant, we examine "the purpose and flagrancy of the official misconduct." In evaluating these factors, we assume without deciding (because the State conceded the point) that Officer Fackrell lacked reasonable suspicion to initially stop Strieff. And, because we ultimately conclude that the warrant breaks the causal chain, we also have no need to decide whether the warrant's existence alone would make the initial stop constitutional even if Officer Fackrell was unaware of its existence.

1

The first factor, temporal proximity between the initially unlawful stop and the search, favors suppressing the evidence. Our precedents have declined to find that this factor favors attenuation unless "substantial time" elapses between an unlawful act and when the evidence is obtained. Here, however, Officer Fackrell discovered drug contraband on Strieff's person only minutes after the illegal stop. As the Court explained in *Brown*, such a short time interval counsels in favor of suppression; there, we found that the confession should be suppressed, relying in part on the "less than two hours" that separated the unconstitutional arrest and the confession.

In contrast, the second factor, the presence of intervening circumstances, strongly favors the State. In *Segura*, the Court addressed similar facts to those here and found sufficient intervening circumstances to allow the admission of evidence. There, agents had probable cause to believe that apartment occupants were dealing cocaine. They sought a warrant. In the meantime, they entered the apartment, arrested an occupant, and discovered evidence of drug activity during a limited search for security reasons. The next evening, the Magistrate Judge issued the search warrant. This Court deemed the evidence admissible notwithstanding the illegal search because the information supporting the warrant was "wholly unconnected with the [arguably illegal] entry and was known to the agents well before the initial entry."

Segura, of course, applied the independent source doctrine because the unlawful entry "did not contribute in any way to discovery of the evidence seized under the warrant." But the *Segura* Court suggested that the existence of a valid warrant favors finding that the connection between unlawful conduct and the discovery of evidence is "sufficiently attenuated to dissipate the taint." That principle applies here.

In this case, the warrant was valid, it predated Officer Fackrell's investigation, and it was entirely unconnected with the stop. And once Officer Fackrell discovered the warrant, he had an obligation to arrest Strieff. "A warrant is a judicial mandate to an officer to conduct a search or make an arrest, and the officer has a sworn duty to carry out its provisions." Officer Fackrell's arrest of Strieff thus was a ministerial act that was independently compelled by the pre-existing warrant. And once Officer Fackrell was authorized to arrest Strieff, it was undisputedly lawful to search Strieff as an incident of his arrest to protect Officer Fackrell's safety.

Finally, the third factor, "the purpose and flagrancy of the official misconduct," also strongly favors the State. The exclusionary rule exists to deter police misconduct. The third factor of the attenuation doctrine reflects that rationale by favoring exclusion only when the police misconduct is most in need of deterrence—that is, when it is purposeful or flagrant.

Officer Fackrell was at most negligent. In stopping Strieff, Officer Fackrell made two good-faith mistakes. First, he had not observed what time Strieff entered the suspected drug house, so he did not know how long Strieff had been there. Officer Fackrell thus lacked a sufficient basis to conclude that Strieff was a short-term visitor who may have been consummating a drug transaction. Second, because he lacked confirmation that Strieff was a short-term visitor, Officer Fackrell should have asked Strieff whether he would speak with him, instead of demanding that Strieff do so. Officer Fackrell's stated purpose was to "find out what was going on [in] the house." Nothing prevented him from approaching Strieff simply to ask. But these errors in judgment hardly rise to a purposeful or flagrant violation of Strieff's Fourth Amendment rights.

While Officer Fackrell's decision to initiate the stop was mistaken, his conduct thereafter was lawful. The officer's decision to run the warrant check was a "negligibly burdensome precautio[n]" for officer safety. And Officer Fackrell's actual search of Strieff was a lawful search incident to arrest.

Moreover, there is no indication that this unlawful stop was part of any systemic or recurrent police misconduct. To the contrary, all the evidence suggests that the stop was an isolated instance of negligence that occurred in connection with a bona fide investigation of a suspected drug house. Officer Fackrell saw Strieff leave a suspected drug house. And his suspicion about the house was based on an anonymous tip and his personal observations.

Applying these factors, we hold that the evidence discovered on Strieff's person was admissible because the unlawful stop was sufficiently attenuated by the pre-existing arrest warrant. Although the illegal stop was close in time to Strieff's arrest, that consideration is outweighed by two factors supporting the State. The outstanding arrest warrant for Strieff's arrest is a critical intervening circumstance that is wholly independent of the illegal stop. The discovery of that warrant broke the causal chain between the unconstitutional stop and the discovery of evidence by compelling Officer Fackrell to arrest Strieff. And, it is especially significant that there is no evidence that Officer Fackrell's illegal stop reflected flagrantly unlawful police misconduct.

We find Strieff's counterarguments unpersuasive.

First, he argues that the attenuation doctrine should not apply because the officer's stop was purposeful and flagrant. He asserts that Officer Fackrell stopped him solely to fish for evidence of suspected wrongdoing. But Officer Fackrell sought information from Strieff to find out what was happening inside a house whose occupants were legitimately suspected of dealing drugs. This was not a suspicionless fishing expedition "in the hope that something would turn up."

Strieff argues, moreover, that Officer Fackrell's conduct was flagrant because he detained Strieff without the necessary level of cause (here, reasonable suspicion). But that conflates the standard for an illegal stop with the standard for flagrancy. For the violation to be flagrant, more severe police misconduct is required than the mere absence of proper cause for the seizure. Neither the officer's alleged purpose nor the flagrancy of the violation rise to a level of misconduct to warrant suppression.

Second, Strieff argues that, because of the prevalence of outstanding arrest warrants in many jurisdictions, police will engage in dragnet searches if the exclusionary rule is not applied. We think that this outcome is unlikely. Such wanton conduct would expose police to civil liability. And in any event, the *Brown* factors take account of the purpose and flagrancy of police misconduct. Were evidence of a dragnet search presented here, the application of the *Brown* factors could be different. But there is no evidence that the concerns that Strieff raises with the criminal justice system are present in South Salt Lake City, Utah.

• • •

We hold that the evidence Officer Fackrell seized as part of his search incident to arrest is admissible because his discovery of the arrest warrant attenuated the connection between the unlawful stop and the evidence seized from Strieff incident to arrest. The judgment of the Utah Supreme Court, accordingly, is reversed.

It is so ordered.

Justice SOTOMAYOR, with whom Justice GINSBURG joins as to Parts I, II, and III, dissenting.

The Court today holds that the discovery of a warrant for an unpaid parking ticket will forgive a police officer's violation of your Fourth Amendment rights. Do not be soothed by the opinion's technical language: This case allows the police to stop you on the street, demand your identification, and check it for outstanding traffic warrants — even if you are doing nothing wrong. If the officer discovers a warrant for a fine you forgot to pay, courts will now excuse his illegal stop and will admit into evidence anything he happens to find by searching you after arresting you on the warrant. Because the Fourth Amendment should prohibit, not permit, such misconduct, I dissent.

I

Minutes after Edward Strieff walked out of a South Salt Lake City home, an officer stopped him, questioned him, and took his identification to run it through a police database. The officer did not suspect that Strieff had done anything wrong. Strieff just happened to be the first person to leave a house that the officer thought might contain "drug activity."

As the State of Utah concedes, this stop was illegal. The Fourth Amendment protects people from "unreasonable searches and seizures." An officer breaches that protection when he detains a pedestrian to check his license without any evidence that the person is engaged in a crime. The officer deepens the breach when he prolongs the detention just to fish further for evidence of wrongdoing. In his search for lawbreaking, the officer in this case himself broke the law.

The officer learned that Strieff had a "small traffic warrant." Pursuant to that warrant, he arrested Strieff and, conducting a search incident to the arrest, discovered methamphetamine in Strieff's pockets.

Utah charged Strieff with illegal drug possession. Before trial, Strieff argued that admitting the drugs into evidence would condone the officer's misbehavior. The methamphetamine, he reasoned, was the product of the officer's illegal stop. Admitting it would tell officers that unlawfully discovering even a "small traffic warrant" would give them license to search for evidence of unrelated offenses. The Utah Supreme Court unanimously agreed with Strieff. A majority of this Court now reverses.

II

It is tempting in a case like this, where illegal conduct by an officer uncovers illegal conduct by a civilian, to forgive the officer. After all, his instincts, although unconstitutional, were correct. But a basic principle lies at the heart of the Fourth Amendment: Two wrongs don't make a right. When "lawless police conduct" uncovers evidence of lawless civilian conduct, this Court has long required later criminal trials to exclude the illegally obtained evidence. For example, if an officer breaks into a home and finds a forged check lying around, that check may not be used to prosecute the homeowner for bank fraud. We would describe the check as "'fruit of the poisonous tree.'" Fruit that must be cast aside includes not only evidence directly found by an illegal search but also evidence "come at by exploitation of that illegality."

This "exclusionary rule" removes an incentive for officers to search us without proper justification. It also keeps courts from being "made party to lawless invasions of the constitutional rights of citizens by permitting unhindered governmental use of the fruits of such invasions." When courts admit only lawfully obtained evidence, they encourage "those who formulate law enforcement polices, and the officers who implement them, to incorporate Fourth Amendment ideals into their value system." But when courts admit illegally obtained evidence as well, they reward "manifest neglect if not an open defiance of the prohibitions of the Constitution."

Applying the exclusionary rule, the Utah Supreme Court correctly decided that Strieff's drugs must be excluded because the officer exploited his illegal stop to discover them. The officer found the drugs only after learning of Strieff's traffic violation; and he learned of Strieff's traffic violation only because he unlawfully stopped Strieff to check his driver's license.

The court also correctly rejected the State's argument that the officer's discovery of a traffic warrant unspoiled the poisonous fruit. The State analogizes finding the warrant to one of our earlier decisions, *Wong Sun v. United States*. There, an officer illegally arrested a person who, days later, voluntarily returned to the station to confess to committing a crime. Even though the person would not have confessed "but for the illegal actions of the police," we noted that the police did not exploit their illegal arrest to obtain the confession. Because the confession was obtained by "means sufficiently distinguishable" from the constitutional violation, we held that it could be admitted into evidence. The State contends that the search incident to the warrant-arrest here is similarly distinguishable from the illegal stop.

But *Wong Sun* explains why Strieff's drugs must be excluded. We reasoned that a Fourth Amendment violation may not color every investigation that follows but it certainly stains the actions of officers who exploit the infraction. We distinguished evidence obtained by innocuous means from evidence obtained by exploiting misconduct after considering a variety of factors: whether a long time passed, whether there were "intervening circumstances," and whether the purpose or flagrancy of the misconduct was "calculated" to procure the evidence. *Brown v. Illinois* (1975).

These factors confirm that the officer in this case discovered Strieff's drugs by exploiting his own illegal conduct. The officer did not ask Strieff to volunteer his name only to find out, days later, that Strieff had a warrant against him. The officer illegally stopped Strieff and immediately ran a warrant check. The officer's discovery of a warrant was not some intervening surprise that he could not have anticipated. Utah lists over 180,000 misdemeanor warrants in its database, and at the time of the arrest, Salt Lake County had a "backlog of outstanding warrants" so large that it faced the "potential for civil liability." The officer's violation was also calculated to procure evidence. His sole reason for stopping Strieff, he acknowledged, was investigative—he wanted to discover whether drug activity was going on in the house Strieff had just exited.

The warrant check, in other words, was not an "intervening circumstance" separating the stop from the search for drugs. It was part and parcel of the officer's illegal "expedition for evidence in the hope that something might turn up." Under our precedents, because the officer found Strieff's drugs by exploiting his own constitutional violation, the drugs should be excluded.

III

A

The Court sees things differently. To the Court, the fact that a warrant gives an officer cause to arrest a person severs the connection between illegal policing and the resulting discovery of evidence. This is a remarkable proposition: The mere existence of a warrant not only gives an officer legal cause to arrest and search a person, it also forgives an officer who, with no knowledge of the warrant at all, unlawfully stops that person on a whim or hunch.

To explain its reasoning, the Court relies on *Segura*. There, federal agents applied for a warrant to search an apartment but illegally entered the apartment to secure it before the judge issued the warrant. After receiving the warrant, the agents then searched the apartment for drugs. The question before us was what to do with the evidence the agents then discovered. We declined to suppress it because "[t]he illegal entry into petitioners' apartment did not contribute in any way to discovery of the evidence seized under the warrant."

According to the majority, *Segura* involves facts "similar" to this case and "suggest[s]" that a valid warrant will clean up whatever illegal conduct uncovered it. It is difficult to understand this interpretation. In *Segura*, the agents' illegal conduct in entering the apartment had nothing to do with their procurement of a search warrant. Here, the officer's illegal conduct in stopping Strieff was essential to his discovery of an arrest warrant. Segura would be similar only if the agents used information they illegally obtained from the apartment to procure a search warrant or discover an arrest warrant. Precisely because that was not the case, the Court admitted the untainted evidence.

The majority likewise misses the point when it calls the warrant check here a "'negligibly burdensome precautio[n]'" taken for the officer's "safety." Remember, the officer stopped Strieff without suspecting him of committing any crime. By his own account, the officer did not fear Strieff. Moreover, the safety rationale we discussed in *Rodriguez*, an opinion about highway patrols, is conspicuously absent here. A warrant check on a highway "ensur[es] that vehicles on the road are operated safely and responsibly." We allow such checks during legal traffic stops because the legitimacy of a person's driver's license has a "close connection to roadway safety." A warrant check of a pedestrian on a sidewalk, "by contrast, is a measure aimed at 'detect[ing] evidence of ordinary criminal wrongdoing.'" Surely we would not allow officers to warrant-check random joggers, dog walkers, and lemonade vendors just to ensure they pose no threat to anyone else.

The majority also posits that the officer could not have exploited his illegal conduct because he did not violate the Fourth Amendment on purpose. Rather, he made "good-faith mistakes." Never mind that the officer's sole purpose was to fish for evidence. The majority casts his unconstitutional actions as "negligent" and therefore incapable of being deterred by the exclusionary rule. Ibid.

But the Fourth Amendment does not tolerate an officer's unreasonable searches and seizures just because he did not know any better. Even officers prone to negligence can learn from courts that exclude illegally obtained evidence. Indeed, they are perhaps the most in need of the education, whether by the judge's opinion, the prosecutor's future guidance, or an updated manual on criminal procedure. If the officers are in doubt about what the law requires, exclusion gives them an "incentive to err on the side of constitutional behavior."

B

Most striking about the Court's opinion is its insistence that the event here was "isolated," with "no indication that this unlawful stop was part of any systemic or recurrent police misconduct." Respectfully, nothing about this case is isolated.

Outstanding warrants are surprisingly common. When a person with a traffic ticket misses a fine payment or court appearance, a court will issue a warrant. When a person on probation drinks alcohol or breaks curfew, a court will issue a warrant. The States and Federal Government maintain databases with over 7.8 million outstanding warrants, the vast majority of which appear to be for minor offenses. Even these sources may not track the "staggering" numbers of warrants, "'drawers and drawers'" full, that many cities issue for traffic violations and ordinance infractions. The county in this case has had a "backlog" of such warrants. The Department of Justice recently reported that in the town of Ferguson, Missouri, with a population of 21,000, 16,000 people had outstanding warrants against them.

Justice Department investigations across the country have illustrated how these astounding numbers of warrants can be used by police to stop people without cause. In a single year in New Orleans, officers "made nearly 60,000 arrests, of which about 20,000 were of people with outstanding traffic or misdemeanor warrants from neighboring parishes for such infractions as unpaid tickets." In the St. Louis metropolitan area, officers "routinely" stop people — on the street, at bus stops, or even in court — for no reason other than "an officer's desire to check whether the subject had a municipal arrest warrant pending." In Newark, New Jersey, officers stopped 52,235 pedestrians within a 4-year period and ran warrant checks on 39,308 of them. The Justice Department analyzed these warrant-checked stops and reported that "approximately 93% of the stops would have been considered unsupported by articulated reasonable suspicion."

I do not doubt that most officers act in "good faith" and do not set out to break the law. That does not mean these stops are "isolated instance[s] of negligence," however. Many are the product of institutionalized training procedures. The New York City Police Department long trained officers to, in the words of a District Judge, "stop and question first, develop reasonable suspicion later." The Utah Supreme Court described as "'routine procedure' or 'common practice'" the decision of Salt Lake City police officers to run warrant checks on pedestrians they detained without reasonable suspicion. In the related context of traffic stops, one widely followed police manual instructs officers looking for drugs to "run at least a warrants check on all drivers you stop. Statistically, narcotics offenders are . . . more likely to fail to appear on simple citations, such as traffic or trespass violations, leading to the issuance of bench warrants. Discovery of an outstanding warrant gives you cause for an immediate custodial arrest and search of the suspect." C. Remsberg, Tactics for Criminal Patrol 205-206 (1995); C. Epp et al., Pulled Over 23, 33-36 (2014).

The majority does not suggest what makes this case "isolated" from these and countless other examples. Nor does it offer guidance for how a defendant can prove that his arrest was the result of "widespread" misconduct. Surely it should not take a federal investigation of Salt Lake County before the Court would protect someone in Strieff's position.

IV

Writing only for myself, and drawing on my professional experiences, I would add that unlawful "stops" have severe consequences much greater than the inconvenience suggested by the name. This Court has given officers an array of instruments to probe and examine you. When we condone officers' use of these devices without adequate cause, we give them reason to target pedestrians in an arbitrary manner. We also risk treating members of our communities as second-class citizens.

Although many Americans have been stopped for speeding or jaywalking, few may realize how degrading a stop can be when the officer is looking for more. This Court has allowed an officer to stop you for whatever reason he wants — so long as he can point to a pretextual justification after the fact. That justification must provide specific reasons why the officer suspected you were breaking the law, but it may factor in your ethnicity, where you live, what you were wearing, and how you behaved. The officer does not even need to know which law you might have broken so long as he can later point to any possible infraction — even one that is minor, unrelated, or ambiguous.

The indignity of the stop is not limited to an officer telling you that you look like a criminal. The officer may next ask for your "consent" to inspect your bag or purse without telling you that you can decline. Regardless of your answer, he may order you to stand "helpless, perhaps facing a wall with [your] hands raised." If the officer thinks you might be dangerous, he may then "frisk" you for weapons. This involves more than just a pat down. As onlookers pass by, the officer may "'feel with sensitive fingers every portion of [your] body. A thorough search [may] be made of [your] arms and armpits, waistline and back, the groin and area about the testicles, and entire surface of the legs down to the feet.'"

The officer's control over you does not end with the stop. If the officer chooses, he may handcuff you and take you to jail for doing nothing more than speeding, jaywalking, or "driving [your] pickup truck . . . with [your] 3-year-old son and 5-year-old daughter . . . without [your] seatbelt fastened." At the jail, he can fingerprint you, swab DNA from the inside of your mouth, and force you to "shower with a delousing agent" while you "lift [your] tongue, hold out [your] arms, turn around, and lift [your] genitals." Even if you are innocent, you will now join the 65 million Americans with an arrest record and experience the "civil death" of discrimination by employers, landlords, and whoever else conducts a background check. And, of course, if you fail to pay bail or appear for court, a judge will issue a warrant to render you "arrestable on sight" in the future.

This case involves a suspicionless stop, one in which the officer initiated this chain of events without justification. As the Justice Department notes, supra, at 2068-2069, many innocent people are subjected to the humiliations of these unconstitutional searches. The white defendant in this case shows that anyone's dignity can be violated in this manner. But it is no secret that people of color are disproportionate victims of this type of scrutiny. For generations, black and brown parents have given their children "the talk" — instructing them never to run down the street; always keep your hands where they can be seen; do not even think of talking back to a stranger — all out of fear of how an officer with a gun will react to them.

By legitimizing the conduct that produces this double consciousness, this case tells everyone, white and black, guilty and innocent, that an officer can verify your legal status at any time. It says that your body is subject to invasion while courts excuse the violation of your rights. It implies that you are not a citizen of a democracy but the subject of a carceral state, just waiting to be cataloged.

We must not pretend that the countless people who are routinely targeted by police are "isolated." They are the canaries in the coal mine whose deaths, civil and literal, warn us that no one can breathe in this atmosphere. They are the ones who recognize that unlawful police stops corrode all our civil liberties and threaten all our lives. Until their voices matter too, our justice system will continue to be anything but.

I dissent.

NOTES AND QUESTIONS

1. Edward Strieff probably did not know that there was a warrant out for his arrest on a traffic violation, and that he could be searched incident to that arrest. But still, why didn't he just walk away when approached by the police officer? Did they not have a course on Street Law in his high school?

2. Even Justice Sotomayor seems to concede that the police officer's conduct was only negligent. Do you agree? Was there anything close to reasonable suspicion? Was the officer's purpose in approaching Strieff — "to find out what was going on in the house" — truly

Edward J. Strieff Jr.

benign? Wasn't the officer interested in whether Strieff was implicated in whatever was going on in the house?

3. Did the officer truly have an "obligation" to arrest Strieff because of the existence of an outstanding bench warrant for a traffic violation? Does it seem suspicious that the only support cited for this proposition is *Leon*, which involved a search warrant? *See* Nirej Sekhon, *Dangerous Warrants*, 93 Wash. L. Rev. 967, 998-1000 (2018) (observing that whether to arrest someone based solely on the existence of a warrant is an act of enforcement discretion similar to many other police functions).

4. Doesn't the *Strieff* decision provide exactly the perverse incentive *Strieff* warns of — that police will be free to do "dragnet" searches in the hopes of discovering people with outstanding warrants who can be arrested? Although those incentives may exist regardless of *Strieff* based on the data from the DOJ investigations noted by Justice Sotomayor.

5. For an interesting look into the varying uses of narrative in *Strieff, see* Danielle Hayes, *He Say, She Say: Utah v. Strieff and the Role of Narrative in Judicial Decisions*, 61 Howard L.J. 611 (2018).

D. STANDING

Who has the right to file a motion to suppress evidence? Anyone against whom illegally acquired evidence might be admitted at trial? The next cases explore this issue.

Jones v. United States
362 U.S. 257 (1960)

Mr. Justice FRANKFURTER delivered the opinion of the Court.

This is a prosecution for violation of federal narcotics laws. In the first count of a two-count indictment petitioner was charged with having "purchased, sold, dispensed and distributed" narcotics in violation of 26 U.S.C. § 4704(a), 26 U.S.C.A. § 4704(a), that is, not in or from the "original stamped package." In the second count petitioner was charged under 21 U.S.C. § 174, 21 U.S.C.A. § 174, with having "facilitated the concealment and sale of" the same narcotics, knowing them to have been imported illegally into the United States. Petitioner was found guilty on both counts and sentenced to seven years' imprisonment. The Court of Appeals, one judge dissenting, affirmed the conviction. Since the case presented important questions in the administration of criminal justice, more particularly a defendant's standing to challenge the legality of a search in the circumstances of this case, as well as the legality of the particular search should standing be established, we granted certiorari.

Both statutory provisions under which petitioner was prosecuted permit conviction upon proof of the defendant's possession of narcotics, and in the case of 26 U.S.C. § 4704(a), 26

U.S.C.A. § 4704(a), of the absence of the appropriate stamps. Possession was the basis of the Government's case against petitioner. The evidence against him may be briefly summarized. He was arrested in an apartment in the District of Columbia by federal narcotics officers, who were executing warrant to search for narcotics. Those officers found narcotics, without appropriate stamps, and narcotics paraphernalia in a bird's nest in an awning just outside a window in the apartment. Another officer, stationed outside the building, had a short time before seen petitioner put his hand on the awning. Upon the discovery of the narcotics and the paraphernalia petitioner had admitted to the officers that some of these were his and that he was living in the apartment.

Prior to trial petitioner duly moved to suppress the evidence obtained through the execution of the search warrant on the ground that the warrant had been issued without a showing of probable cause. The Government challenged petitioner's standing to make this motion because petitioner alleged neither ownership of the seized articles nor an interest in the apartment greater than that of an "invitee or guest." The District Court agreed to take evidence on the issue of petitioner's standing. Only petitioner gave evidence. On direct examination he testified that the apartment belonged to a friend, Evans, who had given him the use of it, and a key, with which petitioner had admitted himself on the day of the arrest. On cross-examination petitioner testified that he had a suit and shirt at the apartment, that his home was elsewhere, that he paid nothing for the use of the apartment, that Evans had let him use it "as a friend," that he had slept there "maybe a night," and that at the time of the search Evans had been away in Philadelphia for about five days.

Solely on the basis of petitioner's lack of standing to make it, the district judge denied petitioner's motion to suppress. When the case came on for trial before a different judge, the motion to suppress was renewed and was denied on the basis of the prior ruling. An unsuccessful objection was made when the seized items were offered in evidence at the trial.

In affirming petitioner's conviction the Court of Appeals agreed with the District Court that petitioner lacked standing, but proceeded to rule that even if it were to find that petitioner had standing, it would hold the evidence to have been lawfully received. A challenge to the search which petitioner had not made in the District Court, namely, that the method of executing the warrant had been illegal, was considered by the Court of Appeals and rejected, while the contention petitioner had made below, that there had been insufficient cause to issue the warrant, was rejected without discussion.

The issue of petitioner's standing is to be decided with reference to Rule 41(e) of the Federal Rules of Criminal Procedure, 18 U.S.C.A. This is a statutory direction governing the suppression of evidence acquired in violation of the conditions validating a search. It is desirable to set forth the Rule.

> A person aggrieved by an unlawful search and seizure may move the district court for the district in which the property was seized for the return of the property and to suppress for use as evidence anything so obtained on the ground that (1) the property was illegally seized without warrant, or (2) the warrant is insufficient on its face, or (3) property seized is not that described in the warrant, or (4) there was not probable cause for believing the existence of the grounds on which the warrant was issued, or (5) the warrant was illegally executed. The judge shall receive evidence on any issue of fact necessary to the decision of the motion. If the motion is granted the property shall be restored unless otherwise subject to lawful detention and it shall not be admissible in evidence at any hearing or trial. The motion to suppress evidence may also be made in the district where the trial is to be had. The motion shall be made before trial or hearing unless opportunity therefor did not exist or the defendant was not aware of the grounds for the motion, but the court in its discretion may entertain the motion at the trial or hearing.

In order to qualify as a "person aggrieved by an unlawful search and seizure" one must have been a victim of a search or seizure, one against whom the search was directed, as distinguished from one who claims prejudice only through the use of evidence gathered as a consequence of a search or seizure directed at someone else. Rule 41(e) applies the general principle that a party will not be heard to claim a constitutional protection unless he "belongs to the class for whose sake the constitutional protection is given." The restrictions upon searches and seizures were obviously designed for protection against official invasion of privacy and the security of property. They are not exclusionary provisions against the admission of kinds of evidence deemed inherently unreliable or prejudicial. The exclusion in federal trials of evidence otherwise competent but gathered by federal officials in violation of the Fourth Amendment is a means for making effective the protection of privacy.

Ordinarily, then, it is entirely proper to require of one who seeks to challenge the legality of a search as the basis for suppressing relevant evidence that he allege, and if the allegation be disputed that he establish, that he himself was the victim of an invasion of privacy. But prosecutions like this one have presented a special problem. To establish "standing," Courts of Appeals have generally required that the movant claim either to have owned or possessed the seized property or to have had a substantial possessory interest in the premises searched. Since narcotics charges like those in the present indictment may be established through proof solely of possession of narcotics, a defendant seeking to comply with what has been the conventional standing requirement has been forced to allege facts the proof of which would tend, if indeed not be sufficient, to convict him. At the least, such a defendant has been placed in the criminally tendentious position of explaining his possession of the premises. He has been faced, not only with the chance that the allegations made on the motion to suppress may be used against him at the trial, although that they may is by no means an inevitable holding, but also with the encouragement that he perjure himself if he seeks to establish "standing" while maintaining a defense to the charge of possession.

The dilemma that has thus been created for defendants in cases like this has been pointedly put by Judge Learned Hand:

> Men may wince at admitting that they were the owners, or in possession, of contraband property; may wish at one to secure the remedies of a possessor, and avoid the perils of the part; but equivocation will not serve. If they come as victims, they must take on that role, with enough detail to cast them without question. The petitioners at bar shrank from that predicament; but they were obliged to choose one horn of the dilemma.

Following this holding, several Courts of Appeals have pinioned a defendant within this dilemma. A District Court has held otherwise. The Government urges us to follow the body of Court of Appeals' decisions and to rule that the lower courts, including the courts below, have been right in barring a defendant in a case like this from challenging a search because of his failure, when making his motion to suppress, to allege either that he owned or possessed the property seized or that he had a possessory interest in the premises searched greater than the interest of an "invitee or guest."

Judge Hand's dilemma is not inescapable. It presupposes requirements of "standing" which we do not find compelling. Two separate lines of thought effectively sustain defendant's standing in this case. (1) The same element in this prosecution which has caused a dilemma, i.e., that possession both convicts and confers standing, eliminates any necessity for a preliminary showing of an interest in the premises searched or the property seized, which ordinarily is required when standing is challenged. (2) Even were this not a prosecution turning on illicit possession, the legally requisite interest in the premises was here satisfied, for it need not be as extensive a property interest as was required by the courts below.

As to the first ground, we are persuaded by this consideration: to hold to the contrary, that is, to hold that petitioner's failure to acknowledge interest in the narcotics or the premises prevented his attack upon the search, would be to permit the Government to have the advantage of contradictory positions as a basis for conviction. Petitioner's conviction flows from his possession of the narcotics at the time of the search. Yet the fruits of that search, upon which the conviction depends, were admitted into evidence on the ground that petitioner did not have possession of the narcotics at that time. The prosecution here thus subjected the defendant to the penalties meted out to one in lawless possession while refusing him the remedies designed for one in that situation. It is not consonant with the amenities, to put it mildly, of the administration of criminal justice to sanction such squarely contradictory assertions of power by the Government. The possession on the basis of which petitioner is to be and was convicted suffices to give him standing under any fair and rational conception of the requirements of Rule 41(e).

The Government's argument to the contrary essentially invokes elegantia juris. In the interest of normal procedural orderliness, a motion to suppress, under Rule 41(e), must be made prior to trial, if the defendant then has knowledge of the grounds on which to base the motion. The Government argues that the defendant therefore must establish his standing to suppress the evidence at that time through affirmative allegations and may not wait to rest standing upon the Government's case at the trial. This provision of Rule 41(e), requiring the motion to suppress to be made before trial, is a crystallization of decisions of this Court requiring that procedure, and is designed to eliminate from the trial disputes over police conduct not immediately relevant to the question of guilt. As codified, the rule is not a rigid one, for under Rule 41(e) "the court in its discretion may entertain the motion (to suppress) at the trial or hearing." This qualification proves that we are dealing with carrying out an important social policy and not a narrow, finicky procedural requirement. This underlying policy likewise precludes application of the Rule so as to compel the injustice of an internally inconsistent conviction. In cases where the indictment itself charges possession, the defendant in a very real sense is revealed as a "person aggrieved by an unlawful search and seizure" upon a motion to suppress evidence prior to trial. Rule 41(e) should not be applied to allow the Government to deprive the defendant of standing to bring a motion to suppress by framing the indictment in general terms, while prosecuting for possession.

As a second ground sustaining "standing" here we hold that petitioner's testimony on the motion to suppress made out a sufficient interest in the premises to establish him as a "person aggrieved" by their search. That testimony established that at the time of the search petitioner was present in the apartment with the permission of Evans, whose apartment it was. The Government asserts that such an interest is insufficient to give standing. The Government does not contend that only ownership of the premises may confer standing. It would draw distinctions among various classes of possessors, deeming some, such as "guests" and "invitees" with only the "use" of the premises, to have too "tenuous" an interest although concededly having "some measure of control" through their "temporary presence," while conceding that others, who in a "realistic sense, have dominion of the apartment" or who are "domiciled" there, have standing. Petitioner, it is insisted, by his own testimony falls in the former class.

While this Court has never passed upon the interest in the searched premises necessary to maintain a motion to suppress, the Government's argument closely follows the prevailing view in the lower courts. They have denied standing to "guests" and "invitees" and employees, who though in "control" or "occupancy" lacked possession. The necessary quantum of interest has been distinguished as being, variously, "ownership in or right to possession of the premises," the interest of a "lessee or licensee," or of one with "dominion." We do not lightly depart from this course of decisions by the lower courts. We are persuaded, however, that it is unnecessary and ill-advised to import into the law surrounding the constitutional right to be free from unreasonable searches and seizures subtle distinctions, developed and refined by the common law in evolving the body of private properly law which, more than almost any other branch of law, has been shaped by distinctions whose validity is largely historical. Even in the area

516   Chapter V The Exclusionary Rule, its Exceptions, and Suppression Hearings

from which they derive, due consideration has led to the discarding of these distinctions in the homeland of the common law. Distinctions such as those between "lessee," "licensee," "invitee" and "guest," often only of gossamer strength, ought not to be determinative in fashioning procedures ultimately referable to constitutional safeguards.

We rejected such distinctions as inappropriate to the law of maritime torts. We found there to be a duty of ordinary care to one rightfully on the ship, regardless of whether he was a "licensee" rather than an "invitee." "For the admiralty law at this late date to import such conceptual distinctions would be foreign to its traditions of simplicity and practicality." A fortiori we ought not to bow to them in the fair administration of the criminal law. To do so would not comport with our justly proud claim of the procedural protections accorded to those charged with crime. No just interest of the Government in the effective and rigorous enforcement of the criminal law will be hampered by recognizing that anyone legitimately on premises where a search occurs may challenge its legality by way of a motion to suppress, when its fruits are proposed to be used against him. This would of course not avail those who, by virtue of their wrongful presence, cannot invoke the privacy of the premises searched. As petitioner's testimony established Evans' consent to his presence in the apartment, he was entitled to have the merits of his motion to suppress adjudicated. . . .

NOTES AND QUESTIONS

1. Note the Court's reliance on Rule 41(e) of the Federal Rules of Criminal Procedure, which by statute gave a right to challenge a search and seizure to any person "aggrieved by" the intrusion. What is the range of possible interpretations of the quoted language?

2. Note that *Jones* was decided one year before *Mapp v. Ohio*, and is thus establishing a standing rule for federal courts only. Is it surprising that the Supreme Court, 46 years after *Weeks*, had never previously addressed the issue?

3. Here is the entirety of the probable cause showing that led to the issuance of the warrant. Under the general rule that an informant tip can only establish probable cause if the tip is corroborated, should this warrant have even been authorized?

> Affidavit in Support of a U.S. Commissioners Search Warrant for Premises 1436 Meridian Place, N.W., Washington, D.C., apartment including window spaces of said apartment. Occupied by Cecil Jones and Earline Richardson.
>
> In the late afternoon of Tuesday, August 20, 1957, I, Detective Thomas Didone, Jr. received information that Cecil Jones and Earline Richardson were involved in the illicit narcotic traffic and that they kept a ready supply of heroin on hand in the above mentioned apartment. The source of information also relates that the two aforementioned persons kept these same narcotics either on their person, under a pillow, on a dresser or on a window ledge in said apartment. The source of information goes on to relate that on many occasions the source of information has gone to said apartment and purchased narcotic drugs from the abovementioned persons and that the narcotics were secreated (sic) in the above mentioned places. The last time being August 20, 1957.
>
> Both the aforementioned persons are familiar to the undersigned and other members of the Narcotic Squad. Both have admitted to the use of narcotic drugs and display needle marks as evidence of same.
>
> This same information, regarding the illicit narcotic traffic, conducted by Cecil Jones and Earline Richardson, has been given to the undersigned and to other officers of the narcotic squad by other sources of information.
>
> Because the source of information mentioned in the opening paragraph has given information to the undersigned on previous occasion and which was correct, and because this same

D. Standing   **517**

information is given by other sources does believe that there is now illicit narcotic drugs being secreted (sic) in the above apartment by Cecil Jones and Earline Richardson.

Det. Thomas Didone, Jr.,
Narcotic Squad, MPDC.

Given the D.C. Circuit precedent—denying standing to guests and invitees—if the agents knew Jones did not live in the apartment, would they have needed to get a warrant in the first place?

4. How much of an improvement over the "subtle distinctions" of the common law is the "legitimately on premises" test?

The *Jones* standard was explicitly repudiated by the Supreme Court in *Rakas v. Illinois*, 439 U.S. 128 (1978). A police officer on routine patrol received word of the robbery of a clothing store, including a description of the getaway car—we are not told anything about the level of detail in the description—and had stopped a car that "he thought might be the getaway car." The stop and subsequent search yielded a gun and shells. The Court found that none of the car's passengers had standing to contest the search as they had no "possessory" interest in the car and thus lacked a legitimate expectation of privacy. Dissenting, along with Justices Brennan, Marshall, and Stevens, Justice White pointed out, among other things, that the Court's decision "invites police to engage in unreasonable searches every time an automobile has more than one occupant." *Id.* at 169.

What are the implications of *Rakas* where multiple people occupy not an automobile but an apartment?

Minnesota v. Carter
523 U.S. 83 (1998)

Chief Justice REHNQUIST delivered the opinion of the Court.

Respondents and the lessee of an apartment were sitting in one of its rooms, bagging cocaine. While so engaged they were observed by a police officer, who looked through a drawn window blind. The Supreme Court of Minnesota held that the officer's viewing was a search that violated respondents' Fourth Amendment rights. We hold that no such violation occurred.

James Thielen, a police officer in the Twin Cities' suburb of Eagan, Minnesota, went to an apartment building to investigate a tip from a confidential informant. The informant said that he had walked by the window of a ground-floor apartment and had seen people putting a white powder into bags. The officer looked in the same window through a gap in the closed blind and observed the bagging operation for several minutes. He then notified headquarters, which began preparing affidavits for a search warrant while he returned to the apartment building. When two men left the building in a previously identified Cadillac, the police stopped the car. Inside were respondents Carter and Johns. As the police opened the door of the car to let Johns out, they observed a black, zippered pouch and a handgun, later determined to be loaded, on the vehicle's floor. Carter and Johns were arrested, and a later police search of the vehicle the next day discovered pagers, a scale, and 47 grams of cocaine in plastic sandwich bags.

After seizing the car, the police returned to Apartment 103 and arrested the occupant, Kimberly Thompson, who is not a party to this appeal. A search of the apartment pursuant to a warrant revealed cocaine residue on the kitchen table and plastic baggies similar to those found in the Cadillac. Thielen identified Carter, Johns, and Thompson as the three people he had observed placing the powder into baggies. The police later learned that while Thompson was the lessee of the apartment, Carter and Johns lived in Chicago and had come to the apartment for the sole purpose of packaging the cocaine. Carter and Johns had never been to the apartment before and were only in the apartment for approximately 2½ hours. In return for the use of the apartment, Carter and Johns had given Thompson one-eighth of an ounce of the cocaine.

Carter and Johns were charged with conspiracy to commit a controlled substance crime in the first degree and aiding and abetting in a controlled substance crime in the first degree, in violation of Minn. Stat. §§ 152.021, subds. 1(1), 3(a), 609.05 (1996). They moved to suppress all evidence obtained from the apartment and the Cadillac, as well as to suppress several postarrest incriminating statements they had made. They argued that Thielen's initial observation of their drug packaging activities was an unreasonable search in violation of the Fourth Amendment and that all evidence obtained as a result of this unreasonable search was inadmissible as fruit of the poisonous tree. The Minnesota trial court held that since, unlike the defendant in *Minnesota v. Olson* (1990), Carter and Johns were not overnight social guests but temporary out-of-state visitors, they were not entitled to claim the protection of the Fourth Amendment against the government intrusion into the apartment. The trial court also concluded that Thielen's observation was not a search within the meaning of the Fourth Amendment. After a trial, Carter and Johns were each convicted of both offenses. The Minnesota Court of Appeals held that respondent Carter did not have "standing" to object to Thielen's actions because his claim that he was predominantly a social guest was "inconsistent with the only evidence concerning his stay in the apartment, which indicates that he used it for a business purpose-to package drugs." In a separate appeal, the Court of Appeals also affirmed Johns' conviction, without addressing what it termed the "standing" issue.

A divided Minnesota Supreme Court reversed, holding that respondents had "standing" to claim the protection of the Fourth Amendment because they had "'a legitimate expectation of privacy in the invaded place.'" We granted certiorari, and now reverse.

The Minnesota courts analyzed whether respondents had a legitimate expectation of privacy under the rubric of "standing" doctrine, an analysis that this Court expressly rejected 20 years ago in *Rakas*. In that case, we held that automobile passengers could not assert the protection of the Fourth Amendment against the seizure of incriminating evidence from a vehicle where they owned neither the vehicle nor the evidence. Central to our analysis was the idea that in determining whether a defendant is able to show the violation of his (and not someone else's) Fourth Amendment rights, the "definition of those rights is more properly placed within the purview of substantive Fourth Amendment law than within that of standing." Thus, we held that in order to claim the protection of the Fourth Amendment, a defendant must demonstrate that he personally has an expectation of privacy in the place searched, and that his expectation is reasonable; i.e., one that has "a source outside of the Fourth Amendment, either by reference to concepts of real or personal property law or to understandings that are recognized and permitted by society."

The Fourth Amendment guarantees: "The right of the people to be secure in their persons, houses, papers, and effects, against unreasonable searches and seizures, shall not be violated, and no Warrants shall issue, but upon probable cause, supported by Oath or affirmation, and particularly describing the place to be searched, and the persons or things to be seized." The Amendment protects persons against unreasonable searches of "their persons [and] houses" and thus indicates that the Fourth Amendment is a personal right that must be invoked by an individual. But the extent to which the Fourth Amendment protects people may depend upon where those people are. We have held that "capacity to claim the protection of the Fourth Amendment depends . . . upon whether the person who claims the protection of the Amendment has a legitimate expectation of privacy in the invaded place."

The text of the Amendment suggests that its protections extend only to people in "their" houses. But we have held that in some circumstances a person may have a legitimate expectation of privacy in the house of someone else. In *Minnesota v. Olson* (1990), for example, we decided that an overnight guest in a house had the sort of expectation of privacy that the Fourth Amendment protects. We said:

> To hold that an overnight guest has a legitimate expectation of privacy in his host's home merely recognizes the every day expectations of privacy that we all share. Staying overnight in another's home is a longstanding social custom that serves functions recognized as valuable by society. We stay in others' homes when we travel to a strange city for business or pleasure, when we visit our parents, children, or more distant relatives out of town, when we are in between jobs or homes, or when we house-sit for a friend. . . .
>
> From the overnight guest's perspective, he seeks shelter in another's home precisely because it provides him with privacy, a place where he and his possessions will not be disturbed by anyone but his host and those his host allows inside. We are at our most vulnerable when we are asleep because we cannot monitor our own safety or the security of our belongings. It is for this reason that, although we may spend all day in public places, when we cannot sleep in our own home we seek out another private place to sleep, whether it be a hotel room, or the home of a friend.

In *Jones v. United States* (1960), the defendant seeking to exclude evidence resulting from a search of an apartment had been given the use of the apartment by a friend. He had clothing in the apartment, had slept there "'maybe a night,'" and at the time was the sole occupant of the apartment. But while the holding of *Jones*—that a search of the apartment violated the defendant's Fourth Amendment rights—is still valid, its statement that "anyone legitimately on the premises where a search occurs may challenge its legality," was expressly repudiated in *Rakas*. Thus, an overnight guest in a home may claim the protection of the Fourth Amendment, but one who is merely present with the consent of the householder may not.

Respondents here were obviously not overnight guests, but were essentially present for a business transaction and were only in the home a matter of hours. There is no suggestion that they had a previous relationship with Thompson, or that there was any other purpose to their visit. Nor was there anything similar to the overnight guest relationship in *Olson* to suggest a degree of acceptance into the household. While the apartment was a dwelling place for Thompson, it was for these respondents simply a place to do business.

Property used for commercial purposes is treated differently for Fourth Amendment purposes from residential property. "An expectation of privacy in commercial premises, however, is different from, and indeed less than, a similar expectation in an individual's home." And while it was a "home" in which respondents were present, it was not their home. Similarly, the Court has held that in some circumstances a worker can claim Fourth Amendment protection over his own workplace. But there is no indication that respondents in this case had nearly as significant a connection to Thompson's apartment as the worker in O'Connor had to his own private office.

If we regard the overnight guest in *Minnesota v. Olson* as typifying those who may claim the protection of the Fourth Amendment in the home of another, and one merely "legitimately on the premises" as typifying those who may not do so, the present case is obviously somewhere in between. But the purely commercial nature of the transaction engaged in here, the relatively short period of time on the premises, and the lack of any previous connection between respondents and the householder, all lead us to conclude that respondents' situation is closer to that of one simply permitted on the premises. We therefore hold that any search which may have occurred did not violate their Fourth Amendment rights.

Chapter V The Exclusionary Rule, its Exceptions, and Suppression Hearings

Because we conclude that respondents had no legitimate expectation of privacy in the apartment, we need not decide whether the police officer's observation constituted a "search." The judgments of the Supreme Court of Minnesota are accordingly reversed, and the cause is remanded for proceedings not inconsistent with this opinion.

It is so ordered.

Justice GINSBURG, with whom Justice STEVENS and Justice SOUTER join, dissenting.

The Court's decision undermines not only the security of short-term guests, but also the security of the home resident herself. In my view, when a homeowner or lessee personally invites a guest into her home to share in a common endeavor, whether it be for conversation, to engage in leisure activities, or for business purposes licit or illicit, that guest should share his host's shelter against unreasonable searches and seizures.

I do not here propose restoration of the "legitimately on the premises" criterion stated in *Jones v. United States*, for the Court rejected that formulation in *Rakas* as it did the "automatic standing rule" in *United States v. Salvucci* (1980). First, the disposition I would reach in this case responds to the unique importance of the home — the most essential bastion of privacy recognized by the law. Second, even within the home itself, the position to which I would adhere would not permit "a casual visitor who has never seen, or been permitted to visit, the basement of another's house to object to a search of the basement if the visitor happened to be in the kitchen of the house at the time of the search." Further, I would here decide only the case of the homeowner who chooses to share the privacy of her home and her company with a guest, and would not reach classroom hypotheticals like the milkman or pizza deliverer.

My concern centers on an individual's choice to share her home and her associations there with persons she selects. Our decisions indicate that people have a reasonable expectation of privacy in their homes in part because they have the prerogative to exclude others.

A homedweller places her own privacy at risk, the Court's approach indicates, when she opens her home to others, uncertain whether the duration of their stay, their purpose, and their "acceptance into the household" will earn protection. It remains textbook law that "[s]earches and seizures inside a home without a warrant are presumptively unreasonable absent exigent circumstances." The law in practice is less secure. Human frailty suggests that today's decision will tempt police to pry into private dwellings without warrant, to find evidence incriminating guests who do not rest there through the night. *Rakas* tolerates that temptation with respect to automobile searches. As I see it, people are not genuinely "secure in their . . . houses . . . against unreasonable searches and seizures," if their invitations to others increase the risk of unwarranted governmental peering and prying into their dwelling places.

Through the host's invitation, the guest gains a reasonable expectation of privacy in the home. *Minnesota v. Olson* (1990) so held with respect to an overnight guest. The logic of that decision extends to shorter term guests as well. Visiting the home of a friend, relative, or business associate, whatever the time of day, "serves functions recognized as valuable by society." One need not remain overnight to anticipate privacy in another's home, "a place where [the guest] and his possessions will not be disturbed by anyone but his host and those his host allows inside." In sum, when a homeowner chooses to share the privacy of her home and her company with a short-term guest, the twofold requirement "emerg[ing] from prior decisions" has been satisfied: Both host and guest "have exhibited an actual (subjective) expectation of privacy"; that "expectation [is] one [our] society is prepared to recognize as 'reasonable.'"

NOTES AND QUESTIONS

1. What about Kimberly Thompson? It appears she cooperated against Carter and Johns. Is that why the record is so murky? There is no suggestion that Carter and Johns disputed that they were solely in the apartment in connection with drug dealing and had no real relationship with Thompson. Is this the result of bad lawyering? Certainly after *Olson* there was no guaranty that mere presence would confer standing.

2. Officer Thielen tried to do the right thing here and get a warrant after corroborating the informant's tip. Will he even bother next time?

3. Justice Ginsburg's dissent notes that an aspect of the privacy in the home is that the owner or occupant can receive guests and be confident in the guests' security. Should this notion confer an associated protectable privacy interest in the guest?

Byrd v. United States
584 U.S. 395 (2018)

Justice KENNEDY delivered the opinion of the Court.

In September 2014, Pennsylvania State Troopers pulled over a car driven by petitioner Terrence Byrd. Byrd was the only person in the car. In the course of the traffic stop the troopers learned that the car was rented and that Byrd was not listed on the rental agreement as an authorized driver. For this reason, the troopers told Byrd they did not need his consent to search the car, including its trunk where he had stored personal effects. A search of the trunk uncovered body armor and 49 bricks of heroin.

The evidence was turned over to federal authorities, who charged Byrd with distribution and possession of heroin with the intent to distribute in violation of 21 U.S.C. § 841(a)(1) and possession of body armor by a prohibited person in violation of 18 U.S.C. § 931(a)(1). Byrd moved to suppress the evidence as the fruit of an unlawful search. The United States District Court for the Middle District of Pennsylvania denied the motion, and the Court of Appeals for the Third Circuit affirmed. Both courts concluded that, because Byrd was not listed on the rental agreement, he lacked a reasonable expectation of privacy in the car. Based on this conclusion, it appears that both the District Court and Court of Appeals deemed it unnecessary to consider whether the troopers had probable cause to search the car.

This Court granted certiorari to address the question whether a driver has a reasonable expectation of privacy in a rental car when he or she is not listed as an authorized driver on the rental agreement. The Court now holds that, as a general rule, someone in otherwise lawful possession and control of a rental car has a reasonable expectation of privacy in it even if the rental agreement does not list him or her as an authorized driver.

The Court concludes a remand is necessary to address in the first instance the Government's argument that this general rule is inapplicable because, in the circumstances here, Byrd had no greater expectation of privacy than a car thief. If that is so, our cases make clear he would lack a legitimate expectation of privacy. It is necessary to remand as well to determine whether, even if Byrd had a right to object to the search, probable cause justified it in any event.

I

On September 17, 2014, petitioner Terrence Byrd and Latasha Reed drove in Byrd's Honda Accord to a Budget car-rental facility in Wayne, New Jersey. Byrd stayed in the parking lot in the Honda while Reed went to the Budget desk and rented a Ford Fusion. The agreement Reed signed required her to certify that she had a valid driver's license and had not committed certain vehicle-related offenses within the previous three years. An addendum to the agreement, which Reed initialed, provides the following restriction on who may drive the rental car:

> I understand that the only ones permitted to drive the vehicle other than the renter are the renter's spouse, the renter's co-employee (with the renter's permission, while on company business),

Chapter V The Exclusionary Rule, its Exceptions, and Suppression Hearings

or a person who appears at the time of the rental and signs an Additional Driver Form. These other drivers must also be at least 25 years old and validly licensed.

PERMITTING AN UNAUTHORIZED DRIVER TO OPERATE THE VEHICLE IS A VIOLATION OF THE RENTAL AGREEMENT. THIS MAY RESULT IN ANY AND ALL COVERAGE OTHERWISE PROVIDED BY THE RENTAL AGREEMENT BEING VOID AND MY BEING FULLY RESPONSIBLE FOR ALL LOSS OR DAMAGE, INCLUDING LIABILITY TO THIRD PARTIES.

In filling out the paperwork for the rental agreement, Reed did not list an additional driver.

With the rental keys in hand, Reed returned to the parking lot and gave them to Byrd. The two then left the facility in separate cars — she in his Honda, he in the rental car. Byrd returned to his home in Patterson, New Jersey, and put his personal belongings in the trunk of the rental car. Later that afternoon, he departed in the car alone and headed toward Pittsburgh, Pennsylvania.

After driving nearly three hours, or roughly half the distance to Pittsburgh, Byrd passed State Trooper David Long, who was parked in the median of Interstate 81 near Harrisburg, Pennsylvania. Long was suspicious of Byrd because he was driving with his hands at the "10 and 2" position on the steering wheel, sitting far back from the steering wheel, and driving a rental car. Long knew the Ford Fusion was a rental car because one of its windows contained a barcode. Based on these observations, he decided to follow Byrd and, a short time later, stopped him for a possible traffic infraction.

When Long approached the passenger window of Byrd's car to explain the basis for the stop and to ask for identification, Byrd was "visibly nervous" and "was shaking and had a hard time obtaining his driver's license." He handed an interim license and the rental agreement to Long, stating that a friend had rented the car. Long returned to his vehicle to verify Byrd's license and noticed Byrd was not listed as an additional driver on the rental agreement. Around this time another trooper, Travis Martin, arrived at the scene. While Long processed Byrd's license, Martin conversed with Byrd, who again stated that a friend had rented the vehicle. After Martin walked back to Long's patrol car, Long commented to Martin that Byrd was "not on the renter agreement," to which Martin replied, "yeah, he has no expectation of privacy."

A computer search based on Byrd's identification returned two different names. Further inquiry suggested the other name might be an alias and also revealed that Byrd had prior convictions for weapons and drug charges as well as an outstanding warrant in New Jersey for a probation violation. After learning that New Jersey did not want Byrd arrested for extradition, the troopers asked Byrd to step out of the vehicle and patted him down.

Long asked Byrd if he had anything illegal in the car. When Byrd said he did not, the troopers asked for his consent to search the car. At that point Byrd said he had a "blunt" in the car and offered to retrieve it for them. The officers understood "blunt" to mean a marijuana cigarette. They declined to let him retrieve it and continued to seek his consent to search the car, though they stated they did not need consent because he was not listed on the rental agreement. The troopers then opened the passenger and driver doors and began a thorough search of the passenger compartment.

Martin proceeded from there to search the car's trunk, including by opening up and taking things out of a large cardboard box, where he found a laundry bag containing body armor. At this point, the troopers decided to detain Byrd. As Martin walked toward Byrd and said he would be placing him in handcuffs, Byrd began to run away. A third trooper who had arrived on the scene joined Long and Martin in pursuit. When the troopers caught up to Byrd, he surrendered and admitted there was heroin in the car. Back at the car, the troopers resumed their search of the laundry bag and found 49 bricks of heroin.

In pretrial proceedings Byrd moved to suppress the evidence found in the trunk of the rental car, arguing that the search violated his Fourth Amendment rights. Although Long contended at a suppression hearing that the troopers had probable cause to search the car after Byrd stated it contained marijuana, the District Court denied Byrd's motion on the ground that Byrd lacked "standing" to contest the search as an initial matter. Byrd later entered a conditional guilty plea, reserving the right to appeal the suppression ruling.

The Court of Appeals affirmed in a brief summary opinion. As relevant here, the Court of Appeals recognized that a "circuit split exists as to whether the sole occupant of a rental vehicle has a Fourth Amendment expectation of privacy when that occupant is not named in the rental agreement"; but it noted that Circuit precedent already had "spoken as to this issue . . . and determined such a person has no expectation of privacy and therefore no standing to challenge a search of the vehicle." The Court of Appeals did not reach the probable-cause question.

This Court granted Byrd's petition for a writ of certiorari to address the conflict among the Courts of Appeals over whether an unauthorized driver has a reasonable expectation of privacy in a rental car.

II

Few protections are as essential to individual liberty as the right to be free from unreasonable searches and seizures. The Framers made that right explicit in the Bill of Rights following their experience with the indignities and invasions of privacy wrought by "general warrants and warrantless searches that had so alienated the colonists and had helped speed the movement for independence." Ever mindful of the Fourth Amendment and its history, the Court has viewed with disfavor practices that permit "police officers unbridled discretion to rummage at will among a person's private effects."

This concern attends the search of an automobile. The Court has acknowledged, however, that there is a diminished expectation of privacy in automobiles, which often permits officers to dispense with obtaining a warrant before conducting a lawful search.

Whether a warrant is required is a separate question from the one the Court addresses here, which is whether the person claiming a constitutional violation "has had his own Fourth Amendment rights infringed by the search and seizure which he seeks to challenge." *Rakas v. Illinois* (1978). Answering that question requires examination of whether the person claiming the constitutional violation had a "legitimate expectation of privacy in the premises" searched. "Expectations of privacy protected by the Fourth Amendment, of course, need not be based on a common-law interest in real or personal property, or on the invasion of such an interest." Still, "property concepts" are instructive in "determining the presence or absence of the privacy interests protected by that Amendment."

Indeed, more recent Fourth Amendment cases have clarified that the test most often associated with legitimate expectations of privacy, which was derived from the second Justice Harlan's concurrence in *Katz v. United States* (1967), supplements, rather than displaces, "the traditional property-based understanding of the Fourth Amendment." *Florida v. Jardines* (2013). Perhaps in light of this clarification, Byrd now argues in the alternative that he had a common-law property interest in the rental car as a second bailee that would have provided him with a cognizable Fourth Amendment interest in the vehicle. But he did not raise this argument before the District Court or Court of Appeals, and those courts did not have occasion to address whether Byrd was a second bailee or what consequences might follow from that determination. In those courts he framed the question solely in terms of the *Katz* test noted above. Because this is "a court of review, not of first view," *Cutter v. Wilkinson*, it is generally unwise to consider arguments in the first instance, and the Court declines to reach Byrd's contention that he was a second bailee.

524 Chapter V The Exclusionary Rule, its Exceptions, and Suppression Hearings

Reference to property concepts, however, aids the Court in assessing the precise question here: Does a driver of a rental car have a reasonable expectation of privacy in the car when he or she is not listed as an authorized driver on the rental agreement?

III

A

One who owns and possesses a car, like one who owns and possesses a house, almost always has a reasonable expectation of privacy in it. More difficult to define and delineate are the legitimate expectations of privacy of others.

On the one hand, as noted above, it is by now well established that a person need not always have a recognized common-law property interest in the place searched to be able to claim a reasonable expectation of privacy in it.

On the other hand, it is also clear that legitimate presence on the premises of the place searched, standing alone, is not enough to accord a reasonable expectation of privacy, because it "creates too broad a gauge for measurement of Fourth Amendment rights."

Although the Court has not set forth a single metric or exhaustive list of considerations to resolve the circumstances in which a person can be said to have a reasonable expectation of privacy, it has explained that "[l]egitimation of expectations of privacy by law must have a source outside of the Fourth Amendment, either by reference to concepts of real or personal property law or to understandings that are recognized and permitted by society." The two concepts in cases like this one are often linked. "One of the main rights attaching to property is the right to exclude others," and, in the main, "one who owns or lawfully possesses or controls property will in all likelihood have a legitimate expectation of privacy by virtue of the right to exclude." This general property-based concept guides resolution of this case.

B

Here, the Government contends that drivers who are not listed on rental agreements always lack an expectation of privacy in the automobile based on the rental company's lack of authorization alone. This per se rule rests on too restrictive a view of the Fourth Amendment's protections. Byrd, by contrast, contends that the sole occupant of a rental car always has an expectation of privacy in it based on mere possession and control. There is more to recommend Byrd's proposed rule than the Government's; but, without qualification, it would include within its ambit thieves and others who, not least because of their lack of any property-based justification, would not have a reasonable expectation of privacy.

1

Stripped to its essentials, the Government's position is that only authorized drivers of rental cars have expectations of privacy in those vehicles. This position is based on the following syllogism: Under *Rakas*, passengers do not have an expectation of privacy in an automobile glove compartment or like places; an unauthorized driver like Byrd would have been the passenger had the renter been driving; and the unauthorized driver cannot obtain greater protection when he takes the wheel and leaves the renter behind. The flaw in this syllogism is its major premise, for it is a misreading of *Rakas*.

The Court in *Rakas* did not hold that passengers cannot have an expectation of privacy in automobiles. To the contrary, the Court disclaimed any intent to hold "that a passenger lawfully in an automobile may not invoke the exclusionary rule and challenge a search of that vehicle unless he happens to own or have a possessory interest in it." The Court instead rejected the argument that legitimate presence alone was sufficient to assert a Fourth Amendment interest, which was fatal to the petitioners' case there because they had "claimed only that they were 'legitimately on [the] premises' and did not claim that they had any legitimate expectation of privacy in the areas of the car which were searched."

What is more, the Government's syllogism is beside the point, because this case does not involve a passenger at all but instead the driver and sole occupant of a rental car. As Justice Powell observed in his concurring opinion in *Rakas*, a "distinction . . . may be made in some circumstances between the Fourth Amendment rights of passengers and the rights of an individual who has exclusive control of an automobile or of its locked compartments." This situation would be similar to the defendant in *Jones*, supra, who, as *Rakas* notes, had a reasonable expectation of privacy in his friend's apartment because he "had complete dominion and control over the apartment and could exclude others from it." Justice Powell's observation was also consistent with the majority's explanation that "one who owns or lawfully possesses or controls property will in all likelihood have a legitimate expectation of privacy by virtue of [the] right to exclude," an explanation tied to the majority's discussion of *Jones*.

The Court sees no reason why the expectation of privacy that comes from lawful possession and control and the attendant right to exclude would differ depending on whether the car in question is rented or privately owned by someone other than the person in current possession of it, much as it did not seem to matter whether the friend of the defendant in Jones owned or leased the apartment he permitted the defendant to use in his absence. Both would have the expectation of privacy that comes with the right to exclude. Indeed, the Government conceded at oral argument that an unauthorized driver in sole possession of a rental car would be permitted to exclude third parties from it, such as a carjacker.

2

The Government further stresses that Byrd's driving the rental car violated the rental agreement that Reed signed, and it contends this violation meant Byrd could not have had any basis for claiming an expectation of privacy in the rental car at the time of the search. As anyone who has rented a car knows, car-rental agreements are filled with long lists of restrictions. Examples include prohibitions on driving the car on unpaved roads or driving while using a handheld cellphone. Few would contend that violating provisions like these has anything to do with a driver's reasonable expectation of privacy in the rental car—as even the Government agrees.

Despite this concession, the Government argues that permitting an unauthorized driver to take the wheel of a rental car is a breach different in kind from these others, so serious that the rental company would consider the agreement "void" the moment an unauthorized driver takes the wheel. To begin with, that is not what the contract says. It states: "Permitting an unauthorized driver to operate the vehicle is a violation of the rental agreement. This may result in any and all coverage otherwise provided by the rental agreement being void and my being fully responsible for all loss or damage, including liability to third parties."

Putting the Government's misreading of the contract aside, there may be countless innocuous reasons why an unauthorized driver might get behind the wheel of a rental car and drive it—perhaps the renter is drowsy or inebriated and the two think it safer for the friend to drive them to their destination. True, this constitutes a breach of the rental agreement, and perhaps a serious one, but the Government fails to explain what bearing this breach of contract, standing alone, has on expectations of privacy in the car. Stated in different terms, for Fourth Amendment purposes there is no meaningful difference between the authorized-driver provision and the other provisions the Government agrees do not eliminate an expectation of privacy, all of which concern risk allocation between private parties—violators might pay additional fees, lose insurance coverage, or assume liability for damage resulting from the breach. But that risk allocation has little to do with whether one would have a reasonable expectation of privacy in the rental car if, for example, he or she otherwise has lawful possession of and control over the car.

3

The central inquiry at this point turns on the concept of lawful possession, and this is where an important qualification of Byrd's proposed rule comes into play. *Rakas* makes clear that "'wrongful' presence at the scene of a search would not enable a defendant to object to the legality of the search." "A burglar plying his trade in a summer cabin during the off season," for example, "may have a thoroughly justified subjective expectation of privacy, but it is not one which the law recognizes as 'legitimate.'" Likewise, "a person present in a stolen automobile at the time of the search may [not] object to the lawfulness of the search of the automobile." No matter the degree of possession and control, the car thief would not have a reasonable expectation of privacy in a stolen car.

On this point, in its merits brief, the Government asserts that, on the facts here, Byrd should have no greater expectation of privacy than a car thief because he intentionally used a third party as a strawman in a calculated plan to mislead the rental company from the very outset, all to aid him in committing a crime. This argument is premised on the Government's inference that Byrd knew he would not have been able to rent the car on his own, because he would not have satisfied the rental company's requirements based on his criminal record, and that he used Reed, who had no intention of using the car for her own purposes, to procure the car for him to transport heroin to Pittsburgh.

It is unclear whether the Government's allegations, if true, would constitute a criminal offense in the acquisition of the rental car under applicable law. And it may be that there is no reason that the law should distinguish between one who obtains a vehicle through subterfuge of the type the Government alleges occurred here and one who steals the car outright.

The Government did not raise this argument in the District Court or the Court of Appeals, however. It relied instead on the sole fact that Byrd lacked authorization to drive the car. And it is unclear from the record whether the Government's inferences paint an accurate picture of what occurred. Because it was not addressed in the District Court or Court of Appeals, the Court declines to reach this question. The proper course is to remand for the argument and potentially further factual development to be considered in the first instance by the Court of Appeals or by the District Court.

IV

The Government argued in its brief in opposition to certiorari that, even if Byrd had a Fourth Amendment interest in the rental car, the troopers had probable cause to believe it contained evidence of a crime when they initiated their search. If that were true, the troopers may have been permitted to conduct a warrantless search of the car in line with the Court's cases concerning the automobile exception to the warrant requirement. The Court of Appeals did not reach this question because it concluded, as an initial matter, that Byrd lacked a reasonable expectation of privacy in the rental car.

It is worth noting that most courts analyzing the question presented in this case, including the Court of Appeals here, have described it as one of Fourth Amendment "standing," a concept the Court has explained is not distinct from the merits and "is more properly subsumed under substantive Fourth Amendment doctrine."

The concept of standing in Fourth Amendment cases can be a useful shorthand for capturing the idea that a person must have a cognizable Fourth Amendment interest in the place searched before seeking relief for an unconstitutional search; but it should not be confused with Article III standing, which is jurisdictional and must be assessed before reaching the merits. Because Fourth Amendment standing is subsumed under substantive Fourth Amendment doctrine, it is not a jurisdictional question and hence need not be addressed before addressing other aspects of the merits of a Fourth Amendment claim. On remand, then, the Court of Appeals is not required to assess Byrd's reasonable expectation of privacy in the rental car before, in its discretion, first addressing whether there was probable cause for the search, if it finds the latter argument has been preserved.

V

Though new, the fact pattern here continues a well-traveled path in this Court's Fourth Amendment jurisprudence. Those cases support the proposition, and the Court now holds, that the mere fact that a driver in lawful possession or control of a rental car is not listed on the rental agreement will not defeat his or her otherwise reasonable expectation of privacy. The Court leaves for remand two of the Government's arguments: that one who intentionally uses a third party to procure a rental car by a fraudulent scheme for the purpose of committing a crime is no better situated than a car thief; and that probable cause justified the search in any event. The Court of Appeals has discretion as to the order in which these questions are best addressed.

* * *

The judgment of the Court of Appeals is vacated, and the case is remanded for further proceedings consistent with this opinion.

It is so ordered.

NOTES AND QUESTIONS

1. The Court criticizes the government's argument about the significance of the language in the rental agreement as well as its factual argument about Byrd's alleged use of a straw person to rent the car because he was ineligible to do so because of his criminal record. Do you think the fact that the government overplayed its hand might have contributed to the result here?

2. On remand, Byrd will have to deal with the argument that his admission that there was marijuana in the car gave the police probable cause to search the entire car. Is there also a case for the good faith exception to the exclusionary rule? Is the police officer's comment about Byrd's "reasonable expectation of privacy" relevant to this inquiry?

3. Does the result here depend on the fact that Byrd was the only occupant and the driver of the rental car? What if he had been a passenger at the time of the stop, and a listed driver on the rental agreement, but the renter was driving? What if he had been driving but the renter was a passenger with him?

4. Is Trooper Long's explanation of the reasons why he began following Byrd believable? Did he have reasonable suspicion to stop Byrd prior to identifying "a possible traffic infraction"? Isn't this obviously a pretextual stop? The Court, needless to say, glosses over the basis for the stop and makes no mention of the fact that Byrd was Black. *See* Tracey Maclin, Byrd v. United States: *Unauthorized Drivers of Rental Cars Have Fourth Amendment Rights? Not as Evident as It Seems*, 2018 Sup. Ct. Rev. 81, 91 n.55 (2019).

5. The Ford Fusion Terrence Byrd was driving when he was stopped by police was rented from a Budget facility in Wayne, New Jersey. Wayne is best known as the location of the lawn ornament store Fountains of Wayne (closed in 2009), from which the eponymous rock band took its name in 1995. In episode 5 of season 3 of *The Sopranos*, "Another Toothpick," Tony visits Fountains of Wayne and interacts with a Black police officer, Leon Wilmore, who had recently given him a speeding ticket.

Fountains of Wayne   Tony Soprano at Fountains of Wayne

E. IMPEACHMENT

Can the government use information obtained illegally to impeach a testifying defendant even if it cannot use the evidence directly against the defendant in its case-in-chief? Would this allow the government to profit from its constitutional violation? Should the answer depend on the nature of the constitutional violation? The cases below explore this issue.

Walder v. United States
347 U.S. 62 (1954)

Mr. Justice FRANKFURTER delivered the opinion of the Court.

In May 1950, petitioner was indicted in the United States District Court for the Western District of Missouri for purchasing and possessing one grain of heroin. Claiming that the heroin capsule had been obtained through an unlawful search and seizure, petitioner moved to suppress it. The motion was granted, and shortly thereafter, on the Government's motion, the case against petitioner was dismissed.

In January of 1952, petitioner was again indicted, this time for four other illicit transactions in narcotics. The Government's case consisted principally of the testimony of two drug addicts who claimed to have procured the illicit stuff from petitioner under the direction of federal agents. The only witness for the defense was the defendant himself, petitioner here. He denied any narcotics dealings with the two Government informers and attributed the testimony against him to personal hostility.

Early on his direct examination petitioner testified as follows:

> **Q.** Now, first, Mr. Walder, before we go further in your testimony, I want to you (sic) tell the Court and jury whether, not referring to these informers in this case, but whether you have ever sold any narcotics to anyone. A. I have never sold any narcotics to anyone in my life.
>
> **Q.** Have you ever had any narcotics in your possession, other than what may have been given to you by a physician for an ailment? A. No.
>
> **Q.** Now, I will ask you one more thing. Have you ever handed or given any narcotics to anyone as a gift or in any other manner without the receipt of any money or any other compensation? A. I have not.
>
> **Q.** Have you ever even acted as, say, have you acted as a conduit for the purpose of handling what you knew to be a narcotic from one person to another? A. No, Sir.

On cross-examination, in response to a question by Government counsel making reference to this direct testimony, petitioner reiterated his assertion that he had never purchased, sold or possessed any narcotics. Over the defendant's objection, the Government then questioned him about the heroin capsule unlawfully seized from his home in his presence back in February 1950. The defendant stoutly denied that any narcotics were taken from him at that time. The Government then put on the stand one of the officers who had participated in the unlawful search and seizure and also the chemist who had analyzed the heroin capsule there seized. The trial judge admitted this evidence, but carefully charged the jury that it was not to be used to determine whether the defendant had committed the crimes here charged, but solely for the purpose of impeaching the defendant's credibility. The defendant was convicted and the Court of Appeals for the Eighth Circuit affirmed, one judge dissenting. The question which divided that court, and the sole issue here, is whether the defendant's assertion on direct examination that he had never possessed any narcotics opened the door, solely for the purpose of attacking the defendant's credibility, to evidence of the heroin unlawfully seized in connection with the earlier proceeding. Because this question presents a novel aspect of the scope of the doctrine of *Weeks v. United States*, we granted certiorari.

The Government cannot violate the Fourth Amendment—in the only way in which the Government can do anything, namely through its agents—and use the fruits of such unlawful conduct to secure a conviction. *Weeks v. United States, supra.* Nor can the Government make indirect use of such evidence for its case, or support a conviction on evidence obtained through leads from the unlawfully obtained evidence. All these methods are outlawed, and convictions obtained by means of them are invalidated, because they encourage the kind of society that is obnoxious to free men.

It is one thing to say that the Government cannot make an affirmative use of evidence unlawfully obtained. It is quite another to say that the defendant can turn the illegal method by which evidence in the Government's possession was obtained to his own advantage, and provide himself with a shield against contradiction of his untruths. Such an extension of the *Weeks* doctrine would be a perversion of the Fourth Amendment.

Take the present situation. Of his own accord, the defendant went beyond a mere denial of complicity in the crimes of which he was charged and made the sweeping claim that he had never dealt in or possessed any narcotics. Of course, the Constitution guarantees a defendant the fullest opportunity to meet the accusation against him. He must be free to deny all the elements of the case against him without thereby giving leave to the Government to introduce by way of rebuttal evidence illegally secured by it, and therefore not available for its case in chief. Beyond that, however, there is hardly justification for letting the defendant affirmatively resort to perjurious testimony in reliance on the Government's disability to challenge his credibility.

The situation here involved is to be sharply contrasted with that presented by *Agnello v. United States*. There the Government, after having failed in its efforts to introduce the tainted evidence in its case in chief, tried to smuggle it in on cross-examination by asking the accused the broad question "Did you ever see narcotics before?" After eliciting the expected denial, it sought to introduce evidence of narcotics located in the defendant's home by means of an unlawful search and seizure, in order to discredit the defendant. In holding that the Government could no more work in this evidence on cross-examination than it could in its case in chief, the Court foreshadowed, perhaps unwittingly, the result we reach today:

> And the contention that the evidence of the search and seizure was admissible in rebuttal is without merit. In his direct examination, Agnello was not asked and did not testify concerning

Chapter V The Exclusionary Rule, its Exceptions, and Suppression Hearings

the can of cocaine. In cross-examination, in answer to a question permitted over his objection, he said he had never seen it. He did nothing to waive his constitutional protection or to justify cross-examination in respect of the evidence claimed to have been obtained by the search.

The judgment is affirmed.

NOTES AND QUESTIONS

1. Are you curious about the relationship between the 1950 and the 1952 prosecutions of Walder? It would appear that the government agents within a year or so of Walder's successful motion to suppress in the 1950 indictment were sending informants after Walder. Should that affect the result here? Was there anything Walder could have done otherwise?

2. The result here had to have been the result of reckless lawyering. Could defense counsel really have been confident that he could get away with having Walder make a blanket denial of involvement in narcotics? Would reading *Agnello* have helped? Was the sought-after testimony even necessary?

3. Is it essential to the result here that Walder "opened the door"? Would these questions have also opened the door:

- Mr. Walder, do you deny all the allegations against you?
- Mr. Walder, are you opposed to those who use and sell narcotics?
- Mr. Walder, do you deny that you are a narcotics dealer?

The next case considers whether information obtained from a *Miranda* violation can be used to impeach a testifying defendant. It is generally regarded as one of the first of many instances where the Court found exceptions to the *Miranda* doctrine.

Harris v. New York
401 U.S. 222 (1971)

Mr. Chief Justice BURGER delivered the opinion of the Court.

We granted the writ in this case to consider petitioner's claim that a statement made by him to police under circumstances rendering it inadmissible to establish the prosecution's case in chief under *Miranda* may not be used to impeach his credibility.

The State of New York charged petitioner in a two-count indictment with twice selling heroin to an undercover police officer. At a subsequent jury trial the officer was the State's chief witness, and he testified as to details of the two sales. A second officer verified collateral details of the sales, and a third offered testimony about the chemical analysis of the heroin.

Petitioner took the stand in his own defense. He admitted knowing the undercover police officer but denied a sale on January 4, 1966. He admitted making a sale of contents of a glassine bag to the officer on January 6 but claimed it was baking powder and part of a scheme to defraud the purchaser.

On cross-examination petitioner was asked seriatim whether he had made specified statements to the police immediately following his arrest on January 7 — statements that partially contradicted petitioner's direct testimony at trial. In response to the cross-examination, petitioner testified that he could not remember virtually any of the questions or answers recited by the prosecutor. At the request of petitioner's counsel the written statement from which the prosecutor had read questions and answers in his impeaching process was placed in the record for possible use on appeal; the statement was not shown to the jury.

E. Impeachment 531

The trial judge instructed the jury that the statements attributed to petitioner by the prosecution could be considered only in passing on petitioner's credibility and not as evidence of guilt. In closing summations both counsel argued the substance of the impeaching statements. The jury then found petitioner guilty on the second count of the indictment.

At trial the prosecution made no effort in its case in chief to use the statements allegedly made by petitioner, conceding that they were inadmissible under *Miranda*. The transcript of the interrogation used in the impeachment, but not given to the jury, shows that no warning of a right to appointed counsel was given before questions were put to petitioner when he was taken into custody. Petitioner makes no claim that the statements made to the police were coerced or involuntary.

Some comments in the *Miranda* opinion can indeed be read as indicating a bar to use of an uncounseled statement for any purpose, but discussion of that issue was not at all necessary to the Court's holding and cannot be regarded as controlling. *Miranda* barred the prosecution from making its case with statements of an accused made while in custody prior to having or effectively waiving counsel. It does not follow from *Miranda* that evidence inadmissible against an accused in the prosecution's case in chief is barred for all purposes, provided of course that the trustworthiness of the evidence satisfies legal standards.

In *Walder v. United States* (1954), the Court permitted physical evidence, inadmissible in the case in chief, to be used for impeachment purposes.

> It is one thing to say that the Government cannot make an affirmative use of evidence unlawfully obtained. It is quite another to say that the defendant can turn the illegal method by which evidence in the Government's possession was obtained to his own advantage, and provide himself with a shield against contradiction of his untruths. Such an extension of the *Weeks* doctrine would be a perversion of the Fourth Amendment.
>
> (T)here is hardly justification for letting the defendant affirmatively resort to perjurious testimony in reliance on the Government's disability to challenge his credibility.

It is true that Walder was impeached as to collateral matters included in his direct examination, whereas petitioner here was impeached as to testimony bearing more directly on the crimes charged. We are not persuaded that there is a difference in principle that warrants a result different from that reached by the Court in *Walder*. Petitioner's testimony in his own behalf concerning the events of January 7 contrasted sharply with what he told the police shortly after his arrest. The impeachment process here undoubtedly provided valuable aid to the jury in assessing petitioner's credibility, and the benefits of this process should not be lost, in our view, because of the speculative possibility that impermissible police conduct will be encouraged thereby. Assuming that the exclusionary rule has a deterrent effect on proscribed police conduct, sufficient deterrence flows when the evidence in question is made unavailable to the prosecution in its case in chief.

Every criminal defendant is privileged to testify in his own defense, or to refuse to do so. But that privilege cannot be construed to include the right to commit perjury. Having voluntarily taken the stand, petitioner was under an obligation to speak truthfully and accurately, and the prosecution here did no more than utilize the traditional truth-testing devices of the adversary process. Had inconsistent statements been made by the accused to some third person, it could hardly be contended that the conflict could not be laid before the jury by way of cross-examination and impeachment.

The shield provided by *Miranda* cannot be perverted into a license to use perjury by way of a defense, free from the risk of confrontation with prior inconsistent utterances. We hold, therefore, that petitioner's credibility was appropriately impeached by use of his earlier conflicting statements.

Affirmed.

[Justices Brennan, Marshall, and Douglas dissented.]

NOTES AND QUESTIONS

1. Why is the opinion so opaque? Was the trial testimony not transcribed? What was the defendant's testimony and what was the statement he made upon being arrested? How is the reader of this opinion to determine how much this case resembles *Walder*?

2. So the trial judge gave a limiting instruction to the effect that the cross-examination of the defendant—which the Court conceded bore "more directly [than the cross in *Walder*] on the crimes charged"—was to be considered only in evaluating the defendant's credibility. And, remarkably, the Court doubled down on this instruction as a palliative, stating without any sign of irony that "the impeachment process here undoubtedly provided valuable aid to the jury in assessing petitioner's credibility."

Can this be taken seriously? The futility of limiting instructions was not a novel concept in 1972. As Justice Jackson had observed decades previously: "The naive assumption that prejudicial effects can be overcome by instructions to the jury, all practicing lawyers know to be unmitigated fiction." *Krulewitch v. United States*, 336 U.S. 440, 453 (1949) (Jackson, J., concurring).

3. The Court dismisses the possibility that "impermissible police conduct will be encouraged" by its decision as "a speculative possibility." Maybe that notion was purely speculative in 1972. But what if it were to turn out that police officers would in fact be encouraged to violate *Miranda* in order to generate impeachment material? *See* Chapter III *supra*.

4. The dissent distinguishes the cross-examination in *Walder* as "completely unrelated" to the charges at issue in the case. Is this a legitimate distinction?

5. Was it necessary to the result in *Harris* that the statement made by the defendant appears to have been made voluntarily? Recall that in *New Jersey v. Portash*, 440 U.S. 450 (1979), the Court would hold that a defendant could not be impeached based on immunized testimony he had given in the grand jury as that testimony was the result of a state compulsion order and was therefore not voluntary.

United States v. Havens
466 U.S. 620 (1980)

Mr. Justice WHITE delivered the opinion of the Court.

The petition for certiorari filed by the United States in this criminal case presented a single question: whether evidence suppressed as the fruit of an unlawful search and seizure may nevertheless be used to impeach a defendant's false trial testimony, given in response to proper cross-examination, where the evidence does not squarely contradict the defendant's testimony on direct examination. We issued the writ.

I

Respondent was convicted of importing, conspiring to import, and intentionally possessing a controlled substance, cocaine. According to the evidence at his trial, Havens and John McLeroth, both attorneys from Ft. Wayne, Ind., boarded a flight from Lima, Peru, to Miami, Fla. In Miami, a customs officer searched McLeroth and found cocaine sewed into makeshift pockets in a T-shirt he was wearing under his outer clothing. McLeroth implicated respondent, who had previously cleared customs and who was then arrested. His luggage was seized and searched without a warrant. The officers found no drugs but seized a T-shirt from which pieces had been cut that matched the pieces that had been sewn to McLeroth's T-shirt. The T-shirt and other evidence seized in the course of the search were suppressed on motion prior to trial.

Both men were charged in a three-count indictment, but McLeroth pleaded guilty to one count and testified against Havens. Among other things, he asserted that Havens had supplied him with the altered T-shirt and had sewed the makeshift pockets shut. Havens took the stand in his own defense and denied involvement in smuggling cocaine. His direct testimony included the following:

Q. And you heard Mr. McLeroth testify earlier as to something to the effect that this material was taped or draped around his body and so on, you heard that testimony?

A. Yes, I did.

Q. Did you ever engage in that kind of activity with Mr. McLeroth and Augusto or Mr. McLeroth and anyone else on that fourth visit to Lima, Peru?

A. I did not.

On cross-examination, Havens testified as follows:

Q. Now, on direct examination, sir, you testified that on the fourth trip you had absolutely nothing to do with the wrapping of any bandages or tee shirts or anything involving Mr. McLeroth; is that correct?

A. I don't—I said I had nothing to do with any wrapping or bandages or anything, yes. I had nothing to do with anything with McLeroth in connection with this cocaine matter.

Q. And your testimony is that you had nothing to do with the sewing of the cotton swatches to make pockets on that tee shirt?

A. Absolutely not.

Q. Sir, when you came through Customs, the Miami International Airport, on October 2, 1977, did you have in your suitcase Size 38-40 medium tee shirts? Id., at 35.

An objection to the latter question was overruled and questioning continued:

Q. On that day, sir, did you have in your luggage a Size 38-40 medium man's tee shirt with swatches of clothing missing from the tail of that tee shirt?

A. Not to my knowledge.

Q. Mr. Havens, I'm going to hand you what is Government's Exhibit 9 for identification and ask you if this tee shirt was in your luggage on October 2nd, 1975 [sic]?

A. Not to my knowledge. No.

Respondent Havens also denied having told a Government agent that the T-shirts found in his luggage belonged to McLeroth.

On rebuttal, a Government agent testified that Exhibit 9 had been found in respondent's suitcase and that Havens claimed the T-shirts found in his bag, including Exhibit 9, belonged to McLeroth. Over objection, the T-shirt was then admitted into evidence, the jury being instructed that the rebuttal evidence should be considered only for impeaching Havens' credibility.

The Court of Appeals reversed, relying on *Agnello v. United States* (1925), and *Walder v. United States* (1954). The court held that illegally seized evidence may be used for impeachment only if the evidence contradicts a particular statement made by a defendant in the course of his direct examination. We reverse.

II

In *Agnello v. United States*, supra, a defendant charged with conspiracy to sell a package of cocaine testified on direct examination that he had possessed the packages involved but did not know what was in them. On cross-examination, he denied ever having seen narcotics and ever having seen a can of cocaine which was exhibited to him and which had been illegally seized from his apartment. The can of cocaine was permitted into evidence on rebuttal. Agnello was convicted and his conviction was affirmed by the Court of Appeals. This Court reversed, holding that the Fourth Amendment required exclusion of the evidence. The Court pointed out that "[i]n his direct examination, Agnello was not asked and did not testify concerning the can of cocaine" and "did nothing to waive his constitutional protection or to justify cross-examination in respect of the evidence claimed to have been obtained by the search." The Court also said, that the exclusionary rule not only commands that illegally seized evidence "shall not be used before the Court but that it shall not be used at all."

The latter statement has been rejected in our later cases, however, and *Agnello* otherwise limited. In *Walder*, the use of evidence obtained in an illegal search and inadmissible in the Government's case in chief was admitted to impeach the direct testimony of the defendant.

These cases were understood by the Court of Appeals to hold that tainted evidence, inadmissible when offered as part of the Government's main case, may not be used as rebuttal evidence to impeach a defendant's credibility unless the evidence is offered to contradict a particular statement made by a defendant during his direct examination; a statement made for the first time on cross-examination may not be so impeached. This approach required the exclusion of the T-shirt taken from Havens' luggage because, as the Court of Appeals read the record, Havens was asked nothing on his direct testimony about the incriminating T-shirt or about the contents of his luggage; the testimony about the T-shirt, which the Government desired to impeach first appeared on cross-examination, not on direct.

In reversing the District Court in the case before us, the Court of Appeals did not stop to consider how closely the cross-examination about the T-shirt and the luggage was connected with matters gone into in direct examination. If these questions would have been suggested to a reasonably competent cross-examiner by Havens' direct testimony, they were not "smuggled in"; and forbidding the Government to impeach the answers to these questions by using contrary and reliable evidence in its possession fails to take account of our cases, particularly *Harris* and *Hass*. In both cases, the Court stressed the importance of arriving at the truth in criminal trials, as well as the defendant's obligation to speak the truth in response to proper questions. We rejected the notion that the defendant's constitutional shield against having illegally seized evidence used against him could be "perverted into a license to use perjury by way of a defense, free from the risk of confrontation with prior inconsistent utterances." Both cases also held that the deterrent function of the rules excluding unconstitutionally obtained evidence is sufficiently served by denying its use to the government on its direct case. It was only a "speculative possibility" that also making it unavailable to the government for otherwise proper impeachment would contribute substantially in this respect.

Neither *Harris* nor *Hass* involved the impeachment of assertedly false testimony first given on cross-examination, but the reasoning of those cases controls this one. There is no gainsaying that arriving at the truth is a fundamental goal of our legal system. We have repeatedly insisted that when defendants testify, they must testify truthfully or suffer the consequences. This is true even though a defendant is compelled to testify against his will. It is essential, therefore, to the proper functioning of the adversary system that when a defendant takes the stand, the government be permitted proper and effective cross-examination in an attempt to elicit the truth. The defendant's obligation to testify truthfully is fully binding on him when he is cross-examined. His privilege against self-incrimination does not shield him from proper questioning. He would unquestionably be subject to a perjury prosecution if he knowingly lies on cross-examination. In terms of impeaching a defendant's seemingly false statements with his prior inconsistent utterances or with other reliable evidence available to the government, we see no difference of constitutional magnitude between the defendant's statements on direct examination and his answers to questions put to him on cross-examination that are

E. Impeachment

535

plainly within the scope of the defendant's direct examination. Without this opportunity, the normal function of cross-examination would be severely impeded.

We also think that the policies of the exclusionary rule no more bar impeachment here than they did in *Walder, Harris*, and *Hass*. In those cases, the ends of the exclusionary rules were thought adequately implemented by denying the government the use of the challenged evidence to make out its case in chief. The incremental furthering of those ends by forbidding impeachment of the defendant who testifies was deemed insufficient to permit or require that false testimony go unchallenged, with the resulting impairment of the integrity of the factfinding goals of the criminal trial. We reaffirm this assessment of the competing interests, and hold that a defendant's statements made in response to proper cross-examination reasonably suggested by the defendant's direct examination are subject to otherwise proper impeachment by the government, albeit by evidence that has been illegally obtained and that is inadmissible on the government's direct case, or otherwise, as substantive evidence of guilt.

In arriving at its judgment, the Court of Appeals noted that in response to defense counsel's objection to the impeaching evidence on the ground that the matter had not been "covered on direct," the trial court had remarked that "[i]t does not have to be covered on direct." The Court of Appeals thought this was error since in its view illegally seized evidence could be used only to impeach a statement made on direct examination. As we have indicated, we hold a contrary view; and we do not understand the District Court to have indicated that the Government's question, the answer to which is sought to be impeached, need not be proper cross-examination in the first instance. The Court of Appeals did not suggest that either the cross-examination or the impeachment of Havens would have been improper absent the use of illegally seized evidence, and we cannot accept respondent's suggestions that because of the illegal search and seizure, the Government's questions about the T-shirt were improper cross-examination. McLeroth testified that Havens had assisted him in preparing the T-shirt for smuggling. Havens, in his direct testimony, acknowledged McLeroth's prior testimony that the cocaine "was taped or draped around his body and so on" but denied that he had "ever engage[d] in that kind of activity with Mr. McLeroth. . . . " This testimony could easily be understood as a denial of any connection with McLeroth's T-shirt and as a contradiction of McLeroth's testimony. Quite reasonably, it seems to us, the Government on cross-examination called attention to his answers on direct and then asked whether he had anything to do with sewing the cotton swatches on McLeroth's T-shirt. This was cross-examination growing out of Havens' direct testimony; and, as we hold above, the ensuing impeachment did not violate Havens' constitutional rights.

We reverse the judgment of the Court of Appeals and remand the case to that court for further proceedings consistent with this opinion.

NOTES AND QUESTIONS

1. Defense counsel here was playing with fire. Plus he asked a really bad question. Consider the full exchange:

Q. And you heard Mr. McLeroth testify earlier as to something to the effect that this material was taped or draped around his body and so on, you heard that testimony?

A. Yes, I did.

Q. Did you ever engage in that kind of activity with Mr. McLeroth and Augusto or Mr. McLeroth and anyone else on that fourth visit to Lima, Peru?

A. I did not.

536 Chapter V The Exclusionary Rule, its Exceptions, and Suppression Hearings

The "engage in that kind of activity" formulation is just too loose. Could a more precise question have neutralized the cooperator's testimony more narrowly and not exposed Havens to cross-examination? How about: "You didn't have anything taped or draped on your body in the airport, did you?"

2. Having this important a rule turn on the allowable scope of cross-examination seems unwise. Wouldn't the cleanest and most understandable rule be one that simply prohibits the government from any use of illegally obtained evidence at trial in any way? Do you think the ambiguity in *Havens* could deter defendants from testifying?

3. In any event, was Havens's denial of "engaging in that kind of activity" false?

4. Note: Whenever the description of a trial is described, as here, as a "search for the truth," the defendant is likely to lose.

———

The next case considers the government's attempt to exploit a particularly egregious constitutional violation under the impeachment exception.

———

James v. Illinois
493 U.S. 307 (1990)

Justice Brennan delivered the opinion of the Court.

The impeachment exception to the exclusionary rule permits the prosecution in a criminal proceeding to introduce illegally obtained evidence to impeach the defendant's own testimony. The Illinois Supreme Court extended this exception to permit the prosecution to impeach the testimony of all defense witnesses with illegally obtained evidence. Finding this extension inconsistent with the balance of values underlying our previous applications of the exclusionary rule, we reverse.

I

On the night of August 30, 1982, eight young boys returning home from a party were confronted by a trio of other boys who demanded money. When the eight boys refused to comply, one member of the trio produced a gun and fired into the larger group, killing one boy and seriously injuring another. When the police arrived, the remaining members of the larger group provided eyewitness accounts of the event and descriptions of the perpetrators.

The next evening, two detectives of the Chicago Police Department took 15-year-old Darryl James into custody as a suspect in the shooting. James was found at his mother's beauty parlor sitting under a hair dryer; when he emerged, his hair was black and curly. After placing James in their car, the detectives questioned him about his prior hair color. He responded that the previous day his hair had been reddish brown, long, and combed straight back. The detectives questioned James again later at the police station, and he further stated that he had gone to the beauty parlor in order to have his hair "dyed black and curled in order to change his appearance."

The State subsequently indicted James for murder and attempted murder. Prior to trial, James moved to suppress the statements regarding his hair, contending that they were the fruit of a Fourth Amendment violation because the detectives lacked probable cause for his warrantless arrest. After an evidentiary hearing, the trial court sustained this motion and ruled that the statements would be inadmissible at trial.

At trial, five members of the larger group of boys testified for the State, and each made an in-court identification of the defendant. Each testified that the person responsible for the shooting had "reddish" hair, worn shoulder length in a slicked-back "butter" style. Each also recalled having seen James several weeks earlier at a parade, at which time James had the aforementioned hair color and style. At trial, however, his hair was black and worn in a "natural" style. Despite the discrepancy between the witnesses' description and his present appearance, the witnesses stood firm in their conviction that James had been present and had fired the shots.

James did not testify in his own defense. He called as a witness Jewel Henderson, a friend of his family. Henderson testified that on the day of the shooting she had taken James to register for high school and that, at that time, his hair was black. The State then sought, over James' objection, to introduce his illegally obtained statements as a means of impeaching the credibility of Henderson's testimony. After determining that the suppressed statements had been made voluntarily, the trial court overruled James' objection. One of the interrogating detectives then reported James' prior admissions that he had reddish hair the night of the shooting and he dyed and curled his hair the next day in order to change his appearance. James ultimately was convicted of both murder and attempted murder and sentenced to 30 years' imprisonment.

On appeal, the Illinois Appellate Court reversed James' convictions and ordered a new trial. The appellate court held that the exclusionary rule barred admission of James' illegally obtained statements for the purpose of impeaching a defense witness' testimony and that the resulting constitutional error was not harmless. However, the Illinois Supreme Court reversed. The court reasoned that, in order to deter the defendant from engaging in perjury "by proxy," the impeachment exception to the exclusionary rule ought to be expanded to allow the State to introduce illegally obtained evidence to impeach the testimony of defense witnesses other than the defendant himself. The court therefore ordered James' convictions reinstated. We granted certiorari.

II

"There is no gainsaying that arriving at the truth is a fundamental goal of our legal system." *United States v. Havens* (1980). But various constitutional rules limit the means by which government may conduct this search for truth in order to promote other values embraced by the Framers and cherished throughout our Nation's history. "Ever since its inception, the rule excluding evidence seized in violation of the Fourth Amendment has been recognized as a principal mode of discouraging lawless police conduct. . . . [W]ithout it the constitutional guarantee against unreasonable searches and seizures would be a mere 'form of words.'" The occasional suppression of illegally obtained yet probative evidence has long been considered a necessary cost of preserving overriding constitutional values: "[T]here is nothing new in the realization that the Constitution sometimes insulates the criminality of a few in order to protect the privacy of us all."

This Court has carved out exceptions to the exclusionary rule, however, where the introduction of reliable and probative evidence would significantly further the truthseeking function of a criminal trial and the likelihood that admissibility of such evidence would encourage police misconduct is but a "speculative possibility." One exception to the rule permits prosecutors to introduce illegally obtained evidence for the limited purpose of impeaching the credibility of the defendant's own testimony. This Court first recognized this exception in *Walder v. United States*, (1954), permitting the prosecutor to introduce into evidence heroin obtained through an illegal search to undermine the credibility of the defendant's claim that he had never possessed narcotics. The Court explained that a defendant

must be free to deny all the elements of the case against him without thereby giving leave to the Government to introduce by way of rebuttal evidence illegally secured by it, and therefore not available for its case in chief. Beyond that, however, there is hardly justification for letting the defendant affirmatively resort to perjurious testimony in reliance on the Government's disability to challenge his credibility.

In *Harris* and *Hass*, the Court applied the exception to permit prosecutors to impeach defendants using incriminating yet voluntary and reliable statements elicited in violation of *Miranda* requirements. Finally, in *Havens* the Court expanded the exception to permit prosecutors to introduce illegally obtained evidence in order to impeach a defendant's "answers to questions put to him on cross-examination that are plainly within the scope of the defendant's direct examination."

This Court insisted throughout this line of cases that "evidence that has been illegally obtained . . . is inadmissible on the government's direct case, or otherwise, as substantive evidence of guilt." However, because the Court believed that permitting the use of such evidence to impeach defendants' testimony would further the goal of truth-seeking by preventing defendants from perverting the exclusionary rule "'into a license to use perjury by way of a defense,'" and because the Court further believed that permitting such use would create only a "speculative possibility that impermissible police conduct will be encouraged thereby," the Court concluded that the balance of values underlying the exclusionary rule justified an exception covering impeachment of defendants' testimony.

III

In this case, the Illinois Supreme Court held that our balancing approach in *Walder* and its progeny justifies expanding the scope of the impeachment exception to permit prosecutors to use illegally obtained evidence to impeach the credibility of defense witnesses. We disagree. Expanding the class of impeachable witnesses from the defendant alone to all defense witnesses would create different incentives affecting the behavior of both defendants and law enforcement officers. As a result, this expansion would not promote the truthseeking function to the same extent as did creation of the original exception, and yet it would significantly undermine the deterrent effect of the general exclusionary rule. Hence, we believe that this proposed expansion would frustrate rather than further the purposes underlying the exclusionary rule.

The previously recognized exception penalizes defendants for committing perjury by allowing the prosecution to expose their perjury through impeachment using illegally obtained evidence. Thus defendants are discouraged in the first instance from "affirmatively resort[ing] to perjurious testimony." But the exception leaves defendants free to testify truthfully on their own behalf; they can offer probative and exculpatory evidence to the jury without opening the door to impeachment by carefully avoiding any statements that directly contradict the suppressed evidence. The exception thus generally discourages perjured testimony without discouraging truthful testimony.

In contrast, expanding the impeachment exception to encompass the testimony of all defense witnesses would not have the same beneficial effects. First, the mere threat of a subsequent criminal prosecution for perjury is far more likely to deter a witness from intentionally lying on a defendant's behalf than to deter a defendant, already facing conviction for the underlying offense, from lying on his own behalf. Hence the Illinois Supreme Court's underlying premise that a defendant frustrated by our previous impeachment exception can easily find a witness to engage in "perjury by proxy" is suspect.

More significantly, expanding the impeachment exception to encompass the testimony of all defense witnesses likely would chill some defendants from presenting their best defense and sometimes any defense at all — through the testimony of others. Whenever police obtained evidence illegally, defendants would have to assess prior to trial the likelihood that the evidence would be admitted to impeach the otherwise favorable testimony of any witness they call. Defendants might reasonably fear that one or more of their witnesses, in a position to offer truthful and favorable testimony, would also make some statement in sufficient tension with the tainted evidence to allow the prosecutor to introduce that evidence for impeachment. First, defendants sometimes need to call "reluctant" or "hostile" witnesses to provide reliable and probative exculpatory testimony, and such witnesses likely will not share the defendants' concern for avoiding statements that invite impeachment through contradictory evidence. Moreover, defendants often cannot trust even "friendly" witnesses to testify without subjecting themselves to impeachment, simply due to insufficient care or attentiveness. This concern is magnified in those occasional situations when defendants must call witnesses to testify despite having had only a limited opportunity to consult with or prepare them in advance. For these reasons, we have recognized in a variety of contexts that a party "cannot be absolutely certain that his witnesses will testify as expected." As a result, an expanded impeachment exception likely would chill some defendants from calling witnesses who would otherwise offer probative evidence.

This realization alters the balance of values underlying the current impeachment exception governing defendants' testimony. Our prior cases make clear that defendants ought not be able to "pervert" the exclusion of illegally obtained evidence into a shield for perjury, but it seems no more appropriate for the State to brandish such evidence as a sword with which to dissuade defendants from presenting a meaningful defense through other witnesses. Given the potential chill created by expanding the impeachment exception, the conceded gains to the truth-seeking process from discouraging or disclosing perjured testimony would be offset to some extent by the concomitant loss of probative witness testimony. Thus, the truth-seeking rationale supporting the impeachment of defendants in *Walder* and its progeny does not apply to other witnesses with equal force.

Moreover, the proposed expansion of the current impeachment exception would significantly weaken the exclusionary rule's deterrent effect on police misconduct. This Court has characterized as a mere "speculative possibility," the likelihood that permitting prosecutors to impeach defendants with illegally obtained evidence would encourage police misconduct. Law enforcement officers will think it unlikely that the defendant will first decide to testify at trial and will also open the door inadvertently to admission of any illegally obtained evidence. Hence, the officers' incentive to acquire evidence through illegal means is quite weak.

In contrast, expanding the impeachment exception to all defense witnesses would significantly enhance the expected value to the prosecution of illegally obtained evidence. First, this expansion would vastly increase the number of occasions on which such evidence could be used. Defense witnesses easily outnumber testifying defendants, both because many defendants do not testify themselves and because many if not most defendants call multiple witnesses on their behalf. Moreover, due to the chilling effect identified above, illegally obtained evidence holds even greater value to the prosecution for each individual witness than for each defendant. The prosecutor's access to impeachment evidence would not just deter perjury; it would also deter defendants from calling witnesses in the first place, thereby keeping from the jury much probative exculpatory evidence. For both of these reasons, police officers and their superiors would recognize that obtaining evidence through illegal means stacks the deck heavily in the prosecution's favor. It is thus far more than a "speculative possibility" that police misconduct will be encouraged by permitting such use of illegally obtained evidence.

The United States argues that this result is constitutionally acceptable because excluding illegally obtained evidence solely from the prosecution's case in chief would still provide a quantum of deterrence sufficient to protect the privacy interests underlying the exclusionary rule. We disagree. Of course, a police officer might in certain situations believe that obtaining particular evidence through illegal means, resulting in its suppression from the case in chief, would prevent the prosecution from establishing a prima facie case to take to a jury. In such situations, the officer likely would be deterred from obtaining the evidence illegally for fear of jeopardizing the entire case. But much if not most of the time, police officers confront opportunities to obtain evidence illegally after they have already legally obtained (or know that they have other means of legally obtaining) sufficient evidence to sustain a prima facie case. In these situations, a rule requiring exclusion of illegally obtained evidence from only the government's case in chief would leave officers with little to lose and much to gain by overstepping constitutional limits on evidence gathering. Narrowing the exclusionary rule in this manner, therefore, would significantly undermine the rule's ability "to compel respect for the constitutional guaranty in the only effectively available way — by removing the incentive to disregard it." So long as we are committed to protecting the people from the disregard of their constitutional rights during the course of criminal investigations, inadmissibility of illegally obtained evidence must remain the rule, not the exception.

IV

The cost to the truth-seeking process of evidentiary exclusion invariably is perceived more tangibly in discrete prosecutions than is the protection of privacy values through deterrence of future police misconduct. When defining the precise scope of the exclusionary rule, however, we must focus on systemic effects of proposed exceptions to ensure that individual liberty from arbitrary or oppressive police conduct does not succumb to the inexorable pressure to introduce all incriminating evidence, no matter how obtained, in each and every criminal case. Our previous recognition of an impeachment exception limited to the testimony of defendants reflects a careful weighing of the competing values. Because expanding the exception to encompass the testimony of all defense witnesses would not further the truth-seeking value with equal force but would appreciably undermine the deterrent effect of the exclusionary rule, we adhere to the line drawn in our previous cases.

Accordingly, we hold that the Illinois Supreme Court erred in affirming James' convictions despite the prosecutor's use of illegally obtained statements to impeach a defense witness' testimony. The court's judgment is reversed, and the case is remanded for further proceedings not inconsistent with this opinion.

NOTES AND QUESTIONS

1. Note the egregiousness of the misconduct here: The police essentially seized a 15-year old boy and absconded with him without probable cause or a warrant. Even if the nature of the misconduct does not affect the impeachment issue, it undoubtedly contributed to the result.

2. Why was the prosecutor here so greedy? How badly did the prosecutor need the rebuttal testimony from the police officer? He had five eyewitnesses who were able to identify the defendant as the shooter. And the prosecutor must have had some way to get into evidence — through Jewel Henderson, the family friend, perhaps — that James's mother had a beauty parlor.

F. SUPPRESSION HEARINGS

Suppression hearings are the vehicles for defendants to attempt to vindicate their constitutional rights before a judge and attempt to have illegally obtained evidence excluded in advance of their trial. In many cases the result of the suppression hearing will determine whether there will be a trial — success might mean the case is dropped while failure might lead to the conclusion that a guilty plea is in order. Suppression hearings often turn on competing versions of the

F. Suppression Hearings   541

facts leading up to a search, seizure, or other police encounter. And it is sometimes necessary for defendants to testify at suppression hearings.

Although the Supreme Court has held that a defendant's testimony at a suppression hearing cannot be used against the defendant on the question of guilt or innocence, *Simmons v. United States*, 390 U.S. 27 (1968), it can be used to impeach the credibility of a testifying defendant. *See supra.*

There are other risks as well, especially since the introduction of the United States Sentencing Guidelines, *see* Chapter XVI *infra,* as the next case shows.

United States v. Matos
907 F.2d 274 (2d Cir. 1990)

MESKILL, Circuit Judge:

This is an appeal from a judgment of conviction entered in the United States District Court for the Southern District of New York, Haight, J. Defendant-appellant was found guilty after a bench trial on stipulated facts of falsely making, forging and counterfeiting United States Federal Reserve Notes in violation of 18 U.S.C. §§ 471 and 2. He was subsequently sentenced under the Sentencing Guidelines (Guidelines) to twenty-four months imprisonment, two years supervised release and a $50 special assessment. On appeal, he contends that the district court erred in increasing his offense level by two points for obstruction of justice under Guidelines § 3C1.1 on the basis of his false testimony at a suppression hearing.

The facts relevant to the resolution of this appeal may be summarized as follows. On February 26, 1988, Secret Service Agents arrested appellant at his print shop on counterfeiting charges. After being advised of his constitutional rights, appellant admitted printing counterfeit currency and stated that he had given the counterfeit money along with the plates and negatives to someone named "Carmello." He was again advised of his rights and consented to a search of his print shop and his apartment.

After the searches, the agents took appellant to the Secret Service's New York Field Office. Special Agent James Figliuolo advised appellant of his constitutional rights, this time using a one page printed waiver form. Figliuolo wrote the date and time on the form, and appellant signed it. In response to questions that followed, appellant restated that he had printed the counterfeit money but had given the money, plates and negatives to "Carmello." Appellant thereafter agreed to take a polygraph test. Before the test, Figliuolo again advised appellant of his rights, using a two page printed waiver form on which appellant marked his initials and wrote the time and date. The results of the polygraph examination showed evidence of deception. After additional questioning, appellant finally admitted that he had given the counterfeit money to his girlfriend. He then signed and dated a three page statement detailing his counterfeiting activities.

At a pretrial suppression hearing, appellant testified, in contradiction to the testimony of the agents involved, that he had not been advised of his constitutional rights until after he had made his various oral and written statements, that he had been forced to sign the waiver forms with the times and dates left blank, and that the agents backdated the time on the forms. He also testified that he asked to consult a lawyer at the print shop and that his request was ignored. The district court discredited appellant's testimony, finding that his rendition of the events was "inherently implausible" and that his claim that his request for an attorney was ignored was nothing more than "an effort to shore up his motion."

Appellant was found guilty after a bench trial on stipulated facts. At sentencing, the district court added two points to the calculation of appellant's offense level for obstruction of

542 Chapter V The Exclusionary Rule, its Exceptions, and Suppression Hearings

justice under Guidelines § 3C1.1 on the ground that he had testified falsely at the suppression hearing.

Guidelines § 3C1.1 provides:

> If the defendant willfully impeded or obstructed, or attempted to impede or obstruct the administration of justice during the investigation or prosecution of the instant offense, increase the offense level by 2 levels.

Application Note 1(c) to this section specifically identifies "testifying untruthfully . . . concerning a material fact" during any judicial proceeding as within the scope of section 3C1.1. Appellant nevertheless argues that the district court erred in increasing his offense level by two points absent a finding that his testimony was motivated by an intent to deceive. In support of his position, appellant relies on Application Note 2 to section 3C1.1, which provides that "[i]n applying [section 3C1.1], suspect testimony and statements should be evaluated in a light most favorable to the defendant." Viewed in this light, appellant contends, his testimony can be seen as the product of confusion rather than an intent to deceive. He further argues that, if such testimony is not viewed in the light most favorable to the defendant, section 3C1.1 will have a chilling effect on a defendant's decision to testify.

We find these claims to be meritless. The district court specifically found that appellant's testimony contained a "basic and bald untruth on an important aspect of the [suppression] motion" and that his false testimony constituted willful obstruction. Application Note 2 "simply instructs the sentencing judge to resolve in favor of the defendant those conflicts about which the judge, after weighing the evidence, has no firm conviction." The district court without question found that appellant testified falsely with the purpose of affecting the outcome of the suppression hearing. This finding is not clearly erroneous.

This result does not, as appellant contends, unconstitutionally chill the exercise of the right to testify. A defendant has no protected right to testify falsely. When, as here, the district court comes away with the firm conviction that the defendant testified falsely with the intent of impeding the disposition of the criminal charges, there is no constitutional bar to an enhanced sentence.

The judgment of the district court is therefore affirmed.

NOTES AND QUESTIONS

1. Does Matos's version of the police interrogation suggest the officers might have been using the successive interrogation technique that was blessed by the Supreme Court in *Oregon v. Elstad*? Why would the district court—presumably well aware of *Elstad*—have found Matos's testimony "inherently implausible"?

2. A two-level guideline increase would probably have added six months to Matos's sentence. Do you agree with his argument about this adjustment having a "chilling effect" on defendants considering testifying at suppression hearings?

3. A trial judge's conclusion on the credibility of a witness is always going to be viewed deferentially on appeal. Given the high stakes in a context such as this one, would it serve any purpose to require the trial judge to make specific findings as to credibility?

4. It seems as if the judge's credibility comments were made at the hearing denying the suppression motion. Why in the world, then, did the defendant waive his right to a jury trial?

Testilying. The credibility of the defendant is hardly the only credibility issue relevant to suppression motions. A substantial body of literature exists on the subject of police perjury, much of it originating in the findings of the Mollen Commission, named after Judge Milton

Mollen, who led an investigation into corruption in the New York City Police Department in the 1990s. The Commission found the following:

> Officers reported a litany of manufactured tales. For example, when officers unlawfully stop and search a vehicle because they believe it contains drugs or guns, officers will falsely claim in police reports and under oath that the car ran a red light (or committed some other traffic violation) and that they subsequently saw contraband in the car in plain view. To conceal an unlawful search of an individual who officers believe is carrying drugs or a gun, they will falsely assert that they saw a bulge in the person's pocket or saw drugs and money changing hands. To justify unlawfully entering an apartment where officers believe narcotics or cash can be found, they pretend to have information from an unidentified civilian informant or claim they saw the drugs in plain view after responding to the premises on a radio run. To arrest people they suspect are guilty of dealing drugs, they falsely assert that the defendants had drugs in their possession when, in fact, the drugs were found elsewhere where the officers had no lawful right to be.

Commission to Investigate Allegations of Police Corruption and the Anti-Corruption Procedures of the Police Dept., City of New York, Commission Report 36 (1994) (Milton Mollen, Chair) (hereinafter Mollen Report). The phenomenon of police perjury was so widespread in some places that the police themselves came up with a name for it — "testilying." *Id.*

The problem of police perjury is most prevalent in suppression hearings, perhaps because in this context police officers see themselves as the righteous defenders of the fight against crime in a theater populated by factually guilty defendants, sleazy defense attorneys, permissive judges, and legal technicalities. *See* Carl B. Klockars, *Blue Lies and Police Placebos*, 27 Am. Behav. Sci. 529, 540 (1984) (Police lie at suppression hearings because they see search-and-seizure rules, and other evidentiary rules, as procedural rules "the violation of which does not affect a perpetrator's factual guilt."). Myron W. Orfield Jr., *Deterrence, Perjury, and the Heater Factor: An Exclusionary Rule in the Chicago Criminal Courts*, 63 U. Colo. L. Rev. 75, 107 (1992) (survey of prosecutors, defense attorneys, and judges indicates a belief that, on average, perjury occurs 20 percent of the time, with defense attorneys estimating it occurs 53 percent of the time in connection with Fourth Amendment issues; only 8 percent believe that police never, or almost never, lie in court).

The problem of police perjury had been in existence for decades when the Mollen Commission did its work, as the next case shows.

People v. McMurty
64 Misc. 2d 63 (1970)

IRVING YOUNGER, J.

For several years now, lawyers concerned with the administration of criminal justice have been troubled by the problem of "dropsy" testimony. This case shows why.

The facts are simple. On July 23, 1970, Patrolman Charles Frisina arrested defendant James McMurty on a charge of possession of marijuana. McMurty moved to suppress the marijuana for use as evidence, and, in due course, a hearing was held. Frisina took the stand. In condensed but substantially verbatim form, he testified as follows:

> At 8:30 p.m. on July 23, 1970, I was on duty driving a patrol car. While stopped for a light at West 3rd Street and Broadway, I observed two men in a doorway of the building at 677 Broadway. One of these men — James McMurty, as I later learned — saw the patrol car and stepped out of the doorway. From his right hand he let drop a small plastic container. I got out of the patrol car and retrieved it. In my opinion, based upon a fair amount of experience, its contents were marijuana. I approached McMurty, who had begun to walk away, and asked him if the container was his. He said no. I said that I had seen him drop it and placed him under arrest.

Chapter V The Exclusionary Rule, its Exceptions, and Suppression Hearings

Then McMurty took the stand. In condensed but substantially verbatim form, he testified as follows:

> On July 23, 1970, at 8:30 p.m., I was walking on Broadway near West 3rd Street when I saw Patrolman Frisina coming toward me. I knew that I had a container of marijuana in my pocket. I also knew, after twelve years of involvement with drugs and four or five prior convictions, that illegal-search-and-seizure was my only defense. The last thing I would do is drop the marijuana to the ground. I simply left it in my pocket. Frisina told me to get into a doorway. I obeyed, hoping that he would search me. He did just that, found the marijuana, and arrested me.

The prosecutor stands on Frisina's testimony. Since the marijuana had been abandoned, he argues, its seizure was lawful. Defense counsel stands on McMurty's testimony. The arrest occurred when McMurty was ordered into the doorway, he argues, and since the officer then had no probable cause to arrest, the search which followed was unlawful.

Were this the first time a policeman had testified that a defendant dropped a packet of drugs to the ground, the matter would be unremarkable. The extraordinary thing is that each year in our criminal courts policemen give such testimony in hundreds, perhaps thousands, of cases — and that, in a nutshell, is the problem of "dropsy" testimony. It disturbs me now, and it disturbed me when I was at the Bar.

Policemen see themselves as fighting a two-front war — against criminals in the street and against "liberal" rules of law in court. All's fair in this war, including the use of perjury to subvert "liberal" rules of law that might free those who "ought" to be jailed. . . . It is a peculiarity of our legal system that the police have unique opportunities (and unique temptations) to give false testimony. When the Supreme Court lays down a rule to govern the conduct of the police, the rule does not enforce itself. Some further proceeding . . . is almost always necessary to determine what actually happened. In *Mapp v. Ohio*, for example, the Supreme Court laid down the rule that evidence obtained by the police through an unreasonable search and seizure may not be used in a state criminal prosecution. But before applying the rule to any particular case, a hearing must be held to establish the facts. Then the judge decides whether those facts constitute an unreasonable search and seizure. . . . The difficulty arises when one stands back from the particular case and looks at a series of cases. It then becomes apparent that policemen are committing perjury at least in some of them, and perhaps in nearly all of them.

Narcotics prosecutions in New York City can be so viewed. Before *Mapp*, the policeman typically testified that he stopped the defendant for little or no reason, searched him, and found narcotics on his person. This had the ring of truth. It was an illegal search (not based upon "probable cause"), but the evidence was admissible because *Mapp* had not yet been decided. Since it made no difference, the policeman testified truthfully. After the decision in *Mapp*, it made a great deal of difference. For the first few months, New York policemen continued to tell the truth about the circumstances of their searches, with the result that evidence was suppressed. Then the police made the great discovery that if the defendant drops the narcotics on the ground, after which the policeman arrests him, the search is reasonable and the evidence is admissible.

Spend a few hours in the New York City Criminal Court nowadays, and you will hear case after case in which a policeman testifies that the defendant dropped the narcotics on the ground, whereupon the policeman arrested him. Usually the very language of the testimony is identical from one case to another. This is now known among defense lawyers and prosecutors as "dropsy" testimony. The judge has no reason to disbelieve it in any particular case, and of course the judge must decide each case on its own evidence, without regard to the testimony in other cases. Surely, though, not in every case was the defendant unlucky enough to drop his narcotics at the feet of a policeman. It follows that at least in some of these cases the police are lying.

So far as I know, there has been only one statistical study of "dropsy" complaints. It confirms my impressions (pp. 556-557): "In the period after *Mapp*, the number of complaints alleging that the suspect dropped the contraband increased for all groups of officers. The Narcotics Squad showed the smallest percentages increase (45.3 per cent), although the rise in the number of their "dropsies" (93, from 205 to 298) was the largest. The plainclothesmen recorded a 71.8 per cent rise in complaints based on this circumstance, an increase from 32 to 55; while the uniformed officers showed the highest percentage increase (79.6 per cent), with the number of complaints alleging drops rising from 69 to 128."

Beyond any doubt, then, the problem exists. Its solution, I suppose, is prosecutors' work. The courts can only deplore. They are ill-equipped to persuade the police to change their practices or alter their philosophy. In Judge Wright's words, "the time is ripe for some soul searching in the prosecutor's office before it offers any more ['dropsy' testimony]."

Withal, Judges must decide the cases that come before them. In this case, my reasoning has taken four steps.

First. "Dropsy" testimony should be scrutinized with especial caution.

I am aware that Judge (as he then was) Burger wrote, with respect to narcotics policemen: "But it would be a dismal reflection on society to say that when the guardians of its security are called to testify in court under oath, their testimony must be viewed with suspicion."

With all possible deference, I disagree. When there are grounds for believing that "the guardians of its security" sometimes give deliberately false testimony, it is no "dismal reflection on society" for Judges to acknowledge what all can see. If courage is the secret of liberty, the first task of free men is to call things by their right name.

Second. Should the policeman's testimony seem inherently unreal, it will forthwith be rejected. This is a consequence of the first consideration.

Here, the evidence given by neither witness strikes me as against the grain of human experience. If Frisina's testimony stood alone, I could believe it. If McMurty's testimony stood alone, I could believe it.

Third. The slightest independent contradiction of the policeman's testimony or corroboration of the defendant's testimony will warrant suppression of the evidence. This too is a consequence of the first consideration.

Here, there was no independent contradiction of Frisina and no independent corroboration of McMurty. The testimony of each remains poised in the balance.

Fourth. Determine whether the burden of proof has been carried.

Had the issue been open, I would hold that the People must prove beyond a reasonable doubt that the seizure was lawful. But the issue is closed. The Court of Appeals declares the burden of proof to be the defendant's. Where the testimony on one side balances the testimony on the other, as here, it is the People who prevail. Defendant's motion to suppress is therefore denied.

I come to this decision reluctantly. Our refusal to face up to the "dropsy" problem soils the rectitude of the administration of justice. One is tempted to deal with it now by suppressing "dropsy" evidence out of hand; yet I cannot. Reason and settled rules of law lead the other way, and Judge serve the integrity of the means, not the attractiveness of the end.

Somehow, policemen must be made to understand that their duty is no different.

NOTES AND QUESTIONS

1. Why are prosecutors largely getting off the hook here? Their most fundamental ethical obligation is to not present perjured testimony.

2. Does this case come out the right way? Is this really a perfect credibility tie, with the government winning the tiebreaker because the burden of proof is on the defendant?

Irving Younger

3. Judge Irving Younger, a former assistant U.S. attorney in the Southern District of New York, was a practicing lawyer and law professor before and after being a judge, and was widely known for his writings and lectures on trial practice. Most trial lawyers to this day regard his "The Ten Commandments of Cross-Examination" as gospel.

Judge Younger attributes dropsy testimony to *Mapp*. This is a standard account, although there are variations on the theme. Professor Bennett Capers, for example, notes that police perjury has an ancient pedigree but that, echoing Judge Younger, the police had little reason to lie and began doing so once the exclusionary rule became applicable. I. Bennett Capers, *Crime, Legitimacy, and Testilying*, 83 Ind. L.J. 835, 868 (2008). Professor Morgan Cloud notes longstanding evidence of police corruption uncovered by the Wickersham Commission in the 1930s, and links testilying to the decisions of the Warren Court. *See* Morgan Cloud, *Judges, "Testilying," and the Constitution*, 69 S. Cal. L. Rev. 1341, 1342-43, 1350-53 (1996); Morgan Cloud, *The Dirty Little Secret*, 43 Emory L.J. 1311, 1314-21 (1994) ("The change in police testimony about investigative practices can be traced to the Supreme Court's decisions constitutionalizing criminal procedure.").

United States v. Restrepo
890 F. Supp. 180 (E.D.N.Y. 1995)

WEINSTEIN, Senior District Judge.

I. INTRODUCTION

Alberto Caro, Jose Francisco Guevara and Christian John Restrepo seek to suppress statements and other evidence of a drug conspiracy. They are charged with conspiring to distribute and to possess with intent to distribute, and with possessing with intent to distribute, cocaine. 21 U.S.C. §§ 841(a)(1) & 841(b)(1)(A)(ii)(II). They move to suppress the following statements and other evidence: Guevara: evidence and statements obtained by law enforcement officials following a traffic stop, on grounds of a series of alleged Fourth Amendment violations; Caro: tapes of conversations between himself and Guevara on the ground that the statutorily required consents to the recordings were not obtained; and Restrepo: evidence obtained as a result of a "security sweep" of his house.

Guevara's motion is granted: law enforcement officials violated his constitutional rights, starting with an illegal stop and search of his car.

* * *

II. GUEVARA'S MOTION TO SUPPRESS
A. Facts

An officer of the Memphis Police Department stopped Guevara, a swarthy Hispanic-appearing male driving a Cadillac with California license plates on an interstate highway in Tennessee. Guevara's eleven-year-old son, Rodolfo, was in the front passenger seat and his wife and two younger children were in the rear.

At a full evidentiary hearing in the Eastern District of New York, the officer testified that Guevara was speeding—driving 65 miles per hour in a 55 miles per hour zone. Guevara and Rodolfo both testified that Guevara was driving slowly because the family was seeking a place to stop for breakfast. Guevara also stated that he was driving at less than 55 miles per hour because he did not want to be intercepted while he was carrying drugs. Rodolfo testified that as they passed the police car he noticed that the car's speedometer read 47-50 miles per hour and that his mother had just chided his father for driving too slowly.

Because Guevara does not speak English, the officer used Rodolfo as an interpreter for communicating with Guevara during the stop.

Rodolfo testified that the officer stated that the reason for the stop was that Guevara was driving too closely behind a tractor trailer. Guevara testified that the officer never told him, through Rodolfo, the reason for the stop. He did, however, acknowledge driving within five or six meters of a tractor trailer. He also believes that at some point during the stop, Rodolfo told him that the officer had mentioned tailgating. The "traffic courtesy warning" issued by the officer states that Guevara was "speeding 65 MPH in a 55 MPH zone."

The officer sought and received Guevara's driver's license which he used to fill out a "courtesy warning." Guevara did not ask his son to translate the courtesy warning, believing that it was not important and that after signing it, he would be permitted to depart.

As the officer filled out the courtesy warning, he questioned Guevara and Rodolfo about their trip. According to Guevara, the officer was "burning time while he filled out the courtesy ticket, he was continuing to ask me questions." Guevara explained that the family was headed to Queens, New York for three days' vacation. Rodolfo testified that the officer also asked Guevara if he is "Mexican."

The officer testified that during this conversation, he noticed that Guevara was growing "more and more nervous," that "[h]is hands were quivering," and that Mrs. Guevara "kept looking back like, you know, nervously every time I would talk to [Guevara,] . . . a real nervous type reaction to me." Under cross examination he explained that general conversation is used to elicit signs of possible criminal activity independent of a traffic violation.

As or immediately after the officer issued the courtesy warning, a second officer arrived. According to the first officer, the second officer happened upon the scene. The second testified, however, that he had been radioed by the first, and Guevara testified that the first used the radio in his patrol car after taking Guevara's license and registration. The second officer asked Guevara many of the same questions that the first had already asked, and received consistent answers.

After Guevara signed the courtesy warning, the second officer asked if he could speak with Mrs. Guevara, and Guevara agreed. The second officer stayed with Guevara while the first went to open the driver's side door. As he opened it, he "observed that the door was overly heavy for a regular door. Felt like it was heavy to me." Then, according to the first officer, he realized that traffic was coming and that it would be better for Mrs. Guevara to exit from the other side; he shut the door and walked back to the squad car, while the second officer walked over to the passenger side door.

Through the open window of the car, the second officer attempted to communicate with Mrs. Guevara in Spanish. In response to his questions, Mrs. Guevara explained that the family was headed to New York, that they were to be gone a week, and that the trip's purpose was to visit relatives.

Based on the observed nervousness of Mr. and Mrs. Guevara, the fact of the heavy door, and what they felt were discrepancies in the Guevaras' replies to questions about the length and purpose of the trip, the officers decided to request permission to search the car. According to the first officer, it "[a]ppeared like it was more than just a speeding violation at that time. We didn't know what it was."

The second officer asked Guevara in Spanish if he had any guns or illegal drugs in the car and if he would consent to a search. According to the first, Guevara denied that there was anything illegal in the car but agreed to the search.

The second officer asked Guevara to sign a written consent-to-search form. He testified that he first explained the form in English. When Guevara looked confused, this officer flipped the form over to the Spanish side whereupon Guevara "scann[ed] the form with his eyes it looked to me like line-by-line." According to the first officer, Guevara "signed the English side first and then the Spanish side I believe." Both officers testified that the blanks on both sides of the form had already been filled in when it was presented to Guevara.

The first officer testified that the officers did not specify in their request a particular part of the car for the search, such as the trunk or glove compartment. The pre-typed portion of the consent form authorizes "a complete search" of the car.

According to the officers' account, after Mrs. Guevara and the remaining children exited the car, the search of the car commenced. While the second officer stayed with the family, the first opened the driver's side door, "popped" the panel and some additional plastic covering, and observed "a bundle of possibly some type of narcotic."

Guevara's and Rodolfo's testimony contradicted that of the officers. Guevara denied that he was asked whether there was anything illegal in the car. He testified that the blanks on the consent-to-search form were not filled in when it was handed to him to sign and that the officers asked only to search the trunk. He testified that he could not read the English-language consent-to-search form, and that he did not ask his son to translate because he believed it merely authorized a search of the trunk, after which he would be permitted to leave. Guevara's signature appears on both sides of the form. Guevara testified that he signed where the officer pointed, without ever holding the form in his hands. He recognized his signature on the Spanish-language side of the form but did not recall signing that side, noting that the process happened "very fast." He claimed that he did not feel free to leave, but he hoped he would be allowed to if he consented to the search of the trunk.

Rodolfo also testified that the officers stated only that they were going to search the trunk. He denied that the officers asked for or received permission to search the inside of the car. He testified that in response to the officers' request, Guevara agreed to open the trunk, and did so, whereupon it was searched by both officers. One of the officers then went on to search the glove compartment, and then pulled apart the plastic paneling on the driver's door.

After discovering a bundle in the door panel, the officer pointed his gun at Guevara and told him to drop to his knees and put his hands behind his back. Guevara complied and was handcuffed. The children and Mrs. Guevara were directed to the back of a squad car. One of the officers retrieved the package. It tested positive for cocaine.

The first officer then informed Guevara that he was under arrest for possession of cocaine. According to the officers' testimony, both of them recited *Miranda* rights to Guevara — the first in English from memory, and the second in English and then Spanish from a card when Guevara appeared confused. The second officer testified that Guevara shook his head in the affirmative when asked whether he would answer questions. Neither officer made a record that the *Miranda* warnings were given. Guevara denied receiving *Miranda* warnings at his arrest.

The second officer then asked Guevara how much cocaine was in the car. Guevara responded "sixty" in English. Ultimately 60 1-kilogram bricks of cocaine were found secreted within the side panels of the car.

Two additional officers, one a Lieutenant, joined the scene. Upon learning at this time that Mrs. Guevara was a Colombian, Rodolfo testified that the second officer responded, "No wonder." The family and their car were taken to the Memphis Police Department.

• • •

The court finds the defendant, Guevara, his son, Rodolfo, and the attorney, April Ferguson, credible. It finds that the first and second officer at the scene of the stop lied. Where there are material inconsistencies between the three defense witnesses' testimony and that of the government's witnesses, the court credits the defense version. The court also finds that Guevara truthfully described his language ability; the government's argument that he understands English is unsupported. These assessments of credibility are based upon the court's observations of the witnesses and all other factors normally utilized in assessing credibility. See, e.g., 1 Leonard B. Sand, John S. Siffert, Walter P. Loughlin & Steven A. Reiss, Modern Federal Jury Instructions: Criminal ¶ 7.01 (1994) ("Witness Credibility").

NOTES AND QUESTIONS

1. This is an outlier case. Judges are notoriously reluctant to openly question the credibility of a testifying police officer. Cloud, *The Dirty Little Secret, supra* at 1311, 1321-24. Crediting police testimony is almost another aspect of the deference that the Supreme Court has told federal judges over and over again that they should give to police expertise. *See generally* Anna Lvovsky, *The Judicial Presumption of Police Expertise*, 130 Harv. L. Rev. 1995 (2017) (describing the historical arc of police reform efforts).

2. Was there probable cause to stop Guevara for tailgating? Does it matter that the police identified the stop as based on speeding? Would the stop of Guevara's car have been legal after *Whren*?

For an argument that the remarkable thing about police lying is not that it happens but that the Supreme Court shows little skepticism about it, *see* Adam M. Gershowitz & Caroline E. Lewis, *Laundering Police Lies*, 2023 Wis. L. Rev. 1187, 1189-90 (2023). For creative proposals for solutions to the police perjury problem, *see generally* Vida B. Johnson, *Bias in Blue: Instructing Jurors to Consider the Testimony of Police Officer Witnesses with Caution*, 44 Pepp. L. Rev. 245 (2017) (proposing jury instruction on the biases and interests of testifying police officers); David N. Dorfman, *Proving the Lie: Litigating Police Credibility*, 26 Am. J. Crim. L. 455 (1998) (proposing expanded discovery into materials regarding police credibility).

CHAPTER VI

ADDRESSING POLICE MISCONDUCT

What to do about police misconduct? It is generally accepted that most police officers discharge their difficult responsibilities honestly and without resort to undue force, yet some police officers—be they rogues or otherwise—all too often beat or kill civilians. *See, e.g.*, Paul Chevigny, Edge of the Knife: Police Violence in the Americas 97 (1995) (stating that generally, a small number of officers appear to be responsible for most of the misconduct). Yet the problem of police misconduct persists, and is apparently impervious to reform from within on any broad basis.

There would appear to be a federal statute that aims to address this problem, 42 U.S.C. § 1983, originally part of the Ku Klux Klan Act of 1871. It provides:

> Every person who, under color of any statute, ordinance, regulation, custom or usage, of any State or Territory, subjects, or causes to be subjected, any citizen of the United States or other person within the jurisdiction thereof to the deprivation of any rights, privileges, or immunities secured by the Constitution and laws, shall be liable to the party injured in an action at law, suit in equity, or other proper proceeding for redress.

Police misconduct sure seems to be "under color" of law. When police use unreasonable force or conduct illegal searches or impermissibly interrogate persons, they "deprive" persons of federal rights. And the statute promises not only money damages but also equitable relief.

But the Supreme Court has hamstrung § 1983 in several ways that have rendered the statute, despite its apparent textual fit, a poor remedial device for addressing police misconduct. Those barriers will be explored below. Two other potential avenues for deterring police misconduct, each with challenges of its own, are specifically addressed elsewhere in this book. Chapter V *supra* examines the exclusionary rule, which aims to deter police misconduct by preventing the admissibility of evidence derived from illegal police activity, and Chapter X *infra* explores the Department of Justice's use of criminal civil rights statutes to prosecute police officers for deprivations of constitutional rights. Neither of these avenues provides for the compensation of victims, however.

Section A below focuses on the reawakening of § 1983 from a long period of dormancy. *Monroe v. Pape*, 365 U.S. 167 (1961), recognized a damages cause of action against defendant police officers under § 1983, but held that their municipality employers were not proper defendants under the statute. Just 17 years later, in *Monell v. Dept. of Social Services of the City of New York*, 436 U.S. 658 (1978), the Court reversed *Monroe*'s holding shielding municipalities from suit, but at the same time rejected municipal liability under a theory of respondeat superior. Section B addresses what remains of municipal liability under § 1983 after *Monell*, including the cases and doctrine that make not only damages but also injunctive relief against police department defendants generally so unobtainable. Section C looks at § 1983 litigation directed at individual police officers, and how the judicially created doctrine of "qualified immunity"

Chapter VI Addressing Police Misconduct

undermines that potential avenue of redress. Section D looks at an entirely different federal remedy, 42 U.S.C. § 14141, which authorizes the Department of Justice to bring actions against police departments that engage in a "pattern or practice" of police misconduct.

A. AWAKENING OF § 1983

Prior to *Monroe*, § 1983 was rarely used. Between 1871 and 1920, only 21 cases were brought under § 1983, and the statute was still rarely used into the 1950s. *See Developments in the Law — Section 1983 and Federalism*, 90 Harv. L. Rev. 1137, 1161 & n.39 (1977). At least some of this impotence was because most of the expansion of constitutional rights (via incorporation of the Bill of Rights into the Fourteenth Amendment) occurred beginning in the 1950s. *See* Jack Beermann, *The History of Civil Rights Legislation, Fifty Years Later*, 34 Conn. L. Rev. 98, 1003-04 (2002). For example, the Fourth Amendment, the violation of which is the basis for James Monroe's claim below, was not held applicable to the states until 1949. *Wolf v. Colorado*, 338 U.S. 25 (1949). The Harvard Law Review editors were not being hyperbolic when they declared that "*Monroe v. Pape* resurrected section 1983 from ninety years of obscurity." *Developments in the Law, supra* at 1137, 1169.

<hr>

Monroe v. Pape
365 U.S. 167 (1961)

Mr. Justice DOUGLAS delivered the opinion of the Court.

This case presents important questions concerning the construction of [42 U.S.C. s 1983], which reads as follows:

> Every person who, under color of any statute, ordinance, regulation, custom or usage, of any State or Territory, subjects, or causes to be subjected, any citizen of the United States or other person within the jurisdiction thereof to the deprivation of any rights, privileges, or immunities secured by the Constitution and laws, shall be liable to the party injured in an action at law, suit in equity, or other proper proceeding for redress.

The complaint alleges that 13 Chicago police officers broke into petitioners' home in the early morning, routed them from bed, made them stand naked in the living room, and ransacked every room, emptying drawers and ripping mattress covers. It further alleges that Mr. Monroe was then taken to the police station and detained on "open" charges for 10 hours, while he was interrogated about a two-day-old murder, that he was not taken before a magistrate, though one was accessible, that he was not permitted to call his family or attorney, that he was subsequently released without criminal charges being preferred against him. It is alleged that the officers had no search warrant and no arrest warrant and that they acted "under color of the statutes, ordinances, regulations, customs and usages" of Illinois and of the City of Chicago. Federal jurisdiction was asserted under, which we have set out above.

The City of Chicago moved to dismiss the complaint on the ground that it is not liable under the Civil Rights Acts nor for acts committed in performance of its governmental functions. All defendants moved to dismiss, alleging that the complaint alleged no cause of action under those Acts or under the Federal Constitution. The District Court dismissed the complaint. The Court of Appeals affirmed. The case is here on a writ of certiorari which we granted because of a seeming conflict of that ruling with our prior cases.

Petitioners claim that the invasion of their home and the subsequent search without a warrant and the arrest and detention of Mr. Monroe without a warrant and without arraignment constituted a deprivation of their "rights, privileges, or immunities secured by the

Constitution" within the meaning of [§ 1983]. It has been said that when 18 U.S.C. s 241, 18 U.S.C.A. s 241, made criminal a conspiracy "to injure, oppress, threaten, or intimidate any citizen in the free exercise or enjoyment of any right or privilege secured to him by the Constitution," it embraced only rights that an individual has by reason of his relation to the central government, not to state governments. But the history of the section of the Civil Rights Act presently involved does not permit such a narrow interpretation.

Section [1983] came onto the books as s 1 of the Ku Klux Act of April 20, 1871. 17 Stat. 13. It was one of the means whereby Congress exercised the power vested in it by s 5 of the Fourteenth Amendment to enforce the provisions of that Amendment.

Its purpose is plain from the title of the legislation, "An Act to enforce the Provisions of the Fourteenth Amendment to the Constitution of the United States, and for other Purposes." Allegation of facts constituting a deprivation under color of state authority of a right guaranteed by the Fourteenth Amendment satisfies to that extent the requirement of the statute. So far petitioners are on solid ground. For the guarantee against unreasonable searches and seizures contained in the Fourth Amendment has been made applicable to the States by reason of the Due Process Clause of the Fourteenth Amendment. *Wolf v. People of State of Colorado.*

• • •

There can be no doubt at least since *Ex parte Virginia* that Congress has the power to enforce provisions of the Fourteenth Amendment against those who carry a badge of authority of a State and represent it in some capacity, whether they act in accordance with their authority or misuse it. The question with which we now deal is the narrower one of whether Congress meant to give a remedy to parties deprived of constitutional rights, privileges and immunities by an official's abuse of his position. *Williams*; *Screws*; *Classic*. We conclude that it did so intend.

It is argued that "under color of" enumerated state authority excludes acts of an official or policeman who can show no authority under state law, state custom, or state usage to do what he did. In this case it is said that these policemen, in breaking into petitioners' apartment, violated the Constitution and laws of Illinois. It is pointed out that under Illinois law a simple remedy is offered for that violation and that, so far as it appears, the courts of Illinois are available to give petitioners that full redress which the common law affords for violence done to a person; and it is earnestly argued that no "statute, ordinance, regulation, custom or usage" of Illinois bars that redress.

The Ku Klux Act grew out of a message sent to Congress by President Grant on March 23, 1871, reading:

> A condition of affairs now exists in some States of the Union rendering life and property insecure and the carrying of the mails and the collection of the revenue dangerous. The proof that such a condition of affairs exists in some localities is now before the Senate. That the power to correct these evils is beyond the control of State authorities I do not doubt; that the power of the Executive of the United States, acting within the limits of existing laws, is sufficient for present emergencies is not clear. Therefore, I urgently recommend such legislation as in the judgment of Congress shall effectually secure life, liberty, and property, and the enforcement of law in all parts of the United States.
>
> The legislation—in particular the section with which we are now concerned—had several purposes. There are threads of many thoughts running through the debates. One who reads them in their entirety sees that the present section had three main aims.
>
> First, it might, of course, override certain kinds of state laws. . . .
>
> Second, it provided a remedy where state law was inadequate.

But the purposes were much broader. The third aim was to provide a federal remedy where the state remedy, though adequate in theory, was not available in practice. The opposition to the measure complained that "It overrides the reserved powers of the States," just as they argued that the second section of the bill "absorb(ed) the entire jurisdiction of the State over their local and domestic affairs."

This Act of April 20, 1871, sometimes called "the third force bill," was passed by a Congress that had the Klan "particularly in mind."

The debates are replete with references to the lawless conditions existing in the South in 1871. There was available to the Congress during these debates a report, nearly 600 pages in length, dealing with the activities of the Klan and the inability of the state governments to cope with it. This report was drawn on by many of the speakers. It was not the unavailability of state remedies but the failure of certain States to enforce the laws with an equal hand that furnished the powerful momentum behind this "force bill.". . .

* * *

Although the legislation was enacted because of the conditions that existed in the South at that time, it is cast in general language and is as applicable to Illinois as it is to the States whose names were mentioned over and again in the debates. It is no answer that the State has a law which if enforced would give relief. The federal remedy is supplementary to the state remedy, and the latter need not be first sought and refused before the federal one is invoked. Hence the fact that Illinois by its constitution and laws outlaws unreasonable searches and seizures is no barrier to the present suit in the federal court.

We had before us in *Classic* 18 U.S.C. s 242, which provides a criminal punishment for anyone who "under color of any law, statute, ordinance, regulation, or custom" subjects any inhabitant of a State to the deprivation of "any rights, privileges, or immunities secured or protected by the Constitution or laws of the United States." The right involved in the *Classic* case was the right of voters in a primary to have their votes counted. The laws of Louisiana required the defendants "to count the ballots, to record the result of the count, and to certify the result of the election." But according to the indictment they did not perform their duty. In an opinion written by Mr. Justice (later Chief Justice) Stone, in which Mr. Justice Roberts, Mr. Justice Reed, and Mr. Justice Frankfurter joined, the Court ruled, "Misuse of power, possessed by virtue of state law and made possible only because the wrongdoer is clothed with the authority of state law, is action taken 'under color of' state law."

That view of the meaning of the words "under color of" state law, 18 U.S.C. s 242, was reaffirmed in *Screws*. The acts there complained of were committed by state officers in performance of their duties, viz., making an arrest effective. It was urged there, as it is here, that "under color of" state law should not be construed to duplicate in federal law what was an offense under state law. It was said there, as it is here, that the ruling in the *Classic* case as to the meaning of "under color of" state law was not in focus and was ill-advised. It was argued there, as it is here, that "under color of" state law included only action taken by officials pursuant to state law. We rejected that view.

We adhered to that view in *Williams*.

* * *

Thus, it is beyond doubt that this phrase should be accorded the same construction in both statutes—in [§ 1983] and in 18 U.S.C. s 242.

Since the *Screws* and *Williams* decisions, Congress has had several pieces of civil rights legislation before it. [Though vigorously debated there was no criticism of the phrase "under color of" state law as previously construed by the Court.] If the results of our construction of "under color of" law were as horrendous as now claimed, if they were as disruptive of our federal scheme as now urged, if they were such an unwarranted invasion of States' rights as pretended, surely the voice of the opposition would have been heard in those Committee reports. Their silence and the new uses to which "under color of" law have recently been given reinforce our conclusion that our prior decisions were correct on this matter of construction.

We conclude that the meaning given "under color of" law in the *Classic* case and in the *Screws* and Williams cases was the correct one; and we adhere to it.

In the *Screws* case we dealt with a statute that imposed criminal penalties for acts "wilfully" done. We construed that word in its setting to mean the doing of an act with "a specific intent to deprive a person of a federal right." We do not think that gloss should be placed on [§ 1983] which we have here. The word "wilfully" does not appear in [§ 1983]. Moreover, [§ 1983]. provides a civil remedy, while in the *Screws* case we dealt with a criminal law challenged on the ground of vagueness. Section [1983] should be read against the background of tort liability that makes a man responsible for the natural consequences of his actions.

So far, then, the complaint states a cause of action. There remains to consider only a defense peculiar to the City of Chicago.

• • •

The City of Chicago asserts that it is not liable under [§ 1983]. We do not stop to explore the whole range of questions tendered us on this issue at oral argument and in the briefs. For we are of the opinion that Congress did not undertake to bring municipal corporations within the ambit of [§ 1983].

• • •

The response of the Congress to the proposal to make municipalities liable for certain actions being brought within federal purview by the Act of April 20, 1871, was so antagonistic that we cannot believe that the word "person" was used in this particular Act to include them. Accordingly we hold that the motion to dismiss the complaint against the City of Chicago was properly granted. But since the complaint should not have been dismissed against the officials the judgment must be and is reversed.

Reversed.

[Justices Harlan and Stewart concurred; Justice Frankfurter dissented.]

NOTES AND QUESTIONS

1. The methodology of *Monroe* is odd. There is almost no discussion of any precedent discussing or applying § 1983. The Court acknowledges that the Seventh Circuit affirmed the district court's dismissal of the complaint but says nothing whatsoever about the court's reasoning or whether other circuits are in agreement. As to why it granted certiorari, the Court states only that the Seventh Circuit's decision conflicted "with our prior cases."

2. Those "prior cases" appear to be two criminal cases: *Screws v. United States*, 325 U.S. 91 (1945), and *United States v. Classic*, 313 U.S. 299 (1941), both of which interpreted related Reconstruction era statutes containing the same "under color of law" language as in § 1983. *See* Chapter X *infra*.

Is it obvious that the language in § 1983 should be interpreted the same as it was in *Screws* and *Classic*?

Is it relevant to the interpretation question that *Screws* and *Classic* were criminal cases?

Is the failure of congressional opponents of then-recent civil rights legislation to object to the "under color of law" language in those bills persuasive?

Why does the Court even address the issue of the requirement in 18 U.S.C. § 242 that a violation must be done "willfully," inasmuch as that adverb is not in § 1983?

3. The Court rejects the view that § 1983 should only apply where the state has no remedy for the misconduct at issue, which is part of the basis for Justice Frankfurter's dissenting opinion. "The federal remedy is supplementary to the state remedy." 365 U.S. at 184.

William A. Dunning

This is not surprising, as the Court may have had the question of the adequacy of state law remedies on its radar. Four months after *Monroe* was decided the Court would issue its decision in *Mapp v. Ohio*, 367 U.S. 643 (1961), *see supra*, overruling *Wolf v. Colorado*, 338 U.S. 25 (1949), and holding the federal exclusionary rule applicable to the states. A key reason for the decision in *Mapp* was the conclusion that the state remedies for Fourth Amendment violations that the Court had previously relied on for its decision in *Wolf* were largely ineffective. *Id.* at 653.

4. The Court devotes a substantial amount of attention to the legislative history of the Ku Klux Klan Act, which is mostly omitted here. By contrast the decisions in *Screws* and *Classic* paid almost no attention to that same legislative history. The dissenters in *Screws*, moreover, vilified Reconstruction era legislation: "It is familiar history that much of this legislation was born of that vengeful spirit which to no small degree envenomed the Reconstruction era." This history is apparently so familiar that the dissenters felt no obligation to cite any authority for it.

They could have, though. The *Screws* dissenters were not inaccurately reflecting the conventional, white supremacist view of the "Dunning School" of Reconstruction historiography, which was predominant into the 1960s. On this view, named after Columbia professor William Dunning and his students, the Reconstruction era was condemned as producing corrupt rule by "uncivilized Negroes" in the South and radical Republicans at the national level. *See* Eric Foner, The Second Founding: How the Civil War and Reconstruction Remade the Constitution xxi-xxiv (2019). Professor Foner has observed that the portrait of Reconstruction advanced by the Dunning School provided "an intellectual foundation for Jim Crow, the racial system of the South and in many ways the United States as a whole, from the 1890s until the civil rights era of the 1960s." *Id.* at xxii. One notable exception to the view of the Dunning School was W.E.B. DuBois's *Black Reconstruction in America 1860-1880* (1935). Although largely ignored by contemporary historians, the message of DuBois's work was largely embraced by Eric Foner's seminal *Reconstruction: America's Unfinished Revolution, 1863-1877* (1988).

W.E.B. DuBois

Professor Eric Foner

A. Awakening of § 1983 **557**

The Dunning School still held sway in 1961 when *Monroe* was decided. It is to the Court's credit that it relied on the legislative history directly, unmediated by the then prevailing academic perspective.

5. In deciding that municipalities do not fall under the term "person" in the statute, the Court acknowledges the policy considerations favoring municipal liability: "It is said that doubts should be resolved in favor of municipal liability because private remedies against officers for illegal searches and seizures are conspicuously ineffective, and because municipal liability will not only afford plaintiffs responsible defendants but cause those defendants to eradicate abuses that exist at the police level."

What other policy considerations favor municipal liability?

What about constitutional violations by federal law enforcement officers? Section 1983 does not apply to them.

Just a few years after James Monroe's mistreatment by Chicago police a similar fate befell a man named Webster Bivens in New York City. Agents of the now defunct Federal Bureau of Narcotics entered his home with weapons drawn, searched his apartment, threatened his family, arrested him on narcotics charges, and subjected him to a strip search upon booking at the federal courthouse in Brooklyn. After the criminal complaint against him was dismissed, Bivens filed a pro se complaint in the Eastern District of New York, seeking $15,000 in damages against each of the six officers for allegedly violating his Fourth Amendment right to be free of unreasonable search and seizure. Bivens did not know the officers' names, hence the case's wonderful title — *Bivens v. Six Unknown Named Agents of Federal Bureau of Narcotics*. 403 U.S. 388 (1971). In *Bivens*, the Supreme Court held for the first time that federal officials could be sued individually for damages for violations of the Fourth Amendment. In finding an implied private right of action under the Fourth Amendment, the Court reasoned that damages are the "ordinary remedy for an invasion of personal interests in liberty," that nothing warranted hesitation in the absence of affirmative action by Congress, and that the alternative of a patchwork of varying and less effective state remedies was undesirable. *Id.* at 397.

The Court relied on *Bivens* in recognizing a right of action for two other federal rights in the subsequent decade. *See Davis v. Passman*, 442 U.S. 228 (1979) (former congressional staffer's Fifth Amendment sex-discrimination claim); *Carlson v. Green*, 446 U.S. 14 (1980) (federal prisoner's inadequate-care claim under the Eighth Amendment). But it's been downhill ever since. Since *Carlson* the Court has refused to infer a private right of action for other constitutional violations at least a dozen times, most recently in *Egbert v. Boule*, 596 U.S. 482, 486 (2022). In *Egbert*, the Court refused to recognize a *Bivens* action for a First Amendment retaliation claim where a U.S. Border Patrol agent in a remote part of Washington state near the Canadian border retaliated against the plaintiff, who complained about the agent's use of excessive force against him. The agent retaliated by persuading the IRS, the Social Security Administration, and state authorities to investigate the plaintiff's business. The Court also refused to recognize the original *Bivens* right of action under the Fourth Amendment in the context of an excessive force case with "national security" implications. *Id.* at 494-97. The Court frankly acknowledged that it did not overrule *Bivens* in *Egbert* only because it didn't need to. *Id.* at 502.

The current Court has limited the § 1983 remedy primarily through application of the qualified immunity doctrine, discussed in Section C below. But it has also narrowly interpreted the term "law" in the statute, finding that a *Miranda* violation did not amount to a deprivation of a right secured by "the Constitution and laws" under § 1983. *Vega v. Tekoh*, 142 S. Ct. 2095 (2022). The plaintiff in *Vega* was investigated for sexual assault and was interrogated without being given *Miranda* warnings. After being tried twice (the jury hung in the first trial) and found not guilty, he brought suit against the interrogating officer under § 1983. By a 6-3 vote, in an opinion that purported to cast doubt on the legitimacy of *Miranda* itself, *see* Chapter III *supra*, the Court held that inasmuch as *Miranda* was only a constitutionally derived "prophylactic" rule it was not part of the "law" referred to in § 1983. Recall that the Court had earlier held that § 1983 afforded no remedy where an illegally obtained confession was not used against a defendant at trial because the Fifth Amendment was only a "trial right." *Chavez v. Martinez*, 528 U.S. 760 (2003).

B. SECTION 1983 ACTIONS AGAINST MUNICIPALITIES

Monell v. Department of Social Services of the City of New York
436 U.S. 658 (1978)

Mr. Justice BRENNAN delivered the opinion of the Court.

Petitioners, a class of female employees of the Department of Social Services and of the Board of Education of the city of New York, commenced this action under 42 U.S.C. § 1983 in July 1971. The gravamen of the complaint was that the Board and the Department had as a matter of official policy compelled pregnant employees to take unpaid leaves of absence before such leaves were required for medical reasons. The suit sought injunctive relief and backpay for periods of unlawful forced leave. Named as defendants in the action were the Department and its Commissioner, the Board and its Chancellor, and the city of New York and its Mayor. In each case, the individual defendants were sued solely in their official capacities.

On cross-motions for summary judgment, the District Court for the Southern District of New York held moot petitioners' claims for injunctive and declaratory relief since the City of New York and the Board, after the filing of the complaint, had changed their policies relating to maternity leaves so that no pregnant employee would have to take leave unless she was medically unable to continue to perform her job. No one now challenges this conclusion. The court did conclude, however, that the acts complained of were unconstitutional under *LaFleur*, supra. Nonetheless plaintiffs' prayers for backpay were denied because any such damages would come ultimately from the City of New York and, therefore, to hold otherwise would be to "circumven[t]" the immunity conferred on municipalities by *Monroe v. Pape*.

On appeal, petitioners renewed their arguments that the Board of Education was not a "municipality" within the meaning of *Monroe v. Pape* and that, in any event, the District Court had erred in barring a damages award against the individual defendants. The Court of Appeals for the Second Circuit rejected both contentions. The court first held that the Board of Education was not a "person" under § 1983 because "it performs a vital governmental function . . ., and, significantly, while it has the right to determine how the funds appropriated to it shall be spent . . ., it has no final say in deciding what its appropriations shall be." The individual defendants, however, were "persons" under § 1983, even when sued solely in their official capacities. Yet, because a damages award would "have to be paid by a city that was held not to be amenable to such an action in *Monroe v. Pape*," a damages action against officials sued in their official capacities could not proceed.

We granted certiorari in this case to consider:

> Whether local governmental officials and/or local independent school boards are "persons" within the meaning of 42 U.S.C. § 1983 when equitable relief in the nature of back pay is sought against them in their official capacities?

Although, after plenary consideration, we have decided the merits of over a score of cases brought under § 1983 in which the principal defendant was a school board — and, indeed,

B. Section 1983 Actions Against Municipalities

in some of which § 1983 and its jurisdictional counterpart, 28 U.S.C. § 1343, provided the only basis for jurisdiction—we indicated last Term that the question presented here was open and would be decided "another day." That other day has come and we now overrule *Monroe v. Pape,* insofar as it holds that local governments are wholly immune from suit under § 1983.

• • •

Our analysis of the legislative history of the Civil Rights Act of 1871 compels the conclusion that Congress did intend municipalities and other local government units to be included among those persons to whom § 1983 applies. Local governing bodies, therefore, can be sued directly under § 1983 for monetary, declaratory, or injunctive relief where, as here, the action that is alleged to be unconstitutional implements or executes a policy statement, ordinance, regulation, or decision officially adopted and promulgated by that body's officers. Moreover, although the touchstone of the § 1983 action against a government body is an allegation that official policy is responsible for a deprivation of rights protected by the Constitution, local governments, like every other § 1983 "person," by the very terms of the statute, may be sued for constitutional deprivations visited pursuant to governmental "custom" even though such a custom has not received formal approval through the body's official decisionmaking channels. As Mr. Justice Harlan, writing for the Court, said in *Adickes v. S. H. Kress & Co.:* "Congress included customs and usages [in § 1983] because of the persistent and widespread discriminatory practices of state officials. . . . Although not authorized by written law, such practices of state officials could well be so permanent and well settled as to constitute a 'custom or usage' with the force of law."

On the other hand, the language of § 1983, read against the background of the same legislative history, compels the conclusion that Congress did not intend municipalities to be held liable unless action pursuant to official municipal policy of some nature caused a constitutional tort. In particular, we conclude that a municipality cannot be held liable solely because it employs a tortfeasor—or, in other words, a municipality cannot be held liable under § 1983 on a respondeat superior theory.

We begin with the language of § 1983 as originally passed:

> [*A*]*ny person who,* under color of any law, statute, ordinance, regulation, custom, or usage of any State, *shall subject, or cause to be subjected,* any person . . . to the deprivation of any rights, privileges, or immunities secured by the Constitution of the United States, shall, any such law, statute, ordinance, regulation, custom, or usage of the State to the contrary notwithstanding, be liable to the party injured in any action at law, suit in equity, or other proper proceeding for redress. . . .

The italicized language plainly imposes liability on a government that, under color of some official policy, "causes" an employee to violate another's constitutional rights. At the same time, that language cannot be easily read to impose liability vicariously on governing bodies solely on the basis of the existence of an employer-employee relationship with a tortfeasor. Indeed, the fact that Congress did specifically provide that A's tort became B's liability if B "caused" A to subject another to a tort suggests that Congress did not intend § 1983 liability to attach where such causation was absent.

Equally important, creation of a federal law of respondeat superior would have raised all the constitutional problems associated with the obligation to keep the peace, an obligation Congress chose not to impose because it thought imposition of such an obligation unconstitutional. To this day, there is disagreement about the basis for imposing liability on an employer for the torts of an employee when the sole nexus between the employer and the tort is the fact of the employer-employee relationship. See W. Prosser, Law of Torts § 69, p. 459 (4th ed. 1971). Nonetheless, two justifications tend to stand out. First is the common-sense notion that no matter how blameless an employer appears to be in an individual

560   Chapter VI Addressing Police Misconduct

case, accidents might nonetheless be reduced if employers had to bear the cost of accidents. See, e.g., ibid.; 2 F. Harper & F. James, Law of Torts, § 26.3, pp. 1368-1369 (1956). Second is the argument that the cost of accidents should be spread to the community as a whole on an insurance theory. See, e.g., id., § 26.5; Prosser, supra, at 459.

The first justification is of the same sort that was offered for statutes like the Sherman amendment: "The obligation to make compensation for injury resulting from riot is, by arbitrary enactment of statutes, affirmatory law, and the reason of passing the statute is to secure a more perfect police regulation." This justification was obviously insufficient to sustain the amendment against perceived constitutional difficulties and there is no reason to suppose that a more general liability imposed for a similar reason would have been thought less constitutionally objectionable. The second justification was similarly put forward as a justification for the Sherman amendment: "we do not look upon [the Sherman amendment] as a punishment. . . . It is a mutual insurance." Again, this justification was insufficient to sustain the amendment.

We conclude, therefore, that a local government may not be sued under § 1983 for an injury inflicted solely by its employees or agents. Instead, it is when execution of a government's policy or custom, whether made by its lawmakers or by those whose edicts or acts may fairly be said to represent official policy, inflicts the injury that the government as an entity is responsible under § 1983. Since this case unquestionably involves official policy as the moving force of the constitutional violation found by the District Court, we must reverse the judgment below. In so doing, we have no occasion to address, and do not address, what the full contours of municipal liability under § 1983 may be. We have attempted only to sketch so much of the § 1983 cause of action against a local government as is apparent from the history of the 1871 Act and our prior cases, and we expressly leave further development of this action to another day.

[Justices Stevens and Powell concurred; Chief Justice Burger and Justice Rehnquist dissented.]

NOTES AND QUESTIONS

1. *Monell* is not a Fifth Amendment case but at its heart are two notable confessions. First, the Court confesses that it misinterpreted the legislative history of § 1983 in holding in *Monroe* that municipalities were not "persons" under the statute. Second, the Court confesses that despite what it said in *Monroe* it had been routinely deciding school desegregation lawsuits that had been brought against school districts (many of them municipalities) under § 1983. One of these decisions was issued the same year *Monroe* was decided; another one, which you will have heard of, *Brown v. Board of Education*, 347 U.S. 483 (1954), was decided seven years before *Monroe*.

2. In rejecting its previous interpretation of legislative history in *Monroe*, the Court does an exhaustive canvassing of the legislative history of § 1983, even more exhaustive than in *Monroe*, which is not reproduced here. Two dissenters disagree with the Court's analysis of that legislative history. And a noted law professor and Reconstruction scholar disagrees with both the majority and the dissent. *See* Robert J. Kaczorowski, *Reflections on* Monell's *Analysis of the Legislative History of § 1983*, 31 Urb. Law. 407, 408 (1999) (the evidence that Congress intended municipalities to be sued under § 1983 is "far from compelling" but, if they were amenable to suit the evidence is that they would have been "vicariously liable" for the actions of their agents).

3. In rejecting a respondeat superior basis for municipal liability, the Court looks at the language of the statute and the legislative history. The Court does not look at the extent to

B. Section 1983 Actions Against Municipalities **561**

which the principle of respondeat superior liability—a doctrine that is at least old enough to have a Latin name—was part of the common law in 1871, when the statute was enacted. One commentator argues that common law principles of respondeat superior liability would have been well known to the members of Congress, and that those members would have expected those principles to be operative in litigation under § 1983. *See* David Jacks Achtenberg, *Taking History Seriously: Municipal Liability Under § 1983 and the Debate over Respondeat Superior,* 73 Fordham L. Rev. 2183, 2196-97 (2005).

This oversight by the Supreme Court may have been the result of the fact that the full scope of municipal liability was not even at issue in *Monell,* as the leave policy challenged by the plaintiff class was an official municipal policy, and there was no need to delve into whether liability could be "vicarious." *See* 436 U.S. at 714 (Stevens, J., concurring in part) (not joining the parts of the opinion on respondeat superior liability as they are "merely advisory"). Justice Stevens later pointed out in dissenting from an opinion that applied the respondeat superior aspect of *Monell* as precedent, that "the commentary on respondeat superior in *Monell* was not responsive to any argument advanced by either party and was not even relevant to the Court's actual holding." *City of Oklahoma City v. Tuttle,* 471 U.S. 808, 842 (1985).

4. The Court notes a contemporary "disagreement" about the wisdom of respondeat superior liability. Is any such disagreement reflected in your understanding of contemporary tort law principles? Did you learn that such a disagreement existed 45 years ago?

Although the Court in *Monell* gratuitously rejected a respondeat superior theory of liability, it did not address "the full contours of municipal liability" under § 1983. 436 U.S. at 695. In *Monell*'s wake, four narrow paths to municipal liability have emerged: liability based on a formal municipal policy (as in *Monell* itself); liability based on a custom (the word is in the statute and cannot be avoided), a settled practice that amounts to the force of law even if not officially adopted; liability based on a failure to train or supervise municipal employees that amounts to a "deliberate indifference" to the rights of the citizens the employees will interact with; and a very limited liability for hiring an employee where an adequate screening or interview process would have shown the hiree's subsequent violation of rights was likely. Achtenberg, *Taking History Seriously, supra* at 2183, 2187-90.

The narrowness of these pathways cannot be overemphasized. The standards for municipal liability under § 1983 are not only stricter than the standards for private employer liability, they are stricter than the standards for awarding *punitive damages* against private employers. *Id.* at 2191. "*Monell* confines entity liability in a manner that is unique to § 1983 and exists in no other area of the law." *Id.*

The next two cases consider these narrow pathways.

Canton v. Harris
489 U.S. 378 (1989)

Justice WHITE delivered the opinion of the Court.

In this case, we are asked to determine if a municipality can ever be liable under 42 U.S.C. § 1983 for constitutional violations resulting from its failure to train municipal employees. We hold that, under certain circumstances, such liability is permitted by the statute.

In April 1978, respondent Geraldine Harris was arrested by officers of the Canton Police Department. Mrs. Harris was brought to the police station in a patrol wagon.

When she arrived at the station, Mrs. Harris was found sitting on the floor of the wagon. She was asked if she needed medical attention, and responded with an incoherent remark.

Chapter VI Addressing Police Misconduct

After she was brought inside the station for processing, Mrs. Harris slumped to the floor on two occasions. Eventually, the police officers left Mrs. Harris lying on the floor to prevent her from falling again. No medical attention was ever summoned for Mrs. Harris. After about an hour, Mrs. Harris was released from custody, and taken by an ambulance (provided by her family) to a nearby hospital. There, Mrs. Harris was diagnosed as suffering from several emotional ailments; she was hospitalized for one week and received subsequent outpatient treatment for an additional year.

Some time later, Mrs. Harris commenced this action alleging many state-law and constitutional claims against the city of Canton and its officials. Among these claims was one seeking to hold the city liable under 42 U.S.C. § 1983 for its violation of Mrs. Harris' right, under the Due Process Clause of the Fourteenth Amendment, to receive necessary medical attention while in police custody.

A jury trial was held on Mrs. Harris' claims. Evidence was presented that indicated that, pursuant to a municipal regulation, shift commanders were authorized to determine, in their sole discretion, whether a detainee required medical care. In addition, testimony also suggested that Canton shift commanders were not provided with any special training (beyond first-aid training) to make a determination as to when to summon medical care for an injured detainee.

At the close of the evidence, the District Court submitted the case to the jury, which rejected all of Mrs. Harris' claims except one: her § 1983 claim against the city resulting from its failure to provide her with medical treatment while in custody. In rejecting the city's subsequent motion for judgment notwithstanding the verdict, the District Court explained the theory of liability as follows:

> The evidence construed in a manner most favorable to Mrs. Harris could be found by a jury to demonstrate that the City of Canton had a custom or policy of vesting complete authority with the police supervisor of when medical treatment would be administered to prisoners. Further, the jury could find from the evidence that the vesting of such carte blanche authority with the police supervisor without adequate training to recognize when medical treatment is needed was grossly negligent or so reckless that future police misconduct was almost inevitable or substantially certain to result.

On appeal, the Sixth Circuit affirmed this aspect of the District Court's analysis, holding that "a municipality is liable for failure to train its police force, [where] the plaintiff . . . prove[s] that the municipality acted recklessly, intentionally, or with gross negligence." The Court of Appeals also stated that an additional prerequisite of this theory of liability was that the plaintiff must prove "that the lack of training was so reckless or grossly negligent that deprivations of persons' constitutional rights were substantially certain to result." Thus, the Court of Appeals found that there had been no error in submitting Mrs. Harris' "failure to train" claim to the jury. However, the Court of Appeals reversed the judgment for respondent, and remanded this case for a new trial, because it found that certain aspects of the District Court's jury instructions might have led the jury to believe that it could find against the city on a mere respondeat superior theory. Because the jury's verdict did not state the basis on which it had ruled for Mrs. Harris on her § 1983 claim, a new trial was ordered.

The city petitioned for certiorari, arguing that the Sixth Circuit's holding represented an impermissible broadening of municipal liability under § 1983. We granted the petition.

• • •

In *Monell* we decided that a municipality can be found liable under § 1983 only where the municipality itself causes the constitutional violation at issue. Respondeat superior or vicarious liability will not attach under § 1983. "It is only when the 'execution of the government's policy or custom . . . inflicts the injury' that the municipality may be held liable under § 1983."

B. Section 1983 Actions Against Municipalities 563

Thus, our first inquiry in any case alleging municipal liability under § 1983 is the question whether there is a direct causal link between a municipal policy or custom and the alleged constitutional deprivation. The inquiry is a difficult one; one that has left this Court deeply divided in a series of cases that have followed *Monell*; one that is the principal focus of our decision again today.

Based on the difficulty that this Court has had defining the contours of municipal liability in these circumstances, petitioner urges us to adopt the rule that a municipality can be found liable under § 1983 only where "the policy in question [is] itself unconstitutional." Whether such a rule is a valid construction of § 1983 is a question the Court has left unresolved. Under such an approach, the outcome here would be rather clear: we would have to reverse and remand the case with instructions that judgment be entered for petitioner. There can be little doubt that on its face the city's policy regarding medical treatment for detainees is constitutional. The policy states that the city jailer "shall . . . have [a person needing medical care] taken to a hospital for medical treatment, with permission of his supervisor. . . ." It is difficult to see what constitutional guarantees are violated by such a policy.

Nor, without more, would a city automatically be liable under § 1983 if one of its employees happened to apply the policy in an unconstitutional manner, for liability would then rest on respondeat superior. The claim in this case, however, is that if a concededly valid policy is unconstitutionally applied by a municipal employee, the city is liable if the employee has not been adequately trained and the constitutional wrong has been caused by that failure to train. For reasons explained below, we conclude, as have all the Courts of Appeals that have addressed this issue, that there are limited circumstances in which an allegation of a "failure to train" can be the basis for liability under § 1983. Thus, we reject petitioner's contention that only unconstitutional policies are actionable under the statute.

Though we agree with the court below that a city can be liable under § 1983 for inadequate training of its employees, we cannot agree that the District Court's jury instructions on this issue were proper, for we conclude that the Court of Appeals provided an overly broad rule for when a municipality can be held liable under the "failure to train" theory. Unlike the question whether a municipality's failure to train employees can ever be a basis for § 1983 liability — on which the Courts of Appeals have all agreed — there is substantial division among the lower courts as to what degree of fault must be evidenced by the municipality's inaction before liability will be permitted. We hold today that the inadequacy of police training may serve as the basis for § 1983 liability only where the failure to train amounts to deliberate indifference to the rights of persons with whom the police come into contact. This rule is most consistent with our admonition in *Monell* that a municipality can be liable under § 1983 only where its policies are the "moving force [behind] the constitutional violation." Only where a municipality's failure to train its employees in a relevant respect evidences a "deliberate indifference" to the rights of its inhabitants can such a shortcoming be properly thought of as a city "policy or custom" that is actionable under § 1983. "[M]unicipal liability under § 1983 attaches where — and only where — a deliberate choice to follow a course of action is made from among various alternatives" by city policymakers. Only where a failure to train reflects a "deliberate" or "conscious" choice by a municipality — a "policy" as defined by our prior cases — can a city be liable for such a failure under § 1983.

Monell's rule that a city is not liable under § 1983 unless a municipal policy causes a constitutional deprivation will not be satisfied by merely alleging that the existing training program for a class of employees, such as police officers, represents a policy for which the city is responsible. That much may be true. The issue in a case like this one, however, is whether that training program is adequate; and if it is not, the question becomes whether such inadequate training can justifiably be said to represent "city policy." It may seem contrary to common sense to assert that a municipality will actually have a policy of not taking reasonable steps to train its employees. But it may happen that in light of the duties assigned to specific officers or employees the need for more or different training is so obvious, and the inadequacy so likely to result in the violation of constitutional rights, that the policymakers of the city can reasonably be said to have been deliberately indifferent to the need. In that event, the failure to provide proper training may fairly be said to represent a policy for which the city is responsible, and for which the city may be held liable if it actually causes injury.

In resolving the issue of a city's liability, the focus must be on adequacy of the training program in relation to the tasks the particular officers must perform. That a particular officer may be unsatisfactorily trained will not alone suffice to fasten liability on the city, for the officer's shortcomings may have resulted from factors other than a faulty training program. It may be, for example, that an otherwise sound program has occasionally been negligently administered. Neither will it suffice to prove that an injury or accident could have been avoided if an officer had had better or more training, sufficient to equip him to avoid the particular injury-causing conduct. Such a claim could be made about almost any encounter resulting in injury, yet not condemn the adequacy of the program to enable officers to respond properly to the usual and recurring situations with which they must deal. And plainly, adequately trained officers occasionally make mistakes; the fact that they do says little about the training program or the legal basis for holding the city liable.

Moreover, for liability to attach in this circumstance the identified deficiency in a city's training program must be closely related to the ultimate injury. Thus in the case at hand, respondent must still prove that the deficiency in training actually caused the police officers' indifference to her medical needs. Would the injury have been avoided had the employee been trained under a program that was not deficient in the identified respect? Predicting how a hypothetically well-trained officer would have acted under the circumstances may not be an easy task for the factfinder, particularly since matters of judgment may be involved, and since officers who are well trained are not free from error and perhaps might react very much like the untrained officer in similar circumstances. But judge and jury, doing their respective jobs, will be adequate to the task.

To adopt lesser standards of fault and causation would open municipalities to unprecedented liability under § 1983. In virtually every instance where a person has had his or her constitutional rights violated by a city employee, a § 1983 plaintiff will be able to point to something the city "could have done" to prevent the unfortunate incident. Thus, permitting cases against cities for their "failure to train" employees to go forward under § 1983 on a lesser standard of fault would result in de facto respondeat superior liability on municipalities—a result we rejected in *Monell*, It would also engage the federal courts in an endless exercise of second-guessing municipal employee-training programs. This is an exercise we believe the federal courts are ill suited to undertake, as well as one that would implicate serious questions of federalism.

Consequently, while claims such as respondent's—alleging that the city's failure to provide training to municipal employees resulted in the constitutional deprivation she suffered—are cognizable under § 1983, they can only yield liability against a municipality where that city's failure to train reflects deliberate indifference to the constitutional rights of its inhabitants.

IV

The final question here is whether this case should be remanded for a new trial, or whether, as petitioner suggests, we should conclude that there are no possible grounds on which respondent can prevail. It is true that the evidence in the record now does not meet the standard of § 1983 liability we have set forth above. But, the standard of proof the District Court ultimately imposed on respondent (which was consistent with Sixth Circuit precedent) was a

B. Section 1983 Actions Against Municipalities   **565**

lesser one than the one we adopt today. Whether respondent should have an opportunity to prove her case under the "deliberate indifference" rule we have adopted is a matter for the Court of Appeals to deal with on remand.

Consequently, for the reasons given above, we vacate the judgment of the Court of Appeals and remand this case for further proceedings consistent with this opinion.

NOTES AND QUESTIONS

1. Do these seem like strong or weak facts for establishing a failure-to-train violation? Consider in your analysis the nature of the injuries suffered, the existence of any municipal policy, the nature of any training that would be necessary to prevent the injury, and the likelihood of harm from the lack of training. As a plaintiff's lawyer, how would you attempt to develop evidence of deliberate indifference? As a lawyer for the city, how would you try to disprove deliberate indifference?

2. This case was tried to a jury. The court of appeals reversed because the jury instruction "might have led the jury to believe that it could find against the city on a mere respondeat superior theory." *Id.* at 383. How could the court have made such an error so many years after *Monell?* Weak lawyering by the city? Weak law clerks? Assuming the city had filed a motion for summary judgment, as typically happens in a civil case, does the trial court's jury instruction explain why that motion may have been denied?

3. How much different is the "deliberate indifference" standard announced by the Court than the standard applied by the Sixth Circuit, which held that liability requires that in failing to train a municipality must have "acted recklessly, intentionally, or with gross negligence" and "that the lack of training was so reckless or grossly negligent that deprivations of persons' constitutional rights were substantially certain to result"? *Id.* at 382. Can you imagine a set of facts where a jury could find all of the elements required by the Sixth Circuit formulation yet ultimately conclude that the city was not deliberately indifferent to the potential harms?

4. The Court emphasizes that whether inadequate training rises to the level of a city "policy" relates to the duties of the city officials involved. It gives the following hypothetical example in footnote 10:

> For example, city policymakers know to a moral certainty that their police officers will be required to arrest fleeing felons. The city has armed its officers with firearms, in part to allow them to accomplish this task. Thus, the need to train officers in the constitutional limitations on the use of deadly force, see *Tennessee v. Garner*, 471 U.S. 1, 105 S. Ct. 1694, 85 L. Ed. 2d 1 (1985), can be said to be "so obvious," that failure to do so could properly be characterized as "deliberate indifference" to constitutional rights.

Does the need to train police station employees on how to determine whether an arrestee needs medical attention meet this standard?

5. The Court goes into full hyperbole mode at the end of its opinion, claiming that "permitting cases against cities for their 'failure to train' employees to go forward under § 1983 on a lesser standard of fault would result in de facto respondeat superior liability on municipalities—a result we rejected in *Monell*." Do you agree? Consider the facts of *Harris* with this variation: The police department supervisor in charge of the station when Harris was arrested had been properly trained on when to seek medical attention for arrestees but had misinterpreted Harris's symptoms and failed to get her medical attention. Result under respondeat superior? Result under a lower standard of "reckless failure to train"?

Note that the jury rejected all of Harris's state law claims but found for her on her § 1983 claim. Might this be responsible for the Court's closing observation, where it decries federal

566   Chapter VI Addressing Police Misconduct

courts engaging "in an endless exercise of second-guessing employee-training programs"? Were the congressmen who voted in favor of the Ku Klux Klan Act concerned about federal courts second-guessing state administrators?

Please ignore the fact that the next case is not about "police misconduct" but rather "prosecutor misconduct" and so arguably doesn't belong in this chapter. *See* Chapter IX *infra* (discussing prosecutor's obligation to disclose exculpatory information to defense). But it is important nonetheless.

Connick v. Thompson
563 U.S. 51 (2011)

Justice THOMAS delivered the opinion of the Court.

The Orleans Parish District Attorney's Office now concedes that, in prosecuting respondent John Thompson for attempted armed robbery, prosecutors failed to disclose evidence that should have been turned over to the defense under *Brady v. Maryland* (1963). Thompson was convicted. Because of that conviction Thompson elected not to testify in his own defense in his later trial for murder, and he was again convicted. Thompson spent 18 years in prison, including 14 years on death row. One month before Thompson's scheduled execution, his investigator discovered the undisclosed evidence from his armed robbery trial. The reviewing court determined that the evidence was exculpatory, and both of Thompson's convictions were vacated.

After his release from prison, Thompson sued petitioner Harry Connick, in his official capacity as the Orleans Parish district attorney, for damages under 42 U.S.C. § 1983. Thompson alleged that Connick had failed to train his prosecutors adequately about their duty to produce exculpatory evidence and that the lack of training had caused the nondisclosure in Thompson's robbery case. The jury awarded Thompson $14 million, and the Court of Appeals for the Fifth Circuit affirmed by an evenly divided en banc court. We granted certiorari to decide whether a district attorney's office may be held liable under § 1983 for failure to train based on a single *Brady* violation. We hold that it cannot.

• • •

In early 1985, John Thompson was charged with the murder of Raymond T. Liuzza, Jr., in New Orleans. Publicity following the murder charge led the victims of an unrelated armed robbery to identify Thompson as their attacker. The district attorney charged Thompson with attempted armed robbery.

As part of the robbery investigation, a crime scene technician took from one of the victims' pants a swatch of fabric stained with the robber's blood. Approximately one week before Thompson's armed robbery trial, the swatch was sent to the crime laboratory. Two days before the trial, Assistant District Attorney Bruce Whittaker received the crime lab's report, which stated that the perpetrator had blood type B. There is no evidence that the prosecutors ever had Thompson's blood tested or that they knew what his blood type was. Whittaker claimed he placed the report on Assistant District Attorney James Williams' desk, but Williams denied seeing it. The report was never disclosed to Thompson's counsel.

Williams tried the armed robbery case with Assistant District Attorney Gerry Deegan. On the first day of trial, Deegan checked all of the physical evidence in the case out of the police property room, including the bloodstained swatch. Deegan then checked all of the evidence but the swatch into the courthouse property room. The prosecutors did not mention the swatch or the crime lab report at trial, and the jury convicted Thompson of attempted armed robbery.

A few weeks later, Williams and Special Prosecutor Eric Dubelier tried Thompson for the Liuzza murder. Because of the armed robbery conviction, Thompson chose not to testify in his own defense. He was convicted and sentenced to death. In the 14 years following Thompson's murder conviction, state and federal courts reviewed and denied his challenges to the conviction and sentence. The State scheduled Thompson's execution for May 20, 1999.

In late April 1999, Thompson's private investigator discovered the crime lab report from the armed robbery investigation in the files of the New Orleans Police Crime Laboratory. Thompson was tested and found to have blood type O, proving that the blood on the swatch was not his. Thompson's attorneys presented this evidence to the district attorney's office, which, in turn, moved to stay the execution and vacate Thompson's armed robbery conviction. The Louisiana Court of Appeal then reversed Thompson's murder conviction, concluding that the armed robbery conviction unconstitutionally deprived Thompson of his right to testify in his own defense at the murder trial. In 2003, the district attorney's office retried Thompson for Liuzza's murder. The jury found him not guilty.

Thompson then brought this action against the district attorney's office, Connick, Williams, and others, alleging that their conduct caused him to be wrongfully convicted, incarcerated for 18 years, and nearly executed. The only claim that proceeded to trial was Thompson's claim under § 1983 that the district attorney's office had violated *Brady* by failing to disclose the crime lab report in his armed robbery trial. Thompson alleged liability under two theories: (1) The *Brady* violation was caused by an unconstitutional policy of the district attorney's office; and (2) the violation was caused by Connick's deliberate indifference to an obvious need to train the prosecutors in his office in order to avoid such constitutional violations.

Before trial, Connick conceded that the failure to produce the crime lab report constituted a *Brady* violation. Accordingly, the District Court instructed the jury that the "only issue" was whether the nondisclosure was caused by either a policy, practice, or custom of the district attorney's office or a deliberately indifferent failure to train the office's prosecutors.

Although no prosecutor remembered any specific training session regarding *Brady* prior to 1985, it was undisputed at trial that the prosecutors were familiar with the general *Brady* requirement that the State disclose to the defense evidence in its possession that is favorable to the accused. Prosecutors testified that office policy was to turn crime lab reports and other scientific evidence over to the defense. They also testified that, after the discovery of the undisclosed crime lab report in 1999, prosecutors disagreed about whether it had to be disclosed under *Brady* absent knowledge of Thompson's blood type.

The jury rejected Thompson's claim that an unconstitutional office policy caused the *Brady* violation, but found the district attorney's office liable for failing to train the prosecutors. The jury awarded Thompson $14 million in damages, and the District Court added more than $1 million in attorney's fees and costs.

After the verdict, Connick renewed his objection — which he had raised on summary judgment — that he could not have been deliberately indifferent to an obvious need for more or different Brady training because there was no evidence that he was aware of a pattern of similar *Brady* violations. The District Court rejected this argument for the reasons that it had given in the summary judgment order. In that order, the court had concluded that a pattern of violations is not necessary to prove deliberate indifference when the need for training is "so obvious." Relying on *Canton v. Harris*, the court had held that Thompson could demonstrate deliberate indifference by proving that "the DA's office knew to a moral certainty that assistan[t] [district attorneys] would acquire *Brady* material, that without training it is not always obvious what *Brady* requires, and that withholding *Brady* material will virtually always lead to a substantial violation of constitutional rights."

Chapter VI Addressing Police Misconduct

A panel of the Court of Appeals for the Fifth Circuit affirmed. The panel acknowledged that Thompson did not present evidence of a pattern of similar *Brady* violations, but held that Thompson did not need to prove a pattern. According to the panel, Thompson demonstrated that Connick was on notice of an obvious need for *Brady* training by presenting evidence "that attorneys, often fresh out of law school, would undoubtedly be required to confront *Brady* issues while at the DA's Office, that erroneous decisions regarding *Brady* evidence would result in serious constitutional violations, that resolution of *Brady* issues was often unclear, and that training in *Brady* would have been helpful."

The Court of Appeals sitting en banc vacated the panel opinion, granted rehearing, and divided evenly, thereby affirming the District Court. We granted certiorari.

The *Brady* violation conceded in this case occurred when one or more of the four prosecutors involved with Thompson's armed robbery prosecution failed to disclose the crime lab report to Thompson's counsel. Under Thompson's failure-to-train theory, he bore the burden of proving both (1) that Connick, the policymaker for the district attorney's office, was deliberately indifferent to the need to train the prosecutors about their *Brady* disclosure obligation with respect to evidence of this type and (2) that the lack of training actually caused the *Brady* violation in this case. Connick argues that he was entitled to judgment as a matter of law because Thompson did not prove that he was on actual or constructive notice of, and therefore deliberately indifferent to, a need for more or different *Brady* training. We agree.

• • •

In limited circumstances, a local government's decision not to train certain employees about their legal duty to avoid violating citizens' rights may rise to the level of an official government policy for purposes of § 1983. A municipality's culpability for a deprivation of rights is at its most tenuous where a claim turns on a failure to train. To satisfy the statute, a municipality's failure to train its employees in a relevant respect must amount to "deliberate indifference to the rights of persons with whom the [untrained employees] come into contact."

"'[D]eliberate indifference' is a stringent standard of fault, requiring proof that a municipal actor disregarded a known or obvious consequence of his action." Thus, when city policymakers are on actual or constructive notice that a particular omission in their training program causes city employees to violate citizens' constitutional rights, the city may be deemed deliberately indifferent if the policymakers choose to retain that program.

A pattern of similar constitutional violations by untrained employees is "ordinarily necessary" to demonstrate deliberate indifference for purposes of failure to train. Policymakers' "continued adherence to an approach that they know or should know has failed to prevent tortious conduct by employees may establish the conscious disregard for the consequences of their action—the 'deliberate indifference'—necessary to trigger municipal liability." Without notice that a course of training is deficient in a particular respect, decisionmakers can hardly be said to have deliberately chosen a training program that will cause violations of constitutional rights.

Although Thompson does not contend that he proved a pattern of similar *Brady* violations, he points out that, during the 10 years preceding his armed robbery trial, Louisiana courts had overturned four convictions because of *Brady* violations by prosecutors in Connick's office. Those four reversals could not have put Connick on notice that the office's *Brady* training was inadequate with respect to the sort of *Brady* violation at issue here. None of those cases involved failure to disclose blood evidence, a crime lab report, or physical or scientific evidence of any kind. Because those incidents are not similar to the violation at issue here, they could not have put Connick on notice that specific training was necessary to avoid this constitutional violation.

Instead of relying on a pattern of similar *Brady* violations, Thompson relies on the "single-incident" liability that this Court hypothesized in *Canton*. He contends that the

Brady violation in his case was the "obvious" consequence of failing to provide specific *Brady* training, and that this showing of "obviousness" can substitute for the pattern of violations ordinarily necessary to establish municipal culpability.

In *Canton*, the Court left open the possibility that, "in a narrow range of circumstances," a pattern of similar violations might not be necessary to show deliberate indifference. The Court posed the hypothetical example of a city that arms its police force with firearms and deploys the armed officers into the public to capture fleeing felons without training the officers in the constitutional limitation on the use of deadly force. Given the known frequency with which police attempt to arrest fleeing felons and the "predictability that an officer lacking specific tools to handle that situation will violate citizens' rights," the Court theorized that a city's decision not to train the officers about constitutional limits on the use of deadly force could reflect the city's deliberate indifference to the "highly predictable consequence," namely, violations of constitutional rights. The Court sought not to foreclose the possibility, however rare, that the unconstitutional consequences of failing to train could be so patently obvious that a city could be liable under § 1983 without proof of a pre-existing pattern of violations.

Failure to train prosecutors in their *Brady* obligations does not fall within the narrow range of *Canton*'s hypothesized single-incident liability. The obvious need for specific legal training that was present in the *Canton* scenario is absent here. Armed police must sometimes make split-second decisions with life-or-death consequences. There is no reason to assume that police academy applicants are familiar with the constitutional constraints on the use of deadly force. And, in the absence of training, there is no way for novice officers to obtain the legal knowledge they require. Under those circumstances there is an obvious need for some form of training. In stark contrast, legal "[t]raining is what differentiates attorneys from average public employees."

Attorneys are trained in the law and equipped with the tools to interpret and apply legal principles, understand constitutional limits, and exercise legal judgment. Before they may enter the profession and receive a law license, all attorneys must graduate from law school or pass a substantive examination; attorneys in the vast majority of jurisdictions must do both. These threshold requirements are designed to ensure that all new attorneys have learned how to find, understand, and apply legal rules.

Nor does professional training end at graduation. Most jurisdictions require attorneys to satisfy continuing-education requirements. Even those few jurisdictions that do not impose mandatory continuing-education requirements mandate that attorneys represent their clients competently and encourage attorneys to engage in continuing study and education. Before Louisiana adopted continuing-education requirements, it imposed similar general competency requirements on its state bar.

Attorneys who practice with other attorneys, such as in district attorney's offices, also train on the job as they learn from more experienced attorneys. For instance, here in the Orleans Parish District Attorney's Office, junior prosecutors were trained by senior prosecutors who supervised them as they worked together to prepare cases for trial, and trial chiefs oversaw the preparation of the cases. Senior attorneys also circulated court decisions and instructional memoranda to keep the prosecutors abreast of relevant legal developments.

In addition, attorneys in all jurisdictions must satisfy character and fitness standards to receive a law license and are personally subject to an ethical regime designed to reinforce the profession's standards. Trial lawyers have a "duty to bring to bear such skill and knowledge as will render the trial a reliable adversarial testing process." Prosecutors have a special "duty to seek justice, not merely to convict. Among prosecutors' unique ethical obligations is the duty to produce *Brady* evidence to the defense. An attorney who violates his or her ethical obligations is subject to professional discipline, including sanctions, suspension, and disbarment.

In light of this regime of legal training and professional responsibility, recurring constitutional violations are not the "obvious consequence" of failing to provide prosecutors with formal in-house training about how to obey the law. Prosecutors are not only equipped but are also ethically bound to know what *Brady* entails and to perform legal research when they are uncertain. A district attorney is entitled to rely on prosecutors' professional training and ethical obligations in the absence of specific reason, such as a pattern of violations, to believe that those tools are insufficient to prevent future constitutional violations in "the usual and recurring situations with which [the prosecutors] must deal." A licensed attorney making legal judgments, in his capacity as a prosecutor, about *Brady* material simply does not present the same "highly predictable" constitutional danger as *Canton*'s untrained officer.

A second significant difference between this case and the example in *Canton* is the nuance of the allegedly necessary training. The *Canton* hypothetical assumes that the armed police officers have no knowledge at all of the constitutional limits on the use of deadly force. But it is undisputed here that the prosecutors in Connick's office were familiar with the general *Brady* rule. Thompson's complaint therefore cannot rely on the utter lack of an ability to cope with constitutional situations that underlies the *Canton* hypothetical, but rather must assert that prosecutors were not trained about particular *Brady* evidence or the specific scenario related to the violation in his case. That sort of nuance simply cannot support an inference of deliberate indifference here. As the Court said in *Canton*, "[i]n virtually every instance where a person has had his or her constitutional rights violated by a city employee, a § 1983 plaintiff will be able to point to something the city 'could have done' to prevent the unfortunate incident."

Thompson suggests that the absence of any formal training sessions about *Brady* is equivalent to the complete absence of legal training that the Court imagined in Canton. But failure-to-train liability is concerned with the substance of the training, not the particular instructional format. The statute does not provide plaintiffs or courts carte blanche to micromanage local governments throughout the United States.

We do not assume that prosecutors will always make correct *Brady* decisions or that guidance regarding specific *Brady* questions would not assist prosecutors. But showing merely that additional training would have been helpful in making difficult decisions does not establish municipal liability. "[P]rov[ing] that an injury or accident could have been avoided if an [employee] had had better or more training, sufficient to equip him to avoid the particular injury-causing conduct" will not suffice. The possibility of single-incident liability that the Court left open in *Canton* is not this case.

The dissent rejects our holding that *Canton*'s hypothesized single-incident liability does not, as a legal matter, encompass failure to train prosecutors in their *Brady* obligation. It would instead apply the *Canton* hypothetical to this case, and thus devotes almost all of its opinion to explaining why the evidence supports liability under that theory. But the dissent's attempt to address our holding—by pointing out that not all prosecutors will necessarily have enrolled in criminal procedure class—misses the point. The reason why the *Canton* hypothetical is inapplicable is that attorneys, unlike police officers, are equipped with the tools to find, interpret, and apply legal principles.

By the end of its opinion, however, the dissent finally reveals that its real disagreement is not with our holding today, but with this Court's precedent. The dissent does not see "any reason," post, for the Court's conclusion in *Bryan County* that a pattern of violations is "ordinarily necessary" to demonstrate deliberate indifference for purposes of failure to train. As our precedent makes clear, proving that a municipality itself actually caused a constitutional violation by failing to train the offending employee presents "difficult problems of proof," and we must adhere to a "stringent standard of fault," lest municipal liability under § 1983 collapse into respondeat superior.

The role of a prosecutor is to see that justice is done. *Berger v. United States* (1935). "It is as much [a prosecutor's] duty to refrain from improper methods calculated to produce a wrongful conviction as it is to use every legitimate means to bring about a just one." By their own admission, the prosecutors who tried Thompson's armed robbery case failed to carry out that responsibility. But the only issue before us is whether Connick, as the policymaker for the district attorney's office, was deliberately indifferent to the need to train the attorneys under his authority.

We conclude that this case does not fall within the narrow range of "single-incident" liability hypothesized in *Canton* as a possible exception to the pattern of violations necessary to prove deliberate indifference in § 1983 actions alleging failure to train. The District Court should have granted Connick judgment as a matter of law on the failure-to-train claim because Thompson did not prove a pattern of similar violations that would "establish that the 'policy of inaction' [was] the functional equivalent of a decision by the city itself to violate the Constitution."

The judgment of the United States Court of Appeals for the Fifth Circuit is reversed.

It is so ordered.

NOTES AND QUESTIONS

1. Do not let the impact of the *Brady* violation here get lost in the shuffle. Thompson was convicted of armed robbery in a trial where the prosecution never turned over to the defense a swatch of fabric stained with the robber's blood, which a crime lab report determined was blood type B. Thompson had blood type O. Because of that conviction Thompson did not take the stand in his murder trial, and was convicted and sentenced to death.

When he was retried on the murder case after the exculpatory evidence was disclosed and both convictions vacated, he took the stand in his own defense. He was found not guilty.

2. Note how the Court attempts to add ever more burdensome glosses onto the "deliberate indifference" proof standard it set forth in *Harris*. The failure-to-train theory is only available "in limited circumstances." A municipality's liability "is at its most tenuous" in a failure-to-train case.

None of these quoted phrases are quotes from *Harris* or other cases, but they are plainly being framed so that they can be used as quotes in subsequent cases, e.g., "As we held in *Connick*, municipality liability 'is at its most tenuous'. . . ."

3. Why should it be necessary that Thompson prove a pattern of "similar" *Brady* violations? Isn't Thompson's allegation that Connick failed to train his prosecutors adequately about their *Brady* obligations generally, and that as a result the exculpatory evidence was not disclosed in Thompson's armed robbery case? Shouldn't the four reversals of convictions for *Brady* violations by Connick's prosecutors have put Connick on notice of the need for *Brady* training as a general matter?

Brady and its progeny are covered in Chapter IX *infra* but one observation on *Brady* is warranted here. *Brady* violations resulting in reversals of convictions are rare. A particular nondisclosure is only "material" for *Brady* purposes "if there is a reasonable probability that, had the evidence been disclosed to the defense, the result of the proceeding would have been different." *United States v. Bagley*, 473 U.S. 667, 682 (1985). When this standard is applied after a conviction, and a full evidentiary record has been established that supports that conviction, courts rarely find that the *Bagley* materiality standard has been met.

In other words, the four reversals by Connick's prosecutors were likely the result of very serious *Brady* violations.

4. The hypothetical from footnote 10 in *Harris*—about the need for training police officers about the use of deadly force in pursuing fleeing felons—gets a surprising amount of attention in *Connick*. How analogous do you find the need to provide prosecutors with training on their *Brady* obligations? Are the consequences of a misuse of deadly force and a failure to observe *Brady* requirements equally likely to result in a deprivation of constitutional rights?

5. What do you make of the Court's point that Connick was entitled to rely on the fact that the prosecutors in his office, by virtue of their legal education, training, and professional responsibilities, would have been aware of their *Brady* obligations? Was the jury entitled to reach a different conclusion based on the abundant evidence that Connick and other prosecutors misunderstood their *Brady* obligations?

6. Connick's reaction to the Supreme Court's decision in *Kyles v. Whitley*, 514 U.S. 419 (1995)—a seminal case on *Brady* violations made in a capital prosecution by Connick's own office, *see infra*—is especially shocking. As pointed out by Justice Ginsburg in her dissent, when he was questioned about *Kyles* at trial Connick told the jury he was satisfied with his office's practices and saw no need to make any changes as a result of the decision. Not only should the case have warranted some level of soul-searching or at least introspection by any reasonable prosecutor, *Kyles* clarified two aspects of *Brady* obligations that every prosecutor needed to understand going forward: (a) *Brady* is violated where the cumulative effect of non-disclosures is material, that is, pieces of exculpatory information cannot be viewed in isolation, and (b) a prosecutor's *Brady* obligations extend to "agents" of the prosecution, that is, the prosecutor is responsible for information contained in police files. *See* Chapter IX *infra*.

7. Defendant Harry F. Connick, the father of American musician Harry Connick Jr., was the district attorney in New Orleans from 1973 to 2003. He won two cases in the Supreme Court on entirely unrelated issues. In addition to *Connick v. Thompson*, he was also the prevailing party in *Connick v. Myers*, 461 U.S. 138 (1983), where the Supreme Court upheld his decision to fire a prosecutor for internally circulating a questionnaire on office morale, finding no First Amendment violation because the questionnaire was not primarily focused on matters of "public concern." Connick was indicted on federal racketeering charges in 1989 but found not guilty at trial.

The deliberate indifference standard is not the only barrier to liability under § 1983. Additional hurdles confront § 1983 plaintiffs who seek injunctive relief against allegedly unconstitutional action by law enforcement. In *O'Shea v. Littleton*, 414 U.S. 488 (1974), Black residents sought class certification and injunctive relief against several different local law enforcement defendants, including a judge and magistrate, alleging a litany of discriminatory practices in setting bail conditions, sentencing, and charging fees for jury trials. *Id.* at 491-92. The Supreme Court held that the case should have been dismissed because, inasmuch as none of the 19 named plaintiffs had been injured by the allegedly discriminatory practices, there was no "case or controversy." *Id.* at 495-96. The Court also implied that equitable relief might be inappropriate for the independent reasons that the injunction sought was "intrusive and unworkable" and offensive to concerns of "equity, comity, and federalism." *Id.* at 499-500.

Two years later, in *Rizzo v. Goode*, 423 U.S. 362 (1976), the Supreme Court reversed a district court's award of injunctive relief against Philadelphia city officials that mandated procedures for improving the handling of complaints of police misconduct. The Court found, as it had in *O'Shea*, the lack of a "case or controversy" and also found § 1983 did not provide for liability under a "failure to act" theory. *Id.* at 372-76. The Court also found that "important considerations of federalism are additional factors weighing against" injunctive relief, and that federal courts must be constantly mindful of the "special delicacy of the adjustment to be preserved between federal equitable power and State administration of its own law." *Id.* at 378.

B. Section 1983 Actions Against Municipalities   **573**

O'Shea and *Rizzo* paved the way for the following even sharper curtailment of § 1983's utility as a vehicle for obtaining injunctive relief against a municipality.

City of Los Angeles v. Lyons
461 U.S. 95 (1983)

Justice WHITE delivered the opinion of the Court.

The issue here is whether respondent Lyons satisfied the prerequisites for seeking injunctive relief in the federal district court.

I

This case began on February 7, 1977, when respondent, Adolph Lyons, filed a complaint for damages, injunction, and declaratory relief in the United States District Court for the Central District of California. The defendants were the City of Los Angeles and four of its police officers. The complaint alleged that on October 6, 1976, at 2 a.m., Lyons was stopped by the defendant officers for a traffic or vehicle code violation and that although Lyons offered no resistance or threat whatsoever, the officers, without provocation or justification, seized Lyons and applied a "chokehold" — either the "bar arm control" hold or the "carotid-artery control" hold or both — rendering him unconscious and causing damage to his larynx. Counts I through IV of the complaint sought damages against the officers and the City. Count V, with which we are principally concerned here, sought a preliminary and permanent injunction against the City barring the use of the control holds. That count alleged that the city's police officers, "pursuant to the authorization, instruction and encouragement of defendant City of Los Angeles, regularly and routinely apply these choke holds in innumerable situations where they are not threatened by the use of any deadly force whatsoever," that numerous persons have been injured as the result of the application of the chokeholds, that Lyons and others similarly situated are threatened with irreparable injury in the form of bodily injury and loss of life, and that Lyons "justifiably fears that any contact he has with Los Angeles police officers may result in his being choked and strangled to death without provocation, justification or other legal excuse." Lyons alleged the threatened impairment of rights protected by the First, Fourth, Eighth and Fourteenth Amendments. Injunctive relief was sought against the use of the control holds "except in situations where the proposed victim of said control reasonably appears to be threatening the immediate use of deadly force." Count VI sought declaratory relief against the City, i.e., a judgment that use of the chokeholds absent the threat of immediate use of deadly force is a per se violation of various constitutional rights.

The District Court, by order, granted the City's motion for partial judgment on the pleadings and entered judgment for the City on Count V and VI. The Court of Appeals reversed the judgment for the City on Count V and VI, holding Lyons had standing to seek relief against the application of the chokeholds. The Court of Appeals held that there was a sufficient likelihood that Lyons would again be stopped and subjected to the unlawful use of force to constitute a case or controversy and to warrant the issuance of an injunction, if the injunction was otherwise authorized. We denied certiorari.

On remand, Lyons applied for a preliminary injunction. Lyons pressed only the Count V claim at this point. The motion was heard on affidavits, depositions and government records. The District Court found that Lyons had been stopped for a traffic infringement and that without provocation or legal justification the officers involved had applied a "department-authorized chokehold which resulted in injuries to the plaintiff." The court further found that the department authorizes the use of the holds in situations where no one is threatened by death or grievous bodily harm, that officers are insufficiently trained, that the use of the holds involves a high risk of injury or death as then employed, and that their continued use in situations where neither death nor serious bodily injury is threatened "is unconscionable in a civilized society." The court concluded that such use violated Lyons' substantive due process rights under the Fourteenth Amendment. A preliminary injunction was entered enjoining "the use of both the carotid-artery and bar arm holds under circumstances which do not threaten death or serious bodily injury." An improved training program and regular reporting and record keeping were also ordered. The Court of Appeals affirmed in a brief per curiam opinion stating that the District Court had not abused its discretion in entering a preliminary injunction. We granted certiorari, and now reverse.

II

Since our grant of certiorari, circumstances pertinent to the case have changed. Originally, Lyons' complaint alleged that at least two deaths had occurred as a result of the application of chokeholds by the police. His first amended complaint alleged that 10 chokehold-related deaths had occurred. By May, 1982, there had been five more such deaths. On May 6, 1982, the Chief of Police in Los Angeles prohibited the use of the bar-arm chokehold in any circumstances. A few days later, on May 12, 1982, the Board of Police Commissioners imposed a six-month moratorium on the use of the carotid-artery chokehold except under circumstances where deadly force is authorized.

Based on these events, on June 3, 1982, the City filed in this Court a Memorandum Suggesting a Question of Mootness, reciting the facts but arguing that the case was not moot. Lyons in turn filed a motion to dismiss the writ of certiorari as improvidently granted. We denied that motion but reserved the question of mootness for later consideration.

In his brief and at oral argument, Lyons has reasserted his position that in light of changed conditions, an injunctive decree is now unnecessary because he is no longer subject to a threat of injury. He urges that the preliminary injunction should be vacated. The City, on the other hand, while acknowledging that subsequent events have significantly changed the posture of this case, again asserts that the case is not moot because the moratorium is not permanent and may be lifted at any time.

We agree with the City that the case is not moot, since the moratorium by its terms is not permanent. Intervening events have not "irrevocably eradicated the effects of the alleged violation." We nevertheless hold, for another reason, that the federal courts are without jurisdiction to entertain Lyons' claim for injunctive relief.

III

It goes without saying that those who seek to invoke the jurisdiction of the federal courts must satisfy the threshold requirement imposed by Article III of the Constitution by alleging an actual case or controversy.

In *O'Shea v. Littleton* we dealt with a case brought by a class of plaintiffs claiming that they had been subjected to discriminatory enforcement of the criminal law. Among other things, a county magistrate and judge were accused of discriminatory conduct in various respects, such as sentencing members of plaintiff's class more harshly than other defendants. The Court of Appeals reversed the dismissal of the suit by the District Court, ruling that if the allegations were proved, an appropriate injunction could be entered.

We reversed for failure of the complaint to allege a case or controversy. Although it was claimed in that case that particular members of the plaintiff class had actually suffered from the alleged unconstitutional practices, we observed that "[p]ast exposure to illegal conduct does not in itself show a present case or controversy regarding injunctive relief . . .

B. Section 1983 Actions Against Municipalities

if unaccompanied by any continuing, present adverse effects." Past wrongs were evidence bearing on "whether there is a real and immediate threat of repeated injury." But the prospect of future injury rested "on the likelihood that [plaintiffs] will again be arrested for and charged with violations of the criminal law and will again be subjected to bond proceedings, trial, or sentencing before petitioners." The most that could be said for plaintiffs' standing was "that if [plaintiffs] proceed to violate an unchallenged law and if they are charged, held to answer, and tried in any proceedings before petitioners, they will be subjected to the discriminatory practices that petitioners are alleged to have followed." We could not find a case or controversy in those circumstances: the threat to the plaintiffs was not "sufficiently real and immediate to show an existing controversy simply because they anticipate violating lawful criminal statutes and being tried for their offenses. . . ." It was to be assumed "that [plaintiffs] will conduct their activities within the law and so avoid prosecution and conviction as well as exposure to the challenged course of conduct said to be followed by petitioners."

We further observed that case or controversy considerations "obviously shade into those determining whether the complaint states a sound basis for equitable relief," and went on to hold that even if the complaint presented an existing case or controversy, an adequate basis for equitable relief against petitioners had not been demonstrated:

> [Plaintiffs] have failed, moreover, to establish the basic requisites of the issuance of equitable relief in these circumstances — the likelihood of substantial and immediate irreparable injury, and the inadequacy of remedies at law. We have already canvassed the necessarily conjectural nature of the threatened injury to which [plaintiffs] are allegedly subjected. And if any of the [plaintiffs] are ever prosecuted and face trial, or if they are illegally sentenced, there are available state and federal procedures which could provide relief from the wrongful conduct alleged.

Another relevant decision for present purposes is *Rizzo v. Goode* (1976), a case in which plaintiffs alleged widespread illegal and unconstitutional police conduct aimed at minority citizens and against City residents in general. The Court reiterated the holding in *O'Shea* that past wrongs do not in themselves amount to that real and immediate threat of injury necessary to make out a case or controversy. The claim of injury rested upon "what one or a small, unnamed minority of policemen might do to them in the future because of that unknown policeman's perception" of departmental procedures. This hypothesis was "even more attenuated than those allegations of future injury found insufficient in *O'Shea* to warrant [the] invocation of federal jurisdiction." The Court also held that plaintiffs' showing at trial of a relatively few instances of violations by individual police officers, without any showing of a deliberate policy on behalf of the named defendants, did not provide a basis for equitable relief.

Golden v. Zwickler (1969), a case arising in an analogous situation, is directly apposite. Congressman Zwickler sought a declaratory judgment that a New York statute prohibiting anonymous handbills directly pertaining to election campaigns was unconstitutional. Although Zwickler had once been convicted under the statute, he was no longer a Congressman apt to run for reelection. A unanimous Court held that because it was "most unlikely" that Zwickler would again be subject to the statute, no case or controversy of "sufficient immediacy and reality" was present to allow a declaratory judgment. Just as Zwickler's assertion that he could be a candidate for Congress again was "hardly a substitute for evidence that this is a prospect of 'immediacy and reality,'" Lyons' assertion that he may again be subject to an illegal chokehold does not create the actual controversy that must exist for a declaratory judgment to be entered.

IV

No extension of *O'Shea* and *Rizzo* is necessary to hold that respondent Lyons has failed to demonstrate a case or controversy with the City that would justify the equitable relief sought.

Lyons' standing to seek the injunction requested depended on whether he was likely to suffer future injury from the use of the chokeholds by police officers. Count V of the complaint alleged the traffic stop and choking incident five months before. That Lyons may have been illegally choked by the police on October 6, 1976, while presumably affording Lyons standing to claim damages against the individual officers and perhaps against the City, does nothing to establish a real and immediate threat that he would again be stopped for a traffic violation, or for any other offense, by an officer or officers who would illegally choke him into unconsciousness without any provocation or resistance on his part. The additional allegation in the complaint that the police in Los Angeles routinely apply chokeholds in situations where they are not threatened by the use of deadly force falls far short of the allegations that would be necessary to establish a case or controversy between these parties.

In order to establish an actual controversy in this case, Lyons would have had not only to allege that he would have another encounter with the police but also to make the incredible assertion either, (1) that all police officers in Los Angeles always choke any citizen with whom they happen to have an encounter, whether for the purpose of arrest, issuing a citation or for questioning or, (2) that the City ordered or authorized police officers to act in such manner. Although Count V alleged that the City authorized the use of the control holds in situations where deadly force was not threatened, it did not indicate why Lyons might be realistically threatened by police officers who acted within the strictures of the City's policy. If, for example, chokeholds were authorized to be used only to counter resistance to an arrest by a suspect, or to thwart an effort to escape, any future threat to Lyons from the City's policy or from the conduct of police officers would be no more real than the possibility that he would again have an encounter with the police and that either he would illegally resist arrest or detention or the officers would disobey their instructions and again render him unconscious without any provocation.

Under *O'Shea* and *Rizzo*, these allegations were an insufficient basis to provide a federal court with jurisdiction to entertain Count V of the complaint. This was apparently the conclusion of the District Court in dismissing Lyons' claim for injunctive relief. Although the District Court acted without opinion or findings, the Court of Appeals interpreted its action as based on lack of standing, i.e., that under *O'Shea* and *Rizzo*, Lyons must be held to have made an "insufficient showing that the police were likely to do this to the plaintiff again." For several reasons — each of them infirm, in our view — the Court of Appeals thought reliance on *O'Shea* and *Rizzo* was misplaced and reversed the District Court.

First, the Court of Appeals thought that Lyons was more immediately threatened than the plaintiffs in those cases since, according to the Court of Appeals, Lyons need only be stopped for a minor traffic violation to be subject to the strangleholds. But even assuming that Lyons would again be stopped for a traffic or other violation in the reasonably near future, it is untenable to assert, and the complaint made no such allegation, that strangleholds are applied by the Los Angeles police to every citizen who is stopped or arrested regardless of the conduct of the person stopped. We cannot agree that the "odds" that Lyons would not only again be stopped for a traffic violation but would also be subjected to a chokehold without any provocation whatsoever are sufficient to make out a federal case for equitable relief. We note that five months elapsed between October 6, 1976, and the filing of the complaint, yet there was no allegation of further unfortunate encounters between Lyons and the police.

Of course, it may be that among the countless encounters between the police and the citizens of a great city such as Los Angeles, there will be certain instances in which strangleholds will be illegally applied and injury and death unconstitutionally inflicted on the victim. As we have said, however, it is no more than conjecture to suggest that in every instance of a traffic stop, arrest, or other encounter between the police and a citizen, the police will act unconstitutionally and inflict injury without provocation or legal excuse. And it is surely no more than speculation to assert either that Lyons himself will again be involved in one of those unfortunate instances, or that he will be arrested in the future and provoke the use of a chokehold by resisting arrest, attempting to escape, or threatening deadly force or serious bodily injury.

Second, the Court of Appeals viewed *O'Shea* and *Rizzo* as cases in which the plaintiffs sought "massive structural" relief against the local law enforcement systems and therefore that the holdings in those cases were inapposite to cases such as this where the plaintiff, according to the Court of Appeals, seeks to enjoin only an "established," "sanctioned" police practice assertedly violative of constitutional rights. *O'Shea* and *Rizzo*, however, cannot be so easily confined to their facts. If Lyons has made no showing that he is realistically threatened by a repetition of his experience of October, 1976, then he has not met the requirements for seeking an injunction in a federal court, whether the injunction contemplates intrusive structural relief or the cessation of a discrete practice.

The Court of Appeals also asserted that Lyons "had a live and active claim" against the City "if only for a period of a few seconds" while the stranglehold was being applied to him and that for two reasons the claim had not become moot so as to disentitle Lyons to injunctive relief: First, because under normal rules of equity, a case does not become moot merely because the complained of conduct has ceased; and second, because Lyons' claim is "capable of repetition but evading review" and therefore should be heard. We agree that Lyons had a live controversy with the City. Indeed, he still has a claim for damages against the City that appears to meet all Article III requirements. Nevertheless, the issue here is not whether that claim has become moot but whether Lyons meets the preconditions for asserting an injunctive claim in a federal forum. The equitable doctrine that cessation of the challenged conduct does not bar an injunction is of little help in this respect, for Lyons' lack of standing does not rest on the termination of the police practice but on the speculative nature of his claim that he will again experience injury as the result of that practice even if continued.

The rule that a claim does not become moot where it is capable of repetition, yet evades review, is likewise inapposite. Lyons' claim that he was illegally strangled remains to be litigated in his suit for damages; in no sense does that claim "evade" review. Furthermore, the capable-of-repetition doctrine applies only in exceptional situations, and generally only where the named plaintiff can make a reasonable showing that he will again be subjected to the alleged illegality. As we have indicated, Lyons has not made this demonstration.

The record and findings made on remand do not improve Lyons' position with respect to standing. The District Court, having been reversed, did not expressly address Lyons' standing to seek injunctive relief, although the City was careful to preserve its position on this question. There was no finding that Lyons faced a real and immediate threat of again being illegally choked. The City's policy was described as authorizing the use of the strangleholds "under circumstances where no one is threatened with death or grievous bodily harm." That policy was not further described, but the record before the court contained the department's existing policy with respect to the employment of chokeholds. Nothing in that policy, contained in a Police Department manual, suggests that the chokeholds, or other kinds of force for that matter, are authorized absent some resistance or other provocation by the arrestee or other suspect. On the contrary, police officers were instructed to use chokeholds only when lesser degrees of force do not suffice and then only "to gain control of a suspect who is violently resisting the officer or trying to escape."

Our conclusion is that the Court of Appeals failed to heed *O'Shea*, *Rizzo*, and other relevant authority, and that the District Court was quite right in dismissing Count V.

V

Lyons fares no better if it be assumed that his pending damages suit affords him Article III standing to seek an injunction as a remedy for the claim arising out of the October 1976 events.

The equitable remedy is unavailable absent a showing of irreparable injury, a requirement that cannot be met where there is no showing of any real or immediate threat that the plaintiff will be wronged again—a "likelihood of substantial and immediate irreparable injury." The speculative nature of Lyons' claim of future injury requires a finding that this prerequisite of equitable relief has not been fulfilled.

Nor will the injury that Lyons allegedly suffered in 1976 go unrecompensed; for that injury, he has an adequate remedy at law. Contrary to the view of the Court of Appeals, it is not at all "difficult" under our holding "to see how anyone can ever challenge police or similar administrative practices." The legality of the violence to which Lyons claims he was once subjected is at issue in his suit for damages and can be determined there.

Absent a sufficient likelihood that he will again be wronged in a similar way, Lyons is no more entitled to an injunction than any other citizen of Los Angeles; and a federal court may not entertain a claim by any or all citizens who no more than assert that certain practices of law enforcement officers are unconstitutional. This is not to suggest that such undifferentiated claims should not be taken seriously by local authorities. Indeed, the interest of an alert and interested citizen is an essential element of an effective and fair government, whether on the local, state or national level. A federal court, however, is not the proper forum to press such claims unless the requirements for entry and the prerequisites for injunctive relief are satisfied.

We decline the invitation to slight the preconditions for equitable relief; for as we have held, recognition of the need for a proper balance between state and federal authority counsels restraint in the issuance of injunctions against state officers engaged in the administration of the states' criminal laws in the absence of irreparable injury which is both great and immediate *Mitchum v. Foster* (1972) held that suits brought under 42 U.S.C. § 1983 are exempt from the flat ban against the issuance of injunctions directed at state court proceedings. But this holding did not displace the normal principles of equity, comity and federalism that should inform the judgment of federal courts when asked to oversee state law enforcement authorities. In exercising their equitable powers federal courts must recognize "[t]he special delicacy of the adjustment to be preserved between federal equitable power and State administration of its own law." The Court of Appeals failed to apply these factors properly and therefore erred in finding that the District Court had not abused its discretion in entering an injunction in this case.

As we noted in *O'Shea*, withholding injunctive relief does not mean that the "federal law will exercise no deterrent effect in these circumstances." If Lyons has suffered an injury barred by the Federal Constitution, he has a remedy for damages under § 1983. Furthermore, those who deliberately deprive a citizen of his constitutional rights risk conviction under the federal criminal laws.

Beyond these considerations the state courts need not impose the same standing or remedial requirements that govern federal court proceedings. The individual states may permit their courts to use injunctions to oversee the conduct of law enforcement authorities on a continuing basis. But this is not the role of a federal court absent far more justification than Lyons has proffered in this case.

The judgment of the Court of Appeals is accordingly
Reversed.

[Justices Marshall, Brennan, Blackmun, and Stevens dissented.]

NOTES AND QUESTIONS

1. *Lyons* was in one sense an easier kind of § 1983 case than either *Harris* or *Connick* because the challenge was to a city policy and there was therefore no need to proceed on a "failure to train" theory and demonstrate "deliberate indifference. The district court found, and it was not disputed on appeal, that the city permitted officers to use chokeholds even when they were not in situations where death or serious harm were threatened. Accordingly, the policy was in violation of the Fourth Amendment, as the Supreme Court held in *Tennessee v. Garner*, 471 U.S. 1 (1985).

2. The Court's use of the standing doctrine in *Lyons* was unprecedented. As the dissent points out, the Court had never before "fragmented" the concept of standing to require a separate type of standing for injunctive relief on top of the standing Lyons undeniably had—he was subjected to an unconstitutional chokehold—with respect to his damages claims.

Chokehold representation

3. The doctrine of standing flows from the Article III requirement that the judicial power can only be exercised in a "case or controversy." Professor Richard Fallon has observed that the conception of standing in *Lyons*, which he labels "remedial standing," is inconsistent with traditional understandings of the term "case," which the Court has held includes all claims arising out of "a common nucleus of operative fact." *UMW v. Gibbs*, 333 U.S. 715 (1966) (a federal court having federal question jurisdiction can exercise pendent jurisdiction over state law claims arising out of the same facts, as the state claims are part of the same "case" for Article III purposes). *See* Richard H. Fallon Jr., *Of Justiciability, Remedies, and Public Law Litigation: Notes on the Jurisprudence of Lyons*, 59 N.Y.U. L. Rev. 1, 22 & n.115 (1984).

4. The Court says that Lyons is no more likely than anyone else in Los Angeles to be subjected to an unconstitutional chokehold. Does this mean that literally no one could bring the injunctive claim Lyons brought?

Further, does this framing simply ignore the disproportionate use of chokeholds on Black people? Does it ignore that Lyons has also alleged an equal protection claim?

5. The Court claims that *O'Shea* and *Rizzo* support the result in *Lyons*. Do you see meaningful distinctions between *Lyons* and those cases?

Was the nature of the equitable relief sought by Lyons distinguishable from the relief sought by the plaintiffs in *O'Shea* and *Rizzo*?

Chapter VI Addressing Police Misconduct

Was the nature of Lyons's "case" as a whole distinguishable from the cases of the plaintiffs in *O'Shea* and *Rizzo*?

6. Professor Vicki Jackson asks an interesting "what if" about *Lyons* and the professed virtues of equitable restraint that it endorsed. It was less than eight years after the decision in *Lyons* that Rodney King was savagely beaten by Los Angeles police officers, which lead to a state court trial in which the officers were acquitted, precipitating riots, 45 deaths, and hundreds of injuries. It also resulted in a federal criminal prosecution of the officers. *See* Chapter X *infra*. Might any of this have been avoided if in the 1980s the Los Angeles Police Department had been under some period of federal court supervision or monitoring of its operations through an injunctive decree? *See* Vicki C. Jackson, *Standing and the Role of Federal Courts: Triple Error Decisions in* Clapper v. Amnesty International USA *and* City of Los Angeles v. Lyons, 23 Wm. & Mary Bill Rts. J. 127, 122, 134 (2014).

Shortly after the Rodney King beating an independent commission headed by Warren Christopher issued a searing report on the LAPD, finding rampant use of excessive force, racist attitudes at all ranks in the department, and an utter failure to investigate and discipline officer misconduct. *Id. See generally* Warren Christopher et al., Report of the Independent Commission on the Los Angeles Police Department (1991).

7. The Court concludes its opinion in *Lyons* with this penultimate paragraph:

As we noted in *O'Shea*, . . . withholding injunctive relief does not mean that the "federal law will exercise no deterrent effect in these circumstances." If Lyons has suffered an injury barred by the Federal Constitution, he has a remedy for damages under § 1983. Furthermore, those who deliberately deprive a citizen of his constitutional rights risk conviction under the federal criminal laws. *Ibid.*

461 U.S. at 112. Is it clear that Lyons has a remedy for damages here? Could the city defend against liability on the basis that the chokehold policy was not implemented at a high enough level in the police department to be attributable to the city under *Monell*?

The passage in *O'Shea* the Court cites makes specific reference to 18 U.S.C. § 242, which authorizes federal criminal prosecutions for deprivations of constitutional rights. *See* Chapter X *infra*. Indeed, this is the statute under which the LAPD officers responsible for the beating of Rodney King were prosecuted and convicted in the federal trial. Does the Court mean to suggest that the federal criminal prosecution of a local police officer is less offensive to principles of federalism than a federal injunction?

In the next case a federal district judge is able to overcome the high hurdles imposed by *Monell* and *Lyons* in a class action challenging the New York City Police Department's stop-and-frisk policies.

Floyd v. City of New York
959 F. Supp. 2d 540 (S.D.N.Y. 2013)

SHIRA A. SCHEINDLIN, District Judge:

I. INTRODUCTION

New Yorkers are rightly proud of their city and seek to make it as safe as the largest city in America can be. New Yorkers also treasure their liberty. Countless individuals have come to New York in pursuit of that liberty. The goals of liberty and safety may be in tension, but they can coexist—indeed the Constitution mandates it.

This case is about the tension between liberty and public safety in the use of a proactive policing tool called "stop and frisk." The New York City Police Department ("NYPD") made 4.4 million stops between January 2004 and June 2012. Over 80% of these 4.4 million stops were of blacks or Hispanics. In each of these stops a person's life was interrupted. The person was detained and questioned, often on a public street. More than half of the time the police subjected the person to a frisk.

Plaintiffs—blacks and Hispanics who were stopped—argue that the NYPD's use of stop and frisk violated their constitutional rights in two ways: (1) they were stopped without a legal basis in violation of the Fourth Amendment, and (2) they were targeted for stops because of their race in violation of the Fourteenth Amendment. Plaintiffs do not seek to end the use of stop and frisk. Rather, they argue that it must be reformed to comply with constitutional limits. Two such limits are paramount here: first, that all stops be based on "reasonable suspicion" as defined by the Supreme Court of the United States; and second, that stops be conducted in a racially neutral manner.

I emphasize at the outset, as I have throughout the litigation, that this case is not about the effectiveness of stop and frisk in deterring or combating crime. This Court's mandate is solely to judge the constitutionality of police behavior, not its effectiveness as a law enforcement tool. Many police practices may be useful for fighting crime—preventive detention or coerced confessions, for example—but because they are unconstitutional they cannot be used, no matter how effective. "The enshrinement of constitutional rights necessarily takes certain policy choices off the table."

This case is also not primarily about the nineteen individual stops that were the subject of testimony at trial. Rather, this case is about whether the City has a policy or custom of violating the Constitution by making unlawful stops and conducting unlawful frisks.

The Supreme Court has recognized that "the degree of community resentment aroused by particular practices is clearly relevant to an assessment of the quality of the intrusion upon reasonable expectations of personal security." In light of the very active and public debate on the issues addressed in this Opinion—and the passionate positions taken by both sides—it is important to recognize the human toll of unconstitutional stops. While it is true that any one stop is a limited intrusion in duration and deprivation of liberty, each stop is also a demeaning and humiliating experience. No one should live in fear of being stopped whenever he leaves his home to go about the activities of daily life. Those who are routinely subjected to stops are overwhelmingly people of color, and they are justifiably troubled to be singled out when many of them have done nothing to attract the unwanted attention. Some plaintiffs testified that stops make them feel unwelcome in some parts of the City, and distrustful of the police. This alienation cannot be good for the police, the community, or its leaders. Fostering trust and confidence between the police and the community would be an improvement for everyone.

Plaintiffs requested that this case be tried to the Court without a jury. Because plaintiffs seek only injunctive relief, not damages, the City had no right to demand a jury. As a result, I must both find the facts and articulate the governing law. I have endeavored to exercise my judgment faithfully and impartially in making my findings of fact and conclusions of law based on the nine-week trial held from March through May of this year.

I begin with an Executive Summary of the most important points in the Opinion. Next, I address the legal standards governing the ability of police to conduct stops and frisks. I provide a statistical overview of the 4.4 million stops made between January 2004 and June 2012, followed by a discussion of the expert analyses of those stops. I then address the question of whether the City had notice of allegations of racial profiling in the conduct of stops and frisks, and the institutional response to that notice in terms of monitoring, supervision, training, and discipline. After addressing these big picture issues, I make findings of fact with respect to each of the nineteen stops of the twelve class members who provided testimony at trial.

Finally, I present my conclusions of law based on my findings of fact. I will address the question of remedies in a separate opinion, because the remedies overlap with a different case involving stop and frisk in which I have already found that preliminary injunctive relief is warranted.

It is important that this Opinion be read synergistically. Each section of the Opinion is only a piece of the overall picture. Some will quarrel with the findings in one section or another. But, when read as a whole, with an understanding of the interplay between each section, I hope that this Opinion will bring more clarity and less disagreement to this complex and sensitive issue.

II. EXECUTIVE SUMMARY

Plaintiffs assert that the City, and its agent the NYPD, violated both the Fourth Amendment and the Equal Protection Clause of the Fourteenth Amendment of the United States Constitution. In order to hold a municipality liable for the violation of a constitutional right, plaintiffs "must prove that 'action pursuant to official municipal policy' caused the alleged constitutional injury." "Official municipal policy includes the decisions of a government's lawmakers, the acts of its policymaking officials, and practices so persistent and widespread as to practically have the force of law."

The Fourth Amendment protects all individuals against unreasonable searches or seizures. The Supreme Court has held that the Fourth Amendment permits the police to "stop and briefly detain a person for investigative purposes if the officer has a reasonable suspicion supported by articulable facts that criminal activity 'may be afoot,' even if the officer lacks probable cause." "Reasonable suspicion is an objective standard; hence, the subjective intentions or motives of the officer making the stop are irrelevant." The test for whether a stop has taken place in the context of a police encounter is whether a reasonable person would have felt free to terminate the encounter. "'[T]o proceed from a stop to a frisk, the police officer must reasonably suspect that the person stopped is armed and dangerous.'"

The Equal Protection Clause of the Fourteenth Amendment guarantees to every person the equal protection of the laws. It prohibits intentional discrimination based on race. Intentional discrimination can be proved in several ways, two of which are relevant here. A plaintiff can show: (1) that a facially neutral law or policy has been applied in an intentionally discriminatory manner; or (2) that a law or policy expressly classifies persons on the basis of race, and that the classification does not survive strict scrutiny. Because there is rarely direct proof of discriminatory intent, circumstantial evidence of such intent is permitted. "The impact of the official action — whether it bears more heavily on one race than another — may provide an important starting point."

The following facts, discussed in greater detail below, are uncontested:

- Between January 2004 and June 2012, the NYPD conducted over 4.4 million *Terry* stops.
- The number of stops per year rose sharply from 314,000 in 2004 to a high of 686,000 in 2011.
- 52% of all stops were followed by a protective frisk for weapons. A weapon was found after 1.5% of these frisks. In other words, in 98.5% of the 2.3 million frisks, no weapon was found.
- 8% of all stops led to a search into the stopped person's clothing, ostensibly based on the officer feeling an object during the frisk that he suspected to be a weapon, or immediately perceived to be contraband other than a weapon. In 9% of these searches, the felt object was in fact a weapon. 91% of the time, it was not. In 14% of these searches, the felt object was in fact contraband. 86% of the time it was not.

B. Section 1983 Actions Against Municipalities

- 6% of all stops resulted in an arrest, and 6% resulted in a summons. The remaining 88% of the 4.4 million stops resulted in no further law enforcement action.
- In 52% of the 4.4 million stops, the person stopped was black, in 31% the person was Hispanic, and in 10% the person was white.
- In 2010, New York City's resident population was roughly 23% black, 29% Hispanic, and 33% white.
- In 23% of the stops of blacks, and 24% of the stops of Hispanics, the officer recorded using force. The number for whites was 17%.
- Weapons were seized in 1.0% of the stops of blacks, 1.1% of the stops of Hispanics, and 1.4% of the stops of whites.
- Contraband other than weapons was seized in 1.8% of the stops of blacks, 1.7% of the stops of Hispanics, and 2.3% of the stops of whites.
- Between 2004 and 2009, the percentage of stops where the officer failed to state a specific suspected crime rose from 1% to 36%.

Both parties provided extensive expert submissions and testimony that is also discussed in detail below. Based on that testimony and the uncontested facts, I have made the following findings with respect to the expert testimony.

With respect to plaintiffs' Fourth Amendment claim, I begin by noting the inherent difficulty in making findings and conclusions regarding 4.4 million stops. Because it is impossible to individually analyze each of those stops, plaintiffs' case was based on the imperfect information contained in the NYPD's database of forms ("UF-250s") that officers are required to prepare after each stop. The central flaws in this database all skew toward underestimating the number of unconstitutional stops that occur: the database is incomplete, in that officers do not prepare a UF-250 for every stop they make; it is one-sided, in that the UF-250 only records the officer's version of the story; the UF-250 permits the officer to merely check a series of boxes, rather than requiring the officer to explain the basis for her suspicion; and many of the boxes on the form are inherently subjective and vague (such as "furtive movements"). Nonetheless, the analysis of the UF-250 database reveals that at least 200,000 stops were made without reasonable suspicion.

The actual number of stops lacking reasonable suspicion was likely far higher, based on the reasons stated above, and the following points: (1) Dr. Fagan was unnecessarily conservative in classifying stops as "apparently unjustified." For example, a UF-250 on which the officer checked only Furtive Movements (used on roughly 42% of forms) and High Crime Area (used on roughly 55% of forms) is not classified as "apparently unjustified." The same is true when only Furtive Movements and Suspicious Bulge (used on roughly 10% of forms) are checked. Finally, if an officer checked only the box marked "other" on either side of the form (used on roughly 26% of forms), Dr. Fagan categorized this as "ungeneralizable" rather than "apparently unjustified." (2) Many UF-250s did not identify any suspected crime (36% of all UF-250s in 2009). (3) The rate of arrests arising from stops is low (roughly 6%), and the yield of seizures of guns or other contraband is even lower (roughly 0.1% and 1.8% respectively). (4) "Furtive Movements," "High Crime Area," and "Suspicious Bulge" are vague and subjective terms. Without an accompanying narrative explanation for the stop, these checkmarks cannot reliably demonstrate individualized reasonable suspicion.

With respect to plaintiffs' Fourteenth Amendment claim, I reject the testimony of the City's experts that the race of crime suspects is the appropriate benchmark for measuring racial bias in stops. The City and its highest officials believe that blacks and Hispanics should be stopped at the same rate as their proportion of the local criminal suspect population. But this reasoning is flawed because the stopped population is overwhelmingly innocent — not criminal. There is no basis for assuming that an innocent population shares the same characteristics

584 Chapter VI Addressing Police Misconduct

as the criminal suspect population in the same area. Instead, I conclude that the benchmark used by plaintiffs' expert—a combination of local population demographics and local crime rates (to account for police deployment) is the most sensible.

Based on the expert testimony I find the following: (1) The NYPD carries out more stops where there are more black and Hispanic residents, even when other relevant variables are held constant. The racial composition of a precinct or census tract predicts the stop rate above and beyond the crime rate. (2) Blacks and Hispanics are more likely than whites to be stopped within precincts and census tracts, even after controlling for other relevant variables. This is so even in areas with low crime rates, racially heterogenous populations, or predominately white populations. (3) For the period 2004 through 2009, when any law enforcement action was taken following a stop, blacks were 30% more likely to be arrested (as opposed to receiving a summons) than whites, for the same suspected crime. (4) For the period 2004 through 2009, after controlling for suspected crime and precinct characteristics, blacks who were stopped were about 14% more likely—and Hispanics 9% more likely—than whites to be subjected to the use of force. (5) For the period 2004 through 2009, all else being equal, the odds of a stop resulting in any further enforcement action were 8% lower if the person stopped was black than if the person stopped was white. In addition, the greater the black population in a precinct, the less likely that a stop would result in a sanction. Together, these results show that blacks are likely targeted for stops based on a lesser degree of objectively founded suspicion than whites.

With respect to both the Fourth and Fourteenth Amendment claims, one way to prove that the City has a custom of conducting unconstitutional stops and frisks is to show that it acted with deliberate indifference to constitutional deprivations caused by its employees—here, the NYPD. The evidence at trial revealed significant evidence that the NYPD acted with deliberate indifference.

As early as 1999, a report from New York's Attorney General placed the City on notice that stops and frisks were being conducted in a racially skewed manner. Nothing was done in response. In the years following this report, pressure was placed on supervisors to increase the number of stops. Evidence at trial revealed that officers have been pressured to make a certain number of stops and risk negative consequences if they fail to achieve the goal. Without a system to ensure that stops are justified, such pressure is a predictable formula for producing unconstitutional stops. As one high ranking police official noted in 2010, this pressure, without a comparable emphasis on ensuring that the activities are legally justified, "could result in an officer taking enforcement action for the purpose of meeting a quota rather than because a violation of the law has occurred."

In addition, the evidence at trial revealed that the NYPD has an unwritten policy of targeting "the right people" for stops. In practice, the policy encourages the targeting of young black and Hispanic men based on their prevalence in local crime complaints. This is a form of racial profiling. While a person's race may be important if it fits the description of a particular crime suspect, it is impermissible to subject all members of a racially defined group to heightened police enforcement because some members of that group are criminals. The Equal Protection Clause does not permit race-based suspicion.

Much evidence was introduced regarding inadequate monitoring and supervision of unconstitutional stops. Supervisors routinely review the productivity of officers, but do not review the facts of a stop to determine whether it was legally warranted. Nor do supervisors ensure that an officer has made a proper record of a stop so that it can be reviewed for constitutionality. Deficiencies were also shown in the training of officers with respect to stop and frisk and in the disciplining of officers when they were found to have made a bad stop or frisk. Despite the mounting evidence that many bad stops were made, that officers failed to make adequate records of stops, and that discipline was spotty or non-existent, little has been done to improve the situation.

B. Section 1983 Actions Against Municipalities 585

One example of poor training is particularly telling. Two officers testified to their understanding of the term "furtive movements." One explained that "furtive movement is a very broad concept," and could include a person "changing direction," "walking in a certain way," "[a]cting a little suspicious," "making a movement that is not regular," being "very fidgety," "going in and out of his pocket," "going in and out of a location," "looking back and forth constantly," "looking over their shoulder," "adjusting their hip or their belt," "moving in and out of a car too quickly," "[t]urning a part of their body away from you," "[g]rabbing at a certain pocket or something at their waist," "getting a little nervous, maybe shaking," and "stutter[ing]." Another officer explained that "usually" a furtive movement is someone "hanging out in front of [a] building, sitting on the benches or something like that" and then making a "quick movement," such as "bending down and quickly standing back up," "going inside the lobby . . . and then quickly coming back out," or "all of a sudden becom[ing] very nervous, very aware." If officers believe that the behavior described above constitutes furtive movement that justifies a stop, then it is no surprise that stops so rarely produce evidence of criminal activity.

I now summarize my findings with respect to the individual stops that were the subject of testimony at trial. Twelve plaintiffs testified regarding nineteen stops. In twelve of those stops, both the plaintiffs and the officers testified. In seven stops no officer testified, either because the officers could not be identified or because the officers dispute that the stop ever occurred. I find that nine of the stops and frisks were unconstitutional—that is, they were not based on reasonable suspicion. I also find that while five other stops were constitutional, the frisks following those stops were unconstitutional. Finally, I find that plaintiffs have failed to prove an unconstitutional stop (or frisk) in five of the nineteen stops. The individual stop testimony corroborated much of the evidence about the NYPD's policies and practices with respect to carrying out and monitoring stops and frisks.

In making these decisions I note that evaluating a stop in hindsight is an imperfect procedure. Because there is no contemporaneous recording of the stop (such as could be achieved through the use of a body-worn camera), I am relegated to finding facts based on the often conflicting testimony of eyewitnesses. This task is not easy, as every witness has an interest in the outcome of the case, which may consciously or unconsciously affect the veracity of his or her testimony. Nonetheless, a judge is tasked with making decisions and I judged the evidence of each stop to the best of my ability. I am also aware that a judge deciding whether a stop is constitutional, with the time to reflect and consider all of the evidence, is in a far different position than officers on the street who must make split-second decisions in situations that may pose a danger to themselves or others. I respect that police officers have chosen a profession of public service involving dangers and challenges with few parallels in civilian life.

In conclusion, I find that the City is liable for violating plaintiffs' Fourth and Fourteenth Amendment rights. The City acted with deliberate indifference toward the NYPD's practice of making unconstitutional stops and conducting unconstitutional frisks. Even if the City had not been deliberately indifferent, the NYPD's unconstitutional practices were sufficiently widespread as to have the force of law. In addition, the City adopted a policy of indirect racial profiling by targeting racially defined groups for stops based on local crime suspect data. This has resulted in the disproportionate and discriminatory stopping of blacks and Hispanics in violation of the Equal Protection Clause. Both statistical and anecdotal evidence showed that minorities are indeed treated differently than whites. For example, once a stop is made, blacks and Hispanics are more likely to be subjected to the use of force than whites, despite the fact that whites are more likely to be found with weapons or contraband. I also conclude that the City's highest officials have turned a blind eye to the evidence that officers are conducting stops in a racially discriminatory manner. In their zeal to defend a policy that they believe to be effective, they have willfully ignored overwhelming proof that the policy of targeting "the right people" is racially discriminatory and therefore violates the United States Constitution. One NYPD official has even suggested that it is permissible to stop racially defined groups just to instill fear in them that they are subject to being stopped at any time for any reason—in the hope that this fear will deter them from carrying guns in the streets. The goal of deterring crime is laudable, but this method of doing so is unconstitutional.

I recognize that the police will deploy their limited resources to high crime areas. This benefits the communities where the need for policing is greatest. But the police are not permitted to target people for stops based on their race. Some may worry about the implications of this decision. They may wonder: if the police believe that a particular group of people is disproportionately responsible for crime in one area, why should the police not target that group with increased stops? Why should it matter if the group is defined in part by race? Indeed, there are contexts in which the Constitution permits considerations of race in law enforcement operations. What is clear, however, is that the Equal Protection Clause prohibits the practices described in this case. A police department may not target a racially defined group for stops in general—that is, for stops based on suspicions of general criminal wrongdoing—simply because members of that group appear frequently in the police department's suspect data. The Equal Protection Clause does not permit the police to target a racially defined group as a whole because of the misdeeds of some of its members.

To address the violations that I have found, I shall order various remedies including, but not limited to, an immediate change to certain policies and activities of the NYPD, a trial program requiring the use of body-worn cameras in one precinct per borough, a community-based joint remedial process to be conducted by a court-appointed facilitator, and the appointment of an independent monitor to ensure that the NYPD's conduct of stops and frisks is carried out in accordance with the Constitution and the principles enunciated in this Opinion, and to monitor the NYPD's compliance with the ordered remedies.

NOTES AND QUESTIONS

1. *Floyd* arose out of New York City's notorious stop-and-frisk police tactics (Stop and Frisk) that began as early as the 1990s in response to surging crime rates. Rudolph Giuliani was elected mayor in 1993 and appointed William Bratton as police commissioner. Bratton famously implemented a "broken windows" theory of policing that involved pouring resources into policing minor offenders (e.g., subway fare evaders) in the hope that a decrease in low-level disorder will result in a decrease of more serious crime. In connection with but not directly related to this policing theory, the NYPD in the 1990s also began aggressively conducting investigative stops to detect and deter the carrying of guns. Aggressive use of stop and frisk correlated with significant lowered crime and incarceration rates in New York in the first decade of the twenty-first century. *See generally* Jeffrey Bellin, *The Inverse Relationship Between the Constitutionality and Effectiveness of Stop and Frisk*, 94 B.U. L. Rev. 1495, 1496-99 (2014). This relationship may have been recognized by Judge Scheindlin, who notes in the introduction to her opinion that "this case is not about the effectiveness of stop and frisk in deterring or combating crime." 959 F. Supp. 2d at 557.

2. Consider the raw data on the 4.4 million stops in the UF-250 database. Do you agree with the district court that the expert's analysis of the database underestimated the number of unconstitutional stops, that is, stops unjustified by "reasonable suspicion" under *Terry v. Ohio*, 392 U.S. 1 (1968)?

What do you make of the fact that only 6 percent of stops result in arrests?

Note that 36 percent of the forms do not identify a "suspected crime." Why does the form require the officer to identify a "suspected crime"?

Copy of blank UF-250 Form used by the NYPD

3. As was expected, the defendants contested the standing of the named plaintiffs based on *Lyons*. The standing of only a single named plaintiff was necessary to meet the "case or controversy" requirement, and as to plaintiff David Ourlicht, the district court was able to distinguish *Lyons*; significantly, unlike Lyons's single chokehold experience, plaintiff Ourlicht had been stopped three times in 2008 and once after the lawsuit was filed in 2010, and thus recurring injury was not "speculative." The court also distinguished the 10 deaths attributed to the LAPD's chokehold policy from the NYPD's 2.8 million stops over 6 years, of which at least 60,000 were unconstitutional (30 facially unconstitutional stops a day). The court also noted that Mr. Ourlicht was stopped while just going about his day — on the sidewalk, in a park, getting into a car — and thus unlike Lyons did not need to disobey the law to suffer a recurrent injury. *See Floyd v. City of New York*, 283 F.R.D. 153, 169-70 (S.D.N.Y. 2012) (finding New York City liable under § 1983 for NYPD's racially motivated stop-and-frisk policies that violated plaintiff's Fourteenth and Fifth Amendment rights).

Floyd was settled before the Second Circuit was called on to pass on the case's merits. Do you think the district court's standing decision would have held up on appeal?

4. Note that liability under *Monell* was also a hotly litigated issue in *Floyd*. The Court notes in its executive summary that the plaintiffs established "deliberate indifference" under *Monell* and *Harris* through a combination of a report from the attorney general's office that put the city on notice of illegal stop and frisks, widespread pressure by supervisors to increase

588 Chapter VI Addressing Police Misconduct

officers' number of stops, poor training of officers on performing and documenting stops, and failure to discipline officers for improper stops.

How do you think the plaintiffs were able to use the discovery process and other investigative means to put together the type of factual record necessary to support these conclusions?

5. The district court found an equal protection violation based on the NYPD's admitted but unwritten policy to target for stops "the right people," who were young Black and Hispanic men based on their prevalence in local criminal complaints.

Is it a defense that the officers honestly believed, based on their own experiences, that young Black and Hispanic men were more likely to be carrying guns than whites?

6. The merits of Judge Scheindlin's decision never made it to the Second Circuit. William DiBlasio was elected mayor in 2012 and the case was settled, with reforms implemented. The case was reassigned to another judge after Judge Scheindlin made statements at a hearing in a related case and in media interviews that caused the Second Circuit to conclude that the "appearance of impartiality" had been compromised such that "reassignment is advisable to preserve the appearance of justice." *Ligon v. City of New York*, 736 F.3d 118, 129 (2d Cir. 2013). And that didn't end the legal drama either. Several police unions attempted to intervene in the case to prevent the settlement, which required another trip to the Second Circuit affirming the denial of their intervention motion. *Floyd v. City of New York*, 770 F.3d 1051, 1056 (2d Cir. 2014).

C. QUALIFIED IMMUNITY

The next set of cases considers the Supreme Court's creation of a doctrine of qualified immunity to protect state and federal public official defendants, including police officers, from suit and liability under both § 1983 and in "*Bivens* actions." The doctrine seemed benign in its original incarnation but eventually became an unruly beast, cutting potentially meritorious lawsuits off at their knees and developing a strange, symbiotic relationship with traditional procedural rules as the Supreme Court took increasingly more extreme measures to protect individual police officers and other public officials from liability and even from litigation.

Pierson v. Ray
386 U.S. 547 (1967)

Mr. Chief Justice WARREN delivered the opinion of Court.

These cases present issues involving the liability of local police officers and judges under s 1 of the Civil Rights Act of 1871, now 42 U.S.C. s 1983. Petitioners in No. 79 were members of a group of 15 white and Negro Episcopal clergymen who attempted to use segregated facilities at an interstate bus terminal in Jackson, Mississippi, in 1961. They were arrested by respondents Ray, Griffith, and Nichols, policemen of the City of Jackson, and charged with violating s 2087.5 of the Mississippi Code, which makes guilty of a misdemeanor anyone who congregates with others in a public place under circumstances such that a breach of the peace may be occasioned thereby, and refuses to move on when ordered to do so by a police officer. Petitioners waived a jury trial and were convicted of the offense by respondent Spencer, a municipal police justice. They were each given the maximum sentence of four months in jail and a fine of $200. On appeal petitioner Jones was accorded a trial de novo in the County Court, and after the city produced its evidence the court granted his motion for a directed verdict. The cases against the other petitioners were then dropped.

Having been vindicated in the County Court, petitioners brought this action for damages in the United States District Court for the Southern District of Mississippi, Jackson Division, alleging that respondents had violated s 1983, supra, and that respondents were liable at common law for false arrest and imprisonment. A jury returned verdicts for respondents on both counts. On appeal, the Court of Appeals for the Fifth Circuit held that respondent Spencer was immune from liability under both s 1983 and the common law of Mississippi for acts committed within his judicial jurisdiction. As to the police officers, the court noted that s 2087.5 of the Mississippi Code was held unconstitutional as applied to similar facts in *Thomas v. Mississippi*. Although Thomas was decided years after the arrest involved in this trial, the court held that the policemen would be liable in a suit under s 1983 for an unconstitutional arrest even if they acted in good faith and with probable cause in making an arrest under a state statute not yet held invalid. The court believed that this stern result was required by *Monroe v. Pape* (1961). Under the count based on the common law of Mississippi, however, it held that the policemen would not be liable if they had probable cause to believe that the statute had been violated, because Mississippi law does not require police officers to predict at their peril which state laws are constitutional and which are not. Apparently dismissing the common-law claim, the Court of Appeals reversed and remanded for a new trial on the s 1983 claim against the police officers because defense counsel had been allowed to cross-examine the ministers on various irrelevant and prejudicial matters, particularly including an alleged convergence of their views on racial justice with those of the Communist Party. At the new trial, however, the court held that the ministers could not recover if it were proved that they went to Mississippi anticipating that they would be illegally arrested because such action would constitute consent to the arrest under the principle of volenti non fit injuria, he who consents to a wrong cannot be injured.

We granted certiorari in No. 79 to consider whether a local judge is liable for damages under s 1983 for an unconstitutional conviction and whether the ministers should be denied recovery against the police officers if they acted with the anticipation that they would be illegally arrested. We also granted the police officers' petition in No. 94 to determine if the Court of Appeals correctly held that they could not assert the defense of good faith and probable cause to an action under s 1983 for unconstitutional arrest.

The evidence at the federal trial showed that petitioners and other Negro and white Episcopal clergymen undertook a "prayer pilgrimage" in 1961 from New Orleans to Detroit. The purpose of the pilgrimage was to visit church institutions and other places in the North and South to promote racial equality and integration, and, finally, to report to a church convention in Detroit. Letters from the leader of the group to its members indicate that the clergymen intended from the beginning to go to Jackson and attempt to use segregated facilities at the bus terminal there, and that they fully expected to be arrested for doing so. The group made plans based on the assumption that they would be arrested if they attempted peacefully to exercise their right as interstate travelers to use the waiting rooms and other facilities at the bus terminal, and the letters discussed arrangements for bail and other matters relevant to arrests.

The ministers stayed one night in Jackson, and went to the bus terminal the next morning to depart for Chattanooga, Tennessee. They entered the waiting room, disobeying a sign at the entrance that announced "White Waiting Room Only — By Order of the Police Department." They then turned to enter the small terminal restaurant but were stopped by two Jackson police officers, respondents Griffith and Nichols, who had been awaiting their arrival and who ordered them to "move on." The ministers replied that they wanted to eat and refused to move on. Respondent Ray, then a police captain and now the deputy chief of police, arrived a few minutes later. The ministers were placed under arrest and taken to the jail.

All witnesses including the police officers agreed that the ministers entered the waiting room peacefully and engaged in no boisterous or objectionable conduct while in the "White

Only" area. There was conflicting testimony on the number of bystanders present and their behavior. Petitioners testified that there was no crowd at the station, that no one followed them into the waiting room, and that no one uttered threatening words or made threatening gestures. The police testified that some 25 to 30 persons followed the ministers into the terminal, that persons in the crowd were in a very dissatisfied and ugly mood, and that they were mumbling and making unspecified threatening gestures. The police did not describe any specific threatening incidents, and testified that they took no action against any persons in the crowd who were threatening violence because they "had determined that the ministers was the cause of the violence if any might occur," although the ministers were concededly orderly and polite and the police did not claim that it was beyond their power to control the allegedly disorderly crowd. The arrests and convictions were followed by this lawsuit.

We find no difficulty in agreeing with the Court of Appeals that Judge Spencer is immune from liability for damages for his role in these convictions. The record is barren of any proof or specific allegation that Judge Spencer played any role in these arrests and convictions other than to adjudge petitioners guilty when their cases came before his court. Few doctrines were more solidly established at common law than the immunity of judges from liability for damages for acts committed within their judicial jurisdiction, as this Court recognized when it adopted the doctrine, in *Bradley v. Fisher* (1872). This immunity applies even when the judge is accused of acting maliciously and corruptly, and it "is not for the protection or benefit of a malicious or corrupt judge, but for the benefit of the public, whose interest it is that the judges should be at liberty to exercise their functions with independence and without fear of consequences." It is a judge's duty to decide all cases within his jurisdiction that are brought before him, including controversial cases that arouse the most intense feelings in the litigants. His errors may be corrected on appeal, but he should not have to fear that unsatisfied litigants may hound him with litigation charging malice or corruption. Imposing such a burden on judges would contribute not to principled and fearless decisionmaking but to intimidation.

We do not believe that this settled principle of law was abolished by s 1983, which makes liable "every person" who under color of law deprives another person of his civil rights. The legislative record gives no clear indication that Congress meant to abolish wholesale all common-law immunities. Accordingly, this Court held in *Tenney v. Brandhove* (1951), that the immunity of legislators for acts within the legislative role was not abolished. The immunity of judges for acts within the judicial role is equally well established, and we presume that Congress would have specifically so provided had it wished to abolish the doctrine.

The common law has never granted police officers an absolute and unqualified immunity, and the officers in this case do not claim that they are entitled to one. Their claim is rather that they should not be liable if they acted in good faith and with probable cause in making an arrest under a statute that they believed to be valid. Under the prevailing view in this country a peace officer who arrests someone with probable cause is not liable for false arrest simply because the innocence of the suspect is later proved. Restatement, Second, Torts s 121 (1965); 1 Harper & James, The Law of Torts s 3.18, at 277-278 (1956); *State of Missouri ex rel. and to Use of, Ward v. Fidelity & Deposit Co. of Maryland* (C.A. 8th Cir. 1950). A policeman's lot is not so unhappy that he must choose between being charged with dereliction of duty if he does not arrest when he has probable cause, and being mulcted in damages if he does. Although the matter is not entirely free from doubt, the same consideration would seem to require excusing him from liability for acting under a statute that he reasonably believed to be valid but that was later held unconstitutional on its face or as applied.

The Court of Appeals held that the officers had such a limited privilege under the common law of Mississippi, and indicated that it would have recognized a similar privilege under s 1983 except that it felt compelled to hold otherwise by our decision in *Monroe v. Pape*. *Monroe v. Pape* presented no question of immunity, however, and none was decided. The

C. Qualified Immunity 591

complaint in that case alleged that "13 Chicago police officers broke into petitioners' home in the early morning, routed them from bed, made them stand naked in the living room, and ransacked every room, emptying drawers and ripping mattress covers. It further allege(d) that Mr. Monroe was then taken to the police station and detained on 'open' charges for 10 hours, while he was interrogated about a two-day-old murder, that he was not taken before a magistrate, though one was accessible, that he was not permitted to call his family or attorney, that he was subsequently released without criminal charges being preferred against him." The police officers did not choose to go to trial and defend the case on the hope that they could convince a jury that they believed in good faith that it was their duty to assault Monroe and his family in this manner. Instead, they sought dismissal of the complaint, contending principally that their activities were so plainly illegal under state law that they did not act "under color of any statute, ordinance, regulation, custom, or usage, of any State or Territory" as required by s 1983. In rejecting this argument we in no way intimated that the defense of good faith and probable cause was foreclosed by the statute. We also held that the complaint should not be dismissed for failure to state that the officers had "a specific intent to deprive a person of a federal right," but this holding, which related to requirements of pleading, carried no implications as to which defenses would be available to the police officers. As we went on to say in the same paragraph, s 1983 "should be read against the background of tort liability that makes a man responsible for the natural consequences of his actions." Part of the background of tort liability, in the case of police officers making an arrest, is the defense of good faith and probable cause.

We hold that the defense of good faith and probable cause, which the Court of Appeals found available to the officers in the common-law action for false arrest and imprisonment, is also available to them in the action under s 1983. This holding does not, however, mean that the count based thereon should be dismissed. The Court of Appeals ordered dismissal of the common-law count on the theory that the police officers were not required to predict our decision in *Thomas v. Mississippi*. We agree that a police officer is not charged with predicting the future course of constitutional law. But the petitioners in this case did not simply argue that they were arrested under a statute later held unconstitutional. They claimed and attempted to prove that the police officers arrested them solely for attempting to use the "White Only" waiting room, that no crowd was present, and that no one threatened violence or seemed about to cause a disturbance. The officers did not defend on the theory that they believed in good faith that it was constitutional to arrest the ministers solely for using the waiting room. Rather, they claimed and attempted to prove that they did not arrest the ministers for the purpose of preserving the custom of segregation in Mississippi, but solely for the purpose of preventing violence. They testified, in contradiction to the ministers, that a crowd gathered and that imminent violence was likely. If the jury believed the testimony of the officers and disbelieved that of the ministers, and if the jury found that the officers reasonably believed in good faith that the arrest was constitutional, then a verdict for the officers would follow even though the arrest was in fact unconstitutional. The jury did resolve the factual issues in favor of the officers but, for reasons previously stated, its verdict was influenced by irrelevant and prejudicial evidence. Accordingly, the case must be remanded to the trial court for a new trial.

It is necessary to decide what importance should be given at the new trial to the substantially undisputed fact that the petitioners went to Jackson expecting to be illegally arrested. We do not agree with the Court of Appeals that they somehow consented to the arrest because of their anticipation that they would be illegally arrested, even assuming that they went to the Jackson bus terminal for the sole purpose of testing their rights to unsegregated public accommodations. The case contains no proof or allegation that they in any way tricked or goaded the officers into arresting them. The petitioners had the right to use the waiting room of the

Jackson bus terminal, and their deliberate exercise of that right in a peaceful, orderly, and inoffensive manner does not disqualify them from seeking damages under s 1983.

The judgment of the Court of Appeals is affirmed in part and reversed in part, and the cases are remanded for further proceedings consistent with this opinion.

NOTES AND QUESTIONS

1. Note the materials the Court purports to rely on as a basis for finding immunity for the police officers: two treatises on tort law and a federal case applying Missouri law. Would the legislative history of § 1983—discussed at length in *Monroe v. Pape* and relied on by Justice Douglas in his dissent here on judicial immunity—be informative? Note also the Court's reference to "the background of tort liability," which it claims to have relied on before in *Monroe* and again here in finding police officer immunity.

Shouldn't this "background of tort liability" have led the Court to adopt the well-settled "background" principles of respondeat superior liability when that issue came up in *Monell* or other cases? *See supra*.

And wouldn't the operative "background" immunity question have required an analysis of the extent of immunity for police officers in 1871, when § 1983 was enacted?

Segregated bus terminal in Memphis, Tennessee, circa 1943

C. Qualified Immunity 593

2. The plaintiffs' theory of liability for the police officers at trial was that the officers arrested them for attempting to use the "whites only" waiting room and not because they believed the plaintiffs were violating the Mississippi ordinance under which they were charged. Is it relevant to the officers' defense in the retrial that 14 of the 15 plaintiffs pleaded guilty to the charges under the ordinance? Are the reasons why the charges were dropped relevant in the retrial? Is it relevant whether a prosecutor was involved in deciding whether to make and/or drop the charges?

3. The Court does not state definitively whether the "good faith and probable cause" immunity defense that it adopts applies outside of the "false arrest" variety of § 1983 violations, although it implies that this might have been available to the officers in *Monroe v. Pape*. How would the defense work in the Fourth Amendment context? For example, how would it have worked in *Monroe* itself?

How would the defense work in a Fifth Amendment context where a plaintiff is challenging police officers' use of coercive interrogation techniques?

4. The Mississippi ordinance at issue here was, as the Court notes, held unconstitutional in 1965, four years after the charges here were made. But that decision, *Thomas v. Mississippi*, 380 U.S. 524 (1965), is a per curiam opinion containing one sentence: "The petition for writ of certiorari is granted and the judgments are reversed," followed by a cite to *Boynton v. Virginia*, 364 U.S. 454 (1960). Does this suggest that the unconstitutionality of the Mississippi ordinance should have been readily apparent to the officers and to Judge Spencer as of when *Boynton* was decided, which was before the events here took place? Does the scope of the judicial immunity recognized by the Court cover judicial enforcement of a statute that a judge knew or should have known was unconstitutional? Would it insulate from liability a judge who judicially enforced a statute even after that very statute was declared unconstitutional by a higher court?

Justice Douglas dissents from the Court's holding on judicial immunity based on language in the legislative history of § 1983 indicating that Congress was concerned about state judges being involved in civil rights violations. The Court would later hold that the doctrine of absolute judicial immunity should not mean that the "federal law will exercise no deterrent effect" on lawless judges, whose immunity would not protect them from criminal exposure under 18 U.S.C. § 242, which criminalizes deprivations of rights "under color of law." *O'Shea v. Littleton*, 414 U.S. 488, 503 (1974). *See* Chapter X *infra*.

5. Note that the only policy reason identified by the Court as supporting immunity for police officers is to prevent them from "being mulcted in damages." And although the Court does use the word "immunity," it leaves no doubt that "good faith and probable cause" is a defense that police officers must assert and prove. Indeed, the Court remands for a new trial where the officers will be able to use the defense.

The Supreme Court would not return to the issue of police officer immunity under § 1983 for over two decades. In the meantime, amid the tumult of the war in Vietnam and the Nixon Administration, several questions of immunity for other executive branch personnel came before the Court. In *Scheuer v. Rhodes*, 416 U.S. 232 (1974), the estates of students slain by the Ohio National Guard in the 1970 massacre at Kent State University brought a § 1983 action against Ohio governor James Rhodes and his top aides. The Court rejected the defendants' assertion of absolute immunity and held that they were sufficiently protected by a qualified immunity. *Id.* at 247-48. In *Butz v. Economou*, 438 U.S. 478 (1978), similarly, the Court rejected the absolute immunity claims of Department of Agriculture officials who allegedly commenced an administrative proceeding against a plaintiff in retaliation for his criticism of the agency. The Court found that qualified immunity was sufficient protection, and again expressed confidence in district judges' ability to use the Federal Rules of Civil Procedure to

Chapter VI Addressing Police Misconduct

protect defendants against frivolous lawsuits. Both cases mentioned *Pierson v. Ray* only in passing, perhaps because the duties of police officers were so different than those of the defendants in these cases.

These cases set the stage for the next case, also arising out of alleged misconduct by officials in the Nixon Administration, and also resting on allegations of retaliation.

Harlow v. Fitzgerald
457 U.S. 800 (1982)

Justice POWELL delivered the opinion of the Court.

The issue in this case is the scope of the immunity available to the senior aides and advisers of the President of the United States in a suit for damages based upon their official acts.

I

In this suit for civil damages petitioners Bryce Harlow and Alexander Butterfield are alleged to have participated in a conspiracy to violate the constitutional and statutory rights of the respondent A. Ernest Fitzgerald. Respondent avers that petitioners entered the conspiracy in their capacities as senior White House aides to former President Richard M. Nixon. As the alleged conspiracy is the same as that involved in *Nixon v. Fitzgerald*, the facts need not be repeated in detail.

Respondent claims that Harlow joined the conspiracy in his role as the Presidential aide principally responsible for congressional relations. At the conclusion of discovery the supporting evidence remained inferential. As evidence of Harlow's conspiratorial activity respondent relies heavily on a series of conversations in which Harlow discussed Fitzgerald's dismissal with Air Force Secretary Robert Seamans. The other evidence most supportive of Fitzgerald's claims consists of a recorded conversation in which the President later voiced a tentative recollection that Harlow was "all for canning" Fitzgerald.

Disputing Fitzgerald's contentions, Harlow argues that exhaustive discovery has adduced no direct evidence of his involvement in any wrongful activity. He avers that Secretary Seamans advised him that considerations of efficiency required Fitzgerald's removal by a reduction in force, despite anticipated adverse congressional reaction. Harlow asserts he had no reason to believe that a conspiracy existed. He contends that he took all his actions in good faith.

Petitioner Butterfield also is alleged to have entered the conspiracy not later than May 1969. Employed as Deputy Assistant to the President and Deputy Chief of Staff to H. R. Haldeman, Butterfield circulated a White House memorandum in that month in which he claimed to have learned that Fitzgerald planned to "blow the whistle" on some "shoddy purchasing practices" by exposing these practices to public view. Fitzgerald characterizes this memorandum as evidence that Butterfield had commenced efforts to secure Fitzgerald's retaliatory dismissal. As evidence that Butterfield participated in the conspiracy to conceal his unlawful discharge and prevent his reemployment, Fitzgerald cites communications between Butterfield and Haldeman in December 1969 and January 1970. After the President had promised at a press conference to inquire into Fitzgerald's dismissal, Haldeman solicited Butterfield's recommendations. In a subsequent memorandum emphasizing the importance of "loyalty," Butterfield counseled against offering Fitzgerald another job in the administration at that time.

For his part, Butterfield denies that he was involved in any decision concerning Fitzgerald's employment status until Haldeman sought his advice in December 1969 — more than a

C. Qualified Immunity   595

month after Fitzgerald's termination had been scheduled and announced publicly by the Air Force. Butterfield states that he never communicated his views about Fitzgerald to any official of the Defense Department. He argues generally that nearly eight years of discovery have failed to turn up any evidence that he caused injury to Fitzgerald.

Together with their codefendant Richard Nixon, petitioners Harlow and Butterfield moved for summary judgment on February 12, 1980. In denying the motion the District Court upheld the legal sufficiency of Fitzgerald's *Bivens* claim under the First Amendment and his "inferred" statutory causes of action under 5 U.S.C. § 7211 and 18 U.S.C. § 1505. The court found that genuine issues of disputed fact remained for resolution at trial. It also ruled that petitioners were not entitled to absolute immunity.

Independently of former President Nixon, petitioners invoked the collateral order doctrine and appealed the denial of their immunity defense to the Court of Appeals for the District of Columbia Circuit. The Court of Appeals dismissed the appeal without opinion. Never having determined the immunity available to the senior aides and advisers of the President of the United States, we granted certiorari.

As we reiterated today in *Nixon v. Fitzgerald*, our decisions consistently have held that government officials are entitled to some form of immunity from suits for damages. As recognized at common law, public officers require this protection to shield them from undue interference with their duties and from potentially disabling threats of liability.

Our decisions have recognized immunity defenses of two kinds. For officials whose special functions or constitutional status requires complete protection from suit, we have recognized the defense of "absolute immunity." The absolute immunity of legislators, in their legislative functions, and of judges, in their judicial functions, now is well settled. Our decisions also have extended absolute immunity to certain officials of the Executive Branch. These include prosecutors and similar officials, executive officers engaged in adjudicative functions and the President of the United States.

For executive officials in general, however, our cases make plain that qualified immunity represents the norm. Without discounting the adverse consequences of denying high officials an absolute immunity from private lawsuits alleging constitutional violations, we emphasized our expectation that insubstantial suits need not proceed to trial:

> Insubstantial lawsuits can be quickly terminated by federal courts alert to the possibilities of artful pleading. Unless the complaint states a compensable claim for relief . . ., it should not survive a motion to dismiss. Moreover, the Court recognized in *Scheuer* that damages suits concerning constitutional violations need not proceed to trial, but can be terminated on a properly supported motion for summary judgment based on the defense of immunity. . . . In responding to such a motion, plaintiffs may not play dog in the manger; and firm application of the Federal Rules of Civil Procedure will ensure that federal officials are not harassed by frivolous lawsuits.

Butz continued to acknowledge that the special functions of some officials might require absolute immunity. But the Court held that "federal officials who seek absolute exemption from personal liability for unconstitutional conduct must bear the burden of showing that public policy requires an exemption of that scope." This we reaffirmed today in *Nixon v. Fitzgerald*.

• • •

Even if they cannot establish that their official functions require absolute immunity, petitioners assert that public policy at least mandates an application of the qualified immunity standard that would permit the defeat of insubstantial claims without resort to trial. We agree.

The resolution of immunity questions inherently requires a balance between the evils inevitable in any available alternative. In situations of abuse of office, an action for damages may offer the only realistic avenue for vindication of constitutional guarantees. It is this recognition that has required the denial of absolute immunity to most public officers. At the same time, however, it cannot be disputed seriously that claims frequently run against the innocent as well as the guilty—at a cost not only to the defendant officials, but to society as a whole. These social costs include the expenses of litigation, the diversion of official energy from pressing public issues, and the deterrence of able citizens from acceptance of public office. Finally, there is the danger that fear of being sued will "dampen the ardor of all but the most resolute, or the most irresponsible [public officials], in the unflinching discharge of their duties."

In identifying qualified immunity as the best attainable accommodation of competing values, we relied on the assumption that this standard would permit "[i]nsubstantial lawsuits [to] be quickly terminated." Yet petitioners advance persuasive arguments that the dismissal of insubstantial lawsuits without trial—a factor presupposed in the balance of competing interests struck by our prior cases—requires an adjustment of the "good faith" standard established by our decisions.

Qualified or "good faith" immunity is an affirmative defense that must be pleaded by a defendant official. Decisions of this Court have established that the "good faith" defense has both an "objective" and a "subjective" aspect. The objective element involves a presumptive knowledge of and respect for "basic, unquestioned constitutional rights." The subjective component refers to "permissible intentions." Characteristically the Court has defined these elements by identifying the circumstances in which qualified immunity would not be available. Referring both to the objective and subjective elements, we have held that qualified immunity would be defeated if an official "knew or reasonably should have known that the action he took within his sphere of official responsibility would violate the constitutional rights of the [plaintiff], or if he took the action with the malicious intention to cause a deprivation of constitutional rights or other injury. . . ."

The subjective element of the good-faith defense frequently has proved incompatible with our admonition in *Butz* that insubstantial claims should not proceed to trial. Rule 56 of the Federal Rules of Civil Procedure provides that disputed questions of fact ordinarily may not be decided on motions for summary judgment. And an official's subjective good faith has been considered to be a question of fact that some courts have regarded as inherently requiring resolution by a jury.

In the context of *Butz*' attempted balancing of competing values, it now is clear that substantial costs attend the litigation of the subjective good faith of government officials. Not only are there the general costs of subjecting officials to the risks of trial—distraction of officials from their governmental duties, inhibition of discretionary action, and deterrence of able people from public service. There are special costs to "subjective" inquiries of this kind. Immunity generally is available only to officials performing discretionary functions. In contrast with the thought processes accompanying "ministerial" tasks, the judgments surrounding discretionary action almost inevitably are influenced by the decisionmaker's experiences, values, and emotions. These variables explain in part why questions of subjective intent so rarely can be decided by summary judgment. Yet they also frame a background in which there often is no clear end to the relevant evidence. Judicial inquiry into subjective motivation therefore may entail broad-ranging discovery and the deposing of numerous persons, including an official's professional colleagues. Inquiries of this kind can be peculiarly disruptive of effective government.

Consistently with the balance at which we aimed in *Butz*, we conclude today that bare allegations of malice should not suffice to subject government officials either to the costs of trial or to the burdens of broad-reaching discovery. We therefore hold that government officials performing discretionary functions generally are shielded from liability for civil damages insofar as their conduct does not violate clearly established statutory or constitutional rights of which a reasonable person would have known.

C. Qualified Immunity   597

Reliance on the objective reasonableness of an official's conduct, as measured by reference to clearly established law, should avoid excessive disruption of government and permit the resolution of many insubstantial claims on summary judgment. On summary judgment, the judge appropriately may determine, not only the currently applicable law, but whether that law was clearly established at the time an action occurred. If the law at that time was not clearly established, an official could not reasonably be expected to anticipate subsequent legal developments, nor could he fairly be said to "know" that the law forbade conduct not previously identified as unlawful. Until this threshold immunity question is resolved, discovery should not be allowed. If the law was clearly established, the immunity defense ordinarily should fail, since a reasonably competent public official should know the law governing his conduct. Nevertheless, if the official pleading the defense claims extraordinary circumstances and can prove that he neither knew nor should have known of the relevant legal standard, the defense should be sustained. But again, the defense would turn primarily on objective factors.

By defining the limits of qualified immunity essentially in objective terms, we provide no license to lawless conduct. The public interest in deterrence of unlawful conduct and in compensation of victims remains protected by a test that focuses on the objective legal reasonableness of an official's acts. Where an official could be expected to know that certain conduct would violate statutory or constitutional rights, he should be made to hesitate; and a person who suffers injury caused by such conduct may have a cause of action. But where an official's duties legitimately require action in which clearly established rights are not implicated, the public interest may be better served by action taken "with independence and without fear of consequences." *Pierson v. Ray* (1967).

In this case petitioners have asked us to hold that the respondent's pretrial showings were insufficient to survive their motion for summary judgment. We think it appropriate, however, to remand the case to the District Court for its reconsideration of this issue in light of this opinion. The trial court is more familiar with the record so far developed and also is better situated to make any such further findings as may be necessary.

The judgment of the Court of Appeals is vacated, and the case is remanded for further action consistent with this opinion.

NOTES AND QUESTIONS

1. This case has an abstract quality about it. The underlying legal claim is barely explained; all that the Court seems to want the reader to know about the lawsuit is that it was "insubstantial" and that defendant's summary judgment motion nonetheless was denied, perhaps because of disputed factual issues about defendant's state of mind (although that's not clear either). The companion lawsuit of *Nixon v. Fitzgerald*, 457 U.S. 731 (1982), explains that the plaintiff, a management analyst in the Department of the Air Force, was allegedly retaliated against by President Nixon and other executive officials after he testified before a congressional subcommittee about enormous cost overruns on a military air transport project. His discharge sufficiently concerned Congress that it held hearings about his discharge after it occurred.

Might there be better candidates than *Harlow* for a case in which to make out of whole cloth a new standard for qualified immunity premised on the protection of officials from frivolous lawsuits?

2. The Court quite candidly admits that it is changing the substantive rules of qualified immunity in order to permit defendants to more easily obtain summary judgment under Fed. R. Civ. P. 56. In doing so, the Court — again candidly — relies on nothing other than pure policy reasons, costs to "society as a whole," that support a more robust immunity. The Court identifies four specific costs engendered by "insubstantial" lawsuits "against the innocent": the diversion of executive energy from public affairs, the expense of litigation, the deterrence of persons from public service, and diminished aggressiveness by public officials.

Which of these social costs seem most persuasive? Least persuasive?

Why do you think the Court doesn't explicitly mention liability exposure as a social cost? Is it implicit in any of the others? Recall the Court's explicit reference in *Pierson* to the possibility of a police officer being "mulcted in damages" absent immunity.

3. The Court's overarching concern is with the "subjective good faith" element of the existing qualified immunity standard. Due to the aforementioned "social costs," and the concerns about allowing for summary judgment, the Court simply eliminates that component and redefines qualified immunity to exist based solely on the "objective reasonableness" of the official's conduct, good faith or not.

Could the goal have been accomplished by simply tweaking rather than eliminating the intent element? If so, how?

4. Summing up, the Court concludes that "bare allegations of malice should not suffice to subject government officials to either the costs of trial or to the burdens of far-reaching discovery." This formulation of the holding reflects at least one and probably two misunderstandings about civil procedure, at least based on civil procedure as you have learned it. What are they?

5. *Harlow* is a "*Bivens* action," inasmuch as the plaintiff's claims are levied against federal officials and not against state officials under § 1983. Should the Court have more latitude in determining the metes and bounds of an immunity defense to a *Bivens* claim than it does to a claim brought under § 1983? Why or why not?

In a footnote the Court notes that in *Butz v. Economou* it had previously held that it would be "untenable to draw a distinction for purposes of immunity law between suits brought against state officials under § 1983 and suits brought directly under the Constitution against federal officials." 438 U.S. at 504. Why would such a result be untenable?

Alexander Butterfield

6. Is it clear that the holding of *Harlow*—that officials enjoy immunity insofar as their conduct "does not violate clearly established statutory or constitutional rights of which a reasonable person would have known"—applies to police officers? Note that *Pierson v. Ray* is only mentioned once at the tail end of the opinion and very much in passing.

How would the *Harlow* immunity formulation apply to the police officers in *Pierson*?

7. One of Bryce Harlow's co-defendants was Alexander Butterfield, deputy assistant to President Richard Nixon. Butterfield transformed the Watergate investigation into the Nixon White House when he acknowledged in Senate testimony in July 1973 that White House communications involving President Nixon were routinely tape-recorded. Butterfield was never charged with any wrongdoing in connection with the Watergate scandal.

The Court returned to the issue of police officer immunity under § 1983 in the next case, where plaintiffs alleged that the defendant officers violated the statute in connection with submitting affidavits to a magistrate upon which arrest warrants were based.

C. Qualified Immunity 599

Malley v. Briggs
475 U.S. 335 (1986)

Justice WHITE delivered the opinion of the Court.

This case presents the question of the degree of immunity accorded a defendant police officer in a damages action under 42 U.S.C. § 1983 when it is alleged that the officer caused the plaintiffs to be unconstitutionally arrested by presenting a judge with a complaint and a supporting affidavit which failed to establish probable cause.

In December 1980, the Rhode Island State Police were conducting a court-authorized wiretap on the telephone of one Paul Driscoll, an acquaintance of respondents' daughter. On December 20, the police intercepted a call to Driscoll from an unknown individual who identified himself as "Dr. Shogun." The police logsheet summarizes the call as follows: "General conversation re. a party they went to last night . . . caller says I can't believe I was token [sic] in front of Jimmy Briggs — caller states he passed it to Louisa . . . Paul says Nancy was sitting in his lap rolling her thing."

Petitioner Edward Malley (hereafter petitioner) was the Rhode Island state trooper in charge of the investigation of Driscoll. After reviewing the logsheet for December 20, petitioner decided that the call from "Dr. Shogun" was incriminating, because in drug parlance "toking" means smoking marihuana and "rolling her thing" refers to rolling a marihuana cigarette. Petitioner also concluded that another call monitored the same day showed that the party discussed by Driscoll and "Dr. Shogun" took place at respondents' house. On the basis of these two calls, petitioner drew up felony complaints charging that respondents and Paul Driscoll "did unlawfully conspire to violate the uniform controlled substance act of the State of Rhode Island by having [marihuana] in their possession. . . ." These complaints were presented to a State District Court Judge in February 1981, after the wiretap of Driscoll's phone had been terminated. Accompanying the complaints were unsigned warrants for each respondent's arrest, and supporting affidavits describing the two intercepted calls and petitioner's interpretation of them. The judge signed warrants for the arrest of respondents and 20 other individuals charged by petitioner as a result of information gathered through the wiretap.

Respondents were arrested at their home shortly before six o'clock on the morning of March 19, 1981. They were taken to a police station, booked, held for several hours, arraigned, and released. Local and statewide newspapers published the fact that respondents, who are prominent members of their community, had been arrested and charged with drug possession. The charges against respondents were subsequently dropped when the grand jury to which the case was presented did not return an indictment.

Respondents brought an action under 42 U.S.C. § 1983 in the United States District Court for the District of Rhode Island charging, inter alia, that petitioner, in applying for warrants for their arrest, violated their rights under the Fourth and Fourteenth Amendments. The case was tried to a jury, and at the close of respondents' evidence, petitioner moved for and was granted a directed verdict. The District Court's primary justification for directing a verdict was that the act of the judge in issuing the arrest warrants for respondents broke the causal chain between petitioner's filing of a complaint and respondents' arrest. The court also stated that an officer who believes that the facts stated in his affidavit are true and who submits them to a neutral magistrate may thereby be entitled to immunity under the "objective reasonableness" standard of *Harlow v. Fitzgerald* (1982).

The United States Court of Appeals for the First Circuit reversed, holding that an officer who seeks an arrest warrant by submitting a complaint and supporting affidavit to a judge is not entitled to immunity unless the officer has an objectively reasonable basis for believing that the facts alleged in his affidavit are sufficient to establish probable cause. We granted certiorari in order to review the First Circuit's application of the "objective reasonableness" standard in this context. We affirm.

II

Petitioner urges reversal on two grounds: first, that in this context, he is absolutely immune from liability for damages; second, that he is at least entitled to qualified immunity in this case. We reject both propositions and address first the absolute immunity issue.

A

Our general approach to questions of immunity under § 1983 is by now well established. Although the statute on its face admits of no immunities, we have read it "in harmony with general principles of tort immunities and defenses rather than in derogation of them." Our initial inquiry is whether an official claiming immunity under § 1983 can point to a common-law counterpart to the privilege he asserts. If "an official was accorded immunity from tort actions at common law when the Civil Rights Act was enacted in 1871, the Court next considers whether § 1983's history or purposes nonetheless counsel against recognizing the same immunity in § 1983 actions." Thus, while we look to the common law for guidance, we do not assume that Congress intended to incorporate every common-law immunity into § 1983 in unaltered form.

Our cases also make plain that "[f]or executive officers in general, . . . qualified immunity represents the norm." Like federal officers, state officers who "seek absolute exemption from personal liability for unconstitutional conduct must bear the burden of showing that public policy requires an exemption of that scope."

B

Although we have previously held that police officers sued under § 1983 for false arrest are qualifiedly immune, *Pierson*, petitioner urges that he should be absolutely immune because his function in seeking an arrest warrant was similar to that of a complaining witness. The difficulty with this submission is that complaining witnesses were not absolutely immune at common law. In 1871, the generally accepted rule was that one who procured the issuance of an arrest warrant by submitting a complaint could be held liable if the complaint was made maliciously and without probable cause. Given malice and the lack of probable cause, the complainant enjoyed no immunity. The common law thus affords no support for petitioner.

Nor are we moved by petitioner's argument that policy considerations require absolute immunity for the officer applying for a warrant. As the qualified immunity defense has evolved, it provides ample protection to all but the plainly incompetent or those who knowingly violate the law. At common law, in cases where probable cause to arrest was lacking, a complaining witness' immunity turned on the issue of malice, which was a jury question. Under the *Harlow* standard, on the other hand, an allegation of malice is not sufficient to defeat immunity if the defendant acted in an objectively reasonable manner. The *Harlow* standard is specifically designed to "avoid excessive disruption of government and permit the resolution of many insubstantial claims on summary judgment," and we believe it sufficiently serves this goal. Defendants will not be immune if, on an objective basis, it is obvious that no reasonably competent officer would have concluded that a warrant should issue; but if officers of reasonable competence could disagree on this issue, immunity should be recognized.

C

As an alternative ground for claiming absolute immunity, petitioner draws an analogy between an officer requesting a warrant and a prosecutor who asks a grand jury to indict a suspect. Like the prosecutor, petitioner argues, the officer must exercise a discretionary judgment based on the evidence before him, and like the prosecutor, the officer may not exercise his best judgment if the threat of retaliatory lawsuits hangs over him. Thus, petitioner urges us to read § 1983 as giving the officer the same absolute immunity enjoyed by the prosecutor.

We reemphasize that our role is to interpret the intent of Congress in enacting § 1983, not to make a freewheeling policy choice, and that we are guided in interpreting Congress' intent by the common-law tradition. In *Imbler, supra*, we concluded that at common law "[t]he general rule was, and is, that a prosecutor is absolutely immune from suit for malicious prosecution." We do not find a comparable tradition of absolute immunity for one whose complaint causes a warrant to issue. While this observation may seem unresponsive to petitioner's policy argument, it is, we believe, an important guide to interpreting § 1983. Since the statute on its face does not provide for any immunities, we would be going far to read into it an absolute immunity for conduct which was only accorded qualified immunity in 1871.

Even were we to overlook the fact that petitioner is inviting us to expand what was a qualified immunity at common law into an absolute immunity, we would find his analogy between himself and a prosecutor untenable. We have interpreted § 1983 to give absolute immunity to functions "intimately associated with the judicial phase of the criminal process," not from an exaggerated esteem for those who perform these functions, and certainly not from a desire to shield abuses of office, but because any lesser degree of immunity could impair the judicial process itself. We intend no disrespect to the officer applying for a warrant by observing that his action, while a vital part of the administration of criminal justice, is further removed from the judicial phase of criminal proceedings than the act of a prosecutor in seeking an indictment. Furthermore, petitioner's analogy, while it has some force, does not take account of the fact that the prosecutor's act in seeking an indictment is but the first step in the process of seeking a conviction. Exposing the prosecutor to liability for the initial phase of his prosecutorial work could interfere with his exercise of independent judgment at every phase of his work, since the prosecutor might come to see later decisions in terms of their effect on his potential liability. Thus, we shield the prosecutor seeking an indictment because any lesser immunity could impair the performance of a central actor in the judicial process.

In the case of the officer applying for a warrant, it is our judgment that the judicial process will on the whole benefit from a rule of qualified rather than absolute immunity. We do not believe that the *Harlow* standard, which gives ample room for mistaken judgments, will frequently deter an officer from submitting an affidavit when probable cause to make an arrest is present. True, an officer who knows that objectively unreasonable decisions will be actionable may be motivated to reflect, before submitting a request for a warrant, upon whether he has a reasonable basis for believing that his affidavit establishes probable cause. But such reflection is desirable, because it reduces the likelihood that the officer's request for a warrant will be premature. Premature requests for warrants are at best a waste of judicial resources; at worst, they lead to premature arrests, which may injure the innocent or, by giving the basis for a suppression motion, benefit the guilty.

Furthermore, it would be incongruous to test police behavior by the "objective reasonableness" standard in a suppression hearing, while exempting police conduct in applying for an arrest or search warrant from any scrutiny whatsoever in a § 1983 damages action. While we believe the exclusionary rule serves a necessary purpose, it obviously does so at a considerable cost to society as a whole, because it excludes evidence probative of guilt. On the other hand, a damages remedy for an arrest following an objectively unreasonable request for a warrant imposes a cost directly on the officer responsible for the unreasonable request, without the side effect of hampering a criminal prosecution. Also, in the case of the § 1983 action, the likelihood is obviously greater than at the suppression hearing that the remedy is benefiting the victim of police misconduct one would think most deserving of a remedy — the person who in fact has done no wrong, and has been arrested for no reason, or a bad reason.

Accordingly, we hold that the same standard of objective reasonableness that we applied in the context of a suppression hearing in *Leon*, supra, defines the qualified immunity accorded an officer whose request for a warrant allegedly caused an unconstitutional arrest. Only where the warrant application is so lacking in indicia of probable cause as to render official belief in its existence unreasonable, will the shield of immunity be lost.

III

We also reject petitioner's argument that if an officer is entitled to only qualified immunity in cases like this, he is nevertheless shielded from damages liability because the act of applying for a warrant is per se objectively reasonable, provided that the officer believes that the facts alleged in his affidavit are true. Petitioner insists that he is entitled to rely on the judgment of a judicial officer in finding that probable cause exists and hence issuing the warrant. This view of objective reasonableness is at odds with our development of that concept in *Harlow* and *Leon*. In *Leon*, we stated that "our good-faith inquiry is confined to the objectively ascertainable question whether a reasonably well-trained officer would have known that the search was illegal despite the magistrate's authorization." The analogous question in this case is whether a reasonably well-trained officer in petitioner's position would have known that his affidavit failed to establish probable cause and that he should not have applied for the warrant. If such was the case, the officer's application for a warrant was not objectively reasonable, because it created the unnecessary danger of an unlawful arrest. It is true that in an ideal system an unreasonable request for a warrant would be harmless, because no judge would approve it. But ours is not an ideal system, and it is possible that a magistrate, working under docket pressures, will fail to perform as a magistrate should. We find it reasonable to require the officer applying for the warrant to minimize this danger by exercising reasonable professional judgment.

The judgment of the Court of Appeals is affirmed, and the case is remanded for further proceedings consistent with this opinion.

NOTES AND QUESTIONS

1. The Court acknowledges *Pierson v. Ray* but makes no effort to apply *Pierson*'s immunity formulation to the case at hand, treating the case as if it, at most, retains utility in the limited context of an allegedly false arrest. *Harlow* is the new sheriff in town; any doubt about whether *Harlow* applies to police officers is removed.

Is there an argument that the type of immunity *Harlow* recognized for senior executive branch officials is not necessarily appropriate for police officers in the field, whose day-to-day duties are much different than such executives?

2. In rejecting the defendant officer's claim for absolute immunity, the Court trumpets the virtues of qualified immunity under *Harlow*, as if to say "who needs absolute immunity when you've got qualified immunity under *Harlow*?" To put a bow on the point, the Court says that the qualified immunity defense under *Harlow* "provides ample protection to all but the plainly incompetent or those who knowingly violate the law."

Having said this, the Court affirms the First Circuit's reversal of the district court's granting of a directed verdict to the defendant police officer, impliedly finding that the jury could have found that the defendant was either "plainly incompetent" or "knowingly violated" the law.

Seriously: How should the district judge instruct the jury on defendant's qualified immunity defense?

C. Qualified Immunity   603

3. *Malley* has an abstract air about it similar to *Harlow*. We know the following: the plaintiffs were arrested on marijuana charges on the basis of arrest warrants issued by a judge that were, in turn, based on complaints submitted by Officer Malley; plaintiffs' arrest received widespread press coverage; the charges were dropped after the grand jury (presumably applying the same probable cause standard as would be applicable to the arrest warrants) refused to indict plaintiffs. What we don't know, critically, is what the complaints submitted by Officer Malley *actually said*. We also aren't told anything about the evidence at the § 1983 trial.

The Court holds that the complaint and supplemental affidavit did not establish probable cause. Can you tell why from the opinion? Was it because the facts in the complaints were false or exaggerated (and the grand jury later found that this was the case)? Was it because the facts in the complaints were true but failed to rise to a sufficient level to establish probable cause? Was it because the officer failed to appreciate a relevant legal standard?

4. The district judge, in granting a directed verdict for Officer Malley, found that the state judge's issuance of the arrest warrants "broke the causal chain" between the officer's complaint and the plaintiffs' arrest. Is that necessarily the case? What is a scenario in which it would be the case?

5. In the interim between *Pierson* and *Harlow* the Court had held in *Imbler v. Pachtman*, 424 U.S. 409 (1976), that prosecutors were generally entitled to absolute immunity from suits under § 1983 when acting within the scope of their duties in initiating a prosecution. Isn't initiating a prosecution a fair description of what Trooper Malley did here? Why shouldn't he receive the same protection as a prosecutor? Suppose that an assistant district attorney had reviewed the complaints before they were presented to the judge. What immunity defenses would Trooper Malley and the ADA have in that scenario?

6. What do you make of the Court's comment, in rejecting defendant's argument for qualified immunity, that: "We reemphasize that our role is to interpret the intent of Congress in enacting § 1983, not to make a freewheeling policy choice, and that we are guided in interpreting Congress' intent by the common-law tradition."

7. Note that the result in *Malley* is a remand for a new trial where, presumably, the jury will decide the qualified immunity issue. This result was itself unremarkable at the time. But as Professor William Baude noted in 2018, in the 30 times the Supreme Court applied the *Harlow* objective reasonableness standard between 1982 and 2017, *Malley* is one of only four cases that counts as even an arguable victory for a plaintiff. William Baude, *Is Qualified Immunity Unlawful?*, 106 Calif. L. Rev. 45, 82-83 (2018).

Anderson v. Creighton
483 U.S. 635 (1987)

Justice SCALIA delivered the opinion of the Court.

The question presented is whether a federal law enforcement officer who participates in a search that violates the Fourth Amendment may be held personally liable for money damages if a reasonable officer could have believed that the search comported with the Fourth Amendment.

I

Petitioner Russell Anderson is an agent of the Federal Bureau of Investigation. On November 11, 1983, Anderson and other state and federal law enforcement officers conducted a warrantless search of the home of respondents, the Creighton family. The search was conducted because Anderson believed that Vadaain Dixon, a man suspected of a bank robbery committed earlier that day, might be found there. He was not.

The Creightons later filed suit against Anderson in a Minnesota state court, asserting among other things a *Bivens* claim for money damages under the Fourth Amendment. After removing the suit to Federal District Court, Anderson filed a motion to dismiss or for summary judgment, arguing that the *Bivens* claim was barred by Anderson's qualified immunity from civil damages liability. Before any discovery took place, the District Court granted summary judgment on the ground that the search was lawful, holding that the undisputed facts revealed that Anderson had had probable cause to search the Creighton's home and that his failure to obtain a warrant was justified by the presence of exigent circumstances.

The Creightons appealed to the Court of Appeals for the Eighth Circuit, which reversed. The Court of Appeals held that the issue of the lawfulness of the search could not properly be decided on summary judgment, because unresolved factual disputes made it impossible to determine as a matter of law that the warrantless search had been supported by probable cause and exigent circumstances. The Court of Appeals also held that Anderson was not entitled to summary judgment on qualified immunity grounds, since the right Anderson was alleged to have violated — the right of persons to be protected from warrantless searches of their home unless the searching officers have probable cause and there are exigent circumstances — was clearly established.

Anderson filed a petition for certiorari, arguing that the Court of Appeals erred by refusing to consider his argument that he was entitled to summary judgment on qualified immunity grounds if he could establish as a matter of law that a reasonable officer could have believed the search to be lawful. We granted the petition to consider that important question.

II

When government officials abuse their offices, "action[s] for damages may offer the only realistic avenue for vindication of constitutional guarantees." On the other hand, permitting damages suits against government officials can entail substantial social costs, including the risk that fear of personal monetary liability and harassing litigation will unduly inhibit officials in the discharge of their duties. Our cases have accommodated these conflicting concerns by generally providing government officials performing discretionary functions with a qualified immunity, shielding them from civil damages liability as long as their actions could reasonably have been thought consistent with the rights they are alleged to have violated. Somewhat more concretely, whether an official protected by qualified immunity may be held personally liable for an allegedly unlawful official action generally turns on the "objective legal reasonableness" of the action assessed in light of the legal rules that were "clearly established" at the time it was taken.

The operation of this standard, however, depends substantially upon the level of generality at which the relevant "legal rule" is to be identified. For example, the right to due process of law is quite clearly established by the Due Process Clause, and thus there is a sense in which any action that violates that Clause (no matter how unclear it may be that the particular action is a violation) violates a clearly established right. Much the same could be said of any other constitutional or statutory violation. But if the test of "clearly established law" were to be applied at this level of generality, it would bear no relationship to the "objective legal reasonableness" that is the touchstone of *Harlow*. Plaintiffs would be able to convert the rule of qualified immunity that our cases plainly establish into a rule of virtually unqualified liability simply by alleging violation of extremely abstract rights. *Harlow* would be transformed from a guarantee of immunity into a rule of pleading. Such an approach, in sum, would destroy "the balance that our cases strike between the interests in vindication of citizens' constitutional rights and in public officials' effective performance of their duties," by making it impossible for officials "reasonably [to] anticipate when their conduct may give rise to liability for damages." It should not be surprising, therefore, that our cases establish that the right the official is alleged to have violated must have been "clearly established" in a more particularized, and hence more relevant, sense: The contours of the right must be sufficiently clear that a reasonable official would understand that what he is doing violates that right. This is not to say that an official action is protected by qualified immunity unless the very action in question has previously been held unlawful, but it is to say that in the light of pre-existing law the unlawfulness must be apparent.

Anderson contends that the Court of Appeals misapplied these principles. We agree. The Court of Appeals' brief discussion of qualified immunity consisted of little more than an assertion that a general right Anderson was alleged to have violated—the right to be free from warrantless searches of one's home unless the searching officers have probable cause and there are exigent circumstances—was clearly established. The Court of Appeals specifically refused to consider the argument that it was not clearly established that the circumstances with which Anderson was confronted did not constitute probable cause and exigent circumstances. The previous discussion should make clear that this refusal was erroneous. It simply does not follow immediately from the conclusion that it was firmly established that warrantless searches not supported by probable cause and exigent circumstances violate the Fourth Amendment that Anderson's search was objectively legally unreasonable. We have recognized that it is inevitable that law enforcement officials will in some cases reasonably but mistakenly conclude that probable cause is present, and we have indicated that in such cases those officials—like other officials who act in ways they reasonably believe to be lawful—should not be held personally liable. The same is true of their conclusions regarding exigent circumstances.

It follows from what we have said that the determination whether it was objectively legally reasonable to conclude that a given search was supported by probable cause or exigent circumstances will often require examination of the information possessed by the searching officials. But contrary to the Creightons' assertion, this does not reintroduce into qualified immunity analysis the inquiry into officials' subjective intent that *Harlow* sought to minimize. The relevant question in this case, for example, is the objective (albeit fact-specific) question whether a reasonable officer could have believed Anderson's warrantless search to be lawful, in light of clearly established law and the information the searching officers possessed. Anderson's subjective beliefs about the search are irrelevant.

The principles of qualified immunity that we reaffirm today require that Anderson be permitted to argue that he is entitled to summary judgment on the ground that, in light of the clearly established principles governing warrantless searches, he could, as a matter of law, reasonably have believed that the search of the Creightons' home was lawful.

III

In addition to relying on the reasoning of the Court of Appeals, the Creightons advance three alternative grounds for affirmance. All of these take the same form, i.e., that even if Anderson is entitled to qualified immunity under the usual principles of qualified immunity law we have just described, an exception should be made to those principles in the circumstances of this case. We note at the outset the heavy burden this argument must sustain to be successful. We have emphasized that the doctrine of qualified immunity reflects a balance that has been struck "across the board." Although we have in narrow circumstances provided officials with an absolute immunity, we have been unwilling to complicate qualified immunity analysis by making the scope or extent of immunity turn on the precise nature of various officials' duties or the precise character of the particular rights alleged to have been violated. An immunity that has as many variants as there are modes of official action and types of rights would not give conscientious officials that assurance of protection that it is the object of the doctrine to provide. With that observation in mind, we turn to the particular arguments advanced by the Creightons.

First, and most broadly, the Creightons argue that it is inappropriate to give officials alleged to have violated the Fourth Amendment—and thus necessarily to have unreasonably searched or seized—the protection of a qualified immunity intended only to protect reasonable official action. It is not possible, that is, to say that one "reasonably" acted unreasonably. The short answer to this argument is that it is foreclosed by the fact that we have previously extended qualified immunity to officials who were alleged to have violated the Fourth Amendment. Even if that were not so, however, we would still find the argument unpersuasive. Its surface appeal is attributable to the circumstance that the Fourth Amendment's guarantees have been expressed in terms of "unreasonable" searches and seizures. Had an equally serviceable term, such as "undue" searches and seizures been employed, what might be termed the "reasonably unreasonable" argument against application of *Harlow* to the Fourth Amendment would not be available—just as it would be available against application of *Harlow* to the Fifth Amendment if the term "reasonable process of law" had been employed there. The fact is that, regardless of the terminology used, the precise content of most of the Constitution's civil-liberties guarantees rests upon an assessment of what accommodation between governmental need and individual freedom is reasonable, so that the Creightons' objection, if it has any substance, applies to the application of *Harlow* generally. We have frequently observed, and our many cases on the point amply demonstrate, the difficulty of determining whether particular searches or seizures comport with the Fourth Amendment. Law enforcement officers whose judgments in making these difficult determinations are objectively legally reasonable should no more be held personally liable in damages than should officials making analogous determinations in other areas of law.

Finally, we reject the Creightons' narrowest and most procrustean proposal: that no immunity should be provided to police officers who conduct unlawful warrantless searches of innocent third parties' homes in search of fugitives. Although it is true that we have observed that our determinations as to the scope of official immunity are made in the light of the "common-law tradition," we have never suggested that the precise contours of official immunity can and should be slavishly derived from the often arcane rules of the common law. That notion is plainly contradicted by *Harlow*, where the Court completely reformulated qualified immunity along principles not at all embodied in the common law, replacing the inquiry into subjective malice so frequently required at common law with an objective inquiry into the legal reasonableness of the official action. As we noted before, *Harlow* clearly expressed the understanding that the general principle of qualified immunity it established would be applied "across the board."

The general rule of qualified immunity is intended to provide government officials with the ability "reasonably [to] anticipate when their conduct may give rise to liability for damages." Where that rule is applicable, officials can know that they will not be held personally liable as long as their actions are reasonable in light of current American law. That security would be utterly defeated if officials were unable to determine whether they were protected by the rule without entangling themselves in the vagaries of the English and American common law. We are unwilling to Balkanize the rule of qualified immunity by carving exceptions at the level of detail the Creightons propose. We therefore decline to make an exception to the general rule of qualified immunity for cases involving allegedly unlawful warrantless searches of innocent third parties' homes in search of fugitives.

For the reasons stated, we vacate the judgment of the Court of Appeals and remand the case for further proceedings consistent with this opinion.

[Justices Stevens, Marshall, and Brennan dissented.]

NOTES AND QUESTIONS

1. Why would law enforcement officers not be incentivized to go to the trouble of getting a search warrant for the search of a home where, as here, they believed a suspect in a case unrelated to the occupants of the home could be found?

2. The district court granted summary judgment for the defendant FBI agent Anderson, before any discovery had occurred, on the ground that the "undisputed facts" showed that he had probable cause to search the home based on exigent circumstances. The court of appeals reversed, finding factual disputes regarding both the probable cause and exigent circumstances inquiries.

How could the facts be undisputed prior to any discovery taking place?

3. The Eighth Circuit also rejected Anderson's qualified immunity claim because the right allegedly violated by defendant—the right of persons to be protected from warrantless searches of their homes absent probable cause and exigent circumstances—was a "clearly established" right within the meaning of *Harlow*.

Why was this conclusion erroneous? Why doesn't the Supreme Court identify the appropriate level of generality at which the "objective legal reasonableness" of Anderson's conduct should be considered? Is this determination purely a function of case law? What case law?

4. The Court here identifies an additional "social cost" of suits against public officials, not mentioned in *Harlow*: "the risk that fear of personal monetary liability . . . will unduly inhibit officials in the discharge of their duties." To the extent this is an important underpinning of the qualified immunity doctrine, should it matter whether any liability (as well as litigation expense) is actually borne by the official as opposed to the employer? *See infra.*

And on the subject of "social costs," aren't these more properly a subject for legislatures to evaluate and not courts?

5. The Court makes an impressively packaged concession in connection with rejecting an argument plaintiffs made based on English precedent: "[W]e have never suggested that the precise contours of official immunity can and should be slavishly derived from the often arcane rules of the common law." What is the Court trying to say here? That we're just making this up as we go along?

6. The dissent makes the point that the Court's decision requires applying a "double standard of reasonableness" in cases such as this one, determining whether a police officer acted reasonably in making the required Fourth Amendment evaluation. Is the standard objectionable as a matter of logic as well as because it unduly insulates police officers from liability?

The "double standard of reasonableness" issue will recur in § 1983 and *Bivens* claims based on police use of excessive force, which the Supreme Court definitively identified as a Fourth Amendment violation in *Graham v. Connor*, 490 U.S. 386 (1989). In the meantime, however, the Court was making sure that civil rights action defendants were given special procedural protections not enjoyed by other litigants.

In 1985, shortly after *Harlow* but before *Malley* and *Anderson*, the Court concluded that the normally applicable procedural rules—which *Harlow* changed the immunity doctrine to avoid—still weren't doing enough to protect § 1983 defendants. It saw an opportunity in *Mitchell v. Forsyth*, 472 U.S. 511 (1985), a claim against former Nixon Administration Attorney General John Mitchell alleging illegal wiretapping under 18 U.S.C. § 2511(3), a provision in Title III of the Omnibus Crime Control and Safe Streets Act of 1968, 18 U.S.C. §§ 2510-2520, a federal statute that for the first time had established comprehensive standards governing the use of wiretaps and electronic surveillance by both governmental and private agents.

Chapter VI Addressing Police Misconduct

In *Mitchell*, the Court repurposed qualified immunity as "an immunity from suit rather than a mere defense to liability." And under this reasoning the Court held that federal district court summary judgment decisions denying a defendant's claim of qualified immunity—though interlocutory—could be immediately appealed under the "collateral order" exception to the final judgment rule. *Id.* at 530. It so held despite such claims not being "conceptually distinct" from the merits, the usual requirement for the exception, and despite its characterization just three years earlier as an "affirmative defense," which normally must be asserted and proven at trial. Indeed, the Court continued even after *Mitchell* to describe qualified immunity as an affirmative defense. *See Corr. Servs. Corp. v. Malesko*, 534 U.S. 61, 69 (2001) (describing qualified immunity as an "affirmative defense"); *Siegert v. Gilley*, 500 U.S. 226, 231 (1991) ("Qualified immunity is a defense that must be pleaded by a defendant official.").

So just to review: In *Harlow* the Court completely transforms the substance of qualified immunity to make it easier for defendants to prevail on summary judgment under Rule 56. And then five years later in *Mitchell* the Court loosens the contours of the collateral order doctrine to allow defendants to circumvent the normal appellate rules.

The interplay between the qualified immunity doctrine and procedural norms was not over. In *Wyatt v. Cole*, 504 U.S. 158 (1992), in a concurring opinion, Justice Kennedy acknowledged that *Harlow* had "depart[ed] from history in the name of policy," and implied that that departure may have been premature inasmuch as just four years after *Harlow* the Court clarified that summary judgment can be granted even in cases where state-of-mind issues such as good faith can be dispositive. *Id.* at 171-72 (citing *Celotex Corp. v. Catrett*, 477 U.S. 317, 322 (1986)).

Many commentators, moreover, attribute the heightened pleading standards imposed by the Supreme Court in *Ashcroft v. Iqbal*, 556 U.S. 662 (2009), to the fact that the underlying claim was a *Bivens* action potentially implicating qualified immunity. *See, e.g.*, John M. Greabe, Iqbal, al-Kidd *and Pleading Past Qualified Immunity: What the Cases Mean and How They Demonstrate a Need to Eliminate the Immunity Doctrines from Constitutional Tort Law*, 20 Wm. & Mary Bill Rts. J. 1, 7-12 (2011).

In the next case the Supreme Court also imposes an unusual procedural requirement. In addressing qualified immunity for the first time in the context of a Fourth Amendment excessive force claim, the Court dictates to district courts the precise sequence in which issues should be decided.

Saucier v. Katz
533 U.S. 194 (2001)

Justice KENNEDY delivered the opinion of the Court.

In this case a citizen alleged excessive force was used to arrest him. The arresting officer asserted the defense of qualified immunity. The matter we address is whether the requisite analysis to determine qualified immunity is so intertwined with the question whether the officer used excessive force in making the arrest that qualified immunity and constitutional violation issues should be treated as one question, to be decided by the trier of fact. The Court of Appeals held the inquiries do merge into a single question. We now reverse and hold that the ruling on qualified immunity requires an analysis not susceptible of fusion with the question whether unreasonable force was used in making the arrest.

I

In autumn of 1994, the Presidio Army Base in San Francisco was the site of an event to celebrate conversion of the base to a national park. Among the speakers was Vice President

C. Qualified Immunity

Albert Gore, Jr., who attracted several hundred observers from the military and the general public. Some in attendance were not on hand to celebrate, however. Respondent Elliot Katz was concerned that the Army's Letterman Hospital would be used for conducting experiments on animals. (Katz was president of a group called In Defense of Animals. Although both he and the group are respondents here, the issues we discuss center upon Katz, and we refer to him as "respondent.") To voice opposition to the possibility that the hospital might be used for experiments, respondent brought with him a cloth banner, approximately 4 by 3 feet, that read "Please Keep Animal Torture Out of Our National Parks." In the past, as respondent was aware, members of the public had been asked to leave the military base when they engaged in certain activities, such as distributing handbills; and he kept the banner concealed under his jacket as he walked through the base.

The area designated for the speakers contained seating for the general public, separated from the stage by a waist-high fence. Respondent sat in the front row of the public seating area. At about the time Vice President Gore began speaking, respondent removed the banner from his jacket, started to unfold it, and walked toward the fence and speakers' platform.

Petitioner Donald Saucier is a military police officer who was on duty that day. He had been warned by his superiors of the possibility of demonstrations, and respondent had been identified as a potential protester. Petitioner and Sergeant Steven Parker—also a military police officer, but not a party to the suit—recognized respondent and moved to intercept him as he walked toward the fence. As he reached the barrier and began placing the banner on the other side, the officers grabbed respondent from behind, took the banner, and rushed him out of the area. Each officer had one of respondent's arms, half-walking, half-dragging him, with his feet "barely touching the ground." Respondent was wearing a visible, knee-high leg brace, although petitioner later testified he did not remember noticing it at the time. Saucier and Parker took respondent to a nearby military van, where, respondent claims, he was shoved or thrown inside. Id., at 25. The reason for the shove remains unclear. It seems agreed that respondent placed his feet somewhere on the outside of the van, perhaps the bumper, but there is a dispute whether he did so to resist. As a result of the shove, respondent claims, he fell to the floor of the van, where he caught himself just in time to avoid any injury. The officers drove respondent to a military police station, held him for a brief time, and then released him. Though the details are not clear, it appears that at least one other protester was also placed into the van and detained for a brief time.

Respondent brought this action in the United States District Court for the Northern District of California against petitioner and other officials pursuant to *Bivens*, alleging, inter alia, that defendants had violated respondent's Fourth Amendment rights by using excessive force to arrest him. The District Court granted the defendants' motions for summary judgment on the grounds of qualified immunity on all claims other than the excessive force claim against Saucier. It held a dispute on a material fact existed concerning whether excessive force was used to remove respondent from the crowd and place him into the van. The District Court held that the law governing excessive force claims was clearly established at the time of the arrest, and that "[i]n the Fourth Amendment context, the qualified immunity inquiry is the same as the inquiry made on the merits." As a result, it ruled, petitioner was not entitled to summary judgment.

In the United States Court of Appeals for the Ninth Circuit petitioner filed an interlocutory appeal from the denial of qualified immunity. The Court of Appeals affirmed, noting at the outset its two-part analysis for qualified immunity questions. First, the Court of Appeals considers "whether the law governing the official's conduct was clearly established." If it was not, that ends the matter, and the official is entitled to immunity. If, however, the law was clearly established when the conduct occurred, the Court of Appeals' second step is to determine if a reasonable officer could have believed, in light of the clearly established law, that his conduct was lawful. As to the first step of its analysis, the court observed that *Graham v. Connor*, 490 U.S. 386 (1989), sets forth the objective reasonableness test for evaluating excessive force claims, a principle the Court of Appeals concluded was clearly established for qualified immunity purposes. The court then concluded that the second step of the qualified immunity inquiry and the merits of the Fourth Amendment excessive force claim are identical, since both concern the objective reasonableness of the officer's conduct in light of the circumstances the officer faced on the scene. On this reasoning, summary judgment based on qualified immunity was held inappropriate.

Saucier, represented by the Government of the United States, sought review here, arguing the Court of Appeals erred in its view that the qualified immunity inquiry is the same as the constitutional inquiry and so becomes superfluous or duplicative when excessive force is alleged. We granted certiorari.

II

The Court of Appeals ruled first that the right was clearly established; and second that the reasonableness inquiry into excessive force meant that it need not consider aspects of qualified immunity, leaving the whole matter to the jury. This approach cannot be reconciled with *Anderson v. Creighton* (1987), however, and was in error in two respects. As we shall explain, the first inquiry must be whether a constitutional right would have been violated on the facts alleged; second, assuming the violation is established, the question whether the right was clearly established must be considered on a more specific level than recognized by the Court of Appeals.

In a suit against an officer for an alleged violation of a constitutional right, the requisites of a qualified immunity defense must be considered in proper sequence. Where the defendant seeks qualified immunity, a ruling on that issue should be made early in the proceedings so that the costs and expenses of trial are avoided where the defense is dispositive. Qualified immunity is "an entitlement not to stand trial or face the other burdens of litigation." The privilege is "an immunity from suit rather than a mere defense to liability; and like an absolute immunity, it is effectively lost if a case is erroneously permitted to go to trial." As a result, "we repeatedly have stressed the importance of resolving immunity questions at the earliest possible stage in litigation."

A court required to rule upon the qualified immunity issue must consider, then, this threshold question: Taken in the light most favorable to the party asserting the injury, do the facts alleged show the officer's conduct violated a constitutional right? This must be the initial inquiry. In the course of determining whether a constitutional right was violated on the premises alleged, a court might find it necessary to set forth principles which will become the basis for a holding that a right is clearly established. This is the process for the law's elaboration from case to case, and it is one reason for our insisting upon turning to the existence or nonexistence of a constitutional right as the first inquiry. The law might be deprived of this explanation were a court simply to skip ahead to the question whether the law clearly established that the officer's conduct was unlawful in the circumstances of the case.

If no constitutional right would have been violated were the allegations established, there is no necessity for further inquiries concerning qualified immunity. On the other hand, if a violation could be made out on a favorable view of the parties' submissions, the next, sequential step is to ask whether the right was clearly established. This inquiry, it is vital to note, must be undertaken in light of the specific context of the case, not as a broad general proposition; and it too serves to advance understanding of the law and to allow officers to avoid the burden of trial if qualified immunity is applicable.

In this litigation, for instance, there is no doubt that *Graham v. Connor, supra*, clearly establishes the general proposition that use of force is contrary to the Fourth Amendment if

C. Qualified Immunity   **611**

it is excessive under objective standards of reasonableness. Yet that is not enough. Rather, we emphasized in Anderson "that the right the official is alleged to have violated must have been 'clearly established' in a more particularized, and hence more relevant, sense: The contours of the right must be sufficiently clear that a reasonable official would understand that what he is doing violates that right." The relevant, dispositive inquiry in determining whether a right is clearly established is whether it would be clear to a reasonable officer that his conduct was unlawful in the situation he confronted.

The approach the Court of Appeals adopted—to deny summary judgment any time a material issue of fact remains on the excessive force claim—could undermine the goal of qualified immunity to "avoid excessive disruption of government and permit the resolution of many insubstantial claims on summary judgment." If the law did not put the officer on notice that his conduct would be clearly unlawful, summary judgment based on qualified immunity is appropriate.

This is not to say that the formulation of a general rule is beside the point, nor is it to insist the courts must have agreed upon the precise formulation of the standard. Assuming, for instance, that various courts have agreed that certain conduct is a constitutional violation under facts not distinguishable in a fair way from the facts presented in the case at hand, the officer would not be entitled to qualified immunity based simply on the argument that courts had not agreed on one verbal formulation of the controlling standard.

The Court of Appeals concluded that qualified immunity is merely duplicative in an excessive force case, eliminating the need for the second step where a constitutional violation could be found based on the allegations. In *Anderson*, a warrantless search case, we rejected the argument that there is no distinction between the reasonableness standard for warrantless searches and the qualified immunity inquiry. We acknowledged there was some "surface appeal" to the argument that, because the Fourth Amendment's guarantee was a right to be free from "unreasonable" searches and seizures, it would be inconsistent to conclude that an officer who acted unreasonably under the constitutional standard nevertheless was entitled to immunity because he "'reasonably' acted unreasonably." This superficial similarity, however, could not overcome either our history of applying qualified immunity analysis to Fourth Amendment claims against officers or the justifications for applying the doctrine in an area where officers perform their duties with considerable uncertainty as to "whether particular searches or seizures comport with the Fourth Amendment." With respect, moreover, to the argument made in *Anderson* that an exception should be made for Fourth Amendment cases, we observed "the heavy burden this argument must sustain to be successful," since "the doctrine of qualified immunity reflects a balance that has been struck 'across the board.'" We held that qualified immunity applied in the Fourth Amendment context just as it would for any other claim of official misconduct.

Faced, then, with the heavy burden of distinguishing *Anderson* and of carving out an exception to the typical qualified immunity analysis applied in other Fourth Amendment contexts, the primary submission by respondent in defense of the Court of Appeals' decision is that our decision in *Graham v. Connor* somehow changes matters. *Graham*, in respondent's view, sets forth an excessive force analysis indistinguishable from qualified immunity, rendering the separate immunity inquiry superfluous and inappropriate. Respondent asserts that, like the qualified immunity analysis applicable in other contexts, the excessive force test already affords officers latitude for mistaken beliefs as to the amount of force necessary, so that "*Graham* has addressed for the excessive force area most of the concerns expressed in *Anderson*." Respondent points out that *Graham* did not address the interaction of excessive force claims and qualified immunity, since the issue was not raised; and respondent seeks to distinguish *Anderson* on the theory that the issue of probable cause implicates evolving legal standards and resulting legal uncertainty, a subject raising recurrent questions of qualified immunity. By contrast, respondent says, excessive force is governed by the standard established in *Graham*, a standard providing ample guidance for particular situations. Finally, respondent adopts the suggestion made by one Court of Appeals that the relevant distinction is that probable cause is an ex post inquiry, whereas excessive force, like qualified immunity, should be evaluated from an ex ante perspective.

These arguments or attempted distinctions cannot bear the weight respondent seeks to place upon them. *Graham* did not change the qualified immunity framework explained in *Anderson*. The inquiries for qualified immunity and excessive force remain distinct, even after *Graham*.

In *Graham*, we held that claims of excessive force in the context of arrests or investigatory stops should be analyzed under the Fourth Amendment's "objective reasonableness standard," not under substantive due process principles. Because "police officers are often forced to make split-second judgments — in circumstances that are tense, uncertain, and rapidly evolving — about the amount of force that is necessary in a particular situation," the reasonableness of the officer's belief as to the appropriate level of force should be judged from that on-scene perspective. We set out a test that cautioned against the "20/20 vision of hindsight" in favor of deference to the judgment of reasonable officers on the scene. *Graham* sets forth a list of factors relevant to the merits of the constitutional excessive force claim, "requir[ing] careful attention to the facts and circumstances of each particular case, including the severity of the crime at issue, whether the suspect poses an immediate threat to the safety of the officers or others, and whether he is actively resisting arrest or attempting to evade arrest by flight." If an officer reasonably, but mistakenly, believed that a suspect was likely to fight back, for instance, the officer would be justified in using more force than in fact was needed.

The qualified immunity inquiry, on the other hand, has a further dimension. The concern of the immunity inquiry is to acknowledge that reasonable mistakes can be made as to the legal constraints on particular police conduct. It is sometimes difficult for an officer to determine how the relevant legal doctrine, here excessive force, will apply to the factual situation the officer confronts. An officer might correctly perceive all of the relevant facts but have a mistaken understanding as to whether a particular amount of force is legal in those circumstances. If the officer's mistake as to what the law requires is reasonable, however, the officer is entitled to the immunity defense.

Graham does not always give a clear answer as to whether a particular application of force will be deemed excessive by the courts. This is the nature of a test which must accommodate limitless factual circumstances. This reality serves to refute respondent's claimed distinction between excessive force and other Fourth Amendment contexts; in both spheres the law must be elaborated from case to case. Qualified immunity operates in this case, then, just as it does in others, to protect officers from the sometimes "hazy border between excessive and acceptable force," and to ensure that before they are subjected to suit, officers are on notice their conduct is unlawful.

Graham and *Anderson* refute the excessive force/probable cause distinction on which much of respondent's position seems to depend. The deference owed officers facing suits for alleged excessive force is not different in some qualitative respect from the probable-cause inquiry in *Anderson.* Officers can have reasonable, but mistaken, beliefs as to the facts establishing the existence of probable cause or exigent circumstances, for example, and in those situations courts will not hold that they have violated the Constitution. Yet, even if a court were to hold that the officer violated the Fourth Amendment by conducting an unreasonable, warrantless search, *Anderson* still operates to grant officers immunity for reasonable mistakes as to the legality of their actions. The same analysis is applicable in excessive force cases, where in addition to the deference officers receive on the underlying constitutional claim, qualified immunity can apply in the event the mistaken belief was reasonable.

III

The case was presented to the Court of Appeals on the assumption that respondent's seizure and brief detention did not violate clearly established First Amendment privileges and did not violate the Fourth Amendment right to be free from arrest without probable cause, as distinct from the force used to detain. The sole question, then, is whether the force used violated a clearly established Fourth Amendment protection so that petitioner was not entitled to immunity.

Our instruction to the district courts and courts of appeals to concentrate at the outset on the definition of the constitutional right and to determine whether, on the facts alleged, a constitutional violation could be found is important. As we have said, the procedure permits courts in appropriate cases to elaborate the constitutional right with greater degrees of specificity. Because we granted certiorari only to determine whether qualified immunity was appropriate, however, and because of the limits imposed upon us by the questions on which we granted review, we will assume a constitutional violation could have occurred under the facts alleged based simply on the general rule prohibiting excessive force, then proceed to the question whether this general prohibition against excessive force was the source for clearly established law that was contravened in the circumstances this officer faced. There was no contravention under this standard. Though it is doubtful that the force used was excessive, we need not rest our conclusion on that determination. The question is what the officer reasonably understood his powers and responsibilities to be, when he acted, under clearly established standards.

Respondent's excessive force claim for the most part depends upon the "gratuitously violent shove" allegedly received when he was placed into the van, although respondent notes as well that the alleged violation resulted from the "totality of the circumstances," including the way he was removed from the speaking area.

These circumstances, however, disclose substantial grounds for the officer to have concluded he had legitimate justification under the law for acting as he did. In *Graham* we noted that "[o]ur Fourth Amendment jurisprudence has long recognized that the right to make an arrest or investigatory stop necessarily carries with it the right to use some degree of physical coercion or threat thereof to effect it." A reasonable officer in petitioner's position could have believed that hurrying respondent away from the scene, where the Vice President was speaking and respondent had just approached the fence designed to separate the public from the speakers, was within the bounds of appropriate police responses.

Petitioner did not know the full extent of the threat respondent posed or how many other persons there might be who, in concert with respondent, posed a threat to the security of the Vice President. There were other potential protesters in the crowd, and at least one other individual was arrested and placed into the van with respondent. In carrying out the detention, as it has been assumed the officers had the right to do, petitioner was required to recognize the necessity to protect the Vice President by securing respondent and restoring order to the scene. It cannot be said there was a clearly established rule that would prohibit using the force petitioner did to place respondent into the van to accomplish these objectives.

As for the shove respondent received when he was placed into the van, those same circumstances show some degree of urgency. We have approved the observation that "[n]ot every push or shove, even if it may later seem unnecessary in the peace of a judge's chambers,

614   Chapter VI Addressing Police Misconduct

violates the Fourth Amendment." Ibid. (citations omitted). Pushes and shoves, like other police conduct, must be judged under the Fourth Amendment standard of reasonableness.

In the circumstances presented to this officer, which included the duty to protect the safety and security of the Vice President of the United States from persons unknown in number, neither respondent nor the Court of Appeals has identified any case demonstrating a clearly established rule prohibiting the officer from acting as he did, nor are we aware of any such rule. Our conclusion is confirmed by the uncontested fact that the force was not so excessive that respondent suffered hurt or injury. On these premises, petitioner was entitled to qualified immunity, and the suit should have been dismissed at an early stage in the proceedings.

The judgment of the Court of Appeals is reversed, and the case is remanded for further proceedings consistent with this opinion.

NOTES AND QUESTIONS

1. Does the Court's description of the excessive force claim here — an uncalled-for "shove" — telegraph how this case is going to come out?

2. *Saucier* resolved a circuit split over how to analyze qualified immunity in the context of excessive force claims under *Graham v. Connor*, 490 U.S. 386 (1989). Prior to *Saucier*, a majority of circuits had held that a qualified immunity defense was unavailable in excessive force cases under the theory that the substantive reasonableness component of the merits claim is coterminous with the reasonableness standard in the defense. *See, e.g., Jackson v. Hoylman*, 933 F.2d 401, 402-03 (6th Cir. 1991) (affirming the district court's determination that "qualified immunity turns on the same objective reasonableness standard that the claim of excessive force turns on . . ."); *see generally* Osagie K. Obasogie & Anna Zaret, *Plainly Incompetent: How Qualified Immunity Became an Exculpatory Doctrine of Police Excessive Force*, 170 U. Pa. L. Rev. 407 (2022) (discussing qualified immunity in excessive force cases).

3. In siding with the minority side of the circuit split the Court endorses a "double standard of reasonableness" similar to the one it found appropriate in *Anderson v. Creighton, supra*. Are there meaningful distinctions between a police officer's actions in assessing probable cause and in exercising force that could justify a different outcome in the latter context? Put differently, in which context should police officers be entitled to a greater amount of leeway?

4. In decreeing the sequence in which lower courts must decide the merits and immunity issues, the Court suggests that the purpose of this requirement is the development of a body of constitutional law. Is this a sufficient justification for imposing such a burden on the lower courts?

If a district court or a court of appeals finds (a) that a complaint adequately alleges a violation of a constitutional right but also finds (b) that the right was not "clearly established," is the former decision dicta?

Is the Court's decree inconsistent with the general rule that constitutional questions should be avoided where possible?

5. The sequencing aspect of *Saucier* was effectively overruled just eight years later in *Pearson v. Callahan*, 555 U.S. 223, 227 (2009), where the Court held that the sequencing it had decreed in *Saucier* was no longer mandatory. Among other things, the Court noted that the opinions resulting from adherence to *Saucier* "often fail to make a meaningful contribution" to the development of constitutional precedent.

Why is that not surprising?

In the next case the Court considers the application of qualified immunity in the context of a police officer's use of deadly force.

C. Qualified Immunity

Mullenix v. Luna
577 U.S. 7 (2015)

PER CURIAM.

On the night of March 23, 2010, Sergeant Randy Baker of the Tulia, Texas Police Department followed Israel Leija, Jr., to a drive-in restaurant, with a warrant for his arrest. When Baker approached Leija's car and informed him that he was under arrest, Leija sped off, headed for Interstate 27. Baker gave chase and was quickly joined by Trooper Gabriel Rodriguez of the Texas Department of Public Safety (DPS).

Leija entered the interstate and led the officers on an 18-minute chase at speeds between 85 and 110 miles per hour. Twice during the chase, Leija called the Tulia Police dispatcher, claiming to have a gun and threatening to shoot at police officers if they did not abandon their pursuit. The dispatcher relayed Leija's threats, together with a report that Leija might be intoxicated, to all concerned officers.

As Baker and Rodriguez maintained their pursuit, other law enforcement officers set up tire spikes at three locations. Officer Troy Ducheneaux of the Canyon Police Department manned the spike strip at the first location Leija was expected to reach, beneath the overpass at Cemetery Road. Ducheneaux and the other officers had received training on the deployment of spike strips, including on how to take a defensive position so as to minimize the risk posed by the passing driver.

DPS Trooper Chadrin Mullenix also responded. He drove to the Cemetery Road overpass, initially intending to set up a spike strip there. Upon learning of the other spike strip positions, however, Mullenix began to consider another tactic: shooting at Leija's car in order to disable it. Mullenix had not received training in this tactic and had not attempted it before, but he radioed the idea to Rodriguez. Rodriguez responded "10-4," gave Mullenix his position, and said that Leija had slowed to 85 miles per hour. Mullenix then asked the DPS dispatcher to inform his supervisor, Sergeant Byrd, of his plan and ask if Byrd thought it was "worth doing." Before receiving Byrd's response, Mullenix exited his vehicle and, armed with his service rifle, took a shooting position on the overpass, 20 feet above I-27. Respondents allege that from this position, Mullenix still could hear Byrd's response to "stand by" and "see if the spikes work first."

As Mullenix waited for Leija to arrive, he and another officer, Randall County Sheriff's Deputy Tom Shipman, discussed whether Mullenix's plan would work and how and where to shoot the vehicle to best carry it out. Shipman also informed Mullenix that another officer was located beneath the overpass.

Approximately three minutes after Mullenix took up his shooting position, he spotted Leija's vehicle, with Rodriguez in pursuit. As Leija approached the overpass, Mullenix fired six shots. Leija's car continued forward beneath the overpass, where it engaged the spike strip, hit the median, and rolled two and a half times. It was later determined that Leija had been killed by Mullenix's shots, four of which struck his upper body. There was no evidence that any of Mullenix's shots hit the car's radiator, hood, or engine block.

Respondents sued Mullenix under 42 U.S.C. § 1983, alleging that he had violated the Fourth Amendment by using excessive force against Leija. Mullenix moved for summary judgment on the ground of qualified immunity, but the District Court denied his motion, finding that "[t]here are genuine issues of fact as to whether Trooper Mullenix acted recklessly, or acted as a reasonable, trained peace officer would have acted in the same or similar circumstances."

Mullenix appealed, and the Court of Appeals for the Fifth Circuit affirmed. The court agreed with the District Court that the "immediacy of the risk posed by Leija is a disputed fact that a reasonable jury could find either in the plaintiffs' favor or in the officer's favor, precluding us from concluding that Mullenix acted objectively reasonably as a matter of law."

Judge King dissented. She described the "'fact issue' referenced by the majority" as "simply a restatement of the objective reasonableness test that applies to Fourth Amendment excessive force claims," which, she noted, the Supreme Court has held "'is a pure question of law.'" Turning to that legal question, Judge King concluded that Mullenix's actions were objectively reasonable. When Mullenix fired, she emphasized, he knew not only that Leija had threatened to shoot the officers involved in his pursuit, but also that Leija was seconds away from encountering such an officer beneath the overpass. Judge King also dismissed the notion that Mullenix should have given the spike strips a chance to work. She explained that because spike strips are often ineffective, and because officers operating them are vulnerable to gunfire from passing cars, Mullenix reasonably feared that the officers manning them faced a significant risk of harm.

We address only the qualified immunity question, not whether there was a Fourth Amendment violation in the first place, and now reverse.

• • •

In this case, Mullenix confronted a reportedly intoxicated fugitive, set on avoiding capture through high-speed vehicular flight, who twice during his flight had threatened to shoot police officers, and who was moments away from encountering an officer at Cemetery Road. The relevant inquiry is whether existing precedent placed the conclusion that Mullenix acted unreasonably in these circumstances "beyond debate." The general principle that deadly force requires a sufficient threat hardly settles this matter.

Far from clarifying the issue, excessive force cases involving car chases reveal the hazy legal backdrop against which Mullenix acted. In *Brosseau* itself, the Court held that an officer did not violate clearly established law when she shot a fleeing suspect out of fear that he endangered "other officers on foot who [she] believed were in the immediate area," "the occupied vehicles in [his] path," and "any other citizens who might be in the area." The threat Leija posed was at least as immediate as that presented by a suspect who had just begun to drive off and was headed only in the general direction of officers and bystanders. By the time Mullenix fired, Leija had led police on a 25-mile chase at extremely high speeds, was reportedly intoxicated, had twice threatened to shoot officers, and was racing towards an officer's location.

This Court has considered excessive force claims in connection with high-speed chases on only two occasions since *Brosseau*. In *Scott v. Harris*, the Court held that an officer did not violate the Fourth Amendment by ramming the car of a fugitive whose reckless driving "posed an actual and imminent threat to the lives of any pedestrians who might have been present, to other civilian motorists, and to the officers involved in the chase." And in *Plumhoff v. Rickard* (2014), the Court reaffirmed *Scott* by holding that an officer acted reasonably when he fatally shot a fugitive who was "intent on resuming" a chase that "pose[d] a deadly threat for others on the road." The Court has thus never found the use of deadly force in connection with a dangerous car chase to violate the Fourth Amendment, let alone to be a basis for denying qualified immunity. Leija in his flight did not pass as many cars as the drivers in *Scott* or *Plumhoff*; traffic was light on I-27. At the same time, the fleeing fugitives in *Scott* and *Plumhoff* had not verbally threatened to kill any officers in their path, nor were they about to come upon such officers. In any event, none of our precedents "squarely governs" the facts here. Given Leija's conduct, we cannot say that only someone "plainly incompetent" or who "knowingly violate[s] the law" would have perceived a sufficient threat and acted as Mullenix did.

• • •

Because the constitutional rule applied by the Fifth Circuit was not "'beyond debate,'" we grant Mullenix's petition for certiorari and reverse the Fifth Circuit's determination that Mullenix is not entitled to qualified immunity.

NOTES AND QUESTIONS

1. The Court emphasizes multiple times that Leija had stated to the dispatcher that he would kill police officers, a fact that may have been necessary to bring the defendant's conduct within the ambit of the rule announced by the Court in *Tennessee v. Garner*, 471 U.S. 1 (1985).

Would the result here have been different if those threats had not been made?

What if Mullenix had admitted at his deposition that he was unaware of those threats? Or that he would have done everything the same even if those threats had not been made?

2. Justice Scalia, concurring, rejects the formulation of the facts here as "application of deadly force." Do you agree? Is it dispositive of this issue that Mullenix fired shots from his rifle in order to stop the car and not to hit the driver?

3. In finding that the defendant had violated clearly established law the Fifth Circuit had relied in part on one of its precedents — *Lytle v. Bexar County*, 560 F.3d 404 (5th Cir. 2009), where it had denied qualified immunity to an officer who had fired at a fleeing car and killed a passenger. The Supreme Court rejects the notion that this precedent did not make what Mullenix did a violation of clearly established law because the car in this case was not fleeing but coming at him.

What does this tell you about the Court's view of the appropriate level of generality at which the immunity inquiry must take place?

Lower courts have no choice against this backdrop but to look for precedent that is right on point. *See Baxter v. Bracey*, 751 F. App'x 869, 870 (6th Cir. 2018), *cert. denied*, 140 S. Ct. 1862 (2020) (defendant officer entitled to qualified immunity in excessive force case for decision to release a police dog on a defendant who was surrendering with his hands up because the nearest precedent only found a violation where police had released their dog on an individual who was lying down).

4. In dissent in *Mullenix* Justice Sotomayor offers an additional fact that she concedes has no significance to the appropriate legal analysis in the case but does have "big picture" import:

> When Mullenix confronted his superior officer after the shooting, his first words were, "How's that for proactive?" (Mullenix was apparently referencing an earlier counseling session in which Byrd suggested that he was not enterprising enough. [577 U.S. at 25-26]) The glib comment does not impact our legal analysis; an officer's actual intentions are irrelevant to the Fourth Amendment's "objectively reasonable" inquiry. But the comment seems to me revealing of the culture this Court's decision supports when it calls it reasonable — or even reasonably reasonable — to use deadly force for no discernible gain and over a supervisor's express order to "stand by." By sanctioning a "shoot first, think later" approach to policing, the Court renders the protections of the Fourth Amendment hollow.

The Supreme Court seems to have singled out cases involving uses of deadly force, such as *Mullenix*, for particular deference in recent years. *See, e.g., Brosseau v. Haugen*, 543 U.S. 194, 195-97 (2004) (per curiam) (overturning lower court decision denying qualified immunity to a police officer who shot plaintiff in the back); *Plumhoff v. Rickard*, 572 U.S. 765, 768-70 (2014) (granting qualified immunity to police officers who shot and killed the driver and passenger in a "dangerous" fleeing car); *City and County of San Francisco v. Sheehan*, 575 U.S. 600, 603-06, 617 (2015) (granting qualified immunity to officers who shot a mentally ill woman in her group home when she would not drop a knife); *White v. Pauly*, 580 U.S. 73 (2017) (per curiam) (granting immunity to an officer who shot an armed home occupant during a standoff); *Kisela v. Hughes*, 584 U.S. 100, 101-08 (2018) (per curiam) (granting immunity to an officer who shot a mentally ill woman armed with a kitchen knife). *But see City of Escondido v. Emmons*, 586 U.S. 38, 39-44 (2019) (per curiam) (reversing lower court decision to grant immunity to an officer who forcibly took a man to the ground as

618 Chapter VI Addressing Police Misconduct

he attempted to walk past them); *City of Tahlequah v. Bond*, 595 U.S. 9, 10-11 (2021) (per curiam) (reversing lower court decision to deny qualified immunity to police who shot man wielding a hammer). *See Kisela*, 584 U.S. at 121 (Sotomayor, J., dissenting) (noting the Court has "unflinching willingness to summarily reverse courts for wrongly denying officers the protection of qualified immunity but rarely intervene[s] where courts wrongly afford officers the benefit of qualified immunity in these same cases").

Notwithstanding all of the above, a leading academic on the subject has suggested there may be "cracks in qualified immunity's armor." Joanna C. Schwartz, *The Case Against Qualified Immunity*, 93 Notre Dame L. Rev. 1797 (2018). Perhaps the most significant crack is the following concurring opinion by Justice Thomas.

Ziglar v. Abbasi
582 U.S. 120 (2017)

THOMAS, J., concurring.

As for respondents' claims under 42 U.S.C. § 1985(3), I join Part V of the Court's opinion, which holds that respondents are entitled to qualified immunity. The Court correctly applies our precedents, which no party has asked us to reconsider. I write separately, however, to note my growing concern with our qualified immunity jurisprudence.

The Civil Rights Act of 1871, of which § 1985(3) and the more frequently litigated § 1983 were originally a part, established causes of action for plaintiffs to seek money damages from Government officers who violated federal law. Although the Act made no mention of defenses or immunities, "we have read it in harmony with general principles of tort immunities and defenses rather than in derogation of them." We have done so because "[c]ertain immunities were so well established in 1871 . . . that 'we presume that Congress would have specifically so provided had it wished to abolish' them." Immunity is thus available under the statute if it was "historically accorded the relevant official" in an analogous situation "at common law," unless the statute provides some reason to think that Congress did not preserve the defense.

In some contexts, we have conducted the common-law inquiry that the statute requires. For example, we have concluded that legislators and judges are absolutely immune from liability under § 1983 for their official acts because that immunity was well established at common law in 1871. *Tenney v. Brandhove* (1951) (legislators); *Pierson v. Ray* (1967) (judges). We have similarly looked to the common law in holding that a prosecutor is immune from suits relating to the "judicial phase of the criminal process." *Imbler.*

In developing immunity doctrine for other executive officers, we also started off by applying common-law rules. In *Pierson*, we held that police officers are not absolutely immune from a § 1983 claim arising from an arrest made pursuant to an unconstitutional statute because the common law never granted arresting officers that sort of immunity. Rather, we concluded that police officers could assert "the defense of good faith and probable cause" against the claim for an unconstitutional arrest because that defense was available against the analogous torts of "false arrest and imprisonment" at common law.

In further elaborating the doctrine of qualified immunity for executive officials, however, we have diverged from the historical inquiry mandated by the statute. In the decisions following *Pierson*, we have "completely reformulated qualified immunity along principles not at all embodied in the common law." *Anderson v. Creighton* (1987) (discussing *Harlow v. Fitzgerald* (1982)). Instead of asking whether the common law in 1871 would have accorded immunity to an officer for a tort analogous to the plaintiff's claim under § 1983, we instead grant immunity to any officer whose conduct "does not violate clearly established statutory or constitutional rights of which a reasonable person would have known." We apply this "clearly established" standard "across the board" and without regard to "the precise nature of the various officials' duties or the precise character of the particular rights alleged to have been violated." We have not attempted to locate that standard in the common law as it existed in 1871, however, and some evidence supports the conclusion that common-law immunity as it existed in 1871 looked quite different from our current doctrine. *See generally* Baude, Is Qualified Immunity Unlawful? 106 Cal. L. Rev. (forthcoming 2018).

Because our analysis is no longer grounded in the common-law backdrop against which Congress enacted the 1871 Act, we are no longer engaged in "interpret[ing] the intent of Congress in enacting" the Act. Our qualified immunity precedents instead represent precisely the sort of "freewheeling policy choice[s]" that we have previously disclaimed the power to make. We have acknowledged, in fact, that the "clearly established" standard is designed to "protec[t] the balance between vindication of constitutional rights and government officials' effective performance of their duties." The Constitution assigns this kind of balancing to Congress, not the Courts.

In today's decision, we continue down the path our precedents have marked. We ask "whether it would have been clear to a reasonable officer that the alleged conduct was unlawful in the situation he confronted," rather than whether officers in petitioners' positions would have been accorded immunity at common law in 1871 from claims analogous to respondents'. Even if we ultimately reach a conclusion consistent with the common-law rules prevailing in 1871, it is mere fortuity. Until we shift the focus of our inquiry to whether immunity existed at common law, we will continue to substitute our own policy preferences for the mandates of Congress. In an appropriate case, we should reconsider our qualified immunity jurisprudence.

Another significant potential "crack" in qualified immunity's armor is that two of the most important policy reasons that led the Supreme Court to create the doctrine in the first place — protecting police officers and other officials from the expense of litigation and judgments — have proven over time to be fallacious. In a study of dozens of police departments Professor Schwartz concluded that police officers almost never pay for defense counsel or damages, sometimes because of their employer's indemnification obligations and sometimes because of custom and practice. Schwartz, *The Case Against Qualified Immunity, supra* at 1804-07. *See Richardson v. McKnight*, 521 U.S. 399, 408-12 (1997) (rejecting qualified immunity claim of prison guards at a private, for-profit prison in part because the private character of the guards' employer "increases the likelihood of employee indemnification"). The other policy reasons the Court identified in *Harlow* as justifications for robust immunity — not discouraging people from public service, and ensuring that public officials are not unduly timid — are largely a function of the expense issue. That leaves only the "distraction of litigation" as a valid policy justification. If the President of the United States is required to defend against civil litigation while in office, *Clinton v. Jones*, 520 U.S. 681 (1997), why shouldn't police officers be required to do the same?

There is also a remote possibility of legislative reform. In the wake of the George Floyd murder in 2020, the House passed several bills modifying or eliminating qualified immunity. *See* Qualified Immunity Act of 2021, H.R. 288, 117th Cong. (2021); Ending Qualified Immunity Act, H.R. 1470, 117th Cong. (2021); Ending Qualified Immunity Act, S. 492, 117th Cong. (2021).

D. THE DEPARTMENT OF JUSTICE AND STRUCTURAL REFORM LITIGATION

Why can't the Department of Justice—Justice!—do something about local police misconduct besides just occasionally prosecuting police officers for constitutional violations? After all, such one-off criminal prosecutions are crude vehicles for changing the behavior of police departments, where misconduct may be endemic. It's not that it hasn't tried. In the 1970s the DOJ filed a civil action against Philadelphia alleging a litany of abusive and racist police practices that deprived persons of their due process rights. *United States v. City of Philadelphia*, 644 F.2d 187 (3d Cir. 1980). As authority for its suit, the Department claimed an implied right of action based on 18 U.S.C. §§ 241 and 242 and/or its authority under Article II, § 3 of the Constitution to "take care that the laws be faithfully executed," citing *Bivens* among other things. The Third Circuit rejected both arguments and dismissed the lawsuit.

Eleven years later there was videotape. On March 3, 1991, LAPD officers were captured on videotape viciously beating Black motorist Rodney King and landing dozens of blows even after King was submissive and then motionless. A grainy black-and-white videotape of the beating, which began recording after King had resisted the officers and the beatings had begun, was made with an early version of a "camcorder" by plumber George Holliday, a resident of an apartment complex across the street from where King was apprehended, who just happened to be out on his balcony. After being rebuffed by the local branch of the LAPD, Holliday took the tape to Los Angeles news station KTLA, which immediately aired the videotape, as eventually did television stations around the world. *See* Chapter X *infra*.

Congress was spurred into action, and the consequence was the passage of 42 U.S.C. § 14141. The statute authorizes the Department of Justice to seek equitable or declaratory relief, *id.* § 14141(b), against any government authority or agent of such authority that engages in a "pattern or practice" of conduct that violates the Constitution or laws of the United States, *id.* § 14141(a). The statute was praised by scholars as a potentially revolutionary reform. *See, e.g.*, Barbara E. Armacost, *Organizational Culture and Police Misconduct*, 72 Geo. Wash. L. Rev. 453, 464-65 (2004) (describing § 14141 as "perhaps the most promising legal mechanism" for reducing police misconduct); William J. Stuntz, *The Pathological Politics of Criminal Law*, 100 Mich. L. Rev. 505, 538-39 n.134 (2001) (describing § 14141 as possibly "more significant, in the long run, than *Mapp v. Ohio*"). (42 U.S.C. § 14141 has been reclassified as § 12601 of Title 34 of the United States Code. To remain consistent with cited works and to avoid confusion, § 14141 will be used throughout this section.)

For reasons that will be explained below, there is almost never litigation under the statute. The City of Columbus, Ohio, however, did bring an early challenge to the department's authority under the statute, and the decision rejecting the challenge nicely explains the statute's text and backdrop.

United States v. City of Columbus
2000 WL 1133166 (S.D. Ohio Aug. 3, 2000)

REPORT AND RECOMMENDATION

KING, Magistrate J.

This is an action for injunctive and declaratory relief, instituted under the provisions of 42 U.S.C. § 14141, in which the United States alleges that officers of the Columbus Division of Police have engaged in a pattern or practice of conduct violative of federal law and that the

D. The Department of Justice and Structural Reform Litigation

621

defendant city has tolerated the alleged misconduct by failing to implement adequate policies, training, supervision, monitoring and incident investigation procedures. This matter is now before the Court on the motion to dismiss filed by the defendant city and on the motion for judgment on the pleadings filed by the defendant-intervenor, the Fraternal Order of Police, City Lodge No. 9.

In their motions, the movants argue, first, that the Court is without subject matter jurisdiction over the claims asserted in the action because Congress exceeded its constitutional authority in promulgating the statute upon which the complaint is based, 42 U.S.C. § 14141. Movants argue, in the alternative, that the original complaint fails to state a claim upon which relief can be granted because it purports to impose vicarious liability on the defendant city, because it fails to allege with specificity the claimed wrongdoing of the defendant city or its police officers, and because its allegations are, in whole or in part, untimely. Although plaintiff has filed a motion for leave to amend the complaint in order to assert an additional claim of racially discriminatory conduct, that motion remains pending. The Court will therefore consider the movants' motions solely by reference to the original complaint.

· · ·

II. THE ORIGINAL COMPLAINT

The original complaint alleges that Columbus police officers have engaged in, and continue to engage in, a pattern or practice of using excessive force, Complaint, ¶ 6, falsely arresting individuals, Id., ¶ 7, and falsifying official reports and conducting searches either without lawful authority or in an improper manner. Id., ¶ 8(a), (b). The complaint further alleges that the City of Columbus has "tolerated the misconduct of individual officers," Id., ¶ 9, by failing "to implement a policy on use of force that appropriately guides the actions of individual officers," Id., ¶ 9(a), by failing to adequately "train," "supervise," and "monitor" officers, Id., ¶ 9(b)-(d), and by failing to "establish a procedure whereby citizen complaints are adequately investigated," Id., ¶ 9(e), "investigate adequately incidents in which a police officer uses lethal or non-lethal force," Id., ¶ 9(f), "fairly and adequately adjudicate or review citizen complaints, and incidents in which an officer uses lethal or non-lethal force," Id., ¶ 9(g), and "discipline adequately . . . officers who engage in misconduct." Id., ¶ 9(h). The complaint seeks a declaration that the city "is engaged in a pattern or practice by . . . officers of depriving persons of rights, privileges, or immunities secured or protected by the Constitution or laws of the United States," and asks that the Court enjoin the city "from engaging in any of the predicate acts forming the basis of the pattern or practice of conduct as described . . ." and order the city "to adopt and implement policies, practices, and procedures to remedy the pattern or practice of conduct described . . . and to prevent officers from depriving persons of rights, privileges or immunities secured or protected by the Constitution or laws of the United States. . . ."

III. THE STATUTE

The original complaint asserts claims under 42 U.S.C. § 14141. That statute, enacted as part of the Violent Crime Control and Law Enforcement Act of 1994, reads in full as follows:

Cause of Action

(a) Unlawful Conduct

It shall be unlawful for any governmental authority, or any agent thereof, or any person acting on behalf of a governmental authority, to engage in a pattern or practice of conduct by law enforcement officers or by officials or employees of any governmental agency with responsibility for the administration of juvenile justice or the incarceration of juveniles that deprives persons of rights, privileges, or immunities secured or protected by the Constitution or laws of the United States.

(b) Civil Action by Attorney General

Whenever the Attorney General has reasonable cause to believe that a violation of paragraph (1) has occurred, the Attorney General, for or in the name of the United States, may in a civil action obtain appropriate equitable and declaratory relief to eliminate the pattern or practice.

The parties agree that § 14141, which has no direct legislative history and which has never been construed by any court, is a successor to an earlier, nearly identical, provision of the Omnibus Crime Control Act of 1991, which was never actually promulgated. All parties also refer to the legislative history of that provision in their discussion of 42 U.S.C. § 14141.

Like § 14141, the earlier statute was intended to confer standing on the United States Attorney General to obtain civil injunctive relief against governmental authorities for patterns or practices of unconstitutional police practices. In considering the need for such legislation, the House Subcommittee on Civil and Constitutional Rights held two days of hearings and, in its report, the Committee on the Judiciary specifically referred to the Rodney King incident in Los Angeles, and to alleged misconduct within the Boston, New York City and Reynoldsburg, Ohio, Police Departments. Although recognizing that police misconduct violates the United States Constitution and, under 18 U.S.C. §§ 241, 242, can give rise to federal criminal liability, the Committee also noted that, under *United States v. City of Philadelphia*, 644 F.2d 187 (3d Cir. 1980), the United States had neither statutory nor constitutional authority to sue a police department itself "to correct the underlying policy." The problem was compounded, the Committee concluded, by the Supreme Court's holding, in *Los Angeles v. Lyons*, 461 U.S. 95 (1983), that, although a private citizen victimized by police misconduct could recover monetary relief under 42 U.S.C. § 1983, future injunctive relief remained unavailable absent a showing of likely future harm to that particular plaintiff. The proposed statute, the committee stated in its report, "would close this gap in the law, authorizing the Attorney General . . . to sue for injunctive relief against abusive police practices." Significantly, the Committee went on to explain:

> The Act does not increase the responsibilities of police departments or impose any new standards of conduct on police officers. The standards of conduct under the Act are the same as those under the Constitution, presently enforced in damage actions under section 1983. The Act merely provides another tool for a court to use, after a police department is held responsible for a pattern or practice of misconduct that violates the Constitution or laws of the United States.
>
> Because the Act imposes no new standard of conduct on law enforcement agencies, it should not increase the amount of litigation against police departments. Individuals aggrieved by the use of excessive force already can and do sue under 42 U.S.C. § 1983 for monetary damages. With adoption of this section, such persons will be able to seek injunctive relief as well, if their injury is the product of a pattern or practice of misconduct. [N.B. A provision in the statute authorizing private individuals to enforce it was removed from the final version after opposition from police groups and the George H. W. Bush administration. Marshall Miller, Note, Police Brutality, 17 Yale L. & Policy Rev. 149, 163 (1998).]

This provision may in fact decrease the number of lawsuits against police departments. Currently, changes in a police department's policy are prompted by successive criminal cases or damage actions; the cumulative weight of convictions or adverse monetary judgments may lead the police leadership to conclude that change is necessary. This is an inefficient way to enforce the Constitution and is not always effective. Some police departments have shown they are willing to absorb millions of dollars of damage payments per year without changing

D. The Department of Justice and Structural Reform Litigation

their policies. If there is a pattern of abuse, this section can bring it to an end with a single legal action.

IV. CONGRESSIONAL AUTHORITY TO PROMULGATE § 14141

• • •

As the House Committee report makes clear, and as all parties to this action appear to concede, the grant of authority to the Attorney General reflected in both the Police Accountability Act of 1991 and in § 14141 was drafted in light of and was intended to remedy the inadequacies of 42 U.S.C. § 1983. That statute provides in pertinent part:

> Every person who, under color of any statute, ordinance, regulation, custom, or usage, of any State or Territory or the District of Columbia subjects, or causes to be subjected, any citizen of the United States or other person within the jurisdiction thereof to the deprivation of any rights, privileges, or immunities secured by the Constitution and laws, shall be liable to the party injured in an action at law, suit in equity, or other proper proceeding for redress.

Section 1983 does not impose vicarious liability solely on the basis of an employment relationship between a governmental agency and a tortfeasor. Before a city can be held liable under § 1983, some "action pursuant to official municipal policy of some nature [must have] caused a constitutional tort." *Monell.* Simply put, cities are not subject to liability under § 1983 on a theory of respondeat superior.

That having been said, cities can nevertheless be held liable under § 1983 for more than just the most direct and egregious violations of an individual's Fourteenth Amendment rights. For example, if the constitutional violation is the result of inadequate police training, the city may be held liable under § 1983 if "the failure to train amounts to deliberate indifference to the rights of persons with whom the police come into contact." Liability under § 1983 can be imposed on a municipality where "'a deliberate choice to follow a course of action is made from among various alternatives' by city policy makers."

The Supreme Court based its relatively narrow construction of § 1983 on the express language of the statute, its legislative history, *Monell,* and "perceived constitutional difficulties" on the part of the drafters of the statute.

This Court concludes that § 14141 is properly construed to similar effect. Its language does not unambiguously contemplate the possibility of vicarious liability and such legislative history as exists manifests a congressional intent to conform its substantive provisions to the standards of § 1983.

As so construed, the Court concludes that § 14141 is a valid and proper exercise of congressional authority under § 5 of the Fourteenth Amendment. As the House Committee report makes clear, the authority conferred on the Attorney General by § 14141 was intended to "close [the] gap in the law" as it had developed in litigation under § 1983 by providing the remedy of broad injunctive relief where "appropriate." The remedy authorized by § 14141 is clearly responsive to the constitutional harm identified in the House Committee report and is no more expansive than is necessary to address that harm. The statute therefore reflects a valid exercise of Congress' constitutional mandate to identify, remedy and even prevent substantive violations of the Fourteenth Amendment. As so construed, § 14141 is neither incongruent nor disproportionate to Congress' constitutional prerogative and responsibility.

To the extent that the complaint seeks to posit liability against the City of Columbus on a theory of respondeat superior, the original complaint is deficient. However, the United States asks that, in such event, "the Court grant the United States sufficient time to amend the complaint to remedy any identified deficiency." The Court will grant that request.

NOTES AND QUESTIONS

1. Does it make sense for the court to interpret § 14141 in light of interpretations of § 1983 simply because they are aimed at the same evil? Is it relevant that the two statutes were enacted 123 years apart?

2. Does the limitation on municipal liability that the court reads into the statute, based on *Monell*, necessarily hamper DOJ's use of § 14141?

3. If *Monell* had recognized traditional respondeat superior liability under § 1983, would § 14141 be necessary? Would the doctrine of qualified immunity be necessary?

The DOJ selects its target police departments from a number of sources. *See generally* Stephen Rushin, *Federal Enforcement of Police Reform*, 82 Fordham L. Rev. 3189, 3219-24 (2014) (identifying sources based on interviews with stakeholders in the "structural police reform process," including former DOJ employees). These include existing civil litigation or investigations initiated by private interest groups; media reports of police misconduct; research studies; police department whistleblowers; and extreme individual examples of police misconduct. *Id.* Based on such sources, the DOJ will start with what it calls a "preliminary inquiry," to determine whether there is reason to believe the police department was or is engaging in systemic misconduct. *Id.* at 3225. If so, a formal investigation will be opened, a step DOJ does not take lightly as formal investigations have proven to be expensive and time-consuming. *Id.* at 3226-28.

Formal investigations usually result in settlement agreements, often with the nominal filing of a lawsuit and the entry of a settlement agreement that is embodied into a consent decree that is judicially enforceable. No one wants to litigate under § 14141. DOJ has resource and financial concerns, and the only remedy it can seek and cares about is essentially accomplished by a settlement agreement embodied in a consent decree. Police departments, similarly, prefer to avoid the expense of litigation as well as the bad publicity it can engender. Settlement agreements typically require police departments to undergo significant reforms in areas such as officer use of force, complaint management, training, bias-free policing, community-oriented policing, line-up procedures, canine deployment, and crisis intervention. Stephen Rushin & Griffin Edwards, *De-Policing*, 102 Cornell L. Rev. 721, 749 (2017). Between its enactment in 1994 through 2016, DOJ has investigated 61 police departments and reached settlements with 31 of them, including large cities such as New York, Los Angeles, Chicago, Washington, D.C., Seattle, Albuquerque, Cincinnati, New Orleans, Newark, Buffalo, Columbus, Pittsburgh, and Cleveland. *Id.* There are approximately 18,000 separate police departments in the United States, *id.*; some may have little need for DOJ intervention.

One issue that comes up in connection with settling investigations under § 14141, even when litigation is unnecessary, is ensuring a meaningful role for nonparty police departments and community organizations. Recall that in the City of Columbus litigation described above as well as in the *Floyd* litigation involving the NYPD, police departments intervened under Fed. R. Civ. P. 24 in litigation against the city. *See generally* Kami Chavis Simmons, *The Politics of Policing: Ensuring Stakeholder Collaboration in the Federal Reform of Local Law Enforcement Agencies*, 98 J. Crim. L. & Criminology 489 (2008) (advocating for inclusion of all stakeholders in the settlement process); Alexandra Holmes, *Bridging the Information Gap: The Department of Justice's "Pattern or Practice" Suits and Community Organizations*, 92 Tex. L. Rev. 1241 (2014) (similar).

Unsurprisingly different presidential administrations have varied in the vigor with which they use § 14141. Rushin, *Federal Enforcement*, *supra* at 3233-36. The Clinton and Obama Administrations aggressively lobbied for increased funding and personnel for these actions. The George W. Bush Administration preferred the use of nonbinding "technical assistance letters" to full-blown investigations. The Trump Administration renounced the use of § 14141 altogether. On March 31, 2017, Attorney General Jeff Sessions issued a two-page memorandum declaring that "[i]t is not the responsibility of the federal government to manage non-federal law enforcement agencies." It declared the "[t]he misdeeds of individual bad actors should not impugn or undermine the legitimate and honorable work that law enforcement officers and agencies perform in keeping American communities safe." And, it ordered the deputy attorney general and associate attorney general to begin a review of existing and contemplated agreements that the DOJ had reached with American police departments during the Obama Administration.

Section 14141 is not without its critics, although most advocate for better and more effective use of this potent weapon. Professor Rushin argues for a more transparent case selection process, Rushin, *Federal Enforcement, supra* at 3240, as does Professor Rachel Harmon. *See* Rachel A. Harmon, *Promoting Civil Rights Through Proactive Policing Reform*, 62 Stan. L. Rev. 1, 27 (2009). Professor Rushin also argues for grafting a private right of action onto the statute as a means for increasing the number of cases, although he cautions that this approach may be precluded by *Lyons, Federal Enforcement, supra*. Professor Monica Bell suggests that DOJ should include in § 14141 settlement agreements remedies aimed at promoting "anti-segregation" policing. Monica C. Bell, *Anti-Segregation Policing*, 95 N.Y.U. L. Rev. 650, 756-57 (2020).

A student commentator suggests allowing potential misconduct victims to make use in private litigation of the factfinding generated under § 14144 investigations, although acknowledging this would not increase the number of police departments investigated and would be a disincentive to settlement. Matthew J. Silveira, Comment, *An Unexpected Application of 42 U.S.C. § 14141: Using Investigative Findings for § 1983 Litigation*, 52 UCLA L. Rev. 601 (2004).

The most interesting suggestion is Professor Harmon's. Her proposal for getting more bang for the buck out of § 14141 centers on a "safe harbor" enforcement model. Under this approach, police departments that have been targeted by DOJ through preliminary inquiries could voluntarily opt in to an agreed-upon set of "best practice" reforms, perhaps less draconian than those typically reached after an investigation, and thereby avoid the expense and disruption of a plenary investigation. The proposal would require the development of a national database that could allow DOJ to identify the most deficient departments, as well as a means of enforcing the safe harbor set of reforms. *See* Rachel A. Harmon, *Promoting Civil Rights Through Proactive Policing Reform, supra* at 2-7.

CHAPTER VII

GRAND JURY

The grand jury, in a constitutional sense, is associated with a "right," a right expressly spelled out in the Bill of Rights no less. The Fifth Amendment provides that "[n]o person shall be held to answer for a capital, or otherwise infamous crime, unless on a presentment or indictment of a Grand Jury." Yet the "right" to indictment only by a grand jury is the only core criminal procedural right in the Bill of Rights that has not been "incorporated," via the Due Process Clause of the Fourteenth Amendment, so as to apply to the States. *Hurtado v. California*, 110 U.S. 516 (1884). No matter how the different attributes of incorporation-worthy rights have been articulated over the years—rights "so rooted in the traditions and conscience of our people so as to be ranked as fundamental," rights that are "the very essence of a scheme of ordered liberty," rights essential to "a fair and enlightened system of justice"—the grand jury right has not passed muster. *See* Roger A. Fairfax Jr., *Interrogating the Nonincorporation of the Grand Jury Clause*, 43 Cardozo L. Rev. 855 (2022).

The grand jury right, in short, is the ugly duckling of the Bill of Rights.

The truth is that Americans soured on the grand jury over the course of the nineteenth century, finding it inefficient and cumbersome, antidemocratic in its traditional secrecy requirements, and a threat to individual liberty in its inquisitorial powers. John F. Decker, *Legislating New Federalism: The Call for Grand Jury Reform in the States*, 58 Okla. L. Rev. 341, 346-47 (2005). Even before *Hurtado* some states had eliminated the grand jury requirement altogether, permitting prosecutions to be commenced by either grand jury indictment or by the prosecutor filing charges with the court that were contained in a document called an "information," which would be reviewed by a magistrate in a preliminary examination. *Id.* After *Hurtado*, the next six states admitted to the union did not guarantee the right to grand jury indictment in their constitutions. *Id.* Today, there is no grand jury indictment requirement in approximately half of the states, and in those states charges can be brought by information or an equivalent procedure. *Id.* at 354-55. In the remaining half, a grand jury indictment is required for the commencement of at least certain types of crimes. *Id.*

Ugly duckling or not, where it exists the grand jury is a critical part of the criminal process. Federally, and in many states as well, a grand jury indictment is the necessary first step in a criminal prosecution. And in the federal system and in many states the grand jury's investigative ability—to subpoena witnesses and documents, to confer immunity from prosecution—is its true power. The term "its power" is used loosely—as will be seen the grand jury is in essence a tool of the prosecutor, and the powers "it" has are in truth enjoyed by and deployed by the prosecutor. So not only does the grand jury have a sort of junior varsity status in the Bill of Rights, it is of interest less as a source of "rights" than as a source of "power"—and powers, no less, that are not really its own.

Section A of this chapter is introductory, further reflecting on the grand jury's second-tier constitutional status. Section B looks at the issue of race and the composition of the grand jury. Section C explores two central attributes of the grand jury—its historic independence and informality—attributes that are still recognized today, and which make it a particularly

628 Chapter VII Grand Jury

powerful investigative force in service of the prosecutor. Section D takes a close look at the grand jury's power to subpoena documents and other records, power that is virtually unfettered in comparison to other public bodies or to a private litigant's ability to get information from an adversary through the discovery process. Section E considers the rules of grand jury secrecy, which are often misconstrued by prosecutors and the public alike. Section F examines the rights, if any, of grand jury witnesses, including the Department of Justice's policies on grand jury witnesses. Section G looks into how the government can abuse the grand jury power for improper purposes. Section H looks at the grand jury's output—indictments. And finally, Section I takes a brief look at the grand jury's role in police misconduct cases.

Almost all of the cases in this section are federal. Where it exists under state law, the grand jury in most respects functions in substance similarly to its federal counterpart. There are numerous administrative variances among state grand juries and as compared to federal practice, however. For example, in federal grand jury practice, governed to a significant extent by Rule 6 of the Federal Rules of Criminal Procedure, there are 23 people on a federal grand jury with 16 votes required for an indictment; state grand jury sizes range from 5 to 23, with the percentage requirements for an indictment varying from a simple majority to near unanimity. Decker, *Legislating New Federalism, supra* at 341, 354-55.

A. INTRODUCTION: GRAND JURY MYTHOS

As if to compensate for the grand jury's exile from the land of incorporation, the Supreme Court has consistently exalted the grand jury in hagiographic terms, describing its historical conception and function in passages that read like—pick your term—paeans, odes, love songs, hosannas. This excerpt from *United States v. Calandra*, 414 U.S. 338 (1974), is representative:

> The institution of the grand jury is deeply rooted in Anglo-American history. In England, the grand jury served for centuries both as a body of accusers sworn to discover and present for trial persons suspected of criminal wrongdoing and as a protector of citizens against arbitrary and oppressive governmental action. In this country the Founders thought the grand jury so essential to basic liberties that they provided in the Fifth Amendment that federal prosecution for serious crimes can only be instituted by "a presentment or indictment of a Grand Jury." The grand jury's historic functions survive to this day. Its responsibilities continue to include both the determination whether there is probable cause to believe a crime has been committed and the protection of citizens against unfounded criminal prosecutions.
>
> Traditionally the grand jury has been accorded wide latitude to inquire into violations of criminal law. No judge presides to monitor its proceedings. It deliberates in secret and may determine alone the course of its inquiry. The grand jury may compel the production of evidence or the testimony of witnesses as it considers appropriate, and its operation generally is unrestrained by the technical procedural and evidentiary rules governing the conduct of criminal trials. It is a grand inquest, a body with powers of investigation and inquisition, the scope of whose inquiries is not to be limited narrowly by questions of propriety or forecasts of the probable result of the investigation, or by doubts whether any particular individual will be found properly subject to an accusation of crime.

Id. at 342-43. By retelling this and other versions of the grand jury myth the Court seems to give itself permission to ignore how the grand jury operates in the real world, particularly with respect to its independence. For example, it has been common knowledge for decades that the grand jury is essentially a tool of the prosecutor. *United States v. Mara*, 410 U.S. 19, 23 (1973) (Douglas, J., dissenting). *See generally* Wayne L. Morse, *A Survey of the Grand Jury System*, 10 Or. L. Rev. 101, 101 (1931) (noting the criticism that the grand jury was "merely a rubber stamp for the district attorney"). Yet the Court has never stopped insisting upon the grand jury's independence, and deciding cases based upon that fiction.

The Court's mythologizing also serves to obscure the formidable power of a prosecutor-led grand jury. "Save for torture, it would be hard to find a more effective tool of tyranny than the power of unlimited and unchecked ex parte examination." *United States v. Remington*, 208 F. 2d 567, 573 (2d Cir. 1953) (L. Hand, J., dissenting), *cert. denied*, 347 U.S. 913 (1954). Yet as in the above passage from *Calandra*, the Court's hosannas consistently sing of the grand jury's dual functions as "sword" and "shield." The cases before the Court, however, almost always focus only on the sword—the grand jury's role as an investigatory or inquisitory body.

B. RACE AND GRAND JURY COMPOSITION

As was the case with its fancier-named cousin the petit jury, the grand jury historically in the United States excluded minorities. The next two cases look at how that began to change.

Castaneda v. Partida
430 U.S. 482 (1977)

Mr. Justice BLACKMUN delivered the opinion of the Court.

The sole issue presented in this case is whether the State of Texas, in the person of petitioner, the Sheriff of Hidalgo County, successfully rebutted respondent prisoner's prima facie showing of discrimination against Mexican-Americans in the state grand jury selection process. In his brief, petitioner, in claiming effective rebuttal, asserts:

> This list (of the grand jurors that indicted respondent) indicates that 50 percent of the names appearing thereon were Spanish. The record indicates that 3 of the 5 jury commissioners, 5 of the grand jurors who returned the indictment, 7 of the petit jurors, the judge presiding at the trial, and the Sheriff who served notice on the grand jurors to appear had Spanish surnames.

I

This Court on prior occasions has considered the workings of the Texas system of grand jury selection. Texas employs the "key man" system, which relies on jury commissioners to select prospective grand jurors from the community at large. The procedure begins with the state district judge's appointment of from three to five persons to serve as jury commissioners. The commissioners then "shall select not less than 15 nor more than 20 persons from the citizens of different portions of the county" to compose the list from which the actual grand jury will be drawn. When at least 12 of the persons on the list appear in court pursuant to summons, the district judge proceeds to "test their qualifications." . . . A grand juror must be a citizen of Texas and of the county, be a qualified voter in the county, be "of sound mind and good moral character," be literate, have no prior felony conviction, and be under no pending indictment "or other legal accusation for theft or of any felony." Interrogation under oath is the method specified for testing the prospective juror's qualifications. . . . After the court finds 12 jurors who meet the statutory qualifications, they are impaneled as the grand jury.

II

Respondent, Rodrigo Partida, was indicted in March 1972 by the grand jury of the 92d District Court of Hidalgo County for the crime of burglary of a private residence at night with intent to rape. Hidalgo is one of the border counties of southern Texas. After a trial before a petit jury, respondent was convicted and sentenced to eight years in the custody of the Texas Department of Corrections. He first raised his claim of discrimination in the grand jury selection process on a motion for new trial in the State District Court. In support of his motion, respondent testified about the general existence of discrimination against Mexican-Americans in that area of Texas and introduced statistics from the 1970 census and the Hidalgo County grand jury records. The census figures show that in 1970, the population of Hidalgo County was 181,535. Persons of Spanish language or Spanish surname totaled 143,611. On the assumption that all the persons of Spanish language or Spanish surname were Mexican-Americans, these figures show that 79.1% of the county's population was Mexican-American.

Respondent's data compiled from the Hidalgo County grand jury records from 1962 to 1972 showed that over that period, the average percentage of Spanish-surnamed grand jurors was 39%. In the 2½-year period during which the District Judge who impaneled the jury that indicted respondent was in charge, the average percentage was 45.5%. On the list from which the grand jury that indicted respondent was selected, 50% were Spanish surnamed. The last set of data that respondent introduced, again from the 1970 census, illustrated a number of ways in which Mexican-Americans tend to be underprivileged, including poverty-level incomes, less desirable jobs, substandard housing, and lower levels of education. The State offered no evidence at all either attacking respondent's allegations of discrimination or demonstrating that his statistics were unreliable in any way. The State District Court, nevertheless, denied the motion for a new trial.

On appeal, the Texas Court of Criminal Appeals affirmed the conviction. Reaching the merits of the claim of grand jury discrimination, the court held that respondent had failed to make out a prima facie case. In the court's view, he should have shown how many of the females who served on the grand juries were Mexican-Americans married to men with Anglo-American surnames, how many Mexican-Americans were excused for reasons of age or health, or other legal reasons, and how many of those listed by the census would not have met the statutory qualifications of citizenship, literacy, sound mind, moral character, and lack of criminal record or accusation. Quite beyond the uncertainties in the statistics, the court found it impossible to believe that discrimination could have been directed against a Mexican-American, in light of the many elective positions held by Mexican-Americans in the county and the substantial representation of Mexican-Americans on recent grand juries. In essence, the court refused to presume that Mexican-Americans would discriminate against their own kind.

After exhausting his state remedies, respondent filed his petition for habeas corpus in the Federal District Court, alleging a denial of due process and equal protection, guaranteed by the Fourteenth Amendment, because of gross under-representation of Mexican-Americans on the Hidalgo County grand juries. At a hearing at which the state transcript was introduced, petitioner presented the testimony of the state judge who selected the jury commissioners who had compiled the list from which respondent's grand jury was taken. The judge first reviewed the State's grand jury selection process. In selecting the jury commissioners, the judge stated that he tried to appoint a greater number of Mexican-Americans than members of other ethnic groups. He testified that he instructed the commissioners about the qualifications of a grand juror and the exemptions provided by law. The record is silent, however, with regard to instructions dealing with the potential problem of discrimination directed against any identifiable group. The judge admitted that the actual results of the selection process had not produced grand jury lists that were "representative of the ethnic balance in the community." The jury commissioners themselves, who were the only ones in a position to explain the apparent substantial underrepresentation of Mexican-Americans and to provide information on the actual operation of the selection process, were never called.

On the basis of the evidence before it, the court concluded that respondent had made out a "bare prima facie case" of invidious discrimination with his proof of "a long continued disproportion in the composition of the grand juries in Hidalgo County." Based on an examination of the reliability of the statistics offered by respondent, however, despite the lack of evidence in the record justifying such an inquiry, the court stated that the prima facie case was weak. The court believed that the census statistics did not reflect the true situation accurately, because of recent changes in the Hidalgo County area and the court's own impression of the demographic characteristics of the Mexican-American community. On the other hand, the court recognized that the Texas key-man system of grand jury selection was highly subjective, and was "archaic and inefficient," and that this was a factor arguing for less tolerance in the percentage differences. On balance, the court's doubts about the reliability of the statistics, coupled with its opinion that Mexican-Americans constituted a "governing majority" in the county, caused it to conclude that the prima facie case was rebutted. The "governing majority" theory distinguished respondent's case from all preceding cases involving similar disparities. On the basis of those findings, the court dismissed the petition.

The United States Court of Appeals for the Fifth Circuit reversed. It agreed with the District Court that respondent had succeeded in making out a prima facie case. It found, however, that the State had failed to rebut that showing. The "governing majority" theory contributed little to the State's case in the absence of specific proof to explain the disparity. In light of the State's abdication of its responsibility to introduce controverting evidence, the court held that respondent was entitled to prevail.

We granted certiorari to consider whether the existence of a "governing majority" in itself can rebut a prima facie case of discrimination in grand jury selection, and, if not, whether the State otherwise met its burden of proof.

III

A

This Court has long recognized that "it is a denial of the equal protection of the laws to try a defendant of a particular race or color under an indictment issued by a grand jury . . . from which all persons of his race or color have, solely because of that race or color, been excluded by the State." While the earlier cases involved absolute exclusion of an identifiable group, later cases established the principle that substantial underrepresentation of the group constitutes a constitutional violation as well, if it results from purposeful discrimination. Recent cases have established the fact that an official act is not unconstitutional solely because it has a racially disproportionate impact. Nevertheless, as the Court recognized in *Arlington Heights*, "(s)ometimes a clear pattern, unexplainable on grounds other than race, emerges from the effect of the state action even when the governing legislation appears neutral on its face." In *Washington v. Davis*, the application of these principles to the jury cases was considered:

> It is also clear from the cases dealing with racial discrimination in the selection of juries that the systematic exclusion of Negroes is itself such an "unequal application of the law . . . as to show intentional discrimination." . . . A prima facie case of discriminatory purpose may be proved as well by the absence of Negroes on a particular jury combined with the failure of the jury commissioners to be informed of eligible Negro jurors in a community, . . . or with racially non-neutral selection procedures. . . . With a prima facie case made out, "the burden of proof shifts to the State to rebut the presumption of unconstitutional action by showing that permissible racially neutral selection criteria and procedures have produced the monochromatic result."

Thus, in order to show that an equal protection violation has occurred in the context of grand jury selection, the defendant must show that the procedure employed resulted in substantial underrepresentation of his race or of the identifiable group to which he belongs. The first step is to establish that the group is one that is a recognizable, distinct class, singled out for different treatment under the laws, as written or as applied. Next, the degree of underrepresentation must be proved, by comparing the proportion of the group in the total population to the proportion called to serve as grand jurors, over a significant period of time. This method of proof, sometimes called the "rule of exclusion," has been held to be available as a method of proving discrimination in jury selection against a delineated class. Finally, as noted above, a selection procedure that is susceptible of abuse or is not racially neutral supports the presumption of discrimination raised by the statistical showing. Once the defendant has shown substantial underrepresentation of his group, he has made out a prima facie case of discriminatory purpose, and the burden then shifts to the State to rebut that case.

B

In this case, it is no longer open to dispute that Mexican-Americans are a clearly identifiable class. The statistics introduced by respondent from the 1970 census illustrate disadvantages to which the group has been subject. Additionally, the selection procedure is not racially neutral with respect to Mexican-Americans; Spanish surnames are just as easily identifiable as race was from the questionnaires in *Alexander* or the notations and card colors in *Whitus v. Georgia* and *Avery v. Georgia*.

The disparity proved by the 1970 census statistics showed that the population of the county was 79.1% Mexican-American, but that, over an 11-year period, only 39% of the persons summoned for grand jury service were Mexican-American. This difference of 40% is greater than that found [in other cases]. Since the State presented no evidence showing why the 11-year period was not reliable, we take it as the relevant base for comparison. The mathematical disparities that have been accepted by this Court as adequate for a prima facie case have all been within the range presented here. For example, in *Whitus v. Georgia* (1967), the number of Negroes listed on the tax digest amounted to 27.1% of the taxpayers, but only 9.1% of those on the grand jury venire. The disparity was held to be sufficient to make out a prima facie case of discrimination. We agree with the District Court and the Court of Appeals that the proof in this case was enough to establish a prima facie case of discrimination against the Mexican-Americans in the Hidalgo County grand jury selection.

Supporting this conclusion is the fact that the Texas system of selecting grand jurors is highly subjective. The facial constitutionality of the key-man system, of course, has been accepted by this Court. Nevertheless, the Court has noted that the system is susceptible of abuse as applied. Additionally, as noted, persons with Spanish surnames are readily identifiable.

The showing made by respondent therefore shifted the burden of proof to the State to dispel the inference of intentional discrimination. Inexplicably, the State introduced practically no evidence. The testimony of the State District Judge dealt principally with the selection of the jury commissioners and the instructions given to them. The commissioners themselves were not called to testify. A case such as *Swain v. Alabama* illustrates the potential usefulness of such testimony, when it sets out in detail the procedures followed by the commissioners. The opinion of the Texas Court of Criminal Appeals is particularly revealing as to the lack of rebuttal evidence in the record:

> How many of those listed in the census figures with Mexican-American names were not citizens of the state, but were so-called "wet-backs" from the south side of the Rio Grande; how many were migrant workers and not residents of Hidalgo County; how many were illiterate and could not read and write; how many were not of sound mind and good moral character, how many had been convicted of a felony or were under indictment or legal accusation for theft or a felony; none of these facts appear in the record.

In fact, the census figures showed that only a small part of the population reported for Hidalgo County was not native born. Without some testimony from the grand jury commissioners

B. Race and Grand Jury Composition

about the method by which they determined the other qualifications for grand jurors prior to the statutory time for testing qualifications, it is impossible to draw any inference about literacy, sound mind and moral character, and criminal record from the statistics about the population as a whole. These are questions of disputed fact that present problems not amenable to resolution by an appellate court. We emphasize, however, that we are not saying that the statistical disparities proved here could never be explained in another case; we are simply saying that the State did not do so in this case.

C

In light of our holding that respondent proved a prima facie case of discrimination that was not rebutted by any of the evidence presently in the record, we have only to consider whether the District Court's "governing majority" theory filled the evidentiary gap. In our view, it did not dispel the presumption of purposeful discrimination in the circumstances of this case. Because of the many facets of human motivation, it would be unwise to presume as a matter of law that human beings of one definable group will not discriminate against other members of their group. . . . The problem is a complex one, about which widely differing views can be held, and, as such, it would be somewhat precipitate to take judicial notice of one view over another on the basis of a record as barren as this.

Furthermore, the relevance of a governing majority of elected officials to the grand jury selection process is questionable. The fact that certain elected officials are Mexican-American demonstrates nothing about the motivations and methods of the grand jury commissioners who select persons for grand jury lists. The only arguably relevant fact in this record on the issue is that three of the five jury commissioners in respondent's case were Mexican-American. Knowing only this, we would be forced to rely on the reasoning that we have rejected that human beings would not discriminate against their own kind in order to find that the presumption of purposeful discrimination was rebutted. Without the benefit of this simple behavioral presumption, discriminatory intent can be rebutted only with evidence in the record about the way in which the commissioners operated and their reasons for doing so. It was the State's burden to supply such evidence, once respondent established his prima facie case. The State's failure in this regard leaves unchallenged respondent's proof of purposeful discrimination.

Finally, even if a "governing majority" theory has general applicability in cases of this kind, the inadequacy of the record in this case does not permit such an approach. Among the evidentiary deficiencies are the lack of any indication of how long the Mexican-Americans have enjoyed "governing majority" status, the absence of information about the relative power inherent in the elective offices held by Mexican-Americans, and the uncertain relevance of the general political power to the specific issue in this case. Even for the most recent time period, when presumably the political power of Mexican-Americans was at its greatest, the discrepancy between the number of Mexican-Americans in the total population and the number on the grand jury lists was substantial. Thus, under the facts presented in this case, the "governing majority" theory is not developed fully enough to satisfy the State's burden of rebuttal.

IV

Rather than relying on an approach to the jury discrimination question that is as faintly defined as the "governing majority" theory is on this record, we prefer to look at all the facts that bear on the issue, such as the statistical disparities, the method of selection, and any other relevant testimony as to the manner in which the selection process was implemented. Under this standard, the proof offered by respondent was sufficient to demonstrate a prima facie case

634   Chapter VII   Grand Jury

of discrimination in grand jury selection. Since the State failed to rebut the presumption of purposeful discrimination by competent testimony, despite two opportunities to do so, we affirm the Court of Appeals' holding of a denial of equal protection of the law in the grand jury selection process in respondent's case.

It is so ordered.

NOTES AND QUESTIONS

1. Consider the operation of Texas's "key man" system for the selection of grand jurors. The Court notes that while the facial constitutionality of such a system has been upheld, the system is "highly subjective" and "is susceptible to abuse as applied." How many different layers of discretion are built into the system?

2. The Court finds that the defendant made out a "prima facie case" of discrimination in violation of the Equal Protection Clause. What is the significance of a "prima facie case" in this context? Is this methodology an alternative to proving intentional discrimination? What are the components of defendant's prima facie case? What does the Court mean by "the rule of exclusion"?

3. In response to defendant's federal habeas challenge the state offered only testimony from the state district judge who selected the jury commissioners in the key man system, and not from the commissioners themselves or the persons the commissioners enlisted to compile juror lists. The Court finds the state's response "inexplicabl[e]," *id.* at 498. What might the explanation be? What showing by the state might be sufficient to rebut the statistical force of the prima facie case?

4. The district court found that the defendant had made out a "weak" prima facie case of discrimination but dismissed the claim nonetheless, in part because Mexican Americans constituted a "governing majority" in the county in light of their substantial presence in elective positions. Both the Court and Justice Marshall, concurring, strongly criticize reliance on this factor. Can you imagine a scenario where such evidence might be relevant, for example, if the jury commissioners themselves were Mexican Americans?

5. While it does not acknowledge the racist diatribe by the Texas Court of Criminal Appeals, *id.* at 498, which the majority opinion calls "revealing," the dissenting opinion of Justice Burger also faults the defendant for not providing a "meaningful statistical disparity" in that there is no showing that "disproportionately large numbers of eligible individuals were excluded systematically from grand jury service." *Id.* at 505. What is eligibility supposed to mean in this context? How could such a statistical disparity be demonstrated?

Vasquez v. Hillery
474 U.S. 254 (1986)

Justice MARSHALL delivered the opinion of the Court.

The Warden of San Quentin State Prison asks this Court to retire a doctrine of equal protection jurisprudence first announced in 1880. The time has come, he urges, for us to abandon the rule requiring reversal of the conviction of any defendant indicted by a grand jury from which members of his own race were systematically excluded.

I

In 1962, the grand jury of Kings County, California, indicted respondent, Booker T. Hillery, for a brutal murder. Before trial in Superior Court, respondent moved to quash the indictment on the ground that it had been issued by a grand jury from which blacks

B. Race and Grand Jury Composition   **635**

had been systematically excluded. A hearing on respondent's motion was held by Judge Meredith Wingrove, who was the sole Superior Court Judge in the county and had personally selected all grand juries, including the one that indicted respondent, for the previous seven years. Absolving himself of any discriminatory intent, Judge Wingrove refused to quash the indictment. Respondent was subsequently convicted of first-degree murder.

For the next 16 years, respondent pursued appeals and collateral relief in the state courts, raising at every opportunity his equal protection challenge to the grand jury that indicted him. Less than one month after the California Supreme Court foreclosed his final avenue of state relief in 1978, respondent filed a petition for a writ of habeas corpus in federal court, raising that same challenge. The District Court concluded that respondent had established discrimination in the grand jury, and granted the writ.

II

. . .

Several affidavits challenged here as "new" evidence supported respondent's allegations that no black had ever served on the grand jury in Kings County and that qualified blacks in the county were available to serve, which he had pressed in his pretrial motion to quash in Superior Court and throughout the state proceedings. The California Supreme Court found that the total absence of blacks from the grand jury in the history of Kings County was an undisputed fact. That fact was entitled, therefore, to a presumption of correctness on federal review. The California Supreme Court also discussed Judge Wingrove's consideration of blacks' qualifications, and found that blacks had served as petit jurors, minimum eligibility requirements for which were substantially the same as for grand jurors. . . .

The remaining "new" evidence under attack, a computer analysis submitted in response to the District Court's request, assessed the mathematical probability that chance or accident could have accounted for the exclusion of blacks from the Kings County grand jury over the years at issue. Petitioner would have us conclude that the "sophisticated computer techniques" rendered respondent's claim a "wholly different animal." These statistical estimates, however, added nothing to the case that this Court has not considered intrinsic to the consideration of any grand jury discrimination claim. As early as 1942, this Court rejected a contention that absence of blacks on the grand jury was insufficient to support an inference of discrimination, summarily asserting that "chance or accident could hardly have accounted for the continuous omission of negroes from the grand jury lists for so long a period as sixteen years or more." This proposition, which the Court derived solely on the basis of judicial intuition, is precisely what respondent sought to establish by methods now considered somewhat more reliable.

More recently, in reviewing a habeas corpus proceeding, this Court independently applied general statistical principles to the evidence on the record in order to assess the role of chance in the exclusion of Mexican-Americans from a grand jury in Texas. *Castaneda v. Partida* (1977). Form would indeed triumph over substance were we to allow the question of exhaustion to turn on whether a federal judge has relied on educated conjecture or has sought out a more sophisticated interpretative aid to accomplish the same objective.

We emphasize that the District Court's request for further information was evidently motivated by a responsible concern that it provide the meaningful federal review of constitutional claims that the writ of habeas corpus has contemplated throughout its history. Respondent had initially submitted only the evidence that had been considered in state court, and subsequently complied with the court's request by furnishing materials no broader than necessary to meet the needs of the court. Accordingly, the circumstances present no occasion for the Court to consider a case in which the prisoner has attempted to expedite federal review by deliberately withholding essential facts from the state courts. We hold merely that the supplemental evidence presented by respondent did not fundamentally alter the legal claim already

Chapter VII Grand Jury

considered by the state courts, and, therefore, did not require that respondent be remitted to state court for consideration of that evidence.

III

On the merits, petitioner urges this Court to find that discrimination in the grand jury amounted to harmless error in this case, claiming that the evidence against respondent was overwhelming and that discrimination no longer infects the selection of grand juries in Kings County. Respondent's conviction after a fair trial, we are told, purged any taint attributable to the indictment process. Our acceptance of this theory would require abandonment of more than a century of consistent precedent.

In 1880, this Court reversed a state conviction on the ground that the indictment charging the offense had been issued by a grand jury from which blacks had been excluded. We reasoned that deliberate exclusion of blacks "is practically a brand upon them, affixed by the law, an assertion of their inferiority, and a stimulant to that race prejudice which is an impediment to securing to individuals of the race that equal justice which the law aims to secure to all others." *Strauder v. West Virginia* (1880).

Thereafter, the Court has repeatedly rejected all arguments that a conviction may stand despite racial discrimination in the selection of the grand jury. Only six years ago, the Court explicitly addressed the question whether this unbroken line of case law should be reconsidered in favor of a harmless-error standard, and determined that it should not. We reaffirmed our conviction that discrimination on the basis of race in the selection of grand jurors "strikes at the fundamental values of our judicial system and our society as a whole," and that the criminal defendant's right to equal protection of the laws has been denied when he is indicted by a grand jury from which members of a racial group purposefully have been excluded.

Petitioner argues here that requiring a State to retry a defendant, sometimes years later, imposes on it an unduly harsh penalty for a constitutional defect bearing no relation to the fundamental fairness of the trial. Yet intentional discrimination in the selection of grand jurors is a grave constitutional trespass, possible only under color of state authority, and wholly within the power of the State to prevent. Thus, the remedy we have embraced for over a century — the only effective remedy for this violation — is not disproportionate to the evil that it seeks to deter. If grand jury discrimination becomes a thing of the past, no conviction will ever again be lost on account of it.

Nor are we persuaded that discrimination in the grand jury has no effect on the fairness of the criminal trials that result from that grand jury's actions. The grand jury does not determine only that probable cause exists to believe that a defendant committed a crime, or that it does not. In the hands of the grand jury lies the power to charge a greater offense or a lesser offense; numerous counts or a single count; and perhaps most significant of all, a capital offense or a noncapital offense — all on the basis of the same facts. Moreover, "[t]he grand jury is not bound to indict in every case where a conviction can be obtained." Thus, even if a grand jury's determination of probable cause is confirmed in hindsight by a conviction on the indicted offense, that confirmation in no way suggests that the discrimination did not impermissibly infect the framing of the indictment and, consequently, the nature or very existence of the proceedings to come.

When constitutional error calls into question the objectivity of those charged with bringing a defendant to judgment, a reviewing court can neither indulge a presumption of regularity nor evaluate the resulting harm. Accordingly, when the trial judge is discovered to have had some basis for rendering a biased judgment, his actual motivations are hidden from review, and we must presume that the process was impaired. Similarly, when a petit jury has been selected upon improper criteria or has been exposed to prejudicial publicity, we have required reversal of the conviction because the effect of the violation cannot be ascertained. Like these fundamental flaws, which never have been thought harmless, discrimination in the grand jury undermines the structural integrity of the criminal tribunal itself, and is not amenable to harmless-error review.

Just as a conviction is void under the Equal Protection Clause if the prosecutor deliberately charged the defendant on account of his race, a conviction cannot be understood to cure the taint attributable to a charging body selected on the basis of race. Once having found discrimination in the selection of a grand jury, we simply cannot know that the need to indict would have been assessed in the same way by a grand jury properly constituted. The overriding imperative to eliminate this systemic flaw in the charging process, as well as the difficulty of assessing its effect on any given defendant, requires our continued adherence to a rule of mandatory reversal.

The judgment of the Court of Appeals, accordingly, is affirmed.

• • •

It is so ordered.

NOTES AND QUESTIONS

1. The factual findings relevant here are set forth in an opinion of the district court. *See Hillery v. Pulley*, 563 F. Supp. 1228 (E.D. Cal. 1983). The population of Kings County was 4 percent Black in 1950 and 5 percent Black in 1960. *Id.* at 1231. No Black person had ever served on a Kings County grand jury. *Id.* The state court judge who had personally selected all of the county's grand jurors during the relevant period testified at the state court hearing on defendant's motion. He denied any prejudice or any attempt to exclude Black people; he said he just tried to select grand jurors of "the better type" of people. *Id.* The district court found, following *Castaneda*, that this methodology was "susceptible to abuse as applied." A statistician testified that the probability that the total exclusion of Black jurors was due to chance was 2 in 1,000. *Id.* at 1242.

2. The Court rejects the state's argument that reversal of the conviction is unwarranted because any discrimination in the grand jury selection process was harmless error inasmuch as the defendant was convicted at trial and thus any "taint" was purged. The premise of this argument seems to be that if defendant was convicted by a petit jury in a trial requiring a unanimous verdict under a reasonable doubt standard, then, as a matter of logic, he necessarily would have been indicted by any grand jury on a probable cause standard, even one including Black jurors, where unanimity was not required.

Is this premise unassailable?

3. The Court rejects the defendant's harmless error argument on essentially three grounds: (a) that reversal is "the only effective remedy for this violation"; (b) that discrimination in the grand jury may have infected the framing of the indictment, independent of its effect on the finding of probable cause; and (c) that the error undermines the structural integrity of the criminal process and is thus not amenable to harmless error analysis.

Which of these arguments do you find most and least persuasive? What does the Court mean by the "structural integrity" of the criminal process? What other types of improper influences on the grand jury might undermine the "structural integrity" of the criminal process?

4. The State argues, with some support from the dissent, that it is unfair to require it to retry the defendant 24 years after the fact. The Court responds that "intentional discrimination in the selection of grand jurors is a grave constitutional trespass, possible only under color

638 Chapter VII Grand Jury

of state authority, and wholly within the power of the State to prevent." *Id.* at 262. What else might the Court have said in response to the state's "unfairness" argument?

C. GRAND JURY INDEPENDENCE AND INFORMALITY

Many of the Supreme Court's passages on the grand jury laud its independence, noting that it is not technically a part of any of the three branches of the federal government. In a similar vein, praise is given to the free-spirited nature of its inquiries, unburdened by legal formalities and technicalities. Consider as you read the next set of cases whether these descriptions are accurate and, to the extent they are, whether these are virtues or vices.

United States v. Costello
350 U.S. 359 (1956)

Mr. Justice BLACK delivered the opinion of the Court.

We granted certiorari in this case to consider a single question: "May a defendant be required to stand trial and a conviction be sustained where only hearsay evidence was presented to the grand jury which indicted him?"

Petitioner, Frank Costello, was indicted for wilfully attempting to evade payment of income taxes due the United States for the years 1947, 1948 and 1949. The charge was that petitioner falsely and fraudulently reported less income than he and his wife actually received during the taxable years in question. Petitioner promptly filed a motion for inspection of the minutes of the grand jury and for a dismissal of the indictment. His motion was based on an affidavit stating that he was firmly convinced there could have been no legal or competent evidence before the grand jury which indicted him since he had reported all his income and paid all taxes due. The motion was denied. At the trial which followed the Government offered evidence designed to show increases is Costello's net worth in an attempt to prove that he had received more income during the years in question than he had reported. To establish its case the Government called and examined 144 witnesses and introduced 368 exhibits. All of the testimony and documents related to business transactions and expenditures by petitioner and his wife. The prosecution concluded its case by calling three government agents. Their investigations had produced the evidence used against petitioner at the trial. They were allowed to summarize the vast amount of evidence already heard and to introduce computations showing, if correct, that petitioner and his wife had received far greater income than they had reported. We have held such summarizations admissible in a "net worth" case like this.

Counsel for petitioner asked each government witness at the trial whether he had appeared before the grand jury which returned the indictment. This cross-examination developed the fact that the three investigating officers had been the only witnesses before the grand jury. After the Government concluded its case, petitioner again moved to dismiss the indictment on the ground that the only evidence before the grand jury was "hearsay," since the three officers had no firsthand knowledge of the transactions upon which their computations were based. Nevertheless the trial court again refused to dismiss the indictment, and petitioner was convicted. The Court of Appeals affirmed, holding that the indictment was valid even though the sole evidence before the grand jury was hearsay. Petitioner here urges: (1) that an indictment based solely on hearsay evidence violates that part of the Fifth Amendment providing that "No person shall be held to answer for a capital, or otherwise infamous crime, unless on a presentment or indictment of a Grand Jury . . ." and (2) that if the Fifth Amendment does not invalidate an indictment based solely on hearsay we should now lay down such a rule for the guidance of federal courts.

C. Grand Jury Independence and Informality

The Fifth Amendment provides that federal prosecutions for capital or otherwise infamous crimes must be instituted by presentments or indictments of grand juries. But neither the Fifth Amendment nor any other constitutional provision prescribes the kind of evidence upon which grand juries must act. The grand jury is an English institution, brought to this country by the early colonists and incorporated in the Constitution by the Founders. There is every reason to believe that our constitutional grand jury was intended to operate substantially like its English progenitor. The basic purpose of the English grand jury was to provide a fair method for instituting criminal proceedings against persons believed to have committed crimes. Grand jurors were selected from the body of the people and their work was not hampered by rigid procedural or evidential rules. In fact, grand jurors could act on their own knowledge and were free to make their presentments or indictments on such information as they deemed satisfactory. Despite its broad power to institute criminal proceedings the grand jury grew in popular favor with the years. It acquired an independence in England free from control by the Crown or judges. Its adoption in our Constitution as the sole method for preferring charges in serious criminal cases shows the high place it held as an instrument of justice. And in this country as in England of old the grand jury has convened as a body of laymen, free from technical rules, acting in secret, pledged to indict no one because of prejudice and to free no one because of special favor. As late as 1927 an English historian could say that English grand juries were still free to act on their own knowledge if they pleased to do so. And in 1852 Mr. Justice Nelson on circuit could say "No case has been cited, nor have we been able to find any, furnishing an authority for looking into and revising the judgment of the grand jury upon the evidence, for the purpose of determining whether or not the finding was founded upon sufficient proof. . . ."

In *Holt v. United States*, this Court had to decide whether an indictment should be quashed because supported in part by incompetent evidence. Aside from the incompetent evidence "there was very little evidence against the accused." The Court refused to hold that such an indictment should be quashed, pointing out that "The abuses of criminal practice would be enhanced if indictments could be upset on such a ground." The same thing is true where as here all the evidence before the grand jury was in the nature of "hearsay." If indictments were to be held open to challenge on the ground that there was inadequate or incompetent evidence before the grand jury, the resulting delay would be great indeed. The result of such a rule would be that before trial on the merits a defendant could always insist on a kind of preliminary trial to determine the competency and adequacy of the evidence before the grand jury. This is not required by the Fifth Amendment. An indictment returned by a legally constituted and unbiased grand jury, like an information drawn by the prosecutor, if valid on its face, is enough to call for trial of the charge on the merits. The Fifth Amendment requires nothing more.

Petitioner urges that this Court should exercise its power to supervise the administration of justice in federal courts and establish a rule permitting defendants to challenge indictments on the ground that they are not supported by adequate or competent evidence. No persuasive reasons are advanced for establishing such a rule. It would run counter to the whole history of the grand jury institution, in which laymen conduct their inquiries unfettered by technical rules. Neither justice nor the concept of a fair trial requires such a change. In a trial on the merits, defendants are entitled to a strict observance of all the rules designed to bring about a fair verdict. Defendants are not entitled, however, to a rule which would result in interminable delay but add nothing to the assurance of a fair trial.

Affirmed.

Mr. Justice CLARK and Mr. Justice HARLAN took no part in the consideration or decision of this case.

Mr. Justice BURTON, concurring.

I agree with the denial of the motion to quash the indictment. In my view, however, this case does not justify the breadth of the declarations made by the Court. I assume that this Court would not preclude an examination of grand-jury action to ascertain the existence of bias or prejudice in an indictment. Likewise, it seems to me that if it is shown that the grand jury had before it no substantial or rationally persuasive evidence upon which to base its indictment, that indictment should be quashed. To hold a person to answer to such an empty indictment for a capital or otherwise infamous federal crime robs the Fifth Amendment of much of its protective value to the private citizen.

Here, as in *Holt v. United States*, substantial and rationally persuasive evidence apparently was presented to the grand jury. We may fairly assume that the evidence before that jury included much of the testimony later given at the trial by the three government agents who said that they had testified before the grand jury. At the trial, they summarized financial transactions of the accused about which they were not qualified to testify of their own knowledge. To use Justice Holmes' phrase in the *Holt* case, such testimony, standing alone, was "incompetent by circumstances," and yet it was rationally persuasive of the crime charged and provided a substantial basis for the indictment. At the trial, with preliminary testimony laying the foundation for it, the same testimony constituted an important part of the competent evidence upon which the conviction was obtained.

To sustain this indictment under the above circumstances is well enough, but I agree with Judge Learned Hand that "if it appeared that no evidence had been offered that rationally established the facts, the indictment ought to be quashed; because then the grand jury would have in substance abdicated." Accordingly, I concur in this judgment, but do so for the reasons stated in the opinion of the Court of Appeals and subject to the limitations there expressed.

NOTES AND QUESTIONS

1. Note that defendant was unable before trial to get access to the transcripts of grand jury testimony. Had he been prosecuted just two years later, he would have been able to get access to the grand jury testimony at least of the witnesses who testified against him at trial under the Jencks Act. *See* Chapter IX *infra*. Yet that may not have been as useful as he likely expected inasmuch as the only witnesses who testified in the grand jury were law enforcement agents.

Why would the prosecutors have proceeded this way, putting their entire case to the grand jury by way of hearsay in the form of summary witness testimony? *See* Fed. R. Evid. 1006 (authorizing use of summary exhibits or testimony). What are the pros and cons from a prosecutor's perspective of calling percipient witnesses to testify in the grand jury as opposed to relying on hearsay, as they did in *Costello*?

2. As usual, the Court provides background on the history of the grand jury "institution." This particular ode to the grand jury focuses on its independence and informality, its amateurish quality—"a body of laymen, free from technical rules." The Court even claims that recently "grand juries were still free to act on their own knowledge."

Isn't it especially ironic that the Court relies on this myth based on the facts of *Costello*? Is the rule against hearsay a "technical rule"?

3. Defendant Frank Costello was at the time of his indictment in this case the boss of the Lucky Luciano branch of New York's organized crime families. Might this have influenced how the prosecutors approached their decision making about which witnesses they called into the grand jury?

On the tax evasion charge at issue here Costello was convicted and sentenced to five years in prison. Costello later served 18 months in federal prison on a contempt of Congress charge

Frank Costello testifying before Congress in 1950 or 1951

arising out of his testimony before Senate hearings investigating organized crime. After he was released from prison, Vito Genovese ordered his assassination in 1957. Although Costello survived the attempt, he subsequently took early retirement, relinquishing power to the Genovese family.

4. The Court notes that permitting challenges to indictments on hearsay grounds would result in "delay." What sort of delay does the Court seem to have in mind? Are there even more serious issues than delay from the prosecution's perspective? The concurrence suggests that an indictment could be challenged where "no evidence had been offered that rationally established the facts." *Id.* at 365. What might this mean? How could such a rule be enforced?

5. As it does in other contexts, the Court relies on the grand jury/trial dichotomy to support its position, noting that "neither justice nor the concept of a fair trial" require permitting challenges to indictments based on hearsay.

Why does the Court view fairness as something to be reserved only for trials?

Does a fair trial extinguish unfairness in the grand jury?

6. The Court does seem to acknowledge that an indictment could be susceptible to challenge if it is not "valid on its face." What do you think this means? Note that current Fed. R. Crim. P. 12(b)(3)(B)(v) contemplates the filing of a pretrial motion challenging an indictment's "failure to state an offense."

The next case addresses whether a judicially imposed requirement that exculpatory evidence be presented to the grand jury would compromise the grand jury's historical mission.

United States v. Williams
504 U.S. 36 (1992)

Justice SCALIA delivered the opinion of the Court.

The question presented in this case is whether a district court may dismiss an otherwise valid indictment because the Government failed to disclose to the grand jury "substantial exculpatory evidence" in its possession.

I

On May 4, 1988, respondent John H. Williams, Jr., a Tulsa, Oklahoma, investor, was indicted by a federal grand jury on seven counts of "knowingly mak[ing] [a] false statement or report . . . for the purpose of influencing . . . the action [of a federally insured financial institution]," in violation of 18 U.S.C. § 1014 (1988 ed., Supp. II). According to the indictment, between September 1984 and November 1985 Williams supplied four Oklahoma banks with "materially false" statements that variously overstated the value of his current assets and interest income in order to influence the banks' actions on his loan requests.

Williams' misrepresentation was allegedly effected through two financial statements provided to the banks, a "Market Value Balance Sheet" and a "Statement of Projected Income and Expense." The former included as "current assets" approximately $6 million in notes receivable from three venture capital companies. Though it contained a disclaimer that these assets were carried at cost rather than at market value, the Government asserted that listing them as "current assets"—i.e., assets quickly reducible to cash—was misleading, since Williams knew that none of the venture capital companies could afford to satisfy the notes in the short term. The second document—the Statement of Projected Income and Expense—allegedly misrepresented Williams' interest income, since it failed to reflect that the interest payments received on the notes of the venture capital companies were funded entirely by Williams' own loans to those companies. The Statement thus falsely implied, according to the Government, that Williams was deriving interest income from "an independent outside source."

Shortly after arraignment, the District Court granted Williams' motion for disclosure of all exculpatory portions of the grand jury transcripts. Upon reviewing this material, Williams demanded that the District Court dismiss the indictment, alleging that the Government had failed to fulfill its obligation under the Tenth Circuit's prior decision in *United States v. Page* (1987), to present "substantial exculpatory evidence" to the grand jury (emphasis omitted). His contention was that evidence which the Government had chosen not to present to the grand jury—in particular, Williams' general ledgers and tax returns, and Williams' testimony in his contemporaneous Chapter 11 bankruptcy proceeding—disclosed that, for tax purposes and otherwise, he had regularly accounted for the "notes receivable" (and the interest on them) in a manner consistent with the Balance Sheet and the Income Statement. This, he contended, belied an intent to mislead the banks, and thus directly negated an essential element of the charged offense.

The District Court initially denied Williams' motion, but upon reconsideration ordered the indictment dismissed without prejudice. It found, after a hearing, that the withheld evidence was "relevant to an essential element of the crime charged," created "'a reasonable doubt about [respondent's] guilt,'" and thus "render[ed] the grand jury's decision to indict gravely suspect." Upon the Government's appeal, the Court of Appeals affirmed the District Court's order, following its earlier decision in *Page*, supra. It first sustained as not "clearly erroneous" the District Court's determination that the Government had withheld "substantial exculpatory evidence" from the grand jury. It then found that the Government's behavior "'substantially influence[d]'" the grand jury's decision to indict, or at the very least raised a "'grave doubt that the decision to indict was free from such substantial influence.'" Under these circumstances, the Tenth Circuit concluded, it was not an abuse of discretion for the District Court to require the Government to begin anew before the grand jury.

• • •

III

Respondent does not contend that the Fifth Amendment itself obliges the prosecutor to disclose substantial exculpatory evidence in his possession to the grand jury. Instead, building on our statement that the federal courts "may, within limits, formulate procedural rules not specifically required by the Constitution or the Congress," he argues that imposition of the Tenth Circuit's disclosure rule is supported by the courts' "supervisory power." We think not. *Hasting*, and the cases that rely upon the principle it expresses, deal strictly with the courts' power to control their own procedures. That power has been applied not only to improve the truth-finding process of the trial, but also to prevent parties from reaping benefit or incurring harm from violations of substantive or procedural rules (imposed by the Constitution or laws) governing matters apart from the trial itself. Thus, *Bank of Nova Scotia v. United States* (1988), makes clear that the supervisory power can be used to dismiss an indictment because of misconduct before the grand jury, at least where that misconduct amounts to a violation of one of those "few, clear rules which were carefully drafted and approved by this Court and by Congress to ensure the integrity of the grand jury's functions."

We did not hold in *Bank of Nova Scotia*, however, that the courts' supervisory power could be used, not merely as a means of enforcing or vindicating legally compelled standards of prosecutorial conduct before the grand jury, but as a means of prescribing those standards of prosecutorial conduct in the first instance—just as it may be used as a means of establishing standards of prosecutorial conduct before the courts themselves. It is this latter exercise that respondent demands. Because the grand jury is an institution separate from the courts, over whose functioning the courts do not preside, we think it clear that, as a general matter at least, no such "supervisory" judicial authority exists, and that the disclosure rule applied here exceeded the Tenth Circuit's authority.

A

"[R]ooted in long centuries of Anglo–American history," the grand jury is mentioned in the Bill of Rights, but not in the body of the Constitution. It has not been textually assigned, therefore, to any of the branches described in the first three Articles. It "'is a constitutional fixture in its own right.'" In fact the whole theory of its function is that it belongs to no branch of the institutional Government, serving as a kind of buffer or referee between the Government and the people. Although the grand jury normally operates, of course, in the courthouse and under judicial auspices, its institutional relationship with the Judicial Branch has traditionally been, so to speak, at arm's length. Judges' direct involvement in the functioning of the grand jury has generally been confined to the constitutive one of calling the grand jurors together and administering their oaths of office.

The grand jury's functional independence from the Judicial Branch is evident both in the scope of its power to investigate criminal wrongdoing and in the manner in which that power is exercised. "Unlike [a] [c]ourt, whose jurisdiction is predicated upon a specific case or controversy, the grand jury 'can investigate merely on suspicion that the law is being violated, or even because it wants assurance that it is not.'" It need not identify the offender it suspects, or even "the precise nature of the offense" it is investigating. The grand jury requires no authorization from its constituting court to initiate an investigation, nor does the prosecutor require leave of court to seek a grand jury indictment. And in its day-to-day functioning, the grand jury generally operates without the interference of a presiding judge. It swears in its own witnesses, and deliberates in total secrecy.

True, the grand jury cannot compel the appearance of witnesses and the production of evidence, and must appeal to the court when such compulsion is required. And the court will refuse to lend its assistance when the compulsion the grand jury seeks would override rights accorded by the Constitution, or even testimonial privileges recognized by the common law. Even in this setting, however, we have insisted that the grand jury remain "free to pursue its investigations unhindered by external influence or supervision so long as it does not trench upon the legitimate rights of any witness called before it." Recognizing this tradition of independence, we have said that the Fifth Amendment's "constitutional guarantee presupposes an investigative body 'acting independently of either prosecuting attorney or judge'. . . ."

No doubt in view of the grand jury proceeding's status as other than a constituent element of a "criminal prosecutio[n]," U.S. Const., Amdt. 6, we have said that certain constitutional protections afforded defendants in criminal proceedings have no application before that body. The Double Jeopardy Clause of the Fifth Amendment does not bar a grand jury from returning an indictment when a prior grand jury has refused to do so. We have twice suggested, though not held, that the Sixth Amendment right to counsel does not attach when an individual is summoned to appear before a grand jury, even if he is the subject of the investigation. And although "the grand jury may not force a witness to answer questions in violation of [the Fifth Amendment's] constitutional guarantee" against self-incrimination, our cases suggest that an indictment obtained through the use of evidence previously obtained in violation of the privilege against self-incrimination "is nevertheless valid."

Given the grand jury's operational separateness from its constituting court, it should come as no surprise that we have been reluctant to invoke the judicial supervisory power as a basis for prescribing modes of grand jury procedure. Over the years, we have received many requests to exercise supervision over the grand jury's evidence-taking process, but we have refused them all, including some more appealing than the one presented today. In *United States v. Calandra*, a grand jury witness faced questions that were allegedly based upon physical evidence the Government had obtained through a violation of the Fourth Amendment; we rejected the proposal that the exclusionary rule be extended to grand jury proceedings, because of "the potential injury to the historic role and functions of the grand jury." In *Costello* we declined to enforce the hearsay rule in grand jury proceedings, since that "would run counter to the whole history of the grand jury institution, in which laymen conduct their inquiries unfettered by technical rules."

These authorities suggest that any power federal courts may have to fashion, on their own initiative, rules of grand jury procedure is a very limited one, not remotely comparable to the power they maintain over their own proceedings. It certainly would not permit judicial reshaping of the grand jury institution, substantially altering the traditional relationships between the prosecutor, the constituting court, and the grand jury itself. As we proceed to discuss, that would be the consequence of the proposed rule here.

B

Respondent argues that the Court of Appeals' rule can be justified as a sort of Fifth Amendment "common law," a necessary means of assuring the constitutional right to the judgment "of an independent and informed grand jury." Respondent makes a generalized appeal to functional notions: Judicial supervision of the quantity and quality of the evidence relied upon by the grand jury plainly facilitates, he says, the grand jury's performance of its twin historical responsibilities, i.e., bringing to trial those who may be justly accused and shielding the innocent from unfounded accusation and prosecution. We do not agree. The rule would neither preserve nor enhance the traditional functioning of the institution that the Fifth Amendment demands. To the contrary, requiring the prosecutor to present exculpatory as well as inculpatory evidence would alter the grand jury's historical role, transforming it from an accusatory to an adjudicatory body.

It is axiomatic that the grand jury sits not to determine guilt or innocence, but to assess whether there is adequate basis for bringing a criminal charge. That has always been so; and to make the assessment it has always been thought sufficient to hear only the prosecutor's side. As Blackstone described the prevailing practice in 18th-century England, the grand jury was "only to hear evidence on behalf of the prosecution[,] for the finding of an indictment is only in the nature of an enquiry or accusation, which is afterwards to be tried and determined So also in the United States. According to the description of an early American court, three years before the Fifth Amendment was ratified, it is the grand jury's function not "to enquire . . . upon what foundation [the charge may be] denied," or otherwise to try the suspect's defenses, but only to examine "upon what foundation [the charge] is made" by the prosecutor. As a consequence, neither in this country nor in England has the suspect under investigation by the grand jury ever been thought to have a right to testify or to have exculpatory evidence presented.

Imposing upon the prosecutor a legal obligation to present exculpatory evidence in his possession would be incompatible with this system. If a "balanced" assessment of the entire matter is the objective, surely the first thing to be done—rather than requiring the prosecutor to say what he knows in defense of the target of the investigation—is to entitle the target to

C. Grand Jury Independence and Informality

tender his own defense. To require the former while denying (as we do) the latter would be quite absurd. It would also be quite pointless, since it would merely invite the target to circumnavigate the system by delivering his exculpatory evidence to the prosecutor, whereupon it would have to be passed on to the grand jury—unless the prosecutor is willing to take the chance that a court will not deem the evidence important enough to qualify for mandatory disclosure.

Respondent acknowledges (as he must) that the "common law" of the grand jury is not violated if the grand jury itself chooses to hear no more evidence than that which suffices to convince it an indictment is proper. Thus, had the Government offered to familiarize the grand jury in this case with the five boxes of financial statements and deposition testimony alleged to contain exculpatory information, and had the grand jury rejected the offer as pointless, respondent would presumably agree that the resulting indictment would have been valid. Respondent insists, however, that courts must require the modern prosecutor to alert the grand jury to the nature and extent of the available exculpatory evidence, because otherwise the grand jury "merely functions as an arm of the prosecution." We reject the attempt to convert a nonexistent duty of the grand jury itself into an obligation of the prosecutor. The authority of the prosecutor to seek an indictment has long been understood to be "coterminous with the authority of the grand jury to entertain [the prosecutor's] charges." If the grand jury has no obligation to consider all "substantial exculpatory" evidence, we do not understand how the prosecutor can be said to have a binding obligation to present it.

There is yet another respect in which respondent's proposal not only fails to comport with, but positively contradicts, the "common law" of the Fifth Amendment grand jury. Motions to quash indictments based upon the sufficiency of the evidence relied upon by the grand jury were unheard of at common law in England. And the traditional American practice was described by Justice Nelson, riding circuit in 1852, as follows:

> No case has been cited, nor have we been able to find any, furnishing an authority for looking into and revising the judgment of the grand jury upon the evidence, for the purpose of determining whether or not the finding was founded upon sufficient proof, or whether there was a deficiency in respect to any part of the complaint.

We accepted Justice Nelson's description in *Costello*, where we held that "[i]t would run counter to the whole history of the grand jury institution" to permit an indictment to be challenged "on the ground that there was inadequate or incompetent evidence before the grand jury." And we reaffirmed this principle recently in *Bank of Nova Scotia*, where we held that "the mere fact that evidence itself is unreliable is not sufficient to require a dismissal of the indictment," and that "a challenge to the reliability or competence of the evidence presented to the grand jury" will not be heard. It would make little sense, we think, to abstain from reviewing the evidentiary support for the grand jury's judgment while scrutinizing the sufficiency of the prosecutor's presentation. A complaint about the quality or adequacy of the evidence can always be recast as a complaint that the prosecutor's presentation was "incomplete" or "misleading." Our words in *Costello* bear repeating: Review of facially valid indictments on such grounds "would run counter to the whole history of the grand jury institution[,] [and] [n]either justice nor the concept of a fair trial requires [it]."

Echoing the reasoning of the Tenth Circuit in *United States v. Page*, respondent argues that a rule requiring the prosecutor to disclose exculpatory evidence to the grand jury would, by removing from the docket unjustified prosecutions, save valuable judicial time. That depends, we suppose, upon what the ratio would turn out to be between unjustified prosecutions eliminated and grand jury indictments challenged—for the latter as well as the former consume "valuable judicial time." We need not pursue the matter; if there is an advantage to the proposal, Congress is free to prescribe it. For the reasons set forth above, however, we conclude that courts have no authority to prescribe such a duty pursuant to their inherent supervisory authority over their own proceedings. The judgment of the Court of Appeals is accordingly reversed, and the cause is remanded for further proceedings consistent with this opinion.

So ordered.

Justice STEVENS, with whom Justice BLACKMUN and Justice O'CONNOR join, and with whom Justice THOMAS joins as to Parts II and III, dissenting.

• • •

II

Like the Hydra slain by Hercules, prosecutorial misconduct has many heads. Some are cataloged in Justice Sutherland's classic opinion for the Court in *Berger*:

> That the United States prosecuting attorney overstepped the bounds of that propriety and fairness which should characterize the conduct of such an officer in the prosecution of a criminal offense is clearly shown by the record. He was guilty of misstating the facts in his cross-examination of witnesses; of putting into the mouths of such witnesses things which they had not said; of suggesting by his questions that statements had been made to him personally out of court, in respect of which no proof was offered; of pretending to understand that a witness had said something which he had not said and persistently cross-examining the witness upon that basis; of assuming prejudicial facts not in evidence; of bullying and arguing with witnesses; and in general, of conducting himself in a thoroughly indecorous and improper manner. . . .
> The prosecuting attorney's argument to the jury was undignified and intemperate, containing improper insinuations and assertions calculated to mislead the jury.

This, of course, is not an exhaustive list of the kinds of improper tactics that overzealous or misguided prosecutors have adopted in judicial proceedings. The reported cases of this Court alone contain examples of the knowing use of perjured testimony, the suppression of evidence favorable to an accused person, and misstatements of the law in argument to the jury, to name just a few.

Nor has prosecutorial misconduct been limited to judicial proceedings: The reported cases indicate that it has sometimes infected grand jury proceedings as well. The cases contain examples of prosecutors presenting perjured testimony, questioning a witness outside the presence of the grand jury and then failing to inform the grand jury that the testimony was exculpatory, failing to inform the grand jury of its authority to subpoena witnesses, operating under a conflict of interest, misstating the law, and misstating the facts on cross-examination of a witness.

Justice Sutherland's identification of the basic reason why that sort of misconduct is intolerable merits repetition:

> "The United States Attorney is the representative not of an ordinary party to a controversy, but of a sovereignty whose obligation to govern impartially is as compelling as its obligation to govern at all; and whose interest, therefore, in a criminal prosecution is not that it shall win a case, but that justice shall be done. As such, he is in a peculiar and very definite sense the servant of the law, the twofold aim of which is that guilt shall not escape or innocence suffer. He may prosecute with earnestness and vigor — indeed, he should do so. But, while he may strike hard blows, he is not at liberty to strike foul ones. It is as much his duty to refrain from improper methods calculated to produce a wrongful conviction as it is to use every legitimate means to bring about a just one." *Berger v. United States.*

It is equally clear that the prosecutor has the same duty to refrain from improper methods calculated to produce a wrongful indictment. Indeed, the prosecutor's duty to protect the

C. Grand Jury Independence and Informality   **647**

fundamental fairness of judicial proceedings assumes special importance when he is presenting evidence to a grand jury. As the Court of Appeals for the Third Circuit recognized, "the costs of continued unchecked prosecutorial misconduct" before the grand jury are particularly substantial because there

> the prosecutor operates without the check of a judge or a trained legal adversary, and virtually immune from public scrutiny. The prosecutor's abuse of his special relationship to the grand jury poses an enormous risk to defendants as well. For while in theory a trial provides the defendant with a full opportunity to contest and disprove the charges against him, in practice, the handing up of an indictment will often have a devastating personal and professional impact that a later dismissal or acquittal can never undo. Where the potential for abuse is so great, and the consequences of a mistaken indictment so serious, the ethical responsibilities of the prosecutor, and the obligation of the judiciary to protect against even the appearance of unfairness, are correspondingly heightened.

In his dissent in *United States v. Ciambrone* (CA2 1979), Judge Friendly also recognized the prosecutor's special role in grand jury proceedings:

> As the Supreme Court has noted, "the Founders thought the grand jury so essential to basic liberties that they provided in the Fifth Amendment that federal prosecution for serious crimes can only be instituted by 'a presentment or indictment of a Grand Jury.'" Before the grand jury the prosecutor has the dual role of pressing for an indictment and of being the grand jury adviser. In case of conflict, the latter duty must take precedence.
>
> The ex parte character of grand jury proceedings makes it peculiarly important for a federal prosecutor to remember that, in the familiar phrase, the interest of the United States "in a criminal prosecution is not that it shall win a case, but that justice shall be done."

The standard for judging the consequences of prosecutorial misconduct during grand jury proceedings is essentially the same as the standard applicable to trials. In *United States v. Mechanik* (1986), we held that there was "no reason not to apply [the harmless error rule] to 'errors, defects, irregularities, or variances' occurring before a grand jury just as we have applied it to such error occurring in the criminal trial itself." We repeated that holding in *Bank of Nova Scotia v. United States* (1988), when we rejected a defendant's argument that an indictment should be dismissed because of prosecutorial misconduct and irregularities in proceedings before the grand jury. Referring to the prosecutor's misconduct before the grand jury, we "concluded that our customary harmless-error inquiry is applicable where, as in the cases before us, a court is asked to dismiss an indictment prior to the conclusion of the trial." Moreover, in reviewing the instances of misconduct in that case, we applied precisely the same standard to the prosecutor's violations and to his violations of the general duty of fairness that applies to all judicial proceedings. This point is illustrated by the Court's comments on the prosecutor's abuse of a witness:

> The District Court found that a prosecutor was abusive to an expert defense witness during a recess and in the hearing of some grand jurors. Although the Government concedes that the treatment of the expert tax witness was improper, the witness himself testified that his testimony was unaffected by this misconduct. The prosecutors instructed the grand jury to disregard anything they may have heard in conversations between a prosecutor and a witness, and explained to the grand jury that such conversations should have no influence on its deliberations. In light of these ameliorative measures, there is nothing to indicate that the prosecutor's conduct toward this witness substantially affected the grand jury's evaluation of the testimony or its decision to indict.

Unquestionably, the plain implication of that discussion is that if the misconduct, even though not expressly forbidden by any written rule, had played a critical role in persuading the jury to return the indictment, dismissal would have been required.

In an opinion that I find difficult to comprehend, the Court today repudiates the assumptions underlying these cases and seems to suggest that the court has no authority to supervise the conduct of the prosecutor in grand jury proceedings so long as he follows the dictates of the Constitution, applicable statutes, and Rule 6 of the Federal Rules of Criminal Procedure. The Court purports to support this conclusion by invoking the doctrine of separation of powers and citing a string of cases in which we have declined to impose categorical restraints on the grand jury. Needless to say, the Court's reasoning is unpersuasive.

Although the grand jury has not been "textually assigned" to "any of the branches described in the first three Articles" of the Constitution, it is not an autonomous body completely beyond the reach of the other branches. Throughout its life, from the moment it is convened until it is discharged, the grand jury is subject to the control of the court. As Judge Learned Hand recognized over 60 years ago, "a grand jury is neither an officer nor an agent of the United States, but a part of the court." This Court has similarly characterized the grand jury:

> A grand jury is clothed with great independence in many areas, but it remains an appendage of the court, powerless to perform its investigative function without the court's aid, because powerless itself to compel the testimony of witnesses. It is the court's process which summons the witness to attend and give testimony, and it is the court which must compel a witness to testify if, after appearing, he refuses to do so.

This Court has, of course, long recognized that the grand jury has wide latitude to investigate violations of federal law as it deems appropriate and need not obtain permission from either the court or the prosecutor. Correspondingly, we have acknowledged that "its operation generally is unrestrained by the technical procedural and evidentiary rules governing the conduct of criminal trials." But this is because Congress and the Court have generally thought it best not to impose procedural restraints on the grand jury; it is not because they lack all power to do so.

To the contrary, the Court has recognized that it has the authority to create and enforce limited rules applicable in grand jury proceedings. Thus, for example, the Court has said that the grand jury "may not itself violate a valid privilege, whether established by the Constitution, statutes, or the common law." And the Court may prevent a grand jury from violating such a privilege by quashing or modifying a subpoena, or issuing a protective order forbidding questions in violation of the privilege. Moreover, there are, as the Court notes, a series of cases in which we declined to impose categorical restraints on the grand jury. In none of those cases, however, did we question our power to reach a contrary result.

Although the Court recognizes that it may invoke its supervisory authority to fashion and enforce privilege rules applicable in grand jury proceedings, ibid., and suggests that it may also invoke its supervisory authority to fashion other limited rules of grand jury procedure, it concludes that it has no authority to prescribe "standards of prosecutorial conduct before the grand jury," because that would alter the grand jury's historic role as an independent, inquisitorial institution. I disagree.

We do not protect the integrity and independence of the grand jury by closing our eyes to the countless forms of prosecutorial misconduct that may occur inside the secrecy of the grand jury room. After all, the grand jury is not merely an investigatory body; it also serves as a "protector of citizens against arbitrary and oppressive governmental action." Explaining why the grand jury must be both "independent" and "informed," the Court wrote in *Wood v. Georgia* (1962):

> Historically, this body has been regarded as a primary security to the innocent against hasty, malicious and oppressive persecution; it serves the invaluable function in our society of standing between the accuser and the accused, whether the latter be an individual, minority group, or

C. Grand Jury Independence and Informality 649

other, to determine whether a charge is founded upon reason or was dictated by an intimidating power or by malice and personal ill will.

It blinks reality to say that the grand jury can adequately perform this important historic role if it is intentionally misled by the prosecutor — on whose knowledge of the law and facts of the underlying criminal investigation the jurors will, of necessity, rely.

Unlike the Court, I am unwilling to hold that countless forms of prosecutorial misconduct must be tolerated — no matter how prejudicial they may be, or how seriously they may distort the legitimate function of the grand jury — simply because they are not proscribed by Rule 6 of the Federal Rules of Criminal Procedure or a statute that is applicable in grand jury proceedings. Such a sharp break with the traditional role of the federal judiciary is unprecedented, unwarranted, and unwise. Unrestrained prosecutorial misconduct in grand jury proceedings is inconsistent with the administration of justice in the federal courts and should be redressed in appropriate cases by the dismissal of indictments obtained by improper methods.

III

What, then, is the proper disposition of this case? I agree with the Government that the prosecutor is not required to place all exculpatory evidence before the grand jury. A grand jury proceeding is an ex parte investigatory proceeding to determine whether there is probable cause to believe a violation of the criminal laws has occurred, not a trial. Requiring the prosecutor to ferret out and present all evidence that could be used at trial to create a reasonable doubt as to the defendant's guilt would be inconsistent with the purpose of the grand jury proceeding and would place significant burdens on the investigation. But that does not mean that the prosecutor may mislead the grand jury into believing that there is probable cause to indict by withholding clear evidence to the contrary. I thus agree with the Department of Justice that "when a prosecutor conducting a grand jury inquiry is personally aware of substantial evidence which directly negates the guilt of a subject of the investigation, the prosecutor must present or otherwise disclose such evidence to the grand jury before seeking an indictment against such a person." U.S. Dept. of Justice, United States Attorneys' Manual ¶ 9-11.233, p. 88 (1988).

Although I question whether the evidence withheld in this case directly negates respondent's guilt, I need not resolve my doubts because the Solicitor General did not ask the Court to review the nature of the evidence withheld. Instead, he asked us to decide the legal question whether an indictment may be dismissed because the prosecutor failed to present exculpatory evidence. Unlike the Court and the Solicitor General, I believe the answer to that question is yes, if the withheld evidence would plainly preclude a finding of probable cause. I therefore cannot endorse the Court's opinion.

NOTES AND QUESTIONS

1. Note the charge and the government's theory of the case against defendant. Does this strike you as a particularly strong case for the government? What weaknesses do you see? Why do you think the Court bothers to explain the charge and theory?

2. How does Williams get access to the grand jury transcripts? What is his argument that the prosecution has violated the Tenth Circuit's rule in *Page*? Is this argument persuasive?

3. The district court dismissed the indictment without prejudice, that is, it ruled that the government was free to attempt to re-indict Willams but it would have to re-present its case, along with the exculpatory evidence, to the grand jury. Why do you think the government did not take advantage of that opportunity, especially given that its pursuit of appeals in the Tenth Circuit and the Supreme Court delayed the prosecution by several years? Did the government fear that the grand jury might not return an indictment if the exculpatory evidence were presented to it? Why might a reasonable prosecutor have been willing to present this exculpatory evidence to the grand jury?

4. The Court emphasizes the grand jury's "operational separateness" in holding that the supervisory power does not authorize a federal court to prescribe modes of prosecutorial conduct before the grand jury. Does the Court exaggerate the grand jury's "operational separateness"? Is it accurate to say, as the Court does, that "[j]udges' direct involvement in the functioning of the grand jury has generally been confined to the constitutive one of calling the grand jurors together and administering their oaths of office"? Is it more accurate to call the grand jury an "appendage of the court" as the dissent does? Outside the narrow context of the exercise of judicial supervisory power, is the entire argument about the grand jury's relationship to the judiciary a red herring in view of the grand jury's total dependence on the prosecutor?

5. The Court also claims that requiring a grand jury to consider exculpatory evidence would alter its historical role as an "accusatory body." The dissent responds by recalling the sword/ shield nature of the grand jury's historical powers, citing dicta from *Calandra* that the grand jury also functions as a "protector of citizens against arbitrary and oppressive action." *Id.* at 68. In any event, isn't the grand jury an accusatory body primarily in the sense that its output is accusations as opposed to determinations? Is there something inherently wrong with an "accusatory body" considering more than one version of events before it levels its accusations?

6. The dissent notes that the ethical obligations of a prosecutor to "do justice" are heightened by the one-sided nature of grand jury proceedings. If anything, the dissent understates this point. In the grand jury the prosecutor is omnipotent: no judge presides; the witnesses do not have counsel, and no one can object to the prosecutor's questions; the prosecutor decides what witnesses to call, what to ask them, and what documents to show them; and the grand jurors are simply a captive witness until the prosecutor lets them go home.

7. Note the difference between the "substantial exculpatory evidence" standard in the *Page* rule and the DOJ rule requiring disclosure of "substantial evidence that directly negates guilt." What are the practical differences between the two rules? Did the undisclosed evidence here satisfy either standard? Both standards?

8. The Tenth Circuit's decision in *United States v. Page*, 808 F.2d 723, 728 (10th Cir. 1987), only required disclosure of exculpatory evidence the government "discovered in" the course of its investigation, obviating the dissent's concern about requiring the government to "ferret out" such evidence. Having said that, aren't responsible prosecutors always going to be on the lookout for potential exculpatory evidence if, for no other reason, so they won't be surprised at trial?

Presentments. The Fifth Amendment provides that "[n]o person shall be held to answer for a capital, or otherwise infamous crime, unless on a *presentment* or indictment of a Grand Jury." A presentment, historically, was a public charge the grand jury would bring on its own, independent of the prosecutor, often against government officials. The prosecutor would have to sign or otherwise ratify the presentment document in order to commence a prosecution. Presentments were famously issued by grand juries in connection with two different investigations of Aaron Burr, who was suspected of treason by his political enemies. Grand juries in Kentucky and Mississippi were empaneled at the instigation of those enemies, and both declined to indict Burr. The Kentucky grand jury issued a written declaration to the court criticizing the lack of evidence against Burr and the Mississippi grand jury returned presentments condemning the accusations against Burr as vindictive. *See* Roger Roots, *If It's Not a Runaway It's Not a Real Grand Jury*, 33 Creighton L. Rev. 821, 840-41 (2000).

Notwithstanding that the word "presentment" is right there in the text of the Fifth Amendment, presentments are now almost entirely of historical interest, as in 1946 the Federal Rules of Criminal Procedure consigned them to the ashbin of history. Rule 7, governing indictments and informations—the means by which federal prosecutions normally begin—makes no mention of presentments. The Advisory Committee's Notes state that "[p]resentment is not included as an additional type of formal accusation, since presentments as a method of initiating prosecutions are obsolete, at least as concerns the Federal courts." Some commentators believe the Rules overstate the obsolescence of presentments, and have urged their return. *See* Roots, *If It's Not a Runaway, supra*; Renee Lettow, *Reviving Grand Jury Presentments*, 103 Yale L.J. 1333 (1994). Another commentator observed, shortly after the Rules were enacted, that retention of the presentment power "might encourage the use of the 'run-away' grand jury as the grand jury could act from their own knowledge or observation and not only from charges made by the United States attorney." Lester B. Oldfeld, *The Federal Grand Jury*, 22 F.R.D. 343, 346 (1958).

Runaway Grand Juries. Despite their banishment by the Federal Rules, presentments and also runaway grand juries reentered the public discourse briefly during the 1990s. A special grand jury was empaneled to investigate environmental crimes at a Rockwell International plutonium trigger manufacturing plant in Rocky Flats, Colorado, a Denver suburb. The plant was on land owned by the Department of Energy, and Rockwell made parts for use in nuclear weapons under a federal contract. After a lengthy investigation the grand jurors were unhappy with the decision of the lead assistant U.S. attorney not to recommend the indictment of individual officials of Rockwell or DOE. When the grand jury rejected a proposed indictment of the corporation only, the AUSA proceeded by way of a criminal information (often used when a defendant is pleading guilty and will waive indictment), bypassing the grand jury, under which Rockwell pled guilty and paid an $18.5 million fine. End of case.

Not so easy. The grand jurors went rogue. They did legal research. They found a prosecutor's manual, and proceeded to draft "indictments" against five Rockwell employees and three DOE officials. They also issued those charges as "presentments" and wrote a report criticizing the prosecutors. The district court sealed all these documents pursuant to Rule 6, but the jurors leaked information to the press, which published accounts of the grand jury proceedings. Then things got even more adversarial: The district court asked the Justice Department to investigate the jurors for violations of their secrecy oath; the jurors wrote to then-President-elect Clinton requesting appointment of a special prosecutor to investigate the AUSA; jurors held press conferences on the courthouse steps; and the jurors hired a lawyer, a Georgetown law professor. A congressional investigation was commenced. Immunity deals for the grand jurors were negotiated. *See generally* Lettow, *Reviving Grand Jury Presentments, supra* at 1333.

The reasons the Rocky Flats grand jury turned into a runaway are complex but by no means so singular as to not recur. By all accounts it was a cocktail of prosecutorial arrogance, some generalized antigovernment populist sentiment, a charismatic foreperson, and a collection of jurors who took both themselves and their mission seriously. For example, the grand jurors pointedly recalled their initial instruction when they were sworn in by the district court: "You must remember that you are not the prosecutor's agent. . . . You must not yield your powers nor forgo your independence of spirit. . . . You would perform a disservice if you did not indict where the evidence warranted an indictment." The grand jurors' spirit was summed up by the grand jury foreperson, rancher Wesley McKinley, who declared at one point: "If you're going to let one government chickenshit lawyer tell you what to do, you're not part of America." It's also worth considering whether the dynamics of a "special grand jury"—empaneled to investigate one case only, and doing so for two and a half years—contributed to the grand jurors' aggressiveness, a dynamic sometimes shared by special prosecutors. *See generally* Lettow, *Reviving Grand Jury Presentments, supra* at 1333, 1349-53.

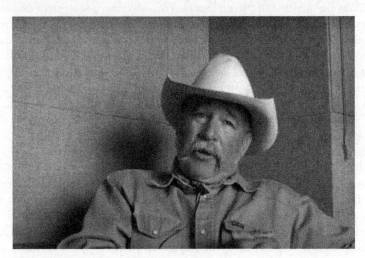

Wesley McKinley

Courts' commitment to the grand jury's independence can be somewhat situational even in less dramatic contexts than a runaway. In *United States v. Marcucci*, 299 F.3d 1156 (9th Cir. 2002), defendants appealed on the ground that the grand jury that indicted them was not instructed that it could refuse to indict even if probable cause existed. Rather, it was instructed in part as follows:

> [Y]our task is to determine whether the government's evidence as presented to you is sufficient to cause you to conclude that there is probable cause to believe that the accused is guilty of the offense charged. To put it another way, you should vote to indict where the evidence presented to you is sufficiently strong to warrant a reasonable person's believing that the accused is probably guilty of the offense with which the accused is charged.

Id. at 1158. Defendants relied on dicta in *Vasquez v. Hillery*, 474 U.S. 254, 263 (1986), where the Supreme Court had stated that "[t]he grand jury is not bound to indict in every case where a conviction can be obtained." A divided panel of the Ninth Circuit found that whatever historical independence the grand jury may have once had in earlier British and American times was no longer an actual feature of its function. Further, the instruction that it was given afforded the grand jury some discretion by charging only that it "should" indict—not "must" or "shall" indict—on a showing of probable cause.

As we have seen and will continue to see, the Supreme Court decides most grand jury issues on the basis of the institution's historical conception, and not on present-day realities. What harm could come from instructing the grand jury in accordance with its historical pedigree?

The next case considers an entirely different angle on grand jury independence, and the respective relationships of the executive and the judiciary vis-à-vis the grand jury. The context is the civil rights movement and litigation in federal court in Mississippi.

United States v. Cox
342 F.2d 167 (5th Cir. 1965)

Jones, Circuit Judge:

On October 22, 1964, an order of the United States District Court for the Southern District of Mississippi, signed by Harold Cox, a judge of that Court, was entered. The order, with caption and formal closing omitted, is as follows:

> THE GRAND JURY, duly elected, impaneled and organized, for the Southern District of Mississippi, reconvened on order of the Court at 9:00 a.m., October 21, 1964, in Court Room Number 2 in Jackson, Mississippi, for the general dispatch of its business. The grand jury was fully instructed as to their duties, powers and responsibilities and retired to the grand jury room number 538 in the Federal Building at Jackson to do its work. The United States Attorney (and one of his assistants) sat with the grand jury throughout the day on October 21 and explained in detail to the grand jury the perjury laws and the Court's construction of such laws for their information. The grand jury heard witnesses throughout the day on October 21, 1964. On the morning of October 22, 1964, the grand jury, through its foreman, made known to the Court in open court that they had requested Robert E. Hauberg, United States Attorney, to prepare certain indictments which they desired to bring against some of the persons under consideration and about which they had heard testimony, and the United States Attorney refused to draft or sign any such indictments on instructions of the Acting Attorney General of the United States; whereupon the Court ordered and directed said United States Attorney to draft such true bills or no bills as the grand jury may have duly voted and desired to report and to sign such instruments as required by law under penalty of contempt. The United States Attorney was afforded one hour within which to decide as to whether or not he would abide by the instructions and order of the Court in such respect. At the end of such time, the Court re-convened and the United States Attorney was specifically asked in open court as to whether or not he intended to conform with the order and direction of the Court in said respects whereupon the United States Attorney answered that he respectfully declined to do so on instructions from Nicholas deB. Katzenbach, Acting Attorney General. He was thereupon duly adjudged by the Court to be in civil contempt of the Court and was afforded an opportunity to make any statement which he desired to make to the Court before sentence; whereupon the United States Attorney reiterated his inability to comply with the order of the Court upon express and direct instructions from Nicholas deB. Katzenbach, Acting Attorney General of the United States.
>
> WHEREFORE, IT IS ORDERED AND ADJUDGED by the Court that Robert E. Hauberg, United States Attorney, is guilty of civil contempt of this Court and in the presence of the Court for his said refusal to obey its said order and he is ordered into custody of the United States Marshal to be confined by him in the Hinds County, Mississippi, jail, there to remain until he purges himself of this contempt by agreeing to conform to said order by performing his official duty for the grand jury as requested in the several (about five) pending cases before them on October 21 and October 22, 1964.
>
> IT IS FURTHER ORDERED by the Court that a citation issue to Nicholas deB. Katzenbach, Acting Attorney General of the United States, directing him to appear before this Court and show cause why he should not be adjudged guilty of contempt of this Court for his instructions and directions to the United States Attorney to disregard and disobey the orders of this Court in the respects stated.
>
> The United States Attorney requested a stay of enforcement of this order and further proceedings herein for five days after this date to enable him to apply to the United States Court of Appeals for the Fifth Circuit for a writ of prohibition and such request is granted; and these proceedings and enforcement of this order in its entirety is stayed for five days, subject to the further orders of the United States Court of Appeals on said application; and for the enforcement of all of which, let proper process issue.

The United States Attorney, Robert E. Hauberg, and the Acting Attorney General, Nicholas deB. Katzenbach, have appealed from the order and they, joined by the United States, seek a writ of prohibition against the District Judge from enforcing the Court's order, and from asserting jurisdiction to require the Attorney General or the United States Attorney "to institute criminal prosecutions or to take any steps in regard thereto." The facts recited in the order are uncontroverted. No further facts are essential to a decision of the issues before this Court. Although the issues here presented arose, in part at least, as an incident of a civil rights matter, no civil rights questions are involved in the rather broad inquiry which we are called upon to make.

The constitutional requirement of an indictment or presentment as a predicate to a prosecution for capital or infamous crimes has for its primary purpose the protection of the individual from jeopardy except on a finding of probable cause by a group of his fellow citizens, and is designed to afford a safeguard against oppressive actions of the prosecutor or a court. The constitutional provision is not to be read as conferring on or preserving to the grand jury, as such, any rights or prerogatives. The constitutional provision is, as has been said, for the benefit of the accused. The constitutional provision is not to be read as precluding, as essential to the validity of an indictment, the inclusion of requisites which did not exist at common law.

Traditionally, the Attorney for the United States had the power to enter a nolle prosequi of a criminal charge at any time after indictment and before trial, and this he could have done without the approval of the court or the consent of the accused. It may be doubted whether, before the adoption of the Federal Rules of Criminal Procedure, he had any authority to prevent the return of an indictment by a grand jury. There would be no constitutional barrier to a requirement that the signature of a United States Attorney upon an indictment is essential to its validity.

It is now provided by the Federal Rules of Criminal Procedure that the Attorney General or the United States Attorney may by leave of court file a dismissal of an indictment. Rule 48(a) Fed. Rules Crim. Proc. 18 U.S.C.A. In the absence of the Rule, leave of court would not have been required. The purpose of the Rule is to prevent harassment of a defendant by charging, dismissing and re-charging without placing a defendant in jeopardy. Rule 7 eliminates the necessity for the inclusion in an indictment of many of the technical and prolix averments which were required at common law, by providing that the indictment shall be a plain, concise and definite written statement of the essential facts constituting the offense charged. The Rule also provides that "It shall be signed by the attorney for the government." Rule 7(c) Fed. Rules Crim. Proc. 18 U.S.C.A.

The judicial power of the United States is vested in the federal courts, and extends to prosecutions for violations of the criminal laws of the United States. The executive power is vested in the President of the United States, who is required to take care that the laws be faithfully executed. The Attorney General is the hand of the President in taking care that the laws of the United States in legal proceedings and in the prosecution of offenses, be faithfully executed. The role of the grand jury is restricted to a finding as to whether or not there is probable cause to believe that an offense has been committed. The discretionary power of the attorney for the United States in determining whether a prosecution shall be commenced or maintained may well depend upon matters of policy wholly apart from any question of probable cause. Although as a member of the bar, the attorney for the United States is an officer of the court, he is nevertheless an executive official of the Government, and it is as an officer of the executive department that he exercises a discretion as to whether or not there shall be a prosecution in a particular case. It follows, as an incident of the constitutional separation of powers, that the courts are not to interfere with the free exercise of the discretionary powers of the attorneys of the United States in their control over criminal prosecutions. The provision of Rule 7, requiring the signing of the indictment by the attorney for the Government, is a recognition of the power of Government counsel to permit or not to permit the bringing of an indictment. If the attorney refuses to sign, as he has the discretionary power of doing, we conclude that there is no valid indictment. It is not to be supposed that the signature of counsel is merely an attestation of the act of the grand jury. The signature of the foreman performs that function. It is not to be supposed that the signature of counsel is a certificate that the indictment is in proper form to charge an offense. The sufficiency of the indictment may be tested before the court. Rather, we think, the requirement of the signature is for the purpose of evidencing the joinder of the attorney for the United States with the grand jury in instituting a criminal proceeding in the court. Without the signature there can be no criminal proceeding brought upon an indictment. Substantial compliance rather than technical exactness meets the requirement of the rule. There seems to be no authority for the statement that the absence of a signature is not fatal.

If it were not for the discretionary power given to the United States Attorney to prevent an indictment by withholding his signature, there might be doubt as to the constitutionality of the requirement of Rule 48 for leave of court for a dismissal of a pending prosecution.

Because, as we conclude, the signature of the Government attorney is necessary to the validity of the indictment and the affixing or withholding of the signature is a matter of executive discretion which cannot be coerced or reviewed by the courts, the contempt order must be reversed. It seems that, since the United States Attorney cannot be required to give validity to an indictment by affixing his signature, he should not be required to indulge in an exercise of futility by the preparation of the form of an indictment which he is unwilling to vitalize with his signature. Therefore he should not be required to prepare indictments which he is unwilling and under no duty to sign.

Judges Tuttle, Jones, Brown and Wisdom join in the conclusion that the signature of the United States Attorney is essential to the validity of an indictment. Judge Brown, as appears in his separate opinion, is of the view that the United States Attorney is required, upon the request of the grand jury, to draft forms of indictments in accordance with its desires. The order before us for review is in the conjunctive; it requires the United States Attorney to prepare and sign. A majority of the court, having decided that the direction to sign is erroneous, the order on appeal will be reversed.

• • •

WISDOM, Circuit Judge (concurring specially):

The dissenters show judicial craftsmanship of the highest order in writing persuasively about "the traditional sphere" of the grand jury while not turning up one case holding that a court may compel a prosecutor to prepare and sign a bill of indictment requested by a grand jury. Not one case in all the years between 1166 and 1965. I submit that the result reached in the dissent is the product of a misunderstanding of the historical meaning of "presentment and indictment," a failure to give effect to the difference between the sword and the shield of the grand jury, and an abstract approach that disregards the factual setting in which the issue is presented.

Nothing in the position of any of the judges in the majority "ignores" or tends to diminish the purely inquisitorial role of the federal grand jury. But when that role goes beyond inquiry and report and becomes accusatorial, no aura of traditional or constitutional sanctity surrounds the grand jury. The Grand Jury earned its place in the Bill of Rights by its shield, not by its sword.

• • •

II

Because recognition of the grand jury's shield-like function is lodged in the Bill of Rights, the bedrock of basic rights, it is fair to say that national policy favors a liberal construction of the power of the grand jury to protect the individual against official tyranny. No such policy favors the grand jury in its accusatorial role. Accordingly, we look for and should expect to find a check on its unjust accusations similar to the grand jury's check on the government's unjust accusations.

If there is one aspect of the doctrine of Separation of Powers that the Founding Fathers agreed upon, it is the principle, as Montesquieu stated it: "To prevent the abuse of power, it is necessary that by the very disposition of things, power should be a check to power." Taking their institutions as they found them, the framers wove a web of checks and balances designed to prevent abuse of power, regardless of the age, origin, and character of the institution. At the same time, the framers were too sophisticated to believe that the three branches of government were absolutely separate, air-tight departments. It does not matter, therefore, whether the grand jury is regarded as an arm of the court, as the Federal Grand Jury Handbook states, or is regarded as a sui generis institution derived from the people. What does matter is that the power of the executive not to prosecute, and therefore not to take steps necessarily leading to prosecution, is the appropriate curb on a grand jury in keeping with the constitutional theory of checks and balances. Such a check is especially necessary, if there is any question of the grand jury's and the district court's being in agreement; if they differ, of course the district court may dismiss the grand jury. The need is rendered more acute if there is a possibility that community hostility against the suspected offenders, individually or as a race, may jeopardize justice before the petit jury. In short, if we give the same meaning to "presentment or indictment" that Madison and others gave to these terms when Madison introduced the Bill of Rights in the First Congress, the grand jury provision in the Bill of Rights cuts both ways: it prevents harassment and intimidation and oppression through unjust prosecution—by the Grand Jury or by the Government.

III

The prosecution of offenses against the United States is an executive function within the exclusive prerogative of the Attorney General. "There shall be at the seat of government an executive department to be known as the Department of Justice, and an Attorney General, who shall be the head thereof." 5 U.S.C. § 291. That official, the chief law-enforcement officer of the Federal Government is "the hand of the president in taking care that the laws of the United States in protection of the interests of the United States in legal proceedings and in the prosecution of offenses be faithfully executed." He "has the authority, and it is made his duty, to supervise the conduct of all suits brought by or against the United States," including the authority "to begin criminal prosecution." He "is invested with the general superintendence of all such suits, and all the district attorneys who do bring them in the various courts in the country are placed under his immediate direction and control."

"The district attorney has absolute control over criminal prosecutions, and can dismiss or refuse to prosecute, any of them at his discretion. The responsibility is wholly his." The determination of whether and when to prosecute "is a matter of policy for the prosecuting officer and not for the determination of the courts." As another court has stated it:

> All of these considerations point up the wisdom of vesting broad discretion in the United States Attorney. The federal courts are powerless to interfere with his discretionary power. The Court cannot compel him to prosecute a complaint, or even an indictment, whatever his reasons for

not acting. The remedy for any dereliction of his duty lies, not with the courts, but, with the executive branch of our government and ultimately with the people.

• • •

The functions of prosecutor and judge are incompatible. In *United States v. Thompson*, for example, the Supreme Court reversed a lower court for attempting to prevent a United States Attorney from instituting criminal prosecution by resubmitting the matter to a grand jury. The Court's decision was expressly based upon "the absolute right of the United States to prosecute," and upon "the right of the Government to initiate prosecutions for crime," a right not subject to control by judicial discretion. Similarly, the Court has held that a district court was without jurisdiction to refuse to issue a warrant of arrest upon an indictment by a grand jury upon the application of the United States Attorney, because such refusal would bar "the absolute right of the United States to prosecute" and would bar "the lawful authority of the United States Attorney."

In *Goldberg v. Hoffman*, a petition for mandamus was filed against the Attorney General, an Assistant Attorney General, and the United States Attorney, to compel them to relieve the petitioner of an indictment. The Court of Appeals dismissed as to the Attorney General and Assistant Attorney General for lack of jurisdiction:

> Our adjudication of the issues raised must be guided by considerations inherent in the well-settled principle of the separation of the powers vested in the three branches of government, which is the keynote of our constitutional mandate. We must bear in mind that the United States Attorney is an officer of the executive branch responsible primarily to the President, and, through him, to the electorate, and that the remedy sought against Tieken is a broad one, to-wit, a direct mandate from this court compelling him to take, or refrain from taking, a specific course of action with respect to the indictment pending against petitioner. More specifically, we are asked to review the exercise of administrative discretion, overrule the decision of the executive and direct the course which that discretion must take. We think such judicial control of an executive officer is beyond the power of this court.

• • •

Rule 48(a) does not directly apply to the present case, because there has been no indictment, information, or complaint, but since the rule preserves the prosecutor's discretion to dismiss a complaint before indictment, the drafters of the Rules must have intended to preserve the discretion not to prosecute. In this case, the prosecutor cannot move to dismiss; there is nothing to dismiss. What he can do, however, is to refuse to prepare and sign the indictment. Under this theory, Rule 7(c), requiring that the indictment be signed by the United States Attorney, preserves the prosecutor's traditional discretion as to whether to initiate prosecution.

The reason for vesting discretion to prosecute in the Executive, acting through the Attorney General is two-fold. First, in the interests of justice and the orderly, efficient administration of the law, some person or agency should be able to prevent an unjust prosecution. The freedom of the petit jury to bring in a verdict of not guilty and the progressive development of the law in the direction of making more meaningful the guarantees of an accused person's constitutional rights give considerable protection to the individual before and after trial. They do not protect against a baseless prosecution. This is a harassment to the accused and an expensive strain on the machinery of justice. The appropriate repository for authority to prevent a baseless prosecution is the chief law-enforcement officer whose duty, unlike the grand jury's duty, is to collect evidence on both sides of a case.

Second, when, within the context of law-enforcement, national policy is involved, because of national security, conduct of foreign policy, or a conflict between two branches of government, the appropriate branch to decide the matter is the executive branch. The executive is charged with carrying out national policy on law-enforcement and, generally speaking, is informed on more levels than the more specialized judicial and legislative branches. In such a situation, a decision not to prosecute is analogous to the exercise of executive privilege. The executive's absolute and exclusive discretion to prosecute may be rationalized as an illustration of the doctrine of separation of powers, but it would have evolved without the doctrine and exists in countries that do not purport to accept this doctrine.

IV

This brings me to the facts. They demonstrate, better than abstract principles or legal dicta, the imperative necessity that the United States, through its Attorney General, have uncontrollable discretion to prosecute.

The crucial fact here is that Goff and Kendrick, two Negroes, testified in a suit by the United States against the Registrar of Clarke County, Mississippi, and the State of Mississippi, to enforce the voting rights of Negroes under the Fourteenth Amendment and the Civil Rights Act.

Goff and Kendrick testified that some seven years earlier at Stonewall, Mississippi, the registrar had refused to register them or give them application forms. They said that they had seen white persons registering, one of whom was a B. Floyd Jones. Ramsey, the registrar, testified that Jones had not registered at that time or place, but had registered the year before in Enterprise, Mississippi. He testified also that he had never discriminated against Negro applicants for registration. Jones testified that he was near the registration table in Stonewall in 1955, had talked with the registrar, and had shaken hands with him. The presiding judge, Judge W. Harold Cox, stated from the bench that Goff and Kendrick should be "bound over to await the action of the grand jury for perjury."

In January 1963 attorneys of the Department of Justice requested the Federal Bureau of Investigation to investigate the possible perjury. The FBI completed a full investigation in March 1963 and referred the matter to the Department's Criminal Division. In June 1963 the Criminal Division advised the local United States Attorney, Mr. Hauberg, that the matter presented "no basis for a perjury prosecution." Mr. Hauberg informed Judge Cox of the Department's decision. Judge Cox stated that in his view the matter was clearly one for the grand jury and that he would be inclined, if necessary, to appoint an outside attorney to present the matter to the grand jury. (I find no authority for a federal judge to displace the United States Attorney by appointing a special prosecutor.) On receiving this information, the Criminal Division again reviewed its files and concluded that the charge of perjury could not be sustained. General Katzenbach, then Deputy Attorney General, after reviewing the files, concurred in the Criminal Division's decision. In September 1963 General Katzenbach called on Judge Cox as a courtesy to explain why the Department had arrived at the conclusion that no perjury was involved. Judge Cox, unconvinced, requested the United States Attorney to present to the grand jury the Goff and Kendrick cases, which he regarded as cases of "palpable perjury."

In October 1963 Goff and Kendrick were arrested, jailed for two days, and placed on a $3,000 bond for violations of State law for falsely testifying in federal court. After their indictment by a state grand jury, the Department of Justice filed suit against the State District Attorney, United States v. Warner, (Civ. No. 1219, S.D. Miss.), seeking to enjoin the state prosecution on the grounds that: (1) the States have no authority to prosecute for alleged perjury committed while testifying in a federal court; (2) the purpose and effect of the State's prosecution was to threaten and intimidate Goff and Kendrick and to inhibit them and other Negroes from registering to vote. The district court (per Mize, J.) ruled in favor of the United States.

C. Grand Jury Independence and Informality

The Federal Grand Jury, originally convened on September 9, 1963, was reconvened on September 21, 1964. September 28, 1964, the Foreman of the Grand Jury advised the Government Attorney who was presenting matters to the Grand Jury that Judge Cox had asked the Foreman to hear several witnesses. September 29, 1964, Mr. Riddell, attorney for the Registrar, and the district attorney for the Second Circuit District for the State of Mississippi, Mr. Holleman, came to the courthouse to appear before the Grand Jury. Judge Mize, in a special charge to the Grand Jury stated—in open court— that Judge Cox had informed him, before leaving for his vacation, that:

> . . . he wanted the Grand Jury to call before it Mr. Boyce Holleman of Gulfport, Mississippi and Mr. Talley Riddell of Quitman, Mississippi as witnesses, because it was his impression that they had some matters that ought to be investigated at least and that they should be permitted to appear.

Judge Mize stated that he was not familiar with the matters "other than just what Judge Cox requested me to do, to see to it that these two witnesses had an opportunity to appear before the Grand Jury." Judge Mize advised the Grand Jury that they had a right to hear the testimony of Messrs. Riddell and Holleman, but requested them not to do so until October 21, 1964, the day after Judge Cox was to return from his vacation.

October 20 Mr. Katzenbach talked with Judge Cox by telephone, reiterating the Department's position. He also instructed Mr. Hauberg not to prepare or sign indictments. October 22 the foreman of the grand jury in open court informed Judge Cox that Mr. Hauberg had declined to assist in preparing true bills. The United States Attorney stated that "the Department of Justice and the United States felt as if that the law and the fact was not sufficient to constitute perjury and that an indictment thereon would be no good." Judge Cox said:

> I here and now order and direct you to disregard your instructions from the Department of Justice and to prepare true bills or no bills as this Grand Jury may direct you to do and to sign those bills or no bills, as the Grand Jury may decide under penalty of contempt. . . ."

Judge Cox recessed court for one hour. During this recess Mr. Hauberg and Mr. Katzenbach conferred by telephone; the Attorney General directed the United States Attorney not to prepare or sign perjury indictments of Goff and Kendrick. Court reopened. Mr. Hauberg respectfully declined to comply with the court's order. Judge Cox forthwith adjudged him "guilty of civil contempt," ordered him confined to a jail in Hinds County, ordered the issuance of a citation to the Acting Attorney General to appear before the court to show cause why he should not be held in contempt; and stayed the order for a period of five days.

Against the backdrop of Mississippi versus the Nation in the field of civil rights, we have a heated but bona fide difference of opinion between Judge Cox and the Attorney General as to whether two Negroes, Goff and Kendrick, should be prosecuted for perjury. Taking a narrow view of the case, we would be justified in holding that the Attorney General's implied powers, by analogy to the express powers of Rule 48(a), give him discretion to prosecute. Here there was a bona fide, reasonable exercise of discretion made after a full investigation and long consideration of the case—both sides of the case, not just the evidence tending to show guilt. If the grand jury is dissatisfied with that administrative decision, it may exercise its inquisitorial power and make a presentment in open court. It could be said, that is all there is to the case. But there is more to the case.

This Court, along with everyone else, knows that Goff and Kendrick, if prosecuted, run the risk of being tried in a climate of community hostility. They run the risk of a punishment that may not fit the crime. The Registrar, who provoked the original litigation, runs no risk, notwithstanding the fact that the district court, in effect, found that Ramsay did not tell the truth on the witness stand. In these circumstances, the very least demands of

660 Chapter VII Grand Jury

justice require that the discretion to prosecute be lodged with a person or agency insulated from local prejudices and parochial pressures. This is not the hard case that makes bad law. This is the type of case that comes up, in one way or another, whenever the customs, beliefs, or interests of a region collide with national policy as fixed by the Constitution or by Congress. It is not likely that the men who devised diversity jurisdiction expected to turn over to local juries the discretionary power to bring federal prosecutions. This case is unusual only for the clarity with which the facts, speaking for themselves, illuminate the imperative necessity in American Federalism that the discretion to prosecute be lodged in the Attorney General of United States.

The decision not to prosecute represents the exercise of a discretion analogous to the exercise of executive privilege. As a matter of law, the Attorney General has concluded that there is not sufficient evidence to prove perjury. As a matter of fact, the Attorney General has concluded, as he pleaded in *United States v. Warner*, that trial for perjury would have the effect of inhibiting not only Goff and Kendrick but other Negroes in Mississippi from registering to vote. There is a conflict, therefore, between society's interest in law enforcement (diluted in this case by the Attorney General's conclusion that the evidence does not support the charge of guilt) and the national policy, set forth in the Constitution and the Civil Rights Acts, of outlawing racial discrimination. It is unthinkable that resolution of this important conflict affecting the whole Nation should lie with a majority of twenty-three members of a jury chosen from the Southern District of Mississippi. The nature of American Federalism, looking to the differences between the Constitution and the Articles of Confederation, requires that the power to resolve this question lie in the unfettered discretion of the President of United States or his deputy for law enforcement, the Attorney General.

My memory, too, goes back to the days, pointedly referred to by the dissenters, when we had "an Attorney General suspected of being corrupt." But I am not aware that we have had more lawless Attorneys General than lawless juries.

NOTES AND QUESTIONS

1. Judge Cox's order, the subject of the appeal, purports to require the United States attorney to draft and sign the bills requested by the grand jury. The order also reveals that Judge Cox appears to have had other involvement with this particular grand jury. How else does he seem to have been involved? Was such involvement permissible? What additional involvement is revealed in Judge Wisdom's opinion? Does a district court judge have any legitimate recourse if he believes a witness is committing perjury in his courtroom?

2. Rule 7(c) of the Federal Rules of Criminal Procedure appears to address purely matters of form, dispensing with technical requirements (much like its civil analogue, Fed. R. Civ. P. 8) and providing, seemingly by way of housekeeping, that it "shall be signed an attorney for the government." Was this rule really intended to carry the weight the court assigns it here?

3. Note that the opinion of the court does not address the underlying facts. Why not?

4. Judge Wisdom opens his opinion by declaring that "[t]he grand jury earned its place in the Bill of Rights by its shield, not its sword." What point is he trying to make here? In the same passage he contrasts the "inquisitorial" and "accusatorial" roles of the grand jury, and notes that in the latter role "no aura of traditional or constitutionality sanctity surrounds the grand jury." *Id.* at 186. How does this compare with the Supreme Court's view of the grand jury decades later in *Williams*?

5. Judge Wisdom finds ample legal authority for the proposition that the prosecution of federal crimes is the "exclusive prerogative" of the executive function, further expressed by statute in Rules 7(c) and 48(a) of the Federal Rules of Criminal Procedure. *See* Chapter IX *infra*. He also views this allocation as wise insofar as the executive branch is the best-suited body for making prosecutorial decisions when matters of "national policy" are involved. What sort of "national policy" is he referring to? Does this sentiment amount to an endorsement of a role for politics in prosecutorial decision making?

6. Here, the DOJ concluded that there was no basis for a perjury prosecution of Goff and Kendrick. (That is not surprising, as it was fellow DOJ lawyers who elicited their testimony.) What if instead the DOJ had doubts about the veracity of their testimony, and believed they may have committed perjury? Was nonprosecution nonetheless justified because of the chilling effect such a prosecution might have on other potential government witnesses in voting rights cases? Was nonprosecution justified by the "lawless juries" likely to be empaneled for such a prosecution?

7. Judge Wisdom states that if the grand jury is dissatisfied with the prosecutor's decision not to indict, its recourse is to "exercise its inquisitorial power and make a presentment in open court." *Id.* at 196. Do you agree that the grand jury has that power?

The presiding district court judge here, Harold Cox, was roommates at the University of Mississippi with James Eastland, who would go on to be a United States senator from Mississippi from 1943 to 1978, leading southern resistance to integration for four decades. Supposedly, President Kennedy's nomination of Cox to a federal judgeship in the early 1960s was a quid pro quo for Eastland's agreement not to oppose Thurgood Marshall's contemporaneous nomination to the Second Circuit. Iconic NAACP civil rights lawyer and future federal judge Constance Baker Motley, who spent much of her life in the early 1960s litigating in federal court in Mississippi, including in connection with James Meredith's efforts to gain admission to the University of Mississippi, called Judge Cox "the most openly racist judge to ever sit on a federal court bench." Constance Baker Motley, Equal Justice Under Law: An Autobiography 180 (1999).

U.S. District Court Judge Harold Cox

Nicholas Katzenbach

662   Chapter VII Grand Jury

D. GRAND JURY SUBPOENA POWER

The grand jury does its work through subpoenas. Grand jury subpoenas for documents are analogous to their civil counterparts—*see* Fed. R. Civ. P. 34 & 45—in that they purport to require the recipient to produce materials at the location of the grand jury room at a specified date. The similarities largely end there. There are no geographical limits on the grand jury's service of subpoenas, and there is no provision in the Federal Rules for "objecting" to grand jury subpoenas, although most prosecutors—remember, these are really the prosecutors' subpoenas—will usually be reasonable about the terms of compliance. The next two cases consider the breadth of the grand jury's subpoena power.

United States v. Dionisio
410 U.S. 1 (1973)

Mr. Justice STEWART delivered the opinion of the Court.

A special grand jury was convened in the Northern District of Illinois in February 1971, to investigate possible violations of federal criminal statutes relating to gambling. In the course of its investigation, the grand jury received in evidence certain voice recordings that had been obtained pursuant to court orders.

The grand jury subpoenaed approximately 20 persons, including the respondent Dionisio, seeking to obtain from them voice exemplars for comparison with the recorded conversations that had been received in evidence. Each witness was advised that he was a potential defendant in a criminal prosecution. Each was asked to examine a transcript of an intercepted conversation, and to go to a nearby office of the United States Attorney to read the transcript into a recording device. The witnesses were advised that they would be allowed to have their attorneys present when they read the transcripts. Dionisio and other witnesses refused to furnish the voice exemplars, asserting that these disclosures would violate their rights under the Fourth and Fifth Amendments.

The Government then filed separate petitions in the United States District Court to compel Dionisio and the other witnesses to furnish the voice exemplars to the grand jury. The petitions stated that the exemplars were "essential and necessary" to the grand jury investigation, and that they would "be used solely as a standard of comparison in order to determine whether or not the witness is the person whose voice was intercepted. . . ."

Following a hearing, the District Judge rejected the witnesses' constitutional arguments and ordered them to comply with the grand jury's request. He reasoned that voice exemplars, like handwriting exemplars or fingerprints, were not testimonial or communicative evidence, and that consequently the order to produce them would not compel any witness to testify against himself. The District Judge also found that there would be no Fourth Amendment violation, because the grand jury subpoena did not itself violate the Fourth Amendment, and the order to produce the voice exemplars would involve no unreasonable search and seizure within the proscription of that Amendment:

> The witnesses are lawfully before the grand jury pursuant to subpoena. The Fourth Amendment prohibition against unreasonable search and seizure applies only where identifying physical characteristics, such as fingerprints, are obtained as a result of unlawful detention of a suspect, or when an intrusion into the body, such as a blood test, is undertaken without a warrant, absent an emergency situation.

When Dionisio persisted in his refusal to respond to the grand jury's directive, the District Court adjudged him in civil contempt and ordered him committed to custody until he obeyed the court order, or until the expiration of 18 months.

D. Grand Jury Subpoena Power

The Court of Appeals for the Seventh Circuit reversed. It agreed with the District Court in rejecting the Fifth Amendment claims, but concluded that to compel the voice recordings would violate the Fourth Amendment. In the court's view, the grand jury was "seeking to obtain the voice exemplars of the witnesses by the use of its subpoena powers because probable cause did not exist for their arrest or for some other, less unusual, method of compelling the production of the exemplars." The court found that the Fourth Amendment applied to grand jury process, and that "under the fourth amendment law enforcement officials may not compel the production of physical evidence absent a showing of the reasonableness of the seizure."

In *Davis* this Court held that it was error to admit the petitioner's fingerprints into evidence at his trial for rape, because they had been obtained during a police detention following a lawless wholesale roundup of the petitioner and more than 20 other youths. Equating the procedures followed by the grand jury in the present case to the fingerprint detentions in Davis, the Court of Appeals reasoned that "(t)he dragnet effect here, where approximately twenty persons were subpoenaed for purposes of identification, has the same invidious effect on fourth amendment rights as the practice condemned in *Davis*."

I

The Court of Appeals correctly rejected the contention that the compelled production of the voice exemplars would violate the Fifth Amendment. It has long been held that the compelled display of identifiable physical characteristics infringes no interest protected by the privilege against compulsory self-incrimination. In *Holt v. United States*, Mr. Justice Holmes, writing for the Court, dismissed as an "extravagant extension of the Fifth Amendment" the argument that it violated the privilege to require a defendant to put on a blouse for identification purposes. He explained that "the prohibition of compelling a man in a criminal court to be witness against himself is a prohibition of the use of physical or moral compulsion to extort communications from him, not an exclusion of his body as evidence when it may be material."

More recently, in *Schmerber* we relied on *Holt*, and noted that:

> (B)oth federal and state courts have usually held that (the privilege) it offers no protection against compulsion to submit to fingerprinting, photographing, or measurements, to write or speak for identification, to appear in court, to stand, to assume a stance, to walk, or to make a particular gesture. The distinction which has emerged, often expressed in different ways, is that the privilege is a bar against compelling "communications" or "testimony," but that compulsion which makes a suspect or accused the source of "real or physical evidence" does not violate it.

The Court held that the extraction and chemical analysis of a blood sample involved no "shadow of testimonial compulsion upon or enforced communication by the accused."

These cases led us to conclude in *Gilbert v. California* that handwriting exemplars were not protected by the privilege against compulsory self-incrimination. While "(o)ne's voice and handwriting are, of course, means of communication," we held that a "mere handwriting exemplar, in contrast to the content of what is written, like the voice or body itself, is an identifying physical characteristic outside its protection." And similarly in *United States v. Wade* we found no error in compelling a defendant accused of bank robbery to utter in a lineup words that had allegedly been spoken by the robber. The accused there was "required to use his voice as an identifying physical characteristic, not to speak his guilt."

Wade and *Gilbert* definitively refute any contention that the compelled production of the voice exemplars in this case would violate the Fifth Amendment. The voice recordings were to be used solely to measure the physical properties of the witnesses' voices, not for the testimonial or communicative content of what was to be said.

II

The Court of Appeals held that the Fourth Amendment required a preliminary showing of reasonableness before a grand jury witness could be compelled to furnish a voice exemplar, and that in this case the proposed "seizures" of the voice exemplars would be unreasonable because of the large number of witnesses summoned by the grand jury and directed to produce such exemplars. We disagree.

The Fourth Amendment guarantees that all people shall be "secure in their persons, houses, papers, and effects, against unreasonable searches and seizures. . . ." Any Fourth Amendment violation in the present setting must rest on a lawless governmental intrusion upon the privacy of "persons" rather than on interference with "property relationships or private papers." In *Terry v. Ohio* the Court explained the protection afforded to "persons" in terms of the statement in *Katz v. United States*, that "the Fourth Amendment protects people, not places," and concluded that "wherever an individual may harbor a reasonable 'expectation of privacy,' . . . he is entitled to be free from unreasonable governmental intrusion."

As the Court made clear in *Schmerber*, supra, the obtaining of physical evidence from a person involves a potential Fourth Amendment violation at two different levels — the "seizure" of the "person" necessary to bring him into contact with government agents, and the subsequent search for and seizure of the evidence. In *Schmerber*, we found the initial seizure of the accused justified as a lawful arrest, and the subsequent seizure of the blood sample from his body reasonable in light of the exigent circumstances. And in *Terry*, we concluded that neither the initial seizure of the person, an investigatory "stop" by a policeman, nor the subsequent search, a "patdown" of his outer clothing for weapons, constituted a violation of the Fourth and Fourteenth Amendments. The constitutionality of the compulsory production of exemplars from a grand jury witness necessarily turns on the same dual inquiry — whether either the initial compulsion of the person to appear before the grand jury, or the subsequent directive to make a voice recording is an unreasonable "seizure" within the meaning of the Fourth Amendment.

It is clear that a subpoena to appear before a grand jury is not a "seizure" in the Fourth Amendment sense, even though that summons may be inconvenient or burdensome. Last Term we again acknowledged what has long been recognized, that "(c)itizens generally are not constitutionally immune from grand jury subpoenas. . . ." We concluded that:

> Although the powers of the grand jury are not unlimited and are subject to the supervision of a judge, the longstanding principle that "the public . . . has a right to every man's evidence," except for those persons protected by a constitutional, common law, or statutory privilege is particularly applicable to grand jury proceedings.

These are recent reaffirmations of the historically grounded obligation of every person to appear and give his evidence before the grand jury. "The personal sacrifice involved is a part of the necessary contribution of the individual to the welfare of the public." And while the duty may be "onerous" at times, it is "necessary to the administration of justice."

The compulsion exerted by a grand jury subpoena differs from the seizure effected by an arrest or even an investigative "stop" in more than civic obligation. For, as Judge Friendly wrote for the Court of Appeals for the Second Circuit:

> The latter is abrupt, is effected with force or the threat of it and often in demeaning circumstances, and, in the case of arrest, results in a record involving social stigma. A subpoena is served in the same manner as other legal process; it involves no stigma whatever; if the time for appearance is inconvenient, this can generally be altered; and it remains at all times under the control and supervision of a court.

Thus the Court of Appeals for the Seventh Circuit correctly recognized in a case subsequent to the one now before us, that a "grand jury subpoena to testify is not that kind of governmental intrusion on privacy against which the Fourth Amendment affords protection once the Fifth Amendment is satisfied."

This case is thus quite different from *Davis v. Mississippi*, supra, on which the Court of Appeals primarily relied. For in *Davis* it was the initial seizure — the lawless dragnet detention — that violated the Fourth and Fourteenth Amendments, not the taking of the fingerprints. We noted that "(i)nvestigatory seizures would subject unlimited numbers of innocent persons to the harassment and ignominy incident to involuntary detention," and we left open the question whether, consistently with the Fourth and Fourteenth Amendments, narrowly circumscribed procedures might be developed for obtaining fingerprints from people when there was no probable cause to arrest them. *Davis* is plainly inapposite to a case where the initial restraint does not itself infringe the Fourth Amendment.

This is not to say that a grand jury subpoena is some talisman that dissolves all constitutional protections. The grand jury cannot require a witness to testify against himself. It cannot require the production by a person of private books and records that would incriminate him. The Fourth Amendment provides protection against a grand jury subpoena duces tecum too sweeping in its terms "to be regarded as reasonable." *Hale v. Henkel.* And last Term, in the context of a First Amendment claim, we indicated that the Constitution could not tolerate the transformation of the grand jury into an instrument of oppression: "Official harassment of the press undertaken not for purposes of law enforcement but to disrupt a reporter's relationship with his news sources would have no justification. Grand juries are subject to judicial control and subpoenas to motions to quash. We do not expect courts will forget that grand juries must operate within the limits of the First Amendment as well as the Fifth."

But we are here faced with no such constitutional infirmities in the subpoena to appear before the grand jury or in the order to make the voice recordings. There is, as we have said, no valid Fifth Amendment claim. There was no order to produce private books and papers, and no sweeping subpoena duces tecum. And even if *Branzburg* be extended beyond its First Amendment moorings and tied to a more generalized *due* process concept, there is still no indication in this case of the kind of harassment that was of concern there.

The Court of Appeals found critical significance in the fact that the grand jury had summoned approximately 20 witnesses to furnish voice exemplars. We think that fact is basically irrelevant to the constitutional issues here. The grand jury may have been attempting to identify a number of voices on the tapes in evidence, or it might have summoned the 20 witnesses in an effort to identify one voice. But whatever the case, "(a) grand jury's investigation is not fully carried out until every available clue has been run down and all witnesses examined in every proper way to find if a crime has been committed. . . ." As the Court recalled last Term, "Because its task is to inquire into the existence of possible criminal conduct and to return only well-founded indictments, its investigative powers are necessarily broad." The grand jury may well find it desirable to call numerous witnesses in the course of an investigation. It does not follow that each witness may resist a subpoena on the ground that too many witnesses have been called. Neither the order to Dionisio to appear nor the order to make a voice recording was rendered unreasonable by the fact that many others were subjected to the same compulsion.

But the conclusion that Dionisio's compulsory appearance before the grand jury was not an unreasonable "seizure" is the answer to only the first part of the Fourth Amendment inquiry here. Dionisio argues that the grand jury's subsequent directive to make the voice recording was itself an infringement of his rights under the Fourth Amendment. We cannot accept that argument.

In *Katz v. United States* we said that the Fourth Amendment provides no protection for what "a person knowingly exposes to the public, even in his own home or office. . . ." The physical characteristics of a person's voice, its tone and manner, as opposed to the content of a specific conversation, are constantly exposed to the public. Like a man's facial characteristics, or handwriting, his voice is repeatedly produced for others to hear. No person can have a reasonable expectation that others will not know the sound of his voice, any more than he can reasonably expect that his face will be a mystery to the world. As the Court of Appeals for the Second Circuit stated:

> Except for the rare recluse who chooses to live his life in complete solitude, in our daily lives we constantly speak and write, and while the content of a communication is entitled to Fourth Amendment protection . . . the underlying identifying characteristics — the constant factor throughout both public and private communications — are open for all to see or hear. There is no basis for constructing a wall of privacy against the grand jury which does not exist in casual contacts with strangers. Hence no intrusion into an individual's privacy results from compelled execution of handwriting or voice exemplars; nothing is being exposed to the grand jury that has not previously been exposed to the public at large.

The required disclosure of a person's voice is thus immeasurably further removed from the Fourth Amendment protection than was the intrusion into the body effected by the blood extraction in *Schmerber*. "The interests in human dignity and privacy which the Fourth Amendment protects forbid any such intrusions on the mere chance that desired evidence might be obtained." Similarly, a seizure of voice exemplars does not involve the "severe, though brief, intrusion upon cherished personal security," effected by the "pat down" in *Terry* — "surely . . . an annoying, frightening, and perhaps humiliating experience." Rather, this is like the fingerprinting in *Davis*, where, though the initial dragnet detentions were constitutionally impermissible, we noted that the fingerprinting itself "involves none of the probing into an individual's private life and thoughts that marks an interrogation or search."

Since neither the summons to appear before the grand jury nor its directive to make a voice recording infringed upon any interest protected by the Fourth Amendment, there was no justification for requiring the grand jury to satisfy even the minimal requirement of "reasonableness" imposed by the Court of Appeals. A grand jury has broad investigative powers to determine whether a crime has been committed and who has committed it. The jurors may act on tips, rumors, evidence offered by the prosecutor, or their own personal knowledge. No grand jury witness is "entitled to set limits to the investigation that the grand jury may conduct." And a sufficient basis for an indictment may only emerge at the end of the investigation when all the evidence has been received.

> It is impossible to conceive that . . . the examination of witnesses must be stopped until a basis is laid by an indictment formally preferred, when the very object of the examination is to ascertain who shall be indicted.

Since Dionisio raised no valid Fourth Amendment claim, there is no more reason to require a preliminary showing of reasonableness here than there would be in the case of any witness who, despite the lack of any constitutional or statutory privilege, declined to answer a question or comply with a grand jury request. Neither the Constitution nor our prior cases justify any such interference with grand jury proceedings.

The Fifth Amendment guarantees that no civilian may be brought to trial for an infamous crime "unless on a presentment or indictment of a Grand Jury." This constitutional guarantee presupposes an investigative body "acting independently of either prosecuting attorney or judge," *Stirone v. United States*, whose mission is to clear the innocent, no less than to bring to trial those who may be guilty. Any holding that would saddle a grand jury with minitrials and preliminary showings would assuredly impede its investigation and frustrate the public's interest in the fair and expeditious administration of the criminal laws. The grand jury may not always serve its historic role as a protective bulwark standing solidly between the ordinary citizen and an overzealous prosecutor, but if it is even to approach the proper performance of its constitutional mission, it must be free to pursue its investigations unhindered by external

D. Grand Jury Subpoena Power   **667**

influence or supervision so long as it does not trench upon the legitimate rights of any witness called before it.

Since the Court of Appeals found an unreasonable search and seizure where none existed, and imposed a preliminary showing of reasonableness where none was required, its judgment is reversed and this case is remanded to that court for further proceedings consistent with this opinion.

It is so ordered.

Judgment reversed and case remanded.

NOTES AND QUESTIONS

1. No specific Rule of the Federal Rules of Criminal Procedure governs grand jury subpoenas, an issue that we consider more thoroughly in connection with *United States v. R. Enterprises, Inc.*, 498 U.S. 292 (1991), *infra*. But consider exactly what the grand jury subpoenas here purport to require of the witnesses: reading from a transcript at a United States attorney's office. The witnesses are not even appearing personally before the grand jury. Does the grand jury have the power to require a witness to testify before another person? Should it?

The government apparently was sensitive to the odd nature of this request as it permitted the witnesses' attorneys to be present during the reading, which would normally be a violation of grand jury secrecy laws governing who may be present during grand jury testimony. *See infra*. And in its motion to compel enforcement of the subpoenas the government had no problem telling the court exactly why it needed the voice exemplars, information prosecutors often refuse to disclose in court due to "grand jury secrecy" concerns. Is the government's description of the basic nature of an investigation really a violation of grand jury secrecy?

2. The Court rejects the defendant's Fifth Amendment argument that the compelled voice exemplars violated his right against self-incrimination, reasoning that they were not "testimonial" but merely "the compelled display of physical characteristics." Do you agree? Is the compelled reading of a transcript (of unknown length) simply a revealing of a physical characteristic? Both of the dissenters disagree with the "testimonial" limit on Fifth Amendment compulsion, but do you have to go that far to disagree with the majority in this case? Are the witnesses here being asked merely for "exemplars"?

3. The Court also rejects the argument that a grand jury subpoena is a "seizure" for Fourth Amendment purposes, and in particular rejects the analogy to the "investigative seizure" condemned by the Court in *Davis v. Mississippi*, 394 U.S. 721 (1969). Justice Douglas's dissent in a companion case to *Dionisio, United States v. Mara*, 410 U.S. 19 (1973), on the other hand, finds the "dragnet effect" at issue to be "just the kind of invasion that the *Davis* case sought to prevent." *Id*. at 26-27. Do you agree? Is it relevant to this issue that Dionisio and Mara were among 20 people that were subpoenaed?

4. In rejecting the seizure argument the Court concedes that the Fourth Amendment at least provides protection against grand jury subpoenas that are unreasonably broad. *Dionisio*, 410 U.S. at 11-12. In reaching this conclusion the Court relied on the venerable case of *Hale v. Henkel*, 201 U.S. 43, 77 (1906), which held that a subpoena lacking in particularity is "equally indefensible as a search warrant would be if couched in similar terms," and that in such cases a showing of "some necessity" may be required of the government.

How is any such overbreadth argument to be analyzed in the typical case where the government has revealed little about the subject of the grand jury's investigation? Were the subpoenas here unreasonably broad, either individually or when analyzed as a group of 20?

5. Justice Douglas begins his *Mara* dissent with the following quotation from United States District Court Judge William Campbell, who has been on the federal court in Chicago for over 32 years:

> This great institution of the past has long ceased to be the guardian of the people for which purpose it was created at Runnymede. Today it is but a convenient tool for the prosecutor—too often used solely for publicity. Any experienced prosecutor will admit that he can indict anybody at any time for almost anything before any grand jury.

Mara, 410 U.S. at 23. This is the earliest public acknowledgment by a Supreme Court Justice that the federal grand jury—no matter how it was conceived or envisioned by the Founders—may not be what the Court says it is. Yet the love songs continued well after *Dionisio*.

United States v. R. Enterprises, Inc.
498 U.S. 292 (1991)

Justice O'CONNOR delivered the opinion of the Court.

This case requires the Court to decide what standards apply when a party seeks to avoid compliance with a subpoena duces tecum issued in connection with a grand jury investigation.

I

Since 1986, a federal grand jury sitting in the Eastern District of Virginia has been investigating allegations of interstate transportation of obscene materials. In early 1988, the grand jury issued a series of subpoenas to three companies—Model Magazine Distributors, Inc. (Model), R. Enterprises, Inc., and MFR Court Street Books, Inc. (MFR). Model is a New York distributor of sexually oriented paperback books, magazines, and videotapes. R. Enterprises, which distributes adult materials, and MFR, which sells books, magazines, and videotapes, are also based in New York. All three companies are wholly owned by Martin Rothstein. The grand jury subpoenas sought a variety of corporate books and records and, in Model's case, copies of 193 videotapes that Model had shipped to retailers in the Eastern District of Virginia. All three companies moved to quash the subpoenas, arguing that the subpoenas called for production of materials irrelevant to the grand jury's investigation and that the enforcement of the subpoenas would likely infringe their First Amendment rights.

The District Court, after extensive hearings, denied the motions to quash. As to Model, the court found that the subpoenas for business records were sufficiently specific and that production of the videotapes would not constitute a prior restraint. As to R. Enterprises, the court found a "sufficient connection with Virginia for further investigation by the grand jury." The court relied in large part on the statement attributed to Rothstein that the three companies were "all the same thing, I'm president of all three." Ibid. Additionally, the court explained in denying MFR's motion to quash that it was "inclined to agree" with "the majority of the jurisdictions," which do not require the Government to make a "threshold showing" before a grand jury subpoena will be enforced. Even assuming that a preliminary showing of relevance was required, the court determined that the Government had made such a showing. It found sufficient evidence that the companies were "related entities," at least one of which "certainly did ship sexually explicit material into the Commonwealth of Virginia." Ibid. The court concluded that the subpoenas in this case were "fairly standard business subpoenas" and "ought to be complied with." Notwithstanding these findings, the companies refused to comply with the subpoenas. The District Court found each in contempt and fined them $500 per day, but stayed imposition of the fine pending appeal.

The Court of Appeals for the Fourth Circuit upheld the business records subpoenas issued to Model, but remanded the motion to quash the subpoena for Model's videotapes. Of particular relevance here, the Court of Appeals quashed the business records subpoenas issued to R. Enterprises and MFR. In doing so, it applied the standards set out by this Court in *United States v. Nixon* (1974). The court recognized that *Nixon* dealt with a trial subpoena, not a grand jury subpoena, but determined that the rule was "equally applicable" in the grand jury context. Accordingly, it required the Government to clear the three hurdles that *Nixon* established in the trial context—relevancy, admissibility, and specificity—in order to enforce the grand jury subpoenas. The court concluded that the challenged subpoenas did not satisfy the *Nixon* standards, finding no evidence in the record that either company had ever shipped materials into, or otherwise conducted business in, the Eastern District of Virginia. The Court of Appeals specifically criticized the District Court for drawing an inference that, because Rothstein owned all three businesses and one of them had undoubtedly shipped sexually explicit materials into the Eastern District of Virginia, there might be some link between the Eastern District of Virginia and R. Enterprises or MFR. It then noted that "any evidence concerning Mr. Rothstein's alleged business activities outside of Virginia, or his ownership of companies which distribute allegedly obscene materials outside of Virginia, would most likely be inadmissible on relevancy grounds at any trial that might occur," and that the subpoenas therefore failed "to meet the requirements [sic] that any documents subpoenaed under [Federal] Rule [of Criminal Procedure] 17(c) must be admissible as evidence at trial." The Court of Appeals did not consider whether enforcement of the subpoenas duces tecum issued to respondents implicated the First Amendment.

We granted certiorari to determine whether the Court of Appeals applied the proper standard in evaluating the grand jury subpoenas issued to respondents. We now reverse.

II

The grand jury occupies a unique role in our criminal justice system. It is an investigatory body charged with the responsibility of determining whether or not a crime has been committed. Unlike this Court, whose jurisdiction is predicated on a specific case or controversy, the grand jury "can investigate merely on suspicion that the law is being violated, or even just because it wants assurance that it is not." The function of the grand jury is to inquire into all information that might possibly bear on its investigation until it has identified an offense or has satisfied itself that none has occurred. As a necessary consequence of its investigatory function, the grand jury paints with a broad brush. "A grand jury investigation 'is not fully carried out until every available clue has been run down and all witnesses examined in every proper way to find if a crime has been committed.'"

A grand jury subpoena is thus much different from a subpoena issued in the context of a prospective criminal trial, where a specific offense has been identified and a particular defendant charged. "[T]he identity of the offender, and the precise nature of the offense, if there be one, normally are developed at the conclusion of the grand jury's labors, not at the beginning." In short, the Government cannot be required to justify the issuance of a grand jury subpoena by presenting evidence sufficient to establish probable cause because the very purpose of requesting the information is to ascertain whether probable cause exists.

This Court has emphasized on numerous occasions that many of the rules and restrictions that apply at a trial do not apply in grand jury proceedings. This is especially true of evidentiary restrictions. The same rules that, in an adversary hearing on the merits, may increase the likelihood of accurate determinations of guilt or innocence do not necessarily advance the mission of a grand jury, whose task is to conduct an ex parte investigation to determine whether or not there is probable cause to prosecute a particular defendant. In *Costello* this

Court declined to apply the rule against hearsay to grand jury proceedings. Strict observance of trial rules in the context of a grand jury's preliminary investigation "would result in interminable delay but add nothing to the assurance of a fair trial." In *Calandra* we held that the Fourth Amendment exclusionary rule does not apply to grand jury proceedings. Permitting witnesses to invoke the exclusionary rule would "delay and disrupt grand jury proceedings" by requiring adversary hearings on peripheral matters, and would effectively transform such proceedings into preliminary trials on the merits. The teaching of the Court's decisions is clear: A grand jury "may compel the production of evidence or the testimony of witnesses as it considers appropriate, and its operation generally is unrestrained by the technical procedural and evidentiary rules governing the conduct of criminal trials."

This guiding principle renders suspect the Court of Appeals' holding that the standards announced in *Nixon* as to subpoenas issued in anticipation of trial apply equally in the grand jury context. The multifactor test announced in *Nixon* would invite procedural delays and detours while courts evaluate the relevancy and admissibility of documents sought by a particular subpoena. We have expressly stated that grand jury proceedings should be free of such delays. "Any holding that would saddle a grand jury with minitrials and preliminary showings would assuredly impede its investigation and frustrate the public's interest in the fair and expeditious administration of the criminal laws. Additionally, application of the *Nixon* test in this context ignores that grand jury proceedings are subject to strict secrecy requirements. See Fed. Rule Crim. Proc. 6(e). Requiring the Government to explain in too much detail the particular reasons underlying a subpoena threatens to compromise "the indispensable secrecy of grand jury proceedings." Broad disclosure also affords the targets of investigation far more information about the grand jury's internal workings than the Federal Rules of Criminal Procedure appear to contemplate.

III

A

The investigatory powers of the grand jury are nevertheless not unlimited. Grand juries are not licensed to engage in arbitrary fishing expeditions, nor may they select targets of investigation out of malice or an intent to harass. In this case, the focus of our inquiry is the limit imposed on a grand jury by Federal Rule of Criminal Procedure 17(c), which governs the issuance of subpoenas duces tecum in federal criminal proceedings. The Rule provides that "[t]he court on motion made promptly may quash or modify the subpoena if compliance would be unreasonable or oppressive."

This standard is not self-explanatory. As we have observed, "what is reasonable depends on the context." In *Nixon*, this Court defined what is reasonable in the context of a jury trial. We determined that, in order to require production of information prior to trial, a party must make a reasonably specific request for information that would be both relevant and admissible at trial. But, for the reasons we have explained above, the *Nixon* standard does not apply in the context of grand jury proceedings. In the grand jury context, the decision as to what offense will be charged is routinely not made until after the grand jury has concluded its investigation. One simply cannot know in advance whether information sought during the investigation will be relevant and admissible in a prosecution for a particular offense.

To the extent that Rule 17(c) imposes some reasonableness limitation on grand jury subpoenas, however, our task is to define it. In doing so, we recognize that a party to whom a grand jury subpoena is issued faces a difficult situation. As a rule, grand juries do not announce publicly the subjects of their investigations. A party who desires to challenge a grand jury subpoena thus may have no conception of the Government's purpose in seeking production of the requested information. Indeed, the party will often not know whether he or she is

D. Grand Jury Subpoena Power   **671**

a primary target of the investigation or merely a peripheral witness. Absent even minimal information, the subpoena recipient is likely to find it exceedingly difficult to persuade a court that "compliance would be unreasonable." As one pair of commentators has summarized it, the challenging party's "unenviable task is to seek to persuade the court that the subpoena that has been served on [him or her] could not possibly serve any investigative purpose that the grand jury could legitimately be pursuing."

Our task is to fashion an appropriate standard of reasonableness, one that gives due weight to the difficult position of subpoena recipients but does not impair the strong governmental interests in affording grand juries wide latitude, avoiding minitrials on peripheral matters, and preserving a necessary level of secrecy. We begin by reiterating that the law presumes, absent a strong showing to the contrary, that a grand jury acts within the legitimate scope of its authority. Consequently, a grand jury subpoena issued through normal channels is presumed to be reasonable, and the burden of showing unreasonableness must be on the recipient who seeks to avoid compliance. Indeed, this result is indicated by the language of Rule 17(c), which permits a subpoena to be quashed only "on motion" and "if *compliance* would be unreasonable" (emphasis added). To the extent that the Court of Appeals placed an initial burden on the Government, it committed error. Drawing on the principles articulated above, we conclude that where, as here, a subpoena is challenged on relevancy grounds, the motion to quash must be denied unless the district court determines that there is no reasonable possibility that the category of materials the Government seeks will produce information relevant to the general subject of the grand jury's investigation. Respondents did not challenge the subpoenas as being too indefinite nor did they claim that compliance would be overly burdensome. The Court of Appeals accordingly did not consider these aspects of the subpoenas, nor do we.

B

It seems unlikely, of course, that a challenging party who does not know the general subject matter of the grand jury's investigation, no matter how valid that party's claim, will be able to make the necessary showing that compliance would be unreasonable. After all, a subpoena recipient "cannot put his whole life before the court in order to show that there is no crime to be investigated." Consequently, a court may be justified in a case where unreasonableness is alleged in requiring the Government to reveal the general subject of the grand jury's investigation before requiring the challenging party to carry its burden of persuasion. We need not resolve this question in the present case, however, as there is no doubt that respondents knew the subject of the grand jury investigation pursuant to which the business records subpoenas were issued. In cases where the recipient of the subpoena does not know the nature of the investigation, we are confident that district courts will be able to craft appropriate procedures that balance the interests of the subpoena recipient against the strong governmental interests in maintaining secrecy, preserving investigatory flexibility, and avoiding procedural delays. For example, to ensure that subpoenas are not routinely challenged as a form of discovery, a district court may require that the Government reveal the subject of the investigation to the trial court in camera, so that the court may determine whether the motion to quash has a reasonable prospect for success before it discloses the subject matter to the challenging party.

IV

Applying these principles in this case demonstrates that the District Court correctly denied respondents' motions to quash. It is undisputed that all three companies — Model, R. Enterprises, and MFR — are owned by the same person, that all do business in the same area, and that one of the three, Model, has shipped sexually explicit materials into the Eastern District of Virginia. The District Court could have concluded from these facts that there was a reasonable possibility that the business records of R. Enterprises and MFR would produce information relevant to the grand jury's investigation into the interstate transportation of obscene materials. Respondents' blanket denial of any connection to Virginia did not suffice to render the District Court's conclusion invalid. A grand jury need not accept on faith the self-serving assertions of those who may have committed criminal acts. Rather, it is entitled to determine for itself whether a crime has been committed.

Both in the District Court and in the Court of Appeals, respondents contended that these subpoenas sought records relating to First Amendment activities, and that this required the Government to demonstrate that the records were particularly relevant to its investigation. The Court of Appeals determined that the subpoenas did not satisfy Rule 17(c) and thus did not pass on the First Amendment issue. We express no view on this issue and leave it to be resolved by the Court of Appeals.

The judgment is reversed insofar as the Court of Appeals quashed the subpoenas issued to R. Enterprises and MFR, and the case is remanded for further proceedings consistent with this opinion.

It is so ordered.

NOTES AND QUESTIONS

Attorney General Edwin Meese

1. The investigation at issue in *R. Enterprises* was part of the effort of the Reagan Administration's Department of Justice, led by Attorney General Edwin Meese, to crack down on the child pornography industry. *See* Jim Duffy & Brian McGee, Main Justice: The Men and Women Who Enforce the Nation's Laws and Guard Its Liberties 279-300 (1996). As part of this effort the DOJ changed its internal guidelines for commencing actions in multiple jurisdictions against the same party.

Is its prioritizing this issue an example of the DOJ being improperly "political"?

2. The Fourth Circuit can be rightly criticized for relying on the trial subpoena standard of *United States v. Nixon*, 418 U.S. 683 (1974), in analyzing a motion to quash a grand jury subpoena, as the three-part showing required in that case—"relevancy, admissibility, and specificity," *id*. at 699-700—makes little sense in the grand jury context, where there is no charged crime, no defendant, and not even any defined facts or issues. And in fact, *Nixon* was addressing the standard for a subpoena returnable "prior to trial," as opposed to at or during trial, making the analogy even weaker.

But isn't the Supreme Court's reliance on Rule 17 of the Federal Rules of Criminal Procedure equally mystifying? Look at its language. Isn't Rule 17 also designed to govern procedures for trial subpoenas and not grand jury subpoenas?

3. The *R. Enterprises* version of the grand jury love song emphasizes the breadth of the grand jury's investigative powers, an aspect that has been touched on but was never the primary focus of earlier versions. In so doing, the Court relies on dicta from two cases that were themselves supported by no precedent whatsoever. First, the Court observes that the grand jury "can investigate merely on suspicion that the law is being violated, or even just because it wants assurance that it is not" (citing *United States v. Morton Salt Co.*, 338 U.S. 632, 642-43

(1950)). *Id.* at 296. The quote is accurate but *Morton Salt* has nothing to do with the grand jury; the Court was simply analogizing to the grand jury in justifying the Federal Trade Commission's authority to require corporations to file reports demonstrating their compliance with a consent decree. And isn't this observation flatly contradicted in *R. Enterprises* itself by the Court's subsequent statement, *id.* at 302, that grand juries "are not licensed to engage in arbitrary fishing expeditions"?

Isn't an investigation to obtain "assurance" that the law is not being violated in substance a description of a fishing exhibition? If the Court's "assurance" language is taken literally, is there any substantive limit to grand jury subpoenas?

4. The Court also relies on dicta from a Second Circuit case, cited by the Court in *Branzburg v. Hayes*, 408 U.S. 665 (1972): "A grand jury investigation 'is not fully carried out until every available clue has been run down and all witnesses examined in every proper way to find if a crime has been committed.'" *Id.* at 701 (quoting *United States v. Stone*, 429 F.2d 138, 140 (2d Cir. 1970)). *Stone* was a two-page decision that included the quoted statement, without any citation, in responding to an argument by the defendant (Sam Stone) that his perjury conviction should be reversed because his false testimony was not "material" to the grand jury.

Doesn't this language also condone fishing exhibitions?

5. It is on the backs of these ill-conceived and never-applied conceptions of the grand jury — as an amorphous and omnivorous investigative blob — that the Court proceeds to determine what "reasonableness" requires under Rule 17. Accordingly, the Court fashions the following test for challenging a grand jury subpoena on relevance grounds: "the motion to quash must be denied unless the district court determines that there is no reasonable possibility that the category of materials the Government seeks will produce information relevant to the general subject of the grand jury's investigation." *Id.* at 301. But of course that definition must also be informed by Rule 6's secrecy requirements, which prevent the government from "explain[ing] in too much detail the particular reasons underlying a subpoena."

6. Did the district court properly deny the motions to quash on relevance grounds under this standard? What does the Court mean by saying that the "grand jury need not accept on faith" the respondents' blanket denial of any connection to Virginia? Does the district court have the discretion in ruling on a motion to quash to simply reject factual contentions made by the movant? Consider the dissent's comments on the relationship between "unreasonable" and "oppressive" under Rule 17. How would you make a combined relevance and burdensomeness argument on these facts?

Note that the superficially straightforward term "grand jury subpoena" is somewhat misleading. On the one hand, it is true that a grand jury subpoena is a document with a court caption that requires the production of materials under the authority of the grand jury's powers. On the other hand, a grand jury subpoena is usually entirely the product of the prosecutor: it is issued by the prosecutor, requiring no approval by the court or even by the grand jury itself; the grand jury may not even be aware of the subpoena's existence; and the grand jury may never even be shown the documents that were produced in response to the subpoena.

E. GRAND JURY SECRECY

Grand jury secrecy has, among its purposes, the protection from public knowledge of the identities of persons who testify in the grand jury as well as the identities of persons under investigation who end up not being charged with a crime. These purposes are important. But sometimes prosecutors invoke the concept of grand jury secrecy overbroadly to impermissibly shield their investigations from public scrutiny.

674 Chapter VII Grand Jury

United States v. Sells Engineering, Inc.
463 U.S. 418 (1983)

BRENNAN, Justice.

The question in this case is under what conditions attorneys for the Civil Division of the Justice Department, their paralegal and secretarial staff, and all other necessary assistants, may obtain access to grand jury materials, compiled with the assistance and knowledge of other Justice Department attorneys, for the purpose of preparing and pursuing a civil suit. We hold that such access is permissible only when the Government moves for court-ordered disclosure under Federal Rule of Criminal Procedure 6(e)(3)(C)(i) and makes the showing of particularized need required by that Rule.

I

Respondents Peter A. Sells and Fred R. Witte were officers of respondent Sells Engineering, Inc. That company had contracts with the United States Navy to produce airborne electronic devices designed to interfere with enemy radar systems. In 1974, a Special Agent of the Internal Revenue Service began a combined criminal and civil administrative investigation of respondents. The Agent issued administrative summonses for certain corporate records of Sells Engineering. When the corporation refused to comply, the Agent obtained a district court order enforcing the summonses. Enforcement was stayed, however, pending appeal.

While the enforcement case was pending in the Court of Appeals, a federal grand jury was convened to investigate charges of criminal fraud on the Navy and of evasion of federal income taxes. The grand jury subpoenaed, and respondents produced, many of the same materials that were the subject of the IRS administrative summonses. The grand jury indicted all three respondents on two counts of conspiracy to defraud the United States and nine counts of tax fraud. Respondents moved to dismiss the indictment, alleging grand jury misuse for civil purposes. Before the motion was decided, however, the parties reached a plea bargain. The individual respondents each pleaded guilty to one count of conspiracy to defraud the Government by obstructing an IRS investigation. All other counts were dismissed, and respondents withdrew their charges of grand jury misuse.

Thereafter, the Government moved for disclosure of all grand jury materials to attorneys in the Justice Department's Civil Division, their paralegal and secretarial assistants, and certain Defense Department experts, for use in preparing and conducting a possible civil suit against respondents under the False Claims Act, 31 U.S.C. § 231 et seq. Respondents opposed the disclosure, renewing their allegations of grand jury misuse. The District Court granted the requested disclosure, concluding that attorneys in the Civil Division are entitled to disclosure as a matter of right under Rule 6(e)(3)(A)(i). The Court also stated that disclosure to Civil Division attorneys and their non-attorney assistants was warranted because the Government had shown particularized need for disclosure. The Court of Appeals vacated and remanded, holding that Civil Division attorneys could obtain disclosure only by showing particularized need under Rule 6(e)(3)(C)(i), and that the District Court had not applied a correct standard of particularized need.

We granted certiorari. We now affirm.

II

A

The grand jury has always occupied a high place as an instrument of justice in our system of criminal law — so much so that it is enshrined in the Constitution. It serves the "dual function of determining if there is probable cause to believe that a crime has been committed and of protecting citizens against unfounded criminal prosecutions." It has always been extended extraordinary powers of investigation and great responsibility for directing its own efforts:

> Traditionally the grand jury has been accorded wide latitude to inquire into violations of criminal law. No judge presides to monitor its proceedings. It deliberates in secret and may determine alone the course of its inquiry. The grand jury may compel the production of evidence or the testimony of witnesses as it considers appropriate, and its operation generally is unrestrained by the technical procedural and evidentiary rules governing the conduct of criminal trials. "It is a grand inquest, a body with powers of investigation and inquisition, the scope of whose inquiries is not to be limited narrowly by questions of propriety or forecasts of the probable result of the investigation, or by doubts whether any particular individual will be found properly subject to an accusation of crime."

These broad powers are necessary to permit the grand jury to carry out both parts of its dual function. Without thorough and effective investigation, the grand jury would be unable either to ferret out crimes deserving of prosecution, or to screen out charges not warranting prosecution.

The same concern for the grand jury's dual function underlies the "long-established policy that maintains the secrecy of the grand jury proceedings in the federal courts."

> We consistently have recognized that the proper functioning of our grand jury system depends upon the secrecy of grand jury proceedings. In particular, we have noted several distinct interests served by safeguarding the confidentiality of grand jury proceedings. First, if preindictment proceedings were made public, many prospective witnesses would be hesitant to come forward voluntarily, knowing that those against whom they testify would be aware of that testimony. Moreover, witnesses who appeared before the grand jury would be less likely to testify fully and frankly, as they would be open to retribution as well as to inducements. There also would be the risk that those about to be indicted would flee, or would try to influence individual grand jurors to vote against indictment. Finally, by preserving the secrecy of the proceedings, we assure that persons who are accused but exonerated by the grand jury will not be held up to public ridicule.

Grand jury secrecy, then, is "as important for the protection of the innocent as for the pursuit of the guilty." Both Congress and this Court have consistently stood ready to defend it against unwarranted intrusion. In the absence of a clear indication in a statute or Rule, we must always be reluctant to conclude that a breach of this secrecy has been authorized.

B

Rule 6(e) of the Federal Rules of Criminal Procedure codifies the traditional rule of grand jury secrecy. Paragraph 6(e)(2) provides that grand jurors, government attorneys and their assistants, and other personnel attached to the grand jury are forbidden to disclose matters occurring before the grand jury. Witnesses are not under the prohibition unless they also happen to fit into one of the enumerated classes. Paragraph 6(e)(3) sets forth four exceptions to this nondisclosure rule.

Subparagraph 6(e)(3)(A) contains two authorizations for disclosure as a matter of course, without any court order. First, under subparagraph 6(e)(3)(A)(i), disclosure may be made without a court order to "an attorney for the government for use in the performance of such attorney's duty" (referred to hereinafter as "(A)(i) disclosure"). "Attorney for the government" is defined in Rule 54(c) in such broad terms as potentially to include virtually every attorney in the Department of Justice. Second, under subparagraph 6(e)(3)(A)(ii), grand jury materials may likewise be provided to "government personnel . . . [who] assist an attorney for the government in the performance of such attorney's duty to enforce federal criminal law" ("(A) (ii) disclosure"). Subparagraph 6(e)(3)(B) further regulates (A)(ii) disclosure, forbidding use of grand jury materials by "government personnel" for any purpose other than assisting an attorney for the Government in his enforcement of criminal law, and requiring that the names of such personnel be provided to the district court.

Subparagraph 6(e)(3)(C) also authorizes courts to order disclosure. Under subparagraph 6(e)(3)(C)(i), a court may order disclosure "preliminarily to or in connection with a judicial proceeding" (a "(C)(i) order"). Under subparagraph 6(e)(3)(C)(ii), a court may order disclosure under certain conditions at the request of a defendant.

The main issue in this case is whether attorneys in the Justice Department may obtain automatic (A)(i) disclosure of grand jury materials for use in a civil suit, or whether they must seek a (C)(i) court order for access. If a (C)(i) order is necessary, we must address the dependent question of what standards should govern issuance of the order.

<h2 style="text-align:center">III</h2>

The Government contends that all attorneys in the Justice Department qualify for automatic disclosure of grand jury materials under (A)(i), regardless of the nature of the litigation in which they intend to use the materials. We hold that (A)(i) disclosure is limited to use by those attorneys who conduct the criminal matters to which the materials pertain. This conclusion is mandated by the general purposes and policies of grand jury secrecy, by the limited policy reasons why government attorneys are granted access to grand jury materials for criminal use, and by the legislative history of Rule 6(e).

<h2 style="text-align:center">A</h2>

The Government correctly contends that attorneys for the Civil Division of the Justice Department are within the class of "attorneys for the government" to whom (A)(i) allows disclosure without a court order. Rule 54(c) defines the phrase expansively, to include "authorized assistants to the Attorney General"; 28 U.S.C. § 515(a) provides that the Attorney General may direct any attorney employed by the Department to conduct "any kind of legal proceeding, civil or criminal, including grand jury proceedings. . . ." *See also* § 518(b). In short, as far as Rules 6 and 54 are concerned, it is immaterial that certain attorneys happen to be assigned to a unit called the Civil Division, or that their usual duties involve only civil cases. If, for example, the Attorney General (for whatever reason) were to detail a Civil Division attorney to conduct a criminal grand jury investigation, nothing in Rule 6 would prevent that attorney from doing so; he need not secure a transfer out of the Civil Division.

It does not follow, however, that any Justice Department attorney is free to rummage through the records of any grand jury in the country, simply by right of office. Disclosure under (A)(i) is permitted only "in the performance of such attorney's duty." The heart of the primary issue in this case is whether performance of duty, within the meaning of (A)(i), includes preparation and litigation of a civil suit by a Justice Department attorney who had no part in conducting the related criminal prosecution.

Given the strong historic policy of preserving grand jury secrecy, one might wonder why government attorneys are given any automatic access at all. The draftsmen of the original Rule 6 provided the answer:

> Government attorneys are entitled to disclosure of grand jury proceedings, other than the deliberations and the votes of the jurors, inasmuch as they may be present in the grand jury room during the presentation of evidence. The rule continues this practice.

Advisory Committee's Notes on Federal Rule of Criminal Procedure 6(e), 18 U.S.C. App., p. 1411.

This is potent evidence that Rule 6(e) was never intended to grant free access to grand jury materials to attorneys not working on the criminal matters to which the materials pertain.

The Advisory Committee's explanation strongly suggests that automatic access to grand jury materials is available only to those attorneys for the Government who would be entitled to appear before the grand jury. But government attorneys are allowed into grand jury rooms, not for the general and multifarious purposes of the Department of Justice, but because both the grand jury's functions and their own prosecutorial duties require it. As the Advisory Committee suggested, the same reasoning applies to disclosure of grand jury materials outside the grand jury room.

The purpose of the grand jury requires that it remain free, within constitutional and statutory limits, to operate "independently of either prosecuting attorney or judge." Nevertheless, a modern grand jury would be much less effective without the assistance of the prosecutor's office and the investigative resources it commands. The prosecutor ordinarily brings matters to the attention of the grand jury and gathers the evidence required for the jury's consideration. Although the grand jury may itself decide to investigate a matter or to seek certain evidence, it depends largely on the prosecutor's office to secure the evidence or witnesses it requires. The prosecutor also advises the lay jury on the applicable law. The prosecutor in turn needs to know what transpires before the grand jury in order to perform his own duty properly. If he considers that the law and the admissible evidence will not support a conviction, he can be expected to advise the grand jury not to indict. He must also examine indictments, and the basis for their issuance, to determine whether it is in the interests of justice to proceed with prosecution.

None of these considerations, however, provides any support for breaching grand jury secrecy in favor of government attorneys other than prosecutors — either by allowing them into the grand jury room, or by granting them uncontrolled access to grand jury materials. An attorney with only civil duties lacks both the prosecutor's special role in supporting the grand jury, and the prosecutor's own crucial need to know what occurs before the grand jury.

Of course, it would be of substantial help to a Justice Department civil attorney if he had free access to a storehouse of evidence compiled by a grand jury; but that is of a different order from the prosecutor's need for access. The civil lawyer's need is ordinarily nothing more than a matter of saving time and expense. The same argument could be made for access on behalf of any lawyer in another government agency, or indeed, in private practice. We have consistently rejected the argument that such savings can justify a breach of grand jury secrecy. In most cases, the same evidence that could be obtained from the grand jury will be available through ordinary discovery or other routine avenues of investigation.

Not only is disclosure for civil use unjustified by the considerations supporting prosecutorial access, but it threatens to do affirmative mischief. The problem is threefold.

First, disclosure to government bodies raises much the same concerns that underlie the rule of secrecy in other contexts. Not only does disclosure increase the number of persons to whom the information is available (thereby increasing the risk of inadvertent or illegal release to others), but it renders considerably more concrete the threat to the willingness of witnesses to come forward and to testify fully and candidly. If a witness knows or fears that his testimony before the grand jury will be routinely available for use in governmental civil litigation or administrative action, he may well be less willing to speak for fear that he will get himself into trouble in some other forum.

Second, because the Government takes an active part in the activities of the grand jury, disclosure to government attorneys for civil use poses a significant threat to the integrity of the grand jury itself. If prosecutors in a given case knew that their colleagues would be free to use the materials generated by the grand jury for a civil case, they might be tempted to manipulate the grand jury's powerful investigative tools to root out additional evidence useful in the civil suit, or even to start or continue a grand jury inquiry where no criminal prosecution seemed likely. Any such use of grand jury proceedings to elicit evidence for use in a civil case is improper per se. We do not mean to impugn the professional characters of Justice

678 Chapter VII Grand Jury

Department lawyers in general; nor do we express any view on the allegations of misuse that have been made in this case. Our concern is based less on any belief that grand jury misuse is in fact widespread than on our concern that, if and when it does occur, it would often be very difficult to detect and prove. Moreover, as the legislative history discussed infra shows our concern over possible misappropriation of the grand jury itself was shared by Congress when it enacted the present version of Rule 6(e). Such a potential for misuse should not be allowed absent a clear mandate in the law.

Third, use of grand jury materials by government agencies in civil or administrative settings threatens to subvert the limitations applied outside the grand jury context on the Government's powers of discovery and investigation. While there are some limits on the investigative powers of the grand jury, there are few if any other forums in which a governmental body has such relatively unregulated power to compel other persons to divulge information or produce evidence. Other agencies, both within and without the Justice Department, operate under specific and detailed statutes, rules, or regulations conferring only limited authority to require citizens to testify or produce evidence. Some agencies have been granted special statutory powers to obtain information and require testimony in pursuance of their duties. Others (including the Civil Division) are relegated to the usual course of discovery under the Federal Rules of Civil Procedure. In either case, the limitations imposed on investigation and discovery exist for sound reasons—ranging from fundamental fairness to concern about burdensomeness and intrusiveness. If government litigators or investigators in civil matters enjoyed unlimited access to grand jury material, though, there would be little reason for them to resort to their usual, more limited avenues of investigation. To allow these agencies to circumvent their usual methods of discovery would not only subvert the limitations and procedural requirements built into those methods, but would grant to the Government a virtual ex parte form of discovery, from which its civil litigation opponents are excluded unless they make a strong showing of particularized need. In civil litigation as in criminal, "it is rarely justifiable for the [Government] to have exclusive access to a storehouse of relevant fact." We are reluctant to conclude that the draftsmen of Rule 6 intended so remarkable a result.

In short, if grand juries are to be granted extraordinary powers of investigation because of the difficulty and importance of their task, the use of those powers ought to be limited as far as reasonably possible to the accomplishment of the task. The policies of Rule 6 require that any disclosure to attorneys other than prosecutors be judicially supervised rather than automatic.

NOTES AND QUESTIONS

1. The love song to the grand jury in *Sells* is different than some we have seen as it explicitly focuses on the "dual function" of the grand jury. Neither function is necessarily implicated by the specific disclosure questions at issue in *Sells*, although the Court does note that both "sword" and "shield" interests are served by the grand jury's secrecy requirements.

Which of the "several distinct interests" for secrecy that are noted by the Court are most compelling? Least compelling?

2. Note that witnesses in the grand jury are not among the persons bound by Rule 6(e)'s secrecy requirements. Bear this in mind next time you read about "grand jury leaks." Sometimes information about grand jury proceedings becomes public by perfectly legal disclosures from a witness or witness's counsel. Why do you think witnesses are exempted from the secrecy requirements?

3. The Court interprets the disclosure-permitting language in Rule 6(e)(3)(A)(i) to permit disclosure only to DOJ attorneys conducting criminal matters. Is this a defensible interpretation of the Rule's language? The Court advances three reasons why permitting disclosure to DOJ non-prosecutors "threatens to do affirmative mischief": (a) witnesses will be less truthful if they believe their testimony will be routinely available for noncriminal purposes; (b) it abuses the grand jury to use it as an adjunct to aid civil enforcement; and (c) civil enforcement lawyers might take advantage of the breadth of grand jury powers to subvert discovery limitations in civil matters.

Are each of these reasons equally persuasive? How does the Court's consciously naïve description of the role of prosecutors in grand jury proceedings advance its argument?

4. *Sells* was a tax case, investigated by agents of the Internal Revenue Service, an agency that has both criminal and civil investigative authority. Note that the investigation appears to have begun as a civil investigation, which stalled due to litigation of a civil discovery dispute, during which time a grand jury investigation was commenced regarding issues that were related, at a minimum, to the civil investigation. Is this the sort of fact pattern that suggests the potential for the second variety of "affirmative mischief" noted above?

5. Tax is an area of the law, like many areas — antitrust, securities fraud, health care fraud, etc. — where the same or substantially similar conduct can violate both civil and criminal laws. Does the existence of these areas of substantive overlap militate for more or less ease of criminal-civil disclosure? *See United States v. Procter & Gamble*, 356 U.S. 677 (1958) (reversing district court's order granting broad disclosure of grand jury testimony to defendants in civil antitrust action, which apparently was made due to the district court's belief that the government had used the grand jury to develop evidence for the civil case; Court noted, however, that it would have been illegal for the government to have used the grand jury for a purpose other than criminal investigation).

While *Sells* is a case about who can rightfully gain access to grand jury materials there is often litigation about what constitutes "a matter occurring before the grand jury" within the meaning of Rule 6(e)(2)(B). For example, in *Hodge v. FBI*, 703 F.3d 575 (D.C. Cir. 2013), a prisoner brought a claim under the federal Freedom of Information Act (FOIA) seeking documents relating to the federal investigation that led to his prosecution. In interpreting one of the FOIA exemptions that cross-references Rule 6(e), the D.C. Circuit found that Rule 6(e) applies if the disclosed material would "tend to reveal some secret aspect of the grand jury's investigation," including "the identities of witnesses or jurors, the substance of testimony, the strategy or direction of the investigation," or "the deliberations or questions of jurors." *Id.* at 580. Prosecutors will often unfurl the banner of "grand jury secrecy" when they don't want to inform a witness or even a court about the nature of an investigation, but cases like *Hodge* make clear that Rule 6(e) sweeps less broadly.

Consider the following hypothetical:

> An investigation of ABC corporation begins with a grand jury subpoena of the company for documents. The documents are produced by ABC to the government and reviewed and analyzed by the prosecution team. As a result of that review, twenty individuals who are current or former employees of ABC are served with grand jury subpoenas. Ten of these individuals show up pursuant to their subpoenas and testify in the grand jury. The other ten, after negotiations between their counsel and the prosecutor, are interviewed by the prosecutor and agents outside the presence of the grand jury. All twenty witnesses are examined about the subjects reflected in the documents produced in response to the grand jury subpoena.

Which of these witnesses were questioned in the "grand jury investigation"?

Would a statement by the AUSA to the press that "we've talked to many company employees" be a Rule 6(e) violation?

United States v. Bryant
655 F.3d 232 (3d Cir. 2011)

Амвко, Circuit Judge.

This case involves the federal crimes of honest services fraud, mail fraud, and bribery. Appellants Wayne Bryant and R. Michael Gallagher were charged with six counts of honest services fraud, in violation of 18 U.S.C. §§ 1341, 1343 and 1346 (the "honest services fraud counts"), and one count each of bribery in connection with a state agency that receives federal funds, in violation of 18 U.S.C. § 666(a) (the "bribery counts"), all in connection with a scheme to defraud the citizens of the State of New Jersey of Bryant's honest services as a State Senator. Counts 9-13 charged Bryant with mail fraud, in violation of 18 U.S.C. § 1341, in connection with a second scheme involving his state pension application. A jury convicted Bryant on all counts and Gallagher on all counts but one, which dealt with the mailing of Bryant's 2003 Financial Disclosure statement. Their sentences included imprisonment—48 months for Bryant and 18 months for Gallagher—and joint restitution in the amount of $113,167. For the reasons that follow, we affirm their convictions and the restitution order.

I. BACKGROUND

Gallagher was formerly Dean of the School of Osteopathic Medicine ("SOM") of the University of Medicine and Dentistry of New Jersey ("UMDNJ"). Bryant, as noted, was a New Jersey State Senator. They were indicted in 2007. The charges stemmed from an alleged quid pro quo arrangement in which Gallagher gave Bryant a "low-show" job at SOM (meaning he provided only minimal or nominal services) as a "Program Support Coordinator," in which position he received an annual salary of $35,000 (and a $5,000 bonus), in exchange for Bryant's efforts as Chairman of the Senate Appropriations Committee to funnel State funding to SOM. The quo was a "success": during Bryant's tenure at SOM, the institution gained an additional $10 million in funding over three years. Based on that same scheme, Bryant and Gallagher were also charged under the federal bribery statute—Bryant for corruptly soliciting and demanding the SOM salary and Gallagher for corruptly giving the salary.

In a second scheme, involving only Bryant, the Government alleged that he also attempted to use a "no-show" job (meaning he personally provided no services at all) as an attorney for the Gloucester County Board of Social Services (the "Social Services Board") to increase his pension benefits. Specifically, the Government introduced evidence at trial showing that Bryant falsely reported that he had worked numerous hours providing legal services to the Social Services Board when he had not provided those services at all but had delegated his work to associates at his private law firm. In other words, Bryant claimed pensionable time credit for work he did not do. In New Jersey, the amount of pension benefits for which a public servant is eligible depends on the number of public sector jobs held. Thus, by accumulating public sector jobs, but not actually performing the duties commensurate with the positions, the Government argued that Bryant fraudulently inflated his pension eligibility.

After Appellants' convictions in November 2008, the District Court denied their motions for a judgment of acquittal or a new trial and this appeal followed. The District Court had jurisdiction under 18 U.S.C. § 3231. We have jurisdiction under 28 U.S.C. § 1291.

Appellants challenge their convictions on the following grounds: they argue that the Government violated their due process rights by interfering with their access to potential witnesses in the pretrial phase of the case. . . .

II. DISCUSSION

A. The Prosecutorial Misconduct Claim

During its investigation of Appellants, the Government issued grand jury subpoenas to potential witnesses with the following language placed on the front of each subpoena:

> Disclosure of the nature and existence of this subpoena could obstruct and impede a criminal investigation into alleged violations of federal law. Therefore, the United States Attorney requests that you do not disclose the existence of this subpoena.

Appellants argued to the District Court that this language, and the Government's requests during the grand jury proceedings that witnesses voluntarily not disclose "any matters" that occur during those proceedings, interfered with the defense's access to witnesses. They claim that this violated due process and Federal Rule of Criminal Procedure 6(e)(2)(A), which prohibits the Government from imposing an obligation of secrecy on witnesses. The District Court denied their pretrial motion to dismiss the indictment on those grounds. Instead, it ordered the Government to write to the witnesses and inform them that they were under no legal obligation to keep the subpoena secret.

On appeal, Appellants again argue that the Government's conduct — including both the subpoena language and its requests to witnesses to preserve the secrecy of the proceeding — violated Rule 6(e)(2)(A) and due process. They claim that the Government's actions restricted the "free choice" of potential witnesses to speak to defense counsel and effectively imposed an obligation of secrecy on those witnesses. We disagree.

We review a district court's decision regarding a motion to dismiss an indictment because of prosecutorial misconduct for abuse of discretion. Generally, because witnesses "belong" neither to the defense nor to the prosecution, both must have equal access to witnesses before trial. If the prosecution impermissibly interferes with the defense's access to a witness during a criminal trial, that conduct violates due process insofar as it undermines the fundamental fairness of the proceeding. In connection with a grand jury proceeding, Rule 6(e)(2) also provides that the Government may not impose an obligation of secrecy on a witness absent limited exceptions, none of which applies here.

However, there is an important difference between requesting nondisclosure and discretion on the part of witnesses and artificially restricting defense counsel's access to witnesses by, for example, instructing the latter not to communicate with the former. Merely requesting that witnesses practice discretion does not violate a defendant's due process rights. Here, the record demonstrates that the Government requested, but never required, witnesses not to disclose the subpoena or the grand jury proceedings. Aside from those requests, it took no affirmative steps to restrict or stop witnesses from conferring with the defense.

Appellants argue that the language, emblazoned on the subpoena, gave an appearance of a judicial imprimatur that suggested to witnesses they were legally obligated to comply with the Government's secrecy request. Certainly, many forthright citizens would comply with such a request, given the context in which it was made. However, we will not say what occurred here imposed an obligation of secrecy.

Nor do we think that the Government's actions infected the fairness of the proceeding. Notably, Appellants did not identify to the District Court (nor do they now) any witnesses who claim that they would have spoken to the defense but were deterred from doing so because of the Government's nondisclosure requests. Rather, those witnesses who declined to speak with the defense did so on the advice of counsel. But "[n]o right of a defendant is violated when a potential witness freely chooses not to talk; a witness may of his own free will refuse to be interviewed by either the prosecution or the defense."

Even if there were witnesses (about whom we do not know) with the mistaken impression that they could not speak to the defense, the District Court took measures to clarify such a misunderstanding well before trial. In response to Appellants' motion to dismiss, the Court instructed the Government to send a letter to all subpoena recipients five months before the start of trial, stating that the witnesses had "an absolute right to speak to anyone . . . about anything [they] know about any of the matters under investigation, including the fact that [they] were subpoenaed and . . . testified before the grand jury." In particular, that letter confirmed that the Government "[would] not take any adverse action against [the witness] or [his or her] employer because [he or she chose] to speak to the defense or anyone else about these matters."

In these circumstances, we believe that Appellants have not shown that, because of the Government's conduct, there was an "absence of . . . fairness [that] fatally infected the trial." Accordingly, we conclude that Appellants were not denied due process of law or the protections of Rule 6(e)(2)(A) and we decline to vacate their convictions for those reasons.

NOTES AND QUESTIONS

1. This is an especially overt example of the government attempting to convert the limited secrecy provisions of Rule 6 into a means of intimidating grand jury witnesses from sharing information about the investigation with others, specifically, the defense team. Note that the broad language on the subpoena could even conceivably deter a witness from seeking legal advice regarding the subpoena. Was the district court's order sufficient to cure the prosecutor's violation? Short of dismissing the indictment, what more could it have done?

2. The Third Circuit notes that the government merely requested, but never required, that the witness not disclose the existence of the subpoena. Is there a meaningful difference in this context? Presumably the most important witnesses in this investigation — a classic public corruption case — were those who worked closely with the defendants and had firsthand knowledge about the allegedly illicit arrangements. These would of course have been the same people who had concern about their own criminal exposure. How firmly did they need to be told about the government's "request" for secrecy? Do you think the prosecutor's "corrective" letter had any effect on them?

3. The Third Circuit also faults the defendants for failing to identify any witnesses who would have spoken to them but for the prosecution's interference. Is this realistic? How could the defense possibly have made that showing?

4. The Court cites other cases where federal prosecutors have improperly instructed grand jury witnesses to keep the proceedings secret. Should the fact that this is recurring misconduct by DOJ prosecutors have affected the district court's remedy or the court of appeals' decision? Could the district court have enlisted Fed. R. Crim. P. 15, which (in its current form) permits a party to "move that a prospective witness be deposed in order to preserve testimony for trial." The court may grant the motion because of exceptional circumstances and in the interest of justice.

F. WITNESSES IN THE GRAND JURY

The next two cases consider whether a witness who faces potential criminal exposure by testifying in the grand jury has a right to receive any sort of warnings — akin to *Miranda* warnings — from the prosecutor before testifying. The *Miranda* analogy is imperfect: The grand jury setting may be coercive but it is not custodial in the classical sense, and a witness's attendance at the grand jury is compelled by subpoena but not (at least initially) by force.

F. Witnesses in the Grand Jury   **683**

The Department of Justice responded to these cases by issuing internal policies regulating the treatment of certain witnesses in the grand jury, which will be discussed after the cases.

United States v. Mandujano
425 U.S. 564 (1976)

Mr. Chief Justice BURGER announced the judgment of the Court in an opinion in which Mr. Justice WHITE, Mr. Justice POWELL, and Mr. Justice REHNQUIST join.

This case presents the question whether the warnings called for by *Miranda*, must be given to a grand jury witness who is called to testify about criminal activities in which he may have been personally involved; and whether, absent such warnings, false statements made to the grand jury must be suppressed in a prosecution for perjury based on those statements.

(1)

During the course of a grand jury investigation into narcotics traffic in San Antonio, Tex., federal prosecutors assigned to the Drug Enforcement Administration Task Force learned of an undercover narcotics officer's encounter with respondent in March 1973. At that time, the agent had received information that respondent, who was employed as a bartender at a local tavern, was dealing in narcotics. The agent, accompanied by an informant, met respondent at the tavern and talked for several hours. During the meeting, respondent agreed to obtain heroin for the agent, and to that end placed several phone calls from the bar. He also requested and received $650 from the agent to make the purchase. Respondent left the tavern with the money so advanced to secure the heroin. However, an hour later respondent returned to the bar without the narcotics and returned the agent's money. Respondent instructed the agent to telephone him at the bar that evening to make arrangements for the transaction. The agent tried but was unable to contact respondent as directed. The record provides no explanation for respondent's failure to keep his appointment. No further action was taken by the agent, and the investigatory file on the matter was closed. The agent did, however, report the information to federal prosecutors. At that time, the Government was seeking information on local drug traffic to present to a special grand jury investigating illicit traffic in the area.

Respondent was subpoenaed to testify before the grand jury on May 2, 1973; this was approximately six weeks after the abortive narcotics transaction at the tavern where respondent was employed. When called into the grand jury room and after preliminary statements, the following colloquy occurred between the prosecutor and respondent:

Q. . . . Now, you are required to answer all the questions that I ask you except for the ones that you feel would tend to incriminate you. Do you understand that?

A. Do I answer all the questions you ask?

Q. You have to answer all the questions except for those you think will incriminate you in the commission of a crime. Is that clear?

A. Yes, sir.

Q. You don't have to answer questions which would incriminate you. All other questions you have to answer openly and truthfully. And, of course, if you do not answer those (questions) truthfully, in other words if you lie about certain questions, you could possibly be charged with perjury. Do you understand that?

A. Yes, sir.

Q. Have you contacted a lawyer in this matter?

A. I don't have one. I don't have the money to get one.

Q. Well, if you would like to have a lawyer, he cannot be inside this room. He can only be outside. You would be free to consult with him if you so chose. Now, if during the course of this investigation, the questions that we ask you, if you feel like you would like to have a lawyer outside to talk to, let me know.

During the questioning respondent admitted that he had previously been convicted of distributing drugs, that he had recently used heroin himself, and that he had purchased heroin as recently as five months previously. Despite this admitted experience with San Antonio's heroin traffic, respondent denied knowledge of the identity of any dealers, save for a streetcorner source named Juan. Respondent steadfastly denied either selling or attempting to sell heroin since the time of his conviction 15 years before.

Respondent specifically disclaimed having discussed the sale of heroin with anyone during the preceding year and stated that he would not even try to purchase an ounce of heroin for $650. Respondent refused to amplify on his testimony when directly confronted by the prosecutor:

Q. Mr. Mandujano, our information is that you can tell us more about the heroin business here in San Antonio than you have today. Is there anything you would like to add telling us more about who sells heroin?

A. Well, sir, I couldn't help you because, you know, I don't get along with the guys and I just can't tell you, you know.

Following this appearance, respondent was charged by a grand jury on June 13, 1973, in a two-count indictment with attempting to distribute heroin in violation of 21 U.S.C. ss 841(a)(1), 846, and for willfully and knowingly making a false material declaration to the grand jury in violation of 18 U.S.C. s 1623. The falsity of his statements was conceded; his sole claim was that the testimony before the grand jury should be suppressed because the Government failed to provide the warnings called for by *Miranda*. Following an evidentiary hearing, the District Court granted respondent's motion to suppress. The court held that respondent was a "putative" or "virtual" defendant when called before the grand jury; respondent had therefore been entitled to full *Miranda* warnings.

The Court of Appeals affirmed. It recognized that certain warnings had in fact been given to respondent at the outset of his grand jury appearance. But the court agreed with the District Court that "full *Miranda* warnings should have been accorded Mandujano who was in the position of a virtual or putative defendant." The essence of the Court of Appeals' holding is:

> In order to deter the prosecuting officers from bringing a putative or virtual defendant before the grand jury, for the purpose of obtaining incriminating or perjur(i)ous testimony, the accused must be adequately apprised of his rights, or all of his testimony, incriminating and perjur(i)ous, will be suppressed.

In so ruling, the court undertook to distinguish its own holding in *United States v. Orta* (1958), in which Judge Rives, speaking for the court, stated:

> (A grand jury witness) might answer truthfully and thereafter assert the constitutional guaranty. Under no circumstances, however, could he commit perjury and successfully claim that the Constitution afforded him protection from prosecution for that crime. ". . .[T]he immunity afforded by the constitutional guaranty relates to the past, and does not endow the person who testifies with a license to commit perjury."

In the *Orta* opinion, Judge Rives went on to observe:

> The only debatable question is one of the supervision of the conduct of Government representatives in the interest of fairness. In *United States v. Scully*, the Court of Appeals for the Second Circuit held:

> the mere possibility that the witness may later be indicted furnishes no basis for requiring
> that he be advised of his rights under the Fifth Amendment, when summoned to give testi-
> mony before a Grand Jury.
>
> That holding is applicable to the present record. There is no showing that the Grand Jury before
> which Orta testified was seeking to indict him or any other person already identified.

The Court of Appeals concluded that the "totality of the circumstances" commanded suppression of all the testimony on which the charge of perjury rested.

We agree with the views expressed by Judge Rives in *Orta*, supra, and disagree with the
Court of Appeals in the instant case; accordingly, we reverse.

(2)

The grand jury is an integral part of our constitutional heritage which was brought to this
country with the common law. The Framers, most of them trained in the English law and
traditions, accepted the grand jury as a basic guarantee of individual liberty; notwithstanding
periodic criticism, much of which is superficial, overlooking relevant history, the grand jury
continues to function as a barrier to reckless or unfounded charges. "Its adoption in our Constitution as the sole method for preferring charges in serious criminal cases shows the high
place it held as an instrument of justice." Its historic office has been to provide a shield against
arbitrary or oppressive action, by insuring that serious criminal accusations will be brought
only upon the considered judgment of a representative body of citizens acting under oath and
under judicial instruction and guidance.

Earlier we noted that the law vests the grand jury with substantial powers, because "(t)
he grand jury's investigative power must be broad if its public responsibility is adequately to
be discharged. Indispensable to the exercise of its power is the authority to compel the attendance and the testimony of witnesses, and to require the production of evidence.

When called by the grand jury, witnesses are thus legally bound to give testimony. This
principle has long been recognized. In *United States v. Burr*, Mr. Chief Justice Marshall drew
on English precedents, aptly described by Lord Chancellor Hardwicke in the 18th century,
and long accepted in America as a hornbook proposition: "The public has a right to every
man's evidence." This Court has repeatedly invoked this fundamental proposition when dealing with the powers of the grand jury.

The grand jury's authority to compel testimony is not, of course, without limits. The
same Amendment that establishes the grand jury also guarantees that "no person . . . shall be
compelled in any criminal case to be a witness against himself. . . ." The duty to give evidence
to a grand jury is therefore conditional; every person owes society his testimony, unless some
recognized privilege is asserted.

Under settled principles, the Fifth Amendment does not confer an absolute right to
decline to respond in a grand jury inquiry; the privilege does not negate the duty to testify
but simply conditions that duty. The privilege cannot, for example, be asserted by a witness
to protect others from possible criminal prosecution. Nor can it be invoked simply to protect
the witness' interest in privacy. "Ordinarily, of course, a witness has no right of privacy before
the grand jury."

The very availability of the Fifth Amendment privilege to grand jury witnesses, recognized
by this Court in *Counselman v. Hitchcock* (1892), suggests that occasions will often arise when
potentially incriminating questions will be asked in the ordinary course of the jury's investigation. Probing questions to all types of witnesses is the stuff that grand jury investigations
are made of; the grand jury's mission is, after all, to determine whether to make a presentment or return an indictment. "The basic purpose of the English grand jury was to provide a
fair method for instituting criminal proceedings against persons believed to have committed
crimes."

It is in keeping with the grand jury's historic function as a shield against arbitrary accusations to call before it persons suspected of criminal activity, so that the investigation can be complete. This is true whether the grand jury embarks upon an inquiry focused upon individuals suspected of wrongdoing, or is directed at persons suspected of no misconduct but who may be able to provide links in a chain of evidence relating to criminal conduct of others, or is centered upon broader problems of concern to society. It is entirely appropriate indeed imperative to summon individuals who may be able to illuminate the shadowy precincts of corruption and crime. Since the subject matter of the inquiry is crime, and often organized, systematic crime as is true with drug traffic it is unrealistic to assume that all of the witnesses capable of providing useful information will be pristine pillars of the community untainted by criminality.

The Court has never ignored this reality of law enforcement. Speaking for the Court in *Kastigar v. United States*, Mr. Justice Powell said:

> (M)any offenses are of such a character that the only persons capable of giving useful testimony are those implicated in the crime.

Mr. Justice White made a similar observation in the context of a state investigation:

> (T)he very fact that a witness is called . . . is likely to be based upon knowledge, or at least a suspicion based on some information, that the witness is implicated in illegal activities. . . .

Moreover, the Court has expressly recognized that "(t)he obligation to appear is no different for a person who may himself be the subject of the grand jury inquiry."

There is nothing new about the Court's recognition of this reality of grand jury inquiries. In one of the early cases dealing with the Fifth Amendment privilege, the Court observed: "(I)t is only from the mouths of those having knowledge of the (unlawful conduct) that the facts can be ascertained."

Accordingly, the witness, though possibly engaged in some criminal enterprise, can be required to answer before a grand jury, so long as there is no compulsion to answer questions that are self-incriminating; the witness can, of course, stand on the privilege, assured that its protection "is as broad as the mischief against which it seeks to guard." The witness must invoke the privilege, however, as the "Constitution does not forbid the asking of criminative questions."

> The (Fifth) Amendment speaks of compulsion. It does not preclude a witness from testifying voluntarily in matters which may incriminate him. If, therefore, he desires the protection of the privilege, he must claim it or he will not be considered to have been "compelled" within the meaning of the Amendment.

Absent a claim of the privilege, the duty to give testimony remains absolute.

The stage is therefore set when the question is asked. If the witness interposes his privilege, the grand jury has two choices. If the desired testimony is of marginal value, the grand jury can pursue other avenues of inquiry; if the testimony is thought sufficiently important, the grand jury can seek a judicial determination as to the bona fides of the witness' Fifth Amendment claim, in which case the witness must satisfy the presiding judge that the claim of privilege is not a subterfuge. If in fact "'there is reasonable ground to apprehend danger to the witness from his being compelled to answer,'" the prosecutor must then determine whether the answer is of such overriding importance as to justify a grant of immunity to the witness.

If immunity is sought by the prosecutor and granted by the presiding judge, the witness can then be compelled to answer, on pain of contempt, even though the testimony would implicate the witness in criminal activity. The reason for this is not hard to divine; Mr. Justice

Frankfurter indicated as much in observing that immunity is the quid pro quo for securing an answer from the witness: "Immunity displaces the danger. Based on this recognition, federal statutes conferring immunity on witnesses in federal judicial proceedings, including grand jury investigations, are so familiar that they have become part of our "'constitutional fabric.'" Immunity is the Government's ultimate tool for securing testimony that otherwise would be protected; unless immunity is conferred, however, testimony may be suppressed, along with its fruits, if it is compelled over an appropriate claim of privilege. On the other hand, when granted immunity, a witness once again owes the obligation imposed upon all citizens the duty to give testimony since immunity substitutes for the privilege.

In this constitutional process of securing a witness' testimony, perjury simply has no place whatever. Perjured testimony is an obvious and flagrant affront to the basic concepts of judicial proceedings. Effective restraints against this type of egregious offense are therefore imperative. The power of subpoena, broad as it is, and the power of contempt for refusing to answer, drastic as that is and even the solemnity of the oath cannot insure truthful answers. Hence, Congress has made the giving of false answers a criminal act punishable by severe penalties; in no other way can criminal conduct be flushed into the open where the law can deal with it.

Similarly, our cases have consistently indeed without exception allowed sanctions for false statements or perjury; they have done so even in instances where the perjurer complained that the Government exceeded its constitutional powers in making the inquiry.

In *Bryson*, a union officer was required by federal labor law to file an affidavit averring that he was not a Communist. The affidavit was false in material statements. In a collateral attack on his conviction, Bryson argued that since the statute required him either to incriminate himself or lie, he could not lawfully be imprisoned for failure to comply. This Court rejected the contention:

> (I)t cannot be thought that as a general principle of our law a citizen has a privilege to answer fraudulently a question that the Government should not have asked. Our legal system provides methods for challenging the Government's right to ask questions lying is not one of them.

Even where a statutory scheme granted blanket immunity from further use of testimony, the Court has found perjured statements to fall outside the grant. In *Glickstein*, a bankrupt was indicted for perjury committed in the course of a bankruptcy proceeding. The Bankruptcy Act expressly conferred broad immunity on a bankrupt: "(N)o testimony given by him shall be offered in evidence against him in any criminal proceeding." The Court rejected the bankrupt's literalistic interpretation of the statute as conferring immunity from prosecution for perjury:

> (T)he sanction of an oath and the imposition of a punishment for false swearing are inherently a part of the power to compel the giving of testimony, they are included in that grant of authority and are not prohibited by the immunity as to self-incrimination. . . . (I)t cannot be conceived that there is power to compel the giving of testimony where no right exists to require that the testimony shall be given under such circumstances and safeguards as to compel it to be truthful. . . . (T)he immunity afforded by the constitutional guarantee relates to the past and does not endow the person who testifies with a license to commit perjury.

(3)

In this case, the Court of Appeals required the suppression of perjured testimony given by respondent, as a witness under oath, lawfully summoned before an investigative grand jury and questioned about matters directly related to the grand jury's inquiry. The court reached this result because the prosecutor failed to give *Miranda* warnings at the outset of Mandujano's interrogation. Those warnings were required, in the Court of Appeals' view, because Mandujano was a "virtual" or "putative" defendant that is, the prosecutor had specific information concerning Mandujano's participation in an attempted sale of heroin and the focus of the grand jury interrogation, as evidenced by the prosecutor's questions, centered on Mandujano's involvement in narcotics traffic. The fundamental error of the prosecutor, in the court's view, was to treat respondent in such a way as to "'smack' of entrapment"; as a consequence, the court concluded that "elemental fairness" required the perjured testimony to be suppressed.

The court's analysis, premised upon the prosecutor's failure to give *Miranda* warnings, erroneously applied the standards fashioned by this Court in *Miranda*. Those warnings were aimed at the evils seen by the Court as endemic to police interrogation of a person in custody. *Miranda* addressed extrajudicial confessions or admissions procured in a hostile, unfamiliar environment which lacked procedural safeguards. The decision expressly rested on the privilege against compulsory self-incrimination; the prescribed warnings sought to negate the "compulsion" thought to be inherent in police station interrogation. But the *Miranda* Court simply did not perceive judicial inquiries and custodial interrogation as equivalents: "(T)he compulsion to speak in the isolated setting of the police station may well be greater than in courts or other official investigations, where there are often impartial observers to guard against intimidation or trickery."

The Court thus recognized that many official investigations, such as grand jury questioning, take place in a setting wholly different from custodial police interrogation. Indeed, the Court's opinion in *Miranda* reveals a focus on what was seen by the Court as police "coercion" derived from "factual studies (relating to) police violence and the 'third degree' . . . physical brutality beating, hanging, whipping and to sustained and protracted questioning incommunicado in order to extort confessions. . . . " To extend these concepts to questioning before a grand jury inquiring into criminal activity under the guidance of a judge is an extravagant expansion never remotely contemplated by this Court in *Miranda*; the dynamics of constitutional interpretation do not compel constant extension of every doctrine announced by the Court.

The marked contrasts between a grand jury investigation and custodial interrogation have been commented on by the Court from time to time. Mr. Justice Marshall observed that the broad coercive powers of a grand jury are justified, because "in contrast to the police it is not likely that (the grand jury) will abuse those powers."

(4)

The warnings volunteered by the prosecutor to respondent in this case were more than sufficient to inform him of his rights and his responsibilities and particularly of the consequences of perjury. To extend the concepts of *Miranda*, as contemplated by the Court of Appeals, would require that the witness be told that there was an absolute right to silence, and obviously any such warning would be incorrect, for there is no such right before a grand jury. Under *Miranda*, a person in police custody has, of course, an absolute right to decline to answer any question, incriminating or innocuous, whereas a grand jury witness, on the contrary, has an absolute duty to answer all questions, subject only to a valid Fifth Amendment claim. And even when the grand jury witness asserts the privilege, questioning need not cease, except as to the particular subject to which the privilege has been addressed. Other lines of inquiry may properly be pursued.

Respondent was also informed that if he desired he could have the assistance of counsel, but that counsel could not be inside the grand jury room. That statement was plainly a correct recital of the law. No criminal proceedings had been instituted against respondent, hence the Sixth Amendment right to counsel had not come into play. A witness "before a grand jury cannot insist, as a matter of constitutional right, on being represented by his counsel. . . ."

Under settled principles the witness may not insist upon the presence of his attorney in the grand jury room. Fed. Rule Crim. Proc. 6(d).

Respondent, by way of further explanation, was also warned that he could be prosecuted for perjury if he testified falsely. Since respondent was already under oath to testify truthfully, this explanation was redundant; it served simply to emphasize the obligation already imposed by the oath.

> Once a witness swears to give truthful answers, there is no requirement to "warn him not to commit perjury or, conversely to direct him to tell the truth." It would render the sanctity of the oath quite meaningless to require admonition to adhere to it.

Similarly, a witness subpoenaed to testify before a petit jury and placed under oath has never been entitled to a warning that, if he violates the solemn oath to "tell the truth," he may be subject to a prosecution for perjury, for the oath itself is the warning. Nor has any case been cited to us holding that the absence of such warnings before a petit jury provides a shield against use of false testimony in a subsequent prosecution for perjury or in contempt proceedings.

In any event, a witness sworn to tell the truth before a duly constituted grand jury will not be heard to call for suppression of false statements made to that jury, any more than would be the case with false testimony before a petit jury or other duly constituted tribunal. In another context, this Court has refused to permit a witness to protect perjured testimony by proving a *Miranda* violation. In *Harris v. New York* (1971), the Court held that notwithstanding a *Miranda* violation

> (The Fifth Amendment) privilege cannot be construed to include the right to commit perjury.

More recently, the Court reaffirmed this salutary principle:

> (T)he shield provided by *Miranda* is not to be perverted to a license to testify inconsistently, or even perjuriously, free from the risk of confrontation with prior inconsistent utterances.

The fact that here the grand jury interrogation had focused on some of respondent's specific activities does not require that these important principles be jettisoned; nothing remotely akin to "entrapment" or abuse of process is suggested by what occurred here. Assuming arguendo, that respondent, was indeed a "putative defendant," that fact would have no bearing on the validity of a conviction for testifying falsely.

The grand jury was appropriately concerned about the sources of narcotics in the San Antonio area. The attempted heroin sale by respondent provided ample reason to believe that he had knowledge about local heroin suppliers. It was, therefore, entirely proper to question him with respect to his knowledge of narcotics trafficking. Respondent was free at every stage to interpose his constitutional privilege against self-incrimination, but perjury was not a permissible option. As the Tenth Circuit has held, the law provides "other methods for challenging the government's right to ask questions."

The judgment of the Court of Appeals is therefore reversed, and the cause is remanded for further proceedings consistent with this opinion.

NOTES AND QUESTIONS

1. Judging by the questioning reproduced in the opinion, what was the government's primary purpose in subpoenaing Mandujano to testify in the grand jury?

2. Mandujano apparently conceded the falsity of his grand jury testimony. Did he have to? What's the strongest case for defending against the perjury charge on the ground that the testimony was not false?

3. The court of appeals held that Mandujano should have been given full-blown *Miranda* warnings because he was a "putative or virtual" defendant. What does that mean? How does this status compare to that of a suspect in a custodial interrogation setting where *Miranda* warnings are required? Do you agree that he was a "putative or virtual" defendant? Should this status require *Miranda* warnings?

4. The grand jury love song here, again unironically, focuses on the "shield" role of the grand jury. *Id.* at 571-73. The Court observes:

> It is in keeping with the grand jury's historic function as a shield against arbitrary accusations to call before it persons suspected of criminal activity, so that the investigation can be complete. This is true whether the grand jury embarks upon an inquiry focused upon individuals suspected of wrongdoing, or is directed at persons suspected of no misconduct but who may be able to provide links in a chain of evidence relating to criminal conduct of others, or is centered upon broader problems of concern to society.

Id. at 573. However accurate this historic description may be, how does it reflect the grand jury's function "as a shield"? Who's being shielded in this scenario? Aren't those people who can "provide links in a chain" as to the criminality of others likely to themselves have some degree of criminal exposure?

5. No one is a proponent of perjury. It is, and should be, a federal crime, such as the one Mandujano was prosecuted under, 18 U.S.C. § 1623. But the Court here seems almost morally offended by the fact that the defendant lied in the grand jury.

> In this constitutional process of securing a witness' testimony, perjury simply has no place whatever. Perjured testimony is an obvious and flagrant affront to the basic concepts of judicial proceedings.

Id. at 577. Does the fact of defendant's perjury affect the result here? Does this case possibly come out differently if the Court was confronted only with the abstract issue whether a person the government intends to indict must be given *Miranda* warnings if he is subpoenaed to the grand jury? Note that the Court seems to concede that some warnings must be given in this context. *Id.* at 580.

6. In a concurring opinion Justice Brennan proposes a caveat to the Court's rule for situations where the government calls before a grand jury a person whom "it has probable cause . . . to suspect of committing a crime" to testify regarding that crime. *Id.* at 599. In such cases, Justice Brennan opines, there must be some form of "intentional and intelligent waiver" of the right against self-incrimination. *Id.* Is this rule enforceable? And why is this a concurrence and not a dissent?

United States v. Washington
431 U.S. 181 (1977)

Mr. Chief Justice BURGER delivered the opinion of the Court.

The question presented in this case is whether testimony given by a grand jury witness suspected of wrongdoing may be used against him in a later prosecution for a substantive criminal offense when the witness was not informed in advance of his testimony that he was a potential defendant in danger of indictment.

(1)

The facts are not in dispute. Zimmerman and Woodard were driving respondent's van truck when a Washington, D.C., policeman stopped them for a traffic offense. Seeing a motorcycle in the rear of the van which he identified as stolen, the officer arrested both men and impounded respondent's vehicle. When respondent came to reclaim the van, he told police that Zimmerman and Woodard were friends who were driving the van with his permission.

He explained the presence of the stolen motorcycle by saying that while driving the van himself he had stopped to assist an unknown motorcyclist whose machine had broken down. Respondent then allowed the motorcycle to be placed in his van to take it for repairs. Soon after this the van stalled and he walked to a nearby gasoline station to call Zimmerman and Woodard for help, leaving the van with the unknown motorcyclist. After reaching Zimmerman by phone, respondent waited at the gasoline station for his friends, then returned to the spot he had left the van when they failed to appear; by that time the van had disappeared. Respondent said he was not alarmed, assuming his friends had repaired the van and driven it away. Shortly thereafter, Zimmerman and Woodard were arrested with the stolen motorcycle in the van.

Not surprisingly, the officer to whom respondent related this tale was more than a little skeptical; he told respondent he did not believe his story, and advised him not to repeat it in court, "because you're liable to be in trouble if you (do so)." The officer also declined to release the van. Respondent then repeated this story to an Assistant United States Attorney working on the case. The prosecutor, too, was dubious of the account; nevertheless, he released the van to respondent. At the same time, he served respondent with a subpoena to appear before the grand jury investigating the motorcycle theft.

When respondent appeared before the grand jury, the Assistant United States Attorney in charge had not yet decided whether to seek an indictment against him. The prosecutor was aware of respondent's explanation, and was also aware of the possibility that respondent could be indicted by the grand jury for the theft if his story was not believed.

The prosecutor did not advise respondent before his appearance that he might be indicted on a criminal charge in connection with the stolen motorcycle. But respondent, after reciting the usual oath to tell the truth, was given a series of other warnings, as follows:

> **Q.** . . . .
> You have a right to remain silent. You are not required to say anything to us in this Grand Jury at any time or to answer any question.
> Anything you say can be used against you in Court.
> You have the right to talk to a lawyer for advice before we question you and have him outside the Grand Jury during any questioning.
> If you cannot afford a lawyer and want one a lawyer will be provided for you.
> If you want to answer questions now without a lawyer present you will still have the right to stop answering at any time.
> You also have the right to stop answering at any time until you talk to a lawyer.
> Now, do you understand those rights, sir?
> **A.** Yes, I do.
> **Q.** And do you want to answer questions of the Grand Jury in reference to a stolen motorcycle that was found in your truck?
> **A.** Yes, sir.
> **Q.** And do you want a lawyer here or outside the Grand Jury room while you answer those questions?
> **A.** No, I don't think so.

In response to questions, respondent again related his version of how the stolen motorcycle came to be in the rear of his van. Subsequently, the grand jury indicted respondent, Zimmerman, and Woodard for grand larceny and receiving stolen property.

Respondent moved to suppress his testimony and quash the indictment, arguing that it was based on evidence obtained in violation of his Fifth Amendment privilege against compelled self-incrimination. The Superior Court for the District of Columbia suppressed the testimony and dismissed the indictment, holding that before the Government could use respondent's grand jury testimony at trial, it had first to demonstrate that respondent had knowingly waived his privilege against compelled self-incrimination. Notwithstanding the comprehensive warnings described earlier, the court found no effective waiver had been made, holding that respondent was not properly advised of his Fifth Amendment rights. The court thought the Constitution required, at a minimum, that

> inquiry be made of the suspect to determine what his educational background is, and what his formal education is and whether or not he understands that this is a constitutional privilege and whether he fully understands the consequences of what might result in the event that he does waive his constitutional right and in the event that he does make incriminatory statements. . . .

The court also held that respondent should have been told that his testimony could lead to his indictment by the grand jury before which he was testifying, and could then be used to convict him in a criminal prosecution.

The District of Columbia Court of Appeals affirmed the suppression order. That court also took the position that "the most significant failing of the prosecutor was in not advising (respondent) that he was a potential defendant. Another shortcoming was in the prosecutor's waiting until after administering the oath in the cloister of the grand jury before undertaking to furnish what advice was given."

(2)

The implicit premise of the District of Columbia Court of Appeals' holding is that a grand jury inquiry, like police custodial interrogation, is an "interrogation of persons suspected or accused of crime (that) contains inherently compelling pressures which work to undermine the individual's will to resist and to compel him to speak where he would not otherwise do so freely." But this Court has not decided that the grand jury setting presents coercive elements which compel witnesses to incriminate themselves. Nor have we decided whether any Fifth Amendment warnings whatever are constitutionally required for grand jury witnesses; moreover, we have no occasion to decide these matters today, for even assuming that the grand jury setting exerts some pressures on witnesses generally or on those who may later be indicted, the comprehensive warnings respondent received in this case plainly satisfied any possible claim to warnings. Accordingly, respondent's grand jury testimony may properly be used against him in a subsequent trial for theft of the motorcycle.

Although it is well settled that the Fifth Amendment privilege extends to grand jury proceedings, it is also axiomatic that the Amendment does not automatically preclude self-incrimination, whether spontaneous or in response to questions put by government officials. "It does not preclude a witness from testifying voluntarily in matters which may incriminate him," for "those competent and freewilled to do so may give evidence against the whole world, themselves included." Indeed, far from being prohibited by the Constitution, admissions of guilt by wrongdoers, if not coerced, are inherently desirable. In addition to guaranteeing the right to remain silent unless immunity is granted, the Fifth Amendment proscribes only self-incrimination obtained by a "genuine compulsion of testimony." Absent some officially coerced self-accusation, the Fifth Amendment privilege is not violated by even the most damning admissions. Accordingly, unless the record reveals some compulsion, respondent's incriminating testimony cannot conflict with any constitutional guarantees of the privilege.

The Constitution does not prohibit every element which influences a criminal suspect to make incriminating admissions. Of course, for many witnesses the grand jury room engenders an atmosphere conducive to truth telling, for it is likely that upon being brought before such a body of neighbors and fellow citizens, and having been placed under a solemn oath to tell the truth, many witnesses will feel obliged to do just that. But it does not offend the guarantees of the Fifth Amendment if in that setting a witness is more likely to tell the truth than in less solemn surroundings. The constitutional guarantee is only that the witness be not compelled to give self-incriminating testimony. The test is whether, considering the totality of the circumstances, the free will of the witness was overborne.

(3)

After being sworn, respondent was explicitly advised that he had a right to remain silent and that any statements he did make could be used to convict him of crime. It is inconceivable that such a warning would fail to alert him to his right to refuse to answer any question which might incriminate him. This advice also eliminated any possible compulsion to self-incrimination which might otherwise exist. To suggest otherwise is to ignore the record and reality. Indeed, it seems self-evident that one who is told he is free to refuse to answer questions is in a curious posture to later complain that his answers were compelled. Moreover, any possible coercion or unfairness resulting from a witness' misimpression that he must answer truthfully even questions with incriminatory aspects is completely removed by the warnings given here. Even in the presumed psychologically coercive atmosphere of police custodial interrogation, *Miranda* does not require that any additional warnings be given simply because the suspect is a potential defendant; indeed, such suspects are potential defendants more often than not.

Respondent points out that unlike one subject to custodial interrogation, whose arrest should inform him only too clearly that he is a potential criminal defendant, a grand jury witness may well be unaware that he is targeted for possible prosecution. While this may be so in some situations, it is an overdrawn generalization. In any case, events here clearly put respondent on notice that he was a suspect in the motorcycle theft. He knew that the grand jury was investigating that theft and that his involvement was known to the authorities. Respondent was made abundantly aware that his exculpatory version of events had been disbelieved by the police officer, and that his friends, whose innocence his own story supported, were to be prosecuted for the theft. The interview with the prosecutor put him on additional notice that his implausible story was not accepted as true. The warnings he received in the grand jury room served further to alert him to his own potential criminal liability. In sum, by the time he testified respondent knew better than anyone else of his potential defendant status.

However, all of this is largely irrelevant, since we do not understand what constitutional disadvantage a failure to give potential defendant warnings could possibly inflict on a grand jury witness, whether or not he has received other warnings. It is firmly settled that the prospect of being indicted does not entitle a witness to commit perjury, and witnesses who are not grand jury targets are protected from compulsory self-incrimination to the same extent as those who are. Because target witness status neither enlarges nor diminishes the constitutional protection against compelled self-incrimination, potential-defendant warnings add nothing of value to protection of Fifth Amendment rights.

Respondent suggests he must prevail under *Garner v. United States*. There, the petitioner was charged with a gambling conspiracy. As part of its case, the Government introduced Garner's income tax returns, in one of which he had identified his occupation as "professional gambler," and in all of which he had reported substantial income from wagering. The Court recognized that Garner was indeed compelled by law to file a tax return, but held that this did not constitute compelled self-incrimination. The Court noted that Garner did not claim his Fifth Amendment privilege, instead making the incriminating disclosure that he was a professional gambler. *Garner* holds that the Self-Incrimination Clause is violated only when the Government compels disclosures which it knows will incriminate the declarant that is, only when it intentionally places the individual under "compulsions to incriminate, not merely

694 Chapter VII Grand Jury

compulsions to make unprivileged disclosures." But the distinction between compulsion to incriminate and compulsion to disclose what the Government is entitled to know is of no help to respondent; in this case there was no compulsion to do either.

In *Beckwith v. United States*, decided shortly after *Garner*, we reaffirmed the need for showing overbearing compulsion as a prerequisite to a Fifth Amendment violation. There, the Government agent interrogated the taxpayer for the explicit purpose of securing information that would incriminate him. There, as here, the interrogation was not conducted in an inherently coercive setting; hence the claim of compelled self-incrimination was rejected.

(4)

Since warnings were given, we are not called upon to decide whether such warnings were constitutionally required. However, the District of Columbia Court of Appeals held that whatever warnings are required are insufficient if given "in the cloister of the grand jury." That court gave no reason for its view that warnings must be given outside the presence of the jury, but respondent now advances two justifications. First, it could be thought that warnings given to respondent before the grand jury came too late, because of the short time to assimilate their significance, and because of the presence of the grand jurors. But respondent does not contend that he did not understand the warnings given here. In any event, it is purely speculative to attribute any such effects to warnings given in the presence of the jury immediately before taking the stand. If anything, the proximity of the warnings to respondent's testimony and the solemnity of the grand jury setting seem likely to increase their effectiveness.

Second, respondent argues that giving the oath in the presence of the grand jury undermines assertion of the Fifth Amendment privilege by placing the witness in fear that the grand jury will infer guilt from invocation of the privilege. But this argument entirely overlooks that the grand jury's historic role is an investigative body; it is not the final arbiter of guilt or innocence. Moreover, it is well settled that invocation of the Fifth Amendment privilege in a grand jury proceeding is not admissible in a criminal trial, where guilt or innocence is actually at stake.

The judgment of the Court of Appeals is reversed, and the cause is remanded for further proceedings not inconsistent with this opinion.

Reversed and remanded.

Mr. Justice BRENNAN, with whom Mr. Justice MARSHALL joins, dissenting.

The general rule that a witness must affirmatively claim the privilege against compulsory self-incrimination must in my view admit of an exception in the case of a grand jury witness whom the prosecutor interrogates with the express purpose of getting evidence upon which to base a criminal charge against him. In such circumstances, even warnings, before interrogation, of his right to silence do not suffice. The privilege is emptied of substance unless the witness is further advised by the prosecutor that he is a potential defendant. Only if the witness then nevertheless intentionally and intelligently waives his right to be free from compulsory self-incrimination and submits to further interrogation should use of his grand jury testimony against him be sanctioned. As I stated in *United States v. Mandujano*:

> I would hold that, in the absence of an intentional and intelligent waiver by the individual of his known right to be free from compulsory self-incrimination, the Government may not call before a grand jury one whom it has probable cause as measured by an objective standard to suspect of committing a crime, and by use of judicial compulsion compel him to testify with regard to that crime. In the absence of such a waiver, the Fifth Amendment requires that any testimony obtained in this fashion be unavailable to the Government for use at trial. Such a waiver could readily be demonstrated by proof that the individual was warned prior to questioning that he is currently subject to possible criminal prosecution for the commission of a stated crime. . . .

In this case, although respondent Washington was advised of his rights to silence and to talk to a lawyer before he appeared before the grand jury, he was "only told that he was needed as a witness in prosecuting the two who were occupants of the van at the time of its impoundment." He was never told that he was in danger of being indicted himself, even though "at the time of his grand jury appearance respondent was a potential defendant whose indictment was considered likely by the prosecution."

The ancient privilege of a witness against being compelled to incriminate himself is precious to free men as a shield against high-handed and arrogant inquisitorial practices. It has survived centuries of controversies, periodically kindled by popular impatience that its protection sometimes allows the guilty to escape punishment. But it has endured as a wise and necessary protection of the individual against arbitrary power, and the price of occasional failures of justice is paid in the larger interest of general personal security.

I would hold that a failure to warn the witness that he is a potential defendant is fatal to an indictment of him when it is made unmistakably to appear, as here, that the grand jury inquiry became an investigation directed against the witness and was pursued with the purpose of compelling him to give self-incriminating testimony upon which to indict him. I would further hold that without such prior warning and the witness' subsequent voluntary waiver of his privilege, there is such gross encroachment upon the witness' privilege as to render worthless the values protected by it unless the self-incriminating testimony is unavailable to the Government for use at any trial brought pursuant to even a valid indictment.

It should be remarked that, of course, today's decision applies only to application of the privilege against self-incrimination secured by the Fifth Amendment to the United States Constitution. The holding does not affect the authority of state courts to construe counterpart provisions of state constitutions even identically phrased provisions "to give the individual greater protection than is provided" by the federal provision. . . . See generally Brennan, State Constitutions and the Protection of Individual Rights, 90 Harv. L. Rev. 489 (1977).

A number of state courts have recognized that a defendant or potential defendant called before a grand jury is privileged against the State's using his self-incriminating testimony to procure an indictment or using it to introduce against him at trial, even in the absence of an affirmative claim of his privilege against self-incrimination. . . . One court has specifically held that interrogating a potential defendant "under (the) guise of examining him as to the guilt of someone else" is a violation of the defendant's privilege against self-incrimination. The rationale of these decisions which I would find applicable to the case now before us is that where the grand jury investigation is in fact a proceeding against the witness, or even if begun as a general investigation it becomes a proceeding against the witness, the encroachment upon the witness' privilege requires that a court deny to the prosecution the use of the witness' self-incriminating testimony.

NOTES AND QUESTIONS

1. According to the Court, at the time Washington was brought before the grand jury, the AUSA "had not yet decided whether to seek an indictment against him." *Id.* at 183. Assuming that was so, what might have been the prosecutor's purpose or purposes in subpoenaing Washington to the grand jury? Do you think it would have affected the prosecutor's decision if Washington had taken the Fifth?

2. Note that unlike the defendant in *Mandujano*, Washington was advised "[a]nything you say can be used against you in Court." Washington argues that notwithstanding the warnings' content, which he admits he understood, the warnings were deficient because (a) they were given in the presence of the grand jury and (b) they were given after he was sworn in to testify.

Is either argument persuasive as a matter of human nature? Should this matter legally?

3. The Court rejects Washington's arguments about the effectiveness of the warnings. Drawing on some unknown fount of psychological expertise, the Court states that "[i]f anything, the proximity of the warnings to respondent's testimony and the solemnity of the grand jury setting seem likely to increase their effectiveness." Effectiveness at what? The Court also observes, as to Washington's argument that the presence of the grand jurors inhibited his willingness to invoke the Fifth Amendment, "the argument entirely overlooks that the grand jury's historic role is an investigative body; it is not the final arbiter of guilt or innocence."

Whatever you think of Washington's arguments, are the Court's arguments dismissing his concerns persuasive?

4. On the psychological expertise front, note the Court's bizarre observation that "for many witnesses the grand jury room engenders an atmosphere conducive to truth telling, for it is likely that upon being brought before such a body of neighbors and fellow citizens, and having been placed under a solemn oath to tell the truth, many witnesses will feel obliged to do just that." *Id.* at 188.

One can't help wondering if anyone on the Court had ever been in a "grand jury room" or, for that matter, ever been accused of wrongdoing.

The context in the opinion for this sentiment is somewhat confusing. Does the Court seem to be contemplating witnesses who have committed crimes, and will willingly and righteously confess their sins to their "neighbors and fellow citizens"? Has the Court forgotten that a federal prosecutor, whose job is to charge people with crimes, will also be in the room?

5. The dissent reasserts the position of the dissent in *Mandujano*, and would require that a witness in Washington's position—who was "likely" to be indicted—must be warned that he "is a potential defendant." What does this add to the warnings Washington actually received? Is it relevant that a police officer who had some affiliation with the case told Washington that he disbelieved his story and warned him not to repeat it in court? Does this mean anything other than that Washington was foolish?

6. The dissent notes a fact omitted in the Court's opinion: that Washington was not told he was a potential defendant but "was only told that he was needed as a witness in prosecuting the two who were occupants of the van at the time of its impoundment." How should this statement factor into the analysis? It is unclear whether it was the prosecutor or a police officer who said this, and it matters: Prosecutors, as lawyers, are ethically bound not to make misrepresentations, while police and agents have no such obligations and often traffic in misrepresentations. Was Washington's story so inherently farfetched that he shouldn't have believed that he was only a witness regardless of what he was told?

7. In a companion case to *Washington, United States v. Wong*, 431 U.S. 174 (1977), the Court held that a witness who lied in the grand jury could be prosecuted for perjury based on that testimony even where the district court found that the witness was a native of China and had not understood the Fifth Amendment warnings she had been given in the grand jury.

Does nothing else matter if a witness commits perjury? Does a person who lies forfeit all rights? Is the take-away that no warning could possibly lead a witness to believe they could lie?

Department of Justice Grand Jury Policies. Notwithstanding the results in *Mandujano*, *Washington*, and *Wong*, the Department of Justice has developed internal policies regarding appropriate practices in this area, which are codified in the DOJ Justice Manual. One of these is JM § 9-11.150, "Subpoenaing Targets of the Investigation." The DOJ definition of "target," in turn, is found in JM 9-11.151: "a person as to whom the prosecutor or the grand jury has substantial evidence linking him or her to the commission of a crime and who, in the judgment of the prosecutor, is a putative defendant."

Do you think the DOJ really means "putative" or is just using that word because it has been used in the case law? Are any dictionary definitions of "putative" helpful here? Under the DOJ definition would you say that Mandujano was a "target" at the time of his grand jury appearance? Was Washington?

As far as subpoenaing targets to the grand jury, the Justice Manual provides:

> A grand jury may properly subpoena a subject or a target of the investigation and question the target about his or her involvement in the crime under investigation. *See United States v. Wong*, 431 U.S. 174, 179 n. 8 (1977); *United States v. Washington*, 431 U.S. 181, 190 n.6 (1977); *United States v. Mandujano*, 425 U.S. 564, 573-75 and 584 n.9 (1976); *United States v. Dionisio*, 410 U.S. 1, 10 n.8 (1973). However, in the context of particular cases such a subpoena may carry the appearance of unfairness. Because the potential for misunderstanding is great, before a known "target" (as defined in JM 9-11.151) is subpoenaed to testify before the grand jury about his or her involvement in the crime under investigation, an effort should be made to secure the target's voluntary appearance. If a voluntary appearance cannot be obtained, the target should be subpoenaed only after the United States Attorney or the responsible Assistant Attorney General have approved the subpoena.

The JM goes on to suggest that approval of such a subpoena should be based on factors such as the need for the testimony in the overall scheme of the investigation and whether the questioning likely implicates any privileges.

Given that by definition a "target" already has exhibited "substantial evidence" of criminality, what factors could account for a "need" for the target's testimony?

Note that the Justice Manual acknowledges the "appearance" of unfairness. How effective do you think this policy would be in limiting the subpoenaing of targets into the grand jury? Suppose you were a supervising AUSA and a junior colleague came to you and requested approval to subpoena Mandujano to the grand jury, based on the facts as recounted in the case prior to the grand jury appearance. How would you analyze the issue?

Why does the policy require an effort to secure the target's voluntary appearance? How likely is it that a target, who was aware of that status, would "voluntarily appear" before the grand jury?

The Justice Manual also has a policy regarding "Advice of 'Rights" to Grand Jury Witnesses," set forth at JM § 9-11.151:

> It is the policy of the Department of Justice to advise a grand jury witness of his or her rights if such witness is a "target" or "subject" of a grand jury investigation.
>
> A "target" [see definition above]
>
> A "subject" of an investigation is a person whose conduct is within the scope of the grand jury's investigation.
>
> The Supreme Court declined to decide whether a grand jury witness must be warned of his or her Fifth Amendment privilege against compulsory self-incrimination before the witness's grand jury testimony can be used against the witness. *See United States v. Washington*, 431 U.S. 181, 186 and 190-191 (1977); *United States v. Wong*, 431 U.S. 174 (1977); *United States v. Mandujano*, 425 U.S. 564, 582 n.7. (1976). In *Mandujano* the Court took cognizance of the fact that Federal prosecutors customarily warn "targets" of their Fifth Amendment rights before grand jury questioning begins. Similarly, in *Washington*, the Court pointed to the fact that Fifth Amendment warnings were administered as negating "any possible compulsion to self-incrimination which might otherwise exist" in the grand jury setting. *See Washington*, 431 U.S. at 188.
>
> Notwithstanding the lack of a clear constitutional imperative, it is the policy of the Department that an "Advice of Rights" form be appended to all grand jury subpoenas to be served on any "target" or "subject" of an investigation. See advice of rights below.
>
> In addition, these "warnings" should be given by the prosecutor on the record before the grand jury and the witness should be asked to affirm that the witness understands them.
>
> Although the Court in *Washington, supra*, held that "targets" of the grand jury's investigation are entitled to no special warnings relative to their status as "potential defendant(s)," the

698   Chapter VII Grand Jury

Department of Justice continues its longstanding policy to advise witnesses who are known "targets" of the investigation that their conduct is being investigated for possible violation of Federal criminal law. This supplemental advice of status of the witness as a target should be repeated on the record when the target witness is advised of the matters discussed in the preceding paragraphs.

When a district court insists that the notice of rights not be appended to a grand jury subpoena, the advice of rights may be set forth in a separate letter and mailed to or handed to the witness when the subpoena is served.

Advice of Rights:

The grand jury is conducting an investigation of possible violations of Federal criminal laws involving: (State here the general subject matter of inquiry, e.g., conducting an illegal gambling business in violation of 18 U.S.C. § 1955).

You may refuse to answer any question if a truthful answer to the question would tend to incriminate you.

Anything that you do say may be used against you by the grand jury or in a subsequent legal proceeding.

If you have retained counsel, the grand jury will permit you a reasonable opportunity to step outside the grand jury room to consult with counsel if you so desire.

Additional Advice to be Given to Targets: If the witness is a target, the above advice should also contain a supplemental warning that the witness's conduct is being investigated for possible violation of federal criminal law.

JM § 9-11.151. How much does the additional advice for targets add to the advice given to subjects? Under the DOJ's own definitions, is the additional advice for targets equally applicable to persons categorized as subjects?

Much of the content in these particular Justice Manual provisions is academic. Targets almost never testify in the grand jury. But the DOJ definitions of "target" and "subject"—and by negative implication a third category of "witness," persons of interest only as sources of information about others—are part of the everyday discourse between defense counsel and AUSAs.

The first question a defense attorney will ask an AUSA about a client who has received a grand jury subpoena is what is the witness's status: that is, is the client a target, subject, or witness? The answer to this question, although often heavily caveated (e.g., "just a witness for now"), will guide defense counsel's advice to the client about how to respond to the subpoena.

If the client is a target, the advice is simple: Do not testify. Take the Fifth if the AUSA insists on an appearance.

Next simplest is the "witness" category. If the client is truly just a witness—based on the AUSA's representation, which defense counsel is able to confirm by interviewing the client and perhaps from other sources of information—it may be permissible for the client simply to appear and testify in response to the subpoena. This is never a good idea unless there is 100 percent confidence the client is only a witness (e.g., a recordkeeper from a bank).

The client who is a "subject"—that is, the client's "conduct is within the scope of the grand jury's investigation"—is more complicated.

Can you negotiate an immunity grant for the client? This is always the ideal solution. But the AUSA will be reluctant to grant immunity if the client has significant exposure (and the AUSA believes the client should plead guilty) or if the AUSA is unsure the client can help the investigation, usually by implicating others in criminal conduct.

Take the Fifth? This strategy will often be necessary when the client is a subject. But this is risky. Sometimes AUSAs will require the client to assert the Fifth on a question-by-question basis. The client will be in the grand jury alone, and asserting the Fifth too broadly can result in collateral litigation over the scope of the privilege, while asserting it too narrowly can result in waiver or exposure.

G. PROSECUTORIAL ABUSE OF THE GRAND JURY'S POWERS

Negotiate a proffer agreement? Under such an arrangement, the client can be interviewed informally by the AUSA and agents outside the grand jury, with a very limited form of immunity. Sometimes this is better than simply taking the Fifth. Sometimes it isn't.

G. PROSECUTORIAL ABUSE OF THE GRAND JURY'S POWERS

The next cases focus on prosecutors' use of the grand jury for an improper purpose, that is, a purpose other than investigating whether a crime has been committed. We saw a variation on this theme in *Sells Engineering, supra*, where the Court was concerned about the grand jury being used to develop evidence for use in a civil suit. The following cases consider whether the grand jury may be used to develop evidence to use in a case that has already been indicted and whether the grand jury can be used to induce a person to commit perjury in the grand jury.

United States v. Doe
455 F.2d 1270 (1st Cir. 1972)

IN THE MATTER OF GRAND JURY PROCEEDING: APPLICATION OF DANIEL ELLSBERG FOR PROTECTIVE ORDER

COFFIN, Circuit Judge.

Daniel Ellsberg, a defendant in a pending criminal prosecution initiated by an indictment in the Central District of California, seeks a protective order barring a grand jury sitting in the District of Massachusetts (Boston) from gathering evidence which would be relevant to his trial in California. The district court denied the motion, basing its decision on the prosecution's representation "that its purpose in calling witnesses [in Boston] is not to obtain testimony or other evidence tending to prove the charge or charges [in California] but to determine whether any offense or offenses against the United States may have been committed within the District of Massachusetts." Movant now asks for a stay of the denial pending appeal.

The California indictment charges Ellsberg with unlawful possession of classified government documents (18 U.S.C. § 793(e)) and with unlawful conversion of such documents to his own use (18 U.S.C. § 641). In addition, Ellsberg, Anthony Russo and "others unknown" are charged with entering into a conspiracy with two other named but unindicted co-conspirators "to defraud the United States . . . [by] defeating its lawful governmental function of controlling the dissemination of classified Government studies," more specifically, by receiving the Pentagon Papers, copying them, and communicating them to unauthorized persons. Trial is scheduled to commence in from six to ten weeks.

The protective order which movant seeks would bar the prosecution from asking any witness subpoenaed to testify before the Boston grand jury questions bearing on the charge that he, Ellsberg, had conspired to communicate the Pentagon Papers to unauthorized persons, as broadly charged in the California indictment. The request is based on movant's assertion that use of the powerful and essentially unreviewable grand jury process in Boston to aid preparation of the government's case in California would subvert the protections accorded a defendant by the Federal Rules of Criminal Procedure and would consequently jeopardize his right to a fair trial on the pending charges. Although movant's argument, so put, contains due process elements, he appeals principally for an exercise of this court's general supervisory powers.

Although the attorneys for the government—the same three being responsible for both the presentation before the Boston grand jury and the California trial jury—have stated that the principal purpose of the Boston proceedings is to ascertain whether offenses against the United States, other than those already charged in the California indictment, have been committed and have expressly disavowed any intent to utilize the Boston grand jury "to extract testimony for use . . . in Los Angeles," they candidly admit that the investigation here may turn up some evidence relevant to the California proceedings. As long as such evidence remains a necessary — though usable — byproduct of the Boston investigation and is not allowed to disturb the focus of that investigation, however, the government contends that such evidence is properly usable in the California trial. It also believes that the Boston grand jury is not foreclosed from inquiring into events in Boston which "suggest other aspects" of the conspiracy alleged in the California indictment or "separate conspiracies involving Daniel Ellsberg as a central figure."

* * *

The nature of movant's claim is a large and compendious one. The rule, as accurately stated by Professor Moore, does not differ markedly from the general position staked out by the government: "It is improper to use the grand jury for the purpose of preparing an already pending indictment for trial. But the courts have generally held that where another purpose is predominant, the fact that the government may derive incidental benefit from a grand jury proceeding does not preclude its use." The classic case dealt with a grand jury subpoenaing the same witnesses and documents as had a prior grand jury which issued an indictment, where the court's compelled conclusion was that the "dominating, if not the only, object" was to prepare for trial of the earlier indictment. In another case, the Supreme Court refused to interfere with government use of a grand jury transcript in the preparation of a civil suit, even though no indictment was returned, in the absence of a finding that the grand jury had been used as a short cut or that criminal procedure had been subverted. In *United States v. Dardi* (1964), the test was thus stated: "It is improper to utilize a Grand Jury for the sole or dominating purpose of preparing an already pending indictment for trial."

Movant's claim of taint, therefore, would be the expansive one that the Boston grand jury, as a whole, had, as its sole or dominating purpose, preparation for trial of the California criminal prosecution. This claim could be tested only by a comprehensive viewing of the entire Boston grand jury minutes. But Rule 6(e) of the Federal Rules of Criminal Procedure gives movant no right to disclosure, except upon a showing of grounds for dismissal of the indictment. Moreover, the 1970 amendments to the Jencks Act, 18 U.S.C. § 3500, make clear that a defendant has no right to compel pre-trial disclosure of grand jury minutes. And, we cannot envisage the California District Court, even in camera, reviewing months of testimony.

But the same problem of immensity of claim that inclines us to take appellate jurisdiction also poses the most serious problem in structuring an intervention in such a way as to respect the independent role of the grand jury while at the same time giving absolute protection to movant. We cannot, for example, subscribe to the protective order requested and attempt to bar the grand jury from inquiring of a witness whether movant communicated the Pentagon Papers to an unauthorized person. In the first place, such a transaction could be a separate crime committed in Massachusetts, implicating additional prospective defendants, as well as being germane to the California trial. In the second place, we give credence to the government attorneys when they say that they do not know in advance what testimony will be forthcoming from a witness. And, finally, we recognize the futility both of barring questions which might occur to the jurors themselves and of policing the questions which could be put. . . .

We recognize, in short, that grand jury proceedings cannot be policed in any detail. It is a price we pay for grand jury independence that sometimes people are indicted on the basis of evidence tainted in part by hearsay, or of illegally obtained evidence. Nor is a grand jury narrowly confined in its objectives. And, even when a grand jury produces evidence but does not return an indictment, that is insufficient to embargo its fruits.

On the other hand, we are sensitive to the possibilities of abuse of the grand jury process which are inherent in the present situation. As Moore has observed, "The government has at its disposal one of the most effective discovery mechanisms yet devised—the grand jury. This body may call witnesses under compulsory process and examine them in secret under oath, unhampered by the rules of evidence or an adversary counsel's cross-examination, or in the case of a 'prospective defendant' by Fifth Amendment immunity [citations omitted]."

The problem is akin to that of using the wide-ranging discovery procedure available under the Federal Rules of Civil Procedure to gather evidence for a criminal prosecution. This practice has been the subject of critical comment but is not easily forbidden. The Court in *Kordel*, however, specifically noted that the issue there faced was not one in which the government brought a civil action "solely to obtain evidence for its criminal prosecution." Here we confront not only a broadly-phrased indictment in California, and a grand jury inquiry on the home ground of the movant, but an identity of prosecutors in the two proceedings. The difficulties they face in not confusing their roles, with the consequent potential for distortion of the role of the grand jury, cannot be dismissed as unreal.

We conclude that there is a modest though necessarily incomplete, protection which we can give movant, consistent with our respect for the integrity of the Boston grand jury. While, in the absence of a compelling showing of the probability of abuse, a total review, either here or there, of that jury's proceedings before movant's trial in California is not warranted, the record will be available here in the event that disciplinary action against the prosecutors should ever be called for. More important from the movant's point of view is the possibility of the California trial court's own scrutiny, pre-trial, of the testimony of such witnesses before the Boston grand jury as are expected to be called as witnesses at the California trial.

It is of course clear that the recent amendments to the Jencks Act, the restrictions surrounding the disclosure of grand jury proceedings in Rule 6(e), F. R. Crim. P., and even the proposed amendment to Rule 6(a)(3) give a defendant no right in the ordinary course to grand jury minutes. But Rule 6(e) itself authorizes a court "preliminarily to or in connection with a judicial proceeding" to direct disclosure. The Supreme Court in *Dennis v. United States* (1966), referring to this power, quoted the statement, "after the grand jury's functions are ended, disclosure is wholly proper where the ends of justice require it."

Were transcripts of the Boston grand jury testimony available to the California trial court, it would be possible for such pre-trial scrutiny to be made, in camera. Cf. Rule 16(e), F. R. Crim. P.; 18 U.S.C. § 3500. In the unlikely event that scrutiny of a number of witnesses' transcripts led the court to suspect that the Boston grand jury might in fact have been used dominantly to prepare for the California trial, it could conduct a more comprehensive review. The court might at some point conclude that the ends of justice would be served by such full disclosure. Short of this, the court could proscribe the calling of a witness whose testimony in Boston appeared to have been elicited chiefly for its contribution to the trial in California. This partial proscription would have been the result in *United States v. Dardi* (1964), had the trial court concluded that a witness had been called before a grand jury largely to gather evidence for an ongoing trial. To be sure, such an inquiry may not uncover fruits stemming from Boston disclosures, but, as the Second Circuit observed a motion for suppression of evidence may seek to encompass such fruits, "which is often quite as difficult of ascertainment as the benefits of the Government's allegedly improper discovery would be here."

In saying what we have said, we most particularly do not wish to be understood as asserting any competence to advise another federal court about the conduct of its business. All we seek is to assure the availability of testimony to the California court if it should see fit to make use of it. We do have and therefore exercise our power here to require the prosecutors who are presenting matters to the Boston grand jury to make available to the District Court of Central California the transcripts of testimony of each witness, if any, whom the government intends to call at trial in California, as seasonably as feasible. This will allow that court the opportunity, if it wishes to avail itself of it, to survey the proposed testimony to judge whether, at least as to the putative witnesses, the Boston grand jury was decoyed into serving primarily as a discovery device for the government's trial preparation.

Subject to this requirement, we deny the motion for stay.

NOTES AND QUESTIONS

1. The court describes "the rule" at issue in this case as straightforward: "It is improper to use the grand jury for the purpose of preparing an already pending indictment for trial." Easily stated, but what aspect or aspects of the grand jury's historic function make this use improper? How is such use inconsistent with the grand jury's broad inquisitorial and investigative powers?

2. Suppose a defendant is indicted but is tipped off and flees the jurisdiction before he can be arrested. The defendant, in other words, is a fugitive. Would it be permissible to use the grand jury to obtain testimony from the defendant's known acquaintances and family members in an attempt to find information regarding the defendant's whereabouts so he can be apprehended? Are there other reasons why these witnesses could be subpoenaed to the grand jury? *See* 18 U.S.C. § 1071 (criminalizing the harboring of a fugitive).

3. The court takes the defendant's allegations of potential grand jury abuse here quite seriously, despite its acknowledged lack of ability or authority to police the grand jury in any meaningful way. How important was it that the same three AUSAs were responsible for both the California trial and the presentation to the Boston grand jury? Note the high quality of the lawyering on both sides here. The defense attorneys make an aggressive and creative argument based on a hardly obvious attribute of the grand jury. And the prosecutors, while claiming they intend to use the Boston grand jury proceedings to investigate crimes other than those charged in California, candidly admit that the Boston grand jury investigation might unearth evidence that is relevant to the California trial.

Can the prosecutors properly use the Boston grand jury to investigate whether other additional crimes or additional persons should be added to the California charges?

4. The civil outcome of Daniel Ellsberg's famous leak of the Pentagon Papers is well known: The Supreme Court ruled in *New York Times v. United States*, 403 U.S. 713 (1971), that the *New York Times* and *Washington Post* could not be enjoined from publishing them. Ellsberg's subsequent indictment by the Nixon Justice Department, at issue here, is less well known. Ultimately, the federal court in California dismissed the Ellsberg indictment on multiple grounds of prosecutorial misconduct. *See* Melville B. Nimmer, *National Security Secrets v. Free Speech: The Issues Left Undecided in the Ellsberg Case*, 26 Stan. L. Rev. 311 (1973).

Somewhat analogous to the improper use of the grand jury to find evidence for an existing indictment is the use of the grand jury for the sole or primary — which adjective applies is unclear — purpose of inducing a witness to commit perjury in the grand jury. Using the grand jury for this purpose is sometimes called a "perjury trap." *See generally* Bennett L. Gershman, *The Perjury Trap*, 129 U. Pa. L. Rev. 624, 683 (1981) ("The prosecutor's use of the grand jury, not to uncover antecedent crime, but to cause perjury to be committed, implicates fundamental notions of fairness. The awesome powers of investigating grand juries, the limited rights of witnesses, the secrecy of the interrogation, and the harsh intolerance of perjured testimony, all provide a natural setting for oppression and deceit. In such circumstances, the protections offered by the due process clause seem especially appropriate, and perhaps necessary.").

G. Prosecutorial Abuse of the Grand Jury's Powers

People v. Tyler
385 N.E.2d 1224 (N.Y. Ct. App. 1978)

BREITEL, Chief Judge.

Based on testimony he gave before a Grand Jury, defendant, a Supreme Court Justice, was convicted after jury trial on three counts of perjury in the first degree (Penal Law, s 210.15). He was sentenced to probation. The Special Prosecutor appeals from the Appellate Division's unanimous reversal and dismissal of the indictment.

There should be an affirmance.

Involved are defendant's false answers to questions limited to the outward details of place and time of a single meeting between defendant and a reputed criminal character. The primary issue is whether a prosecution for perjury may be based on such false answers where the prosecutor, in his questioning, demonstrated no palpable interest in eliciting facts material to the authorized substantive investigation of antecedent crime or official misconduct. A secondary issue is whether the false answers about peripheral details of the single meeting may support a perjury prosecution without the prosecutor laying enough of a foundation to recall to the witness' mind what, without some prodding, may have in truth escaped the witness' recollection. In resolving the issues it is concluded that the conviction may not stand, and the indictment was properly dismissed as a matter of law.

First elected to the Civil Court in 1967, defendant became a Supreme Court Justice in January, 1970. Admitted to the Bar sometime after World War II, for the 18 years before he became a Judge defendant had been a lawyer practicing largely on his own and devoting about 50% of his time to criminal matters.

In February, 1975 an Extraordinary Grand Jury was charged, among other things, with investigating the relationship of defendant with certain known gambling figures. The inquiry, which included 20 sessions at which 22 witnesses were heard, was not concluded until October, 1976. Among the gamblers was one Raymond Marquez, also known as "Spanish" Raymond, the reputed head of one of the largest illegal gambling operations in New York. The Grand Jury was informed that Marquez, who was released from Federal prison in April, 1975, had been convicted of both Federal and State crimes, including interstate racketeering, gambling policy, and contempt.

Each of the counts charged in the instant indictment for perjury before the Grand Jury arises out of defendant's answers to questions concerning a single meeting with Marquez. According to the acting forewoman of the Grand Jury, the inquiry was aimed at uncovering any bribery, bribe receiving, or official misconduct.

Three police officers involved in an extensive personal surveillance of defendant testified to the Grand Jury that on May 16, 1975, after the Grand Jury had been convened, they saw Marquez in defendant's company. According to the officers, after some activity that suggested he may have been waiting for someone, defendant met Marquez and his wife near Lincoln Center in Manhattan. They drove about 10 blocks in defendant's automobile to Patsy's Restaurant on West 56th Street, and remained there for over an hour. Upon leaving, defendant and Marquez allegedly spoke for 10 minutes, while Mrs. Marquez sat in defendant's automobile. Defendant then drove the two back to where their own automobile was garaged. Substantially the same testimony was given by the officers at trial.

Defendant appeared before the Grand Jury on four occasions, and on two was questioned about Marquez. Other areas of inquiry were defendant's background and how he came to be a Judge, defendant's acquaintance with other reputed gamblers, and bail applications granted by defendant out of the ordinary courtroom setting.

Chapter VII Grand Jury

On March 2, 1976, defendant's second appearance, defendant testified that he knew Marquez as a man who had been convicted "some years ago for policy," and recalled representing him as a lawyer "in the fifties" in a case that "had something to do with gambling." When asked about contacts with Marquez since defendant had become a Supreme Court Justice, defendant denied communicating with him. He remembered, however, that as he was going to his courthouse chambers one day he saw Marquez being escorted by Marshals to Federal court.

Marquez was not mentioned when defendant appeared before the Grand Jury for the third time on May 18, 1976. In his final appearance two days later, however, Marquez was again the subject of inquiry. This time, when asked about communications with Marquez, defendant, who later explained at trial that a discussion he had had with his wife following his earlier appearance had refreshed his recollection, recalled the May 16 meeting:

Q. (Y)ou testified before that you saw him on occasion when he was being transported by federal marshals. You said that was the only time you'd seen him since you'd become a judge. Is that the occasion you're talking about?

A. No, that's not the occasion I'm talking about.

Q. What is the occasion that you're talking about?

A. I saw him on an occasion when he was with his wife on 58th Street in Manhattan.

Q. When was that?

A. I couldn't fix the dates. Probably somewhere around May. May of '75, somewhere around there.

Q. Can you describe that in any more detail, that meeting or encounter or whatever it was on 58th Street?

A. Yes. It was outside of Patsy's Restaurant. I think that's where it was.

Q. What were you doing? Were you walking down the street, driving, in the restaurant? What was

A. I was on my way into Patsy's.

Q. What happened?

A. I saw him and his wife.

Q. What did you do?

A. We greeted each other, asked him how he was. He asked me how I was. Asked me how things were getting along, and I asked him the same thing.

Q. This was out on the street?

A. That was on the street.
Then they walked into Patsy's and I walked into Patsy's.

Q. Were you alone or with anyone else?

A. I was alone. I was waiting for my daughter.

Q. What happened after you went into Patsy's?

A. I think I had a drink.

Q. Was there a bar there, or did you have it at the table?

A. Sitting right at the entrance of the door, I had a drink at the door.

Q. Did you have a drink alone?

A. No. He and his wife sat down.

Q. How long did that take?

A. About ten or fifteen minutes.

Q. What happened then?

A. I got up and left.

Q. And they remained in the place?

A. I believe so.

G. Prosecutorial Abuse of the Grand Jury's Powers

Q. Did you have a previous arrangement to meet with Mr. Marquez at that location?

A. No, sir.

Q. It was purely chance?

A. Yes, sir.

Q. When you arrived there did you withdrawn. What did you discuss during the course of that meeting with Mr. Marquez?

A. How he was, basically.

Q. Had he recently come out of prison?

A. I understood that he had, yes.

Q. Was that part of the discussion?

A. Yes.

Q. Anything else except his health?

A. That's all. Health and what he planned to do.

Q. Did he tell you what he planned to do?

A. He said he intended to take it easy.

Q. And that was the extent of the conversation?

A. In substance.

Q. Can you remember anything else that was discussed?

A. No, I can't, because it was just chit-chat.

Q. Did he discuss with you any matters that were in the courts at that time?

A. No, sir.

Q. Did you discuss any of the did he discuss the fact that the people in his organization had been arrested?

A. No, sir.

At this final appearance, defendant also corrected his earlier testimony to reflect that his former representation of Marquez related not to gambling, but to a violation of probation arising out of an assault.

A four-count indictment for perjury in the first degree followed. As noted, the charges are entirely based on defendant's answers to questions about the single meeting with Marquez. The first count charges defendant with falsely stating that he had not "talked to Marquez" since becoming a Supreme Court Justice. That count, presumably because of defendant's later recantation, resulted in an acquittal, but defendant was convicted of the three remaining counts. Count two alleges that "upon being asked where he saw Marquez for the first time on May 16, 1975 (defendant) testified that it was in front of Patsy's Restaurant." Under count three, it is asserted that defendant testified that his meeting with Marquez "had lasted about ten to fifteen minutes." The fourth count alleges that "upon being asked what happened after conversing with Marquez in Patsy's Restaurant, (defendant) testified that . . . he exited the Restaurant and left Marquez inside the premises." The surveillance team, as observed earlier, had testified that defendant, after driving the couple 10 blocks to the restaurant, talked to them there for over an hour, and upon leaving, but before driving them to their garage, spoke to Mr. Marquez while Mrs. Marquez waited in defendant's automobile.

Among the grounds for reversal adopted by the Appellate Division were that in counts two and three the materiality necessary to a conviction for perjury in the first degree was lacking and that in counts two and four the falsity of the statements alleged was insufficiently proved. Since the challenged interrogation amounted, on the whole, to an impermissible "perjury trap," neither ambiguity nor insufficiency of evidence, usually issues of fact resolvable by the jury, need be discussed. Nor need materiality be discussed.

The primary function of the Grand Jury is to uncover crimes and misconduct in public office for the purpose of prosecution. False testimony before the Grand Jury, then, especially by the holder of public office, is a grave matter affecting the public interest and the administration of justice. It is not properly a principal aim of the Grand Jury, however, to "create" new crimes in the course of its proceedings. Thus, where a prosecutor exhibits no palpable interest in eliciting facts material to a substantive investigation of crime or official misconduct and substantially tailors his questioning to extract a false answer, a valid perjury prosecution should not lie. Since no legitimate investigatory function is discernible in questioning designed primarily or solely to support a perjury prosecution against the witness, it cannot be said that the responsive testimony, albeit false, frustrates any authorized purpose of the Grand Jury.

It is not unprecedented for an improper purpose to invalidate that which is otherwise lawful. There is an analogy in the tort field. Where there is an "abuse of process," that is, a "misuse or perversion of regularly issued legal process for a purpose not justified by the nature of the process," a cause of action will lie. It has also been suggested that abuse of the power of the Grand Jury to investigate and indict for criminal acts may fatally infect the proceeding. Recognized is that it is not just the target of the abuse who is offended, but the administration of justice.

The absence of a legitimate purpose to the inquiry also makes suspect the administration of the oath to the defendant. It is elementary that there must be a validly administered oath to establish perjury. Where the questioning is not intended to further the Grand Jury investigation, but, instead, is aimed substantially at trapping the witness into giving false testimony, the validity of the oath previously administered is questionable.

Ordinarily, whether a trap primarily or solely to support a prosecution for perjury against the witness was set by the prosecutor raises a question of fact. The questioning in the instant case, however, was an unmitigated effort to trap the witness on minor outward details of a single meeting with a reputed criminal figure. There was no attempt to establish that the meeting was pertinent to a proper substantive goal of Grand Jury investigation. The meeting might well have been a chance encounter at which the former lawyer chatted with his ex-client. Or, it might have been planned to discuss matters inappropriate between one now a Judge and the other a convicted gambler, even if he were a former client. More to the point, the meeting would then have had more of a suspect character and probably would have related to the substantive criminal investigatory goals of the Grand Jury.

The prosecutor evinced minimal or no interest in establishing the materiality of the meeting. Almost as if he were conducting only a quiz to test memory or recall, he devoted most of his questions, as the excerpt quoted earlier indicates, to the logistical details of the May 16 encounter, facts contemporaneously documented by the surveillance team.

It is true that after an extended series of questions about where defendant and Marquez met, how long they were together, and how they parted, defendant was asked what they spoke about. And, some directed, if isolated, questions, such as whether they discussed matters then in the courts or that people in "the organization" had been arrested, were posed. Seemingly content with defendant's description of an innocuous encounter, however, at no time did the prosecutor, either by repetition, restatement, or elaboration, press defendant into giving a convincing narrative of what indeed went on at the restaurant. Yet, it is the content of the meeting which would determine whether the outward details were of any significance and, more important, whether substantive inquiry should be pursued. In sum, there is demonstrated no palpable effort to establish, either from the Grand Jury testimony or from the evidence at the trial, that the meeting was material to the Grand Jury investigation. In such a context, false answers to questions limited to peripheral details of time and place may not support a prosecution for perjury.

Also critical is that, upon hearing defendant's version of the outward details of the May 16 meeting, the prosecutor failed to confront defendant, or otherwise stimulate his memory, if only by limited cues, with some of the contrary facts acquired from the surveillance team. Such cues are not to inform the witness of the information already acquired, but to make certain that the witness is not failing sincerely to recall details of no memorable significance. To establish that defendant's assertion that he first met Marquez "outside of Patsy's Restaurant" was knowingly false, and not just a lapse in memory, some slight effort to stimulate defendant's recollection should have been made. The same may be said of defendant's assertion that he sat with the Marquezes for only 10 or 15 minutes, and that when he left the restaurant the Marquez couple remained.

It is not so much that the witness deserves an opportunity to refresh his recollection; it is that the foundation established by stimulation of recollection bears on resolution of the ultimate issue: whether defendant is deliberately falsifying. Indeed, if the meeting were no more than benign but questionable socializing between former lawyer and client, details would not likely be remembered or easily recalled. This does not mean that the kind of foundation required to impeach a witness with a prior inconsistent statement is indicated. Much less is indicated, simply enough to exclude the innocent lack of recollection or memory of a peripheral detail not likely to be memorable.

That is not to say that a witness suspected of falsifying must be wetnursed, or that in every case a "last clear chance" to tell the truth must be afforded. A rigid rule would deny the prosecutor the right to exercise judgment. In inquisitorial investigations particularly, just as on trial cross-examination, indirect questioning is characteristic and permissible. But the nature, and especially the intrinsic significance, or insignificance, of the event to be recalled will, almost invariably, be critical in determining the cues, if any, the prosecutor should provide for the witness, if it is the truth that is being sought.

It is true that when defendant met with Marquez, the Grand Jury investigation had already been underway, and inquiry concerning bail applications handled by defendant was being made by the State Commission on Judicial Conduct. That is hardly enough to compel the conclusion that the meeting, albeit between a Supreme Court Justice and a recently released Federal prisoner, was other than harmless, even if perhaps indiscreet. And no more was established by the prosecutor. But even if the encounter between former lawyer and client should have been memorable, either because it involved a transaction of significance, or because it was at that point so unusual for defendant in light of his then experience and associations, it is unrealistic to expect defendant's recollection of the surrounding details to equal that of the surveillance officers who were making contemporaneous notes of defendant's every step.

Put another way, it is not suggested that full disclosure of the information known to the prosecutor must have been made to defendant, especially if disclosure would reveal too much of how the investigation was conducted and how far it has proceeded. Yet, the examiner has an inescapable burden to provide a transcript which demonstrates that the witness is testifying falsely intentionally, rather than mistakenly, whether it is with respect to surrounding neutral details or to substantive matters relevant to an authorized investigation. The record in this case does not establish either intentional falsity or purposeful substantive inquiry. Thus, the only rational explanation for the tactics employed is the unacceptable one: that a perjury indictment, rather than the ascertainment of facts leading to substantive goals, was the object.

Nor is it suggested that defendant would have answered a more disciplined interrogation differently. That cannot be known. Nor should it be supposed that the mere anticipation of perjury in an inquiry would invalidate an indictment for the anticipated perjury. That would be unrealistic, and a boon to which perjurers are not entitled. How defendant might otherwise have responded, or whether a prosecutor could reasonably have hoped for more illuminating testimony, is not what ultimately determines the issues. Dispositive in this case is that the preoccupation with trapping defendant into committing perjury is unmitigated by substantive

708   Chapter VII Grand Jury

investigative goals. There was not even that little which might have presented a question of fact for the jury to decide. Dismissal of the indictment as a matter of law was thus proper.

• • •

Accordingly, the order of the Appellate Division should be affirmed, and the indictment stand dismissed.

NOTES AND QUESTIONS

1. "It is not properly a principal aim of the Grand Jury, however, to 'create' new crimes in the course of its proceedings." If there was ever any doubt about whether a pure perjury trap was a legitimate use of the grand jury, this delightfully understated sentence would seem to eliminate it. The court finds in *Tyler* that the grand jury examination of the defendant had "no legitimate investigatory function." What does that mean? Is there any whiff in the examination of legitimate investigation? How easy would it have been for the prosecutor here, if his intention was to get the defendant to commit perjury, to fake some "legitimate investigatory function"? How would the prosecutor have done so?

2. Apart from the prosecutor's apparent apathy about the content of the defendant's meeting with Marquez, the court also sees it as important "that, upon hearing defendant's version of the outward details of the May 16 meeting, the prosecutor failed to confront defendant, or otherwise stimulate his memory, if only by limited cues, with some of the contrary facts acquired from the surveillance team." How could this have been done without tipping the prosecutor's hand, for example, by suggesting that the defendant had been (and might still be) under surveillance? Is the Court suggesting that the prosecutor's willingness to be satisfied with a weak perjury case is probative of a perjury trap?

3. Consider again the facts of *Mandujano*. What are the arguments for and against a perjury trap defense based on the grand jury testimony in the opinion?

4. *Tyler* is one of the few reported cases upholding a perjury trap defense. Might it have been relevant — either as a matter of experience, institutional fidelity, or motivation — that the prosecutor in *Tyler* was a "Special Counsel," presenting a case to an Extraordinary Grand Jury?

Many federal courts have acknowledged the potential existence of a "perjury trap" defense, but the defense has rarely been litigated and has apparently never succeeded in federal court. *See United States v. Regan*, 103 F.3d 1072, 1079 (2d Cir. 1997) ("[W]e find that the facts of this case 'render the perjury trap defense inapplicable' and thus do not decide whether this defense is available in the Second Circuit."); *United States v. Chevoor*, 526 F.2d 178, 185 (1st Cir. 1975) ("We cannot say that calling Chevoor in these circumstances even in the anticipation that he would perjure himself is beyond the pale of permissible prosecutorial conduct."); *United States v. Nickels*, 502 F.2d 1173, 1176 (7th Cir. 1974) ("Since the questions were material to the grand jury's investigation, we doubt that we can inquire into the motivation for asking them."); *United States v. Lazaros*, 480 F.2d 174, 177 (6th Cir. 1973) ("Regardless of the actual beliefs of the United States Attorney, the grand jury was entitled to hear Lazaros's testimony."). *See* Billy Joe McLain, *Debunking the Perjury-Trap Myth*, 88 Tex. L. Rev. 883 (2010) (arguing inter alia that since a necessary element of the perjury trap defense — the immateriality of the allegedly perjured testimony — is also a defense to perjury on the merits, the perjury trap defense is superfluous).

As for the difficulties of establishing a viable perjury trap defense in a specific case, consider *United States v. Chen*, 933 F.3d 793 (9th Cir. 1991). In a grand jury investigation of potential corruption within the Public Utility Agency of Guam, two agency employees testified they had been paid bribes by one Chen. When Chen was subsequently subpoenaed before the grand jury, he denied paying the bribes and, subsequently, was indicted for perjury on the basis of that testimony.

Chen had one strong fact in his favor: The statute of limitations on any bribe charges had already run at the time he testified in the grand jury. So he raised the defense of perjury trap, arguing that he had been called to testify in the grand jury only for the purpose of eliciting false testimony for which he could be indicted. On appeal, the court acknowledged the theoretical availability of the defense but rejected it, finding that the scope of the grand jury's investigation was wider than just the relationship between Chen and the two agency employees he had testified about, and that the questioning had a legitimate investigative purpose.

H. THE INDICTMENT

An indictment is, above all, a document. As a written instrument, the indictment is critical to a defendant's Sixth Amendment right to be "informed of the nature and cause of the accusation." *Hamling v. United States*, 418 U.S. 87 (1974). Yet the legal requirements of a sufficient indictment are minimal. The Court further stated in *Hamling*: "It is generally sufficient that an indictment set forth the offense in the words of the statute itself . . . provided that it also includes such a statement of the facts and circumstances as will inform the accused of the specific offence, coming under the general description, with which he is charged." Rule 7(c)(1) of the Federal Rules of Criminal Procedure, similarly, merely states that "[t]he indictment or information must be a plain, concise, and definite written statement of the essential facts constituting the offense charged."

Note the similarity between Fed. R. Crim. P. 7(c)(1) and Fed. R. Civ. P. 8(a)(2), which requires only that a complaint set forth "a short and plain statement of the claim showing that the pleader is entitled to relief." In the civil context, however, unlike the criminal, the Supreme Court has by case law aggressively fortified such notice requirements. *See Ashcroft v. Iqbal*, 556 U.S. 662 (2009) (complaint that offers labels and conclusions or formulaic recitation of elements of cause of action will not do, nor does complaint suffice if it tenders naked assertions devoid of further factual enhancement). *Bell Atlantic Corp. v. Twombly*, 550 U.S. 544 (2007) (complaint must "plausibly" allege a claim). Labels, conclusions, and naked assertions are the standard fare of indictments. How is it that a civil defendant is entitled to more notice of the allegations against him than a criminal defendant?

In a similar vein, under Fed. R. Civ. P. 9(b) allegations of fraud must be stated "with particularity." Fed. R. Crim. P. 7 has no equivalent provision pertaining to an indictment's allegations of fraud, which, of course, are the heart of indictments charging defendants with violating one of the many federal criminal fraud statutes (mail, wire, bank, health care, securities, etc.). Rule 9(b) is a potent weapon for civil defendants in all manner of cases premised on fraud, from securities fraud to claims under the federal False Claims Act. *See, e.g., U.S. ex rel. Clausen v. Lab. Corp. of Am.*, 290 F.3d 1301 (11th Cir. 2002). Civil Rule 9(b)'s tepid criminal counterpart, if you can call it that, is Fed. R. Crim. P. 7(f), which provides that the court "may" direct the government to file a bill of particulars, fleshing out the details of an indictment's generalized allegations. Bills of particulars are totally within the trial court's discretion, however, and a decision denying a motion for a bill of particulars will be reviewed only for an abuse of that discretion. *United States v. Mejia*, 448 U.S. 436 (D.C. Cir. 2006).

The grand jury's indictment decision must be based on a finding of probable cause. But given how that finding of probable cause may be arrived at, as we have seen, should that finding have any collateral consequences? The next case considers this issue in the criminal forfeiture context.

Kaley v. United States
571 U.S. 320 (2014)

Justice KAGAN delivered the opinion of the Court.

A federal statute, 21 U.S.C. § 853(e), authorizes a court to freeze an indicted defendant's assets prior to trial if they would be subject to forfeiture upon conviction. In *United States v. Monsanto* (1989) we approved the constitutionality of such an order so long as it is "based on a finding of probable cause to believe that the property will ultimately be proved forfeitable." And we held that standard to apply even when a defendant seeks to use the disputed property to pay for a lawyer.

In this case, two indicted defendants wishing to hire an attorney challenged a pre-trial restraint on their property. The trial court convened a hearing to consider the seizure's legality under *Monsanto*. The question presented is whether criminal defendants are constitutionally entitled at such a hearing to contest a grand jury's prior determination of probable cause to believe they committed the crimes charged. We hold that they have no right to relitigate that finding.

I

A

Criminal forfeitures are imposed upon conviction to confiscate assets used in or gained from certain serious crimes. *See* 21 U.S.C. § 853(a). Forfeitures help to ensure that crime does not pay: They at once punish wrongdoing, deter future illegality, and "lessen the economic power" of criminal enterprises. The Government also uses forfeited property to recompense victims of crime, improve conditions in crime-damaged communities, and support law enforcement activities like police training. Accordingly, "there is a strong governmental interest in obtaining full recovery of all forfeitable assets."

In line with that interest, § 853(e)(1) empowers courts to enter pre-trial restraining orders or injunctions to "preserve the availability of [forfeitable] property" while criminal proceedings are pending. Such an order, issued "[u]pon application of the United States," prevents a defendant from spending or transferring specified property, including to pay an attorney for legal services. In *Monsanto*, our principal case involving this procedure, we held a pre-trial asset restraint constitutionally permissible whenever there is probable cause to believe that the property is forfeitable. That determination has two parts, reflecting the requirements for forfeiture under federal law: There must be probable cause to think (1) that the defendant has committed an offense permitting forfeiture, and (2) that the property at issue has the requisite connection to that crime. See § 853(a). The *Monsanto* Court, however, declined to consider "whether the Due Process Clause requires a hearing" to establish either or both of those aspects of forfeitability.

Since *Monsanto*, the lower courts have generally provided a hearing to any indicted defendant seeking to lift an asset restraint to pay for a lawyer. In that hearing, they have uniformly allowed the defendant to litigate the second issue stated above: whether probable cause exists to believe that the assets in dispute are traceable or otherwise sufficiently related to the crime charged in the indictment. But the courts have divided over extending the hearing to the first issue. Some have considered, while others have barred, a defendant's attempt to challenge the probable cause underlying a criminal charge. This case raises the question whether an indicted defendant has a constitutional right to contest the grand jury's prior determination of that matter.

B

The grand jury's indictment in this case charges a scheme to steal prescription medical devices and resell them for profit. The indictment accused petitioner Kerri Kaley, a sales representative for a subsidiary of Johnson & Johnson, and petitioner Brian Kaley, her husband, with transporting stolen medical devices across state lines and laundering the proceeds of that activity. The Kaleys have contested those allegations throughout this litigation, arguing that the medical devices at issue were unwanted, excess hospital inventory, which they could lawfully take and market to others.

Immediately after obtaining the indictment, the Government sought a restraining order under § 853(e)(1) to prevent the Kaleys from transferring any assets traceable to or involved in the alleged offenses. Included among those assets is a $500,000 certificate of deposit that the Kaleys intended to use for legal fees. The District Court entered the requested order. Later, in response to the Kaleys' motion to vacate the asset restraint, the court denied a request for an evidentiary hearing and confirmed the order, except as to $63,000 that it found (based on the parties' written submissions) was not connected to the alleged offenses.

On interlocutory appeal, the Eleventh Circuit reversed and remanded for further consideration of whether some kind of evidentiary hearing was warranted. The District Court then concluded that it should hold a hearing, but only as to "whether the restrained assets are traceable to or involved in the alleged criminal conduct." The Kaleys informed the court that they no longer disputed that issue; they wished to show only that the "case against them is 'baseless.'" Accordingly, the District Court affirmed the restraining order, and the Kaleys took another appeal. The Eleventh Circuit this time affirmed, holding that the Kaleys were not entitled at a hearing on the asset freeze "to challenge the factual foundation supporting the grand jury's probable cause determination[ ]" — that is, "the very validity of the underlying indictment."

We granted certiorari in light of the Circuit split on the question presented, and we now affirm the Eleventh Circuit.

II

This Court has twice considered claims, similar to the Kaleys', that the Fifth Amendment's right to due process and the Sixth Amendment's right to counsel constrain the way the federal forfeiture statute applies to assets needed to retain an attorney. We begin with those rulings not as mere background, but as something much more. On the single day the Court decided both those cases, it cast the die on this one too.

In *Caplin & Drysdale*, we considered whether the Fifth and Sixth Amendments exempt from forfeiture money that a convicted defendant has agreed to pay his attorney. We conceded a factual premise of the constitutional claim made in the case: Sometimes "a defendant will be unable to retain the attorney of his choice," if he cannot use forfeitable assets. Still, we held, the defendant's claim was "untenable." "A defendant has no Sixth Amendment right to spend another person's money" for legal fees — even if that is the only way to hire a preferred lawyer. Consider, we submitted, the example of a "robbery suspect" who wishes to "use funds he has stolen from a bank to retain an attorney to defend him if he is apprehended." That money is "not rightfully his." Accordingly, we concluded, the Government does not violate the Constitution if, pursuant to the forfeiture statute, "it seizes the robbery proceeds and refuses to permit the defendant to use them" to pay for his lawyer.

And then, we confirmed in *Monsanto* what our "robbery suspect" hypothetical indicated: Even prior to conviction (or trial) — when the presumption of innocence still applies — the Government could constitutionally use § 853(e) to freeze assets of an indicted defendant "based on a finding of probable cause to believe that the property will ultimately be proved forfeitable." In *Monsanto*, too, the defendant wanted to use the property at issue to pay a lawyer, and maintained that the Fifth and Sixth Amendments entitled him to do so. We disagreed. We first noted that the Government may sometimes "restrain persons where there is a finding of probable cause to believe that the accused has committed a serious offense." Given that power, we could find "no constitutional infirmity in § 853(e)'s authorization of a similar restraint on [the defendant's] property" in order to protect "the community's interest" in recovering "ill-gotten gains." Nor did the defendant's interest in retaining a lawyer with the disputed assets change the equation. Relying on *Caplin & Drysdale*, we reasoned: "[I]f the Government may, post-trial, forbid the use of forfeited assets to pay an attorney, then surely no constitutional violation occurs when, after probable cause is adequately established, the Government obtains an order barring a defendant from frustrating that end by dissipating his assets prior to trial." So again: With probable cause, a freeze is valid.

The Kaleys little dispute that proposition; their argument is instead about who should have the last word as to probable cause. A grand jury has already found probable cause to think that the Kaleys committed the offenses charged; that is why an indictment issued. No one doubts that those crimes are serious enough to trigger forfeiture. Similarly, no one contests that the assets in question derive from, or were used in committing, the offenses. The only question is whether the Kaleys are constitutionally entitled to a judicial re-determination of the conclusion the grand jury already reached: that probable cause supports this criminal prosecution (or alternatively put, that the prosecution is not "baseless," as the Kaleys believe). And that question, we think, has a ready answer, because a fundamental and historic commitment of our criminal justice system is to entrust those probable cause findings to grand juries.

This Court has often recognized the grand jury's singular role in finding the probable cause necessary to initiate a prosecution for a serious crime. "[A]n indictment 'fair upon its face,' and returned by a 'properly constituted grand jury,'" we have explained, "conclusively determines the existence of probable cause" to believe the defendant perpetrated the offense alleged. And "conclusively" has meant, case in and case out, just that. We have found no "authority for looking into and revising the judgment of the grand jury upon the evidence, for the purpose of determining whether or not the finding was founded upon sufficient proof." To the contrary, "the whole history of the grand jury institution" demonstrates that "a challenge to the reliability or competence of the evidence" supporting a grand jury's finding of probable cause "will not be heard." The grand jury gets to say — without any review, oversight, or second-guessing — whether probable cause exists to think that a person committed a crime.

And that inviolable grand jury finding, we have decided, may do more than commence a criminal proceeding (with all the economic, reputational, and personal harm that entails); the determination may also serve the purpose of immediately depriving the accused of her freedom. If the person charged is not yet in custody, an indictment triggers "issuance of an arrest warrant without further inquiry" into the case's strength. Alternatively, if the person was arrested without a warrant, an indictment eliminates her Fourth Amendment right to a prompt judicial assessment of probable cause to support any detention. In either situation, this Court — relying on the grand jury's "historical role of protecting individuals from unjust persecution" — has "let [that body's] judgment substitute for that of a neutral and detached magistrate." The grand jury, all on its own, may effect a pre-trial restraint on a person's liberty by finding probable cause to support a criminal charge.

The same result follows when, as here, an infringement on the defendant's property depends on a showing of probable cause that she committed a crime. If judicial review of the grand jury's probable cause determination is not warranted (as we have so often held) to put a defendant on trial or place her in custody, then neither is it needed to freeze her property. The grand jury that is good enough — reliable enough, protective enough — to inflict those other grave consequences through its probable cause findings must needs be adequate to impose this one too. Indeed, *Monsanto* already noted the absence of any reason to hold property seizures to different rules: As described earlier, the Court partly based its adoption of the probable cause standard on the incongruity of subjecting an asset freeze to any stricter requirements than apply to an arrest or ensuing detention. By similar token, the probable cause standard, once selected, should work no differently for the single purpose of freezing assets than for all others. So the longstanding, unvarying rule of criminal procedure we have just described applies here as well: The grand jury's determination is conclusive.

And indeed, the alternative rule the Kaleys seek would have strange and destructive consequences. The Kaleys here demand a do-over, except with a different referee. They wish a judge to decide anew the exact question the grand jury has already answered—whether there is probable cause to think the Kaleys committed the crimes charged. But suppose the judge performed that task and came to the opposite conclusion. Two inconsistent findings would then govern different aspects of one criminal proceeding: Probable cause would exist to bring the Kaleys to trial (and, if otherwise appropriate, hold them in prison), but not to restrain their property. And assuming the prosecutor continued to press the charges, the same judge who found probable cause lacking would preside over a trial premised on its presence. That legal dissonance, if sustainable at all, could not but undermine the criminal justice system's integrity—and especially the grand jury's integral, constitutionally prescribed role. For in this new world, every prosecution involving a pre-trial asset freeze would potentially pit the judge against the grand jury as to the case's foundational issue.

The Kaleys counter that apparently inconsistent findings are not really so, because the prosecutor could have presented scantier evidence to the judge than he previously offered the grand jury. Suppose, for example, that at the judicial hearing the prosecutor put on only "one witness instead of all five"; then, the Kaleys maintain, the judge's decision of no probable cause would mean only that "the Government did not satisfy its burden[ ] on that one day in time." But we do not think that hypothetical solves the problem. As an initial matter, it does not foreclose a different fact pattern: A judge could hear the exact same evidence as the grand jury, yet respond to it differently, thus rendering what even the Kaleys must concede is a contradictory finding. And when the Kaleys' hypothetical is true, just what does it show? Consider that the prosecutor in their example has left home some of the witnesses he took to the grand jury—presumably because, as we later discuss, he does not yet wish to reveal their identities or likely testimony. The judge's ruling of no probable cause therefore would not mean that the grand jury was wrong: As the Kaleys concede, the grand jury could have heard more than enough evidence to find probable cause that they committed the crimes charged. The Kaleys would win at the later hearing despite, not because of, the case's true merits. And we would then see still less reason for a judge to topple the grand jury's (better supported) finding of probable cause.

Our reasoning so far is straightforward. We held in *Monsanto* that the probable cause standard governs the pre-trial seizure of forfeitable assets, even when they are needed to hire a lawyer. And we have repeatedly affirmed a corollary of that standard: A defendant has no right to judicial review of a grand jury's determination of probable cause to think a defendant committed a crime. In combination, those settled propositions signal defeat for the Kaleys because, in contesting the seizure of their property, they seek only to relitigate such a grand jury finding.

* * *

Chief Justice ROBERTS, with whom Justice BREYER and Justice SOTOMAYOR join, dissenting.

An individual facing serious criminal charges brought by the United States has little but the Constitution and his attorney standing between him and prison. He might readily give all he owns to defend himself.

We have held, however, that the Government may effectively remove a defendant's primary weapon of defense—the attorney he selects and trusts—by freezing assets he needs to pay his lawyer. That ruling is not at issue. But today the Court goes further, holding that a defendant may be hobbled in this way without an opportunity to challenge the Government's decision to freeze those needed assets. I cannot subscribe to that holding and respectfully dissent.

I

The facts of this case are important. They highlight the significance to a defendant of being able to hire his counsel of choice, and the potential for unfairness inherent in giving the prosecutor the discretion to take that right away. Kerri Kaley worked as a sales representative for a Johnson & Johnson subsidiary, selling prescription medical devices. Kaley and other sales representatives occasionally obtained outmoded or surplus devices from staff members at the medical facilities they served, when, for example, those devices were no longer needed because they had been superseded by newer models. Kaley sold the unwanted devices to a Florida company, dividing the proceeds among the sales representatives.

Kaley learned in January 2005 that a federal grand jury was investigating those activities as a conspiracy to sell stolen prescription medical devices. Kaley and her husband (who allegedly helped ship the products to Florida) retained counsel, who immediately set to work preparing their defense against any impending charges. Counsel regularly discussed the investigation with the Kaleys, helped review documents demanded by the grand jury, and met with prosecutors in an attempt to ward off an indictment. Nonetheless preparing for the worst, the Kaleys applied for a $500,000 equity line of credit on their home to pay estimated legal fees associated with a trial. They used that money to purchase a $500,000 certificate of deposit, which they set aside until it would be needed to pay their attorneys for the trial.

In February 2007, the grand jury returned a seven-count indictment charging the Kaleys and another sales representative, Jennifer Gruenstrass, with violations of federal law. The indictment alleged that a "money judgment" of over $2 million and the $500,000 certificate of deposit were subject to forfeiture under 18 U.S.C. § 981(a)(1)(C) because those assets constituted "proceeds" of the alleged crimes. Armed with this indictment, the prosecution obtained an ex parte order pursuant to 21 U.S.C. § 853(e), thereby freezing all of the Kaleys' assets listed in the indictment, including the certificate of deposit set aside for legal fees. The Government did not seek to freeze any of Gruenstrass's assets.

The Kaleys moved to vacate the order, requesting a hearing at which they could argue that there was no probable cause to believe their assets were forfeitable, because their alleged conduct was not criminal. They argued they were entitled to such a hearing because the restraining order targeted funds they needed and had set aside to retain for trial the same counsel who had been preparing their defense for two years. And they contended that the prosecution was baseless because the Government could not identify anyone who claimed ownership of the medical devices alleged to have been "stolen." During a telephone conference with a Magistrate Judge on the motion, the prosecution conceded that it had been able to trace only $140,000 in allegedly criminal proceeds to the Kaleys, which led the Magistrate Judge to question the lawfulness of restraining the listed assets.

Just two business days after that conference, the Government obtained a superseding indictment that added a count of conspiracy to commit money laundering under 18 U.S.C. § 1956(h). Adding that charge enabled the Government to proceed under a much broader forfeiture provision than the one in the original indictment. While the civil forfeiture provision in § 981(a)(1)(C) authorized forfeiture of property that "constitutes or is derived from proceeds traceable to" a qualifying criminal violation, the criminal forfeiture provision now invoked by the Government—§ 982(a)(1)—authorizes forfeiture of property "involved in" a qualifying offense, or "any property traceable to such property." The superseding indictment alleged that a sum of more than $2 million, the certificate of deposit reserved to pay legal expenses, and now the Kaleys' home were subject to forfeiture. And again, the Government sought an order freezing substantially all those assets.

The Kaleys objected, repeating the arguments they had previously raised, and also contending that the prosecutors were being vindictive in adding the money laundering charge and seeking broader forfeiture. The District Court nonetheless entered the broader order requested by the Government, and the restraint on the Kaleys' assets remains in place.

While the Kaleys' appeal from that denial was pending, the Government proceeded to trial separately against their codefendant Gruenstrass. As the Government had not sought to freeze Gruenstrass's assets, she was represented by her chosen counsel. Her counsel argued that the Government was pitching a fraud without a victim, because no Government witness took the stand to claim ownership of the allegedly stolen devices. The jury acquitted Gruenstrass on all charges in less than three hours—a good omen for the Kaleys and their counsel as they prepared for their own trial.

II

The issues at stake here implicate fundamental constitutional principles. The Sixth Amendment provides that "[i]n all criminal prosecutions, the accused shall enjoy the right . . . to have the Assistance of Counsel for his defence." In many ways, this is the most precious right a defendant has, because it is his attorney who will fight for the other rights the defendant enjoys. And more than 80 years ago, we found it "hardly necessary to say that, the right to counsel being conceded, a defendant should be afforded a fair opportunity to secure counsel of his own choice."

Indeed, we recently called the "right to select counsel of one's choice . . . the root meaning of the constitutional guarantee" of the Sixth Amendment. *United States v. Gonzalez-Lopez* (2006). The Amendment requires "that a particular guarantee of fairness be provided—to wit, that the accused be defended by the counsel he believes to be best." An individual's right to counsel of choice is violated "whenever the defendant's choice is wrongfully denied," and such error "pervades the entire trial." A violation of this right is therefore a "structural error," that is, one of the very few kinds of errors that "undermine the fairness of a criminal proceeding as a whole." *United States v. Davila* (2013).

It is of course true that the right to counsel of choice is (like most rights) not absolute. A defendant has no right to choose counsel he cannot afford, counsel who is not a member of the bar, or counsel with an impermissible conflict of interest. And a district court need not always shuffle its calendar to accommodate a defendant's preferred counsel if it has legitimate reasons not to do so. But none of those limitations is imposed at the unreviewable discretion of a prosecutor—the party who wants the defendant to lose at trial.

This Court has held that the prosecution may freeze assets a defendant needs to retain his counsel of choice upon "a finding of probable cause to believe that the assets are forfeitable." The Kaleys do not challenge that holding here. But the Court in *Monsanto* acknowledged and reserved the crucial question whether a defendant had the right to be heard before the Government could take such action.

There was good reason for that caution. The possibility that a prosecutor could elect to hamstring his target by preventing him from paying his counsel of choice raises substantial concerns about the fairness of the entire proceeding. "A fair trial in a fair tribunal is a basic requirement of due process." Issues concerning the denial of counsel of choice implicate the overall fairness of the trial because they "bear[ ] directly on the 'framework within which the trial proceeds.'"

III

Notwithstanding the substantial constitutional issues at stake, the majority believes that syllogistic-type reasoning effectively resolves this case. The majority's reasoning goes like this: First, to freeze assets prior to trial, the Government must show probable cause to believe that a defendant has committed an offense giving rise to forfeiture. Second, grand jury determinations of probable cause are nonreviewable. Therefore, the Kaleys cannot "relitigate [the] grand jury finding" of probable cause to avoid a pretrial restraint of assets they need to retain their counsel of choice. I do not view the matter as nearly so "straightforward," and neither did the multiple Courts of Appeals since *Monsanto* that have granted defendants the type of hearing the Kaleys request.

To begin with, the majority's conclusion is wrong on its own terms. To freeze assets prior to trial, the Government must show probable cause to believe both that (1) a defendant has committed an offense giving rise to forfeiture and (2) the targeted assets have the requisite connection to the alleged criminal conduct. 21 U.S.C. § 853(e)(1)(A). The Solicitor General concedes—and all Courts of Appeals to have considered the issue have held—that "defendants are entitled to show that the assets that are restrained are not actually the proceeds of the charged criminal offense," that is, that the second prong of the required showing is not satisfied. But by listing property in the indictment and alleging that it is subject to forfeiture—as required to restrain assets before trial under § 853(e)(1)(A)—the grand jury found probable cause to believe those assets were linked to the charged offenses, just as it found probable cause to believe the Kaleys committed the underlying crimes. Neither the Government nor the majority gives any reason why the District Court may reconsider the grand jury's probable cause finding as to traceability—and in fact constitutionally must, if asked—but may not do so as to the underlying charged offenses.

In any event, the hearing the Kaleys seek would not be mere relitigation of the grand jury proceedings. At that hearing, the District Court would consider the merits of the prosecution to determine whether there is probable cause to believe the Kaleys' assets are forfeitable, not to determine whether the Kaleys may be tried at all. If the judge agrees with the Kaleys, he will merely hold that the Government has not met its burden at that hearing to justify freezing the assets the Kaleys need to pay their attorneys. The Government may proceed with the prosecution, but the Kaleys will have their chosen counsel at their side.

Even though the probable cause standard applies at both the indictment stage and the pretrial asset restraint hearing, the judge's determination will be based on different evidence than that previously presented to the grand jury. For its part, the Government may choose to put on more or less evidence at the hearing than it did before the grand jury. And of course the Kaleys would have the opportunity to tell their side of the story—something the grand jury never hears. Here, much of what the Kaleys want to present comes from Gruenstrass's trial—evidence that the grand jury obviously could not have considered. So even if the judge determined that probable cause to justify the pretrial asset restraint had not been adequately established, that determination would not in any way amount to "looking into and revising the judgment of the grand jury upon the evidence, for the purpose of determining whether or not the finding was founded upon sufficient proof." The judge's decision based on the evidence presented at the hearing would have no necessary legal or logical consequence for the underlying prosecution because it would be based on different evidence and used for a different purpose.

The majority warns that allowing a judge to consider the underlying merits of the prosecution for purposes of determining whether a defendant's assets may be restrained pretrial could create "legal dissonance" with the grand jury's indictment, which "could not but undermine the criminal justice system's integrity." But as explained, such a judicial finding based

H. The Indictment   717

on different evidence with both sides present would not contradict the grand jury's probable cause finding based on what was before it. That finding would still suffice to accomplish its purpose—to call for a trial on the merits of the charges. Rather than creating "dissonance," the traditional roles of the principal actors in our justice system would remain respected: The grand jury decides whether a defendant should be required to stand trial, the judge decides pretrial matters and how the trial should proceed, and the jury decides whether the defendant is guilty of the crime.

Indeed, in the bail context—the pretrial determination that is perhaps the closest analogue to the pretrial restraint of assets at issue here—we allow judicial inquiries into the underlying merits of the indicted charges, without concern about intruding into the province of the grand jury. An indictment charging sufficiently serious crimes gives rise to a rebuttable presumption that a defendant is not eligible for pretrial release. See 18 U.S.C. §§ 3142(e)(3) and (f). Such a defendant is nonetheless entitled to an evidentiary hearing at which he may contest (among other things) "the weight of the evidence against" him, § 3142(g)(2). Yet no one would say that the district court encroached on the grand jury's role if the court determined that it would not authorize pretrial detention because of the weakness of the prosecution's case. That makes sense, because the district court has considered the underlying merits of the charges based on different information and for a different purpose than the grand jury did. Such a defendant would be granted pretrial release, but would still have to show up for trial.

In any event, few things could do more to "undermine the criminal justice system's integrity" than to allow the Government to initiate a prosecution and then, at its option, disarm its presumptively innocent opponent by depriving him of his counsel of choice—without even an opportunity to be heard. That is the result of the Court's decision in this case, and it is fundamentally at odds with our constitutional tradition and basic notions of fair play.

NOTES AND QUESTIONS

1. The Court and the government concede that a defendant has a right to a hearing on the issue of whether there is probable cause to believe restrained property is forfeitable, the second of the two questions deferred in *Monsanto*, even though the grand jury indictment makes allegations both in this regard as well as alleging the commission of a crime. Is the Court's description of the restraint allegations as "a technical matter far removed from the grand jury's core competence" persuasive? Does Chief Justice Roberts's dissenting opinion have the better view of this issue? What is the "core competence" of this body of laypersons?

2. The Court notes that since the grand jury's finding of probable cause is sufficient in itself to justify a person's arrest and to create a presumption of pretrial detention it should therefore also be enough to justify a pretrial asset restraint. Do you agree? How is a pretrial asset restraint distinguishable?

3. Chief Justice Roberts says in dissent that "[t]he facts of this case are important." Of course they are. They always are. But he has a point: It is hard to imagine a better set of facts—a specified bucket of prospective legal fees, a defense counsel known to the prosecution, a not guilty verdict at the trial of a codefendant, a reactive and potentially vindictive action by the prosecutor with regard to forfeiture—on which to litigate this issue. What is the significance of each of these facts?

4. The Court states that if the issue of probable cause could be litigated in the asset restraint context, every such case "would potentially pit the judge against the grand jury as to the case's foundational issue." Do you agree?

Do jury trials likewise "pit" the petit jury against the grand jury on a foundational issue, and in an even starker competition?

Are the defendants really requesting a "do over," as the Court puts it?

Would a contrary judicial finding as to probable cause truly "undermine the criminal justice system's integrity"?

Did the not guilty verdict of the Kaleys' codefendant at trial similarly undermine the criminal justice system's integrity inasmuch as she, too, was indicted by a grand jury?

5. Whether "probable cause" was the original Founding-era standard for the commencement of criminal charges — as has long been assumed, *see Kaley*, 571 U.S. at 328 — has been called into question by Professor William Ortman. William Ortman, *Probable Cause Revisited*, 68 Stan. L. Rev. 511 (2015). Professor Ortman presents a strong case that many Founding-era grand juries were instructed to return indictments only upon a higher evidentiary showing (sometimes a "certainty") due to the summary nature of criminal trials at the time. *Id.* at 514-15. Probable cause appeared to emerge as the governing standard over the course of the nineteenth century as a corollary of the formalization of the criminal trial during the same period. *Id.* at 515. The probable cause standard endured, paradoxically, even as plea bargaining and not trials became the predominant means of resolving criminal cases over the second half of the nineteenth century. *Id.* at 515-16.

6. Suppose the Supreme Court were to embrace Professor Ortmann's "originalist" understanding of the grand jury probable cause requirement. What would be the practical consequences of such a shift?

I. THE GRAND JURY AND INVESTIGATION OF POLICE MISCONDUCT

Among the recent criticisms of the grand jury has been that it has selectively exercised its "shield" function to protect police officers charged with racial violence. Roger A. Fairfax Jr., *Interrogating the Nonincorporation of the Grand Jury Clause*, 43 Cardozo L. Rev. 855, 909-12 (2022). *See also* Roger A. Fairfax Jr., *The Grand Jury and Police Violence Against Black Men*, in Policing the Black Man 209-33 (Angela J. Davis ed., 2017). Grand juries have failed to return indictments against police officers in several high-profile cases, including the killings of Michael Brown (shot and killed by former officer Darren Wilson), Eric Garner (killed by a chokehold administered by former officer Daniel Pantaleo), Tamir Rice (shot and killed by former officer Tim Loehman), and Breonna Taylor (shot and killed by multiple Louisville police officers).

It is impossible to know exactly why grand juries did not indict these police officers. Grand jury secrecy rules make such proceedings largely invisible; note that in many cases misconduct that occurred in the grand jury is uncovered only due to the prosecutor's obligation, at trial, to disclose the prior testimony of witnesses. When a grand jury does not indict, there is no trial and no disclosure obligation ever arises. We do know, of course, that grand jury investigations of police misconduct, like all grand jury investigations, are normally led by prosecutors, who work with and rely on the police officers under investigation. At a minimum, such prosecutors will find it awkward to seek a grand jury indictment of a police officer.

Several other institutional factors make grand jury indictments of police officers difficult. First, member of the general public — that is, grand jurors — tend to respect and sympathize with police officers, public servants who have dangerous jobs. Second, police officers are experienced in the criminal process and are unlikely to make the sort of unforced errors — for example, talking to investigators without lawyering up — that can make indictment and prosecution easy. *See* Kate Levine, *How We Prosecute the Police*, 104 Geo. L.J. 745, 762-63 (2016). Third, and perhaps most important, in a typical police misconduct case — use of excessive force, for example — it is extremely unlikely that any other police officers at the scene will corroborate the victim's version of events. *See, e.g.*, Gabriel J. Chin & Scott C. Wells, *The "Blue Wall of Silence" as Evidence of Bias and Motive to Lie: A New Approach to Police Perjury*, 59 U. Pitt. L. Rev. 233, 237 (1998) ("Police officers . . . lie under oath because of the 'blue wall of silence,' an unwritten code in many departments which prohibits . . . testifying truthfully if the facts would implicate the conduct of a fellow officer.").

It also seems that prosecutors tend to be atypically "thorough" in grand jury investigations of police officers. Levine, *How We Prosecute the Police*, *supra* at 762-66. This was actually confirmed to be the case in the investigation of the killing of Michael Brown by Ferguson, Missouri, police officer Darren Wilson. In that case, St. Louis County prosecuting attorney Robert McCulloch took the unusual step of releasing the grand jury transcripts after the decision not to indict had been made. What the transcripts showed was a grand jury process that was anything but business as usual. Far from the wholly inquisitory and often imbalanced inquiry you have become familiar with throughout this chapter, the investigation of Darren Wilson was exhaustive, stretching over months and involving 62 witnesses. *Id.* at 766. Two things in particular stuck out from the transcripts. One, Darren Wilson testified at some length but was not cross-examined by the prosecutor, although the prosecutor cross-examined many other witnesses. Two, the grand jury was told at the outset that it would be presented with "every statement" and "every bit of evidence" and that the proceeding would be "like a trial." *Id.*

What inference might the grand jurors have drawn from the prosecutor's failure to cross-examine Darren Wilson? How might the instruction that the proceeding would be "like a trial" have affected the grand jury's deliberations?

The point is not necessarily that the Ferguson grand jury was wrong. Indeed, the Department of Justice reached a similar conclusion. *See* Dept. of Justice, Report Regarding the Criminal Investigation into the Shooting Death of Michael Brown by Ferguson, Missouri Police Officer Darren Wilson 86. *But see* Chapter X *infra*. The point is that putative police officer defendants appear to be getting preferential treatment in the grand jury process.

Michael Brown

An unusual civil lawsuit in the aftermath of Ferguson sheds light on this point. In *Doe v. McCulloch*, 2015 WL 2092492 (E.D. Mo. 2015), a woman who had served on the St. Louis County grand jury investigating Officer Wilson sued the county prosecuting attorney, seeking a declaration that Missouri laws that criminalized a juror's disclosure of information about her experience on the state grand jury violated her free speech rights. *Id.* at *1. Specifically, the woman apparently wanted the freedom to speak publicly about the differential manner in the presentation of evidence between other investigations and the investigation of Officer Wilson. She noted that the presentation to the grand jury was different in significant ways from previous cases; the investigation had a stronger emphasis on the victim than in other cases; and the "presentation of the law to which the grand jurors were to apply the facts was made in a muddled and untimely manner." *Id.* at *2. The lawsuit was dismissed on abstention grounds.

A good example of differential process by legislative command — not just prosecutorial choice — can be seen in Georgia law prior to 2016. *See* Roger A. Fairfax Jr., *The Grand*

Jury's Role in the Prosecution of Unjustified Police Killings — Challenges and Solutions, 52 Harv. C.R.-C.L. L. Rev. 397, 413-14 (2017). Georgia had an especially dismal record on fatal police shootings: Half of the over 180 people shot and killed by police between 2010 and 2015 were either unarmed or were shot by police in the back; in only 9 of those cases did the prosecutor ask for an indictment; in only one case was an indictment returned. *Id.* The explanation may be at least partially found in Georgia law that gave police officers the right to be present during the entirety of the grand jury proceeding and listen to and observe — in person — all of the witness testimony against them, and at the conclusion of the grand jury presentation, to make a statement to the grand jurors without any rebuttal by the prosecutor. *Id.*

CHAPTER VIII

RIGHT TO COUNSEL AND THE DEFENSE FUNCTION

In an adversary system of criminal justice, there is no right more essential than the right to the assistance of counsel.

Lakeside v. Oregon, 435 U.S. 333, 341 (1978)

Of all of the rights that an accused person has, the right to be represented by counsel is by far the most pervasive, for it affects his ability to assert any other rights he may have.

Walter V. Schaefer, *Federalism and State Criminal Procedure*, 70 Harv. L Rev. 1, 8 (1956)

This chapter considers several aspects of the right to counsel. Section A explores the scope of the right to counsel, charting the historical development of that right after *Powell v. Alabama*, 287 U.S. 45 (1932), *see* Chapter II *supra*, and into the twenty-first century. Section B considers the consequences of being represented by counsel in terms of ongoing government investigation. Sections C and D consider two aspects of the right to effective assistance of counsel: Section C focuses on the performance standards by which claims of ineffective assistance are evaluated; Section D looks at some of the challenges of meeting those standards due to a lack of public funding for indigent criminal defense. Section E explores the requirements and limits of the "zealous advocacy" obligations of defense counsel.

A. SCOPE OF THE RIGHT TO COUNSEL

In *Johnson v. Zerbst*, 304 U.S. 458 (1938), the Supreme Court held that an indigent defendant in a federal criminal case has a right to appointed counsel where there is a risk of imprisonment. In *Johnson*, two codefendants on leave from military duty and far from home were arrested on counterfeiting offenses, held without bail for over two months until they were indicted and, two days later, arraigned, tried, convicted and sentenced to four and a half years' imprisonment. Quoting the passage in Justice Sutherland's opinion in *Powell v. Alabama* about the legal skills and experience—"the guiding hand of counsel"—necessary to defend against criminal charges, the Court found that the Sixth Amendment required the result.

In the next case the Court considers whether the rule of *Johnson v. Zerbst* applies in a non-capital state criminal trial.

Chapter VIII Right to Counsel and the Defense Function

Betts v. Brady
316 U.S. 455 (1942)

Mr. Justice ROBERTS delivered the opinion of the Court.

The petitioner was indicted for robbery in the Circuit Court of Carroll County, Maryland. Due to lack of funds he was unable to employ counsel, and so informed the judge at his arraignment. He requested that counsel be appointed for him. The judge advised him that this could not be done as it was not the practice in Carroll County to appoint counsel for indigent defendants save in prosecutions for murder and rape.

Without waiving his asserted right to counsel the petitioner pleaded not guilty and elected to be tried without a jury. At his request witnesses were summoned in his behalf. He cross-examined the State's witnesses and examined his own. The latter gave testimony tending to establish an alibi. Although afforded the opportunity, he did not take the witness stand. The judge found him guilty and imposed a sentence of eight years.

* * *

Was the petitioner's conviction and sentence a deprivation of his liberty without due process of law, in violation of the Fourteenth Amendment, because of the court's refusal to appoint counsel at his request?

The Sixth Amendment of the national Constitution applies only to trials in federal courts. The due process clause of the Fourteenth Amendment does not incorporate, as such, the specific guarantees found in the Sixth Amendment although a denial by a state of rights or privileges specifically embodied in that and others of the first eight amendments may, in certain circumstances, or in connection with other elements, operate, in a given case, to deprive a litigant of due process of law in violation of the Fourteenth. Due process of law is secured against invasion by the federal Government by the Fifth Amendment and is safeguarded against state action in identical words by the Fourteenth. The phrase formulates a concept less rigid and more fluid than those envisaged in other specific and particular provisions of the Bill of Rights. Its application is less a matter of rule. Asserted denial is to be tested by an appraisal of the totality of facts in a given case. That which may, in one setting, constitute a denial of fundamental fairness, shocking to the universal sense of justice, may, in other circumstances, and in the light of other considerations, fall short of such denial. In the application of such a concept there is always the danger of falling into the habit of formulating the guarantee into a set of hard and fast rules the application of which in a given case may be to ignore the qualifying factors therein disclosed.

The petitioner, in this instance, asks us, in effect, to apply a rule in the enforcement of the due process clause. He says the rule to be deduced from our former decisions is that, in every case, whatever the circumstances, one charged with crime, who is unable to obtain counsel, must be furnished counsel by the state. Expressions in the opinions of this court lend color to the argument, but, as the petitioner admits, none of our decisions squarely adjudicates the question now presented.

In *Powell v. Alabama*, ignorant and friendless negro youths, strangers in the community, without friends or means to obtain counsel, were hurried to trial for a capital offense without effective appointment of counsel on whom the burden of preparation and trial would rest, and without adequate opportunity to consult even the counsel casually appointed to represent them. This occurred in a State whose statute law required the appointment of counsel for indigent defendants prosecuted for the offense charged. Thus the trial was conducted in disregard of every principle of fairness and in disregard of that which was declared by the law of the State a requisite of fair trial. This court held the resulting convictions were without due process of law. It said that, in the light of all the facts, the failure of the trial court to afford the defendants reasonable time and opportunity to secure counsel was a clear denial of due process. The court stated further that "under the circumstances . . . the necessity of counsel was so vital and imperative that the failure of the trial court to make an effective appointment of counsel was likewise a denial of due process," but added: "whether this would be so in other criminal prosecutions, or under other circumstances, we need not determine. All that it is necessary now to decide, as we do decide, is that in a capital case, where the defendant is unable to employ counsel, and is incapable adequately of making his own defense because of ignorance, feeblemindedness, illiteracy, or the like, it is the duty of the court, whether requested or not, to assign counsel for him as a necessary requisite of due process of law. . . ."

Likewise, in *Avery v. Alabama*, the state law required the appointment of counsel. The claim which we felt required examination, as in the *Powell* case, was that the purported compliance with this requirement amounted to mere lip service. Scrutiny of the record disclosed that counsel had been appointed and the defendant had been afforded adequate opportunity to prepare his defense with the aid of counsel. We, therefore, overruled the contention that due process had been denied.

In *Smith v. O'Grady*, the petition for habeas corpus alleged a failure to appoint counsel but averred other facts which, if established, would prove that the trial was a mere sham and pretense, offensive to the concept of due process. There also, state law required the appointment of counsel for one on trial for the offence involved.

Those cases, which are the petitioner's chief reliance, do not rule this. The question we are now to decide is whether due process of law demands that in every criminal case, whatever the circumstances, a state must furnish counsel to an indigent defendant. Is the furnishing of counsel in all cases whatever dictated by natural, inherent, and fundamental principles of fairness? The answer to the question may be found in the common understanding of those who have lived under the Anglo-American system of law. By the Sixth Amendment the people ordained that, in all criminal prosecutions, the accused should "enjoy the right . . . to have the Assistance of Counsel for his defence." We have construed the provision to require appointment of counsel in all cases where a defendant is unable to procure the services of an attorney, and where the right has not been intentionally and competently waived. Though, as we have noted, the amendment lays down no rule for the conduct of the states, the question recurs whether the constraint laid by the amendment upon the national courts expresses a rule so fundamental and essential to a fair trial, and so, to due process of law, that it is made obligatory upon the states by the Fourteenth Amendment. Relevant data on the subject are afforded by constitutional and statutory provisions subsisting in the colonies and the states prior to the inclusion of the Bill of Rights in the national Constitution, and in the constitutional, legislative, and judicial history of the states to the present date. These constitute the most authoritative sources for ascertaining the considered judgment of the citizens of the states upon the question.

• • •

This material demonstrates that, in the great majority of the states, it has been the considered judgment of the people, their representatives and their courts that appointment of counsel is not a fundamental right, essential to a fair trial. On the contrary, the matter has generally been deemed one of legislative policy. In the light of this evidence we are unable to say that the concept of due process incorporated in the Fourteenth Amendment obligates the states, whatever may be their own views, to furnish counsel in every such case. Every court has power, if it deems proper, to appoint counsel where that course seems to be required in the interest of fairness.

Chapter VIII Right to Counsel and the Defense Function

The practice of the courts of Maryland gives point to the principle that the states should not be straight-jacketed in this respect, by a construction of the Fourteenth Amendment. Judge Bond's opinion states, and counsel at the bar confirmed the fact, that in Maryland the usual practice is for the defendant to waive a trial by jury. This the petitioner did in the present case. Such trials, as Judge Bond remarks, are much more informal than jury trials and it is obvious that the judge can much better control the course of the trial and is in a better position to see impartial justice done than when the formalities of a jury trial are involved.

In this case there was no question of the commission of a robbery. The State's case consisted of evidence identifying the petitioner as the perpetrator. The defense was an alibi. Petitioner called and examined witnesses to prove that he was at another place at the time of the commission of the offence. The simple issue was the veracity of the testimony for the State and that for the defendant. As Judge Bond says, the accused was not helpless, but was a man forty-three years old, of ordinary intelligence and ability to take care of his own interests on the trial of that narrow issue. He had once before been in a criminal court, pleaded guilty to larceny and served a sentence and was not wholly unfamiliar with criminal procedure. It is quite clear that in Maryland, if the situation had been otherwise and it had appeared that the petitioner was, for any reason, at a serious disadvantage by reason of the lack of counsel, a refusal to appoint would have resulted in the reversal of a judgment of conviction. Only recently the Court of Appeals has reversed a conviction because it was convinced on the whole record that an accused tried without counsel had been handicapped by the lack of representation.

To deduce from the due process clause a rule binding upon the states in this matter would be to impose upon them, as Judge Bond points out, a requirement without distinction between criminal charges of different magnitude or in respect of courts of varying jurisdiction. As he says: "Charges of small crimes tried before justices of the peace and capital charges tried in the higher courts would equally require the appointment of counsel. Presumably it would be argued that trials in the Traffic Court would require it." And indeed it was said by petitioner's counsel both below and in this court, that as the Fourteenth Amendment extends the protection of due process to property as well as to life and liberty, if we hold with the petitioner logic would require the furnishing of counsel in civil cases involving property.

As we have said, the Fourteenth Amendment prohibits the conviction and incarceration of one whose trial is offensive to the common and fundamental ideas of fairness and right, and while want of counsel in a particular case may result in a conviction lacking in such fundamental fairness, we cannot say that the amendment embodies an inexorable command that no trial for any offense, or in any court, can be fairly conducted and justice accorded a defendant who is not represented by counsel.

The judgment is affirmed.

Affirmed.

Mr. Justice BLACK, dissenting, with whom Mr. Justice DOUGLAS and Mr. Justice MURPHY concur.

To hold that the petitioner had a constitutional right to counsel in this case does not require us to say that "no trial for any offense, or in any court, can be fairly conducted and justice accorded a defendant who is not represented by counsel." This case can be determined by resolution of a narrower question: whether in view of the nature of the offense and the circumstances of his trial and conviction, this petitioner was denied the procedural protection which is his right under the federal constitution. I think he was.

The petitioner, a farm hand, out of a job and on relief, was indicted in a Maryland state court on a charge of robbery. He was too poor to hire a lawyer. He so informed the court and requested that counsel be appointed to defend him. His request was denied. Put to trial without a lawyer, he conducted his own defense, was found guilty, and was sentenced to eight years'

A. Scope of the Right to Counsel 725

imprisonment. The court below found that the petitioner had "at least an ordinary amount of intelligence." It is clear from his examination of witnesses that he was a man of little education.

If this case had come to us from a federal court, it is clear we should have to reverse it, because the Sixth Amendment makes the right to counsel in criminal cases inviolable by the federal government. I believe that the Fourteenth Amendment made the sixth applicable to the states. But this view, although often urged in dissents, has never been accepted by a majority of this Court and is not accepted today. A statement of the grounds supporting it is, therefore, unnecessary at this time. I believe, however, that under the prevailing view of due process, as reflected in the opinion just announced, a view which gives this Court such vast supervisory powers that I am not prepared to accept it without grave doubts, the judgment below should be reversed.

This Court has just declared that due process of law is denied if a trial is conducted in such manner that it is "shocking to the universal sense of justice" or "offensive to the common and fundamental ideas of fairness and right." On another occasion this Court has recognized that whatever is "implicit in the concept of ordered liberty" and "essential to the substance of a hearing" is within the procedural protection afforded by the constitutional guaranty of due process.

The right to counsel in a criminal proceeding is "fundamental." It is guarded from invasion by the sixth amendment, adopted to raise an effective barrier against arbitrary or unjust deprivation of liberty by the federal government.

An historical evaluation of the right to a full hearing in criminal cases and the dangers of denying it were set out in the *Powell* case where this Court said: "What . . . does a hearing include? Historically and in practice, in our own country at least, it has always included the right to the aid of counsel when desired and provided by the party asserting the right. . . . Even the intelligent and educated layman . . . lacks both the skill and knowledge adequately to prepare his defense, even though he have a perfect one. He requires the guiding hand of counsel in every step in the proceedings against him. Without it, though he be not guilty, he faces the danger of conviction because he does not know how to establish his innocence." *Powell v. Alabama.*

A practice cannot be reconciled with "common and fundamental ideas of fairness and right," which subjects innocent men to increased dangers of conviction merely because of their poverty. Whether a man is innocent cannot be determined from a trial in which, as here, denial of counsel has made it impossible to conclude, with any satisfactory degree of certainty, that the defendant's case was adequately presented. No one questions that due process requires a hearing before conviction and sentence for the serious crime of robbery. As the Supreme Court of Wisconsin said in 1859, ". . . would it not be a little like mockery to secure to a pauper these solemn constitutional guaranties for a fair and full trial of the matters with which he was charged, and yet say to him when on trial, that he must employ his own counsel, who could alone render these guaranties of any real permanent value to him. . . . Why this great solicitude to secure him a fair trial if he cannot have the benefit of counsel?"

Denial to the poor of the request for counsel in proceedings based on charges of serious crime has long been regarded as shocking to the "universal sense of justice" throughout this country. In 1854, for example, the Supreme Court of Indiana said: "It is not to be thought of, in a civilized community, for a moment, that any citizen put in jeopardy of life or liberty should be debarred of counsel because he was too poor to employ such aid. No Court could be respected, or respect itself, to sit and hear such a trial. The defence of the poor, in such cases, is a duty resting somewhere, which will be at once conceded as essential to the accused, to the Court, and to the public." And most of the other states have shown their agreement by constitutional provisions, statutes, or established practice judicially approved which assure that no man shall be deprived of counsel merely because of his poverty. Any other practice seems to me to defeat the promise of our democratic society to provide equal justice under the law.

NOTES AND QUESTIONS

1. The Court purports to justify the lack of counsel for Betts by providing an almost cartoonish oversimplification of Betts's trial.

> In this case there was no question of the commission of a robbery. The State's case consisted of evidence identifying the petitioner as the perpetrator. The defense was an alibi. Petitioner called and examined witnesses to prove that he was at another place at the time of the commission of the offence. The simple issue was the veracity of the testimony for the State and that for the defendant. As Judge Bond says, the accused was not helpless, but was a man forty-three years old, of ordinary intelligence and ability to take care of his own interests on the trial of that narrow issue. He had once before been in a criminal court, pleaded guilty to larceny and served a sentence and was not wholly unfamiliar with criminal procedure.

What does the Court mean that "there was no question of the commission of a robbery"? Is the Court inferring from Betts's pursuit of an alibi defense that the evidence of an actual robbery was undisputed? Did Betts have the wherewithal to consider all available defenses? Betts, of course, was probably not aware that multiple defenses can sometimes be pursued in the same trial.

2. As to the "evidence identifying [Betts] as the perpetrator," how well do you think Betts was able to cross-examine these identification witnesses as to their viewpoint, motive, credibility, etc.? As to his own witnesses, how well do you think he was able to establish their credibility, their neutrality, and their confidence in the testimony they gave in support of his alibi? As to the Court's comment that the "simple issue was the veracity of the testimony"—suffice it to say that many trial lawyers would tell you that enhancing or undermining the "veracity of testimony" is what being a trial lawyer is all about. Finally, how is defendant's previous experience as a criminal defendant—on a guilty plea no less—in any way relevant to his ability to represent himself at trial?

3. In lauding the diversity of state policies on the issue of appointment of counsel, a diversity that somehow cuts against finding a federal due process right, the Court discusses the Maryland practice whereby defendants often waive their right to a jury trial, and proceedings are thus more informal. *Id.* at 472. How might the lack of formality be advantageous to a layperson representing himself in a criminal proceeding? Does anything about the informality of a proceeding assist the defendant in terms of selecting, preparing, and presenting a defense? What advantages might a defendant forfeit in trying his case to a judge instead of a jury?

4. The Court makes the predictable floodgates argument, stating that recognition of a due process right for Betts—who was sentenced to eight years' imprisonment!—would inevitably require appointed counsel for "small crimes tried before justices of the peace" and for "civil cases involving property." Are there any logical toeholds on the slippery slope between *Betts* and an appointed counsel right to indigent parties in civil cases? What are they?

5. In declaring what would become known as the "special circumstances" rule, the Court noted that the Due Process Clause "formulates a concept less rigid and more fluid than those envisaged in other specific and particular provisions in the Bill of Rights." Counterintuitively, however, that "fluidity" counseled against an expanded reading of the term but rather justified an entirely ad hoc case-by-case approach. "Asserted denial (of due process) is to be tested by an appraisal of the totality of facts in a given case. That which may, in one setting, constitute a denial of fundamental fairness, shocking to the universal sense of justice, may, in other circumstances, and in the light of other considerations, fall short of such denial." How are lower courts to apply this standard in considering requests for appointed counsel after *Betts*?

6. The dissent, though in favor of a decision that would fully incorporate the guarantees of the Sixth Amendment (and thus the holding of *Johnson v. Zerbst*) against the states, also argues that even under a due process approach like the one in *Powell v. Alabama* Betts should have been entitled to appointed counsel. What factors did the dissent think weighed in Betts's favor in such a due process approach? Is this argument persuasive?

A. Scope of the Right to Counsel 727

7. To what extent is the dissent driven by, in so many words, equal protection concerns as well as due process concerns?

In the next case the Court takes a step toward serious consideration of the concern Justice Black expressed in his *Betts* dissent that "no man shall be deprived of counsel merely because of his poverty."

Griffin v. Illinois
351 U.S. 12 (1956)

Mr. Justice BLACK announced the judgment of the Court and an opinion in which THE CHIEF JUSTICE, Mr. Justice DOUGLAS, and Mr. Justice CLARK, join.

Illinois law provides that "Writs of error in all criminal cases are writs of right and shall be issued of course." The question presented here is whether Illinois may, consistent with the Due Process and Equal Protection Clauses of the Fourteenth Amendment, administer this statute so as to deny adequate appellate review to the poor while granting such review to all others.

The petitioners Griffin and Crenshaw were tried together and convicted of armed robbery in the Criminal Court of Cook County, Illinois. Immediately after their conviction they filed a motion in the trial court asking that a certified copy of the entire record, including a stenographic transcript of the proceedings, be furnished them without cost. They alleged that they were "poor persons with no means of paying the necessary fees to acquire the Transcript and Court Records needed to prosecute an appeal. . . ." These allegations were not denied. Under Illinois law in order to get full direct appellate review of alleged errors by a writ of error it is necessary for the defendant to furnish the appellate court with a bill of exceptions or report of proceedings at the trial certified by the trial judge. As Illinois concedes, it is sometimes impossible to prepare such bills of exceptions or reports without a stenographic transcript of the trial proceedings. Indigent defendants sentenced to death are provided with a free transcript at the expense of the county where convicted. In all other criminal cases defendants needing a transcript, whether indigent or not, must themselves buy it. The petitioners contended in their motion before the trial court that failure to provide them with the needed transcript would violate the Due Process and Equal Protection Clauses of the Fourteenth Amendment. The trial court denied the motion without a hearing.

Griffin and Crenshaw then filed a petition under the Illinois Post-Conviction Hearing Act. Only questions arising under the Illinois or Federal Constitution may be raised in proceedings under this Act. A companion state act provides that indigent petitioners under the Post-Conviction Act may, under some circumstances, obtain a free transcript. The effect is that indigents may obtain a free transcript to obtain appellate review of constitutional questions but not of other alleged trial errors such as admissibility and sufficiency of evidence. In their Post-Conviction proceeding petitioners alleged that there were manifest nonconstitutional errors in the trial which entitled them to have their convictions set aside on appeal and that the only impediment to full appellate review was their lack of funds to buy a transcript. These allegations have not been denied. Petitioners repeated their charge that refusal to afford full appellate review solely because of poverty was a denial of due process and equal protection. This petition like the first was dismissed without hearing any evidence. The Illinois Supreme Court affirmed the dismissal solely on the ground that the charges raised no substantial state or federal constitutional questions — the only kind of questions which may be raised in Post-Conviction proceedings. We granted certiorari.

Counsel for Illinois concedes that these petitioners needed a transcript in order to get adequate appellate review of their alleged trial errors. There is no contention that petitioners were dilatory in their efforts to get appellate review, or that the Illinois Supreme Court denied review on the ground that the allegations of trial error were insufficient. We must therefore assume for purposes of this decision that errors were committed in the trial which would merit reversal, but that the petitioners could not get appellate review of those errors solely because they were too poor to buy a stenographic transcript. Counsel for Illinois denies that this violates either the Due Process or the Equal Protection Clause, but states that if it does, the Illinois Post-Conviction statute entitles petitioners to a free transcript. The sole question for us to decide, therefore, is whether due process or equal protection has been violated.

Providing equal justice for poor and rich, weak and powerful alike is an age-old problem. People have never ceased to hope and strive to move closer to that goal. This hope, at least in part, brought about in 1215 the royal concessions of Magna Charta: "To no one will we sell, to no one will we refuse, or delay, right or justice. . . . No free man shall be taken or imprisoned, or disseised, or outlawed, or exiled, or anywise destroyed; nor shall we go upon him nor send upon him, but by the lawful judgment of his peers or by the law of the land." These pledges were unquestionably steps toward a fairer and more nearly equal application of criminal justice. In this tradition, our own constitutional guaranties of due process and equal protection both call for procedures in criminal trials which allow no invidious discriminations between persons and different groups of persons. Both equal protection and due process emphasize the central aim of our entire judicial system—all people charged with crime must, so far as the law is concerned, "stand on an equality before the bar of justice in every American court." *Chambers v. Florida*; *Yick Wo v. Hopkins*.

Surely no one would contend that either a State or the Federal Government could constitutionally provide that defendants unable to pay court costs in advance should be denied the right to plead not guilty or to defend themselves in court. Such a law would make the constitutional promise of a fair trial a worthless thing. Notice, the right to be heard, and the right to counsel would under such circumstances be meaningless promises to the poor. In criminal trials a State can no more discriminate on account of poverty than on account of religion, race, or color. Plainly the ability to pay costs in advance bears no rational relationship to a defendant's guilt or innocence and could not be used as an excuse to deprive a defendant of a fair trial. Indeed, a provision in the Constitution of Illinois of 1818 provided that every person in Illinois "ought to obtain right and justice freely, and without being obliged to purchase it, completely and without denial, promptly and without delay, conformably to the laws."

There is no meaningful distinction between a rule which would deny the poor the right to defend themselves in a trial court and one which effectively denies the poor an adequate appellate review accorded to all who have money enough to pay the costs in advance. It is true that a State is not required by the Federal Constitution to provide appellate courts or a right to appellate review at all. But that is not to say that a State that does grant appellate review can do so in a way that discriminates against some convicted defendants on account of their poverty. Appellate review has now become an integral part of the Illinois trial system for finally adjudicating the guilt or innocence of a defendant. Consequently at all stages of the proceedings the Due Process and Equal Protection Clauses protect persons like petitioners from invidious discriminations.

All of the States now provide some method of appeal from criminal convictions, recognizing the importance of appellate review to a correct adjudication of guilt or innocence. Statistics show that a substantial proportion of criminal convictions are reversed by state appellate courts. Thus to deny adequate review to the poor means that many of them may lose their life, liberty or property because of unjust convictions which appellate courts would set aside. Many States have recognized this and provided aid for convicted defendants who have a right to appeal and need a transcript but are unable to pay for it. A few have not. Such a denial is a misfit in a country dedicated to affording equal justice to all and special privileges to none in the administration of its criminal law. There can be no equal justice where the kind of trial a man gets depends on the amount of money he has. Destitute defendants must be afforded as adequate appellate review as defendants who have money enough to buy transcripts.

The Illinois Supreme Court denied these petitioners relief under the Post-Conviction Act because of its holding that no constitutional rights were violated. In view of our holding to the contrary the State Supreme Court may decide that petitioners are now entitled to a transcript, as the State's brief suggests. We do not hold, however, that Illinois must purchase a stenographer's transcript in every case where a defendant cannot buy it. The Supreme Court may find other means of affording adequate and effective appellate review to indigent defendants. For example, it may be that bystanders' bills of exceptions or other methods of reporting trial proceedings could be used in some cases. The Illinois Supreme Court appears to have broad power to promulgate rules of procedure and appellate practice. We are confident that the State will provide corrective rules to meet the problem which this case lays bare.

The judgment of the Supreme Court of Illinois is vacated and the cause is remanded to that court for further action not inconsistent with the foregoing paragraph. Mr. Justice Frankfurter joins in this disposition of the case.

Vacated and remanded.

NOTES AND QUESTIONS

1. One premise for the decision in *Griffin* is that the right to pursue an appeal is inextricably connected to the right to a fair trial. "The right to an appeal from a conviction for crime is today so established that this leads to the easy assumption that it is fundamental to the protection of life and liberty and therefore a necessary ingredient of due process of law." *Id.* at 20.

How can this view be reconciled with the Court's prior holding—recognized here—that a state has no federal constitutional obligation to provide for appellate review? And is the Court's holding necessarily applicable nationwide? The Court expressly notes that "appellate review has become an integral part of the *Illinois* trial system" and that "a substantial proportion of criminal convictions are reversed by state appellate courts," *id.* at 18-19, but for the latter point the Court cites only an Illinois-specific study.

2. The Court analogizes the transcript cost to a requirement that defendants must pay court costs in advance of defending themselves at trial. Is this a fair analogy?

3. The Court states, grandly, that "[i]n criminal trials a State can no more discriminate on account of poverty than on account of religion, race or color." Doesn't the practice condoned in *Betts v. Brady* amount to discrimination "on account of poverty"? Interestingly none of the several opinions in *Griffin* cite to *Betts v. Brady*.

Betts v. Brady had been widely criticized from its inception, and by the early 1960s, shortly after *Griffin* was decided, the Supreme Court was finding "special circumstances" justifying appointment of counsel more and more frequently. For example, in *Hamilton v. Alabama*, 368 U.S. 52, 55 (1961), the Court had held that special circumstances exist in all capital cases; in *Chewing v. Cunningham*, 369 U.S. 443, 447 (1962), it had found special circumstances where a defendant faced "potential prejudice" in defending against the application of a Virginia recidivist statute without counsel. *See* A. Lewis, Gideon's Trumpet 118-22 (1964). Accordingly it was hardly surprising that when the Supreme Court granted leave to Clarence Gideon to proceed in forma pauperis, it explicitly asked whether *Betts v. Brady* should be reconsidered.

Gideon v. Wainwright
372 U.S. 335 (1963)

Mr. Justice BLACK delivered the opinion of the Court.

Petitioner was charged in a Florida state court with having broken and entered a poolroom with intent to commit a misdemeanor. This offense is a felony under Florida law. Appearing in court without funds and without a lawyer, petitioner asked the court to appoint counsel for him, whereupon the following colloquy took place:

The COURT:	Mr. Gideon, I am sorry, but I cannot appoint Counsel to represent you in this case. Under the laws of the State of Florida, the only time the Court can appoint Counsel to represent a Defendant is when that person is charged with a capital offense. I am sorry, but I will have to deny your request to appoint Counsel to defend you in this case.
The DEFENDANT:	The United States Supreme Court says I am entitled to be represented by Counsel.

Put to trial before a jury, Gideon conducted his defense about as well as could be expected from a layman. He made an opening statement to the jury, cross-examined the State's witnesses, presented witnesses in his own defense, declined to testify himself, and made a short argument "emphasizing his innocence to the charge contained in the Information filed in this case." The jury returned a verdict of guilty, and petitioner was sentenced to serve five years in the state prison. Later, petitioner filed in the Florida Supreme Court this habeas corpus petition attacking his conviction and sentence on the ground that the trial court's refusal to appoint counsel for him denied him rights "guaranteed by the Constitution and the Bill of Rights by the United States Government." Treating the petition for habeas corpus as properly before it, the State Supreme Court, "upon consideration thereof" but without an opinion, denied all relief. Since 1942, when *Betts v. Brady* was decided by a divided Court, the problem of a defendant's federal constitutional right to counsel in a state court has been a continuing source of controversy and litigation in both state and federal courts. To give this problem another review here, we granted certiorari. Since Gideon was proceeding in forma pauperis, we appointed counsel to represent him and requested both sides to discuss in their briefs and oral arguments the following: "Should this Court's holding in *Betts v. Brady* be reconsidered?"

I

The facts upon which Betts claimed that he had been unconstitutionally denied the right to have counsel appointed to assist him are strikingly like the facts upon which Gideon here bases his federal constitutional claim. Betts was indicted for robbery in a Maryland state court. On arraignment, he told the trial judge of his lack of funds to hire a lawyer and asked the court to appoint one for him. Betts was advised that it was not the practice in that county to appoint counsel for indigent defendants except in murder and rape cases. He then pleaded not guilty, had witnesses summoned, cross-examined the State's witnesses, examined his own, and chose not to testify himself. He was found guilty by the judge, sitting without a jury, and sentenced to eight years in prison. Like Gideon, Betts sought release by habeas corpus, alleging that he had been denied the right to assistance of counsel in violation of the Fourteenth Amendment. Betts was denied any relief, and on review this Court affirmed. It was held that a refusal to appoint counsel for an indigent defendant charged with a felony did not necessarily violate the Due Process Clause of the Fourteenth Amendment, which for reasons given the Court deemed to be the only applicable federal constitutional provision. The Court said:

A. Scope of the Right to Counsel 731

> Asserted denial (of due process) is to be tested by an appraisal of the totality of facts in a given case. That which may, in one setting, constitute a denial of fundamental fairness, shocking to the universal sense of justice, may, in other circumstances, and in the light of other considerations, fall short of such denial.

Treating due process as "a concept less rigid and more fluid than those envisaged in other specific and particular provisions of the Bill of Rights," the Court held that refusal to appoint counsel under the particular facts and circumstances in the *Betts* case was not so "offensive to the common and fundamental ideas of fairness" as to amount to a denial of due process. Since the facts and circumstances of the two cases are so nearly indistinguishable, we think the *Betts v. Brady* holding if left standing would require us to reject Gideon's claim that the Constitution guarantees him the assistance of counsel. Upon full reconsideration we conclude that *Betts v. Brady* should be overruled.

II

The Sixth Amendment provides, "In all criminal prosecutions, the accused shall enjoy the right . . . to have the Assistance of Counsel for his defence." We have construed this to mean that in federal courts counsel must be provided for defendants unable to employ counsel unless the right is competently and intelligently waived. Betts argued that this right is extended to indigent defendants in state courts by the Fourteenth Amendment. In response the Court stated that, while the Sixth Amendment laid down "no rule for the conduct of the states, the question recurs whether the constraint laid by the amendment upon the national courts expresses a rule so fundamental and essential to a fair trial, and so, to due process of law, that it is made obligatory upon the states by the Fourteenth Amendment." In order to decide whether the Sixth Amendment's guarantee of counsel is of this fundamental nature, the Court in *Betts* set out and considered "(r)elevant data on the subject . . . afforded by constitutional and statutory provisions subsisting in the colonies and the states prior to the inclusion of the Bill of Rights in the national Constitution, and in the constitutional, legislative, and judicial history of the states to the present date." On the basis of this historical data the Court concluded that "appointment of counsel is not a fundamental right, essential to a fair trial." It was for this reason the *Betts* Court refused to accept the contention that the Sixth Amendment's guarantee of counsel for indigent federal defendants was extended to or, in the words of that Court, "made obligatory upon the states by the Fourteenth Amendment." Plainly, had the Court concluded that appointment of counsel for an indigent criminal defendant was "a fundamental right, essential to a fair trial," it would have held that the Fourteenth Amendment requires appointment of counsel in a state court, just as the Sixth Amendment requires in a federal court.

We think the Court in *Betts* had ample precedent for acknowledging that those guarantees of the Bill of Rights which are fundamental safeguards of liberty immune from federal abridgment are equally protected against state invasion by the Due Process Clause of the Fourteenth Amendment. This same principle was recognized, explained, and applied in *Powell v. Alabama*, a case upholding the right of counsel, where the Court held that despite sweeping language to the contrary in *Hurtado*, the Fourteenth Amendment "embraced" those "fundamental principles of liberty and justice which lie at the base of all our civil and political institutions," even though they had been "specifically dealt with in another part of the Federal Constitution." In many cases other than *Powell* and *Betts*, this Court has looked to the fundamental nature of original Bill of Rights guarantees to decide whether the Fourteenth Amendment makes them obligatory on the States. Explicitly recognized to be of this "fundamental nature" and therefore made immune from state invasion by the Fourteenth, or some part of it, are the First Amendment's freedoms of speech, press, religion, assembly, association, and petition for redress of grievances. For the same reason, though not always in precisely the same terminology, the Court has made obligatory on the States the Fifth

Amendment's command that private property shall not be taken for public use without just compensation, the Fourth Amendment's prohibition of unreasonable searches and seizures, and the Eighth's ban on cruel and unusual punishment. On the other hand, this Court in *Palko v. Connecticut* (1937) refused to hold that the Fourteenth Amendment made the double jeopardy provision of the Fifth Amendment obligatory on the States. In so refusing, however, the Court, speaking through Mr. Justice Cardozo, was careful to emphasize that "immunities that are valid as against the federal government by force of the specific pledges of particular amendments have been found to be implicit in the concept of ordered liberty, and thus, through the Fourteenth Amendment, become valid as against the states" and that guarantees "in their origin . . . effective against the federal government alone" had by prior cases "been taken over from the earlier articles of the Federal Bill of Rights and brought within the Fourteenth Amendment by a process of absorption."

We accept *Betts v. Brady*'s assumption, based as it was on our prior cases, that a provision of the Bill of Rights which is "fundamental and essential to a fair trial" is made obligatory upon the States by the Fourteenth Amendment. We think the Court in *Betts* was wrong, however, in concluding that the Sixth Amendment's guarantee of counsel is not one of these fundamental rights. Ten years before *Betts v. Brady*, this Court, after full consideration of all the historical data examined in Betts, had unequivocally declared that "the right to the aid of counsel is of this fundamental character." *Powell v. Alabama.* While the Court at the close of its *Powell* opinion did by its language, as this Court frequently does, limit its holding to the particular facts and circumstances of that case, its conclusions about the fundamental nature of the right to counsel are unmistakable. Several years later, in 1936, the Court reemphasized what it had said about the fundamental nature of the right to counsel in this language:

> We concluded that certain fundamental rights, safeguarded by the first eight amendments against federal action, were also safeguarded against state action by the due process of law clause of the Fourteenth Amendment, and among them the fundamental right of the accused to the aid of counsel in a criminal prosecution.

And again in 1938 this Court said:

> (The assistance of counsel) is one of the safeguards of the Sixth Amendment deemed necessary to insure fundamental human rights of life and liberty. . . . The Sixth Amendment stands as a constant admonition that if the constitutional safeguards it provides be lost, justice will not "still be done."

In light of these and many other prior decisions of this Court, it is not surprising that the *Betts* Court, when faced with the contention that "one charged with crime, who is unable to obtain counsel, must be furnished counsel by the state," conceded that "(e)xpressions in the opinions of this court lend color to the argument. . . ." The fact is that in deciding as it did—that "appointment of counsel is not a fundamental right, essential to a fair trial"—the Court in *Betts v. Brady* made an abrupt break with its own well-considered precedents. In returning to these old precedents, sounder we believe than the new, we but restore constitutional principles established to achieve a fair system of justice. Not only these precedents but also reason and reflection require us to recognize that in our adversary system of criminal justice, any person haled into court, who is too poor to hire a lawyer, cannot be assured a fair trial unless counsel is provided for him. This seems to us to be an obvious truth. Governments, both state and federal, quite properly spend vast sums of money to establish machinery to try defendants accused of crime. Lawyers to prosecute are everywhere deemed essential to protect the public's interest in an orderly society. Similarly, there are few defendants charged with crime, few indeed, who fail to hire the best lawyers they can get to prepare and present their defenses. That government hires lawyers to prosecute and defendants who have the money hire lawyers to defend are the strongest indications of the wide—spread belief that lawyers in criminal courts are necessities, not luxuries. The right of one charged with crime to counsel may not be deemed fundamental and essential to fair trials in some countries, but it is in ours. From the very beginning, our state and national constitutions and laws have laid great emphasis on procedural and substantive safeguards designed to assure fair trials before impartial tribunals in which every defendant stands equal before the law. This noble ideal cannot be realized if the poor man charged with crime has to face his accusers without a lawyer to assist him. A defendant's need for a lawyer is nowhere better stated than in the moving words of Mr. Justice Sutherland in *Powell v. Alabama*:

> The right to be heard would be, in many cases, of little avail if it did not comprehend the right to be heard by counsel. Even the intelligent and educated layman has small and sometimes no skill in the science of law. If charged with crime, he is incapable, generally, of determining for himself whether the indictment is good or bad. He is unfamiliar with the rules of evidence. Left without the aid of counsel he may be put on trial without a proper charge, and convicted upon incompetent evidence, or evidence irrelevant to the issue or otherwise inadmissible. He lacks both the skill and knowledge adequately to prepare his defense, even though he have a perfect one. He requires the guiding hand of counsel at every step in the proceedings against him. Without it, though he be not guilty, he faces the danger of conviction because he does not know how to establish his innocence.

The Court in *Betts v. Brady* departed from the sound wisdom upon which the Court's holding in *Powell v. Alabama* rested. Florida, supported by two other States, has asked that *Betts v. Brady* be left intact. Twenty-two States, as friends of the Court, argue that Betts was "an anachronism when handed down" and that it should now be overruled. We agree.

The judgment is reversed and the cause is remanded to the Supreme Court of Florida for further action not inconsistent with this opinion.

Reversed.

NOTES AND QUESTIONS

1. The Court begins its decision by reproducing the exchange between the Florida state trial court judge in which the unrepresented Gideon requests the appointment of counsel and, in response to the judge's patient though arguably incorrect denial, Gideon famously — and also incorrectly — states "[t]he United States Supreme Court says I am entitled to be represented by Counsel." *Id.* at 336-37. Given the state of the law at the time of Gideon's trial, how should the trial judge have responded to Gideon's request? And why is Gideon's response likely incorrect?

2. Is this exchange included at the beginning of the opinion purely for dramatic effect, or did Gideon's explicit request for counsel actually matter? Note that the issue of a defendant's waiver of any right to appointed counsel, or failure to request counsel, had often been an issue in cases during this time period, a problem exacerbated by the uncertain availability of transcripts and unclear law on the standard for finding waiver. In a book review of *Gideon's Trumpet*, the award-winning book about the case by *New York Times* journalist Anthony Lewis, Professor Yale Kamisar observes:

> And we do not know or would rather forget that even in some of our federal courts, where the "absolute right" to counsel was supposedly won a full generation ago, two-thirds or more of all indigent defendants were "waiving" this right as late as 1961, which means, I submit, that they were not really waiving it at all — at least not "understandingly and knowingly," not "unequivocally and specifically," not the way appellate courts say constitutional rights are supposed to be waived.

Kamisar, Book Review, Gideon's Trumpet *by Anthony Lewis (1964)*, 78 Harv. L. Rev. 478, 483 (1964) (citations omitted).

The made-for-TV movie *Gideon's Trumpet*, based on Anthony Lewis's eponymous book, was nominated for several Emmys. The cast included not only Henry Fonda as Clarence Gideon but also John Houseman as Earl Warren, Jose Ferrer as Abe Fortas, and Fay Wray as Edna Curtis.

3. The Court's decision wastes little time in going right after *Betts v. Brady*. The Court says *Betts* "was wrong" and that in *Betts* the Court "made an abrupt break with its own well-considered precedents." (Naturally the Court says nothing about the substantial changes in the Court's membership in the 21 years since *Betts* was decided.) In a concurring opinion, Justice Harlan, though agreeing with the majority on the merits, advocates for a more "respectful burial" of *Betts*. In essence, he reasons that *Betts* rested on a reasonable reading of *Powell v. Alabama*, and was not an "abrupt break" with the Court's precedents. Is this a fair criticism of the majority opinion in *Gideon*? What obligations should the Supreme Court have in overruling a precedent?

4. Justice Harlan also makes the point that *Betts* has had a "troubled journey," inasmuch as the Supreme Court has found "special circumstances" in relatively straightforward matters, and that "*Betts v. Brady* is no longer a reality." *Id.* at 351. Are there costs to the Supreme Court's "legitimacy" when it drains a precedent of meaning without explicitly overruling it? Justice Harlan notes that the Supreme Court's "evolution" in the recognition of "special circumstances" has not been recognized by state courts, which was the central point of the ACLU's amicus brief in *Gideon*. Brief of the American Civil Liberties Union and the Florida Civil Liberties Union, Amici Curiae, 1962 WL 115121. Can the state courts' failure to "evolve|" along with the Supreme Court be explained as a function of the Court paying only "lip service," as Justice Harlan puts it, to *Betts*? Can it also be explained as a function of the nature of the totality-of-the-circumstances rule created in *Betts*?

5. The Court properly notes the imbalance of resources in cases such as Gideon's: "Governments, both state and federal, quite properly spend vast sums of money to establish machinery to try defendants accused of crime. Lawyers to prosecute are everywhere deemed essential to protect the public's interest in an orderly society."

By the time Gideon's case had reached the Supreme Court, however, the resources tables had turned. The Court had appointed Abe Fortas, future Supreme Court Justice, and his law firm, Arnold Fortas & Porter, to represent Gideon, an effort that was aided by a summer law student intern at the firm, John Hart Ely, who himself became a noted constitutional law scholar at Yale, Harvard, and Stanford law schools. Lewis, Gideon's Trumpet, *supra* at 51, 127. At the Supreme Court, the state of Florida was represented by a single, inexperienced 27-year old assistant attorney general, Bruce Jacob, who was handling his first case before the U.S. Supreme Court. *Id.* at 147-48.

6. That the result in *Gideon* and the overruling of *Betts v. Brady* were neither unexpected nor unwelcome by the states is demonstrated by Jacob's unsuccessful efforts to recruit amicus support. Jacob reached out to the other 49 states' attorneys general and, while some expressed sympathy for Florida's position, only one state, Alabama, ended up filing a supporting amicus brief. But 23 other states, in an effort led by Minnesota's attorney general (and future U.S. Vice President under Jimmy Carter) Walter Mondale, filed an amicus brief *in support of* Gideon, arguing that *Betts* should be overruled. Lewis, Gideon's Trumpet, *supra* at 149-55.

Abe Fortas, Clarence Gideon's lawyer and future Supreme Court Justice, with his longtime client, President Johnson

736   Chapter VIII Right to Counsel and the Defense Function

As to Gideon's actual trial when he represented himself, the Court states that "Gideon conducted his trial about as well as could be expected from a layman," and notes a handful of lawyerly sounding tasks that Gideon performed. *Id.* at 337. Fair enough. But for any competent trial lawyer, Gideon's defense was pathetic. A comparison of Gideon's first trial when he was unrepresented and his retrial with counsel, based on the detailed summaries in *Gideon's Trumpet*, is illuminating.

GIDEON'S TWO TRIALS

First Trial. Gideon conducted no voir dire of the jury and made no challenges to jurors. The government's case consisted of just two witnesses.

First, Henry Cook, like Gideon a local Panama City resident, testified that through a window he saw Gideon inside the Bay Harbor Poolroom at 5:30 a.m., subsequently saw Gideon leave the poolroom with a bottle of wine and get in a cab, and then he (Cook) went in to the poolroom and saw it had been broken into.

Second, Ira Strickland, the owner of the poolroom, testified that he closed the poolroom the night before and when he returned the next morning he found it in disarray, with a broken window, the cigarette machine and jukebox broken into, and liquor missing.

Gideon conducted ineffectual and meandering cross-examinations of both of these witnesses and then called eight witnesses of his own, for no apparent reason except in an attempt to establish that he was not a drunk. When the prosecutor on cross elicited from one of these witnesses that he thought Gideon "worked at" the poolroom Gideon didn't follow up. Gideon declined to testify, the judge instructed the jury (without describing the elements of the crime or giving a reasonable doubt instruction), and the jury shortly returned a verdict of guilty. *See* Lewis, Gideon's Trumpet, *supra* at 59-64.

Retrial. On retrial after the Supreme Court's decision Gideon ended up with an appointed local attorney, Fred Turner, after refusing for unexplained reasons to be represented by lawyers from the ACLU, who had parachuted into Panama City from Miami for that purpose. Turner spent time before trial interviewing witnesses and getting the lay of the land, things Gideon had been unable to do when he had been in jail before trial. Turner struck two of the six jurors based on information he had developed prior to trial, one because he was anti-alcohol and one because he had a local reputation as "a convicter."

The government called Henry Cook as its first witness again. Turner was able to get Cook to admit that he had lied about his criminal record in the first trial, that the inside of the poolroom could not be seen through windows from Cook's claimed vantage point, and that Cook had never contacted the police about the break-in. By getting Cook also to concede that he and his friends had left a party early that morning in search of liquor, Turner planted the seed that Cook and his friends had been the burglars.

The government's second witness, Ira Strickland, now the former owner of Bay Harbor, admitted that Gideon worked at the poolroom occasionally. The government's third witness, the arresting officer, detailed everything that Strickland told him had been taken from the poolroom ($65 in change from the machines, 12 cans of beer, 4 bottles of wine, and 12 bottles of Coca-Cola). The officer admitted that when he arrested Gideon he only had $28 in change on him and none of the stolen beverages.

The first defense witness was the cabdriver who gave Gideon a ride home, who testified that Gideon paid him in change but that Gideon was sober and had no wine, beer, or Coca-Cola with him. The defense also called the proprietor of a nearby grocery store, who said that Henry Cook had come in to the store that morning and told him that "the law had picked him up for questioning" about the break-in and that he told the police he had seen someone inside but that "he wasn't sure who it was." Gideon took the stand in his own defense and testified, among other things," that he ran card games around town (including at the poolroom) and in that regard often carried large amounts of change with him. The jury returned a verdict of not guilty after about an hour of deliberation. Lewis, Gideon's Trumpet, *supra* at 240-49.

Bay County Courthouse (left) in Panama City, Florida, where both of Clarence Gideon's trials took place. Still in use today, it is Bay County's first and only courthouse. The marker (right) placed on the courthouse lawn in 2003 commemorates *Gideon v. Wainwright*. It reads: "This is the site of the landmark Gideon case, after which the Public Defender system was established in Florida and throughout the nation."

Much has been written about the significance of *Gideon*. Two narratives predominate. One is that despite the fanfare—literally, with trumpets—*Gideon* was largely of ceremonial value and had little practical effect outside a handful of southern states. *See* Justin Driver, *Constitutional Outliers*, 81 U. Chi. L. Rev. 929, 939-40 (2014) ("[T]he overwhelming majority of the nation already adhered to the rule that *Gideon* would articulate even before the Court issued its landmark decision."); William J. Stuntz, The Collapse of American Criminal Justice 222 (2011) ("*Gideon* mattered chiefly in the South."); Donald A. Dripps, *Why* Gideon *Failed: Politics and Feedback Loops in the Reform of Criminal Justice*, 70 Wash. & Lee L. Rev. 883, 895 (2013) ("By 1963, only a few states, concentrated in the south, did not appoint counsel for all felony defendants.").

A second is that *Gideon*'s story is essentially one of unfulfilled potential due to a combination of underfunding of indigent defense and underenforcement of the Sixth Amendment right to effective assistance of counsel. *See infra*. *See* Stephanos Bibas, *Shrinking* Gideon *and Expanding Alternatives to Lawyers*, 70 Wash. & Lee L. Rev. 1287, 1288 (2013) (describing indigent defense as "Potemkin lawyering . . . far removed from *Gideon*'s vision"); Stephen B. Bright & Sia M. Sanneh, *Fifty Years of Defiance and Resistance After* Gideon v. Wainwright, 122 Yale L.J. 2150, 2152 (2013) ("Every day in thousands of courtrooms . . . the right to counsel is violated.").

Douglas v. California
372 U.S. 353 (1963)

Mr. Justice DOUGLAS delivered the opinion of the Court.

Petitioners, Bennie Will Meyes and William Douglas, were jointly tried and convicted in a California court on an information charging them with 13 felonies. A single public defender was appointed to represent them. At the commencement of the trial, the defender moved for a continuance, stating that the case was very complicated, that he was not as prepared as he felt he should be because he was handling a different defense every day, and that there was a conflict of interest between the petitioners requiring the appointment of separate counsel for each of them. This motion was denied. Thereafter, petitioners dismissed the defender, claiming he was unprepared, and again renewed motions for separate counsel and for a continuance. These motions also were denied, and petitioners were ultimately convicted by a jury of all 13 felonies, which included robbery, assault with a deadly weapon, and assault with intent to commit murder. Both were given prison terms. Both appealed as of right to the California District Court of Appeal. That court affirmed their convictions. Both Meyes and Douglas then petitioned for further discretionary review in the California Supreme Court, but their petitions were denied without a hearing. We granted certiorari.

Although several questions are presented in the petition for certiorari, we address ourselves to only one of them. The record shows that petitioners requested, and were denied, the assistance of counsel on appeal, even though it plainly appeared they were indigents. In denying petitioners' requests, the California District Court of Appeal stated that it had "gone through" the record and had come to the conclusion that "no good whatever could be served by appointment of counsel." The District Court of Appeal was acting in accordance with a California rule of criminal procedure which provides that state appellate courts, upon the request of an indigent for counsel, may make "an independent investigation of the record and determine whether it would be of advantage to the defendant or helpful to the appellate court to have counsel appointed. . . . After such investigation, appellate courts should appoint counsel if in their opinion it would be helpful to the defendant or the court, and should deny the appointment of counsel only if in their judgment such appointment would be of no value to either the defendant or the court."

We agree, however, with Justice Traynor of the California Supreme Court, who said that the "(d)enial of counsel on appeal (to an indigent) would seem to be a discrimination at least as invidious as that condemned in *Griffin*." In *Griffin v. Illinois*, we held that a State may not grant appellate review in such a way as to discriminate against some convicted defendants on account of their poverty. There the right to a free transcript on appeal was in issue. Here the issue is whether or not an indigent shall be denied the assistance of counsel on appeal. In either case the evil is the same: discrimination against the indigent. For there can be no equal justice where the kind of an appeal a man enjoys "depends on the amount of money he has."

In spite of California's forward treatment of indigents, under its present practice the type of an appeal a person is afforded in the District Court of Appeal hinges upon whether or not he can pay for the assistance of counsel. If he can the appellate court passes on the merits of his case only after having the full benefit of written briefs and oral argument by counsel. If he cannot the appellate court is forced to prejudge the merits before it can even determine whether counsel should be provided. At this stage in the proceedings only the barren record speaks for the indigent, and, unless the printed pages show that an injustice has been committed, he is forced to go without a champion on appeal. Any real chance he may have had of showing that his appeal has hidden merit is deprived him when the court decides on an ex parte examination of the record that the assistance of counsel is not required.

A. Scope of the Right to Counsel

We are not here concerned with problems that might arise from the denial of counsel for the preparation of a petition for discretionary or mandatory review beyond the stage in the appellate process at which the claims have once been presented by a lawyer and passed upon by an appellate court. We are dealing only with the first appeal, granted as a matter of right to rich and poor alike, from a criminal conviction. We need not now decide whether California would have to provide counsel for an indigent seeking a discretionary hearing from the California Supreme Court after the District Court of Appeal had sustained his conviction, or whether counsel must be appointed for an indigent seeking review of an appellate affirmance of his conviction in this Court by appeal as of right or by petition for a writ of certiorari which lies within the Court's discretion. But it is appropriate to observe that a State can, consistently with the Fourteenth Amendment, provide for differences so long as the result does not amount to a denial of due process or an "invidious discrimination." But where the merits of the one and only appeal an indigent has as of right are decided without benefit of counsel, we think an unconstitutional line has been drawn between rich and poor.

When an indigent is forced to run this gantlet of a preliminary showing of merit, the right to appeal does not comport with fair procedure. In the federal courts, on the other hand, an indigent must be afforded counsel on appeal whenever he challenges a certification that the appeal is not taken in good faith. The federal courts must honor his request for counsel regardless of what they think the merits of the case may be; and "representation in the role of an advocate is required." In California, however, once the court has "gone through" the record and denied counsel, the indigent has no recourse but to prosecute his appeal on his own, as best he can, no matter how meritorious his case may turn out to be. The present case, where counsel was denied petitioners on appeal, shows that the discrimination is not between "possibly good and obviously bad cases," but between cases where the rich man can require the court to listen to argument of counsel before deciding on the merits, but a poor man cannot. There is lacking that equality demanded by the Fourteenth Amendment where the rich man, who appeals as of right, enjoys the benefit of counsel's examination into the record, research of the law, and marshalling of arguments on his behalf, while the indigent, already burdened by a preliminary determination that his case is without merit, is forced to shift for himself. The indigent, where the record is unclear or the errors are hidden, has only the right to a meaningless ritual, while the rich man has a meaningful appeal.

We vacate the judgment of the District Court of Appeal and remand the case to that court for further proceedings not inconsistent with this opinion. It is so ordered.

[Justices Clark, Harlan, and Stewart dissented.]

NOTES AND QUESTIONS

1. The Court says almost nothing about the California District Court of Appeal's conclusion, under the "independent investigation" mandated by the state's procedural rule, that "it had 'gone through' the record and had come to the conclusion that 'no good whatever could be served by appointment of counsel.'" Why doesn't the Court address this conclusion? Are the circumstances of the case irrelevant? Regardless of the Court's silence on this point, is there anything about the facts in *Douglas* that make it a compelling vehicle for the Court to find a right to appointed appellate counsel?

2. Why is the Court so skeptical of the California appellate appointment procedure at issue? After all, it appears as if the same judges who would review the record to determine whether counsel should be appointed would be the decision makers in any appeal. Would

740 Chapter VIII Right to Counsel and the Defense Function

the result here be different if the screening process were used to determine whether an appeal could be taken at all, rather than whether counsel should be appointed? Recall that states have no constitutional obligation to provide for appellate review. *McKane v. Durston*, 153 U.S. 684 (1894).

3. Is the Court's point about the "barren record" persuasive? Aren't all appeals confined to the content of the record, barren or not? If an appeal has only "hidden merit," might that mean those meritorious issues have not been preserved?

4. Is the result in *Douglas* dictated by *Gideon*? Put differently, is there anything fundamentally different about the roles of trial counsel and appellate counsel?

Argersinger v. Hamlin
407 U.S. 25 (1972)

Mr. Justice DOUGLAS delivered the opinion of the Court.

Petitioner, and indigent, was charged in Florida with carrying a concealed weapon, an offense punishable by imprisonment up to six months, a $1,000 fine, or both. The trial was to a judge, and petitioner was unrepresented by counsel. He was sentenced to serve 90 days in jail, and brought this habeas corpus action in the Florida Supreme Court, alleging that, being deprived of his right to counsel, he was unable as an indigent layman properly to raise and present to the trial court good and sufficient defenses to the charge for which he stands convicted. The Florida Supreme Court by a four-to-three decision, in ruling on the right to counsel, followed the line we marked out in *Duncan v. Louisiana*, as respects the right to trial by jury and held that the right to court-appointed counsel extends only to trials "for non-petty offenses punishable by more than six months imprisonment."

The case is here on a petition for certiorari, which we granted. We reverse.

The Sixth Amendment, which in enumerated situations has been made applicable to the States by reason of the Fourteenth, provides specified standards for "all criminal prosecutions."

One is the requirement of a "public trial." *In re Oliver, supra*, held that the right to a "public trial" was applicable to a state proceeding even though only a 60-day sentence was involved.

Another guarantee is the right to be informed of the nature and cause of the accusation. Still another, the right of confrontation. *Pointer v. Texas, supra*. And another, compulsory process for obtaining witnesses in one's favor. *Washington v. Texas, supra*. We have never limited these rights to felonies or to lesser but serious offenses.

In *Washington v. Texas, supra*, we said, "We have held that due process requires that the accused have the assistance of counsel for his defense, that he be confronted with the witnesses against him, and that he have the right to a speedy and public trial." Respecting the right to a speedy and public trial, the right to be informed of the nature and cause of the accusation, the right to confront and cross-examine witnesses, the right to compulsory process for obtaining witnesses, it was recently stated, "It is simply not arguable, nor has any court ever held, that the trial of a petty offense may be held in secret, or without notice to the accused of the charges, or that in such cases the defendant has no right to confront his accusers or to compel the attendance of witnesses in his own behalf."

District of Columbia v. Clawans illustrates the point. There, the offense was engaging without a license in the business of dealing in second-hand property, an offense punishable by a fine of $300 or imprisonment for not more than 90 days. The Court held that the offense was a "petty" one and could be tried without a jury. But the conviction was reversed and a new trial ordered, because the trial court had prejudicially restricted the right of cross-examination, a right guaranteed by the Sixth Amendment.

The right to trial by jury, also guaranteed by the Sixth Amendment by reason of the Fourteenth, was limited by *Duncan v. Louisiana, supra,* to trials where the potential punishment was imprisonment for six months or more. But the right to trial by jury has a different genealogy and is brigaded with a system of trial to a judge alone. As stated in *Duncan*:

> Providing an accused with the right to be tried by a jury of his peers gave him an inestimable safeguard against the corrupt or overzealous prosecutor and against the complaint, biased, or eccentric judge. If the defendant preferred the common-sense judgment of a jury to the more tutored but perhaps less sympathetic reaction of the single judge, he was to have it. Beyond this, the jury trial provisions in the Federal and State Constitutions reflect a fundamental decision about the exercise of official power—a reluctance to entrust plenary powers over the life and liberty of the citizen to one judge or to a group of judges. Fear of unchecked power, so typical of our State and Federal Governments in other respects, found expression in the criminal law in this insistence upon community participation in the determination of guilt or innocence. The deep commitment of the Nation to the right of jury trial in serious criminal cases as a defense against arbitrary law enforcement qualifies for protection under the Due Process Clause of the Fourteenth Amendment, and must therefore be respected by the States.

While there is historical support for limiting the "deep commitment" to trial by jury to "serious criminal cases," there is no such support for a similar limitation on the right to assistance of counsel:

> Originally, in England, a person charged with treason or felony was denied the aid of counsel, except in respect of legal questions which the accused himself might suggest. At the same time parties in civil cases and persons accused of misdemeanors were entitled to the full assistance of counsel. . . .
>
> (It) appears that in at least twelve of the thirteen colonies the rule of the English common law, in the respect now under consideration, had been definitely rejected and the right to counsel fully recognized in all criminal prosecutions, save that in one or two instances the right was limited to capital offenses or to the more serious crimes. . . .

The Sixth Amendment thus extended the right to counsel beyond its common-law dimensions. But there is nothing in the language of the Amendment, its history, or in the decisions of this Court, to indicate that it was intended to embody a retraction of the right in petty offenses wherein the common law previously did require that counsel be provided.

We reject, therefore, the premise that since prosecutions for crimes punishable by imprisonment for less than six months may be tried without a jury, they may also be tried without a lawyer.

The assistance of counsel is often a requisite to the very existence of a fair trial. The Court in *Powell v. Alabama*—a capital case—said:

> The right to be heard would be, in many cases, of little avail if it did not comprehend the right to be heard by counsel. Even the intelligent and educated layman has small and sometimes no skill in the science of law. If charged with crime, he is incapable, generally, of determining for himself whether the indictment is good or bad. He is unfamiliar with the rules of evidence. Left without the aid of counsel he may be put on trial without a proper charge, and convicted upon incompetent evidence, or evidence irrelevant to the issue or otherwise inadmissible. He lacks both the skill and knowledge adequately to prepare his defense, even though he have a perfect one. He requires the guiding hand of counsel at every step in the proceedings against him. Without it, though he be not guilty, he faces the danger of conviction because he does not know how to establish his innocence. If that be true of men of intelligence, how much more true is it of the ignorant and illiterate, or those of feeble intellect.

Chapter VIII Right to Counsel and the Defense Function

In *Gideon* we dealt with a felony trial. But we did not so limit the need of the accused for a lawyer. We said:

> (I)n our adversary system of criminal justice, any person haled into court, who is too poor to hire a lawyer, cannot be assured a fair trial unless counsel is provided for him. This seems to us to be an obvious truth. Governments, both state and federal, quite properly spend vast sums of money to establish machinery to try defendants accused of crime. Lawyers to prosecute are everywhere deemed essential to protect the public's interest in an orderly society. Similarly, there are few defendants charged with crime, few indeed, who fail to hire the best lawyers they can get to prepare and present their defenses. That government hires lawyers to prosecute and defendants who have the money hire lawyers to defend are the strongest indications of the widespread belief that lawyers in criminal courts are necessities, not luxuries. The right of one charged with crime to counsel may not be deemed fundamental and essential to fair trials in some countries, but it is in ours. From the very beginning, our state and national constitutions and laws have laid great emphasis on procedural and substantive safeguards designed to assure fair trials before impartial tribunals in which every defendant stands equal before the law. This noble ideal cannot be realized if the poor man charged with crime has to face his accusers without a lawyer to assist him.

Both *Powell* and *Gideon* involved felonies. But their rationale has relevance to any criminal trial, where an accused is deprived of his liberty. *Powell* and *Gideon* suggest that there are certain fundamental rights applicable to all such criminal prosecutions, even those, such as *In re Oliver, supra*, where the penalty is 60 days' imprisonment:

> A person's right to reasonable notice of a charge against him, and an opportunity to be heard in his defense — a right to his day in court — are basic in our system of jurisprudence; and these rights include, as a minimum, a right to examine the witnesses against him, to offer testimony, and to be represented by counsel.

The requirement of counsel may well be necessary for a fair trial even in a petty-offense prosecution. We are by no means convinced that legal and constitutional questions involved in a case that actually leads to imprisonment even for a brief period are any less complex than when a person can be sent off for six months or more.

The trial of vagrancy cases is illustrative. While only brief sentences of imprisonment may be imposed, the cases often bristle with thorny constitutional questions. *See Papachristou.*

In re Gault dealt with juvenile delinquency and an offense which, if committed by an adult, would have carried a fine of $5 to $50 or imprisonment in jail for not more than two months, but which when committed by a juvenile might lead to his detention in a state institution until he reached the age of 21. We said that "(t)he juvenile needs the assistance of counsel to cope with problems of law, to make skilled inquiry into the facts, to insist upon regularity of the proceedings, and to ascertain whether he has a defense and to prepare and submit it. The child 'requires the guiding hand of counsel at every step in the proceedings against him,' citing *Powell v. Alabama*. The premise of *Gault* is that even in prosecutions for offenses less serious than felonies, a fair trial may require the presence of a lawyer."

Beyond the problem of trials and appeals is that of the guilty plea, a problem which looms large in misdemeanor as well as in felony cases. Counsel is needed so that the accused may know precisely what he is doing, so that he is fully aware of the prospect of going to jail or prison, and so that he is treated fairly by the prosecution.

In addition, the volume of misdemeanor cases, far greater in number than felony prosecutions, may create an obsession for speedy dispositions, regardless of the fairness of the result. The Report by the President's Commission on Law Enforcement and Administration of Justice, The Challenge of Crime in a Free Society 128 (1967), states:

> For example, until legislation last year increased the number of judges, the District of Columbia Court of General Sessions had four judges to process the preliminary stages of more than 1,500

felony cases, 7,500 serious misdemeanor cases, and 38,000 petty offenses and an equal number of traffic offenses per year. An inevitable consequence of volume that large is the almost total preoccupation in such a court with the movement of cases. The calendar is long, speed often is substituted for care, and casually arranged out-of-court compromise too often is substituted for adjudication. Inadequate attention tends to be given to the individual defendant, whether in protecting his rights, sifting the facts at trial, deciding the social risk he presents, or determining how to deal with him after conviction. The frequent result is futility and failure. As Dean Edward Barrett recently observed:

> Wherever the visitor looks at the system, he finds great numbers of defendants being processed by harassed and overworked officials. Police have more cases than they can investigate. Prosecutors walk into courtrooms to try simple cases as they take their initial looks at the files. Defense lawyers appear having had no more than time for hasty conversations with their clients. Judges face long calendars with the certain knowledge that their calendars tomorrow and the next day will be, if anything longer, and so there is no choice but to dispose of the cases.
>
> Suddenly it becomes clear that for most defendants in the criminal process, there is scant regard for them as individuals. They are numbers on dockets, faceless ones to be processed and sent on their way. The gap between the theory and the reality is enormous.
>
> Very little such observation of the administration of criminal justice in operation is required to reach the conclusion that it suffers from basic ills.

That picture is seen in almost every report. "The misdemeanor trial is characterized by insufficient and frequently irresponsible preparation on the part of the defense, the prosecution, and the court. Everything is rush, rush."

There is evidence of the prejudice which results to misdemeanor defendants from this "assembly-line justice." One study concluded that "(m)isdemeanants represented by attorneys are five times as likely to emerge from police court with all charges dismissed as are defendants who face similar charges without counsel."

We must conclude, therefore, that the problems associated with misdemeanor and petty offenses often require the presence of counsel to insure the accused a fair trial. Mr. Justice Powell suggests that these problems are raised even in situations where there is no prospect of imprisonment. We need not consider the requirements of the Sixth Amendment as regards the right to counsel where loss of liberty is not involved, however, for here petitioner was in fact sentenced to jail. And, as we said in *Baldwin v. New York*, "the prospect of imprisonment for however short a time will seldom be viewed by the accused as a trivial or 'petty' matter and may well result in quite serious repercussions affecting his career and his reputation."

We hold, therefore, that absent a knowing and intelligent waiver, no person may be imprisoned for any offense, whether classified as petty, misdemeanor, or felony, unless he was represented by counsel at his trial.

We do not sit as an ombudsman to direct state courts how to manage their affairs but only to make clear the federal constitutional requirement. How crimes should be classified is largely a state matter. The fact that traffic charges technically fall within the category of "criminal prosecutions" does not necessarily mean that many of them will be brought into the class where imprisonment actually occurs.

The American Bar Association Project on Standards for Criminal Justice states:

> As a matter of sound judicial administration it is preferable to disregard the characterization of the offense as felony, misdemeanor or traffic offense. Nor is it adequate to require the provision of defense services for all offenses which carry a sentence to jail or prison. Often, as a practical matter, such sentences are rarely if ever imposed for certain types of offenses, so that for all intents and purposes the punishment they carry is at most a fine. Thus, the standard seeks to distinguish those classes of cases in which there is real likelihood that incarceration may follow conviction from those types in which there is no such likelihood. It should be noted that the standard does not recommend a determination of the need for counsel in terms of the facts of

744 Chapter VIII Right to Counsel and the Defense Function

each particular case; it draws a categorical line at those types of offenses for which incarceration as a punishment is a practical possibility.

Under the rule we announce today, every judge will know when the trial of a misdemeanor starts that no imprisonment may be imposed, even though local law permits it, unless the accused is represented by counsel. He will have a measure of the seriousness and gravity of the offense and therefore know when to name a lawyer to represent the accused before the trial starts.

The run of misdemeanors will not be affected by today's ruling. But in those that end up in the actual deprivation of a person's liberty, the accused will receive the benefit of "the guiding hand of counsel" so necessary when one's liberty is in jeopardy.

Reversed.

NOTES AND QUESTIONS

1. The Florida Supreme Court in *Argersinger* had interpreted *Gideon* as only requiring the appointment of counsel in "trials of non-petty offenses punishable by more than six months' imprisonment," *id.* at 26, reasoning from the Supreme Court's holding in *Duncan v. Louisiana*, 381 U.S. 45, 159 (1968), *see* Chapter XIII *infra*, that the Sixth Amendment only requires jury trials for this category of offenses. The Supreme Court rejects this analogy, contrasting the jury trial right with other Sixth Amendment rights such as the right to confront witnesses, the right to notice of the charges, the right to compulsory process, and the right to a speedy and public trial. Although the Court notes that there is "historical support" for limiting the jury trial right to "serious" crimes, are there also meaningful distinctions between the jury trial right and the other Sixth Amendment rights the Court acknowledges? Are these rights equally "essential to a fair trial"?

2. The Court finally seems willing to recognize that the "complexity" of a case — and hence the need for counsel — does not necessarily depend on the statutorily permissible term of imprisonment. 407 U.S. at 33. Indeed the "complexity" of a case will most often turn not on the essential nature of the charge or the authorized prison term but on such purely factual issues as, for example, the vulnerability of the state's witnesses to cross-examination. Having said this, the Court picks an excellent lead example to make this point, namely, vagrancy prosecutions, where the penalties are comparatively small but the level of sophistication needed for a defense is large, given the constitutional vulnerability of such statutes. See Chapter II *supra*. How could even an educated layman try to defend against a prosecution under the vagrancy statute at issue in *Papachristou v. Jacksonville*, 405 U.S. 156 (1972), decided just two years before *Argersinger*?

3. *Argersinger* is one of the earliest Supreme Court cases to acknowledge the "mill" aspect of the criminal justice system, which it calls "assembly line justice," in which an enormous volume of low-level criminal cases are resolved, many by guilty pleas, under a system that lacks the capacity for reflective disposition. Why do these systemic factors make the need for appointed counsel for misdemeanors even more acute? How might the lack of criminal defense expertise of appointed counsel exacerbate this problem?

4. In defining the contours of the *Gideon* right, the Court draws the line at imprisonment, regardless of how a state chooses to classify crimes, holding that the appointment of counsel is required wherever defendant faces the prospect of imprisonment. 407 U.S. at 37. It is undeniable that a bright line appears to exist between imprisonment and other sanctions, and that a bright line is needed in this context. Are there any other places where a reasonable line of universal applicability could be drawn? Solely from a feasibility perspective, what would the advantages be of limiting the *Gideon* right to felonies?

A. Scope of the Right to Counsel 745

5. The Court trumpets the administrative feasibility of its rule: "Under the rule we announce today, every judge will know when the trial of a misdemeanor starts that no imprisonment may be imposed, even though local law permits it, unless the accused is represented by counsel." Is this as easy as it sounds? How is the determination of whether a defendant faces the "prospect of imprisonment" to be made? When will it be made? And, perhaps more importantly, who is to make that determination? The court? The prosecutor? What information will be available to the prosecutor and the court at the time that this determination needs to be made? Note the Court's observation that in the maw of "assembly line justice" there is pressure not just on defendants and their counsel but also on prosecutors, who may "walk into courtrooms to try simple cases as they take their initial looks at the file." *Id.* at 35.

6. In a concurring opinion Justice Brennan suggests that the inevitable drain on legal resources occasioned by *Argersinger* can be alleviated in part by the use of supervised law students in clinical programs as a source of legal representation for indigent defendants. *Id.* at 44. Do you agree? What amount of training and supervision do you believe would be necessary for law students to take primary responsibility for handling a criminal case?

7. In another concurring opinion Justice Powell notes the sometimes debilitating non-imprisonment consequences of a criminal conviction, such as the effect of a criminal record on employment opportunity, moral stigma, or the loss of a driver's license. *See, e.g.*, Michelle Alexander, The New Jim Crow xxvii-xxviii (2012) (pointing out the non-imprisonment consequences of mass incarceration). Accordingly, or perhaps regardless, Justice Powell proposes that the right to appointed counsel in petty-offense cases be determined by the trial court on a case-by-case basis, considering factors such as the complexity of the charge, the likely sentence, and "individual factors" relevant to the case (such as the capability of the defendant and the significance of collateral consequences), and with the judge playing an active oversight role when defendants are unrepresented. What are the pros and cons of such an individualized approach? Does such an approach seem administratively feasible? What sort of a colloquy with the defendant would the judge need to undertake to make this determination?

Alabama v. Shelton
535 U.S. 654 (2002)

Justice GINSBURG delivered the opinion of the Court.

This case concerns the Sixth Amendment right of an indigent defendant charged with a misdemeanor punishable by imprisonment, fine, or both, to the assistance of court-appointed counsel. Two prior decisions control the Court's judgment. First, in *Argersinger* this Court held that defense counsel must be appointed in any criminal prosecution whether classified as petty, misdemeanor, or felony, that actually leads to imprisonment even for a brief period. Later, in *Scott v. Illinois* (1979), the Court drew the line at "actual imprisonment," holding that counsel need not be appointed when the defendant is fined for the charged crime, but is not sentenced to a term of imprisonment.

Defendant-respondent LeReed Shelton, convicted of third-degree assault, was sentenced to a jail term of 30 days, which the trial court immediately suspended, placing Shelton on probation for two years. The question presented is whether the Sixth Amendment right to appointed counsel, as delineated in *Argersinger* and *Scott*, applies to a defendant in Shelton's situation. We hold that a suspended sentence that may "end up in the actual deprivation of a person's liberty" may not be imposed unless the defendant was accorded "the guiding hand of counsel" in the prosecution for the crime charged.

I

After representing himself at a bench trial in the District Court of Etowah County, Alabama, Shelton was convicted of third-degree assault, a class A misdemeanor carrying a maximum punishment of one year imprisonment and a $2,000 fine. He invoked his right to a new trial before a jury in Circuit Court, where he again appeared without a lawyer and was again convicted. The court repeatedly warned Shelton about the problems self-representation entailed, but at no time offered him assistance of counsel at state expense.

The Circuit Court sentenced Shelton to serve 30 days in the county prison. As authorized by Alabama law, the court suspended that sentence and placed Shelton on two years' unsupervised probation.

• • •

Applying the "actual imprisonment" rule to the case before us, we take up first the question we asked amicus to address: Where the State provides no counsel to an indigent defendant, does the Sixth Amendment permit activation of a suspended sentence upon the defendant's violation of the terms of probation? We conclude that it does not. A suspended sentence is a prison term imposed for the offense of conviction. Once the prison term is triggered, the defendant is incarcerated not for the probation violation, but for the underlying offense. The uncounseled conviction at that point "result[s] in imprisonment"; it "end[s] up in the actual deprivation of a person's liberty." This is precisely what the Sixth Amendment does not allow.

Amicus resists this reasoning primarily on two grounds. First, he attempts to align this case with our decisions in *Nichols* and *Gagnon v. Scarpelli*. We conclude that Shelton's case is not properly bracketed with those dispositions.

Nichols presented the question whether the Sixth Amendment barred consideration of a defendant's prior uncounseled misdemeanor conviction in determining his sentence for a subsequent felony offense. Nichols pleaded guilty to federal felony drug charges. Several years earlier, unrepresented by counsel, he was fined but not incarcerated for the state misdemeanor of driving under the influence (DUI). Including the DUI conviction in the federal Sentencing Guidelines calculation allowed the trial court to impose a sentence for the felony drug conviction "25 months longer than if the misdemeanor conviction had not been considered." We upheld this result, concluding that "an uncounseled misdemeanor conviction, valid under Scott because no prison term was imposed, is also valid when used to enhance punishment at a subsequent conviction." In *Gagnon*, the question was whether the defendant, who was placed on probation pursuant to a suspended sentence for armed robbery, had a due process right to representation by appointed counsel at a probation revocation hearing. We held that counsel was not invariably required in parole or probation revocation proceedings; we directed, instead, a "case-by-case approach" turning on the character of the issues involved.

Gagnon and *Nichols* do not stand for the broad proposition amicus would extract from them. The dispositive factor in those cases was not whether incarceration occurred immediately or only after some delay. Rather, the critical point was that the defendant had a recognized right to counsel when adjudicated guilty of the felony offense for which he was imprisoned. Unlike this case, in which revocation of probation would trigger a prison term imposed for a misdemeanor of which Shelton was found guilty without the aid of counsel, the sentences imposed in *Nichols* and *Gagnon* were for felony convictions—a federal drug conviction in *Nichols*, and a state armed robbery conviction in *Gagnon*—for which the right to counsel is unquestioned.

Amicus also contends that "practical considerations clearly weigh against" the extension of the Sixth Amendment appointed-counsel right to a defendant in Shelton's situation. He cites figures suggesting that although conditional sentences are commonly imposed, they are rarely activated. Based on these estimations, amicus argues that a rule requiring appointed counsel in every case involving a suspended sentence would unduly hamper the States' attempts to impose effective probationary punishment. A more "workable solution," he contends, would permit imposition of a suspended sentence on an uncounseled defendant and require appointment of counsel, if at all, only at the probation revocation stage, when incarceration is imminent.

Amicus observes that probation is "now a critical tool of law enforcement in low level cases." Even so, it does not follow that preservation of that tool warrants the reduction of the Sixth Amendment's domain that would result from the regime amicus hypothesizes. Amicus does not describe the contours of the hearing that, he suggests, might precede revocation of a term of probation imposed on an uncounseled defendant. In Alabama, however, the character of the probation revocation hearing currently afforded is not in doubt. The proceeding is an "informal" one, at which the defendant has no right to counsel, and the court no obligation to observe customary rules of evidence.

More significant, the sole issue at the hearing — apart from determinations about the necessity of confinement — is whether the defendant breached the terms of probation. The validity or reliability of the underlying conviction is beyond attack.

We think it plain that a hearing so timed and structured cannot compensate for the absence of trial counsel, for it does not even address the key Sixth Amendment inquiry: whether the adjudication of guilt corresponding to the prison sentence is sufficiently reliable to permit incarceration. Deprived of counsel when tried, convicted, and sentenced, and unable to challenge the original judgment at a subsequent probation revocation hearing, a defendant in Shelton's circumstances faces incarceration on a conviction that has never been subjected to "the crucible of meaningful adversarial testing." The Sixth Amendment does not countenance this result.

In a variation on amicus' position, the dissent would limit review in this case to the question whether the imposition of Shelton's suspended sentence required appointment of counsel, answering that question "plainly no" because such a step "does not deprive a defendant of his personal liberty." Only if the sentence is later activated, the dissent contends, need the Court "ask whether the procedural safeguards attending the imposition of [Shelton's] sentence comply with the Constitution."

Severing the analysis in this manner makes little sense. One cannot assess the constitutionality of imposing a suspended sentence while simultaneously walling off the procedures that will precede its activation. The dissent imagines a set of safeguards Alabama might provide at the probation revocation stage sufficient to cure its failure to appoint counsel prior to sentencing, including, perhaps, "complete retrial of the misdemeanor violation with assistance of counsel." But there is no cause for speculation about Alabama's procedures; they are established by Alabama statute and decisional law, and they bear no resemblance to those the dissent invents in its effort to sanction the prospect of Shelton's imprisonment on an uncounseled conviction. Assessing the issue before us in light of actual circumstances, we do not comprehend how the procedures Alabama in fact provides at the probation revocation hearing could bring Shelton's sentence within constitutional bounds.

Nor do we agree with amicus or the dissent that our holding will "substantially limit the states' ability" to impose probation. Most jurisdictions already provide a state-law right to appointed counsel more generous than that afforded by the Federal Constitution. All but 16 States, for example, would provide counsel to a defendant in Shelton's circumstances, either because he received a substantial fine or because state law authorized incarceration for the charged offense or provided for a maximum prison term of one year. There is thus scant reason to believe that a rule conditioning imposition of a suspended sentence on provision of appointed counsel would affect existing practice in the large majority of the States. And

Chapter VIII Right to Counsel and the Defense Function

given the current commitment of most jurisdictions to affording court-appointed counsel to indigent misdemeanants while simultaneously preserving the option of probationary punishment, we do not share amicus' concern that other States may lack the capacity and resources to do the same.

Moreover, even if amicus is correct that "some courts and jurisdictions at least [can]not bear" the costs of the rule we confirm today, those States need not abandon probation or equivalent measures as viable forms of punishment. Although they may not attach probation to an imposed and suspended prison sentence, States unable or unwilling routinely to provide appointed counsel to misdemeanants in Shelton's situation are not without recourse to another option capable of yielding a similar result.

That option is pretrial probation, employed in some form by at least 23 States. Under such an arrangement, the prosecutor and defendant agree to the defendant's participation in a pretrial rehabilitation program, which includes conditions typical of post-trial probation. The adjudication of guilt and imposition of sentence for the underlying offense then occur only if and when the defendant breaches those conditions.

Like the regime urged by amicus, this system reserves the appointed-counsel requirement for the "small percentage" of cases in which incarceration proves necessary, thus allowing a State to "supervise a course of rehabilitation" without providing a lawyer every time it wishes to pursue such a course. Unlike amicus' position, however, pretrial probation also respects the constitutional imperative that "no person may be imprisoned for any offense . . . unless he was represented by counsel at his trial."

* * *

Satisfied that Shelton is entitled to appointed counsel at the critical stage when his guilt or innocence of the charged crime is decided and his vulnerability to imprisonment is determined, we affirm the judgment of the Supreme Court of Alabama.

It is so ordered.

[Justices Scalia, Kennedy, and Thomas and the Chief Justice dissented.]

NOTES AND QUESTIONS

1. The Court notes that the Alabama probation revocation proceeding that could result in the imposition of a suspended sentence is informal, with no right to counsel and no obligation to observe the rules of evidence; that the sole issue in such a hearing is whether defendant violated a term of his probation; and that there is no opportunity to collaterally attack the underlying offense of conviction. *Id.* at 667. These procedures are by no means unusual. The Supreme Court has held that parole and probation revocation hearings are not "criminal proceedings," and require only minimal due process requirements such as a preliminary hearing, notice of the alleged violations, disclosure of evidence, and an opportunity to be heard and cross-examine the government's witnesses. *Morrissey v. Brewer*, 408 U.S. 471 (1972).

2. The amicus and dissent claim the Court's decision will make the use of suspended sentences prohibitively expensive for states inasmuch as judges will henceforth be unable to impose a suspended sentence without appointing counsel for a defendant. Amicus also speculates that "hundreds of thousands" of defendants receive suspended sentences but that only "thousands" are incarcerated on those sentences pursuant to a probation revocation. The Court suggests that a state could avoid these problems by the use of "pretrial probation" as an alternative measure. 535 U.S. at 671. What are the pros and cons of this alternative, as it is explained by the Court? How else could a state modify its procedures to avoid the financial and administrative burden of appointing counsel in cases where suspended sentences might be imposed? Why might a defendant resolving a case through a plea agreement that includes a term of probation and a suspended sentence be in special need of legal advice?

3. To what extent does *Shelton* effectively extend *Argersinger* to the "authorized imprisonment" standard? In other words, after *Shelton*, what category of defendants remains that will not need appointed counsel from the outset?

4. Amicus argues that only proceedings that result in "immediate actual imprisonment" require appointment of counsel, and points to *Gagnon v. Scarpelli*, 411 U.S. 778 (1973), where the Court held that there is no absolute right to appointed counsel at a probation revocation hearing, even where imprisonment could result, but rather that appointment should be decided on a case-by-case basis. The Court finds *Gagnon* inapt because in that case defendant was represented at the trial of his underlying bank robbery charge and thus when his probation was revoked he was imprisoned "for that offense," that is, the bank robbery. Is this distinction satisfactory? Are *Gagnon* and *Argersinger* inconsistent?

5. The dissent describes the burden the Court's decision imposes on states as "not only the cost of providing state-paid counsel in cases of such insignificance that even financially prosperous defendants sometimes forego the expense of hired counsel, but also the cost of enabling courts and prosecutors to respond to the 'over-lawyering' of even minor cases."

Does the dissent's position account for the realities of probationary sentences? Where, as in *Shelton*, a probation violation can lead directly to imprisonment in the event of a violation of the terms of probation, can a vigorous defense on the underlying charge fairly be considered "over-lawyering"?

B. CONSEQUENCES OF REPRESENTATION BY COUNSEL

The cases in the previous section all dealt with the scope of the Sixth Amendment right to counsel in the trial or appellate context. The Supreme Court has consistently held since 1972 that a defendant's Sixth Amendment right to counsel "does not attach" — that is, come into existence — "until a prosecution is commenced." *Rothgery v. Gillespie Cnty.*, 554 U.S. 191, 198 (2008). A prosecution commences only upon "the initiation of adversary proceedings — whether by way of formal charge, preliminary hearing, indictment, information, or arraignment." *Id.* (quoting *United States v. Gouveia*, 467 U.S. 180, 188 (1984)).

In a trio of cases — one of which was retroactively deemed to be only a Fifth Amendment and not a Sixth Amendment case, *see Escobedo v. Illinois*, 378 U.S. 478 (1964), Chapter IV *supra* — the Court considered what it means for a defendant to be represented by counsel.

The second of these cases was *Massiah v. United States*, 377 U.S. 201 (1964), which is a Sixth Amendment case that is reproduced in full in Chapter III inasmuch as its focus is on the right to counsel in the context of an interrogation. Massiah was indicted along with an alleged conspirator for narcotics offenses. *Id.* at 202. A retained lawyer appeared for Massiah at the arraignment. *Id.* Subsequently, Massiah's codefendant, unbeknownst to Massiah, began cooperating with the government. *Id.* In connection with that cooperation, the codefendant lured Massiah to his automobile where a radio transmitter had been installed. *Id.* at 203. Massiah ultimately made incriminating statements that were listened to by a government agent stationed nearby who was equipped with a receiving device. *Id.* The statements were introduced at trial and Massiah was convicted. *Id.*

The Supreme Court held that the statements should have been suppressed as violations of the Sixth Amendment. It stated that "under our system of justice the most elemental concepts of due process contemplate that an indictment be followed by a trial, 'in an orderly courtroom, presided over by a judge, open to the public, and protected by all the procedural

750 Chapter VIII Right to Counsel and the Defense Function

safeguards of the law.'" *Id.* at 204 (citing and quoting from *Spano v. New York*, 360 U.S. 315, 327 (1959), *see* Chapter III *supra*).

In reading the next case, consider not only the right to counsel but also the meaning of "interrogation" under the *Miranda* line of cases.

Brewer v. Williams
430 U.S. 387 (1977)

Mr. Justice STEWART delivered the opinion of the Court.

An Iowa trial jury found the respondent, Robert Williams, guilty of murder. The judgment of conviction was affirmed in the Iowa Supreme Court by a closely divided vote. In a subsequent habeas corpus proceeding a Federal District Court ruled that under the United States Constitution Williams is entitled to a new trial, and a divided Court of Appeals for the Eighth Circuit agreed. The question before us is whether the District Court and the Court of Appeals were wrong.

I

On the afternoon of December 24, 1968, a 10-year-old girl named Pamela Powers went with her family to the YMCA in Des Moines, Iowa, to watch a wrestling tournament in which her brother was participating. When she failed to return from a trip to the washroom, a search for her began. The search was unsuccessful.

Robert Williams, who had recently escaped from a mental hospital, was a resident of the YMCA. Soon after the girl's disappearance Williams was seen in the YMCA lobby carrying some clothing and a large bundle wrapped in a blanket. He obtained help from a 14-year-old boy in opening the street door of the YMCA and the door to his automobile parked outside. When Williams placed the bundle in the front seat of his car the boy "saw two legs in it and they were skinny and white." Before anyone could see what was in the bundle Williams drove away. His abandoned car was found the following day in Davenport, Iowa, roughly 160 miles east of Des Moines. A warrant was then issued in Des Moines for his arrest on a charge of abduction.

On the morning of December 26, a Des Moines lawyer named Henry McKnight went to the Des Moines police station and informed the officers present that he had just received a long-distance call from Williams, and that he had advised Williams to turn himself in to the Davenport police. Williams did surrender that morning to the police in Davenport, and they booked him on the charge specified in the arrest warrant and gave him the warnings required by *Miranda*. The Davenport police then telephoned their counterparts in Des Moines to inform them that Williams had surrendered. McKnight, the lawyer, was still at the Des Moines police headquarters, and Williams conversed with McKnight on the telephone. In the presence of the Des Moines chief of police and a police detective named Leaming, McKnight advised Williams that Des Moines police officers would be driving to Davenport to pick him up, that the officers would not interrogate him or mistreat him, and that Williams was not to talk to the officers about Pamela Powers until after consulting with McKnight upon his return to Des Moines. As a result of these conversations, it was agreed between McKnight and the Des Moines police officials that Detective Leaming and a fellow officer would drive to Davenport to pick up Williams, that they would bring him directly back to Des Moines, and that they would not question him during the trip.

In the meantime Williams was arraigned before a judge in Davenport on the outstanding arrest warrant. The judge advised him of his *Miranda* rights and committed him to jail.

B. Consequences of Representation by Counsel   751

Before leaving the courtroom, Williams conferred with a lawyer named Kelly, who advised him not to make any statements until consulting with McKnight back in Des Moines.

Detective Leaming and his fellow officer arrived in Davenport about noon to pick up Williams and return him to Des Moines. Soon after their arrival they met with Williams and Kelly, who, they understood, was acting as Williams' lawyer. Detective Leaming repeated the *Miranda* warnings, and told Williams:

> (W)e both know that you're being represented here by Mr. Kelly and you're being represented by Mr. McKnight in Des Moines, and . . . I want you to remember this because we'll be visiting between here and Des Moines.

Williams then conferred again with Kelly alone, and after this conference Kelly reiterated to Detective Leaming that Williams was not to be questioned about the disappearance of Pamela Powers until after he had consulted with McKnight back in Des Moines. When Leaming expressed some reservations, Kelly firmly stated that the agreement with McKnight was to be carried out that there was to be no interrogation of Williams during the automobile journey to Des Moines. Kelly was denied permission to ride in the police car back to Des Moines with Williams and the two officers.

The two detectives, with Williams in their charge, then set out on the 160-mile drive. At no time during the trip did Williams express a willingness to be interrogated in the absence of an attorney. Instead, he stated several times that "(w)hen I get to Des Moines and see Mr. McKnight, I am going to tell you the whole story." Detective Leaming knew that Williams was a former mental patient, and knew also that he was deeply religious.

The detective and his prisoner soon embarked on a wide-ranging conversation covering a variety of topics, including the subject of religion. Then, not long after leaving Davenport and reaching the interstate highway, Detective Leaming delivered what has been referred to in the briefs and oral arguments as the "Christian burial speech." Addressing Williams as "Reverend," the detective said:

> I want to give you something to think about while we're traveling down the road. . . . Number one, I want you to observe the weather conditions, it's raining, it's sleeting, it's freezing, driving is very treacherous, visibility is poor, it's going to be dark early this evening. They are predicting several inches of snow for tonight, and I feel that you yourself are the only person that knows where this little girl's body is, that you yourself have only been there once, and if you get a snow on top of it you yourself may be unable to find it. And, since we will be going right past the area on the way into Des Moines, I feel that we could stop and locate the body, that the parents of this little girl should be entitled to a Christian burial for the little girl who was snatched away from them on Christmas (E)ve and murdered. And I feel we should stop and locate it on the way in rather than waiting until morning and trying to come back out after a snow storm and possibly not being able to find it at all.

Williams asked Detective Leaming why he thought their route to Des Moines would be taking them past the girl's body, and Leaming responded that he knew the body was in the area of Mitchellville a town they would be passing on the way to Des Moines. Leaming then stated: "I do not want you to answer me. I don't want to discuss it any further. Just think about it as we're riding down the road."

As the car approached Grinnell, a town approximately 100 miles west of Davenport, Williams asked whether the police had found the victim's shoes. When Detective Leaming replied that he was unsure, Williams directed the officers to a service station where he said he had left the shoes; a search for them proved unsuccessful. As they continued towards Des Moines, Williams asked whether the police had found the blanket, and directed the officers to a rest area where he said he had disposed of the blanket. Nothing was found. The car continued towards Des Moines, and as it approached Mitchellville, Williams said that he

752 Chapter VIII Right to Counsel and the Defense Function

would show the officers where the body was. He then directed the police to the body of Pamela Powers.

Williams was indicted for first-degree murder. Before trial, his counsel moved to suppress all evidence relating to or resulting from any statements Williams had made during the automobile ride from Davenport to Des Moines. After an evidentiary hearing the trial judge denied the motion. He found that "an agreement was made between defense counsel and the police officials to the effect that the Defendant was not to be questioned on the return trip to Des Moines," and that the evidence in question had been elicited from Williams during "a critical stage in the proceedings requiring the presence of counsel on his request." The judge ruled, however, that Williams had "waived his right to have an attorney present during the giving of such information."

The evidence in question was introduced over counsel's continuing objection at the subsequent trial. The jury found Williams guilty of murder, and the judgment of conviction was affirmed by the Iowa Supreme Court, a bare majority of whose members agreed with the trial court that Williams had "waived his right to the presence of his counsel" on the automobile ride from Davenport to Des Moines. The four dissenting justices expressed the view that "when counsel and police have agreed defendant is not to be questioned until counsel is present and defendant has been advised not to talk and repeatedly has stated he will tell the whole story after he talks with counsel, the state should be required to make a stronger showing of intentional voluntary waiver than was made here."

Williams then petitioned for a writ of habeas corpus in the United States District Court for the Southern District of Iowa. Counsel for the State and for Williams stipulated that "the case would be submitted on the record of facts and proceedings in the trial court, without taking of further testimony." The District Court made findings of fact as summarized above, and concluded as a matter of law that the evidence in question had been wrongly admitted at Williams' trial.

• • •

[T]he judgment before us must in any event be affirmed upon the ground that Williams was deprived of a different constitutional right—the right to the assistance of counsel.

There can be no doubt in the present case that judicial proceedings had been initiated against Williams before the start of the automobile ride from Davenport to Des Moines. A warrant had been issued for his arrest, he had been arraigned on that warrant before a judge in a Davenport courtroom, and he had been committed by the court to confinement in jail. The State does not contend otherwise.

There can be no serious doubt, either, that Detective Leaming deliberately and designedly set out to elicit information from Williams just as surely as and perhaps more effectively than if he had formally interrogated him. Detective Leaming was fully aware before departing for Des Moines that Williams was being represented in Davenport by Kelly and in Des Moines by McKnight. Yet he purposely sought during Williams' isolation from his lawyers to obtain as much incriminating information as possible. Indeed, Detective Leaming conceded as much when he testified at Williams' trial:

> **Q.** In fact, Captain, whether he was a mental patient or not, you were trying to get all the information you could before he got to his lawyer, weren't you?
>
> **A.** I was sure hoping to find out where that little girl was, yes, sir.
>
> **Q.** Well, I'll put it this way: You was (sic) hoping to get all the information you could before Williams got back to McKnight, weren't you?
>
> **A.** Yes, sir.

The state courts clearly proceeded upon the hypothesis that Detective Leaming's "Christian burial speech" had been tantamount to interrogation. Both courts recognized that

Williams had been entitled to the assistance of counsel at the time he made the incriminating statements. Yet no such constitutional protection would have come into play if there had been no interrogation.

The circumstances of this case are thus constitutionally indistinguishable from those presented in *Massiah*. The petitioner in that case was indicted for violating the federal narcotics law. He retained a lawyer, pleaded not guilty, and was released on bail. While he was free on bail a federal agent succeeded by surreptitious means in listening to incriminating statements made by him. Evidence of these statements was introduced against the petitioner at his trial, and he was convicted. This Court reversed the conviction, holding "that the petitioner was denied the basic protections of that guarantee (the right to counsel) when there was used against him at his trial evidence of his own incriminating words, which federal agents had deliberately elicited from him after he had been indicted and in the absence of his counsel."

That the incriminating statements were elicited surreptitiously in the *Massiah* case, and otherwise here, is constitutionally irrelevant. Rather, the clear rule of *Massiah* is that once adversary proceedings have commenced against an individual, he has a right to legal representation when the government interrogates him. It thus requires no wooden or technical application of the *Massiah* doctrine to conclude that Williams was entitled to the assistance of counsel guaranteed to him by the Sixth and Fourteenth Amendments.

III

. . .

The District Court and the Court of Appeals were correct in the view that the question of waiver was not a question of historical fact, but one which, in the words of Mr. Justice Frankfurter, requires "application of constitutional principles to the facts as found. . . ."

The District Court and the Court of Appeals were also correct in their understanding of the proper standard to be applied in determining the question of waiver as a matter of federal constitutional law — that it was incumbent upon the State to prove "an intentional relinquishment or abandonment of a known right or privilege." That standard has been reiterated in many cases. We have said that the right to counsel does not depend upon a request by the defendant, and that courts indulge in every reasonable presumption against waiver. This strict standard applies equally to an alleged waiver of the right to counsel whether at trial or at a critical stage of pretrial proceedings.

We conclude, finally that the Court of Appeals was correct in holding that, judged by these standards, the record in this case falls far short of sustaining petitioner's burden. It is true that Williams had been informed of and appeared to understand his right to counsel. But waiver requires not merely comprehension but relinquishment, and Williams' consistent reliance upon the advice of counsel in dealing with the authorities refutes any suggestion that he waived that right. He consulted McKnight by long-distance telephone before turning himself in. He spoke with McKnight by telephone again shortly after being booked. After he was arraigned, Williams sought out and obtained legal advice from Kelly. Williams again consulted with Kelly after Detective Leaming and his fellow officer arrived in Davenport. Throughout, Williams was advised not to make any statements before seeing McKnight in Des Moines, and was assured that the police had agreed not to question him. His statements while in the car that he would tell the whole story after seeing McKnight in Des Moines were the clearest expressions by Williams himself that he desired the presence of an attorney before any interrogation took place. But even before making these statements, Williams had effectively asserted his right to counsel by having secured attorneys at both ends of the automobile trip, both of whom, acting as his agents, had made clear to the police that no interrogation

754   Chapter VIII Right to Counsel and the Defense Function

was to occur during the journey. Williams knew of that agreement and, particularly in view of his consistent reliance on counsel, there is no basis for concluding that he disavowed it.

Despite Williams' express and implicit assertions of his right to counsel, Detective Leaming proceeded to elicit incriminating statements from Williams. Leaming did not preface this effort by telling Williams that he had a right to the presence of a lawyer, and made no effort at all to ascertain whether Williams wished to relinquish that right. The circumstances of record in this case thus provide no reasonable basis for finding that Williams waived his right to the assistance of counsel.

The Court of Appeals did not hold, nor do we, that under the circumstances of this case Williams could not, without notice to counsel, have waived his rights under the Sixth and Fourteenth Amendments. It only held, as do we, that he did not.

IV

The crime of which Williams was convicted was senseless and brutal, calling for swift and energetic action by the police to apprehend the perpetrator and gather evidence with which he could be convicted. No mission of law enforcement officials is more important. Yet "(d)isinterested zeal for the public good does not assure either wisdom or right in the methods it pursues." Although we do not lightly affirm the issuance of a writ of habeas corpus in this case, so clear a violation of the Sixth and Fourteenth Amendments as here occurred cannot be condoned. The pressures on state executive and judicial officers charged with the administration of the criminal law are great, especially when the crime is murder and the victim a small child. But it is precisely the predictability of those pressures that makes imperative a resolute loyalty to the guarantees that the Constitution extends to us all.

The judgment of the Court of Appeals is affirmed.

It is so ordered.

Mr. Justice MARSHALL, concurring.

I concur wholeheartedly in my Brother Stewart's opinion for the Court, but add these words in light of the dissenting opinions filed today. The dissenters have, I believe, lost sight of the fundamental constitutional backbone of our criminal law. They seem to think that Detective Leaming's actions were perfectly proper, indeed laudable, examples of "good police work." In my view, good police work is something far different from catching the criminal at any price. It is equally important that the police, as guardians of the law, fulfill their responsibility to obey its commands scrupulously. For "in the end life and liberty can be as much endangered from illegal methods used to convict those thought to be criminals as from the actual criminals themselves." *Spano v. New York*.

In this case, there can be no doubt that Detective Leaming consciously and knowingly set out to violate Williams' Sixth Amendment right to counsel and his Fifth Amendment privilege against self-incrimination, as Leaming himself understood those rights. Leaming knew that Williams had been advised by two lawyers not to make any statements to police until he conferred in Des Moines with his attorney there, Mr. McKnight. Leaming surely understood, because he had overheard McKnight tell Williams as much, that the location of the body would be revealed to police. Undoubtedly Leaming realized the way in which that information would be conveyed to the police: McKnight would learn it from his client and then he would lead police to the body. Williams would thereby be protected by the attorney-client privilege from incriminating himself by directly demonstrating his knowledge of the body's location, and the unfortunate Powers child could be given a "Christian burial."

Of course, this scenario would accomplish all that Leaming sought from his investigation except that it would not produce incriminating statements or actions from Williams.

B. Consequences of Representation by Counsel 755

Accordingly, Leaming undertook his charade to pry such evidence from Williams. After invoking the no-passengers rule to prevent attorney Kelly from accompanying the prisoner, Leaming had Williams at his mercy: during the three- or four-hour trip he could do anything he wished to elicit a confession. The detective demonstrated once again "that the efficiency of the rack and the thumbscrew can be matched, given the proper subject by more sophisticated modes of 'persuasion.'"

Leaming knowingly isolated Williams from the protection of his lawyers and during that period he intentionally "persuaded" him to give incriminating evidence. It is this intentional police misconduct not good police practice that the Court rightly condemns. The heinous nature of the crime is no excuse, as the dissenters would have it, for condoning knowing and intentional police transgression of the constitutional rights of a defendant. If Williams is to go free and given the ingenuity of Iowa prosecutors on retrial or in a civil commitment proceeding, I doubt very much that there is any change a dangerous criminal will be loosed on the streets, the bloodcurdling cries of the dissents notwithstanding it will hardly be because he deserves it. It will be because Detective Leaming, knowing full well that he risked reversal of Williams' conviction, intentionally denied Williams the right of every American under the Sixth Amendment to have the protective shield of a lawyer between himself and the awesome power of the State.

I think it appropriate here to recall the closing words of Mr. Justice Brandeis' great dissent in *Olmstead v. United States*:

> In a government of laws, existence of the government will be imperilled if it fails to observe the law scrupulously. Our Government is the potent, the omnipresent teacher. For good or for ill, it teaches the whole people by its example. Crime is contagious. If the Government becomes a lawbreaker, it breeds contempt for law; it invites every man to become a law unto himself; it invites anarchy. To declare that in the administration of the criminal law the end justifies the means to declare that the Government may commit crimes in order to secure the conviction of a private criminal would bring terrible retribution. Against that pernicious doctrine this Court should resolutely set its face.

NOTES AND QUESTIONS

1. There is discussion about an "agreement" between Williams's counsel and Des Moines police to the effect that Williams would not be "questioned" by the Des Moines police after they picked him up in Davenport and drove him back to Des Moines. What were the terms of the agreement in light of Detective Leaming's comment — in the Davenport meeting that included Williams's lawyer — that Leaming and Williams would "be visiting" between Davenport and Des Moines? Was the agreement broken by the police? Why wouldn't such an agreement be enforceable?

2. Detective Leaming candidly admits that he was trying to take advantage of the fact that Williams was not in the presence of counsel during the ride from Davenport to Des Moines, and that he was trying to thread a needle he perceived between "visiting" and "interrogation." In a concurring opinion, Justice Marshall criticizes the views of some of the dissenters who appear to view Leaming's "Christian burial speech" as good police work. *Id.* at 408. He states "there can be no doubt that Detective Leaming consciously and knowingly set out to violate Williams's Sixth Amendment right to counsel and his Fifth Amendment privilege against self-incrimination, as Leaming himself understood these rights." *Id.* Do you agree?

3. The Court finds that "the circumstances of this case are constitutionally indistinguishable" from *Massiah*. What is the strongest argument for distinguishing *Massiah*?

Obituary notice for Detective Cleatus Leaming of "Christian burial speech" fame/infamy

4. The Court's finding that Williams did not waive his right to counsel relies in part on the burden of proof, that is, that it is the state's burden to prove "an intentional relinquishment or abandonment of a known right or privilege." *Id.* at 404 (citing *Johnson v. Zerbst*). Why is this framing of the legal standard for waiver important here? Why is it important that, as the Court says, waiver is "not a question of historical fact but rather "an application of constitutional principles to the facts as found"? *Id.* at 403. What could Detective Leaming have done, if anything, under these standards to "get" Williams to waive his right to counsel?

5. The Court continues to emphasize that the time between charge and trial is a "critical period" of the proceedings, and cites language from *Powell v. Alabama* that it is during this stage "when consultation, thoroughgoing investigation and preparation," 287 U.S. at 45, are vitally important. Is this a good faith use of *Powell*?

Notwithstanding *Massiah* and *Brewer* the government continued to attempt to obtain incriminating statements from defendants even after they had been charged. In *Michigan v. Jackson*, 475 U.S. 26 (1986), the defendants were indicted for murder, were arraigned, requested counsel, and counsel was appointed. *Id.* at 627-28. Before defendants had an opportunity to consult with counsel, they were approached by police, given *Miranda* warnings, and agreed to be interrogated, whereupon they made incriminating statements. *Id.* The statements were introduced at trial and defendants were convicted. *Id.* The Supreme Court found a violation of both the Sixth Amendment right established in *Massiah* as well as the Fifth Amendment right established in *Edwards v. Arizona*, 451 U.S. 477 (1981).

In a case just two years later, *Patterson v. Illinois*, 487 U.S. 285 (1986), the Court found both *Jackson* and *Edwards* inapplicable on unusual facts where defendant had been indicted while in custody but had yet to be arraigned. *Id.* at 287-88. The Court found that defendant's waiver of his *Miranda* rights was a sufficient waiver of his right to counsel and that *Jackson* and *Edwards* had relied on a defendant's affirmative request for counsel, which had not happened here. *Id.* at 290-91. *Jackson* was eventually overruled explicitly in *Montejo v. Louisiana*, 556 U.S. 778 (2009), where the Court held that the variety of state practices in appointing counsel—some involving requests by defendants, others not—make *Jackson* administratively untenable and, in any event, unnecessary in light of the protections provided by *Miranda* and *Edwards*.

C. EFFECTIVE ASSISTANCE OF COUNSEL: STANDARD OF PERFORMANCE

So per *Gideon* and subsequent cases the Sixth Amendment guarantees an indigent defendant the right to "assistance of counsel" at trial, and sometimes earlier, at least where imprisonment

C. Effective Assistance of Counsel: Standard of Performance 757

is imposed. But what is the content of the right to "assistance of counsel"? As far back as *Powell v. Alabama* the Supreme Court made clear that the simple fact of "having counsel" was insufficient, and in 1970 the Court stated, albeit in a footnote, that "the right to counsel is the right to effective assistance of counsel." *McMann v. Richardson*, 397 U.S. 759, 771 n.14 (1970). But it would be another 14 years—21 years after *Gideon*—that the Court would decree a standard for ineffective counsel claims in *Strickland v. Washington*, 466 U.S. 668 (1984). David Cole makes the point that where Clarence Gideon may have made a strong case on the optics for establishing a Sixth Amendment right to counsel in felony cases, the optics attending the ineffective assistance of counsel claim of David Leroy Washington cut the other way:

> On a two-week crime spree in September 1976, Washington robbed and killed a minister because he was a homosexual; robbed and killed a woman in her home while her three elderly sisters-in-law watched while bound and gagged, and then shot all three of the sisters-in-law in the head; and kidnaped a man, stabbed him repeatedly and eventually killed him.
>
> When arrested and charged with capital murder and multiple related counts of robbery, breaking and entering, and kidnapping Washington was appointed a public defender, Bill Tunkey. For a court-appointed lawyer, Tunkey was relatively experienced. He'd been a prosecutor for three years and a defense attorney for three and a half more. During that period, he estimated that he had handled over 1,000 cases as trial attorney. The judge who presided over Washington's post-conviction proceeding called Tunkey "one of the leading criminal defense attorneys in Dade County." . . .
>
> Washington was, to put it mildly, a difficult client. He repeatedly disregarded Tunkey's advice. Tunkey told him not to talk to the police, but Washington disregarded that advice and confessed to all three murders. Tunkey recommended that Washington choose a jury trial, but Washington waived his jury trial right and pleaded guilty. And when Tunkey recommend that Washington invoke his right under Florida law to an advisory jury for capital sentencing, Washington again rejected the advice and waived the right as well.

David Cole, Gideon v. Wainright *and* Strickland v. Washington: *Broken Promises*, in Criminal Procedure Stories 108-09 (Carol Steiker ed., 2006). *See id.* at 102 ("the real story of the right to counsel is not Gideon's but that of David Leroy Washington").

Strickland v. Washington
466 U.S. 668 (1984)

Justice O'CONNOR delivered the opinion of the Court.

This case requires us to consider the proper standards for judging a criminal defendant's contention that the Constitution requires a conviction or death sentence to be set aside because counsel's assistance at the trial or sentencing was ineffective.

• • •

During a 10-day period in September 1976, respondent planned and committed three groups of crimes, which included three brutal stabbing murders, torture, kidnaping, severe assaults, attempted murders, attempted extortion, and theft. After his two accomplices were arrested, respondent surrendered to police and voluntarily gave a lengthy statement confessing to the third of the criminal episodes. The State of Florida indicted respondent for kidnaping and murder and appointed an experienced criminal lawyer to represent him.

Counsel actively pursued pretrial motions and discovery. He cut his efforts short, however, and he experienced a sense of hopelessness about the case, when he learned that, against his specific advice, respondent had also confessed to the first two murders. By the date set for trial, respondent was subject to indictment for three counts of first-degree murder and multiple

Chapter VIII Right to Counsel and the Defense Function

counts of robbery, kidnaping for ransom, breaking and entering and assault, attempted murder, and conspiracy to commit robbery. Respondent waived his right to a jury trial, again acting against counsel's advice, and pleaded guilty to all charges, including the three capital murder charges.

In the plea colloquy, respondent told the trial judge that, although he had committed a string of burglaries, he had no significant prior criminal record and that at the time of his criminal spree he was under extreme stress caused by his inability to support his family. He also stated, however, that he accepted responsibility for the crimes. The trial judge told respondent that he had "a great deal of respect for people who are willing to step forward and admit their responsibility" but that he was making no statement at all about his likely sentencing decision.

Counsel advised respondent to invoke his right under Florida law to an advisory jury at his capital sentencing hearing. Respondent rejected the advice and waived the right. He chose instead to be sentenced by the trial judge without a jury recommendation.

In preparing for the sentencing hearing, counsel spoke with respondent about his background. He also spoke on the telephone with respondent's wife and mother, though he did not follow up on the one unsuccessful effort to meet with them. He did not otherwise seek out character witnesses for respondent. Nor did he request a psychiatric examination, since his conversations with his client gave no indication that respondent had psychological problems.

Counsel decided not to present and hence not to look further for evidence concerning respondent's character and emotional state. That decision reflected trial counsel's sense of hopelessness about overcoming the evidentiary effect of respondent's confessions to the gruesome crimes. It also reflected the judgment that it was advisable to rely on the plea colloquy for evidence about respondent's background and about his claim of emotional stress: the plea colloquy communicated sufficient information about these subjects, and by forgoing the opportunity to present new evidence on these subjects, counsel prevented the State from cross-examining respondent on his claim and from putting on psychiatric evidence of its own.

Counsel also excluded from the sentencing hearing other evidence he thought was potentially damaging. He successfully moved to exclude respondent's "rap sheet." Because he judged that a presentence report might prove more detrimental than helpful, as it would have included respondent's criminal history and thereby would have undermined the claim of no significant history of criminal activity, he did not request that one be prepared.

At the sentencing hearing, counsel's strategy was based primarily on the trial judge's remarks at the plea colloquy as well as on his reputation as a sentencing judge who thought it important for a convicted defendant to own up to his crime. Counsel argued that respondent's remorse and acceptance of responsibility justified sparing him from the death penalty. Counsel also argued that respondent had no history of criminal activity and that respondent committed the crimes under extreme mental or emotional disturbance, thus coming within the statutory list of mitigating circumstances. He further argued that respondent should be spared death because he had surrendered, confessed, and offered to testify against a codefendant and because respondent was fundamentally a good person who had briefly gone badly wrong in extremely stressful circumstances. The State put on evidence and witnesses largely for the purpose of describing the details of the crimes. Counsel did not cross-examine the medical experts who testified about the manner of death of respondent's victims.

The trial judge found several aggravating circumstances with respect to each of the three murders. He found that all three murders were especially heinous, atrocious, and cruel, all involving repeated stabbings. All three murders were committed in the course of at least one other dangerous and violent felony, and since all involved robbery, the murders were for pecuniary gain. All three murders were committed to avoid arrest for the accompanying crimes and to hinder law enforcement. In the course of one of the murders, respondent knowingly

C. Effective Assistance of Counsel: Standard of Performance

subjected numerous persons to a grave risk of death by deliberately stabbing and shooting the murder victim's sisters-in-law, who sustained severe—in one case, ultimately fatal—injuries.

With respect to mitigating circumstances, the trial judge made the same findings for all three capital murders. First, although there was no admitted evidence of prior convictions, respondent had stated that he had engaged in a course of stealing. In any case, even if respondent had no significant history of criminal activity, the aggravating circumstances "would still clearly far outweigh" that mitigating factor. Second, the judge found that, during all three crimes, respondent was not suffering from extreme mental or emotional disturbance and could appreciate the criminality of his acts. Third, none of the victims was a participant in, or consented to, respondent's conduct. Fourth, respondent's participation in the crimes was neither minor nor the result of duress or domination by an accomplice. Finally, respondent's age (26) could not be considered a factor in mitigation, especially when viewed in light of respondent's planning of the crimes and disposition of the proceeds of the various accompanying thefts.

In short, the trial judge found numerous aggravating circumstances and no (or a single comparatively insignificant) mitigating circumstance. With respect to each of the three convictions for capital murder, the trial judge concluded: "A careful consideration of all matters presented to the court impels the conclusion that there are insufficient mitigating circumstances . . . to outweigh the aggravating circumstances." He therefore sentenced respondent to death on each of the three counts of murder and to prison terms for the other crimes. The Florida Supreme Court upheld the convictions and sentences on direct appeal.

. . .

III

A convicted defendant's claim that counsel's assistance was so defective as to require reversal of a conviction or death sentence has two components. First, the defendant must show that counsel's performance was deficient. This requires showing that counsel made errors so serious that counsel was not functioning as the "counsel" guaranteed the defendant by the Sixth Amendment. Second, the defendant must show that the deficient performance prejudiced the defense. This requires showing that counsel's errors were so serious as to deprive the defendant of a fair trial, a trial whose result is reliable. Unless a defendant makes both showings, it cannot be said that the conviction or death sentence resulted from a breakdown in the adversary process that renders the result unreliable.

A

As all the Federal Courts of Appeals have now held, the proper standard for attorney performance is that of reasonably effective assistance.

More specific guidelines are not appropriate. The Sixth Amendment refers simply to "counsel," not specifying particular requirements of effective assistance. It relies instead on the legal profession's maintenance of standards sufficient to justify the law's presumption that counsel will fulfill the role in the adversary process that the Amendment envisions. The proper measure of attorney performance remains simply reasonableness under prevailing professional norms.

Representation of a criminal defendant entails certain basic duties. Counsel's function is to assist the defendant, and hence counsel owes the client a duty of loyalty, a duty to avoid conflicts of interest. From counsel's function as assistant to the defendant derive the overarching duty to advocate the defendant's cause and the more particular duties to consult with the defendant on important decisions and to keep the defendant informed of important developments in the course of the prosecution. Counsel also has a duty to bring to bear such skill and knowledge as will render the trial a reliable adversarial testing process.

These basic duties neither exhaustively define the obligations of counsel nor form a checklist for judicial evaluation of attorney performance. In any case presenting an ineffectiveness claim, the performance inquiry must be whether counsel's assistance was reasonable considering all the circumstances. Prevailing norms of practice as reflected in American Bar Association standards and the like, e.g., ABA Standards for Criminal Justice 4-1.1 to 4-8.6 (2d ed. 1980) ("The Defense Function"), are guides to determining what is reasonable, but they are only guides. No particular set of detailed rules for counsel's conduct can satisfactorily take account of the variety of circumstances faced by defense counsel or the range of legitimate decisions regarding how best to represent a criminal defendant. Any such set of rules would interfere with the constitutionally protected independence of counsel and restrict the wide latitude counsel must have in making tactical decisions. Indeed, the existence of detailed guidelines for representation could distract counsel from the overriding mission of vigorous advocacy of the defendant's cause. Moreover, the purpose of the effective assistance guarantee of the Sixth Amendment is not to improve the quality of legal representation, although that is a goal of considerable importance to the legal system. The purpose is simply to ensure that criminal defendants receive a fair trial.

Judicial scrutiny of counsel's performance must be highly deferential. It is all too tempting for a defendant to second-guess counsel's assistance after conviction or adverse sentence, and it is all too easy for a court, examining counsel's defense after it has proved unsuccessful, to conclude that a particular act or omission of counsel was unreasonable. A fair assessment of attorney performance requires that every effort be made to eliminate the distorting effects of hindsight, to reconstruct the circumstances of counsel's challenged conduct, and to evaluate the conduct from counsel's perspective at the time. Because of the difficulties inherent in making the evaluation, a court must indulge a strong presumption that counsel's conduct falls within the wide range of reasonable professional assistance; that is, the defendant must overcome the presumption that, under the circumstances, the challenged action "might be considered sound trial strategy." There are countless ways to provide effective assistance in any given case. Even the best criminal defense attorneys would not defend a particular client in the same way.

The availability of intrusive post-trial inquiry into attorney performance or of detailed guidelines for its evaluation would encourage the proliferation of ineffectiveness challenges. Criminal trials resolved unfavorably to the defendant would increasingly come to be followed by a second trial, this one of counsel's unsuccessful defense. Counsel's performance and even willingness to serve could be adversely affected. Intensive scrutiny of counsel and rigid requirements for acceptable assistance could dampen the ardor and impair the independence of defense counsel, discourage the acceptance of assigned cases, and undermine the trust between attorney and client.

Thus, a court deciding an actual ineffectiveness claim must judge the reasonableness of counsel's challenged conduct on the facts of the particular case, viewed as of the time of counsel's conduct. A convicted defendant making a claim of ineffective assistance must identify the acts or omissions of counsel that are alleged not to have been the result of reasonable professional judgment. The court must then determine whether, in light of all the circumstances, the identified acts or omissions were outside the wide range of professionally competent assistance. In making that determination, the court should keep in mind that counsel's function, as elaborated in prevailing professional norms, is to make the adversarial testing process work in the particular case. At the same time, the court should recognize that counsel is strongly presumed to have rendered adequate assistance and made all significant decisions in the exercise of reasonable professional judgment.

These standards require no special amplification in order to define counsel's duty to investigate, the duty at issue in this case. As the Court of Appeals concluded, strategic choices made after thorough investigation of law and facts relevant to plausible options are virtually unchallengeable; and strategic choices made after less than complete investigation are reasonable precisely to the extent that reasonable professional judgments support the limitations on investigation. In other words, counsel has a duty to make reasonable investigations or to make a reasonable decision that makes particular investigations unnecessary. In any ineffectiveness case, a particular decision not to investigate must be directly assessed for reasonableness in all the circumstances, applying a heavy measure of deference to counsel's judgments.

The reasonableness of counsel's actions may be determined or substantially influenced by the defendant's own statements or actions. Counsel's actions are usually based, quite properly, on informed strategic choices made by the defendant and on information supplied by the defendant. In particular, what investigation decisions are reasonable depends critically on such information. For example, when the facts that support a certain potential line of defense are generally known to counsel because of what the defendant has said, the need for further investigation may be considerably diminished or eliminated altogether. And when a defendant has given counsel reason to believe that pursuing certain investigations would be fruitless or even harmful, counsel's failure to pursue those investigations may not later be challenged as unreasonable. In short, inquiry into counsel's conversations with the defendant may be critical to a proper assessment of counsel's investigation decisions, just as it may be critical to a proper assessment of counsel's other litigation decisions.

B

An error by counsel, even if professionally unreasonable, does not warrant setting aside the judgment of a criminal proceeding if the error had no effect on the judgment. The purpose of the Sixth Amendment guarantee of counsel is to ensure that a defendant has the assistance necessary to justify reliance on the outcome of the proceeding. Accordingly, any deficiencies in counsel's performance must be prejudicial to the defense in order to constitute ineffective assistance under the Constitution.

In certain Sixth Amendment contexts, prejudice is presumed. Actual or constructive denial of the assistance of counsel altogether is legally presumed to result in prejudice. So are various kinds of state interference with counsel's assistance. Prejudice in these circumstances is so likely that case-by-case inquiry into prejudice is not worth the cost. Moreover, such circumstances involve impairments of the Sixth Amendment right that are easy to identify and, for that reason and because the prosecution is directly responsible, easy for the government to prevent.

One type of actual ineffectiveness claim warrants a similar, though more limited, presumption of prejudice. In *Cuyler* the Court held that prejudice is presumed when counsel is burdened by an actual conflict of interest. In those circumstances, counsel breaches the duty of loyalty, perhaps the most basic of counsel's duties. Moreover, it is difficult to measure the precise effect on the defense of representation corrupted by conflicting interests. Given the obligation of counsel to avoid conflicts of interest and the ability of trial courts to make early inquiry in certain situations likely to give rise to conflicts, see, e.g., Fed. Rule Crim. Proc. 44(c), it is reasonable for the criminal justice system to maintain a fairly rigid rule of presumed prejudice for conflicts of interest. Even so, the rule is not quite the per se rule of prejudice that exists for the Sixth Amendment claims mentioned above. Prejudice is presumed only if the defendant demonstrates that counsel "actively represented conflicting interests" and that "an actual conflict of interest adversely affected his lawyer's performance."

Conflict of interest claims aside, actual ineffectiveness claims alleging a deficiency in attorney performance are subject to a general requirement that the defendant affirmatively prove prejudice. The government is not responsible for, and hence not able to prevent, attorney errors that will result in reversal of a conviction or sentence. Attorney errors come in an infinite variety and are as likely to be utterly harmless in a particular case as they are to be prejudicial. They cannot be classified according to likelihood of causing prejudice. Nor can they be defined with sufficient precision to inform defense attorneys correctly just what conduct to avoid. Representation is an art, and an act or omission that is unprofessional in one case may be sound or even brilliant in another. Even if a defendant shows that particular errors of counsel were unreasonable, therefore, the defendant must show that they actually had an adverse effect on the defense.

It is not enough for the defendant to show that the errors had some conceivable effect on the outcome of the proceeding. Virtually every act or omission of counsel would meet that test, and not every error that conceivably could have influenced the outcome undermines the reliability of the result of the proceeding. Respondent suggests requiring a showing that the errors "impaired the presentation of the defense." That standard, however, provides no workable principle. Since any error, if it is indeed an error, "impairs" the presentation of the defense, the proposed standard is inadequate because it provides no way of deciding what impairments are sufficiently serious to warrant setting aside the outcome of the proceeding.

On the other hand, we believe that a defendant need not show that counsel's deficient conduct more likely than not altered the outcome in the case. This outcome-determinative standard has several strengths. It defines the relevant inquiry in a way familiar to courts, though the inquiry, as is inevitable, is anything but precise. The standard also reflects the profound importance of finality in criminal proceedings. Moreover, it comports with the widely used standard for assessing motions for new trial based on newly discovered evidence. Nevertheless, the standard is not quite appropriate.

Even when the specified attorney error results in the omission of certain evidence, the newly discovered evidence standard is not an apt source from which to draw a prejudice standard for ineffectiveness claims. The high standard for newly discovered evidence claims presupposes that all the essential elements of a presumptively accurate and fair proceeding were present in the proceeding whose result is challenged. An ineffective assistance claim asserts the absence of one of the crucial assurances that the result of the proceeding is reliable, so finality concerns are somewhat weaker and the appropriate standard of prejudice should be somewhat lower. The result of a proceeding can be rendered unreliable, and hence the proceeding itself unfair, even if the errors of counsel cannot be shown by a preponderance of the evidence to have determined the outcome.

Accordingly, the appropriate test for prejudice finds its roots in the test for materiality of exculpatory information not disclosed to the defense by the prosecution, and in the test for materiality of testimony made unavailable to the defense by Government deportation of a witness. The defendant must show that there is a reasonable probability that, but for counsel's unprofessional errors, the result of the proceeding would have been different. A reasonable probability is a probability sufficient to undermine confidence in the outcome.

In making the determination whether the specified errors resulted in the required prejudice, a court should presume, absent challenge to the judgment on grounds of evidentiary insufficiency, that the judge or jury acted according to law. An assessment of the likelihood of a result more favorable to the defendant must exclude the possibility of arbitrariness, whimsy, caprice, "nullification," and the like. A defendant has no entitlement to the luck of a lawless decisionmaker, even if a lawless decision cannot be reviewed. The assessment of prejudice should proceed on the assumption that the decisionmaker is reasonably, conscientiously, and impartially applying the standards that govern the decision. It should not depend on the idiosyncrasies of the particular decisionmaker, such as unusual propensities toward harshness or leniency. Although these factors may actually have entered into counsel's selection of strategies and, to that limited extent, may thus affect the performance inquiry, they are irrelevant to the prejudice inquiry. Thus, evidence about the actual process of decision, if not part of the record of the proceeding under review, and evidence about, for example, a particular judge's sentencing practices, should not be considered in the prejudice determination.

The governing legal standard plays a critical role in defining the question to be asked in assessing the prejudice from counsel's errors. When a defendant challenges a conviction, the question is whether there is a reasonable probability that, absent the errors, the factfinder would have had a reasonable doubt respecting guilt. When a defendant challenges a death sentence such as the one at issue in this case, the question is whether there is a reasonable probability that, absent the errors, the sentencer—including an appellate court, to the extent it independently reweighs the evidence—would have concluded that the balance of aggravating and mitigating circumstances did not warrant death.

In making this determination, a court hearing an ineffectiveness claim must consider the totality of the evidence before the judge or jury. Some of the factual findings will have been unaffected by the errors, and factual findings that were affected will have been affected in different ways. Some errors will have had a pervasive effect on the inferences to be drawn from the evidence, altering the entire evidentiary picture, and some will have had an isolated, trivial effect. Moreover, a verdict or conclusion only weakly supported by the record is more likely to have been affected by errors than one with overwhelming record support. Taking the unaffected findings as a given, and taking due account of the effect of the errors on the remaining findings, a court making the prejudice inquiry must ask if the defendant has met the burden of showing that the decision reached would reasonably likely have been different absent the errors.

IV

A number of practical considerations are important for the application of the standards we have outlined. Most important, in adjudicating a claim of actual ineffectiveness of counsel, a court should keep in mind that the principles we have stated do not establish mechanical rules. Although those principles should guide the process of decision, the ultimate focus of inquiry must be on the fundamental fairness of the proceeding whose result is being challenged. In every case the court should be concerned with whether, despite the strong presumption of reliability, the result of the particular proceeding is unreliable because of a breakdown in the adversarial process that our system counts on to produce just results.

To the extent that this has already been the guiding inquiry in the lower courts, the standards articulated today do not require reconsideration of ineffectiveness claims rejected under different standards. In particular, the minor differences in the lower courts' precise formulations of the performance standard are insignificant: the different formulations are mere variations of the overarching reasonableness standard. With regard to the prejudice inquiry, only the strict outcome-determinative test, among the standards articulated in the lower courts, imposes a heavier burden on defendants than the tests laid down today. The difference, however, should alter the merit of an ineffectiveness claim only in the rarest case.

Although we have discussed the performance component of an ineffectiveness claim prior to the prejudice component, there is no reason for a court deciding an ineffective assistance claim to approach the inquiry in the same order or even to address both components of the inquiry if the defendant makes an insufficient showing on one. In particular, a court need not determine whether counsel's performance was deficient before examining the prejudice suffered by the defendant as a result of the alleged deficiencies. The object of an ineffectiveness claim is not to grade counsel's performance. If it is easier to dispose of an ineffectiveness claim on the ground of lack of sufficient prejudice, which we expect will often be so, that course should be followed. Courts should strive to ensure that ineffectiveness claims not become so burdensome to defense counsel that the entire criminal justice system suffers as a result.

764 Chapter VIII Right to Counsel and the Defense Function

The principles governing ineffectiveness claims should apply in federal collateral proceedings as they do on direct appeal or in motions for a new trial. As indicated by the "cause and prejudice" test for overcoming procedural waivers of claims of error, the presumption that a criminal judgment is final is at its strongest in collateral attacks on that judgment. An ineffectiveness claim, however, as our articulation of the standards that govern decision of such claims makes clear, is an attack on the fundamental fairness of the proceeding whose result is challenged. Since fundamental fairness is the central concern of the writ of habeas corpus, no special standards ought to apply to ineffectiveness claims made in habeas proceedings.

• • •

V

Having articulated general standards for judging ineffectiveness claims, we think it useful to apply those standards to the facts of this case in order to illustrate the meaning of the general principles. The record makes it possible to do so. There are no conflicts between the state and federal courts over findings of fact, and the principles we have articulated are sufficiently close to the principles applied both in the Florida courts and in the District Court that it is clear that the factfinding was not affected by erroneous legal principles.

Application of the governing principles is not difficult in this case. The facts as described above, make clear that the conduct of respondent's counsel at and before respondent's sentencing proceeding cannot be found unreasonable. They also make clear that, even assuming the challenged conduct of counsel was unreasonable, respondent suffered insufficient prejudice to warrant setting aside his death sentence.

With respect to the performance component, the record shows that respondent's counsel made a strategic choice to argue for the extreme emotional distress mitigating circumstance and to rely as fully as possible on respondent's acceptance of responsibility for his crimes. Although counsel understandably felt hopeless about respondent's prospects, nothing in the record indicates, as one possible reading of the District Court's opinion suggests, that counsel's sense of hopelessness distorted his professional judgment. Counsel's strategy choice was well within the range of professionally reasonable judgments, and the decision not to seek more character or psychological evidence than was already in hand was likewise reasonable.

The trial judge's views on the importance of owning up to one's crimes were well known to counsel. The aggravating circumstances were utterly overwhelming. Trial counsel could reasonably surmise from his conversations with respondent that character and psychological evidence would be of little help. Respondent had already been able to mention at the plea colloquy the substance of what there was to know about his financial and emotional troubles. Restricting testimony on respondent's character to what had come in at the plea colloquy ensured that contrary character and psychological evidence and respondent's criminal history, which counsel had successfully moved to exclude, would not come in. On these facts, there can be little question, even without application of the presumption of adequate performance, that trial counsel's defense, though unsuccessful, was the result of reasonable professional judgment.

With respect to the prejudice component, the lack of merit of respondent's claim is even more stark. The evidence that respondent says his trial counsel should have offered at the sentencing hearing would barely have altered the sentencing profile presented to the sentencing judge. As the state courts and District Court found, at most this evidence shows that numerous people who knew respondent thought he was generally a good person and that a psychiatrist and a psychologist believed he was under considerable emotional stress that did not rise to the level of extreme disturbance. Given the overwhelming aggravating factors, there is no reasonable probability that the omitted evidence would have changed the conclusion that the aggravating circumstances outweighed the mitigating circumstances and, hence, the sentence imposed. Indeed, admission of the evidence respondent now offers might even have been harmful to his case: his "rap sheet" would probably have been admitted into evidence, and the psychological reports would have directly contradicted respondent's claim that the mitigating circumstance of extreme emotional disturbance applied to his case.

Our conclusions on both the prejudice and performance components of the ineffectiveness inquiry do not depend on the trial judge's testimony at the District Court hearing. We therefore need not consider the general admissibility of that testimony, although, that testimony is irrelevant to the prejudice inquiry. Moreover, the prejudice question is resolvable, and hence the ineffectiveness claim can be rejected, without regard to the evidence presented at the District Court hearing. The state courts properly concluded that the ineffectiveness claim was meritless without holding an evidentiary hearing.

Failure to make the required showing of either deficient performance or sufficient prejudice defeats the ineffectiveness claim. Here there is a double failure. More generally, respondent has made no showing that the justice of his sentence was rendered unreliable by a breakdown in the adversary process caused by deficiencies in counsel's assistance. Respondent's sentencing proceeding was not fundamentally unfair.

We conclude, therefore, that the District Court properly declined to issue a writ of habeas corpus. The judgment of the Court of Appeals is accordingly

Reversed.

[Justices Brennan and Marshall dissented.]

NOTES AND QUESTIONS

David Leroy Washington

1. The Court cannot say often enough that the bar for establishing that counsel's performance was ineffective is a high one. Judicial scrutiny of counsel's performance must be "highly deferential"; a court must indulge a "strong presumption" that counsel's performance was adequate; and counsel is "strongly presumed" to have been effective. Why the heavy-handed approach, apart from discouraging ineffective assistance claims?

2. The Court invokes several different images of defense counsel's role in a criminal case. One is that of an independent professional tactician. The Court refers to the "constitutionally protected independence of counsel," and worries that "intensive scrutiny" of counsel's performance "could dampen the ardor and impair the independence of defense counsel, discourage the acceptance of assigned cases, and undermine the trust between attorney and client." *Id*. at 689-91. In what ways are defense attorneys more "independent" than other professionals? The Court notes that "there are countless ways to provide effective assistance in any given case." Does this seem accurate? Were there countless ways to represent Washington at his sentencing hearing? The Court also notes a "strong presumption" that a challenged action "might be considered sound trial strategy."

3. The Court also notes, somewhat paradoxically, that defense counsel's function is as an "assistant to the defendant," offering only the proverbial "guiding hand." How can

these two images — guide and independent professional — be reconciled? Plainly counsel's independence and guidance were both compromised in *Strickland* by the unilateral actions taken by counsel's client. But in a more representative case how do you see the twin roles of guide and independent professional operating?

4. The elephant in the room, called out by Justice Marshall's dissent, is money. While the Court notes that "[l]imitations of time and money" can dictate defense counsel's strategic choices, *id.* at 681, Justice Marshall wonders whether the "reasonably competent attorney" standard is the same for an appointed attorney as for a privately paid attorney.

5. The majority refers three times to the "hopelessness" felt by defense counsel. *Id.* at 671, 673, 700. Does the Court mean anything by this? Is hopelessness a mitigating factor in evaluating defense counsel's performance?

6. While some lower courts had applied various codified practice standards in adopting tests for ineffective assistance claims, the Supreme Court pointedly rejects such an approach, instead stating that "reasonableness under prevailing professional norms" shall be the barometer of performance. *Id.* at 689. Isn't this tantamount to self-regulation?

7. The Court further observes that any such standards could only serve as "guides to what is reasonable" lest they restrict "the wide latitude counsel must have in making tactical decisions." *Id.* at 689. How much of defense counsel's work actually consists of "tactical decision making"? The dissent observes that for some aspects of defense counsel practice such wide latitude is unnecessary, and points to areas where uniform standards could be useful, such as preparing for trial, applying for bail, client conferences, trial objections, and filing appeals. *Id.* at 710. What sort of standards can you see governing these tasks? Wouldn't the use of some standards make it easier for courts to filter out weak ineffective assistance claims as opposed to the entirely general standardless test the Court adopts?

In adopting a prejudice standard for ineffective assistance claims, the Court adopts the same standard applicable where the government has failed to disclose material exculpatory information to the defense. *Id.* at 694. (This subject will be addressed in detail in Chapter IX *infra.*) Under this test, the claimant must establish that but for the ineffective assistance of counsel there is a reasonable probability the result of the proceeding would have been different. *Id.* The dissent criticizes this formulation on two different grounds. First, the dissent argues that the cold record of the proceedings may well not reveal the evidence or argument that might have made a difference, especially when the alleged errors of counsel are errors of omission. By contrast, in the nondisclosure of exculpatory information context, the claimant at least can point to the information that was not disclosed in framing an argument. Fair point? Second, the dissent argues that the test for prejudice should be whether the proceedings were fundamentally fair, as the Sixth Amendment right to a fair trial is violated, regardless of result, whenever that is not the case. Which of these two arguments is more persuasive? Is there a workable prejudice standard somewhere between the views of the majority and the dissent?

The *Strickland* standard has been widely criticized by judges, lawyers, and commentators. One prominent example is Judge Alvin Rubin's concurring opinion in *Riles v. McCotter*, 799 F.3d 947 (5th Cir. 1986), a capital case in which defense counsel failed to appeal from the trial court's improper exclusion of certain venire members, failed to object to and appeal from the trial court's improper and prejudicial voir dire examination, and failed to object to the improper introduction of the state's psychiatric evidence. *Id.* at 954. Judge Rubin stated:

> I concur in the opinion because, as a judge of an inferior court, I am bound by the decisions of the Supreme Court, and, as a judge of this court, I am bound by the law of this circuit. If I were free to do so, I would order an evidentiary hearing on the effectiveness of counsel. To me, a sufficient showing has been made that trial counsel did not provide this accused with the quality of defense essential to adequate representation in any serious felony case, and particularly in a capital case.

C. Effective Assistance of Counsel: Standard of Performance

It is probably true that any error made by court-appointed counsel in the guilt-innocence phase of the trial was harmless in the sense that it does not appear likely to have affected the result. The briefs and argument of current counsel, however, together with the record, indicate that, if Riles' trial counsel had been able, the jury might not have imposed the death penalty.

Precedent requires me to agree that this is not enough to justify a certificate of probable cause. The Constitution, as interpreted by the courts, does not require that the accused, even in a capital case, be represented by able or effective counsel. It requires representation only by a lawyer who is not ineffective under the standard set by *Strickland v. Washington*. Proof that the lawyer was ineffective requires proof not only that the lawyer bungled but also that his errors likely affected the result. Ineffectiveness is not measured against the standards set by good lawyers but by the average—"reasonableness under prevailing professional norms"—and "judicial scrutiny of counsel's performance must be highly differential." Consequently, accused persons who are represented by "not-legally-ineffective" lawyers may be condemned to die when the same accused, if represented by effective counsel.

Id. at 955 (footnotes omitted). David Cole emphatically agrees with Judge Rubin:

The *Strickland* standard has proved virtually impossible to meet. Courts have declined to find ineffective assistance where defense counsel slept during portions of the trial, where counsel used heroin and cocaine throughout the trial, where counsel allowed his client to wear the same sweatshirt and shoes in court that the perpetrator was alleged to have worn on the day of the crime, where counsel stated prior to trial that he was not prepared on the law or facts of the case, and where counsel appointed in a capital case could not name a single Supreme Court decision on the death penalty. . . .

David Cole, Gideon v. Wainright *and* Strickland v. Washington: *Broken Promises*, in Criminal Procedure Stories 114-15 (Carol Steiker ed., 2006).

Facts for ineffective assistance claims don't get much worse than in this next case from California.

People v. Garrison
47 Cal. 3d 746 (1989)

PANELLI, J.

Defendant Richard William Garrison was convicted on two counts of murder in the first degree, one count of robbery, and one count of burglary.

For reasons hereafter stated, we affirm the judgment of guilt and three of the special circumstance findings. We reverse the penalty under compulsion of and deny the petition for a writ of habeas corpus.

• • •

Defendant's petition for habeas corpus raises additional issues relative to the effectiveness of counsel. We issued an order to show cause limited to the following: "1) whether or not the alcohol dependency of defendant's court-appointed counsel, Blendon Beardsley, deprived defendant of due process or effective assistance of counsel; and 2) whether Beardsley's failure to undertake essential research and investigation denied defendant effective assistance of counsel."

Responding to the first issue, defendant contends that he was denied effective assistance because Beardsley's performance was per se deficient due to his alcoholism. As to the second issue, defendant claims Beardsley's performance was deficient because he called only one witness at the penalty phase and failed to contact other individuals who could have testified.

Inasmuch as we hereafter reverse the penalty judgment on other grounds, we will not reach the second issue.

The claim of ineffective assistance of counsel involves two components, a showing that counsel's performance was deficient and proof of actual prejudice.

Although it is uncontested that Beardsley was an alcoholic at the time of trial and that he has since died of the disease, defendant has failed to prove that Beardsley's performance was deficient. His reliance on a per se rule of deficiency for alcoholic attorneys is contrary to settled law. We hereafter conclude, therefore, that defendant was not denied his right to effective assistance of counsel.

Blendon Beardsley was court-appointed counsel for defendant from February of 1980 until judgment of death was entered in January of 1981. It is undisputed that Beardsley was an alcoholic at the time of his representation and that he consumed large amounts of alcohol each day of the trial. The declarations in the petition and traverse indicate that Beardsley drank in the morning, during court recesses, and throughout the evening. Although these declarations confirm that Beardsley was an alcoholic, they do not address whether Beardsley's addiction adversely affected his courtroom performance to such an extent that defendant was denied effective assistance of counsel.

Statements made by the bailiff and the trial judge provide insight into the quality of Beardsley's representation. The bailiff, Hector Delgadillo, declares that he was in close contact with Beardsley throughout the trial, that Beardsley always smelled of alcohol, but that Delgadillo "could never really tell for sure to what extent Mr. Beardsley was under the influence of alcohol because he always seemed to act the same," and that he did not see Beardsley stagger or sleep in court.

The trial judge was in the best position to evaluate Beardsley's condition and performance. The judge was put on notice of Beardsley's alcohol problem when, on the second day of jury selection, Beardsley was arrested for driving to the courthouse with a .27 percent blood-alcohol content. On the following day, the judge made a detailed inquiry of the matter and repeatedly asked defendant if he wanted the court to appoint new counsel. Defendant insisted that he wished to continue with Beardsley. The judge stated that Beardsley's courtroom behavior had not given him any reason to believe that Beardsley should not continue and told defendant, "I personally can assure you that you probably have one of the finest defense counsel in this county."

The judge was apparently satisfied with Beardsley's competence and allowed him to continue. In fact, at the conclusion of the penalty phase the judge praised Beardsley for his effort, stating to defendant: "Let me tell you this. I'm not going to try to convince you that the representation that you had in this case was carried on with as much vigor and dedication as any trial I have witnessed because being in your position at this point you certainly are not ready to accept that, and I'm not going to spend a lot of time telling you that. Mr. Beardsley, as I expressed to you earlier in these proceedings, has been one of the better defense attorneys in this county and certainly the amount of effort that he expended in your case is commendable, although the results in your position are not."

In support of his petition for habeas corpus, defendant submits the declaration of Dr. H. Westley Clark. Dr. Clark declares that a chronic alcoholic loses the ability to think through new problems or tasks and often cannot make judgment calls. Defendant concludes from Dr. Clark's analysis that attorneys who are chronic alcoholics should be held ineffective as a matter of law.

Defendant's position cannot be sustained, however, because it would render irrelevant Beardsley's actual performance in court. Our review of the facts indicate that Beardsley did a fine job in this case. Indeed, defendant concedes that Beardsley outwardly appeared

C. Effective Assistance of Counsel: Standard of Performance   **769**

competent, but argues that inwardly Beardsley was "a shell of a man." That may be true, but there is no authority for the type of per se rule espoused by defendant. He must still prove specific deficiency.

We find one authority which addresses this novel issue, *Fowler v. Parratt*. There the court rejected defendant's claim that a rebuttable presumption of ineffectiveness should apply where counsel was an alcoholic. The court concluded that defendant failed to show that counsel's drinking problem resulted in prejudice.

Prejudice is presumed, however, where counsel's performance was so deficient that a breakdown in the adversarial process occurred. "When a true adversarial criminal trial has been conducted—even if defense counsel may have made demonstrable errors—the kind of testing envisioned by the Sixth Amendment has occurred. But if the process loses its character as a confrontation between adversaries, the constitutional guarantee is violated." The case before us is not such a case.

At present, a presumption exists in favor of the effectiveness of counsel. A defendant has the burden of showing by a preponderance of the evidence that counsel's representation was deficient. A per se rule would create a presumption against the competence of attorneys with drinking problems and would invite defendants to challenge their convictions on the basis of speculation about the drinking habits of their attorneys, rather than on the basis of the attorney's actual performance in court.

Furthermore, any bright-line definition of alcoholism itself would be arbitrary and impractical to administer. We therefore decline to adopt a per se rule of deficiency on the mere showing of alcohol abuse.

NOTES AND QUESTIONS

1. What other options did the trial judge have during the colloquy with the defendant after defense counsel was arrested for DUI while driving to court for jury selection? The record is silent as to what position, if any, the prosecution took at this hearing. What should the prosecutor have done?

2. What do you make of the praise the trial judge bestowed upon defense counsel in addressing defendant at the conclusion of the penalty phase (at which the jury found aggravating circumstances sufficient for imposition of the death penalty)?

3. Do you agree with the court's decision not to adopt a per se rule of deficiency based on, as the court puts it, "mere showing of alcohol abuse"? How about when defense counsel actually abuses alcohol when representing a defendant at trial during the time when court is in session?

In 2000 the Court seemed to be lowering the high bar it had set for at least the "performance" prong of the *Strickland* test, at least judging by a trio of death penalty cases. In the first of these, *Williams v. Taylor*, 529 U.S. 362 (2000), the Court found ineffective a defense attorney who failed to do any investigation for mitigating factors until one week before the penalty phase of the trial, rejecting the claim that the delay had been a "tactical decision." *Id.* at 395-96. In the second, *Wiggins v. Smith*, 539 U.S. 510 (2003), the Court reached a similar conclusion in a death penalty failure-to-investigate case, and relied in reaching its conclusion on the ABA Standards for Criminal Justice, which required adequate investigation of a client's background. *Id.* at 524-25.

The third case follows, continuing the trend.

Chapter VIII Right to Counsel and the Defense Function

Rompilla v. Beard
545 U.S. 374 (2005)

Justice SOUTER delivered the opinion of the Court.

This case calls for specific application of the standard of reasonable competence required on the part of defense counsel by the Sixth Amendment. We hold that even when a capital defendant's family members and the defendant himself have suggested that no mitigating evidence is available, his lawyer is bound to make reasonable efforts to obtain and review material that counsel knows the prosecution will probably rely on as evidence of aggravation at the sentencing phase of trial.

I

On the morning of January 14, 1988, James Scanlon was discovered dead in a bar he ran in Allentown, Pennsylvania, his body having been stabbed repeatedly and set on fire. Ronald Rompilla was indicted for the murder and related offenses, and the Commonwealth gave notice of intent to ask for the death penalty. Two public defenders were assigned to the case.

The jury at the guilt phase of trial found Rompilla guilty on all counts, and during the ensuing penalty phase, the prosecutor sought to prove three aggravating factors to justify a death sentence: that the murder was committed in the course of another felony; that the murder was committed by torture; and that Rompilla had a significant history of felony convictions indicating the use or threat of violence. The Commonwealth presented evidence on all three aggravators, and the jury found all proven. Rompilla's evidence in mitigation consisted of relatively brief testimony: five of his family members argued in effect for residual doubt, and beseeched the jury for mercy, saying that they believed Rompilla was innocent and a good man. Rompilla's 14-year-old son testified that he loved his father and would visit him in prison. The jury acknowledged this evidence to the point of finding, as two factors in mitigation, that Rompilla's son had testified on his behalf and that rehabilitation was possible. But the jurors assigned the greater weight to the aggravating factors, and sentenced Rompilla to death. The Supreme Court of Pennsylvania affirmed both conviction and sentence.

· · ·

We granted certiorari and now reverse.

II

Under 28 U.S.C. § 2254, Rompilla's entitlement to federal habeas relief turns on showing that the state court's resolution of his claim of ineffective assistance of counsel under *Strickland v. Washington, supra*, "resulted in a decision that was contrary to, or involved an unreasonable application of, clearly established Federal law, as determined by the Supreme Court of the United States," § 2254(d)(1). An "unreasonable application" occurs when a state court "'identifies the correct governing legal principle from this Court's decisions but unreasonably applies that principle to the facts' of petitioner's case." That is, "the state court's decision must have been [not only] incorrect or erroneous [but] objectively unreasonable."

Ineffective assistance under *Strickland* is deficient performance by counsel resulting in prejudice, with performance being measured against an "objective standard of reasonableness," "under prevailing professional norms." This case, like some others recently, looks to norms of adequate investigation in preparing for the sentencing phase of a capital trial, when defense counsel's job is to counter the State's evidence of aggravated culpability with evidence in mitigation. In judging the defense's investigation, as in applying *Strickland* generally, hindsight is

C. Effective Assistance of Counsel: Standard of Performance

discounted by pegging adequacy to "counsel's perspective at the time" investigative decisions are made, and by giving a "heavy measure of deference to counsel's judgments."

A

A standard of reasonableness applied as if one stood in counsel's shoes spawns few hard-edged rules, and the merits of a number of counsel's choices in this case are subject to fair debate. This is not a case in which defense counsel simply ignored their obligation to find mitigating evidence, and their workload as busy public defenders did not keep them from making a number of efforts, including interviews with Rompilla and some members of his family, and examinations of reports by three mental health experts who gave opinions at the guilt phase. None of the sources proved particularly helpful.

Rompilla's own contributions to any mitigation case were minimal. Counsel found him uninterested in helping, as on their visit to his prison to go over a proposed mitigation strategy, when Rompilla told them he was "bored being here listening" and returned to his cell. To questions about childhood and schooling, his answers indicated they had been normal, ibid., save for quitting school in the ninth grade. There were times when Rompilla was even actively obstructive by sending counsel off on false leads.

The lawyers also spoke with five members of Rompilla's family (his former wife, two brothers, a sister-in-law, and his son), and counsel testified that they developed a good relationship with the family in the course of their representation. The state postconviction court found that counsel spoke to the relatives in a "detailed manner," attempting to unearth mitigating information, although the weight of this finding is qualified by the lawyers' concession that "the overwhelming response from the family was that they didn't really feel as though they knew him all that well since he had spent the majority of his adult years and some of his childhood years in custody." Defense counsel also said that because the family was "coming from the position that [Rompilla] was innocent . . . they weren't looking for reasons for why he might have done this."

The third and final source tapped for mitigating material was the cadre of three mental health witnesses who were asked to look into Rompilla's mental state as of the time of the offense and his competency to stand trial. But their reports revealed "nothing useful" to Rompilla's case, and the lawyers consequently did not go to any other historical source that might have cast light on Rompilla's mental condition.

When new counsel entered the case to raise Rompilla's postconviction claims, however, they identified a number of likely avenues the trial lawyers could fruitfully have followed in building a mitigation case. School records are one example, which trial counsel never examined in spite of the professed unfamiliarity of the several family members with Rompilla's childhood, and despite counsel's knowledge that Rompilla left school after the ninth grade. Other examples are records of Rompilla's juvenile and adult incarcerations, which counsel did not consult, although they were aware of their client's criminal record. And while counsel knew from police reports provided in pretrial discovery that Rompilla had been drinking heavily at the time of his offense, and although one of the mental health experts reported that Rompilla's troubles with alcohol merited further investigation, counsel did not look for evidence of a history of dependence on alcohol that might have extenuating significance.

Before us, trial counsel and the Commonwealth respond to these unexplored possibilities by emphasizing this Court's recognition that the duty to investigate does not force defense lawyers to scour the globe on the off chance something will turn up; reasonably diligent counsel may draw a line when they have good reason to think further investigation would be a waste. The Commonwealth argues that the information trial counsel gathered from Rompilla and the other sources gave them sound reason to think it would have been pointless to spend time and money on the additional investigation espoused by postconviction counsel, and we

772   Chapter VIII Right to Counsel and the Defense Function

can say that there is room for debate about trial counsel's obligation to follow at least some of those potential lines of enquiry. There is no need to say more, however, for a further point is clear and dispositive: the lawyers were deficient in failing to examine the court file on Rompilla's prior conviction.

B

There is an obvious reason that the failure to examine Rompilla's prior conviction file fell below the level of reasonable performance. Counsel knew that the Commonwealth intended to seek the death penalty by proving Rompilla had a significant history of felony convictions indicating the use or threat of violence, an aggravator under state law. Counsel further knew that the Commonwealth would attempt to establish this history by proving Rompilla's prior conviction for rape and assault, and would emphasize his violent character by introducing a transcript of the rape victim's testimony given in that earlier trial. There is no question that defense counsel were on notice, since they acknowledge that a "plea letter," written by one of them four days prior to trial, mentioned the prosecutor's plans. Ibid. It is also undisputed that the prior conviction file was a public document, readily available for the asking at the very courthouse where Rompilla was to be tried.

It is clear, however, that defense counsel did not look at any part of that file, including the transcript, until warned by the prosecution a second time. In a colloquy the day before the evidentiary sentencing phase began, the prosecutor again said he would present the transcript of the victim's testimony to establish the prior conviction.

[DEFENSE]:	I would also like to review whatever he's going to read from.
[PROSECUTOR]:	Well, I told you that I was going to do this a long time ago. You certainly had the opportunity to review the Transcript.

• • •

[DEFENSE]:	Well, I would like a copy of this.
[PROSECUTOR]:	I don't think that's my duty to provide you with a copy. That's a public record, and you could have gotten that Transcript at any time prior to this Trial. I made one copy for myself, and I'd like to have it now.
[DEFENSE]:	Well, Judge, then I'm going to need to get a copy of it. I'm going to need to get a copy of it.

At the postconviction evidentiary hearing, Rompilla's lawyer confirmed that she had not seen the transcript before the hearing in which this exchange took place, and crucially, even after obtaining the transcript of the victim's testimony on the eve of the sentencing hearing, counsel apparently examined none of the other material in the file.

With every effort to view the facts as a defense lawyer would have done at the time, it is difficult to see how counsel could have failed to realize that without examining the readily available file they were seriously compromising their opportunity to respond to a case for aggravation. The prosecution was going to use the dramatic facts of a similar prior offense, and Rompilla's counsel had a duty to make all reasonable efforts to learn what they could about the offense. Reasonable efforts certainly included obtaining the Commonwealth's own readily available file on the prior conviction to learn what the Commonwealth knew about the crime, to discover any mitigating evidence the Commonwealth would downplay, and to anticipate the details of the aggravating evidence the Commonwealth would emphasize. Without making reasonable efforts to review the file, defense counsel could have had no hope of knowing whether the prosecution was quoting selectively from the transcript, or whether

C. Effective Assistance of Counsel: Standard of Performance   **773**

there were circumstances extenuating the behavior described by the victim. The obligation to get the file was particularly pressing here owing to the similarity of the violent prior offense to the crime charged and Rompilla's sentencing strategy stressing residual doubt. Without making efforts to learn the details and rebut the relevance of the earlier crime, a convincing argument for residual doubt was certainly beyond any hope.

The notion that defense counsel must obtain information that the State has and will use against the defendant is not simply a matter of common sense. As the District Court points out, the American Bar Association Standards for Criminal Justice in circulation at the time of Rompilla's trial describes the obligation in terms no one could misunderstand in the circumstances of a case like this one:

> It is the duty of the lawyer to conduct a prompt investigation of the circumstances of the case and to explore all avenues leading to facts relevant to the merits of the case and the penalty in the event of conviction. The investigation should always include efforts to secure information in the possession of the prosecution and law enforcement authorities. The duty to investigate exists regardless of the accused's admissions or statements to the lawyer of facts constituting guilt or the accused's stated desire to plead guilty.

1 ABA Standards for Criminal Justice 4-4.1 (2d ed. 1982 Supp.).

"[W]e long have referred [to these ABA Standards] as 'guides to determining what is reasonable.'" and the Commonwealth has come up with no reason to think the quoted standard impertinent here.

At argument the most that Pennsylvania (and the United States as amicus) could say was that defense counsel's efforts to find mitigating evidence by other means excused them from looking at the prior conviction file. And that, of course, is the position taken by the state postconviction courts. Without specifically discussing the prior case file, they too found that defense counsel's efforts were enough to free them from any obligation to enquire further.

We think this conclusion of the state court fails to answer the considerations we have set out, to the point of being an objectively unreasonable conclusion. It flouts prudence to deny that a defense lawyer should try to look at a file he knows the prosecution will cull for aggravating evidence, let alone when the file is sitting in the trial courthouse, open for the asking. No reasonable lawyer would forgo examination of the file thinking he could do as well by asking the defendant or family relations whether they recalled anything helpful or damaging in the prior victim's testimony. Nor would a reasonable lawyer compare possible searches for school reports, juvenile records, and evidence of drinking habits to the opportunity to take a look at a file disclosing what the prosecutor knows and even plans to read from in his case. Questioning a few more family members and searching for old records can promise less than looking for a needle in a haystack, when a lawyer truly has reason to doubt there is any needle there. But looking at a file the prosecution says it will use is a sure bet: whatever may be in that file is going to tell defense counsel something about what the prosecution can produce.

The dissent thinks this analysis creates a "rigid, per se" rule that requires defense counsel to do a complete review of the file on any prior conviction introduced but that is a mistake. Counsel fell short here because they failed to make reasonable efforts to review the prior conviction file, despite knowing that the prosecution intended to introduce Rompilla's prior conviction not merely by entering a notice of conviction into evidence but by quoting damaging testimony of the rape victim in that case. The unreasonableness of attempting no more than they did was heightened by the easy availability of the file at the trial courthouse, and the great risk that testimony about a similar violent crime would hamstring counsel's chosen defense of residual doubt. It is owing to these circumstances that the state courts were objectively unreasonable in concluding that counsel could reasonably decline to make any effort to review the file. Other situations, where a defense lawyer is not charged with knowledge that the prosecutor intends to use a prior conviction in this way, might well warrant a different assessment.

• • •

Since counsel's failure to look at the file fell below the line of reasonable practice, there is a further question about prejudice, that is, whether "there is a reasonable probability that, but for counsel's unprofessional errors, the result of the proceeding would have been different." Because the state courts found the representation adequate, they never reached the issue of prejudice, and so we examine this element of the *Strickland* claim de novo, and agree with the dissent in the Court of Appeals. We think Rompilla has shown beyond any doubt that counsel's lapse was prejudicial; Pennsylvania, indeed, does not even contest the claim of prejudice.

If the defense lawyers had looked in the file on Rompilla's prior conviction, it is uncontested they would have found a range of mitigation leads that no other source had opened up. In the same file with the transcript of the prior trial were the records of Rompilla's imprisonment on the earlier conviction, which defense counsel testified she had never seen. The prison files pictured Rompilla's childhood and mental health very differently from anything defense counsel had seen or heard. An evaluation by a corrections counselor states that Rompilla was "reared in the slum environment of Allentown, Pa. vicinity. He early came to [the] attention of juvenile authorities, quit school at 16, [and] started a series of incarcerations in and out Penna. often of assaultive nature and commonly related to over-indulgence in alcoholic beverages." The same file discloses test results that the defense's mental health experts would have viewed as pointing to schizophrenia and other disorders, and test scores showing a third grade level of cognition after nine years of schooling.

The accumulated entries would have destroyed the benign conception of Rompilla's upbringing and mental capacity defense counsel had formed from talking with Rompilla himself and some of his family members, and from the reports of the mental health experts. With this information, counsel would have become skeptical of the impression given by the five family members and would unquestionably have gone further to build a mitigation case. Further effort would presumably have unearthed much of the material postconviction counsel found, including testimony from several members of Rompilla's family, whom trial counsel did not interview. Judge Sloviter summarized this evidence:

> Rompilla's parents were both severe alcoholics who drank constantly. His mother drank during her pregnancy with Rompilla, and he and his brothers eventually developed serious drinking problems. His father, who had a vicious temper, frequently beat Rompilla's mother, leaving her bruised and black-eyed, and bragged about his cheating on her. His parents fought violently, and on at least one occasion his mother stabbed his father. He was abused by his father who beat him when he was young with his hands, fists, leather straps, belts and sticks. All of the children lived in terror. There were no expressions of parental love, affection or approval. Instead, he was subjected to yelling and verbal abuse. His father locked Rompilla and his brother Richard in a small wire mesh dog pen that was filthy and excrement filled. He had an isolated background, and was not allowed to visit other children or to speak to anyone on the phone. They had no indoor plumbing in the house, he slept in the attic with no heat, and the children were not given clothes and attended school in rags.

The jury never heard any of this and neither did the mental health experts who examined Rompilla before trial. While they found "nothing helpful to [Rompilla's] case," their postconviction counterparts, alerted by information from school, medical, and prison records that trial counsel never saw, found plenty of "'red flags'" pointing up a need to test further. When they tested, they found that Rompilla "suffers from organic brain damage, an extreme mental disturbance significantly impairing several of his cognitive functions." They also said that "Rompilla's problems relate back to his childhood, and were likely caused by fetal alcohol syndrome [and that] Rompilla's capacity to appreciate the criminality of his conduct or to conform his conduct to the law was substantially impaired at the time of the offense."

These findings in turn would probably have prompted a look at school and juvenile records, all of them easy to get, showing, for example, that when Rompilla was 16 his mother "was missing from home frequently for a period of one or several weeks at a time." The same report noted that his mother "has been reported . . . frequently under the influence of alcoholic beverages, with the result that the children have always been poorly kept and on the filthy side which was also the condition of the home at all times." School records showed Rompilla's IQ was in the mentally retarded range.

This evidence adds up to a mitigation case that bears no relation to the few naked pleas for mercy actually put before the jury, and although we suppose it is possible that a jury could have heard it all and still have decided on the death penalty, that is not the test. It goes without saying that the undiscovered "mitigating evidence, taken as a whole, 'might well have influenced the jury's appraisal' of [Rompilla's] culpability," and the likelihood of a different result if the evidence had gone in is "sufficient to undermine confidence in the outcome" actually reached at sentencing.

The judgment of the Third Circuit is reversed, and Pennsylvania must either retry the case on penalty or stipulate to a life sentence.

It is so ordered.

NOTES AND QUESTIONS

1. The Court in *Strickland* had suggested that defense counsel's choices in a capital penalty-phase investigation should be informed, and may be limited, by information received from the client: "when a defendant has given counsel reason to believe that pursuing certain investigations would be fruitless or even harmful, counsel's failure to pursue those investigations may not later be challenged as unreasonable." 466 U.S. at 691. *Rompilla* limits that principle, however, as the Court suggests that counsel should have more aggressively explored defendant's school records and juvenile criminal records even though Rompilla and his own family described his upbringing and background as "normal." 545 U.S. at 381-82. Are there reasons why information from the client might not be the best source of mitigation evidence? Is Rompilla himself a good example of why clients might be unreliable narrators of their own lives?

2. The petty dispute between the prosecutor and the defense attorney over access to the transcript of the victim's testimony is an embarrassment to the legal profession. Having said that, wasn't it in the prosecution's interest to simply give defense counsel a copy of the transcript? If the prosecutor had reviewed the entire case file of Rompilla's prior conviction, and had come across the various "mitigation leads," would she have been obligated to disclose them to defense counsel?

3. Did trial counsel's ineffectiveness turn on the prosecutor's announced intention to read from the transcript of the victim's testimony from the prior conviction? Even without such notice, did defense counsel have an obligation to review the case file of the prior conviction? Did this obligation depend on defendant's pursuit of a "residual doubt" theory, that is, a defense that lingering doubt about a conviction, even if not "reasonable," militates against a death sentence? Does the simple fact of a conviction for rape and assault demonstrate the statutory aggravating factor of "a significant history of felony indications indicating the use or threat of violence"?

4. The dissent accuses the majority of imposing a "per se rule requiring counsel in every case to review the records of prior convictions use by the State as aggravation evidence," and

Chapter VIII Right to Counsel and the Defense Function

says such a requirement is inconsistent with *Strickland*'s emphasis on the "wide latitude" defense counsel must be afforded and its rejection of reliance on the sort of ABA standards the majority cites. *Id.* at 399-400. Are the standards cited even necessary? Is there any tactical approach defense counsel could take that would make it unnecessary to explore one of the three factual bases for the death penalty (and the only one of the three that is independent of the trial itself)?

5. The majority finds prejudice based on the assumption that if counsel had reviewed the prior conviction file they would have discovered "mitigation leads" in "prison files" relating to the conviction that would have, in turn, lead them to develop the strong mitigation showing summarized by the court of appeals. *Id.* at 391-92. The dissent describes this prejudice theory as resting on "serendipity," inasmuch as the defendant failed to demonstrate that the leads could not have gone unnoticed. *Id.* at 406-07. Fair point?

D. EFFECTIVE ASSISTANCE OF COUNSEL: INDIGENT DEFENSE PROBLEMS

Inasmuch as *Strickland* has prevented or at least hampered the development of a robust body of effective assistance case law, an even more serious problem for the adequacy of indigent criminal defense is the inability and/or unwillingness of state and local governments in many parts of the country to adequately fund their *Gideon* obligations. This happens both in the failure of governments to appropriate funding for public defender offices sufficient for them to reasonably staff cases and also by failing to compensate privately appointed counsel at sufficient rates that will enable a locality to have a critical mass of experienced criminal defense lawyers available for such appointments.

Most indigent defense counsel do an excellent job under extremely difficult circumstances. The next case considers a claim of ineffective assistance by appointed counsel in the representation of a juvenile, which holds special challenges and obligations for defense counsel.

State v. A.N.J.
225 P.3d 956 (Wash. 2012)

CHAMBERS, J.
In 2004, when A.N.J. was 12 years old, he pleaded guilty to first degree child molestation. Almost immediately, he moved to withdraw his plea upon realizing his juvenile sex offense criminal history would remain on his record once he was an adult, that he might have to register as a sex offender for the rest of his life, that he would have to notify his school, and that he would probably be shadowed by an adult while he was at the school. A.N.J. contends his court appointed counsel was ineffective because he failed to do an adequate investigation, failed to consult with experts, failed to fully inform him of the consequences of his plea, and failed to form a confidential relationship with him independent of his parents. He also argues that the trial judge did not adequately confirm that he understood the elements of the crime. He argues that under the facts of this case, his plea was not knowing, voluntary and intelligent, and that he should have been allowed to withdraw it. We conclude several of A.N.J.'s contentions have merit and remand to the trial court with directions that A.N.J. be allowed to withdraw his plea.

The right of effective counsel and the right of review are fundamental to, and implicit in, any meaningful modern concept of ordered liberty. More than 45 years ago Clarence Earl Gideon told his trial judge, "'The United States Supreme Court says I am entitled to be represented by Counsel.'" *Gideon v. Wainwright*. The trial judge disagreed, and without counsel at his side, Gideon was convicted and sentenced to five years in prison. The United States Supreme Court granted Gideon's handwritten petition and concluded that the right to appointed counsel was implicit in the Bill of Rights.

* * *

Yet 45 years after *Gideon*, we continue our efforts to fulfill *Gideon*'s promise. While the vast majority of public defenders do sterling and impressive work, in some times and places, inadequate funding and troublesome limits on indigent counsel have made the promise of effective assistance of counsel more myth than fact, more illusion than substance. Public funds for appointed counsel are sometimes woefully inadequate, and public contracts have imposed statistically impossible case loads on public defenders and require that the costs of experts, investigators, and conflict counsel must come out of the defenders' own already inadequate compensation. Such public contracts for public defenders discourage appropriate investigation, testing of evidence, research, and trial preparation, and literally reward the public defender financially for every guilty plea the defender delivers. Such public defender systems have been called "'meet 'em, greet 'em and plead 'em'" justice. It is clear, even if not calculated, that the prosecution benefits from a system that discourages vigorous defense and creates an economic incentive for indigent defense lawyers to plea bargain.

This case challenges the constitutional adequacy of the prior indigent criminal defense that was provided by Grant County under a previous public defender contract. Since this case, public defense in Grant County was reorganized and improved in response to changes to the Rules of Professional Conduct that addressed several of the troublesome structural components of the system.

A.N.J.

On April 7, 2004, Deputy Matney received a report that five-year-old T.M. of Moses Lake had been sexually molested by another child. On May 3, Deputy Matney interviewed T.M., who reported that his neighbor, A.N.J., had touched him and his four-year-old sister "over and under [their] clothing."

Eleven days later, the deputy called A.N.J.'s parents. Apparently, after speaking with an unnamed attorney, A.N.J.'s parents agreed to have their son talk to the police. According to A.N.J., five-year-old T.M. had attempted to instigate a game of "Icky Poke-U," which, it seems, involves putting one's hands down another's pants. A.N.J. told the deputy he had declined to play and had touched neither child. The deputy noted in his report that he did not believe A.N.J. because he stopped making eye contact and started crying.

A.N.J. was charged with one count of first degree child molestation and assigned a public defender, Douglas Anderson. Anderson had contracted with Grant County to provide public defender services in juvenile cases, among other things, for a flat fee. A 2000 version of the contract set the fee at $162,000 per year. Under the contract, Anderson was required to pay for "expert witnesses, investigators and other service necessary to an adequate . . . defense . . . except for extraordinary cases." Additionally, if conflict counsel was required, it was Anderson's responsibility to notify the court and pay for that counsel out of his flat fee. Under recent revisions of the rules governing attorneys' professional conduct, it is now unethical for an attorney to sign a public defender contract to deliver public defense if the contract requires the attorney to pay for conflict counsel, expert witness, or investigative costs out of a lump fee. The year he represented A.N.J., Anderson represented 263 clients under this contract. Additionally, he carried an average of 30-40 active dependency cases at any one time, and about another 200 cases. Anderson's only assistant was his wife, who had been home with a sick child at the time he was representing A.N.J.

Anderson filed a notice of appearance on behalf of A.N.J. on July 29, 2004. He met with his 12-year-old client and his client's parents once before the August 2, 2004, arraignment for about five minutes, and then briefly before the arraignment itself. Client and lawyer did not meet again before the pretrial conference on September 14, 2004, though A.N.J.'s father called in weekly. Anderson did little if any investigation or research into the case. Despite being given the names of witnesses who might have been able to testify that the victim had been abused by others, which could have provided an alternative explanation for T.M.'s report and knowledge, Anderson called these witnesses only once, did not reach them, and did not follow up. He never spoke to the investigating officer. He made no requests for discovery and filed no motions. At the pretrial conference, Anderson spent 5 to 10 minutes with A.N.J. and his parents.

The day after the pretrial conference, the State offered a deal. If A.N.J. would plead guilty to one count of first degree child molestation, the State would recommend a special sex offender disposition alternative program (SSODA). If A.N.J. successfully finished treatment, the charge would be reduced to second degree child molestation. Anderson believed the State's offer was a good deal and would have the added benefit to A.N.J. that he would not be charged with molesting T.M.'s younger sister.

On September 17, 2004, Anderson met with A.N.J.'s family to discuss the plea offer. Before this meeting, the evidence suggests Anderson had met with A.N.J. three times and spent somewhere between 20 and 30 minutes with them. A.N.J.'s parents estimated 5 to 10 minutes. At first, Anderson testified that he had a copy of the plea agreement at the September 17 meeting but later admitted that he did not. Anderson testified that he spent "well over a half hour" discussing the plea offer. A.N.J.'s parents estimated it was between 5 and 10 minutes. On September 22, just before the plea hearing, A.N.J. saw the plea documents for the first time. Anderson estimated that he saw A.N.J. for only about 5 minutes before the plea hearing. Anderson did not read the entire statement on plea to A.N.J.; instead he "just explained a couple of brief things regarding registering as a sex offender and the fact that [A.N.J.] could not own a firearm or have contact with the victim." The statement on the guilty plea recites the elements of the crime and gives the standard range sentence as 15-36 weeks. It also says that A.N.J. must register as a sex offender, though it says nothing about whether there is, or is not, the possibility of having the registration requirement removed. The box next to "school notification" is not checked.

Based on Anderson's testimony as a whole, it appears that he spent as little as 55 minutes with A.N.J. before the plea hearing, did no independent investigation, did not carefully review the plea agreement, and consulted with no experts. Based upon the testimony of A.N.J.'s parents, Anderson spent between 35 and 40 minutes with their son before the plea.

A.N.J. did not make a statement at his plea hearing. The judge reviewed the record and found that there was a factual basis to accept the plea. Before accepting the plea, the judge asked A.N.J. if his attorney had read him the statement, whether he understood it, and whether he understood that he could serve up to 36 weeks, not attend the same school as the victim, have to pay a fine, and register as a sex offender. A.N.J. said that he did. A.N.J. also said he had no questions. The judge did not review the elements of the crime with A.N.J. on the record. The trial judge checked a box on the form that said that "[t]he Respondent asserted that . . . [t]he respondent's lawyer has previously read to [him] the entire statement above and that [he] understood it in full."

In November 2004, A.N.J. hired a new lawyer and within five weeks moved to withdraw his guilty plea. His parents submitted declarations in support stating that Anderson had not contacted any of the witnesses they supplied, did not return their calls, and met with them only briefly. His mother also said that she "specifically asked Mr. Anderson when this charge would be dropped from [A.N.J.'s] record." According to A.N.J.'s mother, Anderson said, "'[T]he laws change every year and I'll have to look into it, but it can be done either

D. Effective Assistance of Counsel: Indigent Defense Problems

when [A.N.J.] turns eighteen (18) or twenty-one (21).'" Both parents testified they were not told that A.N.J.'s school would be informed or what the SSODA would entail. A.N.J. did not testify or submit a declaration. Anderson also initially submitted a declaration in support of A.N.J.'s motion. He acknowledged he had done no investigation, that he had not read the plea agreement to A.N.J. or had him do so, and that he had told A.N.J.'s parents that he "believed" the convictions could be removed from A.N.J.'s record when he turned 18 or 21.

However, in a subsequent declaration and at the hearing on A.N.J.'s motion to withdraw his plea, Anderson waffled on his signed declaration. A.N.J. unsuccessfully moved to limit Anderson's testimony on the ground that he had not generally waived attorney/client privilege. The judge concluded that A.N.J. had completely waived attorney/client confidentiality by moving to withdraw his guilty plea based on ineffective assistance of counsel. During the hearing, Anderson acknowledged that he probably did not review the mandatory minimum sentence with A.N.J., or the requirement that he inform his school that he was a sex offender. Anderson also acknowledged that he did not talk to the investigating officers himself and had not used an investigator during the contract year. However, he denied misleading A.N.J. about the consequences of the plea.

A.N.J. also assembled experts. Dr. Tasha Boychuk-Spears, an expert in interviewing children, submitted a declaration stating that the police detective's investigation was "insufficient" in a variety of ways, mostly because it did not take into account the suggestibility of young children. Seattle University School of Law Professor John A. Strait also submitted a declaration and testified pro bono as an expert witness in support of allowing A.N.J. to withdraw his plea. Professor Strait flatly concluded that Anderson's representation did not meet Sixth Amendment standards because, among other things, he did not do an adequate investigation, did not develop a rapport with A.N.J. individually, and did not spend sufficient time.

The court was not impressed. The trial judge did not explicitly reach in his ruling whether A.N.J. had been misinformed that the child molestation conviction could ever be stricken from his record. He found that A.N.J. had acknowledged the facts. The judge did find that A.N.J. was not informed that he would be shadowed while at school, but concluded that was a collateral consequence that did not justify withdrawing a plea. He also explicitly found that A.N.J. had not shown ineffective assistance of counsel. At sentencing, which took place on August 29, 2006, the prosecutor did not recommend a SSODA, on the ground that "[A.N.J.] has not evidenced amenability to that type of alternative disposition." The record suggests that A.N.J. had declined to be evaluated for SSODA pending final resolution on his motion to withdraw his guilty plea. Nearly two years after his plea, A.N.J. was sentenced to 15-36 weeks in custody, and required to undergo HIV (human immunodeficiency virus) and DNA (deoxyribonucleic acid) testing, and to register as a sex offender. The Court of Appeals affirmed.

• • •

INEFFECTIVE ASSISTANCE OF COUNSEL

Most of A.N.J.'s challenges are to the effectiveness of his counsel's representation. He bears the burden of showing (1) that his counsel's performance fell below an objective standard of reasonableness and, if so, (2) that counsel's poor work prejudiced him. While generally the trial judge's decision on whether to allow a defendant to withdraw a guilty plea is reviewed for abuse of discretion, "[b]ecause claims of ineffective assistance of counsel present mixed questions of law and fact, we review them de novo."

1. Adequacy of Investigation

A.N.J. challenges the adequacy of Anderson's investigation and his failure to consult with an expert witness. Anderson did no meaningful investigation. He called two witnesses provided by A.N.J.'s parents who might have testified that the complaining witness had been sexually abused before making these allegations against A.N.J. When he did not reach them on his first try, it appears he made no follow up attempts. While no binding opinion of this court has held an investigation is required, a defendant's counsel cannot properly evaluate the merits of a plea offer without evaluating the State's evidence.

The Washington Defender Association (WDA) has established standards for adequate representation. The State essentially argues that we should not consider these standards because they have not been adopted by the court. We disagree. We accept the State's point that professional standards do not establish minimum Sixth Amendment standards. However, while not binding, relevant standards are often useful to courts in evaluating things like effective assistance of counsel. We note that state law now requires each county or city providing public defense to adopt such standards, guided by standards endorsed by the Washington State Bar Association. While we do not adopt the WDA Standards for Public Defense Services, we hold they, and certainly the bar association's standards, may be considered with other evidence concerning the effective assistance of counsel.

The State essentially argues that Anderson, categorically, had no duty to investigate once he believed his client "began to admit" guilt. We disagree. First, we have already held that the failure to investigate, at least when coupled with other defects, can amount to ineffective assistance of counsel. Second, and more importantly, the fact that Anderson seemed to believe that his client was going to confess, or even was guilty, was not enough to excuse some investigation. False confessions (especially by children), mistaken eyewitness identifications, and the fallibility of child testimony are well documented. A criminal defense lawyer owes a duty to defend even a guilty client. Counsel has a duty to assist a defendant in evaluating a plea offer. Effective assistance of counsel includes assisting the defendant in making an informed decision as to whether to plead guilty or to proceed to trial. The degree and extent of investigation required will vary depending upon the issues and facts of each case, but we hold that at the very least, counsel must reasonably evaluate the evidence against the accused and the likelihood of a conviction if the case proceeds to trial so that the defendant can make a meaningful decision as to whether or not to plead guilty.

A.N.J. also argues the Grant County public defender contract in place at the time created an incentive for attorneys not to investigate their clients' cases or hire experts. We agree. Entering such contracts is now a violation of the Rules of Professional Conduct. The system effectively paid a bounty for every guilty plea delivered by assigned defense counsel to the county prosecutor. This was a dysfunctional system. We do not, at this time, go so far as the Arizona Supreme Court in holding that the system itself violates a defendant's constitutional rights to due process and right to counsel. However, we hold that if a public defender contract requires the defender to pay investigative, expert, and conflict counsel fees out of the defender's fee, the contract may be considered as evidence of ineffective assistance of counsel. We further hold that depending on the nature of the charge and the issues presented, effective assistance of counsel may require the assistance of expert witnesses to test and evaluate the evidence against a defendant.

2. Attorney's Duty to Form Confidential Relationship with Client

A.N.J. was always accompanied by his parents when he met with Anderson. Citing Washington State Bar Association (WSBA), American Bar Association (ABA) and local defense bar standards, A.N.J. criticizes Anderson for not meeting with him privately and creating a confidential attorney/client relationship with him. A.N.J. contends that the WSBA standards have been incorporated by reference into Washington statutes, which currently state that "[t]he standards endorsed by the Washington state bar association for the provision of public defense services should serve as guidelines to local legislative authorities in adopting

D. Effective Assistance of Counsel: Indigent Defense Problems

standards." That is a strong reading of the text. At the time that A.N.J. pleaded guilty, the statute merely said that bar endorsed standards "may serve as guidelines." We conclude that the professional standards are evidence of what should be done, no more.

Professor Strait condemned the constant presence of A.N.J.'s parents in both his declaration (attached to the petitioner's supplemental brief) and in testimony at the motion hearing itself. A child, it is argued, may be more candid with his lawyer and more willing to express his own view if his parents are not present. Professor Strait contends, among many other things, that "[c]andor cannot be accomplished . . . when the meeting is held jointly with the parents. There is a substantial risk that the child defer to the parents under such circumstances when advice on the decision to plead guilty or to go to trial is being provided." Thus, he suggests, by failing to establish a confidential relationship with A.N.J., Anderson undermined the attorney/client relationship, undermined client autonomy, and potentially waived attorney/client privilege. Id. A juvenile client should be given the opportunity to consult with and confide in his attorney without his parents present. We hold that the failure to provide that opportunity to a juvenile defendant is a factor that may be considered by a court when considering whether a plea was knowingly, voluntarily, and intelligently made but is not dispositive in this case.

. . .

CONCLUSION

A.N.J. seeks to withdraw his plea largely because of ineffective assistance of counsel and because he was misinformed of the consequences of the plea. To do so, he must establish manifest injustice. While "manifest injustice" has not been definitively defined, this court has clearly held that a defendant may withdraw a guilty plea if it was not knowing, voluntary, and intelligent. "A guilty plea is not knowingly made when it is based on misinformation of sentencing consequences."

We conclude that court appointed counsel's representation fell below the objective standard guaranteed by the constitution and that A.N.J. was prejudiced. When asked about the "record," Anderson responded by saying the registration requirement could be removed. This misled A.N.J. to the consequences of his plea. Considering the contractual constraints under which Anderson was working, the limited time he spent with his client before the plea, the fact he spent just a few minutes with A.N.J. to go over the statement on plea, A.N.J.'s prompt motion to withdraw his plea upon discovering the consequences of the plea, and Anderson's declaration that there was some "confusion" about when the charge could be removed and that Anderson "believed" the conviction could be removed from A.N.J.'s record when he turned 18 or 21, we conclude that A.N.J. has established that he was misinformed as to the consequences of his plea.

Due process requires that a guilty plea may be accepted only upon a showing the accused understands the nature of the charge and enters the plea intelligently and voluntarily. CrR 4.2(d) prohibited the court from accepting a plea without first assuring the defendant understood the "nature of the charge and the consequences of the plea." A.N.J. was charged with first degree child molestation. Sexual contact for the purposes of that crime must be done for gratifying sexual desire. There is nothing in the colloquy with the court, the charging documents, or any other record before this court to show that A.N.J. was informed that mere contact with another was insufficient to constitute the crime. His plea should not have been accepted.

Having concluded that because of ineffective assistance of counsel, A.N.J. was misinformed of the consequences of his plea and was not adequately informed of the nature of the charge against him, we find it unnecessary to reach the remainder of his claims. We reverse and remand to the trial court with directions that A.N.J. be allowed to withdraw his plea.

NOTES AND QUESTIONS

1. Defense counsel's performance here was shockingly unacceptable in multiple respects. But how else did the system break down? Was there really a sufficient basis for a charge of first-degree child molestation here simply because, without much more investigation (that we are told about), a 5-year old made an allegation against 12-year old A.N.J. and a police officer found A.N.J. not credible when he cried in denying the allegation? Further, how could the trial judge have taken A.N.J.'s plea under these circumstances, that is, without achieving a much higher degree of certainty that there was a factual basis for A.N.J.'s guilt and that he was aware of the consequences of his plea?

2. That a plea, especially one by a juvenile, could be handled so cavalierly is shocking, especially when considered in tandem with the high hurdle under Washington law for succeeding on a motion to withdraw a plea: that a withdrawal is "necessary to correct a manifest injustice." *Id.* at 964. The Washington standard is not an outlier—all jurisdictions place a heavy value on finality—as we explore further in Chapter XI *infra*.

3. Defense counsel stated that at one point A.N.J. "began to admit guilt," whatever that means, and the state argues that this admission excused counsel from any subsequent duty to investigate. *Id.* at 966. Why does the court so vehemently reject this argument? Does this mean that a defense lawyer can never rely on his client's admission of guilt in representing the client?

4. The court finds defense counsel ineffective for, among other reasons, failing to establish a confidential attorney-client relationship with A.N.J. as required uniformly by multiple bar standards. *Id.* at 967. Why was that so important in this case? How could the existence of a mandatory bar standard be helpful to a defense lawyer who may be facing resistance from a juvenile's parents in forming such a relationship with a juvenile client?

5. Note that one element of the charge A.N.J. pleaded guilty to is making "sexual contact" with a child "for the purpose of gratifying sexual disclosure." *Id.* at 969. Although the court discusses this issue only in the context of the adequacy of the plea hearing, was it also ineffective for defense counsel not to at least explore a defense based on this element?

6. In considering whether defense counsel has a duty to investigate, the court acknowledges that no precedent requires such a duty and that the bar standards imposing such a duty have not been "adopted" by the court. *Id.* at 965. Yet the Court holds that such a duty does exist, and declares bar standards to be "useful." In so doing the court emphatically (if implicitly) renounces the original *Strickland* anti-standard view ("reasonableness based on prevailing professional norms") and does so partially on the basis of tort law stalwart *The T.J. Hooper*, 60 F.2d 737, 740 (2d Cir. 1932), which stands generally for the idea that courts, rather than the players in a particular industry, should set standards of care. *See* Lauren Johnson, *Revisiting* The T.J. Hooper: *Stating What Is Constitutionally Required of Defense Attorneys Under the* Strickland *Evaluation of Attorney Performance*, 87 S. Cal. L. Rev. 805, 842-45 (2014) (noting trends away from self-regulation in legal and medical fields).

Professor Peter Joy has reflected on the challenges and stakes of indigent defense in *Rationing Justice by Rationing Lawyers*, 37 Wash. U. J.L. & Pol'y 205 (2011):

> As [leading death penalty lawyer] Stephen Bright has argued, caring about the quality of justice system we have for indigent criminal defendants is not about being soft or tough on crime. It is about equal justice under the law. It is an issue that everyone, especially members of the legal profession, should care about. It is about whether we have a justice system that inspires confidence in its decisions of guilt or innocence. It is about whether we can have a criminal justice system where a public defender, who is subject to the same ethics rules as every other licensed lawyer, has the ability to say "I can't take on another case and represent my clients ethically," and the courts will actually listen.

D. Effective Assistance of Counsel: Indigent Defense Problems

In recent years, the media has emphasized how the criminal justice system at the state level is in crisis because of the enormous caseloads burdening many state public defenders. This crisis occurs because there is not enough funding to support the amount of lawyers needed to serve the number of clients. Due to excessive caseloads, our society rations justice by rationing lawyers in almost every state.

More than forty years ago, the National Advisory Commission on Criminal Justice Standards and Goals set the following caseload guidelines for full-time public defenders: a maximum of 150 felonies, or 400 misdemeanors, or 200 juvenile cases, or 200 mental health matters, or 25 appeals per year. But hearings and studies reveal that these caseload limits are exceeded in almost every jurisdiction in the United States. Data collected by the Department of Justice's Bureau of Justice Statistics demonstrate that 70 percent of county-based public defender offices exceed these caseload guidelines, and fifteen of nineteen reporting state public defender programs exceeded the maximum caseload guidelines.

• • •

In a speech at the Seventy-Fifth Anniversary of the Legal Aid Society of New York, Judge Learned Hand coined the famous phrase that inspired the title for this Article: "If we are to keep our democracy, there must be one commandment: Thou shalt not ration justice." While that statement applies to all of the legal needs for the poor, Judge Hand directed the warning specifically at the lack of lawyers for those accused of crimes in state courts. Without effective, ethical representation no one accused of a crime in this country has real access to justice.

Id. at 206-09.

Many of the most serious funding problems are in states that also feature the double whammy of high poverty rates and the death penalty. Since at least the 1970s, as the full impact of *Gideon* was experienced, lawyers and bar associations and other actors have been forced to turn to litigation to seek institutional reforms — often in terms of funding — to enforce the Sixth Amendment right to effective assistance of counsel. Here are two examples of litigation growing out of these funding crises.

State v. Wigley
624 So. 2d 425 (La. 1993)

CALOGERO, Chief Justice.

We granted writs in this case to decide whether the uncompensated appointment of attorneys to represent indigent criminal defendants in unrelated cases, consolidated in this Court, violated the attorneys' constitutional rights.

Uncompensated representation of indigents, when reasonably imposed, is a professional obligation burdening the privilege of practicing law in this state, and does not violate the constitutional rights of attorneys. However, because of the changing environment in the practice of criminal law and the legal profession generally in recent decades, the practices the *Clifton* court allowed as no more than a permissible burden, now, in some cases, "constitute an abusive extension of [attorneys'] professional obligations" which *Clifton* lamented. We find that the instant appointments were unreasonable and oppressive, in retrospect at least, because the attorneys were not assured reimbursement, nor have they yet been reimbursed for their properly incurred expenses, including costs and overhead. Additionally exercising our supervisory jurisdiction, we order that the attorneys be reimbursed.

Pennie Wigley and Robert Earle Higginbotham were each charged with capital murder in unrelated cases in the 14th Judicial District, Calcasieu Parish, for homicides arising out of separate armed robberies. Since both defendants are indigent, attorneys Alcide L. Gray and Anna R. Gray were appointed to represent Wigley, and attorneys Mark A. Delphin and

David F. Dwight to represent Higginbotham. The attorneys' names had appeared on a list of nonvolunteer attorneys. Three of these attorneys were civil practitioners with little criminal law experience. The 14th Judicial District Indigent Defender Board informed the attorneys that it would not be able to pay them for their services or reimburse them for their out-of-pocket expenses. Before trial, the attorneys filed a motion for payment of expenses and compensation. After a hearing, the trial court denied the motion. Each of the defendants eventually pled guilty to manslaughter and was sentenced to prison terms. The attorneys' writ applications from the trial court ruling denying their motion for payment and compensation prompted this Court to grant writs and remand the case to the court of appeal for briefing and argument. The court of appeal thereupon held that to require an attorney "to defend without fee" violates an attorney's right to substantive due process and violates La. Const. art. I, § 13. The court of appeal then determined that $1,000 is the maximum payment allowable and ordered that the attorneys be paid $1,000 each.

Judges have been appointing attorneys to represent indigent defendants in Louisiana for over 100 years. Although the practice has occasioned some controversy, in general the bar has willingly shouldered this burden. When this Court last addressed the issue directly, we endorsed the view that

> [t]he professional obligations assumed by attorneys in this State require that a reasonable amount of time and effort be devoted to promoting the cause of justice, including the defense of indigent accused without compensation. The high purpose and traditions of the legal profession require that this burden be shouldered by its members. So long as the burden is not oppressive and is fairly shared among the members of the bar to which they belong there is no cause for complaint.

We see no reason to depart from the principle announced in *Clifton*. No provision of the state or federal constitutions requires us to do so.

However, the practices this Court approved in *Clifton*—requiring the appointed uncompensated attorneys "to bear the stenographic, secretarial, and out-of-pocket expense required" in connection with an assigned representation—are, by now, outmoded, and no longer comport with the requirement that the burden placed on attorneys be "reasonable" and "not oppressive." First, according to testimony at the district court, as the practice of criminal law has become more specialized and technical, and as the standards for what constitutes reasonably effective assistance of counsel have changed, the time an appointed attorney must devote to an indigent's defense has increased considerably. This is especially true in capital cases like these. The attorneys in these two cases presented testimony which established that three of the four of them had spent between 80 and 140 hours each, even before the hearing which was held on the motion for compensation. Had the cases proceeded through trial, they no doubt would have spent many more hours on them. Second, according to testimony at the district court, as the practice of criminal law has become more specialized and technical, the funds required for investigation, experts, and scientific tests have increased considerably. The attorneys testified that they had incurred hundreds of dollars in out-of-pocket expenses, again, even before the hearing on the motion for compensation. Finally, according to testimony at the district court, the practice of law in general has changed enough so that simply maintaining a modern office requires a significant level of expenditure. One of the attorneys introduced evidence that his overhead costs prorated over each of his billable hours in a year was about $30 per hour.

To require that attorneys represent indigents with no recompense while bearing the expenses of the representation, when the attorneys must maintain their own practices and continue to meet their other professional and financial obligations in today's changed legal marketplace, "is so onerous that it constitutes an abusive extension of their professional obligations." This institutionalized "abusive extension" cannot be perpetuated. As was said in

Smith v. State, "the profession must be relieved of this burden and . . . the burden must pass to the citizens."

However, we also believe "that the bar should continue to contribute something more" to the defense of indigents than the citizenry in general. Time and the changing practice of law have not altered the fact that "[t]he duty of the lawyer to serve is both traditional and specific."

We find that in order to be reasonable and not oppressive, any assignment of counsel to defend an indigent defendant must provide for reimbursement to the assigned attorney of properly incurred and reasonable out-of-pocket expenses and overhead costs. However, a fee for services need not be paid, as long as the time the attorney must devote to cases for which he does not receive a fee does not reach unreasonable levels. What is unreasonable in this context is to be determined by the trial judge in the exercise of his discretion. Such a system will strike a balance between the attorney's ethical duty to provide services pro bono publico and his or her practical need to continue to perform his or her other obligations.

We fully appreciate that the sources of funds from which appointed counsel may be reimbursed are limited. In future cases it will therefore be the district judge's responsibility to determine before he appoints counsel that funds sufficient to cover the anticipated expenses and overhead are likely to be available to reimburse counsel in the manner outlined above, whether the funds come from the Indigent Defender Board, from the state, from one court fund or another, from the local government subdivision pursuant to La. Rev. Stat. Ann. § 15:304 (West 1992), or from any other available source. If the district judge determines that funds are not available to reimburse appointed counsel, he should not appoint members of the private bar to represent indigents.

We realize that this solution may impair the functioning of the indigent defense system in those judicial districts which rely substantially on assigned uncompensated counsel. However, budget exigencies cannot serve as an excuse for the oppressive and abusive extension of attorneys' professional responsibilities. As we noted in *State v. Peart*, "[i]f legislative action is not forthcoming and indigent defense reform does not take place, this Court, in the exercise of its constitutional and inherent power and supervisory jurisdiction, may find it necessary to employ the more intrusive and specific measures it has thus far avoided. . . . We decline at this time to undertake these more intrusive and specific measures because this Court should not lightly tread in the affairs of other branches of government and because the legislature ought to assess such measures in the first instance."

DECREE

We affirm the court of appeal judgment insofar as it held that appointing attorneys without reimbursement for expenses constitutes an unreasonable extension of their professional obligations. We reverse the court of appeal decision insofar as it held that to require an attorney to defend without fee violates an attorney's right to substantive due process and violates La. Const. art. I sec. 13. We also reverse the court of appeal's order that these attorneys be paid only $1,000. We remand this case to the district court with instructions to hold a hearing at which the attorneys may present evidence to establish their reasonable overhead costs and reasonable expenses incurred in the course of the assigned representation. The district judge is to exercise sound discretion and set the level of reimbursement to these attorneys in conformance with the principles set out above, and order payment from such funds as are available.

JUDGMENT AFFIRMED IN PART, REVERSED IN PART; CASE REMANDED TO THE DISTRICT COURT.

. . .

DENNIS, Justice, concurring.

Chapter VIII Right to Counsel and the Defense Function

I respectfully concur in the majority opinion's holding that "any assignment of counsel to defend an indigent defendant must provide for reimbursement to the assigned attorney of properly incurred and reasonable out-of-pocket expenses and overhead costs." However in a capital case an attorney should also receive a reasonable fee for his services and time.

Representing a defendant who faces execution is the most awesome responsibility an attorney will undertake in his professional career. Adding to this responsibility is the more complex nature of practicing criminal law today in regards to both constitutional and procedural issues. In addition, there is an increased need for complex scientific and psychological evidence in today's capital trial. Representing a defendant in a capital case requires literally hundreds of hours of the attorney's time and requires the attorney's utmost attention and ability. Furthermore the weight of such a responsibility surely infects every part of the attorney's daily life. To place this burden on an attorney without the concomitant compensation that should accompany such a burden is simply unfair to the attorney and is intrinsically an abusive extension of the attorney's professional obligations.

The United States Supreme Court held in *Gideon* and its progeny, that the State is constitutionally required to provide indigent defendants with counsel. The Court did not hold that it is the bar's constitutional duty to provide indigent defendants with counsel. While the bar does have a professional obligation to provide their services, and courts have the inherent power to appoint attorneys with or without compensation since they are officers of the court, when the State seeks to end a human being's life by executing him, the State must be willing to pay, at the very least, to ensure that the scales of justice are weighted evenly. Refusing to compensate an attorney for his services in a capital case fails to meet this responsibility. "The relationship between an attorney's compensation and the quality of his or her representation cannot be ignored." An uncompensated attorney is forced to decide how much time he can spend on the appointed case rather than on the paying clients' cases, on the basis of its economic feasibility in relation to keeping his or her practice open. Furthermore, the magnitude of the resources expended by the investigative and prosecutorial forces in capital cases so far exceeds the wherewithal of uncompensated, private attorneys as to amount to a per se, self-evident travesty of the adversarial system of justice.

Capital punishment is an extremely costly institution which places heavy monetary and non-monetary costs upon the legal system and the public. Its primary justification is the benefit that society in general receives by exacting retribution from capital murderers for their offenses. Therefore, the cost of implementing the capital punishment system is clearly a charge that should be paid by the public rather than the private bar. It is not appropriate for the government to finance a major component of the cost of the public's capital punishment system by requiring extreme pecuniary sacrifices of a few individual attorneys. The burden imposed on the relatively few attorneys called upon to handle such cases far exceeds the incidental professional burdens that an attorney should be expected to assume with his or her privilege of practicing law. For the State to pass its burden of providing counsel to indigent defendants, over to the bar, without compensation, is, at least in capital cases, a per se abusive extension of the attorney's professional obligations. It matters not whether the case goes to trial or is pleaded down to a lesser offense, for all of the above concerns are implicated the moment the attorney is faced with defending a person charged with a capital crime.

NOTES AND QUESTIONS

1. The court in *Wigley* in a footnote explicitly disclaims any relationship between compensation for appointed counsel and the adequacy of the legal representation of indigent criminal defendants. Is this naïve? Can claims of ineffective assistance really be handled effectively on a "case by case basis" where appointed attorneys receive no fee whatsoever?

D. Effective Assistance of Counsel: Indigent Defense Problems

2. Note that three of the four lawyers appointed to defend the capital defendants in *Wigley* were civil practitioners with little criminal law experience, and their names were selected from a list of "nonvolunteer attorneys" that was tapped only if no attorneys from the "volunteer list" were available. Imagine these attorneys' initial conversations with their clients. These attorneys proceeded to engage in pretrial litigation over their right to fees, including a trip to the appeals court, while their clients presumably remained in jail. Imagine these attorneys' conversations with their clients about this strategy.

3. In their fee petition the attorneys claimed to have worked between 80 and 140 hours each (perhaps including the work on the fee litigation?) and incurred hundreds of dollars in out-of-pocket expenses. Does this seem like a lot for a capital case, particularly if you have no criminal experience? After the attorneys lost their fee claim on appeal, and the case was remanded, their clients pleaded guilty to manslaughter and were sentenced to prison. On its face a plea to a manslaughter charge seems like a good result in a capital case. But what story do the optics tell here? Suppose defendants won the lottery while in prison and hired you to bring an ineffective assistance claim against their appointed lawyers. What would you look into? How would you summarize the introduction to the performance part of your argument in three sentences? How would you attempt to establish prejudice under *Strickland*?

4. The court quotes approvingly from a 1965 case, decided two years after *Gideon*, establishing that all attorneys in Louisiana have a professional obligation to devote "a reasonable amount of time and effort to promoting the cause of justice, including the defense of indigent accuseds without compensation." *Id.* at 428. Is this realistic given the Sixth Amendment? Has the passage of time affected this assessment?

5. "Representing a defendant who faces execution is the most awesome responsibility an attorney will undertake in his professional career." *Id.* at 430 (Dennis, J., concurring). Justice Dennis makes a compelling case that "death is different," and even if it is generally permissible to compensate appointed counsel only for their expenses and overhead they must be paid a reasonable fee in capital cases. Are any of his arguments in support of this point unique to capital cases?

Missouri v. Pratte
298 S.W.3d 870 (Mo. 2009)

MICHAEL A. WOLFF, Judge.

INTRODUCTION

These writ proceedings raise the question of the role of the courts, the public defender commission and the legal profession in fulfilling Missouri's constitutional obligation to provide attorneys to represent indigent defendants facing incarceration for their alleged crimes.

There is an apocryphal story in legal circles that a well-known prosecutor some years ago voiced his support for the state to provide attorneys for those accused of serious crimes, noting that without legal representation, an accused cannot be tried: "I can't fry 'em if I can't try 'em."

The quip lacks good taste, but it highlights the state's problem. These cases are about public safety as well as constitutional rights. An adequate supply of lawyers available to represent indigent defendants is as important to the functioning of the criminal justice system as are adequate resources for law enforcement, prosecutors and the courts.

The public defender brought these writ proceedings after the respondent judges appointed public defenders in three cases, contrary to rules established by the commission to control the caseload of the statewide public defender program.

These cases are three of more than 83,000 in the most recent fiscal year in which a public defender was assigned to defend indigent persons charged with crimes that carried potential for incarceration.

The constitution protects the right of an accused to an attorney; the state of Missouri, through its executive and the General Assembly, provides the funds to meet this obligation. The problem that the commission confronts is that the resources provided for indigent defense are inadequate.

The statewide public defender system, under rules adopted by the commission, had the capacity last fiscal year to spend only 7.7 hours per case, including trial, appellate and capital cases.

After the commission adopted the rules to control its caseload, the disputes arose that are the subjects of these three writ proceedings. In St. Francois County, respondent Judge Kenneth W. Pratte appointed the public defender in violation of a provision in the commission's rules that denied services to indigent defendants who at some point had retained private counsel. In Boone County, respondent Judge Gary Oxenhandler appointed the public defender to defend a person accused of a probation violation; his order countermanded the public defender's designation of its district office as being of limited availability, under which the office declined to take cases of alleged probation violations, because the office caseload exceeded its maximum allowable cases. In the other Boone County case, respondent Judge Gene Hamilton appointed a full-time public defender in the lawyer's private capacity as a member of the local bar to represent an indigent person accused of a probation violation.

These three writ proceedings raise questions as to the validity of the commission's rules governing caseload management. Before dealing with the specific problems presented by these three writ cases, it is useful to review the constitutional right to counsel and the history and current status of the public defender system to understand the overall problem these cases represent.

THE CONSTITUTIONAL RIGHT TO COUNSEL

• • •

Under *Argersinger*, trial judges have an obligation to ensure that every person's right to counsel is met if he or she faces the prospect of imprisonment. It is then the duty of the court to appoint counsel if a defendant is found to be indigent. Even if counsel is not appointed at the defendant's first appearance, the rule states that the court shall appoint counsel if the court determines, "at any stage of the proceedings, [that] the failure to appoint counsel may result in injustice to the defendant."

Beyond simply ensuring that counsel is appointed to assist every defendant who faces the possibility of imprisonment, a judge also must ensure that the defendant has effective assistance of counsel.

Effective representation under the Sixth Amendment requires appropriate investigation, preparation and presentation of the client's case by counsel.

HISTORY OF THE OFFICE OF STATE PUBLIC DEFENDER

When a defendant is found to be indigent in Missouri, the defendant's Sixth Amendment right to counsel is usually met by the judge appointing the "Office of State Public Defender." The public defender's office, however, currently is facing significant case overload problems. Its lawyers and its staff are overworked.

Following the *Gideon* decision in 1963, Missouri's indigent defendants were represented by unpaid court-appointed attorneys. But in 1971, this Court held that it would no longer

D. Effective Assistance of Counsel: Indigent Defense Problems

"compel the attorneys of Missouri to discharge alone 'a duty which constitutionally is the burden of the State.'" The Missouri legislature in 1972 enacted legislation establishing a public defender commission and creating a "blended system of local public defender offices and appointed counsel programs."

By 1981, however, the funding appropriated by the legislature was running out before the end of each fiscal year. In *State ex rel. Wolff* the Court was asked to compel the state to pay attorneys for their work. At that time, this Court said that it did not have the power to do so but that it did have the power to turn to The Missouri Bar and compel lawyers to represent indigent defendants. As a result, the Court directed that the members of the legal profession represent indigent defendants until the legislature chose to fix the lack of funding.

One year later, in 1982, the General Assembly created the Office of State Public Defender under the control of the public defender commission. The legislation authorized the director of the office to determine if an accused was indigent and, if so, to appoint private counsel to take the case for a set contract fee.

Finally, in 1989, in response "to the rising cost of the contract counsel program and the increasing difficulty finding private practitioners willing to take on indigent cases for the fees paid by the State Public Defender System, the system was reorganized. . . ." The new system gave the director "the authority to hire assistant public defenders, as well as contract with private attorneys, in order to provide defense services 'by means of a centrally administered organization.'" This is the system currently in use.

During the last two decades, the number of persons sentenced for felonies in Missouri has nearly tripled. The public defender represents about 80 percent of those charged with crimes that carry the potential for incarceration. Since 1985, the number of offenders convicted of drug offenses (possession, distribution and trafficking) has increased by nearly 650 percent, while non-drug sentencing has increased by nearly 230 percent.

When the state established the public defender system in the early 1980s, one in 97 Missourians was under correctional control—either in jail or prison or on probation or parole. In 2007, by contrast, one in 36 was under correctional control, and 32 percent of those were incarcerated in prison or jail.

During the decade of the 1990s, the population of Missouri grew by 9.3 percent, while the prison population grew by 184 percent. Recent data show more than 56,000 individuals on probation; nearly 20,000 on parole (supervision that follows a prison term); more than 10,000 in Missouri jails (many of whom are awaiting trial) and about 30,000 in state prisons.

The state's vast increases in criminal prosecutions have not included commensurately increasing resources for the public defender. Much of Missouri's law enforcement and prosecutorial budgets are from local sources, while the public defender system is funded by the state government.

CURRENT STATUS OF THE OFFICE OF STATE PUBLIC DEFENDER

Although the General Assembly's creation of the public defender's office may have lessened the problems that were occurring at the time this Court decided *Wolff*, the office once again is facing inadequate resources, largely as a result of the increasing caseloads generated by the increasing numbers of persons charged with crimes. In January 2006, an interim committee of the Missouri Senate issued a "Report on the Missouri State Public Defender System." The committee found that although the public defender's office had had no addition to its staff in six years, its caseload had risen by more than 12,000 cases. The report cited an assessment of the system stating that " 'the probability that public defenders are failing to provide effective

790 Chapter VIII Right to Counsel and the Defense Function

assistance of counsel and are violating their ethical obligations to their clients increases every day.'" At the same time, however, the Senate committee stated that the office had no way to control or reduce its workload except to refuse cases and "throw the state of Missouri into federal court for constitutionally violating the right of indigent clients to effective assistance of counsel." Despite the Senate committee's report, the "caseload crisis" of the public defender's office has continued to grow.

The commission enacted 18 CSR 10-4.010 in December 2007 to limit the number of cases each public defender district could take. The rule authorizes the commission to "maintain a caseload standards protocol identifying the maximum caseload each district office can be assigned without compromising effective representation." The protocol, authorized by the rule and developed by the public defender commission, modifies the maximum recommended caseload standards developed by the National Advisory Council of the United States Department of Justice Task Force on the Courts in 1972, in which the National Advisory Council determined the maximum number of cases one lawyer could handle each year based on each type of case. The commission gives each case a weight based on how many hours a lawyer can be expected to work on the case. This is distinguishable from the National Advisory Council, which gives each case a weight based on the number of each type of case a lawyer can be expected to handle in a year.

The commission determined that each lawyer has 2,340 hours per year, or 45 hours per week, available. Yet other factors must be taken into account, which are subtracted from that number: (1) 216 hours of annual personal and holiday leave; (2) sick leave; and (3) 13.4 percent of total available attorney hours are used for non-case-related tasks such as continuing legal education, waiting in court for cases to be called and administrative tasks. After subtracting these factors from 2,340 hours, the result is 1,752 available hours per attorney per year. This number does not include a reduction for travel time and management/supervisory time of 1.5 hours per week for each employee supervised, because that number must be calculated separately for each district. The number of available hours per attorney per year (1,752 minus travel time and management time) then is multiplied by the number of lawyers in a district office to determine the district office's maximum-allowable caseload standard.

To determine whether a district office has exceeded its caseload standard, the commission determines the number of cases assigned to the office in each category of case types. Each case then is multiplied by the number of hours that a lawyer should need to devote to the case and then totaled to determine the total number of hours needed for attorneys to handle the caseload assigned to that district. This is done based on the number of cases in three-month intervals. If the number of hours needed to handle the caseload is greater than the number of available attorney hours, the district is placed on "limited availability" status pursuant to 18 CSR 10-4.010(2).

When that determination is made, the director must file a certification of limited availability with the presiding judge of each circuit court or chief judge of each appellate district affected. This certification must be accompanied by statistical verification that the office has exceeded its maximum-allowable caseload for at least three consecutive months. Notice that an office is at risk of limited availability also must be provided to each presiding or chief judge at least one month before limiting the availability of the district office. After notice is given, the rule requires the district defender and other members of the public defender management personnel to consult with the court and prosecutors to determine which categories of cases are to be excluded from representation when the district is designated as having limited availability. Once a district office is certified as having limited availability, the district defender must file with the court a final list of categories of cases that it no longer will take. 18 CSR 10-4.010(2). After certification, the public defender must provide the presiding or chief judge with a caseload report each month verifying that the district's availability remains limited. The district office is reinstated to full availability when the caseload has fallen below the maximum for two consecutive months. 18 CSR 10-4.010(3).

As of July 2009, every Missouri public defender office was over its calculated capacity under 18 CSR 10-4.010. Beyond the constitutional problems this may be creating for indigent defendants in Missouri, the public defenders themselves are risking their own professional lives. The American Bar Association has stated that there is "no exception [to the Model Rules of Professional Responsibility] for lawyers who represent indigent persons charged with crimes." Nor has this Court created an exception in the Code of Professional Responsibility, Rule 4, which governs all Missouri lawyers.

The excessive number of cases to which the public defender's offices currently are being assigned calls into question whether any public defender fully is meeting his or her ethical duties of competent and diligent representation in all cases assigned. The cases presented here to this Court show both the constitutional and ethical dilemmas currently facing the Office of State Public Defender and its clients.

NOTES AND QUESTIONS

1. The court notes that courts must ensure defendants' right to effective assistance of counsel. *Id.* at 875. What does this mean? Appointing only qualified attorneys to represent indigent defendants? Monitoring appointed attorneys' performance? If so, how is this to be done?

2. The description of Missouri's efforts to meet the challenges of *Gideon, id.* at 875-78, is not necessarily typical of states' efforts in this regard, but it does reflect the essential hybrid nature of this country's approach to indigent defense: a combination of unpaid or low-paid court-appointed attorneys and underfunded state and/or local public defender offices, sometimes with both systems operating in the same jurisdiction. The increasing burdens on such systems due to the war on drugs is also familiar.

3. The litigation before the court involves three instances where court appointments had violated rules the Missouri public defender system had enacted to control its caseload in order to ensure defendants' right to effective assistance of counsel. Do each of these three rules make sense? What options did the judges have in these cases, other than making the appointments they did, to discharge their own obligation to ensure effective assistance of counsel?

4. Recall that in *Argersinger* the Supreme Court held that the Sixth Amendment right to counsel applies only in prosecutions where a sentence of imprisonment might be imposed. How could judges use this case to decrease the burdens on public defender offices? How might the legislature respond?

The struggle exemplified in these cases is ongoing, and litigation of various kinds is often pursued where and because other efforts have failed. *See* Mary Sue Backus & Paul Marcus, *The Right to Counsel in Criminal Cases: Still a National Crisis?*, 86 Geo. Wash. L. Rev. 1564, 1589-97 (2018) (describing successful litigation efforts in New York, Idaho, and Pennsylvania). The authors of this article answer the title question affirmatively, by the way. *Id.* at 1566.

E. ZEALOUS ADVOCACY

The next case explores the extent to which basic attorney ethical rules can or should intersect with a defense attorney's obligation to zealously advocate for her client.

Chapter VIII Right to Counsel and the Defense Function

Nix v. Whiteside
475 U.S. 157 (1986)

Chief Justice BURGER delivered the opinion of the Court.

We granted certiorari to decide whether the Sixth Amendment right of a criminal defendant to assistance of counsel is violated when an attorney refuses to cooperate with the defendant in presenting perjured testimony at his trial.

• • •

Whiteside was convicted of second-degree murder by a jury verdict which was affirmed by the Iowa courts. The killing took place on February 8, 1977, in Cedar Rapids, Iowa. Whiteside and two others went to one Calvin Love's apartment late that night, seeking marihuana. Love was in bed when Whiteside and his companions arrived; an argument between Whiteside and Love over the marihuana ensued. At one point, Love directed his girlfriend to get his "piece," and at another point got up, then returned to his bed. According to Whiteside's testimony, Love then started to reach under his pillow and moved toward Whiteside. Whiteside stabbed Love in the chest, inflicting a fatal wound.

Whiteside was charged with murder, and when counsel was appointed he objected to the lawyer initially appointed, claiming that he felt uncomfortable with a lawyer who had formerly been a prosecutor. Gary L. Robinson was then appointed and immediately began an investigation. Whiteside gave him a statement that he had stabbed Love as the latter "was pulling a pistol from underneath the pillow on the bed." Upon questioning by Robinson, however, Whiteside indicated that he had not actually seen a gun, but that he was convinced that Love had a gun. No pistol was found on the premises; shortly after the police search following the stabbing, which had revealed no weapon, the victim's family had removed all of the victim's possessions from the apartment. Robinson interviewed Whiteside's companions who were present during the stabbing, and none had seen a gun during the incident. Robinson advised Whiteside that the existence of a gun was not necessary to establish the claim of self-defense, and that only a reasonable belief that the victim had a gun nearby was necessary even though no gun was actually present.

Until shortly before trial, Whiteside consistently stated to Robinson that he had not actually seen a gun, but that he was convinced that Love had a gun in his hand. About a week before trial, during preparation for direct examination, Whiteside for the first time told Robinson and his associate Donna Paulsen that he had seen something "metallic" in Love's hand. When asked about this, Whiteside responded:

> [I]n Howard Cook's case there was a gun. If I don't say I saw a gun, I'm dead.

Robinson told Whiteside that such testimony would be perjury and repeated that it was not necessary to prove that a gun was available but only that Whiteside reasonably believed that he was in danger. On Whiteside's insisting that he would testify that he saw "something metallic" Robinson told him, according to Robinson's testimony:

> [W]e could not allow him to [testify falsely] because that would be perjury, and as officers of the court we would be suborning perjury if we allowed him to do it; . . . I advised him that if he did do that it would be my duty to advise the Court of what he was doing and that I felt he was committing perjury; also, that I probably would be allowed to attempt to impeach that particular testimony.

Robinson also indicated he would seek to withdraw from the representation if Whiteside insisted on committing perjury.

Whiteside testified in his own defense at trial and stated that he "knew" that Love had a gun and that he believed Love was reaching for a gun and he had acted swiftly in self-defense. On cross-examination, he admitted that he had not actually seen a gun in Love's hand. Robinson presented evidence that Love had been seen with a sawed-off shotgun on other occasions, that the police search of the apartment may have been careless, and that the victim's family had removed everything from the apartment shortly after the crime. Robinson presented this evidence to show a basis for Whiteside's asserted fear that Love had a gun.

The jury returned a verdict of second-degree murder, and Whiteside moved for a new trial, claiming that he had been deprived of a fair trial by Robinson's admonitions not to state that he saw a gun or "something metallic." The trial court held a hearing, heard testimony by Whiteside and Robinson, and denied the motion. The trial court made specific findings that the facts were as related by Robinson.

The Supreme Court of Iowa affirmed respondent's conviction. That court held that the right to have counsel present all appropriate defenses does not extend to using perjury, and that an attorney's duty to a client does not extend to assisting a client in committing perjury. Relying on DR 7-102(A)(4) of the Iowa Code of Professional Responsibility for Lawyers, which expressly prohibits an attorney from using perjured testimony, and Iowa Code § 721.2 (now Iowa Code § 720.3 (1985)), which criminalizes subornation of perjury, the Iowa court concluded that not only were Robinson's actions permissible, but were required. The court commended "both Mr. Robinson and Ms. Paulsen for the high ethical manner in which this matter was handled."

• • •

In *Strickland v. Washington*, we held that to obtain relief by way of federal habeas corpus on a claim of a deprivation of effective assistance of counsel under the Sixth Amendment, the movant must establish both serious attorney error and prejudice. To show such error, it must be established that the assistance rendered by counsel was constitutionally deficient in that "counsel made errors so serious that counsel was not functioning as 'counsel' guaranteed the defendant by the Sixth Amendment." To show prejudice, it must be established that the claimed lapses in counsel's performance rendered the trial unfair so as to "undermine confidence in the outcome" of the trial.

In *Strickland*, we acknowledged that the Sixth Amendment does not require any particular response by counsel to a problem that may arise. Rather, the Sixth Amendment inquiry is into whether the attorney's conduct was "reasonably effective." To counteract the natural tendency to fault an unsuccessful defense, a court reviewing a claim of ineffective assistance must "indulge a strong presumption that counsel's conduct falls within the wide range of reasonable professional assistance." In giving shape to the perimeters of this range of reasonable professional assistance, *Strickland* mandates that

> [p]revailing norms of practice as reflected in American Bar Association Standards and the like, . . . are guides to determining what is reasonable, but they are only guides.

Under the Strickland standard, breach of an ethical standard does not necessarily make out a denial of the Sixth Amendment guarantee of assistance of counsel. When examining attorney conduct, a court must be careful not to narrow the wide range of conduct acceptable under the Sixth Amendment so restrictively as to constitutionalize particular standards of professional conduct and thereby intrude into the state's proper authority to define and apply the standards of professional conduct applicable to those it admits to practice in its courts. In some future case challenging attorney conduct in the course of a state-court trial, we may need to define with greater precision the weight to be given to recognized canons of ethics, the standards established by the state in statutes or professional codes, and the Sixth Amendment,

794 Chapter VIII Right to Counsel and the Defense Function

in defining the proper scope and limits on that conduct. Here we need not face that question, since virtually all of the sources speak with one voice.

C

We turn next to the question presented: the definition of the range of "reasonable professional" responses to a criminal defendant client who informs counsel that he will perjure himself on the stand. We must determine whether, in this setting, Robinson's conduct fell within the wide range of professional responses to threatened client perjury acceptable under the Sixth Amendment.

In *Strickland*, we recognized counsel's duty of loyalty and his "overarching duty to advocate the defendant's cause." Plainly, that duty is limited to legitimate, lawful conduct compatible with the very nature of a trial as a search for truth. Although counsel must take all reasonable lawful means to attain the objectives of the client, counsel is precluded from taking steps or in any way assisting the client in presenting false evidence or otherwise violating the law. This principle has consistently been recognized in most unequivocal terms by expositors of the norms of professional conduct since the first Canons of Professional Ethics were adopted by the American Bar Association in 1908. The 1908 Canon 32 provided:

> No client, corporate or individual, however powerful, nor any cause, civil or political, however important, is entitled to receive nor should any lawyer render any service or advice involving disloyalty to the law whose ministers we are, or disrespect of the judicial office, which we are bound to uphold, or corruption of any person or persons exercising a public office or private trust, or deception or betrayal of the public. . . . He must . . . observe and advise his client to observe the statute law. . . .

Of course, this Canon did no more than articulate centuries of accepted standards of conduct. Similarly, Canon 37, adopted in 1928, explicitly acknowledges as an exception to the attorney's duty of confidentiality a client's announced intention to commit a crime:

> The announced intention of a client to commit a crime is not included within the confidences which [the attorney] is bound to respect.

These principles have been carried through to contemporary codifications of an attorney's professional responsibility. Disciplinary Rule 7-102 of the Model Code of Professional Responsibility (1980), entitled "Representing a Client Within the Bounds of the Law," provides:

> (A) In his representation of a client, a lawyer shall not:
> (4) Knowingly use perjured testimony or false evidence.
> (7) Counsel or assist his client in conduct that the lawyer knows to be illegal or fraudulent.

This provision has been adopted by Iowa, and is binding on all lawyers who appear in its courts. See Iowa Code of Professional Responsibility for Lawyers (1985). The more recent Model Rules of Professional Conduct (1983) similarly admonish attorneys to obey all laws in the course of representing a client:

RULE 1.2 Scope of Representation
> (d) A lawyer shall not counsel a client to engage, or assist a client, in conduct that the lawyer knows is criminal or fraudulent. . . .

Both the Model Code of Professional Responsibility and the Model Rules of Professional Conduct also adopt the specific exception from the attorney-client privilege for disclosure of perjury that his client intends to commit or has committed. Both the Model Code and the Model Rules do not merely authorize disclosure by counsel of client perjury; they require such disclosure.

These standards confirm that the legal profession has accepted that an attorney's ethical duty to advance the interests of his client is limited by an equally solemn duty to comply with the law and standards of professional conduct; it specifically ensures that the client may not use false evidence. This special duty of an attorney to prevent and disclose frauds upon the court derives from the recognition that perjury is as much a crime as tampering with witnesses or jurors by way of promises and threats, and undermines the administration of justice.

The offense of perjury was a crime recognized at common law, and has been made a felony in most states by statute, including Iowa. An attorney who aids false testimony by questioning a witness when perjurious responses can be anticipated risks prosecution for subornation of perjury under Iowa Code § 720.3 (1985).

It is universally agreed that at a minimum the attorney's first duty when confronted with a proposal for perjurious testimony is to attempt to dissuade the client from the unlawful course of conduct. A statement directly in point is found in the commentary to the Model Rules of Professional Conduct under the heading "False Evidence":

> When false evidence is offered by the client, however, a conflict may arise between the lawyer's duty to keep the client's revelations confidential and the duty of candor to the court. Upon ascertaining that material evidence is false, the lawyer should seek to persuade the client that the evidence should not be offered or, if it has been offered, that its false character should immediately be disclosed.

The commentary thus also suggests that an attorney's revelation of his client's perjury to the court is a professionally responsible and acceptable response to the conduct of a client who has actually given perjured testimony. Similarly, the Model Rules and the commentary, as well as the Code of Professional Responsibility adopted in Iowa, expressly permit withdrawal from representation as an appropriate response of an attorney when the client threatens to commit perjury. Withdrawal of counsel when this situation arises at trial gives rise to many difficult questions including possible mistrial and claims of double jeopardy.

The essence of the brief amicus of the American Bar Association reviewing practices long accepted by ethical lawyers is that under no circumstance may a lawyer either advocate or passively tolerate a client's giving false testimony. This, of course, is consistent with the governance of trial conduct in what we have long called "a search for truth." The suggestion sometimes made that "a lawyer must believe his client, not judge him" in no sense means a lawyer can honorably be a party to or in any way give aid to presenting known perjury.

• • •

Considering Robinson's representation of respondent in light of these accepted norms of professional conduct, we discern no failure to adhere to reasonable professional standards that would in any sense make out a deprivation of the Sixth Amendment right to counsel. Whether Robinson's conduct is seen as a successful attempt to dissuade his client from committing the crime of perjury, or whether seen as a "threat" to withdraw from representation and disclose the illegal scheme, Robinson's representation of Whiteside falls well within accepted standards of professional conduct and the range of reasonable professional conduct acceptable under *Strickland*.

The Court of Appeals' holding that Robinson's "action deprived [Whiteside] of due process and effective assistance of counsel" is not supported by the record since Robinson's action, at most, deprived Whiteside of his contemplated perjury. Nothing counsel did in any way undermined Whiteside's claim that he believed the victim was reaching for a gun. Similarly, the record gives no support for holding that Robinson's action "also impermissibly compromised [Whiteside's] right to testify in his own defense by conditioning continued representation . . . and confidentiality upon [Whiteside's] restricted testimony." The record in fact shows the contrary: (a) that Whiteside did testify, and (b) he was "restricted" or restrained only from testifying falsely and was aided by Robinson in developing the basis for the fear that Love was reaching for a gun. Robinson divulged no client communications until he was compelled to do so in response to Whiteside's post-trial challenge to the quality of his performance. We see this as a case in which the attorney successfully dissuaded the client from committing the crime of perjury.

Paradoxically, even while accepting the conclusion of the Iowa trial court that Whiteside's proposed testimony would have been a criminal act, the Court of Appeals held that Robinson's efforts to persuade Whiteside not to commit that crime were improper, first, as forcing an impermissible choice between the right to counsel and the right to testify; and, second, as compromising client confidences because of Robinson's threat to disclose the contemplated perjury.

Whatever the scope of a constitutional right to testify, it is elementary that such a right does not extend to testifying falsely.

Robinson's admonitions to his client can in no sense be said to have forced respondent into an impermissible choice between his right to counsel and his right to testify as he proposed for there was no permissible choice to testify falsely. For defense counsel to take steps to persuade a criminal defendant to testify truthfully, or to withdraw, deprives the defendant of neither his right to counsel nor the right to testify truthfully.

On this record, the accused enjoyed continued representation within the bounds of reasonable professional conduct and did in fact exercise his right to testify; at most he was denied the right to have the assistance of counsel in the presentation of false testimony. Similarly, we can discern no breach of professional duty in Robinson's admonition to respondent that he would disclose respondent's perjury to the court. The crime of perjury in this setting is indistinguishable in substance from the crime of threatening or tampering with a witness or a juror. A defendant who informed his counsel that he was arranging to bribe or threaten witnesses or members of the jury would have no "right" to insist on counsel's assistance or silence. Counsel would not be limited to advising against that conduct. In short, the responsibility of an ethical lawyer, as an officer of the court and a key component of a system of justice, dedicated to a search for truth, is essentially the same whether the client announces an intention to bribe or threaten witnesses or jurors or to commit or procure perjury. No system of justice worthy of the name can tolerate a lesser standard.

The rule adopted by the Court of Appeals, which seemingly would require an attorney to remain silent while his client committed perjury, is wholly incompatible with the established standards of ethical conduct and the laws of Iowa and contrary to professional standards promulgated by that State. The position advocated by petitioner, on the contrary, is wholly consistent with the Iowa standards of professional conduct and law, with the overwhelming majority of courts, and with codes of professional ethics. Since there has been no breach of any recognized professional duty, it follows that there can be no deprivation of the right to assistance of counsel under the *Strickland* standard.

E

We hold that, as a matter of law, counsel's conduct complained of here cannot establish the prejudice required for relief under the second strand of the *Strickland* inquiry. Although a defendant need not establish that the attorney's deficient performance more likely than not altered the outcome in order to establish prejudice under *Strickland*, a defendant must show that "there is a reasonable probability that, but for counsel's unprofessional errors, the result of the proceeding would have been different." According to *Strickland*, "[a] reasonable probability is a probability sufficient to undermine confidence in the outcome." The *Strickland* Court noted that the "benchmark" of an ineffective-assistance claim is the fairness of the adversary proceeding, and that in judging prejudice and the likelihood of a different outcome, "[a] defendant has no entitlement to the luck of a lawless decisionmaker."

Whether he was persuaded or compelled to desist from perjury, Whiteside has no valid claim that confidence in the result of his trial has been diminished by his desisting from the contemplated perjury. Even if we were to assume that the jury might have believed his perjury, it does not follow that Whiteside was prejudiced.

In his attempt to evade the prejudice requirement of *Strickland*, Whiteside relies on cases involving conflicting loyalties of counsel.

Here, there was indeed a "conflict," but of a quite different kind; it was one imposed on the attorney by the client's proposal to commit the crime of fabricating testimony without which, as he put it, "I'm dead." If a "conflict" between a client's proposal and counsel's ethical obligation gives rise to a presumption that counsel's assistance was prejudicially ineffective, every guilty criminal's conviction would be suspect if the defendant had sought to obtain an acquittal by illegal means. Can anyone doubt what practices and problems would be spawned by such a rule and what volumes of litigation it would generate?

Whiteside's attorney treated Whiteside's proposed perjury in accord with professional standards, and since Whiteside's truthful testimony could not have prejudiced the result of his trial, the Court of Appeals was in error to direct the issuance of a writ of habeas corpus and must be reversed.

Reversed.

Justice BRENNAN, concurring in the judgment.

This Court has no constitutional authority to establish rules of ethical conduct for lawyers practicing in the state courts. Nor does the Court enjoy any statutory grant of jurisdiction over legal ethics.

Accordingly, it is not surprising that the Court emphasizes that it "must be careful not to narrow the wide range of conduct acceptable under the Sixth Amendment so restrictively as to constitutionalize particular standards of professional conduct and thereby intrude into the state's proper authority to define and apply the standards of professional conduct applicable to those it admits to practice in its courts." I read this as saying in another way that the Court cannot tell the States or the lawyers in the States how to behave in their courts, unless and until federal rights are violated.

Unfortunately, the Court seems unable to resist the temptation of sharing with the legal community its vision of ethical conduct. But let there be no mistake: the Court's essay regarding what constitutes the correct response to a criminal client's suggestion that he will perjure himself is pure discourse without force of law. . . . Lawyers, judges, bar associations, students, and others should understand that the problem has not now been "decided."

I join Justice Blackmun's concurrence because I agree that respondent has failed to prove the kind of prejudice necessary to make out a claim under *Strickland*.

NOTES AND QUESTIONS

1. Do you agree with defense attorney Robinson's conclusion that Whiteside's anticipated testimony that "he saw something metallic in Love's hand" would amount to perjury? What's the strongest fact suggesting perjury? What's the strongest fact against perjury? Relatedly, if Whiteside had testified to that effect, would Robinson have "knowingly use[d] perjured testimony" at trial in violation of DR 7-102 of the Model Code of Professional Responsibility?

2. The Court notes that the provision above — DR 7-102 — "has been adopted in Iowa and is binding on all lawyers who appear in its courts," *id.*, but it cites and refers to a hodgepodge of other ethical rules, comments, and norms without specifically describing them as "binding" on Iowa attorneys. To the extent these other provisions are in the nature of guidelines only, should this alter the analysis? Does it matter that all of these cited disciplinary rules are applicable in both civil and criminal contexts? Do you agree with Justice Brennan that "the Court's essay regarding what constitutes the correct response to a criminal client's suggestion that he will perjure himself is pure discourse without the force of law"? *Id.* at 177.

3. *Nix* was decided just two years after *Strickland*. Do the two cases express similar views about the relevance of bar standards and rules in evaluating Sixth Amendment ineffective assistance cases?

4. The Court works its way into its analysis of the ethical issues by noting that a defense counsel's obligations are limited to "conduct compatible with the very nature of a trial as a search for the truth." *Id.* at 166. Does the fact that a trial may be described as a "search for the truth" necessarily mean that a defense attorney's conduct must also be consistent with a "search for the truth"? Is it ethical for a defense attorney to attempt to discredit a witness that the attorney believes is testifying truthfully? Are there situations where a defense attorney *must* attempt to discredit a witness that the attorney believes is testifying truthfully?

For example, consider a bank employee eyewitness in a bank robbery prosecution who testifies that she saw the defendant rob the bank, but her story has varied from interview to interview. The defense attorney "knows" that his client was at the bank and participated in the robbery, as the defendant admitted as much in a confession to police that was suppressed because of a *Miranda* violation. Does the defense attorney nonetheless have the right — or the obligation — to attempt to discredit the eyewitness's testimony?

5. The defense at trial was that the victim, Calvin Love, did indeed have a gun, whether it was seen by Whiteside or not. In addition to the testimony of Whiteside and other witnesses that during the argument Love had asked his girlfriend to "get his piece," the defense put on evidence that Love had been seen with a gun on other occasions, had been convicted of gun possession, and by suggesting through cross-examination of government witnesses that the initial police search had been too cursory to discover the gun. Neither of Whiteside's companions testified that they saw Love with a gun that night. Knowing that this was the defense, should Robinson have handled the pretrial prep session with Whiteside differently?

6. Justice Brennan concurs but only because he believes Whiteside failed to establish prejudice within the meaning of *Strickland*. Does analysis of the prejudice issue turn on whether you believe Whiteside's desired testimony would have been perjurious?

7. The Eighth Circuit found that prejudice did not need to be proven but could be presumed because of a conflict of interest between Robinson's ethical duties and duty of loyalty to his client. What's the case for prejudice?

8. The specific ethical issue in *Whiteside* — can a lawyer elicit testimony from a client or other witness that the lawyer knows will be false — was not always a settled matter. *See* Monroe H. Freedman, *Professional Responsibility of the Criminal Defense Lawyer: The Three Hardest Questions*, 64 Mich. L. Rev. 1469 (1966) (noting that this is one of the titular "three hardest questions").

The next case considers the risks a defense attorney runs by not observing — for tactical reasons or otherwise — court discovery rules.

Taylor v. Illinois
484 U.S. 400 (1988)

Justice STEVENS delivered the opinion of the Court.

As a sanction for failing to identify a defense witness in response to a pretrial discovery request, an Illinois trial judge refused to allow the undisclosed witness to testify. The question presented is whether that refusal violated the petitioner's constitutional right to obtain the testimony of favorable witnesses. We hold that such a sanction is not absolutely prohibited by the Compulsory Process Clause of the Sixth Amendment and find no constitutional error on the specific facts of this case.

* * *

A jury convicted petitioner in 1984 of attempting to murder Jack Bridges in a street fight on the south side of Chicago on August 6, 1981. The conviction was supported by the testimony of Bridges, his brother, and three other witnesses. They described a 20-minute argument between Bridges and a young man named Derrick Travis, and a violent encounter that occurred over an hour later between several friends of Travis, including petitioner, on the one hand, and Bridges, belatedly aided by his brother, on the other. The incident was witnessed by 20 or 30 bystanders. It is undisputed that at least three members of the group which included Travis and petitioner were carrying pipes and clubs that they used to beat Bridges. Prosecution witnesses also testified that petitioner had a gun, that he shot Bridges in the back as he attempted to flee, and that, after Bridges fell, petitioner pointed the gun at Bridges' head but the weapon misfired.

Two sisters, who are friends of petitioner, testified on his behalf. In many respects their version of the incident was consistent with the prosecution's case, but they testified that it was Bridges' brother, rather than petitioner, who possessed a firearm and that he had fired into the group hitting his brother by mistake. No other witnesses testified for the defense.

Well in advance of trial, the prosecutor filed a discovery motion requesting a list of defense witnesses. In his original response, petitioner's attorney identified the two sisters who later testified and two men who did not testify. On the first day of trial, defense counsel was allowed to amend his answer by adding the names of Derrick Travis and a Chicago police officer; neither of them actually testified.

On the second day of trial, after the prosecution's two principal witnesses had completed their testimony, defense counsel made an oral motion to amend his "Answer to Discovery" to include two more witnesses, Alfred Wormley and Pam Berkhalter. In support of the motion, counsel represented that he had just been informed about them and that they had probably seen the "entire incident."

In response to the court's inquiry about defendant's failure to tell him about the two witnesses earlier, counsel acknowledged that defendant had done so, but then represented that he had been unable to locate Wormley. After noting that the witnesses' names could have been supplied even if their addresses were unknown, the trial judge directed counsel to bring them in the next day, at which time he would decide whether they could testify. The judge indicated that he was concerned about the possibility "that witnesses are being found that really weren't there."

The next morning Wormley appeared in court with defense counsel. After further colloquy about the consequences of a violation of discovery rules, counsel was permitted to make an offer of proof in the form of Wormley's testimony outside the presence of the jury. It developed that Wormley had not been a witness to the incident itself. He testified that prior to the incident he saw Jack Bridges and his brother with two guns in a blanket, that he heard them say "they were after Ray [petitioner] and the other people," and that on his way home he "happened to run into Ray and them" and warned them "to watch out because they got weapons." On cross-examination, Wormley acknowledged that he had first met defendant "about four months ago" (i.e., over two years after the incident). He also acknowledged that defense counsel had visited him at his home on the Wednesday of the week before the trial began. Thus, his testimony rather dramatically contradicted defense counsel's representations to the trial court.

After hearing Wormley testify, the trial judge concluded that the appropriate sanction for the discovery violation was to exclude his testimony. The judge explained:

> **THE COURT:** All right, I am going to deny Wormley an opportunity to testify here. He is not going to testify. I find this is a blatent [sic] violation of the discovery rules, willful violation of the rules. I also feel that defense attorneys have been violating discovery in this courtroom in the last three or four cases blatantly and I am going to put a stop to it and this is one way to do so.
>
> Further, for whatever value it is, because this is a jury trial, I have a great deal of doubt in my mind as to the veracity of this young man that testified as to whether he was an eyewitness on the scene, sees guns that are wrapped up. He doesn't know Ray but he stops Ray.
>
> At any rate, Mr. Wormley is not going to testify, be a witness in this courtroom.

The Illinois Appellate Court affirmed petitioner's conviction. It held that when "discovery rules are violated, the trial judge may exclude the evidence which the violating party wishes to introduce" and that "[t]he decision of the severity of the sanction to impose on a party who violates discovery rules rests within the sound discretion of the trial court." The court concluded that in this case "the trial court was within its discretion in refusing to allow the additional witnesses to testify."

In this Court petitioner makes two arguments. He first contends that the Sixth Amendment bars a court from ever ordering the preclusion of defense evidence as a sanction for violating a discovery rule. Alternatively, he contends that even if the right to present witnesses is not absolute, on the facts of this case the preclusion of Wormley's testimony was constitutional error. Before addressing these contentions, we consider the State's argument that the Compulsory Process Clause of the Sixth Amendment is merely a guarantee that the accused shall have the power to subpoena witnesses and simply does not apply to rulings on the admissibility of evidence.

· · ·

Petitioner's claim that the Sixth Amendment creates an absolute bar to the preclusion of the testimony of a surprise witness is just as extreme and just as unacceptable as the State's position that the Amendment is simply irrelevant. The accused does not have an unfettered right to offer testimony that is incompetent, privileged, or otherwise inadmissible under standard rules of evidence. The Compulsory Process Clause provides him with an effective weapon, but it is a weapon that cannot be used irresponsibly.

There is a significant difference between the Compulsory Process Clause weapon and other rights that are protected by the Sixth Amendment—its availability is dependent entirely on the defendant's initiative. Most other Sixth Amendment rights arise automatically on the initiation of the adversary process and no action by the defendant is necessary to make them active in his or her case. While those rights shield the defendant from potential prosecutorial abuses, the right to compel the presence and present the testimony of witnesses provides the defendant with a sword that may be employed to rebut the prosecution's case. The decision whether to employ it in a particular case rests solely with the defendant. The very nature of the right requires that its effective use be preceded by deliberate planning and affirmative conduct.

The principle that undergirds the defendant's right to present exculpatory evidence is also the source of essential limitations on the right. The adversary process could not function effectively without adherence to rules of procedure that govern the orderly presentation of facts and arguments to provide each party with a fair opportunity to assemble and submit evidence to contradict or explain the opponent's case. The trial process would be a shambles if either party had an absolute right to control the time and content of his witnesses' testimony. Neither may insist on the right to interrupt the opposing party's case, and obviously there is no absolute right to interrupt the deliberations of the jury to present newly discovered evidence. The State's interest in the orderly conduct of a criminal trial is sufficient to justify the imposition and enforcement of firm, though not always inflexible, rules relating to the identification and presentation of evidence.

The defendant's right to compulsory process is itself designed to vindicate the principle that the "ends of criminal justice would be defeated if judgments were to be founded on a partial or speculative presentation of the facts." Rules that provide for pretrial discovery of an opponent's witnesses serve the same high purpose. Discovery, like cross-examination, minimizes the risk that a judgment will be predicated on incomplete, misleading, or even deliberately fabricated testimony. The "State's interest in protecting itself against an eleventh-hour defense" is merely one component of the broader public interest in a full and truthful disclosure of critical facts.

To vindicate that interest we have held that even the defendant may not testify without being subjected to cross-examination. Moreover, in *United States v. Nobles* we upheld an order excluding the testimony of an expert witness tendered by the defendant because he had refused to permit discovery of a "highly relevant" report. Writing for the Court, Justice Powell explained:

> The court's preclusion sanction was an entirely proper method of assuring compliance with its order. Respondent's argument that this ruling deprived him of the Sixth Amendment rights to compulsory process and cross-examination misconceives the issue. The District Court did not bar the investigator's testimony. It merely prevented respondent from presenting to the jury a partial view of the credibility issue by adducing the investigator's testimony and thereafter refusing to disclose the contemporaneous report that might offer further critical insights. The Sixth Amendment does not confer the right to present testimony free from the legitimate demands of the adversarial system; one cannot invoke the Sixth Amendment as a justification for presenting what might have been a half-truth. Deciding, as we do, that it was within the court's discretion to assure that the jury would hear the full testimony of the investigator rather than a truncated portion favorable to respondent, we think it would be artificial indeed to deprive the court of the power to effectuate that judgment. Nor do we find constitutional significance in the fact that the court in this instance was able to exclude the testimony in advance rather than receive it in evidence and thereafter charge the jury to disregard it when respondent's counsel refused, as he said he would, to produce the report.

Petitioner does not question the legitimacy of a rule requiring pretrial disclosure of defense witnesses, but he argues that the sanction of preclusion of the testimony of a previously undisclosed witness is so drastic that it should never be imposed. He argues, correctly, that a less drastic sanction is always available. Prejudice to the prosecution could be minimized by granting a continuance or a mistrial to provide time for further investigation; moreover, further violations can be deterred by disciplinary sanctions against the defendant or defense counsel.

It may well be true that alternative sanctions are adequate and appropriate in most cases, but it is equally clear that they would be less effective than the preclusion sanction and that there are instances in which they would perpetuate rather than limit the prejudice to the State and the harm to the adversary process. One of the purposes of the discovery rule itself is to minimize the risk that fabricated testimony will be believed. Defendants who are willing to fabricate a defense may also be willing to fabricate excuses for failing to comply with a discovery requirement. The risk of a contempt violation may seem trivial to a defendant facing the threat of imprisonment for a term of years. A dishonest client can mislead an honest attorney, and there are occasions when an attorney assumes that the duty of loyalty to the client outweighs elementary obligations to the court.

We presume that evidence that is not discovered until after the trial is over would not have affected the outcome. It is equally reasonable to presume that there is something suspect about a defense witness who is not identified until after the 11th hour has passed. If a pattern of discovery violations is explicable only on the assumption that the violations were designed to conceal a plan to present fabricated testimony, it would be entirely appropriate to exclude the tainted evidence regardless of whether other sanctions would also be merited.

In order to reject petitioner's argument that preclusion is never a permissible sanction for a discovery violation it is neither necessary nor appropriate for us to attempt to draft a comprehensive set of standards to guide the exercise of discretion in every possible case. It is elementary, of course, that a trial court may not ignore the fundamental character of the defendant's right to offer the testimony of witnesses in his favor. But the mere invocation of that right cannot automatically and invariably outweigh countervailing public interests. The integrity of the adversary process, which depends both on the presentation of reliable evidence and the rejection of unreliable evidence, the interest in the fair and efficient administration of justice, and the potential prejudice to the truth-determining function of the trial process must also weigh in the balance.

A trial judge may certainly insist on an explanation for a party's failure to comply with a request to identify his or her witnesses in advance of trial. If that explanation reveals that the omission was willful and motivated by a desire to obtain a tactical advantage that would minimize the effectiveness of cross-examination and the ability to adduce rebuttal evidence, it would be entirely consistent with the purposes of the Compulsory Process Clause simply to exclude the witness' testimony.

The simplicity of compliance with the discovery rule is also relevant. As we have noted, the Compulsory Process Clause cannot be invoked without the prior planning and affirmative conduct of the defendant. Lawyers are accustomed to meeting deadlines. Routine preparation involves location and interrogation of potential witnesses and the serving of subpoenas on those whose testimony will be offered at trial. The burden of identifying them in advance of trial adds little to these routine demands of trial preparation.

It would demean the high purpose of the Compulsory Process Clause to construe it as encompassing an absolute right to an automatic continuance or mistrial to allow presumptively perjured testimony to be presented to a jury. We reject petitioner's argument that a preclusion sanction is never appropriate no matter how serious the defendant's discovery violation may be.

• • •

Petitioner argues that the preclusion sanction was unnecessarily harsh in this case because the voir dire examination of Wormley adequately protected the prosecution from any possible prejudice resulting from surprise. Petitioner also contends that it is unfair to visit the sins of the lawyer upon his client. Neither argument has merit.

More is at stake than possible prejudice to the prosecution. We are also concerned with the impact of this kind of conduct on the integrity of the judicial process itself. The trial judge found that the discovery violation in this case was both willful and blatant. In view of the fact that petitioner's counsel had actually interviewed Wormley during the week before the trial began and the further fact that he amended his Answer to Discovery on the first day of trial without identifying Wormley while he did identify two actual eyewitnesses whom he did not place on the stand, the inference that he was deliberately seeking a tactical advantage is inescapable. Regardless of whether prejudice to the prosecution could have been avoided in this particular case, it is plain that the case fits into the category of willful misconduct in which the severest sanction is appropriate. After all, the court, as well as the prosecutor, has a vital interest in protecting the trial process from the pollution of perjured testimony. Evidentiary rules which apply to categories of inadmissible evidence—ranging from hearsay to the fruits of illegal searches—may properly be enforced even though the particular testimony being offered is not prejudicial. The pretrial conduct revealed by the record in this case gives rise to a sufficiently strong inference that "witnesses are being found that really weren't there," to justify the sanction of preclusion.

The argument that the client should not be held responsible for his lawyer's misconduct strikes at the heart of the attorney-client relationship. Although there are basic rights that the attorney cannot waive without the fully informed and publicly acknowledged consent of the client, the lawyer has—and must have—full authority to manage the conduct of the trial. The adversary process could not function effectively if every tactical decision required client approval. Moreover, given the protections afforded by the attorney-client privilege and the fact that extreme cases may involve unscrupulous conduct by both the client and the lawyer, it would be highly impracticable to require an investigation into their relative responsibilities before applying the sanction of preclusion. In responding to discovery, the client has a duty to be candid and forthcoming with the lawyer, and when the lawyer responds, he or she speaks for the client. Putting to one side the exceptional cases in which counsel is ineffective, the client must accept the consequences of the lawyer's decision to forgo cross-examination, to decide not to put certain witnesses on the stand, or to decide not to disclose the identity of certain witnesses in advance of trial. In this case, petitioner has no greater right to disavow his lawyer's decision to conceal Wormley's identity until after the trial had commenced than he has to disavow the decision to refrain from adducing testimony from the eyewitnesses who were identified in the Answer to Discovery. Whenever a lawyer makes use of the sword provided by the Compulsory Process Clause, there is some risk that he may wound his own client.

The judgment of the Illinois Appellate Court is
Affirmed.

NOTES AND QUESTIONS

1. Usually witness disclosure would not even attract the court's attention unless raised by one of the parties. Yet there is no discussion of whether the prosecution was prejudiced by the late disclosure of witnesses by the defense on the first and second days of trial. How could the prosecution be prejudiced by late witness disclosure? How could the defense justify such late disclosure, apart from the way they did here? Why would defense counsel want to delay disclosure of defense witnesses as long as possible other than to gain a "tactical advantage"?

2. Why is the trial judge suspicious that the late-disclosed witnesses "really weren't there"? Shouldn't the prosecution be able to figure that out and/or cross-examine the defense witnesses as necessary?

804   Chapter VIII Right to Counsel and the Defense Function

3. What authority does the trial court have to conclude, as it does, that it doubts the "veracity" of Wormley and therefore to exclude him from testifying? What is the most disturbing thing about the court's explanation of its exclusion decision?

4. The Court eloquently explains how the "adversary process could not function effectively without adherence to rules of procedure that govern the orderly presentation of facts and arguments to provide each party with an opportunity to assemble and submit evidence to contradict or explain the opponent's case." *Id.* at 411. But no one is disputing this point. The issue, rather, is whether exclusion of a witness is an appropriate sanction for a violation of a discovery rule where the lawyer lied about the reason for the late disclosure. The Court states that the inference that the rule was violated to obtain a "tactical advantage is inescapable." Do you agree? Precisely what was the tactical advantage?

5. Why isn't any prejudice to the prosecution alleviated by the "less drastic sanction" of a short continuance or a mistrial? If such a sanction were imposed, are there ways for the trial court to discipline defense counsel without punishing the client as well?

6. The dissent would require a lesser sanction than preclusion for discovery violations unless the defendant is responsible for the violation. *Id.* at 419. Is such a rule workable? Are the majority's concerns about attorney-client privilege and the dissent's concerns about conflicts of interest both valid?

What are a defense attorney's obligations when she has a fundamental disagreement with the client about a strategic issue? What about when the disagreement goes beyond strategy?

McCoy v. Louisiana
584 U.S. 414 (2018)

Justice GINSBURG delivered the opinion of the Court.

In *Florida v. Nixon* this Court considered whether the Constitution bars defense counsel from conceding a capital defendant's guilt at trial "when [the] defendant, informed by counsel, neither consents nor objects." In that case, defense counsel had several times explained to the defendant a proposed guilt-phase concession strategy, but the defendant was unresponsive. We held that when counsel confers with the defendant and the defendant remains silent, neither approving nor protesting counsel's proposed concession strategy, "[no] blanket rule demand[s] the defendant's explicit consent" to implementation of that strategy.

In the case now before us, in contrast to *Nixon*, the defendant vociferously insisted that he did not engage in the charged acts and adamantly objected to any admission of guilt. Yet the trial court permitted counsel, at the guilt phase of a capital trial, to tell the jury the defendant "committed three murders. . . . [H]e's guilty." We hold that a defendant has the right to insist that counsel refrain from admitting guilt, even when counsel's experienced-based view is that confessing guilt offers the defendant the best chance to avoid the death penalty. Guaranteeing a defendant the right "to have the Assistance of Counsel for his defence," the Sixth Amendment so demands. With individual liberty — and, in capital cases, life — at stake, it is the defendant's prerogative, not counsel's, to decide on the objective of his defense: to admit guilt in the hope of gaining mercy at the sentencing stage, or to maintain his innocence, leaving it to the State to prove his guilt beyond a reasonable doubt.

• • •

On May 5, 2008, Christine and Willie Young and Gregory Colston were shot and killed in the Youngs' home in Bossier City, Louisiana. The three victims were the mother, stepfather, and son of Robert McCoy's estranged wife, Yolanda. Several days later, police arrested McCoy in Idaho. Extradited to Louisiana, McCoy was appointed counsel from the public defender's office. A Bossier Parish grand jury indicted McCoy on three counts of first-degree murder, and the prosecutor gave notice of intent to seek the death penalty. McCoy pleaded not guilty. Throughout the proceedings, he insistently maintained he was out of State at the time of the killings and that corrupt police killed the victims when a drug deal went wrong. At defense counsel's request, a court-appointed sanity commission examined McCoy and found him competent to stand trial.

In December 2009 and January 2010, McCoy told the court his relationship with assigned counsel had broken down irretrievably. He sought and gained leave to represent himself until his parents engaged new counsel for him. In March 2010, Larry English, engaged by McCoy's parents, enrolled as McCoy's counsel. English eventually concluded that the evidence against McCoy was overwhelming and that, absent a concession at the guilt stage that McCoy was the killer, a death sentence would be impossible to avoid at the penalty phase. McCoy, English reported, was "furious" when told, two weeks before trial was scheduled to begin, that English would concede McCoy's commission of the triple murders. McCoy told English "not to make that concession," and English knew of McCoy's "complet[e] oppos[ition] to [English] telling the jury that [McCoy] was guilty of killing the three victims"; instead of any concession, McCoy pressed English to pursue acquittal.

At a July 26, 2011 hearing, McCoy sought to terminate English's representation, and English asked to be relieved if McCoy secured other counsel. With trial set to start two days later, the court refused to relieve English and directed that he remain as counsel of record. "[Y]ou are the attorney," the court told English when he expressed disagreement with McCoy's wish to put on a defense case, and "you have to make the trial decision of what you're going to proceed with."

At the beginning of his opening statement at the guilt phase of the trial, English told the jury there was "no way reasonably possible" that they could hear the prosecution's evidence and reach "any other conclusion than Robert McCoy was the cause of these individuals' death." McCoy protested; out of earshot of the jury, McCoy told the court that English was "selling [him] out" by maintaining that McCoy "murdered [his] family." The trial court reiterated that English was "representing" McCoy and told McCoy that the court would not permit "any other outbursts." Continuing his opening statement, English told the jury the evidence is "unambiguous," "my client committed three murders." McCoy testified in his own defense, maintaining his innocence and pressing an alibi difficult to fathom. In his closing argument, English reiterated that McCoy was the killer. On that issue, English told the jury that he "took [the] burden off of [the prosecutor]." The jury then returned a unanimous verdict of guilty of first-degree murder on all three counts. At the penalty phase, English again conceded "Robert McCoy committed these crimes," but urged mercy in view of McCoy's "serious mental and emotional issues." The jury returned three death verdicts.

Represented by new counsel, McCoy unsuccessfully moved for a new trial, arguing that the trial court violated his constitutional rights by allowing English to concede McCoy "committed three murders," over McCoy's objection. The Louisiana Supreme Court affirmed the trial court's ruling that defense counsel had authority so to concede guilt, despite the defendant's opposition to any admission of guilt. The concession was permissible, the court concluded, because counsel reasonably believed that admitting guilt afforded McCoy the best chance to avoid a death sentence.

We granted certiorari in view of a division of opinion among state courts of last resort on the question whether it is unconstitutional to allow defense counsel to concede guilt over the defendant's intransigent and unambiguous objection.

. . .

The Sixth Amendment guarantees to each criminal defendant "the Assistance of Counsel for his defence." At common law, self-representation was the norm. As the laws of England and the American Colonies developed, providing for a right to counsel in criminal cases, self-representation remained common and the right to proceed without counsel was recognized. Even now, when most defendants choose to be represented by counsel, an accused may insist upon representing herself — however counterproductive that course may be. As this Court explained, "[t]he right to defend is personal," and a defendant's choice in exercising that right "must be honored out of 'that respect for the individual which is the lifeblood of the law.'"

The choice is not all or nothing: To gain assistance, a defendant need not surrender control entirely to counsel. For the Sixth Amendment, in "grant[ing] to the accused personally the right to make his defense," "speaks of the 'assistance' of counsel, and an assistant, however expert, is still an assistant." Trial management is the lawyer's province: Counsel provides his or her assistance by making decisions such as "what arguments to pursue, what evidentiary objections to raise, and what agreements to conclude regarding the admission of evidence." Some decisions, however, are reserved for the client — notably, whether to plead guilty, waive the right to a jury trial, testify in one's own behalf, and forgo an appeal.

Autonomy to decide that the objective of the defense is to assert innocence belongs in this latter category. Just as a defendant may steadfastly refuse to plead guilty in the face of overwhelming evidence against her, or reject the assistance of legal counsel despite the defendant's own inexperience and lack of professional qualifications, so may she insist on maintaining her innocence at the guilt phase of a capital trial. These are not strategic choices about how best to achieve a client's objectives; they are choices about what the client's objectives in fact are.

Counsel may reasonably assess a concession of guilt as best suited to avoiding the death penalty, as English did in this case. But the client may not share that objective. He may wish to avoid, above all else, the opprobrium that comes with admitting he killed family members. Or he may hold life in prison not worth living and prefer to risk death for any hope, however small, of exoneration. When a client expressly asserts that the objective of "his defence" is to maintain innocence of the charged criminal acts, his lawyer must abide by that objective and may not override it by conceding guilt.

Preserving for the defendant the ability to decide whether to maintain his innocence should not displace counsel's, or the court's, respective trial management roles. Counsel, in any case, must still develop a trial strategy and discuss it with her client, explaining why, in her view, conceding guilt would be the best option. In this case, the court had determined that McCoy was competent to stand trial, i.e., that McCoy had "sufficient present ability to consult with his lawyer with a reasonable degree of rational understanding." If, after consultations with English concerning the management of the defense, McCoy disagreed with English's proposal to concede McCoy committed three murders, it was not open to English to override McCoy's objection. English could not interfere with McCoy's telling the jury "I was not the murderer," although counsel could, if consistent with providing effective assistance, focus his own collaboration on urging that McCoy's mental state weighed against conviction.

* * *

Florida v. Nixon is not to the contrary. Nixon's attorney did not negate Nixon's autonomy by overriding Nixon's desired defense objective, for Nixon never asserted any such objective. Nixon "was generally unresponsive" during discussions of trial strategy, and "never verbally approved or protested" counsel's proposed approach. Nixon complained about the admission of his guilt only after trial. McCoy, in contrast, opposed English's assertion of his guilt at every opportunity, before and during trial, both in conference with his lawyer and in open court. If a client declines to participate in his defense, then an attorney may permissibly guide the defense pursuant to the strategy she believes to be in the defendant's best interest. Presented with express statements of the client's will to maintain innocence, however, counsel may not steer the ship the other way.

The Louisiana Supreme Court concluded that English's refusal to maintain McCoy's innocence was necessitated by Louisiana Rule of Professional Conduct 1.2(d) (2017), which provides that "[a] lawyer shall not counsel a client to engage, or assist a client, in conduct that the lawyer knows is criminal or fraudulent." Presenting McCoy's alibi defense, the court said, would put English in an "ethical conundrum," implicating English in perjury. But McCoy's case does not resemble *Nix*, where the defendant told his lawyer that he intended to commit perjury. There was no such avowed perjury here. English harbored no doubt that McCoy believed what he was saying; English simply disbelieved McCoy's account in view of the prosecution's evidence. English's express motivation for conceding guilt was not to avoid suborning perjury, but to try to build credibility with the jury, and thus obtain a sentence lesser than death. Louisiana's ethical rules might have stopped English from presenting McCoy's alibi evidence if English knew perjury was involved. But Louisiana has identified no ethical rule requiring English to admit McCoy's guilt over McCoy's objection.

The dissent describes the conflict between English and McCoy as "rare" and "unlikely to recur." Yet the Louisiana Supreme Court parted ways with three other State Supreme Courts that have addressed this conflict in the past twenty years. In each of the three cases, as here, the defendant repeatedly and adamantly insisted on maintaining his factual innocence despite counsel's preferred course: concession of the defendant's commission of criminal acts and pursuit of diminished capacity, mental illness, or lack of premeditation defenses. These were not strategic disputes about whether to concede an element of a charged offense; they were intractable disagreements about the fundamental objective of the defendant's representation. For McCoy, that objective was to maintain "I did not kill the members of my family." In this stark scenario, we agree with the majority of state courts of last resort that counsel may not admit her client's guilt of a charged crime over the client's intransigent objection to that admission.

• • •

Because a client's autonomy, not counsel's competence, is in issue, we do not apply our ineffective-assistance-of-counsel jurisprudence, to McCoy's claim. To gain redress for attorney error, a defendant ordinarily must show prejudice. Here, however, the violation of McCoy's protected autonomy right was complete when the court allowed counsel to usurp control of an issue within McCoy's sole prerogative.

Violation of a defendant's Sixth Amendment-secured autonomy ranks as error of the kind our decisions have called "structural"; when present, such an error is not subject to harmless-error review. An error may be ranked structural, we have explained, "if the right at issue is not designed to protect the defendant from erroneous conviction but instead protects some other interest," such as "the fundamental legal principle that a defendant must be allowed to make his own choices about the proper way to protect his own liberty. An error might also count as structural when its effects are too hard to measure, as is true of the right to counsel of choice, or where the error will inevitably signal fundamental unfairness, as we have said of a judge's failure to tell the jury that it may not convict unless it finds the defendant's guilt beyond a reasonable doubt.

Under at least the first two rationales, counsel's admission of a client's guilt over the client's express objection is error structural in kind. Such an admission blocks the defendant's right to make the fundamental choices about his own defense. And the effects of the admission would be immeasurable, because a jury would almost certainly be swayed by a lawyer's concession of his client's guilt. McCoy must therefore be accorded a new trial without any need first to show prejudice.

Larry English was placed in a difficult position; he had an unruly client and faced a strong government case. He reasonably thought the objective of his representation should be avoidance of the death penalty. But McCoy insistently maintained: "I did not murder my family." Once he communicated that to court and counsel, strenuously objecting to English's proposed strategy, a concession of guilt should have been off the table. The trial court's allowance of English's admission of McCoy's guilt despite McCoy's insistent objections was incompatible with the Sixth Amendment. Because the error was structural, a new trial is the required corrective.

For the reasons stated, the judgment of the Louisiana Supreme Court is reversed, and the case is remanded for further proceedings not inconsistent with this opinion.

[Justices Alito, Thomas, and Gorsuch dissented.]

NOTES AND QUESTIONS

1. Consider the dilemma of defense counsel on the eve of trial. His client has rejected his recommended strategy; he doesn't believe his client's alibi defense; his motion to withdraw has been denied; he is aware of the *Florida v. Nixon* case; and the trial judge has told him that it's his "trial decision" whether to contest guilt. Was there anything he could have done that would not be disastrous? It's unclear if he told the judge he had a conflict of interest in moving to withdraw. Did he have a conflict?

2. The Court divides the universe of legal defense into two neat compartments: trial management, the lawyer's responsibility, and the objective of the defense (including such decisions as to whether to plead guilty or to testify), the client's responsibility. Is it always going to be clear who has the responsibility for a decision? Might it be the client's decision whether and how aggressively to cross-examine a witness who is a family member, for example? *See Schriro*

Robert McCoy (left) and Larry English, McCoy's counsel (right)

v. Landrigan, 550 U.S. 465 (2007) (defense counsel not ineffective in capital case for heeding client's instruction not to present mitigating evidence from his ex-wife and birth mother).

3. The Louisiana Supreme Court found that counsel had no choice but to concede guilt due to the same essential disciplinary rule that was at issue in *Nix v. Whiteside*. The Supreme Court essentially overrules that court on the ethical responsibilities of Louisiana lawyers, concluding that the ethical rule is inapplicable because there was "no such avowed perjury here . . . [and defense counsel] harbored no doubt that McCoy believed what he was saying . . . [but] simply disbelieved McCoy's account in view of the prosecution's evidence." 584 U.S. at 425. Is this a persuasive distinction? Recall the dissent's point in *Nix* about the lack of federal judicial power over state ethical rules.

4. Hovering over this case is the Supreme Court's decision in *Faretta v. California*, 422 U.S. 806 (1975), cited throughout *McCoy*, which held that an accused has a Sixth Amendment right to represent himself at trial upon an unequivocal request and a knowing and intelligent waiver of the right to have counsel. The Court's decision in *Faretta* was based on a combination of precedent, the presence of the word "assistance" in the text of the Sixth Amendment, and the "respect for the individual which is the lifeblood of the law," a value the Court relies on so heavily here. Indeed, because McCoy's "autonomy" rights were violated the Court doesn't even review for prejudice under *Strickland* but rather reverses for "structural error." The logic of this conclusion makes sense, but doesn't it seem that defendants whose counsel have been deficient have been denied something that should be on a constitutional par with "autonomy"?

CHAPTER IX

THE PROSECUTION FUNCTION

Professor Angela J. Davis makes no bones about it: "Prosecutors are the most powerful officials in the criminal justice system." Angela J. Davis, Arbitrary Justice: The Power of the American Prosecutor 5 (2007). Their power over the initiation, direction, and outcome of criminal cases, moreover, is "totally discretionary and virtually unreviewable." *Id.* Professor Davis's assertions reflect the consensus view that the prosecution has become the most powerful, and maybe the "most dangerous branch," in the criminal justice system. *See, e.g.,* Samuel W. Buell, *Is the White Collar Offender Privileged?*, 63 Duke L.J. 823, 882 (2014) ("Criminal law scholars are in near complete agreement that prosecutorial discretion now dominates the path that a particular case follows in the criminal justice system"). Prosecutors' discretion exists at every step of the criminal process. Two specific exercises of that discretion—in plea bargaining and sentencing—are considered in Chapters XI and XVI *infra.*

Only in America are prosecutors elected. Just four states—Connecticut, New Jersey, Delaware, and Rhode Island—have appointed rather than elected district attorneys. By contrast, the United States attorney general, and the U.S. attorneys overseeing federal prosecution in the nation's 94 federal judicial districts, are appointed by the President. The reasons the vast majority of states have elected prosecutors are largely historical, the product of a three-decade burst of Jacksonian populism in the middle third of the nineteenth century. *See* Michael J. Ellis, *The Origins of the Elected Prosecutor*, 121 Yale L.J. 1528, 1530-36 & n.3 (2012).

Notwithstanding their power and discretionary authority, the criminal justice system assigns important specific and general responsibilities to prosecutors that are in tension with their law enforcement mission. Most important, by virtue of *Brady v. Maryland*, 373 U.S. 83 (1963), and its progeny, prosecutors are responsible for disclosing exculpatory information and other materials to the defense—their adversary—in furtherance of the Constitution's due process guarantee. Less specifically, and less authoritatively, prosecutors are obliged to "Do Justice," not simply produce convictions, inasmuch as they are not just lawyers for a party but representatives of the state.

This chapter addresses different aspects of the powers and responsibilities of the prosecution though an overarching three-part structure: Discretion (Section A), Disclosure Obligations (Section B), and Ethics and Accountability (Section C). Subsection A.1 is introductory in nature, looking at various manifestations of the discretion "problem." Subsection A.2 looks at discretion in the specific context of prosecutorial charging decisions, including the extent to which race may affect those decisions. Subsection A.3 looks at the wide latitude given prosecutors to use unsavory witnesses and tactics to advance their law enforcement ends.

The subsections of Section B consider three aspects of the prosecutor's disclosure obligations. Subsection B.1 addresses the prosecutor's constitutionally imposed *Brady* obligations, as noted above. Subsection B.2 looks at the prosecutor's discovery obligations under discovery rules. And subsection B.3 considers the prosecutor's statutory obligations, often overlapping with constitutional and discovery obligations, to disclose witness statements.

Chapter IX The Prosecution Function

Subsection C.1 examines the general ethical obligations of prosecutors, obligations generally regarded as different than those of other lawyers. Subsection C.2 considers the general lack of accountability of prosecutors for their errors in exercising the above responsibilities. Finally, subsection C.3 looks at a few selected instances of litigated prosecutorial misconduct.

A. DISCRETION

1. The Concern About Discretion

Prosecutorial discretion is often deemed necessary, if less than ideal, because criminal statutes are numerous and broad, and it would be unrealistic to attempt to prosecute all violations of them. Davis, Arbitrary Justice, *supra* at 12-13 ("Prosecutorial discretion is essential to the operation of our criminal justice system, despite the potential for abuse."). And, further, none of us would want to live in a state where the machinery existed that would allow for the prosecution of 100 percent of illegal conduct. Thankfully, a scarcity in prosecutorial resources also mandates a wide zone of discretion for prosecutors. *Id.* at 13-14.

The broad discretion enjoyed by prosecutors draws recurrent criticism. Professor Vorenberg's critique remains a classic, at least as valid today as it was when made in 1981, as prosecutors' discretionary powers have only increased in the ensuing decades and the "possibility of trial" as a "check" on prosecutors has been all but extinguished inasmuch as more than 95 percent of cases are resolved by guilty pleas:

> The most important reforms in criminal justice in recent years have been the limits imposed on the exercise of discretionary power.
>
> During Chief Justice Warren's tenure, the United States Supreme Court imposed new restrictions on when and how the police may take suspects into custody and seek information by search and by interrogation. Large federal subsidies from the Law Enforcement Assistance Administration during the 1970's encouraged the nation's police agencies to impose greater centralized direction and more civilized standards of conduct on individual officers. Magistrates' power to set bail and other terms for pretrial release has become subject to new statutory controls. Legislatures have limited the leeway accorded sentencing judges and parole boards. Even the largely uncontrolled power that correctional officials once exercised over prisoners has been sharply limited by a series of court decisions since the late 1960's that have imposed substantive and procedural limitations on official discretion.
>
> Prosecutors, however, have been spared this shrinking of discretionary authority. In fact, as the powers of other criminal justice officials have contracted, those of prosecutors have expanded. The fate of most of those accused of crime is determined by prosecutors, but typically this determination takes place out of public view — in the hallways of the courthouse, in the prosecutors' offices, or on the telephone. There is a broad and rather casual acceptance of the fact that prosecutors often exercise greater control over the administration of criminal justice than do other officials.
>
> The attack on discretion in criminal administration was, in part, a reflection of a broader demand that those who exercise authority in public institutions should operate with a higher degree of visibility and accountability. It also drew special strength from efforts over two decades to make the criminal justice system fairer and more effective. It thus seems anomalous at best that, in a system dedicated to due process, great and essentially unreviewable powers are vested in the prosecutor.
>
> To be sure, the divergence between our stated ideal for criminal justice and the actual operation of that system should not be overstated. The ultimate protection for one accused of crime is his "day in court," the confrontation with his accuser. The accused's freedom is guaranteed unless the state can convince a judge or jury of his guilt beyond a reasonable doubt. The drama of a criminal trial has a strong hold on public imagination, but what happens in court is not theater; it is the core of a system of justice that aims to protect the innocent from the consequences

of a false conviction, and the innocent and guilty alike from affronts to their dignity. The trial is open to the public both to protect the defendant against prejudice and abuse and to serve the public's interest in knowing how officials deal with those accused of crime.

The possibility of trial defines the terms of the relationship between prosecution and defense in much the same way that the threat of war affects diplomatic dealings between nations. But the existence of trials cannot check prosecutorial powers not dependent on trial. These powers include the prosecutor's wide discretion in making decisions about charging, plea bargaining, and allocating investigative resources.

James Vorenberg, *Decent Restraint of Prosecutorial Power*, 94 Harv. L. Rev. 1521, 1522-24 (1981).

In response to similar criticisms, the Department of Justice in 1980 announced the promulgation of the Principles of Federal Prosecution, which were intended to, inter alia, "bolster public confidence in the administration of [criminal] justice." Benjamin R. Civiletti, U.S. Attorney Gen., Remarks at the Ninth Circuit Judicial Conference 7-8 (July 14, 1980). The Principles ultimately were incorporated into the United States Attorneys' Manual, rebranded in 2018 as the "Justice Manual," the DOJ's main policy organ.

The Principles are not shy about the breadth of prosecutorial discretion. The Preamble notes seven specific areas in which government attorneys exercise discretion: initiating and declining prosecution; selecting charges; taking a position on detention or release pending trial; entering into plea agreements; opposing offers to plead nolo contendere; entering into non-prosecution agreements in return for cooperation; and participating in sentencing. Justice Manual, Principles of Federal Prosecution, § 9-27.110 (Purpose).

This list of areas in which prosecutors make discretionary decisions could easily be doubled or tripled, as prosecutors exercise discretion every day in numerous other important areas outside the "check" of trials: deciding whether to obtain a grant of immunity for a witness who intends to assert the Fifth Amendment; deciding what pretrial disclosures to make to defendants, and when to make them; deciding what criminal witnesses to use as cooperators, and whether they potentially warrant a recommendation of leniency and, if so, how much; and deciding on the quantum and character of evidence the grand jury should receive before being asked to return an indictment. The list could go on.

The Preamble proceeds to confirm the constitutionality of the Department of Justice's wide discretion, reflects on the constitutional source of that discretion and then, more humbly, notes that "it is desirable, in the interest of the fair and effective administration of justice, that all federal prosecutors be guided by a general statement of principles that summarizes appropriate considerations to be weighed, and desirable practices to be followed, in discharging their prosecutorial responsibilities."

Post-preamble the Justice Manual goes on to address the exercise of discretion in a few dozen specific areas. As a representative example, the provision titled "Plea Agreements Generally," provides as follows:

These agreements are governed by the same fundamental principles as are charging decisions: prosecutors will generally seek a plea to the most serious offense that is consistent with the nature and full extent of the defendant's conduct and likely to result in a sustainable conviction, informed by an individualized assessment of all of the facts and circumstances of each particular case.

Id. § 9-27.400. Does anything here provide a significant limitation on prosecutorial discretion in entering into a plea agreement? And even if the provision were more limiting by its terms, prosecutors "may modify or depart from the principles set forth herein as necessary in the interests of fair and effective law enforcement," *id.* § 9-27.140 (Modification or

814 Chapter IX The Prosecution Function

Departure). Plus, all of the provisions of the Justice Manual are for internal use only: They "are not intended to create a substantive or procedural right or benefit, enforceable at law, and may not be relied upon by a party to litigation with the United States." *Id.* § 9-27.150.

The department's efforts to craft prosecution principles was certainly laudable. And there is no doubt that the Principles are consulted internally by the DOJ in debating close calls. But the Principles' generalized language and external nonenforceability make them virtually toothless as a "check" on prosecutors' exercises of discretion.

Are meaningful principles of prosecution realistic? What would they look like? How could they overcome the heavily caveated nature of the DOJ Principles of Prosecution?

Another classic expression of concerns about prosecutorial discretion is found in Justice Scalia's dissenting opinion in the next case.

Morrison v. Olson
487 U.S. 654 (1988)

Chief Justice REHNQUIST delivered the opinion of the Court.

This case presents us with a challenge to the independent counsel provisions of the Ethics in Government Act of 1978, 28 U.S.C. §§ 49, 591 et seq. (1982 ed., Supp. V). We hold today that these provisions of the Act do not violate the Appointments Clause of the Constitution, Art. II, § 2, cl. 2, or the limitations of Article III, nor do they impermissibly interfere with the President's authority under Article II in violation of the constitutional principle of separation of powers.

I

Briefly stated, Title VI of the Ethics in Government Act (Title VI or the Act), 28 U.S.C. §§ 591-599 (1982 ed., Supp. V), allows for the appointment of an "independent counsel" to investigate and, if appropriate, prosecute certain high-ranking Government officials for violations of federal criminal laws. The Act requires the Attorney General, upon receipt of information that he determines is "sufficient to constitute grounds to investigate whether any person [covered by the Act] may have violated any Federal criminal law," to conduct a preliminary investigation of the matter. When the Attorney General has completed this investigation, or 90 days has elapsed, he is required to report to a special court (the Special Division) created by the Act "for the purpose of appointing independent counsels." 28 U.S.C. § 49 (1982 ed., Supp. V). If the Attorney General determines that "there are no reasonable grounds to believe that further investigation is warranted," then he must notify the Special Division of this result. In such a case, "the division of the court shall have no power to appoint an independent counsel." § 592(b)(1). If, however, the Attorney General has determined that there are "reasonable grounds to believe that further investigation or prosecution is warranted," then he "shall apply to the division of the court for the appointment of an independent counsel." The Attorney General's application to the court "shall contain sufficient information to assist the [court] in selecting an independent counsel and in defining that independent counsel's prosecutorial jurisdiction." § 592(d). Upon receiving this application, the Special Division "shall appoint an appropriate independent counsel and shall define that independent counsel's prosecutorial jurisdiction." § 593(b).

With respect to all matters within the independent counsel's jurisdiction, the Act grants the counsel "full power and independent authority to exercise all investigative and

A. Discretion 815

prosecutorial functions and powers of the Department of Justice, the Attorney General, and any other officer or employee of the Department of Justice." § 594(a). The functions of the independent counsel include conducting grand jury proceedings and other investigations, participating in civil and criminal court proceedings and litigation, and appealing any decision in any case in which the counsel participates in an official capacity. §§ 594(a)(1)-(3). Under § 594(a)(9), the counsel's powers include "initiating and conducting prosecutions in any court of competent jurisdiction, framing and signing indictments, filing informations, and handling all aspects of any case, in the name of the United States." The counsel may appoint employees, § 594(c), may request and obtain assistance from the Department of Justice, § 594(d), and may accept referral of matters from the Attorney General if the matter falls within the counsel's jurisdiction as defined by the Special Division, § 594(e). The Act also states that an independent counsel "shall, except where not possible, comply with the written or other established policies of the Department of Justice respecting enforcement of the criminal laws." § 594(f). In addition, whenever a matter has been referred to an independent counsel under the Act, the Attorney General and the Justice Department are required to suspend all investigations and proceedings regarding the matter. § 597(a). An independent counsel has "full authority to dismiss matters within [his or her] prosecutorial jurisdiction without conducting an investigation or at any subsequent time before prosecution, if to do so would be consistent" with Department of Justice policy. § 594(g).7

• • •

SCALIA, J., dissenting.

• • •

V

The purpose of the separation and equilibration of powers in general, and of the unitary Executive in particular, was not merely to assure effective government but to preserve individual freedom. Those who hold or have held offices covered by the Ethics in Government Act are entitled to that protection as much as the rest of us, and I conclude my discussion by considering the effect of the Act upon the fairness of the process they receive.

Only someone who has worked in the field of law enforcement can fully appreciate the vast power and the immense discretion that are placed in the hands of a prosecutor with respect to the objects of his investigation. Justice Robert Jackson, when he was Attorney General under President Franklin Roosevelt, described it in a memorable speech to United States Attorneys, as follows:

> There is a most important reason why the prosecutor should have, as nearly as possible, a detached and impartial view of all groups in his community. Law enforcement is not automatic. It isn't blind. One of the greatest difficulties of the position of prosecutor is that he must pick his cases, because no prosecutor can even investigate all of the cases in which he receives complaints. If the Department of Justice were to make even a pretense of reaching every probable violation of federal law, ten times its present staff will be inadequate. We know that no local police force can strictly enforce the traffic laws, or it would arrest half the driving population on any given morning. What every prosecutor is practically required to do is to select the cases for prosecution and to select those in which the offense is the most flagrant, the public harm the greatest, and the proof the most certain.
>
> If the prosecutor is obliged to choose his case, it follows that he can choose his defendants. Therein is the most dangerous power of the prosecutor: that he will pick people that he thinks

he should get, rather than cases that need to be prosecuted. With the law books filled with a great assortment of crimes, a prosecutor stands a fair chance of finding at least a technical violation of some act on the part of almost anyone. In such a case, it is not a question of discovering the commission of a crime and then looking for the man who has committed it, it is a question of picking the man and then searching the law books, or putting investigators to work, to pin some offense on him. It is in this realm — in which the prosecutor picks some person whom he dislikes or desires to embarrass, or selects some group of unpopular persons and then looks for an offense, that the greatest danger of abuse of prosecuting power lies. It is here that law enforcement becomes personal, and the real crime becomes that of being unpopular with the predominant or governing group, being attached to the wrong political views, or being personally obnoxious to or in the way of the prosecutor himself.

R. Jackson, The Federal Prosecutor, Address Delivered at the Second Annual Conference of United States Attorneys, April 1, 1940.

Under our system of government, the primary check against prosecutorial abuse is a political one. The prosecutors who exercise this awesome discretion are selected and can be removed by a President, whom the people have trusted enough to elect. Moreover, when crimes are not investigated and prosecuted fairly, nonselectively, with a reasonable sense of proportion, the President pays the cost in political damage to his administration. If federal prosecutors "pick people that [they] thin[k] [they] should get, rather than cases that need to be prosecuted," if they amass many more resources against a particular prominent individual, or against a particular class of political protesters, or against members of a particular political party, than the gravity of the alleged offenses or the record of successful prosecutions seems to warrant, the unfairness will come home to roost in the Oval Office. I leave it to the reader to recall the examples of this in recent years. That result, of course, was precisely what the Founders had in mind when they provided that all executive powers would be exercised by a single Chief Executive. As Hamilton put it, "[t]he ingredients which constitute safety in the republican sense are a due dependence on the people, and a due responsibility." Federalist No. 70, p. 424. The President is directly dependent on the people, and since there is only one President, he is responsible. The people know whom to blame, whereas "one of the weightiest objections to a plurality in the executive . . . is that it tends to conceal faults and destroy responsibility."

That is the system of justice the rest of us are entitled to, but what of that select class consisting of present or former high-level Executive Branch officials? If an allegation is made against them of any violation of any federal criminal law (except Class B or C misdemeanors or infractions) the Attorney General must give it his attention. That in itself is not objectionable. But if, after a 90-day investigation without the benefit of normal investigatory tools, the Attorney General is unable to say that there are "no reasonable grounds to believe" that further investigation is warranted, a process is set in motion that is not in the full control of persons "dependent on the people," and whose flaws cannot be blamed on the President. An independent counsel is selected, and the scope of his or her authority prescribed, by a panel of judges. What if they are politically partisan, as judges have been known to be, and select a prosecutor antagonistic to the administration, or even to the particular individual who has been selected for this special treatment? There is no remedy for that, not even a political one. Judges, after all, have life tenure, and appointing a surefire enthusiastic prosecutor could hardly be considered an impeachable offense. So if there is anything wrong with the selection, there is effectively no one to blame. The independent counsel thus selected proceeds to assemble a staff. As I observed earlier, in the nature of things this has to be done by finding lawyers who are willing to lay aside their current careers for an indeterminate amount of time, to take on a job that has no prospect of permanence and little prospect for promotion. One thing is certain, however: it involves investigating and perhaps prosecuting a particular individual. Can one imagine a less equitable manner of fulfilling the executive responsibility to investigate and prosecute? What would be the reaction if, in an area not covered by this statute, the Justice Department posted a public notice inviting applicants to assist in an investigation and possible prosecution of a certain prominent person? Does this not invite what Justice Jackson described as "picking the man and then searching the law books, or putting investigators to work, to pin some offense on him"? To be sure, the investigation must relate to the area of criminal offense specified by the life-tenured judges. But that has often been (and nothing prevents it from being) very broad—and should the independent counsel or his or her staff come up with something beyond that scope, nothing prevents him or her from asking the judges to expand his or her authority or, if that does not work, referring it to the Attorney General, whereupon the whole process would recommence and, if there was "reasonable basis to believe" that further investigation was warranted, that new offense would be referred to the Special Division, which would in all likelihood assign it to the same independent counsel. It seems to me not conducive to fairness. But even if it were entirely evident that unfairness was in fact the result—the judges hostile to the administration, the independent counsel an old foe of the President, the staff refugees from the recently defeated administration—there would be no one accountable to the public to whom the blame could be assigned.

I do not mean to suggest that anything of this sort (other than the inevitable self-selection of the prosecutory staff) occurred in the present case. I know and have the highest regard for the judges on the Special Division, and the independent counsel herself is a woman of accomplishment, impartiality, and integrity. But the fairness of a process must be adjudged on the basis of what it permits to happen, not what it produced in a particular case. It is true, of course, that a similar list of horribles could be attributed to an ordinary Justice Department prosecution—a vindictive prosecutor, an antagonistic staff, etc. But the difference is the difference that the Founders envisioned when they established a single Chief Executive accountable to the people: the blame can be assigned to someone who can be punished.

The above described possibilities of irresponsible conduct must, as I say, be considered in judging the constitutional acceptability of this process. But they will rarely occur, and in the average case the threat to fairness is quite different. As described in the brief filed on behalf of three ex-Attorneys General from each of the last three administrations:

> "The problem is less spectacular but much more worrisome. It is that the institutional environment of the Independent Counsel—specifically, her isolation from the Executive Branch and the internal checks and balances it supplies—is designed to heighten, not to check, all of the occupational hazards of the dedicated prosecutor; the danger of too narrow a focus, of the loss of perspective, of preoccupation with the pursuit of one alleged suspect to the exclusion of other interests." Brief for Edward H. Levi, Griffin B. Bell, and William French Smith as Amici Curiae.

It is, in other words, an additional advantage of the unitary Executive that it can achieve a more uniform application of the law. Perhaps that is not always achieved, but the mechanism to achieve it is there. The mini-Executive that is the independent counsel, however, operating in an area where so little is law and so much is discretion, is intentionally cut off from the unifying influence of the Justice Department, and from the perspective that multiple responsibilities provide. What would normally be regarded as a technical violation (there are no rules defining such things), may in his or her small world assume the proportions of an indictable offense. What would normally be regarded as an investigation that has reached the level of pursuing such picayune matters that it should be concluded, may to him or her be an investigation that ought to go on for another year. How frightening it must be to have your own independent counsel and staff appointed, with nothing else to do but to investigate you until investigation is no longer worthwhile—with whether it is worthwhile not depending upon what such judgments usually hinge on, competing responsibilities. And to have that counsel and staff decide, with no basis for comparison, whether what you have done is bad enough, willful enough, and provable enough, to warrant an indictment. How admirable the constitutional system that provides the means to avoid such a distortion. And how unfortunate the judicial decision that has permitted it.

The notion that every violation of law should be prosecuted, including—indeed, especially—every violation by those in high places, is an attractive one, and it would be risky to argue in an election campaign that that is not an absolutely overriding value. Fiat justitia, ruat coelum. Let justice be done, though the heavens may fall. The reality is, however, that it is not an absolutely overriding value, and it was with the hope that we would be able to acknowledge and apply such realities that the Constitution spared us, by life tenure, the necessity of election campaigns. I cannot imagine that there are not many thoughtful men and women in Congress who realize that the benefits of this legislation are far outweighed by its harmful effect upon our system of government, and even upon the nature of justice received by those men and women who agree to serve in the Executive Branch. But it is difficult to vote not to enact, and even more difficult to vote to repeal, a statute called, appropriately enough, the Ethics in Government Act. If Congress is controlled by the party other than the one to which the President belongs, it has little incentive to repeal it; if it is controlled by the same party, it dare not. By its shortsighted action today, I fear the Court has permanently encumbered the Republic with an institution that will do it great harm.

Worse than what it has done, however, is the manner in which it has done it. A government of laws means a government of rules. Today's decision on the basic issue of fragmentation of executive power is ungoverned by rule, and hence ungoverned by law. It extends into the very heart of our most significant constitutional function the "totality of the circumstances" mode of analysis that this Court has in recent years become fond of. Taking all things into account, we conclude that the power taken away from the President here is not really too much. The next time executive power is assigned to someone other than the President we may conclude, taking all things into account, that it is too much. That opinion, like this one, will not be confined by any rule. We will describe, as we have today (though I hope more accurately) the effects of the provision in question, and will authoritatively announce: "The President's need to control the exercise of the [subject officer's] discretion is so central to the functioning of the Executive Branch as to require complete control." This is not analysis; it is ad hoc judgment. And it fails to explain why it is not true that—as the text of the Constitution seems to require, as the Founders seemed to expect, and as our past cases have uniformly assumed—all purely executive power must be under the control of the President.

The ad hoc approach to constitutional adjudication has real attraction, even apart from its work-saving potential. It is guaranteed to produce a result, in every case, that will make a majority of the Court happy with the law. The law is, by definition, precisely what the majority thinks, taking all things into account, it ought to be. I prefer to rely upon the judgment of the wise men who constructed our system, and of the people who approved it, and of two centuries of history that have shown it to be sound. Like it or not, that judgment says, quite plainly, that "[t]he executive Power shall be vested in a President of the United States."

NOTES AND QUESTIONS

1. The Ethics in Government Act of 1978 was passed by Congress in response to the turbulent final years of the Nixon Administration, in which President Nixon ordered successive acting attorneys general to fire Watergate Special Prosecutor Archibald Cox. Congress plainly was desirous of providing for an Independent Counsel that was truly insulated as much as was constitutionally possible from the President. *See* Ken Gormley, *An Original Model of the*

Independent Counsel Statute, 97 Mich. L. Rev. 601 (1998). The Supreme Court upheld the constitutionality of the independent counsel provision in *Morrison* on various separation of powers grounds that will not be explored here.

2. Attorney General Jackson's address quoted by Justice Scalia in his dissent is cited as often as anything with the possible exception of *Berger v. United States, see infra*, on the subject of prosecutorial discretion. In the passage quoted here he speaks to its risks. Is prosecutorial discretion a necessary evil? Is the only alternative to relying on the judgment of prosecutors to live in a state that is so heavily policed that it is a feasible goal to prosecute all known criminal violations?

Attorney General Robert H. Jackson in his office at the Justice Department. Jackson had previously served as solicitor general, arguing 44 cases before the Supreme Court with such distinction that Justice Brandeis said Jackson should be "Solicitor General for Life." Jackson was the last Supreme Court Justice who did not have a law degree.

3. Do you agree with the sentiment that "almost everyone" could be prosecuted for at least a "technical violation" of some crime if enough investigative effort were brought to bear? Bear in mind that according to some estimates there are approximately 4,500 federal criminal statutes and tens of thousands of crimes located in federal criminal regulations.

4. Justice Scalia states that "the primary check against prosecutorial abuse is a political one." Do you agree? What other checks are there? If it is the "primary check," is it an effective one? To what extent is "prosecutorial abuse" an issue that registers with voters, particularly where the abused are in the minority or otherwise disfavored?

5. Justice Scalia seems especially worried about the Independent Counsel's not having "the perspective that multiple responsibilities provide." What does he mean by this? Is it important that prosecutors and law enforcement agents have too much to do?

6. Consider Justice Scalia's comment about the Independent Counsel's assembling of a staff. Is this concern equally applicable to the actual Independent Counsel?

There has been no shortage of academic commentary on the Independent Counsel statute, *Morrison*, and investigations undertaken under this authority. Two of the more interesting are from Professors Angela J. Davis and Paul Butler. *See* Angela J. Davis, *The American Prosecutor: Independence, Power and the Threat of Tyranny*, 86 Iowa L. Rev. 393 (2001) (arguing that the purported abuses by the Independent Counsel are largely reflective of abuses by "regular prosecutors"); Paul Butler, *Starr Is to Clinton as Regulator Prosecutors Are to Blacks*, 40 B.C. L. Rev. 705 (1999) (criticism of Independent Counsel Kenneth Starr's pursuit of President Clinton—in its selective prosecution, abuse of discretion, and zeal for punishment—is equally applicable to "regular" prosecutors' pursuit of African Americans).

2. Prosecutorial Discretion in Charging Decisions and the Influence of Race

a. Race and Charging Discretion

Professor Angela Davis explains how racial bias can influence charging decisions, even in situations where race is not a conscious consideration of the prosecutor. Davis, Arbitrary Justice, *supra* at 34-40. For example, one superficially "objective" factor that might influence a prosecutor's decision whether to prosecute, or what charges to bring, is the potential defendant's criminal history. Arguably, a potential defendant with a significant criminal history is more in need of the specific deterrence effect of the criminal sanction than a first offender or someone with a trivial criminal history. Of course that criminal history is not truly an objective factor, but rather—particularly as it reflects arrests and charges as opposed to just convictions—a function of the well-chronicled racial disparities in the stopping, investigation, and prosecution of Black people and other minorities. *Id.* at 38.

Consider a second purportedly objective factor counseling in factor of prosecution—the "victim's interest in the prosecution." Prosecutors vary widely in their solicitude for the victims of crimes, but at the margin, at least, prosecutors often consider the victim's interest in the prosecution of the defendant, especially to the extent the victim is a necessary witness. Davis, Arbitrary Justice, *supra* at 65. Professor Davis contrasts the level of "interest" in two hypothesized victims of equally straightforward burglaries. Victim A appears to live in a rundown apartment building in an area with a high crime rate. She doesn't return the prosecutor's calls, and may not have a phone. The prosecutor worries that she will not be reachable for scheduling court appearances, grand jury, or trial. She doesn't call the prosecutor's office to inquire about the case. The prosecutor concludes the victim lacks interest in the prosecution. Victim B, on the other hand, lives in a single-family home in a middle-class neighborhood. Victim B answers or returns all the prosecutor's calls. She is still angry about the offense. She sounds educated and articulate on the phone. The prosecutor senses that if charges are not brought Victim B will figure out how to complain to his supervisor. The prosecutor concludes that Victim B has a strong interest in the case.

The prosecutor will likely lean toward prosecuting the Victim B robbery over the Victim A robbery. In evaluating the different levels of interest Victim A and Victim B have in the prosecution, the prosecutor is not intentionally or consciously considering race or class, but the so-called objective factors can easily serve as proxies for race or class. Davis, Arbitrary Justice, *supra* at 37.

These same proxies can bleed into the prosecutor's consideration of a third objective factor, the strength of the prosecutor's case. This factor necessarily affects almost every exercise of prosecutorial discretion. Due to the scarcity of resources, prosecutors have little incentive to pursue weak cases. Often, a key determinant of the strength of a case is the extent to which the victim is sympathetic, likeable, and believable. These characteristics, in turn, can sometimes be a function of educational level and background, and will almost always be a function of the victim's availability for witness preparation sessions and court appearances.

The above are comparatively easily explainable examples of how ostensibly objective factors are often freighted with bias. As research on implicit bias continues to develop, more and less intuitive examples will surely continue to emerge. *See* Robert J. Smith & Justin D. Levinson, *The Impact of Implicit Racial Bias on the Exercise of Prosecutorial Discretion*, 35 Seattle U. L. Rev. 795, 822 (2012) (noting that prosecutorial discretion provides "compelling reasons to believe that prosecutors unwittingly display implicit racial bias at a variety of decision points"); James Babikian, Note, *Cleaving the Gordian Knot: Implicit Bias, Selective Prosecution, and Charging Guidelines*, 42 Am. J. Crim. L. 139, 152 (2015). For example, Professors Smith and Levinson point out how research data from the administration of Implicit Association Tests (IATs) on the association of Black males with guns and other weapons can affect charging decisions in homicide cases where self-defense is an issue. *See* Smith & Levinson, The Impact of Implicit Racial Bias on the Exercise of Prosecutorial Discretion, *supra* at 806-08.

Statistical studies tend to support the influence of race on charging decisions. For example, Professors Adams and Cutshall studied 745 shoplifting arrests in the District of Columbia between 1974 and 1975, and concluded that prosecutors were more likely to dismiss charges against white shoplifters than black shoplifters. Kenneth Adams & Charles R. Cutshall, *Refusing to Prosecute Minor Offenses: The Relative Influence of Legal and Extralegal Factors*, 4 Just. Q. 595, 604, 606 (1987). Similarly, in a study of 54,266 juvenile offenders detained in Florida between 1979 and 1981, Professors Bishop and Frazier found that Black youths were more likely than white youths to be recommended for formal processing, although this effect was weaker for more severe offenses. Donna M. Bishop & Charles E. Frazier, *The Influence of Race in Juvenile Justice Processing*, 25 J. Rev. Crime & Delinq. 242, 252-59 (1988). The race of both the defendant and the victim can also affect not just whether to charge but also the severity of the charges. For example, a study of Florida homicide cases between 1973 and 1977 demonstrated that prosecutors were significantly more likely to charge Black-on-white homicides as felony homicides than they were white-on-white or Black-on-Black homicides. Michael L. Radelet & Glenn L. Pierce, *Race and Prosecutorial Discretion in Homicide Cases*, 19 Law & Soc'y Rev. 587, 601 (1985).

b. The Prosecutor's Plenary Charging Power and Discretion

The expansion and proliferation of criminal statutes, and the tough-on-crime regime of mandatory minimum and otherwise standardized sentences, trends beginning in the 1970s and 1980s, have only enhanced the power of prosecutors vis-à-vis the other branches of government. *See, e.g.*, Rachel Barkow, Prisoners of Politics: Breaking the Cycle of Mass Incarceration 129-30 (2019). Given the variety of options prosecutors have in making charging decisions, some commentators have observed that their power—in picking from a menu of charging possibilities—has become quasi-legislative. *See* William J. Stuntz, *The Pathological Politics of Criminal Law*, 100 Mich. L. Rev. 505, 506 (2001) ("The definition of crimes and defenses plays a different and much smaller role in the allocation of criminal punishment than we usually suppose. In general, the role it plays is to empower prosecutors, who are the criminal justice system's real lawmakers."); M. Elizabeth Magill, *The Real Separation in Separation of Powers Law*, 86 Va. L. Rev. 1127, 1193 (2000) ("[D]ecisions by prosecutors about how to enforce a statute are indistinguishable from lawmaking. That is, given that the range of permissible enforcement actions under criminal laws (and many other laws) is extremely broad, it is the prosecutors' pattern of decisions that shape the meaning of law, not the underlying statute itself.").

Prosecutorial powers also encroach on judicial authority. The prosecutor's decision to charge a defendant under a statute with a mandatory minimum sentence, or to allege facts in an indictment that place a sentence within a mandatory or even a quasi-mandatory guideline

820

Chapter IX The Prosecution Function

range, can dictate or at least heavily influence the sentence, reducing any palliative power of the judiciary. *See, e.g.,* Marc L. Miller, *Domination and Dissatisfaction: Prosecutors as Sentencers,* 56 Stan. L. Rev. 1211, 1252 (2004) ("The overwhelming and dominant fact of the federal sentencing system, beyond the Commission and the guidelines and mandatory penalties, is the virtually absolute power the system has given prosecutors over federal prosecution and sentencing.").

This view that the accretion of prosecutorial power has affected traditional separation-of-powers principles is widespread. *See* Erik Luna & Marianne Wade, *Prosecutors as Judges,* 67 Wash. & Lee L. Rev. 1413, 1415 (2010) ("In many (if not most) American jurisdictions, the prosecutor is the criminal justice system."); Adam M. Gershowitz, *Consolidating Local Criminal Justice: Should Prosecutors Control the Jails?,* 51 Wake Forest L. Rev. 677, 677-78 (2016) ("No serious observer disputes that prosecutors drive sentencing and hold most of the power in the United States criminal justice system.").

For a dissenting view, and for an interesting take on prosecutors' wholly discretionary powers of *nonprosecution, see* Jeffrey Bellin, *Reassessing Prosecutorial Power Through the Lens of Mass Incarceration,* 116 Mich. L. Rev. 835 (2018):

> Contrary to the consensus, prosecutors are not the most powerful actors in the criminal justice system.
>
> Prosecutors wield real power in deciding whether to bring charges and, relatedly, in deciding how to charge a suspect whose actions are forbidden by multiple laws. It is important to recognize, however, that the prosecutor's power is at its apex in deciding not to bring charges. A prosecutor's decision to file a felony charge triggers a number of formal and informal checks. The opposite is true when the prosecutor declines to bring a case. As a result, when we think about American prosecutors wielding "unfettered, unreviewable" charging discretion we should primarily be thinking about dismissals.
>
> American prosecutors dismiss many of the cases recommended for prosecution by police.

Id. at 845-46.

The plenary power to prosecute and dismiss that prosecutors enjoy, or believe they should be able to enjoy, largely occurs in the dark. But occasionally the separation-of-powers issues raised by that discretion are contested in court. The judiciary, especially federal district court judges, often bridles at prosecutors' exercises of power, as the next case shows.

United States v. Fokker Services B.V.

818 F.3d 733 (D.C. Cir. 2016)

SRINIVASAN, Circuit Judge:

The Constitution allocates primacy in criminal charging decisions to the Executive Branch. The Executive's charging authority embraces decisions about whether to initiate charges, whom to prosecute, which charges to bring, and whether to dismiss charges once brought. It has long been settled that the Judiciary generally lacks authority to second-guess those Executive determinations, much less to impose its own charging preferences. The courts instead take the prosecution's charging decisions largely as a given, and assume a more active role in administering adjudication of a defendant's guilt and determining the appropriate sentence.

In certain situations, rather than choose between the opposing poles of pursuing a criminal conviction or forgoing any criminal charges altogether, the Executive may conclude that the public interest warrants the intermediate option of a deferred prosecution agreement (DPA). Under a DPA, the government formally initiates prosecution but agrees to dismiss all charges if the defendant abides by negotiated conditions over a prescribed period of time. Adherence to the conditions enables the defendant to demonstrate compliance with the law. If the defendant fails to satisfy the conditions, the government can then pursue the charges based on facts admitted in the agreement.

This case arises from the interplay between the operation of a DPA and the running of time limitations under the Speedy Trial Act. Because a DPA involves the formal initiation of criminal charges, the agreement triggers the Speedy Trial Act's time limits for the commencement of a criminal trial. In order to enable the government to assess the defendant's satisfaction of the DPA's conditions over the time period of the agreement — with an eye towards potential dismissal of the charges — the Speedy Trial Act specifically allows for a court to suspend the running of the time within which to commence a trial for any period during which the government defers prosecution under a DPA.

In this case, appellant Fokker Services voluntarily disclosed its potential violation of federal sanctions and export control laws. After extensive negotiations, the company and the government entered into an 18-month DPA, during which Fokker would continue cooperation with federal authorities and implementation of a substantial compliance program. In accordance with the DPA, the government filed criminal charges against the company, together with a joint motion to suspend the running of time under the Speedy Trial Act pending assessment of the company's adherence to the agreement's conditions. The district court denied the motion because, in the court's view, the prosecution had been too lenient in agreeing to, and structuring, the DPA. Among other objections, the court disagreed with prosecutors' decision to forgo bringing any criminal charges against individual company officers.

We vacate the district court's denial of the joint motion to exclude time under the Speedy Trial Act. We hold that the Act confers no authority in a court to withhold exclusion of time pursuant to a DPA based on concerns that the government should bring different charges or should charge different defendants. Congress, in providing for courts to approve the exclusion of time pursuant to a DPA, acted against the backdrop of long-settled understandings about the independence of the Executive with regard to charging decisions. Nothing in the statute's terms or structure suggests any intention to subvert those constitutionally rooted principles so as to enable the Judiciary to second-guess the Executive's exercise of discretion over the initiation and dismissal of criminal charges.

In vacating the district court order, we have no occasion to disagree (or agree) with that court's concerns about the government's charging decisions in this case. Rather, the fundamental point is that those determinations are for the Executive — not the courts — to make. We therefore grant the government's petition for a writ of mandamus and remand for further proceedings consistent with this opinion.

I

A

The Speedy Trial Act establishes time limits for the completion of various stages of a criminal prosecution. See 18 U.S.C. §§ 3161-3174. For instance, the Act requires the commencement of trial within seventy days of the filing of an information or indictment by the government. Id. § 3161(c)(1). The Act also excludes various pretrial periods from the running of that seventy-day time clock. Of particular relevance, the Act excludes "[a]ny period of delay during which prosecution is deferred by the attorney for the Government pursuant to written agreement with the defendant, with the approval of the court, for the purpose of allowing the defendant to demonstrate his good conduct." Id. § 3161(h)(2).

That exemption exists to enable prosecutors to resolve cases through DPAs. DPAs, along with their out-of-court analogues, non-prosecution agreements (NPAs), afford a middle-ground

824 Chapter IX The Prosecution Function

option to the prosecution when, for example, it believes that a criminal conviction may be difficult to obtain or may result in unwanted collateral consequences for a defendant or third parties, but also believes that the defendant should not evade accountability altogether. Both DPAs and NPAs generally include an admitted statement of facts, require adherence to "conditions designed . . . to promote compliance with applicable law and to prevent recidivism," and remain in effect for a period of one to three years. U.S. Attorney's Manual § 9-28.1000 (2015). During that period, if the defendant fails to abide by the terms of the agreement, the government can prosecute based on the admitted facts. While prosecutors at one time seldom relied on NPAs and DPAs, their use has grown significantly in recent years.

DPAs differ from NPAs primarily with regard to the filing of criminal charges. With an NPA, "formal charges are not filed and the agreement is maintained by the parties rather than being filed with a court." A DPA, by contrast, "is typically predicated upon the filing of a formal charging document by the government."

For that reason, a DPA's viability depends on the specific exclusion of time for such agreements set forth in the Speedy Trial Act, 18 U.S.C. § 3161(h)(2). The filing of an information or indictment would ordinarily trigger the Act's seventy-day clock within which trial must commence. See id. § 3161(c)(1). But in the case of a DPA, if the defendant were to fulfill the agreement's conditions, the prosecution would move to dismiss all charges with prejudice at the end of the specified time period, ordinarily one to three years. Without the statutory exclusion of time for DPAs provided in § 3161(h)(2), the government would relinquish its ability to prosecute based on the conceded facts if the defendant were to violate the agreement after seventy days. That would largely eliminate the leverage that engenders the defendant's compliance with a DPA's conditions. The statutory exclusion of time for DPAs therefore is essential to the agreements' effective operation.

B

Fokker Services, a Dutch aerospace services company, provides technical and logistical support to owners of aircraft manufactured by its predecessor company. In 2010, Fokker voluntarily disclosed to the United States Departments of Treasury and Commerce that it had potentially violated federal sanctions and export control laws concerning Iran, Sudan, and Burma. At the time Fokker came forward, no government agency had initiated any investigation focused on the company.

Over the course of the next four years, Fokker cooperated in the wide-ranging investigation conducted by federal authorities. The company facilitated interviews of relevant witnesses, expedited the government's requests to Dutch authorities for documents under the Mutual Legal Assistance Treaty, and initiated its own internal investigation. Fokker's internal investigation revealed that, from 2005 to 2010, the company had participated in 1,147 illicit transactions through which it earned some $21 million in gross revenue. The company instituted remedial measures to improve its sanctions compliance program, adopting a set of procedures to track parts and bolstering its employee training requirements. It also fired its president and demoted or reassigned other employees who had been involved in the violations. The company's compliance efforts have been described by government officials as "a model to be followed by other corporations."

In light of Fokker's cooperation, remediation efforts, and other mitigating factors, federal agencies negotiated a global settlement with the company. The settlement included, as an integral component, an 18-month DPA. During the DPA's 18-month period, Fokker was to: continue full cooperation with the government, implement its new compliance policy, and pay fines and penalties totaling $21 million (a sum equaling the gross revenues gained by the company from the illicit transactions). Fokker also accepted responsibility for the acts described in the stipulated factual statement accompanying the DPA.

On June 5, 2014, pursuant to the agreement, the government filed with the district court a one-count information against Fokker, together with the DPA. The information charged Fokker with conspiracy to violate the International Emergency Economic Powers Act. See 18 U.S.C. § 371; 50 U.S.C. § 1705. The same day, the government and Fokker filed a joint motion for the exclusion of time under the Speedy Trial Act, in order to "allow [the company] to demonstrate its good conduct and implement certain remedial measures."

The district court then held a series of status conferences, during which it repeatedly emphasized its concerns about the absence of any criminal prosecution of individual company officers. The court requested several additional written submissions from the government. The government was asked to explain why the interests of justice supported the court's approval of the deal embodied by the DPA, and also to address whether Fokker's initial disclosures to the government had in fact been voluntary. In response, the government described why the "proposed resolution with Fokker Services is fair and is an appropriate exercise of the government's discretion," and affirmed the absence of any indication "that Fokker Services was motivated to make its disclosures out of fear about a nonexistent U.S. government investigation," The district court later expressed that it might still reject the DPA because it was "too good a deal for the defendant."

On February 5, 2015, the district court denied the joint motion for the exclusion of time. In explaining the reasons for its decision, the court criticized the government for failing to prosecute any "individuals . . . for their conduct." According to the court, approval of an agreement in which the defendant had been "prosecuted so anemically for engaging in such egregious conduct for such a sustained period of time and for the benefit of one of our country's worst enemies" would "promote disrespect for the law." The court further noted that certain employees had been permitted to remain with the company; that the DPA contained no requirement for an independent monitor; and that the amount of the fine failed to exceed the revenues Fokker gained from the illegal transactions. Based on those considerations, the court rejected the DPA as an "[in]appropriate exercise of prosecutorial discretion."

The district court's order marks the first time any federal court has denied a joint request by the parties to exclude time pursuant to a DPA. Both parties filed a timely notice of appeal. Because both parties seek to overturn the district court's denial of their joint motion to exclude time, we appointed an amicus curiae to present arguments defending the district court's action.

II

. . .

By rejecting the DPA based primarily on concerns about the prosecution's charging choices, the district court exceeded its authority under the Speedy Trial Act. The Act excludes any period of time "during which prosecution is deferred by the attorney for the Government pursuant to written agreement with the defendant, with the approval of the court, for the purpose of allowing the defendant to demonstrate his good conduct." 18 U.S.C. § 3161(h)(2). While the exclusion of time is subject to "the approval of the court," there is no ground for reading that provision to confer free-ranging authority in district courts to scrutinize the prosecution's discretionary charging decisions. Rather, we read the statute against the background of settled constitutional understandings under which authority over criminal charging decisions resides fundamentally with the Executive, without the involvement of—and without oversight power in—the Judiciary. So understood, the statute's "approval of the court" requirement did not empower the district court to disapprove the DPA based on the court's view that the prosecution had been too lenient.

A

The Executive's primacy in criminal charging decisions is long settled. That authority stems from the Constitution's delegation of "take Care" duties, U.S. Const. art. II, § 3, and the pardon power, id. § 2, to the Executive Branch. Decisions to initiate charges, or to dismiss charges once brought, "lie[ ] at the core of the Executive's duty to see to the faithful execution of the laws." The Supreme Court thus has repeatedly emphasized that "[w]hether to prosecute and what charge to file or bring before a grand jury are decisions that generally rest in the prosecutor's discretion." *United States v. Batchelder* (1979); see *Bordenkircher v. Hayes* (1978).

Correspondingly, "judicial authority is . . . at its most limited" when reviewing the Executive's exercise of discretion over charging determinations. The decision whether to prosecute turns on factors such as "the strength of the case, the prosecution's general deterrence value, the [g]overnment's enforcement priorities, and the case's relationship to the [g]overnment's overall enforcement plan." *Wayte v. United States* (1985). The Executive routinely undertakes those assessments and is well equipped to do so. By contrast, the Judiciary, as the Supreme Court has explained, generally is not "competent to undertake" that sort of inquiry. Indeed, "[f]ew subjects are less adapted to judicial review than the exercise by the Executive of his discretion in deciding when and whether to institute criminal proceedings, or what precise charge shall be made, or whether to dismiss a proceeding once brought." "Judicial supervision in this area" would also "entail[ ] systemic costs." It could "chill law enforcement," cause delay, and "impair the performance of a core executive constitutional function." As a result, "the presumption of regularity" applies to "prosecutorial decisions and, in the absence of clear evidence to the contrary, courts presume that [prosecutors] have properly discharged their official duties."

B

Those settled principles counsel against interpreting statutes and rules in a manner that would impinge on the Executive's constitutionally rooted primacy over criminal charging decisions. Of particular salience, Rule 48(a) of the Federal Rules of Criminal Procedure requires a prosecutor to obtain "leave of court" before dismissing charges against a criminal defendant. Fed. R. Crim. P. 48(a). That language could conceivably be read to allow for considerable judicial involvement in the determination to dismiss criminal charges. But decisions to dismiss pending criminal charges—no less than decisions to initiate charges and to identify which charges to bring—lie squarely within the ken of prosecutorial discretion. To that end, the Supreme Court has declined to construe Rule 48(a)'s "leave of court" requirement to confer any substantial role for courts in the determination whether to dismiss charges. Rather, the "principal object of the 'leave of court' requirement" has been understood to be a narrow one—"to protect a defendant against prosecutorial harassment . . . when the [g]overnment moves to dismiss an indictment over the defendant's objection." *Rinaldi v. United States*, 434 U.S. 22, 29 n. 15 (1977). A court thus reviews the prosecution's motion under Rule 48(a) primarily to guard against the prospect that dismissal is part of a scheme of "prosecutorial harassment" of the defendant through repeated efforts to bring—and then dismiss—charges. Id.

So understood, the "leave of court" authority gives no power to a district court to deny a prosecutor's Rule 48(a) motion to dismiss charges based on a disagreement with the prosecution's exercise of charging authority. For instance, a court cannot deny leave of court because of a view that the defendant should stand trial notwithstanding the prosecution's desire to dismiss the charges, or a view that any remaining charges fail adequately to redress the gravity of the defendant's alleged conduct. The authority to make such determinations remains with the Executive.

The same considerations have informed our understanding of the respective roles of the Executive and the courts with regard to the acceptance of certain civil consent decrees proposed by enforcement agencies. . . .

* * *

C

The same considerations govern our interpretation of the Speedy Trial Act provision at issue here. That provision, as noted, allows for excluding "[a]ny period of delay during which prosecution is deferred by the attorney for the Government pursuant to [a DPA], with the approval of the court, for the purpose of allowing the defendant to demonstrate his good conduct." 18 U.S.C. § 3161(h)(2). As with the "leave of court" language in Rule 48(a) and the "public interest" authority in the Tunney Act, we construe the "approval of the court" language in § 3161(h)(2) in a manner that preserves the Executive's long-settled primacy over charging decisions and that denies courts substantial power to impose their own charging preferences.

As an initial matter, the context of a DPA, like that of Rule 48(a), concerns the prosecution's core prerogative to dismiss criminal charges. While dismissal under a DPA follows from the defendant's adherence to agreed-upon conditions over a specified period, the decision to seek dismissal pursuant to a DPA — as under Rule 48(a) — ultimately stems from a conclusion that additional prosecution or punishment would not serve the public interest. Dismissal in either situation thereby fulfills the Executive's duty under Article II to see that the laws are faithfully executed.

We see no reason to recognize a substantially broader authority for courts to scrutinize prosecutorial charging choices in the context of a DPA than in the context of Rule 48(a). Just as Rule 48(a)'s "leave of court" authority does not allow a court to withhold approval of a motion to dismiss charges based on a belief that more serious charges should be brought against the defendant (or against a third party), § 3161(h)(2)'s "approval of the court" authority does not permit a court to withhold approval of a motion to exclude time under a DPA based on that same belief. In either situation, the court's withholding of approval would amount to a substantial and unwarranted intrusion on the Executive Branch's fundamental prerogatives. And the Judiciary's lack of competence to review the prosecution's initiation and dismissal of charges equally applies to review of the prosecution's decision to pursue a DPA and the choices reflected in the agreement's terms. As with conventional charging decisions, a DPA's provisions manifest the Executive's consideration of factors such as the strength of the government's evidence, the deterrence value of a prosecution, and the enforcement priorities of an agency, subjects that are ill-suited to substantial judicial oversight.

To be sure, the criminal charges filed as part of a DPA remain on the court's docket throughout the time of the agreement (i.e., pending assessment of whether the defendant has satisfied the agreement's conditions, upon which the prosecution seeks dismissal of the charges). But the existence of charges on the court's docket suggests no greater power on the part of the court to second-guess the underlying charging decisions than under Rule 48(a): there, too, criminal charges remain on the court's docket until dismissed. The key point is that, although charges remain pending on the court's docket under a DPA, the court plays no role in monitoring the defendant's compliance with the DPA's conditions. For instance, defendants who violate the conditions of their DPA face no court-ordered repercussions. Rather, the prosecution — and the prosecution alone — monitors a defendant's compliance with the agreement's conditions and determines whether the defendant's conduct warrants dismissal of the pending charges. Just as is the case under Rule 48(a), the prosecution, after taking stock of the circumstances, concludes that continued pursuit of a criminal conviction is unwarranted.

A comparison to civil consent decrees is also instructive in this regard. Civil consent decrees not only remain on a court's docket, but the court—unlike with a DPA—can enforce the decree's terms through exercise of the contempt power. . . . And as a general matter, Executive independence is assumed to be even more pronounced in the context of criminal charging decisions than in the context of civil enforcement decisions. In that light, we perceive no basis for concluding that courts have greater power to second-guess charging decisions when reviewing the terms of a DPA than when reviewing any other Executive exercise of criminal charging authority, including dismissals of charges under Rule 48(a).

The text of § 3161(h)(2) does not dictate any contrary conclusion. The statutory language ties the "approval of the court" requirement to the DPA's "purpose of allowing the defendant to demonstrate his good conduct." 18 U.S.C. § 3161(h)(2). We thus understand a court's approval authority for the exclusion of time under a DPA to have a particular focus: i.e., to assure that the DPA in fact is geared to enabling the defendant to demonstrate compliance with the law, and is not instead a pretext intended merely to evade the Speedy Trial Act's time constraints. Whatever may be the precise contours of that authority of a court to confirm that a DPA's conditions are aimed to assure the defendant's good conduct, it does not permit the court to impose its own views about the adequacy of the underlying criminal charges. Rather, as under Rule 48(a), those core charging decisions remain the province of the Executive.

The Senate Committee Report accompanying the Speedy Trial Act reinforces that circumscribed understanding of a district court's "approval" authority under § 3161(h)(2). The report describes the phrase, "with the approval of the court," as designed to "assure[] that the court will be involved in the decision to divert and that the procedure will not be used by prosecutors and defense counsel to avoid the speedy trial time limits." That statement suggests that the judicial-approval requirement was not intended to impinge on the Executive's traditional independence over charging decisions. Rather, the requirement enables courts to assure that a DPA does not exist merely to allow evasion of speedy trial time limits, but instead serves the bona fide purpose of confirming a defendant's good conduct and compliance with law. The Senate Committee Report further describes § 3161(h)(2) as generally intended to "encourage the current trend among United States attorneys" of holding criminal charges in abeyance while defendants participate in rehabilitation programs. Interpreting § 3161(h)(2) to empower courts to scrutinize the prosecution's underlying charging decisions would tend to discourage—not encourage—the prosecution's use of DPAs, contradicting the provision's apparent overarching object.

D

In defending the notion that § 3161(h)(2)'s "approval of the court" language gives district courts substantial authority to second-guess the prosecution's charging decisions, amicus seeks to analogize a court's review of a DPA under § 3161(h)(2) to a court's review of a proposed plea agreement under Rule 11 of the Federal Rules of Criminal Procedure. That argument fails.

To begin with, even in the context of reviewing a proposed plea agreement under Rule 11, a district court lacks authority to reject a proposed agreement based on mere disagreement with a prosecutor's underlying charging decisions. Rule 11 states that a district court may "accept the agreement, reject it, or defer a decision until the court has reviewed the presentence report." Fed. R. Crim. P. 11(c)(3)(A). Although "district courts must exercise discretion in deciding whether to accept or reject a guilty plea, that discretion is not unfettered." In particular, we have explained, "trial judges are not free to withhold approval of guilty pleas . . . merely because their conception of the public interest differs from that of the prosecuting attorney."

A. Discretion 829

In addition, a district court's authority to "accept" or "reject" a proposed plea agreement under Rule 11 is rooted in the Judiciary's traditional power over criminal sentencing, as the Rule itself indicates in permitting the court to "defer a decision until the court has reviewed the presentence report." Fed. R. Crim. P. 11(c)(3)(A). Plea agreements can take roughly two forms: (i) charge bargains, in which a defendant agrees to plead guilty to certain charges in exchange for the dismissal of other charges; and (ii) sentence bargains, in which the defendant agrees to plead guilty to a particular charge after the parties agree upon a sentence, which the prosecution then recommends to the sentencing court. In light of the Executive's traditional power over charging decisions and the Judiciary's traditional authority over sentencing decisions, some of our sister circuits have concluded that district courts have more limited authority to reject charge bargains than sentence bargains. Regardless, even in the case of a charge bargain, the court reviews the defendant's admitted conduct and enters a judgment of conviction, which in turn carries immediate sentencing implications.

The context of a DPA is markedly different. Unlike a plea agreement — and more like a dismissal under Rule 48(a) — a DPA involves no formal judicial action imposing or adopting its terms. Whereas a district court enters a judgment of conviction and then imposes a sentence in the case of a plea agreement, the court takes no such actions in the case of a DPA. Rather, the entire object of a DPA is to enable the defendant to avoid criminal conviction and sentence by demonstrating good conduct and compliance with the law. And a DPA's provisions are agreed to by the parties, not the court, with no occasion for the court to adopt the agreement's terms as its own. The court never exercises its coercive power by entering a judgment of conviction or imposing a sentence. It instead merely approves the prosecution's judgment that further pursuit of criminal charges is unwarranted, as it does when it approves a prosecutor's motion to dismiss charges under Rule 48(a). And as is the case when confronted with a motion to dismiss charges under Rule 48(a), a district court lacks authority to disapprove a DPA under § 3161(h)(2) on the ground that the prosecution has been too lenient in its exercise of charging discretion.

E

Judged by those principles, the district court in this case erred in denying the parties' motion for exclusion of time under § 3161(h)(2). There is no indication that the parties entered into the DPA to evade speedy trial limits rather than to enable Fokker to demonstrate its good conduct and compliance with law. Rather, the district court denied the exclusion of time based on its view that the prosecution should have brought different charges or sought different remedies. In doing so, the court exceeded its authority under § 3161(h)(2).

From the first status conference concerning the DPA, the district court repeatedly criticized the government for failing to bring charges against individual company officers. Noting its belief that illegal conduct had been "orchestrated at the highest levels of the company" and unpersuaded by the government's efforts to ground its charging decisions in traditional prosecutorial considerations such as the strength of the evidence and the value of pursuing of different charges, the district court questioned why no individuals would be held separately accountable. The court also faulted the government for "not requiring Fokker Services to pay as its fine a penny more than the $21 million in revenue it collected from its illegal transactions." In addition, the court thought the prosecution should have required an independent monitor as part of the DPA's terms. The district court denied the motion for the exclusion of time for those reasons.

Even if the district court's criticisms of the prosecution's exercise of charging authority were entirely meritorious — an issue we have no occasion to address — the court should not have "assume[d] the role of Attorney General." Rather, the court should have confined its inquiry to examining whether the DPA served the purpose of allowing Fokker to demonstrate

830 Chapter IX The Prosecution Function

its good conduct, as contemplated by § 3161(h)(2). There is no reason to question the DPA's bona fides in that regard, and the district court made no suggestion otherwise. And insofar as a court has authority to reject a DPA if it contains illegal or unethical provisions, the district court again made no such suggestion here. The court instead denied the exclusion of time under § 3161(h)(2) based on a belief that the prosecution had been unduly lenient in its charging decisions and in the conditions agreed to in the DPA. The court significantly overstepped its authority in doing so.

NOTES AND QUESTIONS

1. The D.C. Circuit refers to the "primacy" of the role of the executive branch in criminal charging decisions, and cites a litany of Supreme Court case law to that effect. And it observes that the exercise of prosecutorial discretion in making such decisions turns on factors such as "the strength of the case, the prosecution's general deterrence value, the Government's enforcement priorities, and the case's relationship to the Government's overall enforcement plan."

Constitutionally speaking, per the court, the primacy of the prosecutorial power is due to the location of certain specific powers in Article II, including the power to "take care" that the laws be executed. But the Court suggests that this allocation of power vis-à-vis the judiciary is also a matter of institutional competence. Do you agree? Are courts inherently less equipped than the executive to evaluate the discretionary factors identified in the Court's opinion?

2. Some commentators have observed that in practice federal prosecution was not a classic executive function at least until the creation of the Department of Justice in 1870, as until then the attorney general's duties were quite limited and the federal prosecuting attorneys that existed were largely unsupervised. Other commentators disagree. The debate is discussed in Davis, *The American Prosecutor*, *supra* at 393, 451-55. In other words, there is arguably an "originalist" perspective on prosecutorial power in which separation-of-powers principles don't always run in favor of prosecutorial discretion. Consider, as you progress through this chapter, how such a perspective might affect existing doctrine.

3. The Speedy Trial Act provision at issue here, 18 U.S.C. § 3161(h)(2), speaks to deferral of prosecution "for the purpose of allowing the defendant to demonstrate *his* good conduct." Does this provision even contemplate deferred prosecution of a corporate defendant such as Fokker? Does the DOJ need statutory authority to enter into a deferred prosecution agreement like the one here?

4. Deferred Prosecution Agreements (DPAs) and Non-Prosecution Agreements (NPAs) are attractive to the government because these mechanisms enable it to exact its pound of flesh, avoid the risks and costs of trial, and exert some degree of prospective control over a corporate defendant. They are also attractive to corporate targets who find themselves in harm's way, and who fear the so-called collateral consequences of unalloyed indictment and possible conviction. These collateral consequences can include not just reputational harm but, more concretely, an inability to obtain government contacts and hardship to often blameless employees, shareholders, and consumers. The total collapse of the accounting firm Arthur Andersen within months of its indictment in the Enron scandal has led some to refer to indictment, dramatically, as the corporate death penalty. *See* Peter Spivack & Sujit Raman, *Regulating the "New Regulators": Current Trends in Deferred Prosecution Agreements*, 45 Am. Crim. L. Rev. 159, 165-66 (2008) (discussing Arthur Andersen demise).

5. However useful the DOJ and corporate targets have found DPAs and NPAs in resolving disputes, such agreements are largely a matter of private contract, operating outside the mainstream of the federal criminal process. No federal statute or rule specifically authorizes such agreements. The Federal Rules of Criminal Procedure, to the contrary, contemplate defendants being charged (by way of indictment or information under Rule 7) and either pleading guilty (under Rule 11) or going to trial (as governed by Rules 18-31). Does the essentially private nature of these agreements affect how the "approval of court" language in § 3161(h)(2) should be interpreted? Does it shed light on why the district judge in this case clamors for a piece of the action — input into the terms of the DPA?

6. Given the apparent lack of applicable legal precedent shedding light on the meaning of § 3161(h)(2), the court by analogy looks to Rule 48(a) of the Federal Rules of Criminal Procedure, which provides that the government can dismiss a case with "leave of Court." The court reasons that since the "leave of court" provision under Rule 48(a) has also been interpreted not to provide any substantive role for the judiciary so should it be with § 3161(h)(2).

Are there any policy reasons why the executive branch should have less "primacy" in making decisions in dismissing a case than it has in charging a case? If so, how can such asymmetry be defended?

7. The district court refused to approve the joint motion to exclude time because the court thought the DPA was an "inappropriate exercise of prosecutorial discretion." How do you think that this choice of words affected the district court's chances of being upheld on appeal?

Consider each of the district court's expressed concerns about the DPA. Are they all just different ways of saying that Fokker got a sweetheart deal? Was the district court in a position to judge whether individual corporate officers also should have been charged, or whether additional employees should have been fired, or whether the fine was too small, or whether a monitor should have been required? Did the district court even meet the Fokkers? How deep into the weeds of the Fokker investigation would the district court have needed to go in order to be able to credibly weigh in on these issues?

8. Why would DOJ choose not to charge individual officers or employees who were complicit in the conduct that led to their employer entering into a DPA or NPA? What discretionary factors might counsel against such prosecution? What special difficulties do you see in charging and convicting individual corporate officers in this context?

While the district court might not have been able to determine which corporate employees or officers should have been charged here, he certainly had reason to believe that some of them had criminal exposure. Under federal law, a sufficient predicate for the criminal responsibility — that is, guilt — of a corporation is that a corporate employee acting within the scope of his duties and intending to benefit the corporation committed a crime. *See N.Y. Cent. & Hudson River R.R. Co. v. United States*, 212 U.S. 481, 491-95 (1909) (approving corporate criminal liability under a respondeat superior standard).

So from the district court's perspective, even without a deep factual dive, a corporate guilty plea necessarily means that individual corporate employees have committed crimes. Despite this logic, it is a demonstrable fact that, much to the consternation of the district court here and the judiciary as a whole, as well as to many academics, in a large number of corporate resolutions via DPAs or NPAs no charges at all are brought against individual officers. *See* Brandon L. Garrett, *The Corporate Criminal as Scapegoat*, 101 Va. L. Rev. 1789, 1790-92 (2015).

Fokker holds that there is no reviewability whatsoever of a prosecutor's decision *not* to charge someone with a crime. But criticisms of this view have recently been heard in some academic circles in response to certain blanket nonprosecution positions taken by so-called progressive prosecutors. *See* Judith L. Ritter, *Making a Case for No Case: Judicial Oversight of Prosecutorial Choices — From Michael Flynn to Progressive Prosecutors*, 26 Berkeley J. Crim. L. 31, 54 (2021) (noting that state prosecutors who decide as a matter of policy not to prosecute certain kinds of crimes are accused of "usurping" legislative power or "nullifying" legislative

832 Chapter IX The Prosecution Function

enactments); Robert J. Delahunty & John C. Yoo, *Dream On: The Obama Administration's Nonenforcement of Immigration Laws, the DREAM Act, and the Take Care Clause*, 91 Tex. L. Rev. 781, 783-84 (2013) (noting Obama Administration's refusal to enforce certain federal drug and immigration laws as an exercise of "prosecutorial discretion," and arguing that the Take Care Clause in Article II requires the Department of Justice to enforce all constitutionally valid acts of Congress).

Do you agree that prosecutorial "nullification" is a potential problem? Is it a problem that has a solution other than a political one?

3. The Prosecutor's Discretion to Use Unsavory and Unreliable Witnesses and Tactics

Prosecutors often must — or say they must — use criminals to convict criminals, sometimes the criminal confederates of the same criminals they prosecute. Prosecutors also have to use — or say they have to use — informants and undercover law enforcement agents to develop evidence of clandestine criminal operations. This seamy side of prosecution is largely tolerated. As Judge Learned Hand put it: "Courts have countenanced the use of informers from time immemorial; in cases of conspiracy, or in other cases when the crime consists of preparing for another crime, it is usually necessary to rely on them or upon accomplices because the criminals will almost certainly proceed covertly." *United States v. Dennis*, 183 F.2d 201, 224 (2d Cir. 1950), *aff'd*, 341 U.S. 494 (1951).

While the necessity of using such witnesses can be debated — both generally and in any particular case — their use raises concerns about the reliability and integrity of the criminal process. The Supreme Court has long recognized that "[t]he use of informers, accessories, accomplices, false friends, or any of the other betrayals which are 'dirty business' may raise serious questions of credibility." *On Lee v. United States*, 343 U.S. 747, 755 (1952).

The next two cases explore these reliability issues in the context of the entrapment doctrine.

Sherman v. United States
356 U.S. 369 (1958)

Mr. Chief Justice WARREN delivered the opinion of the Court.

The issue before us is whether petitioner's conviction should be set aside on the ground that as a matter of law the defense of entrapment was established. Petitioner was convicted under an indictment charging three sales of narcotics in violation of 21 U.S.C. § 174, 21 U.S.C.A. § 174. A previous conviction had been reversed on account of improper instructions as to the issue of entrapment. In the second trial, as in the first, petitioner's defense was a claim of entrapment: an agent of the Federal Government induced him to take part in illegal transactions when otherwise he would not have done so.

In late August 1951, Kalchinian, a government informer, first met petitioner at a doctor's office where apparently both were being treated to be cured of narcotics addition. Several accidental meetings followed, either at the doctor's office or at the pharmacy where both filled their prescriptions from the doctor. From mere greetings, conversation progressed to a discussion of mutual experiences and problems, including their attempts to overcome addiction to narcotics. Finally Kalchinian asked petitioner if he knew of a good source of narcotics. He asked petitioner to supply him with a source because he was not responding to treatment. From the first, petitioner tried to avoid the issue. Not until after a number of repetitions of the request, predicated on Kalchinian's presumed suffering, did petitioner finally acquiesce. Several times thereafter he obtained a quantity of narcotics which he shared with Kalchinian. Each time petitioner told Kalchinian that the total cost of narcotics he obtained was twenty-five dollars and that Kalchinian owed him fifteen dollars. The informer thus bore the cost of his share of the narcotics plus the taxi and other expenses necessary to obtain the drug. After several such sales Kalchinian informed agents of the Bureau of Narcotics that he had another seller for them. On three occasions during November 1951. Government agents observed petitioner give narcotics to Kalchinian in return for money supplied by the Government.

At the trial the factual issue was whether the informer had convinced an otherwise unwilling person to commit a criminal act or whether petitioner was already predisposed to commit the act and exhibited only the natural hesitancy of one acquainted with the narcotics trade. The issue of entrapment went to the jury, and a conviction resulted. Petitioner was sentenced to imprisonment for ten years. The Court of Appeals for the Second Circuit affirmed. We granted certiorari.

In *Sorrells v. United States* this Court firmly recognized the defense of entrapment in the federal courts. The intervening years have in no way detracted from the principles underlying that decision. The function of law enforcement is the prevention of crime and the apprehension of criminals. Manifestly, that function does not include the manufacturing of crime. Criminal activity is such that stealth and strategy are necessary weapons in the arsenal of the police officer. However, a different question is presented when the criminal design originates with the officials of the government, and they implant in the mind of an innocent person the disposition to commit the alleged offense and induce its commission in order that they may prosecute. The stealth and strategy become as objectionable police methods as the coerced confession and the unlawful search. Congress could not have intended that its statutes were to be enforced by tempting innocent persons into violations.

However, the fact that government agents "merely afford opportunities or facilities for the commission of the offense does not" constitute entrapment. Entrapment occurs only when the criminal conduct was "the product of the creative activity" of law-enforcement officials. To determine whether entrapment has been established, a line must be drawn between the trap for the unwary innocent and the trap for the unwary criminal. The principles by which the courts are to make this determination were outlined in *Sorrells*. On the one hand, at trial the accused may examine the conduct of the government agent; and on the other hand, the accused will be subjected to an "appropriate and searching inquiry into his own conduct and predisposition" as bearing on his claim of innocence.

We conclude from the evidence that entrapment was established as a matter of law. In so holding, we are not choosing between conflicting witnesses, nor judging credibility. Aside from recalling Kalchinian, who was the Government's witness, the defense called no witnesses. We reach our conclusion from the undisputed testimony of the prosecution's witnesses.

It is patently clear that petitioner was induced by Kalchinian. The informer himself testified that, believing petitioner to be undergoing a cure for narcotics addiction, he nonetheless sought to persuade petitioner to obtain for him a source of narcotics. In Kalchinian's own words we are told of the accidental, yet recurring, meetings, the ensuing conversations concerning mutual experiences in regard to narcotics addiction, and then of Kalchinian's resort to sympathy. On request was not enough, for Kalchinian tells us that additional ones were necessary to overcome, first, petitioner's refusal, then has evasiveness, and then his hesitancy in order to achieve capitulation. Kalchinian not only procured a source of narcotics but apparently also induced petitioner to return to the habit. Finally, assured of a catch, Kalchinian informed the authorities so that they could close the net. The Government cannot disown Kalchinian and insist it is not responsible for his actions. Although he was not being paid, Kalchinian was an active government informer who had but recently been the instigatory of at least two other prosecutions. Undoubtedly the impetus for such achievements was the fact that in 1951 Kalchinian was himself under criminal charges for illegally selling narcotics and had not yet been sentenced. It makes no difference that the sales for which petitioner was convicted occurred after a series of sales. They were not independent acts subsequent to the inducement but part of a course of conduct which was the product of the inducement. In his testimony the federal agent in charge of the case admitted that he never bothered to question Kalchinian about the way he had made contact with petitioner. The Government cannot make such use of an informer and then claim disassociation through ignorance.

The Government sought to overcome the defense of entrapment by claiming that petitioner evinced a "ready complaisance" to accede to Kalchinian's request. Aside from a record of past convictions, which we discuss in the following paragraph, the Government's case is unsupported. There is no evidence that petitioner himself was in the trade. When his apartment was searched after arrest, no narcotics were found. There is no significant evidence that petitioner even made a profit on any sale to Kalchinian. The Government's characterization of petitioner's hesitancy to Kalchinian's request as the natural wariness of the criminal cannot fill the evidentiary void.

The Government's additional evidence in the second trial to show that petitioner was ready and willing to sell narcotics should the opportunity present itself was petitioner's record of two past narcotics convictions. In 1942 petitioner was convicted of illegally selling narcotics; in 1946 he was convicted of illegally possessing them. However, a nine-year-old sales conviction and a five-year-old possession conviction are insufficient to prove petitioner had a readiness to sell narcotics at the time Kalchinian approached him, particularly when we must assume from the record he was trying to overcome the narcotics habit at the time.

The case at bar illustrates an evil which the defense of entrapment is designed to overcome. The government informer entices someone attempting to avoid narcotics not only into carrying out an illegal sale but also into returning to the habit of use. Selecting the proper time, the informer then tells the government agent. The set-up is accepted by the agent without even a question as to the manner in which the informer encountered the seller. Thus the Government plays on the weaknesses of an innocent party and beguiles him into committing crimes which he otherwise would not have attempted. Law enforcement does not require methods such as this.

It has been suggested that in overturning this conviction we should reassess the doctrine of entrapment according to principles announced in the separate opinion of Mr. Justice Roberts in *Sorrells*. To do so would be to decide the case on grounds rejected by the majority in *Sorrells* and, so far as the record shows, not raised here or below by the parties before us. We do not ordinarily decide issues not presented by the parties and there is good reason not to vary that practice in this case.

At least two important issues of law enforcement and trial procedure would have to be decided without the benefit of argument by the parties, one party being the Government. Mr. Justice Roberts asserted that although the defendant could claim that the Government had induced him to commit the crime, the Government could not reply by showing that the defendant's criminal conduct was due to his own readiness and not to the persuasion of government agents. The handicap thus placed on the prosecution is obvious. Furthermore, it was the position of Mr. Justice Roberts that the factual issue of entrapment — now limited to the question of what the government agents did — should be decided by the judge, not the jury. Not only was this rejected by the Court in *Sorrells*, but where the issue has been presented to them, the Courts of Appeals have since *Sorrells* unanimously concluded that unless it can be decided as a matter of law, the issue of whether a defendant has been entrapped is for the jury as part of its function of determining the guilt or innocence of the accused.

A. Discretion   **835**

To dispose of this case on the ground suggested would entail both overruling a leading decision of this Court and brushing aside the possibility that we would be creating more problems than we would supposedly be solving.

The judgment of the Court of Appeals is reversed and the case is remanded to the District Court with instructions to dismiss the indictment.

Reversed and remanded.

NOTES AND QUESTIONS

1. *Sherman* relies on the principles of entrapment set forth in *Sorrels v. United States*, 287 U.S. 435 (1932), another conviction for what was essentially a victimless crime: possessing and selling a half gallon of whisky for $5 in violation of the National Prohibition Act. The Court notes, as it did in *Sorrels, id.* at 442-43, that "stealth and strategy are necessary weapons in the arsenal of the police officer." Even if that may be the case generally, or sometimes, is it true in *Sherman*? Suppose Sherman had acceded at once to the informant's request to obtain drugs for him, and no entrapment defense were available. Should such a prosecution be encouraged? Tolerated?

2. As a basis for the entrapment doctrine, *Sherman* relies on a theory of legislative intent — that is, the legislature could not have intended that the statute it drafted would be applied where innocent persons were seduced into violations. The dissent calls this theory a "sheer fiction." Do you agree? Is it a fiction that is necessary out of deference to the executive branch's responsibility for enforcement of the criminal law? Does this mean that Congress could eliminate the doctrine by legislation?

3. The government appears to base the entirety of its case for "predisposition" on Sherman's two previous convictions: a five-year-old possession conviction and a nine-year-old sales conviction. What if Sherman had not been in a treatment program? Would these prior convictions at least be enough to leave the decision in the hands of the jury, and not decide the entrapment issue as a matter of law? What if the convictions were only two and four years old?

4. Justice Frankfurter, in a concurring opinion joined by Justices Douglas, Harlan, and Brennan, essentially wants to abandon the "predisposition" element of the entrapment doctrine because it requires the defendant to put his reputation and criminal record, if any, at issue in order to raise the defense and thereby risk a conviction tainted by prejudice. Is this a good enough reason to abandon the predisposition requirement? What about the dissent's argument that entrapment should be a matter for the court to decide — like the suppression of evidence — rather than the jury?

5. Note that Sherman was tried twice for this offense, his prior trial being reversed based on an erroneous jury instruction on entrapment. Why was he tried once, let alone twice? Shouldn't it have been perfectly clear to the prosecutor from his preparation of the informant — whose testimony supplied all the facts establishing entrapment — that Sherman was a sympathetic defendant who was aggressively induced by the informant? Did the prosecutor believe he could bank on Sherman's prior convictions to get him a guilty verdict, either as evidence of predisposition or for their prejudicial effect? Note that the jury convicted Sherman even though they were somehow made aware — this was 14 years before *Giglio* — that the informant had received a suspended sentence on pending narcotics charges due to his cooperation against Sherman.

6. Who bears ultimate responsibility for this prosecution? The informant, who testified on cross-examination that his "job" was to "induce people to sell him drugs"? The federal agent in charge of the case, who admitted he never supervised or questioned the informant

Chapter IX The Prosecution Function

about how he contacted or interacted with Sherman? The prosecutor who indicted and tried the case?

In *United States v. Russell*, 411 U.S. 423 (1973), the Supreme Court rejected an extension of the entrapment doctrine to cover situations, in which some lower courts had found entrapment applicable, where the government had actively participated or had become "enmeshed" in the criminal activity. In *Russell*, a government agent had supplied an essential ingredient necessary to sustain the manufacturing operations of a methamphetamine lab. The Court noted that entrapment was a "very limited defense," and again noted the necessity of covert government strategies:

> The illicit manufacture of drugs is not a sporadic, isolated criminal incident, but a continuing, though illegal, business enterprise. In order to obtain convictions for illegally manufacturing drugs, the gathering of evidence of past unlawful conduct frequently proves to be an all but impossible task. Thus in drug-related offenses law enforcement personnel have turned to one of the only practicable means of detection: the infiltration of drug rings and a limited participation in their unlawful present practices. Such infiltration is a recognized and permissible means of investigation; if that be so, then the supply of some item of value that the drug ring requires must, as a general rule, also be permissible. For an agent will not be taken into the confidence of the illegal entrepreneurs unless he has something of value to offer them.

Id. at 432. The Court's deference to the executive could hardly have been clearer: "the defense of entrapment enunciated in [*Sorrels* and *Sherman*] was not intended to give the federal judiciary a 'chancellor's foot' veto over law enforcement practices of which it did not approve. The execution of the federal laws under our Constitution is confined primarily to the Executive Branch of the Government. . . ."

The next case considers the government's aggressive use of "stealth and strategy" to snare defendants in the pornography context, a prosecution priority in President Ronald Reagan's Department of Justice under Attorney General Edwin Meese. *See* Chapter VII *infra*.

Jacobson v. United States
503 U.S. 540 (1992)

Justice WHITE delivered the opinion of the Court.

On September 24, 1987, petitioner Keith Jacobson was indicted for violating a provision of the Child Protection Act of 1984 (Act), Pub. L. 98-292, 98 Stat. 204, which criminalizes the knowing receipt through the mails of a "visual depiction [that] involves the use of a minor engaging in sexually explicit conduct. . . ." 18 U.S.C. § 2252(a)(2)(A). Petitioner defended on the ground that the Government entrapped him into committing the crime through a series of communications from undercover agents that spanned the 26 months preceding his arrest. Petitioner was found guilty after a jury trial. The Court of Appeals affirmed his conviction, holding that the Government had carried its burden of proving beyond reasonable doubt that petitioner was predisposed to break the law and hence was not entrapped.

Because the Government overstepped the line between setting a trap for the "unwary innocent" and the "unwary criminal," *Sherman v. United States* (1958), and as a matter of law failed to establish that petitioner was independently predisposed to commit the crime for which he was arrested, we reverse the Court of Appeals' judgment affirming his conviction.

I

In February 1984, petitioner, a 56-year-old veteran-turned-farmer who supported his elderly father in Nebraska, ordered two magazines and a brochure from a California adult bookstore. The magazines, entitled Bare Boys I and Bare Boys II, contained photographs of nude preteen and teenage boys. The contents of the magazines startled petitioner, who testified that he had expected to receive photographs of "young men 18 years or older." Tr. 425. On cross-examination, he explained his response to the magazines:

> **[PROSECUTOR]:** [Y]ou were shocked and surprised that there were pictures of very young boys without clothes on, is that correct?
>
> **[JACOBSON]:** Yes, I was.
>
> **[PROSECUTOR]:** Were you offended?
>
> • • •
>
> **[JACOBSON]:** I was not offended because I thought these were a nudist type publication. Many of the pictures were out in a rural or outdoor setting. There was—I didn't draw any sexual connotation or connection with that.

The young men depicted in the magazines were not engaged in sexual activity, and petitioner's receipt of the magazines was legal under both federal and Nebraska law. Within three months, the law with respect to child pornography changed; Congress passed the Act illegalizing the receipt through the mails of sexually explicit depictions of children. In the very month that the new provision became law, postal inspectors found petitioner's name on the mailing list of the California bookstore that had mailed him Bare Boys I and II. There followed over the next 2 ½ years repeated efforts by two Government agencies, through five fictitious organizations and a bogus pen pal, to explore petitioner's willingness to break the new law by ordering sexually explicit photographs of children through the mail.

The Government began its efforts in January 1985 when a postal inspector sent petitioner a letter supposedly from the American Hedonist Society, which in fact was a fictitious organization. The letter included a membership application and stated the Society's doctrine: that members had the "right to read what we desire, the right to discuss similar interests with those who share our philosophy, and finally that we have the right to seek pleasure without restrictions being placed on us by outdated puritan morality." Petitioner enrolled in the organization and returned a sexual attitude questionnaire that asked him to rank on a scale of one to four his enjoyment of various sexual materials, with one being "really enjoy," two being "enjoy," three being "somewhat enjoy," and four being "do not enjoy." Petitioner ranked the entry "[p] re-teen sex" as a two, but indicated that he was opposed to pedophilia.

For a time, the Government left petitioner alone. But then a new "prohibited mailing specialist" in the Postal Service found petitioner's name in a file, and in May 1986, petitioner received a solicitation from a second fictitious consumer research company, "Midlands Data Research," seeking a response from those who "believe in the joys of sex and the complete awareness of those lusty and youthful lads and lasses of the neophite [sic] age." The letter never explained whether "neophite" referred to minors or young adults. Petitioner responded: "Please feel free to send me more information, I am interested in teenage sexuality. Please keep my name confidential."

Petitioner then heard from yet another Government creation, "Heartland Institute for a New Tomorrow" (HINT), which proclaimed that it was "an organization founded to protect and promote sexual freedom and freedom of choice. We believe that arbitrarily

838   Chapter IX The Prosecution Function

imposed legislative sanctions restricting your sexual freedom should be rescinded through the legislative process." The letter also enclosed a second survey. Petitioner indicated that his interest in "[p]reteen sex-homosexual" material was above average, but not high. In response to another question, petitioner wrote: "Not only sexual expression but freedom of the press is under attack. We must be ever vigilant to counter attack right wing fundamentalists who are determined to curtail our freedoms."

HINT replied, portraying itself as a lobbying organization seeking to repeal "all statutes which regulate sexual activities, except those laws which deal with violent behavior, such as rape. HINT is also lobbying to eliminate any legal definition of 'the age of consent.' " These lobbying efforts were to be funded by sales from a catalog to be published in the future "offering the sale of various items which we believe you will find to be both interesting and stimulating." HINT also provided computer matching of group members with similar survey responses; and, although petitioner was supplied with a list of potential "pen pals," he did not initiate any correspondence.

Nevertheless, the Government's "prohibited mailing specialist" began writing to petitioner, using the pseudonym "Carl Long." The letters employed a tactic known as "mirroring," which the inspector described as "reflect[ing] whatever the interests are of the person we are writing to." Petitioner responded at first, indicating that his interest was primarily in "male-male items." Inspector "Long" wrote back:

> My interests too are primarily male-male items. Are you satisfied with the type of VCR tapes available? Personally, I like the amateur stuff better if its [sic] well produced as it can get more kinky and also seems more real. I think the actors enjoy it more.

Petitioner responded:

> As far as my likes are concerned, I like good looking young guys (in their late teens and early 20's) doing their thing together.

Petitioner's letters to "Long" made no reference to child pornography. After writing two letters, petitioner discontinued the correspondence.

By March 1987, 34 months had passed since the Government obtained petitioner's name from the mailing list of the California bookstore, and 26 months had passed since the Postal Service had commenced its mailings to petitioner. Although petitioner had responded to surveys and letters, the Government had no evidence that petitioner had ever intentionally possessed or been exposed to child pornography. The Postal Service had not checked petitioner's mail to determine whether he was receiving questionable mailings from persons—other than the Government—involved in the child pornography industry.

At this point, a second Government agency, the Customs Service, included petitioner in its own child pornography sting, "Operation Borderline," after receiving his name on lists submitted by the Postal Service. Using the name of a fictitious Canadian company called "Produit Outaouais," the Customs Service mailed petitioner a brochure advertising photographs of young boys engaging in sex. Petitioner placed an order that was never filled.

The Postal Service also continued its efforts in the Jacobson case, writing to petitioner as the "Far Eastern Trading Company Ltd." The letter began:

> As many of you know, much hysterical nonsense has appeared in the American media concerning "pornography" and what must be done to stop it from coming across your borders. This brief letter does not allow us to give much comments; however, why is your government spending millions of dollars to exercise international censorship while tons of drugs, which makes yours the world's most crime ridden country are passed through easily.

The letter went on to say:

> [W]e have devised a method of getting these to you without prying eyes of U.S. Customs seizing your mail. . . . After consultations with American solicitors, we have been advised that

once we have posted our material through your system, it cannot be opened for any inspection without authorization of a judge.

The letter invited petitioner to send for more information. It also asked petitioner to sign an affirmation that he was "not a law enforcement officer or agent of the U.S. Government acting in an undercover capacity for the purpose of entrapping Far Eastern Trading Company, its agents or customers." Petitioner responded. A catalog was sent, and petitioner ordered Boys Who Love Boys, a pornographic magazine depicting young boys engaged in various sexual activities. Petitioner was arrested after a controlled delivery of a photocopy of the magazine.

When petitioner was asked at trial why he placed such an order, he explained that the Government had succeeded in piquing his curiosity:

> Well, the statement was made of all the trouble and the hysteria over pornography and I wanted to see what the material was. It didn't describe the—I didn't know for sure what kind of sexual action they were referring to in the Canadian letter.

In petitioner's home, the Government found the Bare Boys magazines and materials that the Government had sent to him in the course of its protracted investigation, but no other materials that would indicate that petitioner collected, or was actively interested in, child pornography.

Petitioner was indicted for violating 18 U.S.C. § 2252(a)(2)(A). The trial court instructed the jury on the petitioner's entrapment defense, petitioner was convicted, and a divided Court of Appeals for the Eighth Circuit, sitting en banc, affirmed, concluding that "Jacobson was not entrapped as a matter of law."

II

There can be no dispute about the evils of child pornography or the difficulties that laws and law enforcement have encountered in eliminating it. Likewise, there can be no dispute that the Government may use undercover agents to enforce the law. "It is well settled that the fact that officers or employees of the Government merely afford opportunities or facilities for the commission of the offense does not defeat the prosecution. Artifice and stratagem may be employed to catch those engaged in criminal enterprises."

In their zeal to enforce the law, however, Government agents may not originate a criminal design, implant in an innocent person's mind the disposition to commit a criminal act, and then induce commission of the crime so that the Government may prosecute. Where the Government has induced an individual to break the law and the defense of entrapment is at issue, as it was in this case, the prosecution must prove beyond reasonable doubt that the defendant was disposed to commit the criminal act prior to first being approached by Government agents.

Thus, an agent deployed to stop the traffic in illegal drugs may offer the opportunity to buy or sell drugs and, if the offer is accepted, make an arrest on the spot or later. In such a typical case, or in a more elaborate "sting" operation involving government-sponsored fencing where the defendant is simply provided with the opportunity to commit a crime, the entrapment defense is of little use because the ready commission of the criminal act amply demonstrates the defendant's predisposition. Had the agents in this case simply offered petitioner the opportunity to order child pornography through the mails, and petitioner—who must be presumed to know the law—had promptly availed himself of this criminal opportunity, it is unlikely that his entrapment defense would have warranted a jury instruction.

But that is not what happened here. By the time petitioner finally placed his order, he had already been the target of 26 months of repeated mailings and communications from Government agents and fictitious organizations. Therefore, although he had become predisposed to break the law by May 1987, it is our view that the Government did not prove that this predisposition was independent and not the product of the attention that the Government had directed at petitioner since January 1985.

The prosecution's evidence of predisposition falls into two categories: evidence developed prior to the Postal Service's mail campaign, and that developed during the course of the investigation. The sole piece of pre-investigation evidence is petitioner's 1984 order and receipt of the Bare Boys magazines. But this is scant if any proof of petitioner's predisposition to commit an illegal act, the criminal character of which a defendant is presumed to know. It may indicate a predisposition to view sexually oriented photographs that are responsive to his sexual tastes; but evidence that merely indicates a generic inclination to act within a broad range, not all of which is criminal, is of little probative value in establishing predisposition.

Furthermore, petitioner was acting within the law at the time he received these magazines. Receipt through the mails of sexually explicit depictions of children for noncommercial use did not become illegal under federal law until May 1984, and Nebraska had no law that forbade petitioner's possession of such material until 1988. Evidence of predisposition to do what once was lawful is not, by itself, sufficient to show predisposition to do what is now illegal, for there is a common understanding that most people obey the law even when they disapprove of it. This obedience may reflect a generalized respect for legality or the fear of prosecution, but for whatever reason, the law's prohibitions are matters of consequence. Hence, the fact that petitioner legally ordered and received the Bare Boys magazines does little to further the Government's burden of proving that petitioner was predisposed to commit a criminal act. This is particularly true given petitioner's unchallenged testimony that he did not know until they arrived that the magazines would depict minors.

The prosecution's evidence gathered during the investigation also fails to carry the Government's burden. Petitioner's responses to the many communications prior to the ultimate criminal act were at most indicative of certain personal inclinations, including a predisposition to view photographs of preteen sex and a willingness to promote a given agenda by supporting lobbying organizations. Even so, petitioner's responses hardly support an inference that he would commit the crime of receiving child pornography through the mails. Furthermore, a person's inclinations and "fantasies . . . are his own and beyond the reach of government. . . ."

On the other hand, the strong arguable inference is that, by waving the banner of individual rights and disparaging the legitimacy and constitutionality of efforts to restrict the availability of sexually explicit materials, the Government not only excited petitioner's interest in sexually explicit materials banned by law but also exerted substantial pressure on petitioner to obtain and read such material as part of a fight against censorship and the infringement of individual rights. For instance, HINT described itself as "an organization founded to protect and promote sexual freedom and freedom of choice" and stated that "the most appropriate means to accomplish [its] objectives is to promote honest dialogue among concerned individuals and to continue its lobbying efforts with State Legislators." These lobbying efforts were to be financed through catalog sales. Mailings from the equally fictitious American Hedonist Society and the correspondence from the nonexistent Carl Long endorsed these themes.

Similarly, the two solicitations in the spring of 1987 raised the spectre of censorship while suggesting that petitioner ought to be allowed to do what he had been solicited to do. The mailing from the Customs Service referred to "the worldwide ban and intense enforcement on this type of material," observed that "what was legal and commonplace is now an 'underground' and secretive service," and emphasized that "[t]his environment forces us to take extreme measures" to ensure delivery. The Postal Service solicitation described the concern about child pornography as "hysterical nonsense," decried "international censorship," and assured petitioner, based on consultation with "American solicitors," that an order that had been posted could not be opened for inspection without authorization of a judge. It further asked petitioner to affirm that he was not a Government agent attempting to entrap the mail order company or its customers. In these particulars, both Government solicitations suggested that receiving this material was something that petitioner ought to be allowed to do.

Petitioner's ready response to these solicitations cannot be enough to establish beyond reasonable doubt that he was predisposed, prior to the Government acts intended to create predisposition, to commit the crime of receiving child pornography through the mails. The evidence that petitioner was ready and willing to commit the offense came only after the Government had devoted 2 ½ years to convincing him that he had or should have the right to engage in the very behavior proscribed by law. Rational jurors could not say beyond a reasonable doubt that petitioner possessed the requisite predisposition prior to the Government's investigation and that it existed independent of the Government's many and varied approaches to petitioner. As was explained in Sherman, where entrapment was found as a matter of law, "the Government [may not] pla[y] on the weaknesses of an innocent party and beguil[e] him into committing crimes which he otherwise would not have attempted."

Law enforcement officials go too far when they "implant in the mind of an innocent person the disposition to commit the alleged offense and induce its commission in order that they may prosecute." Like the *Sorrells* Court, we are "unable to conclude that it was the intention of the Congress in enacting this statute that its processes of detection and enforcement should be abused by the instigation by government officials of an act on the part of persons otherwise innocent in order to lure them to its commission and to punish them." When the Government's quest for convictions leads to the apprehension of an otherwise law-abiding citizen who, if left to his own devices, likely would have never run afoul of the law, the courts should intervene.

Because we conclude that this is such a case and that the prosecution failed, as a matter of law, to adduce evidence to support the jury verdict that petitioner was predisposed, independent of the Government's acts and beyond a reasonable doubt, to violate the law by receiving child pornography through the mails, we reverse the Court of Appeals' judgment affirming the conviction of Keith Jacobson.

It is so ordered.

NOTES AND QUESTIONS

1. We are told immediately that the defendant is "a 56-year old veteran-turned farmer who supported his elderly father in Nebraska." Who's going to win here?

2. The crime here is reprehensible — hardly victimless — and it appears that the only way for defendant to raise his entrapment defense is to take the stand in his defense, waive his Fifth Amendment rights, and expose himself to cross-examination. Can you imagine how an entrapment defense can be raised — particularly the lack of predisposition component — without the defendant testifying? Bear in mind that to even persuade the court to give an entrapment instruction to the jury a defendant would have to put forward at least "some evidence" that would warrant a jury's finding of entrapment.

3. The length and intensity of the government's inducement efforts here are shocking: repeated efforts by two government agencies over 30 months using multiple artifices to obtain a single count of conviction of a lonely middle-aged man who was in no position to cooperate against anyone else. Presumably the government was engaged in similar efforts against every other person on the mailing list of the California "adult book store." But consider the "necessity" rationales advanced in *Sorrels, Sherman,* and *Russell.* Were these concerted efforts necessary? Why not, instead, simply mail a catalog offering child pornographic material to everyone on the mailing list and prosecute those recipients who order something from the catalog? Is the concern that the catalog recipients wouldn't order anything without a little courtship?

842   Chapter IX The Prosecution Function

4. Relatedly, when is the point at which "predisposition" is to be assessed? Is it permissible for law enforcement, through extended foreplay, to create a predisposition for criminality that did not exist at the outset of the relationship? The dissent says that the majority's reasoning "introduces a new requirement that Government sting operations have a reasonable suspicion of illegal activity before contacting a suspect." Does it? Would that be a bad thing?

5. The majority asserts that the government "exerted substantial pressure on [Jacobson] to obtain and read [sexually explicit] material as part of a fight against censorship and the infringement of individual rights." Do you think the government's efforts with respect to Jacobson amounted to "substantial pressure"?

6. The dirty tricks here are done by law enforcement agents, not the prosecutor. And prosecutors are not the supervisors of law enforcement agents. But they are responsible for the quality and character of the prosecutions they bring and what they present in court. What obstacles do you see that the prosecutor would have had in declining to prosecute Jacobson?

The next case considers the use of a criminal informant to attempt to develop a criminal case against a defendant who might charitably be described as "politically unpopular."

Hoffa v. United States
385 U.S. 293 (1966)

Mr. Justice STEWART delivered the opinion of the Court.

Over a period of several weeks in the late autumn of 1962 there took place in a federal court in Nashville, Tennessee, a trial by jury in which James Hoffa was charged with violating a provision of the Taft-Hartley Act. That trial, known in the present record as the Test Fleet trial, ended with a hung jury. The petitioners now before us—James Hoffa, Thomas Parks, Larry Campbell, and Ewing King—were tried and convicted in 1964 for endeavoring to bribe members of that jury. The convictions were affirmed by the Court of Appeals. A substantial element in the Government's proof that led to the convictions of these four petitioners was contributed by a witness named Edward Partin, who testified to several incriminating statements which he said petitioners Hoffa and King had made in his presence during the course of the Test Fleet trial. Our grant of certiorari was limited to the single issue of whether the Government's use in this case of evidence supplied by Partin operated to invalidate these convictions.

The specific question before us, as framed by counsel for the petitioners, is this:

> Whether evidence obtained by the Government by means of deceptively placing a secret informer in the quarters and councils of a defendant during one criminal trial so violates the defendant's Fourth, Fifth and Sixth Amendment rights that suppression of such evidence is required in a subsequent trial of the same defendant on a different charge.

At the threshold the Government takes issue with the way this question is worded, refusing to concede that it "placed" the informer anywhere, much less that it did so "deceptively." In the view we take of the matter, however, a resolution of this verbal controversy is unnecessary to a decision of the constitutional issues before us. The basic facts are clear enough, and a lengthy discussion of the detailed minutiae to which a large portion of the briefs and oral arguments was addressed would serve only to divert attention from the real issues before us.

The controlling facts can be briefly stated. The Test Fleet trial, in which James Hoffa was the sole individual defendant, was in progress between October 22 and December 23, 1962, in Nashville, Tennessee. James Hoffa was president of the International Brotherhood of Teamsters. During the course of the trial he occupied a three-room suite in the Andrew Jackson Hotel in Nashville. One of his constant companions throughout the trial was the petitioner King, president of the Nashville local of the Teamsters Union. Edward Partin, a resident of Baton Rouge, Louisiana, and a local Teamsters Union official there, made repeated visits to Nashville during the period of the trial. On these visits he frequented the Hoffa hotel suite, and was continually in the company of Hoffa and his associates, including King, in and around the hotel suite, the hotel lobby, the courthouse, and elsewhere in Nashville. During this period Partin made frequent reports to a federal agent named Sheridan concerning conversations he said Hoffa and King had had with him and with each other, disclosing endeavors to bribe members of the Test Fleet jury. Partin's reports and his subsequent testimony at the petitioners' trial unquestionably contributed, directly or indirectly, to the convictions of all four of the petitioners.

The chain of circumstances which led Partin to be in Nashville during the Test Fleet trial extended back at least to September of 1962. At that time Partin was in jail in Baton Rouge on a state criminal charge. He was also under a federal indictment for embezzling union funds, and other indictments for state offenses were pending against him. Between that time and Partin's initial visit to Nashville on October 22 he was released on bail on the state criminal charge, and proceedings under the federal indictment were postponed. On October 8, Partin telephoned Hoffa in Washington, D.C., to discuss local union matters and Partin's difficulties with the authorities. In the course of this conversation Partin asked if he could see Hoffa to confer about these problems, and Hoffa acquiesced. Partin again called Hoffa on October 18 and arranged to meet him in Nashville. During this period Partin also consulted on several occasions with federal law enforcement agents, who told him that Hoffa might attempt to tamper with the Test Fleet jury, and asked him to be on the lookout in Nashville for such attempts and to report to the federal authorities any evidence of wrongdoing that he discovered. Partin agreed to do so.

After the Test Fleet trial was completed, Partin's wife received four monthly installment payments of $300 from government funds, and the state and federal charges against Partin were either dropped or not actively pursued.

Reviewing these circumstances in detail, the Government insists the fair inference is that Partin went to Nashville on his own initiative to discuss union business and his own problems with Hoffa, that Partin ultimately cooperated closely with federal authorities only after he discovered evidence of jury tampering in the Test Fleet trial, that the payments to Partin's wife were simply in partial reimbursement of Partin's subsequent out-of-pocket expenses, and that the failure to prosecute Partin on the state and federal charges had no necessary connection with his services as an informer. The findings of the trial court support this version of the facts, and these findings were accepted by the Court of Appeals as "supported by substantial evidence." But whether or not the Government "placed" Partin with Hoffa in Nashville during the Test Fleet trial, we proceed upon the premise that Partin was a government informer from the time he first arrived in Nashville on October 22, and that the Government compensated him for his services as such. It is upon that premise that we consider the constitutional issues presented.

• • •

I

It is contended that only by violating the petitioner's rights under the Fourth Amendment was Partin able to hear the petitioner's incriminating statements in the hotel suite, and that Partin's testimony was therefore inadmissible under the exclusionary rule of *Weeks*. The argument is that Partin's failure to disclose his role as a government informer vitiated the consent that the petitioner gave to Partin's repeated entries into the suite, and that by listening to the petitioner's statements Partin conducted an illegal "search" for verbal evidence.

The preliminary steps of this argument are on solid ground. A hotel room can clearly be the object of Fourth Amendment protection as much as a home or an office. The Fourth Amendment can certainly be violated by guileful as well as by forcible intrusions into a constitutionally protected area. And the protections of the Fourth Amendment are surely not limited to tangibles, but can extend as well to oral statements.

Where the argument falls is in its misapprehension of the fundamental nature and scope of Fourth Amendment protection. What the Fourth Amendment protects is the security a man relies upon when he places himself or his property within a constitutionally protected area, be it his home or his office, his hotel room or his automobile. There he is protected from unwarranted governmental intrusion. And when he puts something in his filing cabinet, in his desk drawer, or in his pocket, he has the right to know it will be secure from an unreasonable search or an unreasonable seizure. So it was that the Fourth Amendment could not tolerate the warrantless search of the hotel room in *Jeffers*, the purloining of the petitioner's private papers in *Gouled*, or the surreptitious electronic surveillance in *Silverman*. Countless other cases which have come to this Court over the years have involved a myriad of differing factual contexts in which the protections of the Fourth Amendment have been appropriately invoked. No doubt the future will bring countless others. By nothing we say here do we either foresee or foreclose factual situations to which the Fourth Amendment may be applicable.

In the present case, however, it is evident that no interest legitimately protected by the Fourth Amendment is involved. It is obvious that the petitioner was not relying on the security of his hotel suite when he made the incriminating statements to Partin or in Partin's presence. Partin did not enter the suite by force or by stealth. He was not a surreptitious eavesdropper. Partin was in the suite by invitation, and every conversation which he heard was either directed to him or knowingly carried on in his presence. The petitioner, in a word, was not relying on the security of the hotel room; he was relying upon his misplaced confidence that Partin would not reveal his wrongdoing. As counsel for the petitioner himself points out, some of the communications with Partin did not take place in the suite at all, but in the "hall of the hotel," in the "Andrew Jackson Hotel lobby," and "at the courthouse."

Neither this Court nor any member of it has ever expressed the view that the Fourth Amendment protects a wrongdoer's misplaced belief that a person to whom he voluntarily confides his wrongdoing will not reveal it. Indeed, the Court unanimously rejected that very contention less than four years ago in *Lopez v. United States*. In that case the petitioner had been convicted of attempted bribery of an internal revenue agent named Davis. The Court was divided with regard to the admissibility in evidence of a surreptitious electronic recording of an incriminating conversation Lopez had had in his private office with Davis. But there was no dissent from the view that testimony about the conversation by Davis himself was clearly admissible.

As the Court put it, "Davis was not guilty of an unlawful invasion of petitioner's office simply because his apparent willingness to accept a bribe was not real. He was in the office with petitioner's consent, and while there he did not violate the privacy of the office by seizing something surreptitiously without petitioner's knowledge. The only evidence obtained consisted of statements made by Lopez to Davis, statements which Lopez knew full well could be used against him by Davis if he wished. In the words of the dissenting opinion in *Lopez*, "The risk of being overheard by an eavesdropper or betrayed by an informer or deceived as to the identity of one with whom one deals is probably inherent in the conditions of human society. It is the kind of risk we necessarily assume whenever we speak."

Adhering to these views, we hold that no right protected by the Fourth Amendment was violated in the present case.

· · ·

NOTES AND QUESTIONS

Attorney General Bobby Kennedy

Jimmy Hoffa

1. The Department of Justice's pursuit of Jimmy Hoffa in the 1960s by Attorney General Robert Kennedy, younger brother of the President, is perhaps the epitome of the risk warned of by Justice Jackson, that the prosecutor may "pick people that he thinks he should get," *see supra*, and look for an offense. Bobby Kennedy's feud with Hoffa dated back to his days working on Senate investigative committees in the 1950s, and only accelerated when he became attorney general in 1961. Kennedy assembled what became known as the "Get Hoffa Squad" in DOJ, consisting of dozens of lawyers and agents. The Test Fleet prosecution underlying Hoffa's jury-tampering conviction at issue here, which lasted for two months, was a prosecution for a misdemeanor violation of the Taft-Hartley Act. *See generally* Tracey Maclin, Hoffa v. United States: *Secret Agents in Private Spaces* 181-87, in Criminal Procedure Stories (Carol Steiker ed., 2006).

2. The Court minimizes any Fourth Amendment concerns about the government's use of the informant under what is essentially an "assumption of the risk" theory. But it also notes that Partin did not enter the hotel suite "by force or by stealth." Putting aside whether his entrance was in fact by "stealth," as his informant status was concealed, does this matter? Should it matter? Is the government conduct ameliorated by the fact Partin was a colleague of Hoffa's? Wouldn't Hoffa's "assumption of risk" have been greater if he had carelessly let a stranger operating under some pretext into the defense camp?

3. Professor Maclin has raised the possibility of treating the government's use of informants like wiretaps or bugs and applying Fourth Amendment standards to their use. Is that workable? If that were the case, could the government have gotten a warrant here? Are there any facts in the case indicating that before the trial the government had probable cause to suspect that Hoffa would tamper with the jury?

4. *Hoffa* was decided just a few months before the decision in *Katz*, where the Court famously stated that the Fourth Amendment "protects people not places," and held that a warrant was required for recording phone calls made from a public telephone booth, in which defendant enjoyed a "reasonable expectation of privacy." Are *Hoffa* and *Katz* inconsistent?

5. In response to the defendant's argument that the totality of the government's conduct violated due process, the Court ultimately concludes that prosecutions based on the testimony of informants—as this one was virtually in its entirety—are constitutional inasmuch as the defendant has the right to cross-examination and the jury is instructed on witness credibility. Does that seem reasonable? The Court notes in a footnote that Partin was on cross-examination for a full week, although it is unclear to what effect. In particular, it is unclear whether the jury was aware that federal and state criminal charges would (or might be) be dropped and that payments were (or would be) made to his wife. It would be another several years before the Court would hold in *Giglio v. United States*, 405 U.S. 150 (1972), *see infra*, that the government was obligated to disclose to defendant any promises, rewards, or inducements given to government witnesses.

6. Chief Justice Warren dissented, analogizing the government's use of Partin to "a bugging device which moved wherever Hoffa went," and thought the conviction should be vacated as an exercise of the Court's supervisory powers. The Chief Justice stated: "'The government of a strong and free nation does not need convictions based upon such testimony. It cannot afford to abide with them.'" (quoting *Mesarosh v. United States*, 352 U.S. 1, 14 (1956).

Would whether government action was "an affront to the quality and fairness of federal law enforcement be a desirable standard for judicial evaluation of the government's use of informants and undercover agents"?

Teamster informant Edward Partin

7. The Court also rejected two Sixth Amendment arguments by Hoffa: (a) that the government had probable cause to arrest *Hoffa* early in the trial and, had it done so, it could thereafter not have used an informant against him under the rule of *Massiah, see* Chapter III *supra*; and (b) that Partin essentially became a "spy in the defense camp" as he sat in on conversations with Hoffa's lawyers. The first argument was frivolous — there is no right to be arrested — the second deadly serious, although ultimately rejected by the Court based on the district court's factual findings that Partin only communicated one aspect of potentially privileged conversations to his FBI handler. It is inconceivable that a prosecution that was not driven by a vendetta like Bobby Kennedy's would have used an informant like Partin at all, and at a minimum would not have let him near the target's attorneys.

Sherman, Jacobson, and *Hoffa* all involve the outer periphery of the government's use of unsavory tactics and or witnesses in an attempt to obtain a conviction. But the government uses the testimony of cooperating witnesses in court every day, and every time it does the integrity of the system is implicated.

The issue of truthful testimony preoccupies prosecutors in dealing with cooperating witnesses. Truthful testimony at trial, to the prosecutor, means testimony that is consistent with the witness's prior grand jury testimony and with whatever statements he has previously made to the prosecution team. The prosecutor knows that any deviations from those statements will be ruthlessly exploited by the defense on cross-examination.

But consider the cooperating witness's incentives on the front end of the process that ultimately results in the cooperator's trial testimony and, with luck, leniency at sentencing. In his initial meeting with the prosecutor — consider it an audition — the potential cooperating witness knows two things: (1) that he needs to demonstrate that he has information that will help the prosecutor convict others and (2) that he can never deviate from that original story lest he be viewed as untruthful.

Due to these motivations, former prosecutor and now Ninth Circuit Judge Stephen Trott cautions prosecutors using cooperating witnesses to never forget that "[c]riminals are likely to say and do almost anything to get what they want, especially when what they want is to get out of trouble with the law." Hon. Stephen Trott, *Words of Warning for Prosecutors Using Criminals as Witnesses*, 47 Hastings. L.J. 1381, 1382 (1996).

Judge Trott offers several other rules of thumb for prosecutors using cooperating witnesses: use little fish to get big fish; drive a hard deal; stay in control; keep your distance from admitted his participation in the crime, but he claimed that Boblit did the actual killing. And, in his summation to the jury, Brady's counsel conceded that Brady was guilty of murder in the first degree, asking only that the jury return that verdict "without capital punishment." Prior to the trial petitioner's counsel had requested the prosecution to allow him to examine Boblit's extrajudicial statements. Several of those statements were shown to him; but one dated July 9, 1958, in which Boblit admitted the actual homicide, was withheld by the prosecution and did not come to petitioner's notice until after he had been tried, convicted, and sentenced, and after his conviction had been affirmed.

Petitioner moved the trial court for a new trial based on the newly discovered evidence that had been suppressed by the prosecution. Petitioner's appeal from a denial of that motion was dismissed by the Court of Appeals without prejudice to relief under the Maryland Post Conviction Procedure Act. The petition for post-conviction relief was dismissed by the trial court; and on appeal the Court of Appeals held that suppression of the evidence by the prosecution denied petitioner due process of law and remanded the case for a retrial of the question of punishment, not the question of guilt.

The crime in question was murder committed in the perpetration of a robbery. Punishment for that crime in Maryland is life imprisonment or death, the jury being empowered to restrict the punishment to life by addition of the words "without capital punishment." In Maryland, by reason of the state constitution, the jury in a criminal case are "the Judges of Law, as well as of fact." Art. XV, § 5. The question presented is whether petitioner was denied a federal right when the Court of Appeals restricted the new trial to the question of punishment.

We agree with the Court of Appeals that suppression of this confession was a violation of the Due Process Clause of the Fourteenth Amendment. The Court of Appeals relied in the main on two decisions from the Third Circuit Court of Appeals, which, we agree, state the correct constitutional rule.

This ruling is an extension of *Mooney v. Holohan* where the Court ruled on what nondisclosure by a prosecutor violates due process:

> It is a requirement that cannot be deemed to be satisfied by mere notice and hearing if a state has contrived a conviction through the pretense of a trial which in truth is but used as a means of depriving a defendant of liberty through a deliberate deception of court and jury by the presentation of testimony known to be perjured. Such a contrivance by a state to procure the conviction and imprisonment of a defendant is as inconsistent with the rudimentary demands of justice as is the obtaining of a like result by intimidation.

In *Pyle v. Kansas* we phrased the rule in broader terms:

> Petitioner's papers are inexpertly drawn, but they do set forth allegations that his imprisonment resulted from perjured testimony, knowingly used by the State authorities to obtain his conviction, and from the deliberate suppression by those same authorities of evidence favorable to him. These allegations sufficiently charge a deprivation of rights guaranteed by the Federal Constitution, and, if proven, would entitle petitioner to release from his present custody.

The Third Circuit in the *Baldi* case construed that statement in *Pyle v. Kansas* to mean that the "suppression of evidence favorable" to the accused was itself sufficient to amount to a denial of due process. In *Napue v. Illinois* we extended the test formulated in *Mooney* when we said: "The same result obtains when the State, although not soliciting false evidence, allows it to go uncorrected when it appears."

We now hold that the suppression by the prosecution of evidence favorable to an accused upon request violates due process where the evidence is material either to guilt or to punishment, irrespective of the good faith or bad faith of the prosecution.

The principle of *Mooney* is not punishment of society for misdeeds of a prosecutor but avoidance of an unfair trial to the accused. Society wins not only when the guilty are convicted

850   Chapter IX The Prosecution Function

but when criminal trials are fair; our system of the administration of justice suffers when any accused is treated unfairly. An inscription on the walls of the Department of Justice states the proposition candidly for the federal domain: "The United States wins its point whenever justice is done its citizens in the courts. A prosecution that withholds evidence on demand of an accused which, if made available, would tend to exculpate him or reduce the penalty helps shape a trial that bears heavily on the defendant. That casts the prosecutor in the role of an architect of a proceeding that does not comport with standards of justice, even though, as in the present case, his action is not 'the result of guile,' to use the words of the Court of Appeals."

NOTES AND QUESTIONS

1. The undisclosed information here—a written admission by defendant's accomplice that he committed the charged murder—is inarguably exculpatory. But a determination whether a piece of evidence is exculpatory will not always be so easy, especially when you factor in that such a determination must be made by a prosecutor, who by disposition is not wired to view information as exculpatory. And such a determination will be made not just by any prosecutor, but by the very prosecutor who has already made the decision to indict the defendant.

Are prosecutors inherently ill-suited to make determinations as to whether evidence in their own cases is exculpatory? Do you see any alternatives to having this crucial task be the responsibility of the prosecutor?

2. The Court does not explain how defendant learned of the exculpatory statement. It appears the statement had all along been in the prosecutor's possession, together with other statements by the accomplice that, by contrast, were shown to defense counsel. That may not always be the case. Exculpatory evidence may be in the possession not of the prosecutor but of the police or another investigative agency. Consider, for example, the modern paradigm where many types of criminal activity, including drug and gun crimes, are investigated by joint federal-state task forces consisting of both federal agents and local police departments. What are the prosecutor's *Brady* obligations in that scenario? Can she rely on representations from agents or police that they are not aware of the existence of any exculpatory information?

3. The Court is unusually explicit about the parameters of its decision, leaving nothing to the imagination: "We now hold that the suppression by the prosecution of evidence favorable to an accused upon request violates due process where the evidence is material either to guilt or to punishment, irrespective of the good faith or bad faith of the prosecution." Why would the Court choose to be so explicit? Without this language, how might future courts or lawyers have tried to read *Brady* narrowly?

4. The Court describes its ruling as an "extension" of precedents finding due process violations where the government knowingly used or failed to correct perjured testimony to obtain a conviction. Are the affirmative obligations created by *Brady* truly an "extension" of these previous precedents? What are the similarities and differences between these precedents and the decision in *Brady*?

5. The Court specifies that its holding does not require any showing of "bad faith" by the prosecution, and describes the nondisclosure in this case as "not the result of guile."

Do you agree with this assessment of the prosecutor's failure to disclose the statement at issue? Why might the Court want to describe its holding this way?

6. The Court states that a trial where favorable evidence has been withheld "casts the prosecutor in the role of an *architect* of a proceeding that does not comport with standards of

B. Prosecutor's Disclosure Obligations   **851**

justice." In what sense is this metaphor accurate? How does the "architect" metaphor inform the prosecutor's obligations?

The next case considers a specific and critical type of exculpatory material: information bearing on a government witness's credibility. Although both *Brady* and *Giglio* deal with exculpatory information, judges and lawyers often refer to "*Brady* material" and "*Giglio* material" as if they were two separate categories.

Giglio v. United States
405 U.S. 150 (1972)

Mr. Chief Justice BURGER delivered the opinion of the Court.

Petitioner was convicted of passing forged money orders and sentenced to five years' imprisonment. While appeal was pending in the Court of Appeals, defense counsel discovered new evidence indicating that the Government had failed to disclose an alleged promise made to its key witness that he would not be prosecuted if he testified for the Government. We granted certiorari to determine whether the evidence not disclosed was such as to require a new trial under the due process criteria of . . . *Brady v. Maryland* (1963).

The controversy in this case centers around the testimony of Robert Taliento, petitioner's alleged coconspirator in the offense and the only witness linking petitioner with the crime. The Government's evidence at trial showed that in June 1966 officials at the Manufacturers Hanover Trust Co. discovered that Taliento, as teller at the bank, had cashed several forged money orders. Upon questioning by FBI agents, he confessed supplying petitioner with one of the bank's customer signature cards used by Giglio to forge $2,300 in money orders; Taliento then processed these money orders through the regular channels of the bank. Taliento related this story to the grand jury and petitioner was indicted; thereafter, he was named as a coconspirator with petitioner but was not indicted.

Trial commenced two years after indictment. Taliento testified, identifying petitioner as the instigator of the scheme. Defense counsel vigorously cross-examined, seeking to discredit his testimony by revealing possible agreements or arrangements for prosecutorial leniency:

(Counsel.)   Did anybody tell you at any time that if you implicated somebody else in this case that you yourself would not be prosecuted?

(Taliento.)   Nobody told me I wouldn't be prosecuted.

Q.   They told you you might not be prosecuted?

A.   I believe I still could be prosecuted.

. . .

Q.   Were you ever arrested in this case or charged with anything in connection with these money orders that you testified to?

A.   Not at that particular time.

Q.   To this date, have you been charged with any crime?

A.   Not that I know of, unless they are still going to prosecute.

In summation, the Government attorney stated, "(Taliento) received no promises that he would not be indicted."

The issue now before the Court arose on petitioner's motion for new trial based on newly discovered evidence. An affidavit filed by the Government as part of its opposition to a new trial confirms petitioner's claim that a promise was made to Taliento by one assistant, DiPaola, that if he testified before the grand jury and at trial he would not be prosecuted. DiPaola presented the Government's case to the grand jury but did not try the case in the District Court, and Golden, the assistant who took over the case for trial, filed an affidavit stating that DiPaola assured him before the trial that no promises of immunity had been made to Taliento. The United States Attorney, Hoey, filed an affidavit stating that he had personally consulted with Taliento and his attorney shortly before trial to emphasize that Taliento would definitely be prosecuted if he did not testify and that if he did testify he would be obliged to rely on the "good judgment and conscience of the Government" as to whether he would be prosecuted.

The District Court did not undertake to resolve the apparent conflict between the two Assistant United States Attorneys, DiPaola and Golden, but proceeded on the theory that even if a promise had been made by DiPaola it was not authorized and its disclosure to the jury would not have affected its verdict. We need not concern ourselves with the differing versions of the events as described by the two assistants in their affidavits. The heart of the matter is that one Assistant United States Attorney — the first one who dealt with Taliento — now states that he promised Taliento that he would not be prosecuted if he cooperated with the Government.

As long ago as *Mooney v. Holohan* (1935), this Court made clear that deliberate deception of a court and jurors by the presentation of known false evidence is incompatible with "rudimentary demands of justice." This was reaffirmed in *Pyle v. Kansas* (1942). In *Napue v. Illinois* (1959), we said, "(t)he same result obtains when the State, although not soliciting false evidence, allows it to go uncorrected when it appears." Thereafter *Brady* held that suppression of material evidence justifies a new trial "irrespective of the good faith or bad faith of the prosecution." See American Bar Association, Project on Standards for Criminal Justice, Prosecution Function and the Defense Function § 3.11(a). When the "reliability of a given witness may well be determinative of guilt or innocence," nondisclosure of evidence affecting credibility falls within this general rule. We do not, however, automatically require a new trial whenever "a combing of the prosecutors' files after the trial has disclosed evidence possibly useful to the defense but not likely to have changed the verdict." A finding of materiality of the evidence is required. A new trial is required if "the false testimony could . . . in any reasonable likelihood have affected the judgment of the jury."

In the circumstances shown by this record, neither DiPaola's authority nor his failure to inform his superiors or his associates is controlling. Moreover, whether the nondisclosure was a result of negligence or design, it is the responsibility of the prosecutor. The prosecutor's office is an entity and as such it is the spokesman for the Government. A promise made by one attorney must be attributed, for these purposes, to the Government. To the extent this places a burden on the large prosecution offices, procedures and regulations can be established to carry that burden and to insure communication of all relevant information on each case to every lawyer who deals with it.

Here the Government's case depended almost entirely on Taliento's testimony; without it there could have been no indictment and no evidence to carry the case to the jury. Taliento's credibility as a witness was therefore an important issue in the case, and evidence of any understanding or agreement as to a future prosecution would be relevant to his credibility and the jury was entitled to know of it.

For these reasons, the due process requirements enunciated in *Napue* and the other cases cited earlier require a new trial, and the judgment of conviction is therefore reversed and the case is remanded for further proceedings consistent with this opinion.

NOTES AND QUESTIONS

1. Why would the prosecution name Taliento as a coconspirator if it wasn't going to indict him? *See* Fed. R. Evid. 801(d)(2)(E).

2. Consider the cross-examination of Taliento. What do you think of the first and third questions noted in the opinion? How should they have been asked? Why doesn't the defense attorney appear to follow up on the answer "Not at that particular time"? What follow-up question or line of questioning should have been asked?

3. Is *Giglio*'s holding limited by the caveat that a due process violation will be found "[w]hen the reliability of a given witness may well be determinative of guilt or innocence"? Is this really the only scenario where the rule applies? Does the rule not apply where, for example, another witness could confirm the testimony of the witness whose information on lack of credibility has been withheld? Two other witnesses? No other witnesses but documentary evidence? How is the prosecutor to discharge this disclosure obligation prospectively, in advance of trial, when it may be less than certain how witnesses will testify?

4. Is "false testimony" a requisite for a violation, as the Court seems to suggest? Suppose that in *Giglio* defense counsel had made a request before trial for evidence of any "promises, rewards, or inducements" to witnesses, and was told there was no such evidence. Accordingly, defense counsel made the wise strategic decision not to cross-examine Taliento on this subject. No false testimony, but still a due process violation?

5. In making a point about materiality, the Court makes a seemingly derogatory reference to a "combing of the prosecutors' files." Isn't a "combing" of the prosecutor's files—or even a more rigorous search—exactly what *Brady* and *Giglio* require?

Disclosure Obligations After **Brady** *and* **Giglio.** Recall that the original *Brady* rule was limited to situations where the exculpatory material was "requested" by defendant. The request requirement was eliminated in *United States v. Bagley*, 473 U.S. 667 (1985), after it had been previously watered down in *United States v. Agurs*, 427 U.S. 97, 103-07 (1976). Why do you think the request requirement was eliminated?

Many experienced defense attorneys make specific requests for certain types of *Brady* material even though requests are not required. Why do you think they would do that?

Bagley is significant for two other reasons: (1) the Court disavowed any difference between exculpatory and impeachment evidence for *Brady* purposes and (2) the Court described a nondisclosure as "material" for *Brady* purposes "if there is a reasonable probability that, had the evidence been disclosed to the defense, the result of the proceeding would have been different." 473 U.S. at 682. A "reasonable probability" of a different result is accordingly shown when the government's evidentiary suppression "undermines confidence in the outcome of the trial." *Id.* at 678.

Dissenting, Justice Marshall took issue with the definition of "materiality" insofar as it served to limit the prosecutor's disclosures from a prospective viewpoint:

> The Court's standard also encourages the prosecutor to assume the role of the jury, and to decide whether certain evidence will make a difference. In our system of justice, that decision properly and wholly belongs to the jury. The prosecutor, convinced of the guilt of the defendant and of the truthfulness of his witnesses, may all too easily view as irrelevant or unpersuasive evidence that draws his own judgments into question. Accordingly he will decide the evidence need not be disclosed. But the ideally neutral trier of fact, who approaches the case from a wholly different perspective, is by the prosecutor's decision denied the opportunity to consider the evidence. The reviewing court, faced with a verdict of guilty, evidence to support that

854 Chapter IX The Prosecution Function

verdict, and pressures, again understandable, to finalize criminal judgments, is in little better position to review the withheld evidence than the prosecutor.

Id. at 702. This phenomenon is only exacerbated by the fact that at the time the prosecutor makes *Brady* determinations he may know little or nothing about the defense theory. Still, does Justice Marshall exaggerate the prosecutor's inability to fairly evaluate his own case? Won't a good prosecutor, for reasons of his own self-interest if nothing else, endeavor to anticipate a defendant's potential defenses?

Justice Marshall also remarks on the flip side of this point — the inherent difficulty of analyzing a nondisclosure through the retrospective lens of appellate review:

> Without doubt, defense counsel develops his trial strategy based on the available evidence. A missing piece of information may well preclude the attorney from pursuing a strategy that potentially would be effective. His client might consequently be convicted even though nondisclosed information might have offered an additional or alternative defense, if not pure exculpation. Under such circumstances, a reviewing court must be sure not to focus on the amount of evidence supporting the verdict to determine whether the trier of fact reasonably would reach the same conclusion. Instead, the court must decide whether the prosecution has shown beyond a reasonable doubt that the new evidence, if disclosed and developed by reasonably competent counsel, would not have affected the outcome of trial.

Id. at 708.

Kyles v. Whitley, 514 U.S. 419 (1995), was the Supreme Court's fourth and, if not final, at least most recent attempt to articulate the contours of *Brady*. *Kyles* clarified that, in determining whether nondisclosures of information were "material" under *Brady*, courts are to consider the cumulative effect of withheld information; the cumulative effect in *Kyles* would have made a different result "reasonably probable" and was therefore a *Brady* violation. It also made clear that the prosecutor's *Brady* obligations extended to "agents" of the prosecution, that is, the prosecutor is responsible for information contained in police files. As for Justice Marshall's point in *Bagley* about the prosecutor's prospective *Brady* decision making, the Court states that "the prosecution, which alone can know what is undisclosed, must be assigned the consequent responsibility to gauge the likely net effect of all such evidence and make disclosure when the point of reasonable probability" is reached.

Note that the line of cases from *Brady* through *Kyles* all arose in the context of an appeal from a conviction at trial, and the cases' analysis of prejudice all look at materiality from a retrospective vantage point — that is, was the undisclosed evidence "material" in the context of a trial that had already occurred and resulted in a conviction. In the next case the Supreme Court considers *Brady* obligations in the context of a case that was resolved before trial by a guilty plea.

United States v. Ruiz
536 U.S. 622 (2002)

Justice BREYER delivered the opinion of the Court.

In this case we primarily consider whether the Fifth and Sixth Amendments require federal prosecutors, before entering into a binding plea agreement with a criminal defendant, to disclose "impeachment information relating to any informants or other witnesses." We hold that the Constitution does not require that disclosure.

I

After immigration agents found 30 kilograms of marijuana in Angela Ruiz's luggage, federal prosecutors offered her what is known in the Southern District of California as a "fast track" plea bargain. That bargain—standard in that district—asks a defendant to waive indictment, trial, and an appeal. In return, the Government agrees to recommend to the sentencing judge a two-level departure downward from the otherwise applicable United States Sentencing Guidelines sentence. In Ruiz's case, a two-level departure downward would have shortened the ordinary Guidelines-specified 18-to-24-month sentencing range by 6 months, to 12-to-18 months.

The prosecutors' proposed plea agreement contains a set of detailed terms. Among other things, it specifies that "any [known] information establishing the factual innocence of the defendant" "has been turned over to the defendant," and it acknowledges the Government's "continuing duty to provide such information." At the same time it requires that the defendant "waiv[e] the right" to receive "impeachment information relating to any informants or other witnesses" as well as the right to receive information supporting any affirmative defense the defendant raises if the case goes to trial. Because Ruiz would not agree to this last-mentioned waiver, the prosecutors withdrew their bargaining offer. The Government then indicted Ruiz for unlawful drug possession. And despite the absence of any agreement, Ruiz ultimately pleaded guilty.

At sentencing, Ruiz asked the judge to grant her the same two-level downward departure that the Government would have recommended had she accepted the "fast track" agreement. The Government opposed her request, and the District Court denied it, imposing a standard Guideline sentence instead.

Relying on 18 U.S.C. § 3742, Ruiz appealed her sentence to the United States Court of Appeals for the Ninth Circuit. The Ninth Circuit vacated the District Court's sentencing determination. The Ninth Circuit pointed out that the Constitution requires prosecutors to make certain impeachment information available to a defendant before trial. It decided that this obligation entitles defendants to receive that same information before they enter into a plea agreement. The Ninth Circuit also decided that the Constitution prohibits defendants from waiving their right to that information. And it held that the prosecutors' standard "fast track" plea agreement was unlawful because it insisted upon that waiver. The Ninth Circuit remanded the case so that the District Court could decide any related factual disputes and determine an appropriate remedy.

The Government sought certiorari. It stressed what it considered serious adverse practical implications of the Ninth Circuit's constitutional holding. And it added that the holding is unique among courts of appeals. We granted the Government's petition.

. . .

III

The constitutional question concerns a federal criminal defendant's waiver of the right to receive from prosecutors exculpatory impeachment material—a right that the Constitution provides as part of its basic "fair trial" guarantee. See U.S. Const., Amdts. 5, 6. See also *Brady v. Maryland* (1963) (Due process requires prosecutors to "avoi[d] . . . an unfair trial" by making available "upon request" evidence "favorable to an accused . . . where the evidence is material either to guilt or to punishment"); *United States v. Agurs* (1976) (defense request unnecessary); *Kyles v. Whitley* (1995) (exculpatory evidence is evidence the suppression of which would

856   Chapter IX The Prosecution Function

"undermine confidence in the verdict"); *Giglio v. United States* (1972) (exculpatory evidence includes "evidence affecting" witness "credibility," where the witness' "reliability" is likely "determinative of guilt or innocence").

When a defendant pleads guilty he or she, of course, forgoes not only a fair trial, but also other accompanying constitutional guarantees. Given the seriousness of the matter, the Constitution insists, among other things, that the defendant enter a guilty plea that is "voluntary" and that the defendant must make related waivers "knowing[ly], intelligent[ly], [and] with sufficient awareness of the relevant circumstances and likely consequences."

In this case, the Ninth Circuit in effect held that a guilty plea is not "voluntary" (and that the defendant could not, by pleading guilty, waive her right to a fair trial) unless the prosecutors first made the same disclosure of material impeachment information that the prosecutors would have had to make had the defendant insisted upon a trial. We must decide whether the Constitution requires that preguilty plea disclosure of impeachment information. We conclude that it does not.

First, impeachment information is special in relation to the fairness of a trial, not in respect to whether a plea is voluntary ("knowing," "intelligent," and "sufficient[ly] aware"). Of course, the more information the defendant has, the more aware he is of the likely consequences of a plea, waiver, or decision, and the wiser that decision will likely be. But the Constitution does not require the prosecutor to share all useful information with the defendant. And the law ordinarily considers a waiver knowing, intelligent, and sufficiently aware if the defendant fully understands the nature of the right and how it would likely apply in general in the circumstances—even though the defendant may not know the specific detailed consequences of invoking it. A defendant, for example, may waive his right to remain silent, his right to a jury trial, or his right to counsel even if the defendant does not know the specific questions the authorities intend to ask, who will likely serve on the jury, or the particular lawyer the State might otherwise provide.

It is particularly difficult to characterize impeachment information as critical information of which the defendant must always be aware prior to pleading guilty given the random way in which such information may, or may not, help a particular defendant. The degree of help that impeachment information can provide will depend upon the defendant's own independent knowledge of the prosecution's potential case—a matter that the Constitution does not require prosecutors to disclose.

Second, we have found no legal authority embodied either in this Court's past cases or in cases from other circuits that provides significant support for the Ninth Circuit's decision. To the contrary, this Court has found that the Constitution, in respect to a defendant's awareness of relevant circumstances, does not require complete knowledge of the relevant circumstances, but permits a court to accept a guilty plea, with its accompanying waiver of various constitutional rights, despite various forms of misapprehension under which a defendant might labor. It is difficult to distinguish, in terms of importance, (1) a defendant's ignorance of grounds for impeachment of potential witnesses at a possible future trial from (2) the varying forms of ignorance at issue in these cases.

Third, due process considerations, the very considerations that led this Court to find trial-related rights to exculpatory and impeachment information in *Brady* and *Giglio*, argue against the existence of the "right" that the Ninth Circuit found here. This Court has said that due process considerations include not only (1) the nature of the private interest at stake, but also (2) the value of the additional safeguard, and (3) the adverse impact of the requirement upon the Government's interests. Here, as we have just pointed out, the added value of the Ninth Circuit's "right" to a defendant is often limited, for it depends upon the defendant's independent awareness of the details of the Government's case. And in any case, as the proposed plea agreement at issue here specifies, the Government will provide "any information establishing the factual innocence of the defendant" regardless. That fact, along with other guilty-plea safeguards, see Fed. Rule Crim. Proc. 11, diminishes the force of Ruiz's concern that, in the absence of impeachment information, innocent individuals, accused of crimes, will plead guilty.

At the same time, a constitutional obligation to provide impeachment information during plea bargaining, prior to entry of a guilty plea, could seriously interfere with the Government's interest in securing those guilty pleas that are factually justified, desired by defendants, and help to secure the efficient administration of justice. The Ninth Circuit's rule risks premature disclosure of Government witness information, which, the Government tells us, could "disrupt ongoing investigations" and expose prospective witnesses to serious harm. And the careful tailoring that characterizes most legal Government witness disclosure requirements suggests recognition by both Congress and the Federal Rules Committees that such concerns are valid. *See, e.g.,* 18 U.S.C. § 3432 (witness list disclosure required in capital cases three days before trial with exceptions); § 3500 (Government witness statements ordinarily subject to discovery only after testimony given); Fed. Rule Crim. Proc. 16(a)(2) (embodies limitations of 18 U.S.C. § 3500).

Consequently, the Ninth Circuit's requirement could force the Government to abandon its "general practice" of not "disclos[ing] to a defendant pleading guilty information that would reveal the identities of cooperating informants, undercover investigators, or other prospective witnesses." It could require the Government to devote substantially more resources to trial preparation prior to plea bargaining, thereby depriving the plea-bargaining process of its main resource-saving advantages. Or it could lead the Government instead to abandon its heavy reliance upon plea bargaining in a vast number — 90% or more — of federal criminal cases. We cannot say that the Constitution's due process requirement demands so radical a change in the criminal justice process in order to achieve so comparatively small a constitutional benefit.

These considerations, taken together, lead us to conclude that the Constitution does not require the Government to disclose material impeachment evidence prior to entering a plea agreement with a criminal defendant.

In addition, we note that the "fast track" plea agreement requires a defendant to waive her right to receive information the Government has regarding any "affirmative defense" she raises at trial. We do not believe the Constitution here requires provision of this information to the defendant prior to plea bargaining — for most (though not all) of the reasons previously stated. That is to say, in the context of this agreement, the need for this information is more closely related to the fairness of a trial than to the voluntariness of the plea; the value in terms of the defendant's added awareness of relevant circumstances is ordinarily limited; yet the added burden imposed upon the Government by requiring its provision well in advance of trial (often before trial preparation begins) can be serious, thereby significantly interfering with the administration of the plea-bargaining process.

For these reasons the judgment of the Court of Appeals for the Ninth Circuit is Reversed.

NOTES AND QUESTIONS

1. Take a close look at Justice Breyer's first sentence in Part III of the opinion, where the substantive legal analysis begins: "The constitutional question concerns a federal criminal defendant's waiver of the right to receive from prosecutors exculpatory impeachment material — a right that the Constitution provides as part of its basic 'fair trial' guarantee. See U.S. Const., Amdts. 5, 6." *Id.* at 628 (citations omitted).

Did you understand *Brady* and *Giglio* to be cases about "fair trial" rights as opposed to "due process" rights? While it is true that the Supreme Court's important cases exploring the scope of *Brady* obligations came to the Court on appeals after trials, does anything in the discussion of those obligations in *Brady* and *Giglio* suggest they were limited to the trial context?

2. Consider the deal offered to the defendant here under the "fast track" plea arrangement. On its face, as described by the Court, the defendant gets a one-third sentence reduction for a waiver of the right to receive impeachment information (as well as the rights to indictment, trial, appeal, etc.). Suppose you represent a defendant like Ruiz, who—to simplify—has admitted to you to possessing the marijuana. How do you analyze the plea offer in advising your client? Do you have a defense? Is there a possible suppression motion? What if the police report says Ruiz consented to a search of her luggage and Ruiz tells you she did not, such that a suppression hearing would likely be a swearing contest between Ruiz and the arresting officer, raising the possibility that *Giglio* material regarding that officer would be important? Can the defendant make a knowing and intelligent decision about pleading guilty without that impeachment information?

Suppose further that the arresting officer is something of a rogue cop. He has been found to have been untruthful in court on several occasions, including on issues of consent, and the prosecutor is aware of this. Does the prosecutor have an obligation, under the terms of the plea agreement, to turn over information on the officer's lack of credibility? Is it "impeachment information" under terms of the plea agreement? Is it "information establishing the factual innocence of the defendant"?

Does the plea agreement address all information that might be either *Brady* or *Giglio* material?

3. In discussing background legal principles the Court cites *Giglio* as follows:

> *Giglio v. United States*, 405 U.S. 150, 154 (1972) (exculpatory evidence includes "evidence affecting" witness "credibility," where the witness' "reliability" is likely "determinative of guilt or innocence").

That may have been an accurate description of *Giglio*'s holding when the case was decided. Should these caveats still apply?

4. The Court has little trouble finding that a defendant can waive a right to *Giglio* material, and points out (a) that any guilty plea requires a waiver of myriad constitutional rights and (b) that guilty pleas have been enforced even where defendant or defendant's counsel has misapprehended the government's case.

Is there anything different about the right to disclosure of impeachment information from the other constitutional rights waived in pleading guilty? The Court notes that the government claims there are compelling reasons not to disclose the identity of witnesses—which would be part and parcel of turning over impeachment information—until shortly before trial. Are these reasons persuasive? Are they equally applicable in all cases? Could the government be required to make an *in camera* showing of these concerns in individual cases?

5. Is the holding of *Ruiz* limited to its facts, where the defendant waived a right to receive impeachment information? Or does it stand for the more general proposition that there is no constitutional right to receive impeachment information prior to pleading guilty? Regardless of the "holding" of *Ruiz*, is there any reason the government cannot insist on impeachment waivers in all of its plea agreements, fast track or otherwise?

6. What does *Ruiz* portend for the government's nonimpeachment *Brady* obligations prior to entering plea agreements? On the one hand, in response to the expressed concern that absent impeachment information innocent people may plead guilty, the Court notes that the fast-track plea agreement requires the disclosure of information establishing defendant's "factual innocence." And the government's concerns about the disclosure of witness's identities isn't necessarily implicated by nonimpeachment *Brady* material. On the other hand, is the Court's waiver analysis as applicable to nonimpeachment *Brady* material as it is to impeachment material?

The federal courts of appeals have split on whether the government must disclose nonimpeachment *Brady* material prior to entering plea agreements, and the Supreme Court in 2019 declined to address the split. Four circuits take the position that *Ruiz* can only mean there is no such requirement. *Alvarez v. City of Brownsville*, 904 F.3d 382, 385-86 (5th Cir. 2018), *cert. denied*, 139 S. Ct. 2690 (2019); *United States v. Mathur*, 624 F.3d 498 (1st Cir. 2010); *Friedman v. Rehal*, 618 F.3d 142, 154 (2d Cir. 2010) (*Ruiz* applies equally to exculpatory and impeachment evidence as the Supreme Court equated the two categories in *Bagley*); *United States v. Moussaoui*, 591 F.3d 263, 286 (4th Cir. 2010). Three circuits disagree, for various reasons. *See Mann v. Mangialardi*, 337 F.3d 782 (7th Cir. 2003) (noting *Ruiz*'s point that the plea agreement upheld there still required the disclosure of "factual innocence" information); *Smith v. Baldwin*, 510 F.3d 1127, 1148 (9th Cir. 2007) (ignoring *Ruiz* and relying on Ninth Circuit precedent that evidence that would cause a defendant to reject a plea must be turned over at the plea-bargaining stage); *United States v. Ohiri*, 133 F. App'x 555, 562 (10th Cir. 2005) (*Brady* material must be turned over where defendant entered plea agreement during jury voir dire).

Two things are noteworthy about the circuit court cases resisting the gravitational pull of *Ruiz*. First, the Ninth Circuit precedent relied on in *Smith v. Baldwin* significantly waters down the *Brady* materiality requirement. Why? To decrease the burden on the prosecutor? Does it significantly lessen the burden on the prosecutor to search only for information that will cause the defendant to reject a plea offer and not also for information that might "undermine confidence" in the trial result if not disclosed?

Second, the Supreme Court's decisions sometimes give the impression that plea bargaining is a specific, delimited stage of a criminal case, like the discovery stage of a civil case, that has a beginning, middle, and end. *Ohiri* shows that is not always the case. While it is true that there usually comes a specific point when the parties enter their proverbial bunkers and prepare for trial, the possibility of a plea agreement is never finally eliminated, as *Ohiri* shows. Sometimes it is during the crucible of trial preparation that the parties are best able to recognize the strengths and weaknesses of their positions and the chances of an agreement increase.

For a discussion of the post-*Ruiz* circuit split and a compelling argument that *Brady* should apply during plea negotiations, *see* Cameron Casey, *Lost Opportunity: Supreme Court Declines to Resolve Circuit Split on* Brady *Obligations During Plea-Bargaining*, 61 B.C. L. Rev. E. Supp. II. 73, II. 82-83 (2020). *See also* Michael N. Petegorsky, *Plea Bargaining in the Dark: The Duty to Disclose Exculpatory* Brady *Evidence During Plea Bargaining*, 81 Fordham L. Rev. 3599, 3647-49 (2013) (arguing that *Brady* should apply during plea bargaining for similar reasons to those that led the court to extend the effective assistance of counsel guarantee to plea bargaining, including that 97 percent of criminal cases are resolved by pleas, as the Court recognized in *Missouri v. Frye*, 566 U.S. 134, 143 (2012)). *See* Chapter XI *infra*.

The next case considers the application of *Brady* and *Giglio* in the context of serious police misconduct.

Milke v. Ryan
711 F.3d 998 (9th Cir. 2013)

KOZINSKI, Chief Judge:

In 1990, a jury convicted Debra Milke of murdering her four-year-old son, Christopher. The judge sentenced her to death. The trial was, essentially, a swearing contest between Milke and Phoenix Police Detective Armando Saldate, Jr. Saldate testified that Milke, twenty-five at the time, had confessed when he interviewed her shortly after the murder; Milke protested her innocence and denied confessing. There were no other witnesses or direct evidence linking Milke to the crime. The judge and jury believed Saldate, but they didn't know about Saldate's long history of lying under oath and other misconduct. The state knew about this misconduct but didn't disclose it, despite the requirements of *Brady* and *Giglio*. Some of the misconduct wasn't disclosed until the case came to federal court and, even today, some evidence relevant to Saldate's credibility hasn't been produced, perhaps because it's been destroyed. In the balance hangs the life of Milke, who has been on Arizona's death row for twenty-two years.

FACTS

On the last evening of his short life, Christopher Milke saw Santa Claus at the mall. He woke up the next morning begging his mother to let him go again. Debra agreed and sent Christopher to the mall with her roommate, James Styers. On the way, Styers picked up his friend, Roger Scott. But instead of heading to the mall, the two men drove the boy out of town to a secluded ravine, where Styers shot Christopher three times in the head. Styers and Scott then drove to the mall, where they reported Christopher as missing.

Sunday morning, less than a day into the missing-child investigation, police began to suspect Styers and Scott. It was supposed to be Detective Saldate's day off, but the homicide sergeant in charge of the case called him in. A veteran of the police force, Saldate was confident he could get the truth out of anyone he interrogated. At headquarters he started in on Styers almost immediately, while his partner, Detective Bob Mills, worked on Scott. Shortly before 1 p.m., Saldate joined Mills in interrogating Scott. According to Saldate, Mills and other officers were happy to let a suspect talk, but Saldate's "style," as he described it, was "a little different"—he preferred a frontal assault. "I knew that I was going to be straightforward with [Scott], I was going to be very truthful with him, but I was going to make sure that whatever he told me was going to jive with the facts."

Soon after Saldate's appearance, Scott broke. He led the detectives to Christopher's body and told them where he and Styers had thrown the unspent ammunition. According to Saldate, Scott said along the way that Debra Milke had been involved. Detective Saldate seized on the statement and flew by helicopter to Florence, Arizona, where Milke had gone to stay with her father and step-family after she learned of Christopher's disappearance.

In Florence, a deputy sheriff invited Milke to headquarters to wait for Saldate. Saldate found Milke waiting in a 15-by-15-foot room of the Pinal County jail. She hadn't been arrested, nor had she been told anything about Christopher. Saldate pushed into the room and introduced himself. He pulled his chair close to Milke, a forearm's length at most, and leaned in even closer. That's when he told her that the police had found her son—dead.

"What, what," Saldate testified Milke said. Saldate also reported that Milke started yelling and "seemed to try crying." But the detective saw through the ploy: "When someone is told that their child was murdered and they start to sob and no tears come to their eyes, it's obviously a way for her to try to make me feel for her, and I didn't buy it. I didn't buy it. . . ."

Saldate placed Milke under arrest and read out her *Miranda* rights. According to Saldate, when Milke started to tell him that she'd complained about Christopher to Styers but never

B. Prosecutor's Disclosure Obligations

realized Styers would hurt the boy, Saldate shut her down: "I immediately, of course, told her that wasn't the truth and I told her I wasn't going to tolerate that, that I wasn't there to listen to lies, nor did I have the time."

With that, Saldate claims, Milke opened up to him about the most intimate details of her life. He testified that, in the span of just thirty minutes, Milke knowingly waived her rights to silence and counsel, reminisced about her high school years when she was "in love with life," feigned tears, calmed down, narrated her failed marriage to Mark Milke — his drug and alcohol abuse and his arrests — recounted how she'd gotten pregnant while on birth control and contemplated an abortion, even making an appointment for one, discussed her fear that Christopher was becoming like his father, confessed to a murder conspiracy, characterized the conspiracy as a "bad judgment call" and solicited Saldate's opinion about whether her family would ever understand. (His view: No.)

By the end of the interview, Saldate had more than just cinched the case against Milke; he'd helped her emotionally. According to Saldate, Milke said she was "starting to feel better and was starting to get some of her self-esteem back." Saldate also testified that Milke asked whether she would be released that night, and when he said she wouldn't be, she asked whether the court could give her "probation for life" if "she could have her tubes tied and never have children again."

Milke has always denied involvement in the murder, and her account of the interrogation differs substantially from Saldate's. Milke testified that she told Saldate she didn't understand the *Miranda* warnings and that, when Saldate asked if she wanted the interrogation taped, she said: "No, I need a lawyer." According to Milke, Saldate ignored her request, instead putting his hands on her knees and proceeding with the interrogation; he then embellished and twisted Milke's statements to make it sound like she had confessed.

The jury had no independent way of verifying these divergent accounts. Saldate didn't record the interrogation, even though his supervisor instructed him to do so. Saldate didn't bring a tape recorder to the interview, nor did he ask anyone to witness the interrogation by sitting in the room or watching through a two-way mirror. Saldate also skipped the basic step of having Milke sign a *Miranda* waiver. Not even Saldate's interview notes made it into court: Saldate testified that he destroyed them after writing his official report three days after the interrogation.

The jury thus had nothing more than Saldate's word that Milke confessed. Everything the state claims happened in the interrogation room depends on believing Saldate's testimony. Without Saldate's testimony, the prosecution had no case against Milke, as there was no physical evidence linking her to the crime and neither of her supposed co-conspirators — Styers and Scott — would testify against her. But Saldate was an experienced witness and his account of Milke's purported confession proved convincing. The jury found Milke guilty of murder, conspiracy to commit murder, child abuse and kidnapping. The judge sentenced her to death.

• • •

Normally that would be the end of the matter. Right or wrong, a jury's credibility determinations are entitled to respect. But the Constitution requires a fair trial, and one essential element of fairness is the prosecution's obligation to turn over exculpatory evidence. This never happened in Milke's case, so the jury trusted Saldate without hearing of his long history of lies and misconduct.

The Appendix contains summaries of some of Saldate's misconduct and the accompanying court orders and disciplinary action. This history includes a five-day suspension for taking "liberties" with a female motorist and then lying about it to his supervisors; four court cases where judges tossed out confessions or indictments because Saldate lied under oath; and four cases where judges suppressed confessions or vacated convictions because Saldate had violated the Fifth Amendment or the Fourth Amendment in the course of interrogations. And it is far from clear that this reflects a full account of Saldate's misconduct as a police officer. All of this information should have been disclosed to Milke and the jury, but the state remained unconstitutionally silent.

• • •

Due process imposes an "inescapable" duty on the prosecutor "to disclose known, favorable evidence rising to a material level of importance." Favorable evidence includes both exculpatory and impeachment material that is relevant either to guilt or punishment. The prosecutor is charged with knowledge of any *Brady* material of which the prosecutor's office or the investigating police agency is aware.

A *Brady* violation has three elements. First, there must be evidence that is favorable to the defense, either because it is exculpatory or impeaching. Second, the government must have willfully or inadvertently failed to produce the evidence. Third, the suppression must have prejudiced the defendant.

Favorable evidence. Any evidence that would tend to call the government's case into doubt is favorable for *Brady* purposes. Saldate's personnel file contained an internal investigation report showing he had been suspended for five days. The report explains that Saldate stopped a female motorist who had a faulty taillight and possibly an outstanding warrant. He let her go without checking her warrant. Let her go isn't quite accurate. Saldate suggested they move to a less conspicuous spot and then followed her to it. Once there, he leaned into her car, "took liberties" with her and acted in a manner "unbecoming an officer." She offered to meet him later for an "act of sexual intercourse." Saldate showed up for the rendezvous, but the woman didn't. Instead, someone — perhaps the woman, once she got free of Saldate — reported Saldate's misconduct to the police.

Questioned by investigators, Saldate steadfastly lied about the incident until he failed a polygraph test. "[Y]our image of honesty, competency, and overall reliability must be questioned," one of Saldate's supervisors wrote in a report signed by the city manager and the chief of police. The facts of Saldate's misconduct, his lies to the investigators and this assessment by his supervisor would certainly have been useful to a jury trying to decide whether Saldate or Milke was telling the truth. Not only does the report show that Saldate has no compunction about lying during the course of his official duties, it discloses a misogynistic attitude toward female civilians and a willingness to abuse his authority to get what he wants. All of this is highly consistent with Milke's account of the interrogation.

The court orders Milke's lawyers uncovered are also favorable evidence that was available to the state but the prosecution did not disclose. As Milke argued to the state post-conviction court, the orders show that Saldate "has lied under oath in order to secure a conviction or to further a prosecution." Those cases all involved the Maricopa County Attorney's Office and the Phoenix Police Department — the same agencies involved in prosecuting Milke:

- *State v. King.* On direct, Saldate told Maricopa County prosecutor Paul Rood that the defendant hadn't been unwilling to answer questions during the interrogation. On cross, the defense counsel read back Saldate's own report showing that the defendant had, in fact, said he wasn't going to answer any more questions. The trial judge threw out the portion of the confession that followed the suspect's request to end the interview: "[T]he statements made up to the time when the defendant advised the detective he no longer wished to answer his questions are admissible. Thereafter they're not admissible."
- *State v. Reynolds.* The judge found that Saldate's false statements to the grand jury "denied [the defendant] his right to due process and a fair and impartial presentation of the evidence." Two false statements particularly worried the judge: Saldate told the grand jury that the victim's son couldn't remember at what time he saw defendant enter the house, drag the victim upstairs and then leave; the son could say only that it was late at night, according to Saldate. That statement was false. In fact, the son told detectives that the defendant left the apartment about 8 p.m.; the son knew this because defendant turned

B. Prosecutor's Disclosure Obligations
863

off the Garry Shandling Show on the way out. Saldate's omission was critical because other witnesses had seen the victim alive after midnight; if the defendant left around 8 p.m., it proved he hadn't killed the victim in their fight.

In the same case, the grand jury asked Saldate whether the defendant was drunk at the time of the crime, which bore on whether the defendant could form the specific intent for first-degree murder. Saldate testified that defendant had said he was drinking but not drunk. However, defendant had told Saldate that he'd been drinking beer and smoking marijuana, and was too drunk to remember some of the events from that night. The judge found that "a fair presentation was not made in connection with the evidence concerning the identification of the defendant by the victim's son," and that "the evidence was not fully and fairly presented with regard to defendant's possible intoxication." Based largely on Saldate's two false statements, the judge threw out the finding of probable cause.

- *State v. Rodriguez.* Saldate told a grand jury that the murder victim had been shot four times, even though it was, as the judge wrote, "undisputed" that the victim was shot only once. The Maricopa County Attorney's Office said it had never intended to claim there was more than one shot. Instead of blaming Saldate for the false statement, the prosecution "[took] issue with the transcription of the grand jury proceeding, for surely the testifying detective, Armando Saldate, of the Phoenix Police Department, and/or this State's attorney would have caught and corrected such an incorrect representation."

    The trial judge didn't buy it. He found that the "reporter's notes and the transcript of the Grand Jury" were accurate and that Saldate had, in fact, said there were four shots. As a result of this false statement, the judge ordered a redetermination of probable cause.
- *State v. Rangel.* A judge agreed with defendant's claim that Saldate and a prosecutor (Lawrence Turoff) misled a grand jury by selectively recounting defendant's statements. The judge held that Saldate's and the prosecutor's statements had materially affected the grand jury's deliberation and remanded the case for a new finding of probable cause.

The above orders make out a *Giglio* violation on their own, but Milke also presented additional Giglio evidence — documents from four cases where courts found Saldate had violated the Fifth Amendment or the Fourth Amendment in the course of his interrogations. Again, those cases all involved the Maricopa County Attorney's Office and the Phoenix Police Department:

- *State v. Yanes.* Saldate admitted interrogating a suspect who was strapped to a hospital bed, incoherent after apparently suffering a skull fracture. When interviewed by doctors, the suspect didn't know his own name, the current year or the name of the president, but the prosecutor nonetheless presented the suspect's statement to Saldate at trial. The court vacated the conviction and ordered a new trial. Id. At the suppression hearing for the new trial, the court suppressed "those statements made by the defendant to Armando Saldate."
- *State v. Conde.* Saldate interrogated a suspect in intensive care who was intubated and connected to intravenous lines. Saldate testified that the suspect was drifting "in and out" of consciousness; several times, Saldate had to shake him "to get his attention." Nonetheless, Saldate read him the *Miranda* warnings and went on with the interrogation. "I really don't know whether he wasn't responding because he didn't understand his rights or wasn't responding because of the medication he was on," Saldate testified. By Saldate's own admission, "it was obvious that [the defendant] was in pain." The nurse told the suspect that she couldn't give him more pain medicine until after he finished talking to Saldate. When the case came to trial in 1989, the court held the statement from this interrogation "involuntary and inadmissible," as the Arizona Court of Appeals noted in a published opinion three years later.
- *State v. King.* Saldate kept asking questions long after the defendant indicated he no longer wanted to answer. The court ruled that those statements were inadmissible. This is the same case discussed earlier in the context of Saldate's false statements.

864   Chapter IX The Prosecution Function

- *State v. Jones*. In the course of a murder investigation, Saldate directed an officer to place a juvenile by himself in an interrogation room, where the juvenile was handcuffed to a table. This, despite the fact that, in the trial court's view, "the police clearly had no information linking the Defendant to the murder or disappearance of [the victim]," and even the Maricopa County Attorney's Office conceded that it had no probable cause for the detention. The court suppressed the murder confession as "the fruit of the illegal arrest" and condemned the juvenile's illegal detention and the interrogation that followed as "a show of flagrant misconduct."

The court order suppressing the confession was dated November 29, 1990, just after Milke's October 12, 1990, conviction but before her January 18, 1991, sentencing. Though too late to affect the jury's verdict, this order should have been produced under *Giglio* because Saldate's credibility remained a live issue. On the day of sentencing, the court entertained Milke's motions for a new trial and for judgment notwithstanding the verdict. The judge denied both motions, explaining that there was no error in allowing Saldate's statement about the confession. The judge said she "does not believe that the Defendant made a request for an attorney prior to or during her questioning by Detective Saldate" and that, while "a good deal of time and effort was expended by the defense to discredit the reports made by Detective Saldate as to other witnesses[, t]hose efforts to discredit his note-taking and report-writing and accuracy were not successful." Had the Maricopa County Attorney's Office produced the suppression order in Jones, Milke could have used it in support of her motions for a new trial and for judgment notwithstanding the verdict, and the outcome might well have been different.

The *Jones* order—and the other orders that the state failed to produce—would likely also have affected the judge's decision whether to sentence Milke to death. As the Supreme Court made clear in *Brady* itself, evidence must be disclosed if it is "material either to guilt or to punishment." Saldate's credibility certainly was material to punishment. For example, Milke's sentencing allocution went into detail about the legal errors that led to her conviction. In pleading for her life, she was particularly critical of Saldate. She said: "I'm disappointed that the Court allowed the use of a purported confession to be used against me when there wasn't any evidence to prove this alleged confession." Milke continued:

> Although Mr. Saldate testified that he follows laws and guidelines, he does not. He didn't follow a direct order from a sergeant to tape-record an interview with me. An[] officer with over 20 years of experience should also know better than to interview a female suspect in a closed room without a witness. . . . This crime was very serious and I feel Mr. Saldate was extremely irresponsible. It is true my *Miranda* rights were read to me and I was apprised of my Fifth Amendment privilege to have counsel present. However, when I requested such a privilege, he immediately ignored me as if I said nothing.

Had Milke been able to present Saldate's menagerie of lies and constitutional violations, her allocution may well have resonated with the sentencing judge and persuaded her to spare Milke's life. Indeed, the trial judge herself acknowledged that she was considering "legitimate questions concerning guilt" as a mitigating factor, only to find she had no such questions about guilt. Had the judge known about Saldate's documented misconduct, she may well have developed such "legitimate questions concerning guilt."

Suppression. The second element of a *Brady* violation is the willful or inadvertent failure of the prosecutor to disclose evidence favorable to the defendant. We have long held that the government has a *Brady* obligation "to produce any favorable evidence in the personnel records" of an officer. A defendant doesn't have to make a request for exculpatory or impeachment evidence: "[T]he duty to disclose [exculpatory] evidence is applicable even though there has been no request by the accused, and . . . the duty encompasses impeachment evidence as well as exculpatory evidence." We've also held that "the government has a duty to examine personnel files upon a defendant's request for their production." If the prosecution isn't sure whether material in a personnel file rises to the *Brady* threshold, "it may submit the information to the trial court for an in camera inspection." As the Supreme Court held in *Kyles v. Whitley*, "a prosecutor anxious about tacking too close to the wind will disclose a favorable piece of evidence."

The state is charged with the knowledge that there was impeachment material in Saldate's personnel file. After all, the state eventually produced some of this evidence in federal habeas proceedings and has never claimed that it could not have disclosed it in time for Milke's trial. There can be no doubt that the state failed in its constitutional obligation of producing this material without any request by the defense.

The state also had an obligation to produce the documents showing Saldate's false and misleading statements in court and before grand juries, as well as the documents showing the Fifth Amendment and Fourth Amendment violations he committed during interrogations. The prosecutor's office no doubt knew of this misconduct because it had harmed criminal prosecutions. The police must have known, too.

Indeed, the timing of the suppression order in Jones underscores the cavalier attitude of the Maricopa County Attorney's Office toward its constitutional duty to disclose impeachment evidence. The prosecution argued against the Jones suppression motion on November 16, 1990, and lost, resulting in the suppression of the murder confession. The prosecutor's office then began preparing for a second hearing, which would determine whether key physical evidence — "the body, shell casings, and shovel" — would also be suppressed. All this was happening between the time of Milke's conviction on October 12, 1990, and her sentencing on January 18, 1991. That means even as Milke's attorney was working hard to stave off a death sentence and win a new trial or judgment notwithstanding the verdict, the prosecutor's office and the police were actively dealing with Saldate's misconduct in another murder case.

When the Jones court suppressed the murder confession, this must surely have reminded the Maricopa County Attorney's Office and the Phoenix Police Department of Saldate's propensity to commit misconduct. Indeed, Paul Rood, the prosecutor in Jones, was also the prosecutor in *King*, where in June 1990, Saldate had been caught in a lie about violating *Miranda*. And, at about the same time as *King*, Rood also received a suppression motion in *State v. Mahler*, a Saldate case in which the defendant made what the Arizona Court of Appeals called "an unequivocal invocation to remain silent." In that case, Saldate kept speaking with the defendant after the invocation, claiming that "he [Saldate] did not want an admission but that he just wanted Mahler's side of the story." The Arizona Court of Appeals held that "Officer Saldate's intent was clear . . . he wanted additional statements from Mahler. This conduct violated Mahler's right to remain silent." The trial court didn't suppress the confession, and the defendant was convicted. But the Court of Appeals held that the confession should not have been admitted and remanded the case.

Because the Court of Appeals in *Mahler* didn't hand down its decision until 1992, after Milke's trial, we don't count this case as *Brady* material. But *Mahler* is still significant because the suppression motion, filed on May 30, 1990, came just about the time that Rood was handling Saldate's misconduct in *King*. The fact that Rood was litigating yet another instance of Saldate's misconduct in the summer of 1990 — albeit one where the trial court went the state's way, before being reversed — is all the more reason to conclude that Rood and his colleagues in the Maricopa County Attorney's Office were intimately familiar with Saldate's pattern of misconduct.

And, as the state absorbed the loss of the Jones confession in November 1990 and prepared arguments to save the physical evidence in Jones from suppression, it must have occurred to Rood or someone in the prosecutor's office or the police department (or both) that Saldate was also the key witness in the high-profile case against Debra Milke — a case where the defendant was still at trial, actively fighting for her life. Yet no one saw fit to disclose this or any of the other instances of Saldate's misconduct to Milke's lawyer.

Even if there somehow weren't actual knowledge of Saldate's misconduct, inadvertent failure to disclose is enough for a *Brady* violation. That the court documents showing Saldate's misconduct were available in the public record doesn't diminish the state's obligation to produce them under *Brady*. In determining whether evidence has been suppressed for purposes of *Brady*, our court has asked whether the defendant "has enough information to be able to ascertain the supposed *Brady* material on his own." If so, there's no *Brady* violation. Where a defendant doesn't have enough information to find the *Brady* material with reasonable diligence, the state's failure to produce the evidence is considered suppression.

Milke was able to discover the court documents detailing Saldate's misconduct only after a team of approximately ten researchers in post-conviction proceedings spent nearly 7000 hours sifting through court records. Milke's post-conviction attorney sent this team to the clerk of court's offices to search for Saldate's name in every criminal case file from 1982 to 1990. The team worked eight hours a day for three and a half months, turning up 100 cases involving Saldate. Another researcher then spent a month reading motions and transcripts from those cases to find examples of Saldate's misconduct. A reasonably diligent lawyer couldn't possibly have found these records in time to use them at Milke's trial. Thus, the documents describing Saldate's lies and his *Miranda* and other constitutional violations during the course of interrogations were suppressed.

Indeed, suppression of the personnel file and suppression of the court documents run together. Had Milke been given the full run of evaluations in Saldate's personnel file, she would have found cases Saldate worked on. For example, the 1989 evaluation — one of just two evaluations turned over — lists six high-profile cases Saldate handled. In addition, the personnel file could have disclosed cases so corrupted by Saldate's misconduct that they were unfit for court. As Milke argued, the court records she found in post-conviction proceedings were just "the 'tip of the iceberg' of Detective Saldate's interrogation/interview practices." But without the full personnel file, we can't know, even now, the full extent of the misconduct that could have been used to impeach Saldate.

Prejudice. To find prejudice under *Brady* and *Giglio*, it isn't necessary to find that the jury would have come out differently. It suffices that there be "a reasonable probability of a different result" as to either guilt or penalty. Prejudice exists "when the government's evidentiary suppression undermines confidence in the outcome of the trial."

Milke's alleged confession, as reported by Saldate, was the only direct evidence linking Milke to the crime. But the confession was only as good as Saldate's word, as he's the only one who claims to have heard Milke confess and there's no recording, written statement or any other evidence that Milke confessed. Saldate's credibility was crucial to the state's case against Milke. It's hard to imagine anything more relevant to the jury's — or the judge's — determination whether to believe Saldate than evidence that Saldate lied under oath and trampled the constitutional rights of suspects in discharging his official duties. If even a single juror had found Saldate untrustworthy based on the documentation that he habitually lied under oath or that he took advantage of women he had in his power, there would have been at least a hung jury. Likewise, if this evidence had been disclosed, it may well have led the judge to order a new trial, enter judgment notwithstanding the verdict or, at least, impose a sentence less than death. The prosecution did its best to impugn Milke's credibility. It wasn't entitled, at the same time, to hide the evidence that undermined Saldate's credibility.

Also at issue was Saldate's claim — again, unsupported by evidence — that Milke waived her *Miranda* rights and didn't ask for a lawyer. Beyond its effect on Saldate's credibility, evidence of Saldate's falsifications and his disregard of *Miranda*, would have been highly relevant to the determination of whether Milke's alleged confession had been lawfully obtained. The suppression of evidence of Saldate's lies and misconduct thus qualifies as prejudicial for purposes of *Brady* and *Giglio*.

B. Prosecutor's Disclosure Obligations

III. CONCLUSION

Milke is entitled to habeas relief. We therefore REVERSE the decision of the district court and REMAND with instructions to GRANT a conditional writ of habeas corpus setting aside her convictions and sentences.

NOTES AND QUESTIONS

1. Consider the evidence at trial regarding Milke's alleged confession. Would you have found Milke guilty beyond a reasonable doubt based on that evidence alone?

2. The incident with the female motorist was found to be *Brady* material apparently because Officer Saldate lied about it to his superiors during an internal investigation. Would it have been *Brady* material if he had simply admitted to the incident? Does the Ninth Circuit's view that the evidence "discloses a misogynistic attitude toward female civilians and a willingness to abuse his authority to get what he wants" make the evidence *Brady* material independent of its bearing on credibility? If so, would it be *Brady* material in some cases — for example, a case with a female defendant — but not others?

3. Note that of the four documented instances of Officer Saldate's lies, three were in the grand jury, where the lie might never have come to light. If, for example, the case were resolved by a plea, or if Officer Saldate were not a trial witness, the grand jury transcript might not have been required to have been disclosed to the defense. If a police officer has been caught in lies under oath four times without any apparent repercussions, how many times do you think he must have lied under oath altogether? Twenty? A hundred? More?

4. Three of the four noncredibility instances of *Brady* violations involve abusive conduct during interrogations.

Do these incidents qualify as *Brady* material here only because the interrogation of Milke, after she was allegedly Mirandized, is so central to this case?

5. Recall how in *Giglio* the Court casually observed that prosecutor's offices would be responsible for implementing procedures to prevent the sort of miscommunications between prosecutors that may have caused the violation in that case:

> A promise made by one attorney must be attributed, for these purposes, to the Government. See Restatement (Second) of Agency § 272. *See also* American Bar Association, Project on Standards for Criminal Justice, Discovery and Procedure Before Trial § 2.1(d). To the extent this places a burden on the large prosecution offices, procedures and regulations can be established to carry that burden and to insure communication of all relevant information on each case to every lawyer who deals with it.

405 U.S. at 154. Twenty-five years later, with *Brady* obligations extended to the files of any police or other agents on the prosecution team, establishing satisfactory procedures can be a daunting task for prosecutors and their sometimes recalcitrant law enforcement allies. For an exploration of this dynamic, and related issues regarding the prosecutor's access to police personnel files, *see* Jonathan Abel, Brady's *Blind Spot: Impeachment Evidence in Police Personnel Files and the Battle Splitting the Prosecution Team*, 67 Stan. L. Rev. 743 (2015).

6. In connection with the last paragraph of the opinion, *see* Chapter VIII *supra*, discussing DOJ authority to initiate actions against police departments under 42 U.S.C. § 14141. *See also* Chapter X *infra*, discussing criminal prosecution of police officers under 18 U.S.C. § 242.

The DOJ first adopted an internal "*Giglio* policy" shortly after *Kyles v. Whitley* was decided in 1996, reflecting that decision by explicitly extending the prosecutor's searching obligations

868 Chapter IX The Prosecution Function

under *Brady* to the files of all relevant law enforcement agents. The current version of the policy, set forth at Justice Manual § 9-5.100, requires all DOJ investigative agencies (FBI, DEA, ATF, etc.) to disclose the following to the prosecutor:

i) any finding of misconduct that reflects upon the truthfulness or possible bias of the employee, including a finding of lack of candor during a criminal, civil, or administrative inquiry or proceeding;

ii) any past or pending criminal charge brought against the employee;

iii) any allegation of misconduct bearing upon truthfulness, bias, or integrity that is the subject of a pending investigation;

iv) prior findings by a judge that an agency employee has testified untruthfully, made a knowing false statement in writing, engaged in an unlawful search or seizure, illegally obtained a confession, or engaged in other misconduct;

v) any misconduct finding or pending misconduct allegation that either casts a substantial doubt upon the accuracy of any evidence — including witness testimony — that the prosecutor intends to rely on to prove an element of any crime charged, or that might have a significant bearing on the admissibility of prosecution evidence. Accordingly, agencies and employees should disclose findings or allegations that relate to substantive violations concerning:

(1) failure to follow legal or agency requirements for the collection and handling of evidence, obtaining statements, recording communications, and obtaining consents to search or to record communications;

(2) failure to comply with agency procedures for supervising the activities of a cooperating person . . .;

(3) failure to follow mandatory protocols with regard to the forensic analysis of evidence;

vi) information that may be used to suggest that the agency employee is biased for or against a defendant; and

vii) information that reflects that the agency employee's ability to perceive and recall truth is impaired.

Id. at 4. Do you see any holes in these categories? Does each category of potential *Giglio* information need to be disclosed in every case?

The DOJ policy does not specifically acknowledge racial bias, and its general reference to bias may be limited to a showing of racial bias in connection with a "proceeding." A few cases touch on the issue of bias and witness credibility. *See United States v. Figueroa*, 548 F.3d 222, 229 (2d Cir. 2008) (defendant minority group member entitled to cross-examine witness on two tattoos depicting swastikas inasmuch as such symbols might indicate witness's animus against racial or ethnic minorities); *State v. Williams*, 956 A.2d 375 (Sup. Ct. N.J., App. Div. 2008) (affirming trial court's requirement that information regarding a nontestifying senior prosecutor's use of a racial epithet in describing defendant be disclosed). *See generally* Vida B. Johnson, *KKK in the PD: White Supremacist Police and What to Do About It*, 23 Lewis & Clark L. Rev. 205, 233-38 (2019) (arguing that *Brady* imposes an affirmative duty on prosecutors to investigate police for racial basis, including affiliation with white supremacist organizations).

2. Discovery Obligations

The obligations *Brady* and *Giglio* impose on the government are constitutional. They should not be confused with "discovery" obligations of the government, which are generally imposed by court or legislative rules, although the terminology in this area can sometimes be imprecise. The Supreme Court has said that "[t[here is no general constitutional right to discovery in a criminal case. . . ." *Weatherford v. Bursery*, 429 U.S. 545, 559 (1977). One could imagine that the demands of due process might impose some sort of basic obligation on the government to disclose information about its case in advance. The Supreme Court has never so held, however, perhaps because it hasn't had to reconsider the issue inasmuch as discovery has been required by the federal rules since the 1960s.

B. Prosecutor's Disclosure Obligations **869**

Criminal discovery was slow to come to the United States. Long after liberal civil discovery rules were adopted, resistance to criminal discovery remained strong. Ironically, arguments against criminal discovery were often premised on the fundamental difference between civil and criminal litigation, inasmuch as the stakes in the latter were so much higher. The argument went — not that criminal defendants had a greater need for discovery due to the higher stakes — but that because of those stakes defendants simply couldn't be trusted with advance information lest they suborn perjury, bribe and intimidate witnesses, fabricate alibis, and otherwise wreak havoc. One version of these arguments is set forth in *State v. Tune*, 13 N.J. 203, 98 A.2d 881 (1953). Versions of these same arguments recur today in government opposition to early disclosure of *Brady* and other discoverable information, as seen in *Ruiz, supra*.

The Federal Rules of Criminal Procedure govern discovery in federal criminal cases. Most states have something similar, whether by rule or statute. Fed. R. Crim. P. 16 is the general discovery provision in the Federal Rules of Criminal Procedure. It was adopted in a rough approximation of its current form in 1966. Witness statement disclosure had been governed by a federal statute, the Jencks Act, since 1957.

The heart of Rule 16 is subsection (a)(1)(E), which requires the government to disclose to the defendant three categories of documents and objects: those that are material to preparing the defense; those that the government intends to use in its case-in-chief at trial; and those that were obtained from or belong to the defendant. Subsection (b)(1)(B) imposes obligations on the defendant that largely mirror the first two categories. Other parts of Rule 16 require disclosure of any statements by the defendant, Rule 16(a)(1)(A), (B), and exempt from disclosure information that is essentially government work-product.

District courts have discretion in regulating the timing of such disclosures, and often will require the parties to exchange witness and exhibit lists before trial, as a matter of fairness to the defense as well as a way to anticipate and/or eliminate evidentiary disputes.

Reciprocal Discovery. Note that Rule 16 requires reciprocal discovery of the defendant. But should the prosecutor also be entitled to discovery? Why should the defendant have to disclose information that might implicate his defense?

Rule 16's discovery obligations were not always reciprocal. That was not always the case. As adopted in 1966, the Rule only imposed discovery obligations on the government. Due to "one way street" complaints by federal prosecutors, in 1974 the Rule was amended to require reciprocal discovery despite Fifth Amendment arguments to the contrary.

State court discovery moved roughly in parallel with the Federal Rules. The next case considers a reciprocal discovery obligation on a defendant under a Florida statute, a variation of which was subsequently included in the 1974 version of the Federal Rules of Criminal Procedure.

Williams v. Florida
399 U.S. 78 (1970)

Mr. Justice WHITE delivered the opinion of the Court.

Prior to his trial for robbery in the State of Florida, petitioner filed a "Motion for a Protective Order," seeking to be excused from the requirements of Rule 1.200 of the Florida Rules of Criminal Procedure, 33 F.S.A. That rule requires a defendant, on written demand of the prosecuting attorney, to give notice in advance of trial if the defendant intends to claim an alibi, and to furnish the prosecuting attorney with information as to the place where he claims to have been and with the names and addresses of the alibi witnesses he intends to use. In his motion petitioner openly declared his intent to claim an alibi, but objected to the further disclosure requirements on the ground that the rule "compels the Defendant in a criminal case to be a witness against himself" in violation of his Fifth and Fourteenth Amendment rights. The motion was denied. Petitioner also filed a pretrial motion to impanel a 12-man jury instead of the six-man jury provided by Florida law in all but capital cases. That motion too was denied. Petitioner was convicted as charged and was sentenced to life imprisonment. The District Court of Appeal affirmed, rejecting petitioner's claims that his Fifth and Sixth Amendment rights had been violated. We granted certiorari.

I

Florida's notice-of-alibi rule is in essence a requirement that a defendant submit to a limited form of pretrial discovery by the State whenever he intends to rely at trial on the defense of alibi. In exchange for the defendant's disclosure of the witnesses he proposes to use to establish that defense, the State in turn is required to notify the defendant of any witnesses it proposes to offer in rebuttal to that defense. Both sides are under a continuing duty promptly to disclose the names and addresses of additional witnesses bearing on the alibi as they become available. The threatened sanction for failure to comply is the exclusion at trial of the defendant's alibi evidence — except for his own testimony — or, in the case of the State, the exclusion of the State's evidence offered in rebuttal of the alibi.

In this case, following the denial of his Motion for a Protective Order, petitioner complied with the alibi rule and gave the State the name and address of one Mary Scotty. Mrs. Scotty was summoned to the office of the State Attorney on the morning of the trial, where she gave pretrial testimony. At the trial itself, Mrs. Scotty, petitioner, and petitioner's wife all testified that the three of them had been in Mrs. Scotty's apartment during the time of the robbery. On two occasions during cross-examination of Mrs. Scotty, the prosecuting attorney confronted her with her earlier deposition in which she had given dates and times that in some respects did not correspond with the dates and times given at trial. Mrs. Scotty adhered to her trial story, insisting that she had been mistaken in her earlier testimony. The State also offered in rebuttal the testimony of one of the officers investigating the robbery who claimed that Mrs. Scotty had asked him for directions on the afternoon in question during the time when she claimed to have been in her apartment with petitioner and his wife.

We need not linger over the suggestion that the discovery permitted the State against petitioner in this case deprived him of "due process" or a "fair trial." Florida law provides for liberal discovery by the defendant against the State, and the notice-of-alibi rule is itself carefully hedged with reciprocal duties requiring state disclosure to the defendant. Given the ease with which an alibi can be fabricated, the State's interest in protecting itself against an eleventh-hour defense is both obvious and legitimate. Reflecting this interest, notice-of-alibi provisions, dating at least from 1927, are now in existence in a substantial number of States. The adversary system of trial is hardly an end in itself; it is not yet a poker game in which players enjoy an absolute right always to conceal their cards until played. We find ample room in that system, at least as far as "due process" is concerned, for the instant Florida rule, which is designed to enhance the search for truth in the criminal trial by insuring both the defendant and the State ample opportunity to investigate certain facts crucial to the determination of guilt or innocence.

Petitioner's major contention is that he was "compelled . . . to be a witness against himself" contrary to the commands of the Fifth and Fourteenth Amendments because the notice-of-alibi rule required him to give the State the name and address of Mrs. Scotty in advance of trial and thus to furnish the State with information useful in convicting him. No pretrial statement of petitioner was introduced at trial; but armed with Mrs. Scotty's name and address and the knowledge that she was to be petitioner's alibi witness, the State was able to

B. Prosecutor's Disclosure Obligations   871

take her deposition in advance of trial and to find rebuttal testimony. Also, requiring him to reveal the elements of his defense is claimed to have interfered with his right to wait until after the State had presented its case to decide how to defend against it. We conclude, however, as has apparently every other court that has considered the issue, that the privilege against self-incrimination is not violated by a requirement that the defendant give notice of an alibi defense and disclose his alibi witnesses.

The defendant in a criminal trial is frequently forced to testify himself and to call other witnesses in an effort to reduce the risk of conviction. When he presents his witnesses, he must reveal their identity and submit them to cross-examination which in itself may prove incriminating or which may furnish the State with leads to incriminating rebuttal evidence. That the defendant faces such a dilemma demanding a choice between complete silence and presenting a defense has never been thought an invasion of the privilege against compelled self-incrimination. The pressures generated by the State's evidence may be severe but they do not vitiate the defendant's choice to present an alibi defense and witnesses to prove it, even though the attempted defense ends in catastrophe for the defendant. However "testimonial" or "incriminating" the alibi defense proves to be, it cannot be considered "compelled" within the meaning of the Fifth and Fourteenth Amendments.

Very similar constraints operate on the defendant when the State requires pretrial notice of alibi and the naming of alibi witnesses. Nothing in such a rule requires the defendant to rely on an alibi or prevents him from abandoning the defense; these matters are left to his unfettered choice. That choice must be made, but the pressures that bear on his pretrial decision are of the same nature as those that would induce him to call alibi witnesses at the trial: the force of historical fact beyond both his and the State's control and the strength of the State's case built on these facts. Response to that kind of pressure by offering evidence or testimony is not compelled self-incrimination transgressing the Fifth and Fourteenth Amendments.

In the case before us, the notice-of-alibi rule by itself in no way affected petitioner's crucial decision to call alibi witnesses or added to the legitimate pressures leading to that course of action. At most, the rule only compelled petitioner to accelerate the timing of his disclosure, forcing him to divulge at an earlier date information that the petitioner from the beginning planned to divulge at trial. Nothing in the Fifth Amendment privilege entitles a defendant as a matter of constitutional right to await the end of the State's case before announcing the nature of his defense, any more than it entitles him to await the jury's verdict on the State's case-in-chief before deciding whether or not to take the stand himself.

Petitioner concedes that absent the notice-of-alibi rule the Constitution would raise no bar to the court's granting the State a continuance at trial on the ground of surprise as soon as the alibi witness is called. Nor would there be self-incrimination problems if, during that continuance, the State was permitted to do precisely what it did here prior to trial: take the deposition of the witness and find rebuttal evidence. But if so utilizing a continuance is permissible under the Fifth and Fourteenth Amendments, then surely the same result may be accomplished through pretrial discovery, as it was here, avoiding the necessity of a disrupted trial. We decline to hold that the privilege against compulsory self-incrimination guarantees the defendant the right to surprise the State with an alibi defense.

· · ·

Mr. Justice BLACK, with whom Mr. Justice DOUGLAS joins, concurring in part and dissenting in part.

· · ·

872   Chapter IX The Prosecution Function

The Court also holds that a State can require a defendant in a criminal case to disclose in advance of trial the nature of his alibi defense and give the names and addresses of witnesses he will call to support that defense. This requirement, the majority says, does not violate the Fifth Amendment prohibition against compelling a criminal defendant to be a witness against himself. Although this case itself involves only a notice-of-alibi provision, it is clear that the decision means that a State can require a defendant to disclose in advance of trial any and all information he might possibly use to defend himself at trial. This decision, in my view, is a radical and dangerous departure from the historical and constitutionally guaranteed right of a defendant in a criminal case to remain completely silent, requiring the State to prove its case without any assistance of any kind from the defendant himself.

I

The core of the majority's decision is an assumption that compelling a defendant to give notice of an alibi defense before a trial is no different from requiring a defendant, after the State has produced the evidence against him at trial, to plead alibi before the jury retires to consider the case. This assumption is clearly revealed by the statement that "the pressures that bear on (a defendant's) pre-trial decision are of the same nature as those that would induce him to call alibi witnesses at the trial: the force of historical fact beyond both his and the State's control and the strength of the State's case built on these facts." That statement is plainly and simply wrong as a matter of fact and law, and the Court's holding based on that statement is a complete misunderstanding of the protections provided for criminal defendants by the Fifth Amendment and other provisions of the Bill of Rights.

A

When a defendant is required to indicate whether he might plead alibi in advance of trial, he faces a vastly different decision from that faced by one who can wait until the State has presented the case against him before making up his mind. Before trial the defendant knows only what the State's case might be. Before trial there is no such thing as the "strength of the State's case"; there is only a range of possible cases. At that time there is no certainty as to what kind of case the State will ultimately be able to prove at trial. Therefore any appraisal of the desirability of pleading alibi will be beset with guesswork and gambling far greater than that accompanying the decision at the trial itself. Any lawyer who has actually tried a case knows that, regardless of the amount of pretrial preparation, a case looks far different when it is actually being tried than when it is only being thought about.

The Florida system, as interpreted by the majority, plays upon this inherent uncertainty in predicting the possible strength of the State's case in order effectively to coerce defendants into disclosing an alibi defense that may never be actually used. Under the Florida rule, a defendant who might plead alibi must, at least 10 days before the date of trial, tell the prosecuting attorney that he might claim an alibi or else the defendant faces the real threat that he may be completely barred from presenting witnesses in support of his alibi. According to the Court, however, if he gives the required notice and later changes his mind "(n)othing in such a rule requires (him) to rely on an alibi or prevents him from abandoning the defense; these matters are left to his unfettered choice." Thus in most situations defendants with any possible thought of pleading alibi are in effect compelled to disclose their intentions in order to preserve the possibility of later raising the defense at trial. Necessarily few defendants and their lawyers will be willing to risk the loss of that possibility by not disclosing the alibi. Clearly the pressures on defendants to plead an alibi created by this procedure are not only quite different from the pressures operating at the trial itself, but are in fact significantly greater. Contrary to the majority's assertion, the pretrial decision cannot be analyzed as simply a matter of "timing," influenced by the same factors operating at the trial itself.

B. Prosecutor's Disclosure Obligations   873

The Court apparently also assumes that a defendant who has given the required notice can abandon his alibi without hurting himself. Such an assumption is implicit in and necessary for the majority's argument that the pretrial decision is no different from that at the trial itself. I, however, cannot so lightly assume that pretrial notice will have no adverse effects on a defendant who later decides to forgo such a defense. Necessarily the defendant will have given the prosecutor the names of persons who may have some knowledge about the defendant himself or his activities. Necessarily the prosecutor will have every incentive to question these persons fully, and in doing so he may discover new leads or evidence. Undoubtedly there will be situations in which the State will seek to use such information — information it would probably never have obtained but for the defendant's coerced cooperation.

B

It is unnecessary for me, however, to engage in any such intellectual gymnastics concerning the practical effects of the notice-of-alibi procedure, because the Fifth Amendment itself clearly provides that "(n)o person . . . shall be compelled in any criminal case to be a witness against himself." If words are to be given their plain and obvious meaning, that provision, in my opinion, states that a criminal defendant cannot be required to give evidence, testimony, or any other assistance to the State to aid it in convicting him of crime. *Cf. Schmerber v. California* (1966) (Black, J., dissenting). The Florida notice-of-alibi rule in my opinion is a patent violation of that constitutional provision because it requires a defendant to disclose information to the State so that the State can use that information to destroy him. It seems to me at least slightly incredible to suggest that this procedure may have some beneficial effects for defendants. There is no need to encourage defendants to take actions they think will help them. The fear of conviction and the substantial cost or inconvenience resulting from criminal prosecutions are more than sufficient incentives to make defendants want to help themselves. If a defendant thinks that making disclosure of an alibi before trial is in his best interest, he will obviously do so. And the only time the State needs the compulsion provided by this procedure is when the defendant has decided that such disclosure is likely to hurt his case.

It is no answer to this argument to suggest that the Fifth Amendment as so interpreted would give the defendant an unfair element of surprise, turning a trial into a "poker game" or "sporting contest," for that tactical advantage to the defendant is inherent in the type of trial required by our Bill of Rights. The Framers were well aware of the awesome investigative and prosecutorial powers of government and it was in order to limit those powers that they spelled out in detail in the Constitution the procedure to be followed in criminal trials. A defendant, they said, is entitled to notice of the charges against him, trial by jury, the right to counsel for his defense, the right to confront and cross-examine witnesses, the right to call witnesses in his own behalf, and the right not to be a witness against himself. All of these rights are designed to shield the defendant against state power. None are designed to make convictions easier and taken together they clearly indicate that in our system the entire burden of proving criminal activity rests on the State. The defendant, under our Constitution, need not do anything at all to defend himself, and certainly he cannot be required to help convict himself. Rather he has an absolute, unqualified right to compel the State to investigate its own case, find its own witnesses, prove its own facts, and convince the jury through its own resources. Throughout the process the defendant has a fundamental right to remain silent, in effect challenging the State at every point to: "Prove it!"

The Bill of Rights thus sets out the type of constitutionally required system that the State must follow in order to convict individuals of crime. That system requires that the State itself must bear the entire burden without any assistance from the defendant. This requirement is clearly indicated in the Fifth Amendment itself, but it is equally apparent when all the specific provisions of the Bill of Rights relating to criminal prosecutions are considered together. And when a question concerning the constitutionality of some aspect of criminal procedure

874   Chapter IX The Prosecution Function

arises, this Court must consider all those provisions and interpret them together. The Fifth Amendment prohibition against compelling a defendant to be a witness against himself is not an isolated, distinct provision. It is part of a system of constitutionally required procedures, and its true meaning can be seen only in light of all those provisions. "Strict construction" of the words of the Constitution does not mean that the Court can look only to one phrase, clause, or sentence in the Constitution and expect to find the right answer. Each provision has clear and definite meaning, and various provisions considered together may have an equally clear and definite meaning. It is only through sensitive attention to the specific words, the context in which they are used, and the history surrounding the adoption of those provisions that the true meaning of the Constitution can be discerned.

This constitutional right to remain absolutely silent cannot be avoided by superficially attractive analogies to any so-called "compulsion" inherent in the trial itself that may lead a defendant to put on evidence in his own defense. Obviously the Constitution contemplates that a defendant can be "compelled" to stand trial, and obviously there will be times when the trial process itself will require the defendant to do something in order to try to avoid a conviction. But nothing in the Constitution permits the State to add to the natural consequences of a trial and compel the defendant in advance of trial to participate in any way in the State's attempt to condemn him.

A criminal trial is in part a search for truth. But it is also a system designed to protect "freedom" by insuring that no one is criminally punished unless the State has first succeeded in the admittedly difficult task of convincing a jury that the defendant is guilty. That task is made more difficult by the Bill of Rights, and the Fifth Amendment may be one of the most difficult of the barriers to surmount. The Framers decided that the benefits to be derived from the kind of trial required by the Bill of Rights were well worth any loss in "efficiency" that resulted. Their decision constitutes the final word on the subject, absent some constitutional amendment. That decision should not be set aside as the Court does today.

• • •

NOTES AND QUESTIONS

1. The Court describes the Florida notice-of-alibi rule as "designed to enhance the search for truth." Is that what criminal trials are for? Justice Black, dissenting, partially rejects this view, stating that an equally important aspect of the criminal justice system is to ensure that "no one is punished unless the State has first succeeded in the admittedly difficult task of convincing a jury that the defendant is guilty." Are these two views compatible? Is Justice Black endorsing "unfair surprise"?

2. The majority views the notice requirement as essentially a matter of timing, only requiring the defendant to disclose in advance what he would have to disclose at trial in any event. Justice Black vehemently disagrees, and states that the decision whether to assert an alibi defense is a "vastly different" one if it must be made prior to trial rather than after the government has rested its case. Are you persuaded by Justice Black? What is the harm in early disclosure, if there is no obligation to actually present the defense?

3. This is a particularly harsh application of the notice requirement inasmuch as Florida law permitted the government to require Ms. Scotty, once her identity was disclosed, to be forced to submit to a deposition before the trial. What could the police have done if the deposition option were not available?

Suppose that instead of the notice requirement there was a court practice—such practices are commonplace—whereby each side had to disclose their witnesses in advance? So Williams would have had to have given the government, at least before putting on his own case, and perhaps earlier, Ms. Scotty's name. Would this practice also violate the Fifth Amendment under Justice Black's logic?

4. The Court notes that the notice requirement is part of a quid pro quo discovery arrangement, the price the defendant pays for enjoying liberal discovery of the government's case. Just three years later this quid pro quo was constitutionalized. *See Wardius v. Oregon,* 412 U.S. 470, 472 (1973) ("the Due Process Clause of the Fourteenth Amendment forbids enforcement of alibi notice rules unless reciprocal discovery rights are given to criminal defendants").

5. The Federal Rules of Criminal Procedure have three provisions requiring advance notice by defendants of certain defenses: Rule 12.1 (alibi); Rule 12.2 (insanity); and 12.3 ("public authority" essentially, that defendant was acting on behalf of law enforcement when the alleged crime was committed).

What do these defenses have in common?

Are there any constitutional limits on the types of defenses that a legislature could make subject to advance notice requirements?

Expert Discovery. An especially fraught aspect of Rule 16 is the scant obligation it imposes with respect to expert witness disclosures. Prior to a 2020 amendment, Rule 16(a)(1)(G) required disclosure only of a "written summary" of an expert's anticipated testimony, including a description of "the witness's opinions, the bases and reasons for those opinions, and the witness's qualifications."

The next case illustrates this phenomenon.

Williams v. United States
900 F.3d 486 (7th Cir. 2018)

[AMY CONEY] BARRETT, Circuit Judge.

Jaboree Williams argues that his conviction was tainted by improperly admitted expert testimony. He maintains that the government violated the expert disclosure rules by giving him inadequate notice of what its expert planned to say at trial. Moreover, he says that the government used the expert's testimony to make an argument that the Federal Rules of Evidence prohibit: that he had the character of a sex trafficker and was therefore likely to have committed sex-trafficking crimes.

While the government did not violate the rules prohibiting the use of character evidence, it probably did violate the expert disclosure requirement. Nonetheless, we affirm Williams' conviction because any error was harmless. The evidence of his guilt was so overwhelming that the jury would surely have convicted him even if the government's expert had not testified.

I

Jaboree Williams was accused of myriad offenses relating primarily to a wide-ranging sex-trafficking scheme. We won't recount every sordid detail of Williams' scheme; suffice it to say that he lured women in desperate circumstances into prostitution by convincing them that he would take care of them. He then maintained control over these women through brutal physical abuse. He was indicted on numerous charges relating to sex trafficking, prostitution, heroin, obstruction of justice, and extortion.

876   Chapter IX The Prosecution Function

Before trial, the government filed a notice of its intent to call Amy Mentzel, an FBI agent, as an expert witness. The notice adequately described Mentzel's credentials and her career with the FBI. But its summary of her anticipated testimony was sparse: it listed a series of broad topics without any explanation of what she would say about each. For example, it stated that she would testify about "the recruiting processes used by pimps," "the methods pimps and those they prostitute use to advertise their services and acquire customers," and "other aspects of human sex trade involving adults and juveniles." It offered no detail about what Mentzel would say about recruiting, advertising, or any other aspect of the sex trade.

Williams moved to exclude Mentzel from testifying on the ground that the expert disclosure was inadequate and her testimony would not help the jury. The district court deferred consideration of that motion, and when the government introduced Mentzel as a witness at trial, Williams renewed his objections. He repeated his argument that the expert disclosure had been inadequate under Federal Rule of Criminal Procedure 16(a)(1)(G), which requires that the disclosure contain "a written summary of any [expert] testimony that the government intends to use" in its case-in-chief. And he again insisted that Mentzel's testimony would not help the jury — the court's jury instructions would define the crime of human trafficking for the jurors, so he said that they would need no additional guidance on that point. He also referred the district court back to the motion he had originally filed to exclude Mentzel on the ground that her testimony would be impermissible character evidence.

The court overruled these objections, and Mentzel testified. She told the jury about how a human trafficker preys on vulnerable young women and makes them think that they're in a "boyfriend/girlfriend type of relationship" before having them go on prostitution "dates." She talked about how pimps coerce their victims through fraud and force, how they handle money, how they punish their victims to ensure obedience, how they organize their operations, what certain terminology means (like "trick" and "incall"), and the sorts of rules they set for their victims. Mentzel did not testify about Williams or his actions, as she had not been involved in his case.

Mentzel's expert testimony was a small part of a trial in which the lay testimony was substantial. Three of Williams' victims testified about how Williams recruited them to prostitution, set up prostitution "dates" in numerous states, laid down rules for those "dates," controlled and kept any payment, violently punished them for breaking any of his rules, and threatened them to ensure obedience. One victim testified that Williams knew about her addiction to Percocet and withheld the drug as a means of controlling her. There was also testimony that Williams choked one victim to the point of unconsciousness, stomped on one in a bathtub, beat one with a belt, punched one in the face, broke one victim's nose, and more. A woman named Heller, who was romantically linked to Williams but did not engage in prostitution, testified that Williams admitted to prostituting several of the testifying victims. Heller often picked Williams and his victims up from hotels where Williams had forced them to service his clients. She also listened as Williams physically abused one of his victims. Another witness, one of Williams' longtime friends, told the jury that Williams had both introduced one of the testifying victims as his prostitute and bragged about his pimping activities.

The documentary evidence was similarly ample. There were pictures of injuries that Williams had inflicted on his victims. There were online prostitution ads for each of the testifying victims, all linked to Williams' email addresses. There were text messages and Facebook messages in which Williams admitted that he was a pimp and referred to the same victims who later testified at his trial. In short, the evidence against Williams was overwhelming.

The jury convicted Williams of almost all of the charged crimes, and he now appeals that conviction.

II

Williams argues that the court should have excluded Mentzel's testimony, because the government's expert disclosure was insufficient. Federal Rule of Criminal Procedure 16(a)(1)(G) requires the government to provide a "written summary" of the expert testimony it intends to introduce, and the government cannot satisfy that obligation by merely providing a "list of topics." To help the defendant prepare for trial, the disclosure must summarize what the expert will actually say about those topics. The government's disclosure of Mentzel's testimony was plainly inadequate under that standard, because it did no more than list a series of topics that she planned to cover.

The government, however, argues that this standard does not apply. According to the government, a written summary must include more than a list of topics only when an expert provides opinion testimony. And Mentzel did not provide opinion testimony; she provided "background, educational testimony." Thus, the government says, the list it provided was enough to satisfy Rule 16(a)(1)(G).

There are serious reasons to doubt the government's position. The "written summary" requirement of Rule 16(a)(1)(G) applies to "any testimony that the government intends to use under Rule[] 702," and Rule 702 governs both experts who offer an opinion and those who don't. And in defining the phrase "written summary," we have stated broadly and unequivocally that Rule 16(a)(1)(G) "requires a summary of the expected testimony, not a list of topics." Neither the rule nor our interpretation of it suggests that "written summary" means something different for non-opinion experts.

That said, any deficiency in the written summary was harmless. As an initial matter, Williams has not shown that the lack of detail affected his ability to present a defense. For example, he has not shown that he was "unduly surprised" by Mentzel's testimony. His opening brief does say in passing that the vague notice made it impossible for him to evaluate whether he needed an expert witness of his own to rebut Mentzel's testimony. But he does not assert, let alone show, that he actually would have considered having his own expert testify had the notice been more detailed. He also argues that the sparse notice made it difficult for him to make, and for the district court to assess, other arguments against the admission of the testimony. Yet his substantive objection to the testimony is meritless — we will say more about that below — so any impediment to making that objection was harmless.

Moreover, any error in admitting Mentzel's testimony "could not have made any difference" to the outcome. To evaluate whether an error was harmless, we consider "whether the prosecution's case would have been significantly less persuasive in the mind of the average juror if the erroneously admitted evidence had been excluded." Williams has conceded that the testimony of his victims was more than adequate to convince the jury that he was guilty of the charges for which he was convicted, and "[t]he question for the trial was whether the women should be believed." Nothing in Mentzel's testimony bore on whether the women who testified should be believed, and we see no reason that an average juror would find the prosecution's case less compelling without Mentzel's description of how sex trafficking works.

NOTES AND QUESTIONS

1. *Williams* is a classic illustration of the government's capacity for abusing expert testimony disclosure obligations. The government flouts its Rule 16 obligations by simply providing notice of an intent to use expert testimony, a c.v. (it would appear) of the expert, and a list of anticipated generic "topics" the expert will address. Even when called on these deficiencies prior to trial the government makes no attempt to comply with the Rule. And the government gets away with it. The district court deferred (ignored) the defense motion, even though the government's noncompliance was obvious, and although the deficiency is ever so softly recognized (by then Seventh Circuit Judge Amy Coney Barrett) on appeal (the government "probably did violate the expert disclosure requirement"), it is already harmless error time.

2. But consider how little the government could have gotten away with here to satisfy Rule 16(a)(1)(G), given the skimpiness of the "written summary" requirement. The government probably could have just disclosed a version of the Seventh Circuit's summary of the expert's testimony: human traffickers prey on vulnerable young women and makes them think that they're in a "boyfriend/girlfriend type of relationship" before having them go on prostitution "dates"; pimps coerce their victims through fraud and force, handling their money, and punishing their victims to ensure obedience, etc.

While it is unclear here that expert testimony was even necessary, in a closer case where the evidence was less clearcut, would this sort of disclosure give defendant enough information to do a meaningful cross-examination of the expert?

3. The government's laissez-faire approach to expert disclosures is exacerbated by the type of expert the government uses here, a law enforcement officer who testifies as a "background" expert on a particular genre of criminality, sex trafficking in this case. This type of witness has become more common in the last couple of decades, as the government seeks to cloak agents with experience in a particular field with a patina of "expertise." *See United States v. Mejia*, 543 F.3d 179, 189 (2d Cir. 2008) (describing government's trend of using law enforcement "expert" witnesses as "de facto" anthropologists, explaining subjects such as the organization and structure of La Cosa Nostra organized crime families and street gangs, and the use of jargon in narcotics trafficking circles). With such witnesses, where their purported expertise is based on their training and experience in law enforcement, it is critical that the defendant be given sufficient information to evaluate "the bases" for the expert-officer's opinions. The weak expert disclosure requirements in Rule 16 are just one example of the irony that the defendant in a criminal case is entitled to much less discovery than the parties in a civil case. The two biggest examples at the federal level and in the vast majority of states are the lack of depositions (except to preserve testimony) and interrogatories in criminal cases, but there are countless other examples as well. *See United States v. Gupta*, 848 F. Supp. 2d 491, 495 (S.D.N.Y. 2012) (noting the differences between civil and criminal discovery obligations); Richard M. Strassberg & Yvonne M. Cristovici, *Criminal Discovery: Reform to Level the Playing Field?*, N.Y. L.J., Sept. 14, 2010, at 1, available at http://NYLJ.com ("The difference in the discovery requirements between criminal and civil litigation has long been the subject of heated debate among attorneys, judges and legal scholars. The more limited disclosure in criminal cases, when a defendant's liberty is at risk, stands in marked contrast to the fulsome disclosure afforded parties in a civil litigation, when only money is typically at issue.").

On the expert front, happily, Rule 16(a)(1)(G) was amended in 2020 to more closely resemble the requirements of Rule 26 of the Federal Rules of Civil Procedure, which requires detailed expert reports and permits depositions. The Rule now provides:

(iii) Contents of the Disclosure. The disclosure for each expert witness must contain:

- a complete statement of all opinions that the government will elicit from the witness in its case-in-chief, or during its rebuttal to counter testimony that the defendant has timely disclosed under (b)(1)(C);
- the bases and reasons for them;
- the witness's qualifications, including a list of all publications authored in the previous 10 years; and
- a list of all other cases in which, during the previous 4 years, the witness has testified as an expert at trial or by deposition.

B. Prosecutor's Disclosure Obligations

The Rule 16 Advisory Committee Notes explain the amendment as follows: "The amendment addresses two shortcomings of the prior provisions on expert witness disclosure: the lack of adequate specificity regarding what information must be disclosed, and the lack of an enforceable deadline for disclosure. . . . Although the language of some of these provisions is drawn from Civil Rule 26, the amendment is not intended to replicate all aspects of practice under the civil rule in criminal cases, which differ in many significant ways from civil cases. The amendment requires a complete statement of all opinions the expert will provide, but does not require a verbatim recitation of the testimony the expert will give at trial."

3. Witness Statements

So if you think of "discovery" in its most general sense—as material the government must turn over to defendants in a criminal case—there is both a constitutional dimension (*Brady* and *Giglio*) and a Fed. R. Crim. P. "rule" dimension (Rule 16, for example) to the government's obligations. There is also a statutory component to these obligations, regarding witness statements under the Jencks Act, which this subsection explores. These different obligations are of course interrelated. For example, consider an important government witness who testified multiple times, with some inconsistencies, in the grand jury. The grand jury transcripts of that witness's testimony are likely both *Brady* and *Giglio* material and are also covered, as we shall see, by the Jencks Act. To round out the "source" issue, the important question of timing—when all of these disclosures must be made—is often addressed by local rules promulgated by district courts. *See, e.g.*, LR, D. Mass. 116.2 (deadlines for "Disclosure of Exculpatory Evidence").

The case whose holding was subsequently more or less codified by Congress in the Jencks Act arose out of a McCarthy era prosecution of a union official and political activist, Clinton Jencks, who the FBI suspected of Communist Party affiliation.

United States v. Jencks
353 U.S. 657 (1957)

Mr. Justice BRENNAN delivered the opinion of the Court.

On April 28, 1950, the petitioner, as president of Amalgamated Bayard District Union, Local 890, International Union of Mine, Mill & Smelter Workers, filed an "Affidavit of Non-Communist Union Officer" with the National Labor Relations Board, pursuant to § 9(h) of the National Labor Relations Act. He has been CONVICTED under a two-count indictment charging that he violated 18 U.S.C. § 1001, 18 U.S.C.A. § 10012 by falsely swearing in that affidavit that he was not on April 28, 1950, a member of the Communist Party or affiliated with such Party. The Court of Appeals for the Fifth Circuit affirmed the conviction, and also an order of the District Court denying the petitioner's motion for a new trial. This Court granted certiorari.

Two alleged trial errors are presented for our review. Harvey F. Matusow and J. W. Ford, the Government's principal witnesses, were Communist Party members paid by the Federal Bureau of Investigation contemporaneously to make oral or written reports of Communist Party activities in which they participated. They made such reports to the F.B.I. of activities allegedly participated in by the petitioner, about which they testified at the trial. Error is asserted in the denial by the trial judge of the petitioner's motions to direct the Government to produce these reports for inspection and use in cross-examining Matusow and Ford. Error is also alleged in the instructions given to the jury on membership, affiliation, and the credibility of informers.

Former Party members testified that they and the petitioner, as members of the Communist Party of New Mexico, had been expressly instructed to conceal their membership and not to carry membership cards. They also testified that the Party kept no membership records or minutes of membership meetings, and that such meetings were secretly arranged and clandestinely held. One of the witnesses said that special care was taken to conceal the Party membership of members, like the petitioner, "occupying strategic and important positions in labor unions and other organizations where public knowledge of their membership to non-Communists would jeopardize their position in the organization." Accordingly, the Government did not attempt to prove the petitioner's alleged membership in the Communist Party on April 28, 1950, with any direct admissions by the petitioner of membership, by proof of his compliance with Party membership requirements, or that his name appeared upon a membership roster, or that he carried a membership card.

The evidence relied upon by the Government was entirely circumstantial. It consisted of testimony of conduct of the petitioner from early 1946 through October 15, 1949, and of Matusow's testimony concerning alleged conversations between him and the petitioner at a vacation ranch in July or August 1950, and concerning a lecture delivered by the petitioner at the ranch. The Government also attached probative weight to the action of the petitioner in executing and filing an Affidavit of Non-Communist Union Officer on October 15, 1949, because of the events surrounding the filing of that affidavit. The Government bridged the gap between October 15, 1949, and July or August 1950 with the testimony of Ford that, during that period, the Party took no disciplinary action against the petitioner for defection or deviation, and did not replace the petitioner in the Party office which Ford testified the petitioner held as a member of the Party State Board.

The first alleged Party activity of the petitioner preceded his union employment. A witness, who was a Party member in the spring of 1946, testified that, at that time, he and the petitioner were present at a closed Party meeting at the home of the Party chairman for Colorado, where the petitioner, a veteran of World War II, led in urging that veterans who were Party members spread out into several veterans' organizations and not all join the same one, the better to further Party work.

Later in 1946 the petitioner was employed by the International Union of Mine, Mill & Smelter Workers as business agent for several local unions in the Silver City-Bayard, New Mexico, area. It was testified that one of the petitioner's first acts was to meet with the International Union's then Regional Director for the Southwest, a Communist Party member, and with the Communist Party organizer for the area, to develop plans for organizing a Party group within each of those locals, which later merged to form Amalgamated Local 890 under the petitioner's presidency.

J. W. Ford was a member of the Communist Party of New Mexico from 1946 to September 1950 and, from 1948, was a member of the State Board and a Party security officer. He said that in 1948 he became a paid undercover agent for the F.B.I. and reported regularly upon Party activities and meetings. He testified that the petitioner was also a Party and a State Board member, and he related in detail occurrences at five closed Party meetings which he said the petitioner attended.

At the first meeting, in August 1948, Ford said the Party members worked out a plan to support the petitioner's candidacy for Congress on the ticket of the Progressive Party. At the second meeting, in February 1949, Ford said that the petitioner and other Communist Party members were appointed delegates to a meeting of the Mexican-American Association in Phoenix, Arizona, to further a Party plan to infiltrate that organization and to use it for the Party's purposes. At the third meeting, in April 1949, Ford said that the Party's state organization was completed, and the petitioner was appointed to the State Board and the Party leader in the southern half of the State. At the fourth meeting, in May 1949, Ford said that the

B. Prosecutor's Disclosure Obligations 881

petitioner gave a progress report upon his success in recruiting Party members among labor groups, and offered to use Local 890's newspaper, "The Union Worker," which he edited, to support issues of Party interest. At the fifth meeting, in August 1949, Ford said that preparations were made for another meeting later in that month of the Mexican-American Association in Albuquerque, and that the delegates, including the petitioner, were instructed to give vigorous support to the meeting but to take care not to make themselves conspicuous in the proceedings.

Ford's duties as a Party security officer were to keep watch on all Party members and to report "any particular defections from the Communist philosophy or any peculiar actions, statements or associations, which would endanger the security of the Communist Party of the state." If any defection reported by a security officer were considered important, the member "would be called in and would be either severely reprimanded or criticized, or disciplined. If he refused to accept such discipline he would either be suspended or expelled." Ford testified that, between August 1949 and September 1950, when Ford ceased his activities with the New Mexico Party, there was no disciplinary action taken against the petitioner and, to his knowledge, the petitioner was not replaced in his position on the State Board of the Communist Party.

The events leading up to the petitioner's execution and filing, on October 15, 1949, of an Affidavit of Non-Communist Union Officer were testified to by a former International Union representative, a Communist Party member during 1947 to 1949. He said that, about 17 months before, in May or June 1948, a meeting of Party members, holding offices in locals of the International Union of Mine, Mill & Smelter Workers, was held in Denver to formulate plans for combatting a movement, led by non-Communists, to secede from the International Union. He said that the Party members, including the petitioner, were informed of Party policy not to sign affidavits required by § 9(h) of the then recently enacted Taft-Hartley Act. There was no testimony that that policy changed before October 15, 1949.

The affidavit was filed shortly before a C.I.O. convention was scheduled to expel the Mine-Mill International and other unions from its membership. After filing the affidavit, the petitioner and other Local 890 officers published an article in "The Union Worker" charging that the contemplated C.I.O. action was part of a program of "right-wing unions . . . gobbling up chunks of militant unions. . . . Our International Union and its officers have swallowed a lot of guff, a lot of insults. But that is not the point. . . . Now that our Union has signed the phony affidavits we can defend ourselves . . . in case of raids. We do not fear attack from that quarter any longer."

Matusow was a member of the Communist Party of New York and was a paid undercover agent for the F.B.I. before he went to New Mexico. In July or August 1950, he spent a 10-day vacation on a ranch near Taos, New Mexico, with the petitioner and a number of other people. He testified to several conversations with the petitioner there. He said he twice told the petitioner of his desire to transfer his membership from the New York to the New Mexico Party, and that on both occasions the petitioner applauded the idea and told him, "we can use you out here, we need more active Party members." On one of these occasions, Matusow said, the petitioner asked him for suggestions for a lecture the petitioner was preparing for delivery at the ranch, particularly as to what the New York Communists were doing about the Stockholm Peace Appeal. Matusow described to the petitioner a "do-day" program adopted in New York when the Party members were doers, not talkers, and performed some activity, such as painting signs around a baseball stadium urging support for the Peace Appeal. He testified that the petitioner showed great interest in the idea and said he might bring it back to his fellow Party members in Silver City.

Matusow testified that the petitioner delivered his planned lecture, informed his audience of the "do-day" idea, praised the Soviet Union's disarmament plan, referred to the United

States as the aggressor in Korea, and urged all to read the "Daily People's World," identified by Matusow as the "West Coast Communist Party newspaper." Another witness, an expelled member of Amalgamated Local 890, testified that petitioner, during 1950, 1951 and 1952, repeatedly urged at union meetings that the union members read that paper.

Matusow also testified that, in one of their conversations, the petitioner told him of a program he was developing with leaders of the Mexican Miners Union to negotiate simultaneous expiration dates of collective bargaining agreements, to further a joint action of Mexican and American workers to cut off production to slow down the Korean War effort. Matusow also testified that when he told the petitioner that he had joined the Taos Chapter of the Mexican-American Association, the petitioner told him that this was proper Communist work because the Association was a key organization, controlled by the Party, for Communist activities in New Mexico and and that he, the petitioner, was active in the Association in the Silver City area.

Ford and Matusow were subjected to vigorous cross-examination about their employment as informers for the F.B.I. Ford testified that in 1948 he went to the F.B.I. and offered his services, which were accepted. He thereafter regularly submitted reports to the FB.I., "sometimes once a week, sometimes once a month, and at various other times; maybe three or four times a week, depending on the number of meetings . . . (he) attended and the distance between the meetings." He said that his reports were made immediately following each meeting, while the events were still fresh in his memory. He could not recall, however, which reports were oral and which in writing.

The petitioner moved "for an order directing an inspection of reports of the witness Ford to the Federal Bureau of Investigation dealing with each of the meetings which he said that he attended with the defendant Jencks in the years 1948 and 1949." The trial judge, without stating reasons, denied the motion.

Matusow, on his cross-examination, testified that he made both oral and written reports to the F.B.I. on events at the ranch, including his conversations with the petitioner. The trial judge, again without reasons, denied the motion to require 'the prosecution to produce in Court the reports submitted to the F.B.I. by this witness (Matusow) concerning matters which he saw or heard at the . . . Ranch during the period that he was a guest there. . . .

The Government opposed petitioner's motions at the trial upon the sole ground that a preliminary foundation was not laid of inconsistency between the contents of the reports and the testimony of Matusow and Ford. The Court of Appeals rested the affirmance primarily upon that ground.

Both the trial court and the Court of Appeals erred. We hold that the petitioner was not required to lay a preliminary foundation of inconsistency, because a sufficient foundation was established by the testimony of Matusow and Ford that their reports were of the events and activities related in their testimony.

The reliance of the Court of Appeals upon *Gordon v. United States* is misplaced. It is true that one fact mentioned in this Court's opinion was that the witness admitted that the documents involved contradicted his testimony. However, to say that *Gordon* held a preliminary showing of inconsistency a prerequisite to an accused's right to the production for inspection of documents in the Government's possession, is to misinterpret the Court's opinion. The necessary essentials of a foundation, emphasized in that opinion, and present here, are that "(t)he demand was for production of . . . specific documents and did not propose any broad or blind fishing expedition among documents possessed by the Government on the chance that something impeaching might turn up. Nor was this a demand for statements taken from persons or informants not offered as witnesses." We reaffirm and re-emphasize these essentials. "For production purposes, it need only appear that the evidence is relevant, competent, and outside of any exclusionary rule. . . ."

B. Prosecutor's Disclosure Obligations

The crucial nature of the testimony of Ford and Matusow to the Government's case is conspicuously apparent. The impeachment of that testimony was singularly important to the petitioner. The value of the reports for impeachment purposes was highlighted by the admissions of both witnesses that they could not remember what reports were oral and what written, and by Matusow's admission: "I don't recall what I put in my reports two or three years ago, written or oral, I don't know what they were."

Every experienced trial judge and trial lawyer knows the value for impeaching purposes of statements of the witness recording the events before time dulls treacherous memory. Flat contradiction between the witness' testimony and the version of the events given in his reports is not the only test of inconsistency. The omission from the reports of facts related at the trial, or a contrast in emphasis upon the same facts, even a different order of treatment, are also relevant to the cross-examining process of testing the credibility of a witness' trial testimony.

Requiring the accused first to show conflict between the reports and the testimony is actually to deny the accused evidence relevant and material to his defense. The occasion for determining a conflict cannot arise until after the witness has testified, and unless he admits conflict, as in Gordon, the accused is helpless to know or discover conflict without inspecting the reports. A requirement of a showing of conflict would be clearly incompatible with our standards for the administration of criminal justice in the federal courts and must therefore be rejected. For the interest of the United States in a criminal prosecution ". . . is not that it shall win a case, but that justice shall be done. . . ." *Berger v. United States.*

This Court held in *Goldman v. United States* that the trial judge had discretion to deny inspection when the witness ". . . does not use his notes or memoranda (relating to his testimony) in court. . . ." We now hold that the petitioner was entitled to an order directing the Government to produce for inspection all reports of Matusow and Ford in its possession, written and, when orally made, as recorded by the F.B.I., touching the events and activities as to which they testified at the trial. We hold, further, that the petitioner is entitled to inspect the reports to decide whether to use them in his defense. Because only the defense is adequately equipped to determine the effective use for purpose of discrediting the Government's witness and thereby furthering the accused's defense, the defense must initially be entitled to see them to determine what use may be made of them. Justice requires no less.

The practice of producing government documents to the trial judge for his determination of relevancy and materiality, without hearing the accused, is disapproved. Relevancy and materiality for the purposes of production and inspection, with a view to use on cross-examination, are established when the reports are shown to relate to the testimony of the witness. Only after inspection of the reports by the accused, must the trial judge determine admissibility — e.g., evidentiary questions of inconsistency, materiality and relevancy — of the contents and the method to be employed for the elimination of parts immaterial or irrelevant.

In the courts below the Government did not assert that the reports were privileged against disclosure on grounds of national security, confidential character of the reports, public interest or otherwise. In its brief in this Court, however, the Government argues that, absent a showing of contradiction, "(t)he rule urged by petitioner . . . disregards the legitimate interest that each party — including the Government — has in safeguarding the privacy of its files, particularly where the documents in question were obtained in confidence. Production of such documents, even to a court, should not be compelled in the absence of a preliminary showing by the party making the request." The petitioner's counsel, believing that Court of Appeals' decisions imposed such a qualification, restricted his motions to a request for production of the reports to the trial judge for the judge's inspection and determination whether and to what extent the reports should be made available to the petitioner.

It is unquestionably true that the protection of vital national interests may militate against public disclosure of documents in the Government's possession. This has been recognized in

Chapter IX The Prosecution Function

decisions of this Court in civil causes where the Court has considered the statutory authority conferred upon the departments of government to adopt regulations "not inconsistent with law, for . . . use . . . of the records, papers . . . appertaining" to his department. The Attorney General has adopted regulations pursuant to this authority declaring all Justice Department records confidential and that no disclosure, including disclosure in response to subpoena, may be made without his permission.

But this Court has noticed the holdings of the Court of Appeals for the Second Circuit that, in criminal causes ". . . the Government can invoke its evidentiary privileges only at the price of letting the defendant go free. The rationale of the criminal cases is that, since the Government which prosecutes an accused also has the duty to see that justice is done, it is unconscionable to allow it to undertake prosecution and then invoke its governmental privileges to deprive the accused of anything which might be material to his defense. . . ."

In *United States v. Andolschek* Judge Learned Hand said:

> . . . While we must accept it as lawful for a department of the government to suppress documents, even when they will help determine controversies between third persons, we cannot agree that this should include their suppression in a criminal prosecution, founded upon those very dealings to which the documents relate, and whose criminality they will, or may, tend to exculpate. So far as they directly touch the criminal dealings, the prosecution necessarily ends any confidential character the documents may possess; it must be conducted in the open, and will lay bare their subject matter. The government must choose; either it must leave the transactions in the obscurity from which a trial will draw them, or it must expose them fully. Nor does it seem to us possible to draw any line between documents whose contents bears directly upon the criminal transactions, and those which may be only indirectly relevant. Not only would such a distinction be extremely difficult to apply in practice, but the same reasons which forbid suppression in one case forbid it in the other, though not, perhaps, quite so imperatively. . . .

We hold that the criminal action must be dismissed when the Government, on the ground of privilege, elects not to comply with an order to produce, for the accused's inspection and for admission in evidence, relevant statements or reports in its possession of government witnesses touching the subject matter of their testimony at the trial. The burden is the Government's, not to be shifted to the trial judge, to decide whether the public prejudice of allowing the crime to go unpunished is greater than that attendant upon the possible disclosure of state secrets and other confidential information in the Government's possession.

Reversed.

NOTES AND QUESTIONS

1. A federal labor statute in effect at the time, 29 U.S.C. § 159(h), required union officials such as Jencks to submit the affidavit upon which this alleged violation of 18 U.S. § 1001 was based. To prove the falsity element under § 1001 the government was thus required to prove either that defendant was a "member" of the Communist Party or was "affiliated" with the Communist Party. What difficulties do you see in proving either of these two facts? Is the term "affiliated" too vague to be the basis for a criminal conviction?

2. Consider all of the testimony of the two informants, as described by the Court. Does any of the informants' testimony establish that Jencks was a Communist Party member? That he was "affiliated" with the Communist Party? Or does it show at most, in the argot of the Cold War, that he was a "Communist sympathizer"? Why do you think the prosecution was eager to elicit evidence from the informants that party leaders "expressly instructed [them] to conceal their membership and not to carry membership cards"? Is there an argument that evidence of this instruction should be inadmissible at trial?

3. The Court rejects the notion that defendant's rights could be adequately preserved by the district judge's screening of the informants' statements for impeachment value beforehand. Why wouldn't that be an adequate solution?

4. The Court also rejects the notion that a defendant must make a preliminary showing of "conflict" between a witness's current and former testimony before being entitled to review the prior statements. Naturally, very few witnesses will admit to a conflict between their current testimony and what they previously said or wrote, especially when they cannot be confronted with their former statements. "Conflict," moreover, should not be the standard in any event, as Justice Brennan — at his lawyerly finest — makes clear:

> Every experienced trial judge and trial lawyer knows the value for impeaching purposes of statements of the witness recording the events before time dulls treacherous memory. Flat contradiction between the witness' testimony and the version of the events given in his reports is not the only test of inconsistency. The omission from the reports of facts related at the trial, or a contrast in emphasis upon the same facts, even a different order of treatment, are also relevant to the cross-examining process of testing the credibility of a witness' trial testimony.

This passage sheds light on the related issue, *see supra*, of prosecutors' difficulty recognizing *Brady* and impeachment material: The exercise of wringing every ounce of omission, emphasis, de-emphasis, and terminology differences out of competing statements is the quintessence of cross-examination, a task that prosecutors seldom have to perform.

5. Was it necessary to the decision that both witnesses admitted that they did not recall exactly what they had disclosed in their written and oral reports? That they had submitted dozens of reports?

6. What is the source of the rule announced in *Jencks*? Is it a constitutional rule? An evidentiary rule? Does the cite to *Berger* shed light on the answer to this question?

7. Harvey Matusow not only testified against Clinton Jencks in this prosecution but also before the House Un-American Activities Committee, implicating dozens of people in Communist Party activities, including folksinger Pete Seeger. In 1955 he recanted most of his testimony and was charged with and convicted of perjury, serving 44 months in prison. Clinton Jencks played a character based on himself in the 1954 movie *The Salt of the Earth*, an activist organizing miners in New Mexico. The screenwriter, producer, and director of the movie had all been blacklisted by the Hollywood establishment for alleged Communist party involvement.

Clinton Jencks in *The Salt of the Earth* (1954)   Harvey Matusow

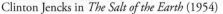

Later in the same year as the Court's decision in *Jencks*, 1957, Congress enacted the Jencks Act, essentially codifying the result in *Jencks* that defendants are entitled to any previous statement

of a testifying witness that "relates to the subject matter of the testimony." 18 U.S.C. § 3500. Because of concerns about "witness intimidation, subordination of perjury, and other threats to the integrity of the trial process," *United States v. Tarantino*, 847 F.2d 1384, 1414 (D.C. Cir. 1988), Congress decreed that such statements need not be produced until after the witness has testified at trial. To alleviate any prejudice to the defense by the timing of the disclosure, the act authorizes the court to recess for a reasonable time to permit the defense to prepare for cross-examination. Federal prosecutors often will turn over "Jencks material" in advance of trial, if they have no actual witness intimidation concerns, to avoid interruptions during the presentation of their case.

Rule 26.2 of the Federal Rules of Criminal Procedure, adopted in 1979, codified the Jencks Act in the procedural rules and made it applicable at suppression and other hearings. The Rule also made the Jencks Act disclosure obligations applicable to the defense. The symmetry is consistent with Rule 16 but also somewhat illusory, as defendants—who don't have any pretrial ability to compel someone to give a statement—rarely have any "statements" to turn over.

Consider again the facts of *Jencks*. If the Jencks Act had been the law in *Jencks*, would the defense have been entitled to statements the informants had made about *other* targets they were investigating? Do such reports "relate to the subject matter" of their testimony? How might these other reports be useful to the defense? What confidentiality arguments might the government raise about producing them? How are courts to resolve such assertions of confidentiality, per the opinion's concluding paragraphs?

Prosecutors sometimes, particularly in white collar cases where witness interference concerns may be low, provide "open file discovery," where they literally share the entire contents of their investigative files—purged of attorney work-product—with the defense. This has the advantage of simplifying the prosecutor's obligations and heading off defense motions and arguments, as in one fell swoop *Brady, Giglio, Jencks,* and Rule 16 materials are turned over.

Some states require open file discovery in certain types of cases. *See, e.g.,* N.C. Gen. Stat. § 15A-903(a)(1) (2012) ("Upon motion of the defendant, the court must order: The State to make available to the defendant the complete files of all law enforcement agencies, investigatory agencies, and prosecutors' offices involved in the investigation of the crimes committed or the prosecution of the defendant."); Fla. R. Crim. P. 3.220(b)(1) ("[T]he prosecutor shall . . . disclose to the defendant . . . a list of the names and addresses of all persons known to the prosecutor to have information that may be relevant . . . [and] the statement of any [such] person . . . [plus other information such as that which] has been provided by a confidential informant . . . whether there has been any electronic surveillance . . . reports or statements of experts . . . and any tangible papers or objects that the prosecuting attorney intends to use in the hearing or trial and that were not obtained from or that did not belong to the defendant.").

C. ETHICS AND ACCOUNTABILITY

1. General Ethical Obligations of Prosecutors

Because of their substantial discretion and broad powers, it is generally agreed that prosecutors have special ethical obligations, different than other lawyers. The next case and the Notes and Questions that follow consider why this is so, and what these extra obligations might entail.

C. Ethics and Accountability

Berger v. United States
295 U.S. 78 (1935)

Mr. Justice SUTHERLAND delivered the opinion of the Court.

Petitioner was indicted in a federal district court charged with having conspired with seven other persons named in the indictment to utter counterfeit notes purporting to be issued by designated federal reserve banks, with knowledge that they had been counterfeited. The indictment contained eight additional counts alleging substantive offenses. Among the persons named in the indictment were Katz, Rice, and Jones. Rice and Jones were convicted by the jury upon two of the substantive counts and the conspiracy count. Petitioner was convicted upon the conspiracy count only. Katz pleaded guilty to the conspiracy count, and testified for the government upon an arrangement that a nolle prosequi as to the substantive counts would be entered. It is not necessary now to refer to the evidence further than to say that it tended to establish not a single conspiracy as charged, but two conspiracies — one between Rice and Katz and another between Berger, Jones and Katz. The only connecting link between the two was that Katz was in both conspiracies and the same counterfeit money had to do with both. There was no evidence that Berger was a party to the conspiracy between Rice and Katz. During the trial, the United States attorney who prosecuted the case for the government was guilty of misconduct, both in connection with his cross-examination of witnesses and in his argument to the jury, the particulars of which we consider at a later point in this opinion. At the conclusion of the evidence, Berger moved to dismiss the indictment as to the conspiracy count, on the ground that the evidence was insufficient to support the charge. That motion was denied. Petitioner, Rice, Katz, and Jones were sentenced to terms of imprisonment.

The Circuit Court of Appeals, affirming the judgment, held that there was a variance between the allegations of the conspiracy count and the proof, but that it was not prejudicial; and that the conduct of the prosecuting attorney, although to be condemned, was not sufficiently grave to affect the fairness of the trial. We brought the case here on certiorari because of a conflict with other Circuit Courts of Appeals in respect of the effect of the alleged variance.

• • •

That the United States prosecuting attorney overstepped the bounds of that propriety and fairness which should characterize the conduct of such an officer in the prosecution of a criminal offense is clearly shown by the record. He was guilty of misstating the facts in his cross-examination of witnesses; of putting into the mouths of such witnesses things which they had not said; of suggesting by his questions that statements had been made to him personally out of court, in respect of which no proof was offered; of pretending to understand that a witness had said something which he had not said and persistently cross-examining the witness upon that basis; of assuming prejudicial facts not in evidence; of bullying and arguing with witnesses; and, in general, of conducting himself in a thoroughly indecorous and improper manner. We reproduce in the margin a few excerpts from the record illustrating some of the various points of the foregoing summary. It is impossible, however, without reading the testimony at some length, and thereby obtaining a knowledge of the setting in which the objectionable matter occurred, to appreciate fully the extent of the misconduct. The trial judge, it is true, sustained objections to some of the questions, insinuations and misstatements, and instructed the jury to disregard them. But the situation was one which called for stern rebuke and repressive measures and, perhaps, if these were not successful, for the granting of a mistrial. It is impossible to say that the evil influence upon the jury of these acts of misconduct was removed by such mild judicial action as was taken.

The prosecuting attorney's argument to the jury was undignified and intemperate, containing improper insinuations and assertions calculated to mislead the jury. A reading of the entire argument is necessary to an appreciation of these objectionable features. The following is an illustration: A witness by the name of Goldie Goldstein had been called by the prosecution to identify the petitioner. She apparently had difficulty in doing so. The prosecuting attorney, in the course of his argument, said:

> Mrs. Goldie Goldstein takes the stand. She says she knows Jones, and you can bet your bottom dollar she knew Berger. She stood right where I am now and looked at him and was afraid to go over there, and when I waved my arm everybody started to holler, "Don't point at him." You know the rules of law. Well, it is the most complicated game in the world. I was examining a woman that I knew knew Berger and could identify him, she was standing right here looking at him, and I couldn't say, "Isn't that the man?" Now, imagine that! But that is the rules of the game, and I have to play within those rules.

The jury was thus invited to conclude that the witness Goldstein knew Berger well but pretended otherwise; and that this was within the personal knowledge of the prosecuting attorney.

Again, at another point in his argument, after suggesting that defendants' counsel had the advantage of being able to charge the district attorney with being unfair "of trying to twist a witness," he said:

> But, oh, they can twist the questions, . . . they can sit up in their offices and devise ways to pass counterfeit money; but don't let the Government touch me, that is unfair; please leave my client alone.

The United States Attorney is the representative not of an ordinary party to a controversy, but of a sovereignty whose obligation to govern impartially is as compelling as its obligation to govern at all; and whose interest, therefore, in a criminal prosecution is not that it shall win a case, but that justice shall be done. As such, he is in a peculiar and very definite sense the servant of the law, the twofold aim of which is that guilt shall not escape or innocence suffer. He may prosecute with earnestness and vigor — indeed, he should do so. But, while he may strike hard blows, he is not at liberty to strike foul ones. It is as much his duty to refrain from improper methods calculated to produce a wrongful conviction as it is to use every legitimate means to bring about a just one.

It is fair to say that the average jury, in a greater or less degree, has confidence that these obligations, which so plainly rest upon the prosecuting attorney, will be faithfully observed. Consequently, improper suggestions, insinuations, and, especially, assertions of personal knowledge are apt to carry much weight against the accused when they should properly carry none. The court below said that the case against Berger was not strong; and from a careful examination of the record we agree. Indeed, the case against Berger, who was convicted only of conspiracy and not of any substantive offense as were the other defendants, we think may properly be characterized as weak — depending, as it did, upon the testimony of Katz, an accomplice with a long criminal record.

In these circumstances prejudice to the cause of the accused is so highly probable that we are not justified in assuming its nonexistence. If the case against Berger had been strong, or, as some courts have said, the evidence of his guilt "overwhelming," a different conclusion might be reached. Moreover, we have not here a case where the misconduct of the prosecuting attorney was slight or confined to a single instance, but one where such misconduct was pronounced and persistent, with a probable cumulative effect upon the jury which cannot be disregarded as inconsequential. A new trial must be awarded.

Judgment reversed.

NOTES AND QUESTIONS

1. The Court summarizes the prosecutor's misconduct as follows:

He was guilty of misstating the facts in his cross-examination of witnesses; of putting into the mouths of such witnesses things which they had not said; of suggesting by his questions that statements had been made to him personally out of court, in respect of which no proof was offered; of pretending to understand that a witness had said something which he had not said and persistently cross-examining the witness upon that basis; of assuming prejudicial facts not in evidence; of bullying and arguing with witnesses; and, in general, of conducting himself in a thoroughly indecorous and improper manner.

Bullying and arguing with witnesses might be described as "indecorous and improper." The other conduct described here, exemplified by the Goldie Goldstein closing excerpt, is of a different character entirely, as it amounts to an outright distortion of the factual record. How is it possible that a trial judge allowed this conduct? That a court of appeals found the conduct improper but not prejudicial? And that the Supreme Court might have reached a different result if the evidence had been stronger? How could you even evaluate the record evidence in view of the prosecutor's distortions of the record?

2. The Court suggests that prosecutors enjoy a sort of presumption of good faith in the eyes of the jury, and thus "improper suggestions, insinuations, and, especially, assertions of personal knowledge are apt to carry much weight against the accused when they should properly carry none." Do you agree that prosecutors have this status in the eyes of the jury? Is this status the source of their higher ethical obligations?

3. Westlaw's tab for "Citing References" indicates that *Berger* has been cited 21,252 times as of January 10, 2023. All such citations are presumably to, in whole or in part, this passage:

The United States Attorney is the representative not of an ordinary party to a controversy, but of a sovereignty whose obligation to govern impartially is as compelling as its obligation to govern at all; and whose interest, therefore, in a criminal prosecution is not that it shall win a case, but that justice shall be done. As such, he is in a peculiar and very definite sense the servant of the law, the twofold aim of which is that guilt shall not escape or innocence suffer. He may prosecute with earnestness and vigor—indeed, he should do so. But, while he may strike hard blows, he is not at liberty to strike foul ones. It is as much his duty to refrain from improper methods calculated to produce a wrongful conviction as it is to use every legitimate means to bring about a just one.

Justice Robert Jackson famously made the same point in a speech he made while he was attorney general. *See* Robert H. Jackson, *The Federal Prosecutor*, 31 J. Crim. L. & Criminology 3 (1940) ("Although the government technically loses its case, it has really won if justice has been done"). If the government "technically" loses a case does that mean the case should not have been brought? Should the government ever indict a case where it does not believe with near certainty it can prove it beyond a reasonable doubt?

4. The Court singles out as representative of the prosecutor's misconduct the testimony of Goldie Goldstein, who had trouble identifying Berger. The prosecutor improperly suggests that but for those pesky "rules of law" she would have been able to identify him. Though the term was not used in *Berger*, this is a variation of an unfortunately common species of prosecutorial misconduct known as "vouching" for a witness. *See* Rajan S. Trehan, *An "Unfortunate Bit of Legal Jargon": Prosecutorial Vouching Applied to Cooperating Witnesses*, 114 Colum. L. Rev. 997, 1002 (2014) (describing *Berger* as an early example of the prohibition on vouching). The rationale for the prohibition on vouching is that the determination of the credibility of witnesses is the core function of the jury, the criminal justice system's "lie detector." *United States v. Scheffer*, 523 U.S. 303, 313 (1998) (emphasis omitted) (quoting *United States v. Barnard*, 490 F.2d 907, 912 (9th Cir. 1973)).

That prosecutors are supposed to "do justice" is a given. But the why and the how of that axiom are the subject of debate. Are they supposed to "do justice" because, as noted in *Berger*, they represent the government? Is it because prosecutors, unlike other lawyers in the adversary system, do not have an individual client to whom they owe undivided loyalty? Is it because they enjoy a resource advantage over defendants?

Consider the following hypothetical:

ROGUE COP?

Trevor is indicted for drug possession in connection with a search of his car near the border that uncovered a large quantity of marijuana. The report by the Border Patrol agent states that Trevor consented to a search of his car. The AUSA believes the agent is telling the truth on this occasion but is aware that the agent has previously been found by a court to have lied about a consent issue. In that case, which is not published, the evidence was suppressed. Defense counsel approaches the prosecutor shortly after indictment about the possibility of her client pleading guilty to a drug possession charge. Trevor has denied giving consent to the search, although defense counsel is not totally convinced he is telling the truth.

Should the prosecutor disclose the information about the police officer's previous testimony even though under *Ruiz* there is no legal obligation to do so?

Must the prosecutor disclose the information?

Does the prosecutor have an obligation to the U.S. Attorney's Office, his employer, *not* to disclose the information in the absence of a clear legal obligation?

Berger was about a prosecutor's conduct at trial, and the avoidance of striking foul blows — like prosecutor's blows in *Berger* — is a comparatively straightforward task in that context. The applicable ethical rules largely do not address trial conduct, but focus instead on charging decisions and pretrial matters. Rule 3.8 of the ABA Model Rules of Professional Conduct, approximate versions of which are applicable in most states, has a rule titled "Special Responsibilities of a Prosecutor," which provides:

The prosecutor in a criminal case shall:

(a) refrain from prosecuting a charge that the prosecutor knows is not supported by probable cause;

(b) make reasonable efforts to assure that the accused has been advised of the right to, and the procedure for obtaining, counsel and has been given reasonable opportunity to obtain counsel;

(c) not seek to obtain from an unrepresented accused a waiver of important pretrial rights, such as the right to a preliminary hearing;

(d) make timely disclosure to the defense of all evidence or information known to the prosecutor that tends to negate the guilt of the accused or mitigates the offense, and, in connection with sentencing, disclose to the defense and to the tribunal all unprivileged mitigating information known to the prosecutor, except when the prosecutor is relieved of this responsibility by a protective order of the tribunal;

(e) not subpoena a lawyer in a grand jury or other criminal proceeding to present evidence about a past or present client unless the prosecutor reasonably believes: (1) the information sought is not protected from disclosure by any applicable privilege; (2) the evidence sought is essential to the successful completion of an ongoing investigation or prosecution; and (3) there is no other feasible alternative to obtain the information;

(f) except for statements that are necessary to inform the public of the nature and extent of the prosecutor's action and that serve a legitimate law enforcement purpose, refrain from making extrajudicial comments that have a substantial likelihood of heightening public condemnation of the accused and exercise reasonable care to prevent investigators, law enforcement personnel, employees or other persons assisting or associated with the prosecutor in a criminal case from making an extrajudicial statement that the prosecutor would be prohibited from making under Rule 3.6 or this Rule.

(g) When a prosecutor knows of new, credible and material evidence creating a reasonable likelihood that a convicted defendant did not commit an offense of which the defendant was convicted, the prosecutor shall: (1) promptly disclose that evidence to an appropriate court or authority, and (2) if the conviction was obtained in the prosecutor's jurisdiction, (i) promptly disclose that evidence to the defendant unless a court authorizes delay, and (ii) undertake further investigation, or make reasonable efforts to cause an investigation, to determine whether the defendant was convicted of an offense that the defendant did not commit.

(h) When a prosecutor knows of clear and convincing evidence establishing that a defendant in the prosecutor's jurisdiction was convicted of an offense that the defendant did not commit, the prosecutor shall seek to remedy the conviction.

Do any of these requirements seem controversial? Note that Rule 3.8(g) imposes an obligation on the prosecutor even after he is done with a case.

How does a prosecutor's obligation to "do justice" apply at trial? Does a prosecutor have an obligation to attempt to "level the playing field" in a situation where defense counsel's performance is substandard? One distinguished commentator says yes:

> [Doing] "justice" has two fairly limited prongs: (1) prosecutors should not prosecute unless they have a good faith belief that the defendant is guilty; and, (2) prosecutors must ensure that the basic elements of the adversary system exist at trial.

Fred C. Zacharias, *Structuring the Ethics of Prosecutorial Trial Practice: Can Prosecutors Do Justice?*, 44 Vand. L. Rev. 45, 49 (1991). How could a prosecutor carry out an obligation to "ensure that the basic elements of the adversary system exist at trial"? Must she do so if it endangers a conviction she believes is just? Suppose it becomes clear early in a trial that defense counsel is both unprepared and a poor cross-examiner. The prosecutor knows that one of the government's witnesses would, if cross-examined competently, provide information helpful to the defendant. Should the prosecutor bring out the information in her direct examination? Must she?

It is largely because of the difficulty of questions like this one that most affirmative ethical obligations of prosecutors focus on disclosure and other pretrial obligations.

2. Prosecutors' Lack of Accountability

The breadth of the prosecutor's discretion is rivaled only by the prosecutor's virtually total lack of accountability. As Professor Davis points out, other criminal justice players who wield discretionary power often come under public fire when things go wrong: police officers who make improper stops, judges who fail to detain defendants who commit crimes upon their release, parole boards who grant early release to prisoners who reoffend, governors and even Presidents who grant pardons to unpopular defendants. Davis, Arbitrary Justice, *supra* at 7-8. By contrast, prosecutors are only rarely held accountable for their abuses of discretion.

One reason for this is the harmless error doctrine. "Where a reviewing court can find that the record developed at trial establishes guilt beyond a reasonable doubt, the interest in fairness has been satisfied and the judgment should be affirmed." *Rose v. Clark*, 478 U.S. 570, 579 (1986). This standard insulates from review most trial misconduct by prosecutors, as an error would have to be particularly egregious for an appellate court—looking back on a case where the jury has already returned a conviction — to find that the misconduct would have caused a different result. Application of the harmless error rule not only insulates prosecutors from accountability, it arguably emboldens them:

> Every time an error is declared harmless in a particular situation, it diminishes the risk to the prosecutor in the use of the evidence or the technique. The lessening of the risk is added into a formula which favors risk-taking based upon the doctrine alone. In a sense, the doctrine encourages the prosecutor to use the evidence or the technique in every case. Initially, there are three possibilities: (1) the evidence or technique does not involve any error, (2) if the evidence or technique involves error, it will be harmless, and (3) the evidence or technique involves error that will cause a reversal because the remainder of the evidence is not "overwhelming." What should the intelligent and conscientious risk assessor do? The first two possibilities present no question. If there is no error there is no problem, and if the error is harmless the only problem is the time and expense of an appeal. The result is the same: a legal conviction. Convictions which are legal are, after all, what the society pays the prosecutor to obtain. The third choice is the problem. The court has defined a doctrine of harmless constitutional error which says to a prosecutor that if the case is not overwhelming any error will cause a reversal, and if it is overwhelming, no worry. The prosecutor then looks at the case and determines that it is not very strong. Use of the evidence or technique has two chances of success — no error and harmless — and one chance of failure. By the Court's definition of "harmless," that one chance of failure demands that the evidence or technique be crucial to the prosecutor's case. The prosecutor has no advocate's choice which mitigates in favor of not using the evidence or technique. Even if the prosecutor believes the case is strong, the likelihood is that the evidence or technique will be used. The odds are still two-to-one. Further, the advocate's predilection to cover every base is reinforced by the doctrine's admonition: if the evidence or technique is not needed by the advocate it is not likely to cause a reversal.

Steven H. Goldberg, *Harmless Error: Constitutional Sneak Thief*, J. Crim. L. & Criminology 421, 439-40 (1980).

The Court has also cut back on federal courts' abilities to use their "supervisory powers" to formulate standards of procedure for federal prosecutors. *United States v. Russell*, 411 U.S. 423 (1973), *supra*, was a case where the district court had used its supervisory powers to find entrapment where the government had actively participated or had become "enmeshed" in the criminal activity. The Court made it very clear that the supervisory power should not be employed as a "chancellor's foot" veto over law enforcement practices of which it did not approve. And in *United States v. Hasting*, 461 U.S. 499 (1983), the Court held that the supervisory power could not be used, where any error was harmless, to reverse a conviction based on the prosecutor's violation of the *Griffin* "no comment" rule in closing argument. Davis, Arbitrary Justice, *supra* at 128.

Prosecutors are rarely held accountable through other avenues, either. Although a prosecutor's deprivation of a person's rights is an action taken "under color of law," and theoretically subject to redress under § 1983, the Supreme Court has held that prosecutors enjoy absolute immunity from § 1983 liability. *Imbler v. Pachtman*, 424 U.S. 409 (1976). *See* Chapter VI *supra*. Prosecutors are rarely disciplined or even reprimanded by bar authorities or other bodies. Davis, Arbitrary Justice, *supra* at 135-36. And even though prosecutors are most often elected, and despite Justice Scalia's views in *Morrison*, *supra*, local district attorney elections too often are uncontested and low-information affairs. *Id.* at 166-69.

3. Prosecutorial Misconduct Examples

The next two cases are exceptions that prove the general rule of prosecutorial unaccountability. In both cases, one a common arena for misconduct and one more unusual, the First Circuit Court of Appeals takes prosecutorial misconduct seriously, even though the misconduct, on a superficial level, may not seem particularly egregious.

C. Ethics and Accountability

United States v. Hardy
37 F.3d 753 (1st Cir. 1994)

TORRUELLA, Circuit Judge.

A grand jury returned a five-count indictment alleging various firearm related charges against defendant/appellant Frederick Hardy and his co-defendant Raymond Moreno, Jr. A trial was held and the jury found both defendants guilty on all counts. Moreno challenged his conviction in a separate appeal. In this appeal, Hardy claims that the government made several impermissible arguments at trial, including improperly commenting in its closing on Hardy's decision not to testify at trial. We believe that the government's comment on Hardy's silence at trial violated the Fifth Amendment, and that this error, coupled with other improper arguments, deprived Hardy of a fair trial. We therefore vacate Hardy's convictions and order a new trial.

I. BACKGROUND

A. Facts

We are concerned here not with a claim of insufficient evidence, but with a case in which we find that the government improperly commented on Hardy's right not to testify and made other inappropriate remarks during the course of the trial. Accordingly, our description of the facts is not limited in this case to evidence and inferences most favorable to the government, but rather it is designed to provide a balanced picture of the evidence appropriate for determining whether the comments and remarks were harmless or prejudicial.

On the evening of April 18, 1991, a group of five law enforcement officers, while on foot patrol in the Lenox Street Housing Development in Boston, Massachusetts, heard a series of gunshots coming from another area within the development. Three of the officers, Officers Garvey, Perkins and Devane, ran in the direction of the shots; the other two, Officer Murphy and Trooper Drummy, returned to a parked cruiser.

As Officers Garvey, Perkins, and Devane were running down Hammond Street, they observed three black males emerge from a courtyard in the direction of the gunshots, run across Hammond Street, and disappear near a cluster of buildings across the street. One of the officers described the three men as running in a line in a "hunched over" manner. The men then disappeared from view. Almost at once, two of the three officers, joined by Officer Murphy (who had left his cruiser to assist in the foot pursuit), saw three men running through a parking lot behind the cluster of buildings, and gave chase.

The officers saw one of the three men veer off from the other two and run in a separate direction. The second and third men were then seen by the officers to come together briefly and appeared to pass an object between them. Officer Murphy, who was closest to the two individuals, described the item being exchanged as a dark object about one to one-and-a-half feet long. The individual who took this object then ran off through a grass courtyard. The individual who passed on the object, Raymond Moreno, Jr., immediately stopped, raised his arms and surrendered.

Another police officer, Paul MacIsaac, aided in the pursuit. Upon arriving at the scene, Officer Murphy, who had Moreno in custody, directed Officer MacIsaac to head in the direction where the other man, to whom Moreno had passed the object, had run. Officer MacIsaac followed these directions, and came across two black males at a nearby intersection, standing on a sidewalk, looking into an adjacent field. Officer MacIsaac questioned the two men, conducted a pat-frisk, and then placed the two men in the back of his cruiser. The officer eventually took them to the station for questioning and they were later released.

894   Chapter IX The Prosecution Function

Officer Garvey testified that in order to cut off any escape route that the fleeing suspect might use, he had circled around to the opposite end of the grass courtyard. Officer Garvey soon saw a black male, wearing dark clothes, who was later identified as Frederick Hardy, enter the courtyard. The officer testified that he never saw Hardy with any weapon in his possession. After telling Hardy several times to stop, Officer Garvey testified that as Hardy raised his arms — first his right, then his left — over his head, he heard a soft thud on the ground nearby. Despite being only two to three feet away from Hardy, however, Officer Garvey did not see any object leave Hardy's hands. Hardy was then arrested. Hardy did not possess any firearms when he was arrested. After Officer Garvey took Hardy to a police cruiser, he returned to the area. A search of the area revealed a .32 caliber pistol about five to eight feet from where Hardy had stopped.

The officers searched the path between the area of Moreno's arrest and the spot at which Officer Garvey first observed Hardy. The officers found a double-barreled sawed-off shotgun with a 12½ inch barrel, fully loaded with ammunition, hidden in bushes along that route.

While Moreno and Hardy were being arrested, Officer Devane was in search of the first of the three runners, who had gone off in a separate direction. Officer Devane discovered a black male, Steven Fernándes, sweating and out of breath, hiding in some bushes. After arresting Fernándes and placing him in the cruiser, Officer Devane found a semi-automatic pistol on the ground near where Fernándes had been hiding.

After receiving his Miranda warning at the police station, Hardy said that he had been at the development by himself to visit his niece and ran when he heard shots. Hardy denied knowing Moreno or Fernándes. At trial, however, a resident of the housing development testified that he had seen Hardy together with Moreno and Fernándes a number of times during the prior year. Additionally, Officer Dreary of the Boston Police Department testified that in March 1991, he had stopped a red Isuzu Trooper, and that Hardy was the driver and Moreno was a passenger in the front seat.

B. Proceedings Below

The grand jury returned a five-count indictment against Hardy and Moreno on June 25, 1991. Count One charged Hardy with being a felon-in-possession of a firearm, and Count Four charged Hardy with being a felon-in-possession of ammunition, both of which were in violation of 18 U.S.C. § 922(g). Count Two charged Hardy with possessing a firearm, a short-barreled Stevens 12 gauge, double barrel shotgun, in violation of 26 U.S.C. § 5861(d). Counts Three and Five charged Moreno with possession of the same short-barreled shotgun and being a felon-in-possession of ammunition.

The trial took place over ten days from October 28, 1991 to November 14, 1991. The jury returned guilty verdicts on all five counts.

The court then sentenced Hardy to 262 months' incarceration. Hardy appealed both his conviction and his sentence, and on November 5, 1992, this Court, while retaining jurisdiction, remanded the case to the district court with respect to some sentencing issues. The district court then reaffirmed Hardy's sentence, and Hardy again appealed. This second appeal was then consolidated with the first appeal.

II. STANDARD OF REVIEW

Hardy argues that the prosecutor improperly commented on his failure to testify at trial, and that this comment constituted a violation of his Fifth Amendment privilege against self-incrimination, which unduly prejudiced his ability to obtain a fair trial. We will utilize a de novo standard to review the legal question of whether the prosecutor's argument constituted constitutional error. We will review the trial court's decision to deny Hardy's motion for a mistrial, based on this alleged constitutional violation, for an abuse of discretion.

III. THE PROSECUTOR'S COMMENT ON THE DEFENDANTS' SILENCE

A. Did the Prosecutor's Comment Violate the Fifth Amendment?

The most serious argument that Hardy raises in this appeal concerns the prosecutor's closing argument at trial. In *Griffin v. California*, 380 U.S. 609 (1965), the United States Supreme Court held that the Fifth Amendment's self-incrimination clause forbids the prosecution from commenting on an accused's failure to take the stand and testify during a trial. A prosecutor's comment is improper where, under the circumstances of the case, "the language used was manifestly intended or was of such character that the jury would naturally and necessarily take it to be a comment on the failure of the accused to testify." A prosecutor's comment does not therefore need to be direct; rather, a prosecutor may run afoul of the rule in *Griffin* by making such comments inferentially.

We believe that here, the prosecutor improperly called attention to the failure of Hardy to take the stand and testify at trial. The prosecutor stated:

> Ladies and gentlemen, the evidence here, the only reasonable conclusion that can come from this evidence is that Mr. Hardy possessed that caliber pistol loaded, Mr. Moreno possessed the sawed-off shotgun loaded, and that during the course of the chase, Mr. Moreno passed it off to Mr. Hardy so that he could get rid of it. What the evidence shows is that these two defendants that night were running and hiding. They'd been involved in that incident and then they unfortunately had the misfortune of running right into the police who just happened to be in the area, and they were running and hiding, running from the police and hiding the evidence from the police. *They're still running and hiding today. The time has come for them to stop running and stop hiding. The time has come for them to be held accountable for the wrongful acts that they committed on the night of April 18th, 1991 in Boston.* That time is now and only you can hold them accountable. Thank you (emphasis added).

Defense counsel objected and requested a limiting instruction. The district court was initially concerned that such an instruction might hurt rather than help, because the jury might not have construed the prosecutor's remark as a comment on defendants' silence. The court then asked the government:

Tell me this:	In what other sense can the Government argue that [the defendants] are running and hiding even at this time?
The government replied:	Because, your Honor, I'm just drawing an analogy between their running and hiding on that night and the Government's burden of proving guilt beyond a reasonable doubt.
The court stated:	I'm going to give the limiting instruction. It doesn't satisfy me.
The court then gave the following instruction to the jury:	Members of the jury, I sustain the objection to the argument . . . that even today the defendants are running and hiding. You will disregard that argument and not consider it in any respect in your consideration of the evidence in this case.

The court then asked defense counsel if they requested further instructions, and they replied no. The defendants moved for a mistrial, and the court denied these motions.

The prosecutor's comment during his closing set up an analogy between what the defendants were allegedly doing on the night of the crime—running and hiding—and what the prosecutor believed they were doing during the trial—running and hiding. Of course, the defendants were not literally running from the trial or hiding during the trial. Rather, they were both in custody and were sitting silently during each day of the proceeding. Neither defendant testified on his own behalf. The natural and necessary implication of the prosecutor's remark was therefore that the defendants were running from the evidence presented against them, and hiding behind their right to silence during the trial. The prosecutor's comment therefore violated the Fifth Amendment.

B. Is a New Trial Required?

Where it appears that the prosecutor has made an improper argument to the jury, this Circuit has established a standard to evaluate whether a new trial is required.

Although we have used slightly varying terminology in describing [the relevant] factors, the common denominators are (1) the severity of the misconduct; (2) the context in which it occurred; (3) whether the judge gave any curative instructions and the likely effect of such instructions; and (4) the strength of the evidence against the defendant.

We treat these factors in order, to determine if the prosecutor's comment was harmless.

First, as we discussed above, we believe that the prosecutor's argument constituted a violation of the *Griffin* rule. Additionally, we believe that the comments were, in a sense, deliberate. In his closing argument, the prosecutor had constructed an analogy based on the facts of the case, with certain rhetoric significantly repeated, which appeared to be planned. We do not believe that the prosecutor intentionally intended to influence the jury by commenting on Hardy's silence, and we hope that our belief is not misplaced. We do believe, however, that when preparing or reviewing his proposed closing, the prosecutor should have known that such a comment was improper.

Second, we point out that this comment was made against a backdrop where the possibility that Hardy would receive a fair trial was already in danger — that is, the prosecutor's closing was not an isolated instance of misconduct. In *Moreno*, we addressed several arguments, (two in the majority opinion, two more in the dissent) which Hardy has also raised in this appeal, relating to improper arguments made by the government during trial. Our conclusions in *Moreno* are equally applicable to this case.

In *Moreno*, we noted that in the prosecutor's opening remarks, he stated, "the evidence will show that [the police officers] were doing their jobs protecting the community that has been plagued by violence, senseless violence, shootings and killings. That's why they were there and that's why we're here today." We concluded that because there was no evidence in the case about "senseless violence" or "shootings and killings," it was patently improper for the prosecutor to make those remarks. The remarks played upon the jury's emotional reaction to neighborhood violence and was outside the bounds of legitimate argument.

We were equally disturbed by a second argument by the prosecutor which not only reiterated the senseless violence theme, but also established a second departure from the "straight and narrow." The prosecutor argued in his closing that the shotgun was not just tossed away but deliberately concealed, and continued: "Forget about the fact that maybe Mr. Hooker [who lived nearby] or his wife or his three kids might come out and look at the gun and get their heads blown off. But I'm sure Mr. Hardy had other things on his mind going through there, like getting away from the cops." Although we found that both of these arguments were improper, we found that the errors were harmless as they related to *Moreno*.

The dissent found two more arguments made by the prosecutors to be troublesome. The prosecutor vouched for a government witness, intimating that that witness possessed some information beyond the evidence presented. The prosecutor also improperly disparaged defense counsel, by stating that they were paid to see things in a different way, defense counsel was talking out of both sides of his mouth, and that one defense argument was meant to divert the jury's attention. The jury was therefore exposed to a number of emotional and prejudicial arguments which potentially interfered with its ability to appraise the evidence objectively and dispassionately.

Third, while the trial court gave a limiting instruction, and Hardy's counsel did not request a stronger instruction, we do not believe that the curative effect of the judge's

C. Ethics and Accountability   **897**

instruction negated the effects of the prosecutor's constitutional indiscretion. Whether a curative instruction is sufficient to avoid prejudice depends on the impact of the remark taken in the context of the whole of the evidence, including any other aggravating remarks or circumstances that may increase the risk that the improper remark did affect the outcome. An improper comment that may seem insignificant where the evidence is overwhelming can assume a very different aspect in a close case. This is such a close case.

Finally, the strength of the evidence proffered against Hardy was not overwhelming. First, the government's case against Hardy largely rested on the credibility of Officer Garvey. Therefore, if the jury disbelieved, or had questions about, Officer Garvey's testimony, we do not believe that Hardy would have been convicted. Second, the jury was required to draw a number of inferences in order to convict Hardy. No officer ever saw Hardy possess either the pistol or the sawed-off shotgun. While Officer Garvey testified that after he stopped Hardy, he heard a soft thud as Hardy raised his arms, Garvey never saw a gun in Hardy's hand, or fall from his hand, despite the fact that he was only two to three feet away from Hardy. Rather, the officers found the pistol later, in the area where Hardy was stopped. Additionally, other officers found the shotgun hidden in an area that Hardy had seemingly passed through, but nobody saw Hardy dispose of the weapon there. There were also other men stopped in the area who could have somehow been responsible for the guns. We do not believe that this circumstantial evidence, which for the most part rested on Officer Garvey's credibility, clearly established Hardy's guilt. Moreover, in light of the prosecution's comment, the jury may very well have wondered, either consciously or subconsciously, what Hardy had to say about the extent of his involvement, and concluded that he must have had something to hide because of his failure to testify.

The district court did not evaluate these relevant factors on the record to determine if a new trial was warranted in light of the prosecutor's improper closing argument, when Hardy moved for a mistrial. Because all of these factors cut in favor of a new trial, we believe that the district court abused its discretion when it denied Hardy's motion. The government improperly commented on Hardy's failure to testify, and in light of the government's other improper comments and the evidence presented, we believe that this constituted reversible error.

For the foregoing reasons, we vacate Hardy's convictions and order a new trial.

NOTES AND QUESTIONS

1. The court goes out of its way, it says, to provide a more "balanced" picture of the evidence than it would in a case challenging the sufficiency of the evidence, where the preamble to the facts section of the opinion would usually begin, in words or substance, "a reasonable jury could have found the following." But does it? What facts are either omitted or absent in the court's description that a good defense lawyer would have investigated and made part of the record as appropriate? (What is "foot patrol"? How many other people did the police see or interact with during their patrol that evening? What was the visibility at every stage of the patrol?)

2. Under First Circuit precedent at the time, a violation of the Fifth Amendment self-incrimination clause will be found in prosecutorial comment where "the language used was manifestly intended or was of such character that the jury would naturally and necessarily take it to be a comment on the failure of the accused to testify."

Do you agree that the prosecutor's comment about "running and hiding" amounted to such a violation? If so, is that because of how the comment was intended or how it was likely understood?

3. What do you make of the trial judge's reaction that a limiting instruction might hurt the defense rather than help it? How might it hurt rather than help? If you were the defense

Chapter IX The Prosecution Function

counsel, would you have wanted a more robust instruction, perhaps something saying that the comment by the prosecutor was improper and reemphasizing that the defendant has no burden to put on any evidence at all and that the burden of proof always remains with the prosecution?

4. What do you make of this colloquy between the judge and the prosecutor:

The court then asked the government:	Tell me this: In what other sense can the Government argue that [the defendants] are running and hiding even at this time?
The government replied:	Because, your Honor, I'm just drawing an analogy between their running and hiding on that night and the Government's burden of proving guilt beyond a reasonable doubt.

Does the prosecutor's response even make sense? While respecting the fact that this stage of a trial — closing arguments — is fraught with stress and emotion, and not an occasion ripe for sober reflection, could the prosecutor have avoided reversal by falling on his sword here and admitted to making a mistake rather than being disingenuous? What would falling on his sword have entailed?

5. The standard for whether a prosecutor's improper comment will amount to anything besides "disapproval," usually, as here, without the trial prosecutors being named, is a demanding one. Here, however, as to the "context" of the remark, the court is able to point to several other examples of misconduct in the same case.

Why are the references to "senseless violence" and "shootings and killings" in the prosecutor's opening improper? If the "foot patrol" was a police response to a recent flurry of shootings in the Lenox Street project, and that information had made its way into evidence, would the comment still have been improper?

6. The court also notes that the prosecutor impermissibly "vouched" for a witness. *See supra.* In discussing the "cylindrical object" that appellant passed on to another individual, the prosecutor warranted that the police "knew what it was, but they're not overstating their testimony." He later asserted that "[t]hey knew what the object was. They were going to find it."

In what way does this constitute improper vouching? What is objectionable about this statement wholly apart from its vouching aspect?

7. The Court also found that the prosecutor "improperly disparaged defense counsel, by stating that they were paid to see things in a different way, defense counsel was talking out of both sides of his mouth, and that one defense argument was meant to divert the jury's attention."

Can't all of these points be made by the prosecutor without personally impugning defense counsel? Recall that disparagement of defense counsel was one of the many objectionable comments made by the prosecutor in *Berger*, a case that every prosecutor should be familiar with.

United States v. Coast of Maine Lobster Co.
538 F.2d 899 (1st Cir. 1976)

ALDRICH, Senior Circuit Judge.

Defendants were convicted following a jury trial at Portland, Maine, on some 20 counts of mail and wire fraud, 18 U.S.C. ss 1341, 1343, involving false promises to ship Maine lobsters nationwide. On appeal the assigned errors all concern matters occurring during trial.

C. Ethics and Accountability 899

Only one appears of any stature. It presents a novel and borderline question of potential prejudice arising from prominent publicity given during trial to statements of the prosecutor's immediate supervisor which, though not referring to a trial in progress, could reasonably be thought to have bearing on it. Because the hazard, being one step removed from that arising from direct comment on a case, is both so resistant to a search for proven prejudice and so easily prevented, we deem this a proper occasion for the exercise of our supervisory power, intending not so much to criticize unthinking conduct in the past as to assure more sensitive conduct in the future.

In the case at hand, defendants had been on trial for a week. The case was to go to the jury on a Monday. On the day before, a Sunday, the United States Attorney, Peter Mills, appeared on a local television broadcast, "At Issue," which had been taped the previous Thursday, the fourth day of trial. In the broadcast, an interview, he expressed his opinion, inter alia, that "(p)eople who commit so-called white collar crimes are not considered very apt candidates for much time in jail." Monday morning, the Portland Press Herald, the widely read local newspaper, carried a conspicuous headline across the top of the front page, "Mills: White Collar Criminals Get Off Easy," together with a picture of Mills. There was a byline, "United Press International." The first half of the article, appearing on the front page, was principally addressed to Mills' opinion that white collar criminals, such as those convicted of income tax evasion, received inadequate jail sentences. While expressing his "utmost respect" for the district judge, Mills felt he could properly make known his differences.

Defendant moved for a mistrial. The court thereupon inquired of the jury, collectively, in open court. It first asked if jurors had seen an article in Saturday's newspaper, not here relevant, and reminded the jurors of its instruction not to read any articles. There being no response to this query, it asked if any juror had heard the Sunday "At Issue" broadcast, and again received no response. It then inquired if any juror had seen that morning's Portland Press Herald. Again the record indicates "(No response)." The court then asked if any juror had read any article reporting on the United States Attorney's appearance on the Sunday telecast. The vice foreman acknowledged that he had read about it in the morning paper. Another juror then said that she had not read the article but had seen the picture. Further inquiry revealed that "a fair number," estimated by the court to be seven or eight, had seen the front page and the picture. At this point the court twice asked the jurors whether anyone had read the article, and whether seeing "the picture or anything else" would have any influence on them, and received no response.

So far as the jurors' collective disclaimers are concerned, the record provides no strong basis for confidence that the message of the headline had not been received. Their silent responses, given the total picture, might be thought based less upon full candor than upon a reaction to the court's reminder of their instructions not to read the newspapers. The eventual admission that seven or eight had seen the picture and the front page, which necessarily included the headline, gives us pause. We may well wonder under the circumstances how many, after seeing the head, resolutely put the paper down.

Our analysis of the out of court publicity in this case is aided by no precise parallel in other cases. The article made no reference to the defendants or to the pending trial. We confidently assume that this was not an occasion where a prosecutor was seeking a public forum in which to try to influence the jury's verdict. The gist of the article itself was concerned with sentencing, the judge's function. Nor are we implying that prosecutors should not have different views from those of the district judge, or express them publicly and in critical terms.

Here, however, we deal with publicity over which the chief prosecutor had control both as to subject matter and timing. In this case the prosecution of the defendants was the only federal criminal proceeding taking place in the district, and had been so for a week. The alleged crime was mail fraud, a white collar crime. The United States Attorney was well known to the

Chapter IX The Prosecution Function

jurors, who had been in service since January, the instant trial being held in July. The banner headline "White Collar Criminals Get Off Easy," accompanied by the picture, had the potential (a) of making a juror think of the case before him as one of a class in which there had been excessive leniency, and a challenge to exhibit appropriate toughness; (b) of perhaps increasing a juror's willingness to convict if he thought a lenient sentence might be imposed; and (c) of making a juror feel that public attention, because of the article, would be more sharply and critically directed to the ultimate verdict in the case at hand. Had a juror read the article itself, as the vice foreman at one point said he had, he might also be tempted, by the assertion of one's right to differ from the judge, not to follow faithfully the instructions. All of this is in the conjectural area of potential for prejudice. But the danger of prejudice can best be avoided if prosecutors are more sensitive to the possible impact of any public statements made by them during a trial.

The ABA Standards Relating to the Prosecution Function and the Defense Function, Approved Draft, 1971, set forth the following standards as to public statements, § 1.3: "(a) The prosecutor should not exploit his office by means of personal publicity connected with a case before trial, during trial and thereafter. (b) The prosecutor should comply with the ABA Standards on Fair Trial and Free Press." The ABA Standards Relating to Fair Trial and Free Press, Approved Draft, 1968, § 1.1, recommended that "During the trial of any criminal matter . . . no lawyer associated with the prosecution or defense shall give or authorize any extrajudicial statement or interview, relating to the trial or the parties or issues in the trial. . . ." The commentary on this section, reads: "The reasons for this broad prohibition on the attorney as an officer of the court should be readily apparent. His proper function at this point is to present his case in the courtroom, not to make extrajudicial statements interpreting or explaining the evidence, anticipating his own or his adversary's strategy, or attempting to build a favorable climate of opinion. Moreover, the period of trial in a case that has aroused public attention is the most critical from the standpoint of potential prejudice." See, generally *Berger v. United States.*

While "issues in the trial" and "build a favorable climate" apply most obviously to references to the concrete facts and issues of a particular case, the potential for prejudice can also be triggered by a publicized opinion on an issue, more generally expressed but likely to be associated in the public mind with the issues posed by a trial in progress. For example, a prosecutor's views on mercy killings would not likely be insulated by the absence of specific reference to an active prosecution against a doctor.

We do not hold that the article, in spite of its timing, was sufficiently prejudicial to cause the trial to be constitutionally unfair. There was no certainty, perhaps no more than a possibility, that the jury would be affected. We realize that our opinion may be construed by prosecutors as chilling their own freedom of speech and by defense counsel as a hunting license to seek out any published statements, present or past, of anyone associated, however indirectly, with the prosecution of his client. It therefore behooves us to emphasize the narrowness of the rule we announce today and clearly to state the conditions under which we will exercise our supervisory power and set aside a conviction in a case similar to the one at bar. The following factors are critical: the timing of the statement, the relationship of the prosecutor to the criminal trial, the prominence of the public statement, and the relationship of the published views to the issues in the prosecution.

The timing of the prosecutor's statement is particularly critical. We do not intend to foreclose a prosecutor from making public statements regarding questions of law enforcement when he is not associated with a pending criminal trial. We say this even though we recognize that a newspaper always may resurrect one of prosecutor's previous statements at a poignant moment. Statements that a prosecutor makes while a trial is pending and which foreseeably may be made public while the trial is pending, however, stand on a different footing. Because of the prosecutor's sensitive position and his duty to ensure a fair trial, we think that any statements made under such conditions must be carefully examined.

It follows that the rule we announce is necessarily confined to the statements of a prosecutor who is closely associated with the particular case, either because of his actual participation in it or because he is known by the jury to be an immediate supervisor of it. To take an extreme example, the Attorney General of the United States is not required to keep silent until such time as no criminal cases are being tried anywhere in the country. The world does not come to a halt because a criminal case is being tried. It is only those who are intimately associated with the ongoing prosecution who are under an obligation to take exceptional steps to avoid prejudicing it.

The final two factors go to the prejudicial effect of the statement as published. The prominence of the publicity is important because it, more than anything else, affects the likelihood of prejudice to the criminal defendant. An obscure item on the inside pages of a newspaper, it needs hardly be said, is less likely to place pressure on a jury than a banner headline on the front page. Finally, the nexus between the views as published and the issues in the pending trial must be close enough so that a reasonable person might see an obvious connection. If the views are general or the nexus remote or strained, the potential for prejudice is not realistic.

Here, the supervising prosecutor, who was known as such to the jury, made a public statement in the media while the trial was pending; the statement was given even further prominence in the newspaper during the trial and communicated to the majority of the jury; and it singled out for tougher treatment the very species of criminal cases that the jury was being called upon to decide. We think the integrity of the trial was needlessly impugned. In such circumstances the chief prosecutor goes public during trial at considerable risk. A majority of this court, as previously constituted, tolerated it once. Once was enough. In the exercise of our supervisory power we vacate the judgment and order a new trial.

Vacated and remanded.

PER CURIAM.

The government has filed a petition for rehearing. It concludes,

> If the prosecutor had known that the Singer case was going to the jury on Monday, and if the prosecutor had known that the Portland Press Herald was going to make a front-page story out of his remarks, and if the prosecutor had known that the story would focus on "white-collar crime," and if the prosecutor had known that his reference to that phrase would later be coupled to the Singer case, one would have to say that the prosecutor's control was indiscreet, to say the least. We submit, however, that none of these conditions applied here and that the timing of the regrettable publicity was wholly beyond the prosecutor's control.

We divide this in two parts.

Timing. It appears from the petition that the trial commenced on Monday, July 14; that on Thursday, July 17, the chief prosecutor, Mr. Mills, was interviewed as a "guest personality" by members of the media; that the interview was taped for subsequent broadcast; that Mr. Mills expected, or concededly, should have expected, that the broadcast "probably" would occur on Sunday, July 20; that the case went to the jury on Monday, following the newspaper publication; that on one occasion, six months prior, the court had submitted a case to the jury on a Saturday morning.

On this basis, with all due respect to the government, we cannot accept the claim that the "timing . . . was wholly beyond the prosecutor's control." There was no obligation on Mr. Mills' part, at least vis-a-vis the government, to appear as a guest speaker on this particular Thursday. On his own concession, release the following Sunday was probable, and, obviously, the next morning was when the broadcast would be reported in the press. There

902 Chapter IX The Prosecution Function

is no suggestion in the petition that he thought on Thursday that the case would go to the jury on Friday. Courts do not normally sit Saturdays. There is no suggestion that he in fact thought there would be an exception made in this case. Hence, rather than being beyond control, the timing of what the government concedes was regrettable publicity, was entirely foreseeable.

Subject Matter. The petition alleges that Mr. Mills "had . . . only minimal or incidental control over the televised interview." But clearly he had control over whether he gave the interview or not. Nor can it be thought that he did not have control over what he said. Equally difficult to understand is the allegation that he "had no control over the subject matter of the newspaper publicity." There is no claim of misquotation. The only contention is that the newspaper emphasized ("zeroed in on") some particular remarks. One would be highly unsophisticated to suppose that a paper does not find some remarks more newsworthy than others.

In sum, the petition does not support its above quoted conclusion, either as to timeliness, or as to subject matter. The most that could be said is that Mr. Mills may not have expected front page publicity. But we would be the last to suggest that a newspaper, assuming that something is printable, cannot choose the place and the manner. The petition almost suggests that we are interfering with a free press. A careful reading of our opinion shows that we said the reverse. It is because of the rights of the press that the prosecutor must choose a time to speak that will not interfere with his obligation of fairness to defendants.

This would be the end of the matter were it not for the content of a memorandum filed by the Department of Justice and the United States Attorneys elsewhere in this circuit which shows a misconception of what we have held. There is a vast difference between a United States Attorney's "keeping the public informed on the general administration of federal criminal justice in his district," and telling a jury that a particular judge before whom it is sitting imposes inadequate sentences in the type of case they are hearing. It is hornbook law that a judge cannot inform a jury in advance of the sentence he will impose. For reasons pointed out in our opinion, it may be even worse for the prosecutor to state that the sentence will be too small.

To answer the Department's memorandum, we would say the same thing, whether it be in a small district, or a large one. But by the same token, on rereading our opinion, we see no basis for saying that we have imposed a "gag rule" in any district. A United States Attorney is free at any time, for example, to state that the government is going to make a point of prosecuting white collar crimes. The difficulty came from what he added.

Axiomatically, as reflected in the American Bar Association Standards cited in our main opinion, a prosecutor must "not give . . . any extrajudicial statement or interview, relating to the trial or the parties or issues in the trial." In our opinion we have merely applied this proscription to views which, though not explicit references, are fraught with the same possibility of influencing the jury. This must include possibly jury-influencing statements about the judge. We cannot believe the government's memorandum that in a large district there may never be a time when such remarks may be made, but if that is so a prosecutor's obligation to provide a fair trial is more important than a right to publicize his opinions.

The petition for rehearing is denied.

NOTES AND QUESTIONS

1. Ah, newspapers. This case probably only makes sense if you are able to imagine or have heard about a time when most people learned of "the news" through newspapers;

C. Ethics and Accountability   **903**

that newspapers were read on a daily basis by most people; and that in some areas of the country—like Portland, Maine—a single local newspaper dominated a market and provided a common daily text for a significant portion of the community.

2. Was the district judge's voir dire adequate? Any indication that the trial judge's response to the defense motion reflected the fact that the judge felt personally disparaged by the United States attorney's comments in the interview? The First Circuit does not directly criticize the voir dire conducted by the district court but nonetheless concludes that the record does not eliminate the possibility that the "message of the headline" was received, and is skeptical that the jurors did not read the article.

3. Should the trial judge have pressed the jurors—maybe individually as opposed to collectively—on exactly how they came across the newspaper? Consider, if you can, the many different ways in which someone can "see" the front page of a newspaper, and even notice a picture or headline, without having either possession of the paper or the ability to read it. You could see the front page of the paper in your driveway or front porch or steps, delivered but unopened; you could see it displayed in a newsstand or vending machine; you could see the paper in someone else's hands as they read the interior. Shouldn't the trial judge have probed further?

4. The court notes three potential prejudicial effects of the headline "White Collar Criminals Get Off Easy":

> (a) of making a juror think of the case before him as one of a class in which there had been excessive leniency, and a challenge to exhibit appropriate toughness; (b) of perhaps increasing a juror's willingness to convict if he thought a lenient sentence might be imposed; and (c) of making a juror feel that public attention, because of the article, would be more sharply and critically directed to the ultimate verdict in the case at hand.

Do you see these risks as equally likely? As equally concerning?

5. The court emphasizes the narrowness of its decision, including that—apparently due to the functioning of the District of Maine's jury summonsing process—the jury had been in service for over six months and had, as a result, some direct contact with the U.S. attorney. Why is this factor important?

6. Why do you think the DOJ felt the need to move for a rehearing, with the support of Main Justice and all New England United States attorneys? What do you make of DOJ's argument that in large districts, with much more frequent trials, there may never be a time when a U.S. attorney can comment on "the general administration of federal criminal justice in his district"? What do you make of the court's response?

7. It is generally accepted that some level of publicity is appropriate for prosecutors under the "general deterrence" theory of criminal justice. For example, the DOJ through its U.S. Attorney's Offices generally issues a press release whenever an indictment is returned or a conviction is obtained by plea or verdict, and sometimes arrests or appellate victories are also publicized. These releases usually provide barebones information about the defendant (name, age, address), a summary of the charges and the event being publicized, and the identification of the prosecuting attorneys and law enforcement agencies involved.

8. Consider the text of the following press release, taken verbatim (except defendant's name is redacted) from the DOJ website on April 18, 2024:

> An Illinois man made his initial appearance today on an indictment returned by a federal grand jury in Chicago charging him with 21 counts of preparing false tax returns for others.
>
> According to the indictment, [REDACTED], of Homewood, allegedly operated We Are Taxes Inc., a return preparation business. For tax years 2017 through 2020, Taylor allegedly prepared returns for clients that contained false information resulting in the clients claiming refunds to which they were not entitled. The false information allegedly included, among other

things, fraudulent business losses and false deductions – including medical and dental expenses, gifts to charity and state and local real estate taxes – and unreimbursed employee expenses.

If convicted, [REDACTED] faces a maximum penalty of three years in prison for each count. A federal district court judge will determine any sentence after considering the U.S. Sentencing Guidelines and other statutory factors.

Acting Deputy Assistant Attorney General Stuart M. Goldberg of the Justice Department's Tax Division made the announcement. IRS Criminal Investigation is investigating the case. Assistant Chief Matthew J. Kluge and Trial Attorney Boris Bourget of the Tax Division are prosecuting the case.

An indictment is merely an allegation. All defendants are presumed innocent until proven guilty beyond a reasonable doubt in a court of law.

What do you make of the two sentences regarding potential punishment? Is the disclaimer regarding an indictment adequate? Need it include that an indictment is made by the grand jury? Need it include that the standard for an indictment is only probable cause?

CHAPTER X

THE DEPARTMENT OF JUSTICE AND THE PROSECUTION OF CIVIL RIGHTS CRIMES

Lawyers and others sometime think of "civil rights law" as the body of statutes and case law aimed at preventing and redressing discrimination. *Brown v. Board of Education. Loving v. Virginia.* The Civil Rights Act of 1964. Yet there also exists a body of civil rights law authorizing the federal prosecution of persons for civil rights violations, often called "civil rights crimes." Sometimes the same statutes that prohibit a certain type of civil rights offense, and authorize civil equitable relief and/or damages, also provide a criminal enforcement mechanism. In a related context, in regard to the federal Antipeonage Act, Justice Robert Jackson called Congress's use of this combination as raising "both a sword and a shield" in the civil rights cause. *Pollock v. Williams*, 322 U.S. 4, 7 (1942). *See* Chapter II *supra*

This chapter is largely and necessarily historical. It looks at the Department of Justice's history in the area of criminal civil rights enforcement. The department's track record in this regard is, frankly, underwhelming. To be fair, the department has not always had the best statutory weaponry available to it — the blame for this falls on the Supreme Court and Congress — but it has often been overly timid with what weaponry it has had or, worse, simply indifferent to civil rights enforcement. We will look at the department's intermittent flashes of energy and consider the reasons for its timidity and indifference.

Section A looks at the Reconstruction era legislation that enabled civil rights prosecutions. Section B considers the Grant Administration's valiant but short-lived efforts to enforce some of those statutes to protect former slaves from white supremacist terrorism during Reconstruction, a distant reminder of the potential for vigorous civil rights enforcement. Section C turns to the Supreme Court's role in rolling back the capacity of much Reconstruction legislation with a series of decisions beginning in the 1870s. Section D jumps ahead to a period of revival, again short-lived, of the Department of Justice's civil rights enforcement interest around the time of World War II, including the use of §§ 241 and 242 of Title 18, and the DOJ's experience in *Screws v. United States*, a case whose unfortunate legacy may still linger, justifiably or not. Section E considers the role of the Double Jeopardy Clause in the context of successive prosecutions, including civil rights prosecutions, and zeroes in on how the legacy of *Screws* and related discretionary principles bear on the use and potential use of 18 U.S.C. § 242 in recent high-profile police violence cases.

A. RECONSTRUCTION ERA CONGRESSIONAL CRIMINAL LEGISLATION

Professor Frederick Lawrence posits three categories of civil rights crimes: (1) bias crimes, that is, statutes that criminalize or provide enhanced punishment for crimes motivated by bias; (2) crimes prohibiting interference with the exercise of certain political or civil rights, or "rights-interference" crimes; and (3) unjustifiable official use of force crimes, for example, police brutality. *See generally* Frederick M. Lawrence, *Civil Rights and Criminal Wrongs: The Mens Rea of Civil Rights Crimes*, 67 Tul. L. Rev. 2116-17, 2133 (1993).

The second two categories of crimes were very much the focus of legislative attention by the Reconstruction Congress in the 1860s and 1870s. And while the Supreme Court substantially dismantled much of that Congress's work on both the civil and criminal fronts between 1873 and 1906, two of those Reconstruction era statutes — presently codified as 18 U.S.C. §§ 241 and 242 — have survived over the years and remain in use today.

The Civil Rights Act of 1866, Ch. 31, 14 Stat. 27. Section 2 of the Civil Rights Act of 1866 made it a federal crime for a person acting "under color of law" to deprive another of "any right secured or protected by the Constitution or laws of the United States." Section 2 is the precursor to the statute now codified at 18 U.S.C. § 242. The legislation was bitterly opposed by congressional Democrats on the grounds of both vagueness and federalism. President Johnson vetoed the bill, and for the first time in American history Congress overrode a presidential veto of a major statute. Lawrence, *Civil Rights and Criminal Wrongs, supra* at 2129-33.

The Enforcement Act of 1870, Ch. 114, 16 Stat. 140. Violence toward Black people and white southern unionists was endemic in the South after the Civil War. The Black Codes had begun to be installed. In 1866, racial altercations in New Orleans and Memphis escalated into wholesale massacres of Black people by white mobs. Violence was often visited upon Black people in connection with their attempts to vote. Accordingly, the focus of the Enforcement Act of 1870, including its 1871 amendment, Ch. 99, 16 Stat. 433, was voting rights. Criminal penalties were attached to several different forms of interference with the exercise of voting rights. For example, § 6 established the "rights interference" crime of conspiring to "injure, oppress, threaten or intimidate any citizen with intent to prevent or hinder his free exercise and enjoyment of any [federal] right or privilege." This provision was the precursor to 18 U.S.C. § 241.

The Ku Klux Klan Act of 1871, Ch. 22, 17 Stat. 13. This statute was Congress's response to the ever-increasing reign of terror in southern states by the Klan and other loosely aligned white supremacist organizations. Section 2 provided federal criminal sanctions for conspiracies to interfere with a long list of rights. Section 1 provided a civil damages remedy; it was the precursor to 42 U.S.C. § 1983. *See* Chapter VI *supra.*

Civil Rights Act of 1875, Ch. 114, 18 Stat. 335. This statute provided civil and criminal remedies for denial of access to public accommodations. It thus criminalized behavior that was neither "under color of law" nor directed at the exercise of a federal right. At the time of this statute's enactment the judicial dismantling of Reconstruction legislation had begun and the appetite for federal enforcement of civil rights legislation had declined. The statute was largely symbolic. Lawrence, *Civil Rights and Criminal Wrongs, supra* at 2162.

B. FEDERAL CRIMINAL ENFORCEMENT DURING RECONSTRUCTION

Prior to 1870 there was no Department of Justice. The post of attorney general had been created by the Judiciary Act of 1789, but the responsibilities of that job were modest (advising the President on legal issues and representing the United States in the Supreme Court), part-time (most attorneys general also had a private law practice), and the attorney general had no supervisory responsibility over the regional United States attorneys, sometimes called district attorneys. No one did, really. At times some authority was exercised over the U.S. attorneys by the Treasury Department, but for the most part they had discretion to bring or not bring prosecutions under (the very few) existing federal criminal statutes. *See generally* Jed Handelsman Shugarman, *The Creation of the Department of Justice: Professionalization Without Civil Rights or Civil Service*, 66 Stan. L. Rev. 121, 128-32 (2014).

Some have suggested that the Department of Justice was created for the purpose of protecting and enforcing the civil rights of former slaves, that is, that the DOJ's origins were part and parcel of Reconstruction. *See* Norman W. Spaulding, *Independence and Experimentalism in the Department of Justice*, 63 Stan. L. Rev. 409, 438 (2011); Seth P. Waxman, *Twins at Birth: Civil Rights and the Role of the Solicitor General*, 75 Ind. L.J. 1297, 1297, 1300-01 (2000). Others disagree. *See* Handelsman, *The Creation of the Department of Justice, supra* (disputing this theory and contending the department was created as part of an effort to professionalize legal practice).

Whatever the purpose motivating its creation, the new Department of Justice was born in the midst of a civil rights crisis. The late 1860s and early 1870s saw a significant increase in the Ku Klux Klan's reign of terror on Black people in the South. It was as if the Civil War was being continued by other means. The violence only worsened after the 1870 congressional elections, in which six Black persons were elected to Congress. State law enforcement authorities were unable or unwilling to exert control, and many state governors appealed directly to President Grant for federal law enforcement assistance under the new federal statutes. Grant was determined not to let the federal government be simply an observer to this retrenchment. Grant sent federal troops (back) into South Carolina in 1870 and later suspended the writ of habeas corpus in several South Carolina counties. Grant personally appeared before Congress to lobby for the passage of the 1871 Ku Klux Klan Act.

Grant also made two critical appointments. Just weeks after the Department of Justice was created in May 1870, he appointed Amos Akerman as attorney general and, shortly thereafter, appointed Benjamin Bristow to the newly created post of solicitor general, the number two position in the department. Both were southern Republicans. Akerman was from Georgia, although he had been born and raised in New Hampshire; Bristow was from Louisville, Kentucky, a so-called Kentucky Bluejay, who had served with Grant during the Civil War, including at the Battle of Shiloh. Appointed as a regional U.S. attorney after the war ended, he had developed a strong reputation on racial issues in bringing cases in Kentucky under the Civil Rights Act of 1866. Both Akerman and Bristow were as committed to staving off the Klan threat as Grant was.

Among the challenges facing Akerman and Bristow would be leading and directing the regional United States attorneys in the enforcement campaign, lawyers who until weeks earlier had been roving federal free agents unaccustomed to direction or oversight. Akerman wasted no time. Just weeks after taking office he wrote to all U.S. attorneys, federal marshals, and other federal personnel ordering them to "make[] it your special duty to initiate proceedings against all violators of [the Enforcement Act of 1870]. You will, therefore, whenever you receive from any source credible information that the law has been violated, take prompt measures for the arrest and effectual prosecution of the guilty party." R. Kaczorowski, The Politics

Amos T. Akerman   Benjamin Bristow

of Judicial Interpretation: The Federal Courts, Department of Justice, and Civil Rights, 1866-1876, at 64 (1985).

The challenges to aggressive enforcement of civil rights statutes in the southern states were substantial. The enthusiasm for the effort shared by Grant, Akerman, and Bristow was not uniform among all U.S. attorneys or even all federal judges. Witnesses, both Black and white, were afraid to testify. Grand juries were afraid to indict. Petit juries were afraid to convict. Federal resources were scarce; one impact of the new statute creating the Department of Justice was to implement cost-cutting measures on federal attorneys, including restrictions on the use of outside counsel. To meet these and other challenges, federal prosecutors began resorting to the practice, commonplace today, of providing immunity from prosecution for Klan members who cooperated in federal investigations and identified other Klan members.

There were some signs of success. Over three thousand indictments were returned and over a thousand convictions were obtained. Many sentences were short, or even suspended, however. The conviction success rate is not as low as it appears, though; in the chaos of the campaign many prosecutions were brought in haste and had to be dismissed, and when the prosecution effort subsided in 1874 many cases were simply abandoned. A collateral positive byproduct of the investigations and prosecutions was that most of the grand and petit juries that sat in them were racially mixed, as the Ku Klux Klan Act of 1871 prohibited from jury service persons who had been members of any conspiracy to deny the civil rights of Black people. Kermit L. Hall, *Political Power and Constitutional Legitimacy: The South Carolina Ku Klux Klan Trials, 1871-72*, 33 Emory L.J. 921, 938 & n.68 (1984).

Grant ultimately just ran out of gas and the enforcement campaign was abandoned. The campaign had always been expensive, and fiscal pressures on his administration mounted. Other political problems plagued him after his reelection in 1872. Still, order was restored

C. THE SUPREME COURT AND RECONSTRUCTION LEGISLATION

for a time, elections were safer for a time, and the Klan's power was diminished. As Senator Adelbert Ames, a Mississippi Republican, wrote:

> Had it not been for the Ku Klux law . . . we would not have had any showing at this election. At one time, just previous to the passage of that law, the K.K. organizations were being perfected in every county in the state. It is believed by our friends that had the law not been passed, not one of them would have been safe outside of the larger cities. As it is, the K.K.'s cowards as they are, have for a time at least suspended their operations in all but the Eastern parts of the state. Recent convictions in North Carolina and the President's action in putting a part of South Carolina under martial law has had a very subduing effect all over the South. It is perceptible here.

Ron Chernow, Grant 709-10 (2017). Chernow wrote that "the imperishable story of Grant's presidency was his campaign to crush the Klan." It was a noble effort that was abandoned too soon, although it is impossible to know how much more in the way of resources would have been necessary to make a material difference in the course of southern history.

For more on the Grant Administration's enforcement efforts *see generally* Ron Chernow, Grant, *supra* at xxiii, 700-11; E. Foner, Reconstruction: America's Unfinished Revolution 1863-1877, at 457-460 (1988); Hall, *Political Power and Constitutional Legitimacy, supra* at 921; Kaczorowski, The Politics of Judicial Interpretation, *supra*.

C. THE SUPREME COURT AND RECONSTRUCTION LEGISLATION

In a series of cases beginning in 1873, the Supreme Court proceeded to dismantle much of the work of the Reconstruction Congress. By the end of the decade, the promise of robust federal civil rights enforcement that had characterized the five-year period from 1866 to 1871 — or at least the legal capacity for such enforcement — was gone, and by the end of the century much of the work of all Reconstruction legislation had been dismantled.

This retrenchment was not a fait accompli. Professor Kaczorowski contends that prior to the Supreme Court's intervention most lower federal courts acknowledged the national re-ordering reflected in Reconstruction legislation. *See* Kaczorowski, The Politics of Judicial Interpretation, *supra* at 4-20.

> Regardless of whether judges approved or disapproved of the Civil Rights Act, they shared a common understanding of its intended objectives and scope. Judges expressed the belief that the act's congressional supporters intended to confer upon the federal courts complete authority directly and effectively to secure civil rights as federally enforceable rights of American citizenship.

Id. at 7.

The Slaughter-House Cases, **83 U.S. (16 Wall.) 36 (1873).** This was not a criminal case and did not arise under any of the Reconstruction statutes, yet its conception of federalism set the stage for cases to follow. Butchers in Louisiana brought a challenge under the Thirteenth and Fourteenth Amendments to a statute that created a state-chartered monopoly over cattle-slaughtering facilities in New Orleans. The butchers claimed that this arrangement created a condition of "involuntary servitude" under the Thirteenth Amendment inasmuch as it restricted their freedom to work, and also infringed on their "privileges and immunities" under the Fourteenth Amendment. The Court rejected both arguments, holding that the Fourteenth Amendment protected only rights pertaining purely to national citizenship, such as the access to navigable waterways or the right to run for national office.

United States v. Cruikshank, 92 U.S. 542 (1876). This case made clear the ramifications of *The Slaughter-House Cases* for federal criminal enforcement. In connection with a contested state election in Louisiana in 1872, and the establishment of parallel Democrat and Republican governments in the state, a group of armed whites in the village of Colfax invaded the enclave of the Republican government and massacred as many as 280 Black persons. The Colfax Massacre was of such moment that the Department of Justice, even though it had begun to de-escalate its criminal enforcement campaign, investigated the matter and obtained 97 indictments under the Enforcement Act of 1870. Nine defendants (many had fled) were found and tried, with only limited success, and even that was short-lived. The Supreme Court ultimately found all of the indictments invalid on one of two grounds: (1) the indictments failed to specifically allege racial animus or, more fatally, (2) they were beyond the government's constitutional powers, which are limited to protecting against state interference with federal rights. The Court's opinion is notable in that it says virtually nothing about the language, purpose, or context of the Enforcement Act, nor did it acknowledge that there had been a Civil War.

United States v. Reese, 92 U.S. 214 (1876). Decided the same day as *Cruikshank, Reese* invalidated a conviction under the Enforcement Act of 1870 based on an allegation that Lexington, Kentucky voting officials had interfered with the voting rights of Black people in its administration of a poll tax. The Court held that the Fifteenth Amendment did not guarantee a right to vote per se, but only prohibited discrimination in the exercise of the right based on race. Accordingly, the Court found that the provisions of the Enforcement Act criminalizing interference with voting rights, generally, were unconstitutional.

The Civil Rights Cases, 109 U.S. 3 (1883). The Court here held that both the criminal and civil provisions of the Civil Rights Act of 1875 were unconstitutional inasmuch as they regulated private conduct. Writing for the Court, Justice Bradley held forth on his personal views of Reconstruction legislation:

> When a man has emerged from slavery, and by the aid of beneficent legislation has shaken off the inseparable concomitants of that state, there must be some stage in the progress of his elevation when he takes the rank of a mere citizen, and ceases to be the special favorite of the laws, and when his rights as a citizen, or a man, are to be protected in the ordinary modes by which other men's rights are protected.

Id. at 25. Justice Bradley wrote this sentence 18 years after the end of the Civil War. For a different perspective on Black people "shaking it off," consider President Johnson's 1965 remarks 82 years later at Howard University's commencement:

> That beginning is freedom; and the barriers to that freedom are tumbling down. Freedom is the right to share, share fully and equally, in American society — to vote, to hold a job, to enter a public place, to go to school. . . . But freedom is not enough. You do not wipe away the scars of centuries by saying: Now you are free to go where you want, and do as you desire, and choose the leaders you please. You do not take a person who, for years, has been hobbled by chains and liberate him, bring him up to the starting line of a race and then say, "you are free to compete with all the others," and still justly believe that you have been completely fair. Thus it is not enough just to open the gates of opportunity. All our citizens must have the ability to walk through those gates.

Lyndon B. Johnson, Commencement Address at Howard University: To Fulfill These Rights, LBJ Presidential Library (June 4, 1965), http://www.lbjlib.utexas.edu/johnson/archives.hom /speeches.hom/650604.asp.

Justice Harlan wrote a dissenting opinion in *The Civil Rights Cases* that rivaled his more famous dissent to come 13 years later in *Plessy v. Ferguson,* 163 U.S. 537 (1896). In his view, the Thirteenth Amendment empowered the federal government to protect the freed slaves even if doing so encroached upon traditional spheres of state sovereignty. Justice Harlan also argued that the federal power to do so should be as extensive as constitutional power had previously been in protecting the institution of slavery. 109 U.S. at 36-40. Professor Kaczorowski has suggested that Justice Harlan's perspective may have been influenced by his work as a special prosecutor in *United States v. Reese. See* Kaczorowski, The Politics of Judicial Interpretation, *supra* at 201.

United States v. Harris, 106 U.S. 29 (1883). In *Harris,* the Court struck down, on reasoning similar to that in *The Civil Rights Cases,* § 2 of the Ku Klux Klan Act, which had criminalized conspiring to deprive another of the "equal protection of the laws."

And so things stood as the century drew to a close. There was precious little federal prosecution of civil rights offenses between the Grant and Franklin Roosevelt Administrations. To some extent this was a matter of statutory weaponry, or lack thereof, due to the Supreme Court cases described above and Congress's consistent failure to pass anti-lynching legislation or any other civil rights enforcement legislation. The few cases that were brought under the statutory survivors of the Reconstruction era featured egregious facts and violations of rights that were specifically and unambiguously federal in nature, such as serving on juries or voting in federal elections. *See, e.g., Ex parte Virginia,* 100 U.S. 339, 349 (1880) (affirming conviction of state judge for denying Black citizens the right to serve as jurors in state court); *Ex parte Yarbrough,* 110 U.S. 651, 655-57 (1884) (upholding the conviction of nine white men under the Enforcement Act of 1870 for beating a Black man because he had voted in a federal congressional election); *United States v. Waddell,* 112 U.S. 76, 80-81 (1884) (affirming conviction for deprivation of right to establish claim to federal lands under Homestead Act); *United States v. Mosley,* 238 U.S. 383, 386-88 (1915) (upholding indictments of Oklahoma officials for conspiring to skew results in a federal congressional election). *See generally* Lawrence, *Civil Rights and Criminal Wrongs, supra* at 2133, 2166-69.

An exception to the 70 years of underenforcement was a flurry of investigations and prosecutions in the first two decades of the twentieth century under the Antipeonage Act of 1867, a federal statute enacted in connection with the acquisition of the New Mexico territory. *See* Chapter II *supra.* The statute aimed to eliminate the system of vassalage that had evolved under Spanish rule in New Mexico, whereby workers were held in conditions of involuntary servitude in liquidation of debts or other monetary obligations. The language of the act was broad enough to cover peonage-like relationships that had led to the virtual reenslavement of Black people in the South after the Civil War. When the peonage practices in the South were exposed around the turn of the century by progressive journalists, a handful of progressive southern judges and the Department of Justice, intermittently, brought some prosecutions. *See generally* Benno C. Schmidt Jr., *Principle and Prejudice in the Progressive Era. Part 2: The Peonage Cases,* 82 Colum. L. Rev. 646 (1983).

D. THE DEPARTMENT OF JUSTICE CIVIL RIGHTS SECTION AND THE DISAPPOINTMENT OF *SCREWS v. UNITED STATES*

In 1939 Roosevelt appointed progressive Frank Murphy of Michigan to be his attorney general. Murphy had been a federal prosecutor in Michigan during Prohibition, as well as mayor of Detroit and governor of Michigan, and as a state court trial judge had famously presided over the trials of Ossian and Henry Sweet, two Black brothers who were acquitted by an all-white jury of murder charges based on their firing of a gun into a crowd of white rioters storming their home.

Ossian Sweet

Ossian Sweet home

In his one year as attorney general before being appointed to the Supreme Court, Murphy was responsible for the creation of the Civil Rights Section within the Department of Justice. In the order establishing the section (originally called the Civil Liberties Unit but renamed in 1941 to avoid confusion with the ACLU), Murphy stated:

> The function and purpose of this unit will be to make a study of the provisions of the Constitution of the United States and Acts of Congress relating to civil rights with reference to present conditions, and to direct, supervise and conduct prosecutions of violations of the provisions of the Constitution or Acts of Congress guaranteeing civil rights to individuals.

Order of the Attorney General No. 3204, February 3, 1939. The reference to "mak[ing] a study" of the relevant law suggests that the Department's civil rights project was starting, if not from scratch, at least anew.

One of the section's first prosecutions arose out of alleged voting irregularities in the Louisiana Democratic primary in connection with a special election held after the 1935 assassination of Senator Huey Long, the populist Roosevelt opponent and potential 1936 presidential candidate.

United States v. Classic
313 U.S. 299 (1941)

Mr. Justice STONE delivered the opinion of the Court.

Two counts of an indictment found in a federal district court charged that appellees, Commissioners of Elections, conducting a primary election under Louisiana law, to nominate a candidate of the Democratic Party for representative in Congress, willfully altered and falsely counted and certified the ballots of voters cast in the primary election. The questions for decision are whether the right of qualified voters to vote in the Louisiana primary and to have their ballots counted is a right "secured . . . by the Constitution" within the meaning of ss 19 and 20 of the Criminal Code, and whether the acts of appellees charged in the indictment violate those sections.

On September 25, 1940, appellees were indicted in the District Court for Eastern Louisiana for violations of ss 19 and 20 of the Criminal Code, 18 U.S.C. ss 51, 52, 18 U.S.C.A. § 51, 52. The first count of the indictment alleged that a primary election was held on September 10,

D. The Department of Justice Civil Rights Section and the Disappointment of *Screws v. United States* **913**

1940, for the purpose of nominating a candidate of the Democratic Party for the office of Representative in Congress for the Second Congressional District of Louisiana, to be chosen at an election to be held on November 10th; that in that district nomination as a candidate of the Democratic Party is and always has been equivalent to an election; that appellees were Commissioners of Election, selected in accordance with the Louisiana law to conduct the primary in the Second Precinct of the Tenth Ward of New Orleans, in which there were five hundred and thirty-seven citizens and qualified voters.

The charge based on these allegations, was that the appellees conspired with each other and with others unknown, to injure and oppress citizens in the free exercise and enjoyment of rights and privileges secured to them by the Constitution and Laws of the United States, namely, (1) the right of qualified voters who cast their ballots in the primary election to have their ballots counted as cast for the candidate of their choice, and (2) the right of the candidates to run for the office of Congressman and to have the votes in favor of their nomination counted as cast. The overt acts alleged were that the appellees altered eighty-three ballots cast for one candidate and fourteen cast for another, marking and counting them as votes for a third candidate, and that they falsely certified the number of votes cast for the respective candidates to the chairman of the Second Congressional District Committee.

The second count, repeating the allegations of fact already detailed, charged that the appellees, as Commissioners of Election willfully and under color of law subjected registered voters at the primary who were inhabitants of Louisiana to the deprivation of rights, privileges and immunities secured and protected by the Constitution and Laws of the United States, namely their right to cast their votes for the candidates of their choice and to have their votes counted as cast. It further charged that this deprivation was effected by the willful failure and refusal of defendants to count the votes as cast, by their alteration of the ballots, and by their false certification of the number of votes cast for the respective candidates in the manner already indicated.

The District Court sustained a demurrer to counts 1 and 2 on the ground that ss 19 and 20 of the Criminal Code under which the indictment was drawn do not apply to the state of facts disclosed by the indictment and that, if applied to those facts, ss 19 and 20 are without constitutional sanction.

Section 19 of the Criminal Code condemns as a criminal offense any conspiracy to injure a citizen in the exercise "of any right or privilege secured to him by the Constitution or laws of the United States." Section 20 makes it a penal offense for anyone who, "acting under color of any law" "willfully subjects, or causes to be subjected, any inhabitant of any State . . . to the deprivation of any rights, privileges, or immunities secured or protected by the Constitution and laws of the United States." The Government argues that the right of a qualified voter in a Louisiana congressional primary election to have his vote counted as cast is a right secured by Article I, ss 2 and 4 of the Constitution, and that a conspiracy to deprive the citizen of that right is a violation of § 19, and also that the willful action of appellees as state officials, in falsely counting the ballots at the primary election and in falsely certifying the count, deprived qualified voters of that right and of the equal protection of the laws guaranteed by the Fourteenth Amendment, all in violation of § 20 of the Criminal Code.

• • •

Unless the constitutional protection of the integrity of "elections" extends to primary elections, Congress is left powerless to effect the constitutional purpose, and the popular choice of representatives is stripped of its constitutional protection save only as Congress, by taking over the control of state elections, may exclude from them the influence of the state primaries. Such an expedient would end that state autonomy with respect to elections which the Constitution contemplated that Congress should be free to leave undisturbed, subject only to such minimum regulation as it should find necessary to insure the freedom and integrity of the choice. Words, especially those of a constitution, are not to be read with such stultifying narrowness. The words of ss 2 and 4 of Article I, read in the sense which is plainly permissible and in the light of the constitutional purpose, require us to hold that a primary election which involves a necessary step in the choice of candidates for election as representatives in Congress, and which in the circumstances of this case controls that choice, is an election within the meaning of the constitutional provision and is subject to congressional regulation as to the manner of holding it.

Not only does § 4 of Article I authorize Congress to regulate the manner of holding elections, but by Article I, § 8, Clause 18, Congress is given authority "To make all Laws which shall be necessary and proper for carrying into Execution the foregoing Powers and all other Powers vested by this Constitution in the Government of the United States, or in any Department or Officer thereof." This provision leaves to the Congress the choice of means by which its constitutional powers are to be carried into execution. "Let the end be legitimate, let it be within the scope of the constitution, and all means which are appropriate, which are plainly adapted to that end, which are not prohibited, but consist with the letter and spirit of the constitution, are constitutional." *McCulloch v. Maryland.* That principle has been consistently adhered to and liberally applied, and extends to the congressional power by appropriate legislation to safeguard the right of choice by the people of representatives in Congress secured by § 2 of Article I.

There remains the question whether ss 19 and 20 are an exercise of the congressional authority applicable to the acts with which appellees are charged in the indictment. Section 19 makes it a crime to conspire to "injure" or "oppress" any citizen "in the free exercise of any right or privilege secured to him by the Constitution." In *Ex parte Yarbrough, supra*, and in *Mosley, supra*, as we have seen, it was held that the right to vote in a congressional election is a right secured by the Constitution, and that a conspiracy to prevent the citizen from voting or to prevent the official count of his ballot when cast, is a conspiracy to injure and oppress the citizen in the free exercise of a right secured by the Constitution within the meaning of § 19. In reaching this conclusion the Court found no uncertainty or ambiguity in the statutory language, obviously devised to protect the citizen "in the free exercise . . . of any right or privilege secured to him by the Constitution," and concerned itself with the question whether the right to participate in choosing a representative is so secured. Such is our function here. Conspiracy to prevent the official count of a citizen's ballot, held in *Mosley, supra*, to be a violation of § 19 in the case of a congressional election, is equally a conspiracy to injure and oppress the citizen when the ballots are cast in a primary election prerequisite to the choice of party candidates for a congressional election. In both cases the right infringed is one secured by the Constitution. The injury suffered by the citizen in the exercise of the right is an injury which the statute describes and to which it applies in the one case as in the other.

The suggestion that § 19, concededly applicable to conspiracies to deprive electors of their votes at congressional elections, is not sufficiently specific to be deemed applicable to primary elections, will hardly bear examination. Section 19 speaks neither of elections nor of primaries. In unambiguous language it protects "any right or privilege secured . . . by the Constitution," a phrase which as we have seen extends to the right of the voter to have his vote counted in both the general election and in the primary election, where the latter is a part of the election machinery, as well as to numerous other constitutional rights which are wholly unrelated to the choice of a representative in Congress.

In the face of the broad language of the statute, we are pointed to no principle of statutory construction and to no significant legislative history which could be thought to sanction our saying that the statute applies any the less to primaries than to elections, where in one as in the other it is the same constitutional right which is infringed. It does not avail to attempt to distinguish the protection afforded by § 1 of the Civil Rights Act of 1871, to the right to participate in primary as well as general elections, secured to all citizens by the Constitution on the ground that in those cases the injured citizens were Negroes whose rights were clearly protected by the Fourteenth Amendment. At least since *Ex parte Yarbrough, supra,* and no member of the Court seems ever to have questioned it, the right to participate in the choice of representatives in Congress has been recognized as a right protected by Art. I, ss 2 and 4 of the Constitution. Differences of opinion have arisen as to the effect of the primary in particular cases on the choice of representatives. But we are troubled by no such doubt here. Hence, the right to participate through the primary in the choice of representatives in Congress — a right clearly secured by the Constitution — is within the words and purpose of § 19 in the same manner and to the same extent as the right to vote at the general election. *Mosley.* It is no extension of the criminal statute, as it was not of the civil statute in *Nixon v. Herndon, supra,* to find a violation of it in a new method of interference with the right which its words protect. For it is the constitutional right, regardless of the method of interference, which is the subject of the statute and which in precise terms it protects from injury and oppression.

It is hardly the performance of the judicial function to construe a statute, which in terms protects a right secured by the Constitution, here the right to choose a representative in Congress, as applying to an election whose only function is to ratify a choice already made at the primary but as having no application to the primary which is the only effective means of choice. To withdraw from the scope of the statute, an effective interference with the constitutional right of choice, because other wholly different situations not now before us may not be found to involve such an interference is to say that acts plainly within the statute should be deemed to be without it because other hypothetical cases may later be found not to infringe the constitutional right with which alone the statute is concerned.

If a right secured by the Constitution may be infringed by the corrupt failure to include the vote at a primary in the official count, it is not significant that the primary, like the voting machine, was unknown when § 19 was adopted. Abuse of either may infringe the right and therefore violate § 19. Nor does the fact that in circumstances not here present there may be difficulty in determining whether the primary so affects the right of the choice as to bring it within the constitutional protection, afford any ground for doubting the construction and application of the statute once the constitutional question is resolved. That difficulty is inherent in the judicial administration of every federal criminal statute, for none, whatever its terms, can be applied beyond the reach of the congressional power which the Constitution confers.

The right of the voters at the primary to have their votes counted is, as we have stated, a right or privilege secured by the Constitution, and to this § 20 also gives protection. The alleged acts of appellees were committed in the course of their performance of duties under the Louisiana statute requiring them to count the ballots, to record the result of the count, and to certify the result of the election. Misuse of power, possessed by virtue of state law and made possible only because the wrongdoer is clothed with the authority of state law, is action taken 'under color of' state law. Here the acts of appellees infringed the constitutional right and deprived the voters of the benefit of it within the meaning of § 20, unless by its terms its application is restricted to deprivations "on account of (an) inhabitant being an alien, or by reason of his color, or race."

The last clause of § 20 protects inhabitants of a state from being subjected to different punishments, pains or penalties by reason of alienage, color or race, than are prescribed for the punishment of citizens. That the qualification with respect to alienage, color and race, refers only to differences in punishment and not to deprivations of any rights or privileges secured by the Constitution, is evidenced by the structure of the section and the necessities of the practical application of its provisions. The qualification as to alienage, color and race, is a parenthetical phrase in the clause penalizing different punishments "than are prescribed for . . . citizens" and in the common use of language could refer only to the subject matter of the clause and not to that of the earlier one relating to the deprivation of rights to which it makes no reference in terms.

Moreover the prohibited differences of punishment on account of alienage, color or race, are those referable to prescribed punishments which are to be compared with those prescribed for citizens. A standard is thus set up applicable to differences in prescribed punishments on account of alienage, color or race, which it would be difficult if not impossible to apply to the willful deprivations of constitutional rights or privileges, in order to determine whether they are on account of alienage, color or race. We think that § 20 authorizes the punishment of two different offenses. The one is willfully subjecting any inhabitant to the deprivation of rights secured by the Constitution; the other is willfully subjecting any inhabitant to different punishments on account of his color or race, than are prescribed for the punishment of citizens. The meager legislative history of the section supports this conclusion.

So interpreted § 20 applies to deprivation of the constitutional rights of qualified voters to choose representatives in Congress. The generality of the section made applicable as it is to deprivations of any constitutional right, does not obscure its meaning or impair its force within the scope of its application, which is restricted by its terms to deprivations which are willfully inflicted by those acting under color of any law, statute and the like.

We do not discuss the application of § 20 to deprivations of the right to equal protection of the laws guaranteed by the Fourteenth Amendment, a point apparently raised and discussed for the first time in the Government's brief in this Court. The point was not specially considered or decided by the court below, and has not been assigned as error by the Government. Since the indictment on its face does not purport to charge a deprivation of equal protection to voters or candidates, we are not called upon to construe the indictment in order to raise a question of statutory validity or construction which we are alone authorized to review upon this appeal.

Reversed.

NOTES AND QUESTIONS

1. The defendants in *Classic* were prosecuted under §§ 19 and 20 of Title 18 of the United States Code, the statutory precursors to 18 U.S.C. §§ 241 and 242. The bulk of the majority's opinion focused on whether federal voting rights encompassed the right to vote in the state-administered Democratic primary election, which would determine the candidate for the general election, and thereby fell within the conduct proscribed by §§ 19 and 20. As a practical matter in Louisiana at the time, the Democratic primary winner would be the general election winner. How much does this political reality matter to the Court's result?

2. The Court ultimately answers the question regarding federal voting rights in the affirmative, channeling (but not citing) *Marbury v. Madison* and urging the reader to "remember that it is a constitution we are expounding," and that the Constitution's words are not to be read as "legislative codes." Great. But isn't it also a "legislative code," namely, §§ 19 and 20, that are really — or at least also — being interpreted here? Does the Court not take seriously enough the argument — based on the principle of fair notice — that the statutes are not sufficiently specific to cover state-administered primary elections? Is it plausible that a local Louisiana election official working in a state primary would not comprehend that his misconduct would violate a federal right? Is proof of that mental state — knowledge of the violation of a federal law — necessary for a conviction?

3. The Court elegantly dispatches the defendants' argument that their actions were not "under color of law":

> The alleged acts of appellees were committed in the course of their performance of duties under the Louisiana statute requiring them to count the ballots, to record the result of the count, and to certify the result of the election. Misuse of power, possessed by virtue of state law and made possible only because the wrongdoer is clothed with the authority of state law, is action taken "under color of" state law.

The Court's primary support for this proposition was the prosecution and conviction it had upheld 50 years previously in *Ex parte Virginia*, 100 U.S. 339, 349 (1880), where a state court judge was prosecuted and convicted for refusing to empanel a Black juror. The Court also held, as to the objection that §§ 19 and 20 swept too broadly, that the "under color of law" language restricted the statutes' application.

What are the implications of judges having criminal exposure under these federal civil rights statutes? While the conviction in *Ex parte Virginia* was based on a defiant breach of legal obligation, what problems do you see lurking in the gray area of a federal statute that criminalizes judicial conduct?

4. Justice Douglas wrote a dissenting opinion, joined by Justices Black and Murphy, focusing mainly on the specificity issue. While he did not take the position that the purely federal voting cases in the past (e.g., *Yarborough* and *Mosley*) had been wrongly decided, he thought the inference necessary to extend that federal right to state primary elections was too attenuated.

5. Justice Douglas also noted the "perilous territory" the Court was entering here inasmuch as in the United States there are no common law criminal offenses. Why are common law offenses prohibited? Can §§ 19 and 20 be characterized as creating what are essentially common law offenses?

Classic, though important in its reaffirmation of the vitality of §§ 19 and 20 of Title 18, and in the breadth of its interpretation of "under color of law," was something of a warm-up for the new Civil Rights Section. As fascism advanced in Europe in the 1930s, many Americans were awakened to their own country's shortcomings on civil rights. Tom C. Clark, *A Federal Prosecutor Looks at the Civil Rights Statutes*, 47 Colum. L. Rev. 176, 180 (1947). Attorney General Murphy had created the section in order "to send the message that the full authority of federal law enforcement was poised to protect the civil rights of oppressed minorities." Robert K. Carr, Federal Protection of Civil Rights: Quest for a Sword 25 n.37 (1947). It was the civil rights of these "oppressed minorities" that were intended to be the section's focus.

President Roosevelt himself, although previously ambivalent on civil rights, was under wartime pressure during the early 1940s due to Axis propaganda about the sorry state of American race relations. Accordingly, the President personally encouraged the Department of Justice under Francis Biddle and the FBI under J. Edgar Hoover to investigate and prosecute police brutality and lynching cases in the South. Beverly Gage, G-Man: J. Edgar Hoover and the Making of the American Century 311 (2022). While Hoover was no proponent of racial equality, lynching and police misconduct were offensive to his sense of order and his dislike of vigilantism, and the FBI made some reasonably good faith efforts to investigate racial violence in the South. *Id.* at 304-11. But investigations in Brownsville, Texas (of the murder of an NAACP official), and of the lynching of prisoners in state custody in Sikeston, Missouri, and Shubuta, Mississippi, all failed due to what would become familiar factors: a lack of cooperation from local law enforcement; witnesses' reluctance to cooperate, including Black witnesses who feared retaliation; grand juries' refusals to indict; and trial juries' refusals to convict. These were some of the same factors hindering federal civil rights criminal enforcement in the South in the 1870s.

Chapter X The Department of Justice and the Prosecution of Civil Rights Crimes

A rare exception to the FBI's dismal record in the 1940s was the 1945 case of Georgia sheriff Claude Screws. Sheriff Screws brutally beat and murdered one Robert Hall—perhaps due to a longstanding grievance, perhaps due to Hall's civil rights activity, but brutally murdered him nonetheless. This was a perfect test case for the Civil Rights Section, the civil rights "sword" it had long been looking for. Carr, Federal Protection of Civil Rights, *supra* at 25. In what many hoped was a breakthrough win for the FBI and the Department of Justice, Sheriff Screws was indicted by a federal grand jury of Georgians and convicted at trial by a federal petit jury of Georgians. The conviction was affirmed by the Fifth Circuit on appeal.

It was too good to be true.

Screws v. United States
325 U.S. 91 (1945)

Mr. Justice DOUGLAS announced the judgment of the Court and delivered the following opinion, in which THE CHIEF JUSTICE, Mr. Justice BLACK, and Mr. Justice REED, concur.

This case involves a shocking and revolting episode in law enforcement. Petitioner Screws was sheriff of Baker County, Georgia. He enlisted the assistance of petitioner Jones, a policeman, and petitioner Kelley, a special deputy, in arresting Robert Hall, a citizen of the United States and of Georgia. The arrest was made late at night at Hall's home on a warrant charging Hall with theft of a tire. Hall, a young negro about thirty years of age, was handcuffed and taken by car to the court house. As Hall alighted from the car at the court house square, the three petitioners began beating him with their fists and with a solid-bar blackjack about eight inches long and weighing two pounds. They claimed Hall had reached for a gun and had used insulting language as he alighted from the car. But after Hall, still handcuffed, had been knocked to the ground they continued to beat him from fifteen to thirty minutes until he was unconscious. Hall was then dragged feet first through the court house yard into the jail and thrown upon the floor dying. An ambulance was called and Hall was removed to a hospital where he died within the hour and without regaining consciousness. There was evidence that Screws held a grudge against Hall and had threatened to "get" him.

An indictment was returned against petitioners—one count charging a violation of § 20 of the Criminal Code, 18 U.S.C. § 52, 18 U.S.C.A. § 52, and another charging a conspiracy to violate § 20 contrary to § 37 of the Criminal Code, 18 U.S.C. § 88, 18 U.S.C.A. § 88. Sec. 20 provides:

> Whoever, under color of any law, statute, ordinance, regulation, or custom, will-fully subjects, or causes to be subjected, any inhabitant of any State, Territory, or District to the deprivation of any rights, privileges, or immunities secured or protected by the Constitution and laws of the United States, or to different punishments, pains, or penalties, on account of such inhabitant being an alien, or by reason of his color, or race, than are prescribed for the punishment of citizens, shall be fined not more than $1,000, or imprisoned not more than one year, or both.

The indictment charged that petitioners, acting under color of the laws of Georgia, "willfully" caused Hall to be deprived of "rights, privileges, or immunities secured or protected" to him by the Fourteenth Amendment—the right not to be deprived of life without due process of law; the right to be tried, upon the charge on which he was arrested, by due process of law and if found guilty to be punished in accordance with the laws of Georgia; that is to say that petitioners "unlawfully and wrongfully did assault, strike and beat the said Robert Hall about the head with human fists and a blackjack causing injuries" to Hall "which were the proximate and immediate cause of his death." A like charge was made in the conspiracy count.

D. The Department of Justice Civil Rights Section and the Disappointment of *Screws v. United States* **919**

The case was tried to a jury. The court charged the jury that due process of law gave one charged with a crime the right to be tried by a jury and sentenced by a court. On the question of intent it charged that ". . . if these defendants, without its being necessary to make the arrest effectual or necessary to their own personal protection, beat this man, assaulted him or killed him while he was under arrest, then they would be acting illegally under color of law, as stated by this statute, and would be depriving the prisoner of certain constitutional rights guaranteed to him by the Constitution of the United States and consented to by the State of Georgia."

The jury returned a verdict of guilty and a fine and imprisonment on each count was imposed. The Circuit Court of Appeals affirmed the judgment of conviction, one judge dissenting. The case is here on a petition for a writ of certiorari which we granted because of the importance in the administration of the criminal laws of the questions presented.

I

We are met at the outset with the claim that § 20 is unconstitutional, in so far as it makes criminal acts in violation of the due process clause of the Fourteenth Amendment. The argument runs as follows: It is true that this Act as construed in *Classic*, was upheld in its application to certain ballot box frauds committed by state officials. But in that case the constitutional rights protected were the rights to vote specifically guaranteed by Art. I, § 2 and § 4 of the Constitution. Here there is no ascertainable standard of guilt. There have been conflicting views in the Court as to the proper construction of the due process clause. The majority have quite consistently construed it in broad general terms. Thus it was stated in *Twining*, that due process requires that "no change in ancient procedure can be made which disregards those fundamental principles, to be ascertained from time to time by judicial action, which have relation to process of law, and protect the citizen in his private right, and guard him against the arbitrary action of government." In *Snyder v. Massachusetts*, it was said that due process prevents state action which "offends some principle of justice so rooted in the traditions and conscience of our people as to be ranked as fundamental." And the same idea was recently phrased as follows: "The phrase formulates a concept less rigid and more fluid than those envisaged in other specific and particular provisions of the Bill of Rights. Its application is less a matter of rule. Asserted denial is to be tested by an appraisal of the totality of facts in a given case. That which may, in one setting, constitute a denial of fundamental fairness, shocking to the universal sense of justice, may, in other circumstances, and in the light of other considerations, fall short of such denial." *Betts v. Brady*.

It is said that the Act must be read as if it contained those broad and fluid definitions of due process and that if it is so read it provides no ascertainable standard of guilt. It is pointed out that in *United States v. L. Cohen Grocery Co.*, an Act of Congress was struck down, the enforcement of which would have been "the exact equivalent of an effort to carry out a statute which in terms merely penalized and punished all acts detrimental to the public interest when unjust and unreasonable in the estimation of the court and jury." In that case the act declared criminal was the making of "any unjust or unreasonable rate or charge in handling or dealing in or with any necessaries." The Act contained no definition of an "unjust or unreasonable rate" nor did it refer to any source where the measure of "unjust or unreasonable" could be ascertained. In the instant case the decisions of the courts are, to be sure, a source of reference for ascertaining the specific content of the concept of due process. But even so the Act would incorporate by reference a large body of changing and uncertain law. That law is not always reducible to specific rules, is expressible only in general terms, and turns many times on the facts of a particular case. Accordingly, it is argued that such a body of legal principles lacks the basic specificity necessary for criminal statutes under our system of government. Congress did not define what it desired to punish but referred the citizen to a comprehensive law library in order to ascertain what acts were prohibited. To enforce such a statute would be like sanctioning the practice of Caligula who "published the law, but it was written in a very small hand, and posted up in a corner, so that no one could make a copy of it." Suetonius, Lives of the Twelve Caesars, p. 278.

The serious character of that challenge to the constitutionality of the Act is emphasized if the customary standard of guilt for statutory crimes is taken. As we shall see specific intent is at times required. But the general rule was stated as follows: "If a man intentionally adopts certain conduct in certain circumstances known to him, and that conduct is forbidden by the law under those circumstances, he intentionally breaks the law in the only sense in which the law ever considers intent." Under that test a local law enforcement officer violates § 20 and commits a federal offense for which he can be sent to the penitentiary if he does an act which some court later holds deprives a person of due process of law. And he is a criminal though his motive was pure and though his purpose was unrelated to the disregard of any constitutional guarantee. The treacherous ground on which state officials—police, prosecutors, legislators, and judges—would walk is indicated by the character and closeness of decisions of this Court interpreting the due process clause of the Fourteenth Amendment. A confession obtained by too long questioning (*Ashcraft v. Tennessee*); the enforcement of an ordinance requiring a license for the distribution of religious literature (*Murdock v. Pennsylvania*); the denial of the assistance of counsel in certain types of cases (*Cf. Powell v. Alabama*); the enforcement of certain types of anti-picketing statutes (*Thornhill v. Alabama*); the enforcement of state price control laws (*Olsen v. Nebraska*); the requirement that public school children salute the flag (*West Virginia State Board of Education v. Barnette*)—these are illustrative of the kind of state action which might or might not be caught in the broad reaches of § 20 dependent on the prevailing view of the Court as constituted when the case arose. Those who enforced local law today might not know for many months (and meanwhile could not find out) whether what they did deprived some one of due process of law. The enforcement of a criminal statute so construed would indeed cast law enforcement agencies loose at their own risk on a vast uncharted sea.

If such a construction is not necessary, it should be avoided. This Court has consistently favored that interpretation of legislation which supports its constitutionality. That reason is impelling here so that if at all possible § 20 may be allowed to serve its great purpose—the protection of the individual in his civil liberties.

Sec. 20 was enacted to enforce the Fourteenth Amendment. It derives from § 2 of the Civil Rights Act of April 9, 1866, 14 Stat. 27. Senator Trumbull, chairman of the Senate Judiciary Committee which reported the bill, stated that its purpose was "to protect all persons in the United States in their civil rights, and furnish the means of their vindication." Cong. Globe, 39th Cong., 1st Sess., p. 211. In origin it was an antidiscrimination measure (as its language indicated), framed to protect negroes in their newly won rights. It was amended by § 17 of the Act of May 31, 1870, 16 Stat. 144, 18 U.S.C.A. § 52,6 and made applicable to "any inhabitant of any State or Territory." The prohibition against the "deprivation of any rights, privileges, or immunities, secured or protected by the Constitution and laws of the United States" was introduced by the revisers in 1874. R.S. § 5510, 18 U.S.C.A. § 52. Those words were taken over from § 1 of the Act of April 20, 1871, 17 Stat. 13 (the so-called Ku-Klux Act) which provided civil suits for redress of such wrongs. The 1874 revision was applicable to any person who under color of law, etc., "subjects, or causes to be subjected" any inhabitant to the deprivation of any rights, etc. The requirement for a "willful" violation was introduced by the draftsmen of the Criminal Code of 1909. Act of March 4, 1909, 35 Stat. 1092. And we are told "willfully" was added to § 20 in order to make the section "less severe."

D. The Department of Justice Civil Rights Section and the Disappointment of *Screws v. United States*　　**921**

We hesitate to say that when Congress sought to enforce the Fourteenth Amendment in this fashion it did a vain thing. We hesitate to conclude that for 80 years this effort of Congress, renewed several times, to protect the important rights of the individual guaranteed by the Fourteenth Amendment has been an idle gesture. Yet if the Act falls by reason of vagueness so far as due process of law is concerned, there would seem to be a similar lack of specificity when the privileges and immunities clause and the equal protection clause of the Fourteenth Amendment are involved. Only if no construction can save the Act from this claim of unconstitutionality are we willing to reach that result. We do not reach it, for we are of the view that if § 20 is confined more narrowly than the lower courts confined it, it can be preserved as one of the sanctions to the great rights which the Fourteenth Amendment was designed to secure.

II

We recently pointed out that "willful" is a word "of many meanings, its construction often being influenced by its context." At times, as the Court held in *United States v. Murdock*, the word denotes an act which is intentional rather than accidental. But "when used in a criminal statute, it generally means an act done with a bad purpose." In that event something more is required than the doing of the act proscribed by the statute. An evil motive to accomplish that which the statute condemns becomes a constituent element of the crime. And that issue must be submitted to the jury under appropriate instructions.

An analysis of the cases in which "willfully" has been held to connote more than an act which is voluntary or intentional would not prove helpful as each turns on its own peculiar facts. Those cases, however, make clear that if we construe "willfully" in § 20 as connoting a purpose to deprive a person of a specific constitutional right, we would introduce no innovation. The Court, indeed, has recognized that the requirement of a specific intent to do a prohibited act may avoid those consequences to the accused which may otherwise render a vague or indefinite statute invalid. The constitutional vice in such a statute is the essential injustice to the accused of placing him on trial for an offense, the nature of which the statute does not define and hence of which it gives no warning. But where the punishment imposed is only for an act knowingly done with the purpose of doing that which the statute prohibits, the accused cannot be said to suffer from lack of warning or knowledge that the act which he does is a violation of law. The requirement that the act must be willful or purposeful may not render certain, for all purposes, a statutory definition of the crime which is in some respects uncertain. But it does relieve the statute of the objection that it punishes without warning an offense of which the accused was unaware. That was pointed out by Mr. Justice Brandeis speaking for the Court in *Omaechevarria v. Idaho*. An Idaho statute made it a misdemeanor to graze sheep "upon any range usually occupied by any cattle grower." The argument was that the statute was void for indefiniteness because it failed to provide for the ascertainment of boundaries of a "range" or for determining what length of time was necessary to make a prior occupation a "usual" one. The Court ruled that "any danger to sheepmen which might otherwise arise from indefiniteness, is removed by section 6314 of Revised Codes, which provides that: 'In every crime or public offence there must exist a union, or joint operation, of act and intent, or criminal negligence.'" A similar ruling was made in *Hygrade Provision Co. v. Sherman*. The charge was that a criminal statute which regulated the sale of "kosher" meat or products "sanctioned by the orthodox Hebrew religious requirements," Penal Law N.Y. § 435, subd. 4, was unconstitutional for want of any ascertainable standard of guilt. The Court speaking through Mr. Justice Sutherland stated, ". . . since the statutes require a specific intent to defraud in order to encounter their prohibitions, the hazard of prosecution which appellants fear loses whatever substantial foundation it might have in the absence of such a requirement." In *United States v. Ragen, supra*, we took that course in a prosecution for willful evasion of a federal income tax where it was alleged that the defendant had deducted more than "reasonable" allowances for salaries. By construing the statute to require proof of bad faith we avoided the serious question which the rule of *United States v. L. Cohen Grocery Co., supra,* might have presented. We think a like course is appropriate here.

Moreover, the history of § 20 affords some support for that narrower construction. As we have seen, the word "willfully" was not added to the Act until 1909. Prior to that time it may be that Congress intended that he who deprived a person of any right protected by the Constitution should be liable without more. That was the pattern of criminal legislation which has been sustained without any charge or proof of scienter. And the present Act in its original form would have been susceptible of the same interpretation apart from the equal protection clause of the Fourteenth Amendment, where "purposeful discriminatory" action must be shown. But as we have seen, the word "willfully" was added to make the section "less severe." We think the inference is permissible that its severity was to be lessened by making it applicable only where the requisite bad purpose was present, thus requiring specific intent not only where discrimination is claimed but in other situations as well. We repeat that the presence of a bad purpose or evil intent alone may not be sufficient. We do say that a requirement of a specific intent to deprive a person of a federal right made definite by decision or other rule of law saves the Act from any charge of unconstitutionality on the grounds of vagueness.

Once the section is given that construction, we think that the claim that the section lacks an ascertainable standard of guilt must fail. The constitutional requirement that a criminal statute be definite serves a high function. It gives a person acting with reference to the statute fair warning that his conduct is within its prohibition. This requirement is met when a statute prohibits only "willful" acts in the sense we have explained. One who does act with such specific intent is aware that what he does is precisely that which the statute forbids. He is under no necessity of guessing whether the statute applies to him for he either knows or acts in reckless disregard of its prohibition of the deprivation of a defined constitutional or other federal right. Nor is such an act beyond the understanding and comprehension of juries summoned to pass on them. The Act would then not become a trap for law enforcement agencies acting in good faith. "A mind intent upon willful evasion is inconsistent with surprised innocence."

It is said, however, that this construction of the Act will not save it from the infirmity of vagueness since neither a law enforcement official nor a trial judge can know with sufficient definiteness the range of rights that are constitutional. But that criticism is wide of the mark. For the specific intent required by the Act is an intent to deprive a person of a right which has been made specific either by the express terms of the Constitution or laws of the United States or by decisions interpreting them. Take the case of a local officer who persists in enforcing a type of ordinance which the Court has held invalid as violative of the guarantees of free speech or freedom of worship. Or a local official continues to select juries in manner which flies in the teeth of decisions of the Court. If those acts are done willfully, how can the officer possibly claim that he had no fair warning that his acts were prohibited by the statute? He violates the statute not merely because he has a bad purpose but because he acts in defiance of announced rules of law. He who defies a decision interpreting the Constitution knows precisely what he is doing. If sane, he hardly may be heard to say that he knew not what he did. Of course, willful conduct cannot make definite that which is undefined. But willful violators of constitutional requirements, which have been defined, certainly are in no position to say that they had no adequate advance notice that they would be visited with punishment. When they act willfully in the sense in which we use the word, they act in open defiance or in reckless disregard of a constitutional requirement which has been made specific and definite. When they are convicted for so acting, they are not punished for violating an unknowable something.

The Act so construed has a narrower range in all its applications than if it were interpreted in the manner urged by the government. But the only other alternative, if we are to

D. The Department of Justice Civil Rights Section and the Disappointment of *Screws v. United States* 923

avoid grave constitutional questions, is to construe it as applicable only to those acts which are clearly marked by the specific provisions of the Constitution as deprivations of constitutional rights, privileges, or immunities, and which are knowingly done within the rule of *Ellis v. United States*, supra. But as we have said that course would mean that all protection for violations of due process of law would drop out of the Act. We take the course which makes it possible to preserve the entire Act and save all parts of it from constitutional challenge. If Congress desires to give the Act wider scope, it may find ways of doing so. Moreover, here we are dealing with a situation where the interpretation of the Act which we adopt does not preclude any state from punishing any act made criminal by its own laws. Indeed, the narrow construction which we have adopted more nearly preserves the traditional balance between the States and the national government in law enforcement than that which is urged upon us.

United States v. Classic, supra, met the test we suggest. In that case we were dealing merely with the validity of an indictment, not with instructions to the jury. The indictment was sufficient since it charged a willful failure and refusal of the defendant-election officials to count the votes cast, by their alteration of the ballots and by their false certification of the number of votes cast for the respective candidates. The right so to vote is guaranteed by Art. I, § 2 and § 4 of the Constitution. Such a charge is adequate since he who alters ballots or without legal justification destroys them would be acting willfully in the sense in which § 20 uses the term. The fact that the defendants may not have been thinking in constitutional terms is not material where their aim was not to enforce local law but to deprive a citizen of a right and that right was protected by the Constitution. When they so act they at least act in reckless disregard of constitutional prohibitions or guarantees. Likewise, it is plain that basic to the concept of due process of law in a criminal case is a trial—a trial in a court of law, not a "trial by ordeal." *Brown v. Mississippi.* It could hardly be doubted that they who "under color of any law, statute, ordinance, regulation, or custom" act with that evil motive violate § 20. Those who decide to take the law into their own hands and act as prosecutor, jury, judge, and executioner plainly act to deprive a prisoner of the trial which due process of law guarantees him. And such a purpose need not be expressed; it may at times be reasonably inferred from all the circumstances attendant on the act.

The difficulty here is that this question of intent was not submitted to the jury with the proper instructions. The court charged that petitioners acted illegally if they applied more force than was necessary to make the arrest effectual or to protect themselves from the prisoner's alleged assault. But in view of our construction of the word "willfully" the jury should have been further instructed that it was not sufficient that petitioners had a generally bad purpose. To convict it was necessary for them to find that petitioners had the purpose to deprive the prisoner of a constitutional right, e.g. the right to be tried by a court rather than by ordeal. And in determining whether that requisite bad purpose was present the jury would be entitled to consider all the attendant circumstance—the malice of petitioners, the weapons used in the assault, its character and duration, the provocation, if any, and the like.

It is true that no exception was taken to the trial court's charge. Normally we would under those circumstances not take note of the error. And where the error is so fundamental as not to submit to the jury the essential ingredients of the only offense on which the conviction could rest, we think it is necessary to take note of it on our own motion. Even those guilty of the most heinous offenses are entitled to a fair trial. Whatever the degree of guilt, those charged with a federal crime are entitled to be tried by the standards of guilt which Congress has prescribed.

III

It is said, however, that petitioners did not act "under color of any law" within the meaning of § 20 of the Criminal Code. We disagree. We are of the view that petitioners acted under 'color' of law in making the arrest of Robert Hall and in assaulting him. They were officers of the law who made the arrest. By their own admissions they assaulted Hall in order to protect themselves and to keep their prisoner from escaping. It was their duty under Georgia law to make the arrest effective. Hence, their conduct comes within the statute.

Some of the arguments which have been advanced in support of the contrary conclusion suggest that the question under § 20 is whether Congress has made it a federal offense for a state officer to violate the law of his State. But there is no warrant for treating the question in state law terms. The problem is not whether state law has been violated but whether an inhabitant of a State has been deprived of a federal right by one who acts under "color of any law." He who acts under "color" of law may be a federal officer or a state officer. He may act under "color" of federal law or of state law. The statute does not come into play merely because the federal law or the state law under which the officer purports to act is violated. It is applicable when and only when some one is deprived of a federal right by that action. The fact that it is also a violation of state law does not make it any the less a federal offense punishable as such. Nor does its punishment by federal authority encroach on state authority or relieve the state from its responsibility for punishing state offenses.

We agree that when this statute is applied to the action of state officials, it should be construed so as to respect the proper balance between the States and the federal government in law enforcement. Violation of local law does not necessarily mean that federal rights have been invaded. The fact that a prisoner is assaulted, injured, or even murdered by state officials does not necessarily mean that he is deprived of any right protected or secured by the Constitution or laws of the United States. The Fourteenth Amendment did not alter the basic relations between the States and the national government. Our national government is one of delegated powers alone. Under our federal system the administration of criminal justice rests with the States except as Congress, acting within the scope of those delegated powers, has created offenses against the United States. "It is no more the duty or within the power of the United States to punish for a conspiracy to falsely imprison or murder within a State, than it would be to punish for false imprisonment or murder itself." It is only state action of a "particular character" that is prohibited by the Fourteenth Amendment and against which the Amendment authorizes Congress to afford relief. Thus Congress in § 20 of the Criminal Code did not undertake to make all torts of state officials federal crimes. It brought within § 20 only specified acts done "under color" of law and then only those acts which deprived a person of some right secured by the Constitution or laws of the United States.

This section was before us in *Classic*, where we said: "Misuse of power, possessed by virtue of state law and made possible only because the wrongdoer is clothed with the authority of state law, is action taken 'under color of' state law." In that case state election officials were charged with failure to count the votes as cast, alteration of the ballots, and false certification of the number of votes cast for the respective candidates. We stated that those acts of the defendants "were committed in the course of their performance of duties under the Louisiana statute requiring them to count the ballots, to record the result of the count, and to certify the result of the election." In the present case, as we have said, the defendants were officers of the law who had made an arrest and [who assaulted Hall to protect] themselves and to keep the prisoner from escaping, i.e. to make the arrest effective. That was a duty they had under Georgia law. *Classic* is, therefore, indistinguishable from this case so far as "under color of" state law is concerned. In each officers of the State were performing official duties; in each the power which they were authorized to exercise was misused. We cannot draw a distinction between them unless we are to say that § 20 is not applicable to police officers. But the broad sweep of its language leaves no room for such an exception. It is said that we should abandon the holding of the *Classic* case. It is suggested that the present problem was not clearly in focus in that case and that its holding was ill-advised. A reading of the opinion makes plain that the question was squarely involved and squarely met. It followed the rule announced in

D. The Department of Justice Civil Rights Section and the Disappointment of *Screws v. United States*   **925**

Ex parte Commonwealth of Virginia, that a state judge who in violation of state law discriminated against negroes in the selection of juries violated the Act of March 1, 1875, 18 Stat. 336. It is true that that statute did not contain the words under "color" of law. But the Court in deciding what was state action within the meaning of the Fourteenth Amendment held that it was immaterial that the state officer exceeded the limits of his authority ". . . as he acts in the name and for the State, and is clothed with the State's power, his act is that of the State. This must be so, or the constitutional prohibition has no meaning. Then the State has clothed one of its agents with power to annul or to evade it." The *Classic* case recognized, without dissent, that the contrary view would defeat the great purpose which § 20 was designed to serve. Reference is made to statements of Senator Trumbull in his discussion of § 2 of the Civil Rights Act of 1866, 14 Stat. 27, and to statements of Senator Sherman concerning the 1870 Act as supporting the conclusion that "under color of any law" was designed to include only action taken by officials pursuant to state law. But those statements in their context are inconclusive on the precise problem involved in the *Classic* case and in the present case. We are not dealing here with a case where an officer not authorized to act nevertheless takes action. Here the state officers were authorized to make an arrest and to take such steps as were necessary to make the arrest effective. They acted without authority only in the sense that they used excessive force in making the arrest effective. It is clear that under "color" of law means under "pretense" of law. Thus acts of officers in the ambit of their personal pursuits are plainly excluded. Acts of officers who undertake to perform their official duties are included whether they hew to the line of their authority or overstep it. If, as suggested, the statute was designed to embrace only action which the State in fact authorized, the words "under color of any law" were hardly apt words to express the idea.

But beyond that is the problem of stare decisis. The construction given § 20 in the *Classic* case formulated a rule of law which has become the basis of federal enforcement in this important field. The rule adopted in that case was formulated after mature consideration. It should be good for more than one day only. We do not have here a situation comparable to *Mahnich v. Southern*, where we overruled a decision demonstrated to be a sport in the law and inconsistent with what preceded and what followed. The *Classic* case was not the product of hasty action or inadvertence. It was not out of line with the cases which preceded. It was designed to fashion the governing rule of law in this important field. We are not dealing with constitutional interpretations which throughout the history of the Court have wisely remained flexible and subject to frequent re-examination. The meaning which the Classic case gave to the phrase "under color of any law" involved only a construction of the statute. hence if it states a rule undesirable in its consequences, Congress can change it. We add only to the instability and uncertainty of the law if we revise the meaning of § 20 to meet the exigencies of each case coming before us.

Since there must be a new trial, the judgment below is reversed.

• • •

Mr. Justice MURPHY, dissenting.

I dissent. Robert Hall, a Negro citizen, has been deprived not only of the right to be tried by a court rather than by ordeal. He has been deprived of the right of life itself. That right belonged to him not because he was a Negro or a member of any particular race or creed. That right was his because he was an American citizen, because he was a human being. As such, he was entitled to all the respect and fair treatment that befits the dignity of man, a dignity that is recognized and guaranteed by the Constitution. Yet not even the semblance of due process has been accorded him. He has been cruelly and unjustifiably beaten to death by local police officers acting under color of authority derived from the state. It is difficult to believe that such an obvious and necessary right is indefinitely guaranteed by the Constitution or is foreign to the knowledge of local police officers so as to cast any reasonable doubt on the conviction under Section 20 of the Criminal Code of the perpetrators of this "shocking and revolting episode in law enforcement."

The Constitution and Section 20 must be read together inasmuch as Section 20 refers in part to certain provisions of the Constitution. Section 20 punishes any one, acting under color of any law, who willfully deprives any person of any right, privilege or immunity secured or protected by the Constitution or laws of the United States. The pertinent part of the Constitution in this instance is Section 1 of the Fourteenth Amendment, which firmly and unmistakably provides that no state shall deprive any person of life without due process of law. Translated in light of this specific provision of the Fourteenth Amendment, Section 20 thus punishes any one, acting under color of state law, who willfully deprives any person of life without due process of law. Such is the clear statutory provision upon which this conviction must stand or fall.

A grave constitutional issue, however, is said to lurk in the alleged indefiniteness of the crime outlawed by Section 20. The rights, privileges and immunities secured or protected by the Constitution or laws of the United States are claimed to be so uncertain and flexible, dependent upon changeable legal concepts, as to leave a state official confused and ignorant as to what actions of his might run afoul of the law. The statute, it is concluded, must be set aside for vagueness.

It is axiomatic, of course, that a criminal statute must give a clear and unmistakable warning as to the acts which will subject one to criminal punishment. And courts are without power to supply that which Congress has left vague. But this salutary principle does not mean that if a statute is vague as to certain criminal acts but definite as to others the entire statute must fall. Nor does it mean that in the first case involving the statute to come before us we must delineate all the prohibited acts that are obscure and all those that are explicit.

Thus it is idle to speculate on other situations that might involve Section 20 which are not now before us. We are unconcerned here with state officials who have coerced a confession from a prisoner, denied counsel to a defendant or made a faulty tax assessment. Whatever doubt may exist in those or in other situations as to whether the state officials could reasonably anticipate and recognize the relevant constitutional rights is immaterial in this case. Our attention here is directed solely to three state officials who, in the course of their official duties, have unjustifiably beaten and crushed the body of a human being, thereby depriving him of trial by jury and of life itself. The only pertinent inquiry is whether Section 20, by its reference to the Fourteenth Amendment guarantee that no state shall deprive any person of life without due process of law, gives fair warning of state officials that they are criminally liable for violating this right to life.

Common sense gives an affirmative answer to that problem. The reference in Section 20 to rights protected by the Constitution is manifest and simple. At the same time, the right not to be deprived of life without due process of law is distinctly and lucidly protected by the Fourteenth Amendment. There is nothing vague or indefinite in these references to this most basic of all human rights. Knowledge of a comprehensive law library is unnecessary for officers of the law to know that the right to murder individuals in the course of their duties is unrecognized in this nation. No appreciable amount of intelligence or conjecture on the part of the lowliest state official is needed for him to realize that fact; nor should it surprise him to find out that the Constitution protects persons from his reckless disregard of human life and that statutes punish him therefor. To subject a state official to punishment under Section 20 for such acts is not to penalize him without fair and definite warning. Rather it is to uphold elementary standards of decency and to make American principles of law and our constitutional guarantees mean something more than pious rhetoric.

D. The Department of Justice Civil Rights Section and the Disappointment of *Screws v. United States*

Under these circumstances it is unnecessary to send this case back for a further trial on the assumption that the jury was not charged on the matter of the willfulness of the state officials, an issue that was not raised below or before us. The evidence is more than convincing that the officials willfully, or at least with wanton disregard of the consequences, deprived Robert Hall of his life without due process of law. A new trial could hardly make that fact more evident; the failure to charge the jury on willfulness was at most an inconsequential error. Moreover, the presence or absence of willfulness fails to decide the constitutional issue raised before us. Section 20 is very definite and certain in its reference to the right to life as spelled out in the Fourteenth Amendment quite apart from the state of mind of the state officials. A finding of willfulness can add nothing to the clarity of that reference.

It is an illusion to say that the real issue in this case is the alleged failure of Section 20 fully to warn the state officials that their actions were illegal. The Constitution, Section 20 and their own consciences told them that. They knew that they lacked any mandate or authority to take human life unnecessarily or without due process of law in the course of their duties. They knew that their excessive and abusive use of authority would only subvert the ends of justice. The significant question, rather, is whether law enforcement officers and those entrusted with authority shall be allowed to violate with impunity the clear constitutional rights of the inarticulate and the friendless. Too often unpopular minorities, such as Negroes, are unable to find effective refuge from the cruelties of bigoted and ruthless authority. States are undoubtedly capable of punishing their officers who commit such outrages. But where, as here, the states are unwilling for some reason to prosecute such crimes the federal government must step in unless constitutional guarantees are to become atrophied.

This necessary intervention, however, will be futile if courts disregard reality and misuse the principle that criminal statutes must be clear and definite. Here state officers have violated with reckless abandon a plain constitutional right of an American citizen. The two courts below have found and the record demonstrates that the trial was fair and the evidence of guilt clear. And Section 20 unmistakably outlaws such actions by state officers. We should therefore affirm the judgment.

• • •

NOTES AND QUESTIONS

1. The conviction of Screws was vacated because the jury instruction did not adequately capture the intent element of the statute as the plurality opinion fashioned it. Yet the instruction was not objected to and, as the plurality notes, the Court had quite recently affirmed a conviction where the defendant had not objected to an erroneous instruction. Why couldn't the Court have weighed in on the jury instruction issue, providing guidance for future cases, while at the same time affirming the conviction of this evil defendant?

2. The plurality's analysis of the statute's requirement that it be violated "willfully," and that some specie of specific intent must therefore be inferred from this word, is befuddling on multiple levels. For one thing, the Court had interpreted the term "willfully" in a criminal statute just four years earlier. In that case, *Browder v. United States*, 312 U.S. 335 (1941), the Court interpreted a statute that criminalized "willfully and knowingly us[ing]" a passport secured by a false statement. The Court held that the adverb meant simply "deliberately and with knowledge and not something which is merely careless or negligent or inadvertent." *Id.* at 341. There was no requirement that a defendant be aware that his conduct was illegal. This analysis is consistent with the Court's subsequent analyses of willfulness requirements in criminal statutes. *See Cheek v. United States*, 498 U.S. 192, 209 (1991) (the term "willfully" in criminal law generally "refers to consciousness of the act but not to consciousness that the act is unlawful") (Scalia, J., concurring in judgment). Is there anything about the statute at issue in *Screws* that might justify a deviation from this standard practice of interpreting the adverb "willfully"?

3. It is also confusing how the plurality opinion believed inferring a specific intent requirement from the word "willfully" could solve the specificity problem, that is, the lack of "an ascertainable standard of guilt." Does a knowledge-of-illegality requirement address any concern that the acts the statute purports to make illegal are insufficiently specified? If, say, it is unclear whether a pre-arrest beating of a criminal suspect is covered by the "deprivation of rights" language in the statute, does it become fair to prosecute that defendant if the jury is instructed the defendant must have known that his actions were unlawful?

4. To the extent the plurality means to impose some sort of specific intent requirement, it either intentionally or inadvertently waters down that requirement in two respects. First, the plurality states that it is not material that "the defendants may not have been thinking in constitutional terms." If not, then what exactly is the willfulness requirement? Do defendants need to have acted with some sub-constitutional sense of illegality? Second, the plurality goes on to say that defendants must have acted "at least in reckless disregard of constitutional prohibitions or guarantees." But "reckless regard" is the least culpable formulation of intent, bordering on negligence. How many different mens rea requirements are floating around in the plurality opinion?

5. The specificity issue, as seen both by the plurality opinion and the dissenters, is purportedly a product of the 1945 status of the Court's Fourteenth Amendment jurisprudence. The incorporation doctrine was in an immature stage in 1945 and, as the plurality notes, there is some open-ended, if not mealymouthed, language in some of the Court's recent cases describing due process:

> The phrase [due process] formulates a concept less rigid and more fluid than those envisaged in other specific and particular provisions of the Bill of Rights. Its application is less a matter of rule. Asserted denial is to be tested by an appraisal of the totality of facts in a given case. That which may, in one setting, constitute a denial of fundamental fairness, shocking to the universal sense of justice, may, in other circumstances, and in the light of other considerations, fall short of such denial.

Id. at 95 (quoting *Betts v. Brady*, 316 U.S. 455, 462 (1938)).

6. Both Justice Rutledge, concurring, and Justice Murphy, dissenting, have little patience for the plurality's agonizing over the specificity issue. Justice Murphy is emphatic: "the right not to be deprived of life without due process of law [as Hall was] is distinctly and lucidly protected by the Fourteenth Amendment," and "a comprehensive law library is unnecessary for officers of the law to know that the right to murder individuals in the course of their duties is unrecognized in this nation." Justice Rutledge makes this point too, and adds, less dramatically, that the constitutional specificity requirement has two purposes: fair warning of what is prohibited and sufficient notice to the accused in order that he can prepare his defense. As to the latter, Justice Rutledge notes that the indictment particularized "the rights infringed and the acts infringing them" and that defendants could have requested a bill of particulars if they believed they needed further specification, which they did not do.

If Justices Rutledge and Murphy are correct here, then what about a case where the scope of the constitutional right at issue is genuinely ambiguous? For example, consider the case of a police officer who, a year before *Miranda* is decided, extracts a confession from an unrepresented suspect by way of nonphysical but psychologically coercive tactics?

7. Justice Rutledge also makes the point that the Court has blessed any number of vague criminal statutes, and gives the Sherman Act as "the most obvious illustration." That statute,

D. The Department of Justice Civil Rights Section and the Disappointment of *Screws v. United States*

currently codified at 15 U.S.C. §§ 1-2, criminalized then, as it does now, agreements "in restraint of trade or commerce." A robust body of common law has grown up around this statute, and for that you would definitely need Justice Murphy's law library in order to steer clear of violations. Is Justice Douglas's concern in *Classic* about the prohibition against criminal common law a silent factor animating his views in *Screws* just as it did in *Classic*? Is the specificity concern in *Screws*, at least in part, a separation-of-powers issue?

8. The dissenters frame the "practical question" posed by *Screws* as whether "the States should be relieved from responsibility to bring their law officers to book for homicide." The dissenters answer this question, actually more of a rhetorical question than a practical one, in the negative. They do so even though they acknowledge the abject local failure in *Screws*; the applicable Georgia prosecutor received no complaint regarding the Hall murder and had no means to investigate the matter in any event, as that would have been the responsibility of the defendants themselves and their colleagues. Despite this acknowledgment, the dissenters state that "the cure is a re-invigoration of State responsibility."

How could such a "reinvigoration" be accomplished by any part of the federal government? What could the Supreme Court do? What could the Department of Justice do? It is worth noting that the Department of Justice's files on the *Screws* case show the department made diligent efforts to persuade Georgia authorities to prosecute Screws before presenting the case to a federal grand jury. Robert K. Carr, Screws v. United States: *The Georgia Police Brutality Case*, 31 Cornell L.Q. 48, 52 (1945).

9. The dissenters also brush off the department's prospective assurances about its anticipated disciplined and moderate use of the criminal civil rights statutes, and other structural safeguards against overuse of the statute. Are the dissenters right to be skeptical about the DOJ's commitment to self-discipline? Are the dissenters' related concerns about the Court's ceding its power over federal-state relations to juries reasonable? The dissenters go out of their way to disparage juries — "whose function is to resolve factual questions"! — and are unwilling to acknowledge that the members of the grand jury that indicted Screws and the petit jury that convicted him are as representative of the state of Georgia as any local prosecutor. Is the dissent, at bottom, anti-democratic?

10. The statutes at issue here, in and of themselves, draw the dissenters' ire. The dissenters state, with respect to Congress's efforts to enforce the Fourteenth Amendment, that "[i]t is familiar history that much of this legislation was born of that vengeful spirit which to no small degree envenomed the Reconstruction era." This history is apparently so familiar that the dissenters felt no obligation to cite any authority for it. They could have, though.

The dissenters are not inaccurately reflecting the conventional, white supremacist view of the "Dunning School" of Reconstruction historiography, which was predominant into the 1960s. On this view, named after Columbia professor William Dunning and his students, the Reconstruction era was condemned as producing corrupt rule by "uncivilized Negroes" in the South and radical Republicans at the national level. *See* Eric Foner, The Second Founding: How the Civil War and Reconstruction Remade the Constitution xxi-xxiv (2019). Professor Foner has observed that the portrait of Reconstruction advanced by the Dunning School provided "an intellectual foundation for Jim Crow, the racial system of the South and in many ways the United States as a whole, from the 1890s until the civil rights era of the 1960s." *Id.* at xxii. *See* Chapter VI *supra*.

Claude Screws was retried in 1946 and found not guilty. On remand, the trial judge struggled, as would any judge, with how to incorporate the plurality's internally inconsistent statements about intent into something digestible by a jury. The trial judge's charge included the following language: "if this incident was no more than an unlawful homicide . . . which

Post-mortem photograph of Robert Hall's bludgeoned body

should be remedied by the State Courts of Georgia" then it is not a federal offense. Harry H. Shapiro, *Limitations in Prosecuting Civil Rights Violations*, 46 Cornell L.Q. 532, 535 (1961) (citing charge of the court in *Screws v. United States*, No. 1300 Cr., M.D. Ga., Nov. 1, 1945, obtained from the Civil Rights Division, at 18).

Did the trial judge go too far in attempting to capture the gist of the Supreme Court's decision? What does the "no more than an unlawful homicide" language say to the jury where the evidence showed that Screws had a longstanding dispute with Hall and used his power as sheriff to execute his private vengeance? Why the distinction in the instruction between state and federal courts? Did this language give jurors permission to base their verdict on a vague and inchoate notion of states' rights?

The prosecutor, naturally, blamed the defeat on the bulked-up jury instruction. Carr, Federal Protection of Civil Rights, *supra* at 115. Professor Shapiro, *Limitations*, *supra* at 353 n.25, reports that the jury foreman in the *Screws* retrial stated that the jurors were convinced the defendant was guilty of manslaughter or second-degree murder, and that the state should do something about it, but that they felt bound by the judge's instructions to acquit. The head of the DOJ Civil Rights Section confirmed the line prosecutor's sentiment that the willfulness instruction was "very damaging," and opined further that the Supreme Court's decision was going to be an obstacle to the Section's work. Carr, Federal Protection of Civil Rights, *supra* at 138-39. As for Screws himself, he parlayed his victory in the retrial into sufficient local celebrity that he was later elected to the Georgia state senate. David Dante Troutt, *Screws, Koon, and Routine Aberrations: The Use of Fictional Narratives in Federal Police Brutality Prosecutions*, 74 N.Y.U. L. Rev. 18, 52 (1999).

The rate of lynchings and police brutality actually accelerated after the end of World War II, as did the FBI's futility. Especially embarrassing were the cases where Black veterans,

D. The Department of Justice Civil Rights Section and the Disappointment of *Screws v. United States*

returning home after their service ended, were murdered and terrorized. In Batesburg, South Carolina, Sergeant Isaac Woodard was dragged off an interstate bus and beaten so badly he was blinded. While the FBI diligently investigated the case, and was able to identify Woodard's principal assailant as the local police chief and to obtain his indictment, an all-white federal jury acquitted him. Gage, G-Man, *supra* at 312. In Monroe, Georgia, a white mob pulled two Black couples, including an army veteran, out of a car and shot them near Moore's Ford Bridge. Suspecting the complicity of local law enforcement—the car was coming directly from picking up one of the victims at the local jail—Hoover spared no resources. *Id.* at 313. The FBI interviewed 2,790 people in the Monroe area and, after months of investigation that resulted in more than 10,000 pages of memoranda, presented 106 witnesses to a federal grand jury over 16 days. *Id.* The yield? One indictment on a charge of lying to the FBI. *Id.* For more on the FBI's failure to bring charges in connection with the murder of Black veterans after World War II, *see generally* Margaret Burnham, By Hands Now Known: Jim Crow's Legal Executioners (2022).

The legacy of *Screws* is complicated, at best. *Screws* undoubtedly caused the DOJ to become conservative, if not timid, about bringing police brutality charges under § 242. *See* Mia Teitelbaum, *Willful Intent:* U.S. v. Screws *and the Legal Strategies of the Department of Justice*, U. Pa. J.L. & Soc. Change 185, 193, 203-05 (2017). And the DOJ's timidity harmed its relationship with the NAACP, which grew frustrated with DOJ's reluctance to act on cases the NAACP referred to it. *Id.* at 207-12. As for the FBI, Hoover testified before President Truman's Committee on Civil Rights in 1947, and cited as two impediments to civil rights prosecutions the "hostility of local officials and communities" and "vaguely worded" federal statutes. Gage, G-Man, *supra* at 318. On the other hand, § 242 emerged from the scrutiny of the Supreme Court bloodied but unbowed. Federal civil rights prosecutions were still possible. *See* Hon. Paul Watford, Screws v. United States *and the Birth of Federal Rights Civil Rights Enforcement*, 98 Marq. L. Rev. 465 (2014) ("The most important legacy of *Screws* is that Section 242 survived.").

The next few cases show that prosecutions for civil rights crimes were still possible after *Screws*.

United States v. Crews
160 F.2d 746 (5th Cir. 1947)

WALLER, Circuit Judge.

The beautiful Suwannee River—the mention of which calls to memory a plaintive melody of strumming banjos, humming bees, childhood's playful hours, a hut among the bushes, and a longing to go back to the place where the old folks stay—was the scene of the cruel and revolting crime that provoked the gesture of dealing out justice that is this case.

The defendant, although guilty of a cruel and inexcusable homicide, was indicted and convicted merely of having deprived his helpless victim of a constitutional right, under strained constructions of an inadequate Federal statute, and given the maximum sentence under that statute of one year in prison and a fine of $1,000.

Sam McFadden—"Puddin" he was customarily called—was missing for some time from the little village of Branford on the banks of the Suwannee River in the country that bears the river's name. Some knew that he had gone away but none knew where until his bleached and putrescent corpse was discovered by fishermen against the overhanging willows at the edge of a little island in the middle of the river.

932 Chapter X The Department of Justice and the Prosecution of Civil Rights Crimes

It would have been better for the country's reputation for law and order among justice-loving men had this piece of decaying flotsam drifted out into the sea and into oblivion and the facts of its venomous and vicious slaying had never come to light. But the willows arranged otherwise and held it until the fishermen came.

Tom A. Crews, the defendant, was the Town Marshal of Branford and also the Constable of the District that embraced the Town. He was "the law," twice fortified. Four or five months before the occasion involved in the present case, the Constable was said to have had trouble with McFadden when the latter seized a shot gun and threatened to kill the officer as he was attempting to arrest another person. The deceased was arrested at that time and taken before the County Judge who declined to comply with the Constable's request that McFadden be charged with an assault with a deadly weapon, or some kindred felony. Instead the County Judge charged McFadden merely with the misdemeanor of having been drunk and disorderly. It was said to have come thereafter to the defendant's ears that McFadden had stated on more than one occasion that he intended to kill defendant, and it was in evidence that he attempted to buy a pistol with the expressed purpose of getting in readiness to carry out that threat.

The defendant, nursing his wrath, and being resentful of certain vile and opprobrious epithets which McFadden was said to have applied several times to him, and being also apprehensive of Harm at McFadden's hands, and perhaps deeming the law, as administered by the County Judge, inadequate—so it is argued—took matters into his own hands.

Riding with his nephew in an automobile belonging to the latter, on the night of September 21, 1945, he stated, according to that nephew, that he was "going to get McFadden if he was drunk." Later that night he located the Negro, took him by the arm, guided him without effort or resistance to the nephew's car, and had him take the rear seat. The nephew, who testified that McFadden "looked like he was drunk," declined to swear positively whether he was or not. Other witnesses saw no evidence whatsoever of inebriation on the part of the deceased.

We shall skip the shocking details of the beating that Crews administered with a bull whip after the taking of McFadden into custody and come to the ultimate act of personal venom and hate, or of the vicious exercise of official despotism and cruelty—depending upon how one views the evidence.

After directing his nephew to drive the automobile toward Live Oak, the county site, Crews also directed him to stop at the home of one Cribbs, who lived outside Branford on the road to Live Oak. Cribbs then became a passenger in the car. Instead of placing McFadden in jail when they reached Live Oak, the defendant directed his nephew to drive to a highway bridge several miles up the river from Branford. Before reaching the bridge the defendant stated that he was going to give McFadden, a fifty-fifty chance, but notwithstanding McFadden's protestations that he could not swim, the Constable forced him to jump from the high bridge into the deep, swift current of the river, from which he never came out until he was taken from the water and the willows by the undertaker.

There was evidence that, as Town Marshal, the appellant, when on duty, regularly wore a cap denoting his position, and that at the time of taking McFadden into custody he was without this cap, which he considered as the symbol of his official authority and without which, it was argued, he considered that he was not on duty. There was evidence that Crews, unofficially, or without formal or official sanction from the Town, frequently procured one Lee to take his place, during which period, it was also asserted, Crews considered himself not to be on duty as Town Marshal. There is also evidence that Crews had on no uniform or badge as the Town ordinance was said to require, and that he was riding in no official police car. From these circumstances it was argued that Crews considered he was off duty at the time. As Constable there was no requirement of cap, bade, or uniform, nor limitation of hours. He was always on call.

It was not shown that Crews accused McFadden of being drunk at the time of taking him into custody, nor that he ever stated to the deceased that he was under arrest. He had

D. The Department of Justice Civil Rights Section and the Disappointment of *Screws v. United States*

no warrant for the arrest of McFadden. None was necessary if he were drunk in the officer's presence.

Counsel for the appellant concedes that the evidence is sufficient to establish the commission of the homicide of McFadden by Crews with all of its heartless cruelty; but he earnestly and ably insists that the act was solely one of personal vengeance and entirely devoid of official character or authority and, therefore, not within the purview of the statute under which the indictment was drawn. He insists that the following testimony by Barber, the Constable's nephew, as they rode in the automobile of the latter in the earlier part of the night in question,

> Q. What, if anything, did he say to you just before you started out with reference to McFadden?
> A. I believe he told me he was going to get him if he was drunk

plus the testimony of Barber that McFadden "looked like he was drunk," was all of the testimony on the vital question of whether defendant was acting under color of law, and that such evidence was wholly insufficient, in the light of all the other facts in the case, to justify the jury in making the requisite finding that Crews was acting under "color of law."

It is also vigorously urged upon us that the vital question of whether or not the defendant was acting under color of law in the deprivation of the constitutional right of McFadden to life or liberty or to a fair trial under due processes of law rather than a trial by ordeal, is supported only by circumstantial evidence of too weak a character to overcome every other reasonable hypothesis other than that the defendant was acting under color of law.

With equal earnestness defendant's counsel also impresses upon us that this same circumstantial evidence entirely fails to meet the standard set by the Supreme Court in *Screws v. United States*, supra (325 U.S. 91, 65 S. Ct. 1038), wherein that court said:

> But in view of our construction of the word "willfully" the jury should have been further instructed that it was not sufficient that petitioners had a generally bad purpose. To convict it was necessary for them to find that petitioners had the purpose to deprive the prisoner of a constitutional right, e.g. the right to be tried by a court rather than by ordeal. And in determining whether that requisite bad purpose was present the jury would be entitled to consider all the attendant circumstances — the malice of petitioners, the weapons used in the assault, its character and duration, the provocation, if any, and the like.

It is unnecessary for us to enter into an extended discussion of the legal principles involved in this case for they have been set forth by the Supreme Court in a recent decision in *Screws v. United States*, supra.

Concededly, the defendant was actuated by a spirit of revenge, of personal malice, perhaps of fear of personal harm at the hands of McFadden. His chastisement of the deceased with the bull whip until he broke it, prior to the time he forced McFadden to jump to his death, furnishes convincing evidence that Crew's personal anger and desire for vengeance were intense. Nevertheless, if he, as Constable or as Town Marshal, arrested McFadden or took him into custody because he was drunk, or because he believed that he was drunk, or if he, while acting under color of his authority as Town Marshal or Constable, took McFadden into custody on the pretense that he believed him to be drunk, and, while having him in such custody, determined that instead of granting to his prisoner the constitutional right of a lawful trial he should be tried by ordeal, and in pursuance of which he committed the acts alleged, the offense charged would be complete even though the defendant was also actuated by personal anger, hate, malice, and a desire for revenge. If in the use of his official authority under color of law an officer vents his malice upon a prisoner and deprives him of a constitutional right, this manifestation and use of personal spleen need not necessarily negative the fact that such officer might at the same time have also acted with the conscious and willful purpose of depriving the prisoner of constitutional rights. Conversely, one cannot willfully deprive another of the constitutional right to life without having the willful intent to slay.

There is direct evidence: (a) That Crews intended to arrest McFadden if he were drunk; (b) that McFadden looked like he was drunk; (c) that Crews, upon finding McFadden, took him into custody and thereafter did not place him in jail, prefer any charge against him, nor take him before any judicial officer or tribunal. Instead, he put his prisoner through an ordeal that brought about the latter's death.

An officer of the law should not be permitted to divest himself of his official authority in actions taken by him wherein he acts, or purports, or pretends, to act pursuant to his authority, and where one, known by another to be an officer, takes the other into custody in a manner which appears on its face to be in the exercise of authority of law, without making to the other any disclosure to the contrary, such officer thereby justifies the conclusion that he was acting under color of law in making such an arrest.

It was the function of the jury, as the fact-finding body of the Court, to consider all the facts and circumstances in evidence, meanwhile weighing preponderances, drawing inferences, comparing presumptions, probing intent, and balancing hypotheses. It is not necessary, in order to uphold a jury's verdict, that this Court concur in every fact found by the jury but merely that it determine that a jury question was involved and that there was competent and substantial evidence to support the jury's verdict.

The question of intent in a case of this sort must of necessity be one for the jury to determine from all the facts and circumstances in evidence. It is not given to a jury to look into a man's mind and read its purposes, but the jury may probe into his words, his knowledge, his experience, his surroundings, his acts and doings and their results, in order to decide the question of intent. An officer of the law undoubtedly knows that a person arrested by him for an offense has the constitutional right to a trial under the law, and if the jury should believe from the evidence beyond a reasonable doubt that such an officer willfully failed to accord to one arrested by him the opportunity for such a trial but substituted instead his own trial by ordeal, such jury would be justified in finding that such a denial of such constitutional right was consciously and willfully made. One is generally presumed to have intended the normal and reasonable consequences of his acts. A deprivation of the right to life is an inexorable and concomitant consequence of a willful homicide.

We think the charge of the lower Court was fair, full, and able, in the giving of which the Court followed with unfaltering accuracy the law as laid down by the Supreme Court in *Screws v. United States*, supra.

The other specifications of error are not such as in our opinion require a reversal of this case. The judgment of the lower Court is affirmed.

NOTES AND QUESTIONS

1. As in *Screws*, the defense in *Crews* is simple: It was "only" murder. The defendant police officer, as in *Screws*, put on evidence of his long-simmering dispute with the victim, and argued that whatever had happened between them was personal, not business. That a case could be defended in this manner says something about the arrogance of the defendant as well as his opinion of the members of his community who would serve on his jury.

2. As to the "under color of law" element, the defense tried to convince the jury he was "off duty" when the incident occurred, and thus not acting under the color or even the "pretense of law," as Justice Douglas had described it in *Screws*. When the jury rejected this defense, the defendant argued that the evidence he acted "under color of law" was entirely circumstantial and insufficient to sustain the verdict. What is the Fifth Circuit panel's response to this argument? Does the evidence suggest not that Crews was actually "off duty" but rather

D. The Department of Justice Civil Rights Section and the Disappointment of *Screws v. United States* 935

that he was attempting to conceal the outward manifestations of his authority? How does such evidence cut?

3. Compare the panel's description of the jury's role in the opinion's penultimate paragraph with the dissenters' implicit disparagement of juries in *Screws*. In that same paragraph the panel has no patience for the specificity issue that paralyzed the *Screws* plurality, finding that a policeman "undoubtedly knows that a person arrested by him has the constitutional right to a trial under the law."

4. The panel doesn't even mention *Screws* in the body of its opinion until the last sentence, where it states that the lower court's charge to the jury was consistent with *Screws*. This conclusion is interesting, as *Screws* was internally inconsistent about what the intent element required, but inasmuch as there were multiple ways to interpret the *Screws* plurality opinion perhaps this method — conclusory affirmance — was the best way to deal with the jury instruction issue.

Fourteen years later, Justice Frankfurter, one of the dissenters in *Screws*, in making a related dissent in *Monroe v. Pape*, 365 U.S. 167 (1961) (recognizing a federal civil cause of action under 42 U.S.C. § 1983), cited the Fifth Circuit's decision in *Crews* as an example of the lower courts not paying sufficient fealty to *Screws*. *See id.* at 207 & n.7 (Frankfurter, J., dissenting) ("lower courts in applying [*Screws*] have allowed inference of the requisite specific intent from evidence, it would appear, of malevolence alone").

In the next case the Court addresses a § 242 prosecution based on a different type of alleged constitutional violation — an allegedly coerced confession.

Williams v. United States
341 U.S. 97 (1951)

Mr. Justice DOUGLAS delivered the opinion of the Court.

The question in this case is whether a special police officer who in his official capacity subjects a person suspected of crime to force and violence in order to obtain a confession may be prosecuted under § 20 of the Criminal Code, 18 U.S.C. (1946 ed.) § 52, now 18 U.S.C.A. § 242.

Section 20 provides in pertinent part: "Whoever, under color of any law, statute, ordinance, regulation, or custom, willfully subjects, or causes to be subjected, any inhabitant of any State, Territory, or District to the deprivation of any rights, privileges, or immunities secured or protected by the Constitution and laws of the United States . . . shall be fined not more than $1,000, or imprisoned not more than one year, or both."

The facts are these: The Lindsley Lumber Co. suffered numerous thefts and hired petitioner, who operated a detective agency, to ascertain the identity of the thieves. Petitioner held a special police officer's card issued by the City of Miami, Florida, and had taken an oath and qualified as a special police officer. Petitioner and others over a period of three days took four men to a paint shack on the company's premises and used brutal methods to obtain a confession from each of them. A rubber hose, a pistol, a blunt instrument, a sash cord and other implements were used in the project. One man was forced to look at a bright light for fifteen minutes; when he was blinded, he was repeatedly hit with a rubber hose and a sash cord and finally knocked to the floor. Another was knocked from a chair and hit in the stomach again and again. He was put back in the chair and the procedure was repeated. One was backed against the wall and jammed in the chest with a club. Each was beaten, threatened, and unmercifully punished for several hours until he confessed. One Ford, a policeman, was sent by his superior to lend authority to the proceedings. And petitioner, who committed the assaults, went about flashing his badge.

The indictment charged among other things that petitioner acting under color of law used force to make each victim confess to his guilt and implicate others, and that the victims were denied the right to be tried by due process of law and if found guilty to be sentenced and punished in accordance with the laws of the state. Petitioner was found guilty by a jury under instructions which conformed with the rulings of the Court in *Screws*. The Court of Appeals affirmed.

We think it clear that petitioner was acting "under color" of law within the meaning of § 20, or at least that the jury could properly so find. We interpreted this phrase of § 20 in *Classic*. "Misuse of power, possessed by virtue of state law and made possible only because the wrongdoer is clothed with the authority of state law, is action taken 'under color of' state law." It is common practice, as we noted in *Jones & Laughlin*, for private guards or detectives to be vested with policemen's powers. We know from the record that that is the policy of Miami, Florida. Moreover, this was an investigation conducted under the aegis of the State, as evidenced by the fact that a regular police officer was detailed to attend it. We need go no further to conclude that the lower court, to whom we give deference on local law matters, was correct in holding that petitioner was no mere interloper but had a semblance of policeman's power from Florida. There was, therefore, evidence that he acted under authority of Florida law; and the manner of his conduct of the interrogations makes clear that he was asserting the authority granted him and not acting in the role of a private person. In any event the charge to the jury drew the line between official and unofficial conduct which we explored in *Screws* and gave petitioner all of the protection which "color of" law as used in § 20 offers.

The main contention is that the application of § 20 so as to sustain a conviction for obtaining a confession by use of force and violence is unconstitutional. The argument is the one that a clear majority of the Court rejected in *Screws*, and runs as follows:

Criminal statutes must have an ascertainable standard of guilt or they fall for vagueness. Section 20, it is argued, lacks the necessary specificity when rights under the Due Process Clause of the Fourteenth Amendment are involved. We are pointed to the course of decisions by this Court under the Due Process Clause as proof of the vague and fluid standard for "rights, privileges, or immunities secured or protected by the Constitution" as used in § 20. We are referred to decisions where we have been closely divided on whether state action violated due process. More specifically we are cited many instances where the Court has been conspicuously in disagreement on the illegal character of confessions under the Due Process Clause. If the Court cannot agree as to what confessions violate the Fourteenth Amendment, how can one who risks criminal prosecutions for his acts be sure of the standard? Thus it is sought to show that police officers such as petitioner walk on ground far too treacherous for criminal responsibility.

Many criminal statutes might be extended to circumstances so extreme as to make their application unconstitutional. Conversely, as we held in *Screws*, a close construction will often save an act from vagueness that is fatal. The present case is as good an illustration as any. It is as plain as a pikestaff that the present confessions would not be allowed in evidence whatever the school of thought concerning the scope and meaning of the Due Process Clause. This is the classic use of force to make a man testify against himself. The result is as plain as if the rack, the wheel, and the thumb screw—the ancient methods of securing evidence by torture, *Brown v. State of Mississippi, Chambers v. State of Florida*, were used to compel the confession. Some day the application of § 20 to less obvious methods of coercion may be presented and doubts as to the adequacy of the standard of guilt may be presented. There may be a similar doubt when an officer is tried under § 20 for beating a man to death. That was a doubt stirred in the Screws case; and it was the reason we held that the purpose must be plain, the deprivation of the constitutional right willful. But where police take matters in their own hands, seize victims, beat and pound them until they confess, there cannot be the slightest doubt that the police have deprived the victim of a right under the Constitution. It is the right of the accused to be tried by a legally constituted court, not by a kangaroo court. Hence when officers wring

D. The Department of Justice Civil Rights Section and the Disappointment of *Screws v. United States* 937

confessions from the accused by force and violence, they violate some of the most fundamental, basic, and well-established constitutional rights which every citizen enjoys. Petitioner and his associates acted willfully and purposely; their aim was precisely to deny the protection that the Constitution affords. It was an arrogant and brutal deprivation of rights which the Constitution specifically guarantees. Section 20 would be denied the high service for which it was designed if rights so palpably plain were denied its protection. Only casuistry could make vague and nebulous what our constitutional scheme makes so clear and specific.

An effort, however, is made to free Williams by an extremely technical construction of the indictment and charge, so as to condemn the application of § 20 on the grounds of vagueness.

The indictment charged that petitioners deprived designated persons of rights and privileges secured to them by the Fourteenth Amendment. These deprivations were defined in the indictment to include "illegal" assault and battery. But the meaning of these rights in the context of the indictment was plain, viz. immunity from the use of force and violence to obtain a confession. Thus count 2 of the indictment charges that the Fourteenth Amendment rights of one Purnell were violated in the following respects: ". . . the right and privilege not to be deprived of liberty without due process of law, the right and privilege to be secure in his person while in the custody of the State of Florida, the right and privilege not to be subjected to punishment without due process of law, the right and privilege to be immune, while in the custody of persons acting under color of the laws of the State of Florida, from illegal assault and battery by any person exercising the authority of said State, and the right and privilege to be tried by due process of law and if found guilty to be sentenced and punished in accordance with the laws of the State of Florida; that is to say, on or about the 28th day of March, 1947, the defendants arrested and detained and caused to be arrested and detained the said Frank J. Purnell, Jr., and brought and caused him to be brought to and into a certain building sometimes called a shack on the premises of the Lindsley Lumber Co., at or near 3810 N.W. 17th Avenue, in said City of Miami, Florida, and did there detain the said Frank J. Purnell, Jr., and while he was so detained the defendants did then and there illegally strike, bruise, batter, beat, assault and torture the said Frank J. Purnell, Jr., in order illegally to coerce and force the said Frank J. Purnell, Jr., to make an admission and confession of his guilt in connection with the alleged theft of personal property, alleged to be the property of said Lindsley Lumber Co., and in order illegally to coerce and force the said Frank J. Purnell, Jr., to name and accuse other persons as participants in alleged thefts of personal property, alleged to be the property of the said Lindsley Lumber Co., and for the purpose of imposing illegal summary punishment upon the said Frank J. Purnell, Jr."

The trial judge in his charge to the jury summarized Count 2 as meaning that the defendants beat Purnell "for the purpose of forcing him to make a confession and for the purpose of imposing illegal summary punishment upon him." He further made clear that the defendants were "not here on trial for a violation of any law of the State of Florida for assault" nor "for assault under any laws of the United States." There cannot be the slightest doubt from the reading of the indictment and charge as a whole that the defendants were charged with and tried for one of the most brutal deprivations of constitutional rights that can be imagined. It therefore strains at technicalities to say that any issue of vagueness of § 20 as construed and applied is present in the case. Our concern is to see that substantial justice is done, not to search the record for possible errors which will defeat the great purpose of Congress in enacting § 20.

Affirmed.

Experience in the effort to apply the doctrine of *Screws v. United States*, 325 U.S. 91, 65 S. Ct. 1031, 89 L. Ed. 1495, leads Mr. Justice FRANKFURTER, Mr. Justice JACKSON and Mr. Justice MINTON to dissent for the reasons set forth in dissent in that case.

NOTES AND QUESTIONS

1. The Court says without irony that the lower court's jury instructions "conformed" with *Screws*. It does not reproduce the charge, although it's hard to imagine that it wasn't a ground for the defendant's appeal. The Court does state that the jury was instructed that the charged crime was beating the defendant to induce a confession and not for assault under either state or federal law. Does this satisfy even a strict reading of *Screws*'s intent requirements?

2. What is it about confession-induced beatings that makes this an easier case than *Screws*, at least for Justice Douglas if not for Justices Frankfurter and Jackson? Is it factual, in that the beatings here were administered to each victim "until he confessed," making their unconstitutional object more obvious? Is it legal, in that the Supreme Court as of the time of the misconduct had several decisions on the books holding torture-induced confessions unconstitutional? Note that Justice Douglas seems to view confession-induced beatings to present much more clearcut constitutional violations — "plain as a pikestaff" — than the murder of persons under arrest.

3. What facts are essential here to establishing the "under color of law" element? Should it matter that Williams appears to have been retained for this matter by the lumber company in his capacity as a private detective, and not assigned to the case by the City of Miami in his capacity as a Special Police Officer? The Court does not say whether the victims had been arrested. What if they were employees, and were on the premises in that capacity and not under arrest? How significant is it that the city sent an actual police officer to observe the proceedings, although the Court does not say whether he participated in the beatings. Does it matter who the "others" were who administered the beatings? What is the significance of the fact that Williams flashed his badge? From whose perspective is the "under color of law" element measured?

The next case, involving the infamous murder of civil rights activists in Philadelphia, Mississippi, is one of two federal criminal prosecutions arising out of the civil rights movement to reach the Supreme Court. Civil rights activists were largely on their own in the South, without federal protection and subject to hostilities from local communities that were ignored and sometimes abetted by local law enforcement. Hoover was not personally supportive of the civil rights movement, and the FBI was notoriously reluctant to provide "protection" for civil rights activists in the South. Gage, G-Man, *supra* at 495. Hoover viewed that protection as the responsibility of local law enforcement, *id.*, much in the same way the *Screws* dissenters viewed the prosecution of Sheriff Screws as a matter of local responsibility. The FBI was generally willing, on the other hand, to investigate crimes after the fact if it believed there was a basis for federal jurisdiction.

United States v. Price
383 U.S. 787 (1966)

Mr. Justice FORTAS delivered the opinion of the Court.

These are direct appeals from the dismissal in part of two indictments returned by the United States Grand Jury for the Southern District of Mississippi. The indictments allege assaults by the accused persons upon the rights of the asserted victims to due process of law under the Fourteenth Amendment. The indictment in No. 59 charges 18 persons with violations of 18 U.S.C. § 241 (1964 ed.). In No. 60, the same 18 persons are charged with offenses based upon 18 U.S.C. § 242 (1964 ed.). These are among the so-called civil rights statutes which have come to us from Reconstruction days, the period in our history which also produced the Thirteenth, Fourteenth, and Fifteenth Amendments to the Constitution.

The sole question presented in these appeals is whether the specified statutes make criminal the conduct for which the individuals were indicted. It is an issue of construction, not of constitutional power. We have no doubt of "the power of Congress to enforce by appropriate criminal sanction every right guaranteed by the Due Process Clause of the Fourteenth Amendment."

The events upon which the charges are based, as alleged in the indictments, are as follows: On June 21, 1964, Cecil Ray Price, the Deputy Sheriff of Neshoba County, Mississippi, detained Michael Henry Schwerner, James Earl Chaney and Andrew Goodman in the Neshoba County jail located in Philadelphia, Mississippi. He released them in the dark of that night. He then proceeded by automobile on Highway 19 to intercept his erstwhile wards. He removed the three men from their automobile, placed them in an official automobile of the Neshoba County Sheriff's office, and transported them to a place on an unpaved road.

These acts, it is alleged, were part of a plan and conspiracy whereby the three men were intercepted by the 18 defendants, including Deputy Sheriff Price, Sheriff Rainey and Patrolman Willis of the Philadelphia, Mississippi, Police Department. The purpose and intent of the release from custody and the interception, according to the charge, were to "punish" the three men. The defendants, it is alleged, "did wilfully assault, shoot and kill" each of the three. And, the charge continues, the bodies of the three victims were transported by one of the defendants from the rendezvous on the unpaved road to the vicinity of the construction site of an earthen dam approximately five miles southwest of Philadelphia, Mississippi.

These are federal and not state indictments. They do not charge as crimes the alleged assaults or murders. The indictments are framed to fit the stated federal statutes, and the question before us is whether the attempt of the draftsman for the Grand Jury in Mississippi has been successful: whether the indictments charge offenses against the various defendants which may be prosecuted under the designated federal statutes.

We shall deal first with the indictment in No. 60, based on § 242 of the Criminal Code and then with the indictment in No. 59, under § 241. We do this for ease of exposition and because § 242 was enacted by the Congress about four years prior to § 241. Section 242 was enacted in 1866; § 241 in 1870.

I. No. 60

Section 242 defines a misdemeanor, punishable by fine of not more than $1,000 or imprisonment for not more than one year, or both. So far as here significant, it provides punishment for "Whoever, under color of any law, statute, ordinance, regulation, or custom, willfully subjects any inhabitant of any State . . . to the deprivation of any rights, privileges, or immunities secured or protected by the Constitution or laws of the United States. . . ."

The indictment in No. 60 contains four counts, each of which names as defendants the three officials and 15 nonofficial persons. The First Court charges, on the basis of allegations substantially as set forth above, that all of the defendants conspired "to wilfully subject" Schwerner, Chaney and Goodman "to the deprivation of their right, privilege and immunity secured and protected by the Fourteenth Amendment to the Constitution of the United States not to be summarily punished without due process of law by persons acting under color of the laws of the State of Mississippi." This is said to constitute a conspiracy to violate § 242, and therefore an offense under 18 U.S.C. § 371 (1964 ed.). The latter section, the general conspiracy statute, makes it a crime to conspire to commit any offense against the United States. The penalty for violation is the same as for direct violation of § 242 — that is, it is a misdemeanor.

On a motion to dismiss, the District Court sustained this First Court as to all defendants. As to the sheriff, deputy sheriff and patrolman, the court recognized that each was clearly alleged to have been acting "under color of law" as required by § 242. As to the private persons, the District Court held that "(I)t is immaterial to the conspiracy that these private individuals were not acting under color of law" because the count charges that they were conspiring with persons who were so acting.

The court necessarily was satisfied that the indictment, in alleging the arrest, detention, release, interception and killing of Schwerner, Chaney and Goodman, adequately stated as the purpose of the conspiracy, a violation of § 242, and that this section could be violated by "wilfully subject(ing the victims) . . . to the deprivation of their right, privilege and immunity" under the Due Process Clause of the Fourteenth Amendment.

No appeal was taken by the defendants from the decision of the trial court with respect to the First Count and it is not before us for adjudication.

The Second, Third and Fourth Counts of the indictment in No. 60 charge all of the defendants, not with conspiracy, but with substantive violations of § 242. Each of these counts charges that the defendants, acting "under color of the laws of the State of Mississippi," "did wilfully assault, shoot and kill" Schwerner, Chaney and Goodman, respectively, "for the purpose and with the intent" of punishing each of the three and that the defendants "did thereby wilfully deprive" each "of rights, privileges and immunities secured and protected by the Constitution and the laws of the United States" — namely, due process of law.

The District Court held these counts of the indictment valid as to the sheriff, deputy sheriff and patrolman. But it dismissed them as against the nonofficial defendants because the counts do not charge that the latter were "officers in fact, or de facto in anything allegedly done by them 'under color of law.'"

We note that by sustaining these counts against the three officers, the court again necessarily concluded that an offense under § 242 is properly stated by allegations of willful deprivation, under color of law, of life and liberty without due process of law. We agree. No other result would be permissible under the decisions of this Court.

But we cannot agree that the Second, Third or Fourth Counts may be dismissed as against the nonofficial defendants. Section 242 applies only where a person indicted has acted "under color" of law. Private persons, jointly engaged with state officials in the prohibited action, are acting "under color" of law for purposes of the statute. To act "under color" of law does not require that the accused be an officer of the State. It is enough that he is a willful participant in joint activity with the State or its agents.

In the present case, according to the indictment, the brutal joint adventure was made possible by state detention and calculated release of the prisoners by an officer of the State. This action, clearly attributable to the State, was part of the monstrous design described by the indictment. State officers participated in every phase of the alleged venture: the release from jail, the interception, assault and murder. It was a joint activity, from start to finish. Those who took advantage of participation by state officers in accomplishment of the foul purpose alleged must suffer the consequences of that participation. In effect, if the allegations are true, they were participants in official lawlessness, acting in willful concert with state officers and hence under color of law.

Appellees urge that the decision of the District Court was based upon a construction of the indictment to the effect that it did not charge the private individuals with acting "under color" of law. Consequently, they urge us to affirm in No. 60. In any event, they submit, since the trial court's decision was based on the inadequacy of the indictment and not on construction of the statute, we have no jurisdiction to review it on direct appeal. We do not agree. Each count of the indictment specifically alleges that all of the defendants were acting "under color of the laws of the State of Mississippi." The fault lies not in the indictment, but in the

D. The Department of Justice Civil Rights Section and the Disappointment of *Screws v. United States*

District Court's view that the statute requires that each offender be an official or that he act in an official capacity. We have jurisdiction to consider this statutory question on direct appeal and, as we have shown, the trial court's determination of it is in error. Since each of the private individuals is indictable as a principal acting under color of law, we need not consider whether he might be held to answer as an "aider or abettor" under 18 U.S.C. § 2 (1964 ed.), despite omission to include such a charge in the indictment.

Accordingly, we reverse the dismissal of the Second, Third and Fourth Counts of the indictment in No. 60 and remand for trial.

II. No. 59

No. 59 charges each of the 18 defendants with a felony—a violation of § 241. This indictment is in one count. It charges that the defendants "conspired together . . . to injure, oppress, threaten and intimidate" Schwerner, Chaney and Goodman "in the free exercise and enjoyment of the right and privilege secured to them by the Fourteenth Amendment to the Constitution of the United States not to be deprived of life or liberty without due process of law by persons acting under color of the laws of Mississippi." The indictment alleges that it was the purpose of the conspiracy that Deputy Sheriff Price would release Schwerner, Chaney and Goodman from custody in the Neshoba County jail at such time that Price and the other 17 defendants "could and would intercept" them "and threaten, assault, shoot and kill them." The penalty under § 241 is a fine of not more than $5,000, or imprisonment for not more than 10 years, or both.

Section 241 is a conspiracy statute. It reads as follows:

If two or more persons conspire to injure, oppress, threaten, or intimidate any citizen in the free exercise or enjoyment of any right or privilege secured to him by the Constitution or laws of the United States, or because of his having so exercised the same; or

If two or more persons go in disguise on the highway, or on the premises of another, with intent to prevent or hinder his free exercise or enjoyment of any right or privilege so secured—

They shall be fined not more than $5,000 or imprisoned not more than ten years, or both.

The District Court dismissed the indictment as to all defendants. In effect, although § 241 includes rights or privileges secured by the Constitution or laws of the United States without qualification or limitation, the court held that it does not include rights protected by the Fourteenth Amendment.

It will be recalled that in No. 60 the District Court held that § 242 included the denial of Fourteenth Amendment rights—the same right to due process involved in the indictment under § 241. Both include rights or privileges secured by the Constitution or laws of the United States. Neither is qualified or limited. Each includes, presumably, all of the Constitution and laws of the United States. To the reader of the two sections, versed only in the English language, it may seem bewildering that the two sections could be so differently read.

But the District Court purported to read the statutes with the gloss of *Williams I*. In that case, the only case in which this Court has squarely confronted the point at issue, the Court did in fact sustain dismissal of an indictment under § 241. But it did not, as the District Court incorrectly assumed, hold that § 241 is inapplicable to Fourteenth Amendment rights. The Court divided equally on the issue. Four Justices, in an opinion by Mr. Justice Frankfurter, were of the view that § 241 "only covers conduct which interferes with rights arising from the substantive powers of the Federal Government"—rights "which Congress can beyond doubt constitutionally secure against interference by private individuals." Four other Justices, in an opinion by Mr. Justice Douglas, found no support for Mr. Justice Frankfurter's view in the language of the section, its legislative history, or its judicial interpretation up to that time. They read the statute as plainly covering conspiracies to injure others in the

Chapter X The Department of Justice and the Prosecution of Civil Rights Crimes

exercise of the Fourteenth Amendment rights. They could see no obstacle to using it to punish deprivations of such rights. Dismissal of the indictment was affirmed because Mr. Justice Black voted with those who joined Mr. Justice Frankfurter. He did so, however, for an entirely different reason—that the prosecution was barred by res judicata—and he expressed no view on the issue whether "s 241, as applied, is too vague and uncertain in scope to be consistent with the Fifth Amendment." Williams I thus left the proper construction of § 241, as regards its applicability to protect Fourteenth Amendment rights, an open question.

In view of the detailed opinions in *Williams I*, it would be supererogation to track the arguments in all of their intricacy. On the basis of an extensive re-examination of the question, we conclude that the District Court erred; that § 241 must be read as it is written—to reach conspiracies "to injure . . . any citizen in the free exercise or enjoyment of any right or privilege secured to him by the Constitution or laws of the United States . . ."; that this language includes rights or privileges protected by the Fourteenth Amendment; that whatever the ultimate coverage of the section may be, it extends to conspiracies otherwise within the scope of the section participated in by officials alone or in collaboration with private persons; and that the indictment in No. 59 properly charges such a conspiracy in violation of § 241. We shall confine ourselves to a review of the major considerations which induce our conclusion.

1

There is no doubt that the indictment in No. 59 sets forth a conspiracy within the ambit of the Fourteenth Amendment. Like the indictment in No. 60, supra, it alleges that the defendants acted "under color of law" and that the conspiracy included action by the State through its law enforcement officers to punish the alleged victims without due process of law in violation of the Fourteenth Amendment's direct admonition to the States.

The indictment specifically alleges that the sheriff, deputy sheriff and a patrolman participated in the conspiracy; that it was a part of the "plan and purpose of the conspiracy" that Deputy Sheriff Price, "while having (the three victims) . . . in his custody in the Neshoba County Jail . . . would release them from custody at such time that he (and others of the defendants) . . . could and would intercept (the three victims) . . . and threaten, assault, shoot and kill them."

This is an allegation of state action which, beyond dispute, brings the conspiracy within the ambit of the Fourteenth Amendment. It is an allegation of official, state participation in murder, accomplished by and through its officers with the participation of others. It is an allegation that the State, without the semblance of due process of law as required of it by the Fourteenth Amendment, used its sovereign power and office to release the victims from jail so that they were not charged and tried as required by law, but instead could be intercepted and killed. If the Fourteenth Amendment forbids denial of counsel, it clearly denounces denial of any trial at all.

As we have consistently held "The Fourteenth Amendment protects the individual against state action, not against wrongs done by individuals." In the present case, the participation by law enforcement officers, as alleged in the indictment, is clearly state action, as we have discussed, and it is therefore within the scope of the Fourteenth Amendment.

2

The argument, however, of Mr. Justice Frankfurter's opinion in *Williams I*, upon which the District Court rests its decision, cuts beneath this. It does not deny that the accused conduct is within the scope of the Fourteenth Amendment, but it contends that in enacting § 241, the Congress intended to include only the rights and privileges conferred on the citizen by reason of the "substantive" powers of the Federal Government—that is, by reason of federal power operating directly upon the citizen and not merely by means of prohibitions of state action.

D. The Department of Justice Civil Rights Section and the Disappointment of *Screws v. United States*   **943**

As the Court of Appeals for the Fifth Circuit in *Williams I*, relied upon in the opinion below, put it, "the Congress had in mind the federal rights and privileges which appertain to citizens as such and not the general rights extended to all persons by the . . . Fourteenth Amendment." We do not agree.

The language of § 241 is plain and unlimited. As we have discussed, its language embraces all of the rights and privileges secured to citizens by all of the Constitution and all of the laws of the United States. There is no indication in the language that the sweep of the section is confined to rights that are conferred by or "flow from" the Federal Government, as distinguished from those secured or confirmed or guaranteed by the Constitution. We agree with the observation of Mr. Justice Holmes in *United States v. Mosley*, that

> The source of this section in the doings of the Ku Klux and the like is obvious, and acts of violence obviously were in the mind of Congress. Naturally Congress put forth all its powers. . . . (T)his section dealt with Federal rights, and with all Federal rights, and protected them in the lump. . . . (It should not be construed so) as to deprive citizens of the United States of the general protection which on its face § 19 (now § 241) most reasonably affords.

We believe, with Mr. Justice Holmes, that the history of the events from which § 241 emerged illuminates the purpose and means of the statute with an unmistakable light. We think that history leaves no doubt that, if we are to give § 241 the scope that its origins dictate, we must accord it a sweep as broad as its language. We are not at liberty to seek ingenious analytical instruments for excluding from its general language the Due Process Clause of the Fourteenth Amendment — particularly since the violent denial of legal process was one of the reasons motivating enactment of the section.

Section 241 was enacted as part of what came to be known as the Enforcement Act of 1870, 16 Stat. 140.10 The Act was passed on May 31, 1870, only a few months after ratification of the Fifteenth Amendment. In addition to the new § 241, it included a re-enactment of a provision of the Civil Rights Act of 1866 which is now § 242. The intended breadth of § 241 is emphasized by contrast with the narrowness of § 242 as it then was. Section 242 forbade the deprivation, "under color of any law," of "any right secured or protected by this act." The rights protected by the Act were narrow and specific: "to make and enforce contracts, to sue, be parties, give evidence, and to the full and equal benefit of all laws and proceedings for the security of person and property as is enjoyed by white citizens (and to) be subject to like punishment, pains, penalties, taxes, licenses, and exactions of every kind, and none other." Act of May 31, 1870, § 16, 16 Stat. 144, re-enacting with minor changes Act of April 9, 1866, § 1, 14 Stat. 27. Between 1866 and 1870 there was much agitated criticism in the Congress and in the Nation because of the continued denial of rights to Negroes, sometimes accompanied by violent assaults. In response to the demands for more stringent legislation Congress enacted the Enforcement Act of 1870. Congress had before it and re-enacted § 242 which was explicitly limited as we have described. At the same time, it included § 241 in the Act using broad language to cover not just the rights enumerated in § 242, but all rights and privileges under the Constitution and laws of the United States.

It was not until the statutory revision of 1874 that the specific enumeration of protected rights was eliminated from § 242. The section was then broadened to include as wide a range of rights as § 241 already did: "any rights, privileges, or immunities, secured or protected by the Constitution or laws of the United States." The substantial change thus effected was made with the customary stout assertions of the codifiers that they had merely clarified and reorganized without changing substance. Section 241 was left essentially unchanged, and neither in the 1874 revision nor in any subsequent re-enactment has there been the slightest indication of a congressional intent to narrow or limit the original broad scope of § 241. It is clear, therefore, that § 241, from original enactment through subsequent codifications, was intended to deal, as Mr. Justice Holmes put it, with conspiracies to interfere with "Federal rights, and with all Federal rights." We find no basis whatsoever for a judgment of Solomon which would give to the statute less than its words command.

The purpose and scope of the 1866 and 1870 enactments must be viewed against the events and passions of the time. The Civil War had ended in April 1865. Relations between Negroes and whites were increasingly turbulent. Congress had taken control of the entire governmental process in former Confederate States. It had declared the governments in 10 "unreconstructed" States to be illegal and had set up federal military administrations in their place. Congress refused to seat representatives from these States until they had adopted constitutions guaranteeing Negro suffrage, and had ratified the Fourteenth Amendment. Constitutional conventions were called in 1868. Six of the 10 States fulfilled Congress' requirements in 1868, the other four by 1870.

For a few years "radical" Republicans dominated the governments of the Southern States and Negroes played a substantial political role. But countermeasures were swift and violent. The Kr Klux Klan was organized by southern whites in 1866 and a similar organization appeared with the romantic title of the Knights of the White Camellia. In 1868 a wave of murders and assaults was launched including assassinations designed to keep Negroes from the polls. The States themselves were helpless, despite the resort by some of them to extreme measures such as making it legal to hunt down and shoot any disguised man.

Within the Congress pressures mounted in the period between the end of the war and 1870 for drastic measures. A few months after the ratification of the Thirteenth Amendment on December 6, 1865, Congress, on April 9, 1866, enacted the Civil Rights Act of 1866, which, as we have described, included § 242 in its originally narrow form. On June 13, 1866, the Fourteenth Amendment was proposed, and it was ratified in July 1868. In February 1869 the Fifteenth Amendment was proposed, and it was ratified in February 1870. On May 31, 1870, the Enforcement Act of 1870 was enacted.

In this context, it is hardly conceivable that Congress intended § 241 to apply only to a narrow and relatively unimportant category of rights. We cannot doubt that the purpose and effect of § 241 was to reach assaults upon rights under the entire Constitution, including the Thirteenth, Fourteenth and Fifteenth Amendments, and not merely under part of it.

This is fully attested by the only statement explanatory of § 241 in the recorded congressional proceedings relative to its enactment. We refer to the speech of Senator Pool of North Carolina who introduced the provisions as an amendment to the Enforcement Act of 1870. The Senator's remarks are printed in full in the Appendix to this opinion. He urged that the section was needed in order to punish invasions of the newly adopted Fourteenth and Fifteenth Amendments to the Constitution. He acknowledged that the States as such were beyond the reach of the punitive process, and that the legislation must therefore operate upon individuals. He made it clear that "It matters not whether those individuals be officers or whether they are acting upon their own responsibility." We find no evidence whatever that Senator Pool intended that § 241 should not cover violations of Fourteenth Amendment rights, or that it should not include state action or actions by state officials.

We conclude, therefore, that it is incumbent upon us to read § 241 with full credit to its language. Nothing in the prior decisions of this Court or of other courts which have considered the matter stands in the way of that conclusion.

The present application of the statutes at issue does not raise fundamental questions of federal-state relationships. We are here concerned with allegations which squarely and indisputably involve state action in direct violation of the mandate of the Fourteenth Amendment—that no State shall deprive any person of life or liberty without due process of law. This is a direct, traditional concern of the Federal Government. It is an area in which the federal interest has existed for at least a century, and in which federal participation has intensified as part of a renewed emphasis upon civil rights. Even as recently as 1951, when *Williams I* was

D. The Department of Justice Civil Rights Section and the Disappointment of *Screws v. United States*   945

decided, the federal role in the establishment and vindication of fundamental rights—such as the freedom to travel, nondiscriminatory access to public areas and nondiscriminatory educational facilities—was neither as pervasive nor as intense as it is today. Today, a decision interpreting a federal law in accordance with its historical design, to punish denials by state action of constitutional rights of the person can hardly be regarded as adversely affecting "the wise adjustment between State responsibility and national." In any event, the problem, being statutory and not constitutional, is ultimately, as it was in the beginning, susceptible of congressional disposition.

Reversed and remanded.

NOTES AND QUESTIONS

1. The facts underlying *Price* are familiar: the arrest and subsequent "disappearance" of three civil rights workers near Philadelphia, Mississippi, during the "Freedom Summer" of 1964, and the subsequent discovery by the FBI of their torched car and, later, their bodies, 14 feet below an earthen dam on a local farm. The 1988 movie *Mississippi Burning* focused on the FBI investigation. Throughout the early 1960s, the Justice Department under Bobby Kennedy and the FBI under Hoover were criticized for their failure to provide advance federal protection for civil rights workers in the Deep South. Michael R. Belknap, *The Vindication of Burke Marshall: The Southern Legal System and the Anti-Civil Rights Violence of the 1960s*, 33 Emory L.J. 93, 99-100 (1984).

FBI Poster

Loosely based on the missing civil rights workers in Philadelphia, Mississippi, *Mississippi Burning* starred Gene Hackman, Willem Dafoe, and Frances McDormand.

2. Unlike *Screws* and *Williams, Price* comes to the Court not as an appeal from a verdict but rather as an appeal from the district court's dismissal of an indictment. The Court, curiously, frames the question before it as whether "the draftsman for the Grand Jury in Mississippi" has successfully brought the case within the scope of §§ 241 and 242. Why, in 1966, is the Court still indulging the fiction that the grand jury is independently drafting indictments through its appointed "draftsman"?

3. The district court here had dismissed the substantive (i.e., non-conspiracy) counts against the defendants who were not public officials on the ground that those defendants were not acting "under color of law." Rejecting this view, the Court observes that the indictment charges a "brutal joint adventure," with the Mississippi public officials' calculated release of their prisoners to a bloodthirsty mob that was poised to slaughter them, and that the mob was thereby "in willful concert with state officers and hence under color of law." Could the private defendants alternatively be charged and convicted as aiders and abettors under 18 U.S.C. § 2, on the theory that they "intended to facilitate the commission of a crime by another"?

4. The Court's discussion of the legislative history of § 241 reveals an entirely different take on the Reconstruction era than that of the *Screws* dissenters, 20 years earlier, who had criticized the "vengeful spirit" of that period. In its analysis the Court twice cites in footnotes the recently published *The Era of Reconstruction: 1865-77* (1965) by University of California historian Kenneth Stampp, one of the first major historical works to cast Reconstruction in a positive light, unlike the prevailing view of the Dunning School. In his foreword, Stampp noted that at present—that is, 1965—"the leaders of the resistance to civil rights legislation and racial integration have evoked the hobgoblins of reconstruction to advance their cause," and notes that the pejorative perspective on Reconstruction "lives on" even in liberal circles. *Id.* at vii.

5. On remand in *Price*, 5 of the 18 defendants—including Sheriff Cecil Ray Price—were convicted at trial. It was the first time Mississippi jurors had convicted a white man charged with a significant racial killing. *See* Belknap, *The Vindication of Burke Marshall, supra* at 93, 112.

6. The federal district court judge who dismissed the grand jury indictments in *Price* was Harold Cox, the notoriously racist Mississippi judge who also strong-armed a grand jury into indicting for perjury Black witnesses who testified in a voting rights case and then held in contempt the DOJ attorneys who refused to sign the indictment. *United States v. Cox*, 342 F.2d 167 (1965). *See* Chapter VII *supra*.

On at least two occasions in the 1960s, both in high-profile cases where there was public pressure, the Department of Justice brought civil rights prosecutions even where state prosecutors, unlike the Georgia authorities in *Screws*, had brought prosecutions but had been unable to secure convictions. One example was the federal prosecution of the Klansmen who had murdered Black army reservist Lemuel Penn in 1964. Penn, returning to his home in Washington, D.C., from reserve training at Fort Benning in Georgia, was gunned down in his car just outside Athens, Georgia. After a Georgia state court jury including other Klansmen and their sympathizers acquitted the defendants, the DOJ brought federal charges under § 241 and obtained convictions, which were affirmed in *Myers v. United States*, 377 F.2d 412 (5th Cir. 1967). For a thorough accounting of the two trials and overhanging legal issues and developments, *see* Michael R. Belknap, *The Legal Legacy of Lemuel Penn*, 25 How. L.J. 467 (1982).

Another example was the successful federal prosecution of the murderers of Michigan civil rights activist Viola Liuzzo. Liuzzo, a mother of five, was gunned down in her car by Klansmen as she was shuttling other activists between Montgomery and Selma in connection with the Selma-Montgomery voting rights march in 1965. One of the Klansmen was tried twice in state court, the first trial ending in a hung jury and the second in an acquittal. Subsequently,

D. The Department of Justice Civil Rights Section and the Disappointment of *Screws v. United States*   **947**

three of the four Klansmen were convicted in federal court under § 241. *See Liuzzo v. United States*, 485 F. Supp. 1274, 1276 (E.D. Mich. 1980) (recounting prosecution history in civil suit).

The "fourth Klansmen," who was not charged in the federal indictment, turned out to be an FBI agent who had infiltrated the Klan and was in the car with the shooters who killed Liuzzo. He testified for the government in all three trials and, naturally, was the focus of vigorous cross-examination by defense counsel. *Id.* It was all to the great embarrassment of the FBI, as the day after Liuzzo's murder President Johnson had gone on national television and praised the FBI and Hoover by name for so promptly solving the case. *Id.* Liuzzo's children ultimately sued the FBI under the Federal Tort Claims Act for causing, or at least failing to prevent, their mother's murder.

The Supreme Court has only sporadically addressed §§ 241 and 242 since *Price* and its companion case *United States v. Guest*, 383 U.S. 745 (1966). Congress has amended § 242 three times to increase its maximum penalties, although since 1987 sentences have been largely determined by the United States Sentencing Guidelines. The statutes have often been utilized in civil rights prosecutions outside the police brutality context, such as sexual harassment and abuse by public officials. One court of appeals decision and one Supreme Court decision do warrant special attention, however.

In a case arising out the Watergate scandals of the Nixon Administration, White House counsel and senior domestic advisor John D. Ehrlichmann was prosecuted for his role in an effort to discredit Daniel Ellsberg, who in 1971 had leaked to the press the "Pentagon Papers," a confidential Defense Department study that was highly critical of U.S. military efforts in Southeast Asia and Vietnam. Ehrlichman and others consequently conspired to burglarize the office of Daniel Ellsberg's psychiatrist in an effort to find information damaging to Ellsberg's credibility. *United States v. Ehrlichman*, 546 F.2d 910, 914-16 (D.C. Cir. 1976). Charged under 18 U.S.C. § 241, which the Supreme Court had interpreted in *Guest* as having the same specific intent requirement as § 242, Ehrlichman defended on the ground that he had a good faith belief, mistaken or not, that the executive had a constitutional prerogative to authorize a warrantless Fourth Amendment search for national security purposes. *Id.* at 916. The D.C. Circuit rejected that defense. It held that although "some of the language in *Screws* can be read more broadly," § 242's intent requirement has two components: Is the right allegedly violated "clearly delineated"? Did the defendant act with the intent to deprive the victim of the enjoyment of the interests protected by that right? *Id.* at 921. "If both requirements are met, even if the defendant did not in fact recognize the unconstitutionality of his act," he has acted willfully. *Id.*

The Supreme Court itself reached a similar conclusion on § 242's intent requirement 20 years later in *United States v. Lanier*, 520 U.S. 259 (1997). Tennessee state probate court judge David Lanier was prosecuted and convicted under § 242 for sexually assaulting multiple women in his chambers, including court employees and a woman who had legal proceedings before his court. The Sixth Circuit ultimately reversed the conviction on the ground that § 242 failed to give "fair warning" that "sexual assault" was within its coverage. *Id.* at 263. Writing for a unanimous Court, Justice Souter held that the "fair warning" requirement of § 242, as interpreted in *Screws*, required only that the right at issue be "clearly established," and analogized the requirement to the similar requirement in applications of qualified immunity under 42 U.S.C. § 1983. *Id.* at 269-71. The Court explicitly rejected the Sixth Circuit's view that the right at issue must be established by Supreme Court precedent, as opposed to precedent of lower courts, and must have been previously applied in a "fundamentally similar" context. *Id.*

Two caveats must be noted regarding *Lanier*. First, the Court did not explicitly address or even mention the "willfully" element. It seems unlikely, however, inasmuch as *Screws*'s interpretation(s) of the "willfully" requirement arose from the same "fair warning" concerns as in *Lanier*, that the adverb imposes requirements beyond those described in *Lanier*. Second, as observed in Chapter VI *supra*, the Supreme Court has made the defense of qualified immunity increasingly easier to prove, in part by requiring greater specificity in the factual application of the right at issue. This expansion of the scope of qualified immunity has been driven largely by policy reasons that are not necessarily applicable in the criminal context.

Of course, the "federal rights" cross-referenced in §§ 241 and 242 have evolved since *Price* and *Guest*, and thereby the scope of the statutes. In 1989, notably, in *Graham v. O'Connor*, 490 U.S. 386, 396-97 (1989), the Supreme Court held that the Fourth Amendment's prohibition on unreasonable seizures creates a right to be free from a police officer's "objectively unreasonable" use of force. Accordingly, the Department of Justice has been willing to use § 242 in police brutality cases, including in its 1992 prosecution of Los Angeles police officers for the beating of Rodney King. That prosecution and others are considered in the next sections, along with the Department of Justice policies on federal civil rights prosecutions in the context of federalism principles and the law of double jeopardy.

As prelude, we look at the law of double jeopardy and the Constitution's surprising tolerance for successive prosecutions.

E. DOUBLE JEOPARDY, SUCCESSIVE PROSECUTIONS, AND FEDERAL CIVIL RIGHTS ENFORCEMENT

Abbate v. United States
359 U.S. 187 (1959)

Mr. Justice BRENNAN delivered the opinion of the Court.

During a strike against the Southern Bell Telephone and Telegraph Company, the petitioners and one McLeod were solicited in Chicago, Illinois, by a union official, Shelby, to dynamite facilities of the telephone company located in the States of Mississippi, Tennessee, and Louisiana. The four men met in Chicago where Shelby gave the petitioners and McLeod the plans of the facilities to be dynamited and instructed them as to the method to be used. After Shelby left Chicago the petitioners told McLeod that they would not go through with the plan. McLeod, however, obtained dynamite and went to Mississippi to destroy telephone company facilities located there. The petitioners thereupon disclosed the plot to the telephone company and the Chicago police.

The petitioners, with Shelby and McLeod, were subsequently indicted by the State of Illinois for violating an Illinois statute making it a crime to conspire to injure or destroy the property of another. The indictment describes the property as "communication facilities belonging to the Southern Bell Telephone & Telegraph Company" and "belonging to the American Telephone and Telegraph Company." The petitioners entered pleas of guilty to the indictment and were each sentenced to three months' imprisonment.

Thereafter indictments were returned in the United States District Court for the Southern District of Mississippi against the petitioners and Shelby, and also against one Perry who pointed out to McLeod the property to be dynamited. This indictment does not refer to the facilities as belonging to the telephone companies, but charges the offense of violating 18 U.S.C. § 371, 18 U.S.C.A. § 3712 by conspiring to destroy, contrary to 18 U.S.C. § 1362, 18 U.S.C.A. § 1362, "certain works, property and material known as coaxial repeater stations and micro-wave towers . . . located in the States of Mississippi, Tennessee and Louisiana . . . which were essential and integral parts of systems and means of communication

E. Double Jeopardy, Successive Prosecutions, and Federal Civil Rights Enforcement 949

operated and controlled by the United States." McLeod confessed to his part in the conspiracy and testified on the federal trial to petitioners' acts of participation in the conspiracy. These same acts were the basis of the Illinois convictions. The Government also introduced proof that the Strategic Air Command, the Civil Aeronautics Administration, the Navy and other federal agencies have the exclusive use of some of the circuits within the coaxial cables carried by the repeater stations and micro-wave towers that were to be destroyed. The federal jury found the four defendants guilty as charged. On appeal the Fifth Circuit Court of Appeals reversed the convictions of Shelby and Perry for error in the admission of evidence, but affirmed the convictions of the petitioners. We granted certiorari limited to consideration of the claim that the federal prosecutions, based on the same acts as were the prior state convictions, placed petitioners twice in jeopardy contrary to the Fifth Amendment.

In *Bartkus v. People of Illinois*, the order of the prosecutions was the reverse of the order in this case. Here the federal prosecution came after the Illinois convictions. Thus this case squarely raises the question whether a federal prosecution of defendants already prosecuted for the same acts by a State subjects those defendants "for the same offense to be twice put in jeopardy of life or limb" in violation of the Fifth Amendment.

We do not write on a clean slate in deciding this question. As early as 1820 in *Houston v. Moore*, it was recognized that this issue would arise from the concurrent application of state and federal laws. During the following three decades a number of state courts reached differing conclusions as to whether a state prosecution would bar a subsequent federal prosecution of the same person for the same acts. Against this background this Court thoroughly considered the question in three cases between 1847 and 1852. In *Fox v. State of Ohio*, the petitioner had been convicted of passing a counterfeit coin of the United States within the State of Ohio in violation of a state statute. She contended that the Fifth Amendment prohibited successive state and federal prosecutions for the same acts, and therefore that a prosecution under the Ohio statute would prevent federal authorities from prosecuting the same act under the federal counterfeiting laws. Thus, the argument continued, the Court should declare the Ohio statute unconstitutional under the Supremacy Clause in order to preserve the effectiveness of federal law enforcement. *Houston v. Moore* and some of the leading state authorities bearing on whether the Fifth Amendment applied to successive state and federal prosecutions were argued to the Court. All members of the Court agreed that the Fifth Amendment would not prohibit a federal prosecution even though based on the same act of passing the counterfeit coin that resulted in the state prosecution. There was a division, however, as to what disposition of the case was required by this conclusion. The majority reasoned that since the Ohio prosecution would not render the Federal Government powerless to enforce its counterfeit laws there was no basis for declaring the Ohio statute unconstitutional under the Supremacy Clause, Const. art. 6. Mr. Justice McLean, dissenting, thought that since "the punishment under the State law would be no bar to a prosecution under the law of Congress," this undesirable result should be avoided by declaring the state statute unconstitutional, for, he said, "Nothing can be more repugnant . . . than two punishments for the same act." Three years later, in *United States v. Marigold*, a unanimous Court affirmed a conviction under the federal counterfeiting statute that was discussed in *Fox*. The Court, in holding that a state and a federal statute could both apply to the same conduct, accepted the conclusion of *Fox* that "the same act might . . . constitute an offense against both the State and Federal governments, and might draw to its commission the penalties denounced by either. . . ."

The third case, *Moore v. People of State of Illinois*, gave clear expression to the emerging principle that the Fifth Amendment did not apply to a federal prosecution subsequent to a state prosecution of the same person for the same acts. That case involved a conviction of Moore under an Illinois statute for harboring an escaped slave. A federal statute outlawed the same act as an interference with the rights of the owner of the slave. Moore urged that the

950 Chapter X The Department of Justice and the Prosecution of Civil Rights Crimes

Illinois statute was void "as it subjects the delinquent to a double punishment for a single offence." The Court rejected this argument, saying:

> Every citizen of the United States is also a citizen of a State or territory. He may be said to owe allegiance to two sovereigns, and may be liable to punishment for an infraction of the laws of either. The same act may be an offence or transgression of the laws of both. . . . That either or both may (if they see fit) punish such an offender, cannot be doubted. Yet it cannot be truly averred that the offender has been twice punished for the same offence; but only that by one act he has committed two offences, for each of which he is justly punishable. He could not plead the punishment by one in bar to a conviction by the other; consequently, this court has decided, in the case of *Fox v. State of Ohio*, . . . that a State may punish the offence of uttering or passing false coin, as a cheat or fraud practised on its citizens; and, in the case of the *United States v. Marigold*, . . . that Congress, in the proper exercise of its authority, may punish the same act as an offence against the United States.

Justice McLean again dissented on the ground of his dissent in *Fox*, namely, that the state law should be declared invalid for the very reason that "the conviction and punishment under the State law would be no bar to a prosecution under the law of Congress."

The reasoning of the Court in these three cases was subsequently accepted by this Court, in dictum, in the following cases: *United States v. Cruikshank*. . . . Typical of the statements adopting the principle is that of Chief Justice Taney, on circuit, in *United States v. Amy*, that "from the nature of our government, the same act may be an offence against the laws of the United States and also of a state, and be punishable in both."

Culminating this development was *United States v. Lanza*, where the issue was directly presented to this Court. Lanza was convicted by the State of Washington for "manufacturing, transporting, and having in possession" a quantity of liquor in violation of a state statute. He was subsequently convicted in a Federal District Court of violating the Volstead Act, for performing the same acts with regard to the same liquor. The Court held that the prior state conviction did not bar the federal prosecution. It pointed out that the State could constitutionally make Lanza's acts criminal under its original powers reserved by the Tenth Amendment, and the Federal Government could constitutionally prohibit the acts under the Eighteenth Amendment. Thus this case presented the situation hypothesized in *Fox v. State of Ohio* and other early cases; two sovereigns had, within their constitutional authority, prohibited the same acts, and each was punishing a breach of its prohibition. A unanimous Court, in an opinion by Chief Justice Taft, held:

> We have here two sovereignties, deriving power from different sources, capable of dealing with the same subject-matter within the same territory. . . . Each government in determining what shall be an offense against its peace and dignity is exercising its own sovereignty, not that of the other.
>
> It follows that an act denounced as a crime by both national and state sovereignties is an offense against the peace and dignity of both and may be punished by each. The Fifth Amendment, like all the other guaranties in the first eight amendments, applies only to proceedings by the federal government, . . . and the double jeopardy therein forbidden is a second prosecution under authority of the federal government after a first trial for the same offense under the same authority.

The *Lanza* principle has been accepted without question in *Hebert v. State of Louisiana*, also a Volstead Act case, and in the following cases in this Court arising under other statutes. . . . Similarly, *Lanza* has been considered in many cases in the Courts of Appeals to have established the general principle that a federal prosecution is not barred by a prior state prosecution of the same person for the same acts.

Petitioner asks us to overrule *Lanza*. We decline to do so. No consideration or persuasive reason not presented to the Court in the prior cases is advanced why we should depart from

E. Double Jeopardy, Successive Prosecutions, and Federal Civil Rights Enforcement 951

its firmly established principle. On the contrary, undesirable consequences would follow if Lanza were overruled. The basic dilemma was recognized over a century ago in *Fox v. State of Ohio*. As was there pointed out, if the States are free to prosecute criminal acts violating their laws, and the resultant state prosecutions bar federal prosecutions based on the same acts, federal law enforcement must necessarily be hindered. For example, the petitioners in this case insist that their Illinois convictions resulting in three months' prison sentences should bar this federal prosecution which could result in a sentence of up to five years. Such a disparity will very often arise when, as in this case, the defendants' acts impinge more seriously on a federal interest than on a state interest. But no one would suggest that, in order to maintain the effectiveness of federal law enforcement, it is desirable completely to displace state power to prosecute crimes based on acts which might also violate federal law. This would bring about a marked change in the distribution of powers to administer criminal justice, for the States under our federal system have the principal responsibility for defining and prosecuting crimes. *See Screws v. United States*. . . . Thus, unless the federal authorities could somehow insure that there would be no state prosecutions for particular acts that also constitute federal offenses, the efficiency of federal law enforcement must suffer if the Double Jeopardy Clause prevents successive state and federal prosecutions. Needless to say, it would be highly impractical for the federal authorities to attempt to keep informed of all state prosecutions which might bear on federal offenses.

The conclusion is therefore compelled that the prior Illinois conviction of the petitioners did not bar the instant federal prosecution.

Affirmed.

• • •

Mr. Justice BLACK, with whom THE CHIEF JUSTICE and Mr. Justice DOUGLAS concur, dissenting.

Petitioners, Abbate and Falcone, were convicted in an Illinois State Court of conspiracy to blow up certain property located in Mississippi and adjoining States. After receiving prison sentences in Illinois they were indicted and convicted of the same conspiracy in the Federal District Court of Mississippi and again sentenced to prison. The Court now affirms their second sentences over the contention that the federal conviction violates the double jeopardy provision of the Fifth Amendment.

In support of its affirmance, the Court points to *United States v. Lanza*. In that case, this Court sustained Lanza's conviction for handling liquor contrary to federal law, after Lanza had been convicted under state law of handling the same liquor at the same time and place. Some writers have explained *Lanza* as justified by the broad language of the Prohibition Amendment which was then in effect and which gave the States and the Federal Government concurrent power to control liquor traffic. The Court's opinion, in *Lanza*, however, seemed rather to rely on dicta in a number of past cases in this Court. These had assumed that identical conduct of an accused might be prosecuted twice, once by a State and once by the Federal Government, because the "offense" punished by each is in some, meaningful, sense different. The legal logic used to prove one thing to be two is too subtle for me to grasp.

I am also not convinced that a State and the Nation can be considered two wholly separate sovereignties for the purpose of allowing them to do together what, generally, neither can do separately. In the first place, I cannot conceive that our States are more distinct from the Federal Government than are foreign nations from each other. And it has been recognized that most free countries have accepted a prior conviction elsewhere as a bar to a second trial in their jurisdiction. In the second place, I believe the Bill of Rights' safeguard against double jeopardy was intended to establish a broad national policy against federal courts trying or

Chapter X The Department of Justice and the Prosecution of Civil Rights Crimes

punishing a man a second time after acquittal or conviction in any court. It is just as much an affront to human dignity and just as dangerous to human freedom for a man to be punished twice for the same offense, once by a State and once by the United States, as it would be for one of these two Governments to throw him in prison twice for the offense. Perhaps a belief that this is true was responsible for the fact that a proposed amendment to the Double Jeopardy Clause was rejected in our First Congress while the Bill of Rights was being considered. If that amendment had been adopted the Clause apparently would have barred double prosecutions for "the same offense" only if brought under "any law of the United States." I fear that this limitation on the scope of the Double Jeopardy Clause, which Congress refused to accept, is about to be firmly established as the constitutional rule by the Court's holding in this case and in *Bartkus*.

I would reverse both convictions.

NOTES AND QUESTIONS

1. The Court quotes bedrock language from ancient cases — the foundation for its double jeopardy analysis—to the effect that a person owes "an allegiance to two sovereigns" and that the same conduct might "constitute an offense against both the States and the Federal governments." Are these phrases anything more than legal fictions? Has anyone in the real world—even putting aside putative criminal offenders—ever thought of themselves as owing "allegiance" to two different "sovereigns"?

2. Shouldn't the Double Jeopardy Clause be more defendant-focused like its constitutional neighbors in the Fifth Amendment such as the privilege against self-incrimination? Justice Black, dissenting, questions the "legal logic" behind the notion of dual sovereignty: "It is just as much an affront to human dignity and just as dangerous to human freedom for a man to be punished twice for the same offense, once by a State and once by the United States, as it would be for one of these two Governments to throw him in prison twice for the offense."

3. Justice Black's defendant-focused perspective had commanded a (bare) majority just two years earlier in *Green v. United States*, 355 U.S. 184 (1957), where, in a "single sovereignty" context, the Court had found a successive federal first-degree murder charge barred by a prior acquittal on the same charge. Justice Black explained "the underlying idea" of the Double Jeopardy Clause:

> that the State with all its resources and power should not be allowed to make repeated attempts to convict an individual for an alleged offense, thereby subjecting him to embarrassment, expense, and ordeal and compelling him to live in a continuing state of anxiety and insecurity, as well as enhancing the possibility that even though innocent he may be found guilty.

Id. at 187-88.

4. The Court in *Abbate* observes that states have the principal responsibility for "defining and prosecuting crimes," a proposition for which it cites *Screws*. If that is so, why isn't the consequence of that proposition that Illinois's prosecution and sentencing of the defendants in *Abbate* for the bombing conspiracy the end of the matter? Why shouldn't DOJ be required to accept Illinois's judgment that a fair resolution of this unexecuted crime was guilty pleas and three months' imprisonment?

5. The Court accepts uncritically the government's argument that the defendants' actions here "impinge more seriously" on federal interests than state interests. Are there reasons to be skeptical of the government's argument? Does the federal interest appear to be contrived? Does it matter that defendants presumably had no intention of compromising any federal interest? Their target was the telephone company buildings—surely they were unaware that the "coaxial repeater stations and micro-wave towers" in those buildings were operated by the federal government. Isn't it more likely that DOJ simply thought the defendants got a sweetheart deal in state court and wanted to exact more significant punishment? Should that be enough to justify a successive prosecution?

Note the tension between the dual sovereignty doctrine and the entire animating principle of the Supreme Court's Eighth Amendment jurisprudence, namely, that federal courts should almost always defer to state judgments about the appropriate criminal punishment for a particular crime. *See, e.g., Harmelin v. Michigan*, 501 U.S. 957 (1991). Why not require federal prosecutors in successive prosecutions to articulate an independent federal interest, judicially reviewable, to justify their action? Would such a requirement be inconsistent with the separation of powers? Could Congress legislate such a requirement as a general matter, or at least for specific statutes?

6. *United States v. Lanza*, 260 U.S. 377 (1922), was the most recent and most on point Supreme Court dual sovereignty precedent when *Abbate* was decided, so on point that the defendants argued in *Abbate* that it should be overruled. *Lanza* was a Prohibition case, and it carries that historical baggage as well as the potential complication that the Eighteenth Amendment gave the states "concurrent power" to enforce the Amendment's liquor prohibitions. But *Lanza* is otherwise even a weaker case than *Abbate* for application of the dual sovereignty doctrine. In *Lanza* the state and federal substantive interests — prohibiting the manufacture, transporting, possessing, etc. of alcohol — were indisputably identical, and the government made no argument to the contrary.

In Washington state court the defendants in *Lanza* had pleaded guilty to liquor offenses and were only fined — no jail time. On the basis of those state convictions, the federal district court dismissed on double jeopardy grounds a subsequent federal indictment under the Volstead Act. In reversing that dismissal, the Supreme Court relied on the standard "two sovereigns" and "two different offenses" principles but also explicitly noted the differential punishment issue:

> If a state were to punish the manufacture, transportation and sale of intoxicating liquor by small or nominal fines, the race of offenders to the courts of that state to plead guilty and secure immunity from federal prosecution for such acts would not make for respect for the federal statute or for its deterrent effect.

Id. at 385. Putting aside the low likelihood of "a race of offenders" to plead guilty in state court, is a prosecution to secure a harsher punishment under these circumstances a legitimate effort to vindicate a specific federal interest?

In a companion case to *Abbate* decided the same day, *Bartkus v. Illinois*, 355 U.S. 902 (1959), the Court dealt with the reverse order of prosecutions as in *Abbate*. In *Bartkus*, the federal bank robbery prosecution went first, and defendant was acquitted. Thereafter, the state of Illinois convicted him of bank robbery under state law. As in *Abbate*, the Court rejected the double jeopardy argument by the same 5-4 margin.

As you might imagine given the appearance of injustice and the lack of compelling recent precedent — *Lanza*, after all, was a World War, a Great Depression, and a New Deal ago — negative public reaction to the 1959 announcement of the *Abbate* and *Bartkus* decisions was immediate. (In the 1950s it was still possible for elected representatives to be critical of law enforcement with little electoral peril.) Congress introduced a bill to bar most federal prosecutions where a state had previously prosecuted a defendant for the same conduct. *See* A Bill to Amend Title 18, United States Code, Entitled "Crimes and Criminal Procedure," H.R. 6176, 86th Cong. (1959). *See* Adam Harris Kurland, *The Enduring Virtues of Deferential Federalism: The Federal Government's Proper Role in Prosecuting Law Enforcement Officers for Civil Rights Offenses*, 70 Hastings L.J. 771, 797 (2019).

Chapter X The Department of Justice and the Prosecution of Civil Rights Crimes

Attorney General William Rogers tried to seize control of the narrative. Approximately a week after the decisions in *Abbate* and *Bartkus* he issued a press release — an unusual means, at the time, to communicate DOJ policy — directing all United States attorneys to "continue" to "sparingly" use the federal power to successively prosecute defendants for the same conduct already prosecuted by the state. *Id.* Rogers urged cooperation between federal and state prosecutors, and imposed a requirement that all successive prosecutions be approved by Main Justice and brought to his personal attention. Kurland, *The Enduring Virtues of Deferential Federalism, supra* at 797-99.

This policy soon became known as the *Petite* Policy, named after the next case, and as it has evolved over the years the *Petite* Policy has been an enduring factor — at least optically — in DOJ's decision making regarding successive federal civil rights prosecutions.

Petite v. United States
361 U.S. 529 (1960)

PER CURIAM.

Petitioner was indicted, with others, in the Eastern District of Pennsylvania for conspiring to make false statements to an agency of the United States at hearings held in Philadelphia and Baltimore under proceedings for the deportation of an alien. Petitioner was also separately indicted for suborning perjury at the Philadelphia hearings. Petitioner's co-defendants pleaded guilty to the conspiracy charged. Petitioner went to trial on both indictments, but at the close of the Government's case he changed his plea to nolo contendere to the conspiracy charge, and the Government dismissed the subornation indictment. He was fined $500 and sentenced to two months' imprisonment, which he served. Petitioner was subsequently indicted in the District of Maryland for suborning the perjury of two witnesses at the Baltimore hearings. Among the overt acts which had been relied upon in the Pennsylvania conspiracy indictment was the testimony of these two witnesses. Because of this, petitioner moved to dismiss the Maryland indictment on the ground of double jeopardy, but his motion was denied and the conviction which resulted was affirmed by the Court of Appeals for the Fourth Circuit.

Thereupon a petition for a writ of certiorari was filed with the double jeopardy issue as the single question presented, and certiorari was granted. The Government did not oppose the granting of this petition, but informed the Court that the case was under consideration by the Department of Justice to determine whether the second prosecution in the District of Maryland was consistent with the sound policy of the Department in discharging its responsibility for the control of government litigation wholly apart from the question of the legal validity of the claim of double jeopardy.

In due course the Government filed this motion for an order vacating the judgment below and remanding the case to the United States District Court for the District of Maryland with directions to dismiss the indictment. It did so on the ground that it is the general policy of the Federal Government "that several offenses arising out of a single transaction should be alleged and tried together and should not be made the basis of multiple prosecutions, a policy dictated by considerations both of fairness to defendants and of efficient and orderly law enforcement." The Solicitor General on behalf of the Government represents this policy as closely related to that against duplicating federal-state prosecutions, which was formally defined by the Attorney General of the United States in a memorandum to the United States Attorneys. (Department of Justice Press Release, Apr. 6, 1959.) Counsel for petitioner "joins in and consents" to the Government's motion.

E. Double Jeopardy, Successive Prosecutions, and Federal Civil Rights Enforcement   **955**

The case is remanded to the Court of Appeals to vacate its judgment and to direct the District Court to vacate its judgment and to dismiss the indictment. In the interest of justice, the Court is clearly empowered thus to dispose of the matter, 28 U.S.C. § 2106, 28 U.S.C.A. § 2106, and we do so with due regard for the settled rule that the Court will not "anticipate a question of constitutional law in advance of the necessity of deciding it." By thus disposing of the matter, we are of course not to be understood as remotely intimating in any degree an opinion on the question of double jeopardy sought to be presented by the petition for certiorari.

Case remanded with directions.

Mr. Chief Justice WARREN, concurring.

I concur with the judgment of the Court, but desire to record my reasons for so doing.

The Solicitor General, who has statutory authority to conduct litigation in this Court, has requested us to vacate the judgment and remand for dismissal in the interests of justice. The petitioner has consented. Under these circumstances, I believe that 28 U.S.C. § 2106, 28 U.S.C.A. § 2106, empowers us to entertain the motion.

Authority to grant this type of motion is one thing, however, and determination of the considerations relevant to a proper exercise of that authority is another. As I believe that the Court should not deny all such motions peremptorily, so do I believe that we should not automatically grant them through invocation of the policy of avoiding decision of constitutional issues. There are circumstances in which our responsibility of definitively interpreting the law of the land and of supervising its judicial application would dictate that we dispose of a case on its merits. In a situation, for example, where the invalidity of the judgment is clear and the motion to vacate and remand is obviously a means of avoiding an adjudication, I think we would be remiss in our duty were we to grant the motion.

But this is not such a case. Although a full hearing might well establish petitioner's contention that his conviction violated the Double Jeopardy Clause of the Constitution, Amend. 5, no devious purpose can be ascribed to the Government, which asserts that the prosecution of petitioner "was . . . by inadvertence," and that it "does not intend to take (such action) in the future." Its representation with respect to future practice is given support by the Attorney General's memorandum to United States Attorneys which establishes a closely related policy against successive federal-state prosecutions; and the reasonableness of its request is demonstrated by the fact that this memorandum was issued after the prosecution, the conviction, and the judgment of the Court of Appeals in this case. For these reasons the action requested is, in the words of § 2106, "just under the circumstances."

Mr. Justice BRENNAN, with whom Mr. Justice BLACK and Mr. Justice DOUGLAS join.

The Government has commendably done the just and right thing in asking us to wipe the slate clean of this second federal conviction for the same criminal conduct. But with all deference, I do not see how our duty can be fully performed in this case if our action stops with simply giving effect to a "policy" of the Government—a policy whose only written expression does not even cover the case at bar. Even where the Government confesses error, this Court examines the case on the merits itself, and one would not have thought our duty less in this case—particularly where the Government has reserved the right to apply or not apply its "policy" in its discretion. Presumably this reservation would apply to cases at the appellate level as well. "(T)he proper administration of the criminal law cannot be left merely to the stipulation of parties." I believe that the Double Jeopardy Clause of the Fifth Amendment was an insurmountable barrier to this second prosecution. My reasons supporting this view have been detailed in my separate opinion in *Abbate v. United States*. On this basis I agree that the judgment of the Court of Appeals is not to stand; but I would reverse it on the merits.

NOTES AND QUESTIONS

1. The Department of Justice asserts that its successive prosecution of Petite was "inadverten[t]." Is this believable? Why wasn't the "inadvertence" of the successive Maryland federal prosecution acknowledged by DOJ when Petite moved to dismiss his indictment in the trial court on double jeopardy grounds? Or when he raised the issue on appeal to the Fourth Circuit? Doesn't the truth more likely lie in the fact that the Fourth Circuit decision rejecting Petite's double jeopardy argument was dated January 3, 1959, three months *before Abbate* and *Bartkus* were decided and the attendant public backlash that led to the DOJ policy announcement and congressional activity?

2. Why does the Court bend over backwards to accept the DOJ's questionable claim of "inadvertence" and decide not to reach the merits? Is Justice Brennan correct that the better course would have been to decide the case on the merits? What are the pros and cons of doing so? Note that nothing in the DOJ "policy" precludes it from taking a different position in a future case, and that the situation in *Petite* — successive federal prosecutions for the same conduct — is not even addressed by the public directive from Attorney General Rogers.

3. Chief Justice Warren, concurring, accepts the government's inadvertence excuse but also states that "no devious purpose can be ascribed to the government." What sort of devious purpose could be attributed to the government such that the Court would deny its dismissal motion?

The earliest version of the sentiments underlying the *Petite* Policy were expressed in connection with the broad federal civil rights enforcement powers given to federal prosecutors — there was no Department of Justice yet — regarding the Civil Rights Act of 1866. According to Professor Kaczorowski, U.S. Attorney Benjamin Bristow of Kentucky, who was virtually alone in pursuing civil rights violations under the Andrew Johnson Administration, instructed federal officers not to pursue federal charges under the act unless and until Black defendants were denied justice in state courts. Kaczorowski, The Politics of Judicial Interpretation, *supra* at 41.

The *Petite* Policy, which still exists today in the DOJ's Justice Manual, evolved over time. It generally encouraged cooperation with state and local authorities; generally permitted subsequent federal prosecution only where necessary to vindicate a specific federal interest; and at times specifically called out civil rights prosecutions as being in service of a uniquely federal interest. Kurland, *The Enduring Virtues of Deferential Federalism, supra* at 798-807. In each incarnation, as with all DOJ policies, it was never binding on the DOJ. Nor did that lack of enforceability really matter, as the policy was always articulated with sufficient qualifications and vagueness that it could not be a true source of accountability.

Throughout its various forms, and its sporadic recognition of a specific federal interest in civil rights prosecutions, the Petite Policy has never taken the position that the federal government should be the primary means of civil rights enforcement. Rather, the federal role the policy has consistently envisioned is as a "backstop," waiting in the wings in the event that state prosecution efforts are inadequate. *See* Kurland, *The Enduring Virtues of Deferential Federalism, supra* at 775-76, 796-808.

Is such deference to states as the "primary" law enforcement sovereign still necessary? Can you imagine scenarios where a state might welcome federal prosecutors taking the lead in a civil rights prosecution?

The dual sovereignty doctrine underpinning the Supreme Court's double jeopardy jurisprudence has always been sharply criticized. Much of that criticism was in the spirit of Justice Black's dissent in *Abbate* and *Bartkus*, to the effect that from a defendant's perspective the

E. Double Jeopardy, Successive Prosecutions, and Federal Civil Rights Enforcement

difference between two sovereigns is both immaterial and somewhat metaphysical. The successive state and federal trials in the early 1990s of the Los Angeles police officers who brutally beat Rodney King, where officers acquitted in a state trial were subsequently convicted federally, cast a national spotlight on the issue of successive prosecutions.

Rodney King: His Beating and Its Recording. On March 3, 1991, LAPD officers were captured on videotape viciously beating Black motorist Rodney King and landing dozens of blows even after King was submissive and then motionless. King had been apprehended by the officers after a high-speed chase, during which, according to a defense witness at trial, King had driven up to 80 miles per hour and had failed to yield when police activated their overhead lights and siren.

A grainy black-and-white videotape of the beating, which began recording after King had resisted the officers and the beatings had begun, was made with an early version of a "camcorder" by plumber George Holliday, a resident of an apartment complex across the street from where King was apprehended, who just happened to be out on his balcony. The next day Holliday tried to discuss what he had recorded with the local branch of the LAPD but got nowhere, and therefore refused to surrender the videotape. He had more luck with news station KTLA, which immediately aired the videotape, as eventually did television stations around the world, shocking a global audience. This was 16 years before the 2007 release of the iPhone, which irrevocably changed the documentation of police brutality.

This Sony Handycam 8 CCD-F401 camcorder is likely the model used to film the Rodney King beating.

See generally Laurie L. Levenson, *The Future of State and Federal Civil Rights Prosecutions: The Lessons of the Rodney King Trial,* 41 UCLA L. Rev. 509, 516-20 (1994).

Rodney King: State Court Proceedings. Within two weeks of the beating, on March 14, 1991, a Los Angeles County grand jury returned an indictment charging the officers with state crimes focused on, inter alia, excessive use of force. The defendants moved for a change of venue from Los Angeles County based on the extensive pretrial publicity surrounding the case. Although the trial judge denied the motion, the defendants successfully appealed that ruling, and the case was transferred to state court in Simi Valley in Ventura County, a suburban community popular with retired Los Angeles police officers.

Trial commenced in Simi Valley before a predominantly white jury containing no African-American jurors. The prosecution relied almost exclusively on the videotape: it presented no expert use-of-force testimony in its case-in-chief; did not present any testimony from civilian witnesses to the beating; did not call Rodney King himself as a witness; and presented no evidence about the cause of King's injuries (15 facial fractures). The defense presented two LAPD use-of-force experts who reviewed the videotape and explained to the jury, frame by frame, why King's behavior justified the officers' actions and that those actions were consistent with LAPD policy. Two of the officers testified, consistently with the use-of-force experts, that they believed King was a threat and that their use of force was necessary.

The jury acquitted all defendants except one.

Chapter X The Department of Justice and the Prosecution of Civil Rights Crimes

See generally Levenson, *The Future of State and Federal Civil Rights Prosecutions, supra* at 526-27.

Rodney King: Aftermath of the State Court Acquittals. Immediately after the state court verdict, Los Angeles erupted in four days of looting and violence. When the riots ended, at least 45 people had died and Los Angeles had suffered $1 billion in property damage. During the riots, which like the beating videotape were also televised around the world, President George H. W. Bush announced on television that he was "stunned" by the verdict and did not see how it "could possibly square with the video." He committed to a federal review of the matter. *Id.* at 527-28.

Attorney General William Barr — in his first stint at the job — stated publicly that "[i]t's important for people to remember . . . that the verdicts . . . on state charges are not the end of the process" and that the standard whether to bring a second federal prosecution is "whether or not we believe the federal interest has been vindicated by the state proceeding." Although this was plainly a reference to the *Petite* Policy, if not the policy's words at least its substance, the department never made public any analysis under that policy. Kurland, *The Enduring Virtues of Deferential Federalism, supra* at 818.

On August 4, 1992, three months after the state court acquittals, the federal grand jury for the Central District of California returned an indictment against all four officers for civil rights violations. Each defendant was charged with a single count of violating Rodney King's civil rights in violation of 18 U.S.C. § 242. Levenson, *The Future of State and Federal Civil Rights Prosecutions, supra* at 528.

Rodney King: Federal Court Proceedings. There were several interesting pretrial motions in the federal case. The prosecution sought to introduce evidence of prior misconduct by the defendants (denied), to limit the defendants' expert use-of-force testimony (deferred), and to try the case to an anonymous and sequestered jury (granted). Defendants sought to dismiss the case both on double jeopardy grounds (denied) and for violations of the *Petite* Policy (denied). *United States v. Koon*, 833 F. Supp. 769, 790 (C.D. Cal. 1993), *aff'd in relevant part*, 34 F.3d 1416, 1438 (9th Cir. 1994). Trial commenced on February 16, 1993, and lasted seven weeks.

Having learned from the failures of the state trial — that is, taking full advantage of the proverbial second bite at the apple — federal prosecutors tried their case differently than the state prosecutors. They still focused on the Holliday videotape, but the federal prosecutors also presented:

- civilian witnesses to the beating, who testified to hearing King's screams and the officers' talking and laughing;
- an LAPD use-of-force expert, who testified that the blows administered during the first 31 seconds of the videotape were necessary to subdue King, but that each of the dozens of blows in the 51 seconds thereafter were excessive and also violated LAPD policy;
- a medical expert who testified that the fractures to King's head and face from the blows left those bones "reduced to a very fine powder, like sand"; and
- a biomechanic expert, who testified that King's head and facial injuries were consistent with being beaten by a police baton, and inconsistent with a fall to the road (the defendants' theory) as there was no evidence of abrasions that a fall on asphalt would have caused.

The prosecutors also called King as a witness, a decision that critically attached a human face to the grainy footage in the videotape. Prosecutors also were ready and able to impeach potential defense witnesses, who they had been able to identify from the first trial and other sources.

Prosecutors had subpoenaed those potential defense witnesses to the grand jury as a defensive maneuver—to get a preview of, and to lock in, any testimony they might be called on to give that was helpful to defendants.

After one week of deliberations, on a Saturday morning—while the Los Angeles Police Department was on full-city tactical alert—the federal jury returned its verdicts. The jury found two of the defendants guilty of violating § 242 and acquitted the other two.

See generally Levenson, *The Future of State and Federal Civil Rights Prosecutions, supra* at 529-30.

Rodney King: The Double Jeopardy Aftermath, the ACLU, and the Case for a Civil Rights Exception. The Supreme Court had never before considered the application of the dual sovereignty doctrine in the exact context of the Rodney King trials, that is, where a successive federal prosecution followed a state court acquittal. But it is extremely doubtful the successive federal prosecution of the Los Angeles police officers in the Rodney King beating was barred by applicable double jeopardy law wholly irrespective of the dual sovereignty doctrine. While the federal prosecution under § 242 required as an "element" the proof of a deprivation of a federal right, none of the several California statutes the officers had been charged with—assault with a deadly weapon, unlawful use of excessive force, filing false reports, and accessories after the fact—required such proof. Accordingly, under the so-called separate element test of *Blockburger v. United States*, 284 U.S. 299 (1932), none of the charged state crimes and the charged federal crime were the "same offense" under the Double Jeopardy Clause regardless of sovereign.

The Edward R. Roybal Federal Courthouse in the Civic Center section of Los Angeles, where the second "Rodney King trial" was held in 1993.

But the extensive public debate over double jeopardy did not turn on such legal niceties. *See* Paul Hoffman, *Double Jeopardy Wars: The Case for a Civil Rights Exception*, 41 UCLA L. Rev. 649, 650 (1994). It was more visceral. Were the police officer defendants treated fairly? Did the federal government have an obligation to right the "wrong" of an ineffectual state court prosecution in a defendant-contrived venue that was hostile to the prosecution? Didn't the videotape plainly demonstrate the defendants' guilt? Was the second prosecution "political"? Was it "politically correct"? Laypersons naturally wondered why this wasn't a violation of the double jeopardy rule they had read about in high school or college. Liberals and civil libertarians, including some who had roundly criticized the dual sovereignty doctrine, argued for a "civil rights exception" to a properly conceived understanding of double jeopardy.

Against the background of this public hue and cry, the American Civil Liberties Union was undergoing introspective agony. In 1990, after over a decade of study, debate, and discussion, the ACLU had adopted its own position on double jeopardy: (1) it rejected the dual sovereignty theory; (2) it rejected the *Blockburger* "element" test and instead defined "same offense" as the same conduct or transaction; and (3) it rejected a civil rights exception to this reconfigured doctrine. Susan N. Herman, *Double Jeopardy All Over Again: Dual Sovereignty, Rodney King and the ACLU*, 41 UCLA L. Rev. 609, 615 (1994). In adopting this absolutist position, the ACLU reasoned that Congress or federal prosecutors could take other steps to vindicate the federal interest in civil rights enforcement, such as preempting state prosecutions in certain situations, providing for the removal of some state prosecutions to federal court, enhancing federal-state cooperation to increase the likelihood of state court success, and using civil suits for damages and injunctive relief to deter constitutional violations. *Id.*

Then came Rodney King. The Southern California chapter of the ACLU went rogue, advocating for federal prosecution of the LAPD officers after the state court acquittals, notwithstanding ACLU national policy. *Id.* at 616. The ACLU board commenced another round of study, debate, and discussion and ultimately—amid public accusations of waffling—retained its original position, as difficult as that must have been in view of the ACLU's consistent commitment to federal enforcement of civil rights. *Id.* at 617-18.

Rodney King in April 2012, shortly before his death at age 47

To those who would advocate for a civil rights "exception" to double jeopardy, and there certainly are strong historical arguments in favor of an exception even putting doctrine aside, it is fair to ask the following questions:

- Is the exception necessary because federal civil rights prosecutions are inherently superior to state civil rights prosecutions?
- Is the exception necessary so the federal government will have a second bite at the apple if the state prosecution, in some way to be defined (e.g., acquittal, mistrial, unacceptably light sentence) fails?
- Should the federal prosecution option presumptively operate as a "backstop," with the state authorities going first?

As to the first of these questions, Professor Laurie Levenson explored—against the backdrop of the Rodney King prosecutions—the pros and cons of state and federal prosecutions of civil rights crimes. Levenson, *The Future of State and Federal Civil Rights Prosecutions*, *supra* at 542-49. After an exhaustive analysis she finds no decisive overall advantage either way but does note some specific federal advantages (no necessary reliance on local law enforcement for investigative power, federal prosecutors more experienced in using grand juries as an investigative tool) as well as some specific state advantages (better and more statutory charging options, state prosecutors' familiarity with local judges whereas federal prosecutions likely tried by DOJ Civil Rights Division lawyers based in Washington).

Dual Sovereignty in the Twenty-First Century. The dual sovereignty doctrine has been criticized since its twentieth-century reincarnation in *Lanza*, a time when legal commentary was in its infancy. *See* J.A.C. Grant, *The* Lanza *Rule of Successive Prosecutions*, 32 Colum. L. Rev. 1309, 1331 (1932) (describing the dual sovereignty doctrine as a "metaphysical subtlety"). *See* Herman, *Double Jeopardy All Over Again*, *supra* at 609, 618 & n.32 (citing critical commentary); Eleuthera Ocerton Sa, Note, *The Limits of Dual Sovereignty*, 97 N.Y.U. L. Rev. 798, 800 & nn.20-22 (2022) (same). Accordingly, when certiorari was granted in 2016 in *Gamble v. United States*, there was a stirring of hope that the Court might be willing to reconsider the dual sovereignty doctrine, perhaps even on the basis of an originalist interpretation. *Cf. Puerto Rico v. Sánchez Valle*, 579 U.S. 59 (2016) (Ginsburg, J., joined by Thomas, J., concurring) ("The double jeopardy proscription is intended to shield individuals from the harassment of multiple prosecutions for the same misconduct. Current 'separate sovereigns' doctrine hardly serves that objective.").

Gamble v. United States
587 U.S. 678 (2019)

Justice ALITO delivered the opinion of the Court.

We consider in this case whether to overrule a longstanding interpretation of the Double Jeopardy Clause of the Fifth Amendment. That Clause provides that no person may be "twice put in jeopardy" "for the same offence." Our double jeopardy case law is complex, but at its core, the Clause means that those acquitted or convicted of a particular "offence" cannot be tried a second time for the same "offence." But what does the Clause mean by an "offence"?

We have long held that a crime under one sovereign's laws is not "the same offence" as a crime under the laws of another sovereign. Under this "dual-sovereignty" doctrine, a State may prosecute a defendant under state law even if the Federal Government has prosecuted him for the same conduct under a federal statute.

Or the reverse may happen, as it did here. Terance Gamble, convicted by Alabama for possessing a firearm as a felon, now faces prosecution by the United States under its own felon-in-possession law. Attacking this second prosecution on double jeopardy grounds, Gamble asks us to overrule the dual-sovereignty doctrine. He contends that it departs from the founding-era understanding of the right enshrined by the Double Jeopardy Clause. But the historical evidence assembled by Gamble is feeble; pointing the other way are the Clause's text, other historical evidence, and 170 years of precedent. Today we affirm that precedent, and with it the decision below.

I

In November 2015, a local police officer in Mobile, Alabama, pulled Gamble over for a damaged headlight. Smelling marijuana, the officer searched Gamble's car, where he found a loaded 9-mm handgun. Since Gamble had been convicted of second-degree robbery, his possession of the handgun violated an Alabama law providing that no one convicted of "a crime of violence" "shall own a firearm or have one in his or her possession." Ala. Code § 13A-11-72(a) (2015); see § 13A-11-70(2) (defining "crime of violence" to include robbery). After Gamble pleaded guilty to this state offense, federal prosecutors indicted him for the same instance of possession under a federal law—one forbidding those convicted of "a crime punishable by imprisonment for a term exceeding one year . . . to ship or transport in interstate or foreign commerce, or possess in or affecting commerce, any firearm or ammunition." 18 U.S.C. § 922(g)(1).

Gamble moved to dismiss on one ground: The federal indictment was for "the same offence" as the one at issue in his state conviction and thus exposed him to double jeopardy. But because this Court has long held that two offenses "are not the 'same offence'" for double jeopardy purposes if "prosecuted by different sovereigns," the District Court denied Gamble's motion to dismiss. Gamble then pleaded guilty to the federal offense while preserving his right to challenge the denial of his motion to dismiss on double jeopardy grounds. But on appeal the Eleventh Circuit affirmed, citing the dual-sovereignty doctrine. We granted certiorari to determine whether to overturn that doctrine.

II

Gamble contends that the Double Jeopardy Clause must forbid successive prosecutions by different sovereigns because that is what the founding-era common law did. But before turning to that historical claim, see Part III infra, we review the Clause's text and some of the cases Gamble asks us to overturn.

A

We start with the text of the Fifth Amendment. Although the dual-sovereignty rule is often dubbed an "exception" to the double jeopardy right, it is not an exception at all. On the contrary, it follows from the text that defines that right in the first place. "[T]he language of the Clause . . . protects individuals from being twice put in jeopardy 'for the same offence,' not for the same conduct or actions," *Grady v. Corbin*, (1990), as Justice Scalia wrote in a soon-vindicated dissent, see *United States v. Dixon* (1993) (overruling *Grady*). And the term "'[o]ffence' was commonly understood in 1791 to mean 'transgression,' that is, 'the Violation or Breaking of a Law.'" As originally understood, then, an "offence" is defined by a law, and each law is defined by a sovereign. So where there are two sovereigns, there are two laws, and two "offences."

Faced with this reading, Gamble falls back on an episode from the Double Jeopardy Clause's drafting history. The first Congress, working on an earlier draft that would have banned "'more than one trial or one punishment for the same offence,'" voted down a

E. Double Jeopardy, Successive Prosecutions, and Federal Civil Rights Enforcement **963**

proposal to add "'by any law of the United States.'" 1 Annals of Cong. 753 (1789). In rejecting this addition, Gamble surmises, Congress must have intended to bar successive prosecutions regardless of the sovereign bringing the charge.

Even if that inference were justified — something that the Government disputes — it would count for little. The private intent behind a drafter's rejection of one version of a text is shoddy evidence of the public meaning of an altogether different text.

Besides, if we allowed conjectures about purpose to inform our reading of the text, the Government's conjecture would prevail. The Government notes that the Declaration of Independence denounced King George III for "protecting [British troops] by a mock Trial, from punishment for any Murders which they should commit on the Inhabitants of these States." ¶ 17. The Declaration was alluding to "the so-called Murderers' Act, passed by Parliament after the Boston Massacre," Amar, Sixth Amendment First Principles, 84 Geo. L.J. 641, 687, n. 181 (1996), a law that allowed British officials indicted for murder in America to be "'tried in England, beyond the control of local juries.'" Ibid. (quoting J. Blum et al., The National Experience 95 (3d ed. 1973)). "During the late colonial period, Americans strongly objected to . . . [t]his circumvention of the judgment of the victimized community." Amar, 84 Geo. L. Rev., at 687, n. 181. Yet on Gamble's reading, the same Founders who quite literally revolted against the use of acquittals abroad to bar criminal prosecutions here would soon give us an Amendment allowing foreign acquittals to spare domestic criminals. We doubt it.

We see no reason to abandon the sovereign-specific reading of the phrase "same offence," from which the dual-sovereignty rule immediately follows.

B

Our cases reflect the same reading. A close look at them reveals how fidelity to the Double Jeopardy Clause's text does more than honor the formal difference between two distinct criminal codes. It honors the substantive differences between the interests that two sovereigns can have in punishing the same act.

The question of successive federal and state prosecutions arose in three antebellum cases implying and then spelling out the dual-sovereignty doctrine. The first, *Fox v. Ohio*, involved an Ohio prosecution for the passing of counterfeit coins. The defendant argued that since Congress can punish counterfeiting, the States must be barred from doing so, or else a person could face two trials for the same offense, contrary to the Fifth Amendment. We rejected the defendant's premise that under the Double Jeopardy Clause "offences falling within the competency of different authorities to restrain or punish them would not properly be subjected to the consequences which those authorities might ordain and affix to their perpetration." Indeed, we observed, the nature of the crime or its effects on "public safety" might well "deman[d]" separate prosecutions. Generalizing from this point, we declared in a second case that "the same act might, as to its character and tendencies, and the consequences it involved, constitute an offence against both the State and Federal governments, and might draw to its commission the penalties denounced by either, as appropriate to its character in reference to each." *United States v. Marigold*.

A third antebellum case, *Moore v. Illinois*, expanded on this concern for the different interests of separate sovereigns, after tracing it to the text in the manner set forth above. Recalling that the Fifth Amendment prohibits double jeopardy not "for the same ac[t]" but "for the same offence," and that "[a]n offence, in its legal signification, means the transgression of a law," we drew the now-familiar inference: A single act "may be an offence or transgression of the laws of" two sovereigns, and hence punishable by both. Then we gave color to this abstract principle — and to the diverse interests it might vindicate — with an example. An assault on a United States marshal, we said, would offend against the Nation and a State:

the first by "hindering" the "execution of legal process," and the second by "breach[ing]" the "peace of the State." Ibid. That duality of harm explains how "one act" could constitute "two offences, for each of which [the offender] is justly punishable."

This principle comes into still sharper relief when we consider a prosecution in this country for crimes committed abroad. If, as Gamble suggests, only one sovereign may prosecute for a single act, no American court — state or federal — could prosecute conduct already tried in a foreign court. Imagine, for example, that a U.S. national has been murdered in another country. That country could rightfully seek to punish the killer for committing an act of violence within its territory. The foreign country's interest lies in protecting the peace in that territory rather than protecting the American specifically. But the United States looks at the same conduct and sees an act of violence against one of its nationals, a person under the particular protection of its laws. The murder of a U.S. national is an offense to the United States as much as it is to the country where the murder occurred and to which the victim is a stranger. That is why the killing of an American abroad is a federal offense that can be prosecuted in our courts, see 18 U.S.C. § 2332(a)(1), and why customary international law allows this exercise of jurisdiction.

There are other reasons not to offload all prosecutions for crimes involving Americans abroad. We may lack confidence in the competence or honesty of the other country's legal system. Less cynically, we may think that special protection for U.S. nationals serves key national interests related to security, trade, commerce, or scholarship. Such interests might also give us a stake in punishing crimes committed by U.S. nationals abroad — especially crimes that might do harm to our national security or foreign relations. See, e.g., § 2332a(b) (bombings). These examples reinforce the foundation laid in our antebellum cases: that a crime against two sovereigns constitutes two offenses because each sovereign has an interest to vindicate.

We cemented that foundation 70 years after the last of those antebellum cases, in a decision upholding a federal prosecution that followed one by a State. *See United States v. Lanza*. And for decades more, we applied our precedent without qualm or quibble. When petitioners in 1959 asked us twice to reverse course, we twice refused, finding "[n]o consideration or persuasive reason not presented to the Court in the prior cases" for disturbing our "firmly established" doctrine.

C

We briefly address two objections to this analysis.

First, the dissents contend that our dual-sovereignty rule errs in treating the Federal and State Governments as two separate sovereigns when in fact sovereignty belongs to the people. This argument is based on a non sequitur. Yes, our Constitution rests on the principle that the people are sovereign, but that does not mean that they have conferred all the attributes of sovereignty on a single government. Instead, the people, by adopting the Constitution, " 'split the atom of sovereignty.' " As we explained last Term:

> When the original States declared their independence, they claimed the powers inherent in sovereignty. . . . The Constitution limited but did not abolish the sovereign powers of the States, which retained "a residuary and inviolable sovereignty." The Federalist No. 39, p. 245 (C. Rossiter ed. 1961). Thus, both the Federal Government and the States wield sovereign powers, and that is why our system of government is said to be one of "dual sovereignty."

It is true that the Republic is " 'ONE WHOLE.' " But there is a difference between the whole and a single part, and that difference underlies decisions as foundational to our legal system as *McCulloch v. Maryland* (1819). There, in terms so directly relevant as to seem presciently tailored to answer this very objection, Chief Justice Marshall distinguished precisely between "the people of a State" and "[t]he people of all the States," between the "sovereignty which

E. Double Jeopardy, Successive Prosecutions, and Federal Civil Rights Enforcement   **965**

the people of a single state possess" and the sovereign powers "conferred by the people of the United States on the government of the Union," and thus between "the action of a part" and "the action of the whole." In short, McCulloch's famous holding that a State may not tax the national bank rested on a recognition that the States and the Nation have different "interests" and "right[s]." One strains to imagine a clearer statement of the premises of our dual-sovereignty rule, or a more authoritative source. The United States is a federal republic; it is not, contrary to Justice Gorsuch's suggestion, a unitary state like the United Kingdom.

Gamble and the dissents lodge a second objection to this line of reasoning. They suggest that because the division of federal and state power was meant to promote liberty, it cannot support a rule that exposes Gamble to a second sentence. This argument fundamentally misunderstands the governmental structure established by our Constitution. Our federal system advances individual liberty in many ways. Among other things, it limits the powers of the Federal Government and protects certain basic liberties from infringement. But because the powers of the Federal Government and the States often overlap, allowing both to regulate often results in two layers of regulation. Taxation is an example that comes immediately to mind. It is also not at all uncommon for the Federal Government to permit activities that a State chooses to forbid or heavily restrict—for example, gambling and the sale of alcohol. And a State may choose to legalize an activity that federal law prohibits, such as the sale of marijuana. So while our system of federalism is fundamental to the protection of liberty, it does not always maximize individual liberty at the expense of other interests. And it is thus quite extraordinary to say that the venerable dual-sovereignty doctrine represents a " 'desecrat[ion]' " of federalism.

* * *

IV

Besides appealing to the remote past, Gamble contends that recent changes—one doctrinal, one practical—blunt the force of stare decisis here. They do not.

A

If historical claims form the chorus of Gamble's argument, his refrain is "incorporation." In Gamble's telling, the recognition of the Double Jeopardy Clause's incorporation against the States washed away any theoretical foundation for the dual-sovereignty rule. But this incorporation-changes-everything argument trades on a false analogy.

The analogy Gamble draws is to the evolution of our doctrine on the Fourth Amendment right against unreasonable searches and seizures. We have long enforced this right by barring courts from relying on evidence gathered in an illegal search. Thus, in *Weeks v. United States* (1914), the Court held that federal prosecutors could not rely on the fruits of an unreasonable search undertaken by federal agents. But what if state or local police conducted a search that would have violated the Fourth Amendment if conducted by federal agents? Before incorporation, the state search would not have violated the Federal Constitution, so federal law would not have barred admission of the resulting evidence in a state prosecution. But by the very same token, under what was termed "the silver-platter doctrine," state authorities could hand such evidence over to federal prosecutors for use in a federal case.

Once the Fourth Amendment was held to apply to the States as well as the Federal Government, however, the silver-platter doctrine was scuttled. Now the fruits of unreasonable state searches are inadmissible in federal and state courts alike.

Gamble contends that the incorporation of the Double Jeopardy Clause should likewise end the dual-sovereignty rule, but his analogy fails. The silver-platter doctrine was based on the fact that the state searches to which it applied did not at that time violate federal law. Once the Fourth Amendment was incorporated against the States, the status of those state searches changed. Now they did violate federal law, so the basis for the silver-platter doctrine was gone.

By contrast, the premises of the dual-sovereignty doctrine have survived incorporation intact. Incorporation meant that the States were now required to abide by this Court's interpretation of the Double Jeopardy Clause. But that interpretation has long included the dual-sovereignty doctrine, and there is no logical reason why incorporation should change it. After all, the doctrine rests on the fact that only same-sovereign successive prosecutions are prosecutions for the "same offense," see Part II, supra—and that is just as true after incorporation as before.

B

If incorporation is the doctrinal shift that Gamble invokes to justify a departure from precedent, the practical change he cites is the proliferation of federal criminal law. Gamble says that the resulting overlap of federal and criminal codes heightens the risk of successive prosecutions under state and federal law for the same criminal conduct. Thus, Gamble contends, our precedent should yield to "'far-reaching systemic and structural changes'" that make our "earlier error all the more egregious and harmful." But unlike Gamble's appeal to incorporation, this argument obviously assumes that the dual-sovereignty doctrine was legal error from the start. So the argument is only as strong as Gamble's argument about the original understanding of double jeopardy rights, an argument that we have found wanting.

Insofar as the expansion of the reach of federal criminal law has been questioned on constitutional rather than policy grounds, the argument has focused on whether Congress has overstepped its legislative powers under the Constitution. Eliminating the dual-sovereignty rule would do little to trim the reach of federal criminal law, and it would not even prevent many successive state and federal prosecutions for the same criminal conduct unless we also overruled the long-settled rule that an "offence" for double jeopardy purposes is defined by statutory elements, not by what might be described in a looser sense as a unit of criminal conduct. Perhaps believing that two revolutionary assaults in the same case would be too much, Gamble has not asked us to overrule *Blockburger* along with the dual-sovereignty rule.

The judgment of the Court of Appeals for the Eleventh Circuit is affirmed.

It is so ordered.

• • •

Justice GINSBURG, dissenting.

Terance Martez Gamble pleaded guilty in Alabama state court to both possession of a firearm by a person convicted of "a crime of violence" and drug possession, and was sentenced to ten years' imprisonment, all but one year suspended. Apparently regarding Alabama's sentence as too lenient, federal prosecutors pursued a parallel charge, possession of a firearm by a convicted felon, in violation of federal law. Gamble again pleaded guilty and received nearly three more years in prison.

Had either the Federal Government or Alabama brought the successive prosecutions, the second would have violated Gamble's right not to be "twice put in jeopardy . . . for the same offence." U.S. Const., Amdt. 5, cl. 2. Yet the Federal Government was able to multiply Gamble's time in prison because of the doctrine that, for double jeopardy purposes, identical criminal laws enacted by "separate sovereigns" are different "offence[s]."

I dissent from the Court's adherence to that misguided doctrine. Instead of "fritter[ing] away [Gamble's] libert[y] upon a metaphysical subtlety, two sovereignties I would hold that the Double Jeopardy Clause bars "successive prosecutions [for the same offense] by parts of the whole USA."

E. Double Jeopardy, Successive Prosecutions, and Federal Civil Rights Enforcement 967

I

A

Gamble urges that the Double Jeopardy Clause incorporates English common law. That law, he maintains, recognized a foreign acquittal or conviction as a bar to retrial in England for the same offense. The Court, in turn, strives mightily to refute Gamble's account of the common law. This case, however, does not call for an inquiry into whether and when an 18th-century English court would have credited a foreign court's judgment in a criminal case. Gamble was convicted in both Alabama and the United States, jurisdictions that are not foreign to each other. English court decisions regarding the respect due to a foreign nation's judgment are therefore inapposite.

B

In *United States v. Lanza* (1922), this Court held that "an act denounced as a crime by both national and state sovereignties is an offense against the peace and dignity of both and may be punished by each." Decades later, a sharply divided Court reaffirmed this separate-sovereigns doctrine. *Abbate v. United States*. I would not cling to those ill-advised decisions.

1

Justification for the separate-sovereigns doctrine centers on the word "offence": An "offence," the argument runs, is the violation of a sovereign's law, the United States and each State are separate sovereigns, ergo successive state and federal prosecutions do not place a defendant in "jeopardy . . . for the same offence."

This "compact syllogism" is fatally flawed. The United States and its constituent States, unlike foreign nations, are "kindred systems," "parts of ONE WHOLE." The Federalist No. 82, p. 493 (C. Rossiter ed. 1961) (A. Hamilton). They compose one people, bound by an overriding Federal Constitution. Within that "WHOLE," the Federal and State Governments should be disabled from accomplishing together "what neither government [could] do alone — prosecute an ordinary citizen twice for the same offence." Amar & Marcus, Double Jeopardy Law After Rodney King, 95 Colum. L. Rev. 1, 2 (1995).

The notion that the Federal Government and the States are separate sovereigns overlooks a basic tenet of our federal system. The doctrine treats governments as sovereign, with state power to prosecute carried over from years predating the Constitution. In the system established by the Federal Constitution, however, "ultimate sovereignty" resides in the governed. Insofar as a crime offends the "peace and dignity" of a sovereign, that "sovereign" is the people, the "original fountain of all legitimate authority," The Federalist No. 22, at 152 (A. Hamilton). States may be separate, but their populations are part of the people composing the United States.

In our "compound republic," the division of authority between the United States and the States was meant to operate as "a double security [for] the rights of the people." The Federalist No. 51, at 323 (J. Madison). The separate-sovereigns doctrine, however, scarcely shores up people's rights. Instead, it invokes federalism to withhold liberty. See Bartkus (Black, J., dissenting).

It is the doctrine's premise that each government has — and must be allowed to vindicate — a distinct interest in enforcing its own criminal laws. That is a peculiar way to look at the Double Jeopardy Clause, which by its terms safeguards the "person" and restrains the government. The Double Jeopardy Clause embodies a principle, "deeply ingrained" in our system of justice,

> that the State with all its resources and power should not be allowed to make repeated attempts to convict an individual for an alleged offense, thereby subjecting him to embarrassment, expense and ordeal and compelling him to live in a continuing state of anxiety and insecurity, as well as enhancing the possibility that even though innocent he may be found guilty.

"Looked at from the standpoint of the individual who is being prosecuted," the liberty-denying potential of successive prosecutions, when Federal and State Governments prosecute in tandem, is the same as it is when either prosecutes twice. *Bartkus* (Black, J., dissenting).

. . .

The expansion of federal criminal law has exacerbated the problems created by the separate-sovereigns doctrine. Ill effects of the doctrine might once have been tempered by the limited overlap between federal and state criminal law. In the last half century, however, federal criminal law has been extended pervasively into areas once left to the States. This new "age of 'cooperative federalism,' [in which] the Federal and State Governments are waging a united front against many types of criminal activity," provides new opportunities for federal and state prosecutors to "join together to take a second bite at the apple," This situation might be less troublesome if successive prosecutions occurred only in "instances of peculiar enormity, or where the public safety demanded extraordinary rigor." The run-of-the-mill felon-in-possession charges Gamble encountered indicate that, in practice, successive prosecutions are not limited to exceptional circumstances.

. . .

Against all this, there is little to be said for keeping the separate-sovereigns doctrine. Gamble's case "do[es] not implicate the reliance interests of private parties." The closest thing to a reliance interest would be the interest Federal and State Governments have in avoiding avulsive changes that could complicate ongoing prosecutions. As the Court correctly explains, however, overruling the separate-sovereigns doctrine would not affect large numbers of cases. In prosecutions based on the same conduct, federal and state prosecutors will often charge offenses having different elements, charges that, under Blockburger, will not trigger double jeopardy protection.

Notably, the Federal Government has endeavored to reduce the incidence of "same offense" prosecutions. Under the Petite policy adopted by the Department of Justice, the Department will pursue a federal prosecution "based on substantially the same act(s) or transaction(s)" previously prosecuted in state court only if the first prosecution left a "substantial federal interest . . . demonstrably unvindicated" and a Department senior official authorizes the prosecution. Dept. of Justice, Justice Manual § 9-2.031(A) (rev. July 2009).

At oral argument, the Government estimated that it authorizes only "about a hundred" Petite prosecutions per year. Some of these prosecutions will not implicate double jeopardy, as the Petite policy uses a same-conduct test that is broader than the Blockburger same-elements test. And more than half the States forbid successive prosecutions for all or some offenses previously resolved on the merits by a federal or state court. In short, it is safe to predict that eliminating the separate-sovereigns doctrine would spark no large disruption in practice.

. . .

The separate-sovereigns doctrine, especially since *Bartkus* and *Abbate*, has been subject to relentless criticism by members of the bench, bar, and academy. Nevertheless, the Court reaffirms the doctrine, thereby diminishing the individual rights shielded by the Double Jeopardy Clause. Different parts of the "WHOLE" United States should not be positioned to prosecute a defendant a second time for the same offense. I would reverse Gamble's federal conviction.

E. Double Jeopardy, Successive Prosecutions, and Federal Civil Rights Enforcement 969

NOTES AND QUESTIONS

1. Note the majority's uncritical assessment in the first paragraph of Part I of the facts that led to the state prosecution: a traffic stop for what would at most be a minor civil infraction; a search of Gamble's car based on either consent or probable cause, we can only guess; and a state court prosecution followed by a federal prosecution, without any explanation of how or why federal prosecutors got involved. We are told later, in Justice Ginsburg's dissent, that the likely explanation is that the federal conviction and sentence added three years to Gamble's ten-year state sentence.

None of this is directly relevant to the Court's double jeopardy analysis, except to the extent it sheds light on the consequences of sanctioning successive prosecutions for a single episode of criminal conduct.

2. Are different interests being vindicated by the state and federal prosecutions here? Is this case more like *Lanza* or more like *Abbate*?

3. The Court uses the example of taxation to make the point that dual systems of regulation are commonplace in "our federal system." Is that a good analogy? What are the purposes of state taxation as opposed to federal taxation? Do the state and federal governments have analogous sovereign-specific interests in incarcerating persons convicted of crimes in their own prisons or supervising their probation by their own probation officers?

4. The wall of precedent the Court recites is indeed long — originating in three antebellum cases — but in the federal-state context the wall crumbles at the latest in the 1970s, apart from *Puerto Rico v. Sánchez Valle*, 579 U.S. 59 (2016), which held only that Puerto Rico and the United States are not separate sovereigns for dual sovereignty purposes. Both Justices Ginsburg and Gorsuch, dissenting, are mindful of this history and point to the proliferation of federal criminal offenses in recent decades, a development the precedent has never reckoned with, as a reason for reconsidering dual sovereignty. *See* 587 U.S. 758-59 (Gorsuch, J., dissenting) ("In the era when the separate sovereigns exception first emerged, the federal criminal code was new, thin, modest and restrained. Today, it can make none of those boasts. Some . . . estimate that the U.S. Code contains more than 4500 criminal statutes. . . .").

Justice Ginsburg also points to the modern predominance of "cooperative federalism," where state and federal governments are often operating as a united front against many kinds of criminal activity, as another development undermining the "separate sovereigns" ideal. Indeed, Gamble's federal prosecution may well have been an example of such cooperation, as state and federal law enforcement have historically cooperated on felon-in-possession cases. Or, as Justice Gorsuch described such cooperation in his dissenting opinion: "A free society does not allow its government to try the same individual for the same crime until it's happy with the result." *Id.* at 737.

How should these structural developments in the federal criminal process inform the claims of stare decisis on the dual sovereignty doctrine? Is the majority's response to these arguments adequate?

5. Should it matter to the survival of the dual sovereignty doctrine that federal-state coordination on matters of overlapping jurisdiction should be logistically seamless today, as in this age of "cooperative federalism" each of the country's 94 U.S. attorneys is already presumably in regular communication with the state prosecutors in her federal judicial district? Recall that in 1959, in *Abbate*, the Court scoffed at the feasibility of such coordination: "Needless to say, it would be highly impractical for the federal authorities to attempt to keep informed of all state prosecutions which might bear on federal offenses." 359 U.S. at 187, 195 (1959).

6. Apropos of "cooperative federalism," none of the opinions in *Gamble* address what lower courts call the "*Bartkus* exception" to dual sovereignty, a creature — perhaps mythological, as no one has ever seen one — derived from language in *Bartkus* to the effect that a subsequent prosecution that was "merely a tool" of the original prosecuting authorities would be barred by the Double Jeopardy Clause. *Id.* at 123-24. In *Bartkus*, a federal jury acquitted Bartkus of bank robbery and he was subsequently convicted in a state bank robbery prosecution in which federal authorities solicited the state to act, assured the attendance of witnesses, unearthed additional evidence, and actively participated in trial preparation. *Id.* at 165.

Lower courts have thrilled at the idea of a *Bartkus* exception but have never gone so far as to actually find one. This is not surprising, as it's hard to imagine a more "toolish" successive prosecution than the one in *Bartkus* itself. *See* Eleuthera Ocerton Sa, Note, *The Limits of Dual Sovereignty*, *supra* at 798, 818-25 (discussing *Bartkus* exception). Both the trial court and the Ninth Circuit rejected the defendants' *Bartkus* exception argument in the federal Rodney King prosecution. *United States v. Koon*, 833 F. Supp. 769, 790 (C.D. Cal. 1993), *aff'd in relevant part*, 34 F.3d 1416, 1438 (9th Cir. 1994).

7. The Court and Justice Gorsuch in dissent disagree about the Framers' intent with respect to double jeopardy, including the original understanding of the term "offense." Just a friendly reminder that originalism is not a secret potion unlocking the meaning of the Constitution but rather just one among many methods of interpretation and argument.

Twenty-First Century DOJ Prosecution Decisions. The themes this chapter has explored are still with us. Section 242 remains the primary vehicle of choice for the federal prosecution of civil rights crimes. The Department of Justice still struggles with decisions whether to bring federal prosecutorial authority to bear in situations where a state has (or has not) acted, and what if anything it should publicly state about its decision making in those situations. Judges and lawyers continue to debate, and to disagree, about how jury instructions should capture § 242's "willfully" element. *See* Aneri Shah, Comment, *Reinvigorating the Federal Government's Role in Civil Rights Enforcement Under 18 U.S.C. Section 242: The George Floyd Justice in Policing Act's Not So Reckless Proposal*, 52 Seton Hall L. Rev. 1601, 1613-16 (2022) (describing a three-way circuit split on interpretation of the "willfully" element in § 242).

Recent DOJ decisions in high-profile civil rights cases are revealing. The DOJ has sometimes decided to prosecute.

Walter Scott. Walter Scott, a 50-year old Black man, was pulled over by North Charleston, South Carolina police officer Michael Slager for an allegedly faulty brake light. A cellphone recording shows Scott running away from the officer, who fired eight shots at him as he ran. Scott died at the scene. Officer Slager was charged under § 242 with depriving Walter Scott of his federal "right to be free from the use of unreasonable force by a law enforcement officer." *United States v. Slager*, Crim. No. 216-cr-00378 (D.S.C. May 10, 2016) (Indictment).

At the time of his federal indictment, Slager had already been indicted for murder by South Carolina authorities, although the case had not gone to trial. The state case proceeded to trial first, and resulted in a mistrial. Before the state court retrial, with

Walter Scott, age 50, in a photograph posted by his brother shortly after he was killed

E. Double Jeopardy, Successive Prosecutions, and Federal Civil Rights Enforcement   971

cooperation from the South Carolina authorities, Slager pleaded guilty in federal court to the § 242 count and the remaining federal charges and state murder charge were dismissed.

Should DOJ have waited to do its investigation and seek an indictment until the state proceeding had run its course? What risks does that approach entail?

George Floyd. George Floyd was killed when Minneapolis police officer Derek Chauvin put his knee on Floyd's neck for several minutes while Floyd was handcuffed, not resisting arrest, and, ultimately, nonresponsive. Chauvin and three other Minneapolis police officers were charged under § 242 with depriving Floyd of his federal right "to be free from an unreasonable seizure, which includes the right to be free from the use of unreasonable force by a police officer." *United States v. Chauvin*, Cr. 21.108 (D. Minn. May 6, 2001) (Indictment).

At the time of his federal indictment, Chauvin had already been convicted—but had not been sentenced—on state court murder charges. The federal prosecution of Chauvin thus seems analogous to the "backstop" role envisioned under the DOJ *Petite* Policy, an insurance policy if something unforeseen were to happen at sentencing or on appeal. Chauvin ultimately pleaded guilty to the federal charges and received a sentence that was approximately equivalent to his 22-year state court sentence.

Is Chauvin's guilty plea on federal § 242 charges a sufficient vindication of federal interests? Was a federal plea necessary to that end?

George Floyd

Breonna Taylor. Breonna Taylor, a 26-year old Black woman, was fatally shot in her apartment by Louisville, Kentucky police officers who were executing a no-knock search warrant in connection with a drug investigation centered on her live-in boyfriend. After Taylor's boyfriend fired one warning shot at the officers, the officers fired 34 shots in response, 6 of which hit Taylor and killed her. After developing evidence that the affidavit upon which the search warrant was based contained falsehoods, the DOJ chose not to charge the officers with an unreasonable use of force, as they had in the Scott and Floyd cases. They instead charged two of them, again under § 242, with depriving Taylor of the federal right "to be free from unreasonable searches and seizures" insofar as they were aware that "the affidavit contained false and misleading statements, omitted material information, relied on stale information, and was not supported by probable cause." *United States v. Jaynes*, No. 3:22-CR-85-CRS (W.D. Ky. Aug. 3, 2022) (Indictment). No state proceedings have been brought against the police officers. The City of Louisville banned no-knock search warrants after her killing, and several states have followed suit.

Breonna Taylor, on the occasion of her graduation from EMT school

Ahmaud Arbery. Ahmaud Arbery was jogging unarmed through a residential neighborhood in Brunswick, Georgia, when he was followed then pursued by three armed men in trucks, who boxed him in, shot him dead, and left him in the street. The three men were charged federally not under § 242, but rather under the more rarely used § 245(b)(2)(B), which prohibits "interference" with certain specified rights on the basis of race. Unlike § 242, this statute requires proof of racial motivation. Accordingly, the indictment charged the men with interfering "with Ahmaud Arbery, an African-American man, because of Arbery's race and color, and because he was and had been enjoying a facility provided and administered by a state and a subdivision thereof . . . a public street in the Satilia Shores neighborhood of Brunswick, Georgia." *United States v. McMichael*, No. CR 221-022 (S.D. Ga. Apr. 28, 2021) (Indictment).

After a state court trial and convictions and the imposition of life sentences (two without the possibility of parole) of the three men on earlier-filed state charges, federal prosecutors negotiated plea deals with defendants on the federal charges. But the trial judge refused to accept the pleas because of objections from the victim's family. After a two-week trial all of the defendants were convicted under § 245, with the prosecution proving the defendants' racial motivation through a combination of the defendants' social media posts, text messages, and racist comments.

Was a separate federal trial important to vindicate a separate federal interest here? Should the prosecutors have negotiated guilty pleas with the defendants? Should the judge have accepted the defendants' plea agreements notwithstanding the objections from Arbery's family?

Ahmaud Arbery

Sometimes, on the other hand, the DOJ decides not to prosecute. The Department of Justice has over the years typically refrained from making any public comment on ongoing investigations or decisions not to prosecute. The policy is not without exceptions, however, and for the last decade the department has more often than not commented publicly about high-profile civil rights cases in which it decided not to bring federal charges. One thing all of the DOJ commentary on nonprosecution decisions has in common is that it emphasizes, often defensively, the heavy burden the government would have in proving that the defendant acted "willfully."

A recent example of this trend was DOJ's decision not to prosecute George Zimmerman in connection with his fatal shooting of **Travon Martin** in Sanford, Florida. On July 15, 2013, two days after Zimmerman, a private citizen on a "neighborhood watch," was found not guilty by a Florida state jury, the Department of Justice issued a press release announcing that it was continuing to investigate the matter. Its announcement was heavily caveated, however. The release stated that DOJ was looking into "whether the evidence reveals a prosecutable violation of any of the limited federal criminal civil rights statutes" available, and whether prosecution would be appropriate in accordance with "the Department's policy governing successive federal prosecution following a state court trial." DOJ Press Release, Justice Department Statement on the Trayvon Martin-George Zimmerman Case (July 15, 2013).

Over 18 months later, DOJ announced that it would not be bringing federal charges, inasmuch as "the matter cannot be prosecuted federally." DOJ Press Release, Federal Officials Close Investigation into Death of Trayvon Martin (Feb. 24, 2015). Because Zimmerman was not a police officer, he could not have been prosecuted under § 242. Nonetheless DOJ noted that it had considered the possibility of hate crime charges under 18 U.S.C. § 249, which requires that defendant acted willfully, which "is one of the highest standards of intent imposed by law." *Id.*

The following month, the DOJ announced that it would not be bringing federal charges against Darren Wilson, the Ferguson, Missouri police officer who had fatally shot **Michael Brown**. This announcement came not merely in a press release, but in a publicly released 86-page report that contained a detailed account of the evidence the DOJ reviewed, as well as DOJ's factual and legal analysis. U.S. Dept. of Justice Civil Rights Div., Report Regarding the Criminal Investigation into the Shooting of Michael Brown by Ferguson Police Officer, Darren Wilson (2015). As noted in Chapter VII *supra*, a state grand jury had declined to indict Wilson on any charges in connection with Brown's shooting. The report devoted almost three full pages to the challenging nature of the "willfully" requirement, citing the *Screws* opinion no fewer than nine times. *See* Paul Savoy, *Reopening Ferguson and Rethinking Civil Rights Prosecutions*, 41 N.Y.U. Rev. L. & Soc. Change 277, 283 (2017) (criticizing legal analysis in the DOJ report).

In September 2017, DOJ announced it would not be bringing federal charges against Baltimore, Maryland police officers in connection with the death of **Freddie Gray**. DOJ, Federal Officials Decline Prosecution in the Death of Freddie Gray (Sept. 12, 2017). Gray had died in police custody after being placed in the back deck of a police van without being restrained by seat belts and transported through the city. His death precipitated several days of rioting in Baltimore. Six officers were charged by the state: one trial resulted in a hung jury; three officers were acquitted in bench trials; and state prosecutors thereafter dismissed all remaining charges against all officers. Kurland, *The Enduring Virtues of Deferential Federalism, supra* at 829.

The DOJ Press Release reviewed the evidence in detail. The government concluded that, in light of the evidence, it would not be able to sustain its "heavy burden" of proving willfulness under § 242, which is "one of the highest standards of intent imposed by law."

The press releases announcing the decisions declining to prosecute the police officers involved in the deaths of **Tamir Rice** in Cleveland and **Eric Garner** in Staten Island are similar. They provided a detailed review of the evidence, and concluded that DOJ would likely be unable to satisfy its burden under § 242 of proving defendants acted willfully, "one of the highest intent standards imposed by law."

Is DOJ's concern about prosecutors' ability to satisfy the willfully requirement in § 242 justified? Might it instead, or also, be a convenient cover for nonintervention? To be fair, the DOJ is not alone in its views of § 242's challenges. Many commentators have also pointed to the statute's intent requirement as an impediment to the vindication of civil rights through federal criminal prosecution. *See* Rachael A. Harmon, *Promoting Civil Rights Through Proactive Policing Reform*, 62 Stan. L. Rev. 1, 9 (2000) ("Federal criminal civil rights prosecutions face significant legal and practical obstacles, including that federal law imposes an onerous intent requirement on civil rights crimes"); John V. Jacobi, *Prosecuting Police Misconduct*, 2000 Wis. L. Rev. 789, 806-11 (discussing § 242's mens rea requirement as an impediment to federal prosecution).

Congress, too, has recognized the challenge of § 242's intent requirement. The George Floyd Justice in Policing Act of 2020, H.R. 7120, 116th Cong. (2020), which passed the House by a wide margin but failed in the Senate, has proposed replacing the term "willfully" in § 242 with "knowingly or recklessly." *Id.* at 7-8.

It is not clear, however, that the "willfully" requirement in § 242 imposes—or should impose, if aggressively and successively litigated—as onerous a burden as DOJ and commentators ascribe to it. First of all, there is *Lanier. See supra.* Although DOJ's statements about the onerous intent requirement of §§ 241 and 242 are not necessarily "wrong," there is a decent chance that *Lanier* more accurately describes that burden.

Second, the Supreme Court's most recent general analysis of a criminal statute's willfulness requirement is not hopeless. In *United States v. Bryan*, 524 U.S. 184 (1998), the Court considered the Firearms Owners' Protection Act's addition of 18 U.S.C. § 924(a)(1)(D) to the Criminal Code, which prohibited anyone from "willfully" violating, inter alia, § 922(a)(1)(A), which forbids dealing in firearms without a federal license. In *Bryan*, the Court acknowledged that while the word "willfully" can have different meanings depending on context, *id.* at 191, it normally means simply that an action was taken with a "bad purpose"—in other words, that the defendant knew his conduct "was unlawful." *Id.* at 193. The word does not, however, require knowledge of any particular illegality—it is not "an exception to the traditional rule that ignorance of the law is no excuse," *id.* at 194—only a generalized knowledge that the conduct was unlawful.

In prosecutions of police officers for civil rights violations, how much does this intent requirement really add to the—very considerable—challenges of such prosecutions? Consider a classic form of civil rights violation: a police brutality case involving the alleged use of unreasonable force by a police officer in making an arrest. If the government can prove that the use of force was unreasonable, the government's burden in any event, is there room left for the defendant to contend that he was unaware that his use of force, while unreasonable, was unlawful? Police officers have known for decades that unreasonable uses of force are unlawful. Police brutality cases are difficult for many reasons, not the least of which is that juries may well sympathize with the public servants who are making split-second decisions while facing personal danger from a potentially armed defendant. But a properly interpreted "willfully" requirement would not seem to materially increase that difficulty.

Consider also potential civil rights prosecutions for deprivations of other kinds of federal rights. Recall that in *Williams v. United States*, 341 U.S. 97 (1951), the Court had no trouble upholding a civil rights conviction based on a coercive interrogation—it's "plain as a pikestaff"—given the settled law on the subject. In a modern variation on that dynamic, could police officers who fail to give a suspect *Miranda* warnings—as they sometimes do, for collateral investigative reasons, *see* Chapter III *supra*—defend against a § 242 charge on the basis they did not know their conduct was unlawful? Also, as noted above, two of the Louisville police officers involved in preparing the affidavit in support of the search warrant application for Breonna Taylor's apartment were charged under § 242 with falsifying the affidavit. Could those officers really defend the § 242 charges against them on the basis that they didn't know their conduct—falsifying information in an affidavit submitted to court—was unlawful?

Along these lines, it is worth asking whether the DOJ Civil Rights Division shouldn't devote more energy generally to deprivations of rights other than the Fourth Amendment right to be free of excessive force. Motions to suppress searches and confessions are not easy to win, but they are commonplace. Among the universe of successful motions, those featuring the most egregious police misconduct should provide substantial fodder for investigation—with the suppression decision as a starting point—into possible federal civil rights prosecutions. These cases won't be easy either—among other problems would be the role of the prosecutor in approving a search warrant affidavit—but the context, unlike excessive force prosecutions, is not necessarily one in which juries will naturally sympathize with police defendants.

CHAPTER XI

PLEAS AND PLEA BARGAINING

The Supreme Court announced—finally!—in 2012 that plea bargaining "is not some adjunct to the criminal justice system; it *is* the criminal justice system." *Missouri v. Frye*, 566 U.S. 134, 144 (2012) (emphasis added). As support for this news flash the Court quoted from a law review article that was then 20 years old. *Id.* (quoting Robert E. Scott & William J. Stuntz, *Plea Bargaining as Contract*, 101 Yale L.J. 1909, 1912 (1992)). Professors Scott and Stuntz, for their part, did not purport to be breaking news but rather were applying classic contract theory in considering the arguments of the supporters and opponents of the long-settled practice of plea bargaining. In making this acknowledgment the Court pointed to recent DOJ statistics that 97 percent of federal convictions and 94 percent of state convictions are the result of pleas. *Frye*, 566 U.S. at 143.

We begin with some plea-bargaining fundamentals, based on standard practices in most jurisdictions. The output of plea bargaining is a deal, usually called a plea agreement, between the defendant and the prosecutor whereby the defendant agrees to plead guilty in court in exchange for concessions that will ensure or at least make more likely a lower sentence than if the defendant were to be convicted at trial. In short, the price of the plea "bargain" is that the defendant gives up his right to go to trial. The agreement is often but not always memorialized in writing. The actual guilty "plea" is a statement in court by the defendant ("I plead guilty"), which takes place in a court proceeding subsequent to the negotiation of the plea agreement between the defendant's attorney and the prosecutor. At the plea hearing, the terms of the plea agreement are considered and almost always accepted by the court and, more importantly, the court determines, based upon a colloquy with the defendant, that there is a factual basis for the plea and that the plea is a voluntary, knowing, and intelligent waiver of the constitutional right to go to trial. Upon these two findings, the court formally "accepts" the defendant's guilty plea. Sentencing usually comes later, depending on the jurisdiction.

These fundamentals are important to bear in mind, even though the separate parts of this chapter do not track neatly onto them. Section A is largely introductory. It examines how racial bias can affect the plea-bargaining process and also looks at the history of plea bargaining, a history that is significant mostly insofar as it was largely ignored until it was too late. Section B explores the "waiver" aspect of a guilty plea—a guilty plea is above all a waiver of the constitutional right to a jury trial—and a court's obligation to ensure that a defendant pleading guilty understands what he is giving up. Section C focuses specifically on the requirement that the waiver of rights in a guilty plea be voluntary. Section D examines plea bargaining, the controversial process by which the criminal justice system churns out the guilty pleas that keep it afloat. Section E looks at the Supreme Court's belated recent discovery—for the second time—of the prevalence of plea bargaining, and the Court's recognition that attorney conduct in plea bargaining must be governed by the Sixth Amendment's effective assistance of counsel requirement. Section F looks at the enforceability of plea agreements, particularly as to the collateral waivers the government is fond of requiring.

A. INTRODUCTION: THE PLEA-BARGAINING CONTROVERSY

1. Race and Plea Bargaining

As with charging decisions, *see* Chapter IX *supra*, implicit biases can affect the prosecutor's negotiation of a plea agreement. If anything, in plea bargaining prosecutors have even more discretion than they do in making charging decisions. The range of outcomes of plea agreements, subject to statutory requirements and office policy, is wide—from dismissal or probation or suspended sentence, on the low end, up to varying degrees of jail time on the other. In dealing with defense counsel, the prosecutor can make no plea offer at all. Prosecutors can make a single "take it or leave it" offer. They can engage in lengthy back and forth communication with defense counsel about the case's strengths and weaknesses and the defendant's characteristics. They can engage with defense counsel shortly after charges are brought, closer to trial, or even during trial. There is no judicial scrutiny over any aspect of this process, which is subject only to the policies of the prosecutor's office regarding acceptable outcomes. Nor will there be any meaningful judicial scrutiny of the terms of any deal that is ultimately reached—the court's scrutiny at the plea hearing will normally be limited to determining whether there is a minimal factual basis for the plea, based on the prosecutor's abbreviated summary of the anticipated proof, and whether the defendant's guilty plea is voluntary, knowing, and intelligent.

As with charging decisions, the prosecutor's exercise of her discretion will typically be guided by ostensibly objective factors. For example, in deciding what sort of resolution is appropriate the prosecutor is likely to take into consideration the need for specific deterrence of the defendant. This will entail a review of the defendant's criminal record, which, as we saw with respect to charging decisions, may not truly be a race-neutral factor. Angela J. Davis, Arbitrary Justice: The Power of the American Prosecutor 47 (2007). Similarly, the victim's interest in the case will again be a factor in determining an acceptable outcome and, as we saw earlier, may not be race-neutral.

Professors Smith and Levinson point out that one of the factors the Department of Justice singles out for consideration in plea bargaining is "the seriousness of the offense charged." *See* Chapter IX *supra*. They argue that the implicit bias concept of "in-group favoritism" might well lead a prosecutor to view a crime with a victim of the same race as the prosecutor as more "serious" than a crime with a victim of another race. Robert J. Smith & Justin D. Levinson, *The Impact of Implicit Racial Bias on the Exercise of Prosecutorial Discretion*, 35 Seattle U. L. Rev. 795, 816-17 (2012). They also observe that a similar phenomenon could be at work in a prosecutor's evaluation of another DOJ factor, "the public interest in having the case tried instead of being disposed of by a guilty plea":

> Imagine a prosecutor trying to determine whether to offer a defendant a plea to manslaughter (and thus a term of years) or to proceed to trial to try to obtain a second-degree murder conviction (and thus, in many jurisdictions, life without parole). Whether "the public interest" is satisfied by a plea bargain (as opposed to going to trial where the defendant could receive a harsher sentence) and whether "the expense of trial" is worth it turn on how the prosecutor views the defendant. Is this person dangerous and thus likely to commit a future crime? As a white prosecutor reviews the case file of a young white defendant, the prosecutor might be unknowingly affected by positive implicit stereotypes relating to lawfulness and trustworthiness. This could lead to a more lenient evaluation of the defendant—troubled, but not a bad person, for example—and thus a plea offer is more likely to follow. As we have well-covered by now, the opposite will be true when the prosecutor views a black defendant; the prosecutor's mind will likely trigger automatic associations between the defendant and the concepts of violence and hostility.

Id. at 817.

Another DOJ factor is "the defendant's remorse or contrition and his willingness to assume responsibility." Assessments of remorse or contrition are entirely subjective, as is the even vaguer concept of assumption of responsibility. A prosecutor will inevitably bring his own cultural background and expectations to an assessment of this factor. *See* M. Eve Hanan, *Remorse Bias*, 83 Mo. L. Rev. 301 (2018) (exploring the racial bias against Black men in remorse assessments for sentencing purposes).

There is not a lot of data demonstrating the existence of racial bias in plea bargaining. One exception is a dataset from court records in Dane County, Wisconsin, which was analyzed by Professor Carlos Berdejó. *See* Carlos Berdejó, *Criminalizing Race: Racial Disparities in Plea Bargaining*, 59 B.C. L. Rev. 1187 (2018). Professor Berdejo studied the results in approximately 50,000 plea-bargained cases that were resolved during 1999-2006. Among his findings:

- White defendants are twenty-five percent more likely than black defendants to have their most serious initial charge dropped or reduced to a less severe charge.
- White defendants initially charged with misdemeanors are approximately seventy-five percent more likely than black defendants to be convicted for crimes carrying no possible incarceration, or not to be convicted at all.
- Racial disparities in plea-bargaining outcomes appear to be driven by cases in which defendants have no prior convictions. In cases involving defendants with prior convictions there are no significant racial disparities in plea-bargaining outcomes.
- Racial disparities in plea-bargaining outcomes are greater in cases involving misdemeanors and low-level felonies relative to cases involving more severe offenses.
- Black defendants are significantly more likely to receive a prison sentence than white defendants. The incarceration rate for black defendants is 51.99%, substantially higher than that of white defendants, 34.88%.
- Additionally, black defendants receive sentences that are on average two months longer than those received by white defendants (4.85 months versus 2.84 months).

See id. at 1191-93, 1205-09.

2. Plea Bargaining History

It is generally agreed that plea bargaining became widespread in the United States in the second half of the nineteenth century. *See* William Ortman, *When Plea Bargaining Became Normal*, 100 B.U. L. Rev. 1435, 1441 (2020). Prohibition spurred the growth of plea bargaining during the 1920s as both state and federal courts were flooded with cases needing resolution, which made bargaining a legal and practical necessity. Albert W. Alschuler, *Plea Bargaining and Its History*, 79 Colum. L. Rev. 1, 28 (1979). Between the early twentieth century and 1925, pleas increased from 50 to 90 percent. Emory Bruckner was the United States Attorney for the Southern District of New York during the throes of Prohibition. In an effort to manage the crushing backlog of pending Volstead Act cases, his office would publicize so-called bargain days, when hundreds of cases would be resolved for reduced penalties in a single proceeding.

At least by the time of Prohibition the prevalence of plea bargaining was no secret on the ground. The judges, lawyers, and defendants—the players in the criminal justice system—were well aware of plea bargaining's significance. But the pervasiveness of plea bargaining was not understood or acknowledged by the legal profession at large until it was "discovered" in the 1920s and 1930s in connection with the crime commission movement of that era, some of which—like the Wickersham Commission—was focused on Prohibition. Ortman, *When Plea Bargaining Became Normal*, *supra* at 1455-59. The commissions generally found that

Emory Bruckner, U.S. Attorney for the Southern District of New York, federal enforcer of the Volstead Act

Andrew Volstead, Republican congressman from Minnesota, 1903-1923, sponsor of the eponymous federal legislation implementing the Eighteenth Amendment

this pervasiveness was the result of compromises between prosecutors and defendants, where defendants received leniency (shorter sentence, suspended sentence, probation) in exchange for pleading guilty and lightening the prosecutor's burden. *Id.* at 1458-59.

Reformers considering the commissions' results were displeased. Their two main responses to the discovery of the pervasiveness of plea bargaining were negative: Criminals were escaping justice and prosecutors were corruptly aiding and abetting them in doing so. *Id.* at 1460-62. The reformers and discoverers expressed little if any concern about the coerciveness of plea bargaining, the main focus of critics today. Alschuler, *Plea Bargaining and Its History*, *supra* at 30-32 They clearly seemed to view the typical exchange as a "plea discount" rather than a "trial penalty," and often a corrupt discount at that. The reformers' reactions were not far afield from the general public's view of "plea bargaining" today, as a vaguely distasteful and dishonorable process in which all participants share the blame. *See* Ortman, *When Plea Bargaining Became Normal*, *supra* at 1439 (the public "has never really understood plea bargaining and . . . has certainly never accepted it"); Davis, Arbitrary Justice, *supra* at 43 ("The term 'plea bargaining' usually evokes negative reactions" from the public). In any event, the efficiencies of plea bargaining eventually won out, and by the time the Supreme Court first publicly acknowledged plea bargaining's pervasiveness in or about 1970, it was a firmly established and apparently indispensable part of the criminal justice system.

The triumph of plea bargaining raises important concerns about coercion. Those will be discussed below in Section D. But for practicing lawyers it also means a different way of life. Professor Fisher puts it well:

> There is no glory in plea bargaining. In place of a noble clash for truth, plea bargaining gives us a skulking truce. Opposing lawyers shrink from battle, and the jury's empty box signals the system's disappointment. But though its victory merits no fanfare, plea bargaining has triumphed. Bloodlessly and clandestinely, it has swept across the penal landscape and driven our vanquished jury into small pockets of resistance. Plea bargaining may be, as some chroniclers claim, the invading barbarian. But it has won all the same.

George Fisher, *Plea Bargaining's Triumph*, 109 Yale L.J. 857 (2000). Professor Fisher's comment on the "ingloriousness" of plea bargaining may be a lawyerly conceit, but it is a conceit lawyers uniformly embrace. Every trial has a story or two, but no prosecutor or defense lawyer has ever told a decent story about a guilty plea. Plea bargains come, plea bargains go, and they are soon forgotten.

Practicing lawyers often get nostalgic about a supposed former golden age of trials. In 2003 the Litigation Section of the ABA held a symposium titled "The Vanishing Trial." But this should not have been news in 2002. Raymond Moley, a political scientist at Case Western Reserve University and the impetus for the Cleveland Foundation's study of criminal justice in Cleveland in the 1920s, wrote a law review article in 1927 about the commission's discovery of the prevalence of plea bargaining titled "The Vanishing Jury." Raymond Moley, *The Vanishing Jury*, 2 S. Cal. L. Rev. 97, 105 (1928).

B. THE PLEA HEARING: WAIVER AND CONSEQUENCES

Guilty plea hearings are governed by Rule 11 of the Federal Rules of Criminal Procedure. The Rule has been often amended to reflect Supreme Court decisions on the constitutional requirements of such hearings; such interplay between the Rules and Supreme Court doctrine is common. The next case is part of that dynamic.

Boykin v. Alabama
395 U.S. 238 (1969)

Mr. Justice DOUGLAS delivered the opinion of the Court.

In the spring of 1966, within the period of a fortnight, a series of armed robberies occurred in Mobile, Alabama. The victims, in each case, were local shopkeepers open at night who were forced by a gunman to hand over money. While robbing one grocery store, the assailant fired his gun once, sending a bullet through a door into the ceiling. A few days earlier in a drugstore, the robber had allowed his gun to discharge in such a way that the bullet, on ricochet from the floor, struck a customer in the leg. Shortly thereafter, a local grand jury returned five indictments against petitioner, a 27-year-old Negro, for common law robbery—an offense punishable in Alabama by death.

Before the matter came to trial, the court determined that petitioner was indigent and appointed counsel to represent him. Three days later, at his arraignment, petitioner pleaded guilty to all five indictments. So far as the record shows, the judge asked no questions of petitioner concerning his plea, and petitioner did not address the court.

Trial strategy may of course make a plea of guilty seem the desirable course. But the record is wholly silent on that point and throws no light on it.

Alabama provides that when a defendant pleads guilty, "the court must cause the punishment to be determined by a jury" (except where it is required to be fixed by the court) and may "cause witnesses to be examined, to ascertain the character of the offense." Ala. Code, Tit. 15, § 277 (1958). In the present case a trial of that dimension was held, the prosecution presenting its case largely through eyewitness testimony. Although counsel for petitioner engaged in cursory cross-examination, petitioner neither testified himself nor presented testimony concerning his character and background. There was nothing to indicate that he had a prior criminal record.

In instructing the jury, the judge stressed that petitioner had pleaded guilty in five cases of robbery, defined as "the felonious taking of money . . . from another against his will . . . by

Chapter XI Pleas and Plea Bargaining

violence or by putting him in fear . . . (carrying) from ten years minimum in the penitentiary to the supreme penalty of death by electrocution." The jury, upon deliberation, found petitioner guilty and sentenced him severally to die on each of the five indictments.

Taking an automatic appeal to the Alabama Supreme Court, petitioner argued that a sentence of death for common-law robbery was cruel and unusual punishment within the meaning of the Federal Constitution, a suggestion which that court unanimously rejected. On their own motion, however, four of the seven justices discussed the constitutionality of the process by which the trial judge had accepted petitioner's guilty plea. From the order affirming the trial court, three justices dissented on the ground that the record was inadequate to show that petitioner had intelligently and knowingly pleaded guilty. The fourth member concurred separately, conceding that "a trial judge should not accept a guilty plea unless he has determined that such a plea was voluntarily and knowingly entered by the defendant," but refusing "(f)or aught appearing" to presume that the trial judge failed to do his duty. We granted certiorari.

Respondent does not suggest that we lack jurisdiction to review the voluntary character of petitioner's guilty plea because he failed to raise that federal question below and the state court failed to pass upon it. But the question was raised on oral argument and we conclude that it is properly presented. The very Alabama statute that provides automatic appeal in capital cases also requires the reviewing court to comb the record for "any error prejudicial to the appellant, even though not called to our attention in brief of counsel." The automatic appeal statute "is the only provision under the Plain Error doctrine of which we are aware in Alabama criminal appellate review." In the words of the Alabama Supreme Court:

> Perhaps it is well to note that in reviewing a death case under the automatic appeal statute, . . . we may consider any testimony that was seriously prejudicial to the rights of the appellant and may reverse thereon, even though no lawful objection or exception was made thereto. Our review is not limited to the matters brought to our attention in brief of counsel.

It was error, plain on the face of the record, for the trial judge to accept petitioner's guilty plea without an affirmative showing that it was intelligent and voluntary. That error, under Alabama procedure, was properly before the court below and considered explicitly by a majority of the justices and is properly before us on review.

A plea of guilty is more than a confession which admits that the accused did various acts; it is itself a conviction; nothing remains but to give judgment and determine punishment. Admissibility of a confession must be based on a "reliable determination on the voluntariness issue which satisfies the constitutional rights of the defendant." The requirement that the prosecution spread on the record the prerequisites of a valid waiver is no constitutional innovation. In *Carnley v. Cochran*, we dealt with a problem of waiver of the right to counsel, a Sixth Amendment right. We held: "Presuming waiver from a silent record is impermissible. The record must show, or there must be an allegation and evidence which show, that an accused was offered counsel but intelligently and understandingly rejected the offer. Anything less is not waiver."

We think that the same standard must be applied to determining whether a guilty plea is voluntarily made. For, as we have said, a plea of guilty is more than an admission of conduct; it is a conviction. Ignorance, incomprehension, coercion, terror, inducements, subtle or blatant threats might be a perfect cover-up of unconstitutionality. The question of an effective waiver of a federal constitutional right in a proceeding is of course governed by federal standards.

Several federal constitutional rights are involved in a waiver that takes place when a plea of guilty is entered in a state criminal trial. First, is the privilege against compulsory self-incrimination guaranteed by the Fifth Amendment and applicable to the States by reason of the Fourteenth. Second, is the right to trial by jury. Third, is the right to confront one's accusers. We cannot presume a waiver of these three important federal rights from a silent record.

What is at stake for an accused facing death or imprisonment demands the utmost solicitude of which courts are capable in canvassing the matter with the accused to make sure he has a full understanding of what the plea connotes and of its consequence. When the judge discharges that function, he leaves a record adequate for any review that may be later sought, and forestalls the spin-off of collateral proceedings that seek to probe murky memories.

The three dissenting justices in the Alabama Supreme Court stated the law accurately when they concluded that there was reversible error "because the record does not disclose that the defendant voluntarily and understandingly entered his pleas of guilty."

Reversed.

Mr. Justice HARLAN, whom Mr. Justice BLACK joins, dissenting.

The Court today holds that petitioner Boykin was denied due process of law, and that his robbery convictions must be reversed outright, solely because "the record (is) inadequate to show that petitioner . . . intelligently and knowingly pleaded guilty." The Court thus in effect fastens upon the States, as a matter of federal constitutional law, the rigid prophylactic requirements of Rule 11 of the Federal Rules of Criminal Procedure. It does so in circumstances where the Court itself has only very recently held application of Rule 11 to be unnecessary in the federal courts. Moreover, the Court does all this at the behest of a petitioner who has never at any time alleged that his guilty plea was involuntary or made without knowledge of the consequences. I cannot possibly subscribe to so bizarre a result.

I

In June 1966, an Alabama grand jury returned five indictments against petitioner Boykin, on five separate charges of common-law robbery. He was determined to be indigent, and on July 11 an attorney was appointed to represent him. Petitioner was arraigned three days later. At that time, in open court and in the presence of his attorney, petitioner pleaded guilty to all five indictments. The record does not show what inquiries were made by the arraigning judge to confirm that the plea was made voluntarily and knowingly.

Petitioner was not sentenced immediately after the acceptance of his plea. Instead, pursuant to an Alabama statute, the court ordered that "witnesses . . . be examined, to ascertain the character of the offense," in the presence of a jury which would then fix petitioner's sentence. That proceeding occurred some two months after petitioner pleaded guilty. During that period, petitioner made no attempt to withdraw his plea. Petitioner was present in court with his attorney when the witnesses were examined. Petitioner heard the judge state the elements of common-law robbery and heard him announce that petitioner had pleaded guilty to that offense and might be sentenced to death. Again, petitioner made no effort to withdraw his plea.

On his appeal to the Alabama Supreme Court, petitioner did not claim that his guilty plea was made involuntarily or without full knowledge of the consequences. In fact, petitioner raised no questions at all concerning the plea. In his petition and brief in this Court, and in oral argument by counsel, petitioner has never asserted that the plea was coerced or made in ignorance of the consequences.

II

Against this background, the Court holds that the Due Process Clause of the Fourteenth Amendment requires the outright reversal of petitioner's conviction. This result is wholly unprecedented. There are past holdings of this Court to the effect that a federal habeas corpus petitioner who makes sufficiently credible allegations that his state guilty plea was involuntary is entitled to a hearing as to the truth of those allegations. These holdings suggest that if equally convincing allegations were made in a petition for certiorari on direct review, the petitioner might in some circumstances be entitled to have a judgment of affirmance vacated and the case remanded for a state hearing on voluntariness. However, as has been noted, this petitioner makes no allegations of actual involuntariness.

The Court's reversal is therefore predicated entirely upon the failure of the arraigning state judge to make an "adequate" record. In holding that this is a ground for reversal, the Court quotes copiously from *McCarthy v. United States* (1969), in which we held earlier this Term that when a federal district judge fails to comply in every respect with the procedure for accepting a guilty plea which is prescribed in Rule 11 of the Federal Rules of Criminal Procedure, the plea must be set aside and the defendant permitted to replead, regardless of lower-court findings that the plea was in fact voluntary. What the Court omits to mention is that in *McCarthy* we stated that our decision was based "solely upon our construction of Rule 11," and explicitly disavowed any reliance upon the Constitution. Thus *McCarthy* can provide no support whatever for today's constitutional edict.

III

So far as one can make out from the Court's opinion, what is now in effect being held is that the prophylactic procedures of Criminal Rule 11 are substantially applicable to the States as a matter of federal constitutional due process. If this is the basis upon which Boykin's conviction is being reversed, then the Court's disposition is plainly out of keeping with a sequel case to *McCarthy*, decided only last month. For the Court held in *Halliday v. United States* (1969), that "in view of the large number of constitutionally valid convictions that may have been obtained without full compliance with Rule 11, we decline to apply *McCarthy* retroactively. The Court quite evidently found Halliday's conviction to be 'constitutionally valid,'" for it affirmed the conviction even though Halliday's guilty plea was accepted in 1954 without any explicit inquiry into whether it was knowingly and understandingly made, as now required by present Rule 11. In justification, the Court noted that two lower courts had found in collateral proceedings that the plea was voluntary. The Court declared that:

> (A) defendant whose plea has been accepted without full compliance with Rule 11 may still resort to appropriate post-conviction remedies to attack his plea's voluntariness. Thus, if his plea was accepted prior to our decision in McCarthy, he is not without a remedy to correct constitutional defects in his conviction.

It seems elementary that the Fifth Amendment due process to which petitioner Halliday was entitled must be at least as demanding as the Fourteenth Amendment process due petitioner Boykin. Yet petitioner Halliday's federal conviction has been affirmed as "constitutionally valid," despite the omission of any judicial inquiry of record at the time of his plea, because he initiated collateral proceedings which revealed that the plea was actually voluntary. Petitioner Boykin, on the other hand, today has his Alabama conviction reversed because of exactly the same omission, even though he too "may . . . resort to appropriate post-conviction remedies to attack his plea's voluntariness" and thus "is not without a remedy to correct constitutional defects in his conviction." In short, I find it utterly impossible to square today's holding with what the Court has so recently done.

I would hold that petitioner Boykin is not entitled to outright reversal of his conviction simply because of the "inadequacy" of the record pertaining to his guilty plea. Further, I would not vacate the judgment below and remand for a state-court hearing on voluntariness. For even if it is assumed for the sake of argument that petitioner would be entitled to such a hearing if he had alleged that the plea was involuntary, a matter which I find it unnecessary to decide, the fact is that he has never made any such claim. Hence, I consider that petitioner's present arguments relating to his guilty plea entitle him to no federal relief.

B. The Plea Hearing: Waiver and Consequences   **983**

NOTES AND QUESTIONS

1. The Court states that a "plea of guilty is more than a confession which admits that the accused did various acts; it is itself a conviction, nothing remains but to give judgment and determine punishment." What does it mean that a guilty plea is "a conviction"? How is that "more" than a confession? Do you think of a guilty plea as a "conviction" in the colloquial sense?

2. What is the constitutional basis for the Court's holding in *Boykin*?

3. What does it mean that a defendant who pleads guilty waives his Fifth Amendment privilege against self-incrimination?

4. The Court spends much of the short opinion discussing waiver but at one point states the plea colloquy must also ensure the defendant "has a full understanding of what the plea connotes and its consequence." Does the term "consequence" merely refer to the things that are waived by the plea (e.g., right to a jury trial) or something else? Note that in a footnote at this point the Court identifies "the permissible range of sentences." Does an "intelligent" waiver of constitutional rights by a guilty plea require an understanding of the sentencing consequences of that decision?

5. Consider the performance of Boykin's appointed counsel. Do you see much discernable difference between counsel's performance here and counsel's performance in *Powell v. Alabama*, Chapter VIII, *supra*? Is *Boykin* really a case about the Sixth Amendment right to counsel? Would counsel's performance in *Boykin* have been ineffective under *Strickland*?

6. The dissent claims that petitioner "made no attempt to withdraw his plea" before he was sentenced and even on appeal "makes no allegations of actual involuntariness." Judging by the apparent local standards for appointed counsel, are either of these shortcomings surprising? And isn't the point of *Boykin* to make it the responsibility of the court to ensure voluntariness and not to leave it up to the vagaries of defendant's counsel?

7. *Boykin* was not writing on a totally blank slate. The Court had recognized the bare constitutional requirements of a guilty plea in federal court decades earlier. *See Kercheval v. United Sates*, 274 U.S. 220, 224 (1927) ("Out of just consideration for persons accused of crime, courts are careful that a plea of guilty shall not be accepted unless made voluntarily after proper advice and with full understanding of the consequences."). And earlier in the same year *Boykin* was decided, the Court decided *McCarthy v. United States*, 394 U.S. 459 (1969), holding that a federal district court must scrupulously comply with the requirements of Rule 11 of the Federal Rules of Criminal Procedure for a guilty plea to be valid.

As originally enacted in 1944, Rule 11 simply provided:

> A defendant may plead not guilty, guilty or, with consent of the court, nolo contendere. The court may refuse to accept a plea of guilty, and shall not accept the plea without first determining that the plea is made voluntarily with understanding of the nature of the charge. If a defendant refuses to plead or if the court refuses to accept a plea of guilty or if a defendant corporation fails to appear, the court shall enter a plea of not guilty.

Fed. R. Crim. P. 11. In 1966, the Rule was amended to require that the court find a factual basis for the plea, and in response to *Boykin* the Rule was amended in 1975 to include acknowledgments of the specific waivers addressed in that case. The Rule has been amended in several respects since then to require additional acknowledgments and advisements.

Don't confuse the court's duty to determine that there is a "factual basis" for the plea, currently codified at Rule 11(b)(3), with a duty to inquire into the substantive fairness of the plea. The Advisory Committee Notes to the 1966 amendments to Rule 11 make clear that the purpose of this subsection is to ensure that the conduct to which the defendant admits establishes the elements of the crime to which he is pleading guilty. It is not to determine the strength of the government's case.

In two cases decided shortly after *Boykin*, the Court returned to the question of the consequences of the fact that a guilty plea is "more than a conviction." *McMann v. Richardson*, 397 U.S. 759 (1970), involved three New York defendants who had pleaded guilty but on appeal claimed that their guilty pleas were the result of coerced confessions that, at the time of their pleas, would have been litigated at trial under a procedure later found to be unconstitutional. The Court upheld the guilty pleas. It drew a sharp distinction between coerced confessions that contribute to a guilty verdict at trial and those that may induce a guilty plea. Unlike a jury verdict, the Court reasoned, a guilty plea is based on a defendant's admission that the defendant committed the charged crime, and not is independent of and subsequent to any antecedent violation. Similarly, in *Tollett v. Henderson*, 411 U.S. 258 (1973), the defendant pleaded guilty to a murder charge but later petitioned for habeas relief claiming that Black people had been excluded from the grand jury that indicted him. As in *McMann*, the Court found that the guilty plea in *Tollett* likewise foreclosed inquiry into the grand jury selection claim.

C. GUILTY PLEAS AND VOLUNTARINESS

At the same time it was beginning to examine the consequences of plea hearings, and what was constitutionally required in terms of their memorialization, the Supreme Court also continued to address the requirement that a valid plea be voluntary.

The statutory context in which the next case arose was the Federal Kidnapping Act, 18 U.S.C. § 1201(a), one of the first federal statutes to federally criminalize conduct that was also illegal under state law. It was passed largely in response to public outcry over the kidnaping and murder of the toddler son of American aviation hero Charles Lindbergh. The theory behind the law's enactment was that state and local law enforcement would be unable to pursue kidnaping suspects across state lines. The federal statute authorized a death sentence, but such a sentence could only be imposed by a jury, not the judge. If the defendant waived a jury trial, the maximum sentence the judge could impose was life imprisonment. Bruno Hauptmann, a German-born carpenter, was ultimately prosecuted for the Lindbergh baby's abduction under New Jersey law. He was convicted and executed. Several books have been written challenging the conviction.

Bruno Hauptmann

C. Guilty Pleas and Voluntariness **985**

In 1968, the death penalty provision of the Federal Kidnapping Act was ruled unconstitutional in *United States v. Jackson*, 390 U.S. 570 (1968), because it unduly discouraged defendants from asserting their Sixth Amendment right to a trial by jury. In *Brady*, which follows, the defendant claimed his pre-*Jackson* guilty plea was involuntary because it was coerced by the risk of receiving the death penalty if he elected for a trial by jury.

Brady v. United States
397 U.S. 742 (1970)

Mr. Justice WHITE delivered the opinion of the Court.

In 1959, petitioner was charged with kidnaping in violation of 18 U.S.C. § 1201(a). Since the indictment charged that the victim of the kidnaping was not liberated unharmed, petitioner faced a maximum penalty of death if the verdict of the jury should so recommend. Petitioner, represented by competent counsel throughout, first elected to plead not guilty. Apparently because the trial judge was unwilling to try the case without a jury, petitioner made no serious attempt to reduce the possibility of a death penalty by waiving a jury trial. Upon learning that his codefendant, who had confessed to the authorities, would plead guilty and be available to testify against him, petitioner changed his plea to guilty. His plea was accepted after the trial judge twice questioned him as to the voluntariness of his plea. Petitioner was sentenced to 50 years' imprisonment, later reduced to 30.

In 1967, petitioner sought relief under 28 U.S.C. § 2255, claiming that his plea of guilty was not voluntarily given because § 1201(a) operated to coerce his plea, because his counsel exerted impermissible pressure upon him, and because his plea was induced by representations with respect to reduction of sentence and clemency. It was also alleged that the trial judge had not fully complied with Rule 11 of the Federal Rules of Criminal Procedure.

After a hearing, the District Court for the District of New Mexico denied relief. According to the District Court's findings, petitioner's counsel did not put impermissible pressure on petitioner to plead guilty and no representations were made with respect to a reduced sentence or clemency. The court held that § 1201(a) was constitutional and found that petitioner decided to plead guilty when he learned that his codefendant was going to plead guilty: petitioner pleaded guilty "by reason of other matters and not by reason of the statute" or because of any acts of the trial judge. The court concluded that "the plea was voluntarily and knowingly made."

The Court of Appeals for the Tenth Circuit affirmed, determining that the District Court's findings were supported by substantial evidence and specifically approving the finding that petitioner's plea of guilty was voluntary. We granted certiorari, to consider the claim that the Court of Appeals was in error in not reaching a contrary result on the authority of this Court's decision in *United States v. Jackson* (1968). We affirm.

I

In *United States v. Jackson* the defendants were indicted under § 1201(a). The District Court dismissed the § 1201(a) count of the indictment, holding the statute unconstitutional because it permitted imposition of the death sentence only upon a jury's recommendation and thereby made the risk of death the price of a jury trial. This Court held the statute valid, except for the death penalty provision; with respect to the latter, the Court agreed with the trial court "that the death penalty provision . . . imposes an impermissible burden upon the exercise of a constitutional right. . . ." The problem was to determine "whether the Constitution permits the establishment of such a death penalty, applicable only to those defendants who assert the right to contest their guilt before a jury." The inevitable effect of the provision was said

Chapter XI Pleas and Plea Bargaining

to be to discourage assertion of the Fifth Amendment right not to plead guilty and to deter exercise of the Sixth Amendment right to demand a jury trial. Because the legitimate goal of limiting the death penalty to cases in which a jury recommends it could be achieved without penalizing those defendants who plead not guilty and elect a jury trial, the death penalty provision "needlessly penalize(d) the assertion of a constitutional right," and was therefore unconstitutional.

Since the "inevitable effect" of the death penalty provision of § 1201(a) was said by the Court to be the needless encouragement of pleas of guilty and waivers of jury trial, Brady contends that *Jackson* requires the invalidation of every plea of guilty entered under that section, at least when the fear of death is shown to have been a factor in the plea. Petitioner, however, has read far too much into the *Jackson* opinion.

The Court made it clear in *Jackson* that it was not holding § 1201(a) inherently coercive of guilty pleas: "the fact that the Federal Kidnaping Act tends to discourage defendants from insisting upon their innocence and demanding trial by jury hardly implies that every defendant who enters a guilty plea to a charge under the Act does so involuntarily." Cited in support of this statement was *Laboy v. New Jersey* (D.C.N.J. 1967), where a plea of guilty (non vult) under a similar statute was sustained as voluntary in spite of the fact, as found by the District Court, that the defendant was greatly upset by the possibility of receiving the death penalty.

Moreover, the Court in *Jackson* rejected a suggestion that the death penalty provision of § 1201(a) be saved by prohibiting in capital kidnaping cases all guilty pleas and jury waivers, "however clear (the defendants') guilt and however strong their desire to acknowledge it in order to spare themselves and their families the spectacle and expense of protracted courtroom proceedings." "(T)hat jury waivers and guilty pleas may occasionally be rejected" was no ground for automatically rejecting all guilty pleas under the statute, for such a rule "would rob the criminal process of much of its flexibility."

Plainly, it seems to us, *Jackson* ruled neither that all pleas of guilty encouraged by the fear of a possible death sentence are involuntary pleas nor that such encouraged pleas are invalid whether involuntary or not. *Jackson* prohibits the imposition of the death penalty under § 1201(a), but that decision neither fashioned a new standard for judging the validity of guilty pleas nor mandated a new application of the test theretofore fashioned by courts and since reiterated that guilty pleas are valid if both "voluntary" and "intelligent." *See Boykin v. Alabama* (1969).

That a guilty plea is a grave and solemn act to be accepted only with care and discernment has long been recognized. Central to the plea and the foundation for entering judgment against the defendant is the defendant's admission in open court that he committed the acts charged in the indictment. He thus stands as a witness against himself and he is shielded by the Fifth Amendment from being compelled to do so — hence the minimum requirement that his plea be the voluntary expression of his own choice. But the plea is more than an admission of past conduct; it is the defendant's consent that judgment of conviction may be entered without a trial — a waiver of his right to trial before a jury or a judge. Waivers of constitutional rights not only must be voluntary but must be knowing, intelligent acts done with sufficient awareness of the relevant circumstances and likely consequences. On neither score was Brady's plea of guilty invalid.

II

The trial judge in 1959 found the plea voluntary before accepting it; the District Court in 1968, after an evidentiary hearing, found that the plea was voluntarily made; the Court of Appeals specifically approved the finding of voluntariness. We see no reason on this record to disturb the judgment of those courts. Petitioner, advised by competent counsel, tendered his plea after his codefendant, who had already given a confession, determined to plead guilty and became available to testify against petitioner. It was this development that the District Court found to have triggered Brady's guilty plea.

The voluntariness of Brady's plea can be determined only by considering all of the relevant circumstances surrounding it. One of these circumstances was the possibility of a heavier sentence following a guilty verdict after a trial. It may be that Brady, faced with a strong case against him and recognizing that his chances for acquittal were slight, preferred to plead guilty and thus limit the penalty to life imprisonment rather than to elect a jury trial which could result in a death penalty. But even if we assume that Brady would not have pleaded guilty except for the death penalty provision of § 1201(a), this assumption merely identifies the penalty provision as a "but for" cause of his plea. That the statute caused the plea in this sense does not necessarily prove that the plea was coerced and invalid as an involuntary act.

The State to some degree encourages pleas of guilty at every important step in the criminal process. For some people, their breach of a State's law is alone sufficient reason for surrendering themselves and accepting punishment. For others, apprehension and charge, both threatening acts by the Government, jar them into admitting their guilt. In still other cases, the post-indictment accumulation of evidence may convince the defendant and his counsel that a trial is not worth the agony and expense to the defendant and his family. All these pleas of guilty are valid in spite of the State's responsibility for some of the factors motivating the pleas; the pleas are no more improperly compelled than is the decision by a defendant at the close of the State's evidence at trial that he must take the stand or face certain conviction.

Of course, the agents of the State may not produce a plea by actual or threatened physical harm or by mental coercion overbearing the will of the defendant. But nothing of the sort is claimed in this case; nor is there evidence that Brady was so gripped by fear of the death penalty or hope of leniency that he did not or could not, with the help of counsel, rationally weigh the advantages of going to trial against the advantages of pleading guilty. Brady's claim is of a different sort: that it violates the Fifth Amendment to influence or encourage a guilty plea by opportunity or promise of leniency and that a guilty plea is coerced and invalid if influenced by the fear of a possibly higher penalty for the crime charged if a conviction is obtained after the State is put to its proof.

Insofar as the voluntariness of his plea is concerned, there is little to differentiate Brady from (1) the defendant, in a jurisdiction where the judge and jury have the same range of sentencing power, who pleads guilty because his lawyer advises him that the judge will very probably be more lenient than the jury; (2) the defendant, in a jurisdiction where the judge alone has sentencing power, who is advised by counsel that the judge is normally more lenient with defendants who plead guilty than with those who go to trial; (3) the defendant who is permitted by prosecutor and judge to plead guilty to a lesser offense included in the offense charged; and (4) the defendant who pleads guilty to certain counts with the understanding that other charges will be dropped. In each of these situations, as in Brady's case, the defendant might never plead guilty absent the possibility or certainty that the plea will result in a lesser penalty than the sentence that could be imposed after a trial and a verdict of guilty. We decline to hold, however, that a guilty plea is compelled and invalid under the Fifth Amendment whenever motivated by the defendant's desire to accept the certainty or probability of a lesser penalty rather than face a wider range of possibilities extending from acquittal to conviction and a higher penalty authorized by law for the crime charged.

The issue we deal with is inherent in the criminal law and its administration because guilty pleas are not constitutionally forbidden, because the criminal law characteristically extends to judge or jury a range of choice in setting the sentence in individual cases, and because both the State and the defendant often find it advantageous to preclude the possibility of the maximum penalty authorized by law. For a defendant who sees slight possibility of acquittal, the advantages of pleading guilty and limiting the probable penalty are obvious—his exposure is reduced, the correctional processes can begin immediately, and the practical burdens of a trial are eliminated. For the State there are also advantages—the more promptly imposed punishment after an admission of guilt may more effectively attain the objectives of punishment; and with the avoidance of trial, scarce judicial and prosecutorial resources are conserved for those cases in which there is a substantial issue of the defendant's guilt or in which there is substantial doubt that the State can sustain its burden of proof. It is this mutuality of advantage that perhaps explains the fact that at present well over three-fourths of the criminal convictions in this country rest on pleas of guilty, a great many of them no doubt motivated at least in part by the hope or assurance of a lesser penalty than might be imposed if there were a guilty verdict after a trial to judge or jury.

Of course, that the prevalence of guilty pleas is explainable does not necessarily validate those pleas or the system which produces them. But we cannot hold that it is unconstitutional for the State to extend a benefit to a defendant who in turn extends a substantial benefit to the State and who demonstrates by his plea that he is ready and willing to admit his crime and to enter the correctional system in a frame of mind that affords hope for success in rehabilitation over a shorter period of time than might otherwise be necessary.

A contrary holding would require the States and Federal Government to forbid guilty pleas altogether, to provide a single invariable penalty for each crime defined by the statutes, or to place the sentencing function in a separate authority having no knowledge of the manner in which the conviction in each case was obtained. In any event, it would be necessary to forbid prosecutors and judges to accept guilty pleas to selected counts, to lesser included offenses, or to reduced charges. The Fifth Amendment does not reach so far.

Bram v. United States (1897) held that the admissibility of a confession depended upon whether it was compelled within the meaning of the Fifth Amendment. To be admissible, a confession must be "free and voluntary: that is, must not be extracted by any sort of threats or violence, nor obtained by any direct or implied promises, however slight, nor by the exertion of any improper influence." More recently, *Malloy v. Hogan* (1964), carried forward the *Bram* definition of compulsion in the course of holding applicable to the States the Fifth Amendment privilege against compelled self-incrimination.

Bram is not inconsistent with our holding that Brady's plea was not compelled even though the law promised him a lesser maximum penalty if he did not go to trial. *Bram* dealt with a confession given by a defendant in custody, alone and unrepresented by counsel. In such circumstances, even a mild promise of leniency was deemed sufficient to bar the confession, not because the promise was an illegal act as such, but because defendants at such times are too sensitive to inducement and the possible impact on them too great to ignore and too difficult to assess. But *Bram* and its progeny did not hold that the possibly coercive impact of a promise of leniency could not be dissipated by the presence and advice of counsel, any more than *Miranda v. Arizona* (1966), held that the possibly coercive atmosphere of the police station could not be counteracted by the presence of counsel or other safeguards.

Brady's situation bears no resemblance to Bram's. Brady first pleaded not guilty; prior to changing his plea to guilty he was subjected to no threats or promises in face-to-face encounters with the authorities. He had competent counsel and full opportunity to assess the advantages and disadvantages of a trial as compared with those attending a plea of guilty; there was no hazard of an impulsive and improvident response to a seeming but unreal advantage. His plea of guilty was entered in open court and before a judge obviously sensitive to the requirements of the law with respect to guilty pleas. Brady's plea, unlike Bram's confession, was voluntary.

C. Guilty Pleas and Voluntariness   **989**

The standard as to the voluntariness of guilty pleas must be essentially that defined by Judge Tuttle of the Court of Appeals for the Fifth Circuit:

> (A) plea of guilty entered by one fully aware of the direct consequences, including the actual value of any commitments made to him by the court, prosecutor, or his own counsel, must stand unless induced by threats (or promises to discontinue improper harassment), misrepresentation (including unfulfilled or unfulfillable promises), or perhaps by promises that are by their nature improper as having no proper relationship to the prosecutor's business (e.g. bribes).

Under this standard, a plea of guilty is not invalid merely because entered to avoid the possibility of a death penalty.

III

The record before us also supports the conclusion that Brady's plea was intelligently made. He was advised by competent counsel, he was made aware of the nature of the charge against him, and there was nothing to indicate that he was incompetent or otherwise not in control of his mental faculties; once his confederate had pleaded guilty and became available to testify, he chose to plead guilty, perhaps to ensure that he would face no more than life imprisonment or a term of years. Brady was aware of precisely what he was doing when he admitted that he had kidnaped the victim and had not released her unharmed.

It is true that Brady's counsel advised him that § 1201(a) empowered the jury to impose the death penalty and that nine years later in *United States v. Jackson* the Court held that the jury had no such power as long as the judge could impose only a lesser penalty if trial was to the court or there was a plea of guilty. But these facts do not require us to set aside Brady's conviction.

Often the decision to plead guilty is heavily influenced by the defendant's appraisal of the prosecution's case against him and by the apparent likelihood of securing leniency should a guilty plea be offered and accepted. Considerations like these frequently present imponderable questions for which there are no certain answers; judgments may be made that in the light of later events seem improvident, although they were perfectly sensible at the time. The rule that a plea must be intelligently made to be valid does not require that a plea be vulnerable to later attack if the defendant did not correctly assess every relevant factor entering into his decision. A defendant is not entitled to withdraw his plea merely because he discovers long after the plea has been accepted that his calculus misapprehended the quality of the State's case or the likely penalties attached to alternative courses of action. More particularly, absent misrepresentation or other impermissible conduct by state agents, a voluntary plea of guilty intelligently made in the light of the then applicable law does not become vulnerable because later judicial decisions indicate that the plea rested on a faulty premise. A plea of guilty triggered by the expectations of a competently counseled defendant that the State will have a strong case against him is not subject to later attack because the defendant's lawyer correctly advised him with respect to the then existing law as to possible penalties but later pronouncements of the courts, as in this case, hold that the maximum penalty for the crime in question was less than was reasonably assumed at the time the plea was entered.

The fact that Brady did not anticipate *United States v. Jackson* does not impugn the truth or reliability of his plea. We find no requirement in the Constitution that a defendant must be permitted to disown his solemn admissions in open court that he committed the act with which he is charged simply because it later develops that the State would have had a weaker case than the defendant had thought or that the maximum penalty then assumed applicable has been held inapplicable in subsequent judicial decisions.

This is not to say that guilty plea convictions hold no hazards for the innocent or that the methods of taking guilty pleas presently employed in this country are necessarily valid in all

Chapter XI Pleas and Plea Bargaining

respects. This mode of conviction is no more foolproof than full trials to the court or to the jury. Accordingly, we take great precautions against unsound results, and we should continue to do so, whether conviction is by plea or by trial. We would have serious doubts about this case if the encouragement of guilty pleas by offers of leniency substantially increased the likelihood that defendants, advised by competent counsel, would falsely condemn themselves. But our view is to the contrary and is based on our expectations that courts will satisfy themselves that pleas of guilty are voluntarily and intelligently made by competent defendants with adequate advice of counsel and that there is nothing to question the accuracy and reliability of the defendants' admissions that they committed the crimes with which they are charged. In the case before us, nothing in the record impeaches Brady's plea or suggests that his admissions in open court were anything but the truth.

Although Brady's plea of guilty may well have been motivated in part by a desire to avoid a possible death penalty, we are convinced that his plea was voluntarily and intelligently made and we have no reason to doubt that his solemn admission of guilt was truthful.

Affirmed.

NOTES AND QUESTIONS

1. The Court accepts the lower court's finding that Brady pleaded guilty after his codefendant had confessed and pleaded guilty and thus became available to testify against Brady. And the Court places considerable stock in the fact that the trial judge questioned Brady not once but twice about the voluntariness of his plea. The second colloquy is reproduced in footnote 2:

THE COURT:	Having read the presentence report and the statement you made to the probation officer, I want to be certain that you know what you are doing and you did know when you entered a plea of guilty the other day. Do you want to let that plea of guilty stand, or do you want to withdraw it and plead not guilty?
DEFENDANT BRADY:	I want to let that plea stand, sir.
THE COURT:	You understand that in doing that you are admitting and confessing the truth of the charge contained in the indictment and that you enter a plea of guilty voluntarily, without persuasion, coercion of any kind? Is that right?
DEFENDANT BRADY:	Yes, your Honor.
THE COURT:	And you do that?
DEFENDANT BRADY:	Yes, I do.
THE COURT:	You plead guilty to the charge?
DEFENDANT BRADY:	Yes, I do.

That's it for voluntariness? Are you impressed by the rigor of this colloquy? What more should the judge have done? Should the judge have asked questions that would have elicited the defendant's specific concerns about the codefendant's cooperation?

How important is it that Brady had counsel?

2. The dissent notes that a determination whether the death penalty scheme exercised "its pernicious influence" requires a "consideration of the factors that actually motivated the defendant to plead guilty." *Id.* at 808. At some point, however, does such a colloquy inevitably encroach upon the attorney-client privilege? What would happen to a defendant whose plea was rejected because the court found that the defendant was in fact "coerced" by the death penalty provision? Note that if a plea is withdrawn or not accepted statements made by defendant at the plea hearing can be admissible at any subsequent trial.

3. The Court states: "That a guilty plea is a grave and solemn act to be accepted only with care and discernment has long been recognized. Central to the plea and the foundation for entering judgment against the defendant is the defendant's admission in open court that he committed the acts charged in the indictment." *Id.* at 747.

Is there any suggestion in the colloquy that in accepting Brady's plea the lower court required such factual admissions? The Court cites nothing for the proposition that the defendant's "admission" is central to a guilty plea's validity, and it appears that Brady pleaded guilty prior to the 1966 amendment to Fed. R. Crim. P. 11, which added the requirement that the court must find a factual basis for the plea. *Boykin* says nothing about this aspect of a valid plea, and the court there apparently made no effort to find a factual basis for Boykin's guilt at the plea hearing. Why is it important that a court find a factual basis for a plea before accepting it?

4. The Court is quite blunt in its analysis of the inherently coercive nature of the criminal process: "The State to some degree encourages pleas of guilty at every important step in the criminal process." Is this overstated? Does the fact that capital punishment was at issue make Brady different? The dissent suggests that it does, and that the nature of the death penalty distinguishes this case from garden-variety coercion. *Id.* at 808. Do you agree?

5. The Court seems to view the system by which guilty pleas are offered and accepted as a necessary evil of the criminal justice system, and notes that "a contrary holding" would be unworkable. *Id.* at 753. As the Court notes in a footnote, by this time — 1970 — 90 to 95 percent of criminal convictions were being resolved by guilty pleas. Was it just too late to care about coercion?

6. The Court fairly notes that guilty plea convictions are no more "foolproof" than trials, and that "great precautions against unsound results must be taken in all cases." It then notes that it would have a higher level of concern "if the encouragement of guilty pleas by offers of leniency substantially increased the likelihood that defendants, advised by competent counsel, would falsely condemn themselves." *Id.* at 758.

Two things stick out in this passage. The first is the conception, rooted in the vocabulary of leniency, that plea offers are tantamount to "discounts," acts of beneficence by the government for which the defendant should be grateful. Is this accurate? What other reasons might a prosecutor make a plea offer? The second notable aspect of this passage is the binary view of the universe of defendants — they are either innocent or guilty. The Court genuinely doubts that defendants who are "actually innocent" plead guilty. But even if that were right, and it most surely is not, what about defendants whose cases are "triable," as defense lawyers say, but are afraid to take any significant trial risk for fear of draconian penalties?

7. The Court elsewhere confirms that the constitutionality of plea bargaining is to some degree dependent on the notion of leniency: "[W]e cannot hold that it is unconstitutional for the State to extend a benefit to a defendant who in turn extends a substantial benefit to the State."

8. In discussing a defendant's rational decision to plead guilty to avoid a harsher sentence, the Court drops the following footnote:

> We here make no reference to the situation where the prosecutor or judge, or both, deliberately employ their charging and sentencing powers to induce a particular defendant to tender a plea of guilty. In Brady's case there is no claim that the prosecutor threatened prosecution on a charge not justified by the evidence or that the trial judge threatened Brady with a harsher sentence if convicted after trial in order to induce him to plead guilty.

Id. at 751 n.8. How can these hypothesized scenarios be distinguished from what happened here? Or from the normal back-and-forth of plea bargaining?

North Carolina v. Alford
400 U.S. 25 (1970)

Mr. Justice WHITE delivered the opinion of the Court.

On December 2, 1963, Alford was indicted for first-degree murder, a capital offense under North Carolina law. The court appointed an attorney to represent him, and this attorney questioned all but one of the various witnesses who appellee said would substantiate his claim of innocence. The witnesses, however, did not support Alford's story but gave statements that strongly indicated his guilt. Faced with strong evidence of guilt and no substantial evidentiary support for the claim of innocence. Alford's attorney recommended that he plead guilty, but left the ultimate decision to Alford himself. The prosecutor agreed to accept a plea of guilty to a charge of second-degree murder, and on December 10, 1963, Alford pleaded guilty to the reduced charge.

Before the plea was finally accepted by the trial court, the court heard the sworn testimony of a police officer who summarized the State's case. Two other witnesses besides Alford were also heard. Although there was no eyewitness to the crime, the testimony indicated that shortly before the killing Alford took his gun from his house, stated his intention to kill the victim, and returned home with the declaration that he had carried out the killing. After the summary presentation of the State's case, Alford took the stand and testified that he had not committed the murder but that he was pleading guilty because he faced the threat of the death penalty if he did not do so. In response to the questions of his counsel, he acknowledged that his counsel had informed him of the difference between second- and first-degree murder and of his rights in case he chose to go to trial. The trial court then asked appellee if, in light of his denial of guilt, he still desired to plead guilty to second-degree murder and appellee answered, "Yes, sir. I plead guilty on — from the circumstances that he (Alford's attorney) told me." After eliciting information about Alford's prior criminal record, which was a long one, the trial court sentenced him to 30 years' imprisonment, the maximum penalty for second-degree murder.

Alford sought post-conviction relief in the state court. Among the claims raised was the claim that his plea of guilty was invalid because it was the product of fear and coercion. After a hearing, the state court in 1965 found that the plea was "willingly, knowingly, and understandingly" made on the advice of competent counsel and in the face of a strong prosecution case. Subsequently, Alford petitioned for a writ of habeas corpus, first in the United States District Court for the Middle District of North Carolina, and then in the Court of Appeals for the Fourth Circuit. Both courts denied the writ on the basis of the state court's findings that Alford voluntarily and knowingly agreed to plead guilty. In 1967, Alford again petitioned for a writ of habeas corpus in the District Court for the Middle District of North Carolina. That court, without an evidentiary hearing, again denied relief on the grounds that the guilty plea was voluntary and waived all defenses and nonjurisdictional defects in any prior stage of the proceedings and that the findings of the state court in 1965 clearly required rejection of Alford's claim that that he was denied effective assistance of counsel prior to pleading guilty. On appeal, a divided panel of the Court of Appeals for the Fourth Circuit reversed on the ground that Alford's guilty plea was made involuntarily. In reaching its conclusion, the Court of Appeals relied heavily on *United States v. Jackson* (1968), which the court read to require invalidation of the North Carolina statutory framework for the imposition of the death penalty because North Carolina statutes encouraged defendants to waive constitutional rights by the promise of no more than life imprisonment if a guilty plea was offered and accepted. Conceding that *Jackson* did not require the automatic invalidation of pleas of guilty entered under the North Carolina statutes, the Court of Appeals ruled that Alford's guilty plea was

C. Guilty Pleas and Voluntariness

involuntary because its principal motivation was fear of the death penalty. By this standard, even if both the judge and the jury had possessed the power to impose the death penalty for first-degree murder or if guilty pleas to capital charges had not been permitted, Alford's plea of guilty to second-degree murder should still have been rejected because impermissibly induced by his desire to eliminate the possibility of a death sentence. We noted probable jurisdiction. We vacate the judgment of the Court of Appeals and remand the case for further proceedings.

We held in *Brady v. United States* (1970) that a plea of guilty which would not have been entered except for the defendant's desire to avoid a possible death penalty and to limit the maximum penalty to life imprisonment or a term of years was not for that reason compelled within the meaning of the Fifth Amendment. *Jackson* established no new test for determining the validity of guilty pleas. The standard was and remains whether the plea represents a voluntary and intelligent choice among the alternative courses of action open to the defendant. That he would not have pleaded except for the opportunity to limit the possible penalty does not necessarily demonstrate that the plea of guilty was not the product of a free and rational choice, especially where the defendant was represented by competent counsel whose advice was that the plea would be to the defendant's advantage. The standard fashioned and applied by the Court of Appeals was therefore erroneous and we would, without more, vacate and remand the case for further proceedings with respect to any other claims of Alford which are properly before that court, if it were not for other circumstances appearing in the record which might seem to warrant an affirmance of the Court of Appeals.

As previously recounted after Alford's plea of guilty was offered and the State's case was placed before the judge, Alford denied that he had committed the murder but reaffirmed his desire to plead guilty to avoid a possible death sentence and to limit the penalty to the 30-year maximum provided for second-degree murder. Ordinarily, a judgment of conviction resting on a plea of guilty is justified by the defendant's admission that he committed the crime charged against him and his consent that judgment be entered without a trial of any kind. The plea usually subsumes both elements, and justifiably so, even though there is no separate, express admission by the defendant that he committed the particular acts claimed to constitute the crime charged in the indictment. Here Alford entered his plea but accompanied it with the statement that he had not shot the victim.

If Alford's statements were to be credited as sincere assertions of his innocence, there obviously existed a factual and legal dispute between him and the State. Without more, it might be argued that the conviction entered on his guilty plea was invalid, since his assertion of innocence negatived any admission of guilt, which, as we observed last Term in *Brady*, is normally "(c)entral to the plea and the foundation for entering judgment against the defendant."

In addition to Alford's statement, however, the court had heard an account of the events on the night of the murder, including information from Alford's acquaintances that he had departed from his home with his gun stating his intention to kill and that he had later declared that he had carried out his intention. Nor had Alford wavered in his desire to have trial court determine his guilt without a jury trial. Although denying the charge against him, he nevertheless preferred the dispute between him and the State to be settled by the judge in the context of a guilty plea proceeding rather than by a formal trial. Thereupon, with the State's telling evidence and Alford's denial before it, the trial court proceeded to convict and sentence Alford for second-degree murder.

State and lower federal courts are divided upon whether a guilty plea can be accepted when it is accompanied by protestations of innocence and hence contains only a waiver of trial but no admission of guilt. Some courts, giving expression to the principle that "(o)ur law only authorizes a conviction where guilt is shown," require that trial judges reject such pleas. But others have concluded that they should not "force any defense on a defendant in a criminal case," particularly when advancement of the defense might "end in disaster. . . ."

They have argued that, since "guilt, or the degree of guilt, is at times uncertain and elusive," "(a)n accused, though believing in or entertaining doubts respecting his innocence, might reasonably conclude a jury would be convinced of his guilt and that he would fare better in the sentence by pleading guilty. As one state court observed nearly a century ago, '(r)easons other than the fact that he is guilty may induce a defendant to so plead, . . . (and) (h)e must be permitted to judge for himself in this respect.'"

This Court has not confronted this precise issue, but prior decisions do yield relevant principles. In *Lynch v. Overholser* (1962), Lynch, who had been charged in the Municipal Court of the District of Columbia with drawing and negotiating bad checks, a misdemeanor punishable by a maximum of one year in jail, sought to enter a plea of guilty, but the trial judge refused to accept the plea since a psychiatric report in the judge's possession indicated that Lynch had been suffering from "a manic depressive psychosis, at the time of the crime charged," and hence might have been not guilty by reason of insanity. Although at the subsequent trial Lynch did not rely on the insanity defense, he was found not guilty by reason of insanity and committed for an indeterminate period to a mental institution. On habeas corpus, the Court ordered his release, construing the congressional legislation seemingly authorizing the commitment as not reaching a case where the accused preferred a guilty plea to a plea of insanity. The Court expressly refused to rule that Lynch had an absolute right to have his guilty plea accepted, but implied that there would have been no constitutional error had his plea been accepted even though evidence before the judge indicated that there was a valid defense.

The issue in *Hudson v. United States* (1926) was whether a federal court has power to impose a prison sentence after accepting a plea of nolo contendere, a plea by which a defendant does not expressly admit his guilt, but nonetheless waives his right to a trial and authorizes the court for purposes of the case to treat him as if he were guilty. The Court held that a trial court does have such power, and except for the cases which were rejected in *Hudson*, the federal courts have uniformly followed this rule, even in cases involving moral turpitude. Implicit in the nolo contendere cases is a recognition that the Constitution does not bar imposition of a prison sentence upon an accused who is unwilling expressly to admit his guilt but who, faced with grim alternatives, is willing to waive his trial and accept the sentence.

These cases would be directly in point if Alford had simply insisted on his plea but refused to admit the crime. The fact that his plea was denominated a plea of guilty rather than a plea of nolo contendere is of no constitutional significance with respect to the issue now before us, for the Constitution is concerned with the practical consequences, not the formal categorizations, of state law. Thus, while most pleas of guilty consist of both a waiver of trial and an express admission of guilt, the latter element is not a constitutional requisite to the imposition of criminal penalty. An individual accused of crime may voluntarily, knowingly, and understandingly consent to the imposition of a prison sentence even if he is unwilling or unable to admit his participation in the acts constituting the crime.

Nor can we perceive any material difference between a plea that refuses to admit commission of the criminal act and a plea containing a protestation of innocence when, as in the instant case, a defendant intelligently concludes that his interests require entry of a guilty plea and the record before the judge contains strong evidence of actual guilt. Here the State had a strong case of first-degree murder against Alford. Whether he realized or disbelieved his guilt, he insisted on his plea because in his view he had absolutely nothing to gain by a trial and much to gain by pleading. Because of the overwhelming evidence against him, a trial was precisely what neither Alford nor his attorney desired. Confronted with the choice between a trial for first-degree murder, on the one hand, and a plea of guilty to second-degree murder, on the other, Alford quite reasonably chose the latter and thereby limited the maximum penalty to a 30-year term. When his plea is viewed in light of the evidence against him, which substantially negated his claim of innocence and which further provided a means by which the judge could test whether the plea was being intelligently entered, its validity cannot be seriously questioned. In view of the strong factual basis for the plea demonstrated by the State and Alford's clearly expressed desire to enter it despite his professed belief in his innocence, we hold that the trial judge did not commit constitutional error in accepting it.

Relying on *United States v. Jackson*, Alford now argues in effect that the State should not have allowed him this choice but should have insisted on proving him guilty of murder in the first degree. The States in their wisdom may take this course by statute or otherwise and may prohibit the practice of accepting pleas to lesser included offenses under any circumstances. But this is not the mandate of the Fourteenth Amendment and the Bill of Rights. The prohibitions against involuntary or unintelligent pleas should not be relaxed, but neither should an exercise in arid logic render those constitutional guarantees counterproductive and put in jeopardy the very human values they were meant to preserve.

The Court of Appeals for the Fourth Circuit was in error to find Alford's plea of guilty invalid because it was made to avoid the possibility of the death penalty. That court's judgment directing the issuance of the writ of habeas corpus is vacated and the case is remanded to the Court of Appeals for further proceedings consistent with this opinion.

It is so ordered.

Vacated and remanded.

* * *

Mr. Justice BRENNAN, with whom Mr. Justice DOUGLAS and Mr. Justice MARSHALL join, dissenting.

Last Term, this Court held, over my dissent, that a plea of guilty may validly be induced by an unconstitutional threat to subject the defendant to the risk to death, so long as the plea is entered in open court and the defendant is represented by competent counsel who is aware of the threat, albeit not of its unconstitutionality. *Brady v. United States* (1970). Today the Court makes clear that its previous holding was intended to apply even when the record demonstrates that the actual effect of the unconstitutional threat was to induce a guilty plea from a defendant who was unwilling to admit his guilt.

I adhere to the view that, in any given case, the influence of such an unconstitutional threat "must necessarily be given weight in determining the voluntariness of a plea." And, without reaching the question whether due process permits the entry of judgment upon a plea of guilty accompanied by a contemporaneous denial of acts constituting the crime, I believe that at the very least such a denial of guilt is also a relevant factor in determining whether the plea was voluntarily and intelligently made. With these factors in mind, it is sufficient in my view to state that the facts set out in the majority opinion demonstrate that Alford was "so gripped by fear of the death penalty" that his decision to plead guilty was not voluntary but was "the product of duress as much so as choice reflecting physical constraint." Accordingly, I would affirm the judgment of the Court of Appeals.

NOTES AND QUESTIONS

1. The factual basis for Alford's plea here is robust, perhaps because there had been preplea communications among the prosecutor, defense counsel, and the court about the nature of Alford's anticipated plea.

Yet note the intrusions into the attorney-client privilege and attorney confidentiality requirement necessitated by Alford's claim for post-conviction relief on the basis that his guilty plea was the product of coercion. It is revealed that none of the witnesses Alford thought would substantiate his claims of innocence would do so. We also learn that Alford's appointed attorney recommended that he plead guilty. We are even told, gratuitously, that Alford's lawyer "left the ultimate decision to Alford himself." Maybe, just a few years into the *Gideon* era, this is meant as a compliment to the lawyer, to counteract the impression that legions of appointed attorneys were just churning out guilty pleas. But even then it should have been clear that the decision to plead guilty is always the client's decision.

2. The Court acknowledges that a judgment of conviction by guilty plea normally includes both an admission of guilt and consent to judgment without trial, and that the former is lacking here. Does the factual basis for Alford's guilt somehow compensate for that deficit here, even though Alford made no admissions at the plea hearing and there were no eyewitnesses to the crime? If the evidence were weaker, would the result be different?

3. What does the Court mean when it expresses skepticism as to the "sincerity" of Alford's assertions of innocence? How can the Court gauge sincerity from a dry record? What if Alford actually had articulated a viable defense—an alibi perhaps, accompanied by his anticipated testimony that his statements about the murder were just made to appear tough—but still did not want to risk the death penalty? Would his decision still have been "voluntary and intelligent"?

4. The Court ultimately finds no constitutional error in accepting Alford's plea notwithstanding the lack of any admitted factual basis for the charge. Without explicitly saying so, the Court seems influenced by concerns for personal autonomy similar to those that would lead to the recognition of a right to self-representation in *Faretta v. California*, 422 U.S. 806 (1975). *See* Chapter VIII *supra*. The Court does state that "arid logic" should not "put in jeopardy the very human values [that constitutional principles] were meant to preserve." 400 U.S. at 39. Why is the Court being coy here? What "human values" are being implied here?

5. The dissent finds Alford's plea to be involuntary under the same reasoning as in the concurring opinion in *Brady*, as on this record it is absolutely clear—unlike in *Brady*—that Alford was pleading guilty only or at least mainly to avoid the death penalty. *Id.* at 39-40. As to the lack of an admitted factual basis for guilt, and indeed the defendant's denial of guilt, the dissent found that that fact was a relevant factor in determining whether the plea was voluntarily and intelligently made. *Id.* Do you agree with the majority's characterization of the dissent's position as resting on "arid logic"?

So-called *Alford* pleas remain a recognizable, albeit rare, method of guilty plea—a plea where the defendant pleads guilty but maintains his innocence or at the very least does not admit guilt. The states vary on the use of *Alford pleas*: Currently they are frequently used in Louisiana, Missouri, Ohio, and Pennsylvania, but are forbidden in Indiana and New Jersey. *See* Jenny Elayne Ronis, *The Pragmatic Plea: Expanding Use of the* Alford *Plea to Promote Traditionally Conflicting Interests of the Criminal Justice System*, 82 Temp. L. Rev. 1389, 1390 (2010). *See also* Michael Conklin, *The* Alford *Plea Turns Fifty: Why It Deserves Another Fifty Years*, 54 Creighton L. Rev. 1 (2020) (offering a full-throated endorsement of *Alford* pleas).

The *Alford* plea is not acknowledged in the Federal Rules of Criminal Procedure, although Rule 11 does not require that the factual basis for the plea come from the defendant or that the defendant otherwise admit guilt. *See* Fed. R. Crim. P. 11(b)(3) ("Before entering judgment on a guilty plea, the court must determine that there is a factual basis for the plea."). Rule 11(a)(3), on the other hand, specifically contemplates the *Alford* plea's cousin, the plea of nolo contendere, with the permission of the Court. The difference between the two pleas is slight. A defendant pleading nolo contendere only refuses to admit guilt, whereas a defendant making an *Alford* plea, like Alford himself, claims he is innocent. And a nolo plea, but not an *Alford* plea, lacks estoppel effect in any follow-on civil litigation. Stephanos Bibas, *Harmonizing Substantive-Criminal-Law Values and Criminal Procedure: The Case of* Alford *and Nolo Contendere Pleas*, 88 Cornell L. Rev. 1361, 1373 (2003).

Critics of *Alford* and nolo contendere pleas argue, among other things, that such pleas disserve the interests of victims looking for closure, permit guilty defendants to engage in psychological denial, and erode public confidence in plea bargaining by suggesting that innocent people may be pleading guilty. *See* Bibas, *Harmonizing Substantive-Criminal-Law Values and Criminal Procedure, supra* at 1361, 1379-80. Defenders of the pleas, including almost all defense lawyers, view them as a practical tool of last resort for convincing a difficult client to do what is in his best interests while avoiding whatever sense of shame or embarrassment keeps him from admitting guilt. *Id.* at 1377-80.

D. PLEA BARGAINING, THE CONSTITUTION, AND COERCION

Enter the barbarian. Professor Rachel Barkow has been quoted by Emily Bazelon as describing the next case, *Bordenkircher*, as "the single biggest wrong turn the Supreme Court has taken in criminal law. . . . If you asked me what's the one thing the Supreme Court could do to fix our current system I'd say it would be to overturn it." Emily Bazelon, Charged 137-38 (2019).

Bordenkircher v. Hayes
434 U.S. 357 (1978)

Mr. Justice STEWART delivered the opinion of the Court.

The question in this case is whether the Due Process Clause of the Fourteenth Amendment is violated when a state prosecutor carries out a threat made during plea negotiations to reindict the accused on more serious charges if he does not plead guilty to the offense with which he was originally charged.

I

The respondent, Paul Lewis Hayes, was indicted by a Fayette County, Ky., grand jury on a charge of uttering a forged instrument in the amount of $88.30, an offense then punishable by a term of 2 to 10 years in prison. After arraignment, Hayes, his retained counsel, and the Commonwealth's Attorney met in the presence of the Clerk of the Court to discuss a possible plea agreement. During these conferences the prosecutor offered to recommend a sentence of five years in prison if Hayes would plead guilty to the indictment. He also said that if Hayes did not plead guilty and "save[d] the court the inconvenience and necessity of a trial," he would return to the grand jury to seek an indictment under the Kentucky Habitual Criminal Act, then Ky. Rev. Stat. § 431.190 (1973) (repealed 1975), which would subject Hayes to a mandatory sentence of life imprisonment by reason of his two prior felony convictions. Hayes chose not to plead guilty, and the prosecutor did obtain an indictment charging him under the Habitual Criminal Act. It is not disputed that the recidivist charge was fully justified by the evidence, that the prosecutor was in possession of this evidence at the time of the original indictment, and that Hayes' refusal to plead guilty to the original charge was what led to his indictment under the habitual criminal statute.

A jury found Hayes guilty on the principal charge of uttering a forged instrument and, in a separate proceeding, further found that he had twice before been convicted of felonies. As required by the habitual offender statute, he was sentenced to a life term in the penitentiary. The Kentucky Court of Appeals rejected Hayes' constitutional objections to the enhanced sentence, holding in an unpublished opinion that imprisonment for life with the possibility of parole was constitutionally permissible in light of the previous felonies of which Hayes had been convicted, and that the prosecutor's decision to indict him as a habitual offender was a legitimate use of available leverage in the plea-bargaining process.

On Hayes' petition for a federal writ of habeas corpus, the United States District Court for the Eastern District of Kentucky agreed that there had been no constitutional violation in the sentence or the indictment procedure, and denied the writ. The Court of Appeals for the Sixth Circuit reversed the District Court's judgment. While recognizing "that plea bargaining now plays an important role in our criminal justice system," the appellate court thought that the prosecutor's conduct during the bargaining negotiations had violated the principles of *Blackledge v. Perry*, which "protect[ed] defendants from the vindictive exercise of a prosecutor's discretion." Accordingly, the court ordered that Hayes be discharged "except for his confinement under a lawful sentence imposed solely for the crime of uttering a forged instrument." We granted certiorari to consider a constitutional question of importance in the administration of criminal justice.

II

It may be helpful to clarify at the outset the nature of the issue in this case. While the prosecutor did not actually obtain the recidivist indictment until after the plea conferences had ended, his intention to do so was clearly expressed at the outset of the plea negotiations. Hayes was thus fully informed of the true terms of the offer when he made his decision to plead not guilty. This is not a situation, therefore, where the prosecutor without notice brought an additional and more serious charge after plea negotiations relating only to the original indictment had ended with the defendant's insistence on pleading not guilty. As a practical matter, in short, this case would be no different if the grand jury had indicted Hayes as a recidivist from the outset, and the prosecutor had offered to drop that charge as part of the plea bargain.

The Court of Appeals nonetheless drew a distinction between "concessions relating to prosecution under an existing indictment," and threats to bring more severe charges not contained in the original indictment — a line it thought necessary in order to establish a prophylactic rule to guard against the evil of prosecutorial vindictiveness. Quite apart from this chronological distinction, however, the Court of Appeals found that the prosecutor had acted vindictively in the present case since he had conceded that the indictment was influenced by his desire to induce a guilty plea. The ultimate conclusion of the Court of Appeals thus seems to have been that a prosecutor acts vindictively and in violation of due process of law whenever his charging decision is influenced by what he hopes to gain in the course of plea bargaining negotiations.

III

We have recently had occasion to observe: "[W]hatever might be the situation in an ideal world, the fact is that the guilty plea and the often concomitant plea bargain are important components of this country's criminal justice system. Properly administered, they can benefit all concerned." The open acknowledgment of this previously clandestine practice has led this Court to recognize the importance of counsel during plea negotiations, the need for a public record indicating that a plea was knowingly and voluntarily made, and the requirement that a prosecutor's plea-bargaining promise must be kept. The decision of the Court of Appeals in the present case, however, did not deal with considerations such as these, but held that the substance of the plea offer itself violated the limitations imposed by the Due Process Clause of the Fourteenth Amendment. For the reasons that follow, we have concluded that the Court of Appeals was mistaken in so ruling.

IV

This Court held in *North Carolina v. Pearce* that the Due Process Clause of the Fourteenth Amendment "requires that vindictiveness against a defendant for having successfully attacked his first conviction must play no part in the sentence he receives after a new trial." The same principle was later applied to prohibit a prosecutor from reindicting a convicted misdemeanant on a felony charge after the defendant had invoked an appellate remedy, since in this situation there was also a "realistic likelihood of 'vindictiveness.'" *Blackledge v. Perry*.

In those cases the Court was dealing with the State's unilateral imposition of a penalty upon a defendant who had chosen to exercise a legal right to attack his original conviction—a situation "very different from the give-and-take negotiation common in plea bargaining between the prosecution and defense, which arguably possess relatively equal bargaining power." The Court has emphasized that the due process violation in cases such as *Pearce* and *Perry* lay not in the possibility that a defendant might be deterred from the exercise of a legal right, but rather in the danger that the State might be retaliating against the accused for lawfully attacking his conviction.

To punish a person because he has done what the law plainly allows him to do is a due process violation of the most basic sort, and for an agent of the State to pursue a course of action whose objective is to penalize a person's reliance on his legal rights is "patently unconstitutional." But in the "give-and-take" of plea bargaining, there is no such element of punishment or retaliation so long as the accused is free to accept or reject the prosecution's offer.

Plea bargaining flows from "the mutuality of advantage" to defendants and prosecutors, each with his own reasons for wanting to avoid trial. *Brady v. United States*. Defendants advised by competent counsel and protected by other procedural safeguards are presumptively capable of intelligent choice in response to prosecutorial persuasion, and unlikely to be driven to false self-condemnation. Indeed, acceptance of the basic legitimacy of plea bargaining necessarily implies rejection of any notion that a guilty plea is involuntary in a constitutional sense simply because it is the end result of the bargaining process. By hypothesis, the plea may have been induced by promises of a recommendation of a lenient sentence or a reduction of charges, and thus by fear of the possibility of a greater penalty upon conviction after a trial.

While confronting a defendant with the risk of more severe punishment clearly may have a "discouraging effect on the defendant's assertion of his trial rights, the imposition of these difficult choices [is] an inevitable"—and permissible—"attribute of any legitimate system which tolerates and encourages the negotiation of pleas." It follows that, by tolerating and encouraging the negotiation of pleas, this Court has necessarily accepted as constitutionally legitimate the simple reality that the prosecutor's interest at the bargaining table is to persuade the defendant to forgo his right to plead not guilty.

It is not disputed here that Hayes was properly chargeable under the recidivist statute, since he had in fact been convicted of two previous felonies. In our system, so long as the prosecutor has probable cause to believe that the accused committed an offense defined by statute, the decision whether or not to prosecute, and what charge to file or bring before a grand jury, generally rests entirely in his discretion. Within the limits set by the legislature's constitutionally valid definition of chargeable offenses, "the conscious exercise of some selectivity in enforcement is not in itself a federal constitutional violation" so long as "the selection was [not] deliberately based upon an unjustifiable standard such as race, religion, or other arbitrary classification." To hold that the prosecutor's desire to induce a guilty plea is an "unjustifiable standard," which, like race or religion underlie the concept of plea bargaining itself. Moreover, a rigid constitutional rule that would prohibit a prosecutor from acting forthrightly in his dealings with the defense could only invite unhealthy subterfuge that would drive the practice of plea bargaining back into the shadows from which it has so recently emerged.

There is no doubt that the breadth of discretion that our country's legal system vests in prosecuting attorneys carries with it the potential for both individual and institutional abuse. And broad though that discretion may be, there are undoubtedly constitutional limits upon its exercise. We hold only that the course of conduct engaged in by the prosecutor in this case, which no more than openly presented the defendant with the unpleasant alternatives of forgoing trial or facing charges on which he was plainly subject to prosecution, did not violate the Due Process Clause of the Fourteenth Amendment.

Accordingly, the judgment of the Court of Appeals is

Reversed.

Mr. Justice BLACKMUN, with whom Mr. Justice BRENNAN and Mr. Justice MARSHALL join, dissenting.

I feel that the Court, although purporting to rule narrowly (that is, on "the course of conduct engaged in by the prosecutor in this case," ante, this page), is departing from, or at least restricting, the principles established in *North Carolina v. Pearce* (1969), and in *Blackledge v. Perry* (1974). If those decisions are sound and if those principles are salutary, as I must assume they are, they require, in my view, an affirmance, not a reversal, of the judgment of the Court of Appeals in the present case.

In *Pearce*, as indeed the Court notes, it was held that "vindictiveness against a defendant for having successfully attacked his first conviction must play no part in the sentence he receives after a new trial." Accordingly, if on the new trial, the sentence the defendant receives from the court is greater than that imposed after the first trial, it must be explained by reasons "based upon objective information concerning identifiable conduct on the part of the defendant occurring after the time of the original sentencing proceeding," other than his having pursued the appeal or collateral remedy. On the other hand, if the sentence is imposed by the jury and not by the court, if the jury is not aware of the original sentence, and if the second sentence is not otherwise shown to be a product of vindictiveness, *Pearce* has no application.

Then later, in *Perry*, the Court applied the same principle to prosecutorial conduct where there was a "realistic likelihood of 'vindictiveness.'" It held that the requirement of Fourteenth Amendment due process prevented a prosecutor's reindictment of a convicted misdemeanant on a felony charge after the defendant had exercised his right to appeal the misdemeanor conviction and thus to obtain a trial de novo. It noted the prosecution's "considerable stake" in discouraging the appeal.

The Court now says, however, that this concern with vindictiveness is of no import in the present case, despite the difference between five years in prison and a life sentence, because we are here concerned with plea bargaining where there is give-and-take negotiation, and where, it is said, "there is no such element of punishment or retaliation so long as the accused is free to accept or reject the prosecution's offer." Yet in this case vindictiveness is present to the same extent as it was thought to be in *Pearce* and in *Perry*; the prosecutor here admitted that the sole reason for the new indictment was to discourage the respondent from exercising his right to a trial. Even had such an admission not been made, when plea negotiations, conducted in the face of the less serious charge under the first indictment, fail, charging by a second indictment a more serious crime for the same conduct creates "a strong inference" of vindictiveness. As then Judge McCree aptly observed, in writing for a unanimous panel of the Sixth Circuit, the prosecutor initially "makes a discretionary determination that the interests of the state are served by not seeking more serious charges." I therefore do not understand why, as in *Pearce*, due process does not require that the prosecution justify its action on some basis other than discouraging respondent from the exercise of his right to a trial.

Prosecutorial vindictiveness, it seems to me, in the present narrow context, is the fact against which the Due Process Clause ought to protect. I perceive little difference between

D. Plea Bargaining, the Constitution, and Coercion

vindictiveness after what the Court describes, as the exercise of a "legal right to attack his original conviction," and vindictiveness in the "'give-and-take negotiation common in plea bargaining.'" Prosecutorial vindictiveness in any context is still prosecutorial vindictiveness. The Due Process Clause should protect an accused against it, however it asserts itself. The Court of Appeals rightly so held, and I would affirm the judgment.

It might be argued that it really makes little difference how this case, now that it is here, is decided. The Court's holding gives plea bargaining full sway despite vindictiveness. A contrary result, however, merely would prompt the aggressive prosecutor to bring the greater charge initially in every case, and only thereafter to bargain. The consequences to the accused would still be adverse, for then he would bargain against a greater charge, face the likelihood of increased bail, and run the risk that the court would be less inclined to accept a bargained plea. Nonetheless, it is far preferable to hold the prosecution to the charge it was originally content to bring and to justify in the eyes of its public.

Mr. Justice Powell, dissenting.

Although I agree with much of the Court's opinion, I am not satisfied that the result in this case is just or that the conduct of the plea bargaining met the requirements of due process.

Respondent was charged with the uttering of a single forged check in the amount of $88.30. Under Kentucky law, this offense was punishable by a prison term of from 2 to 10 years, apparently without regard to the amount of the forgery. During the course of plea bargaining, the prosecutor offered respondent a sentence of five years in consideration of a guilty plea. I observe, at this point, that five years in prison for the offense charged hardly could be characterized as a generous offer. Apparently respondent viewed the offer in this light and declined to accept it; he protested that he was innocent and insisted on going to trial. Respondent adhered to this position even when the prosecutor advised that he would seek a new indictment under the State's Habitual Criminal Act which would subject respondent, if convicted, to a mandatory life sentence because of two prior felony convictions.

The prosecutor's initial assessment of respondent's case led him to forgo an indictment under the habitual criminal statute. The circumstances of respondent's prior convictions are relevant to this assessment and to my view of the case. Respondent was 17 years old when he committed his first offense. He was charged with rape but pleaded guilty to the lesser included offense of "detaining a female." One of the other participants in the incident was sentenced to life imprisonment. Respondent was sent not to prison but to a reformatory where he served five years. Respondent's second offense was robbery. This time he was found guilty by a jury and was sentenced to five years in prison, but he was placed on probation and served no time. Although respondent's prior convictions brought him within the terms of the Habitual Criminal Act, the offenses themselves did not result in imprisonment; yet the addition of a conviction on a charge involving $88.30 subjected respondent to a mandatory sentence of imprisonment for life. Persons convicted of rape and murder often are not punished so severely.

No explanation appears in the record for the prosecutor's decision to escalate the charge against respondent other than respondent's refusal to plead guilty. The prosecutor has conceded that his purpose was to discourage respondent's assertion of constitutional rights, and the majority accepts this characterization of events.

It seems to me that the question to be asked under the circumstances is whether the prosecutor reasonably might have charged respondent under the Habitual Criminal Act in the first place. The deference that courts properly accord the exercise of a prosecutor's discretion perhaps would foreclose judicial criticism if the prosecutor originally had sought an indictment under that Act, as unreasonable as it would have seemed. But here the prosecutor evidently made a reasonable, responsible judgment not to subject an individual to a mandatory life sentence when his only new offense had societal implications as limited as those accompanying the uttering of a single $88 forged check and when the circumstances of his prior convictions confirmed the inappropriateness of applying the habitual criminal statute. I think it may be inferred that the prosecutor himself deemed it unreasonable and not in the public interest to put this defendant in jeopardy of a sentence of life imprisonment.

There may be situations in which a prosecutor would be fully justified in seeking a fresh indictment for a more serious offense. The most plausible justification might be that it would have been reasonable and in the public interest initially to have charged the defendant with the greater offense. In most cases a court could not know why the harsher indictment was sought, and an inquiry into the prosecutor's motive would neither be indicated nor likely to be fruitful. In those cases, I would agree with the majority that the situation would not differ materially from one in which the higher charge was brought at the outset.

But this is not such a case. Here, any inquiry into the prosecutor's purpose is made unnecessary by his candid acknowledgment that he threatened to procure and in fact procured the habitual criminal indictment because of respondent's insistence on exercising his constitutional rights. We have stated in unequivocal terms, in discussing *United States v. Jackson* (1968) and *North Carolina v. Pearce* (1969), that "*Jackson* and *Pearce* are clear and subsequent cases have not dulled their force: if the only objective of a state practice is to discourage the assertion of constitutional rights it is 'patently unconstitutional.'" And in *Brady v. United States* (1970) we drew a distinction between the situation there approved and the "situation where the prosecutor or judge, or both, deliberately employ their charging and sentencing powers to induce a particular defendant to tender a plea of guilty."

The plea-bargaining process, as recognized by this Court, is essential to the functioning of the criminal-justice system. It normally affords genuine benefits to defendants as well as to society. And if the system is to work effectively, prosecutors must be accorded the widest discretion, within constitutional limits, in conducting bargaining. This is especially true when a defendant is represented by counsel and presumably is fully advised of his rights. Only in the most exceptional case should a court conclude that the scales of the bargaining are so unevenly balanced as to arouse suspicion. In this case, the prosecutor's actions denied respondent due process because their admitted purpose was to discourage and then to penalize with unique severity his exercise of constitutional rights. Implementation of a strategy calculated solely to deter the exercise of constitutional rights is not a constitutionally permissible exercise of discretion. I would affirm the opinion of the Court of Appeals on the facts of this case.

NOTES AND QUESTIONS

1. The Court distinguishes both *North Carolina v. Pearce*, 395 U.S. 711 (1969), and *Blackledge v. Perry*, 417 U.S. 357 (1978), on the ground that whereas those cases involved the unilateral imposition of a penalty on a defendant who had elected to exercise a legal right, *Bordenkircher* involved "the give-and-take negotiation common in plea bargaining between the government and defense, which arguably possess relatively equal bargaining power." 434 U.S. at 362.

This is a case that makes it easy to be cynical about terms such as "give-and-take" and "bargaining power," however accurately such phrases may describe some sort of plea-bargaining ideal. In fact *Bordenkircher* vividly illustrates what is more often than not the case: that the term "plea bargain" is wholly inapt, in both senses of the term "bargain." In *Bordenkircher*, there was certainly no "bargain" as in "discount" nor was there any "bargain" as in "negotiation."

2. The dissent notes that the vindictiveness that was essentially presumed in *Pearce* and *Blackledge* was actually admitted here, as the prosecutor made no attempt to conceal that his decision to indict Hayes under the habitual offender statute was made because Hayes refused to plead guilty to the uttering charge. *Id.* at 358. Does this matter? The majority seems at most ambivalent on this score, referring to the "unhealthy subterfuge" of the previously "clandestine practice" of plea bargaining. Would this have been an unremarkable case if the plea discussions had not been memorialized by the court clerk? Should all such discussions be memorialized by a public official?

3. The prosecutor's candor seems to have been totally uninhibited by the fact that the plea negotiations were held in the presence of the clerk of the court.

Why do you think the prosecutor was willing to be so candid about his intentions notwithstanding the presence of a third party, and a representative of the judiciary at that? Could he have been mindful of *Blackledge* and *Pearce*? Of at least the gist of the Supreme Court's statement in footnote 8 in *Brady*, which purported to distinguish that case from "the situation where the prosecutor or judge, or both, deliberately employ their charging and sentencing powers to induce a particular defendant to tender a plea of guilty"?

4. Why at trial did the prosecutor cross-examine Hayes about his refusal to "plead guilty to five years . . . and save the court the inconvenience and necessity of a trial"? Note that the jury was presumably unaware of the life imprisonment penalty under the habitual offender statute, in keeping with the customary division of authority between court and jury. Should the jury have been informed of the consequences of finding Hayes guilty? *See* Chapter XIII *infra.*

5. The Court acknowledges the breadth of prosecutorial discretion in "our system," limited only by whether the prosecutor has "probable cause to believe that the accused committed an offense defined by statute." *Id.* at 364. It also notes that the breadth of that discretion "carries with it the potential for both individual and institutional abuse." *Id.* at 365. But if that discretion must remain immunized from scrutiny, does the same need to be true of the legislative decisions that confer and permit that wide discretion? Shouldn't those at least be subject to constitutional scrutiny?

Is the real issue here not simply prosecutorial power but rather the Eighth Amendment? If there is no constitutionally principled way to limit plea bargaining, does the solution lie elsewhere? Note Justice Powell's dissent, which finds a due process violation, relying on footnote 8 from *Brady*, because the prosecutor's "admitted purpose was to discourage and then to penalize with *unique severity* his exercise of constitutional rights." *Id.* at 372-73. Is the severity the real issue?

Five years after *Bordenkircher*, in *Solem v. Helm*, 463 U.S. 277 (1983), the Court held that South Dakota's habitual offender statute violated the Eighth Amendment's "proportionality principle." That statute provided for a life sentence without parole (South Dakota had abolished parole) where a defendant was convicted of a felony and had three prior felony convictions. The proportionality principle of *Solem* was effectively gutted just eight years later in *Harmelin v. Michigan*, 501 U.S. 957 (1991).

6. The habitual offender statute under which Hayes was charged—an early precursor to the notorious "three strikes" laws that proliferated in the 1980s and 1990s—was also a function of increased crime rates. Yet Hayes fell within the statute's cross-hairs most unfortunately: The statute was enacted prior to Hayes's offense but was revised shortly afterwards to change the mandatory life sentence upon conviction to a term of 10 to 20 years. In other words, at the time of Hayes's sentencing, neither the prosecutor nor even the legislature thought that someone like Hayes should receive a life sentence on these facts.

7. The Court's opinion has a somber, almost fatalistic tone, as if the Court recognized the injustice of the situation but did not see a way to come out differently without bringing down the entire plea-bargaining edifice that it was "tolerating" and has "necessarily accepted as legitimate." The dissent, too, recognizes that a "contrary result, however, merely would prompt the aggressive prosecutor to bring the greatest charge initially in every case and only thereafter to bargain." 434 U.S. at 368.

Is this necessarily the case? Would defendants likely be better or worse off in a world where prosecutors are incentivized to bring the maximum available charge at the outset of a case?

It may seem odd that as "early" as 1978 the Court is so fatalistic about the inevitability of plea bargaining. After all, it had first used the term "plea bargain" in a decision, and in quotation marks no less, just seven years earlier in *Santobello*. Was unfettered plea bargaining by this point—1978—so embedded beyond repair in the criminal justice system? It might have seemed so from the Court's perspective. By 1978 crime rates were on the rise and prosecutors' offices had enormous caseloads that were not being met by associated budget increases. In any event, the Court had acknowledged the inevitability of plea bargaining eight years earlier in *Brady*.

On the one hand, this case isn't only about the defendant, Paul Hayes, but about other defendants in his position—perhaps with triable cases—who were sufficiently cowed by the prosecutor's threat of a life sentence that they pleaded guilty. Still, one can't help wonder about Hayes's decision to reject the offer to plead guilty, and the advice of his counsel in making that decision. The facts do not reveal a defense to the uttering charge. Hayes had a not insubstantial criminal record, which would have made it difficult for him to testify. And Hayes, a 28-year old Black man, would likely be tried by an all-white jury in Kentucky, a former slave state with a history of segregation. In the 1970s, moreover, a prosecutor would have been legally able to use all of his peremptory challenges to eliminate Black persons from the jury just like the prosecutor of James Batson down the road in Louisville would do a few years later. *See* Chapter XV *infra*.

There is no mention of race in *Bordenkircher*. And race may have had nothing to do with the deal Paul Hayes was offered. Yet the breadth of discretion afforded law enforcement always raises concerns about whether that discretion is exercised without regard to race. *See* Angela J. Davis, *Prosecution and Race: The Power and Privilege of Discretion*, 67 Fordham L. Rev. 13, 34-38 (1998) (describing how unconscious racism may permeate facially race-neutral prosecutorial decisions).

Everyone has always been late on plea bargaining. When the reformers in the 1920s and 1930s "discovered" plea bargaining, it had been mainstream for over 50 years. When the Supreme Court first took up plea bargaining in 1970, in *Brady*, it was already too late: Over 90 percent of cases were being resolved by pleas. Similarly, plea bargaining's coercive nature did not become well recognized by commentators until it was too late. When Professor Langbein famously compared plea bargaining to torture it was in 1979—not just *Brady* but also *Bordenkircher* had already been decided. *See generally* Ortman, *When Plea Bargaining Became Normal*, *supra* at 1439, 1497.

In theory plea bargaining should be as benignly efficacious as the resolution of civil lawsuits by settlement agreement. After all, civil cases, like their criminal counterparts, rarely go to trial. In civil cases, reasonable and well-informed counsel clinically analyze the likely outcome at trial (say, $1-1.5 million in damages), discount the trial result by plaintiff's likelihood of success (say, 60-80%), and reach a compromise result somewhere near the midpoint of a settlement zone of $600,000 to $1.25m. The perfect compromise is where both sides are equally unhappy. *See* Stephanos Bibas, *Plea Bargaining Outside the Shadow of Trial*, 117 Harv. L. Rev. 2463, 2464 (2004) ("Plea-bargaining literature predicts that parties strike plea bargains in the shadow of expected trial outcomes."). In theory, criminal cases are similarly amenable to resolution based on the lawyers' rational evaluation of the comparative strength of the evidence and defenses and so on.

But there are two major differences between plea bargaining and civil settlement negotiations. First is the information deficit. Whereas civil cases normally have a lengthy discovery period, where both sides have robust and equal access to documents and witnesses, "discovery" in a criminal case—much more limited in any event—typically occurs only at the back end, shortly before trial. And, even more important, the government has no obligation to turn over discovery materials, even exculpatory information and witness statements, prior to entering into a plea agreement. Not only does this mean that defendants and their counsel have to assess their case based on sparse and imperfect information, they are often under pressure to do so quickly, as prosecutors sometimes will only consider plea agreements during the time period before they have to invest resources in a case and prepare for trial. Other influences also skewing the plea-bargaining market, taking it "outside the shadow of trial," are lawyer quality and the pressures imposed by pretrial detention. *See* Bibas, *Plea Bargaining Outside the Shadow of Trial, supra* at 2463, 2468.

Second, and even more important, since the proliferation of minimum mandatory sentences and rigid guidelines sentencing regimes in the 1970s through the 1990s, the prosecutor is often able to realistically threaten a defendant with a truly draconian trial outcome if the defendant will not agree to plead guilty to a lesser charge. The delta in outcomes at the prosecutor's disposal is unlike anything in a civil case, where opposing counsel may well disagree on the likelihood of success on the merits and likely damages but usually only to an arithmetic, not a geometric, degree. For example, in *Bordenkircher* the prosecutor had the nuclear weaponry of a "habitual offender" statute at his disposal and was able to credibly threaten a defendant with a sentence after trial of life imprisonment if he did not agree to plead guilty to a five-year prison term.

So defendants often plead guilty based on imperfect information or to avoid a realistic but worst-case-scenario result. The data emphatically support the proposition that defendants who plead guilty receive lower sentences than those who go to trial. *See* Rachel E. Barkow, *Institutional Design and the Policing of Prosecutors: Lessons from Administrative Law*, 61 Stan. L. Rev. 869, 881 (2009) ("At the federal level, defendants who refuse to waive their right to a jury trial receive an average sentence three times longer than those who plead.").

The most dramatic consequence of this dynamic is that people who are actually innocent plead guilty. *See* Jed S. Rakoff, Why Do Innocent People Plead Guilty and the Guilty Go Free: And Other Paradoxes of Our Broken Legal System 28-29 (2021) (citing statistics from the Innocence Project and National Registry of Exonerations on people exonerated by DNA evidence who had pleaded guilty). In an only slightly less dramatic sense, defendants who have triable (i.e., potentially winnable) cases will be coerced into pleading guilty by draconian sentencing threats from prosecutors. A defendant faced with the alternatives of, say, a 60 percent chance of losing at trial and receiving a five-year sentence and a 30 percent chance of losing at trial and receiving a sentence of life imprisonment is no longer a rational actor. *See* Lucian E. Dervan, *Bargained Justice: Plea Bargaining's Innocence Problem and the* Brady *Safety Valve*, 2012 Utah L. Rev. 51, 65-82 ("At some point, the sentencing differential becomes so large that it destroys the defendant's ability to act freely and decide in a rational manner whether to accept or reject the government's offer.").

The criminal justice system plainly tolerates a high degree of coercion, whether wielded by the legislature (*Brady*) or the prosecutor (*Bordenkircher*). It should not be shocking, therefore, that prosecutorial threats to bring criminal charges against a defendant's family members are tolerated as well. *See Bontkowski v. United States*, 850 F.2d 306, 313 (7th Cir. 1988) (holding that threats to prosecute a defendant's pregnant wife were not sufficient to render his plea involuntary); *United States v. Buckley*, 847 F.2d 991, 1000 n.6 (1st Cir. 1988) (stating that a family member threatened with indictment is not sufficient to render a plea involuntary).

Chapter XI Pleas and Plea Bargaining

United States v. Goodwin
457 U.S. 368 (1982)

Justice STEVENS delivered the opinion of the Court.

This case involves presumptions. The question presented is whether a presumption that has been used to evaluate a judicial or prosecutorial response to a criminal defendant's exercise of a right to be retried after he has been convicted should also be applied to evaluate a prosecutor's pretrial response to a defendant's demand for a jury trial.

After the respondent requested a trial by jury on pending misdemeanor charges, he was indicted and convicted on a felony charge. Believing that the sequence of events gave rise to an impermissible appearance of prosecutorial retaliation against the defendant's exercise of his right to be tried by jury, the United States Court of Appeals for the Fourth Circuit reversed the felony conviction. Because this case presents an important question concerning the scope of our holdings in *North Carolina v. Pearce* and *Blackledge v. Perry* we granted the Government's petition for certiorari.

I

Respondent Goodwin was stopped for speeding by a United States Park Policeman on the Baltimore-Washington Parkway. Goodwin emerged from his car to talk to the policeman. After a brief discussion, the officer noticed a clear plastic bag underneath the armrest next to the driver's seat of Goodwin's car. The officer asked Goodwin to return to his car and to raise the armrest. Respondent did so, but as he raised the armrest he placed the car into gear and accelerated rapidly. The car struck the officer, knocking him first onto the back of the car and then onto the highway. The policeman returned to his car, but Goodwin eluded him in a high-speed chase.

The following day, the officer filed a complaint in the District Court charging respondent with several misdemeanor and petty offenses, including assault. Goodwin was arrested and arraigned before a United States Magistrate. The Magistrate set a date for trial, but respondent fled the jurisdiction. Three years later Goodwin was found in custody in Virginia and was returned to Maryland.

Upon his return, respondent's case was assigned to an attorney from the Department of Justice, who was detailed temporarily to try petty crime and misdemeanor cases before the Magistrate. The attorney did not have authority to try felony cases or to seek indictments from the grand jury. Respondent initiated plea negotiations with the prosecutor, but later advised the Government that he did not wish to plead guilty and desired a trial by jury in the District Court.

The case was transferred to the District Court and responsibility for the prosecution was assumed by an Assistant United States Attorney. Approximately six weeks later, after reviewing the case and discussing it with several parties, the prosecutor obtained a four-count indictment charging respondent with one felony count of forcibly assaulting a federal officer and three related counts arising from the same incident. A jury convicted respondent on the felony count and on one misdemeanor count.

Respondent moved to set aside the verdict on the ground of prosecutorial vindictiveness, contending that the indictment on the felony charge gave rise to an impermissible appearance of retaliation. The District Court denied the motion, finding that "the prosecutor in this case has adequately dispelled any appearance of retaliatory intent."

Although the Court of Appeals readily concluded that "the prosecutor did not act with actual vindictiveness in seeking a felony indictment," it nevertheless reversed. Relying on our decisions in *Pearce* [and] *Blackledge*, the court held that the Due Process Clause of the Fifth Amendment prohibits the Government from bringing more serious charges against a defendant after he has invoked his right to a jury trial, unless the prosecutor comes forward with objective evidence to show that the increased charges could not have been brought before the defendant exercised his rights. Because the court believed that the circumstances surrounding the felony indictment gave rise to a genuine risk of retaliation, it adopted a legal presumption designed to spare courts the "unseemly task" of probing the actual motives of the prosecutor.

II

To punish a person because he has done what the law plainly allows him to do is a due process violation "of the most basic sort." *Bordenkircher v. Hayes.* In a series of cases beginning with *North Carolina v. Pearce* and culminating in *Bordenkircher v. Hayes*, the Court has recognized this basic — and itself uncontroversial — principle. For while an individual certainly may be penalized for violating the law, he just as certainly may not be punished for exercising a protected statutory or constitutional right.

The imposition of punishment is the very purpose of virtually all criminal proceedings. The presence of a punitive motivation, therefore, does not provide an adequate basis for distinguishing governmental action that is fully justified as a legitimate response to perceived criminal conduct from governmental action that is an impermissible response to noncriminal, protected activity. Motives are complex and difficult to prove. As a result, in certain cases in which action detrimental to the defendant has been taken after the exercise of a legal right, the Court has found it necessary to "presume" an improper vindictive motive. Given the severity of such a presumption, however — which may operate in the absence of any proof of an improper motive and thus may block a legitimate response to criminal conduct — the Court has done so only in cases in which a reasonable likelihood of vindictiveness exists.

In *North Carolina v. Pearce*, the Court held that neither the Double Jeopardy Clause nor the Equal Protection Clause prohibits a trial judge from imposing a harsher sentence on retrial after a criminal defendant successfully attacks an initial conviction on appeal. The Court stated, however, that "[i]t can hardly be doubted that it would be a flagrant violation [of the Due Process Clause] of the Fourteenth Amendment for a state trial court to follow an announced practice of imposing a heavier sentence upon every reconvicted defendant for the explicit purpose of punishing the defendant for his having succeeded in getting his original conviction set aside." The Court continued:

> Due process of law, then, requires that vindictiveness against a defendant for having successfully attacked his first conviction must play no part in the sentence he receives after a new trial. And since the fear of such vindictiveness may unconstitutionally deter a defendant's exercise of the right to appeal or collaterally attack his first conviction, due process also requires that a defendant be freed of apprehension of such a retaliatory motivation on the part of the sentencing judge.

In order to assure the absence of such a motivation, the Court concluded:

> [W]henever a judge imposes a more severe sentence upon a defendant after a new trial, the reasons for his doing so must affirmatively appear. Those reasons must be based upon objective information concerning identifiable conduct on the part of the defendant occurring after the time of the original sentencing proceeding. And the factual data upon which the increased sentence is based must be made part of the record, so that the constitutional legitimacy of the increased sentence may be fully reviewed on appeal.

In sum, the Court applied a presumption of vindictiveness, which may be overcome only by objective information in the record justifying the increased sentence.

Chapter XI Pleas and Plea Bargaining

In *Blackledge v. Perry*, the Court confronted the problem of increased punishment upon retrial after appeal in a setting different from that considered in *Pearce*. *Perry* was convicted of assault in an inferior court having exclusive jurisdiction for the trial of misdemeanors. The court imposed a 6-month sentence. Under North Carolina law, Perry had an absolute right to a trial de novo in the Superior Court, which possessed felony jurisdiction. After Perry filed his notice of appeal, the prosecutor obtained a felony indictment charging him with assault with a deadly weapon. Perry pleaded guilty to the felony and was sentenced to a term of five to seven years in prison.

In reviewing Perry's felony conviction and increased sentence, this Court first stated the essence of the holdings in *Pearce* and the cases that had followed it:

> The lesson that emerges from *Pearce* . . . is that the Due Process Clause is not offended by all possibilities of increased punishment upon retrial after appeal, but only by those that pose a realistic likelihood of "vindictiveness."

The Court held that the opportunities for vindictiveness in the situation before it were such "as to impel the conclusion that due process of law requires a rule analogous to that of the *Pearce* case." Ibid. It explained:

> A prosecutor clearly has a considerable stake in discouraging convicted misdemeanants from appealing and thus obtaining a trial de novo in the Superior Court, since such an appeal will clearly require increased expenditures of prosecutorial resources before the defendant's conviction becomes final, and may even result in a formerly convicted defendant's going free. And, if the prosecutor has the means readily at hand to discourage such appeals—by "upping the ante" through a felony indictment whenever a convicted misdemeanant pursues his statutory appellate remedy—the State can insure that only the most hardy defendants will brave the hazards of a de novo trial.

The Court emphasized in *Blackledge* that it did not matter that no evidence was present that the prosecutor had acted in bad faith or with malice in seeking the felony indictment. As in *Pearce*, the Court held that the likelihood of vindictiveness justified a presumption that would free defendants of apprehension of such a retaliatory motivation on the part of the prosecutor.

Both *Pearce* and *Blackledge* involved the defendant's exercise of a procedural right that caused a complete retrial after he had been once tried and convicted. The decisions in these cases reflect a recognition by the Court of the institutional bias inherent in the judicial system against the retrial of issues that have already been decided. The doctrines of stare decisis, res judicata, the law of the case, and double jeopardy all are based, at least in part, on that deep-seated bias. While none of these doctrines barred the retrials in *Pearce* and *Blackledge*, the same institutional pressure that supports them might also subconsciously motivate a vindictive prosecutorial or judicial response to a defendant's exercise of his right to obtain a retrial of a decided question.

In *Bordenkircher v. Hayes*, the Court for the first time considered an allegation of vindictiveness that arose in a pretrial setting. In that case the Court held that the Due Process Clause of the Fourteenth Amendment did not prohibit a prosecutor from carrying out a threat, made during plea negotiations, to bring additional charges against an accused who refused to plead guilty to the offense with which he was originally charged. The prosecutor in that case had explicitly told the defendant that if he did not plead guilty and "save the court the inconvenience and necessity of a trial" he would return to the grand jury to obtain an additional charge that would significantly increase the defendant's potential punishment. The defendant refused to plead guilty and the prosecutor obtained the indictment. It was not disputed that the additional charge was justified by the evidence, that the prosecutor was in possession of this evidence at the time the original indictment was obtained, and that the prosecutor sought the additional charge because of the accused's refusal to plead guilty to the original charge.

D. Plea Bargaining, the Constitution, and Coercion

In finding no due process violation, the Court in *Bordenkircher* considered the decisions in *Pearce* and *Blackledge*, and stated:

> In those cases the Court was dealing with the State's unilateral imposition of a penalty upon a defendant who had chosen to exercise a legal right to attack his original conviction — a situation "very different from the give-and-take negotiation common in plea bargaining between the prosecution and defense, which arguably possess relatively equal bargaining power."

The Court stated that the due process violation in *Pearce* and *Blackledge* "lay not in the possibility that a defendant might be deterred from the exercise of a legal right . . . but rather in the danger that the State might be retaliating against the accused for lawfully attacking his conviction."

The Court held, however, that there was no such element of punishment in the "give-and-take" of plea negotiation, so long as the accused "is free to accept or reject the prosecution's offer." The Court noted that, by tolerating and encouraging the negotiation of pleas, this Court had accepted as constitutionally legitimate the simple reality that the prosecutor's interest at the bargaining table is to persuade the defendant to forgo his constitutional right to stand trial. The Court concluded:

> We hold only that the course of conduct engaged in by the prosecutor in this case, which no more than openly presented the defendant with the unpleasant alternatives of forgoing trial or facing charges on which he was plainly subject to prosecution, did not violate the Due Process Clause of the Fourteenth Amendment.

The outcome in *Bordenkircher* was mandated by this Court's acceptance of plea negotiation as a legitimate process. In declining to apply a presumption of vindictiveness, the Court recognized that "additional" charges obtained by a prosecutor could not necessarily be characterized as an impermissible "penalty." Since charges brought in an original indictment may be abandoned by the prosecutor in the course of plea negotiation — in often what is clearly a "benefit" to the defendant — changes in the charging decision that occur in the context of plea negotiation are an inaccurate measure of improper prosecutorial "vindictiveness." An initial indictment — from which the prosecutor embarks on a course of plea negotiation — does not necessarily define the extent of the legitimate interest in prosecution. For just as a prosecutor may forgo legitimate charges already brought in an effort to save the time and expense of trial, a prosecutor may file additional charges if an initial expectation that a defendant would plead guilty to lesser charges proves unfounded.

III

This case, like *Bordenkircher*, arises from a pretrial decision to modify the charges against the defendant. Unlike *Bordenkircher*, however, there is no evidence in this case that could give rise to a claim of actual vindictiveness; the prosecutor never suggested that the charge was brought to influence the respondent's conduct. The conviction in this case may be reversed only if a presumption of vindictiveness — applicable in all cases — is warranted.

There is good reason to be cautious before adopting an inflexible presumption of prosecutorial vindictiveness in a pretrial setting. In the course of preparing a case for trial, the prosecutor may uncover additional information that suggests a basis for further prosecution or he simply may come to realize that information possessed by the State has a broader significance. At this stage of the proceedings, the prosecutor's assessment of the proper extent of prosecution may not have crystallized. In contrast, once a trial begins — and certainly by the time a conviction has been obtained — it is much more likely that the State has discovered and assessed all of the information against an accused and has made a determination, on the basis of that information, of the extent to which he should be prosecuted. Thus, a change in the charging decision made after an initial trial is completed is much more likely to be improperly motivated than is a pretrial decision.

In addition, a defendant before trial is expected to invoke procedural rights that inevitably impose some "burden" on the prosecutor. Defense counsel routinely file pretrial motions to suppress evidence; to challenge the sufficiency and form of an indictment; to plead an affirmative defense; to request psychiatric services; to obtain access to government files; to be tried by jury. It is unrealistic to assume that a prosecutor's probable response to such motions is to seek to penalize and to deter. The invocation of procedural rights is an integral part of the adversary process in which our criminal justice system operates.

Thus, the timing of the prosecutor's action in this case suggests that a presumption of vindictiveness is not warranted. A prosecutor should remain free before trial to exercise the broad discretion entrusted to him to determine the extent of the societal interest in prosecution. An initial decision should not freeze future conduct. As we made clear in *Bordenkircher*, the initial charges filed by a prosecutor may not reflect the extent to which an individual is legitimately subject to prosecution.

The nature of the right asserted by the respondent confirms that a presumption of vindictiveness is not warranted in this case. After initially expressing an interest in plea negotiation, respondent decided not to plead guilty and requested a trial by jury in District Court. In doing so, he forced the Government to bear the burdens and uncertainty of a trial. This Court in *Bordenkircher* made clear that the mere fact that a defendant refuses to plead guilty and forces the government to prove its case is insufficient to warrant a presumption that subsequent changes in the charging decision are unjustified. Respondent argues that such a presumption is warranted in this case, however, because he not only requested a trial—he requested a trial by jury.

We cannot agree. The distinction between a bench trial and a jury trial does not compel a special presumption of prosecutorial vindictiveness whenever additional charges are brought after a jury is demanded. To be sure, a jury trial is more burdensome than a bench trial. The defendant may challenge the selection of the venire; the jury itself must be impaneled; witnesses and arguments must be prepared more carefully to avoid the danger of a mistrial. These matters are much less significant, however, than the facts that before either a jury or a judge the State must present its full case against the accused and the defendant is entitled to offer a full defense. As compared to the complete trial de novo at issue in *Blackledge*, a jury trial—as opposed to a bench trial—does not require duplicative expenditures of prosecutorial resources before a final judgment may be obtained. Moreover, unlike the trial judge in *Pearce*, no party is asked "to do over what it thought it had already done correctly." A prosecutor has no "personal stake" in a bench trial and thus no reason to engage in "self-vindication" upon a defendant's request for a jury trial. Perhaps most importantly, the institutional bias against the retrial of a decided question that supported the decisions in *Pearce* and *Blackledge* simply has no counterpart in this case.

There is an opportunity for vindictiveness, as there was in *Colten* and *Chaffin*. Those cases demonstrate, however, that a mere opportunity for vindictiveness is insufficient to justify the imposition of a prophylactic rule. As *Blackledge* makes clear, "the Due Process Clause is not offended by all possibilities of increased punishment . . . but only by those that pose a realistic likelihood of 'vindictiveness.'" The possibility that a prosecutor would respond to a defendant's pretrial demand for a jury trial by bringing charges not in the public interest that could be explained only as a penalty imposed on the defendant is so unlikely that a presumption of vindictiveness certainly is not warranted.

IV

In declining to apply a presumption of vindictiveness, we of course do not foreclose the possibility that a defendant in an appropriate case might prove objectively that the prosecutor's charging decision was motivated by a desire to punish him for doing something that the law plainly allowed him to do. In this case, however, the Court of Appeals stated: "On this record we readily conclude that the prosecutor did not act with actual vindictiveness in seeking a felony indictment." Respondent does not challenge that finding. Absent a presumption of vindictiveness, no due process violation has been established.

The judgment of the Court of Appeals is reversed. The case is remanded for further proceedings consistent with this opinion.

It is so ordered.

NOTES AND QUESTIONS

1. The factual record here seems very undeveloped for a case in which certiorari would be granted by the Supreme Court. How much is this case really like *Bordenkircher*? What do we know about the plea negotiations here, compared to the very specific memorialization of those discussions in *Bordenkircher*? We are told only that the defendant "initiated plea negotiations with the prosecutor" but later advised the government that he wished a jury trial in district court. Was defendant offered any kind of a plea deal to the pending misdemeanor charges? Why does that matter?

2. The original complaint alleging minor offenses — filed the day after the traffic encounter by the officer, without any evident involvement by a prosecutor — has the feel of a placeholder charge that was filed promptly by the officer in order to obtain an arrest warrant, given that the defendant had (rather dramatically) left the scene of the traffic stop. Why no discussion of whether it would have been normal practice for these charges to have been superseded in some fashion in any event, but for defendant's flight? Why no discussion of whether it would have been normal practice to permit a defendant to plead guilty — under a plea deal or otherwise — to misdemeanor charges that were filed three years before the defendant was captured as a fugitive?

3. In analyzing the retaliation issue, the court of appeals applied a "presumption of vindictiveness," which was not rebutted by the government, yet also found that "the prosecutor did not act with actual vindictiveness in seeking a felony indictment." The circuit court reasoned that the presumption could only be rebutted by "objective evidence to show that the increased charges could not have been brought before the defendant exercised his rights." What objective evidence could pass this test?

4. The Supreme Court ultimately declines to apply a presumption of vindictiveness, reasoning in part that a defendant's actions leading up to trial — filing motions! — may "burden" the prosecutor, *id.* at 381, and that a response to such actions should not be viewed as punitive. Why not? Aren't those actions intrinsically bound up with exercising the right to go to trial? Inasmuch as every trial will "burden" the prosecutor who has to prepare for it, does this mean that no increase of charges based on a defendant's decision to go to trial can be found to be vindictive?

5. The dissent distinguishes *Bordenkircher* on the ground that the increased charges here were not part of the "give-and-take negotiation common in plea bargaining." 434 U.S. at 362. Is this persuasive?

E. THE SUPREME COURT DISCOVERS PLEA AGREEMENTS AGAIN

The next two full cases reflect the Supreme Court's rediscovery — 40 years after its initial discovery in *Brady* — of the pervasiveness of plea bargaining. The Court ultimately accepts the

1012   Chapter XI Pleas and Plea Bargaining

proposition that defense counsel's role in the resolution of a case by a guilty plea, the manner in which 95 percent of all criminal cases are resolved, should be subject to the constitutional guarantee of effective assistance of counsel.

Padilla v. Kentucky
599 U.S. 356 (2010)

Justice STEVENS delivered the opinion of the Court.

Petitioner Jose Padilla, a native of Honduras, has been a lawful permanent resident of the United States for more than 40 years. Padilla served this Nation with honor as a member of the U.S. Armed Forces during the Vietnam War. He now faces deportation after pleading guilty to the transportation of a large amount of marijuana in his tractor-trailer in the Commonwealth of Kentucky.

In this postconviction proceeding, Padilla claims that his counsel not only failed to advise him of this consequence prior to his entering the plea, but also told him that he "'did not have to worry about immigration status since he had been in the country so long.'" Padilla relied on his counsel's erroneous advice when he pleaded guilty to the drug charges that made his deportation virtually mandatory. He alleges that he would have insisted on going to trial if he had not received incorrect advice from his attorney.

Assuming the truth of his allegations, the Supreme Court of Kentucky denied Padilla postconviction relief without the benefit of an evidentiary hearing. The court held that the Sixth Amendment's guarantee of effective assistance of counsel does not protect a criminal defendant from erroneous advice about deportation because it is merely a "collateral" consequence of his conviction. In its view, neither counsel's failure to advise petitioner about the possibility of removal, nor counsel's incorrect advice, could provide a basis for relief.

We granted certiorari to decide whether, as a matter of federal law, Padilla's counsel had an obligation to advise him that the offense to which he was pleading guilty would result in his removal from this country. We agree with Padilla that constitutionally competent counsel would have advised him that his conviction for drug distribution made him subject to automatic deportation. Whether he is entitled to relief depends on whether he has been prejudiced, a matter that we do not address.

I

The landscape of federal immigration law has changed dramatically over the last 90 years. While once there was only a narrow class of deportable offenses and judges wielded broad discretionary authority to prevent deportation, immigration reforms over time have expanded the class of deportable offenses and limited the authority of judges to alleviate the harsh consequences of deportation. The "drastic measure" of deportation or removal, is now virtually inevitable for a vast number of noncitizens convicted of crimes.

The Nation's first 100 years was "a period of unimpeded immigration." An early effort to empower the President to order the deportation of those immigrants he "judge[d] dangerous to the peace and safety of the United States" was short lived and unpopular. It was not until 1875 that Congress first passed a statute barring convicts and prostitutes from entering the country. In 1891, Congress added to the list of excludable persons those "who have been convicted of a felony or other infamous crime or misdemeanor involving moral turpitude."

The Immigration Act of 1917 (1917 Act) brought "radical changes" to our law. For the first time in our history, Congress made classes of noncitizens deportable based on conduct committed on American soil. Section 19 of the 1917 Act authorized the deportation of "any

E. The Supreme Court Discovers Plea Agreements Again

1013

alien who is hereafter sentenced to imprisonment for a term of one year or more because of conviction in this country of a crime involving moral turpitude, committed within five years after the entry of the alien to the United States. . . ." And § 19 also rendered deportable non-citizen recidivists who commit two or more crimes of moral turpitude at any time after entry. Congress did not, however, define the term "moral turpitude."

While the 1917 Act was "radical" because it authorized deportation as a consequence of certain convictions, the Act also included a critically important procedural protection to minimize the risk of unjust deportation: At the time of sentencing or within 30 days thereafter, the sentencing judge in both state and federal prosecutions had the power to make a recommendation "that such alien shall not be deported." This procedure, known as a judicial recommendation against deportation, or JRAD, had the effect of binding the Executive to prevent deportation; the statute was "consistently . . . interpreted as giving the sentencing judge conclusive authority to decide whether a particular conviction should be disregarded as a basis for deportation." Thus, from 1917 forward, there was no such creature as an automatically deportable offense. Even as the class of deportable offenses expanded, judges retained discretion to ameliorate unjust results on a case-by-case basis.

Although narcotics offenses—such as the offense at issue in this case—provided a distinct basis for deportation as early as 1922, the JRAD procedure was generally available to avoid deportation in narcotics convictions. Except for "technical, inadvertent and insignificant violations of the laws relating to narcotics," it appears that courts treated narcotics offenses as crimes involving moral turpitude for purposes of the 1917 Act's broad JRAD provision.

In light of both the steady expansion of deportable offenses and the significant ameliorative effect of a JRAD, it is unsurprising that, in the wake of *Strickland v. Washington* (1984), the Second Circuit held that the Sixth Amendment right to effective assistance of counsel applies to a JRAD request or lack thereof. In its view, seeking a JRAD was "part of the sentencing" process, Janvier, even if deportation itself is a civil action. Under the Second Circuit's reasoning, the impact of a conviction on a noncitizen's ability to remain in the country was a central issue to be resolved during the sentencing process—not merely a collateral matter outside the scope of counsel's duty to provide effective representation.

However, the JRAD procedure is no longer part of our law. Congress first circumscribed the JRAD provision in the 1952 Immigration and Nationality Act (INA), and in 1990 Congress entirely eliminated it. In 1996, Congress also eliminated the Attorney General's authority to grant discretionary relief from deportation, an authority that had been exercised to prevent the deportation of over 10,000 noncitizens during the 5-year period prior to 1996. Under contemporary law, if a noncitizen has committed a removable offense after the 1996 effective date of these amendments, his removal is practically inevitable but for the possible exercise of limited remnants of equitable discretion vested in the Attorney General to cancel removal for noncitizens convicted of particular classes of offenses. Subject to limited exceptions, this discretionary relief is not available for an offense related to trafficking in a controlled substance.

These changes to our immigration law have dramatically raised the stakes of a noncitizen's criminal conviction. The importance of accurate legal advice for noncitizens accused of crimes has never been more important. These changes confirm our view that, as a matter of federal law, deportation is an integral part—indeed, sometimes the most important part—of the penalty that may be imposed on noncitizen defendants who plead guilty to specified crimes.

II

Before deciding whether to plead guilty, a defendant is entitled to "the effective assistance of competent counsel." The Supreme Court of Kentucky rejected Padilla's ineffectiveness claim on the ground that the advice he sought about the risk of deportation concerned only

Chapter XI Pleas and Plea Bargaining

collateral matters, i.e., those matters not within the sentencing authority of the state trial court. In its view, "collateral consequences are outside the scope of representation required by the Sixth Amendment," and, therefore, the "failure of defense counsel to advise the defendant of possible deportation consequences is not cognizable as a claim for ineffective assistance of counsel." The Kentucky high court is far from alone in this view.

We, however, have never applied a distinction between direct and collateral consequences to define the scope of constitutionally "reasonable professional assistance" required. Whether that distinction is appropriate is a question we need not consider in this case because of the unique nature of deportation.

We have long recognized that deportation is a particularly severe "penalty," but it is not, in a strict sense, a criminal sanction. Although removal proceedings are civil in nature, deportation is nevertheless intimately related to the criminal process. Our law has enmeshed criminal convictions and the penalty of deportation for nearly a century. And, importantly, recent changes in our immigration law have made removal nearly an automatic result for a broad class of noncitizen offenders. Thus, we find it "most difficult" to divorce the penalty from the conviction in the deportation context. Moreover, we are quite confident that noncitizen defendants facing a risk of deportation for a particular offense find it even more difficult.

Deportation as a consequence of a criminal conviction is, because of its close connection to the criminal process, uniquely difficult to classify as either a direct or a collateral consequence. The collateral versus direct distinction is thus ill suited to evaluating a *Strickland* claim concerning the specific risk of deportation. We conclude that advice regarding deportation is not categorically removed from the ambit of the Sixth Amendment right to counsel. *Strickland* applies to Padilla's claim.

III

Under *Strickland*, we first determine whether counsel's representation "fell below an objective standard of reasonableness." Then we ask whether "there is a reasonable probability that, but for counsel's unprofessional errors, the result of the proceeding would have been different." The first prong—constitutional deficiency—is necessarily linked to the practice and expectations of the legal community: "The proper measure of attorney performance remains simply reasonableness under prevailing professional norms." We long have recognized that "[p]revailing norms of practice as reflected in American Bar Association standards and the like . . . are guides to determining what is reasonable. . . ." Although they are "only guides," and not "inexorable commands," these standards may be valuable measures of the prevailing professional norms of effective representation, especially as these standards have been adapted to deal with the intersection of modern criminal prosecutions and immigration law.

The weight of prevailing professional norms supports the view that counsel must advise her client regarding the risk of deportation. "[A]uthorities of every stripe—including the American Bar Association, criminal defense and public defender organizations, authoritative treatises, and state and city bar publications—universally require defense attorneys to advise as to the risk of deportation consequences for non-citizen clients. . . ."

We too have previously recognized that "'[p]reserving the client's right to remain in the United States may be more important to the client than any potential jail sentence.'" Likewise, we have recognized that "preserving the possibility of" discretionary relief from deportation "would have been one of the principal benefits sought by defendants deciding whether to accept a plea offer or instead to proceed to trial." We expected that counsel who were unaware of the discretionary relief measures would "follo[w] the advice of numerous practice guides" to advise themselves of the importance of this particular form of discretionary relief.

In the instant case, the terms of the relevant immigration statute are succinct, clear, and explicit in defining the removal consequence for Padilla's conviction. See 8 U.S.C. § 1227(a)

E. The Supreme Court Discovers Plea Agreements Again 1015

(2)(B)(i) ("Any alien who at any time after admission has been convicted of a violation of (or a conspiracy or attempt to violate) any law or regulation of a State, the United States or a foreign country relating to a controlled substance . . ., other than a single offense involving possession for one's own use of 30 grams or less of marijuana, is deportable"). Padilla's counsel could have easily determined that his plea would make him eligible for deportation simply from reading the text of the statute, which addresses not some broad classification of crimes but specifically commands removal for all controlled substances convictions except for the most trivial of marijuana possession offenses. Instead, Padilla's counsel provided him false assurance that his conviction would not result in his removal from this country. This is not a hard case in which to find deficiency: The consequences of Padilla's plea could easily be determined from reading the removal statute, his deportation was presumptively mandatory, and his counsel's advice was incorrect.

Immigration law can be complex, and it is a legal specialty of its own. Some members of the bar who represent clients facing criminal charges, in either state or federal court or both, may not be well versed in it. There will, therefore, undoubtedly be numerous situations in which the deportation consequences of a particular plea are unclear or uncertain. The duty of the private practitioner in such cases is more limited. When the law is not succinct and straightforward (as it is in many of the scenarios posited by Justice Alito), a criminal defense attorney need do no more than advise a noncitizen client that pending criminal charges may carry a risk of adverse immigration consequences. But when the deportation consequence is truly clear, as it was in this case, the duty to give correct advice is equally clear.

Accepting his allegations as true, Padilla has sufficiently alleged constitutional deficiency to satisfy the first prong of *Strickland*. Whether Padilla is entitled to relief on his claim will depend on whether he can satisfy *Strickland*'s second prong, prejudice, a matter we leave to the Kentucky courts to consider in the first instance.

IV

The Solicitor General has urged us to conclude that *Strickland* applies to Padilla's claim only to the extent that he has alleged affirmative misadvice. In the United States' view, "counsel is not constitutionally required to provide advice on matters that will not be decided in the criminal case . . .," though counsel is required to provide accurate advice if she chooses to discusses these matters.

Respondent and Padilla both find the Solicitor General's proposed rule unpersuasive, although it has support among the lower courts. Kentucky describes these decisions isolating an affirmative misadvice claim as "result-driven, incestuous . . . [, and] completely lacking in legal or rational bases." We do not share that view, but we agree that there is no relevant difference "between an act of commission and an act of omission" in this context.

A holding limited to affirmative misadvice would invite two absurd results. First, it would give counsel an incentive to remain silent on matters of great importance, even when answers are readily available. Silence under these circumstances would be fundamentally at odds with the critical obligation of counsel to advise the client of "the advantages and disadvantages of a plea agreement." When attorneys know that their clients face possible exile from this country and separation from their families, they should not be encouraged to say nothing at all. Second, it would deny a class of clients least able to represent themselves the most rudimentary advice on deportation even when it is readily available. It is quintessentially the duty of counsel to provide her client with available advice about an issue like deportation and the failure to do so "clearly satisfies the first prong of the *Strickland* analysis."

We have given serious consideration to the concerns that the Solicitor General, respondent, and amici have stressed regarding the importance of protecting the finality of convictions obtained through guilty pleas. We confronted a similar "floodgates" concern in *Hill*, but nevertheless applied *Strickland* to a claim that counsel had failed to advise the client regarding his parole eligibility before he pleaded guilty.

A flood did not follow in that decision's wake. Surmounting *Strickland*'s high bar is never an easy task. Moreover, to obtain relief on this type of claim, a petitioner must convince the court that a decision to reject the plea bargain would have been rational under the circumstances. There is no reason to doubt that lower courts — now quite experienced with applying *Strickland* — can effectively and efficiently use its framework to separate specious claims from those with substantial merit.

It seems unlikely that our decision today will have a significant effect on those convictions already obtained as the result of plea bargains. For at least the past 15 years, professional norms have generally imposed an obligation on counsel to provide advice on the deportation consequences of a client's plea. We should, therefore, presume that counsel satisfied their obligation to render competent advice at the time their clients considered pleading guilty.

Likewise, although we must be especially careful about recognizing new grounds for attacking the validity of guilty pleas, in the 25 years since we first applied *Strickland* to claims of ineffective assistance at the plea stage, practice has shown that pleas are less frequently the subject of collateral challenges than convictions obtained after a trial. Pleas account for nearly 95% of all criminal convictions. But they account for only approximately 30% of the habeas petitions filed. The nature of relief secured by a successful collateral challenge to a guilty plea — an opportunity to withdraw the plea and proceed to trial — imposes its own significant limiting principle: Those who collaterally attack their guilty pleas lose the benefit of the bargain obtained as a result of the plea. Thus, a different calculus informs whether it is wise to challenge a guilty plea in a habeas proceeding because, ultimately, the challenge may result in a less favorable outcome for the defendant, whereas a collateral challenge to a conviction obtained after a jury trial has no similar downside potential.

Finally, informed consideration of possible deportation can only benefit both the State and noncitizen defendants during the plea-bargaining process. By bringing deportation consequences into this process, the defense and prosecution may well be able to reach agreements that better satisfy the interests of both parties. As in this case, a criminal episode may provide the basis for multiple charges, of which only a subset mandate deportation following conviction. Counsel who possess the most rudimentary understanding of the deportation consequences of a particular criminal offense may be able to plea bargain creatively with the prosecutor in order to craft a conviction and sentence that reduce the likelihood of deportation, as by avoiding a conviction for an offense that automatically triggers the removal consequence. At the same time, the threat of deportation may provide the defendant with a powerful incentive to plead guilty to an offense that does not mandate that penalty in exchange for a dismissal of a charge that does.

In sum, we have long recognized that the negotiation of a plea bargain is a critical phase of litigation for purposes of the Sixth Amendment right to effective assistance of counsel. The severity of deportation — "the equivalent of banishment or exile" — only underscores how critical it is for counsel to inform her noncitizen client that he faces a risk of deportation.

V

It is our responsibility under the Constitution to ensure that no criminal defendant — whether a citizen or not — is left to the "mercies of incompetent counsel." To satisfy this responsibility, we now hold that counsel must inform her client whether his plea carries a risk of deportation. Our longstanding Sixth Amendment precedents, the seriousness of deportation as a consequence of a criminal plea, and the concomitant impact of deportation on families living lawfully in this country demand no less.

E. The Supreme Court Discovers Plea Agreements Again   **1017**

Taking as true the basis for his motion for postconviction relief, we have little difficulty concluding that Padilla has sufficiently alleged that his counsel was constitutionally deficient. Whether Padilla is entitled to relief will depend on whether he can demonstrate prejudice as a result thereof, a question we do not reach because it was not passed on below.

The judgment of the Supreme Court of Kentucky is reversed, and the case is remanded for further proceedings not inconsistent with this opinion.

It is so ordered.

NOTES AND QUESTIONS

1. The Court in *Padilla* notes that it had previously—25 years earlier—held the *Strickland* ineffectiveness test inapplicable in the context of a guilty plea, rejecting a claim based on an allegation of improper advice about parole eligibility because the claimant had not alleged prejudice, that is, that but for the erroneous advice he would not have pleaded guilty. *Hill v. Lockhart* (1985). Are there any other ways to interpret *Strickland*'s prejudice component in the context of a guilty plea? Can you see why courts might be suspicious of such claims?

2. Padilla does make the necessary prejudice allegation—that he would not have pleaded guilty if he was properly advised of the plea's immigration consequences—and the case is remanded to the state court to make a factual determination on this issue. How might Padilla attempt to prove his allegation of prejudice on remand? Might he need to waive the attorney-client privilege? How will the state try to disprove prejudice? Will any plea discussions the parties had be relevant? *See* Fed. R. Crim. P. 11(f); Fed. R. Evid. 410.

3. The Court makes no apologies for its reliance on memorialized "professional norms," citing all manner of guidelines, practice manuals, and bar standards on the issue of immigration consequences, consistent with the trend that began in death penalty cases such as *Wiggins v. Smith*, 539 U.S. 510 (2003), and *Williams v. Taylor*, 529 U.S. 362 (2000). *See* Chapter VIII *supra*. In his concurring opinion Justice Alito points out that some of these standards, etc., may be only "aspirational" and not reflective of the norms of actual practice; recall also that the Court stated explicitly in *Strickland* that the ineffective assistance rule it announced in that case was not intended to be a means of improving lawyers' standards of practice. Does *Padilla* signal a retreat from that view? In particular, does the Court's refusal to limit its holding to "affirmative misadvice" suggest it is willing to impose rules that might effectively raise practice standards?

4. *Padilla* was an easy case in one sense as the attorney's advice on immigration consequences was so egregiously and carelessly wrong ("don't worry about it," essentially). But the actual scope of the duty imposed on defense counsel by the Court's decision is unclear. How long must the attorney spend researching the potential immigration consequences of a particular charged crime before concluding that the answer is "unclear or uncertain," and that he can therefore acquit himself with a generalized warning to the client as to "potential adverse immigration consequences"? It is to be hoped, of course, that the result of *Padilla* will be an increased focus on immigration consequences by both individual lawyers and the institutionalized defense bar, and that the black, white, and gray areas surrounding the issues will become more readily ascertainable.

5. One alternative, or supplement, to an ineffective assistance remedy for erroneous advice on immigration consequences would be to require the court in taking a plea to inform a defendant on the record during the plea colloquy about potential adverse immigration consequences. (Note that in 2013 Rule 11 was amended to require this additional advice. Fed. R. Crim. P. 11(b)(1)(O).) What are the pros and cons of this solution? It is easy to see this part of the colloquy not going well. What if the defendant, asked about his awareness of potential immigration consequences, says "no, I wasn't aware of that" or "what consequences"? Could a plea still be accepted in such a scenario? If not, does the plea hearing need to be continued so the lawyer can look into the immigration consequences? And what if at the rescheduled hearing the lawyer has concluded that the immigration consequences are "unclear" and so advised the client. Can the plea be accepted? Is a guilty plea by a noncitizen who has no knowledge of any potential immigration consequences knowing and intelligent?

6. In his concurring opinion, Justice Alito contends that immigration law is sufficiently complex that a defense lawyer, to be effective, must advise the client that a conviction could have immigration consequences and that if the client wants advice on the issue, the client should consult an immigration lawyer. 599 U.S. at 375. Is this realistic, given that a high percentage of defendants rely on court-appointed counsel for their defense, and may have no means of acquiring, or at least paying for, separate immigration advice? Further, is it obvious that an immigration lawyer with no criminal expertise is better able to advise a client on this issue than a criminal defense lawyer with no immigration law expertise?

The Court takes great pains to emphasize that there is something extraordinary about deportation. "We have long recognized that deportation is a particularly severe 'penalty,'" *Fong Yue Ting v. United States* (1893). "The severity of deportation — 'the equivalent of banishment or exile,' *Delgadillo v. Carmichael* (1947) — only underscores how critical it is for counsel to inform her noncitizen client that he faces a risk of deportation.'" The Court does so not only to limit its holding but also because it is aware of all of the other "collateral" consequences of conviction, a few of which are identified in Justice Alito's concurrence: "civil commitment, civil forfeiture, the loss of the right to vote, disqualification from public benefits, ineligibility to possess firearms, dishonorable discharge from the Armed Forces, and loss of business or professional licenses." Are any of these consequences sufficiently serious generally, or in certain contexts, to rival deportation as a collateral consequence that an effective defense lawyer should be expected to advise the client about? *See* Carlie Malone, *Plea Bargaining and Collateral Consequences: An Experimental Analysis*, 73 Vand. L. Rev. 1161 (2020) (suggesting that a plea colloquy should require advice to defendants on collateral consequences of guilty pleas such as a loss of public housing).

Padilla was a noteworthy case for the Supreme Court, which had not often before entered the realm of guilty pleas. The Court's recognition that 95 percent of all convictions are guilty pleas was surely a contributing factor in its granting of certiorari. One commentator saw *Padilla* as significant for just this reason:

> The U.S. Supreme Court's decision last year in *Padilla v. Kentucky* marks a watershed in the Court's approach to regulating plea bargains. *Padilla* held that, before a guilty plea, criminal defense counsel must advise clients not only about the plea's direct criminal consequences, but also about one of its chief collateral civil consequences, deportation. While *Padilla*'s holding is limited to deportation, its reasoning could reach much further. *Padilla* is a landmark interpretation of the Sixth Amendment's right to effective assistance of counsel, but it is much more than that. The Court began to move beyond its fixation upon the handful of cases that go to jury trials. It recognized that the other 95 percent of adjudicated cases resolved by guilty pleas matter greatly, and began in earnest to regulate plea bargains the way it has long regulated jury trials. Though the Court's shift in emphasis is nascent, it is long overdue and welcome.
>
> To understand *Padilla*'s grand implications, one must first appreciate the Court's historical focus on jury trials. In recent decades, the Supreme Court has promulgated exacting procedures to regulate jury trials. For example, prosecutors must now produce live witnesses in court (instead of routine lab reports) and prove aggravating facts to juries beyond a reasonable doubt. But even as trial procedures hypertrophied, plea bargaining remained all but unregulated, a free market that sometimes resembled a Turkish bazaar.

E. The Supreme Court Discovers Plea Agreements Again

The Court's indifference to pleas reflected both practicality and principle. The judicial system had grown addicted to plea bargaining, relying on guilty pleas to resolve the vast majority of criminal cases, and could not afford to stifle this trade. Courts, assuming that innocent defendants would not plead guilty and that parties plea bargain in the shadows of expected trial outcomes, counted on jury trials as backstops to protect defendants. Additionally, the Bill of Rights provided no explicit protections for plea bargaining.

Much criminal procedure thus resembled a Potemkin village, a fine-looking facade inhabited by few. The Court trusted the shadows cast by trials to regulate plea outcomes, even though few defendants dared risk the huge penalties for going to trial. And because most guilty pleas waive defendants' rights to appeal, few typical guilty-plea cases ever reached the Supreme Court. The Court continued to filigree procedures for atypical jury trials, heedless of their effects on the overwhelming majority of cases resolved by plea.

Stephanos Bibas, *Regulating the Plea-Bargaining Market: From Caveat Emptor to Consumer Protection*, 99 Calif. L. Rev. 1117, 1118-19 (2011).

The Court relied on *Padilla* as precedent in two subsequent cases involving ineffective assistance claims arising out of the plea-bargaining context. *See Missouri v. Frye*, 566 U.S. 134, 138-39 (2012) (ineffective assistance of counsel not to communicate plea offer to client); *Lafler v. Cooper*, 566 U.S. 156, 161-68 (2012) (ineffective assistance of counsel to give erroneous advice on plea offer).

Missouri v. Frye
566 U.S. 134 (2012)

Justice KENNEDY delivered the opinion of the Court.

The Sixth Amendment, applicable to the States by the terms of the Fourteenth Amendment, provides that the accused shall have the assistance of counsel in all criminal prosecutions. The right to counsel is the right to effective assistance of counsel. This case arises in the context of claimed ineffective assistance that led to the lapse of a prosecution offer of a plea bargain, a proposal that offered terms more lenient than the terms of the guilty plea entered later. The initial question is whether the constitutional right to counsel extends to the negotiation and consideration of plea offers that lapse or are rejected. If there is a right to effective assistance with respect to those offers, a further question is what a defendant must demonstrate in order to show that prejudice resulted from counsel's deficient performance. Other questions relating to ineffective assistance with respect to plea offers, including the question of proper remedies, are considered in a second case decided today.

I

In August 2007, respondent Galin Frye was charged with driving with a revoked license. Frye had been convicted for that offense on three other occasions, so the State of Missouri charged him with a class D felony, which carries a maximum term of imprisonment of four years.

On November 15, the prosecutor sent a letter to Frye's counsel offering a choice of two plea bargains. The prosecutor first offered to recommend a 3-year sentence if there was a guilty plea to the felony charge, without a recommendation regarding probation but with a recommendation that Frye serve 10 days in jail as so-called "shock" time. The second offer was to reduce the charge to a misdemeanor and, if Frye pleaded guilty to it, to recommend a 90-day sentence. The misdemeanor charge of driving with a revoked license carries a maximum term

1020 Chapter XI Pleas and Plea Bargaining

of imprisonment of one year. The letter stated both offers would expire on December 28. Frye's attorney did not advise Frye that the offers had been made. The offers expired.

Frye's preliminary hearing was scheduled for January 4, 2008. On December 30, 2007, less than a week before the hearing, Frye was again arrested for driving with a revoked license. At the January 4 hearing, Frye waived his right to a preliminary hearing on the charge arising from the August 2007 arrest. He pleaded not guilty at a subsequent arraignment but then changed his plea to guilty. There was no underlying plea agreement. The state trial court accepted Frye's guilty plea. The prosecutor recommended a 3-year sentence, made no recommendation regarding probation, and requested 10 days shock time in jail. The trial judge sentenced Frye to three years in prison.

Frye filed for postconviction relief in state court. He alleged his counsel's failure to inform him of the prosecution's plea offer denied him the effective assistance of counsel. At an evidentiary hearing, Frye testified he would have entered a guilty plea to the misdemeanor had he known about the offer.

A state court denied the postconviction motion, but the Missouri Court of Appeals reversed. It determined that Frye met both of the requirements for showing a Sixth Amendment violation under *Strickland*. First, the court determined Frye's counsel's performance was deficient because the "record is void of any evidence of any effort by trial counsel to communicate the Offer to Frye during the Offer window." The court next concluded Frye had shown his counsel's deficient performance caused him prejudice because "Frye pled guilty to a felony instead of a misdemeanor and was subject to a maximum sentence of four years instead of one year."

To implement a remedy for the violation, the court deemed Frye's guilty plea withdrawn and remanded to allow Frye either to insist on a trial or to plead guilty to any offense the prosecutor deemed it appropriate to charge. This Court granted certiorari.

II

A

It is well settled that the right to the effective assistance of counsel applies to certain steps before trial. The "Sixth Amendment guarantees a defendant the right to have counsel present at all 'critical' stages of the criminal proceedings." Critical stages include arraignments, postindictment interrogations, postindictment lineups, and the entry of a guilty plea.

With respect to the right to effective counsel in plea negotiations, a proper beginning point is to discuss two cases from this Court considering the role of counsel in advising a client about a plea offer and an ensuing guilty plea: *Hill v. Lockhart* (1985); and *Padilla v. Kentucky* (2010).

Hill established that claims of ineffective assistance of counsel in the plea bargain context are governed by the two-part test set forth in *Strickland*. As noted above, in Frye's case, the Missouri Court of Appeals, applying the two part test of *Strickland*, determined first that defense counsel had been ineffective and second that there was resulting prejudice.

In *Hill*, the decision turned on the second part of the *Strickland* test. There, a defendant who had entered a guilty plea claimed his counsel had misinformed him of the amount of time he would have to serve before he became eligible for parole. But the defendant had not alleged that, even if adequate advice and assistance had been given, he would have elected to plead not guilty and proceed to trial. Thus, the Court found that no prejudice from the inadequate advice had been shown or alleged.

In *Padilla*, the Court again discussed the duties of counsel in advising a client with respect to a plea offer that leads to a guilty plea. *Padilla* held that a guilty plea, based on a plea offer, should be set aside because counsel misinformed the defendant of the immigration consequences of the conviction. The Court made clear that "the negotiation of a plea bargain is a critical phase of litigation for purposes of the Sixth Amendment right to effective assistance of counsel." It also rejected the argument made by petitioner in this case that a knowing and voluntary plea supersedes errors by defense counsel.

In the case now before the Court the State, as petitioner, points out that the legal question presented is different from that in *Hill* and *Padilla*. In those cases the claim was that the prisoner's plea of guilty was invalid because counsel had provided incorrect advice pertinent to the plea. In the instant case, by contrast, the guilty plea that was accepted, and the plea proceedings concerning it in court, were all based on accurate advice and information from counsel. The challenge is not to the advice pertaining to the plea that was accepted but rather to the course of legal representation that preceded it with respect to other potential pleas and plea offers.

To give further support to its contention that the instant case is in a category different from what the Court considered in *Hill* and *Padilla*, the State urges that there is no right to a plea offer or a plea bargain in any event. It claims Frye therefore was not deprived of any legal benefit to which he was entitled. Under this view, any wrongful or mistaken action of counsel with respect to earlier plea offers is beside the point.

The State is correct to point out that *Hill* and *Padilla* concerned whether there was ineffective assistance leading to acceptance of a plea offer, a process involving a formal court appearance with the defendant and all counsel present. Before a guilty plea is entered the defendant's understanding of the plea and its consequences can be established on the record. This affords the State substantial protection against later claims that the plea was the result of inadequate advice. At the plea entry proceedings the trial court and all counsel have the opportunity to establish on the record that the defendant understands the process that led to any offer, the advantages and disadvantages of accepting it, and the sentencing consequences or possibilities that will ensue once a conviction is entered based upon the plea. *Hill* and *Padilla* both illustrate that, nevertheless, there may be instances when claims of ineffective assistance can arise after the conviction is entered. Still, the State, and the trial court itself, have had a substantial opportunity to guard against this contingency by establishing at the plea entry proceeding that the defendant has been given proper advice or, if the advice received appears to have been inadequate, to remedy that deficiency before the plea is accepted and the conviction entered.

When a plea offer has lapsed or been rejected, however, no formal court proceedings are involved. This underscores that the plea-bargaining process is often in flux, with no clear standards or timelines and with no judicial supervision of the discussions between prosecution and defense. Indeed, discussions between client and defense counsel are privileged. So the prosecution has little or no notice if something may be amiss and perhaps no capacity to intervene in any event. And, as noted, the State insists there is no right to receive a plea offer. For all these reasons, the State contends, it is unfair to subject it to the consequences of defense counsel's inadequacies, especially when the opportunities for a full and fair trial, or, as here, for a later guilty plea albeit on less favorable terms, are preserved.

The State's contentions are neither illogical nor without some persuasive force, yet they do not suffice to overcome a simple reality. Ninety-seven percent of federal convictions and ninety-four percent of state convictions are the result of guilty pleas. The reality is that plea bargains have become so central to the administration of the criminal justice system that defense counsel have responsibilities in the plea bargain process, responsibilities that must be met to render the adequate assistance of counsel that the Sixth Amendment requires in the criminal process at critical stages. Because ours "is for the most part a system of pleas, not a system of trials," it is insufficient simply to point to the trial as a backstop that inoculates any errors in the pretrial process. "To a large extent . . . horse trading [between prosecutor and defense counsel] determines who goes to jail and for how long. That is what plea bargaining is. It is not some adjunct to the criminal justice system; it is the criminal justice system." Scott &

Stuntz, Plea Bargaining as Contract, 101 Yale L.J. 1909, 1912 (1992). See also Barkow, Separation of Powers and the Criminal Law, 58 Stan. L. Rev. 989, 1034 (2006) ("[Defendants] who do take their case to trial and lose receive longer sentences than even Congress or the prosecutor might think appropriate, because the longer sentences exist on the books largely for bargaining purposes. This often results in individuals who accept a plea bargain receiving shorter sentences than other individuals who are less morally culpable but take a chance and go to trial" (footnote omitted)). In today's criminal justice system, therefore, the negotiation of a plea bargain, rather than the unfolding of a trial, is almost always the critical point for a defendant.

To note the prevalence of plea bargaining is not to criticize it. The potential to conserve valuable prosecutorial resources and for defendants to admit their crimes and receive more favorable terms at sentencing means that a plea agreement can benefit both parties. In order that these benefits can be realized, however, criminal defendants require effective counsel during plea negotiations. "Anything less . . . might deny a defendant 'effective representation by counsel at the only stage when legal aid and advice would help him.'"

B

The inquiry then becomes how to define the duty and responsibilities of defense counsel in the plea bargain process. This is a difficult question. "The art of negotiation is at least as nuanced as the art of trial advocacy, and it presents questions further removed from immediate judicial supervision." Bargaining is, by its nature, defined to a substantial degree by personal style. The alternative courses and tactics in negotiation are so individual that it may be neither prudent nor practicable to try to elaborate or define detailed standards for the proper discharge of defense counsel's participation in the process.

This case presents neither the necessity nor the occasion to define the duties of defense counsel in those respects, however. Here the question is whether defense counsel has the duty to communicate the terms of a formal offer to accept a plea on terms and conditions that may result in a lesser sentence, a conviction on lesser charges, or both.

This Court now holds that, as a general rule, defense counsel has the duty to communicate formal offers from the prosecution to accept a plea on terms and conditions that may be favorable to the accused. Any exceptions to that rule need not be explored here, for the offer was a formal one with a fixed expiration date. When defense counsel allowed the offer to expire without advising the defendant or allowing him to consider it, defense counsel did not render the effective assistance the Constitution requires.

Though the standard for counsel's performance is not determined solely by reference to codified standards of professional practice, these standards can be important guides. The American Bar Association recommends defense counsel "promptly communicate and explain to the defendant all plea offers made by the prosecuting attorney," ABA Standards for Criminal Justice, Pleas of Guilty 14-3.2(a) (3d ed. 1999), and this standard has been adopted by numerous state and federal courts over the last 30 years. The standard for prompt communication and consultation is also set out in state bar professional standards for attorneys.

The prosecution and the trial courts may adopt some measures to help ensure against late, frivolous, or fabricated claims after a later, less advantageous plea offer has been accepted or after a trial leading to conviction with resulting harsh consequences. First, the fact of a formal offer means that its terms and its processing can be documented so that what took place in the negotiation process becomes more clear if some later inquiry turns on the conduct of earlier pretrial negotiations. Second, States may elect to follow rules that all offers must be in writing, again to ensure against later misunderstandings or fabricated charges. Third, formal offers can be made part of the record at any subsequent plea proceeding or before a trial on the merits, all to ensure that a defendant has been fully advised before those further proceedings commence. At least one State often follows a similar procedure before trial.

E. The Supreme Court Discovers Plea Agreements Again   **1023**

Here defense counsel did not communicate the formal offers to the defendant. As a result of that deficient performance, the offers lapsed. Under *Strickland*, the question then becomes what, if any, prejudice resulted from the breach of duty.

C

To show prejudice from ineffective assistance of counsel where a plea offer has lapsed or been rejected because of counsel's deficient performance, defendants must demonstrate a reasonable probability they would have accepted the earlier plea offer had they been afforded effective assistance of counsel. Defendants must also demonstrate a reasonable probability the plea would have been entered without the prosecution canceling it or the trial court refusing to accept it, if they had the authority to exercise that discretion under state law. To establish prejudice in this instance, it is necessary to show a reasonable probability that the end result of the criminal process would have been more favorable by reason of a plea to a lesser charge or a sentence of less prison time.

This application of *Strickland* to the instances of an uncommunicated, lapsed plea does nothing to alter the standard laid out in *Hill*. In cases where a defendant complains that ineffective assistance led him to accept a plea offer as opposed to proceeding to trial, the defendant will have to show "a reasonable probability that, but for counsel's errors, he would not have pleaded guilty and would have insisted on going to trial." *Hill* was correctly decided and applies in the context in which it arose. *Hill* does not, however, provide the sole means for demonstrating prejudice arising from the deficient performance of counsel during plea negotiations. Unlike the defendant in *Hill*, Frye argues that with effective assistance he would have accepted an earlier plea offer (limiting his sentence to one year in prison) as opposed to entering an open plea (exposing him to a maximum sentence of four years' imprisonment). In a case, such as this, where a defendant pleads guilty to less favorable terms and claims that ineffective assistance of counsel caused him to miss out on a more favorable earlier plea offer, *Strickland*'s inquiry into whether "the result of the proceeding would have been different," requires looking not at whether the defendant would have proceeded to trial absent ineffective assistance but whether he would have accepted the offer to plead pursuant to the terms earlier proposed.

In order to complete a showing of *Strickland* prejudice, defendants who have shown a reasonable probability they would have accepted the earlier plea offer must also show that, if the prosecution had the discretion to cancel it or if the trial court had the discretion to refuse to accept it, there is a reasonable probability neither the prosecution nor the trial court would have prevented the offer from being accepted or implemented. This further showing is of particular importance because a defendant has no right to be offered a plea, nor a federal right that the judge accept it. In at least some States, including Missouri, it appears the prosecution has some discretion to cancel a plea agreement to which the defendant has agreed. The Federal Rules, some state rules including in Missouri, and this Court's precedents give trial courts some leeway to accept or reject plea agreements. It can be assumed that in most jurisdictions prosecutors and judges are familiar with the boundaries of acceptable plea bargains and sentences. So in most instances it should not be difficult to make an objective assessment as to whether or not a particular fact or intervening circumstance would suffice, in the normal course, to cause prosecutorial withdrawal or judicial nonapproval of a plea bargain. The determination that there is or is not a reasonable probability that the outcome of the proceeding would have been different absent counsel's errors can be conducted within that framework.

III

These standards must be applied to the instant case. As regards the deficient performance prong of *Strickland*, the Court of Appeals found the "record is void of any evidence of any effort by trial counsel to communicate the [formal] Offer to Frye during the Offer window, let alone any evidence that Frye's conduct interfered with trial counsel's ability to do so." On this record, it is evident that Frye's attorney did not make a meaningful attempt to inform the defendant of a written plea offer before the offer expired. The Missouri Court of Appeals was correct that "counsel's representation fell below an objective standard of reasonableness."

The Court of Appeals erred, however, in articulating the precise standard for prejudice in this context. As noted, a defendant in Frye's position must show not only a reasonable probability that he would have accepted the lapsed plea but also a reasonable probability that the prosecution would have adhered to the agreement and that it would have been accepted by the trial court. Frye can show he would have accepted the offer, but there is strong reason to doubt the prosecution and the trial court would have permitted the plea bargain to become final.

There appears to be a reasonable probability Frye would have accepted the prosecutor's original offer of a plea bargain if the offer had been communicated to him, because he pleaded guilty to a more serious charge, with no promise of a sentencing recommendation from the prosecutor. It may be that in some cases defendants must show more than just a guilty plea to a charge or sentence harsher than the original offer. For example, revelations between plea offers about the strength of the prosecution's case may make a late decision to plead guilty insufficient to demonstrate, without further evidence, that the defendant would have pleaded guilty to an earlier, more generous plea offer if his counsel had reported it to him. Here, however, that is not the case. The Court of Appeals did not err in finding Frye's acceptance of the less favorable plea offer indicated that he would have accepted the earlier (and more favorable) offer had he been apprised of it; and there is no need to address here the showings that might be required in other cases.

The Court of Appeals failed, however, to require Frye to show that the first plea offer, if accepted by Frye, would have been adhered to by the prosecution and accepted by the trial court. Whether the prosecution and trial court are required to do so is a matter of state law, and it is not the place of this Court to settle those matters. The Court has established the minimum requirements of the Sixth Amendment as interpreted in *Strickland*, and States have the discretion to add procedural protections under state law if they choose. A State may choose to preclude the prosecution from withdrawing a plea offer once it has been accepted or perhaps to preclude a trial court from rejecting a plea bargain. In Missouri, it appears "a plea offer once accepted by the defendant can be withdrawn without recourse" by the prosecution. The extent of the trial court's discretion in Missouri to reject a plea agreement appears to be in some doubt.

We remand for the Missouri Court of Appeals to consider these state-law questions, because they bear on the federal question of *Strickland* prejudice. If, as the Missouri court stated here, the prosecutor could have canceled the plea agreement, and if Frye fails to show a reasonable probability the prosecutor would have adhered to the agreement, there is no *Strickland* prejudice. Likewise, if the trial court could have refused to accept the plea agreement, and if Frye fails to show a reasonable probability the trial court would have accepted the plea, there is no Strickland prejudice. In this case, given Frye's new offense for driving without a license on December 30, 2007, there is reason to doubt that the prosecution would have adhered to the agreement or that the trial court would have accepted it at the January 4, 2008, hearing, unless they were required by state law to do so.

It is appropriate to allow the Missouri Court of Appeals to address this question in the first instance. The judgment of the Missouri Court of Appeals is vacated, and the case is remanded for further proceedings not inconsistent with this opinion.

It is so ordered.

Justice SCALIA, with whom THE CHIEF JUSTICE, Justice THOMAS, and Justice ALITO join, dissenting.

This is a companion case to *Lafler v. Cooper.* The principal difference between the cases is that the fairness of the defendant's conviction in *Lafler* was established by a full trial and jury verdict, whereas Frye's conviction here was established by his own admission of guilt, received by the court after the usual colloquy that ensured it was voluntary and truthful. In *Lafler* all that could be said (and as I discuss there it was quite enough) is that the fairness of the conviction was clear, though a unanimous jury finding beyond a reasonable doubt can sometimes be wrong. Here it can be said not only that the process was fair, but that the defendant acknowledged the correctness of his conviction. Thus, as far as the reasons for my dissent are concerned, this is an a fortiori case. I will not repeat here the constitutional points that I discuss at length in *Lafler*, but I will briefly apply those points to the facts here and comment upon a few statements in the Court's analysis.

Galin Frye's attorney failed to inform him about a plea offer, and Frye ultimately pleaded guilty without the benefit of a deal. Counsel's mistake did not deprive Frye of any substantive or procedural right; only of the opportunity to accept a plea bargain to which he had no entitlement in the first place. So little entitlement that, had he known of and accepted the bargain, the prosecution would have been able to withdraw it right up to the point that his guilty plea pursuant to the bargain was accepted.

The Court acknowledges, moreover, that Frye's conviction was untainted by attorney error: "[T]he guilty plea that was accepted, and the plea proceedings concerning it in court, were all based on accurate advice and information from counsel." Given the "ultimate focus" of our ineffective-assistance cases on "the fundamental fairness of the proceeding whose result is being challenged," that should be the end of the matter. Instead, here, as in *Lafler*, the Court mechanically applies an outcome-based test for prejudice, and mistakes the possibility of a different result for constitutional injustice. As I explain in *Lafler*, that approach is contrary to our precedents on the right to effective counsel, and for good reason.

The Court announces its holding that "as a general rule, defense counsel has the duty to communicate formal offers from the prosecution" as though that resolves a disputed point; in reality, however, neither the State nor the Solicitor General argued that counsel's performance here was adequate. The only issue was whether the inadequacy deprived Frye of his constitutional right to a fair trial. In other cases, however, it will not be so clear that counsel's plea-bargaining skills, which must now meet a constitutional minimum, are adequate. "[H]ow to define the duty and responsibilities of defense counsel in the plea bargain process," the Court acknowledges, "is a difficult question," since "[b]argaining is, by its nature, defined to a substantial degree by personal style." Indeed. What if an attorney's "personal style" is to establish a reputation as a hard bargainer by, for example, advising clients to proceed to trial rather than accept anything but the most favorable plea offers? It seems inconceivable that a lawyer could compromise his client's constitutional rights so that he can secure better deals for other clients in the future; does a hard-bargaining "personal style" now violate the Sixth Amendment? The Court ignores such difficulties, however, since "[t]his case presents neither the necessity nor the occasion to define the duties of defense counsel in those respects." Perhaps not. But it does present the necessity of confronting the serious difficulties that will be created by constitutionalization of the plea-bargaining process. It will not do simply to announce that they will be solved in the sweet by-and-by.

While the inadequacy of counsel's performance in this case is clear enough, whether it was prejudicial (in the sense that the Court's new version of *Strickland* requires) is not. The Court's description of how that question is to be answered on remand is alone enough to show how unwise it is to constitutionalize the plea-bargaining process. Prejudice is to be determined, the Court tells us, by a process of retrospective crystal-ball gazing posing as legal analysis. First of all, of course, we must estimate whether the defendant would have accepted the earlier plea bargain. Here that seems an easy question, but as the Court acknowledges, it will not always be. Next, since Missouri, like other States, permits accepted plea offers to be withdrawn by the prosecution (a reality which alone should suffice, one would think, to demonstrate that Frye had no entitlement to the plea bargain), we must estimate whether the prosecution would have withdrawn the plea offer. And finally, we must estimate whether the trial court would have approved the plea agreement. These last two estimations may seem easy in the present case, since Frye committed a new infraction before the hearing at which the agreement would have been presented; but they assuredly will not be easy in the mine run of cases.

The Court says "[i]t can be assumed that in most jurisdictions prosecutors and judges are familiar with the boundaries of acceptable plea bargains and sentences." Assuredly it can, just as it can be assumed that the sun rises in the west; but I know of no basis for the assumption. Virtually no cases deal with the standards for a prosecutor's withdrawal from a plea agreement beyond stating the general rule that a prosecutor may withdraw any time prior to, but not after, the entry of a guilty plea or other action constituting detrimental reliance on the defendant's part. And cases addressing trial courts' authority to accept or reject plea agreements almost universally observe that a trial court enjoys broad discretion in this regard. Of course after today's opinions there will be cases galore, so the Court's assumption would better be cast as an optimistic prediction of the certainty that will emerge, many years hence, from our newly created constitutional field of plea-bargaining law. Whatever the "boundaries" ultimately devised (if that were possible), a vast amount of discretion will still remain, and it is extraordinary to make a defendant's constitutional rights depend upon a series of retrospective mind-readings as to how that discretion, in prosecutors and trial judges, would have been exercised.

The plea-bargaining process is a subject worthy of regulation, since it is the means by which most criminal convictions are obtained. It happens not to be, however, a subject covered by the Sixth Amendment, which is concerned not with the fairness of bargaining but with the fairness of conviction. "The Constitution . . . is not an all-purpose tool for judicial construction of a perfect world; and when we ignore its text in order to make it that, we often find ourselves swinging a sledge where a tack hammer is needed." In this case and its companion, the Court's sledge may require the reversal of perfectly valid, eminently just, convictions. A legislature could solve the problems presented by these cases in a much more precise and efficient manner. It might begin, for example, by penalizing the attorneys who made such grievous errors. That type of sub-constitutional remedy is not available to the Court, which is limited to penalizing (almost) everyone else by reversing valid convictions or sentences. Because that result is inconsistent with the Sixth Amendment and decades of our precedent, I respectfully dissent.

NOTES AND QUESTIONS

1. *Frye* illustrates three distinct plea-bargaining phenomena — "overcharging," "sentence bargaining," and "charge bargaining" — and how they can operate in the same case. The prosecutor "overcharges" by charging Frye with a Class D felony carrying a four-year maximum prison term. We know it is an overcharge because without any intervening developments (to speak of) the prosecutor offers plea deals well under the charged maximum, an admission that Frye doesn't "deserve" four years in prison. The prosecutor's first alternative offer is an example of "sentence bargaining," an offered sentencing recommendation under the charged statute. The second alternative offer is a "charge bargain" — an offer to drop the charged statute in exchange for a plea to a misdemeanor. The original charge here, in other words, acts essentially as leverage, to deter defendant from taking the risk of going to trial.

2. The state contends that because there is no right to a plea offer or plea bargain that defendant has not been deprived of anything to which he was entitled on account of counsel's errors, and therefore there has been no Sixth Amendment violation. *Id.* at 142. The state also argues that because it has no visibility into the relationship between client and defense counsel it is unfair to subject the State — presumably by having to defend ineffective assistance claims — to the consequences of defense counsel's shortcomings. The Court describes these two arguments by the state as "neither illogical nor without some persuasive force." Do you agree?

3. The Court's response to these arguments is to rely on the fact that almost all cases are resolved by pleas, not trials, and that plea bargaining, as Professors Scott and Stuntz aptly put it, "is not some adjunct to the criminal justice system, it is the criminal justice system." *Id.* at 144 (citation omitted). This is, of course, the undeniable reality of the modern criminal justice system. But is it a satisfying response to the state's arguments? Should defense counsel's plea-advising conduct be immune from constitutional scrutiny if only 50 percent of cases were resolved by plea bargaining? On the other hand, should defense counsel's trial conduct be immune from scrutiny because only 3 percent of cases go to trial?

Note that the Court also cites a law review article by Rachel Barkow, and her point not about the prevalence of plea bargaining but rather about its coercive effect. Notwithstanding Professor's Barkow's point, and notwithstanding the obvious overcharging in this case, the Court does not comment on any coercive aspects of plea bargaining.

4. In *Frye* there is no need to prescribe defense counsel's responsibilities in the plea-bargaining context as it was essentially undisputed that defense counsel did not communicate the state's plea offer to the client. But the Court nonetheless muses, channeling *Strickland, see* Chapter VIII *supra*, about how negotiation might be judicially regulated, declaring that it is "a matter of personal style" and an "art" that is "at least as nuanced as the art of trial strategy." *Id.* at 144-45. Is this really what ineffective assistance analysis in the plea-advising context is about? Shouldn't the focus be, rather, on counsel's communication to, explanation of, and legal advice regarding plea offers to the client? The dissent pounces on the reference to "personal style," positing a defense counsel with a "hard-bargaining" personal style. Cheap shot or legitimate criticism?

5. The Court holds that "as a general rule, defense counsel has the duty to communicate formal offers from the prosecution to accept a plea on terms and conditions that may be favorable to the accused." *Id.* at 145. Can you think of potential exceptions to this general rule? What about a defendant who tells counsel initially that he is innocent and will never plead guilty? Why the caveat language — "on terms and conditions favorable to the accused" — in the Court's articulation of the general rule? Isn't it "the accused" who is the ultimate arbiter of whether the plea offer is "favorable"?

6. Consider the three elements a defendant must show to demonstrate prejudice in the context of an uncommunicated plea offer: that he would have accepted the offer (easy here, as he accepted a worse offer); that the prosecutor would have honored the offer; and that the judge would have accepted the deal that was the subject of the offer. Each of these elements does involve a degree of "retrospective crystal-gazing," as the dissent puts it. *Id.* at 154. But does this "show how unwise it is to constitutionalize the plea-bargaining process"? Is it the Court, or the Constitution, with its "assistance of counsel" guarantee, that "constitutionalizes" the plea-bargaining process? The dissent concedes that "the plea-bargaining process is a subject worthy of regulation, since it is the means by which most criminal convictions are obtained." What would such nonjudicial regulation look like? Like the professional standards the majority cites? *Id.* at 145-46. Why would such regulation be preferable to litigation?

7. In a companion case to *Frye, Lafler v. Cooper*, 566 U.S. 156 (2012), the Court applied the *Strickland* standard where a defendant rejected a plea offer based on erroneous advice from his lawyer and was subsequently convicted at trial. Defendant was charged under Michigan law with assault with intent to commit murder, among other crimes, and rejected a plea offer of a sentence of 51 to 85 months based on his counsel's advice that the government could not prove the intent element because the victim was shot below the waist. *Id.* at 161. After being convicted defendant was sentenced to 185 to 360 months. The performance prong of *Strickland* was easily satisfied as trial counsel conceded his advice was erroneous. As for prejudice, the Court held that a defendant would need to establish at a minimum that but for counsel's errors he would have accepted the plea. Does this rule involve as much or more crystal ball-gazing as the rule in *Frye*?

A decade after *Frye* and *Lafler*, the Supreme Court denied certiorari in a case where the defendant, who was sentenced to 160 years' imprisonment after trial on a series of robberies he committed when he was 19, alleged that his lawyer was ineffective for failing to initiate any plea negotiations with the prosecutor. Dissenting from that ruling, Justice Jackson, joined by Justice Sotomayor, found that the case was a good opportunity to resolve a circuit split among courts of appeals that have differed as to whether "prejudice" can be shown under *Strickland* where the government has not made a plea offer. *Davis v. United States*, 598 U.S. ___ (2023) (No. 22-5364, Feb. 21, 2023). Davis had alleged that each of his five codefendants, who were charged with the same series of robberies, had negotiated favorable plea agreements that permitted sentencing below the mandatory minimum. They had received sentences of less than 40 years, and Davis's sentencing judge stated that he believed 40 years was also an appropriate sentence for Davis were he not bound by the mandatory minimum.

What are the pros and cons of permitting an ineffectiveness claim based on the facts of *Davis*? Shouldn't the job of defense counsel include monitoring developments in the cases of similarly situated defendants, and certainly of the cases of co-defendants?

F. THE ENFORCEABILITY OF PLEA AGREEMENTS: BREACH AND COLLATERAL WAIVERS

The Supreme Court seldom addressed the subject of guilty pleas and plea bargaining until the late 1960s. Its criminal procedure focus prior to that time had been almost entirely on trial issues. Indeed, in this next case the term "plea bargaining" requires quotation marks around it.

Santobello v. New York
404 U.S. 257 (1971)

Mr. Chief Justice Burger delivered the opinion of the Court.

We granted certiorari in this case to determine whether the State's failure to keep a commitment concerning the sentence recommendation on a guilty plea required a new trial.

The facts are not in dispute. The State of New York indicted petitioner in 1969 on two felony counts. Petitioner first entered a plea of not guilty to both counts. After negotiations, the Assistant District Attorney in charge of the case agreed to permit petitioner to plead guilty to a lesser-included offense, conviction of which would carry a maximum prison sentence of one year. The prosecutor agreed to make no recommendation as to the sentence.

On June 16, 1969, petitioner accordingly withdrew his plea of not guilty and entered a plea of guilty to the lesser charge. Petitioner represented to the sentencing judge that the plea was voluntary and that the facts of the case, as described by the Assistant District Attorney, were true. The court accepted the plea and set a date for sentencing. A series of delays followed, owing primarily to the absence of a pre-sentence report, so that by September 23,

1969, petitioner had still not been sentenced. By that date petitioner acquired new defense counsel.

Petitioner's new counsel moved immediately to withdraw the guilty plea. In an accompanying affidavit, petitioner alleged that he did not know at the time of his plea that crucial evidence against him had been obtained as a result of an illegal search. The accuracy of this affidavit is subject to challenge since petitioner had filed and withdrawn a motion to suppress, before pleading guilty. In addition to his motion to withdraw his guilty plea, petitioner renewed the motion to suppress and filed a motion to inspect the grand jury minutes.

These three motions in turn caused further delay until November 26, 1969, when the court denied all three and set January 9, 1970, as the date for sentencing. On January 9 petitioner appeared before a different judge, the judge who had presided over the case to this juncture having retired. Petitioner renewed his motions, and the court again rejected them. The court then turned to consideration of the sentence.

At this appearance, another prosecutor had replaced the prosecutor who had negotiated the plea. The new prosecutor recommended the maximum one-year sentence. In making this recommendation, he cited petitioner's criminal record and alleged links with organized crime. Defense counsel immediately objected on the ground that the State had promised petitioner before the plea was entered that there would be no sentence recommendation by the prosecution. He sought to adjourn the sentence hearing in order to have time to prepare proof of the first prosecutor's promise. The second prosecutor, apparently ignorant of his colleague's commitment, argued that there was nothing in the record to support petitioner's claim of a promise, but the State, in subsequent proceedings, has not contested that such a promise was made.

The sentencing judge ended discussion, with the following statement, quoting extensively from the pre-sentence report:

> Mr. Aronstein (Defense Counsel), I am not at all influenced by what the District Attorney says, so that there is no need to adjourn the sentence, and there is no need to have any testimony. It doesn't make a particle of difference what the District Attorney says he will do, or what he doesn't do.
>
> I have here, Mr. Aronstein, a probation report. I have here a history of a long, long serious criminal record. I have here a picture of the life history of this man. . . .
>
> "He is unamenable to supervision in the community. He is a professional criminal." This is in quotes. "And a recidivist. Institutionalization—"; that means, in plain language, just putting him away, "is the only means of halting his anti-social activities," and protecting you, your family, me, my family, protecting society. "Institutionalization." Plain language, put him behind bars.
>
> Under the plea, I can only send him to the New York City Correctional Institution for men for one year, which I am hereby doing.

The judge then imposed the maximum sentence of one year.

Petitioner sought and obtained a certificate of reasonable doubt and was admitted to bail pending an appeal. The Supreme Court of the State of New York, Appellate Division, First Department, unanimously affirmed petitioner's conviction, and petitioner was denied leave to appeal to the New York Court of Appeals. Petitioner then sought certiorari in this Court. Mr. Justice Harlan granted bail pending our disposition of the case.

This record represents another example of an unfortunate lapse in orderly prosecutorial procedures, in part, no doubt, because of the enormous increase in the workload of the often understaffed prosecutor's offices. The heavy workload may well explain these episodes, but it does not excuse them. The disposition of criminal charges by agreement between the prosecutor and the accused, sometimes loosely called "plea bargaining," is an essential component of the administration of justice. Properly administered, it is to be encouraged. If every criminal charge were subjected to a full-scale trial, the States and the Federal Government would need to multiply by many times the number of judges and court facilities.

Chapter XI Pleas and Plea Bargaining

Disposition of charges after plea discussions is not only an essential part of the process but a highly desirable part for many reasons. It leads to prompt and largely final disposition of most criminal cases; it avoids much of the corrosive impact of enforced idleness during pre-trial confinement for those who are denied release pending trial; it protects the public from those accused persons who are prone to continue criminal conduct even while on pretrial release; and, by shortening the time between charge and disposition, it enhances whatever may be the rehabilitative prospects of the guilty when they are ultimately imprisoned.

However, all of these considerations presuppose fairness in securing agreement between an accused and a prosecutor. It is now clear, for example, that the accused pleading guilty must be counseled, absent a waiver. Fed. Rule Crim. Proc. 11, governing pleas in federal courts, now makes clear that the sentencing judge must develop, on the record, the factual basis for the plea, as, for example, by having the accused describe the conduct that gave rise to the charge. The plea must, of course, be voluntary and knowing and if it was induced by promises, the essence of those promises must in some way be made known. There is, of course, no absolute right to have a guilty plea accepted. A court may reject a plea in exercise of sound judicial discretion.

This phase of the process of criminal justice, and the adjudicative element inherent in accepting a plea of guilty, must be attended by safeguards to insure the defendant what is reasonably due in the circumstances. Those circumstances will vary, but a constant factor is that when a plea rests in any significant degree on a promise or agreement of the prosecutor, so that it can be said to be part of the inducement or consideration, such promise must be fulfilled.

On this record, petitioner "bargained" and negotiated for a particular plea in order to secure dismissal of more serious charges, but also on condition that no sentence recommendation would be made by the prosecutor. It is now conceded that the promise to abstain from a recommendation was made, and at this stage the prosecution is not in a good position to argue that its inadvertent breach of agreement is immaterial. The staff lawyers in a prosecutor's office have the burden of "letting the left hand know what the right hand is doing" or has done. That the breach of agreement was inadvertent does not lessen its impact.

We need not reach the question whether the sentencing judge would or would not have been influenced had he known all the details of the negotiations for the plea. He stated that the prosecutor's recommendation did not influence him and we have no reason to doubt that. Nevertheless, we conclude that the interests of justice and appropriate recognition of the duties of the prosecution in relation to promises made in the negotiation of pleas of guilty will be best served by remanding the case to the state courts for further consideration. The ultimate relief to which petitioner is entitled we leave to the discretion of the state court, which is in a better position to decide whether the circumstances of this case require only that there be specific performance of the agreement on the plea, in which case petitioner should be resentenced by a different judge, or whether, in the view of the state court, the circumstances require granting the relief sought by petitioner, i.e., the opportunity to withdraw his plea of guilty. We emphasize that this is in no sense to question the fairness of the sentencing judge; the fault here rests on the prosecutor, not on the sentencing judge.

The judgment is vacated and the case is remanded for reconsideration not inconsistent with this opinion.

* * *

Mr. Justice MARSHALL, with whom Mr. Justice BRENNAN and Mr. Justice STEWART join, concurring in part and dissenting in part.

F. The Enforceability of Plea Agreements: Breach and Collateral Waivers

I agree with much of the majority's opinion, but conclude that petitioner must be permitted to withdraw his guilty plea. This is the relief petitioner requested and, on the facts set out by the majority, it is a form of relief to which he is entitled.

There is no need to belabor the fact that the Constitution guarantees to all criminal defendants the right to a trial by judge or jury, or, put another way, the "right not to plead guilty." This and other federal rights may be waived through a guilty plea, but such waivers are not lightly presumed and, in fact, are viewed with the "utmost solicitude." Given this, I believe that where the defendant presents a reason for vacating his plea and the government has not relied on the plea to its disadvantage, the plea may be vacated and the right to trial regained at least where the motion to vacate is made prior to sentence and judgment. In other words, in such circumstances I would not deem the earlier plea to have irrevocably waived the defendant's federal constitutional right to a trial.

Here, petitioner never claimed any automatic right to withdraw a guilty plea before sentencing. Rather, he tendered a specific reason why, in his case, the plea should be vacated. His reason was that the prosecutor had broken a promise made in return for the agreement to plead guilty. When a prosecutor breaks the bargain, he undercuts the basis for the waiver of constitutional rights implicit in the plea. This, it seems to me, provides the defendant ample justification for rescinding the plea. Where a promise is "unfulfilled," *Brady v. United States* (1970), specifically denies that the plea "must stand." Of course, where the prosecutor has broken the plea agreement, it may be appropriate to permit the defendant to enforce the plea bargain. But that is not the remedy sought here. Rather, it seems to me that a breach of the plea bargain provides ample reason to permit the plea to be vacated.

It is worth noting that in the ordinary case where a motion to vacate is made prior to sentencing, the government has taken no action in reliance on the previously entered guilty plea and would suffer no harm from the plea's withdrawal. More pointedly, here the State claims no such harm beyond disappointed expectations about the plea itself. At least where the government itself has broken the plea bargain, this disappointment cannot bar petitioner from withdrawing his guilty plea and reclaiming his right to a trial.

I would remand the case with instructions that the plea be vacated and petitioner given an opportunity to replead to the original charges in the indictment.

NOTES AND QUESTIONS

1. Guilty pleas were a familiar part of the federal criminal justice landscape by the 1971 decision in *Santobello*, well known to the Supreme Court. Even by this time it was commonly understood that a substantial majority of federal criminal cases were resolved by guilty pleas, and the dissenters cite statistics from the Report of Director of Administrative Office of U.S. Courts to the effect that 90.2 percent of federal convictions had been resolved by guilty plea in 1964 and that 85 percent of federal convictions had been resolved by plea in 1970. *Id.* at n.1a. But the process by which these guilty pleas came about had received less attention, although the Court notes that they are an "essential part of the administration of justice." *Id.* at 261. And despite this recognition, the Court had only recently begun to weigh in on how state courts should determine whether guilty pleas were knowing and voluntary waivers of constitutional rights. *See Boykin v. Alabama*, 395 U.S. 238 (1969), *supra*.

2. Both the majority and the dissent analogize the plea agreement to a contract, breached by the government in this case, and differ only as to remedy. The dissent, invoking the contractual concept of rescission, argues that the defendant should be able to have his plea agreement vacated, while the majority would defer to the state court on what remedy — specific performance or vacatur — is appropriate. Does the defendant get a windfall here if he is

1032   Chapter XI Pleas and Plea Bargaining

allowed to vacate his plea entirely? Recall the evidence of "buyer's remorse" here inasmuch as defendant moved to withdraw his original guilty plea shortly after it was made and months before the successor prosecutor breached the plea agreement. Should that fact be relevant to the remedy? Is analyzing a plea agreement in contractual terms appropriate?

3. The dissent favors a liberal approach to presentencing withdrawals of pleas generally, even absent breach by the government, *id.* at 501-02, inasmuch as the government will rarely be prejudiced by such a withdrawal. What limits, if any, should be placed on such a right? What reasons should suffice for being able to withdraw a guilty plea? Note that Rule 32(e) of the Federal Rules of Criminal Procedure provides that a guilty plea can be withdrawn before sentencing for a "fair and just reason."

4. Note also that Santobello's sentencing was deferred in order that a "pre-sentence report" could be prepared, and it was the substance of the presentence report that resulted in his maximum sentence. Deferring final sentence until a presentence report is prepared remains common practice today, notwithstanding improved access to criminal records. *See* Fed. R. Crim. P. 32(d) (prescribing information that must be contained in presentence report). It appears that the original prosecutor had not been aware of Mr. Santobello's background when he agreed to drop charges and not make a sentencing recommendation. Is it likely that Santobello relied on the prosecutor's promise not to make a sentencing recommendation in entering into the plea agreement?

In the 1990s the Department of Justice aggressively began to attempt to require defendants to waive their appellate rights as part of plea bargains. This effort was almost entirely a result of the United States Sentencing Guidelines, the effect of which on appellate practice in the guilty plea context cannot be overstated. Indeed, as the court notes in the next case, *Raynor*, there was really no such thing as "appellate practice" in the guilty plea context before the Sentencing Guidelines. The government had little right to appeal a sentence, and even for defendants there was nothing really to appeal from, as sentencing judges had unbridled discretion in imposing sentences within the statutory range and thus enjoyed "virtually unconditional deference on appeal." *See Mistretta v. United States*, 488 U.S. 361, 364 (1989) (describing pre-Guidelines sentencing regime). The Guidelines changed all that, as the Sentencing Reform Act afforded both parties significant appellate rights as part of the overarching goal to make sentencing more uniform. *See* Chapter XVI *infra.*

United States v. Raynor
989 F. Supp. 43 (D.D.C. 1997)

PAUL L. FRIEDMAN, District Judge.

Defendants Terry Leon Raynor and Cynthia D. Lewis entered into plea agreements with the government that initially contained the following language:

> Your client understands and acknowledges that Title 18, United States Code, Section 3742 affords a defendant the right to appeal the sentence imposed after a plea of guilty or trial. After consultation with counsel, and in exchange for the concessions made by this Office in this plea agreement, your client voluntarily and knowingly waives the right to appeal any sentence within the maximum provided in the statute(s) of conviction, or the manner in which that sentence was determined, on the grounds set forth in Title 18, United States Code, Section 3742 or on any ground whatever. Your client also voluntarily and knowingly waives your client's right to challenge the sentence or the manner in which it was determined in any collateral attack, including but not limited to a motion brought under Title 28, United States Code,

Section 2255. Your client further acknowledges and agrees that this agreement does not limit the Government's right to appeal a sentence, as set forth in Title 18, United States Code, Section 3742(b).

Plea Agreement at 4.

The Court refused to accept the pleas, concluding that the government may not condition its agreement to a plea on a defendant's waiving his or her right to appeal a sentence that has yet to be imposed — a sentence that may ultimately be illegal, unconstitutional or otherwise improper. The Court explained its reasons from the Bench and memorializes them here.

The obligation of the Court under Rule 11 of the Federal Rules of Criminal Procedure is to assure that a plea is voluntary and that whatever rights the defendant waives incident to the plea are waived knowingly, intelligently and voluntarily. It is this Court's view that a defendant can never knowingly and intelligently waive the right to appeal or collaterally attack a sentence that has not yet been imposed. Such a waiver is by definition uninformed and unintelligent and cannot be voluntary and knowing. Until the sentence is imposed, the defendant cannot possibly know what it is he or she is waiving. A plea that requires such a waiver of unknown rights cannot comport with Rule 11 or the Constitution.

The waiver sought by the government in this case contrasts with every other waiver provision typically included in a plea agreement. Every other right that normally is relinquished is a known, well-defined right, and the quid pro quo is understandable. For example, when a defendant gives up the right to trial in favor of a plea, he or she knows that there will no longer be twelve jurors sitting in judgment, that there will no longer be live testimony and the right to confront witnesses, and that there will be no speedy and public trial. The defendant also understands that he or she is giving up the privilege against self-incrimination because the defendant must acknowledge guilt before the plea can be accepted. Moreover, when a defendant waives the right to a trial by jury in exchange for a plea to fewer counts or a lesser offense, the defendant not only gives up any advantages that may come with a jury trial but also is relieved of the uncertainties that may result from exercising the right to trial.

When a defendant waives the right to appeal a sentence, however, he or she is freed of none of the uncertainties that surround the sentencing process in exchange for giving up the right to later challenge a possibly erroneous application or interpretation of the Sentencing Guidelines or a sentencing statute. For example, when it comes time for sentencing in this case, this Court could make incorrect, unsupportable factual findings with respect to the amount of drugs involved, the nature of the relevant conduct to be considered or whether either of these defendants was involved in more than minimal planning with respect to the narcotics conspiracy to which they pled. Under the plea agreement proffered by the government, the defendants would have no right to ask the court of appeals to correct the illegal or unconstitutional ramifications of such sentencing errors.

Suppose a case where the facts support embezzlement in the amount of $100,000, but a court, by mistake or on whim, finds that the amount embezzled was one million dollars. Suppose a case where the amount of cocaine base or crack involved was five grams, but the court, by mistake, makes a factual finding (perhaps because of a grave mathematical error) that there were 50 grams. The sentencing range under the Guidelines would be increased drastically and unjustifiably, and the statutory mandatory minimum sentence would be ten years instead of five; yet, there would be no right to appeal because that right had been irrevocably waived at the time of the plea. Or suppose that a defendant has two prior convictions that ought to be counted towards his or her criminal history points, but the probation officer in preparing the presentence investigation report erroneously concludes that there are five offenses that should be considered, and the court adopts the probation officer's mistaken conclusion. The defendant would be placed in Criminal History Category IV, V or VI, instead of II or III and would receive a much more substantial sentence as a result; yet he or she would have no right to appeal. Barring the possibility of a clairvoyant defendant, in none of these cases could there be a knowing and intelligent waiver of the right to appeal and to collaterally attack such sentences.

The very concerns expressed by this Court have also been expressed by the Justice Department, which has provided guidance to prosecutors to guard against "lawless district courts" that might disregard the Sentencing Guidelines to the disadvantage of the government. See United States Department of Justice Memorandum for All United States Attorneys from John C. Keeney, Acting Assistant Attorney General ("Keeney Memo") at 3 (Oct. 4, 1995). The Justice Department warns its lawyers:

> The disadvantage of the broad sentencing appeal waiver is that it could result in guideline-free sentencing of defendants in guilty plea cases, and it could encourage a lawless district court to impose sentences in violation of the guidelines. It is imperative to guard against the use of waivers of appeal to promote circumvention of the sentencing guidelines. . . .

Indeed, the Justice Department, jealously guarding its own appellate rights, recommends that its attorneys file appeals in certain cases even where both the government and the defendant have ostensibly waived their rights to appeal:

> Use of waiver of appeal rights in a manner resulting in sentences in violation of the sentencing guidelines could prompt a court of appeals to reconsider its decision to uphold the validity of a sentencing appeal waiver. Alternatively, the reviewing court could construe a sentencing appeal waiver narrowly in order to correct an obvious miscarriage of justice. To avoid these concerns, we recommend that, in a case involving an egregiously incorrect sentence, the prosecutor consider electing to disregard the waiver and to argue the merits of the appeal. That would avoid confronting the court of appeals with the difficult decision of enforcing a sentencing appeal waiver that might result in a miscarriage of justice.

Id.

To avoid problems for the government in the future, the Justice Department suggests that, as a prophylactic measure, the preferred practice is to make the waiver of the right to appeal a one-way street: plea agreements should be drafted so that only the defendant must abandon the right to appeal. Keeney Memo at 3. In that way, when a "miscarriage of justice" results from erroneous sentences, only the defendant will be left in the awkward position of attempting to raise appellate rights that have supposedly been waived at the trial level. Meanwhile, Justice Department lawyers will enjoy an unobstructed path to the courts of appeals.

The Justice Department values its right to appeal erroneous sentences for a reason. Before the Guidelines, the government had virtually no right to appeal a sentence. Sentencing was in the discretion of the trial judge and, except where provided expressly by Congress, there was no appeal by the government. Now much of sentencing judgment and policy is within the discretion of the Sentencing Commission. And because of the prosecutor's traditional charging discretion and added leverage in sentence bargaining and charge bargaining in the post-Guidelines world, the discretion to cabin the parameters of the sentence is very much in the control of the prosecutor rather than the court.

To the extent that Congress has endorsed this new balance of power by statute, the courts must and will apply the law. To the extent that the government seeks methods and means of avoiding appellate review of the exercise of prosecutorial power in the sentencing context, effectively circumventing what Congress intended, however, it is plainly the responsibility of the judiciary to uphold and protect the criminal justice process from such manipulation.

The Sentencing Reform Act of 1984 established the respective rights of the parties to appeal a sentence in a criminal case. 18 U.S.C. § 3742(a) sets forth the circumstances in which a defendant may appeal a sentence, while Section 3742(b) is a parallel provision giving the government a right to appeal, thus providing a congressionally-mandated symmetry and an equal opportunity to appeal sentences in criminal cases. With plea agreements like the one presented in this case, however, the government seeks unilaterally to undermine the statutory balance by requiring defendants to give up their traditional right to appeal, while the government would retain the full range of its newly-granted appellate rights under Section 3742. Thus, the government, but not the defendant, would have the right to seek to correct erroneous factual findings, to correct erroneous Guideline calculations, and to argue to the court of appeals that the district court has misinterpreted or disregarded the Guidelines, or imposed an unreasonable sentence through erroneous departure decisions, or a sentence in violation of law. 18 U.S.C. § 3742(b). For the future, this would mean that every Sentencing Guideline case considered by the courts of appeals would be a case brought by the government to correct errors that favor defendants. The appellate courts would never again decide a sentencing case brought by a defendant. Not only is that inherently unfair, but it also eliminates the symmetry Congress intended by Section 3742.

The waiver provision demanded by the government in this case also would insulate from review by the district courts and the courts of appeals matters relating to the ineffectiveness of counsel in the plea process. Suppose, for example, that a lawyer has been ineffective in the representation of a client in negotiating a plea, or in advising a defendant of his or her rights with respect to a plea. Suppose that a lawyer was drunk or using drugs when he or she engaged in those negotiations or advised clients of their rights. Suppose a lawyer had a conflict of interest at the time or, in advising a client, was not really recommending what was best for the client but what was best for the drug kingpin or some other interested person who was paying the lawyer's fee. Under the government's proposal, the defendant is required to give up the right to raise challenges on appeal even in these cases.

The waiver provision also requires defendants to give up their rights under 28 U.S.C. § 2255. Section 2255 is an extraordinary remedy, and there are not many successful Section 2255 petitions after trial or plea; but the statute enacted by Congress nevertheless serves important functions. If a court imposes a sentence in violation of the Constitution or laws of the United States, or in excess of the time allowed by law, one is entitled to bring a Section 2255 action. But not in this jurisdiction any longer if this plea agreement were accepted. Through its superior bargaining power, the government would have defendants give up the rights Congress has provided them under both 18 U.S.C. § 3742 and 28 U.S.C. § 2255.

Interestingly, the government itself concedes that certain of defendants' rights were not meant to be waived, and it therefore admits that the waiver provision in the plea agreements in this case is not even an accurate statement of the law. Despite the unforgiving language of the waiver provision, the government acknowledges that such provisions do not in fact waive all rights to appeal. It does not concede, however, that this fact should be spelled out in the agreement or explained to defendants. As the Keeney memorandum states:

> A sentencing appeal waiver provision does not waive all claims on appeal. The courts of appeals have held that certain constitutional and statutory claims survive a sentencing appeal waiver in a plea agreement. For example, a defendant's claim that he was denied the effective assistance of counsel at sentencing, that he was sentenced on the basis of his race, or that his sentence exceeded the statutory maximum, will be reviewed on the merits by a court of appeals despite the existence of a sentencing appeal waiver in a plea agreement.

Keeney Memo at 2.2.

Thus, the government asks the Court to assume that a defendant who, by the government's own admission, is misinformed about his or her rights and the extent of the waiver in a plea letter and at a plea proceeding nevertheless understands those rights and can knowingly and intelligently waive them by virtue of the language of the proposed paragraph in the plea agreements. The government asks this of the Court, when in fact, the paragraph is not an accurate statement of the law, and neither the plea agreement nor the Rule 11 colloquy can assure that a defendant knows what his or her rights are and what is purportedly being waived.

While our court of appeals has not yet addressed this issue, Judge Harold Greene of this Court recently did so in an opinion that is most persuasive. As Judge Greene pointed out:

> [I]t is only after the judge has sentenced the defendant that the latter knows which rights he waived, and whether those rights included the right to appeal a sentence in which the court may have erroneously applied the Guidelines or otherwise ordered an illegal or even unconstitutional sentence. The waiver could be regarded as knowing only if it be assumed that the appeal rights need not stand regardless of the grossness of the error of the sentencing court or the court's intent and purpose.

By contrast, the decisions of the courts of appeals cited by the government in support of its proposed appeal waiver provision are not convincing. Some fail to reach the fundamental question of whether a defendant can knowingly and intelligently waive an unknown right, or whether the rights involved can be understood, while others do not involve waiver provisions as sweeping as the one before this Court. The one voice of reason is Judge Parker's concurring opinion in *United States v. Melancon:* A defendant can never "knowingly and intelligently waive, as part of a plea agreement, the right to appeal a sentence that has yet to be imposed at the time he or she enters into the plea agreement; such a 'waiver' is inherently uninformed and unintelligent."

If the government wishes to "reduc[e] the burden of appellate and collateral litigation involving sentencing issues," see Keeney Memo at 1, it already has a way to do so through a method endorsed by Congress; it can simply negotiate a different kind of plea under Rule 11(e)(1)(C) of the Federal Rules of Criminal Procedure. Under Rule 11(e)(1)(C), the government has the right to enter into a plea agreement that requires the defendant to give up the right to appeal—but only in limited circumstances. Specifically, in exchange for a defendant giving up the right to appeal, the government agrees to the imposition of a specific sentence at the time the plea agreement is entered. If the court agrees with that sentence, the defendant is precluded from filing a notice of appeal; if not, the plea does not go forward or the defendant is permitted to withdraw it. Rule 11(e)(1)(C), (e)(2)-(4), Fed. R. Crim. P. With this type of plea agreement, a defendant is not forced to accept a future sentence about which he or she knows virtually nothing, because it allows the defendant to clearly see what is being gained and what is being given up. As Congress recognized in 18 U.S.C. § 3742(c), if the government wishes to reduce sentencing appeals by defendants, Rule 11(e)(1)(C) is the proper vehicle, not forcing defendants to blindly give up their statutory rights and requiring courts to abdicate their responsibilities under the Federal Rules and the Constitution.

If the purpose of the waiver proffered by the government is to eliminate frivolous appeals, see Keeney Memo at 1, the government is engaging in overkill. There are not very many frivolous appeals of sentences after pleas in this jurisdiction, and, if there were, the United States Attorney could develop a standard motion to dismiss the appeal on grounds of frivolousness. 18 U.S.C. § 3742 lists those few bases on which Congress thought it appropriate to preserve the government's and the defendant's right to appeal. Those appeals that do not fall within the statutory bases undoubtedly could be dismissed in short order.

The very purpose for the Sentencing Guidelines was to assure more uniformity in criminal sentencing. That was the intent of Congress and the intent of the Guidelines. What the government seeks to do through the appeal waiver provision is inconsistent with the goals and intent of Congress and the goals and intent of the Sentencing Commission. It will insulate from appellate review erroneous factual findings, interpretations and applications of the Guidelines by trial judges and thus, ultimately, it will undermine uniformity. The integrity of the system depends on the ability of appellate courts to correct sentencing errors, but the waiver provision at issue here inevitably will undermine the important role of the courts of appeals to correct errors in sentencing, a role that Congress has specifically set out for them.

The condition sought to be imposed by the government is inherently unfair; it is a one-sided contract of adhesion; it will undermine the error correcting function of the courts of appeals in sentencing; it will create a sentencing regime where courts of appeals will never have the opportunity to review an illegal or unconstitutional sentence, or a sentence that has no basis in fact, unless those sentencing errors work to the disadvantage of the government. Such a result is inconsistent with what Congress intended when it created the Sentencing Commission and the Sentencing Guidelines. It is inconsistent with the express terms of 18 U.S.C. § 3742, and it is inconsistent with the scheme of Rule 11 of the Federal Rules of Criminal Procedure. A defendant cannot knowingly, intelligently and voluntarily give up the right to appeal a sentence that has not yet been imposed and about which the defendant has no knowledge as to what will occur at the time of sentencing. This Court therefore will accept no plea agreements containing waiver provisions of this kind.

SO ORDERED.

NOTES AND QUESTIONS

1. Note that the waiver language from Raynor's written plea agreement that is reproduced in the opinion recites that the appellate waiver is being made "in exchange for concessions made by this Office in this plea agreement." Yet doesn't it appear from the DOJ's Keeney Memo that appellate waivers are being requested or required as a matter of course by the DOJ? If so, are there government "concessions" that are specifically linked to this waiver or are those concessions just folded in to whatever plea deal is being offered? The court seems skeptical that the waiver provision is truly "bargained for," and describes it as instead being "imposed by the government." *Id.* at 49. Does this sound accurate?

2. The court distinguishes between the waiver of appellate rights and the waiver of the other rights that are inherent in a guilty plea (right to trial by jury, etc.) by describing the latter as "a known, well-defined right, and the *quid pro quo* is understandable." *Id.* at 44. Is this a persuasive basis for distinguishing between these two types of rights? Do you agree with the sentiment of Judge Parker, quoted in *Raynor*, that a defendant cannot knowingly and intelligently waive the right to appeal a sentence that has yet to be imposed?

3. Does it strike you as odd that as a general matter defendants plead guilty without knowing what their sentences will be? The court notes that the parties have the option of negotiating a plea under Rule 11(c)(1)(C) whereby the parties agree to a specific sentence that the court must accept or else the plea can be withdrawn. Such pleas are not common because prosecutors dislike their uncertainty, and judges dislike such pleas because they deprive them of their sentencing discretion.

4. The plea agreement language requires a waiver of an appeal "on any ground whatever," *id.* at 43, even though the DOJ concedes in the Keeney Memo that such a provision does not, as a matter of law, waive all claims on appeal.

Why would the DOJ include such a broadly worded waiver, even if it knows the term is unenforceable? How should the judge handle this issue in the plea colloquy? Is it grounds for not accepting the plea agreement?

Chapter XI Pleas and Plea Bargaining

United States v. Guillen
561 F.3d 527 (D.C. Cir. 2009)

GINSBURG, Circuit Judge:

As part of her agreement to plead guilty to one count of wire fraud, Maribel Guillen waived her right to appeal her sentence if it was within the range indicated by the United States Sentencing Guidelines. Guillen received such a sentence but appeals nonetheless, contending the waiver is not enforceable. We join the eleven other circuits with jurisdiction over criminal appeals in holding such waivers are generally enforceable.

I. BACKGROUND

Guillen entered into an agreement with the Government whereby she would plead guilty to one count of wire fraud, which she committed as part of a scheme to embezzle funds from her former employer. The agreement also provided she

> [W]aives the right to appeal her sentence or the manner in which it was to be determined pursuant to 18 U.S.C. § 3742, except to the extent that (a) the Court sentences Ms. Guillen to a period of imprisonment longer than the statutory maximum or (b) the Court departs upward from the applicable Sentencing Guideline range.

Guillen duly pled guilty. During the plea colloquy, the court told Guillen "you would always have the right to take an appeal if you thought my sentence was illegal." The court also explained the method it would use to sentence Guillen, which "start[s] with a presumption that [a sentence within the Guideline range] is reasonable." Later in the hearing, the court said:

> I do want to talk about [the waiver provision]. As I understand this . . . and this paragraph is a little bit different than the usual one, [Guillen] is giving up her right to appeal any sentence she receives unless I sentence her to a period longer than 20 years or unless I depart upwards from the guideline range.

Then, in light of Guillen's waiver, the court corrected its prior statement that Guillen "would always have the right" to appeal an illegal sentence. Guillen said she understood the waiver provision and the court accepted her plea.

The court later determined the applicable Guideline range was 15 to 21 months imprisonment. At a sentencing hearing the court considered Guillen's arguments that she ought to receive a sentence below the Guideline range, but concluded a sentence within "the guideline range is reasonable and meets the requirements of 18 U.S.C. § 3553." The court thereupon sentenced Guillen to the minimum Guideline sentence of 15 months imprisonment and to two years of supervised release and ordered her to pay restitution. Guillen appealed the sentence.

II. ANALYSIS

• • •

We do not consider these arguments because, as explained below, we agree with the Government that Guillen validly waived her right to appeal a sentence within the Guideline range.

A. General Validity of Pre-Sentence Waivers

As the First Circuit has observed, "The basic argument against presentence waivers of appellate rights is that such waivers are anticipatory." Accordingly, Guillen argues a defendant cannot knowingly waive his right to appeal a sentence that has not yet been imposed. All eleven other courts of appeals with criminal jurisdiction (including the First) have rejected this argument and held such waivers are presumptively valid. This court has enforced a waiver of the right to appeal a yet-to-be-imposed sentence on two occasions, but we have not yet determined "whether such waivers are valid as a general matter."

We now agree with our sister circuits that such waivers generally may be enforced. A defendant may waive his right to appeal his sentence as long as his decision is knowing, intelligent, and voluntary. An anticipatory waiver — that is, one made before the defendant knows what the sentence will be — is nonetheless a knowing waiver if the defendant is aware of and understands the risks involved in his decision. If "the record [shows] that [the defendant] knows what he is doing and his choice is made with eyes open," then the Court will enforce an anticipatory waiver.

In addition, we note the right to appeal a sentence is a creature of statute. See 18 U.S.C. § 3742. It would make little sense to hold a criminal defendant, who may waive basic rights guaranteed by the Constitution, may not waive a right created by statute and hence revocable at will by the Congress. The defendant cannot be certain of the consequences of waiving his constitutional right to trial by jury or to be represented by counsel any more than he can be certain of the consequences of waiving his right to appeal his sentence. In each situation, he must evaluate the possibilities open to him and their associated probabilities and, with the help of counsel, choose the most favorable alternative. A defendant who waives trial by pleading guilty, for example, believes the sentence he is likely to receive as a result (with credit for accepting responsibility) is more attractive than facing the range of possibilities — from acquittal on all counts to conviction and the maximum sentence on all counts — discounted by their corresponding probabilities. Pleading guilty allows the defendant to narrow the range of possible penalties. The calculation a defendant makes in waiving his right to appeal his yet-to-be-imposed sentence is fundamentally similar and ought not to be treated differently.

Allowing a defendant to waive the right to appeal his sentence also gives him an additional bargaining chip to use in negotiating a plea agreement with the Government. For example, the prosecutor might be willing to dismiss a count in exchange for the defendant's waiver of his right to appeal his sentence. Indeed, in certain circumstances an agreement may not be possible if the defendant may not waive his right to appeal. Allowing the defendant to waive this right therefore improves the defendant's bargaining position and increases the probability he will reach a satisfactory plea agreement with the Government.

B. When a Pre-Sentence Waiver Is Not Enforceable

By waiving the right to appeal his sentence, the defendant does not agree to accept any defect or error that may be thrust upon him by either an ineffective attorney or an errant sentencing court. Rather, the defendant waives his right to contest only a sentence within the statutory range and imposed under fair procedures; his waiver relieves neither his attorney nor the district court of their obligations to satisfy applicable constitutional requirements. Drawing upon the experience of sister circuits, therefore, we mention some circumstances that may lead a reviewing court not to enforce a pre-sentence waiver.

Most obvious, a waiver should not be enforced insofar as the defendant makes a colorable claim he received ineffective assistance of counsel in agreeing to the waiver. If such a claim is upheld, it follows that, because the defendant's attorney failed to ensure the defendant understood the consequences of his waiver, the waiver was not knowing, intelligent, and voluntary. If, however "a defendant's complaints of his counsel's inadequacy plainly lack merit, a court cannot allow itself to be manipulated" into voiding a bargained-for waiver of the right to appeal.

Nor should a waiver be enforced if the sentencing court's failure in some material way to follow a prescribed sentencing procedure results in a miscarriage of justice. If, for example, the district court utterly fails to advert to the factors in 18 U.S.C. § 3553(a), then this court may disregard the waiver and consider the defendant's argument that the district court imposed an unlawful sentence. In the same vein, a defendant does not waive his right to appeal a sentence that is unlawful because it exceeds the statutory maximum. Finally, we note a waiver does not shield from review a sentence colorably alleged to rest upon a constitutionally impermissible factor, such as the defendant's race or religion.

C. Guillen's Waiver Is Valid

We turn now to Guillen's claim her waiver of the right to appeal her sentence was not knowing, intelligent, and voluntary. As with the validity of a defendant's waiver of the right to counsel, our review is de novo.

In this case, the transcript of the plea hearing demonstrates that Guillen's waiver was knowing, intelligent, and voluntary. Guillen argues her waiver was not made knowingly because the district court initially said she "would always have the right to take an appeal if [she] thought [the] sentence was illegal." As the Government points out, however, the court later corrected this statement in light of Guillen's waiver. The court explained to Guillen she was waiving her right to appeal her sentence unless it was above the statutory maximum or was an upward departure from the Guideline range. Guillen then said she understood that, which leaves us with no reason to doubt Guillen's waiver was knowing, intelligent, and voluntary.

Guillen makes no argument that the district court failed to follow a prescribed sentencing procedure resulting in a miscarriage of justice. Instead, Guillen makes several arguments that have little relevance to our analysis.

First, Guillen argues the district court voided the waiver agreement when it told her, at the end of the sentencing hearing, "You do have the right to take an appeal from this sentence. If you want to do so you should tell [your attorney], and you have to let him know within ten days." This statement does not undermine the waiver agreement because it is correct; Guillen was entitled to appeal her sentence if it was above the statutory maximum or departed upward from the Guideline range. More important, a statement made at the sentencing hearing could not have informed (or misinformed) Guillen's decision to waive her right to appeal because that decision was made at the earlier plea hearing.

Next, Guillen argues she is entitled to appeal because she waived her right to appeal only under 18 U.S.C. § 3742 and not under 28 U.S.C. § 1291. Unlike § 3742, however, § 1291 does not give a criminal defendant a right to appeal. Rather, § 1291 gives the circuit courts subject matter jurisdiction over final orders of the district courts, including sentencing orders.

Finally, Guillen argues her waiver should not be enforced because the district court impermissibly presumed any sentence within the Guideline range was reasonable. Here Guillen points to the district court's statement at the plea hearing that it "starts with a presumption" that a sentence within the Guideline range is reasonable. Guillen's argument that the court impermissibly applied a presumption of reasonableness to a sentence within the Guideline range is of the kind a reviewing court need not consider when the defendant has waived his right to appeal a sentence or the manner in which it was determined. As stated above, we will disregard a waiver agreement on account of a district court's procedural error only if the error results in a miscarriage of justice; that the district court presumed any sentence within the Guideline range would be reasonable deprived Guillen of no element essential to a lawful sentence. Guillen points to three decisions holding it impermissible for a district court to presume a sentence within the Guideline range is reasonable. Notably, however, none of these cases involved a defendant who had waived his right to appeal his sentence.

From our review of the transcript of Guillen's sentencing hearing, it is apparent the district court identified the correct Guideline range, considered the factors in § 3553(a), and chose a sentence within the Guideline range. Pursuant to the terms of the waiver agreement and the concomitantly limited scope of our review, we do not consider whether the district court erred by applying a presumption of reasonableness to a sentence within that range. Moreover, because we hold Guillen's waiver was knowing, intelligent, and voluntary, we do not consider her arguments that the sentence was substantively unreasonable because the district court failed to give sufficient weight to her poor health, her personal history, and her cooperation with authorities.

III. CONCLUSION

Guillen waived her right to appeal any sentence below the statutory maximum and within the Guideline range. She appealed anyway but advances no argument that would cause us to disregard her waiver: She makes no claim she received ineffective assistance of counsel and she has not shown that the district court worked a miscarriage of justice by failing to follow an essential procedure or relied upon a constitutionally impermissible factor in determining her sentence. We therefore enforce the waiver agreement and hold she waived her right to appeal her sentence. Her appeal is, accordingly,

Dismissed.

NOTES AND COMMENTS

1. The D.C. Circuit here effectively overrules the district court's decision in *Raynor*, holding that "anticipatory" waivers generally are enforceable. Is the court's reasoning persuasive? Do you believe the enforceability of such waivers "improves the defendant's bargaining position" in practice? What do you make of the observation that "an agreement may not be possible if the defendant may not waive his right to appeal"?

2. The court glosses over the trial judge's mistake in the colloquy regarding the defendant's appellate rights, noting only that it was "corrected." Are you satisfied that the correction was adequate? Are you convinced on this record that Guillen's waiver of her appellate rights was knowing, intelligent, and voluntary?

3. Note that the government and defendant here have reached substantial agreement on the application of the sentencing guidelines, and that Guillen is essentially waiving only her right to appeal a sentence that exceeds the 19-month ceiling of the agreed-upon guideline range. Would a broader waiver of appellate rights require a more searching colloquy? Consider, for example, a defendant who pleads guilty without any plea agreement at all, and thus the range of possible sentences is enormous. In such a scenario, where the guilty plea itself does little to "narrow the range of penalties," would the court in the Rule 11 hearing need to approach an appellate waiver—or perhaps the entire colloquy—more rigorously?

4. In describing the sorts of waivers that are not enforceable notwithstanding the agreement's broad language, the court notes a "colorable claim" alleging "ineffective assistance of counsel in agreeing to the waiver." *Id.* at 530. What does the limitation to "colorable" claims mean? Why wouldn't a claim alleging ineffective assistance generally—as opposed to regarding the waiver—be nonenforceable? And why the distinction between waivability and enforceability?

5. For examinations of the constitutional and contractual issues in appellate waivers, *see* Robert K. Calhoun, *Waiver of the Right to Appeal*, 23 Hastings Const. L.Q. 127, 174-77 (1995); Alexandra W. Reimelt, Note, *An Unjust Bargain: Plea Bargains and Waiver of the Right to Appeal*, 51 B.C. L. Rev. 871, 877-79 (2010).

1042 Chapter XI Pleas and Plea Bargaining

The next two cases involve DOJ's even more aggressive attempt to require defendants to waive their right to collaterally attack a conviction. Although DOJ partially retreated from enforcing such waivers in 2014, and stopped including them in plea agreements in 2020, the vestiges of some waivers still remain operative. These waivers illustrate the lengths to which DOJ will go in its quest for finality.

Watson v. United States
682 F.3d 740 (8th Cir. 2012)

BYE, Circuit Judge.

Pursuant to 28 U.S.C. § 2255, Charles Watson, Jr., filed a motion to vacate the 165-month sentence he received after he pleaded guilty to a drug conspiracy charge. The district court summarily denied the motion because Watson waived the right to bring a § 2255 motion in his plea agreement. We granted a certificate of appealability on the issue of whether the waiver was enforceable to the extent Watson claimed ineffective assistance of counsel in matters directly related to his plea agreement. We now affirm.

I

On October 5, 2008, Watson delivered heroin to Joseph Vanhoe in Iowa City, Iowa. Within a few hours, Vanhoe was found dead in his apartment. Vanhoe had a fresh needle mark in his arm. Police found two hypodermic needles with liquid inside them near Vanhoe's body, along with several baggie corners containing heroin residue. An autopsy concluded Vanhoe died from ethanol and heroin poisoning.

A federal grand jury indicted Watson with: (1) conspiring to distribute cocaine base and heroin resulting in death in violation of 21 U.S.C. §§ 841(a)(1), (b)(1)(A), (b)(1)(C), and 846; (2) distribution of heroin resulting in death in violation of 21 U.S.C. § 841(a)(1) and (b)(1)(C); and (3) distribution of heroin in violation of 21 U.S.C. § 841(a)(1) and (b)(1)(C). Watson pleaded guilty to the conspiracy count pursuant to a written plea agreement. The conspiracy count carried a mandatory minimum sentence of 240 months due to the allegation that death resulted from the distribution of the controlled substances involved in the conspiracy.

In the plea agreement, Watson waived the right to file a direct appeal of his sentence. He also waived the right to collaterally attack his sentence. The relevant provision in the plea agreement stated:

> *Waiver of Right to Collateral Attack.* The defendant also understands that he has a right to attack his conviction, and/or the sentence imposed, collaterally on the grounds that it was imposed in violation of the Constitution or laws of the United States; that the defendant received ineffective assistance from his attorney; that the Court was without proper jurisdiction; or that the conviction and/or sentence were otherwise subject to collateral attack. The defendant understands that such an attack is usually brought through a motion pursuant to 28 U.S.C. § 2255. The defendant and the defendant's attorney have reviewed Section 2255, and the defendant understands applicable rights under the statute. The defendant's attorney has fully discussed and explained the defendant's right to attack the conviction and/or sentence collaterally with the defendant. Understanding those rights, and having thoroughly discussed those rights with his attorney, the defendant knowingly and voluntarily waives the right to collaterally attack his conviction and/or sentence. The defendant specifically acknowledges that the decision to waive the right to challenge any later claim of the ineffectiveness of his counsel was made by him alone notwithstanding any advice he may or may not have received from his attorney regarding that right. Regardless of any advice the defendant's attorney may have given him, in exchange for

F. The Enforceability of Plea Agreements: Breach and Collateral Waivers   **1043**

the concessions made by the United States in this Agreement, the defendant hereby knowingly and voluntarily waives the right to collaterally attack the conviction and/or sentence. The rights waived by the defendant include the right to challenge the amount of any fine or restitution in any collateral attack including, but not limited to, a motion brought under Section 2255.

Plea Agreement at ¶ 14.

During Watson's plea hearing, the district court discussed the collateral attack waiver with Watson. The following colloquy took place:

THE COURT: People who get done appealing, going as far as they can go, ordinarily have a right for a period of one year to bring a limited attack on their conviction. Sometimes it is called post conviction relief, sometimes it is referred to by the criminal code Section 2255 that it is filed under usually in Federal Court. I see in Paragraph 14 of the Plea Agreement that you have given up that as well. In the Plea Agreement it says that you understand that you have that right, that you and your lawyer have discussed that right, and that understanding the right to bring that limited attack, you knowingly and voluntarily waive or give up the right to collaterally attack your conviction or sentence. Oftentimes this right is used to bring a claim that your lawyer rendered ineffective assistance of counsel, that your lawyer just wasn't up to the task or left something out or did something wrong along the way. Here in the Plea Agreement it says, "The defendant specifically acknowledges that the decision to waive the right to challenge any later claim of ineffective assistance of his counsel was made by him alone, notwithstanding any advice he may or may not have received from his attorney regarding that right." So you don't get to bring a claim later that Mr. Ingram was ineffective in recommending this plea agreement. Do you understand that?

THE DEFENDANT: Yes, sir.

The district court later sentenced Watson to 165 months of imprisonment, departing below the 240-month mandatory minimum after granting the government's motion for a substantial assistance departure under 18 U.S.C. § 3553(e). The other two counts against Watson were dismissed pursuant to the plea agreement.

Within a year after being sentenced, Watson filed a motion to vacate his sentence under 28 U.S.C. § 2255. The motion alleged four grounds for setting aside the conviction and sentence: (1) the sentence was illegal because it was based upon a finding Watson was responsible for fifty grams or more of cocaine base even though the presentence report (PSR) only attributed 1.6 grams of cocaine base directly to Watson; (2) the sentence was illegal due to the enhancement based on Joseph Vanhoe's death; (3) the receipt of improper advice from his attorney with regard to entering into the cooperation agreement with the government; and (4) ineffective assistance of counsel, including ineffective advice Watson received regarding the plea agreement itself.

The district court denied the section 2255 motion without an evidentiary hearing, enforcing the collateral attack waiver in Watson's plea agreement. The district court also later denied Watson's request for a certificate of appealability. Watson renewed his request for a certificate of appealability in our court. We granted Watson's request in part, limiting it "to the question whether the district court correctly enforced Watson's waiver of his right to attack his conviction and sentence in a proceeding under 28 U.S.C. § 2255 based on ineffective assistance of counsel." This appeal followed.

II

We review issues related to plea agreements de novo, including the interpretation of a waiver of appellate rights or a waiver of the right to collaterally attack a sentence and conviction.

Citing *DeRoo v. United States* (8th Cir. 2000), Watson argues the district court erred in enforcing the collateral attack waiver in his plea agreement because he alleged in his section 2255 motion that the guilty plea itself was tainted by ineffective assistance of counsel in violation of his Sixth Amendment rights. In *DeRoo*, we stated the "[d]ismissal of a section 2255 motion on the basis of a waiver in the plea agreement is inappropriate when the defendant's claims of ineffective assistance relate to the negotiation of, and entry into, the plea agreement and waiver." We determined a "decision to enter into a plea agreement cannot be knowing and voluntary when the plea agreement itself is the result of advice outside 'the range of competence demanded of attorneys in criminal cases.'" Thus, "justice dictates that a claim of ineffective assistance of counsel in connection with the negotiation of a cooperation agreement cannot be barred by the agreement itself—the very product of the alleged ineffectiveness."

Our court subsequently noted the tension between a broad reading of *DeRoo* and the Supreme Court's long recognition of a defendant's ability to waive rights guaranteed by the Sixth Amendment, including the right to effective assistance of counsel. In *Chesney*, we explained:

> If a criminal defendant is able to negotiate substantial concessions from the prosecution, but only on the condition that the defendant waive a potential future claim of ineffective assistance of counsel, does "justice" really dictate that this court refuse to enforce such an agreement in all circumstances? If the government cannot obtain the benefit of avoiding collateral litigation under section 2255, then the government may not be willing to offer certain concessions, and a defendant may be unable to secure the bargain most favorable to his interests. To require that conclusion would seem, in Justice Frankfurter's famous words, "to imprison a man in his privileges and call it the Constitution."

Chesney suggested that perhaps *DeRoo* should be refined to stand for the following proposition:

> [A] general waiver of the right to bring post-conviction or post-sentencing claims under section 2255 would not be sufficient to waive such a claim of ineffective assistance of counsel, but an explicit waiver of the Sixth Amendment right to counsel—which explained the concept of ineffective assistance of counsel and the basic ramifications of waiving a claim that ineffectiveness influenced the signing of the waiver—would be considered knowing and voluntary. *Cf. Faretta v. California* (1975). Under the law of this circuit, so long as such a waiver of Sixth Amendment rights did not result in a "miscarriage of justice," the waiver would be enforceable.

Chesney ultimately did not adopt such a refinement of *DeRoo* because "Chesney's waiver did not specifically mention the Sixth Amendment or the right to effective assistance of counsel, and the colloquy with the court at the time of sentencing was no more specific than the general written waiver." The government nonetheless urges us to adopt *Chesney*'s dicta as a holding in this case because the collateral attack provision in Watson's plea agreement explicitly referred to the right to bring a claim for ineffective assistance of counsel, and the district court specifically discussed the waiver with Watson during the plea colloquy.

We are not inclined to decide whether to adopt *Chesney*'s refinement of *DeRoo* in this particular case, however, because the parties failed to address an issue we find difficult to ignore in determining whether Watson knowingly and voluntarily waived his right to bring an ineffective assistance claim with respect to matters directly related to the plea agreement. Ethics opinions from various states have addressed whether a defendant's attorney labors under a conflict of interest when advising a client to waive an ineffective assistance of counsel claim, with conflicting results. Watson does not claim his counsel labored under a conflict of interest when advising him to enter the plea agreement, and the parties did not brief this issue. We therefore believe it prudent to forego the issue of whether *DeRoo* should be refined by *Chesney*'s suggestions until this related issue on a potential conflict of interest is fully aired by the adversarial process.

Instead, we accept the government's invitation to determine whether the district court should be affirmed in any event because Watson's ineffective assistance claim fails on the merits. In order to satisfy the prejudice prong of the *Strickland* test in the guilty plea context, a defendant must establish a reasonable probability that he would have exercised his right to a trial but for counsel's ineffectiveness. On appeal, Watson never directly contends he would not have pleaded guilty and would have insisted on going to trial but for his counsel's alleged deficiencies. Instead, he claims he can show prejudice because his section 2255 motion challenges "the aspects of his conviction which led to his 20 year mandatory minimum sentence—the allegations that he was involved in a conspiracy to distribute more than 50 grams of cocaine, and that his involvement in the alleged distribution of heroin led to the death of Joseph Vanhoe."

Watson's contention that he faced a mandatory minimum sentence of 240 months because the conspiracy involved fifty grams or more of cocaine base is incorrect. As we stated above, Watson faced a mandatory minimum sentence of 240 months because the conspiracy involved a death resulting from the distribution of heroin. Thus, Watson's admission that the conspiracy involved fifty grams or more of cocaine had no bearing on the mandatory minimum sentence he faced. As a result, he cannot establish any prejudice due to any advice he may have received from his counsel in that regard.

With respect to Watson's second contention—that his counsel failed to investigate Watson's involvement in Vanhoe's death—the record establishes "Watson admitted he delivered heroin to Vanhoe on the day of Vanhoe's death[.]" The autopsy report indicated Vanhoe died from heroin poisoning. In addition, one of Watson's codefendants, Reginald Penro, was shown the heroin seized from Vanhoe's residence and "stated it appeared to be the same substance he and Watson delivered to Vanhoe on the day of Vanhoe's death." Watson fails to address the strength of this evidence or otherwise explain how his trial counsel was ineffective in failing to further investigate whether Watson's conduct resulted in Vanhoe's death. We therefore conclude that Watson cannot establish he was prejudiced by his counsel's alleged ineffective assistance, and thus the district court did not abuse its discretion in denying the relief Watson requested without holding an evidentiary hearing.

III

We affirm the district court.

NOTES AND QUESTIONS

1. DOJ is working hard to ensure the enforceability of its collateral attack waiver here, packing lots of language into this term of the plea agreement. What is the purpose of the sentence in the waiver provision that says "[t]he defendant specifically acknowledges that the decision to waive the right to challenge any later claim of ineffectiveness of his counsel was made by him alone notwithstanding any advice he may or may not have received from counsel"? Should the district court accept an agreement containing such a term? Putting aside the DOJ ethical issues this term implicates, should the court bless a representation that is most likely untrue?

1046   Chapter XI Pleas and Plea Bargaining

2. The district court does a more admirable job than many in explaining this waiver to the defendant, trying to use ordinary language in spots. Consider, by contrast, this colloquy from *United States v. Lemaster*, 403 F.3d 216, 218 (4th Cir. 2005):

> **Q:** And as to a collateral attack, you understand the same thing applies, that in the absence of the plea agreement you would have a right to file a collateral attack?
> **A:** Yes.
> **Q:** And do you understand by signing this plea agreement you're agreeing to waive that right?
> **A:** Yeah.

3. Note that defendant receives an almost one-third reduction off his sentence for rendering "substantial assistance" to the government, that is, becoming a cooperating witness. 682 F.3d at 742. Imagine the pressure the availability of such a potential reduction puts on defendants to provide testimony and other information implicating their co-conspirators. *See* Chapter XVI *infra*.

4. Are ineffective assistance waivers ethical? It is hardly surprising that the government "failed to address" the ethical issues that led the court ultimately to avoid deciding the enforceability of the collateral attack waiver and, rather, to decide the collateral attack on the merits. For the government, recognizing such ethical issues could undermine its continuing attempt to include such waivers in its plea agreements. As to those ethical issues, consider Model Rule 1.7(a)(2), which states that "a lawyer shall not represent a client if . . . there is a significant risk that the representation . . . will be materially limited by the lawyer's responsibilities to another client, a former client or a third person or by a personal interest of the lawyer."

Is this rule applicable in the context of advising a client on waiving his right to collateral attack? How about Model Rule 8.4(a), which states that a lawyer shall not "violate or attempt to violate the Rules of Professional Conduct, knowingly assist or induce another to do so, or do so through the acts of another"? Could these two rules in combination be applicable *to the prosecutor* in this context?

Hurlow v. United States
726 F.3d 958 (7th Cir. 2013)

BAUER, Circuit Judge.

Petitioner Thomas Hurlow pleaded guilty to multiple drug and firearm offenses after law enforcement officials discovered drugs and a firearm in the home Hurlow shared with his fiancée. In a written plea agreement, Hurlow waived his right to challenge his conviction under 28 U.S.C. § 2255. He has done just that, though, alleging in a § 2255 petition that he advised his trial counsel of events that suggested that the search of his home was in violation of *Georgia v. Randolph* (2006), but that counsel failed to investigate those events and instead persuaded Hurlow to plead guilty. The district court denied Hurlow's request for an evidentiary hearing and concluded that his § 2255 motion was barred by the waiver in his plea agreement. Because the § 2255 waiver in his plea agreement does not bar his claim that his trial counsel was ineffective in negotiating the plea agreement, we remand the matter to the district court for an evidentiary hearing on that claim.

I. BACKGROUND

On December 16, 2008, a case worker from the Indiana Department of Child Services and two detectives from the Vigo County Drug Task Force arrived at the home Hurlow shared with his fiancée, Tina Funk, to conduct a welfare check on Funk's children. According to Hurlow, he objected to the presence of the detectives and requested that they leave unless they had a valid search warrant. The detectives instead asked Funk for her permission to search the house. The detectives told Funk that her children would be taken from her if she did not agree to the search; Funk gave her written consent to the search over Hurlow's objections.

During the search that followed, the detectives found a substance containing detectable amounts of methamphetamine, marijuana, drug paraphernalia, and a handgun. After being taken into custody and read his *Miranda* warnings, Hurlow told the detectives that all of the illegal items found belonged to him and that Funk had no knowledge that the drugs were in the home.

According to Hurlow, he told his appointed trial counsel the circumstances surrounding the search of the home that led to his arrest. He also informed counsel that his "rights ha[d] been violated" by the search and "requested that [counsel] advocate that as a defense." Hurlow contends, though, that counsel "failed to listen to Hurlow's version of events," "fail[ed] to investigate" the events surrounding the search, and otherwise failed to make "any attempt" to pursue Hurlow's claim that the search was illegal. Instead, counsel persuaded Hurlow to plead guilty to avoid a sentence of "30 years to life imprisonment."

Based on counsel's advice, Hurlow entered into a plea agreement with the government and pleaded guilty to all of the charges against him. Like many plea agreements, this one contained a provision noting Hurlow's agreement not to contest his conviction or sentence in a collateral attack under 28 U.S.C. § 2255. In addition to the plea agreement, the parties submitted a stipulated factual basis for the plea to the district court. Regarding the December 2008 search that led to Hurlow's arrest, the document states that "Funk granted [the detectives] consent to search [the home] in writing."

During his change of plea hearing on July 28, 2009, the district court conducted a Rule 11 colloquy, and Hurlow affirmed the factual basis for the plea, including that Funk consented to the search. He also affirmed that he was satisfied with his counsel's representation and that he had "had sufficient time to talk with him and to work with him to try to consider any options that [Hurlow] might have in this case[.]" Hurlow agreed that there was not anything that he wanted his counsel "to do in regards to this case that he failed to do[.]" The district court concluded that Hurlow's plea was "knowing and voluntary," and ultimately sentenced him to 248 months' imprisonment.

On September 9, 2010, Hurlow filed a motion for postconviction relief pursuant to 28 U.S.C. § 2255, arguing, among other claims, that his plea agreement was involuntary because it resulted from the ineffective assistance of trial counsel. Hurlow alleged that he informed his trial counsel of the facts surrounding the search of the home he shared with Funk but that counsel failed to listen to Hurlow, conduct any investigation regarding the search, or file a motion to suppress that would have been successful under *Georgia v. Randolph*. He instead persuaded Hurlow to plead guilty.

The district court rejected Hurlow's request for an evidentiary hearing and denied his § 2255 motion, concluding that Hurlow had "waived his opportunity to challenge his conviction pursuant to § 2255." The district court reasoned that the waiver in the plea agreement barred Hurlow's motion because Hurlow had not alleged that his counsel was "ineffective with regard to negotiation of the waiver" and his statements at his plea colloquy indicated that "his plea was knowing, intelligent, and voluntary." The district court accordingly denied Hurlow's § 2255 motion, denied a certificate of appealability, and entered judgment on September 26, 2011.

· · ·

1048 Chapter XI Pleas and Plea Bargaining

II. DISCUSSION

This appeal does not involve the merits of Hurlow's ineffective assistance of counsel claim. Rather, the appeal presents us with two issues that go to whether Hurlow should be heard on that claim: the timeliness of his appeal and the effect of the § 2255 waiver in his plea agreement. We address each in turn.

• • •

B. Hurlow's § 2255 Motion

We now turn to the issue of whether Hurlow's § 2255 challenge to his conviction is barred by the collateral review waiver in his plea agreement. We review de novo the enforceability of a plea agreement's waiver of direct or collateral review. It is well-settled that waivers of direct and collateral review in plea agreements are generally enforceable. Nevertheless, because a plea agreement is a contract and generally governed by ordinary contract law principles, waivers contained in the agreements are unenforceable in certain circumstances akin to those in which a contract would be unenforceable, such as when the government has materially breached the agreement or the dispute falls outside the scope of the waiver.

Though disputes over plea agreements are "usefully viewed through the lens of contract law," we have recognized that the application of ordinary contract law principles to plea agreements, "must be tempered by recognition of limits that the Constitution places on the criminal process, limits that have no direct counterparts in the sphere of private contracting." For example, "while a contracting party is bound by the mistakes of his lawyer, however egregious (his only remedy being a suit for malpractice), the Constitution entitles defendants entering plea agreements to effective assistance of counsel." We have therefore repeatedly recognized that appellate and collateral review waivers cannot be invoked against claims that counsel was ineffective in the negotiation of the plea agreement.

Despite our precedent indicating that a collateral review waiver does not prevent a habeas petitioner from being heard on claims that his plea agreement was the product of ineffective assistance of counsel, the government argues, and the district court concluded, that this avenue of relief from waiver is not applicable to Hurlow because he has not alleged that his counsel was ineffective in the negotiation of the waiver provision of his plea agreement, as opposed to the agreement as a whole. In support, the government relies upon *Jones v. United States*, in which we stated that collateral review "waivers are enforceable as a general rule; the right to mount a collateral attack pursuant to § 2255 survives only with respect to those discrete claims which relate directly to the negotiation of the waiver." But a more complete reading of *Jones* does not support the government's interpretation: we stated that "[t]he right to appeal survives where the agreement is involuntary" and reasoned that "[j]ustice dictates that a claim of ineffective assistance of counsel in connection with the negotiation of a cooperation agreement cannot be barred by the agreement itself — the very product of the alleged ineffectiveness." And we enforced the waiver provision in *Jones* not because the defendant failed to show ineffectiveness with regards to the negotiation of the waiver provision, but because the defendant made no showing whatsoever with respect to his "naked assertions that he was denied effective assistance of counsel and that the agreement was involuntary."

While we have repeated the less-than-artful phrase in *Jones* regarding the "negotiation of the waiver," we have never held that the waiver is unenforceable only when counsel is ineffective in negotiating the specific waiver provision. Instead, our cases since *Jones* have affirmed that an attorney's ineffectiveness with regard to the plea agreement as a whole, and not just the specific waiver provision at issue, renders the waiver unenforceable. This is because a "claim[] that the plea agreement was involuntary or the result of ineffective assistance of

F. The Enforceability of Plea Agreements: Breach and Collateral Waivers

counsel . . . concern[s] the validity of the plea agreement," and so it "would knock out the waiver . . . along with the rest of the promises" if successful. Thus, "a waiver stands or falls with the plea bargain of which it is a part." We accordingly reaffirm that a direct or collateral review waiver does not bar a challenge regarding the validity of a plea agreement (and necessarily the waiver it contains) on grounds of ineffective assistance of counsel; Hurlow need not have alleged that his counsel was ineffective in the negotiation of the waiver provision of his plea agreement specifically.

Our inquiry does not end here, however. Not every claim of ineffective assistance of counsel can overcome a waiver in a plea agreement. We have rejected broad, unsupported assertions of ineffective assistance, as well as "garden variety attacks . . . raise[d] in the guise of a claim of ineffective assistance of counsel." We therefore must determine whether Hurlow's claims of ineffective assistance of counsel are sufficient to overcome the waiver in his plea agreement.

Our analysis here is informed by cases in which a defendant has pleaded guilty unconditionally, which, like a direct or collateral review waiver, generally "forecloses any opportunity to contest any alleged antecedent constitutional deprivations." In *Tollett v. Henderson*, the Supreme Court explained the reasoning behind this principle:

> [A] guilty plea represents a break in the chain of events which has preceded it in the criminal process. When a criminal defendant has solemnly admitted in open court that he is in fact guilty of the offense with which he is charged, he may not thereafter raise independent claims relating to the deprivation of constitutional rights that occurred prior to the entry of the guilty plea.

The Supreme Court recognized, though, that a criminal defendant can bring claims "attack[ing] the voluntary and intelligent character of the guilty plea[,]" such as claims that the defendant "plead[ed] guilty on the advice of counsel" that "was not 'within the range of competence demanded of attorneys in criminal cases[.]'" This includes cases in which counsel has "fail[ed] to evaluate properly facts giving rise to a constitutional claim, or [failed to] inform himself [properly] of facts that would have shown the existence of a constitutional claim[.]" The Supreme Court emphasized, however, that while the habeas petitioner "must, of course, prove that some constitutional infirmity occurred in the proceedings[,]" the "focus of federal habeas inquiry is the nature of the advice and the voluntariness of the plea, not the existence as such of an antecedent constitutional infirmity." Nevertheless, while claims of prior constitutional deprivations "are not themselves independent grounds for federal collateral relief[,]" they "may play a part in evaluating the advice rendered by counsel[.]"

The same is true for a petitioner such as Hurlow who seeks to overcome the waiver provision in his plea agreement based on ineffective assistance of counsel: he cannot just assert that a constitutional violation preceded his decision to plead guilty or that his trial counsel was ineffective for failing to raise the constitutional claim. Rather, he must allege that he entered the plea agreement based on advice of counsel that fell below constitutional standards. In other words, he must allege that the plea agreement was "the product of ineffective assistance of counsel," or "tainted by ineffective assistance of counsel." For example, in *United States v. Cieslowski*, the defendant's plea agreement contained a waiver of direct and collateral review, but the defendant claimed that his decision to enter into that plea agreement was the product of his attorney's ineffectiveness in "fail[ing] to file two suppression motions[.]" Because this claim was the sort that, "if successful, would result in setting aside the plea agreement as a whole," we considered (and ultimately rejected) the defendant's ineffective assistance of counsel argument on the merits.

Turning to Hurlow's allegations in his § 2255 petition, we similarly conclude that they are sufficient to overcome the waiver in his plea agreement. First, he alleged that his trial counsel was ineffective by failing to recognize that the detectives who obtained the critical evidence

Chapter XI Pleas and Plea Bargaining

against him did so in violation of the Fourth Amendment: even though Hurlow apprised him of facts that indicated that the search violated *Georgia v. Randolph*, counsel refused to listen or investigate further. Second, Hurlow alleged that his decision to plead guilty resulted from counsel's ineffectiveness. According to Hurlow, counsel failed to inform him that a challenge to the search was possible, and instead "persuaded" and "cajoled" him into pleading guilty by telling him "that if [he] did not plead guilty, that [he] would [receive] 30 years to life imprisonment." Hurlow alleged that had he known he could "contest the unconstitutional and unreasonable search[,]" he "would not have entered into the one-sided government authorized plea agreement" or "pled guilt[.]" Thus, Hurlow is saying that he would not have agreed to the terms of the plea agreement had his counsel informed him of his potentially meritorious Fourth Amendment claim. This is sufficient to overcome the collateral review waiver in his plea agreement.

Seeking to avoid this result, the government argues that Hurlow affirmed his satisfaction with counsel when he "knowingly and voluntarily" pleaded guilty after a "thorough Rule 11 colloquy." But as we discuss above, a plea, even one that complies with Rule 11, cannot be "knowing and voluntary" if it resulted from ineffective assistance of counsel. It is not surprising that Hurlow said he was satisfied with counsel; when he told his counsel about the facts surrounding the search, his lawyer ignored him. Thus, his statement to the district court was made against the backdrop of his ignorance regarding the possibility of a successful motion to suppress.

Moreover, aside from his dissatisfaction with counsel, Hurlow's allegations in his § 2255 petition are not inconsistent with the factual basis for his plea or the statements he made under oath during the Rule 11 colloquy. Hurlow does not dispute that Funk gave her written consent to the search. Rather, he claims Funk's consent resulted from a coercive police threat and that he objected to the search prior to Funk's consent. Thus, nothing we have said in any way undercuts the fact that representations made to a court during "a plea colloquy are presumed to be true."

In reaching the conclusion that the collateral review waiver in Hurlow's plea agreement does not bar his claim that his guilty plea resulted from ineffective assistance of counsel, we offer no opinion regarding the veracity of Hurlow's allegations or the ultimate outcome of his collateral attack. Our inquiry here is focused on whether Hurlow's allegations entitle him to an evidentiary hearing on his § 2255 motion. We conclude that they do, and accordingly remand the case to the district court for a hearing on Hurlow's Sixth Amendment claim.

NOTES AND QUESTIONS

1. Consider closely the law school exam fact pattern here. Why were narcotics detectives accompanying state regulatory agency inspectors on a family home visit welfare check? Assuming the regulators had statutory authorization to conduct the visit, and that continued child custody might require such a visit, did *the narcotics detectives* have any authority to threaten Tina Funk as they did? Was her consent to the detectives' search voluntary? Why did Hurlow—who appears to be something of a legal eagle—admit to the detectives that he owned the drugs and other seized evidence?

2. Does it surprise you that both the prosecutor and defense counsel were apparently unaware of *Georgia v. Randolph*, 547 U.S. 103 (2006), a significant Supreme Court case decided just a couple of years before the search and arrest? *See* Chapter IV *supra*. Recall that in that case the Court held that a consent to search jointly occupied premises by one occupant of the premises does not overcome a refusal to consent by a physically present co-occupant. If the prosecutor had been aware of that case, should he have drafted the factual stipulation the parties submitted differently? Was the language regarding Funk's consent sufficient from the prosecutor's perspective? Would this case have come out differently, for example, if Hurlow had agreed in the factual stipulation that Funk "freely, knowingly, and intelligently" consented to the search of the house?

3. The court in *Hurlow* weighs in on the issue alluded to in *Guillen*, namely, whether a collateral attack waiver can be overcome by an allegation of ineffective assistance in advice regarding the plea agreement generally as opposed to advice regarding the waiver. It holds that it can, as the waiver is part of the plea agreement and therefore "stands or falls with the plea bargain of which it is a part." 926 F.3d at 965 (citation omitted). The court notes that the analogy between contracts and plea agreements only goes so far — whereas a party to a contract will normally be bound by his lawyer's mistakes, a defendant is entitled to effective assistance of counsel.

4. The government argues that Hurlow's claims of ineffectiveness are belied by his statements at the colloquy to the effect that he was satisfied with counsel's performance. The court has little trouble concluding that those statements were not "knowing" inasmuch as Hurlow was unaware at that time that he had a potentially successful motion to suppress. Does it matter in this regard that Hurlow suggested to his lawyer that he believed his rights were violated by the search? Did his counsel have an independent obligation to investigate the circumstances of the search regardless of Hurlow's suggestion? Would a competent investigation have uncovered the basis for a motion to suppress?

5. The court expresses no opinion on "the veracity of Hurlow's allegations or the ultimate outcome of his collateral attack." *Id.* at 968. What do you think the outcome should be if Hurlow's allegations are found credible?

6. Assume the detectives' incident report acknowledged that the detectives had been accompanying the social worker on the welfare check, but stated only, without elaboration, that Tina Funk had consented to the search. Did the prosecutor have an ethical obligation to interview Tina Funk about the nature of her consent? To interview the social worker about the nature of the detectives' presence?

Suppose further that the incident report stated that Tina Funk refused to consent to the search, and that after the plea agreement was signed but before the hearing the prosecutor was alerted to the significance of *Georgia v. Randolph*. What are the prosecutor's ethical obligations? Would they be any different if the plea agreement had not been signed?

Shortly after *Hurlow* the DOJ changed its policy on enforcement of ineffective assistance waivers. *See* Memorandum from James M. Cole, Deputy Attorney General, to All Federal Prosecutors (Oct. 14, 2014), available at http://pdfserver.amlaw.com/nlj/DOJ — Ineffective — Assistance — Counsel.pdf ("For cases in which a defendant's ineffective assistance claim would be barred by a previously executed waiver, prosecutors should decline to enforce the waiver when defense counsel rendered ineffective assistance resulting in prejudice or when the defendant's ineffective assistance claim raises a serious debatable issue that a court should resolve.").

Does this mean that the prosecutor needs to judge the merits of the ineffective assistance claim before deciding whether to seek to enforce the waiver? In 2020, DOJ reiterated its 2014 policy and also, prospectively, prohibited prosecutors from seeking to include such waivers in plea agreements. Justice Manual § 9-16.330, Plea Agreements and Waivers of Effective Assistance of Counsel.

The next case illustrates how various sources of legal authority intersect in the law of guilty pleas: constitutional, statutory (Rule 11), and contractual (the plea agreement). Here, the

1052 Chapter XI Pleas and Plea Bargaining

Court has to consider whether the appellate right at issue was waived "inherently" by the constitutional law of guilty pleas, by virtue of the Rule 11 colloquy, and/or by the parties' written plea agreement.

Class v. United States
583 U.S. 174 (2018)

Justice BREYER delivered the opinion of the Court.

Does a guilty plea bar a criminal defendant from later appealing his conviction on the ground that the statute of conviction violates the Constitution? In our view, a guilty plea by itself does not bar that appeal.

I

In September 2013, a federal grand jury indicted petitioner, Rodney Class, for possessing firearms in his locked jeep, which was parked in a lot on the grounds of the United States Capitol in Washington, D.C. See 40 U.S.C. § 5104(e)(1) ("An individual . . . may not carry . . . on the Grounds or in any of the Capitol Buildings a firearm"). Soon thereafter, Class, appearing pro se, asked the Federal District Court for the District of Columbia to dismiss the indictment. As relevant here, Class alleged that the statute, § 5104(e), violates the Second Amendment. He also raised a due process claim, arguing that he was denied fair notice that weapons were banned in the parking lot. Following a hearing, the District Court denied both claims.

Several months later, Class pleaded guilty to "Possession of a Firearm on U.S. Capitol Grounds, in violation of 40 U.S.C. § 5104(e)." The Government agreed to drop related charges.

A written plea agreement set forth the terms of Class' guilty plea, including several categories of rights that he expressly agreed to waive. Those express waivers included: (1) all defenses based upon the statute of limitations; (2) several specified trial rights; (3) the right to appeal a sentence at or below the judicially determined, maximum sentencing guideline range; (4) most collateral attacks on the conviction and sentence; and (5) various rights to request or receive information concerning the investigation and prosecution of his criminal case. At the same time, the plea agreement expressly enumerated categories of claims that Class could raise on appeal, including claims based upon (1) newly discovered evidence; (2) ineffective assistance of counsel; and (3) certain statutes providing for sentence reductions. Finally, the plea agreement stated under the heading "Complete Agreement":

> No agreements, promises, understandings, or representations have been made by the parties or their counsel other than those contained in writing herein, nor will any such agreements . . . be made unless committed to writing and signed. . . .

The agreement said nothing about the right to raise on direct appeal a claim that the statute of conviction was unconstitutional.

The District Court held a plea hearing during which it reviewed the terms of the plea agreement (with Class present and under oath) to ensure the validity of the plea. After providing Class with the required information and warnings, the District Court accepted his guilty plea. Class was sentenced to 24 days imprisonment followed by 12 months of supervised release.

Several days later, Class appealed his conviction to the Court of Appeals for the District of Columbia Circuit. Class was appointed an amicus to aid him in presenting his arguments. He repeated his constitutional claims, namely, that the statute violates the Second Amendment

F. The Enforceability of Plea Agreements: Breach and Collateral Waivers

and the Due Process Clause because it fails to give fair notice of which areas fall within the Capitol Grounds where firearms are banned. The Court of Appeals held that Class could not raise his constitutional claims because, by pleading guilty, he had waived them. Class filed a petition for certiorari in this Court asking us to decide whether in pleading guilty a criminal defendant inherently waives the right to challenge the constitutionality of his statute of conviction. We agreed to do so.

II

The question is whether a guilty plea by itself bars a federal criminal defendant from challenging the constitutionality of the statute of conviction on direct appeal. We hold that it does not. Class did not relinquish his right to appeal the District Court's constitutional determinations simply by pleading guilty. As we shall explain, this holding flows directly from this Court's prior decisions.

Fifty years ago this Court directly addressed a similar claim (a claim that the statute of conviction was unconstitutional). And the Court stated that a defendant's "plea of guilty did not . . . waive his previous [constitutional] claim." Though Justice Harlan's opinion for the Court offered little explanation for this statement, subsequent decisions offered a rationale that applies here.

In *Blackledge v. Perry* (1974), North Carolina indicted and convicted Jimmy Seth Perry on a misdemeanor assault charge. When Perry exercised his right under a North Carolina statute to a de novo trial in a higher court, the State reindicted him, but this time the State charged a felony, which carried a heavier penalty, for the same conduct. Perry pleaded guilty. He then sought habeas relief on the grounds that the reindictment amounted to an unconstitutional vindictive prosecution. The State argued that Perry's guilty plea barred him from raising his constitutional challenge. But this Court held that it did not.

The Court noted that a guilty plea bars appeal of many claims, including some "'antecedent constitutional violations' " related to events (say, grand jury proceedings) that had "'occurred prior to the entry of the guilty plea.'" While *Tollett* claims were "of constitutional dimension," the Court explained that "the nature of the underlying constitutional infirmity is markedly different" from a claim of vindictive prosecution, which implicates "the very power of the State" to prosecute the defendant. Accordingly, the Court wrote that "the right" Perry "asserts and that we today accept is the right not to be haled into court at all upon the felony charge" since "[t]he very initiation of the proceedings" against Perry "operated to deprive him due process of law."

A year and a half later, in *Menna v. New York* (1975) (per curiam), this Court repeated what it had said and held in *Blackledge*. After Menna served a 30-day jail term for refusing to testify before the grand jury on November 7, 1968, the State of New York charged him once again for (what Menna argued was) the same crime. Menna pleaded guilty, but subsequently appealed arguing that the new charge violated the Double Jeopardy Clause. U.S. Const., Amdt. The lower courts held that Menna's constitutional claim had been "waived" by his guilty plea.

This Court reversed. Citing *Blackledge*, the Court held that "a plea of guilty to a charge does not waive a claim that—judged on its face—the charge is one which the State may not constitutionally prosecute." Menna's claim amounted to a claim that "the State may not convict" him "no matter how validly his factual guilt is established." Menna's "guilty plea, therefore, [did] not bar the claim."

These holdings reflect an understanding of the nature of guilty pleas which, in broad outline, stretches back nearly 150 years. In 1869 Justice Ames wrote for the Supreme Judicial Court of Massachusetts:

> The plea of guilty is, of course, a confession of all the facts charged in the indictment, and also of the evil intent imputed to the defendant. It is a waiver also of all merely technical and formal objections of which the defendant could have availed himself by any other plea or motion. But if the facts alleged and admitted do not constitute a crime against the laws of the Commonwealth, the defendant is entitled to be discharged.

Decisions of federal and state courts throughout the 19th and 20th centuries reflect a similar view of the nature of a guilty plea. We refer to these cases because it was against this background that Justice Harlan in his opinion for the Court made the statement to which we originally referred, namely, that a defendant's "plea of guilty did not, of course, waive his previous [constitutional] claim."

In more recent years, we have reaffirmed the *Menna–Blackledge* doctrine and refined its scope. In *United States v. Broce* (1989), the defendants pleaded guilty to two separate indictments in a single proceeding which "on their face" described two separate bid-rigging conspiracies. They later sought to challenge their convictions on double jeopardy grounds, arguing that they had only admitted to one conspiracy. Citing *Blackledge* and *Menna*, this Court repeated that a guilty plea does not bar a claim on appeal "where on the face of the record the court had no power to enter the conviction or impose the sentence." However, because the defendants could not "prove their claim by relying on those indictments and the existing record" and "without contradicting those indictments," this Court held that their claims were "foreclosed by the admissions inherent in their guilty pleas."

Unlike the claims in *Broce*, Class' constitutional claims here, as we understand them, do not contradict the terms of the indictment or the written plea agreement. They are consistent with Class' knowing, voluntary, and intelligent admission that he did what the indictment alleged. Those claims can be "resolved without any need to venture beyond that record."

Nor do Class' claims focus upon case-related constitutional defects that "'occurred prior to the entry of the guilty plea.'" They could not, for example, "have been 'cured' through a new indictment by a properly selected grand jury." Because the defendant has admitted the charges against him, a guilty plea makes the latter kind of constitutional claim "irrelevant to the constitutional validity of the conviction." But the cases to which we have referred make clear that a defendant's guilty plea does not make irrelevant the kind of constitutional claim Class seeks to make.

In sum, the claims at issue here do not fall within any of the categories of claims that Class' plea agreement forbids him to raise on direct appeal. They challenge the Government's power to criminalize Class' (admitted) conduct. They thereby call into question the Government's power to "'constitutionally prosecute'" him. A guilty plea does not bar a direct appeal in these circumstances.

III

We are not convinced by the three basic arguments that the Government and the dissent make in reply.

First, the Government contends that by entering a guilty plea, Class inherently relinquished his constitutional claims. The Government is correct that a guilty plea does implicitly waive some claims, including some constitutional claims. However, as we explained in Part II, supra, Class' valid guilty plea does not, by itself, bar direct appeal of his constitutional claims in these circumstances.

As an initial matter, a valid guilty plea "forgoes not only a fair trial, but also other accompanying constitutional guarantees." While those "simultaneously" relinquished rights include the privilege against compulsory self-incrimination, the jury trial right, and the right to confront accusers, they do not include "a waiver of the privileges which exist beyond the confines

F. The Enforceability of Plea Agreements: Breach and Collateral Waivers 1055

of the trial." Here, Class' statutory right directly to appeal his conviction "cannot in any way be characterized as part of the trial."

A valid guilty plea also renders irrelevant—and thereby prevents the defendant from appealing—the constitutionality of case-related government conduct that takes place before the plea is entered. Neither can the defendant later complain that the indicting grand jury was unconstitutionally selected. But, as we have said, those kinds of claims are not at issue here.

Finally, a valid guilty plea relinquishes any claim that would contradict the "admissions necessarily made upon entry of a voluntary plea of guilty." But the constitutional claim at issue here is consistent with Class' admission that he engaged in the conduct alleged in the indictment. Unlike the defendants in *Broce*, Class' challenge does not in any way deny that he engaged in the conduct to which he admitted. Instead, like the defendants in *Blackledge* and *Menna*, he seeks to raise a claim which, "'judged on its face'" based upon the existing record, would extinguish the government's power to "'constitutionally prosecute'" the defendant if the claim were successful.

Second, the Government and the dissent point to Rule 11(a)(2) of the Federal Rules of Criminal Procedure, which governs "conditional" guilty pleas. The Rule states:

> Conditional Plea. With the consent of the court and the government, a defendant may enter a conditional plea of guilty or nolo contendere, reserving in writing the right to have an appellate court review an adverse determination of a specified pretrial motion. A defendant who prevails on appeal may then withdraw the plea.

The Government and the dissent argue that Rule 11(a)(2) means that "a defendant who pleads guilty cannot challenge his conviction on appeal on a forfeitable or waivable ground that he either failed to present to the district court or failed to reserve in writing." They support this argument by pointing to the notes of the Advisory Committee that drafted the text of Rule 11(a)(2). In particular, the dissent points to the suggestion that an unconditional guilty plea constitutes a waiver of "nonjurisdictional defects," while the Government points to the drafters' statement that they intended the Rule's "conditional plea procedure . . . to conserve prosecutorial and judicial resources and advance speedy trial objectives," while ensuring "much needed uniformity in the federal system on this matter. The Government adds that its interpretation of the Rule furthers these basic purposes. And, the argument goes, just as defendants must use Rule 11(a)(2)'s procedures to preserve, for instance, Fourth Amendment unlawful search-and-seizure claims, so must they use it to preserve the constitutional claims at issue here.

The problem with this argument is that, by its own terms, the Rule itself does not say whether it sets forth the exclusive procedure for a defendant to preserve a constitutional claim following a guilty plea. At the same time, the drafters' notes acknowledge that the "Supreme Court has held that certain kinds of constitutional objections may be raised after a plea of guilty." The notes then specifically refer to the "*Menna–Blackledge* doctrine." They add that the Rule "should not be interpreted as either broadening or narrowing [that] doctrine or as establishing procedures for its application." And the notes state that Rule 11(a)(2) "has no application" to the "kinds of constitutional objections" that may be raised under that doctrine. The applicability of the *Menna–Blackledge* doctrine is at issue in this case. We therefore hold that Rule 11(a)(2) cannot resolve this case.

Third, the Government argues that Class "expressly waived" his right to appeal his constitutional claim. The Government concedes that the written plea agreement, which sets forth the "Complete Agreement" between Class and the Government, does not contain this waiver. Rather, the Government relies on the fact that during the Rule 11 plea colloquy, the District Court Judge stated that, under the written plea agreement, Class was "giving up [his] right to appeal [his] conviction." *Id.*, at 76. And Class agreed.

We do not see why the District Court Judge's statement should bar Class' constitutional claims. It was made to ensure Class understood "the terms of any plea-agreement provision waiving the right to appeal or to collaterally attack the sentence." Fed. Rule Crim. Proc. 11(b)(1)(N). It does not expressly refer to a waiver of the appeal right here at issue. And if it is interpreted as expressly including that appeal right, it was wrong, as the Government acknowledged at oral argument. Under these circumstances, Class' acquiescence neither expressly nor implicitly waived his right to appeal his constitutional claims.

• • •

For these reasons, we hold that Rodney Class may pursue his constitutional claims on direct appeal. The contrary judgment of the Court of Appeals for the District of Columbia Circuit is reversed, and the case is remanded for further proceedings consistent with this opinion.

It is so ordered.

NOTES AND QUESTIONS

1. Note the difference between the waiver provisions in Class's plea agreement and those in the above cases. For one thing, the agreement did not require a collateral attack waiver, although this was likely due less to the DOJ's generosity than to the fact that Class was acting pro se when he pleaded guilty. For another thing, while some appellate rights were expressly waived, others were expressly preserved. As to others the agreement was silent. Accordingly, as the Court observes, "[t]he agreement said nothing about the right to raise on direct appeal a claim that the statute of conviction was unconstitutional." *Id.* at 177.

Would the inclusion of the sort of broad and general appellate waiver like the one in *Guillen* have barred Class's appeal?

Why do you think Class, a pro se litigant, was able to negotiate a plea agreement that was so lacking in finality as compared to the plea agreements DOJ normally insists on?

2. Is the Court's conclusion that Class's guilty plea does not "inherently" waive his right to challenge the state's power to prosecute persuasive as a matter of precedent? How about as a matter of logic? Is it essential that Class's challenge to the statute of conviction was constitutional? What if defendant had been indicted for mail fraud and argued that the conduct alleged in the indictment did not violate the mail fraud statute? If defendant ultimately pleaded guilty, and the agreement was silent on the subject, would the issue be preserved for appeal?

3. Shame on the government for not interceding to correct the trial court when it misdescribed the plea agreement during the plea colloquy with Class, stating that he was waiving all appeal rights, to which Class mistakenly agreed. HE WAS PRO SE! And an even deeper shame on the government for arguing on appeal that Class "expressly waived" his appellate right by such mistaken agreement. Did the AUSA have an ethical obligation to correct the trial court's mistake during the plea colloquy?

4. Note that the Court's description of the plea agreement's waivers appears to include a waiver of the "right to request or receive information concerning the investigation and prosecution about the case," which appears to be a reference to the Freedom of Information Act (FOIA). While the Court had made very clear that all constitutional rights are waivable, is there nonetheless an argument that a FOIA waiver should be analyzed differently?

Both the Court's mistaken description of the plea arrangement, and Class's confused acquiescence to it, shed light on the supposed sacred ritual of the Rule 11 colloquy. Here, the plea agreement included a very complex appellate waiver provision, including some appeals, excluding some appeals, and remaining silent on others. Yet the trial judge, perhaps reading off a boilerplate Rule 11 checklist, totally botched the description of the waiver. And Class, who apparently placed a high value on the constitutional issue he wanted to appeal, agreed with this mischaracterization. There is plenty of room for error in Rule 11 colloquies, and this case illustrates why the colloquies are worth exacting appellate scrutiny.

Judges are often less than vigilant in discharging their Rule 11 responsibilities. As Judge Rakoff has explained:

> In theory . . . the judge is supposed to question the defendant about the facts underlying his confession of guilt. But in practice, most judges, happy for reasons of their own to avoid a time-consuming trial, will hardly question the defendant beyond the bare bones of his assertion of guilt, relying instead on the prosecutor's statement (untested by any cross-examination) of what the underlying facts are.

Rakoff, Why Do Innocent People Plead Guilty and the Guilty Go Free, *supra* at 29-30.

Typically, the judge will simply ask the prosecutor to summarize the evidence that would be proven at trial, which will often be given in a cursory, narrative format without any inkling of how these facts would be proven or any weaknesses in the proof. After the prosecutor's statement, the defendant will simply be asked by the judge something to the effect of "do you agree?" And that's the factual basis. This is obviously a process that relies almost entirely on the integrity of prosecutors and the diligence and competence of defense counsel.

CHAPTER XII

DISCRIMINATORY ENFORCEMENT

This chapter looks at what the cases often call selective prosecution, the prosecution of persons based on impermissible considerations such as race or political viewpoint. Both parts of the term "selective prosecution" can be troublesome. First, the term "selective" can mislead inasmuch as the government action that is prohibited under the doctrine is more aptly called "discriminatory" prosecution. Indeed, one of the main Supreme Court cases on the subject unhelpfully condones some unidentified forms of "selectivity" in prosecutorial decision making. Second, the term "prosecution" can also be problematic. In its narrowest sense, prosecution can refer to the decisions prosecutors make as to who to prosecute; but the term "prosecution" can also, more broadly, include the investigation aspect of the process that may result in prosecution — that is, the actions of law enforcement agents and other executive officials in producing to the prosecutor persons, or a pool of persons, who are potential defendants. For convenience's sake this chapter will usually use the generic term "selective prosecution" unless a more nuanced usage is necessary in a particular context.

Indeed, in some contexts the terminology makes a difference. In a series of cases in the Seventh Circuit arising out of the employment of "fake stash house stings" by the Bureau of Alcohol, Tobacco, Firearms and Explosives (ATF), *see infra*, courts have considered whether the merits and discovery standards for "selective prosecution" claims differ depending on whether the allegedly impermissible selectivity is done by prosecutors or law enforcement agents. Arguably, greater deference is owed to prosecutors, whose decisions are often said to enjoy a "presumption of regularity," than to police and other law enforcement agents, whose actions are not cloaked with such a presumption and are not bound by the norms of legal ethics.

The chapter progresses largely chronologically. Section A considers *Yick Wo v. Hopkins*, the too-good-to-be-true case from the late nineteenth century that established a Platonic ideal of selective prosecution, and *Oyler v. Boles*, a case that — 80 years later — grudgingly confirmed that the prosecution of persons based on impermissible factors can be unconstitutional. Section B examines a series of lower court cases from the 1960s and 1970s that consider, and acknowledge the viability of, selective prosecution claims in the context of viewpoint discrimination. Section C examines two Supreme Court cases in which the Court, employing recently announced equal protection principles, significantly raised the bar for selective prosecution claims. Section D, parsing the difference between prosecution and investigation, examines cases where the alleged offensive discrimination took place entirely in the investigative stage of the case, including the remarkable and improbable 1961 case of *California v. Harris*.

Chapter XII Discriminatory Enforcement

A. DISCRIMINATORY PROSECUTION: THE PERFECTION OF *YICK WO V. HOPKINS*

Yick Wo v. Hopkins
118 U.S. 356 (1886)

These two cases were argued as one, and depend upon precisely the same state of facts; the first coming here upon a writ of error to the supreme court of the state of California, the second on appeal from the circuit court of the United States for that district.

The plaintiff in error, Yick Wo, on August 24, 1885, petitioned the supreme court of California for the writ of habeas corpus, alleging that he was illegally deprived of his personal liberty by the defendant as sheriff of the city and county of San Francisco. The sheriff made return to the writ that he held the petitioner in custody by virtue of a sentence of the police judge's court No. 2 of the city and county of San Francisco, whereby he was found guilty of a violation of certain ordinances of the board of supervisors of that county, and adjudged to pay a fine of $10, and, in default of payment, be imprisoned in the county jail at the rate of one day for each dollar of fine until said fine should be satisfied; and a commitment in consequence of non-payment of said fine.

The ordinances for the violation of which he had been found guilty are set out as follows:

Order No. 1,569, passed May 26, 1880, prescribing the kind of buildings in which laundries may be located.

The people of the city and county of San Francisco do ordain as follows:

Section 1. It shall be unlawful, from and after the passage of this order, for any person or persons to establish, maintain, or carry on a laundry, within the corporate limits of the city and county of San Francisco, without having first obtained the consent of the board of supervisors, except the same be located in a building constructed either of brick or stone.

Sec. 2. It shall be unlawful for any person to erect, build, or maintain, or cause to be erected, built, or maintained, over or upon the roof of any building now erected, or which may hereafter be erected, within the limits of said city and county, any scaffolding, without first obtaining the written permission of the board of supervisors, which permit shall state fully for what purpose said scaffolding is to be erected and used, and such scaffolding shall not be used for any other purpose than that designated in such permit.

Sec. 3. Any person who shall violate any of the provisions of this order shall be deemed guilty of a misdemeanor, and upon conviction thereof shall be punished by a fine of not more than one thousand dollars, or by imprisonment in the county jail not more than six months, or by both such fine and imprisonment.

Order No. 1,587, passed July 28, 1880, the following section:

Sec. 68. It shall be unlawful, from and after the passage of this order, for any person or persons to establish, maintain, or carry on a laundry within the corporate limits of the city and county of San Francisco without having first obtained the consent of the board of supervisors, except the same be located in a building constructed either of brick or stone

The following facts are also admitted on the record: That petitioner is a native of China, and came to California in 1861, and is still a subject of the emperor of China; that he has been engaged in the laundry business in the same premises and building for 22 years last past; that he had a license from the board of fire-wardens, dated March 3, 1884, from which it appeared "that the above-described premises have been inspected by the board of fire-wardens, and upon such inspection said board found all proper arrangements for carrying on the business; that the stoves, washing and drying apparatus, and the appliances for heating smoothing-irons, are in good condition, and that their use is not dangerous to the surrounding property from fire, and that all proper precautions have been taken to comply with the provisions of order No. 1,617, defining 'the fire limits of the city and county of San Francisco, and making regulations concerning the erection and use of buildings in said city and county,' and of order No. 1,670, 'prohibiting the kindling, maintenance, and use of open fires in houses;' that he had a certificate from the health officer that the same premises had been inspected by him, and that he found that they were properly and sufficiently drained, and that all proper arrangements for carrying on the business of a laundry, without injury to the sanitary condition of the neighborhood, had been complied with; that the city license of the petitioner was in force, and expired October 1, 1885; and that the petitioner applied to the board of supervisors, June 1, 1885, for consent of said board to maintain and carry on his laundry, but that said board, on July 1, 1885, refused said consent." It is also admitted to be true, as alleged in the petition, that on February 24, 1880, "there were about 320 laundries in the city and county of San Francisco, of which about 240 were owned and conducted by subjects of China, and of the whole number, viz., 320, about 310 were constructed of wood, the same material that constitutes nine tenths of the houses in the city of San Francisco. The capital thus invested by the subjects of China was not less than two hundred thousand dollars, and they paid annually for rent, license, taxes, gas, and water about one hundred and eighty thousand dollars." It is alleged in the petition that "your petitioner, and more than one hundred and fifty of his countrymen, have been arrested upon the charge of carrying on business without having such special consent, while those who are not subjects of China, and who are conducting eighty odd laundries under similar conditions, are left unmolested, and free to enjoy the enhanced trade and profits arising from this hurtful and unfair discrimination. The business of your petitioners, and of those of his countrymen similarly situated, is greatly impaired, and in many cases practically ruined, by this system of oppression to one kind of men, and favoritism to all others."

The statement therein contained as to the arrest, etc., is admitted to be true, with the qualification only that the 80-odd laundries referred to are in wooden buildings without scaffolds on the roofs. It is also admitted "that petitioner and 200 of his countrymen similarly situated petitioned the board of supervisors for permission to continue their business in the various houses which they had been occupying and using for laundries for more than twenty years, and such petitions were denied, and all the petitions of those who were not Chinese, with one exception of Mrs. Mary Meagles, were granted."

MATTHEWS, J.

In the case of the petitioner, brought here by writ of error to the supreme court of California, our jurisdiction is limited to the question whether the plaintiff in error has been denied a right in violation of the constitution, laws, or treaties of the United States. The question whether his imprisonment is illegal, under the constitution and laws of the state, is not open to us. And although that question might have been considered in the circuit court in the application made to it, and by this court on appeal from its order, yet judicial propriety is best consulted by accepting the judgment of the state court upon the points involved in that inquiry. That, however, does not preclude this court from putting upon the ordinances of the supervisors of the county and city of San Francisco an independent construction; for the determination of the question whether the proceedings under these ordinances, and in enforcement of them, are in conflict with the constitution and laws of the United States, necessarily involves the meaning of the ordinances, which, for that purpose, we are required to ascertain and adjudge.

We are consequently constrained, at the outset, to differ from the supreme court of California upon the real meaning of the ordinances in question. That court considered these ordinances as vesting in the board of supervisors a not unusual discretion in granting or withholding their assent to the use of wooden buildings as laundries, to be exercised in reference to the circumstances of each case, with a view to the protection of the public against the dangers of fire. We are not able to concur in that interpretation of the power conferred upon the supervisors. There is nothing in the ordinances which points to such a regulation of the business of keeping and conducting laundries. They seem intended to confer, and actually to confer, not a discretion to be exercised upon a consideration of the circumstances of each case, but a naked and arbitrary power to give or withhold consent, not only as to places, but as to persons; so that, if an applicant for such consent, being in every way a competent and qualified person, and having complied with every reasonable condition demanded by any public interest, should, failing to obtain the requisite consent of the supervisors to the prosecution of his business, apply for redress by the judicial process of mandamus to require the supervisors to consider and act upon his case, it would be a sufficient answer for them to say that the law had conferred upon them authority to withhold their assent, without reason and without responsibility. The power given to them is not confided to their discretion in the legal sense of that term, but is granted to their mere will. It is purely arbitrary, and acknowledges neither guidance nor restraint.

This erroneous view of the ordinances in question led the supreme court of California into the further error of holding that they were justified by the decisions of this court in the cases of *Barbier v. Connelly* and *Soon Hing v. Crowley*. In both of these cases the ordinance involved was simply a prohibition to carry on the washing and ironing of clothes in public laundries and wash houses, within certain prescribed limits of the city and county of San Francisco, from 10 o'clock at night until 6 o'clock in the morning of the following day. This provision was held to be purely a police regulation, within the competency of any municipality possessed of the ordinary powers belonging to such bodies, — a necessary measure of precaution in a city composed largely of wooden buildings, like San Francisco, in the application of which there was no invidious discrimination against any one within the prescribed limits; all persons engaged in the same business being treated alike, and subject to the same restrictions, and entitled to the same privileges, under similar conditions. For these reasons that ordinance was adjudged not to be within the prohibitions of the fourteenth amendment to the constitution of the United States, which, it was said in the first case cited, "undoubtedly intended, not only that there should be no arbitrary deprivation of life or liberty, or arbitrary spoliation of property, but that equal protection and security should be given to all under like circumstances in the enjoyment of their personal and civil rights; that all persons should be equally entitled to pursue their happiness, and acquire and enjoy property; that they should have like access to the courts of the country for the protection of their persons and property, the prevention and redress of wrongs, and the enforcement of contracts; that no impediment should be interposed to the pursuits of any one, except as applied to the same pursuits by others under like circumstances; that no greater burdens should be laid upon one than are laid upon others in the same calling and condition; and that, in the administration of criminal justice, no different or higher punishment should be imposed upon one than such as is prescribed to all for like offenses. . . . Class legislation, discriminating against some and favoring others, is prohibited; but legislation which, in carrying out a public purpose, is limited in its application, if, within the sphere of its operation, it affects alike all persons similarly situated, is not within the amendment."

The ordinance drawn in question in the present case is of a very different character. It does not prescribe a rule and conditions, for the regulation of the use of property for laundry purposes, to which all similarly situated may conform. It allows, without restriction, the use for such purposes of buildings of brick or stone; but, as to wooden buildings, constituting nearly all those in previous use, it divides the owners or occupiers into two classes, not having respect to their personal character and qualifications for the business, nor the situation and nature and adaptation of the buildings themselves, but merely by an arbitrary line, on one side of which are those who are permitted to pursue their industry by the mere will and consent of the supervisors, and on the other those from whom that consent is withheld, at their mere will and pleasure. And both classes are alike only in this: that they are tenants at will, under the supervisors, of their means of living. The ordinance, therefore, also differs from the not unusual case where discretion is lodged by law in public officers or bodies to grant or withhold licenses to keep taverns, or places for the sale of spirituous liquors, and the like, when one of the conditions is that the applicant shall be a fit person for the exercise of the privilege, because in such cases the fact of fitness is submitted to the judgment of the officer, and calls for the exercise of a discretion of a judicial nature.

The rights of the petitioners, as affected by the proceedings of which they complain, are not less because they are aliens and subjects of the emperor of China. By the third article of the treaty between this government and that of China, concluded November 17, 1880 (22 St. 827), it is stipulated: "If Chinese laborers, or Chinese of any other class, now either permanently or temporarily residing in the territory of the United States, meet with ill treatment at the hands of any other persons, the government of the United States will exert all its powers to devise measures for their protection, and to secure to them the same rights, privileges, immunities, and exemptions as may be enjoyed by the citizens or subjects of the most favored nation, and to which they are entitled by treaty." The fourteenth amendment to the constitution is not confined to the protection of citizens. It says: "Nor shall any state deprive any person of life, liberty, or property without due process of law; nor deny to any person within its jurisdiction the equal protection of the laws." These provisions are universal in their application, to all persons within the territorial jurisdiction, without regard to any differences of race, of color, or of nationality; and the equal protection of the laws is a pledge of the protection of equal laws. It is accordingly enacted by section 1977 of the Revised Statutes that "all persons within the jurisdiction of the United States shall have the same right, in every state and territory, to make and enforce contracts, to sue, be parties, give evidence, and to the full and equal benefit of all laws and proceedings for the security of persons and property as is enjoyed by white citizens, and shall be subject to like punishment, pains, penalties, taxes, licenses, and exactions of every kind, and to no other." The questions we have to consider and decide in these cases, therefore, are to be treated as involving the rights of every citizen of the United States equally with those of the strangers and aliens who now invoke the jurisdiction of the court.

It is contended on the part of the petitioners that the ordinances for violations of which they are severally sentenced to imprisonment are void on their face, as being within the prohibitions of the fourteenth amendment, and, in the alternative, if not so, that they are void by reason of their administration, operating unequally, so as to punish in the present petitioners what is permitted to others as lawful, without any distinction of circumstances, — an unjust and illegal discrimination, it is claimed, which, though not made expressly by the ordinances, is made possible by them.

When we consider the nature and the theory of our institutions of government, the principles upon which they are supposed to rest, and review the history of their development, we are constrained to conclude that they do not mean to leave room for the play and action of purely personal and arbitrary power. Sovereignty itself is, of course, not subject to law, for it is the author and source of law; but in our system, while sovereign powers are delegated to the agencies of government, sovereignty itself remains with the people, by whom and for whom all government exists and acts. And the law is the definition and limitation of power. It is, indeed, quite true that there must always be lodged somewhere, and in some person or body, the authority of final decision; and in many cases of mere administration, the responsibility is purely political, no appeal lying except to the ultimate tribunal of the public judgment, exercised either in the pressure of opinion, or by means of the suffrage. But the fundamental rights to life, liberty, and the pursuit of happiness, considered as individual possessions, are secured by those maxims of constitutional law which are the monuments showing the victorious progress of the race in securing to men the blessings of civilization under the reign of just and equal laws, so that, in the famous language of the Massachusetts bill of rights, the government of the commonwealth "may be a government of laws and not of men." For the very idea that one man may be compelled to hold his life, or the means of living, or any material right essential to the enjoyment of life, at the mere will of another, seems to be intolerable in any country where freedom prevails, as being the essence of slavery itself.

• • •

In the present cases, we are not obliged to reason from the probable to the actual, and pass upon the validity of the ordinances complained of, as tried merely by the opportunities which their terms afford, of unequal and unjust discrimination in their administration; for the cases present the ordinances in actual operation, and the facts shown establish an administration directed so exclusively against a particular class of persons as to warrant and require the conclusion that, whatever may have been the intent of the ordinances as adopted, they are applied by the public authorities charged with their administration, and thus representing the state itself, with a mind so unequal and oppressive as to amount to a practical denial by the state of that equal protection of the laws which is secured to the petitioners, as to all other persons, by the broad and benign provisions of the fourteenth amendment to the constitution of the United States. Though the law itself be fair on its face, and impartial in appearance, yet, if it is applied and administered by public authority with an evil eye and an unequal hand, so as practically to make unjust and illegal discriminations between persons in similar circumstances, material to their rights, the denial of equal justice is still within the prohibition of the constitution. This principle of interpretation has been sanctioned by this court.

The present cases, as shown by the facts disclosed in the record, are within this class. It appears that both petitioners have complied with every requisite deemed by the law, or by the public officers charged with its administration, necessary for the protection of neighboring property from fire, or as a precaution against injury to the public health. No reason whatever, except the will of the supervisors, is assigned why they should not be permitted to carry on, in the accustomed manner, their harmless and useful occupation, on which they depend for a livelihood; and while this consent of the supervisors is withheld from them, and from 200 others who have also petitioned, all of whom happen to be Chinese subjects, 80 others, not Chinese subjects, are permitted to carry on the same business under similar conditions. The fact of this discrimination is admitted. No reason for it is shown, and the conclusion cannot be resisted that no reason for it exists except hostility to the race and nationality to which the petitioners belong, and which, in the eye of the law, is not justified. The discrimination is therefore illegal, and the public administration which enforces it is a denial of the equal protection of the laws, and a violation of the fourteenth amendment of the constitution. The imprisonment of the petitioners is therefore illegal, and they must be discharged. To this end the judgment of the supreme court of California in the Case of Yick Wo, and that of the circuit court of the United States for the district of California in the Case of Wo Lee, are severally reversed, and the cases remanded, each to the proper court, with directions to discharge the petitioners from custody and imprisonment.

NOTES AND QUESTIONS

1. *Yick Wo* is an almost perfect case: facts that seem like they must have been made up; an exhaustive factual record, apparently compiled without any formal right to "discovery," and belying the saw that such records will normally be only in the government's possession; and further, a chorus of truth that is quoted with a fidelity and regularity similar to Justice Sutherland's passage on the right to counsel in *Powell v. Alabama*:

> Though the law itself be fair on its face, and impartial in appearance, yet, if it is applied and administered by public authority with an evil eye and an unequal hand, so as practically to make unjust and illegal discriminations between persons in similar circumstances, material to their rights, the denial of equal justice is still within the prohibition of the constitution.

Id. at 373-74.

2. *Yick Wo* is often characterized as a landmark case insofar as it recognized an equal protection right against "selective prosecution." *See, e.g.,* Richard H. McAdams, *Race and Selective Prosecution: Discovering the Pitfalls of* Armstrong, 73 Chi.-Kent L. Rev. 605, 615 (1998) (referring to "the pathbreaking nineteenth-century equal protection case"). At the risk of indulging in semantics, is that characterization technically accurate? What was selective about the *prosecution* of Yick Wo?

3. The administration of the ordinance at issue in *Yick Wo* was just one manifestation of decades of legally sanctioned racism against Chinese immigrants in the nineteenth century. *See generally* Charles McClain, In Search of Equality: The Chinese Struggle Against Discrimination in Nineteenth-Century America (1994). During the nineteenth century and into the twentieth century, there was substantial litigation in state and federal court over racial issues regarding the Chinese, and the Supreme Court was by no means a consistent ally of the Chinese immigrants. *See* Marie A. Failinger, Yick Wo *at 125: Four Simple Lessons for the Contemporary Supreme Court*, 17 Mich. J. Race & L. 217, 252-53 (2012).

4. To cite one important example from 20 years after *Yick Wo*, in *Ah Sin v. Whitman*, 198 U.S. 500 (1905), the Court rejected a challenge to the City of San Francisco's execution of police raids that "solely and exclusively" targeted Chinese gambling houses but not white-run gambling houses. The Court held such allegations were insufficient to establish a claim where there was no allegation or proof that gambling "did not exist exclusively among the Chinese, or that there were other offenders against whom it was not enforced." *Id.* at 507-08.

How would a factual record establishing this necessary predicate—that white gambling houses existed yet were ignored by the police—be created without the ability to get some discovery from the government?

Yick Wo's influence was hardly instantaneous. It was not until 1944 that the Supreme Court held that the principle of *Yick Wo* was generally applicable in the context of discriminatory state civil regulation. *Snowden v. Hughes*, 321 U.S. 1, 11 (1944). And it was not until 18 years after that that the Warren Court found *Yick Wo* applicable, without much enthusiasm, in a challenge to a criminal statute in *Oyler v. Boles*, 386 U.S. 448 (1962).

The eponymous Yick Wo Elementary School in San Francisco serves the neighborhoods of North Beach, Chinatown, and Russian Hill.

Chapter XII Discriminatory Enforcement

Oyler v. Boles
368 U.S. 448 (1962)

Mr. Justice CLARK delivered the opinion of the Court.

The petitioners in these consolidated cases are serving life sentences imposed under West Virginia's habitual criminal statute. This Act provides for a mandatory life sentence upon the third conviction "of a crime punishable by confinement in a penitentiary." The increased penalty is to be invoked by an information filed by the prosecuting attorney "immediately upon conviction and before sentence." Alleging that this Act had been applied without advance notice and to only a minority of those subject to its provisions, in violation respectively of the Due Process and Equal Protection Clauses of the Fourteenth Amendment, the petitioners filed separate petitions for writs of habeas corpus in the Supreme Court of Appeals of West Virginia. Both of their petitions were denied without opinion. Unlike *Chewning v. Cunningham,* here each of the petitioners was represented by counsel at the time he was sentenced. Finding the cases representative of the many recidivist cases that have been docketed in this Court the past few Terms, we granted certiorari. We now affirm the judgment in each case.

William Oyler, the petitioner in No. 56, was convicted of murder in the second degree on February 5, 1953, which offense carried a penalty of from 5 to 18 years' imprisonment. Sentence was deferred, and on February 11 his motion for a new trial was overruled. On that same date the Prosecuting Attorney requested and was granted leave to file an information in writing alleging that Oyler was the same person who had suffered three prior convictions in Pennsylvania which were punishable by confinement in a penitentiary. After being cautioned as to the effect of such information, Oyler, accompanied by his counsel, acknowledged in open court that he was the person named in the information. The court then determined that the defendant had thrice been convicted of crimes punishable by confinement in a penitentiary and sentenced him to life imprisonment. In so doing the court indicated that the life sentence was mandatory under the statute and recommended that Oyler be paroled as soon as he was eligible. In 1960 Oyler filed a habeas corpus application in the Supreme Court of Appeals alleging a denial of due process under the Fourteenth Amendment in that he had not been given advance notice of his prosecution as a recidivist which prevented him from showing the inapplicability of the habitual criminal law. The statute was alleged to be inapplicable because he had never been sentenced to imprisonment in a penitentiary although he had been convicted of crimes subjecting him to the possibility of such sentence. He also attacked his sentence on the equal protection ground previously set forth.

In 1957 Paul Crabtree, the petitioner in No. 57, pleaded guilty to forging a $35 check, which offense carried a penalty of from 2 to 10 years' imprisonment. Sentence was deferred, and a week later the Prosecuting Attorney informed the court that Crabtree had suffered two previous felony convictions, one in the State of Washington and one in West Virginia. The trial judge, after cautioning Crabtree of the effect of the information and his rights under it, inquired if he was in fact the accused person. Crabtree, who had been represented by counsel throughout, admitted in open court that he was such person. Upon this admission and the accused's further statement that he had nothing more to say, the court proceeded to sentence him to life imprisonment. In 1960 Crabtree sought habeas corpus relief in the Supreme Court of Appeals claiming denial of due process because of the absence of notice which prevented him from showing he had never been convicted in Walla Walla County, Washington, as had been alleged in the information. Like Oyler, he also raised the equal protection ground.

• • •

II

Petitioners also claim they were denied the equal protection of law guaranteed by the Fourteenth Amendment. In his petition for a writ of habeas corpus to the Supreme Court of Appeals of West Virginia, Oyler stated:

> Petitioner was discriminated against as an Habitual Criminal in that from January, 1940, to June, 1955, there were six men sentenced in the Taylor County Circuit Court who were subject to prosecution as Habitual offenders, Petitioner was the only man thus sentenced during this period. It is a matter of record that the five men who were not prosecuted as Habitual Criminals during this period, all had three or more felony convictions and sentences as adults, and Petitioner's former convictions were a result of Juvenile Court actions.
>
> The Petitioner was discriminated against by selective use of a mandatory State Statute, in that 904 men who were known offenders throughout the State of West Virginia were not sentenced as required by the mandatory Statutes, Chapter 61, Article 11, Sections 18 and 19 of the Code. Equal Protection and Equal Justice was (sic) denied.

Statistical data based on prison records were appended to the petition to support the latter allegation. Crabtree in his petition included similar statistical support and alleged:

> The said Statute are (sic) administered and applied in such a manner as to be in violation of Equal Protection and Equal Justice therefor in conflict with the Fourteenth Amendment to the Constitution of the United States.

Thus petitioners' contention is that the habitual criminal statute imposes a mandatory duty on the prosecuting authorities to seek the severer penalty against all persons coming within the statutory standards but that it is done only in a minority of cases. This, petitioners argue, denies equal protection to those persons against whom the heavier penalty is enforced. We note that it is not stated whether the failure to proceed against other three-time offenders was due to lack of knowledge of the prior offenses on the part of the prosecutors or was the result of a deliberate policy of proceeding only in a certain class of cases or against specific persons. The statistics merely show that according to penitentiary records a high percentage of those subject to the law have not been proceeded against. There is no indication that these records of previous convictions, which may not have been compiled until after the three-time offenders had reached the penitentiary, were available to the prosecutors. Hence the allegations set out no more than a failure to prosecute others because of a lack of knowledge of their prior offenses. This does not deny equal protection due petitioners under the Fourteenth Amendment.

Moreover, the conscious exercise of some selectivity in enforcement is not in itself a federal constitutional violation. Even though the statistics in this case might imply a policy of selective enforcement, it was not stated that the selection was deliberately based upon an unjustifiable standard such as race, religion, or other arbitrary classification. Therefore grounds supporting a finding of a denial of equal protection were not alleged. *Snowden v. Hughes* (1944).

Affirmed.

NOTES AND QUESTIONS

1. The factual basis for Oyler's claim, though perhaps conceptually flawed, is impressively documented: prison records showing that 904 prisoners had not been sentenced, as Oyler had been, to mandatory life sentences as required by the West Virginia habitual offender statute. How do you think it was possible for Oyler to create this factual record? Does the Court accept the truth of Oyler's evidence?

1068 Chapter XII Discriminatory Enforcement

Is it really plausible, as the Court finds, and finds significant, that the prosecution might not have had knowledge of the prior convictions of these other potential habitual offenders at the time of the offense that brought them within the scope of the habitual offender statute?

Should state life imprisonment sentences really depend on whether a defendant's criminal record was accurately maintained and readily accessible to prosecutors, perhaps prosecutors (as here) in another jurisdiction?

2. Is it fair to characterize Oyler's argument as the Court does, namely, "that the habitual criminal statute imposes a mandatory duty on the prosecuting authorities to seek the severer penalty against all persons coming within the statutory standards"? What is a better way to describe the claim that Oyler is making?

3. The Court implies that the case might have come out differently had there been evidence of selectivity "based upon an unjustifiable standard such as race, religion or other arbitrary classification."

4. What sort of "arbitrary classification"—as opposed to a classification based on race or religion—would run afoul of the Equal Protection Clause in this context?

5. What do you make of the Court's comment that "the conscious exercise of some selectivity in enforcement is not in itself a federal constitutional violation"? What examples of benign or permissible selectivity in identifying targets for prosecution come to mind? Bear in mind that the author of the opinion, Justice Thomas Clark, was an experienced state and federal prosecutor and served as U.S. attorney general from 1945 to 1949.

For example, would it be permissible for a court to "select" someone for prosecution based on the fact that the person had a substantial criminal record?

How about because the person was a well-known public figure and the prosecution would be widely publicized, thereby increasing the deterrent effect of the prosecution?

B. LOWER COURTS AND SELECTIVE PROSECUTION CLAIMS

After *Oyler*, several lower courts in the 1960s and 1970s showed some receptivity to selective prosecution claims based on *Oyler* and/or on *Yick Wo. Robinson* was the first of these.

United States v. Robinson
311 F. Supp. 1063 (W.D. Mo. 1969)

BECKER, Chief Judge.

In this criminal action, a private detective was convicted of an obviously illegal wiretap (interception and divulgence) of telephone calls of an unfaithful wife of a client of defendant.

In the information filed herein on July 12, 1966, the defendant, a private investigator, was charged in 12 counts with 12 separate violations of Section 2, Title 18, U.S.C., and Sections 501 and 605, Title 47, U.S.C. (Prior to trial only private persons have been prosecuted for violations of these statutes.) The separate counts charged 12 acts of intercepting (by wire tap) and divulging of the communications intercepted thereby. The communications alleged to have been intercepted and divulged were telephone conversations all between one Saundra Jane Lloyd at one end of the line and Eugene G. Peterson, L. E. Shepard, Bessie, Koller, Stephen, J. Pratt, and Alfred E. Couch on the other end. Defendant plead not guilty to all counts on July 25, 1966. On April 3, 1967, Counts II, IV, X and XIII of the information were dismissed by the Government pursuant to Rule 48(a), F. R. Crim. P. Counts III, IX and XI were subsequently dismissed under the same rule on April 5, 1967. Trial by jury was subsequently had in this Court. On April 7, 1967, the jury under the instructions properly returned verdicts of guilty on Counts I, V, VII and VIII and a verdict of not guilty on Count VI.

The defendant's counsel attempted to submit to the jury the defense of unconstitutional systematic discrimination against private person in enforcement of the statutes but was not permitted to do so. With leave of Court the question, which may have been waived under Rule 12, F. R. Crim. P., was permitted by the Court to be reserved as a ground for a motion for judgment of acquittal.

Thereafter, the defendant filed a motion for judgment of acquittal under Rule 29(c), F. R. Crim. P., or in the alternative, for a new trial under Rule 33, with respect to the counts on which verdicts of guilty had been returned.

Except for denial of the motion for acquittal there was no error in the trial. So the motion for new trial should be denied.

The acts charged in the counts upon which defendant was found guilty by the jury were alleged in the information to have taken place on August 16, 1964; August 17, 1964; and August 18, 1964. Much documentary evidence has been adduced by defendant on his motion for acquittal or for new trial to show that, during this time, and before and after, the Government itself, while it was not explicitly exempt itself from the operation of the statute, engaged in its systematic violation. This evidence proves that at least from May 21, 1940, when wire tapping was advised by President Franklin D. Roosevelt in a message to Attorney General Jackson as an acceptable method of protecting the national security (See Long, The Intruders (Praeger Publications, 1967) at page 89), through the time in question here, the agencies of the federal government did in fact engage in extensive wire tapping activities in violation of Sections 605 and 501, which come within the prohibition of the same statutes under which the defendant in the case at bar has been charged. These activities have continued right up to the time of the alleged offense in the case at bar. *See Katz v. United States; Alderman v. United States; Desist v. United States;* and *Olmstead v. United States.* In *Alderman v. United States*, the Supreme Court of the United States held that a defendant may require production by the Government of transcripts of any illegal electronic surveillance or wire taps of his conversations, or those of people on his premises. The Government was thus obliged to yield records of FBI surveillance of James Hoffa, Cassius Clay, Martin Luther King, Jr., and Elijah Muhammad, among many others. The abundance of other materials which tend to prove the systematic violation by the Government of the wire tapping statute is great. The necessary conclusion from this evidence is that there has been systematic discrimination in the enforcement of the act against the defendant in this case, which renders the prosecution invalid. As Professor Moreland has said in his work cited above:

> I do not feel that the Department of Justice can, in good conscience, prosecute persons for a practice engaged in by the Department itself and regarded as legal by the Department.

Further, the American Bar Association Project on Minimum Standards for Criminal Justice noted in its Standards Relating to Electronic Surveillance (Tentative Draft, June 1968) at 18, n. 30:

> No prosecution, however, has ever been brought under the statute, and no public justification has been offered why the past and present practice of the United States Department of Justice is not in violation of the statute.

Although an act or statute may be valid on its face, intentional discriminatory enforcement thereof can render its discriminatory enforcement constitutionally invalid. In *Yick Wo v. Hopkins*, the United States Supreme Court held:

> Though the law itself be fair on its face, and impartial in appearance, yet, if it is applied and administered by public authority with an . . . unequal hand, so as practically to make unjust and illegal discriminations between persons in similar circumstances, material to their rights, the denial of equal justice is still within the prohibition of the constitution.

The similarity of circumstances of the interception and divulgence by defendant and the Government in wire tapping operations are readily apparent. While the Government attempts to justify its wire tapping operations in the paramount interests of public safety and on an unsound definition of "divulgence," the statute in question contains no such exceptions. Thus, no reasonable basis for systematic discriminatory enforcement of the statute can be found. Nor does the use by the Government of electronic microphones which do not penetrate the wire or property of others differentiate its activity from that of the defendant in contemplation of law. While it has been formerly held that a microphonic device did not constitute "interception" within the terms of § 605, the idea that a device does not "intercept" simply because it does not penetrate the communications medium has been discredited by the United States Supreme Court decision in *Katz*. While that case defined "protected persons" for Fourteenth Amendment purposes, it is apparent that, in the context of this case, the purposes of the Fourth Amendment and those of § 605 are much the same. As the court stated in *Katz*, "the Government's activities in electronically listening to and recording the petitioner's words violated the privacy upon which he justifiably relied while using the telephone booth." Similarly, "the purpose of section 605 is to prohibit blatant public or private encroachments on the privacy of messages and the integrity of the communications system." In *Katz*, the Government relied on the district court decision in *Borgese* to support its contention that a microphone attached to a telephone booth did not violate this purpose. The Supreme Court held that attached microphone methods of interception were in law no different from interception by actual penetration into the line of communication. Thus, there can be no rational distinction between the activity of the Government and that of the defendant in the case at bar. Therefore, the application of the statutes here involved to the defendant in the case at bar represented a systematic fixed and continuous policy of unjust discrimination in their enforcement in violation of the Fifth Amendment to the Constitution of the United States.

Moreover, there is no showing that the Government during the relevant period refrained from penetration and cutting of wires to effect taps.

For the foregoing reasons, it is

Ordered that defendant's motion for acquittal under Rule 29(c), F. R. Crim. P., be, and the same is hereby, granted.

NOTES AND QUESTIONS

1. It's hard not to love the implicit chutzpah of the premise of Robinson's claim: that a private detective illegally tapping the phones of his client's allegedly unfaithful wife is "similarly situated" to FBI agents illegally tapping phones in the service (supposedly) of national security.

2. Note that Robinson's attorney sought to litigate his selective prosecution claim before the jury, as opposed to the court in a pretrial motion. At the time there was no clear-cut procedure for bringing any type of pretrial challenge to a prosecution or indictment. The 1974 Amendments to Fed. R. Crim. P. 12 added a requirement that certain motions must be made before trial, including "selective or vindictive prosecution." Fed. R. Crim. P. 12 (b)(3)(A)(iv).

Strategically, why do you think Robinson's lawyer would have preferred litigation of the issue to the jury? Would there also have been advantages to submitting the issue to the court?

3. Note that the district court does not cite *Oyler* as support for a selective prosecution claim but goes directly to *Yick Wo*. How could Robinson have framed his "selectivity" claim based on the "arbitrary classification" formulation set forth in *Oyler*? Is a distinction between private persons and law enforcement agents an "arbitrary classification"? Put differently, chutzpah aside, are the law enforcement agents whose illegal wiretapping was uncovered in the case law Robinson cites "similarly situated" to Robinson? Are there reasons why the government would have preferred not to have to defend against a selective prosecution claim on these facts?

4. Professor Moreland, cited by the district court, describes the problem with the prosecution of private persons for conduct engaged in by federal agents as an issue of "good conscience" as opposed to an issue of equal protection.

What kind of a legal defense might be fashioned based on the government's taking a position that it cannot take "in good conscience"?

5. *Robinson* was distinguished by another federal district court in *United States v. Perkins*, 383 F. Supp. 922 (N.D. Ohio 1974), due to the intervening enactment of the Omnibus Crime Control Act of 1968, a federal statute that for the first time authorized and heavily regulated wiretapping by the government. The district court found that the enactment of this statute "removed the taint which affected the *Robinson* case."

The district court in *Perkins* went on to give a full-throated endorsement of prosecutors' virtually unreviewable power over criminal charges, citing and quoting from *United States v. Cox*, 342 F.2d 167

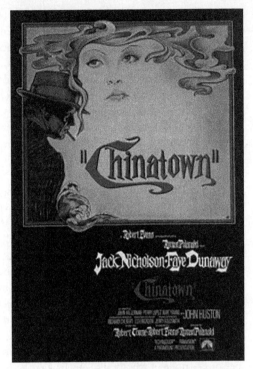

In the 1974 movie *Chinatown*, the private investigator Jake Gittes, played by Jack Nicholson, like the defendant in *United States v. Robinson*, earned a living unearthing the infidelity of his clients' spouses.

(5th Cir. 1965), *see* Chapter VII *supra*, where the Fifth Circuit headed off district judge Harold Cox's attempt to manipulate the grand jury into an indictment the Department of Justice opposed:

> The discretionary power of the attorney for the United States in determining whether a prosecution shall be commenced or maintained may well depend upon matters of policy wholly apart from any question of probable cause. Although as a member of the bar, the attorney for the United States is an officer of the court, he is nevertheless an executive official of the Government, and it is as an officer of the executive department that he exercises a discretion as to whether or not there shall be a prosecution in a particular case. It follows, as an incident of the constitutional separation of powers, that the courts are not to interfere with the free exercise of the discretionary powers of the attorneys of the United States in their control over criminal prosecutions.

Id. at 171. *Cox*, as you will recall, dealt specifically with the question whether the grand jury had an independent right to bring criminal charges that the Department of Justice did not approve of. Does the district court in *Perkins* read *Cox* too broadly? Are there circumstances where a court may "interfere" with the free exercise of the discretionary powers of federal prosecutors?

In the early 1970s three circuit courts of appeals addressed potential selective prosecution claims based on a defendant's expression of an antigovernment viewpoint, two involving

Chapter XII Discriminatory Enforcement

antiwar protesters and one involving an anti-census protester. In the first case of this "trilogy," *United States v. Crowthers*, 456 F.2d 1074 (4th Cir. 1972), defendants held what they called "masses for peace" on the Pentagon concourse, a publicly accessible outdoor space on the Pentagon grounds where other political and religious ceremonies had been held in the past. Defendants were charged criminally under federal regulations prohibiting "disorderly conduct" on the property. Their convictions were reversed, as the court found — based in part on evidence of equal or greater "disorderliness" at other events — that the regulations were "selectively and discriminatorily enforced" against defendants based on their expression of an "unpopular viewpoint." As in *Robinson*, the Court cited *Yick Wo* but not *Oyler* as authority for the equal protection point.

The second case in the trilogy was *United States v. Steele*, 461 F.2d 1148 (9th Cir. 1972), where the defendant was charged with violating a federal statute that criminalized the failure to provide information to census takers. The lawyering by Steele's counsel was superb. The government called a senior local census official in its case-in-chief. In cross-examination of this official, Steele's lawyer was able to establish almost his entire case: (1) that only four people in the state (Hawaii) had been prosecuted under this statute; (2) all four were "hard core [census] resisters," who were active in encouraging others to not comply with the census for privacy reasons; (3) that the census official had compiled background dossiers on the four resisters, a procedure that he had not followed with any of the other, numerous, offenders; and (4) that the official's organization had been "very concerned" about the census resistance movement.

As to the existence of persons similarly situated, Steele presented evidence of six other persons — none of whom, like Steele, were active, vocal anti-census "resisters" — who had also refused to cooperate with the census takers but were not prosecuted. Although it did not use the term "prima facie case," the court found that Steele's showing required the government to produce some valid explanation for its selection of the particular defendants, even if the selection was just random, which the government could not or would not do. Accordingly, the convictions were reversed.

Is *Steele* a case of selective prosecution or selective enforcement? Does *Steele* shed light on why the government routinely opposes having to produce witnesses to testify about its decisions as to what cases should be prosecuted, or what cases investigators should refer for prosecution?

The third case in the trilogy is *United States v. Falk*, 479 F.2d 616 (7th Cir. 1974) (en banc), another case involving alleged discrimination based upon defendant's expression of an antiwar viewpoint.

United States v. Falk
479 F.2d 616 (7th Cir. 1974) (en banc)

SPRECHER, Circuit Judge.

This appeal reheard en banc requires us to focus closely upon the dividing line between presumptive regularity in the enforcement of penal laws and impermissible prosecutorial selectivity.

Jeffrey Falk was charged in a four-count indictment with refusing to submit to induction into the Armed Forces and with failure to possess a registration card or his 1968 and 1969 I-A classification cards, all in violation of 50 U.S.C. App. § 462. The defendant filed a pretrial motion to dismiss those counts of the indictment charging him with failure to possess the proper cards on the ground that the prosecution sought the indictment for the improper purpose of chilling the exercise of rights guaranteed by the First Amendment and to punish him for participation in a draft counseling organization. The trial judge denied the motion without holding an evidentiary hearing. At trial, an offer of proof based on the same contention was similarly rejected. A jury found Falk guilty on all four counts, but the district court granted a post-trial motion for acquittal on count one on the ground that there had been no basis in fact for denying Falk classification as a conscientious objector. He received three consecutive one year sentences on the card-carrying counts.

On appeal, a panel of this court affirmed Falk's conviction, one judge dissenting. A petition for rehearing en banc was granted, in which the principal issue was the alleged discriminatory prosecutorial purpose in seeking the indictment. We have concluded that Falk is entitled to a hearing on his charge of an improper purpose. We accordingly reverse.

The Fourteenth Amendment prohibits any state from taking action which would "deny to any person within its jurisdiction the equal protection of the laws." This admonition is applicable to the federal government through the Fifth Amendment. The promise of equal protection of the laws is not limited to the enactment of fair and impartial legislation, but necessarily extends to the application of these laws. The basic principle was stated long ago in *Yick Wo v. Hopkins* (1886):

> Though the law itself be fair on its face and impartial in appearance, yet, if it is applied and administered by public authority with an evil eye and an unequal hand, so as practically to make unjust and illegal discriminations between persons in similar circumstances, material to their rights, the denial of equal justice is still within the prohibition of the Constitution.

The city ordinance for which violation *Yick Wo* was convicted made it unlawful for any person to maintain a laundry in the city of San Francisco without first obtaining the permission of the board of supervisors unless the laundry were located in a building constructed of brick or stone. Although the statute was, on its face, a fair and reasonable exercise of the police power, the facts showed that principally Chinese were refused permission to continue using wooden facilities. The Supreme Court held that criminal enforcement of the law was therefore illegal.

Yick Wo was concerned with an abuse of discretion in the administration of a public ordinance by a city licensing board, and not with the activities of law enforcement officials who presumably prosecuted all Chinese who violated the commands of the licensing board. The underlying principle has nevertheless been properly held to apply to the actions of prosecutors and police officials.

Despite the seemingly undeniable application of *Yick Wo* to discriminatory prosecutions, two questions have troubled various courts and appear to be the source of the disagreement between the majority and dissenters on this court. The first of these arises from the decision in *Oyler v. Boles* (1962), in which the Court noted that the "conscious exercise of some selectivity in enforcement is not in itself a federal constitutional violation," and went on to state that since it had not been alleged "that the selection was deliberately based upon an unjustifiable standard such as race, religion, or other arbitrary classification" there were no grounds to support a finding that the equal protection clause had been violated. From this it is argued that a person attempting to defend against the discriminatory enforcement of a law must show that he is a member of a class against which the law is being selectively enforced. We agree with Judge Lumbard in *Moss v. Hornig* that *Oyler* does not preclude the granting of relief against intentional or purposeful discrimination against an individual. No intentional discrimination against the petitioner as an individual was alleged by *Oyler* and he merely attempted to show, by statistical evidence, that fewer than all multiple offenders were given heavier sentences. In the present case intentional discrimination is alleged.

Falk's allegations indicate that he was singled out for selective and discriminatory treatment on the basis of activities which form an unjustifiable standard for selectivity in prosecution. Falk was an active member of a draft counseling organization known as the Chicago Area Draft Resisters. In his pretrial motion and again in his offer of proof he asserted that the prosecution against him for violation of the card carrying requirements was brought not because he had violated the statute but to punish him for and stifle his and others' participation in protected First Amendment activities in opposition to the draft and the war in Vietnam. There can be no doubt but that the expression of views opposing this country's foreign policy with regard to Vietnam is protected by the First Amendment. And, just as discrimination on the basis of religion or race is forbidden by the Constitution, so is discrimination on the basis of the exercise of protected First Amendment activities, whether done as an individual or, as in this case, as a member of a group unpopular with the government.

Similar results have been reached in two recent cases. The most recent, *United States v. Steele* (9th Cir. 1972), involved a conviction for refusing to answer questions in a census report in violation of 13 U.S.C. § 221(a). The defendant argued that he had been deliberately selected for prosecution because of his participation in a census resistance movement. The Court of Appeals for the Ninth Circuit agreed that there was evidence that Steele had been singled out for prosecution on the basis of his exercise of First Amendment rights and concluded that his conviction could not stand under *Oyler* and *Yick Wo.*

Convictions were also reversed in *United States v. Crowthers* (4th Cir. 1972), on a finding that an unlawful and discriminatory purpose precipitated the indictments. The arrests in that case were for violations of a disorderly conduct regulation which prohibited loud and unusual noise and obstruction of passageways and a regulation forbidding the distribution of handbills without prior permission of the federal agency in whose space the material was to be distributed.

The second source of disagreement among some courts and within this court concerns the problem of proof. Certainly, the prospect of government prosecutors being called to the stand by every criminal defendant for cross-examination as to their motives in seeking an indictment is to be avoided. That does not mean that a criminal defendant is never to be afforded an opportunity to prove that the prosecution stems from an improper prosecutorial design or that he may never question a prosecutor under oath. The presumption is always that a prosecution for violation of a criminal law is undertaken in good faith and in nondiscriminatory fashion for the purpose of fulfilling a duty to bring violators to justice. However, when a defendant alleges intentional purposeful discrimination and presents facts sufficient to raise a reasonable doubt about the prosecutor's purpose, we think a different question is raised.

Defendant in this case twice attempted to present evidence which would have shown an impermissible prosecutorial purpose. In his pretrial motion for dismissal of those counts of the indictment charging violations of the card possession requirements, the defendant expressed his belief that over 25,000 Selective Service registrants had dispossessed themselves of their draft cards without criminal sanction, and sought an evidentiary hearing at which he would submit evidence in proof of his allegations. In his motion for acquittal at the close of the government's case, Falk again attempted to show that the government was aware of many violations and that others were not being prosecuted, citing the policy statement of Lt. General Louis B. Hershey, Director, Selective Service System, Legal Aspects of

Selective Service 47 (January 1, 1969, U.S. Government Printing Office), which states in relevant part:

> The escalation of the United States military involvement in Vietnam increased the draft calls, and there was an upsurge of public demonstrations in protest. Some of these protests took the form of turning "draft" cards in to various public officials of the Department of Justice, the State or National Headquarters of Selective Service System, or directly to local boards. By agreement with the Department of Justice, registrants who turned in cards (as contrasted to those who burned cards) were not prosecuted under Section 12(a) of the Military Selective Service Law of 1967, but were processed administratively by the local boards.

The Hershey statement goes on to say that many of these protesters were classified I-A, a policy which the Supreme Court found unacceptable in *Gutknecht v. United States* (1970). It is, of course, possible that following the *Gutknecht* decision, the government changed its policy on non-prosecution. However, in view of its admitted policy not to prosecute prior to that decision we believe that in the particular circumstances of the instant case it was incumbent upon the government to come forward with evidence that it had in fact changed its policy generally or otherwise to explain why Falk was being singled out for prosecution in contravention of the government's own procedures.

The particular circumstances of this case which we believe compelled the government to accept the burden of proving nondiscriminatory enforcement of the law are several. Falk was, as noted earlier, actively involved in advising others on methods of legally avoiding military service and in protesting American actions in Vietnam. Similar circumstances, in which a vocal dissenter appeared to have been singled out for prosecution, led the court in *United States v. Steele* to hold that "[a]n enforcement procedure that focuses upon the vocal offender is inherently suspect, since it is vulnerable to the charge that those chosen for prosecution are being punished for their expression of ideas, a constitutionally protected right." In the present case there are several indications that this was exactly the purpose of the prosecution. At the close of the trial Falk's attorney asked that the Assistant United States Attorney who tried the case be called as a witness, and offered to prove that the Assistant United States Attorney had told Falk's attorney at a meeting in December, 1970, that he knew of defendant's draft counseling activities, that a good deal of their trouble in enforcing the draft laws came from people such as Falk, that few indictments were brought for non-possession of draft cards, that defendant's draft-counseling activity was one of the reasons why the prosecution for non-possession of draft cards was brought, and that the government would not dismiss the card-carrying counts of the indictment even though Falk agreed to carry the cards in the future. The court refused the offer of proof but did allow the Assistant United States Attorney to make a reply. We think the unsolicited reply is itself some evidence that Falk was singled out for special prosecution. Apparently in an effort to show that his own participation in the process of deciding to prosecute was inconsequential, the Assistant noted that the indictment against Falk was approved not only by him, but also by the Chief of the Criminal Division of the United States Attorney's Office, the First Assistant United States Attorney, the United States Attorney and the Department of Justice in Washington. It is difficult to believe that the usual course of proceedings in a draft case requires such careful consideration by such a distinguished succession of officials prior to a formal decision to prosecute.

The particular circumstances of this case which overcome the initial presumption of legal regularity in enforcement of penal laws also includes the lengthy delay in bringing the indictment. Falk returned his registration card to the Department of Justice on December 4, 1967, mailed his I-A classification notice to Federal District Judge Hubert Will in

Chapter XII Discriminatory Enforcement

October, 1968 and sent a later notice of classification to his draft board in May, 1969. The government therefore had notice of his violations of the regulations from December, 1967. Yet the indictment charging violations of the card possession requirements was not returned until almost three years had passed, in October of 1970, following Falk's refusal to submit to induction in May of that year. Some explanation for the delay in prosecution for the earlier offenses may be found in a statement of policy by the Director of the Selective Service System:

> Selective Service Regulations are designed to delay the prosecution of a violator of the law until after he has failed to report for or refused to submit to induction or assigned civilian work. This is to prevent, wherever possible, prosecutions for minor infractions of rules during his selective service processing, thereby reducing the number of cases that reach the courts and also giving the registrant, before being prosecuted, an opportunity to report for service in the armed forces. Since the purpose of the law is to provide men for the military establishment rather than for the penitentiaries, it would seem that when a registrant is willing to be inducted, he should not be prosecuted for minor offenses committed during his processing. The result of this procedure is that the great majority of prosecutions involve the failure to report for or refusal to submit to induction or assigned civilian work.

Although this statement would seem to provide a valid, and even in some cases benevolent, explanation for a delay of up to three years in bringing the indictment, it also adds forceful weight to defendant's contention that the prosecution in this case was for the purpose of punishing Falk for his exercise of First Amendment rights. According to this statement, it is government policy to prosecute only a portion of those who commit "minor infractions of rules"; whether a violator is one of those prosecuted depends upon whether he accepts or refuses induction. We may assume, at least for purposes of this case, that a general decision to prosecute those who refuse induction on grounds which will support a conviction to the exclusion of those who agree to cooperate with the Selective Service in the future is within the prosecutor's discretion. The problem in this case, however, is that Falk was found to have been justified in refusing induction in that he was entitled to classification as a conscientious objector. The result is that he faces three years' imprisonment because his local draft board arbitrarily and without grounds to so act refused his claim as a conscientious objector and he was forced to refuse induction in order to assert a valid claim, thereby also incurring prosecution for prior "minor infractions." The conclusion would seem to be compelling that, in the admitted policy of the Selective Service officials and apart from whether Falk's draft counseling activities were involved in the decision to prosecute, he was indicted and prosecuted for violation of the card possession requirements only because he exercised his First Amendment privilege to claim a statutory right as a conscientious objector. But "[i]t is clearly unconstitutional to enable a public official to determine which expressions of view will be permitted and which will not or to engage in invidious discrimination among persons or groups . . . by selective enforcement of an extremely broad prohibitory statute."

Punishment of Falk, however valid otherwise, only because he chose to assert his right as a conscientious objector, is very similar to the conduct of city officials who reinstated criminal charges for alleged traffic violations following the defendant's action in filing an official complaint charging police misconduct in *Dixon v. District of Columbia* (1968). Chief Judge Bazelon, in reversing the defendant's conviction on those charges, stated:

> The Government may not prosecute for the purpose of deterring people from exercising their right to protest official misconduct and petition for redress of grievances. Moreover, a prosecution under such circumstances would be barred by the equal protection clause, since the Government employs an impermissible classification when it punishes those who complain against police misconduct and excuses those who do not.

Similarly, the government is not free to punish those who refuse to acquiesce in a local draft board's irrational refusal to give a conscientious objector his proper classification while it

B. Lower Courts and Selective Prosecution Claims 1077

excuses those who, however much their decision may conflict with moral principles, agree to submit to induction.

To summarize, the combination in this case of the published government policy not to prosecute violators of the card possession regulations, Falk's status as an active and vocal dissenter to United States policy with regard to the draft and the Vietnam War, the Assistant United States Attorney's statement that officials ranging from an Assistant Attorney to the Department of Justice in Washington participated in the decision to prosecute Falk, the untimely delay in bringing the indictment and the government's stated policy to prosecute only those who refuse induction while absolving those who submit to the will of the authorities, lead us to conclude that the district court erred in refusing a hearing on the offer of proof. The unrebutted evidence before the court, including the admission of the Assistant United States Attorney and the two published statements by the Selective Service officials which contradict the propriety of the action taken in this case, made out at least a prima facie case of improper discrimination in enforcing the law. We will therefore remand the case, to a different judge, for a hearing at which time Falk may question the Assistant United States Attorney as to the content of his previous statements to defendant's counsel and present any additional evidence he wishes on the issue of other alleged violators and the government's lack of general enforcement. In accordance with our holding that a prima facie case has already been presented, and in agreement with *United States v. Crowthers*, supra, however, the burden of going forward with proof of nondiscrimination will then rest on the government. Particularly with regard to the seemingly inherent discrimination against Falk in prosecuting him for insisting on his claim as a conscientious objector, we think the government will be required to present compelling evidence to the contrary if its burden is to be met. If the district court finds that the prosecution was not the result of a purpose to punish Falk for exercising First Amendment rights as a draft counselor and Vietnam protestor and is also satisfied that the government has not made an invidious discrimination between violators who acquiesce to the power of the Selective Service System and those who continue to assert their rights to be classified as conscientious objectors, the conviction will stand. If the court finds that Falk would not have been prosecuted for violation of the card possession requirements except for his assertion of a conscientious objector claim or his draft counseling and lawful protest activities, the indictment must be dismissed.

In conclusion, we wish to note our disapproval of the apparently frequent, and often too easy, practice of simply dismissing all allegations of illegal discrimination in the enforcement of criminal laws with a reference to *Oyler v. Boles*, supra, and its statement that the conscious exercise of some selectivity in the enforcement of laws does not violate the Constitution. That correct principle does not in many cases answer the question whether selective enforcement in a given case is invidious discrimination which cannot be reconciled with the principles of equal protection. As Judge Cummings reminded us in *Stamler v. Willis* (7th Cir. 1969), "[t]he judiciary has always borne the basic responsibility for protecting individuals against unconstitutional invasions of their rights by all branches of the Government."

• • •

Judgment of conviction vacated and cause remanded.

FAIRCHILD, Circuit Judge (concurring).

I agree that there has been a sufficient showing to warrant judicial inquiry into the motives of the prosecutor. This is indeed an exceptional area of national life where conscientious opposition to government policy has been intertwined with violations of the laws which implement the policy.

I would add one further point, with respect to the sentence imposed. Defendant was given an aggregate three year sentence for his card violations, as much as or more than he would probably have received if his induction order had been lawful. The judge apparently considered an ill-advised and offensive remark defendant made to his Board. In any event, the sentence appears grossly disproportionate to the circumstances of the offenses. I would readily concede that one who knowingly commits an offense as a means of protest deliberately risks the penalty. In a sense his exposure to sacrifice is a means of making his protest meaningful. On the other hand, the card offenses here can not be considered serious, nor to have threatened, under the circumstances, the government's legitimate objective in requiring the possession of cards.

Even if the prosecution were deemed lawful on remand, I believe the aggregate sentence must be substantially reduced.

NOTES AND QUESTIONS

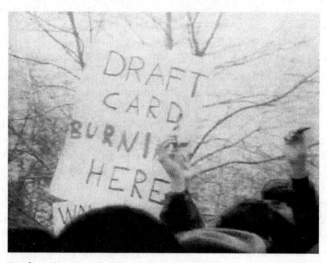

Draft card protest during the Vietnam War

1. The district court in *Falk* refused to even hold a pretrial evidentiary hearing on Falk's selective prosecution claim. Is that surprising? Recall that at that time of Falk's indictment (1970) the only federal case to have upheld a selective prosecution claim was the district court's decision in *Robinson*, which was hardly on point. So all *Falk* had to go on in arguing for a hearing was 85-year old *Yick Wo* itself and *Oyler*. Did the language in *Oyler* make clear that Falk had a potentially viable selective prosecution claim such that a hearing should have been granted? Would singling out people like Falk for prosecution have been an "arbitrary classification" as the term was used in *Oyler*?

2. By the time of the en banc decision in *Falk*, however, the Seventh Circuit had the advantage of the federal appellate decisions in *Crowthers* and *Steele*. By the third paragraph of the opinion the court was already quoting the magic of *Yick Wo*:

> Though the law itself be fair on its face, and impartial in appearance, yet, if it is applied and administered by public authority with an evil eye and an unequal hand, so as practically to make unjust and illegal discriminations between persons in similar circumstances, material to their rights, the denial of equal justice is still within the prohibition of the constitution.

188 U.S. at 373-74. The Seventh Circuit easily distinguishes the facts of *Oyler*, as the discrimination alleged by Falk — that he was singled out for prosecution based on his draft

counseling activities — was protected by the First Amendment and thereby analogous to the sort of impermissible enforcement based on race or religion that was acknowledged as the basis for a claim in *Oyler*.

3. The court goes out of its way to criticize lower courts' expansive reading of the dicta in *Oyler* as condoning selectivity, deriding

> the apparently frequent, and often too easy, practice of simply dismissing all allegations of illegal discrimination in the enforcement of criminal laws with a reference to *Oyler v. Boles* . . . and its statement that the conscious exercise of some selectivity in the enforcement of laws does not violate the Constitution. That correct principle does not in many cases answer the question whether selective enforcement in a given case is invidious discrimination which cannot be reconciled with the principles of equal protection.

Id. at 624. Is this criticism fair? Can you see how lower courts might be understandably reluctant to view *Oyler* as a green light for selective prosecution claims?

4. The Seventh Circuit may not have faulted the trial judge for not holding an evidentiary hearing. But at least one member of the court was alarmed by the harsh (three-year) sentence the trial judge imposed; the rebuke by Judge Fairchild, in a sentencing era of almost standardless discretion and extremely deferential appellate review, is almost unheard of. Note also that the Seventh Circuit took the unusual step of remanding the case to a different judge.

5. The offer of proof Falk made by way of pretrial motion and also at the close of evidence as a motion for judgment of acquittal consisted of the following:

> 25,000 registrants had not been prosecuted for dispossessing their draft cards as Falk had; Falk was actively involved in advising registrants on draft noncompliance; and the AUSA who prosecuted Falk told Falk's attorney before trial that Falk had been targeted in part due to his draft-counseling activity.

Id. at 621-22. The court did not say explicitly whether this showing was enough to establish a prima facie case and therefore entitle Falk to a hearing. But it found that Falk's original showing, in combination with the lengthy chain of approval authorizing his prosecution — evidence put forth by the AUSA at trial in order to minimize his own role in that process — and the delay in bringing that prosecution, was sufficient to warrant a hearing. *Id.* at 623.

Which of these pieces of evidence is most compelling? Least compelling?

Which evidence do you think is most susceptible to being countered or neutralized by the government in the evidentiary hearing that is to take place on remand?

6. The court refers to the "presumptive regularity" of criminal enforcement and adds that the "presumption is always that a prosecution for violation of a criminal law is undertaken in good faith and in nondiscriminatory fashion for the purpose of fulfilling a duty to bring violators to justice." What does this mean? Does it mean anything other than that the defendant has the burden of proving selective prosecution? Does it imply that the burden of proving selective discrimination is higher than a preponderance standard?

7. The court recognizes that "the prospect of government prosecutors being called to the stand by every criminal defendant for cross-examination as to their motives in seeking an indictment is to be avoided." Yet in remanding for an evidentiary hearing the Court explicitly states that the AUSA who spoke to Falk's attorney must testify. Was this necessary? Was this conversation an essential part of Falk's prima facie case? What are the downsides of requiring testimony from the prosecutor, both in this case and generally? Given that Falk's indictment was approved at several different levels in the U.S. Attorney's Office, as well as by Main Justice, should all the government lawyers in the approval process be obliged to testify?

Chapter XII Discriminatory Enforcement

In the next case the defendant alleges a different, more attenuated kind of viewpoint discrimination. The defendant Teamster official claims he was targeted for prosecution by the Department of Justice in the Nixon Administration because of his outspoken support for George McGovern in the 1972 presidential election that was won by Richard Nixon, and because of his efforts to unionize the Marriott restaurant chain, an organization with close ties to President Nixon.

United States v. Berrios
501 F.2d 1207 (2d Cir. 1974)

MANSFIELD, Circuit Judge:

At issue on this appeal by the government is the question of whether the district court, after the defendant Pablo Berrios alleged that in this case he had been the victim of selective and discriminatory prosecution by the government, acted properly and within its powers in dismissing the indictment against all defendants because of the government's refusal to turn over to the court for disclosure to defense counsel a memorandum that had been sent by the prosecutor to the United States Department of Justice recommending that prosecution of the defendants be initiated. We vacate the district court's order and remand the case for further proceedings consistent with this opinion.

Some eighty years ago, the Supreme Court observed that the administration of laws "with an evil eye and an unequal hand, so as practically to make unjust and illegal discrimination between persons in similar circumstances" constitutes a denial of equal protection. *Yick Wo v. Hopkins* (1886). Nothing can corrode respect for a rule of law more than the knowledge that the government looks beyond the law itself to arbitrary considerations, such as race, religion, or control over the defendant's exercise of his constitutional rights, as the basis for determining its applicability. *Oyler v. Boles* (1962). Selective prosecution then can become a weapon used to discipline political foe and the dissident, see, e.g., *United States v. Falk* (7th Cir. 1973); *United States v. Steele* (9th Cir. 1972). The prosecutor's objective is then diverted from the public interest to the punishment of those harboring beliefs with which the administration in power may disagree. This case involves such allegations.

In an indictment filed on January 8, 1973, appellee Berrios stands accused of holding union office in violation of 29 U.S.C. § 504, which provides that no person who has been convicted of the crime of arson, among others, shall within five years of such conviction serve as an officer or employee of a labor organization. Berrios, it is alleged, was convicted of the crime of arson by the Supreme Court of New York in 1971 and, notwithstanding that conviction, within five years thereafter became Trustee and a member of the Executive Board of Teamsters Union Local 840. His success in achieving these positions is the cause of his present plight. The other appellees (Nuchow, Principe and Zaretsky) were later charged with violating § 504 by willfully and knowingly permitting Berrios to hold union office after his conviction.

Berrios contends that he was chosen for prosecution because he was counted among the few Teamster officials who were in 1972 outspoken in their support of Senator McGovern for President as against President Nixon and because he was at that time spearheading an effort to unionize the Marriott Restaurant Chain, an enterprise that apparently enjoys close ties with President Nixon and his family. In support of his charge of selective prosecution, Berrios submitted the affidavit of his counsel, Martin Garbus, Esq., which states that he and his client "believe" that (1) there have been only three prosecutions under § 504 since 1969; (2) Mr. Marriott has been a close friend of the President and a substantial contributor to his political campaign; (3) Donald Nixon, the President's brother, is a vice-president of Marriott;

B. Lower Courts and Selective Prosecution Claims   **1081**

(4) Herbert Kalmbach, attorney for Marriott, was also the President's personal attorney; (5) Charles Colson, formerly counsel to the President and later counsel to the Teamsters Union was a "prime mover in the prosecution," and (6) there are hundreds of unions with officers who have prison records. Although Berrios' counsel later pointed to newspaper articles as the basis for some of these beliefs, no evidence or facts were offered to show the basis of his belief that numerous other violations of 29 U.S.C. § 504 had gone unprosecuted. Nevertheless, on the strength of the affidavit, Berrios moved for a hearing on his defense of selective prosecution.

Upon oral argument, which was conducted by the court for the purpose of determining whether a hearing was required, counsel for Berrios urged that he had shown enough to warrant further exploration by way of a hearing. As might be anticipated, the government took the opposite view, pointing out the vagueness of Berrios' allegations and explaining that the prosecutor had learned of Berrios' criminal record while investigating a charge of arson lodged against him for an attempted firebomb attack on a Marriott restaurant. (Berrios was acquitted of this charge after a jury trial before Judge Judd on February 7, 1973.) Judge Judd suggested that the charge of selective prosecution might be resolved without a hearing if the government would turn over a copy of the letter from the prosecutor to his superiors, which originally sought authorization for the prosecution of Berrios. At first the government resisted this idea on the ground that the material sought was confidential. Eventually, however, the United States Attorney proposed a compromise: let the judge view the memorandum in camera and, if he should determine that there was nothing to support Berrios' claim, return it to the government without disclosure to the defense. Defense counsel, dissatisfied with the notion of a completely in camera inspection, prevailed upon the judge to order that the defendants should have access to the memorandum which would be redacted only to the extent necessary to protect against disclosure of any confidential grand jury testimony.

When the government declined to comply with the disclosure order Judge Judd, acting upon Berrios' motion for dismissal of the indictment, filed an opinion and order on January 7, 1974, directing that the indictment be dismissed unless the government within thirty days submitted the memorandum to the court for its study and for release to the defendants of any portions thereof which the court should determine "are not required to be kept confidential." In his opinion Judge Judd held that Berrios' allegations warranted a hearing on the selective prosecution issue and that Berrios' "offer of proof" was sufficient to create a prima facie case of selective prosecution. Upon the government's refusal to produce the memorandum on the terms specified by Judge Judd, the court, on February 8, 1974, dismissed the indictment, from which the Government appeals.

DISCUSSION

To support a defense of selective or discriminatory prosecution, a defendant bears the heavy burden of establishing, at least prima facie, (1) that, while others similarly situated have not generally been proceeded against because of conduct of the type forming the basis of the charge against him, he has been singled out for prosecution, and (2) that the government's discriminatory selection of him for prosecution has been invidious or in bad faith, i.e., based upon such impermissible considerations as race, religion, or the desire to prevent his exercise of constitutional rights. These two essential elements are sometimes referred to as "intentional and purposeful discrimination." Mere "conscious exercise of some selectivity in enforcement is not in itself a federal constitutional violation." *Oyler v. Boles* (1962).

In the present case, in an effort to support his defense of selective prosecution, Berrios sought a hearing and disclosure of certain government records solely upon the basis of his counsel's affidavit to the effect that he and his clients "believe" that facts indicating a vindictive

Chapter XII Discriminatory Enforcement

motive on the part of the government exist (as outlined above) and their further belief that "there are hundreds of unions who have men with prison records sitting as officers." In support of the latter claim, although Berrios introduced a letter from the Department of Justice to the effect that there had been three indictments of others for violations of § 504 since July 1969, he neither named any unprosecuted violators nor identified any of the unions in which they allegedly held office.

Clearly the defendants are not entitled under Rule 16, F. R. Crim. P., to disclosure of the government records sought by them, since Rule 16(b) expressly exempts from discovery "reports, memoranda, or other internal government documents made by government agents in connection with the investigation and prosecution of the case. . . ." Upon an adequate preliminary showing of relevancy, however, the district court may hold a hearing upon a motion raising defenses or objections, Rule 12(b)(4), F. R. Crim. P., and issue a subpoena directing the government to produce books, papers or records for introduction at the hearing, Rule 17(c), F. R. Crim. P. Upon the meagre preliminary showing made here, we doubt whether we would have granted a hearing or ordered the production of evidence for such a hearing, since Berrios appears frankly to have embarked upon a fishing expedition. The effect could be to encourage use of the defense of selective prosecution, however baseless, as a means of obtaining discovery to which the defense would not otherwise be entitled. In order to show what has been described by the Third Circuit as a "colorable basis" entitling the defense to subpoena documentary evidence required to establish a selective prosecution defense, we would first require some evidence tending to show the existence of the essential elements of the defense and that the documents in the government's possession would indeed be probative of these elements. In this case, Berrios has not pointed to the existence of a single unprosecuted violation of § 504 on the part of others, even though proof of this essential element would not necessarily be in the government's exclusive control. Nor has Berrios represented that the government's files, including the prosecutor's recommendation that prosecution be initiated, will in fact support his beliefs.

Notwithstanding the apparent weakness of Berrios' claim, we recognize that the decision to permit a hearing and, in anticipation thereof, to authorize a subpoena of evidence in the government's possession, lies largely in the trial judge's discretion. As the Supreme Court has just stated in *United States v. Nixon* (1974):

> Enforcement of a pretrial subpoena duces tecum must necessarily be committed to the sound discretion of the trial court since the necessity for the subpoena most often turns upon a determination of factual issues. Without a determination of arbitrariness or that the trial court finding was without record support, an appellate court will not ordinarily disturb a finding that the applicant for a subpoena complied with Rule 17(c).

Although we might have proceeded differently in this case, we cannot on this record say that Judge Judd abused his discretion in ordering the government to turn over to him for "study" its memorandum recommending prosecution. However, his opinion and order filed January 7, 1974, went too far in directing the government to surrender the memorandum "for release to the defendants of any portions thereof which the court shall determine are not required to be kept confidential."

Although Berrios does not object to redaction of any portions of the prosecutor's memorandum found by the court to be entitled to protection from disclosure on the grounds of confidentiality (e.g., the substance of grand jury testimony, see Rule 6(e), F. R. Crim. P.)he would at most be entitled under Rule 17(c), F. R. Crim. P. to introduce at a hearing only material that is demonstrably relevant, i.e., which would tend to establish the elements of his defense of selective and discriminatory prosecution. Even under the district court's liberal ruling the test for disclosure should be the relevancy of the evidence to the specific defense for

B. Lower Courts and Selective Prosecution Claims   **1083**

which it is sought, not its lack of confidentiality. The government is entitled to have withheld from the defendants all material in the memorandum which does not relate to the defense of selective prosecution. On the other hand, the government is not entitled, on a mere claim of generalized confidentiality, to withhold material that is relevant to the defense.

The order of the district court is vacated and the case is remanded for proceedings consistent with this opinion. Against the possibility that, upon remand, a difference might arise between the court and the government regarding the relevancy of any portions of the memorandum which the court proposes to release to the defendants, we retain jurisdiction for the purpose of review of the court's ruling. Should Judge Judd decide, on the other hand, not to release all or any part of the memorandum to the defendants, we direct that the entire memorandum be sealed and retained by the court so that it will be available for such review after trial as may become necessary. *United States v. Nixon*, supra.

NOTES AND QUESTIONS

1. The second paragraph of the court's opinion beautifully sums up both the evils of selective prosecution and the state of the law on the subject. Do you see selective prosecution primarily as a "rule of law" concern, as reflected in this passage, as opposed to a "fairness" concern? Obviously all of the defendants raising selective prosecution claims believe it is "unfair" for them to be prosecuted when others who are similarly situated are not.

2. The court specifies a two-part test for establishing a prima facie case of selective prosecution: (a) defendant has been singled out for prosecution while others who are similarly situated to defendant have not been prosecuted and (b) the government's "selection of him for prosecution has been invidious or in bad faith, i.e., based upon such impermissible considerations as race, religion, or the desire to prevent his exercise of constitutional rights."

Are the words "invidious or in bad faith, i.e." necessary to this formulation? Do they add anything? Could a prosecution be brought in "bad faith" but not be based on "impermissible considerations"? Does the Second Circuit's formulation of the test align with *Oyler*? With the *Crowthers-Steele-Falk* trilogy? And what, under this standard, constitutes a prima facie case? Evidence that if unrebutted will establish the defense? Less than that? Does the basis for a prima facie case need to be admissible evidence?

3. The issue in *Berrios* is not whether defendant established a prima facie case sufficient to require an evidentiary hearing—it seems largely undisputed that he did not—but rather whether he has demonstrated a "colorable basis" for issuance of a subpoena under Rule 17. The Second Circuit seems dubious, stating that "Berrios appears frankly to have embarked upon a fishing expedition." Do you agree? What are the strongest and weakest parts of Berrios's showing? Is this a "colorable basis" for discovery? Is the comparative weakness of his "similarly situated" evidence overcome by the comparative strength of his "impermissible considerations" evidence?

4. The specific discovery at issue appears to be "a letter from the prosecutor to his superiors, which originally sought authorization for the prosecution of Berrios." (In U.S. attorney parlance this document is usually known as a "prosecution memorandum.") Why did the defense reject the trial judge's compromise suggestion of in camera review? Was this a reasonable objection? Can you think of a more modest discovery request that would have been more narrowly tailored to the specific weakness in Berrios's claim? Is the prosecution memorandum likely to address the "similarly situated" issue?

5. Note that the government hadn't entirely stiffed Berrios prior to the subpoena dispute. Among other things, the prosecutor disclosed that he had learned of Berrios's criminal record

1084 Chapter XII Discriminatory Enforcement

(an element of the charged offense) while investigating an arson charge against him for an attempted firebombing of a Marriott restaurant. Do you think the fact that Berrios had been acquitted of the arson charge in a trial before Judge Judd, the same trial judge who authorized the issuance of the subpoena, affected the analysis of Berrios's selective prosecution claim?

6. Ultimately the Second Circuit defers to Judge Judd, as such matters as whether to hold a hearing and/or issue a subpoena are normally within the trial judge's discretion under *United States v. Nixon*, 418 U.S. 683 (1974), decided earlier that summer. Still, requiring the government to turn over its prosecution memorandum is sufficiently novel and "legal" that it is surprising the court did not reverse. Should it factor into the court's deference to Judge Judd that he had experience with the government's previous prosecution of Berrios? By contrast, in *Falk* the Seventh Circuit made no mention of an abuse-of-discretion standard in finding that the trial judge erred in not holding a hearing. The *Berrios* court does find that Judge Judd had abused his discretion in holding that the prosecution memorandum would be turned over to defendants subject to confidentiality constraints, and notes that defendants are entitled to only those portions of the memorandum that tend to establish their selective prosecution defense. Do you agree that decision was an abuse of discretion?

C. THE SUPREME COURT STEPS BACK IN

The Supreme Court reentered the selective prosecution waters in 1985, in another antidraft viewpoint discrimination case. By this point the Court was armed with a recently formed body of equal protection law that made all manner of discrimination claims extremely difficult to prove.

Wayte v. United States
470 U.S. 598 (1985)

Justice POWELL delivered the opinion of the Court.

The question presented is whether a passive enforcement policy under which the Government prosecutes only those who report themselves as having violated the law, or who are reported by others, violates the First and Fifth Amendments.

I

On July 2, 1980, pursuant to his authority under § 3 of the Military Selective Service Act, the President issued Presidential Proclamation No. 4771, 3 CFR 82 (1981). This Proclamation directed male citizens and certain male residents born during 1960 to register with the Selective Service System during the week of July 21, 1980. Petitioner fell within that class but did not register. Instead, he wrote several letters to Government officials, including the President, stating that he had not registered and did not intend to do so.

Petitioner's letters were added to a Selective Service file of young men who advised that they had failed to register or who were reported by others as having failed to register. For reasons we discuss, Selective Service adopted a policy of passive enforcement under which it would investigate and prosecute only the cases of nonregistration contained in this file. In furtherance of this policy, Selective Service sent a letter on June 17, 1981, to each reported violator who had not registered and for whom it had an address. The letter explained the duty to register, stated that Selective Service had information that the person was required to register but had not done so, requested that he either comply with the law by filling out an enclosed

C. The Supreme Court Steps Back In   **1085**

registration card or explain why he was not subject to registration, and warned that a violation could result in criminal prosecution and specified penalties. Petitioner received a copy of this letter but did not respond.

On July 20, 1981, Selective Service transmitted to the Department of Justice, for investigation and potential prosecution, the names of petitioner and 133 other young men identified under its passive enforcement system — all of whom had not registered in response to the Service's June letter. At two later dates, it referred the names of 152 more young men similarly identified. After screening out the names of those who appeared not to be in the class required to register, the Department of Justice referred the remaining names to the Federal Bureau of Investigation for additional inquiry and to the United States Attorneys for the districts in which the nonregistrants resided. Petitioner's name was one of those referred.

Pursuant to Department of Justice policy, those referred were not immediately prosecuted. Instead, the appropriate United States Attorney was required to notify identified nonregistrants by registered mail that, unless they registered within a specified time, prosecution would be considered. In addition, an FBI agent was usually sent to interview the nonregistrant before prosecution was instituted. This effort to persuade nonregistrants to change their minds became known as the "beg" policy. Under it, young men who registered late were not prosecuted, while those who never registered were investigated further by the Government. Pursuant to the "beg" policy, the United States Attorney for the Central District of California sent petitioner a letter on October 15, 1981, urging him to register or face possible prosecution. Again petitioner failed to respond.

On December 9, 1981, the Department of Justice instructed all United States Attorneys not to begin seeking indictments against nonregistrants until further notice. On January 7, 1982, the President announced a grace period to afford nonregistrants a further opportunity to register without penalty. This grace period extended until February 28, 1982. Petitioner still did not register.

Over the next few months, the Department decided to begin prosecuting those young men who, despite the grace period and "beg" policy, continued to refuse to register. It recognized that under the passive enforcement system those prosecuted were "liable to be vocal proponents of nonregistration" or persons "with religious or moral objections." Memorandum of March 17, 1982, from Lawrence Lippe, Chief, General Litigation and Legal Advice Section, Criminal Division, Department of Justice, to D. Lowell Jensen, Assistant Attorney General, Criminal Division, App. 301. It also recognized that prosecutions would "undoubtedly result in allegations that the [case was] brought in retribution for the nonregistrant's exercise of his first amendment rights." The Department was advised, however, that Selective Service could not develop a more "active" enforcement system for quite some time. Because of this, the Department decided to begin seeking indictments under the passive system without further delay. On May 21, 1982, United States Attorneys were notified to begin prosecution of nonregistrants. On June 28, 1982, FBI agents interviewed petitioner, and he continued to refuse to register. Accordingly, on July 22, 1982, an indictment was returned against him for knowingly and willfully failing to register with the Selective Service in violation of §§ 3 and 12(a) of the Military Selective Service Act. This was one of the first indictments returned against any individual under the passive policy.

II

Petitioner moved to dismiss the indictment on the ground of selective prosecution. He contended that he and the other indicted nonregistrants were "vocal" opponents of the registration program who had been impermissibly targeted (out of an estimated 674,000 nonregistrants) for prosecution on the basis of their exercise of First Amendment rights. After a hearing, the District Court for the Central District of California granted petitioner's broad request for discovery and directed the Government to produce certain documents and make certain officials available to testify. The Government produced some documents and agreed to make some Government officials available but, citing executive privilege, it withheld other documents and testimony. On October 29, 1982, the District Court ordered the Government to produce the disputed documents and witness. The Government declined to comply and on November 5, 1982, asked the District Court to dismiss the indictment in order to allow an appeal challenging the discovery order. Petitioner asked for dismissal on several grounds, including discriminatory prosecution.

On November 15, 1982, the District Court dismissed the indictment on the ground that the Government had failed to rebut petitioner's prima facie case of selective prosecution. Following precedents of the Court of Appeals for the Ninth Circuit, the District Court found that in order to establish a prima facie case petitioner had to prove that (i) others similarly situated generally had not been prosecuted for conduct similar to petitioner's and (ii) the Government's discriminatory selection was based on impermissible grounds such as race, religion, or exercise of First Amendment rights. Petitioner satisfied the first requirement, the District Court held, because he had shown that all those prosecuted were "vocal" nonregistrants and because "[t]he inference is strong that the Government could have located non-vocal non-registrants, but chose not to." The District Court found the second requirement satisfied for three reasons. First, the passive enforcement program was "'inherently suspect'" because "'it focuse[d] upon the vocal offender . . . [and was] vulnerable to the charge that those chosen for prosecution [were] being punished for their expression of ideas, a constitutionally protected right.'" Second, the Government's awareness that a disproportionate number of vocal nonregistrants would be prosecuted under the passive enforcement system indicated that petitioner was prosecuted because of his exercise of First Amendment rights. Finally, the involvement of high Government officials in the prosecution decisions "strongly suggest[ed] impermissible selective prosecution." The District Court then held that the Government had failed to rebut the prima facie case.

The Court of Appeals reversed. Applying the same test, it found the first requirement satisfied but not the second. The first was satisfied by petitioner's showing that out of the estimated 674,000 nonregistrants the 13 indicted had all been vocal nonregistrants. As to the second requirement, the Court of Appeals held that petitioner had to show that the Government focused its investigation on him because of his protest activities. Petitioner's evidence, however, showed only that the Government was aware that the passive enforcement system would result in prosecutions primarily of two types of men — religious and moral objectors and vocal objectors — and that the Government recognized that the latter type would probably make claims of selective prosecution. Finding no evidence of impermissible governmental motivation, the court held that the District Court's finding of a prima facie case of selective prosecution was clearly erroneous. The Court of Appeals also found two legitimate explanations for the Government's passive enforcement system: (i) the identities of nonreported nonregistrants were not known, and (ii) nonregistrants who expressed their refusal to register made clear their willful violation of the law.

Recognizing both the importance of the question presented and a division in the Circuits, we granted certiorari on the question of selective prosecution. We now affirm.

III

In our criminal justice system, the Government retains "broad discretion" as to whom to prosecute. "[S]o long as the prosecutor has probable cause to believe that the accused committed an offense defined by statute, the decision whether or not to prosecute, and what charge to file or bring before a grand jury, generally rests entirely in his discretion." *Bordenkircher v. Hayes* (1978). This broad discretion rests largely on the recognition that the decision to prosecute is particularly ill-suited to judicial review. Such factors as the strength of the case, the prosecution's general deterrence value, the Government's enforcement priorities, and the case's relationship to the Government's overall enforcement plan are not readily susceptible to the kind of analysis the courts are competent to undertake. Judicial supervision in this area, moreover, entails systemic costs of particular concern. Examining the basis of a prosecution delays the criminal proceeding, threatens to chill law enforcement by subjecting the prosecutor's motives and decisionmaking to outside inquiry, and may undermine prosecutorial effectiveness by revealing the Government's enforcement policy. All these are substantial concerns that make the courts properly hesitant to examine the decision whether to prosecute.

As we have noted in a slightly different context, however, although prosecutorial discretion is broad, it is not "'unfettered.' Selectivity in the enforcement of criminal laws is . . . subject to constitutional constraints." In particular, the decision to prosecute may not be "'deliberately based upon an unjustifiable standard such as race, religion, or other arbitrary classification,'" *Bordenkircher v. Hayes*, quoting *Oyler v. Boles* (1962).

It is appropriate to judge selective prosecution claims according to ordinary equal protection standards. *See Oyler v. Boles*. Under our prior cases, these standards require petitioner to show both that the passive enforcement system had a discriminatory effect and that it was motivated by a discriminatory purpose. *Personnel Administrator of Massachusetts v. Feeney* (1979); *Arlington Heights v. Metropolitan Housing Development Corp.* (1977); *Washington v. Davis* (1976). All petitioner has shown here is that those eventually prosecuted, along with many not prosecuted, reported themselves as having violated the law. He has not shown that the enforcement policy selected nonregistrants for prosecution on the basis of their speech. Indeed, he could not have done so given the way the "beg" policy was carried out. The Government did not prosecute those who reported themselves but later registered. Nor did it prosecute those who protested registration but did not report themselves or were not reported by others. In fact, the Government did not even investigate those who wrote letters to Selective Service criticizing registration unless their letters stated affirmatively that they had refused to comply with the law. The Government, on the other hand, did prosecute people who reported themselves or were reported by others but who did not publicly protest. These facts demonstrate that the Government treated all reported nonregistrants similarly. It did not subject vocal nonregistrants to any special burden. Indeed, those prosecuted in effect selected themselves for prosecution by refusing to register after being reported and warned by the Government.

Even if the passive policy had a discriminatory effect, petitioner has not shown that the Government intended such a result. The evidence he presented demonstrated only that the Government was aware that the passive enforcement policy would result in prosecution of vocal objectors and that they would probably make selective prosecution claims. As we have noted, however: "'[D]iscriminatory purpose' . . . implies more than . . . intent as awareness of consequences. It implies that the decisionmaker . . . selected or reaffirmed a particular course of action at least in part 'because of,' not merely 'in spite of,' its adverse effects upon an identifiable group." In the present case, petitioner has not shown that the Government prosecuted him because of his protest activities. Absent such a showing, his claim of selective prosecution fails.

• • •

V

We conclude that the Government's passive enforcement system together with its "beg" policy violated neither the First nor Fifth Amendment. Accordingly, we affirm the judgment of the Court of Appeals.

It is so ordered.

NOTES AND QUESTIONS

1. The Court lists the time-honored factors informing prosecutorial discretion—strength of the case, etc.—and notes that "the decision to prosecute is ill-suited to judicial review." *See* Chapter IX *supra*. Why are these considerations not "suitable" for judicial review? For example, is a court, as a matter of institutional capability, competent to evaluate the general deterrence value of a prosecution? Does the Court mean to say that these are considerations that under separation-of-powers principles are assigned to the executive branch and it would be improper for a court to second-guess the prosecution?

2. Are the "systemic costs" of judicial scrutiny of prosecutors that the Court identifies in the same paragraph equally compelling? How does the existence of a "selective prosecution" defense as set forth in, say, *Berrios* unduly "chill law enforcement"? As to the Court's reference to the possible disclosure of "the Government's enforcement policy," how would a permissible enforcement policy be relevant to the government's establishing a selective prosecution defense? Would the costs be sufficiently lowered if the initial review was conducted by the court in camera?

3. Recall the facts of *Berrios*. Suppose the government had decided to prioritize, as a matter of enforcement policy, the prosecution of (a) union officers who served jail time as a result of their convictions, (b) officers of the unions with the most members, and (c) officers of unions that had been cited by the NLRB for unfair practices. Suppose further that these priorities were spelled out in a prosecution memorandum like the one at issue in *Berrios*. Should defendants be entitled to see these portions of the memo after in camera review by the trial judge?

4. Wayte was able to support his claim with a tremendous amount of information about the government's enforcement policies even without getting any discovery, by subpoena or otherwise. This includes information on the government's "passive enforcement" policy and the "beg" sub-policy. Wayte also managed to get what appears to be an internal DOJ memorandum anticipating allegations of selective prosecution. What is the significance of this internal memorandum in the trial judge's decision to allow discovery and an evidentiary hearing?

5. The Court rejects the defendant's claim essentially because defendant showed only the government's awareness of a discriminatory effect—as evidenced by the DOJ memo anticipating equal protection claims—and did not show that the government intended to discriminate. The Court wholly ignores the effective procedural posture of the case—an appeal of a dismissal caused by the government's failure to comply with a discovery order—and never mentions the appropriate legal standard for obtaining discovery or for reviewing a trial court's discovery order. The dissent concludes that defendant had established at least the requisite "colorable basis" for discovery and that the district court had not abused its discretion in ordering the discovery it did.

Neither party devotes much attention to the elephant in the room: that the trial judge's discovery order required the testimony of Attorney General Edwin Meese. Is this a district court judge run amok? Even if all of the three reasons the Court cites for the need for the testimony are true, and even if the attorney general possesses relevant information on the subject, is it conceivable that the testimony of the attorney general was necessary? Could the district court have proceeded more incrementally? By overplaying his hand, and giving traction to appellate courts' fears of judicial scrutiny of prosecutorial decisions, the trial judge likely not only doomed Wayte's case but also may have harmed the development of the selective prosecution doctrine.

C. The Supreme Court Steps Back In   **1089**

In discussing the defendant's failure to prove intentional discrimination, the Court states that selective prosecution claims are subject to ordinary equal protection standards, and proceeds to cite *Oyler* and three cases decided in the late 1970s: *Personnel Administrator of Massachusetts v. Feeney*, 442 U.S. 256 (1979); *Arlington Heights v. Metropolitan Housing Development Corp.*, 429 U.S. 252 (1977); *Washington v. Davis*, 426 U.S. 229 (1976). This trilogy of cases steadfastly requires evidence of discriminatory intent for a viable equal protection claim, and has effectively operated to preclude all manner of such claims, especially claims based on racial discrimination.

For commentary on race and equal protection doctrine, *see* David Sklansky, *Cocaine, Race and Equal Protection*, 47 Stan. L. Rev. 1283 (1995); Charles Lawrence, *The Id, the Ego and Equal Protection: Reckoning with Unconscious Racism*, 39 Stan. L. Rev. 317 (1987); Sheri Lynn Johnson, *Unconscious Racism and the Criminal Law*, 73 Cornell L. Rev. 1016 (1988).

The Supreme Court returned to the issue of discriminatory prosecution just over a decade later in the next case, *United States v. Armstrong*, which involves allegations of race-based prosecution decisions similar to those made in *Yick Wo*. As in *Falk*, *Berrios*, and *Wayte*, the precise issue for decision is not the necessary merits of such a claim but rather the showing that a defendant must make to be entitled to discovery.

The legal and cultural context in which *Armstrong* arose — largely ignored by the other Justices — is set forth in Justice Stevens's dissent: the crack vs. cocaine sentencing disparity in federal court. *See* Chapter XV *infra*.

United States v. Armstrong
517 U.S. 456 (1996)

Chief Justice REHNQUIST delivered the opinion of the Court.

In this case, we consider the showing necessary for a defendant to be entitled to discovery on a claim that the prosecuting attorney singled him out for prosecution on the basis of his race. We conclude that respondents failed to satisfy the threshold showing: They failed to show that the Government declined to prosecute similarly situated suspects of other races.

In April 1992, respondents were indicted in the United States District Court for the Central District of California on charges of conspiring to possess with intent to distribute more than 50 grams of cocaine base (crack) and conspiring to distribute the same, in violation of 21 U.S.C. §§ 841 and 846 (1988 ed. and Supp. IV), and federal firearms offenses. For three months prior to the indictment, agents of the Federal Bureau of Alcohol, Tobacco, and Firearms and the Narcotics Division of the Inglewood, California, Police Department had infiltrated a suspected crack distribution ring by using three confidential informants. On seven separate occasions during this period, the informants had bought a total of 124.3 grams of crack from respondents and witnessed respondents carrying firearms during the sales. The agents searched the hotel room in which the sales were transacted, arrested respondents Armstrong and Hampton in the room, and found more crack and a loaded gun. The agents later arrested the other respondents as part of the ring.

In response to the indictment, respondents filed a motion for discovery or for dismissal of the indictment, alleging that they were selected for federal prosecution because they are black. In support of their motion, they offered only an affidavit by a "Paralegal Specialist," employed by the Office of the Federal Public Defender representing one of the respondents. The only allegation in the affidavit was that, in every one of the 24 § 841 or § 846 cases closed by the office during 1991, the defendant was black. Accompanying the affidavit was a "study" listing the 24 defendants, their race, whether they were prosecuted for dealing cocaine as well as crack, and the status of each case.

The Government opposed the discovery motion, arguing, among other things, that there was no evidence or allegation "that the Government has acted unfairly or has prosecuted non-black defendants or failed to prosecute them." The District Court granted the motion. It ordered the Government (1) to provide a list of all cases from the last three years in which the Government charged both cocaine and firearms offenses, (2) to identify the race of the defendants in those cases, (3) to identify what levels of law enforcement were involved in the investigations of those cases, and (4) to explain its criteria for deciding to prosecute those defendants for federal cocaine offenses.

The Government moved for reconsideration of the District Court's discovery order. With this motion it submitted affidavits and other evidence to explain why it had chosen to prosecute respondents and why respondents' study did not support the inference that the Government was singling out blacks for cocaine prosecution. The federal and local agents participating in the case alleged in affidavits that race played no role in their investigation. An Assistant United States Attorney explained in an affidavit that the decision to prosecute met the general criteria for prosecution, because

> there was over 100 grams of cocaine base involved, over twice the threshold necessary for a ten year mandatory minimum sentence; there were multiple sales involving multiple defendants, thereby indicating a fairly substantial crack cocaine ring; . . . there were multiple federal firearms violations intertwined with the narcotics trafficking; the overall evidence in the case was extremely strong, including audio and videotapes of defendants; . . . and several of the defendants had criminal histories including narcotics and firearms violations.

The Government also submitted sections of a published 1989 Drug Enforcement Administration report which concluded that "[l]arge-scale, interstate trafficking networks controlled by Jamaicans, Haitians and Black street gangs dominate the manufacture and distribution of crack."

In response, one of respondents' attorneys submitted an affidavit alleging that an intake coordinator at a drug treatment center had told her that there are "an equal number of caucasian users and dealers to minority users and dealers." Respondents also submitted an affidavit from a criminal defense attorney alleging that in his experience many nonblacks are prosecuted in state court for crack offenses, and a newspaper article reporting that federal "crack criminals . . . are being punished far more severely than if they had been caught with powder cocaine, and almost every single one of them is black."

The District Court denied the motion for reconsideration. When the Government indicated it would not comply with the court's discovery order, the court dismissed the case.

A divided three-judge panel of the Court of Appeals for the Ninth Circuit reversed, holding that, because of the proof requirements for a selective-prosecution claim, defendants must "provide a colorable basis for believing that 'others similarly situated have not been prosecuted'" to obtain discovery. The Court of Appeals voted to rehear the case en banc, and the en banc panel affirmed the District Court's order of dismissal, holding that "a defendant is not required to demonstrate that the government has failed to prosecute others who are similarly situated." We granted certiorari to determine the appropriate standard for discovery for a selective-prosecution claim.

Neither the District Court nor the Court of Appeals mentioned Federal Rule of Criminal Procedure 16, which by its terms governs discovery in criminal cases. Both parties now discuss the Rule in their briefs, and respondents contend that it supports the result reached by the Court of Appeals. Rule 16 provides, in pertinent part:

> Upon request of the defendant the government shall permit the defendant to inspect and copy or photograph books, papers, documents, photographs, tangible objects, buildings or

place, or copies or portions thereof, which are within the possession, custody or control of the government, and which are material to the preparation of the defendant's defense or are intended for use by the government as evidence in chief at the trial, or were obtained from or belong to the defendant.

Respondents argue that documents "within the possession . . . of the government" that discuss the Government's prosecution strategy for cocaine cases are "material" to respondents' selective-prosecution claim. Respondents argue that the Rule applies because any claim that "results in nonconviction" if successful is a "defense" for the Rule's purposes, and a successful selective-prosecution claim has that effect.

We reject this argument, because we conclude that in the context of Rule 16 "the defendant's defense" means the defendant's response to the Government's case in chief. While it might be argued that as a general matter, the concept of a "defense" includes any claim that is a "sword," challenging the prosecution's conduct of the case, the term may encompass only the narrower class of "shield" claims, which refute the Government's arguments that the defendant committed the crime charged. Rule 16(a)(1)(C) tends to support the "shield-only" reading. If "defense" means an argument in response to the prosecution's case in chief, there is a perceptible symmetry between documents "material to the preparation of the defendant's defense," and, in the very next phrase, documents "intended for use by the government as evidence in chief at the trial."

If this symmetry were not persuasive enough, subdivision (a)(2) of Rule 16 establishes beyond peradventure that "defense" in subdivision (a)(1)(C) can refer only to defenses in response to the Government's case in chief. Rule 16(a)(2), as relevant here, exempts from defense inspection "reports, memoranda, or other internal government documents made by the attorney for the government or other government agents in connection with the investigation or prosecution of the case."

Under Rule 16(a)(1)(C), a defendant may examine documents material to his defense, but, under Rule 16(a)(2), he may not examine Government work product in connection with his case. If a selective-prosecution claim is a "defense," Rule 16(a)(1)(C) gives the defendant the right to examine Government work product in every prosecution except his own. Because respondents' construction of "defense" creates the anomaly of a defendant's being able to examine all Government work product except the most pertinent, we find their construction implausible. We hold that Rule 16(a)(1)(C) authorizes defendants to examine Government documents material to the preparation of their defense against the Government's case in chief, but not to the preparation of selective-prosecution claims.

In *Wade v. United States* (1992), we considered whether a federal court may review a Government decision not to file a motion to reduce a defendant's sentence for substantial assistance to the prosecution, to determine whether the Government based its decision on the defendant's race or religion. In holding that such a decision was reviewable, we assumed that discovery would be available if the defendant could make the appropriate threshold showing, although we concluded that the defendant in that case did not make such a showing. We proceed on a like assumption here.

A selective-prosecution claim is not a defense on the merits to the criminal charge itself, but an independent assertion that the prosecutor has brought the charge for reasons forbidden by the Constitution. Our cases delineating the necessary elements to prove a claim of selective prosecution have taken great pains to explain that the standard is a demanding one. These cases afford a "background presumption," that the showing necessary to obtain discovery should itself be a significant barrier to the litigation of insubstantial claims.

A selective-prosecution claim asks a court to exercise judicial power over a "special province" of the Executive. The Attorney General and United States Attorneys retain "'broad discretion'" to enforce the Nation's criminal laws. *Wayte v. United States* (1985). They have this latitude because they are designated by statute as the President's delegates to help him discharge his constitutional responsibility to "take Care that the Laws be faithfully executed." U.S. Const., Art. II, § 3; see 28 U.S.C. §§ 516, 547. As a result, "[t]he presumption of regularity supports" their prosecutorial decisions and, "in the absence of clear evidence to the contrary, courts presume that they have properly discharged their official duties." In the ordinary case, "so long as the prosecutor has probable cause to believe that the accused committed an offense defined by statute, the decision whether or not to prosecute, and what charge to file or bring before a grand jury, generally rests entirely in his discretion." *Bordenkircher v. Hayes* (1978).

Of course, a prosecutor's discretion is "subject to constitutional constraints." One of these constraints, imposed by the equal protection component of the Due Process Clause of the Fifth Amendment, is that the decision whether to prosecute may not be based on "an unjustifiable standard such as race, religion, or other arbitrary classification," *Oyler v. Boles* (1962). A defendant may demonstrate that the administration of a criminal law is "directed so exclusively against a particular class of persons . . . with a mind so unequal and oppressive" that the system of prosecution amounts to "a practical denial" of equal protection of the law. *Yick Wo v. Hopkins* (1886).

In order to dispel the presumption that a prosecutor has not violated equal protection, a criminal defendant must present "clear evidence to the contrary." We explained in *Wayte* why courts are "properly hesitant to examine the decision whether to prosecute." Judicial deference to the decisions of these executive officers rests in part on an assessment of the relative competence of prosecutors and courts. "Such factors as the strength of the case, the prosecution's general deterrence value, the Government's enforcement priorities, and the case's relationship to the Government's overall enforcement plan are not readily susceptible to the kind of analysis the courts are competent to undertake." It also stems from a concern not to unnecessarily impair the performance of a core executive constitutional function. "Examining the basis of a prosecution delays the criminal proceeding, threatens to chill law enforcement by subjecting the prosecutor's motives and decisionmaking to outside inquiry, and may undermine prosecutorial effectiveness by revealing the Government's enforcement policy."

The requirements for a selective-prosecution claim draw on "ordinary equal protection standards." The claimant must demonstrate that the federal prosecutorial policy "had a discriminatory effect and that it was motivated by a discriminatory purpose." To establish a discriminatory effect in a race case, the claimant must show that similarly situated individuals of a different race were not prosecuted. This requirement has been established in our case law since *Ah Sin v. Wittman* (1905). Ah Sin, a subject of China, petitioned a California state court for a writ of habeas corpus, seeking discharge from imprisonment under a San Francisco County ordinance prohibiting persons from setting up gambling tables in rooms barricaded to stop police from entering. He alleged in his habeas petition "that the ordinance is enforced 'solely and exclusively against persons of the Chinese race and not otherwise.'" We rejected his contention that this averment made out a claim under the Equal Protection Clause, because it did not allege "that the conditions and practices to which the ordinance was directed did not exist exclusively among the Chinese, or that there were other offenders against the ordinance than the Chinese as to whom it was not enforced."

The similarly situated requirement does not make a selective-prosecution claim impossible to prove. Twenty years before *Ah Sin*, we invalidated an ordinance, also adopted by San Francisco, that prohibited the operation of laundries in wooden buildings. *Yick Wo.* The plaintiff in error successfully demonstrated that the ordinance was applied against Chinese nationals but not against other laundry-shop operators. The authorities had denied the applications of 200 Chinese subjects for permits to operate shops in wooden buildings, but granted the applications of 80 individuals who were not Chinese subjects to operate laundries in wooden buildings "under similar conditions." We explained in *Ah Sin* why the similarly situated requirement is necessary:

C. The Supreme Court Steps Back In

> No latitude of intention should be indulged in a case like this. There should be certainty to every intent. Plaintiff in error seeks to set aside a criminal law of the State, not on the ground that it is unconstitutional on its face, not that it is discriminatory in tendency and ultimate actual operation as the ordinance was which was passed on in the *Yick Wo* case, but that it was made so by the manner of its administration. This is a matter of proof, and no fact should be omitted to make it out completely, when the power of a Federal court is invoked to interfere with the course of criminal justice of a State.

Although *Ah Sin* involved federal review of a state conviction, we think a similar rule applies where the power of a federal court is invoked to challenge an exercise of one of the core powers of the Executive Branch of the Federal Government, the power to prosecute.

Respondents urge that cases such as *Batson v. Kentucky* (1986) cut against any absolute requirement that there be a showing of failure to prosecute similarly situated individuals. We disagree. In *Hunter*, we invalidated a state law disenfranchising persons convicted of crimes involving moral turpitude. Our holding was consistent with ordinary equal protection principles, including the similarly situated requirement. There was convincing direct evidence that the State had enacted the provision for the purpose of disfranchising blacks, and indisputable evidence that the state law had a discriminatory effect on blacks as compared to similarly situated whites: Blacks were "'by even the most modest estimates at least 1.7 times as likely as whites to suffer disfranchisement under'" the law in question." *Hunter* thus affords no support for respondents' position.

In *Batson*, we considered "[t]he standards for assessing a prima facie case in the context of discriminatory selection of the venire" in a criminal trial. We required a criminal defendant to show "that the prosecutor has exercised peremptory challenges to remove from the venire members of the defendant's race" and that this fact, the potential for abuse inherent in a peremptory strike, and "any other relevant circumstances raise an inference that the prosecutor used that practice to exclude the veniremen from the petit jury on account of their race." During jury selection, the entire res gestae take place in front of the trial judge. Because the judge has before him the entire venire, he is well situated to detect whether a challenge to the seating of one juror is part of a "pattern" of singling out members of a single race for peremptory challenges. He is in a position to discern whether a challenge to a black juror has evidentiary significance; the significance may differ if the venire consists mostly of blacks or of whites. Similarly, if the defendant makes out a prima facie case, the prosecutor is called upon to justify only decisions made in the very case then before the court. The trial judge need not review prosecutorial conduct in relation to other venires in other cases.

Having reviewed the requirements to prove a selective-prosecution claim, we turn to the showing necessary to obtain discovery in support of such a claim. If discovery is ordered, the Government must assemble from its own files documents which might corroborate or refute the defendant's claim. Discovery thus imposes many of the costs present when the Government must respond to a prima facie case of selective prosecution. It will divert prosecutors' resources and may disclose the Government's prosecutorial strategy. The justifications for a rigorous standard for the elements of a selective-prosecution claim thus require a correspondingly rigorous standard for discovery in aid of such a claim.

The parties, and the Courts of Appeals which have considered the requisite showing to establish entitlement to discovery, describe this showing with a variety of phrases, like "colorable basis," "substantial threshold showing," "substantial and concrete basis," or "reasonable likelihood." However, the many labels for this showing conceal the degree of consensus about the evidence necessary to meet it. The Courts of Appeals "require some evidence tending to show the existence of the essential elements of the defense," discriminatory effect and discriminatory intent.

In this case we consider what evidence constitutes "some evidence tending to show the existence" of the discriminatory effect element. The Court of Appeals held that a defendant may establish a colorable basis for discriminatory effect without evidence that the Government has failed to prosecute others who are similarly situated to the defendant. We think it was mistaken in this view. The vast majority of the Courts of Appeals require the defendant to produce some evidence that similarly situated defendants of other races could have been prosecuted, but were not, and this requirement is consistent with our equal protection case law. As the three-judge panel explained, "'[s]elective prosecution' implies that a selection has taken place."

The Court of Appeals reached its decision in part because it started "with the presumption that people of all races commit all types of crimes—not with the premise that any type of crime is the exclusive province of any particular racial or ethnic group." It cited no authority for this proposition, which seems contradicted by the most recent statistics of the United States Sentencing Commission. Those statistics show: More than 90% of the persons sentenced in 1994 for crack cocaine trafficking were black, United States Sentencing Comm'n, 1994 Annual Report 107 (Table 45); 93.4% of convicted LSD dealers were white, ibid.; and 91% of those convicted for pornography or prostitution were white, id., at 41 (Table 13). Presumptions at war with presumably reliable statistics have no proper place in the analysis of this issue.

The Court of Appeals also expressed concern about the "evidentiary obstacles defendants face." But all of its sister Circuits that have confronted the issue have required that defendants produce some evidence of differential treatment of similarly situated members of other races or protected classes. In the present case, if the claim of selective prosecution were well founded, it should not have been an insuperable task to prove that persons of other races were being treated differently than respondents. For instance, respondents could have investigated whether similarly situated persons of other races were prosecuted by the State of California and were known to federal law enforcement officers, but were not prosecuted in federal court. We think the required threshold—a credible showing of different treatment of similarly situated persons—adequately balances the Government's interest in vigorous prosecution and the defendant's interest in avoiding selective prosecution.

In the case before us, respondents' "study" did not constitute "some evidence tending to show the existence of the essential elements of" a selective-prosecution claim. The study failed to identify individuals who were not black and could have been prosecuted for the offenses for which respondents were charged, but were not so prosecuted. This omission was not remedied by respondents' evidence in opposition to the Government's motion for reconsideration. The newspaper article, which discussed the discriminatory effect of federal drug sentencing laws, was not relevant to an allegation of discrimination in decisions to prosecute. Respondents' affidavits, which recounted one attorney's conversation with a drug treatment center employee and the experience of another attorney defending drug prosecutions in state court, recounted hearsay and reported personal conclusions based on anecdotal evidence. The judgment of the Court of Appeals is therefore reversed, and the case is remanded for proceedings consistent with this opinion.

It is so ordered.

Justice SOUTER, concurring.

Justice BREYER, concurring in part and concurring in the judgment.

I write separately because, in my view, Federal Rule of Criminal Procedure 16 does not limit a defendant's discovery rights to documents related to the Government's case in chief. The Rule says that "the government shall permit the defendant to inspect and copy" certain physical items (I shall summarily call them "documents") "which are material to the preparation of the defendant's defense." Fed. Rule Crim. Proc. 16(a)(1)(C). A "defendant's defense" can take many forms, including (1) a simple response to the Government's case in chief, (2) an affirmative defense unrelated to the merits (such as a Speedy Trial Act claim), (3) an unrelated claim of constitutional right, (4) a foreseeable surrebuttal to a likely Government rebuttal, and others. The Rule's language does not limit its scope to the first item on this list. To interpret the Rule in this limited way creates a legal distinction that, from a discovery perspective, is arbitrary. It threatens to create two full parallel sets of criminal discovery principles. And, as far as I can tell, the interpretation lacks legal support.

The Court bases its interpretation upon what it says is a "perceptible symmetry" between two phrases in Rule 16(a)(1)(C) — the phrase "material to the preparation of the defendant's defense," and the next phrase, "intended for use by the government as evidence in chief at the trial." To test the Court's argument, consider these two phrases in context. The Rule says:

> Upon request of the defendant the government shall permit the defendant to inspect and copy [documents and other items] . . . which [1] are material to the preparation of the defendant's defense or [2] are intended for use by the government as evidence in chief at the trial, or [3] were obtained from or belong to the defendant.

Fed. Rule Crim. Proc. 16(a)(1)(C).

Though symmetry may reside in the eye of the beholder, I can find no relevant symmetry here. Rather, the language suggests a simple three-part categorization of the documents and other physical items that the Rule requires the Government to make available to the defendant. From a purely linguistic perspective, there is no more reason to import into the first category a case-in-chief-related limitation (from the second category) than some kind of defendant's-belongings-related limitation (from the third category).

Rule 16 creates these three categories for a reason that belies "symmetry" — namely, to specify two sets of items (the Government's case in chief evidence, the defendant's belongings) that the Government must make available to the defendant without a preliminary showing of "materiality." The Rule's first category creates a residual classification (items "material to the preparation of the defendant's defense") that require a preliminary "materiality" showing. The Committee thought, however, that "[l]imiting the rule to situations in which the defendant can show that the evidence is material seems unwise. . . . For this reason subdivision (a)(1)(C) also contains language to compel disclosure if the government intends to use the property as evidence at the trial or if the property was obtained from or belongs to the defendant." Nothing in the Notes, or in the Rule's language, suggests that the residual category of items "material to the preparation of the defendant's defense," means to cover only those items related to the case in chief.

The only other reason the majority advances in support of its "case in chief" limitation concerns a later part of the Rule, subdivision 16(a)(2). As relevant here, that subdivision exempts Government attorney work product from certain of Rule 16's disclosure requirements. In the majority's view, since (1) a defendant asserting a valid "selective prosecution" defense would likely need prosecution work product to make his case, but (2) the Rule exempts prosecution work product from discovery, then (3) the Rule must have some kind of implicit limitation (such as a "case in chief" limitation) that makes it irrelevant to defense efforts to assert "selective prosecution" defenses.

The majority's conclusion, however, does not follow from its premises. For one thing, Rule 16's work-product exception may itself contain implicit exceptions. After all, "[t]he privilege derived from the work-product doctrine is not absolute." *United States v. Nobles* (1975). To the extent such a reading permits a defendant to obtain "work product" in an appropriate case (say, with a strong prima facie showing of selective prosecution), the Court's problem does not exist. Of course, to read the work-product exception as containing some such implicit exception itself represents a departure from the Rule's literal language. But, is it not far easier to believe the Rule's authors intended some such small implicit exception to an exception, consistent with the language and purpose of the Rule, than that they intended the very large exception created by the Court?

For another thing, even if one reads the work-product exception literally, the Court's problem disappears as long as courts can supplement Rule 16 discovery with discovery based upon other legal principles. The language of the work-product exception suggests the possibility of such supplementation, for it says, not that work product is "exemp[t]" from discovery, but that "this rule" does not authorize discovery of the prosecutor's work product. Fed. Rule Civ. Proc. 16(a)(2). The Advisory Committee's Notes make clear that the Committee believed that other rules of law may authorize (or require) discovery not mentioned in the Rule. Of course, the majority, in a sense, reads the Rule as permitting supplementation, but it does more. It goes well beyond the added (say, constitutionally related) rule supplementation needed to overcome its problem; instead, it shrinks the Rule by unnecessarily creating a major limitation on its scope.

Finally, and in any event, here the defendants sought discovery of information that is not work product. Thus, we need not decide whether in an appropriate case it would be necessary to find an implicit exception to the language of Rule 16(a)(2), or to find an independent constitutional source for the discovery, or to look for some other basis.

In sum, neither the alleged "symmetry" in the structure of Rule 16(a)(1)(C), nor the work-product exception of Rule 16(a)(2), supports the majority's limitation of discovery under Rule 16(a)(1)(C) to documents related to the Government's "case in chief." Rather, the language and legislative history make clear that the Rule's drafters meant it to provide a broad authorization for defendants' discovery, to be supplemented if necessary in an appropriate case. Whether or not one can also find a basis for this kind of discovery in other sources of law, Rule 16(a)(1)(C) provides one such source, and we should consider whether the defendants' discovery request satisfied the Rule's requirement that the discovery be "material to the preparation of the defendant's defense."

I believe that the defendants' request did not satisfy this threshold. Were the "selective prosecution" defense valid in this case — i.e., were there "clear evidence," *United States v. Chemical Foundation, Inc.* (1926), that the Federal Government's prosecutorial policy "had a discriminatory effect and . . . was motivated by a discriminatory purpose," *Wayte v. United States*, (1985), it should have been fairly easy for the defendants to find, not only instances in which the Federal Government prosecuted African-Americans, but also some instances in which the Federal Government did not prosecute similarly situated caucasians. The defendants' failure to do so, for the reasons the Court sets forth, amounts to a failure to make the necessary threshold showing in respect to materiality

Justice STEVENS, dissenting.

Federal prosecutors are respected members of a respected profession. Despite an occasional misstep, the excellence of their work abundantly justifies the presumption that "they have properly discharged their official duties." Nevertheless, the possibility that political or racial animosity may infect a decision to institute criminal proceedings cannot be ignored. *Oyler v. Boles* (1962). For that reason, it has long been settled that the prosecutor's broad discretion to determine when criminal charges should be filed is not completely unbridled. As the Court notes, however, the scope of judicial review of particular exercises of that discretion is not fully defined.

The United States Attorney for the Central District of California is a member and an officer of the bar of that District Court. As such, she has a duty to the judges of that Court to maintain the standards of the profession in the performance of her official functions. If a District Judge has reason to suspect that she, or a member of her staff, has singled out particular defendants for prosecution on the basis of their race, it is surely appropriate for the judge to determine whether there is a factual basis for such a concern. I agree with the Court that Rule 16 of the Federal Rules of Criminal Procedure is not the source of the District Court's power to make the necessary inquiry. I disagree, however, with its implicit assumption that a different, relatively rigid rule needs to be crafted to regulate the use of this seldom-exercised inherent judicial power. *See* Advisory Committee's Notes on Rule 16 (Rule 16 is "not intended to limit the judge's discretion to order broader discovery in appropriate cases").

The Court correctly concludes that in this case the facts presented to the District Court in support of respondents' claim that they had been singled out for prosecution because of their race were not sufficient to prove that defense. Moreover, I agree with the Court that their showing was not strong enough to give them a right to discovery, either under Rule 16 or under the District Court's inherent power to order discovery in appropriate circumstances. Like Chief Judge Wallace of the Court of Appeals, however, I am persuaded that the District Judge did not abuse her discretion when she concluded that the factual showing was sufficiently disturbing to require some response from the United States Attorney's Office. Perhaps the discovery order was broader than necessary, but I cannot agree with the Court's apparent conclusion that no inquiry was permissible.

The District Judge's order should be evaluated in light of three circumstances that underscore the need for judicial vigilance over certain types of drug prosecutions. First, the Anti–Drug Abuse Act of 1986 and subsequent legislation established a regime of extremely high penalties for the possession and distribution of so-called "crack" cocaine. Those provisions treat one gram of crack as the equivalent of 100 grams of powder cocaine. The distribution of 50 grams of crack is thus punishable by the same mandatory minimum sentence of 10 years in prison that applies to the distribution of 5,000 grams of powder cocaine. The Sentencing Guidelines extend this ratio to penalty levels above the mandatory minimums: For any given quantity of crack, the guideline range is the same as if the offense had involved 100 times that amount in powder cocaine. These penalties result in sentences for crack offenders that average three to eight times longer than sentences for comparable powder offenders. United States Sentencing Commission, Special Report to Congress: Cocaine and Federal Sentencing Policy 145 (Feb. 1995).

Second, the disparity between the treatment of crack cocaine and powder cocaine is matched by the disparity between the severity of the punishment imposed by federal law and that imposed by state law for the same conduct. For a variety of reasons, often including the absence of mandatory minimums, the existence of parole, and lower baseline penalties, terms of imprisonment for drug offenses tend to be substantially lower in state systems than in the federal system. The difference is especially marked in the case of crack offenses. The majority of States draw no distinction between types of cocaine in their penalty schemes; of those that do, none has established as stark a differential as the Federal Government. For example, if respondent Hampton is found guilty, his federal sentence might be as long as a mandatory life term. Had he been tried in state court, his sentence could have been as short as 12 years, less worktime credits of half that amount.

Finally, it is undisputed that the brunt of the elevated federal penalties falls heavily on blacks. While 65% of the persons who have used crack are white, in 1993 they represented only 4% of the federal offenders convicted of trafficking in crack. Eighty-eight percent of such defendants were black. During the first 18 months of full guideline implementation, the sentencing disparity between black and white defendants grew from preguideline levels: Blacks on average received sentences over 40% longer than whites. Those figures represent a major threat to the integrity of federal sentencing reform, whose main purpose was the elimination of disparity (especially racial) in sentencing. The Sentencing Commission acknowledges that the heightened crack penalties are a "primary cause of the growing disparity between sentences for Black and White federal defendants."

The extraordinary severity of the imposed penalties and the troubling racial patterns of enforcement give rise to a special concern about the fairness of charging practices for crack offenses. Evidence tending to prove that black defendants charged with distribution of crack in the Central District of California are prosecuted in federal court, whereas members of other races charged with similar offenses are prosecuted in state court, warrants close scrutiny by the federal judges in that district. In my view, the District Judge, who has sat on both the federal and the state benches in Los Angeles, acted well within her discretion to call for the development of facts that would demonstrate what standards, if any, governed the choice of forum where similarly situated offenders are prosecuted.

Respondents submitted a study showing that of all cases involving crack offenses that were closed by the Federal Public Defender's Office in 1991, 24 out of 24 involved black defendants. To supplement this evidence, they submitted affidavits from two of the attorneys in the defense team. The first reported a statement from an intake coordinator at a local drug treatment center that, in his experience, an equal number of crack users and dealers were caucasian as belonged to minorities. App. 138. The second was from David R. Reed, counsel for respondent Armstrong. Reed was both an active court-appointed attorney in the Central District of California and one of the directors of the leading association of criminal defense lawyers who practice before the Los Angeles County courts. Reed stated that he did not recall "ever handling a [crack] cocaine case involving non-black defendants" in federal court, nor had he even heard of one. He further stated that "[t]here are many crack cocaine sales cases prosecuted in state court that do involve racial groups other than blacks."

The majority discounts the probative value of the affidavits, claiming that they recounted "hearsay" and reported "personal conclusions based on anecdotal evidence." But the Reed affidavit plainly contained more than mere hearsay; Reed offered information based on his own extensive experience in both federal and state courts. Given the breadth of his background, he was well qualified to compare the practices of federal and state prosecutors. In any event, the Government never objected to the admission of either affidavit on hearsay or any other grounds. It was certainly within the District Court's discretion to credit the affidavits of two members of the bar of that Court, at least one of whom had presumably acquired a reputation by his frequent appearances there, and both of whose statements were made on pains of perjury.

The criticism that the affidavits were based on "anecdotal evidence" is also unpersuasive. I thought it was agreed that defendants do not need to prepare sophisticated statistical studies in order to receive mere discovery in cases like this one. Certainly evidence based on a drug counselor's personal observations or on an attorney's practice in two sets of courts, state and federal, can "'ten[d] to show the existence'" of a selective prosecution.

Even if respondents failed to carry their burden of showing that there were individuals who were not black but who could have been prosecuted in federal court for the same offenses, it does not follow that the District Court abused its discretion in ordering discovery. There can be no doubt that such individuals exist, and indeed the Government has never denied the same. In those circumstances, I fail to see why the District Court was unable to take judicial notice of this obvious fact and demand information from the Government's files to support or refute respondents' evidence. The presumption that some whites are prosecuted in state court is not "contradicted" by the statistics the majority cites, which show only that high percentages of blacks are convicted of certain federal crimes, while high percentages of whites are convicted of other federal crimes. Those figures are entirely consistent with the allegation of selective prosecution. The relevant comparison, rather, would be with the percentages of

C. The Supreme Court Steps Back In   1099

blacks and whites who commit those crimes. But, as discussed above, in the case of crack far greater numbers of whites are believed guilty of using the substance. The District Court, therefore, was entitled to find the evidence before it significant and to require some explanation from the Government.

In sum, I agree with the Sentencing Commission that "[w]hile the exercise of discretion by prosecutors and investigators has an impact on sentences in almost all cases to some extent, because of the 100-to-1 quantity ratio and federal mandatory minimum penalties, discretionary decisions in cocaine cases often have dramatic effects." The severity of the penalty heightens both the danger of arbitrary enforcement and the need for careful scrutiny of any colorable claim of discriminatory enforcement. In this case, the evidence was sufficiently disturbing to persuade the District Judge to order discovery that might help explain the conspicuous racial pattern of cases before her court. I cannot accept the majority's conclusion that the District Judge either exceeded her power or abused her discretion when she did so. I therefore respectfully dissent.

NOTES AND QUESTIONS

1. Defendants' claim is not exactly that they were selected for prosecution because they were Black. Rather, it is that they were selected for *federal* prosecution—and thus to the federal court punishment disparity Justice Stevens refers to—because they were Black. In this regard, what is the significance of the fact that the investigation that led to defendants' arrests was a joint investigation by federal (ATF) and state (Inglewood police department) agents? Does the fact this prosecution arose out of the work of such a task force lend credence to defendants' claims?

2. Is the Court's analysis of Fed. R. Crim. P. 16 persuasive? Are the materials the district court ordered the government to produce covered by Rule 16(a)(2)? Can you think of any exceptions to the Rule 16(a)(2) exemption? Consider, for example, an interview memorandum prepared by the FBI of a witness who contradicts a key government witness's eyewitness account of the crime.

3. Suppose the government had simply complied with the district court's order and produced responsive documents. Suppose further that the government's response showed that it had prosecuted a hundred crack/firearms cases in the last three years, all the defendants were Black, only line level DEA agents were involved in the investigations that led to those charges, and that the prosecution criteria it used in all cases were those identified in its response to the defendants' motion. Should a motion to dismiss for selective prosecution succeed—on the merits—on these facts? If not, what other discovery should the defendants have sought to obtain? Presumably the defendants' counsel had, or would have been able to establish, a cooperative relationship with local state public defender organizations, which would have been able to establish whether whites were prosecuted in state court for crack offenses. What do you make of this gap in the defendants' showing?

4. The Court states that because the standard for selective prosecution claims is "a demanding one," it follows that a "showing necessary to obtain discovery should itself be a significant barrier to the litigation of insubstantial claims." Does this follow as a matter of logic? Does it follow from this point that if a claim were comparatively easy to prove the standard for obtaining discovery to support such a claim should be lower than usual? Note that the discovery rules in both the criminal and civil rules of federal procedure are generally symmetrical, and are intended to apply regardless of the type of claim at issue.

The point is weak legally as well. The Court describes this purported claim-discovery relationship as a "background presumption," from "our cases," although the only case it is able to cite (and only by a *cf.* signal) on this point, *United States v. Mezzanatto*, 513 U.S. 196, 203 (1995), uses the term only in reference to the "background presumption" that evidentiary arguments can be waived by trial stipulations.

5. The Court ultimately adopts the following as the showing required to obtain discovery for a selective prosecution claim: "some evidence tending to show the existence of the essential elements of the defense." This formulation would seem to mean that a heavy showing on one element — say 100 out of 100 crack defendants were Black — could never make up for a weaker showing on another element. Does this make sense? In applying this standard to what it calls the "discriminatory effect" or "similarly situated" element of the claim, the Court discounts entirely as "hearsay" and "anecdotal" the affidavits from the drug treatment center employee (both whites and Blacks use and deal crack) and state court defense attorney (whites are prosecuted for crack offenses in state court). This qualitative component seems at odds with the "some evidence tending to show" formulation. Don't the affidavits, even if anecdotal, "tend" to show the more general points? And why should the evidentiary rules against hearsay be applicable in this context, where defendants are not presenting evidence in court but are merely trying to show that they should be entitled to discovery?

6. Ironically the Court cites and quotes from *Berrios* as the source of the "some evidence tending to show the existence of the essential elements of the defense" discovery standard. It is ironic, first, because the only evidence Berrios adduced on the "similarly situated" element was a newspaper article, classic hearsay, and second, because in *Berrios* the Second Circuit deferred to the trial judge under an abuse-of-discretion standard, a standard not even discussed by the majority in *Armstrong*.

7. The Court, as solace to defendants, points out that selective prosecution claims are not "impossible to prove," and in support of that proposition cites *Yick Wo*. Is it a tribute to the Court's self-awareness that it defends the standard it announces as "not impossible to prove"? Is this *Yick Wo*'s true legacy, as an unattainable ideal of an equal protection claim, that the Supreme Court can point to as precedent? Is *Yick Wo* to the Supreme Court what God was to Voltaire — if he did not exist it would have been necessary to invent him?

But it is no surprise that the only example the Court can point to was over a hundred years old. In the era of *Yick Wo*, there was comparatively no shame or stigma in admitting to racism. Indeed, the City of San Francisco did not even contest Yick Wo's factual allegations, just as the state in *Neal v. Delaware*, 130 U.S. 370 (1880), six years earlier, conceded that no Black persons had ever served on grand or petit juries in the state courts of Delaware. *See* Chapter I *supra*. Obviously, by the time of *Armstrong*, at least, few public officials were admitting to any racist motivations they were conscious that they had, and by definition were unaware of any unconscious racism they harbored.

8. Consider again the Court's statement that the "showing necessary to obtain discovery should itself be a significant barrier to the litigation of insubstantial claims." But isn't the difficulty of the required showing also a barrier to the litigation of *substantial* claims as well? Consider *Ah Sin v. Whitman*, 198 U.S. 500 (1905), which the Court cites to demonstrate the venerability of the similarly situated requirement, and assume further that defendant's claim there was factually valid, that is, that Chinese illegal gambling operations were investigated by the police but that similarly illegal white gambling operations were not. How would the defendants in *Ah Sin* realistically have been able to demonstrate "some evidence" as to the "similarly situated" element? Consider further that such evidence could neither be "hearsay" nor "anecdotal."

Does the Court simply doubt that many substantial claims exist? Is part of the majority's homage to prosecutorial propriety, for which it relies heavily on *Wayte*, based on skepticism that prosecutors would misbehave? Even Justice Stevens, in dissent, joins this party: "Federal prosecutors are respected members of a respected profession. Despite an occasional misstep,

C. The Supreme Court Steps Back In   **1101**

the excellence of their work abundantly justifies the presumption that 'they have properly discharged their official duties.'" Is there any reason to believe that the people who are federal prosecutors are not representative of America and may harbor conscious and unconscious biases?

9. What if discovery had demonstrated that 100 percent of the defendants who were referred to the U.S. Attorney's Office for potential prosecution for crack and firearms offenses by the DEA were Black, and that the U.S. Attorney's Office had no role in or knowledge of the DEA's selection criteria. Putting aside whether an arrangement granting the DEA carte blanche referral powers would have been irresponsible by the U.S. Attorney's Office, inasmuch as the DEA is part of the Department of Justice, should a motion for discovery of information from the DEA be governed by the same standard as in *Armstrong*?

The Court invokes the "special province" of the executive to prosecute criminal cases, and disavows any role for the judiciary in second-guessing those decisions, subject to constitutional constraints. But is the same degree of judicial deference owed to law enforcement agents as to prosecutors?

10. In footnote 3 the Court says this: "We reserve the question whether a defendant must satisfy the similarly situated requirement in a case 'involving direct admissions by [prosecutors] of discriminatory purpose.'" Why would the similarly situated requirement even be relevant where the prosecutor made such an admission? Of course the government could dispute the consequences of the admission—the prosecutor didn't say it, didn't mean it, it was a joke, etc.—but if the court finds that such a statement was said and meant what's left to litigate? Haven't both discriminatory purpose and effect been established?

Professor Randall Kennedy posits that there are no reported cases in federal or state court ruling that a prosecutor selectively discriminated on the basis of race. Randall Kennedy, Race, Crime, and the Law 354-55 n.* (1997). He correctly points out, as the Court also did in *Falk*, that the discrimination in *Yick Wo* was actually done by the county board of supervisors, not the prosecutors. *Id.* He rejects a case sometimes cited as an example of a successful claim because the case was dismissed not on the merits of a selective prosecution defense but for failure to comply with a discovery order. *People v. Ochoa*, 212 Cal. Rptr. 4 (Ct. App. 1985). As an example of a case that comes closest to this category Professor Kennedy notes the injunction against the retrial of Paul Duncan in *Duncan v. Perez*, 445 F.2d 557 (5th Cir. 1971), *see* Chapter XIV *infra*, due to the racial overtones of the original prosecution.

In *United States v. Al Jibori*, 90 F.3d 22 (2d Cir. 1996), the Second Circuit reversed a district court's denial of a motion for discovery on a selective prosecution claim. The facts are unique. Defendant Al Jibori, an Iraqi living in Romania, presented a false Swedish passport bearing the name "Lundkvist" upon entry to the United States at Kennedy Airport. He was charged under a rarely used statute, 18 U.S.C § 1543, which criminalized use of a false passport. To fend off the defendant's discovery motion the government submitted an affidavit stating that one reason Al Mijori was charged was because he was from a part of the world (the Middle East) that had been the source of terrorist activity. The Second Circuit reversed the district court's denial of the discovery motion, finding that the government had essentially admitted it had charged the defendant in part based on his national origin, an issue—the role of prosecutor's admissions—that *Armstrong* chose not to address. The Court noted that had the government simply remained silent the discovery motion would properly have been denied.

Courts have also dealt with selective prosecution claims in the wake of 9/11 and the prosecution of suspected terrorists. In *United States v. Khan*, 461 F.3d 477 (4th Cir. 2006), for example, several defendants were charged with violations of, inter alia, the Neutrality Act,

1102   Chapter XII Discriminatory Enforcement

which generally prohibits assisting any military actions against a nation with which the United States is "at peace." The charges centered around the defendants' involvement in certain terrorist training camps, some of which were involved in operations against Indian troops in Kashmir. Defendants claimed selective prosecution based on their being "Muslim in a post 9/11 world" and pointed to the government's failure to prosecute other quasi-terrorist organizations under the Neutrality Act, namely, the Cambodian Freedom Fighters (CFF) and the Irish Republican Army (IRA), who were indirectly involved in operations against Cambodia and England. The Fourth Circuit held that these other putative defendants were not "similarly situated" inasmuch as the organizations with which defendants were affiliated were overtly hostile to the United States, which served as a legitimate prosecutorial factor that distinguished them from the CFF and the IRA.

D. SELECTIVE INVESTIGATION

The next three cases consider what might be called pure cases of selective investigation. In these cases the pool of potential defendants is determined by allegedly discriminatory decision making by investigative agencies prior to any involvement by a prosecutor. These cases invite the question whether the standard for selective prosecution claims — or at least for obtaining discovery in pursuit of such claims — should be the same where the impermissible "selecting" is done not by prosecutors but by the police or other law enforcement agents.

People v. Harris
182 Cal. App. 2d Supp. 837 (1961)

HULS, J.

This and 10 other cases are cognate cases and being appeals from judgments of conviction of violation of Penal Code, section 330 (gambling), and the other eight, from judgments of conviction of violation of Pasadena Ordinance Number 453-3 ½ (knowingly being present at a place where gambling was being conducted). The facts of the gambling (playing "21" for money) and being present thereat, were stipulated to, provided that the defendants be permitted to make an offer of proof as to the constitutional question of deliberate and intentional discrimination and unequal treatment in the enforcement of the applicable statute and ordinance, by reason of race and color. "Offers of proof" were made by defendants and argued to the court, which rejected the offers and found each defendant guilty as charged, and fined each $26.25.

From all the trial court's comments in the transcript, we believe that he rejected the offers because he was of the opinion that the evidence if admitted would not prove intentional and deliberate discriminatory enforcement, "even though there may be some slight inference even on the very small scale the offer of proof is made, it falls far short of showing deliberate, intentional, discriminatory practice."

We are not considering the affidavits brought up to us on respondent's motion to augment the record, for the reason that there is nothing in the record to show that they were before the trial court which heard the evidence and the offers of proof. The contents of the affidavits might have become the subject of evidence in rebuttal by the prosecution had the court determined that any or all of the offers of proof should have been granted. The real questions before us are as to the admissibility of such evidence, not as to its ultimate weight or effect, and whether the trial court committed prejudicial error in rejecting them.

The offers of proof were:

1. Racial population figures and percentages in Pasadena.

D. Selective Investigation 1103

2. Record of Pasadena gambling arrests showing for the year 1957, 16 white persons arrested, 276 Negroes; 1958, 9 white, 82 Negroes; 1959, all persons arrested, Negroes.
3. Existence of gambling for years in three men's clubs, all members of which were white, and no arrests made. That the chief of police was a member of one of the clubs and aware of the gambling.
4. One of the arresting officers would testify the routine city police procedure was to patrol the colored section and, on finding grouped parked cars, prowl the private premises for gambling, with no like patrol in the white section and no investigation made when cars were so parked in white areas. That no arrests were made when, shortly before the instant arrests, police found white men gambling, some of them city police officers.

5 and 6. Somewhat similar testimony by an arresting officer, and another officer.

The question before us is whether the offered proof was admissible as tending to show deliberate and intentional racial discriminatory enforcement of the criminal laws in violation of the equal protection guarantee of the 14th Amendment to the Constitution of the United States and of article I, section 11, of the Constitution of the State of California.

The question has been raised in actions for injunction, by habeas corpus and as a defense on appeal from judgments of conviction in criminal cases.

A pleading alleging intentional and deliberate discrimination in the enforcement of a criminal ordinance fair on its face was held to be within the principle announced in *Yick Wo v. Hopkins* (1886) and followed in [state cases]. The plaintiff there was seeking injunctive relief and the court also held the pleading to be squarely within the rule announced in . . . *Snowden v. Hughes* (1943). *People v. Gordon* (1951) was another case involving injunctive relief. . . .

If equity will intervene to prevent discriminatory enforcement of an ordinance valid on its face, it would seem to be unnecessary to require such intervention as a prerequisite, when the constitutional question has been squarely raised and the objection to prosecution made as a defense in a criminal proceeding.

The question here raised was before the court on a petition for habeas corpus in the cases of *Ah Sin v. Wittman* (1905) and *Ex parte Fiske* (1887). The court in the latter case, with respect to the ordinance there under consideration, after discussing the *Yick Wo* case, supra, said, "Neither the face of the ordinance, nor its administration, shows any intent to discriminate against a class of persons, or against any person."

The *Yick Wo* case has been extensively cited in cases involving laws both valid and invalid on their face. While a distinction may be attempted on this disparity, it should be noted that in *East Coast Lumber Terminal, Inc. v. Babylon* (C.A.2d N.Y., 1949) the federal court observed: "It has indeed been the law for over sixty years that the Amendment covers the unequal enforcement of valid laws, as well as any enforcement of invalid laws." *See also Concordia F. Ins. Co. v. Illinois* (1934) "The purpose of the equal protection clause of the 14th Amendment is to secure every person within the state's jurisdiction against intentional and arbitrary discrimination, whether occasioned by express terms of a statute or by its improper execution through duly constituted agents." An actual discrimination arising from the method of administering a law is as potential in creating a denial of equality of rights as discrimination made by law. "The guaranty was aimed at undue favor and individual or class privilege, on the one hand, and at hostile discrimination or the oppression of inequality, on the other. It sought an equality of treatment of all persons, even though all enjoyed the protection of due process."

In reversing a judgment of conviction of a violation of an ordinance for illegally obstructing a public sidewalk, *People v. Amdur* (1954), recognizing the principles above referred to, stated "Fundamental personal rights are not less sacred and not less entitled to injunctive protection than are property rights" and ordered a new trial with directions to admit all competent evidence offered on the issue of the unconstitutional application of the ordinance in question.

Convictions of Negroes, after trial upon indictments returned by grand juries from which Negroes had been systematically excluded, have been reversed on the grounds of a denial of equal protection.

An unconstitutional application of an ordinance is always available as a defense to prosecution for violation thereof. Similarly, conviction of members of a religious sect warranted the application of the equal protection guarantee.

> Upon trial, defendants are entitled to present proof, if any, that there has been intentional discrimination, based on any improper consideration. Discriminatory law enforcement, to constitute a want of due process of law, and a denial of the equal protection of the laws, must be intentional, and purposeful. It will not be presumed, and before it can be established, proof thereof must be judicially made.

The appellants should have been permitted to introduce any evidence they offered which tended to show actual intentional discrimination in the enforcement of the statute and ordinance in this instance. We are not holding that the offered evidence proves the defense of discriminatory enforcement; we are merely holding that it was admissible in appellants' efforts to prove that defense. It is wholly unsatisfactory to determine whether that defense was sufficient merely on an offer of proof.

The judgment is reversed. A new trial is ordered, with directions to admit all competent evidence not inconsistent with this opinion on the issue of the unconstitutional application of the statute and ordinance in question.

SWAIN, P.J., and SMITH, J., concurred.

NOTES AND QUESTIONS

1. Defendants' offer of proof is critical in *Harris*. Indeed, defendants in the consolidated cases abandoned any other factual defenses they may have had—I wasn't there; it wasn't gambling; I didn't see it—and stipulated to facts that would establish their guilt in exchange for the opportunity to present their offer of proof. (It is unclear why they had to make this concession. A defendant has a right to make an offer of proof.)

An offer of proof is a statement of counsel on the record outside the presence of the jury describing certain evidence that the lawyer wants to introduce but has not yet been found admissible, or has been ruled inadmissible. It can be an opportunity to persuade the trial judge to admit the evidence but it is usually done for appellate purposes after the trial court has excluded the evidence, so an appellate court can decide whether the exclusion of the evidence requires that the verdict of the trial court be set aside or reversed. *See* Fed. R. Evid. 103(a)(2) (a claim of error in the exclusion of evidence requires that a party "informs the court of its substance by an offer of proof, unless the substance was apparent from the context").

2. Assume that the defendants in the ordered retrial are able to introduce competent evidence in support of all of the points in their offer of proof, which was excluded in the first trial. The appellate court expresses no opinion on whether the evidence is sufficient to establish a selective enforcement defense.

What do you think? On this evidence would defendants have made out a viable selective enforcement claim under even the unforgiving standards developed later in *Armstrong* and *Wayte*? What, if anything, are they missing?

3. If you represented the city, how would you try respond to defendants' evidence? What if you could marshal evidence that the city did not have the resources to police both Black and white neighborhoods and focused on the Black neighborhoods because they tended to find more violations there? What if there was evidence the city received more citizen complaints about gambling from residents of the Black neighborhoods?

4. It is interesting that the Court cites *Ah Sin v. Whitman*, 198 U.S. 500 (1905), *see supra.* In *Harris*, the defendants are able to make the sort of allegations, apparently with evidentiary support, that were found lacking in *Ah Sin*: that whites were engaged in the same illegal conduct the minority defendants had been charged with; and that the minorities were investigated for the misconduct but that whites were not. How do you think that the defendants were able to develop the factual support they point to for this part of their offer of proof? Is it realistic to expect all defendants bringing such challenges to be able to develop this sort of factual support?

5. *Harris* is a remarkable case. For its factual record, for one thing (assuming the offer of proof is supportable). For its legal foresight, for another. Not only was it decided two years before the Supreme Court recognized a selective prosecution claim in *Oyler*, it was also decided at a time when many courts had refused to recognize a selective enforcement claim in the context of criminal prosecutions, *see* Note, *The Right to Nondiscriminatory Enforcement of State Penal Laws*, 61 Colum. L. Rev. 1103, 1104 & n.12 (1961), and when no courts had recognized such a claim where the selectivity was based on race.

Professor David Cole, echoing Professor Kennedy, stated in 1999 that since *Yick Wo* there has been no reported federal or state case where a court dismissed a prosecution because a prosecutor acted for racial reasons. David Cole, No Equal Justice 159 (1999). Professor Gabriel Chin describes *Harris* as being the closest thing there is to such a case. Gabriel J. Chin, *Inexplicable on Grounds of Race: Doubts About* Yick Wo, 2008 U. Ill. L. Rev. 1359, 1361 n.11.

The next case considers allegations of discriminatory enforcement, also at the police department level, of liquor laws in Portsmouth, Virginia, in the 1970s. The case is not an appeal from a conviction—the underlying criminal case was dismissed—but is a civil rights action based on the same underlying police conduct.

Butler v. Cooper
554 F.2d 645 (4th Cir. 1977)

K.K. HALL, Circuit Judge:

The plaintiff, Esther Butler, filed this action pro se in the United States District Court for the Eastern District of Virginia. Her complaint alleged that the defendants, various officials and police officers of the City of Portsmouth, Virginia, conspired to deprive her and all Black Americans in the City of Portsmouth of equal protection of the laws by disproportionate and racially selective enforcement of Virginia's liquor laws. Under 42 U.S.C. § 1983, she sought injunctive and declaratory relief and monetary relief in the amount of $250,000 compensatory damages and $250,000 exemplary damages. The district court granted defendants' motions for summary judgment, finding the plaintiff's allegations of denial of equal protection to be "vague and conclusory" and "unsupported by factual allegations." We agree and affirm.

The fourteenth amendment equal protection clause embraces a right to be free from racially discriminatory enforcement of a state's criminal laws. *Rizzo v. Goode* (1976); *Yick Wo*

1106 Chapter XII Discriminatory Enforcement

v. Hopkins (1886). The plaintiff correctly stated that in alleging discrimination, one must do more than allege and prove that others have violated the law and are not being prosecuted. *See, e.g., Oyler v. Boles* (1962). Before a claim of unlawful discrimination in the enforcement of criminal laws can be established, the plaintiff must allege and prove a deliberate selective process of enforcement based upon race (or other arbitrary classification).

Butler pleaded the requisite allegations, however, no substantial proof was offered in support thereof. The defendants allegedly conspired to deprive the plaintiff and other blacks of equal protection of the laws by enforcing Virginia liquor laws primarily against members of the black race in order to obtain court fines and city revenue. After finding that the plaintiff's complaint failed to state a cause of action against defendants, the district court granted her leave to submit "whatever additional material she . . . (thought) relevant and necessary." In response, the plaintiff merely stated:

> That the gist of my facts to support the conspiracy allegation is as follows: That 98% of the people arrested under 4-58 A.B.C. Code are members of the Black race. As a result, 4-58 A.B.C. Code is being used to disproportionately, capriciously, and arbitrarily arrest the Plaintiff and other members of the Black race.

Defendants submitted certified copies of offense reports of the Portsmouth Police Department from September of 1973 through April of 1975 which arrest records disclosed that approximately 84% of all persons arrested for violating Virginia's Alcoholic Beverage Control Act during this period were Black Americans. In addition, the defendants filed affidavits in connection with their motions for summary judgment denying the substance of the plaintiff's claim that they had engaged in a conspiracy to enforce the Commonwealth's liquor laws in a discriminatory manner.

Judge Kellam was right when he said, "Assuming . . . that plaintiff's contention is true (that 98% of these arrests were of blacks), that fact alone is wholly inadequate to support the conspiracy charge in this case. (S)he offers no other factual material of any type in support of her allegations. . . ."

Moreover, the alleged purpose of the conspiracy must fail on its face. The Virginia liquor laws (including Va. Code § 4-58) are criminal statutes of the Commonwealth of Virginia. The City of Portsmouth receives no revenue from fines paid for violations of these laws. These court fines are paid directly into the treasury of the state.

In determining whether summary judgment is appropriate, a court must view the record in the light most favorable to the party opposing the motion. All inferences of fact from the proofs submitted must be drawn against the movant and in favor of the opposing party. The lower court construed the plaintiff's pro se pleadings and affidavits liberally. Given these liberal standards in favor of the plaintiff, the record as viewed on appeal is totally devoid of a meritorious claim based on 42 U.S.C. § 1983 or § 1985. At best, this court can only recognize that approximately 84% of the persons arrested for liquor law violations in Portsmouth during the given period were members of the black race. Nothing in the record supports a theory of conspiracy to racially discriminate in the enforcement of these laws, least of all, not a naked allegation of percentage of black arrests.

It is significant that in *Rizzo v. Goode*, supra, the Supreme Court of the United States denied injunctive relief under 42 U.S.C. § 1983 against local police officials who failed to correct their subordinate officers' violations of constitutional rights of individuals. In reversing the judgment of the Court of Appeals for the 3rd Circuit, the Court stated that an aggrieved party could not enjoin officials from certain conduct absent a showing that the violation of constitutional rights by the subordinate policeman resulted from an affirmative policy or plan of the official.

Moreover, the court in *Rizzo* held that the mere existence of a "statistical pattern" of police violations was not, in any event, sufficient to make the defendant city and police authorities liable under § 1983 for their failure to take corrective measures.

It is evident from the pleadings and affidavits that there was never a showing of an affirmative policy or plan linking the plaintiff's alleged deprivation of constitutional rights with actions by any of the defendants. The plaintiff's arrests for violations of Virginia's liquor laws began back in 1946 as shown by her arrest record which was filed in district court. Her arrests and convictions have been numerous. Without more proof, we cannot permit this plaintiff to pursue an unfounded grudge in federal court.

There is no genuine issue of any material fact. The district court properly granted summary judgment.

AFFIRMED.

BUTZNER, Circuit Judge, dissenting:

I dissent because the record discloses a genuine issue of material fact within the meaning of Rule 56 of the Federal Rules of Civil Procedure. Therefore, the district court erred in granting summary judgment.

In *Yick Wo v. Hopkins* (1886), the court said:

> Though the law itself be fair on its face and impartial in appearance, yet, if it is applied and administered by public authority with an evil eye and an unequal hand, so as practically to make unjust and illegal discriminations between persons in similar circumstances, material to their rights, the denial of equal justice is still within the prohibition of the Constitution.

The allegations of racial discrimination in Esther Butler's pro se complaint, supplemented by the records of the Portsmouth police department and her affidavits, disclose facts which, if proven at trial, would constitute a violation of the fourteenth amendment's equal protection clause as interpreted in *Yick Wo*.

The police arrested Butler, a fifty-year-old widow, for selling two cans of beer in her home. She was charged with selling alcoholic beverages in violation of state law and with maintaining a disorderly house in violation of a city ordinance. On three occasions she appeared in court, accompanied by her counsel and a privately engaged court reporter. Each time, the case was continued on motion of the prosecution over her objection. After the last continuance, a police officer suggested that she plead guilty to a lesser offense. Upon her refusal, she was convicted in the magistrate's court, fined $200, and sentenced to 60 days in jail. Ultimately, the case was dismissed on appeal because the police failed to file the search warrant as required by law. She charged that the prosecution was conducted in bad faith because of her support for civil rights. She alleged that the continuances were typical of trial delays forced on black defendants to coerce them to plead guilty to lesser charges.

In her complaint, Butler asserted a class action on behalf of all black persons similarly situated in Portsmouth. She alleged that approximately one-third of the city's population of 117,000 are black. She charged that despite this ratio, 98% of the people arrested for the sale of legal whiskey without a license are black. Amplifying this charge, she explained:

> Members of the Black race have their own social clubs such as the Elk's Club, Masonic Temple, American Legion, etc. Members of the White race have their own social clubs such as the Elk's Club, Masonic Temple, American Legion, etc. Black undercover police officers are used to infiltrate the Black operated social clubs, especially the American Legion for Blacks, in order to obtain violations of 4-58 ABC Code. As a result, many Blacks are arrested in social clubs and placed in jail for violation of 4-58 ABC Code. Since the inception of the Portsmouth Police Department, the Police Department has never infiltrated and arrested any members of the White race in an Elk's Masonic or American Legion Club operated by members of the White race for violation of the 4-58 ABC Code. As a result, 4-58 ABC Code is being used

Chapter XII Discriminatory Enforcement

to disapportionately, capriciously and arbitrarily arrest the Plaintiff and other members of the Black race.

The police records corroborate Butler's charge of disparity in the enforcement of liquor laws. Over a 20-month period, approximately 84% of the persons arrested for violating these laws were black. Moreover, in many months, the ratio approached or exceeded 98%, as Butler alleges. For example, in October, 1973, all 39 people arrested for running a disorderly house were black. Similarly, in April, 1974, all 45 people arrested for this offense were black, and in June, 1974, all 57 arrested were black. Arrests for violations of the state ABC laws show a similar disparity. Thus, in November, 1973, all six of the persons arrested for violating these laws were black. The next month, all 13 arrested were black, and in January, 1974, only one out of the 17 persons arrested was white. The next month, all 16 of the persons arrested were black.

In contrast, the records show that for other crimes, including such related offenses as drunk driving and public drunkenness, there is no marked disparity between the number of black and white citizens arrested.

The appellees denied that they conspired to discriminate against Butler or members of her class. They have not explained, however, the disproportionate number of black people arrested for the unlicensed sale of legal whiskey.

In *American Fidelity and Casualty Co. v. The London and Edinburgh Insurance Co.* (4th Cir. 1965), the court said with respect to granting a motion for summary judgment:

> Not merely must the historic facts be free of controversy but also there must be no controversy as to the inferences to be drawn from them. It is often the case that although the basic facts are not in dispute, the parties nevertheless disagree as to the inferences which may properly be drawn. Under such circumstances the case is not one to be decided on a motion for summary judgment.

That principle of law is applicable to this case where the parties disagree as to the inferences which may reasonably be drawn from the pleadings, affidavits, and exhibits. Furthermore, there is a direct conflict between the charge and the denial of utilizing undercover agents for the selective prosecution of black citizens.

Under the principles set forth in *Yick Wo*, Butler has established a cognizable claim that the police infringed rights secured by the equal protection clause. Therefore, she should be allowed to proceed to discovery.

Rizzo v. Goode (1976), on which the appellees rely, is not to the contrary. In that case, the district court held a full evidentiary hearing. The Supreme Court noted that 250 witnesses were heard. It explained:

> As the facts developed, there was no affirmative link between the occurrence of the various incidents of police misconduct and the adoption of any plan or policy by petitioners express or otherwise showing their authorization or approval of such misconduct.

Rizzo does not hold that statistics indicating a pattern of discrimination are insufficient to defeat a motion for summary judgment. Rather, in *Rizzo* the complainants failed to prove their allegations after a full evidentiary hearing. Unlike the complainants in *Rizzo*, Butler has not even been given a chance to proceed to discovery, much less to prove her case at trial.

Despite the suggestion to the contrary, *Oyler v. Boles* (1962), does not support the grant of summary judgment. The Supreme Court described the deficiency of the complaint in that case as follows:

> It is not stated whether the failure to proceed against other three-time offenders was due to lack of knowledge of the prior offenses on the part of the prosecutors or was the result of a deliberate policy of proceeding only in a certain class of cases or against specific persons.

D. Selective Investigation   **1109**

In contrast, Butler has alleged and reaffirmed in subsequently filed affidavits that the appellees' selective prosecution of black persons resulted from a deliberate policy of racially motivated enforcement.

Never before have we required proof of racial discrimination before permitting a plaintiff to go to trial in a § 1983 action. Rather, we have adhered to the sound principle that trial should be ordered, and summary judgment denied, when the record discloses a genuine issue as to any material facts, or to the inferences that may reasonably be drawn from them about such discrimination. Butler has satisfied this test. Therefore, I would vacate the judgment of the district court and remand the case for further proceedings, including disposition of the defenses of privilege. Butler's allegations, if true, would prove a serious violation of the constitutional rights of many people. For this reason, I would direct the district court to appoint a lawyer to represent her, if she is unable to retain one, so that her evidence can be intelligently marshalled and presented to the court.

NOTES AND QUESTIONS

1. Unlike the other selective prosecution claimants we have encountered in this chapter, Esther Butler brings her claim affirmatively under 42 U.S.C. § 1983 and Fed. R. Civ. P. 23, and not as a defense to a criminal prosecution. We are told she was acquitted on the criminal charges against her due to an error by the government in assembling the appellate record. *Id.* at 645 n.2. So the issue here is the validity of her claim that defendants deprived her and others similarly situated pursuant to Rule 23 of their constitutional rights. To be more precise, the issue on appeal is whether the district court correctly ruled, in granting summary judgment for defendants under Fed. R. Civ. P. 56, that defendants met their burden of showing "there is no genuine dispute as to any material fact" and that they are "entitled to judgment as a matter of law."

2. To further flesh out the procedural context: Butler brought her civil claim in federal court pro se, although she had counsel on appeal; her complaint was dismissed once under Rule 12(b)(6) because no "substantial proof" was offered in support of her allegations; she was allowed to amend her complaint, and did so by adding conclusory statistical allegations; defendants supported their motion for summary judgment with affidavits from city officials denying liability and arrest records of the Portsmouth Police Department showing that 84 percent of persons arrested for ABC Act violations were Black.

Assuming the Fourth Circuit accurately described it, was the district court's original dismissal of Butler's claim correct?

If you had represented Butler, what moves would you have made in response to the city's summary judgment motion? *See* Fed. R. Civ. P. 56(d).

3. In the footnote (not reproduced here) explaining the reason for her acquittal due to the government's procedural error, the court notes, gratuitously, that the district court reviewed the warrant and found it to be valid. Gratuitous remarks such as this one often speak volumes. What other gratuitous remarks are in the Court's opinion?

4. The court plainly understands the law applicable to Butler's claim, which it accurately describes as one of "racially selective enforcement." It cites *Yick Wo* and *Oyler*. Why does the court not engage with Butler's allegations regarding selective investigation of ABC violations by police, which were not—as far as the opinion reports—responded to or factually refuted by the city? As noted earlier, *Yick Wo* itself, while usually described as a case of selective prosecution, is most precisely understood as an example of selective enforcement. What about

1110 Chapter XII Discriminatory Enforcement

Butler's allegation that she was targeted for prosecution because of her civil rights advocacy? Does that allegation need to be addressed on summary judgment?

5. The dissent notes that Butler should at least be entitled to discovery on her claims. What additional discovery does she need?

Both *Harris* and *Butler*, as well as *Ah Sin* for that matter, bring home the obvious yet overlooked point that, with respect to claims of discriminatory investigation, "[t]here is an important correlation between looking for things and finding them." Paul Butler, *Starr Is to Clinton as Regulator Prosecutors Are to Blacks*, 40 B.C. L. Rev. 705, 709 (1999); *see also* Angela J. Davis, *Prosecution and Race: The Power and Privilege of Discretion*, 67 Fordham L. Rev. 13, 37 (1998) ("policy decisions about where police officers should be deployed and what offenses they should investigate have racial ramifications").

The next case considers whether the discovery standard should be lower than the standard decreed in *Armstrong* in a case of "discrimination enforcement," that is, where the alleged discrimination is being done not by prosecutors but by police officers.

United States v. Conley
5 F.4th 781 (7th Cir. 2021)

HAMILTON, Circuit Judge.

Tracy Conley has invoked 28 U.S.C. § 2255 to vacate convictions arising from his participation in a "fake stash house" sting orchestrated by the Bureau of Alcohol, Tobacco, Firearms, and Explosives (ATF). Conley asserts that his convictions were obtained unlawfully through racially selective law enforcement and outrageous government conduct, in violation of his Fifth Amendment equal protection and due process rights, respectively. The district court denied Conley's motion, and we affirm. We disagree with the district court's decision to require "clear and convincing" evidence for Conley's selective enforcement claim, but his evidence cannot meet even the less-demanding standard of preponderance of the evidence. This circuit has not recognized a defense for "outrageous government conduct," and even if we did, ATF's conduct in Conley's case would not satisfy the standard other circuits have applied. Regardless of the wisdom of this fake stash house sting, it did not violate Conley's constitutional rights.

I. BACKGROUND

Our opinion affirming Conley's convictions on direct appeal sets out the facts of his case. Here we focus on the facts relevant to his selective enforcement and outrageous conduct theories. On November 1, 2011, Conley found himself stranded at a gas station without money for gas. There he ran into three acquaintances—Anthony Adams, David Flowers, and Anwar Trapp—who successfully recruited Conley to help rob a cocaine stash house later that day. Adams, David, and Trapp had themselves been recruited recently for the robbery by David's brother, Myreon Flowers.

Myreon had been tipped off a week earlier about the supposed stash house by a man claiming to be a disgruntled courier for a drug cartel. The courier told Myreon that the stash house contained fifty kilograms of cocaine, and that to steal it, Myreon should assemble an armed team to overpower the cartel guards. Myreon jumped at the opportunity, bragging about how easy the robbery would be compared to others he had pulled off. Myreon quickly assembled a crew, recruiting his brother David Flowers and their cousins Anwar Trapp and Dwayne Jones. David also recruited Anthony Adams, who in turn suggested recruiting Conley.

The supposed cartel courier was an undercover ATF agent. There was no stash house or real drugs, just a convincing ruse designed to ensnare Myreon and his crew in a conspiracy to steal fifty kilograms of cocaine at gunpoint. It turns out the FBI had originally focused on Myreon through an investigation into the Belizean Bloods, a Chicago street gang. Confidential sources had told the FBI that Myreon was an active member of a Belizean Bloods armed robbery crew, as well as a murder suspect. Based on that information, the FBI had referred Myreon to the ATF as a potential target for a stash house sting, and the ATF obliged.

On November 1, Myreon's group, including Conley, met in Adams's basement to plan the robbery. Conley not only agreed to participate but volunteered for a frontline role as one of two armed robbers who would confront the guards and steal the cocaine. Conley even asked the group whether they should kill the cartel courier (i.e., the undercover agent) but fortunately was told not to harm him. Later that day, the group met the undercover agent at a secluded parking lot near the supposed stash house. Conley and the others were dressed in dark clothing, wearing latex gloves, and equipped with walkie-talkies and a toolbox containing three guns for the robbery. Myreon told Conley, Adams, and another member to get into a van that would take them to the stash house for the robbery. As soon as they were all in the van, the undercover agent gave the arrest signal.

A jury convicted Conley of conspiring and attempting to possess with intent to distribute more than five kilograms of cocaine, in violation of 21 U.S.C. §§ 841(a)(1) and 846; possessing a firearm in furtherance of a drug trafficking offense, in violation of 18 U.S.C. § 924(c)(1)(A); and being a felon in possession of a firearm in violation of 18 U.S.C. § 922(g)(1). The district court sentenced Conley to fifteen years in prison, which included a ten-year mandatory minimum based on the large amount of non-existent drugs he agreed to steal — an amount the ATF made up just to trigger that ten-year minimum.

On direct appeal, we affirmed the denial of Conley's motion for acquittal. We found that sufficient evidence supported his convictions and that he could not argue entrapment because the ATF recruited neither Conley nor those who recruited him.

Conley then filed his § 2255 motion in the district court seeking to set aside his convictions on two new grounds. First, he asserts that federal agents intentionally targeted him for the sting because he is Black, in violation of the equal protection component of the Fifth Amendment. Second, Conley asserts that even though he cannot show entrapment, the ATF's conduct in executing this fake stash house sting was so outrageous that prosecuting him violated his due process rights. The district court denied Conley's § 2255 motion but granted a certificate of appealability on both claims.

Judge Coleman denied Conley's selective-enforcement claim by relying exclusively on then-Chief Judge Castillo's denial of a nearly identical claim brought by fake stash house defendants in *United States v. Brown* (N.D. Ill. 2018). Judge Coleman certified the issue for appeal, however, "based on the uncertainty of the applicable evidentiary standard" governing a selective-enforcement claim in this circuit. As for outrageous government conduct, Judge Coleman denied Conley's claim because this circuit has repeatedly rejected the existence of such a defense. Again, however, Judge Coleman certified Conley's appeal on this issue: "If there ever was a situation in which the conduct of law enforcement agents was so outrageous that a criminal defendant's due process rights have been violated, this is it."

While this appeal was pending, Judge Coleman granted Conley's motion for compassionate release under 18 U.S.C. § 3582(c)(1)(A)(i). Conley's release from prison does not remove our jurisdiction over his § 2255 motion or render it moot. A movant under § 2255 must be "in custody." 28 U.S.C. § 2255(a). But Conley "was in custody when he filed [his] motion" for § 2255 relief, "and that is all that is required. . . ." Moreover, despite his release from prison, Conley is still subject to a three-year term of supervised release, which is "a form of custody," and carries collateral consequences sufficient to prevent his motion from being moot.

II. CONTROVERSY SURROUNDING FAKE STASH HOUSE STINGS

Before turning to the merits, we provide some background on the ATF's controversial and now-abandoned practice of conducting fake stash house stings in Chicago. As we noted in Conley's direct appeal, there is a "substantial body of criticism of similar stash house cases both from this circuit and others." We have described the tactic as "'tawdry,' noting in particular how these operations are 'directed at unsophisticated, and perhaps desperate defendants' like Conley who easily take the all-too-tempting bait put out for them by the government."

These stings are troubling in several ways. First, the agents in these stings blindly encourage the initial target to rope in a large group of co-conspirators who otherwise may have stayed out of trouble.

Second, the vast majority of defendants caught in these stings have been poor people of color. *United States v. Black*, 750 F.3d 1053, 1057 (9th Cir. 2014) (Reinhardt, J., dissenting from denial of rehearing en banc) ("In this era of mass incarceration, in which we already lock up more of our population than any other nation on Earth, it is especially curious that the government feels compelled to invent fake crimes and imprison people for long periods of time for agreeing to participate in them. . . .").

Third, these stings give law enforcement free rein to manipulate sentences by setting imaginary drug amounts. *See United States v. Briggs* (9th Cir. 2010) (criticizing ability to manipulate sentences with fake drug amounts).

Fourth, economic analysis suggests that fake stash house stings may actually facilitate the illegal drug trade. They make real stash houses more secure by deterring potential robbers. These problems have led jurists to question whether fake stash house stings comport with "the pride we take in presenting American criminal justice as a system that treats defendants fairly and equally."

Amid this controversy, many defendants in Chicago have challenged the ATF's fake stash house stings as racially selective. Sitting en banc in 2015, we laid out principles for granting discovery in these cases. Various stash house cases then progressed on different timelines. In December 2017, the matter culminated in a unique two-day evidentiary hearing in the Northern District of Illinois before nine district judges presiding over twelve similar stash house cases. Statistical experts testified to whether the ATF's fake stash house program was racially discriminatory.

Following that hearing, Judge Castillo issued a careful opinion denying defendants' selective-enforcement claims due to flaws and limits in the statistical analysis performed by the court's appointed expert, Columbia University Law Professor Jeffrey Fagan. The opinion criticized the ATF's fake stash house stings as a matter of policy, and it took pains to clarify that the court was not deciding whether these stings "are honorable or fair," but only "whether law enforcement agents violated the Due Process Clause of the Fifth Amendment in pursuing these investigations."

This history forms the backdrop of Conley's appeal. In particular, Judge Castillo's analysis in *Brown* is critical here because Conley relies on the statistics in the Fagan Report to prove his selective-enforcement claim. We now turn to the merits of that claim.

III. SELECTIVE ENFORCEMENT

Conley asserts that the ATF targeted him for the sting because he is Black. Conley did not raise this selective-enforcement claim until his § 2255 motion. But we may consider it because, as the district court noted, the government chose not to raise procedural default as a defense to this claim.

Because Conley himself was not the initial target of the sting, his theory is that the ATF first targeted Myreon Flowers because of his race, with further hopes that Myreon would recruit other Black people like Conley as co-conspirators. If proven, that would amount to purposeful discrimination in violation of the Fifth Amendment's equal protection component. *See Whren v. United States* (1996) ("[T]he Constitution prohibits selective enforcement of the law based on considerations such as race. . . . [T]he constitutional basis for objecting to intentionally discriminatory application of laws is the Equal Protection Clause").

Racially selective law enforcement is a quintessential equal protection violation. One of the Supreme Court's earliest equal protection opinions granted habeas corpus relief to petitioners who alleged selective enforcement of building codes against Chinese-owned laundries in San Francisco. *Yick Wo v. Hopkins* (1886). The *Yick Wo* petitioners showed that authorities had denied the applications of two hundred Chinese people for permits to operate laundries in wooden buildings but granted the applications of eighty non-Chinese people "under similar conditions." The Court made clear that, in such a situation, law enforcement can be "directed so exclusively against a particular class of persons . . . with a mind so unequal and oppressive as to amount to a practical denial by the state of that equal protection of the laws which is secured to the petitioners . . . by the broad and benign provisions of the fourteenth amendment. . . ." Today, *Yick Wo* is seen as providing historical roots not only for selective enforcement claims but also for selective-prosecution claims. *See United States v. Armstrong* (1996) (discussing *Yick Wo* as one source of selective-prosecution claims).

Selective prosecution occurs when, from among the pool of people referred by police, a prosecutor pursues similar cases differently based on race. Selective enforcement occurs when police investigate people of one race but not similarly-situated people of a different race. Hence, with selective enforcement, "the constitutional problem . . . precede[s] the prosecutor's role." It does not matter if prosecutors then pursue each case equally because the pool of defendants itself was racially selected.

As equal protection claims, both selective prosecution and selective enforcement require proof "that the defendants' actions had a discriminatory effect and were motivated by a discriminatory purpose." A plaintiff must show discriminatory purpose "in his case." And discriminatory purpose "implies more than . . . awareness of consequences. It implies that the decisionmaker . . . selected or reaffirmed a particular course of action at least in part 'because of,' not merely 'in spite of,' its adverse effects upon an identifiable group."

A. Standard of Proof

The first issue we confront is the standard of proof Conley must meet to prove his selective-enforcement claim. The district court granted a certificate of appealability on this claim "because reasonable jurists could debate that his claim should have been resolved in a different manner based on the uncertainty of the applicable evidentiary standard." We review this legal issue de novo. The government argues that Conley must meet the same "clear evidence" standard that governs selective-prosecution claims. *See Armstrong* ("In order to dispel the presumption that a prosecutor has not violated equal protection, a criminal defendant must present 'clear evidence to the contrary.'" Conley counters that the reasons for *Armstrong*'s clear-evidence standard are specific to prosecutors, so that selective-enforcement claims against police need be proven by only a preponderance of the evidence. The district court agreed with the government's view, as did Judge Castillo in *Brown*. We disagree, however, and hold that racially selective-enforcement claims must be proven by a preponderance of the evidence.

Our analysis proceeds as follows. First, in Part III-A-1, we explain Armstrong's clear-evidence standard and why its rationale does not extend to selective-enforcement claims. In Part III-A-2, we explain why *McCleskey v. Kemp* does not require a heightened standard of proof. Finally, in Part III-A-3, we draw connections to other doctrines showing that a preponderance standard fits better into the broader legal landscape.

1. *Armstrong* Does Not Set the Standard of Proof

a. *Armstrong's Clear-Evidence Standard*

Equal protection claims generally must be proven by a preponderance of the evidence. (1985) (citing with approval circuit court's statement that "plaintiffs must prove by a preponderance of the evidence that racial discrimination was a substantial or motivating factor").

Selective-prosecution claims, however, must be proven by "clear evidence." In *Armstrong*, the Supreme Court reversed a grant of discovery in a selective-prosecution case despite evidence that "every defendant in every crack-cocaine prosecution filed by a particular United States Attorney's office and assigned to the public defender was black." The Supreme Court held that, because a "selective-prosecution claim asks a court to exercise judicial power over a 'special province' of the Executive," the plaintiffs needed further evidence showing that comparators of another race were not prosecuted before a court could even order discovery against the prosecutor's office.

The Court derived that discovery requirement from a heightened "clear-evidence" standard governing the merits of a selective prosecution claim. *Armstrong*'s "clear-evidence" standard is based in turn on the need to preserve prosecutorial discretion and on the "presumption of regularity" that applies to federal prosecutors as officers of the Executive Branch:

> The Attorney General and United States Attorneys retain "'broad discretion'" to enforce the Nation's criminal laws. They have this latitude because they are designated by statute as the President's delegates to help him discharge his constitutional responsibility to "take Care that the Laws be faithfully executed." As a result, "[t]he presumption of regularity supports" their prosecutorial decisions and, "in the absence of clear evidence to the contrary, courts presume that they have properly discharged their official duties."

· · ·

In order to dispel the presumption that a prosecutor has not violated equal protection, a criminal defendant must present "clear evidence to the contrary."

b. *Armstrong's Rationale Does Not Extend to Selective Enforcement*

The reasons underlying *Armstrong*'s clear-evidence standard for selective-prosecution claims simply do not extend to selective-enforcement claims brought against police. As the above passage shows, *Armstrong*'s "clear-evidence" standard invokes language from *Chemical Foundation*, a bedrock presumption-of-regularity case. The presumption of regularity is a deference doctrine that limits judicial scrutiny of procedures and motivations supporting certain Executive Branch decisions. The presumption is driven by separation-of-powers concerns, which increase as courts venture closer to core executive activity. The presumption has been applied to different degrees depending on "the Court's assessment of the relevant decision-making scheme across several dimensions: procedural fairness, accountability, and degree of discretion, as well as complexity. . . ." The presumption of regularity is an analytic tool, not

D. Selective Investigation   1115

an excuse to rubberstamp any and all executive action as lawful absent clear evidence to the contrary.

In *Armstrong*, the court applied the presumption to prosecutorial decision-making. And in *Reno v. American-Arab Anti-Discrimination Committee*, the Court extended that logic to federal deportation decisions, which, like prosecutorial decisions, implicate core executive strategy that courts should not over-scrutinize. The Court has not extended the presumption of regularity, however, to street-level police investigations. Few police officers are high-level executive officers. And while their decisions certainly reflect law enforcement priorities, judicial inquiry into their motives is routine. We therefore see no persuasive reason to extend Armstrong's heightened standard to selective-enforcement claims.

Our en banc opinion in *Davis* took this limited approach to *Armstrong*. Like this case, *Davis* arose in the context of a fake stash house sting. But the issue there concerned *Armstrong's* discovery standard. The district court had granted broad discovery against the prosecutor's office, ATF, FBI, and others based on the fact that the prosecution had "brought at least twenty purported phony stash house cases, with the overwhelming majority of the defendants named being individuals of color." The government argued that, under *Armstrong*, that was an insufficient showing of racial discrimination to authorize discovery.

We agreed with respect to discovery from the prosecutor's office, but we disagreed with respect to discovery from the ATF and FBI for selective enforcement because "the sort of considerations that led to the outcome in *Armstrong* do not apply to a contention that agents of the FBI or ATF engaged in racial discrimination when selecting targets for sting operations, or when deciding which suspects to refer for prosecution." "*Armstrong* was about prosecutorial discretion," and unlike prosecutors, "Agents of the ATF and FBI are not protected by a powerful privilege or covered by a presumption of constitutional behavior." On the contrary, police officers are regularly called before courts to justify their tactics. Accordingly, *Davis* found that *Armstrong's* requirement to show comparators before granting discovery did not apply to the plaintiffs' selective-enforcement claims.

The government in this appeal asks us not to extend *Davis's* reasoning when it comes to the standard of proof. But given that *Armstrong* imposed its "rigorous standard for discovery" only to match the correspondingly "rigorous standard for the elements of a selective-prosecution claim," the distinction we drew in *Davis* for discovery naturally extends to the standard of proof. Indeed, we recognized in *Chavez* that *Armstrong* does not govern at least one aspect of proving discriminatory effect in a selective-enforcement case. There, we affirmed summary judgment on a selective-enforcement claim on the merits without suggesting a standard of proof higher than preponderance applied. Rather, we rejected plaintiffs' need to satisfy *Armstrong's* burden to identify comparators to prove discriminatory effect on the merits. We did so for the same reasons we rejected the need for comparators at the discovery stage in *Davis*: "[T]he instant case involves police conduct, not prosecutorial discretion, and is in a civil, not criminal, context. This case is thus not like *Armstrong*."

•   •   •

Even in criminal cases, many affirmative defenses are provable by a preponderance of the evidence. Even the way the entrapment defense operates in fake stash house cases like this one shows defendants need not present "clear" evidence to prove their defenses. Rather, so long as the defendant puts forth enough evidence to show that a reasonable jury could find he was entrapped, the judge must submit the defense to the jury with an instruction that, to convict, the jury must find beyond a reasonable doubt that the defendant was not entrapped. *Jacobson v. United States* (1992). So, given that accused defendants can secure release through other affirmative defenses that use preponderance standards (or standards even more favorable to defendants), there should be no concern about applying a preponderance standard to Conley's selective enforcement defense. For these reasons, we hold that Conley could prove his selective enforcement claim by a preponderance of the evidence.

• • •

AFFIRMED.

NOTES AND QUESTIONS

1. The Seventh Circuit, showing a gift for understatement, describes the ATF's fake stash house stings as "tawdry." Of the four objections to these stings that the Court notes which do you find most apt?

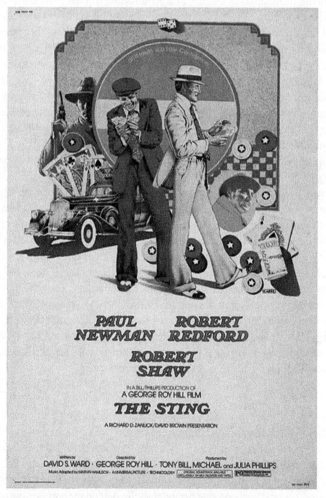

The investigative term "sting" was popularized in popular culture by the 1973 movie *The Sting*, starring Paul Newman, Robert Redford, and Robert Shaw. It won Oscars for Best Picture and Best Director (George Roy Hill).

2. While these stings were conceived and operated by the ATF, with help from the FBI, any resultant prosecutions had to be brought by prosecutors in U.S. Attorney's Offices, which—like the ATF and the FBI—were part of the Department of Justice.

Why didn't senior leadership in the DOJ rein in the ATF?

3. Are you persuaded by the court's distinction between selective prosecution and selective enforcement? The distinction obviously matters in *Conley*, but as a general matter does the distinction seem overly technical, perhaps because the term "enforcement" is the more general term of the two, and is broad enough to encompass both the investigative and prosecutorial aspects of "law enforcement"? The distinction has real-world consequences in at least one other case, however. In *United States v. Cannon*, 987 F.3d 924 (11th Cir. 2021), defendant charged in a fake stash house sting case sought discovery from both the U.S. Attorney's Office and ATF regarding their recruitment selection criteria in an attempt to establish what he labeled a "selective prosecution" defense. His discovery motion was denied, and on appeal the Eleventh Circuit only considered his discovery motion as to the U.S. Attorney's Office, and not the FBI, finding that by using only the term "selective prosecution" on appeal he had waived his right to appeal of his "selective enforcement" claim.

4. The line between investigation and prosecution may not always be crystal clear. Suppose the DOJ was concerned about bad publicity from the fake stash house stings and therefore provided guidelines for ATF to use in implementing the stings and assigned AUSAs to monitor compliance with these guidelines. How would the burden of proof be determined in this context?

5. Defendants in the fake stash house sting cases usually asserted entrapment as well as selective enforcement defenses. Why were the entrapment defenses almost always unsuccessful? *See* Chapter IX *supra*.

6. In *Conley*, in finding that *Armstrong*'s rigorous discovery standard does not apply in the "selective enforcement" context, the Seventh Circuit relied on its earlier decision in *United States v. Davis*, 793 F.3d 712, 720 (7th Cir. 2015) (en banc). Two other circuits have followed *Davis* in this regard. *See United States v. Washington*, 869 F.3d 193, 220-21 (3d Cir. 2017); *United States v. Sellers*, 906 F.3d 848, 855-56 (9th Cir. 2018). *See* Alison Siegler & William Admussen, *Discovering Racial Discrimination by the Police*, 115 Nw. U. L. Rev. 987, 1004-26 (2021) (distinguishing *Armstrong* and advocating for the lower discovery standard adopted in *Davis*).

7. In *United States v. Lopez*, 415 F. Supp. 3d 422, 426 (S.D.N.Y. 2019), the district court held that the *Armstrong* standard did not apply and permitted defendants, who alleged they were targeted by the DEA in a fake stash house sting case because of their race, to receive limited discovery. Specifically, the district court allowed defendants to receive discovery of DEA manuals, etc., about the investigative program as well as information about how these defendants were selected.

CHAPTER XIII

THE JURY I: SCOPE OF THE RIGHT AND OTHER ISSUES

Representative government and trial by jury are the heart and lungs of liberty. Without them we have no other fortification against being ridden like horses, fleeced like sheep, worked like cattle, and fed and clothed like swine and hounds.

John Adams, The Revolutionary Writings of John Adams 55
(C. Bradley Thompson ed., 2000)

Juries are enshrined in the Constitution four times. The Fifth Amendment requires presentment or indictment by a grand jury; the Seventh Amendment mandates the right to a jury trial in a civil case; and both the Sixth Amendment and Article III guarantee the right to a jury trial in a criminal case. As a commentator and now federal judge put it, "[t]he Constitution is obsessed with juries." Joan L. Larsen, *Ancient Juries and Modern Judges: Originalism's Uneasy Relationship with the Jury*, 71 Ohio St. L.J. 959, 964 (2010).

This chapter addresses several different aspects of juries and jury trials. Section A considers the scope and dimension of the right to a jury trial, including the kind of a jury the Constitution requires. Sections B and C examine two important powers the jury currently does not have, but arguably should have under an "originalist" understanding of juries: the right to "nullify" or disregard the court's instructions on the law and the right to be informed of a defendant's potential punishment. Section D looks at three specific types of jury instructions: the reasonable doubt instruction, which is given in almost every criminal case; the "*Allen* charge," a dangerous instruction sometimes given to juries that report they are deadlocked; and an instruction on "implicit bias" that one former federal judge routinely used.

A. SCOPE OF THE RIGHT TO TRIAL BY JURY

In the first case we consider, the Supreme Court finds that the right to a jury trial is a "fundamental" right applicable to the states under the Fourteenth Amendment's due process requirement. This is not the last case involving Louisiana's jury trial system that would reach the Supreme Court.

Duncan v. Louisiana
391 U.S. 145 (1968)

Mr. Justice WHITE delivered the opinion of the Court.

Appellant, Gary Duncan, was convicted of simple battery in the Twenty-fifth Judicial District Court of Louisiana. Under Louisiana law simple battery is a misdemeanor, punishable by a maximum of two years' imprisonment and a $300 fine. Appellant sought trial by jury, but because the Louisiana Constitution grants jury trials only in cases in which capital punishment or imprisonment at hard labor may be imposed the trial judge denied the request. Appellant was convicted and sentenced to serve 60 days in the parish prison and pay a fine of $150. Appellant sought review in the Supreme Court of Louisiana, asserting that the denial of jury trial violated rights guaranteed to him by the United States Constitution. The Supreme Court, finding "(n)o error of law in the ruling complained of," denied appellant a writ of certiorari. Pursuant to 28 U.S.C. s 1257(2) appellant sought review in this Court, alleging that the Sixth and Fourteenth Amendments to the United States Constitution secure the right to jury trial in state criminal prosecutions where a sentence as long as two years may be imposed. We noted probable jurisdiction, and set the case for oral argument.

Appellant was 19 years of age when tried. While driving on Highway 23 in Plaquemines Parish on October 18, 1966, he saw two younger cousins engaged in a conversation by the side of the road with four white boys. Knowing his cousins, Negroes who had recently transferred to a formerly all-white high school, had reported the occurrence of racial incidents at the school, Duncan stopped the car, got out, and approached the six boys. At trial the white boys and a white onlooker testified, as did appellant and his cousins. The testimony was in dispute on many points, but the witnesses agreed that appellant and the white boys spoke to each other, that appellant encouraged his cousins to break off the encounter and enter his car, and that appellant was about to enter the car himself for the purpose of driving away with his cousins. The whites testified that just before getting in the car appellant slapped Herman Landry, one of the white boys, on the elbow. The Negroes testified that appellant had not slapped Landry, but had merely touched him. The trial judge concluded that the State had proved beyond a reasonable doubt that Duncan had committed simple battery, and found him guilty.

I

The Fourteenth Amendment denies the States the power to "deprive any person of life, liberty, or property, without due process of law." In resolving conflicting claims concerning the meaning of this spacious language, the Court has looked increasingly to the Bill of Rights for guidance; many of the rights guaranteed by the first eight Amendments to the Constitution have been held to be protected against state action by the Due Process Clause of the Fourteenth Amendment. That clause now protects the right to compensation for property taken by the State; the rights of speech, press, and religion covered by the First Amendment; the Fourth Amendment rights to be free from unreasonable searches and seizures and to have excluded from criminal trials any evidence illegally seized; the right guaranteed by the Fifth Amendment to be free of compelled self-incrimination; and the Sixth Amendment rights to counsel, to a speedy and public trial, to confrontation of opposing witnesses, and to compulsory process for obtaining witnesses.

The test for determining whether a right extended by the Fifth and Sixth Amendments with respect to federal criminal proceedings is also protected against state action by the Fourteenth Amendment has been phrased in a variety of ways in the opinions of this Court. The question has been asked whether a right is among those " 'fundamental principles of liberty and justice which lie at the base of all our civil and political institutions,' " whether it is "basic in our system of jurisprudence," and whether it is "a fundamental right, essential to a fair trial." The claim before us is that the right to trial by jury guaranteed by the Sixth Amendment meets these tests. The position of Louisiana, on the other hand, is that the Constitution imposes upon the States no duty to give a jury trial in any criminal case, regardless of the seriousness of the crime or the size of the punishment which may be imposed. Because we believe that trial by jury in criminal cases is fundamental to the American scheme of justice, we hold that the Fourteenth Amendment guarantees a right of jury trial in all criminal cases which — were they to be tried in a federal court — would come within the Sixth Amendment's guarantee. Since we consider the appeal before us to be such a case, we hold that the Constitution was violated when appellant's demand for jury trial was refused.

The history of trial by jury in criminal cases has been frequently told. It is sufficient for present purposes to say that by the time our Constitution was written, jury trial in criminal cases had been in existence in England for several centuries and carried impressive credentials traced by many to Magna Carta Its preservation and proper operation as a protection against arbitrary rule were among the major objectives of the revolutionary settlement which was expressed in the Declaration and Bill of Rights of 1689. In the 18th century Blackstone could write:

> Our law has therefore wisely placed this strong and two-fold barrier, of a presentment and a trial by jury, between the liberties of the people and the prerogative of the crown. It was necessary, for preserving the admirable balance of our constitution, to vest the executive power of the laws in the prince: and yet this power might be dangerous and destructive to that very constitution, if exerted without check or control, by justices of oyer and terminer occasionally named by the crown; who might then, as in France or Turkey, imprison, dispatch, or exile any man that was obnoxious to the government, by an instant declaration that such is their will and pleasure. But the founders of the English law have, with excellent forecast, contrived that . . . the truth of every accusation, whether preferred in the shape of indictment, information, or appeal, should afterwards be confirmed by the unanimous suffrage of twelve of his equals and neighbours, indifferently chosen and superior to all suspicion.

Jury trial came to America with English colonists, and received strong support from them. Royal interference with the jury trial was deeply resented. Among the resolutions adopted by the First Congress of the American Colonies (the Stamp Act Congress) on October 19, 1765 — resolutions deemed by their authors to state "the most essential rights and liberties of the colonists" — was the declaration:

> That trial by jury is the inherent and invaluable right of every British subject in these colonies.

The First Continental Congress, in the resolve of October 14, 1774, objected to trials before judges dependent upon the Crown alone for their salaries and to trials in England for alleged crimes committed in the colonies; the Congress therefore declared:

> That the respective colonies are entitled to the common law of England, and more especially to the great and inestimable privilege of being tried by their peers of the vicinage, according to the course of that law.

The Declaration of Independence stated solemn objections to the King's making "judges dependent on his will alone, for the tenure of their offices, and the amount and payment of their salaries," to his "depriving us in many cases, of the benefits of Trial by Jury," and to his "transporting us beyond Seas to be tried for pretended offenses." The Constitution itself, in Art. III, s 2, commanded:

> The Trial of all Crimes, except in Cases of Impeachment, shall be by Jury; and such Trial shall be held in the State where the said Crimes shall have been committed.

Objections to the Constitution because of the absence of a bill of rights were met by the immediate submission and adoption of the Bill of Rights. Included was the Sixth Amendment which, among other things, provided:

> In all criminal prosecutions, the accused shall enjoy the right to a speedy and public trial, by an impartial jury of the State and district wherein the crime shall have been committed.

Chapter XIII The Jury I: Scope of the Right and Other Issues

The constitutions adopted by the original States guaranteed jury trial. Also, the constitution of every State entering the Union thereafter in one form or another protected the right to jury trial in criminal cases.

Even such skeletal history is impressive support for considering the right to jury trial in criminal cases to be fundamental to our system of justice, an importance frequently recognized in the opinions of this Court. For example, the Court has said:

> Those who emigrated to this country from England brought with them this great privilege "as their birthright and inheritance, as a part of that admirable common law which had fenced around and interposed barriers on every side against the approaches of arbitrary power."

Jury trial continues to receive strong support. The laws of every State guarantee a right to jury trial in serious criminal cases; no State has dispensed with it; nor are there significant movements underway to do so. Indeed, the three most recent state constitutional revisions, in Maryland, Michigan, and New York, carefully preserved the right of the accused to have the judgment of a jury when tried for a serious crime.

We are aware of prior cases in this Court in which the prevailing opinion contains statements contrary to our holding today that the right to jury trial in serious criminal cases is a fundamental right and hence must be recognized by the States as part of their obligation to extend due process of law to all persons within their jurisdiction. . . . None of these cases, however, dealt with a State which had purported to dispense entirely with a jury trial in serious criminal cases. *Maxwell* held that no provision of the Bill of Rights applied to the States—a position long since repudiated—and that the Due Process Clause of the Fourteenth Amendment did not prevent a State from trying a defendant for a noncapital offense with fewer than 12 men on the jury. It did not deal with a case in which no jury at all had been provided. In neither *Palko* nor *Snyder* was jury trial actually at issue, although both cases contain important dicta asserting that the right to jury trial is not essential to ordered liberty and may be dispensed with by the States regardless of the Sixth and Fourteenth Amendments. These observations, though weighty and respectable, are nevertheless dicta, unsupported by holdings in this Court that a State may refuse a defendant's demand for a jury trial when he is charged with a serious crime. Perhaps because the right to jury trial was not directly at stake, the Court's remarks about the jury in *Palko* and *Snyder* took no note of past or current developments regarding jury trials, did not consider its purposes and functions, attempted no inquiry into how well it was performing its job, and did not discuss possible distinctions between civil and criminal cases. In *Malloy v. Hogan*, supra, the Court rejected *Palko*'s discussion of the self-incrimination clause. Respectfully, we reject the prior dicta regarding jury trial in criminal cases.

The guarantees of jury trial in the Federal and State Constitutions reflect a profound judgment about the way in which law should be enforced and justice administered. A right to jury trial is granted to criminal defendants in order to prevent oppression by the Government. Those who wrote our constitutions knew from history and experience that it was necessary to protect against unfounded criminal charges brought to eliminate enemies and against judges too responsive to the voice of higher authority. The framers of the constitutions strove to create an independent judiciary but insisted upon further protection against arbitrary action. Providing an accused with the right to be tried by a jury of his peers gave him an inestimable safeguard against the corrupt or overzealous prosecutor and against the compliant, biased, or eccentric judge. If the defendant preferred the common-sense judgment of a jury to the more tutored but perhaps less sympathetic reaction of the single judge, he was to have it. Beyond this, the jury trial provisions in the Federal and State Constitutions reflect a fundamental decision about the exercise of official power—a reluctance to entrust plenary powers over the life and liberty of the citizen to one judge or to a group of judges. Fear of unchecked power, so typical of our State and Federal Governments in other respects, found expression in the criminal law in this insistence upon community participation in the determination of guilt or innocence. The deep commitment of the Nation to the right of jury trial in serious criminal cases as a defense against arbitrary law enforcement qualifies for protection under the Due Process Clause of the Fourteenth Amendment, and must therefore be respected by the States.

Of course jury trial has "its weaknesses and the potential for misuse." We are aware of the long debate, especially in this century, among those who write about the administration of justice, as to the wisdom of permitting untrained laymen to determine the facts in civil and criminal proceedings. Although the debate has been intense, with powerful voices on either side, most of the controversy has centered on the jury in civil cases. Indeed, some of the severest critics of civil juries acknowledge that the arguments for criminal juries are much stronger. In addition, at the heart of the dispute have been express or implicit assertions that juries are incapable of adequately understanding evidence or determining issues of fact, and that they are unpredictable, quixotic, and little better than a roll of dice. Yet, the most recent and exhaustive study of the jury in criminal cases concluded that juries do understand the evidence and come to sound conclusions in most of the cases presented to them and that when juries differ with the result at which the judge would have arrived, it is usually because they are serving some of the very purposes for which they were created and for which they are now employed.

The State of Louisiana urges that holding that the Fourteenth Amendment assures a right to jury trial will cast doubt on the integrity of every trial conducted without a jury. Plainly, this is not the import of our holding. Our conclusion is that in the American States, as in the federal judicial system, a general grant of jury trial for serious offenses is a fundamental right, essential for preventing miscarriages of justice and for assuring that fair trials are provided for all defendants. We would not assert, however, that every criminal trial—or any particular trial—held before a judge alone is unfair or that a defendant may never be as fairly treated by a judge as he would be by a jury. Thus we hold no constitutional doubts about the practices, common in both federal and state courts, of accepting waivers of jury trial and prosecuting petty crimes without extending a right to jury trial. However, the fact is that in most places more trials for serious crimes are to juries than to a court alone; a great many defendants prefer the judgment of a jury to that of a court. Even where defendants are satisfied with bench trials, the right to a jury trial very likely serves its intended purpose of making judicial or prosecutorial unfairness less likely.

II

Louisiana's final contention is that even if it must grant jury trials in serious criminal cases, the conviction before us is valid and constitutional because here the petitioner was tried for simple battery and was sentenced to only 60 days in the parish prison. We are not persuaded. It is doubtless true that there is a category of petty crimes or offenses which is not subject to the Sixth Amendment jury trial provision and should not be subject to the Fourteenth Amendment jury trial requirement here applied to the States. Crimes carrying possible penalties up to six months do not require a jury trial if they otherwise qualify as petty offenses. But the penalty authorized for a particular crime is of major relevance in determining whether it is serious or not and may in itself, if severe enough, subject the trial to the mandates of the Sixth Amendment. The penalty authorized by the law of the locality may be taken "as a gauge of its social and ethical judgments" of the crime in question. In *Clawans* the defendant was jailed for 60 days, but it was the 90-day authorized punishment on which the Court focused in determining that the offense was not one for which the Constitution assured trial by jury. In the case before us the Legislature of Louisiana has made simple battery a criminal offense punishable by imprisonment for up to two years and a fine. The question, then, is whether a crime carrying such a penalty is an offense which Louisiana may insist on trying without a jury.

Chapter XIII The Jury I: Scope of the Right and Other Issues

We think not. So-called petty offenses were tried without juries both in England and in the Colonies and have always been held to be exempt from the otherwise comprehensive language of the Sixth Amendment's jury trial provisions. There is no substantial evidence that the Framers intended to depart from this established common-law practice, and the possible consequences to defendants from convictions for petty offenses have been thought insufficient to outweigh the benefits to efficient law enforcement and simplified judicial administration resulting from the availability of speedy and inexpensive nonjury adjudications. These same considerations compel the same result under the Fourteenth Amendment. Of course the boundaries of the petty offense category have always been ill-defined, if not ambulatory. In the absence of an explicit constitutional provision, the definitional task necessarily falls on the courts, which must either pass upon the validity of legislative attempts to identify those petty offenses which are exempt from jury trial or, where the legislature has not addressed itself to the problem, themselves face the question in the first instance. In either case it is necessary to draw a line in the spectrum of crime, separating petty from serious infractions. This process, although essential, cannot be wholly satisfactory, for it requires attaching different consequences to events which, when they lie near the line, actually differ very little.

In determining whether the length of the authorized prison term or the seriousness of other punishment is enough in itself to require a jury trial, we are counseled by *Clawans,* supra, to refer to objective criteria, chiefly the existing laws and practices in the Nation. In the federal system, petty offenses are defined as those punishable by no more than six months in prison and a $500 fine. In 49 of the 50 States crimes subject to trial without a jury, which occasionally include simple battery, are punishable by no more than one year in jail. Moreover, in the late 18th century in America crimes triable without a jury were for the most part punishable by no more than a six-month prison term, although there appear to have been exceptions to this rule. We need not, however, settle in this case the exact location of the line between petty offenses and serious crimes. It is sufficient for our purposes to hold that a crime punishable by two years in prison is, based on past and contemporary standards in this country, a serious crime and not a petty offense. Consequently, appellant was entitled to a jury trial and it was error to deny it.

The judgment below is reversed and the case is remanded for proceedings not inconsistent with this opinion.

NOTES AND QUESTIONS

1. The second paragraph of the Court's opinion speaks volumes. It says three things. First, this is a case about race. Second, the trial in this case turned solely on the issue of the credibility of the eyewitnesses to the alleged assault (a slap on the elbow). Third, the trial judge—the finder of fact here—chose to believe the white witnesses and not the Black witnesses. But step back for a moment. Is it fair to ask what the Court, or the civil rights lawyers who represented Paul Duncan, thought victory would mean in this case? Was Paul Duncan better off with a trial by a jury in a case such as this one with clear racial overtones? The jury would almost surely be all white, and legally so, as the Supreme Court just three years earlier in *Swain v. Alabama,* 380 U.S. 82 (1965), had blessed the prosecution's use of peremptory challenges to strike Black persons from juries. *See* Chapter XV *infra.*

2. *Duncan* was indeed a case about race. Plaquemines Parish, Louisiana, was ruled by political boss Leander Perez, a notorious racist and segregationist who made a special point of intimidating and sometimes incarcerating civil rights workers ("outside agitators"). *See* Nancy J. King, Duncan v. Louisiana: *How Bigotry in the Bayou Led to the Federal Regulation of State*

Juries 261-64, in Criminal Procedure Stories (Carol S. Steiker ed., 2006). At the time of Paul Duncan's altercation with the white youths in October 1966, the parish had just been sued by the Department of Justice over its public school segregationist policies. Perez had responded to the suit by transferring all public school property (textbooks, buses, athletic equipment, etc.) to the parish council, establishing a new private school for whites, and firing all the white public school teachers and rehiring them at the white private schools. The lawsuit had been reported in the *New York Times*, and Perez's reputation had been widely reported in the national media throughout the 1960s. *Id.* at 264-65.

3. The Court recognizes the historical significance of the right to a jury trial as a vehicle to "prevent oppression by the Government." It notes that the Framers of the Constitution had sought to impose this safeguard against the overreaching of both the "overzealous prosecutor and against the compliant, biased, or eccentric judge." Why is the "right" to indictment by a grand jury so rarely invoked as part of this generalized salute to the Framers' efforts to curb the abuse of official authority?

4. The Court focuses almost exclusively on colonial history in finding the fundamental nature of the right to trial by jury. It could have found equally strong support in the nineteenth century. Much of the controversy over the federal Fugitive Slave Acts (of both 1793 and 1850) focused on the statutes' authorizing the return of a person to bondage by a wholly summary process, without a jury determination of such central facts as "is the person a slave." Southern proponents of the summary process aspect of the legislation thought northern advocates for the jury trial right just wanted to provide the opportunity for jury nullification opportunities. James Forman, *Juries and Race in the Nineteenth Century*, 113 Yale L.J. 895, 898-909 (2004).

5. The Court holds that the test for whether a defendant has a right to a jury trial—which it does not precisely specify here—shall be determined not by the actual sentence received (60 days in Paul Duncan's case) but rather by the statutorily authorized maximum, here two years. Recall that the Court in *Argersinger v. Hamlin*, 407 U.S. 25 (1972), *see* Chapter VIII *supra*, would reject *Duncan*'s use of the authorized term of imprisonment as the test for determining the scope of the right to counsel, opting instead for a touchstone of "actual imprisonment." Is there a case to be made that the two rights should be coterminous, that is, that right to counsel and the right to a jury trial should apply in the exact same situations? Is the need for counsel more acute in jury trials than in bench trials?

6. Duncan's brief in the Supreme Court was explicitly based on an appeal to racial justice. After explaining the trial judge's crediting of the white witnesses' testimony over that of the Black witnesses, Duncan argued:

> It is plain that in cases such as this—where the personal and political leanings of the trial judge will often be antagonistic to the defendant—the potential for a factual determination that is influenced by considerations other than the evidence of record is very great. This situation, particularly in civil rights related prosecutions in the Deep South, is not uncommon.

Duncan v. Louisiana, Brief of Appellant 23.

The Court's announcement of its decision in *Duncan* received front page coverage in both the *New York Times* and the *New Orleans Times-Picayune*, the leading newspapers in two of the three states that denied jury trials to defendants facing more than six months' incarceration. King, Duncan v. Louisiana, *supra* at 281. State officials in these three states predicted disaster for their criminal justice systems. Two things forestalled the doom and gloom. The legislatures in Louisiana and New Jersey (the third state) immediately passed statutes reducing the penalties for some crimes to six months. And the Supreme Court ultimately ruled that *Duncan* did not apply retroactively. *DeStefano v. Woods*, 392 U.S. 631 (1968). Two years later, in *Baldwin v. New York*, 399 U.S. 66 (1970), the Court announced the bright line rule it declined to impose in *Duncan*, holding that the right to a jury trial existed wherever the charged offense authorized more than six months' imprisonment.

On remand Perez sought to retry Duncan, again without a jury because the penalty for battery had been reduced in the meantime. Perez had also filed criminal charges against one of Duncan's trial counsel, civil rights lawyer Richard Sobol, for practicing law without a Louisiana license. Both prosecutions were ultimately enjoined by United States District Judge Fred James Cassibry, who concluded as follows:

> First, that the proceeding against Duncan in state court is maintained by the defendant in bad faith and for purposes of harassment. The multiple arrests, the unusually high bond on the battery charge, the unusually high sentence on the battery conviction, the unlawful demand that double bond be posted, the arrest of Sobol, and the comments of the defendant and the state district judge, all taken together, established that these authorities are personally hostile to Duncan and have altered established principles of criminal procedure in an effort to punish Duncan for his exercise of federally secured rights.
>
> Second, there is no legitimate state interest in the reprosecution of Duncan. Without attempting to resolve the disputed issue of whether Duncan slapped or simply touched the white youth on the arm, it is clear beyond dispute that any violation that may have occurred was so slight and technical as to be generally reserved for law school hypotheticals rather than criminal prosecutions. The white boy was not hurt and displayed no bruise minutes after the incident. De minimus "batteries" of this kind occur repeatedly in Plaquemines Parish and elsewhere and do not become the subject of criminal proceedings. The factors bearing on the question of harassment, considered together with the nature of the conduct on which the charge is based, convince the court that the charge against Duncan would not have been prosecuted, and certainly not reprosecuted, were it not for the civil rights context out of which the case arose, for Duncan's selection of civil rights attorneys to represent him, and for the vigor of his defense.
>
> Third, the reprosecution of Duncan would deter and suppress the exercise of federally secured rights by Negroes in Plaquemines Parish. The various stages of the Duncan and Sobol cases have been thoroughly publicized in the New Orleans papers, which the parties have stipulated are the only daily newspapers generally read by residents of Plaquemines Parish. Duncan has waged an unprecedented four year fight to avoid conviction and incarceration on the charges against him. Not only did the charge against him relate to the occasional racial violence that accompanied the integration of the Boothville-Venice School, the civil rights overtones of the case were underscored by the participation of civil rights attorneys, by the appeal to the Supreme Court of the United States, and by the arrest of Sobol and the extensive proceedings which followed. If Duncan were required to face retrial, it would constitute an unmistakable message to Negroes in Plaquemines Parish that it is unprofitable to step outside familiar patterns and to seek to rely on federal rights to oppose the policies of certain parish officials. The destructive effect on the exercise of federal rights could not be corrected by Duncan's possible subsequent success in state or federal court.

USDJ Fred James Cassibry

Duncan v. Perez, 321 F. Supp. 181, 184-85 (E.D. La. 1970), *aff'd,* 445 F.2d 557 (5th Cir. 1971). Professor Randall Kennedy contends that *Duncan v. Perez* is perhaps the only reported case where a court has found that a prosecutor abused his discretion on grounds of racial discrimination. Randall Kennedy, Race, Crime, and the Law 354 n* (1997).

A. Scope of the Right to Trial by Jury **1127**

A loose end that *Duncan* did not address, among others, was whether the Sixth and Fourteenth Amendments mandated a particular minimum jury size. In *Williams v. Florida*, 399 U.S. 78 (1970), the Court found constitutional Florida's use of a six-person jury for non-capital cases. The Court found that the traditional size of common law juries at the time of the Founding was twelve, but that number was nothing but "a historical accident, unrelated to the great purposes which gave rise to the jury in the first place." *Id.* at 100. It held that a jury of six was "large enough to promote group deliberation, free from outside attempts at intimidation, and to provide a fair possibility of obtaining a representative cross-section of the community." *Id.* The Court brushed aside the argument that a jury of twelve doubles the defendant's chance of finding a juror who will insist on a finding of not guilty and that, as to whether a jury of six will be sufficiently diverse, it observed that since twelve persons will not represent every voice in the community, six will do just fine. *Id.* at 101-02.

Eight years later, besieged by data showing the inferiority of smaller juries—in reliability, in consistency, and in having (to the detriment of defendants) a demonstrably lower frequency of hung juries—the Court invalidated a conviction by a five-person jury in Georgia, drawing a bright if arbitrary constitutional line at six. *Ballew v. Georgia*, 435 U.S. 223 (1978).

How do you think a Supreme Court committed to an "originalist" perspective on constitutional interpretation would react to the sentiment expressed in *Williams* that the common law tradition of twelve-man juries was merely "a historical accident, unrelated to the great purposes which gave rise to the jury in the first place"?

Juries are often instructed by the judge, in words or substance, "you are the judges of the facts, in the same way I am the judge of the law." This seems straightforward. But the next case considers precisely what facts in a criminal case must be decided by the jury.

United States v. Gaudin
515 U.S. 506 (1995)

Justice SCALIA delivered the opinion of the Court.

In the trial at issue here, respondent was convicted of making material false statements in a matter within the jurisdiction of a federal agency, in violation of 18 U.S.C. § 1001. The question presented is whether it was constitutional for the trial judge to refuse to submit the question of "materiality" to the jury.

I

In the 1980's, respondent engaged in a number of real estate transactions financed by loans insured by the Federal Housing Administration (FHA), an agency within the Department of Housing and Urban Development (HUD). Respondent would purchase rental housing, renovate it, obtain an inflated appraisal, and sell it to a "straw buyer" (a friend or relative), for whom respondent would arrange an FHA-insured mortgage loan. Then, as prearranged, respondent would repurchase the property (at a small profit to the straw buyer) and assume the mortgage loan. Twenty-nine of these ventures went into default.

Respondent was charged by federal indictment with, among other things, multiple counts of making false statements on federal loan documents in violation of 18 U.S.C. § 1001. Two of these counts charged that respondent had made false statements on HUD/FHA form 92800-5 by knowingly inflating the appraised value of the mortgaged property. The other false-statement counts charged that respondent had made misrepresentations on HUD/FHA form HUD-1, the settlement form used in closing the sales of the properties. Line 303 of this form requires disclosure of the closing costs to be paid or received by the borrower/buyer and the seller. The forms executed by respondent showed that the buyer was to pay some of the closing costs, whereas in fact he, the seller, had arranged to pay all of them. To prove the materiality of these false statements, the Government offered the testimony of several persons charged with administering FHA/HUD programs, who explained why the requested information was important.

At the close of the evidence, the United States District Court for the District of Montana instructed the jury that, to convict respondent, the Government was required to prove, inter alia, that the alleged false statements were material to the activities and decisions of HUD. But, the court further instructed, "[t]he issue of materiality . . . is not submitted to you for your decision but rather is a matter for the decision of the court. You are instructed that the statements charged in the indictment are material statements." The jury convicted respondent of the § 1001 charges.

A panel of the Court of Appeals for the Ninth Circuit reversed these convictions because Circuit precedent dictated that materiality in a § 1001 prosecution be decided by the jury. On rehearing en banc, the Court of Appeals stood by this precedent. It held that taking the question of materiality from the jury denied respondent a right guaranteed by the Fifth and Sixth Amendments to the United States Constitution. We granted certiorari.

II

Section 1001 of Title 18 provides:

> Whoever, in any matter within the jurisdiction of any department or agency of the United States knowingly and willfully falsifies, conceals or covers up by any trick, scheme, or device a material fact, or makes any false, fictitious or fraudulent statements or representations, or makes or uses any false writing or document knowing the same to contain any false, fictitious or fraudulent statement or entry, shall be fined not more than $10,000 or imprisoned not more than five years, or both.

It is uncontested that conviction under this provision requires that the statements be "material" to the Government inquiry, and that "materiality" is an element of the offense that the Government must prove. The parties also agree on the definition of "materiality": The statement must have "a natural tendency to influence, or [be] capable of influencing, the decision of the decisionmaking body to which it was addressed." The question for our resolution is whether respondent was entitled to have this element of the crime determined by the jury.

The Fifth Amendment to the United States Constitution guarantees that no one will be deprived of liberty without "due process of law"; and the Sixth, that "[i]n all criminal prosecutions, the accused shall enjoy the right to a speedy and public trial, by an impartial jury." We have held that these provisions require criminal convictions to rest upon a jury determination that the defendant is guilty of every element of the crime with which he is charged, beyond a reasonable doubt. The right to have a jury make the ultimate determination of guilt has an impressive pedigree. Blackstone described "trial by jury" as requiring that "the truth of every accusation, whether preferred in the shape of indictment, information, or appeal, should afterwards be confirmed by the unanimous suffrage of twelve of [the defendant's] equals and neighbors. . . ." Justice Story wrote that the "trial by jury" guaranteed by the Constitution was "generally understood to mean . . . a trial by a jury of twelve men, impartially selected, who must unanimously concur in the guilt of the accused before a legal conviction can be had." This right was designed "to guard against a spirit of oppression and tyranny on the part of rulers," and "was from very early times insisted on by our ancestors in the parent country, as the great bulwark of their civil and political liberties." *See also Duncan v. Louisiana* (1968).

III

Thus far, the resolution of the question before us seems simple. The Constitution gives a criminal defendant the right to demand that a jury find him guilty of all the elements of the crime with which he is charged; one of the elements in the present case is materiality; respondent therefore had a right to have the jury decide materiality. To escape the force of this logic, the Government offers essentially three arguments. Having conceded the minor premise — that materiality is an element of the offense — the Government argues first, that the major premise is flawed; second, that (essentially) a page of history is worth a volume of logic, and uniform practice simply excludes the element of materiality from the syllogism; and third, that stare decisis requires the judgment here to be reversed.

A

As to the first, the Government's position is that "materiality," whether as a matter of logic or history, is a "legal" question, and that although we have sometimes spoken of "requiring the jury to decide 'all the elements of a criminal offense,' the principle actually applies to only the factual components of the essential elements." The Government claims that this understanding of the jury's role dates back to *Sparf v. United States* (1895), and is reaffirmed by recent decisions of this Court.

By limiting the jury's constitutionally prescribed role to "the factual components of the essential elements" the Government surely does not mean to concede that the jury must pass upon all elements that contain some factual component, for that test is amply met here. Deciding whether a statement is "material" requires the determination of at least two subsidiary questions of purely historical fact: (a) "what statement was made?" and (b) "what decision was the agency trying to make?" The ultimate question: (c) "whether the statement was material to the decision," requires applying the legal standard of materiality (quoted above) to these historical facts. What the Government apparently argues is that the Constitution requires only that (a) and (b) be determined by the jury, and that (c) may be determined by the judge. We see two difficulties with this. First, the application-of-legal-standard-to-fact sort of question posed by (c), commonly called a "mixed question of law and fact," has typically been resolved by juries. Indeed, our cases have recognized in other contexts that the materiality inquiry, involving as it does "delicate assessments of the inferences a 'reasonable [decisionmaker]' would draw from a given set of facts and the significance of those inferences to him . . . [is] peculiarly on[e] for the trier of fact." *TSC Industries, Inc. v. Northway, Inc.* (1976) (securities fraud).

The second difficulty with the Government's position is that it has absolutely no historical support. If it were true, the lawbooks would be full of cases, regarding materiality and innumerable other "mixed-law-and-fact" issues, in which the criminal jury was required to come forth with "findings of fact" pertaining to each of the essential elements, leaving it to the judge to apply the law to those facts and render the ultimate verdict of "guilty" or "not guilty." We know of no such case. Juries at the time of the framing could not be forced to produce mere "factual findings," but were entitled to deliver a general verdict pronouncing the defendant's guilt or innocence. Justice Chase's defense to one of the charges in his 1805 impeachment trial was that "he well knows, that it is the right of juries in criminal cases, to give a general verdict of acquittal, which cannot be set aside on account of its being contrary to law, and that hence results the power of juries, to decide on the law as well as on the facts, in all criminal cases. This power he holds to be a sacred part of our legal privileges. . . ."

Sparf, supra, the case on which the Government relies, had nothing to do with the issue before us here. The question there was whether the jury could be deprived of the power to determine, not only historical facts, not only mixed questions of fact and law, but pure

1130 Chapter XIII The Jury I: Scope of the Right and Other Issues

questions of law in a criminal case. As the foregoing quotation from Justice Chase suggests, many thought the jury had such power. We decided that it did not. In criminal cases, as in civil, we held, the judge must be permitted to instruct the jury on the law and to insist that the jury follow his instructions. But our decision in no way undermined the historical and constitutionally guaranteed right of criminal defendants to demand that the jury decide guilt or innocence on every issue, which includes application of the law to the facts. To the contrary, Justice Harlan, writing for the Court, explained the many judicial assertions of the jury's right to determine both law and fact as expressions of "the principle, that when the question is compounded of law and fact, a general verdict, ex necessitate, disposes of the case in hand, both as to law and fact." He gave as an example the 1807 treason trial of Aaron Burr in which Chief Justice Marshall charged the jury that " 'levying war is an act compounded of law and fact; of which the jury, aided by the court must judge. . . . [And] hav[ing] now heard the opinion of the court on the law of the case[,] [t]hey will apply that law to the facts, and will find a verdict of guilty or not guilty as their own consciences may direct.' " Other expressions of the same principle abound. As Thayer wrote at the end of the 19th century: "From the beginning . . . it was perceived that any general verdict, such as . . . not guilty, involved a conclusion of law, and that the jury did, in a sense, in such cases answer a question of law."

The more modern authorities the Government cites also do not support its concept of the criminal jury as mere factfinder. Although each contains language discussing the jury's role as factfinder, each also confirms that the jury's constitutional responsibility is not merely to determine the facts, but to apply the law to those facts and draw the ultimate conclusion of guilt or innocence. The point is put with unmistakable clarity in *Allen,* which involved the constitutionality of statutory inferences and presumptions. Such devices, *Allen* said, can help

> the trier of fact to determine the existence of an element of the crime — that is, an "ultimate" or "elemental" fact — from the existence of one or more "evidentiary" or "basic" facts. . . . Nonetheless, in criminal cases, the ultimate test of any device's constitutional validity in a given case remains constant: the device must not undermine the factfinder's responsibility at trial, based on evidence adduced by the State, to find the ultimate facts beyond a reasonable doubt.

B

The Government next argues that, even if the jury is generally entitled to pass on all elements of a crime, there is a historical exception for materiality determinations in perjury prosecutions. We do not doubt that historical practice is relevant to what the Constitution means by such concepts as trial by jury, and it is precisely historical practice that we have relied on in concluding that the jury must find all the elements. The existence of a unique historical exception to this principle — and an exception that reduces the power of the jury precisely when it is most important, i.e., in a prosecution not for harming another individual, but for offending against the Government itself — would be so extraordinary that the evidence for it would have to be convincing indeed. It is not so.

The practice of having courts determine the materiality of false statements in perjury prosecutions is neither as old, nor as uniform, as the Government suggests. In England, no pre-Revolution cases appear to have addressed the question, and the judges reached differing results when the issue finally arose in the mid-19th century. It was not until 1911, 120 years after the adoption of our Bill of Rights, that the rule the Government argues for was finally adopted in England — not by judicial decision but by Act of Parliament.

Much more importantly, there was also no clear practice of having the judge determine the materiality question in this country at or near the time the Bill of Rights was adopted. The Government cites *Power v. Price* (N.Y. 1836), as "[t]he earliest reported case on the question" whether "materiality in perjury prosecutions is a question for the court rather than the jury," claiming that there "New York's highest court held that a trial judge had correctly reserved the question of materiality to itself." *Power* held nothing even close to this. *Power* was not a perjury case; indeed, it was not even a criminal prosecution. It was a civil action in which Price sued Power for the slander of imputing to him the crime of perjury. The Court of Appeals held that Price did not need to prove the materiality of the alleged false statement in order to make out a prima facie case; but that Power could raise immateriality as an affirmative defense negating intent to impute perjury. It then said that the trial court "was clearly right in instructing the jury that the testimony given on the former trial was proved to be material," since "it merely decided a question of law, arising upon the proof of facts as to which there was no dispute or contrariety of testimony." But the courts' power to resolve mixed-law-and-fact questions in civil cases is not at issue here; civil and criminal juries' required roles are obviously not identical, or else there could be no directed verdicts for civil plaintiffs. The other early case relied upon by the Government, *Steinman v. McWilliams* (1847), another slander case, is inapt for the same reason. The earliest American case involving the point that we have been able to find places the Government itself in opposition to its position here. In *United States v. Cowing* (CC DC 1835), the United States argued that materiality in a perjury prosecution was a matter for the jury's consideration, citing an unpublished decision of the General Court of Virginia. The federal court, however, did not address the issue.

State and federal cases appear not to have addressed the question until the latter part of the 19th century, at which time they do not display anything like the "virtual unanimity" claimed by the Government. Some of the opinions cited by the Government, asserting that materiality was a question of "law" for the judge, appear to have involved either demurrers to the indictment or appeals from convictions in which the case for materiality was so weak that no reasonable juror could credit it — so that even on our view of the matter the case should not have gone to the jury. (The prosecution's failure to provide minimal evidence of materiality, like its failure to provide minimal evidence of any other element, of course raises a question of "law" that warrants dismissal.) And some of the other cited cases involve the convicted defendant's claim that materiality should not have been decided by the jury, so that even if the issue was not one of the prosecution's failure to make a threshold case, it did not arise in a context in which the defendant's right to jury trial was at issue.

Even assuming, however, that all the Government's last-half-of-the-19th-century cases fully stand for the proposition that the defendant has no right to jury determination of materiality, there are cases that support the other view. At most there had developed a division of authority on the point, as the treatise writers of the period amply demonstrate. . . .

In sum, we find nothing like a consistent historical tradition supporting the proposition that the element of materiality in perjury prosecutions is to be decided by the judge. Since that proposition is contrary to the uniform general understanding (and we think the only understanding consistent with principle) that the Fifth and Sixth Amendments require conviction by a jury of all elements of the crime, we must reject those cases that have embraced it. Though uniform post-ratification practice can shed light upon the meaning of an ambiguous constitutional provision, the practice here is not uniform, and the core meaning of the constitutional guarantees is unambiguous.

• • •

NOTES AND QUESTIONS

1. The statute at issue, § 1001 of Title 18, is one of the federal prosecutor's favorite weapons inasmuch as it criminalizes, among other things, virtually any false statement made by a witness during an interview by a federal agent. Thus the statute's *in terrorem* power is huge. Recall that Trump's National Security Advisor Michael Flynn was prosecuted under § 1001 in 2017 prior to withdrawing his guilty plea and being pardoned. *Gaudin* is a good example of the breadth of the statute, as the HUD-1 form that was the vehicle for defendant's misstatements is a garden-variety piece of paperwork required in connection with real estate transactions involving a federally insured loan.

2. Note also the substantive weakness of the statute's materiality requirement: A statement need only "be capable of influencing the decisionmaking body to which it was addressed." In the context of false statements to law enforcement, the bar is particularly low given the amorphous nature of any investigation in which such an interview occurs. *See United States v. Lupton*, 620 F.3d 790 (7th Cir. 2010) (defendant's exculpatory denials to the FBI were material under § 1001 even though agents had secretly recorded tapes of defendant making contrary statements and defendant's statements had no actual impact on the investigation). In short, the breadth of § 1001 is one of the reasons why it is almost never a good idea to voluntarily talk to the FBI.

3. The prosecution in *Gaudin* is based on a violation of the first clause of § 1001, which explicitly references a "material fact." As a matter of statutory interpretation, should all three clauses of § 1001 be interpreted to have a materiality requirement?

4. The key to *Gaudin* was the classification of materiality, an issue the parties agreed on, as an "element" of § 1001. The government argues that materiality is more of a "legal question" than a factual one that must be decided by the jury. In what sense is materiality, as the standard is defined in *Gaudin*, a legal question? In responding to this argument the Court notes that the jury is not a "mere factfinder" but has as its mission to determine the facts and also "to apply the law to those facts and draw the ultimate conclusion of guilt or innocence." What does this mean? Are there no limits on the jury's ability to "draw the ultimate conclusion of guilt or innocence"? In quoting from the jury charge in the trial of Aaron Burr—the jury will apply the law to the facts and find a verdict of guilty or not guilty "as their own consciences may direct"—does the Court really mean the jurors' "consciences" are the ultimate touchstone of guilt or innocence?

Do the historical lessons set forth in *Gaudin*—the impeachment trial of Justice Chase, the treason trial of Aaron Burr—suggest there may be an originalist argument for jury nullification? *See* Section B *infra*.

5. As to elements: Are elements something that are organically part of particular crimes or are they purely a product of a written statute? Can the existence or nonexistence of elements be decreed (manipulated) by the legislative drafters of statutes? The concurring opinion, seeking to soften the blow of *Gaudin*, suggests that elements are emphatically up to the legislature's discretion, and that, for example, legislatures can "reallocate burdens of proof" by labeling elements as affirmative defenses or sentencing factors. Are there limits to this view? How does such "reallocation" affect the government's burden to prove each element of the offense beyond a reasonable doubt? The Court came to address these and related questions in a series of cases in the sentencing context, shortly after *Gaudin*, beginning with *Apprendi v. New Jersey*, 530 U.S. 466 (2000). This line of cases is considered in Chapter XVI *infra*.

Back to Louisiana. Like *Duncan*, the next case, *Ramos,* is about juries with a strong racial sub-plot.

A. Scope of the Right to Trial by Jury · 1133

Ramos v. Louisiana
590 U.S. 83 (2020)

Justice GORSUCH announced the judgment of the Court and delivered the opinion of the Court with respect to Parts I, II-A, III, and IV-B-1, an opinion with respect to Parts II-B, IV-B-2, and V, in which Justice GINSBURG, Justice BREYER, and Justice SOTOMAYOR join, and an opinion with respect to Part IV-A, in which Justice GINSBURG and Justice BREYER join.

Accused of a serious crime, Evangelisto Ramos insisted on his innocence and invoked his right to a jury trial. Eventually, 10 jurors found the evidence against him persuasive. But a pair of jurors believed that the State of Louisiana had failed to prove Mr. Ramos's guilt beyond reasonable doubt; they voted to acquit.

In 48 States and federal court, a single juror's vote to acquit is enough to prevent a conviction. But not in Louisiana. Along with Oregon, Louisiana has long punished people based on 10-to-2 verdicts like the one here. So instead of the mistrial he would have received almost anywhere else, Mr. Ramos was sentenced to life in prison without the possibility of parole.

Why do Louisiana and Oregon allow nonunanimous convictions? Though it's hard to say why these laws persist, their origins are clear. Louisiana first endorsed nonunanimous verdicts for serious crimes at a constitutional convention in 1898. According to one committee chairman, the avowed purpose of that convention was to "establish the supremacy of the white race," and the resulting document included many of the trappings of the Jim Crow era: a poll tax, a combined literacy and property ownership test, and a grandfather clause that in practice exempted white residents from the most onerous of these requirements.

Nor was it only the prospect of African-Americans voting that concerned the delegates. Just a week before the convention, the U.S. Senate passed a resolution calling for an investigation into whether Louisiana was systemically excluding African-Americans from juries. Seeking to avoid unwanted national attention, and aware that this Court would strike down any policy of overt discrimination against African-American jurors as a violation of the Fourteenth Amendment, the delegates sought to undermine African-American participation on juries in another way. With a careful eye on racial demographics, the convention delegates sculpted a "facially race-neutral" rule permitting 10-to-2 verdicts in order "to ensure that African-American juror service would be meaningless."

Adopted in the 1930s, Oregon's rule permitting nonunanimous verdicts can be similarly traced to the rise of the Ku Klux Klan and efforts to dilute "the influence of racial, ethnic, and religious minorities on Oregon juries." In fact, no one before us contests any of this; courts in both Louisiana and Oregon have frankly acknowledged that race was a motivating factor in the adoption of their States' respective nonunanimity rules.

We took this case to decide whether the Sixth Amendment right to a jury trial—as incorporated against the States by way of the Fourteenth Amendment—requires a unanimous verdict to convict a defendant of a serious offense. Louisiana insists that this Court has never definitively passed on the question and urges us to find its practice consistent with the Sixth Amendment. By contrast, the dissent doesn't try to defend Louisiana's law on Sixth or Fourteenth Amendment grounds; tacitly, it seems to admit that the Constitution forbids States from using nonunanimous juries. Yet, unprompted by Louisiana, the dissent suggests our precedent requires us to rule for the State anyway. What explains all this? To answer the puzzle, it's necessary to say a bit more about the merits of the question presented, the relevant precedent, and, at last, the consequences that follow from saying what we know to be true.

I

The Sixth Amendment promises that "[i]n all criminal prosecutions, the accused shall enjoy the right to a speedy and public trial, by an impartial jury of the State and district wherein the crime shall have been committed, which district shall have been previously ascertained by law." The Amendment goes on to preserve other rights for criminal defendants but says nothing else about what a "trial by an impartial jury" entails.

Still, the promise of a jury trial surely meant something — otherwise, there would have been no reason to write it down. Nor would it have made any sense to spell out the places from which jurors should be drawn if their powers as jurors could be freely abridged by statute. Imagine a constitution that allowed a "jury trial" to mean nothing but a single person rubber-stamping convictions without hearing any evidence — but simultaneously insisting that the lone juror come from a specific judicial district "previously ascertained by law." And if that's not enough, imagine a constitution that included the same hollow guarantee twice — not only in the Sixth Amendment, but also in Article III. No: The text and structure of the Constitution clearly suggest that the term "trial by an impartial jury" carried with it some meaning about the content and requirements of a jury trial.

One of these requirements was unanimity. Wherever we might look to determine what the term "trial by an impartial jury trial" meant at the time of the Sixth Amendment's adoption — whether it's the common law, state practices in the founding era, or opinions and treatises written soon afterward — the answer is unmistakable. A jury must reach a unanimous verdict in order to convict.

The requirement of juror unanimity emerged in 14th century England and was soon accepted as a vital right protected by the common law. As Blackstone explained, no person could be found guilty of a serious crime unless "the truth of every accusation . . . should . . . be confirmed by the unanimous suffrage of twelve of his equals and neighbors, indifferently chosen, and superior to all suspicion." A " 'verdict, taken from eleven, was no verdict' " at all.

This same rule applied in the young American States. Six State Constitutions explicitly required unanimity. Another four preserved the right to a jury trial in more general terms. But the variations did not matter much; consistent with the common law, state courts appeared to regard unanimity as an essential feature of the jury trial.

It was against this backdrop that James Madison drafted and the States ratified the Sixth Amendment in 1791. By that time, unanimous verdicts had been required for about 400 years. If the term "trial by an impartial jury" carried any meaning at all, it surely included a requirement as long and widely accepted as unanimity.

Influential, postadoption treatises confirm this understanding. For example, in 1824, Nathan Dane reported as fact that the U.S. Constitution required unanimity in criminal jury trials for serious offenses. A few years later, Justice Story explained in his Commentaries on the Constitution that "in common cases, the law not only presumes every man innocent, until he is proved guilty; but unanimity in the verdict of the jury is indispensable." Similar statements can be found in American legal treatises throughout the 19th century.

Nor is this a case where the original public meaning was lost to time and only recently recovered. This Court has, repeatedly and over many years, recognized that the Sixth Amendment requires unanimity. As early as 1898, the Court said that a defendant enjoys a "constitutional right to demand that his liberty should not be taken from him except by the joint action of the court and the unanimous verdict of a jury of twelve persons." A few decades later, the Court elaborated that the Sixth Amendment affords a right to "a trial by jury as understood and applied at common law, . . . includ[ing] all the essential elements as they were recognized in this country and England when the Constitution was adopted." And, the Court observed, this includes a requirement "that the verdict should be unanimous." In all,

A. Scope of the Right to Trial by Jury 1135

this Court has commented on the Sixth Amendment's unanimity requirement no fewer than 13 times over more than 120 years.

There can be no question either that the Sixth Amendment's unanimity requirement applies to state and federal criminal trials equally. This Court has long explained that the Sixth Amendment right to a jury trial is "fundamental to the American scheme of justice" and incorporated against the States under the Fourteenth Amendment. This Court has long explained, too, that incorporated provisions of the Bill of Rights bear the same content when asserted against States as they do when asserted against the federal government. So if the Sixth Amendment's right to a jury trial requires a unanimous verdict to support a conviction in federal court, it requires no less in state court.

II

A

How, despite these seemingly straightforward principles, have Louisiana's and Oregon's laws managed to hang on for so long? It turns out that the Sixth Amendment's otherwise simple story took a strange turn in 1972. That year, the Court confronted these States' unconventional schemes for the first time—in *Apodaca v. Oregon* and a companion case, *Johnson v. Louisiana*. Ultimately, the Court could do no more than issue a badly fractured set of opinions. Four dissenting Justices would not have hesitated to strike down the States' laws, recognizing that the Sixth Amendment requires unanimity and that this guarantee is fully applicable against the States under the Fourteenth Amendment. But a four-Justice plurality took a very different view of the Sixth Amendment. These Justices declared that the real question before them was whether unanimity serves an important "function" in "contemporary society." Then, having reframed the question, the plurality wasted few words before concluding that unanimity's costs outweigh its benefits in the modern era, so the Sixth Amendment should not stand in the way of Louisiana or Oregon.

The ninth Member of the Court adopted a position that was neither here nor there. On the one hand, Justice Powell agreed that, as a matter of "history and precedent, . . . the Sixth Amendment requires a unanimous jury verdict to convict." But, on the other hand, he argued that the Fourteenth Amendment does not render this guarantee against the federal government fully applicable against the States. In this way, Justice Powell doubled down on his belief in "dual-track" incorporation—the idea that a single right can mean two different things depending on whether it is being invoked against the federal or a state government.

Justice Powell acknowledged that his argument for dual-track incorporation came "late in the day." Late it was. The Court had already, nearly a decade earlier, "rejected the notion that the Fourteenth Amendment applies to the States only a 'watered-down, subjective version of the individual guarantees of the Bill of Rights.'" It's a point we've restated many times since, too, including as recently as last year. Still, Justice Powell frankly explained, he was "unwillin[g]" to follow the Court's precedents. So he offered up the essential fifth vote to uphold Mr. Apodaca's conviction—if based only on a view of the Fourteenth Amendment that he knew was (and remains) foreclosed by precedent.

B

In the years following *Apodaca*, both Louisiana and Oregon chose to continue allowing nonunanimous verdicts. But their practices have always stood on shaky ground. After all, while Justice Powell's vote secured a favorable judgment for the States in *Apodaca*, it's never been clear what rationale could support a similar result in future cases. Only two possibilities exist: Either the Sixth Amendment allows nonunanimous verdicts, or the Sixth Amendment's guarantee of a jury trial applies with less force to the States under the Fourteenth Amendment. Yet, as we've

1136   Chapter XIII The Jury I: Scope of the Right and Other Issues

seen, both bear their problems. In *Apodaca* itself, a majority of Justices—including Justice Powell—recognized that the Sixth Amendment demands unanimity, just as our cases have long said. And this Court's precedents, both then and now, prevent the Court from applying the Sixth Amendment to the States in some mutated and diminished form under the Fourteenth Amendment. So what could we possibly describe as the "holding" of *Apodaca*?

Really, no one has found a way to make sense of it. In later cases, this Court has labeled *Apodaca* an "exception," "unusual," and in any event "not an endorsement" of Justice Powell's view of incorporation. At the same time, we have continued to recognize the historical need for unanimity. We've been studiously ambiguous, even inconsistent, about what *Apodaca* might mean. To its credit, Louisiana acknowledges the problem. The State expressly tells us it is not "asking the Court to accord Justice Powell's solo opinion in *Apodaca* precedential force." Instead, in an effort to win today's case, Louisiana embraces the idea that everything is up for grabs. It contends that this Court has never definitively ruled on the propriety of nonunanimous juries under the Sixth Amendment—and that we should use this case to hold for the first time that nonunanimous juries are permissible in state and federal courts alike.

III

Louisiana's approach may not be quite as tough as trying to defend Justice Powell's dual-track theory of incorporation, but it's pretty close. How does the State deal with the fact this Court has said 13 times over 120 years that the Sixth Amendment does require unanimity? Or the fact that five Justices in *Apodaca* said the same? The best the State can offer is to suggest that all these statements came in dicta. But even supposing (without granting) that Louisiana is right and it's dicta all the way down, why would the Court now walk away from many of its own statements about the Constitution's meaning? And what about the prior 400 years of English and American cases requiring unanimity—should we dismiss all those as dicta too?

Sensibly, Louisiana doesn't dispute that the common law required unanimity. Instead, it argues that the drafting history of the Sixth Amendment reveals an intent by the framers to leave this particular feature behind. The State points to the fact that Madison's proposal for the Sixth Amendment originally read: "The trial of all crimes . . . shall be by an impartial jury of freeholders of the vicinage, with the requisite of unanimity for conviction, of the right of challenge, and other accustomed requisites. . . ." Louisiana notes that the House of Representatives approved this text with minor modifications. Yet, the State stresses, the Senate replaced "impartial jury of freeholders of the vicinage" with "impartial jury of the State and district wherein the crime shall have been committed" and also removed the explicit references to unanimity, the right of challenge, and "other accustomed requisites." In light of these revisions, Louisiana would have us infer an intent to abandon the common law's traditional unanimity requirement.

But this snippet of drafting history could just as easily support the opposite inference. Maybe the Senate deleted the language about unanimity, the right of challenge, and "other accustomed prerequisites" because all this was so plainly included in the promise of a "trial by an impartial jury" that Senators considered the language surplusage. The truth is that we have little contemporaneous evidence shedding light on why the Senate acted as it did. So rather than dwelling on text left on the cutting room floor, we are much better served by interpreting the language Congress retained and the States ratified. And, as we've seen, at the time of the Amendment's adoption, the right to a jury trial meant a trial in which the jury renders a unanimous verdict.

Further undermining Louisiana's inference about the drafting history is the fact it proves too much. If the Senate's deletion of the word "unanimity" changed the meaning of the text that remains, then the same would seemingly have to follow for the other deleted words as well. So it's not just unanimity that died in the Senate, but all the "other accustomed requisites" associated with the common law jury trial right—i.e., everything history might have taught us about what it means to have a jury trial. Taking the State's argument from drafting history to its logical conclusion would thus leave the right to a "trial by jury" devoid of meaning. A right mentioned twice in the Constitution would be reduced to an empty promise. That can't be right.

Faced with this hard fact, Louisiana's only remaining option is to invite us to distinguish between the historic features of common law jury trials that (we think) serve "important enough" functions to migrate silently into the Sixth Amendment and those that don't. And, on the State's account, we should conclude that unanimity isn't worthy enough to make the trip.

But to see the dangers of Louisiana's overwise approach, there's no need to look any further than Apodaca itself. There, four Justices, pursuing the functionalist approach Louisiana espouses, began by describing the "'essential'" benefit of a jury trial as "'the interposition . . . of the commonsense judgment of a group of laymen'" between the defendant and the possibility of an "'overzealous prosecutor.'" And measured against that muddy yardstick, they quickly concluded that requiring 12 rather than 10 votes to convict offers no meaningful improvement. Meanwhile, these Justices argued, States have good and important reasons for dispensing with unanimity, such as seeking to reduce the rate of hung juries.

Who can profess confidence in a breezy cost-benefit analysis like that? Lost in the accounting are the racially discriminatory reasons that Louisiana and Oregon adopted their peculiar rules in the first place. What's more, the plurality never explained why the promised benefit of abandoning unanimity—reducing the rate of hung juries—always scores as a credit, not a cost. But who can say whether any particular hung jury is a waste, rather than an example of a jury doing exactly what the plurality said it should—deliberating carefully and safeguarding against overzealous prosecutions? And what about the fact, too, that some studies suggest that the elimination of unanimity has only a small effect on the rate of hung juries? Or the fact that others profess to have found that requiring unanimity may provide other possible benefits, including more open-minded and more thorough deliberations? It seems the *Apodaca* plurality never even conceived of such possibilities.

Our real objection here isn't that the *Apodaca* plurality's cost-benefit analysis was too skimpy. The deeper problem is that the plurality subjected the ancient guarantee of a unanimous jury verdict to its own functionalist assessment in the first place. And Louisiana asks us to repeat the error today, just replacing *Apodaca's* functionalist assessment with our own updated version. All this overlooks the fact that, at the time of the Sixth Amendment's adoption, the right to trial by jury included a right to a unanimous verdict. When the American people chose to enshrine that right in the Constitution, they weren't suggesting fruitful topics for future cost-benefit analyses. They were seeking to ensure that their children's children would enjoy the same hard-won liberty they enjoyed. As judges, it is not our role to reassess whether the right to a unanimous jury is "important enough" to retain. With humility, we must accept that this right may serve purposes evading our current notice. We are entrusted to preserve and protect that liberty, not balance it away aided by no more than social statistics.

. . .

Justice SOTOMAYOR, concurring.

. . .

Finally, the majority vividly describes the legacy of racism that generated Louisiana's and Oregon's laws. Although Ramos does not bring an equal protection challenge, the history is worthy of this Court's attention. That is not simply because that legacy existed in the first place—unfortunately, many laws and policies in this country have had some history of racial animus—but also because the States' legislatures never truly grappled with the laws' sordid history in reenacting them. *See generally United States v. Fordice* (1992) (policies that are "traceable" to a State's de jure racial segregation and that still "have discriminatory effects" offend the Equal Protection Clause).

Where a law otherwise is untethered to racial bias—and perhaps also where a legislature actually confronts a law's tawdry past in reenacting it—the new law may well be free of discriminatory taint. That cannot be said of the laws at issue here. While the dissent points to the "legitimate" reasons for Louisiana's reenactment, Louisiana's perhaps only effort to contend with the law's discriminatory purpose and effects came recently, when the law was repealed altogether.

Today, Louisiana's and Oregon's laws are fully—and rightly—relegated to the dustbin of history. And so, too, is *Apodaca*. While overruling precedent must be rare, this Court should not shy away from correcting its errors where the right to avoid imprisonment pursuant to unconstitutional procedures hangs in the balance.

Justice ALITO, with whom THE CHIEF JUSTICE joins, and with whom Justice KAGAN joins as to all but Part III-D, dissenting.

* * *

To add insult to injury, the Court tars Louisiana and Oregon with the charge of racism for permitting nonunanimous verdicts—even though this Court found such verdicts to be constitutional and even though there are entirely legitimate arguments for allowing them.

* * *

I

Too much public discourse today is sullied by ad hominem rhetoric, that is, attempts to discredit an argument not by proving that it is unsound but by attacking the character or motives of the argument's proponents. The majority regrettably succumbs to this trend. At the start of its opinion, the majority asks this rhetorical question: "Why do Louisiana and Oregon allow nonunanimous convictions?" And the answer it suggests? Racism, white supremacy, the Ku Klux Klan. Non-unanimous verdicts, the Court implies, are of a piece with Jim Crow laws, the poll tax, and other devices once used to disfranchise African-Americans.

If Louisiana and Oregon originally adopted their laws allowing non-unanimous verdicts for these reasons, that is deplorable, but what does that have to do with the broad constitutional question before us? The answer is: nothing.

For one thing, whatever the reasons why Louisiana and Oregon originally adopted their rules many years ago, both States readopted their rules under different circumstances in later years. Louisiana's constitutional convention of 1974 adopted a new, narrower rule, and its stated purpose was "judicial efficiency." "In that debate no mention was made of race." The people of Louisiana ratified the new Constitution. The majority makes no effort to show either that the delegates to the constitutional convention retained the rule for discriminatory purposes or that proponents of the new Constitution made racial appeals when approval was submitted to the people. The same is true for Oregon's revisions and reenactments.

The more important point, however, is that today's decision is not limited to anything particular about Louisiana or Oregon. The Court holds that the Sixth Amendment requires jury unanimity in all state criminal trials. If at some future time another State wanted to allow non-unanimous verdicts, today's decision would rule that out—even if all that State's lawmakers were angels.

For this reason, the origins of the Louisiana and Oregon rules have no bearing on the broad constitutional question that the Court decides. That history would be relevant if there were no legitimate reasons why anyone might think that allowing non-unanimous verdicts is good policy. But that is undeniably false.

Some years ago the British Parliament enacted a law allowing non-unanimous verdicts. Was Parliament under the sway of the Klan? The Constitution of Puerto Rico permits non-unanimous verdicts. Were the framers of that Constitution racists? Non-unanimous verdicts were once advocated by the American Law Institute and the American Bar Association. Was their aim to promote white supremacy? And how about the prominent scholars who have taken the same position? Racists all? Of course not. So all the talk about the Klan, etc., is entirely out of place. We should set an example of rational and civil discourse instead of contributing to the worst current trends.

• • •

NOTES AND QUESTIONS

1. *Ramos* includes several long opinions (none included in full here) on the extent to which the doctrine of stare decisis counsels for or against the overruling of *Apodaca v. Oregon*, 406 U.S. 404 (1975), which had upheld, in a divided opinion, the constitutionality of a nonunanimous verdict in a criminal case. 2020 was a good year for the Justices to test drive their views on stare decisis, prepping them for what might be down the road. And to be sure, *Apodaca* was not the Court's finest hour; it was red meat for those inclined to overrule. But is the savage-cum-glib treatment of Justice Powell's opinion by the majority necessary?

2. Justice Alito, dissenting, lambastes the majority for engaging in "ad hominem rhetoric." But he's not talking about the majority's characterization of Justice Powell's opinion in *Apodaca*. Rather, his ire is directed at the Court's frank acknowledgment of the racist origins of Louisiana's and Oregon's approval of nonunanimous verdicts in criminal cases. Isn't it healthy for a court—or for any governmental or social institution for that matter—to recognize such historical origins? And do Louisiana and Oregon really deserve credit for re-adopting their nonunanimous verdict rules decades later in circumstances where there was no acknowledgment of present or former racial rationales? And aren't the origins of these rules relevant to the Court's decision insofar as Louisiana and Oregon are now trying to defend the rules based on alternative arguments?

3. As in *Florida v. Williams*, there is discussion in *Ramos* on the effect of a particular type of jury on the incidence of hung juries. The majority notes that a plurality of the Court in *Apodaca* justified the rationale for permitting 10-2 verdicts for conviction on the ground, among others, that such a rule will reduce the rate of hung juries. But isn't this argument essentially a variation—call it a facially neutral version—of the racist rationale for nonunanimous verdicts in the first place? Wasn't the original adoption of the 10-2 rule designed to regulate away the potential power of the occasional Black persons that might find their way on to a criminal jury to defeat unanimity and cause a hung jury?

4. And at a higher level, why is it that hung juries are seen as system failures? Isn't the majority right that a hung jury is not necessarily a waste but rather "an example of a jury doing exactly what the [*Apodaca*] plurality said it should—deliberating carefully and safeguarding against overzealous prosecutions"? Justice Alito does not seem to share this view. In noting that one of the "legitimate reasons" for nonunanimous verdicts is preventing hung juries, he posits the paradigmatic hung jury as the result, not of a conscientious juror sticking

Evangelisto Ramos, after he was found NOT GUILTY by a unanimous jury of 12 in his retrial subsequent to the Supreme Court's decision

to her guns, but rather of "a single rogue juror, that is, a juror who refuses to pay attention at trial, expressly defies the law, or spurns deliberations." 590 U.S. at 142 & n.3.

5. Note carefully Louisiana's drafting history argument and the majority's response to it. *Id.* at 1400. The majority's response is a wonderful weapon for a lawyer to use whenever they want to argue that a subsequent version of a document—be it a constitution, a statute, a contract, a letter, etc.—does not have the same detail about a term or a concept or an undertaking. In response to an argument along the lines of "the drafter eliminated facts x, y and z because they weren't important" one can always argue that these facts were eliminated because they were "plainly included" in the term, etc.

6. The Court shortly after deciding *Ramos* declined to give the decision retroactive effect. *Edwards v. Vannoy*, 593 U.S. 255, 302 (2021).

B. JURY NULLIFICATION

The Supreme Court has not spoken on the subject of jury nullification since rejecting the concept as anything more than an unspoken extralegal power of the jury in *Sparf v. United States*, 156 U.S. 51 (1895). The opinions in *United States v. Dougherty*, 473 F.2d 1113 (D.C. Cir. 1972), explore this secret power and the arguments for and against it.

United States v. Dougherty
473 F.2d 1113 (D.C. Cir. 1972)

LEVENTHAL, Circuit Judge:

Seven of the so-called "D.C. Nine" bring this joint appeal from convictions arising out of their unconsented entry into the Washington offices of the Dow Chemical Company, and their destruction of certain property therein. Appellants, along with two other defendants who subsequently entered pleas of nolo contendere, were tried before District Judge

B. Jury Nullification 1141

John H. Pratt and a jury on a three count indictment alleging, as to each defendant, one count of second degree burglary, and two counts of malicious destruction of property valued in excess of $100. On February 11, 1970, after a six-day trial, the seven were each convicted of two counts of malicious destruction. The jury acquitted on the burglary charges but convicted on the lesser-included offense of unlawful entry.

Appellants urge three grounds for reversal as follows: (1) The trial judge erred in denying defendants' timely motions to dispense with counsel and represent themselves. (2) The judge erroneously refused to instruct the jury of its right to acquit appellants without regard to the law and the evidence, and refused to permit appellants to argue that issue to the jury. (3) The instructions actually given by the court coerced the jury into delivering a verdict of guilty. On the basis of defendants' first contention we reverse and remand for new trial. To provide an appropriate mandate governing the new trial, we consider the second and third contentions, and conclude that these cannot be accepted.

III. THE ISSUE OF JURY NULLIFICATION

[Appellants] say that the jury has a well-recognized prerogative to disregard the instructions of the court even as to matters of law, and that they accordingly have the legal right that the jury be informed of its power. We turn to this matter in order to define the nature of the new trial permitted by our mandate.

There has evolved in the Anglo-American system an undoubted jury prerogative-in-fact, derived from its power to bring in a general verdict of not guilty in a criminal case, that is not reversible by the court. The power of the courts to punish jurors for corrupt or incorrect verdicts, which persisted after the medieval system of attaint by another jury became obsolete, was repudiated in 1670 when *Bushell's Case* (C.P. 1670) discharged the jurors who had acquitted William Penn of unlawful assembly. Juries in civil cases became subject to the control of ordering a new trial; no comparable control evolved for acquittals in criminal cases.

The pages of history shine on instances of the jury's exercise of its prerogative to disregard uncontradicted evidence and instructions of the judge. Most often commended are the 18th century acquittal of Peter Zenger of seditious libel, on the plea of Andrew Hamilton, and the 19th century acquittals in prosecutions under the fugitive slave law. The values involved drop a notch when the liberty vindicated by the verdict relates to the defendant's shooting of his wife's paramour, or purchase during Prohibition of alcoholic beverages.

Even the notable Dean Pound commented in 1910 on positive aspects of "such jury lawlessness." These observations of history and philosophy are underscored and illuminated, in terms of the current place of the jury in the American system of justice, by the empirical information and critical insights and analyses blended so felicitously in H. Kalven and H. Zeisel, The American Jury.

Reflective opinions upholding the necessity for the jury as a protection against arbitrary action, such as prosecutorial abuse of power, stress fundamental features like the jury "common sense judgment" and assurance of "community participation in the determination of guilt or innocence." Human frailty being what it is, a prosecutor disposed by unworthy motives could likely establish some basis in fact for bringing charges against anyone he wants to book, but the jury system operates in fact so that the jury will not convict when they empathize with the defendant, as when the offense is one they see themselves as likely to commit, or consider generally acceptable or condonable under the mores of the community.

The existence of an unreviewable and unreversible power in the jury, to acquit in disregard of the instructions on the law given by the trial judge, has for many years co-existed with legal practice and precedent upholding instructions to the jury that they are required to follow the instructions of the court on all matters of law. There were different soundings in colonial days

Chapter XIII The Jury I: Scope of the Right and Other Issues

and the early days of our Republic. We are aware of the number and variety of expressions at that time from respected sources—John Adams; Alexander Hamilton; prominent judges—that jurors had a duty to find a verdict according to their own conscience, though in opposition to the direction of the court; that their power signified a right; that they were judges both of law and of fact in a criminal case, and not bound by the opinion of the court.

The rulings did not run all one way, but rather precipitated "a number of classic exchanges on the freedom and obligations of the criminal jury." This was, indeed, one of the points of clash between the contending forces staking out the direction of the government of the newly established Republic, a direction resolved in political terms by reforming but sustaining the status of the courts, without radical change. As the distrust of judges appointed and removable by the king receded, there came increasing acceptance that under a republic the protection of citizens lay not in recognizing the right of each jury to make its own law, but in following democratic processes for changing the law.

The crucial legal ruling came in *United States v. Battiste* (C.C.D. Mass. 1835). Justice Story's strong opinion supported the conception that the jury's function lay in accepting the law given to it by the court and applying that law to the facts. This considered ruling of an influential jurist won increasing acceptance in the nation. The youthful passion for independence accommodated itself to the reality that the former rebels were now in control of their own destiny, that the practical needs of stability and sound growth outweighed the abstraction of centrifugal philosophy, and that the judges in the courts, were not the colonial appointees projecting royalist patronage and influence but were themselves part and parcel of the nation's intellectual mainstream, subject to the checks of the common law tradition and professional opinion, and capable, in Roscoe Pound's words, of providing "true judicial justice" standing in contrast with the colonial experience.

The tide was turned by *Battiste*, but there were cross-currents. At midcentury the country was still influenced by the precepts of Jacksonian democracy, which spurred demands for direct selection of judges by the people through elections, and distrust of the judge-made common law which enhanced the movement for codification reform. But by the end of the century, even the most prominent state landmarks had been toppled; and the Supreme Court settled the matter for the Federal courts in *Sparf v. United States* (1895) after exhaustive review in both majority and dissenting opinions. The jury's role was respected as significant and wholesome, but it was not to be given instructions that articulated a right to do whatever it willed. The old rule survives today only as a singular relic.

The breadth of the continuing prerogative of the jury, however, perseveres, as appears from the rulings permitting inconsistent verdicts. These reflect, in the words of Justice Holmes, an acknowledgment that "the jury has the power to bring in a verdict in the teeth of both law and facts," or as Judge Learned Hand said: "We interpret the acquittal as no more than their assumption of a power which they had no right to exercise, but to which they were disposed through lenity."

Since the jury's prerogative of lenity, again in Learned Hand's words, introduces a "slack into the enforcement of law, tempering its rigor by the mollifying influence of current ethical conventions," it is only just, say appellants, that the jurors be so told. It is unjust to withhold information on the jury power of "nullification," since conscientious jurors may come, ironically, to abide by their oath as jurors to render verdicts offensive to their individual conscience, to defer to an assumption of necessity that is contrary to reality.

This so-called right of jury nullification is put forward in the name of liberty and democracy, but its explicit avowal risks the ultimate logic of anarchy. This is the concern voiced by Judge Sobeloff in *United States v. Moylan* (4th Cir. 1969):

> To encourage individuals to make their own determinations as to which laws they will obey and which they will permit themselves as a matter of conscience to disobey is to invite chaos. No legal system could long survive if it gave every individual the option of

disregarding with impunity any law which by his personal standard was judged morally untenable. Toleration of such conduct would not be democratic, as appellants claim, but inevitably anarchic.

The statement that avowal of the jury's prerogative runs the risk of anarchy, represents, in all likelihood, the habit of thought of philosophy and logic, rather than the prediction of the social scientist. But if the statement contains an element of hyperbole, the existence of risk and danger, of significant magnitude, cannot be gainsaid. In contrast, the advocates of jury "nullification" apparently assume that the articulation of the jury's power will not extend its use or extent, or will not do so significantly or obnoxiously. Can this assumption fairly be made? We know that a posted limit of 60 m.p.h. produces factual speeds 10 or even 15 miles greater, with an understanding all around that some "tolerance" is acceptable to the authorities, assuming conditions warrant. But can it be supposed that the speeds would stay substantially the same if the speed limit were put: Drive as fast as you think appropriate, without the posted limit as an anchor, a point of departure?

Our jury system is a resultant of many vectors, some explicit, and some rooted in tradition, continuity and general understanding without express formulation. A constitution may be meaningful though it is unwritten, as the British have proved for 900 years.

The jury system has worked out reasonably well overall, providing "play in the joints" that imparts flexibility and avoid undue rigidity. An equilibrium has evolved—an often marvelous balance—with the jury acting as a "safety valve" for exceptional cases, without being a wild-cat or runaway institution. There is reason to believe that the simultaneous achievement of modest jury equity and avoidance of intolerable caprice depends on formal instructions that do not expressly delineate a jury charter to carve out its own rules of law. We have taken due and wry note that those whose writings acclaim and invoke Roscoe Pound's 1910 recognition of the value of the jury as safety valve, omit mention of the fact that in the same article he referred to "the extreme decentralization that allows a local jury or even a local prosecutor to hold up instead of uphold the law of the state" as one of the conditions that "too often result in a legal paralysis of legal administration," that his writings of that period are expressly concerned with the evils of the "extravagant powers" of juries, and that in 1931 he joined the other distinguished members of the Wickersham Commission in this comment:

> In a number of jurisdictions juries are made judges of the law in criminal cases, thus inviting them to dispense with the rules of law instead of finding the facts. The juror is made judge of the law not to ascertain what it is, but to judge of its conformity to his personal ideals and ascertain its validity on that basis. . . . It is significant that there is most satisfaction with criminal juries in those jurisdictions which have interfered least with the conception of a trial of the facts unburdened with further responsibility and instructed as to the law and advised as to the facts by the judge.

The way the jury operates may be radically altered if there is alteration in the way it is told to operate. The jury knows well enough that its prerogative is not limited to the choices articulated in the formal instructions of the court. The jury gets its understanding as to the arrangements in the legal system from more than one voice. There is the formal communication from the judge. There is the informal communication from the total culture—literature (novel, drama, film, and television); current comment (newspapers, magazines and television); conversation; and, of course, history and tradition. The totality of input generally convey adequately enough the idea of prerogative, of freedom in an occasional case to depart from what the judge says. Even indicators that would on their face seem too weak to notice—like the fact that the judge tells the jury it must acquit (in case of reasonable doubt) but never tells the jury in so many words that it must convict—are a meaningful part of the jury's total input. Law is a system, and it is also a language, with secondary meanings that may be unrecorded yet are part of its life.

When the legal system relegates the information of the jury's prerogative to an essentially informal input, it is not being duplicitous, chargeable with chicane and intent to deceive. The limitation to informal input is, rather a governor to avoid excess: the prerogative is reserved for the exceptional case, and the judge's instruction is retained as a generally effective constraint. We "recognize a constraint as obligatory upon us when we require not merely reason to defend our rule departures, but damn good reason." The practicalities of men, machinery and rules point up the danger of articulating discretion to depart from a rule, that the breach will be more often and casually invoked. We cannot gainsay that occasionally jurors uninstructed as to the prerogative may feel themselves compelled to the point of rigidity. The danger of the excess rigidity that may now occasionally exist is not as great as the danger of removing the boundaries of constraint provided by the announced rules.

We should also note the inter-relation of the unanimity requirement for petit juries, which was applicable to this trial, and is still the general rule though no longer constitutionally required for state courts. This is an additional reason—a material consideration, though neither a necessary nor sufficient condition—to brake the wheels of those who would tell the petit jurors they are to determine the rules of law, either directly or by telling them they are free to disregard the judge's statement of the rules. The democratic principle would not be furthered, as proponents of jury nullification claim, it would be disserved by investing in a jury that must be unanimous the function not merely of determining facts, hard enough for like-minded resolution, but of determining the rules of law.

Rules of law or justice involve choice of values and ordering of objectives for which unanimity is unlikely in any society, or group representing the society, especially a society as diverse in cultures and interests as ours. To seek unity out of diversity, under the national motto, there must be a procedure for decision by vote of a majority or prescribed plurality—in accordance with democratic philosophy. To assign the role of mini-legislature to the various petit juries, who must hang if not unanimous, exposes criminal law and administration to paralysis, and to a deadlock that betrays rather than furthers the assumptions of viable democracy.

Moreover, to compel a juror involuntarily assigned to jury duty to assume the burdens of mini-legislator or judge, as is implicit in the doctrine of nullification, is to put untoward strains on the jury system. It is one thing for a juror to know that the law condemns, but he has a factual power of lenity. To tell him expressly of a nullification prerogative, however, is to inform him, in effect, that it is he who fashions the rule that condemns. That is an overwhelming responsibility, an extreme burden for the jurors' psyche. And it is not inappropriate to add that a juror called upon for an involuntary public service is entitled to the protection, when he takes action that he knows is right, but also knows is unpopular, either in the community at large or in his own particular grouping, that he can fairly put it to friends and neighbors that he was merely following the instructions of the court.

In the last analysis, our rejection of the request for jury nullification doctrine is a recognition that there are times when logic is not the only or even best guide to sound conduct of government. For machines, one can indulge the person who likes to tinker in pursuit of fine tuning. When men and judicial machinery are involved, one must attend to the many and complex mechanisms and reasons that lead men to change their conduct—when they know they are being studied; when they are told of the consequences of their conduct; and when conduct exercised with restraint as an unwritten exception is expressly presented as a legitimate option.

What makes for health as an occasional medicine would be disastrous as a daily diet. The fact that there is widespread existence of the jury's prerogative, and approval of its existence as a "necessary counter to casehardened judges and arbitrary prosecutors," does not establish as an imperative that the jury must be informed by the judge of that power. On the contrary, it is pragmatically useful to structure instructions in such wise that the jury must feel

B. Jury Nullification 1145

strongly about the values involved in the case, so strongly that it must itself identify the case as establishing a call of high conscience, and must independently initiate and undertake an act in contravention of the established instructions. This requirement of independent jury conception confines the happening of the lawless jury to the occasional instance that does not violate, and viewed as an exception may even enhance, the over-all normative effect of the rule of law. An explicit instruction to a jury conveys an implied approval that runs the risk of degrading the legal structure requisite for true freedom, for an ordered liberty that protects against anarchy as well as tyranny.

Finally, we are aware that the denial of defendants' request for a nullification instruction will be considered by them to negative some, or perhaps most, of the value of the right of pro se representation which we have recognized. This point could be answered in terms of logic: The right of self-representation is given for reasons recognized by the law, and cannot be a springboard to establish the validity of other advantages or conditions that lie in its tactical wake. Thus, a defendant's ability to present his demeanor and often even a kind of testimony, without exposure to impeachment or cross-examination, may be a tactical consequence of pro se representation, and even a moving cause of its invocation, but this is not to say it is an objective of the law. But defendants' position merits a more spacious answer, that lies outside the domain of formal logic. It is this. The jury system provides flexibility for the consideration of interests of justice outside the formal rules of law. This embraces whatever extra the defendant conveys by personal representation, whether through demeanor or sincerity of justification. But it is subject to the overriding consideration that what is tolerable or even desirable as an informal, self-initiated exception, harbors grave dangers to the system if it is opened to expansion and intensification through incorporation in the judge's instruction.

• • •

BAZELON, Chief Judge, concurring in part and dissenting in part:

• • •

My disagreement with the Court concerns the issue of jury nullification. As the Court's opinion clearly acknowledges, there can be no doubt that the jury has "an unreviewable and unreversible power . . . to acquit in disregard of the instructions on the law given by the trial judge. . . ." More important, the Court apparently concedes — although in somewhat grudging terms — that the power of nullification is a "necessary counter to case-hardened judges and arbitrary prosecutors," and that exercise of the power may, in at least some instances, "enhance, the over-all normative effect of the rule of law." We could not withhold that concession without scoffing at the rationale that underlies the right to jury trial in criminal cases, and belittling some of the most legendary episodes in our political and jurisprudential history.

The sticking point, however, is whether or not the jury should be told of its power to nullify the law in a particular case. Here, the trial judge not only denied a requested instruction on nullification, but also barred defense counsel from raising the issue in argument before the jury. The majority affirms that ruling. I see no justification for, and considerable harm in, this deliberate lack of candor.

At trial, the defendants made no effort to deny that they had committed the acts charged. Their defense was designed to persuade the jury that it would be unconscionable to convict them of violating a statute whose general validity and applicability they did not challenge. An instruction on nullification — or at least some argument to the jury on that issue — was, therefore, the linchpin of the defense.

At the outset it is important to recognize that the trial judge was not simply neutral on the question of nullification. His instruction, set out in part in the margin, emphatically denied the existence of a "legal defense" based on "sincere religious motives" or a belief that action was justified by "some higher law." That charge was not directly inconsistent with the theory of jury nullification. Nullification is not a "defense" recognized by law, but rather a mechanism that permits a jury, as community conscience, to disregard the strict requirements of law where it finds that those requirements cannot justly be applied in a particular case. Yet the impact of the judge's instruction, whatever his intention, was almost surely to discourage the jury from measuring the defendants' action against community concepts of blameworthiness.

Thus, we are left with a doctrine that may "enhance the over-all normative effect of the rule of law," but, at the same time, one that must not only be concealed from the jury, but also effectively condemned in the jury's presence. Plainly, the justification for this sleight-of-hand lies in a fear that an occasionally noble doctrine will, if acknowledged, often be put to ignoble and abusive purposes — or, to borrow the Court's phrase, will "run the risk of anarchy." A breakdown of the legal order is not a result I would knowingly encourage or enjoy. But the question cannot be resolved, at least at this stage of the argument, by asking if we are for or against anarchy, or if we are willing to tolerate a little less law and order so that we can permit a little more jury nullification. No matter how horrible the effect feared by the Court, the validity of its reasoning depends on the existence of a demonstrable connection between the alleged cause (a jury nullification instruction or argument to the jury on that issue) and that effect. I am unable to see a connection.

To be sure, there are abusive purposes, discussed below, to which the doctrine might be put. The Court assumes that these abuses are most likely to occur if the doctrine is formally described to the jury by argument or instruction. That assumption, it should be clear, does not rest on any proposition of logic. It is nothing more or less than a prediction of how jurors will react to the judge's instruction or argument by counsel. And since we have no empirical data to measure the validity of the prediction, we must rely on our own rough judgments of its plausibility.

The Court reasons that a jury uninformed of its power to nullify will invoke that power only where it "feel[s] strongly about the values involved in the case, so strongly that it [will] itself identify the case as establishing a call of high conscience. . . ." In other words, the spontaneous and unsolicited act of nullification is thought less likely, on the whole, to reflect bias and a perverse sense of values than the act of nullification carried out by a jury carefully instructed on its power and responsibility.

It seems substantially more plausible to me to assume that the very opposite is true. The juror motivated by prejudice seems to me more likely to make spontaneous use of the power to nullify, and more likely to disregard the judge's exposition of the normally controlling legal standards. The conscientious juror, who could make a careful effort to consider the blameworthiness of the defendant's action in light of prevailing community values, is the one most likely to obey the judge's admonition that the jury enforce strict principles of law.

Moreover, if it were true that nullification which arises out of ignorance is in some sense more worthy than nullification which arises out of knowledge, the Court would have to go much further. For under the Court's assumption, the harm does not arise because a jury is told of its power to disregard the law, but because it knows of its power. Logically construed, the Court's opinion would seem to require the disqualification at voir dire of any prospective juror who admitted to knowledge of the doctrine. By excluding jurors with knowledge of the doctrine the Court could insure that its invocation would be spontaneous. And yet, far from requiring the exclusion of jurors who are aware of the power, the Court takes comfort in the fact that informal communication to the jury "generally convey[s] adequately enough the idea of prerogative, of freedom in an occasional case to depart from what the judge says." One cannot, it seems to me, have the argument both ways. If, as the Court appears to concede, awareness is preferable to ignorance, then I simply do not understand the justification for relying on a haphazard process of informal communication whose effectiveness is likely to depend, to a large extent, on whether or not any of the jurors are so well-educated and astute that they are able to receive the message. If the jury should know of its power to disregard the law, then the power should be explicitly described by instruction of the court or argument of counsel.

My own view rests on the premise that nullification can and should serve an important function in the criminal process. I do not see it as a doctrine that exists only because we lack the power to punish jurors who refuse to enforce the law or to re-prosecute a defendant whose acquittal cannot be justified in the strict terms of law. The doctrine permits the jury to bring to bear on the criminal process a sense of fairness and particularized justice. The drafters of legal rules cannot anticipate and take account of every case where a defendant's conduct is "unlawful" but not blameworthy, any more than they can draw a bold line to mark the boundary between an accident and negligence. It is the jury—as spokesman for the community's sense of values—that must explore that subtle and elusive boundary.

Admittedly, the concept of blameworthiness does not often receive explicit recognition in the criminal process. But it comes very close to breaking through the surface in cases where the responsibility defense is raised, and it is implicit in every case where criminal sanctions are imposed. More than twenty-five years ago this Court recognized that "[o]ur collective conscience does not allow punishment where it cannot impose blame." And the Supreme Court, in a well-known opinion by Justice Jackson, has pointed out that

> courts of various jurisdictions, and for the purposes of different offenses, have devised working formulae, if not scientific ones, for the instruction of juries around such terms as "felonious intent," "criminal intent," "malice aforethought," "guilty knowledge," "fraudulent intent," "wilfulness," "scienter," to denote guilty knowledge, or "mens rea," to signify an evil purpose or mental culpability. By use or combination of these various tokens, they have sought to protect those who were not blameworthy in mind from conviction of infamous common-law crimes.

The very essence of the jury's function is its role as spokesman for the community conscience in determining whether or not blame can be imposed.

I do not see any reason to assume that jurors will make rampantly abusive use of their power. Trust in the jury is, after all, one of the cornerstones of our entire criminal jurisprudence, and if that trust is without foundation we must re-examine a great deal more than just the nullification doctrine. Nevertheless, some abuse can be anticipated. If a jury refuses to apply strictly the controlling principles of law, it may—in conflict with values shared by the larger community —convict a defendant because of prejudice against him, or acquit a defendant because of sympathy for him and prejudice against his victim. Our fear of unjust conviction is plainly understandable. But it is hard for me to see how a nullification instruction could enhance the likelihood of that result. The instruction would speak in terms of acquittal, not conviction, and it would provide no comfort to a juror determined to convict a defendant in defiance of the law or the facts of the case. Indeed, unless the jurors ignored the nullification instruction they could not convict on the grounds of prejudice alone. Does the judge's recitation of the instruction increase the likelihood that the jury will ignore the limitation that lies at its heart? I hardly think so.

As for the problem of unjust acquittal, it is important to recognize the strong internal check that constrains the jury's willingness to acquit. Where defendants seem dangerous, juries are unlikely to exercise their nullification power, whether or not an explicit instruction is offered. Of course, that check will not prevent the acquittal of a defendant who may be blameworthy and dangerous except in the jaundiced eyes of a jury motivated by a perverse and sectarian sense of values. But whether a nullification instruction would make such acquittals more common is problematical, if not entirely inconceivable. In any case, the real problem in this situation is not the nullification doctrine, but the values and prejudice that prompt the acquittal. And the solution is not to condemn the nullification power, but to spotlight the prejudice and parochial values that underlie the verdict in the hope that public outcry will force a re-examination of those values, and deter their implementation in subsequent cases. Surely nothing is gained by the pretense that the jurors lack the power to nullify, since that pretense deprives them of the opportunity to hear the very instruction that might compel them to confront their responsibility.

One often-cited abuse of the nullification power is the acquittal by bigoted juries of whites who commit crimes (lynching, for example) against blacks. That repellent practice cannot be directly arrested without jeopardizing important constitutional protections — the double jeopardy bar and the jury's power of nullification. But the revulsion and sense of shame fostered by that practice fueled the civil rights movement, which in turn made possible the enactment of major civil rights legislation. That same movement spurred on the revitalization of the equal protection clause and, in particular, the recognition of the right to be tried before a jury selected without bias. The lessons we learned from these abuses helped to create a climate in which such abuses could not so easily thrive.

Moreover, it is not only the abuses of nullification that can inform our understanding of the community's values and standards of blameworthiness. The noble uses of the power — the uses that "enhance the over-all normative effect of the rule of law" — also provide an important input to our evaluation of the substantive standards of the criminal law. The reluctance of juries to hold defendants responsible for unmistakable violations of the prohibition laws told us much about the morality of those laws and about the "criminality" of the conduct they proscribed. And the same can be said of the acquittals returned under the fugitive slave law as well as contemporary gaming and liquor laws. A doctrine that can provide us with such critical insights should not be driven underground.

On remand the trial judge should grant defendants' request for a nullification instruction. At the very least, I would require the trial court to permit defendants to argue the question before the jury. But it is not at all clear that defendants would prevail even with the aid of an instruction or argument. After all, this case is significantly different from the classic, exalted cases where juries historically invoked the power to nullify. Here, the defendants have no quarrel with the general validity of the law under which they have been charged. They did not simply refuse to obey a government edict that they considered illegal, and whose illegality they expected to demonstrate in a judicial proceeding. Rather, they attempted to protest government action by interfering with others — specifically, the Dow Chemical Company. This is a distinction which could and should be explored in argument before the jury. If revulsion against the war in Southeast Asia has reached a point where a jury would be unwilling to convict a defendant for commission of the acts alleged here, we would be far better advised to ponder the implications of that result than to spend our time devising stratagems which let us pretend that the power of nullification does not even exist.

• • •

NOTES AND QUESTIONS

1. The majority states that in the American jury system the jury has a recognized "prerogative" to disregard the instructions of the court, even on matters of law, that is "derived from its power to bring in a general verdict of not guilty in a criminal case that is not reversible by the court." How is this prerogative "derived" from the jury's general verdict and finality powers? What does the Court mean when it describes this power as a "prerogative-in-fact"? Is the

B. Jury Nullification 1149

Court simply saying that the jury has this prerogative because there is no way to enforce the jury's obligation to follow the court's instructions?

2. Judge Learned Hand had this to say about jury nullification in *United States ex rel. McCann v. Adams*, 126 F.2d 774 (2d Cir. 1942):

> The institution of trial by jury — especially in criminal cases–has its hold upon public favor chiefly for two reasons. The individual can forfeit his liberty — to say nothing of his life — only at the hands of those who, unlike any official, are in no wise accountable, directly or indirectly, for what they do, and who at once separate and melt anonymously in the community from which they came. Moreover, since if they acquit their verdict is final, no one is likely to suffer of whose conduct they do not morally disapprove; and this introduces a slack into the enforcement of law, tempering its rigor by the mollifying influence of current ethical conventions.

Id. at 775-76. The notion of more "slack" in the law sounds appealing. But is "slack" a two-way street? Is the power to disregard the court's instructions a power that can lead as easily to "lawless" convictions as well as lawless acquittals? At least a lawless conviction can be challenged on appeal on some grounds; a lawless acquittal is final. Is there a way to make jury nullification a one-way street where the jury could only "nullify" a court's instructions for the benefit of the defendant?

3. The majority cites from *United States v. Moylan*, 417 F.2d 1002, 1009 (4th Cir. 1969), *cert. denied*, 397 U.S. 910 (1970), where the Fourth Circuit affirmed the district court's refusal to instruct the jury on nullification in a case, similar to *Dougherty*, where defendants committed various property crimes at a draft board office as part of a protest against the war in Vietnam. Do you agree with the *Dougherty* majority that the sentiment quoted from *Moylan* is hyperbolic? Could an instruction on nullification be crafted to permit the jury to disregard the trial court's instructions only in narrow circumstances for specific reasons? If they were so instructed, do you think jurors would seek out opportunities to disregard the court's instructions or, rather, would generally be content to defer to the judge?

4. The majority insists that the jury is aware of its nullification "prerogative" — from inputs from the "total culture" among other things — without being explicitly advised by the judge that it has this power. Do you agree? Were you aware of this prerogative? And even if true, how does this cut? If the jury has a generalized awareness from the "total culture," isn't it even more important to instruct on the metes and bounds of that prerogative? What are those metes and bounds? Do you agree with the majority that requiring the jury to independently initiate nullification — rather than be instructed on it — is important to prevent overuse of nullification?

5. Should prospective jurors be subject to voir dire on any propensity they may have for nullification? For example, should a prospective juror be stricken for cause based on his answers to the following questions:

> The judge will be instructing the jury on its obligations in reaching a verdict once all the evidence has been admitted in this case. Is there any reason you would not be willing or able to follow those instructions?
>
> Do you believe the jury has the power to render a verdict in disregard of the court's instructions? Can you be fair and impartial regardless of this belief?

How else might appropriate voir dire questions be framed?

If jurors can be stricken for cause based on how they answer such questions, what remains of the historical "prerogative"?

6. The majority states that instructing the jury on nullification would unfairly increase the burden on juries, requiring each juror to act as a "mini-legislator or judge" and to "fashion[] the rule that condemns." Is this criticism exaggerated? Is to be instructed on the power of nullification equivalent to being conscripted as "judges both of law and fact," as juries were in the early days of the nation's history?

What would be the likely effect on the deliberation dynamics in the jury room if the jury were instructed on nullification? Is it fair to subject jurors not only to the heavy burden of deciding innocence or guilt but also to attendance at an amateur-led political science seminar?

7. Is there a downside to instructing on jury nullification other than some number of "unjust acquittals" (that is, acquittals where reasonable people would all agree the prosecution proved its case beyond a reasonable doubt)? What volume of such acquittals would be unacceptable? Consider in this regard that prosecutors have virtually unreviewable power to decide who they will prosecute. For various institutional reasons there is literally no legal mechanism to ensure that all persons similarly situated will be charged with a crime. Could the volume of "slack" that jurors extend to charged defendants ever approximate the volume of "slack" received by persons that do not get charged by prosecutors?

8. Most courts' pattern (standard use) jury instructions tell the jury that it is not to decide the case based on sympathy or prejudice. The following from Pattern Crim. J. Instr. 1st Cir. 3.01 (1998) is representative:

> It is your duty to find the facts from all the evidence admitted in this case. To those facts you must apply the law as I give it to you. The determination of the law is my duty as the presiding judge in this court. It is your duty to apply the law exactly as I give it to you, whether you agree with it or not. You must not be influenced by any personal likes or dislikes, prejudices or sympathy. That means that you must decide the case solely on the evidence before you and according to the law. You will recall that you took an oath promising to do so at the beginning of the case.

Does this instruction go too far in eliminating the nullification prerogative? Isn't rendering a verdict based on "sympathy" essential to the exercise of the prerogative? Does the sympathy prohibition mean that the jurors are not entitled to be sympathetic to victim witnesses?

The jury's historic exercises of its nullification powers are not uncontroversial. The majority notes the examples of nullification in the fields of seditious libel and the fugitive slave laws. *See, e.g., United States v. Morris*, 26 F. Cas. 1323 (C.C.D. Mass. 1851) (No. 15,815) (in prosecution under the Fugitive Slave Act in Massachusetts defense attorney argued to the jury that "if any of them believed [the statute] to be unconstitutional they were bound by their oaths to disregard any direction to the contrary which the court might give them").

On the other hand, Judge Bazelon properly acknowledges acquittals of whites charged with racial violence against Black people. *See* Chapter X *supra*. At the same time, Judge Bazelon also recognizes the important service jury nullification can play as a sort of feedback loop on "the substantive standards of the criminal law," illustrated by how acquittals for clear-cut violations of Prohibition laws hastened the demise of those laws. He observes that a "doctrine that can provide us with such insights should not be driven underground."

Although the Supreme Court has not spoken directly on the subject of jury nullification since *Sparf*, the courts of appeals almost uniformly reflect the view of the majority in *Dougherty*, that is, that juries have the power to nullify but should not be instructed on that power. *See Sparf*, 156 U.S. at 74 (juries have the power to disregard the law but that "the duty of the jury is to follow the law as laid down by the court"; accused persons have the right to be tried by a law that is certain and what the jury believes it to be). But the history set forth in both *Sparf* and *Dougherty* suggests strongly that at the time of the ratification of the Sixth Amendment the jury had at least overt nullification powers and may well have been the judges of both fact and law.

What does this portend for the doctrine of jury nullification if the current Supreme Court, populated by advocates of "originalism," elects to revisit the issue? Recall that in the Court's decision in *Ramos* in 2019 the inquiry into the existence of a jury unanimity requirement focused on the Founders' understanding of the dimensions of a right to a jury trial at the time of the founding. *See* Larsen, *Ancient Juries and Modern Judges, supra* at 959, 961-62 (suggesting that much of the Supreme Court's law on juries is inconsistent with an originalist perspective).

As the next case illustrates, clever defense attorneys will always try to get the jury to understand its nullification prerogative.

United States v. Sepulveda
15 F.3d 1161 (1st Cir. 1993)

SELYA, Circuit Judge.

These appeals, arising out of the drug-trafficking convictions of a dozen New Hampshire residents, suggest that while two New Hampshire men might once have been a match for Satan, see Stephen Vincent Benet, The Devil and Daniel Webster (1937), times have changed. The tale follows.

• • •

VIII. JURY NULLIFICATION

The defendants invoked the specter of jury nullification during final arguments. Labrie's lawyer, in particular, invited the jury to "send out a question" concerning this doctrine. Three non-events followed; the government did not object to this soliloquy, the district court did not intervene sua sponte, and the court's charge did not broach the subject. Nevertheless, the deliberating jury took the invitation literally and asked the judge to "[c]larify the law on jury nullification." The court responded by telling the jury:

> Federal trial judges are forbidden to instruct on jury nullification, because they are required to instruct only on the law which applies to a case. As I have indicated to you, the burden in each instance which is here placed upon the Government is to prove each element of the offenses . . . beyond a reasonable doubt, and in the event the Government fails to sustain its burden of proof beyond a reasonable doubt as to any essential element of any offense charged against each defendant, it has then failed in its burden of proof as to such defendant and that defendant is to be acquitted. In short, if the Government proves its case against any defendant, you should convict that defendant. If it fails to prove its case against any defendant you must acquit that defendant.

Appellants objected to this supplemental instruction. They now argue that the instruction amounted to a wrongful repudiation of the time-honored concept of jury nullification.

The applicable rule is that, although jurors possess the raw power to set an accused free for any reason or for no reason, their duty is to apply the law as given to them by the court. Accordingly, while jurors may choose to flex their muscles, ignoring both law and evidence in a gadarene rush to acquit a criminal defendant, neither the court nor counsel should encourage jurors to exercise this power. A trial judge, therefore, may block defense attorneys' attempts to serenade a jury with the siren song of nullification, and, indeed, may instruct the jury on the dimensions of their duty to the exclusion of jury nullification.

To the extent that appellants, during closing argument, managed to mention nullification, they received more than was their due. Having pocketed this gratuity, appellants now complain that they were not allowed to capitalize on it. When the jurors rose to the bait, appellants say, Judge Devine should have assured them that nullification is an "historical

1152 Chapter XIII The Jury I: Scope of the Right and Other Issues

prerogative" of juries from time immemorial. We disagree. Though jury nullification has a long and sometimes storied past, the case law makes plain that a judge may not instruct the jury anent its history, vitality, or use. This proscription is invariant; it makes no difference that the jury inquired, or that an aggressive lawyer managed to pique a particular jury's curiosity by mentioning the subject in closing argument, or that a napping prosecutor failed to raise a timely objection to that allusion. Thus, the district court appropriately scotched appellants' suggested jury instruction.

Appellants' fallback position — that the district court, if disinclined to sing the praises of jury nullification, should have refrained from giving any supplemental instruction and, instead, should have stonewalled — is not well conceived. The objection focuses on the district court's opening comment that "[f]ederal trial judges are forbidden to instruct on jury nullification," interpreting this as a judicial prohibition against the jury's use of its inherent power. The objection fails for several reasons, most noticeably because the quoted statement conveys no such chilling effect.

Taken literally, the judge's comment is an accurate recitation of the law and an appropriate rejoinder to the jury's question on nullification (a question that appellants prompted). The district court explained why it could not answer the jury's request for more information on nullification. The court went on to repeat its earlier instruction that if the government proved its case the jury "should" convict, while if the government failed to carry its burden the jury "must" acquit. This contrast in directives, together with the court's refusal to instruct in any detail about the doctrine of jury nullification, left pregnant the possibility that the jury could ignore the law if it so chose. Whether the jury perceived this possibility or not, no error infiltrated the court's supplemental instruction.

• • •

NOTES AND QUESTIONS

1. How important to the result here was it that the defense counsel essentially induced the jury to inquire about jury nullification?

2. The First Circuit finds something of a coded message to the jury at the end of the judge's clarifying instruction: "In short, if the Government proves its case against any defendant, you *should convict* that defendant. If it fails to prove its case against any defendant you *must acquit* that defendant." It is unclear if the jury received a paper copy of this instruction. Do you think this is too subtle for the jury to absorb on the fly? Is there a message — one way or another — in the judge's opening comment that "federal judges are forbidden to instruct on jury nullification"?

3. If the jury had raised the issue differently — say, without prompting and by simply asking, are you permitted to tell us about jury nullification — could the result have been different? What should the judge have done in this scenario? Must the jury's independent initiation of its nullification prerogative be done wholly extrajudicially?

4. Do you agree that the first sentence of the judge's supplemental instruction did not have an overly chilling effect?

Professor Paul Butler, a former federal prosecutor, believes that Black jurors should consider nullification where Black persons are prosecuted for certain nonviolent crimes:

> I was a Special Assistant United States Attorney in the District of Columbia in 1990. I prosecuted people accused of misdemeanor crimes, mainly the drug and gun cases that overwhelm

the local courts of most American cities. As a federal prosecutor, I represented the United States of America and used that power to put people, mainly African-American men, in prison. I am also an African-American man. While at the U.S. Attorney's office, I made two discoveries that profoundly changed the way I viewed my work as a prosecutor and my responsibilities as a black person.

The first discovery occurred during a training session for new Assistants conducted by experienced prosecutors. We rookies were informed that we would lose many of our cases, despite having persuaded a jury beyond a reasonable doubt that the defendant was guilty. We would lose because some black jurors would refuse to convict black defendants who they knew were guilty.

The second discovery was related to the first, but was even more unsettling. It occurred during the trial of Marion Barry, then the second-term mayor of the District of Columbia. Barry was being prosecuted by my office for drug possession and perjury. I learned, to my surprise, that some of my fellow African-American prosecutors hoped that the mayor would be acquitted, despite the fact that he was obviously guilty of at least one of the charges—he had smoked cocaine on FBI videotape. These black prosecutors wanted their office to lose its case because they believed that the prosecution of Barry was racist.

Federal prosecutors in the nation's capital hear many rumors about prominent officials engaging in illegal conduct, including drug use. Some African-American prosecutors wondered why, of all those people, the government chose to "set up" the most famous black politician in Washington, D.C. They also asked themselves why, if crack is so dangerous, the FBI had allowed the mayor to smoke it. Some members of the predominantly black jury must have had similar concerns: They convicted the mayor of only one count of a fourteen-count indictment, despite the trial judge's assessment that he had "'never seen a stronger government case.'" Some African-American prosecutors thought that the jury, in rendering its verdict, jabbed its black thumb in the face of a racist prosecution, and that idea made those prosecutors glad.

As such reactions suggest, lawyers and judges increasingly perceive that some African-American jurors vote to acquit black defendants for racial reasons, a decision sometimes expressed as the juror's desire not to send yet another black man to jail. This Essay examines the question of what role race should play in black jurors' decisions to acquit defendants in criminal cases. Specifically, I consider trials that include both African-American defendants and African-American jurors. I argue that the race of a black defendant is sometimes a legally and morally appropriate factor for jurors to consider in reaching a verdict of not guilty or for an individual juror to consider in refusing to vote for conviction.

My thesis is that, for pragmatic and political reasons, the black community is better off when some nonviolent lawbreakers remain in the community rather than go to prison. The decision as to what kind of conduct by African-Americans ought to be punished is better made by African-Americans themselves, based on the costs and benefits to their community, than by the traditional criminal justice process, which is controlled by white lawmakers and white law enforcers. Legally, the doctrine of jury nullification gives the power to make this decision to African-American jurors who sit in judgment of African-American defendants. Considering the costs of law enforcement to the black community and the failure of white lawmakers to devise significant nonincarcerative responses to black antisocial conduct, it is the moral responsibility of black jurors to emancipate some guilty black outlaws.

P. Butler, *Racially Based Jury Nullification: Black Power in the Criminal Justice System*, 105 Yale L.J. 677, 678-89 (1995).

C. JURY KNOWLEDGE OF POTENTIAL PUNISHMENT

Jurors are not informed of the potential punishment, or ranges of punishment, that will be imposed on a defendant they find guilty. Does this strike you as counterintuitive? Are there good reasons for this prohibition? How might knowledge of the potential punishment affect the jury?

Rogers v. United States
422 U.S. 35 (1975)

Mr. Chief Justice BURGER delivered the opinion of the Court.

Petitioner was convicted by a jury on five counts of an indictment charging him with knowingly and willfully making oral threats "to take the life of or to inflict bodily harm upon the President of the United States," in violation of 18 U.S.C. s 871(a). The Court of Appeals affirmed, and we granted certiorari to resolve an apparent conflict among the Courts of Appeals concerning the elements of the offense proscribed by s 871(a). After full briefing and argument, however, we find it unnecessary to reach that question, since certain circumstances of petitioner's trial satisfy us that the conviction must be reversed.

The record reveals that the jury retired for deliberation at 3 p.m. on the second day of petitioner's trial. Approximately two hours later, at 4:55 p.m., the jury sent a note, signed by the foreman, to the trial judge, inquiring whether the court would "accept the Verdict — 'Guilty as charged with extreme mercy of the Court.'" Without notifying petitioner or his counsel, the court instructed the marshal who delivered the note "to advise the jury that the Court's answer was in the affirmative." Five minutes later at 5 p.m., the jury returned, and the record contains the following account of the acceptance of its verdict:

> **THE COURT:** We understand from a note you sent to the Court the verdict finds him guilty on all five counts but that you wish to recommend extreme mercy; is that correct?
>
> **THE FOREMAN:** Yes, Your Honor.
>
> **THE COURT:** Will you please poll the jury. (Whereupon the jury was polled and all jurors answered in the affirmative.)
>
> **THE COURT:** Let the verdict be entered as the judgment of the Court. Certainly the Court will take into consideration your recommendation of mercy, but before we can act upon the case, we will have the Probation Officer make a pre-sentence investigation report. We do not know whether the man has a prior criminal record or not and we will certainly take into account what you have recommended.

Generally, a recommendation of leniency made by a jury without statutory authorization does not affect the validity of the verdict and may be disregarded by the sentencing judge. However in *Cook,* the Court of Appeals held that an exception to this general rule, requiring further inquiry by the trial court, arises where the circumstances of the recommendation cast doubt upon the unqualified nature of the verdict. Assuming the validity of the exception, we need not decide whether either the factual differences between the recommendation in *Cook* and that in the instant case, or petitioner's failure to request further inquiry prior to the recording of the verdict, see Fed. Rule Crim. Proc. 31(d), would suffice to distinguish the cases for purposes of appropriate appellate relief. We deal here not merely with a potential defect in the verdict.

In *Fillippon v. Albion Vein Slate Co.* (1919), the Court observed "that the orderly conduct of a trial by jury, essential to the proper protection of the right to be heard, entitles the parties who attend for the purpose to be present in person or by counsel at all proceedings from the time the jury is impaneled until it is discharged after rendering the verdict." In applying that principle, the Court held that the trial judge in a civil case had "erred in giving a supplementary instruction to the jury in the absence of the parties and without affording them an opportunity either to be present or to make timely objection to the instruction."

In *Shields v. United States* (1927), the Court had occasion to consider the implications of the "orderly conduct of a trial by jury" in a criminal case. The trial judge had replied to a written communication from the jury, indicating its inability to agree as to the guilt or innocence of the defendant, by sending a written direction that it must find the defendant "guilty or not guilty." The communications were not made in open court while the defendant and his counsel were present nor were they advised of them. The jury thereupon found Shields guilty of one count with a recommendation of mercy. This Court held that a previous request by counsel for Shields and the Government that the trial judge hold the jury in deliberation until they had agreed upon a verdict "did not justify exception to the rule of orderly conduct of jury trial entitling the defendant, especially in a criminal case, to be present from the time the jury is impaneled until its discharge after rendering the verdict."

As in *Shields*, the communication from the jury in this case was tantamount to a request for further instructions. However, we need not look solely to our prior decisions for guidance as to the appropriate procedure in such a situation. Federal Rule Crim. Proc. 43 guarantees to a defendant in a criminal trial the right to be present "at every stage of the trial including the impaneling of the jury and the return of the verdict." Cases interpreting the Rule make it clear, if our decisions prior to the promulgation of the Rule left any doubt, that the jury's message should have been answered in open court and that petitioner's counsel should have been given an opportunity to be heard before the trial judge responded.

Although a violation of Rule 43 may in some circumstances be harmless error, see Fed. Rule Crim. Proc. 52(a), the nature of the information conveyed to the jury, in addition to the manner in which it was conveyed, does not permit that conclusion in this case. The trial judge should not have confined his response to the jury's inquiry to an indication of willingness to accept a verdict with a recommendation of "extreme mercy." At the very least, the court should have reminded the jury that the recommendation would not be binding in any way. In addition, the response should have included the admonition that the jury had no sentencing function and should reach its verdict without regard to what sentence might be imposed. *See United States v. Louie Gim* (CA2 1957); *United States v. Glick* (CA2 1972).

The fact that the jury, which had been deliberating for almost two hours without reaching a verdict, returned a verdict of "guilty with extreme mercy" within five minutes "after being told unconditionally and unequivocally that it could recommend leniency," strongly suggests that the trial judge's response may have induced unanimity by giving members of the jury who had previously hesitated about reaching a guilty verdict the impression that the recommendation might be an acceptable compromise. We acknowledge that the comments of the trial judge upon receiving the verdict may be said to have put petitioner's counsel on notice that the jury had communicated with the court, but the only indication that the court had unilaterally communicated with the jury comes from the note itself, which the court correctly ordered to be filed in the record, with a notation as to the time of receipt and the court's response. It appears, however, that petitioner's counsel was not aware of the court's communication until after we granted the petition for certiorari. In such circumstances, and particularly in light of the difficult task of the factfinder in a prosecution under s 871(a), we conclude that the combined effect of the District Court's errors was so fraught with potential prejudice as to require us to notice them notwithstanding petitioner's failure to raise the issue in the Court of Appeals or in this Court.

Reversed and remanded.

Mr. Justice MARSHALL, with whom Mr. Justice DOUGLAS joins, concurring.

George Rogers, a 34-year-old unemployed carpenter with a 10-year history of alcoholism, wandered into the coffee shop of a Holiday Inn in Shreveport, La., early one morning, behaving in a loud and obstreperous manner. He accosted several customers and waitresses, telling them, among other things, that he was Jesus Christ and that he was opposed to President Nixon's visiting China because the Chinese had a bomb that only he knew about, which might be used against the people of this country. In the course of his various outbursts, Rogers announced that he was going to go to Washington to "whip Nixon's ass," or to "kill him in order to save the United States."

The local police were soon called to remove Rogers from the Holiday Inn. When the arresting officer arrived, he asked Rogers whether he had threatened the President. Rogers replied that he didn't like the idea of the President's going to China and making friends with the Chinese, our enemies. He told the officer, "I'm going to Washington and I'm going to beat his ass off. Better yet, I will go kill him." Rogers added that he intended to "walk" to Washington because he didn't like cars. Rogers was not charged with any state-law crimes, but the police reported the incident to a local Secret Service agent, who subsequently had petitioner arrested on a federal warrant.

This sad set of circumstances resulted in a five-count indictment under the "threats against the President" statute, 18 U.S.C. s 871(a). After a jury trial, petitioner was convicted under that statute and sentenced to five years' imprisonment, to be followed by five years of supervised probation. The Court of Appeals for the Fifth Circuit affirmed petitioner's conviction in a brief per curiam opinion, holding that the District Court had properly instructed the jury under s 871, and that the evidence against petitioner was sufficient to sustain a conviction under that statute as properly construed.

After we granted certiorari, and after the petitioner's brief was filed here, the Solicitor General confessed error, but on a point that had not been raised either here, in the Court of Appeals, or at trial. The Court today seizes on that point to reverse the conviction, leaving unresolved the issue that we granted certiorari to consider. Although I do not disagree with the Court's treatment of the question on which it bases its reversal today, I would reach the merits and reverse petitioner's conviction on the grounds pressed in the Court of Appeals and in the petition for certiorari.

* * *

NOTES AND QUESTIONS

1. Was the judge's failure to have counsel and the defendant present to address the jury's note to the judge prejudicial? What should defense counsel have argued had they been present? What should the prosecutor have argued? Defense counsel presumably was present when the judge referred, just prior to the polling of the jury, to "a note that you sent to the Court." What should defense counsel have done at this point? What should the prosecutor have done? Bear in mind that both lawyers have just learned of the verdict and are standing in the courtroom before a jury that believes its work is over and that it is about to walk out of the courtroom and go home.

2. The Court notes that upon receiving the note the trial judge, at a minimum, should have instructed the jury that it "had no sentencing function and should reach its verdict without regard to what sentence might be imposed." *Id.* at 40. What else should the court have done? What were its options? Would it have been permissible for the court to take the jury's recommendation into account in imposing sentence after reviewing the presentence report? Was the court obligated to do so? Note that this case was before the sentencing guidelines and therefore the judge had almost unlimited discretion in imposing sentence and no obligation to explain his reasoning. Does the five-year sentence suggest the jury's recommendation resonated with the judge?

3. Note the lack of any compelling authority for the proposition that the jury has "no sentencing function." All three of the cases cited — the Second Circuit's decisions in *Gim Hall*

C. Jury Knowledge of Potential Punishment   **1157**

and *Glick* and the D.C. Circuit's decision in *Patrick, id.*—were cases where convictions were reversed because trial judges improperly suggested to juries that the judge could or would take their sentence recommendations into account, which appeared in each case to have "unlocked" a hung jury. While the courts noted in their rulings that juries should focus on guilt and not punishment, the three cases—as with *Rogers* itself—had to do more with the effect of the judge's response on the juror's deliberations rather than the appropriate division of labor between the judge and the jury.

4. The Court observes: "The fact that the jury, which had been deliberating for almost two hours without reaching a verdict, returned a verdict of 'guilty with extreme mercy' within five minutes 'after being told unconditionally and unequivocally that it could recommend leniency,' . . . *strongly suggests* that the trial judge's response may have induced unanimity by giving members of the jury who had previously hesitated about reaching a guilty verdict the impression that the recommendation might be an acceptable compromise." *Id.* (emphasis added) Understatement? Was this timing issue necessary to the Court's conclusion of plain error? Do you think the Court would have found plain error on the basis of the Rule 43 violation alone if the jury had deliberated for another two hours before reaching its verdict?

5. The interpretation of 18 U.S.C. § 871, which then and now criminalizes threats against the President, is the subject of Justice Marshall's concurrence. The issue has nothing to do with whether the jury should be informed about punishment. Having said that, if you were a juror, and were instructed that the statute requires that the alleged threatener intended for his statement to be construed as a threat, how would you have voted? Would your vote be the same if you were instructed that the statute only required the making of a statement that could reasonably be understood as a threat?

The next case considers whether a jury confronting an insanity defense should be instructed on the consequences of a finding that the defendant is not guilty by reason of insanity.

Shannon v. United States
512 U.S. 573 (1994)

Justice THOMAS delivered the opinion of the Court.

In this case, we consider whether a federal district court is required to instruct the jury regarding the consequences to the defendant of a verdict of "not guilty by reason of insanity," either under the Insanity Defense Reform Act of 1984 or as a matter of general federal practice. We conclude that such an instruction is not required, and therefore affirm.

I

A

Prior to the enactment of the Insanity Defense Reform Act of 1984 (IDRA or Act), 18 U.S.C. §§ 17, 4241-4247, federal courts generally did not recognize a verdict of "not guilty by reason of insanity" (NGI). Defendants who mounted a successful insanity defense—that is, those who raised a reasonable doubt as to their sanity at the time of the offense—were simply found "not guilty." In addition, there was no general federal civil commitment procedure available to ensure that an insanity acquittee would receive proper care and treatment. Only in the District of Columbia was a defendant who successfully presented an insanity defense to a federal criminal charge subject to a federal commitment process—a process governed

1158   Chapter XIII The Jury I: Scope of the Right and Other Issues

by a 1955 congressional enactment. Elsewhere, federal authorities were forced to rely on the willingness of state authorities to institute civil commitment proceedings. Reliance on state cooperation was "at best a partial solution to a serious problem," however, and federal courts "[t]ime and again . . . decried this gaping statutory hole."

Before the IDRA was enacted, the Federal Courts of Appeals generally disapproved of instructing the jury concerning the post-trial consequences of an insanity acquittal. Thus, jurors typically were given no information with regard to what would happen to a defendant acquitted by reason of insanity. The courts in general gave two reasons for disapproving such instructions. First, they pointed out that, given the absence of a federal commitment procedure, the consequences of an insanity acquittal were far from certain. Second, they concluded that such instructions would run afoul of the well-established principle that a jury is to base its verdict on the evidence before it, without regard to the possible consequences of the verdict.

The only Court of Appeals to endorse the practice of instructing the jury regarding the consequences of an insanity acquittal was the District of Columbia Circuit. In *Lyles,* the District of Columbia Circuit addressed the jury instruction question in the context of D.C. Code Ann. § 24-301 (1951 ed., Supp. V), which, unlike generally applicable federal law, provided for a special verdict of NGI and, as noted above, a civil commitment procedure. The *Lyles* court recognized the "well established and sound" doctrine "that the jury has no concern with the consequences" of a verdict, but stated that the doctrine "d[id] not apply" to the situation before it. According to the court, although jurors generally were "aware of the meanings of verdicts of guilty and not guilty," they were unfamiliar with the meaning of an NGI verdict. The court concluded that jurors had "a right to know" the meaning of an NGI verdict "as accurately as [they] kno[w] by common knowledge the meaning of the other two possible verdicts."

The acquittal of John Hinckley on all charges stemming from his attempt on President Reagan's life, coupled with the ensuing public focus on the insanity defense, prompted Congress to undertake a comprehensive overhaul of the insanity defense as it operated in the federal courts. The result of this effort was the IDRA. In the IDRA, Congress made insanity an affirmative defense to be proved by the defendant by clear and convincing evidence, and created a special verdict of "not guilty only by reason of insanity." 18 U.S.C. §§ 17 and 4242(b). In addition, Congress filled the "statutory hole" that had been identified by federal courts by creating a comprehensive civil commitment procedure. § 4243. Under that procedure, a defendant found NGI is held in custody pending a court hearing, which must occur within 40 days of the verdict. § 4243(c). At the conclusion of the hearing, the court determines whether the defendant should be hospitalized or released. §§ 4243(d), (e).

B

At about 4 a.m. on August 25, 1990, a police officer stopped petitioner Terry Lee Shannon, a convicted felon, on a street in Tupelo, Mississippi. For reasons not explained in the record before us, the officer asked Shannon to accompany him to the station house to speak with a detective. After telling the officer that he did not want to live anymore, Shannon walked across the street, pulled a pistol from his coat, and shot himself in the chest.

Shannon survived his suicide attempt and was indicted for unlawful possession of a firearm by a felon in violation of 18 U.S.C. § 922(g)(1). At trial, he raised the insanity defense, and asked the District Court to instruct the jury that he would be involuntarily committed if the jury returned an NGI verdict. The District Court refused to give Shannon's proposed charge. Instead, it instructed the jury "to apply the law as [instructed] regardless of the consequence," and that "punishment . . . should not enter your consideration or discussion." The jury returned a guilty verdict.

The Court of Appeals for the Fifth Circuit affirmed Shannon's conviction. The court noted that under its pre-IDRA precedent, juries were not to be instructed concerning the consequences of an insanity acquittal. Turning to the text of the IDRA, the court observed that Congress had "said nothing about informing juries of the consequences" of an NGI verdict. Because there was no "statutory requirement" to the contrary, the court "adhere[d] to the established axiom that it is inappropriate for a jury to consider or be informed about the consequences of its verdict."

We granted certiorari in order to consider whether federal district courts are required to instruct juries with regard to the consequences of an NGI verdict.

II

It is well established that when a jury has no sentencing function, it should be admonished to "reach its verdict without regard to what sentence might be imposed." *Rogers v. United States* (1975). The principle that juries are not to consider the consequences of their verdicts is a reflection of the basic division of labor in our legal system between judge and jury. The jury's function is to find the facts and to decide whether, on those facts, the defendant is guilty of the crime charged. The judge, by contrast, imposes sentence on the defendant after the jury has arrived at a guilty verdict. Information regarding the consequences of a verdict is therefore irrelevant to the jury's task. Moreover, providing jurors sentencing information invites them to ponder matters that are not within their province, distracts them from their factfinding responsibilities, and creates a strong possibility of confusion.

Despite these familiar precepts, Shannon contends that an instruction informing the jury of the consequences of an NGI verdict is required under the IDRA whenever requested by the defendant. He also argues that such an instruction is required as a matter of general federal criminal practice. We address each argument in turn.

A

To determine whether Congress intended courts to depart from the principle that jurors are not to be informed of the consequences of their verdicts, we turn first, as always, to the text of the statute. The IDRA refers to the subject of jury instructions only once, and that reference occurs in its description of the possible verdicts a jury may return. Under the Act, "the jury shall be instructed to find . . . the defendant — (1) guilty; (2) not guilty; or (3) not guilty only by reason of insanity." 18 U.S.C. § 4242(b). The text of the Act gives no indication that jurors are to be instructed regarding the consequences of an NGI verdict. As the court below observed, the Act "leaves the jury solely with its customary determination of guilt or innocence." The Act's text thus gives no support to Shannon's contention that an instruction informing the jury of the consequences of an NGI verdict is required.

Shannon asserts, however, that an express statutory directive is not necessary because, by modeling the IDRA on D.C. Code Ann. § 24-301 (1981), Congress impliedly adopted the District of Columbia Circuit's decision in *Lyles* and the practice endorsed by that decision of instructing the jury as to the consequences of an NGI verdict. For this argument he relies on *Capital Traction Co. v. Hof* (1899), in which we stated:

> By a familiar canon of interpretation, heretofore applied by this court whenever Congress . . . has borrowed from the statutes of a State provisions which had received in that State a known and settled construction before their enactment by Congress, that construction must be deemed to have been adopted by Congress together with the text which it expounded, and the provisions must be construed as they were understood at the time in the State.

The canon of interpretation upon which Shannon relies, however, is merely a "presumption of legislative intention" to be invoked only "under suitable conditions." We believe that the

Chapter XIII The Jury I: Scope of the Right and Other Issues

"conditions" are not "suitable" in this case. Indeed, although Congress may have had the District of Columbia Code in mind when it passed the IDRA, it did not, in the language of *Hof*, "borrow" the terms of the IDRA from the District of Columbia Code. Rather, Congress departed from the scheme embodied in D.C. Code Ann. § 24-301 in several significant ways.

The IDRA, for example, requires a defendant at trial to prove insanity by clear and convincing evidence, 18 U.S.C. § 17(b); the District of Columbia statute, by contrast, employs a preponderance standard. A commitment hearing must be held under the IDRA within 40 days of an NGI verdict, 18 U.S.C. § 4243(c); the period is 50 days under the District of Columbia scheme. Under the IDRA, a defendant whose offense involved bodily injury to another or serious damage to another's property, or the substantial risk thereof, must demonstrate at the hearing by clear and convincing evidence that he is entitled to release, 18 U.S.C. § 4243(d); under the District of Columbia scheme, an acquittee, regardless of the character of his offense, need only meet the preponderance standard. The IDRA provides that an acquittee, once committed, may be released when he no longer presents a substantial risk of harm to others or to their property, 18 U.S.C. § 4243(f); an acquittee under the District of Columbia system may be released from commitment when he "will not in the reasonable future be dangerous to himself or others." Finally, in the IDRA, Congress rejected the broad test for insanity that had been utilized under the District of Columbia provision, and instead adopted a more restrictive formulation under which a person is deemed insane if he is unable "to appreciate the nature and quality or the wrongfulness of his acts." We believe that these significant differences between the IDRA and D.C. Code Ann. § 24-301 render the canon upon which Shannon relies inapplicable in this case.

Alternatively, Shannon contends that a provision explicitly requiring the instruction is unnecessary for a different reason: namely, that Congress made its intention to adopt the *Lyles* practice crystal clear in the IDRA's legislative history. In particular, Shannon points to the following statement in the Senate Report:

> The Committee endorses the procedure used in the District of Columbia whereby the jury, in a case in which the insanity defense has been raised, may be instructed on the effect of a verdict of not guilty by reason of insanity. If the defendant requests that the instruction not be given, it is within the discretion of the court whether to give it or not.

Members of this Court have expressed differing views regarding the role that legislative history should play in statutory interpretation. We are not aware of any case, however (and Shannon does not bring one to our attention), in which we have given authoritative weight to a single passage of legislative history that is in no way anchored in the text of the statute. On its face, the passage Shannon identifies does not purport to explain or interpret any provision of the IDRA. Rather, it merely conveys the Committee's "endorsement" of the *Lyles* "procedure"—a procedure that Congress did not include in the text of the Act. To give effect to this snippet of legislative history, we would have to abandon altogether the text of the statute as a guide in the interpretative process. We agree with the District of Columbia Circuit that "courts have no authority to enforce [a] principl[e] gleaned solely from legislative history that has no statutory reference point." We thus conclude that there is no support in the Act for the instruction Shannon seeks.

B

Setting the Act aside, Shannon argues that the instruction he proposes is required as a matter of general federal criminal practice. Presumably, Shannon asks us to invoke our supervisory power over the federal courts. According to Shannon, the instruction is necessary because jurors are generally unfamiliar with the consequences of an NGI verdict, and may erroneously believe that a defendant who is found NGI will be immediately released into society.

Jurors who are under this mistaken impression, Shannon continues, may also fear that the defendant, if released, would pose a danger to the community. Shannon concludes that such jurors, in order to ensure that the defendant will not be released, may be tempted to return a guilty verdict in a case in which an NGI verdict would be appropriate.

Even assuming Shannon is correct that some jurors will harbor the mistaken belief that defendants found NGI will be released into society immediately—an assumption that is open to debate—the jury in his case was instructed "to apply the law as [instructed] regardless of the consequence," and that "punishment . . . should not enter your consideration or discussion." That an NGI verdict was an option here gives us no reason to depart from "the almost invariable assumption of the law that jurors follow their instructions." Indeed, although it may take effort on a juror's part to ignore the potential consequences of the verdict, the effort required in a case in which an NGI defense is raised is no different from that required in many other situations. For example, if the Government fails to meet its burden of proof at trial, our judicial system necessarily assumes that a juror will vote to acquit, rather than to convict, even if he is convinced the defendant is highly dangerous and should be incarcerated. We do not believe that the situation involving an NGI verdict should be treated any differently.

We also are not persuaded that the instruction Shannon proposes would allay the fears of the misinformed juror about whom Shannon is concerned. "[I]f the members of a jury are so fearful of a particular defendant's release that they would violate their oaths by convicting [the defendant] solely in order to ensure that he is not set free, it is questionable whether they would be reassured by anything short of an instruction strongly suggesting that the defendant, if found NGI, would very likely be civilly committed for a lengthy period." An accurate instruction about the consequences of an NGI verdict, however, would give no such assurance. Under the IDRA, a postverdict hearing must be held within 40 days to determine whether the defendant should be released immediately into society or hospitalized. Thus, the only mandatory period of confinement for an insanity acquittee is the period between the verdict and the hearing. Instead of encouraging a juror to return an NGI verdict, as Shannon predicts, such information might have the opposite effect—that is, a juror might vote to convict in order to eliminate the possibility that a dangerous defendant could be released after 40 days or less. Whether the instruction works to the advantage or disadvantage of a defendant is, of course, somewhat beside the point. Our central concern here is that the inevitable result of such an instruction would be to draw the jury's attention toward the very thing—the possible consequences of its verdict—it should ignore.

Moreover, Shannon offers us no principled way to limit the availability of instructions detailing the consequences of a verdict to cases in which an NGI defense is raised. Jurors may be as unfamiliar with other aspects of the criminal sentencing process as they are with NGI verdicts. But, as a general matter, jurors are not informed of mandatory minimum or maximum sentences, nor are they instructed regarding probation, parole, or the sentencing range accompanying a lesser included offense. Because it is conceivable that some jurors might harbor misunderstandings with regard to these sentencing options, a district court, under Shannon's reasoning, might be obligated to give juries information regarding these possibilities as well. In short, if we pursue the logic of Shannon's position, the rule against informing jurors of the consequences of their verdicts would soon be swallowed by the exceptions.

Finally, Congress' recent action in this area counsels hesitation in invoking our supervisory powers. As noted above, the IDRA was the product of a thorough and exhaustive review of the insanity defense as used in the federal courts. Given the comprehensive nature of the task before it, Congress certainly could have included a provision requiring the instruction Shannon seeks. For whatever reason, Congress chose not to do so. Under these circumstances, we are reluctant to depart from well-established principles of criminal practice without more explicit guidance from Congress.

III

Although we conclude that the IDRA does not require an instruction concerning the consequences of an NGI verdict, and that such an instruction is not to be given as a matter of general practice, we recognize that an instruction of some form may be necessary under certain limited circumstances. If, for example, a witness or prosecutor states in the presence of the jury that a particular defendant would "go free" if found NGI, it may be necessary for the district court to intervene with an instruction to counter such a misstatement. The appropriate response, of course, will vary as is necessary to remedy the specific misstatement or error. We note this possibility merely so that our decision will not be misunderstood as an absolute prohibition on instructing the jury with regard to the consequences of an NGI verdict. Our observations in this regard are not applicable to Shannon's situation, however, for there is no indication that any improper statement was made in the presence of the jury during his trial.

• • •

Because the District Court properly refused to give the instruction Shannon requested, we affirm.

NOTES AND QUESTIONS

1. The facts of this case are disturbing, beginning with the lack of any explanation in the record as to why the police officer asked Shannon to accompany him to the police station, why Shannon did so, and how and why this altercation precipitated Shannon's suicide attempt. Nonetheless it is a strange case for an insanity defense as the government can prove a violation of the felon-in-possession statute simply by presenting evidence of defendant's possession of a firearm and the fact of a prior conviction. What do you think Shannon and his lawyer may have had in mind?

2. As in *Rogers*, the Court's attempt to marshal legal support for the proposition that the jury should not be informed about punishment is anemic. Despite describing the issue as "well settled" it cites just *Rogers* and a 1967 Fifth Circuit case. Its description of the status quo is nothing more than a description, untethered to logic or precedent:

> The principle that juries are not to consider the consequences of their verdicts is a reflection of the basic division of labor in our legal system between judge and jury. The jury's function is to find the facts and to decide whether, on those facts, the defendant is guilty of the crime charged. The judge, by contrast, imposes sentence on the defendant after the jury has arrived at a guilty verdict. Information regarding the consequences of a verdict is therefore irrelevant to the jury's task. Moreover, providing jurors sentencing information invites them to ponder matters that are not within their province, distracts them from their factfinding responsibilities, and creates a strong possibility of confusion.

Id. at 579. The Court makes no attempt to explain why information about punishment operates as a distraction from the jury's factfinding function or confuses the jury in discharging that duty. Nor does the Court make any attempt to identify any historical origins for the purported prohibition on providing sentencing information to the jury. Nor could it. To the contrary, there is historical evidence that juries in eighteenth-century Britain and colonial America were aware of punishment options and factored them into their verdicts. *See* Daniel Epps & William Ortman, *The Informed Jury*, 75 Vand. L. Rev. 823, 840-48 (2022).

3. The trial court in *Shannon* instructed the jury specifically that "punishment . . . should not enter your consideration or discussion." Assuming this instruction is followed literally

C. Jury Knowledge of Potential Punishment 1163

by the jury, doesn't this diminish the historical role of the jury as envisioned in cases such as *Duncan v. Louisiana*? Is the jury to wholly ignore that the case they are deciding is a criminal case, where liberty—at least—is at stake? Note that most states have pattern instructions to similar effect. Epps & Ortman, *The Informed Jury, supra* at 823, 831-32 & nn.42-44 (2022). According to Professors Epps and Ortman, all but two states effectively prohibit informing the jury about punishment: Louisiana, which requires the jury be informed about mandatory minimum punishments and gives judges the discretion to inform them about other punishments; and North Carolina, where a state statute requires juries to be informed of prescribed punishments.

4. The Court discounts the risk that jurors may be concerned that someone who is found not guilty by reason of insanity will be released even though dangerous, relying on the presumption that jurors will follow their instructions. That is a necessary presumption for many reasons. But why make it necessary to a proper result here when the alternative is so easy? Is there a single downside to instructing on the consequences of an NGI verdict? Is the Court's slippery slope argument a persuasive reason to refuse to give the instruction here? The dissent notes that the *Lyles* case on NGI verdict consequences has been the law in the District of Columbia for decades without swallowing the general rule.

5. The Court's analysis of the language of the text and legislative history of the IDRA suggests that Congress certainly had the power to require courts to give a jury instruction on the consequences of an NGI verdict. Are there any limits to this power? For example, could Congress pass a general statute, not tied to a specific crime, requiring federal district courts to instruct the jury on the range of punishment possibilities that might follow from a conviction for a federal crime?

The next case holds that it is so important that the jury not understand the consequences of its verdict—that it not be informed, even indirectly, about potential punishment—that a defendant's constitutional Confrontation Clause rights must suffer.

United States v. Trent
863 F.3d 699 (7th Cir. 2017)

KANNE, Circuit Judge.

Defendant-Appellant Phil Trent distributed heroin that killed Tyler Corzette. He was charged in a five-count indictment, which included two counts related to Corzette's death.

At trial, Trent objected to testimony of two of the government's witnesses: Kyle Hull and Curtis Land. Like Trent, these witnesses had also been charged with distribution of heroin resulting in Corzette's death, but each pled guilty to that charge pursuant to a plea agreement.

Trent sought to impeach Hull and Land based on their plea agreements. Specifically, he wanted to question them about the twenty-year mandatory minimum associated with the heroin-distribution-resulting-in-death charges. But because Trent had also been charged with distribution resulting in Corzette's death, he faced the same twenty-year mandatory minimum if convicted.

The district court noted that, if the jury became aware of the exact length of Hull's and Land's mandatory minimum, it would also know the minimum penalty that Trent would have to serve—which could improperly sway the jury's decision in Trent's case. To avoid this situation, the court prevented Trent from asking Hull and Land about the mandatory minimum's exact length but permitted him to describe the mandatory minimum as "substantial."

Trent now argues that this limitation violated his Sixth Amendment right to confrontation and was an abuse of discretion. We disagree and hold that the court committed no error in its ruling.

• • •

I. BACKGROUND

Trent was a heroin supplier in Rock Island, Illinois. Hull was a heroin addict who often purchased heroin from Trent and his dealers. On August 29, 2014, Hull planned to attend a local music festival with one of his friends, Corzette, who was also a heroin addict. The two decided to purchase heroin before they went to the festival. Hull called Trent and ordered three "bags" of heroin (each of which contained a tenth of a gram), one bag for Corzette and two bags for another friend, Jacob Thompson. Hull did not order any heroin for himself because he was already high from using heroin earlier that day — heroin that he had also purchased from Trent. Trent set the price at $90 for the three bags and told Hull to contact Land, one of Trent's dealers.

Hull then called Land, and they arranged a meeting. Hull, Corzette, and Thompson rode together to that meeting, and once they arrived, Hull purchased the bags of heroin from Land for the agreed-upon price. After the deal, Thompson took his two bags of heroin and went home.

Hull and Corzette then went to a nearby park where Hull helped Corzette cook and inject the heroin. Soon thereafter, Corzette passed out. Hull, who later testified that he was not initially worried about Corzette because he had seen this happen before with heroin use, left Corzette in the car and attended the music festival.

After the festival, Hull returned to the car and found Corzette still unconscious and with vomit on his clothes. Hull checked Corzette's pulse and, still believing him to be fine, left Corzette in the car for the night. When Hull returned the following morning, he found Corzette dead in the car.

Hull panicked. He took the syringe from Corzette's hand and threw it in the grass next to the car. He then went to work. But after spending only an hour at work, Hull returned to the park and called the police. Rock Island Police Officer Christopher Sloan responded to the call. When he arrived, he spoke with Hull, who claimed that Corzette was dead. Officer Sloan called an ambulance and confirmed that Corzette was in fact dead. He then discovered the syringe that Hull had thrown in the grass. A forensic pathologist later concluded that Corzette had died of adverse effects from heroin.

A. Investigation and Arrest of Trent

Later on August 30, Hull agreed to cooperate with the police department in its investigation. In particular, Hull agreed to participate in a controlled purchase of three additional bags of heroin from Land that same day. This controlled purchase led to Land's arrest, after which Land also agreed to cooperate. The police department then arranged for an undercover officer to make two purchases of heroin from Trent. After the second purchase, the police department obtained an arrest warrant for Trent, and Trent was arrested on October 3, 2014.

The Rock Island Police Department later learned that the Illinois State Police had also been engaged in an undercover investigation of Trent in August of 2014. During that investigation, Sergeant Rieck communicated with Trent both in person and by telephone. He also purchased $50 of heroin from one of Trent's dealers. Sergeant Rieck attempted to arrange a second purchase of heroin from Trent, but Trent refused after discovering that Rieck was an undercover officer.

C. Jury Knowledge of Potential Punishment

1165

B. Trent's Jury Trial

A grand jury returned a five-count indictment, charging Trent with one count of heroin distribution resulting in death, three counts of heroin distribution, and one count of conspiracy to distribute and possess with intent to distribute heroin resulting in death. These charges stemmed from both the Rock Island Police Department's investigation and the Illinois State Police's investigation of Trent. During a five-day jury trial, the government called numerous witnesses, including Hull, Land, and Sergeant Rieck.

1. Testimony and Impeachment of Hull and Land

Hull and Land testified about their interactions with Trent on and before August 29, 2014—the day that Corzette took the drugs that ultimately killed him. Hull said that he had been a heroin user since the summer of 2013 and that Trent was his regular heroin supplier. He further stated that he had used heroin with Corzette on several occasions before August 29. Hull then claimed that he called Trent to purchase heroin on August 29 and that Trent told him to arrange a meeting with Land. Next, Hull testified that, when he met with Land, he saw "what [he] thought was [Trent's] vehicle." He then recounted his purchase of three bags of heroin from Land and his subsequent trip to the park to help Corzette inject heroin from one of those bags. Hull finally testified about his actions (or, perhaps more appropriately, his inaction) after Corzette began suffering from an apparent overdose.

Land testified that he had been a heroin user for over twenty years and that he had used heroin with Trent on several occasions since the summer of 2014. He then stated that he began selling heroin for Trent shortly after they met. He described their relationship in detail, stating that he would take six or seven bags of heroin from Trent each day, that Trent would set the price for that heroin, and that Land would sell those bags to Trent's customers. Land also claimed that he would return to Trent any heroin that he did not sell on any particular day.

Land then corroborated Hull's story about the August 29 drug sale. Specifically, Land testified that Trent dropped him off at a local gas station that afternoon and that he received calls from "a number of customers," including Hull. According to Land, he met with Hull at the gas station and sold Hull the drugs that eventually killed Corzette. Land reiterated that the drugs he sold to Hull came from Trent. Land then testified that Trent "came and got the money" after the sale.

Next, both Hull and Land—who were also arrested and charged with distribution of heroin resulting in Corzette's death—testified about their cooperation with the government. They stated that, in exchange for their cooperation, their truthful testimony at Trent's trial, and their pleas of guilty to a charge of distribution resulting in death, the government had agreed to file motions to reduce their sentences.

During the trial, Trent's defense counsel sought to impeach Hull and Land based on the details of their plea agreements. In particular, he wanted to question them about the exact mandatory minimum—twenty years—that they faced if they refused to cooperate and about how their cooperation could lead to a reduction of their sentences below that mandatory minimum.

The government sought to limit this impeachment to a more general questioning: although it agreed that Trent's counsel should be permitted to question Hull and Land about their cooperation and about their plea agreements, the government argued that Trent's counsel should be limited to discussing a substantial mandatory minimum rather than the exact length in years of that mandatory minimum.

Because Trent had been charged with the same crime to which Hull and Land had pled guilty—distribution resulting in death—he faced the same twenty-year mandatory minimum. The government thus sought to limit Trent's counsel's impeachment of Hull and Land to prevent the jury from learning the exact minimum penalty that Trent faced if convicted on the distribution-resulting-in-death charge.

The district court ruled in favor of the government and permitted Trent's counsel to question Hull and Land about the "substantial mandatory minimum" each faced "without quantifying the exact amount." On cross-examination, Trent's counsel did just that: he impeached Hull and Land by asking a variety of questions about the mandatory minimum without referring to its twenty-year term.

$$\cdots$$

At the end of the five-day trial, a jury convicted Trent on all five charges. The district court sentenced Trent to an aggregate term of 300 months' imprisonment. This appeal followed.

II. ANALYSIS

On appeal, Trent repeats two arguments that he made at trial. First, he contends that the district court abused its discretion and violated his Sixth Amendment right to confrontation when it refused to permit him to question Hull and Land about the specific length of the mandatory minimum each faced after pleading guilty. Next, Trent argues that the district court abused its discretion when it overruled his objections to Sergeant Rieck's testimony about his phone conversations with Trent. We address each argument in turn.

A. Limitation on Cross-Examination

Trent first argues that the court should have permitted him to cross-examine Hull and Land about the exact length — twenty years — of the mandatory minimum each faced on a distribution-resulting-in-death charge. Our standard of review when a district court limits the defendant's cross-examination depends on whether the court's limit "directly implicates the 'core values of the Confrontation Clause.'" If so, we review the limit de novo. If not, we review the limit only for abuse of discretion. Id.

The Sixth Amendment "guarantees a defendant an opportunity for effective cross-examination." Id. But that doesn't mean that the Sixth Amendment requires a district court to permit a defendant to question witnesses "in whatever way, and to whatever extent, the defense might wish." Instead, a district court has discretion to place reasonable limits on cross-examination, especially when necessary to prevent irrelevant or confusing evidence from being presented to the jury.

Federal juries don't sentence defendants in noncapital cases. We have thus permitted district courts to prevent juries from learning information from which they could infer defendants' potential sentences, holding that inclusion of this information might confuse or mislead the juries in their true task: deciding defendants' guilt or innocence. That is precisely what the district court did here: it limited Trent's cross-examination of Hull and Land to prevent the jury from learning the exact penalty that Trent himself faced on conviction.

Nonetheless, Trent contends that the term "substantial" — as the district court permitted Trent to describe the mandatory minimum in lieu of using the exact term of years — was too "nebulous" to give the jury a full impression of the witnesses' incentives to testify. He asserts that, had the precise "magnitude" of Hull's and Land's potential sentences been made known to the jury, "the jury might have received a substantially different impression of their credibility." Because the district court did not permit Trent to question Hull and Land about the exact length of the mandatory minimum, Trent maintains that his Sixth Amendment rights were violated.

True enough, the "ability to expose a witness's motivation for testifying, his bias, or his possible incentives to lie" is a core value of the Sixth Amendment's Confrontation Clause.

C. Jury Knowledge of Potential Punishment 1167

But that value is only offended when "the defense is completely forbidden from exposing the witness's bias." When the defense is given a reasonable opportunity to question witnesses about their biases, the Sixth Amendment is not implicated. "In other words, merely having the chance to present a motive to lie is sufficient to satisfy the core values of the confrontation right."

Here, Trent was not prohibited from cross-examining Hull and Land about their potential biases or motives to lie. Rather, the district court permitted Trent to vigorously cross-examine them. For instance, Trent's counsel asked Hull the following questions:

- And you have a rather substantial mandatory minimum sentence, don't you?
- And it's a pretty long time, isn't it?
- You know that the judge who decides — who sentences you cannot give you a sentence below that substantial mandatory minimum unless the prosecutors file a motion and ask the judge to go below that mandatory minimum?
- So, you certainly want one of [the two prosecutors] to be happy with your testimony so they'll file that motion [reducing your sentence], don't you?
- And that's why you're here, is to get your sentence reduced, isn't it?
- That's why you entered into the plea agreement, so you'd get an opportunity to get your sentence reduced below the mandatory minimum, correct?
- Because you don't want to serve that much time in prison if you can avoid it, correct?

Trent's counsel similarly asked Land the following questions:

- Now, because of the charge that you pled guilty to, you are facing a substantial mandatory minimum sentence; is that fair? Is that correct?
- And you don't really want to serve that much time, do you?
- And the only way you can get less than that substantial mandatory minimum sentence is if one of [the two prosecutors] right here files a motion to ask the judge to reduce your sentence below that mandatory minimum; is that correct?
- And you know that it's by you cooperating with this plea agreement that you signed with the government that you can get your sentence reduced if they believe that your testimony was helpful?
- And you want them to believe that [your testimony was helpful]?
- Because you told us nobody would want to serve that mandatory minimum, right?

In response to the questioning, Hull and Land admitted that they were testifying under plea agreements and that the government agreed to file motions to reduce their sentences if they agreed to testify truthfully. They also admitted that, without the government's motion, they would have to serve the duration of the substantial mandatory minimum.

Because the court allowed Trent to engage in this thorough cross-examination, which readily exposed any of Hull's or Land's biases and incentives to testify adversely to Trent, the court did not offend the core values of the Confrontation Clause. We therefore review the district court's limitation only for abuse of discretion.

To determine whether the court abused its discretion, we must decide "whether the jury had sufficient information to make a discriminating appraisal of the witness's motives and biases." Trent contends that the jury couldn't make a "discriminating appraisal" without knowing the mandatory minimum's exact length. We disagree.

Based on the answers to Trent's extensive cross-examination of both Hull and Land, we hold that the jury had ample information to make a discriminating appraisal of the motives of those two witnesses.

Trent's argument that the court's limitation precluded him from portraying the full magnitude of Hull's and Land's biases is unavailing. Although the court did not permit Trent to mention the mandatory minimum's twenty-year term, it did allow him to describe the term as "substantial." And Trent probed in painstaking detail each witness's incentives to lie.

Hull admitted to the jury that the mandatory minimum was a "pretty long time" and Land averred that "nobody would" want to serve the entire length of the mandatory minimum. Moreover, the court instructed the jury to consider the overall testimony of Hull and Land "with caution and great care."

Although "[t]he jury might not have possessed all the information [Trent] wanted it to have, . . . it certainly had sufficient information to evaluate [Hull's and Land's] testimony." Given the court's very real and well-founded concerns about misleading or confusing the jury, we hold that the court did not err, let alone abuse its discretion, by limiting Trent's cross-examination of Hull and Land in the manner that it did.

• • •

For the foregoing reasons, we AFFIRM the district court's judgment of conviction.

NOTES AND QUESTIONS

1. Despite the sketchy provenance of the prohibition on informing the jury about punishment, the Seventh Circuit here finds it sufficiently important to be enforced at the expense of an explicit Sixth Amendment right. *See Davis v. Alaska*, 415 U.S. 308, 316-17 (1974) ("the exposure of a witness' motivation in testifying is a proper and important function of the constitutionally protected right of cross-examination"). And all the court can offer to justify this incursion is the observation that allowing a defense attorney to reference the actual punishment facing the government's cooperating witnesses absent their cooperation would "confuse or mislead the juries in their true task: deciding defendants' guilt or innocence."

Is this language code for something else? Of course the defense lawyer wants to be able to refer to the witness's actual sentence to maximize the impact of his cross-examination. But doesn't the defense lawyer also want to suggest to the jury that his client will be receiving that sentence—here, 20 years—if convicted in order to make sure the jury understands the consequences of its actions? And doesn't the prosecutor want to keep that information from the jurors to prevent them from realizing those same consequences?

Is the prosecutor really concerned about the jury being confused or misled?

2. Does the court's restriction on the defense's freedom to refer to the cooperator's potential sentence really matter? Take a look at the first few lines of the cross-examination of Hull. Does the reference to a "substantial mandatory minimum sentence" have the same bite as a "20-year sentence"? (The reference in the next line to "a pretty long time" is poor cross-examination regardless.) And consider also that a specific 20-year sentence can be used in ways on cross-examination that a nonspecific "substantial" sentence cannot. "So you're 28? Your kids are 2 and 4? If you are sentenced to 20 years you'll miss all their soccer games? First Communions? High school graduations? Maybe weddings?" And so forth.

3. There is a circuit split on a variation of this issue as some courts permit cross-examination on the specific sentences cooperators hope to avoid in circumstances where—as in *Trent*—the sentence is a mandatory minimum and there is no judicial discretion or other uncertainty as to the sentence. *See United States v. Larson*, 495 F.3d 1094, 1106 (9th Cir. 2007) (en banc).

C. Jury Knowledge of Potential Punishment 1169

Professors Epps and Ortman offer a compelling argument for informing the jury of potential punishment, a proposal that is both radical yet also consistent with the jury's historical role.

No institution in American law is more exalted in rhetoric, yet less revered in actual practice, than the criminal jury. We are told that the criminal jury is a "defense against arbitrary law enforcement," "an indispensable protection against the possibility of governmental oppression," and a "tangible implementation of the principle that the law comes from the people"; perhaps even "the spinal column of American democracy." But this rhetoric is utterly detached from reality. Only a tiny fraction of criminal cases see a trial, much less a jury trial. While the Constitution guarantees defendants a jury, courts permit prosecutors to coerce defendants, using the threat of severe punishment, into giving up this right and pleading guilty. In the handful of cases that do actually go to trial, jurors often discover that their job is merely to answer narrow factual questions. In short, twenty-first century criminal juries have vanishingly few opportunities to "check . . . governmental power" and almost none to participate in the normative project of criminal justice.

This state of affairs is nothing less than a tragedy. The demise of the criminal jury has exacerbated major problems in our criminal legal system, and it is deeply inconsistent with our constitutional traditions. The American criminal jury could, and should, regain the importance rhetoric claims for it. This Article proposes a surprisingly simple change to the procedure of jury trials that would help restore the jury to its proper role at the heart of the criminal legal system. The proposal's basic outline is simple: In every criminal case, the judge should disclose the defendant's sentencing exposure to the jury for each count. That means that the judge would tell the jury the maximum sentence authorized by statute, whether there was a mandatory minimum, and whether the sentence would (or could) run consecutively with other sentences.

There is good reason to expect that juries possessing that information would, at least on the margins, decide cases differently than juries without it. Theory, empirical studies, and especially historical evidence all support the idea that when juries know that a defendant may face excessive punishment if found guilty, they become less likely to convict. Jury nullification is part of the story, as criminal juries may conclude that a punishment is too severe for even an obviously guilty defendant. But nullification is not the whole story. Informed jurors also deploy a more demanding standard of proof when they know that harsh punishment is waiting for the defendant on the other side of a guilty verdict. Even when they are not inclined to nullify, in other words, they take the government's burden to prove its case beyond a reasonable doubt more seriously.

Informed juries are thus more prone to acquit defendants than ignorant juries when they perceive the potential punishment to be excessive. That would certainly matter for individual cases, but why do we say that adopting informed juries would reinvigorate the jury as a criminal justice institution? There are two principal reasons.

The first is that our proposal would make juries catalysts of criminal law reform. Informing juries about punishment would enable a virtuous political feedback loop that could make our extraordinarily punitive criminal legal system less severe. In a world with punishment-informed juries, legislators and prosecutors would want to avoid the acquittals that could occur when juries learned about harsh sentencing consequences. The only way they could do so would be by steering clear of harsh punishments in the first place. That means less overcharging by prosecutors. Even more importantly, it means that legislators would have an incentive to enact statutes that accord with common sense notions of justice. They would, that is, have good cause to avoid enacting mandatory minimums, excessively severe recidivism enhancements (e.g., "three strikes" laws), and statutory maximum sentences designed to scare defendants into guilty pleas. Informing the jury would thus go some ways towards restoring an equilibrium that our system lacks today. And because harsh criminal statutes and prosecutorial overcharging are the underpinning of our system of pleas, disrupting them would make plea bargaining—which accounts for the vast majority of criminal convictions—less coercive.

The second principal reason why our proposal would reinvigorate the criminal jury is that it would enable juries to perform their core political function in criminal cases: authorizing state punishment. Although many observers have recognized the truth of Alexis de

1170   Chapter XIII The Jury I: Scope of the Right and Other Issues

Tocqueville's observation that the jury is a political institution, not merely a factfinding body, our system today has lost sight of that important part of the jury's role. The jury cannot meaningfully exercise its political responsibility for adjudicating criminal cases — and authorizing punishment — unless it knows the entire range of legal consequences of a decision to convict.

Restoring the jury to its proper role in our democracy is particularly pressing at this moment in time. There is growing consensus that our system faces an ongoing crisis of mass incarceration in which millions of Americans languish in jail and prison, at great human cost and without any clear benefit to society. Moreover, few who look at how our system works in practice can miss the deep racial disparities our machinery of punishment produces, in which the brunt of harm is borne by Black and Brown Americans. Informed criminal juries cannot solve these problems completely, but we hope to show they could go some ways towards ameliorating them.

To be sure, our proposal is very much contrary to existing law. Federal courts (including the Supreme Court) and nearly all state courts embrace what we call an "iron law" of jury ignorance. But we are not the first to recognize that as a problem. Indeed, in recent years a number of federal district judges have chafed against it. We hope to persuade our readers that the appellate courts that resisted their efforts, like the Supreme Court before them, got it wrong — and grievously so. Indeed, we hope to show that our judicial system has lost sight of the original promise of a jury guaranteed in our Constitution.

See Epps & Ortman, *The Informed Jury, supra* at 823, 824-27.

D. JURY INSTRUCTION ISSUES: REASONABLE DOUBT, THE *ALLEN* CHARGE, AND IMPLICIT BIAS

Judges usually give two distinct sets of instructions to the jury, as well as miscellaneous instructions along the way (E.g., "I instruct you not to consider the witness's last response.").

At the beginning of the trial, as well as informing the jury about logistics and the nature of the case, the judge will give preliminary instruction to the members of the jury about how to do their job, that is, about how they are supposed to consider the evidence they will be hearing during the trial. These instructions are usually boilerplate and do not vary from case to case, for example, "what the lawyers say is not evidence."

At the end of the trial the judge will instruct the jury about its deliberations and the specific elements of the charges that the government must prove. One of those instructions will be on the burden of proof, usually including some sort of explanation of the concept of "proof beyond a reasonable doubt."

1. Reasonable Doubt

Sandoval v. California
511 U.S. 1 (1994)

Justice O'CONNOR delivered the opinion of the Court.

The government must prove beyond a reasonable doubt every element of a charged offense. *In re Winship* (1970). Although this standard is an ancient and honored aspect of our criminal justice system, it defies easy explication. In these cases, we consider the constitutionality of two attempts to define "reasonable doubt."

I

The beyond a reasonable doubt standard is a requirement of due process, but the Constitution neither prohibits trial courts from defining reasonable doubt nor requires them to do so as a matter of course. Indeed, so long as the court instructs the jury on the necessity that the defendant's guilt be proved beyond a reasonable doubt, the Constitution does not require that any particular form of words be used in advising the jury of the government's burden of proof. Rather, "taken as a whole, the instructions [must] correctly conve[y] the concept of reasonable doubt to the jury."

In only one case have we held that a definition of reasonable doubt violated the Due Process Clause. *Cage v. Louisiana* (1990). There, the jurors were told:

> [A reasonable doubt] is one that is founded upon a real tangible substantial basis and not upon mere caprice and conjecture. *It must be such doubt as would give rise to a grave uncertainty*, raised in your mind by reasons of the unsatisfactory character of the evidence or lack thereof. A reasonable doubt is not a mere possible doubt. *It is an actual substantial doubt.* It is a doubt that a reasonable man can seriously entertain. What is required is not an absolute or mathematical certainty, but a *moral certainty*.

We held that the highlighted portions of the instruction rendered it unconstitutional:

> It is plain to us that the words "substantial" and "grave," as they are commonly understood, suggest a higher degree of doubt than is required for acquittal under the reasonable doubt standard. When those statements are then considered with the reference to "moral certainty," rather than evidentiary certainty, it becomes clear that a reasonable juror could have interpreted the instruction to allow a finding of guilt based on a degree of proof below that required by the Due Process Clause.

In a subsequent case, we made clear that the proper inquiry is not whether the instruction "could have" been applied in an unconstitutional manner, but whether there is a reasonable likelihood that the jury did so apply it. The constitutional question in the present cases, therefore, is whether there is a reasonable likelihood that the jury understood the instructions to allow conviction based on proof insufficient to meet the *Winship* standard. Although other courts have held that instructions similar to those given at petitioners' trials violate the Due Process Clause, both the Nebraska and the California Supreme Courts held that the instructions were constitutional. We granted certiorari and now affirm both judgments.

II

On October 14, 1984, petitioner Sandoval shot three men, two of them fatally, in a gang-related incident in Los Angeles. About two weeks later, he entered the home of a man who had given information to the police about the murders and shot him dead; Sandoval then killed the man's wife because she had seen him murder her husband. Sandoval was convicted on four counts of first degree murder. The jury found that Sandoval personally used a firearm in the commission of each offense, and found the special circumstance of multiple murder. He was sentenced to death for murdering the woman and to life in prison without possibility of parole for the other three murders. The California Supreme Court affirmed the convictions and sentences.

The jury in Sandoval's case was given the following instruction on the government's burden of proof:

> A defendant in a criminal action is presumed to be innocent until the contrary is proved, and in case of a reasonable doubt whether his guilt is satisfactorily shown, he is entitled to a verdict of not guilty. This presumption places upon the State the burden of proving him guilty beyond a reasonable doubt.

> Reasonable doubt is defined as follows: It is not a mere possible doubt; because everything relating to human affairs, and *depending on moral evidence*, is open to some possible or imaginary doubt. It is that state of the case which, after the entire comparison and consideration of all the evidence, leaves the minds of the jurors in that condition that they cannot say they feel an abiding conviction, *to a moral certainty*, of the truth of the charge.

The California Supreme Court rejected Sandoval's claim that the instruction, particularly the highlighted passages, violated the Due Process Clause.

The instruction given in Sandoval's case has its genesis in a charge given by Chief Justice Shaw of the Massachusetts Supreme Judicial Court more than a century ago:

> [W]hat is reasonable doubt? It is a term often used, probably pretty well understood, but not easily defined. It is not mere possible doubt; because every thing relating to human affairs, and depending on moral evidence, is open to some possible or imaginary doubt. It is that state of the case, which, after the entire comparison and consideration of all the evidence, leaves the minds of jurors in that condition that they cannot say they feel an abiding conviction, to a moral certainty, of the truth of the charge. The burden of proof is upon the prosecutor. All the presumptions of law independent of evidence are in favor of innocence; and every person is presumed to be innocent until he is proved guilty. If upon such proof there is reasonable doubt remaining, the accused is entitled to the benefit of it by an acquittal. For it is not sufficient to establish a probability, though a strong one arising from the doctrine of chances, that the fact charged is more likely to be true than the contrary; but the evidence must establish the truth of the fact to a reasonable and moral certainty; a certainty that convinces and directs the understanding, and satisfies the reason and judgment, of those who are bound to act conscientiously upon it. This we take to be proof beyond reasonable doubt.

The *Webster* charge is representative of the time when "American courts began applying [the beyond a reasonable doubt standard] in its modern form in criminal cases." In *People v. Strong* (1866), the California Supreme Court characterized the *Webster* instruction as "probably the most satisfactory definition ever given to the words 'reasonable doubt' in any case known to criminal jurisprudence." In *People v. Paulsell* (1896), the court cautioned state trial judges against departing from that formulation. And in 1927, the state legislature adopted the bulk of the Webster instruction as a statutory definition of reasonable doubt. Indeed, the California Legislature has directed that "the court may read to the jury [the applicable] section . . . of this code, and no further instruction on the subject of the presumption of innocence or defining reasonable doubt need be given." The statutory instruction was given in Sandoval's case.

· · ·

A

Sandoval's primary objection is to the use of the phrases "moral evidence" and "moral certainty" in the instruction. As noted, this part of the charge was lifted verbatim from Chief Justice Shaw's Webster decision; some understanding of the historical context in which that instruction was written is accordingly helpful in evaluating its continuing validity.

By the beginning of the Republic, lawyers had borrowed the concept of "moral evidence" from the philosophers and historians of the 17th and 18th centuries. James Wilson, who was instrumental in framing the Constitution and who served as one of the original Members of this Court, explained in a 1790 lecture on law that "evidence . . . is divided into two species — demonstrative and moral." Wilson went on to explain the distinction thus:

> Demonstrative evidence has for its subject abstract and necessary truths, or the unchangeable relations of ideas. Moral evidence has for its subject the real but contingent truths and connections, which take place among things actually existing. . . .

D. Jury Instruction Issues: Reasonable Doubt, the *Allen* Charge, and Implicit Bias

> In moral evidence, there not only may be, but there generally is, contrariety of proofs: in demonstrative evidence, no such contrariety can take place. . . . [T]o suppose that two contrary demonstrations can exist, is to suppose that the same proposition is both true and false: which is manifestly absurd. With regard to moral evidence, there is, for the most part, real evidence on both sides. On both sides, contrary presumptions, contrary testimonies, contrary experiences must be balanced.

A leading 19th century treatise observed that "[m]atters of fact are proved by moral evidence alone; . . . [i]n the ordinary affairs of life, we do not require demonstrative evidence, . . . and to insist upon it would be unreasonable and absurd."

The phrase "moral certainty" shares an epistemological pedigree with moral evidence. Moral certainty was the highest degree of certitude based on such evidence. In his 1790 lecture, James Wilson observed:

> In a series of moral evidence, the inference drawn in the several steps is not necessary; nor is it impossible that the premises should be true, while the conclusion drawn from them is false.
> . . . In moral evidence, we rise, by an insensible gradation, from possibility to probability, and from probability to the highest degree of moral certainty.

At least one early treatise explicitly equated moral certainty with proof beyond a reasonable doubt:

> Evidence which satisfies the minds of the jury of the truth of the fact in dispute, to the entire exclusion of every reasonable doubt, constitutes full proof of the fact. . . .
> Even the most direct evidence can produce nothing more than such a high degree of probability as amounts to moral certainty. From the highest degree it may decline, by an infinite number of gradations, until it produce in the mind nothing more than a mere preponderance of assent in favour of the particular fact.

Thus, when Chief Justice Shaw penned the *Webster* instruction in 1850, moral certainty meant a state of subjective certitude about some event or occurrence. As the Massachusetts Supreme Judicial Court subsequently explained:

> Proof "beyond a reasonable doubt" . . . is proof "to a moral certainty," as distinguished from an absolute certainty. As applied to a judicial trial for crime, the two phrases are synonymous and equivalent; each has been used by eminent judges to explain the other; and each signifies such proof as satisfies the judgment and consciences of the jury, as reasonable men, and applying their reason to the evidence before them, that the crime charged has been committed by the defendant, and so satisfies them as to leave no other reasonable conclusion possible.

Indeed, we have said that "[p]roof to a 'moral certainty' is an equivalent phrase with 'beyond a reasonable doubt.'"

We recognize that the phrase "moral evidence" is not a mainstay of the modern lexicon, though we do not think it means anything different today than it did in the 19th century. The few contemporary dictionaries that define moral evidence do so consistently with its original meaning.

Moreover, the instruction itself gives a definition of the phrase. The jury was told that "everything relating to human affairs, and depending on moral evidence, is open to some possible or imaginary doubt"—in other words, that absolute certainty is unattainable in matters relating to human affairs. Moral evidence, in this sentence, can only mean empirical evidence offered to prove such matters—the proof introduced at trial.

This conclusion is reinforced by other instructions given in Sandoval's case. The judge informed the jurors that their duty was "to determine the facts of the case from the evidence received in the trial and not from any other source." The judge continued: "Evidence consists of testimony of witnesses, writings, material objects, or anything presented to the senses and offered to prove the existence or non-existence of a fact." The judge also told the jurors that "you must not be influenced by pity for a defendant or by prejudice against him," and that "[y]ou must not be swayed by mere sentiment, conjecture, sympathy, passion, prejudice, public opinion or public feeling." These instructions correctly pointed the jurors' attention to the facts of the case before them, not (as Sandoval contends) the ethics or morality of Sandoval's criminal acts. Accordingly, we find the reference to moral evidence unproblematic.

We are somewhat more concerned with Sandoval's argument that the phrase "moral certainty" has lost its historical meaning, and that a modern jury would understand it to allow conviction on proof that does not meet the beyond a reasonable doubt standard. Words and phrases can change meaning over time: A passage generally understood in 1850 may be incomprehensible or confusing to a modern juror. And although some contemporary dictionaries contain definitions of moral certainty similar to the 19th century understanding of the phrase, we are willing to accept Sandoval's premise that "moral certainty," standing alone, might not be recognized by modern jurors as a synonym for "proof beyond a reasonable doubt." But it does not necessarily follow that the California instruction is unconstitutional.

Sandoval first argues that moral certainty would be understood by modern jurors to mean a standard of proof lower than beyond a reasonable doubt. In support of this proposition, Sandoval points to contemporary dictionaries that define moral certainty in terms of probability. But the beyond a reasonable doubt standard is itself probabilistic. "[I]n a judicial proceeding in which there is a dispute about the facts of some earlier event, the factfinder cannot acquire unassailably accurate knowledge of what happened. Instead, all the factfinder can acquire is a belief of what probably happened." The problem is not that moral certainty may be understood in terms of probability, but that a jury might understand the phrase to mean something less than the very high level of probability required by the Constitution in criminal cases.

Although in this respect moral certainty is ambiguous in the abstract, the rest of the instruction given in Sandoval's case lends content to the phrase. The jurors were told that they must have "an abiding conviction, to a moral certainty, of the truth of the charge." An instruction cast in terms of an abiding conviction as to guilt, without reference to moral certainty, correctly states the government's burden of proof. And the judge had already informed the jury that matters relating to human affairs are proved by moral evidence, giving the same meaning to the word moral in this part of the instruction, moral certainty can only mean certainty with respect to human affairs. As used in this instruction, therefore, we are satisfied that the reference to moral certainty, in conjunction with the abiding conviction language, "impress[ed] upon the factfinder the need to reach a subjective state of near certitude of the guilt of the accused." Accordingly, we reject Sandoval's contention that the moral certainty element of the California instruction invited the jury to convict him on proof below that required by the Due Process Clause.

Sandoval's second argument is a variant of the first. Accepting that the instruction requires a high level of confidence in the defendant's guilt, Sandoval argues that a juror might be convinced to a moral certainty that the defendant is guilty even though the government has failed to prove his guilt beyond a reasonable doubt. A definition of moral certainty in a widely used modern dictionary lends support to this argument, and we do not gainsay its force. As we have noted, "[t]he constitutional standard recognized in the *Winship* case was expressly phrased as one that protects an accused against a conviction except on 'proof beyond a reasonable doubt.'" Indeed, in *Cage* we contrasted "moral certainty" with "evidentiary certainty"

But the moral certainty language cannot be sequestered from its surroundings. In the *Cage* instruction, the jurors were simply told that they had to be morally certain of the defendant's guilt; there was nothing else in the instruction to lend meaning to the phrase. Not so here. The jury in Sandoval's case was told that a reasonable doubt is "that state of the case which, after the entire comparison and consideration of all the evidence, leaves the minds of the jurors in that condition that they cannot say they feel an abiding conviction, to a moral certainty, of the truth of the charge." The instruction thus explicitly told the jurors that their conclusion had to be based on the evidence in the case. Other instructions reinforced this message. The jury was told "to determine the facts of the case from the evidence received in the trial and not from any other source." The judge continued that "you must not be influenced by pity for a defendant or by prejudice against him. . . . You must not be swayed by mere sentiment, conjecture, sympathy, passion, prejudice, public opinion or public feeling." Accordingly, there is no reasonable likelihood that the jury would have understood moral certainty to be disassociated from the evidence in the case.

We do not think it reasonably likely that the jury understood the words "moral certainty" either as suggesting a standard of proof lower than due process requires or as allowing conviction on factors other than the government's proof. At the same time, however, we do not condone the use of the phrase. As modern dictionary definitions of moral certainty attest, the common meaning of the phrase has changed since it was used in the *Webster* instruction, and it may continue to do so to the point that it conflicts with the *Winship* standard. Indeed, the definitions of reasonable doubt most widely used in the federal courts do not contain any reference to moral certainty. But we have no supervisory power over the state courts, and in the context of the instructions as a whole we cannot say that the use of the phrase rendered the instruction given in Sandoval's case unconstitutional.

B

Finally, Sandoval objects to the portion of the charge in which the judge instructed the jury that a reasonable doubt is "not a mere possible doubt." The *Cage* instruction included an almost identical reference to "not a mere possible doubt," but we did not intimate that there was anything wrong with that part of the charge. That is because "[a] 'reasonable doubt,' at a minimum, is one based upon 'reason.'" A fanciful doubt is not a reasonable doubt. As Sandoval's defense attorney told the jury: "Anything can be possible. . . . [A] planet could be made out of blue cheese. But that's really not in the realm of what we're talking about." That this is the sense in which the instruction uses "possible" is made clear from the final phrase of the sentence, which notes that everything "is open to some possible or imaginary doubt." We therefore reject Sandoval's challenge to this portion of the instruction as well.

· · ·

Justice GINSBURG, concurring in part and concurring in the judgment.

I agree with the Court that the reasonable doubt instructions given in these cases, read as a whole, satisfy the Constitution's due process requirement. As the Court observes, the instructions adequately conveyed to the jurors that they should focus exclusively upon the evidence, and that they should convict only if they had an "abiding conviction" of the defendant's guilt. I agree, further, with the Court's suggestion that the term "moral certainty," while not in itself so misleading as to render the instructions unconstitutional, should be avoided as an unhelpful way of explaining what reasonable doubt means.

Similarly unhelpful, in my view, are two other features of the instruction given in Victor's case. That instruction begins by defining reasonable doubt as "such a doubt as would cause a reasonable and prudent person, in one of the graver and more important transactions of life, to pause and hesitate before taking the represented facts as true and relying and acting thereon." A committee of distinguished federal judges, reporting to the Judicial Conference of the United States, has criticized this "hesitate to act" formulation because the analogy it uses seems misplaced. In the decisions people make in the most important of their own affairs, resolution of conflicts about past events does not usually play a major role. Indeed, decisions we make in the most important affairs of our lives — choosing a spouse, a job, a place to live, and the like — generally involve a very heavy element of uncertainty and risk-taking. They are wholly unlike the decisions jurors ought to make in criminal cases.

More recently, Second Circuit Chief Judge Jon O. Newman observed:

> Although, as a district judge, I dutifully repeated [the "hesitate to act" standard] to juries in scores of criminal trials, I was always bemused by its ambiguity. If the jurors encounter a doubt that would cause them to "hesitate to act in a matter of importance," what are they to do then? Should they decline to convict because they have reached a point of hesitation, or should they simply hesitate, then ask themselves whether, in their own private matters, they would resolve the doubt in favor of action, and, if so, continue on to convict?

Even less enlightening than the "hesitate to act" formulation is the passage of the Victor instruction counseling: "[The jury] may find an accused guilty upon the strong probabilities of the case, *provided such probabilities are strong enough to exclude any doubt of his guilt that is reasonable.*" If the italicized words save this part of the instruction from understating the prosecution's burden of proof, they do so with uninstructive circularity. Jury comprehension is scarcely advanced when a court "defines" reasonable doubt as "doubt . . . that is reasonable."

These and similar difficulties have led some courts to question the efficacy of any reasonable doubt instruction. At least two of the Federal Courts of Appeals have admonished their District Judges not to attempt a definition. This Court, too, has suggested on occasion that prevailing definitions of "reasonable doubt" afford no real aid. But we have never held that the concept of reasonable doubt is undefinable, or that trial courts should not, as a matter of course, provide a definition. Nor, contrary to the Court's suggestion, have we ever held that the Constitution does not require trial courts to define reasonable doubt.

Because the trial judges in fact defined reasonable doubt in both jury charges we review, we need not decide whether the Constitution required them to do so. Whether or not the Constitution so requires, however, the argument for defining the concept is strong. While judges and lawyers are familiar with the reasonable doubt standard, the words "beyond a reasonable doubt" are not self-defining for jurors. Several studies of jury behavior have concluded that "jurors are often confused about the meaning of reasonable doubt" when that term is left undefined. Thus, even if definitions of reasonable doubt are necessarily imperfect, the alternative — refusing to define the concept at all — is not obviously preferable.

Fortunately, the choice need not be one between two kinds of potential juror confusion — on one hand, the confusion that may be caused by leaving "reasonable doubt" undefined, and on the other, the confusion that might be induced by the anachronism of "moral certainty," the misplaced analogy of "hesitation to act," or the circularity of "doubt that is reasonable." The Federal Judicial Center has proposed a definition of reasonable doubt that is clear, straightforward, and accurate. That instruction reads:

> [T]he government has the burden of proving the defendant guilty beyond a reasonable doubt. Some of you may have served as jurors in civil cases, where you were told that it is only necessary to prove that a fact is more likely true than not true. In criminal cases, the government's proof must be more powerful than that. It must be beyond a reasonable doubt.
>
> Proof beyond a reasonable doubt is proof that leaves you firmly convinced of the defendant's guilt. There are very few things in this world that we know with absolute certainty, and in criminal cases the law does not require proof that overcomes every possible doubt. If, based on your consideration of the evidence, you are firmly convinced that the defendant is guilty of the crime charged, you must find him guilty. If on the other hand, you think there is a real possibility that he is not guilty, you must give him the benefit of the doubt and find him not guilty.

D. Jury Instruction Issues: Reasonable Doubt, the *Allen* Charge, and Implicit Bias **1177**

This instruction plainly informs the jurors that the prosecution must prove its case by more than a mere preponderance of the evidence, yet not necessarily to an absolute certainty. The "firmly convinced" standard for conviction, repeated for emphasis, is further enhanced by the juxtaposed prescription that the jury must acquit if there is a "real possibility" that the defendant is innocent. This model instruction surpasses others I have seen in stating the reasonable doubt standard succinctly and comprehensibly.

I recognize, however, that this Court has no supervisory powers over the state courts, and that the test we properly apply in evaluating the constitutionality of a reasonable doubt instruction is not whether we find it exemplary; instead, we inquire only whether there is a "reasonable likelihood that the jury understood the instructio[n] to allow conviction based on proof insufficient to meet" the reasonable doubt standard. . . .

. . .

NOTES AND QUESTIONS

1. "Reasonable doubt" is one of the most important concepts in American criminal law. It purports to distinguish criminal proceedings, where life or liberty are at stake, from lower-stakes civil proceedings that are only about money. And while the Constitution requires this high standard of proof for criminal cases, the Supreme Court has never dictated how the concept should be explained to juries. Do you agree with the sentiment expressed by Chief Justice Shaw of Massachusetts in 1850, that reasonable doubt "is a term often used, probably pretty well understood, but not easily defined"?

2. The Court is relatively untroubled by the use of the term "moral evidence" in the lower court's instruction, although conceding that it "is not a mainstay of the modern lexicon." Why does the Court spend so much time discussing the "epistemological pedigrees" of the terms "moral evidence" and "moral certainty"? How do you think the term "moral evidence" could be misunderstood by modern jurors? Does this misunderstanding favor the defense or the government? How about "moral certainty"?

3. Consider the "hesitate to act" portion of the instruction reproduced in Justice Ginsburg's opinion. Do you agree with Judge Newman's comment on the "ambiguity" of this phraseology? Is the usage of this term simply "unhelpful," as Justice Ginsburg notes, or does it favor either the government or the defense?

4. Some courts do not provide any instruction on reasonable doubt. *See, e.g., United States v. Adkins*, 937 F.2d 947, 950 (4th Cir. 1991) ("This circuit has repeatedly warned against giving the jury definitions of reasonable doubt, because definitions tend to impermissibly lessen the burden of proof. . . . The only exception to our categorical disdain for definition is when the jury specifically requests it.").

Does this make sense to you?

2. The *Allen* Charge

The next case considers the notorious "*Allen* charge," an instruction that is given to juries who have reported to the court that they are deadlocked. The goal of an *Allen* charge is to encourage the jury to continue to deliberate and reach a verdict if reasonably possible, yet not to encourage any members of the jury to abandon their positions.

The concept of such a charge was first sanctioned by the Supreme Court in *Allen v. United States*, 164 U.S. 492 (1896). The Court has subsequently reversed one *Allen*-inspired conviction where as part of the charge the judge told the jury "[y]ou have got to reach a decision

1178 Chapter XIII The Jury I: Scope of the Right and Other Issues

in this case," *Jenkins v. United States*, 380 U.S. 445, 446 (1965) (per curiam), but has more recently recognized the continuing validity of *Allen* charges. *Lowenfield v. Phelps*, 484 U.S. 231, 237-38 (1988).

Because of their coercive potential, *Allen* charges are extremely controversial in both federal and state courts. In many jurisdictions they are discouraged or limited, in whole or in part, although in only a few states are they outright prohibited. *See* Samantha P. Bateman, Comment, *Blast It All:* Allen *Charges and the Danger of Playing with Dynamite*, 32 U. Haw. L. Rev. 323, 329-33 (2010) (noting state efforts to limit the use of *Allen* charges). The Supreme Court of California banned *Allen* charges in 1977, holding in *People v. Gainer*, 566 P.2d 997, 1004-05 (Cal. 1977), that "the admonition to minority jurors . . . constitutes . . . excessive pressure on the dissenting jurors to acquiesce in a verdict" and that the "open encouragement given by the charge to such acquiescence is manifestly incompatible with the requirement of independently achieved jury unanimity."

United States v. Paniagua-Ramos
135 F.3d 193 (1st Cir. 1998)

DiClerico, District Judge.

After a conviction by a federal jury for conspiracy to possess with intent to distribute a controlled substance and an acquittal on a charge of aiding and abetting possession of a controlled substance, the defendant-appellee, Daniel Paniagua-Ramos, was granted a new trial by the trial judge on the ground that the district court's jury charge was prejudicial. On appeal, the government asserts that the district court abused its discretion by finding plain error in its charge and granting a new trial. Because we find that the district court did not abuse its discretion in concluding that its charge was improper, we affirm.

FACTUAL AND PROCEDURAL BACKGROUND

This is an appeal from an order entered January 15, 1997, by the district court granting a new trial. The government prosecuted the appellee, Daniel Paniagua-Ramos, for conspiracy to possess 400 kilograms of cocaine with the intent to distribute it, and for aiding and abetting the possession of the cocaine in violation of 18 U.S.C. § 2 and 21 U.S.C. §§ 841(a)(1), 846.

The case was tried in district court from Tuesday, December 3, 1996, to Friday, December 6, 1996. On Friday, December 6, the jury retired to deliberate for three hours, after which they requested leave to continue on Monday, December 9. On Monday morning they began deliberating at approximately 9:30 a.m., but at 10:30 a.m. they forwarded a note to the court stating: "We have not reached an unanimous decision, and will not be changed." The court instructed the jury to continue trying to decide. After lunch, they continued deliberations. The jury sent another note to the court at 4:16 p.m. stating: "We still don't have a unanimous verdict, and none wants to change its decision." At 4:33 p.m. the jury sent yet another note to the court, stating: "We suggest to retire our position as a juror for the case of Mr. Daniel Paniagua. Due to no unanimous verdict between all jurors." The court then gave the jury a charge based in part on the modified *Allen* charge found in a draft of proposed criminal law pattern jury instructions under consideration for use as an aid to the district courts of the First Circuit. The court instructed the jury as follows:

> Members of the jury, I have seen your two notes but I want you to listen carefully to what I have to say and, of course, this is an additional instruction. I want all of you to pay careful attention to this instruction that I am going to give you.

In trials, such as this one that you participated in, absolute certainty can neither be expected nor attained. And that happens, I would say, in the majority of the trials. You should consider that you are selected or you were selected in this case in the same manner and from the same source as any future jury will be selected. In other words, the fact that you have not agreed doesn't mean that this is the end of the case. The case will have to be tried again if you cannot agree. The point I am making is this: There is no reason to suppose that this case would be ever [sic] submitted to 12 jurors different from you people who are either more intelligent or more capable or more impartial or more competent than the 12 of you. And they are going to hear the same evidence that you have heard.

The point that I am trying to make is that you, the 12 of you, have to make a conscious effort to try to decide this case if you can do so without doing violence to your individual judgment.

I know by experience in dealing with collective decisions, because I have sat, for example, on the Court of Appeals many times and then it is three judges deciding, that the three judges or the many judges may have different views on something. But when you have different views you have to look calmly at the issues and calmly assess them to see whether there is any way of bringing about a solution.

You have to pay respect to each other's opinions. You have to listen with a mind open to be convinced of other people's arguments. Thus, where there is disagreement, jurors that are presently favoring acquittal should consider whether a doubt in their own mind is a reasonable one when it makes no impression upon the minds of the other equally honest and intelligent jurors who have heard the same evidence with the same degree of attention and with the same desire to arrive at the truth under the sanction of the same oath.

On the other hand, jurors favoring conviction ought to seriously ask themselves whether they should not distrust the weight or sufficiency of the evidence which fails to dispel reasonable doubt in the minds of their fellow jurors.

Not only should jurors in the minority re-examine their positions, but jurors in the majority should also do so to see whether they have given careful consideration and sufficient weight to the evidence that has favorably impressed the persons in disagreement with them.

Remember that I gave you a charge on Friday and I gave you this morning the charge for you to have in writing. The burden of proof instruction is a legal tool that will help you to decide this case.

The law imposes upon the prosecution a high burden of proof. The prosecution has the burden to establish with respect to each count each essential element of the offense and to establish that essential element beyond a reasonable doubt. And with respect to any element of any count that you are left in reasonable doubt, then the defendant is entitled to the benefit of such doubt and must be acquitted.

It is your duty to decide the case if you can do so without doing violence to your individual judgment. But remember, as I said before, that your indecision is not going to be the end of this. Because in the long run I have to take your indecisive verdict, that is no verdict, and I will have to simply try this case again, as I said, and get 12 jurors that may be worse equipped, they are going to hear the same evidence, and they are going to go through the same exercise.

So the point that I am trying to make is that if you put all of your 12 minds to work and all of you make an honest effort not to fight with each other, for example, but to honestly listen to each other, I am pretty sure that you will be able to agree on a verdict.

Remember something that I said before, and if I did not, I think I did say it in the preliminary instructions that I gave you, you are not parties to this case. You do not work for the government. You are not related to the defendant. You are strangers to this controversy the same way that I am. Our mission is to try to resolve this case, to decide this case on the basis of the instructions and on the basis of the applicable law. That is what the system requires. That is the only system that we have.

So with that in mind, I am going to beg you to go back and give it a try because I am pretty sure that you can.

No objections to the charge were made after the charge was given and before the jury retired to deliberate. See Fed. R. Crim. P. 30. No copies of the pattern charge were provided to counsel at the time the charge was given to the jury. Immediately after instructing the jury, the court informed counsel that the charge given was the proposed pattern charge. At approximately 6:40 p.m. the jury returned a verdict finding the defendant guilty on the conspiracy charge and not guilty on the substantive charge of aiding and abetting.

On December 13, 1996, the defendant received a copy of the proposed pattern jury instruction pursuant to his request. On December 16, 1996, after contrasting the proposed pattern instruction with the instruction as given by the district court, the defendant filed a timely request for a new trial. See Fed. R. Crim. P. 33. The defendant argued that the court's *Allen* charge was defective and coerced the jury into reaching a verdict. Since the defendant failed to object to the charge before the jury retired to deliberate, the district court reviewed the charge for plain error. The court rejected the government's arguments opposing a new trial and ordered a new trial. The government appeals this decision, arguing that the court abused its discretion in ordering a new trial on the basis that the *Allen* charge constituted plain error.

DISCUSSION

It is within the discretion of the district court to set aside a jury verdict and order a new trial, but this remedy must be "sparingly used, and then only where there would be a miscarriage of justice." "[A]n appellate court must sustain the granting of a new trial unless there was an abuse of discretion." A review for abuse of discretion is deferential to the district court, as the court was present at the trial and had the opportunity first hand to observe the evidence, the witnesses, and the jury. However, there are several components to the abuse of discretion standard. While a court of appeals need not defer to the district court in reviewing questions of law, findings of fact are often subjected to clear error review.

Because the defendants in this case failed to object to the *Allen* charge in a timely fashion, a reviewing court may not take notice of the error unless the error meets the requirements of Fed. R. Crim. P. 52(b). In *United States v. Olano*, the Supreme Court articulated the proper analysis to be employed in reviewing for plain error. First, an error must have been committed. Second, the error must be "plain," which has been interpreted as "obvious" or "clear under current law." Third, the error must affect substantial rights. Finally, once these three elements are satisfied, the court may in its discretion take notice of the plain error if it is appropriate to do so. We will address these elements seriatim.

A. The Error

In the past, we have referred to the *Allen* charge as the "dynamite charge" and noted that it should be used with "great caution, and only when absolutely necessary." A defendant may be prejudiced by an *Allen* charge in a number of ways. Therefore, we have instructed district courts to include three elements in the substance of an *Allen* charge to ameliorate its potentially prejudicial effect. *See United States v. Manning* (1st Cir. 1996). "A district court should instruct jurors in substance that (1) members of both the majority and the minority should reexamine their positions, (2) a jury has the right to fail to agree, and (3) the burden of proving guilt beyond a reasonable doubt remains with the government." We have further instructed trial courts to avoid substantive departures from approved formulations of the *Allen* charge, and to avoid using language that might heighten its coercive effect. In situations where the substance of these elements was not communicated to the jury, this court has found reversible error without further inquiry. At issue in this case is the second element.

The trial court stated that agreement should not come at the cost of doing violence to a juror's independent judgment, and that an indecisive verdict will require a new trial. While the court determined that it had failed to include in its *Allen* charge the substance of the jury's

D. Jury Instruction Issues: Reasonable Doubt, the *Allen* Charge, and Implicit Bias

right to fail to agree, it indicated that implicit in the charge given was the jury's right to fail to agree. This court has refrained from offering definite wording for an *Allen* charge, and in *Vachon* we held that a court's failure to include the specific language "a jury has the right to disagree" did not necessitate a new trial.

However, the case at hand is readily distinguished from *Vachon*. Here, the language the court used to communicate the jury's right to fail to agree was insufficient when considered in the coercive context in which it was given, i.e., the jury had already informed the court on three occasions that it could not reach a unanimous verdict. Moreover, any force behind the implicitly communicated right to fail to agree was negated by the court's other statements in which it was embedded. The court summarized the "point" of the *Allen* charge given by stating "if you put all of your 12 minds to work and all of you make an honest effort not to fight with each other, for example, but to honestly listen to each other, I am pretty sure that you will be able to agree on a verdict." This statement inevitably created an atmosphere of coercion that minimized the significance of the positions held by the individual jurors and in effect compelled unanimity. Referring to a juror's attempts to maintain his or her individual judgment as a "fight" undermined the admonition that jurors should not do violence to their individual judgment. The coercive nature of this language was enhanced by the court's statement that the "mission" was to "try to resolve this case, to decide this case. . . . That is what the system requires. That is the only system that we have. . . . I am going to beg you to go back and give it a try because I am pretty sure that you can." These statements infer that it would be reasonable, perhaps even expected, for the jurors to come to a decision on the evidence submitted, and that our system of justice required and depended on their arriving at such a decision. Finally, the aura of compulsion was intensified by the court's implicit dissatisfaction with an indecisive verdict. The court emphasized that the jury's indecision "is no verdict" and "is not going to be the end of this" and that "in the long run" "I will have to simply try this case again."

These statements in the context in which they appear run counter to our instruction that "in all events, the court should be careful to . . . avoid language which might heighten" the coercive effect of an *Allen* charge. This court has expressly disapproved of statements that "directly imply[ ] that it would be reasonable for the jury to reach a decision on the evidence before them."

Moreover, because the jury's weakly enunciated right to deliver an indecisive verdict was closely intertwined with language that strongly compelled a jury agreement, the charge failed to communicate adequately the substance of the jury's right to fail to agree. We therefore find that the lower court's determination that its instruction was legally insufficient was correct under the circumstances.

The government fails in its attempt to characterize the trial court's order for a new trial as being premised solely upon the court's failure to state expressly that the jury had a "right to fail to agree." The trial court's order focused on the First Circuit's requirement that "the substance of the jury's right" be communicated. The court found that it had "failed to communicate the notion that the jury has a 'right' to deliver an inconclusive verdict," and that the charge lacked "complete accuracy in communicating the extent of the jury's obligations and rights." Second, given the facts of this case, we disagree with the government's contention that the defendant's failure to object in a timely manner indicates the charge was not in error. The parties were not provided with a copy of the draft pattern charge. Immediately after the jury was excused, the court said to the parties "[b]efore you say anything, let me say this . . ." and informed the parties that the instruction given was a proposed pattern *Allen* charge that the First Circuit was considering for publication. We agree with the district court that the failure of the parties to object was understandable in these circumstances.

B. The Clarity of the Error

The second requirement of Rule 52(b) is that the error be plain or clear. Here, the court's error in its instruction constituted clear error under current law. We established as early as

1973 that the failure to instruct the jury on the substance of the three elements was reversible error, without further inquiry as to the coerciveness of the charge. The error committed by the trial court is therefore "plain error" under Rule 52(b).

C. Substantial Rights Affected

Finally, we must address the third requirement of Rule 52(b), whether the plain error affected substantial rights. In most instances, this requires that the error be prejudicial. Here, the jury sent three notes to the court over a six hour period indicating that the jury was deadlocked, and ultimately suggested that the jury be allowed to "retire." A reasonable inference is that the jurors were divided and deeply entrenched in their opinions. The court then instructed the jury with the *Allen* charge at issue, using language that we have found to be coercive in the context in which it was given. The jury returned its verdict approximately an hour and forty minutes later. Its verdict was split. It acquitted the defendant of the substantive charge, but convicted the defendant of the conspiracy charge. The district court found it likely that the modified *Allen* charge "intimated [the jury] into a decision" and "tainted this jury's deliberation." The trial court's findings on the prejudicial effect of the *Allen* charge are entitled to deference, and we find them to be reasonable under the circumstances.

The government argues, however, that the verdict was free from undue influence, and that the charge did not have a prejudicial effect on the defendant. It asserts that the verdict was not inconsistent, and that the court erred when it considered the inconsistency of the verdict as evidence of coercion. Although an inconsistent verdict in itself is not grounds to vacate a conviction, an inconsistent verdict can be probative of whether a jury was confused or coerced into rendering a compromise verdict. Furthermore, we do not disagree with the district court that "given the nature of the evidence in this case, the logical verdicts would have been that [the defendant] was guilty of both the substantive charge and the conspiracy charge or that he was innocent of both charges." To bolster its contentions, the government again argues that neither party objected to the charge, an issue we have already addressed supra, and need not revisit. Finally, the government urges that the polling of the jurors failed to indicate any coercion. Polling is useful to indicate an irregularity in a verdict. However, the failure of a poll to indicate coercion is not conclusive as to whether coercion actually existed.

D. Miscarriage of Justice

We find that the three elements required by Rule 52(b) are therefore satisfied in this case. However, Rule 52(b) is discretionary. Even when plain error is found that affects substantial rights, a reviewing court must determine whether the error " 'seriously affect[s] the fairness, integrity or public reputation of the judicial proceedings' " before exercise of its discretion is appropriate. Under this standard, a reviewing court should exercise its discretion when failure to take notice of the error would result in a miscarriage of justice.

Here, the government's case relied upon the testimony of a cooperating witness. The trial court found the credibility of this witness to be "substantially compromised by impeachment through cross examination and by the testimony of a probation officer." The court determined that it was likely this led to the "severe deadlock broken only by the *Allen* charge" which "intimidated [the jury] into a decision." This court forewarned against this precise situation in *Angiulo* when we expressed our concern that an *Allen* charge may prejudice a defendant by depriving the defendant of "whatever safeguard he might have had in a hung jury [or] a declaration of mistrial." In this case the jury verdict may be attributed at least in part to coercion by the court. We agree with the district court's implicit determination that a failure to order a new trial would result in a miscarriage of justice. We find no abuse of discretion.

Affirmed.

NOTES AND QUESTIONS

1. In *Paniagua-Ramos*, for reasons that are unexplained, the court simply read to the jury a very long version of an *Allen* charge without giving counsel an opportunity to object or comment on the charge before reading it. And neither lawyer objected to the charge after it was given, perhaps because the judge immediately informed them—inaccurately—that he had simply given the proposed pattern instruction. Regardless, both lawyers should have objected based on existing First Circuit precedent, which required that an *Allen* charge include a statement about jurors' right to disagree, which was plainly missing from the charge based on even just a close listen. But for this easily correctible mistake—by the judge and both lawyers—a retrial might have been avoided. Why was it the responsibility of both lawyers to object, given that the missing ingredient of the charge was favorable to the defense?

2. In analyzing for plain error, the court concludes that the defendant's failure to object was "understandable in these circumstances." Does the court let the defendant off too lightly? Consider all of the circumstances: the trial was only about three days long; the jury deliberated for three hours on Friday before going home for the weekend; the jury announced it was deadlocked after one hour of deliberations on Monday; they confirmed they were still deadlocked at 4:16 and 4:33 p.m. on Monday; and shortly thereafter the judge gave the *Allen* charge. From 10:30 a.m. on, in short, the jury appeared potentially deadlocked and, therefore, there was a substantial risk the judge would attempt to break the deadlock by giving an *Allen* charge. Some judges might have had more patience and waited longer but it was a very short trial and counsel should have been ready. After 10:30 a.m. on Monday, counsel should have immediately made sure they were up to speed on the latest First Circuit law on *Allen* charges. Had they done so, they could not have missed the First Circuit case decided just nine months earlier, *United States v. Manning*, 79 F.2d 212, 222 (1st Cir. 1996), which set forth the three necessary elements of an *Allen* charge.

3. Look closely at the charge the judge gave. What do you make of the language that "[y]ou are strangers to this controversy the same way that I am"?

The First Circuit notes all the aspects of the charge that make it overly coercive. Does that same language, as well as other language, also suggest that a hung jury is a failure? How so? Why isn't a hung jury (after a reasonable amount of time) seen simply as a failed prosecution, where the government could not persuade a jury of defendant's guilt beyond a reasonable doubt? *See Huffman v. United States*, 297 F.2d 754, 759 (5th Cir. 1962) (Brown, J., dissenting) (advocating for abolition of *Allen* charges and describing a hung jury as a "safeguard of liberty").

4. In what way was the verdict "inconsistent"? Why does this inconsistency tend to show that the error was prejudicial?

5. In *The Sopranos*, the jury in Uncle Junior's trial was given an *Allen* charge, much to Uncle Junior's consternation, although the mob-intimidated juror continued to hold out and a mistrial was declared. Season 4, episode 13, "Whitecaps."

Uncle Junior, played by Dominic Chianese

3. Implicit Bias Instruction

In a 2010 article, former Judge Mark W. Bennett of the Northern District of Iowa discusses the role of implicit bias in jury selection. *See* Mark W. Bennett, *Unraveling the Gordian Knot of Implicit Bias in Jury Selection: The Problems of Judge-Dominated Voir Dire, the Failed Promise of* Batson, *and Proposed Solutions*, 4 Harv. L. & Pol'y Rev. 149 (2010). He advocates for increased attorney involvement in jury voir dire and the abolition of peremptory challenges, *see* Chapter XV *infra*, among other things. He also routinely gives the following instruction to jurors on implicit bias:

> As we discussed in jury selection, growing scientific research indicates each one of us has "implicit biases," or hidden feelings, perceptions, fears and stereotypes in our subconscious. These hidden thoughts often impact how we remember what we see and hear and how we make important decisions. While it is difficult to control one's subconscious thoughts, being aware of these hidden biases can help counteract them. As a result, I ask you to recognize that all of us may be affected by implicit biases in the decisions that we make. Because you are making very important decisions in this case, I strongly encourage you to critically evaluate the evidence and resist any urge to reach a verdict influenced by stereotypes, generalizations, or implicit biases.

Id. at 169 n.35. Judge Bennett states that many of his colleagues are unreceptive to giving such an instruction, ostensibly due to a concern that calling attention to implicit biases will exacerbate them.

Do you agree? What do you see as the pros and cons of giving such an instruction? Should this instruction be used in only certain types of cases? Conversely, should it be used in all cases, and should the judge tell the jury that he gives the instruction in every case?

CHAPTER XIV

EYEWITNESS IDENTIFICATION

[T]here is almost nothing more convincing than a live human being who takes the stand, points a finger at the defendant and says "That's the one!"

Watkins v. Sowders, 449 U.S. 341, 352 (1981) (Brennan, J., dissenting)

So convincing, yet so unreliable. As of 2020, of the 375 DNA exonerations documented by the Innocence Project, 69 percent have involved an eyewitness identification. The Supreme Court has long recognized the fallibility of eyewitness identification yet has struggled with how to address the issue and how if at all to incorporate the ongoing developments of the social science on the subject into its case law.

Section A of this chapter considers eyewitness identification and the extent to which a criminal suspect or defendant has a right to counsel in connection with an investigative proceeding at which he or a photograph of him is presented to a putative trial witness for identification. Section B examines what limitations due process guarantees may impose on the admissibility of identification evidence at trial.

A. EYEWITNESS IDENTIFICATION AND THE RIGHT TO COUNSEL

United States v. Wade
388 U.S. 218 (1967)

Mr. Justice BRENNAN delivered the opinion of the Court.

The question here is whether courtroom identifications of an accused at trial are to be excluded from evidence because the accused was exhibited to the witnesses before trial at a post-indictment lineup conducted for identification purposes without notice to and in the absence of the accused's appointed counsel.

The federally insured bank in Eustace, Texas, was robbed on September 21, 1964. A man with a small strip of tape on each side of his face entered the bank, pointed a pistol at the female cashier and the vice president, the only persons in the bank at the time, and forced them to fill a pillowcase with the bank's money. The man then drove away with an accomplice who had been waiting in a stolen car outside the bank. On March 23, 1965, an indictment was returned against respondent, Wade, and two others for conspiring to rob the bank, and against Wade and the accomplice for the robbery itself. Wade was arrested on April 2, and counsel was appointed to represent him on April 26. Fifteen days later an FBI agent, without notice to Wade's lawyer, arranged to have the two bank employees observe a lineup made up of Wade and five or six other prisoners and conducted in a courtroom of the local county courthouse. Each person in the line wore strips of tape such as allegedly worn by the robber and upon direction each said something like "put the money in the bag," the words allegedly uttered by the robber. Both bank employees identified Wade in the lineup as the bank robber.

At trial the two employees, when asked on direct examination if the robber was in the courtroom, pointed to Wade. The prior lineup identification was then elicited from both employees on cross-examination. At the close of testimony, Wade's counsel moved for a judgment of acquittal or, alternatively, to strike the bank officials' courtroom identifications on the ground that conduct of the lineup, without notice to and in the absence of his appointed counsel, violated his Fifth Amendment privilege against self-incrimination and his Sixth Amendment right to the assistance of counsel. The motion was denied, and Wade was convicted. The Court of Appeals for the Fifth Circuit reversed the conviction and ordered a new trial at which the in-court identification evidence was to be excluded, holding that, though the lineup did not violate Wade's Fifth Amendment rights, "the lineup, held as it was, in the absence of counsel, already chosen to represent appellant, was a violation of his Sixth Amendment rights." We granted certiorari and set the case for oral argument with *Gilbert* and *Stovall*. We reverse the judgment of the Court of Appeals and remand to that court with direction to enter a new judgment vacating the conviction and remanding the case to the District Court for further proceedings consistent with this opinion.

* * *

II

The fact that the lineup involved no violation of Wade's privilege against self-incrimination does not, however, dispose of his contention that the courtroom identifications should have been excluded because the lineup was conducted without notice to and in the absence of his counsel. Our rejection of the right to counsel claim in *Schmerber* rested on our conclusion in that case that "(n)o issue of counsel's ability to assist petitioner in respect of any rights he did possess is presented." In contrast, in this case it is urged that the assistance of counsel at the lineup was indispensable to protect Wade's most basic right as a criminal defendant — his right to a fair trial at which the witnesses against him might be meaningfully cross-examined.

The Framers of the Bill of Rights envisaged a broader role for counsel than under the practice then prevailing in England of merely advising his client in "matters of law," and eschewing any responsibility for "matters of fact." The constitutions in at least 11 of the 13 States expressly or impliedly abolished this distinction. *Powell v. State of Alabama*. "Though the colonial provisions about counsel were in accord on few things, they agreed on the necessity of abolishing the facts-law distinction; the colonists appreciated that if a defendant were forced to stand alone against the state, his case was foredoomed." This background is reflected in the scope given by our decisions to the Sixth Amendment's guarantee to an accused of the assistance of counsel for his defense. When the Bill of Rights was adopted, there were no organized police forces as we know them today. The accused confronted the prosecutor and the witnesses against him, and the evidence was marshalled, largely at the trial itself. In contrast, today's law enforcement machinery involves critical confrontations of the accused by the prosecution at pretrial proceedings where the results might well settle the accused's fate and reduce the trial itself to a mere formality. In recognition of these realities of modern criminal prosecution, our cases have construed the Sixth Amendment guarantee to apply to "critical" stages of the proceedings. The guarantee reads: "In all criminal prosecutions, the accused shall enjoy the right . . . to have the Assistance of Counsel for his defence." The plain wording of this guarantee thus encompasses counsel's assistance whenever necessary to assure a meaningful "defence."

A. Eyewitness Identification and the Right to Counsel

As early as *Powell v. State of Alabama, supra,* we recognized that the period from arraignment to trial was "perhaps the most critical period of the proceedings," during which the accused "requires the guiding hand of counsel," if the guarantee is not to prove an empty right. That principle has since been applied to require the assistance of counsel at the type of arraignment — for example, that provided by Alabama — where certain rights might be sacrificed or lost: "What happens there may affect the whole trial. Available defenses may be irretrievably lost, if not then and there asserted. . . ." The principle was also applied in *Massiah*, where we held that incriminating statements of the defendant should have been excluded from evidence when it appeared that they were overheard by federal agents who, without notice to the defendant's lawyer, arranged a meeting between the defendant and an accomplice turned informant. We said that "(a)nything less . . . might deny a defendant 'effective representation by counsel at the only stage when legal aid and advice would help him.'"

In *Escobedo*, we drew upon the rationale of *Hamilton* and *Massiah* in holding that the right to counsel was guaranteed at the point where the accused, prior to arraignment, was subjected to secret interrogation despite repeated requests to see his lawyer. We again noted the necessity of counsel's presence if the accused was to have a fair opportunity to present a defense at the trial itself:

> The rule sought by the State here, however, would make the trial no more than an appeal from the interrogation; and the "right to use counsel at the formal trial (would be) a very hollow thing (if), for all practical purposes, the conviction is already assured by pretrial examination." . . . "One can imagine a cynical prosecutor saying: 'Let them have the most illustrious counsel, now. They can't escape the noose. There is nothing that counsel can do for them at the trial.'"

Finally in *Miranda*, the rules established for custodial interrogation included the right to the presence of counsel. The result was rested on our finding that this and the other rules were necessary to safeguard the privilege against self-incrimination from being jeopardized by such interrogation.

Of course, nothing decided or said in the opinions in the cited cases links the right to counsel only to protection of Fifth Amendment rights. Rather those decisions "no more than (reflect) a constitutional principle established as long ago as *Powell v. Alabama*. . . ." *Massiah v. United States*. It is central to that principle that in addition to counsel's presence at trial, the accused is guaranteed that he need not stand alone against the State at any stage of the prosecution, formal or informal, in court or out, where counsel's absence might derogate from the accused's right to a fair trial. The security of that right is as much the aim of the right to counsel as it is of the other guarantees of the Sixth Amendment — the right of the accused to a speedy and public trial by an impartial jury, his right to be informed of the nature and cause of the accusation, and his right to be confronted with the witnesses against him and to have compulsory process for obtaining witnesses in his favor. The presence of counsel at such critical confrontations, as at the trial itself, operates to assure that the accused's interests will be protected consistently with our adversary theory of criminal prosecution.

In sum, the principle of *Powell v. Alabama* and succeeding cases requires that we scrutinize any pretrial confrontation of the accused to determine whether the presence of his counsel is necessary to preserve the defendant's basic right to a fair trial as affected by his right meaningfully to cross-examine the witnesses against him and to have effective assistance of counsel at the trial itself. It calls upon us to analyze whether potential substantial prejudice to defendant's rights inheres in the particular confrontation and the ability of counsel to help avoid that prejudice.

III

The Government characterizes the lineup as a mere preparatory step in the gathering of the prosecution's evidence, not different — for Sixth Amendment purposes — from various other preparatory steps, such as systematized or scientific analyzing of the accused's fingerprints, blood sample, clothing, hair, and the like. We think there are differences which preclude such stages being characterized as critical stages at which the accused has the right to the presence of his counsel. Knowledge of the techniques of science and technology is sufficiently available, and the variables in techniques few enough, that the accused has the opportunity for a meaningful confrontation of the Government's case at trial through the ordinary processes of cross-examination of the Government's expert witnesses and the presentation of the evidence of his own experts. The denial of a right to have his counsel present at such analyses does not therefore violate the Sixth Amendment; they are not critical stages since there is minimal risk that his counsel's absence at such stages might derogate from his right to a fair trial.

IV

But the confrontation compelled by the State between the accused and the victim or witnesses to a crime to elicit identification evidence is peculiarly riddled with innumerable dangers and variable factors which might seriously, even crucially, derogate from a fair trial. The vagaries of eyewitness identification are well-known; the annals of criminal law are rife with instances of mistaken identification. Mr. Justice Frankfurter once said: "What is the worth of identification testimony even when uncontradicted? The identification of strangers is proverbially untrustworthy. The hazards of such testimony are established by a formidable number of instances in the records of English and American trials. These instances are recent — not due to the brutalities of ancient criminal procedure." The Case of Sacco and Vanzetti 30 (1927). A major factor contributing to the high incidence of miscarriage of justice from mistaken identification has been the degree of suggestion inherent in the manner in which the prosecution presents the suspect to witnesses for pretrial identification. A commentator has observed that "(t)he influence of improper suggestion upon identifying witnesses probably accounts for more miscarriages of justice than any other single factor — perhaps it is responsible for more such errors than all other factors combined." Suggestion can be created intentionally or unintentionally in many subtle ways. And the dangers for the suspect are particularly grave when the witness' opportunity for observation was insubstantial, and thus his susceptibility to suggestion the greatest.

Moreover, "(i)t is a matter of common experience that, once a witness has picked out the accused at the line-up, he is not likely to go back on his word later on, so that in practice the issue of identity may (in the absence of other relevant evidence) for all practical purposes be determined there and then, before the trial."

The pretrial confrontation for purpose of identification may take the form of a lineup, also known as an "identification parade" or "showup," as in the present case, or presentation of the suspect alone to the witness, as in *Stovall v. Denno, supra*. It is obvious that risks of suggestion attend either form of confrontation and increase the dangers inhering in eyewitness identification. But as is the case with secret interrogations, there is serious difficulty in depicting what transpires at lineups and other forms of identification confrontations. "Privacy results in secrecy and this in turn results in a gap in our knowledge as to what in fact goes on. . . ." *Miranda*. For the same reasons, the defense can seldom reconstruct the manner and mode of lineup identification for judge or jury at trial. Those participating in a lineup with the accused may often be police officers; in any event, the participants' names are rarely recorded or divulged at trial. The impediments to an objective observation are increased when the victim is the witness. Lineups are prevalent in rape and robbery prosecutions and present a particular hazard that a victim's understandable outrage may excite vengeful or spiteful motives. In any event, neither witnesses nor lineup participants are apt to be alert for conditions prejudicial to the suspect. And if they were, it would likely be of scant benefit to the suspect since neither witnesses nor lineup participants are likely to be schooled in the detection of suggestive influences. Improper influences may go undetected by a suspect, guilty or not, who experiences the emotional tension which we might expect in one being confronted with potential accusers. Even when he does observe abuse, if he has a criminal record he may be reluctant to take the stand and open up the admission of prior convictions. Moreover any protestations by the suspect of the fairness of the lineup made at trial are likely to be in vain; the jury's choice is between the accused's unsupported version and that of the police officers present. In short, the accused's inability effectively to reconstruct at trial any unfairness that occurred at the lineup may deprive him of his only opportunity meaningfully to attack the credibility of the witness' courtroom identification.

What facts have been disclosed in specific cases about the conduct of pretrial confrontations for identification illustrate both the potential for substantial prejudice to the accused at that stage and the need for its revelation at trial. A commentator provides some striking examples:

> In a Canadian case . . . the defendant had been picked out of a lineup of six men, of which he was the only Oriental. On other cases, a black-haired suspect was placed among a group of light-haired persons, tall suspects have been made to stand with short nonsuspects, and, in a case where the perpetrator of the crime was known to be a youth, a suspect under twenty was placed in a lineup with five other persons, all of whom were forty or over.

Similarly state reports, in the course of describing prior identifications admitted as evidence of guilt, reveal numerous instances of suggestive procedures, for example, that all in the lineup but the suspect were known to the identifying witness, that the other participants in a lineup were grossly dissimilar in appearance to the suspect, that only the suspect was required to wear distinctive clothing which the culprit allegedly wore, that the witness is told by the police that they have caught the culprit after which the defendant is brought before the witness alone or is viewed in jail, that the suspect is pointed out before or during a lineup, and that the participants in the lineup are asked to try on an article of clothing which fits only the suspect.

The potential for improper influence is illustrated by the circumstances, insofar as they appear, surrounding the prior identifications in the three cases we decide today. In the present case, the testimony of the identifying witnesses elicited on cross-examination revealed that those witnesses were taken to the courthouse and seated in the courtroom to await assembly of the lineup. The courtroom faced on a hallway observable to the witnesses through an open door. The cashier testified that she saw Wade "standing in the hall" within sight of an FBI agent. Five or six other prisoners later appeared in the hall. The vice president testified that he saw a person in the hall in the custody of the agent who "resembled the person that we identified as the one that had entered the bank."

The lineup in *Gilbert, supra,* was conducted in an auditorium in which some 100 witnesses to several alleged state and federal robberies charged to Gilbert made wholesale identifications of Gilbert as the robber in each other's presence, a procedure said to be fraught with dangers of suggestion. And the vice of suggestion created by the identification in *Stovall, supra,* was the presentation to the witness of the suspect alone handcuffed to police officers. It is hard to imagine a situation more clearly conveying the suggestion to the witness that the one presented is believed guilty by the police.

The few cases that have surfaced therefore reveal the existence of a process attended with hazards of serious unfairness to the criminal accused and strongly suggest the plight of the more numerous defendants who are unable to ferret out suggestive influences in the secrecy of the confrontation. We do not assume that these risks are the result of police procedures intentionally designed to prejudice an accused. Rather we assume they derive from the dangers inherent in eyewitness identification and the suggestibility inherent in the context of the pretrial identification. Williams & Hammelmann, in one of the most comprehensive studies of such forms of identification, said, "(T)he fact that the police themselves have, in a given case, little or no doubt that the man put up for identification has committed the offense, and that their chief pre-occupation is with the problem of getting sufficient proof, because he has not 'come clean,' involves a danger that this persuasion may communicate itself even in a doubtful case to the witness in some way. . . ."

Insofar as the accused's conviction may rest on a courtroom identification in fact the fruit of a suspect pretrial identification which the accused is helpless to subject to effective scrutiny at trial, the accused is deprived of that right of cross-examination which is an essential safeguard to his right to confront the witnesses against him. And even though cross-examination is a precious safeguard to a fair trial, it cannot be viewed as an absolute assurance of accuracy and reliability. Thus in the present context, where so many variables and pitfalls exist, the first line of defense must be the prevention of unfairness and the lessening of the hazards of eyewitness identification at the lineup itself. The trial which might determine the accused's fate may well not be that in the courtroom but that at the pretrial confrontation, with the State aligned against the accused, the witness the sole jury, and the accused unprotected against the overreaching, intentional or unintentional, and with little or no effective appeal from the judgment there rendered by the witness— "that's the man."

Since it appears that there is grave potential for prejudice, intentional or not, in the pretrial lineup, which may not be capable of reconstruction at trial, and since presence of counsel itself can often avert prejudice and assure a meaningful confrontation at trial, there can be little doubt that for Wade the postindictment lineup was a critical stage of the prosecution at which he was "as much entitled to such aid (of counsel) . . . as at the trial itself." Thus both Wade and his counsel should have been notified of the impending lineup, and counsel's presence should have been a requisite to conduct of the lineup, absent an "intelligent waiver." No substantial countervailing policy considerations have been advanced against the requirement of the presence of counsel. Concern is expressed that the requirement will forestall prompt identifications and result in obstruction of the confrontations. As for the first, we note that in the two cases in which the right to counsel is today held to apply, counsel had already been appointed and no argument is made in either case that notice to counsel would have prejudicially delayed the confrontations. Moreover, we leave open the question whether the presence of substitute counsel might not suffice where notification and presence of the suspect's own counsel would result in prejudicial delay. And to refuse to recognize the right to counsel for fear that counsel will obstruct the course of justice is contrary to the basic assumptions upon which this Court has operated in Sixth Amendment cases. We rejected similar logic in *Miranda*, concerning presence of counsel during custodial interrogation:

> (A)n attorney is merely exercising the good professional judgment he has been taught. This is not cause for considering the attorney a menace to law enforcement. He is merely carrying out what he is sworn to do under his oath—to protect to the extent of his ability the rights of his client. In fulfilling this responsibility the attorney plays a vital role in the administration of criminal justice under our Constitution.

In our view counsel can hardly impede legitimate law enforcement; on the contrary, for the reasons expressed, law enforcement may be assisted by preventing the infiltration of taint in the prosecution's identification evidence. That result cannot help the guilty avoid conviction but can only help assure that the right man has been brought to justice.

Legislative or other regulations, such as those of local police departments, which eliminate the risks of abuse and unintentional suggestion at lineup proceedings and the impediments to meaningful confrontation at trial may also remove the basis for regarding the stage as "critical." But neither Congress nor the federal authorities have seen fit to provide a solution. What

A. Eyewitness Identification and the Right to Counsel

we hold today "in no way creates a constitutional straitjacket which will handicap sound efforts at reform, nor is it intended to have this effect." *Miranda.*

V

We come now to the question whether the denial of Wade's motion to strike the courtroom identification by the bank witnesses at trial because of the absence of his counsel at the lineup required, as the Court of Appeals held, the grant of a new trial at which such evidence is to be excluded. We do not think this disposition can be justified without first giving the Government the opportunity to establish by clear and convincing evidence that the in-court identifications were based upon observations of the suspect other than the lineup identification. Where, as here, the admissibility of evidence of the lineup identification itself is not involved, a per se rule of exclusion of courtroom identification would be unjustified. A rule limited solely to the exclusion of testimony concerning identification at the lineup itself, without regard to admissibility of the courtroom identification, would render the right to counsel an empty one. The lineup is most often used, as in the present case, to crystallize the witnesses' identification of the defendant for future reference. We have already noted that the lineup identification will have that effect. The State may then rest upon the witnesses' unequivocal courtroom identifications, and not mention the pretrial identification as part of the State's case at trial. Counsel is then in the predicament in which Wade's counsel found himself — realizing that possible unfairness at the lineup may be the sole means of attack upon the unequivocal courtroom identification, and having to probe in the dark in an attempt to discover and reveal unfairness, while bolstering the government witness' courtroom identification by bringing out and dwelling upon his prior identification. Since counsel's presence at the lineup would equip him to attack not only the lineup identification but the courtroom identification as well, limiting the impact of violation of the right to counsel to exclusion of evidence only of identification at the lineup itself disregards a critical element of that right.

We think it follows that the proper test to be applied in these situations is that quoted in *Wong Sun*: "(W)hether, granting establishment of the primary illegality, the evidence to which instant objection is made has been come at by exploitation of that illegality or instead by means sufficiently distinguishable to be purged of the primary taint." Application of this test in the present context requires consideration of various factors; for example, the prior opportunity to observe the alleged criminal act, the existence of any discrepancy between any pre-lineup description and the defendant's actual description, any identification prior to lineup of another person, the identification by picture of the defendant prior to the lineup, failure to identify the defendant on a prior occasion, and the lapse of time between the alleged act and the lineup identification. It is also relevant to consider those facts which, despite the absence of counsel, are disclosed concerning the conduct of the lineup.

We doubt that the Court of Appeals applied the proper test for exclusion of the in-court identification of the two witnesses. The court stated that "it cannot be said with any certainty that they would have recognized appellant at the time of trial if this intervening lineup had not occurred," and that the testimony of the two witnesses "may well have been colored by the illegal procedure (and) was prejudicial." Moreover, the court was persuaded, in part, by the "compulsory verbal responses made by Wade at the instance of the Special Agent." This implies the erroneous holding that Wade's privilege against self-incrimination was violated so that the denial of counsel required exclusion.

On the record now before us we cannot make the determination whether the in-court identifications had an independent origin. This was not an issue at trial, although there is some evidence relevant to a determination. That inquiry is most properly made in the District Court. We therefore think the appropriate procedure to be followed is to vacate the conviction pending a hearing to determine whether the in-court identifications had an independent source, or whether, in any event, the introduction of the evidence was harmless error, and for the District Court to reinstate the conviction or order a new trial, as may be proper.

The judgment of the Court of Appeals is vacated and the case is remanded to that court with direction to enter a new judgment vacating the conviction and remanding the case to the District Court for further proceedings consistent with this opinion. It is so ordered.

THE CHIEF JUSTICE joins the opinion of the Court except for Part I, from which he dissents for the reasons expressed in the opinion of Mr. Justice FORTAS.

Mr. Justice DOUGLAS joins the opinion of the Court except for Part I. On that phase of the case he adheres to the dissenting views in *Schmerber*, since he believes that compulsory lineup violates the privilege against self-incrimination contained in the Fifth Amendment.

Mr. Justice WHITE, whom Mr. Justice HARLAN and Mr. Justice STEWART join, dissenting in part and concurring in part.

The Court has again propounded a broad constitutional rule barring the use of a wide spectrum of relevant and probative evidence, solely because a step in its ascertainment or discovery occurs outside the presence of defense counsel. This was the approach of the Court in *Miranda*. I objected then to what I thought was an uncritical and doctrinaire approach without satisfactory factual foundation. I have much the same view of the present ruling and therefore dissent from the judgment and from Parts II, IV, and V of the Court's opinion.

The Court's opinion is far-reaching. It proceeds first by creating a new per se rule of constitutional law: a criminal suspect cannot be subjected to a pretrial identification process in the absence of his counsel without violating the Sixth Amendment. If he is, the State may not buttress a later courtroom identification, of the witness by any reference to the previous identification. Furthermore, the courtroom identification is not admissible at all unless the State can establish by clear and convincing proof that the testimony is not the fruit of the earlier identification made in the absence of defendant's counsel—admittedly a heavy burden for the State and probably an impossible one. To all intents and purposes, courtroom identifications are barred if pretrial identifications have occurred without counsel being present.

The rule applies to any lineup, to any other techniques employed to produce an identification and a fortiori to a face-to-face encounter between the witness and the suspect alone, regardless of when the identification occurs, in time or place, and whether before or after indictment or information. It matters not how well the witness knows the suspect, whether the witness is the suspect's mother, brother, or long-time associate, and no matter how long or well the witness observed the perpetrator at the scene of the crime. The kidnap victim who has lived for days with his abductor is in the same category as the witness who has had only a fleeting glimpse of the criminal. Neither may identify the suspect without defendant's counsel being present. The same strictures apply regardless of the number of other witnesses who positively identify the defendant and regardless of the corroborative evidence showing that it was the defendant who had committed the crime.

The premise for the Court's rule is not the general unreliability of eyewitness identifications nor the difficulties inherent in observation, recall, and recognition. The Court assumes a narrower evil as the basis for its rule—improper police suggestion which contributes to erroneous identifications. The Court apparently believes that improper police procedures are so widespread that a broad prophylactic rule must be laid down, requiring the presence of counsel at all pretrial identifications, in order to detect recurring instances of police misconduct. I do not share this pervasive distrust of all official investigations. None of the materials the Court relies upon supports it. Certainly, I would bow to solid fact, but the Court quite obviously does not have before it any reliable, comprehensive survey of current police practices on which to base its new rule. Until it does, the Court should avoid excluding relevant evidence from state criminal trials.

The Court goes beyond assuming that a great majority of the country's police departments are following improper practices at pretrial identifications. To find the lineup a "critical" stage of the proceeding and to exclude identifications made in the absence of counsel, the Court must also assume that police "suggestion," if it occurs at all, leads to erroneous rather than accurate identifications and that reprehensible police conduct will have an unavoidable and largely undiscoverable impact on the trial. This in turn assumes that there is now no adequate source from which defense counsel can learn about the circumstances of the pretrial identification in order to place before the jury all of the considerations which should enter into an appraisal of courtroom identification evidence. But these are treacherous and unsupported assumptions resting as they do on the notion that the defendant will not be aware, that the police and the witnesses will forget or prevaricate, that defense counsel will be unable to bring out the truth and that neither jury, judge, nor appellate court is a sufficient safeguard against unacceptable police conduct occurring at a pretrial identification procedure. I am unable to share the Court's view of the willingness of the police and the ordinary citizen witness to dissemble, either with respect to the identification of the defendant or with respect to the circumstances surrounding a pretrial identification.

There are several striking aspects to the Court's holding. First, the rule does not bar courtroom identifications where there have been no previous identifications in the presence of the police, although when identified in the courtroom, the defendant is known to be in custody and charged with the commission of a crime. Second, the Court seems to say that if suitable legislative standards were adopted for the conduct of pretrial identifications, thereby lessening the hazards in such confrontations, it would not insist on the presence of counsel. But if this is true, why does not the Court simply fashion what it deems to be constitutionally acceptable procedures for the authorities to follow? Certainly the Court is correct in suggesting that the new rule will be wholly inapplicable where police departments themselves have established suitable safeguards.

Third, courtroom identification may be barred, absent counsel at a prior identification, regardless of the extent of counsel's information concerning the circumstances of the previous confrontation between witness and defendant—apparently even if there were recordings or sound-movies of the events as they occurred. But if the rule is premised on the defendant's right to have his counsel know, there seems little basis for not accepting other means to inform. A disinterested observer, recordings, photographs—any one of them would seem adequate to furnish the basis for a meaningful cross-examination of the eyewitness who identifies the defendant in the courtroom.

I share the Court's view that the criminal trial, at the very least, should aim at truthful factfinding, including accurate eyewitness identifications. I doubt, however, on the basis of our present information, that the tragic mistakes which have occurred in criminal trials are as much the product of improper police conduct as they are the consequence of the difficulties inherent in eyewitness testimony and in resolving evidentiary conflicts by court or jury. I doubt that the Court's new rule will obviate these difficulties, or that the situation will be measurably improved by inserting defense counsel into the investigative processes of police departments everywhere.

But, it may be asked, what possible state interest militates against requiring the presence of defense counsel at lineups? After all, the argument goes, he may do some good, he may upgrade the quality of identification evidence in state courts and he can scarcely do any harm. Even if true, this is a feeble foundation for fastening an ironclad constitutional rule upon state criminal procedures. Absent some reliably established constitutional violation, the processes by which the States enforce their criminal laws are their own prerogative. The States do have an interest in conducting their own affairs, an interest which cannot be displaced simply by saying that there are no valid arguments with respect to the merits of a federal rule emanating from this Court.

Beyond this, however, requiring counsel at pretrial identifications as an invariable rule trenches on other valid state interests. One of them is its concern with the prompt and efficient enforcement of its criminal laws. Identifications frequently take place after arrest but before an indictment is returned or an information is filed. The police may have arrested a suspect on probable cause but may still have the wrong man. Both the suspect and the State have every interest in a prompt identification at that stage, the suspect in order to secure his immediate release and the State because prompt and early identification enhances accurate identification and because it must know whether it is on the right investigative track. Unavoidably, however, the absolute rule requiring the presence of counsel will cause significant delay and it may very well result in no pretrial identification at all. Counsel must be appointed and a time arranged convenient for him and the witnesses. Meanwhile, it may be necessary to file charges against the suspect who may then be released on bail, in the federal system very often on his own recognizance, with neither the State nor the defendant having the benefit of a properly conducted identification procedure.

Nor do I think the witnesses themselves can be ignored. They will now be required to be present at the convenience of counsel rather than their own. Many may be much less willing to participate if the identification stage is transformed into an adversary proceeding not under the control of a judge. Others may fear for their own safety if their identity is known at an early date, especially when there is no way of knowing until the lineup occurs whether or not the police really have the right man.

Finally, I think the Court's new rule is vulnerable in terms of its own unimpeachable purpose of increasing the reliability of identification testimony.

Law enforcement officers have the obligation to convict the guilty and to make sure they do not convict the innocent. They must be dedicated to making the criminal trial a procedure for the ascertainment of the true facts surrounding the commission of the crime. To this extent, our so-called adversary system is not adversary at all; nor should it be. But defense counsel has no comparable obligation to ascertain or present the truth. Our system assigns him a different mission. He must be and is interested in preventing the conviction of the innocent, but, absent a voluntary plea of guilty, we also insist that he defend his client whether he is innocent or guilty. The State has the obligation to present the evidence. Defense counsel need present nothing, even if he knows what the truth is. He need not furnish any witnesses to the police, or reveal any confidences of his client, or furnish any other information to help the prosecution's case. If he can confuse a witness, even a truthful one, or make him appear at a disadvantage, unsure or indecisive, that will be his normal course. Our interest in not convicting the innocent permits counsel to put the State to its proof, to put the State's case in the worst possible light, regardless of what he thinks or knows to be the truth. Undoubtedly there are some limits which defense counsel must observe but more often than not, defense counsel will cross-examine a prosecution witness, and impeach him if he can, even if he thinks the witness is telling the truth, just as he will attempt to destroy a witness who he thinks is lying. In this respect, as part of our modified adversary system and as part of the duty imposed on the most honorable defense counsel, we countenance or require conduct which in many instances has little, if any, relation to the search for truth.

I would not extend this system, at least as it presently operates, to police investigations and would not require counsel's presence at pretrial identification procedures. Counsel's interest is in not having his client placed at the scene of the crime, regardless of his whereabouts. Some counsel may advise their clients to refuse to make any movements or to speak any words in a lineup or even to appear in one. To that extent the impact on truthful factfinding

A. Eyewitness Identification and the Right to Counsel

is quite obvious. Others will not only observe what occurs and develop possibility for later cross-examination but will hover over witnesses and begin their cross-examination then, menacing truthful factfinding as thoroughly as the Court fears the police now do. Certainly there is an implicit invitation to counsel to suggest rules for the lineup and to manage and produce it as best he can. I therefore doubt that the Court's new rule, at least absent some clearly defined limits on counsel's role, will measurably contribute to more reliable pretrial identifications. My fears are that it will have precisely the opposite result. It may well produce fewer convictions, but that is hardly a proper measure of its long-run acceptability. In my view, the State is entitled to investigate and develop its case outside the presence of defense counsel. This includes the right to have private conversations with identification witnesses, just as defense counsel may have his own consultations with these and other witnesses without having the prosecutor present.

Whether today's judgment would be an acceptable exercise of supervisory power over federal courts is another question. But as a constitutional matter, the judgment in this case is erroneous and although I concur in Parts I and III of the Court's opinion I respectfully register this dissent.

NOTES AND QUESTIONS

1. The Court notes that the rule it fashions in *Wade* might be displaced in the future by "[l]egislative or other regulations, such as those of local police departments, which eliminate the risks of abuse at lineup proceedings and the impediments to real confrontation at trial." What does this mean? That the rule in *Wade* is not constitutionally required? If not, what is the rule's source?

The dissent, in response to this point, asks, "[I]f this is true, why does not the Court simply fashion what it deems to be constitutionally acceptable procedures for the authorities to follow?" As we have seen, that is exactly what the Court had done the previous term in *Miranda*, prescribing standards for custodial interrogations. What reasons—either practical or institutional—might make the Court more hesitant to fashion standards in *Wade* than it was in *Miranda*?

2. The real problem at issue in *Wade*, of course, is not suggestive lineup identification procedures in themselves but rather the consequences of such procedures for witness identification at trial. As the Court puts it, "it is a matter of common sense that, once a witness has picked the accused at the lineup, he is not likely to go back on his word later on [i.e., in a subsequent lineup or at trial], so that in practice the issue of identity may (in the absence of other relevant evidence) for all practical purposes be determined then, before the trial."

Do you agree that this is simply a matter of common sense? Could defense counsel effectively cross-examine a witness to make this point? Should a defendant be entitled to a jury instruction to this effect?

The dissent also points out that nothing in *Wade* prevents "courtroom identifications where there have been no previous identifications in the presence of the police, although when identified in the courtroom, the defendant is known to be in custody and charged with the commission of a crime." Would a prosecutor be likely to gamble on a key witness's ability to identify the defendant, perhaps a stranger, for the first time in the courtroom years after the fact? What can defense counsel do to ensure the witness is not reflexively identifying the person in the courtroom who appears to be the defendant?

3. The dissent also notes, in decrying the burden the decision imposes on the prosecution, that the requirement of the presence of defense counsel applies no matter "how well the witness knows the suspect, whether the witness is the suspect's mother, brother or long-time associate." What do you make of this argument?

4. What exactly is the expected function of defense counsel at a pretrial lineup? The dissent plainly believes that defense counsel will attempt to obstruct the lineup proceedings. Are those fears realistic? What risks does defense counsel run in engaging in the sort of obstructionist tactics described by the dissent, especially in front of the witness? Is defense counsel's role at a lineup simply to act both as a deterrent to the police's use of suggestible procedures and also as a witness to any suggestible procedures that might take place? Does a defense lawyer really want to be a witness? Note that under ABA Model Rule 3.7 lawyers can be subject to disqualification at trial if they are material witnesses on factual issues.

5. The Court stresses that the problem it addresses is not necessarily one of intentionally prejudicial procedures but rather the "dangers inherent in eyewitness identification and the suggestibility inherent in the context of the pretrial identification." The dissent emphatically disagrees, noting that it does "not share [the Court's] pervasive distrust of all official investigations." Consider the facts of the *Wade* lineup. What exactly was the suggestibility problem? Was this problem the result of an intentionally prejudicial procedure or the suggestibility inherent in a pretrial lineup?

6. The Court remands the case so the trial court can make a determination whether, notwithstanding the suggestibility in the lineup procedure, the witness's in-court identification had an "independent origin." What does this mean? What factors would be relevant to this inquiry?

Gilbert v. California
388 U.S. 263 (1967)

Mr. Justice BRENNAN delivered the opinion of the Court.

This case was argued with *Wade*, and presents the same alleged constitutional error in the admission in evidence of in-court identifications there considered. . . .

Petitioner was convicted in the Superior Court of California of the armed robbery of the Mutual Savings and Loan Association of Alhambra and the murder of a police officer who entered during the course of the robbery. There were separate guilt and penalty stages of the trial before the same jury, which rendered a guilty verdict and imposed the death penalty. The California Supreme Court affirmed. We granted certiorari and set the case for argument with *Wade* and with *Stovall v. Denno*. If our holding today in *Wade* is applied to this case, the issue whether admission of the in-court and lineup identifications is constitutional error which requires a new trial could be resolved on this record only after further proceedings in the California courts. We must therefore first determine whether petitioner's other contentions warrant any greater relief.

• • •

Since none of the petitioner's other contentions warrants relief, the issue becomes what relief is required by application to this case of the principles today announced in *United States v. Wade, supra.*

Three eyewitnesses to the Alhambra crimes who identified Gilbert at the guilt stage of the trial had observed him at a lineup conducted without notice to his counsel in a Los Angeles auditorium 16 days after his indictment and after appointment of counsel. The manager of the apartment house in which incriminating evidence was found, and in which Gilbert allegedly resided, identified Gilbert in the courtroom and also testified, in substance, to her prior lineup identification on examination by the State. Eight witnesses who identified him in the courtroom at the penalty stage were not eyewitnesses to the Alhambra crimes but to other robberies allegedly committed by him. In addition to their in-court identifications, these witnesses also testified that they identified Gilbert at the same lineup.

The line-up was on a stage behind-bright lights which prevented those in the line from seeing the audience. Upwards of 100 persons were in the audience, each an eyewitness to one of the several robberies charged to Gilbert. The record is otherwise virtually silent as to what occurred at the lineup.

At the guilt stage, after the first witness, a cashier of the savings and loan association, identified Gilbert in the courtroom, defense counsel moved, out of the presence of the jury, to strike her testimony on the ground that she identified Gilbert at the pretrial lineup conducted in the absence of counsel in violation of the Sixth Amendment made applicable to the States by the Fourteenth Amendment. He requested a hearing outside the presence of the jury to present evidence supporting his claim that her in-court identification was, and others to be elicited by the State from other eyewitnesses would be, "predicated at least in large part upon their identification or purported identification of Mr. Gilbert at the showup. . . ." The trial judge denied the motion as premature. Defense counsel then elicited the fact of the cashier's lineup identification on cross-examination and again moved to strike her identification testimony. Without passing on the merits of the Sixth Amendment claim, the trial judge denied the motion on the ground that, assuming a violation, it would not in any event entitle Gilbert to suppression of the in-court identification. Defense counsel thereafter elicited the fact of lineup identifications from two other eyewitnesses who on direct examination identified Gilbert in the courtroom. Defense counsel unsuccessfully objected at the penalty stage, to the testimony of the eight witnesses to the other robberies that they identified Gilbert at the lineup.

The admission of the in-court identifications without first determining that they were not tainted by the illegal lineup but were of independent origin was constitutional error. *United States v. Wade, supra.* We there held that a post-indictment pretrial lineup at which the accused is exhibited to identifying witnesses is a critical stage of the criminal prosecution; that police conduct of such a lineup without notice to and in the absence of his counsel denies the accused his Sixth Amendment right to counsel and calls in question the admissibility at trial of the in-court identifications of the accused by witnesses who attended the lineup. However, as in *Wade*, the record does not permit an informed judgment whether the in-court identifications at the two stages of the trial had an independent source. Gilbert is therefore entitled only to a vacation of his conviction pending the holding of such proceedings as the California Supreme Court may deem appropriate to afford the State the opportunity to establish that the in-court identifications had an independent source, or that their introduction in evidence was in any event harmless error.

Quite different considerations are involved as to the admission of the testimony of the manager of the apartment house at the guilt phase and of the eight witnesses at the penalty stage that they identified Gilbert at the lineup. That testimony is the direct result of the illegal lineup "come at by exploitation of (the primary) illegality." The State is therefore not entitled to an opportunity to show that that testimony had an independent source. Only a per se exclusionary rule as to such testimony can be an effective sanction to assure that law enforcement authorities will respect the accused's constitutional right to the presence of his counsel at the critical lineup. In the absence of legislative regulations adequate to avoid the hazards to a fair trial which inhere in lineups as presently conducted, the desirability of deterring the constitutionally objectionable practice must prevail over the undesirability of excluding relevant evidence. That conclusion is buttressed by the consideration that the witness' testimony of his lineup identification will enhance the impact of his in-court identification on the jury and seriously aggravate whatever derogation exists of the accused's right to a fair trial.

Judgment and conviction vacated and case remanded with directions.

NOTES AND QUESTIONS

1. As in *Wade*, the Court in *Gilbert* remands to the trial court for a determination whether the in-court identification by the cashier and two other employees of the bank allegedly robbed by Gilbert had an "independent origin." The Court reaches a different result as to the testimony of nine other witnesses who testified at the penalty stage. Why? On remand, with the benefit of the Court's decisions in *Wade* and *Gilbert*, what might the prosecutor do at the penalty stage to try to introduce the testimony of the witnesses to the other bank robberies?

2. What is the most disturbing aspect of the lineup procedure in *Gilbert*? Are there any other facts necessary to fully understand the procedure that was used? What do you make of the fact that the auditorium where the lineup was conducted was "used for that purpose by the Los Angeles police"?

3. Note the trial court's apparently indifferent reaction to defense counsel's efforts to exclude the eyewitnesses' in-court identifications, despite the extreme suggestibility of the lineup procedures. It appears that defense counsel may have only argued that the in-court identifications should be suppressed because of the lack of counsel at the pretrial lineup. Any theories as to why the argument was so limited?

Shortly after the decisions in *Wade* and *Gilbert*, the Court drew back from their full implication, limiting the right to counsel to post-indictment identification procedures.

Kirby v. Illinois
406 U.S. 682 (1972)

Mr. Justice STEWART announced the judgment of the Court and an opinion in which THE CHIEF JUSTICE, Mr. Justice BLACKMUN, and Mr. Justice REHNQUIST join.

In *Wade* and *Gilbert*, this Court held "that a post-indictment pretrial lineup at which the accused is exhibited to identifying witnesses is a critical stage of the criminal prosecution; that police conduct of such a lineup without notice to and in the absence of his counsel denies the accused his Sixth (and Fourteenth) Amendment right to counsel and calls in question the admissibility at trial of the in-court identifications of the accused by witnesses who attended the lineup." Those cases further held that no "in-court identifications" are admissible in evidence if their "source" is a lineup conducted in violation of this constitutional standard. "Only a per se exclusionary rule as to such testimony can be an effective sanction," the Court said, "to assure that law enforcement authorities will respect the accused's constitutional right to the presence of his counsel at the critical lineup." In the present case we are asked to extend the *Wade-Gilbert* per se exclusionary rule to identification testimony based upon a police station showup that took place before the defendant had been indicted or otherwise formally charged with any criminal offense.

On February 21, 1968, a man named Willie Shard reported to the Chicago police that the previous day two men had robbed him on a Chicago street of a wallet containing, among other things, traveler's checks and a Social Security card. On February 22, two police officers stopped the petitioner and a companion, Ralph Bean, on West Madison Street in Chicago. When asked for identification, the petitioner produced a wallet that contained three traveler's checks and a Social Security card, all bearing the name of Willie Shard. Papers with Shard's name on them were also found in Bean's possession. When asked to explain his possession of Shard's property, the petitioner first said that the traveler's checks were "play money," and then told the officers that he had won them in a crap game. The officers then arrested the petitioner and Bean and took them to a police station.

A. Eyewitness Identification and the Right to Counsel

Only after arriving at the police station, and checking the records there, did the arresting officers learn of the Shard robbery. A police car was then dispatched to Shard's place of employment, where it picked up Shard and brought him to the police station. Immediately upon entering the room in the police station where the petitioner and Bean were seated at a table, Shard positively identified them as the men who had robbed him two days earlier. No lawyer was present in the room, and neither the petitioner nor Bean had asked for legal assistance, or been advised of any right to the presence of counsel.

More than six weeks later, the petitioner and Bean were indicted for the robbery of Willie Shard. Upon arraignment, counsel was appointed to represent them, and they pleaded not guilty. A pretrial motion to suppress Shard's identification testimony was denied, and at the trial Shard testified as a witness for the prosecution. In his testimony he described his identification of the two men at the police station on February 22, and identified them again in the courtroom as the men who had robbed him on February 20. He was cross-examined at length regarding the circumstances of his identification of the two defendants. The jury found both defendants guilty, and the petitioner's conviction was affirmed on appeal. The Illinois appellate court held that the admission of Shard's testimony was not error, relying upon an earlier decision of the Illinois Supreme Court, holding that the *Wade-Gilbert* per se exclusionary rule is not applicable to preindictment confrontations. We granted certiorari, limited to this question.

I

We note at the outset that the constitutional privilege against compulsory self-incrimination is in no way implicated here. The Court emphatically rejected the claimed applicability of that constitutional guarantee in *Wade* itself:

> Neither the lineup itself nor anything shown by this record that *Wade* was required to do in the lineup violated his privilege against self-incrimination. We have only recently reaffirmed that the privilege "protects an accused only from being compelled to testify against himself, or otherwise provide the State with evidence of a testimonial or communicative nature. . . ."
>
> We have no doubt that compelling the accused merely to exhibit his person for observation by a prosecution witness prior to trial involves no compulsion of the accused to give evidence having testimonial significance. It is compulsion of the accused to exhibit his physical characteristics, not compulsion to disclose to any knowledge he might have. . . .

It follows that the doctrine of *Miranda* has no applicability whatever to the issue before us; for the *Miranda* decision was based exclusively upon the Fifth and Fourteenth Amendment privilege against compulsory self-incrimination, upon the theory that custodial interrogation is inherently coercive.

The *Wade-Gilbert* exclusionary rule, by contrast, stems from a quite different constitutional guarantee — the guarantee of the right to counsel contained in the Sixth and Fourteenth Amendments. Unless all semblance of principled constitutional adjudication is to be abandoned, therefore, it is to the decisions construing that guarantee that we must look in determining the present controversy.

In a line of constitutional cases in this Court stemming back to the Court's landmark opinion in *Powell v. Alabama*, it has been firmly established that a person's Sixth and Fourteenth Amendment right to counsel attaches only at or after the time that adversary judicial proceedings have been initiated against him.

This is not to say that a defendant in a criminal case has a constitutional right to counsel only at the trial itself. The *Powell* case makes clear that the right attaches at the time of arraignment, and the Court has recently held that it exists also at the time of a preliminary hearing. But the point is that, while members of the Court have differed as to existence of the right to counsel in the contexts of some of the above cases, all of those cases have involved points of time at or after the initiation of adversary judicial criminal proceedings—whether by way of formal charge, preliminary hearing, indictment, information, or arraignment.

The only seeming deviation from this long line of constitutional decisions was *Escobedo*. But *Escobedo* is not apposite here for two distinct reasons. First, the Court in retrospect perceived that the "prime purpose" of *Escobedo* was not to vindicate the constitutional right to counsel as such, but, like *Miranda*, "to guarantee full effectuation of the privilege against self-incrimination." Secondly, and perhaps even more important for purely practical purposes, the Court has limited the holding of *Escobedo* to its own facts, and those facts are not remotely akin to the facts of the case before us.

The initiation of judicial criminal proceedings is far from a mere formalism. It is the starting point of our whole system of adversary criminal justice. For it is only then that the government has committed itself to prosecute, and only then that the adverse positions of government and defendant have solidified. It is then that a defendant finds himself faced with the prosecutorial forces of organized society, and immersed in the intricacies of substantive and procedural criminal law. It is this point, therefore, that marks the commencement of the "criminal prosecutions" to which alone the explicit guarantees of the Sixth Amendment are applicable.

In this case we are asked to import into a routine police investigation an absolute constitutional guarantee historically and rationally applicable only after the onset of formal prosecutorial proceedings. We decline to do so. Less than a year after *Wade* and *Gilbert* were decided, the Court explained the rule of those decisions as follows: "The rationale of those cases was that an accused is entitled to counsel at any 'critical stage of the prosecution,' and that a post-indictment lineup is such a 'critical stage.'" We decline to depart from that rationale today by imposing a per se exclusionary rule upon testimony concerning an identification that took place long before the commencement of any prosecution whatever.

II

What has been said is not to suggest that there may not be occasions during the course of a criminal investigation when the police do abuse identification procedures. Such abuses are not beyond the reach of the Constitution. As the Court pointed out in *Wade* itself, it is always necessary to "scrutinize any pretrial confrontation." The Due Process Clause of the Fifth and Fourteenth Amendments forbids a lineup that is unnecessarily suggestive and conducive to irreparable mistaken identification. When a person has not been formally charged with a criminal offense, *Stovall* strikes the appropriate constitutional balance between the right of a suspect to be protected from prejudicial procedures and the interest of society in the prompt and purposeful investigation of an unsolved crime.

The judgment is affirmed.

[Chief Justice Burger and Justice Powell concurred.]

[Justices Brennan, Marshall, and Douglas dissented.]

NOTES AND QUESTIONS

1. We are told in a footnote that Kirby and Bean were stopped and questioned because the police believed Kirby was a man named Hampton who had been involved in a different offense. Did Kirby and Bean have a legal obligation to respond to the officers' questions? Putting aside the questionable strategy of Kirby's provision of information relating to a crime victim, did the two men have a legal obligation to produce identification? From the facts disclosed, was there probable cause for their arrest? If so, for what crime?

A. Eyewitness Identification and the Right to Counsel

2. The suggestiveness of the identification procedure used by the police here is undeniable, and the Court makes no effort to defend it. Oddly, there is no discussion about the extraordinary circumstances by which Shard came to identify the defendants in the police station and the conversations between Shard and the police officers in that regard. Neglect by defense counsel? How would you cross-examine Shard in order to bring out the suggestiveness of his identification?

3. Once the Court gets *Escobedo* out of the way, a move the dissent does not significantly quarrel with, it has no problem rejecting Kirby's claim on the ground that the right to counsel only attaches "after the initiation of adversary proceedings," which it observes is "far from a mere formalism." Do you agree? Can you think of situations in which the government may have "committed itself to prosecute" prior to formally charging a person?

4. The Court describes Shard's identification as occurring during a "routine police investigation," and also notes the defendants were not indicted until six weeks after the identification. The Court does not say whether they were released after the identification or held in jail on their original arrest. Does it matter? Would the result here have been any different if the defendants had been indicted the day after the identification?

5. The dissent points out that nothing in *Wade* turned on the fact that the identification procedure used there was post-indictment, and that "an arrest evidences the belief of the police that the perpetrator has been caught." *Id.* at 698. Is this generally true? Was it true in *Kirby*? The dissent also notes that a "post-arrest confrontation for identification is not a mere preparatory step in the gathering of the prosecution's evidence." *Id.* How burdensome would it be on the police to allow arrestees a right to counsel in such situations? How burdensome would it have been in *Kirby*?

Should *Wade* apply when a witness is asked to identify a suspect or defendant in a photo array, that is, an identification procedure where a witness is asked to identify a potential or actual defendant from a group of photographs?

United States v. Ash
413 U.S. 300 (1973)

Mr. Justice BLACKMUN delivered the opinion of the Court.

In this case the Court is called upon to decide whether the Sixth Amendment grants an accused the right to have counsel present whenever the Government conducts a post-indictment photographic display, containing a picture of the accused, for the purpose of allowing a witness to attempt an identification of the offender. The United States Court of Appeals for the District of Columbia Circuit, sitting en banc, held, by a 5-to-4 vote, that the accused possesses this right to counsel. The court's holding is inconsistent with decisions of the courts of appeals of nine other circuits. We granted certiorari to resolve the conflict and to decide this important constitutional question. We reverse and remand.

I

On the morning of August 26, 1965, a man with a stocking mask entered a bank in Washington, D.C., and began waving a pistol. He ordered an employee to hang up the telephone and instructed all others present not to move. Seconds later a second man, also wearing a stocking mask, entered the bank, scooped up money from tellers' drawers into a bag, and left. The gunman followed, and both men escaped through an alley. The robbery lasted three or four minutes.

Chapter XIV Eyewitness Identification

A Government informer, Clarence McFarland, told authorities that he had discussed the robbery with Charles J. Ash, Jr., the respondent here. Acting on this information, an FBI agent, in February 1966, showed five black-and-white mug shots of Negro males of generally the same age, height, and weight, one of which was of Ash, to four witnesses. All four made uncertain identifications of Ash's picture. At this time Ash was not in custody and had not been charged. On April 1, 1966, an indictment was returned charging Ash and a codefendant, John L. Bailey, in five counts related to this bank robbery.

Trial was finally set for May 1968, almost three years after the crime. In preparing for trial, the prosecutor decided to use a photographic display to determine whether the witnesses he planned to call would be able to make in-court identifications. Shortly before the trial, an FBI agent and the prosecutor showed five color photographs to the four witnesses who previously had tentatively identified the black-and-white photograph of Ash. Three of the witnesses selected the picture of Ash, but one was unable to make any selection. None of the witnesses selected the picture of Bailey which was in the group. This post-indictment identification provides the basis for respondent Ash's claim that he was denied the right to counsel at a "critical stage" of the prosecution.

No motion for severance was made, and Ash and Bailey were tried jointly. The trial judge held a hearing on the suggestive nature of the pretrial photographic displays. The judge did not make a clear ruling on suggestive nature, but held that the Government had demonstrated by "clear and convincing" evidence that in-court identifications would be "based on observation of the suspect other than the intervening observation."

At trial, the three witnesses who had been inside the bank identified Ash as the gunman, but they were unwilling to state that they were certain of their identifications. None of these made an in-court identification of Bailey. The fourth witness, who had been in a car outside the bank and who had seen the fleeing robbers after they had removed their masks, made positive in-court identifications of both Ash and Bailey. Bailey's counsel then sought to impeach this in-court identification by calling the FBI agent who had shown the color photographs to the witnesses immediately before trial. Bailey's counsel demonstrated that the witness who had identified Bailey in court had failed to identify a color photograph of Bailey. During the course of the examination, Bailey's counsel also, before the jury, brought out the fact that this witness had selected another man as one of the robbers. At this point the prosecutor became concerned that the jury might believe that the witness had selected a third person when, in fact, the witness had selected a photograph of Ash. After a conference at the bench, the trial judge ruled that all five color photographs would be admitted into evidence. The Court of Appeals held that this constituted the introduction of a post-indictment identification at the prosecutor's request and over the objection of defense counsel.

McFarland testified as a Government witness. He said he had discussed plans for the robbery with Ash before the event and, later, had discussed the results of the robbery with Ash in the presence of Bailey. McFarland was shown to possess an extensive criminal record and a history as an informer.

The jury convicted Ash on all counts. It was unable to reach a verdict on the charges against Bailey, and his motion for acquittal was granted. Ash received concurrent sentences on the several counts, the two longest being 80 months to 12 years.

The five-member majority of the Court of Appeals held that Ash's right to counsel, guaranteed by the Sixth Amendment, was violated when his attorney was not given the opportunity to be present at the photographic displays conducted in May 1968 before the trial.

The majority did not reach the issue of suggestiveness; their opinion implies, however, that they would order a remand for additional findings by the District Court. The majority refrained from deciding whether the in-court identifications could have independent bases, but expressed doubt that the identifications at the trial had independent origins.

A. Eyewitness Identification and the Right to Counsel

Dissenting opinions, joined by four judges, disagreed with the decision of the majority that the photographic identification was a "critical stage" requiring counsel, and criticized the majority's suggestion that the in-court identifications were tainted by defects in the photographic identifications.

. . .

III

Although the Court of Appeals' majority recognized the argument that "a major purpose behind the right to counsel is to protect the defendant from errors that he himself might make if he appeared in court alone," the court concluded that "other forms of prejudice," mentioned and recognized in *Wade*, could also give rise to a right to counsel. These forms of prejudice were felt by the court to flow from the possibilities for mistaken identification inherent in the photographic display.

We conclude that the dangers of mistaken identification, mentioned in *Wade*, were removed from context by the Court of Appeals and were incorrectly utilized as a sufficient basis for requiring counsel. Although *Wade* did discuss possibilities for suggestion and the difficulty for reconstructing suggestivity, this discussion occurred only after the Court had concluded that the lineup constituted a trial-like confrontation, requiring the "Assistance of Counsel" to preserve the adversary process by compensating for advantages of the prosecuting authorities.

The above discussion of *Wade* has shown that the traditional Sixth Amendment test easily allowed extension of counsel to a lineup. The similarity to trial was apparent, and counsel was needed to render "Assistance" in counterbalancing any "overreaching" by the prosecution.

After the Court in *Wade* held that a lineup constituted a trial-like confrontation requiring counsel, a more difficult issue remained in the case for consideration. The same changes in law enforcement that led to lineups and pretrial hearings also generated other events at which the accused was confronted by the prosecution. The Government had argued in *Wade* that if counsel was required at a lineup, the same forceful considerations would mandate counsel at other preparatory steps in the "gathering of the prosecution's evidence," such as, for particular example, the taking of fingerprints or blood samples.

The Court concluded that there were differences. Rather than distinguishing these situations from the lineup in terms of the need for counsel to assure an equal confrontation at the time, the Court recognized that there were times when the subsequent trial would cure a one-sided confrontation between prosecuting authorities and the uncounseled defendant. In other words, such stages were not "critical." Referring to fingerprints, hair, clothing, and other blood samples, the Court explained:

> Knowledge of the techniques of science and technology is sufficiently available, and the variables in techniques few enough, that the accused has the opportunity for a meaningful confrontation of the Government's case at trial through the ordinary processes of cross-examination of the Government's expert witnesses and the presentation of the evidence of his own experts.

The structure of *Wade*, viewed in light of the careful limitation of the Court's language to "confrontations," makes it clear that lack of scientific precision and inability to reconstruct an event are not the tests for requiring counsel in the first instance. These are, instead, the tests to determine whether confrontation with counsel at trial can serve as a substitute for counsel at the pretrial confrontation. If accurate reconstruction is possible, the risks inherent in any confrontation still remain, but the opportunity to cure defects at trial causes the confrontation to cease to be "critical." The opinion of the Court even indicated that changes in procedure might cause a lineup to cease to be a "critical" confrontation:

> Legislative or other regulations, such as those of local police departments, which eliminate the risks of abuse and unintentional suggestion at lineup proceedings and the impediments to meaningful confrontation at trial may also remove the basis for regarding the stage as "critical."

The Court of Appeals considered its analysis complete after it decided that a photographic display lacks scientific precision and ease of accurate reconstruction at trial. That analysis, under *Wade*, however, merely carries one to the point where one must establish that the trial itself can provide no substitute for counsel if a pretrial confrontation is conducted in the absence of counsel. Judge Friendly, writing for the Second Circuit in *United States v. Bennett* (1969), recognized that the "criticality" test of *Wade*, if applied outside the confrontation context, would result in drastic expansion of the right to counsel:

> None of the classical analyses of the assistance to be given by counsel, suggests that counsel must be present when the prosecution is interrogating witnesses in the defendant's absence even when, as here, the defendant is under arrest; counsel is rather to be provided to prevent the defendant himself from falling into traps devised by a lawyer on the other side and to see to it that all available defenses are proffered. Many other aspects of the prosecution's interviews with a victim or a witness to a crime afford just as much opportunity for undue suggestion as the display of photographs; so, too, do the defense's interviews, notably with alibi witnesses.

We now undertake the threshold analysis that must be addressed.

IV

A substantial departure from the historical test would be necessary if the Sixth Amendment were interpreted to give Ash a right to counsel at the photographic identification in this case. Since the accused himself is not present at the time of the photographic display, and asserts no right to be present, no possibility arises that the accused might be misled by his lack of familiarity with the law or overpowered by his professional adversary. Similarly, the counsel guarantee would not be used to produce equality in a trial-like adversary confrontation. Rather, the guarantee was used by the Court of Appeals to produce confrontation at an event that previously was not analogous to an adversary trial.

Even if we were willing to view the counsel guarantee in broad terms as a generalized protection of the adversary process, we would be unwilling to go so far as to extend the right to a portion of the prosecutor's trial-preparation interviews with witnesses. Although photography is relatively new, the interviewing of witnesses before trial is a procedure that predates the Sixth Amendment. In England in the 16th and 17th centuries counsel regularly interviewed witnesses before trial. The traditional counterbalance in the American adversary system for these interviews arises from the equal ability of defense counsel to seek and interview witnesses himself.

That adversary mechanism remains as effective for a photographic display as for other parts of pretrial interviews. No greater limitations are placed on defense counsel in constructing displays, seeking witnesses, and conducting photographic identifications than those applicable to the prosecution. Selection of the picture of a person other than the accused, or the inability of a witness to make any selection, will be useful to the defense in precisely the same manner that the selection of a picture of the defendant would be useful to the prosecution. In this very case, for example, the initial tender of the photographic display was by Bailey's counsel, who sought to demonstrate that the witness had failed to make a photographic identification. Although we do not suggest that equality of access to photographs removes all potential for abuse, it does remove any inequality in the adversary process itself and thereby fully satisfies the historical spirit of the Sixth Amendment's counsel guarantee.

A. Eyewitness Identification and the Right to Counsel **1205**

The argument has been advanced that requiring counsel might compel the police to observe more scientific procedures or might encourage them to utilize corporeal rather than photographic displays. This Court has recognized that improved procedures can minimize the dangers of suggestion. Commentators have also proposed more accurate techniques.

Pretrial photographic identifications, however, are hardly unique in offering possibilities for the actions of the prosecutor unfairly to prejudice the accused. Evidence favorable to the accused may be withheld; testimony of witnesses may be manipulated; the results of laboratory tests may be contrived. In many ways the prosecutor, by accident or by design, may improperly subvert the trial. The primary safeguard against abuses of this kind is the ethical responsibility of the prosecutor, who, as so often has been said, may "strike hard blows" but not "foul ones." If that safeguard fails, review remains available under due process standards. These same safeguards apply to misuse of photographs.

We are not persuaded that the risks inherent in the use of photographic displays are so pernicious that an extraordinary system of safeguards is required.

We hold, then, that the Sixth Amendment does not grant the right to counsel at photographic displays conducted by the Government for the purpose of allowing a witness to attempt an identification of the offender. This holding requires reversal of the judgment of the Court of Appeals.

Reversed and remanded.

[Justices Brennan, Douglas, and Marshall dissented.]

NOTES AND QUESTIONS

1. The Court attempts to distinguish *Wade* on the ground, among others, that unlike a photo array, the pretrial lineup in *Wade* was a "trial-like confrontation." Was this aspect of *Wade* important to the result? In what ways—apart from the presence of the defendant—is a pretrial lineup identification any more "trial-like" than a photo array identification? Does even the presence of the accused at a pretrial lineup make it any more trial-like than a photo array identification?

2. The trial in *Ash* was substantially an identification case, as the only other evidence against defendants was the testimony of a jailhouse informant, whose testimony was freighted with that fact as well as specific rewards and inducements he had received from the government. So identification evidence was critical to the prosecution.

Accordingly, what inferences, if any, do you draw from the fact that the prosecution deliberately chose not to do an in-person lineup, even though one of the witnesses specifically asked to see the defendant in person, a fact that defense counsel was presumably able to use effectively on cross-examination? Could it have been the obligation—clearcut by the time, as *Wade* was decided a year before the trial in *Ash*—that the presence of defense counsel would have been required at such an in-person lineup, whereas the law was unsettled as to whether the same was true as to photo array identifications? And given that the law was unsettled at the time with respect to photo arrays—nine circuits eventually had held by the time of the *Ash* decision that counsel's presence was not required at photo arrays but none had done so by the time of the trial in *Ash*—why do you think the prosecution did not give defense counsel the opportunity to attend the photo array identification?

3. Consider closely the facts of *Ash*: (1) the bank robbers wore stocking masks; (2) the crime lasted three to four minutes; (3) none of the witnesses was able, on the day of the crime, to provide a description of the robbers' facial characteristics; (4) five months later, pre-indictment, none of the witnesses was able to positively identify Ash from a black-and-white photo array that included his picture; (5) over two years after that photo array, on the literal eve of trial, three of the four witnesses suddenly were able to identify Ash from an array of color photos.

Chapter XIV Eyewitness Identification

What possible explanation, aside from the use of suggestive procedures, is there for the witnesses' newfound ability to identify Ash? Further, the witnesses who identified Ash from the eve-of-trial photo array were certainly aware that the trial was starting the next day and that they would be government witnesses. How might this dynamic have affected their susceptibility to suggestiveness? Any theories as to why the government waited until the eve of trial to do the second photo array?

4. Should the prosecutor have asked the grand jury to indict Ash based on the status of the investigation available at the time of indictment, that is, when there was not any identification evidence to corroborate the jailhouse informant's testimony? A prosecutor has no ethical obligation to put before the grand jury exculpatory evidence—that is, the lack of eyewitness testimony identifying Ash—and presumably the prosecutor did not do so here. Why might a prosecutor choose to put exculpatory evidence before the grand jury even if not required to do so?

5. The Court does not seriously dispute that pretrial photo array identifications have significant potential for suggestiveness. Instead it points out that many other aspects of the government's pretrial activities—preparing witnesses, for example—are as fraught with the potential for subversion as photo array identifications, and the principal safeguard against such abuse is the prosecutor's ethical obligations. Do you agree that witness preparation has the same potential for subversion as photo array identifications?

And what do you make of the Court's "counterbalance" point, that the government's unfettered right to interview witnesses before trial corresponds to "the equal ability of defense counsel to seek and interview witnesses himself"?

6. As the Court notes, neither defendant moved for a severance, that is, that the two defendants be tried separately. This led to an interesting bit of lawyering during the examination of the so-called fourth witness, who observed the robbers not in the bank but from a car outside the bank after the robbers—in the course of flight—had removed their masks. Only this witness was able to identify Bailey in court and, like the others, had been unable to identify Bailey from the photo array. Was it ethical for Bailey's counsel to leave the jury with the impression that the fourth witness was unable to identify Bailey at the photo array and had in fact identified someone else? Was the trial judge's cure appropriate?

B. EYEWITNESS IDENTIFICATION AND DUE PROCESS

The three cases in the preceding section involved the applicability of what might be regarded as a conventional criminal procedure remedy—whether the Sixth Amendment right to the assistance of counsel required that defense counsel's presence be permitted at a particular stage of the proceedings. The same day the Court decided *Wade* and *Gilbert*, however, the Court also decided *Stovall v. Denno*, 388 U.S. 293 (1967), which required the Court to consider whether, and under what circumstances, the Fourteenth Amendment Due Process Clause on its own terms precluded the admission of an in-court identification that was tainted by an impermissibly suggestive out-of-court pretrial identification.

Stovall v. Denno
388 U.S. 293 (1967)

Mr. Justice BRENNAN delivered the opinion of the Court.

This federal habeas corpus proceeding attacks collaterally a state criminal conviction for the same alleged constitutional errors in the admission of allegedly tainted identification evidence that were before us on direct review of the convictions involved in *Wade* and *Gilbert*.

This case therefore provides a vehicle for deciding the extent to which the rules announced in *Wade* and *Gilbert* — requiring the exclusion of identification evidence which is tainted by exhibiting the accused to identifying witnesses before trial in the absence of his counsel — are to be applied retroactively. A further question is whether in any event, on the facts of the particular confrontation involved in this case, petitioner was denied due process of law in violation of the Fourteenth Amendment.

Dr. Paul Behrendt was stabbed to death in the kitchen of his home in Garden City, Long Island, about midnight August 23, 1961. Dr. Behrendt's wife, also a physician, had followed her husband to the kitchen and jumped at the assailant. He knocked her to the floor and stabbed her 11 times. The police found a shirt on the kitchen floor and keys in a pocket which they traced to petitioner. They arrested him on the afternoon of August 24. An arraignment was promptly held but was postponed until petitioner could retain counsel.

Mrs. Behrendt was hospitalized for major surgery to save her life. The police, without affording petitioner time to retain counsel, arranged with her surgeon to permit them to bring petitioner to her hospital room about noon of August 25, the day after the surgery. Petitioner was handcuffed to one of five police officers who, with two members of the staff of the District Attorney, brought him to the hospital room. Petitioner was the only Negro in the room. Mrs. Behrendt identified him from her hospital bed after being asked by an officer whether he "was the man" and after petitioner repeated at the direction of an officer a "few words for voice identification." None of the witnesses could recall the words that were used. Mrs. Behrendt and the officers testified at the trial to her identification of the petitioner in the hospital room, and she also made an in-court identification of petitioner in the courtroom.

Petitioner was convicted and sentenced to death. The New York Court of Appeals affirmed without opinion. Petitioner pro se sought federal habeas corpus in the District Court for the Southern District of New York. He claimed that among other constitutional rights allegedly denied him at his trial, the admission of Mrs. Behrendt's identification testimony violated his rights under the Fifth, Sixth, and Fourteenth Amendments because he had been compelled to submit to the hospital room confrontation without the help of counsel and under circumstances which unfairly focused the witness' attention on him as the man believed by the police to be the guilty person. The District Court dismissed the petition after hearing argument on an unrelated claim of an alleged invalid search and seizure. On appeal to the Court of Appeals for the Second Circuit a panel of that court initially reversed the dismissal after reaching the issue of the admissibility of Mrs. Behrendt's identification evidence and holding it inadmissible on the ground that the hospital room identification violated petitioner's constitutional right to the assistance of counsel. The Court of Appeals thereafter heard the case en banc, vacated the panel decision, and affirmed the District Court. We granted certiorari, and set the case for argument with *Wade* and *Gilbert*. We hold that *Wade* and *Gilbert* affect only those cases and all future cases which involve confrontations for identification purposes conducted in the absence of counsel after this date. The rulings of *Wade* and *Gilbert* are therefore inapplicable in the present case. We think also that on the facts of this case petitioner was not deprived of due process of law in violation of the Fourteenth Amendment. The judgment of the Court of Appeals is, therefore, affirmed.

· · ·

II

We turn now to the question whether petitioner, although not entitled to the application of *Wade* and *Gilbert* to his case, is entitled to relief on his claim that in any event the confrontation conducted in this case was so unnecessarily suggestive and conducive to irreparable mistaken identification that he was denied due process of law. This is a recognized ground of

Chapter XIV Eyewitness Identification

attack upon a conviction independent of any right to counsel claim. The practice of showing suspects singly to persons for the purpose of identification, and not as part of a lineup, has been widely condemned. However, a claimed violation of due process of law in the conduct of a confrontation depends on the totality of the circumstances surrounding it, and the record in the present case reveals that the showing of Stovall to Mrs. Behrendt in an immediate hospital confrontation was imperative. The Court of Appeals, en banc, stated:

> Here was the only person in the world who could possibly exonerate Stovall. Her words, and only her words, "He is not the man" could have resulted in freedom for Stovall. The hospital was not far distant from the courthouse and jail. No one knew how long Mrs. Behrendt might live. Faced with the responsibility of identifying the attacker, with the need for immediate action and with the knowledge that Mrs. Behrendt could not visit the jail, the police followed the only feasible procedure and took Stovall to the hospital room. Under these circumstances, the usual police station line-up, which Stovall now argues he should have had, was out of the question.

The judgment of the Court of Appeals is affirmed. It is so ordered.

NOTES AND QUESTIONS

1. As for Stovall's due process claim, the Court notes that showing suspects singly to a witness—often called "show-ups"—"has been widely condemned," although it cites no case law in support of that point but only scholarly works, and the Court cites only one Fourth Circuit case as support for the general proposition that an "unnecessarily suggestive" identification procedure can be challenged on due process grounds. Perhaps this dearth of case law explains why the Court, in announcing that such a due process violation depends on the "totality of circumstances" says nothing about what the relevant circumstances are or about how the different circumstances are to be evaluated. What are the factors that should be considered? Can you imagine a set of considerations that would support a due process violation based on the facts of *Stovall*?

2. One factor that is plainly relevant to any conceivable test would be the existence of any "exigent circumstances" confronting the police, that is, circumstances that would make a lineup with or without the inclusion of counsel impractical. Those seem to exist here, as the only witness to the crime was on the brink of "major surgery to save her life."

So why does the Court pretend that the purpose of the hospital show-up was to potentially exonerate Stovall? If another factor in the "totality of circumstances" is the law enforcement need for the lineup, how does it factor in to such an analysis that the police were able to locate Stovall the next day based on materials from the crime scene? How does it factor in that there is no apparent reason why the police could not have assembled a photo array to present to the victim in the 18 to 24 hours between the arrest and the show-up?

Manson v. Brathwaite
432 U.S. 98 (1977)

Mr. Justice BLACKMUN delivered the opinion of the Court.

This case presents the issue as to whether the Due Process Clause of the Fourteenth Amendment compels the exclusion, in a state criminal trial, apart from any consideration of reliability, of pretrial identification evidence obtained by a police procedure that was both suggestive and unnecessary.

I

Jimmy D. Glover, a full-time trooper of the Connecticut State Police, in 1970 was assigned to the Narcotics Division in an undercover capacity. On May 5 of that year, about 7:45 p.m., e.d.t., and while there was still daylight, Glover and Henry Alton Brown, an informant, went to an apartment building at 201 Westland, in Hartford, for the purpose of purchasing narcotics from "Dickie Boy" Cicero, a known narcotics dealer. Cicero, it was thought, lived on the third floor of that apartment building. Glover and Brown entered the building, observed by back-up Officers D'Onofrio and Gaffey, and proceeded by stairs to the third floor. Glover knocked at the door of one of the two apartments served by the stairway. The area was illuminated by natural light from a window in the third floor hallway. The door was opened 12 to 18 inches in response to the knock. Glover observed a man standing at the door and, behind him, a woman. Brown identified himself. Glover then asked for "two things" of narcotics. The man at the door held out his hand, and Glover gave him two $10 bills. The door closed. Soon the man returned and handed Glover two glassine bags. While the door was open, Glover stood within two feet of the person from whom he made the purchase and observed his face. Five to seven minutes elapsed from the time the door first opened until it closed the second time.

Glover and Brown then left the building. This was about eight minutes after their arrival. Glover drove to headquarters where he described the seller to D'Onofrio and Gaffey. Glover at that time did not know the identity of the seller. He described him as being "a colored man, approximately five feet eleven inches tall, dark complexion, black hair, short Afro style, and having high cheekbones, and of heavy build. He was wearing at the time blue pants and a plaid shirt." D'Onofrio, suspecting from this description that respondent might be the seller, obtained a photograph of respondent from the Records Division of the Hartford Police Department. He left it at Glover's office. D'Onofrio was not acquainted with respondent personally but did know him by sight and had seen him "(s)everal times" prior to May 5. Glover, when alone, viewed the photograph for the first time upon his return to headquarters on May 7; he identified the person shown as the one from whom he had purchased the narcotics.

The toxicological report on the contents of the glassine bags revealed the presence of heroin. The report was dated July 16, 1970.

Respondent was arrested on July 27 while visiting at the apartment of a Mrs. Ramsey on the third floor of 201 Westland. This was the apartment at which the narcotics sale had taken place on May 5.

Respondent was charged, in a two-count information, with possession and sale of heroin. At his trial in January 1971, the photograph from which Glover had identified respondent was received in evidence without objection on the part of the defense. Glover also testified that, although he had not seen respondent in the eight months that had elapsed since the sale, "there (was) no doubt whatsoever" in his mind that the person shown on the photograph was respondent. Glover also made a positive in-court identification without objection.

No explanation was offered by the prosecution for the failure to utilize a photographic array or to conduct a lineup.

Respondent, who took the stand in his own defense, testified that on May 5, the day in question, he had been ill at his Albany Avenue apartment ("a lot of back pains, muscle spasms . . . a bad heart . . . high blood pressure . . . neuralgia in my face, and sinus,"), and that at no time on that particular day had he been at 201 Westland. His wife testified that she recalled, after her husband had refreshed her memory, that he was home all day on May 5. Doctor Wesley M. Vietzke, an internist and assistant professor of medicine at the University of Connecticut, testified that respondent had consulted him on April 15, 1970, and that he took a medical history from him, heard his complaints about his back and facial pain, and discovered that he had high blood pressure. The physician found respondent, subjectively, "in great discomfort." Respondent in fact underwent surgery for a herniated disc at L5 and S1 on August 17.

The jury found respondent guilty on both counts of the information. He received a sentence of not less than six nor more than nine years. His conviction was affirmed per curiam by the Supreme Court of Connecticut. That court noted the absence of an objection to Glover's in-court identification and concluded that respondent "has not shown that substantial injustice resulted from the admission of this evidence." Under Connecticut law, substantial injustice must be shown before a claim of error not made or passed on by the trial court will be considered on appeal.

Fourteen months later, respondent filed a petition for habeas corpus in the United States District Court for the District of Connecticut. He alleged that the admission of the identification testimony at his state trial deprived him of due process of law to which he was entitled under the Fourteenth Amendment. The District Court, by an unreported written opinion based on the court's review of the state trial transcript, dismissed respondent's petition. On appeal, the United States Court of Appeals for the Second Circuit reversed, with instructions to issue the writ unless the State gave notice of a desire to retry respondent and the new trial occurred within a reasonable time to be fixed by the District Judge.

In brief summary, the court felt that evidence as to the photograph should have been excluded, regardless of reliability, because the examination of the single photograph was unnecessary and suggestive. And, in the court's view, the evidence was unreliable in any event. We granted certiorari.

• • •

III

In the present case the District Court observed that the "sole evidence tying Brathwaite to the possession and sale of the heroin consisted in his identifications by the police undercover agent, Jimmy Glover." On the constitutional issue, the court stated that the first inquiry was whether the police used an impermissibly suggestive procedure in obtaining the out-of-court identification. . . . The court concluded that there was no substantial likelihood of irreparable misidentification. It referred to the facts: Glover was within two feet of the seller. The duration of the confrontation was at least a "couple of minutes." There was natural light from a window or skylight and there was adequate light to see clearly in the hall. Glover "certainly was paying attention to identify the seller." He was a trained police officer who realized that later he would have to find and arrest the person with whom he was dealing. He gave a detailed description to D'Onofrio. The reliability of this description was supported by the fact that it enabled D'Onofrio to pick out a single photograph that was thereafter positively identified by Glover. Only two days elapsed between the crime and the photographic identification. Despite the fact that another eight months passed before the in-court identification, Glover had "no doubt" that Brathwaite was the person who had sold him heroin.

The Court of Appeals [stated] that the exhibition of the single photograph to Glover was "impermissibly suggestive," and felt that, in addition, "it was unnecessarily so." There was no emergency and little urgency. . . . The court also concluded that for post-*Stovall* identifications, *Biggers* had not changed the existing rule. Thus: "Evidence of an identification unnecessarily obtained by impermissibly suggestive means must be excluded under *Stovall*. . . . No rules less stringent than these can force police administrators and prosecutors to adopt procedures that will give fair assurance against the awful risks of misidentification." Finally, the court said, even if this conclusion were wrong, the writ, nevertheless, should issue. It took

B. Eyewitness Identification and Due Process

judicial notice that on May 5, 1970, sunset at Hartford was at 7:53 p.m. It characterized Glover's duty as an undercover agent as one "to cause arrests to be made," and his description of the suspect as one that "could have applied to hundreds of Hartford black males." The in-court identification had "little meaning," for Brathwaite was at the counsel table. The fact that respondent was arrested in the very apartment where the sale was made was subject to a "not implausible" explanation from the respondent, "although evidently not credited by the jury." And the court was troubled by "the long and unexplained delay" in the arrest. It was too great a danger that the respondent was convicted because he was a man D'Onofrio had previously observed near the scene, was thought to be a likely offender, and was arrested when he was known to be in Mrs. Ramsey's apartment, rather than because Glover "really remembered him as the seller."

IV

Petitioner at the outset acknowledges that "the procedure in the instant case was suggestive (because only one photograph was used) and unnecessary" (because there was no emergency or exigent circumstance). The respondent, in agreement with the Court of Appeals, proposes a per se rule of exclusion that he claims is dictated by the demands of the Fourteenth Amendment's guarantee of due process. He rightly observes that this is the first case in which this Court has had occasion to rule upon strictly post-*Stovall* out-of-court identification evidence of the challenged kind.

• • •

The respondent here stresses the same theme and the need for deterrence of improper identification practice, a factor he regards as pre-eminent. Photographic identification, it is said, continues to be needlessly employed. He notes that the legislative regulation the Court had hoped *Wade* would engender has not been forthcoming. He argues that a totality rule cannot be expected to have a significant deterrent impact; only a strict rule of exclusion will have direct and immediate impact on law enforcement agents. Identification evidence is so convincing to the jury that sweeping exclusionary rules are required. Fairness of the trial is threatened by suggestive confrontation evidence, and thus, it is said, an exclusionary rule has an established constitutional predicate.

There are, of course, several interests to be considered and taken into account. . . . Usually the witness must testify about an encounter with a total stranger under circumstances of emergency or emotional stress. The witness' recollection of the stranger can be distorted easily by the circumstances or by later actions of the police. Thus, *Wade* and its companion cases reflect the concern that the jury not hear eyewitness testimony unless that evidence has aspects of reliability. It must be observed that both approaches before us are responsive to this concern. The per se rule, however, goes too far since its application automatically and peremptorily, and without consideration of alleviating factors, keeps evidence from the jury that is reliable and relevant.

The second factor is deterrence. Although the per se approach has the more significant deterrent effect, the totality approach also has an influence on police behavior. The police will guard against unnecessarily suggestive procedures under the totality rule, as well as the per se one, for fear that their actions will lead to the exclusion of identifications as unreliable.

The third factor is the effect on the administration of justice. Here the per se approach suffers serious drawbacks. Since it denies the trier reliable evidence, it may result, on occasion, in the guilty going free. Also, because of its rigidity, the per se approach may make error by the trial judge more likely than the totality approach. And in those cases in which the admission of identification evidence is error under the per se approach but not under the

Chapter XIV Eyewitness Identification

totality approach cases in which the identification is reliable despite an unnecessarily suggestive identification procedure reversal is a Draconian sanction. Certainly, inflexible rules of exclusion that may frustrate rather than promote justice have not been viewed recently by this Court with unlimited enthusiasm.

We therefore conclude that reliability is the linchpin in determining the admissibility of identification testimony for both pre- and post-*Stovall* confrontations. The factors to be considered . . . include the opportunity of the witness to view the criminal at the time of the crime, the witness' degree of attention, the accuracy of his prior description of the criminal, the level of certainty demonstrated at the confrontation, and the time between the crime and the confrontation. Against these factors is to be weighed the corrupting effect of the suggestive identification itself.

V

We turn, then, to the facts of this case and apply the analysis:

1. The opportunity to view. Glover testified that for two to three minutes he stood at the apartment door, within two feet of the respondent. The door opened twice, and each time the man stood at the door. The moments passed, the conversation took place, and payment was made. Glover looked directly at his vendor. It was near sunset, to be sure, but the sun had not yet set, so it was not dark or even dusk or twilight. Natural light from outside entered the hallway through a window. There was natural light, as well, from inside the apartment.

2. The degree of attention. Glover was not a casual or passing observer, as is so often the case with eyewitness identification. Trooper Glover was a trained police officer on duty and specialized and dangerous duty when he called at the third floor of 201 Westland in Hartford on May 5, 1970. Glover himself was a Negro and unlikely to perceive only general features of "hundreds of Hartford black males," as the Court of Appeals stated. It is true that Glover's duty was that of ferreting out narcotics offenders and that he would be expected in his work to produce results. But it is also true that, as a specially trained, assigned, and experienced officer, he could be expected to pay scrupulous attention to detail, for he knew that subsequently he would have to find and arrest his vendor. In addition, he knew that his claimed observations would be subject later to close scrutiny and examination at any trial.

3. The accuracy of the description. Glover's description was given to D'Onofrio within minutes after the transaction. It included the vendor's race, his height, his build, the color and style of his hair, and the high cheekbone facial feature. It also included clothing the vendor wore. No claim has been made that respondent did not possess the physical characteristics so described. D'Onofrio reacted positively at once. Two days later, when Glover was alone, he viewed the photograph D'Onofrio produced and identified its subject as the narcotics seller.

4. The witness' level of certainty. There is no dispute that the photograph in question was that of respondent. Glover, in response to a question whether the photograph was that of the person from whom he made the purchase, testified: "There is no question whatsoever." This positive assurance was repeated.

5. The time between the crime and the confrontation. Glover's description of his vendor was given to D'Onofrio within minutes of the crime. The photographic identification took place only two days later. We do not have here the passage of weeks or months between the crime and the viewing of the photograph.

These indicators of Glover's ability to make an accurate identification are hardly outweighed by the corrupting effect of the challenged identification itself. Although identifications arising

B. Eyewitness Identification and Due Process   1213

from single-photograph displays may be viewed in general with suspicion, we find in the instant case little pressure on the witness to acquiesce in the suggestion that such a display entails. D'Onofrio had left the photograph at Glover's office and was not present when Glover first viewed it two days after the event. There thus was little urgency and Glover could view the photograph at his leisure. And since Glover examined the photograph alone, there was no coercive pressure to make an identification arising from the presence of another. The identification was made in circumstances allowing care and reflection.

Although it plays no part in our analysis, all this assurance as to the reliability of the identification is hardly undermined by the facts that respondent was arrested in the very apartment where the sale had taken place, and that he acknowledged his frequent visits to that apartment.

Surely, we cannot say that under all the circumstances of this case there is "a very substantial likelihood of irreparable misidentification." Short of that point, such evidence is for the jury to weigh. We are content to rely upon the good sense and judgment of American juries, for evidence with some element of untrustworthiness is customary grist for the jury mill. Juries are not so susceptible that they cannot measure intelligently the weight of identification testimony that has some questionable feature.

Of course, it would have been better had D'Onofrio presented Glover with a photographic array including "so far as practicable . . . a reasonable number of persons similar to any person then suspected whose likeness is included in the array." The use of that procedure would have enhanced the force of the identification at trial and would have avoided the risk that the evidence would be excluded as unreliable. But we are not disposed to view D'Onofrio's failure as one of constitutional dimension to be enforced by a rigorous and unbending exclusionary rule. The defect, if there be one, goes to weight and not to substance.

We conclude that the criteria laid down in *Biggers* are to be applied in determining the admissibility of evidence offered by the prosecution concerning a post-*Stovall* identification, and that those criteria are satisfactorily met and complied with here.

The judgment of the Court of Appeals is reversed.

It is so ordered.

NOTES AND QUESTIONS

1. Do you agree with the Court's analysis of the five reliability factors with respect to Officer Glover's identification of the defendant?

2. As to the opportunity to view, doesn't the Court gloss over the fact that during most of the 5- to 7-minute interaction with the defendant the door to the apartment was closed, and that when open it was only cracked 12 to 18 inches? Does it make sense that the officer looked directly at the vendor? Does this seem like how an undercover officer—hoping to deflect any suspicion—would behave?

3. As to the accuracy of the description, isn't this essentially a generic description of a Black man except for the "high cheekbones" and clothing description, which of course is largely irrelevant under the circumstances here?

4. As to the level of certainty, isn't the level of confidence the officer showed at trial likely attributable to the fact that he was "locked in" to his earlier identification? As the Court specifically noted in *Wade*, this is one of the problems with suggestive lineup procedures. Do you think a police officer or a civilian witness is more likely to question their earlier identification?

5. Note that at trial defense counsel made no objection to the admission of Glover's in-court identification, and therefore may have not even cross-examined Glover on the reliability factors the decision ultimately turns on. As a consequence the evidence about Glover's description of the defendant, the "natural light," etc., came in just as the prosecution wanted it. Nor was there any development of the relationship between Officer Glover and Officer D'Onofrio, why D'Onofrio had access to a picture of defendant handy and why he suspected him, and why there was no attempt at any point to conduct a photo array or a lineup. How might exploration of these issues have helped development of a stronger case for exclusion?

6. In explaining its rejection of the "per se" test for a "reliability" test, the Court expresses confidence in "the good sense and judgment of American juries, for evidence of untrustworthiness is customary grist for the jury's mill." Certainly this is true as far as it goes. But wasn't part of the concern expressed by the Court in *Wade* due to the fact that eyewitness testimony is often so compelling to a jury notwithstanding its unreliability?

7. Suppose the per se test had been the law at the time of the investigation in *Manson*. How would the police (assuming they were well advised) have handled the investigation differently if that was the case? How burdensome would such compliance have been?

8. The Court notes that the district court found that "the sole evidence tying Brathwaite to the possession and sale of the heroin consisted in his identification by the police undercover agent, Jimmy Glover." Is this legally relevant to the application of either the per se or reliability tests? Might this lack of other evidence relate to the fact that the defendant was not arrested until almost three months after the undercover buy?

As noted by Professor Brandon Garrett, writing in 2012, in the decades since *Manson* the social science of eyewitness testimony has continued to develop in ways that cast doubt on *Manson's* reliability factors:

> Eyewitness identifications are designed to be a test of a witness's memory. Pioneering psychologists Elizabeth Loftus and Gary Wells, followed by many others, realized beginning in the late 1970s that eyewitness memory can be tested in lab experiments, and now a vast body of social science research has demonstrated that most of the five *Manson* "reliability" factors do not correlate at all with the reliability of an eyewitness's identification.

* * *

> A series of studies has shown that jurors rely strongly on the confidence of the eyewitness. Yet, confidence is not highly correlated with accuracy. The correlation is highly variable. In fact, a mistaken eyewitness may appear particularly confident. Why? A factor that strongly affects confidence is suggestion by the administrator. Expectations of the administrator affect the confidence of the eyewitness even if the suggestion is unconscious. The eyewitness may perceive cues that the police never intended to convey. That is why social scientists have long recommended that police administer double-blind lineups where the police officer does not know who is the suspect, and the eyewitness knows that the officer does not know. The way that police construct the lineup can enhance confidence. If police stack the lineup so that one photo stands out, the eyewitness not only will be more likely to identify the person highlighted, but the eyewitness will predictably be more certain. Feedback or reinforcement after the identification can also have a dramatic effect on confidence. If police say, "Good job, you picked the right one," then the eyewitness will tend to be far more certain. If police tell the eyewitness that a suspect had been arrested and would be present in the lineup, the eyewitness will likewise tend to be far more certain. Finally, studies suggest that repeated identification procedures create an enhanced risk that a witness will identify an innocent suspect. Even permitting more than one "lap" or viewing of a photo array increases the risk of errors. Likewise, routine preparation for trial, or even the suggestion that an eyewitness will later be cross-examined concerning an identification, has the effect of making an eyewitness more certain.

B. Eyewitness Identification and Due Process   **1215**

Brandon L. Garrett, *Eyewitness and Exclusion*, 65 Vand. L. Rev. 451, 468-71 (2012) (citations omitted).

In the next case the Court considers the admissibility of an out-of-court identification made under suggestive circumstances that were not attributable to any action by law enforcement.

Perry v. New Hampshire
565 U.S. 228 (2012)

Justice GINSBURG delivered the opinion of the Court.

In our system of justice, fair trial for persons charged with criminal offenses is secured by the Sixth Amendment, which guarantees to defendants the right to counsel, compulsory process to obtain defense witnesses, and the opportunity to cross-examine witnesses for the prosecution. Those safeguards apart, admission of evidence in state trials is ordinarily governed by state law, and the reliability of relevant testimony typically falls within the province of the jury to determine. This Court has recognized, in addition, a due process check on the admission of eyewitness identification, applicable when the police have arranged suggestive circumstances leading the witness to identify a particular person as the perpetrator of a crime.

An identification infected by improper police influence, our case law holds, is not automatically excluded. Instead, the trial judge must screen the evidence for reliability pretrial. If there is "a very substantial likelihood of irreparable misidentification," the judge must disallow presentation of the evidence at trial. But if the indicia of reliability are strong enough to outweigh the corrupting effect of the police-arranged suggestive circumstances, the identification evidence ordinarily will be admitted, and the jury will ultimately determine its worth.

We have not extended pretrial screening for reliability to cases in which the suggestive circumstances were not arranged by law enforcement officers. Petitioner requests that we do so because of the grave risk that mistaken identification will yield a miscarriage of justice. Our decisions, however, turn on the presence of state action and aim to deter police from rigging identification procedures, for example, at a lineup, showup, or photograph array. When no improper law enforcement activity is involved, we hold, it suffices to test reliability through the rights and opportunities generally designed for that purpose, notably, the presence of counsel at postindictment lineups, vigorous cross-examination, protective rules of evidence, and jury instructions on both the fallibility of eyewitness identification and the requirement that guilt be proved beyond a reasonable doubt.

I

A

Around 3 a.m. on August 15, 2008, Joffre Ullon called the Nashua, New Hampshire, Police Department and reported that an African-American male was trying to break into cars parked in the lot of Ullon's apartment building. Officer Nicole Clay responded to the call. Upon arriving at the parking lot, Clay heard what "sounded like a metal bat hitting the ground." She then saw petitioner Barion Perry standing between two cars. Perry walked toward Clay, holding two car-stereo amplifiers in his hands. A metal bat lay on the ground behind him. Clay asked Perry where the amplifiers came from. "[I] found them on the ground," Perry responded.

Meanwhile, Ullon's wife, Nubia Blandon, woke her neighbor, Alex Clavijo, and told him she had just seen someone break into his car. Clavijo immediately went downstairs to

1216   Chapter XIV Eyewitness Identification

the parking lot to inspect the car. He first observed that one of the rear windows had been shattered. On further inspection, he discovered that the speakers and amplifiers from his car stereo were missing, as were his bat and wrench. Clavijo then approached Clay and told her about Blandon's alert and his own subsequent observations.

By this time, another officer had arrived at the scene. Clay asked Perry to stay in the parking lot with that officer, while she and Clavijo went to talk to Blandon. Clay and Clavijo then entered the apartment building and took the stairs to the fourth floor, where Blandon's and Clavijo's apartments were located. They met Blandon in the hallway just outside the open door to her apartment.

Asked to describe what she had seen, Blandon stated that, around 2:30 a.m., she saw from her kitchen window a tall, African-American man roaming the parking lot and looking into cars. Eventually, the man circled Clavijo's car, opened the trunk, and removed a large box.

Clay asked Blandon for a more specific description of the man. Blandon pointed to her kitchen window and said the person she saw breaking into Clavijo's car was standing in the parking lot, next to the police officer. Perry's arrest followed this identification.

About a month later, the police showed Blandon a photographic array that included a picture of Perry and asked her to point out the man who had broken into Clavijo's car. Blandon was unable to identify Perry.

B

Perry was charged in New Hampshire state court with one count of theft by unauthorized taking and one count of criminal mischief. Before trial, he moved to suppress Blandon's identification on the ground that admitting it at trial would violate due process. Blandon witnessed what amounted to a one-person showup in the parking lot, Perry asserted, which all but guaranteed that she would identify him as the culprit.

The New Hampshire Superior Court denied the motion. To determine whether due process prohibits the introduction of an out-of-court identification at trial, the Superior Court said, this Court's decisions instruct a two-step inquiry. First, the trial court must decide whether the police used an unnecessarily suggestive identification procedure. If they did, the court must next consider whether the improper identification procedure so tainted the resulting identification as to render it unreliable and therefore inadmissible.

Perry's challenge, the Superior Court concluded, failed at step one: Blandon's identification of Perry on the night of the crime did not result from an unnecessarily suggestive procedure "manufacture[d] . . . by the police." Blandon pointed to Perry "spontaneously," the court noted, "without any inducement from the police." Clay did not ask Blandon whether the man standing in the parking lot was the man Blandon had seen breaking into Clavijo's car. Nor did Clay ask Blandon to move to the window from which she had observed the break-in.

The Superior Court recognized that there were reasons to question the accuracy of Blandon's identification: The parking lot was dark in some locations; Perry was standing next to a police officer; Perry was the only African-American man in the vicinity; and Blandon was unable, later, to pick Perry out of a photographic array. But "[b]ecause the police procedures were not unnecessarily suggestive," the court ruled that the reliability of Blandon's testimony was for the jury to consider.

At the ensuing trial, Blandon and Clay testified to Blandon's out-of-court identification. The jury found Perry guilty of theft and not guilty of criminal mischief.

On appeal, Perry repeated his challenge to the admissibility of Blandon's out-of-court identification. The trial court erred, Perry contended, in requiring an initial showing that the police arranged the suggestive identification procedure. Suggestive circumstances alone, Perry argued, suffice to trigger the court's duty to evaluate the reliability of the resulting identification before allowing presentation of the evidence to the jury.

B. Eyewitness Identification and Due Process   1217

The New Hampshire Supreme Court rejected Perry's argument and affirmed his conviction. Only where the police employ suggestive identification techniques, that court held, does the Due Process Clause require a trial court to assess the reliability of identification evidence before permitting a jury to consider it.

We granted certiorari to resolve a division of opinion on the question whether the Due Process Clause requires a trial judge to conduct a preliminary assessment of the reliability of an eyewitness identification made under suggestive circumstances not arranged by the police.

· · ·

Perry concedes that, in contrast to every case in the *Stovall* line, law enforcement officials did not arrange the suggestive circumstances surrounding Blandon's identification. He contends, however, that it was mere happenstance that each of the *Stovall* cases involved improper police action. The rationale underlying our decisions, Perry asserts, supports a rule requiring trial judges to prescreen eyewitness evidence for reliability any time an identification is made under suggestive circumstances. We disagree.

Perry's argument depends, in large part, on the Court's statement in *Brathwaite* that "reliability is the linchpin in determining the admissibility of identification testimony." If reliability is the linchpin of admissibility under the Due Process Clause, Perry maintains, it should make no difference whether law enforcement was responsible for creating the suggestive circumstances that marred the identification.

Perry has removed our statement in *Brathwaite* from its mooring, and thereby attributes to the statement a meaning a fair reading of our opinion does not bear. [T]he *Brathwaite* Court's reference to reliability appears in a portion of the opinion concerning the appropriate remedy when the police use an unnecessarily suggestive identification procedure. The Court adopted a judicial screen for reliability as a course preferable to a per se rule requiring exclusion of identification evidence whenever law enforcement officers employ an improper procedure. The due process check for reliability, *Brathwaite* made plain, comes into play only after the defendant establishes improper police conduct. The very purpose of the check, the Court noted, was to avoid depriving the jury of identification evidence that is reliable, notwithstanding improper police conduct.

Perry's contention that improper police action was not essential to the reliability check *Brathwaite* required is echoed by the dissent. Both ignore a key premise of the *Brathwaite* decision: A primary aim of excluding identification evidence obtained under unnecessarily suggestive circumstances, the Court said, is to deter law enforcement use of improper lineups, showups, and photo arrays in the first place. Alerted to the prospect that identification evidence improperly obtained may be excluded, the Court reasoned, police officers will "guard against unnecessarily suggestive procedures." This deterrence rationale is inapposite in cases, like Perry's, in which the police engaged in no improper conduct.

· · ·

Perry and the dissent place significant weight on *Wade*, describing it as a decision not anchored to improper police conduct. In fact, the risk of police rigging was the very danger to which the Court responded in Wade when it recognized a defendant's right to counsel at postindictment, police-organized identification procedures. . . .

Perry's argument, reiterated by the dissent, thus lacks support in the case law he cites. Moreover, his position would open the door to judicial preview, under the banner of due process, of most, if not all, eyewitness identifications. External suggestion is hardly the only factor that casts doubt on the trustworthiness of an eyewitness' testimony. As one of Perry's amici points out, many other factors bear on "the likelihood of misidentification"—for example, the passage of time between exposure to and identification of the defendant, whether the witness was under stress when he first encountered the suspect, how much time the witness had to observe the suspect, how far the witness was from the suspect, whether the suspect carried a weapon, and the race of the suspect and the witness. There is no reason why an identification made by an eyewitness with poor vision, for example, or one who harbors a grudge against the defendant, should be regarded as inherently more reliable, less of a "threat to the fairness of trial," than the identification Blandon made in this case. To embrace Perry's view would thus entail a vast enlargement of the reach of due process as a constraint on the admission of evidence.

Perry maintains that the Court can limit the due process check he proposes to identifications made under "suggestive circumstances." Even if we could rationally distinguish suggestiveness from other factors bearing on the reliability of eyewitness evidence, Perry's limitation would still involve trial courts, routinely, in preliminary examinations. Most eyewitness identifications involve some element of suggestion. Indeed, all in-court identifications do. Out-of-court identifications volunteered by witnesses are also likely to involve suggestive circumstances. For example, suppose a witness identifies the defendant to police officers after seeing a photograph of the defendant in the press captioned "theft suspect," or hearing a radio report implicating the defendant in the crime. Or suppose the witness knew that the defendant ran with the wrong crowd and saw him on the day and in the vicinity of the crime. Any of these circumstances might have "suggested" to the witness that the defendant was the person the witness observed committing the crime.

C

In urging a broadly applicable due process check on eyewitness identifications, Perry maintains that eyewitness identifications are a uniquely unreliable form of evidence. We do not doubt either the importance or the fallibility of eyewitness identifications. Indeed, in recognizing that defendants have a constitutional right to counsel at postindictment police lineups, we observed that "the annals of criminal law are rife with instances of mistaken identification."

We have concluded in other contexts, however, that the potential unreliability of a type of evidence does not alone render its introduction at the defendant's trial fundamentally unfair. We reach a similar conclusion here: The fallibility of eyewitness evidence does not, without the taint of improper state conduct, warrant a due process rule requiring a trial court to screen such evidence for reliability before allowing the jury to assess its creditworthiness.

Our unwillingness to enlarge the domain of due process as Perry and the dissent urge rests, in large part, on our recognition that the jury, not the judge, traditionally determines the reliability of evidence. We also take account of other safeguards built into our adversary system that caution juries against placing undue weight on eyewitness testimony of questionable reliability. These protections include the defendant's Sixth Amendment right to confront the eyewitness. Another is the defendant's right to the effective assistance of an attorney, who can expose the flaws in the eyewitness' testimony during cross-examination and focus the jury's attention on the fallibility of such testimony during opening and closing arguments. Eyewitness-specific jury instructions, which many federal and state courts have adopted, likewise warn the jury to take care in appraising identification evidence. The constitutional requirement that the government prove the defendant's guilt beyond a reasonable doubt also impedes convictions based on dubious identification evidence.

State and Federal Rules of Evidence, moreover, permit trial judges to exclude relevant evidence if its probative value is substantially outweighed by its prejudicial impact or potential for misleading the jury. In appropriate cases, some States also permit defendants to present expert testimony on the hazards of eyewitness identification evidence.

Many of the safeguards just noted were at work at Perry's trial. During her opening statement, Perry's court-appointed attorney cautioned the jury about the vulnerability of

Blandon's identification. While cross-examining Blandon and Officer Clay, Perry's attorney constantly brought up the weaknesses of Blandon's identification. She highlighted: (1) the significant distance between Blandon's window and the parking lot, (2) the lateness of the hour, (3) the van that partly obstructed Blandon's view, (4) Blandon's concession that she was "so scared [she] really didn't pay attention" to what Perry was wearing, (5) Blandon's inability to describe Perry's facial features or other identifying marks, (6) Blandon's failure to pick Perry out of a photo array, and (7) Perry's position next to a uniformed, gun-bearing police officer at the moment Blandon made her identification. Perry's counsel reminded the jury of these frailties during her summation: Blandon "wasn't able to tell you much about who she saw.... She couldn't pick [Perry] out of a lineup, out of a photo array.... [Blandon said] [t]hat guy that was with the police officer, that's who was circling. Again, think about the context with the guns, the uniforms. Powerful, powerful context clues."

After closing arguments, the trial court read the jury a lengthy instruction on identification testimony and the factors the jury should consider when evaluating it. The court also instructed the jury that the defendant's guilt must be proved beyond a reasonable doubt, and specifically cautioned that "one of the things the State must prove [beyond a reasonable doubt] is the identification of the defendant as the person who committed the offense."

Given the safeguards generally applicable in criminal trials, protections availed of by the defense in Perry's case, we hold that the introduction of Blandon's eyewitness testimony, without a preliminary judicial assessment of its reliability, did not render Perry's trial fundamentally unfair.

Affirmed.

NOTES AND QUESTIONS

Barion Perry

1. Note that the Court acknowledges that the defendant was a Black man, as were the defendants in *Stovall* and *Manson*. Here, as in *Stovall*, the Court acknowledges the defendant's race without any additional comment, whereas in *Manson* the Court makes the observation in connection with noting that the police officer who identified the defendant was also Black. In both *Stovall* and *Perry*, how would you argue that the defendant's race could have contributed to the suggestibility of the witness's identification? What additional facts would you need?

2. In rejecting Perry's claim the Court reasons that "[a] primary aim of excluding identification evidence obtained under unnecessarily suggestive circumstances is to deter law enforcement use of improper procedures in the first place." The dissent sharply disagrees: "Our precedents make no distinction between intentional and unintentional suggestion." Who has the better of this argument? Recall the back and forth in *Wade* between the majority and dissent about distrust of law enforcement.

3. The dissent purports to bolster its position by referring to the facts of the lineup at issue in *Wade* itself, and notes that in "underscoring these hazards, we made no mention of whether the encounter had been arranged; indeed the facts suggest that it was not." Is the goal of a deterrence remedy limited to preventing only intentional misconduct?

4. If the Court had held that the *Manson* reliability test was applicable here, how would Blandon's identification fare on *Manson's* five-factor test? Do you agree with the dissent that "[t]here are many reasons why Perry's particular situation might not violate due process"?

5. Did the prosecution need Blandon's out-of-court identification of Perry in order to convict him? How would you have presented the case for the prosecution without using such testimony? How far could the prosecution have gotten with just the testimony of Officer Clay and Blandon's neighbor, Alex Clavijo? Given that at the time of Perry's trial it was unsettled law—at least in the Supreme Court—whether "police-arranged" susceptibility was required for exclusion of an identification, why would the prosecution jeopardize its case by relying on Blandon's identification?

6. The Court makes a classic "floodgates" argument, noting that there are innumerable ways in which eyewitness testimony can be unreliable, and even many ways that it can be unreliable due to suggestibility unrelated to any law enforcement activity, and that excluding all such testimony would essentially turn the Due Process Clause into a rule of evidence. Is this a fair point?

7. The Court gives short shrift to Perry's argument that eyewitness identification testimony is "uniquely" unreliable, and points to a litany of other safeguards—cross-examination, jury instructions, rules of evidence—available to mitigate the effect of unreliable eyewitness evidence. What, if anything, is "uniquely" unreliable about eyewitness testimony? For example, is there something about eyewitness testimony that is inherently different in its unreliability than, say, the testimony of a cooperating witness who may get a reduced sentence in exchange for his testimony?

8. The dissent by Justice Sotomayor points out that the majority essentially ignores that in the 50 years since the Court first expressed concerns about eyewitness testimony in *Wade* the social science case against its reliability has strengthened substantially:

> Over the past three decades, more than 2,000 studies related to eyewitness identification have been published. One State Supreme Court recently appointed a Special Master to conduct an exhaustive survey of the current state of the scientific evidence and concluded that "[t]he research . . . is not only extensive," but "it represents the 'gold standard in terms of the applicability of social science research to the law.'" "Experimental methods and findings have been tested and retested, subjected to scientific scrutiny through peer-reviewed journals, evaluated through the lens of meta-analyses, and replicated at times in real-world settings."
>
> The empirical evidence demonstrates that eyewitness misidentification is "'the single greatest cause of wrongful convictions in this country.'" Researchers have found that a staggering 76% of the first 250 convictions overturned due to DNA evidence since 1989 involved eyewitness misidentification. Study after study demonstrates that eyewitness recollections are highly susceptible to distortion by post event information or social cues; that jurors routinely overestimate the accuracy of eyewitness identifications; that jurors place the greatest weight on eyewitness confidence in assessing identifications even though confidence is a poor gauge of accuracy; and that suggestiveness can stem from sources beyond police-orchestrated procedures. The majority today nevertheless adopts an artificially narrow conception of the dangers of suggestive identifications at a time when our concerns should have deepened.

565 U.S. at 262-66 (citations omitted). Why doesn't the Court even acknowledge the state of the social science?

In view of this continuous march of social science through the decades, the Department of Justice in 2017 revised its guidelines for DOJ prosecutors and agents conducting eyewitness identification photo arrays. Memorandum for Heads of Department Law Enforcement Components Re: Eyewitness Identification: Procedures for Photo Arrays (DOJ 2017). While these guidelines are sometimes merely suggestive in nature, and generally apply only

B. Eyewitness Identification and Due Process 1221

where "practicable," they nonetheless contain important provisions aimed at minimizing suggestiveness, including the following: (a) a photo array should include at least five photographs of non-suspects; (b) the non-suspect photographs should generally fit the witness's description of the perpetrator; (c) the array should be presented to the witness by an "administrator" who is not involved in the investigation and does not know what the suspect looks like; (d) when such "blind" administration of the array is impracticable the procedure should be "blinded" so that the administrator is unable to see which photograph the witness is viewing at any particular time; (e) the witness should be instructed that the array "may or may not" include a photo of the perpetrator and that it is okay if the witness does not recognize anyone; and (f) that the administrator video-record or audio-record the proceedings or at the least prepare a thorough record of everything that transpired, including, where the witness makes an identification, the witness's level of confidence in that identification.

An Appendix to the guidelines notes the importance of the "confidence statement" of the witness, and cites new research in a 2016 study finding that a witness's confidence in an initial identification is a reliable indicator of accuracy, a finding at odds with the studies referenced in the dissent in *Perry*. Without exploring the merits of the competing studies, do you think as a matter of common sense that confidence in an identification is an indicator of accuracy? How could you cross-examine a witness who says "I am confident my identification was accurate"?

As with almost all DOJ guidelines of this nature, there is a standard caveat that this document "is not intended to create, does not create, and may not be relied upon to create any rights, substantive or procedural, enforceable at law by any party in any matter civil or criminal." What does this mean? Could a federal defendant successfully move to exclude an identification performed in a manner that deviates from these guidelines? Even if that is not the case, are there ways for a good defense attorney to use such a deviation from these guidelines to his client's advantage at trial?

The dissent in *Perry* makes references to various state court attempts to mitigate the effects of the unreliability of eyewitness testimony through jury instructions. The next case looks at the efforts of the Supreme Judicial Court of Massachusetts in this regard. In this excerpt from the opinion the court identifies five principles of eyewitness identification that should be used when applicable to the facts of the case.

Commonwealth v. Gomes
470 Mass. 352 (2015)

GANTS, C.J.

In the early morning of September 10, 2011, the defendant slashed the face of the victim, Zachary Sevigny, with a box cutter while the victim was sitting in the driver's seat of his vehicle. A Superior Court jury found the defendant guilty of [state crimes]. On appeal, the defendant claims that the judge erred by giving the model jury instruction regarding eyewitness identification that we [previously adopted] rather than the instruction he requested, which would have informed the jury about various scientific principles regarding eyewitness identification. We conclude that the judge did not err by declining to instruct the jury about these principles where the defendant offered no expert testimony, scholarly articles, or treatises that established that these principles were "so generally accepted that . . . a standard jury instruction stating [those principles] would be appropriate." Therefore, we affirm the convictions.

However, now that we have the benefit of the Report and Recommendations of the Supreme Judicial Court Study Group on Eyewitness Evidence (Study Group Report), and the comments in response to it, we conclude that there are scientific principles regarding eyewitness identification that are "so generally accepted" that it is appropriate in the future to instruct juries regarding these principles so that they may apply the principles in their evaluation of eyewitness identification evidence.

Background. At approximately 1:30 a.m. on September 10, 2011, the defendant, who appeared intoxicated, walked into a gasoline station convenience store in Pittsfield, bumped into a customer, Lindsay Holtzman, and asked the employee who was working the cash register, Jordan Wilson, for a box of matches. Wilson asked the defendant to apologize to Holtzman. In response, the defendant cursed and stared at Wilson, and challenged him to a fight. Wilson laughed and gave the defendant a box of matches. The defendant left the store, but continued to yell at Wilson to meet him outside to fight.

When the defendant left the store, the victim and his friend, Gerald Mortensen, were sitting in the victim's automobile, parked in a well-lit portion of the store's parking lot, approximately ten to fifteen feet from the front door of the store. The victim was in the driver's seat with the window down. After the victim and the defendant made eye contact, the defendant approached the vehicle and said to the victim, "What the fuck are you looking at, tough guy?" The victim responded, "I'm not looking at anything." The defendant then pulled a box cutter from his back pocket, reached inside the vehicle with his left arm, and slashed the victim with the blade behind the victim's ear and down his face.

Mortensen, who was sitting on the passenger's side, ran inside the store, said that his friend had been cut, and told a store clerk to call for help. Mortensen and Holtzman then left the store and watched as the defendant walked backwards toward a corner of the parking lot, still staring at the victim. The victim was taken to a hospital where he received approximately thirty stitches.

On September 15, Wilson went to the Pittsfield police station to meet with Detective Timothy Koenig. Wilson said that he had seen the person who injured the victim before and could identify him. Detective Koenig created a pool of 975 archived photographs that fit Wilson's description of the person. Wilson used a computer, which displayed twelve photographs per page, to look through the pool. He eventually selected the defendant's photograph. When he made the identification, he reported that he was "110 per cent positive."

Detective Koenig then created a simultaneous array containing eight photographs, one of which depicted the defendant, and presented the array that same day to Mortensen and the victim separately. Mortensen stated that none of the photographs showed the assailant. The victim said that he did not think the assailant "[wa]s anyone in these photos," but added that if he had to choose somebody, it would be the man with a chin similar to that of the assailant; that man was the defendant. Holtzman did not view a photographic array, although Detective Koenig attempted to reach her by telephone more than once to do so.

On September 18, Holtzman, Mortensen, and the victim were driving together, and stopped for gasoline at a different service station in Pittsfield. Holtzman and the victim entered the convenience store while Mortensen stayed inside the victim's vehicle. The victim testified that he briefly left the store to retrieve exact change from his automobile to purchase drinks and cigarettes. When he reentered the store, he immediately saw the defendant and recognized him as the assailant. After he put down his change, the victim and Holtzman left the store together, and confirmed with each other that the man in the store was the assailant. The victim then told Mortensen that the defendant was inside the store. When the defendant left the store, Mortensen agreed that the defendant was the assailant and the victim called the police on his cellular telephone.

As the victim spoke with the police, the defendant left the gasoline station in someone's automobile. The victim and Mortensen followed the defendant to an apartment complex in Pittsfield, with the victim communicating the defendant's location to the police as he was

B. Eyewitness Identification and Due Process   **1223**

driving. Shortly thereafter, the police arrived at the apartment complex and asked the victim and Mortensen to perform a showup identification; they identified the defendant as the assailant. After the defendant's arrest, Detective Koenig interviewed Holtzman, who confirmed that the person in the convenience store on September 18 had been the same person she saw at the other convenience store on September 10.

Before trial, the defendant filed motions to suppress Holtzman's and the victim's pretrial identification of the defendant. The trial judge denied the motions. At trial, the defendant argued that he had been mistakenly identified as the assailant, and offered the testimony of his father, Earl Kirchner, who said that he lived with the defendant and that the defendant did not leave his apartment on the evening of the attack.

• • •

b. *Five generally accepted principles regarding eyewitness identification.* We turn now to the five principles at issue in this case that we determine to have achieved a near consensus in the relevant scientific community and therefore are "so generally accepted" that it is appropriate that they now be included in a revised model jury instruction regarding eyewitness identification. We also summarize the research that informed our conclusions as to each generally accepted principle.

i. *Human memory does not function like a video recording but is a complex process that consists of three stages: acquisition, retention, and retrieval.* The central principle that has emerged from over 2,000 published studies over the past thirty years is that "memory does not function like a videotape, accurately and thoroughly capturing and reproducing a person, scene or event. . . . Memory is, rather[,] a constructive, dynamic and selective process." Rather, memories are made through a three-stage process: "acquisition — 'the perception of the original event'; retention [or storage] — 'the period of time that passes between the event and the eventual recollection of a particular piece of information'; and retrieval — the 'stage during which a person recalls stored information.'"

ii. *An eyewitness's expressed certainty in an identification, standing alone, may not indicate the accuracy of the identification, especially where the witness did not describe that level of certainty when the witness first made the identification.* We have long questioned the reliability of a witness's certainty as a reflection of accuracy. Our doubts are now supported by the research. "[S]tudies show that, under most circumstances, witness confidence or certainty is not a good indicator of identification accuracy."

This does not mean that eyewitness certainty is never correlated with accuracy; it means simply that the existence and strength of the correlation depends on the circumstances. After viewing the crime but before the identification procedure, an eyewitness's expressed level of certainty does not correlate with accuracy. Where an eyewitness makes a positive identification and expresses a level of certainty immediately after the identification procedure, there is some correlation between certainty and accuracy, but there is not yet a near consensus regarding the strength of that correlation. There is, however, a near consensus in the research that, where an eyewitness during an identification procedure did not express certainty when first asked to make an identification, a subsequent claim of certainty by that witness deserves little weight in evaluating the accuracy of that identification.

Although the research regarding the correlation (or lack of correlation) between eyewitness certainty and accuracy is complex and still evolving, it is necessary to inform a jury about this tenuous relationship because there is a near consensus that jurors tend to give more weight to a witness's certainty in evaluating the accuracy of an identification than is warranted by the research. Therefore, it is necessary to inform the jury that an eyewitness's expressed certainty in an identification, standing alone, may not indicate the accuracy of an identification, and that this is especially true where the witness did not describe that level of certainty when the witness first made an identification.

Chapter XIV Eyewitness Identification

iii. *High levels of stress can reduce an eyewitness's ability to make an accurate identification.* There is "considerable support for the hypothesis that high levels of stress negatively impact both accuracy of eyewitness identification as well as accuracy of recall of crime-related details." This principle is counterintuitive to the "common misconception that faces seen in highly stressful situations can be 'burned into' a witness's memory." Therefore, it is important to inform the jury of this principle lest they evaluate an identification made under high stress based on the "common misconception."

iv. *Information that is unrelated to the initial viewing of the event, which an eyewitness receives before or after making an identification, can influence the witness's later recollection of the memory or of the identification.* "An extensive body of studies demonstrates that the memories of witnesses for events and faces, and witnesses' confidence in their memories, are highly malleable and can readily be altered by information received by witnesses both before and after an identification procedure." This outside information, known as "feedback," affects witnesses' memory differently depending on whether the witness receives feedback before or after making an identification. "Jurors, however, tend to be unaware of . . . how susceptible witness certainty is to manipulation by suggestive procedures or confirming feedback."

Preidentification feedback may contaminate the witness's memory. For instance, suggestive wording and leading questions prior to participating in an identification procedure can influence the process of forming a memory. Postidentification feedback is information unrelated to the witness's actual memory that suggests to the witness that he or she correctly identified the suspect. This confirmatory information may boost the witness's level of certainty without increasing the likelihood of an accurate identification.

Although police officers are common potential sources of feedback, feedback from cowitnesses and other private actors can also influence a witness's memory. "When a witness is permitted to discuss the event with other witnesses or views another witness's identification decision, the witness may alter his or her own memory or identification decision to conform to that of the cowitness."

v. *A prior viewing of a suspect at an identification procedure may reduce the reliability of a subsequent identification procedure in which the same suspect is shown.* A prior viewing of a suspect in an identification procedure raises doubts about the reliability of a subsequent identification procedure involving the same suspect. "[S]uccessive views of the same person can make it difficult to know whether the later identification stems from a memory of the original event or a memory of the earlier identification procedure."

One form of this source memory problem is "mugshot exposure," where a witness's viewing of an innocent suspect's mugshot can heighten the chances of a later misidentification. A meta-analysis of eleven published articles showed that "prior mugshot exposure decreases accuracy at a subsequent lineup, both in terms of reductions in rates for hits and correct rejections as well as in terms of increases in the rate for false alarms."

. . .

We expect the new model instruction will provide at least one source of reliable information in cases where expert testimony is not offered. Jury instructions offer certain advantages over expert testimony: "they are focused and concise, authoritative (in that juries hear them from the trial judge, not a witness called by one side), and cost-free; they avoid possible confusion to jurors created by dueling experts; and they eliminate the risk of an expert invading the jury's role or opining on an eyewitness'[s] credibility."

Nevertheless, our provisional instruction is not intended in any way to preclude expert testimony regarding eyewitness identification or to discourage judges from exercising their discretion to permit such expert testimony. Expert testimony may be important to elaborate on the generally accepted principles in a model instruction and to explain how other variables

B. Eyewitness Identification and Due Process 1225

relevant to the particular case can affect the accuracy of the identification. A judge may also allow an expert to challenge the generally accepted principles we incorporated, and, where the judge finds the expert's challenge to be persuasive, the judge may modify the model instruction accordingly.

NOTES AND QUESTIONS

1. Note the court's comparison of expert testimony and jury instructions—two of the conventional tools for coping with the eyewitness problem cited in *Perry*—as alternative means of highlighting the eyewitness issue for the jury. Do you see other pros and cons of these alternatives?

2. The court states that one of the reasons for its new model instruction is that "common sense is not enough to accurately discern the reliable eyewitness identification from the unreliable because many of the results of the research are not commonly known, and some are counterintuitive." What aspects of the principles the court sets forth for the model instruction are counterintuitive?

3. Suppose that the principles the court describes were contained in an instruction used in *Gomes*. If you were not able to have the identification evidence suppressed pretrial, what would your strongest arguments in closing be as to why the jury should reject the eyewitness testimony?

4. As noted in the discussion of *Wade* above, the focus of the court's identification cases is not on the suggestiveness of a pretrial identification procedure itself but rather—given the "lock in" dynamic—that a suggestive pretrial procedure will inevitably taint a subsequent courtroom identification. But what can defense counsel do, if anything, about the extreme suggestiveness of courtroom identifications, where the defendant is sitting at counsel table next to defense counsel? Sometimes not much, as many judges view their courtrooms as sacred places where reliability can only be enhanced and won't take such claims seriously. Defense counsel can try to persuade the judge that an in-person lineup should be required inside or outside the courtroom.

5. Brandon Garrett proposes the radical solution that courtroom identifications should be presumptively excluded:

> I argue that courtroom identifications should be per se excluded, perhaps with a heavy burden on the prosecution to show why it is absolutely necessary. After all, as courts acknowledge, "the in-court testimony of an eyewitness can be devastatingly persuasive," and "of all the evidence that may be presented to a jury, a witness'[s] in-court statement that he is the one is probably the most dramatic and persuasive."
>
> Perhaps the eyewitness could still identify the defendant's photo as the one previously identified in a photo array. Then again, the police officer could just as readily authenticate the photo array as the one administered and describe which photo was that of the defendant. Particularly important is that the eyewitness would not be permitted make an in-court identification of the defendant or additional testify about confidence at the time of trial that the identification is correct. As discussed, confidence on the day of trial is not a sound measure of accuracy and is prejudicial. Allowing the eyewitness to point to the defendant in the courtroom permits a display of such confidence.
>
> If the prior identification is not suppressed as unduly suggestive, the eyewitness should be permitted to describe the out-of-court identification and be cross-examined concerning any suggestion or unreliability of that procedure. As Justice Marshall put it, dissenting in *Manson*, "[T]he issue is whether the witness is identifying the defendant solely on the basis of his memory of events at the time of the crime, or whether he is merely remembering the person he picked out in a pretrial procedure."

1226 Chapter XIV Eyewitness Identification

> Such a rule would give police strong incentives to conduct lineups and identification procedures before the trial. Regardless, police have every reason to test an eyewitness's memory to be sure that they have the right person. Indeed, in a typical case, they may not be able to make an arrest since, without an eyewitness identification, they would lack probable cause. Further, although judges do not often order lineup procedures at a trial, as noted, when they do, it is typically because the police did not conduct an identification procedure before trial.

Garrett, *Eyewitness and Exclusion, supra* at 489-90.

The next case considers one lawyer's attempt to combat the pernicious effect of the courtroom identification.

United States v. Thoreen
653 F.2d 1332 (9th Cir. 1981)

EUGENE A. WRIGHT, Circuit Judge:

I. INTRODUCTION

The issue before us is whether an attorney may be found in criminal contempt for pursuing a course of aggressive advocacy while representing his client in a criminal proceeding such that, without the court's permission or knowledge, he substitutes someone for his client at counsel table with the intent to cause a misidentification, resulting in the misleading of the court, counsel, and witnesses; a delay while the government reopened its case to identify the defendant; and violation of a court order and custom.

We affirm the district court's finding of criminal contempt. The conclusion that this appeal was untimely is reversed.

II. FACTS

By February 1980, Thoreen, an attorney, had practiced law for almost five years. He was a member of the bars of the State of Washington and of the Western District of Washington. He had made numerous court appearances and participated in one trial and several pretrial appearances before Judge Jack E. Tanner of the Western District of Washington.

In February 1980, he represented Sibbett, a commercial fisher, during Sibbett's non-jury trial before Judge Tanner for criminal contempt for three violations of a preliminary injunction against salmon fishing. In preparing for trial, Thoreen hoped that the government agent who had cited Sibbett could not identify him. He decided to test the witness's identification.

He placed next to him at counsel table Clark Mason, who resembled Sibbett and had Mason dressed in outdoor clothing denims, heavy shoes, a plaid shirt, and a jacket-vest.

Sibbett wore a business suit, large round glasses, and sat behind the rail in a row normally reserved for the press.

Thoreen neither asked the court's permission for, nor notified it or government counsel of, the substitution.

On Thoreen's motion at the start of the trial, the court ordered all witnesses excluded from the courtroom. Mason remained at counsel table.

Throughout the trial, Thoreen made and allowed to go uncorrected numerous misrepresentations. He gestured to Mason as though he was his client and gave Mason a yellow legal pad on which to take notes. The two conferred. Thoreen did not correct the court when it expressly referred to Mason as the defendant and caused the record to show identification of Mason as Sibbett.

B. Eyewitness Identification and Due Process   **1227**

Because of the conduct, two government witnesses misidentified Mason as Sibbett. Following the government's case, Thoreen called Mason as a witness and disclosed the substitution. The court then called a recess.

When the trial resumed, the government reopened and recalled the government agent who had cited Sibbett for two of the violations. He identified Sibbett, who was convicted of all three violations.

On February 20, 1980, Thoreen was ordered to appear on February 27 and show cause why he should not be held in criminal contempt. At the hearing, Judge Tanner found him in criminal contempt.

III. DISCUSSION

• • •

B. Contempt

Judge Tanner found Thoreen in criminal contempt for the substitution because it was imposed on the court and counsel without permission or prior knowledge; the claimed identification issue did not exist; it disrupted the trial; it deceived the court and frustrated its responsibility to administer justice; and it violated a court custom. He found Mason's presence in the courtroom after giving the order excluding witnesses another ground for contempt because Thoreen planned that Mason would testify when the misidentification occurred.

Thoreen's principal defense is that his conduct was a good faith tactic in aid of cross-examination and falls within the protected realm of zealous advocacy. He argues that as defense counsel he has no obligation to ascertain or present the truth and may seek to confuse witnesses with misleading questions, gestures, or appearances. *See United States v. Wade.*

He argues also that (1) in the absence of a court rule controlling who may sit at counsel table, his failure to give notice of the substitution is not misbehavior within 18 U.S.C. § 401(1) (1976); (2) he did not intend to deceive; and (3) the exclusion order was not directed at Mason.

1. Zealous Advocacy

While we agree that defense counsel should represent his client vigorously, regardless of counsel's view of guilt or innocence, we conclude that Thoreen's conduct falls outside this protected behavior.

Vigorous advocacy by defense counsel may properly entail impeaching or confusing a witness, even if counsel thinks the witness is truthful, and refraining from presenting evidence even if he knows the truth. *Wade, supra.* When we review this conduct and find that the line between vigorous advocacy and actual obstruction is close, our doubts should be resolved in favor of the former.

The latitude allowed an attorney is not unlimited. He must represent his client within the bounds of the law. As an officer of the court, he must "preserve and promote the efficient operation of our system of justice."

Thoreen's view of appropriate cross-examination, which encompasses his substitution, crossed over the line from zealous advocacy to actual obstruction because, as we discuss later, it impeded the court's search for truth, resulted in delays, and violated a court custom and rule. Moreover, this conduct harms rather than enhances an attorney's effectiveness as an advocate.

It is fundamental that in relations with the court, defense counsel must be scrupulously candid and truthful in representations of any matter before the court. This is not only a basic ethical requirement, but it is essential if the lawyer is to be effective in the role of advocate, for if the lawyer's reputation for veracity is suspect, he or she will lack the confidence of the court when it is needed most to serve the client.

1228 Chapter XIV Eyewitness Identification

2. Criminal Contempt

18 U.S.C. § 401 (1976) provides

> A court of the United States shall have power to punish by fine or imprisonment, at its discretion, such contempt of its authority, and none other, as
>
> (1) Misbehavior of any person in its presence or so near thereto as to obstruct the administration of justice;
>
> (3) Disobedience or resistance to its lawful writ, process, order, rule, decree, or command.

Contumacious misbehavior punishable under section 401(1) must be willful, and must "'actually obstruct'" the district judge in the performance of his judicial duties.

One may be found in contempt for disobeying an order pursuant to section 401(3) "only if the order is clear and definite, and the contemnor has knowledge of it."

a. Contumacious Misbehavior and Obstruction of Justice

Because Thoreen's conduct was in the court's presence, our inquiry turns to whether it constituted contumacious misbehavior that obstructed the administration of justice.

Misbehavior punishable under section 401(1) has been defined as "conduct inappropriate to the particular role of the actor, be he judge, juror, party, witness, counsel or spectator." *United States v. Seale.* Requiring adherence to these roles ensures "that a judicial proceeding (will be) confined to a rational search for truth in the context of defined legal issues." *Seale.*

Contumacious misbehavior by an attorney includes disobeying a court's rulings or instructions, *Gustafson,* supra, and deceiving the court. Examples of contumacious deceptive behavior are misrepresenting oneself as a practicing attorney; an attorney's swearing to and filing of admittedly false affidavits and supplemental complaint, plus the pursuit of meritless litigation; and an attorney's presentation of false evidence.

Making misrepresentations to the court is also inappropriate and unprofessional behavior under ethical standards that guide attorneys' conduct. These guidelines, in effect in Washington and elsewhere, decree explicitly that an attorney's participation in the presentation or preservation of false evidence is unprofessional and subjects him to discipline.

Substituting a person for the defendant in a criminal case without a court's knowledge has been noted as an example of unethical behavior by the ABA Committee on Professional Ethics. See Informal Opinion No. 914, 2/24/66 (decided under the former ABA Code of Professional Responsibility).

Ethical standards establish the outermost limits of appropriate and sanctioned attorney conduct. While we acknowledge that a court's power to discipline or disbar an attorney "'proceeds upon very different grounds' from those which support a court's power to punish for contempt," we consider and apply ethical benchmarks when determining whether an attorney's conduct is inappropriate to his role and thus constitutes contumacious misbehavior.

Counsel's conduct must cause an actual obstruction of justice before criminal contempt lies. The standard is whether the obstruction or disruption is material.

The seriousness of the misbehavior has some bearing on whether the conduct is materially obstructive. *Seale, supra.* Mere disrespect, insult, or an affront to a court's sense of dignity are insufficient.

The record supports Judge Tanner's conclusion that Thoreen's substitution was misbehavior that obstructed justice. It was inappropriate because it was done without consent, and violated a court custom to allow only counsel, parties, and others having the court's permission to sit forward of the rail. This conduct is deemed unprofessional and may subject an attorney to disciplinary measures in Washington.

• • •

We AFFIRM the contempt conviction.

NOTES AND QUESTIONS

1. The Ninth Circuit criticizes Thoreen for conducting his identification scheme without the permission or knowledge of the court or, perhaps, even the knowledge of the prosecutor. Do you think it is relevant that the trial was a bench trial? What other creative options—that is, other than cross-examination or requesting a jury instruction—did Thoreen have for testing the identification testimony of the government witnesses? What should Thoreen have done if the court had refused any and all such options for challenging the government witnesses' identification testimony?

2. The Ninth Circuit held that "Sibbert's identification was not an issue" and that therefore there was no need for Thoreen to use a ruse to attempt to impeach the testimony of the government witnesses who identified Sibbert. What does it mean that "identification" was not an issue?

Bobby Seale, co-founder of the Black Panther Party

3. The Ninth Circuit frames the test for criminal contempt under 18 U.S.C. § 401(1) as requiring "actual obstruction of justice." 653 F.2d at 1340. Do you agree that Thoreen's ruse amounted to "obstruction of justice" because it "delayed" the proceedings and "frustrated the rational search for the truth"?

4. Note that in analyzing the contempt issues the Ninth Circuit relies heavily on *United States v. Seale*, 461 F.2d 345 (7th Cir. 1972), where Black Panther leader Bobby Seale was found in contempt and bound and gagged during the notorious trial of the "Chicago Seven." In Aaron Sorkin's 2020 movie adaptation, *The Trial of the Chicago Seven*, Bobby Seale is played by Yahya Abdul-Mateen II.

CHAPTER XV

THE JURY II: RACE AND JURIES

This second chapter on juries focuses on selected ways in which racial issues affect both the composition of the jury and trial proceedings before the jury. Section A looks at the Sixth Amendment's fair cross-section requirement. Section B explores the use of voir dire challenges in attempting to eliminate from jury service persons who may harbor racial bias. Section C examines the use of peremptory challenges to strike jurors on the basis of race, and the Supreme Court's attempt to preclude that practice in *Batson v. Kentucky*, a well-intended solution that is widely considered to have been ineffective. Section D considers the perils of cross-racial witness identification, and remedies courts have designed to moderate its potential harm.

A. RACE AND THE SIXTH AMENDMENT'S FAIR CROSS-SECTION REQUIREMENT

Ironically, given this heading, both of the Supreme Court's leading cases on this subject are claims alleging that juries wrongfully excluded women. But this is nonetheless a largely untapped avenue for obtaining more racially diverse juries.

Taylor v. Louisiana
419 U.S. 522 (1975)

Mr. Justice WHITE delivered the opinion of the Court.

When this case was tried, Art. VII, s 41, of the Louisiana Constitution, and Art. 402 of the Louisiana Code of Criminal Procedure provided that a woman should not be selected for jury service unless she had previously filed a written declaration of her desire to be subject to jury service. The constitutionality of these provisions is the issue in this case.

I

Appellant, Billy J. Taylor, was indicted by the grand jury of St. Tammany Parish, in the Twenty-second Judicial District of Louisiana, for aggravated kidnaping. On April 12, 1972, appellant moved the trial court to quash the petit jury venire drawn for the special criminal term beginning with his trial the following day. Appellant alleged that women were systematically excluded from the venire and that he would therefore be deprived of what he claimed to be his federal constitutional right to "a fair trial by jury of a representative segment of the community. . . ."

The Twenty-second Judicial District comprises the parishes of St. Tammany and Washington. The appellee has stipulated that 53% of the persons eligible for jury service in these parishes were female, and that no more than 10% of the persons on the jury wheel in St. Tammany Parish were women. During the period from December 8, 1971, to November 3, 1972, 12 females were among the 1,800 persons drawn to fill petit jury venires in St. Tammany Parish. It was also stipulated that the discrepancy between females eligible for jury service and those actually included in the venire was the result of the operation of La. Const., Art. VII, s 41, and La. Code Crim. Proc., Art. 402. In the present case, a venire totaling 175 persons was drawn for jury service beginning April 13, 1972. There were no females on the venire.

Appellant's motion to quash the venire was denied that same day. After being tried, convicted, and sentenced to death, appellant sought review in the Supreme Court of Louisiana, where he renewed his claim that the petit jury venire should have been quashed. The Supreme Court of Louisiana, recognizing that this claim drew into question the constitutionality of the provisions of the Louisiana Constitution and Code of Criminal Procedure dealing with the service of women on juries, squarely held, one justice dissenting, that these provisions were valid and not unconstitutional under federal law.

Appellant appealed from that decision to this Court. We noted probable jurisdiction to consider whether the Louisiana jury-selection system deprived appellant of his Sixth and Fourteenth Amendment right to an impartial jury trial. We hold that it did and that these Amendments were violated in this case by the operation of La. Const., Art. VII, s 41, and La. Code Crim. Proc., Art. 402. In consequence, appellant's conviction must be reversed.

II

The Louisiana jury-selection system does not disqualify women from jury service, but in operation its conceded systematic impact is that only a very few women, grossly disproportionate to the number of eligible women in the community, are called for jury service. In this case, no women were on the venire from which the petit jury was drawn. The issue we have, therefore, is whether a jury-selection system which operates to exclude from jury service an identifiable class of citizens constituting 53% of eligible jurors in the community comports with the Sixth and Fourteenth Amendments.

The State first insists that Taylor, a male, has no standing to object to the exclusion of women from his jury. But Taylor's claim is that he was constitutionally entitled to a jury drawn from a venire constituting a fair cross section of the community and that the jury that tried him was not such a jury by reason of the exclusion of women. Taylor was not a member of the excluded class; but there is no rule that claims such as Taylor presents may be made only by those defendants who are members of the group excluded from jury service. In *Peters v. Kiff* (1972), the defendant, a white man, challenged his conviction on the ground that Negroes had been systematically excluded from jury service. Six Members of the Court agreed that petitioner was entitled to present the issue and concluded that he had been deprived of his federal rights. Taylor, in the case before us, was similarly entitled to tender and have adjudicated the claim that the exclusion of women from jury service deprived him of the kind of factfinder to which he was constitutionally entitled.

III

The background against which this case must be decided includes our holding in *Duncan v. Louisiana* (1968), that the Sixth Amendment's provision for jury trial is made binding on the States by virtue of the Fourteenth Amendment. Our inquiry is whether the presence of a fair cross section of the community on venires, panels, of lists from which petit juries are drawn is essential to the fulfillment of the Sixth Amendment's guarantee of an impartial jury trial in criminal prosecutions.

The Court's prior cases are instructive. Both in the course of exercising its supervisory powers over trials in federal courts and in the constitutional context, the Court has unambiguously declared that the American concept of the jury trial contemplates a jury drawn from a fair cross section of the community. A unanimous Court stated in *Smith v. Texas* (1940), that "(i)t is part of the established tradition in the use of juries as instruments of public justice that the jury be a body truly representative of the community." To exclude racial groups from jury service was said to be "at war with our basic concepts of a democratic society and a representative government." A state jury system that resulted in systematic exclusion of Negroes as jurors was therefore held to violate the Equal Protection Clause of the Fourteenth Amendment. *Glasser v. United States* (1942), in the context of a federal criminal case and the Sixth Amendment's jury trial requirement, stated that "(o)ur notions of what a proper jury is have developed in harmony with our basic concepts of a democratic system and representative government," and repeated the Court's understanding that the jury "be a body truly representative of the community . . . and not the organ of any special group or class."

A federal conviction by a jury from which women had been excluded, although eligible for service under state law. Noting the federal statutory "design to make the jury 'a cross-section of the community'" and the fact that women had been excluded, the Court exercised its supervisory powers over the federal courts and reversed the conviction. In *Brown v. Allen* (1953), the Court declared that "(o)ur duty to protect the federal constitutional rights of all does not mean we must or should impose on states our conception of the proper source of jury lists, so long as the source reasonably reflects a cross-section of the population suitable in character and intelligence for that civic duty."

Some years later in *Carter v. Jury Comm'n* (1970), the Court observed that the exclusion of Negroes from jury service because of their race "contravenes the very idea of a jury — a body truly representative of the community.' At about the same time it was contended that the use of six-man juries in noncapital criminal cases violated the Sixth Amendment for failure to provide juries drawn from a cross section of the community. In the course of rejecting that challenge, we said that the number of persons on the jury should "be large enough to promote group deliberation, free from outside attempts at intimidation, and to provide a fair possibility for obtaining a representative cross-section of the community." In like vein, in *Apodaca v. Oregon* (1972) (plurality opinion), it was said that "a jury will come to such a (commonsense) judgment as long as it consists of a group of laymen representative of a cross section of the community who have the duty and the opportunity to deliberate . . . on the question of a defendant's guilt." Similarly, three Justices in *Peters v. Kiff* observed that the Sixth Amendment comprehended a fair possibility for obtaining a jury constituting a representative cross section of the community.

The unmistakable import of this Court's opinions, at least since 1940, *Smith v. Texas, supra*, and not repudiated by intervening decisions, is that the selection of a petit jury from a representative cross section of the community is an essential component of the Sixth Amendment right to a jury trial. Recent federal legislation governing jury selection within the federal court system has a similar thrust. Shortly prior to this Court's decision in *Duncan v. Louisiana, supra*, the Federal Jury Selection and Service Act of 1968 was enacted. In that Act, Congress stated "the policy of the United States that all litigants in Federal courts entitled to trial by jury shall have the right to grand and petit juries selected at random from a fair cross section of the community in the district or division wherein the court convenes." 28 U.S.C. s 1861. In that Act, Congress also established the machinery by which the stated policy was to be implemented. 28 U.S.C. ss 1862-1866. In passing this legislation, the Committee Reports of both the House and the Senate recognized that the jury plays a political function in the administration of the law and that the requirement of a jury's being chosen from a fair cross section of the community is fundamental to the American system of justice. Debate on the floors of the House and Senate on the Act invoked the Sixth Amendment, the Constitution generally, and prior decisions of this Court in support of the Act.

We accept the fair-cross-section requirement as fundamental to the jury trial guaranteed by the Sixth Amendment and are convinced that the requirement has solid foundation. The purpose of a jury is to guard against the exercise of arbitrary power — to make available the commonsense judgment of the community as a hedge against the overzealous or mistaken prosecutor and in preference to the professional or perhaps overconditioned or biased response of a judge. *Duncan v. Louisiana.* This prophylactic vehicle is not provided if the jury pool is made up of only special segments of the populace or if large, distinctive groups are excluded from the pool. Community participation in the administration of the criminal law, moreover, is not only consistent with our democratic heritage but is also critical to public confidence in the fairness of the criminal justice system. Restricting jury service to only special groups or excluding identifiable segments playing major roles in the community cannot be squared with the constitutional concept of jury trial. "Trial by jury presupposes a jury drawn from a pool broadly representative of the community as well as impartial in a specific case. . . . (T)he broad representative character of the jury should be maintained, partly as assurance of a diffused impartiality and partly because sharing in the administration of justice is a phase of civic responsibility."

IV

We are also persuaded that the fair-cross-section requirement is violated by the systematic exclusion of women, who in the judicial district involved here amounted to 53% of the citizens eligible for jury service. This conclusion necessarily entails the judgment that women are sufficiently numerous and distinct from men and that if they are systematically eliminated from jury panels, the Sixth Amendment's fair-cross-section requirement cannot be satisfied. This very matter was debated in *Ballard v. United States, supra*. Positing the fair-cross-section rule — there said to be a statutory one — the Court concluded that the systematic exclusion of women was unacceptable. The dissenting view that an all-male panel drawn from various groups in the community would be as truly representative as if women were included, was firmly rejected:

> The thought is that the factors which tend to influence the action of women are the same as those which influence the action of men — personality, background, economic status — and not sex. Yet it is not enough to say that women when sitting as jurors neither act nor tend to act as a class. Men likewise do not act as a class. But, if the shoe were on the other foot, who would claim that a jury was truly representative of the community if all men were intentionally and systematically excluded from the panel? The truth is that the two sexes are not fungible; a community made up exclusively of one is different from a community composed of both; the subtle interplay of influence one on the other is among the imponderables. To insulate the courtroom from either may not in a given case make an iota of difference. Yet a flavor, a distinct quality is lost if either sex is excluded. The exclusion of one may indeed make the jury less representative of the community than would be true if an economic or racial group were excluded.

In this respect, we agree with the Court in *Ballard*: If the fair-cross-section rule is to govern the selection of juries, as we have concluded it must, women cannot be systematically excluded from jury panels from which petit juries are drawn. This conclusion is consistent with the current judgment of the country, now evidenced by legislative or constitutional provisions in every State and at the federal level qualifying women for jury service.

V

There remains the argument that women as a class serve a distinctive role in society and that jury service would so substantially interfere with that function that the State has ample justification for excluding women from service unless they volunteer, even though the result is that

A. Race and the Sixth Amendment's Fair Cross-Section Requirement   **1235**

almost all jurors are men. It is true that *Hoyt v. Florida* (1961), held that such a system did not deny due process of law or equal protection of the laws because there was a sufficiently rational basis for such an exemption. But *Hoyt* did not involve a defendant's Sixth Amendment right to a jury drawn from a fair cross section of the community and the prospect of depriving him of that right if women as a class are systematically excluded. The right to a proper jury cannot be overcome on merely rational grounds. There must be weightier reasons if a distinctive class representing 53% of the eligible jurors is for all practical purposes to be excluded from jury service. No such basis has been tendered here.

The States are free to grant exemptions from jury service to individuals in case of special hardship or incapacity and to those engaged in particular occupations the uninterrupted performance of which is critical to the community's welfare. It would not appear that such exemptions would pose substantial threats that the remaining pool of jurors would not be representative of the community. A system excluding all women, however, is a wholly different matter. It is untenable to suggest these days that it would be a special hardship for each and every woman to perform jury service or that society cannot spare any women from their present duties. This may be the case with many, and it may be burdensome to sort out those who should be exempted from those who should serve. But that task is performed in the case of men, and the administrative convenience in dealing with women as a class is insufficient justification for diluting the quality of community judgment represented by the jury in criminal trials.

VI

Although this judgment may appear a foregone conclusion from the pattern of some of the Court's cases over the past 30 years, as well as from legislative developments at both federal and state levels, it is nevertheless true that until today no case had squarely held that the exclusion of women from jury venires deprives a criminal defendant of his Sixth Amendment right to trial by an impartial jury drawn from a fair cross section of the community. It is apparent that the first Congress did not perceive the Sixth Amendment as requiring women on criminal jury panels; for the direction of the First Judiciary Act of 1789 was that federal jurors were to have the qualifications required by the States in which the federal court was sitting and at the time women were disqualified under state law in every State. Necessarily, then, federal juries in criminal cases were all male, and it was not until the Civil Rights Act of 1957, 71 Stat. 638, 28 U.S.C. s 1861 (1964 ed.), that Congress itself provided that all citizens, with limited exceptions, were competent to sit on federal juries. Until that time, federal courts were required by statute to exclude women from jury duty in those States where women were disqualified. Utah was the first State to qualify women for juries; it did so in 1898. Moreover, *Hoyt v. Florida* was decided and has stood for the proposition that, even if women as a group could not be constitutionally disqualified from jury service, there was ample reason to treat all women differently from men for the purpose of jury service and to exclude them unless they volunteered.

Accepting as we do, however, the view that the Sixth Amendment affords the defendant in a criminal trial the opportunity to have the jury drawn from venires representative of the community, we think it is no longer tenable to hold that women as a class may be excluded to given automatic exemptions based solely on sex if the consequence is that criminal jury venires are almost totally male. To this extent we cannot follow the contrary implications of the prior cases, including *Hoyt v. Florida*. If it was ever the case that women were unqualified to sit on juries or were so situated that none of them should be required to perform jury service, that time has long since passed. If at one time it could be held that Sixth Amendment juries must be drawn from a fair cross section of the community but that this requirement permitted the almost total exclusion of women, this is not the case today. Communities differ at different times and places. What is a fair cross section at one time or place is not necessarily a fair cross section at another time or a different place. Nothing persuasive has been presented to us in this case suggesting that all-male venires in the parishes involved here are fairly representative of the local population otherwise eligible for jury service.

VII

Our holding does not augur or authorize the fashioning of detailed jury selection codes by federal courts. The fair-cross-section principle must have much leeway in application. The States remain free to prescribe relevant qualifications for their jurors and to provide reasonable exemptions so long as it may be fairly said that the jury lists or panels are representative of the community. *Carter v. Jury Comm'n, supra,* as did *Brown v. Allen, supra; Rawlins v. Georgia, supra,* and other cases, recognized broad discretion in the States in this respect. We do not depart from the principles enunciated in *Carter.* But, as we have said, Louisiana's special exemption for women operates to exclude them from petit juries, which in our view is contrary to the command of the Sixth and Fourteenth Amendments.

It should also be emphasized that in holding that petit juries must be drawn from a source fairly representative of the community we impose no requirement that petit juries actually chosen must mirror the community and reflect the various distinctive groups in the population. Defendants are not entitled to a jury of any particular composition, but the jury wheels, pools of names, panels, or venires from which juries are drawn must not systematically exclude distinctive groups in the community and thereby fail to be reasonably representative thereof.

The judgment of the Louisiana Supreme Court is reversed and the case remanded to that court for further proceedings not inconsistent with this opinion.

So ordered.

NOTES AND QUESTIONS

1. The challenge to Louisiana's jury system whereby women had to affirmatively opt in to be selected for jury service was brought by a white male defendant in a kidnapping case.

Why does the Court find that Taylor has standing to bring a claim challenging this provision? Why might Taylor have thought a jury including women would be in his interest?

2. The Court holds, referring to several precedents, that Louisiana's exclusion policy runs afoul of the Sixth Amendment's requirement that "a representative cross section of the community is an essential component of the Sixth Amendment right to a jury trial." The Court makes no attempt to find the source of this requirement in the language of the Sixth Amendment. That Amendment provides:

> In all criminal prosecutions, the accused shall enjoy the right to a speedy and public trial, by an impartial jury of the State and district wherein the crime shall have been committed, which district shall have been previously ascertained by law, and to be informed of the nature and cause of the accusation; to be confronted with the witnesses against him; to have compulsory process for obtaining witnesses in his favor, and to have the Assistance of Counsel for his defence.

What part, if any, of the Sixth Amendment comes closest to suggesting a fair cross-section requirement? Can the right to a jury composed of a fair cross-section of the community be seen as something inherent in the nature of a jury?

A. Race and the Sixth Amendment's Fair Cross-Section Requirement

3. The Court traces the source of the right to comments it had made in cases such as *Duncan v. Louisiana* and *Williams v. Florida, supra*, in which it had highlighted the jury's purpose to guard against the exercise of arbitrary power—to make available the "commonsense judgment of the community as a hedge against the overzealous or mistaken prosecutor and in preference to the professional or perhaps overconditioned or biased response of a judge." The Court also noted the recently enacted Federal Jury Selection and Service Act of 1968, which also recognized a fair cross-section right.

4. Just five years prior to *Taylor*, in *Carter v. Jury Commission*, 396 U.S. 320 (1970), the Court had recognized the validity of a class action claim by Black residents of Greene County, Alabama, alleging that they had been excluded from jury service by operation of the state's jury commission system. The Court had no trouble finding that the plaintiff class members—just like criminal defendants—had a "cognizable legal interest in nondiscriminatory jury selection," but the Court was silent on whether the basis for the claim was the Equal Protection Clause or the fair cross-section requirement.

Duren v. Missouri
439 U.S. 357 (1979)

Mr. Justice WHITE delivered the opinion of the Court.

In *Taylor v. Louisiana* (1975), this Court held that systematic exclusion of women during the jury-selection process, resulting in jury pools not "reasonably representative" of the community, denies a criminal defendant his right, under the Sixth and Fourteenth Amendments, to a petit jury selected from a fair cross section of the community. Under the system invalidated in *Taylor*, a woman could not serve on a jury unless she filed a written declaration of her willingness to do so. As a result, although 53% of the persons eligible for jury service were women, less than 1% of the 1,800 persons whose names were drawn from the jury wheel during the year in which appellant Taylor's jury was chosen were female.

At the time of our decision in *Taylor* no other State provided that women could not serve on a jury unless they volunteered to serve. However, five States, including Missouri, provided an automatic exemption from jury service for any women requesting not to serve.

Subsequent to *Taylor*, three of these States eliminated this exemption. Only Missouri, respondent in this case, and Tennessee continue to exempt women from jury service upon request. Today we hold that such systematic exclusion of women that results in jury venires averaging less than 15% female violates the Constitution's fair-cross-section requirement.

I

Petitioner Duren was indicted in 1975 in the Circuit Court of Jackson County, Mo., for first-degree murder and first-degree robbery. In a pretrial motion to quash his petit jury panel and again in a post-conviction motion for a new trial, he contended that his right to trial by a jury chosen from a fair cross section of his community was denied by provisions of Missouri law granting women who so request an automatic exemption from jury service. Both motions were denied.

At hearings on these motions, petitioner established that the jury-selection process in Jackson County begins with the annual mailing of a questionnaire to persons randomly selected from the Jackson County voter registration list. Approximately 70,000 questionnaires were mailed in 1975. The questionnaire contains a list of occupations and other categories which are the basis under Missouri law for either disqualification or exemption from jury service. Included on the questionnaire is a paragraph prominently addressed "TO WOMEN" that states in part:

> Any woman who elects not to serve will fill out this paragraph and mail this questionnaire to the jury commissioner at once.

A similar paragraph is addressed "TO MEN OVER 65 YEARS OF AGE," who are also statutorily exempt upon request.

The names of those sent questionnaires are placed in the master jury wheel for Jackson County, except for those returning the questionnaire who indicate disqualification or claim an applicable exemption. Summonses are mailed on a weekly basis to prospective jurors randomly drawn from the jury wheel. The summons, like the questionnaire, contains special directions to men over 65 and to women, this time advising them to return the summons by mail if they desire not to serve. The practice also is that even those women who do not return the summons are treated as having claimed exemption if they fail to appear for jury service on the appointed day. Other persons seeking to claim an exemption at this stage must make written or personal application to the court.

Petitioner established that according to the 1970 census, 54% of the adult inhabitants of Jackson County were women. He also showed that for the periods June-October 1975 and January-March 1976, 11,197 persons were summoned and that 2,992 of these or 26.7%, were women. Of those summoned, 741 women and 4,378 men appeared for service. Thus, 14.5% (741 of 5,119) of the persons on the postsummons weekly venires during the period in which petitioner's jury was chosen were female. In March 1976, when petitioner's trial began, 15.5% of those on the weekly venires were women (110 of 707). Petitioner's jury was selected from a 53-person panel on which there were 5 women; all 12 jurors chosen were men. None of the foregoing statistical evidence was disputed.

In affirming petitioner's conviction, the Missouri Supreme Court questioned two aspects of his statistical presentation. First, it considered the census figures inadequate because they were six years old and might not precisely mirror the percentage of women registered to vote. Second, petitioner had not unequivocally demonstrated the extent to which the low percentage of women appearing for jury service was due to the automatic exemption for women, rather than to sex-neutral exemptions such as that for persons over age 65.

The court went on to hold, however, that even accepting petitioner's statistical proof, "the number of female names in the wheel, those summoned and those appearing were well above acceptable constitutional standards." We granted certiorari, because of concern that the decision below is not consistent with our decision in *Taylor*.

II

We think that in certain crucial respects the Missouri Supreme Court misconceived the nature of the fair-cross-section inquiry set forth in *Taylor*. In holding that "petit juries must be drawn from a source fairly representative of the community," we explained that

> jury wheels, pools of names, panels, or venires from which juries are drawn must not systematically exclude distinctive groups in the community and thereby fail to be reasonably representative thereof.

In order to establish a prima facie violation of the fair-cross-section requirement, the defendant must show (1) that the group alleged to be excluded is a "distinctive" group in the community; (2) that the representation of this group in venires from which juries are selected is not fair and reasonable in relation to the number of such persons in the community; and (3) that this underrepresentation is due to systematic exclusion of the group in the jury-selection process.

A

With respect to the first part of the prima facie test, *Taylor* without doubt established that women "are sufficiently numerous and distinct from men" so that "if they are systematically eliminated from jury panels, the Sixth Amendment's fair-cross-section requirement cannot be satisfied."

B

The second prong of the prima facie case was established by petitioner's statistical presentation. Initially, the defendant must demonstrate the percentage of the community made up of the group alleged to be underrepresented, for this is the conceptual benchmark for the Sixth Amendment fair-cross-section requirement. In *Taylor*, the State had stipulated that 53% of the population eligible for jury service was female, while petitioner Duren has relied upon a census measurement of the actual percentage of women in the community (54%). In the trial court, the State of Missouri never challenged these data. Although the Missouri Supreme Court speculated that changing population patterns between 1970 and 1976 and unequal voter registration by men and women rendered the census figures a questionable frame of reference, there is no evidence whatsoever in the record to suggest that the 1970 census data significantly distorted the percentage of women in Jackson County at the time of trial. Petitioner's presentation was clearly adequate prima facie evidence of population characteristics for the purpose of making a fair-cross-section violation.

Given petitioner's proof that in the relevant community slightly over half of the adults are women, we must disagree with the conclusion of the court below that jury venires containing approximately 15% women are "reasonably representative" of this community. If the percentage of women appearing on jury pools in Jackson County had precisely mirrored the percentage of women in the population, more than one of every two prospective jurors would have been female. In fact, less than one of every six prospective jurors was female; 85% of the average jury was male. Such a gross discrepancy between the percentage of women in jury venires and the percentage of women in the community requires the conclusion that women were not fairly represented in the source from which petit juries were drawn in Jackson County.

C

Finally, in order to establish a prima facie case, it was necessary for petitioner to show that the underrepresentation of women, generally and on his venire, was due to their systematic exclusion in the jury-selection process. Petitioner's proof met this requirement. His undisputed demonstration that a large discrepancy occurred not just occasionally but in every weekly venire for a period of nearly a year manifestly indicates that the cause of the underrepresentation was systematic—that is, inherent in the particular jury-selection process utilized.

Petitioner Duren's statistics and other evidence also established when in the selection process the systematic exclusion took place. There was no indication that underrepresentation of women occurred at the first stage of the selection process—the questionnaire canvass of persons randomly selected from the relevant voter registration list. The first sign of a systematic discrepancy is at the next stage—the construction of the jury wheel from which persons are randomly summoned for service. Less than 30% of those summoned were female, demonstrating that a substantially larger number of women answering the questionnaire claimed either ineligibility or exemption from jury service. Moreover, at the summons stage women were not only given another opportunity to claim exemption, but also were presumed to have claimed exemption when they did not respond to the summons. Thus, the percentage of women at the final, venire, stage (14.5%) was much lower than the percentage of women who were summoned for service (26.7%).

The resulting disproportionate and consistent exclusion of women from the jury wheel and at the venire stage was quite obviously due to the system by which juries were selected. Petitioner demonstrated that the underrepresentation of women in the final pool of prospective jurors was due to the operation of Missouri's exemption criteria—whether the automatic exemption for women or other statutory exemptions—as implemented in Jackson County. Women were therefore systematically underrepresented within the meaning of *Taylor*.

III

The demonstration of a prima facie fair-cross-section violation by the defendant is not the end of the inquiry into whether a constitutional violation has occurred. We have explained that "States remain free to prescribe relevant qualifications for their jurors and to provide reasonable exemptions so long as it may be fairly said that the jury lists or panels are representative of the community." However, we cautioned that "[t]he right to a proper jury cannot be overcome on merely rational grounds." Rather, it requires that a significant state interest be manifestly and primarily advanced by those aspects of the jury-selection process, such as exemption criteria, that result in the disproportionate exclusion of a distinctive group.

The Supreme Court of Missouri suggested that the low percentage of women on jury venires in Jackson County may have been due to a greater number of women than of men qualifying for or claiming permissible exemptions, such as those for persons over 65, teachers, and government workers. Respondent further argues that petitioner has not proved that the exemption for woman had "any effect" on or was responsible for the underrepresentation of women on venires.

However, once the defendant has made a prima facie showing of an infringement of his constitutional right to a jury drawn from a fair cross section of the community, it is the State that bears the burden of justifying this infringement by showing attainment of a fair cross section to be incompatible with a significant state interest. Assuming, arguendo, that the exemptions mentioned by the court below would justify failure to achieve a fair community cross section on jury venires, the State must demonstrate that these exemptions caused the underrepresentation complained of. The record contains no such proof, and mere suggestions or assertions to that effect are insufficient.

The other possible cause of the disproportionate exclusion of women on Jackson County jury venires is, of course, the automatic exemption for women. Neither the Missouri Supreme Court nor respondent in its brief has offered any substantial justification for this exemption. In response to questioning at oral argument, counsel for respondent ventured that the only state interest advanced by the exemption is safeguarding the important role played by women in home and family life. But exempting all women because of the preclusive domestic responsibilities of some women is insufficient justification for their disproportionate exclusion on jury venires. What we stated in *Taylor* with respect to the system there challenged under which women could "opt in" for jury service is equally applicable to Missouri's "opt out" exemption:

> It is untenable to suggest these days that it would be a special hardship for each and every woman to perform jury service or that society cannot spare any women from their present duties. This may be the case with many, and it may be burdensome to sort out those who should be exempted from those who should serve. But that task is performed in the case of men and the administrative convenience in dealing with women as a class is insufficient justification for diluting the quality of community judgment represented by the jury in criminal trials.
>
> If it was ever the case that women were unqualified to sit on juries or were so situated that none of them should be required to perform jury service, that time has long since passed.

We recognize that a State may have an important interest in assuring that those members of the family responsible for the care of children are available to do so. An exemption appropriately tailored to this interest would, we think, survive a fair-cross-section challenge. We stress, however, that the constitutional guarantee to a jury drawn from a fair cross section of the community requires that States exercise proper caution in exempting broad categories of persons from jury service. Although most occupational and other reasonable exemptions may inevitably involve some degree of overinclusiveness or underinclusiveness, any category expressly limited to a group in the community of sufficient magnitude and distinctiveness so as to be within the fair-cross-section requirement — such as women — runs the danger of resulting in underrepresentation sufficient to constitute a prima facie violation of that constitutional requirement. We also repeat the observation made in *Taylor* that it is unlikely that reasonable exemptions, such as those based on special hardship, incapacity, or community needs, "would pose substantial threats that the remaining pool of jurors would not be representative of the community."

The judgment of the Missouri Supreme Court is reversed, and the case is remanded for further proceedings not inconsistent with this opinion.

So ordered.

NOTES AND QUESTIONS

1. Note the Court's formulation of the "systematic exclusion" test for establishing a prima facie violation of the fair cross-section requirement. What is the essential difference between a discriminatory effect, required to establish a prima facie equal protection violation, and a systematic exclusion, required for a prima facie fair cross-section violation? And what are the different rebuttal obligations of the government in each context?

2. In analyzing the state's response to defendant's prima facie case the Court notes that the state has not offered any "proof" that the low percentage of women on jury venires is due to factors other than the exemption for women nor has it attempted to "justify" the exemption beyond stating at oral argument that the exemption protected the role of women in home and family life. Yet the Court leaves the door open for the state to come up with an exemption that would be narrowly tailored to the protection from jury service of those providing child care. Yes, it is the 1970s, but why would the Court make this gratuitous concession? How would such an exemption be handled on a questionnaire of the type used in *Duren*? Could special hardship situations regarding child care, etc., simply be dealt with by the judge once the venire was established?

3. Any argument that the exemption for persons 65 years or over, analogous to the exemption for women, also violates the fair cross-section requirement?

Fair cross-section challenges to jury compositions have been notoriously unsuccessful in the lower courts notwithstanding the demonstrable existence of racial and ethnic disparity in the jury system. *See* Nina W. Chernoff, *Black to the Future: The State Action Doctrine and the White Jury*, 58 Washburn L.J. 103, 103-04:

> There is a significant amount of evidence, however, that jury pools do not reflect a fair cross-section of their communities, in that they underrepresent African-Americans and Latinos. But despite the gap between the robust right to representation and the consistent evidence of underrepresentation, defendants who raise fair cross-section claims almost always lose them. One study of fair cross-section claims in federal and state courts between 2000 and 2010 found that of 167 claims, defendants prevailed in exactly none.

Professor Chernoff has observed that "the underwhelming track record of the fair cross-section right stems from courts' routine [mistaken] importation of equal protection standards

1242   Chapter XV The Jury II: Race and Juries

into the analysis" instead of faithfully applying the Sixth Amendment test set forth in *Duren*. *See* Nina W. Chernoff, *Wrong About the Right: How Courts Undermine the Fair Cross-Section Guarantee by Confusing It with Equal Protection*, 64 Hastings L.J. 141, 148-49 (2012).

A viable fair cross-section claim was recognized in *United States v. Green*, 389 F. Supp. 2d 29 (D. Mass. 2005), *rev'd on other grounds, In re United States*, 426 F.3d 1 (1st Cir. 2005), albeit under the Federal Jury Selection and Service Act of 1968 (JSSA) and not the Sixth Amendment. The United States District Judge Nancy Gertner found, inter alia, that the jury pool selection process for the Eastern Division of Massachusetts relied on inaccurate and outdated resident lists that resulted in a representation of 3 percent African Americans even though the available pool of African Americans in Suffolk County, where the alleged crimes in the case were committed, was 20 percent. *Id.* at 35-37. While for various reasons the *Duren* test for a prima facie violation could not be made, the court found an affirmative obligation under the JSSA to take steps that ensure a "fair cross-section," and ordered remedies aimed at alleviating the inaccurate and outdated address selection process. *Id.* at 38.

B. BIAS CHALLENGES TO POTENTIAL JURORS

The next set of cases involves defendants' attempts to obtain a fair jury by requesting that potential jurors be questioned for racial bias, among other things. Consider whether the result in the next case depends on the specific nature of defendant's theory of defense.

Ham v. South Carolina
409 U.S. 524 (1973)

Mr. Justice REHNQUIST delivered the opinion of the Court.

Petitioner was convicted in the South Carolina trial court of the possession of marihuana in violation of state law. He was sentenced to 18 months' confinement, and on appeal his conviction was affirmed by a divided South Carolina Supreme Court. We granted certiorari limited to the question of whether the trial judge's refusal to examine jurors on voir dire as to possible prejudice against petitioner violated the latter's federal constitutional rights.

Petitioner is a young, bearded Negro who has lived most of his life in Florence County, South Carolina. He appears to have been well known locally for his work in such civil rights activities as the Southern Christian Leadership Conference and the Bi-racial Committee of the City of Florence. He has never previously been convicted of a crime. His basic defense at the trial was that law enforcement officers were "out to get him" because of his civil rights activities, and that he had been framed on the drug charge.

Prior to the trial judge's voir dire examination of prospective jurors, petitioner's counsel requested the judge to ask jurors four questions relating to possible prejudice against petitioner. The first two questions sought to elicit any possible racial prejudice against Negroes; the third question related to possible prejudice against beards; and the fourth dealt with pretrial publicity relating to the drug problem. The trial judge, while putting to the prospective jurors three general questions as to bias, prejudice, or partiality that are specified in the South Carolina statutes, declined to ask any of the four questions posed by petitioner.

The dissenting justices in the Supreme Court of South Carolina thought that this Court's decision in *Aldridge v. United States* (1931), was binding on the State. There a Negro who was being tried for the murder of a white policeman requested that prospective jurors be asked whether they entertained any racial prejudice. This Court reversed the judgment of conviction because of the trial judge's refusal to make such an inquiry. Mr. Chief Justice Hughes,

B. Bias Challenges to Potential Jurors   1243

writing for the Court, stated that the "essential demands of fairness" required the trial judge under the circumstances of that case to interrogate the veniremen with respect to racial prejudice upon the request of counsel for a Negro criminal defendant.

The Court's opinion relied upon a number of state court holdings throughout the country to the same effect, but it was not expressly grounded upon any constitutional requirement. Since one of the purposes of the Due Process Clause of the Fourteenth Amendment is to insure these "essential demands of fairness," and since a principal purpose of the adoption of the Fourteenth Amendment was to prohibit the States from invidiously discriminating on the basis of race, we think that the Fourteenth Amendment required the judge in this case to interrogate the jurors upon the subject of racial prejudice. South Carolina law permits challenges for cause, and authorizes the trial judge to conduct voir dire examination of potential jurors. The State having created this statutory framework for the selection of juries, the essential fairness required by the Due Process Clause of the Fourteenth Amendment requires that under the facts shown by this record the petitioner be permitted to have the jurors interrogated on the issue of racial bias.

We agree with the dissenting justices of the Supreme Court of South Carolina that the trial judge was not required to put the question in any particular form, or to ask any particular number of questions on the subject, simply because requested to do so by petitioner. The Court in *Aldridge* was at pains to point out, in a context where its authority within the federal system of courts allows a good deal closer supervision than does the Fourteenth Amendment, that the trial court "had a broad discretion as to the questions to be asked." The discretion as to form and number of questions permitted by the Due Process Clause of the Fourteenth Amendment is at least as broad. In this context, either of the brief, general questions urged by the petitioner would appear sufficient to focus the attention of prospective jurors on any racial prejudice they might entertain.

The third of petitioner's proposed questions was addressed to the fact that he wore a beard. While we cannot say that prejudice against people with beards might not have been harbored by one or more of the potential jurors in this case, this is the beginning and not the end of the inquiry as to whether the Fourteenth Amendment required the trial judge to interrogate the prospective jurors about such possible prejudice. Given the traditionally broad discretion accorded to the trial judge in conducting voir dire, *Aldridge v. United States, supra,* and our inability to constitutionally distinguish possible prejudice against beards from a host of other possible similar prejudices, we do not believe the petitioner's constitutional rights were violated when the trial judge refused to put this question. The inquiry as to racial prejudice derives its constitutional stature from the firmly established precedent of *Aldridge* and the numerous state cases upon which it relied, and from a principal purpose as well as from the language of those who adopted the Fourteenth Amendment. The trial judge's refusal to inquire as to particular bias against beards, after his inquiries as to bias in general, does not reach the level of a constitutional violation.

Petitioner's final question related to allegedly prejudicial pretrial publicity. But the record before us contains neither the newspaper articles nor any description of the television program in question. Because of this lack of material in the record substantiating any pretrial publicity prejudicial to this petitioner, we have no occasion to determine the merits of his request to have this question posed on voir dire.

Because of the trial court's refusal to make any inquiry as to racial bias of the prospective jurors after petitioner's timely request therefor, the judgment of the Supreme Court of South Carolina is reversed.

Judgment reversed.

Mr. Justice DOUGLAS, concurring in part and dissenting in part.

I concur in that portion of the majority's opinion that holds that the trial judge was constitutionally compelled to inquire into the possibility of racial prejudice on voir dire. I think, however, that it was an abuse of discretion for the trial judge to preclude the defendant from an inquiry by which prospective jurors' prejudice to hair growth could have been explored.

It is unquestioned that a defendant has the constitutional right to a trial by a neutral and impartial jury. Criminal convictions have been reversed when the limitations on voir dire have unreasonably infringed the exercise of this right. *Aldridge v. United States*. Such reversals have not been limited to incidents where the defendant was precluded from inquiring into possible racial prejudice. In both *Morford v. United States* and *Dennis v. United States* defendants were held to have the right to inquire into possible prejudices concerning the defendants' alleged ties with the Communist party. In *Aldridge* this Court made it clear that voir dire aimed at disclosing "prejudices of a serious character" must be allowed.

Prejudices involving hair growth are unquestionably of a "serious character." Nothing is more indicative of the importance currently being attached to hair growth by the general populace than the barrage of cases reaching the courts evidencing the attempt by one segment of society officially to control the plumage of another. On the issue of a student's right to wear long hair alone there are well over 50 reported cases. In addition, the issue of plumage has surfaced in the employment-discrimination context as well as the military area.

The prejudices invoked by the mere sight of non-conventional hair growth are deeply felt. Hair growth is symbolic to many of rebellion against traditional society and disapproval of the way the current power structure handles social problems. Taken as an affirmative declaration of an individual's commitment to a change in social values, nonconventional hair growth may become a very real personal threat to those who support the status quo. For those people, nonconventional hair growth symbolizes an undesirable life-style characterized by unreliability, dishonesty, lack of moral values, communal ("communist") tendencies, and the assumption of drug use. If the defendant, especially one being prosecuted for the illegal use of drugs, is not allowed even to make the most minimal inquiry to expose such prejudices, can it be expected that he will receive a fair trial?

Since hair growth is an outward manifestation by which many people determine whether to apply deep-rooted prejudices to an individual, to deny a defendant the right to examine this aspect of a prospective juror's personality is to deny him his most effective means of voir dire examination.

• • •

NOTES AND QUESTIONS

1. The Court notes that by statute South Carolina requires that generalized questions as to "bias, prejudice, or partiality" be asked of all prospective jurors. Are these sufficient to uncover any possible racial prejudice? Are there any tactical reasons why a defendant such as Ham might not want to propose any specific questions about racial prejudice? Does it matter whether under the particular state practice at issue voir dire questions are posed by the judge or by defense counsel?

2. *Ham* refers to *Aldridge v. United States*, 283 U.S. 308 (1931), where the Court exercised its supervisory powers to reverse the conviction where the trial judge, upon defendant's request, refused to question prospective jurors on racial prejudice in a case where a Black defendant was tried for the murder of a white policeman. *Ham* recognizes a similar requirement, binding on the states, in the Due Process Clause of the Fourteenth Amendment. In

Aldridge the Court rejected the government's argument that such questioning was unseemly: "The argument is advanced on behalf of the Government that it would be detrimental to the administration of the law in the courts of the United States to allow questions to jurors as to racial or religious prejudices. We think that it would be far more injurious to permit it to be thought that persons entertaining a disqualifying prejudice were allowed to serve as jurors and that inquiries designed to elicit the fact of disqualification were barred." *Id.* at 314-15.

3. Note the negligible burden that a ruling such as the ruling in *Ham* or *Aldridge* imposes on the trial judge. Ask a question or two on this subject, ok? Both the majority and the dissent agree that a judge cannot be required to question on a subject in a specific manner or by way of a specific number of questions. This is in part because voir dire is not an end itself but rather a means to an end: to allow the defendant's intelligent exercise of jury challenges to ensure an impartial jury.

4. Defendant's request for voir dire on prejudice against beards surely seems silly from a modern perspective, but Justice Douglas in his concurrence does not at all exaggerate the extent to which "plumage," as he puts it, was a culturally divisive issue in the time frame of Ham's trial. What good reason might the trial judge have had for refusing to ask a voir dire question on this subject? Can you think of present-day personal appearance characteristic that would warrant a defendant's requested voir dire question as to prejudice? Note, as to the anachronistic nature of defendant's requested voir dire question regarding beard prejudice, that another of the defendant's requested voir dire questions was whether the jurors would be influenced by "the use of the term 'black'" to describe persons more commonly described as "Negroes" then (including by the Supreme Court).

5. Note the good lawyering by Ham's defense counsel to tie his voir dire requests to the specifics of his defense, namely, that Ham was targeted by police as a result of his civil rights activities and that he was framed. Apart from this defense, do you believe the mere fact of potential prejudice against a Black defendant by a (presumably) white jury would have been sufficient itself to warrant a voir dire question on racial prejudice under *Aldridge*? How plausible was it to defend Ham on the basis of this defense before a likely all-white jury? Given the nature of Ham's defense, what other specific voir dire questions should Ham have asked?

As for the cultural and geographical context in which Ham's prosecution arose: Two years before Ham's trial and 80 miles away, in Orangeburg, South Carolina, state and local police officers fired into a crowd of protesting students at South Carolina State University (then South Carolina State College), an HBCU institution, killing three and wounding dozens. The protest had arisen out of the refusal of the proprietor of a local bowling alley to provide service to Black students notwithstanding the passage of the 1964 Civil Rights Act. One of the organizers of the protest was Cleveland Sellers, whose son Bakari Sellers became the youngest Black elected official in the country when he was elected to the South Carolina legislature at age 22 in 2006. Cleveland Sellers was wounded by the officers' gunfire and hospitalized; he was arrested in his hospital bed and charged with inciting a riot. He was convicted and ultimately pardoned, decades later.

Nine of the officers who fired into the crowd were charged, tried, and found not guilty in a 1969 trial. There is no evidence indicating that Gene Ham was at the protest in Orangeburg. The "Orangeburg Massacre" drew only fleeting national media attention, even though it was factually similar to the 1970 massacre by the Ohio National Guard of white antiwar protesters at Kent State University. *See generally* Lorraine Boissenault, *In 1968, Three Students Were Killed by Police, Today, Few Remember the Orangeburg Massacre,* Smithsonian Mag. (Feb. 7, 2018).

Cleveland Sellers, shot by police—and also charged criminally—in the Orangeburg Massacre

Ristaino v. Ross
424 U.S. 589 (1976)

Mr. Justice POWELL delivered the opinion of the Court.

Respondent is a Negro convicted in a state court of violent crimes against a white security guard. The trial judge denied respondent's motion that a question specifically directed to racial prejudice be asked during voir dire in addition to customary questions directed to general bias or prejudice. The narrow issue is whether, under our recent decision in *Ham v. South Carolina* (1973), respondent was constitutionally entitled to require the asking of a question specifically directed to racial prejudice. The broader issue presented is whether Ham announced a requirement applicable whenever there may be a confrontation in a criminal trial between persons of different races or different ethnic origins. We answer both of these questions in the negative.

I

Respondent, James Ross, Jr., was tried in a Massachusetts court with two other Negroes for armed robbery, assault and battery by means of a dangerous weapon, and assault and battery with intent to murder. The victim of the alleged crimes was a white man employed by Boston University as a uniformed security guard. The Voir [sic] dire of prospective jurors was to be conducted by the court, which was required by statute to inquire generally into prejudice. Each defendant, represented by separate counsel, made a written motion that the prospective jurors also be questioned specifically about racial prejudice. Each defendant also moved that the veniremen be asked about affiliations with law enforcement agencies.

The trial judge consulted counsel for the defendants about their motions. After tentatively indicating that he "(felt) that no purpose would be accomplished by asking such questions in this instance," the judge invited the views of counsel:

> **THE COURT:** . . . I thought from something Mr. Donnelly (counsel for a codefendant) said, he might have wanted on the record something which was peculiar to this case, or peculiar to the circumstances which we are operating under here which perhaps he didn't want to say in open court.

	Is there anything peculiar about it, Mr. Donnelly?
MR. DONNELLY:	No, just the fact that the victim is white, and the defendants are black.
THE COURT:	This, unfortunately, is a problem with us, and all we can hope and pray for is that the jurors and all of them take their oaths seriously and understand the spirit of their oath and understand the spirit of what the Court says to them this Judge anyway and I am sure all Judges of this Court would take the time to impress upon them before, during, and after the trial, and before their verdict, that their oath means just what it says, that they are to decide the case on the evidence, with no extraneous considerations.
	I believe that that is the best that can be done with respect to the problems which as I said, I regard as extremely important. . . .

Further discussion persuaded the judge that a question about law enforcement affiliations should be asked because of the victim's status as a security guard. But he adhered to his decision not to pose a question directed specifically to racial prejudice.

The Voir dire of five panels of prospective jurors then commenced. The trial judge briefly familiarized each panel with the facts of the case, omitting any reference to racial matters. He then explained to the panel that the clerk would ask a general question about impartiality and a question about affiliations with law enforcement agencies. Consistently with his announced intention to "impress upon (the jurors) . . . that they are to decide the case on the evidence, with no extraneous considerations," the judge preceded the questioning of the panel with an extended discussion of the obligations of jurors. After these remarks the clerk posed the questions indicated to the panel. Panelists answering a question affirmatively were questioned individually at the bench by the judge, in the presence of counsel. This procedure led to the excusing of 18 veniremen for cause on grounds of prejudice, including one panelist who admitted a racial bias.

The jury eventually impaneled convicted each defendant of all counts. On direct appeal Ross contended that his federal constitutional rights were violated by the denial of his request that prospective jurors be questioned specifically about racial prejudice. This contention was rejected by the Supreme Judicial Court of Massachusetts, and Ross sought a writ of certiorari. While his petition was pending, we held in *Ham* that a trial court's failure on request to question veniremen specifically about racial prejudice had denied Ham due process of law. We granted Ross' petition for certiorari and remanded for reconsideration in light of *Ham*; the Supreme Judicial Court again affirmed Ross' conviction. The court reasoned that *Ham* turned on the need for questions about racial prejudice presented by its facts and did not announce "a new broad constitutional principle requiring that (such) questions . . . be put to prospective jurors in all State criminal trials when the defendant is black. . . ." Ross again sought certiorari, but the writ was denied.

In the present case Ross renewed his contention on collateral attack in federal habeas corpus. Relying on *Ham*, the District Court granted a writ of habeas corpus, and the Court of Appeals for the First Circuit affirmed. The Court of Appeals assumed that Ham turned on its facts. But it held that the facts of Ross' case, involving "violence against a white" with "a status close to that of a police officer," presented a need for specific questioning about racial prejudice similar to that in *Ham*. We think the Court of Appeals read *Ham* too broadly.

II

The Constitution does not always entitle a defendant to have questions posed during Voir dire specifically directed to matters that conceivably might prejudice veniremen against him. Voir dire "is conducted under the supervision of the court, and a great deal must, of necessity, be left to its sound discretion." This is so because the "determination of impartiality, in which demeanor plays such an important part, is particularly within the province of the trial judge." Thus, the State's obligation to the defendant to impanel an impartial jury generally can be satisfied by less than an inquiry into a specific prejudice feared by the defendant.

In *Ham*, however, we recognized that some cases may present circumstances in which an impermissible threat to the fair trial guaranteed by due process is posed by a trial court's refusal to question prospective jurors specifically about racial prejudice during Voir dire. *Ham* involved a Negro tried in South Carolina courts for possession of marihuana. He was well known in the locale of his trial as a civil rights activist, and his defense was that law enforcement officials had framed him on the narcotics charge to "get him" for those activities. Despite the circumstances, the trial judge denied Ham's request that the court-conducted Voir dire include questions specifically directed to racial prejudice. We reversed the judgment of conviction because "the essential fairness required by the Due Process Clause of the Fourteenth Amendment requires that under the facts shown by this record the (defendant) be permitted to have the jurors interrogated (during voir dire) on the issue of racial bias."

By its terms *Ham* did not announce a requirement of universal applicability. Rather, it reflected an assessment of whether under all of the circumstances presented there was a constitutionally significant likelihood that, absent questioning about racial prejudice, the jurors would not be as "indifferent as (they stand) unsworn." In this approach *Ham* was consistent with other determinations by this Court that a State had denied a defendant due process by failing to impanel an impartial jury.

The circumstances in *Ham* strongly suggested the need for Voir dire to include specific questioning about racial prejudice. Ham's defense was that he had been framed because of his civil rights activities. His prominence in the community as a civil rights activist, if not already known to veniremen, inevitably would have been revealed to the members of the jury in the course of his presentation of that defense. Racial issues therefore were inextricably bound up with the conduct of the trial. Further, Ham's reputation as a civil rights activist and the defense he interposed were likely to intensify any prejudice that individual members of the jury might harbor. In such circumstances we deemed a Voir dire that included questioning specifically directed to racial prejudice, when sought by Ham, necessary to meet the constitutional requirement that an impartial jury be impaneled.

We do not agree with the Court of Appeals that the need to question veniremen specifically about racial prejudice also rose to constitutional dimensions in this case. The mere fact that the victim of the crimes alleged was a white man and the defendants were Negroes was less likely to distort the trial than were the special factors involved in *Ham*. The victim's status as a security officer, also relied upon by the Court of Appeals, was cited by respective defense counsel primarily as a separate source of prejudice, not as an aggravating racial factor, and the trial judge dealt with it by his question about law-enforcement affiliations. The circumstances thus did not suggest a significant likelihood that racial prejudice might infect Ross' trial. This was made clear to the trial judge when Ross was unable to support his motion concerning Voir dire by pointing to racial factors such as existed in *Ham* or others of comparable significance. In these circumstances, the trial judge acted within the Constitution in determining that the demands of due process could be satisfied by his more generalized but thorough inquiry into the impartiality of the veniremen. Accordingly, the judgment is

Reversed.

. . .

Mr. Justice MARSHALL, with whom Mr. Justice BRENNAN joins, dissenting.

In 1973, the Court refused to review the affirmance on direct appeal of Mr. Ross' conviction. In dissenting from that refusal, I observed that "(t)o deny this petition for certiorari is to see our decision in *Ham* stillborn and to write an epitaph for those 'essential demands of fairness' recognized by this Court 40 years ago in *Aldridge*." Today, in reversing the Court of Appeals' affirmance of the District Court's grant of a writ of habeas corpus, the Court emphatically confirms that the promises inherent in *Ham* and Aldridge will not be fulfilled. For the reasons expressed in my dissent from the earlier denial of certiorari, I cannot join in this confirmation. Accordingly, I respectfully dissent.

NOTES AND QUESTIONS

1. The Court distinguishes *Ham* on the ground that, due to the specifics of Ham's defense, "[r]acial issues therefore were inextricably bound up with the conduct of the trial." Is it too much to say that racial issues are bound up with the conduct of almost every trial, or at least every trial with a Black defendant and white victim? Take another look at *Ham*. Did *Ham* appear to rely on its specific facts? Did the Court really mean to tie the scope of its decision to the existence of a defense that the same Court would dismiss as speculative were it raised otherwise? And why aren't the facts at issue in the trial here — the alleged murder of a white security guard by Black persons — as susceptible to infection by prejudice as those in *Ham*?

2. The Court quotes the trial court's statement in rejecting defense counsel's request for a voir dire on racial prejudice that "all that we can hope and pray for is that the jurors and all of them take their oath seriously." *Id.* at 591. Why not just ask the requested questions instead of agonizing about hopes and prayers? Or do both? Why does the Court include this bit of colloquy in its opinion? Is the trial judge's acknowledgment of the potential for prejudice helpful or harmful to the credibility of the Court's result?

3. The Court emphasizes that voir dire must normally be left to the "sound discretion" of the trial judge and that "the determination of impartiality, in which demeanor plays such an important part, is particularly within the province of the trial judge."

If this is so, why does the trial judge here appear to delegate to the court clerk the "important" function of questioning the panel on impartiality and law enforcement affiliations?

And is it really the case that voir dire is "the province of the trial judge"? While jurors' "demeanor" may be relevant in analyzing potential jurors' responses to the voir dire questions asked of them — and crucial to the lawyers' decisions on exercising strikes — is "demeanor" also relevant to deciding which questions to ask in the first place?

4. In a footnote to its opinion the Court notes the unseemliness of voir dire questioning of jurors on potential prejudice: "In our heterogeneous society policy as well as constitutional considerations militate against the divisive assumption . . . that justice in a court of law may turn upon the pigmentation of skin, the accident of birth, or the choice of religion." *Id.* at 596 n.8. Note that the Court flatly rejected a substantially similar argument by the government in *Aldridge*. Is the Court less willing in 1976 to acknowledge the existence of prejudice than it was in 1931? Does the Court in 1976 think racial prejudice is a thing of the past?

5. In another pair of footnotes the Court distinguishes between voir dire requirements imposed on state courts by the Fourteenth Amendment, as in *Ham*, and those imposed on federal courts under the Court's supervisory power, as in *Aldridge. Id.* at 597 nn.9-10. The Court acknowledges that were its supervisory power applicable it would have required an instruction on racial prejudice in *Ristaino*.

1250 Chapter XV The Jury II: Race and Juries

6. The Court almost blithely reports that 18 veniremen were dismissed "for cause on grounds of prejudice, including one panelist who admitted a racial bias." *Id.* at 592. Does this demonstrate that the trial judge's generalized instruction on impartiality was sufficient? What light do these admissions of prejudice shed on the trial court's statement that "all we can do is hope and pray" that the jurors take their oath seriously?

Turner v. Murray
476 U.S. 28 (1986)

Justice WHITE announced the judgment of the Court and delivered the opinion of the Court with respect to Parts I and III, and an opinion with respect to Parts II and IV, in which Justice BLACKMUN, Justice STEVENS, and Justice O'CONNOR join.

Petitioner is a black man sentenced to death for the murder of a white storekeeper. The question presented is whether the trial judge committed reversible error at voir dire by refusing petitioner's request to question prospective jurors on racial prejudice.

I

On July 12, 1978, petitioner entered a jewelry store in Franklin, Virginia, armed with a sawed-off shotgun. He demanded that the proprietor, W. Jack Smith, Jr., put jewelry and money from the cash register into some jewelry bags. Smith complied with petitioner's demand, but triggered a silent alarm, alerting the Police Department. When Alan Bain, a police officer, arrived to inquire about the alarm, petitioner surprised him and forced him to surrender his revolver.

Having learned that Smith had triggered a silent alarm, petitioner became agitated. He fired toward the rear wall of the store and stated that if he saw or heard any more police officers, he was going to start killing those in the store. When a police siren sounded, petitioner walked to where Smith was stationed behind a counter and without warning shot him in the head with Bain's pistol, wounding Smith and causing him to slump incapacitated to the floor.

Officer Bain attempted to calm petitioner, promising to take him anywhere he wanted to go and asking him not to shoot again. Petitioner angrily replied that he was going to kill Smith for "snitching," and fired two pistol shots into Smith's chest, fatally wounding him. As petitioner turned away from shooting Smith, Bain was able to disarm him and place him under arrest.

A Southampton County, Virginia, grand jury indicted petitioner on charges of capital murder, use of a firearm in the commission of a murder, and possession of a sawed-off shotgun in the commission of a robbery. Petitioner requested and was granted a change of venue to Northampton County, Virginia, a rural county some 80 miles from the location of the murder.

Prior to the commencement of voir dire, petitioner's counsel submitted to the trial judge a list of proposed questions, including the following:

> The defendant, Willie Lloyd Turner, is a member of the Negro race. The victim, W. Jack Smith, Jr., was a white Caucasian. Will these facts prejudice you against Willie Lloyd Turner or affect your ability to render a fair and impartial verdict based solely on the evidence?

The judge declined to ask this question, stating that it "has been ruled on by the Supreme Court." The judge did ask the venire, who were questioned in groups of five in petitioner's presence, whether any person was aware of any reason why he could not render a fair and impartial verdict, to which all answered "no." At the time the question was asked, the prospective jurors had no way of knowing that the murder victim was white.

The jury that was empaneled, which consisted of eight whites and four blacks, convicted petitioner on all of the charges against him. After a separate sentencing hearing on the capital charge, the jury recommended that petitioner be sentenced to death, a recommendation the trial judge accepted.

Petitioner appealed his death sentence to the Virginia Supreme Court. Among other points, he argued that the trial judge deprived him of his constitutional right to a fair and impartial jury by refusing to question prospective jurors on racial prejudice. The Virginia Supreme Court rejected this argument. Relying on our decision in *Restaino*, the court stated that a trial judge's refusal to ask prospective jurors about their racial attitudes, while perhaps not the wisest decision as a matter of policy, is not constitutionally objectionable in the absence of factors akin to those in *Ham v. South Carolina*. The court held that "[t]he mere fact that a defendant is black and that a victim is white does not constitutionally mandate . . . an inquiry [into racial prejudice]."

Having failed in his direct appeal, petitioner sought habeas corpus relief in the Federal District Court for the Eastern District of Virginia. Again he argued without success that the trial judge's refusal to ask prospective jurors about their racial attitudes deprived him of his right to a fair trial. The District Court noted that in *Ristaino*, supra, which involved a crime of interracial violence, we held that inquiry into racial prejudice at voir dire was not constitutionally required because the facts of the case " 'did not suggest a significant likelihood that racial prejudice might infect [the defendant's] trial.' " The court found the present case like *Ristaino* and unlike *Ham* in that "racial issues [are] not 'inextricably bound up with the facts at trial.' "

The United States Court of Appeals for the Fourth Circuit affirmed the District Court's denial of habeas corpus relief for petitioner. Like the Virginia Supreme Court and the District Court, the Fourth Circuit found no "special circumstances" in this case analogous to those in *Ham*. The court rejected the idea that "the nature of the crime or punishment itself is . . . a special circumstance." Relying on *Ristaino*, the court likewise found no special circumstance in the fact that petitioner is black and his victim white.

We granted certiorari to review the Fourth Circuit's decision that petitioner was not constitutionally entitled to have potential jurors questioned concerning racial prejudice. We reverse.

II

The Fourth Circuit's opinion correctly states the analytical framework for evaluating petitioner's argument: "The broad inquiry in each case must be . . . whether under all of the circumstances presented there was a constitutionally significant likelihood that, absent questioning about racial prejudice, the jurors would not be indifferent as [they stand] unsworn." The Fourth Circuit was correct, too, in holding that under *Ristaino* the mere fact that petitioner is black and his victim white does not constitute a "special circumstance" of constitutional proportions. What sets this case apart from *Ristaino*, however, is that in addition to petitioner's being accused of a crime against a white victim, the crime charged was a capital offense.

In a capital sentencing proceeding before a jury, the jury is called upon to make a "highly subjective, 'unique, individualized judgment regarding the punishment that a particular person deserves.' " The Virginia statute under which petitioner was sentenced is instructive of the kinds of judgments a capital sentencing jury must make. First, in order to consider the death penalty, a Virginia jury must find either that the defendant is likely to commit future violent crimes or that his crime was "outrageously or wantonly vile, horrible or inhuman in that it involved torture, depravity of mind or an aggravated battery to the victim." Second, the jury must consider any mitigating evidence offered by the defendant. Mitigating evidence may include, but is not limited to, facts tending to show that the defendant acted under the influence of extreme emotional or mental disturbance, or that at the time of the crime the defendant's capacity "to appreciate the criminality of his conduct or to conform his conduct to the requirements of law was significantly impaired." Finally, even if the jury has found an aggravating factor, and irrespective of whether mitigating evidence has been offered, the jury has discretion not to recommend the death sentence, in which case it may not be imposed.

Virginia's death-penalty statute gives the jury greater discretion than other systems which we have upheld against constitutional challenge. However, our cases establish that every capital sentencer must be free to weigh relevant mitigating evidence before deciding whether to impose the death penalty, and that in the end it is the jury that must make the difficult, individualized judgment as to whether the defendant deserves the sentence of death.

Because of the range of discretion entrusted to a jury in a capital sentencing hearing, there is a unique opportunity for racial prejudice to operate but remain undetected. On the facts of this case, a juror who believes that blacks are violence prone or morally inferior might well be influenced by that belief in deciding whether petitioner's crime involved the aggravating factors specified under Virginia law. Such a juror might also be less favorably inclined toward petitioner's evidence of mental disturbance as a mitigating circumstance. More subtle, less consciously held racial attitudes could also influence a juror's decision in this case. Fear of blacks, which could easily be stirred up by the violent facts of petitioner's crime, might incline a juror to favor the death penalty.

The risk of racial prejudice infecting a capital sentencing proceeding is especially serious in light of the complete finality of the death sentence. "The Court, as well as the separate opinions of a majority of the individual Justices, has recognized that the qualitative difference of death from all other punishments requires a correspondingly greater degree of scrutiny of the capital sentencing determination." We have struck down capital sentences when we found that the circumstances under which they were imposed "created an unacceptable risk that 'the death penalty [may have been] meted out arbitrarily or capriciously' or through 'whim . . . or mistake.'" In the present case, we find the risk that racial prejudice may have infected petitioner's capital sentencing unacceptable in light of the ease with which that risk could have been minimized. By refusing to question prospective jurors on racial prejudice, the trial judge failed to adequately protect petitioner's constitutional right to an impartial jury.

III

We hold that a capital defendant accused of an interracial crime is entitled to have prospective jurors informed of the race of the victim and questioned on the issue of racial bias. The rule we propose is minimally intrusive; as in other cases involving "special circumstances," the trial judge retains discretion as to the form and number of questions on the subject, including the decision whether to question the venire individually or collectively. Also, a defendant cannot complain of a judge's failure to question the venire on racial prejudice unless the defendant has specifically requested such an inquiry.

IV

The inadequacy of voir dire in this case requires that petitioner's death sentence be vacated. It is not necessary, however, that he be retried on the issue of guilt. Our judgment in this case is that there was an unacceptable risk of racial prejudice infecting the capital sentencing proceeding. This judgment is based on a conjunction of three factors: the fact that the crime charged involved interracial violence, the broad discretion given the jury at the death-penalty hearing, and the special seriousness of the risk of improper sentencing in a capital case. At the guilt phase of petitioner's trial, the jury had no greater discretion than it would have had if the crime charged had been noncapital murder. Thus, with respect to the guilt phase of petitioner's trial, we find this case to be indistinguishable from *Ristaino*, to which we continue to adhere.

The judgment of the Court of Appeals is reversed, and the case is remanded for further proceedings consistent with this opinion.

It is so ordered.

Justice BRENNAN, concurring in part and dissenting in part.

The Court's judgment vacates petitioner's sentence of death while refusing to disturb his conviction. Adhering to my view that the death penalty is in all circumstances cruel and unusual punishment prohibited by the Eighth and Fourteenth Amendments, I agree that the death sentence in this case must be vacated. But even if I did not hold that view, I would still find that the sentence was unconstitutionally imposed in this case. In my view, the constitutional right of a defendant to have a trial judge ask the members of the venire questions concerning possible racial bias is triggered whenever a violent interracial crime has been committed. The reality of race relations in this country is such that we simply may not presume impartiality, and the risk of bias runs especially high when members of a community serving on a jury are to be confronted with disturbing evidence of criminal conduct that is often terrifying and abhorrent. In analyzing the question of when the Constitution requires trial judges to accommodate defendants' requests for inquiries into racial prejudice, I, like the Court, am influenced by what the Court correctly describes as the "ease" with which the risk may be minimized.

In any event, I cannot fully join either the Court's judgment or opinion. For in my view, the decision in this case, although clearly half right, is even more clearly half wrong. After recognizing that the constitutional guarantee of an impartial jury entitles a defendant in a capital case involving interracial violence to have prospective jurors questioned on the issue of racial bias—a holding which requires that this case be reversed and remanded for new sentencing—the Court disavows the logic of its own reasoning in denying petitioner Turner a new trial on the issue of his guilt. It accomplishes this by postulating a jury role at the sentencing phase of a capital trial fundamentally different from the jury function at the guilt phase and by concluding that the former gives rise to a significantly greater risk of a verdict tainted by racism. Because I believe that the Court's analysis improperly intertwines the significance of the risk of bias with the consequences of bias, and because in my view the distinction between the jury's role at a guilt trial and its role at a sentencing hearing is a distinction without substance in so far as juror bias is concerned, I join only that portion of the Court's judgment granting petitioner a new sentencing proceeding, but dissent from that portion of the judgment refusing to vacate the conviction.

The Sixth Amendment guarantees criminal defendants an impartial jury. This is not mere exhortation for it has been noted that "the right to an impartial jury carries with it the concomitant right to take reasonable steps designed to insure that the jury is impartial." Among the most important of the means designed to insure an impartial jury is the right to strike those jurors who manifest an inability to try the case solely on the basis of the evidence. This right to exclude incompetent jurors cannot be exercised meaningfully or effectively unless counsel has sufficient information with which to evaluate members of the venire. As Justice White noted for the Court in *Rosales-Lopez v. United States*, "lack of adequate voir dire impairs the defendant's right to exercise peremptory challenges where provided by statute or rule, as it is in the federal courts."

Recognizing this fact, we held long ago that "essential demands of fairness" may require a judge to ask jurors whether they entertain any racial prejudice. More recently, we attempted to refine the analysis, and declared that when there is a showing of a "likelihood" that racial or ethnic prejudice may affect the jurors, the Constitution requires a trial judge to honor a defendant's request to examine the jurors' ability to deal impartially with the evidence adduced at trial. Exercising our supervisory powers over the federal courts, we held in *Rosales-Lopez* that when a violent crime has been committed, and the victim and the accused are of different races, a per se inference of a "reasonable possibility" of prejudice is shown. In the present case, we deal with a criminal case from a state court involving an act of interracial violence, and are faced with the question of what factors and circumstances will elevate this presumptive "reasonable possibility" of prejudice into a constitutionally significant "likelihood" of prejudice.

The Court identifies three factors, the "conjunction" of which in its view entitled petitioner Turner as a matter of constitutional right to have the jury questioned on racial bias. These are (1) the fact that the crime committed involved interracial violence; (2) the broad discretion given the jury at the death penalty hearing; and (3) the "special seriousness of the risk of improper sentencing in a capital case." I agree with the Court that when these three factors are present, as they were at petitioner's sentencing hearing, the trial court commits constitutional error in refusing a defense request to ask the jurors if the race of either the victim or the accused will bear on their ability to render a decision based solely on the evidence. What I cannot accept is that the judge is released from this obligation to insure an impartial jury—or, to put it another way, that the defendant is stripped of this constitutional safeguard—when a capital jury is hearing evidence concerning a crime involving interracial violence but passing "only" on the issue of guilt/innocence, rather than on the appropriate sentence.

The Court's argument is simply untenable on its face. As best I can understand it, the thesis is that since there is greater discretion entrusted to a capital jury in the sentencing phase than in the guilt phase, "there is [in the sentencing hearing] a unique opportunity for racial prejudice to operate but remain undetected." However, the Court's own discussion of the issues demonstrates that the opportunity for racial bias to taint the jury process is not "uniquely" present at a sentencing hearing, but is equally a factor at the guilt phase of a bifurcated capital trial.

According to the Court, a prejudiced juror sitting at a sentencing hearing might be influenced by his racial bias in deciding whether the crime committed involved aggravating factors specified under state law; the Court notes that racial prejudice might similarly cause that juror to be less favorably inclined toward an accused's evidence of mitigating circumstances. Moreover, the Court informs us:

> More subtle, less consciously held racial attitudes could also influence a juror's decision. . . . Fear of blacks, which could easily be stirred up by the violent facts of [a] crime, might incline a juror to favor the death penalty.

The flaw in this "analysis" is that there is simply no connection between the proposition advanced, the support proffered for that thesis, and the conclusion drawn. In other words, it is certainly true, as the Court maintains, that racial bias inclines one to disbelieve and disfavor the object of the prejudice, and it is similarly incontestable that subconscious, as well as express, racial fears and hatreds operate to deny fairness to the person despised; that is why we seek to insure that the right to an impartial jury is a meaningful right by providing the defense with the opportunity to ask prospective jurors questions designed to expose even hidden prejudices. But the Court never explains why these biases should be of less concern at the guilt phase than at the sentencing phase. The majority asserts that "a juror who believes that blacks are violence prone or morally inferior might well be influenced by that belief in deciding whether petitioner's crime involved the aggravating factors specified under Virginia law." But might not that same juror be influenced by those same prejudices in deciding whether, for example, to credit or discredit white witnesses as opposed to black witnesses at the guilt phase? Might not those same racial fears that would incline a juror to favor death not also incline a juror to favor conviction?

A trial to determine guilt or innocence is, at bottom, nothing more than the sum total of a countless number of small discretionary decisions made by each individual who sits in the jury box. The difference between conviction and acquittal turns on whether key testimony is believed or rejected; on whether an alibi sounds plausible or dubious; on whether a character witness appears trustworthy or unsavory; and on whether the jury concludes that the defendant had a motive, the inclination, or the means available to commit the crime charged. A racially biased juror sits with blurred vision and impaired sensibilities and is incapable of fairly making the myriad decisions that each juror is called upon to make in the course of a trial. To put it simply, he cannot judge because he has prejudged. This is equally true at the trial on guilt as at the hearing on sentencing.

To sentence an individual to death on the basis of a proceeding tainted by racial bias would violate the most basic values of our criminal justice system. This the Court understands. But what it seems not to comprehend is that to permit an individual to be convicted by a prejudiced jury violates those same values in precisely the same way. The incongruity of the Court's split judgment is made apparent after it is appreciated that the opportunity for bias to poison decisionmaking operates at a guilt trial in the same way as it does at a sentencing hearing and after one returns to the context of the case before us. Implicit in the Court's judgment is the acknowledgment that there was a likelihood that the jury that pronounced the death sentence acted, in part, on the basis of racial prejudice. But the exact same jury convicted Turner. Does the Court really mean to suggest that the constitutional entitlement to an impartial jury attaches only at the sentencing phase? Does the Court really believe that racial biases are turned on and off in the course of one criminal prosecution?

My sense is that the Court has confused the consequences of an unfair trial with the risk that a jury is acting on the basis of prejudice. In other words, I suspect that what is really animating the Court's judgment is the sense of outrage it rightly experiences at the prospect of a man being sentenced to death on the basis of the color of his skin. Perhaps the Court is slightly less troubled by the prospect of a racially motivated conviction unaccompanied by the death penalty, and I suppose that if, for some unimaginable reason, I had to choose between the two cases, and could only rectify one, I would remedy the case where death had been imposed. But there is no need to choose between the two cases. To state what seems to me obvious, the constitutional right implicated is the right to be judged by an impartial jury, regardless of the sentence, and the constitutional focus thus belongs on whether there is a likelihood of bias, and not on what flows from that bias. In *Ham*, we reversed the conviction of a young black man who was charged with and convicted of possession of marijuana; because the man was known in the community as a civil rights activist, and because we were persuaded that racial issues were inextricably bound up with the conduct of the trial, we concluded that it was likely that any prejudice that individual members of the jury might harbor would be intensified and held that under those circumstances the trial judge was required to oblige the defense request to inquire into the jury's possible racial bias. We did not reject the petitioner's claim in that case because he was sentenced only to 18 months' imprisonment. Surely one has a right to an impartial jury whether one is subject to punishment for a day or a lifetime.

The Court may believe that it is being Solomonic in "splitting the difference" in this case and granting petitioner a new sentencing hearing while denying him the other "half" of the relief demanded. Starkly put, petitioner "wins" in that he gets to be resentenced, while the State "wins" in that it does not lose its conviction. But King Solomon did not, in fact, split the baby in two, and had he done so, I suspect that he would be remembered less for his wisdom than for his hardheartedness. Justice is not served by compromising principles in this way. I would reverse the conviction as well as the sentence in this case to insure compliance with the constitutional guarantee of an impartial jury.

• • •

NOTES AND QUESTIONS

1. "It 'has been ruled on by the Supreme Court.'" What do you make of the trial judge's response to the defendant's request for a voir dire question on racial prejudice? Isn't he saying, more or less, "*Ristaino* says I don't have to and therefore I won't."

Was this judge exercising the "sound discretion" entrusted to him to ensure the fairness of the upcoming trial? What does this reaction suggest to you about the extent to which trial judges should be given wide latitude on voir dire? What do you make of the fact that the judge did not inform the jurors that the murder victim was white before questioning them on impartiality?

2. The Court distinguishes *Ristaino* on the ground that *Turner* is a capital case, and that the kind of judgment a jury must make in the sentencing phase of a capital case is qualitatively different—more individualized, more subjective, more discretionary—than a simple judgment as to guilt or innocence, and that in capital sentencing "there is a unique opportunity for racial prejudice to operate but remain undetected." Accordingly, it reverses the conviction but only as to the sentencing portion of the judgment. It's hard to quarrel with the observation that capital sentencing is different. But isn't there always room for racial prejudice to operate "undetected"? And what are the implications of the Court's apparent suggestion that racial prejudice might actually lead a juror to vote for death in a capital case?

3. Justice Brennan, concurring in part and dissenting in part, describes the majority opinion as "improperly intertwin[ing] the risk of bias with the consequences of bias." *Id.* at 39-40. Is this a fair criticism? He also rejects the majority's distinction between the jury's capital sentencing judgment and the judgment of guilt or innocence:

> A trial to determine guilt or innocence is, at bottom, nothing more than the sum total of a countless number of small discretionary decisions made by each individual who sits in the jury box. The difference between conviction and acquittal turns on whether key testimony is believed or rejected; on whether an alibi sounds plausible or dubious; on whether a character witness appears trustworthy or unsavory; and on whether the jury concludes that the defendant had a motive, the inclination, or the means available to commit the crime charged. A racially biased juror sits with blurred vision and impaired sensibilities and is incapable of fairly making the myriad decisions that each juror is called upon to make in the course of a trial. To put it simply, he cannot judge because he has prejudged. This is equally true at the trial on guilt as at the hearing on sentencing.

Id. at 42-43. Do you agree that there is no material difference between guilt and sentencing determinations in terms of the potential for prejudice to have an effect?

4. The dissent states emphatically that "[n]othing in this record suggests that racial bias played any role in the jurors' obligations." *Id.* at 47. What evidence—other than overtly racist statements by jurors in front of total strangers—would be probative of such bias? Isn't the danger of covert prejudice as real as overt prejudice? The dissent claims that asking a question about racial prejudice in voir dire has "the negative effect of suggesting to the jurors that race is somehow relevant to the case." *Id.* at 48 n.5. Do you agree? Even if there is some risk in crudely asking such a question, aren't trial judges equipped to inquire in a way that would eliminate the risk of such a suggestion?

Professor Sheri Lynn Johnson argues that according to empirical studies of racism the decision in *Turner* is "exactly backward":

> In *Turner*, however, I think we see more than just a pragmatic balancing of values and views. This compromise can be justified; its justification, however, rests upon a false empirical premise. *If* racial bias were an exceptional occurrence and *if* it were largely composed of conscious hostility

towards persons of other races, then we would expect that in an "ordinary" decision determining the "facts" of guilt, prejudice would be much less likely to operate than in a decision regarding how to punish a person. But these assumptions are both empirically wrong: race affects the thinking of virtually everyone in this society, and for more and more people, this influence is neither conscious nor motivated by hostility. Ironically, the empirical evidence says that Justice White got it exactly backward. If we look at mock jury studies examining the effects of the defendant's race on jurors' decisions, it appears that the defendant's race affects guilt determinations more often than it affects sentences; it is the subtle, unconscious alteration of judgment, not the conscious desire to injure, that most threatens the fair administration of the criminal justice system.

Sheri Lynn Johnson, *Unconscious Racism and the Criminal Law*, 73 Cornell L. Rev. 1016, 1022 (1988).

An issue of clearcut, overt prejudice by a juror was considered by the Court in a post-verdict context in *Pena-Rodriguez v. Colorado*, 580 U.S. 206 (2017). A Colorado jury had rendered a verdict finding a Latino defendant guilty of sexual harassment charges based on an incident with two teenage girls. After the jury was discharged two jurors informed defendant's counsel that one of the jurors had expressed anti-Hispanic bias toward the defendant and the defendant's alibi witness. *Id.* at 212. According to the two jurors, the other juror stated the following: that he "believed the defendant was guilty because, in his experience as an ex-law enforcement officer, Mexican men had a bravado that caused them to believe they could do whatever they wanted with women"; that Mexican men are physically controlling of women because of their sense of entitlement; "I think he did it because he's Mexican and Mexican men take whatever they want"; that, in his experience, "nine times out of ten Mexican men were guilty of being aggressive toward women and young girls"; and that he did not find petitioner's alibi witness credible because, among other things, the witness was "an illegal." *Id.* at 213. (In fact, the witness testified during trial that he was a legal resident of the United States.)

The existence of demonstrated racial animus implicated the general jury "no impeachment" rule, recognized at common law and in some form at the federal level and in every state, *see, e.g.*, Fed. R. Evid. 606(b), that prohibited juror testimony about statements made during jury deliberations. In a 6-3 decision, the Court held that the no-impeachment rule must yield for the limited purpose of permitting the trial court to take evidence on whether "racial animus was a significant motivating factor in the juror's vote to convict." *Id.* at 225-26. Is that an appropriate remedy? How should the trial court handle the matter on remand?

In *Love v. Texas*, 590 U.S. _____ (2022), No. 21-5050, 2022 WL 1131367 (Sotomayor, J., dissenting from denial of certiorari), a capital murder trial of a Black defendant, one of the jurors stated in response to a question on a pretrial questionnaire administered by the court that he believed "statistics show that more violent crimes are committed by certain races." Under Texas law one of the specific sentencing issues for the jury to consider was whether the defendant would commit future acts of violence. The trial court refused to strike the juror for cause, without explanation, and defendant had already used all of his peremptory challenges. The Texas appellate court found any error harmless because defendant was previously given two extra peremptory challenges under a Texas procedure intended to cure in advance any error in for-cause challenges. The three dissenters argued that as a matter of federal law the seating of a partial juror could not be harmless, and that the case should be remanded for the state court's consideration of the constitutional issue.

C. RACE AND PEREMPTORY CHALLENGES

The flip side of the defense use of voir dire challenges to probe for bias — with the goal of eliminating bias from the jury — may be the prosecution's historic ability to use peremptory challenges in an effort to preclude Black people from serving on juries.

In *Swain v. Alabama*, 380 U.S. 202 (1965), the Court upheld the prosecutor's use of peremptory challenges to strike Black jurors even though the record indicated there had never been a Black petit juror in Talladega County. The Court allowed for the possibility that a "systematic" practice of excluding Black persons from juries through the use of peremptory challenges—"in case after case, whatever the circumstances, whatever the crime and whoever the defendant or the victim may be"—could conceivably establish a Fourteenth Amendment violation. (The Court's citation to *Yick Wo v. Hopkins* at this point in the opinion was a hint that making such a case will almost surely be impossible.) And the Court concluded that the "record in this case is insufficient" because there is no evidence "of what the prosecutor did or did not do on its own account in any cases other than the one at bar." *Id.* at 224-25.

The Court in *Swain* emphasized the longstanding practice of peremptory challenges not *despite* the potential for their discriminatory use but almost *because* of it. *Id.* at 219-23. The Court openly admitted that peremptories can be and are used on grounds "normally thought irrelevant to legal proceedings" such as race, religion, and nationality. *Id.* at 220. Such challenges, the Court concluded serve a function "in a pluralistic society"—a society with multiple races and nationalities?—and to require their use to be explained would be inconsistent with that function. Accordingly, the Court established a presumption that the prosecutor in any particular case is using peremptory challenges to obtain a fair and impartial jury. *Id.* at 222. Are there any better reasons for peremptory challenges than the ones the Court provides?

Trial lawyers like peremptory challenges because they foster the illusion that lawyers have insight into how jurors behave, but this is hardly a reason justifying their existence. *See* John Paul Stevens, Foreword, *Symposium: The Jury at a Crossroad: The American Experience*, 78 Chi.-Kent L. Rev. 907, 907-08 (2003) ("During my years as a practicing lawyer, I viewed the arbitrary right to exclude individual members of the venire from acting as jurors in particular trials as one of the litigant's fundamental procedural protections. History, tradition, and the adversary character of the trial process supported my view that the peremptory challenge had the status of an inalienable right."). Recall the Court's statement in *Duncan v. Louisiana* that the jury trial was conceived as a safeguard against the overreaching of *both* the "overzealous prosecutor and . . . the compliant, biased, or eccentric judge." Do peremptory challenges serve something of the same function as a safeguard against the second of these evils?

Swain was very much an outlier for the Warren Court, best known for its progressive criminal procedure decisions in cases such as *Gideon*, *Miranda*, and *Mapp*, all decided within a few years of *Swain*. And in perhaps the ultimate irony it was the law-and-order Burger Court that not only ultimately reversed *Swain* but also saved Swain himself, vacating his death sentence in 1972, 408 U.S. 936 (1972), as a consequence of its temporary invalidation of the death penalty in *Furman v. Georgia*, 408 U.S. 238 (1972).

Not long after *Swain* was decided some state courts relied on provisions of their own state constitutions to prohibit the use of race-based peremptory challenges. In *People v. Wheeler*, 22 Cal. 3d 258 (1978), the California Supreme Court held that the use of race-based peremptory challenges violates the right to trial by a jury drawn from a representative cross-section of the community under Cal. Const., art. I, § 16. And in *Commonwealth v. Soares,* 377 Mass. 461 (1979), the Supreme Judicial Court of Massachusetts reached a similar result under the jury trial right afforded by Article 12 of the Massachusetts Constitution, which includes a right to a jury representing a fair cross-section of the community. Both courts noted the Supreme Court's recent "fair cross-section" decision in *Taylor v. Louisiana,* and relied on state counterparts of that provision rather than equal protection cognates.

Swain was argued in the Supreme Court by the NAACP's Constance Baker Motley, and reportedly was the only case she ever lost there in 10 arguments. Tomiko Brown-Nagin, Civil Rights Queen: Constance Baker Motley and the Struggle for Equality 342 (2022).

C. Race and Peremptory Challenges

NAACP litigator and federal judge
Constance Baker Motley

Swain was reconsidered over two decades later by a very conservative version of the Burger Court.

Batson v. Kentucky
476 U.S. 79 (1986)

Justice POWELL delivered the opinion of the Court.

This case requires us to reexamine that portion of *Swain v. Alabama* (1965), concerning the evidentiary burden placed on a criminal defendant who claims that he has been denied equal protection through the State's use of peremptory challenges to exclude members of his race from the petit jury.

I

Petitioner, a black man, was indicted in Kentucky on charges of second-degree burglary and receipt of stolen goods. On the first day of trial in Jefferson Circuit Court, the judge conducted voir dire examination of the venire, excused certain jurors for cause, and permitted the parties to exercise peremptory challenges. The prosecutor used his peremptory challenges to strike all four black persons on the venire, and a jury composed only of white persons was selected. Defense counsel moved to discharge the jury before it was sworn on the ground that the prosecutor's removal of the black veniremen violated petitioner's rights under the Sixth and Fourteenth Amendments to a jury drawn from a cross section of the community, and under the Fourteenth Amendment to equal protection of the laws. Counsel requested a hearing on his motion. Without expressly ruling on the request for a hearing, the trial judge observed that the parties were entitled to use their peremptory challenges to "strike anybody they want to." The judge then denied petitioner's motion, reasoning that the cross-section requirement applies only to selection of the venire and not to selection of the petit jury itself.

The jury convicted petitioner on both counts. On appeal to the Supreme Court of Kentucky, petitioner pressed, among other claims, the argument concerning the prosecutor's use of peremptory challenges. Conceding that *Swain v. Alabama, supra*, apparently foreclosed an equal protection claim based solely on the prosecutor's conduct in this case, petitioner urged the court to follow decisions of other States, *People v. Wheeler* (1978); *Commonwealth v. Soares* (1979), and to hold that such conduct violated his rights under the Sixth Amendment and § 11 of the Kentucky Constitution to a jury drawn from a cross section of the community. Petitioner also contended that the facts showed that the prosecutor had engaged in a "pattern" of discriminatory challenges in this case and established an equal protection violation under *Swain*.

The Supreme Court of Kentucky affirmed. In a single paragraph, the court declined petitioner's invitation to adopt the reasoning of *People v. Wheeler, supra*, and *Commonwealth v. Soares, supra*. The court observed that it recently had reaffirmed its reliance on *Swain*, and had held that a defendant alleging lack of a fair cross section must demonstrate systematic exclusion of a group of jurors from the venire. We granted certiorari, and now reverse.

II

In *Swain v. Alabama*, this Court recognized that a "State's purposeful or deliberate denial to Negroes on account of race of participation as jurors in the administration of justice violates the Equal Protection Clause." This principle has been "consistently and repeatedly" reaffirmed, in numerous decisions of this Court both preceding and following *Swain*. We reaffirm the principle today.

A

More than a century ago, the Court decided that the State denies a black defendant equal protection of the laws when it puts him on trial before a jury from which members of his race have been purposefully excluded. *Strauder v. West Virginia* (1880). That decision laid the foundation for the Court's unceasing efforts to eradicate racial discrimination in the procedures used to select the venire from which individual jurors are drawn. In *Strauder*, the Court explained that the central concern of the recently ratified Fourteenth Amendment was to put an end to governmental discrimination on account of race. Exclusion of black citizens from service as jurors constitutes a primary example of the evil the Fourteenth Amendment was designed to cure.

In holding that racial discrimination in jury selection offends the Equal Protection Clause, the Court in *Strauder* recognized, however, that a defendant has no right to a "petit jury composed in whole or in part of persons of his own race." "The number of our races and nationalities stands in the way of evolution of such a conception" of the demand of equal protection. But the defendant does have the right to be tried by a jury whose members are selected pursuant to nondiscriminatory criteria. The Equal Protection Clause guarantees the defendant that the State will not exclude members of his race from the jury venire on account of race, or on the false assumption that members of his race as a group are not qualified to serve as jurors.

Purposeful racial discrimination in selection of the venire violates a defendant's right to equal protection because it denies him the protection that a trial by jury is intended to secure. "The very idea of a jury is a body . . . composed of the peers or equals of the person whose rights it is selected or summoned to determine; that is, of his neighbors, fellows, associates, persons having the same legal status in society as that which he holds." The petit jury has occupied a central position in our system of justice by safeguarding a person accused of crime against the arbitrary exercise of power by prosecutor or judge. Those on the venire must be "indifferently chosen," to secure the defendant's right under the Fourteenth Amendment to "protection of life and liberty against race or color prejudice."

Racial discrimination in selection of jurors harms not only the accused whose life or liberty they are summoned to try. Competence to serve as a juror ultimately depends on an assessment of individual qualifications and ability impartially to consider evidence presented at a trial. A person's race simply "is unrelated to his fitness as a juror." As long ago as *Strauder*, therefore, the Court recognized that by denying a person participation in jury service on account of his race, the State unconstitutionally discriminated against the excluded juror.

The harm from discriminatory jury selection extends beyond that inflicted on the defendant and the excluded juror to touch the entire community. Selection procedures that purposefully exclude black persons from juries undermine public confidence in the fairness of our system of justice. Discrimination within the judicial system is most pernicious because it is "a stimulant to that race prejudice which is an impediment to securing to [black citizens] that equal justice which the law aims to secure to all others."

B

In *Strauder*, the Court invalidated a state statute that provided that only white men could serve as jurors. We can be confident that no State now has such a law. The Constitution requires, however, that we look beyond the face of the statute defining juror qualifications and also consider challenged selection practices to afford "protection against action of the State through its administrative officers in effecting the prohibited discrimination." Thus, the Court has found a denial of equal protection where the procedures implementing a neutral statute operated to exclude persons from the venire on racial grounds, and has made clear that the Constitution prohibits all forms of purposeful racial discrimination in selection of jurors. While decisions of this Court have been concerned largely with discrimination during selection of the venire, the principles announced there also forbid discrimination on account of race in selection of the petit jury. Since the Fourteenth Amendment protects an accused throughout the proceedings bringing him to justice, the State may not draw up its jury lists pursuant to neutral procedures but then resort to discrimination at "other stages in the selection process."

Accordingly, the component of the jury selection process at issue here, the State's privilege to strike individual jurors through peremptory challenges, is subject to the commands of the Equal Protection Clause. Although a prosecutor ordinarily is entitled to exercise permitted peremptory challenges "for any reason at all, as long as that reason is related to his view concerning the outcome" of the case to be tried, the Equal Protection Clause forbids the prosecutor to challenge potential jurors solely on account of their race or on the assumption that black jurors as a group will be unable impartially to consider the State's case against a black defendant.

III

The principles announced in *Strauder* never have been questioned in any subsequent decision of this Court. Rather, the Court has been called upon repeatedly to review the application of those principles to particular facts. A recurring question in these cases, as in any case alleging a violation of the Equal Protection Clause, was whether the defendant had met his burden of proving purposeful discrimination on the part of the State. That question also was at the heart of the portion of *Swain v. Alabama* we reexamine today.

A

Swain required the Court to decide, among other issues, whether a black defendant was denied equal protection by the State's exercise of peremptory challenges to exclude members of his race from the petit jury. The record in *Swain* showed that the prosecutor had used the State's peremptory challenges to strike the six black persons included on the petit jury venire. While rejecting the defendant's claim for failure to prove purposeful discrimination, the Court nonetheless indicated that the Equal Protection Clause placed some limits on the State's exercise of peremptory challenges.

The Court sought to accommodate the prosecutor's historical privilege of peremptory challenge free of judicial control, and the constitutional prohibition on exclusion of persons from jury service on account of race. While the Constitution does not confer a right to peremptory challenges, those challenges traditionally have been viewed as one means of assuring the selection of a qualified and unbiased jury. To preserve the peremptory nature of the prosecutor's challenge, the Court in *Swain* declined to scrutinize his actions in a particular case by relying on a presumption that he properly exercised the State's challenges.

The Court went on to observe, however, that a State may not exercise its challenges in contravention of the Equal Protection Clause. It was impermissible for a prosecutor to use his challenges to exclude blacks from the jury "for reasons wholly unrelated to the outcome of the particular case on trial" or to deny to blacks "the same right and opportunity to participate in the administration of justice enjoyed by the white population." Accordingly, a black defendant could make out a prima facie case of purposeful discrimination on proof that the peremptory challenge system was "being perverted" in that manner. For example, an inference of purposeful discrimination would be raised on evidence that a prosecutor, "in case after case, whatever the circumstances, whatever the crime and whoever the defendant or the victim may be, is responsible for the removal of Negroes who have been selected as qualified jurors by the jury commissioners and who have survived challenges for cause, with the result that no Negroes ever serve on petit juries." Evidence offered by the defendant in *Swain* did not meet that standard. While the defendant showed that prosecutors in the jurisdiction had exercised their strikes to exclude blacks from the jury, he offered no proof of the circumstances under which prosecutors were responsible for striking black jurors beyond the facts of his own case.

A number of lower courts following the teaching of *Swain* reasoned that proof of repeated striking of blacks over a number of cases was necessary to establish a violation of the Equal Protection Clause. Since this interpretation of *Swain* has placed on defendants a crippling burden of proof, prosecutors' peremptory challenges are now largely immune from constitutional scrutiny. For reasons that follow, we reject this evidentiary formulation as inconsistent with standards that have been developed since *Swain* for assessing a prima facie case under the Equal Protection Clause.

B

Since the decision in *Swain*, we have explained that our cases concerning selection of the venire reflect the general equal protection principle that the "invidious quality" of governmental action claimed to be racially discriminatory "must ultimately be traced to a racially discriminatory purpose. As in any equal protection case, the "burden is, of course," on the defendant who alleges discriminatory selection of the venire "to prove the existence of purposeful discrimination." In deciding if the defendant has carried his burden of persuasion, a court must undertake "a sensitive inquiry into such circumstantial and direct evidence of intent as may be available." Circumstantial evidence of invidious intent may include proof of disproportionate impact. We have observed that under some circumstances proof of discriminatory impact "may for all practical purposes demonstrate unconstitutionality because in various circumstances the discrimination is very difficult to explain on nonracial grounds." For example, "total or seriously disproportionate exclusion of Negroes from jury venires," "is itself such an 'unequal application of the law . . . as to show intentional discrimination.'"

Moreover, since *Swain*, we have recognized that a black defendant alleging that members of his race have been impermissibly excluded from the venire may make out a prima facie case of purposeful discrimination by showing that the totality of the relevant facts gives rise to an inference of discriminatory purpose. Once the defendant makes the requisite showing, the burden shifts to the State to explain adequately the racial exclusion. The State cannot meet this burden on mere general assertions that its officials did not discriminate or that they properly performed their official duties. Rather, the State must demonstrate that "permissible racially neutral selection criteria and procedures have produced the monochromatic result."

The showing necessary to establish a prima facie case of purposeful discrimination in selection of the venire may be discerned in this Court's decisions. The defendant initially must show that he is a member of a racial group capable of being singled out for differential treatment. In combination with that evidence, a defendant may then make a prima facie case by proving that in the particular jurisdiction members of his race have not been summoned for jury service over an extended period of time. Proof of systematic exclusion from the venire raises an inference of purposeful discrimination because the "result bespeaks discrimination."

Since the ultimate issue is whether the State has discriminated in selecting the defendant's venire, however, the defendant may establish a prima facie case "in other ways than by evidence of long-continued unexplained absence" of members of his race "from many panels." In cases involving the venire, this Court has found a prima facie case on proof that members of the defendant's race were substantially underrepresented on the venire from which his jury was drawn, and that the venire was selected under a practice providing "the opportunity for discrimination." This combination of factors raises the necessary inference of purposeful discrimination because the Court has declined to attribute to chance the absence of black citizens on a particular jury array where the selection mechanism is subject to abuse. When circumstances suggest the need, the trial court must undertake a "factual inquiry" that "takes into account all possible explanatory factors" in the particular case.

Thus, since the decision in *Swain*, this Court has recognized that a defendant may make a prima facie showing of purposeful racial discrimination in selection of the venire by relying solely on the facts concerning its selection in his case. These decisions are in accordance with the proposition, articulated in *Arlington Heights v. Metropolitan Housing Department Corp.*, that "a consistent pattern of official racial discrimination" is not "a necessary predicate to a violation of the Equal Protection Clause. A single invidiously discriminatory governmental act" is not "immunized by the absence of such discrimination in the making of other comparable decisions." For evidentiary requirements to dictate that "several must suffer discrimination" before one could object, would be inconsistent with the promise of equal protection to all.

C

The standards for assessing a prima facie case in the context of discriminatory selection of the venire have been fully articulated since *Swain*. These principles support our conclusion that a defendant may establish a prima facie case of purposeful discrimination in selection of the petit jury solely on evidence concerning the prosecutor's exercise of peremptory challenges at the defendant's trial. To establish such a case, the defendant first must show that he is a member of a cognizable racial group, and that the prosecutor has exercised peremptory challenges to remove from the venire members of the defendant's race. Second, the defendant is entitled to rely on the fact, as to which there can be no dispute, that peremptory challenges constitute a jury selection practice that permits "those to discriminate who are of a mind to discriminate." Finally, the defendant must show that these facts and any other relevant circumstances raise an inference that the prosecutor used that practice to exclude the veniremen from the petit jury on account of their race. This combination of factors in the empaneling of the petit jury, as in the selection of the venire, raises the necessary inference of purposeful discrimination.

In deciding whether the defendant has made the requisite showing, the trial court should consider all relevant circumstances. For example, a "pattern" of strikes against black jurors included in the particular venire might give rise to an inference of discrimination. Similarly, the prosecutor's questions and statements during voir dire examination and in exercising his challenges may support or refute an inference of discriminatory purpose. These examples are merely illustrative. We have confidence that trial judges, experienced in supervising voir dire, will be able to decide if the circumstances concerning the prosecutor's use of peremptory challenges creates a prima facie case of discrimination against black jurors.

Once the defendant makes a prima facie showing, the burden shifts to the State to come forward with a neutral explanation for challenging black jurors. Though this requirement imposes a limitation in some cases on the full peremptory character of the historic challenge, we emphasize that the prosecutor's explanation need not rise to the level justifying exercise of a challenge for cause. But the prosecutor may not rebut the defendant's prima facie case of discrimination by stating merely that he challenged jurors of the defendant's race on the assumption — or his intuitive judgment — that they would be partial to the defendant because of their shared race. Just as the Equal Protection Clause forbids the States to exclude black persons from the venire on the assumption that blacks as a group are unqualified to serve as jurors, so it forbids the States to strike black veniremen on the assumption that they will be biased in a particular case simply because the defendant is black. The core guarantee of equal protection, ensuring citizens that their State will not discriminate on account of race, would be meaningless were we to approve the exclusion of jurors on the basis of such assumptions, which arise solely from the jurors' race. Nor may the prosecutor rebut the defendant's case merely by denying that he had a discriminatory motive or "affirm[ing] [his] good faith in making individual selections." If these general assertions were accepted as rebutting a defendant's prima facie case, the Equal Protection Clause "would be but a vain and illusory requirement." The prosecutor therefore must articulate a neutral explanation related to the particular case to be tried. The trial court then will have the duty to determine if the defendant has established purposeful discrimination.

IV

The State contends that our holding will eviscerate the fair trial values served by the peremptory challenge. Conceding that the Constitution does not guarantee a right to peremptory challenges and that *Swain* did state that their use ultimately is subject to the strictures of equal protection, the State argues that the privilege of unfettered exercise of the challenge is of vital importance to the criminal justice system.

While we recognize, of course, that the peremptory challenge occupies an important position in our trial procedures, we do not agree that our decision today will undermine the contribution the challenge generally makes to the administration of justice. The reality of practice, amply reflected in many state- and federal-court opinions, shows that the challenge may be, and unfortunately at times has been, used to discriminate against black jurors. By requiring trial courts to be sensitive to the racially discriminatory use of peremptory challenges, our decision enforces the mandate of equal protection and furthers the ends of justice. In view of the heterogeneous population of our Nation, public respect for our criminal justice system and the rule of law will be strengthened if we ensure that no citizen is disqualified from jury service because of his race.

Nor are we persuaded by the State's suggestion that our holding will create serious administrative difficulties. In those States applying a version of the evidentiary standard we recognize today, courts have not experienced serious administrative burdens, and the peremptory challenge system has survived. We decline, however, to formulate particular procedures to be followed upon a defendant's timely objection to a prosecutor's challenges.

C. Race and Peremptory Challenges

V

In this case, petitioner made a timely objection to the prosecutor's removal of all black persons on the venire. Because the trial court flatly rejected the objection without requiring the prosecutor to give an explanation for his action, we remand this case for further proceedings. If the trial court decides that the facts establish, prima facie, purposeful discrimination and the prosecutor does not come forward with a neutral explanation for his action, our precedents require that petitioner's conviction be reversed.

It is so ordered.

• • •

Justice MARSHALL, concurring.

I join Justice Powell's eloquent opinion for the Court, which takes a historic step toward eliminating the shameful practice of racial discrimination in the selection of juries. The Court's opinion cogently explains the pernicious nature of the racially discriminatory use of peremptory challenges, and the repugnancy of such discrimination to the Equal Protection Clause. The Court's opinion also ably demonstrates the inadequacy of any burden of proof for racially discriminatory use of peremptories that requires that "justice . . . sit supinely by" and be flouted in case after case before a remedy is available. I nonetheless write separately to express my views. The decision today will not end the racial discrimination that peremptories inject into the jury-selection process. That goal can be accomplished only by eliminating peremptory challenges entirely.

I

A little over a century ago, this Court invalidated a state statute providing that black citizens could not serve as jurors. *Strauder v. West Virginia* (1880). State officials then turned to somewhat more subtle ways of keeping blacks off jury venires. *See Swain v. Alabama* (1965) Although the means used to exclude blacks have changed, the same pernicious consequence has continued.

Misuse of the peremptory challenge to exclude black jurors has become both common and flagrant. Black defendants rarely have been able to compile statistics showing the extent of that practice, but the few cases setting out such figures are instructive. An instruction book used by the prosecutor's office in Dallas County, Texas, explicitly advised prosecutors that they conduct jury selection so as to eliminate " 'any member of a minority group.' " In 100 felony trials in Dallas County in 1983-1984, prosecutors peremptorily struck 405 out of 467 eligible black jurors; the chance of a qualified black sitting on a jury was 1 in 10, compared to 1 in 2 for a white.

The Court's discussion of the utter unconstitutionality of that practice needs no amplification. This Court explained more than a century ago that " 'in the selection of jurors to pass upon [a defendant's] life, liberty, or property, there shall be no exclusion of his race, and no discrimination against them, because of their color.' " *Neal v. Delaware* (188). Justice Rehnquist, dissenting, concedes that exclusion of blacks from a jury, solely because they are black, is at best based upon "crudely stereotypical and . . . in many cases hopelessly mistaken" notions. Yet the Equal Protection Clause prohibits a State from taking any action based on crude, inaccurate racial stereotypes — even an action that does not serve the State's interests. Exclusion of blacks from a jury, solely because of race, can no more be justified by a belief that blacks are less likely than whites to consider fairly or sympathetically the State's case against a black defendant than it can be justified by the notion that blacks lack the "intelligence, experience, or moral integrity" to be entrusted with that role.

II

I wholeheartedly concur in the Court's conclusion that use of the peremptory challenge to remove blacks from juries, on the basis of their race, violates the Equal Protection Clause. I would go further, however, in fashioning a remedy adequate to eliminate that discrimination. Merely allowing defendants the opportunity to challenge the racially discriminatory use of peremptory challenges in individual cases will not end the illegitimate use of the peremptory challenge.

Evidentiary analysis similar to that set out by the Court has been adopted as a matter of state law in States including Massachusetts and California. Cases from those jurisdictions illustrate the limitations of the approach. First, defendants cannot attack the discriminatory use of peremptory challenges at all unless the challenges are so flagrant as to establish a prima facie case. This means, in those States, that where only one or two black jurors survive the challenges for cause, the prosecutor need have no compunction about striking them from the jury because of their race. Prosecutors are left free to discriminate against blacks in jury selection provided that they hold that discrimination to an "acceptable" level.

Second, when a defendant can establish a prima facie case, trial courts face the difficult burden of assessing prosecutors' motives. Any prosecutor can easily assert facially neutral reasons for striking a juror, and trial courts are ill equipped to second-guess those reasons. How is the court to treat a prosecutor's statement that he struck a juror because the juror had a son about the same age as defendant, or seemed "uncommunicative," or "never cracked a smile" and, therefore "did not possess the sensitivities necessary to realistically look at the issues and decide the facts in this case"? If such easily generated explanations are sufficient to discharge the prosecutor's obligation to justify his strikes on nonracial grounds, then the protection erected by the Court today may be illusory.

Nor is outright prevarication by prosecutors the only danger here. "[I]t is even possible that an attorney may lie to himself in an effort to convince himself that his motives are legal." A prosecutor's own conscious or unconscious racism may lead him easily to the conclusion that a prospective black juror is "sullen," or "distant," a characterization that would not have come to his mind if a white juror had acted identically. A judge's own conscious or unconscious racism may lead him to accept such an explanation as well supported. As Justice Rehnquist concedes, prosecutors' peremptories are based on their "seat-of-the-pants instincts" as to how particular jurors will vote. Yet "seat-of-the-pants instincts" may often be just another term for racial prejudice. Even if all parties approach the Court's mandate with the best of conscious intentions, that mandate requires them to confront and overcome their own racism on all levels—a challenge I doubt all of them can meet. It is worth remembering that "114 years after the close of the War Between the States and nearly 100 years after *Strauder*, racial and other forms of discrimination still remain a fact of life, in the administration of justice as in our society as a whole."

III

The inherent potential of peremptory challenges to distort the jury process by permitting the exclusion of jurors on racial grounds should ideally lead the Court to ban them entirely from the criminal justice system. Justice Goldberg, dissenting in *Swain*, emphasized that "[w]ere it necessary to make an absolute choice between the right of a defendant to have a jury chosen in conformity with the requirements of the Fourteenth Amendment and the right to challenge peremptorily, the Constitution compels a choice of the former." I believe that this case presents just such a choice, and I would resolve that choice by eliminating peremptory challenges entirely in criminal cases.

Some authors have suggested that the courts should ban prosecutors' peremptories entirely, but should zealously guard the defendant's peremptory as "essential to the fairness of trial by jury." I would not find that an acceptable solution. Our criminal justice system "requires not only freedom from any bias against the accused, but also from any prejudice against his prosecution. Between him and the state the scales are to be evenly held." We can maintain that balance, not by permitting both prosecutor and defendant to engage in racial discrimination in jury selection, but by banning the use of peremptory challenges by prosecutors and by allowing the States to eliminate the defendant's peremptories as well.

Much ink has been spilled regarding the historic importance of defendants' peremptory challenges. The approving comments of the *Lewis* and *Pointer* Courts are noted above; the *Swain* Court emphasized the "very old credentials" of the peremptory challenge and cited the "long and widely held belief that peremptory challenge is a necessary part of trial by jury." But this Court has also repeatedly stated that the right of peremptory challenge is not of constitutional magnitude, and may be withheld altogether without impairing the constitutional guarantee of impartial jury and fair trial. The potential for racial prejudice, further, inheres in the defendant's challenge as well. If the prosecutor's peremptory challenge could be eliminated only at the cost of eliminating the defendant's challenge as well, I do not think that would be too great a price to pay.

I applaud the Court's holding that the racially discriminatory use of peremptory challenges violates the Equal Protection Clause, and I join the Court's opinion. However, only by banning peremptories entirely can such discrimination be ended.

NOTES AND QUESTIONS

1. Note that Batson's counsel objected at trial to the prosecutor's use of peremptory challenges to strike all the Black persons on the venire. Why? *Swain* had been settled law for almost 20 years. As the trial judge stated in response, the prosecution can "strike anybody they want to." In an episode of the podcast *More Perfect* titled "Object Anyway," which focuses on *Batson*, reporter Sean Rameswaram provides the following explanation, based on his interview of the defendant himself, James Kirkland Batson:

> Batson was in the courtroom and watched as [the prosecutor Joe] Guttman used four peremptory challenges to remove all four African-American prospective jurors from the venire. . . . Batson could see that after the four African-American prospective jurors were struck, "[e]verybody in the courtroom was white[,]" except for Batson. Batson's lawyer was white; the prosecutor was white; the judge was white, and after the peremptory challenges, all twelve jurors on his jury were white. Batson described the moment as follows: "And I'm like Ah! That's completely — They struck all the blacks off the jury pool. It ain't right. I told my lawyer, I said object to that. . . ." His lawyer said that he had no basis to object, but Batson insisted. Batson told his lawyer to "object anyway," and that is what his lawyer did. The case was able to reach the Supreme Court because of that objection.

Sean Rameswaram, Object Anyway, Radiolab Presents: More Perfect, WNYC Studios (July 16, 2016), http://www.wnyc.org/story/object-anyway/ [https://perma.cc/NZ6M-YHVA]. *See* Nancy S. Marder, Batson v. Kentucky: *Reflections on a Podcast*, 105 Ky. L.J. 621, 628 (2017).

Rameswaram also reports that Batson had been tried previously on the same burglary charge but the jury had hung, apparently due to a Black juror who thought Batson was innocent. *Id.*

2. Is the trial judge's response to Batson's objection correct, though? Is this a wholly accurate reading of *Swain*? Can you imagine a factual scenario, even under *Swain*, where race-based peremptory challenges in a single case could violate the Fourteenth Amendment?

3. Batson's counsel on appeal rooted his claim in the fair cross-section requirement, rather than equal protection, apparently calculating that it would be easier to get the Court to sidestep *Swain* than to overrule it. And this approach had the added benefit of the ability to exploit the reasoning of *Wheeler* and *Soares*, decisions from two prestigious state high courts that relied on California and Massachusetts constitutional requirements that juries must represent a fair cross-section of the community. Note that the Court's opinion in *Batson* never explicitly acknowledges that it is overruling *Swain*, even though Justice White, who wrote the Court's opinion in *Swain*, says as much in his concurring opinion.

James Batson

4. The Court at one point even mildly defends *Swain*. It ascribes the immunity from review that peremptory challenges enjoy to an "interpretation" of *Swain*:

> A number of lower courts following the teaching of *Swain* reasoned that proof of repeated striking of blacks over a number of cases was necessary to establish a violation of the Equal Protection Clause. Since this interpretation of *Swain* has placed on defendants a crippling burden of proof, prosecutors' peremptory challenges are now largely immune from constitutional scrutiny.

Id. at 92-93. What other interpretation of *Swain* was permissible? Is the "crippling burden of proof" required by *Swain* the function of the equal protection doctrine generally or the facts of *Swain* in particular?

5. The Court eventually proceeds to repudiate *Swain*, relying on a combination of intervening jury venire, equal protection, and employment cases (buried in footnotes) that touch on discriminatory impact and burden shifting. Note that one aspect of the test the Court announces is that the defendant must be "a member" of the "cognizable racial group" that is wrongfully excluded from jury service. Why must that be the case? Is this consistent with the Court's statement that the "harm from discriminatory jury selection extends beyond that inflicted on the defendant and the excluded juror to touch the entire community"?

6. Under the Court's test, the prosecutor can rebut a defendant's showing of discriminatory impact by positing "a neutral explanation for challenging black jurors." *Id.* at 97. The Court explains that this explanation need not be as persuasive as a challenge for cause but must be more than the prosecutor's belief or intuition that the challenged jurors will be partial because of their race. How can prosecutors thread this needle? How much room does this leave the defendant—who carries the ultimate burden of proving purposeful discrimination—to dispute the prosecutor's proffered "neutral explanation"?

James Batson speaks to the law class at Louisville's Central High School taught by *Batson* prosecutor Joe Gutmann

7. In a concurring opinion Justice Marshall applauds the decision as a "historic step" yet is skeptical about the capability of the Court's remedy to snuff out race-based peremptory challenges, and concludes that peremptory challenges should be abolished. Is he too cynical about the integrity of prosecutors? About the ability of judges to ferret out pretextual neutral explanations? How does it affect the analysis that prosecutors are usually assigned to a particular court and will often appear before the same judge with regularity?

8. Although the fruits of the burglary Batson was charged with yielded only $30 at a Louisville pawn shop, he was sentenced to 20 years under a Kentucky statute for being a "persistent felony offender." He was released when the Supreme Court decision was issued and, per the decision, the trial court was required to implement the *Batson* test. How exactly would this be done?

An unsurprising result of *Batson* was a concerted effort by prosecutors to "get around" the Court's decision. Representative of this effort was a training video made by Pennsylvania prosecutor Jack McMahon, still available on YouTube, where he advises lawyers to question Black prospective jurors at length and to make contemporaneous notes of race-neutral reasons so they will "have something" if they are challenged and need it later. As examples, he advises prosecutors to note that a Black juror is "unemployed" or "has a kid about the defendant's age." *See* Marder, Batson v. Kentucky: *Reflections on a Podcast, supra* at 621, 628, 631-32.

Some of *Batson*'s many loose ends were addressed by the Court in relatively short order. In *Powers v. Ohio*, 499 U.S. 400 (1991), the Court held—notwithstanding its formulation of the prima facie case standard in *Batson* itself—that *Batson* applied where a white criminal defendant challenged the prosecutor's use of six of nine peremptory challenges on Black prospective jurors. The first sentence of the opinion gave away the result: "Jury service is an exercise of responsible citizenship by all members of the community, including those who otherwise might not have the opportunity to contribute to our civic life." The Court didn't stop there: It observed that "with the exception of voting, for most citizens the honor and privilege of jury duty is their most significant opportunity to participate in the democratic process"; quoted from several of its various decisions denouncing discrimination in jury

Chapter XV The Jury II: Race and Juries

selection going as far back as *Strauder*; and twice noted that disqualifying a person from jury service on account of race is a federal crime under 18 U.S.C. § 243. As for the standing of the white defendant to make a *Batson* challenge, the Court noted, inter alia, that both the defendant and the excluded jurors have a common interest in excluding racial discrimination from the courtroom.

Edmonson v. Leesville Concrete Co., 500 U.S. 614 (1991), was a civil workplace injury action brought by a Black construction worker against a concrete company. The plaintiff made a *Batson* challenge when the corporate defendant used two of its three peremptory challenges to strike Black prospective jurors. Resolving a circuit split, the Supreme Court found *Batson* applicable. The central issue, on which three Justices dissented, was whether the actions of a private litigant in a civil suit amounted to state action. The Court found state action to exist inasmuch as the exercise of peremptory challenges amounts essentially to assisting the trial court with the governmental function of selecting a jury.

Is that an accurate description of the function of peremptory challenges? Is a lawyer in a civil case in any way acting on behalf of the government? Is it meaningful that in exercising a peremptory challenge a party is not selecting but rather excluding a juror? Is a litigant in a civil case more like a government agent or a consumer of a government resource?

The next case involves the question everyone knew was coming: Does *Batson* apply to a criminal defendant's use of peremptory challenges? The Court explicitly reserved deciding this issue in *Batson* itself, 407 U.S. 79, 89 n.12, although Justice Marshall and two other Justices stated their view that *Batson* should be equally applicable to criminal defendants. *Id.* at 107.

Georgia v. McCollum
505 U.S. 42 (1992)

Justice BLACKMUN delivered the opinion of the Court.

For more than a century, this Court consistently and repeatedly has reaffirmed that racial discrimination by the State in jury selection offends the Equal Protection Clause. Last Term this Court held that racial discrimination in a civil litigant's exercise of peremptory challenges also violates the Equal Protection Clause. Today, we are asked to decide whether the Constitution prohibits a criminal defendant from engaging in purposeful racial discrimination in the exercise of peremptory challenges.

I

On August 10, 1990, a grand jury sitting in Dougherty County, Ga., returned a six-count indictment charging respondents with aggravated assault and simple battery. The indictment alleged that respondents beat and assaulted Jerry and Myra Collins. Respondents are white; the alleged victims are African-Americans. Shortly after the events, a leaflet was widely distributed in the local African-American community reporting the assault and urging community residents not to patronize respondents' business.

Before jury selection began, the prosecution moved to prohibit respondents from exercising peremptory challenges in a racially discriminatory manner. The State explained that it expected to show that the victims' race was a factor in the alleged assault. According to the State, counsel for respondents had indicated a clear intention to use peremptory strikes in a racially discriminatory manner, arguing that the circumstances of their case gave them the right to exclude African-American citizens from participating as jurors in the trial. Observing that 43 percent of the county's population is African-American, the State contended that, if a statistically representative panel is assembled for jury selection, 18 of the potential 42 jurors would be African-American. With 20 peremptory challenges, respondents therefore would be able to remove all the African-American potential jurors. Relying on *Batson*, the Sixth Amendment, and the Georgia Constitution, the State sought an order providing that, if it succeeded in making out a prima facie case of racial discrimination by respondents, the latter would be required to articulate a racially neutral explanation for peremptory challenges.

The trial judge denied the State's motion, holding that "[n]either Georgia nor federal law prohibits criminal defendants from exercising peremptory strikes in a racially discriminatory manner." The issue was certified for immediate appeal.

The Supreme Court of Georgia, by a 4-to-3 vote, affirmed the trial court's ruling. The court acknowledged that in *Edmondson* this Court had found that the exercise of a peremptory challenge in a racially discriminatory manner "would constitute an impermissible injury" to the excluded juror. The court noted, however, that *Edmonson* involved private civil litigants, not criminal defendants. "Bearing in mind the long history of jury trials as an essential element of the protection of human rights," the court "decline[d] to diminish the free exercise of peremptory strikes by a criminal defendant." Three justices dissented, arguing that *Edmonson* and other decisions of this Court establish that racially based peremptory challenges by a criminal defendant violate the Constitution. A motion for reconsideration was denied.

We granted certiorari to resolve a question left open by our prior cases—whether the Constitution prohibits a criminal defendant from engaging in purposeful racial discrimination in the exercise of peremptory challenges.

II

. . .

In deciding whether the Constitution prohibits criminal defendants from exercising racially discriminatory peremptory challenges, we must answer four questions. First, whether a criminal defendant's exercise of peremptory challenges in a racially discriminatory manner inflicts the harms addressed by *Batson*. Second, whether the exercise of peremptory challenges by a criminal defendant constitutes state action. Third, whether prosecutors have standing to raise this constitutional challenge. And fourth, whether the constitutional rights of a criminal defendant nonetheless preclude the extension of our precedents to this case.

III

A

The majority in *Powers* recognized that "*Batson* 'was designed "to serve multiple ends,"' only one of which was to protect individual defendants from discrimination in the selection of jurors." As in *Powers* and *Edmonson*, the extension of *Batson* in this context is designed to remedy the harm done to the "dignity of persons" and to the "integrity of the courts."

As long ago as *Strauder*, this Court recognized that denying a person participation in jury service on account of his race unconstitutionally discriminates against the excluded juror. While "[a]n individual juror does not have a right to sit on any particular petit jury, . . . he or she does possess the right not to be excluded from one on account of race." Regardless of who invokes the discriminatory challenge, there can be no doubt that the harm is the same—in all cases, the juror is subjected to open and public racial discrimination.

But "[t]he harm from discriminatory jury selection extends beyond that inflicted on the defendant and the excluded juror to touch the entire community." One of the goals of our jury system is "to impress upon the criminal defendant and the community as a whole that a verdict of conviction or acquittal is given in accordance with the law by persons who are fair." Selection procedures that purposefully exclude African-Americans from juries undermine that public confidence — as well they should. "The overt wrong, often apparent to the entire jury panel, casts doubt over the obligation of the parties, the jury, and indeed the court to adhere to the law throughout the trial of the cause."

The need for public confidence is especially high in cases involving race-related crimes. In such cases, emotions in the affected community will inevitably be heated and volatile. Public confidence in the integrity of the criminal justice system is essential for preserving community peace in trials involving race-related crimes.

"[B]e it at the hands of the State or the defense," if a court allows jurors to be excluded because of group bias, "[it] is [a] willing participant in a scheme that could only undermine the very foundation of our system of justice — our citizens' confidence in it." Just as public confidence in criminal justice is undermined by a conviction in a trial where racial discrimination has occurred in jury selection, so is public confidence undermined where a defendant, assisted by racially discriminatory peremptory strikes, obtains an acquittal.

B

The fact that a defendant's use of discriminatory peremptory challenges harms the jurors and the community does not end our equal protection inquiry. Racial discrimination, although repugnant in all contexts, violates the Constitution only when it is attributable to state action. Thus, the second question that must be answered is whether a criminal defendant's exercise of a peremptory challenge constitutes state action for purposes of the Equal Protection Clause.

Until *Edmonson*, the cases decided by this Court that presented the problem of racially discriminatory peremptory challenges involved assertions of discrimination by a prosecutor, a quintessential state actor. In *Edmonson*, by contrast, the contested peremptory challenges were exercised by a private defendant in a civil action. In order to determine whether state action was present in that setting, the Court in *Edmonson* used the analytical framework summarized in *Lugar v. Edmondson Oil Co.* (1982).

The first inquiry is "whether the claimed [constitutional] deprivation has resulted from the exercise of a right or privilege having its source in state authority." "There can be no question" that peremptory challenges satisfy this first requirement, as they "are permitted only when the government, by statute or decisional law, deems it appropriate to allow parties to exclude a given number of persons who otherwise would satisfy the requirements for service on the petit jury." As in *Edmonson*, a Georgia defendant's right to exercise peremptory challenges and the scope of that right are established by a provision of state law.

The second inquiry is whether the private party charged with the deprivation can be described as a state actor. In resolving that issue, the Court in *Edmonson* found it useful to apply three principles: (1) "the extent to which the actor relies on governmental assistance and benefits"; (2) "whether the actor is performing a traditional governmental function"; and (3) "whether the injury caused is aggravated in a unique way by the incidents of governmental authority."

As to the first principle, the *Edmonson* Court found that the peremptory challenge system, as well as the jury system as a whole, "simply could not exist" without the "overt, significant participation of the government." Georgia provides for the compilation of jury lists by the board of jury commissioners in each county and establishes the general criteria for service and the sources for creating a pool of qualified jurors representing a fair cross section of the community. State law further provides that jurors are to be selected by a specified process; they are to be summoned to court under the authority of the State; and they are to be paid an expense allowance by the State whether or not they serve on a jury. At court, potential jurors are placed in panels in order to facilitate examination by counsel; they are administered an oath; they are questioned on voir dire to determine whether they are impartial; and they are subject to challenge for cause.

In light of these procedures, the defendant in a Georgia criminal case relies on "governmental assistance and benefits" that are equivalent to those found in the civil context in *Edmonson*. "By enforcing a discriminatory peremptory challenge, the Court 'has . . . elected to place its power, property and prestige behind the [alleged] discrimination.'"

In regard to the second principle, the Court in *Edmonson* found that peremptory challenges perform a traditional function of the government: "Their sole purpose is to permit litigants to assist the government in the selection of an impartial trier of fact." And, as the *Edmonson* Court recognized, the jury system in turn "performs the critical governmental functions of guarding the rights of litigants and 'ensur[ing] continued acceptance of the laws by all of the people.'" These same conclusions apply with even greater force in the criminal context because the selection of a jury in a criminal case fulfills a unique and constitutionally compelled governmental function. The State cannot avoid its constitutional responsibilities by delegating a public function to private parties.

Finally, the *Edmonson* Court indicated that the courtroom setting in which the peremptory challenge is exercised intensifies the harmful effects of the private litigant's discriminatory act and contributes to its characterization as state action. These concerns are equally present in the context of a criminal trial. Regardless of who precipitated the jurors' removal, the perception and the reality in a criminal trial will be that the court has excused jurors based on race, an outcome that will be attributed to the State.

Respondents nonetheless contend that the adversarial relationship between the defendant and the prosecution negates the governmental character of the peremptory challenge. Respondents rely on *Polk County v. Dodson* (1981) in which a defendant sued, under 42 U.S.C. § 1983, the public defender who represented him. The defendant claimed that the public defender had violated his constitutional rights in failing to provide adequate representation. This Court determined that a public defender does not qualify as a state actor when engaged in his general representation of a criminal defendant.

Polk County did not hold that the adversarial relationship of a public defender with the State precludes a finding of state action — it held that this adversarial relationship prevented the attorney's public employment from alone being sufficient to support a finding of state action. Instead, the determination whether a public defender is a state actor for a particular purpose depends on the nature and context of the function he is performing. For example, in *Branti v. Finkel* (1980), this Court held that a public defender, in making personnel decisions on behalf of the State, is a state actor who must comply with constitutional requirements. And the *Polk County* Court itself noted, without deciding, that a public defender may act under color of state law while performing certain administrative, and possibly investigative, functions.

The exercise of a peremptory challenge differs significantly from other actions taken in support of a defendant's defense. In exercising a peremptory challenge, a criminal defendant is wielding the power to choose a quintessential governmental body — indeed, the institution of government on which our judicial system depends. Thus, as we held in *Edmonson*, when "a government confers on a private body the power to choose the government's employees or officials, the private body will be bound by the constitutional mandate of race neutrality."

Lastly, the fact that a defendant exercises a peremptory challenge to further his interest in acquittal does not conflict with a finding of state action. Whenever a private actor's conduct is deemed "fairly attributable" to the government, it is likely that private motives will have animated the actor's decision. Indeed, in *Edmonson*, the Court recognized that the private party's exercise of peremptory challenges constituted state action, even though the motive underlying the exercise of the peremptory challenge may be to protect a private interest.

C

Having held that a defendant's discriminatory exercise of a peremptory challenge is a violation of equal protection, we move to the question whether the State has standing to challenge a defendant's discriminatory use of peremptory challenges. In *Powers*, this Court held that a white criminal defendant has standing to raise the equal protection rights of black jurors wrongfully excluded from jury service. While third-party standing is a limited exception, the *Powers* Court recognized that a litigant may raise a claim on behalf of a third party if the litigant can demonstrate that he has suffered a concrete injury, that he has a close relation to the third party, and that there exists some hindrance to the third party's ability to protect its own interests. In *Edmonson*, the Court applied the same analysis in deciding that civil litigants had standing to raise the equal protection rights of jurors excluded on the basis of their race.

In applying the first prong of its standing analysis, the *Powers* Court found that a criminal defendant suffered cognizable injury "because racial discrimination in the selection of jurors 'casts doubt on the integrity of the judicial process,' and places the fairness of a criminal proceeding in doubt." In *Edmonson*, this Court found that these harms were not limited to the criminal sphere. Surely, a State suffers a similar injury when the fairness and integrity of its own judicial process is undermined.

In applying the second prong of its standing analysis, the *Powers* Court held that voir dire permits a defendant to "establish a relation, if not a bond of trust, with the jurors," a relation that "continues throughout the entire trial." "Exclusion of a juror on the basis of race severs that relation in an invidious way."

The State's relation to potential jurors in this case is closer than the relationships approved in *Powers* and *Edmonson*. As the representative of all its citizens, the State is the logical and proper party to assert the invasion of the constitutional rights of the excluded jurors in a criminal trial. Indeed, the Fourteenth Amendment forbids the State to deny persons within its jurisdiction the equal protection of the laws.

In applying the final prong of its standing analysis, the *Powers* Court recognized that, although individuals excluded from jury service on the basis of race have a right to bring suit on their own behalf, the "barriers to a suit by an excluded juror are daunting." The barriers are no less formidable in this context. Accordingly, we hold that the State has standing to assert the excluded jurors' rights.

D

The final question is whether the interests served by *Batson* must give way to the rights of a criminal defendant. As a preliminary matter, it is important to recall that peremptory challenges are not constitutionally protected fundamental rights; rather, they are but one state-created means to the constitutional end of an impartial jury and a fair trial. This Court repeatedly has stated that the right to a peremptory challenge may be withheld altogether without impairing the constitutional guarantee of an impartial jury and a fair trial.

Yet in *Swain*, the Court reviewed the "very old credentials" of the peremptory challenge and noted the "long and widely held belief that the peremptory challenge is a necessary part of trial by jury." This Court likewise has recognized that "the role of litigants in determining the jury's composition provides one reason for wide acceptance of the jury system and of its verdicts."

We do not believe that this decision will undermine the contribution of the peremptory challenge to the administration of justice. Nonetheless, "if race stereotypes are the price for acceptance of a jury panel as fair," we reaffirm today that such a "price is too high to meet the standard of the Constitution." It is an affront to justice to argue that a fair trial includes the right to discriminate against a group of citizens based upon their race.

Nor does a prohibition of the exercise of discriminatory peremptory challenges violate a defendant's Sixth Amendment right to the effective assistance of counsel. Counsel can ordinarily explain the reasons for peremptory challenges without revealing anything about trial strategy or any confidential client communications. In the rare case in which the explanation for a challenge would entail confidential communications or reveal trial strategy, an in camera discussion can be arranged. In any event, neither the Sixth Amendment right nor the attorney-client privilege gives a criminal defendant the right to carry out through counsel an unlawful course of conduct.

Lastly, a prohibition of the discriminatory exercise of peremptory challenges does not violate a defendant's Sixth Amendment right to a trial by an impartial jury. The goal of the Sixth Amendment is "jury impartiality with respect to both contestants."

We recognize, of course, that a defendant has the right to an impartial jury that can view him without racial animus, which so long has distorted our system of criminal justice. We have, accordingly, held that there should be a mechanism for removing those on the venire whom the defendant has specific reason to believe would be incapable of confronting and suppressing their racism.

But there is a distinction between exercising a peremptory challenge to discriminate invidiously against jurors on account of race and exercising a peremptory challenge to remove an individual juror who harbors racial prejudice. This Court firmly has rejected the view that assumptions of partiality based on race provide a legitimate basis for disqualifying a person as an impartial juror. As this Court stated just last Term in *Powers*, "[w]e may not accept as a defense to racial discrimination the very stereotype the law condemns." "In our heterogeneous society policy as well as constitutional considerations militate against the divisive assumption—as a per se rule—that justice in a court of law may turn upon the pigmentation of skin, the accident of birth, or the choice of religion." We therefore reaffirm today that the exercise of a peremptory challenge must not be based on either the race of the juror or the racial stereotypes held by the party.

IV

We hold that the Constitution prohibits a criminal defendant from engaging in purposeful discrimination on the ground of race in the exercise of peremptory challenges. Accordingly, if the State demonstrates a prima facie case of racial discrimination by the defendants, the defendants must articulate a racially neutral explanation for peremptory challenges. The judgment of the Supreme Court of Georgia is reversed, and the case is remanded for further proceedings not inconsistent with this opinion.

It is so ordered.

NOTES AND QUESTIONS

1. Although Justice Marshall favored the elimination of peremptory challenges altogether, he opposed eliminating only the government's right to peremptory challenges. He stated in his concurring opinion in *Batson*: "I would not find that an acceptable solution. Our criminal justice system requires not only freedom from any bias against the accused, but also from any prejudice against his prosecution. Between him and the state the scales are to be evenly held." 476 U.S. at 107-08.

Do you agree with Justice Marshall? Aren't there other aspects of criminal procedure where the scales are—deliberately—uneven? For example, it is widely recognized that a prosecutor's obligation is to "do justice" while a defense attorney's duty is to do what is in his client's interest. Defendants have no burden of proof. Given these and other examples, would it be shocking for *Batson* to apply only to prosecutors as a matter of policy? Note also the strong historical tradition of allocating peremptory challenges only to the defense. *See* Anna Roberts, *Asymmetry as Fairness: Reversing a Peremptory Trend*, 92 Wash. U. L. Rev. 1503, 1534-35 (2015).

2. The principal doctrinal question here is not whether peremptory challenges should be balanced as a matter of policy but whether a criminal defendant can be seen as exercising the power of the state for purposes of the Fourteenth Amendment. There can be no doubt that the evil of racial exclusion from jury service is as pernicious when the result of action by the defendant as by the prosecutor. As the Court notes, quoting from a New Jersey court's extension of the *Batson* rule to criminal defendants, " '[B]e it at the hands of the State or the defense,' " if a court allows jurors to be excluded because of group bias, "[it] is [a] willing participant in a scheme that could only undermine the very foundation of our system of justice — our citizens' confidence in it." *State v. Alvarado*, 221 N.J. Super. 324, 328, 534 A.2d 440, 442 (1987). This formulation of the principle raises an interesting question: Does a court have an independent obligation to monitor the use of peremptory challenges for bias, irrespective of whether the prosecutor makes a "*Batson* challenge"?

3. The Court relies heavily on *Edmondson v. Leesville* in concluding that *Batson* applies to criminal defendants, quoting its conclusion there that peremptory challenges' "sole purpose is to permit litigants to assist the government in the selection of an impartial trier of fact." Is there a principled distinction between *Leesville* and *McCollum*? Justice O'Connor, who was in the majority in *Leesville*, dissents here. She notes, among other things, that the state and the defendant are in an unequivocally adversarial relationship in a criminal case, where as they are not similarly opposed in a civil case where the state is not a party. Persuasive? Note Justice Scalia's dissent in *Leesville*, predicting that its holding will apply to criminal prosecutions and that *Leesville* "will not necessarily be a net help to minority litigants in obtaining racially diverse juries." 500 U.S. 614, 644 (1991).

4. Justice Thomas, concurring, relies on a more realistic, if not fatalistic, view of racial prejudice. He reasons that one of the premises of *Strauder* itself was the recognition that "securing representation of defendant's race on the jury may help to overcome racial bias and provide the defendant with a better chance of having a fair trial." He finds the Court's decision to be an "inversion of priorities":

> Today's decision, while protecting jurors, leaves defendants with less means of protecting themselves. Unless jurors actually admit prejudice during voir dire, defendants generally must allow them to sit and run the risk that racial animus will affect the verdict. Cf. Fed. Rule Evid. 606(b) (generally excluding juror testimony after trial to impeach the verdict). In effect, we have exalted the right of citizens to sit on juries over the rights of the criminal defendant, even though it is the defendant, not the jurors, who faces imprisonment or even death.

Id. at 61-62. Justice Thomas was not on the Court when *Leesville* was decided. But do you agree with his point about "inversion of priorities"? But isn't it only an "inversion of priorities" if you accept the majority's conclusion on state action? Citizens' rights to sit on juries are improperly exalted only if you believe that a defendant acts as "the state" in excluding them. That only state actors are bound by the Constitution is a legal commonplace. As Justice O'Connor observes in her dissent, "The concept that the government alone must honor constitutional dictates, however, is a fundamental tenet of our legal order, not an obstacle to be circumvented." *Id.* at 68.

Justice O'Connor not only takes on the majority's state action analysis — a "perverse result" — but she affirmatively notes that a Black criminal defendant's best chance to eliminate the likely conscious and unconscious bias that may infect jury deliberations may be to use peremptory challenges to gain at least some minority representation on the jury. *Id. See* Roberts, *Asymmetry as Fairness, supra* at 1503, 1523 & n.132 (collecting sources demonstrating that diverse juries deliberate more carefully and suppress racial bias better than nondiverse juries).

In a similar vein, Professor Sheri Lynn Johnson posits that for *Batson* purposes "racial discrimination in jury selection is any jury selection practice that is intended to increase the likelihood that racial bias will influence the outcome of a particular criminal trial." *See* Sheri Lynn Johnson, *The Language and Culture (Not to Say Race) of Peremptory Challenges,* 35 Wm. & Mary L. Rev. 21, 83-84 (1993). Accordingly, challenges of white jurors intended to increase the jury's diversity and thereby eliminate bias should not be viewed as discriminatory. *Id.*

Professor James Forman Jr. draws on the nineteenth-century experiences of abolitionism and the Reconstruction era for insight into the proper applicability of the scope of *Batson.* James Forman Jr., *Juries and Race in the Nineteenth Century,* 113 Yale L.J. 895, 898-909 (2004). "Almost immediately after the Civil War, the South began a practice that would continue for many decades: All-white juries punished black defendants particularly harshly, while simultaneously refusing to punish violence by whites, including Ku Klux Klan members, against blacks and Republicans." *Id.* at 909-10. As but one example, just in the years 1865 and 1866, all-white juries in Texas decided a total of 500 prosecutions of white defendants charged with killing African Americans. All 500 were acquitted. *Id.* at 916. Accordingly, one of the goals of abolishing obstacles to Black jury service was to protect victims as well as defendants, contrary to Justice Thomas's view that the protection of Black defendants was the sole concern of Reconstruction legislation. *Id.* at 898.

The next case brings home the point Justice Marshall made in his *Batson* concurrence about the difficulty of judging prosecutors' "facially neutral" explanations for peremptory challenges that appear to be based on race (or, in *Hernandez*, ethnicity).

Hernandez v. New York
500 U.S. 352 (1991)

Justice KENNEDY announced the judgment of the Court and delivered an opinion in which THE CHIEF JUSTICE, Justice WHITE, and Justice SOUTER join.

Petitioner Dionisio Hernandez asks us to review the New York state courts' rejection of his claim that the prosecutor in his criminal trial exercised peremptory challenges to exclude Latinos from the jury by reason of their ethnicity. If true, the prosecutor's discriminatory use of peremptory strikes would violate the Equal Protection Clause as interpreted by our decision in *Batson*. We must determine whether the prosecutor offered a race-neutral basis for challenging Latino potential jurors and, if so, whether the state courts' decision to accept the prosecutor's explanation should be sustained.

Petitioner and respondent both use the term "Latino" in their briefs to this Court. The amicus brief employs instead the term "Hispanic," and the parties referred to the excluded jurors by that term in the trial court. Both words appear in the state-court opinions. No attempt has been made at a distinction by the parties and we make no attempt to distinguish the terms in this opinion. We will refer to the excluded venirepersons as Latinos in deference to the terminology preferred by the parties before the Court.

I

The case comes to us on direct review of petitioner's convictions on two counts of attempted murder and two counts of criminal possession of a weapon. On a Brooklyn street, petitioner fired several shots at Charlene Calloway and her mother, Ada Saline. Calloway suffered three gunshot wounds. Petitioner missed Saline and instead hit two men in a nearby restaurant. The victims survived the incident.

The trial was held in the New York Supreme Court, Kings County. We concern ourselves here only with the jury selection process and the proper application of *Batson*, which had been handed down before the trial took place. After 63 potential jurors had been questioned and 9 had been empaneled, defense counsel objected that the prosecutor had used four peremptory challenges to exclude Latino potential jurors. Two of the Latino venirepersons challenged by the prosecutor had brothers who had been convicted of crimes, and the brother of one of those potential jurors was being prosecuted by the same District Attorney's office for a probation violation. Petitioner does not press his *Batson* claim with respect to those prospective jurors, and we concentrate on the other two excluded individuals.

After petitioner raised his *Batson* objection, the prosecutor did not wait for a ruling on whether petitioner had established a prima facie case of racial discrimination. Instead, the prosecutor volunteered his reasons for striking the jurors in question. He explained:

> Your honor, my reason for rejecting the—these two jurors—I'm not certain as to whether they're Hispanics. I didn't notice how many Hispanics had been called to the panel, but my reason for rejecting these two is I feel very uncertain that they would be able to listen and follow the interpreter.

After an interruption by defense counsel, the prosecutor continued:

> We talked to them for a long time; the Court talked to them, I talked to them. I believe that in their heart they will try to follow it, but I felt there was a great deal of uncertainty as to whether they could accept the interpreter as the final arbiter of what was said by each of the witnesses, especially where there were going to be Spanish-speaking witnesses, and I didn't feel, when I asked them whether or not they could accept the interpreter's translation of it, I didn't feel that they could. They each looked away from me and said with some hesitancy that they would try, not that they could, but that they would try to follow the interpreter, and I feel that in a case where the interpreter will be for the main witnesses, they would have an undue impact upon the jury.

Defense counsel moved for a mistrial "based on the conduct of the District Attorney," and the prosecuto1r requested a chance to call a supervisor to the courtroom before the judge's ruling.

Following a recess, defense counsel renewed his motion, which the trial court denied. Discussion of the objection continued, however, and the prosecutor explained that he would have no motive to exclude Latinos from the jury:

> [T]his case, involves four complainants. Each of the complainants is Hispanic. All my witnesses, that is, civilian witnesses, are going to be Hispanic. I have absolutely no reason—there's no reason for me to want to exclude Hispanics because all the parties involved are Hispanic, and I certainly would have no reason to do that.

After further interchange among the judge and attorneys, the trial court again rejected petitioner's claim.

On appeal, the New York Supreme Court, Appellate Division, noted that though the ethnicity of one challenged bilingual juror remained uncertain, the prosecutor had challenged the only three prospective jurors with definite Hispanic surnames. The court ruled that this fact made out a prima facie showing of discrimination. The court affirmed the trial court's rejection of petitioner's *Batson* claim, however, on the ground that the prosecutor had offered race-neutral explanations for the peremptory strikes sufficient to rebut petitioner's prima facie case.

The New York Court of Appeals also affirmed the judgment, holding that the prosecutor had offered a legitimate basis for challenging the individuals in question and deferring to the factual findings of the lower New York courts. Two judges dissented, concluding that on this record, analyzed in the light of standards they would adopt as a matter of state constitutional law, the prosecutor's exclusion of the bilingual potential jurors should not have been permitted. We granted certiorari and now affirm.

II

In *Batson*, we outlined a three-step process for evaluating claims that a prosecutor has used peremptory challenges in a manner violating the Equal Protection Clause. The analysis set forth in *Batson* permits prompt rulings on objections to peremptory challenges without substantial disruption of the jury selection process. First, the defendant must make a prima facie showing that the prosecutor has exercised peremptory challenges on the basis of race. Second, if the requisite showing has been made, the burden shifts to the prosecutor to articulate a race-neutral explanation for striking the jurors in question. Finally, the trial court must determine whether the defendant has carried his burden of proving purposeful discrimination. This three-step inquiry delimits our consideration of the arguments raised by petitioner.

A

The prosecutor defended his use of peremptory strikes without any prompting or inquiry from the trial court. As a result, the trial court had no occasion to rule that petitioner had or had not made a prima facie showing of intentional discrimination. This departure from the normal course of proceeding need not concern us. We explained in the context of employment discrimination litigation under Title VII of the Civil Rights Act of 1964 that "[w]here the defendant has done everything that would be required of him if the plaintiff had properly made out a prima facie case, whether the plaintiff really did so is no longer relevant." The same principle applies under *Batson*. Once a prosecutor has offered a race-neutral explanation for the peremptory challenges and the trial court has ruled on the ultimate question of intentional discrimination, the preliminary issue of whether the defendant had made a prima facie showing becomes moot.

B

Petitioner contends that the reasons given by the prosecutor for challenging the two bilingual jurors were not race neutral. In evaluating the race neutrality of an attorney's explanation, a court must determine whether, assuming the proffered reasons for the peremptory challenges are true, the challenges violate the Equal Protection Clause as a matter of law. A court addressing this issue must keep in mind the fundamental principle that "official action will not be held unconstitutional solely because it results in a racially disproportionate impact. . . . Proof of racially discriminatory intent or purpose is required to show a violation of the Equal Protection Clause." " 'Discriminatory purpose' . . . implies more than intent as volition or intent as awareness of consequences. It implies that the decisionmaker . . . selected . . . a particular course of action at least in part 'because of,' not merely 'in spite of,' its adverse effects upon an identifiable group."

A neutral explanation in the context of our analysis here means an explanation based on something other than the race of the juror. At this step of the inquiry, the issue is the facial validity of the prosecutor's explanation. Unless a discriminatory intent is inherent in the prosecutor's explanation, the reason offered will be deemed race neutral.

Petitioner argues that Spanish-language ability bears a close relation to ethnicity, and that, as a consequence, it violates the Equal Protection Clause to exercise a peremptory challenge on the ground that a Latino potential juror speaks Spanish. He points to the high correlation between Spanish-language ability and ethnicity in New York, where the case was tried. We need not address that argument here, for the prosecutor did not rely on language ability without more, but explained that the specific responses and the demeanor of the two individuals during voir dire caused him to doubt their ability to defer to the official translation of Spanish-language testimony.

The prosecutor here offered a race-neutral basis for these peremptory strikes. As explained by the prosecutor, the challenges rested neither on the intention to exclude Latino or bilingual jurors, nor on stereotypical assumptions about Latinos or bilinguals. The prosecutor's articulated basis for these challenges divided potential jurors into two classes: those whose conduct during voir dire would persuade him they might have difficulty in accepting the translator's rendition of Spanish-language testimony and those potential jurors who gave no such reason for doubt. Each category would include both Latinos and non-Latinos. While the prosecutor's criterion might well result in the disproportionate removal of prospective Latino jurors, that disproportionate impact does not turn the prosecutor's actions into a per se violation of the Equal Protection Clause.

Petitioner contends that despite the prosecutor's focus on the individual responses of these jurors, his reason for the peremptory strikes has the effect of a pure, language-based reason because "[a]ny honest bilingual juror would have answered the prosecutor in the exact same way." Petitioner asserts that a bilingual juror would hesitate in answering questions like those asked by the judge and prosecutor due to the difficulty of ignoring the actual Spanish-language testimony. In his view, no more can be expected than a commitment by a prospective juror to try to follow the interpreter's translation.

But even if we knew that a high percentage of bilingual jurors would hesitate in answering questions like these and, as a consequence, would be excluded under the prosecutor's criterion, that fact alone would not cause the criterion to fail the race-neutrality test. As will be discussed below, disparate impact should be given appropriate weight in determining whether the prosecutor acted with a forbidden intent, but it will not be conclusive in the preliminary race-neutrality step of the *Batson* inquiry. An argument relating to the impact of a classification does not alone show its purpose. Equal protection analysis turns on the intended consequences of government classifications. Unless the government actor adopted a criterion with the intent of causing the impact asserted, that impact itself does not violate the principle of race neutrality. Nothing in the prosecutor's explanation shows that he chose to exclude jurors who hesitated in answering questions about following the interpreter because he wanted to prevent bilingual Latinos from serving on the jury.

If we deemed the prosecutor's reason for striking these jurors a racial classification on its face, it would follow that a trial judge could not excuse for cause a juror whose hesitation convinced the judge of the juror's inability to accept the official translation of foreign-language testimony. If the explanation is not race neutral for the prosecutor, it is no more so for the trial judge. While the reason offered by the prosecutor for a peremptory strike need not rise to the level of a challenge for cause, the fact that it corresponds to a valid for-cause challenge will demonstrate its race-neutral character.

C

Once the prosecutor offers a race-neutral basis for his exercise of peremptory challenges, "[t]he trial court then [has] the duty to determine if the defendant has established purposeful discrimination." While the disproportionate impact on Latinos resulting from the prosecutor's criterion for excluding these jurors does not answer the race-neutrality inquiry, it does have relevance to the trial court's decision on this question. "[A]n invidious discriminatory purpose may often be inferred from the totality of the relevant facts, including the fact, if it is true, that the [classification] bears more heavily on one race than another." If a prosecutor articulates a basis for a peremptory challenge that results in the disproportionate exclusion of members of a certain race, the trial judge may consider that fact as evidence that the prosecutor's stated reason constitutes a pretext for racial discrimination.

In the context of this trial, the prosecutor's frank admission that his ground for excusing these jurors related to their ability to speak and understand Spanish raised a plausible, though not a necessary, inference that language might be a pretext for what in fact were race-based peremptory challenges. This was not a case where by some rare coincidence a juror happened to speak the same language as a key witness, in a community where few others spoke that tongue. If it were, the explanation that the juror could have undue influence on jury deliberations might be accepted without concern that a racial generalization had come into play. But this trial took place in a community with a substantial Latino population, and petitioner and other interested parties were members of that ethnic group. It would be common knowledge in the locality that a significant percentage of the Latino population speaks fluent Spanish, and that many consider it their preferred language, the one chosen for personal communication, the one selected for speaking with the most precision and power, the one used to define the self.

The trial judge can consider these and other factors when deciding whether a prosecutor intended to discriminate. For example, though petitioner did not suggest the alternative to the trial court here, Spanish-speaking jurors could be permitted to advise the judge in a discreet way of any concerns with the translation during the course of trial. A prosecutor's persistence in the desire to exclude Spanish-speaking jurors despite this measure could be taken into account in determining whether to accept a race-neutral explanation for the challenge.

The trial judge in this case chose to believe the prosecutor's race-neutral explanation for striking the two jurors in question, rejecting petitioner's assertion that the reasons were pretextual. In *Batson*, we explained that the trial court's decision on the ultimate question of discriminatory intent represents a finding of fact of the sort accorded great deference on appeal:

> In a recent Title VII sex discrimination case, we stated that "a finding of intentional discrimination is a finding of fact" entitled to appropriate deference by a reviewing court. Since the trial judge's findings in the context under consideration here largely turn on evaluation of credibility, a reviewing court ordinarily should give those findings great deference.

Batson's treatment of intent to discriminate as a pure issue of fact, subject to review under a deferential standard, accords with our treatment of that issue in other equal protection cases. As *Batson*'s citation to *Anderson* suggests, it also corresponds with our treatment of the intent inquiry under Title VII.

Deference to trial court findings on the issue of discriminatory intent makes particular sense in this context because, as we noted in *Batson*, the finding "largely will turn on evaluation of credibility." In the typical peremptory challenge inquiry, the decisive question will be whether counsel's race-neutral explanation for a peremptory challenge should be believed. There will seldom be much evidence bearing on that issue, and the best evidence often will be the demeanor of the attorney who exercises the challenge. As with the state of mind of a juror, evaluation of the prosecutor's state of mind based on demeanor and credibility lies "peculiarly within a trial judge's province."

* * *

We discern no clear error in the state trial court's determination that the prosecutor did not discriminate on the basis of the ethnicity of Latino jurors. We have said that "[w]here there are two permissible views of the evidence, the factfinder's choice between them cannot be clearly erroneous." *Anderson v. Bessemer City* (1985). The trial court took a permissible view of the evidence in crediting the prosecutor's explanation. Apart from the prosecutor's demeanor, which of course we have no opportunity to review, the court could have relied on the facts that the prosecutor defended his use of peremptory challenges without being asked to do so by the judge, that he did not know which jurors were Latinos, and that the ethnicity of the victims and prosecution witnesses tended to undercut any motive to exclude Latinos from the jury. Any of these factors could be taken as evidence of the prosecutor's sincerity. The trial court, moreover, could rely on the fact that only three challenged jurors can with confidence be identified as Latinos, and that the prosecutor had a verifiable and legitimate explanation for two of those challenges. Given these factors, that the prosecutor also excluded one or two Latino venirepersons on the basis of a subjective criterion having a disproportionate impact on Latinos does not leave us with a "definite and firm conviction that a mistake has been committed."

D

Language permits an individual to express both a personal identity and membership in a community, and those who share a common language may interact in ways more intimate than those without this bond. Bilinguals, in a sense, inhabit two communities, and serve to bring them closer. Indeed, some scholarly comment suggests that people proficient in two languages may not at times think in one language to the exclusion of the other. The analogy is that of a high-hurdler, who combines the ability to sprint and to jump to accomplish a third feat with characteristics of its own, rather than two separate functions. This is not to say that the cognitive processes and reactions of those who speak two languages are susceptible of easy generalization, for even the term "bilingual" does not describe a uniform category. It is a simple word for a more complex phenomenon with many distinct categories and subdivisions.

Our decision today does not imply that exclusion of bilinguals from jury service is wise, or even that it is constitutional in all cases. It is a harsh paradox that one may become proficient enough in English to participate in trial, see, e.g., 28 U.S.C. §§ 1865(b)(2), (3) (English-language ability required for federal jury service), only to encounter disqualification because he knows a second language as well. As the Court observed in a somewhat related context: "Mere knowledge of [a foreign] language cannot reasonably be regarded as harmful. Heretofore it has been commonly looked upon as helpful and desirable." *Meyer v. Nebraska* (1923).

Just as shared language can serve to foster community, language differences can be a source of division. Language elicits a response from others, ranging from admiration and respect, to distance and alienation, to ridicule and scorn. Reactions of the latter type all too often result from or initiate racial hostility. In holding that a race-neutral reason for a peremptory challenge means a reason other than race, we do not resolve the more difficult question of the breadth with which the concept of race should be defined for equal protection purposes. We would face a quite different case if the prosecutor had justified his peremptory challenges with the explanation that he did not want Spanish-speaking jurors. It may well be, for certain ethnic groups and in some communities, that proficiency in a particular language, like skin color, should be treated as a surrogate for race under an equal protection analysis. *Meyer v. Nebraska, supra* (striking down law prohibiting grade schools from teaching languages other than English). And, as we make clear, a policy of striking all who speak a given language, without regard to the particular circumstances of the trial or the individual responses of the jurors, may be found by the trial judge to be a pretext for racial discrimination. But that case is not before us.

III

We find no error in the application by the New York courts of the three-step *Batson* analysis. The standard inquiry into the objecting party's prima facie case was unnecessary given the course of proceedings in the trial court. The state courts came to the proper conclusion that the prosecutor offered a race-neutral basis for his exercise of peremptory challenges. The trial court did not commit clear error in choosing to believe the reasons given by the prosecutor.

Affirmed.

• • •

Justice STEVENS, with whom Justice MARSHALL joins, dissenting.

A violation of the Equal Protection Clause requires what our cases characterize as proof of "discriminatory purpose." By definition, however, a prima facie case is one that is established by the requisite proof of invidious intent. Unless the prosecutor comes forward with an explanation for his peremptories that is sufficient to rebut that prima facie case, no additional evidence of racial animus is required to establish an equal protection violation. In my opinion, the Court therefore errs when it concludes that a defendant's *Batson* challenge fails whenever the prosecutor advances a nonpretextual justification that is not facially discriminatory.

I

In *Batson* we held that "a 'pattern' of strikes against black jurors included in the particular venire might give rise to an inference of discrimination" sufficient to satisfy the defendant's burden of proving an equal protection violation. "Once the defendant makes a prima facie showing, the burden shifts to the State to come forward with a neutral explanation." If the prosecutor offers no explanation, the defendant has succeeded in establishing an equal protection violation based on the evidence of invidious intent that gave rise to the prima facie case. If the prosecutor seeks to dispel the inference of discriminatory intent, in order to succeed his explanation "need not rise to the level justifying exercise of a challenge for cause." However, the prosecutor's justification must identify " 'legitimate reasons' " that are "related to the particular case to be tried" and sufficiently persuasive to "rebu[t] a defendant's prima facie case."

An avowed justification that has a significant disproportionate impact will rarely qualify as a legitimate, race-neutral reason sufficient to rebut the prima facie case because disparate impact is itself evidence of discriminatory purpose. An explanation based on a concern that can easily be accommodated by means less drastic than excluding the challenged venireperson from the petit jury will also generally not qualify as a legitimate reason because it is not in fact "related to the particular case to be tried." And, as in any other equal protection challenge to a government classification, a justification that is frivolous or illegitimate should not suffice to rebut the prima facie case.

If any explanation, no matter how insubstantial and no matter how great its disparate impact, could rebut a prima facie inference of discrimination provided only that the explanation itself was not facially discriminatory, "the Equal Protection Clause 'would be but a vain and illusory requirement.' " The Court mistakenly believes that it is compelled to reach this result because an equal protection violation requires discriminatory purpose. The Court overlooks, however, the fact that the "discriminatory purpose" which characterizes violations of the Equal Protection Clause can sometimes be established by objective evidence that is consistent with a decisionmaker's honest belief that his motive was entirely benign. "Frequently the most probative evidence of intent will be objective evidence of what actually happened," including evidence of disparate impact. *See, e.g., Yick Wo v. Hopkins* (1886). The line between discriminatory purpose and discriminatory impact is neither as bright nor as critical as the Court appears to believe.

The Court therefore errs in focusing the entire inquiry on the subjective state of mind of the prosecutor. In jury selection challenges, the requisite invidious intent is established once the defendant makes out a prima facie case. No additional evidence of this intent is necessary unless the explanation provided by the prosecutor is sufficiently powerful to rebut the prima facie proof of discriminatory purpose. By requiring that the prosecutor's explanation itself provide additional, direct evidence of discriminatory motive, the Court has imposed on the defendant the added requirement that he generate evidence of the prosecutor's actual subjective intent to discriminate. Neither *Batson* nor our other equal protection holdings demand such a heightened quantum of proof.

II

Applying the principles outlined above to the facts of this case, I would reject the prosecutor's explanation without reaching the question whether the explanation was pretextual. Neither the Court nor respondent disputes that petitioner made out a prima facie case. Even assuming the prosecutor's explanation in rebuttal was advanced in good faith, the justification proffered was insufficient to dispel the existing inference of racial animus.

The prosecutor's explanation was insufficient for three reasons. First, the justification would inevitably result in a disproportionate disqualification of Spanish-speaking venirepersons. An explanation that is "race neutral" on its face is nonetheless unacceptable if it is merely a proxy for a discriminatory practice. Second, the prosecutor's concern could easily have been accommodated by less drastic means. As is the practice in many jurisdictions, the jury could have been instructed that the official translation alone is evidence; bilingual jurors could have been instructed to bring to the attention of the judge any disagreements they might have with the translation so that any disputes could be resolved by the court. *See, e.g., United States v. Perez* (CA9 1981). Third, if the prosecutor's concern was valid and substantiated by the record, it would have supported a challenge for cause. The fact that the prosecutor did not make any such challenge should disqualify him from advancing the concern as a justification for a peremptory challenge.

Each of these reasons considered alone might not render insufficient the prosecutor's facially neutral explanation. In combination, however, they persuade me that his explanation should have been rejected as a matter of law. Accordingly, I respectfully dissent.

[Justice O'Connor wrote a concurring opinion that Justice Scalia joined.]

NOTES AND QUESTIONS

1. The Court has no trouble holding *Batson* applicable to peremptory challenges based on ethnicity. It would eventually reach the same result as to gender, finding a *Batson* violation in *J.E.B. v. Alabama ex rel. T.B.*, 511 U.S. 127 (1994), where the state used nine of its ten peremptory challenges to strike male prospective jurors in a paternity and child support trial. The Court rejected the state's argument that men might be more sympathetic to the defendant than women, as being based on the very "stereotype that the law condemns." And in *SmithKline Beecham Corp. v. Abbott Labs.*, 740 F.3d 471, 476 (9th Cir. 2014), a panel of the Ninth Circuit found a *Batson* violation where a corporate pharmaceutical company defendant in a case about AIDS medications used a peremptory challenge to strike the only prospective juror who had effectively self-identified as gay during voir dire questioning.

2. The prosecutor in *Hernandez* offered two explanations for striking Hispanic prospective jurors. First, he argued that he didn't believe they would accept the interpreter as the final arbiter of witness testimony, and noted their lack of eye contact when questioned on the subject. Second, after a discussion with his supervisor, he added that all of his civilian witnesses were Hispanic and that therefore he would have had no logical reason to exclude Hispanics. Should the trial judge have even considered the second of these explanations, as it was only offered (contrived) after the fact, most likely due to a suggestion by the prosecutor's supervisor?

Regardless of that intervention, which explanation is more persuasive? Is it realistic to expect bilingual jurors who speak the language of a testifying witness to rely on a court interpreter instead of what they hear the witness actually say with their own two ears?

3. Eye contact is a funny thing. It comes up a lot in *Batson* cases, often as part of the prosecutor's race-neutral explanation for strikes. For one thing, many people have eye contact anxiety, sometimes as a result of nothing but shyness. For another, a "lack of eye contact" in a person can be created: Staring at a person will normally cause a person to look away. Further, a "lack of eye contact" is easy to exaggerate (or to fabricate) and cannot possibly be monitored in real time by the trial judge.

What is the significance of the fact that the trial judge, after questioning the Latino potential jurors, was sufficiently satisfied they would follow the interpreter that he did not excuse them? Did this excuse the prosecutor's failure to attempt to strike them for cause, as the dissent suggests the prosecutor should have done? Why didn't the judge find the prosecutor's argument pretextual, given that the judge had reached the opposite conclusion?

4. Judge Kaye of the New York Court of Appeals dissented from that court's affirmance of the trial court's decision that the prosecutor's explanation was sufficient. He noted that the prosecutor had not asked for any voir dire questioning of any of the non–Hispanic appearing potential jurors as to whether they spoke Spanish.

Does this omission demonstrate that the prosecutor was using language as a proxy for ethnicity?

5. The Supreme Court concludes that the appellate court should not have second-guessed the legitimacy of the prosecutor's proffered neutral explanation for the strikes because the issue turns so heavily on the "credibility" and the "demeanor" of the prosecutor. Do you agree? Is it clear that the trial judge actually relied on the prosecutor's demeanor? Does that matter? What effect might such a rule have on trial judges hearing *Batson* challenges?

6. The concurrence defends the prosecutor's explanation for his challenges in part by noting as follows: "They may have acted like strikes based on race, but they were *not* based on race." 500 U.S. at 375. But isn't how the strikes "act" an important factor in determining whether they are pretextual or, at the very least, insincere or contrived?

7. The dissent claims the prosecutor's explanation was insufficient for three reasons. Are these equally compelling? How does it cut that the best case the prosecutor can find to support his interpreter argument isn't very favorable to his position? Is the dissent's apparent requirement of a for-cause strike here reasonable?

The reviewability of unsuccessful *Batson* challenges after *Hernandez* was reduced even further by *Purkett v. Elem*, 514 U.S. 765 (1995), a case where the prosecutor struck two prospective Black jurors because of their long hair and facial hair. The Court held that the reviewing court erred by considering the "plausibility" of the prosecutor's proffered explanation for the strikes at step two of the *Batson* analysis, which is only concerned with whether the explanation was race-neutral. Plausibility, the Court held, can only be considered at step three, as part of the ultimate determination whether the defendant has proven discriminatory intent. While the holding in *Purkett* seems arcane and purely doctrinal, it has the effect of insulating findings of nonplausibility from review by burying them into the ultimate factual finding, to which "great deference" must be accorded.

In her article Batson v. Kentucky: *Reflections on a Podcast, supra*, Professor Nancy S. Marder reports that statistics compiled by the Equal Justice Initiative (EJI) show that even after *Batson* not a single *Batson* ruling was reversed in a 30-year period in Tennessee and that in Houston County, Alabama, 80 percent of qualified Black persons were struck from capital cases during a five-year period. *Id.* at 632 & nn.90-91. Implausible explanations for peremptory challenges that were upheld, moreover, are legion. Interviewed on the *Object Anyway* podcast, EJI founder Bryan Stevenson recalls making a *Batson* challenge against a prosecutor who said that "he struck an African-American prospective juror because the man said that he was a mason and the prosecutor said that he did not want anybody who belonged to a Masonic lodge on his jury." When Stevenson put the prospective juror back on the stand and asked him if he was a member of a Masonic lodge, the man said: "No. I'm not . . . I'm a brick mason!" Nevertheless, the judge accepted the reason and let the prosecutor strike the man from the jury. *Id.* at 632. *See United States v. Alvarado-Sandoval*, 997 F.2d 491, 491-92 (8th Cir. 1993) (accepting prosecutor's explanation that "I am going to get into an aiding and abetting type theory and just for whatever reason I did not want a cosmetologist").

In part because of the inability or unwillingness of trial judges to do the policing work necessary to ferret out *Batson* violations, and the effective insulation of their rulings from appellate review, *Batson* is widely seen as a failure, and many of its critics have joined the view of Justice Marshall in his *Batson* concurring opinion that peremptory challenges should be abolished. *See* Roberts, *Asymmetry as Fairness, supra* at 1503, 1510-13 & nn.50-67.

One commentator finds a silver lining in *Batson*'s ability to "punch above its weight" on appeal and in post-trial proceedings, where a finding of a *Batson* violation will amount to an automatic reversal and new trial, given that such a violation is "structural error" and thus eludes harmless error analysis. By contrast, a successful *Batson* challenge at trial may mean only that a particular juror is seated rather than excluded, or perhaps a new jury has to be empaneled if it is too late to resurrect the situation. Jonathan Abel, Batson's *Appellate Appeal and Trial Tribulations*, 118 Colum. L. Rev. 713 (2018).

Reform has come at the state level, however. One state high court has substantially modified the requirements of establishing a *Batson* violation though use of its rulemaking authority. In 2018, the Washington Supreme Court promulgated Wash. Ct. Gen. R. 37 (GR 37), which altered the *Batson* framework in two ways.

First, GR 37 rejects *Batson*'s required finding of purposeful discrimination and instead incorporates "implicit, institutional, and unconscious" biases. GR 37(f). The Rule disallows peremptory challenges if an "objective observer could view [a juror's] race or ethnicity as a factor in the use" of the strike. *Id.* 37(e). The Rule defines an objective observer as someone who is "aware that implicit, institutional, and unconscious biases, in addition to purposeful discrimination, have resulted in the unfair exclusion of potential jurors in Washington State." *Id.* 37(f). Second, GR 37 combats the use of common race-neutral reasons that are historically associated with improper discrimination in jury selection. For example, the Rule lists presumptively invalid reasons for a strike including expressing a belief that law enforcement engages in racial profiling, having prior contact with law enforcement, and living in a high-crime neighborhood. GR 37 also makes it more difficult to strike a juror based on a behavioral reason such as failing to make eye contact or exhibiting a "problematic" attitude.

In California, a reform similar to Washington's judicial rule was effected by legislation. Under Assembly Bill 3070, which went into effect in January 2022, factors similar to those under Washington's GR 37 are declared presumptively invalid, and the prosecutor must demonstrate his rebuttal to a *Batson* challenge by clear and convincing evidence that his strike was unrelated to a juror's membership in a protected group or class.

What effect do you think the Washington and California rules are likely to have on prosecutors' use of peremptory challenges?

C. Race and Peremptory Challenges

Arizona went even further, one might say, eliminating peremptory challenges altogether in both criminal and civil cases. Following the recommendation of the Arizona Task Force on Jury Data Collection Practices and Procedures, the Arizona Supreme Court in August 2021 amended Rules 18.4 and 18.5 of the Arizona Rules of Criminal Procedure and Rule 47 of the Arizona Rules of Civil Procedure so as to eliminate peremptory challenges.

Do you think the elimination of peremptory challenges favors the prosecution or the defense?

Speaking of podcasts, in May 2018 American Public Media's *In the Dark* podcast began exploring the state of Mississippi's serial prosecutions of Curtis Flowers, who had been tried six separate times for the alleged murder of four people in a furniture store in Winona, Mississippi. In November 2018 the Supreme Court granted a writ of certiorari on Flowers's *Batson* challenge issue.

The "In the Dark" podcast team

Flowers v. Mississippi
588 U.S. 284 (2019)

Justice KAVANAUGH delivered the opinion of the Court.

In *Batson* this Court ruled that a State may not discriminate on the basis of race when exercising peremptory challenges against prospective jurors in a criminal trial.

In 1996, Curtis Flowers allegedly murdered four people in Winona, Mississippi. Flowers is black. He has been tried six separate times before a jury for murder. The same lead prosecutor represented the State in all six trials.

In the initial three trials, Flowers was convicted, but the Mississippi Supreme Court reversed each conviction. In the first trial, Flowers was convicted, but the Mississippi Supreme Court reversed the conviction due to "numerous instances of prosecutorial misconduct." In the second trial, the trial court found that the prosecutor discriminated on the basis of race in the peremptory challenge of a black juror. The trial court seated the black juror. Flowers was then convicted, but the Mississippi Supreme Court again reversed the conviction because of prosecutorial misconduct at trial. In the third trial, Flowers was convicted, but the Mississippi Supreme Court yet again reversed the conviction, this time because the court concluded that the prosecutor had again discriminated against black prospective jurors in the jury selection process. The court's lead opinion stated: "The instant case presents us with as strong a prima facie case of racial discrimination as we have ever seen in the context of a *Batson* challenge." The opinion further stated that the "State engaged in racially discriminatory practices during the jury selection process" and that the "case evinces an effort by the State to exclude African-Americans from jury service."

The fourth and fifth trials of Flowers ended in mistrials due to hung juries.

In his sixth trial, which is the one at issue here, Flowers was convicted. The State struck five of the six black prospective jurors. On appeal, Flowers argued that the State again violated

Batson in exercising peremptory strikes against black prospective jurors. In a divided 5-to-4 decision, the Mississippi Supreme Court affirmed the conviction. We granted certiorari on the *Batson* question and now reverse.

Four critical facts, taken together, require reversal. First, in the six trials combined, the State employed its peremptory challenges to strike 41 of the 42 black prospective jurors that it could have struck—a statistic that the State acknowledged at oral argument in this Court. Second, in the most recent trial, the sixth trial, the State exercised peremptory strikes against five of the six black prospective jurors. Third, at the sixth trial, in an apparent effort to find pretextual reasons to strike black prospective jurors, the State engaged in dramatically disparate questioning of black and white prospective jurors. Fourth, the State then struck at least one black prospective juror, Carolyn Wright, who was similarly situated to white prospective jurors who were not struck by the State.

We need not and do not decide that any one of those four facts alone would require reversal. All that we need to decide, and all that we do decide, is that all of the relevant facts and circumstances taken together establish that the trial court committed clear error in concluding that the State's peremptory strike of black prospective juror Carolyn Wright was not "motivated in substantial part by discriminatory intent." In reaching that conclusion, we break no new legal ground. We simply enforce and reinforce *Batson* by applying it to the extraordinary facts of this case.

We reverse the judgment of the Supreme Court of Mississippi, and we remand the case for further proceedings not inconsistent with this opinion.

I

The underlying events that gave rise to this case took place in Winona, Mississippi. Winona is a small town in northern Mississippi, just off I-55 almost halfway between Jackson and Memphis. The total population of Winona is about 5,000. The town is about 53 percent black and about 46 percent white.

In 1996, Bertha Tardy, Robert Golden, Derrick Stewart, and Carmen Rigby were murdered at the Tardy Furniture store in Winona. All four victims worked at the Tardy Furniture store. Three of the four victims were white; one was black. In 1997, the State charged Curtis Flowers with murder. Flowers is black. Since then, Flowers has been tried six separate times for the murders. In each of the first two trials, Flowers was tried for one individual murder. In each subsequent trial, Flowers was tried for all four of the murders together. The same state prosecutor tried Flowers each time. The prosecutor is white.

At Flowers' first trial, 36 prospective jurors—5 black and 31 white—were presented to potentially serve on the jury. The State exercised a total of 12 peremptory strikes, and it used 5 of them to strike the five qualified black prospective jurors. Flowers objected, arguing under *Batson* that the State had exercised its peremptory strikes in a racially discriminatory manner. The trial court rejected the *Batson* challenge. Because the trial court allowed the State's peremptory strikes, Flowers was tried in front of an all-white jury. The jury convicted Flowers and sentenced him to death.

On appeal, the Mississippi Supreme Court reversed the conviction, concluding that the State had committed prosecutorial misconduct in front of the jury by, among other things, expressing baseless grounds for doubting the credibility of witnesses and mentioning facts that had not been allowed into evidence by the trial judge. In its opinion, the Mississippi Supreme Court described "numerous instances of prosecutorial misconduct" at the trial. Because the Mississippi Supreme Court reversed based on prosecutorial misconduct at trial, the court did not reach Flowers' *Batson* argument.

At the second trial, 30 prospective jurors—5 black and 25 white—were presented to potentially serve on the jury. As in Flowers' first trial, the State again used its strikes against all five black prospective jurors. But this time, the trial court determined that the State's asserted reason for one of the strikes was a pretext for discrimination. Specifically, the trial court determined that one of the State's proffered reasons—that the juror had been inattentive and was nodding off during jury selection—for striking that juror was false, and the trial court therefore sustained Flowers' *Batson* challenge. The trial court disallowed the strike and sat that black juror on the jury. The jury at Flowers' second trial consisted of 11 white jurors and 1 black juror. The jury convicted Flowers and sentenced him to death.

On appeal, the Mississippi Supreme Court again reversed. The court ruled that the prosecutor had again engaged in prosecutorial misconduct in front of the jury by, among other things, impermissibly referencing evidence and attempting to undermine witness credibility without a factual basis.

At Flowers' third trial, 45 prospective jurors—17 black and 28 white—were presented to potentially serve on the jury. One of the black prospective jurors was struck for cause, leaving 16. The State exercised a total of 15 peremptory strikes, and it used all 15 against black prospective jurors. Flowers again argued that the State had used its peremptory strikes in a racially discriminatory manner. The trial court found that the State had not discriminated on the basis of race. The jury in Flowers' third trial consisted of 11 white jurors and 1 black juror. The lone black juror who served on the jury was seated after the State ran out of peremptory strikes. The jury convicted Flowers and sentenced him to death.

On appeal, the Mississippi Supreme Court yet again reversed, concluding that the State had again violated *Batson* by discriminating on the basis of race in exercising all 15 of its peremptory strikes against 15 black prospective jurors. The court's lead opinion stated: "The instant case presents us with as strong a prima facie case of racial discrimination as we have ever seen in the context of a *Batson* challenge." The opinion explained that although "each individual strike may have justifiably appeared to the trial court to be sufficiently race neutral, the trial court also has a duty to look at the State's use of peremptory challenges in toto." The opinion emphasized that "trial judges should not blindly accept any and every reason put forth by the State, especially" when "the State continues to exercise challenge after challenge only upon members of a particular race." The opinion added that the "State engaged in racially discriminatory practices" and that the "case evinces an effort by the State to exclude African-Americans from jury service."

At Flowers' fourth trial, 36 prospective jurors—16 black and 20 white—were presented to potentially serve on the jury. The State exercised a total of 11 peremptory strikes, and it used all 11 against black prospective jurors. But because of the relatively large number of prospective jurors who were black, the State did not have enough peremptory challenges to eliminate all of the black prospective jurors. The seated jury consisted of seven white jurors and five black jurors. That jury could not reach a verdict, and the proceeding ended in a mistrial.

As to the fifth trial, there is no available racial information about the prospective jurors, as distinct from the jurors who ultimately sat on the jury. The jury was composed of nine white jurors and three black jurors. The jury could not reach a verdict, and the trial again ended in a mistrial.

At the sixth trial, which we consider here, 26 prospective jurors—6 black and 20 white—were presented to potentially serve on the jury. The State exercised a total of six peremptory strikes, and it used five of the six against black prospective jurors, leaving one black juror to sit on the jury. Flowers again argued that the State had exercised its peremptory strikes in a racially discriminatory manner. The trial court concluded that the State had offered race-neutral reasons for each of the five peremptory strikes against the five black prospective jurors. The jury at Flowers' sixth trial consisted of 11 white jurors and 1 black juror. That jury convicted Flowers of murder and sentenced him to death.

In a divided decision, the Mississippi Supreme Court agreed with the trial court on the *Batson* issue and stated that the State's "race-neutral reasons were valid and not merely pretextual." Flowers then sought review in this Court. This Court granted Flowers' petition for a writ of certiorari, vacated the judgment of the Mississippi Supreme Court, and remanded for further consideration in light of the decision in *Foster*. In *Foster,* this Court held that the defendant Foster had established a *Batson* violation.

On remand, the Mississippi Supreme Court by a 5-to-4 vote again upheld Flowers' conviction. Justice King wrote a dissent for three justices. He stated: "I cannot conclude that Flowers received a fair trial, nor can I conclude that prospective jurors were not subjected to impermissible discrimination." According to Justice King, both the trial court and the Mississippi Supreme Court "completely disregard[ed] the constitutional right of prospective jurors to be free from a racially discriminatory selection process." We granted certiorari.

II

A

Other than voting, serving on a jury is the most substantial opportunity that most citizens have to participate in the democratic process.

Jury selection in criminal cases varies significantly based on state and local rules and practices, but ordinarily consists of three phases, which we describe here in general terms. First, a group of citizens in the community is randomly summoned to the courthouse on a particular day for potential jury service. Second, a subgroup of those prospective jurors is called into a particular courtroom for a specific case. The prospective jurors are often questioned by the judge, as well as by the prosecutor and defense attorney. During that second phase, the judge may excuse certain prospective jurors based on their answers. Third, the prosecutor and defense attorney may challenge certain prospective jurors. The attorneys may challenge prospective jurors for cause, which usually stems from a potential juror's conflicts of interest or inability to be impartial. In addition to challenges for cause, each side is typically afforded a set number of peremptory challenges or strikes. Peremptory strikes have very old credentials and can be traced back to the common law. Those peremptory strikes traditionally may be used to remove any potential juror for any reason — no questions asked.

That blanket discretion to peremptorily strike prospective jurors for any reason can clash with the dictates of the Equal Protection Clause of the Fourteenth Amendment to the United States Constitution. This case arises at the intersection of the peremptory challenge and the Equal Protection Clause. And to understand how equal protection law applies to peremptory challenges, it helps to begin at the beginning.

Ratified in 1868 in the wake of the Civil War, the Equal Protection Clause of the Fourteenth Amendment provides that no State shall "deny to any person within its jurisdiction the equal protection of the laws." A primary objective of the Equal Protection Clause, this Court stated just five years after ratification, was "the freedom of the slave race, the security and firm establishment of that freedom, and the protection of the newly-made freeman and citizen from the oppressions of those who had formerly exercised unlimited dominion over him." *Slaughter-House Cases* (1873).

In 1875, to help enforce the Fourteenth Amendment, Congress passed and President Ulysses S. Grant signed the Civil Rights Act of 1875. Among other things, that law made it a criminal offense for state officials to exclude individuals from jury service on account of their race. 18 U.S.C. § 243. The Act provides: "No citizen possessing all other qualifications which are or may be prescribed by law shall be disqualified for service as grand or petit juror in any court of the United States, or of any State on account of race, color, or previous condition of servitude."

In 1880, just 12 years after ratification of the Fourteenth Amendment, the Court decided *Strauder*. That case concerned a West Virginia statute that allowed whites only to serve as jurors. The Court held the law unconstitutional.

C. Race and Peremptory Challenges   1291

In reaching its conclusion, the Court explained that the Fourteenth Amendment required "that the law in the States shall be the same for the black as for the white; that all persons, whether colored or white, shall stand equal before the laws of the States, and, in regard to the colored race, for whose protection the amendment was primarily designed, that no discrimination shall be made against them by law because of their color." In the words of the *Strauder* Court: "The very fact that colored people are singled out and expressly denied by a statute all right to participate in the administration of the law, as jurors, because of their color, though they are citizens, and may be in other respects fully qualified, is practically a brand upon them, affixed by the law, an assertion of their inferiority, and a stimulant to that race prejudice which is an impediment to securing to individuals of the race that equal justice which the law aims to secure to all others." For those reasons, the Court ruled that the West Virginia statute excluding blacks from jury service violated the Fourteenth Amendment.

As the Court later explained in *Brown v. Board of Education* (1954), the Court's decisions in the *Slaughter-House Cases* and *Strauder* interpreted the Fourteenth Amendment "as proscribing all state-imposed discriminations against the Negro race," including in jury service.

In the decades after *Strauder*, the Court reiterated that States may not discriminate on the basis of race in jury selection.

But critical problems persisted. Even though laws barring blacks from serving on juries were unconstitutional after *Strauder*, many jurisdictions employed various discriminatory tools to prevent black persons from being called for jury service. And when those tactics failed, or were invalidated, prosecutors could still exercise peremptory strikes in individual cases to remove most or all black prospective jurors.

In the century after *Strauder*, the freedom to exercise peremptory strikes for any reason meant that "the problem of racial exclusion from jury service" remained "widespread" and "deeply entrenched." 5 U.S. Commission on Civil Rights Report 90 (1961). Simple math shows how that happened. Given that blacks were a minority of the population, in many jurisdictions the number of peremptory strikes available to the prosecutor exceeded the number of black prospective jurors. So prosecutors could routinely exercise peremptories to strike all the black prospective jurors and thereby ensure all-white juries. The exclusion of black prospective jurors was almost total in certain jurisdictions, especially in cases involving black defendants. Similarly, defense counsel could use—and routinely did use—peremptory challenges to strike all the black prospective jurors in cases involving white defendants and black victims.

In the aftermath of *Strauder*, the exclusion of black jurors became more covert and less overt—often accomplished through peremptory challenges in individual courtrooms rather than by blanket operation of law. But as this Court later noted, the results were the same for black jurors and black defendants, as well as for the black community's confidence in the fairness of the American criminal justice system.

Eighty-five years after *Strauder*, the Court decided *Swain v. Alabama*. The defendant Swain was black. Swain was convicted of a capital offense in Talladega County, Alabama, and sentenced to death. Swain presented evidence that no black juror had served on a jury in Talladega County in more than a decade. And in Swain's case, the prosecutor struck all six qualified black prospective jurors, ensuring that Swain was tried before an all-white jury. Swain invoked *Strauder* to argue that the prosecutor in his case had impermissibly discriminated on the basis of race by using peremptory challenges to strike the six black prospective jurors.

This Court ruled that Swain had not established unconstitutional discrimination. Most importantly, the Court held that a defendant could not object to the State's use of peremptory strikes in an individual case. In the Court's words: "[W]e cannot hold that the striking of Negroes in a particular case is a denial of equal protection of the laws." The *Swain* Court reasoned that prosecutors do not always judge prospective jurors individually when exercising peremptory strikes. Instead, prosecutors choose which prospective jurors to strike "in light of the limited knowledge counsel has of them, which may include their group affiliations, in the context of the case to be tried." In the Court's view, the prosecutor could strike prospective jurors on the basis of their group affiliations, including race. In other words, a prosecutor could permissibly strike a prospective juror for any reason, including the assumption or belief that a black prospective juror, because of race, would be favorable to a black defendant or unfavorable to the State.

To be sure, the *Swain* Court held that a defendant could make out a case of racial discrimination by showing that the State "in case after case, whatever the circumstances, whatever the crime and whoever the defendant or the victim may be," had been responsible for the removal of qualified black prospective jurors so that no black jurors "ever serve on petit juries." But *Swain*'s high bar for establishing a constitutional violation was almost impossible for any defendant to surmount, as the aftermath of *Swain* amply demonstrated.

Twenty-one years later, in its 1986 decision in *Batson*, the Court revisited several critical aspects of *Swain* and in essence overruled them. In so doing, the Batson Court emphasized that "the central concern" of the Fourteenth Amendment "was to put an end to governmental discrimination on account of race." The *Batson* Court noted that *Swain* had left prosecutors' peremptory challenges "largely immune from constitutional scrutiny." In his concurrence in Batson, Justice Byron White (the author of *Swain*) agreed that *Swain* should be overruled. He stated: "[T]he practice of peremptorily eliminating blacks from petit juries in cases with black defendants remains widespread, so much so" that "I agree with the Court that the time has come to rule as it has."

Under *Batson*, once a prima facie case of discrimination has been shown by a defendant, the State must provide race-neutral reasons for its peremptory strikes. The trial judge must determine whether the prosecutor's stated reasons were the actual reasons or instead were a pretext for discrimination.

Four parts of *Batson* warrant particular emphasis here.

First, the Batson Court rejected *Swain*'s insistence that a defendant demonstrate a history of racially discriminatory strikes in order to make out a claim of race discrimination. According to the *Batson* Court, defendants had run into "practical difficulties" in trying to prove that a State had systematically "exercised peremptory challenges to exclude blacks from the jury on account of race." The *Batson* Court explained that, in some jurisdictions, requiring a defendant to "investigate, over a number of cases, the race of persons tried in the particular jurisdiction, the racial composition of the venire and petit jury, and the manner in which both parties exercised their peremptory challenges" posed an "insurmountable" burden.

In addition to that practical point, the Court stressed a basic equal protection point: In the eyes of the Constitution, one racially discriminatory peremptory strike is one too many.

For those reasons, the *Batson* Court held that a criminal defendant could show "purposeful discrimination in selection of the petit jury solely on evidence concerning the prosecutor's exercise of peremptory challenges at the defendant's trial."

Second, the *Batson* Court rejected *Swain*'s statement that a prosecutor could strike a black juror based on an assumption or belief that the black juror would favor a black defendant. In some of the most critical sentences in the *Batson* opinion, the Court emphasized that a prosecutor may not rebut a claim of discrimination "by stating merely that he challenged jurors of the defendant's race on the assumption—or his intuitive judgment—that they would be partial to the defendant because of their shared race." The Court elaborated: The Equal Protection Clause "forbids the States to strike black veniremen on the assumption that they will be biased in a particular case simply because the defendant is black. The core guarantee of equal protection, ensuring citizens that their State will not discriminate on account of race, would be meaningless were we to approve the exclusion of jurors on the basis of such assumptions, which arise solely from the jurors' race." In his concurrence, Justice Thurgood Marshall drove the point home: "Exclusion of blacks from a jury, solely because of race, can no more be justified by a belief that blacks are less likely than whites to consider fairly or sympathetically the State's case against a black defendant than it can be justified by the notion that blacks lack the intelligence, experience, or moral integrity to be entrusted with that role."

Third, the *Batson* Court did not accept the argument that race-based peremptories should be permissible because black, white, Asian, and Hispanic defendants and jurors were all "equally" subject to race-based discrimination. The Court stated that each removal of an individual juror because of his or her race is a constitutional violation. Discrimination against one defendant or juror on account of race is not remedied or cured by discrimination against other defendants or jurors on account of race. As the Court later explained: Some say that there is no equal protection violation if individuals "of all races are subject to like treatment, which is to say that white jurors are subject to the same risk of peremptory challenges based on race as are all other jurors. The suggestion that racial classifications may survive when visited upon all persons is no more authoritative today than the case which advanced the theorem, *Plessy v. Ferguson* (1896). This idea has no place in our modern equal protection jurisprudence. It is axiomatic that racial classifications do not become legitimate on the assumption that all persons suffer them in equal degree."

Fourth, the *Batson* Court did not accept the argument that race-based peremptories are permissible because both the prosecution and defense could employ them in any individual case and in essence balance things out. Under the Equal Protection Clause, the Court stressed, even a single instance of race discrimination against a prospective juror is impermissible. Moreover, in criminal cases involving black defendants, the both-sides-can-do-it argument overlooks the percentage of the United States population that is black (about 12 percent) and the cold reality of jury selection in most jurisdictions. Because blacks are a minority in most jurisdictions, prosecutors often have more peremptory strikes than there are black prospective jurors on a particular panel. In the pre-*Batson* era, therefore, allowing each side in a case involving a black defendant to strike prospective jurors on the basis of race meant that a prosecutor could eliminate all of the black jurors, but a black defendant could not eliminate all of the white jurors. So in the real world of criminal trials against black defendants, both history and math tell us that a system of race-based peremptories does not treat black defendants and black prospective jurors equally with prosecutors and white prospective jurors.

B

Equal justice under law requires a criminal trial free of racial discrimination in the jury selection process. Enforcing that constitutional principle, *Batson* ended the widespread practice in which prosecutors could (and often would) routinely strike all black prospective jurors in cases involving black defendants. By taking steps to eradicate racial discrimination from the jury selection process, *Batson* sought to protect the rights of defendants and jurors, and to enhance public confidence in the fairness of the criminal justice system. *Batson* immediately revolutionized the jury selection process that takes place every day in federal and state criminal courtrooms throughout the United States.

In the decades since *Batson*, this Court's cases have vigorously enforced and reinforced the decision, and guarded against any backsliding. Moreover, the Court has extended *Batson* in certain ways. A defendant of any race may raise a *Batson* claim, and a defendant may raise a *Batson* claim even if the defendant and the excluded juror are of different races. Moreover, *Batson* now applies to gender discrimination, to a criminal defendant's peremptory strikes, and to civil cases.

Of particular relevance here, *Batson*'s holding raised several important evidentiary and procedural issues, three of which we underscore.

First, what factors does the trial judge consider in evaluating whether racial discrimination occurred? Our precedents allow criminal defendants raising *Batson* challenges to present a variety of evidence to support a claim that a prosecutor's peremptory strikes were made on the basis of race. For example, defendants may present:

- statistical evidence about the prosecutor's use of peremptory strikes against black prospective jurors as compared to white prospective jurors in the case;
- evidence of a prosecutor's disparate questioning and investigation of black and white prospective jurors in the case;
- side-by-side comparisons of black prospective jurors who were struck and white prospective jurors who were not struck in the case;
- a prosecutor's misrepresentations of the record when defending the strikes during the Batson hearing;
- relevant history of the State's peremptory strikes in past cases; or
- other relevant circumstances that bear upon the issue of racial discrimination.

Second, who enforces *Batson*? As the *Batson* Court itself recognized, the job of enforcing *Batson* rests first and foremost with trial judges. America's trial judges operate at the front lines of American justice. In criminal trials, trial judges possess the primary responsibility to enforce *Batson* and prevent racial discrimination from seeping into the jury selection process.

As the *Batson* Court explained and as the Court later reiterated, once a prima facie case of racial discrimination has been established, the prosecutor must provide race-neutral reasons for the strikes. The trial court must consider the prosecutor's race-neutral explanations in light of all of the relevant facts and circumstances, and in light of the arguments of the parties. The trial judge's assessment of the prosecutor's credibility is often important. The Court has explained that "the best evidence of discriminatory intent often will be the demeanor of the attorney who exercises the challenge." "We have recognized that these determinations of credibility and demeanor lie peculiarly within a trial judge's province." The trial judge must determine whether the prosecutor's proffered reasons are the actual reasons, or whether the proffered reasons are pretextual and the prosecutor instead exercised peremptory strikes on the basis of race. The ultimate inquiry is whether the State was "motivated in substantial part by discriminatory intent."

Third, what is the role of appellate review? An appeals court looks at the same factors as the trial judge, but is necessarily doing so on a paper record. "Since the trial judge's findings in the context under consideration here largely will turn on evaluation of credibility, a reviewing court ordinarily should give those findings great deference." The Court has described the appellate standard of review of the trial court's factual determinations in a *Batson* hearing as "highly deferential." "On appeal, a trial court's ruling on the issue of discriminatory intent must be sustained unless it is clearly erroneous."

III

In accord with the principles set forth in *Batson*, we now address Flowers' case.

The Constitution forbids striking even a single prospective juror for a discriminatory purpose. The question for this Court is whether the Mississippi trial court clearly erred in concluding that the State was not "motivated in substantial part by discriminatory intent" when exercising peremptory strikes at Flowers' sixth trial. Because this case arises on direct review, we owe no deference to the Mississippi Supreme Court, as distinct from deference to the Mississippi trial court.

C. Race and Peremptory Challenges   1295

Four categories of evidence loom large in assessing the *Batson* issue in Flowers' case: (1) the history from Flowers' six trials, (2) the prosecutor's striking of five of six black prospective jurors at the sixth trial, (3) the prosecutor's dramatically disparate questioning of black and white prospective jurors at the sixth trial, and (4) the prosecutor's proffered reasons for striking one black juror (Carolyn Wright) while allowing other similarly situated white jurors to serve on the jury at the sixth trial. We address each in turn.

A

First, we consider the relevant history of the case. Recall that in *Swain*, the Court held that a defendant may prove racial discrimination by establishing a historical pattern of racial exclusion of jurors in the jurisdiction in question. Indeed, under *Swain*, that was the only way that a defendant could make out a claim that the State discriminated on the basis of race in the use of peremptory challenges.

In *Batson*, the Court ruled that *Swain* had imposed too heavy a burden on defendants seeking to prove that a prosecutor had used peremptory strikes in a racially discriminatory manner. *Batson* lowered the evidentiary burden for defendants to contest prosecutors' use of peremptory strikes and made clear that demonstrating a history of discriminatory strikes in past cases was not necessary.

In doing so, however, *Batson* did not preclude defendants from still using the same kinds of historical evidence that *Swain* had allowed defendants to use to support a claim of racial discrimination. Most importantly for present purposes, after *Batson*, the trial judge may still consider historical evidence of the State's discriminatory peremptory strikes from past trials in the jurisdiction, just as *Swain* had allowed. After *Batson*, the defendant may still cast *Swain*'s "wide net" to gather " 'relevant' " evidence. A defendant may rely on "all relevant circumstances."

Here, our review of the history of the prosecutor's peremptory strikes in Flowers' first four trials strongly supports the conclusion that his use of peremptory strikes in Flowers' sixth trial was motivated in substantial part by discriminatory intent. (Recall that there is no record evidence from the fifth trial regarding the race of the prospective jurors.)

The numbers speak loudly. Over the course of the first four trials, there were 36 black prospective jurors against whom the State could have exercised a peremptory strike. The State tried to strike all 36. The State used its available peremptory strikes to attempt to strike every single black prospective juror that it could have struck. Not only did the State's use of peremptory strikes in Flowers' first four trials reveal a blatant pattern of striking black prospective jurors, the Mississippi courts themselves concluded on two separate occasions that the State violated *Batson*. In Flowers' second trial, the trial court concluded that the State discriminated against a black juror. Specifically, the trial court determined that one of the State's proffered reasons — that the juror had been inattentive and was nodding off during jury selection — for striking that juror was false, and the trial court therefore sustained Flowers' *Batson* challenge. In Flowers' next trial — his third trial — the prosecutor used all 15 of its peremptories to strike 15 black prospective jurors. The lead opinion of the Mississippi Supreme Court stated: "The instant case presents us with as strong a prima facie case of racial discrimination as we have ever seen in the context of a *Batson* challenge." The opinion further stated that "the State engaged in racially discriminatory practices during the jury selection process" and that the "case evinces an effort by the State to exclude African-Americans from jury service."

To summarize the most relevant history: In Flowers' first trial, the prosecutor successfully used peremptory strikes against all of the black prospective jurors. Flowers faced an all-white jury. In Flowers' second trial, the prosecutor tried again to strike all of the black prospective jurors, but the trial court decided that the State could not strike one of those jurors. The jury consisted of 11 white jurors and 1 black juror. In Flowers' third trial, there were 17 black prospective jurors. The prosecutor used 15 out of 15 peremptory strikes against black prospective jurors. After one black juror was struck for cause and the prosecutor ran out of strikes, one black juror remained. The jury again consisted of 11 white jurors and 1 black juror. In Flowers' fourth trial, the prosecutor again used 11 out of 11 peremptory strikes against black prospective jurors. Because of the large number of black prospective jurors at the trial, the prosecutor ran out of peremptory strikes before it could strike all of the black prospective jurors. The jury for that trial consisted of seven white jurors and five black jurors, and the jury was unable to reach a verdict. To reiterate, there is no available information about the race of prospective jurors in the fifth trial. The jury for that trial consisted of nine white jurors and three black jurors, and the jury was unable to reach a verdict.

Stretching across Flowers' first four trials, the State employed its peremptory strikes to remove as many black prospective jurors as possible. The State appeared to proceed as if *Batson* had never been decided. The State's relentless, determined effort to rid the jury of black individuals strongly suggests that the State wanted to try Flowers before a jury with as few black jurors as possible, and ideally before an all-white jury. The trial judge was aware of the history. But the judge did not sufficiently account for the history when considering Flowers' *Batson* claim.

The State's actions in the first four trials necessarily inform our assessment of the State's intent going into Flowers' sixth trial. We cannot ignore that history. We cannot take that history out of the case.

B

We turn now to the State's strikes of five of the six black prospective jurors at Flowers' sixth trial, the trial at issue here. As *Batson* noted, a "'pattern' of strikes against black jurors included in the particular venire might give rise to an inference of discrimination."

Flowers' sixth trial occurred in June 2010. At trial, 26 prospective jurors were presented to potentially serve on the jury. Six of the prospective jurors were black. The State accepted one black prospective juror—Alexander Robinson. The State struck the other five black prospective jurors—Carolyn Wright, Tashia Cunningham, Edith Burnside, Flancie Jones, and Dianne Copper. The resulting jury consisted of 11 white jurors and 1 black juror.

The State's use of peremptory strikes in Flowers' sixth trial followed the same pattern as the first four trials, with one modest exception: It is true that the State accepted one black juror for Flowers' sixth trial. But especially given the history of the case, that fact alone cannot insulate the State from a Batson challenge. In *Miller-El II*, this Court skeptically viewed the State's decision to accept one black juror, explaining that a prosecutor might do so in an attempt "to obscure the otherwise consistent pattern of opposition to" seating black jurors. The overall record of this case suggests that the same tactic may have been employed here. In light of all of the circumstances here, the State's decision to strike five of the six black prospective jurors is further evidence suggesting that the State was motivated in substantial part by discriminatory intent.

C

We next consider the State's dramatically disparate questioning of black and white prospective jurors in the jury selection process for Flowers' sixth trial. As *Batson* explained, "the prosecutor's questions and statements during voir dire examination and in exercising his challenges may support or refute an inference of discriminatory purpose."

The questioning process occurred through an initial group voir dire and then more in-depth follow-up questioning by the prosecutor and defense counsel of individual prospective jurors. The State asked the five black prospective jurors who were struck a total of 145 questions. By contrast, the State asked the 11 seated white jurors a total of 12 questions. On average, therefore, the State asked 29 questions to each struck black prospective juror. The State asked an average of one question to each seated white juror.

One can slice and dice the statistics and come up with all sorts of ways to compare the State's questioning of excluded black jurors with the State's questioning of the accepted white jurors. But any meaningful comparison yields the same basic assessment: The State spent far more time questioning the black prospective jurors than the accepted white jurors.

The State acknowledges, as it must under our precedents, that disparate questioning can be probative of discriminatory intent. As *Miller-El I* stated, "if the use of disparate questioning is determined by race at the outset, it is likely [that] a justification for a strike based on the resulting divergent views would be pretextual. In this context the differences in the questions posed by the prosecutors are some evidence of purposeful discrimination."

But the State here argues that it questioned black and white prospective jurors differently only because of differences in the jurors' characteristics. The record refutes that explanation.

For example, Dianne Copper was a black prospective juror who was struck. The State asked her 18 follow-up questions about her relationships with Flowers' family and with witnesses in the case. Pamela Chesteen was a white juror whom the State accepted for the jury. Although the State asked questions of Chesteen during group voir dire, the State asked her no individual follow-up questions about her relationships with Flowers' family, even though the State was aware that Chesteen knew several members of Flowers' family. Similarly, the State asked no individual follow-up questions to four other white prospective jurors who, like Dianne Copper, had relationships with defense witnesses, even though the State was aware of those relationships. Those white prospective jurors were Larry Blaylock, Harold Waller, Marcus Fielder, and Bobby Lester.

Likewise, the State conducted disparate investigations of certain prospective jurors. Tashia Cunningham, who is black, stated that she worked with Flowers' sister, but that the two did not work closely together. To try to disprove that statement, the State summoned a witness to challenge Cunningham's testimony. The State apparently did not conduct similar investigations of white prospective jurors.

It is certainly reasonable for the State to ask follow-up questions or to investigate the relationships of jurors to the victims, potential witnesses, and the like. But white prospective jurors who were acquainted with the Flowers' family or defense witnesses were not questioned extensively by the State or investigated. White prospective jurors who admitted that they or a relative had been convicted of a crime were accepted without apparent further inquiry by the State. The difference in the State's approaches to black and white prospective jurors was stark.

Why did the State ask so many more questions — and conduct more vigorous inquiry — of black prospective jurors than it did of white prospective jurors? No one can know for certain. But this Court's cases explain that disparate questioning and investigation of prospective jurors on the basis of race can arm a prosecutor with seemingly race-neutral reasons to strike the prospective jurors of a particular race. In other words, by asking a lot of questions of the black prospective jurors or conducting additional inquiry into their backgrounds, a prosecutor can try to find some pretextual reason — any reason — that the prosecutor can later articulate to justify what is in reality a racially motivated strike. And by not doing the same for white prospective jurors, by not asking white prospective jurors those same questions, the prosecutor can try to distort the record so as to thereby avoid being accused of treating black and white jurors differently. Disparity in questioning and investigation can produce a record that says little about white prospective jurors and is therefore resistant to characteristic-by-characteristic comparisons of struck black prospective jurors and seated white jurors. Prosecutors can decline to seek what they do not want to find about white prospective jurors.

A court confronting that kind of pattern cannot ignore it. The lopsidedness of the prosecutor's questioning and inquiry can itself be evidence of the prosecutor's objective as much as it is of the actual qualifications of the black and white prospective jurors who are struck or seated. The prosecutor's dramatically disparate questioning of black and white prospective jurors — at least if it rises to a certain level of disparity — can supply a clue that the prosecutor may have been seeking to paper the record and disguise a discriminatory intent.

To be clear, disparate questioning or investigation alone does not constitute a *Batson* violation. The disparate questioning or investigation of black and white prospective jurors may reflect ordinary race-neutral considerations. But the disparate questioning or investigation can also, along with other evidence, inform the trial court's evaluation of whether discrimination occurred.

Here, along with the historical evidence we described above from the earlier trials, as well as the State's striking of five of six black prospective jurors at the sixth trial, the dramatically disparate questioning and investigation of black prospective jurors and white prospective jurors at the sixth trial strongly suggests that the State was motivated in substantial part by a discriminatory intent. We agree with the observation of the dissenting justices of the Mississippi Supreme Court: The "numbers described above are too disparate to be explained away or categorized as mere happenstance."

D

Finally, in combination with the other facts and circumstances in this case, the record of jury selection at the sixth trial shows that the peremptory strike of at least one of the black prospective jurors (Carolyn Wright) was motivated in substantial part by discriminatory intent. As this Court has stated, the Constitution forbids striking even a single prospective juror for a discriminatory purpose.

Comparing prospective jurors who were struck and not struck can be an important step in determining whether a *Batson* violation occurred. The comparison can suggest that the prosecutor's proffered explanations for striking black prospective jurors were a pretext for discrimination. When a prosecutor's "proffered reason for striking a black panelist applies just as well to an otherwise-similar nonblack panelist who is permitted to serve, that is evidence tending to prove purposeful discrimination." Although a defendant ordinarily will try to identify a similar white prospective juror whom the State did not strike, a defendant is not required to identify an identical white juror for the side-by-side comparison to be suggestive of discriminatory intent.

In this case, Carolyn Wright was a black prospective juror who said she was strongly in favor of the death penalty as a general matter. And she had a family member who was a prison security guard. Yet the State exercised a peremptory strike against Wright. The State said it struck Wright in part because she knew several defense witnesses and had worked at Wal-Mart where Flowers' father also worked.

Winona is a small town. Wright had some sort of connection to 34 people involved in Flowers' case, both on the prosecution witness side and the defense witness side. But three white prospective jurors — Pamela Chesteen, Harold Waller, and Bobby Lester — also knew many individuals involved in the case. Chesteen knew 31 people, Waller knew 18 people, and Lester knew 27 people. Yet as we explained above, the State did not ask Chesteen, Waller, and Lester individual follow-up questions about their connections to witnesses. That is a telling statistic. If the State were concerned about prospective jurors' connections to witnesses in the case, the State presumably would have used individual questioning to ask those potential white jurors whether they could remain impartial despite their relationships. A "State's failure to engage in any meaningful voir dire examination on a subject the State alleges it is concerned about is evidence suggesting that the explanation is a sham and a pretext for discrimination."

Both Carolyn Wright and Archie Flowers, who is the defendant's father, had worked at the local Wal-Mart. But there was no evidence that they worked together or were close in any way. Importantly, the State did not ask individual follow-up questions to determine the nature of their relationship. And during group questioning, Wright said she did not know whether Flowers' father still worked at Wal-Mart, which "supports an inference that Wright and Flowers did not have a close working relationship." And white prospective jurors also had relationships with members of Flowers' family. Indeed, white prospective juror Pamela Chesteen stated that she had provided service to Flowers' family members at the bank and that she knew several members of the Flowers family. Likewise, white prospective juror Bobby Lester worked at the same bank and also encountered Flowers' family members. Although Chesteen and Lester were questioned during group voir dire, the State did not ask Chesteen or Lester individual follow-up questions in order to explore the depth of their relationships with Flowers' family. And instead of striking those jurors, the State accepted them for the jury. To be sure, both Chesteen and Lester were later struck by the defense. But the State's acceptance of Chesteen and Lester necessarily informs our assessment of the State's intent in striking similarly situated black prospective jurors such as Wright.

The State also noted that Wright had once been sued by Tardy Furniture for collection of a debt 13 years earlier. Wright said that the debt was paid off and that it would not affect her evaluation of the case. The victims in this case worked at Tardy Furniture. But the State did not explain how Wright's 13-year-old, paid-off debt to Tardy Furniture could affect her ability to serve impartially as a juror in this quadruple murder case. The "State's unsupported characterization of the lawsuit is problematic." In any event, the State did not purport to rely on that reason alone as the basis for the Wright strike, and the State in this Court does not rely on that reason alone in defending the Wright strike.

The State also explained that it exercised a peremptory strike against Wright because she had worked with one of Flowers' sisters. That was incorrect. The trial judge immediately stated as much. But incorrect statements of that sort may show the State's intent: When a prosecutor misstates the record in explaining a strike, that misstatement can be another clue showing discriminatory intent.

That incorrect statement was not the only one made by the prosecutor. The State made apparently incorrect statements to justify the strikes of black prospective jurors Tashia Cunningham, Edith Burnside, and Flancie Jones. The State contradicted Cunningham's earlier statement that she had only a working relationship with Flowers' sister by inaccurately asserting that Cunningham and Flowers' sister were close friends. The State asserted that Burnside had tried to cover up a Tardy Furniture suit. She had not. And the State explained that it struck Jones in part because Jones was Flowers' aunt. That, too, was not true. The State's pattern of factually inaccurate statements about black prospective jurors suggests that the State intended to keep black prospective jurors off the jury.

To be sure, the back and forth of a *Batson* hearing can be hurried, and prosecutors can make mistakes when providing explanations. That is entirely understandable, and mistaken explanations should not be confused with racial discrimination. But when considered with other evidence of discrimination, a series of factually inaccurate explanations for striking black prospective jurors can be telling. So it is here.

The side-by-side comparison of Wright to white prospective jurors whom the State accepted for the jury cannot be considered in isolation in this case. In a different context, the Wright strike might be deemed permissible. But we must examine the whole picture. Our disagreement with the Mississippi courts (and our agreement with Justice King's dissent in the Mississippi Supreme Court) largely comes down to whether we look at the Wright strike in isolation or instead look at the Wright strike in the context of all the facts and circumstances. Our precedents require that we do the latter. As Justice King explained in his dissent in the Mississippi Supreme Court, the Mississippi courts appeared to do the former. As we see it, the overall context here requires skepticism of the State's strike of Carolyn Wright. We must examine the Wright strike in light of the history of the State's use of peremptory strikes in the prior trials, the State's decision to strike five out of six black prospective jurors at Flowers' sixth trial, and the State's vastly disparate questioning of black and white prospective jurors during jury selection at the sixth trial. We cannot just look away. Nor can we focus on the Wright strike in isolation. In light of all the facts and circumstances, we conclude that the trial court clearly erred in ruling that the State's peremptory strike of Wright was not motivated in substantial part by discriminatory intent.

• • •

In sum, the State's pattern of striking black prospective jurors persisted from Flowers' first trial through Flowers' sixth trial. In the six trials combined, the State struck 41 of the 42 black prospective jurors it could have struck. At the sixth trial, the State struck five of six. At the sixth trial, moreover, the State engaged in dramatically disparate questioning of black and white prospective jurors. And it engaged in disparate treatment of black and white prospective jurors, in particular by striking black prospective juror Carolyn Wright.

To reiterate, we need not and do not decide that any one of those four facts alone would require reversal. All that we need to decide, and all that we do decide, is that all of the relevant facts and circumstances taken together establish that the trial court at Flowers' sixth trial committed clear error in concluding that the State's peremptory strike of black prospective juror Carolyn Wright was not motivated in substantial part by discriminatory intent. In reaching that conclusion, we break no new legal ground. We simply enforce and reinforce *Batson* by applying it to the extraordinary facts of this case.

We reverse the judgment of the Supreme Court of Mississippi, and we remand the case for further proceedings not inconsistent with this opinion.

It is so ordered.

NOTES AND QUESTIONS

1. The Court in *Flowers* devotes several pages to its jury selection precedents, a legacy that appears to culminate in *Batson*, when the Court claims that "equal justice under law," *id.* at 301, is finally obtained. The Court even states without irony that "*Batson* ended the widespread practice in which prosecutors could (and often would) routinely strike all black prospective jurors in cases involving black defendants," as if the facts of Curtis Flowers's trials that it has just recounted had happened before *Batson* became law instead of as recently as 2011. If the Court was honestly taking stock of its work in this area, what could and should it also have said about the *Batson* line of cases?

In a similarly smug vein the Court notes that it has "vigorously enforced and reinforced" *Batson* and has extended it to other contexts, *id.*, although the Court does acknowledge that the actual enforcement of *Batson* is done by trial judges and that appellate review of their work is "highly deferential." What else could and should the Court have noted in this regard? Why is the Court so hell-bent on using this occasion for a victory lap?

2. In discussing the types of evidence and argument that can be used to make *Batson* challenges, *id.* at 302, the Court notes, in addition to the prosecutor's history of the use of peremptory challenges in the case at bar and other cases, three other categories, all at issue in *Flowers*: (a) the prosecutor's disparate questioning of white and Black prospective jurors, (b) side-by-side comparisons of Black prospective jurors who were struck and white prospective jurors who were not struck, and (c) the prosecutor's misrepresentation of the record when defending his strikes at the *Batson* hearing. These are all types of proof that became more widely used as *Batson* challenges matured over time, and were at issue in a handful of *Batson* cases that reached the Court in the last 25 years. *See Foster v. Chatman*, 578 U.S. 488 (2016); *Snyder v. Louisiana*, 552 U.S. 472 (2008); *Miller El v. Dretke (Miller-El II)*, 545 U.S. 231 (2005).

C. Race and Peremptory Challenges   **1301**

Why are these types of arguments superior to the sort of "plausibility" arguments made by defendants in cases such as *Hernandez* and *Purkett*? Why are they more likely than plausibility arguments to succeed on appeal even if rejected by the trial judge? Note that the "disparate questioning" of Black jurors that ultimately became a red flag was one of the methods originally recommended by Philadelphia prosecutor Jack McMahon as a way to "get around" *Batson*. How will creative prosecutors try to "get around" *Flowers*?

3. Notwithstanding its claim in the beginning of the opinion about *Batson* "ending" the practice of the discriminatory use of peremptory challenges, the Court does acknowledge eventually, after describing the government's use of peremptories in Flowers's first four trials, that "the State appeared to proceed as if *Batson* had never been decided." *Id.* at 306. And yet it refuses to condemn the prosecutor—it buried the fact that the same individual prosecutor tried Curtis Flowers every time—and only says that the evidence "strongly suggests" that the prosecutor wanted to "try Flowers before a jury with as few black jurors as possible, and ideally before an all-white jury." *Id.* The Court doesn't even call the prosecutor out by name. Why not? Nor does the Court mention whether—or not—the prosecutor, Doug Evans, was ever disciplined by any Mississippi court or bar authority based on his *Batson* recidivism.

So the Court does not condemn the prosecutor for his conduct, even though it concludes that he committed intentional racial discrimination. Nor does the Court treat *Flowers* as a vehicle for advancing, even in incremental ways, the *Batson* doctrine. Indeed, the opposite is true. The Court both begins and ends its analysis with the virtually identical caveats:

> To reiterate, we need not and do not decide that any one of those four facts alone would require reversal. All that we need to decide, and all that we do decide, is that all of the relevant facts and circumstances taken together establish that the trial court at Flowers' sixth trial committed clear error in concluding that the State's peremptory strike of black prospective juror Carolyn Wright was not motivated in substantial part by discriminatory intent. In reaching that conclusion, we break no new legal ground. We simply enforce and reinforce *Batson* by applying it to the extraordinary facts of this case.

Id. at 2251. *See id.* at 2235 (saying essentially the same thing). In case this repetition might elude some readers, Justice Alito, concurring, tries to make the same point in other ways, calling the case "highly unusual" and "likely one of a kind."

Back to the prosecutor, Doug Evans. The Supreme Court's decision in *Flowers* was the third time Evans had been adjudicated to have engaged in racial discrimination in the selection of jurors *in trials of Curtis Flowers alone.* Was this sufficient basis for an investigation of Evans for violations of 18 U.S.C. § 242? *See* Chapter X *supra.*

Professor Paul Butler has written eloquently about *Flowers. See* P. Butler, *Mississippi Goddamn:* Flowers v. Mississippi*'s Cheap Racial Justice,* 2019 Sup. Ct. L. Rev. 73. He worries that the Supreme Court did not acknowledge the actual effect of race in the verdict in Curtis Flowers's six trials. He worries that the facts of *Flowers* are so extreme that less egregious misconduct will not be redressed.

> *Flowers v. Mississippi* raises complex questions about what the law can and should do to remedy race discrimination, what should happen when the constitutional rights of jurors are in tension with the constitutional rights of accused persons, and how far the United States has progressed in eradicating white supremacy from the criminal legal process.
> In contrast, the six trials of Curtis Flowers were painfully simple. Here are the most essential facts.
> In the first trial, with an all-white jury, Mr. Flowers was convicted.
> In the second trial, with a jury of eleven whites and one black, Mr. Flowers was convicted.
> In the third trial, which also had a jury of eleven whites and one black, Mr. Flowers was convicted.

In the fourth trial, with a jury of seven whites and five blacks, a mistrial was declared, because the jurors could not agree on a verdict.

In the fifth trial, with a jury of nine whites and three blacks, another mistrial was declared, because the jury was unable to reach a verdict.

In the sixth trial, with a jury of eleven whites and one black, Mr. Flowers was convicted.

The race of the jurors thus determined the outcome of each trial. If there was an all-white jury or a jury with only one African American, there was a conviction. In juries that had three or more African Americans, there was a mistrial, because the jurors could not arrive at a unanimous decision.

You would not learn this most important fact from a casual read of the majority opinion. Kavanaugh extolled the virtues of colorblindness in a case where color meant everything. The majority opinion is an interracial group fantasy, joined by all the Court's moderates and all but two of its conservatives.

One might have expected that the four moderate Justices knew better. Dissenting in *Utah v. Strieff,* Justice Sotomayor wrote the most powerful racial critique of the U.S. criminal legal process ever to appear in the Supreme Court Reporter. Citing Michelle Alexander's The New Jim Crow and works by James Baldwin and Ta-Nehisi Coates, Sotomayor wrote that "people of color are disproportionate victims" of police abuse, and that "[u]ntil their voices matter too, our justice system will continue to be anything but." Last Term, commenting on the denial of a cert, Sotomayor stated, "racial bias [by jurors] is a familiar and recurring evil . . . racism can and does seep in the jury system."

Yet in *Flowers*, only Justice Thomas was grounded in the "reality" that bias by white jurors can undermine a fair process for a black accused person. On the constitutionality of race-consciousness, the liberal Justices and Clarence Thomas "switch sides."

I want to defend a portion of Thomas's dissent, which has been widely ridiculed. I also want to question the contention that District Attorney Evans is a racist, based simply on his exercise of peremptory challenges against African Americans. My analysis stems, in part, from my own exercise of peremptory challenges when I was a prosecutor. There are cases in which it would come close to legal malpractice for either the prosecutor or the defense to ignore race. Nobody in *Flowers* can or does, not even Justice Kavanaugh in his fantasia about how race does not matter.

Mississippi has particularly vexing issues with regard to racial justice. Mississippi is where, in 1955, Emmet Till, after being falsely accused of flirting with a white woman, was kidnapped from his home by two white men, pistol-whipped, shot, and then dumped into the Tallahatchie River. After two trials and two acquittals, the accused men gave Look magazine a detailed story on how they had done the killing. Mississippi is where, in 1963, NAACP leader Medgar Evers was assassinated by Byron De La Beckwith, a member of the White Citizens' Council. Mississippi is where, in 1964, civil rights activists James Chaney, Andrew Goodman, and Michael Schwerner were abducted and murdered. Mississippi is where, in 1970, the police opened fire on a group of Jackson State University students protesting segregation at a local bowling alley. Two students were killed, and twelve were injured.

Mississippi's population is 40 percent African American, the highest of any state, but it has not elected a black person to a statewide office in 129 years. Mississippi prisons are likely the worst in the country, and they are filled with African Americans.

But the concerns about race and the criminal legal process that this article raises are national. Mississippi is only a particularly egregious example of a broader phenomenon. This was, I think, Nina Simone's meaning when, after noting substantial problems in Alabama and Tennessee, she wrote "Mississippi Goddamn." *Flowers* can be understood to mean that, even by the usual standards of exercising peremptory strikes, an out-of-control district attorney in Winona, Mississippi, went several bridges too far. But this understanding of *Flowers* is troubling because it permits less egregious instances of racial mischief to go unchecked.

See Butler, *Mississippi Goddamn, supra* at 73, 74-77.

The next section considers the problem of cross-racial identification testimony at trials, and some of the steps courts have taken to guard against this potentially unreliable evidence.

D. CROSS-RACIAL IDENTIFICATIONS AT TRIAL

Psychological studies have demonstrated that the risk of error normally attending eyewitness identification, *see* Chapter VIII *supra*, increases when a witness attempts to identify a person who is of a different race than the witness. This is sometimes called "own race bias" (ORB). While there is a consensus about the increased risk of error in cross-racial identifications there is not a similar consensus about the reason for that increased risk. The prevailing view is that witnesses' lack of quality interaction with other races explains or at least contributes to the error. In any event, the consensus includes the view that all races are susceptible to ORB and that ORB is not the result of conscious or unconscious racism. Courts have struggled with whether and, more recently, how to ensure that juries are best equipped to understand this risk in evaluating the reliability of cross-racial identification eyewitness identification evidence. *See generally* Bryan Scott Ryan, Note, *Alleviating Own Race Bias in Cross-Racial Identifications*, 8 Wash. U. Juris. Rev. 115 (2015).

The three cases in this section all consider the advisability of jury instructions and or expert testimony as a means for protecting against the risks of unreliable cross-racial identifications.

United States v. Hines
55 F. Supp. 2d 62 (D. Mass. 1999)

GERTNER, District Judge.

This case raises questions concerning the application of *Daubert v. Merrell Dow Pharmaceuticals, Inc.* (1993) and *Kumho Tire Co. v. Carmichael* (1999) to technical fields, that are not, strictly speaking, science. Two fields are involved: The first is an "old" field, handwriting analysis, which has been the subject of expert testimony for countless years. The second is a comparatively "new" field, the psychology of eyewitness identification. The government maintained that handwriting analysis is "science," meeting the *Daubert* and *Kumho* tests, while the psychology of eyewitness identification is not. Not surprisingly, the defendant insisted that the opposite is true.

Johannes Hines ("Hines") is charged under 18 U.S.C. § 2113 for allegedly robbing the Broadway National Bank in Chelsea, Massachusetts on January 27, 1997. The government's principal evidence consisted of the eyewitness identification of the teller who was robbed, Ms. Jeanne Dunne, and the handwriting analysis of the robbery note. In connection with the latter, the government offered Diana Harrison ("Harrison"), a document examiner with the Federal Bureau of Investigations, to testify as to the authorship of a "stick-up" note found at the scene of the crime.

Hines sought to exclude the handwriting analysis. This testimony, defense claims, notwithstanding its venerable history, does not meet the standards of *Daubert* and *Kumho.* In the alternative, if the court permitted the jury to hear the handwriting testimony, Hines sought to have his expert — Professor Mark Denbeaux ("Denbeaux") — testify as to the weaknesses of the methodology and the basis of Harrison's conclusions. The government, on the other hand, argued for its handwriting expert under the applicable tests, and rejects Denbeaux.

Hines also offered the testimony of Dr. Saul Kassin ("Kassin"), a psychologist who studies perception and memory, and who has been qualified as an eyewitness identification expert in other cases. The government opposed. Should I allow the testimony of either defense's handwriting analysis critic or eyewitness expert, the government seeks counter experts,

Dr. Ebbe B. Ebbesen ("Ebbesen"), on eyewitness identification, and Dr. Moshe Kam ("Kam") on handwriting.

With respect to handwriting analysis, I held a *Daubert/Kumho* hearing at which Denbeaux testified, and the government cross examined. In addition, the government offered several articles as well as the curriculum vitae of its expert, Kam. Harrison did not testify, as she had previously testified during the first trial, but I reviewed her prior testimony. With respect to eyewitness identification, the matter was briefed and argued. After I indicated my intention to admit the testimony, the government focused on the qualifications of Kassin, and the particular conclusions he would be drawing. At the eleventh hour, the government waived its motion for a hearing on this issue.

For the reasons set forth below, I DENIED Hines' motion to exclude handwriting analysis to the extent that it sought to exclude the handwriting expert's entire testimony. I GRANTED the motion in part: I did not permit the handwriting expert to make any ultimate conclusions on the actual authorship of the questioned writing. As a result of this ruling, counsel for Hines made the strategic decision not to call Denbeaux as an expert to critique handwriting analysis at trial. Thus, the government's motion to exclude Denbeaux's testimony (and offer Kam's) was MOOT.

I also DENIED the government's motion to exclude the testimony of Hines' eyewitness expert. Defense presented the testimony; the government presented its own witness.

This trial ended in a hung jury (as did the first). Since the issues noted in this memorandum will recur in the next trial, I outline my reasoning for the reasoning.

I. FRAMEWORK FOR THE ANALYSIS OF EXPERT TESTIMONY

To some, *Daubert/Kumho* have considerably raised the bar for the admissibility of expert testimony. In some ways that is true; in some ways it is not. It is true that *Daubert/Kumho* have focused a great deal of attention on the judge's role as a gatekeeper for expert testimony under Fed. R. Evid. 104(a). To the extent that there is more pre-trial review of expert testimony, there are bound to be more exclusions. In other ways, however, the impact of *Daubert/Kumho* has been the opposite—opening the door to testimony previously excluded.

Our evidentiary rules put a premium on firsthand observations. Opinion testimony is disfavored except under certain circumstances; hearsay is generally excluded. The jury is to draw reasonable inferences from the firsthand data. When an expert witness is called upon to draw those inferences, several concerns are raised. The rules give expert witnesses greater latitude than is afforded other witnesses to testify based on data not otherwise admissible before the jury. In addition, a certain patina attaches to an expert's testimony unlike any other witness; this is "science," a professional's judgment, the jury may think, and give more credence to the testimony than it may deserve.

Accordingly, the trial court is supposed to review expert testimony carefully. The court is to admit the testimony not only where it is relevant to the issues at bar, the usual standard under Fed. R. Evid. 401, but when certain additional requirements are met under Fed. R. Evid. 702.

The first requirement has to do with the necessity for the testimony: expert testimony may be admitted where the inferences that are sought to be drawn are inferences that a jury could not draw on its own. The inferences may be the product of specialized information, for example, beyond the ken of the lay jury. Significantly, *Daubert* also emphasized the fact that expert testimony is admissible where it would "assist" the trier of fact. In the latter case, even if the inferences may be drawn by the lay juror, expert testimony may be admissible as an "aid" in that enterprise. For example, the subject looks like one the jury understands from every day life, but in fact, the inferences the jury may draw are erroneous. (As I describe below, eyewitness identification, and testimony about battered women syndrome fits uniquely into this category.)

The second requirement concerns the nature of the inferences to be drawn. In outlining the standards for admissibility, the *Daubert* Court noted the difference between information gleaned in a scientific setting and information presented in a courtroom. In the former, the decision makers are professionals; there is no need to come to a definitive conclusion; the decision making process comports with certain rules established by the professional scientific community. In the courtroom, the decision makers are lay, a jury; there is a need to come to a definitive conclusion; the decision making process has to satisfy norms of due process and fairness. In our tradition, for example, the adversary system and party examination and cross examination are central. The issue then, is not only how objectively reliable the evidence is, but also the legitimacy of the process by which it is generated. It is not just how valid the data is, but how well the jury can understand it after direct and cross examination, and legal instructions.

It was not surprising, then, that the Court found the rules for admissibility of expert testimony, even with respect to scientific fields, were flexible, bearing in mind their unique setting and purposes. A trial judge could consider some or all of the following factors: (1) whether the expert's technique can be or has been tested; (2) whether the method has been subjected to peer review and publication; (3) the known or potential rate of error of a technique or theory when applied; and, (4) whether there is "general acceptance" within the relevant scientific community, to the extent that one exists.

Significantly, the "general acceptance test" of *Frye v. United States* (1923), although now one of many standards, was still important. *Daubert's* principal focus was necessarily on new science. Its rules were intended to open the door to the admission of theories challenging existing orthodoxies. The petitioners, children born with serious birth defects, allegedly caused by their mothers' ingestion of Bendectin during pregnancy, sought to introduce scientific studies, performed by well credentialed medical experts, that contradicted the existing "generally accepted" theory that Bendectin was not a teratogen (a substance capable of causing malformations in fetuses). *Frye's* "general acceptance" test was inadequate to deal with new theories and approaches. Having relinquished the *Frye* test, the Court was obliged to map other standards.

But the standards articulated by the majority in *Daubert* raised serious concerns. The *Frye* test was perfectly suited to the court's competence. The judge did not have to be a scientist. He or she only had, in effect, to count the "scientific" votes; determine what the majority accepted. *Daubert/Kumho*, however, required a judge, a notable generalist, to second guess a scientist. Thus, by listing the "scientific" standards and encouraging review, the decision pointed in the direction of more rigor. But, by underscoring the uniqueness of the trial setting, the "assist the trier" standard and flexibility, the decision does the opposite.

One way of reconciling the competing vectors is this: Traditional science, generally accepted by judges for decades, may not need the same kind of rigorous analysis as "new" science which lacks the legitimacy of a chorus of sponsors. As to the latter, the *Daubert* analysis is critical, and the court should be an especially vigilant gatekeeper.

Kumho extended *Daubert* to non-scientific fields. In this category, for example, are the fields that are based on observations, not traditional science.

At the same time, the Court plainly recognized the limitations of the *Daubert* approach. It reaffirmed *Daubert's* holding that the court must be the gatekeeper, and must assure the reliability and relevance of testimony with respect to all expert testimony included in Fed.

R. Evid. 702, not just scientific testing. But the nature of the test, notably, how much the *Daubert* standards are modified, was within the court's discretion. And if the *Daubert* standards were flexible when applied to traditional scientific fields, surely they were flexible when applied to nonscientific, technical fields.

Moreover, if the *Daubert* standard takes into account the unique trial setting — how well the lay trier will understand the testimony after examination and instructions — *Kumho* plainly does as well. In fact, cross examination and limiting instructions may be more effective in "technical" fields because they are more accessible to the jury, than fields with the charisma of science.

Again, a mixed message: Apply *Daubert* to technical fields, even though the scientific method may not really fit, but be flexible. Moreover, in this setting, because few technical fields are as firmly established as traditional scientific ones, the new science/old science comparison is less clear. The court is plainly inviting a reexamination even of "generally accepted" venerable, technical fields.

* * *

B. Eyewitness Identification

The government offered the testimony of Jeanne Dunne ("Dunne"), the teller. Dunne, a white woman, gave the following identification moments after the robbery occurred: She identified the man as black with dark skin, a wide nose, and a medium build. Her description was as close to a generic identification of an African American man as one can imagine. Dunne was unable to identify Hines from a book of photographs of African American men shortly after the robbery. She picked out a few photographs, but none of them were as "dark black" as the robber. Working with a police artist, she helped construct a sketch of the robber. Immediately following, she was shown eight photographs, including one of Hines, and indicated that the Hines photograph "resembled" the robber, that it "looked like him," but she was still not sure. (Since the robber was wearing a hat, she tried to envision the man in the photograph with a baseball cap.) Months later Dunne picked Hines out of a lineup.

Hines offered the testimony of Kassin, a psychologist studying human perception at Williams College with substantial credentials, and trial experience. The government offered a similarly credentialed expert, Ebbesen. I allowed the testimony of both.

The Kassin testimony was offered to show, inter alia, the following: the decreased accuracy of cross-racial identification relative to same-race identification, the effect of stress on identification, the effect of time on memory as it relates to identification, the "confidence-accuracy" phenomenon which suggests the absence of any correlation between the amount of confidence expressed by an eyewitness in his or her memory and the accuracy of that witness' identification, the suggestiveness of subtle aspects of the identification process, such as the darkness of a particular photo as compared to others in the array, the fact that the eyewitness knows there is a suspect in the mix, the transference phenomenon by which a witness may believe that a face looks familiar but is unable to say whether her familiarity comes from seeing a previous mug shot, or from the robbery, etc.

On direct examination, Kassin identified those factors in the Dunne identification that were implicated in the studies with which he was familiar, and could undermine accuracy — the cross racial issues, the differences between the photographs of the other men and Hines' in the photo array, the differences between Hines and the other men in the lineup. He noted problems with what he called relative, comparative judgments: The witness would like to resolve the case and so compares the photographs of one man to another in the array, rather than attempting to compare the photographs to the man she saw. On cross, the government brought up the factors that enhanced accuracy, the nature of the lighting, the distance from the robber, the instructions that were given to the witness, especially at the lineup. The government questioned Kassin about the instructions given to Dunne at the lineup. Kassin agreed that those instructions were "ideal."

Unlike handwriting analysis, there is no question as to the scientific underpinnings of Kassin's testimony. They are based on experimental psychological studies, testing the acquisition of memory, retention, and retrieval of memory under different conditions. Indeed, the central debate before the jury, eloquently articulated by Ebbesen, the government's expert, is the polar opposite of the debate in the handwriting field—whether conclusions obtained in an experimental, academic, setting with college students should be applied to a real life setting. Kassin and others believe that these conclusions are appropriately applied to eyewitness identifications in court. Ebbesen disagreed.

The government claimed that the jury did not need this testimony at all, that it was not necessary under Fed. R. Evid. 702 to assist the trier of fact. I disagree. While jurors may well be confident that they can draw the appropriate inferences about eyewitness identification directly from their life experiences, their confidence may be misplaced, especially where cross-racial identification is concerned. Indeed, in this respect the rationale for the testimony tracks that for battered women syndrome experts. The jury, for example, may fault the victim for not leaving an abusive spouse, believing that they are fully capable of putting themselves in the shoes of the defendant. In fact, psychological evidence suggests that the "ordinary" response of an "ordinary" woman are not in play in situations of domestic violence where the victim suffers from "battered women syndrome." Common sense inferences thus may well be way off the mark.

Nor do I agree that this testimony somehow usurps the function of the jury. The function of the expert here is not to say to the jury— "you should believe or not believe the eyewitness." (Indeed, it has far fewer pretensions to conclusions than does handwriting analysis, with far more science attached to it.) All that the expert does is provide the jury with more information with which the jury can then make a more informed decision. And only the expert can do so. In the absence of an expert, a defense lawyer, for example, may try to argue that cross racial identifications are more problematic than identifications between members of the same race, or that stress may undermine accuracy, but his voice necessarily lacks the authority of the scientific studies Kassin cited.

Finally, the fact that the expert has not interviewed the particular eyewitness makes it less likely that the jury will merely accept the expert testimony and more likely that the testimony will be appropriately cabined. The witness can only be providing the jury with the tools to analyze the eyewitness; he has no more specific information. The science makes no pretensions that it can predict whether a particular witness is accurate or mistaken.

In my judgment, the accuracy of these proceedings was enormously enhanced by treating the jury to all sides of the eyewitness debate, rather than assuming there was no controversy, that the issue, notwithstanding this literature is clear.

II. CONCLUSION

Accordingly, the testimony of the government's handwriting expert was limited as described above, to identifying the similarities and dissimilarities of the known writing and the unknown. The defense expert on eyewitness identification was permitted along with the testimony of the government witness.

SO ORDERED.

NOTES AND QUESTIONS

1. From the court's description of the eyewitness's testimony, there appears to be plenty of cross-examination material here wholly apart from the cross-racial identification issue. Suppose the court had ruled that the expert on eyewitness identification could not testify. How could defense counsel go about cross-examining the eyewitness on the perils of cross-racial identification? As defense counsel, how would you handle the government's use of a "police artist" in this case?

2. The court notes that one of the predicates for the admissibility of expert testimony under Fed. R. Evid. 702 is that it must "assist the trier of fact to understand the evidence or to determine a fact in issue." The government argues, in opposing the admission of the defendant's expert's testimony on the decreased accuracy of cross-racial identifications, that such testimony is unnecessary inasmuch as it is known to the jurors from their own life experiences and common sense. Do you agree that this phenomenon is widely known? Did you know about it? Is the court's analogy to battered women syndrome persuasive?

3. The court reasons that the expert testimony does not "usurp the function of the jury" because the testimony simply provides the jury with information it can use in making its own decision. How could defense counsel argue the cross-racial identification issue to the jury without expert testimony on the subject?

4. In the first trial the court also gave a jury instruction on the decreased accuracy of cross-racial identifications, as the last part of a general instruction on eyewitness identification, using a variation of an instruction recognized by the D.C. Circuit in *United States v. Telfaire*, 469 F.2d 552 (D.C. Cir. 1972). Here is the relevant part of the instruction:

> One more thing on identification. In this case, the identifying witness is of a different race than the defendant. In the experience of many, it is more difficult to identify members of a different race than members of one's own. If this is also your own experience, you may consider that in evaluating the witness' testimony. This is one of the elements that you may then consider in evaluating the witness' testimony.

Thoughts on this instruction? Can the instruction be interpreted as attributing the difficulty of cross-racial identifications to conscious or unconscious racism? What are the consequences of such an interpretation? Is there a risk of inconsistency between the court's instruction and the parties' experts?

5. As noted above, the consensus view from the studies is that ORB is not the result of conscious or unconscious racism. Is it necessary or important that this aspect of ORB be included as part of the jury instruction? Should an expert include this as part of his testimony?

Commonwealth v. Bastaldo
32 N.E.3d 873 (Mass. 2015)

GANTS, C.J.

In the parking lot of a night club in Springfield, the defendant, Elvin Bastaldo, punched the victim, Juan Benito, several times in the face using brass knuckles, blinding him in one eye, while the victim was standing near a police officer who was arresting the defendant's brother, Juan Bastaldo (Juan). The defendant was convicted by a Superior Court jury of mayhem and resisting arrest.

On appeal, the defendant claims that he is entitled to a new trial because (1) the judge abused her discretion in denying the defendant's requested cross-racial and cross-ethnic eyewitness identification jury instruction where two of the three eyewitnesses were "Caucasian" and the defendant was a "dark-skinned Hispanic of Dominican descent"; (2) the admission of three in-court eyewitness identifications created a substantial risk of a miscarriage of justice where it was the first time any of them had formally identified the defendant; and (3) the judge committed prejudicial error by giving a consciousness of guilt instruction that suggested to the jury that the defendant was the assailant.

We conclude that because this case was tried before our opinion issued in *Commonwealth v. Gomes* (2015), where we prospectively required that a jury instruction on cross-racial eyewitness identification be given in these circumstances, the judge did not abuse her discretion in declining to give the defendant's requested cross-racial and cross-ethnic instruction. We now revise the content of the provisional model jury instruction regarding cross-racial identification that we issued in *Gomes*, as well as our guidance as to when such an instruction should be given. In criminal trials that commence after the issuance of this opinion, a cross-racial instruction should always be included when giving the model eyewitness identification instruction, unless the parties agree that there was no cross-racial identification. We authorize judges in their discretion to include a cross-ethnic eyewitness identification instruction in appropriate circumstances.

* * *

Background. The jury could have found the following facts from the evidence admitted at trial. At approximately 12:30 a.m. on September 2, 2012, Juan and three companions (not including the defendant) attempted to enter a night club in Springfield. The victim, who, by his description, served as the "doorman, security, [and] host" of the club, denied their entry because the companions with Juan were under twenty-one years of age. A brief verbal and physical altercation ensued in which Juan punched the victim in the chest, and the victim countered by punching Juan below the eye. Springfield police officer Thomas Liebel, who was working a security detail at the club, ordered Juan to leave the area, which he did.

The club closed at 2 a.m. As Liebel walked to his vehicle to leave, Juan and two or three other men appeared from a nearby alleyway and headed toward the main entrance of the club. When they attempted to enter the club, Liebel approached them and ordered them to leave. The victim was standing inside the club near the entrance, along with Ronald Kenniston, a club employee who worked as a "bar back-up." As soon as the victim opened the entrance door, Juan punched the victim in the side of the face.

Liebel moved to arrest Juan, but when Juan "went for" Liebel, Liebel sprayed him with mace. Juan and the other men ran away, but Liebel gave chase and caught Juan. The victim followed to make sure Liebel was all right, and stood near Liebel as he struggled to handcuff Juan. The victim was then suddenly struck in the face. He did not see from where the blow came, but it rendered him dazed and blind in his left eye. When he turned around to defend himself, he saw the defendant, whom he had never seen before, standing a foot or two in front of him. The defendant punched the victim in the face two or three more times.

The defendant then approached Liebel and yelled in English, "I am going to fuck you up, Officer." The defendant came within three feet of Liebel before police sirens sounded and the defendant "bolted." Liebel watched the defendant run through a large parking lot, transmitted a description of the defendant's clothing and location over the police radio, and learned one minute later that the defendant had been arrested. Liebel soon saw the defendant again before he was placed inside a police transport vehicle with Juan, where they threatened and cursed Liebel in English.

Kenniston had been standing approximately fifteen feet away from the victim when a person "came up from behind [the victim] and sucker punched his eye a few times." He identified the defendant at trial as the person who threw the "sucker" punches. Kenniston testified that he got a good look at the defendant's face, and observed a silver object in the defendant's hand that covered three of his fingers. He also watched the defendant throw an object across the street, which sounded like metal when it landed, before the defendant ran away. Kenniston saw police officers catch up to the defendant, tackle him, arrest him, and bring him back to Liebel.

Kenniston then drove the victim to a local hospital. On the way, he passed the police transport vehicle and saw that the defendant was in custody. The victim was later transferred to Massachusetts General Hospital, where he underwent surgery on his eye. At the time of trial, the victim was still blind in his left eye.

The defendant testified at trial that he and Juan had arrived at the club at approximately 9:05 p.m. by themselves and remained inside until 2 a.m. He then left with Juan but Juan stayed near the entrance to talk with someone while the defendant continued walking. The defendant had not walked far when he turned around to see that there was fighting and that a police officer had handcuffed Juan. He saw that Juan had lost a shoe, so he retrieved it and walked over toward him and the officer who had handcuffed him, asking, "What happened?" When the police were about to take Juan away, the defendant walked through a parking lot in the direction of his house. Before he reached the street, he was grabbed by the police and thrown to the ground. The defendant stated that he did not see anyone strike the victim, and did not punch the victim himself.

Discussion. 1. Cross-racial and cross-ethnic eyewitness identification instruction. At the charge conference, the defendant's attorney requested the following cross-racial and cross-ethnic eyewitness identification instruction:

> In this case, the identifying witnesses are of a different race or ethnicity than the defendant. Scientific studies have shown that it is more difficult to identify members of a different race or ethnicity than members of one's own. In addition, studies reveal that even people with no prejudice against other races and substantial contact with persons of other races still experience difficulty in accurately identifying members of a different race or ethnicity. Quite often people do not recognize this difficulty in themselves. You should consider this in evaluating the reliability of the witnesses' identification of the defendant.

As to the race or ethnicity of the eyewitnesses, Kenniston and Liebel testified that they are Caucasian; no evidence was offered regarding their ethnicity. The victim testified that his father is Puerto Rican and his mother is Italian, and he considers himself Hispanic. No evidence was offered regarding the race of the victim; based on his photograph, his skin color appears to be brown.

As to the defendant's race or ethnicity, the defendant testified that he is from the Dominican Republic but did not discuss his racial identity. Liebel testified that the person who struck the victim was Hispanic. Kenniston was also asked if the person who struck the victim was Hispanic, and he responded:

> Yeah. . . . Well, I mean I don't know the classification because . . . I have friends that are . . . black, Puerto Rican, and they can speak two languages, so . . . just because they are a certain color, I'm not going to say they are Spanish or Black. . . . I really need to talk to them to know what they are.

The defendant's written request for a cross-racial and cross-ethnic instruction stated that he is Hispanic. On appeal, he characterizes himself as a "dark-skinned Hispanic of Dominican descent." Based on his photograph, his skin color appears to be black.

D. Cross-Racial Identifications at Trial 1311

The Commonwealth objected to the request and questioned whether the identifications were truly cross-racial or cross-ethnic, as the evidence only showed that the witnesses may have different ethnic backgrounds. The Commonwealth also asked that if a cross-racial or cross-ethnic instruction were given, it not apply to the victim because he was also Hispanic.

The judge declined the defendant's request for an instruction, stating that Kenniston and Liebel are of different ethnicity from the defendant, but "[w]e are not talking about a cross-racial identification here." The judge also stated that, even if she were to assume that the identification was similar to a cross-racial identification, it is "far from settled" that such an instruction should be given, and giving such an instruction "is hardly the standard in the courts at this point." She acknowledged that we were considering the Report and Recommendations of the Supreme Judicial Court Study Group on Eyewitness Evidence (July 25, 2013) (Study Group Report), and that the proposed jury instructions regarding cross-racial identification were "very controversial" in the Superior Court. The judge instead instructed the jury in accordance with the then-existing model eyewitness identification instruction. Because the defendant objected at the close of the instructions to the absence of the requested instruction, we review its denial for prejudicial error.

In *Gomes* we concluded that a principle of eyewitness identification may be appropriate for inclusion in a model jury instruction "where there is a near consensus in the relevant scientific community adopting that principle." Because it was not argued that the identifications in that case were cross-racial, we did not address that issue, but we included an instruction on cross-racial identification in the provisional model jury instruction that we required to be given, where appropriate, in trials that commence after the issuance of that opinion. That instruction provided that, in deciding whether a witness's identification is accurate, a jury should consider "whether the witness and the offender are of different races — research has shown that people of all races may have greater difficulty in accurately identifying members of a different race than they do in identifying members of their own race." Including that instruction reflected our conclusion that this principle had been adopted by a near consensus in the relevant scientific community. But we declined to give the new provisional model jury instruction any retroactive application so it has no bearing on this case, which was tried one year before the issuance of *Gomes*.

Under our case law at the time of trial, a judge was not precluded "in the exercise of discretion from instructing a jury that, in determining the weight to be given eyewitness identification testimony, they may consider the fact of any cross-racial identification and whether the identification by a person of different race from the defendant may be less reliable than identification by a person of the same race." But a defendant "was not entitled to such an instruction." Therefore, the judge did not err in declining to read the requested instruction.

Although it was not error before *Gomes* for the judge to decline to give a cross-racial instruction, such an instruction must be given in trials that commence after Gomes where there is a cross-racial identification. The existence of the "cross-race effect" (CRE) — that people are generally less accurate at identifying members of other races than they are at identifying members of their own race — has reached a near consensus in the relevant scientific community and has been recognized by courts and scholars alike. We remain convinced that jurors who are asked to evaluate the accuracy of an identification should be informed of the CRE.

We take this opportunity, however, to consider when a cross-racial instruction should be given. In *Bly*, we declared that it is within a judge's discretion to give a cross-racial instruction "when warranted by the evidence," and our provisional instruction in *Gomes*, provides that the instruction should be given when the "witness and offender are of different races." But we have yet to discuss when the evidence warrants such an instruction and who, if anyone, should determine whether the witness and the person identified are of different races, perhaps because the cross-racial character of an identification is often not contested.

The social science research establishing the CRE often does not define race. Roy S. Malpass, a leading scholar on the CRE, highlights the difficulty of defining race in this area of research, stating, "There seems to be no good and consistent way to refer to all the various 'races,'" and "the old racial names just don't seem to work, especially in complex multiethnic societies." For example, what is the race of a person whose grandparents on his father's side were an African-American and an Asian-American, and on his mother's side were a Caucasian and a Native American? And what evidence would be admissible to ascertain the person's race?

In facial recognition studies, the person making the identification is generally asked to self-identify his or her race, and that self-identification is accepted as the person's race for purposes of the study; the race of the person who is identified is generally determined based on the physical appearance of the person's face, including but not limited to skin color. Although social scientists "refer to the phenomenon as the [CRE] . . . the operative factor is perceived facial physiognomic characteristics, regardless of racial classification per se." In short, when we speak of cross-racial identification in the context of eyewitness identification, we mean that based on facial appearance, the person who made the identification is likely to have perceived the person identified to be of a different race.

Because differences in race based on facial appearance lie in the eye of the beholder, we shall not ask judges to determine whether a reasonable juror would perceive the identification to be cross-racial. Rather, we shall direct that a cross-racial instruction be given unless all parties agree that there was no cross-racial identification. This obviates any need for the judge to decide whether the identification was actually cross-racial, or whether jurors might perceive it to be. If the jury receive such an instruction but do not think the identification was cross-racial, they may simply treat the instruction as irrelevant to their deliberations. Consequently, we amend our provisional instruction in *Gomes* to the extent that, in criminal trials that commence after the issuance of this opinion, the following instruction should be included when giving the model eyewitness identification instruction, unless all parties agree to its omission:

> If the witness and the person identified appear to be of different races, you should consider that people may have greater difficulty in accurately identifying someone of a different race than someone of their own race.

We also take this opportunity to consider whether a cross-ethnic instruction should be included with the cross-racial instruction. Ethnicity is generally distinct from race; for instance, a person who identifies as Hispanic may be of any race. Yet, in facial recognition studies, the terms "race" and "ethnicity" are often conflated and used interchangeably; when they are defined separately, ethnicity may refer to "the smaller physical differences that exist within a race, such as with ancestry from Norway versus Greece within Europe, or China versus Japan within Asia, or Nigeria versus Ethiopia within Africa." From our review of the social science, we are aware of studies that support the conclusion that people are better at recognizing the faces of persons of the same ethnicity than a different ethnicity. But there is not yet a near consensus in the relevant scientific community that people are generally less accurate at recognizing the face of someone of a different ethnicity than the face of someone of their own ethnicity. In *Romero*, a non-Hispanic Caucasian male identified a Hispanic male that the trial court determined was also Caucasian. The New Jersey Supreme Court investigated the social science research and concluded that "[s]ocial science research does not tie identification unreliability directly to ethnic differences in the same way that racial differences can affect identification reliability."

For now, we leave the decision to add ethnicity to the cross-racial instruction in the judge's sound discretion. Where the persons involved in the identification self-identify as being of the same race but different ethnicity, and look as categorically different as people of different races, a cross-ethnic instruction will generally be appropriate, because the research suggests

D. Cross-Racial Identifications at Trial   **1313**

that cross-ethnic facial recognition in these circumstances has reliability issues similar to the CRE. Ethnicity should also generally be included in the instruction where, for example, a non-Hispanic eyewitness identifies a defendant who is Hispanic and looks multiracial, because the jury may not know whether to attribute the difference in appearance to race or ethnicity or both; an instruction that only references race might inadvertently lead the jury to ignore facial characteristics that are relevant to the CRE. But the addition of ethnicity may not be appropriate where, for example, the witness and the person identified appear to be of the same race, but one is Australian and the other North American. Until the social science reaches a near consensus, we will not require the inclusion of ethnicity in the model instruction but will leave its inclusion to the discretion of the judge based on the circumstances of the identification.

· · ·

NOTES AND QUESTIONS

1. The Supreme Judicial Court (SJC) of Massachusetts had previously announced a model cross-racial eyewitness identification instruction in *Commonwealth v. Gomes*, 470 Mass. 352, 376, 382, 22 N.E.3d 897 (Appendix) (2015):

> [I]n deciding whether a witness's identification is accurate, a jury should consider whether the witness and the offender are of different races — research has shown that people of all races may have greater difficulty in accurately identifying members of a different race than they do in identifying members of their own race.

Id. at 382, 22 N.E.3d 897 (Appendix). In *Bastaldo*, the SJC modified that instruction to address the uncertainties of defining race, replacing it with the following: "If the witness and the person identified appear to be of different races, you should consider that people may have greater difficulty in accurately identifying someone of a different race than someone of their own race."

Note the other differences in the modified instruction. Which version do you think is likely to be more effective? Is the addition of the "appear to be of different races" language helpful?

2. Defense counsel in *Bastaldo* requested the following instruction:

> In this case, the identifying witnesses are of a different race or ethnicity than the defendant. Scientific studies have shown that it is more difficult to identify members of a different race or ethnicity than members of one's own. In addition, studies reveal that even people with no prejudice against other races and substantial contact with persons of other races still experience difficulty in accurately identifying members of a different race or ethnicity. Quite often people do not recognize this difficulty in themselves. You should consider this in evaluating the reliability of the witnesses' identification of the defendant.

What are the pros and cons of this instruction vis-à-vis the original and revised *Gomes* instructions? What objections would you have to this instruction if you were the prosecutor?

3. The court notes that even though there is no scientific consensus as to the reliability of cross-ethnic identifications lower courts have discretion to give a cautionary instruction to that effect. But the instruction it provides the lower courts on exercising that discretion is poorly defined. How are the lower courts to determine how the defendant and the witnesses "self-identify" for these purposes in terms of race and ethnicity? Inasmuch as the SJC seems to be suggesting that the discretion turns largely on appearances, how will the lower courts' decisions be reviewed?

1314   Chapter XV The Jury II: Race and Juries

4. As a prosecutor, how can you conduct the direct examination of an eyewitness to counteract the anticipated implications of a cross-racial identification instruction? What aspects of a witness's background and livelihood might be explored? Why might this get dicey on cross? Consider *State v. Walker*, 8 A.3d 844 (N.J. Super. Ct. App. Div. 2010), where the trial judge refused to give a cross-racial identification cautionary instruction, reasoning that the white eyewitness to the crime worked at an inner-city Blimpie's in Newark and had served time in state prison, and thus had substantial contact with African Americans. *Id.* at 847. The case was reversed on appeal, given the centrality of the identification to the trial and the appellate court's reluctance to find that the witness's exposure reduced or eliminated the cross-racial identification impairment. *Id.* at 848-49.

People v. Boone
91 N.E.3d 1194 (N.Y. Ct. App. 2017)

FAHEY, J.:

In light of the near consensus among cognitive and social psychologists that people have significantly greater difficulty in accurately identifying members of a different race than in accurately identifying members of their own race, the risk of wrongful convictions involving cross-racial identifications demands a new approach. We hold that when identification is an issue in a criminal case and the identifying witness and defendant appear to be of different races, upon request, a party is entitled to a charge on cross-racial identification.

I

On February 16, 2011, a white man in his 20s was walking in Brooklyn when he was approached by a stranger, a short-haired black man. The stranger asked to know the time, and the young man retrieved his cell phone. The stranger snatched the cell phone and fled. The victim gave chase, until the robber pulled out a knife and told him to stay where he was. The victim described his attacker as an African-American man, about six feet tall, weighing about 170 pounds, and wearing a baseball cap and a hooded sweatshirt.

Ten days later, a white teenager was walking in the same neighborhood of Brooklyn, sending a text message from his cell phone, when a man behind him asked the time. The teenager looked back over his shoulder and observed a stranger, a black man, wearing a winter coat and a hat with flaps that covered his ears and the top of his head. The teenager looked at his cell phone and told the stranger the time. The stranger then grabbed the phone. The teenager did not immediately let go, and the robber stabbed him. The robber then took the phone and fled. Before the victim was taken to the hospital, he described the perpetrator to the police as an African-American man, about 18 years old and approximately six feet, two inches tall, and he gave an estimated weight.

Defendant Otis Boone, a black man who was short-haired, 19 years old, and 6 feet tall, and weighed about 170 pounds, was suspected of committing the crimes. On March 14, 2011, defendant was placed in two six-person lineups and the victims separately identified him. The teenager was initially unsure whether defendant was his attacker, but identified him after he spoke the words "What time is it?" Defendant and the fillers in the lineups all wore hats.

Neither cell phone was recovered, and no physical evidence linked defendant to the crimes.

D. Cross-Racial Identifications at Trial   1315

II

Defendant was charged with two counts of robbery in the first degree and other crimes.

At defendant's jury trial in July 2012, during the charge conference, defense counsel requested that the jury be instructed on cross-racial identification. Supreme Court denied the request, on the basis that there had been no expert testimony or cross-examination concerning "a lack of reliability of cross-racial identification." The trial court gave the jury an expanded charge on eyewitness identification, based on the pertinent Criminal Jury Instruction (see CJI 2d [NY] Identification [One Witness]), omitting the part of the pattern instruction addressing cross-racial identification.

The jury found defendant guilty of both robbery counts. On appeal from the judgment of conviction and sentence, defendant argued that Supreme Court denied him a fair trial by refusing to charge the jury on the inaccuracy of cross-racial identification.

The Appellate Division modified the judgment, as to the sentence, and affirmed as modified, holding that Supreme Court had not erred in declining to instruct the jury on cross-racial identification. The Appellate Division reasoned that defendant had not "placed the issue in evidence during the trial."

A Judge of this Court granted defendant leave to appeal from Appellate Division order and we now reverse.

III

Mistaken eyewitness identifications are "the single greatest cause of wrongful convictions in this country, "responsible for more . . . wrongful convictions than all other causes combined." Inaccurate identifications, especially misidentifications by a single eyewitness, play a role in the vast majority of post-conviction DNA-based exonerations in the United States. Indeed, a recent report by the National Academy of Sciences concluded that "at least one mistaken eyewitness identification was present in almost three-quarters" of DNA exonerations. According to amicus The Innocence Project, about 70% of DNA exonerations nationally involve eyewitness This Court has noted in recent years the prevalence of eyewitness misidentifications in wrongful convictions and the danger they pose to the truth-seeking function and integrity of our justice.

Social scientists have found that the likelihood of misidentification is higher when an identification is cross-racial. Generally, people have significantly greater difficulty accurately identifying members of other races than members of their own race. According to a meta-analysis of 39 psychological studies of the phenomenon, participants were "1.56 times more likely to falsely identify a novel other-race face when compared with performance on own-race faces." The phenomenon is known as the cross-race effect or own-race bias.

Our trial level courts have recognized the general scientific acceptance of the cross-race effect. This Court too has had occasion to observe the significance of the effect. In *People v. Abney* we held that a trial court erred in refusing, without the benefit of a *Frye* hearing, to allow an expert witness to testify on cross-racial identification and other factors affecting accuracy of identification.

The cross-race effect is "generally accepted" by experts in the fields of cognitive and social psychology, a point that the People do not dispute. Indeed, in a survey of psychologists with expertise in eyewitness identification, 90% of the experts believed that empirical evidence of the cross-race effect was sufficiently reliable to be presented in court. The phenomenon has been described as "[o]ne of the best documented examples of face recognition errors."

There is, however, a significant disparity between what the psychological research shows and what uninstructed jurors believe. One study showed that only 47% of jurors were familiar with the cross-race effect. A survey of over 1,000 jurors in Washington, D.C., cited by amicus the American Psychological Association, found that "[a] large plurality of the survey respondents (48%) thought cross-race and same-race identifications are of equal reliability, and many of the other [survey] respondents either did not know or thought a cross-racial identification would be more reliable (11%). Only 36% of the survey respondents understand that a cross-racial identification may be less reliable." These findings demonstrate that, while the cross-race effect is a matter of common sense and experience for some jurors, it is by no means a universal belief shared by all. The need for a charge on the cross-race effect is evident. The question becomes how this instruction is best given.

IV

As to each crime of which he was convicted, defendant, who is black, was found guilty entirely on the basis of the testimony of a single white witness identifying defendant as the person who had robbed him. Nevertheless, Supreme Court refused to give the requested charge instructing the jury on the relative inaccuracy of cross-racial identifications. One of Supreme Court's reasons for refusing to give the charge was that such an instruction should not be given if there has been no expert testimony on the subject. We reject this rationale and hold that Supreme Court erred in relying on it. For this reason and because the error was not harmless, we reverse.

Expert testimony on the cross-race effect is not a precondition of a jury charge on the subject. Indeed, the People do not contend that it is, but instead insist, at least in this appeal, that expert testimony on the cross-race effect is a preferable substitute for a jury charge and one that renders the charge superfluous. We disagree.

The decision to grant a request for expert testimony on the subject of cross-racial identification remains within the trial court's discretion. However, expert testimony is not necessary to establish the right to the charge.

A psychological principle such as the cross-race effect may lend itself to expert testimony. "Despite the fact that jurors may be familiar from their own experience with factors relevant to the reliability of eyewitness observation and identification, it cannot be said that psychological studies regarding the accuracy of an identification are within the ken of the typical juror." Contrary to the People's position, this does not mean that the cross-race effect cannot be expressed in a jury charge.

We have recognized that the same psychological principle may be the subject of expert testimony and a jury charge. For example, the pattern jury instructions ask jurors to consider "[f]or what period of time . . . the witness actually observe[d] the perpetrator," because exposure time, the amount of time a witness has to view a perpetrator, affects that person's ability to identify someone accurately as the perpetrator. Yet, we have held that a trial court abused its discretion in refusing to hold a *Frye* hearing with regard to an expert's proposed testimony on the effect of exposure time, among other factors.

Similarly, as noted above, a juror may have a tentative belief, based on his or her ordinary experiences, that cross-racial identifications are often inaccurate, but most jurors will have no knowledge of the research demonstrating the cross-race effect. Expert testimony explaining the studies to the jury is admissible, because "it would help to clarify an issue calling for professional or technical knowledge, possessed by the expert and beyond the ken of the typical juror," with the decision to admit subject to the trial court's discretion. Such expert testimony does not render a charge regarding the cross-race effect superfluous.

In short, the absence of expert testimony on cross-racial identification does not preclude the charge.

V

Supreme Court also erred in assuming that a cross-racial identification charge should be predicated on whether defense counsel cross-examined the People's witnesses about their identifications. An eyewitness is often utterly confident about an identification, expressing the identification or recollection of identification with subjective certainty, and hence entirely unshakable on cross-examination. "[A]s scholars have cautioned, most eyewitnesses think they are telling the truth even when their testimony is inaccurate, and because the eyewitness is testifying honestly (i.e., sincerely), he or she will not display the demeanor of the dishonest or biased witness." Instead, some mistaken eyewitnesses, at least by the time they testify at trial, exude supreme confidence in their identifications. Honesty and accuracy are entirely different categories by which jurors evaluate testimony. It is the fact of a cross-racial identification that should be the basis of the court's charge, not the nature of the questions asked on the examination.

Amici former judges and prosecutors observe that cross-examination that is "aimed at establishing that a witness may have difficulty identifying members of another race may offend the witness and the jury, without any benefit to the examiner." The amici note that "[a]s a society, we do not discuss racial issues easily. Some jurors may deny the existence of the cross-race effect in the misguided belief that it is merely a racist myth . . . while others may believe in the reality of this effect but be reluctant to discuss it in deliberations for fear of being seen as bigots. That, however, makes an instruction all the more essential." As with whether to seek expert testimony, cross-examination should be a decision that counsel makes within the context of an individual case.

VI

High courts in other states have recently considered the significance of the cross-race effect and three have required that trial courts, in appropriate cases, instruct juries regarding the phenomenon.

In 2011, in *State v. Henderson*, the Supreme Court of New Jersey held that a cross-racial identification charge (to be drafted by the state Criminal Practice Committee and Committee on Model Criminal Jury Charges) must be given "whenever cross-racial identification is in issue at trial." The high court adopted the findings of a Special Master, appointed to evaluate scientific and other evidence about eyewitness identifications, who had heard testimony by seven experts and issued an extensive report. The court "anticipate[d] . . . that with enhanced jury instructions, there will be less need for expert testimony. Jury charges offer a number of advantages: they are focused and concise, authoritative (in that juries hear them from the trial judge, not a witness called by one side), and cost-free; they avoid possible confusion to jurors created by dueling experts; and they eliminate the risk of an expert invading the jury's role or opining on an eyewitness' credibility."

The following year, the Supreme Court of Hawaii held that trial courts in criminal cases "must give the jury a specific eyewitness identification instruction whenever identification evidence is a central issue in the case, and it is requested by the defendant," including an instruction that one factor to be considered in evaluating identification testimony is the cross-racial nature of an identification.

In *Commonwealth v. Bastaldo* (2015), the Supreme Judicial Court of Massachusetts, relying on the Report and Recommendations of the Supreme Judicial Court Study Group on Eyewitness Evidence, held that in light of the fact that "the existence of the 'cross-race effect' . . . has reached a near consensus in the relevant scientific community and has been recognized by courts and scholars alike," an instruction on the inaccuracy of cross-racial identification must be given, unless the parties agree that there was no cross-racial identification.

1318 Chapter XV The Jury II: Race and Juries

> [I]n criminal trials that commence after the issuance of this opinion, the following instruction should be included when giving the model eyewitness identification instruction, unless all parties agree to its omission: "If the witness and the person identified appear to be of different races, you should consider that people may have greater difficulty in accurately identifying someone of a different race than someone of their own race."

Defendant urges this Court to require that a jury charge on the cross-race effect be given in all cases unless both parties agree that no cross-racial identification has occurred, or, alternatively, when requested by defense counsel.

VII

In February 2011, the New York State Justice Task Force published Recommendations for Improving Eyewitness Identifications. Under the heading of Pattern Jury Instructions, the Justice Task Force endorsed the substance of the existing pattern Criminal Jury Instructions regarding eyewitness identification, and further recommended "that the jury instructions be revised to include an instruction on cross-racial identifications in cases in which cross-racial identification is an issue." The Justice Task Force suggested the following instruction:

> If you think it is appropriate to do so, you may consider whether the fact that the defendant is of a different race than the witness has affected the accuracy of the witness' original perception or the accuracy of a later identification. You should consider that some people may have greater difficulty in accurately identifying members of a different race than in identifying members of their own race.

The Task Force added that "[t]his instruction should be given in cases in which cross-racial identification is an issue, regardless of whether an expert testifies on the topic of cross-racial identification."

In the same year, the authors of the Criminal Jury Instructions amended the pattern jury instructions for identification, so as to include the following model charge on cross-racial identification:

> You may consider whether there is a difference in race between the defendant and the witness who identified the defendant, and if so, whether that difference affected the accuracy of the witness's identification. Ordinary human experience indicates that some people have greater difficulty in accurately identifying members of a different race than they do in identifying members of their own race. With respect to this issue, you may consider the nature and extent of the witness's contacts with members of the defendant's race and whether such contacts, or lack thereof, affected the accuracy of the witness's identification. . . .

We note that, unlike the Massachusetts Supreme Judicial Court, our Justice Task Force does not suggest that the instruction should always be given unless the parties agree to its omission. Neither do the authors of the Criminal Jury Instructions.

VIII

In light of our discussion of the cross-race effect, which has been accepted by a near consensus in the relevant scientific community of cognitive and social psychologists, and recognizing the very significant part that inaccurate identifications play in wrongful convictions, we reach the following holding: in a case in which a witness's identification of the defendant is at issue, and the identifying witness and defendant appear to be of different races, a trial court is required to give, upon request, during final instructions, a jury charge on the cross-race effect, instructing (1) that the jury should consider whether there is a difference in race between the defendant and the witness who identified the defendant, and (2) that, if so, the jury should consider (a) that some people have greater difficulty in accurately identifying members of a different race than in accurately identifying members of their own race and (b) whether the difference in race affected the accuracy of the witness's identification. The instruction would not be required when there is no dispute about the identity of the perpetrator nor would it be obligatory when no party asks for the charge[.]

NOTES AND QUESTIONS

1. Here, as in *State v. Walker*, eyewitness identification was the centerpiece of the trial. No physical evidence connected the defendant to the alleged crimes and there were no other witnesses besides the victim. The court of appeals does not rely on that fact, however, and announces more broadly that a cautionary instruction must be given upon request whenever a cross-racial identification is at issue in a case. Can you imagine circumstances where a defense attorney might not request an instruction even though entitled to one?

2. The trial court had refused to give an instruction on cross-racial identification, as requested by defendant, in part because there was no expert testimony on the subject and defense counsel did not cross-examine the government's witnesses on the subject. The appellate division affirmed the ruling, finding that defendant hadn't "placed the issue in evidence at trial." There are many reasons why defense counsel might not have retained an expert witness on this subject, including a lack of funds. (Anticipating the court giving a cautionary instruction might have been another.) Apart from expert testimony, how was the defendant supposed to have "placed the issue in evidence during the trial"? Why might counsel have chosen not to do this?

3. The government argues that expert testimony on the subject of cross-racial identifications is preferable to a jury instruction. Why would the government find it advantageous to force the defendant to call an expert rather than have the court instruct the jury on the subject?

4. The court cites data regarding the extent to which the public is aware of the decreased reliability of cross-racial identifications. Is the data persuasive? What if a survey showed that 75 percent of the public was aware of the decreased reliability? Should an instruction still be given? Would it still "assist the trier of fact"?

5. In *Boone* the court of appeals cites three other states that have also required an instruction on the cross-racial effect where applicable. In one of these three cases, *State v. Henderson*, 27 A.3d 872 (2011), the Supreme Court of New Jersey held that the requirement of a cross-racial identification instruction would likely reduce or eliminate the need for expert testimony on the subject. The court noted that jury instructions "offer a number of advantages: they are focused and concise, authoritative (in that juries hear them from the trial judge, not a witness called by one side), and cost-free; they avoid possible confusion to jurors created by dueling experts; and they eliminate the risk of an expert invading the jury's role or opining on an eyewitness' credibility." *Id.* at 925. Do you agree with the reasoning of the court in *Henderson*? Are there other ways to prevent the court's concerns about expert testimony, either in itself or in combination with a jury instruction?

6. *Boone* held that the jury must be instructed as follows in all cases where the defendant and identifying witness appear to be of different races and the instruction is requested:

> that the jury should consider whether there is a difference in race between the defendant and the witness who identified the defendant, and that, if so, the jury should consider that some people have greater difficulty in accurately identifying members of a different race than in accurately identifying members of their own race and whether the difference in race affected the accuracy of the witness's identification.

How could this instruction be improved, based on the similar instructions you have seen in other cases? How might expert testimony still be useful to the jury if this instruction is given?

CHAPTER XVI

INCARCERATION: BAIL, PRETRIAL DETENTION, AND SENTENCING

A generation or two ago criminal procedural courses focused little, if any, attention on sentencing even though sentencing in some form has always been the consequence of the criminal process for the vast majority of defendants entering the system. One of the reasons for this was the absence of any real law on sentencing outside the death penalty context, and even that body of law did not emerge until the 1970s. And the focus on incarceration at the front end of the criminal process—bail and pretrial detention—is an even later arrival.

This chapter attempts to bridge those traditional gaps. Section A is introductory, touching on the phenomenon of mass incarceration, which makes this chapter so indispensable. Section B examines bail and pretrial detention, looking at the statutory changes in pretrial detention policies that have contributed heavily to American incarceration rates. Section C explores the United States Sentencing Guidelines—the sentencing reform movement that lead to their legislative enactment, the essential principles underlying the Guidelines, the functioning of the Guidelines in practice, and the constitutional challenges to the Guidelines. Section D considers the role of race in sentencing, focusing primarily on racial challenges to the administration of the death penalty and to the crack-cocaine sentencing disparity enacted by Congress in 1986.

A. MASS INCARCERATION

Until the 1970s the American criminal justice system had an imprisonment rate roughly similar to the rates of western European countries. Since then the nation's incarceration rate has skyrocketed, increasing steadily until apparently beginning to subside in the early 2010s. Peak rates were five to ten times greater than in other western European countries. And at peak rates during the 1990s Black people were seven times more likely than whites to be incarcerated. Jeremy Travis & Bruce Western, *Poverty, Violence, and Black Incarceration* 301-03, in Policing the Black Man: Arrest, Prosecution and Imprisonment (Angela J. Davis ed., 2017).

The reasons for the spike in imprisonment rates are many, apart from an undeniable increase in crime rates during the 1960s and 1970s: the politicization of crime, beginning with the Nixon presidential campaigns and administration; the media's obsession with crime stories; legislative tough-on-crime sentencing policies; the increased power and aggressiveness of prosecutors; and the decline of parole as a back-end palliative. The increased racial disparities of mass incarceration have been variously attributed to the racial overtones of the "war on drugs," and to the focus and comparative effectiveness of waging that war in poor urban areas where more of daily life, including illegal activity, occurs in public spaces. *See id.* at 298;

1322 Chapter XVI Incarceration: Bail, Pretrial Detention, and Sentencing

Michelle Alexander, The New Jim Crow: Mass Incarceration in the Age of Colorblindness 60 (2020 ed.).

Mass incarceration's costs are enormous. Total annual economic costs are estimated at $80 billion a year. Even worse are the costs to the current and former imprisoned. Due to both the psychic and tangible collateral consequences of a criminal record, Michelle Alexander views the criminal justice system generally, and incarceration specifically, as a "gateway" to a "new caste system," a world of "racial stigmatization and permanent marginalization." *Id.* at xxvii.

> More than 70 million Americans—over 20 percent of the entire U.S. population, overwhelmingly poor and disproportionately people of color—now have criminal records that authorize legal discrimination for life. . . . [I]t is a serious mistake to think of mass incarceration as simply a problem of too many people in prisons and jails. It is that, but also much, much more. Prison statistics barely begin to capture the enormity of the crisis.

Id. at xxix.

B. BAIL AND PRETRIAL DETENTION

A less commonly noted reason for increased rates of mass incarceration is the change in policies regarding bail and pretrial detention over the last few decades, discussed below. Estimates hold that today around 60 to 75 percent of all individuals in jails on any given day are unconvicted—presumed innocent—defendants awaiting trial. Todd D. Minton & Zhen Zeng, Bureau of Justice Statistics, Jail Inmates at Midyear 2014, at 3 (2015). As is the case with overall incarceration rates, persons jailed prior to trial are disproportionately Black and Hispanic. *Id.* at 1. One study has found that "Hispanic and black defendants are more likely to be detained [pretrial] than similarly situated white defendants." *See* Stephen Demuth & Darrell Steffensmeier, *The Impact of Gender and Race-Ethnicity in the Pretrial Release Process*, 51 Soc. Probs. 222 (2004).

Even these shorter periods of incarceration, sometimes only temporary, also have collateral consequences. The economic costs of pretrial detention are estimated at $14 billion annually. The human costs are also prohibitive. As the Supreme Court has recognized, persons detained prior to trial are "handicapped in consulting counsel, searching for evidence and witnesses, and preparing a defense." *Stack v. Boyle*, 342 U.S. 1, 8 (1951). Detainees can lose their jobs, their housing, and custody of their children. Recent studies also show that pretrial detention increases the likelihood of being sentenced to jail and of reoffending in the future. *See generally* Note, *Bail Reform and Risk Assessment: The Cautionary Tale of Federal Sentencing*, 131 Harv. L. Rev. 1128-29 (2018).

The next case considers the issue of bail in a Cold War setting where the Department of Justice and the FBI were focused on prosecuting suspected Communists. The Court's approach to bail is almost casual, a mood that would not last long.

Stack v. Boyle
342 U.S. 1 (1951)

Mr. Chief Justice VINSON delivered the opinion of the Court.

Indictments have been returned in the Southern District of California charging the twelve petitioners with conspiring to violate the Smith Act, 18 U.S.C. (Supp. IV) ss 371, 2385, 18 U.S.C.A. ss 371, 2385. Upon their arrest, bail was fixed for each petitioner in the widely varying amounts of $2,500, $7,500, $75,000 and $100,000. On motion of petitioner

B. Bail and Pretrial Detention

Schneiderman following arrest in the Southern District of New York, his bail was reduced to $50,000 before his removal to California. On motion of the Government to increase bail in the case of other petitioners, and after several intermediate procedural steps not material to the issues presented here, bail was fixed in the District Court for the Southern District of California in the uniform amount of $50,000 for each petitioner.

Petitioners moved to reduce bail on the ground that bail as fixed was excessive under the Eighth Amendment. In support of their motion, petitioners submitted statements as to their financial resources, family relationships, health, prior criminal records, and other information. The only evidence offered by the Government was a certified record showing that four persons previously convicted under the Smith Act in the Southern District of New York had forfeited bail. No evidence was produced relating those four persons to the petitioners in this case. At a hearing on the motion, petitioners were examined by the District Judge and cross-examined by an attorney for the Government. Petitioners' factual statements stand uncontroverted.

After their motion to reduce bail was denied, petitioners filed applications for habeas corpus in the same District Court. Upon consideration of the record on the motion to reduce bail, the writs were denied. The Court of Appeals for the Ninth Circuit affirmed. Prior to filing their petition for certiorari in this Court, petitioners filed with Mr. Justice Douglas an application for bail and an alternative application for habeas corpus seeking interim relief. Both applications were referred to the Court and the matter was set down for argument on specific questions covering the issues raised by this case.

Relief in this type of case must be speedy if it is to be effective. The petition for certiorari and the full record are now before the Court and, since the questions presented by the petition have been fully briefed and argued, we consider it appropriate to dispose of the petition for certiorari at this time. Accordingly, the petition for certiorari is granted for review of questions important to the administration of criminal justice.

First. From the passage of the Judiciary Act of 1789, 1 Stat. 73, 91, to the present Federal Rules of Criminal Procedure, Rule 46(a)(1), 18 U.S.C.A., federal law has unequivocally provided that a person arrested for a non-capital offense shall be admitted to bail. This traditional right to freedom before conviction permits the unhampered preparation of a defense, and serves to prevent the infliction of punishment prior to conviction. Unless this right to bail before trial is preserved, the presumption of innocence, secured only after centuries of struggle, would lose its meaning.

The right to release before trial is conditioned upon the accused's giving adequate assurance that he will stand trial and submit to sentence if found guilty. Like the ancient practice of securing the oaths of responsible persons to stand as sureties for the accused, the modern practice of requiring a bail bond or the deposit of a sum of money subject to forfeiture serves as additional assurance of the presence of an accused. Bail set at a figure higher than an amount reasonably calculated to fulfill this purpose is "excessive" under the Eighth Amendment.

Since the function of bail is limited, the fixing of bail for any individual defendant must be based upon standards relevant to the purpose of assuring the presence of that defendant. The traditional standards as expressed in the Federal Rules of Criminal Procedure are to be applied in each case to each defendant. In this case petitioners are charged with offenses under the Smith Act and, if found guilty, their convictions are subject to review with the scrupulous care demanded by our Constitution. Upon final judgment of conviction, petitioners face imprisonment of not more than five years and a fine of not more than $10,000. It is not denied that bail for each petitioner has been fixed in a sum much higher than that usually imposed for offenses with like penalties and yet there has been no factual showing to justify such action in this case. The Government asks the courts to depart from the norm by assuming, without the introduction of evidence, that each petitioner is a pawn in a conspiracy and will, in obedience to a superior, flee the jurisdiction. To infer from the fact of indictment alone a need for bail in an unusually high amount is an arbitrary act. Such conduct would inject into our own system of government the very principles of totalitarianism which Congress was seeking to guard against in passing the statute under which petitioners have been indicted.

If bail in an amount greater than that usually fixed for serious charges of crimes is required in the case of any of the petitioners, that is a matter to which evidence should be directed in a hearing so that the constitutional rights of each petitioner may be preserved. In the absence of such a showing, we are of the opinion that the fixing of bail before trial in these cases cannot be squared with the statutory and constitutional standards for admission to bail.

• • •

Judgment of Court of Appeals vacated and case remanded to District Court with directions.

By Mr. Justice JACKSON, whom Mr. Justice FRANKFURTER joins.

I think the principles governing allowance of bail have been misunderstood or too casually applied in these cases and that they should be returned to the Circuit Justice or the District Courts for reconsideration in the light of standards which it is our function to determine. We have heard the parties on only four specific questions relating to bail before conviction — two involving considerations of law and of fact which should determine the amount of bail, and two relating to the procedure for correcting any departure therefrom. I consider first the principles which govern release of accused persons upon bail pending their trial.

The practice of admission to bail, as it has evolved in Anglo-American law, is not a device for keeping persons in jail upon mere accusation until it is found convenient to give them a trial. On the contrary, the spirit of the procedure is to enable them to stay out of jail until a trial has found them guilty. Without this conditional privilege, even those wrongly accused are punished by a period of imprisonment while awaiting trial and are handicapped in consulting counsel, searching for evidence and witnesses, and preparing a defense. To open a way of escape from this handicap and possible injustice, Congress commands allowance of bail for one under charge of any offense not punishable by death, Fed. Rules Crim. Proc. 46(a)(1) providing: "A person arrested for an offense not punishable by death shall be admitted to bail . . ." before conviction.

Admission to bail always involves a risk that the accused will take flight. That is a calculated risk which the law takes as the price of our system of justice. We know that Congress anticipated that bail would enable some escapes, because it provided a procedure for dealing with them. Fed. Rules Crim. Proc. 46(f).

In allowance of bail, the duty of the judge is to reduce the risk by fixing an amount reasonably calculated to hold the accused available for trial and its consequence. Fed. Rules Crim. Proc. 46(c). But the judge is not free to make the sky the limit, because the Eighth Amendment to the Constitution says: "Excessive bail shall not be required. . . ."

Congress has reduced this generality in providing more precise standards, stating that ". . . the amount thereof shall be such as in the judgment of the commissioner or court or judge or justice will insure the presence of the defendant, having regard to the nature and circumstances of the offense charged, the weight of the evidence against him, the financial ability of the defendant to give bail and the character of the defendant." Fed. Rules Crim. Proc. 46(c).

These statutory standards are not challenged as unconstitutional, rather the amounts of bail established for these petitioners are alleged to exceed these standards. We submitted no constitutional questions to argument by the parties, and it is our duty to avoid constitutional issues if possible. For me, the record is inadequate to say what amounts would be reasonable in any particular one of these cases and I regard it as not the function of this Court to do so. Furthermore, the whole Court agrees that the remedy pursued in the circumstances of this case is inappropriate to test the question and bring it here. But I do think there is a fair showing that these congressionally enacted standards have not been correctly applied.

It is complained that the District Court fixed a uniform blanket bail chiefly by consideration of the nature of the accusation and did not take into account the difference in circumstances between different defendants. If this occurred, it is a clear violation of Rule 46(c). Each defendant stands before the bar of justice as an individual. Even on a conspiracy charge defendants do not lose their separateness or identity. While it might be possible that these defendants are identical in financial ability, character and relation to the charge — elements Congress has directed to be regarded in fixing bail — I think it violates the law of probabilities. Each accused is entitled to any benefits due to his good record, and misdeeds or a bad record should prejudice only those who are guilty of them. The question when application for bail is made relates to each one's trustworthiness to appear for trial and what security will supply reasonable assurance of his appearance.

Complaint further is made that the courts below have been unduly influenced by recommendations of very high bail made by the grand jury. It is not the function of the grand jury to fix bail, and its volunteered advice is not governing. Since the grand jury is a secret body, ordinarily hearing no evidence but the prosecution's, attended by no counsel except the prosecuting attorneys, it is obvious that it is not in a position to make an impartial recommendation. Its suggestion may indicate that those who have heard the evidence for the prosecution regard it as strongly indicative that the accused may be guilty of the crime charged. It could not mean more than that without hearing the defense, and it adds nothing to the inference from the fact of indictment. Such recommendations are better left unmade, and if made should be given no weight.

But the protest charges, and the defect in the proceedings below appears to be, that, provoked by the flight of certain Communists after conviction, the Government demands and public opinion supports a use of the bail power to keep Communist defendants in jail before conviction. Thus, the amount is said to have been fixed not as a reasonable assurance of their presence at the trial, but also as an assurance they would remain in jail. There seems reason to believe that this may have been the spirit to which the courts below have yielded, and it is contrary to the whole policy and philosophy of bail. This is not to say that every defendant is entitled to such bail as he can provide, but he is entitled to an opportunity to make it in a reasonable amount. I think the whole matter should be reconsidered by the appropriate judges in the traditional spirit of bail procedure.

NOTES AND QUESTIONS

1. The statute allegedly violated here, the Smith Act, was enacted in 1940 after the Nazi invasion of France in World War II, the success of which was thought to be partially attributable to internal disloyalties. The statute generally criminalized advocating for, or belonging to a group advocating for, the violent overthrow of the government. The Smith Act was used aggressively by the DOJ and the FBI to prosecute Communists and suspected Communists during the 1940s and 1950s. *See* Beverly Gage, G-Men: J. Edgar Hoover and the Making of the American Century 238, 348-57 (2022).

2. The arrogance of the government in this case is remarkable. It offered no evidence specific to the charges or the defendants and appeared to argue only that the defendants would flee the jurisdiction prior to trial, as it claims that other Smith Act defendants had done, in response to orders from their Communist superiors. The government offered only this by way of argument, despite the plain language of the operative rule, Fed. R. Crim. P. 46(c), that the amount of bail to require of a defendant shall be established based on "the nature and circumstances of the offense charged, the weight of the evidence against him, the financial ability of the defendant to give bail and the character of the defendant." On top of this, it appears that

1326 Chapter XVI Incarceration: Bail, Pretrial Detention, and Sentencing

the prosecutors asked the grand jury for their thoughts on bail and relayed those thoughts to the court.

3. Does *Stack* hold that there is an Eighth Amendment *right* to bail in a non-capital case? What are the contours of any such right? Is it a right to bail in the minimal amount that will assure the defendant's appearance at trial? Should the case be read more narrowly?

4. Justice Jackson makes the point that the occasional flight of a defendant is essentially the cost of doing business, part and parcel of the natural attrition in a sensible system of criminal justice. This is a remarkably and refreshingly laissez-faire approach for someone who was formerly the Attorney General of the United States. Do you agree? How does this observation square with Justice Jackson's remarks about prosecutorial discretion that are quoted in Justice Scalia's dissent in *Morrison v. Olson*? Are defendants who flee analogous to persons who commit crimes but don't get prosecuted in the first place?

When the Supreme Court reconsidered issues of pretrial detention 36 years later in *United States v. Salerno*, 481 U.S. 739 (1987), the world had changed. Crime rates had increased dramatically in the 1960s and 1970s. During those 20 years the murder rate doubled and the violent crime rate tripled. U.S. Census Bureau, Statistical Abstract of the United States, at HS-23 (2003) ("Crime Rates by Type of Offense": 1960-2002). And, at least as significant as the increased crime rates, crime as an issue had become more politicized than it had previously been. Anti-crime rhetoric featured prominently in Nixon's 1968 presidential campaign and the volume stayed high for decades. As crime rates spiked, Congress became much more active in criminal justice matters, flexing its tough-on-crime muscles.

United States v. Salerno
481 U.S. 739 (1987)

Chief Justice REHNQUIST delivered the opinion of the Court.

The Bail Reform Act of 1984 (Act) allows a federal court to detain an arrestee pending trial if the Government demonstrates by clear and convincing evidence after an adversary hearing that no release conditions "will reasonably assure . . . the safety of any other person and the community." The United States Court of Appeals for the Second Circuit struck down this provision of the Act as facially unconstitutional, because, in that court's words, this type of pretrial detention violates "substantive due process." We granted certiorari because of a conflict among the Courts of Appeals regarding the validity of the Act. We hold that, as against the facial attack mounted by these respondents, the Act fully comports with constitutional requirements. We therefore reverse.

I

Responding to "the alarming problem of crimes committed by persons on release," Congress formulated the Bail Reform Act of 1984, 18 U.S.C. § 3141 et seq., as the solution to a bail crisis in the federal courts. The Act represents the National Legislature's considered response to numerous perceived deficiencies in the federal bail process. By providing for sweeping changes in both the way federal courts consider bail applications and the circumstances under which bail is granted, Congress hoped to "give the courts adequate authority to make release decisions that give appropriate recognition to the danger a person may pose to others if released."

To this end, § 3141(a) of the Act requires a judicial officer to determine whether an arrestee shall be detained. Section 3142(e) provides that "[i]f, after a hearing pursuant to the

B. Bail and Pretrial Detention   **1327**

provisions of subsection (f), the judicial officer finds that no condition or combination of conditions will reasonably assure the appearance of the person as required and the safety of any other person and the community, he shall order the detention of the person prior to trial." Section 3142(f) provides the arrestee with a number of procedural safeguards. He may request the presence of counsel at the detention hearing, he may testify and present witnesses in his behalf, as well as proffer evidence, and he may cross-examine other witnesses appearing at the hearing. If the judicial officer finds that no conditions of pretrial release can reasonably assure the safety of other persons and the community, he must state his findings of fact in writing, § 3142(i), and support his conclusion with "clear and convincing evidence," § 3142(f).

The judicial officer is not given unbridled discretion in making the detention determination. Congress has specified the considerations relevant to that decision. These factors include the nature and seriousness of the charges, the substantiality of the Government's evidence against the arrestee, the arrestee's background and characteristics, and the nature and seriousness of the danger posed by the suspect's release. § 3142(g). Should a judicial officer order detention, the detainee is entitled to expedited appellate review of the detention order. §§ 3145(b), (c).

Respondents Anthony Salerno and Vincent Cafaro were arrested on March 21, 1986, after being charged in a 29-count indictment alleging various Racketeer Influenced and Corrupt Organizations Act (RICO) violations, mail and wire fraud offenses, extortion, and various criminal gambling violations. The RICO counts alleged 35 acts of racketeering activity, including fraud, extortion, gambling, and conspiracy to commit murder. At respondents' arraignment, the Government moved to have Salerno and Cafaro detained pursuant to § 3142(e), on the ground that no condition of release would assure the safety of the community or any person. The District Court held a hearing at which the Government made a detailed proffer of evidence. The Government's case showed that Salerno was the "boss" of the Genovese crime family of La Cosa Nostra and that Cafaro was a "captain" in the Genovese family. According to the Government's proffer, based in large part on conversations intercepted by a court-ordered wiretap, the two respondents had participated in wide-ranging conspiracies to aid their illegitimate enterprises through violent means. The Government also offered the testimony of two of its trial witnesses, who would assert that Salerno personally participated in two murder conspiracies. Salerno opposed the motion for detention, challenging the credibility of the Government's witnesses. He offered the testimony of several character witnesses as well as a letter from his doctor stating that he was suffering from a serious medical condition. Cafaro presented no evidence at the hearing, but instead characterized the wiretap conversations as merely "tough talk."

The District Court granted the Government's detention motion, concluding that the Government had established by clear and convincing evidence that no condition or combination of conditions of release would ensure the safety of the community or any person:

> The activities of a criminal organization such as the Genovese Family do not cease with the arrest of its principals and their release on even the most stringent of bail conditions. The illegal businesses, in place for many years, require constant attention and protection, or they will fail. Under these circumstances, this court recognizes a strong incentive on the part of its leadership to continue business as usual. When business as usual involves threats, beatings, and murder, the present danger such people pose in the community is self-evident.

Respondents appealed, contending that to the extent that the Bail Reform Act permits pretrial detention on the ground that the arrestee is likely to commit future crimes, it is unconstitutional on its face. Over a dissent, the United States Court of Appeals for the Second Circuit agreed. Although the court agreed that pretrial detention could be imposed if the defendants were likely to intimidate witnesses or otherwise jeopardize the trial process, it found "§ 3142(e)'s authorization of pretrial detention [on the ground of future dangerousness] repugnant to the concept of substantive due process, which we believe prohibits the total deprivation of liberty simply as a means of preventing future crimes." The court concluded that the Government could not, consistent with due process, detain persons who had not been accused of any crime merely because they were thought to present a danger to the community. It reasoned that our criminal law system holds persons accountable for past actions, not anticipated future actions. Although a court could detain an arrestee who threatened to flee before trial, such detention would be permissible because it would serve the basic objective of a criminal system — bringing the accused to trial. The court distinguished our decision in *Gerstein v. Pugh* (1975), in which we upheld police detention pursuant to arrest. The court construed *Gerstein* as limiting such detention to the "'administrative steps incident to arrest.'" The Court of Appeals also found our decision in *Schall v. Martin* (1984), upholding postarrest, pretrial detention of juveniles, inapposite because juveniles have a lesser interest in liberty than do adults. The dissenting judge concluded that on its face, the Bail Reform Act adequately balanced the Federal Government's compelling interests in public safety against the detainee's liberty interests.

II

A facial challenge to a legislative Act is, of course, the most difficult challenge to mount successfully, since the challenger must establish that no set of circumstances exists under which the Act would be valid. The fact that the Bail Reform Act might operate unconstitutionally under some conceivable set of circumstances is insufficient to render it wholly invalid, since we have not recognized an "overbreadth" doctrine outside the limited context of the First Amendment. We think respondents have failed to shoulder their heavy burden to demonstrate that the Act is "facially" unconstitutional.

Respondents present two grounds for invalidating the Bail Reform Act's provisions permitting pretrial detention on the basis of future dangerousness. First, they rely upon the Court of Appeals' conclusion that the Act exceeds the limitations placed upon the Federal Government by the Due Process Clause of the Fifth Amendment. Second, they contend that the Act contravenes the Eighth Amendment's proscription against excessive bail. We treat these contentions in turn.

A

The Due Process Clause of the Fifth Amendment provides that "No person shall . . . be deprived of life, liberty, or property, without due process of law. . . ." This Court has held that the Due Process Clause protects individuals against two types of government action. So-called "substantive due process" prevents the government from engaging in conduct that "shocks the conscience," *Rochin v. California* (1952), or interferes with rights "implicit in the concept of ordered liberty," *Palko v. Connecticut* (1937). When government action depriving a person of life, liberty, or property survives substantive due process scrutiny, it must still be implemented in a fair manner. *Mathews v. Eldridge* (1976). This requirement has traditionally been referred to as "procedural" due process.

Respondents first argue that the Act violates substantive due process because the pretrial detention it authorizes constitutes impermissible punishment before trial. The Government, however, has never argued that pretrial detention could be upheld if it were "punishment." The Court of Appeals assumed that pretrial detention under the Bail Reform Act is regulatory, not penal, and we agree that it is.

As an initial matter, the mere fact that a person is detained does not inexorably lead to the conclusion that the government has imposed punishment. To determine whether a

B. Bail and Pretrial Detention

restriction on liberty constitutes impermissible punishment or permissible regulation, we first look to legislative intent. Unless Congress expressly intended to impose punitive restrictions, the punitive/regulatory distinction turns on "'whether an alternative purpose to which [the restriction] may rationally be connected is assignable for it, and whether it appears excessive in relation to the alternative purpose assigned [to it].'"

We conclude that the detention imposed by the Act falls on the regulatory side of the dichotomy. The legislative history of the Bail Reform Act clearly indicates that Congress did not formulate the pretrial detention provisions as punishment for dangerous individuals. Congress instead perceived pretrial detention as a potential solution to a pressing societal problem. There is no doubt that preventing danger to the community is a legitimate regulatory goal.

Nor are the incidents of pretrial detention excessive in relation to the regulatory goal Congress sought to achieve. The Bail Reform Act carefully limits the circumstances under which detention may be sought to the most serious of crimes. The arrestee is entitled to a prompt detention hearing, and the maximum length of pretrial detention is limited by the stringent time limitations of the Speedy Trial Act. See 18 U.S.C. § 3161. Moreover, the conditions of confinement envisioned by the Act "appear to reflect the regulatory purposes relied upon by the" Government. As in *Schall*, the statute at issue here requires that detainees be housed in a "facility separate, to the extent practicable, from persons awaiting or serving sentences or being held in custody pending appeal." We conclude, therefore, that the pretrial detention contemplated by the Bail Reform Act is regulatory in nature, and does not constitute punishment before trial in violation of the Due Process Clause.

The Court of Appeals nevertheless concluded that "the Due Process Clause prohibits pretrial detention on the ground of danger to the community as a regulatory measure, without regard to the duration of the detention." Respondents characterize the Due Process Clause as erecting an impenetrable "wall" in this area that "no governmental interest — rational, important, compelling or otherwise — may surmount."

We do not think the Clause lays down any such categorical imperative. We have repeatedly held that the Government's regulatory interest in community safety can, in appropriate circumstances, outweigh an individual's liberty interest. For example, in times of war or insurrection, when society's interest is at its peak, the Government may detain individuals whom the government believes to be dangerous. Even outside the exigencies of war, we have found that sufficiently compelling governmental interests can justify detention of dangerous persons. Thus, we have found no absolute constitutional barrier to detention of potentially dangerous resident aliens pending deportation proceedings. We have also held that the government may detain mentally unstable individuals who present a danger to the public, and dangerous defendants who become incompetent to stand. We have approved of postarrest regulatory detention of juveniles when they present a continuing danger to the community. Even competent adults may face substantial liberty restrictions as a result of the operation of our criminal justice system. If the police suspect an individual of a crime, they may arrest and hold him until a neutral magistrate determines whether probable cause exists. *Gerstein v. Pugh* (1975). Finally, respondents concede and the Court of Appeals noted that an arrestee may be incarcerated until trial if he presents a risk of flight or a danger to witnesses.

Respondents characterize all of these cases as exceptions to the "general rule" of substantive due process that the government may not detain a person prior to a judgment of guilt in a criminal trial. Such a "general rule" may freely be conceded, but we think that these cases show a sufficient number of exceptions to the rule that the congressional action challenged here can hardly be characterized as totally novel. Given the well-established authority of the government, in special circumstances, to restrain individuals' liberty prior to or even without criminal trial and conviction, we think that the present statute providing for pretrial detention on the basis of dangerousness must be evaluated in precisely the same manner that we evaluated the laws in the cases discussed above.

The government's interest in preventing crime by arrestees is both legitimate and compelling. In *Schall*, we recognized the strength of the State's interest in preventing juvenile crime. This general concern with crime prevention is no less compelling when the suspects are adults. Indeed, "[t]he harm suffered by the victim of a crime is not dependent upon the age of the perpetrator." The Bail Reform Act of 1984 responds to an even more particularized governmental interest than the interest we sustained in *Schall*. The statute we upheld in *Schall* permitted pretrial detention of any juvenile arrested on any charge after a showing that the individual might commit some undefined further crimes. The Bail Reform Act, in contrast, narrowly focuses on a particularly acute problem in which the Government interests are overwhelming. The Act operates only on individuals who have been arrested for a specific category of extremely serious offenses. Congress specifically found that these individuals are far more likely to be responsible for dangerous acts in the community after arrest. Nor is the Act by any means a scattershot attempt to incapacitate those who are merely suspected of these serious crimes. The Government must first of all demonstrate probable cause to believe that the charged crime has been committed by the arrestee, but that is not enough. In a full-blown adversary hearing, the Government must convince a neutral decisionmaker by clear and convincing evidence that no conditions of release can reasonably assure the safety of the community or any person. While the Government's general interest in preventing crime is compelling, even this interest is heightened when the Government musters convincing proof that the arrestee, already indicted or held to answer for a serious crime, presents a demonstrable danger to the community. Under these narrow circumstances, society's interest in crime prevention is at its greatest.

On the other side of the scale, of course, is the individual's strong interest in liberty. We do not minimize the importance and fundamental nature of this right. But, as our cases hold, this right may, in circumstances where the government's interest is sufficiently weighty, be subordinated to the greater needs of society. We think that Congress' careful delineation of the circumstances under which detention will be permitted satisfies this standard. When the Government proves by clear and convincing evidence that an arrestee presents an identified and articulable threat to an individual or the community, we believe that, consistent with the Due Process Clause, a court may disable the arrestee from executing that threat. Under these circumstances, we cannot categorically state that pretrial detention "offends some principle of justice so rooted in the traditions and conscience of our people as to be ranked as fundamental."

Finally, we may dispose briefly of respondents' facial challenge to the procedures of the Bail Reform Act. To sustain them against such a challenge, we need only find them "adequate to authorize the pretrial detention of at least some [persons] charged with crimes," whether or not they might be insufficient in some particular circumstances. We think they pass that test. As we stated in *Schall*, "there is nothing inherently unattainable about a prediction of future criminal conduct."

Under the Bail Reform Act, the procedures by which a judicial officer evaluates the likelihood of future dangerousness are specifically designed to further the accuracy of that determination. Detainees have a right to counsel at the detention hearing. They may testify in their own behalf, present information by proffer or otherwise, and cross-examine witnesses who appear at the hearing. The judicial officer charged with the responsibility of determining the appropriateness of detention is guided by statutorily enumerated factors, which include the nature and the circumstances of the charges, the weight of the evidence, the history and characteristics of the putative offender, and the danger to the community. The Government must prove its case by clear and convincing evidence. Finally, the judicial officer must include written findings of fact and a written statement of reasons for a decision to detain. The Act's review provisions provide for immediate appellate review of the detention decision.

We think these extensive safeguards suffice to repel a facial challenge. The protections are more exacting than those we found sufficient in the juvenile context, and they far exceed what we found necessary to effect limited postarrest detention in *Gerstein*. Given the legitimate and compelling regulatory purpose of the Act and the procedural protections it offers, we conclude that the Act is not facially invalid under the Due Process Clause of the Fifth Amendment.

B

Respondents also contend that the Bail Reform Act violates the Excessive Bail Clause of the Eighth Amendment. The Court of Appeals did not address this issue because it found that the Act violates the Due Process Clause. We think that the Act survives a challenge founded upon the Eighth Amendment.

The Eighth Amendment addresses pretrial release by providing merely that "[e]xcessive bail shall not be required." This Clause, of course, says nothing about whether bail shall be available at all. Respondents nevertheless contend that this Clause grants them a right to bail calculated solely upon considerations of flight. They rely on *Stack v. Boyle* (1951), in which the Court stated that "[b]ail set at a figure higher than an amount reasonably calculated [to ensure the defendant's presence at trial] is 'excessive' under the Eighth Amendment." In respondents' view, since the Bail Reform Act allows a court essentially to set bail at an infinite amount for reasons not related to the risk of flight, it violates the Excessive Bail Clause. Respondents concede that the right to bail they have discovered in the Eighth Amendment is not absolute. A court may, for example, refuse bail in capital cases. And, as the Court of Appeals noted and respondents admit, a court may refuse bail when the defendant presents a threat to the judicial process by intimidating witnesses. Respondents characterize these exceptions as consistent with what they claim to be the sole purpose of bail—to ensure the integrity of the judicial process.

While we agree that a primary function of bail is to safeguard the courts' role in adjudicating the guilt or innocence of defendants, we reject the proposition that the Eighth Amendment categorically prohibits the government from pursuing other admittedly compelling interests through regulation of pretrial release. The above-quoted dictum in *Stack v. Boyle* is far too slender a reed on which to rest this argument. The Court in Stack had no occasion to consider whether the Excessive Bail Clause requires courts to admit all defendants to bail, because the statute before the Court in that case in fact allowed the defendants to be bailed. Thus, the Court had to determine only whether bail, admittedly available in that case, was excessive if set at a sum greater than that necessary to ensure the arrestees' presence at trial.

The holding of *Stack* is illuminated by the Court's holding just four months later in *Carlson v. Landon* (1952). In that case, remarkably similar to the present action, the detainees had been arrested and held without bail pending a determination of deportability. The Attorney General refused to release the individuals, "on the ground that there was reasonable cause to believe that [their] release would be prejudicial to the public interest and would endanger the welfare and safety of the United States." The detainees brought the same challenge that respondents bring to us today: the Eighth Amendment required them to be admitted to bail. The Court squarely rejected this proposition:

> The bail clause was lifted with slight changes from the English Bill of Rights Act. In England that clause has never been thought to accord a right to bail in all cases, but merely to provide that bail shall not be excessive in those cases where it is proper to grant bail. When this clause was carried over into our Bill of Rights, nothing was said that indicated any different concept. The Eighth Amendment has not prevented Congress from defining the classes of cases in which bail shall be allowed in this country. Thus, in criminal cases bail is not compulsory where the punishment may be death. Indeed, the very language of the Amendment fails to say all arrests must be bailable.

Carlson v. Landon was a civil case, and we need not decide today whether the Excessive Bail Clause speaks at all to Congress' power to define the classes of criminal arrestees who shall be admitted to bail. For even if we were to conclude that the Eighth Amendment imposes some substantive limitations on the National Legislature's powers in this area, we would still hold that the Bail Reform Act is valid. Nothing in the text of the Bail Clause limits permissible Government considerations solely to questions of flight. The only arguable substantive limitation of the Bail Clause is that the Government's proposed conditions of release or detention not be "excessive" in light of the perceived evil. Of course, to determine whether the Government's response is excessive, we must compare that response against the interest the Government seeks to protect by means of that response. Thus, when the Government has admitted that its only interest is in preventing flight, bail must be set by a court at a sum designed to ensure that goal, and no more. *Stack v. Boyle*, supra. We believe that when Congress has mandated detention on the basis of a compelling interest other than prevention of flight, as it has here, the Eighth Amendment does not require release on bail.

III

In our society liberty is the norm, and detention prior to trial or without trial is the carefully limited exception. We hold that the provisions for pretrial detention in the Bail Reform Act of 1984 fall within that carefully limited exception. The Act authorizes the detention prior to trial of arrestees charged with serious felonies who are found after an adversary hearing to pose a threat to the safety of individuals or to the community which no condition of release can dispel. The numerous procedural safeguards detailed above must attend this adversary hearing. We are unwilling to say that this congressional determination, based as it is upon that primary concern of every government — a concern for the safety and indeed the lives of its citizens — on its face violates either the Due Process Clause of the Fifth Amendment or the Excessive Bail Clause of the Eighth Amendment.

The judgment of the Court of Appeals is therefore

Reversed.

[Justices Marshall, Brennan, and Stevens dissented.]

NOTES AND QUESTIONS

1. Just 18 years prior to the Bail Reform Act of 1984 that is at issue in *Salerno*, Congress had enacted the Bail Reform Act of 1966, which permitted bail to be required only for the purpose of assuring the defendant's return to court. The act announced its remedial purpose: "The purpose of this Act is to revise the practices relating to bail to assure that all persons, regardless of their financial status, shall not needlessly be detained pending their appearance. . . ."

By 1984, by contrast, the legislative history of the Bail Reform Act bemoaned "the alarming problem of crimes committed by persons on release," and the Court itself posited a "bail crisis in the federal courts."

2. Did Cafaro's indefinite detention cause him to decide to cooperate with the government as a means of securing his release prior to trial? While any such conclusion would be speculative, there is no doubt that detention prior to trial puts extreme pressure on defendants to resolve their cases, normally by guilty pleas. This is especially true of misdemeanor detainees, who are likely to be released — albeit with a conviction on their record — if they plead guilty. *See* Paul Heaton et al., *The Downstream Consequences of Misdemeanor Pretrial Detention*, 69 Stan. L. Rev. 711, 714-16 (2017) (not only is a detained defendant hindered in his ability to develop a defense, "a detained person may plead guilty — even if innocent — simply to get out of jail").

3. The Court concludes that the preventive detention provision does not violate substantive due process because it is "regulatory, not penal." Granted, there is an arguable difference in objective between imposing punishment based on a criminal conviction and detaining someone on dangerousness grounds. But are there any limits to this distinction? Could the government establish facially neutral criteria of dangerousness (convictions for crimes of violence?) and subject persons who meet those criteria — after judicial proceedings like those required under the act — to a finite term of detention as a means of protecting public safety?

4. Looking at it differently, what is the actual significance of the indictment to the preventive detention provision? Does it make sense that a grand jury's finding of probable cause for one of the crimes for which detention is permitted gives the grand jury (i.e., the prosecutor) too much power, notwithstanding the procedural safeguards under the statute? Is the indictment just the necessary step to getting custody over the defendant as an initial matter? Justice Stevens notes in his dissenting opinion that the defendant must have been just as dangerous the day before the indictment was returned and, if so, shouldn't something have been done on that account beforehand. One commentator has even questioned whether defendants, as a class, are more dangerous than nondefendants. Sandra G. Mayson, *Dangerous Defendants*, 127 Yale L.J. 490, 518-20 (2018) (challenging that assumption and its effects on the imposition of conditions and detention).

5. The Court brushes aside its earlier language about excessive bail in *Stack v. Boyle* as dictum. Would a faithful adherence to *Stack* require that the Court find the Bail Reform Act unconstitutional? Would *Stack* prohibit a court from denying bail to a defendant who had threatened and was likely to continue to threaten witnesses?

6. Are the procedural safeguards under the act sufficient? Why not require proof beyond a reasonable doubt, a standard district court judges apply in their courtrooms whenever a defendant elects to waive the right to jury trial?

7. If it is permissible to detain a defendant based on a finding that he is likely to obstruct justice (i.e., to attempt to harass or intimidate witnesses), why shouldn't it be permissible to detain him because he is dangerous more generally in order to protect the community? Is the integrity of the criminal justice system more worthy of protection than the community writ large?

8. The Court notes in justifying the act as regulatory that the period of detention is limited by the "stringent time limitations" of the Speedy Trial Act. Those time limitations are largely illusory in practice, however, as the statute provides that numerous actions in a case amount to "excludable delay" from those limitations, including the time for making and resolving pretrial motions, which in most cases is an absolute requirement of a competent defense. *See* 18 U.S.C. § 3161(h)(1)(D).

The story behind the story in *Salerno*, hinted at in the opening of Justice Marshall's dissent, is as follows. At the time of his arrest on these charges in March 1986, Anthony Salerno was the elderly (74) but still reigning boss of the Genovese crime family. One of Salerno's codefendants, Vincent Cafaro, a Genovese family capo, was also detained on dangerous grounds. While being held, Cafaro began cooperating with the government. In October 1986 — six months after the detention order — Cafaro was released, purportedly "temporarily for medical care and treatment," but in reality on a $1 million personal appearance bond with the consent of the government. The true reason for his release — that he was cooperating — was not made public until the following March, when U.S. Attorney Rudolph Giuliani announced the indictment on drug charges of a defendant set up by Cafaro, a defendant the U.S. attorney called a "major Mafia drug dealer." *See generally* Daniel Richman, United States v. Salerno: *The Constitutionality of Regulatory Detention* 419-28, in Criminal Procedure Stories (Carol S. Steiker ed., 2005).

Anthony "Fat Tony" Salerno, reputed boss of the Genovese family

Both before and especially after *Salerno*, with concerns about the constitutionality of preventive detention having been swept aside, almost all jurisdictions amended their bail requirements to permit pretrial detention on public safety grounds. *See* Heaton et al., *The Downstream Consequences*, *supra* at 711, 720. As noted above, this development has had a significant effect on incarceration levels.

The next case considers whether a defendant's wealth can be a factor in the district court's determination under the Bail Act of "the least restrictive . . . conditions that . . . will reasonable assure the appearance of a person."

United States v. Boustani
932 F.3d 79 (2d Cir. 2019)

JOSÉ A. CABRANES, Circuit Judge:

Defendant-Appellant Jean Boustani ("Boustani") appeals from a March 28, 2019 order of the District Court for the Eastern District of New York (William F. Kuntz, II, Judge) denying Boustani's bail application and directing that he be detained pending trial. We affirmed the District Court's order by order on May 16, 2019. We write to explain that decision and to clarify the circumstances under which the Bail Reform Act permits a District Court to release a defendant pending trial pursuant to a condition under which the defendant would pay for private armed security guards.

I. BACKGROUND

Boustani is charged with conspiracy to commit wire fraud, in violation of 18 U.S.C. §§ 1343 and 1349; conspiracy to commit securities fraud, in violation of 15 U.S.C. §§ 78j(b)

and 78ff and 18 U.S.C. §§ 371; and conspiracy to commit money laundering, in violation of 18 U.S.C. § 1956(a) and (h).

Boustani filed an application for bail pending trial, proposing a set of conditions that included home confinement under the supervision of private armed security guards, to be paid for by Boustani. The Government opposed Boustani's request and argued that he should be detained pending trial because he was a flight risk. The District Court denied Boustani's bail application, and Boustani appealed. We affirmed the District Court's order without prejudice to further bail applications before the District Court. Boustani then filed another bail application, which the District Court again denied on March 28, 2019. Boustani now appeals from the District Court's order denying his second bail application. After oral argument on May 14, 2019, we affirmed the District Court order by order on May 16, 2019.

II. DISCUSSION

We review a district court's order of detention for clear error and will reverse only where "on the entire evidence we are left with the definite and firm conviction that a mistake has been committed."

Under the Bail Reform Act, a court is required to order the pretrial release of a defendant on personal recognizance or after execution of an appearance bond "unless the judicial officer determines that such release will not reasonably assure the appearance of the person as required or will endanger the safety of any other person or the community." If the court finds that a defendant poses a risk of flight, it must release him "subject to the least restrictive further condition, or combination of conditions, that . . . will reasonably assure the appearance of the person." The court must order detention, however, if it "finds that no condition or combination of conditions will reasonably assure the appearance of the person as required and the safety of any other person and the community." In determining whether any condition or combination of conditions is sufficient, a court should consider several factors, including: (1) the nature and circumstances of the charged offense; (2) the weight of the evidence; (3) the history and characteristics of the defendant; and (4) the nature and seriousness of the danger posed by the defendant's release.

The Government bears the burden of proving by a preponderance of the evidence both that the defendant "presents an actual risk of flight" and that "no condition or combination of conditions could be imposed on the defendant that would reasonably assure his presence in court."

We have previously recognized that, in limited circumstances, a court may release a defendant subject to conditions of home confinement in which, among other things, the defendant pays for private armed security guards. In *United States v. Sabhnani*, we first acknowledged that such home confinement, combined with other restrictive conditions, may suffice to reasonably assure the defendant's appearance in court. We noted in that case, however, that we had "no occasion to consider whether it would be contrary to principles of detention and release on bail to allow wealthy defendants to buy their way out by constructing a private jail." We observed that the defendants in that case were likely denied bail because of their wealth and that defendants of "lesser means . . . might have been granted bail in the first place."

Since *Sabhnani*, however, we have highlighted our concerns regarding granting bail to defendants because of their wealth. In non-precedential summary orders, we have observed that pretrial release pursuant to, inter alia, conditions such as supervision by privately hired security guards may not be appropriate for wealthy defendants when similarly situated defendants of lesser means would be detained. And we have noted that district courts need not routinely consider "the retention of self-paid private security guards," which may be best understood as "a less onerous form of detention available only to the wealthy."

We now expressly hold that the Bail Reform Act does not permit a two-tiered bail system in which defendants of lesser means are detained pending trial while wealthy defendants are released to self-funded private jails. It is a fundamental principle of fairness that the law protects "the interests of rich and poor criminals in equal scale, and its hand extends as far to each." To interpret the Bail Reform Act as requiring district courts to permit wealthy defendants to employ privately funded armed guards where an otherwise similarly situated defendant without means would be detained would violate this core principle. Such a two-tiered system would "foster inequity and unequal treatment in favor of a very small cohort of criminal defendants who are extremely wealthy."

That said, the private-security condition we described in *Sabhnani* may be appropriate where the defendant is deemed to be a flight risk primarily because of his wealth. In other words, a defendant may be released on such a condition only where, but for his wealth, he would not have been detained. By contrast, if a similarly situated defendant of lesser means would be detained, a wealthy defendant cannot avoid detention by relying on his personal funds to pay for private detention. Such a limitation on private-security conditions ensures that the standards of the Bail Reform Act are applied equitably to all defendants.

In the instant appeal, Boustani does not challenge the District Court's finding that he poses a risk of flight. Instead, he argues that the District Court erred in finding that no conditions or combination of conditions would reasonably assure his appearance in court.

In ruling on Boustani's initial bail application, the District Court found that he poses a risk of flight based on several factors. First, the District Court noted the seriousness of the charged offenses and the lengthy possible sentence Boustani would face if convicted. Second, without drawing any conclusions about the merits of the case, the District Court found that the evidence against Boustani "appears strong." Third, the Court considered Boustani's personal characteristics, including his "alleged deceptive actions, access to substantial financial resources, frequent international travel, complete lack of ties to the United States, and extensive ties to foreign countries without extradition." Having evaluated "the totality of the circumstances," the District Court found that "the Government has shown by a preponderance of the evidence" that Boustani poses "a serious risk of flight."

The District Court further found that the Government had satisfied its burden of showing that no conditions or combination of conditions could reasonably assure Boustani's appearance in court. The District Court noted, among other considerations, that releasing Boustani to a privately funded jail would lead to disparate treatment between him and his co-defendants, who might pose flight risks for similar reasons but lack the financial resources available to Boustani.

Boustani's amended bail application did not alter the District Court's conclusions that Boustani poses a flight risk and that no conditions or combination of conditions would reasonably assure his appearance in court.

The District Court's findings are not clearly erroneous. It is clear that the District Court did not rely primarily on Boustani's personal wealth in finding that he posed a flight risk. Rather, his wealth was one of many factors the Court considered. A similarly situated defendant of lesser means surely would be detained pending trial, and Boustani is not permitted to avoid such a result by relying on his own financial resources to pay for a private jail.

III. CONCLUSION

For the foregoing reasons, the District Court's order of March 28, 2019, was affirmed by order on May 16, 2019.

NOTES AND QUESTIONS

1. The Second Circuit's August 1, 2019, issuance of its decision in *Boustani*—issued six weeks after it had issued a summary order affirming the district court's denial of defendant's bail application—has been attributed to developments in an unrelated case. On July 6, 2019, jet-set socialite Jeffrey Epstein was arrested and charged with sex trafficking of minors, a crime for which there is a rebuttable presumption of detention under 18 U.S.C. § 3142. His lawyers argued for release conditions that included home detention in Manhattan, electronic monitoring, an extradition waiver, a bond secured by multiple multimillion-dollar properties, permission for pretrial services to randomly access his house, scheduled reporting to pretrial services, a prohibition on anyone other than Epstein and his attorneys entering the home, a trustee or trustees living with him, and more. *See* Cait Barrett, *Liberty and Justice for All: Equalizing Pretrial Detention for Wealthy and Indigent Defendants*, 53 Conn. L. Rev. 473, 479-80 (2021). Epstein's bail application was denied on July 28, 2019, and while his appeal of that decision was pending *Boustani* was issued.

2. In rejecting "a two-tiered bail system in which defendants of lesser means are detained pending trial while wealthy defendants are released to self-funded private jails," the Court relies on *Smith v. Bennett*, 365 U.S. 708, 714 (1961), where the Supreme Court struck down a habeas corpus filing fee as violating the Equal Protection Clause vis-à-vis indigent defendants. Why do you think the Court does not explicitly ground its decision in *Boustani* on the Equal Protection Clause? Is *Bennett* distinguishable from *Boustani*? Would denying bail to defendants *because* of their wealth—that is, because their wealth enabled flight that a person without means would not have available—also violate the Equal Protection Clause?

3. Consider all of the factors the district court relied on in denying bail to Boustani. Are any of those factors proxies for wealth?

Cash Bail. On the subject of two-tiered bail systems, one of the most controversial aspects of the American bail system is the widespread practice of imposing "cash bail" to guarantee a defendant's return to court. Where a judge or magistrate decides against releasing a defendant on a mere promise to return to court (release on personal recognizance), or on conditions (e.g., checking in with pretrial services, drug testing), cash bail is often imposed even for minor crimes and misdemeanors and often regardless of defendants' ability to pay. Cash bail usually means the payment of a secured bond, where the defendant will be released from jail upon paying the bond amount to the court or will retain the services of a wholly private bail bondsman, who will post the bond amount for a nonrefundable fee, often 10 percent of the bail amount. *See generally* Note, *Bail Reform and Risk Assessment*, *supra* at 1125, 1126-27. Many states in the past few years have taken steps to eliminate or reduce cash bail. Emily Bazelon, Charged: The New Movement to Transform American Prosecution and End Mass Incarceration 41-50 (2019).

Sometimes reform of cash bail regimes requires, or is at least augmented by, litigation, as the next case shows.

Odonnell v. Harris County, Texas
251 F. Supp. 3d 1052 (S.D. Tex. 2017)

MEMORANDUM AND OPINION SETTING OUT FINDINGS OF FACT AND CONCLUSIONS OF LAW

LEE H. ROSENTHAL, Chief United States District Judge.

• • •

Introduction

"Twenty years ago, not quite one-third of [Texas's] jail population was awaiting trial. Now the number is three-fourths. Liberty is precious to Americans, and any deprivation must be scrutinized. To protect public safety and ensure that those accused of a crime will appear at trial, persons charged with breaking the law may be detained before their guilt or innocence can be adjudicated, but that detention must not extend beyond its justifications. Many who are arrested cannot afford a bail bond and remain in jail awaiting a hearing. Though presumed innocent, they lose their jobs and families, and are more likely to re-offend. And if all this weren't bad enough, taxpayers must shoulder the cost—a staggering $1 billion per year." The Honorable Nathan L. Hecht, Chief Justice of the Texas Supreme Court, Remarks Delivered to the 85th Texas Legislature, Feb. 1, 2017.

This case requires the court to decide the constitutionality of a bail system that detains 40 percent of all those arrested only on misdemeanor charges, many of whom are indigent and cannot pay the amount needed for release on secured money bail. These indigent arrestees are otherwise eligible for pretrial release, yet they are detained for days or weeks until their cases are resolved, creating the problems that Chief Justice Hecht identified. The question addressed in this Memorandum and Opinion is narrow: whether the plaintiffs have met their burden of showing a likelihood of success on the merits of their claims and the other factors necessary for a preliminary injunction against Harris County's policies and practices of imposing secured money bail on indigent misdemeanor defendants. Maranda Lynn Odonnell, Robert Ryan Ford, and Loetha McGruder sued while detained in the Harris County Jail on misdemeanor charges. They allege that they were detained because they were too poor to pay the amount needed for release on the secured money bail imposed by the County's policies and practices. They ask this court to certify a Rule 23(b)(2) class and preliminarily enjoin Harris County, the Harris County Sheriff, and—to the extent they are State enforcement officers or County policymakers—the Harris County Criminal Court at Law Judges, from maintaining a "wealth-based post-arrest detention scheme."

This case is difficult and complex. The Harris County Jail is the third largest jail in the United States. Although misdemeanor arrestees awaiting trial make up about 5.5 percent of the Harris County Jail population on any given day, about 50,000 people are arrested in Harris County on Class A and Class B misdemeanor charges each year. The arrests are made by a number of law-enforcement agencies, including the Houston Police Department and the police forces of smaller municipalities, the Texas Department of Public Safety, and the Harris County Sheriff's Office. Harris County's bail system is regulated by State law, local municipal codes, informal rules, unwritten customary practices, and the actions of judges in particular cases. The legal issues implicate intertwined Supreme Court and Fifth Circuit precedents on the level of judicial scrutiny in equal protection and due process cases and on the tailoring of sufficient means to legitimate ends.

Bail has a longstanding presence in the Anglo-American common law tradition. Despite this pedigree, the modern bail-bond industry and the mass incarceration on which it thrives present important questions that must be examined against current law and recent developments. Extrajudicial reforms have caused a sea change in American bail practices within the last few years. Harris County is also in the midst of commendable and important efforts to reform its bail system for misdemeanor arrests. The reform effort follows similar work in other cities and counties around the country. This work is informed by recent empirical data about the effects of secured money bail on a misdemeanor defendant's likely appearance at hearings and other law-abiding conduct before trial, as well as the harmful effects on the defendant's life.

The plaintiffs contend that certainly before, and even with, the implemented reforms, Harris County's bail system for misdemeanor arrests will continue to violate the Constitution. This case is one of many similar cases recently filed around the country challenging long-established bail practices. Most have settled because the parties have agreed to significant reform. This case is one of the first, although not the only one, that requires a court to examine in detail the constitutionality of a specific bail system for misdemeanor arrestees. This case is also one of the most thoroughly and skillfully presented by able counsel on all sides, giving the court the best information available to decide these difficult issues.

One other complication is worth noting at the outset. Since this case was filed, the 2016 election replaced the Harris County Sheriff and the presiding County Judge of Criminal Court at Law No. 16. The new Sheriff and County Judge have taken positions adverse to their codefendants, although each continues to oppose certain aspects of the plaintiffs' request for preliminary injunctive relief. Nonparty County officials, including the newly elected Harris County District Attorney and one of the Harris County Commissioners, have filed amicus briefs supporting the plaintiffs. Harris County's Chief Public Defender has filed a declaration supporting the defendants. The lines of affinity and adversity between the defendants and their nonparty County colleagues are not always clear.

Even with the factual and legal complexities, at the heart of this case are two straightforward questions: Can a jurisdiction impose secured money bail on misdemeanor arrestees who cannot pay it, who would otherwise be released, effectively ordering their pretrial detention? If so, what do due process and equal protection require for that to be lawful? Based on the extensive record and briefing, the fact and expert witness testimony, the arguments of able counsel, and the applicable legal standards, the answers are that, under federal and state law, secured money bail may serve to detain indigent misdemeanor arrestees only in the narrowest of cases, and only when, in those cases, due process safeguards the rights of the indigent accused.

Because Harris County does not currently supply those safeguards or protect those rights, the court will grant the plaintiffs' motion for preliminary injunctive relief. The reasons and the precise, limited relief granted are set out in detail below.

More specifically, the court finds that:

- Harris County has a consistent and systematic policy and practice of imposing secured money bail as de facto orders of pretrial detention in misdemeanor cases.
- These de facto detention orders effectively operate only against the indigent, who would be released if they could pay at least a bondsman's premium, but who cannot. Those who can pay are released, even if they present similar risks of nonappearance or of new arrests.
- These de facto detention orders are not accompanied by the protections federal due process requires for pretrial detention orders.
- Harris County has an inadequate basis to conclude that releasing misdemeanor defendants on secured financial conditions is more effective to assure a defendant's appearance or law-abiding behavior before trial than release on unsecured or nonfinancial conditions, or that secured financial conditions of release are reasonably necessary to assure a defendant's appearance or to deter new criminal activity before trial.
- Harris County's policy and practice violates the Equal Protection and Due Process Clauses of the United States Constitution.

The court accordingly orders that:

- Harris County and its policymakers—the County Judges in their legislative and rulemaking capacity and the Harris County Sheriff in his law-enforcement capacity—are enjoined from detaining misdemeanor defendants who are otherwise eligible for release but cannot pay a secured financial condition of release.
- Harris County Pretrial Services must verify a misdemeanor arrestee's inability to pay bail on a secured basis by affidavit.
- The Harris County Sheriff must release on unsecured bail those misdemeanor defendants whose inability to pay is shown by affidavit, who would be released on secured bail if they

could pay, and who have not been released after a probable cause hearing held within 24 hours after arrest.

The court does not order: relief in cases involving felony charges or a mix of misdemeanor and felony charges; the elimination of secured money bail; changes to Texas State law; changes to the written Harris County Criminal Courts at Law Rules of Court; modification of prior federal court orders, including the consent decree in Roberson v. Richardson; or a right to "affordable bail" under the Eighth Amendment. Instead, the relief ordered is consistent with Texas state and Harris County law as written, is required by the Equal Protection and Due Process Clauses, and is justified by the plaintiffs' evidence. The relief is narrow so as not to interfere with the improvements the County is working to implement by July 1, 2017.

The reasons for these rulings are set out in the detailed findings and conclusions below.

• • •

F. THE EFFECTS OF PRETRIAL DETENTION ON MISDEMEANOR DEFENDANTS WHO CANNOT PAY SECURED MONEY BAIL

Recent studies of bail systems in the United States have concluded that even brief pretrial detention because of inability to pay a financial condition of release increases the likelihood that misdemeanor defendants will commit future crimes or fail to appear at future court hearings. A study co-authored by Dr. VanNostrand, who is helping Harris County reform its bail system, found that for misdemeanor defendants, even two to three days of pretrial detention correlated at statistically significant levels with recidivism. Pretrial detention made it more likely that misdemeanor defendants would fail to appear at future hearings. Other studies have confirmed these findings and shown that the likelihood of recidivism and failure to appear correlates with the imposition of secured money bail, not with a particular bail amount.

The Heaton Study found that if, during the six years between 2008 to 2013, Harris County had given early release on unsecured personal bonds to the lowest-risk misdemeanor defendants — those receiving secured bail amounts of $500 or less — 40,000 more people would have been released pretrial; nearly 6,000 convictions and 400,000 days in jail at County expense would have been avoided; those released would have committed 1,600 fewer felonies and 2,400 fewer misdemeanors in the eighteen months following pretrial release; and the County would have saved $20 million in supervision costs alone. Sheriff Gonzalez credibly testified that the research showing the "criminogenic" effects of even a short period of pretrial detention and the high public costs of extended detention is consistent with his own experience as a Harris County law-enforcement officer.

A growing literature examines empirical data on "cumulative disadvantage" in pretrial detention. "Cumulative disadvantage" is a "sequence of undesirable events whereby the occurrence of earlier negative events increases the odds of subsequent negative events." "Bail exacerbates and perpetuates poverty because of course only people who cannot afford the bail assessed or to post a bond — people who are already poor — are held in custody pretrial. As a consequence, they often lose their jobs, may lose their housing, be forced to abandon their education, and likely are unable to make their child support payments."

Money-based pretrial systems exacerbate the racial disparities in pretrial detention and posttrial outcomes. An amicus filing by Harris County Commissioner Rodney Ellis and the NAACP Legal Defense and Educational Fund notes that African-Americans make up 18 percent of Harris County's adult population but 48 percent of the Harris County Jail's adult population. A 2011 study found that in Harris County, 70 percent of white misdemeanor defendants obtain early pretrial release from detention, but only 52 percent of Latino misdemeanor defendants and 45 percent of African-American misdemeanor defendants do so. The defendants did not dispute this data.

• • •

NOTES AND QUESTIONS

1. The court notes its legal conclusion that "secured money bail may serve to detain indigent defendants only in the narrowest of cases, and only when, in those cases, due process safeguards the rights of the accused." What types of cases or circumstances do you think might fall into the "narrowest" category such that cash bail might nonetheless be warranted? What procedural due process protections should a defendant potentially in that category be afforded?

2. What should the "affidavit" Pretrial Services must use to determine inability to pay require? Should the defendant be advised of the affidavit's purpose? Should the affidavit have a temporal component to it? In other words, should the inquiry into indigency focus on how much the defendant can post in the next, say, 48 hours?

3. Are you surprised by the empirical data comparing the effectiveness of secured and unsecured appearance bonds in assuring both future appearance and law-abiding pretrial behavior? Would you expect this data to be similar for felony cases?

4. Why do you think that even a few days of pretrial detention correlates with statistically significant rates of recidivism?

5. Abolition or reduction of cash bail has some bipartisan support, as might be expected given the significant cost savings that would flow from even a modest reduction, as shown by the Heaton Study cited in *Odonnell.* New Jersey all but abolished cash bail in 2017 pursuant to legislation signed by Governor Chris Christie, a Republican and former U.S. attorney. The new law required judges to use a risk evaluation tool called a Public Safety Assessment (PSA) to determine the likelihood of a defendant's failure to appear or commit a crime while on release. The PSA algorithm used nine factors (e.g., age, criminal history, history of defaults, whether there were allegations of violence in the current charge). Defendants found dangerous would be detained; those with lower risk to the public, or at risk to default only, would be released with monitoring conditions (e.g., reporting). *See generally* Craig W. Trainor, *In the Rush to Reform, Prudence Is Among the Highest Duties: How to Responsibly End Cash Bail,* 22 Federalist Soc'y Rev. 118, 124 (2021).

The results in New Jersey were impressive. Only 6 percent of defendants were detained; the pretrial detainee population fell by 30 percent in a year. And crime rates fell. A comparison of the same nine-month period in 2016 to 2018 saw 30+ percent decreases in homicides, robberies, and burglaries, and double-digit percent decreases in rapes and assaults. *Id.*

Many states are using risk assessment tools like PSA in connection with efforts at bail reform. They are no panacea, however, and critics contend that, insofar as they rely on existing crime data, they will likely reflect economic and racial disparities in existing bail systems. *See* Note, *Bail Reform and Risk Assessment, supra* at 1125, 1130-33 (cataloguing critiques of risk assessment tools); Sandra G. Mayson, *Bias In, Bias Out,* 128 Yale L.J. 2218, 2226 (2019) (criticizing likely disparate outcomes due to use of algorithmic risk assessment tools).

C. THE SENTENCING GUIDELINES

Prior to the late 1980s, federal judges enjoyed virtually unfettered discretion in sentencing defendants within the broad maximum limits set by Congress, usually five or ten years. The discretion was broad in two senses: There were no constraints on what sentence to select and no appellate review of that selection. With the introduction of parole in the federal system in 1910 the judiciary's discretion—on the back end—was shared with the executive. Parole boards determined prisoners' actual release dates, which were often at a point where between one-third and two-thirds of the decreed sentence had been served.

An early and vocal critic of the parole system was FBI Director J. Edgar Hoover, even though both the FBI and the federal Parole Commission were both constituent parts of the Department of Justice. Anticipating the hardliners' arguments that would solidify decades later, as early as the 1930s Hoover criticized "sob sister judges" who released defendants from prison early, invariably claimed that FBI agents killed in the line of duty were the victims of criminals on parole, and railed against sentences that, due to parole, "say one thing and mean another." Gage, G-Man, *supra* at 191-93.

J. Edgar Hoover in a 1961 photograph. Hoover was the director of the FBI and its predecessor, the Bureau of Investigation, from 1924 until his death in 1972.

This "indeterminate" sentencing regime came under attack from all sides in the 1970s and 1980s. On the left, critics argued that the disparities in sentences resulting from the discretionary regime were inconsistent with principles of equality under law and were rife with opportunities for racial bias to infect sentencing. Some on the left argued, in particular, that white collar criminals, with privileged backgrounds similar to the judges who sentenced them, were in general treated more leniently than defendants committing "street crime." Samuel W. Buell, *Is the White Collar Offender Privileged?*, 63 Duke L.J. 823, 833 (2014). On the right, and in connection with increasing crime rates in the 1970s and 1980s, critics were dissatisfied with the perceived leniency of judges and parole officials. There was a consensus among critics that the system was plagued by unwarranted disparities, that sentences were not "honest" because of the role of parole, and that the underlying theory of the indeterminate model—the potential for rehabilitation—was or was becoming obsolete. *See generally* Kate Stith & Steve Koh, *The Politics of Sentencing Reform: The Legislative History of the Federal Sentencing Guidelines*, 28 Wake Forest L. Rev. 223, 225-27 (1993); Kate Stith, United States v. Mistretta: *The Constitution and the Sentencing Guidelines*, in Criminal Procedure Stories (Carol Steiker ed., 2006).

Accordingly, Congress took up sentencing reform in earnest in the 1970s. Over the years, the "tough on crime" sentiments on the right began to exert more and more influence, and those sentiments emerged front and center in the ultimate legislation. Stith & Koh, *The Politics of Sentencing Reform*, *supra* at 267-68. The upshot was the Sentencing Reform Act of 1984, which, among many other things, abolished parole, created a sentencing commission to prescribe sentencing ranges—"guidelines"—for all federal crimes, and provided for appellate review of district judges' sentences.

The Sentencing Commission issued its first set of guidelines, more than 250 pages in length, in late 1987. Litigation over the Sentencing Reform Act and the Guidelines was fierce and immediate. Between February and November 1988, 84 federal district courts had issued written decisions addressing the Guidelines' constitutionality. Stith, United States v. Mistretta, *supra* at 460-61. While the Supreme Court found the Guidelines constitutional as a matter of separation of powers in *Mistretta v. United States*, 488 U.S. 361 (1989), the Court just 15 years later held in *Booker v. United States*, 543 U.S. 220 (2005), that to the extent the Guidelines were mandatory they violated defendants' Sixth Amendment rights. But because *Booker* did not invalidate the Guidelines but only rendered them advisory, the Guidelines still dominate the sentencing landscape today.

Below is a heavily abridged version of *Mistretta*, provided not for the various separation of powers issues it addresses (omitted) but for its description of the Sentencing Reform Act and the federal sentencing regime it replaced.

Mistretta v. United States
488 U.S. 361 (1989)

Justice BLACKMUN delivered the opinion of the Court.

In this litigation, we granted certiorari before judgment in the United States Court of Appeals for the Eighth Circuit in order to consider the constitutionality of the Sentencing Guidelines promulgated by the United States Sentencing Commission. The Commission is a body created under the Sentencing Reform Act of 1984 (Act), as amended, 18 U.S.C. § 3551 et seq. The United States District Court for the Western District of Missouri ruled that the Guidelines were constitutional.

I

A. Background

For almost a century, the Federal Government employed in criminal cases a system of indeterminate sentencing. Statutes specified the penalties for crimes but nearly always gave the sentencing judge wide discretion to decide whether the offender should be incarcerated and for how long, whether he should be fined and how much, and whether some lesser restraint, such as probation, should be imposed instead of imprisonment or fine. This indeterminate-sentencing system was supplemented by the utilization of parole, by which an offender was returned to society under the "guidance and control" of a parole officer.

Both indeterminate sentencing and parole were based on concepts of the offender's possible, indeed probable, rehabilitation, a view that it was realistic to attempt to rehabilitate the inmate and thereby to minimize the risk that he would resume criminal activity upon his return to society. It obviously required the judge and the parole officer to make their respective sentencing and release decisions upon their own assessments of the offender's amenability to rehabilitation. As a result, the court and the officer were in positions to exercise, and usually did exercise, very broad discretion. This led almost inevitably to the conclusion on the part of a reviewing court that the sentencing judge "sees more and senses more" than the appellate court; thus, the judge enjoyed the "superiority of his nether position," for that court's determination as to what sentence was appropriate met with virtually unconditional deference on appeal. The decision whether to parole was also "predictive and discretionary." The correction official possessed almost absolute discretion over the parole decision.

Historically, federal sentencing—the function of determining the scope and extent of punishment—never has been thought to be assigned by the Constitution to the exclusive jurisdiction of any one of the three Branches of Government. Congress, of course, has the power to fix the sentence for a federal crime, and the scope of judicial discretion with respect to a sentence is subject to congressional control. Congress early abandoned fixed-sentence rigidity, however, and put in place a system of ranges within which the sentencer could choose the precise punishment. Congress delegated almost unfettered discretion to the sentencing judge to determine what the sentence should be within the customarily wide range so selected. This broad discretion was further enhanced by the power later granted the judge to suspend the sentence and by the resulting growth of an elaborate probation system. Also, with the advent of parole, Congress moved toward a "three-way sharing" of sentencing responsibility by granting corrections personnel in the Executive Branch the discretion to release a prisoner before the expiration of the sentence imposed by the judge. Thus, under the indeterminate-sentence system, Congress defined the maximum, the judge imposed a sentence within the statutory range (which he usually could replace with probation), and the Executive Branch's parole official eventually determined the actual duration of imprisonment.

Serious disparities in sentences, however, were common. Rehabilitation as a sound penological theory came to be questioned and, in any event, was regarded by some as an unattainable goal for most cases. In 1958, Congress authorized the creation of judicial sentencing institutes and joint councils, see 28 U.S.C. § 334, to formulate standards and criteria for sentencing. In 1973, the United States Parole Board adopted guidelines that established a "customary range" of confinement. Congress in 1976 endorsed this initiative through the Parole Commission and Reorganization Act, an attempt to envision for the Parole Commission a role, at least in part, "to moderate the disparities in the sentencing practices of individual judges." That Act, however, did not disturb the division of sentencing responsibility among the three Branches. The judge continued to exercise discretion and to set the sentence within the statutory range fixed by Congress, while the prisoner's actual release date generally was set by the Parole Commission.

This proved to be no more than a way station. Fundamental and widespread dissatisfaction with the uncertainties and the disparities continued to be expressed. Congress had wrestled with the problem for more than a decade when, in 1984, it enacted the sweeping reforms that are at issue here.

Helpful in our consideration and analysis of the statute is the Senate Report on the 1984 legislation. The Report referred to the "outmoded rehabilitation model" for federal criminal sentencing, and recognized that the efforts of the criminal justice system to achieve rehabilitation of offenders had failed. It observed that the indeterminate-sentencing system had two "unjustifi[ed]" and "shameful" consequences. The first was the great variation among sentences imposed by different judges upon similarly situated offenders. The second was the uncertainty as to the time the offender would spend in prison. Each was a serious impediment to an evenhanded and effective operation of the criminal justice system. The Report went on to note that parole was an inadequate device for overcoming these undesirable consequences. This was due to the division of authority between the sentencing judge and the parole officer who often worked at cross purposes; to the fact that the Parole Commission's own guidelines did not take into account factors Congress regarded as important in sentencing, such as the sophistication of the offender and the role the offender played in an offense committed with others, and to the fact that the Parole Commission had only limited power to adjust a sentence imposed by the court.

Before settling on a mandatory-guideline system, Congress considered other competing proposals for sentencing reform. It rejected strict determinate sentencing because it concluded that a guideline system would be successful in reducing sentence disparities while retaining the flexibility needed to adjust for unanticipated factors arising in a particular case. The Judiciary Committee rejected a proposal that would have made the sentencing guidelines only advisory.

B. The Act

The Act, as adopted, revises the old sentencing process in several ways:

1. It rejects imprisonment as a means of promoting rehabilitation, 28 U.S.C. § 994(k), and it states that punishment should serve retributive, educational, deterrent, and incapacitative goals, 18 U.S.C. § 3553(a)(2).
2. It consolidates the power that had been exercised by the sentencing judge and the Parole Commission to decide what punishment an offender should suffer. This is done by creating the United States Sentencing Commission, directing that Commission to devise guidelines to be used for sentencing, and prospectively abolishing the Parole Commission. 28 U.S.C. §§ 991, 994, and 995(a)(1).
3. It makes all sentences basically determinate. A prisoner is to be released at the completion of his sentence reduced only by any credit earned by good behavior while in custody. 18 U.S.C. §§ 3624(a) and (b).
4. It makes the Sentencing Commission's guidelines binding on the courts, although it preserves for the judge the discretion to depart from the guideline applicable to a particular case if the judge finds an aggravating or mitigating factor present that the Commission did not adequately consider when formulating guidelines. §§ 3553(a) and (b). The Act also requires the court to state its reasons for the sentence imposed and to give "the specific reason" for imposing a sentence different from that described in the guideline. § 3553(c).
5. It authorizes limited appellate review of the sentence. It permits a defendant to appeal a sentence that is above the defined range, and it permits the Government to appeal a sentence that is below that range. It also permits either side to appeal an incorrect application of the guideline. §§ 3742(a) and (b).

Thus, guidelines were meant to establish a range of determinate sentences for categories of offenses and defendants according to various specified factors, "among others." 28 U.S.C. §§ 994(b), (c), and (d). The maximum of the range ordinarily may not exceed the minimum by more than the greater of 25% or six months, and each sentence is to be within the limit provided by existing law. §§ 994(a) and (b)(2).

C. The Sentencing Commission

The Commission is established "as an independent commission in the judicial branch of the United States." § 991(a). It has seven voting members (one of whom is the Chairman)

Chapter XVI Incarceration: Bail, Pretrial Detention, and Sentencing

appointed by the President "by and with the advice and consent of the Senate." "At least three of the members shall be Federal judges selected after considering a list of six judges recommended to the President by the Judicial Conference of the United States." No more than four members of the Commission shall be members of the same political party. The Attorney General, or his designee, is an ex officio non-voting member. The Chairman and other members of the Commission are subject to removal by the President "only for neglect of duty or malfeasance in office or for other good cause shown." Except for initial staggering of terms, a voting member serves for six years and may not serve more than two full terms. §§ 992(a) and (b).

D. The Responsibilities of the Commission

In addition to the duty the Commission has to promulgate determinative-sentence guidelines, it is under an obligation periodically to "review and revise" the guidelines. It is to "consult with authorities on, and individual and institutional representatives of, various aspects of the Federal criminal justice system." It must report to Congress "any amendments of the guidelines. It is to make recommendations to Congress whether the grades or maximum penalties should be modified. It must submit to Congress at least annually an analysis of the operation of the guidelines. It is to issue "general policy statements" regarding their application. And it has the power to "establish general policies . . . as are necessary to carry out the purposes" of the legislation; to "monitor the performance of probation officers" with respect to the guidelines; to "devise and conduct periodic training programs of instruction in sentencing techniques for judicial and probation personnel" and others; and to "perform such other functions as are required to permit Federal courts to meet their responsibilities" as to sentencing.

We note, in passing, that the monitoring function is not without its burden. Every year, with respect to each of more than 40,000 sentences, the federal courts must forward, and the Commission must review, the presentence report, the guideline worksheets, the tribunal's sentencing statement, and any written plea agreement.

II. THIS LITIGATION

On December 10, 1987, John M. Mistretta (petitioner) and another were indicted in the United States District Court for the Western District of Missouri on three counts centering in a cocaine sale. Mistretta moved to have the promulgated Guidelines ruled unconstitutional on the grounds that the Sentencing Commission was constituted in violation of the established doctrine of separation of powers, and that Congress delegated excessive authority to the Commission to structure the Guidelines. As has been noted, the District Court was not persuaded by these contentions.

$$\bullet \quad \bullet \quad \bullet$$

NOTES AND QUESTIONS

1. In describing the work of the Sentencing Reform Act, the Court notes that the act "rejects" the rehabilitative model of sentencing. Are statutes allowed to have philosophies? Does this pronouncement have judicially enforceable meaning?

2. The commission's Guidelines are binding on the courts. So why are they called guidelines? Certainly the federal judges, whose comfortably unaccountable sentencing worlds are being upended by the Guidelines, are not going to be fooled by this. Is this sleight of hand for public consumption? What about the concern that sentences in the previous regime had been "dishonest"?

3. The Court states that the act provides for "limited" appellate review. Does the description of the scope of that review—sentences that are too high, sentences that are too low, sentences that misapply the mandatory guidelines—really seem "limited"? Why does the Court feel the need to sugarcoat the act? And, again, for what audience?

4. Location, location, location. The Court insists, noting the language of the act, that the Sentencing Commission is "located" in the judicial branch. What does this mean? Why do eight Justices of the Court accept this statutory characterization, which is plainly at odds with the operation and function of the commission? As the Court notes elsewhere, the commission is "fully accountable to Congress," which can revoke or amend any of the commission's Guidelines within 180 days of their issuance.

5. Professor Stith argues that both the statutory "location" of the commission in the judicial branch, along with the requirement that three of the seven commissioners be federal judges, were essentially part of a congressional con:

> [The provisions] were fig-leaves designed to obscure the usurpation of (heretofore) judicial power, to distract from the radical transformation of federal criminal law effected by the Sentencing Reform Act, to protect the Guidelines from challenge under the Administrative Procedure Act . . . and, most importantly, to clothe the agency with the courts' reputation for impartiality and sentencing expertise.

Stith, United States v. Mistretta, *supra* at 481-82.

6. The Court also says the Guidelines do not "bind or regulate the primary conduct of the public." Really? Consider the commission's fraud guideline, which increases the sentence by the amount of the "loss" occasioned by the fraud. Do you think a defendant who receives an extra period of imprisonment based on the amount of his fraud feels that he is "bound and regulated" by the Sentencing Commission?

The victory of the "tough on crime" sentencing reformers is evident in the examples the Court uses in its nondelegation analysis of the "detailed guidance" Congress gave to the commission (e.g., requiring certain types of sentences to be at or near the statutory maximum). The act also required the commission to use existing sentencing data on average sentences as "the starting point" for its guideline determinations. But given the abolition of parole by the Sentencing Reform Act, those existing averages would already reflect substantially longer periods of incarceration than were actually imposed under the prior regime. In his dissenting opinion, Justice Scalia noted the value-laden early work of the commission: choosing substantial increases over average prior sentences for multiple forms of white collar crime; eliminating previous opportunities for probation sentences; and requiring all nonindigent offenders to pay a fine.

In addition to the nondelegation and separation-of-powers challenges considered here, the Court in *Mistretta* also rejects arguments that the act's provisions for presidential removal of commissioners and for judges sharing power with nonjudges undermines the integrity of the judicial branch. The only other opinion is Justice Scalia's solo dissent, in which he condemns the Sentencing Commission as an unconstitutional "junior varsity congress," an independent agency with lawmaking power that is not accountable to the executive branch as are most administrative agencies.

Many important aspects of the Guidelines as eventually promulgated by the Sentencing Commission are not addressed in *Mistretta*. Some highlights follow.

Individual Characteristics. The Guidelines rejected the use of individualized information about the defendant that had influenced sentencing under the prior regime. Under USSG § 5H1, the commission decreed that the defendant's age, gender, military service, employment

1348 Chapter XVI Incarceration: Bail, Pretrial Detention, and Sentencing

history, education, youthful disadvantage, community service, family ties were either "never relevant" or "not ordinarily" relevant to sentence determination. Note that these Guidelines were promulgated only a decade or so after the Supreme Court had found that a capital defendant had a constitutional right to an individualized sentence. *See* Section D *infra*.

"Real Offense" Conduct. The theory behind the focus on "real offense" conduct — and in keeping with reducing sentencing disparities — was that defendants were to be sentenced based on the entirety of their criminal conduct and not simply the facts that were either agreed to in defendants' plea colloquy or proven at trial. This vision is manifested primarily in the "Relevant Conduct" Guideline, which provides that the defendant shall be sentenced based on all of his own acts and omissions, plus "in the case of a jointly undertaken criminal activity (a criminal plan, scheme, endeavor, or enterprise undertaken by the defendant in concert with others, whether or not charged as a conspiracy), all acts and omissions of others that were . . . in furtherance of that criminal activity." USSG § 1B1.3(a)(1)(B). A comment to this Guideline notes that even conduct for which a defendant had been acquitted at trial could be the source of "relevant conduct" on which a sentence must be based.

Another reason for the focus on "real offense" conduct was to reduce the power of prosecutors over sentencing, eliminating their ability to dictate a sentence based on their charging decisions. The reasoning was short-sighted. The Guidelines were swarming with sentencing factors that increased or decreased the total offense level on which a sentence would be based, and those factors can be the subject of bargaining between a prosecutor and a defendant just as easily as statutes.

How was this "real offense" conduct to be discovered for the purposes of using it at sentencing? The Guidelines assumed this task would be the job of federal probation officers, who under the new system — freed from some of their supervisory responsibilities due to decreased use of probation sentences — would have time on their hands, and could independently determine the "facts relevant to sentencing." The problem was that probation officers were not trained to be criminal investigators and had no power to conduct such investigations. In practice, probation officers ended up relying almost entirely on prosecutors for determining the necessary facts. Kate Stith & Jose A. Cabranes, Fear of Judging: Sentencing Guidelines in the Federal Courts 138-39 (1998) ("The description of the offense in most presentence reports in most districts is prepared largely or exclusively on the basis of information supplied by the government."). Defendants, who had not been sentenced and might be pursuing an appeal, were in no position to discuss their offense conduct with probation officers, as any statements they made might be admissible against them in the event of a retrial or even at sentencing.

Acceptance of Responsibility. In first formulating the Guidelines in 1987 the commission considered an automatic two-level reduction for a defendant who pleaded guilty but rejected it as inconsistent with "the public's perception of justice." William Wilkins, *Plea Negotiation, Acceptance of Responsibility, Role of the Offender, and Departures: Policy Decisions in the Promulgation of the Federal Sentencing Guidelines*, 23 Wake Forest L. Rev. 181, 191 (1988). Instead it promulgated USSG § 3E1.1, which provides a two-level reduction where a defendant "clearly demonstrates acceptance of responsibility for his offense." Initially a guilty plea did not automatically entitle a defendant to this reduction nor did going to trial preclude this reduction. That shortly changed, as the commission added an "application note" providing that "the adjustment is not intended to apply to a defendant who puts the government to its burden of proof at trial."

The same provision also allows for an additional one-level reduction for certain sentences where, upon a motion by the government, the defendant timely notifies the

C. The Sentencing Guidelines 1349

government of his intent to plead guilty and allows the government to avoid preparing for trial. These reductions are not trivial. For example, a defendant with an offense level of 33 who would ordinarily face a sentence of 11 to 14 years can reduce his sentence by four years with a three-level reduction.

You can easily see how these provisions act as the proverbial "trial penalty." Is putting the government to its burden of proof—the exercise of a constitutional right—inherently inconsistent with an "acceptance of responsibility"? Does it depend on the nature of the defense? On the other hand, in what sense is a defendant who pleads guilty to avoid a longer sentence truly "accepting responsibility"? Stepping back even further, why should "acceptance of responsibility" matter?

Substantial Assistance. Another euphemism, another way to avoid draconian Guideline sentences: Defendants who provide "substantial assistance" (i.e., cooperate) to the government are eligible for a downward departure under USSG § 5K1.1. Again, as for a three-level acceptance of responsibility reduction, a motion by the prosecutor is required. But unlike acceptance of responsibility there is no limit on how far a sentence can be reduced under § 5K1.1. In a typical year, between 10 and 15 percent of all federal defendants receive a § 5K1.1 downward departure motion.

The commission's requirement of a government motion changed existing practice. Under Fed. R. Crim. P. 35 defendants had been able to appeal directly to the sentencing judge for leniency, and could receive it, even without the support of the prosecutor. The Guideline, moreover, urges the sentencing judge to defer to the prosecutor. *See* § 5K1.1 (a)(1) (the sentencing judge should consider "the government's evaluation of the assistance rendered"); *id.* Application Note 3 ("substantial weight should be given to the government's evaluation of the extent of the defendant's assistance").

The Sentencing Table. The table on the next page shows how a sentencing range, expressed in months of imprisonment, is determined by the intersection of a defendant's criminal history category and offense level.

Sentencing Hypothetical. Defendant pleads guilty to a wire fraud scheme. The facts show that defendant, a partner in a law firm, encouraged four associates working under him on a case to inflate the amount of time that they spent on that case, the Smith matter, where the partner had reason to believe that the bills would not be scrutinized by in-house counsel, an old friend who he knew had a drinking problem. He knew this because he had inflated his own time in a previous case, the Jones matter. The associates never pushed back because they were afraid of potential negative feedback or other retaliation by the partner.

One of the associates finally reported the partner to firm management, which did an internal investigation. The firm learned that the client overpaid approximately $500,000 in fees on the Smith case and $200,000 on the older, Jones matter, for which the billing occurred outside the statute of limitations for a fraud charge. After the internal investigation was completed, the firm turned the results of its investigation over to the U.S. Attorney's Office. When the defendant learned that one of the associates on the Smith matter had received a grand jury subpoena, the defendant told the associate to "make sure to get yourself a good lawyer" and "if I were you I'd take the Fifth."

Defendant is indicted on the Smith matter and pleads guilty well prior to trial. The Guidelines potentially apply as follows under the 2023 Guidelines Manual (continues on page 1351).

SENTENCING TABLE
(in months of imprisonment)

	Offense Level	Criminal History Category (Criminal History Points)					
		I (0 or 1)	II (2 or 3)	III (4, 5, 6)	IV (7, 8, 9)	V (10, 11, 12)	VI (13 or more)
Zone A	1	0–6	0–6	0–6	0–6	0–6	0–6
	2	0–6	0–6	0–6	0–6	0–6	1–7
	3	0–6	0–6	0–6	0–6	2–8	3–9
	4	0–6	0–6	0–6	2–8	4–10	6–12
	5	0–6	0–6	1–7	4–10	6–12	9–15
	6	0–6	1–7	2–8	6–12	9–15	12–18
	7	0–6	2–8	4–10	8–14	12–18	15–21
	8	0–6	4–10	6–12	10–16	15–21	18–24
Zone B	9	4–10	6–12	8–14	12–18	18–24	21–27
	10	6–12	8–14	10–16	15–21	21–27	24–30
	11	8–14	10–16	12–18	18–24	24–30	27–33
Zone C	12	10–16	12–18	15–21	21–27	27–33	30–37
	13	12–18	15–21	18–24	24–30	30–37	33–41
Zone D	14	15–21	18–24	21–27	27–33	33–41	37–46
	15	18–24	21–27	24–30	30–37	37–46	41–51
	16	21–27	24–30	27–33	33–41	41–51	46–57
	17	24–30	27–33	30–37	37–46	46–57	51–63
	18	27–33	30–37	33–41	41–51	51–63	57–71
	19	30–37	33–41	37–46	46–57	57–71	63–78
	20	33–41	37–46	41–51	51–63	63–78	70–87
	21	37–46	41–51	46–57	57–71	70–87	77–96
	22	41–51	46–57	51–63	63–78	77–96	84–105
	23	46–57	51–63	57–71	70–87	84–105	92–115
	24	51–63	57–71	63–78	77–96	92–115	100–125
	25	57–71	63–78	70–87	84–105	100–125	110–137
	26	63–78	70–87	78–97	92–115	110–137	120–150
	27	70–87	78–97	87–108	100–125	120–150	130–162
	28	78–97	87–108	97–121	110–137	130–162	140–175
	29	87–108	97–121	108–135	121–151	140–175	151–188
	30	97–121	108–135	121–151	135–168	151–188	168–210
	31	108–135	121–151	135–168	151–188	168–210	188–235
	32	121–151	135–168	151–188	168–210	188–235	210–262
	33	135–168	151–188	168–210	188–235	210–262	235–293
	34	151–188	168–210	188–235	210–262	235–293	262–327
	35	168–210	188–235	210–262	235–293	262–327	292–365
	36	188–235	210–262	235–293	262–327	292–365	324–405
	37	210–262	235–293	262–327	292–365	324–405	360–life
	38	235–293	262–327	292–365	324–405	360–life	360–life
	39	262–327	292–365	324–405	360–life	360–life	360–life
	40	292–365	324–405	360–life	360–life	360–life	360–life
	41	324–405	360–life	360–life	360–life	360–life	360–life
	42	360–life	360–life	360–life	360–life	360–life	360–life
	43	life	life	life	life	life	life

C. The Sentencing Guidelines   1351

Base Offense Level Under USSG § 2B1.1:   **6**

Specific Offense Characteristics:

Amount of Loss> $550,000 per § 2B1.1(b): **+14**

Note that this figure is the sum of the intended loss for both the Smith matter (Offense of Conviction) and also the Jones matter (Relevant Conduct).

Adjustments

Vulnerable Victim § 3A1.1:	**+2**
Obstruction of Justice § 3C1 § 3B1.1.1:	**+2**
Organizer/Leader USSG § 3E1.1:	**+4**
Acceptance of Responsibility § 3E1.1:	**−3**
Total Offense Level	**26**

With a Criminal History of Category I, the relevant Guideline range for defendant is **63-78 Months**.

Defendant could negotiate the application of the Guidelines in working out a plea agreement with the prosecutor. For example, the application of both the Obstruction of Justice and Vulnerable Victim adjustments are likely debatable, factually and legally. He could attempt to compromise with the prosecutor, agreeing to the Vulnerable Victim adjustment if the prosecutor drops any claim to the Obstruction adjustment. Or he could try to persuade the prosecutor to litigate one or both of those adjustments at the sentencing hearing, although the prosecutor will normally seek as much finality in the agreement as possible. And there is always a risk that an aggressive probation officer will demand to see the prosecutor's entire case file, which may include interview memoranda that would lead the probation officer to take an independent position on an enhancement even if the prosecutor is willing to forgo it.

The next case considers how a defendant's criminal history affects a guideline sentence, and the possibility for a downward departure under the Guidelines where a defendant's criminal history exaggerates the defendant's culpability.

United States v. Leviner
31 F. Supp. 2d 23 (D. Mass. 1998)

GERTNER, District Judge.

• • •

The sentencing of Alexander Leviner (hereinafter "Leviner") raises two major issues:

• • •

Second, should this Court depart from the Guideline range on the grounds that Leviner's record—overwhelmingly motor vehicle violations and minor drug possession offenses—overstates his culpability and the likelihood of his recidivism? I conclude that Leviner's record does so, and thus I will depart downward. A system for evaluating criminal history, like the Federal Guidelines system, which assigns points for past convictions solely according to the length of sentence the defendant received, necessarily replicates disparities in state sentencing. Furthermore, even more profound concerns are raised where, as here, the defendant is African American, the convictions were largely motor vehicle offenses, for which the defendant was imprisoned. The scholarly and

Chapter XVI Incarceration: Bail, Pretrial Detention, and Sentencing

popular literature strongly suggests that there is racial disparity in the rates at which African Americans are stopped and prosecuted for traffic offenses. That literature, together with the specific facts about Leviner's record and background, compel me to depart from the Guideline range.

Alexander Leviner pled guilty to the charge of Felon in Possession of a Firearm in violation of 18 U.S.C. § 922(g)(1). The indictment charges Leviner with possessing a 9 mm Smith and Wesson, semiautomatic handgun, together with fourteen rounds of ammunition. Leviner, the indictment further charges, had previously been convicted of a crime punishable by a term of imprisonment exceeding one year.

The data on which this sentencing decision is based are as follows: A two-day hearing that was held on Defendant's Motion To Suppress, which described the circumstances of Leviner's arrest; (see Memorandum and Order dated June 29, 1998); the plea colloquy; and a two-day sentencing hearing.

I. FACTS

A. Offense

The car in which Leviner was a passenger was observed by police officers as traveling at a high rate of speed, without headlights, from an area in which shots had reportedly been fired. The officers followed the car and stopped it. The officers reported that the occupants of the car (the driver—Denise Cummings, the front seat passenger—Derrick Johnson, and Leviner, who was seated in the rear) were cooperative, that they produced the requested documentation (license and registration for the driver, identification for the passengers), answered all questions posed to them, and even agreed to be searched. But for the fact that Cumming's registration did not match the car she was driving, the officers were prepared to allow them to leave. As a result of the registration disparity, Leviner and the others were asked to step out of the car. At some point the officers found a holster on Leviner, and he fled. The officers apprehended him almost immediately and found the gun in question on the car floor near where Leviner had been sitting.

The Government has also represented that tests indicate that shots had been fired from Leviner's gun and a shell casing was found on the car floor. There was, however, no indication that the gun was fired at anyone in particular, or even that anyone was threatened by its use. The Government does not even make such an accusation.

The offense is unquestionably a serious one. The Assistant United States Attorney quite appropriately points out that this was not the mere possession of the firearm, but its firing. While the gun was not used to threaten anyone, it was nevertheless used.

B. Offender

Leviner has had a consistent employment record. He is a trained asbestos removal worker, regularly employed over the past ten years. Moreover, he was raised in a stable family situation, and has maintained close ties with his extended family and his children. Impressively, the courtroom was filed with family and friends for each hearing.

Additionally, while Leviner has a relatively long record, it consists almost entirely of motor vehicle offenses, and minor drug possession charges. Except for a conviction for assault when he was seventeen (Leviner is now thirty-three), his record is overwhelmingly non-violent.

If I were to apply the Sentencing Guidelines to this case uncritically, none of these facts would make much of a difference. Instead, what would matter most in determining Leviner's sentence would be two numbers on a grid—the fact that this offender has a relatively high criminal history score—a Category V, without regard to its nature, and the fact this Felon in Possession of a Firearm offense is graded more severely because Leviner has two felony convictions, without regard to the fact that one conviction took place two weeks after Leviner possessed the gun.

While the Sentencing Guidelines were designed to eliminate unwarranted disparities in sentencing, and constrain a judge's discretion, they are not to be applied mechanistically, wholly ignoring fairness, logic, and the underlying statutory scheme.

II. GUIDELINE CALCULATIONS

The Guideline calculations reflected in the Presentence Report, and endorsed by the Government, are the following:

A. The base offense level: Based on Probation's conclusion that Leviner has two prior convictions for controlled substance offenses, under USSG § 2K2.1(a)(2) the offense level is 24.

I reject this interpretation for the reasons described in Section III. Consequently, considering only the one felony conviction within the meaning of the Guidelines — the one that actually occurred prior to the firearm possession — the base offense level is 20.

B. Adjustment for Acceptance of Responsibility: All parties agree that Leviner is entitled to a 3 point reduction for acceptance of responsibility.

C. Total offense level: The offense level is 17.

D. Criminal History: Leviner's criminal history score, according to the Presentence Report, is a Category V, based on a score of 11.

I reject this calculation for the reasons described infra in Section IV. Instead, I conclude that Leviner's criminal history vastly overstates his true culpability and his likelihood of recidivism on this offense. Accordingly, I base my calculations on a criminal history score of 4.

Based on the Sentencing Table, the Guideline imprisonment range is 30 to 37 months. I will sentence this defendant to a term of 30 months.

• • •

IV. WHETHER LEVINER'S CRIMINAL HISTORY OVERSTATES HIS CULPABILITY

Leviner's criminal history category score is 11. It is the second highest category that an offender can receive under the Sentencing Guidelines; a Category V out of a possible VI. If the numerical scores accurately reflect Leviner's likelihood of recidivism, I would be deeply concerned, but they do not. Indeed, Leviner's case acutely demonstrates the limitations of the criminal history rankings under the Guidelines.

Leviner receives seven criminal history points as a result of motor vehicle offenses, all but one of which was operating a motor vehicle after suspension of his license:

1) On January 20, 1994, Leviner used a motor vehicle without authority and illegally possessed marijuana. Charges were brought in the Boston Municipal Court, Leviner was sentenced to three months in the House of Correction, suspended. For this, he received one criminal history point under the Guidelines.

2) On September 21, 1994, he was charged in the Waltham District Court with operating a motor vehicle after his license had been suspended (2d offense). On May 31, 1995, he received a six months House of Correction sentence, suspended. One criminal history point was assigned.

3) On March 2, 1995, he was arrested by the Brookline Police and charged with operating after his license was suspended and operating an uninsured motor vehicle. On November 5, 1997, he received sixty days in the House of Correction. As a result of the sentence, two criminal history points were assigned.

4) On April 21, 1995, he was arrested by the Milton Police Department, and charged with operating a motor vehicle after his license was suspended, and, on the same day, pled guilty to the charge. He was sentenced to ten days in a House of Correction. One criminal history point was assigned.

When the instant offense was committed on September 14, 1997, Leviner was on probation for the motor vehicle convictions in Quincy and Waltham, and the Boston Municipal Court use without authority/marijuana possession case. As a result, two more points were added to his score pursuant to U.S.S.G. § 4A1.1(d), for a total of seven points.

The remaining four criminal history points were for possession of a class B substance (crack cocaine), over nine years ago, when Leviner was twenty-three years old, and for the conviction which followed the instant felon in possession case, on September 30, 1997, for possession with intent to distribute a class D substance, marijuana.

The Commission made certain compromises when it promulgated the criminal history guidelines. Recognizing that those compromises necessarily diluted the validity of the criminal history measure, U.S.S.G. § 4A1.3 authorizes a downward departure when the criminal history category over-represents the "seriousness of the defendant's criminal history or the likelihood that the defendant will commit further crimes." U.S.S.G. § 4A1.3 (1997).

Obviously, trial courts should not make this determination out of thin air. Rather, it is appropriate to analyze the purpose of the criminal history system, its structure and its limitations, and then to determine where this defendant's record fits: Does the record suggest the likelihood of recidivism for a felon in possession charge, as opposed to minor drug possession or motor vehicle offenses? How does the defendant's record compare with other Category V offenders? What does the record teach the Court about the nature of this offender, relative to other information available to the Court?

A. Purpose of the Criminal History System

Criminal history has been described by one commentator as an "anomaly" in the guidelines system. Like traditional offender characteristics, such as employment history and family background which the Commission rejected for the most part in the determination of the sentence, criminal history has no direct relationship to the offender's current offense of conviction. Employment history and family background factors arguably point in opposite directions. Criminal history, so the Commission thought, did not. Instead, criminal history was found to be a strong predictor of recidivism and a good measure of culpability. But while that may be so in general, in particular cases, as with Leviner, the relationship breaks down.

B. The Significance of Measuring Criminal History Points by the Length of Sentence the Prior Conviction Received

The current system scores convictions based on the length of the sentence imposed for the offense. Prior sentences of more than thirteen months receive three points, sentences between six and thirteen months receive two points, and those of less than six months receive one point. See § 4A1.1. The system has three problems, all of which resonate in this case:

1. The criminal history score does not accurately reflect the relatively minor nature of Leviner's record.

The criminal history system of the Guidelines does not accurately account for differences in the seriousness of the defendant's prior convictions. In the case of Leviner's record, for example, his eighteen month term for possession with intent to distribute drugs (the May 13, 1997, charge) would receive the same score as would an eighteen year sentence for murder. Furthermore, the cumulative effect of all the minor convictions and their interrelationships is to put Leviner in the same class as would be a far more serious offender.

2. The criminal history score does not accurately reflect the non-violent nature of Leviner's record.

Since the criminal history system is focused entirely on the sentences received for the prior convictions, it does not make distinctions concerning the kind of offense: Motor vehicle versus fraud, violent versus non-violent. Indeed, the violent/non-violent line, for example, may well be more meaningful in terms of predicting recidivism and evaluating the offender's culpability.

Again, in Leviner's case, except for one offense, at age seventeen, none of the convictions reflect a crime of violence, or indeed, even the use of a gun. The instant charge is the first.

To treat this man as if he were only a point on a grid, the intersection of an offense score of seventeen and a criminal history of Category V, would do violence to the purposes of the Sentencing Guidelines. It would treat someone convicted of Felon in Possession of a Firearm with a minor record, solely because he had a few sentences in the criminal history (1), (2), and, (3) range, the same as someone with multiple, violent crimes, and multiple ten to fifteen year sentences. It would create a new form of disparity, treating offenders that are completely different in a like way.

3. The criminal history score mirrors disparities in state sentencing, and in particular, racial disparities.

By counting the imprisonment that the defendant has received for the prior offenses, the system effectively replicates disparities in sentencing in the state system. This would include not only the ordinary disparities between similarly situated defendants, but racial disparities.

Motor vehicle offenses, in particular, raise deep concerns about racial disparity. Studies from a number of scholars, and articles in the popular literature have focused on the fact that African American motorists are stopped and prosecuted for traffic stops, more than any other citizens. And if that is so, then it is not unreasonable to believe that African Americans would also be imprisoned at a higher rate for these offenses, as well.

Leviner's motor vehicle offenses were mainly for driving while his license was suspended (except for one use without authority) — not one charge involved driving erratically, or violating a traffic law. The distinction is important. While I can make no judgment about what happened specifically with Leviner's motor vehicle charges, surely, the studies described above raise questions about what drew the officer's attention to Leviner in the first place.

Moreover, these stops evolved into "countable" offenses under the Guidelines only because they were offenses for which Leviner received more than thirty days' imprisonment. Again, without knowing the specific facts surrounding each sentence, this record raises concerns at the very least. Would others have received the same sentence who were similarly situated, no matter how often they had been apprehended driving after their license had been suspended?

C. The Defendant's Overall Record Relative to Other Offender Information

Leviner's record shows a man who, until 1997, worked consistently and took care of his family. He had an eleven year period with nothing but operating after suspended license offenses, with two exceptions — a possession with intent conviction arising from a 1985 arrest in which he was found in possession of five $10 bags of marijuana and a 1994 use without authority and possession of marijuana charge.

In 1997 circumstances changed. Leviner believed he was passed over for more responsible work at his place of employment because of his race. More serious offenses followed — possession with intent to distribute marijuana and this Felon in Possession offense. While age and employment records have been rejected by the Commission as not ordinarily relevant, see e.g., USSG §§ 5H1.1 (age); 5H1.5 (employment record); 5H1.6 (family ties and responsibilities), in this case they help to illuminate the relationship between this record and Leviner's likely recidivism and culpability. A succession of non-violent offenses, and minor drug possession charges, mixed in with consistent employment and family obligations suggest someone whose drug problems had never been addressed in the past and thus he continued to re-offend. If the purpose of criminal history computations is to predict recidivism and reflect culpability, this record at the most suggests the likelihood that without help, Leviner will repeat his minor drug and motor vehicle crimes — not gun offenses or crimes of violence.

1356 Chapter XVI Incarceration: Bail, Pretrial Detention, and Sentencing

As noted above, to treat this defendant the same as an offender with a Category V criminal history of violent offenses, no employment history to speak of, or family life, would be to create a new, and even more grotesque disparity than in the past. I will consider Leviner as having a criminal history of four, taking out the seven points attributable to the motor vehicle offenses.

• • •

VI. SENTENCE

In order to deal with Leviner's obvious drug problem and mental issues, I have ordered thirty months' incarceration, at a facility to address those problems. F.C.I. Raybrook has been recommended in order for Leviner to participate in the 500 hour Bureau of Prisons ("BOP") Drug Treatment Program and BOP mental health program. BOP will report the results of this placement to me, on a regular basis, should the Bureau agree.

Supervised release of three years will follow, during which time Leviner will be subject to specific conditions, including mental health and drug counseling.

SO ORDERED.

NOTES AND QUESTIONS

1. Judge Gertner describes some of defendant's personal characteristics and the details of his criminal record as a prelude to stating, "If I were to apply the Sentencing Guidelines uncritically to this case none of these facts would make much of a difference." What does she mean?

2. The district court is not just freelancing here but is sentencing pursuant to a recognized departure for situations where the Guidelines' criminal history calculation overrepresents the "seriousness of the defendant's criminal history or the likelihood that the defendant will commit future crimes." Are the court's three criticisms of the Guidelines' criminal history calculation system equally valid? Should the court have also discounted for the fact that many of the sentences were suspended?

3. The court appears to assume that most of defendant's motor vehicle offenses were the result of traffic stops, and cites to a wealth of scholarly authority on selective enforcement of traffic regulations. Were those laws selectively enforced here? Does that matter? How can the court be sure that the charges did not involve "driving erratically or violating a traffic law"? Should that matter?

4. The court describes criminal history as an "anomaly" in the Guidelines system. What makes criminal history anomalous? What does the court mean when it states that certain offender characteristics — which the Commission largely rejected as relevant to sentencing — "arguably point in opposite directions"?

5. Is the court's consideration of the "not ordinarily relevant" facts of defendant's employment history and family ties in connection with the downward departure simply a clever attempt to do an end run around the Guidelines? Or is it a legitimate effort to consider § 4A1.3's inquiry about likelihood of recidivism? Is it both? Note that the government apparently chose not to appeal from this sentence.

———

At the time *Mistretta* was decided it may not have been clear to the Supreme Court how the Guidelines would actually operate. From the Sentencing Reform Act itself, the focus of Mistretta's separation-of-powers challenge, the degree to which judges would be tasked with extensive factfinding and the sentencing impact of those factual determinations was not obvious—and it might not have mattered. The sentencing backdrop against which the act was passed had two significant features: (1) judges could rely on virtually any sort of information in imposing a sentence and (2) legislatures could label virtually any aspect of criminal conduct as a "sentencing factor" as opposed to an element of the crime.

The first of these characteristics was the result of *Williams v. New York*, 337 U.S. 241 (1949). In *Williams* a New York state court trial judge imposed a death sentence on a murder defendant even though the jury had recommended life imprisonment. The judge's decision was based on information obtained through the presentence report and "through other sources" that were not disclosed including information regarding other crimes for which the defendant had not been convicted and information indicating that the defendant had "a morbid sexuality." In other words, the trial judge both overrode the jury's decision on punishment and also imposed the death penalty based on what appears to be pure and rank hearsay. The Supreme Court nonetheless upheld the sentence, noting without irony that "progressive efforts to improve the administration of justice" and "modern penology" require that probation departments have wide latitude in conducting their investigations in order to enable "individualiz[ed] punishments." Are there no due process rights at a sentencing hearing? Remarkably, *Williams* was cited as good law not only in *Apprendi, Blakely,* and *Booker—see infra*—but as recently as 2022 by Justice Sotomayor, writing for the Court in *Concepcion v. United States*, 597 U.S. 481, 486 (2022).

The notion of a "sentencing factor," a part of the sentencing landscape that predated the Guidelines, is reflected in *McMillan v. Pennsylvania*, 477 U.S. 79, 86 (1986). In *McMillan* the Court considered a challenge to a Pennsylvania statute that provided that anyone convicted of certain felonies would be subject to a mandatory minimum sentence if the judge found, by a preponderance of evidence, that the person "visibly possessed a firearm" in the course of committing the offense. The Court found that the legislature had permissibly defined visible possession as a sentencing factor, rather than an element of the offense, and that this designation authorized the judge, rather than the jury, to find this fact by a preponderance of evidence without violating the Constitution.

Nine years later, the Court decided *United States v. Gaudin*, 515 U.S. 506 (1995), recommitting itself to the power of the jury to decide all elements of a charged crime. The Sixth Amendment was now on a collision course with the Sentencing Guidelines. Do state and federal legislative bodies have unlimited authority to declare conduct that increases a sentence to be a "sentencing factor" or a "sentencing enhancement" and not an element of the crime, and thereby eliminate a defendant's right to have a unanimous jury find that the government had proven that conduct beyond a reasonable doubt?

Booker v. United States
543 U.S. 220 (2005)

Justice STEVENS delivered the opinion of the Court in part.

The question presented in each of these cases is whether an application of the Federal Sentencing Guidelines violated the Sixth Amendment. In each case, the courts below held that binding rules set forth in the Guidelines limited the severity of the sentence that the judge could lawfully impose on the defendant based on the facts found by the jury at his trial. In both cases the courts rejected, on the basis of our decision in *Blakely v. Washington* (2004), the Government's recommended application of the Sentencing Guidelines because the proposed sentences were based on additional facts that the sentencing judge found by a preponderance of the evidence. We hold that both courts correctly concluded that the Sixth Amendment as construed in *Blakely* does apply to the Sentencing Guidelines. In a separate opinion authored by Justice Breyer, the Court concludes that in light of this holding, two provisions of the Sentencing Reform Act of 1984 (SRA) that have the effect of making the Guidelines mandatory must be invalidated in order to allow the statute to operate in a manner consistent with congressional intent.

I

Respondent Booker was charged with possession with intent to distribute at least 50 grams of cocaine base (crack). Having heard evidence that he had 92.5 grams in his duffel bag, the jury found him guilty of violating 21 U.S.C. § 841(a)(1). That statute prescribes a minimum sentence of 10 years in prison and a maximum sentence of life for that offense. § 841(b)(1)(A)(iii).

Based upon Booker's criminal history and the quantity of drugs found by the jury, the Sentencing Guidelines required the District Court Judge to select a "base" sentence of not less than 210 nor more than 262 months in prison. The judge, however, held a post-trial sentencing proceeding and concluded by a preponderance of the evidence that Booker had possessed an additional 566 grams of crack and that he was guilty of obstructing justice. Those findings mandated that the judge select a sentence between 360 months and life imprisonment; the judge imposed a sentence at the low end of the range. Thus, instead of the sentence of 21 years and 10 months that the judge could have imposed on the basis of the facts proved to the jury beyond a reasonable doubt, Booker received a 30-year sentence.

Over the dissent of Judge Easterbrook, the Court of Appeals for the Seventh Circuit held that this application of the Sentencing Guidelines conflicted with our holding in *Apprendi v. New Jersey* (2000), that "[o]ther than the fact of a prior conviction, any fact that increases the penalty for a crime beyond the prescribed statutory maximum must be submitted to a jury, and proved beyond a reasonable doubt." The majority relied on our holding in *Blakely* that "the 'statutory maximum' for *Apprendi* purposes is the maximum sentence a judge may impose solely on the basis of the facts reflected in the jury verdict or admitted by the defendant." The court held that the sentence violated the Sixth Amendment, and remanded with instructions to the District Court either to sentence respondent within the sentencing range supported by the jury's findings or to hold a separate sentencing hearing before a jury.

Respondent Fanfan was charged with conspiracy to distribute and to possess with intent to distribute at least 500 grams of cocaine in violation of 21 U.S.C. §§ 846, 841(a)(1), and 841(b)(1)(B)(ii). He was convicted by the jury after it answered "Yes" to the question "Was the amount of cocaine 500 or more grams?" Under the Guidelines, without additional findings of fact, the maximum sentence authorized by the jury verdict was imprisonment for 78 months.

A few days after our decision in *Blakely*, the trial judge conducted a sentencing hearing at which he found additional facts that, under the Guidelines, would have authorized a sentence in the 188-to-235-month range. Specifically, he found that respondent Fanfan was responsible for 2.5 kilograms of cocaine powder, and 261.6 grams of crack. He also concluded that respondent had been an organizer, leader, manager, or supervisor in the criminal activity. Both findings were made by a preponderance of the evidence. Under the Guidelines, these additional findings would have required an enhanced sentence of 15 or 16 years instead of the 5 or 6 years authorized by the jury verdict alone. Relying not only on the majority opinion in *Blakely*, but also on the categorical statements in the dissenting opinions and in the Solicitor General's brief in *Blakely*, the judge concluded that he could not follow the particular provisions of the Sentencing Guidelines "which involve drug quantity and role enhancement."

Expressly refusing to make "any blanket decision about the federal guidelines," he followed the provisions of the Guidelines that did not implicate the Sixth Amendment by imposing a sentence on respondent "based solely upon the jury verdict in this case."

Following the denial of its motion to correct the sentence in Fanfan's case, the Government filed a notice of appeal in the Court of Appeals for the First Circuit, and a petition in this Court for a writ of certiorari before judgment. Because of the importance of the questions presented, we granted that petition, as well as a similar petition filed by the Government in Booker's case. In both petitions, the Government asks us to determine whether our *Apprendi* line of cases applies to the Sentencing Guidelines, and if so, what portions of the Guidelines remain in effect.

In this opinion, we explain why we agree with the lower courts' answer to the first question. In a separate opinion for the Court, Justice Breyer explains the Court's answer to the second question.

II

It has been settled throughout our history that the Constitution protects every criminal defendant "against conviction except upon proof beyond a reasonable doubt of every fact necessary to constitute the crime with which he is charged." It is equally clear that the "Constitution gives a criminal defendant the right to demand that a jury find him guilty of all the elements of the crime with which he is charged." These basic precepts, firmly rooted in the common law, have provided the basis for recent decisions interpreting modern criminal statutes and sentencing procedures.

In *Jones v. United States* (1999), we considered the federal carjacking statute, which provides three different maximum sentences depending on the extent of harm to the victim: 15 years in jail if there was no serious injury to a victim, 25 years if there was "serious bodily injury," and life in prison if death resulted. In spite of the fact that the statute "at first glance has a look to it suggesting [that the provisions relating to the extent of harm to the victim] are only sentencing provisions," we concluded that the harm to the victim was an element of the crime. That conclusion was supported by the statutory text and structure, and was influenced by our desire to avoid the constitutional issues implicated by a contrary holding, which would have reduced the jury's role "to the relative importance of low-level gatekeeping." Foreshadowing the result we reach today, we noted that our holding was consistent with a "rule requiring jury determination of facts that raise a sentencing ceiling" in state and federal sentencing guidelines systems.

In *Apprendi v. New Jersey* (2000), the defendant pleaded guilty to second-degree possession of a firearm for an unlawful purpose, which carried a prison term of 5-to-10 years. Thereafter, the trial court found that his conduct had violated New Jersey's "hate crime" law because it was racially motivated, and imposed a 12-year sentence. This Court set aside the enhanced sentence. We held: "Other than the fact of a prior conviction, any fact that increases the penalty for a crime beyond the prescribed statutory maximum must be submitted to a jury, and proved beyond a reasonable doubt."

The fact that New Jersey labeled the hate crime a "sentence enhancement" rather than a separate criminal act was irrelevant for constitutional purposes. As a matter of simple justice, it seemed obvious that the procedural safeguards designed to protect Apprendi from punishment for the possession of a firearm should apply equally to his violation of the hate crime statute. Merely using the label "sentence enhancement" to describe the latter did not provide a principled basis for treating the two crimes differently.

In *Ring v. Arizona* (2002), we reaffirmed our conclusion that the characterization of critical facts is constitutionally irrelevant. There, we held that it was impermissible for "the trial

Chapter XVI Incarceration: Bail, Pretrial Detention, and Sentencing

judge, sitting alone" to determine the presence or absence of the aggravating factors required by Arizona law for imposition of the death penalty. "If a State makes an increase in a defendant's authorized punishment contingent on the finding of a fact, that fact—no matter how the State labels it—must be found by a jury beyond a reasonable doubt." Our opinion made it clear that ultimately, while the procedural error in Ring's case might have been harmless because the necessary finding was implicit in the jury's guilty verdict, "the characterization of a fact or circumstance as an 'element' or a 'sentencing factor' is not determinative of the question 'who decides,' judge or jury."

In *Blakely v. Washington* (2004), we dealt with a determinate sentencing scheme similar to the Federal Sentencing Guidelines. There the defendant pleaded guilty to kidnaping, a class B felony punishable by a term of not more than 10 years. Other provisions of Washington law, comparable to the Federal Sentencing Guidelines, mandated a "standard" sentence of 49-to-53 months, unless the judge found aggravating facts justifying an exceptional sentence. Although the prosecutor recommended a sentence in the standard range, the judge found that the defendant had acted with "'deliberate cruelty'" and sentenced him to 90 months.

For reasons explained in *Jones, Apprendi,* and *Ring,* the requirements of the Sixth Amendment were clear. The application of Washington's sentencing scheme violated the defendant's right to have the jury find the existence of "'any particular fact'" that the law makes essential to his punishment. That right is implicated whenever a judge seeks to impose a sentence that is not solely based on "facts reflected in the jury verdict or admitted by the defendant." We rejected the State's argument that the jury verdict was sufficient to authorize a sentence within the general 10-year sentence for class B felonies, noting that under Washington law, the judge was required to find additional facts in order to impose the greater 90-month sentence. Our precedents, we explained, make clear "that the 'statutory maximum' for *Apprendi* purposes is the maximum sentence a judge may impose solely on the basis of the facts reflected in the jury verdict or admitted by the defendant." The determination that the defendant acted with deliberate cruelty, like the determination in *Apprendi* that the defendant acted with racial malice, increased the sentence that the defendant could have otherwise received. Since this fact was found by a judge using a preponderance of the evidence standard, the sentence violated Blakely's Sixth Amendment rights.

As the dissenting opinions in *Blakely* recognized, there is no distinction of constitutional significance between the Federal Sentencing Guidelines and the Washington procedures at issue in that case. This conclusion rests on the premise, common to both systems, that the relevant sentencing rules are mandatory and impose binding requirements on all sentencing judges.

If the Guidelines as currently written could be read as merely advisory provisions that recommended, rather than required, the selection of particular sentences in response to differing sets of facts, their use would not implicate the Sixth Amendment. We have never doubted the authority of a judge to exercise broad discretion in imposing a sentence within a statutory range. *Williams v. New York* (1949). Indeed, everyone agrees that the constitutional issues presented by these cases would have been avoided entirely if Congress had omitted from the SRA the provisions that make the Guidelines binding on district judges; it is that circumstance that makes the Court's answer to the second question presented possible. For when a trial judge exercises his discretion to select a specific sentence within a defined range, the defendant has no right to a jury determination of the facts that the judge deems relevant.

The Guidelines as written, however, are not advisory; they are mandatory and binding on all judges. While subsection (a) of § 3553 of the sentencing statute lists the Sentencing Guidelines as one factor to be considered in imposing a sentence, subsection (b) directs that the court "*shall* impose a sentence of the kind, and within the range" established by the Guidelines, subject to departures in specific, limited cases. (Emphasis added.) Because they

C. The Sentencing Guidelines   1361

are binding on judges, we have consistently held that the Guidelines have the force and effect of laws.

The availability of a departure in specified circumstances does not avoid the constitutional issue, just as it did not in *Blakely* itself. The Guidelines permit departures from the prescribed sentencing range in cases in which the judge "finds that there exists an aggravating or mitigating circumstance of a kind, or to a degree, not adequately taken into consideration by the Sentencing Commission in formulating the guidelines that should result in a sentence different from that described." At first glance, one might believe that the ability of a district judge to depart from the Guidelines means that she is bound only by the statutory maximum. Were this the case, there would be no *Apprendi* problem. Importantly, however, departures are not available in every case, and in fact are unavailable in most. In most cases, as a matter of law, the Commission will have adequately taken all relevant factors into account, and no departure will be legally permissible. In those instances, the judge is bound to impose a sentence within the Guidelines range. It was for this reason that we rejected a similar argument in *Blakely*, holding that although the Washington statute allowed the judge to impose a sentence outside the sentencing range for "'substantial and compelling reasons,'" that exception was not available for Blakely himself. The sentencing judge would have been reversed had he invoked the departure section to justify the sentence.

Booker's case illustrates the mandatory nature of the Guidelines. The jury convicted him of possessing at least 50 grams of crack in violation of 21 U.S.C. § 841(b)(1)(A)(iii) based on evidence that he had 92.5 grams of crack in his duffel bag. Under these facts, the Guidelines specified an offense level of 32, which, given the defendant's criminal history category, authorized a sentence of 210-to-262 months. Booker's is a run-of-the-mill drug case, and does not present any factors that were inadequately considered by the Commission. The sentencing judge would therefore have been reversed had he not imposed a sentence within the level 32 Guidelines range.

Booker's actual sentence, however, was 360 months, almost 10 years longer than the Guidelines range supported by the jury verdict alone. To reach this sentence, the judge found facts beyond those found by the jury: namely, that Booker possessed 566 grams of crack in addition to the 92.5 grams in his duffel bag. The jury never heard any evidence of the additional drug quantity, and the judge found it true by a preponderance of the evidence. Thus, just as in Blakely, "the jury's verdict alone does not authorize the sentence. The judge acquires that authority only upon finding some additional fact." There is no relevant distinction between the sentence imposed pursuant to the Washington statutes in *Blakely* and the sentences imposed pursuant to the Federal Sentencing Guidelines in these cases.

In his dissent, Justice Breyer argues on historical grounds that the Guidelines scheme is constitutional across the board. He points to traditional judicial authority to increase sentences to take account of any unusual blameworthiness in the manner employed in committing a crime, an authority that the Guidelines require to be exercised consistently throughout the system. This tradition, however, does not provide a sound guide to enforcement of the Sixth Amendment's guarantee of a jury trial in today's world.

It is quite true that once determinate sentencing had fallen from favor, American judges commonly determined facts justifying a choice of a heavier sentence on account of the manner in which particular defendants acted. In 1986, however, our own cases first recognized a new trend in the legislative regulation of sentencing when we considered the significance of facts selected by legislatures that not only authorized, or even mandated, heavier sentences than would otherwise have been imposed, but increased the range of sentences possible for the underlying crime. Provisions for such enhancements of the permissible sentencing range reflected growing and wholly justified legislative concern about the proliferation and variety of drug crimes and their frequent identification with firearms offenses.

The effect of the increasing emphasis on facts that enhanced sentencing ranges, however, was to increase the judge's power and diminish that of the jury. It became the judge, not the jury, who determined the upper limits of sentencing, and the facts determined were not required to be raised before trial or proved by more than a preponderance.

As the enhancements became greater, the jury's finding of the underlying crime became less significant. And the enhancements became very serious indeed.

As it thus became clear that sentencing was no longer taking place in the tradition that Justice Breyer invokes, the Court was faced with the issue of preserving an ancient guarantee under a new set of circumstances. The new sentencing practice forced the Court to address the question how the right of jury trial could be preserved, in a meaningful way guaranteeing that the jury would still stand between the individual and the power of the government under the new sentencing regime. And it is the new circumstances, not a tradition or practice that the new circumstances have superseded, that have led us to the answer first considered in *Jones* and developed in *Apprendi* and subsequent cases culminating with this one. It is an answer not motivated by Sixth Amendment formalism, but by the need to preserve Sixth Amendment substance.

III

The Government advances three arguments in support of its submission that we should not apply our reasoning in *Blakely* to the Federal Sentencing Guidelines. It contends that *Blakely* is distinguishable because the Guidelines were promulgated by a Commission rather than the Legislature; that principles of stare decisis require us to follow four earlier decisions that are arguably inconsistent with *Blakely*; and that the application of *Blakely* to the Guidelines would conflict with separation-of-powers principles reflected in *Mistretta v. United States* (1989). These arguments are unpersuasive.

Commission v. Legislature

In our judgment the fact that the Guidelines were promulgated by the Sentencing Commission, rather than Congress, lacks constitutional significance. In order to impose the defendants' sentences under the Guidelines, the judges in these cases were required to find an additional fact, such as drug quantity, just as the judge found the additional fact of serious bodily injury to the victim in *Jones*. As far as the defendants are concerned, they face significantly higher sentences—in Booker's case almost 10 years higher—because a judge found true by a preponderance of the evidence a fact that was never submitted to the jury. Regardless of whether Congress or a Sentencing Commission concluded that a particular fact must be proved in order to sentence a defendant within a particular range, "[t]he Framers would not have thought it too much to demand that, before depriving a man of [ten] more years of his liberty, the State should suffer the modest inconvenience of submitting its accusation to 'the unanimous suffrage of twelve of his equals and neighbours,' rather than a lone employee of the State."

The Government correctly notes that in *Apprendi* we referred to "'any fact that increases the penalty for a crime beyond the prescribed statutory maximum (4)27.'" The simple answer, of course, is that we were only considering a statute in that case; we expressly declined to consider the Guidelines. It was therefore appropriate to state the rule in that case in terms of a "statutory maximum" rather than answering a question not properly before us.

More important than the language used in our holding in *Apprendi* are the principles we sought to vindicate. Those principles are unquestionably applicable to the Guidelines. They are not the product of recent innovations in our jurisprudence, but rather have their genesis in the ideals our constitutional tradition assimilated from the common law. The Framers of the Constitution understood the threat of "judicial despotism" that could arise from "arbitrary punishments upon arbitrary convictions" without the benefit of a jury in criminal cases. The Founders presumably carried this concern from England, in which the right to a jury trial had been enshrined since the Magna Carta. As we noted in *Apprendi*:

> [T]he historical foundation for our recognition of these principles extends down centuries into the common law. "[T]o guard against a spirit of oppression and tyranny on the part of rulers," and "as the great bulwark of [our] civil and political liberties," trial by jury has been understood to require that "the truth of every accusation, whether preferred in the shape of indictment, information, or appeal, should afterwards be confirmed by the unanimous suffrage of twelve of [the defendant's] equals and neighbours. . . ."

Regardless of whether the legal basis of the accusation is in a statute or in guidelines promulgated by an independent commission, the principles behind the jury trial right are equally applicable.

Stare Decisis

The Government next argues that four recent cases preclude our application of *Blakely* to the Sentencing Guidelines. We disagree. In *United States v. Dunnigan* (1993), we held that the provisions of the Guidelines that require a sentence enhancement if the judge determines that the defendant committed perjury do not violate the privilege of the accused to testify on her own behalf. There was no contention that the enhancement was invalid because it resulted in a more severe sentence than the jury verdict had authorized. Accordingly, we found this case indistinguishable from *United States v. Grayson* (1978), a pre-Guidelines case in which we upheld a similar sentence increase. Applying *Blakely* to the Guidelines would invalidate a sentence that relied on such an enhancement if the resulting sentence was outside the range authorized by the jury verdict. Nevertheless, there are many situations in which the district judge might find that the enhancement is warranted, yet still sentence the defendant within the range authorized by the jury. Thus, while the reach of *Dunnigan* may be limited, we need not overrule it.

In *Witte v. United States* (1995), we held that the Double Jeopardy Clause did not bar a prosecution for conduct that had provided the basis for an enhancement of the defendant's sentence in a prior case. "We concluded that 'consideration of information about the defendant's character and conduct at sentencing does not result in "punishment" for any offense other than the one of which the defendant was convicted.' Rather, the defendant is 'punished only for the fact that the present offense was carried out in a manner that warrants increased punishment. . . .'" In *Watts*, relying on *Witte*, we held that the Double Jeopardy Clause permitted a court to consider acquitted conduct in sentencing a defendant under the Guidelines. In neither *Witte* nor *Watts* was there any contention that the sentencing enhancement had exceeded the sentence authorized by the jury verdict in violation of the Sixth Amendment. The issue we confront today simply was not presented.

Finally, in *Edwards v. United States* (1998), the Court held that a jury's general verdict finding the defendants guilty of a conspiracy involving either cocaine or crack supported a sentence based on their involvement with both drugs. Even though the indictment had charged that their conspiracy embraced both, they argued on appeal that the verdict limited the judge's sentencing authority. We recognized that the defendants' statutory and constitutional claims might have had merit if it had been possible to argue that their crack-related activities were not part of the same conspiracy as their cocaine activities. But they failed to make that argument, and, based on our review of the record which showed "a series of interrelated drug transactions involving both cocaine and crack," we concluded that no such claim could succeed.

None of our prior cases is inconsistent with today's decision. Stare decisis does not compel us to limit *Blakely*'s holding.

Separation of Powers

Finally, the Government and, to a lesser extent, Justice Breyer's dissent, argue that any holding that would require Guidelines sentencing factors to be proved to a jury beyond a reasonable doubt would effectively transform them into a code defining elements of criminal offenses. The result, according to the Government, would be an unconstitutional grant to the Sentencing Commission of the inherently legislative power to define criminal elements.

There is no merit to this argument because the Commission's authority to identify the facts relevant to sentencing decisions and to determine the impact of such facts on federal sentences is precisely the same whether one labels such facts "sentencing factors" or "elements" of crimes. Our decision in *Mistretta*, upholding the validity of the delegation of that authority, is unaffected by the characterization of such facts, or by the procedures used to find such facts in particular sentencing proceedings. Indeed, we rejected a similar argument in *Jones*:

> Contrary to the dissent's suggestion, the constitutional proposition that drives our concern in no way "call[s] into question the principle that the definition of the elements of a criminal offense is entrusted to the legislature." The constitutional guarantees that give rise to our concern in no way restrict the ability of legislatures to identify the conduct they wish to characterize as criminal or to define the facts whose proof is essential to the establishment of criminal liability. The constitutional safeguards that figure in our analysis concern not the identity of the elements defining criminal liability but only the required procedures for finding the facts that determine the maximum permissible punishment; these are the safeguards going to the formality of notice, the identity of the factfinder, and the burden of proof.

Our holding today does not call into question any aspect of our decision in *Mistretta*. That decision was premised on an understanding that the Commission, rather than performing adjudicatory functions, instead makes political and substantive decisions. We noted that the promulgation of the Guidelines was much like other activities in the Judicial Branch, such as the creation of the Federal Rules of Evidence, all of which are nonadjudicatory activities. We also noted that "Congress may delegate to the Judicial Branch nonadjudicatory functions that do not trench upon the prerogatives of another Branch and that are appropriate to the central mission of the Judiciary." While we recognized that the Guidelines were more substantive than the Rules of Evidence or other nonadjudicatory functions delegated to the Judicial Branch, we nonetheless concluded that such a delegation did not exceed Congress' powers.

Further, a recognition that the Commission did not exercise judicial authority, but was more properly thought of as exercising some sort of legislative power, ibid., was essential to our holding. If the Commission in fact performed adjudicatory functions, it would have violated Article III because some of the members were not Article III judges. As we explained:

> [T]he "practical consequences" of locating the Commission within the Judicial Branch pose no threat of undermining the integrity of the Judicial Branch or of expanding the powers of the Judiciary beyond constitutional bounds by uniting within the Branch the political or quasi-legislative power of the Commission with the judicial power of the courts. [The Commission's] powers are not united with the powers of the Judiciary in a way that has meaning for separation-of-powers analysis. Whatever constitutional problems might arise if the powers of the Commission were vested in a court, the Commission is not a court, does not exercise judicial power, and is not controlled by or accountable to members of the Judicial Branch.

We have thus always recognized the fact that the Commission is an independent agency that exercises policymaking authority delegated to it by Congress. Nothing in our holding today is inconsistent with our decision in *Mistretta*.

C. The Sentencing Guidelines 1365

IV

All of the foregoing supports our conclusion that our holding in *Blakely* applies to the Sentencing Guidelines. We recognize, as we did in *Jones, Apprendi*, and *Blakely*, that in some cases jury factfinding may impair the most expedient and efficient sentencing of defendants. But the interest in fairness and reliability protected by the right to a jury trial—a common-law right that defendants enjoyed for centuries and that is now enshrined in the Sixth Amendment—has always outweighed the interest in concluding trials swiftly. As Blackstone put it:

> [H]owever convenient these [new methods of trial] may appear at first, (as doubtless all arbitrary powers, well executed, are the most convenient) yet let it be again remembered, that delays, and little inconveniences in the forms of justice, are the price that all free nations must pay for their liberty in more substantial matters; that these inroads upon this sacred bulwark of the nation are fundamentally opposite to the spirit of our constitution; and that, though begun in trifles, the precedent may gradually increase and spread, to the utter disuse of juries in questions of the most momentous concerns.

Accordingly, we reaffirm our holding in *Apprendi*: Any fact (other than a prior conviction) which is necessary to support a sentence exceeding the maximum authorized by the facts established by a plea of guilty or a jury verdict must be admitted by the defendant or proved to a jury beyond a reasonable doubt.

. . .

NOTES AND QUESTIONS

1. The Court charts the rapid development of its case law on jury trial rights in the five years preceding *Booker*. The case that ultimately put the writing on the wall for the federal Sentencing Guidelines, however, was *Blakely*. In *Blakely*, a judge found that a defendant acted with "deliberate cruelty" in the kidnapping of his wife, and based on this finding sentenced defendant to 90 months even though the standard sentence for the offense, recommended by the prosecutor, was 49 to 53 months. The judge did not make his finding of "deliberate cruelty" casually: He held a three-day hearing at which there was testimony from the victim, the defendant's son, police officers, and medical experts. 542 U.S. at 300. The practical upshot of *Blakely*'s holding that the state sentencing enhancement violated the Sixth Amendment was that federal prosecutors began adding to their indictments any enhancement or aggravating factors they expected to rely on at sentencing, and preparing to prove those facts to juries at trial if necessary.

2. There is some irony in the Court's reference to *Gaudin* in its introduction to what it describes as the "basic precepts" of the right to trial by jury. Prior to *Gaudin* the Supreme Court had been largely silent on the scope of the jury trial right since its decisions in *Duncan v. Louisiana*, 391 U.S. 145 (1968), and *Williams v. Florida*, 399 U.S. 78 (1970). And while the decision in *Gaudin* was an affirmance of the Ninth Circuit's requirement that the issue of materiality in an 18 U.S.C. § 1001 prosecution had to be submitted to the jury, every other circuit in the country had previously held—undisturbed by the Supreme Court—that the issue of materiality under § 1001 was for the judge to decide. 515 U.S. at 527 (Rehnquist, C.J., concurring).

3. The Court declares that if the Guidelines were merely advisory that the selection of sentences based on particular facts would not implicate the Sixth Amendment. Do you agree? Was the judge in *Blakely* required under Washington law to impose the sentencing adjustment for "deliberate cruelty"?

4. The Court observes that due to the legislative lust for enacting punishment enhancements the jury's role has diminished vis-à-vis judges, and that in some cases the tail is now wagging the dog. Note that in the two cases on which the Court granted certiorari the Guidelines required increases of 50 percent (*Booker*) and 200 percent (*Fanfan*) over the sentences based solely on the facts to be proven at trial. Apart from the optics, how much does this dynamic matter? Isn't a sentence that is increased 10 percent by a judge-found fact just as unconstitutional as one that is increased 50 percent by a judge-found fact?

At the end of this section the Court states that its holding "is not motivated by Sixth Amendment formalism, but by the need to preserve Sixth Amendment substance." What does it mean by Sixth Amendment formalism? Why is the Court defensive on this score?

5. In summing up its holding, the Court states: "Any fact (other than a prior conviction) which is necessary to support a sentence exceeding the maximum authorized by the facts established by a plea of guilty or a jury verdict must be admitted by the defendant or proved to a jury beyond a reasonable doubt."

Why the exception for a prior conviction? Is this a formalistic or pragmatic exception?

6. The *Booker* punch line, however, is *not* that the Guidelines are null and void. Rather, in a separate remedial majority opinion written by Justice Breyer, sometimes called *Booker II*, the Court rules that the provisions in the Sentencing Reform Act that make the Guidelines mandatory are "severable" from the remainder of the statute, and therefore the Guidelines live on in an "advisory" capacity. The *Booker II* opinion does not sever the parts of the act that provided for appellate review, however. If the Guidelines were truly meant to be only advisory, why would appellate review be necessary?

7. Justice Stevens, the author of *Booker I*, dissents from Justice Breyer's remedial majority opinion and argues that the better solution would simply be for the prosecution, as it had been doing at least since *Blakely* and maybe earlier, to seek indictment on, and prepare to prove to the jury beyond a reasonable doubt, whatever facts it intended to use to support an upward sentencing adjustment.

Which of these two remedial solutions seems better suited to achieving Congress's goal of reducing sentencing disparities? Which solution seems more beneficial to defendants attempting to negotiate a plea bargain with a prosecutor? Which solution poses the most administrative difficulty?

After *Booker*, under Guidelines that were only advisory, defendants were theoretically able to make sentencing arguments directly under 18 U.S.C. § 3553, which provided, among other things, that a sentence shall be "sufficient, but not greater than necessary" to comply with an enumerated list of generic sentencing purposes (e.g., "to afford adequate deterrence to criminal conduct"). Under this statute, some factors that were previously prohibited or discouraged (e.g., the defendant's personal characteristics) could be considered.

In a decision two years after *Booker*, the Supreme Court held that even after *Booker* the Guidelines remain the presumptive "starting point and benchmark" for sentencing decisions, and that judges must still do a Guideline calculation and consider that calculation in imposing a sentence. *Rita v. United States*, 551 U.S. 338, 347-48 (2007). At the same time the Court enhanced the sentencing discretion of the district courts. In *Rita* the defendant faced an advisory Guidelines range of 33 to 41 months based on a conviction for making false statements to a grand jury. *Id.* at 341. Rita argued that he should be sentenced below the Guidelines range based on his work as a government cooperator, his military service, and his poor health. *Id.* at 345. The district court disagreed and sentenced him to 33 months. *Id.* On appeal, the Fourth Circuit rejected Rita's argument that his sentence was unreasonable, and applied a presumption of reasonableness for all within-Guidelines sentences, falling in

C. The Sentencing Guidelines

line with a majority of other circuits that had adopted a similar presumption. *Id.* at 346. The Supreme Court addressed the circuit split by upholding the presumption of reasonableness applied by the Fourth Circuit to Rita's case, but stating that the courts of appeals that did not apply a presumption of reasonableness were not required to do so. *Id.* at 355-56.

Shortly after *Rita*, the Court on the same day decided two other important cases, *Gall v. United States*, 552 U.S. 38 (2007), and *Kimbrough v. United States*, 552 U.S. 85 (2007). Brian Gall sold drugs briefly as a college student but thereafter ceased all drug-related activity, graduated college, and established a career. *Id.* at 41-42. When approached by agents more than three years after his drug involvement had ended, he admitted his illegal activity and agreed to plead guilty. *Id.* at 42-43. Under a written plea agreement with the government, Gall's advisory Guidelines range was 30 to 37 months' imprisonment. *Id.* at 43. The government advocated for a within-Guidelines sentence, but the District Court for the Southern District of Iowa imposed no jail time and a probation period of 36 months, citing Gall's extraordinary pre-indictment rehabilitation and acceptance of responsibility. *Id.* at 44-45. The Court of Appeals for the Eighth Circuit reversed, reasoning that the variance between the sentence imposed and advisory Guideline range could only be justified by "extraordinary circumstances." *Id.* at 45. The Supreme Court reversed, holding that "while the extent of the difference between a particular sentence and the recommended Guidelines range is surely relevant, courts of appeals must review all sentences—whether inside, just outside, or significantly outside the Guidelines range—under a deferential, abuse-of-discretion standard," and found that Gall's sentence was reasonable under the circumstances. *Id.* at 41.

In *Kimbrough*, defendant pleaded guilty to crack cocaine distribution and firearms charges. 552 U.S. at 91. He faced a statutory sentencing range of ten years to life for his three drug offenses and an additional five years to life for his firearm crime. *Id.* at 91-92. As part of his guilty plea, Kimbrough had admitted responsibility for 56 grams of crack cocaine and 92.1 grams of powder cocaine. *Id.* at 92. All in all, including a mandatory 60 months for the gun crime, Kimbrough's final advisory Guidelines range was 228 to 270 months' imprisonment. *Id.* According to the district court, a within-Guidelines sentence would have violated the "parsimony provision," which requires courts to impose sentences "sufficient, but not greater than necessary" to accomplish the purposes set forth in 18 U.S.C. § 3553(a). *Id.* at 92-93. After considering the appropriate sentencing factors, the district court noted that had Kimbrough been responsible for an equivalent quantity of powder cocaine instead of crack cocaine, his advisory Guidelines range would have been only 97 to 106 months' imprisonment. *Id.* at 93. Citing the "disproportionate and unjust effect that crack cocaine guidelines have in sentencing," the district court sentenced Kimbrough to the statutory mandatory minimum of 180 months, a downward variance from his advisory Guidelines range, because such a sentence was "clearly long enough." *Id.*

The Court of Appeals for the Fourth Circuit reversed, reasoning that a sentence "outside the guidelines range is per se unreasonable when it is based on a disagreement with the sentencing disparity for crack and powder cocaine offenses." *Id.* The Supreme Court reversed the Fourth Circuit, holding that a sentencing judge is free to vary categorically from the suggested Guidelines range based on a disagreement with the crack/powder disparity embodied in Guideline § 2D1.1. *Id.* at 109-10. However, the Court found "no occasion for elaborative discussion" of the nature of such disagreements, because the crack cocaine "Guidelines do not exemplify the Commission's exercise of its characteristic institutional role," in that they were not based on empirical study or even the Commission's own policy convictions. *Id.* at 109.

Notwithstanding this ostensible discretion—whether out of habit, inertia, or fear of being reversed—the great majority of federal sentences after *Booker* are within or close to the "advisory" guideline ranges. *See* Frank O. Bowman III, *Loss Revisited: A Guarded Defense of the Centerpiece of the Federal Economic Crime Sentencing Guideline*, 82 Mo. L. Rev. 1, 3 (2017)

1368 Chapter XVI Incarceration: Bail, Pretrial Detention, and Sentencing

(half of all sentences imposed are within the Guideline range and most of the other half are close to that range).

D. RACE AND SENTENCING

The Death Penalty. Race and the death penalty have a long and infamous relationship in the United States. In the South prior to the Civil War most states had separate capital offenses based on both race and slave status. After the Civil War capital punishment was seen as an important tool in the South to punish the crimes of what the white population feared to be a newly freed and lustful and perhaps vengeful Black population. Even after the decline of lynchings—"unofficial capital punishment"—in the first half of the twentieth century, the death penalty remained important in the South. *See generally* Carol S. Steiker & Jordan M. Steiker, *The American Death Penalty and Invisibility of Race*, 82 U. Chi. L. Rev. 243, 248-55 (2015).

The Supreme Court first indicated the possibility of considering the constitutionality of the death penalty in 1963, when Justice Arthur Goldberg dissented from the denial of certiorari in *Rudolph v. Alabama*, 375 U.S. 889 (1963) (Goldberg, J., dissenting from denial of certiorari). *Rudolph* was a death penalty rape case out of Alabama, with a Black defendant and white victim, and Justice Goldberg urged the Court to consider whether imposing the death penalty for rape where there was no endangerment of human life was cruel and unusual punishment barred by the Eighth Amendment. Reportedly, Chief Justice Warren persuaded Justice Goldberg to remove any reference to race in his published opinion. *See* Evan J. Mandery, A Wild Justice: The Death and Resurrection of Capital Punishment in America 3-30 (2013). The NAACP took up the death penalty cause on the heels of *Rudolph*, notwithstanding the lack of a race angle in that opinion. The NAACP launched an ambitious litigation strategy, engaging a prominent criminologist at the University of Pennsylvania, Marvin Wolfgang, to conduct an empirical study that could demonstrate disparate treatment in the imposition of the death penalty in southern rape cases. *See* generally Steiker & Steiker, *The American Death Penalty and Invisibility of Race*, *supra* at 243, 254-55.

Maxwell v. Bishop
398 F.2d 138 (8th Cir. 1968)

BLACKMUN, Circuit Judge.

William L. Maxwell, a Negro and an Arkansas prisoner under sentence of execution on his 1962 conviction for the state crime of rape, as defined by Ark. Stat. Ann. § 41-3401 (Repl. 1964), petitions a second time for a federal writ of habeas corpus and, with its denial, a second time appeals. The points now urged to us are (1) that a prima facie case of racially discriminatory imposition of the death penalty for rape in Arkansas has now been established and remains unrebutted by the State; (2) that Arkansas' single verdict procedure is without appropriate standards, allows the jury to exercise its discretion irrationally, and is impermissible; and (3) that the decisions of the United States Supreme Court since Maxwell's first federal appeal demonstrate the error of our prior holding, adverse to the petitioner, on the jury selection issue.

We again review the background:

1. The offense for which Maxwell was charged was committed in the early morning of November 3, 1961, in the City of Hot Springs, Garland County, Arkansas. Maxwell, who

D. Race and Sentencing   **1369**

was 21 at the time, was arrested within two hours after the offense was committed. His convicting jury did not "render a verdict of life imprisonment in the State penitentiary at hard labor," as it had the option to do (since 1915 (Acts 1915, No. 187, § 1, p. 774)) under §§ 43-2153 and 41-3403 and for which it had been given an alternate verdict form. Accordingly, and in line with the interpretation consistently given the statutes by the Supreme Court of Arkansas, the trial court imposed the death sentence.

2. Maxwell appealed. On this state appeal he challenged the sufficiency of the evidence; his prosecution by information; the constitutionality in application of the penalty statute, § 41-3403; the denial of his motion that his case be removed to federal court; the overruling of certain objections relating to voir dire; the overruling of objections as to latitude in his cross-examination of witnesses; the admission of evidence; the instructions; and aspects of the prosecution's argument to the jury. All these points were decided adversely to the defense and the judgment of conviction was affirmed by a unanimous Supreme Court of Arkansas (one justice not participating). No petition for certiorari was filed with the Supreme Court of the United States.

3. Maxwell, with new counsel, then filed a petition for a writ of habeas corpus in the United States District Court for the Eastern District of Arkansas. In that petition, as twice amended, he alleged the illegality of his arrest; impropriety of the search of his person; impropriety of the search of his home; mistreatment by the police; coerced confessions; an adverse and hostile trial atmosphere; racial discrimination in the selection of his jury; unconstitutional application of § 41-3403; and unconstitutionality of the death penalty for rape. Judge Young decided each point so raised adversely to the defense and denied the petition. His detailed opinion is reported as *Maxwell v. Stephens*.

4. Judge Young, however, granted the certificate of probable cause required by 28 U.S.C. § 2253 and stayed execution. With additional counsel from New York, an appeal was taken to this court. We noted that, except for an early period prior to the state trial, when court-appointed attorneys were in the case, Maxwell had been represented through all the state and federal proceedings by competent, although different, non-court-appointed counsel. The points primarily argued to us were three: (1) that Maxwell was denied due process and equal protection because he was sentenced under statutes which are discriminatorily enforced against Negroes; (2) that he was denied due process and equal protection because the Garland County jury lists revealed race and were compiled from racially designated poll tax books; and (3) that the taking of Maxwell's coat and references to it in testimony at the trial violated his Fourth, Fifth and Fourteenth Amendment rights. In what we thought was an opinion meticulously concerned with the several issues raised by Maxwell, we reached the conclusion that Judge Young's decision was correct. The late Judge Ridge dissented on the search and seizure issue concerning the coat but agreed with all the other conclusions arrived at by the majority.

5. With still another name added to the list of Maxwell's counsel, a petition for certiorari was filed. This was denied, with Mr. Justice Douglas being of the opinion that certiorari should be granted.

6. Execution was rescheduled but was stayed administratively until September 2, 1966.

7. Maxwell's second and present petition for a federal writ of habeas corpus was filed July 21, 1966, in the United States District Court for the Eastern District of Arkansas and came before Chief Judge Henley. The court denied the petition.

8. The district court and a judge of this court successively declined to grant a stay of the execution or to issue a certificate of probable cause. But the Supreme Court granted leave to file a petition for a writ of certiorari, issued the writ, reversed the denial of the application for the certificate, and remanded the cause with directions to issue it. Accordingly, the certificate was issued and the execution stayed, and the case is here on appeal.

Chapter XVI Incarceration: Bail, Pretrial Detention, and Sentencing

As we observed before, Maxwell's guilt or innocence is not in issue before us. So far as the details of the crime itself are concerned, we recite only what we said there:

> The circumstances and details of the crime are, as usual, sordid. They are set forth in the Arkansas opinion and need not be repeated here. It suffices only to say that the victim was a white woman, 35 years old, who lived with her helpless ninety-year-old father; that their home was entered in the early morning by the assailant's cutting or breaking a window screen; that in the ensuing struggle the victim bit her assailant and caused bleeding; and that she was assaulted and bruised, her father injured, and the lives of both threatened. Confessions taken from Maxwell were not employed at the trial. The defense presented no evidence. The jury was out several hours. No question is raised as to the sufficiency of the evidence.

THE STATISTICAL ARGUMENT

Maxwell's present argument that Arkansas discriminates against Negroes in the application of the death penalty for rape, and thus violates the Equal Protection Clause and also 42 U.S.C. § 1981, rests on what is described as newly discovered evidence which became available since this court's disposition of Maxwell's first habeas appeal. It is said, in the words of the petition:

> This evidence consists of the results of a survey of rape convictions during the period 1945-1965 in a representative sample of nineteen counties comprising more than 47% of the population of the State of Arkansas. The survey was conducted in the summer of 1965, as part of a study of the application of the death penalty for rape in eleven southern states. This comprehensive study required the work of 28 law students throughout the summer, the expenditure of more than $35,000 and numerous hours of consultative time by expert criminal lawyers, criminologists and statisticians. Petitioner, who is an indigent, could not have himself at any time during the prior proceedings in his cause conducted such a study.

The record and the evidence. At a pretrial conference the district court was advised that the evidence to be presented on behalf of Maxwell was that which resulted from the survey and study so described, and that it would be presented through the testimony of Marvin Wolfgang, a criminologist-statistician on the faculty of the University of Pennsylvania. It was agreed in pretrial that the survey's individual case schedules would be made available for inspection by counsel for the State. The court ruled that, subject to objections as to relevancy and materiality, Professor Wolfgang would be permitted to testify as an expert and to introduce his report as a summary exhibit. The State filed no objection to any of the individual case schedules. At the ensuing hearing the State agreed that the basic facts of the schedules, "that is, the age of the victim, the race, and so on, of the individual defendants, or the alleged victims," would stand admitted. Dr. Wolfgang then was called as a witness.

Dr. Wolfgang possesses the degree of Doctor of Philosophy in Sociology, with Criminology as a sub-field. He is Professor and graduate chairman of the Department of Sociology at the University of Pennsylvania. He is co-director of the Department's Criminological Center. He obviously is a man of scholastic achievement and of experience in his field. The State concedes that his "qualifications as a criminologist have never been questioned by the respondent."

The witness testified that in 1965 he was asked to participate in a study on capital punishment for rape and that this was suggested "as an appropriate topic for research analysis because of the underlying assumption that there is differential imposition of the death penalty in rape cases in certain states." This was to be "an effort to collect the appropriate kind of data necessary to provide some kind of empirical study, either in support of, or in rejection of, the underlying assumption. The ultimate objective of the study was to give the empirical data the appropriate kind of statistical analysis that would satisfy scientific requirements." He was informed that the result might be used in litigation on behalf of defendants who had been convicted and sentenced to death for rape.

The study was carried out in twelve states. One of these was Arkansas. For the State of Arkansas the period investigated was that from January 1, 1945, to the summer of 1965. Not every Arkansas rape case during that period was included but every case which occurred in the sample counties was included.

The study produced 55 rape convictions in the 19 selected Arkansas counties. The witness prepared a preliminary analysis of the data contained in the schedules the student investigators prepared for these cases. Among the variables considered were race of the defendant, race of the victim, and sentence. The approach was to develop a "null hypothesis" that there is no difference in the distribution of the sentence of death or life imprisonment imposed on negro and white defendants; the calculation of a theoretical frequency which represents the number of defendants expected to be sentenced to death if the null hypothesis is valid; the comparison of this theoretical frequency with the actual frequency in the collected data for each defendant-victim racial combination; and the determination whether the discrepancy between the expected and the observed frequencies is great enough so that, under accepted statistical standards, that discrepancy can be said to be a product of the real phenomena tested rather than of the operation of chance within the testing process. "If that difference reaches a sufficiently high proportion, . . . then the assertion can be made . . . that the difference is significant and could not have occurred by chance."

The data gathering was not limited to the facts of race and sentence. It included other items such as the defendant's age family status, occupation, and prior criminal record; the victim's age, family status, occupation, husband's occupation, and reputation for chastity; aspects of the prior relationship, if any, between the defendant and the victim; the circumstances of the offense such as the number of offenders and victims, the place, the degree of threat or violence, and the injury inflicted; other offenses contemporaneously committed; the presence of third persons and threats or injury to them; the nature of the intercourse; the involvement of alcohol or drugs; and the circumstances of the trial and post-trial proceedings. Data of this general kind were included because they "were felt to be relevant to the imposition of the type of sentence" and "they, rather than race alone, may play a more important role in the disproportionate sentencing to death of Negro defendants convicted of raping white victims." The witness conceded that some data potentially pertinent were not collected as, for example, that "with respect to the strength of the prosecution's case' for 'we had no information of that sort that we could objectively collect."

The study disclosed that, in the 55 Arkansas cases, 34 defendants were Negroes and 21 were whites; that 33 had a previous record; that 26 were known to have been in prison; that 39 victims were whites, 15 were Negroes, and the race of one was unknown; that of the victims, two had prior criminal records and 31 did not; that 16 victims had a good reputation for chastity and 6 bad; that 14 received the death sentence and 41 life; that counsel was appointed in 35 cases and retained in 9; that in 23 cases the offender was known by the victim and in 26 he was unknown; that the offender and the victim had had prior sexual relations in 4 cases; and that in 12 cases a plea of guilty was entered.

From this Arkansas data and his study Dr. Wolfgang concluded:

1. Factors not significantly associated with either the defendant's race or with the sentence were the place of offense, nature of entry, plea, type of counsel, duration of trial, seriousness of injury to the victim, type of prior relationship between defendant and victim, the defendant's previous record, and the victim's having dependent children.
2. Factors not significantly associated with the defendant's race were the commission of a contemporaneous offense and previous imprisonment.
3. Factors not significantly associated with the sentence were the defendant's marital status, his age, the victim's age, the display of a weapon, and the defendant's having dependent children.

Chapter XVI Incarceration: Bail, Pretrial Detention, and Sentencing

4. Factors which were significantly associated with sentence were commission of a contemporaneous offense and previous imprisonment.

5. Factors which were significantly associated with the defendant's race were marital status (a greater percentage of Negroes than whites were not married), display of a weapon (more Negroes than whites used one), the defendant's age (more Negroes were young), the victim's age (the defendants were white more frequently in the older-defendant-younger-victim combination), and the existence of children dependent on the defendant (more whites had them).

6. An analysis of significant association with defendant's race or the sentence was either unnecessary or not possible with respect to the victim's prior record, her reputation for chastity, the force employed, her pregnancy by the offense, prior sexual relations between the defendant and the victim, and the defendant's assertion of the defense of insanity. The study covered other items, too, but the analysis was confined to "those particular items in which there was sufficient information to display statistically and to treat statistically."

The witness then further concluded (1) that the critical variables were race of the offender, race of his victim, and sentence; (2) compared to other rape defendants, negroes convicted of raping white victims were disproportionately sentenced to death; and (3) "no variable of which analysis was possible could account for the observed disproportionate frequency."

On cross-examination Dr. Wolfgang stated that the Arkansas report was "preliminary" in the sense that the other states for which data was being collected would be included in the final report; that the 55 Arkansas cases did include some new trials; that, however, he did not think this disturbed his analysis; that he was only "very little" familiar with Arkansas geography; that he was "gratified the report is as good as it is"; that he used such variables as he could get information on; that if he had had more information, he could have used other variables and his report, accordingly, would have been more extensive; that reputation for chastity was presumed to be of some relevance but "unfortunately, there was not enough information upon which to make the analysis complete"; that as a criminologist he was willing to say "that an analysis of a social system — in this case, the judicial system — operated relative to the decision making regarding rape, is such that it casts considerable doubt upon the quality of justice in those particular cases throughout the system"; and that he has never sat on a jury but has been around them.

It was then agreed that among the 55 schedules there were 4 cases which concerned defendants convicted twice for the same rape as a result of a second trial. A fifth case was not one of repeated convictions but, instead concerned two victims.

Received in evidence was an exhibit prepared by the United States Bureau of Prisons. This showed that, for the years 1930-62, 446 persons were executed under civil authority in the United States for rape and that, of these, only 45 were white but 399 were Negro and 2 were of other races, and that, for the same period, 3,298 were executed for murder and, of these, 1,640 were white, 1,619 were Negro, and 39 were of other races.

The petitioner's second and only other witness was John Monroe, a Philadelphia statistician with 17 years' experience in sampling and surveys. He testified that he was asked by Dr. Wolfgang to design a representative sampling of counties in 12 southern states so that inferences could be drawn for each state and for the region as a whole. Arkansas was included. The 1960 negro population was used as the measure. The sample size was determined largely on speculation as to what area the law students could cover in the time available to them. Nineteen Arkansas Counties were selected. These contained more than 47% of the state's population. Mr. Monroe stated that his sample of Arkansas counties was a very reliable one under the restriction, that is, the number of counties that could be investigated during the time allotted. He went on to say that, so far as the sample is concerned, the inferences drawn from it were valid for Arkansas. Garland County was not one of those selected. This was because "the random number just didn't happen to fall in the population for Garland County." Had that county possessed more than 19,000 negro population it would have been selected. The witness conceded that he was sampling the negro population and not the entire population. This was because of the purpose of the study and, in order to compare negro and white cases, the sample has to provide enough of the former to make the findings valid.

The witness stated that he took the total negro population of Arkansas and divided it by the number of draws allocated to the State. This number turned out to be approximately 19,400. A random number between it and zero was selected. As adjacent county negro population added up to the random number plus 19,400, the county was selected. In this way, counties having more than 19,400 Negroes, or approximately that number, were taken consecutively.

On cross-examination it was pointed out that this method did not result in having the selected counties geographically dispersed throughout the State. Instead, the selected counties for the most part were in the east and south. This is where Arkansas' negro population is primarily located.

The court inquired what there was about the survey that gave it validity in Garland County. The answer was that the inferences drawn from the sample were valid for the State of Arkansas. Counsel then observed that it was not Garland County that convicted Maxwell and sentenced him to death but the State, and that the purpose of Mr. Monroe's testimony was to show that the counties selected were representative of the State.

On further cross-examination, the witness acknowledged that the northwestern part of the State was essentially the white population area, that the southeastern portion was the negro population area, and that Garland County was in the white area.

The State offered no evidence.

Such is the record. It is apparent from a reading of the record that the trial court was generous in its rulings on admissibility. Everything which the petitioner presented came in.

The trial court's conclusions on the statistical argument. Chief Judge Henley, in his opinion, described the statistical argument as the "contention which has been urged most seriously here." He referred to professor Wolfgang as "a well qualified sociologist and criminologist" and to Mr. Monroe as "a qualified statistician." He observed that the investigation showed three categories, namely, rapes of white women by negro men, rapes of negro women by negro men, and rapes of white women by white men, and that there was no conviction of a white man for rape of a negro woman. He noted that Dr. Wolfgang "concluded, and the Court agrees, that the differential could not be due to the operation of the laws of chance." He characterized Dr. Wolfgang's conclusions "to be that a Negro man who is convicted of raping a white woman has about a 50 percent chance of receiving a death sentence, regardless of the facts and circumstances surrounding the crime, whereas a man who is convicted of criminally assaulting a woman of his own race stands about only a 14 percent chance of receiving the death sentence." He acknowledged that "the statistical evidence produced in this case is more extensive and sophisticated than has been produced heretofore." Yet he was not convinced that "it is sufficiently broad, accurate, or precise as to establish satisfactorily that Arkansas juries in general practice unconstitutional racial discrimination in rape cases involving Negro men and white women. . . . The study does not indicate that Negro men convicted of raping white women invariably or even in a majority of cases receive the death penalty. . . . Only 7 Negro men were sentenced to die for raping white women. The case studies, and the number of death sentences imposed are simply too few in number to afford convincing proof of the proposition urged by petitioner." It is not correct, as Dr. Wolfgang said in his report, that the selected Arkansas counties are "representative of the State in urban-rural and white-Negro population rations." The statistics "really reveal very little about the details of the cases" where the death sentence was imposed upon Negroes for raping white women as compared with other racial situations. "On the meager material before it the Court is simply not prepared to convict Arkansas juries of unconstitutional racial discrimination in rape cases." The court went on to observe that "In cases not involving inter-racial situations the issue of consent may be and frequently is very real," but that that issue "is much less likely to be present in cases in which white women have been attacked by Negro men."

The petitioner's argument. The petitioner-appellant characterizes the present proceeding as one presenting "for the first time in any appellate court . . . a record which is the end product of a detailed and exhaustive examination of the practical consequences of the procedures used in making the decision whether a man should live or die." It is stated that the question in this record is one of proof, namely, whether the petitioner has made a sufficient showing of racially discriminatory capital sentencing under Arkansas rape statutes. It is pointed out that on three previous occasions, namely, in the Supreme Court of Arkansas, before Judge Young, and in this court, the answer has been in the negative, "notwithstanding that on each successive occasion the evidence tended in the direction of more depth and completeness." This demonstrates, it is said, "how difficult it is for Negro litigants generally and those without means particularly, to make courts see "the reality of the world, indeed . . . the segregated world" . . . in which they live . . . the law (needs to) "see what all others see."

The heart of the petitioner's statistical argument is then forthcoming. It is that on this record the petitioner has made a prima facie case of racial discrimination in sentencing and that he is entitled to prevail when, as here, the State presents no evidence or presents evidence of insufficient moment to overcome the prima facie case so established.

It is said that the Supreme Court of necessity has developed the doctrine that a prima facie showing of unequal racial treatment, calling state procedures in question, compels the inference that the State is drawing the racial line unless it offers justification in non-racial factors for the disproportion. Jury selection and voting deprival cases such as *Hernandez v. State of Texas* (1954), and *Gomillion v. Lightfoot* (1960), are cited generally. Also cited, however, are other cases which, it is said, show that the prima facie approach has not been restricted to jury selection and voting cases. It is argued that there is no reason why the prima facie approach should not be applied to the present case. If there are factors which offset Dr. Wolfgang's expert conclusion, they were in the power of the State to unearth and prove. "Every justification for shifting the burden of persuasion to the State . . . applies with evident force here."

Finally, it is stated that the district court committed manifest error in its evaluation of the evidence. Counsel would dismiss the trial court's observation that the Arkansas figures contained instances of defendants tried more than once on the ground that each Arkansas jury death sentence is an indication of the application of the Arkansas statute. They would dismiss the trial court's concern with the small number of cases on the ground that the whole purpose of the statistical analysis was to satisfy Dr. Wolfgang as an expert and that he was so satisfied and his conclusions are sustainable under accepted scientific standards. They would dismiss the court's concern with the geographical location of the selected Arkansas counties as unsupportable and improper. And they would dismiss the court's concern with the "issue of consent" as being "plainly the sheerest speculation." The observations are made that "any experienced criminal lawyer in the South . . . well knows that the failure to present the defense of consent in interracial rape cases is itself a product of the discriminatory pattern of Southern justice which petitioner here attacks," and that "Southern jury attitudes . . . have long impressed upon defense counsel the extreme unwisdom of advancing the consent defense on behalf of a Negro defendant where the complainant is white."

The petitioner's argument is an interesting one and we are not disposed to say that it could not have some validity and weight in certain situations. Like the trial court, however, although perhaps not for each and all of the reasons it advanced, we feel that the argument does not have validity and pertinent application to Maxwell's case.

D. Race and Sentencing

It is perhaps well to emphasize initially what the study and Dr. Wolfgang's testimony do not do or purport to do:

1. They do not relate specifically to Garland County where this particular offense was committed and where Maxwell was tried and convicted. They are concerned with 19 other Arkansas counties and with counties in 11 other states.
2. They admittedly do not take every variable into account.
3. They do not show that the petit jury which tried and convicted Maxwell acted in his case with racial discrimination.
4. They do not deny that generally the burden of demonstrating discrimination in penalty imposition is on the one who asserts it.

What we are concerned with here is Maxwell's case and only Maxwell's case. And it is indisputable, from the record before us, that, despite the five references to "free" and "voluntary" in the defense's opening statement at the trial, there is no question, and no hint of one, as to the victim's lack of consent. The facts of the attack, which are not in dispute, which were reviewed by the Arkansas court and which we have again quoted above, include forcible entry of the home, physical assault on both the victim and her aged father, resistance by both, and the infliction of injuries on all three. The petitioner's attack, therefore, to the extent it would concern itself with the issue of consent in rape cases, both interracial and non-interracial, and with allegedly purposeful avoidance of the consent issue by southern defense counsel, has no place here and, in its attempted application, is a straw argument based on speculation.

Further, while it is true that it is in a sense the state which prosecutes, nevertheless the county has a character and a posture too. Inasmuch as Garland County, as it was conceded, is in the predominantly white area of Arkansas, one might expect from the petitioner an argument that alleged southern injustice in interracial rape cases would be more apparent in such a county than in those areas where the negro population is predominant. Yet the Garland County statistics, which we noted and which we have again recited by quotation in footnote 6, supra, afford no local support to the petitioner's statistical argument. The evidence produced at the prior hearing and at this one discloses only Maxwell as a recipient of the death penalty in Garland County for rape.

We are not yet ready to condemn and upset the result reached in every case of a negro rape defendant in the State of Arkansas on the basis of broad theories of social and statistical injustice. This is particularly so on a record so specific as this one. And we are not yet ready to nullify this petitioner's Garland County trial on the basis of results generally, but elsewhere, throughout the South.

We therefore reject the statistical argument in its attempted application to Maxwell's case. Whatever value that argument may have as an instrument of social concern, whatever suspicion it may arouse with respect to southern interracial rape trials as a group over a long period of time, and whatever it may disclose with respect to other localities, we feel that the statistical argument does nothing to destroy the integrity of Maxwell's trial. Although the investigation and study made by Professor Wolfgang in the summer of 1965 is interesting and provocative, we do not, on the basis of that study, upset Maxwell's conviction and, as a necessary consequence, cast serious doubt on every other rape conviction in the state courts of Arkansas.

At oral argument we asked Professor Amsterdam, counsel for Maxwell, whether (apart from any Eighth Amendment argument) his statistical approach would not mean that it would be constitutionally impossible for a negro defendant in Arkansas ever to receive the death penalty upon conviction of the crime of rape of a white woman. The answer given us was in the affirmative, that is, that it would be constitutionally impossible. At the same time it was conceded, in contrast, that it would be possible for a white man to receive the death penalty upon his conviction for rape. When counsel was asked whether this would not be

Chapter XVI Incarceration: Bail, Pretrial Detention, and Sentencing

discriminatory, the reply was that once the negro situation was remedied the white situation "would take care of itself."

The legal logic and the rightness of this totally escape us. If that end result would actually be forthcoming (and we wonder whether this may accurately be forecast), that fact does not, in our view, make it legally right or satisfy constitutional dictates. We still read the first section of the Fourteenth Amendment as proscribing the denial "to any person" within a state's jurisdiction of "the equal protection of the laws." We feel that this means what it seems to require, namely, protection which is equal, and that equal protection is denied if, factually, a member of one race (whether black or white) is subjected, because of his race, to greater or different punishment than a member of another race. The argument therefore turns back upon and defeats the very side which here proposes it. We are not inclined to accept as constitutional doctrine an abstraction which provides equality only through assumed and hoped-for day-to-day practicalities. It is the law, not probabilities or possibilities, which must afford equal protection.

We can understand and appreciate the disappointment and seeming frustration which Maxwell's counsel must feel in again failing to prevail on a still more sophisticated statistical approach. They will ask themselves just how far they are required to go in order to prevail.

We are not certain that, for Maxwell, statistics will ever be his redemption. The facts as to rape charges in Garland County are known and have been recited. Standing by themselves, they disclose nothing from which conclusions of unconstitutionality in application may appropriately be drawn. This situation — the aridity of the Garland County facts on which to claim unequal protection of the laws — forces Maxwell and his counsel to present his case on a state-wide and long-term historical approach, and even on a South-wide one, and to claim that conclusions which, at best, are necessarily general have valid application to Maxwell.

We do not say that there is no ground for suspicion that the death penalty for rape may have been discriminatorily applied over the decades in that large area of states whose statutes provide for it. There are recognizable indicators of this. But, as we have noted before, with respect to the issue of jury selection, improper state practice of the past does not automatically invalidate a procedure of the present. We do say that nothing has been presented in Maxwell's case which convinces us, or causes us seriously to wonder, that, with the imposition of the death penalty, he was the victim of discrimination based on race.

• • •

NOTES AND QUESTIONS

1. The only issues on appeal relate to the imposition of the death penalty. Yet the Eighth Circuit (then-Judge Harry Blackmun writing for the panel) observes gratuitously in the factual background that confessions made by Maxwell were not introduced into evidence and that the jury was out for several hours. What is the point of these observations?

2. Maxwell contended that the statistics and testimony of Dr. Wolfgang established at least a prima facie case of discrimination, and that the state has admitted the basic facts in the schedule of cases that Dr. Wolfgang relies on. How could the state rebut this prima facie case?

3. Note the trial judge's conclusion that it is "not prepared to convict Arkansas juries of unconstitutional racism in rape cases." This sentiment, sometimes implicit, prevails in many discrimination contexts, where courts are reluctant to reach a conclusion that a group or individual has acted in a discriminatory manner. The suggestion is that to label a person or group as racist requires evidence of a higher order. If the notion of "unconscious racism" had widespread acceptance in the law, would this sentiment be tempered? Note the irony of the trial judge's sentiment here, where he is reluctant to reach a conclusion of discriminatory intent for fear of condemning Arkansas juries even though the allegation is that those juries have condemned Black persons to death for discriminatory reasons.

4. While conceding that "it is in a sense the state which prosecutes," the court ultimately concludes that the focus must be on Garland County, where the crime took place, where Maxwell was prosecuted, and where the jurors were from. "What we are concerned with here is Maxwell's case and only Maxwell's case." Does such a focus seal Maxwell's fate, at least on this record? What statistics from Garland County itself would be needed to overcome a focus on a particular defendant's case? How could defense counsel convert the focus from the county to the state in a future case? How can the devastating Bureau of Prison statistics—399 Blacks and only 45 whites executed for rape from 1930 to 1962—be used in a future case?

5. As to the paucity of underlying details in the cases where Black men have been sentenced to death for raping white women, the trial judge points out—apparently as to why such cases were more appropriate than other rape cases for a death sentence—that the defense of consent is less likely to be an issue in such cases. What can he mean? Is this anything other than a twisted and racist endorsement of the virtue of southern women?

Defendant responds by noting that this differential is a matter of defense strategy not fact: "Southern jury attitudes . . . have long impressed upon defense counsel the extreme unwisdom of advancing the defense of consent on behalf of a Negro defendant where the complainant is white." *Id.* at 146. Assuming this is true, and further that trial judges do not recognize this phenomenon, should you even need statistics to invalidate a death sentence in such a case?

Anthony Amsterdam

As if to contradict this assertion by defendant, then-Judge Blackmun, who was from Minnesota, noted in a footnote that trial defense counsel apparently had raised the issue of consent in his opening. Does this refute or confirm the defendant's point about "best practices" in defending a Black defendant in a rape case brought by a white complainant?

6. Anthony Amsterdam, counsel for Maxwell in this appeal, was the chief architect of the NAACP Legal Defense Foundation (LDF)'s capital punishment effort. *See* Steiker & Steiker, *The American Death Penalty and Invisibility of Race, supra* at 243, 257. What do you think of his affirmative response to the question from the bench as to whether his statistical argument meant Arkansas could not constitutionally impose the death penalty on a Black man convicted of the rape of a white woman? How about his response to the follow-up question—Wouldn't it be discriminatory if white men but not Black men could be executed for rape?—that "once the negro situation was remedied the white situation would take care of itself"?

The Supreme Court granted certiorari in *Maxwell* not on the statistical evidence of racial discrimination addressed by the Eighth Circuit but on the issue of the standardless discretion given to Arkansas juries in deciding between death and lesser penalties. The Supreme Court never reached *Maxwell*, however, because in the meantime it decided *Witherspoon v. Illinois*, 391 U.S. 510 (1968), rejecting Illinois's overbroad approach to death-qualifying jurors, and reversed Maxwell's sentence on the basis of *Witherspoon*. *See* Steiker & Steiker, *The American Death Penalty and Invisibility of Race, supra* at 243, 258-59.

Chapter XVI Incarceration: Bail, Pretrial Detention, and Sentencing

In its *Maxwell* petition for certiorari, the NAACP had emphasized an argument similar to the one that it later pursued successfully in *Furman v. Georgia*, 408 U.S. 238 (1972), that the standardless discretion given juries under death penalty statutes permitted them to impose a death sentence for discriminatory reasons. The *Furman* amicus briefs also focused on the racial aspects of capital punishment. Yet none of the five separate opinions in *Furman*, except the opinion of Justice Douglas, focus on the racial angle. *Id.* at 259-65. And four years later, when the Court invalidated a Georgia statute authorizing the death penalty for the rape of an adult woman, *Coker v. Georgia*, 433 U.S. 584 (1976), it seemed to have cherrypicked a case with a white defendant. 408 U.S. at 273.

Why the Court's hesitancy to situate its death penalty jurisprudence at least to some extent in the racial context in which it existed? The Steikers contend, or at least speculate, that the Warren Court was reluctant to jeopardize whatever credibility it still retained after the popular backlash it had received from its seminal criminal procedure decisions and school desegregation decisions of the 1960s. *Id.* at 277-79. For example, a year before *Furman* was decided the Court in *Swann v. Charlotte-Mecklenburg Board of Education*, 402 U.S. 1 (1971), had ruled that court-ordered busing of school children was a permissible way to achieve integration in a public school system.

States responded to *Furman* in one of two ways: (1) limiting jury's discretion by enacting statutes that required juries to find specific factors in order to recommend the death penalty or (2) eliminating the jury's discretion altogether by making the death penalty mandatory for certain crimes. The latter solution was struck down by the Court in *Woodson v. North Carolina*, 428 U.S. 280 (1976), a decision that has profoundly impacted death penalty litigation. *Woodson* held that imposition of the death penalty required the state to provide a defendant with an opportunity to present mitigating evidence, broadly defined to include almost anything about not only the circumstances of the crime but also about the personal circumstances of the defendant himself. As a consequence, a capital defense legal team since *Woodson* has the opportunity—and the obligation—to make a mitigation case for their client, and must include all manner of medical, psychiatric, psychological, and mitigation specialists to obtain, develop, and present such evidence. This judicial commitment to free-form individualized sentencing has resulted in not just the protraction but also the increased expense of death penalty litigation. *See* Steiker & Steiker, *The American Death Penalty and Invisibility of Race*, *supra* at 243, 290-91. *See* Chapter VIII *supra*.

Twenty years after *Maxwell*, the author of the Eighth Circuit's opinion in that case, Harry Blackmun, was on the Supreme Court. Several other Justices had also come to the Court since *Furman*. Statistical methodologies had improved and more data from criminal files was accessible and available. This was the context for the Court's next death penalty case involving race.

McCleskey v. Kemp
481 U.S. 279 (1987)

Justice POWELL delivered the opinion of the Court.

This case presents the question whether a complex statistical study that indicates a risk that racial considerations enter into capital sentencing determinations proves that petitioner McCleskey's capital sentence is unconstitutional under the Eighth or Fourteenth Amendment.

I

McCleskey, a black man, was convicted of two counts of armed robbery and one count of murder in the Superior Court of Fulton County, Georgia, on October 12, 1978. McCleskey's convictions arose out of the robbery of a furniture store and the killing of a white police officer during the course of the robbery. The evidence at trial indicated that McCleskey and three accomplices planned and carried out the robbery. All four were armed. McCleskey entered the front of the store while the other three entered the rear. McCleskey secured the front of the store by rounding up the customers and forcing them to lie face down on the floor. The other three rounded up the employees in the rear and tied them up with tape. The manager was forced at gunpoint to turn over the store receipts, his watch, and $6. During the course of the robbery, a police officer, answering a silent alarm, entered the store through the front door. As he was walking down the center aisle of the store, two shots were fired. Both struck the officer. One hit him in the face and killed him.

Several weeks later, McCleskey was arrested in connection with an unrelated offense. He confessed that he had participated in the furniture store robbery, but denied that he had shot the police officer. At trial, the State introduced evidence that at least one of the bullets that struck the officer was fired from a .38 caliber Rossi revolver. This description matched the description of the gun that McCleskey had carried during the robbery. The State also introduced the testimony of two witnesses who had heard McCleskey admit to the shooting.

The jury convicted McCleskey of murder. At the penalty hearing, the jury heard arguments as to the appropriate sentence. Under Georgia law, the jury could not consider imposing the death penalty unless it found beyond a reasonable doubt that the murder was accompanied by one of the statutory aggravating circumstances. Ga. Code Ann. § 17-10-30(c) (1982). The jury in this case found two aggravating circumstances to exist beyond a reasonable doubt: the murder was committed during the course of an armed robbery, § 17-10-30(b)(2); and the murder was committed upon a peace officer engaged in the performance of his duties, § 17-10-30(b)(8). In making its decision whether to impose the death sentence, the jury considered the mitigating and aggravating circumstances of McCleskey's conduct. § 17-10-2(c). McCleskey offered no mitigating evidence. The jury recommended that he be sentenced to death on the murder charge and to consecutive life sentences on the armed robbery charges. The court followed the jury's recommendation and sentenced McCleskey to death.

On appeal, the Supreme Court of Georgia affirmed the convictions and the sentences. This Court denied a petition for a writ of certiorari. The Superior Court of Fulton County denied McCleskey's extraordinary motion for a new trial. McCleskey then filed a petition for a writ of habeas corpus in the Superior Court of Butts County. After holding an evidentiary hearing, the Superior Court denied relief. The Supreme Court of Georgia denied McCleskey's application for a certificate of probable cause to appeal the Superior Court's denial of his petition, and this Court again denied certiorari.

McCleskey next filed a petition for a writ of habeas corpus in the Federal District Court for the Northern District of Georgia. His petition raised 18 claims, one of which was that the Georgia capital sentencing process is administered in a racially discriminatory manner in violation of the Eighth and Fourteenth Amendments to the United States Constitution. In support of his claim, McCleskey proffered a statistical study performed by Professors David C. Baldus, Charles Pulaski, and George Woodworth, and (the Baldus study) that purports to show a disparity in the imposition of the death sentence in Georgia based on the race of the murder victim and, to a lesser extent, the race of the defendant. The Baldus study is actually two sophisticated statistical studies that examine over 2,000 murder cases that occurred in Georgia during the 1970's. The raw numbers collected by Professor Baldus indicate that defendants charged with killing white persons received the death penalty in 11% of the cases, but defendants charged with killing blacks received the death penalty in only 1% of the cases. The raw numbers also indicate a reverse racial disparity according to the race of the defendant: 4% of the black defendants received the death penalty, as opposed to 7% of the white defendants.

Baldus also divided the cases according to the combination of the race of the defendant and the race of the victim. He found that the death penalty was assessed in 22% of the cases involving black defendants and white victims; 8% of the cases involving white defendants and white victims; 1% of the cases involving black defendants and black victims; and 3% of the cases involving white defendants and black victims. Similarly, Baldus found that prosecutors sought the death penalty in 70% of the cases involving black defendants and white victims; 32% of the cases involving white defendants and white victims; 15% of the cases involving black defendants and black victims; and 19% of the cases involving white defendants and black victims.

Baldus subjected his data to an extensive analysis, taking account of 230 variables that could have explained the disparities on nonracial grounds. One of his models concludes that, even after taking account of 39 nonracial variables, defendants charged with killing white victims were 4.3 times as likely to receive a death sentence as defendants charged with killing blacks. According to this model, black defendants were 1.1 times as likely to receive a death sentence as other defendants. Thus, the Baldus study indicates that black defendants, such as McCleskey, who kill white victims have the greatest likelihood of receiving the death penalty.

The District Court held an extensive evidentiary hearing on McCleskey's petition. Although it believed that McCleskey's Eighth Amendment claim was foreclosed, it nevertheless considered the Baldus study with care. It concluded that McCleskey's "statistics do not demonstrate a prima facie case in support of the contention that the death penalty was imposed upon him because of his race, because of the race of the victim, or because of any Eighth Amendment concern." As to McCleskey's Fourteenth Amendment claim, the court found that the methodology of the Baldus study was flawed in several respects. Because of these defects, the court held that the Baldus study "fail[ed] to contribute anything of value" to McCleskey's claim. Accordingly, the court denied the petition insofar as it was based upon the Baldus study.

The Court of Appeals for the Eleventh Circuit, sitting en banc, carefully reviewed the District Court's decision on McCleskey's claim. It assumed the validity of the study itself and addressed the merits of McCleskey's Eighth and Fourteenth Amendment claims. That is, the court assumed that the study "showed that systematic and substantial disparities existed in the penalties imposed upon homicide defendants in Georgia based on race of the homicide victim, that the disparities existed at a less substantial rate in death sentencing based on race of defendants, and that the factors of race of the victim and defendant were at work in Fulton County." Even assuming the study's validity, the Court of Appeals found the statistics "insufficient to demonstrate discriminatory intent or unconstitutional discrimination in the Fourteenth Amendment context, [and] insufficient to show irrationality, arbitrariness and capriciousness under any kind of Eighth Amendment analysis." The court noted:

> The very exercise of discretion means that persons exercising discretion may reach different results from exact duplicates. Assuming each result is within the range of discretion, all are correct in the eyes of the law. It would not make sense for the system to require the exercise of discretion in order to be facially constitutional, and at the same time hold a system unconstitutional in application where that discretion achieved different results for what appear to be exact duplicates, absent the state showing the reasons for the difference. . . .
>
> The Baldus approach . . . would take the cases with different results on what are contended to be duplicate facts, where the differences could not be otherwise explained, and conclude that the different result was based on race alone. . . . This approach ignores the realities. . . . There are, in fact, no exact duplicates in capital crimes and capital defendants. The type of research submitted here tends to show which of the directed factors were effective, but is of restricted use in showing what undirected factors control the exercise of constitutionally required discretion.

The court concluded:

> Viewed broadly, it would seem that the statistical evidence presented here, assuming its validity, confirms rather than condemns the system. . . . The marginal disparity based on the race of the victim tends to support the state's contention that the system is working far differently from the one which *Furman v. Georgia* (1972) condemned. In pre-*Furman* days, there was no rhyme or reason as to who got the death penalty and who did not. But now, in the vast majority of cases, the reasons for a difference are well documented. That they are not so clear in a small percentage of the cases is no reason to declare the entire system unconstitutional.

The Court of Appeals affirmed the denial by the District Court of McCleskey's petition for a writ of habeas corpus insofar as the petition was based upon the Baldus study, with three judges dissenting as to McCleskey's claims based on the Baldus study. We granted certiorari, and now affirm.

II

McCleskey's first claim is that the Georgia capital punishment statute violates the Equal Protection Clause of the Fourteenth Amendment. He argues that race has infected the administration of Georgia's statute in two ways: persons who murder whites are more likely to be sentenced to death than persons who murder blacks, and black murderers are more likely to be sentenced to death than white murderers. As a black defendant who killed a white victim, McCleskey claims that the Baldus study demonstrates that he was discriminated against because of his race and because of the race of his victim. In its broadest form, McCleskey's claim of discrimination extends to every actor in the Georgia capital sentencing process, from the prosecutor who sought the death penalty and the jury that imposed the sentence, to the State itself that enacted the capital punishment statute and allows it to remain in effect despite its allegedly discriminatory application. We agree with the Court of Appeals, and every other court that has considered such a challenge, that this claim must fail.

A

Our analysis begins with the basic principle that a defendant who alleges an equal protection violation has the burden of proving "the existence of purposeful discrimination." A corollary to this principle is that a criminal defendant must prove that the purposeful discrimination "had a discriminatory effect" on him. *Wayte v. United States* (1985). Thus, to prevail under the Equal Protection Clause, McCleskey must prove that the decisionmakers in his case acted with discriminatory purpose. He offers no evidence specific to his own case that would support an inference that racial considerations played a part in his sentence. Instead, he relies solely on the Baldus study. McCleskey argues that the Baldus study compels an inference that his sentence rests on purposeful discrimination. McCleskey's claim that these statistics are sufficient proof of discrimination, without regard to the facts of a particular case, would extend to all capital cases in Georgia, at least where the victim was white and the defendant is black.

The Court has accepted statistics as proof of intent to discriminate in certain limited contexts. First, this Court has accepted statistical disparities as proof of an equal protection violation in the selection of the jury venire in a particular district. Although statistical proof normally must present a "stark" pattern to be accepted as the sole proof of discriminatory intent under the Constitution, *Arlington Heights v. Metropolitan Housing Dev. Corp.* (1977), "[b]ecause of the nature of the jury-selection task, . . . we have permitted a finding of constitutional violation even when the statistical pattern does not approach [such] extremes." Second, this Court has accepted statistics in the form of multiple-regression analysis to prove statutory violations under Title VII of the Civil Rights Act of 1964.

But the nature of the capital sentencing decision, and the relationship of the statistics to that decision, are fundamentally different from the corresponding elements in the venire-selection or Title VII cases. Most importantly, each particular decision to impose the death penalty is made by a petit jury selected from a properly constituted venire. Each jury is unique in its composition, and the Constitution requires that its decision rest on consideration of innumerable factors that vary according to the characteristics of the individual defendant and the facts of the particular capital offense. Thus, the application of an inference drawn from the general statistics to a specific decision in a trial and sentencing simply is not comparable to the application of an inference drawn from general statistics to a specific venire-selection or Title VII case. In those cases, the statistics relate to fewer entities, and fewer variables are relevant to the challenged decisions.

Another important difference between the cases in which we have accepted statistics as proof of discriminatory intent and this case is that, in the venire-selection and Title VII contexts, the decisionmaker has an opportunity to explain the statistical disparity. Here, the State has no practical opportunity to rebut the Baldus study. "[C]ontrolling considerations of . . . public policy," dictate that jurors "cannot be called . . . to testify to the motives and influences that led to their verdict." Similarly, the policy considerations behind a prosecutor's traditionally "wide discretion" suggest the impropriety of our requiring prosecutors to defend their decisions to seek death penalties, "often years after they were made." *See Imbler v. Pachtman* (1976). Moreover, absent far stronger proof, it is unnecessary to seek such a rebuttal, because a legitimate and unchallenged explanation for the decision is apparent from the record: McCleskey committed an act for which the United States Constitution and Georgia laws permit imposition of the death penalty.

Finally, McCleskey's statistical proffer must be viewed in the context of his challenge. McCleskey challenges decisions at the heart of the State's criminal justice system. "[O]ne of society's most basic tasks is that of protecting the lives of its citizens and one of the most basic ways in which it achieves the task is through criminal laws against murder." Implementation of these laws necessarily requires discretionary judgments. Because discretion is essential to the criminal justice process, we would demand exceptionally clear proof before we would infer that the discretion has been abused. The unique nature of the decisions at issue in this case also counsels against adopting such an inference from the disparities indicated by the Baldus study. Accordingly, we hold that the Baldus study is clearly insufficient to support an inference that any of the decisionmakers in McCleskey's case acted with discriminatory purpose.

B

McCleskey also suggests that the Baldus study proves that the State as a whole has acted with a discriminatory purpose. He appears to argue that the State has violated the Equal Protection Clause by adopting the capital punishment statute and allowing it to remain in force despite its allegedly discriminatory application. But "'[d]iscriminatory purpose' . . . implies more than intent as volition or intent as awareness of consequences. It implies that the decisionmaker, in this case a state legislature, selected or reaffirmed a particular course of action at least in part 'because of,' not merely 'in spite of,' its adverse effects upon an identifiable group." For this claim to prevail, McCleskey would have to prove that the Georgia Legislature enacted or maintained the death penalty statute because of an anticipated racially discriminatory effect. In *Gregg v. Georgia*, supra, this Court found that the Georgia capital sentencing system could operate in a fair and neutral manner. There was no evidence then, and there is none now, that the Georgia Legislature enacted the capital punishment statute to further a racially discriminatory purpose.

Nor has McCleskey demonstrated that the legislature maintains the capital punishment statute because of the racially disproportionate impact suggested by the Baldus study. As legislatures necessarily have wide discretion in the choice of criminal laws and penalties, and as there were legitimate reasons for the Georgia Legislature to adopt and maintain capital punishment, we will not infer a discriminatory purpose on the part of the State of Georgia. Accordingly, we reject McCleskey's equal protection claims.

III

McCleskey also argues that the Baldus study demonstrates that the Georgia capital sentencing system violates the Eighth Amendment. We begin our analysis of this claim by reviewing the restrictions on death sentences established by our prior decisions under that Amendment.

A

The Eighth Amendment prohibits infliction of "cruel and unusual punishments." This Court's early Eighth Amendment cases examined only the "particular methods of execution to determine whether they were too cruel to pass constitutional muster." Subsequently, the Court recognized that the constitutional prohibition against cruel and unusual punishments "is not fastened to the obsolete but may acquire meaning as public opinion becomes enlightened by a humane justice." In *Weems*, the Court identified a second principle inherent in the Eighth Amendment, "that punishment for crime should be graduated and proportioned to offense."

Chief Justice Warren, writing for the plurality in *Trop v. Dulles* (1958), acknowledged the constitutionality of capital punishment. In his view, the "basic concept underlying the Eighth Amendment" in this area is that the penalty must accord with "the dignity of man." In applying this mandate, we have been guided by his statement that "[t]he Amendment must draw its meaning from the evolving standards of decency that mark the progress of a maturing society." Thus, our constitutional decisions have been informed by "contemporary values concerning the infliction of a challenged sanction." In assessing contemporary values, we have eschewed subjective judgment, and instead have sought to ascertain "objective indicia that reflect the public attitude toward a given sanction." First among these indicia are the decisions of state legislatures, "because the . . . legislative judgment weighs heavily in ascertaining" contemporary standards. We also have been guided by the sentencing decisions of juries, because they are "a significant and reliable objective index of contemporary values." Most of our recent decisions as to the constitutionality of the death penalty for a particular crime have rested on such an examination of contemporary values.

B

Two principal decisions guide our resolution of McCleskey's Eighth Amendment claim. In *Furman v. Georgia* (1972), the Court concluded that the death penalty was so irrationally imposed that any particular death sentence could be presumed excessive. Under the statutes at issue in Furman, there was no basis for determining in any particular case whether the penalty was proportionate to the crime: "[T]he death penalty [was] exacted with great infrequency even for the most atrocious crimes and . . . there [was] no meaningful basis for distinguishing the few cases in which it [was] imposed from the many cases in which it [was] not."

In *Gregg*, the Court specifically addressed the question left open in *Furman*—whether the punishment of death for murder is "under all circumstances, 'cruel and unusual' in violation of the Eighth and Fourteenth Amendments of the Constitution." We noted that the imposition of the death penalty for the crime of murder "has a long history of acceptance both in the United States and in England." "The most marked indication of society's endorsement of the death penalty for murder [was] the legislative response to *Furman*." During the 4-year period between *Furman* and *Gregg*, at least 35 States had reenacted the death penalty, and Congress had authorized the penalty for aircraft piracy. The "actions of juries" were "fully compatible with the legislative judgments." We noted that any punishment might be unconstitutionally severe if inflicted without penological justification, but concluded:

Considerations of federalism, as well as respect for the ability of a legislature to evaluate, in terms of its particular State, the moral consensus concerning the death penalty and its social utility as a sanction, require us to conclude, in the absence of more convincing evidence, that the infliction of death as a punishment for murder is not without justification and thus is not unconstitutionally severe.

The second question before the Court in *Gregg* was the constitutionality of the particular procedures embodied in the Georgia capital punishment statute. We explained the fundamental principle of *Furman*, that "where discretion is afforded a sentencing body on a matter so grave as the determination of whether a human life should be taken or spared, that discretion must be suitably directed and limited so as to minimize the risk of wholly arbitrary and capricious action." Numerous features of the then new Georgia statute met the concerns articulated in Furman. The Georgia system bifurcates guilt and sentencing proceedings so that the jury can receive all relevant information for sentencing without the risk that evidence irrelevant to the defendant's guilt will influence the jury's consideration of that issue. The statute narrows the class of murders subject to the death penalty to cases in which the jury finds at least one statutory aggravating circumstance beyond a reasonable doubt. Conversely, it allows the defendant to introduce any relevant mitigating evidence that might influence the jury not to impose a death sentence. The procedures also require a particularized inquiry into "'the circumstances of the offense together with the character and propensities of the offender.'" Thus, "while some jury discretion still exists, 'the discretion to be exercised is controlled by clear and objective standards so as to produce non-discriminatory application.'" Moreover, the Georgia system adds "an important additional safeguard against arbitrariness and caprice" in a provision for automatic appeal of a death sentence to the State Supreme Court. The statute requires that court to review each sentence to determine whether it was imposed under the influence of passion or prejudice, whether the evidence supports the jury's finding of a statutory aggravating circumstance, and whether the sentence is disproportionate to sentences imposed in generally similar murder cases. To aid the court's review, the trial judge answers a questionnaire about the trial, including detailed questions as to "the quality of the defendant's representation [and] whether race played a role in the trial."

C

In the cases decided after *Gregg*, the Court has imposed a number of requirements on the capital sentencing process to ensure that capital sentencing decisions rest on the individualized inquiry contemplated in *Gregg*. In *Woodson v. North Carolina* (1976), we invalidated a mandatory capital sentencing system, finding that the "respect for humanity underlying the Eighth Amendment requires consideration of the character and record of the individual offender and the circumstances of the particular offense as a constitutionally indispensable part of the process of inflicting the penalty of death." Similarly, a State must "narrow the class of murderers subject to capital punishment" by providing "specific and detailed guidance" to the sentencer.

In contrast to the carefully defined standards that must narrow a sentencer's discretion to impose the death sentence, the Constitution limits a State's ability to narrow a sentencer's discretion to consider relevant evidence that might cause it to decline to impose the death sentence. "[T]he sentencer . . . [cannot] be precluded from considering, as a mitigating factor, any aspect of a defendant's character or record and any of the circumstances of the offense that the defendant proffers as a basis for a sentence less than death." Any exclusion of the "compassionate or mitigating factors stemming from the diverse frailties of humankind" that are relevant to the sentencer's decision would fail to treat all persons as "uniquely individual human beings."

Although our constitutional inquiry has centered on the procedures by which a death sentence is imposed, we have not stopped at the face of a statute, but have probed the application of statutes to particular cases. For example, in *Godfrey v. Georgia* (1980), the Court invalidated a Georgia Supreme Court interpretation of the statutory aggravating circumstance that the murder be "outrageously or wantonly vile, horrible or inhuman in that it involved torture, depravity of mind, or an aggravated battery to the victim." Although that court had articulated an adequate limiting definition of this phrase, we concluded that its interpretation in *Godfrey* was so broad that it may have vitiated the role of the aggravating circumstance in guiding the sentencing jury's discretion.

Finally, where the objective indicia of community values have demonstrated a consensus that the death penalty is disproportionate as applied to a certain class of cases, we have established substantive limitations on its application. In *Coker v. Georgia* (1977), the Court held that a State may not constitutionally sentence an individual to death for the rape of an adult woman. In *Enmund v. Florida* (1982), the Court prohibited imposition of the death penalty on a defendant convicted of felony murder absent a showing that the defendant possessed a sufficiently culpable mental state. Most recently, in *Ford v. Wainwright* (1986), we prohibited execution of prisoners who are insane.

D

In sum, our decisions since *Furman* have identified a constitutionally permissible range of discretion in imposing the death penalty. First, there is a required threshold below which the death penalty cannot be imposed. In this context, the State must establish rational criteria that narrow the decisionmaker's judgment as to whether the circumstances of a particular defendant's case meet the threshold. Moreover, a societal consensus that the death penalty is disproportionate to a particular offense prevents a State from imposing the death penalty for that offense. Second, States cannot limit the sentencer's consideration of any relevant circumstance that could cause it to decline to impose the penalty. In this respect, the State cannot channel the sentencer's discretion, but must allow it to consider any relevant information offered by the defendant.

IV

A

In light of our precedents under the Eighth Amendment, McCleskey cannot argue successfully that his sentence is "disproportionate to the crime in the traditional sense." He does not deny that he committed a murder in the course of a planned robbery, a crime for which this Court has determined that the death penalty constitutionally may be imposed. His disproportionality claim "is of a different sort." McCleskey argues that the sentence in his case is disproportionate to the sentences in other murder cases.

On the one hand, he cannot base a constitutional claim on an argument that his case differs from other cases in which defendants did receive the death penalty. On automatic appeal, the Georgia Supreme Court found that McCleskey's death sentence was not disproportionate to other death sentences imposed in the State. The court supported this conclusion with an appendix containing citations to 13 cases involving generally similar murders. Moreover, where the statutory procedures adequately channel the sentencer's discretion, such proportionality review is not constitutionally required.

On the other hand, absent a showing that the Georgia capital punishment system operates in an arbitrary and capricious manner, McCleskey cannot prove a constitutional violation by demonstrating that other defendants who may be similarly situated did not receive the death

1386 Chapter XVI Incarceration: Bail, Pretrial Detention, and Sentencing

penalty. In *Gregg*, the Court confronted the argument that "the opportunities for discretionary action that are inherent in the processing of any murder case under Georgia law," specifically the opportunities for discretionary leniency, rendered the capital sentences imposed arbitrary and capricious. We rejected this contention:

> The existence of these discretionary stages is not determinative of the issues before us. At each of these stages an actor in the criminal justice system makes a decision which may remove a defendant from consideration as a candidate for the death penalty. *Furman*, in contrast, dealt with the decision to impose the death sentence on a specific individual who had been convicted of a capital offense. Nothing in any of our cases suggests that the decision to afford an individual defendant mercy violates the Constitution. *Furman* held only that, in order to minimize the risk that the death penalty would be imposed on a capriciously selected group of offenders, the decision to impose it had to be guided by standards so that the sentencing authority would focus on the particularized circumstances of the crime and the defendant.

Because McCleskey's sentence was imposed under Georgia sentencing procedures that focus discretion "on the particularized nature of the crime and the particularized characteristics of the individual defendant," we lawfully may presume that McCleskey's death sentence was not "wantonly and freakishly" imposed, and thus that the sentence is not disproportionate within any recognized meaning under the Eighth Amendment.

B

Although our decision in *Gregg* as to the facial validity of the Georgia capital punishment statute appears to foreclose McCleskey's disproportionality argument, he further contends that the Georgia capital punishment system is arbitrary and capricious in application, and therefore his sentence is excessive, because racial considerations may influence capital sentencing decisions in Georgia. We now address this claim.

To evaluate McCleskey's challenge, we must examine exactly what the Baldus study may show. Even Professor Baldus does not contend that his statistics prove that race enters into any capital sentencing decisions or that race was a factor in McCleskey's particular case. Statistics at most may show only a likelihood that a particular factor entered into some decisions. There is, of course, some risk of racial prejudice influencing a jury's decision in a criminal case. There are similar risks that other kinds of prejudice will influence other criminal trials. The question "is at what point that risk becomes constitutionally unacceptable," *Turner v. Murray* (1986). McCleskey asks us to accept the likelihood allegedly shown by the Baldus study as the constitutional measure of an unacceptable risk of racial prejudice influencing capital sentencing decisions. This we decline to do.

Because of the risk that the factor of race may enter the criminal justice process, we have engaged in "unceasing efforts" to eradicate racial prejudice from our criminal justice system. *Batson v. Kentucky* (1986). Our efforts have been guided by our recognition that "the inestimable privilege of trial by jury . . . is a vital principle, underlying the whole administration of criminal justice." *See Duncan v. Louisiana* (1968). Thus, it is the jury that is a criminal defendant's fundamental "protection of life and liberty against race or color prejudice." *Strauder v. West Virginia* (1880). Specifically, a capital sentencing jury representative of a criminal defendant's community assures a "'diffused impartiality,'" in the jury's task of "express[ing] the conscience of the community on the ultimate question of life or death."

Individual jurors bring to their deliberations "qualities of human nature and varieties of human experience, the range of which is unknown and perhaps unknowable." The capital sentencing decision requires the individual jurors to focus their collective judgment on the unique characteristics of a particular criminal defendant. It is not surprising that such collective judgments often are difficult to explain. But the inherent lack of predictability of jury decisions does not justify their condemnation. On the contrary, it is the jury's function to make the difficult and uniquely human judgments that defy codification and that "buil[d] discretion, equity, and flexibility into a legal system."

McCleskey's argument that the Constitution condemns the discretion allowed decision-makers in the Georgia capital sentencing system is antithetical to the fundamental role of discretion in our criminal justice system. Discretion in the criminal justice system offers substantial benefits to the criminal defendant. Not only can a jury decline to impose the death sentence, it can decline to convict or choose to convict of a lesser offense. Whereas decisions against a defendant's interest may be reversed by the trial judge or on appeal, these discretionary exercises of leniency are final and unreviewable. Similarly, the capacity of prosecutorial discretion to provide individualized justice is "firmly entrenched in American law." As we have noted, a prosecutor can decline to charge, offer a plea bargain, or decline to seek a death sentence in any particular case. Of course, "the power to be lenient [also] is the power to discriminate," K. Davis, Discretionary Justice 170 (1973), but a capital punishment system that did not allow for discretionary acts of leniency "would be totally alien to our notions of criminal justice."

C

At most, the Baldus study indicates a discrepancy that appears to correlate with race. Apparent disparities in sentencing are an inevitable part of our criminal justice system. The discrepancy indicated by the Baldus study is "a far cry from the major systemic defects identified in *Furman*." As this Court has recognized, any mode for determining guilt or punishment "has its weaknesses and the potential for misuse." Specifically, "there can be 'no perfect procedure for deciding in which cases governmental authority should be used to impose death.'" Despite these imperfections, our consistent rule has been that constitutional guarantees are met when "the mode [for determining guilt or punishment] itself has been surrounded with safeguards to make it as fair as possible." Where the discretion that is fundamental to our criminal process is involved, we decline to assume that what is unexplained is invidious. In light of the safeguards designed to minimize racial bias in the process, the fundamental value of jury trial in our criminal justice system, and the benefits that discretion provides to criminal defendants, we hold that the Baldus study does not demonstrate a constitutionally significant risk of racial bias affecting the Georgia capital sentencing process.

V

Two additional concerns inform our decision in this case. First, McCleskey's claim, taken to its logical conclusion, throws into serious question the principles that underlie our entire criminal justice system. The Eighth Amendment is not limited in application to capital punishment, but applies to all penalties. Thus, if we accepted McCleskey's claim that racial bias has impermissibly tainted the capital sentencing decision, we could soon be faced with similar claims as to other types of penalty. Moreover, the claim that his sentence rests on the irrelevant factor of race easily could be extended to apply to claims based on unexplained discrepancies that correlate to membership in other minority groups, and even to gender. Similarly, since McCleskey's claim relates to the race of his victim, other claims could apply with equally logical force to statistical disparities that correlate with the race or sex of other actors in the criminal justice system, such as defense attorneys, or judges. Also, there is no logical reason that such a claim need be limited to racial or sexual bias. If arbitrary and capricious punishment is the touchstone under the Eighth Amendment, such a claim could — at least in theory — be based upon any arbitrary variable, such as the defendant's facial characteristics, or the physical attractiveness of the defendant or the victim, that some statistical study indicates may be influential in jury decisionmaking. As these examples illustrate, there is no limiting principle to the type of challenge brought by McCleskey. The Constitution does not require that a State eliminate any demonstrable disparity that correlates with a potentially irrelevant factor in order to operate a criminal justice system that includes capital punishment. As we have stated specifically in the context of capital punishment, the Constitution does not "plac[e] totally unrealistic conditions on its use."

Second, McCleskey's arguments are best presented to the legislative bodies. It is not the responsibility — or indeed even the right — of this Court to determine the appropriate punishment for particular crimes. It is the legislatures, the elected representatives of the people, that are "constituted to respond to the will and consequently the moral values of the people." Legislatures also are better qualified to weigh and "evaluate the results of statistical studies in terms of their own local conditions and with a flexibility of approach that is not available to the courts." Capital punishment is now the law in more than two-thirds of our States. It is the ultimate duty of courts to determine on a case-by-case basis whether these laws are applied consistently with the Constitution. Despite McCleskey's wide-ranging arguments that basically challenge the validity of capital punishment in our multiracial society, the only question before us is whether in his case, the law of Georgia was properly applied. We agree with the District Court and the Court of Appeals for the Eleventh Circuit that this was carefully and correctly done in this case.

VI

Accordingly, we affirm the judgment of the Court of Appeals for the Eleventh Circuit.

Justice BRENNAN, with whom Justice MARSHALL joins, and with whom Justice BLACKMUN and Justice STEVENS join in all but Part I, dissenting.

I

Adhering to my view that the death penalty is in all circumstances cruel and unusual punishment forbidden by the Eighth and Fourteenth Amendments, I would vacate the decision below insofar as it left undisturbed the death sentence imposed in this case. The Court observes that "[t]he *Gregg*-type statute imposes unprecedented safeguards in the special context of capital punishment," which "ensure a degree of care in the imposition of the death penalty that can be described only as unique." Notwithstanding these efforts, murder defendants in Georgia with white victims are more than four times as likely to receive the death sentence as are defendants with black victims. Nothing could convey more powerfully the intractable reality of the death penalty: "that the effort to eliminate arbitrariness in the infliction of that ultimate sanction is so plainly doomed to failure that it — and the death penalty — must be abandoned altogether."

Even if I did not hold this position, however, I would reverse the Court of Appeals, for petitioner McCleskey has clearly demonstrated that his death sentence was imposed in violation of the Eighth and Fourteenth Amendments. While I join Parts I through IV-A of Justice Blackmun's dissenting opinion discussing petitioner's Fourteenth Amendment claim, I write separately to emphasize how conclusively McCleskey has also demonstrated precisely the type of risk of irrationality in sentencing that we have consistently condemned in our Eighth Amendment jurisprudence.

II

At some point in this case, Warren McCleskey doubtless asked his lawyer whether a jury was likely to sentence him to die. A candid reply to this question would have been disturbing.

First, counsel would have to tell McCleskey that few of the details of the crime or of McCleskey's past criminal conduct were more important than the fact that his victim was white. Furthermore, counsel would feel bound to tell McCleskey that defendants charged with killing white victims in Georgia are 4.3 times as likely to be sentenced to death as defendants charged with killing blacks. In addition, frankness would compel the disclosure that it was more likely than not that the race of McCleskey's victim would determine whether he received a death sentence: 6 of every 11 defendants convicted of killing a white person would not have received the death penalty if their victims had been black, while, among defendants with aggravating and mitigating factors comparable to McCleskey's, 20 of every 34 would not have been sentenced to die if their victims had been black. Finally, the assessment would not be complete without the information that cases involving black defendants and white victims are more likely to result in a death sentence than cases featuring any other racial combination of defendant and victim. The story could be told in a variety of ways, but McCleskey could not fail to grasp its essential narrative line: there was a significant chance that race would play a prominent role in determining if he lived or died.

The Court today holds that Warren McCleskey's sentence was constitutionally imposed. It finds no fault in a system in which lawyers must tell their clients that race casts a large shadow on the capital sentencing process. The Court arrives at this conclusion by stating that the Baldus study cannot "prove that race enters into any capital sentencing decisions or that race was a factor in McCleskey's particular case." Since, according to Professor Baldus, we cannot say "to a moral certainty" that race influenced a decision, we can identify only "a likelihood that a particular factor entered into some decisions," and "a discrepancy that appears to correlate with race." This "likelihood" and "discrepancy," holds the Court, is insufficient to establish a constitutional violation. The Court reaches this conclusion by placing four factors on the scales opposite McCleskey's evidence: the desire to encourage sentencing discretion, the existence of "statutory safeguards" in the Georgia scheme, the fear of encouraging widespread challenges to other sentencing decisions, and the limits of the judicial role. The Court's evaluation of the significance of petitioner's evidence is fundamentally at odds with our consistent concern for rationality in capital sentencing, and the considerations that the majority invokes to discount that evidence cannot justify ignoring its force.

III

A

It is important to emphasize at the outset that the Court's observation that McCleskey cannot prove the influence of race on any particular sentencing decision is irrelevant in evaluating his Eighth Amendment claim. Since *Furman v. Georgia* (1972), the Court has been concerned with the risk of the imposition of an arbitrary sentence, rather than the proven fact of one. *Furman* held that the death penalty "may not be imposed under sentencing procedures that create a substantial risk that the punishment will be inflicted in an arbitrary and capricious manner." As Justice O'Connor observed in *Caldwell v. Mississippi* (1985), a death sentence must be struck down when the circumstances under which it has been imposed "creat[e] an unacceptable risk that 'the death penalty [may have been] meted out arbitrarily or capriciously' or through 'whim or mistake.'" This emphasis on risk acknowledges the difficulty of divining the jury's motivation in an individual case. In addition, it reflects the fact that concern for arbitrariness focuses on the rationality of the system as a whole, and that a system that features a significant probability that sentencing decisions are influenced by impermissible considerations cannot be regarded as rational. As we said in *Gregg*, "the petitioner looks to the sentencing system as a whole (as the Court did in *Furman* and we do today)": a constitutional violation is established if a plaintiff demonstrates a "pattern of arbitrary and capricious sentencing."

As a result, our inquiry under the Eighth Amendment has not been directed to the validity of the individual sentences before us. In *Godfrey*, for instance, the Court struck down the petitioner's sentence because the vagueness of the statutory definition of heinous crimes created a risk that prejudice or other impermissible influences might have infected the sentencing decision. In vacating the sentence, we did not ask whether it was likely that Godfrey's own sentence reflected the operation of irrational considerations. Nor did we demand a demonstration that such considerations had actually entered into other sentencing decisions involving heinous crimes. Similarly, in *Roberts v. Louisiana* (1976) and *Woodson v. North Carolina* (1976) we struck down death sentences in part because mandatory imposition of the death penalty created the risk that a jury might rely on arbitrary considerations in deciding which persons should be convicted of capital crimes. Such a risk would arise, we said, because of the likelihood that jurors reluctant to impose capital punishment on a particular defendant would refuse to return a conviction, so that the effect of mandatory sentencing would be to recreate the unbounded sentencing discretion condemned in *Furman*. We did not ask whether the death sentences in the cases before us could have reflected the jury's rational consideration and rejection of mitigating factors. Nor did we require proof that juries had actually acted irrationally in other cases.

Defendants challenging their death sentences thus never have had to prove that impermissible considerations have actually infected sentencing decisions. We have required instead that they establish that the system under which they were sentenced posed a significant risk of such an occurrence. McCleskey's claim does differ, however, in one respect from these earlier cases: it is the first to base a challenge not on speculation about how a system might operate, but on empirical documentation of how it does operate.

The Court assumes the statistical validity of the Baldus study, and acknowledges that McCleskey has demonstrated a risk that racial prejudice plays a role in capital sentencing in Georgia. Nonetheless, it finds the probability of prejudice insufficient to create constitutional concern. Close analysis of the Baldus study, however, in light of both statistical principles and human experience, reveals that the risk that race influenced McCleskey's sentence is intolerable by any imaginable standard.

B

The Baldus study indicates that, after taking into account some 230 nonracial factors that might legitimately influence a sentencer, the jury more likely than not would have spared McCleskey's life had his victim been black. The study distinguishes between those cases in which (1) the jury exercises virtually no discretion because the strength or weakness of aggravating factors usually suggests that only one outcome is appropriate; and (2) cases reflecting an "intermediate" level of aggravation, in which the jury has considerable discretion in choosing a sentence. McCleskey's case falls into the intermediate range. In such cases, death is imposed in 34% of white-victim crimes and 14% of black-victim crimes, a difference of 139% in the rate of imposition of the death penalty. In other words, just under 59% — almost 6 in 10 — defendants comparable to McCleskey would not have received the death penalty if their victims had been black.

Furthermore, even examination of the sentencing system as a whole, factoring in those cases in which the jury exercises little discretion, indicates the influence of race on capital sentencing. For the Georgia system as a whole, race accounts for a six percentage point difference in the rate at which capital punishment is imposed. Since death is imposed in 11% of all white-victim cases, the rate in comparably aggravated black-victim cases is 5%. The rate of capital sentencing in a white-victim case is thus 120% greater than the rate in a black-victim case. Put another way, over half — 55% — of defendants in white-victim crimes in Georgia would not have been sentenced to die if their victims had been black. Of the more than 200 variables potentially relevant to a sentencing decision, race of the victim is a powerful explanation for variation in death sentence rates—as powerful as nonracial aggravating factors such as a prior murder conviction or acting as the principal planner of the homicide.

These adjusted figures are only the most conservative indication of the risk that race will influence the death sentences of defendants in Georgia. Data unadjusted for the mitigating or aggravating effect of other factors show an even more pronounced disparity by race. The capital sentencing rate for all white-victim cases was almost 11 times greater than the rate for black-victim cases. Furthermore, blacks who kill whites are sentenced to death at nearly 22 times the rate of blacks who kill blacks, and more than 7 times the rate of whites who kill blacks. In addition, prosecutors seek the death penalty for 70% of black defendants with white victims, but for only 15% of black defendants with black victims, and only 19% of white defendants with black victims. Since our decision upholding the Georgia capital sentencing system in Gregg, the State has executed seven persons. All of the seven were convicted of killing whites, and six of the seven executed were black. Such execution figures are especially striking in light of the fact that, during the period encompassed by the Baldus study, only 9.2% of Georgia homicides involved black defendants and white victims, while 60.7% involved black victims.

McCleskey's statistics have particular force because most of them are the product of sophisticated multiple-regression analysis. Such analysis is designed precisely to identify patterns in the aggregate, even though we may not be able to reconstitute with certainty any individual decision that goes to make up that pattern. Multiple-regression analysis is particularly well suited to identify the influence of impermissible considerations in sentencing, since it is able to control for permissible factors that may explain an apparent arbitrary pattern. While the decisionmaking process of a body such as a jury may be complex, the Baldus study provides a massive compilation of the details that are most relevant to that decision. As we held in the context of Title VII of the Civil Rights Act of 1964 last term in *Bazemore v. Friday* (1986), a multiple-regression analysis need not include every conceivable variable to establish a party's case, as long as it includes those variables that account for the major factors that are likely to influence decisions. In this case, Professor Baldus in fact conducted additional regression analyses in response to criticisms and suggestions by the District Court, all of which confirmed, and some of which even strengthened, the study's original conclusions.

The statistical evidence in this case thus relentlessly documents the risk that McCleskey's sentence was influenced by racial considerations. This evidence shows that there is a better than even chance in Georgia that race will influence the decision to impose the death penalty: a majority of defendants in white-victim crimes would not have been sentenced to die if their victims had been black. In determining whether this risk is acceptable, our judgment must be shaped by the awareness that "[t]he risk of racial prejudice infecting a capital sentencing proceeding is especially serious in light of the complete finality of the death sentence," *Turner v. Murray* (1986), and that "[i]t is of vital importance to the defendant and to the community that any decision to impose the death sentence be, and appear to be, based on reason rather than caprice or emotion." In determining the guilt of a defendant, a State must prove its case beyond a reasonable doubt. That is, we refuse to convict if the chance of error is simply less likely than not. Surely, we should not be willing to take a person's life if the chance that his death sentence was irrationally imposed is more likely than not. In light of the gravity of the interest at stake, petitioner's statistics on their face are a powerful demonstration of the type of risk that our Eighth Amendment jurisprudence has consistently condemned.

C

Evaluation of McCleskey's evidence cannot rest solely on the numbers themselves. We must also ask whether the conclusion suggested by those numbers is consonant with our understanding of history and human experience. Georgia's legacy of a race-conscious criminal justice system, as well as this Court's own recognition of the persistent danger that racial attitudes may affect criminal proceedings, indicates that McCleskey's claim is not a fanciful product of mere statistical artifice.

For many years, Georgia operated openly and formally precisely the type of dual system the evidence shows is still effectively in place. The criminal law expressly differentiated between crimes committed by and against blacks and whites, distinctions whose lineage traced back to the time of slavery. During the colonial period, black slaves who killed whites in Georgia, regardless of whether in self-defense or in defense of another, were automatically executed. A. Higginbotham, In the Matter of Color: Race in the American Legal Process 256 (1978).

By the time of the Civil War, a dual system of crime and punishment was well established in Georgia. The state criminal code contained separate sections for "Slaves and Free Persons of Color" and for all other persons. The code provided, for instance, for an automatic death sentence for murder committed by blacks, but declared that anyone else convicted of murder might receive life imprisonment if the conviction were founded solely on circumstantial testimony or simply if the jury so recommended. The code established that the rape of a free white female by a black "shall be" punishable by death. However, rape by anyone else of a free white female was punishable by a prison term not less than 2 nor more than 20 years. The rape of blacks was punishable "by fine and imprisonment, at the discretion of the court." A black convicted of assaulting a free white person with intent to murder could be put to death at the discretion of the court, but the same offense committed against a black, slave or free, was classified as a "minor" offense whose punishment lay in the discretion of the court, as long as such punishment did not "extend to life, limb, or health." Assault with intent to murder by a white person was punishable by a prison term of from 2 to 10 years. While sufficient provocation could reduce a charge of murder to manslaughter, the code provided that "[o]bedience and submission being the duty of a slave, much greater provocation is necessary to reduce a homicide of a white person by him to voluntary manslaughter, than is prescribed for white persons."

In more recent times, some 40 years ago, Gunnar Myrdal's epochal study of American race relations produced findings mirroring McCleskey's evidence:

> "As long as only Negroes are concerned and no whites are disturbed, great leniency will be shown in most cases. . . . The sentences for even major crimes are ordinarily reduced when the victim is another Negro.
> "For offenses which involve any actual or potential danger to whites, however, Negroes are punished more severely than whites.
> "On the other hand, it is quite common for a white criminal to be set free if his crime was against a Negro." G. Myrdal, An American Dilemma 551-553 (1944).

This Court has invalidated portions of the Georgia capital sentencing system three times over the past 15 years. The specter of race discrimination was acknowledged by the Court in striking down the Georgia death penalty statute in *Furman*. Justice Douglas cited studies suggesting imposition of the death penalty in racially discriminatory fashion, and found the standardless statutes before the Court "pregnant with discrimination." Justice Marshall pointed to statistics indicating that "Negroes [have been] executed far more often than whites in proportion to their percentage of the population. Studies indicate that while the higher rate of execution among Negroes is partially due to a higher rate of crime, there is evidence of racial discrimination." Although Justice Stewart declined to conclude that racial discrimination had been plainly proved, he stated that "[m]y concurring Brothers have demonstrated that, if any basis can be discerned for the selection of these few to be sentenced to die, it is the constitutionally impermissible basis of race." In dissent, Chief Justice Burger acknowledged that statistics "suggest, at least as a historical matter, that Negroes have been sentenced to death with greater frequency than whites in several States, particularly for the crime of interracial rape." Finally, also in dissent, Justice Powell intimated that an Equal Protection Clause argument would be available for a black "who could demonstrate that members of his race were being singled out for more severe punishment than others charged with the same offense." He noted that although the Eighth Circuit had rejected a claim of discrimination in *Maxwell v. Bishop*, the statistical evidence in that case "tend[ed] to show a pronounced disproportion in the number of Negroes receiving death sentences for rape in parts of Arkansas and elsewhere in the South." It is clear that the Court regarded the opportunity for the operation of racial prejudice a particularly troublesome aspect of the unbounded discretion afforded by the Georgia sentencing scheme.

Five years later, the Court struck down the imposition of the death penalty in Georgia for the crime of rape. *Coker v. Georgia* (1977). Although the Court did not explicitly mention race, the decision had to have been informed by the specific observations on rape by both the Chief Justice and Justice Powell in *Furman*. Furthermore, evidence submitted to the Court indicated that black men who committed rape, particularly of white women, were considerably more likely to be sentenced to death than white rapists. For instance, by 1977 Georgia had executed 62 men for rape since the Federal Government began compiling statistics in 1930. Of these men, 58 were black and 4 were white.

Three years later, the Court in *Godfrey* found one of the State's statutory aggravating factors unconstitutionally vague, since it resulted in "standardless and unchanneled imposition of death sentences in the uncontrolled discretion of a basically uninstructed jury. . . ." Justice Marshall, concurring in the judgment, noted that "[t]he disgraceful distorting effects of racial discrimination and poverty continue to be painfully visible in the imposition of death sentences."

This historical review of Georgia criminal law is not intended as a bill of indictment calling the State to account for past transgressions. Citation of past practices does not justify the automatic condemnation of current ones. But it would be unrealistic to ignore the influence of history in assessing the plausible implications of McCleskey's evidence. "[A]mericans share a historical experience that has resulted in individuals within the culture ubiquitously attaching a significance to race that is irrational and often outside their awareness." Lawrence, The Id, The Ego, and Equal Protection: Reckoning With Unconscious Racism, Stan. L. Rev. 327 (1987). See generally id., at 328-344 (describing the psychological dynamics of unconscious racial motivation). As we said in *Rose v. Mitchell* (1979):

> [W]e . . . cannot deny that, 114 years after the close of the War Between the States and nearly 100 years after *Strauder*, racial and other forms of discrimination still remain a fact of life, in the administration of justice as in our society as a whole. Perhaps today that discrimination takes a form more subtle than before. But it is not less real or pernicious.

The ongoing influence of history is acknowledged, as the majority observes, by our "'unceasing efforts' to eradicate racial prejudice from our criminal justice system." These efforts, however, signify not the elimination of the problem but its persistence. Our cases reflect a realization of the myriad of opportunities for racial considerations to influence criminal proceedings: in the exercise of peremptory challenges, *Batson v. Kentucky, supra*; in the selection of the grand jury, *Vasquez v. Hillery* (1986); . . . and in the conscious or unconscious bias of jurors, *Turner v. Murray* (1986), *Ristaino v. Ross* (1976).

The discretion afforded prosecutors and jurors in the Georgia capital sentencing system creates such opportunities. No guidelines govern prosecutorial decisions to seek the death penalty, and Georgia provides juries with no list of aggravating and mitigating factors, nor any standard for balancing them against one another. Once a jury identifies one aggravating factor, it has complete discretion in choosing life or death, and need not articulate its basis for selecting life imprisonment. The Georgia sentencing system therefore provides considerable opportunity for racial considerations, however subtle and unconscious, to influence charging and sentencing decisions.

History and its continuing legacy thus buttress the probative force of McCleskey's statistics. Formal dual criminal laws may no longer be in effect, and intentional discrimination may no longer be prominent. Nonetheless, as we acknowledged in *Turner*, "subtle, less consciously held racial attitudes" continue to be of concern, and the Georgia system gives such attitudes considerable room to operate. The conclusions drawn from McCleskey's statistical evidence are therefore consistent with the lessons of social experience.

The majority thus misreads our Eighth Amendment jurisprudence in concluding that McCleskey has not demonstrated a degree of risk sufficient to raise constitutional concern. The determination of the significance of his evidence is at its core an exercise in human moral judgment, not a mechanical statistical analysis. It must first and foremost be informed by awareness of the fact that death is irrevocable, and that as a result "the qualitative difference of death from all other punishments requires a greater degree of scrutiny of the capital sentencing determination." For this reason, we have demanded a uniquely high degree of rationality in imposing the death penalty. A capital sentencing system in which race more likely than not plays a role does not meet this standard. It is true that every nuance of decision cannot be statistically captured, nor can any individual judgment be plumbed with absolute certainty. Yet the fact that we must always act without the illumination of complete knowledge cannot induce paralysis when we confront what is literally an issue of life and death. Sentencing data, history, and experience all counsel that Georgia has provided insufficient assurance of the heightened rationality we have required in order to take a human life.

IV

The Court cites four reasons for shrinking from the implications of McCleskey's evidence: the desirability of discretion for actors in the criminal justice system, the existence of statutory safeguards against abuse of that discretion, the potential consequences for broader challenges to criminal sentencing, and an understanding of the contours of the judicial role. While these concerns underscore the need for sober deliberation, they do not justify rejecting evidence as convincing as McCleskey has presented.

The Court maintains that petitioner's claim "is antithetical to the fundamental role of discretion in our criminal justice system." It states that "[w]here the discretion that is fundamental to our criminal process is involved, we decline to assume that what is unexplained is invidious."

Reliance on race in imposing capital punishment, however, is antithetical to the very rationale for granting sentencing discretion. Discretion is a means, not an end. It is bestowed in order to permit the sentencer to "trea[t] each defendant in a capital case with that degree of respect due the uniqueness of the individual." The decision to impose the punishment of death must be based on a "particularized consideration of relevant aspects of the character and record of each convicted defendant." Failure to conduct such an individualized moral inquiry "treats all persons convicted of a designated offense not as unique individual human beings, but as members of a faceless, undifferentiated mass to be subjected to the blind infliction of the penalty of death."

Considering the race of a defendant or victim in deciding if the death penalty should be imposed is completely at odds with this concern that an individual be evaluated as a unique human being. Decisions influenced by race rest in part on a categorical assessment of the worth of human beings according to color, insensitive to whatever qualities the individuals in question may possess. Enhanced willingness to impose the death sentence on black defendants, or diminished willingness to render such a sentence when blacks are victims, reflects a devaluation of the lives of black persons. When confronted with evidence that race more likely than not plays such a role in a capital sentencing system, it is plainly insufficient to say that the importance of discretion demands that the risk be higher before we will act—for in such a case the very end that discretion is designed to serve is being undermined.

Our desire for individualized moral judgments may lead us to accept some inconsistencies in sentencing outcomes. Since such decisions are not reducible to mathematical formulae, we are willing to assume that a certain degree of variation reflects the fact that no two defendants are completely alike. There is thus a presumption that actors in the criminal justice system exercise their discretion in responsible fashion, and we do not automatically infer that sentencing patterns that do not comport with ideal rationality are suspect.

As we made clear in *Batson v. Kentucky* (1986), however, that presumption is rebuttable. *Batson* dealt with another arena in which considerable discretion traditionally has been afforded, the exercise of peremptory challenges. Those challenges are normally exercised without any indication whatsoever of the grounds for doing so. The rationale for this deference has been a belief that the unique characteristics of particular prospective jurors may raise concern on the part of the prosecution or defense, despite the fact that counsel may not be able to articulate that concern in a manner sufficient to support exclusion for cause. As with sentencing, therefore, peremptory challenges are justified as an occasion for particularized determinations related to specific individuals, and, as with sentencing, we presume that such challenges normally are not made on the basis of a factor such as race. As we said in *Batson*, however, such features do not justify imposing a "crippling burden of proof," in order to rebut that presumption. The Court in this case apparently seeks to do just that. On the basis of the need for individualized decisions, it rejects evidence, drawn from the most sophisticated capital sentencing analysis ever performed, that reveals that race more likely than not infects capital sentencing decisions. The Court's position converts a rebuttable presumption into a virtually conclusive one.

The Court also declines to find McCleskey's evidence sufficient in view of "the safeguards designed to minimize racial bias in the [capital sentencing] process." *Gregg* upheld the Georgia capital sentencing statute against a facial challenge which Justice White described in his concurring opinion as based on "simply an assertion of lack of faith" that the system could operate in a fair manner (opinion concurring in judgment). Justice White observed that the claim that prosecutors might act in an arbitrary fashion was "unsupported by any facts," and that prosecutors must be assumed to exercise their charging duties properly "[a]bsent facts to the contrary." It is clear that *Gregg* bestowed no permanent approval on the Georgia system. It simply held that the State's statutory safeguards were assumed sufficient to channel discretion without evidence otherwise.

It has now been over 13 years since Georgia adopted the provisions upheld in *Gregg*. Professor Baldus and his colleagues have compiled data on almost 2,500 homicides committed during the period 1973-1979. They have taken into account the influence of 230 nonracial variables, using a multitude of data from the State itself, and have produced striking evidence that the odds of being sentenced to death are significantly greater than average if a defendant is black or his or her victim is white. The challenge to the Georgia system is not speculative or theoretical; it is empirical. As a result, the Court cannot rely on the statutory safeguards in discounting McCleskey's evidence, for it is the very effectiveness of those safeguards that such evidence calls into question. While we may hope that a model of procedural fairness will curb the influence of race on sentencing, "we cannot simply assume that the model works as intended; we must critique its performance in terms of its results."

The Court next states that its unwillingness to regard petitioner's evidence as sufficient is based in part on the fear that recognition of McCleskey's claim would open the door to widespread challenges to all aspects of criminal sentencing. Taken on its face, such a statement seems to suggest a fear of too much justice. Yet surely the majority would acknowledge that if striking evidence indicated that other minority groups, or women, or even persons with blond hair, were disproportionately sentenced to death, such a state of affairs would be repugnant to deeply rooted conceptions of fairness. The prospect that there may be more widespread abuse than McCleskey documents may be dismaying, but it does not justify complete abdication of our judicial role. The Constitution was framed fundamentally as a bulwark against governmental power, and preventing the arbitrary administration of punishment is a basic ideal of any society that purports to be governed by the rule of law.

In fairness, the Court's fear that McCleskey's claim is an invitation to descend a slippery slope also rests on the realization that any humanly imposed system of penalties will exhibit some imperfection. Yet to reject McCleskey's powerful evidence on this basis is to ignore both the qualitatively different character of the death penalty and the particular repugnance of racial discrimination, considerations which may properly be taken into account in determining whether various punishments are "cruel and unusual." Furthermore, it fails to take account of the unprecedented refinement and strength of the Baldus study.

It hardly needs reiteration that this Court has consistently acknowledged the uniqueness of the punishment of death. "Death, in its finality, differs more from life imprisonment than a 100-year prison term differs from one of only a year or two. Because of that qualitative difference, there is a corresponding difference in the need for reliability in the determination that death is the appropriate punishment." Furthermore, the relative interests of the state and the defendant differ dramatically in the death penalty context. The marginal benefits accruing to the state from obtaining the death penalty rather than life imprisonment are considerably less than the marginal difference to the defendant between death and life in prison. Such a disparity is an additional reason for tolerating scant arbitrariness in capital sentencing. Even those who believe that society can impose the death penalty in a manner sufficiently rational to justify its continuation must acknowledge that the level of rationality that is considered satisfactory must be uniquely high. As a result, the degree of arbitrariness that may be adequate to render the death penalty "cruel and unusual" punishment may not be adequate to invalidate lesser penalties. What these relative degrees of arbitrariness might be in other cases need not concern us here; the point is that the majority's fear of wholesale invalidation of criminal sentences is unfounded.

The Court also maintains that accepting McCleskey's claim would pose a threat to all sentencing because of the prospect that a correlation might be demonstrated between sentencing outcomes and other personal characteristics. Again, such a view is indifferent to the considerations that enter into a determination whether punishment is "cruel and unusual." Race is a consideration whose influence is expressly constitutionally proscribed. We have expressed a moral commitment, as embodied in our fundamental law, that this specific characteristic should not be the basis for allotting burdens and benefits. Three constitutional amendments, and numerous statutes, have been prompted specifically by the desire to address the effects of racism. "Over the years, this Court has consistently repudiated '[d]istinctions between citizens solely because of their ancestry' as being 'odious to a free people whose institutions are founded upon the doctrine of equality.'" *Loving v. Virginia* (1967). Furthermore, we have explicitly acknowledged the illegitimacy of race as a consideration in capital sentencing. *Zant v. Stephens* (1983). That a decision to impose the death penalty could be influenced by race is thus a particularly repugnant prospect, and evidence that race may play even a modest role in levying a death sentence should be enough to characterize that sentence as "cruel and unusual."

Certainly, a factor that we would regard as morally irrelevant, such as hair color, at least theoretically could be associated with sentencing results to such an extent that we would regard as arbitrary a system in which that factor played a significant role. As I have said above, however, the evaluation of evidence suggesting such a correlation must be informed not merely by statistics, but by history and experience. One could hardly contend that this Nation has on the basis of hair color inflicted upon persons deprivation comparable to that imposed on the basis of race. Recognition of this fact would necessarily influence the evaluation of data suggesting the influence of hair color on sentencing, and would require evidence of statistical correlation even more powerful than that presented by the Baldus study.

Furthermore, the Court's fear of the expansive ramifications of a holding for McCleskey in this case is unfounded because it fails to recognize the uniquely sophisticated nature of the Baldus study. McCleskey presents evidence that is far and away the most refined data ever assembled on any system of punishment, data not readily replicated through casual effort. Moreover, that evidence depicts not merely arguable tendencies, but striking correlations, all the more powerful because nonracial explanations have been eliminated. Acceptance of petitioner's evidence would therefore establish a remarkably stringent standard of statistical evidence unlikely to be satisfied with any frequency.

The Court's projection of apocalyptic consequences for criminal sentencing is thus greatly exaggerated. The Court can indulge in such speculation only by ignoring its own jurisprudence demanding the highest scrutiny on issues of death and race. As a result, it fails to do justice to a claim in which both those elements are intertwined — an occasion calling for the most sensitive inquiry a court can conduct. Despite its acceptance of the validity of Warren McCleskey's evidence, the Court is willing to let his death sentence stand because it fears that we cannot successfully define a different standard for lesser punishments. This fear is baseless.

Finally, the Court justifies its rejection of McCleskey's claim by cautioning against usurpation of the legislatures' role in devising and monitoring criminal punishment. The Court is, of course, correct to emphasize the gravity of constitutional intervention and the importance that it be sparingly employed. The fact that "[c]apital punishment is now the law in more than two thirds of our States," however, does not diminish the fact that capital punishment is the most awesome act that a State can perform. The judiciary's role in this society counts for little if the use of governmental power to extinguish life does not elicit close scrutiny. It is true that society has a legitimate interest in punishment. Yet, as Alexander Bickel wrote:

> "It is a premise we deduce not merely from the fact of a written constitution but from the history of the race, and ultimately as a moral judgment of the good society, that government should serve not only what we conceive from time to time to be our immediate material needs but also certain enduring values. This in part is what is meant by government under law." The Least Dangerous Branch 24 (1962).

Our commitment to these values requires fidelity to them even when there is temptation to ignore them. Such temptation is especially apt to arise in criminal matters, for those granted constitutional protection in this context are those whom society finds most menacing and opprobrious. Even less sympathetic are those we consider for the sentence of death, for execution "is a way of saying, 'You are not fit for this world, take your chance elsewhere.'"

For these reasons, "[t]he methods we employ in the enforcement of our criminal law have aptly been called the measures by which the quality of our civilization may be judged." Those whom we would banish from society or from the human community itself often speak in too faint a voice to be heard above society's demand for punishment. It is the particular role of courts to hear these voices, for the Constitution declares that the majoritarian chorus may not alone dictate the conditions of social life. The Court thus fulfills, rather than disrupts, the scheme of separation of powers by closely scrutinizing the imposition of the death penalty, for no decision of a society is more deserving of "sober second thought."

V

At the time our Constitution was framed 200 years ago this year, blacks "had for more than a century before been regarded as beings of an inferior order, and altogether unfit to associate with the white race, either in social or political relations; and so far inferior, that they had no rights which the white man was bound to respect." *Dred Scott v. Sandford* (1857). Only 130 years ago, this Court relied on these observations to deny American citizenship to blacks. A mere three generations ago, this Court sanctioned racial segregation, stating that "[i]f one race be inferior to the other socially, the Constitution of the United States cannot put them upon the same plane." *Plessy v. Ferguson* (1896).

In more recent times, we have sought to free ourselves from the burden of this history. Yet it has been scarcely a generation since this Court's first decision striking down racial segregation, and barely two decades since the legislative prohibition of racial discrimination in major domains of national life. These have been honorable steps, but we cannot pretend that in three decades we have completely escaped the grip of a historical legacy spanning centuries. Warren McCleskey's evidence confronts us with the subtle and persistent influence of the past. His message is a disturbing one to a society that has formally repudiated racism, and a frustrating one to a Nation accustomed to regarding its destiny as the product of its own will. Nonetheless, we ignore him at our peril, for we remain imprisoned by the past as long as we deny its influence in the present.

It is tempting to pretend that minorities on death row share a fate in no way connected to our own, that our treatment of them sounds no echoes beyond the chambers in which they die. Such an illusion is ultimately corrosive, for the reverberations of injustice are not so easily confined. "The destinies of the two races in this country are indissolubly linked together," id., at 560 (Harlan, J., dissenting), and the way in which we choose those who will die reveals the depth of moral commitment among the living.

The Court's decision today will not change what attorneys in Georgia tell other Warren McCleskeys about their chances of execution. Nothing will soften the harsh message they must convey, nor alter the prospect that race undoubtedly will continue to be a topic of discussion. McCleskey's evidence will not have obtained judicial acceptance, but that will not affect what is said on death row. However many criticisms of today's decision may be rendered, these painful conversations will serve as the most eloquent dissents of all.

• • •

NOTES AND QUESTIONS

1. Consider McCleskey's sentencing hearing. First, under the statute, the jury is permitted to recommend the death penalty upon finding beyond a reasonable doubt just one of the following aggravating factors set forth in the statute.

> (1) The offense . . . was committed by a person with a prior record of conviction for a capital felony;
>
> (2) The offense . . . was committed while the offender was engaged in the commission of another capital felony or aggravated battery, or the offense of murder was committed while the offender was engaged in the commission of burglary or arson in the first degree;
>
> (3) The offender, by his act of murder . . . knowingly created a great risk of death to more than one person in a public place by means of a weapon or device which would normally be hazardous to the lives of more than one person;

D. Race and Sentencing 1399

(4) The offender committed the offense . . . for himself or another, for the purpose of receiving money or any other thing of monetary value;

(5) The murder of a judicial officer, former judicial officer, district attorney or solicitor, or former district attorney or solicitor was committed during or because of the exercise of his official duties;

(6) The offender caused or directed another to commit murder or committed murder as an agent or employee of another person;

(7) The offense of murder, rape, armed robbery, or kidnapping was outrageously or wantonly vile, horrible, or inhuman in that it involved torture, depravity of mind, or an aggravated battery to the victim;

(8) The offense . . . was committed against any peace officer, corrections employee, or fireman while engaged in the performance of his official duties;

(9) The offense . . . was committed by a person in, or who has escaped from, the lawful custody of a peace officer or place of lawful confinement; or

(10) The murder was committed for the purpose of avoiding, interfering with, or preventing a lawful arrest or custody in a place of lawful confinement, of himself or another.

Ga. Code Ann. § 17-10-30(b) & (c) (1982).

What types of murder can you readily think of that do *not* feature one of those aggravating circumstances? Does such a statute truly eliminate the standardless discretion that *Furman* condemned?

Second, McCleskey "offered no mitigating evidence." None. Now, granted, capital defense lawyering as we now know it was still in its infancy at the time of McCleskey's sentencing, but no mitigating evidence whatsoever? *See* Chapter VIII *supra* (discussing ineffective assistance of counsel in the death penalty litigation context).

Third, as Justice Blackmun points out in his dissenting opinion, the district attorney at a deposition in connection with the habeas proceedings testified that his office had no training other than "on the job" training and no standards or policies whatever for determining when to seek the death penalty. In other words, the decision to decide whether one of the above aggravating factors was applicable and whether as a consequence to seek the death penalty was within the total discretion of an assistant district attorney.

2. In Part IIIA of its equal protection analysis the Court begins by citing *Wayte* and proclaiming that "McCleskey must prove that the decisionmakers in *his* case acted with discriminatory purpose." Doesn't this mean it's over? Are any statistics ever going to prove this? While the next paragraph implies that a "stark" statistical showing sometimes may suffice the case the Court references as an example of this possibility (in a footnote) is *Yick Wo v. Hopkins, see supra*, the unattainable apotheosis of statistical perfection.

3. The Court recognizes that it has sometimes required a less "stark" statistical showing in jury composition cases "because of the nature of the jury-selection task," a proposition for which it cites *Arlington Heights v. Metropolitan Housing Dev. Corp.*, 429 U.S. 252, 266 n.13 (1977). Suffice it to say that *Arlington Heights* did not explain what was unique about the jury selection cases that required special treatment, and the jury selection cases cited in *Arlington Heights* gave no indication they were announcing "special" rules.

But in any event, if there were ever an occasion for relaxation of conventional doctrine, shouldn't it be due to "the nature of" the death penalty task? Isn't death different?

4. In considering the potential applicability of a Title VII burden-shifting methodology, the Court says "the State has no practical opportunity to rebut the Baldus study." Is this true? Why couldn't the state retain its own expert to conduct a study and/or to respond to the Baldus study? This is a garden-variety feature of both civil and criminal litigation.

5. Justice Brennan's dissent notes that the majority's requirement that McCleskey prove that discrimination affected *his* sentence is wrong under the Eighth Amendment and, indeed, is at war with the Court's recent death penalty decisions in cases such as *Furman* and *Gregg*.

481 U.S. at 323-24. These cases and others focus on the state's sentencing system as a whole, and analyze the "risk" that sentencing decisions are influenced by impermissible considerations. Does the Baldus study suggest a risk of the influence of impermissible considerations in the same way that a standardless sentencing regime does?

6. The Court's comments on discretion are bizarre. It seems to view discretion not as a necessary evil, something to be tolerated, but rather as a virtue, or at least as a protective shield. It states that because discretion is "essential" to the criminal justice system the Court would require "exceptionally clear proof" before finding that discretion has been abused. Where does this purported burden come from? The Court cites to nothing for this proposition. Later, the Court says that McCleskey's discrimination argument "is antithetical to the fundamental role of discretion in our criminal justice system," and observes that a jury or prosecutor can show a defendant leniency. Does the fact that a decision maker has wide discretion means the decision maker is insulated from review, that discretion cannot be abused? Does the ability of a prosecutor or jury to bestow leniency mean that it is immune from challenge when it allegedly acts unconstitutionally? Don't appellate courts review district court judges every day for abusing their discretion? As Justice Brennan puts it, citing to *Batson*, the presumption of regularity within a zone of discretion is rebuttable.

Despite its own comments on leniency the Court nonetheless cites Professor Davis's on-point observation that "the power to be lenient [also] is the power to discriminate." K. Davis, Discretionary Justice 170 (1973).

7. The majority's enlistment of *Batson* is curious. Is the Court just being defensive here, as elsewhere in its overview of its work in the death penalty and other areas? Is it saying, in effect, we've taken steps to make juries more integrated, what else do you expect us to do? And what does the Court mean when it says that "the inherent lack of predictability of jury decisions does not justify their condemnation"? Isn't the entire point of the Baldus study to show that in some very important ways juries are predictable?

The Court's "policy" arguments are especially difficult to take seriously. The Court's slippery slope argument—that McCleskey's argument could be extended to all manner of unexplained discrepancies and "even to gender"—ignores the fact that courts are in the business of drawing lines and do so all the time. And it is preposterous to analogize "hair color" to race, or to believe that the statistical force and effort reflected in the Baldus study will be replicated in service of an effort to litigate over frivolous distinctions. It is also true, as Justice Brennan points out in dissent, that the Court's arguments reflect "a fear of too much justice."

Warren McCleskey

The Court also suggests that McCleskey's arguments are best presented to legislative bodies inasmuch as it is improper for courts to "determine the appropriate punishment for particular crimes," and for that point, oddly, cites the dissenting opinion in *Furman v. Georgia*. The rich irony here is that just two years after the decision in *McCleskey*, in *Mistretta v. United States*, 488 U.S. 361 (1989), the Court would uphold the constitutionality of legislative reform that created a federal sentencing commission, purportedly located in the judicial branch, whose sole mission was to "determine the appropriate punishment for particular crimes." *See supra*.

McCleskey is one of the most criticized Supreme Court decisions of the modern era, condemned by journalists and academics alike. *See* Randall Kennedy, McCleskey v. Kemp*: Race, Capital Punishment, and the Supreme Court*, 101 Harv. L. Rev. 1388, 1388-89 & n.11 (1988) (itemizing denunciations).

The next case looks at a federal judge's quixotic effort to find an equal protection violation in Congress's legislated crack-cocaine disparity in the Anti–Drug Abuse Act of 1986. The disparity is fleshed out in the background section of the opinion.

United States v. Clary
846 F. Supp. 768 (E.D. Mo. 1994), rev'd 34 F.3d 709 (8th Cir. 1994)

CAHILL, District Judge.

Defendant Edward Clary was arrested for possession with intent to distribute 67.76 grams of cocaine base. Clary pled guilty to possession with intent to distribute cocaine base ("crack cocaine"), pursuant to 21 U.S.C. § 841(b)(1)(A)(iii) (hereinafter referred to as the "crack statute"), punishable by a mandatory minimum sentence of 10 years imprisonment. Prior to sentencing, Clary, a black male, filed a motion challenging the constitutionality of the crack statute and contended, inter alia, that the sentence enhancement provisions contained in it and United States Sentencing Guidelines (U.S.S.G.) § 2D1.1 violated his equal protection rights guaranteed by the Fifth Amendment.

The Court scheduled this case for hearing on the motion for a downward departure and the motion challenging the constitutionality of the statute. After extended hearings the Court took this matter under advisement and gave it detailed and exhaustive consideration. Upon evaluating the evidence and legal arguments, the Court issues this memorandum.

Specifically, defendant Clary asserts that the penalty differential of the "100 to 1" ratio of cocaine to cocaine base contained in both the crack statute and the United States Sentencing Guidelines has a disproportionate impact on blacks because blacks are more likely to possess cocaine base than whites who are more likely to possess cocaine powder. Therefore, defendant's argument continues, providing longer sentences for possession of cocaine base than for the identical amount of cocaine powder treats a similarly situated defendant in a dissimilar manner, which violates his right to equal protection under the law.

THE PROBLEM BEFORE THE COURT

Before this Court are two different sentencing provisions contained within the same statute for possession and distribution of different forms of the same drug. The difference—the key difference—is that possession and distribution of 50 grams of crack cocaine carries the same mandatory minimum sentence of 10 years imprisonment as possession and distribution of 5000 grams of powder cocaine. Both provisions punish the same drug, but penalize crack cocaine 100 times more than powder cocaine!

Congress tells us that the rationale for this sentencing dichotomy which produces harsher punishment for involvement with crack cocaine is because it is so much more dangerous than powder cocaine. As "proof," Congress relied upon endless media accounts of crack's increased threat to society. While Congress may have had well-intentioned concerns, the Court is equally aware that this one provision, the crack statute, has been directly responsible for incarcerating nearly an entire generation of young black American men for very long periods, usually during the most productive time of their lives. Inasmuch as crack and powder cocaine are really the same drug (powder cocaine is "cooked" with baking soda for about a minute to make crack), it appears likely that race rather than conduct was the determining factor.

Although both statutory provisions purport to punish criminal activity for both crack and powder cocaine, the blacks using crack are punished with much longer sentences than whites using the same amount of powder cocaine. This disparity is so significantly disproportional that it shocks the conscience of the Court and invokes examination.

The Eighth Circuit Court of Appeals has rejected numerous constitutional challenges to the crack statute and the United States Sentencing Guidelines. However, the Eighth Circuit acknowledged the "extraordinary disparity in punishment between possession of cocaine powder and cocaine base."

"With so much at stake, however, in this and other cases, we are reluctant to say that full exploration of the issues is unwarranted . . . in connection with crack cocaine punishments, which continue to perplex many sentencing judges. We do not invite mere repetition of prior rejected arguments, without new facts or legal analysis."

This Court accepts the Eighth Circuit's invitation to present a novel legal analysis of the adverse disparate impact on blacks resulting from the imposition of 21 U.S.C. § 841(b)(1)(A)(iii). Here is the Court's analysis.

CRIME AND THE LEGISLATIVE RESPONSE

Crime!! The very word connotes fear and panic, resulting in a frenzied attempt to control and curtail criminal actions in today's violence-soaked world. Never before have Americans cringed at the thought of becoming victims of random, irrational assaults; never before has the fear and frustration of average citizens grown to such a level that a "lynch mob mentality" becomes the common emotional reaction to crime.

Today there are so many senseless crimes whose gory details are displayed in living color on living room TVs in America that people, inured to the bloodshed, simply retreat in horror from the senseless details. Crime has always been an unpleasant but ever present segment of life in America, but never has it been so brutally and instantaneously reported in repetitive words and pictures from all segments of the media — print, audio, and video. So whether there is more violence, as most believe, or whether the ratio is about the same but appears greater because of the larger population and visual immediacy makes little difference. There is no doubt that the public's perception is so pronounced that the public is prepared — no, anxious — to pay any price to control crime even to the abandonment of traditional constitutional safeguards.

The media has for years kept up a drum beat of repetitious reporting of the most horrendous criminal actions, intruding upon the grief stricken victims, interrogating them while they are in shock and tears, further enraging the public against anyone even accused of a crime. The presumption of innocence is now a legal myth.

Of especial importance is the fact that crime is no longer segregated to the other side of town. People living in the "better parts" of the community are now subject to the random anger and uncontrolled hatred of psychopaths and weak, frustrated individuals unable to cope with the problems of life. When one reads of the brutal murder of elderly persons in the bedrooms of their ransacked homes, of gangland style executions and drive-by shootings, and ravishment of innocent children of tender years, it is understandable that anxious citizens demand action. Legislators, feeling the heat of the public's anger, scramble to comply with the demands of raging infernos caused by the citizens' ire.

For the last few years there has been a feeding frenzy of responses by lawmakers of every stripe and political persuasion, so that both Congress and state legislators fill the hoppers with proposed bills designed to curtail crime (each one more restrictive or Draconian than those before) in the misguided hope of reducing crime, but in the certainty that, effective or not, it will gain votes.

It is true we need the relief demanded by citizens. It is true that we need firm and stern punishment for many crimes, including life imprisonment in appropriate cases. It is true that the scourges of communities saturated with drugs must be corrected. It is true that the police alone cannot correct this destructive societal force. But it is also true that we cannot continue to ignore the "root causes" of crime, such as poverty, racism, unemployment, and poor education.

It is, therefore, with concern that the Court broaches a subject which, no matter how just and fair it may be, will be seen by some as "soft on crime." No matter how onerous its penalty, and more importantly, no matter how unjust and unequal the penalties may be for one class of criminals, unthinking citizens, frustrated and afraid, say simply, "Lock 'em all up and melt the keys."

This Court favors an omnibus of remedies which include lengthy incarceration, speedy trials, and appropriately severe sentences to deter crime. Drug trafficking must be reduced and drug treatment for addicts must be made available. The biggest single factor in the elimination of drug usage, violence, and crime is JOBS. But meaningful jobs and opportunities must be available. In plain and simple terms, we must utilize both carrot and stick to eliminate the scourge of crime.

Therefore, let this be perfectly clear. This Court does not condone crime in any form or by any class or group, and is firmly convinced that, in these times especially, punishment must be severe enough and imposed with such certainty and promptness as to deter further transgression. The Court is well aware that there are individuals who must be separated from society for lengthy periods, even life imprisonment, in order to protect society. Sadly, there are youngsters for whom deterrents must be imposed early and sternly enough to change their behavior. Our society must be protected from the random and senseless violence that is so much a part of contemporary America, especially in our inner cities where most of the victims reside.

This Court recognizes that the control of crime is the most important goal of sentencing, and a firm and certain punishment must be the major goal in criminal justice. However, such punishment must be fair; it must fit the particulars of the offense and must acknowledge characteristics of individuals.

Let it be further understood that this Court would play no role in furthering the belief that drugs are to be condoned or ignored. Naturally, the greatest effectiveness would come from controlling those nearest the source of the drugs, but even the couriers and street peddlers facilitate the distribution of the deadly substances and they, too, must be punished — but to a degree commensurate with their culpability.

The "100 to 1" ratio, coupled with mandatory minimum sentencing provided by federal statute, has created a situation that reeks with inhumanity and injustice. The scales of justice have been turned topsy turvy so that those masterminds, the "kingpins" of drug trafficking, escape detection, while those whose role is minimal, even trivial, are hoisted on the spears of an enraged electorate and at the pinnacle of their youth are imprisoned for years while those most responsible for the evil of the day remain free.

THE CHALLENGE TO THE COURT

Having clearly stated the Court's conviction that crime cannot be reduced without stern and prompt punishment as well as long range plans to reduce criminal activities, the Court now feels emboldened to express a viewpoint designed to eliminate the disproportional punishment for crack, which would enhance the credibility of the government among black citizens and help restore their faith in believing that equal justice is for all.

THE CHALLENGE TO THE COURT

The Court is faced with the task of resolving whether the crack statute violated defendant Clary's equal protection rights. The equal protection component of the Fifth Amendment Due Process clause commands that similarly situated people must be treated alike. The Court's basic understanding of this constitutional rule is that when one group of people violates the same type of laws as other people similar to them, they should be punished in the same manner.

To determine whether a law treats similarly situated people in a dissimilar manner, a violation of equal protection under the U.S. Constitution, the Court must first determine the appropriate type of judicial review to apply. Judicial review is conducted under one of three different levels of scrutiny depending upon the seriousness of the constitutional violation that triggers the review.

The Court conducts the lowest level of constitutional scrutiny, a rational basis review, to determine whether a law that causes disparate treatment among similarly situated persons serves a rational state or governmental purpose. "Equal protection does not require that all persons be dealt with identically . . . [but] it does require that a distinction [that is] made have some relevance to the purpose for which the classification is made."

The next level of review, intermediate scrutiny, applies when the Court must determine whether the classification scheme included in the law must "fairly be viewed as furthering a substantial interest of the state." "Under this standard, although a law does not involve a facially invidious classification, it will be reviewed if it gives rise to recurring constitutional difficulties."

The highest form of constitutional review that the Court evokes, strict scrutiny, is mandated when the legislative classification incorporates presumptively suspect factors, such as race, or fundamental individual liberties, such as religion. In such cases, once the suspect classification is revealed, the government must prove that the classification is narrowly tailored to further a compelling government interest. For example, racist statutes which on their face and in their direct language created segregated facilities such as restrooms and drinking fountains were struck down by the United States Supreme Court under strict scrutiny.

The difficult situation that a Court must face is to determine whether a statute which is facially neutral was enacted for racial reasons and would thereby have a disparate impact on a particular racial group. Whether or not racial discrimination was involved in legislative action that resulted in a law which, although facially neutral, still has a racially disparate impact "demands a sensitive inquiry into such circumstantial evidence of intent as may be available."

Under *Arlington*, the Supreme Court set forth key factors to evaluate whether a law was motivated by racial discrimination. These factors included the presence of disparate impact, the overall historical context of the legislation, the legislative history of the challenged law, and departures from the normal legislative process. Additional legal precedent has provided the Court with more criteria for its review, such as foreseeability of the consequences of the legislation; however, *Arlington* provides the Court with the major benchmark to discover the presence of racial influence in the legislative decision making process.

These various levels of constitutional review evolved as a response to the manner in which racism in America has manifested itself within the legal system. Overt racism, evidenced by

D. Race and Sentencing 1405

such occurrences as "Jim Crow Laws," allowed legislators to enact racist laws without reprisals. As civil rights for all Americans became a reality, continued attempts to maintain racial barriers took on the form of more subtle, covert, facially neutral legislation. Examples of this type of legislation included zoning, voting and housing laws.

Today most legislation would not contain overtly racist referrals and, indeed, would eliminate the slightest allusion to racial factors in the words of the legislation itself. But today, despite the fact that a law may be racially neutral on its face, there still may be factors derived from unconscious racism that affect and infiltrate the legislative result.

A HISTORY OF RACISM IN CRIMINAL PUNISHMENT

That black people have been punished more severely for violating the same law as whites is not a new phenomenon. A dual system of criminal punishment based on racial discrimination can be traced back to the time of slavery. In order to understand the role that racism has played in enacting the penalty enhancement for using crack cocaine, one must first take note of America's history of racially tainted criminal laws, particularly drug laws. Race has often served as a significant contributing factor to the enhancement of penalties for crime.

Early in our nation's history, legislatures were motivated by racial discrimination to differentiate between crimes committed by whites and crimes committed by blacks. For example, "An Act Against Stealing Hogs" provided a penalty of 25 lashes on a bare back or a 10 pound fine for white offenders, while nonwhites (slave and free) would receive 39 lashes, with no chance of paying a fine to avoid the whipping. In 1697, Pennsylvania passed death sentence legislation for black men who raped white women and castrated them for attempted rape. White men who committed the same offense would be fined, whipped, or imprisoned for one year.

During Reconstruction, Southern legislatures sought to maintain control of freed slaves by passing criminal laws directed at blacks that treated petty crimes as serious offenses. A Georgia law passed in 1875 made hog stealing a felony. A Missouri "pig law" defined the theft of property worth more than $10 as grand larceny and provided for punishment of up to five years of hard labor. As a result, Southern prisons swelled and became, for the first time, predominantly black. The prison population in Georgia alone tripled within two years.

Prior to the civil rights era, Congress repeatedly imposed severe criminal sanctions on addictive substances once they became popular with minorities. Historically, a consortium of reactionary media and a subsequently inflamed constituency have combined to influence Congress to impose more severe criminal sanctions for use of narcotics once they became popular with minorities.

Media accounts and inaccurate data influenced public opinion about opium smoking. "Ambivalence and outright hostility" toward Chinese coupled with the concern that opium smoking was spreading to the upper classes, provided the foundation for the passage of the 1909 Smoking Opium Exclusion Act. "Yellow Peril" was a term used in the years between the Great Wars to express the fear that the huge population of the Far East posed a military threat to the West. This fear induced an aversion to the opium usage believed to be prevalent in Chinese communities and foisted anti-opium legislation.

The Harrison Act of 1914, the first federal law to prohibit distribution of cocaine and heroin, was passed on the heels of overblown media accounts depicting heroin-addicted black prostitutes and criminals in the cities. The author of the Act, Representative Francis Harrison, moved to include coca leaves in the bill "since [the leaves] make Coca-Cola and Pepsi-Cola and all those things are sold to Negroes all over the South." At one point the bill appeared to be facing defeat until Dr. Hamilton Wright, the American delegate to the Hague Opium Conference, 1911-1912, submitted an official report in which he warned Congress of the

Chapter XVI Incarceration: Bail, Pretrial Detention, and Sentencing

drug crazed blacks in the South whose drug habits "threaten[ed] to creep into the higher social ranks of the country" The images of narcotics and a black rebellion in the South and images of black addicts involved with white women were central to the hysteria that motivated legislative enactments. His report, amplified and personalized by the news media and photographs, helped to shape public opinion regardless of the factual basis. True or not, the black addict became a stereotype not synonymous with most black men.

The Marijuana Tax Act was signed into law on August 2, 1937, after a successful media campaign orchestrated by Harry J. Anslinger, then the Commissioner of the Treasury Department's Bureau of Narcotics. Using the media as his forum, Anslinger graphically depicted the alleged insane violence which he alleged resulted from marijuana use.

In later decades cocaine became associated with exotic groups such as Hollywood entertainers and jazz musicians. It earned the moniker of the "rich man's drug." In the early 1960s and 1970s, cocaine began to move into mainstream society, and became the "drug of the eighties." Even with the widespread use of powder cocaine, no new drug laws were enacted to further criminalize or penalize cocaine possession. The "war on drugs" with respect to powder cocaine was concentrated on impeding international import of the drug or targeted large scale financiers. The social history is clear that so long as cocaine powder was a popular amusement among young, white professionals, law enforcement policy prohibiting cocaine was weakly enforced.

Almost every major drug has been, at various times in America's history, treated as a threat to the survival of America by some minority segment of society. Panic based on media reports which incited racial fears has been used historically in this country as the catalyst for generating racially biased legislation. The association of illicit drug use with minorities and the threat of it "spreading to the higher ranks" is disturbingly similar to the events which culminated in the "100 to 1" ratio enhancement in the crack statute.

RACISM IN TRANSITION

The mid-1860s marked the eve of the demise of slavery. In both the urban North and South, blacks and whites lived side by side but in segregated arrangements. Free blacks were prohibited from using many public conveniences and conveyances. Blacks were systematically segregated. "Jim Crow" laws, a Northern creation, moved South.

Blacks in the North were made painfully aware of white supremacy and black inferiority. Although blacks had token freedom, white constituencies firmly believed that blacks were intellectually, politically, socially, and physically incapable of assimilating into the white mainstream. Even Abraham Lincoln made a clearly politically expedient statement in 1858 when he said:

> "I will say then that I am not, nor ever have been in favor of bringing about in any way the social and political equality of the white and black races [applause] — that I am not nor ever have been in favor of making voters or jurors of negroes, nor of qualifying them to hold office, nor to intermarry with white people, and I will say in addition to this that there is a physical difference between the black and white races which I believe will for ever forbid the two races living together on terms of social and political equality. And inasmuch as they cannot so live, while they do remain together there must be the position of superior and inferior, and I as much as any other man am in favor of having the superior position assigned to the white race."
> Woodward, C. Vann, The Strange Career of Jim Crow, p. 21.

It would, of course, be unimaginable for a politician today to make such statements. In the context of what was necessary to solicit political support in 1858, utterances like these were comparatively mild. But today or yesterday, Lincoln's speech would, nonetheless, have a harmful impact upon blacks and is a good example of the effect of "unconscious racism" in his day.

D. Race and Sentencing   **1407**

In the anarchy that followed the Civil War, whites became hysterical that blacks would seek insurrectional revenge. As freedmen roamed the countryside and congregated in towns, white reactionary frenzy increasingly put pressure on the federal government to respond. In 1865 President Johnson passed the notorious Black Codes, "intended to establish systems of peonage or apprenticeship resembling slavery." Until the late 1940s, America solidly entrenched institutionally racist laws and forms of behavior into the social fabric of the country.

In 1945, the legal codes of many states openly discriminated against blacks, denying them the freedom to compete for and enjoy the good things of American life. But around 1950, many of these laws began to be struck down by the federal courts in a series of decisions leading up to *Brown v. Board of Education* (1954). Those decisions, however, did not automatically end segregation nor did they move blacks from a position of legal inferiority to one of equality. The legacy of years of slavery and second class citizenship in the wake of emancipation could not be so easily eliminated.

The 1960s were years of great turmoil in America. The assassinations of President John F. Kennedy, Robert Kennedy, and Dr. Martin Luther King left an indelible mark in our nation's history. The civil rights struggle epitomized the inherent principles of American justice and thus provided the moral high ground to those advocating respect for human dignity for all men — black and white alike. It was slowly becoming politically correct and morally right to espouse acceptance of blacks into the American mainstream. Overt discrimination was no longer in vogue and could not be publicly displayed. To accept blacks into hitherto closed areas of society was in style. But for many the years of segregation left their mark — so discrimination, unconscious though it may have been, still lived.

During the 1970s, victories of the civil rights battles had brought new hopes and heightened expectations to many residents of the inner cities. They then saw the opening wedge of success, at least by a few talented individuals who were entering mainstream America and achieving financial, political, and professional success. The dismal days of "American apartheid" or segregation appeared to be over; public accommodations were opening, albeit grudgingly in some instances, and a new day had begun for the forgotten and poor. Retrenchment set in. Challenges to affirmative action programs were being heard everywhere. While employment was available to the educated and trained, there were fewer menial jobs available. The great reduction in pay for jobs in service industries such as restaurants and labor pools in contrast to factories and assembly lines made such employment only suitable for students or retirees.

IMPACT OF THE 80s

The 1980s were times of cataclysmic economic change in America. The smoke-stack industries which furnished considerable highly paid employment to many persons with limited formal education were dead, dying, or moving elsewhere. The major corporations were retreading and making more products with more machines but fewer humans, and finally, a pervasive opinion grew that government had to curtail spending for the poor in order to reduce its own budget deficit. Even the grants of the "military-industrial" complex were affected. Local and state governments were getting less and less money returned by the federal government, and therefore most community projects such as hospitals, playgrounds, emergency shelters, and food pantries were closed. Unemployment reached levels as high as 8 percent nationally but in the inner cities it hovered around 20 percent and in some cases soared to levels of 50 to 60 percent for young black men.

The 80s found many communities bereft of the assistance from institutions financed by the federal government, and with virtually no employment, many young residents of the inner cities lost hope and motivation. In their anger and frustration they turned to the most visible source of immediate financial reward—drug traffic. Because there were so few employment opportunities otherwise available, and because the immense drug market offered huge profits immediately, many persons were attracted to it. This, in turn, brought competition, and in the absence of regulation (usually enforced by government), turf competition developed which led to more and more gang wars in which the use of military type firearms flourished. Desperate to maintain their share of the obscenely lucrative profits from drug peddling, the gangs became more aggressive and exhibited little sympathy for bystanders caught in the crossfire. It must be noted that in the early years of the drug war few paid attention to the escalating violence among these competing gangs because they were then only killing each other or an occasional hapless victim who lived nearby. The media rarely did more than mention the victims who lived in the inner cities. It was only when suburbanites and European tourists became targets of these desperados that the government responded. Then did much of law enforcement concentrate on "controlling crime," mainly by keeping it boxed up in the ghettos.

Acrimonious relations began to grow in many communities, and a tendency simply to contain the crime in a designated area rather than to try to eliminate it began to form. Highways and fences were used to segregate the troubled zones, and police tried to isolate the residents of inner cities, many times by unjustified harassment and unfair arrests. In a recent 1987 incident, the residents of East St. Louis, Illinois, were blocked from crossing the bridge across the Mississippi River to prevent their attendance at the St. Louis Fourth of July celebration until then Chief U.S. District Judge John F. Nangle, E.D. Missouri, ordered the police department to remove the barriers.

In the mid-1980s a sea change of attitudes toward crime itself had coalesced in America. Prior to this era, the predominant view was that crime was caused by deprivation or neglect and that rehabilitation was the main goal of incarceration. When the media (both press and electronic) became able to reveal instantaneously to the entire world graphic details of any crime occurring anywhere in this nation, the general public became aroused and angered as never before. The repetition of the stories on TV, cable, newspaper, and magazines, fanned the flames of anger into an inferno of fiery frenzy. This anger resulted in town hall meetings, TV crime dramas, pitiful photographs, all generating even more notoriety relating to crime and criminals. Most important of all, those parts of a neighborhood believed to be immune to the spread of crime now found that the plague was spreading, first to the edges of the inner cities and then to the affluent suburbs and even to the distant rural towns and villages.

In assessing judgment and determining fault, all facets of the circumstances must be known and weighed. Picture a city where it is easier to buy cocaine than it is to purchase a loaf of bread. Imagine a town that discourages those who could be role models by denying them mortgages and loans to improve their homes. Think of a community where mothers, barely more than children themselves, serve as one-parent heads of households in a world without fathers. Consider a neighborhood without effective leaders because they all have fled to suburbia. Contemplate the facts that markets and malls are nonexistent; dilapidated buildings serve as hideaways for prostitutes and drug dens; sales bulletins, catalogs, and coupons are never delivered to residents because of their mailing zip codes, thus eliminating opportunities for discounts and lower prices. Remember the children who rarely see a doctor, lawyer, or teacher as a neighbor and whose only source of inspiration is a chain bedecked drug peddler.

These portraits of misery and degradation are the daily world of the inner city resident and are all, part and parcel, products of unconscious racism. Is it any wonder that there is no motivation, no happiness, no hope? It is not strange to recognize that with such misery surrounding them they have lost the ambition to work and to fight, but only await the inevitable—death. The terror of long prison terms has little deterrence for them—their life is already a prison of despair.

It has been only a little over 30 years since the "legislative prohibition of racial discrimination in major domains of national life." Although moderate strides have been taken, we cannot fool ourselves into believing that our decisions are free from the influences of this country's legacy of racial subordination and discrimination. If we deny the influences of the vestiges of racism, we will "remain imprisoned by the past."

UNCONSCIOUS RACISM

Thus, the root of racism has been implanted in our collective unconscious and has biased the ideas that Americans accept about the significance of race. Racism goes beyond prejudicial discrimination and bigotry. It arises from outlooks, stereotypes, and fears of which we are vastly unaware. Our historical experience has made racism an integral part of our culture even though society has more recently embraced an ideal that rejects racism as immoral. When an individual experiences conflict between racist ideas and the social ethic that condemns those ideas, the mind excludes his racism from his awareness.

Conjointly, the root of unconscious racism can be found in the latent psyches of white Americans that were inundated for centuries with myths and fallacies of their superiority over the black race. So deeply embedded are these ideas, that their acceptance and socialization from generation to generation have become a mere routine.

Unconscious racism existed in some limited form during slavery. As outright discrimination against blacks became increasingly politically and socially unacceptable, and, in 1954, in some measure illegal, racist actions metamorphized into more subtle forms of discrimination. As more well-educated blacks flowed into America's mainstream, whites even began to differentiate between the kind of blacks who reflected white values and who were not like "those other" blacks akin to the inner city stereotype.

A benign neglect for the harmful impact or fallout upon the black community that might ensue from decisions made by the white community for the "greater good" of society has replaced intentional discrimination. In the "enlightened and politically correct 90s," whites have become indignant at the suggestion that they harbor any ill-will towards blacks or retain any vestiges of racism. After all, they have black friends. They work with black people every day. They enjoy black entertainers on their favorite television programs every night.

Similarly, police and law enforcement authorities responded that they were also protecting black neighborhoods and black citizens from the scourges of crime and drugs by using harsh "get tough" laws to arrest crack dealers and other criminal perpetrators who lurked in the ghetto. Therefore, the logic continued, it really did not matter what happened to those blacks who did not fit the mold as long as white America was kept protected and safe from them. Hardly any law or measure was too harsh to deal with them, including the crack statute.

When counsel first argued that overt racism was really the basis for the discriminatory crack penalties, this Court rejected that approach out-of-hand, for the Court did not believe that such outrageous and outmoded ideas would affect the legislators of this day and age. But upon reflection, the Court recognizes that while intentional discrimination is unlikely today, unconscious feelings of difference and superiority still live on even in well-intentioned minds. There is a realization that most Americans have grown beyond the evils of overt racial malice, but still have not completely shed the deeply rooted cultural bias that differentiates between "them" and "us."

The illustration of unconscious racism is patently evident in the crack cocaine statutes. Had the same type of law been applied to powder cocaine, it would have sentenced droves of young whites to prison for extended terms. Before the enactment of such a law, it would have been much more carefully and deliberately considered. After all, in these days when "toughness on crime" is a political virtue, the simplest and fairest solution would have been to make the severe punishment for powder cocaine the same as for crack cocaine. But when the heavy punishment is inflicted only upon those in the weak and unpopular minority community, it is an example of benign neglect arising from unconscious racism.

Psychoanalytic theory explains the processes which govern the mind and control mental behavior as primary and secondary. The primary process, the Id, consists of wishes, desires and instincts that strive for gratification, and which occur outside of our awareness. The secondary process, the Ego, happens under conscious control and is bound by logic and reason. "The Ego is required to respect the demands of reality and to conform to ethical and moral laws." The thoughts and desires generated by the Id will not reach our conscious control until screened by the Ego where they are "criticized, rejected or modified" by defense measures. In the case of a conflict, the information from the Id will not pass, thereby remaining in the unconscious, or will pass by "disguising forbidden wishes and making them palatable."

Racism is irrational. It is socially and politically unacceptable. Because the "Ego must adapt to cultural order," ideas, attitudes, and behavior based upon racial prejudice will be repressed and relegated to the unconscious by the Ego and not allowed to pass to the conscious until they reshape or restructure to be disguised as morally and socially acceptable. When an individual cannot live up to the aspirations and standards of his own conscience, he will rationalize his unexplained conflict in his emotions with a legitimate reason. Hence, racism is forced into the unconscious mind. A person who feels benign toward blacks will nevertheless make decisions and take actions that will harm minorities "because of" their race and consequently create racial stereotypes.

Cognitive theorists promote that "categorization" is a common source of racial stereotypes. Because too many events occur daily for the mind to address them on an individual basis, the mind categorizes experiences in order to make sense of them. The more particular the categorization of groups of people, the more likely the person is to sharply distinguish the characteristics of individuals belonging to the group. Social categories are created through assimilation, which "entails learning and internalizing preferences and evaluations." Stereotyping, assimilating and internalizing occur early in life, usually from parents or television. Becoming fearful of blacks, perceiving blacks as dangerous, different or subordinate, are lessons learned and internalized completely outside of our awareness, and are reinforced by the media generated stereotyping.

Studies of the impact of race on white decision making nearly always explain disparate effects by focusing on negative assessments of, or undesirable outcomes for, nonwhites, rather than positive results for whites. That is, they adopt a conceptual framework in which unconscious race discrimination is triggered by stereotyping.

Whites are rarely introduced to the image of blacks as criminals through direct experience; generally, the media serves to provide and promote these racial caricatures. A fearful white class afraid to encounter a black man results from never being exposed to positive images of black America. Given the racially segregated nature of American economic and social life, the media has played an important role in the construction of a national image of black male youth as "the criminal" in two significant respects which served to enhance penalties for crack cocaine violators: 1) generating public panic regarding crack cocaine; and 2) associating black males with crack cocaine. Ergo, the decision maker who is unaware of this selection perception that has produced his stereotype will believe that his actions are not motivated by racial prejudice.

The influence of "unconscious racism" on legislative decisions has never been presented to any court in this context. Constitutional redress to racial discrimination has resulted primarily from judicial vigilance directed toward correcting overt and facially discriminatory legislation forged first by slavery and followed by continuing racial animosity toward blacks and other ethnic minorities. Remaining still is a more pernicious, albeit intangible, form of race discrimination in the individual's unconscious thoughts that influences the decision making process. As a result, "individuals . . . ubiquitously attach a significance to race that is irrational and often used outside their awareness."

Consequently, the focus on "purposeful" discrimination is inadequate as a response to more subtle and deeply buried forms of racism. In 1909, the United States Supreme Court acknowledged that "[racial] [b]ias or prejudice is such an elusive condition of the mind that it is most difficult, if not impossible, to always recognize its existence." *Crawford v. United States* (1909). Eighty-three years later, *Crawford* holds: the inquiry to determine racial bias is still "difficult, if not impossible." Without consideration of the influences of unconscious racism, the standard of review set forth in *Washington v. Davis* (1976) is a "crippling burden of proof." *Batson v. Kentucky* (1985).

The concomitant twin of racism is class oppression. Race and class bias have always worked together to reinforce systems of social control and economic distribution. Arguably, most forms of overt racism have been eliminated. However, those who choose to discriminate on the basis of race find it easier to achieve the same results by basing their distinctions on class. Ergo, identification of race bias has become more complex, more divisive, and morally more problematic.

On average, blacks experience significantly worse economic conditions than whites, and historically the criminal justice system has dealt more harshly with those who are economically weak. Black people constitute a disproportionate share of persons who exist in absolute poverty. In 1990, there were 33.6 million persons in poverty in the U.S. Although blacks comprise only 12% of the nation's population, 29% of those poverty stricken were black—2.4 times the rate of the general population. This mixture of race and economic discrimination has diminished the bright line of overt racism. "The . . . distorting effects of racial discrimination and poverty continue to be painfully visible" in decisions to mete out criminal punishment. *Godfrey v. Georgia* (1980) (Marshall, J. concurring).

It is against this background that the Court considers the merits of defendant's challenge.

EQUAL PROTECTION ANALYSIS

A current equal protection analysis must therefore take into account the unconscious predispositions of people, including legislators, who may sincerely believe that they are not making decisions on the basis of race. This predisposition is a pertinent factor in determining the existence of a racially discriminatory motive. Racial influences which unconsciously seeped into the legislative decision making process are no less injurious, reprehensible, or unconstitutional. Although intent per se may not have entered Congress' enactment of the crack statute, its failure to account for a foreseeable disparate impact which would [a]ffect black Americans in grossly disproportionate numbers would, nonetheless, violate the spirit and letter of equal protection.

The equal protection component of the Fifth Amendment Due Process clause commands that similarly situated people be treated alike. A criminal defendant who alleges an equal protection violation must prove that the "invidious quality" of governmental action claimed to be racially discriminatory "must ultimately be traced to a racially discriminatory purpose." Absent direct evidence of intent to discriminate, the defendant can make a prima facie case "by showing [that] the totality of the relevant facts gives rise to an inference of discriminatory purpose." In deciding whether the defendant has carried the burden of persuasion, a court must undertake a "sensitive inquiry into such circumstantial evidence of intent as may be available."

Chapter XVI Incarceration: Bail, Pretrial Detention, and Sentencing

In *Arlington,* the Supreme Court listed circumstantial evidentiary sources for judicial review of legislative or executive motivation to determine whether a racially discriminatory purpose exists. The "subjects of proper inquiry," are:

(1) adverse racial impact of the official action,
(2) historical background of the decisions,
(3) specific sequence of events leading up to the challenged decision,
(4) departures from normal procedure sequence,
(5) substantive departure from routine decisions,
(6) contemporary statements made by the decision makers, and
(7) the inevitability or foreseeability of the consequence of the law.

The Court explicitly stated that the list of evidentiary sources was not exhaustive. Therefore, this Court will proceed with its examination by reviewing the circumstantial evidence, including the *Arlington* factors, to determine whether race influenced the legislature's actions.

ENACTMENT OF THE CRACK STATUTE

Crack cocaine eased into the mainstream of the drug culture about 1985 and immediately absorbed the media's attention. Between 1985 and 1986, over 400 reports had been broadcast by the networks. Media accounts of crack-user horror stories appeared daily on every major channel and in every major newspaper. Many of the stories were racist. Despite the statistical data that whites were prevalent among crack users, rare was the interview with a young black person who had avoided drugs and the drug culture, and even rarer was any media association with whites and crack. Images of young black men daily saturated the screens of our televisions. These distorted images branded onto the public mind and the minds of legislators that young black men were solely responsible for the drug crisis in America. The media created a stereotype of a crack dealer as a young black male, unemployed, gang affiliated, gun toting, and a menace to society. These stereotypical descriptions of drug dealers may be accurate, but not all young black men are drug dealers. The broad brush of uninformed public opinion paints them all as the same.

Legislators used these media accounts as informational support for the enactment of the crack statute. The Congressional Record, prior to enactment of the statute, is replete with news articles submitted by members for their colleagues' consideration which labeled crack dealers as black youths and gangs. Members of Congress also introduced into the record media reports containing language that was either overtly or subtly racist, and which exacerbated white fears that the "crack problem" would spill out of the ghettos.

These stereotypical images undoubtedly served as the touchstone that influenced racial perceptions held by legislators and the public as related to the "crack epidemic." The fear of increased crime as a result of crack cocaine fed white society's fear of the black male as a crack user and as a source of social disruption. The prospect of black crack migrating to the white suburbs led the legislators to reflexively punish crack violators more harshly than their white, suburban, powder cocaine dealing counterparts. The ultimate outcome resulted in the legislators drafting the crack statute with its Draconian punishment.

Arlington decided that departures from normal procedures are relevant in determining the existence of invidious influences. Defendant presented evidence that there were significant departures from prior substantive and procedural sequences, which point toward invidious discriminatory purpose.

The media reports associating blacks with the horrors of crack cocaine caused the Congress to react irrationally and arbitrarily. The evolution of the 100 to 1 crack to powder ratio mandatory minimum sentence was a direct result of a "frenzied" Congress that was moved to action based upon an unconscious racial animus. The "frenzied" state of Congress led members to depart from normal and substantive procedures that are routinely considered a part of the legislative process.

The 1986 Controlled Substances Act followed an extraordinarily hasty and truncated legislative process. As Eric Sterling, then counsel to the House Subcommittee on Crime, has summarized:

> The Controlled Substances Act sentencing provisions were initiated in the [House] Subcommittee on Crime in early August 1986 in a climate in the Congress that some have characterized as frenzied. Speaker O'Neill returned from Boston after the July 4th district work period where he had been bombarded with constituent horror and outrage about the cocaine overdose death of NCAA basketball star Len Bias after signing with the championship Boston Celtics. The Speaker announced that the House Democrats would develop an omnibus anti-drug bill, easing the reelection concerns of many Democratic members of the House by ostensibly preempting the crime and drug issue from the Republicans who had used it very effectively in the 1984 election season. The Speaker set a deadline for the conclusion of all Committee work on this bill as the start of the August recess — five weeks away.
>
> The development of this omnibus bill was extraordinary. Typically Members introduce bills which are referred to a subcommittee, and hearings are held on the bills. Comment is invited from the Administration, the Judicial Conference, and organizations that have expertise on the issue. A markup is held on a bill, and amendments are offered to it. For this omnibus bill much of this procedure was dispensed with. The careful deliberative practices of the Congress were set aside for the drug bill.
>
> Few hearings were held in the House on the enhanced penalties for crack offenders. Despite the lack of fact-gathering about crack, "the 100:1 cocaine to crack ratio . . . was originally a 50:1 ratio in the Crime Subcommittee's bill, H.R. 5394, . . . arbitrarily doubled simply to symbolize redoubled Congressional seriousness."
>
> When the Senate considered the legislation, many Senators fruitlessly cautioned against undue haste in light of the House's abbreviated consideration of the bill, to little avail. Tossing caution to the wind, the Senate conducted a single hearing between 9:40 a.m. to 1:15 p.m., including recesses. Attendance was intermittent.

The Supreme Court has addressed the issue of foreseeability in the disparate impact context as follows:

> [A]ctions having foreseeable and anticipated disparate impact are relevant evidence to prove the ultimate fact, forbidden purpose. . . . Adherence to a particular policy or practice, "with full knowledge of the predictable effects of such adherence upon racial imbalance . . . may be considered by a court in determining whether an inference of [discriminatory] intent should be drawn."

What cannot be clearly gleaned from the transcripts of floor discussions among congressional members may well be inferred from the exhibits that were introduced into the record. Legions of newspaper and magazine articles regarding the crack cocaine epidemic depicted racial imagery of heavy involvement by blacks in crack cocaine. Practically every newspaper account featured a black male either using crack, selling crack, involved in police contact due to crack, or behind bars because of crack.

Media pictures and stories emphasized that the "crack problem" was a "black problem" that needed to be isolated and prevented from "spreading" to white suburban areas. The intent to contain the crack problem and prevent it from entering the "mainstream" or the "suburbs" is evident from the articles cited in the Congressional Record. To keep crack out of suburbia meant to keep crack users and dealers out of suburban neighborhoods. While it may not have been intentional, it was foreseeable that the harsh penalties imposed upon blacks would be clearly disproportional to the far more lenient sentences given whites for use of the same drug — cocaine.

Circumstantial evidence of invidious intent may include proof of disproportionate impact. "Impact of the official action—whether it 'bears more heavily on one race than another'" is important evidence.

Defendant's evidence that the impact of the crack statute "bears more heavily" on blacks than whites is undisputed. 98.2 percent of defendants convicted of crack cocaine charges in the Eastern District of Missouri between the years 1988 and 1992 were black. Nationally, 92.6 percent of the defendants convicted during 1992 of federal crack cocaine violations were black and 4.7 percent of the defendants were white. In comparison, 45.2 percent of defendants sentenced for powder cocaine were white, as opposed to 20.7 percent of black defendants. All of the defendants sentenced for simple possession of crack cocaine were black. The national figures comport to essentially the same percentage as the Missouri statistics.

According to a U.S.A. Today report which investigated the racial disparity caused by the "100 to 1 ratio" and the mandatory minimum sentencing practices in the country, although only 12 percent of the population, blacks accounted for 42 percent of all drug arrests in 1991. The 1992 federal figures indicate that blacks comprise 1.6 million of the illegal drug use population while 8.7 million whites admit to illegal drug use. Yet, blacks are four times as likely as whites to be arrested on drug charges in this country. Notably, in the Eastern District blacks are eight times as likely to be arrested.

According to the U.S. Sentencing Commission, blacks receive sentences at or above the mandatory minimum more often than whites arrested on the same charge. The disparate application appears to be related to race, and the disparity is constant even when variables such as nature of the offense and prior criminal record are considered.

Moreover, overcrowding in the Federal Bureau of Prisons reflects the disparity in a dramatic way. An estimated 90 percent increase in the prison population during the last several years is directly related to the mandatory minimum drug sentences and the sentencing guidelines. As of July 1993, 60.4 percent of the inmates in the Bureau of Prisons are there for drug related offenses. "Attorney General Reno told the Judicial Conference this past summer that the federal prisons are filling faster than new prisons can be built, and the Bureau of Prison faces gridlock within three years."

Clary argues that the statistical disparity is overwhelming proof of discrimination, and that in cases where statistical evidence of disparity is "stark," statistics alone have been accepted as the sole source of proof of an equal protection violation. This Court agrees that the statistical evidence of disparate impact resulting from crack cocaine sentences is compelling. In one of the first in a long line of cases which interpreted the equal protection clause, the Supreme Court ruled that the effect of a law may be so harsh or adverse in its weight against a particular race that an intent to discriminate is not only a permissible inference, but a necessary one. *Yick Wo v. Hopkins* (1886). This appears to be the effect of the crack statute challenged in this court.

Objective evidence supports the belief that racial animus was a motivating factor in enacting the crack statute. Congress' decision was based, in large part, on the racial imagery generated by the media which connected the "crack problem" with blacks in the inner city. Congress deviated from procedural patterns, departed from a thorough, rational discussion of the "crack issue" and reacted to it in a "frenzy" initiated by the media and emotionally charged constituents. Under Arlington, all of these factors may be considered by the Court to infer intent.

PROSECUTORIAL AND LAW ENFORCEMENT DISCRETION

The crack statute in conjunction with the resultant mandatory minimum sentence, standing alone, may not have spawned the kind and degree of racially disparate impact that warrants judicial review but for the manner of its application by law enforcement agencies. The law enforcement practices, charging policies, and sentencing departure decisions by prosecutors constitute major contributing factors which have escalated the disparate outcome.

Prosecutors do have broad discretion in determining who will be charged with a crime. All that is required for the prosecutor to have probable cause is to believe that the accused committed an offense defined by statute. "The decision whether or not to prosecute, and what charge to file . . . generally rests within his discretion." *Bordenkircher v. Hayes*. While the prosecutor does have broad discretion, it is not unlimited. For example, the prosecutor may not base the decision to prosecute upon impermissible factors such as race, religion, or other arbitrary and unjustified classifications.

Prosecutorial discretion as it relates to crack cocaine cases should be exercised in a manner that is responsive to Congress' expressed intent to target "kingpins" and "high level traffickers." It would seem to be economically sensible to devote scarce government resources to reducing the large ingress and wholesale distribution of powder cocaine by major traffickers which would consequently reduce the existence of crack as a derivative product. Without cocaine, there could be no crack.

However, both national and local statistical data do not show that the prosecution is targeting the upper echelons in the drug trade. Few kingpins are prosecuted. Review of the cases that have been prosecuted in this district reflects a clear pattern of disparate impact. Out of 57 convictions in the Eastern District of Missouri, 55 of the defendants were black, one was white, one was Hispanic, and not one kingpin among them. Three of the 56 defendants were jointly charged with having 944 grams, three others had 454 grams between them, and one had 451 grams. The other 50 had a total of less than 2000 grams, averaging less than 40 grams each. Eight defendants had less than 10 grams. Five of them had less than a gram, barely enough to detect or to utilize. The total amount of crack cocaine for 56 of the 57 defendants (the amount for one defendant was not determined) was less than 4,000 grams. Powder cocaine is usually imported into this country by boats, trucks, and planes, and in huge quantities. Kingpin dealers are then able to transport the drug in brick-like packages referred to as "kilos." A kilogram weighs 1,000 grams. Thus, it appears clear that the removal of this small quantity of drugs would hardly reduce the supply of crack cocaine in St. Louis or impede its flow.

The issue of prosecutorial venue is so intertwined with the racial impact flowing from the crack and mandatory minimum statute that it requires careful scrutiny. Generally, federal prosecutions are much more likely to result in conviction, with more severe punishment. In cases where there is joint jurisdiction of similar offenses, careful discernment by conscientious state and federal prosecutors can carefully select among the charges (state and federal) the ones that more nearly result in the most appropriate penalty. There would be inefficiency in double prosecutions, so a choice ought to be made. While various factors would be considered in selecting federal or state actions, certainly a decision based upon race would not be appropriate. And yet—when an examination of the crack cocaine violations in the district court is made, they are nearly all black (55 of 57). Where conviction is a certainty, harsh penalties inevitable, and nearly all defendants are black, suspicion will arise.

The Court notes that a close examination of many of the 57 files involving crack cocaine in this district shows that federal prosecution occurs with both state and federal law officers making the arrests. Generally, those arrested by state officers had very small amounts of crack cocaine. For example, nine of the 57 crack cocaine defendants were assigned to this Court and most of them had only tiny quantities of crack cocaine. All but one was black. All of them, even though arrested by state law officers, were prosecuted in the federal court. Even a disinterested inquirer would wonder why the tremendous expense of federal prosecution and subsequent incarceration should be wasted on relatively minor offenders. The following tables [omitted] are a descriptive list of the 57 persons prosecuted for crack cocaine violations in the Eastern District of Missouri during 1989-92. Fifty-five defendants were black, one was Hispanic, and one was white. Those defendants in boldface were assigned to this Court for trial. That is why this Court can produce greater detail garnered from its own files. The defendants who were assigned to this Court were all arrested by state officials and then transferred to the federal courts when charged.

Perhaps there were other reasons for charging those with "dust amounts," and then, perhaps they were all charged in the federal court because they had crack and were black. The failure by the prosecutors to explain these and other discrepancies adds a telling ingredient to the argument that the crack statute was constitutionally infirm and further exhibited the unconscious racism proffered here, generally, and as applied to this defendant. After all, while the Eastern District of Missouri includes the City of St. Louis with its large black population, it also includes St. Louis County with a white population four or five times larger. Surely if the prosecution were really free of racism, unconscious or not, there would be more than one white defendant convicted for crack violations in the federal courts of the Eastern District of Missouri in three years.

Without explanation, the logical inference to be drawn is that the prosecutors in the federal courts are selectively prosecuting black defendants who were involved with crack, no matter how trivial the amount, and ignoring or diverting whites when they do the same thing.

There may be rational explanations for these disproportionate figures. That is why this Court repeatedly requested the U.S. Attorney's Office to make available its standards or principles for the selection of crack cocaine cases. But the prosecutor refused to divulge this information (an in camera submission would have been sufficient), citing prosecutorial discretion. The Court is not sure that it has the authority to demand such an explanation from the prosecutor. But failure to divulge the standards used during 1989-92 raises an inference that unconscious racism may have influenced the decision to severely punish blacks for violations involving their form of cocaine while hardly touching whites who utilize another form of the same drug—both are forms of cocaine.

The focus on the prosecution of numerous low level crack dealers appears to be part of a national policy, perhaps designed to give the impression of great victories in the War on Drugs. Such a misguided approach to the elimination of drug traffic has resulted in the necessity for expensive prisons, has destroyed the lives of many young first offenders, and most importantly, has not reduced the quantity of drugs saturating the nation. In the St. Louis area there is a greater amount of cocaine available than in 1980 and it is cheaper. Small-time dealers grow like dandelions and are immediately and easily replaced, which further establishes the authority of the drug kingpins and dilutes the police resources available to curtail kingpin drug dealers.

This Court has known and respected the staff of the United States Attorney's Office for many years, and does not believe that overt racism would influence their decisions. The national statistics comport with the data from the Eastern District of Missouri. What is more likely is that the subliminal influence of unconscious racism has permeated federal prosecution throughout the nation. After all, even U.S. prosecutors are not immune from unconscious racism.

• • •

FINDINGS AND CONCLUSIONS

In summary, the Court, after careful consideration, reluctantly concludes that the pertinent sections of 21 U.S.C. § 841 which mandate punishment to be 100 times greater for crack cocaine than for powder cocaine are constitutionally invalid, both generally and as applied in this case. The Court finds that there is no material difference between the chemical properties of crack and powder cocaine, and that they are one and the same drug. The Court further finds that this defendant has been denied equal protection of the laws when the punishment assessed against him is 100 times greater than the punishment assessed for the same violation but involving powder cocaine.

The Court further finds that the "symbolic" action of the Congress in raising the original 50 to 1 ratio to 100 to 1 is yet another indication of its irrational and arbitrary actions, and further evidences the failure of the Congress to narrowly tailor its provisions as required by law in suspect class cases.

The Court further finds that the Congress enacted this law in an arbitrary and irrational manner, without the testimony of adequate scientific and professional advice, and without providing sufficient time for subcommittee hearings and debate.

The Court further finds that the statistics offered by the defendant, both local and national, show that the disparate impact upon blacks is so great as to shock the conscience of the court. Ratios as high as 55 to 1 appear in the Eastern District of Missouri; even greater disparities are evident on the national level. These ratios are apparent in arrest levels, convictions, and the prosecutorial acts which mitigate or eliminate punishment for whites while maximizing punishment for blacks. The Court finds that the actions of Congress and the prosecuting officials were influenced and motivated by unconscious racism, causing great harm and injury to black defendants because of their race inasmuch as whites are rarely arrested, prosecuted, or convicted for crack cocaine offenses.

The Court further finds that the Office of the U.S. Attorney for the Eastern District of Missouri only convicted one white person for crack cocaine violations during the years 1989-92 while convicting 55 blacks and one Hispanic. In the absence of explanation by the prosecutors, these disproportionate figures give rise to a strong inference that only blacks are being prosecuted in the federal courts for crack cocaine violations. Prosecution based on race is obviously discriminatory even if it is occasioned by unconscious racism.

INVALIDATION OF THE CRACK STATUTE

Therefore, this Court concludes that the disproportionate penalties for crack cocaine as specified in all of the pertinent sections of 21 U.S.C. § 841 violate the Equal Protection Clause of the U.S. Constitution generally and as applied in this case. The Court further holds that the prosecutorial selection of cases on the basis of race is constitutionally impermissible as applied to this defendant in this case.

Accordingly, the Court has sentenced the defendant to a prison term in conformity with this memorandum.

Dated this 11th day of February, 1994.

ADDENDUM TO MEMORANDUM RE: IMPOSITION OF SENTENCE

Defendant Edward Clary pleaded guilty to a charge of possessing with intent to distribute 67.76 grams of crack cocaine. He was sentenced to a four year prison term on January 26, 1994, prior to the processing of a lengthy legal memorandum which was filed on February 11, 1994.

The statute requiring a mandatory minimum sentence of 10 years for possessing with intent to distribute 50 grams of crack cocaine was coupled with a Sentencing Guideline Table fixing the range of punishment at 121 to 151 months. Had the cocaine been in powder form instead of crack or cocaine base, the Guidelines provided a punishment range of 21-27 months and even included the possibility of probation.

This defendant was 18 years of age at the time of the offense. He had no prior criminal convictions and therefore had a criminal history category of I per the Sentencing Guidelines.

Inasmuch as the Court has invalidated those pertinent sections of the statute fixing the punishment for crack cocaine offenses at a 100:1 ratio compared to powder cocaine, the 10 year mandatory minimum sentence was not applicable. The Court then decided to impose sentence in accordance with the range of the Sentencing Guidelines for powder cocaine, which would be for 21-27 months, with the possibility of probation.

However, the Court believed that there were aggravating circumstances which ought to be considered. Among those circumstances must be included the travel to California to purchase the cocaine and to return with it to St. Louis where he intended to sell it for profit. Because of this forethought and planning the Court departed upwards from the Sentencing Guidelines and imposed a prison sentence of four years followed by three years of supervised release.

NOTES AND QUESTIONS

1. Judge Cahill was not the only federal district judge to take issue with the disparate crack penalties. Some judges found that the disparity lacked a rational basis and did not enforce it; some downward departed from the applicable Guideline range based on the disparity; some simply expressed outrage and reluctantly followed the law. All judges who did not apply the disparate crack penalties were reversed. The crack penalties were undefeated at the appellate level. *See* Melissa C. Brown, *Equal Protection in a Mean World: Why Judge Cahill Was Right in* United States v. Clary, 11 Notre Dame J.L. Ethics & Pub. Pol'y 307, 318-21 (1997) (describing district court reactions); David A. Sklansky, *Cocaine, Race, and Equal Protection*, 47 Stan. L. Rev. 1283, 1303 & n.93 (1995) (noting defendants' lack of success at the appellate level).

One of the more interesting reactions to the crack-cocaine disparity was that of federal Judge Owen Forrester, in Atlanta, who—incidentally—was the district court judge in *McCleskey v. Kemp* who had aggressively picked nits with the Baldus study in denying McCleskey's habeas petition. As to the crack penalties, Judge Forrester engaged court-appointed chemistry experts who testified at an evidentiary hearing about the similarities of cocaine and cocaine base, and on the basis of this testimony Judge Forrester concluded that the two substances were essentially the same and thus there was no rational basis for the legislative distinction made by Congress. *United States v. Davis*, 864 F. Supp. 1303 (N.D. Ga. 1994).

2. The likelihood of the disparate crack penalties being the product of unconscious racism figured significantly in Judge Cahill's decision. He saw its manifestation in the fact that if a similar type of law would likely have resulted in the lengthy imprisonment of droves of young whites it would have been more "carefully and deliberately considered." Professor Sklansky agrees: "The federal crack penalties provide a paradigmatic case of unconscious racism." Sklansky, *Cocaine, Race, and Equal Protection, supra* at 1283, 1303, 1308 (Congress would have at least been more restrained if the penalties did not apply almost exclusively to Black people).

Do you agree? Given the media portrayal of the crack epidemic, some of which was relied on by at least some members of Congress, was this "unconscious" or "unspoken" racism?

3. Judge Cahill parlays his point about unconscious racism into a rejection of "purposeful discrimination," which is tantamount to a rejection of the Supreme Court's equal protection doctrine. Can racism that is truly "unconscious" also be purposeful? Is there any room for unconscious racism in the conventional equal production doctrine? Would a widespread acceptance of the notion of unconscious racism at least enhance the importance of disparate impacts?

D. Race and Sentencing   **1419**

Individual Supreme Court Justices had recognized the concept of unconscious racism a handful of times as of 1994 but the Court itself had not. *See* Jason A. Gillmer, Note, United States v. Clary: *Equal Protection and the Crack Statute*, 45 Am. U. L. Rev. 497, 550 & n.443 (1995) (providing three examples of references to unconscious racism: *Georgia v. McCollum*, 112 S. Ct. 2348, 2364 (1992) (O'Connor, J., dissenting) (recognizing unconscious racism in the context of peremptory challenges); *McCleskey v. Kemp*, 481 U.S. 279, 328-35 (1987) (Brennan, J., dissenting) (relying on unconscious racism as one factor, together with statistics showing racial disparity, why death penalty was unconstitutional); *Batson v. Kentucky*, 476 U.S. 79, 106 (1986) (Marshall, J., concurring) (invoking unconscious racism where prosecutor challenged potential jurors through peremptory challenges solely on basis of race)).

4. In discussing various descriptions of the "victimization" of Black people by the disparate crack penalties, Professor Randall Kennedy observes, as he does elsewhere, that Black people can be "victimized" both by the underenforcement of criminal law and by its overenforcement:

> When discussing racial issues and the administration of criminal justice, some commentators think immediately and, all too often, solely about invidious criminal prosecution of people of color. There is reason for that. Throughout American history, officials have wielded the criminal law as a weapon with which to intimidate blacks and other people of color. But the flip side of racially invidious over-enforcement of the criminal law is often minimized. Racially invidious under-enforcement purposefully denies African-American victims of violence the things that all persons legitimately expect from the state: civil order and, in the event that crimes are committed, best efforts to apprehend and punish offenders. For most of the nation's history, blacks were denied this public good. The history of anti-black lynching and the failure of the states and the federal government to combat it effectively offers only the most notorious example. In many contexts, in comparison to the treatment accorded to whites, blacks have been denied quite literally the equal protection of the law.

Randall Kennedy, *The State, Criminal Law, and Racial Discrimination: A Comment*, 107 Harv. L. Rev. 1255, 1267-68 (1994).

Against the backdrop of Professor Kennedy's observation about underenforcement, what do you make of the testimony—cited by the Eighth Circuit in reversing Judge Cahill's finding of discrimination—from a supporter of the legislation who stated that the members of Congress did not have racial animus, but rather "racial consciousness," an awareness that the "problem in the inner cities . . . was about to explode into the white part of the country." *United States v. Clary*, 34 F.3d 709, 713 (8th Cir. 1994). Is it a redeeming feature of the crack penalties that action is necessary because the contagion of crack can no longer be kept in the inner cities? Is this also an example of unconscious racism? Judge Cahill notes that this same fear—previously contained minorities' drug use threatening to spill over into white communities—was also an impetus for criminalization of opium smoking and heroin distribution in the early 1900s.

5. Judge Cahill expresses concern about the potential abuse of prosecutorial discretion, and notes that in his district out of 57 crack convictions only one defendant was white. 846 F. Supp. at 788. Although this was two years before *United States v. Armstrong, see supra*, and hundreds of miles away, the underlying facts are similar: prosecution of almost exclusively Black defendants; arrests made by a joint task force of state and federal law enforcement personnel; a judicial request for some explanation of the prosecutors' charging decisions; and the prosecution's refusal to respond to that request on the grounds of prosecutorial discretion. It is a shame that the federal defense bar in St. Louis did not aggressively litigate a request for discovery on this issue and possibly develop a factual record that might have enjoyed more ultimate success than the record established by defense counsel in *Armstrong*.

Do you think this apparent unified nationwide defense by DOJ indicates it was defensive about its crack enforcement policies or just protective of its prosecutorial discretion as a general matter?

6. In February 1995, nine years after the enactment of "the crack statute," the Sentencing Commission sent a report to Congress detailing the discriminatory impact of the disparate crack penalties in the intervening years. It noted, for example, that in 1993 88 percent of convicted crack defendants were Black. The commission proposed that the disparity be eliminated altogether for such reasons, which would have happened automatically on November 1, 1995, absent action by Congress. On October 18, 1995, the House of Representatives voted 332-83 to reject the commission's proposal. *See generally* Brown, *Equal Protection in a Mean World, supra* at 307, 308, 313-17.

Among other things cited by the commission in its report, which found little factual support for the 100:1 disparity, was the example of Len Bias, also noted by Judge Cahill. Len Bias was a star basketball player at the University of Maryland who was drafted by the Boston Celtics with the second pick of the June 1986 NBA draft. In an unspeakable tragedy, in celebrating his achievement on the night of the draft with friends on the Maryland campus, he overdosed on crack cocaine and died. Boston's Larry Bird called Bias's death "the cruelest thing he ever heard of." Bias's tragic experience overdosing on crack was cited multiple times by members of Congress and witnesses in the frantic legislative run-up to the enactment of the crack statute in the fall of 1986.

Len Bias

Except it wasn't true. In the criminal trial of Bias's supplier in 1987 evidence emerged that Bias and his friends were celebrating with powder cocaine, not crack. No less tragic, for sure. But indicative of how the media and others unreliably fueled the crack cocaine frenzy in 1986.

7. Clary was resentenced on remand—151 months—and on an appeal from that sentence challenged as discriminatory the legislative rejection of the Sentencing Commission's 1995 proposal to abolish the 100:1 disparity. The Eighth Circuit summarily rejected this argument. *United States v. Clary*, 97 F.3d 1457 (8th Cir. 1996). Was his case for establishing an equal protection claim strengthened the second time around as a result of the Sentencing Commission's proposal?

State courts, of course, are not bound by federal equal protection law in interpreting analogous provisions in their own constitutions. Accordingly, in *State v. Russell*, 477 N.W.2d 886, 887-91 (1991) (en banc), the Supreme Court of Minnesota sustained an equal protection challenge under Minnesota's constitution to the state's statutory 10:3 cocaine-crack disparity. The court found that the law failed to pass muster under Minnesota's "rational basis" test for equal protection challenges inasmuch as, inter alia, the distinctions between cocaine and crack—in the amounts indicating street-level dealing, in addictiveness, in association with violence—were unpersuasive and/or based on purely anecdotal evidence.

Congress has recently taken steps to reduce the crack-cocaine disparity. In the Fair Sentencing Act, Pub. L. No. 111-220, Aug. 3, 2010, 124 Stat. 2372, the ratio was reduced from 100:1 to 18:1. Eight years later, in the First Step Act, Pub. L. No. 115-391, Dec. 21, 2018, 132 Stat. 5194, Congress made the changes in the Fair Sentencing Act retroactive, authorizing

D. Race and Sentencing

district courts to "impose a reduced sentence" on defendants serving sentences for certain crack-cocaine offenses as if the Fair Sentencing Act were in effect at the time the covered offense was committed. *See Concepcion v. United States*, 597 U.S. 481 (2022) (considering interplay between First Step and Fair Sentencing Acts). A bill to eliminate the disparity entirely, Eliminating a Quantifiably Unjust Application of the Law Act (the EQUAL Act), H.R. 1693, 117th Cong. 2021-22, is currently pending in Congress.

Critics contend that Black offenders are sentenced more harshly than white offenders but such claims are hard to prove. In the next case, the sentencing judge said the quiet part out loud, explicitly basing a sentence on the "superpredator" stereotype, a cultural creation of the 1990s, which resulted in a sentence being vacated decades later.

Belcher v. Connecticut
342 Conn. 1 (2022)

MULLINS, J.

The defendant, Keith Belcher, a juvenile offender, appeals from the trial court's denial of his motion to correct an illegal sentence. After his conviction, the defendant received a total effective sentence of sixty years of incarceration. He claims, inter alia, that the trial court improperly denied his motion to correct on the basis of the court's conclusion that the sentencing court did not impose the sentence in an illegal manner by relying on materially false information.

Our review of the record reveals that the defendant established that the sentencing court substantially relied on materially false information in imposing his sentence, specifically, on the court's view that the defendant was a "charter member" of a mythical group of teenage "superpredators." Therefore, we conclude that the trial court abused its discretion in denying the defendant's motion to correct. Accordingly, we reverse the judgment of the trial court, and the case is remanded with direction to grant the defendant's motion and for resentencing.

The following facts and procedural history are relevant to this appeal. "The defendant was fourteen years of age when, on December 24, 1993, he and a companion approached the victim in front of her apartment in Bridgeport. The victim was unloading groceries from her car when the defendant approached her from behind, pulled out a gun and demanded that she give him her purse. When she informed the defendant that the purse was upstairs, he dragged her up to the apartment to retrieve it, all the time holding the gun on her." While in the apartment, the defendant sexually assaulted the victim twice, attempted to do so a third time, and pistol-whipped her.

Soon thereafter, based on the victim's identification of him from police photographs, the police arrested the defendant. Proceedings against him were initiated in the docket for juvenile matters of the Superior Court. Following a hearing, the court granted the state's motion to transfer the defendant's case to the regular criminal docket of the Superior Court. The state charged the defendant with kidnapping in the first degree, sexual assault in the first degree, attempt to commit sexual assault in the first degree, robbery in the first degree, and burglary in the first degree. The defendant was convicted on all seven counts. The sentencing court imposed a total effective sentence of sixty years of incarceration.

. . .

Relevant to the resolution of this appeal, the defendant claims that the trial court abused its discretion in concluding that the sentencing court did not substantially rely on materially false information, in violation of his right to due process, in sentencing him to a total effective sentence of sixty years of incarceration. Specifically, the defendant claims that his sentence was imposed in an illegal manner because the sentencing court relied on the erroneous and subsequently discredited theory of teenage superpredators in making its sentencing decision. We agree with the defendant and, accordingly, reverse the trial court's ruling.

The following additional facts and procedural history are relevant to this claim. Prior to the defendant's sentencing hearing on January 24, 1997, the sentencing court had reviewed the presentence investigation report (PSI), which the court stated was thorough and included school records and psychological reports. The court heard argument from the prosecutor and defense counsel. In his remarks, the prosecutor emphasized the trauma suffered by the victim, who testified at trial that she would never be the same. The prosecutor also highlighted the defendant's "extensive juvenile record." In fact, when the defendant committed his crimes, he was on a holiday furlough from Long Lane School, which was a facility for delinquent children. School officials indicated that the defendant showed no remorse for his prior actions. The prosecutor referred the sentencing court to the PSI, arguing that the information therein supported a "substantial sentence. . . ."

Defense counsel argued in mitigation that the defendant was only fourteen years old when he committed his crimes, that he came from a "troubled background," and that this was his first conviction as an adult. Counsel acknowledged the defendant's juvenile history but pointed out that, with the exception of one conviction for assault in the second degree, that history involved nonviolent offenses.

The defendant's claim that his sentence was imposed in an illegal manner arises from the sentencing court's brief remarks prior to imposing the sentence. The court began by stating that, in arriving at the defendant's sentence, it relied on the PSI and the evidence presented at trial. Of particular import, the court explained, was the victim's testimony, which the court found "most compelling. . . ." On the basis of the evidence, the court said: "To say that the conduct here was extremely serious and egregious is simply to understate the facts of what happened. The conduct here was just so inhumane as to be considered subhuman. This is despite the fact that, as disclosed in the [PSI], [the defendant's] . . . testing shows average intelligence. He could have chosen another lifestyle, even at his very young age, but deliberately chose not to. Professor John [J. DiIulio, Jr.], of Princeton University has coined the term 'superpredator,' which refers to a group of radically impulsive, brutally remorseless youngsters who assault, rape, rob and burglarize. Mr. Belcher, you are a charter member of that group. You have no fears, from your conduct, of the pains of imprisonment; nor do you suffer from the pangs of conscience. I agree with the [prosecutor], the probation officer, and the victim, who, incidentally, still suffers physically and psychologically from your conduct, who all ask for substantial incarceration to ensure the safety of the community."

In rejecting the defendant's claim that the sentencing court's remarks demonstrated that it had substantially relied on materially false information in sentencing him, the trial court reasoned that the superpredator theory did not constitute "information." Specifically, the trial court observed that the term "superpredator" is descriptive, rather than factual. Additionally, the trial court noted that, although the superpredator theory has since been discredited, at the time of sentencing, the sentencing court had a reasonable basis to rely on the theory. The trial court finally observed both that the evidence supported the conclusion that the defendant fit the definition of a "superpredator," regardless of the truth of the theory, and that the sentencing court's remarks about the superpredator theory were not central to the sentencing decision. The trial court went on to say that "[t]he superpredator reference was just a gloss. This court has no doubt that, had Professor DiIulio repudiated his theory before sentencing, [the sentencing court] would have imposed the same sentence."

We begin by setting forth the legal principles that govern our review of the trial court's denial of the defendant's motion to correct a sentence imposed in an illegal manner. "[A] claim that the trial court improperly denied a defendant's motion to correct an illegal sentence is [typically] reviewed pursuant to the abuse of discretion standard. . . ." We have explained, in pertinent part, that "[s]entences imposed in an illegal manner have been defined as being within the relevant statutory limits but . . . imposed in a way [that] violates [a] defendant's right . . . to be sentenced by a judge relying on accurate information or considerations solely in the record. . . ." (Internal quotation marks omitted.) We have emphasized that the protection against sentencing in an illegal manner "reflects the fundamental proposition that [t]he defendant has a legitimate interest in the character of the procedure [that] leads to the imposition of sentence even if he may have no right to object to a particular result of the sentencing process."

We also have acknowledged that "[a] sentencing judge has very broad discretion in imposing any sentence within the statutory limits and in exercising that discretion he may and should consider matters that would not be admissible at trial. . . . Consistent with due process the trial court may consider responsible unsworn or out-of-court information relative to the circumstances of the crime and to the convicted person's life and circumstance. . . . It is a fundamental sentencing principle that a sentencing judge may appropriately conduct an inquiry broad in scope, and largely unlimited either as to the kind of information he may consider or the source from which it may come. . . . Finally, although a trial court's discretion is not completely unfettered, and information may be considered as a basis for a sentence only if it has some minimal indicium of reliability . . . [a]s long as the sentencing judge has a reasonable, persuasive basis for relying on the information which he uses to fashion his ultimate sentence, an appellate court should not interfere with his discretion."

To prevail on a claim that the sentencing court violated his due process rights by relying on materially false information, a defendant cannot merely allege that the information relied on by the court contained factual inaccuracies or inappropriate information. "[T]he mere reference to information outside of the record does not require a sentence to be set aside unless the defendant shows: (1) that the information was materially false or unreliable; and (2) that the trial court substantially relied on the information in determining the sentence." "A sentencing court demonstrates [substantial] reliance on misinformation when the court gives explicit attention to it, [bases] its sentence at least in part on it, or gives specific consideration to the information before imposing sentence."

We consider each of these factors in turn. First, a review of the superpredator theory and its history demonstrates that the theory constituted materially false and unreliable information. In the mid-1990s, Professor DiIulio of Princeton University coined the term "superpredator." J. DiIulio, "The Coming of the Super-Predators," The Weekly Standard, November 27, 1995. DiIulio, whose work the sentencing court referenced specifically, warned that "the demographic bulge of the next [ten] years will unleash an army of young male predatory street criminals who will make even the leaders of the Bloods and Crips . . . look tame by comparison." DiIulio predicted that this coming wave of superpredators would include "elementary school youngsters who pack guns instead of lunches" and "have absolutely no respect for human life. . . ." He further warned: "On the horizon . . . are tens of thousands of severely morally impoverished juvenile super-predators. They are perfectly capable of committing the most heinous acts of physical violence for the most trivial reasons (for example, a perception of slight disrespect or the accident of being in their path). They fear neither the stigma of arrest nor the pain of imprisonment. They live by the meanest code of the meanest streets, a code that reinforces rather than restrains their violent, hair-trigger mentality. In prison or out, the things that super-predators get by their criminal behavior—sex, drugs, money—are their own immediate rewards. Nothing else matters to them. So for as long as their youthful energies hold out, they will do what comes 'naturally': murder, rape, rob, assault, burglarize, deal deadly drugs, and get high."

These dire predictions centered disproportionately on the demonization of Black male teens. DiIulio warned readers that, although "the trouble will be greatest in [Black, inner city] neighborhoods," those in other areas should expect a "spill over" of morally impoverished, "crime-prone young males." A few months later, in an article about race, crime and law enforcement, DiIulio wrote: "[N]ot only is the number of young [B]lack criminals likely to surge, but also the [B]lack crime rate, both black-on-black and black-on-white, is increasing, so that as many as [one] half of these juvenile super-predators could be young [B]lack males." J. DiIulio, "My Black Crime Problem, and Ours," City Journal, Spring, 1996.

Extensive research data and empirical analysis quickly demonstrated that the superpredator theory was baseless. In fact, contrary to DiIulio's assertion, even at the time that he coined the term in the mid-1990s, juvenile offense rates already had dropped significantly from their peak across demographic groups. The falsity of DiIulio's claim was demonstrated in a 2000 bulletin of the United States Department of Justice, which provided a data-driven assessment of juvenile crime patterns through the 1990s. The bulletin revealed that, although serious juvenile offense rates did peak in the late 1980s into the early 1990s, "by 1995, the rate had returned to its traditional level." The bulletin concluded that, therefore, "[r]ather than providing evidence for development of a juvenile superpredator, the . . . data indicate that, despite a temporary increase, the rate of serious juvenile offending as of the mid-[1990s] was comparable to that of a generation ago."

In 2001, the United States Office of the Surgeon General labeled the superpredator theory a myth. We conclude that the superpredator theory was baseless when it originally was espoused and has since been thoroughly debunked and universally rejected as a myth, and it therefore constituted false and unreliable information that a sentencing court ought not consider in crafting a sentence for a juvenile offender.

In the context of the sentencing of the defendant, a Black teenager, the court's reliance on the materially false superpredator myth is especially detrimental to the integrity of the sentencing procedure for two reasons. First, reliance on that myth invoked racial stereotypes, thus calling into question whether the defendant would have received as lengthy a sentence were he not Black. Second, the use of the superpredator myth supported treating the characteristics of youth as an aggravating, rather than a mitigating, factor. To fully appreciate how the use of this term was not simply a gloss but, rather, an inappropriate sentencing consideration, some historical and sociological context is needed.

The superpredator theory tapped into and amplified racial stereotypes that date back to the founding of our nation. Specifically relevant to the present case, the dehumanization of Black children pervades this country's history. In 1776, when Thomas Jefferson, a slave owner, declared "all men are created equal," in many of the colonies, Black adults and children were property and "were not legally considered human. . . ."

As one legal scholar has observed, throughout the history of our country, our policies have reflected that only some children—white ones—have deserved societal protection. Professor Kenneth B. Nunn explained that the mid-nineteenth century saw the birth of the concept of "adolescence," resulting in a shift from the understanding of children over the age of ten as a labor resource for families to a class of persons deserving of societal protection. A particular part of this shift arose from concerns regarding a rise in childhood poverty and a perception of increasing crime among children. Those concerns prompted social reforms, grounded in the doctrine of parens patriae, aimed at directing "'wayward youth'" to reform schools rather than incarcerating them with adult prisoners. Notably, the protections and progressive social innovations afforded by these reforms were not provided to Black children, who were considered "'unsalvageable and undeserving'" of the "citizen-building ideals" that had prompted the changes. As a result, by 1850, rather than being sent to reform schools, "a disproportionate number of Black youths were jailed in cities with majority white populations."

At the time that adolescence was being recognized as a distinct developmental stage for white children, many Black children remained enslaved and were viewed as subhuman. In contrast to white children in their teens, Black children could be separated from their parents, bought and sold like chattel. The nascent concept of adolescence, therefore, did not apply to them. The historical fiction that Black adolescents are not actually "children," meriting societal protection, stems from the dehumanization of Black Americans and is one of the roots of the disparate treatment of Black teens by the justice system.

Against this backdrop, the superpredator myth employed a particular tool of dehumanization—portraying Black people as animals. A "predator" is defined as "one that preys, destroys, or devours," or "an animal that depends on predation for its food. . . ." The superpredator metaphor invoked images of packs of teens prowling the streets. The news coverage in the mid-1990s, which depicted "young Black males, showing them [handcuffed] and shackled, held down by [the] police, or led into courtrooms wearing orange jumpsuits" left little doubt that the "packs" were Black teens.

The superpredator myth triggered and amplified the fears inspired by these dehumanizing racial stereotypes, thus perpetuating the systemic racial inequities that historically have pervaded our criminal justice system. Looming on the apocalyptic horizon were tens of thousands of these fabricated, subhuman superpredators, who would "do what comes 'naturally': murder, rape, rob, assault, burglarize, deal deadly drugs, and get high." A threat on this scale called for a response. And the response came in the form of a public panic and media frenzy, prompting nearly every state in the country to step up the sentencing and punishment of juveniles. This shift in the law subjected "juvenile offenders to sentencing regimes that were originally conceived for adults. . . ." And the consequences of the changes to juvenile justice fell disproportionately on Black teens.

The second reason the superpredator myth constituted particularly harmful materially false information for sentencing purposes is because it turns upside down the constitutional mandate of *Roper* and its progeny. By labeling a juvenile as a superpredator, the very characteristics of youth that should serve as mitigating factors in sentencing—impulsivity, submission to peer pressure, deficient judgment—are treated instead as aggravating factors justifying harsher punishment. The superpredator theory and the correspondingly harsh punishment of juvenile offenders cannot be reconciled with the recognition in *Roper v. Simmons, supra*, that the medical and social science research demonstrates that "the signature qualities of youth are transient; as individuals mature, the impetuousness and recklessness that may dominate in younger years can subside."

In summary, by invoking the superpredator theory to sentence the young, Black male defendant in the present case, the sentencing court, perhaps even without realizing it, relied on materially false, racial stereotypes that perpetuate systemic inequities—demanding harsher sentences—that date back to the founding of our nation. In addition, contrary to *Roper* and its progeny, in relying on the superpredator myth, the sentencing court counted the characteristics of youth as an aggravating factor against the defendant. Although we do not mean to suggest that the sentencing judge intended to perpetuate a race based stereotype, we cannot overlook the fact that the superpredator myth is precisely the type of materially false information that courts should not rely on in making sentencing decisions. Whether used wittingly or unwittingly, reliance on such a baseless, illegitimate theory calls into question the legitimacy of the sentencing procedure and the sentence.

Having concluded that the superpredator doctrine was materially false information, we next must determine whether the sentencing court substantially relied on the materially false and unreliable superpredator theory in arriving at the defendant's sentence. In other words, we review the record to determine whether the sentencing court gave explicit attention to the superpredator theory, whether that court based its sentence at least in part on it, or whether that court gave specific consideration to the theory before imposing sentence. Because the test is framed in the disjunctive, any of the three conditions would suffice. We conclude that the sentencing court did all three.

We already have observed that the sentencing court's remarks were brief—the court's comments occupied less than one and one-half pages of the sentencing transcript. The court expressly referenced the defendant's supposed status as a "charter member" of the superpredator group, and the court's comments regarding the superpredator theory comprised a substantial portion of its brief remarks. Given that the court's brief remarks were heavily directed at and shaped by the superpredator theory, it is evident that the court gave explicit attention to the theory, gave specific consideration to it and also based its sentence, in part, on the fact that it considered the defendant a superpredator.

Furthermore, the sentencing court's discussion of the superpredator theory throughout its brief remarks demonstrates that the court's view of the defendant was shaped by this theory that there was a group of youths who were destined to live an irredeemable life of violence and that the defendant was a "member" of that group. The sentencing court described the superpredator group as "a group of radically impulsive, brutally remorseless youngsters who assault, rape, rob and burglarize." Echoing DiIulio's description of superpredators, the court stated to the defendant: "You have no fears, from your conduct, of the pains of imprisonment; nor do you suffer from the pangs of conscience." The court went further and called the defendant a "charter member" of that fictitious group. This was more than a mere gloss or broad statement. The court's reliance on the superpredator theory, and its view that it had to protect society from a charter member of this remorseless group, dominated its sentencing remarks. The superpredator theory, and the court's application of that theory to the defendant, was central to the court's sentencing determination. It was the prism through which the court viewed this defendant. The sentencing court's explicit attention to the superpredator theory demonstrates that the court substantially relied on that baseless and now debunked theory when sentencing the defendant. Consequently, we conclude that reliance on the false and pernicious superpredator theory in the present case so infected the sentencing that the sentence was imposed in an illegal manner.

It is axiomatic "that [t]he defendant has a legitimate interest in the character of the procedure which leads to the imposition of sentence Z. . . ." We conclude that, because the superpredator theory constituted materially false, and, therefore, unreliable, evidence on which the sentencing court substantially relied, the trial court abused its discretion in denying the defendant's motion to correct an illegal sentence. The defendant's sentence was imposed in an illegal manner, in violation of his right to due process.

The trial court's decision is reversed and the case is remanded to that court with direction to grant the defendant's motion to correct an illegal sentence and for resentencing.

NOTES AND QUESTIONS

1. The trial court gave three reasons for rejecting defendant's argument: (a) that the superpredator theory was not "information" within the meaning of the "illegal manner" doctrine; (b) that whatever its fate the theory had not been discredited at the time the sentencing judge relied on it; and (c) the superpredator reference was just "gloss" and did not affect the sentence.

Which is the strongest of these arguments? Which is the weakest?

Do you find anything else disturbing in the sentencing judge's remarks aside from his superpredator references?

2. Is the right to not be sentenced in an "illegal manner" entirely procedural in concept? The root of this Connecticut right is that the defendant "has a legitimate interest in the character of the procedure." What sort of misinformation do you think would usually be at issue in cases making this claim? Why doesn't the court give examples from other cases? Whatever you think of the result here, does the opinion lack credibility as a result?

3. Do you agree with the conclusion that the sentencing judge "substantially relied" on the superpredator theory in sentencing Belcher? What if the judge had not said "Mr. Belcher, you are a charter member of that group"?

4. The court notes that the sentencing judge viewed the defendant through the "prism" of the superpredator theory. But isn't it even worse than that? Doesn't the judge simply assume that the defendant has all of the characteristics of the superpredator posited under the theory? Does the sentencing judge ever consider whether Belcher himself has exhibited any remorse for the crime on which he's being sentenced?

5. Is it necessary to the decision that the purported characteristics of a superpredator—remorselessness, lack of conscience, etc.—bear directly on the question of the appropriate length of sentence? Is it necessary to the decision that the superpredator theory "turns upside down" the evolving understandings of adolescence reflected in Supreme Court decisions such as *Roper* and *Miller*?

6. The Court notes in a footnote that DiIulio himself renounced the superpredator theory in the late 1990s. Do not understand this theory, articulated by a Princeton professor, to have existed only in some rarified corner of academia. It was given substantial play in mainstream media.

Imagine how many juvenile judges internalized the superpredator theory and relied on it, consciously or unconsciously—but always tacitly, unlike the sentencing judge here—in their sentencing decisions during the period when the theory was in its ascent?

Imagine how many defendants still are under the yoke of such sentences.

TABLE OF CASES

Principal cases are indicated by italics.

Abbate v. United States, 948, 952, 953, 954, 956, 969

Adams v. Williams, 427

Adkins; United States v., 1177

Agnello v. United States, 530

Aguilar v. Texas, 305, 490

Agurs; United States v., 853

Ah Sin v. Whitman, 1065, 1100, 1105, 1110

Akins v. Texas, 72

Alabama v. Shelton, 745, 748-749

Alabama v. White, 420

Aldridge v. United States, 1244-1245, 1249

Al Jibora; United States v., 1101

Allen v. United States, 1170, 1177, 1178, 1183

Alvarado; State v., 1276

Alvarado-Sandoval; United States v., 1286

Alvarez v. City of Brownsville, 859

Alvarez-Sanchez; United States v., 196

Anderson v. Creighton, 603, 607, 614

Andresen v. Maryland, 91

A.N.J.; State v., 776, 782

Apodaca v. Oregon, 1139

Apprendi v. New Jersey, 1132, 1357

Argersinger v. Hamlin, 740, 744-745, 749, 791, 1125

Arizona v. Evans, 490-491, 497

Arizona v. Fulminante, 117

Arizona v. Gant, 339, 340, 496

Arizona v. Hicks, 306

Arizona v. Johnson, 416, 420

Arkansas v. Sanders, 386

Arlington Heights v. Metro. Hous. Dev. Corp., 1089, 1399

Armstrong; United States v., 1089, 1099-1101, 1104, 1110, 1117, 1419

Arreola; State v., 454

Arvizu; United States v., 421

Ash; United States v., 1201, 1205-1206

Ashcraft v. Tennessee, 104, 108-109

Ashcroft v. al-Kidd, 436

Ashcroft v. Iqbal, 608, 709

Atwater v. City of Lago Vista, 319, 327-329, 339, 349

Bagley; United States v., 571, 853-854, 859

Bailey v. Alabama, 19, 28-29, 30, 34, 35

Baldwin v. New York, 1125

Ballew v. Georgia, 1127

Barnard; United States v., 889

Barron ex rel. Tiernan v. Mayor of Balt., 6

Bartkus v. Illinois, 953, 954, 956, 969-970

Bastaldo; Commonwealth v., 1308, 1313

Batson v. Kentucky, 283, 1231, 1259, 1267-1270, 1275, 1276, 1277, 1284, 1285, 1286, 1287, 1300, 1301, 1400, 1419

Baxter v. Bracey, 617

Baxter v. Palmigiano, 103

Belcher v. Connecticut, 1421, 1426-1427

Bell Atl. Corp. v. Twombly, 709

Bellis v. United States, 91

Berger v. New York, 213, 216, 217

Berger v. United States, 819, 885, 887, 889, 890, 898

Berghuis v. Thompkins, 166

Berkemer v. McCarty, 143, 147, 416, 437

Berrios; United States v., 1080, 1083-1084, 1088, 1089, 1100

Betts v. Brady, 722, 726, 727, 729, 734-735, 928

Birchfield v. North Dakota, 147, 341

Bivens v. Six Unknown Named Agents of the Fed. Bureau of Narcotics, 557, 588, 598, 608

Blackledge v. Perry, 1002, 1003

Blakely v. Washington, 1357, 1365, 1366

Blockburger v. United States, 959, 960

Board of Educ. v. Earls, 375

Bontkowski v. United States, 1005

Booker v. United States, 1343, 1357, 1365, 1366, 1367

Boone; People v., 1314, 1319

Bordenkircher v. Hayes, 997, 1002-1004, 1005, 1011

Boustani; United States v., 1334, 1336-1337

Boyd v. United States (116 U.S. 616), 90-91, 383

Boyd; United States v. (833 F. Supp. 1277), 847

Boykin v. Alabama, 979, 983-984, 991, 1031

Boynton v. Virginia, 593

Brady v. Maryland, 571-572, 811, *848*, 850-851, 853, 854, 858-859, 867, 868, 869, 879, 885, 886
Brady v. United States, 985, 990-991, 996, 1003, 1004, 1011
Branzburg v. Hayes, 673
Braswell v. United States, 91, 103
Brendlin v. California, 420
Brewer v. Williams, 750, 755-756
Brigham City v. Stuart, 356
Brignoni-Ponce; United States v., 430, 434-435, 436
Brinegar v. United States, 383, *384*, 386, 387, 447
Brosseau v. Haugen, 617
Browder v. United States, 927
Brown v. Bd. of Educ., 560, 905
Brown v. Illinois, 497, 503
Brown v. Mississippi (297 U.S. 278), 12, 17, *60*, 64, 65, 66, 104
Brown v. State (36 So. 73), 64
Bryan; United States v., 974
Bryant; United States v., 680, 682
Buckley; United States v., 1005
Butler v. Cooper, 1105, 1109-1110
Butz v. Economou, 593, 598
Byrd v. United States, 521, 527

Calandra; United States v., 628, 629, 650
California v. Acevedo, 386
California v. Beheler, 143
California v. Byers, 81
California v. Carney, 387, 390, 391
California v. Ciraolo, 224, 225
California v. Greenwood, 218
California v. Harris, 1059
California v. Hodari D., 266, 268-269
California v. Prysock, 171
Camara v. Mun. Court of City & Cnty. of S.F., 360
Cannon; United States v., 1117
Canton v. Harris, 561, 565-566, 571, 572, 578, 587
Carlson v. Green, 557
Caro; United States v., 183
Carpenter v. United States, 243, 259, 297, 341
Carroll v. United States, 311, *375*, 383-384, 386-387, 403, 435
Carter v. Jury Comm'n, 1237
Carter v. Texas, 17
Castaneda v. Partida, 629, 634, 637
Celotex Corp. v. Catrett, 608
Chadwick; United States v., 386
Chambers v. Mahoney, 386, 390
Chauvin; United States v., 971
Chavez v. Martinez, 202, 210, 558
Cheek v. United States, 927-928

Chen; United States v., 708-709
Chevoor; United States v., 708
Chewing v. Cunningham, 729
Chimel v. California, 329, 332
City of. *See name of city*
The Civil Rights Cases, 910, 911
Clary; United States v. (97 F.3d 1457), 1420
Clary; United States v. (34 F.3d 709), 1401, 1419
Clary; United States v. (846 F. Supp. 768), 1401, 1418-1419
Class v. United States, 1052, 1056-1057
Classic; United States v., 555, 556, *912*, 916-917, 929
Clausen, United States ex rel., v. Lab. Corp. of Am., 709
Clinton v. Jones, 619
Clyatt v. United States, 34
Coast of Maine Lobster Co.; United States v., 898, 903
Coker v. Georgia, 1378
Collins v. Virginia, 391
Colorado v. Connelly, 117
Colorado v. Spring, 176
Columbus, City of; United States v., 620, 624
Commonwealth v. *See name of defendant*
Comprehensive Drug Testing, Inc. (BALCO); United States v., 297
Concepcion v. United States, 1357, 1421
Conley; United States v., 1110, 1116-1117
Connick v. Myers, 572
Connick v. Thompson, 566, 571-572, 578
Coolidge v. New Hampshire, 296, 306, 310
Coppola v. Powell, 183
Correctional Servs. Corp. v. Malesko, 608
Costello; United States v., 638, 640-641
Counselman v. Hitchcock, 80, 88
County of. *See name of county*
Cox; United States v., 653, 660-661, 946, 1071
Crews; United States v., 931, 934-935
Crocker; United States v., 196
Crowthers; United States v., 1072, 1083
Cruikshank; United States v., 6, 910

Daniels v. New York, 428
Davis v. Alaska, 1168
Davis v. Mississippi, 667
Davis v. Passman, 557
Davis v. United States (598 U.S. ___, 143 S. Ct. 647), 1028
Davis v. United States (554 U.S. 229), 496-497
Davis v. United States (512 U.S. 452), 164-165, 196-197
Davis; United States v. (793 F.3d 712), 1117
Davis; United States v. (864 F. Supp. 1303), 1418
Defore; People v., 480
Delaware v. Prouse, 360-361, 437
Dennis; United States v., 832

Table of Cases 1431

DeStefano v. Woods, 1125
Dickerson v. United States (530 U.S. 428), 104, 134, 138, 176, *197*, 201-202, 209, 210
Dickerson v. United States (166 F.3d 667), 197
Dickerson v. United States (971 F. Supp. 1023), 197
Dionisio; United States v., 662, 667, 668
Di Re; United States v., 383
Disbrow; People v., 8
District of Columbia v. Heller, 7
Doe v. *See name of opposing party*
Doe; United States v. (465 U.S. 605) (Doe I), 91
Doe; United States v. (455 F.2d 1270), 699, 702
Dougherty; United States v., 1140, 1148-1150
Douglas v. California, 738, 739-740
Doyle v. Ohio, 177, 183
Dozier v. United States, 283-284
Drayton; United States v., 269, 275, 276
Duckworth v. Eagan, 171
Dunaway v. New York, 311
Duncan v. Louisiana, 6, 7, 11, 118, 744, *1119*, 1124-1127, 1132, 1163, 1237, 1258, 1365
Duncan v. Perez, 1101, 1126
Duren v. Missouri, 1237, 1241-1242

Easley; United States v., 284
Edmonson v. Leesville Concrete Co., 1270, 1276
Edwards v. Arizona, 161, 164, 165, 756
Edwards v. Vannoy, 1140
Egbert v. Boule, 557
Ehrlichman; United States v., 947
Escobedo v. Illinois, 118, 131, 132, 749, 1201
Escondido, City of, v. Emmons, 617-618

Falk; United States v., 1072, 1078-1079, 1083, 1084, 1089
Fanfan; United States v., 1366
Faretta v. California, 809, 996
Fernandez v. California, 356
Figueroa; United States v., 868
Fisher v. United States, 91, 100
Fletcher v. Weir, 183
Florida v. Bostick, 275, 276, 448
Florida v. Jardines, 239, 243, 391
Florida v. JL, 421
Florida v. Nixon, 808
Florida v. Riley, 218, 224, 225
Florida v. Royer, 265, 429
Florida v. Wells, 340
Florida v. Williams, 1139
Flowers v. Mississippi, 1287, 1300-1302
Floyd v. City of New York (770 F.3d 1051), 588
Floyd v. City of New York (59 F. Supp. 2d 540), 428, *580*, 586, 624
Floyd v. City of New York (283 F.R.D. 153), 587

Fokker Services B.V.; United States v., 822, 830, 831
Folding Carton Antitrust Litig., In re, 104
Fong Yue Ting v. United States, 1018
Foster v. Chatman, 1300
Frank v. Magnum, 43
Frazier v. Cupp, 164
Friedman v. Rehal, 859
Furman v. Georgia, 1258, 1378, 1399, 1401

Gagnon v. Scarpelli, 749
Gainer; People v., 1178
Gall v. United States, 1367
Galpin; United States v., 296, 297
Gamble v. United States, 961, 969
Ganias; United States v., 297
Garrison; People v., 767, 769
Gaudin; United States v., 1127, 1132, 1357, 1365
Georgia v. McCollum, 1270, 1275-1277, 1419
Georgia v. Randolph, 355-356, 1050
Gerstein v. Pugh, 160-161, 165
Gideon v. Wainwright, 6, 11, 117, 118, 392, *730*, 733-737, 740, 744, 756, 757, 776, 783, 791, 996, 1258
Giglio v. United States, 835, 845, *851*, 853, 858, 859, 867, 868, 879, 886
Gilbert v. California, 1196, 1198, 1206
Gim Hall; United States v., 1156
Glick; United States v., 1157
Goldman v. United States, 212
Gomes; Commonwealth v., 1221, 1225, 1313
Gonzales; State v., 9
Goodwin; United States v., 1006, 1011
Gouled v. United States, 91
Gouveia; United States v., 749
Graham v. Connor, 291, 294-295, 607, 614, 948
Green v. United States (355 U.S. 184), 952
Green; United States v. (389 F. Supp. 2d 29), 1242
Gregg v. Georgia, 1399
Griffin v. California, 101, 103, 177, 202, 892
Griffin v. Illinois, 727, 729
Griffin v. Wisconsin, 360
Groh v. Ramirez, 296, 356
Guest; United States v., 947, 948
Guillen; United States v., 1038, 1041
Gupta; United States v., 878
Guzman; United States v., 447, 448

Hale v. Henkel, 667
Ham v. South Carolina, 1242, 1244, 1245, 1249
Hamilton v. Alabama, 729
Hamling v. United States, 709
Hardy; United States v., 893, 897-898
Harlow v. Fitzgerald, 295, *594*, 597-598, 602, 603, 607, 608, 619
Harmelin v. Michigan, 953, 1003

Table of Cases

Harris v. New York, 8, 89, 134, *530*, 532
Harris; People v., 1102, 1104-1105, 1110
Harris; United States v., 911
Hasting; United States v., 892
Havens; United States v., 532, 535-536
Henderson; State v., 1319
Hernandez v. New York, 1277, 1284-1285, 1301
Herring v. United States, 491, 495-496, 497
Hiibel v. Sixth Judicial District Court of Nevada, 81, *411*, 415-416
Hill v. Lockhart, 1017
Hillery v. Pulley, 637
Hines; United States v., 1303, 1308
Hodge v. FBI, 679
Hoffa v. United States, 842, 845, 846
Hoffman v. United States, 103
Holt v. United States, 80, 81
Horton v. California, 306
    Hubbell; United States v. (530 U.S. 27), 92, 99-100
Hubbell; United States v. (11 F. Supp. 2d 25), 99
Hudson v. Michigan, 497, 503
Huffman v. United States, 1183
Hurlow v. United States, 1046, 1050-1051
Hurtado v. California, 6, 627

Illinois v. Gates, 297, 305, 489
Illinois v. Krull, 490
Illinois v. Rodriguez, 350, 355
Illinois v. Wardlow, 424, 426, 427, 428, 429
Imbler v. Pachtman, 603, 892
Indianapolis, City of, v. Edmond, 361, 366
INS v. Delgado, 265-266, 276
INS v. Lopez-Mendoza, 435

Jackson v. Hoylman, 614
Jackson; United States v., 985
Jacobson v. United States, 836, 841-842, 846
James v. Illinois, 536, 540
Jaynes; United States v., 971
J.D.B. v. North Carolina, 151, 156-157, 284
J.E.B. v. Alabama ex rel. T.B., 1284
Jencks; United States v., 879, 884-886
Jenkins v. Anderson, 183
Jenkins v. United States, 1178
Johnson v. United States, 296, 386
Johnson v. Zerbst, 117, 721, 726, 756
Johnson; State v., 8
Johnson; United States v. (874 F.3d 571), 463, 469
Jones v. United States (362 U.S. 257), 512, 516-517
Jones; State v., 276, 284
Jones; United States v. (565 U.S. 400), 230, 239, 243, 259

Kaley v. United States, 710, 717-718
Kansas v. Glover, 421
Karo; United States v., 218

Kastigar v. United States, 81, 88-89, 90, 100, 103, 177
Katz v. United States, 211, 212, *213*, 216, 217, 224, 230, 243, 296, 845
Kentucky v. King, 359
Ker v. California, 356
Kercheval v. United States, 983
Khan; United States v., 1101
Kimbrough v. United States, 1367
Kirby v. Illinois, 1198, 1200-1201
Kisela v. Hughes, 617, 618
Knights; United States v., 284
Knotts; United States v., 218
Knowles v. Iowa, 328
Kolender v. Lawson, 39-40
Koon; United States v., 958, 970
Krulewitch v. United States, 532
Kyles v. Whitley, 572, 854, 867
Kyllo v. United States, 225, 229-230, 243

Ladson; State v., 9, 454
Lafler v. Cooper, 1019, 1027-1028
Lakeside v. Oregon, 721
Lange v. California, 359
Lanier; United States v., 947-948, 974
Lanza; United States v., 953, 961, 969
Larson; United States v., 1168
Laymon; United States v., 438
Lazaros; United States v., 708
Lefkowitz v. Turley, 103
Lemaster; United States v., 1046
Leon; United States v., 8, 269, 305, *481*, 489-490, 512
Leviner; United States v., 1351, 1356
Ligon v. City of New York, 588
Liuzzo v. United States, 947
Long; Commonwealth v., 9
Lopez; United States v., 1117
Los Angeles, City of, v. Lyons, 573, 578-580, 587, 625
Love v. Texas, 1257
Loving v. Virginia, 905
Lowenfield v. Phelps, 1178
Lupton; United States v., 1132
Lyles v. United States, 1163
Lyons v. Oklahoma, 66, 71-72
Lytle v. Bexar Cnty., 617

Malinski v. New York, 1
Malley v. Briggs, 599, 602-603, 607
Malloy v. Hogan, 6, 100, 118
Mandujano; United States v., 683, 689-690, 695, 697, 708
Mann v. Mangialardi, 859
Manning; United States v., 1183
Manson v. Brathwaite, 1208, 1213-1214, 1219, 1220

Mapp v. Ohio, 6, 8, 118, 392, 473, *474*, 480, 481, 496, 516, 546, 556, 1258
Mara; United States v., 628, 667, 668
Marbury v. Madison, 916
Marcucci; United States v., 652
Marron v. United States, 296
Martinez-Fuerte; United States v., 360, 435, 436
Maryland v. Buie, 407
Maryland v. Garrison, 296
Maryland v. Shatzer, 165
Maryland v. Wilson, 420
Massachusetts v. Sheppard, 490
Massiah v. United States, 114, 116, 117, 749, 755, 756, 846
Mathur; United States v., 859
Matlock; United States v., 350, 355
Matos; United States v., 541, 542
Maxwell v. Bishop, 1368, 1376-1378
McCann, United States ex rel., v. Adams, 1149
McCarthy v. United States, 983
McCleskey v. Kemp, 1378, 1398-1401, 1418, 1419
McCoy v. Louisiana, 804, 808, 809
McCulloch; Doe v., 719
McDonald v. City of Chicago, 6, 7
McKane v. Durston, 740
McMann v. Richardson, 757, 984
McMichael; United States v., 972
McMillan v. Pennsylvania, 1357
McMurty; People v., 543, 545
Mejia; United States v., 709, 878
Mendenhall; United States v., 260, 264-265, 268, 276, 284, 436
Mesarosh v. United States, 846
Mezzanatto; United States v., 1100
Michigan v. Chesternut, 266
Michigan v. Jackson, 756
Michigan v. Long, 406
Michigan v. Mosley, 157, 160, 164, 165, 175
Michigan v. Tucker, 138
Michigan v. Tyler, 360
Michigan Dep't of State Police v. Sitz, 361, 366
Milke v. Ryan, 860, 867
Miller v. Alabama, 1427
Miller El v. Dretke, 1300
Minnesota v. Carter, 217, *517*, 520-521
Minnesota v. Dickerson, 407, 411
Minnesota v. Olson, 521
Miranda v. Arizona, 1, 4, 8, 77, 80, 81, 89, 104, 117, *118*, 131-134, 137, 138, 143, 148, 151, 157, 160, 164, 165, 171, 175, 176, 182, 183, 190, 191, 196, 197, 201, 202, 210, 284, 311, 349, 405, 447, 497, 530, 532, 557, 558, 682, 690, 750, 756, 798, 928, 974, 1195, 1258
Missouri v. Frye, 859, 975, *1019*, 1026-1027, 1028

Missouri v. Pratte, 787, 791
Missouri v. Seibert, 104, *191*, 196, 202
Mistretta v. United States, 1032, *1343*, 1346-1347, 1356, 1401
Mitchell v. Forsyth, 607-608
Mitchell v. United States, 103
Monell v. Department of Social Services of the City of New York, 551, *558*, 560-561, 580, 587, 592, 624
Monroe v. Pape, 44, 551, *552*, 555-557, 560, 592, 593, 935
Monsanto; United States v., 717
Montejo v. Louisiana, 756
Montero-Camargo; United States v., 427-428
Moore v. Dempsey, 12, *40*, 44, 52, 65, 66
Moran v. Burbine, 165, 175
Morris; United States v., 1150
Morrison v. Olson, 814, 819, 892, 1326
Morrissey v. Brewer, 748
Morton Salt Co.; United States v., 672-673
Mosley; United States v., 911, 917
Moussaoui; United States v., 859
Moylan; United States v., 1149
Muehler v. Mena, 305
Mullenix v. Luna, 615, 617
Murray v. United States, 497
Myers v. United States, 946

Nardone; United States v. (308 U.S. 338), 212
Nardone; United States v. (302 U.S. 379), 212
Navarette v. California, 421
Neal v. Delaware, 16, 17, 52, 60, 1100
New Jersey v. Portash, 89, 532
New Jersey v. T.L.O., 367, 374
New York v. Belton, 339-340, 496
New York v. Burger, 360, 390
New York v. Quarles, 134, 137-138, 143
New York Cent. & Hudson River R.R. Co. v. United States, 831
New York Times v. United States, 702
Nickels; United States v., 708
Nix v. Whiteside, 792, 797-798, 809
Nix v. Williams, 497
Nixon v. Fitzgerald, 597
Nixon; United States v., 672, 1084
Norris v. Alabama, 12, 16, *54*, 60, 65, 66, 71
North Carolina v. Alford, 992, 995-997
North Carolina v. Butler, 165
North Carolina v. Pearce, 1002, 1003

Ochoa; People v., 1101
Ochoa; State v., 454
Odonnell v. Harris County, Texas, 1337, 1341
Ohio v. Robinette, 350, 437, 447
Ohiri; United States v., 859
Oklahoma City, City of, v. Tuttle, 561
Oliver v. United States, 218

1434   Table of Cases

Olmstead v. United States, 211-212, 217, 224, 480
On Lee v. United States, 832
Oplinger; United States v., 183
Oregon v. Bradshaw, 164, 165
Oregon v. Elstad, 184, 190-191, 196, 201, 202, 542
Oregon v. Mathiason, 143
Ornelas v. United States, 387
O'Shea v. Littleton, 572, 573, 579, 580, 593
Oyler v. Boles, 424, 452, 1059, 1065, *1066*, 1067-1068, 1070, 1072, 1078-1079, 1083, 1089, 1105, 1109

Padilla v. Kentucky, 1012, 1017-1019
Page; United States v., 649, 650
Paniagua-Ramos; United States v., 1178, 1183
Papachristou v. Jacksonville, 35, 39, 404, 744
Patane; United States v., 202
Patrick; United States v., 1157
Patterson v. Illinois, 756
Payton v. New York, 296, *311*, 318
Pearson v. Callahan, 614
Pena-Rodriguez v. Colorado, 1257
Pennsylvania v. Mimms, 406, 420
Pennsylvania v. Muniz, 81
People v. *See name of defendant*
Perkins; United States v., 1071
Perry v. New Hampshire, 1215, 1219-1220, 1221, 1225
Personnel Adm'r of Mass. v. Feeney, 1089
Petite v. United States, 954, 956, 958, 971
Philadelphia, City of; United States v., 620
Pierson v. Ray, 588, 592-593, 594, 598, 602, 603
Plessy v. Ferguson, 910
Plumhoff v. Rickard, 617
Pointer v. Texas, 6
Pollock v. Williams, 30, 34-35, 905
Powell v. Alabama, 6, 12, *45*, 52-53, 65, 66, 117, 721, 726, 734, 756, 757, 983, 1064
Powers v. Ohio, 1269-1270
Price; United States v., 938, 945, 946, 947, 948
Procter & Gamble; United States v., 679
Puerto Rico v. Sánchez Valle, 961, 969
Purkett v. Elem, 1285, 1301

Quarles; People v., 137

Rakas v. Illinois, 517
Ramos v. Louisiana, 7, 1132, *1133*, 1139-1140, 1151
Raynor; United States v., 1032, 1037, 1041
Reese; United States v., 910, 911
Regan; United States v., 708
Remington; United States v., 629
R. Enters., Inc.; United States v., 667, *668*, 672, 673
Restrepo; United States v., 546, 549
Reynolds; United States v., 29-30, 34, 35
Rhode Island v. Innis, 138, 143
Richards v. Wisconsin, 306
Richardson v. McKnight, 619
Riles v. McCotter, 766-767

Riley, Ex parte, 29
Riley v. California, 340
Ristaino v. Ross, 1246, 1249-1250, 1256
Rita v. United States, 1366-1367
Rivas-Lopez; United States v., 196
Rivera; United States v., 183
Riverside, Cnty. of, v. Arizona, 161
Riverside, Cnty. of, v. McLaughlin, 165, 311
Rizzo v. Goode, 572, 573, 579, 580
Robinson; United States v. (414 U.S. 218), 333, 338-339, 340, 341
Robinson; United States v. (311 F. Supp. 1063), 1068, 1070-1071, 1072, 1078
Rodriguez v. United States, 420
Rodriguez; State v., 276
Roe v. Wade, 81
Rogers v. Alabama, 17
Rogers v. United States, 1154, 1156-1157
Rompilla v. Beard, 770, 775-776
Roper v. Simmons, 1427
Rose v. Clark, 891
Ross; United States v., 386
Rothgery v. Gillespie Cnty., 749
Rudolph v. Alabama, 1368
Ruiz; United States v., 854, 857, 858, 859, 869, 890
Russell; State v., 1420
Russell; United States v., 836, 841, 892

Salerno; United States v., 1326, 1332-1334
Salinas v. Texas, 103, *171*, 175, 176, 177, 202
San Francisco, City & Cnty. of, v. Sheehan, 617
Sandoval v. California, 1170, 1177
Santana; United States v., 356, 359
Santobello v. New York, 1004, *1028*, 1031-1032
Saucier v. Katz, 608, 614
Savory, United States ex rel., v. Lane, 183
Scheffer; United States v., 889
Scheuer v. Rhodes, 593
Schmerber v. California, 78, 80-81, 91
Schneckloth v. Bustamonte, 8, *341*, 348-349, 350, 437, 447
Schriro v. Landrigan, 808-809
Scott v. Harris, 291
Screws v. United States v. (325 U.S. 91), 555, 556, 905, 911, *918*, 927-930, 931, 934, 935, 938, 946, 947, 952, 973
Screws; United States v. (M.D. Ga. 1945), 930
Seale; United States v., 1229
Sellers; United States v., 1117
Sells Engineering, Inc.; United States v., 674, 678-679, 699
Sepulveda; United States v., 1151, 1152
Shannon v. United States, 1157, 1162-1163
Shelley v. Kraemer, 44
Sherman v. United States, 832, 835-836, 841, 846
Sibron v. New York, 422
Siegert v. Gilley, 608
Silverman v. United States, 212-213
Silverthorne Lumber Co. v. United States, 473

Simmons v. United States, 265, 541
Skinner v. Ry. Labor Execs.' Ass'n, 375
Slager; United States v., 970
The Slaughter-House Cases, 6, 909, 910
Smith v. Baldwin, 859
Smith v. Bennett, 1337
Smith v. Maryland, 218, 239
Smith; United States v., 284
SmithKline Beecham Corp. v. Abbott Labs., 1284
Snowden v. Hughes, 1065
Snyder v. Louisiana, 1300
Soares; Commonwealth v., 1258, 1268
Solem v. Helm, 1003
Sorrels v. United States, 835, 841
Soto; State v., 454, 462-463
Spano v. New York, 109, 113, 114, 116, 117, 750
Sparf v. United States, 1140, 1150
Spinelli v. United States, 305, 490
Stack v. Boyle, 1322, 1325-1326, 1333
Stansbury v. California, 148, 151, 176
State v. *See name of defendant*
Steagald v. United States, 318-319
Steele; United States v., 1072, 1083
Stone v. Powell, 489
Stone; United States v., 673
Stovall v. Denno, 1206, 1208, 1219
Strauder v. West Virginia, 12, 16, 17, 52, 1276
Strickland v. Washington, 757, 765-766, 769, 775,
    776, 798, 809, 983, 1017, 1027, 1028
Sullivan; United States v., 81
Sum; State v., 277, 283, 284
Swain v. Alabama, 1124, 1258-1259, 1267, 1268
Swann v. Charlotte-Mecklenburg Bd. of Educ.,
    1378

Tahlequah, City of, v. Bond, 618
Tanguay; United States v., 276
Tarantino; United States v., 886
Taylor v. Georgia, 35
Taylor v. Illinois, 799, 803-804
Taylor v. Louisiana, 1231, 1236-1237, 1258
Telfaire; United States v., 1308
Tennessee v. Garner, 285, 290-291, 294, 579, 617
Terry v. Ohio, 35, 147, 148, 211, 239, 264, 339,
    387, 391, *392,* 402-407, 411, 415, 416,
    421-427, 435, 436, 463, 469, 495, 586
Thomas v. Mississippi, 593
Thompson; United States v., 276
Thoreen; United States v., 1226, 1229
Timbs v. Indiana, 7
Tinker v. Des Moines Indep. Cmty. Sch. Dist.,
    367
The T.J. Hooper, 782
Tollett v. Henderson, 984
Torres v. Madrid, 269
Treasury Emps. v. Von Raab, 375
Trent; United States v., 1163, 1168

Tune; State v., 869
Turner v. Murray, 1250, 1256
Twining v. New Jersey, 6
Tyler; People v., 703, 708

UMW v. Gibbs, 579
United States, In re, 1242
United States ex rel. *See name of relator*
United States v. *See name of defendant*
Utah v. Strieff, 340, 415, *503,* 511-512

Vasquez v. Hillery, 634, 637-638, 652
Vega v. Tekoh, 202, 210, 557-558
Vernonia School District 47J v. Acton, 367,
    374-375
Virginia, Ex parte, 911, 917
Virginia v. Moore, 328

Waddell; United States v., 911
Wade; United States v., 91, *1185,* 1195-1196,
    1198, 1201, 1205, 1206, 1213, 1214, 1219,
    1220, 1225
Walder v. United States, 528, 530, 532
Walker; State v., 1314, 1319
Warden v. Hayden, 91
Wardius v. Oregon, 875
Warren; Commonwealth v., 429
Washington v. Davis, 1089
Washington v. Texas, 6
Washington; United States v. (431 U.S. 181), 690,
    695-696
Washington; United States v. (869 F.3d 193 (3d
    Cir. 2017)), 1117
Washington; United States v. (490 F.3d 765 (9th
    Cir. 2007)), 283
Watkins v. Sowders, 1185
Watson v. United States (682 F.3d 740), 1042,
    1045-1046
Watson; United States v. (423 U.S. 41), 311
Watts v. Indiana, 113
Wayte v. United States, 1084, 1088, 1089, 1100,
    1104, 1399
Weatherford v. Bursery, 868
Weaver; United States v., 436
Weeks v. United States, 329, 332, 473, 496, 516
Welsh v. Wisconsin, 356, 359
Wheeler; People v., 1258, 1268
White v. Pauly, 617
White; United States v., 218
Whren v. United States (517 U.S. 806), 9, 328,
    339, 367, 436, *448,* 453-454, 463, 469, 549
Whren; United States v. (53 F.3d 371), 454
Wiggins v. Smith, 769, 1017
Wigley; State v., 783, 786-787
Williams v. Florida, 869, 874-875, 1127, 1237,
    1365
Williams v. New York, 1357

Williams v. Taylor, 769, 1017
Williams v. United States (341 U.S. 97), 935, 938, 946, 974
Williams v. United States (900 F.3d 486), 875, 877-878
Williams; State v., 868
Williams; United States v. (504 U.S. 36), 641, 649-650, 660
Wilson v. Arkansas, 306
Wilson v. United States, 103
Witherspoon v. Illinois, 1377
Wolf v. Colorado, 473, 480, 552, 556
Wong; United States v., 696

Woodson v. North Carolina, 1378
Wyatt v. Cole, 608
Wyoming v. Houghton, 391

Yarbrough, Ex parte, 911, 917
Ybarra v. Illinois, 306
Yick Wo v. Hopkins, 28, 434, 1059, *1060*, 1064-1065, 1068, 1070, 1072, 1078, 1089, 1100, 1101, 1105, 1109, 1258, 1399

Zanabria; United States v., 183
Zapata-Ibarra; United States v., 436
Ziglar v. Abbasi, 618

INDEX

ABA Standards for Criminal Justice, 743, 769, 773, 776

Absolute immunity, 88, 593, 602-603, 892

ACLU. *See* American Civil Liberties Union (ACLU)

Acquittal, 946, 952, 958, 959, 960, 961, 1079, 1109, 1149, 1150, 1302

"Act of production" doctrine, 91-92

Adams, John, 9, 1119

Adams, Kenneth, 821

Administrative searches, 211, 359-375

Aerial surveillance, 217, 218-224

Affirmative defense, 608

Aguilar-Spinelli test, 297-305

Air space, surveillance from, 217, 218-224

Akerman, Amos, 907, 908

Alexander, Michele, 1322

Alford plea, 992-995, 995-997

Alibi defense, 164, 726, 808, 874, 875, 996, 1257

Allen charge, 1177-1183

American Civil Liberties Union (ACLU), 736, 912, 959, 960

American Public Media, 1287

Ames, Adelbert, 909

Amsterdam, Anthony, 1377

Anonymous tips, 224, 503-511
   reasonable suspicion and, 420-421
   search warrants, 297-305

Anti–Drug Abuse Act, 1401-1418

Antipeonage Act, 17-28, 34, 905, 911

Antiwar viewpoint, discrimination based on, 1072-1079, 1084-1088

Appeal
   counsel right on, 727-729, 738-740
   direct, 3
   summary of process, 3

Appellate review
   Batson challenge, 1286, 1300
   counsel appointment procedure, 740
   criminal conviction, 729
   indigent defendants, 727-729, 738-740
   nondisclosure, 854
   probable cause and reasonable suspicion determinations, 387
   sentencing, 1079, 1342, 1343, 1345, 1347, 1366
   states, 740

Arbery, Ahmaud, 972

Arizona, elimination of peremptory challenges in, 1287

Arraignment, summary of process, 1-2

Arrest
   defined, 1
   drunk-driving charges, 341
   probable cause, 160, 311-318
   reasonableness of, 319-329
   search incident to arrest, 211, 311, 328, 329-341
   seizure, as most extreme form of, 259
   summary of process, 1
   warrant, 295, 318-319
   warrantless. *See* Warrantless arrests

Arthur Andersen, demise of, 830

"Assembly line justice," 744

Assistant district attorney, defined, 3

Assistant United States attorneys, defined, 4

Assumption of the risk, 845

ATF. *See* Bureau of Alcohol, Tobacco, Firearms and Explosives (ATF)

Attenuation, 495, 497-512. *See also* Exclusionary rule

Attorney-client privilege, 804, 990, 995, 1017

Automobile exception, warrantless search, 211, 375-391

Automobility exception, 386, 387

Bail, 311, 1322-1341
   cash bail, 1337-1341
   Public Safety Assessment, 1341

Bail Reform Act, 1326-1332
   wealth of defendant, consideration of, 1334-1336

Bailey, Walter, 290, 291

Baldus study on race and death penalty, 1378-1399, 1400, 1418

Bar-Gill, Oren, 470

Barkow, Rachel, 997

Barr, William, 958

Batson, James Kirkland, 1259-1267, 1268, 1269

Battle of Shiloh, 907

Baude, William, 603

Bazelon, Emily, 997, 1150

Beepers, 211, 217, 218

Bell, Monica, 625

Bellin, Jeffrey, 822

Bench trial, 2, 973, 1125, 1229

1437

Bench warrant, 295, 340, 512
Bennett, Mark W., 1184
Berdejó, Carlos, 977
Bias
    cognitive, 424
    crimes, 906
    implicit. *See* Implicit bias
    jurors, challenges to potential, 1242-1257
    own race bias, 1303, 1308
    racial. *See* Racial bias
Bias crimes, 906
Bias, Len, 1420
Biddle, Francis, 917
Bill of Rights, 6, 177, 552, 627
Bird, Larry, 1420
Bishop, Donna M., 821
Bivens actions, 588, 598, 608
Bivens, Webster, 557
Black Codes, 7, 906
Black Panther Party, 1229
Blackmun, Harry, 1376, 1377, 1378
Bland, Sandra, 470
Blood alcohol tests, 341, 356, 359, 391
Bookkeeping error, 491, 496. *See also* Exclusionary
    rule
Border Patrol, 430-436
Border searches, 360, 430-436
Boston Massacre, 9
Bratton, William, 586
Brennan, William, Jr., 8
Bristow, Benjamin, 907, 908, 956
Broken windows policing, 406, 586
Brown, Michael, 718, 719, 973
Bruckner, Emory, 977, 978
Bugging, 213, 845, 846
Bureau of Alcohol, Tobacco, Firearms and Explosives
    (ATF), 1059, 1099, 1116-1117
Bureau of Investigation, 1342
Bureau of Prison statistics, 1377
Burr, Aaron, 650
Bush (George W.) Administration, 625
Butler, Esther, 1109
Butler, Paul, 820, 1152-1153, 1301-1302
Butterfield, Alexander, 598

Cafaro, Vincent, 1326-1333
California, peremptory challenges reform in,
    1286
Cambodian Freedom Fighters (CFF), 1102
Campbell, William, 668
Capers, I. Bennett, 276, 546
Capital cases. *See* Death penalty cases
Caplan, Gerald M., 133
Carbado, Devon W., 284, 350, 403, 424
Carter Administration, 735
Case or controversy, 572, 579, 587
Case Western Reserve University, 979

Cassibry, Fred James, 1126
Castile, Philando, 470
Cell phone records, 243-259
Cellphones, 211
Cell-site location information (CSLI), 243-259
CFF. *See* Cambodian Freedom Fighters (CFF)
Charging decisions, race and, 820-832. *See also*
    Prosecutors
Chauvin, Derek, 971
Chernoff, Nina W., 1241-1242
Child pornography, 672, 836-842
Chin, Gabriel, 1105
Chokeholds, 573-580, 587, 718
Christian burial speech, 750-756
Christie, Chris, 1341
Christopher, Warren, 580
Civil procedure vs. criminal procedure, 5-6
Civil Rights Act of 1866, 906, 956
Civil Rights Act of 1875, 906, 910
Civil Rights Act of 1964, 905, 1245
Civil rights crimes, 905-974
    bias crimes, 906
    categories, 906
    rights-interference crimes, 906
    unjustifiable use of force crimes, 906
Civil rights enforcement, 948-974
Civil War, 7, 17, 28, 906, 907, 910, 911, 1368
Clark, Thomas, 1068
Cleveland Foundation
    criminal justice, study of, 979
Clinton Administration, 624
Clinton, Bill, 820
Cloud, Morgan, 546
Cocaine-crack disparity, sentencing, 1089-1100
Coercion
    confessions, 60-76, 104-113, 935-938
    plea bargaining, 997-1011
    testimony, 89
Cognitive bias, 424
Cold War, 1322
Cole, David, 436, 757, 767, 1105
Collateral consequences, 830
Collateral order exception to final judgment rule,
    608
"Color of law," 551, 552-555, 906, 917, 918-927.
    See also Section 1983 actions
"Colorable claim," 1041
Common authority over premises, consent to search
    of persons with, 355-356, 1050-1051
Communist Party, 58-59
Communists, prosecution of, 1322-1325
Complaint
    criminal charge, 1
    notice requirement, 709
Confessions
    coerced, 60-76, 104-113, 935-938
    voluntariness, 60-76, 104-113, 935-938

Confidentiality, attorney, 995
Confrontation Clause, 1163
Confrontation right, 744
Consent searches, 211, 341-356
Constitution
 Article II, 830, 832
 Article III, 579, 1119
 Confrontation Clause, 1163
 Double Jeopardy Clause, 905, 952, 959, 970
 Due Process Clause. *See* Due Process Clause
 Equal Protection Clause. *See* Equal Protection Clause
 Excessive Fines Clause, 7
 Fifteenth Amendment, 910
 Fifth Amendment. *See* Fifth Amendment
 First Amendment, 6, 557, 572, 1079
 Fourteenth Amendment. *See* Fourteenth Amendment
 Fourth Amendment. *See* Fourth Amendment
 plea bargaining, 997-1011
 Sixth Amendment. *See* Sixth Amendment
 Take Care Clause, 832
 Thirteenth Amendment. *See* Thirteenth Amendment
"Contempt of cop," 406. *See also* Police
Corporate criminal liability, 831
Counsel, right to, 1, 4, 6, 53, 721-809
 on appeal, 727-729, 738-740
 appellate appointment, 738-740
 appointment of counsel, 721-727, 730-733, 738-740
 consequences of representation by counsel, 749-756
 defensive, 116-117
 disagreement with client, 804-808
 discovery rules, nonobservance of, 798-804
 effective assistance of counsel. *See* Effective assistance of counsel
 ethical rules vs. zealous advocacy, 791-798
 eyewitness identification and, 1185-1206
 indigent defense, 721-737, 738-740, 740-745, 756, 776-791
 interrogation context, 114-117
 Miranda and, 161-165
 performance, standard of, 756-776
 post-indictment, eyewitness identification procedures, 1198-1201
 scope of, 721-749
 "special circumstances" rule, 726, 729, 734
 unambiguous request, 164-165, 171
 waiver, 733
 zealous advocacy, 791-809
Court-appointed counsel, types of, 4
Cox, Archibald, 818
Cox, Harold, 661, 946
Crack-cocaine disparity, sentencing, 1089-1100, 1321, 1367, 1401-1421

Crime rates, statistics, 1326
Criminal charge
 forms in which brought, 1
 summary of process, 1
Criminal Code, 974
Criminal contempt, 1226-1229
Criminal forfeiture, 709-718
"Cross-Examination, The Ten Commandments of," 546
Cross-racial identifications
 charge regarding, 1314-1319
 direct examination of eyewitness and, 1314
 expert testimony, 1303-1308, 1319
 jury instructions, 1308-1313, 1314-1319
 reliability of, 1303-1319
CSLI. *See* Cell-site location information (CSLI)
Curtilage, 218-224, 225, 391
Custodial interrogation, 4, 118-132. *See also Miranda*
Cutshall, Charles R., 821

Database errors, effect of, 490-491, 491-496. *See also* Exclusionary rule
Davis, Angela J., 811, 812, 820, 891
Davis, K., 1400
D-Day invasion of Normandy, 108
DEA. *See* Drug Enforcement Administration (DEA)
Deadlocked jury, 1119, 1177, 1183. *See also Allen* charge
Death penalty, 53, 775, 783-786, 985-991, 1250-1256, 1257, 1321
 aggravating factors, 1398-1399
 discretion, role of, 1378-1398, 1399, 1400
 effective assistance of counsel, 769, 782-783, 783-787
 mitigation evidence, 1378
 rape cases, 1368-1378
 sentencing, 1368-1401
 statistical studies on racial disparity in sentencing, 1378-1399
Deferred prosecution agreements (DPAs), 830, 831
Deliberate indifference, 561, 565, 571, 572, 579, 587
Deliberation by jury, 4, 1150, 1257, 1277
Department of Justice (DOJ), *passim, e.g.*, 3, 89, 100, 196-197, 212, 672, 946, 948, 952-956, 970, 972, 971, 1071, 1088, 1117, 1322, 1325, 1342, 1420
 Civil Rights Division, 911-948, 974
 eyewitness identification photo arrays, 1220-1221
 good faith exception to exclusionary rule, 489
 grand jury policies, 683, 696-699
 Justice Manual, 813-814, 868, 956, 1051
 plea bargaining, 976-977
 police departments, actions against, 867
 Principles of Federal Prosecution, 813-814
Deportation, 1012-1018
DiBlasio, William, 588

DiIulio, John J., Jr., 1427
Disclosure obligations, prosecutors, 848-886
Discovery
   expert, 875-879
   prosecutor obligations, 868-879
   reciprocal discovery, 869-875
   review before plea bargaining, 2
   state court, 869-875
Discretion of prosecutors, 812-848, 976, 1004, 1419
Discrimination
   burden-shifting framework 16, 1399
   in enforcement. *See* Selective enforcement
   in investigation. *See* Selective investigation
   prima facie case, 16, 60
   in prosecution, 1060-1068
Disorderly conduct, 360, 406, 1072
DNA evidence, 104, 1005, 1185
Dogs
   drug-sniffing, 239-243, 361-367, 420
   search of home and immediate surroundings by
      police dog, 239-243
DOJ. *See* Department of Justice (DOJ)
Double jeopardy, 948-974
   civil rights exception, case for, 959-961
Double Jeopardy Clause, 905, 952, 959, 970
Double standard of reasonableness, 607, 614
DPAs. *See* Deferred prosecution agreements (DPAs)
Dropsy testimony, 546
Drug checkpoints, 361-367
Drug courier profile, 259, 260-265, 266, 436
Drug Enforcement Administration (DEA), 1101,
   1117
   Operation Pipeline, 437
Drug-sniffing dogs, 239-243, 361-367, 420
Drug trafficking, 448, 1151-1152
Drugs, war on, 448, 791, 1321
Drunk driving
   arrest, 341, 356
   sobriety checkpoint, 361
Dual sovereignty, 952-956, 961-969
DuBois, W.E.B., 65, 556
Due process
   eyewitness identification, 1206-1229
   rights, 6, 116, 726, 848, 858, 875, 1207, 1220,
      1244
Due Process Clause, 6, 726, 848, 875, 1207, 1220,
   1244
Duncan, Paul, 1101, 1119-1125, 1126
"Dunning School" of Reconstruction historiography,
   556-557, 929, 946
Dunning, William, 556, 557, 929
Dyer Bill, 43-44

Eastland, James, 661
Edward R. Roybal Federal Courthouse, 959
Effective assistance of counsel
   alcohol abuse, 767-769

competence of defense counsel, 770-775
death penalty cases, 769, 782-783, 783-787
immigration consequences of plea, erroneous
   advice on, 1012-1018
indigent defense, 756-776, 776-791
juvenile, representation of, 776-782
plea-bargaining context, 1012-1018, 1019-1028
prejudice standard, 757-766
waivers, 1046
Ehrlichmann, John D., 947
Eighth Amendment, 7, 557, 953, 1003, 1326, 1399
Electronic eavesdropping, 213-217
Electronic surveillance, 1, 5, 607
Electronically stored information, search warrant
   for, 297
Eliminating a Quantifiably Unjust Application of
   the Law Act (EQUAL Act), 1421
Ellsberg, Daniel, 702, 947
Ely, John Hart, 735
Emmit Till Act, 44
Enforcement Act, 906, 910, 911
English, Larry, 808
Enron scandal, 830
Entrapment doctrine, 832-836
   government's active participation in criminal
      activity, 836
   predisposition element, 832-835, 841-842
   stealth and strategy, use of, 836-841, 845
Epps, Daniel, 1162, 1163, 1169-1170
Epstein, Jeffrey, 1337
EQUAL Act. *See* Eliminating a Quantifiably Unjust
   Application of the Law Act (EQUAL Act)
Equal Justice Initiative
   lynchings, documentation of, 44
   National Memorial for Peace and Justice, 43
Equal Protection Clause, 284, 290, 453, 634, 1068,
   1237, 1337
Equal protection doctrine, race and, 1089
Ethical obligations of prosecutors, 886-891
Ethics in Government Act, 99, 814-818
Evans, Doug, 1301
Evasive conduct, 428-429
Excessive Fines Clause, 7
Excessive use of force, 284, 291-295, 557, 580, 607,
   608-614, 615-617, 718, 959, 974
Exclusionary rule, 297-305, 329, 340, 473-481
   attenuation, 495, 497-512
   database errors, effect of, 490-491, 491-496
   good faith exception, 355, 481-497
   impeachment exception, 528-540
   negligent bookkeeping error, 491, 496
   standing, 512-528
   suppression hearings, 540-549
Exculpatory evidence, grand jury, 641-650
Exculpatory information, 2, 848-868
   Brady material, 848-851, 853
   disclosure to defense, 766

Giglio material, 851-853
  materiality, 853-854
  prosecutors, 848-868
Exigent circumstances doctrine, 211, 356-359
  exception where exigency created by police
      conduct, 359
  eyewitness identification, 1208
  severity of crime, significance of, 359
  warrantless entry into home to arrest or search,
      211, 311-318, 356-359
Expert witnesses
  cross-racial identifications, 1303-1308, 1319
  disclosure, contents of, 878
  discovery, 875-879
  on use of force, 295
Eye contact, effect of, 1285
Eyewitness identification
  counsel, right to, 1185-1206, 1208
  cross-racial identifications at trial. *See*
      Cross-racial identifications
  due process, 1206-1229
  exigent circumstances, 1208
  in-court identification, 1185-1201, 1206-1213,
      1225-1229
  jury instructions, 1221-1225, 1308-1313,
      1314-1319
  lineup identification, 1185-1201, 1205
  own race bias, 1303, 1308
  "per se" test vs. "reliability" test, 1208-1213,
      1214, 1220
  photo array identifications, 1201-1206, 1208-
      1213, 1214, 1220-1221
  post-indictment procedures, 1198-1200
  psychology of, 1303-1308
  social science of, 1214-1215, 1220
  suggestive out-of-court identification, 1206-
      1208, 1215-1219
  at trial, 1303-1319

Fagan, Jeffrey, 428
Fair cross-section requirement for jury, 5, 1231-1242
Fair Sentencing Act, 1420-1421
"Fair trial" rights, 857-858
Fair warning, 948
Fake stash house stings, 1059, 1117
Fallon, Richard J., Jr., 579
False arrest, 593, 602
False Claims Act, 709
False statements made in federal matter, 1127-1132
FBI (Federal Bureau of Investigation), 918, 930,
      931, 938, 945, 947, 1070, 1117, 1132,
      1322, 1325, 1342
Federal jurisdiction, 938
Federal Jury Selection and Service Act, 1237, 1242
Federal Kidnapping Act, 984, 985
Federal Rules of Civil Procedure, 593
  Rule 8, 660

Rule 8(a)(2), 709
Rule 9(b), 709
Rule 12(b)(6), 1109
Rule 23, 1109
Rule 34, 662
Rule 45, 662
Rule 56, 597, 1109
Rule 56(d), 1109
Federal Rules of Criminal Procedure
  Rule 6, 628, 673, 682
  Rule 6(e), 678, 679
  Rule 6(e)(2)(B), 679
  Rule 6(e)(3)(A)(i), 678
  Rule 7, 651, 709, 831
  Rule 7(c), 660
  Rule 7(c)(1), 709
  Rule 7(f), 709
  Rule 11, 831, 979, 983, 991, 996, 1041,
      1051-1052, 1056-1057
  Rule 11(a)(3), 996
  Rule 11(b)(1)(O), 1017
  Rule 11(b)(3), 983, 996
  Rule 11(c)(1)(C), 1037
  Rule 11(f), 1017
  Rule 12, 1070
  Rule 12(b)(3)(A)(iv), 1070
  Rule 12(b)(3)(B)(v), 641
  Rule 12.1, 875
  Rule 12.2, 875
  Rule 12.3, 875
  Rule 15, 682
  Rule 16, 869, 875, 877, 878, 879, 886, 1099
  Rule 16(a)(1)(A), 869
  Rule 16(a)(1)(B), 869
  Rule 16(a)(1)(E), 869
  Rule 16(a)(1)(G), 875, 878
  Rule 16(a)(2), 1099
  Rule 16(b)(1)(B), 869
  Rule 17, 672, 673
  Rules 18-31, 831
  Rule 26.2, 886
  Rule 32(d), 1032
  Rule 32(e), 1032
  Rule 35, 1349
  Rule 41(e), 516
  Rule 41(f)(B), 297
  Rule 43, 1157
  Rule 46(c), 1325
  Rule 48(a), 660, 831
Federal Rules of Evidence
  admissions against interest, 108
  hearsay rule, 108
  Rule 103(a)(2), 1104
  Rule 410, 1017
  Rule 606(b), 1257
  Rule 702, 1308
  Rule 1006, 640

Federal Tort Claims Act, 947
Federalism
  cooperative, 969-970
  deferential, 953, 954, 956, 958, 973
Field interrogation, 391-392, 406
Fifteenth Amendment, 910
Fifth Amendment, 2, 5, 6, 77-210, 756
  grand jury, 627, 690, 696, 698-699, 1119
  presentment or indictment, 1119
  self-incrimination. *See* Self-incrimination,
    right against
Final judgment rule, 608
Fingerprinting, 80
Firearms Owners' Protection Act, 974
First Amendment, 6, 557, 572, 1079
First Step Act, 1420-1421
Fisher, George, 978-979
"Fleeing felon" rule, 285-290
Flight
  "fleeing felon" rule, 285-290
  headlong flight, 429
  reasonable suspicion, 424-429
Florida, open file discovery in, 886
Flowers, Curtis, 1287-1301
Floyd, George, 619, 971
Flynn, Michael, 1132
FOIA. *See* Freedom of Information Act (FOIA)
Foner, Eric, 556, 929
For-cause challenges, 1257, 1285. *See also*
    Peremptory challenges
Force, use of
  excessive. *See* Excessive use of force
  seizure by police, 265, 284-295
Forfeiture, criminal, 709-718
Forman, James, Jr., 1277
Forrester, Owen, 1418
Fortas, Abe, 735
Fourteenth Amendment, 6-7, 11, 16, 53, 76, 909,
    928, 1119, 1127, 1207, 1244
Fourth Amendment, 5, 8, 80, 90, 91, 118, 211-471,
    947, 948
  informant, use of, 845
  search. *See* Search
  seizure. *See* Seizure
  warrants. *See* Warrants
Fraud cases, 1
Frazier, Charles E., 821
Fred T. Korematsu Center for Law and Equality,
    283
Freedom of Information Act (FOIA), 679, 1056
Free-to-leave analysis, 264, 265-266, 269-276, 284,
    429. *See also* Seizure
Fried, Charles, 134
Friedman, Barry, 6, 470
Frisking. *See* Stop and frisk
Fruit of the poisonous tree, 202, 453, 497
Fugitive Slave Acts, 1125, 1150

Gambling, 213-217, 1065, 1100, 1105
Garner, Eric, 718, 973
Garrett, Brandon, 1214-1215, 1225-1226
George Floyd Justice in Policing Act, 973
Georgia, grand jury role in prosecution of unjustified
    police killings, 719-720
Gertner, Nancy, 1242
Gideon, Clarence, 729-737, 757
Giuliani, Rudolph, 586, 1333
Global positioning system (GPS) tracking, 211,
    230-239
Goldberg, Arthur, 1368
Goldstein, Goldie, 889
Good faith exception, 355, 481-497. *See also*
    Exclusionary rule
GPS devices, 211, 230-239
Grand jury, 1, 5, 627-720
  Black people, exclusion of, 17, 629-638
  composition, 17, 629-638
  disclosure-permitting language, 678-679
  DOJ policies, 683, 696-699
  exculpatory evidence, 641-650
  executive vs. judiciary vis-á-vis grand jury, 652-661
  independence, 638-661
  indictment, 1, 7, 17, 627, 709-718
  informality, 638-661
  investigative powers, breadth of, 668-673
  mythos, 628-629
  perjury before, 682-690, 696, 703-709
  police misconduct, investigation of, 718-720
  powers of, prosecutor abuse of, 699-709
  presentment, 650-651
  prosecutorial abuse of grand jury's powers,
    699-709
  race, 629-638
  runaway, 651-652
  secrecy, 673-682, 718
  "special grand jury," 651-652
  subpoena power, 662-673
  witnesses, 682-699
Grant Administration, 905, 907-909, 911
Gray, Freddie, 973
Great Depression, 953
Grunwald, Ben, 428
Guilty pleas, 2, 5, 979-983, 984-997, 1012-1019,
    1019-1026, 1028-1032
  statistics, 1031
Gutmann, Joe, 1269

Habitual offender statute, 997-1003, 1005,
    1066-1068
Hall, Robert, 918-930
Ham, Gene, 1242-1245
Hand, Learned, 832, 1149
Harmless error doctrine, 637, 891-892, 1257
Harmon, Rachel, 294-295, 329, 625
Hate Crimes Act, 44

Hauptmann, Bruno, 984
Hearsay, indictments based on, 638-641
High crime area, reasonable suspicion, 424-429
High school students
    athletes, drug testing of, 367-375
    extracurricular activity participants, drug testing
        of, 375
    "special needs" warrantless search, 367-375
Hiibel, Larry Dudley, 415, 416, 420
Hill, Henry, 848
Hoffa, Jimmy, 842-846
Holliday, George, 620, 957-958
Home exceptionalism, 243, 311
Hoover, J. Edgar, 917, 1342
Human trafficking, 878
Hung jury, 1133-1140, 1267
Hymon, Elton, 290-291

IATs. *See* Implicit Association Tests (IATs)
ILD. *See* Internal Labor Defense (ILD)
Illegal narcotics, highway checkpoint program,
        361-367
Immigration
    checkpoints, 360, 427, 435
    enforcement, use of ethnicity in, 430-436
    plea, erroneous advice on consequences of,
        1012-1018
Impeachment exception, 528-540. *See also*
        Exclusionary rule
Implicit Association Tests (IATs), 821
Implicit bias, 424, 976, 1119, 1170
    jury instruction, 1184
    prosecutors, 821
Imprisonment rates, spike in, 1321-1322
Incorporation, 6-7, 53
Independent counsel, 90, 99-100, 814-820
Indiana, no *Alford* pleas in, 996
Indictment by grand jury, 1, 7, 17, 627, 709-718
Indigent defendants, 53, 118, 721-737, 738-740,
        740-745, 756, 776-791
    appointed counsel, right to, 721-729, 745-748
    effective assistance of counsel, 756-776, 776-791
Informant. *See* Informers, use of
Information, charge brought by, 1, 627
Informed consent, 8
Informers, use of, 165, 832-836, 842-845, 847, 848
In-group favoritism, 976
Initial appearance, summary of process, 1-2
Injunctive relief, 551, 558-560, 572, 573-580,
        580-586, 960
Innocence Project, 1005, 1185
Insanity defense, 875, 1157-1163
Internal Labor Defense (ILD), 58
Internal Revenue Service, 679
Interrogation, meaning of, 138-143, 750-755
Investigation, summary of process, 1
Irish Republican Army (IRA), 1102

Jackson, Robert, 113-114, 819, 905
Jackson, Vicki, 580
Jacob, Bruce, 735
Jencks Act, 640, 869, 879-886
Jim Crow, 556
Johnson (Andrew) Administration, 956
Johnson, Kevin R., 434-435
Johnson, Lyndon Baines, 735, 910, 947
Johnson, Sheri Lynn, 1256-1257, 1277
Joy, Peter, 782-783
Judiciary Act of 1789, 907
Junkyards, warrantless searches of, 360, 390, 391
Jurisdiction
    federal question, 579
    pendent, 579
Jury, 2, 4
    Allen charge, 1177-1183
    bias challenges to potential jurors, 4, 1242-1257
    charged crime, power to decide elements of,
        1357
    convictions, invalidation of, 12-17
    cross-racial identifications at trial, 1303-1319
    deadlock, 1177. *See also Allen* charge
    deliberation, 4, 1150
    disparity in system, racial and ethnic, 1241
    exclusion of Black people from, 12-17,
        1257-1302
    facts decided by, 1127-1131, 1132
    fair cross-section requirement, 5, 1231-1242
    for-cause challenges, 1257, 1285
    hung jury, 1133-1140, 1267
    implicit bias instruction, 1184
    instructions. *See* Jury instructions
    nonunanimous verdicts, 1133-1140
    nullification, 1140-1153
    panel, 4
    peremptory challenges, 4, 1257-1302
    potential punishment, knowledge of, 1153-1170
    race and, 12-17, 1231-1319
    reasonable doubt, 1170-1177
    right to jury trial, 1119-1229, 1231-1319
    scope of right, 1119-1140, 1365
    selection process, 4, 5
    size, 1127
    "systematic exclusion" test, 1237-1240
    unanimity, 7, 1133-1140
    venire, 4
    verdicts, 1157-1163, 1163-1168
    voir dire, 1149, 1242-1257
    women, exclusion of, 1231-1236, 1237-1240
Jury instructions, 4, 1149, 1150, 1170-1184
    cross-racial identifications, 1308-1313,
        1314-1319
    eyewitness identification, 1221-1225,
        1308-1313, 1314-1319
Justice Department. *See* Department of Justice
        (DOJ)

Justice Manual, 813-814, 868, 956, 1051
Juveniles, representation of, 776-782

Kaczorowski, Robert J., 560, 909, 911, 956
Kamisar, Yale, 132, 733
Katzenbach, Nicholas, 661
Kelling, George, 406
Kennedy, Randall, 1101, 1105, 1126, 1419
Kennedy, Robert, 845, 846, 945
Kent State University antiwar protestors, 1245
King, Martin Luther, Jr., 291
King, Rodney, 580, 620, 948, 957-961
Klarman, Michael J., 12, 43
"Knock and announce" requirement, 306, 497-503.
    See also Search warrants
Korematsu, Fred, 283
Ku Klux Klan, 907, 908, 909, 946-947
Ku Klux Klan Act, 551, 906, 907, 908, 911

Langbein, John H., 1004
Larsen, Joan L., 1119
Law enforcement agencies. *See also* Police
    responsibility of, 3
    selective investigation by. *See* Selective
        investigation
Lawrence, Frederick M., 906
Leaming, Cleatus, 750-756
"Legislative codes," 916
Leibowitz, Samuel, 58, 59
Leong, Nancy, 470
Levenson, Laurie, 961
Levinson, Justin D., 821, 976
Lindbergh, Charles, 984
"Line prosecutors," 3, 4, 930
Lineup identification, 1185-1201, 1205
Liquor laws, 1105-1109
Liuzzo, Viola, 946-947
Long, Huey, 912
Louisiana, *Alford* pleas in, 996
Lying by police, 542-549
Lynching, 40-43, 43-44, 1368

Maclin, Tracey, 103, 276, 405, 421, 496-497, 503,
    845
Mail fraud, 99, 1056
Mandatory minimum sentences, 821, 1005
Marder, Nancy S., 1286
Marshall, Thurgood, 71, 454
Martin, Travon, 972-973
Mass incarceration, 745, 822, 1321-1322
Materiality, exculpatory information, 853-854
Matusow, Henry, 885
McCleskey, Warren, 1378-1400
McCoy, Robert, 808
McCulloch, Robert, 719
McFadden, Martin J., 404, 405, 422-424
McGovern, George, 1080

McKinley, Wesley, 651, 652
McMahon, Jack, 1269, 1301
Meese, Edwin, 134, 672, 836, 1088
Mens rea, 6, 906, 928, 973
Minors
    interrogation of, 151-157
    representation of, 776-782
    "special needs" searches in high schools, 367-375
Miranda, 4, 8, 77, 118-210
    child's age, effect on waiver of rights, 284
    choosing to remain silent without warnings,
        171-177
    as "constitutional rule," 197-202, 209
    content of warnings, 171
    counsel, right to, 4, 161-165
    custody, defined, 143-157
    detention, amount of, 143-157
    durability of, 196-210
    exceptions, 134-138, 530-532
    federal cases, "voluntariness" test in, 196-210
    interrogation, meaning of, 138-143, 750-755
    invocation of rights, 157-183
    minors, interrogation of, 151-157
    as prophylactic rule, 201-202, 202-210
    public safety exception, 134-138, 143
    resumption of questioning after invocation of
        right to counsel, 161-165
    "routine" traffic stops, 143-148
    successive interrogation, unwarned and warned
        phases, 183-196
    summary, 1
    unambiguous assertion of right to remain silent,
        165-171
    violations, consequences of, 183-196
    waiver, 157, 161-165
    witnesses in grand jury, 682-690
Misconduct
    police, 551-625, 718-720, 859-867, 974. *See also*
        Excessive use of force
    prosecutors, 566-572, 887-889, 892-904
Missouri, *Alford* pleas in, 996
Mitchell, John, 607
Mob convictions, 40-60, 65
Model Code of Professional Responsibility
    DR 7-102, 797-798
Model Rules of Professional Conduct (MRPC)
    Rule 1.7(a)(2), 1046
    Rule 3.7, 1196
    Rule 3.8, 890
    Rule 3.8(g), 891
    Rule 8.4(a), 1046
Moley, Raymond, 979
Mollen Commission, 542-543
Mondale, Walter, 735
Monroe, James, 552-557
Moral certainty, 1177
Moral evidence, 1177

Moreland, Professor, 1071
Mosteller, Robert P., 100
Motion in limine, 2
Motley, Constance Baker, 661, 1258-1259
Motor home, search of, 387-390
Motor vehicle stop. *See also* Stop and frisk
    pretextual, 9, 438-448, 463
    search, consent for, 8, 438-448
MRPC. *See* Model Rules of Professional Conduct
    (MRPC)
Municipal liability, 1983 actions, 557, 558-588
Munsch, Christin L., 349-350
Murphy, Frank, 911-912

NAACP, 43, 44, 58, 59, 65, 1258-1259, 1368, 1378
    Legal Defense and Educational Fund, Inc.,
      421-422
    Legal Defense Foundation (LDF), capital
      punishment effort, 1377
Narcotics trafficking, 424-426, 683-698, 878
National Civil Rights Museum, 291
National Memorial for Peace and Justice, 43
National Prohibition Act, 835
National Registry of Exonerations, 1005
Neutrality Act, 1101, 1102
New Deal, 953
New Jersey, no *Alford* pleas in, 996
New York, stop and frisk policies in, 580-588
NGI (not guilty by reason of insanity), 1157-1163
Nichols, Tyre, 470
9/11, 436, 1101-1102
Nixon Administration, 818, 947, 1321, 1326
Nixon, Richard, 1018
"No impeachment" rule, 1257
No-knock search warrant, 306, 971
Nolo contendere plea, 996
Non-prosecution agreements (NPAs), 830, 831
Nonunanimous jury verdicts, 1133-1140
North Carolina, open file discovery in, 886
NPAs. *See* Non-prosecution agreements (NPAs)
Nullification
    jury, 1140-1153
    prosecutors, 832

Obama Administration, 624, 625, 832
Objective reasonableness standard, 9, 225, 598, 603, 614
Obstruction misdemeanor, 406
Obstruction of justice, actual, 1229
Offer of proof, 1104
Ohio, *Alford* pleas in, 996
Omnibus Crime Control Act, 1071
Omnibus Crime Control and Safe Streets Act, 133, 217, 406, 607
"Open fields" doctrine, 218
Orangeburg Massacre, 1245, 1246
ORB. *See* Own race bias (ORB)

Organized crime, 640-641, 878
Originalism, 269, 290, 718, 830, 961, 970, 1119, 1127, 1132, 1150-1151
Ortman, William, 718, 977, 978, 1004, 1162, 1163, 1169-1170
Outside agitators, 1124
Overbreadth
    grand jury subpoena, 667
    warrant, 296
Own race bias (ORB), 1303, 1308. *See also*
    Eyewitness identification

Parking violations, 463-469
Parole Commission, 1342
Parole revocation hearing, 748
Partin, Edward, 846
"Patrol" encounters with police, 391. *See also* Police
Pattern or practice of police misconduct, 552
Payne, Reuben, 423-424
Pedestrian checks, 340
Pen registers, 211, 217-218
Penn, Lemuel, 946
Pennsylvania, *Alford* pleas in, 996
Pentagon Papers, 702, 947
Peonage convictions, 17-40. *See also* Antipeonage
    Act
Peremptory challenges
    criminal defendant's use of, 1270-1275
    elimination in criminal and civil cases in
      Arizona, 1287
    eye contact, effect of, 1285
    facially neutral explanations for race/ethnicity-
      based challenges, 1277-1285
    gender-based, 1284
    misconduct, prosecutorial, numerous instances
      of, 1287-1302
    plausibility of proffered explanation, 1285-1286, 1301
    prosecutor's use of, 1259-1269, 1276, 1277-1285, 1287-1302
    race and, 1257-1302
    state reforms in Washington and California, 1286
    summary, 4
Perez, Leander, 1124-1125, 1126
Perjury
    before grand jury, 682-690, 696, 703-709
    by police, 542-549
Perjury-trap defense, 708-709
Perry, Barion, 1219
Petit jury, 59, 629, 637, 717, 908, 918, 929, 1100, 1258
Petite Policy, 954-956, 958, 971
Photo array identifications, 1201-1206, 1208-1213, 1214, 1220-1221
Pickpocketing, 392-404
Plain error, 1157, 1183

Index

"Plain feel" exception, 407-411. *See also* Stop and frisk
Plain view exception, 211, 306-311. *See also* Search warrants
Players in criminal justice system, 3-5
Plea agreements, 1011-1028
    breach of, 1028-1057
    disclosure of impeachment information, 854-859
    discretion, exercise of, 813
    enforceability of, 1028-1057
    fast track, 858
Plea bargaining, 975-1057
    agreements. *See* Plea agreements
    appellate rights, waiver of, 1032-1037, 1038-1041
    coercion, 997-1011
    collateral consequences, 1012-1018
    collateral waivers, 1028, 1042-1057
    consequences of waiving hearing, 979-984
    Constitution and, 997-1011
    controversy, 976-979
    disclosure of exculpatory evidence, 854-859
    guilty pleas, 979-983, 984-997, 1028-1032
    hearing, 979-984
    history, 977-979
    ineffective assistance of counsel, 1012-1018, 1019-1028
    overcharging, 1016
    plea agreements. *See* Plea agreements
    race and, 976-977
    racial bias in, 977
    statistics on guilty pleas, 1031
    summary of process, 2
    uncommunicated plea offer, 1027
    voluntariness, 984-997
    waiver of plea hearing, 979-984
Pleading standards, heightened, 608
Plenary charging power, prosecutors, 821-832
Podcasts
    In the Dark, 1287
    More Perfect, 1267
    Object Anyway, 1286
Police
    bias against Black persons, 421-422
    brutality, 906, 917, 929, 930, 931, 947, 948, 957, 974
    consensual encounters, 264
    "contempt of cop," 406
    credibility, 549
    custodial interrogation. *See Miranda*; Police interrogation
    deadly force, use of, 285-290, 291, 614-618
    DOJ authority regarding misconduct of, 620-625
    excessive use of force, 284, 291-295, 608-614
    field interrogation, 391
    free-to-leave analysis, 264, 265, 269-276, 284
    grand jury investigation of misconduct, 718-720

implicit racial bias, 424. *See also* Implicit bias
interrogation by. *See Miranda*; Police interrogation
lies by, 171-175, 542-549
misconduct, 551-625, 718-720, 859-867, 974
numbers of, 3
patrol encounters, 391
perjury, 542-549
qualified immunity, 295
responsibility of, 3
selective enforcement, 1105-1110, 1110-1117
selective investigation. *See* Selective investigation
stop and frisk. *See* Stop and frisk
structural reform litigation, 620-625
traffic stops, 437-471
violence, 905
"Police artist," use of, 1308
Police interrogation, 104-117
    Fifth Amendment and, 77-210
    Miranda requirements. *See Miranda*
    voluntariness, 104-117
Poll tax, 910
Polygraph, 164
Ponomarenko, Maria, 6
Post-conviction relief, summary of process, 3
Post-indictment investigation, 116
Pre-sentence report, 1032
Presentments, 650-651
President's Commission on Law Enforcement and Administration of Justice, 421
Pretext
    arrest, 338
    traffic stops, 437-471
    vehicle stops, 328, 338, 438-448, 448-454
Pretrial detention, 1322-1341
Preventive detention, 1333, 1334
Privacy
    reasonable expectation of, 211, 213-218, 224-225, 239, 243, 355
    right of, 80-81
Privileges or Immunities Clause, 6
Probable cause, 1, 216, 259, 341
    exception, 211, 391-421
    grand jury indictment decision, 709-718
    search warrants, 211, 296, 297-305, 306
    Terry doctrine, 211, 391-421
Probation revocation proceeding, 745-748
Probationer, searching home of, 360
Prohibition, 211-212, 382, 977
Proof beyond reasonable doubt. *See* Reasonable doubt
Prophylactic racial profiling, 424
Prosecution memorandum, 1083
Prosecutors, 811-904
    absolute immunity, 603, 892
    accountability, lack of, 891-892
    appointment of, 3-4

assistant district attorney, 3
assistant United States attorneys, 4
charging decisions, race and, 820-832
checks against prosecutorial abuse, 819
commencement of prosecution, 749
disclosure obligations, 848-886
discovery obligations, 868-879
discretion, 812-848, 976, 1004, 1419
discriminatory prosecution, 1060-1068
district attorney, 3
"doing justice," 891
election of, 3
ethical obligations, 886-891
exculpatory information, 848-868
expert discovery, 875-879
grand jury's powers, abuse of, 699-709
implicit bias, 821
judicial authority, encroachment on, 821,
    822-830
"line," 3, 4
misconduct, 566-572, 887-889, 892-904
nonprosecution, power of, 822, 831-832
nullification, 832
plenary charging power, 821-832
politically unpopular defendant, 842-845
power of, 811, 821, 822
racial bias, 820-821
racial discrimination, abuse of discretion on
    grounds of, 1119-1126
reciprocal discovery, 869-875
as sentencers, 822
special responsibilities, 890-891
United States attorneys, appointment of, 3-4
unsavory/unreliable witnesses and tactics, use of,
    832-848
victims of crimes, solicitude for, 820
witness statements, 879-886
"Protective sweep" of premises, 407
PSA. *See* Public Safety Assessment (PSA)
Public air space, surveillance from, 218-224
Public authority, 875
Public defenders, 782-783, 787-791, 1099
Public Safety Assessment (PSA), 1341
Public safety exception, 134-138, 143. *See also*
    Miranda

Qualified immunity, 295, 503, 551-552, 557,
    588-619, 947-948

Race and ethnicity. *See also specific topics throughout
    index*
    charging discretion of prosecutors, 820-832
    equal protection doctrine, 1089
    grand jury, 17, 629-638
    immigration enforcement, 430-436
    influence on perception of police encounter,
        276-284

jury, exclusion from, 12-17, 1257-1302
    police bias, 421-422
    suspicion and, 421-471
Race riots, 406
Racial bias
    in jury, 4, 1242-1257
    in plea bargaining, 977
    in police, 421-422
    in prosecutors, 820-821
Racial profiling, 339
    prophylactic, 424
    search, 430-436
    traffic stops, 454-463
    warrantless search, 360
Racketeering cases, 1, 572
Rader, Jennifer, 496-497, 503
Rakoff, Jed S., 1005, 1057
Rameswaram, Sean, 1267
Ramos, Evangelisto, 1133-1140
Rape cases, death penalty in, 1368-1378
Reagan Administration, 672, 836
Reasonable doubt, 1170-1177
Reasonable expectation of privacy
    rental car, 521-527
    search for Fourth Amendment purposes, 211,
        213-216, 239
Reasonable suspicion, 35, 259, 260, 265, 387,
        402-403, 404, 406, 411, 415, 416-420
    anonymous tips and, 420-421
    factors used as basis for, 433
    flight, 424-429
    high crime area, 424-429
    race and. *See* Suspicion and race
Reciprocal discovery, 869
Reckless disregard, 928
Reconstruction era, 556, 905
    congressional criminal legislation, 905, 906
    federal criminal enforcement during, 907-909
    Supreme Court and legislation, 909-911
Remsberg, Charles, 437
Reno, Janet, 99
Rental car, expectation of privacy in, 521-527
Rescission, 1031
Respondeat superior liability, 551, 560-561, 624, 831
Retaliation, 1011
Rice, Tamir, 718, 973
Rights-interference crimes, 906
Risk assessment tools, 1341
Robbery, armed, 404-405
Rogers, William, 954
Roosevelt (Franklin) Administration, 911
Rubin, Alvin, 766-767
Runaway grand jury, 651-652
Rushin, Stephen, 624, 625

Schauer, Frederick, 201
Scheduling conferences, summary of process, 2

Index

Schmidt, Benno C., Jr., 18-19, 59-60
Schulhofer, Stephen, 133-134
Schwartz, Joanna C., 618, 619
Scott, Robert E., 975
Scott, Walter, 970-971
Seale, Bobby, 1229
Search
    arrest, incident to, 211, 311, 328, 329-341
    border searches, 360, 430-436
    cell phone records, 243-259
    consent search, 211, 341-356
    defined, 211-259
    drug-sniffing dogs, 239-243, 361-367, 420
    GPS. *See* Global positioning system (GPS) tracking
    home and immediate surroundings by police
        dog, 239-243
    racial profiling, 430-436
    suspicionless, 211, 359-375
    technology, 211, 225-239
    warrantless. *See* Warrantless searches
    warrants. *See* Search warrants
Search warrants, 295, 296-306
    anonymous informant's tip, partially
        corroborated, 297-305
    description of place to be searched, 296
    detached and neutral magistrate, issuance by, 490
    electronically stored information, 297
    exceptions, 211, 296, 306-311
    execution of, 305-306
    identification of specific offense, 296
    inadvertent discovery of incriminating evidence,
        306-311
    items to be seized, 296
    "knock and announce" requirement, 306,
        497-503
    no-knock, 306, 971
Second Amendment, 7
Secrecy, grand jury, 673-682, 718
Section 1983 actions, 44, 77, 551, 552-619, 935
    absolute immunity of prosecutors, 892
    civil damages actions, 284
    federal government officials, 594-598
    municipalities, actions against, 558-588
    qualified immunity, 588-619
    text of §1983, 210
Seeger, Pete, 885
Segregated waiting rooms, 592-593
Seizure
    age of child and view of freedom to leave, 284
    arrest. *See* Arrest
    defined, 259-295
    force, use of, by police, 265, 284-295
    free-to-leave analysis, 264, 265-266, 269-276,
        284, 429
    lack of freedom of movement, 269-276
    police encounters and, 260-276
    police use of force, 265, 284-295

race and ethnicity, influence of, on perception of
    police encounter, 276-284
reasonableness of, 284, 948
warrantless arrests. *See* Warrantless arrests
Selective enforcement, 1059-1117
Selective investigation, 1102-1117
Selective prosecution, 1059-1117
    equal protection right against, 1060-1066
    lower courts, 1068-1084
    prima facie case, 1083
    Supreme Court, 1084-1102
Self-incrimination, right against, 6, 78-104, 952.
        See also Silence, right to
    absence of affirmative assertion of right, 171-177
    civil cases, 103
    immunized testimony, 81-90
    "no comment" rule, 103
    scope of right, 78-104
    "testimonial or communicative" conduct, 78-80
    voice exemplars, 667
    waiver of, 690
Sellers, Bakari, 1245
Sellers, Cleveland, 1245, 1246
"Sense enhancing" technology, 225-230, 243
Sentencing, 821-822
    crack-cocaine disparity, 1089-1100, 1321, 1367,
        1401-1421
    death penalty. *See* Death penalty
    discretion in, 1341
    enhancement, 1357
    guidelines. *See* Sentencing Guidelines
    hypothetical, 1349, 1351
    indeterminate, 1342
    life imprisonment, 997, 1003, 1005, 1066-1068,
        1357
    mandatory minimum sentence, 821, 1005
    presentence report, 2
    prosecutors as sentencers, 822
    race and, 1368-1427
    reduction for waiver of right to receive
        impeachment information, 858
    reform, 1343
    summary of process, 2-3
    "superpredator" theory, 1421-1427
Sentencing Commission, 1343-1347, 1420
Sentencing Guidelines, 2, 541-542, 947, 1032,
        1321, 1341-1368, 1418
    acceptance of responsibility, 1348
    criminal history, effect of, 1351-1356
    individual characteristics, 1347-1348
    range, 1349, 1350
    "real offense" conduct, 1348
    relevant conduct, 1348
    Sixth Amendment, violation of, 1357-1365
    starting point and benchmark, 1366
    substantial assistance, 1349
    table, 1349, 1350

Index   **1449**

Sentencing Reform Act, 1343-1347, 1356, 1366
Seo, Sarah A., 383, 384, 386, 403, 470
Separate-sovereignty doctrine, 961-968, 969
Separation of powers, 296, 819, 821, 822, 830, 929, 953, 1088, 1343, 1347, 1356
Sequencing, 614
Sessions, Jeff, 625
Seventh Amendment, jury trial in civil case, 1119
Sex trafficking, 875-878, 1337
Sexual assault, 947
Shapiro, Harry H., 930
Sherman Act, 928-929
Shoplifting, 392-404
Silence. *See also* Self-incrimination, right against
    case-in-chief, use in, 183
    choice to remain silent without *Miranda* warnings, 171-177
    impeachment, use for, 177-183
    post-arrest, 177-183
    pre-arrest, 183
    trial, use at, 177-183
    unambiguous assertion of right to remain silent, 165-171
Sixth Amendment, 2, 5, 7, 53, 118, 1127, 1150, 1168, 1231-1319
    counsel, right to. *See* Counsel, right to
    effective assistance of counsel. *See* Effective assistance of counsel, right to
    jury trial in criminal case, 1119
    Sentencing Guidelines' application and, 1357-1365. *See also* Sentencing Guidelines
Sklansky, David A., 1418
Slager, Michael, 970-971
Smith Act, 1322-1325
Smith, Robert J., 821, 976
Sobol, Richards, 1126
Sobriety checkpoint, 361
"Special needs" searches, 211, 359-375
Specific performance, 1031
Speedy Trial Act, 830-831, 1333
Stages of criminal process, 1-3
Stampp, Kenneth, 946
Standing
    exclusionary rule, 512-528
    federal law, 512-516
    guests and invitees, 516-517, 517-521
    injunctive relief, 573-579
    invitees. *See* guests and invitees, *this heading*
Stare decisis, 340, 969, 1139
Starr, Kenneth, 92, 99, 820
State action doctrine, 44
State constitutional criminal procedure, 7-9
Stevenson, Bryan, 1286
Stith, Kate, 1343, 1347
Stokes, Louis, 422, 423
Stone, Harlan Fiske, 211
Stop and frisk, 35, 148, 339, 391-404

NYPD policies, 580-588
passengers in vehicle at traffic stop, 416-420
reasonable suspicion, 35, 259, 402-403, 404
touch, sense of, 407-411
"Stop and identify" statutes, 411-416
Stored Communications Act, 259
Storey, Moorefield, 44
Street crime, 1342
Strict constructionists, 406
Students
    athletes, drug-testing of, 367-375
    extracurricular activity participants, drug-testing of, 375
    "special needs" warrantless searches, 367-375
Stuntz, William J., 5-6, 975
Subpoena power, grand jury, 662-673
Successive prosecutions, 948-974
Summons to appear, 329
"Superpredator" theory, 1421-1427
Suppression hearing, 143, 160, 176, 191, 196, 224, 265, 276, 310, 340, 390, 403, 405, 422, 423, 429, 434, 453, 540-549. *See also* Exclusionary rule
Suppression of evidence, standing, 512-528
Surveillance
    electronic, 1, 213-216, 607
    from public air space, 218-224
Suspicion
    race, effect of. *See* Suspicion and race
    reasonableness of. *See* Reasonable suspicion
    suspicionless search, 211, 359-375
Suspicion and race, 421-471
    border searches, 430-436
    pretext, 437-471
    profiling, 430-436
    Terry doctrine, 421-429
    traffic stops, 437-471
Sweet, Henry, 911
Sweet, Ossian, 911
"Systematic exclusion" test, 1237-1240

Taft-Hartley Act, 845
Take Care Clause, 830, 832
Tax law, 679
Taylor, Breonna, 718, 971
Technology
    GPS tracking, 211, 230-239
    search, 211, 225-239
    sense-enhancing, 225-230, 243
    thermal imaging, 211, 225-230, 243
Terrorist activities, 138, 436, 1101-1102
Terry, John W., 404
Terry stop. *See* Stop and frisk
Testilying, 542-549
"Testimonial or communicative" conduct, 78-80. *See also* Self-incrimination, right against
Textualism, 177, 229

Index

Thermal imaging, 211, 225-230, 243
Third-party consent to search shared living space, 350-356
Thirteenth Amendment, 12, 29, 30, 909, 910
Thompson, Anthony C., 422, 424
Title VII burden-shifting methodology, 1399
"Tough on crime" sentiments, 1343, 1347
Traffic regulations, selective enforcement of, 1356
Traffic stops, 437-471. *See also* Stop and frisk
    routine stops, 143-148
Training, adequacy of, for §1983 actions, 561-566, 579
Trespass, 230, 239
Trial, summary of process, 2
Trott, Stephen, 846-847
Truman Administration, 931
Trump Administration, 625

Unanimity of jury, 7, 1133-1140
Unconscious racism, 1376, 1418-1419
United States attorneys, appointment of, 3-4
United States Attorneys' Manual, 813. *See also*
    Justice Manual
United States Attorney's Offices, 1117
Unjustifiable use of force crimes, 906

Vacatur, 1031
Vagrancy statutes, 18, 35-39, 404, 744
Vehicle checkpoints, 360-367
Venire, 4, 1241, 1250, 1267, 1268. *See also* Jury
Verdict
    jury, 1157-1163, 1163-1168
    NGI. *See* Insanity defense
Veterans, 930-931
Vicarious liability, 561
Victimization of Black people, 1419
Victims of crimes, prosecutor solicitude for, 820
Viewpoint discrimination, 1072-1079, 1080-1083, 1084-1088
Voice exemplars, self-incrimination, 667
Voir dire, 1149, 1242-1257
Volstead Act, 81, 211, 382, 383, 953, 977-978
Volstead, Andrew, 978
Vorenberg, James, 812-813
Voting rights, 912-916

Waivers
    ineffective assistance of counsel, 1046
    Miranda, 157, 161-165
    plea hearing, 979-984
    self-incrimination, right against, 690
Warrantless arrests, 211, 311-329
    felony charge, 311-318
    misdemeanor charge, 319-329, 375-383
Warrantless searches, 218-224
    administrative searches, 211, 359-375
    arrest, search incident to, 211, 311, 328, 329-341

    automobile exception, 211, 375-391
    border search, 360, 435-436
    common authority over premises, persons with, 355-356, 1050-1051
    consent searches, 211, 341-356
    exigent circumstances. *See* Exigent circumstances doctrine
    high school students, 367-375
    immigration checkpoints, 360, 427, 435
    of junkyards, 360, 390, 391
    of motor home, 387-390
    probationer, home of, 360
    racial profiling, 360
    sobriety checkpoint, 361
    "special needs" searches, 211, 359-375
    third-party consent to search shared living space, 350-356
    vehicle checkpoints, 360-367
Warrants, 295-391
    arrest warrants. *See* Arrest warrants
    bench warrants, 295, 340, 512
    exceptions, 211
    search warrants. *See* Search warrants
Warren, Earl, 11
Washington, David Leroy, 757, 765
Washington, peremptory challenges reforms in, 1286
Watergate, 947
Weisselberg, Charles, 191
White collar criminals, 1342, 1347
White supremacy, 35, 52, 556, 868, 905, 906, 929
White, Walter, 44, 45
Wickersham Commission, 977
Wickersham Report, 108-109
Willfulness, 927-928, 948, 973
Wilson, Darren, 718, 719, 973
Wilson, James Q., 406
Wire fraud, 1349
Wiretapping, 211-212, 213-217, 607, 1070
Witnesses
    cooperating, 1046
    expert. *See* Expert witnesses
    grand jury, 682-699
    statements, 879-886
    unsavory/unreliable, prosecutor use of, 832-848
Wolfgang, Marvin, 1368, 1376
Women, exclusion from juries, 1231-1236, 1237-1240
Woodard, Isaac, 931
World War, 953
World War I, 40
World War II, 905, 930, 1325

Young, Kathryne M., 349
Younger, Irving, 546

Zealous advocacy, 791-809
Zier, Magdalen, 44
Zimmerman, George, 972-973
Zone of privacy, 80-81